ROBERT ALTHANN S.J.

ELENCHUS OF BIBLICA
EXEGESIS
1995

EDITRICE PONTIFICIO ISTITUTO BIBLICO
ROMA 1998

ROBERT ALTHANN S.J.

ELENCHUS OF BIBLICA

EXEGESIS

1995

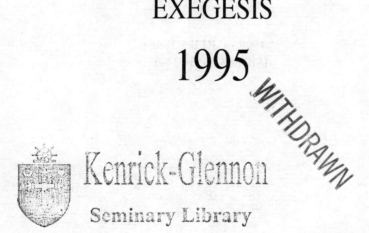
EDITRICE PONTIFICIO ISTITUTO BIBLICO
ROMA 1998

20-066

EDITRICE PONTIFICIO ISTITUTO BIBLICO
Piazza della Pilotta, 35 - 00187 Roma

Urbes editionis — **Cities of publication**

AA	Ann Arbor	Lp	Leipzig
Amst	Amsterdam	Lv(N)	Leuven (L-Neuve)
B	Berlin	LVL	Louisville KY
Ba/BA	Basel/Buenos Aires	M/Mi	Madrid/Milano
Barc	Barcelona	Mkn/Mp	Maryknoll/Minneapolis
Bo/Bru	Bologna/Brussel	Mü/Müns('r)	München/Münster
CasM	Casale Monferrato	N	Napoli
CinB	Cinisello Balsamo	ND	NotreDame IN
C	Cambridge, England	Neuk	Neukirchen/Verlag
CM	Cambridge, Mass.	NHv/Nv	New Haven/Nashville
Ch	Chicago	NY	New York
ColMn	Collegeville MN	Ox	Oxford
Da:Wiss	Darmstadt, WissBuchg	P/Pd	Paris/Paderborn
DG	Downers Grove	Ph	Philadelphia
Dü	Düsseldorf	R/Rg	Roma/Regensburg
E	Edinburgh	S/Sdr	Salamanca/Santander
ENJ	EnglewoodCliffs NJ	SF	San Francisco
F	Firenze	Shf	Sheffield
FrB/FrS	Freiburg-Br/Schweiz	Sto	Stockholm
Fra	Frankfurt/M	Stu	Stuttgart
Gö	Göttingen	T/TA	Torino/Tel Aviv
GR	Grand Rapids MI	Tü	Tübingen
Gü	Gütersloh	U/W	Uppsala/Wien
Ha	Hamburg	WL	Winona Lake IN
Heid	Heidelberg	Wmr	Warminster
Hmw	Harmondsworth	Wsb	Wiesbaden
J	Jerusalem	Wsh	Washington D.C.
K	København	Wsz	Warszawa
L/Lei	London/Leiden	Wu/Wü	Wuppertal/Würzburg
LA	Los Angeles	Z	Zürich

Punctuation: To separate a subtitle from its title, this volume (11/1, see Preface) uses a COLON (:). The *semicolon* (;) serves to separate items that belong together. Hence, at the end of an entry a *semicolon* indicates a link with the following entry. This link may consist in the two entries having the same author or in the case of multiauthor works having the same book title; the author will be mentioned in the first entry of such a group, the common book title in the last entry, that is the one which concludes with a period [fullstop] (.).

Vector (*renvoi*): In this volume, only works to which renvoi is actually made feature in sections A1-2.

Abbreviations: These follow S.M. Schwertner, **IATG**[2] (De Gruyter; Berlin 1992) as far as possible.

The Index of Authors includes editors, authors of book reviews, authors cited in titles and translators. In this volume no indication is given of the category of author to which the index number refers.

Price of books: This is sometimes rounded off ($10 for $9.95).

4

Index systematicus — Contents

As indicated by Father Robert North in the ELENCHUS for 1994 [1997], the 1995 materials will appear in two volumes. The present volume numbered 11/1 contains the exegetical sections in E-F-G. The remaining sections will be in volume 11/2 to appear later. The 1996 materials will again be together in one volume.

I should like in the first place to express thanks to confreres in Rome: Fathers Robert North, Jean-Noël Aletti and Ronald Wozniak for their generous help.

With an annual grant from The Catholic Biblical Association of America, the publication management has been assured by Father Pasquale Puca for the Pontifical Gregorian University Press. The material for this volume has been gathered from the libraries of the Pontifical Biblical Institute, the Pontifical Gregorian University and the University of Innsbruck. I should like here to express my appreciation of the helpfulness of the staff at these libraries. From the library of the Pontifical Biblical Institute many book entries have been made available to the Elenchus in machine readable form. The same service has been rendered by the technical staff of the Departments of Old and New Testament Studies of the University of Innsbruck responsible for 'Biblical Literature Documented in Innsbruck' (BILDI), accessible on the internet, who have also contributed information on articles in numerous periodicals and collected works. Cooperation between the University of Innsbruck and the Elenchus has also resulted in reviews of books listed in this volume of the Elenchus being accessible through BILDI on the internet. The internet address of BILDI is httm://starwww.uibk.ac.at. Reviews from subsequent years too are accessible on the internet through BILDI. It may be added that this service of the University of Innsbruck is free. We wish to continue and develop our cooperation with a view to making the contents of the Elenchus more easily and quickly available to the scholarly community.

R.A.

Acronyms: Periodica - Series (small).
8 fig. = ISSN; *10 fig.* = ISBN.

AASF: Annales Academiae Scientiarum Fennicae; Helsinki.
AASF.DHL: Dissertationes humanarum litterarum.
ÄAT: Ägypten und Altes Testament; Wsb.
AAWG.PH: Abhandlungen der Akademie der Wissenschaften in Gö. Philologisch-historische Klasse.
ABenR: American Benedictine Review; NY.
ABQ: American Baptist Quarterly; Rochester, NY.
ABR: Australian Biblical Review; Melbourne.
Abr-n.: Abr-nahrain; Lei.
AcBib: Acta Pontificii Instituti Biblici; Roma.
ACEBT: Amsterdamse cahiers voor exegese en bijbelse theologie; Kampen.
ACr: Arte cristiana; Mi.
ACR: Australasian Catholic Record; Sydney.
ACra: Analecta Cracoviensia [**P.**]; Kraków.
Acta Patristica et Byzantina; Pretoria.
Acta Theologica; Bloemfontein.
Actualidad Bibliográfica; Barc.
ADAI.K: Abhandlungen des Deutschen Archäologischen Instituts, Kairo. Koptische Reihe; Heid.
Aevum; Mi.
AFH: Archivum franciscanum historicum; F.
AGJU: Arbeiten zur Geschichte des antiken Judentums und des Urchristentums; Lei.
AGLB: Aus der Geschichte der lateinischen Bibel; FrB.
AION: Annali dell'Istituto Universitario Orientale di Napoli; N.
AJBI: Annual of the Japanese Biblical Institute; Tokyo.
AJS: American Journal of Sociology; Ch.
AJTh: Asia Journal of Theology; Singapore.
AKuG: Archiv für Kulturgeschichte; B.

Al-Mushir [**Urdu**]; Rawalpindi.
Aloi.: Aloisiana; N.
Ambrosius. Bolletino liturgico ambrosiano; Mi.
America; NY.
AmUSt.H: American University Studies. History; NY. **P**: Philosophy. **TR**: Theology and Religion.
AnáMnesis; México.
AnBib: Analecta Biblica; R.
AnBoll: Analecta bollandiana; Bru.
AncB: Anchor Bible; NY.
ANETS: Ancient Near Eastern Texts and Studies; Lewiston.
Ang.: Angelicum; R.
Annales Theologici; R.
Annali Chieresi; Chieri.
Annals of Theology [**P.**]; Kråkow.
ANRW: Aufstieg und Niedergang der römischen Welt; B.
ANTJ: Arbeiten zum Neuen Testament und zum Judentum; Fra.
Anton.: Antonianum; R.
ANTT: Arbeiten zur neutestamentlichen Textforschung; B.
AOAT: Alter Orient und Altes Testament; Kevelaer.
Apocrypha; Turnhout.
Archaeology in the Biblical World; Shafter, CA.
ARGU: Arbeiten zur Religion und Geschichte des Urchristentums; Fra.
ASBF: Analecta. Studium Biblicum Franciscanum; J.
AsbTJ: Asbury Theological Journal; Wilmore, KY.
ASEs: Annali di storia dell'esegesi; Bo.
Asp.: Asprenas; N.
ATD: Das Alte Testament Deutsch; Gö.
ATG: Archivo Teologico Granadino; Granada.
ÄthF: Äthiopistische Forschungen; Wsb.
AThR: Anglican Theological Review; NY.
AtK: Ateneum kapłańskie [**P.**]; Włocławek.
ATSAT: Arbeiten zu Text und Sprache im Alten Testament; St. Ottilien.
Atualização; Belo Horizonte.
Aug.: Augustinianum; R.
Aug(L): Augustiniana; Lv.
AugSt: Augustinian Studies; Villanova, Pa.

Augustinus; M.
AulOr: Aula Orientalis; Barc.
AUSS: Andrews University Seminary Studies; Berrien Springs.
AWA: Archiv zur Weimarer Ausgabe der Werke Martin Luthers; Köln.
AzTh: Arbeiten zur Theologie; Stu.
BA: Biblical Archaeologist; New Haven.
BAEO: Boletin de la Asociación Española de Orientalistas; M.
BAG: Beiträge zur alten Geschichte; Lp.
BArR: Biblical Archaeology Review; Wsh.
BASOR: Bulletin of the American Schools of Oriental Research; New Haven.
BBB: Bonner Biblische Beiträge; Bonn.
BCR: Biblioteca di cultura religiosa; R.
BEAT: Beiträge zur Erforschung des Alten Testaments und des antiken Judentums; Fra.
BEB: Biblioteca de espiritualidad biblica; M.
BEL: Bibliotheca 'Ephemerides Liturgicae'; R.
BeO: Bibbia e oriente; Mi.
BET: Beiträge zur biblischen Exegese und Theologie; Fra.
Beth Mikra; J.
BEThL: Bibliotheca Ephemeridum theologicarum Lovaniensium; Lv.
BEvTh: Beiträge zur evangelischen Theologie; Mü.
BGBE: Beiträge zur Geschichte der biblischen Exegese; Tü.
BGrL: Bibliothek der griechischen Literatur; Stu.
BHR: Bibliothèque d'humanisme et renaissance; Genève.
Bib.: Biblica; R.
BiBh: Bible Bhashyam; Kottayam.
Bibl.Interp.: Biblical Interpretation; Lei.
Biblioteca EstB: Biblioteca de Estudios Bíblicos; S.
BibOr: Biblica et Orientalia; R.
BiFe: Biblia y fe; M.
Bijdr.: Bijdragen. Tijdschrift voor philosophie en theologie; Nijmegen.

BiKi: Bibel und Kirche; Stu.
BiLi: Bibel und Liturgie: Klosterneuburg.
BiOr: Bibliotheca orientalis; Lei.
BIOSCS: Bulletin of the International Organization for Septuagint and Cognate Studies.
BiRe: Bible Review; Wsh.
BiSe: Biblical Seminar; Shf.
BiTod: Bible Today; ColMn.
BiTr: Bible Translator; L.
BJRL: Bulletin of the John Rylands Library; Manchester.
BJSt: Brown Judaic Studies; Missoula
BK: Biblischer Kommentar; Neuk.
BLE: Bulletin de littérature ecclésiastique; Toulouse.
BN: Biblische Notizen; Bamberg.
BN.B: Biblische Notizen. Beiheft; Bamberg.
BnS: La bibbia nella storia; Bo.
BNTC: Black's New Testament Commentaries; L.
Bobolanum [P.]; Wsz.
Bogoslovni Vestnik; Ljubljana.
BoL: Book List. Society for Old Testament Study; L.
BolT: Boletín teológico; Buenos Aires.
BPat: Biblioteca patristica; F.
BR: Biblical Research; Ch.
BRoHi.T: Biblioteca románica hispánica. Textos; M.
BRSLR: Biblioteca della Rivista di storia e letteratura religiosa; F.
BRT: The Baptist Review of Theology / La revue baptiste de théologie; Gormely, Ontario.
BS: Bibliotheca Sacra; Dallas.
BSal: Boletín de la Sociedad Arqueológica Luliana; Palma.
BSOAS: Bulletin of the School of Oriental and African Studies; L.
BT: Bibliothèque de théologie; Paris.
BTB: Biblical Theology Bulletin; NY.
BTCon: Biblioteca di teologia contemporanea; Brescia.
BTF: Bangalore Theological Forum; Bangalore.
BThZ: Berliner theologische Zeitschrift; B.
BU: Biblische Untersuchungen; Regensburg.

BuBbgB: Bulletin de bibliographie biblique; Lausanne.

Bulletin de l'Association G. Budé; P.

Bulletin for Biblical Research; WL.

Burg.: Burgense; Burgos.

BurH: Buried History; Melbourne.

BVLI: Bericht des Instituts. Vetus Latina-Institut; Beuron.

BVp: Biblical Viewpoint; Greenville, S.C.

BVV: Biblioteca verdade e vida; Porto.

BWANT: Beiträge zur Wissenschaft vom Alten und Neuen Testament; Stu.

Byz.: Byzantion; Bru.

BZ: Biblische Zeitschrift; Pd.

BZAW: Beihefte zur Zeitschrift für die alttestamentliche Wissenschaft; B.

BZNW: Beihefte zur Zeitschrift für die neutestamentliche Wissenschaft und die Kunde der älteren Kirche; B.

C: in Chinese.

Cahiers de l'Atelier; P.

Cahiers de traduction biblique; Pierrefitte France.

CahPhRel: Cahiers de l'Ecole des Sciences philosophiques et religieuses; Bru.

Carthaginensia; Murcia.

Catechisti parrocchiali; R.

Cathedra; Bogotá.

Cath(P): Catholica; P.

CB: Coniectanea biblica; Lund.

CBFV: Cahiers bibliques de foi et vie; P.

CBi: Collana biblica; T.

CBQ: Catholic Biblical Quarterly; Wsh.

CBQ.MS: Catholic Biblical Quarterly. Monograph Series; Wsh.

CBTJ: Calvary Baptist Theological Journal; Lansdale, Pa.

CChr.CM: Corpus Christianorum. Continuatio mediaevalis; Turnhout. SG: Series Graeca.

CCist: Collectanea Cisterciensia; Forges.

CCMéd: Cahiers de civilisation médiévale; Poitiers.

CDios: Ciudad de Dios; El Escorial.

CEv: Cahiers évangile; P.

CEv(S): Cahiers évangile. (Supplément); P.

CFi: Cogitatio fidei; P.

CFr: Collectanea Franciscana; R.

Chemins de Dialogue; Marseille.

ChFe: Ching feng; Hong Kong.

ChiSt: Chicago Studies; Ch.

ChM: Churchman; L.

Choisir; Genève.

Christus; P.

ChrTo: Christianity Today; Wsh.

Cias; Buenos Aires.

CiSt: Cistercian Studies; Chimay.

CivCatt: Civiltà cattolica; R.

CJ: Classical Journal; Menasha, Wis.

Clar.: Claretianum; R.

CLehre: Die Christenlehre; B.

Coll.: Collationes; Gent.

Colloquium; Brisbane.

Com(F): Communio. Revue catholique internationale; P.

Com(I): Communio. Strumento internazionale per un lavoro teologico; Mi.

Communio; Sevilla [cf. **IKaZ**].

Com(US): Communio. International Catholic Review; Spokane

Comp.: Compostellanum; Santiago de Compostella.

Conc(D): Concilium; Einsiedeln; **(F)** P.; **(GB)** L; **(I)** Brescia.

ConJ: Concordia Journal; St. Louis, Mo.

CoTh: Collectanea theologica; Wsz.

CPB: Christlich-pädagogische Blätter; W.

CRAI: Comptes rendus des séances de l'Académie des Inscriptions et Belles Lettres; P.

CRB: Cahiers de la Revue biblique; P.

CRI: Compendia rerum Iudaicarum ad novum testamentum; Assen.

CritRR: Critical Review of Books in Religion; Atlanta.

Crkva u Svijetu [**Croatian**]; Split.

CrossCur: Cross Currents; NY.

CrSoc: Cristianismo y sociedad; Buenos Aires.

CrSt: Cristianesimo nella storia; Bo.

Crux: Vancouver.
CSB: Collana studi biblici; Brescia.
CSCO.S: Corpus scriptorum christianorum orientalium. Scriptores Syri; R.
CSRT: Courtenay studies in Reformation theology; Appleford.
CStP: Collectània Sant Pacià; Barc.
CTC: Commission on Theological Concerns, Christian Conference of Asia; Hong Kong.
CTePa: Collana di testi patristici; R.
CThMi: Currents in Theology and Mission; St. Louis, Mo.
CTHP: Collection de théologie héritage et projet; Québec.
CTJ: Calvin Theological Journal; GR.
CTom: Ciencia tomista; S.
CTR: Chinese Theological Review; Holland, Mich.
CTUF: Collectanea theologica Universitatis Fujen; Taichung.
CuaBi: Cuadernos biblicos; Valencia.
Cuestion Social, La; Mexico.
CurResB: Currents in Research: Biblical Studies; Shf.
CV: Communio viatorum; Praha.
D.: Director dissertationis.
DBM: Deltio biblikōn meletōn [G.]. Bulletin of Biblical Studies; Athēnai.
Dialog. A Journal of Theology; Mp.
Didascalia; Rosario ARG.
Did(L): Didaskalia; Lisbōa.
Direction; Fresno CA.
DissA: Dissertation Abstracts International; AA/L. -A [= US etc.]: 0419-4209 [C = Europe. 0307-6075].
Div.: Divinitas; R.
DosP: Les Dossiers de la Bible; P.
DR: Downside Review; Bath.
DSD: Dead Sea Discoveries; Lei.
E: Editor, Herausgeber, a cura di.
EdF: Erträge der Forschung; Da.
EE: Estudios eclesiásticos; M.
EeT(O): Église et théologie; Ottawa.
EETS: Early English Text Society; L.
EeV: Esprit et vie; Langres.
Efemérides Mexicana; Tlalpan.

EHPR: Études d'histoire et de philosophie religieuses; P.
EHS.T: Europäische Hochschulschriften. Theologie; Fra.
EK: Evangelische Kommentare; Stu.
EKK: Evangelisch-katholischer Kommentar zum Neuen Testament; Z. ·
EL: Ephemerides liturgicae; Città del Vaticano.
EMISJ: Estudios y monografias. Institución San Jeronimo para la investigación biblica; M.
Emmanuel; St. Meinrads, IN.
Encounter; Indianapolis, IN.
Entschluß; W.
EO: Ecclesia orans; FrB.
EpRe: Epworth Review; L.
ER: Ecumenical Review; Lausanne.
EscrVedat: Escritos del Vedat; Valencia.
EstAg: Estudio agustiniano; Valladolid.
EstB: Estudios bíblicos; M.
EsTe: Estudos teológicos; São Leopoldo.
EstFr: Estudios franciscanos; Barc.
ET: Expository Times; E.
ÉtB: Études bibliques; P.
EThL: Ephemerides theologicae Lovanienses; Lv.
EThSt: Erfurter theologische Studien; Lp.
EtMar: Estudios marianos; M.
ETR: Études théologiques et religieuses; Montpellier.
ETSI Journal; Igbaja, Nigeria.
EuA: Erbe und Auftrag; Beuron.
EurJT: European Journal of Theology; Carlisle.
Evangel; E.
Evangelizzare; Bo.
EvErz: Der evangelische Erzieher; Fra.
EvJo: Evangelical Journal; Myerstown, Pa.
EvQ: Evangelical Quarterly; L.
ExAu: Ex auditu; Allison Park, Pa.
F: Festschrift.
FaF: Faith and Freedom; Leeds.
FAT: Forschungen zum Alten Testament; Tü.

FC: Fontes christiani; FrB.
Feminist Theology; Shf.
FgNT: Filologia Neotestamentaria; Córdoba.
FilTeo: Filosofia et teologia; N.
Firmana; Fermo.
Florensia; S. Giovanni in Fiore (CS).
Folia Theologica; Budapest.
FolOr: Folia orientalia [P.]; Kraków.
Forum. A journal of the foundations & facets of Western culture; Sonoma, CA.
Forum Religion; Stu.
FOTL: The forms of the Old Testament literature; GR.
Franciscanum; Bogotá.
FRLANT: Forschungen zur Religion and Literatur des Alten und Neuen Testaments; Gö.
FrRu: Freiburger Rundbrief; FrB.
FTS: Frankfurter theologische Studien; Fra.
Fundamentum; Basel.
FuSt: Fuldaer Studien; St. Ottilien.
FV: Foi et vie; P.
FzB: Forschung zur Bibel; Stu.
G: in Greek.
Gema; Yogyakarta.
GlLern: Glaube und Lernen; Gö.
Gnomon; Mü.
Gnosis; SF.
GNS: Good news studies; ColMn.
GOF.S: Göttinger Orientforschung. Syriaca; Wsb.
Gr.: Gregorianum; R.
Graphè; Lille.
GThT: Gereformeerd theologisch tijdschrift; Aalten.
GuL: Geist und Leben. Zeitschrift für Aszese und Mystik; Wü.
H: in Hebrew.
HAT: Handbuch zum Alten Testament; Tü.
HBT: Horizons in Biblical Theology; Pittsburg.
HebStud: Hebrew Studies; Madison, Wisc.
Hekima Review; Nairobi.
Helm.: Helmantica; S.
Henoch; T.
HerKorr: Herder-Korrespondenz; FrB.

HeyJ: Heythrop Journal; L.
Hist.: Historia. Zeitschrift für alte Geschichte; Wsb.
History of European Ideas; Ox.
HNT: Handbuch zum Neuen Testament; Tü.
Horeb; Pozzo di Gotto (ME).
HPR: Homiletic and Pastoral Review; NY.
HR: History of Religions; Ch.
HSM: Harvard Semitic Monographs; CM.
HThK: Herders theologische Kommentar; FrB.
HThR: Harvard Theological Review; CM.
HTS: Hervormde teologiese studies; Pretoria.
HTS.S: Hervormde teologiese studies. Supplementum; Pretoria.
HUCA: Hebrew Union College Annual; Cincinatti.
HumTeo: Humanistica e teologia; Porto.
HUTh: Hermeneutische Untersuchungen zur Tehologie; Tü.
HZ: Historische Zeitschrift; Mü.
IBSt: Irish Biblical Studies; Belfast.
ICC: International Critical Commentary; E.
Ichthys IΧΘΥΣ; Aarhus.
IEJ: Israel Exploration Journal; J.
IET: Informatique et étude de textes; Lv.
Igreja e Missão. Revista missionária de cultura e actualidade; Valadares, Cucujaes.
IKaZ: Internationale katholische Zeitschrift [= Communio]; Fra.
IKZ: Internationale kirchliche Zeitschrift; Bern.
IMR: Indian Missiological Review; Shillong.
InfJud: Information Judentum; Neuk.
Insights; Austin, TX.
Inter Fratres; Fabriano (AN).
Interp.: Interpretation. A Journal of Bible and Theology; Richmond, Virg.
FC: Fontes christiani; FrB.
Feminist Theology; Shf.
FgNT: Filologia Neotestamentaria; Córdoba.

FilTeo: Filosofia et teologia; N.

Firmana; Fermo.

Florensia; S. Giovanni in Fiore (CS).

Folia Theologica; Budapest.

FolOr: Folia orientalia [**P**.]; Kraków.

Forum. A journal of the foundations & facets of Western culture; Sonoma, CA.

Forum Religion; Stu.

FOTL: The forms of the Old Testament literature; GR.

Franciscanum; Bogotá.

FRLANT: Forschungen zur Religion and Literatur des Alten und Neuen Testaments; Gö.

FrRu: Freiburger Rundbrief; FrB.

FTS: Frankfurter theologische Studien; Fra.

Fundamentum; Basel.

FuSt: Fuldaer Studien; St. Ottilien.

FV: Foi et vie; P.

FzB: Forschung zur Bibel; Stu.

G: in Greek.

Gema; Yogyakarta.

GlLern: Glaube und Lernen; Gö.

Gnomon; Mü.

Gnosis; SF.

GNS: Good news studies; ColMn.

GOF.S: Göttinger Orientforschung. Syriaca; Wsb.

Gr.: Gregorianum; R.

Graphè; Lille.

GThT: Gereformeerd theologisch tijdschrift; Aalten.

GuL: Geist und Leben. Zeitschrift für Aszese und Mystik; Wü.

H: in Hebrew.

HAT: Handbuch zum Alten Testament; Tü.

HBT: Horizons in Biblical Theology; Pittsburg.

HebStud: Hebrew Studies; Madison, Wisc.

Hekima Review; Nairobi.

Helm.: Helmantica; S.

Henoch; T.

HerKorr: Herder-Korrespondenz; FrB.

HeyJ: Heythrop Journal; L.

Hist.: Historia. Zeitschrift für alte Geschichte; Wsb.

History of European Ideas; Ox.

HNT: Handbuch zum Neuen Testament; Tü.

Horeb; Pozzo di Gotto (ME).

HPR: Homiletic and Pastoral Review; NY.

HR: History of Religions; Ch.

HSM: Harvard Semitic Monographs; CM.

HThK: Herders theologische Kommentar; FrB.

HThR: Harvard Theological Review; CM.

HTS: Hervormde teologiese studies; Pretoria.

HTS.S: Hervormde teologiese studies. Supplementum; Pretoria.

HUCA: Hebrew Union College Annual; Cincinatti.

HumTeo: Humanistica e teologia; Porto.

HUTh: Hermeneutische Untersuchungen zur Tehologie; Tü.

HZ: Historische Zeitschrift; Mü.

IBSt: Irish Biblical Studies; Belfast.

ICC: International Critical Commentary; E.

Ichthys ΙΧΘΥΣ; Aarhus.

IEJ: Israel Exploration Journal; J.

IET: Informatique et étude de textes; Lv.

Igreja e Missão. Revista missionária de cultura e actualidade; Valadares, Cucujaes.

IKaZ: Internationale katholische Zeitschrift [= Communio]; Fra.

IKZ: Internationale kirchliche Zeitschrift; Bern.

IMR: Indian Missiological Review; Shillong.

InfJud: Information Judentum; Neuk.

Insights; Austin, TX.

Inter Fratres; Fabriano (AN).

Interp.: Interpretation. A Journal of Bible and Theology; Richmond, Virg.

Interpretation. Journal of Political Philosophy; Flushing.

IP: Instrumenta patristica; 's-Gravenhage.

Irén.: Irénikon; Chevetogne.

IRM: International Review of Missions; L.

ISBL: Indiana Studies in Biblical Literature; Bloomington.

Isidorianum; Sevilla.

Iter; Caracas.

IThQ: Irish Theological Quarterly; Maynooth.

IThS: Innsbrucker theologische Studien.

Itin.: Itinerarium. Revista franciscana de cultura católica; Buenos Aires.

ITS: Indian Theological Studies; Bangalore.

J: in Japanese.

JAAR: Journal of the American Academy of Religion; Boston.

JAC: Jahrbuch fü Antike und Christentum; Müns.

JAC.E: Jahrbuch für Antike und Christentum. Ergänzungsband; Müns.

JANES: Journal of the Ancient Near Eastern Society; NY.

JAOS: Journal of the American Oriental Society; Baltimore.

JBL: Journal of Biblical Literature; Ph.

JBQ: The Jewish Bible Quarterly; J.

JBS: Jerusalem biblical studies; J.

JBTSA: Journal of Black Theology in South Africa; Atteridgeville.

JDh: Journal of Dharma; Bangalore.

JEarlyC: Journal of Early Christian Studies; Baltimore.

Jeevadhara; Alleppey, Kerala.

JETh: Jahrbuch für evangelische Theologie; Wu.

JETS: Journal of the Evangelical Theological Society; Wheaton, Ill.

JHiC: Journal of Higher Criticism; Montclair, NJ.

Jian Dao [C.]; Hong Kong.

JJS: Journal of Jewish Studies; L.

JK: Junge Kirche; Dortmund.

JLT: Journal of Literature and Theology; Ox.

JNES: Journal of Near Eastern Studies; Ch.

JNSL: Journal of Northwest Semitic Languages; Stellenbosch.

Jota; Lv.

Journal of Medieval History; Amsterdam.

JPentec: Journal of Pentecostal Theology; Shf.

JPersp: Jerusalem Perspective; J.

JProgJud: Journal of Progressive Judaism; Shf.

JPSTC: Jewish Publication Society. The JPS Torah commentary; Ph.

JQR: Jewish Quarterly Review; Ph.

JR: Journal of Religion; Ch.

JRadRef: Journal from the Radical Reformation; Morrow, GA.

JSem: Journal for Semitics; Pretoria.

JSJ: Journal for the Study of Judaism in the Persian, Hellenistic and Roman period; Lei.

JSNT: Journal for the Study of the New Testament; Shf.

JSNT.S: Journal for the Study of the New Testament. Supplementary Series; Shf.

JSOT: Journal for the Study of the Old Testament; Shf.

JSOT.S: Journal for the Study of the Old Testament. Supplementary Series; Shf.

JSPE.S: Journal for the Study of the Pseudepigrapha. Supplementary Series; Shf.

JSSR: Journal for the Scientific Study of Religion; Wsh.

JSSt: Journal of Semitic Studies; Manchester.

JThS: Journal of Theological Studies; Ox.

JTrTL: Journal of Translation and Textlinguistics; Dallas.

JTSA: Journal of Theology for Southern Africa; Rondebosch.

Jud.: Judaism; NY.

JudChr: Judaica et Christiana; Bern.

JudSer : Judaica Series; NY.

JWCI: Journal of the Warburg and Courtauld Institutes; L.

K: in Korean.

Kairós; Zeitschrift für Religionswissenschaft und Theologie; Salzburg.

Kairós. Zeitschrift für Religionswissenschaft und Theologie; Salzburg.

Kairos(G); Guatemala.

KaKe: Katorikku-Kenkyu; Tokyo.
KAT: Kommentar zum Alten Testament; Lp.
KatBl: Katechetische Blätter; Mü.
KEK: Kritisch-exegetischer Kommentar über das Neue Testament; Gö.
Kerux; Escondido, CA.
KeTh: Kerk en theologie; Wageningen.
KiHe: Kirche heute; Graz.
Klerus-Blatt; Salzburg.
KuD: Kerygma und Dogma; Gö.
Landas. Journal of Loyola School of Theology; Manila.
Laós.
LAPO: Littératures anciennes du Proche-Orient; P.
LASBF: Liber annuus. Studium Biblicum Franciscanum; J.
Lat.: Lateranum; R.
Laur.: Laurentianum; R.
LebZeug: Lebendiges Zeugnis; Pd.
LeDiv: Lectio Divina; P.
LexTQ: Lexington Theological Quarterly; Lexington, KY.
LHR: Lectures on the History of Religions; NY.
LiBi: Lire la Bible; P.
Lire et Dire.
Liturgy; Ch.
Living Light; Wsh.
LM: Lutherische Monatshefte; Hamburg.
LoB: Leggere oggi la Bibbia; Brescia.
LouvSt: Louvain Studies; Lv.
LS: Lebendige Seelsorge; FrB.
LThPM: Louvain Theological and Pastoral Monographs; Lv.
LTJ: Lutheran Theological Journal; Adelaide.
Luther Digest; Fort Wayne, IN.
LuThK: Lutherische Theologie und Kirche; Oberursel.
LuthQ: Lutheran Quarterly; Gettysburg, Pa.
LV: Lumen vitae; Wsh.
LV.F: Lumen Vitae. Revue internationale de la formation religieuse; Bru.
LV(L): Lumière et vie; Lyon.
M.: Memorial.
MÂ: Moyen-âge; Bru.

MAe: Medium aevum; Ox.
MAI: Masters Abstracts International; AA: 0898-9095.
Manresa; Barc.
MastJ: Master's Seminary Journal; Sun Valley, CA.
Mayéutica; Marcilla (Navarra).
MCom: Miscelánea Comillas; Comillas, Sdr.
MD: La Maison-Dieu. Revue de pastorale liturgique; P.
MDAI.R: Mitteilungen des Deutschen Archäologischen Instituts. Römische Abteilung; R.
MethT: Method and Theory in the Study of Religion; Toronto.
MF: Miscellanea francescana; R.
MGH: Monumenta Germaniae historica; Hannover.
MillSt: Milltown Studies; Dublin.
MJT: Melanesian Journal of Theology; Lae.
MoBi: Monde de la bible; P.
MoThSt.S: Moraltheologische Studien. Systematische Abteilung; Dü.
MPIL: Monographs of the Peshiṭta Institute; Lei. MS: Monograph Series.
MSR: Mélanges de science religieuse; Lille.
MSSNTS: Monograph Series. Society for New Testament Studies; C.
MSU: Mitteilungen des Septuaginta-Unternehmens; Gö.
MTh: Melita theologica; Valetta.
MThA: Münsteraner theologische Abhandlungen; Altenberge.
MThZ: Münchener theologische Zeitschrift; Mü.
MuK: Musik und Kirche; Kassel.
Muséon, Le. Revue d'études orientales; Lv.
NAC: New American Commentary; Nv.
NCBC: New Century Bible Commentary; GR.
NCeB: New Century Bible; L.
NEB: Neue Echter Bibel; Wü.
NedThT: Nederlands theologisch tijdschrift; 's-Gravenhage.
Nemalah; K.
Neotest.: Neotestamentica; Pretoria.

Neukirchener Theologische Zeitschrift; Neuk.

New Theology Review; Ch.

NGTT: Nederduitse gereformeerde teologiese tydskrif; Kaapstad.

NIBC: New International Biblical Commentary; Peabody.

NIC: New International Commentary; GR.

Nicolaus; Bari.

NIGTC: New International Greek Testament Commentary; Exeter.

NJT: Nigerian Journal of Theology; Owerri.

NotesTrans: Notes on Translation; Dallas.

NRTh: Nouvelle Revue Théologique; Lv.

NT: Novum Testamentum; Lei.

NTA: Neutestamentliche Abhandlungen; Mü.

NTAb: New Testament Abstracts; Weston, Mass.

NTGu: New Testament Guides; Shf.

NThAR: Neuerwerbungen Theologie und allgemeine Religionswissenschaft; Tü.

NTOA: Novum Testamentum et orbis antiquus; FrS.

NTS: New Testament Studies; L.

NT.S: Novum Testamentum. Supplement; Lei.

NTT: Norssk teologisk tidsskrift; Oslo.

NTTRU: New Testament Textual Research Update; Ashfield NSW, Australia. 1320-3037.

NTTS: New Testament Tools and Studies; Lei.

NuMu: Nuevo Mundo; Buenos Aires.

Nuova Umanità; R.

NV: Nova et vetera; Genève.

OBO: Orbis biblicus et orientalis; FrS.

ÖBS: Österreichische biblische Studien; Klosterneuburg.

OCA: Orientalia christiana analecta; R.

OCP: Orientalia christiana periodica; R.

OIRSI: Oriental Institute of Religious Studies, India; Kottayam.

Hokhma; Lausanne.

OLA: Orientalia Lovaniensia analecta; Lv.

OLZ: Orientalistische Literaturzeitung; B.

Omnis Terra; R.

ÖR: Ökumenische Rundschau; Stu.

OrBibChr: Orbis biblicus et christianus; Glückstadt.

OrChr: Oriens christianus; R.

OrdKor: Ordenskorrespondenz; Köln.

Orien.: Orientierung; Z.

Orph.: Orpheus. Rivista di umanità classica e cristiana; Catania.

OTA: Old Testament Abstracts; Wsh.

ÖTBK: Ökumenischer Taschenbuchkommentar zum Neuen Testament; Gü.

OTEs: Old Testament Essays; Pretoria.

OTGu: Old Testament Guides; Shf.

OTL: Old Testament Library; L.

OTM: Oxford Theological Monographs; Ox.

OTS: Oudtestamentische studiën; Lei.

OTSt: Old Testament Studies; E.

P: in Polish.

Pacifica. Australian Theological Studies; Melbourne.

Paginas; Lima.

PaiC.: Paideia Cristiana; Rosario, ARG.

PalCl: Palestra del clero; Rovigo.

Palestjinskji Sbornik [R.]; Moskva.

Parabola; NY.

PastPo: Pastoral Popular; Santiago de Chile.

PaVi: Parole di vita; T.

PBT: Piccola biblioteca teologica; T.

PenCath: Pensée catholique; P.

PEQ: Palestine Exploration Quarterly; L.

PerTeol: Perspectiva teológica; São Leopoldo.

Phase; Barc.

Philosophiques; Montréal.

PIBA: Proceedings of the Irish Biblical Association; Dublin.

POC: Proche-Orient chrétien; J.

PoeT: Poetics Today; Durham, NC.

PosLuth: Positions luthériennes; P.

Presbyterion; St. Louis.

Presbyteri; Trento.

PresPast: Presenza Pastorale, R.

Prism; St. Paul, MN.

ProcGLM: Proceedings of the Eastern Great Lakes and Midwest Bible Societies; Buffalo.

ProEc: Pro ecclesia; Northfield, MN.

Prooftexts; Baltimore.

Protest.: Protestantesimo; R.

ProySal: Proyecto Centro Salesiano de Estudios; Buenos Aires.

PRSt: Perspectives in Religious Studies; Mufreesboro, N.C.

PSB: Princeton Seminary Bulletin; Princeton.

PSV: Parola spirito e vita; Bo.

PSV: Parola spirito et vita; Bo.

PTh: Pastoraltheologie; Gö.

PTMS: Princeton Theological Monograph Series; Allison Park.

PzB: Protokolle zur Bibel; Klosterneuburg.

QD: Quaestiones disputatae; FrB.

QR: Quarterly Review. A Scholarly Journal for Reflection on Ministry; Nv.

Quaderni di azione sociale; R.

Qumran Chronicle; Kraków.

R: in Russian.

R: *recensio*, book-review.

RAMi: Rivista di ascetica e mistica; F.

RAT: Revue africaine de théologie; Kinshasa.

RB: Revue biblique; P.

RBen: Revue bénédictine de critique, d'histoire et de littérature religieuses; Maredsous.

RBL: Ruch biblijny i liturgiczny. De actione biblica et liturgica; Kraków.

RCatT: Revista catalana de teología; Barc.

RCB: Revista de cultura biblica; Rio de Janeiro.

RCI: Rivista del clero italiano; R.

RdQ: Revue de Qumrân; P.

RdT: Rassegna di teologia; R.

Reason and the Faith, The; Kwangju.

REAug: Revue des études augustiniennes; P.

REB: Revista eclesiástica brasileira; Petrópolis.

Recollectio; R.

RefR(H): Reformed Review; Holland, Mich.

REG: Revue des études grecques; P.

ReHe: Religion heute; Menden.

REJ: Revue des études juives; P.

RelCult: Religión y cultura; M.

Religion. A Journal of Religion and Religions; L.

RelT: Religion and Theology; Pretoria.

ResB: Reseña Bíblica; Estella.

REsp: Revista de espiritualidad; M.

RestQ: Restoration Quarterly; Austin, TX.

RET: Revista española de teología; M.

RevBib: Revista bíblica; Buenos Aires.

RevCT: Revista de cultura teológica; São Paulo.

Reviews in Religion and Theology; L.

RevSR: Revue des sciences religieuses; Strasbourg.

Revue d'éthique et de théologie morale; P.

RExp: Review and Expositor; LVL.

RGRW: Religions in the Graeco-Roman World; Lei.

RHEF: Revue d'histoire de l'église de France; P.

RHPhR: Revue d'histoire et de philosophie religieuses; Strasbourg.

rhs: Religionsunterricht an höheren Schulen; Dü.

Ribla: Revista de interpretação biblica latino-americana; Petrópolis.

RICAO: Revue de l'Institut Catholique de l'Afrique de l'Ouest; Abidjan.

RICP: Revue de l'Institut Catholique de Paris; P.

RIL: Rendiconti. Istituto Lombardo di Scienze e Lettere; Mi.

RivBib: Rivista biblica; R.

Roczniki Teologiczne. Annals of Theology; Lublin.

RPäB: Religionspädagogische Beiträge; Kaarst.

RRef: Revue réformée; Saint-Germain-en-Laye.

RSE: Revue des sciences ecclésiastiques; P.

RSPhTh: Revue des sciences philosophiques et théologiques; P.

RSR: Recherches de science religieuse; P.

RStB: Ricerche storico-bibliche; Bo.

RStT: Religious Studies and Theology; Edmonton.

RThAM: Recherches de théologie ancienne et médiévale; Lv.

RThom: Revue thomiste; Bruges.

RTK: Roczniki teologiczno-kanoniczne; Lublin.

RTL: Revue théologique de Louvain; Lv.

RTLi: Revista teológica limense; Lima.

RTR: Reformed Theological Review; Melbourne.

ru: Zeitschrift für die Praxis des Religionsunterrichts; Stu.

RVS: Rivista di vita spirituale; R.

RW: Reformed World; Genève.

S: Supplement.

SAAA: Studies on the Apocryphal Acts of the Apostles; Kampen.

Saeculum Christianum; Wsz.

Sal.: Salesianum; T.

Salm.: Salmanticensis; S.

SalTer: Sal terrae; Sdr.

SBAB: Stuttgarter biblische Aufsatzbände; Stu.

SBB: Stuttgarter biblische Beiträge; Stu.

SBEC: Studies in the Bible and Early Christianity; Lewiston.

SBET: Scottish Bulletin of Evangelical Theology; E.

SBFA: Studii biblici Franciscani analecta; J.

SBL.DS: Society of Biblical Literature. Dissertation Series; Missoula.

SP: Seminar Paper Series.

SBL.SP: Society of Biblical Literature. Seminar Paper Series; Missoula.

SBS: Stuttgarter Bibelstudien; Stu.

SC: Sources chrétiennes: P.

ScEs: Science et esprit; Bruges.

SCJ: Sixteenth Century Journal; St. Charles, Mo.

SCJud: Studies in Christianity and Judaism; Waterloo, Ont.

Scr.: Scriptorium. Revue internationale des études relatives aux manuscrits; Bru.

ScrB: Scripture Bulletin; L.

Scriptura; Stellenbosch.

ScrTh: Scripta theologica; Pamplona.

SCSt: Septuagint and Cognate Studies; CM.

SE: Sacris erudiri; Steenbrugge.

SEÅ: Svensk exegetisk årsbok; Lund.

Search; Dublin.

SEAug: Studia ephemerides 'Augustinianum'; R.

Sedes Sapientiae; Chéméré-le-Roi.

Sef.: Sefarad. Revista de la Escuela de Hebraicos; M.

SelTeol: Selecciones de teología; Barc.

SémBib: Sémiotique et bible; Lyon.

Semeia; Atlanta.

Semiotica; Amst.

Sen.: Sendros; Costa Rica.

Servitium; CasM.

Sève; P.

SFSHJ: South Florida Studies in the History of Judaism; Atlanta.

Shofar; West Lafayette, IN.

SIDIC: Service International de Documentation Judéo-Chrétienne; R.

SIJD: Schriften des Institutum Judaicum Delitzschianum; Stu.

Sinhak Jonmang; Kwangju, S. Korea.

SJ: Studia Judaica; B.

SJ(NY): Studies in Judaica; NY.

SJOT: Scandinavian Journal of the Old Testament; Åarhus.

SJTh: Scottish Journal of Theology; E.

SK: Skrif en Kerk; Pretoria.

SMBen.BE: Serie monografica di 'Benedictina'. Sezione biblico-ecumenica; R.

SMSR: Studi e materiali di storia delle religioni; R.

SNTA: Studiorum Novi Testamenti auxilia; Lv.

SNTU: Studien zum Neuen Testament und seiner Umwelt; Linz.

SOCr: Scritti delle origini christiane; Bo.

Soundings; Nv.

Sources; FrS.

South Pacific Journal of Mission Studies; North Turramurra NSW.

Spiritual Life; Wsh.

Spiritus; P.

SpOr: Spiritualité orientale; Bégrolles-en-Mauges.

SR: Studies in Religion; Toronto.

SSN: Studia semitica Neerlandica; Assen.

St Mark's Review; Canberra.

StAns: Studia Anselmiana; R.

Stauros. Bolletino trimestrale sulla teologia della Croce; Pescara.

StBi: Studi biblici; Brescia.

StFr: Studi francescani; F.

StLeg: Studium legionense; León.

StLi: Studia liturgica; Rotterdam.

StOv: Studium Ovetense; Oviedo.

StPat: Studia patavina. Rivista di filosofia e teologia; Padova.

StRel: Storia delle religioni; Bari.

Strom.: Stromata; San Miguel.

StSp: Studies in Spirituality; Kampen.

StTh: Studia theologica. Scandinavian Journal of Theology; Lund.

Studi di Teologia; R: Istituto Biblico Evangelico.

Studi Fatti Ricerche; Mi.

Studies in World Christianity; E.

Studium; M.

Stulos. Theological Journal; Bandung, Indonesia.

StUNT: Studien zur Umwelt des Neuen Testaments; Gö.

SVigChr: Supplements to Vigiliae Christianae; Amst.

SvTK: Svensk teologisk kvartalskrift; Lund.

SVTQ: St. Vladimir's Theological Quarterly; NY.

SWJT: Southwestern Journal of Theology; Seminary Hill, TX.

Symb.: Symbolon. Jahrbuch für Symbolforschung; Basel.

T: Translator.

TANZ: Texte und Arbeiten zum neutestamentlichen Zeitalter; Tü.

TCNN: Theological College of Northern Nigeria; Bukuru.

TEF.SG: Theological Education Fund. Study Guide; L.

Teocomunicaçâo; Porto Alegre, Brasil.

Teol.: Teología; Pont. Universidad Católica, Buenos Aires.

Teol(Br): Teologia; Brescia.

Ter Herkenning. Tijdschrift voor christenen en joden; 's-Gravenhage.

Ter.: Teresianum; R.

Test.: Testimonia; Dü.

Textus; J.

TFT: Theologische Faculteit Tilburg; Tilburg.

ThBeitr: Theologische Beiträge; Wu.

ThD : Theology Digest; St. Louis.

Themelios; L.

Theol.: Theology; L.

Theologica & Historica; Cagliari.

Theologika; Lima.

Theológos, Ho; Palermo.

Theology for Our Times; Bangalore.

Theotokos; R.

ThG(B): Theologie der Gegenwart; Bergen-Enkheim.

ThGl: Theologie und Glaube; Pd.

ThIK: Theologie im Kontext; Aachen.

ThLZ: Theologische Literaturzeitung; Lp.

ThPh: Theologie und Philosophie; FrB.

ThPQ: Theologisch-praktische Quartalschrift; Linz.

ThQ: Theologische Quartalschrift; Tü.

ThR: Theologische Rundschau; Tü.

ThRv: Theologische Revue; Münster.

ThTo: Theology Today; Notre Dame, Ind.

ThX: Theologica Xaveriana; Bogotá.

ThZ: Theologische Zeitschrift; Basel.

TJT: Toronto Journal of Theology; Toronto.

T&K: Texte und Kontexte; Stu.

TLS: Times Literary Supplement; L.

TOTC: Tyndale Old Testament Commentaries; L.

Tr.: Traditio; NY.

Trinity Journal; Deerfield, IL.

TS: Theological Studies; Wsh.

TSAJ: Texte und Studien zum antiken Judentum; Tü.

TS(I): Terra santa; J.

TSTP: Tübinger Studien zur Theologie und Philosophie; Mainz.

TTE: The Theological Educator; New Orleans.

TTh: Tijdschrift voor theologie; Nijmegen.

TThZ: Trierer theologische Zeitschrift; Trier.

TTK: Tidsskrift for teologi og kirke; Oslo.

TVOA: Testi del Vicino Oriente antico; Brescia.

Tychique; Lyon.

TynB: Tyndale Bulletin; C.

TyV: Teología y vida; Santiago de Chile.

UBS: United Bible Societies; L.

UF: Ugarit-Forschungen; Neuk.

Umat Baru; Yogyakarta, Indonesia.

Una Voce-Korrespondenz; Köln.

USQR: Union Seminary Quarterly Review; NY.

UTB: Uni-Taschenbücher; Heid.

VDI: Vestnik drevnej istorii. Journal of Ancient History; Moskva.

VetChr: Vetera christianorum; Bari.

VF: Verkündigung und Forschung; Mü.

Vie Chrétienne; P.

Vie, La: des communautés religieuses; Montréal.

VigChr: Vigiliae Christianae; Amst.

Vita Sociale; F.

Vivarium; Catanzaro.

Vivens Homo; F.

VJTR: Vidyajyoti Journal of Theological Reflection; Delhi.

VL: Vetus Latina; FrB.

VLAR: Veröffentlichungen der Luther-Akademie Ratzeburg; Erlangen.

VM: Vita monastica; R.

VoxScr: Vox Scripturae; São Paulo.

VS: Vie spirituelle; P.

VT: Vetus Testamentum; Lei.

—S: Supplement; Lei.

Way, The; L.

WBC: Word Biblical Commentary; Waco.

WCC: World Council of Churches; Geneva.

WiWei: Wissenschaft und Weisheit; FrB.

WLQ: Wisconsin Lutheran Quarterly; Milwaukee.

WMANT: Wissenschaftliche Monographien zum Alten und Neuen Testament; Neuk.

Worship; ColMn.

WStB: Wuppertaler Studienbibel; Wu.

WThJ: Westminster Theological Journal; Ph.

WuA(M): Wort und Antwort; Mainz.

WuD: Wort und Dienst; Bielefeld.

WUNT: Wissenschaftliche Untersuchungen zum Neuen Testament; Tü.

WWorld: Word and World; St. Paul.

ZAH: Zeitschrift für Althebraistik; Stu.

ZARBG: Zeitschrift für altorientalische und biblische Rechtsgeschichte; Wsb.

ZAW: Zeitschrift für die alttestamentliche Wissenschaft; B.

ZBK: Zürcher Bibelkommentare; Z.

ZDPV: Zeitschrift des Deutschen Palästina-Vereins; Wsb.

ZID: Zeitschrifteninhaltsdienst Theologie; Tü.

ZKG: Zeitschrift für Kirchengeschichte; Stu.

ZKTh: Zeitschrift für katholische Theologie; Innsbruck.

ZMR: Zeitschrift für Missionswissenschaft und Religionswissenschaft; Müns.

ZNW: Zeitschrift für die neutestamentliche Wissenschaft und die Kunde der älteren Kirche; B.

ZPE: Zeitschrift für Papyrologie und Epigraphik; Bonn.

ZSRG.K: Zeitschrift der Savigny-Stiftung für Rechtsgeschichte, Kanonistische Abteilung; Weimar.

ZThK: Zeitschrift für Theologie und Kirche; Tü.

Bibliographica

A1 *Opera collecta* .1 **Festschriften**, memorials

1 AHLSTRÖM, Gösta W.: The pitcher is broken: memorial essays for Gösta W. Ahlström, ᴱHolloway, Steven W.; Handy, Lowell K.: JSOT.S 190: Shf 1995, Academic 474 pp. £45/$68. 1-85075-525-6.

2 ATKINSON, James: The Bible, the Reformation and the Church: essays in honour of James Atkinson, ᴱStephens, W.P.: JSNT.S 105: Shf 1995, Academic. 340 pp. 1-85075-502-7.

3 BARTA, Winfried: Gedenkschrift für Winfried Barta, ᴱKessler, Dieter; Schulz, Regine: Münchener ägyptologische Untersuchungen 4: Fra 1995, Lang. 3-631-48366-X.

4 BEAUCHAMP, Paul: Ouvrir les écritures: mélanges offerts à Paul Beauchamp à l'occasion de ses soixante-dix ans, ᴱBovati, Pietro; Meynet, Roland: LeDiv 162: P 1995, Cerf. 435 pp. 2-204-05231-0.

5 BECKER Jürgen: Annäherungen: zur urchristlichen Theologiegeschichte und zum Umgang mit ihren Quellen: ausgewählte Aufsätze zum 60. Geburtstag mit einer Bibliographie des Verfassers, ᴱMell, Ulrich: BZNW 76: B 1995, De Gruyter xii; 496 pp. DM178. 3-11-014551-0.

6 BEKER, Johan Christiaan: Biblical theology: problems and perspectives: in honor of J. Christiaan Beker, ᴱOllenburger, Ben C.; Myers, Charles D.; Kraftchick, Steven J.: Nv 1995, Abingdon. 336 pp. portrait. $20. 0-687-03386-1 [OTA 19,522].

7 BULCKENS, Josef: Geloeven als toekomst: Godsdienstpedagogische visies en bijdragen aangeboden aan Professor...bij zijn emeritaat, ᴱLeijssen, L.; Lombaerts, H.; Roebben, B.: Lv 1995, Acco. 640 pp. [EThL 72/2-3, 13*].

8 DONNER, Herbert: Meilenstein: Festgabe für Herbert Donner zum 16. Februar 1995, ᴱWeippert, Manfred: ÄAT 30: Wsb 1995, Harrassowitz. xviii; 361 pp. 3-447-03713-X.

9 EMERTON, John A.: Wisdom in ancient Israel: essays in honour of J.A. Emerton, ᴱDay, John; Gordon, Robert P.; Williamson, H.G.M.: C 1995, CUP xiii; 311 pp. £37.50. 0-521-42013-X.

10 FREEDMAN, David Noel: Fortunate the eyes that see: essays in honor of David Noel Freedman in celebration of his seventieth birthday, ᴱBeck, Astrid B.; Bartelt, Andrew H.; Raabe, Paul R.; Franke, Chris A.: GR 1995, Eerdmans. xx; 672 pp. $45. 0-8028-0790-9.

11 GREENFIELD, Jonas C.: Solving riddles and untying knots: biblical, epigraphic, and Semitic studies in honor of Jonas C. Greenfield,

ᴱZevit, Ziony; Gitin, Seymour; Sokoloff, Michael: WL 1995, Eisenbrauns. xxxiv; 668 pp. portrait, $49.50. 0-931464-93-5.

12 HAMRICK, Emmett Willard: The Yahweh/Baal confrontation and other studies in biblical literature and archaeology: essays in honour of Emmett Willard Hamrick, ᴱO'Brien, Julia M.; Horton, Fred L.: SBEC 35: Lewiston 1995, Mellen. xii; 180 pp. photograph, 0-7734-2426-1.

13 HARL, Marguerite, KATA TOUS O': selon les Septante: trente études sur la Bible grecque des Septante, ᴱDorival, Gilles; Munnich, Olivier: P 1995, Cerf 539 pp. En hommage à Marguerite Harl; photograph. FF450. 2-204-05-75-X.

14 HARTMAN, Lars: Texts and contexts: biblical texts in their textual and situational contexts: essays in honor of Lars Hartman, ᴱFornberg, Tord; Hellholm, David: Oslo 1995, Scandinavian University Press. xxix; 1070 pp. 82-00-22446-5.

15 HEINEMANN, Heribert: Theologia et Jus Canonicum: Festgabe für Heribert Heinemann zur Vollendung seines 70. Lebensjahres. ᴱReinhardt, Heinrich J.F., Essen 1995, Ludgerus xii; 641 pp. port. 3-87497-204-6.

16 HENNESSY, J. Basil: Trade, contact, and the movement of peoples in the eastern Mediterranean: studies in honour of J. Basil Hennessy, ᴱBourke, Stephen; Descoeudres, Jean-Paul: Mediterranean Archaeology Supplement 3: Sydney 1995, Southwood. xix; 339 pp. 0-86758-944-2.

17 JERVELL, Jacob: Mighty minorities?: minorities in early christianity—positions and strategies: essays in honour of Jacob Jervell on his 70th birthday 21 May 1995, ᴱHellholm, David; Moxnes, Halvor; Seim, Turid K.: Oslo 1995, Scandinavian University Press. 242 pp.

18 LIPINSKI, Edward: Immigration and emigration within the ancient Near East, ᴱVan Lerberghe, Karel: OLA 65: Lv 1995, Peeters. xxv; 458 pp. 90-6831-727-X.

19 MATTIOLI, Anselmo: In spiritu et veritate: miscellanea di studi offerti al P. Anselmo Mattioli in occasione del suo 81º anno di età <Italian>, ᴱVolpi, Isidoro: R 1995, Conferenza Italiana Ministri Provinciali Cappuccini Commissione per la Cultura. 718 pp.

20 MEEKS, Wayne A.: The social world of the first Christians: essays in honor of Wayne A. Meeks, ᴱWhite, Michael; Yarbrough, O. Larry: Mp 1995, Fortress. xxix; 418 pp. $54. 0-8006-2585-4.

21 MILGROM, Jacob: Pomegranates and golden bells: studies in biblical, Jewish, and Near Eastern ritual, law, and literature in honor of Jacob Milgrom, ᴱWright, David P.; Freedman, David Noel; Hurvitz, A.: WL 1995, Eisenbrauns. xxxii; 861 pp. $59.50. 0-931464-87-0.

22 RENAUD, Bernard: Ce Dieu qui vient: études sur l'Ancien et le Nouveau Testament offerts au Professeur Bernard Renaud à l'occasion de son soixante-cinquième anniversaire, ᴱKuntzmann, Raymond: LeDiv 159: P 1995, Cerf. 422 pp. 2-204-05083-0.

23 ROGERSON, John: The Bible in human society: essays in honour of John Rogerson, ᴱCarroll R., M. Daniel: JSOT.S 200: Shf 1995, JSOT. 479 pp. 1-85075-568-X <pb>.

24 SAWYER, John F.A.: Words remembered, texts renewed: essays in honour of John F.A. Sawyer, ᴱDavies, John; Harvey, Graham; Watson, Wilfred G.E.: JSOT.S 195: Shf 1995, Academic. 1-85075-542-6.

25 SCHNEIDER Theodor, Vorgeschmack; ökumenische Bemühungen um die Eucharistie. ᴱHilberath, Bernd J; Sattler, Dorothea. Mainz 1995, Grünewald 643 pp. DM58. 3-7867-1837-7 [ThR 91,365].

26 SCHNEIDER, W.: Narrative and comment: contributions to discourse grammar and biblical Hebrew. ᴱTalstra, Eep. Kampen 1995, Kok Pharos. ƒ46.50/£18.20. 90-390-0117-0.

27 SERVOTTE, Herman: Herinnering en hoop: Herman Servotte aangeboden door de universitaire parochie van de K.U. Leuven, ᴱMichiels, R.; Schwall, H.: Averbode 1995, Altiora. 420 pp.

28 SIXDENIER, Guy Dominique: New Samaritan Studies of the Société d'Études Samaritaines III & IV, ᴱCrown, Alan David; Davey, Lucy: SJ(NY) 5: Sydney 1995, Mandelbaum; University of Sydney. 618 pp. Essays in Honour of G.D. Sixdenier; proceedings of the congresses of Oxford 1990, Yarnton Manor and Paris 1992, Collège de France with lectures given at Hong Kong 1993 as participation in the ICANAS Congress. 0-86758-980-9 <pb>.

29 STEGMANN, Franz Josef: Glaube in Politik und Zeitgeschichte: Festschrift für Franz Josef Stegmann zum 65. Geburtstag, ᴱGiegel, G.; Langhorst, P.; Remele, K.: Pd 1995, Schöningh. 328 pp. [EThL 72/2-3, 11*].

30 STRECKER, Georg: Bilanz und Perspektiven gegenwärtiger Auslegung des Neuen Testaments: Symposion zum 65. Geburtstag von Georg Strecker, ᴱHorn, Friedrich W.: BZNW 75: B 1995, De Gruyter. 288 pp. 3-11-014505-7.

31 STROBEL, August: Zurück zu den Anfängen: Beiträge und Schriftenverzeichnis von Professor Dr. August Strobel, ᴱKraus, Wolfgang: Fürth 1995, Flacius-Verlag. 94 pp. Zum 65. Geburtstag. 3-924022-36-4 [RB 103, 119].

32 STUDER, Basil: Mysterium Christi: Symbolgegenwart und theologische Bedeutung: Festschrift für Basil Studer, ᴱLöhrer, M.; Salmann, E.: StAns 116: R 1995, Pontificio Ateneo S. Anselmo. 403 pp. [EThL 72/2-3, 13*].

33 THOMA, Clemens: Tempelkult und Tempelzerstörung (70 n.Chr.): Festschrift für Clemens Thoma zum 60. Geburtstag , ᴱLauer, Simon: JudChr 15: Fra 1995, Lang. 265 pp. 3-906753-46-8.

34 THRAEDE, Klaus, Panchaia: Festschrift für Klaus Thraede. ᴱWacht, Manfred. JAC.E 22. Müns 1995, Aschendorff. 260 pp. port. 3-402-08106-7.

35 TILLARD, Jean-Marie Roger: Communion et réunion: mélanges Jean-Marie Roger Tillard, ᴱEvans, Gillian R.; Gourgues, Michel: BEThL 121: Lv 1995, University Press. xi; 431 pp. 90-6186-699-5.

36 TUCKER, Gene M.: Old Testament interpretation: past, present and future: essays in honour of Gene M. Tucker, ᴱMays, James L.; Petersen, David L.; Richards, Kent H.: OTSt: E 1995, Clark. 304 pp. $20. 0-567-29289-4 <pb>.

37 WAGNER, Siegfried: Von Gott reden: Beiträge zur Theologie und Exegese des Alten Testaments: Festschrift für Siegfried Wagner zum 65. Geburtstag, ᴱVieweger, Dieter: Neuk 1995, Neuk. 307 pp. ill. DM98. 3-7887-1562-6 <pb>.

A1.2 **Miscellanea** *unius* auctoris

38 **Bammel, Caroline P.** Tradition and exegesis in early christian writers. L 1995, Variorum xii; 312 pp. $87.50.

39 **Barrett, Charles K.**, Jesus and the word: and other essays. E 1995, Clark. x; 276 pp. 0-567-29306-8.

40 **Bovon, François**, New Testament traditions and apocryphal narratives. ^T*Haapiseva-Hunter, Jane:* PTMS 36. Allison Park 1995, Pickwick x; 256 pp. $35. 1-55635-024-4. [RB 103, 117].

41 **Brueggemann, Walter**, The Psalms and the life of faith. ^E*Miller, Patrick D.*, Mp 1995, Fortress xviii; 292 pp. $18. 0-8006-2733-4 <pb>.

42 **Clines, David J.A.**, Interested parties: the ideology of writers and readers of the Hebrew Bible. JSOT.S 205; Gender, culture, theory 1. Shf 1995, JSOT 296 pp. 1-85075-570-1/-748-8.

43 **Crenshaw, James L.** Urgent advice and probing questions: collected writings on Old Testament wisdom. Macon, GA 1995, Mercer University Press xiii; 605 pp. $60. 0-86554-483-2.

44 **Dautzenberg, Gerhard** Studien zur Theologie der Jesustradition. SBAB 19. Stu 1995, Kath. Bibelwerk. xi; 423 pp. 3-460-06191-X.

45 **Derrett, J. Duncan M.** Jesus among biblical exegetes. Studies in the New Testament 6. Lei 1995, Brill. x; 251 pp. $80.75. 90-04-10228-0 [RStR 22,66].

46 **Ebach, Jürgen** Hiobs Post: gesammelte Aufsätze zum Hiobbuch zu Themen biblischer Theologie und zur Methodik der Exegese. Neuk 1995, Neuk v; 219 pp. DM68. 3-7887-1486-7.

47 **Evans, Craig A.** Jesus and his contemporaries: comparative studies. AGJU 25. Lei 1995, Brill xiii; 532 pp. $131.50. 90-04-10279-5. ^RCritRR 8 (1995) 399-401 (*Moser, Paul K.*).

48 **Fossum, Jarl E.** The image of the invisible God: essays on the influence of Jewish mysticism on early christology. NTOA 30. FrS/Gö 1995, Universitätsverlag; Vandenhoeck & R 181 pp. 3-7278-1002-5/3-525-53932-0.

49 **Greenberg, Moshe**, Studies in the Bible and Jewish thought. JPS Scholar of distinction series. Ph 1995, Jewish Publication Society of America. xviii; 462 pp. 1 portrait. 0-8276-0504-8.

50 **Hengel, Martin** Studies in early christology. E 1995, Clark xix; 402 pp. 0-567-09705-6.

51 **Hoffmann, Paul** Tradition und Situation: Studien zur Jesusüberlieferung in der Logienquelle und den synoptischen Evangelien. NTA 28. Müns 1995, Aschendorff vii; 390 pp. DM93. 3-402-04776-4.

52 **Hübner, Hans** Biblische Theologie als Hermeneutik: gesammelte Aufsätze. ^E*Labahn, Antje; Labahn, Michael.* Gö 1995, Vandenhoeck & Ruprecht 310 pp. 3-525-53635-6.

53 **Kremer, Jacob** Die Bibel beim Wort genommen: Beiträge zu Exegese und Theologie des Neuen Testaments. ^E*Kühschwelm, Roman; Stowasser, Martin.* FrB 1995, Herder 496 pp. DM88. 3-451-23649-4 <pb>.

54 **Lohfink, Norbert** Studien zum Deuteronomium und zur deuteronomistischen Literatur 3. SBAB.AT 20. Stu 1995, Katholisches Bibelwerk 303 pp. DM79. 3-460-06201-0.

55 **Marböck, Johannes** Gottes Weisheit unter uns: zur Theologie des Buches Sirach. ^E*Fischer, Irmtraud*, Herders Biblische Studien 6. FrB 1995, Herder xi; 196 pp. DM78. 3-451-23744-X.

56 **McKane, William** A late harvest: reflections on the Old Testament. E 1995, Clark x; 182 pp. £20. 0-567-09727-7.

57 **Perlitt, Lothar,** Allein mit dem Wort: theologische Studien, ESpieckermann, Hermann. Gö 1995, Vandenhoeck & Ruprecht 370 pp. 3-525-53634-8.

58 **Stendahl, Krister** Paolo tra ebrei e pagani: e altri saggi. ERibet, Paolo. Piccola collana moderna 74. T 1995, Claudiana 165 pp. 88-7016-206-0.

59 **Talmon, Shemaryahu,** Israels Gedankenwelt in der hebräischen Bibel: gesammelte Aufsätze 3. InfJud 13. Neuk 1995, Neuk viii; 280 pp. DM88. 3-7887-1425-5 [ZAW 108,156].

60 **Thüsing, Wilhelm,** Studien zur neutestamentlichen Theologie, ESöding, Thomas: WUNT 2/82. Tü 1995, Mohr viii; 327 pp. 3-16-146337-4.

A1.3 *Plurium compilationes* biblicae

61 E**Beckwith, Roger T.; Selman, Martin J.,** Sacrifice in the Bible. Carlisle/GR 1995, Paternoster/Baker xii; 186 pp. $18. 0-85364-611-2/0-8010-2044-1 <pb> [NTAb 40,162].

62 E**Bellis, Alice Ogden** Many voices: multicultural responses to the Minor Prophets. Lanham 1995, University Press of America 101 pp. 0-8191-9836-6.

63 **Bianchi, Enzo,** (al.), Il mistero e il ministero della koinonia. PSV 31. Bo 1995, EDB 317 pp.

64 E**Blanchard, Yves-Marie,** Evangelio y reino de Dios. CuaBi 84. Estella 1995, Verbo Divino 68 pp. Ptas575. 84-8169-021-X <pb> [NTAb 40,162].

65 E**Bodine, Walter R.** Discourse analysis of biblical literature: what it is and what it offers. SBL Semeia Studies. Atlanta, Ga. 1995, Scholars x; 264 pp. 0-7885-0010-4/-11-2.

66 E**Bommarius, Alexander** Fand die Auferstehung wirklich statt?: eine Diskussion mit Gerd LUEDEMANN. Dü 1995, Parega 123 pp. 3-930450-04-6.

67 E**Borgen, Peder; Giversen, Søren** The New Testament and Hellenistic Judaism. Aarhus 1995, Aarhus University Press 293 pp. DKR288/$38. 87-7288-458-4.

68 E**Brenner, Athalya** A feminist companion to the latter prophets. The Feminist Companion to the Bible 8. Shf 1995, Academic 384 pp. £16.50; $24.50. 1-85075-515-9 <pb>.

69 E**Brenner, Athalya** A feminist companion to wisdom literature. The Feminist Companion to the Bible 9. Shf 1995, Academic 264 pp. £16.50; $24.50. 1-85075-735-6 <pb>.

70 E**Büchmann, Christina; Spiegel, Celina** Out of the garden: women writers on the Bible. L 1995, Pandora 352 pp. £10. 0-04-440933-8 <pb>.

71 **Caron, Gérald,** (al.), Des femmes aussi faisaient route avec lui: perspectives féministes sur la Bible. Sciences Bibliques: Études/Instruments 1. Montréal 1995, Médiaspaul 230 pp. [EThL 72,10*].

72 E**Charlesworth, James** Qumran questions. BiSe 36. Shf 1995, JSOT 210 pp. 1-85075-770-4.

73 E**Chauvin, Danièle** La Bible, images, mythes et traditions. P 1995, Albin Michel 243 pp.

74 ᴱCipriani, Settimio La lettera ai Romani ieri e oggi. Epifania della Parola 2. Bo 1995, Dehoniane 141 pp. L17.000. 88-10-40228-6 <pb>.

75 ᴱCousin, Hugues La Pâque et le passage de la mer dans les lectures, juives, chrétiennes et musulmanes (Exode 12-14). CEv.S 92. P 1995, Cerf. FF50.

76 ᴱDirksen, Piet B.; Van der Kooij, Arie, The Peshitta as a translation: papers read at the II Peshitta Symposium, held at Leiden, 19-21 August 1993. MPIL 8. Lei 1995, Brill. 240 pp. ƒ131.50/$85. 90-04-10351-1.

77 ᴱDohmen, Christoph; Söding, Thomas Eine Bibel — zwei Testamente: Positionen biblischer Theologie. UTB 1893. Pd 1995, Schöningh 318 pp. DM28.80. 3-506-99471-9.

78 ᴱEbach, Jürgen; Faber, Richard, Bibel und Literatur. Mü 1995, Fink 304 pp. DM48. 3-7705-2974-X <pb>.

79 ᴱEdelman, Diana Vikander The triumph of Elohim: from Yahwisms to Judaisms. Contributions to Biblical Exegesis and Theology 13. Kampen 1995, Kok Pharos 262 pp. 90-390-0124-3.

80 ᴱEsler, Philip Modelling early christianity: social-scientific studies of the New Testament in its context. L 1995, Routledge xv; 349 pp. 0-415-12980-X.

81 ᴱEvans, Craig A.; Porter, Stanley E. The synoptic gospels: a Sheffield reader. BiSe 31. Shf 1995, Academic 313 pp. 1-85075-732-1.

82 ᴱFinan, Thomas; Twomey, Vincent Scriptural interpretation in the Fathers: letter and spirit. Dublin 1995, Four Courts xi; 370 pp. IEP35. 1-85182-162-7.

83 ᴱGordon, Robert P. 'The place is too small for us': the Israelite prophets in recent scholarship. Sources for Biblical and Theological Study 5. WL 1995, Eisenbrauns xviii; 638 pp. 1-57506-000-0.

84 ᴱGourgues, Michel; Laberge, Léo, "De bien des manières": la recherche biblique aux abords du XXIe siècle: actes du cinquantenaire de l'ACEBAC (1943-1993). LeDiv 163. P 1995, Cerf 491 pp. 2-204-01592-6.

85 ᴱGreen, Joel B. Hearing the New Testament: strategies for interpretation. Carlisle/GR 1995, Paternoster/Eerdmans xvi; 439 pp. £16. 0-85364-687-2 (Paternoster).

86 ᴱGroß, Walter Jeremia und die 'deuteronomistische Bewegung'. BBB 98. Weinheim 1995, Beltz Athenäum 397 pp. DM98. 3-89547-068-6.

87 ᴱHaase, Wolfgang Religion: vorkonstantinisches Christentum: Neues Testament. ANRW II,226/2. B 1995, De Gruyter xiv; 816-1933 pp. 3-11-010371-0.

88 ᴱHeubach, Joachim "Ich bin der Herr, dein Gott": das erste Gebot in säkularisierter Zeit. LAR 24. Erlangen 1995, Martin Luther 134 pp. 3-87513-095-2.

89 ᴱHolmgren, Fredrick C., Preaching biblical texts: expositions by Jewish and christian scholars. GR 1995, Eerdmans xvii; 166 pp. 0-8028-0814-X.

90 ᴱHolt, Else K.; Lundager Jensen, Hans J.; Jeppesen, Knud Lov og visdom. Fredriksberg 1995, Anis 104 pp.

91 ᴱJonge, H.J. de; Ruyter, B.W.J. de Totdat hij komt: een discussie over de wederkomst van Jezus Christus. Baarn 1995, Ten Have 138 pp. 90-259-4575-9.

92 ᴱKeck, Leander E.; Petersen, David L.; Long, Thomas G., (al.), General articles on the New Testament, the gospel of Matthew, the

gospel of Mark. NIntB 8. Nv 1995, Abingdon xviii; 744 pp. 0-687-27821-X;

93   The gospel of Luke, the gospel of John. NIntB 9. Nv 1995, Abingdon xviii; 875 pp. 0-687-27822-8.

94   EKloppenborg, John S. Conflict and invention: literary, rhetorical, and social studies on the sayings gospel Q. Valley Forge, Pa. 1995, Trinity ix; 245 pp. $16. 1-56338-123-0.

95   EKrodel, Gerhard The general letters: Hebrews, James, 1-2 Peter, Jude, 1-2-3 John. Proclamation Commentaries. Mp 1995, Fortress xiv; 154 pp. $10. 0-8006-2895-0 [NTAb 40,155].

96   ELorenzani, Massimo, Gli anziani nella bibbia. Studio Biblico Teologico Aquilano 14. L'Aquila 1995, ISSRA xiii; 260 pp.

97   LOGOS: Corso di Studi Biblici 3. Leumann (T) 1995, Elle Di Ci 459 pp. L55.000. 88-01-10472-3. RLASBF 45 (1995) 586-590 (Cortese, Enzo).

98   EMays, James Luther; Achtemeier, Paul J. Interpreting the prophets. Ph 1995, Fortress 336 pp. £13. 0-8006-1932-3.

99   EMoor, Johannes C. de, Synchronic or diachronic?: a debate on method in Old Testament exegesis. OTS 34. Lei 1995, Brill viii; 255 pp. $93.75. 90-04-10342-2.

100 ENiccacci, Alviero, Divine promises to the fathers in the three monotheistic religions. Proceedings of a symposium held in Jerusalem, March 24-25th, 1993. ASBF 40. J 1995, Franciscan Printing Press 220 pp. $25.

101 EPiper, Ronald A. The gospel behind the gospels: current studies on Q. NT.S 75. Lei 1995, Brill xii; 411 pp. $114.50. 90-04-09737-6.

102 EPorter, Stanley E.; Carson, D.A. Discourse analysis and other topics in Biblical Greek. JSNT.S 113. Shf 1995, Academic 227 pp. 1-85075-545-0.

103 EPorter, Stanley E.; Evans, Craig A. The historical Jesus: a reader. BiSe 33. Shf 1995 <1990>, Academic 314 pp. 1-85075-731-3.

104 EPorter, Stanley E.; Evans, Craig A. The Johannine writings. BiSe 34. Shf 1995, Academic 300 pp. £12/$18. 1-85075-729-1 [NTAb 40,147].

105 EPorter, Stanley E.; Evans, Craig A. The Pauline writings. BiSe 34. Shf 1995, Academic 300 pp. £11.95/$18. 1-85075-730-5 [NTAb 40,157].

106 EPorter, Stanley E.; Tombs, David Approaches to New Testament study. JSNT.S 120. Shf 1995, Academic 392 pp. £43. 1-85075-567-1.

107 EReventlow, Henning Graf; Farmer, William Biblical studies and the shifting of paradigms 1850-1914. JSOT.S 192. Shf 1995, Academic 297 pp. $45. 1-85075-532-9.

108 ERichter, Klemens; Kranemann, Benedikt Christologie der Liturgie: der Gottesdienst der Kirche—Christusbekenntnis und Sinaibund. QD 159. FrB 1995, Herder 300 pp. DM48. 3-451-02159-5. <pb>.

109 ERogerson, John William; Davies, Margaret; Carroll R., M. Daniel The Bible in ethics. The second Sheffield Colloquium. JSOT.S 207. Shf 1995, Academic 379 pp. 0-85075-573-6.

110 ERosner, Brian S. Understanding Paul's ethics: twentieth century approaches. GR/Carlisle 1995, Eerdmans/Paternoster xiii; 377 pp. $22. 0-8028-0749-6/0-85364-618-X [NTAb 40,360].

111 ᴱSatterthwaite, Philip E., The Lord's anointed: interpretation of Old Testament messianic texts. Tyndale House Studies. Carlisle 1995, Paternoster x; 320 pp. 0-85364-685-6.

112 ᴱSegovia, Fernando F.; Tolbert, Mary A., Social location and biblical interpretation in the United States. Reading from this place I. Mp 1995, Fortress xiv; 321 pp. 0-8006-2812-8. [OTA 19,524].

113 ᴱSegovia, Fernando F.; Tolbert, Mary A., Social location and biblical interpretation in global perspective. Reading from this place II. Mp 1995, Fortress xv; 365 pp. 0-8006-2949-3. [OTA 19,524].

114 ᴱSmith-Christopher, Daniel, Text and experience: towards a cultural exegesis of the Bible. BiSe 35. Shf 1995, JSOT 354 pp. 1-85075-740-2.

115 ᴱStanton, Graham N. The interpretation of Matthew. Studies in New Testament Interpretation. E ²1995 <1983 ⇒64,4229>, Clark xiv; 219 pp. $20. 0-567-29255-X [NTAb 40,349].

116 ᴱTelford, William R. The interpretation of Mark. Studies in New Testament Interpretation. E ²1995, Clark xiv; 342 pp. $26. 0-567-29256-8.

117 ᴱTrublet, Jacques La sagesse biblique: de l'Ancien au Nouveau Testament. Actes du XVᵉ Congrès de l'ACFEB. LeDiv 160. P 1995, Cerf. 617 pp. FF245. 2-204-05153-5.

118 ᴱVerweyen, Hansjürgen Osterglaube ohne Auferstehung? Diskussion mit Gerd LUEDEMANN. QD 155. Fr/B 1995, Herder 144 pp. DM38. 3-451-02155-2 <pb>.

119 ᴱWilkins, Michael J.; Moreland, J.P. Jesus under fire: modern scholarship reinvents the historical Jesus. GR 1995, Zondervan ix; 243 pp. $17. 0-310-61700-6.

A1.4 *Plurium compilationes* theologicae

120 Forschungsstelle Judentum a.d. Theol. Fak. Leipzig, Mitteilungen und Beiträge 9. Leipzig 1995, Thomas. 3-86174-044-3.

121 ᴱJohnstone, William, William Robertson SMITH: essays in reassessment. JSOT.S 189. Shf 1995, JSOT 403 pp. 1-85075-523-X.

122 ᴱKasper, Walter, Dämon bis Fragmentenstreit. LThK 3. FrB 1995³, Herder 1378 pp. 3-451-22003-2.

123 ᴱKasper, Walter, Franca bis Hermenegild. LThK 4. FrB 1995³, Herder 1450 pp. 3-451-22004-0.

124 ᴱLe Boulluec, Alain, La controverse religieuse et ses formes. Patrimoines. P 1995, Cerf 424 pp. [EThL 72,13*].

125 ᴱMiller, David L. JUNG and the interpretation of the Bible. NY 1995, Continuum 143 pp. 0-8264-0809-5.

126 Origeniana Sexta: ORIGENE et la Bible / ORIGEN and the Bible. ᴱDorival, Gilles; Le Boulluec, Alain. BEThL 118. Lv 1995, Peeters xii; 865 pp. Actes du Colloquium Origenianum Sextum, Chantilly, 30 août - 3 septembre 1993. 90-6180-718-5.

127 ᴱSasson, Jack M.; Baines, John; Beckman, Gary, Civilizations of the ancient Near East. NY 1995, Charles Scribner's Sons. 4 vols. 0-684-19279-9.

128 ᴱSchneider, Theodor Geschieden—Wiederverheiratet—Abgewiesen? Antworten der Theologie. QD 157; Schriften der Europäischen Gesellschaft für Katholische Theologie 2. FrB 1995, Herder 448 pp. DM68. 3-451-02157-9 <pb>.

129 ᴱSugirtharajah, R.S., Voices from the margin: interpreting the Bible in the third world. Mkn ²1995 <1991>, Orbis x; 484 pp. 1-57075-046-7 <pb>.

130 ᴱVan der Horst, Pieter W., Aspects of religious contact and conflict in the ancient world. Utrechtse Theologische Reeks 31. Utrecht 1995, Faculteit der Godgeleerdheid. 166 pp. 90-72235-32-0.

A1.5 *Plurium compilationes* philologicae *vel* archaeologicae

131 Arav, Rami; Freund, Richard A. Bethsaida: a city by the north shore of the Sea of Galilee. The Bethsaida Excavations Project Reports and Contextual Studies 1. Kirksville, Missouri 1995, Jefferson. 0-943549-30-2/-37-X.

132 García Martínez, Florentino; Trebolle Barrera, Julio The people of the Dead Sea Scrolls: their writings, beliefs and practices. Lei 1995, Brill x; 270 pp. ƒ74.50/$47.50. 90-04-10085-7.

A2 Acta *congressuum* .1 biblica

133 Actes du Quatrième Colloque International Bible et informatique: 'Matériel et matière': Amsterdam 15-18 août 1994: l'impact de l'informatique sur les études bibliques. Travaux de linguistique quantitative 57. P 1995, Champion-Slatkine 496 pp. 2-85203-508-1.

134 ᴱBeuken, Willem A.M. The book of Job. BEThL 114. Lv 1994, Peeters x; 462 pp. FB2.400. 90-6831-652-4. ᴿEThL 71 (1995) 209-210 *(Lust, J.)*.
ᴱDirksen, Piet B. *(al.)* The Peshitta as a translation ⇒76.
ᴱDorival, Gilles *(al.)* Origeniana Sexta ⇒126.

135 ᴱEmerton, John A., Congress Volume: Paris 1992. VT.S 61. Lei 1995, Brill viii; 357 pp. International Organization for the Study of the Old Testament 14. Congress. ƒ198/$128. 90-04-10259-0.

136 ᴱGreenspoon, Leonard J.; Munnich, Olivier, VIII Congress of the International Organization for Septuagint and Cognate Studies Paris 1992. SBL.SCSt 41. Atlanta, GA 1995, Scholars xi; 401 pp. $55. 0-7885-0208-5 [CBQ 59, 415].

137 ᴱLovering, Eugene H., Society of Biblical Literature 1995 Seminar Papers: One Hundred Thirty-First Annual Meeting November 18-21, 1995 Philadelphia. SBL.SPS 34. Atlanta, GA 1995, Scholars ix; 721 pp. 0-7885-0156-9.
ᴱMoor, Johannes C. de Synchronic or diachronic? ⇒99.

138 ᴱPadovese, Luigi Atti del III Simposio di Tarso su S. Paolo Apostolo. Turchia: la Chiesa e la sua storia 9. R 1995, Pontificio Ateneo Antoniano 221 pp.

139 ᴱPadovese, Luigi Atti del V Simposio di Efeso su S. Giovanni Apostolo. Turchia: la Chiesa e la sua storia 8. R 1995, Pontificio Ateneo Antoniano vi; 247 pp.
ᴱRogerson, John W. *(al.)* The Bible in ethics: the second Sheffield Colloquium ⇒109.
ᴱTrublet, Jacques La sagesse biblique ⇒117.

Libri historici VT

E1 **Pentateuchus, Tora** .1 *Textus, commentarii*

140 **Antonelli, Judith S.**, In the image of God: a feminist commentary on the Torah. Northvale, NJ 1995, Aronson. xlviii; 558 pp. 1-56821-438-3.

141 **Boorer, Suzanne,** The promise of the land as oath. 1992. ⇒9,1729; 10,1580. RCBQ 57 (1995) 544-546 (*Dozeman, Thomas B.*).

142 *Borbone, Pier G.* Correspondences lexicales entre Peshitta et TM du Pentateuque: les racines verbales. The Peshitta. 1995 ⇒76. 1-16.

143 **Crüsemann, Frank,** Die Tora: Theologie und Sozialgeschichte. 1992. ⇒8,229...10,1581. RBiKi 50/3 (1995) 191-192 (*Schwendemann, Wilhelm*); EvErz 47 (1995) 107-109 (*Grünwaldt, Klaus*).

144 TFox, **Everett,** The five books of Moses: Genesis, Exodus, Leviticus, Numbers, Deuteronomy: a new translation with introduction, commentary, and notes. The Schocken Bible 1. Dallas 1995, Word xxxii; 1024 pp. 0-8052-4061-6.

145 **Hallo, William W.** The book of the people. ⇒7,1710...9,1731. 1991. RCritRR 7 (1994) 121-123 (*Chavalas, Mark W.*); JSSt 40 (1995) 105-108 (*Weinfeld, M.*).

146 EHaudebert, **P.,** Le pentateuque. LeDiv 151. 1992. ⇒8,474...10,1583. RMD 202 (1995) 137-139 (*Auneau, Joseph*).

147 EKeck, **Leander E.; Petersen, David L.; Long, Thomas G.,** General and Old Testament articles: Genesis, Exodus, Leviticus. NIntB 1. 1994. ⇒10,1575. RThTo 52 (1995) 406-410 (*Harrelson, Walter*).

148 *Maori, Yeshayahu* The peshitta version of the pentateuch and early Jewish exegesis. **H.** Perry Foundation...: Jerusalem 1995, Magnes; Hebrew University. 408 pp. 965-223-874-0. [JJS 48, 383].

149 *Tov, Emanuel,* 4QReworked Pentateuch: a synopsis of its contents. RdQ 16/4 (1995) 647-653.

E1 *Pentateuchus* .2 **Introduction; Fontes JEDP**

150 *Barthélemy, Dominique,* Les traditions anciennes de division du texte biblique de la Torah. ⇒13. FHARL, M., 1995, 27-51.

151 *Blenkinsopp, Joseph,* Introduction to the Pentateuch. ⇒147. NIntB 1, 1994, 305-318.

152 *Blenkinsopp, Joseph,* P and J in Genesis 1:1-11:26: an alternative hypothesis. ⇒10. FFREEDMAN D, 1995, 1-15.

153 *David, Robert,* Le pentateuque: tendances actuelles concernant les traditions littéraires. ⇒84. De bien des manières. 17-46.

154 *Dirksen, Piet B.*, Some aspects of the translation technique in P-Chronicles. 1995 ⇒76. The Peshitta. 17-23.

155 **Gleßmer, Uwe,** Einleitung in die Targume zum Pentateuch. TSAJ 48, Tü 1995, Mohr xv; 274 pp. DM138. 3-16-145818-4.

156 *Gnuse, Robert,* Dreams in the night—scholarly mirage or theophanic formula?: the dream report as a motif of the so-called elohist tradition. BZ 39 (1995) 28-53.

157 **Houtman, Cees** Der Pentateuch: die Geschichte seiner Erforschung neben einer Auswertung. ⇒10,1584. 1994. REeT(O) 26 (1995) 257-258 (*Laberge, Léo*); JETh 9 (1995) 153-155 (*Dreytza, Manfred*).

158 **Krapf, T.M.**, Die Priesterschrift und die vorexilische Zeit: Yehez-kiel KAUFMANNS vernachlässigter Beitrag zur Geschichte der bibli-schen Religion. ⟹8,1971...10,1604. 1992. ᴿOTEs 8 (1995) 307-308 (*Tonder, C.A.P. van*).

159 **Levin, Christoph,** Der Jahwist. ⟹9,1747; 10,1591. 1993. ᴿThLZ 120 (1995) 786-790 (*Blum, Erhard*); CBQ 57 (1995) 354-355 (*Carr, David M.*).

160 *Otto, Eckart,* Gesetzesfortschreibung und Pentateuchredaktion. ZAW 107 (1995) 373-392.

161 *Otto, Eckart,* Kritik der Pentateuchkomposition (E. Blum / A.F. Campbell + M.A. O'Brien / C. Levin). ThR 60 (1995) 163-191.

162 *Petersen, David L.,* The formation of the pentateuch. ⟹36. ᶠTUCKER, G., 1995. 31-45.

163 *Rendtorff, Rolf,* El paradigma del pentateuco està cambiando: te-nuoses y esperanzas. ᵀᴱ*Sala, Márius.* SelTeol 34 (1995) 301-311 [sum. of Bibl.Interp. 1 (1993) 34-53].

164 **Schmidt, Ludwig,** Studien zur Priesterschrift. 1993 ⟹10,1608. ᴿOTEs 8 (1995) 147-149 (*Wittenberg, G.H.*); CritRR 8 (1995) 148-149 (*Rendtorff, Rolf*).

165 *Schmidt, Ludwig,* Zur Entstehung des Pentateuch. VF 40/1 (1995) 3-28.

166 **Schmitt, Chr.**, Die Suche nach der Identität des Jahweglaubens im nachexilischen Israel: Bemerkungen zur theologischen Intention der Endredaktion des Pentateuch. Pluralismus und Identität. Veröffentli-chungen der Wissenschaftlichen Gesellschaft für Theologie 8. Gü 1995, Kaiser/Gütersloher Verlagshaus. 0-8006-2733-4. 259-278. [ZAW 108, 318].

167 **Seidel, Bodo,** Karl David ILGEN und die Pentateuchforschung im Umkreis der sogenannten älteren Urkundenhypothese: Studien zur Geschichte der exegetischen Hermeneutik in der späten Aufklärung. Habil.-Diss. ⟹9,1755. B 1993, De Gruyter xii; 363 pp. DM158. ᴿCBQ 57 (1995) 790-791 (*Rogerson, J.W.*); CritRR 8 (1995) 150 (*Lemche, Niels P.*).

168 *Ska, Jean Louis,* De la relative indépendance de l'écrit sacerdotal. Bib. 76 (1995) 396-415. [Exod 12; Num 16; 17].

169 *Steins, Georg,* Elohist. ⟹122. LThK 3. 608-609.

170 **Van Seters, John,** Prologue to history: the Yahwist as historian in Genesis. 1992. ⟹8,1977...10,1611. ᴿBiOr 52/1-2 (1995) 105-107 (*Deurloo, K.A.*); JBL 114 (1995) 127-128 (*Kaminsky, Joel S.*); CBQ 57 (1995) 579-580 (*Thompson, Thomas L.*); ABR 43 (1995) 78-81 (*O'Brien, Mark A.*).

171 **Whybray, R. Norman,** Introduction to the Pentateuch. GR 1995, Eerdmans vii; 146 pp. $12.99. 0-8028-0837-9.

172 **Whybray, R. Norman,** El Pentateuco: estudio metodológico. Bibli-coteca Manuales Desclée 7. Bilbao 1995, Desclée 265 pp. 84-330-1105-7.

E1.3 *Pentateuchus*, **Themata**.

173 **Alexander, T. Desmond,** From paradise to the promised land: an introduction to the main themes of the Pentateuch. Carlisle 1995, Paternoster xxv; 227 pp. £9.99. 0-85364-647-3 [BoL 1996,71].

174 *Beyers, J.; Breytenbach, A.P.B.*, 'n vergelykende studie tussen 'n gedeelte uit die Samaritaanse liturgie en werwante gedeeltes in die Penteug [A comparison between an excerpt from the Samaritan liturgy and corresponding passages in the pentateuch]. HTS 51 (1995) 900-930 [OTA 19, 219].

175 *Clines, David J.A.*, God in the Pentateuch: reading against the grain. ⇒42. Interested parties. 1995. 187-211.

176 *Cortese, Enzo*, Promises and blessings for Jews and Arabs in the Pentateuch. ⇒100. Divine promises to the fathers. 1995. 28-46.

177 **Eskenazi, Tamara C.**, Torah as narrative and narrative as torah. ⇒36. ᶠTUCKER G., 1995. 13-30.

178 *Fanuli, Antonio*, Interessi e disposizioni di un anziano nel pentateuco: i patriarchi, Mosè. ⇒96. Gli anziani nella Bibbia. 1995. 69-92.

179 **Graupner, A.; Delkurt, H.; Ernst, A.B.**, Studien zur Hermeneutik und Methodik: Pentateuch und Prophetie. Vielfalt und Einheit alttestamentlichen Glaubens I. Neuk 1995, Neuk viii; 256 pp. DM68 [ZAW 108, 153].

180 *Greenberg, Moshe*, Three conceptions of the torah in Hebrew scriptures. Studies ⇒49. 1995. 11-24.

181 **Grünwaldt, Klaus**, Exil und Identität: Beschneidung, Passa und Sabbat in der Priesterschrift. BBB 85. ⇒8,1984; 9,1762, 1992. Diss. ᴿZABR 1 (1995) 155-159 (*Gertz, Jan C.*); JBL 114 (1995) 493-495 (*VanderKam, James C.*).

182 **Jenson, P.P.**, Graded holiness...P. ⇒8,1988...10,1603. 1992. ᴿJSSt 40 (1995) 111 (*Budd, P.J.*).

183 *Köckert, Matthias*, Das Land in der priesterlichen Komposition des Pentateuch. ⇒37. ᶠWAGNER, S. 1995. 147-162.

184 **Phillips, Judith A.**, The concept of the holy in the Pentateuch and its implications toward wholeness of being and ethical conduct. Diss. ᴰLeaver, V. Wayne. Walden 1995. 287 pp. AAC 9526510; DAI-A 56,1401.

185 **Pola, Thomas**, Die ursprüngliche Priesterschrift: Beobachtungen zur Literarkritik und Traditionsgeschichte von Pᵍ. WMANT 70. Neuk 1995, Neuk 445 pp. 3-7887-1503-0.

186 *Sacchi, Paolo*, Le pentateuque, le deutéronomiste et SPINOZA. Congress Volume: Paris 1992. VT.S 61. 1995. 275-288.

187 *Ska, Jean Louis*, L'istituzione degli 'anziani' nel pentateuco. ⇒96. Gli anziani nella Bibbia. 1995. 49-67.

188 *Talmon, Shemaryahu*, Hat es ein israelitisches Nationalepos gegeben? ⇒59. Israels Gedankenwelt. InfJud 13. 1995 <1981>. 82-103.

189 *Watts, James*, Rhetorical strategy in the composition of the pentateuch. JSOT 68 (1995) 3-22.

190 *Watts, James W.*, Public readings and Pentateuchal law. VT 45 (1995) 540-557.

E1.4 **Genesis**; *Textus, commentarii.*

191 *Asendorf, Ulrich*, LUTHERS Genesisvorlesung als Paradigma christlicher Weltverantwortung [Luther's lectures on Genesis as paradigm of Christian responsibility in the world]. Luther Digest 3 (1995) 2-5 [Cf. Christentum und Weltverantwortung 19 (1992) 71-94].

192 **Bianchi, E.**, Adamo, dove sei?: commento esegetico-spirituale ai capitoli 1-11 del libro della Genesis. ⇒10,1660. 1994. [R]NRTh 177 (1995) 267-268 *(Ska, Jean Louis)*.

193 **Boecker, Hans Jochen** 1.Mose 25,12-37,1: Isaak und Jakob. 1992. ⇒8,2409...10,1614. [R]ThLZ 120 (1995) 989-990 *(Seidel, Hans)*.

194 **Edele, Blaine A.**, A critical edition of Genesis in Ethiopic. Diss. [D]*Peters, Melvin K. H.; Wintermute, Orval S.*, Duke 1995. 278 pp. [AAC 9606440; DAI-A 56,4428].

195 *Fretheim, Terence E.*, The book of Genesis: introduction, commentary, and reflections. ⇒147. NIntB 1. 1994. 319-674.

196 **Hamilton, Victor P.**, The book of Genesis: chapters 18-50. NIC.OT. GR 1995, Eerdmans xx; 774 pp. $42. 0-8028-2308-4.

197 **Jagersma, H.**, Genesis 1:1-25:11. Verklaring van de Hebreeuwse Bijbel. Nijkerk 1995, Callenbach 288 pp. f44.90. 90-266-0363-0.

198 **Kamesar, Adam,** JEROME, Greek scholarship and the Hebrew bible: a study of the Quaestiones Hebraicae in Genesim. ⇒9,1777; 10,1622. 1993. [R]Orph. 16 (1995) 182-187 *(Sanfilippo, Antonino)*; JSSt 40 (1995) 153-154 *(Langer, Ruth)*; Latomus 54 (1995) 894-897 *(Dorival, G.)*.

199 **Knobloch, Frederick W.**, Hebrew sounds in Greek script: transcriptions and related phenomena in the Septuagint, with special focus on Genesis. Diss. [D]*Tigay, Jeffrey H.*, Pennsylvania 1995, 652 pp. [AAC 9532222; DAI-A 56,1829].

200 [T]**Korsak, Mary Phil,** At the start: Genesis made new: a translation of the Hebrew text. ⇒8,2008...10,1623. 1993. [R]JSSt 40 (1995) 108-109 *(Yudkin, Leon I.)*; AUSS 33/1 (1995) 125-126 *(Running, Leona Glidden)*.

201 *Lienhard, Marc,* LUTHER et sa conception de l'homme: regards sur le Commentaire de la Genèse (1535 à 1545). [Luther and his concept of humanity: observations on the Genesis Commentary (1535 to 1545)]. Luther Digest 3 (1995) 32-34.

202 **Mathews, Kenneth A.**, Genesis 1-11. NAC 1A. Nv 1995, Broadman & Holman 528 pp. 0-8054-0101-6.

203 **Neri, Umberto,** Genesi: versione ufficiale italiana confrontata con ebraico masoretico, greco dei Settanta, siriaco della Peshitta, latino della Vulgata: commenti de autori greci...siriaci...latini...BIBLIA AT 1. Bo 1995, EDB cxlvi; 662 pp. L94.000. 88-10-2058-0.

204 *Puech, Émile,* Un autre manuscrit de la Genèse récemment identifié dans les fragments de la grotte 4 (4QGn[n]). RdQ 16 (1995) 637-640 [34,7-10; 50,3].

205 *Qimron, Elisha; Sivan, Daniel; Bearman, Gregory; Spiro, Sheila,* The hitherto unpublished columns of the Genesis Apocryphon. Abr-n. 33 (1995) 30-54.

206 **Ravasi, Gianfranco,** El libro del Génesis (1-11). ⇒8,2014; 9,1781. 1992. [R]Isidorianum 4 (1995) 283-284 *(Flor, Gonzalo)*.

207 **Ravasi, Gianfranco,** El libro del Génesis (12-50). [T]*Villanueva Salas, Marciano.* Guía Espiritual del Antiguo Testamento. Barc/M 1994, Herder/Ciudad Nueva 310 pp. 84-254-1869-0. [R]Isidorianum 4 (1995) 283-284 *(Flor, Gonzalo)*; Comunidades 24 (1995) 155-156 *(Huarte Osácar, J.)*.

208 **Rösel, Martin,** Übersetzung als Vollendung der Auslegung: Studien zur Genesis Septuaginta. ⇒9,1594; 10,1551. Diss. [D]*Koch, Klaus.* BZAW 223. 1994. [R]CBQ 57 (1995) 784-785 *(Laberge, Léo)*.

209 *Rösel, Martin*, Übersetzung als Vollendung der Auslegung: Studien zur Genesis-Septuaginta. BIOSCS 28 (1995) 42-50 [Sum. <⇒208].
210 ^ET^**Rottzoli, Dirk U.**, Rabbinischer Kommentar zum Buch Genesis: Darstellung der Rezeption des Buches Genesis in Mischna und Talmud unter Angabe targumischer und midraschischer Paralleltexte. ⇒10,1629. SJ 14. 1994. ^R^CBQ 57 (1995) 574-576 (*Basser, H.W.*).
211 **Ruppert, Lothar**, Genesis: 1. Teilband: Gen 1,1-11,26. ⇒8,2015...10,1630. FzB 70. 1992. ^R^EstB 53 (1995) 132-134 (*Arambarri, J.*); RevBib 57 (1995) 58-63 (*Levoratti, A.J.*).
212 *Ruppert, Lothar*, Genesis. LThK 4. ⇒123. 453-454.
213 ^E^**Savoca, Gaetano**, Traduzione interlineare della Genesi sul testo della BHS. ^T^*Di Marco, A. Salvatore* (al.). Messina 1995, ACCT 280 pp. L26.000.
214 **Souzenelle, Annick de**, Alliance de feu: une lecture chrétienne du texte hébreu de la Genèse 1. La bibliothèque spirituelle 3. P 1995, Michel 781 pp. 2-226-07737-5 [NThAR 1996/3,54].
215 *Ter Haar Romeny, R.B.*, Techniques of translation and transmission in the earliest text forms of the Syriac version of Genesis. 1995 ⇒76. The Peshitta. MPIL 8. 177-185.
216 **Westermann, Claus**, Genesis: an introduction. ^T^*Scullion, John J.*, Mp 1992, Fortress viii; 278 pp. Can$15.50; U.S.$12.95. ^R^TJT 11/1 (1995) 87-88 (*Harvey, John E.*).
217 **Westermann, Claus**, Genesi. Theologica. CasM 1995, Piemme 340 pp. 88-384-2009-2.
218 **Wevers, John William**, Notes on the Greek text of Genesis. ⇒9,1786; 10,1636. SCSt 35. 1993. ^R^JR 75/1 (1995) 103-104 (*Hendel, Ronald S.*); ThRv 91 (1995) 310-311 (*Schenker, Adrian*); EThL 71 (1995) 446-447 (*Lust, J.*); JAOS 115 (1995) 721 (*Taylor, Bernard A.*).

E1.5 *Genesis*, **Themata**.

219 *Alexander, T. Desmond*, Messianic ideology in the book of Genesis. ⇒111. The Lord's anointed. 1995. 19-39.
220 *Bailey, Randall C.*, They're nothing but incestuous bastards: the polemical use of sex and sexuality in Hebrew canon narratives. 1995 ⇒112. Reading from this place 1. 121-138 [Gen 12; 20; 26; 19; 9] [OTA 19,406].
221 *Castiñeiras González, Manuel Antonio*, Cycles de la Genèse et calendriers dans l'art roman hispanique: à propos du portail de l'église de Beleña del Sorbe (Guadalajara). CCMéd38 (1995) 307-317.
222 *Davies, Philip R.*, Making it: creation and contradiction in Genesis. ⇒23. ^F^ROGERSON, J., JSOT.S 200. 1995. 249-256 [Gen 1-3].
223 *Derousseaux, Louis*, Commencements: Genèse dans le Nouveau Testament. Graphè 4 (1995) 59-70.
224 **Feuillet, André**, Histoire du salut de l'humanité d'après les premiers chapitres de la Genèse. P 1995, Téqui 96 pp. FF40 [EeV 106,103].
225 ^TE^**Hayward, C.T.R.**, JEROME'S Hebrew questions on Genesis: translated with an introduction and commentary. Ox 1995, OUP xiii; 274 pp. £35. 0-19-826350-3.
226 *Hendel, Ronald S.*, Tangled plots in Genesis. ⇒10. ^F^FREEDMAN, D., 1995. 35-51.

227 **Isabelle de la Source, Soeur,** La Genèse. Lire la Bible avec les Pères 1. P 1995, Médiaspaul. FF66. 2-7122-0305-4.

228 *Johnson, Michael,* From cosmogony to cartography in Genesis 1-13. ProcGLM 15 (1995) 93-112.

229 *Longacre, R.E.,* Genesis as soap opera: some observations about storytelling in the Hebrew bible. JTrTL 7/1 (1995) 1ff [ZID 21,309].

230 *Maraval, Pierre,* "Midi": variations sur un symbole. 1995 ⇒13. FHARL, M., 463-471.

231 *Perlitt, Lothar,* Die Urgeschichte im Werk Gottfried BENNS. ⇒57. Allein mit dem Wort. 1995. 333-360.

232 **Rashkow, Ilona N.,** The phallacy of Genesis: a feminist-psychoanalytic approach. ⇒9,1345; 10,1652. 1993. RTJT 11/1 (1995) 86-87 (*Isaac, Jacqueline R.*);   PSB 16 (1995) 365-366 (*Greenstein, Edward L.*); CBQ 57 (1995) 365-366 (*Williams, James G.*); Bibl.Interp. 3/1 (1995) 116-118 (*Brenner, Athalya*).

233 **Steinberg, Naomi,** Kinship and marriage in Genesis: a household economic perspective. 1993. ⇒9,1799. RCBQ 57 (1995) 791-792 (*Matthews, Victor H.*).

234 **Syrén, Roger,** The forsaken first-born: a study of a recurrent motif in the patriarchal narratives. ⇒9,1801; 10,1654. JSOT.S 133. 1993. RETR 70 (1995) 424-425 (*Römer, Thomas*); JBL 114 (1995) 297-299 (*Ackerman, James S.*).

235 *Wittenberg, G.H.,* Wisdom influences on Genesis 2-11: a contribution to the debate about the 'Yahwistic' primeval history. OTEs 8 (1995) 439-457 [sum. 439].

236 **Wolde, Ellen J. van,** Verhalen over het begin: Genesis 1-11 en andere scheppingsverhalen. Baarn 1995, Ten Have. 275 pp. 90-259-4596-1.

237 **Zornberg, Avivah Gottlieb,** Genesis: the beginning of desire. Philadelphia 1995, Jewish Publication Society of America xix; 456 pp. $34.95. 0-8276-0521-8.

E1.6   **Creatio,** *Genesis 1s..*

238 **Arteaga Natividad, Rodolfo,** La creación en los comentarios de San Agustin al Génesis. ⇒10,1658. 1994. RLat. 61 (1995) 229-230 (*Sanna, Ignazio*); RevAg 36 (1995) 1124-1126 (*Sepulcre, Jaime*).

239 *Baranzke, H.; Lamberty-Zielinski, H.,* Lynn WHITE und das dominium terrae (Gen 1,28b): ein Beitrag zu einer doppelten Wirkungsgeschichte. BN 76 (1995) 32-61.

240 *Bescond, Lucien,* Saint AUGUSTIN: lecteur et interprète de la 'Genèse'. Graphè 4 (1995) 47-57.

241 *Borgen, Pederer A.,* Man's sovereignty over animals and nature according to PHILO of Alexandria. ⇒14. FHARTMAN L. 1995. 369-389.

242 EBørresen, Kari E. Image of God. ⇒7,472. 1991. RCritRR 7 (1994) 528-530 (*Dowd, Sharyn*).

243 **Bossard, Franz; Bossard, Paul,** Die Welt als Gottes Schöpfung: neue Beurteilung des biblischen Schöpfungsberichtes nach den Erfahrungen eines Patentanwaltes und eines Pfarrers. Stein am Rhein 1995, Christiana. 80 pp. DM13. [KiHe 4,36].

244 *Boulogne, Jacques,* La pensée du commencement en Genèse: HESIODE et PLATON. Graphè 4 (1995) 33-46.

245 Bröker, Werner; Lüke, Ulrich, Erschaffung des Menschen. ⇒122. LThK 3. 825-827.

246 **Brown, William P.**, Structure, role, and ideology in the Hebrew and Greek texts of Genesis 1:1-2:3. ⇒9,1810; 10,1664. SBL.DS 132. 1993. RCBQ 57 (1995) 120-121 (Michael, Tony S.L.).

247 EColzani, Gianni, Creazione e male del cosmo: scandalo per l'uomo e sfida per il credente. Padova 1995, Messaggero 195 pp. Associazione Teologica Italiana: studio teologico fiorentino.

248 **Dassmann, Ernst**, "Als Mann und Frau erschuf er sie": Gen 1,27c im Verständnis der Kirchenväter. ⇒34. FTHRAEDE K., JAC.E 22. 1995. 45-60.

249 Dines, Jennifer, Imaging creation: the Septuagint translation of Genesis 1:2. HeyJ 36 (1995) 439-450.

250 Dubuisson, Daniel, Pourquoi et comment parle-t-on des origines?. Graphè 4 (1995) 19-31.

251 Ernst, Josef, Gottesebenbildlichkeit: Neues Testament. ⇒123. LThK 4. 1995. 873-874.

252 Festorazzi, Franco, Il racconto della creazione in Gen 1-2. 1995 ⇒267. Dizionario di spiritualità biblico-patristica 10, 71-82.

253 Gibert, Pierre, Fermeture et ouverture d'un corpus: la multiplicité des textes bibliques de création. Graphè 4 (1995) 11-18.

254 Gross, Walter, Gottesebenbildlichkeit: Altes Testament. ⇒123. LThK 4. 1995. 871-873.

255 **Haag, Herbert**, Am Morgen der Zeit: das Hohelied der Schöpfung: mit Fotografien von Werner Richter. Solothurn 1995, Benziger 119 pp. 3-545-33147-4 [Gen 1-2; Ps 113; 2 Cor 5,17].

256 **Haffner, Paul**, Mystery of creation. Leonminster 1995, Gracewing xvi; 224 pp. £13. 0-85244-316-1.

257 Hart, I., Genesis 1:1-2:3 as a prologue to the book of Genesis. TynB 46 (1995) 315-336.

258 **Jaki, Stanley L.**, Genesis 1. ⇒8,2049...10,1672. 1992. RGr. 76 (1995) 759-760 (Haffner, Paul); CBQ 57 (1995) 140-141 (Patton, Corrine L.).

259 Jaki, Stanley L., The sabbath-rest of the maker of all. AsbTJ 50/1 (1995) 37-49.

260 Kirchschläger, Walter, Ordnung als theologische Bewältigung des Chaos. ThPQ 143 (1995) 279-284.

261 Lefebvre, Philippe, Les mots de la Septante ont-ils trois dimensions? φωστῆρας εἰς ἀρχὰς (Gn 1,16). ⇒13. FHARL, M. Selon les Septante. 1995. 299-320.

262 **Louyot, Yves**, L'homme clefs en mains: relecture pédagogique des sept jours de la Genèse. Saint Maurice 1995 <1890>, Saint-Augustin 230 pp. 2-88011-031-9 [EeV 106,288].

263 **May, Gerhard**, Creatio ex nihilo: the doctrine of "creation out of nothing" in early christian thought. ⇒10,1677. 1994. RVigChr 49 (1995) 306-307 (Winden, J.C.M. van).

264 Müller, Hans-Peter, Neue Parallelen zu Gen 2,7: zur Bedeutung der Religionsgeschichte für die Exegese des Alten Testaments. ⇒18. FLIPINSKI E., OLA 65. 1995. 195-204.

265 O'Loughlin, Thomas, 'The waters above the heavens': Isidore and the Latin tradition. MillSt 36 (1995) 104-117 [Gen 1,7].

266 **Och, Bernard**, Creation and redemption: towards a theology of creation. Jud. 44 (1995) 226-243.

267 ^EPanimolle, Salvatore A., Creazione uomo-donna: nella Bibbia e nel giudaismo antico. Dizionario di spiritualità biblico-patristica 10. R 1995, Borla 184 pp. 88-263-1071-8.

268 *Sharp, Donald B.*, A biblical foundation for an environmental theology: a new perspective on Genesis 1:26-28 and 6:11-13. ScEs 47 (1995) 305-313.

269 **Simkins, Ronald A.**, Creator and creation: nature in the worldview of ancient Israel. ⇒10,1685. 1994. ^ROCP 61 (1995) 588-590 (*Farrugia, E.G.*); NRTh 117 (1995) 903-904 (*Ska, Jean Louis*).

270 **Sousan, André**, Une aide qui correspond à Abel: la création de la femme dans la Genèse. Diss. 1995 Lausanne [BuBbgB 19,9].

271 *Speyer, Wolfgang*, Die Erschaffung von Meer und Erde: Gen 1,9f.13 und DRACONTIUS, De laudibus dei 1,149-166. Religionsgeschichtliche Studien. ^ESpeyer, Wolfgang. Collectanea 15. Hildesheim 1995, Olms. 3-487-09993-4. 152-162.

272 *Strolz, Walter*, Schöpfung als Urbejahung: was sich aus der jüdischen Schriftauslegung lernen läßt. HerKorr 49 (1995) 155-159.

273 *Talmon, Shemaryahu*. Das biblische Verständnis der Schöpfung. ⇒59. Israels Gedankenwelt. InfJud 13. 1995 <1987>. 119-148.

274 **Thomas, Anne**, Only fellow-voyagers: creation stories as guides for the journey. L 1995, Quaker Home Service & Woodbrooke College 145 pp. Swarthmore Lecture 1995. 0-85245-272-1.

275 ^TThomson, Robert W., BASILIUS Caesariensis: the Syriac version of the Hexaemeron. CSCO.S 222-223; CSCO 550-551. Lv 1995, Peeters. 2 volumes. 90-6831-704-0; -705-9.

276 **Tsumura, David T.**, The earth and the waters in Genesis 1 and 2: a linguistic investigation. ⇒5,1978...10,1698. JSOT.S 83. 1989. ^RBiOr 52/1-2 (1995) 107-109 (*Cook, Johann*).

277 *Vannier, Marie-Anne*, ORIGENE et AUGUSTIN, interprètes de la création. ⇒126. Origeniana Sexta. BEThL 118. 1995. 723-736.

278 *Wächter, L.*, Was bedeutet der Herrschaftsauftrag des Menschen von Genesis 1,26-28 im Kontext biblischer Botschaft?. "Macht euch die Erde untertan": Sinn und Problematik eines Bibelwortes. Texte aus der VELDK 60 (1995) 5-27 [ZAW 108,308].

279 ^EWetzel, Christoph, Die Schöpfungsgeschichte nacherzählt in Bildern aus der Biblioteca Apostolica Vaticana: Erläuterungen von...: Stu 1995, Belser 47 pp. DM29.80. 3-7630-5787-0 [ThRv 91,448].

E1.7   *Genesis 1s*: Bible and myth.

280 **Batto, Bernard F.**, Slaying the dragon: mythmaking in the biblical tradition. ⇒9,1867; 10,1716. 1992. ^RJR 75/1 (1995) 102 (*Roberts, J.J.M.*).

281 **Bauks, Michaela**, Die Welt am Anfang: zum Verhältnis von Vorwelt und Weltentstehung in Gen 1 und in der altorientalischen Literatur. Diss. ^D*Janowski*. 1995 Heidelberg. [ThRv 92,ix].

282 **Blumenthal, Elke**, (*al.*), Weisheitstexte, Mythen und Epen: Mythen und Epen 3. Texte aus der Umwelt des Alten Testaments 3/5. Gü 1995, Gü'er 870-1087. 3-579-00082-9.

283 **Callender, Dexter Eugene, Jr.**, The significance and use of primal man traditions in ancient Israel. Diss. ^D*Hackett, Jo Ann*. Harvard 1995. 276 pp. [AAC 9539073; DAI-A 56,2726].

284 **Clifford, Richard J.**, Creation accounts in the ancient Near East and in the Bible. ⇒10,1721*. CBQ.MS 26. 1994. ᴿThLZ 120 (1995) 984-985 (*Neumann, Thomas*).

285 **Diakonoff, Igor M.**, Archaic myths of the orient and the occident. Orientalia Gothoburgensia 10. Göteborg 1995, Acta Universitatis Gothoburgensis 216 pp.

286 *Esterhammer, Angela*, From fiat to 'thou shalt not': reflections on Genesis, romanticism, and language. History of European Ideas 20 (1995) 699-705.

287 *Görg, Manfred*, "Chaos" in ägyptischen und biblischen Kosmogonien. ⇒3. ᴹBARTA W., Münchener ägyptologische Untersuchungen 4. 1995. 159-163.

288 *Lee, Archie C.C.*, The Chinese creation myth of Nu Kua and the biblical narrative in Genesis I-II. ⇒129. Voices from the margin. 1995 <1991>. 368-380.

289 **Pitzele, Peter**, Our fathers' wells: a personal encounter with the myths of Genesis. SF 1995, HarperSanFrancisco 228 pp. $22.

290 **Rohl, David M.**, The bible: from myth to history. A test of time 1. L 1995, Century, Random House iii; 425 pp. 0-7126-5913-7.

291 **Walker, Steven F.**, JUNG and the Jungians on myth: an introduction. Theorists of Myth 4. NY 1995, Garland xiii; 198 pp. 0-8240-3443-0.

E1.8   *Gen 1s, Jos 10,13...*: **The Bible, the Church, Science**.

292 *Alvarez Valdés, A.* Existieron Adán y Eva? Didascalia 5 (1995) 17-21 [Strom. 52,344].

293 **Ganoczy,   Alexandre,**   Chaos—Zufall—Schöpfungsglaube: die Chaostheorie als Herausforderung der Theologie. Mainz 1995, Grünwald 238 pp. [LebZeug 52,310].

294 ᴱGready, Jill, God, cosmos, nature and creativity. E 1995, Scottish Academic Press vii; 102 pp. The Templeton Lectures. £9.95. 0-7073-0745-7. ET 107 (1995-96) 59 (*Polkinghorne, John*).

295 **Haught, John F.**, Science and religion: from conflict to conversation. Mahwah 1995, Paulist 225 pp. 0-8091-3606-6.

296 **Jori, Giacomo**, Le forme della creazione: sulla fortuna del "mondo creato" (secoli XVII e XVIII). BRSLR 6. F 1995, Olschki 159 pp. 88-222-4319-6.

297 **Kaiser, Christopher**, Creation and the history of science. ⇒8,2147...10,1813. 1991. ᴿSJTh 48 (1995) 104-106 (*Murray, Paul*).

298 **Mazhar, Noor Giovanni**, Catholic attitudes to evolution in nineteenth-century Italian literature. Venezia 1995, Istituto Veneto di Scienze, Lettere ed Arti. 284 pp. [Il Futuro dell'Uomo 23,81].

299 **Pelt, Jean-Marie**, Dieu de l'univers: sciences et foi. P 1995, Fayard. 287 pp. [EeV 106,447].

300 *Welker, Michael*, Creation: big bang or the work of seven days? ThTo 52 (1995) 173-187.

301 **Wiskin, Richard** Die Bibel und das Alter der Erde. Stu 1994, Hänssler 80 pp. 75 ill. ᴿJETh 9 (1995) 177-178 (*Pehlke, Helmuth*).

302 **Wright, M.R.**, Cosmology in antiquity. Sciences of Antiquity. L 1995, Routledge x; 201 pp. £40; £12.99 <pb>. 0-415-08372-9; -08183-3 [ClR 47,185].

E1.9 *Peccatum originale*, **The Sin of Eden**, *Genesis 2-3*

303 *Achtemeier, Elizabeth*, Genesis 3:1-34: the story of us all: a christian exposition of Genesis 3. 1995 ⇒89. Preaching biblical texts. 1-10.
304 *Alvarez Valdés, Ariel*, ¿El diablo y el demonio son lo mismo? RevBib 57/4 (1995) 231-238.
305 **Barnum, Thaddeus,** Remember Eve: how the deceiver works in the believer's life. DeBary, Fla. 1995, Longwood 210 pp. 1-883928-13-3.
306 **Barr, James,** The garden of Eden. ⇒9,1990; 10,1884. 1992. ᴿNew Theology Review 8 (1995) 91-92 *(Reid, Barbara)*.
307 **Barr, James,** Éden et la quête de l'immortalité. LiBi 107. P 1995, Cerf 208 pp. FF120. 2-204-05253-1.
308 **Basset, Lytta,** Le pardon originel: de l'abîme du mal au pouvoir de pardonner. LiTh 24. Genève 1995 <1994>, Labor et Fides 500 pp. 2-8309-0720-5.
309 *Baudry, Gérard-Henry*, Liturgie baptismale et péché originel. EeV 105 (1995) 513-525; 536-544.
310 *Baudry, Gérard-Henry*, A propos du péché originel: approches bibliques. EeV 105 (1995) 497-511.
311 *Beach, Eleanor Ferris; Pryor, Frederic L.*, How did Adam and Eve make a living? BiRe 11/2 (1995) 38-42.
312 *Bechtel, Lyn M.*, Genesis 2.4b-3.24: a myth about human maturation. JSOT 67 (1995) 3-26.
313 *Betz, Otto.* Der Garten und der Traum vom Paradies oder: Spuren des nie ganz verlorenen Paradieses. Symb. 12 (1995) 13-25.
314 **Callender, Dexter Eugene Jr.,** The significance and use of primal man traditions in ancient Israel. Diss. ᴰ*Hackett, Jo Ann*. Harvard 1995, 276 pp. DAI-A 56/07,2726.
315 *Cazier, Pierre*, Du serpent et de l'arbre de la connaissance: lectures patristiques (Philon, Grégoire de Nysse, Jean Chrysostome, Augustin). Graphè 4 (1995) 73-103.
316 **Delhez, Charles,** Satan. Que penser de...26. Namur 1995, Fidélité 48 pp. FF65. 0777-141X [RTL 27,254].
317 **Delumeau, Jean,** History of paradise: the garden of Eden in myth and tradition. ᵀ*O'Connell, Matthew*. NY 1995, Continuum x; 276 pp. map. ill.
318 **Drewermann, Eugen,** Le mal: approche psychanalytique du récit yahviste des origines I. P 1995, Desclée de Brouwer 480 pp. FF260. 2-220-03725-8.
319 **Gottfried, Robert R.,** Economics, ecology and the roots of western faith: perspectives from the garden. Lanham, MD 1995, Rowman and Littlefield 165 pp. $18.95.
320 **Jager, Eric,** The tempter's voice: language and fall in medieval literature. Ithaca, NY 1993, Cornell University Press xix; 336 pp. 7 black and white ill. $42.50. ᴿSpec. 70/3 (1995) 636-639 *(Besserman, Lawrence)*.
321 *Johnson, Victor James*, Illustrating evil: the effects of the fall as seen in Genesis 4-11. MJT 11/1-2 (1995) 69-84 [ThIK 18,64].
322 **Kempf, Stephen,** A discourse analysis of Genesis 2:4B-3:24 with implications for interpretation and Bible translation. Diss. ᴰ*Filteau, J.-Cl.*, Laval 1995. 1159 pp. [RTL 27,529].
323 *Kirchschläger, Walter*, Exorzismus: Biblisch. ⇒122. LThK 3. 1995. 1126-1127.

324 *Korsak, Mary Phil,* Eve, malignant or maligned?. CrossCur 44/4 (1994-95) 453-462.

325 **Lang, Bernhard,** DREWERMANN interprête de la Bible: le paradis; la naissance du Christ. ⇒10,1257. Théologies. 1994. ᴿCBQ 57/3 (1995) 560-561 (*Biddle, Mark E.*).

326 **Laurentin, René,** Il demonio: mito o realtà?. ᵀGalli, A., Segno 1995, Massimo 340 pp. L35.000. 88-7282-165-7.

327 **Loh, Johannes,** Mythenlogik als praktisch-theologische Herausforderung biblischer Texte: dargestellt am Paradiesmythos. Diss.-Habil. ᴰ*Schröer.* 1995 Bonn [ThRv 92,III].

328 *Luke, K.,* Original sin in Jewish tradition. BiBh 21/4 (1995) 219-235.

329 *Marks, Herbert,* Biblical naming and poetic etymology. JBL 114/1 (1995) 21-42.

330 *Mazor, Yair,* Scolding aesthetics in biblical literature. SJOT 9/2 (1995) 297-313 [Gen 3; 12; 2 Sam 11].

331 *Neumann, H.,* Political theology?: an interpretation of Genesis (3:5,22). Interpretation (Journal of Political Philosophy) 23 (1995-6) 77-87 [EThL 72,180*].

332 *Niclós, José Vicente,* Génesis 3 como relato de apropiación. EstB 53/2 (1995) 181-200.

333 **Page, Sydney H.T.,** Powers of evil: a biblical study of Satan. GR 1995, Baker 295 pp. $19.99. 0-8010-7137-2.

334 **Pagels, Elaine,** The origin of Satan. NY 1995, Random xi; 214 pp. $23. 0-679401-40-7.

335 *Papageorgiou, Panayiotis,* CHRYSOSTOM and AUGUSTINE on the sin of Adam and its consequences. SVTQ 39/4 (1995) 361-378.

336 **Pricoco, Salvatore,** Il demonio e i suoi complici: dottrine e credenze demonologiche nella tarda antichità. Armarium 6. Soveria Mannelli (Catanzaro) 1995, Rubbettino 321 pp. 88-7284-361-8.

337 *Ravasi, Gianfranco,* Comentarios herméneuticos a Génesis 2-3. ᵀ*Sala, Márius.* SelTeol 34 (1995) 313-320 [<Communio 20,294-304].

338 *Shimoff, Sandra R.,* Gardens: from Eden to Jerusalem. JSJ 26/2 (1995) 145-155.

339 *Stolz, Fritz,* Paradies II: Biblisch. TRE 25 (1995) 708-711.

340 **Stratton, Beverly J.,** Out of Eden: reading, rhetoric, and ideology in Genesis 2-3. Diss. Luther Seminary 1995. ᴰ*Fretheim, Terence.* JSOT.S 208. Shf 1995, Academic 292 pp. £50; $75. 1-85075-575-2 [BoL 1996,69].

341 **Suchocki, Marjorie Hewitt,** The fall to violence: original sin in relational theology. NY 1994, Continuum 168 pp. $18.95. ᴿCritRR 8 (1995) 512-514 (*Bechtel, Daniel R.*).

342 *Taisne, Geneviève de,* La relation pervertie: au regard de Genèse 3. Christus 42 (1995) 431-438.

343 *Theobald, Michael,* Erbsünde, Erbsündenlehre: der Befund der Schrift. ⇒122. LThK 3. 1995. 743-744.

344 *Tuohey, John F.,* The gender distinctions of primeval history and a christian sexual ethic. HeyJ 36 (1995) 173-189.

345 **Vaz, Armindo dos Santos,** A visão das origens em Gen 2,4b-3,24 como coeręncia temática e unidade literária. Diss. excerpt Pont. Univ. Gregoriana. ᴰ*Costacurta, Bruna.* Lisboa 1995, 212 pp.

346 *Ward, Graham,* A postmodern version of paradise. JSOT 65 (1995) 3-12.

347 *Willi-Plein, Ina,* Sprache als Schlüssel zur Schöpfung: Überlegungen
zur sogenannten Sündenfallgeschichte in Gen 3. ThZ 51 (1995) 1-17.
348 *Zhuo, Xinping,* Original sin in the east-west dialogue: a Chinese
view. Studies in World Christianity 1/1 (1995) 80-86 [ThIK 18,84].

E2.1 Cain et Abel; *gigantes, longaevi; Genesis 4s.*

349 *Álvarez, Ariel,* Caín y Abel, y el pecado original "social". T*Rosell,
Enrique.* SelTeol 34 (1995) 321-324 [< Cias 43,122-128].
350 **Böttrich, Christfried,** "Die Vögel des Himmels haben ihn begraben": Überlieferungen zu Abels Bestattung und zur Ätiologie des
Grabes. SIJD 3. Gö 1995, Vandenhoeck & Ruprecht 157 pp. 20 ill.
DM78. 3-525-54203-8.
351 **Boyer,** *Frédéric,* "Depuis le sang d'Abel..." fraternité, violence et
transcendance. ⇒4. F*Beauchamp,* P. Ouvrir les écritures. LeDiv
162. 1995. 53-64.
352 *Herion, Gary A.,* Why God rejected Cain's offering: the obvious
answer. ⇒10. F*Freedman* D., Fortunate the eyes that see. 1995.
52-65.
353 *Külling, S.R.,* Genesis 56: Teil: Gen 5,1ff. Fundamentum 1 (1995)
8-19 [OTA 19,47].
354 *Külling, S.R.,* Bibelerklärung: Genesis 57: Teil: Gen 5,1ff. Fundamentum 2 (1995) 11-16 [OTA 19,47].
355 *Külling, S.R.,* Genesis 58: Teil: Gen 5,1ff. Fundamentum 4/4 (1995)
13-17 [OTA 19,223].
356 *Manicardi, Luciano,* L'omicidio è un fratricidio (Gen 4,1-16). PSV
32 (1995) 11-26.
357 *O'Loughlin, Thomas,* The controversy over Methuselah's death:
proto-chronology and the origins of the western concept of inerrancy. RThAM 62/1 (1995) 182-225 [ZID 21,442].
358 *Plaut, Gunther,* Genesis 4:1-16: Cain and Abel: bible, tradition, and
contemporary reflection. 1995 ⇒89. Preaching biblical texts. 11-16.
359 *Vervenne, Marc,* All they need is love: once more Genesis 6.1-4.
⇒24. F*Sawyer* J., JSOT.S 195. 1995. 19-40.

E2.2 *Diluvium,* The Flood; Gilgameš (Atraḫasis); **Genesis 6...**

360 *Brooke, George J.,* 4Q253: a preliminary edition. JSSt 40/2 (1995)
227-239 [Gen 6-9; Mal 3,16-18].
361 *Davila, James R.,* The Flood hero as king and priest. JNES 54/3
(1995) 199-214.
362 *Findeis, Hans-Jürgen,* Heiden. ⇒123. LThK 4. 1995. 1252-1254.
363 *Gosse, Bernard,* Genèse 8,21 et le "parfum d'apaisement". NRTh
117 (1995) 885-889.
364 *Halpern, Baruch,* What they don't know won't hurt them: Genesis 6-
9. ⇒10. F*Freedman* D., Fortunate the eyes that see. 1995. 16-34.
365 *Hendel, Ronald S.,* 4Q252 and the Flood chronology of Genesis 7-8:
a text-critical solution. DSD 2/1 (1995) 72-79.
366 *Jackson, Jared Judd,* The ark and its making. HBT 17/2 (1995) 117-
122.
367 *Millard, Matthias,* Die rabbinischen noachidischen Gebote und das
biblische Gebot Gottes an Noah: ein Beitrag zur Methodendiskussion. WuD 23 (1995) 71-90.

368 *Schmidt, Brian,* Flood narratives of ancient western Asia. ⇒127. Civilizations...4. 1995. 2337-2351.
369 **Silva Castillo, Jorge,** Gilgamesh, o la angustia por la muerte (poema bibilonio). Mexico City ²1995, Colegio de México 226 pp. [JAOS 117,378].
370 *Singgih, E.G.,* Warum schickt Gott die Sintflut auf die Erde?: zum Verständnis der göttlichen Gewalt im Alten Testament [in Indonesian]. Gema 50 (1995) 1-17 [ThIK 18,45].
371 ᵀᴱTournay, **Raymond Jacques,** L'épopée de Gilgamesh. ⇒10,1989. LAPO 15. ᴿPOC 45/1-2 (1995) 293-294 (*Ternant, P.*).
372 *Vervenne, Marc,* What shall we do with the drunken sailor?: a critical re-examination of Genesis 9.20-27. JSOT 68 (1995) 33-55.
373 **Wiesel, Elie,** Noah oder ein neuer Anfang. Biblische Portraits. FrB 1994, Herder 200 pp. ᴿFrRu NF 2/2 (1995) 145-146 (*Winklehner, Herbert*); GuL 68/3 (1995) 239 (*Brunner, Stephan*).
374 **Young, Davis A.,** The biblical flood: a case study of the Church's response to extrabiblical evidence. GR 1995, Eerdmans xiii; 327 pp. $20. 0-8028-0719-8.

375 *Alvarez Valdés, A.,* La torre de Babel: ¿Cuál es su mensaje? Cias 44 (1995) 475-480 [Strom. 52,344].
376 *Beck, Mordechai,* Speaking in tongues. Parabola 20/3 (1995) 13-15.
377 *Farmer, Kathleen A.,* Genesis 11:1-9: what is "this" they begin to do? 1995 ⇒89. Preaching biblical texts. 17-28.
378 *Sherwin, Byron L.,* The tower of Babel. BiTod 33/2 (1995) 104-109.
379 *Walton, John H.,* The Mesopotamian background of the Tower of Babel account and its implications. Bulletin for Biblical Research 5 (1995) 155-175.

E2.3 Patriarchae, Abraham; *Genesis 12s.*

380 *Agourides, S.,* The religion of the Hebrew patriarchs. G. DBM 14/1 (1995) 5-17.
381 **Brueggemann, Walter,** The land: place as gift, promise and challenge in biblical faith. Overtures to biblical theology. Mp 1995, Fortress xviii; 203 pp. 0-8006-1526-3 [reprint].
382 *Cortese, Enzo,* Patriarchal genealogies: literary, historical and theologico-political criticism. ⇒100. Divine promises to the fathers. ASBF 40. 1995. 11-27.
383 *Davies, Philip R.,* Abraham & Yahweh: a case of male bonding. BiRe 11/4 (1995) 24-33, 44-45 [Gen 12,1-3].
384 *Drave, Elisabeth,* Strukturen jüdischer Bibelauslegung in Thomas MANNs Roman "Joseph und seine Brüder": das Beispiel Abraham. ⇒78. Bibel und Literatur. 1995. 195-213.
385 **Dreifuss, Gustav; Riemer, Judith,** Abraham: the man and the symbol: a Jungian interpretation of the biblical story. Wilmette, Ill 1995, Chiron ix; 148 pp. 0-933029-94-2.
386 *Egron, Agnès,* Abraham devant Dieu selon saint GREGOIRE de Nysse. VS 149 (1995) 433-441.
387 *Finney, Paul Corby,* Abraham and Isaac iconography on late-antique amulets and seals: the western evidence. 6 figures, plates 3/6. JAC 38 (1995) 140-166.
388 **Fischer, Irmtraud,** Die Erzeltern Israels: feministisch-theologische Studien zu Genesis 12-26. ⇒10,2027. BZAW 222. ᴿZKTh 117/1

(1995) 101 (*Bucher-Gillmayr, Susanne*).

389 *Fischer, Irmtraud,* Den Frauen der Kochtopf—den Männern die hohe Politik?: zum Klischee der Geschlechterrollen in der Bibelauslegung am Beispiel der Erzeltern-Erzählungen. CPB 108 (1995) 134-138.

390 *Gilbert, Maurice,* The divine promises to the patriarchs in the deuterocanonical books. ⇒100. Divine promises to the fathers. ASBF 40. 1995. 170-173.

391 *Goshen-Gottstein, Alon,* The promise to the patriarchs in rabbinic literature. ⇒100. Divine promises to the fathers. 1995. 60-97.

392 **Gossai, Hemchand,** Power and marginality in the Abraham narrative. NY 1995, University Press of America xiv; 221 pp. $52; $21 <pb>. 0-8191-9862-5 [OTA 18,632].

393 **Habel, Norman C.,** The land is mine: six biblical land ideologies. Foreword by Walter Brueggemann. Overtures to Biblical Theology. Mp 1995, Fortress xv; 190 pp. $12. 0-8006-2664-8 <pb>.

394 *Helyer, Larry R.,* Abraham's eight crises: the bumpy road to fulfilling God's promise of an heir. BiRe 11/ 5 (1995) 20-27, 44.

395 *Hendel, Ronald S.,* Finding historical memories in the patriarchal narratives. BArR 21/4 (1995) 52-59, 70.

396 *Kitchen, Kenneth A.,* The patriarchal age: myth or history? BArR 21/2 (1995) 48-57, 88.

397 *Kremer, Jacob.* Erscheinungen: Biblisch. ⇒122. LThK 3. 1995. 828-829.

398 *Kronholm, Tryggve,* Abraham the physician: the image of Abraham the patriarch in the genuine hymns of Ephraem Syrus. ⇒11. FGREENFIELD, J., 1995. 107-115.

399 *Lowe, Malcolm,* How were the divine promises to the patriarchs seen in the last decades of the second temple? ⇒100. Divine promises to the fathers. ASBF 40. 1995. 176-188.

400 *März, Klaus-Peter,* Eucharistie, Eucharistiefeier: Neutestamentlich. ⇒122. LThK 3. 1995. 944-946.

401 **Mason, Elizabeth Mary,** Literary reflections of God: the characterization of Yhwh in the Abrahamic saga. Diss. DPolzin, Robert. Carleton 1995, 176 pp. 0-612-02989-1 [MAI 34/03,988].

402 *Milgrom, Jacob,* Bible versus Babel. BiRe 11/2 (1995) 19 [Gen 12,1-3].

ENiccacci, Alviero, Divine promises to the fathers. ⇒100. ASBF 40. 1995.

403 *Noujaim, Halim; Goshen-Gottstein, Alon; Al-Mallah, Yassir,* Comments on the symposium on the divine promises. ⇒100. Divine promises to the fathers. 1995. 189-197.

404 **Pagolu, Augustine,** Patriarchal religion as portrayed in Genesis 12-50: comparison with ancient Near Eastern and later Israelite religions. Diss. DWenham, G.J., Open 1995 [abstract TynB 47/2 (1996) 375-378].

405 *Ruppert, Lothar,* "Zieh fort... in das Land, das ich dir zeigen werde" (Gn 12,1): der wegweisende und erscheinende Gott in Gn 12 und 13. ⇒22. FRENAUD, B., LeDiv 159. 1995. 69-94.

406 *Schenke, Ludger,* Exodus: Exodusmotiv I: Biblisch-historisch: Neues Testament. ⇒122. LThK 3. 1995. 1122-1123.

407 **Ségal, Abraham,** Abraham: enquête sur un patriarche. Le Doigt de Dieu. P 1995, Plon 425 pp. [RHPhR 77,197].

408 *Teugels, Lieve* A matriarchal cycle?: the portrayal of Isaac in Genesis in the light of the presentation of Rebekah. Bijdr. 56/1 (1995) 61-72.

409 *Weisman, Ze'ev,* Societal divergences in the patriarchal narratives. Henoch 17/1-2 (1995) 117-127.
410 *Zakovitch, Yair,* Juxtaposition in the Abraham cycle. ⇒21. FMILGROM, J., 1995. 509-524.

E2.4 Melchisedech, Sodoma; *Genesis 14...19.*

411 *Andersen, Francis I.,* Genesis 14: an enigma. ⇒21. FMILGROM, J., 1995. 497-508.
412 *Aschim, Anders,* Verdens eldste bibelkommentar? Melkisedek-teksten fra Qumran. TTK 66/2 (1995) 85-103.
413 *Manzi, Franco,* La figura di Melchisedek: saggio di bibliografia aggiornata. EL 109/4-5 (1995) 331-349.
414 *Soggin, J.A.,* Abraham and the eastern kings: on Genesis 14. ⇒11. FGREENFIELD, J., 1995. 283-291.
415 *Talmon, Shemaryahu,* rp'jm in der Bibel und rpu/i(m) im Ugaritischen. ⇒59. Israels Gedankenwelt. InfJud 13. 1995 <1983>. 104-118.

E2.5 The Covenant (alliance, Bund); *Foedus, Genesis 15...*

416 *Anderson, Bernhard W.,* Standing on God's promises: covenant and continuity in biblical theology. ⇒6. FBEKER, J., 1995. 145-154.
417 *Bartholomew, Craig G.,* Covenant and creation: covenant overload or covenantal deconstruction. CTJ 30/1 (1995) 11-33.
418 **Bennett, Stephen,** The Abrahamic covenant and the idea of mission. Diss. DCurtis. 1995 Manchester.
419 *Bouwen, Frans,* The divine promises: past, present and future. ⇒100. Divine promises to the fathers. ASBF 40. 1995. 201-204.
420 *Dubarle, André-Marie,* La nouvelle alliance et le Saint-Esprit. Revue d'éthique et de théologie morale 195 (1995) 153-166.
421 **Dumbrell, William J.,** Covenant and creation: a theology of the Old Testament covenants. GR 1993 <1984>, Baker (reprint). ROTEs 8 (1995) 464-466 (*Burden, J.J.*).
422 **Elazar, Daniel J.** The covenant tradition in politics I: covenant polity in biblical Israel: biblical foundations and Jewish expressions. L 1995, Transaction 480 pp. [ASSR 100,82—*Azria, Régine*].
423 *Malamat, Abraham,* A note on the ritual of treaty making in Mari and the bible. IEJ 45/4 (1995) 226-229.
424 **Nordheim, E. von,** Die Selbstbehauptung Israels Gn 15. OBO 115. 1992. ⇒8,2366...10,2043. RVT 45 (1995) 133-134 (*Emerton, John A.E.*).
425 **Rendtorff, Rolf,** Die "Bundesformel": eine exegetisch-theologische Untersuchung. SBS 160. Stu 1995, Katholisches Bibelwerk 104 pp. DM39.80/ÖS311. 3-460-04601-5 [OTA 18,655]. REntschluß 50/9-10 (1995) 50-51 (*Oberforcher, Robert*).
426 *Rofé, Alexander,* Promises and covenant: the promise to the patriarchs in late biblical literature. ⇒100. Divine promises to the fathers. ASBF 40. 1995. 52-59.
427 *Seely, David Rolph,* The raised hand of God as an oath gesture. 1995 ⇒10. FFREEDMAN, D., 411-421.

428 *Starke, Frank,* Zur urkundlichen Charakterisierung neuassyrischer Treueide anhand einschlägiger hethitischer Texte des 13. Jh. ZABRG 1 (1995) 70-82.

429 *Swetnam, James,* The Old Testament and the new and eternal covenant. MTh 46 (1995) 65-78 [OTA 19,497].

430 **Hagelia, Hallvard,** Numbering the stars...Gen 15. CB.OT 39. 1994 ⇒10,2041. ᴿJThS 46 (1995) 575-577 (*Coxon, Peter W.*).

431 *Noort, Edward,* "Land" in the deuteronomistic tradition: Genesis 15: the historical and theological necessity of a diachronic approach. ⇒99. Şynchronic or diachronic? OTS 34. 1995. 129-144.

432 *Soggin, Jan Alberto,* "Fede" e "giustizia" in Abramo, Genesi Cap. 15. ⇒8. ᶠDᴏɴɴᴇʀ, H., AAT 30. 1995. 259-265.

433 *Cohen, Jeffrey M.,* Was Abraham heartless? JBQ 23/3 (1995) 180-187 [Gen 16].

434 *Zuidema, W.; Teugels, L.; Sattar, S.A.B.; Lier, J. van; Hazel, D.,* Hagar en Sara. Jota 7 (1995) 3-61 [EThL 72,181*] [Gen 16].

435 *Bernabò, Massimo,* Agar e Ismaele: varianti non conosciute di Genesi 16 e 21 nella illustrazione bizantina dei Settanta. OCP 61 (1995) 215-222.

436 *Silberman, Lou H.,* Genesis 18: boldness in the service of justice. 1995 ⇒89. Preaching biblical texts. 29-35.

437 **Letellier, Robert Ignatius,** Day in Mamre, night in Sodom: Abraham and Lot in Genesis 18 and 19. Bibl.Interp. 10. Lei 1995, Brill xvi; 296 pp. *f*135; $77.25. 90-04-10250-7.

438 *Loza, José,* Genèse XVIII-XIX: présence ou représentation de Yahvé?: essai sur la critique littéraire et la signification du récit. ⇒135. Congress Volume: Paris 1992. VT.S 61. 1995. 179-192.

439 *Brueggemann, Walter* "Impossibility" and epistemology in the faith tradition of Abraham and Sarah (Genesis 18:1-15). ⇒41. The psalms and the life of faith. 1995. 167-188.

440 *Kurianal, J.,* The birth annunciation narratives in Gen 18,1-15 and Jud 13,2-10. BiBh 21/4 (1995) 250-271.

441 *Godden, M.R.,* The trouble with Sodom: literary responses to biblical sexuality. BJRL 77/3 (1995) 97-119 [Gen 19].

442 *Hart, Thomas M.,* Lot's incest. BiTod 33/5 (1995) 266-271 [Gen 19].

443 **Kunin, Seth Daniel,** The logic of incest: a structuralist analysis of Hebrew mythology. JSOT.S 185. Shf 1995, Academic 297 pp. Diss. £32.50; $52.50. 1-85075-509-4.

444 **Neev, David; Emery, K.O.,** The destruction of Sodom, Gomorrah, and Jericho: geological, climatological, and archaeological background. NY 1995, OUP xii; 175 pp. ill. map. $35. 0-19-509094-2 [Gen 19].

445 *White, Leland J.,* Does the bible speak about gays or same-sex orientation?: a test case in biblical ethics I. BTB 25/1 (1995) 14-23 [Gen 19].

446 *Soggin, J. Alberto,* Abramo e Sara a Gerar—insidia all'antenata: Genesi cap. 20. ⇒18. ᶠLɪᴘɪɴsκɪ, E., OLA 65. 1995. 313-317.

447 *Schwartz, Joshua,* Ishmael at play: on exegesis and Jewish society. HUCA 66 (1995) 203-221 [Gen 21,9].

E2.6 The 'Aqedâ; Isaac, Genesis 22...

448 EManns, Frédéric The sacrifice of Isaac in the three monotheistic religions. ASBF 41. Jerusalem 1995, Franciscan Printing Press 211 pp. Proceedings of a symposium on the interpretation of the Scriptures held in Jerusalem, March 16-17, 1995; 8 fig., $25 [RB 103,457].

449 Bekker, C.J.; Nortjé, S.J. Die gebruik van die 'offer' van Isak as 'n motief vir die verkondiging van Jesus as die lydende Christus [The use of the 'sacrifice' of Isaac as a motif for the proclamation of Jesus as the suffering Christ]. HTS 51 (1995) 454-464 [OTA 19,50].

450 Bregman, Marc The riddle of the ram in Genesis chapter 22: Jewish-Christian contacts in late antiquity. ⇒448. The sacrifice of Isaac. 1995. 127-145 [Gen 22,13].

451 Cignelli, Lino The sacrifice of Isaac in patristic exegesis. ⇒448. The sacrifice of Isaac. ASBF 41. 1995. 123-126 [Gen 22,1-9].

452 Cortese, Enzo Gen 22,1-19: history and theology of the narrative. ⇒448. The sacrifice of Isaac. ASBF 41. 1995. 11-23 [Gen 22,1-19].

453 Doukhan, Jacques The Akedah at the 'crossroad': its significance in the Jewish-Christian-Muslim dialogue. ⇒448. The sacrifice of Isaac. ASBF 41. 1995. 165-176 [Gen 22,1-19].

454 Frindte-Baumann, K. Marlene DUMAS "Ritual mit Puppe": Hinweise zur Gottesdienstgestaltung und Unterricht mit dem Bild (Gen 22,1-19). CLehre 48/6 (1995) 264ff [ZID 21,527].

455 Krupp, Michael Die Bindung Isaaks nach dem Midrasch Bereschit Rabba. T&K 65/66 (1995) 3-59 [OTA 18,511].

456 Kunin, Seth Daniel The death of Isaac: structuralist analysis of Genesis 22. ⇒448. The sacrifice of Isaac. ASBF 41. 1995. 35-58 [Gen 22,1-19].

457 Manns, Frédéric The binding of Isaac in Jewish liturgy. ⇒448. The sacrifice of Isaac. ASBF 41. 1995. 59-80.

458 Niehoff, M.R. The return of myth in Genesis Rabbah on the Akeda. JJS 46/1-2 (1995) 69-87.

459 Paczkowski, Mieczysław The sacrifice of Isaac in early patristic exegesis. ⇒448. The sacrifice of Isaac. ASBF 41. 1995. 101-121 [Gen 22,1-19].

460 Parmentier, Martin Der Satzteil "Jetzt habe ich erkannt..." (Gen.22:12) in jüdischer und christlicher Überlieferung. Bijdr. 56 (1995) 362-368 [Gen 22,12].

461 Raynaud, Christiane Le sacrifice d'Abraham dans quelques représentations de la fin du Moyen Age. Journal of Medieval History 21 (1995) 249-273.

462 Reedijk, W. Izaaks bloed, heidens, joods of christelijk?. Ter Herkenning 23 (1995) 43-51 [EThL 72,181*].

463 Schaalman, Herman E. Genesis 22:1-19: the binding of Isaac. 1995 ⇒89. Preaching biblical texts. 36-45 [Gen 22,1-19].

464 Thordson, Thord The sacrifice of Isaac in Samaritan tradition. ⇒448. The sacrifice of Isaac. ASBF 41. 1995. 25-33.

465 Vervenne, Marc 'To bind or not to bind, that is the question': een exegetische oefening over Genesis 22. 1995 ⇒7. FBULCKENS J., 79-94 [EThL 72,181*].

466 Wieringen, Archibald L.H.M. van The reader in Genesis 22:1-19: textsyntax—textsemantics—textpragmatics. EstB 53/3 (1995) 289-304 [Gen 22,1-19].

467 *Yunis, ʿAmer* The sacrifice of Abraham in Islam. ⇒448. The sacrifice of Isaac. ASBF 41. 1995. 147-157 [Resp. *Noujaim, Halim*; Gen 22,1-19].

468 *Orel, Vladimir* The deal of Machpelah. BeO 37/1 (1995) 3-11 [Gen 23,0-20].

469 *Bucher-Gillmayr, Susanne* The interaction of textual signs and reader response—the meaning and the meanings of a text. ⇒133. Actes du quatrième᷍ Colloque. 1995. 241-254 [Gen 24,1-7].

470 *Rendsburg, Gary A. lāśûah* in Genesis xxiv 63. VT 45/4 (1995) 558-560.

471 *Teugels, Lieve* The anonymous matchmaker: an enquiry into the characterization of the servant of Abraham in Genesis 24. JSOT 65 (1995) 13-23.

472 *Wolde, Ellen J. van* Telling and retelling: the words of the servant in Genesis 24. ⇒99. Synchronic or diachronic?. OTS 34. 1995. 227-244.

E2.7 **Jacob** and Esau: ladder-dream; *Jacob, somnium, Gn 25...*

473 **Dicou, Bert** Edom, Israel's brother and antagonist. ⇒10,2079. JSOT.S 169. 1994. ᴿCBQ 57/3 (1995) 547-548 *(Walsh, Jerome T.)*; JBL 114/4 (1995) 713-714 *(Miller, J. Maxwell)*.

474 **Faes de Mottoni, Barbara** BONAVENTURA e la scala di Giacobbe: letture di angelologia. N 1995, Bibliopolis 329 pp.

475 *Fleischer, G.* Jakob träumt: eine Auseinandersetzung mit Erhard BLlUMs methodischem Ansatz am Beispiel von Gen 28,10-22. BN 76 (1995) 82-102.

476 *Freedman, Harry* Jacob and Esau: their struggle in the second century. JBQ 23/2 (1995) 107-115.

477 **Gese, Hartmut** Jakob, der Betrüger?. ⇒8. ᶠDONNER H., ÄAT 30. 1995. 33-43 [Gen 27].

478 *Kille, D. Andrew* Jacob—a study in individuation. ⇒125. JUNG. 1995. 40-54.

479 *Kugel, James* The ladder of Jacob. HThR 88 (1995) 209-227.

480 *Maritano, Mario* La figura di Giacobbe nei padri della chiesa. PaVi 40/2 (1995) 28-29 [OTA 19,317].

481 *Mazzinghi, Luca* Giacobbe e le sue moglie. PaVi 40/2 (1995) 15-18.

482 *Mello, Alberto* Il sogno a Betʾel. PaVi 40/2 (1995) 12-14.

483 *Neeb, John H.C.* ORIGEN's interpretation of Genesis 28:12 and the rabbis. ⇒126. Origeniana Sexta. BEThL 118. 1995. 71-80.

484 *Perani, Mauro* La figura di Giacobbe nel midrash. PaVi 40/2 (1995) 25-27 [OTA 19,318].

485 **Riebl, Maria** Heilsame Umwege: Betrachtungen zum alttestamentlichen Jakobszyklus aus exegetischer und tiefenpsychologischer Sicht. Innsbruck 1995, Tyrolia 128 pp. 3-7022-1979-X.

486 *Rosso, Stefano* Il patriarca Giacobbe nella liturgia. PaVi 40/2 (1995) 30-33.

487 **Wahl, Harald** Die Jakobserzählungen: Studien zu ihrer mündlichen Überlieferung, Verschriftung und Historizität. Diss. ᴰ*Michel, D.*, 1994-95, Mainz [RTL 27,531].

E2.8 Jacob's wrestling *Gn 31-36 & 38*

488 *Greenberg, Moshe* Another look at Rachel's theft of the teraphim.
⇒49 Studies 1995. 261-272 [Gen 31].

489 *Hayes, C. E.* The midrashic career of the confession of Judah (Genesis xxxviii 26), part I: the extra-canonical texts, targums and other versions; part II: the rabbinic midrashim. VT 45 (1995) 62-81, 174-187.

490 **Menn, Esther Marie** Judah and Tamar (Genesis 38) in ancient Jewish exegesis: studies in literary form and hermeneutics. Diss. DFishbane, Michael, Chicago 1995, 460 pp. DAI-A 56,1830.

491 *Monari, Luciano* Hai combattuto con Dio e con gli uomini. PaVi 40/2 (1995) 19-21 [Gen 32,23-33].

492 **Salm, Eva** Juda und Tamar (Gen 38): eine exegetische Studie. Diss. DRuppert, L., Fribourg 1995 [BZ 39,314].

493 *Sheridan, Mark* Jacob and Israel: a contribution to the history of an interpretation. ⇒32. FSTUDER B., StAns 116. 1995. 219-241 [Gen 32,28].

E2.9 Joseph; Jacob's blessings; *Genesis 37; 39-50.*

494 **Bae, Eun-ju [Sr. Isaac, OSB]** A multiple approach to the Joseph story: with a detailed reading of Genesis 46,31-47,31; 50,1-11.14. Diss. DConroy, Charles, R 1995, Pont. Univ. Gregoriana vii; 152 pp. no. 4117; excerpt. [Gen 46,31-47,31; 50,1-11; 50,14].

495 **Bridges, George** Thomas MANN's "Joseph und seine Brüder" and the phallic theology of the Old Testament. Stanford German Studies 25. B 1995, Lang 283 pp. 3-906755-02-9.

496 **Catastini, Alessandro** L'itinerario di Giuseppe: studio sulla tradizione di *Genesi 37-50*. Studia Semitica 13. R 1995, L'Università degli Studi "La Sapienza" 400 pp.

497 *Catastini, Alessandro* Le testimonianze di MANETONE e la "Storia di Guiseppe" (Genesi 37-50). Henoch 17/3 (1995) 279-300.

498 *Crocker, P.T.* Voluntary slavery for food?: was Joseph's treatment of the Egyptians politically correct?. BurH 31 56-62 [Gen 47,13-26; OTA 18,513]

499 EDeurloo, K.; Veen, W. De gezegende temidden van zijn broeders: Jozef en Juda in Genesis 37-50: studies over Genesis. Baarn 1995, Ten Have 220 pp. [EThL 72,182*].

500 *Deurloo, K.A.* Eerstelingschap en koningschap: Genesis 38 als integrerend onderdeel van de Jozefcyclus. ACEBT 14 (1995) 62-73 [EThL 72,182*].

501 *Deurloo, Karel A.* Genesis 37,2-11 als thematischer Auftakt zum Josef—Juda—Zyklus. ⇒26. FSCHNEIDER W., 1995. 71-81.

502 *Fry, Euan* How was Joseph taken to Egypt? (Genesis 37.12-36). BiTr 46/4 (1995) 445-448.

503 **Goldman, Shalom** The wiles of women/the wiles of men: Joseph and Potiphar's wife in ancient Near Eastern, Jewish and Islamic folklore. Albany 1995, SUNY Press 189 pp. $16.95. 0-7914-2684-X [OTA 19,365].

504 *Hyman, Ronald T.* Power of persuasion: Judah, Abigail, and Hushai. JBQ 23/1 (1995) 9-16 [Gen 44; 1 Sam 25; 2 Sam 16-17].

505 *MacKinlay, J.* Potiphar's wife in conversation. Feminist Theology 10 (1995) 69-80 [Gen 39,6-18].

506 *Macuch, Rudolf* Hermeneutical divergencies between the Samaritan and Jewish versions of the blessings on the patriarchs (Genesis 49 and Deuteronomy 33). ⇒28. ᶠSɪxᴅᴇɴɪᴇʀ G., SJ(NY) 5. 1995. 365-379.

507 *Marx, Alfred* "Jusqu'à ce que vienne Shiloh": pour une interprétation messianique de Genèse 49,8-12. ⇒22. ᶠRᴇɴᴀᴜᴅ B. LeDiv 159. 1995. 95-111.

508 *Matthews, Victor H.* The anthropology of clothing in the Joseph narrative. JSOT 65 (1995) 25-36.

509 **Niehoff, Maren** The figure of Joseph in post-biblical Jewish literature. ⇒8,2444...10,2116. AGJU 16. 1992. ᴿCritRR 8 (1995) 435-437 *(Neusner, Jacob)*.

510 *Nissan, Ephraim; Weiss, Hillel* The hyperJoseph project: part A: hypermedia and knowledge-representation for supporting an analysis of the text and narrative in Genesis 39 and of the respective exegesis and legendary homiletics: part B: a representation syntax for intertextuality, that takes into account translation, editing, and the page layout of given editions. ⇒133. Actes du quatrième Colloque. 1995. 154-162, 163-173.

511 *Oswald, Wolfgang* Text segmentation and pragmatics. ⇒133. Actes du quatrième Colloque. 1995. 140-153. [Gen 22,1; 39,3; 39,8; 39,17; 39,20].

512 **Paap, Carolin** Die Josephsgeschichte Genesis 37-50: Bestimmungen ihrer literarischen Gattung in der zweiten Hälfte des 20. Jahrhunderts. EHS.T 534. Fra 1995, Lang 193 pp. $42.50. 3-631-48571-9.

513 *Péter-Contesse, René* Genèse 37,36; 39,1 Potifar était-il un eunuque?. Cahiers de traduction biblique 23 (1995) 9-14.

514 *Peffley, Francis J.* The two Josephs. HPR 96/3 (1995) 61-64.

515 *Rolla, Armando* La benedizioni di Giacobbe. PaVi 40/2 (1995) 22-24.

516 *Rösel, Martin* Die Interpretation von Genesis 49 in der Septuaginta. BN 79 (1995) 54-70.

517 ᴱ**Schweizer, Harald** Textbeschreibung und -interpretation. Computerunterstützte Textinterpretation I. Textwissenschaft, Theologie, Hermeneutik, Linguistik, Literaturanalyse, Informatik 7/1. Tü 1995, Francke xix; 382 pp.

518 ᴱ**Schweizer, Harald** Anhänge zu den Textanalysen: Arbeitsübersetzung, Datensätze zu Semantik/Pragmatik, tabellarische Befunde. Computerunterstützte Textinterpretation II. Textwissenschaft, Theologie, Hermeneutik, Linguistik, Literaturanalyse, Informatik 7/2. Tü 1995, Francke vi; 313 pp. [EThL 72,182*].

519 ᴱ**Schweizer, Harald** Anhang zur Methodik: Datenbankprogramm JOSEF im Gesamtkonzept SLANG. Computerunterstützte Textinterpretation III: Search for a learning non-normative grammar. Textwissenschaft, Theologie, Hermeneutik, Linguistik, Literaturanalyse, Informatik 7/3. Tü 1995, Francke x; 227 pp. [EThL 72,182*].

520 **Schweizer, Harald** Die Josefsgeschichte. 1991. ⇒7,2122...2118. ᴿBZ 39/1 (1995) 120-122 *(Seidl, Theodor)*.

521 *Schweizer, Harald* Text segmentation and levels of interpretation: reading and rereading the biblical story of Joseph. Semiotica 107/3-4 (1995) 273-292.

522 *Somekh, Alberto* L'interpretazione ebraica della Bibbia nei targumim. La lettura ebraica delle Scritture. ᴱSierra, Sergio BnS 18. Bo 1995, Dehoniane. 59-73 [Gen 49,2-27; BuBbgB 19,17].
523 **Standhartinger, Angela** Das Frauenbild im Judentum der hellenistischen Zeit: ein Beitrag anhand von 'Joseph und Aseneth'. AGJU. Lei 1995, Brill viii; 289 pp. 90-04-10350-3.
524 *Watt, Trevor* Joseph's dreams. ⇒125. Jᴜɴɢ. 1995. 55-70.

E3.1 Exodus event and theme; *textus, commentarii.*

525 ᴱ**Brenner, Athalya,** A feminist companion to Exodus to Deuteronomy. Feminist Companion to the Bible 6. Shf 1994, Academic 269 pp. £16.50/$24.50. ᴿJJS 46/1-2 (1995) 349 *(Harvey, Graham).*
526 **Childs, Brevard S.** Il libro dell'Esodo: commentario criticoteologico. ᵀ*Ferroni, Andrea,* Theologica. CasM 1995, Piemme 83 pp. L120.000. 88-384-2384-9.
527 **Houtman, Cornelis** Exodus I [Eng.]. ᵀ*Rebel, J.; Woudstra, S.,* ⇒10,2141. 1993. ᴿETR 70 (1995) 587-588 *(Macchi, Jean-Daniel);* BiOr 52 (1995) 741-743 *(Wevers, John W.).*
528 **Johnstone, W.** Exodus. OTGu. Sheffield 1995, Academic 120 pp. [reprint; EThL 72,183*].
529 ᵀᴱ**Le Boulluec, Alain; Sandevoir, Pierre** L'Exode. ⇒6,2541...9,2253. Bible d'Alexandrie 2. 1989. ᴿBijdr. 56/1 (1995) 78-79 *(Ruiten, J.T.A.G.M. van);* Igreja e Missã 47 (1995) 305-306 *(Couto, A.).*
530 **Martínez Sáiz, Teresa** Mekilta de Rabbí Ismael: comentario rabínico al libro del Éxodo. Biblioteca Midrásica 16. Estella 1995, Verbo Divino iv; 534 pp. 84-8169-054-6.
531 ᵀᴱ**Salvesen, Alison** The Exodus commentary of St. Eᴘʜʀᴇᴍ. Kottayam 1995, 'Eth'o 67 pp. [OstKSt 46,235].
532 **Schmidt, Werner H.** Exodus (7,1-10,29). BKAT 2/2. Neuk 1995, Neuk 313-392. DM33 [EThL 72,182*].
533 **Spreafico, Ambrogio** El libro del Éxodo. ᵀ*Villanueva Salas, Marciano* Guía espiritual del Antiguo Testamento. M 1995, Ciudad Nueva 217 pp. Ptas1.900. 84-254-1886-0.
534 **Wevers, John William; Quast, U.** Exodus. Septuaginta 2/1. 1991. ⇒7,2155...10,2152. ᴿEeT(O) 26 (1995) 109-111 *(Laberge, Léo);* ThRv 91 (1995) 308-310 *(Schenker, Adrian).*

535 *Adler, Jonathan* Dating the Exodus: a new perspective. JBQ 23/1 (1995) 44-51.
536 *Anbar, Moshe* Les milieux de vie de deux motifs dans le récit de l'exode illustrés par les archives royale de Mari. ⇒18. ꜰLɪᴘɪɴsᴋɪ E., OLA 65. 1995. 11-17 [Exod 13,21-22; 14,19-20; Num 10,31-33; Ps 87,14].
537 *Birch, Bruce C.* Divine character and the formation of moral community in the book of Exodus. ⇒109 The Bible in ethics. JSOT.S 207. 1995. 119-135.
538 *Bogaert, P.* La forme conservée la plus ancienne de Ex 36-40: le Monacensis (VL 104). BVLI 39 (1995) 37-39.
539 *Brueggemann, Walter* The book of Exodus: introduction, commentary, and reflections. ⇒83. NIntB 1. 1995. 675-981.

540 *Collins, John J.* The Exodus and biblical theology. BTB 25 (1995) 152-160.

541 *Duckworth, Robin* Exodus: the myth and the reality. ScrB 25 (1995) 15-23.

542 *Durken, Daniel* My Exodus. BiTod 33 (1995) 88-93.

543 *Ela, Jean-Marc* A black African perspective: an African reading of Exodus. ⇒129. Voices from the margin. 1995 <1991>. 244-254.

544 *Fischer, Georg* Keine Priesterschrift in Ex 1-15? ZKTh 117 (1995) 203-211.

545 **Knohl, Israel** The sanctuary of silence: the priestly torah and the holiness school. Mp 1995, Fortress x; 246 pp. $28. 0-8006-2763-6 [BoL 1996,105].

546 *Moon, Cyris H.S.* A Korean minjung perspective: the Hebrews and the Exodus. ⇒129. Voices from the margin. 1995 <1991>. 228-243.

547 *Nardoni, Enrique* El exodo como acontecimiento de justicia libera-dora. RevBib 57 (1995) 193-222.

548 **Owens, James T.** Narrative criticism and theology in Exodus 1-15. Diss. ^DBegg, C., 1995 Wsh [RTL 27,530].

549 *Roderick, Bradley P.* God's mission to Egypt in the Exodus. TTE 52 (1995) 21-26 [OTA 19,52].

550 **Schmidt, Werner H.** Exodus, Sinai und Mose: Erwägungen zu Ex 1-19 und 24. EdF 191. Da ³1995 <1990>, Wiss viii; 176 pp. DM39.80. 3-460-04601-5 [ThRv 91,534].

551 *Tov, Emanuel* A paraphrase of Exodus: 4Q422. ⇒11. ^FGREENFIELD J., 1995. 351-363.

552 *Weimar, Peter* Exodus, Exodusmotiv: I. Biblisch-historisch: Altes Testament. ⇒122. LThK 3. 1995. 1120-1122.

553 *Wulung, FX. Heryano Wono* Der Befreier-Gott (eine biblische Verkündigung zu Exodus 1-15) [in Indonesian]. Umat Baru 28 (1995) 15-21 [ThIK 17,50].

E3.2 **Moyses** — Pharaoh, Goshen — *Exodus 1...*

554 *Asian Group Work* An Asian feminist perspective: the Exodus story (Exodus 1.8-22; 2.1-10. ⇒129. Voices from the margin. 1995 <1991>. 255-266.

555 *Barbiero, Gianni* Il cammino di fede del giovane Mosè come sintesi dell'esperienza spirituale dell'Esodo. Sal. 57 (1995) 3-23.

556 *Bartelmus, Rüdiger* Begegnung in der Fremde: Anmerkungen zur theologischen Relevanz der topographischen Verortung der Beru-fungsvisionen des Mose und des Ezechiel (Ex 3,1-4,17 bzw. Ez 1,1-3,15). BN 78 (1995) 21-38.

557 *Bartolini, Elena* "Fa' che io passi" Mosè di fronte alla morte. Horeb 12/3 (1995) 23-28. [Exod 4,24-26].

558 *Boadt, Lawrence* Exodus 1-2: divine wonders never cease: the birth of Moses in God's plan of Exodus. 1995 ⇒89. Preaching biblical texts. 46-61.

559 *Brueggemann, Walter* Pharaoh as vassal: a study of a political meta-phor. CBQ 57 (1995) 27-51.

560 *Chandler, T.* À propos de Moïse: deux notes de recherche. Philoso-phiques 22 (1995) 297-299 [EThL 72,183*].

561 *Chapalain, Claude* Notes de lecture: Exode—Chapitres 1 & 2. Sém-Bib 78 (1995) 47-52.

562 **Chouraqui, A.** Moïse: voyage aux confins de'un mystère révélé et d'une utopie réalisable. Monaco 1995, Du Rocher 502 pp. [ETL 72,178*].

563 **Davies, Gordon F.** Israel in Egypt: reading Exodus 1-2. ⇒8,2489...10,2161. JSOT.S 135. 1992. ᴿCritRR 7 (1994) 109-111 *(Jobling, David)*; ScrB 25/1 (1995) 31 *(Duckworth, Robin)*; BO 52 (1995) 456-458 *(Houtman, C.; Kupfer, C.)*; TJT 11/1 (1995) 84-85 *(Eslinger, Lyle)*.

564 *Day, John* The pharaoh of the Exodus, Jᴏsᴇᴘʜᴜs and Jubilees. VT 45 (1995) 377-378.

565 *Delcor, Matthias* La légende de la mort de Moïse dans le Memar Marqah comparée à quelques traditions juives. ⇒28. ᶠSɪxᴅᴇɴɪᴇʀ G., SJ(NY) 5. 1995. 25-45.

566 *Dell'Orto, Giuseppe* "Io sarò con te": una rilettura della vocazione di Mosè. RCI 76 (1995) 271-287.

567 **Dörrfuß, Ernst Michael** Mose in den Chronikbüchern: Garant theokratischer Zukunftserwartung. ⇒10,2162. 1994. ᴿABG 38 (1995) 278-279 [Autor].

568 *Ebach, Jürgen* Die Schwester des Mose: Anmerkungen zu einem "Widerspruch" in Exodus 2,1-10. ⇒46. Hiobs Post. 1995 <1993>. 130-144.

569 **Fleg, Edmond** The life of Moses. ᵀ*Guest, Stephen Haden*, Pasadena, CAL 1995, Hope xii; 209 pp. 0-932727-82-4.

570 *Giacomoni, Silvia* La vita di Mosè. Studi Fatti Ricerche 69 (1995) 13-14.

571 **Giacomoni, Silvia** La vita di Mosè. Narrativa per la scuola. Mi 1995, Signorelli 140 pp. L14.600. 88-304-1137-X.

572 *Isabelle de la Source, Soeur* Le cycle de Moïse. Lire la Bible avec les Pères 2. P 1995, Médiaspaul. F85. 2-7122-0372-0.

573 **Landman, Gerrit Marinus** In de ruimte van de naam: liturgische grondwoorden in het onderricht van Mozes en hun invloid op het Nieuwe Testament en de christelijke eredienst. Diss. Zoetermeer 1995, Boekencentrum xxi; 280 pp. Abstract in English.

574 *Miller, Robert D.* The form-critical problem of Moses' call. ProcGLM 15 113-119 [sum. 113].

575 *Münkler, Herfried* Moses, David und Ahab: biblische Gestalten in der politischen Theorie der frühen Neuzeit. ⇒78. Bibel und Literatur. 1995. 113-136.

576 **Nohrnberg, James** Like unto Moses: the constituting of an interruption. ISBL Bloomington 1995, Indiana University Press xx; 396 pp. $40. 0-253-34090-X [RB 103,316].

577 *North, Robert* State of the published proof that Qantir is Raamses. ⇒16. ᶠHᴇɴɴᴇssʏ J., Mediterranean Archaeology Supplement 3. 1995. 207-217 [Exod 1,11].

578 *Smend, Rudolf* Mose als geschichtliche Gestalt. HZ 260 (1995) 1-19.

579 **Stefani, Piero; Barbaglio, Giuseppe** Davanti a Dio: il cammino spirituale di Mosè, di Elia e di Gesù. Quaderni di Camaldoli—Ricerche 6. Bo 1995, Dehoniane 60 pp. L10.000. 88-10-41105-6. ᴿPresPast 65 (1995) 119-120.

580 **Van Seters, John** The life of Moses: the Yahwist as historian in Exodus-Numbers. Contributions to Biblical Exegesis and Theology

10. 1994. RLouvSt 20 (1995) 79-80 *(Eynikel, Erik)*; BTB 25 (1995) 47-48 *(Gnuse, Robert)*; EeT(O) 26 (1995) 259-260 *(Laberge, Léo)*; Bib. 76 (1995) 419-422 *(Ska, Jean Louis)*; VT 45 (1995) 431-432 *(Williamson, H.G.M.)*; JR 75 (1995) 545-547 *(Dozeman, Thomas B.)*; IThQ 61 (1995) 312-313 *(Maher, Michael)*.

E3.3 Nomen divinum, Tetragrammaton; *Exodus 3,14...*Plagues.

581 *Anderson, Bernhard W.* Taking the Lord's name in vain—which name?. BiRe 11/3 (1995) 17, 48 [Exod 3,13-14].
582 *Ashby, G.W.* The bloody bridegroom: the interpretation of Exodus 4.24-26. ET 106 (1995) 203-205.
583 *Caquot, André* Une contribution ougaritique à la préhistoire du titre divin Shadday. ⇒135. Congress Volume: Paris 1992. VT.S 61. 1-12.
584 *Cazelles, Henri* Yahwisme, ou Yahwé en son peuple. 1995 ⇒21. FRENAUD B., LeDiv 159. 13-29.
585 *Cunningham, David S.* On translating the divine name. TS 56 (1995) 415-440.
586 *Dreyfus, A. Stanley* Exodus 3:1-22: the burning bush through the eyes of midrash: God's word then and now. 1995 ⇒89. Preaching biblical texts. 62-75.
587 *Ebach, Jürgen* "Herr, warum handelst du böse an diesem Volk?" Klage vor Gott und Anklage Gottes in der Erfahrung des Scheiterns. ⇒46. Hiobs Post. 1995 <1990>. 73-83 [Exod 5,22-23].
588 **Gozier, André** Vers le buisson ardent. P 1995, C.L.D. 150 pp. FF85 [EeV 106,69].
589 *Kirchschläger, Walter* Gottesnamen, Gottesepitheta: Neues Testament. ⇒123. LTK 4. 1995. 938-939.
590 *Link, Christian* Die Spur des Namens: zur Funktion und Bedeutung des biblischen Gottesnamens. EvTh 55 (1995) 416-438.
591 *Lubetski, Meir* W.R. SMITH's *'hyeh 'šer 'hyeh*: five score years and eighteen. ⇒121. William Robertson Smith. JSOT.S 189. 1995. 158-163 [Exod 3,14].
592 *Mafico, Temba L.J.* The divine name Yahweh 'Elōhīm from an African perspective. ⇒113. Reading II. 1995. 21-32 [OTA 19,492].
593 *Magonet, Jonathan* The names of God in biblical narratives. ⇒24. FSAWYER J., JSOT.S 195. 1995. 80-96.
594 *Marx, Alfred* La généalogie d'Exode vi 14-25: sa forme, sa fonction. VT 45 (1995) 318-336.
595 **Mettinger, Tryggve N.D.** Buscando a Dios: significado y mensaje de los nombres divinos en la Biblia. ⇒10,2195. 1994. RRF 232 (1995) 121 *(Andrés, Rafael de)*.
596 *Purcell, Michael* Nec tamen consumebatur: Exodus 3 and the non-consumable other in the philosophy of Emmanuel LEVINAS. SJTh 48 (1995) 79-95.
597 *Römer, Thomas* Exode 4,24-26. Lire et Dire 23 (1995) 39-47 [Bulletin of Biblical Bibliography 13,15].
598 **Scriba, Albrecht** Die Geschichte des Motivkomplexes Theophanie: seine Elemente, Einbindung in Geschehensabläufe und Verwendungsweisen in altisraelitischer, frühjüdischer und frühchristlicher Literatur. Diss. Mainz 1992. ⇒9,2295. DBrandenburger, Egon. FRLANT 167. Gö 1995, Vandenhoeck & Ruprecht 274 pp. DM98. 3-525-53850-2. .

599 *Stemberger, Günter* Gottesnamen, Gottesepitheta: Altes Testament u. Judentum. ⇒123. LThK 4. 1995. 936-938.
600 *Thompson, Thomas L.* How Yahweh became God: Exodus 3 and 6 and the heart of the pentateuch. JSOT 68 (1995) 57-74.
601 *Wolters, Al* The tetragrammaton in the Psalms Scroll. Textus 18 (1995) 87-99.

602 *Currid, John D.* The Egyptian setting of the "serpent": confrontation in Exodus 7,8-13. BZ 39 (1995) 203-224.
603 *Greenstein, Edward L.* The firstborn plague and the reading process. ⇒21. FMILGROM J., 1995. 555-569 [Exod 4,22-23].
604 **Kilpatrick, Robert Kirk** Against the gods of Egypt: an examination of the narrative of the ten plagues in the light of Exodus 12:12. Diss. Mid-Amer. Baptist Theol. Sem. 1995, 188 pp. AAC 9533865.
605 *Noegel, Scott B.* The significance of the seventh plague. Bib. 76 (1995) 532-539 [Exod 9,13-19].
606 *Van Seters, John* A context of magicians?: the plague stories in P. ⇒21. FMILGROM J., 1995. 569-580.

E3.4 *Pascha, sanguis, sacrificium:* **Passover, blood, sacrifice,** *Ex 11...*

607 *Alexander, T.D.* The passover sacrifice. ⇒61. Sacrifice. 1995. 1-24.
608 *Bar-On, Shimon* Zur literarkritischen Analyse von Ex 12,21-27. ZAW 107 (1995) 18-30.
609 *Beckwith, Roger T.* The death of Christ as a sacrifice in the teaching of Paul and Hebrews. ⇒61. Sacrifice. 130-135.
610 *Berder, Michel* Exode 12-15 dans la musique occidentale. ⇒75. La Pâque. CEv.S 92. 93-95.
611 **Bradley, Ian** The power of sacrifice. L 1995, Darton, Longman & Todd 328 pp. £11.95. 0-232-52057-7. RET 106 (1994-95) 289-290 *(Rodd, C.S.)*.
612 **Brenner, Martin** The song of the sea: Ex 15:1-21. ⇒7,2531...9,2322. 1991. RBZ 39 (1995) 296-297 *(Mommer, Peter)*.
613 *Brueggemann, Walter* Exodus 11:1-10: a night for crying/weeping. 1995 ⇒89. Preaching biblical texts. 76-89.
614 *Cousin, Hugues* De la Septante au Nouveau Testament 9-24 [Exod 12-14];
ECousin, Hugues, La Pâque et le passage de la mer 1995 ⇒75.
615 *Déclais, Jean-Louis* En Islam, la destruction de Pharaon 84-90 [Exod 12-14];
616 *Delattre, Bertrand; Birnbaum, Michel* La tradition des sages 29-50. 1995 ⇒75. La Pâque. CEv.S 92 [Exod 12-14].
617 *Dietzfelbinger, Rudolf* Ex 17,8-16 und Dt 25,17-19 beim Wort genommen. Sef. 55 (1995) 41-60.
618 Le dossier patristique. 1995 ⇒75. La Pâque. CEv.S 92. 60-83 [Exod 12-14].
619 *Etaix, Raymond* Une prédication médiévale. ⇒75. La Pâque. CEv.S 92. 1995. 91-92 [Exod 12-14].
620 *Görg, Manfred* Nochmals zu Amalek. BN 79 (1995) 15-16 [Exod 17,8-16].
621 *Gruson, Philippe* Les données de l'Ancien Testament 6-8 [Exod 12-14];

622 La lecture liturgique de l'Église romaine 5-9. 1995 ⇒75. La Pâque. CEv.S 92 [Exod 12-14].

623 *Hayward, Robert* Some ancient Jewish reflections on Israel's imminent redemption. ⇒23. F ROGERSON J., JSOT.S 200. 1995. 293-305 [Exod 14,11-12].

624 **Jarne Ubieto, Javier** La tradición del maná: estudio exegético de Ex 16. Diss. D*Varo, F.*, 1995, Pampelune 382 pp. [RTL 27,529].

625 **Lamberty-Zielinski, Hedwig** Das "Schilfmeer": Herkunft, Bedeutung und Funktion eines alttestamentlichen Exodusbegriffs. BBB 78. 1993. ⇒9,2319. R JBL 114 (1995) 299-300 *(Willis, John T.)*.

626 *Marsden, Richard* The death of the messenger: the 'spelboda' in the Old English *Exodus.* BJRL 77/3 (1995) 141-164 [Exod 13-14; Jdt 5,13].

627 *Mello, Alberto* L'alleanza sinaitica: aspetti comunionali (Es 19,1-8). PSV 31 (1995) 25-34.

628 *Meunier, Bernard* PHILON d'Alexandrie. ⇒75. La Pâque. CEv.S 92. 1995. 25-28 [Exod 12-14].

629 *Patterson, Richard D.* The song of redemption. WThJ 57 (1995) 453-461 [Exod 15,1-18].

630 *Prigent, Pierre* La synagogue de Doura Europos. 1995 ⇒75. La Pâque. CEv.S 92. 51-53 [Exod 12-14].

631 **Rooze, Egbert** Amalek geweldig verslagen: een bijbelstheologisch onderzoek naar de vijandschap Israël-Amalek. Diss. Bruxelles, D*Jagersma, H.*. Gorinchem 1995, Narratio 248 pp. ƒ39.50. 90-5263-902-7 [Exod 17,8-16; RTL 27,530].

632 **Saßmann, Christiane Karin** Die Opferbereitschaft Israels: anthropologische und theologische Voraussetzungen des Opferkultes. EHS.T 52. Fra 1995, Lang 280 pp. DM84. 3-631-48247-7.

633 *Schwemer, Daniel* Das alttestamentliche Doppelritual ⟨lwt wšlmym im Horizont der hurritischen Opfertermini *ambašši* und *keldi.* Edith PORADA Memorial Volume. E**Owen, David I.; Wilhelm, Gernot.** Studies in the civilization and culture of Nuzi and the Hurrians 7. Bethesda 1995, CDL x; 159 pp. 81-116 [sum. 81].

634 *Selman, Martin J.* Sacrifice in the ancient Near East. ⇒61. Sacrifice. 1995. 88-104.

635 *Smelik, Klaas A.D.* Moloch, molekh or molk-sacrifice?: a reassessment of the evidence concerning the Hebrew term molekh. SJOT 9 (1995) 133-142.

636 **Talbott, Rick Franklin** Sacred sacrifice: ritual paradigms in Vedic religion and early Christianity. AmUSt.H 150. NY 1995, Lang vii; 356 pp. 0-8204-2322-X.

637 *Tournay, Raymond Jacques* Le chant de victoire d'Exode 15. RB 102 (1995) 522-531.

638 *Vermeylen, Jacques* Théophanie, purification et liturgie: à propos de Ex 19,10-25. ⇒22. F RENAUD B., LeDiv 159. 1995. 113-130.

639 *Vervenne, Marc* Topic and comment: the case of an initial superordinate rs3' clause in Exodus 14:13. ⇒26. F SCHNEIDER W., 1995. 187-198.

640 *Weimar, Peter* Zum Problem der Entstehungsgeschichte von Ex 12,1-14. ZAW 107 (1995) 1-17.

641 *Weimar, Peter* Ex 12,1-14 und die priesterschriftliche Geschichtsdarstellung. ZAW 107 (1995) 196-214.

642 *Wenham, Gordon J.* The theology of Old Testament sacrifice. ⇒61. Sacrifice. 1995. 75-87.

643 *Wodecki, B.* Aspekty soteriologiczne przymierza synajskiego [Soteriological aspects of the Sinai covenant]. **P**. RBL 48 (1995) 1-17 [Mark 6,52-53; OTA 19,308].
644 *Zwickel, Wolfgang* "Opfer der Gerechtigkeit" (Dtn xxxiii 19; Ps. iv 6, li 21). VT 45 (1995) 386-391.

E3.5 **Decalogus,** *Ex 20 = Dt 5; Ex 21ss;* **Ancient Near East Law**

645 *Clines, David J.A.* The ten commandments, reading from left to right. ⇒37. Interested parties. JSOT.S 205. 1995. 26-45.
646 *Graf, F.W.* Die Zehn Gebote als Grundlage christlicher Ethik. LM 34/12 (1995) 11-13 [20,1-17; Dt 5,6-21].
647 *Greenberg, Moshe* The decalogue tradition critically examined. ⇒49 Studies 1995. 279-312.
648 *Gross, Walter* Wandelbares Gesetz—unwandelbarer Dekalog? ThQ 175 (1995) 161-170.
649 *Hossfeld, Frank-Lothar* Dekalog: Altes Testament. ⇒122. LThK 3. 1995. 62-64.
650 *Hunold, Gerfried W.* Wider den Konkurs der Freiheit: vom bleibenden Zeitgespräch des Dekalogs zwischen Vernunft und Sittlichkeit. ThQ 175 (1995) 171-178.
651 *Hvalvik, Reidar* Ordene fra Guds egen munn: Til spørsmål om dekalogens stilling i den antikke jødedom og den tidlige kirke [The decalogue in ancient Judaism and in the early Church]. TTK 66 (1995) 261-274 [20,1-17; Dt 5,6-21; sum. 273].
652 **Koch, Traugott** Zehn Gebote für die Freiheit. Tü 1995, Mohr 139 pp. DM39. 3-16-146178-9.
653 **Lehmann, Paul L.** The decalogue and a human future: the meaning of the commandments for making and keeping human life human. GR 1995, Eerdmans vii; 232 pp. $18. 0-8028-0835-2. ^RCritRR 8 (1995) 246-248 *(Bartel, Michelle J.)*.
654 *Merklein, Helmut* Dekalog: Neues Testament. ⇒122. LThK 3. 64-65.
655 **Niehaus, Jeffrey J.** God at Sinai: covenant and theophany in the Bible and ancient Near East. Studies in Old Testament Biblical Theology. Carlisle; GR 1995, Paternoster; Zondervan 426 pp. £10; $19. 0-85364-649-X; 0-310-49471-0.
656 ^T**Spaeth, Paul J.** St. BONAVENTURE's Collations on the Ten Commandments. Works of Saint Bonaventure 6. St. Bonaventure, NY 1995, Franciscan Institute xvi; 101 pp. $11. 1-57659-005-4.
657 ^T**Tapiero, M.** Les dix paroles. P 1995, Cerf 609 pp. [EThL 72/,184*].
658 **Van Uden, D.; Wilde, N. de; Scholder, H.** Gebeitelde woorden—sprekende taal: verkenning van de Tien Woorden in de joodse traditie. Ga en Leer, Verkenningen in de rabbijnse literatuur 1. Zoetermeer 1995, Boekencentrum 207 pp. *f*25 [GThT 97/4,184].
659 *Wartenberg-Potter, Bärbel* Kraft der Befreiung: die Weisungen von Sinai geben dem Leben Sinn. EK 9 (1995) 515-517.

660 ^E**Baptist-Hlawatsch, Gabriele** ULRICH von Pottenstein: Dekalog-Auslegung: Text und Quellen: das erste Gebot. Texte und Textgeschichte 43. Tü 1995, Niemeyer ix; 662 pp. DM394. 3-484-36043-7 [20,3; Dt 5,7; ThLZ 122,348].

661 *Bayer, Oswald* "Ich bin der Herr, dein Gott ...": das erste Gebot in seiner Bedeutung für die Grundlegung der Ethik 109-120;

662 *Beutel, Albrecht* LUTHERs Auslegung des ersten Gebots 65-108. ⇒88. Das erste Gebot. 1995 [20,2-6; Dt 5,6-10].

663 EDietrich, Walter; Klopfenstein, Martin A. Ein Gott allein?. ⇒10,467*. OBO 139. 1994. REThL 71 (1995) 436-437 *(Lust, J.)*; ET 106 (1994-95) 334-335 *(Mason, Rex)* [20,3].
EHeubach, Joachim "Ich bin der Herr"...erste Gebot 1995 ⇒88.

664 *Patrick, D.* The first commandment in the structure of the pentateuch. VT 45 (1995) 107-118 [20,3-6].

665 *Saebø, Magne* Das erste Gebot im Rahmen der Heiligen Schrift. ⇒88. Das erste Gebot. 1995. 41-63 [20; Dt 5,6-21].

666 *Schmidt, Werner H.* Erwägungen zur Geschichte der Ausschließlichkeit des alttestamentlichen Glaubens. 1995 ⇒135. Congress Volume: Paris 1992. VT.S 61. 289-314.

667 *Ziemer, Jürgen* Der Gottes-Dienst der christlichen Gemeinde in einer pluralistischen Gesellschaft: Überlegungen zur Praxis des ersten Gebots. ⇒88. Das erste Gebot. 1995. 121-134.

668 *Ararat, Nisan* The second commandment: 'thou shalt not bow down unto them, nor serve them, for I the Lord thy God am a jealous God'. Shofar 13 (1995) 44-57 [20,5-6; Dt 5,9-10].

669 *Dohmen, Christoph* Vom Gottesbild zum Menschenbild: Aspekte der innerbiblischen Dynamik des Bilderverbotes. LebZeug 50 (1995) 245-252.

670 *Edelman, Diana* Tracking observance of the aniconic tradition through numismatics. ⇒79. The triumph of Elohim. 1995. 185-225.

671 *Evans, Carl D.* Cult images, royal policies and the origins of aniconism. ⇒1. MAHLSTRÖM G., JSOT.S 190. 1995. 192-212.

672 Mettinger, Tryggve N.D. No graven image?: Israelite aniconism in its ancient Near Eastern context. CB.OT 42. Sto 1995, Almqvist & Wiksell International 250 pp. SEK192. 91-22-01664-3. RThLZ 120 (1995) 986-987 *(Zwickel, Wolfgang)*; SvTK 71 (1995) 178-180 *(Retsö, Jan)*; AulOr 13 (1995) 275-276 *(Heltzer, M.)*.

673 Ndjerareou, Abel Laondoye The theological bases for the prohibitions of idolatry: an exegetical and theological study of the second commandment. Diss. DMerrill, Eugene H., Dallas 1995 360 pp. AAC 9531280; DAI-A 56,1830.

674 EEskenazi, Tamara C.; Harrington, Daniel J.; Shea, William H. The sabbath in Jewish and Christian traditions. ⇒7,431...10,7625. 1991. RJQR 86 (1995) 254-255 *(Spier, Erich)*.

675 *Huffmon, Herbert B.* The fundamental code illustrated: the third commandment. ⇒21. FMILGROM J., 1995. 363-371 [20,7; Dt 5,11].

676 *Greene-McCreight, Kathryn* Restless until we rest in God: the fourth commandment as test case in christian 'plain sense' interpretation. ExAu 11 (1995) 29-41 [20,8; Dt 5,12-15].

677 *Schenker, Adrian* "Ehre Vater und Mutter": das vierte Gebot in der Gesamtordnung des Dekalogs. IKaZ 24/1 (1995) 11ff [[20,12; Dt 5,16; ZID 21,287].

678 *Ben Hayyim, Ze'ev* The tenth commandment in the Samaritan pentateuch. ⇒28. FSIXDENIER G., 1995. 487-492 [20,17].

679 **Barbiero, Gianni** L'asino del nemico: Es 23,4-5; Dt 22,1-4; Lv 19,17-18. ⇒7,2224...10,2273. AnBib 128. RFirmana 11 (1995) 161-164 (*Virgili, Rosanna*).

680 *Brin, Gershon* The formula "if he shall not (do)" and the problem of sanctions in biblical law. ⇒21. FMILGROM J., 1995. 341-362.

681 *Chinitz, Jacob* Eye for eye—an old canard. JBQ 23 (1995) 79-85 [21,23].

682 *Colpe, Carsten* Priesterschrift und Videvdad: ritualistische Gesetzgebung für Israeliten und Iranier. ⇒8. FDONNER H., ÄAT 30. 1995. 9-18.

683 *Gerstenberger, Erhard S.* '...(He/they) shall be put to death': live[sic]-preserving divine threats in Old Testament law. ExAu 11 (1995) 43-61.

684 *Gruber, Mayer I.* Matrilineal determination of Jewishness: biblical and Near Eastern roots. ⇒21. FMILGROM J., 1995. 437-443 [21,4-6].

685 *Harvey, Graham* The suffering of witches and children: uses of the witchcraft passages in the bible. ⇒24. FSAWYER J., JSOT.S 195. 1995. 113-148 [22,17; Lk 18,16].

686 *Lohfink, Norbert* Gibt es eine deuteronomistische Bearbeitung im Bundesbuch? ⇒54. Studien 3. SBAB.AT 20. 1995 <1990>. 39-64.

687 **Marshall, Joy Wade** Israel and the book of the covenant. ⇒9,2364...10,2262. SBL.DS 140. 1993. RIBSt 17 (1995) 188-193 (*Alexander, T.D.*); CBQ 57 (1995) 564-565 (*Benjamin, Don C.*).

688 *Neef, Heinz-Dieter* "Ich selber bin in ihm" (Ex 23,21): exegetische Beobachtungen zur Rede vom "Engel des Herrn" in Ex 23,20-22; 32,34; 33,2; Jdc 2,1-5; 5,23. BZ 39 (1995) 54-75.

689 **Osumi, Yuichi** Die Kompositionsgeschichte des Bundesbuches Exodus 20,22b-23,33. ⇒7,2218...10,2266. OBO 105. 1991. RBZ 39 (1995) 299-300 (*Seebass, Horst*).

690 *Rota Scalabrini, Patrizio* L'originalità della religione di Israele: l'alleanza alla montagna di Dio: teofania, sacrificio e codice dell'alleanza. Ambrosius 71 (1995) 9-47 [EThL 72/,184*].

691 *Schwendemann, Wilhelm* Recht—Grundrecht—Menschenwürde: eine Untersuchung von Ex 21,2-11 im Rahmen theologischer Anthropologie. BN 77 (1995) 34-40.

692 **Sprinkle, Joe M.** 'The book of the covenant': a literary approach. ⇒10,2265. JSOT.S 174. 1994. RThLZ 120 (1995) 328-332 (*Otto, Eckart*); CBQ 57 (1995) 371-372 (*Gnuse, Robert*).

693 *Wittenberg, Gunther H.* Legislating for justice—the social legislation of the Covenant Code and Deuteronomy. Scriptura 54 (1995) 215-228 [OTA 19/,56].

694 *Berthoud, P.* La loi: une perspective biblique. RRef 46 (1995) 19-22.

695 *Bockmuehl, Markus* Natural law in Second Temple Judaism. VT 45 (1995) 17-44.

696 **Bovati, Pietro** Re-establishing justice. JSOT.S 105. 1994 ⇒10,2276. RZABRG 1 (1995) 159-166 (*Otto, Eckart*).

697 **Brin, Gershon** Studies in biblical law. ⇒10,163*. JSOT.S 176. 1994. RThLZ 120 (1995) 324-327 (*Otto, Eckart*); JThS 46 (1995) 592-594 (*Philipps, A.*).

698 **Carmichael, Calum M.** The origins of biblical law. 1992. ⇒8,2543*...10,2236. RJAOS 115 (1995) 165 (*Handy, Lowell K.*).

699 *Greenberg, Moshe* Some postulates of biblical criminal law. ⇒49. Studies. 1995. 25-42.

700 *Hossfeld, Frank-Lothar* Gesetz: Altes Testament. ⇒123. LThK 4. 1995. 580-583.

701 **Houten, Christiana van** The alien in Israelite law. ⇒7,2231... 10,2281. JSOT.S 107. 1991. RJAOS 115 (1995) 722-724 *(Matthews, Victor H.)*.

702 **Lasserre, Guy** Synopse des lois du Pentateuque. ⇒10,2283. VT.S 59. 1994. RETR 70 (1995) 588-589 *(Macchi, Jean-Daniel)*.

703 *McBride, S. Dean* Perspective and context in the study of pentateuchal legislation. ⇒36. FTUCKER G., 1995. 47-59.

704 *McBride, S. Dean* The yoke of torah. ExAu 11 (1995) 1-15.

705 *Otto, Eckart* Biblische Rechtsgeschichte: Ergebnisse und Perspektiven der Forschung. ThRv 91 (1995) 283-292.

706 *Rüterswörden, Udo* Die persische Reichsautorisation der Thora: fact or fiction?. ZABRG 1 (1995) 47-61.

707 **Stahl, Nanette** Law and liminality in the Bible. JSOT.S 202. Shf 1995, Academic 104 pp. £25; $37.50. 0-85075-561-2 [BoL 1996,94].

708 *Willi, Thomas* Tora—Israels Lebensprinzip nach dem Zeugnis des späteren Alten Testamentes. ⇒8. FDONNER H., AAT 30. 1995. 339-348.

709 *Zevit, Ziony* Philology, archaeology, and a terminus a quo for P's ḥaṭṭāʾt legislation. ⇒21. FMILGROM J., 1995. 29-38.

710 EBehrends, Okko; Sellert, Wolfgang Nomos und Gesetz: Ursprünge und Wirkungen des griechischen Gesetzesdenkens. 6. Symposion der Kommission 'Die Funktion des Gesetzes in Geschichte und Gegenwart'. AAWG.PH 209. Gö 1995, Vandenhoeck & Ruprecht 261 pp. DM124 [HZ 265,744].

711 *Greengus, Samuel* Legal and social institutions of ancient Mesopotamia. ⇒127. Civilizations 1. 1995. 469-484.

712 *Haase, Richard* Der Vertrag im Privatrecht der Hethiter: Versuch eines Überblicks. ZABRG 1 (1995) 62-69.

713 *Hoffner, Harry A., Jr.* Legal and social institutions of Hittite Anatolia. ⇒127. Civilizations. 1995. 555-569.

714 ELevinson, Bernard M. Theory and method in biblical and cuneiform law. ⇒10,2284. JSOT.S 181. 1994. RJNSL 21/2 (1995) 128-131 *(Deist, Ferdinand E.)*.

715 *Lorton, David* Legal and social institutions of pharaonic Egypt. ⇒127. Civilizations 1. 1995. 345-362.

716 **Roth, Martha Tobi** Law collections from Mesopotamia and Asia Minor. *Hoffner, Harry A. <collaborator>*. SBL Writings from the Ancient World 6. Atlanta, GA 1995, Scholars xviii; 283 pp. 2 maps. $59.95 ($39.95). 0-7885-0104-6; 0-7885-0126-7 <pb>.

E3.6 Cultus, *Exodus 24-40.*

717 **Cosand, James Robert** The theology of remembrance in the cultus of Israel. Diss. DMagary, Dennis R., 1995, Trinity Evangelical Divinity School 336 pp. AAC 9533047; DAI-A 56,2279.

718 *Dexinger, Ferdinand* Samaritan and Jewish festivals: comparative considerations. ⇒28. FSIXDENIER G., SJ(NY) 5. 1995. 57-78.

719 *Fabry, Heinz-Josef* Feste u. Feiertage: Biblisch. ⇒123. LThK 4. 1995. 1151-1153.
720 *Feliks, Yehuda* The incense of the tabernacle. ⇒21. ᶠMILGROM J., 1995. 125-149.
721 **Coelho Dias, Geraldo** A festa e as festas na Bíblia e na vida. Bíblica: série científica 4. Lisboa 1995, Difusora Bíblica 160 pp.
722 *Fishbane, Michael* Census and intercession in a priestly text (Exodus 30:11-16) and in its midrashic transformation. ⇒21. ᶠMILGROM J., 1995. 103-111.
723 *Fraenkel, Detlef* Übersetzungsnorm und literarische Gestaltung— Spuren individueller Übersetzungstechnik in Exodus 25 ff. + 35 ff. ⇒136. VIII Congress. SCSt 41. 1995. 73-87.
724 *Gowan, Donald E.* Exodus 32:7-14: changing God's mind. 1995 ⇒89. Preaching biblical texts 90-104.
725 *Heinemann, Olliver* Die "Lade" aus Akazienholz—ägyptische Wurzeln eines israelitischen Kultobjekts? BN 80 (1995) 32-40.
726 **Henshaw, Richard A.** Female and male: the cultic personnel: the Bible and the rest of the ancient Near East. PTMS 31. Allison Park 1994, Pickwick xiv; 385 pp. $52. ᴿJBL 114 (1995) 711-712 (*Wiggins, Steve A.*).
727 *Knierim, Rolf P.* Conceptual aspects in Exodus 25:1-9. ⇒21. ᶠMILGROM J., 1995. 113-123.
728 *Knoppers, Gary N.* Aaron's calf and Jeroboam's calves. ⇒10. ᶠFREEDMAN D., 1995. 92-104. [32].
729 *Longacre, Robert E.* Building for the worship of God: Exodus 25:1-30:10. ⇒65. Discourse analysis. SBL Semeia Studies. 1995. 21-49.
730 **Mbachu, Hilary** Berith blood ritual on Mount Sinai (Ex 24,3-8) in Igbo context. Deutsche Hochschulschriften 1052. Egelsbach 1995, Hänsel-Hohenhausen 66 pp. 3-8267-1052-5.
731 *Parisi, Serafino* Feste religiose e fede del popolo in YHWH. Vivarium 3 (1995) 183-203.
732 *Porten, Bezalel* Did the ark stop at Elephantine? BArR 21/3 (1995) 54-57.
733 *Rand, Herbert* The destruction of the golden calf: a reply. JBQ 23 (1995) 242-247 [32,20; <D. Frankel, VT 44 (1994) 330-339].
734 **Rubenstein, Jeffrey L.** The history of Sukkot in the Second Temple and rabbinic periods. BJSt 302. Atlanta 1995, Scholars. 361 pp. 0-7885-0130-5.
735 *Ruiten, Jacques van* The rewriting of Exodus 24:12-18 in Jubilees 1:1-4. BN 79 (1995) 25-29.
736 *Van der Toorn, Karel* Theology, priests, and worship in Canaan and ancient Israel. ⇒127. Civilizations 3. 1995. 2043-2058.
737 **Vicent Saera, Rafael** La fiesta judía de las Cabañas (Sukkot): interpretaciones midrásicas en la Biblia y en el judaísmo antiguo. Biblioteca Midrásica 17. Estella (Navarra) 1995, Verbo Divino 295 pp. 84-8169-074-0.
738 **Willi-Plein, Ina** Opfer und Kult im alttestamentlichen Israel: Textbefragungen und Zwischenergebnisse. ⇒9,2420. SBS 153. 1993. ᴿITS 32 (1995) 278-281 (*Ceresko, Anthony R.*).

E3.7 **Leviticus**

739 *Albertz, R.* Die Tora Gottes gegen die wirtschaftlichen Sachzwänge: die Sabbat- und Jobeljahrgesetzgebung Lev 25 in ihrer Geschichte. OR 44 (1995) 290ff [ZID 21,676].

740 *Beal, Timothy K.; Linafelt, Tod* Sifting for cinders: strange fires in Leviticus 10:1-5. Semeia 69/70 (1995) 19-32.

741 **Bryan, David** Cosmos, chaos and the kosher mentality. JSPE.S 12. Shf 1995, Academic 303 pp. £40; $60. 1-85075-536-1.

742 *Cardellini, Innocenzo* "Possessio" o "dominium bonorum"?: riflessioni sulla proprietà privata e la "rimessa dei debiti" in Levitico 25. Anton. 70 (1995) 333-348.

743 *Carmichael, Calum M.* Forbidden mixtures in Deuteronomy xxii 9-11 and Leviticus xix 19. VT 45 (1995) 433-448.

744 **Chirichigno, Gregory C.** Debt slavery in Israel and the ancient Near East. ⇒9,2466; 10,2346. JSOT.S 141. 1993. RBib. 76 (1995) 254-261 (*Otto, Eckart*).

745 *Douglas, Mary* Poetic structure in Leviticus. ⇒21. FMILGROM J., 1995. 239-256.

746 **Drazin, Israel** Targum Onkelos to Leviticus: an English translation of the text with analysis and commentary: based on the A. SPERBER and A. BERLINER editions. Hoboken, NJ 1994, Ktav xvi; 278 pp. $59.50. RCBQ 57 (1995) 766-767 (*Levine, Baruch A.*).

747 **Fager, Jeffrey A.** Land tenure and the biblical jubilee. ⇒9,2467; 10,2347. 1993. RBiOr 52 (1995) 771-773 (*Otto, Eckart*) [Lev 25].

748 *Fredriksen, Paula* Did Jesus oppose the purity laws? BiRe 11 (1995-June) 19-25, 42-47 [Lev 12-15].

749 *Galpaz-Feller, Pnina* The stela of King Piye: a brief consideration of "clean" and "unclean" in ancient Egypt and the bible. RB 102 (1995) 506-521.

750 **Gerstenberger, Erhard S.** Das dritte Buch Mose: Leviticus. 9,2437; 10,2320. ATD 6. 1993. RCritRR 8 (1995) 121-123 (*Wright, David P.*).

751 *Görg, Manfred* "Asaselologen" unter sich—eine neue Runde?. BN 80 (1995) 25-31 [Lev 16].

752 **Harrington, Hannah K.** The impurity systems of Qumran and the rabbis: biblical foundations. ⇒9,2633; 10,2327. SBL.DS 143. 1993. RCBQ 57 (1995) 136-137 (*Duhaime, Jean*) [12; Lev 11].

753 *Holmgren, Fredrick C.* Leviticus 19:1-37: the way of torah: escape from Egypt. 1995 ⇒89. Preaching biblical texts. 117-128.

754 **Houston, Walter** Purity and monotheism: clean and unclean animals in biblical law. ⇒9,2455; 10,2335. JSOT.S 140. 1993. RCritRR 7 (1994) 123-125 (*Simkins, Ronald A.*); CBQ 57 (1995) 139-140 (*Shafer, Byron E.*); JQR 85 (1995) 443-444 (*Milgrom, Jacob*) [Lev 11; Dt 14].

755 *Jenson, Philip P.* The Levitical sacrificial system. ⇒61. Sacrifice. 1995. 25-40.

756 *Joosten, Jan* Le cadre conceptuel du code de sainteté. RHPhR 75 (1995) 385-398.

757 *Kaiser, Walter C. Jr.* The book of Leviticus: introduction, commentary, and reflections. ⇒93. NintB 1. 1995. 983-1191.

758 *Karff, Samuel E.* Leviticus 10:1-20: silence and weeping before the song. 1995 ⇒89. Preaching biblical texts. 105-116.

759 *Klingbeil, Gerald A.* Ritual space in the ordination ritual of Leviticus 8. JNSL 21/1 (1995) 59-82.
760 **Knierim, Rolf P.** Text and concept in Leviticus 1:1-9. ⇒8,2630... 10,2330. 1992. RJSSt 40 (1995) 109-111 (*Wenham, G.J.*); JAOS 115 (1995) 320 (*Milgrom, Jacob*).
761 **Lane, David J.** The Peshitta of Leviticus. ⇒10,2322. MPIL 6. 1994. RThLZ 120 (1995) 641-642 (*Schwaiger, Wolfgang*).
762 **Levine, Baruch A.** Leviticus. ⇒5,2156... 7,2268. 1989. RJR 75 (1995) 104-106 (*Anderson, Gary A.*).
763 **Levy, Ralph David** The symbolism of the Azazel goat. Diss. DFritz, *H. Ira.* Union Institute 1995, 108 pp. AAC 9537924; DAI-A 56,2728 [Lev 16].
764 **Maier, Gerhard** Das dritte Buch Mose. 1994. RJETh 9 (1995) 161-164 (*Hilbrands, Walter*).
765 **Milgrom, Jacob** Leviticus 1-16. ⇒7,2270... 10,2324. AncB 3. 1991. RGr. 76 (1995) 147-152 (*Prato, Gian Luigi*).
766 *Milgrom, Jacob* The land redeemer and the jubilee. ⇒10. FFREEDMAN D., 1995. 66-69 [21,1-11; Lev 25,33.35-43; Dt 15,12-18].
767 *Neufeld, Ernest* Magical transformations: Sukkoth and the four species. JBQ 23 (1995) 27-32,37 [Lev 23,40].
768 *Nicole, Jacques* Lévitique 25. Lire et Dire 23 (1995) 3-11 [Bulletin of Biblical Bibliography 13,22].
769 *Perrar, H.J.* "Ihr sollt heilig werden..." (Lev 19,2): Annäherungen an Leviticus 19,1-27. ru 25 (1995) 17ff [ZID 21 (1995) 191].
770 *Pralon, Didier* L'allégorie au travail: interprétation de Lévitique X par PHILON d'Alexandrie. ⇒13. FHARL M., 1995. 483-497.
771 *Rendtorff, Rolf* Another prolegomenon to Leviticus 17:11. ⇒21. FMILGROM J., 1995. 23-28.
772 *Seidl, Theodor* Heiligkeitsgesetz. ⇒123. LThK 4. 1995. 1327-1328.
773 *Söding, Thomas* Feindeshaß und Bruderliebe: Beobachtungen zur essenischen Ethik. RdQ 16 (1995) 601-619 [Lev 19,18].
774 *Stallman, Robert C.* Levi and the Levites in the Dead Sea Scrolls. ⇒72. Qumran questions. BiSe 36. 1995. 164-190.
775 *Tov, Emanuel* 4QLevc,e,g(4Q25, 26a, 26b). ⇒21. FMILGROM J., 1995. 257-266 [Lev 1,1-7; 3,16-4,6.12-14.23-28; 5,12-13; 8,26-28; 3,2-4.5-8; 19,34-37; 20,1-3.27-21,4.9-12.21-24; 22,4-6; 22,11-17; 7,19-26].
776 *Virgulin, Stefano* Il sacrificio di comunione. PSV 31 (1995) 35-42.
777 *Werman, Cana* The rules of consuming and covering the blood in priestly and rabbinic law. RdQ 16 (1995) 621-636.
778 *Whitekettle, Richard* Leviticus 12 and the Israelite woman: ritual process, liminality and the womb. ZAW 107 (1995) 393-408.
779 *Wilken, Robert L.* ORIGEN's Homilies on Leviticus and Vayikra Rabbah. 1995 ⇒126. Origeniana Sexta. BEThL 118. 81-91.

E3.8 *Numeri;* **Numbers, Balaam.**

780 **Ashley, Timothy R.** The book of Numbers. ⇒9,2475; 10,2349. NIC. 1993. RJR 75 (1995) 254-255 (*Olson, Dennis T.*).
781 TClarke, **Ernest G.** Targum Pseudo-Jonathan: Numbers: translated with apparatus and notes. The Aramaic Bible 4. Collegeville, MN

1995, Liturgical. $79.95. 0-8146-5483-5 [bound with M. McNamara, Targum Neofiti 1: Numbers; OTA 19,340].

782 **Davies, Eryl W.** Numbers. NCeB. GR; L 1995, Eerdmans; Marshall Pickering lxxiv; 378 pp. $23; £30. 0-8028-0790-9; 0-551-02835-1 [BoL 1996,53].

783 **Dorival, Gilles** Les Nombres. ⇒10,2350. Bible d'Alexandrie 4. 1994. ᴿFV 94/3 (1995) 116-117 (*Flichy, Odile*); EeV 105 (1995) 265-267 (*Cothenet, Édouard*); MSR 52 (1995) 333-334 (*Spanneut, Michel*).

784 *Dorival, Gilles* Les phénomènes d'intertextualité dans le livre grec des Nombres. ⇒13. ᶠHARL M., 1995. 253-285.

785 *Dorival, Gilles* Remarques sur l'originalité du livre grec des nombres. ⇒136. VIII Congress. SCSt 41. 1995. 89-107.

786 **Levine, Baruch A.** Numbers 1-20. ⇒9,2479; 10,2353. AncB 4A. 1993. ᴿJR 75 (1995) 104-106 (*Anderson, Gary A.*); JSSt 40 (1995) 112-114 (*Tomes, Roger*); AUSS 33/1 (1995) 131-132 (*Gane, Roy*); CBQ 57 (1995) 147-148 (*Wright, David P.*); Bijdr. 56 (1995) 451-452 (*Wieringen, Archibald van*).

787 **Licht, Jacob** פירוש על ספר במדבר [A commentary on the book of Numbers (XXII-XXXVI)]. H. Hebrew University Jerusalem 1995, Magnes 15*; 209 pp. $18. 965-223-903-8 [BoL 1996,63].

788 ᵀ**McNamara, Martin** Targum Neofiti 1: Numbers: translated with apparatus and notes. Aramaic Bible 4. ColMn 1995, Liturgical. $80. 0-8146-5483-5 [bound with E.G. Clarke, Targum Pseudo-Jonathan: Numbers; OTA 19,340].

789 **Milgrom, Jacob** Numbers. ⇒6,2768... 10,2355. JPSTC. 1990. ᴿHebStud 36 (1995) 171-174 (*Ehrlich, Carl S.*).

790 **Sakenfeld, Katharine Doob** Journeying with God: a commentary on the book of Numbers. International Theological Commentary. GR 1995, Eerdmans xiv; 194 pp. $13. 0-8028-4126-0.

791 **Scharbert, Josef** Numeri. ⇒8,2652... 10,2356. NEB 27. 1992. CBQ 57 (1995) 787-788 (*Olson, Dennis T.*).

792 **Seebaß, Horst** Numeri (13,1-15,41). BK.AT 4/2. Neuk 1995, Neuk 81-160.

793 **Artus, Olivier** Étude sur le livre des Nombres: récit, histoire et loi en Nombres 13,1-20,13. Diss. ᴰ*Briend, Jacques*. P 1995, L'Institut Catholique de Paris 443 pp. [RICP 57,271-274].

794 **Bell, Richard H.** Sin offerings and sinning with a high hand. JProg-Jud 4 (1995) 25-59 [[Num 15,30-31; NTAb 40,275].

795 **Cartledge, Tony W.** Vows in the Hebrew Bible and the ANE. ⇒8,2655... 10,2364*. JSOT.S 147. 1992. ᴿAJS 20 (1995) 391-392 (*Milgrom, Jacob*).

796 *Crocker, P.T.* May the Lord bless you and keep you...: BurH 31 (1995) 24-29 [Num 6,24-26; OTA 18,517].

797 *Davies, Eryl W.* A mathematical conundrum: the problem of the large numbers in Numbers i and xxvi. VT 45 (1995) 449-469.

798 *Derrett, John Duncan M.* The bronze serpent. Studies 6. ⇒45. Studies 6. 1995 <1991>. 78-96 [Num 21,1-9; John 3,16-21].

799 **Douglas, Mary** In the wilderness: the doctrine of defilement in the book of Numbers. ⇒9,2477; 10,2357. JSOT.S 158. 1993. ᴿBiRe (June 1995) 14, 41 (*Hendel, Ronald S.*); BSOAS 58 (1995) 353-355 (*Weightman, S.C.R.*); JSSt 40 (1995) 326-327 (*Auld, Graeme*); TJT

11 (1995) 230-231 (*Williams, Tyler F.*); CBQ 57 (1995) 124-125 (*Gnuse, Robert*); CritRR 8 (1995) 119-121 (*Anderson, Gary*).
800 *Fishbane, Michael* The priestly blessing and its Aggadic reuse. ⇒83. Israelite prophets. Sources for biblical and theological study 5. 1995 <1985>. 223-229 [Num 6,23-27].
801 *Greenberg, Moshe* Idealism and practicality in Numbers 35:4-5 and Ezekiel 48. 1995 ⇒49. Studies. 313-326.
802 *Hirth, Thomas* Überlegungen zu den Serafim. BN 77 (1995) 17-19 [Num 21,6-8; Isa 6,2-6].
803 *Kero, Kewai* The significance of water in Numbers. MJT 11 (1995) 104-115 [ThIK 18,64].
804 *Lux, Rüdiger* "Und die Erde tat ihren Mund auf...": zum "aktuellen Erzählinteresse" Israels am Konflikt zwischen Mose und Datan und Abiram in Num 16. ⇒37. FWAGNER S., 1995. 187-216.
805 *Malino, Jerome R.* Numbers 19:1-22: the ashes of the red heifer: religious ceremonies and obedience to torah. 1995 ⇒89. Preaching biblical texts. 144-148.
806 *Martin-Achard, Robert* Remarques sur la bénédiction sacerdotale Nb 6/22-27 (I). ETR 70 (1995) 75-84.
807 *Mosconi, Franco* "L'ho forse generato io questo popolo?" (Nm 10 ss). Presbyteri 29 (1995) 731-744.
808 *Oberlinner, Lorenz* Genealogie: Biblisch. ⇒123. LThK 4. 1995. 442-443.
809 **Scolnic, Benjamin E.** Theme and context in biblical lists. SFSHJ 119. Atlanta 1995, Scholars 174 pp. Diss. Jewish Theological Seminary of America. $74.95. 0-7885-0145-3 [BoL 1996,92].
810 *Stuhlmueller, Carroll* Numbers 11:29: "would that all were prophets!" 1995 ⇒89. Preaching biblical texts. 129-143.
811 **Ullmann, Douglas Wayne** Moses' bronze serpent (Numbers 21:4-9) in early Jewish and christian exegesis. Diss. Dallas Theological Seminary, DTaylor, Richard A., Dallas 1995, 285 pp. AAC 9531284; DAI-A 56,1832.
812 **Vieweger, Dieter** Μασχανά. κεῖται δὲ 'πὶ τοῦ 'Αρνωνᾶ: Ergebnisse eines Surveys im Bereich südöstlich von Madeba. ZDPV 111/1 (1995) 49-59 [Num 21,18-19].

813 *Dijkstra, Meindert* The geography of the story of Balaam: synchronic reading as a help to date a biblical text. ⇒99. Synchronic or diachronic?. 1995. 72-97.
814 *Dijkstra, Meindert* Is Balaam also among the prophets?. JBL 114 (1995) 43-64.
815 **Grundke, Christopher Laurie Karl** A literary examination of the Masoretic Balaam cycle. Diss. DAshley, Timothy R., Acadia 1995, 157 pp. 0-612-04605-2. MAI 34,987.
816 *Lust, J.* The Greek version of Balaam's third and fourth oracles: the ANTHRWPOS in Num 24:7 and 17: messianism and lexicography. ⇒136. VIII Congress. SCSt 41. 1995. 233-257 [Num 24].
817 *Seebaß, Horst* Zur literarischen Gestalt der Bileam-Perikope. ZAW 107 (1995) 409-419.
818 *Segert, Stanislav* Bileam, der Sohn Beors. ZAH 8/1 (1995) 71-77.

E3.9 Liber Deuteronomii.

819 **Bovati, Pietro** Il libro del Deuteronomio (1-11). 1994. RCivCatt 146
(1995) 91-92 (*Teani, M.*).
820 **Clifford, Richard** Deuteronomio: con un excursus su alleanza e
legge. TDi *Giovambattista, Fulvio*, LoB.AT 6. Brescia 1995,
Queriniana 193 pp. L25.000. 88-399-1556-7.
821 **Hamlin, E. John** A guide to Deuteronomy. SPCK International
Study Guides 32. L 1995, SPCK x; 214 pp. ill. map. 0-281-04863-0.
822 **Mann, Thomas Wingate** Deuteronomy. Westminster Bible Com- ·
panion. Louisville 1995, Westminster John Knox 169 pp. $16. 0-
664-25266-4 [Interp. 50,304].
823 **Merrill, Eugene H.** Deuteronomy. ⇒10,2390. NAC 4. 1994.
RHebStud 36 (1995) 174-177 (*Dempster, Stephen*).
824 **Nielsen, Eduard** Deuteronomium. HAT 1/6. Tü 1995, Mohr x; 311
pp. DM88. 3-16-146250-5; -6253-X <pb>. RET 107 (1995-96)
371-372 (*Rogerson, John*).
825 **Weinfeld, Moshe** Deuteronomy 1-11. ⇒7,2337...10,2393. AncB 5.
1991. RGr. 76 (1995) 377-380 (*Prato, Gian Luigi*).
826 **Wevers, John William** Notes on the Greek text of Deuteronomy.
SCSt 39. Atlanta 1995, Scholars xxx; 665 pp. $76. 0-7885-0120-8.
RJR 75/1 (1995) 103-104 (*Hendel, Ronald S.*); ThRv 91 (1995) 310-
311 (*Schenker, Adrian*); EThL 71 (1995) 446-447 (*Lust, J.*); ABR 43
(1995) 77-78 (*Jenkins, R.G.*).

827 **Barker, Paul A.** Faithless Israel, faithful Yahweh in Deuteronomy.
Diss. DWenham, G.J., Bristol 1995 [TynB 47,173].
828 EBraulik, **Georg** Bundesdokument und Gesetz: Studien zum
Deuteronomium. Herders Biblische Studien 4. Gö 1995, Herder.
DM82. 3-451-23623-0.
829 *Braulik, Georg* Deuteronomium, Deuteronomist: Geschichtswerk,
Deuteronomist: Schule. ⇒122. LThK 3. 1995. 116-118.
830 *Briend, Jacques* Le Dieu d'Israel reconnu par des étrangers, signe de
l'universalisme du salut. ⇒4. FBEAUCHAMP P., LeDiv 162. 1995.
65-76.
831 EChristensen, **Duane L.** A song of power and the power of song.
⇒9,263. 1993. RAUSS 33 (1995) 110-111 (*Gregor, Zeljko*).
832 EGarcía Martínez, **F.** Studies in Deuteronomy. FLABUSCHAGNE
C., ⇒10,68. VT.S 53. 1994. RJThS 46 (1995) 577-580 (*McConville,
J.G.*); ETR 70 (1995) 425-427 (*Römer, Thomas*); NRTh 117 (1995)
907-908 (*Ska, Jean Louis*); CBQ 57 (1995) 839-840 (*Nelson,
Richard D.*).
833 *Gosse, B.* Les rédactions liées à la mention du sabbat dans le
Deutéronome et le livre d'Ésaïe. ETR 70 (1995) 581-585.
834 *Greenberg, Blu* Deuteronomy 1-34: hear, O Israel: law and love in
Deuteronomy. 1995 ⇒89. Preaching biblical texts. 149-158.
835 *Harl, Marguerite* L'originalité lexicale de la version grecque du
deutéronome (LXX) et la "paraphrase" de Flavius JOSEPHE (A.J.
IV, 176-331). ⇒136. VIII Congress. SCSt 41. 1995. 1-20.
836 *Jensen, Hans J. Lundager* Talen ud af ilden: Deuteronomium, traktat, visdom [The speech out of the fire: Deuteronomy, treaty, wis-
dom]. 1995 ⇒90. Lov og visdom. 58-77 [OTA 19,420].
837 **Keller, Martin** Untersuchungen zur deuteronomisch-deuteronomisti-
schen Namenstheologie. Diss. DSeybold, K., Basel 1995.

838 *Kloppers, M.H.O.* Die 'profeet' in Deuteronomium [The 'prophet' in Deuteronomy]. NGTT 36 (1995) 453-458 [OTA 19,420].

839 *Knight, Douglas A.* Deuteronomy and the deuteronomists. ⇒36. ᶠTUCKER G., 1995. 61-79.

840 *Krebernik, Manfred* M. WEINFELDS Deuteronomiumskommentar aus assyriologischer Sicht. ⇒828. Bundesdokument. 1995. 27-36.

841 *Lohfink, Norbert* Bund als Vertrag im Deuteronomium. ZAW 107 (1995) 215-239.

   Lohfink, Norbert Studien zum Deuteronomium: 3. ⇒54. SBAB.AT 20. 1995:

842 Das deuteronomische Gesetz in der Endgestalt: Entwurf einer Gesellschaft ohne marginale Gruppen 205-218;

843 Das Deuteronomium: Jahwegesetz oder Mosegesetz?: die Subjektzuordnung bei Wörtern für 'Gesetz' im Dtn und in der dtr Literatur <1990> 157-165;

844 Deuteronomium und Pentateuch: zum Stand der Forschung <1992> 13-38;

845 Opferzentralisation, Säkularisierungsthese und mimetische Theorie 219-260.

846 *Lohfink, Norbert* Kultzentralisation und Deuteronomium: zu einem Buch von Eleonore REUTER. ZABRG 1 (1995) 117-148.

847 *Lohfink, Norbert* Zur Fabel des Deuteronomiums. ⇒828. Bundesdokument. 1995. 65-78.

848 **McConville, J. Gordon** Grace in the end: a study in Deuteronomic theology. ⇒9,2532; 10,2404. Studies in Old Testament Biblical Theology. ᴿAUSS 33 (1995) 310-312 *(Duerksen, Paul Dean)*.

849 **McConville, J. Gordon; Millar, J.G.** Time and place in Deuteronomy. ⇒10,2405. JSOT.S 179. 1994. ZABRG 1 (1995) 149-155 *(Achenbach, Reinhard)*.

850 **Millar, J.G.** The ethics of Deuteronomy: an exegetical and theological study of the book of Deuteronomy. 1995, Oxford diss. [sum. TynB 46 (1995) 389-392].

851 *Moore, R. D.* Deuteronomy and the fire of God: a critical charismatic interpretation. JPentec 7 (1995) 11-33.

852 **Nohrnberg, James** Like unto Moses: the constituting of an interruption. ISBL Bloomington 1995, Indiana University Press xx; 396 pp. $40. 0-253-34090-X [RB 103,316].

853 *O'Brien, Mark A.* The book of Deuteronomy. CurResB 3 (1995) 95-128.

854 **Olson, Dennis T.** Deuteronomy and the death of Moses: a theological reading. ⇒10,2450. 1994. ᴿPSB 16 (1995) 243-244 *(Nelson, Richard D.)*.

855 *Olson, Dennis T.* Deuteronomy as de-centering center: reflections on postmodernism and the quest for a theological center of the Hebrew scriptures. Semeia 71 (1995) 119-132.

856 *Otto, Eckart* Von der Programmschrift einer Rechtsreform zum Verfassungsentwurf des Neuen Israel: die Stellung des Deuteronomiums in der Rechtsgeschichte Israels. ⇒828. Bundesdokument. 1995. 93-104.

857 *Patrick, Dale* The rhetoric of collective responsibility in Deuteronomic law. ⇒21. ᶠMILGROM J., 1995. 421-436.

858 **Perlitt, Lothar** Deuteronomium-Studien. ⇒10,214. FAT 8. 1994. ᴿThLZ 120 (1995) 419-421 *(Nielsen, Eduard)*.

859 *Perlitt, Lothar* Der Staatsgedanke im Deuteronomium. ⇒57. Allein mit dem Wort. 1995. 236-248.

860 **Pressler, Carolyn** The view of women found in the Deuteronomic family laws. ⇒9,2536; 10,2407. BZAW 216. 1993. ᴿOLZ 90 (1995) 291-293 *(Herrmann, Wolfram)*; OTEs 8 (1995) 303-305 *(Domeris, William R.)*; JBL 114 (1995) 492-493 *(Blenkinsopp, Joseph)*; CBQ 57 (1995) 363-365 *(Brenner, A.)*.

861 *Römer, Thomas* Approches exégétiques du Deutéronome: brève histoire de la recherche sur le Deutéronome depuis Martin NOTH. RHPhR 75 (1995) 153-175.

862 *Schäfer-Lichtenberger, Christa* Der deuteronomische Verfassungsentwurf: theologische Vorgaben als Gestaltungsprinzipien sozialer Realität. ⇒828. Bundesdokument. 1995. 105-118.

863 *Suzuki, Yoshihide* A new aspect of חרם in Deuteronomy in view of an assimilation policy of King Josiah. AJBI 21 (1995) 3-27.

864 *Tarragon, Jean-Michel de* Witchcraft, magic, and divination in Canaan and ancient Israel. ⇒127. Civilizations 3. 1995. 2071-2081.

865 *Westbrook, Raymond* Riddles in Deuteronomic law. ⇒828. Bundesdokument. 1995. 159-174.

866 **Wilson, Ian** Out of the midst of the fire: divine presence in Deuteronomy. SBLDS 151. Atlanta, GA 1995, Scholars xiv; 257 pp. $30; $20. 0-7885-0160-7; -0161-5 <pb>.

867 *Vanoni, Gottfried* Anspielungen und Zitate innerhalb der hebräischen Bibel: am Beispiel von Dtn 4,29; Dtn 30,3 und Jer 29,13-14. 1995 ⇒86. Jeremia. BBB 98. 383-397.

868 *Levinson, Bernard M.* "But you shall surely kill him!": the text-critical and neo-Assyrian evidence for MT Deuteronomy 13:10. ⇒828. Bundesdokument. 1995. 37-63.

869 *Braulik, Georg* Die dekalogische Redaktion der deuteronomischen Gesetze: ihre Abhängigkeit von Levitikus 19 am Beispiel von Deuteronomium 22,1-12; 24,10-22; 25,13-16 <German>. ⇒828. Bundesdokument und Gesetz. 1995. 1-25 [Lev 19; Deut 22,1-12; 24,10-22; 25,13-16].

870 *Nwachukwu, Fortunatus* The textual differences between the MT and the LXX of Deuteronomy 31: a response to Leo LABERGE. ⇒828. Bundesdokument. 1995. 79-92.

871 *Kallai, Zecharia* Where did Moses speak (Deuteronomy i 1-5)?. VT 45 (1995) 188-197.

872 *Lohfink, Norbert* Zu את סבב in Dtn 2,1.3 <1994> 1995 ⇒54. Studien: 3. 263-268.

873 *Blancy, Alain* Le Shema Israël, coeur de la prière et de la foi juives. FV 94/5 (1995) 65-82 [Deut 6,4].

874 *Loretz, Oswald* Die *Einzigkeit* Jahwes (Dtn 6,4) im Licht des ugaritischen Baal-Mythos: das Argumentationsmodell des altsyrisch-kanaanäischen und biblischen 'Monotheismus'. Vom alten Orient zum Alten Testament: Festschrift für Wolfram Freiherrn von SODEN zum 85. Geburtstag am 19. Juni 1993. ᴱDietrich, Manfried; Loretz, Oswald, AOAT 240. Kevelaer; Neuk 1995, Butzon & Bercker; Neuk 581 pp. 3-7666-9977-6; 3-7887-1534-0. 215-304.

875 *Heintz, Jean-Georges* "Dans la plénitude du coeur": à propos d'une formule d'alliance à Mari, en Assyrie et dans la Bible. ⇒22. ᶠRENAUD B., 1995. 31-44.

876 *Lohfink, Norbert* Deuteronomium 6,24: לְחַיֹּתֵנוּ 'für unseren Unterhalt aufzukommen' <1992> 1995 ⇒54. Studien: 3. 269-278;

877 *Harmsen, H.* Syntactical parsing and actants analysis: the clause as the basic linguistic unit in the discourse structure of Deuteronomy 8. ⇒133. L'impact de l'informatique. 1995. 129-139.

878 *Bosman, Hendrik Jan* Computer assisted clause description of Deuteronomy 8. ⇒133. L'impact de l'informatique. 1995. 76-100.

879 *Veijola, Timo* "Der Mensch lebt nicht vom Brot allein": zur literarischen Schichtung und theologischen Aussage von Deuteronomium 8. ⇒828. Bundesdokument. 1995. 143-158.

880 *Andersen, F.I.; Forbes, A.D.* Opportune parsing: clause analysis of Deuteronomy 8. ⇒133. L'impact de l'informatique. 1995. 49-75.

881 *Talstra, Eep* Deuteronomy 9 and 10: synchronic and diachronic observations. ⇒99. Synchronic or diachronic?. OTS 34. 1995. 187-210.

882 *Cohen, Jeffrey M.* Why Moses smashed the tablets. 1995. JBQ 23/1 (1995) 33-37 [9,17].

883 *Otto, Eckart* Rechtsreformen in Deuteronomium XII-XXVI und im Mittelassyrischen Kodex der Tafel A. (KAV 1). ⇒135. Congress Volume: Paris 1992. VT.S 61. 1995. 239-273.

884 **Reuter, Eleonore** Kultzentralisation: Entstehung und Theologie von Dtn 12. ⇒9,2549. BBB 87. 1993. ᴿZABRG 1 (1995) 117-148 *(Lohfink, Norbert)*.

885 *Houtman, A.D.* 'And there shall cleave nought of the cursed thing in your hand...': a dispute between a gentile and a sage about the interpretation of Deuteronomy 13:18. ⇒130. Aspects of religious contact. 1995. 135-145 [EThL 72,186*].

886 *Veijola, Timo* Wahrheit und Intoleranz nach Deuteronomium 13. ZThK 92 (1995) 287-314.

887 **Morrow, William S.** Scribing the center: organization and redaction in Deuteronomy 14:1-17:13. ᴰ*Dion, Paul Eugene*, SBL.MS 49. Atlanta 1995, Scholars xi; 271 pp. Diss. Toronto 1988 [⇒4,2716]. $50; $34. 0-7885-0064-3; -0065-1 <pb> [RB 103,315].

888 *Houston, Walter* "You shall open your hand to your needy brother": ideology and moral formation in Deut. 15.1-18. ⇒109 The Bible in ethics. 1995. 296-314.

889 *Lasserre, G.* Lutter contre la paupérisation et ses conséquences: lecture rhétorique de Dt 15/12-18. ETR 70 (1995) 481-492 [Deut 15,12-18].

890 *Pearce, Sarah* Josephus as interpreter of Biblical law: the representation of the high court of Deut. 17:8-12 according to Jewish Antiquities 4.218. JJS 46/1-2 (1995) 30-42.

891 **Kim, Yoon-Hee** 'The prophet like Moses': Deut 18:15-22 reexamined within the context of the pentateuch and in light of the final shape of the tanak. Diss. ᴰ*Sailhamer, J.*, 1995, Trinity Evangelical Divinity School 315 pp. AAC 9533055; DAI-A 56,2281.

892 *Frank, Karl Suso* Die 'captiva gentilis' (Dt 21,10-13) in der lateinischen Väterexegese. Aristotelica et Lulliana magistro doctissimo Charles H. LOHR septuagesimum annum feliciter agenti dedicata. ᴱ**Domínguez, Fernando; Imbach, Ruedi; Pindl, Theodor; Walter, Peter**. IP 26. Turnhout 1995, Brepols ix; 598 pp. 1-10.

893 *Lieu, Judith M.* Reading in canon and community: Deuteronomy 21.22-23, a test case for dialogue. ⇒23. ᶠROGERSON J., JSOT.S 200. 1995. 317-334 [Gal 3,10-14].

894 *Tigay, Jeffrey H.* Some archaeological notes on Deuteronomy. ⇒21. FMILGROM J., 1995. 373-380 [Deut 22,2; 24,6; 25,1-4; 32,34].
895 *Christensen, Richard L.* Deuteronomy 26:1-11. Interp. 49/1 (1995) 59-62.
896 *Rendtorff, Rolf* Sihon, Og und das israelitische "Credo". ⇒8. FDONNER H., ÄAT 30. 1995. 198-203 [Num 21,21-23; Deut 26,5-9; 6,20-24; Ps 136].
897 *Blenkinsopp, Joseph* Deuteronomy and the politics of post-mortem existence. VT 45 (1995) 1-16 [Deut 26,14; 18,9-22].
898 *Curtis, John Briggs* The relationship formula of Deuteronomy 26:17-8 and the covenant. ProcGLM 15 (1995) 169-183.
899 *Steymans, Hans Ulrich* Eine assyrische Vorlage für Deuteronomium 28,20-44. ⇒828. Bundesdokument. 1995. 119-141.
900 **Lenchak, Timothy A.** "Choose life!": a rhetorical-critical investigation of Deuteronomy 28,69-30,20. ⇒9,2559; 10,2441. AnBib 129. 1993. RBib. 76 (1995) 93-98 *(Sonnet, Jean-Pierre)*; CBQ 57 (1995) 145-146 *(Nelson, Richard D.)*; CivCatt 146 (1995) 632-633 *(Scaiola, D.)*.
901 *Lohfink, Norbert* Dtn 28,69: Überschrift oder Kolphon? <1992> 1995 ⇒54. Studien: 3. 279-291.
902 **Steymans, Hans Ulrich** Deuteronomium 28 und die *Adê* zur Thronfolgeregelung Asarhaddons: Segen und Fluch im Alten Orient und in Israel. Diss. Wien 1995, DBraulik, Georg, OBO 145. Gö; FrS 1995, Vandenhoeck & Ruprecht; Éditions Universitaires xi; 425 pp. FS125; DM150; SCH1.110. 3-525-53780-8; 2-7278-1038-6 [BZ 39,318; RB 103,479]. RET 107 (1995-96) 371 *(Rogerson, John)*.
903 **Gillen, Jeannot** Umkehr und Wiederherstellung: die bedingte Heilsankündigung in DTN 30 im Vergleich mit verwandten Verheissungen. Diss. DConroy, Charles, 1995. Pont. Univ. Gregoriana.
904 *Lust, Johan* The raised hand of the Lord in Deut 32:40 according to MT, 4QDeut/q, and LXX. Textus 18 (1995) 33-45.
905 **Knight, George A.F.** The song of Moses: a theological quarry. GR 1995, Eerdmans viii; 156 pp. $13. 0-8028-0599-X [Deut 32].
906 *Duncan, Julie A.* New readings for the "Blessing of Moses" from Qumran. JBL 114 (1995) 273-290 [Deut 33,1-29].
907 **Beyerle, Stefan** Der Mosesegen im Deuteronomium: eine text-, kompositions- und formkritische Studie zu Deuteronomium 33. Diss. DSeebass, H., 1995 Bonn [ThRv 92/2,VI].
908 *Tigay, Jeffrey H.* לא נס לחה "he had not become wrinkled" (Deuteronomy 34:7). ⇒11. FGREENFIELD J., 1995. 345-350.
909 **Kushelevsky, Rella** Moses and the angel of death. Diss. DElstein, Yoav, Studies on Themes and Motifs in Literature 4. NY 1995, Lang xxii; 325 pp. $57.95. 0-8204-2147-2 [Deut 34; OTA 19,366].
910 *Haber, Heriberto* Who wrote the story of Moses' death? JBQ 23/1 (1995) 52-53 [Dt 34].

E4.1   *Origo Israelis in Canaan: Deuteronomista;* **Liber Josue.**

911 *Botta, Alejandro Felix* Problemas históricos en torno a los origines de Israel. BolT 57 (1995) 61-70 [OTA 18,497].
912 *Dever, William G.* Ceramics, ethnicity, and the question of Israel's origins. BA 58 (1995) 200-213.

913 **Fischer, Irmtraud** Gottesstreiterinnen: biblische Erzählungen über die Anfänge Israels. Stu 1995, Kohlhammer 200 pp. 3-17-013508-2.
914 *Hasel, Michael G.* Israel in the Merneptah stela. BASOR 296 (1995) 45-61.
915 **Hostetter, Edwin C.** Nations mightier and more numerous: the biblical view of Palestine's pre-Israelite peoples. BIBAL.DS 3. New Richland Hills 1995, BIBAL xiii; 172 pp. Diss. Johns Hopkins. 0-941037-36-3.
916 **Lemche, Niels Peter** The Canaanites and their land. ⇒7,b17... 10,10997. JSOT.S 110. 1991. ᴿBZ 39 (1995) 109-112 (*Albertz, Rainer*); NedThT 49/1 (1995) 72-73 (*Smelik, K.A.D.*).
917 *Levin, Christoph* Das System der zwölf Stämme Israels. ⇒135. Congress Volume: Paris 1992. VT.S 61. 1995. 163-178.
918 *Martín Juárez, Miguel Ángel* Conciencia étnica: el pueblo de Israel. BiFe 61 (1995) 29-53.
919 **Nordheim, E. von** Die Selbstbehauptung Israels. ⇒8,2737... 10,2043. OBO 115. 1992. ᴿVT 45 (1995) 133-134 (*Emerton, John A.E.*).

920 **Alvarez, Miguel** Terminologia deuteronomistica en los libros historicos (Jueces - 2 Reyes). Biblioteca 35. R 1995, Antonianum.
921 *Coggins, Richard* What does "deuteronomistic" mean? ⇒24. ꜰSAWYER J., JSOT.S 195. 1995. 135-148.
922 **Doorly, W.D.** Obsession with justice: the story of the deuteronomists. ⇒10,2459. 1994. CritRR 8 (1995) 118-119 (*Gnuse, Robert*).
923 *Friedman, Richard Elliott* The deuteronomistic school. ⇒10. ꜰFREEDMAN D., 1995. 70-80.
924 *Hoffman, Yair* The deuteronomist and the exile. ⇒21. ꜰMILGROM J., 1995. 659-675.
925 *Laberge, Léo* Le deutéronomiste. ⇒84. De bien des manières. LeDiv 163. 1995. 47-77 [EThL 72/,187*].
926 *Lohfink, Norbert* Gab es eine deuteronomistische Bewegung?. 1995 ⇒86. Jeremia. BBB 98. 313-382.
927 *Lohfink, Norbert* Gab es eine deuteronomistische Bewegung?. ⇒54. Studien 3. SBAB.AT 20. 1995 65-142.
928 **Mullen, E. Theodore** Narrative history and ethnic boundaries: the deuteronomistic historian and the creation of Israelite national identity. ⇒9,2583. SBL.Semeia Studies. 1993. ᴿCBQ 57 (1995) 151-152 (*Miscall, Peter D.*); JBL 114 (1995) 301-302 (*Dearman, J. Andrew*).
929 *Naʾaman, Nadav* The deuteronomist and voluntary servitude to foreign powers. JSOT 65 (1995) 37-53.
930 **O'Brien, Mark A.** The Deuteronomistic History hypothesis. ⇒5,2608... 10,2462. OBO 92. 1989. ᴿBZ 39 (1995) 114-115 (*Gerstenberger, Erhard S.*).
931 *Pleins, J. David* Murderous fathers, manipulative mothers, and rivalrous siblings: rethinking the architecture of Genesis-Kings. ⇒10. ꜰFREEDMAN D., 1995. 121-136.
932 *Stadelmann, A.* Le origini del profetismo nella prospettiva teologica del 'deuteronomista'. ⇒32. ꜰSTUDER B., StAns 116. 1995. 15-38 [EThL 72,188*].
933 *Trebolle, Julio* Histoire du texte des livres historiques et histoire de la composition et de la rédaction deutéronomistes avec une publication préliminaire de 4Q481a, "Apocryphe d'Élisée". ⇒135. Congress Volume: Paris 1992. VT.S 61. 1995. 327-342.

934 **Westermann, Claus** Die Geschichtsbücher des Alten Testaments:
gab es ein deuteronomistisches Geschichtswerk?. ⇒10,2465. 1994.
[R]ThPQ 143 (1995) 91-94 *(Böhmisch, Franz)*; ETR 70 (1995) 112-
114 *(Römer, Thomas)* ThLZ 120 (1995) 332-334 *(Dietrich, Walter)*.
935 *Whitelam, Keith W.* New deuteronomistic heroes and villains: a response to T.L. THOMPSON. SJOT 9 (1995) 97-118.
936 **Würthwein, Ernst** Studien zum Deuteronomistischen Geschichtswerk. 1994 ⇒10,233. BZAW 227. [R]ET 106 (1994-95) 332-333
(Mason, Rex); CBQ 57 (1995) 631-632 *(McKenzie, Steven L.)*.

937 **Aḥituv, Shmuel** Joshua: introduction and commentary. H. Mikra
Leyisra'el. Tel Aviv 1995, Am Oved 408 pp. map. 965-13-1059-6.
938 **Cortese, Enzo** Giosuè. ⇒9,2588. Piccola Biblioteca di Teologia 2.
1992. [R]PaVi 40/4 (1995) 45-47 *(Marocco, Giuseppe)*.
939 **Fritz, Volkmar** Das Buch Josua. ⇒10,2467. HAT 1/7. 1994. [R]ETR
70 (1995) 268-269 *(Römer, Thomas)*.
940 **Hertog, Cornelis den** Studien zur griechischen Übersetzung des
Buches Josua. Diss. [D]*Fritz, V.*, 1995-1996 Giessen [RTL 27,528].
941 *Hertog, Cornelis G. den* Anmerkungen zu MARGOLIS' The book of
Joshua in Greek. BIOSCS 28 (1995) 51-56.
942 *Moatti-Fine, Jacqueline* La "tâche du traducteur" de Josué / Jésus.
⇒13. [F]HARL M., 1995. 321-330.
943 **Moor, Johannes C. de** Joshua. A bilingual concordance to the Targum of the Prophets 1. Lei 1995, Brill x; 413 pp. ƒ199.50; $129.
90-04-10277-9.
944 *Moor, Johannes C. de; Sepmeijer, Floris* The Peshitta and the Targum of Joshua. ⇒76. The Peshitta. MPIL 8. 1995. 129-176.
945 **Navarro Puerto, Mercedes** Los Libros de Josué, Jueces y Rut. Guía
espiritual del Antiguo Testamento. Barc 1995, Herder 172 pp.
Ptas1.500. 84-254-1898-4.

946 *Auld, Graeme* Reading Joshua after Kings. ⇒24. [F]SAWYER J.,
JSOT.S 195. 1995. 167-181.
947 **Bieberstein, Klaus** Lukian und Theodotion im Josuabuch: mit einem
Beitrag zu den Josuarollen von Hirbet Qumran. ⇒10,2473. BN.B 7.
1994. [R]JSJ 26 (1995) 185-187 *(Tov, Emmanuel)*.
948 **Bieberstein, Klaus** Josua—Jordan—Jericho: Archäologie, Geschichte
und Theologie der Landnahmeerzählung Josua 1-6. Diss. Tü, [D]*Groß,
Walter*, OBO 143. FrS 1995, Universitätsverlag xii; 483 pp. FS50.
3-7278-1016-5.
949 *Gottwald, Norman K.* Theological education as a theory-praxis loop:
situating the book of Joshua in a cultural, social ethical, and theological matrix. ⇒109 The Bible in ethics. JSOT.S 207. 1995. 107-118.
950 *Hess, Richard S.* Studies in the book of Joshua. Themelios 20/3
(1995) 12-15 [OTA 19,62].
951 *Lambert, Chiara* La figura di Giosuè nei mosaici di Santa Maria
Maggiore. PaVi 40/4 (1995) 40-41.
952 *Machetta, Domenico* Giosuè: le guerre del Signore. PaVi 40/4
(1995) 38-39.
953 *Marconcini, Benito* L'erede di Mosè. PaVi 40/4 (1995) 6-8.
954 **Mitchell, Gordon** Together in the land: a reading of the book of Joshua. ⇒10,2470. JSOT.S 134. 1993. [R]ETR 70 (1995) 269-270
(Römer, Thomas); CritRR 8 (1995) 137-138 *(Britt, Brian M.)*.

955 *Nardi, Carlo* Giosuè nel primo cristianesimo. PaVi 40/4 (1995) 29-33.

956 **Park, Myon Ki** Toward a theology of land reform ('land division'): a theological study of Joshua 13-21. Diss. Fuller Theological Seminary. ᴰ*Gilliland, Dean S.*, 1995, 169 pp. MAI 33,p.1687.

957 *Perani, Mauro* La figura di Giosuè nei midrashim. PaVi 40/2 (1995) 27-28.

958 *Peroni, Mauro* Giosuè in alcuni testi midrashici. PaVi 40/4 (1995) 27-28.

959 **Schäfer-Lichtenberger, Christa** Josua und Salomo: eine Studie zu Autorität und Legitimität des Nachfolgers im Alten Testament. VT.S 58. Lei 1995, Brill xii; 424 pp. Diss.-Habil. 90-04-10064-4.

960 *Sipilä, Seppo* The renderings of wjhj and whjh as formulas in the LXX of Joshua. ⇒136. VIII Congress. SCSt 41. 1995. 273-289.

961 **Weinfeld, Moshe** From Joshua to Josiah. ⇒8,2579; 9,2579. 1992. ᴿJQR 86 (1995) 205-207 *(Glatt-Gilad, David A.)*.

962 **Winther-Nielsen, Nicolai** A functional discourse grammar of Joshua: a computer-assisted rhetorical structure analysis. CB.OT 40. Sto 1995, Almqvist & Wiksell xii; 353 pp. Diss. Lund 1994. SEK234. 91-22-01658-9. ᴿThQ 175 (1995) 223-224 *(Gross, Walter)*; ΙΧΘΥΣ 22 (1995) 174-183 *(Kofoed, Jens Bruun)*.

963 *Mello, Alberto* Il passagio del Giordano. PaVi 40/4 (1995) 9-12 [Josh 3-4].

964 *Howard, David M. Jr.* All Israel's response to Joshua: a note on the narrative framework of Joshua 1. ⇒10. ᶠFʀᴇᴇᴅᴍᴀɴ D., 1995. 81-91.

965 *Barnes, Peter* Was Rahab's lie a sin? 1995. RTR 54/1 (1995) 1-9 [Josh 2,4-5].

966 *Minde, H. J. van der* Die Überquerung des Jordan oder die Rettung vor den Wassern. IKZ 85 (1995) 34-50 [Josh 3,1-17; Matt 14,22-33].

967 *Millard, A.R.* Back to the iron bed: Og's or Procrustes'?. ⇒135. Congress Volume: Paris 1992. VT.S 61. 1995. 193-203 [Josh 5,2-3; 7,21; 17,16-18; Judg 1,19; 4,3.13].

968 *Jacob, Edmond* Une théophanie mystérieuse: Josué 5,13-15. ⇒22. ᶠRᴇɴᴀᴜᴅ B., LeDiv 159. 1995. 131-135.

969 *Mazor, Lea* A nomistic re-working of the Jericho conquest narrative reflected in the LXX to Joshua 6:1-20. Textus 18 (1995) 47-62.

970 *Rolla, Armando* La presa di Gerico. PaVi 40/4 (1995) 13-16 [Josh 6].

971 *Kaminsky, Joel S.* Joshua 7: a reassessment of Israelite conceptions of corporate punishment. ⇒1. ᴹAʜʟsᴛʀöᴍ G., JSOT.S 190. 1995. 315-346.

972 *Younger, K. L.* The "conquest" of the south (Jos 10,28-39). BZ 39 (1995) 255-264.

973 *Mittmann, Siegfried* Die Gebietsbeschreibung des Stammes Ruben in Josua 13,15-23. ZDPV 111 (1995) 1-27.

974 *Eshel, Hanan* A note on Joshua 15:61-62 and the identification of the city of salt. IEJ 45/1 (1995) 37-40.

975 *Ottosson, Magnus* 'So it was with all these towns' (Jos. 21:42). 1995 ⇒16. ᶠHᴇɴɴᴇssʏ J., 219-231.

976 *Schmitt, Götz* Levitenstädte. ZDPV 111 (1995) 28-48 [Josh 21].

977 *Cortese, Enzo* L'assemblea di Sichem Gs 24,1-27. PaVi 40/4 (1995) 17-21.
978 *Rosso, Stefano* Lettura liturgica dell'assemblea di Sichem. PaVi 40/4 (1995) 34-36 [Josh 24].

E4.2 *Liber Judicum:* Richter, Judges

979 *Bowman, Richard G.* Narrative criticism of Judges. ⇒984. Judges and method. 1995. 17-44.
980 ᴱ**Brenner, Athalya** A feminist companion to Judges. Feminist Companion to the Bible 4. 1994. ᴿJJS 46 (1995) 350-351 *(Harvey, Graham)*.
981 **Holland, Martin; Steinhoff, Volker** Das Buch der Richter und das Buch Rut. WStB.AT. Wuppertal 1995, Brockhaus 316 pp. 3-417-25227-X; -25327-6 <pb>.
982 **Lindars, Barnabas** Judges 1-5: a new translation and commentary. ᴱ*Mayes, A.D.H.*, E 1995, Clark xxxiii; 302 pp. £24.95. 0-567-09696-3 [BoL 1996,64].
    Navarro Puerto, Mercedes Los Libros de Josué, Jueces...⇒945.
983 **Smelik, Willem F.** The targum of Judges. OTS 36. Lei 1995, Brill xii; 681 pp. *f*254; $171. 90-04-10365-1.
984 ᴱ**Yee, Gale A.** Judges and method: new approaches in Biblical studies. Mp 1995, Fortress vii; 186 pp. $17. 0-8006-2745-8.

985 **Becker, Uwe** Richterzeit und Königtum. ⇒6,2883... 9,2625. BZAW 192. 1990. ᴿAnton. 70/2 (1995) 299-301 *(Nobile, Marco)*.
986 *Exum, J. Cheryl* Feminist criticism: whose interests are being served?. ⇒984. Judges and method. 1995. 65-90.
987 *Jobling, David* Structuralist criticism: the text's world of meaning. ⇒984. Judges and method. 1995. 91-118.
988 *Mafico, Temba L.J.* Were the 'Judges' of Israel like African spirit mediums?. ⇒114.. Text and experience. BiSe 35. 1995. 330-343.
989 *Nel, P.J.* Character in the book of Judges. OTEs 8 (1995) 191-204.
990 *Ogden, Graham S.* Some translational issues in the book of Judges. Chinese. Jian Dao 4 (1995) 17-28 [OTA 18,525].
991 *Yee, Gale A.* Introduction: why Judges?. ⇒984. Judges and method. 1995. 1-16.

992 *Younger, K. Lawson* The configuring of judicial preliminaries: Judges 1.1-2.5 and its dependence on the book of Joshua. JSOT 68 (1995) 75-92 [Judg 1,1-2,5].
993 *Fewell, Danna Nolan* Deconstructive criticism: Achsah and the (e)razed city of writing. ⇒984. Judges and method. 1995. 119-145 [Judg 1,11-15].
994 *Van der Kooij, A.* "And I also said": a new interpretation of Judges ii 3. VT 45 (1995) 294-306.
995 *Rösel, Hartmut N.* Ehud und die Ehuderzählung. ⇒8. ᶠDONNER H., ÄAT 30. 1995. 225-233 [Judg 3,12-39].
996 *Perani, Mauro* Debora nei *midrashim.* PaVi 40/5 (1995) 17 [Judg 4-5; OTA 19,514].
997 *Scippa, Vincenzo* Due donne forti dell'AT. PaVi 40/5 (1995) 12-16 [Judg 4-5; OTA 19,426].

998 *Margalit, Baruch* Observations on the Jael-Sisera story (Judges 4-5). ⇒21. FMILGROM J., 1995. 629-641.
999 *Diebner, B.-J.* Wann sang Deborah ihr Lied? Überlegungen zu zwei der ältesten Texte des TNK (Ri 4 und 5). ACEBT 14 (1995) 106-130 [OTA 19,242].
1000 *Neville, Robert Cummings* The last words of Sisera: a libretto. Soundings 78 (1995) 439-462 [Judg 4,19-20].
1001 *Wolde, Ellen van* Ya'el in Judges 4. ZAW 107 (1995) 240-246.
1002 *Kasher, Rimmon* An unknown version of "Targum Yonathan" to the song of Deborah (Judges 5). Textus 18 (1995) 179, 1*-27*.
1003 *Neef, Heinz-Dieter* Der Stil des Deboraliedes (Ri 5). ZAH 8 (1995) 275-293 [Judg 5].
1004 *Fokkelman, Jan P.* The song of Deborah and Barak: its prosodic levels and structure. ⇒21. FMILGROM J., 1995. 595-628 [Judg 5].
1005 **Faranda Bellofiglio, Nunzio** The Gideon and Abimelech narratives: the contribution of form critical analysis to the current debate on the late dating of biblical historiography. Diss. DRichardson. 1995 Manchester [RTL 27,528].
1006 *Steinberg, Naomi* Social scientific criticism: Judges 9 and issues of kinship. ⇒984. Judges and method. 1995. 45-64.
1007 *Ogden, Graham S.* Jotham's fable: its structure and function in Judges 9. BiTr 46 (1995) 301-308.
1008 *Mehlman, Israel* Jephthah. JBQ 23/2 (1995) 73-78 [Judg 10,17-12,7].
1009 *Bartelmus, Rüdiger* Jephtha—Anmerkungen eines Exegeten zu G.F. HANDELs musikalisch-theologischer Deutung einer "entlegenen" alttestamentlichen Tradition. ThZ 51 (1995) 106-127 [Judg 11].
1010 *Alonso Schökel, Luis* La figlia di Jefte. Fortezza, tragedia e inganno: la donna all'epoca dei Giudici. Atti del Seminario invernale Verona 1993. F 1995, Biblia. 43-59 [Judg 11; AcPIB 10/1,30].
1011 *Harlé, Paul* Flavius JOSEPHE et la Septante des Juges. ⇒13. FHARL M., 1995. 129-132 [Judg 12,7; 14,11; 16,7-9.25].
1012 *Gay, D.* Milton's Samson and the figure of the Old Testament giant. JLT 9 (1995) 355-369 [EThL 72,180*].
1013 **Kim, Jichan** The structure of the Samson cycle. ⇒10,2504. 1993. RRTL 26 (1995) 91-92 *(Auwers, J.-M.)*; Bib. 76 (1995) 98-101 *(Groß, Walter)*; CBQ 57 (1995) 144-145 *(Toews, Wesley I.)*; JBL 114 (1995) 495-496 *(Exum, J. Cheryl)*.
1014 *Stipp, Hermann-Josef* Simson, der Nasiräer. VT 45 (1995) 337-369.
1015 **Bader, Winfried** Simson bei Delila. ⇒7,2434. 1991. RZKTh 117 (1995) 82-85 *(Oesch, Josef M.)*.
1016 *Weldon, Fay* Samson and his women. ⇒70. Out of the garden. 1995. 72-81 [Judg 13-16].
1017 *Webb, B.* A serious reading of the Samson story (Judges 13-16). RTR 54/3 (1995) 110-120.
1018 *Koenen, Klaus* "Süßes geht vom Starken aus" (Ri 14,14): Vergleiche zwischen Gott und Tier im Alten Testament. EvTh 55 (1995) 174-197.
1019 *Yee, Gale A.* Ideological criticism: Judges 17-21 and the dismembered body. ⇒984. Judges and method. 1995. 146-170.
1020 *Wilson, Michael K.* "As you like it": the idolatry of Micah and the Danites (Judges 17-18). RTR 54/2 (1995) 1-48 [Judg 17,1-18,31].

1021   *Bauer, Uwe F.W.* Eine synchrone Lesart von Ri 18,13-18. ⇒26.
       FSCHNEIDER W., 1995. 53-63.
1022   *Robert, Philippe de* Jérusalem et Bethléem. ⇒22. FRENAUD B.,
       LeDiv 159. 1995. 155-161 [Judg 19].
1023   *Stone, Ken* Gender and homosexuality in Judges 19: subject-honor,
       object-shame?. JSOT 67 (1995) 87-107.

       E4.3   **Liber Ruth,** *'V Rotuli'*, the Five Scrolls.

1024   TBeattie, D.R.G. The targum of Ruth. ⇒10,2514. The Aramaic
       Bible 19. 1994. RCBQ 57 (1995) 758-759 *(Garber, Zev)*.
1025   EBengtsson, Per A. Two Arabic versions of the book of Ruth: text
       edition and language studies. Studia Orientalia Lundensia 6. Lund
       1995, University Press. xxxiii; 214 pp. 11 pl. SEK221; DM168.
       91-7966-339-7.
1026   EBrenner, Athalya A feminist companion to Ruth. ⇒9,2653. Fe-
       minist Companion to the Bible 3. 1993. RCBQ 57 (1995) 420-422
       (Green, Barbara).
           Holland, Martin; Steinhoff, Volker Das Buch der Richter und
       das Buch Rut. ⇒981.
1027   Luter, A. Boyd; Davis, Barry C. God behind the scene: exposi-
       tions of the books of Ruth and Esther. Expositor's Guide to the
       Historical Books. GR 1995, Baker 377 pp. $17. 0-8010-9000-8
       [OTA 19,535].
1028   Masini, M. "Lectio divina" del libro di Rut. ⇒10,2530. 1994.
       RNRTh 177 (1995) 270-271 *(Ska, Jean Louis)*; Gr. 76 (1995) 761
       (Farahian, Edmond).
           Navarro Puerto, Mercedes Los Libros de Josué, Jueces y Rut.
       ⇒945.
1029   EPoli, E. Il libro di Rut: antica interpretazione ebraica. Sussidi
       biblici 37. Reggio Emilia 1992, San Lorenzo 59 pp. RHenoch
       17/1-2 (1995) 252-253 *(Perani, Mauro)*.
1030   Ravasi, Gianfranco Rut, Giuditta, Ester. Conversazioni Bibliche.
       Bo 1995, Dehoniane 142 pp. L18.000. 88-10-70953-5.
1031   Zakovitz, Yair רות: עם מבוא ופירוש [Ruth: introduction and com-
       mentary]. H. ⇒9,2699; 10,2518. 1990. RJQR 85 (1995) 424-425
       (Eskenazi, Tamara C.).

1032   Carmody, Denise Lardner; Carmody, John Tully Corn & ivy:
       spiritual reading in Ruth and Jonah. Vally Forge, Pa. 1995, Trinity
       Press International x; 180 pp. 1-56338-134-6.
1033   *Ebach, Jürgen* Fremde in Moab—Fremde aus Moab: das Buch
       Ruth als politische Literatur. ⇒78. Bibel und Literatur. 1995. 277-
       304.
1034   *Efthimiadis, H.* Woman to womyn: countering patriarchal stereoty-
       pes in the book of Ruth. JSem 7/1 (1995) 57-78 [sum. 57].
1035   *Falchini, Cecilia* Rut: una donna. PaVi 40/5 (1995) 6-8 [OTA
       19,428].
1036   *Hamlin, E. John* Terms for gender and status in the book of Ruth.
       ProcGLM 15 (1995) 133-143.
1037   *Leutzsch, M.* Solidarität aus biblischer Perspektive. GlLern 10/1
       (1995) 17ff [ZID 21,456].
1038   *Maldonado, Robert D.* Reading MALINCHE reading Ruth: toward
       a hermeneutics of betrayal. Semeia 72 (1995) 91-109.

1039 *Nash, Peter Theodore* Ruth: an exercise in Israelite political correctness or a call to proper conversion?. ⇒1. MAHLSTRÖM G., JSOT.S 190. 1995. 347-354.

1040 **Paschelke, Michael** Das Buch Ruth im Unterricht: ein Beitrag zur Untersuchung der Rezeption des Buches Ruth in Schulbüchern sowie im Bereich deutscher Theologie, Kunst und Pädagogik des 19. und 20. Jahrhunderts unter dem Gesichtspunkt der Verwendbarkeit im Unterricht besonders in der Oberstufe des Gymnasiums. Diss. 1995 Heidelberg [ThRv 92/2,X].

1041 *Ranon, Angelo* Una storia di famiglia. PaVi 40/5 (1995) 9-11 [OTA 19,428].

1042 **Ranta, Kaija Helena Anneli** The biblical book of Ruth: a feminist literary reading. Diss. DAmore, Roy C., Windsor 1995, 136 pp. MAI 34/2,p.547.

1043 Ruth-Judith-Ester-Susanna: trouw door dik en dun. Den Bosch 1995, Katholieke Bijbelstichting 124 pp. ƒ11. 90-6173-938-1 [Str. 64,184].

1044 *Stachowiak, Lech* Der Universalismus und die Bücher Jona und Rut. **P**. Roczniki Teologiczne 42/1 (1995) 17-25 [Zsfg 24].

1045 *Stefani, Piero* Il Libro di Rut. Studi Fatti Ricerche 72 (1995) 4-8.

1046 *Dray, Stephen* Ruth 1:1-22: trust and obey. Evangel 13/2 (1995) 34-36.

1047 *Carasik, Michael* Ruth 2,7: why the overseer was embarrassed. ZAW 107 (1995) 493-494.

1048 *Harm, H.J.* The function of double entendre in Ruth 3. JTrTL 7/1 (1995) 19ff [ZID 21,309].

1049 *Nielsen, Kirsten* Lov og fortaelling i Ruths bog: eller hvordan man kan laese Ruth 4,7-8 intertekstuelt [Law and story in the book of Ruth: or, how one can read Ruth 4,7-8 intertextually]. 1995 ⇒90. Lov og visdom. 78-89 [OTA 19,428].

E4.4 1-2 Samuel.

1050 **Bowes, P.** I libri di Samuele. BT 8. Brescia 1995, Queriniana 190 pp. L20.000 [RdT 36,383].

1051 **Caquot, André; Robert, Philippe de** Les livres de Samuel. ⇒10,2535. Commmentaire de l'Ancien Testament 6. 1994. RETR 70 (1995) 111-112 (*Macchi, Jean-Daniel*); EstAg 30 (1995) 338-339 (*Mielgo, C.*); JThS 46 (1995) 580-583 (*Murray, D.F.*); EeV 105 (1995) 379-381 (*Monloubou, Louis*); Bib. 76 (1995) 422-426 (*Pisano, Stephen*); CBQ 57 (1995) 761-762 (*Toews, Wesley I.*).

1052 **Dietrich, Walter; Naumann, Thomas** Die Samuelbücher. EdF 287. Da 1995, Da:Wiss xii; 340 pp. DM49.80. 3-534-10027-1 [ThRv 91,534].

1053 **Stoebe, Hans-Joachim** Das zweite Buch Samuelis. ⇒10,2545. KAT 8/2. 1994. RThZ 51 (1995) 278-279 (*Kellenberger, Edgar*); ThQ 175 (1995) 222-223 (*Groß, Walter*); JETh 9 (1995) 165-168 (*Klement, Herbert H.*).

1054 *Aejmelaeus, Anneli* The Septuagint of 1 Samuel. ⇒136. VIII Congress. 1995. 109-129.

1055 EBrenner, Athalya A feminist companion to Samuel and Kings. ⇒10,2548. Feminist Companion to the Bible 5. 1994. RJJS 46 (1995) 351-352 (*Harvey, Graham*).

1056 **Conferenza dei religiosi del Brasile** La lettura profetica della storia. La tua Parola è Vita 3. Piccola Editrice 1995, Celleno 247 pp. [Sam. & Kgs].

1057 *Conrad, Joachim* Samuel im Alten und Neuen Testament: Marginalien zur Problematik biblischer Theologie. ⇒37. ᶠWAGNER S., 1995. 83-93.

1058 *Dell'Orto, Giuseppe* Nabi Samuel. PaVi 40/6 (1995) 26-30.

1059 *Doody, Margaret Anne* Infant piety and the infant Samuel 103-122;

1060 **Moenikes, Ansgar** Die grundsätzliche Ablehnung des Königtums in der Hebräischen Bibel: ein Beitrag zur Religionsgeschichte des Alten Israel. Diss. Bonn. ᴰ*Hoheisel, Karl*, BBB 99. Weinheim 1995, Beltz Athenäum 256 pp. DM88. 3-89547-073-2.

1061 *Peranï, Mauro* Samuele nei testi midrashici. PaVi 40/6 (1995) 31-32.

1062 *Riede, Peter* David und der Floh: Tiere und Tiervergleiche in den Samuelbüchern. BN 77 (1995) 86-117.

1063 *Rosso, Stefano* Samuele nei lezionari romani. PaVi 40/6 (1995) 37-39.

1064 *Spencer, John R.* Priestly families (or factions) in Samuel and Kings. ⇒1. ᴹAHLSTRÖM G., JSOT.S 190. 1995. 387-400.

1065 **Wonneberger, R.** Redaktion: Studien zur Textfortschreibung im Alten Testament am Beispiel der Samuel-Überlieferung. ⇒8,2830; 10,2555. FRLANT 156. 1991. ᴿHenoch 17 (1995) 246-247 *(Soggin, J. Alberto)*.

1066 *Mazor, Yair* I Samuel 1-2: when biblical narrative unveils its aesthetics and afterwards. **H.** Beit Mikra 141 (1995) 196-191 [Heb. sum. 190-189].

1067 *Ozick, Cynthia* Hannah and Elkanah: Torah as the matrix. ⇒70. Out of the garden. 1995. 88-93 [1 Sam 1-2].

1068 *Heller, Karin* La madre di Samuele. PaVi 40/6 (1995) 6-9 [1 Sam 1-2].

1069 **Fokkelman, J.P.** Vow and desire (1 Sam 1-12). ⇒9,2684; 10,2556. SSN 31. 1993. ᴿBijdr. 56 (1995) 340-341 *(Beentjes, P.C.)*; CBQ 57 (1995) 130-132 *(McKenzie, Steven L.)*.

1070 **Becker-Spörl, Silvia** "Und Hanna betete und sie sprach...". ⇒8,2640... 10,2559. 1992. ᴿBZ 39 (1995) 119-120 *(Seidl, Theodor)* [1 Sam 2,1-10].

1071 *Falk, Marcia* Reflections on Hannah's prayer. 1995 ⇒70. Out of the garden. 94-102 [1 Sam 2,1-10].

1072 *Auffret, Pierre* Et d'un trône de gloire il les fait hériter: étude structurelle du cantique d'Anne. OTEs 8 (1995) 223-240 [1 Sam 2,1-11].

1073 *Moberly, R.W.L.* To hear the master's voice: revelation and spiritual discernment in the call of Samuel. SJTh 48 (1995) 443-468 [1 Sam 3].

1074 *Orsatti, Mauro* Storia di un incontro (1 Sam 3). PaVi 40/6 (1995) 10-13.

E4.5 *1 Sam 7...Initia potestatis regiae,* **Origins of kingship.**

1075 *Kreuzer, Siegfried* Die Verbindung von Gottesherrschaft und Königtum Gottes im Alten Testament. ⇒135. Congress Volume: Paris 1992. VT.S 61. 1995. 145-161.

1076 *Levinson, Deirdre* The psychopathology of King Saul. ⇒70. Out of the garden. 1995. 123-141.
1077 *Liwak, R.* Der Herrscher als Wohltäter: soteriologische Aspekte in den Königstraditionen des Alten Orients und des Alten Testaments. ⇒37. ^FWagner S., 1995. 163-186.
1078 **Niemann, Hermann Michael** Herrschaft, Königtum und Staat. ⇒9,2705. FAT 6. 1993. ^RThQ 175 (1995) 150-151 (*Niehr, Herbert*); CBQ 57 (1995) 153-154 (*Burden, Terry L.*); JBL 114 (1995) 715-716 (*Handy, Lowell K.*).

1079 *Bailey, Randall C.* The redemption of Yhwh: a literary critical function of the songs of Hannah and David. Bibl.Interp. 3 (1995) 213-231 [1 Sam 2,1-10].
1080 *Paximadi, Georgio* Samuele e Saul (1 Sam 8-9). PaVi 40/6 (1995) 14-17.
1081 **George, Mark Keith** Body works: power, the construction of identity, and gender in the discourse on kingship. Diss. ^D*Olson, Dennis T.*, Princeton Theol. Sem. 1995, 153 pp. AAC 9530821; DAI-A 56,1828 [1 Sam 8].
1082 *Frolof, Serge; Orel, Vladimir* A nameless city. JBQ 23 (1995) 252-256 [1 Sam 9,3-10,16].
1083 *Tsumura, D. T.* Bedan, a copyist's error? (1 Samuel xii 11). VT 45 (1995) 122-123.
1084 *Montagnini, Felice* Il testamento di Samuele (1 Sam 12). PaVi 40/6 (1995) 18-20.
1085 *Bakon, Shimon* Jonathan. JBQ 23 (1995) 143-150 [1 Sam 13-23].
1086 *Wyatt, N.* Jonathan's adventure and a philological conundrum. PEQ 127 (1995) 62-69 [1 Sam 14,4].
1087 *Stone, G.R.* Grasping the fringe. BurH 31 (1995) 4-20, 36-47 [1 Sam 15,27; 24,4-5].
1088 *Vehse, Charles Ted* Long live the king: historical fact and narrative fiction in 1 Samuel 9-10. ⇒1. ^MAhlström G., JSOT.S 190. 1995. 435-444.

E4.6 *1 Sam 16...2 Sam: Accessio Davidis.* **David's Rise.**

1089 **Auld, A. Graeme** Kings without privilege: David and Moses in the story of the Bible's kings. ⇒10,2583. 1994. ^RBSOAS 58 (1995) 544-545 (*Lawson, Jack N.*).
1090 *Avanzinelli, Milka Ventura* David, il "piccolo" dai grandi destini, in alcuni racconti rabbinici. RStB 7/1 (1995) 187-204.
1091 *Bergmeier, Roland* Erfüllung der Gnadenzusagen an David. ZNW 86 (1995) 277-286.
1092 *Bettenzoli, Giuseppe* David nella letteratura profetica. RStB 7/1 (1995) 35-56.
1093 *Boccaccini, Gabriele* La figura di Davide nei giudaismi di età ellenistico-romana. RStB 7/1 (1995) 175-185.
1094 *Cardellini, Innocenzo* Il re David e la "regalità". RStB 7/1 (1995) 103-127.
1095 **Catherwood, Fred** David: poet, warrior, king. Nottingham 1995, IVP. 0-85111-863-6.
1096 *Cimosa, Mario* Davide nei Salmi: modello biblico e prospettive messianiche. 1995. RStB 7/1 (1995) 79-102.

1097   *Clines, David J.A.* David the man: the construction of masculinity in the Hebrew Bible. ⇒37. Interested parties. JSOT.S 205. 1995. 212-243.

1098   **Costacurta, Bruna** Con la cetra e con la fionda: l'ascesa di Davide verso il trono. Collana Biblica. Roma 1995, Dehoniane 265 pp. 88-396-0552-5.

1099   *Cryer, Frederick H.* A 'BETDAWD' miscellany: DWD, DWD' or DWDH?. SJOT 9 (1995) 52-58.

1100   David: groot in het kleine. Den Bosch 1995, Katholieke Bijbelstichting 166 pp. *f*12.50. 90-6173-937-3 [Str. 64,184].

1101   *Garbini, Giovanni* Davide nella storiografia dei libri storici (Sam-Re). RStB 7/1 (1995) 17-33.

1102   *Gelio, Roberto* Davide e la *m*ᵉ*ṣudat Ṣiyyôn*: chi gli avversari?. RStB 7/1 (1995) 129-155.

1103   *Hentschel, Georg* David. ⇒122. LThK 3. 1995. 37-38.

1104   Is this King David's tomb?. BArR 21/1 (1995) 62-67.

1105   *Jucci, Elio* Davide a Qumran. RStB 7/1 (1995) 157-173.

1106   *Knoppers, Gary N.* Images of David in early Judaism: David as repentant sinner in Chronicles. Bib. 76 (1995) 449-470.

1107   *Lehmann, Reinhard G.; Reichel, Marcus* DOD und ASIMA in Tell Dan. BN 77 (1995) 29-31.

1108   **Massie, Allan** King David: a novel. L 1995, Sceptre.

1109   *Meyers, Carol L.; Meyers, Eric M.* The future fortunes of the house of David: the evidence of Second Zechariah. ⇒10. ᶠFʀᴇᴇᴅᴍᴀɴ D., 1995. 207-222 [Zech 9-14].

1110   *Naʾaman, Nadav* Beth-David in the Aramaic stela from Tel Dan. BN 79 (1995) 17-24.

1111   **Pomykala, Kenneth E.** The Davidic dynasty tradition in early Judaism: its history and significance for messianism. SBL Early Judaism and Its Literature 7. Atlanta 1995, Scholars xv; 308 pp. $40; $24.95. 0-7885-0068-6; 69-4 <pb>. ᴿEThL 71 (1995) 442-443 *(Lust, J.)*.

1112   ᴱ**Prato, Gian Luigi** Davide—modelli biblici e prospettive messianiche: atti dell'VIII Convegno di Studi Veterotestamentari (1993): Associazione Biblica Italiana. RStB 7/1. Bo 1995, Dehoniane 204 pp.:

1113   Davide: modelli biblici e prospettive messianiche: introduzione. 5-15.

1114   **Russelliah, Chelliah** The influence of torah upon king David. Diss. ᴰ*Archer, Gleason L.*, Trinity Evang. Div. School 1995, 323 pp. AAC 9533065; DAI-A 56,2282.

1115   *Tagliacarne, Pierfelice* La figura di Davide nei libri delle Cronache. RStB 7/1 (1995) 57-77.

1116   *Thompson, Thomas L.* 'House of David': an eponymic referent to Yahweh as godfather. SJOT 9 (1995) 59-74.

1117   *Meyers, Carol* An ethnoarchaeological analysis of Hannah's sacrifice. ⇒21. ᶠMɪʟɢʀᴏᴍ J., 1995. 77-91 [1 Sam 1,24].

1118   *Satterthwaite, Philip E.* David in the books of Samuel: a Messianic hope?. ⇒111. The Lord's anointed. 1995. 41-65 [1 Sam 2,1-10; 2 Sam 22; 23,1-7; 7,16].

1119   *Dalla Vecchia, Flavio* Samuele e Davide (1 Sam 16,1-13). PaVi 40/6 (1995) 22-25.

1120 *Dietrich, Walter* Der Fall des Riesen Goliat: biblische und nachbiblische Erzählversuche. ⇒78. Bibel und Literatur. 1995. 241-258 [1 Sam 17].

1121 *Fleming, D.E.* New moon celebration once a year: Emar's Ḫidašu of Dagan. ⇒18. FLIPINSKI E., OLA 65. 1995. 57-64 [1 Sam 20].

1122 **Riepl, Christian** Sind David und Saul berechenbar?: von der sprachlichen Analyse zur literarischen Struktur von 1 Sam 21 und 22. ⇒9,2728; 10,2599. ATSAT. 1993. ROLZ 90 (1995) 532-535 *(Stahl, Rainer)*.

1123 *Cogan, Mordechai* The road to En-dor. ⇒21. FMILGROM J., 1995. 319-326 [1 Sam 28].

1124 *Maritano, Mario* Samuele e la maga di Endor. PaVi 40/6 (1995) 33-36 [1 Sam 28].

1125 **Kleiner, Michael** Saul in En-Dor Wahrsagung oder Totenbeschwörung?: eine synchrone und diachrone Untersuchung zu 1 Sam 28. EThSt 66. Lp 1995, Benno xix; 239 pp. DM48; FS46; ÖS355. 3-7462-1116-6.

1126 *Schmidt, Brian B.* The "witch" of En-Dor, 1 Samuel 28, and ancient Near Eastern necromancy. Ancient magic and ritual power. EMeyer, Marvin; Mirecki, Paul, RGRW 129. Lei 1995, Brill. 90-04-10406-2. 111-129.

1127 **Calvin, John** Sermons on 2 Samuel. TKelly, Douglas. Carlisle 1992, Banner of Truth 520 pp. ill. £47. 0-85151-578-9. RSBET 13/1 (1995) 83-84 *(Baxter, Tony)*.

1128 *Green, E. E.* Donne sagge: autorità femminile durante il regno davidico. RivBib 43 (1995) 467-484.

1129 **Polzin, Robert** David and the Deuteronomist: 2 Samuel. ⇒9,2732; 10,2605. 1993. RBib. 76 (1995) 101-105 *(Wénin, André)*; CBQ 57 (1995) 572-573 *(Newsome, James D.)*.

1130 *Willi-Plein, Ina* Frauen um David: Beobachtungen zur Davidshausgeschichte. ⇒8. FDONNER H., ÄAT 30. 1995. 349-361.

1131 **Zaitzow, Michael D.** Biblical parallelism in 2 Samuel. Diss. DPolzin, R., Carleton 1995, 116 pp. MAI 34/1,p.86. 0-315-98561-5.

1132 *Weitzman, Steven* David's lament and the poetics of grief in 2 Samuel. JQR 85 (1995) 341-360 [2 Sam 1,17-27].

1133 *Haelewyck, Jean-Claude* David a-t-il régné du vivant de Saul?: étude littéraire et historique de II Sm 2,1-11. RTL 26 (1995) 165-184.

1134 *Haelewyck, Jean-Claude* La mort d'Abner: 2 Sam 3,1-39. RB 102 (1995) 161-192 [2 Sam 3,1-39].

1135 *Gelio, Roberto* Davide conquista la 'Rocca di Sion' (II Sam 5,6-8//I Cron 11,4-6): la presenza degli ʿwwᵉrîm wepissᵉhîm: un caso di iponimia. Lat. 61/1 (1995) 11-77 [sum. 77];

1136 *Görg, Manfred* Ṣinnor—ein Versuch zur Wortdeutung. BN 76 (1995) 7-13 [2 Sam 5,8].

1137 *Weiss, Raphael* A peculiar textual phenomenon. Textus 18 (1995) 27-32 [2 Sam 6,3-4; 2 Kgs 7,13; 1 Chr 15,18; 16,5; Isa 17,12-13].

1138 *Zwickel, Wolfgang* David als Vorbild für den Glauben: die Veränderung des Davidbildes im Verlauf der alttestamentlichen Geschichte, dargestellt an 2 Sam 6. BN 79 (1995) 88-101.

1139 **Eslinger, Lyle** House of God or house of David: the rhetoric of 2 Samuel 7. ⇒10,2620. JSOT.S 164. 1994. ᴿThLZ 120 (1995) 24-27 (*Naumann, Thomas*); TZ 51 (1995) 88 (*Keller, Martin*); JThS 46 (1995) 210-216 (*Murray, D.F.*); JBL 114 (1995) 135-136 (*Hauser, Alan J.*).

1140 *Santos B.*, *Silva* Davi e Betsabéia (2 Sm 11): história de um amor proibido. Atualizaçâo 25 (1995) 287-306 [Strom. 52,345].

1141 *Petit, Madeleine* La rencontre de David et Bersabée (II Sam. 11, 2-5, 26-27): les interprétations des Pères des premiers siècles. ⇒13. ᶠHᴀʀʟ M., 1995. 473-481.

1142 *Wright, David P.* David autem remansit in Hierusalem: felix coniunctio!. ⇒21. ᶠMɪʟɢʀᴏᴍ J., 1995. 215-230 [2 Sam 11-12].

1143 *Toloni, Giancarlo* Una singolare occorrenza dei yadîd: l'epiteto yᵉdîdyāh (2Sam. 12,25), attestato della predilezione di YHWH. Aevum 69/1 (1995) 15-29.

1144 *Busto Saiz, José Ramón* The Antiochene text in 2 Samuel 22. ⇒136. VIII Congress. SCSt 41. 1995. 131-143.

1145 *Miscall, Peter D.* Texts, more texts, a textual reader and a textual writer. Semeia 69/70 (1995) 247-260 [2 Sam 23,13-17].

1146 *Koorevaar, H.J.* 'Gott' oder 'man' (jemand), 'Satan' oder 'ein Gegner': die Übersetzung der Präfixkonjugation dritte Person maskulin Singular in 2 Sam 24,1 und der Begriff 'Satan' in 1 Chr 21, auf grund eines Vergleiches dieser parallelen Texte miteinander. Fundamentum 3 (1995) 224-235 [OTA 19,66].

1147 *Adler, Joshua J.* David's last sin: was it the census?. JBQ 23/2 (1995) 91-95 [2 Sam 24; 1 Chr 21].

E4.7 *Libri Regum:* Solomon, Temple: 1 Kings...

1148 **Buis, Pierre** El libro de los Reyes. ᵀ*Darrícal, Nicolás.* CuaBi 86. Estella 1995, Verbo Divino 62 pp. 84-8169-026-0.

1149 **Fernández Marcos, Natalio** Scribes and translators: Septuagint and Old Latin in the books of Kings. ⇒10,2636. VT.S 54. 1994. ᴿEThL 71 (1995) 203-204 (*Lust, J.*); Sef. 55/1 (1995) 209-210 (*Spottorno, Victoria*).

1150 *Fernández Marcos, Natalio* The Vetus Latina of 1-2 Kings and the Hebrew. ⇒136. VIII Congress. SCSt 41. 1995. 153-163.

1151 **Fernández Marcos, Natalio; Busto Saiz, J.R.** El texto antioqueno de la Biblia griega II. 1-2 Reyes. ⇒8,2908. 1992. ᴿEM 63/1 (1995) 147-149 (*Morano, Ciriaca*); CBQ 57 (1995) 549-550 (*Davila, James R.*).

1152 **House, Paul R.** 1, 2 Kings. NAC 8. Nv 1995, Broadman and Holman 432 pp. 0-8054-0108-3 [OTA 18,638].

1153 **Laffey, A.** I libri dei Re. BT 9. Brescia 1995, Queriniana 122 pp. L15.000 [RdT 36,512].

1154 **Provan, Iain W.** 1 and 2 Kings. NIBC.OT. Peabody, MA 1995, Hendrickson xiv; 305 pp. $11.95. 1-56563-053-X [OTA 19,342].

1155 *Spottorno, Victoria* Jᴏsᴇᴘʜᴜs' text for 1-2 Kings (3-4 Kingdoms). ⇒136. VIII Congress. SCSt 41. 1995. 145-152.

1156 *Walter, D. M.* The use of sources in the Peshitta of Kings. ⇒76. The Peshitta. 1995.

1157 **Wiseman, Donald John** 1 and 2 Kings. ⇒9,2774; 10,2643. TOTC. 1993. ᴿJETh 9 (1995) 168-171 (*Gugler, Werner*).

1158 **Barnes, William Hamilton** Studies in the chronology of the divided monarchy of Israel. ⇒7,2557... 10,2677. HSM 48. 1991. ᴿIEJ 45/1 (1995) 75-76 (*Cogan, Mordechai*); JAOS 115/1 (1995) 122-123 (*Reade, J.E.*); BZ 39 (1995) 290-293 (*Thiel, Winfried*).

1159 **McKenzie, Steven L.** The trouble with Kings. ⇒7,2534... 10,2645. VT.S 42. 1991. ᴿAJSR 20/1 (1995) 161-163 (*Brettler, Marc*); NedThT 49/1 (1995) 71-72 (*Becking, Bob*); JQR 86/1-2 (1995) 245-247 (*Polzin, Robert*).

1160 *Provan, Iain W.* The Messiah in the books of kings. ⇒111. The Lord's anointed. 1995. 67-85.

1161 *Wilson, Robert R.* The former prophets: reading the books of Kings. ⇒36. ᶠTUCKER G., 1995. 83-96 [2 Kgs 18,13-19,35].

1162 *Young, Ian* The "northernisms" of the Israelite narratives in Kings. ZAH 8 (1995) 63-70.

1163 **Knoppers, Gary N.** The reign of Solomon and the rise of Jeroboam. ⇒9,2807; 10,2637. HSM 52. 1993. ᴿJBL 114 (1995) 302-304 (*Klein, Ralph W.*); CBQ 57 (1995) 351-352 (*Rogers, Jeffrey S.*); ThLZ 120 (1995) 29-30 (*Särkiö, Pekka*).

1164 *Lasine, Stuart* The king of desire: indeterminacy, audience, and the Solomon narrative. Semeia 71 (1995) 85-118.

1165 **Beyer, Rolf** König Salomo: vom Brudermörder zum Friedensfürsten. ⇒9,2777; 10,2648. 1993. ᴿThLZ 120 (1995) 777-780 (*Niemann, Hermann Michael*).

1166 *Sweeney, Marvin A.* The critique of Solomon in the Josianic edition of the deuteronomistic history. JBL 114 (1995) 607-622.

1167 *Gibert, Pierre* Les figures bibliques de la sagesse. MoBi 95 (1995) 17-18.

1168 *Feldman, Louis H.* JOSEPHUS' portrait of Solomon. HUCA 66 (1995) 103-167.

1169 *Lemaire, André* Wisdom in Solomonic historiography. ⇒9. ᶠEMERTON J., 1995. 106-118.

1170 *Provan, Iain W.* Why Barzillai of Gilead (1 Kings 2:7)?: narrative art and the hermeneutics of suspicion in 1 Kings 1-2. TynB 46 (1995) 103-116.

1171 *Walsh, Jerome T.* The characterization of Solomon in First Kings 1-5. CBQ 57 (1995) 471-493.

1172 *Hoop, R. De* The Testament of David: a response to W.T. KOOPMANS. VT 45 (1995) 270-279 [1 Kgs 2,1-10].

1173 *Freund, Yossef* The marriage and the dowry. JBQ 23 (1995) 248-251 [1 Kgs 3,1].

1174 *Wolde, Ellen van* Who guides whom?: embeddedness and perspective in Biblical Hebrew and in 1 Kings 3:16-28. JBL 114 (1995) 623-642.

1175 *Ash, Paul S.* Solomon's? District? List. JSOT 67 (1995) 67-86 [1 Kgs 4,7-19].

1176 *Fritz, Volkmar* Die Verwaltungsgebiete Salomons nach 1Kön 4,7-19. ⇒8. ᶠDONNER H., ÄAT 30. 1995. 19-26.

1177 **Talstra, Ebele** Solomon's prayer. ⇒9,2794; 10,2673. Contributions to Biblical Exegesis and Theology 3. 1993. ᴿJBL 114 (1995) 497-498 (*Knoppers, Gary N.*); CBQ 57 (1995) 372-374 (*Dobbs-Allsopp, F.W.*) [1 Kgs 8,14-61].

1178 *Abadie, Philippe* Entre histoire et légende. MoBi 95 (1995) 16-17 [1 Kgs 10,1-13].

1179   *Boespflug, François; Préville, Agnès de* La reine de Saba dans l'art
       chrétien médiéval. MoBi 95 (1995) 24-29 [1 Kgs 10,1-10.13].
1180   *Pelletier, Anne-Marie* La reine de Saba, ou il y a plus ici qu'une
       anecdote... ⇒4. FBEAUCHAMP P., 1995. 119-132 [1 Kgs 10,1-
       13; 2 Chr 9,1-12].
1181   *Warner, Marina* In and out of the fold: wisdom, danger, and gla-
       mour in the tale of the queen of Sheba. ⇒70. Out of the garden.
       1995. 150-165 [1 Kgs 10,1-13].
1182   *Lassner, Jacob* Ritual purity and political exile: Solomon, the
       Queen of Sheba, and the events of 586 B.C.E. in a Yemenite folk-
       tale. ⇒11. FGREENFIELD J., 1995. 117-136 [1 Kgs 10,1-13].
1183   *Haddad, Michèle* La Bible, la femme et le nu dans la peinture du
       XIXᵉ siècle: la reine de Saba. 1995 ⇒73. La Bible. 217-232 [1 Kgs
       10,1-13; BuBbgB 19,48].
1184   *Edelman, Diana V.* Solomon's adversaries Hadad, Rezon and Jero-
       boam: a trio of "bad guy" characters illustrating the theology of
       immediate retribution. ⇒1. MAHLSTRÖM G., JSOT.S 190. 1995.
       166-191 [1 Kgs 11,14].
1185   *Machinist, Peter* The transfer of kingship: a divine turning. ⇒10.
       FFREEDMAN D., 1995. 105-120 [Num 36,6-7; 2 Sam 3,12;
       14,20; 1 Kgs 12,15; 2 Chr 10,15; Jer 6,12; Hab 2,16].
       Schäfer-Lichtenberger, Christa Josua und Salomo. ⇒959.

Templum.

1186   **Barker, Margaret** On earth as it is in heaven: temple symbolism
       in the New Testament. E 1995, Clark xv; 86 pp. $14.95 0-567-
       29278-9 <pb>.
1187   *Bedford, Peter Ross* Discerning the time: Haggai, Zechariah and
       the "delay" in the rebuilding of the Jerusalem temple. ⇒1.
       MAHLSTRÖM G., JSOT.S 190. 1995. 71-94.
1188   **Bissoli, Giovanni** Il tempio nella letteratura giudaica e neotesta-
       mentaria: studio sulla corrispondenza fra tempio celeste e tempio
       terrestre. SBFA 37. J 1995, Franciscan Printing Press xiv; 239 pp.
       L40.000.
1189   *Brändle, Rudolf* Die Auswirkungen der Zerstörung des Jerusalemer
       Tempels auf Johannes CHRYSOSTOMUS und andere Kirchenväter.
       ⇒33. FTHOMA C., JudChr 15. 1995. 231-246.
1190   *Brodd, Jeffrey* Julian the Apostate and his plan to rebuild the Jeru-
       salem temple. BiRe 11/5 (1995) 32-38, 48.
1191   *Casalini, N.* Il tempio nella letteratura giudaica e neotestamentaria.
       RivBib 43 (1995) 181-210.
1192   *Catron, Janice E.* Temple and bamah: some considerations. ⇒1.
       MAHLSTRÖM G., JSOT.S 190. 1995. 150-165.
1193   TEConnolly, **Sean** BEDE: on the temple. *O'Reilly, Jennifer*
       <introd by>. Translated Texts for Historians 21. Liverpool 1995,
       Liverpool University Press lv; 142 pp. [DR 115,155].
1194   *Dschulnigg, Peter* Die Zerstörung des Tempels in den synoptischen
       Evangelien. ⇒33. FTHOMA C., JudChr 15. 1995. 167-187
       [Mark13,1-4; 14,58].
1195   *Evans, Craig A.* Excursus three: Jesus and predictions of the
       destruction of the Herodian temple. 1995 ⇒47. Jesus and his con-
       temporaries. AGJU 25. 367-380 [Mt 24,1-2].

1196 **Haran, Menahem** Temples and temple-service in ancient Israel. WL 1995 <1985,> Eisenbrauns xviii; 394 pp. reprint ⇒2,2095; map; fig. 0-931464-18-8.

1197 **Hurowitz, Victor** I have built you an exalted house: temple building in the Bible in light of Mesopotamian and Northwest Semitic writings. ⇒8,2929... 10,2666. JSOT.S 115. 1992. AulOr 13/1 (1995) 144-146 (*Olmo Lete, G. del*).

1198 *Hurowitz, Victor Avigdor* Solomon's golden vessels (1 Kings 7:48-50) and the cult of the first temple. ⇒21. ^FMILGROM J., 1995. 151-164.

1199 *Hurvitz, Avi* Terms and epithets relating to the Jerusalem temple compound in the book of Chronicles: the linguistic aspect. ⇒21. ^FMILGROM J., 1995. 165-183.

1200 **Junco Garza, Carlos** La crítica profética ante el templo: teología vetero-testamentaria. ⇒10,2669. Bibliotheca Mexicana 8. 1994. ^RPhase 35 (1995) 435-436 (*Latorre, J.*); NRTh 117 (1995) 910-911 (*Ska, Jean Louis*).

1201 *Knoppers, Gary N.* Prayer and propaganda: Solomon's dedication of the temple and the deuteronomist's program. CBQ 57 (1995) 229-254 [1 Kgs 8,1-13].

1202 *Levine, Lee I.* The second temple of Jerusalem: JOSEPHUS' description and other sources. H. Cathedra 77 (1995) 3-16 [sum. 194].

1203 *Maier, Johann* Zwischen zweitem und drittem Tempel: jüdische Deutungen und Hoffnungen angesichts des zerstörten Tempels. ⇒33. ^FTHOMA C., JudChr 15. 1995. 247-265.

1204 *Rosenkranz, Simone* Vom Paradies zum Tempel. ⇒33. ^FTHOMA C., JudChr 15. 1995. 27-131.

1205 *Schaper, Joachim* The Jerusalem temple as an instrument of the Achaemenid fiscal administration. VT 45 (1995) 528-539.

1206 **Schmidt, Francis** La pensée du temple. ⇒10,2668. 1994. ^RRB 102 (1995) 257-262 (*Nodet, Étienne*); CBQ 57 (1995) 788-789 (*Patton, Corrine*).

1207 *Scott, Bernard Brandon* After the future: from mad Max to the destruction of the temple. Forum 8 (1992) [1995] 313-336 [Mark 13].

1208 **Zwickel, Wolfgang** Der Tempelkult in Kanaan und Israel. ⇒10,2671. FAT 10. 1994. ^RThQ 175 (1995) 369-370 (*Niehr, Herbert*); LASBF 45 (1995) 599-604 (*Cortese, Enzo*).

1 Regum 12ss

1209 **Toews, Wesley I.** Monarchy and religious institution in Israel under Jeroboam I. ⇒9,2806; 10,2686. SBL.MS 47. 1993. ^RJSSt 40 (1995) 92-93 (*Tomes, Roger*); EThL 71 (1995) 443-444 (*Lust, J.*); JBL 114 (1995) 133-134 (*Denning-Bolle, Sara J.*); ABR 43 (1995) 81-82 (*Wynn-Williams, Damian J.*).

1210 **Knoppers, Gary N.** The reign of Jeroboam, the fall of Israel and the reign of Josiah. ⇒10,2637. HSM 53. 1994. ^RThLZ 120 (1995) 29-30 (*Särkiö, Pekka*).

1211 *O'Connor, M.* War and rebel chants in the former prophets. ⇒10. ^FFREEDMAN D., 1995. 322-337 [1 Kgs 8,12-13; 12,16; 2 Kgs 19,21-28].

1212 *Gelinas, Margaret M.* United monarchy-divided monarchy: fact or fiction?. ⇒1. MAHLSTRÖM G., JSOT.S 190. 1995. 227-237 [1 Kgs 11,26-14,30].

1213 *Luciani, Ferdinando* Alcune versioni antiche di 1Re 12,24b e i problemi che ne derivano. RivBib 43 (1995) 31-43.

1214 *Knoppers, Gary N.* Aaron's calf and Jeroboam's calves. ⇒10. FFREEDMAN D., 1995. 92-104 [Exod 32; 1 Kgs 12,25-33; 13; 14,7-18].

1215 *Frolov, Serge* "Days of Shiloh" in the kingdom of Israel. Bib. 76 (1995) 210-218 [1 Kgs 12,26-33].

1216 **Talshir, Zipora** The alternative story of the division of the kingdom: 3 Kingdoms 12:24a-z. ⇒9,2802. JBS 6. 1993. RRTL 26 (1995) 494-496 *(Bogaert, P.-M.)*; CBQ 57 (1995) 792-793 *(Grabbe, Lester L.)*.

1217 *Briend, Jacques* Du message au messager: remarques sur 1 Rois XIII. ⇒135. Congress Volume: Paris 1992. VT.S 61. 1995. 13-24 [1 Kgs 13].

1218 *Liwak, Rüdiger* Omri. TRE 25 (1995) 242-244 [1 Kgs 16,15-28].

        E4.8 *1 Regum 17-22: Elias,* Elijah.

1219 EGrünwaldt, Klaus; Schroeter, Harald Was suchst du hier, Elia?: ein hermeneutisches Arbeitsbuch. Hermeneutica 4. Rheinbach-Merzbach 1994, CMZ 350 pp. DM38. 3-87062-020-X <pb>.

1220 *Ackerman, Jane* Stories of Elijah and medieval Carmelite identity. HR 35 (1995) 124-147.

1221 *Alkier, Stefan* Unmögliche Möglichkeiten: zur Erzählfolge von 1 Kön 16,29-18,46: eine semiotische Lektüre. ⇒1219. 184-195 [1 Kgs 16,29-18,46].

1222 *Bartelmus, Rüdiger* Elia(s): eine Prophetengestalt im Alten Testament und ihre musikalisch-theologische Deutung durch Felix MENDELSOHN Bartholdy. MuK 65 (1995) 182ff [ZID 21,670].

1223 *Beuscher, Bernd* Theologie—unplugged: Elia in neostrukturalistischer Re-lektüre. ⇒1219. Mit einem Anhang von Dietrich Zilleßen. 213-227 [1 Kgs 16,29-18,46].

1224 *Beyerle, Stefan* Erwägungen zu "Utopie" und "Restauration" als Aspekte der Elia-Haggada. ⇒1219. 55-71.

1225 *Blenkinsopp, Joseph* Ahab of Israel and Jehoshaphat of Judah: the Syro-Palestinean corridor in the ninth century. ⇒127. Civilizations 2. 1309-1319.

1226 *Brandner, Doerthe* Zeigefingerprophetie oder: wie sag ich's meinem Kinde? Elia in Kinderbibeln als pädagogische Instanz, Anwalt der Schwachen oder schillernde Persönlichkeit. ⇒1219. 356-363.

1227 **Choi, Anna** La figura di Elia secondo 1 Re 17-19. Diss. DConroy, Charles, R 1995, Pont. Univ. Gregoriana 87 pp. no. 4120; excerpt.

1228 *Erdmann, Jürgen* Elia im Kabarett. ⇒1219. 320-330.

1229 *Fermor, Gotthard; Schroeter, Harald* Sounds of silence: popmusikalische Kontrapunkte zu Elia. ⇒1219. 308-319.

1230 *Funk, Claudia* Elia und die Frauen: eine feministisch-theologische Betrachtung. ⇒1219. Was suchst du hier, Elia?. 1994. 243-252 [1 Kgs 16,29-18,46].

1231 *Grünwaldt, Kerstin* Elia in der bildenden Kunst. ⇒1219. Was suchst du hier, Elia?. 1994. 267-282.

1232 *Grünwaldt, Klaus* Elia zeitgeistlich: eine kleine Forschungsgeschichte. ⇒1219. Was suchst du hier, Elia?. 1994. 17-26.

1233 *Grünwaldt, Klaus* Von den Ver-Wandlungen des Profeten: die Elia-Rezeption im Alten Testament. ⇒1219. Was suchst du hier, Elia?. 1994. 43-54 [2 Chr 21,12-15; Mal 3,22-24].

1234 **Hauser, Alan J.; Gregory, Russell** From Carmel to Horeb: Elijah in crisis. ⇒6,3068... 10,2697. JSOT.S 85. 1990. RVT 45 (1995) 124-126 *(O'Connell, Robert H.)* [1 Kgs 17-19].

1235 *Hentschel, Georg* Elija: Altes Testament. ⇒122. LThK 3. 1995. 595-596.

1236 *Hirschberg, Andreas* Was, Elia, suchst du im Religionsunterricht?. ⇒1219. Was suchst du hier, Elia?. 1994. 364-374.

1237 *Holt, Else K.* "... Urged on by his wife Jezebel": a literary reading of 1 Kgs 18 in context. SJOT 9 (1995) 83-96 [1 Kgs 18].

1238 *Janssen, Wibke* Das Erscheinen des Elia: Spurensuche in der deutschen Literatur *[Rilke, Rainer M.; Buber, Martin].* ⇒1219. Was suchst du hier, Elia?. 1994. 283-294.

1239 *Kellermann, Ulrich* Elia redivivus und die heilszeitliche Auferwekkung der Toten. ⇒1219. Was suchst du hier, Elia?. 1994. 72-84.

1240 *Klein, Ralph W.* Reflections on historiography in the account of Jehoshaphat. ⇒21. FMILGROM J., 1995. 643-657 [1 Kgs 22].

1241 *Koerrenz, Ralf* Elia in der kirchlichen Bildungsarbeit: eine perspektivische Skizze. ⇒1219. Was suchst du hier, Elia?. 1994. 375-387.

1242 *Lange, Eric* Elia in der Musik. ⇒1219. Was suchst du hier, Elia?. 1994. 295-307.

1243 *Lexutt, Athina* Eliae redivivi—LUTHER, MUENTZER und der Prophet Elia: zur Eliadeutung in der Reformationszeit. ⇒1219. Was suchst du hier, Elia?. 1994. 124-131.

1244 *Lillie, Betty Jane* The vocations of Elijah and Elisha. BiTod 33 141-145.

1245 *Löhr, Hermut* Bemerkungen zur Elia-Erwartung in den Evangelien: ausgehend von Mk 9,11-13. ⇒1219. Was suchst du hier, Elia?. 1994. 85-95.

1246 *Lüders, Stephanie; Weingärtler, Claudia* Elia: homem de Deus, homem do povo: Beispiele aus der lateinamerikanischen Befreiungstheologie. ⇒1219. Was suchst du hier, Elia?. 1994. 253-264 [1 Kgs 16,29-18,46].

1247 *Maurer, Ernstpeter* Elia am Horeb: Paradigmen für eine systematisch-theologische Unterscheidungslehre. ⇒1219. Was suchst du hier, Elia?. 1994. 177-183.

1248 **Mitchell, Christine Karen** Remembering Jezebel: reading and rewriting a biblical character. Diss. DPolzin, Robert, Carleton 1995, 121 pp. MAI 34,988. 0-612-02993-X. [1 Kgs 21].

1249 *Müsse, Carola* Von Engeln, Trommelfeuer und Elia: Bericht von einem Bibliodrama zu Elia am Horeb. ⇒1219. Was suchst du hier, Elia?. 1994. 392-397.

1250 *Nützel, Johannes M.* Elija: Neues Testament. ⇒122. LThK 3. 1995. 596-597.

1251   *Ortmann, Volkmar* Elia multiplex: ein Prophet und mehrfacher Schriftsinn: zur Eliadeutung im Mittelalter. ⇒1219. Was suchst du hier, Elia?. 1994. 115-123.

1252   **Poirot, Soeur Éliane** Élie, archétype du moine: pour un ressourcement prophétique de la vie monastique. SpOr 65. Abbaye de Bellefontaine 1995, 275 pp.

1253   *Reitenberger-Hamidi, Dagmar* Der Prophet Elia im Islam: ein Mahner und Bote Gottes. ⇒1219. Was suchst du hier, Elia?. 1994. 96-101.

1254   *Remy, Jochen* Johann Amos COMENIUS: "Clamores Eliae". ⇒1219. Was suchst du hier, Elia?. 1994. 132-144.

1255   *Rinn-Maurer, Angela* 1 Kön 19—Elia in poimenischer Sicht. ⇒1219. Was suchst du hier, Elia?. 1994. 388-391.

1256   *Roesler, Johannes* Elia und GREIMAS auf dem Karmel: semiotische Analyse von 1 Kön 16,29-18,46. ⇒1219. Was suchst du hier, Elia?. 1994. 196-212.

1257   *Schroeter, Harald* Bist du's, Elia? Streiflichter zum homiletischen Gebrauch der Elia-Texte im 20.Jh. ⇒1219. Was suchst du hier, Elia?. 1994. 333-348.

1258   *Schroeter, Harald* Mit Elia Gottesdienst feiern: Anregungen zur liturgischen Gestaltung von Elia-Texten. ⇒1219. Was suchst du hier, Elia?. 1994. 349-355.

1259   *Stipp, Hermann-Josef* Ahabs Buße und die Komposition des deuteronomistischen Geschichtswerks. Bib. 76 (1995) 471-497 [1 Kgs 21,27-29].

1260   *Strauch, Andreas* Die Elia-Predigten Gottfried MENKENS und Friedrich Wilhelm KRUMMACHERS: Elia in Predigten des 19. Jahrhunderts. ⇒1219. Was suchst du hier, Elia?. 1994. 145-163.

1261   *Thiel, Winfried* Die Erkenntnisaussage in den Elia- und Elisa-Überlieferungen. ⇒37. FWAGNER S., 1995. 256-269.

1262   *Thiel, Winfried* Das "Land" in den Elia und Elisa-Überlieferungen. Landgabe: Festschrift für Jan HELLER zum 70. Geburtstag. Kampen 1995, Kok Pharos [ZAW 108,306]. 64-75.

1263   *Thiel, Winfried* Zu Ursprung und Entfaltung der Elia-Tradition. ⇒1219. Was suchst du hier, Elia?. 1994. 27-39.

1264   *Trible, Phyllis* Exegesis for storytellers and other strangers. JBL 114 (1995) 3-19.

1265   *Trible, Phyllis* The odd couple: Elijah and Jezebel. ⇒70. Out of the garden. 1995. 166-179.

1266   *Van der Toorn, Karel* Migration and the spread of local cults. ⇒18. FLIPINSKI E., OLA 65. 1995. 365-377 [1 Kgs 17,29-33; 2 Kgs 17,24-33].

1267   *Wanke, Daniel* Vorläufer, Typus und Asket: Bemerkungen zur Gestalt des Elia in der altchristlichen Literatur. ⇒1219. Was suchst du hier, Elia?. 1994. 102-114.

1268   *Wolf-Withöft, Susanne* Elia in der Trias der Ambivalenzen: ein Prophet im Spiegel psychologischer Auslegung. ⇒1219. Was suchst du hier, Elia?. 1994. 228-242 [1 Kgs 16,29-18,46].

E4.9   2 Reg 1... *Elisaeus,* Elisha... Ezechias, Josias

1269   *Asurmendi, Jesús* Eliseo, justicia y política, y el relato ficticio. EstB 53 (1995) 145-164.

1270 **Baumgart, N.Cl.** Gott, Prophet und Israel: eine synchrone und diachrone Auslegung der Naamanerzählung und ihrer Gehasiepisode (2 Kön 5). ⇒10,2726. EThSt 68. 1994. RNRTh 117 (1995) 911-912 (*Ska, Jean Louis*).

1271 *Fernández Marcos, Natalio* La reanimación del hijo de la Sunamita en el texto antioqueno. ⇒13. FHARL M., 1995. 119-128 [2 Kgs 4,18-37.

1272 *Pippin, Tina* Jezebel re-vamped. Semeia 69/70 (1995) 221-233 [2 Kgs 9; Rev 2,20].

1273 *Rofe, A.* Eliseo a Dotàn (2Re 6,8-23): saggio di critica storica- letteraria coll'ausilio della tradizione giudaica. RivBib 43/1-2 (1995) 45-54.

1274 *Begg, Christopher T.* Ahaziah's fall (2 Kgs 1): the version of JOSEPHUS. Sef. 55 (1995) 25-40 [2 Kgs 1].

1275 *Long, Burke O.* Sacred geography as narrative structure in 2 Kings 11. ⇒21. FMILGROM J., 1995. 231-238.

1276 *Begg, Christopher T.* Jehoahaz, king of Israel according to JOSEPHUS. Sef. 55 (1995) 227-237 [2 Kgs 13,1-9; 13,22-23].

1277 *Begg, Christopher* Amaziah of Judah according to JOSEPHUS. Anton. 70/1 (1995) 3-30 [2 Kgs 14,1-22; 2 Chr 25,1-26,2].

1278 *Begg, Christopher T.* Uzziah (Azariah) according to JOSEPHUS. EstB 53 (1995) 5-24 [2 Kgs 14,21-15,7].

1279 *Naʾaman, Nadav* Rezin of Damascus and the land of Gilead. ZDPV 111 (1995) 105-117 [2 Kgs 16; Isa 7].

1280 **Chang, Sok-Chung** Yhwh's land: a composition analysis of 2 Kgs 17. Diss. DKnierim, Rolf P., Claremont 1995, 270 pp. AAC 9532681; DAI-A 56,2278.

1281 **Camp, Ludger** Hiskija... ⇒5,2866... 8,2985. 1990. RBijdr. 56 (1995) 453-454 (*Eynikel, Erik*) [2 Kgs 18-20].

1282 *Begg, Christopher T.* Hezekiah's illness and visit according to JOSEPHUS. EstB 53 (1995) 365-385 [2 Kgs 18,1-20,21].

1283 *Naʾaman, Nadav* The debated historicity of Hezekiah's reform in the light of historical and archaeological research. ZAW 107 (1995) 179-195 [2 Kgs 18,4.22].

1284 *Galil, Gershon* The last years of the kingdom of Israel and the fall of Samaria. CBQ 57 (1995) 52-65 [2 Kgs 18,9-12; 17,1-24].

1285 *Borowski, Oded* Hezekiah's reforms and the revolt against Assyria. BA 58/3 (1995) 148-155 [2 Kgs 18,13-19,37; 2 Chr 29,15-19].

1286 *Hyman, Ronald T.* The Rabshakeh's speech (II Kg. 18-25 [sic]): a study of rhetorical intimidation. JBQ 23 (1995) 213-220 [2 Kgs 18,19-35].

1287 *Holloway, Steven W.* Harran: cultic geography in the Neo-Assyrian empire and its implications for Sennacherib's "letter to Hezekiah" in 2 Kings. ⇒1. MAHLSTRÖM G., JSOT.S 190. 1995. 276-314 [2 Kgs 18-19].

1288 **Keulen, Percy S.F. van** Manasseh through the eyes of the deuteronomists: the Manasseh account (2 Kings 21:1-18) and the final chapters of the deuteronomistic history. Diss. DVan der Kooij, A., 1995, Leiden 210 pp. 90-04-10666-9 [RTL 27,531].

1289 **Manor, Dale Wallace** An archaeological commentary on the Josianic reforms Diss. DDever, William G., Arizona 1995, 466 pp. AAC 9603373; DAI-A 56,4006.

1290 **Nakanose, Shigeyuki** Josiah's passover: sociology and the liberating Bible. ⇒10,2750. 1993. ᴿCBQ 57 (1995) 359-360 (*Simkins, Ronald A.*); CritRR 8 (1995) 138-140 (*Frick, Frank S.*).

1291 *Niehr, Herbert* Die Reform des Joschija: methodische, historische und religionsgeschichtliche Aspekte. ⇒86. Jeremia. BBB 98. 1995. 33-55.

1292 *Schneider, Tammi* Did King Jehu kill his own family?: new interpretation reconciles biblical text with famous Assyrian inscription. BArR 21/1 (1995) 26-33, 80.

1293 *Uehlinger, Christoph* Gab es eine joschijanische Kultreform? Plädoyer für ein begründetes Minimum. 1995 ⇒86. Jeremia. BBB 98. 57-89.

1294 *Rüterswörden, Udo* Die Prophetin Hulda. ⇒8. ᶠDONNER H., AAT 30. 1995. 234-242 [2 Kgs 22,14-20].

1295 *Handy, Lowell K.* Historical probability and the narrative of Josiah's reform in 2 Kings. ⇒1. ᴹAHLSTRÖM G., JSOT.S 190. 1995. 252-275. [2 Kgs 22-23].

1296 *Lohfink, Norbert* 2 Kön 23,2 und Dtn 6,17. ⇒54. Studien 3. SBAB.AT 20. 1995 <1990>. 145-155.

1297 *Cruz, Hieronymus* Centralization of cult by Josiah: a biblical perspective in relation to globalization. Jeevadhara 25 (1995) 65-71 [2 Kgs 23].

1298 *Lemaire, Andre* Royal signature: name of Israel's last king surfaces in a private collection. BArR 21/6 (1995) 48-52 [2 Kgs 24,17].

E5.2   *Chronicorum libri* — The books of Chronicles.

1299 **Japhet, Sara** I and II Chronicles: a commentary. ⇒9,2861; 10,2754. OTL. 1993. ᴿTS 56 (1995) 151-152 (*Endres, John C.*); JSSt 40 (1995) 122-123 (*Mason, Rex*); WThJ 57/1 (1995) 257-259 (*Konkel, A.H.*); CBQ 57 (1995) 774-775 (*Graham, M. Patrick*); HebStud 36 (1995) 209-212 (*Schniedewind, William M.*).

1300 ᵀᴱ**McIvor, J. Stanley** The targum of Chronicles. ⇒10,2754*. The Aramaic Bible 19. 1994. ᴿJBL 114 (1995) 545-547 (*Rendsburg, Gary A.*).

1301 **Nielsen, Kjeld; Granild, S.** Krønikebøgerne, Ezras bog og Nehemias' bog. København 1995, Det danske Bibelselskab 170 pp. DKR180. 87-7523-3274 [BoL 1996,66].

1302 **Richter, Wolfgang** 1 und 2 Chronik. ⇒9,2864. Biblia Hebraica transcripta 15. ATSAT 33. 1993. ᴿJSSt 40 (1995) 103-105 (*Verheij, Arian J.C.*).

1303 **Thompson, J.A.** 1,2 Chronicles. NAC 9. Nv 1995, Broadman & Holman 411 pp. $28 [JBL 114,577].

1304 **Abadie, Philippe** El libro de las Crónicas. ᵀ*Darrícal, Nicolás*, CuaBi 87. Estella 1995, Verbo Divino. 63 pp. 84-8169-075-9.

1305 *Ben Zvi, Ehud* A sense of proportion: an aspect of the theology of the chronicler. SJOT 9 (1995) 37-51.

      Dörrfuß, Ernst Michael Mose in den Chronikbüchern. ⇒567.

1306 *Kalimi, Isaac* The contribution of the literary study of Chronicles to the solution of its textual problems. Bibl.Interp. 3 (1995) 190-212.

1307 *Kalimi, Isaac* Paronomasia in the book of Chronicles. JSOT 67 (1995) 27-41.

1308 **Kalimi, Isaac** Zur Geschichtsschreibung des Chronisten: literarisch-historiographische Abweichungen der Chronik von ihren Paralleltexten in den Samuel- und Königsbüchern. BZAW 226. B 1995, De Gruyter ix; 400 pp. Diss. Hebrew University 1989. DM188. 3-11-014237-6. ᴿEThL 71 (1995) 440-442 (*Lust, J.*).

1309 *Kelly, Brian* Messianic elements in the Chronicler's work. 1995 ⇒111. The Lord's anointed. 249-264.

1310 **Kleinig, John W.** The Lord's song: the basis, function and significance of choral music in Chronicles. ⇒9,2873; 10,2761. JSOT.S 156. 1993. ᴿCBQ 57 (1995) 350-351 (*Larson-Miller, Lizette*).

1311 **Menchén Carrasco, Joaquín** Historia cronistica: Cronicas, Esdras y Nehemias. El mensaje del Antiguo Testamento 9. M 1995, Atenas 383 pp. map. 84-7020-361-4.

1312 *Richards, Kent Harold* Reshaping Chronicles and Ezra-Nehemiah interpretation. ⇒36. ᶠTucker G., 1995. 211-224.

1313 **Riley, William** King and cultus in Chronicles: worship and the reinterpretation of history. ⇒9,2877; 10,2765. JSOT.S 160. 1993. ᴿJThS 46 (1995) 217-222 (*Schaper, J.L.W.*); JBL 114 (1995) 498-500 (*Throntveit, Mark A.*); CBQ 57 (1995) 783-784 (*Wright, John W.*).

1314 **Steins, Georg** Die Chronik als kanonisches Abschlussphänomen: Studien zur Entstehung und Theologie von 1 / 2 Chronik. BBB 93. Weinheim 1995, Beltz Athenäum 582 pp. 3-89547-030-9.

1315 **Steins, Georg** König—Tempel—Leviten: Untersuchungen zur Entstehung und Theologie der Chronikbücher. Diss. ⇒10,2768. BBB 93. Fra 1995, Hain 582 pp. 3-89547-030-9.

1316 *Weinberg, Joel P.* The 'extracanonical' prophecies in the books of Chronicles. R. Palestjinskji Sbornik 32 (1995) 8-16 [OTA 18,535].

1317 *Ho, C.Y.S.* Conjectures and refutations: is 1 Samuel xxxi 1-13 really the source of 1 Chronicles x 1-12?. VT 45 (1995) 82-106.

1318 *Eskenazi, Tamara C.* A literary approach to Chronicles' ark narrative in 1 Chronicles 13-16. ⇒10. ᶠFreedman D., 1995. 258-274.

1319 *Dirksen, Piet* The development of the text of I Chronicles 15:1-24. Henoch 17 (1995) 267-277.

1320 **Auffret, Pierre** Merveilles à nos yeux: étude structurelle de vingt psaumes dont celui de 1 Ch 16,8-36. BZAW 235. B 1995, De Gruyter xii; 315 pp. 3-11-014666-5 [Pss 68; 89; 97; 98; 99; 102; 107; 109; 115; 118; 121; 135; 140; 141; 142; 143; 144; 149; 150].

1321 *Dirksen, Piet* What are the mᵉḥabbᵉrôt in 1 Chron. 22:3?. BN 80 (1995) 23-24.

1322 *Kuntzmann, Raymond* Dieu vient vers son lieu de repos (2 Ch 6,41). ⇒22. ᶠRenaud B., LeDiv 159. 1995. 205-213.

1323 *Begg, Christopher* Jehoshaphat at mid-career according to AJ 9,1-17. RB 102 (1995) 379-402 [2 Chr 19; 20; 21,1].

1324 *Begg, Christopher* Josephus' portrait of Jehoshaphat: compared with the biblical and rabbinic portrayals. BN 78 (1995) 39-48 [2 Chr 17].

1325 **Strübind, Kim** Tradition als Interpretation in der Chronik: König Josaphat als Paradigma chronistischer Hermeneutik und Theologie.

⇒6,3144... 9,2891. BZAW 201. 1991. ᴿThLZ 120 (1995) 424-425 (*Willi, Thomas*).

E5.4   *Esdrae libri* — **Ezra, Nehemiah.**

1326   **Becker, Joachim** Esra/Nehemia. ⇒6,3147... 8,3040. 1990. ᴿThRv 91 (1995) 380-381 (*Mathys, Hans Peter*).

1327   **Breneman, Mervin** Ezra, Nehemiah, Esther. ⇒10,2778. NAC 10. 1993. ᴿCBQ 57 (1995) 118-120 (*Smith-Christopher, Daniel L.*).

1328   **Burns, R.** Esdra e Neemia. BT 11. Brescia 1995, Queriniana 142 pp. L16.000 [RdT 36,511].

1329   *Gärtig, William G.* The attribution of the Iʙɴ Ezʀᴀ supercommentary Avvat Nefesh to Asʜᴇʀ ben Abraham Crescas reconsidered. HUCA 66 (1995) 239-257.

1330   **Hanhart, Robert** Ein unbekannter Text zur griechischen Esra-Überliefurung: Lothar Perlitt zum 65. Geburtstag am 2. Mai 1995. MSU 22. Gö 1995, Vandenhoeck & Ruprecht 22 pp.

1331   **Lim, David Kyung-Chul** Nehemiah: an interpretive analysis of leadership development. Diss. Fuller Theological Seminary 1995, 144 pp. MAI 34,548.

1332   **Schniedewind, William M.** The word of God in transition: from prophet to exegete in the Second Temple period. Diss. Brandeis 1992 ⇒8,3021. ᴰ*Brettler, M.*, JSOT.S 197. Shf 1995, Academic 275 pp. £27.50/$41. 1-85075-550-7 [BoL 1996,90].

1333   *Talmon, Shemaryahu* Esra-Nehemia: Historiographie oder Theologie? ⇒59. Israels Gedankenwelt. InfJud 13. 1995 <1992>. 218-240.

1334   *Knauf, Ernst Axel* Zum Verhältnis von Esra 1,1 zu 2 Chronik 36,20-23. BN 78 (1995) 16-17.

1335   *Fleishman, Joseph* The investigating commission of Tattenai: the purpose of the investigation and its results. HUCA 66 (1995) 81-102 [Ezra 5,3-4].

1336   *Koch, Klaus* Der Artaxerxes-Erlaß im Esrabuch. ⇒8. ᶠDᴏɴɴᴇʀ H., AAT 30. 1995. 87-98 [Ezra 7,12-26].

1337   **Horn, Siegfried H.; Wood, Lynn H.** Die Chronologie von Esra 7. Wien 1995, Wegweiser 200 pp. 3-900160-06-6.

1338   *Wong, G.C.I.* A note on "joy" in Nehemiah viii 10. VT 45 (1995) 383-386.

1339   *Mathias, Dietmar* Nachexilische Geschichtsrezeption am Beispiel von Nehemia 9,6-31: Hans Seidel zum 65. Geburtstag gewidmet. Mitteilungen und Beiträge 9. ᴱ**Forschungsstelle Judentum a.d. Theol. Fak. Leipzig.** Lp 1995, Thomas-Verlag. 3-86174-044-3. 3-25.

1340   **Boda, Mark J.** Praying the tradition: the origin and use of tradition in Nehemiah 9. Diss. ᴰ*Williamson, H.G.M.*, 1995, Cambridge [TynB 48,179-182].

1341   *Gosse, Bernard* L'alliance avec Levi et l'opposition entre les lignes royale et sacerdotale à l'époque perse. Transeuphratène 10 (1995) 29-33 [Neh 10,1; 13,29; Jer 33,21; Mal 2,4.8].

1342   *Lemaire, André* Ashdodien et Judéen à l'époque perse: Ne 13,24. ⇒18. ᶠLɪᴘɪɴsᴋɪ E., OLA 65. 1995. 153-163 [Neh 13,24].

E5.5 Libri Tobiae, Judith, Esther.

1343 EBrenner, Athalya A feminist companion to Esther, Judith and Susanna. The Feminist Companion to the Bible 7. Shf 1995, Academic 336 pp. £16.50; $24.50. 1-85075-527-2.

1344 Craghan, John Ester, Giuditta, Tobia, Giona. LoB 1/11. Brescia 1995, Queriniana 186 pp. L24.000. 88-399-1561-3.
Ravasi, Gianfranco Rut, Giuditta, Ester ⇒1030.
Ruth-Judith-Ester-Susanna ⇒1043.

1345 *Arzt, Peter; Hampel, Andreas* Tobits Lobgesang: sprachlicher Schlüssel zu Tob 13,1-14,1. PzB 4 (1995) 59-72.

1346 *Fitzmyer, Joseph A.* The Aramaic and Hebrew fragments of Tobit from Qumran Cave 4. CBQ 57 (1995) 655-675.

1347 *McCracken, David* Narration and comedy in the book of Tobit. JBL 114 (1995) 401-418.

1348 *Nowell, Irene* Irony in the book of Tobit. BiTod 33 (1995) 79-83.

1349 *Stagno, Laura* Tobiolo e Tobia nella pittura genovese del primo seicento. ACr 83 (1995) 353-364.

1350 *Craven, Toni* Judith prays for help (Jdt 9:1-14): prayer from Alexander to Constantine: a critical anthology. SBL.SP 34. 208-212.

1351 Demissy, Claude Sagesse et violence: une lecture de Judith. Diss. Strasbourg. DRobert, Ph. de, 1995 [RTL 27,528].

1352 *Di Lella, A.A.* Women in the Wisdom of Ben Sira and the book of Judith: a study in contrasts and reversals. ⇒135. Congress Volume: Paris 1992. VT.S 61. 1995. 39-52.

1353 Haag, Ernst Das Buch Judit. Geistliche Schriftlesung : Erläuterungen zum Alten Testament für die geistliche Lesung 15. Dü 1995, Patmos 200 pp. 3-491-77173-0.

1354 *Henten, Jan Willem van* Judith as alternative leader: a rereading of Judith 7-13. ⇒1343. A feminist companion. 1995. 224-252.

1355 *La Posta, Mara* Giuditta: una donna al servizio di Dio. PaVi 40/5 (1995) 24-28.

1356 *Levine, Amy-Jill* Sacrifice and salvation: otherness and domestication in the book of Judith. ⇒1343. A feminist companion. 1995. 208-223.

1357 *Levison, John R.* Judith 16:14 and the creation of woman. JBL 114 (1995) 467-469.
Luter, A. Boyd; Davis, Barry C. God behind the scene: expositions of the books of Ruth and Esther. ⇒1027.

1358 *Roitman, Adolfo D.* The mystery of Arphaxad (Jdt 1): a new proposal. Henoch 17 (1995) 301-310.

1359 *Shin, Kyo-Seon* A study of the major theological thought of Judith. K. The Reason and the Faith 10 (1995) 53-106 [ThIK 17,54].

1360 *Arzt, Silvia* "Ich finde, daß sehr großer Mut dazugehört, in dieser Zeit nicht einem Mann zu gehorchen: noch dazu dem König": wie Kinder eine biblische Geschichte neu-konstruieren. CPB 108 (1995) 156-158 [Esth 1].

1361 *Bach, Alice* Mirror, mirror in the text: reflections on reading and rereading. ⇒1343. A feminist companion. 1995. 81-86.

1362 Beal, Timothy K. Identity and subversion in Esther. Diss. Emory. DNewson, C.A., 1995 [RTL 27,527].

1363 *Beal, Timothy K.* Tracing Esther's beginnings. ⇒1343. A feminist companion. 1995. 87-110.

1364 *Brenner, Athalya* Looking at Esther through the looking glass, ⇒1343. A feminist companion. 1995. 71-80.

1365 *Bronner, Leila Leah* Esther revisited: an aggadic approach. ⇒1343. A feminist companion. 1995. 176-197.

1366 **Craig, Kenneth M.** Reading Esther: a case for the literary carnivalesque. Literary currents in biblical interpretation. LVL 1995, Westminster John Knox 192 pp. $16. 0-664-25518-3 [CBQ 58,194].

1367 **Day, Linda** Three faces of a queen: characterization in the books of Esther. Diss. JSOT.S 186. Shf 1995, Academic 254 pp. $45. 1-85075-517-5 [RStR 22,59].

1368 *Derby, Josiah* The paradox in the book of Esther. JBQ 23 (1995) 116-119 [Esth 2,10. 20].

1369 *Gitay, Zefira* Esther and the queen's throne. ⇒1343. A feminist companion. 1995. 136-148.

1370 *Hubbard, R.L.* La estrategia de la bella reina Ester: Ester, 3-5. Kairos(G) 17 (1995) 17-22 [Strom. 52,345].

1371 **Jobes, Karen Hill** The Alpha-Text of Esther: its character and relationship to the Masoretic Text. Diss. Westminster Theological Seminary. [D]*Silva, Moises,* 1995 454 pp. DAI-A 56,1829.

1372 *Klein, Lillian R.* Honor and shame in Esther. ⇒1343. A feminist companion. 1995. 149-175.

1373 **Klingbeil, G. A.** *rkš* and Esther 8,10.14: a semantic note. ZAW 107 (1995) 301-303.

1374 *Langenhorst, Georg* "Das aber war nicht Liebe"—Esther im Spiegel moderner Literatur. EuA 71 (1995) 396-412.

1375 **Méroz, Christianne** Esther en exile: pour une spiritualité de la différence. Poliez-le-Grand 1995, Moulin 85 pp. [EstB 55,269].

1376 *Mosala, Itumeleng J.* The implications of the text of Esther for African women's struggle for liberation in South Africa. ⇒129. Voices from the margin. 1995 <1991>. 168-178.

1377 *Niditch, Susan* Esther: folklore, wisdom, feminism and authority. ⇒1343. A feminist companion. 1995. 26-46.

1378 *Niditch, Susan* Short stories: the book of Esther and the theme of woman as a civilizing force. ⇒36. [F]TUCKER G., 1995. 195-209.

1379 **Rodriguez, Angel Manuel** Esther: a theological approach. Berrien Springs, MI 1995, Andrews University Press xii; 162 pp. $17. 1-883925-03-7.

1380 *Scaiola, Donatella* Ester. PaVi 40/5 (1995) 18-23.

1381 **Segal, Eliezer** The Babylonian Esther midrash. ⇒10,2829. BJSt 291-293. 1994. [R]JSJ 26 (1995) 219-225 *(Neusner, Jacob)*.

1382 *Spiegel, Celina* The world remade: the book of Esther. ⇒70. Out of the garden. 1995. 191-203.

1383 **Steck, Odil Hannes; Kottsieper, Ingo; Kratz, Reinhard G.** Das Buch Baruch: zu Esther und Daniel: der Brief Jeremias. ATD. Apokryphen 5. Gö 1995, Vandenhoeck & Ruprecht. DM40. 3-525-51405-0.

1384 *Talmon, Shemaryahu* "Weisheit" im Buch Ester. ⇒59. Israels Gedankenwelt. InfJud 13. 1995 <1963>. 177-217.

1385 *Talmon, Shermaryahu* Was the book of Esther known at Qumran?. DSD 2 (1995) 249-267.

1386 *Troyer, Kristin De* An oriental beauty parlour: an analysis of Esther 2.8-18 in the Hebrew, the Septuagint and the second Greek text. ⇒1343. A feminist companion. 1995. 47-70.

1387 **Walfish, Barry Dov** Esther in medieval garb: Jewish interpretation of the book of Esther in the Middle Ages. ⇒9,2941; 10,2841. 1993. ᴿSR 24 (1995) 371-372 (*Segal, Eliezer*); JAOS 115 (1995) 327-328 (*Levenson, Jon D.*); AJS 20 (1995) 420-422 (*Cohen, Jeremy*).

1388 **Weinreb, Friedrich** Die Rolle Esther: das Buch Esther nach der ältesten jüdischen Überlieferung. Bern ²1995, Origo. FS52.

E5.8 *Machabaeorum libri*, 1-2[-3] Maccabees

1389 *Lee, Stuart* ÆLFRIC's treatment of source material in his homily on the books of the Maccabees. BJRL 77/3 (1995) 165-176.

1390 Libri I-II Macchabeorum cum praefationibus et capitulorum seriebus. Biblia Sacra iuxta Latinam Vulgatam versionem ad codicum fidem iussu Ioannis Pauli PP II cura et studio monachorum... Sancti Hieronymi in Urbe edita 18. Romae 1995, Vaticana lxv; 266 pp.

1391 **Spilly, A.** I libri dei Maccabei. BT 12. Brescia 1995, Queriniana 192 pp. L25.000 [RdT 36,772].

1392 *Enermalm, Agneta* Prayers in wartime: thematic tensions in 1 Maccabees. StTh 49 (1995) 272-286.

1393 *Rappaport, Uriel* The extradition clause in 1 Maccabees, XV, 21. ⇒18. ᶠLIPINSKI E., OLA 65. 1995. 271-283.

1394 *Brown Tkacz, Catherine* The seven Maccabees, the three Hebrews and a newly discovered sermon of St. Augustine (Mayence 50). REAug 41/1 (1995) 59-78 [Dan 3; 2 Macc 7].

1395 *Parente, Fausto* Le témoignage de THEODORE de Mopsueste sur le sort d'Onias III et la fondation du temple de Léontopolis. REJ 154 (1995) 429-436 [2 Macc 3-4].

1396 *Passoni Dell'Acqua, A.* La preghiera del III libro dei Maccabei: genere letterario e tematica. RivBib 43 (1995) 135-179 [3 Macc 2,2-20; 6,1-15].

1397 *Tromp, Johannes* The formation of the third book of Maccabees. Henoch 17 (1995) 311-328.ls 1

Libri didactici VT

E6.1 *Poesis 1.metrica*, **Biblical** and Semitic **versification**.

1398 **Alonso Schökel, Luis** Antologia della poesia biblica. ᵀ*Zappella, Marco*. CasM 1995, Piemme 589 pp. ill.

1399 *Andersen, Francis I.* What biblical scholars might learn from Emily DICKINSON. ⇒24. ᶠSAWYER J., JSOT.S 195. 1995. 52-79.

1400 *Barsch, Achim* Metrics between phonology and theory of literature. PoeT 16 (1995) 411-428.

1401 **Berlin, Adele** Poetics and interpretation of Biblical narrative. WL 1995, Eisenbrauns. $12.95. 0-931464-93-5.
1402 *Bernhart, Walter* How final can a theory of verse be?: toward a pragmatics of metrics. PoeT 16 (1995) 429-444.
1403 **Berry, Donald K.** An introduction to wisdom and poetry of the Old Testament. Nv 1995, Broadman & Holman xvi; 463 pp. 0-8054-1547-5.
1404 *Bjorklund, Beth* Form, anti-form, and informality: reinventing free verse. PoeT 16 (1995) 547-567.
1405 *Cross, Frank Moore* Toward a history of Hebrew prosody. ⇒10. FFREEDMAN D., 1995. 298-309.
1406 *Forceville, Charles* (A)symmetry in metaphor: the importance of extended context. PoeT 16 (1995) 677-708.
1407 **Gillingham, S.E.** The poems and psalms of the Hebrew Bible. ⇒10,2872. 1994. RSJTh 48 (1995) 263-264 (*Goulder, Michael*); CritRR 8 (1995) 124-125 (*Williams, Tyler F.*).
1408 *Irwin, W. H.* Conflicting parallelism in Job 5,13; Isa 30,28, Isa 32,7. Bib. 76 (1995) 72-74
1409 *Küper, Christoph* Metrics today I: an introduction. PoeT 16 (1995) 389-409.
1410 **Lord, A.B.** The singer resumes the tale. ELord, M.L., Myth and Poetics. L 1995, Cornell University Press xiii; 258 pp. £31.50. 0-8014-3103-4 [ClR 47,9].
1411 **Marböck, Johannes** *qw*—Eine Bezeichnung für das hebräische Metrum?. ⇒55. Gottes Weisheit. 1995 <1970>. 144-146.
1412 **Petersen, David L.; Richards, Kent Harold** Interpreting Hebrew poetry. ⇒8,3121... 10,2875. 1992. RCritRR 7 (1994) 130-133 (*Kleven, Terence*).
1413 *Tristram, Hildegard L.C.* Near-sameness in early insular metrics: oral ancestry and aesthetic potential. PoeT 16 (1995) 445-470.
1414 *Vegas Montaner, Luis; Seijas de los Ríos, Guadalupe* A computer assisted syntactical study of poetic biblical texts 1995 ⇒133. Bible et Informatique. 341-355 [Isa 1-39].
1415 *Watts, J.W.* Song and the ancient reader. PRSt 22 (1995) 135-147.

E6.2 **Psalmi, textus.**

1416 De Psalmen. TTromp, N.J., Den Bosch 1995, Katholieke Bijbelstichting 213 pp. Willibrordvertaling; Grote letter editie. *f*47.50. 90-6173-690-0 [Str. 64,184].
1417 *Flint, Peter W.* The Psalms scrolls from the Judaean desert and the Septuagint Psalter. ⇒136. VIII Congress. SCSt 41. 1995. 203-217.
1418 **Gabra, Gawdat** Der Psalter im oxyrhynchitischen (mesokemischen/mittelägyptischen) Dialekt. ADAI.K 4. Heidelberg 1995, Heidelberg Orientverlag 209 pp. Mit Beiträgen von Nasry Iskander, Gerd Mink und John L. Sharp; 20 ill. map. 3-927552-11-9.
1419 *Haney, Kristine E.* The St Albans Psalter: a reconsideration. JWCI 58 (1995) 1-28 [RBen 106,404].
1420 EHeinzer, Felix Der Landgrafenpsalter. ⇒8,3131. 1992. RMAe 64 (1995) 305-307; Scr. 49/1 (1995) 148-152 (*Büttner, F.O.*).
1421 *Jenkins, R.G.* Sunnia and Fretela revisited: reflections on the Hexaplaric Psalter. ⇒136. VIII Congress. SCSt 41. 1995. 219-232.

1422 *Lund, Jerome* Grecisms in the Peshitta Psalms. ⇒76. The Peshitta. MPIL 8. 1995. 85-102.

1423 **Mele, Giampaolo** Hymni. Psalterium-Hymnarium Arborense: il manuscritto P.XIII della cattedrale di Oristano (secolo XIV-XV): studio codicologico, paleografico, testuale, storico, liturgico, gregoriano: trascrizioni. Quaderni di 'Studi Gregoriani' 3. Roma 1994 [=1995], Torre d'Orfeo 401 pp. 47 ill. L45.000 [MF 96,657ss— *Costa, Francesco*).

1424 **Nicole, Émile; Johnston, Philip; Blanchard, Thomas** Tehillîm: les psaumes: aide à la lecture cursive du texte hébreu. Villeurbanne 1995, CLE. FF99. 2-906090-21-2. [ETR 72,604].

1425 **Noel, William** The Harley psalter. Cambridge Studies in Palaeography and Codicology 4. C 1995, University Press xvii; 231 pp. ill. £40. 0-521-46495-1.

1426 **Norton, Gerard J.** The fragments of the Hexapla of the psalter and the preparation of a critical edition of the Hebrew psalter. Origeniana Sexta. ⇒126. BEThL 118. 1995. 187-201.

1427 *Puig i Tàrrech, Armand* Tomàs SUCCONA: primer traductor modern dels Salms en català. RCatT 20 (1995) 277-292 [sum. 292; Acts 3,12-26].

1428 **Rougier, Stan** Montre-moi ton visage: variations sur les Psaumes. Prières. P 1995, Desclée 276 pp. 2-220-03631-6.

1429 *Stanton, Anne Rudloff* Notes on the codicology of the Queen Mary Psalter. Scr. 49 (1995) 250-262.

1430 [ET]**Urvoy, Marie-Thérèse** Le Psautier mozarabe de HAFS le Goth: édition et traduction de... Toulouse 1994, Presses universitaires du Mirail xxii; 462 pp. [R]BLE 96 (1995) 227-228 (*Dagorn, R.*); RThom 95 (1995) 701-702 (*Jomier, Jacques*).

1431 **Wieder, Laurance** The poets' book of Psalms: the complete Psalter as rendered by twenty-five poets from the sixteenth to the twentieth centuries. SF 1995, Harper San Francisco xxiii; 311 pp. 0-06-069284-7.

E6.3 Psalmi, introductio.

1432 **Armellini, Fernando; Moretti, Giuseppe** I salmi: canti della vita. Quaderni di Evangelizzare 9. Bo 1995, EDB 158 pp. 88-10-60709-0.

1433 *Beckwith, Roger T.* The early history of the Psalter. TynB 46 (1995) 1-27.

1434 **Bonhoeffer, Dietrich** Introduction au livre des Psaumes: le livre de prières de la Bible. Turnhout 1995, Brepols [BuBbgB 19,86].

1435 *Chouraqui, André* Liminaire aux psaumes. SIDIC 28/1 (1995) 16.

1436 [E]**Collin, Matthieu** Le livre des Psaumes. Présenté par... CEv 92. P 1995, Cerf 66 pp. FF33.

1437 **Declaisse-Walford, Nancy L.** Reading from the beginning: the shaping of the Hebrew Psalter. Diss. [D]*Bellinger, W. H. Jr.*, Baylor 1995, 228 pp. DAI-A 56,4428.

1438 *Girard, Marc* L'exégèse des psaumes: état de la recherche (1980-1992). ⇒84. De bien des manières. LeDiv 163. 1995. 119-145.

1439 *Grünwaldt, Klaus* Loblied und Laienlyrik: zum exegetischen Verständnis der Psalmen. EvErz 47 (1995) 12-27.

1440 TEHeine, Ronald E. Gregorius Nyssenus: in iscriptiones Psalmorum: GREGORY of Nyssa's treatise on the inscriptions of the
Psalms. Oxford Early Christian Studies. Ox 1995, Clarendon xii;
221 pp. £35. 0-19-826763-0.

1441 Levine, Herbert J. Sing unto God a new song: a contemporary
reading of the Psalms. ISBL. Bloomington 1995, Indiana University Press xvi; 279 pp. $39.95; £35. 0-253-33341-5 [BoL
1996,63].

1442 Lumbreras Meabe, J.M. Salmos cristianos. M 1995, Sociedad de
Educación Atenas 261 pp. [ScrTh 27,1092].

1443 Mays, James Luther The Lord reigns: a theological handbook to
the Psalms. ⇒10,2897. 1994. RTS 56 (1995) 355-356 (Soll, Will);
ThTo 52 (1995) 402-406 (Janzen, J. Gerald); Dialog 34 (1995)
313-316 (Jacobson, Del).

1444 EMcCann, J. Clinton The shape and shaping of the Psalter.
⇒9,395; 10,2895. JSOT.S 159. 1993. RTJT 11/1 (1995) 85-86
(Taylor, J. Glen); CBQ 57 (1995) 214-216 (Ceresko, Anthony R.);
BiOr 52 (1995) 749-751 (Prinsloo, Willem S.).

1445 McCann, J. Clinton A theological introduction to the book of
Psalms: the Psalms as Torah. ⇒10,2896. 1993. RCBQ 57 (1995)
565-566 (Day, Linda); CritRR 8 (1995) 132-134 (Langston, Scott).

1446 Millard, Matthias Die Komposition des Psalters. ⇒10,2901*
[Willard!]. FAT 9. 1994. RRTL 26 (1995) 496-501 (Auwers, Jean-
Marie).

1447 Norris, Kathleen The paradox of the psalms. ⇒70. Out of the garden. 1995. 221-233.

1448 Oemig, Manfred Die Psalmen in Forschung und Verkündigung. VF
40/1 (1995) 28-51.

1449   Psalmen: onvergankelijke poëzie. Den Bosch 1995, Katholieke
Bijbelstichting 92 pp. f8.25. 90-6173-933-0 [Str. 64,184].

1450 Sarna, Nahum M. Songs of the heart: an introduction to the book
of Psalms. ⇒9,2999. 1993. RProoftexts 15 (1995) 202-208
(Lichtenstein, Murray H.); JR 75 (1995) 257-259 (Miller, Patrick
D.); CritRR 8 (1995) 147-148 (McCann, J. Clinton).

1451 Schröer, Henning Kontexte zu den Psalmen der Bibel. EvErz 47
(1995) 98-100.

1452 ESeybold, Klaus; Zenger, Erich Neue Wege der Psalmenfor-
schung. FBEYERLIN W., ⇒10,15. 1994. RTZ 51 (1995) 87
(Weber, Beat); RevBib 57 (1995) 239-246 (Ricciardi, Alberto).

1453 Simon, Uriel Four approaches to the Book of Psalms from
SAADIAH to Abraham IBN EZRA. ⇒7,2747. 1991. RCritRR 7
(1994) 437-439 (Kaminsky, Joel S.).

1454 Stork, Dieter Psalmen—Wort im Bild. EvErz 47 (1995) 27-45.

1455 Tronina, Antoni Teologia Psalmów: wprowadzenie do lektury
Psałterza. Lublin 1995, RW KUL 262 pp.

E6.4 Psalmi, commentarii.

1456 Alves, Manuel Isidro BARTOLOMEU Dos Mártires: Comentário
aos Salmos, edição bilingue: introdução, tradução e anotações.
BVV 14. Fátima 1991, Movimento Bartolomeacno 517 pp.
RHumTeo 16 (1995) 315-316 (Couto, A.); Igreja e Missão 47
(1995) 301-302 (Couto, A.).

1457 **Barratt, Alexandra** The Seven Psalms: a commentary on the penitential psalms. ^T*Hull, Eleanor*, EETS 307. Ox 1995, OUP xli; 326 pp. £30. 0-19-722309-5.

1458 **Blaumeiser, Hubertus** Martin LUTHERs Kreuzestheologie: Schlüssel zu seiner Deutung von Mensch und Wirklichkeit: eine Untersuchung anhand der Operationes in Psalmos (1519-1521). KKTS 60. Paderborn 1995, Bonifatius 576 pp. DM98.

1459 **Brinkman, J.M.** Psalmen I: een praktische bijbelverklaring. Tekst en Toelichting. Kampen 1995, Kok 198 pp. *f*40. 90-242-2215-X [KeTh 47,248].

1460 **Centre d'Analyse et de Documentation Patristiques** Le Psautier chez les Pères. Présenté par *Pierre Maraval,* Cahiers de Biblia Patristica 4. Strasbourg 1994 310 pp. FF170. ^RStPat 42/3 (1995) 164-166 *(Corsato, Celestino)*; ThPh 70 (1995) 578-579 *(Sieben, H.J.)*.

1461 **Cimosa, Mario** Con te non temo alcun male: Salmi 1-25. Lettura esegetica e spirituale della Bibbia 1. R 1995, Dehoniane 342 pp. L28.000. 88-396-0573-8. ^RPalCl 74 (1995) 812 *(Lavarda, Girolamo)*.

1462 ^{TE}**Coppa, Giovanni** ORIGENE-GEROLAMO: 74 omelie sul libro dei Salmi. 1993, ^RCivCatt 146 (1995) 516-518 *(Cremascoli, G.)*.

1463 **Craven, Toni** The book of Psalms. ⇒8,3152. 1992. ^RCritRR 7 (1994) 108-109 *(Ceresko, Anthony R.)*.

1464 **De Simone, G.P.** CASSIODORO e l'*Expositio Psalmorum*: una lettura cristologica dei Salmi. Cosenza 1993, Progetto 2000: 167 pp. ^RVetChr 32/1 (1995) 221-222 *(Bettocchi, Silvia)*.

1465 **Eaton, John H.** Psalms of the way and the kingdom: a conference with the commentators. JSOT.S 199. Shf 1995, Academic 144 pp. £22.50; $33.50. 1-85075-552-3.

1466 **Gerstenberger, Erhard S.** Psalms, 1 [to 60]. ⇒4,3117... 9,3010. FOTL 14. 1988. ^RThLZ 120 (1995) 638-641 *(Janowski, Bernd)*.

1467 **Girard, Marc** Les psaumes redécouverts: de la structure au sens 2-3: 51-100: 101-150. Montréal 1994, Bellarmin 624; 564 pp. $34.95; $32.95. 2-89007-773-X; 2-89007-774-8. ^REeT(O) 26 (1995) 261-263 *(Vogels, Walter)*.

1468 **Hirsch, Samson Raphael** Psalmen: übersetzt und erläutert. Z 1995, Reprint Morascha 850 pp.

1469 **Kraus, Hans-Joachim** Salmos 1-59, 60-150. BEB 53-54. Salamanca 1995, Sígueme 829; 883 pp. ^RTer. 46 (1995) 661-663 *(Pasquetto, Virgilio)*; SalTer 83 (1995) 411-413 *(Ramos, Felipe F.)*; EstTrin 29/1 (1995) 131-132 *(Pikaza, X.)*; Lumen 44 (1995) 517-518 *(Ortiz de Urtaran, Félix)*.

1470 **Mays, James Luther** Psalms. ⇒10,2915. 1994. ^RPSB 16/1 (1995) 84-85 *(Murphy, Roland E.)*; ThTo 52/1 (1995) 146-150 *(Peterson, Eugene H.)*; TS 56 (1995) 355-356 *(Soll, Will)*.

1471 **Murphy, Roland Edmund** The Psalms are yours. ⇒9,3017. 1993. Carmelus 42/1 (1995) 296-298 *(Vella, Alexander)*; OTEs 8 (1995) 311-313 *(Helberg, J.L.)*.

1472 **Schneider, Dieter** Das Buch der Psalmen. WStB.AT. Wu 1995, Brockhaus 3 vols. 1. Teil: Psalm 1 bis 50; 2. Teil: Psalm 51 bis 100; 3. Teil: Psalm 101 bis 150.

1473 **Schumacher, Heinz** Die Psalmen: erklärt und ausgelegt. Hänssler-Bibelwissen 11. Stu 1994, Hänssler 400 pp. DM40. 3-7751-2213-3. ^RJETh 9 (1995) 171-172 *(Pehlke, Helmuth)*.

1474 *Seybold, Klaus* Psalmen-Kommentare 1972-1994. ThR 60 (1995) 113-130.
1475 **Stoffregen Pedersen, Kirsten** Traditional Ethiopian exegesis of the book of Psalms. ÄthF 36. Wsb 1995, Harrassowitz 301 pp. 3-447-03443-2.
1476 **Tate, Marvin E.** Psalms 51-100. ⇒6,3264b... 10,2921. WBC 20. 1990. REstB 53 (1995) 409-411 (*Aparicio, A.*).
1477 Psaumes 31 à 55: traduction et commentaires fondés sur les sources talmudiques, midrachiques et rabbiniques. Tehillim = Les Psaumes 2. P 1995, Colbo [BuBbgB 19,87].

E6.5 **Psalmi, themata.**

1478 *Antomas Oses, I.* La iglesia, cuerpo de Cristo, en las Enarraciones a los salmos de san AGUSTIN. Mayéutica 21 (1995) 9-49.
1479 *Ballhorn, Egbert* "Um deines Knechtes David willen" (Ps 132,10): die Gestalt Davids im Psalter. BN 76 (1995) 16-31.
1480 *Bandstra, Barry L.* Marking turns in poetic text: waw in the Psalms. ⇒26. FSCHNEIDER W., 1995. 45-52.
1481 *Bell, Desmond* Elementar verständliche Texte: Psalmen als Thema biblischer Didaktik. EvErz 47 (1995) 45-55.
1482 *Bezuidenhout, L.C.* Perspektiewe uit die psalms wat lig werp op die wese van die geloofsgemeenskap [Perspectives from the psalms which illuminate the nature of the faith-community]. HTS 51 (1995) 712-719 [OTA 19,255].
1483 *Bohren, Rudolf* Die Bußpsalmen: Lebenserfahrung und Doxologie. PTh 84 (1995) 150-165.
1484 *Bourgeault, Cynthia* The hidden wisdom of psalmody. Gnosis 37 (1995) 22-28.
1485 *Braulik, Georg* Christologisches Verständnis der Psalmen—schon im Alten Testament? ⇒108. Christologie der Liturgie. QD 159. 1995. 57-86 [EThL 72,206*].
1486 *Brueggemann, Walter* Bounded by obedience and praise: the psalms as canon 189-213;
1487 The costly loss of lament 98-111;
1488 The formfulness of grief 84-97;
1489 From hurt to joy, from death to life 67-83;
1490 Praise and the psalms: a politics of glad abandonment 112-132. ⇒41. The psalms. 1995.
1491 **Carmody, John** Psalms for time of trouble. Mystic, Conn 1995, Twenty-Third Publications 163 pp. [CTJ 30,661].
1492 **Carp, B.C.** De actualiteit van de Psalmen. Kampen 1995, Kok Voorhoeve 101 pp. ƒ19.90. 90-297-1308-9 [TTh 36,112].
1493 *Cimosa, Mario* La preghiera dell'anziano 'tu sei la mia fiducia fin dalla giovinezza': la 'terza età' nei salmi. ⇒96. Gli anziani nella Bibbia. 1995. 23-47.
1494 *Courtman, Nigel B.* Sacrifice in the psalms. 1995 ⇒61. Sacrifice. 41-58.
1495 **Dhanaraj, Dharmakkan** Theological significance of the motif of enemies in selected psalms of individual lament. ⇒8,3177. Or-BibChr 4. 1992. RThLZ 120 (1995) 780-782 (*Gerstenberger, Erhard*).
1496 *Dines, Jenny* Les psaumes et l'expérience humaine. SIDIC 28/1 (1995) 9-13.

1497 **Emmendörffer, Michael** Der ferne Gott: Israels Ringen um die Abwesenheit JHWHs in tempelloser Zeit: eine Untersuchung der alttestamentlichen Volksklagelieder auf dem Hintergrund der altorientalischen Literatur. Diss. ^D*Spieckermann, H.*, 1995-1996 Hamburg [RTL 27,528].

1498 *Espinel, José Luis* Los salmos, testigos de una búsqueda de plenitud en Dios. REsp 54 (1995) 245-264.

1499 *Fermor, Gotthard* Psalmen und Popmusik: vom Kult, seiner Musik und Dichtung—damals und heute. EvErz 47 (1995) 63-72.

1500 *Fischer, Balthasar* Gradualpsalmen. ⇒123. LThK 4. 1995. 973-974.

1501 *Fløysvik, Ingvar* When God behaves strangely: a study in the complaint psalms. CJ 21 (1995) 298-304 [OTA 18,539].

1502 **Fuchs, Guido** Psalmdeutung im Lied: die Interpretation der "Feinde" bei Nikolaus SENECKER (1530-1592). Gö 1993, Vandenhoeck & Ruprecht 248 pp. DM68. ^RSCJ 26 (1995) 702-703 (*De Vries, Herman J.*).

1503 **Godet, Jacques-Marie** L'image de Dieu en l'homme dans les Enarrationes in Psalmos de Saint AUGUSTIN. R 1995, Diss. Institutum Patristicum "Augustinianum" ii, a-d, 100 pp.

1504 *Gosse, Bernard* L'usage rédactionnel des oracles contre les nations à l'époque post-exilique. BLE 96 (1995) 219-221.

1505 *Goulder, Michael* Asaph's History of Israel (Elohist Press, Bethel, 725 BCE). JSOT 65 (1995) 71-81.

1506 *Harman, A.M.* The continuity of the covenant curses in the imprecations of the Psalter. RTR 54/2 (1995) 65-72.

1507 **Hauge, Martin Ravndal** Between Sheol and temple: motif structure and function in the I-Psalms. JSOT.S 178. Shf 1995, Academic 314 pp. £45; $67.50. 1-85075-491-8 [BoL 1996,58].

1508 *Häussling, A.A.* Die Psalmen des Alten Testamentes in der Liturgie des neuen Bundes?. ⇒108. Christologie der Liturgie. QD 159. 1995. 87-102 [EThL 72,206*].

1509 *Hengel, Martin* The song about Christ in earliest worship. ⇒50. Studies 1995. 227-291.

1510 *Houston, Walter* David, Asaph and the mighty works of God: theme and genre in the psalm collections. JSOT 68 (1995) 93-111.

1511 *Hsu, Shumei* The religous consciousness of the Psalms. C. CTUF 106 (1995) 479-485 [ThIK 18,27].

1512 **Ishikawa, Ritsu** Der Hymnu Testament und seine kritische Funktion. Diss.-Habil. ^D*Baltzer, K.*, 1995-96 Mü [RTL 27,529].

1513 *Janowski, Bernd* Dem Löwen gleich, gierig nach Raub: zum Feindbild in den Psalmen. EvTh 55 (1995) 155-173.

1514 **Kleer, Martin** "Der liebliche Sänger der Psalmen Israels": Untersuchungen zu David als Dichter und Beter der Psalmen. Diss. ^D*Zenger, E.*, 1995 Müns [ThRv 92/2, XIII].

1515 **Kodithuwakku, Nail Dias** A typology of violence in the Psalter. Diss. ^D*Nogalski, James D.*, Southern Baptist Theological Seminary 1995, 176 pp. MAI 33,1688.

1516 **Kuczynski, Michael P.** Prophetic songs: the Psalms as moral discourse in late medieval England. Ph 1995, University of Pennsylvania Press xxx; 292 pp. $36.95. 0-8122-3271-2.

1517 **Lee, Tai-Hon** Gattungsvergleich der akkadischen Su-ila-Gebete mit den biblischen Lobpsalmen. Diss. ^D*Müller, H.P.*, 1995, Müns [RTL 27,529].

1518 **Lindström, Fredrik** Suffering and sin: interpretations of illness in the individual complaint psalms. ^T*McLamb, Michael*, CB.OT 37. Sto 1994. Almqvist & Wiksell International xii; 500 pp. SEK310. ^RSvTK 71 (1995) 87-89 (*Sæbø, Magne*); ThQ 175 (1995) 148-150 (*Groß, Walter*); JR 75 (1995) 403-404 (*Fretheim, Terence E.*); CBQ 57 (1995) 563-564 (*Brueggemann, Walter*).

1519 **Magonet, Jonathan** A rabbi reads the Psalms. ⇒10,2914. 1994. ^RJBQ 23 (1995) 57-58 (*Berlyn, P.J.*).

1520 *Masini, Mario* La comunione con Dio nei Salmi. PSV 31 (1995) 43-59.

1521 *Mays, James Luther* Past, present, and prospect in psalm study. ⇒36. ^FTUCKER G., 1995. 147-156.

1522 **Mitchell, David Campbell** The message of the psalter: eschatology and the composition of the book of Psalms. Diss. ^D*Provon, I.W.*, 1995, E 332 pp. [RTL 27,530].

1523 *Morales Ríos, J.H.* La pascua de Jesucristo vista a través de los salmos. Franciscanum 109-110 (1995) 13-57 [Strom. 52/3-4, 45].

1524 *Mottu, H.* Les Psaumes et la forme du travail de deuil. ETR 70 (1995) 391-404.

1525 *Prinsloo, W.S.* Die psalms as samehangende boek [The psalter as a cohesive book]. NGTT 36 (1995) 459-469 [OTA 19,443].

1526 **Schaper, Joachim** Eschatology in the Greek Psalter. Diss. ^D*Horbury, W.*, WUNT 2/76. Tü 1995, Mohr xii; 212 pp. DM78. 3-16-146434-6.

1527 **Serna Andres, José** Salmos del siglos XXI. Caminos 2. Bilbao 1995, DDB 248 pp.

1528 **Shepherd, Jerry Eugene** The book of Psalms as the book of Christ: a christo-canonical approach to the book of Psalms. ^D*Longman, Tremper III*, Westminster Theol. Sem. 1995, 672 pp. AAC 9532743; DAI-A 56,1831.

1529 *Souza, Marcelo de Barros* A terra e os céus se casam no louvor: os salmos e a ecologia. Ribla 21 (1995) 186-198 [ThIK 17/2,68].

1530 **Sylva, Dennis** Psalms and the transformation of stress: poetic-communal interpretation and the family. LThPM 16. Lv 1995, Peeters xvi; 267 pp. BEF595.

1531 *Tobias, Alexander* On the musical instruments in Psalms. JBQ 23 (1995) 53-55.

1532 *Trublet, Jacques* Le corpus sapientiel et le Psautier. ⇒117. La sagesse biblique. LeDiv 160. 1995. 139-174.

1533 *Tucker, W. Dennis* Beyond the lament: instruction and theology in Book I of the Psalter. ProcGLM 15 (1995) 121-132.

1534 **Turzyński, Piotr** Il cantico nuova nella teologia di Sant'AGOSTINO: specialmente nelle Enarrationes in psalmos. 1995. Excerpt Diss. Pont. Univ. Gregoriana, R, 112 pp.

1535 **Večko, Terezija Snežna** Divine and human faithfulness: general observations and the place of the concept in the Psalms. *Krašovec, Jože* (collab.). BN.B 10. Mü 1995, Inst. für Bibl. Exegese 133 pp.

1536 *Whybray, R.N.* The wisdom psalms. ⇒9. ^FEMERTON J., 152-160.

1537 **Zenger, Erich** Ein Gott der Rache? Feindpsalmen verstehen. ⇒10,2952. 1994. ^RThQ 175 (1995) 63-64 (*Groß, Walter*).

1538 *Zenger, Erich* Fluchpsalmen. ⇒122. LThK 3. 1995. 1335-1336.

E6.6 *Psalmi: oratio, liturgia* — **Psalms as prayer.**

1539 *Alford, John A.* ROLLE's English Psalter and *lectio divina.* BJRL 77/3 (1995) 47-59.

1540 **Aparicio, A.; Rey Garcia, J.C.** I Salmi, preghiera della community: per celebrare la liturgia delle ore. 1995, Libreria Editrice Vaticana 544 pp.⇒

1541 *Baltruweit, Fritz* Psalmen und neue geistliche Lieder. EvErz 47 (1995) 92-97.

1542 *Bojorge, Horacio* Los Salmos en la liturgia romana: la situación del imaginario orante discernida desde la liturgia: a propósito de un libro reciente. Strom. 51 (1995) 141-151.

1543 **Bonhoeffer, Dietrich** Bidden met Psalmen: met levensbeschrijving door Eberhard BETHGE. Lei 1995, Goen en Zoon 56 pp. *f*14.95 [GTT 96,41].

1544 *Brueggemann, Walter* The psalms as prayer. ⇒36. The psalms. 1995. 33-66.

1545 *Buchinger, Harald G.* Die älteste erhaltene christliche Psalmenhomilie: zu Verwendung und Verständnis des Psalters bei HIPPOLYT. TThZ 104 (1995) 125-144; 272-298.

1546 [E]**Byron, William J.** Take courage: psalms of support and encouragement. Kansas City, MO 1995, Sheed & Ward vi; 186 pp. 1-55612-751-0.

1547 **Coninck, Frédéric de** La prière libéré: à l'école des psaumes. Poliez-le-Grand 1995, Du Moulin 92 pp. FF56 [RHPhR 75,443].

1548 *Franz, Ansgar* Der Psalm im Wortgottesdienst: Einladung zur Besichtigung eines ungeräumten Problemfeldes. BiLi 68 (1995) 198-203.

1549 *Girlanda, A.* I salmi, preghiera cristiana. Catechisti Parrocchiali 6 (1995) 8-11.

1550 *Häußling, Angelus A.* Die Psalmen des Alten Testaments in der Liturgie des neuen Bundes. ⇒108. Christologie der Liturgie. 1995. 87-102.

1551 **Holladay, William L.** The Psalms...prayerbook. ⇒9,3063; 10,2961. 1993. [R]Worship 69 (1995) 180-182 (*Sloyan, Gerard S.*); WThJ 57 (1995) 260-262 (*Belcher, Richard*); HebStud 36 (1995) 194-195 (*Howell, Maribeth*).

1552 **Huonder, Vitus** Die Psalmen in der Liturgia Horarum. ⇒8,3209... 10,2962. [R]EO 12 (1995) 470-472 (*Stadelmann, Andreas*).

1553 **Kampchen, Martin** The holy waters: Indian Psalm meditations. Bangalore 1995, Asian Trading Corporation xv; 142 pp. Rs 40 [JDh 21,228].

1554 *Krieg, Gustav A.* Gesungenes Lob—gesungene Klage: Psalmen als Motivation für den Komponisten. EvErz 47 (1995) 55-63.

1555 *Magnante, Antonio* I Salmi, preghiera eminentemente missionaria. Omnis Terra 13 (1995) 129-137. Omnis Terra(F) 34 (1995) 183-191.

1556 *Martini, Carlo Maria* Quomodo in communi Psalmo oretur?. **P.** RBL 48/2 (1995) 116-120.

1557 **Nowell, Irene** Sing a new song: the psalms in the Sunday lectionary. ⇒9,3071. 1993. [R]CBQ 57 (1995) 154-155 (*Walsh, Jerome T.*).

1558 [TE]**Ortiz V., Pedro** Los Salmos: oración del pueblo de Dios. Colección Biblica. Santafé de Bogotá 1995, San Pablo 253 pp. 958-607-873-6.

1559 ᴱOrtkemper, Franz Josef Psalmen. Neue Predigten zum Alten Testament 4. Stu 1995, Katholisches Bibelwerk 168 pp. DM39.80. 3-460-32994-7 [OrdKom 38,119].

1560 *Petey-Girard, Bruno* Citation psalmique et appropriation éthique: les Méditations sur les Psaumes de Jᴇᴀɴ de Sponde. BHR 57 (1995) 381-393.

1561 **Pleins, J. David** The Psalms: songs of tragedy, hope, and justice. ⇒9,3071*. 1993. ᴿOTEs 8 (1995) 305-307 (*Helberg, J.L.*).
     Rougier, Stan Montre-moi ton visage ⇒1428.

1562 *Schröer, Henning* Zwischen Lyrik und Liturgie: von der Poesie der Psalmen zu den Psalmen der Poesie. EvErz 47 (1995) 72-81.

1563 *Seils, Ruth Margarete* Psalmen im Bibliodrama. EvErz 47 (1995) 82-92.

1564 *Standaert, Benoît* Le moine et les psaumes. SIDIC 28/1 (1995) 14-15.

1565 ᴱSueldo, Gerardo Los Salmos en la liturgia romana: VIII Encuentro de Estudios de la Sociedad Argentina de Liturgia, Comisión Episcopal de Liturgia, Conferencia Episcopal Argentina. 1994, Oficina del Libro 216 pp. ᴿStrom. 51 (1995) 141-151 (*Bojorge, Horacio*).

1566 **The International Commission on English in the Liturgy** The Psalter: a faithful and inclusive rendering from the Hebrew into contemporary English poetry, intended primarily for communal song and recitation. ᴱHuck, Gabe. 1995, Liturgy Training Publications xxxiv; 149 pp. ill. $18; $12. 0-929650-77-8; -88-3 <pb>. ᴿFirst Things 58 (1995) 45-48 (*Alter, Robert*).

1567 **Tournay, Raymond Jacques** Seeing and hearing God with the Psalms. ⇒8,3222... 10,2968. JSOT.S 118. 1991. ᴿJQR 86/1-2 (1995) 233-236 (*Levine, Lee I.*).

1568 **Vidal i Cruañas, Albert** Tu i els salms. Els daus 140. Barc 1995, Claret 127 pp. 84-7263-934-7.

1569 **Vincent, Monique** Saint Aᴜɢᴜsᴛɪɴ maître de prière...EnPs. ⇒6,3338... 9,3074. 1990. ᴿFranciscanum 37 (1995) 239-242

1570 *Vogüé, Adalbert de* Le psaume et l'oraison: nouveau florilège. EO 12 (1995) 325-349.

E6.7 *Psalmi: versiculi* — **Psalms by number and verse.**

1571 **Lee, Simon Sang-Il** Promise and fulfillment: new insights into Psalm 1/3/8/23. K. Spiritual Life 4. Seoul 1995, Institute for Ignatian Spirituality. 161 pp. 89-85528-12-2.

1572 *Wehrle, Josef* Ps 1: Das Tor zum Psalter: Exegese und theologische Schwerpunkte. MThZ 46 (1995) 215-229.

1573 *Weiß, I.* Umgang mit einem Psalm. FoRe (1995/1) 42ff [ZiD 21,258; Ps 1].

1574 *Wénin, André* Le psaume 1 et l'"encadrement" du livre des louanges. ⇒4. ꜰBᴇᴀᴜᴄʜᴀᴍᴘ P., 1995. 151-176.

1575 *Waddell, Chrysogonus* A christological interpretation of Psalm 1?: the psalter and Christian prayer. Com(US) 22 (1995) 502-521.

1576 *Marböck, Johannes* Zur frühen Wirkungsgeschichte von Ps 1. ⇒55. Gottes Weisheit. 1995 <1986>. 88-100 [Sir 14,20-27; 15,1-10].

1577 *Hengel, Martin* The Dionysiac Messiah. ⇒50. Studies 1995. 293-331 [Ps 2,1-11].

1578 *Vang, Carsten* Ps 2,11-12—a new look at an old crux interpretum. SJOT 9 (1995) 163-184.

1579 *Olofsson, Staffan* The crux interpretum in Ps 2,12. SJOT 9 (1995) 185-199.

1580 *Clines, David J. A.* Psalm 2 and the MLF (Moabite Liberation Front). ⇒23. FROGERSON J., JSOT.S 200. 1995. 158-185.

1581 *Bons, Eberhard* Psaume 2: bilan de recherche et essai de réinterprétation (1). RevSR 69 (1995) 147-171.

1582 *Barré, M. L.* Hearts, beds, and repentance in Psalm 4,5 and Hosea 7,14. Bib. 76 (1995) 53-62.

1583 **Kinzig, Wolfram** Erbin Kirche...Ps 5,1 ASTERIUS. ⇒6,3350... 8,3232. 1990. RJThS 46 (1995) 347-349 (*Parvis, P.M.*).

1584 *Auffret, Pierre* "Conduis-moi dans ta justice!": étude structurelle du psaume 5. JANES 23 (1995) 1-28.

1585 **Auffret, Pierre** Quatre Psaumes et un cinquième: étude structurelle des psaumes 7 à 10 et 35. ⇒10,2974. 1992. REstB 53 (1995) 407-408 (*Aparicio, A.*).

1586 *Ravasi, Gianfranco* L'universalismo dei Salmi 8—47—87. RivBib 43 (1995) 77-84.

1587 **Kinzer, Mark Stephen** 'All things under his feet': psalm 8 in the New Testament and in other Jewish literature of late antiquity. Diss. DFossum, Jarl, Michigan 1995, 310 pp. AAC 9542876; DAI-A 56,3165.

1588 *Perlitt, Lothar* Der Mensch nach der Offenbarung des Alten Testaments: eine Auslegung des 8. Psalms. ⇒57. Allein mit dem Wort. 1995. 67-80.

1589 *Prinsloo, G.M.T.* Polarity as dominant textual strategy in Psalm 8. OTEs 8 (1995) 370-387 [sum. 370].

1590 *Brueggemann, Walter* Psalms 9-10: a counter to conventional social reality. ⇒36. The psalms. 1995. 217-234.

1591 *Jurič, Stipe* Great theological experience of the efficacy of prayer (Ps 13). **Croatian**. Crkva u Svijetu 30 (1995) 260-283 [sum. 283-284].

1592 *Irvine, Stuart A.* A note on psalm 14:4. JBL 114 (1995) 463-466.

1593 *Botha, P.J.* Ironie als sleutel tot die verstaan van Psalm 14 [Irony as the key to the interpretation of Psalm 14]. Skrif en Kerk 16 (1995) 14-27 [OTA 19,78].

1594 *Conti, Martino* Stolto e saggio di fronte a Dio secondo il Salmo 14. Anton. 70/2 (1995) 163-185.

1595 *Johnston, Philip S.* 'Left in hell'? Psalm 16, Sheol and the holy one. ⇒111. The Lord's anointed. 1995. 213-222.

1596 *Aparicio Rodríguez, Ángel* Tú eres mi bien: análisis exegético y teológico del Salmo 16. ⇒9,3100; 10,2987. 1993. REstB 53 (1995) 408-409 (*Fraile, A.G.*); Actualidad Bibliográfica 32 (1995) 182-184 (*Queralt, A.*).

1597 *McNamara, Martin* Psalm 16 in the Bible, in earlier and Irish tradition. MillSt 36 (1995) 52-63.

1598 *Auffret, Pierre* "C'est un peuple humilié que tu sauves": études structurelles du psaume 18 (2ème partie). ScÉs 47 (1995) 81-101.

1599 **Berry, Donald K.** The Psalms and their readers: interpretative strategies for Psalm 18. ⇒10,2991. JSOT.S 153. 1993. RCritRR 8 (1995) 110-114 (*Smith, Mark S.*); BiOr 52 (1995) 746-747 (*Prinsloo, Willem S.*).

1600 *Wyatt, N.* The liturgical context of Psalm 19 and its mythical and ritual origins. UF 27 (1995) 559-596.

1601 *Klingbeil, Martin* Una nota iconográfica breve sobre salmo 21:13. Theologika 10 (1995) 223-225 [OTA 19,445].

1602 *Silva, A.A. da* Psalm 21: a poem of association and dissociation. OTEs 8 (1995) 48-60.

1603 *Prinsloo, G.T.M.* Hope against hope—a theological reflection on Psalm 22. OTEs 8 (1995) 61-85.

1604 *Tappy, Ron* Psalm 23: symbolism and structure. CBQ 57 (1995) 255-280.

1605 *Lescow, Theodor* Textübergreifende Exegese: zur Lesung von Ps 24-26 auf redaktioneller Sinnebene. ZAW 107 (1995) 65-79.

1606 *Clines, David J.A.* A world founded on water (psalm 24): reader response, deconstruction and bespoke interpretation. ⇒37. Interested parties. JSOT.S 205. 1995. 172-186.

1607 *Irigoin, Jean* Le psaume 26 dans la Septante: étude de composition rythmique. ⇒13. ᶠHARL M., 1995. 287-297.

1608 **Eriksson, Lars Olov** 'Come... ' Psalm 34. ⇒7,2834... 10,3007. CB.OT 32. 1991. ᴿHebStud 36 (1995) 196-198 (*Nasuti, Harry P.*).

1609 *Janzen, J. Gerald* The root שׁכל and the soul bereaved in Psalm 35. JSOT 65 (1995) 55-69.

1610 ᵀᴱ**Crouzel, Henri; Brésard, Luc** ORIGENE: homélies sur les psaumes 36 à 38. Texte critique établi par *Emanuela Prinzivalli*. SC 411. P 1995, Cerf 494 pp. FF291. 2-204-05338-4.

1611 *Brueggemann, Walter* Psalm 37: conflict of interpretation. ⇒36. The psalms. 1995. 235-257.

1612 *Kaiser, Otto* Psalm 39. ⇒37. ᶠWAGNER S., 1995. 133-145.

1613 *Haag, Ernst* Psalm 40: das Vertrauensbekenntnis eines leidenden Gerechten. TThZ 104 (1995) 56-75.

1614 *Grünbeck, Elisabeth* AUGUSTINS ekklesiologische Christologie im Spiegel seiner Hermeneutik: die Bildstruktur der *Enarratio in Ps 44*. VigChr 49 (1995) 353-378.

1615 **Grünbeck, Elisabeth** Christologische Schriftargumentation...in der patristischen Auslegung des 44. (45.) Psalms. ⇒10,3013. SVigChr 26. 1994. ᴿThPh 70 (1995) 569-571 (*Sieben, H.J.*).

1616 *Kessler, R.* Den Kriegen ein Ende! (Psalm 46). JK 56 (1995) 578-579.

1617 *Cohen, Samuel I.* Psalm 47: numerical and geometrical devices used to emphasize the author's message. JBQ 23 (1995) 258-264.

1618 *Collins, C. John* "Death will be their shepherd" or "death will feed on them"? *māwet yir'ēm* in Psalm 49.15 (EVV v 14). BiTr 46 (1995) 320-326.

1619 *Glazov, Gregory* The invocation of Ps. 51:17 in Jewish and christian morning prayer. JJS 46/1-2 (1995) 167-182.

1620 *Rosenblit, Barbara Ellison* David, Bat Sheva, and the fifty-first psalm. CrossCur 45 (1995) 326-340 [2 Sam 11-12].

1621 *Brooks, Claire Vonk* Psalm 51. Interp. 49/1 (1995) 62-66.

1622 *Weber, Beat* "Fest ist mein Herz, o Gott!": zu Ps 57,8-9 . ZAW 107 (1995) 294-295.

1623 *Wénin, André* Violence et prière: le psaume 58. CahPhRel 18 (1995) 129-146.

1624 **Bellinger, W.H. Jr.** A hermeneutic of curiosity and readings of Psalm 61. Studies in Old Testament Interpretation 1. Macon, GA 1995, Mercer University Press viii; 151 pp. $20. 0-86554-464-6.

1625 *Blocher, H.* Psalm 67: God, our God. EurJT 4 (1995) 19-22.
1626 *Marion, Denis* Un psaume de Pentecôte Ps 68 (67). EeV 105 (1995) 124-127. Un psaume de la passion Ps 69. 52-54, 59-64.
1627 **Tillmann, Norbert** "Das Wasser bis zum Hals": Gestalt...des 69. Psalms. ⇒9,3135. MThA 20. 1993. ^RCBQ 57 (1995) 163-164 (*Holladay, William L.*).
1628 *Marion, Denis* Un psaume de la Passion Ps 69. EeV 105 (1995) 52-54, 59-64.
1629 *Langemeyer, Georg* "Auch wenn ich alt und grau bin, verlaß mich nicht!" (Ps 71,18): zur theologischen Sinndeutung der Altersphase des menschlichen Lebens. ⇒15. ^FHEINEMANN H., 1995. 211-223.
1630 *Heim, Knut M.* The perfect king of Psalm 72: an 'intertextual' inquiry. ⇒111. The Lord's anointed. 1995. 223-248.
1631 *Auffret, Pierre* Et moi sans cesse avec toi—études structurelle du Psaume 73. SJOT 9 (1995) 241-276.
1632 *Cortese, R.* E se il salmo 73 lo recitano i poveri?. RivBib 43 (1995) 55-76.
1633 *Human, D.J.* B^erit in Psalm 74. Skrif en Kerk 16 (1995) 57-66 [OTA 19,83].
1634 *Dijkstra, Meindert* He pours the sweet wine off, only the dregs are for the wicked: an epigraphic note on ZAW 107 (1995) 296-300.
1635 **Weber, Beat** Psalm 77 und sein Umfeld: eine poetologische Studie. BBB 103. Weinheim 1995, Beltz Athenäum xiii; 362 pp. Dissertation Basel 1994. DM98. 3-89547-093-7.
1636 *Brueggemann, Walter* Psalm 77: the turn from self to God. ⇒36. The psalms. 1995. 258-267.
1637 *Hieke, Thomas* "Weitergabe des Glaubens" (Ps 78,1-8): Versuch zu Syntax und Struktur von Ps 78. BN 78 (1995) 49-62.
1638 *Stern, Philip* The eighth century dating of Psalm 78 re-argued. HUCA 66 (1995) 41-65.
1639 *Parker, Simon B.* The beginning of the Reign of God—psalm 82 as myth and liturgy. RB 102 (1995) 532-559.
1640 *Prinsloo, W.S.* Psalm 82: once again, gods or men?. Bib. 76 (1995) 219-228.
1641 *Craig, Kenneth M.* Psalm 82. Interp. 49 (1995) 281-292.
1642 *Human, D.J.* Enkele tradisie-historiese perspektiewe op Psalm 83 [Some traditio-historical perspectives on Psalm 83]. HTS 51 (1995) 175-188 [OTA 19,83].
1643 *Trofimova, M.K.* "Mercy and truth are met together". **R.** VDI 213 (1995) 186-193 [sum. 193] [Ps 85,10-11].
1644 *Ebach, J.* Was anders war, kann anders werden: (Psalm 85). JK 56 (1995) 510ff [ZID 21,700].
1645 *Renaud, Bernard* Le psaume 85 et son caractère théophanique. 1995 ⇒4. ^FBEAUCHAMP P., LeDiv 162. 133-149.
1646 **Volgger, David** Notizen zur Textanalyse von Ps 89. ATSAT 45. St. Ottilien 1995, EOS xi; 258 pp. 3-88096-545-5.
1647 *Renaud, Bernard* La cohérence littéraire et théologique du Psaume 89. RevSR 69 (1995) 419-435.
1648 **Koenen, Klaus** Jahwe wird kommen, zu herrschen über die Erde: Ps 90-100 als Komposition. BBB 101. Weinheim 1995, Beltz Athenäum 140. pp. DM64. 3-89547-091-0 [ThRv 91,534].
1649 *Holt, Else K.* Salme 90: en genlaesning [Psalm 90: a reading]. 1995 ⇒90. Lov og visdom. 49-57 [OTA 19,450].

1650 *Jens, W.* Psalm 90: on transience. LuthQ 9 (1995) 177ff.
1651 *Marion, Denis* Un psaume pour le Carême (ps 91). EeV 105 (1995) 35-39.
1652 *Prinsloo, W.S.* Psalm 95: if only you will listen to his voice!. ⟹23. FROGERSON J. JSOT.S 200. 1995. 393-410.
1653 *Prinsloo, W.S.* Psalm 97: almal moet bly wees, want Jahwe is koning [Psalm 97: all must rejoice for Yahweh is king]. HTS 51 (1995) 1088-1113 [OTA 19,263].
1654 *Leene, H.* Psalm 98 and Deutero-Isaiah: linguistic analogies and literary affinity. ⟹133. Bible et Informatique. 1995. 313-340.
1655 *Schniedewind, W.M.* "Are we his people or not?": biblical interpretation during crisis. Bib. 76 (1995) 540-550.
1656 **Brunert, Gunhild** Ps 102 im Kontext des vierten Psalmenbuches. Diss. 1995, Müns, DZenger, E. [ThRv 92/2,XIII].
1657 *Dittmann, R.* Fire, smoke, and ashes: a remembrance of the holocaust; based on the 102. Psalm. ProEc 4 (1995) 398-403 [ZID 1996,72].
1658 *Sedlmeier, Franz* Zusammengesetzte Nominalsätze und ihre Leistung für Psalm cii. VT 45 (1995) 239-250.
1659 *Metzger, Martin* Lobpreis der Gnade: Erwägungen zu Struktur und Inhalt von Psalm 103. 1995 ⟹8. FDONNER H., ÄAT 30. 1995. 121-133.
1660 *Baarde, T.* "Mogen de zondaren van de aarde vergaan..." Psalm 104:35—een andere manier van lezen?. KeTh 46/2 (1995) 90-92.
1661 *Brueggemann, Walter* Psalm 109: steadfast love as social solidarity. ⟹36. The psalms. 1995. 268-282.
1662 *Hengel, Martin* "Sit at my right hand!": the enthronement of Christ at the right hand of God and Psalm 110:1. ⟹50. Studies 1995. 119-225.
1663 *Dautzenberg, Gerhard* Psalm 110 im Neuen Testament. 1995 ⟹44. Studien. SBAB 19. 63-97.
1664 *Morgan, Fred* Une lecture juive des psaumes: mérite et miracles: le cas du psaume 114. SIDIC 28/1 (1995) 2-8.
1665 *Frettlöh, M.L.* Von der Macht des Segens: Psalm 115. JK 56 (1995) 638-641.
1666 *Booij, Thijs* Psalm 116,10-11: the account of an inner crisis. Bib. 76 (1995) 388-395.
1667 *Spieckermann, Hermann* Lieben und glauben: Beobachtungen in Psalm 116. ⟹8. FDONNER H., ÄAT 30. 1995. 266-275.
1668 *Berder, Michel* "La pierre rejetée par les bâtisseurs": psaume 118,22-23 et son emploi dans les traditions juives et dans le Nouveau Testament. Diss. DSchlosser, J. 1995, Štrasbourg 512 pp. [RTL 27,527].
1669 *O'Connor, Daniel J.* The stone the builders rejected: psalm 118(117):22 in CARAVAGGIO's deposition. IThQ 61 (1995) 2-13.
1670 *Pelland, Gilles* La loi dans le tr.ps. 118 de saint HILAIRE. Gr. 76 (1995) 575-583.
1671 *Zegarra, Felipe* "Diez palabras": el salmo 118. Paginas 20 (1995) 45-52.
1672 **Schröten, Jutta** Entstehung, Komposition und Wirkungsgeschichte des 118. Psalms. BBB 95. Weinheim 1995, Beltz Athenäum 180 pp. 3-89547-063-5.
1673 **Auffret, Pierre** Voyez de nos yeux: étude structurelle de vingt psaumes, dont le psaume 119. ⟹9,3165. VTS 48. 1993. RThRv 91

(1995) 19-21 *(Reventlow, Henning Graf)*; ScEs 47 (1995) 221-222 *(Girard, Marc)*; JBL 114 (1995) 304-305 *(Ceresko, Anthony R.)*.

1674 *Skehan, Patrick W.; Ulrich, Eugene; Flint, Peter W.* Two manuscripts of Psalm 119 from Qumran Cave 4. RdQ 16 (1995) 477-486.

1675 *Milhau, Marc* La version grecque du psaume cxviii par ORIGENE et sa version latine par HILAIRE de Poitiers. ⇒126. Origeniana Sexta. BEThL 118. 1995. 701-707.

1676 *Monloubou, Louis; Robert, Elisabeth* Un trésor dans le champ du psautier, le psaume 119. EeV 105 (1995) 381-384.

1677 *Lehrman, S.M.* Psalm 119. JBQ 23 (1995) 55-56.

1678 *Freedman, David Noel* The structure of psalm 119. FMILGROM J., 1995 ⇒21. 725-756.

1679 **Kaiser, Walter C.** The journey isn't over: the pilgrim psalms. ⇒9,3168. 1993. OTEs 8 (1995) 155-156 *(Helberg, J.L.)*.

1680 *Barker, David G.* "The Lord watches over you": a pilgrimage reading of Psalm 121. BS 152 (1995) 163-181.

1681 *Yao, John* Ps. 122: a commentary and a tasting. C. CTUF 106 (1995) 487-495 [ThIK 18,27].

1682 *Niekerk, Martin J.H. van* Psalms 127 and 128: examples of divergent wisdom views on life. OTEs 8 (1995) 414-424 [sum. 414].

1683 *Fleming, Daniel E.* Psalm 127: sleep for the fearful, and security in sons. ZAW 107 (1995) 435-444.

1684 *Herrmann, Wolfram* Psalm 129. ⇒37. FWAGNER S., 1995. 123-132.

1685 *Patton, Corrine L.* Psalm 132: a methodological inquiry. CBQ 57 (1995) 643-654.

1686 *Miller, Patrick D.* Between text and sermon: psalm 136:1-9, 23-26. Interp. 49 (1995) 390-393.

1687 *Rabe, N.* Des Beters vergessende rechte Hand: zur Textkritik und Übersetzung von Ps 137,5. UF 27 (1995) 429-453.

1688 *Rabe, Norbert* "Tochter Babel, die verwüstete!" (Psalm 137,8)—textkritisch betrachtet. BN 78 (1995) 84-103.

1689 *Isani-Díaz, Ada María* 'By the rivers of Babylon': exile as a way of life. ⇒112. Reading...1. 1995. 149-163 [Ps 137; OTA 19,452].

1690 *Lou, Shibo* Escape, introspection and turning to God: a meditation on Psalm 139. CTR 10 (1995) 167-174 [ThIK 17,28].

1691 *Ho, Catherine* Ps. 143: a curse with rights?. C. CTUF 106 (1995) 497-507 [ThIK 18/1,27].

1692 **Risse, Siegfried** Gut ist es, unserem Gott zu singen: Untersuchungen zu Ps 147. Diss. Müns, DZenger, E., MThA 37. Altenberge 1995, Oros 367 pp. DM66. 3-89375-112-2 [ThRv 91,534].

E7.1   **Job,** *textus, commentarii.*

1693 **Alden, Robert** Job. ⇒9,3178. NAC 11. 1993. RAUSS 33 (1995) 103-104 *(Caesar, Lael)*; WThJ 57 (1995) 259-260 *(Konkel, A.H.)*; CBQ 57 (1995) 757-758 Sermons on Job. ⇒10,3076. 1994. RCTJ 30 (1995) 554-556 *(Beeke, J.R.)*.

1694 **Calvin, John** Sermons on Job. ⇒10,3076. 1994. RCTJ 30 (1995) 554-556 *(Beeke, J.R.)*.

1695 *Crenshaw, James L.* Job. ⇒43. Urgent advice. 1995 <1992>. 426-448.

1696 **Gentry, Peter John** The asterisked materials in the Greek Job. SCSt 38. Atlanta 1995, Scholars xxxvii; 559 pp. $50/$34. 0-7885- 0094-5. ᴿEThL 71 (1995) 449-451 (*Lust, J.*).

1697 ᴱ*Giustiniani, Pasquale* Dal commento "ad litteram" del libro di Giobbe. FilTeo 9 (1995) 371-390.

1698 *Meyvaert, Paul* Uncovering a lost work of GREGORY the Great: fragments of the early commentary on Job. Tr. 50 (1995) 55-74.

1699 ᵀᴱ**Miguélez Baños, C.** CIPRIANO de la Huerga: obras completas 2: comentarios al libro de Job (1. Introducción, edición latina, notas y traducción española. Humanistas españoles 4. León 1992, Secretariado de Publicaciones de la Universidad de León. xxxix; 397 pp. ᴿScrTh 27 (1995) 1070-1071 (*Goñi Gaztambide, J.*).

1700 *Perotto, Lorenzo* Lessicografia tomista nel commento a Giobbe. Annali Chieresi (1995) 7-20.

1701 **Strauss, H.** Hiob [19,1-23,17]. BKAT 16/2, Fasc. 1. Neuk 1995, Neuk 1-80.

1702 **Szpek, Heidi M.** Translation technique in the Peshitta to Job. ⟹8,3332... 10,3087. SBL.DS 137. 1992. ᴿJSSt 40 (1995) 155-157 (*Stec, D.M.*).

1703 **Wolfers, David†** Deep things out of darkness: the book of Job: essays and a new English translation. Kampen/GR 1995, Kok/Eerdmans 552 pp. *f*79. 90-390-0104-9/0-8028-4082-5.

E7.2 *Job: themata,* **Topics...** *Versiculi,* **Verse-numbers.**

1704 **Astell, Ann W.** Job, BOETHIUS, and epic truth . L 1994, Cornell University Press xv; 240 pp. $32.95. ᴿSpec. 70 (1995) 861-871 (*Lerer, Seth*).

1705 *Bechtel, Lyn M.* A feminist approach to the book of Job. ⟹69. A feminist companion to wisdom literature. 1995. 222-251.

1706 *Berg, W.* Arbeit und Soziales im Buch Ijob. ⟹29. ᶠSTEGMANN F., 1995. 151-168 [EThL 72,209*].

1707 *Berges, Ulrich* Der Ijobrahmen (Ijob 1,1-2,10; 42,7-17): theologische Versuche angesichts unschuldigen Leidens. BZ 39 (1995) 225-245.

ᴱ**Beuken, Willem A.M.** The book of Job ⟹134. BEThL 114. 1994.

1708 **Borgonovo, Gianantonio** La notte e il suo sole: luce e tenebre nel libro di Giobbe: analisi simbolica. Diss. Pont. Istituto Biblico. AnBib 135. R 1995, Biblical Institute Press xiv; 498 pp. L56.000. 88-7653-135-1.

1709 *Cañellas, Gabriel* ¿Por qué sufren los justos?: respuesta del libro de Job. BiFe 21 (1995) 184-212.

1710 **Cheney, Michael** Dust, wind and agony: character, speech and genre in Job. ⟹10,3090. CB.OT 36. 1994. ᴿSvTK 71/3 (1995) 129-131 (*Illman, Karl-Johan*).

1711 **Chieregatti, Arrigo** Giobbe: lettura spirituale. Conversazioni bibliche. Bo 1995, EDB 235 pp. 88-10-709552-7.

1712 *Clines, David J.A.* Deconstructing the book of Job. BiRe 11/2 (1995) 30-35, 43-44.

1713 *Clines, David J.A.* Job and the spirituality of the Reformation ⟹2. ᶠATKINSON J., JSNT.S 105. 1995. 49-72.

1714 *Clines, David J.A.* Why is there a book of Job, and what does it do to you if you read it?. ⇒37. Interested parties. JSOT.S 205. 1995. 122-144.

1715 **Course, John E.** Speech and response: a rhetorical analysis of the introductions to the speeches of the book of Job (Chaps. 4-24). CBQ.MS 25. Wsh 1994, The Catholic Biblical Association of America vii; 184 pp. $8.50. 0-915170-24-8. ᴿThLZ 120 (1995) 636-38 *(Wahl, Harald-Martin)*; JThS 46 (1995) 583-584 *(Rodd, C.S.)*.

1716 *Crenshaw, James L.* The high cost of preserving God's honor [1987] 468-476;

1717 Job as drama [1977] 477-480;

1718 Job the silent or Job the affirmer? [1992] 449-454. 1995 ⇒43. Urgent advice.

1719 **Dell, Katharine** Shaking a fist at God: understanding suffering through the book of Job. L 1995, Harper 89 pp. £5. 0-00-627932-5 [BoL 1996,54].

1720 *Ebach, Jürgen* Babel und Bibel oder: das "Heidnische" im Alten Testament [1994] 145-163;

1721 Gott und die Normativität des Faktischen: Plädoyer für die Freunde Hiobs [1991] 55-66;

1722 Vergangene Zeit und Jetztzeit: Walter BENJAMINS Reflexionen als Anfragen an die biblische Exegese und Hermeneutik [1992] 108-129. ⇒46. Hiobs Post. 1995.

1723 **Ebach, Jürgen** Streiten mit Gott—Hiob 1: Hiob 1-20. Kleine Biblische Bibliothek. Neuk 1995, Neuk xix; 177 pp. 3-7887-1485-9.

1724 **Fuchs, Gisela** Mythos und Hiobdichtung. ⇒9,3201; 10,3097. 1993. ᴿThLZ 120 (1995) 27-29 *(Wagner, Siegfried)*; CBQ 57 (1995) 132-133 *(Vall, Gregory)*; JBL 114 (1995) 500-501 *(Lang, Bernhard)*.

1725 *Garbini, Giovanni* La metereologia di Giobbe. RivBib 43 (1995) 85-91.

1726 *Greenberg, Moshe* Job. 335-357;

1727 Reflections on Job's theology 327-334. ⇒49 Studies 1995.

1728 Job: aanklacht en weerwoord. Den Bosch 1995, Katholieke Bijbelstichting 118 pp. ƒ9.50. 90-6173-934-9 [Str. 64,184].

1729 *Klein, Lillian R.* Job and the womb: text about men, subtext about women. ⇒69. A feminist companion to wisdom literature. 1995. 186-200.

1730 **Lamb, Jonathan** The rhetoric of suffering: reading the book of Job in the eighteenth century. Ox 1995, Clarendon xii; 329 pp. ill. $65. 0-19-818264-3 [OTA 19,347].

1731 **Langenhorst, Georg** Hiob unser Zeitgenosse. ⇒10,3101. Theologie und Literatur 10. 1994. Matthias-Grünewald 448 pp. ᴿTThZ 104 (1995) 76-78 *(Mende, Theresia)*; ThPh 70 (1995) 304-306 *(Splett, J.)*; LebZeug 50 (1995) 315-316 *(Petzel, Paul)*; Actualidad Bibliográfica 32 (1995) 215-216 *(Boada, J.)*; rhs 38 (1995) 203-206 *(Ott, Rudi)*.

1732 *Lavoie, Jean-Jacques* Les livres de Job, Qohélet et Proverbes: les enjeux méthodologiques dans l'histoire de la recherche depuis 1980. ⇒84. De bien des manières. LeDiv 163. 1995. 147-180 [EThL 72,209*].

1733 **Leaman, Oliver** Evil and suffering in Jewish philosophy. CSRT 6. C 1995, CUP vii; 257 pp. $60. 0-521-41724-4 [OTA 18,641].

1734 *Lévêque, Jean* Sagesse et paradoxe dans le livre de Job. ⇒117. La sagesse biblique. LeDiv 160. 1995. 99-128.
1735 **Lugt, Pieter van der** Rhetorical criticism and the poetry of the book of Job. OTS 32. Lei 1995, Brill xvi; 548 pp. *f*230; $131. 90-0410326-0.
1736 **Lundberg, Marilyn Jean** 'So that hidden things may be brought to light': a concept analysis of the Yahweh speeches in the book of Job. Diss.   Claremont 1995, 318 pp. AAC 9535491; DAI-A 56,2281.
1737 **Maggioni, Bruno** Job y Cohélet: la contestación sapiencial en la Biblia. Bilbao 1993, Desclée de Brouwer 105 pp. ᴿREsp 54 (1995) 431-432 *(Martínez, Emilio)*.
1738 *Marsden, Richard* Job in his place: the Ezra miniature in the Codex Amiatinus. Scr. 49/1 (1995) 3-15.
1739 **Müller, Hans Peter** Das Hiobproblem: seine Stellung und Entstehung im Alten Orient und im Alten Testament. EdF 84. Da ³1995, Da:Wiss x; 230 pp. 3-534-07265-0.
1740 *Müller, Klaus* Theodizee nach Ijob: eine systematisch-geistliche Betrachtung. ThG(B) 38 (1995) 211-222.
1741 *Newsom, Carol A.* Job and Ecclesiastes. OTSt. ⇒36. ᶠTUCKER G., 1995. 177-194.
1742 *Nicholson, E.W.* The limits of theodicy as a theme of the book of Job. ⇒9. 1995. 71-82.
1743 **Noegel, Scott B.** Janus parallelism and its literary significance in the book of Job with excursuses on the device in extra-Jobian and other ancient Near Eastern literatures. Diss. Cornell 1995, 418 pp. [DissA 55,3827].
1744 **O'Connor, Donald** Job: his wife, his friends, and his God. Maynooth Bicentenary Series. Blackrock 1995, Columba Press 167 pp. IR£9. 1-85607-127-8 [RB 103,478].
1745 *Oorschot, Jürgen van* Tendenzen der Hiobforschung. ThR 60 (1995) 349-388.
1746 **Perdue, Leo G.** Wisdom in revolt...Job. ⇒7,2905... 10,3112. JSOT.S 112. 1991. ᴿJQR 86/1-2 (1995) 202-204 *(Gitay, Yehoshua)*.
1747 *Pury, Albert de* Le Dieu qui vient en adversaire: de quelques différences à propos de la perception de Dieu dans l'Ancien Testament. ⇒22. ᶠRENAUD B., 1995. 45-67.
1748 *Raurell, Frederic* Anthropological meaning of "Doxa" in Job-LXX. EstFr 96 (1995) 197-227.
1749 *Rouillard-Bonraisin, H.* Le livre de Job et ses vraix-faux dialogues. ⇒124. La controverse religieuse. 1995. 47-70 [EThL 72/2-3,13*].
1750 **Schreiner, Susan E.** "Where shall wisdom be found?" CALVIN's exegesis of Job. ⇒10,3084. 1994. ᴿSCJ 26 (1995) 430-431 *(Graham, W. Fred)*.
1751 *Steinmann, Andrew E.* The graded numerical saying in Job. ⇒10. ᶠFREEDMAN D., 1995. 288-297 [5,17-27; 33,13-30; 40,3-5].
1752 *Swados, Elizabeth* Job: he's a clown. Out of the garden. 1995. 204-220.
1753 *Treves, Marco* The book of Job. ZAW 107 (1995) 261-272.
1754 *Viviers, H.* Die funksie van Elihu (Job 32-37) in die boek Job [The function of Elihu (Job 32-37) in the book of Job]. SK 16 (1995) 171-192 [OTA 19,90].

1755 **Vogels, Walter A.** Job, l'homme qui a bien parlé de Dieu. LiBi
104. P 1995, Cerf 268 pp. ᴿSR 24 (1995) 364-366 (*Lavoie, Jean-Jacques*).

1756 *Wilson, L.* The book of Job and the fear of God. TynB 46 (1995)
59-79.

1757 *Wolde, Ellen Van* The development of Job: Mrs Job as catalyst.
⇒69. A feminist companion to wisdom literature. 1995. 201-221.

1758 *Garbini, Giovanni* Le ricchezze di Giobbe. ⇒8. ᶠDONNER H.,
ÄAT 30. 1995. 27-32 [1,3; 42,12].

1759 *Vall, Gregory* The enigma of Job 1,21a. Bib. 76 (1995) 325-342
[Wis 7,1-6; Qoh 5,14; 1 Tim 6,7].

1760 *Gitay, Zefira* The portrayal of Job's wife and her representation in
the visual arts. ⇒10. ᶠFREEDMAN D., 1995. 516-526 [2,9].

1761 *Steinmann, Andrew E.* The graded numerical saying in Job. ⇒10.
ᶠFREEDMAN D., 1995. 288-297 [5,17-27; 33,13-30; 40,3-5].

1762 *Noegel, Scott B.* Another look at Job 18:2,3. JBQ 23 (1995) 159-
161.

1763 *Ebach, Jürgen* Die "Schrift" in Hiob 19,23. ⇒46. Hiobs Post.
1995 <1991>. 32-54.

1764 **Witte, Markus** Philologische Notizen zu Hiob 21-27. BZAW 234.
B 1995, De Gruyter xi; 202 pp. DM128. 3-11-014656-8.

1765 **Witte, Markus** Vom Leiden zur Lehre: der dritte Redegang (Hiob
21-27) und die Redaktionsgeschichte des Hiobbuches. BZAW 230.
B 1994, De Gruyter xi; 333 pp. DM164. 3-11-014375-5. ᴿThLZ
120 (1995) 238-240 (Hört Gott nicht den Schrei der Armen?: exegetische Untersuchungen zu Ijob 24. Diss.   1995 St. Georgen
[ThRv 92/2,VIII].

1766 **Grenzer, Matthias** Hört Gott nicht den Schrei der Armen?: exegetische Untersuchungen zu Ijob 24. Diss. St. Georgen 1995,
ᴰ*Jüngling, Hans-W.*

1767 *Wyatt, Nicolas* Le centre du monde dans les littératures d'Ougarit
et d'Israël. JNSL 21/2 (1995) 123-142 [26,7].

1768 **Kautz, James Richard** A hermeneutical study of Job 29-31. Diss.
Southern Baptist Theological Seminary. Ann Arbor, Michigan
1995 xv; 287pp. [UMI].

1769 *Loader, J.A.* Die moontlikhede van Elihu: wat in Suid-Afrika met
hom gedoen is / kan word. OTEs 8 (1995) 356-369 [32-37; sum.
356].

1770 **Wahl, Harald-Martin** Der gerechte Schöpfer...32-37. ⇒9,3245.
BZAW 207. 1993. ᴿThLZ 120 (1995) 647-649 (*Wagner,
Siegfried*); OTEs 8 (1995) 145-147 (*Loader, J.A.*); JBL 114 (1995)
501-503 (*McLaughlin, John L.*).

1771 *Loader, J.A.* The question of a tiqqun in Job 32:3. JSem 7/1 (1995)
79-86 [sum. 79].

1772 *Crenshaw, James L.* When form and content clash: the theology of
Job 38:1-40:5 [1993]. ⇒43. Urgent advice. 1995. 455-467.

1773 *Vaage, Leif E.* Do meio da tempestado: a resposta de Deus a Jó:
sabedoria bíblica, ecologia moderna, vida marginal: uma leitura de
Jó 38,1-42,6. Ribla 21 (1995) 199-213 [ThIK 17/2,68].

1774 *Vall, Gregory* "From whose womb did the ice come forth?":
procreation images in Job 38:28-29. CBQ 57 (1995) 504-513.

1775 *Ciccarese, Maria Pia* Filippo e i corvi di Giobbe 38,41: alla ricerca di una fonte perduta. Aug. 35 (1995) 137-159.

1776 *Dailey, Thomas F.* Seeing he repents—contemplative consciousness and the wisdom of Job. ABenR 46/1 (1995) 87-101 [40,4-5; 42,2-6].

1777 *Ebach, Jürgen* Hiobs Töchter: zur Lektüre von Hiob 42,13-15 (auch eine Art Brief an Luise SCHOTTROFF). ⇒46. Hiobs Post. 1995 <1994>. 67-72.

E7.3 *Canticum Canticorum*, Song of Songs, Das Hohelied, *textus, comm.*

1778 **Alonso Schökel, Luis** "Steh auf, meine Freundin"... Gedanken zum Hohenlied. ⇒10,3152. 1991. RThRv 91/2 (1995) 124-125 (*Haag, Herbert*);

1779 Cantico dei Cantici: la dignità dell'amore. ⇒6,3492... 9,3251. 1993. <1990>. RCivCatt 146 (1995) 102 (*Scaiola, D.*).

1780 EBlecua, José Manuel Fray Luis de LEON: Cantar de los Cantares. ⇒10,3156. BRoHi.T IV 22. 1994. RRecollectio 18 (1995) 375-376 (*Martínez Cuesta, Ángel*).

1781 **Bloch, Ariel & Chana** The Song of Songs: a new translation with an introduction and commentary. Afterword *Alter, Robert*. NY 1995, Random 253 pp. $27.50.

1782 TBonato, Vincenzo GREGORIO di Nissa: omelie sul Cantico dei cantici. Epifania della Parola 3. Bo 1995, Dehoniane 255 pp. L34.000. 88-10-40225-1.

1783 EBrenner, Athalya A feminist companion to the Song of Songs. 1993 ⇒9,3256. RBiOr 52 (1995) 118-120 (*Korpel, Mario C.A.*).

1784 *Brock, S.P.* Mingana syr. 628: a folio from a revision of the Peshitta Song of Songs. 1995. JSSt 40/1 (1995) 39-56.

1785 **Dünzl, Franz** Braut und Bräutigam: die Auslegung des Canticum durch GREGOR von Nyssa. ⇒9,3259; 10,3160. BGBE 32. 1993. RREAug 41/1 (1995) 157-159 (*Pelletier, Anne-Marie*); TyV 36 (1995) 455 (*Meis, Anneliese*).

1786 TEmery, Pierre-Yves GILBERT de Hoyland: sermons sur le Cantique des Cantiques: Sermons 21 à 47. Pain de Cîteaux 7. Oka, Québec 1995, Abbaye Notre-Dame du Lac [EeV 106,206].

1787 **Engammare, Max** Qu'il me baise...⇒8,3430... 10,3161. 1993. REstFr 96 (1995) 269-271 (*Raurell, Frederic*).

1788 **Faessler, Marc; Carrillo, Francine** L'alliance du désir: le Cantique des cantiques revisité. Genève 1995, Labor et Fides 89 pp. Redistribution dramatique du texte, nouvelle traduction, introduction et notes par M. Faessler. Commentaire à deux voix par Fr. Carrillo et M. Faessler. FF119; FS30. 2-8309-0781-7.

1789 TFernández Tejero, Emilia El cantar más bello. ⇒10,3162. 1994. REE 70 (1995) 251-253 (*Pascual, Enrique*); Sef. 55/1 (1995) 210-212 (*Girón, Luis*).

1790 EGarbini, Giovanni Cantico. ⇒8,3409... 10,3163. 1992. RCBQ 57 (1995) 552-553 (*Althann, Robert*).

1791 **Garrett, Duane A.** Proverbs, Ecclesiastes, Song of Songs. ⇒9,3344; 10,3239. NAC 14. 1993. RRExp 92 (1995) 240-241 (*Bland, David*); HebStud 36 (1995) 201-204 (*Michel, Walter L.*).

1792 EGuérard, Marie-Gabrielle NIL d'Ancyre: commentaire sur le Cantique des Cantiques I. SC 403. 1994 ⇒10,3166. RJThS 46 (1995) 727-729 (*Gould, Graham*); EThL 71 (1995) 448-449 (*Lust, J.*); POC 45 (1995) 300-301 (*Ternant, P.*).

1793 *Harl, Marguerite* La version LXX du Cantique des Cantiques et le groupe Kaige-Theodotion: quelques remarques lexicales. Textus 18 (1995) 101-119.

1794 Hooglied: kom mijn liefste kom. Den Bosch 1995, Katholieke Bijbelstichting 48 pp. *f*8.50. 90-6173-936-5 [Str. 64,184].

1795 ᵀKönig, Hildegard APPONIUS: Lied. 1992 ⇒8,3142... 10,3169. ᴿGnomon 67 (1995) 267-268 (*Doignon, Jean*).

1796 McMonagle, Mother Xavier Love's fugue: translation and commentary on 'the finest Song of all'. L 1995, Hodder & Stoughton x; 133 pp. 0-340-63045-0.

1797 *Meis, Anneliese* ORIGENES y Gregorio de NISA, In Canticum. 1995 ⇒126. Origeniana Sexta. 599-616.

1798 *Moreno García, Abdón* El Cantar de los Cantares traducido por Arias Montano: un manuscrito inédito. EstB 53 (1995) 489-524.

1799 Neusner, Jacob Israel's love affair with God: Song of Songs 1992. ⇒9,3272. ᴿAUSS 33/1 (1995) 140-141 (*Duerksen, Paul D.*); HebStud 36 (1995) 204-206 (*Landy, Francis*).

1800 Pelletier, Anne-Marie El Cantar de los cantares. CuaBi 84. Estella 1995, Verbo Divino. 64 pp.

1801 *Sáenz-Badilos, A.* En torno a dos comentarios al *Cantar de los Cantares*. Helm. 46 (1995) 159-176 [EThL 72/2-3,210*].

1802 *Schepers, Kees* Ps. BONAVENTURA super Cantica Canticorum and its source text: glossa tripartita super Cantica. AFH 88 (1995) 473-496.

1803 *Schlageter, Johannes* Die Bedeutung des Hoheliedkommentars des Franziskanertheologen Petrus Johannes OLIVI (+1298): Argumente für eine neue Edition. WiWei 58 (1995) 137-151.

1804 ᴱSchulz-Flügel, Eva GREGORIUS Eliberritanus... in Canticis Canticorum. ⇒10,3177. AGLB 26. 1994. ᴿJThS 46 (1995) 724-725 (*Wickham, L.R.*).

1805 Snaith, John G. Song of Songs. ⇒9,3277; 10,3178. NCeB. 1993. ᴿCritRR 8 (1995) 151-153 (Landy, Francis).

1806 Speyr, Adrienne von Le Cantique des Cantiques. ᵀ*Laforcade, I. de*, préf. *Balthasar, Hans Urs von*, Adrienne von Speyr 12. Bruxelles 1995, Culture et Vérité 98 pp. [EThL 72/2-3,210*].

1807 Stadelmann, Luís I. Cântico dos Cânticos. Bíblica Loyola 11. São Paolo 1993, Loyola 224 pp. ᴿRCB 19 (1995) 157-158 (*Ribeiro, Ari Luís do Vale*);

1808 Love and politics 1992 ⇒8,3419... 10,3179. ᴿEstB 53 (1995) 549-551 (*Flor, G.*).

1809 *Tov, Emanuel* Three manuscripts (abbreviated texts?) of Canticles from Qumran Cave 4. JJS 46/1-2 (1995) 88-111.

1810 Turner, Denys Eros and allegory: medieval exegesis of the Song of Songs. Cistercian Studies. Kalamazoo, Mich. 1995, Cistercian 471 pp. $50/$30. 0-87907-956-8.

E7.4 Canticum, *themata, versiculi*

1811 *Basson, M.M.J.; Breytenbach, A.P.B.* 'n ondersoek na die teologiese relevansie van die metaforiese spreke in Hooglied [An inquiry into the problem of the theological relevance of the metaphorical language of the Song of Songs]. HTS 51 (1995) 438-453 [OTA 19,94].

1812 *Bennett, R.H.* The song of wisdom in BERNARD's "Sermones Super Cantica Canticorum". CiSt 30/2 (1995) 147ff [ZID 21,659].

1813 *Bertoni Nimtz, Jeni* Análise poético-literária do Cânticos dos Cânticos. RevCT 3 (1995) 117-121 [OTA 18,557].

1814 **Cabrillo, Francine; Faessler, Marc** L'alliance du désir ⇒1788.

1815 **Camisani,** E. Cantico dei cantici: riflessi del Cantico nell'epistolario di S. GIROLAMO. Brescia 1995, Pavoniana 80 pp. [RdT 36,639].

1816 **Castellana, Franco** "Cantico dei cantici": riflessioni teologiche e spirituali. Meditazioni per la vita 5. Mi 1995, Paoline 194 pp. L14.000. 88-315-1041-X. ᴿRAMi 64 (1995) 217-218 (*Turchi, Athos*).

1817 **Chauvin, Jacques** Un amour émerveillé: le Cantique des cantiques. Poliez-le-Grand 1995, Du Moulin 99 pp. FF58 [RHPhR 77,198].

1818 *Clines, David J.A.* Why is there a Song of Songs, and what does it do to you if you read it?. ⇒37. Interested parties. JSOT.S 205. 1995. 94-121.

1819 *Croatto, J.S.* Cantar de los cantares. PastPo 249 (1995) 22 [Strom. 52,345].

1820 **Engammare, Max** Lire le Cantique des cantiques à la Renaissance, suivi de *La violette et le rossignol* et *Les colombes de tes yeux*. La Rochelle 1994, Rumeurs des âges 87 pp. ᴿRHEF 81 (1995) 468-469 (*Bernos, Marcel*).

1821 *Gallazzi, Ana Maria Rizzante* 'Eu sere para ele como aquela que dá a paz'. Ribla 21 (1995) 214-224 [ThIK 17/2,68].

1822 *Girlanda, A.* Il Cantico dei Cantici. Catechisti Parrocchiali 4 (1995) 9-12.

1823 *Lane, David J.* "The curtains of Solomon": some notes on the "Syriacing" of Šir-hašširim. ⇒76. The Peshitta. MPIL 8. 1995. 73-84.

1824 *Lavoie, Jean-Jacques* La femme dans le Cantique des Cantiques. ⇒71. Des femmes. 1995. 103-111 [EThL 72/2-3,211*].

1825 *Lavoie, Jean-Jacques* Festin érotique et tendresse cannibalique dans le Cantique des cantiques. SR 24/2 (1995) 131-146.

1826 *Merkin, Daphne* The women in the balcony: on rereading the Song of Songs. ⇒70. Out of the garden. 1995. 238-251.

1827 *Morris, A.* The Trinity in BERNARD's sermons on the Song of Songs. CiSt 30/1 (1995) 35ff [ZID 21,659].

1828 **Munro, Jill M.** Spikenard and saffron: the imagery of the Song of Songs. JSOT.S 203. Shf 1995, Academic 166 pp. $40. 1-85075-562-0 [OTA 19,350].

1829 *O'Loughlin, Thomas* Seeking the early medieval view of the Song of Songs. PIBA 18 (1995) 94-116.

1830 *Schulz-Flügel, Eva* Zur Darstellung der Rubrikenreihen zum Canticum. BVLI 39 (1995) 17-26.

1831 **Six, Jean-François** Le chant de l'amour: Éros dans la Bible. P 1995, Desclée de Brouwer 270 pp. 2-220-03604-9.

1832 **Vries, Sytze de** Liefde, op het lif geschreven: een wandeling door het Hooglied [Love inscribed on the body: a walk through the Song of Songs]. Zoetermeer 1995, Meinema [OTA 19,350].

1833 *Watson, Wilfred* Some ancient Near Eastern parallels to the Song of Songs ⇒24. ᶠSAWYER J., JSOT.S 195. 1995. 253-271;

1834 —Verse patterns in the Song of Songs. JNSL 21/1 (1995) 111-122.

1835 *Paul, Shalom M.* The "plural of ecstasy" in Mesopotamian and Biblical love poetry. 1995 ⇒11. 585-597 [1,4; 2,15].
1836 *Lundbom, Jack R.* Between text and sermon: Song of Songs 3:1-4. Interp. 49 (1995) 172-175.
1837 *Barbiero, Gianni* Die Liebe der Töchter Jerusalems Hld 3,10b MT im Kontext von 3,6-11. BZ 39 (1995) 96-104.
1838 *Bloch, Ariel A.* The cedar and the palm tree: a paired male/female symbol in Hebrew and Aramaic. ⇒11. 1995. 13-17 [5,10-15].
1839 *LaCocque, André* La Shulamite et les chars d'Aminadab: un essai herméneutique sur Cantique 6,12-7,1. RB 102 (1995) 330-346.
1840 *Brzegowy, Tadeusz* "Miłość mocniejsza niż śmierć": egzegeza Pnp 8,6-7 ["L'amour plus fort que la mort": l'exégèse Pnp 8,6-7]. P. AtK 125 (1995) 26-34 [8,6-7].

E7.5 *Libri sapientiales* — **Wisdom literature.**

1841 *Amsler, Samuel* Gerhard von RAD et la sagesse. ⇒117. La sagesse biblique. LeDiv 160. 1995. 209-216.
       Berry, Donald K. An introduction to wisdom and poetry of the Old Testament. ⇒1403.
1842 **Blenkinsopp, Joseph** Sage, priest, prophet: religious and intellectual leadership in ancient Israel. Library of Ancient Israel. LVL 1995, Westminster xii; 191 pp. $19. 0-664-21954-3 [CBQ 58,397].
1843 **Blenkinsopp, Joseph** Wisdom and law in the Old Testament: the ordering of life in Israel and early Judaism. Oxford Bible Series. Ox 1995, University Press 197 pp. £30; £11. 0-19-875503-1; -504-X <pb>.
       [E]**Brenner, Athalya** A feminist companion to wisdom literature. ⇒69.
1844 *Brenner, Athalya* Introduction to wisdom literature 11-21;
1845 Some observations on the figurations of woman in wisdom literature 50-66. 1995 ⇒69. A feminist companion to wisdom literature.
1846 **Cannizzo, Antonio** L'enigma della sfinge: la sapienza del Qohelet e l'interrogare di Giobbe. RdT books 9. R 1995, AVE 143 pp. 88-8065-086-6.
1847 *Cathcart, Kevin J.* The trees, the beasts and the birds: fables, parables and allegories in the Old Testament. ⇒9. [F]EMERTON J., 1995. 212-221.
1848 *Cazelles, Henri* Aḥiqar, Ummân and Amun, and biblical wisdom texts. ⇒11. [F]GREENFIELD J., 45-55.
1849 *Clements, R. E.* Wisdom, virtue and the human condition. ⇒23. [F]ROGERSON J., JSOT.S 200. 1995. 139-157.
1850 **Clements, R.E.**   Wisdom in theology...1992. ⇒8,3459... 10,3203. [R]CritRR 7 (1994) 106-108 (*Bergant, Dianne*); TJT 11 (1995) 229-230 (*Delsnyder, Robert*); JSJ 26 (1995) 346-349 (*Woude, A.S. van der*).
1851 *Clements, R.E.* Wisdom and Old Testament theology. ⇒9. [F]EMERTON J., 1995. 269-286.
       Crenshaw, James L. Urgent advice and probing questions: collected writings on Old Testament wisdom 1995 ⇒43.

1852   *Crenshaw, James L.* The acquisition of knowledge in Israelite wisdom literature [1987] 292-299;
1853   The concept of God in Old Testament wisdom [1993] 191-205;
1854   The contemplative life [1995] 250-264;
1855   Education in ancient Israel [1985] 235-249;
1856   Impossible questions, sayings, and tasks [1980] 265-278;
1857   Introduction: the shift from theodicy to anthropodicy [1983] 141-154;
1858   Method in determining wisdom influence upon 'historical' literature [1969] 312-325;
1859   Murphy's axiom: every gnomic saying needs a balancing corrective [1987] 344-354;
1860   The restraint of reason, the humility of prayer 206-221;
1861   Studies in ancient Israelite wisdom: prolegomenon [1976] 90-140;
1862   Wisdom [1974] 45-77;
1863   Wisdom and authority: sapiential rhetoric and its warrants [1982] 326-343;
1864   Wisdom in Israel (Gerhard von RAD): a review [1976] 300-311;
1865   The wisdom literature [1985] 14-44;
1866   Wisdom literature: biblical books [1987] 1-13;
1867   Wisdom literature: retrospect and prospect [1993] 78-89. ⇒43. Urgent advice. 1995.
1868   *Davies, G.I.* Were there schools in ancient Israel?. ⇒9. [F]EMERTON J., 1995. 199-211.
       [E]**Day, John**, Wisdom in ancient Israel. [F]EMERTON J., 1995. ⇒9.
1869   *Fontaine, Carole R.* The social roles of women in the world of wisdom. ⇒69. A feminist companion to wisdom literature. 1995. 24-49.
1870   [M]GAMMIE In search of wisdom. [E]**Perdue, Leo G.** ⇒9,50. 1993. [R]VT 45 (1995) 404-405 *(Dell, Katharine J.)*; CBQ 57 (1995) 433-435 *(Asma, Lawrence F.)*.
1871   *Gilbert, Maurice* Qu'en est-il de la Sagesse?. ⇒117. La sagesse biblique. 1995. 19-60.
1872   **Goldsworthy, Graeme** Gospel and wisdom: Israel's wisdom literature in the christian life. Biblical Classics Library. Carlisle 1995, Paternoster 202 pp. 0-85364-651-1.
1873   **Golka, Friedemann W.** The leopard's spots: biblical and African wisdom in proverbs. ⇒9,3312. 1993. [R]VT 45 (1995) 566-567 *(Dell, Katharine J.)*.
1874   *Gordon, Robert P.* A house divided: wisdom in Old Testament narrative traditions. ⇒9. [F]EMERTON J., 1995. 94-105.
1875   *Greenfield, Jonas C.* The wisdom of Ahiqar. ⇒9. [F]EMERTON J., 1995. 43-52.
1876   *Hadley, Judith M.* Wisdom and the goddess. ⇒9. [F]EMERTON J., 1995. 234-243.
1877   *Hannig, Rainer H. G.* Amenemope 5. Kapitel. ⇒3. [M]BARTA W., 1995. 179-198.
1878   **Heaton, E.W.** The school tradition of the Old Testament. Ox 1994, OUP xiv; 210 pp. Bampton Lectures 1994. £25; $55. [R]RStT 13-14 (1995) 92-93 *(Norton, Gerard J.)*.
1879   [E]**Hilten, W. van** Een vreemde vrouw: bevreemding of herkenning: teksten uit Spreuken en andere wijsheidsliteratuur. Serie op reis. Kampen 1995, Kok 103 pp. ƒ24.90. 90-242-8471-6 [TTh 36,299].

E_{Holt, Else K.} Lov og visdom 1995. ⇒90.

1880 *Joncheray, Jean* Actualité de la sagesse. ⇒117. La sagesse biblique. 1995. 503-517.

1881 *Kaiser, Otto* Anknüpfung und Widerspruch: die Antwort der jüdischen Weisheit auf die Herausforderung durch den Hellenismus. Pluralismus und Identität. E^{Mehlhausen, Joachim}, Veröffentlichungen der Wissenschaftlichen Gesellschaft für Theologie 8. Gü 1995, Kaiser 637 pp. DM98; ÖS716; FS92. 3579-00105-1 [BuBbgB 19,125].

1882 *Lambert, W.G.* Some new Babylonic wisdom literature. ⇒9. F_{EMERTON} J., 1995. 30-42.

Lavoie, Jean-Jacques Les livres de Job, Qohélet et Proverbes: recherche depuis 1980. ⇒1732.

1883 *Loader, J.A.* Fools can explain it, wise men never try. OTEs 8 (1995) 129-144.

1884 *Marböck, Johannes* Die jüngere Weisheit im Alten Testament: zu einigen Ansätzen in der neueren Forschungsgeschichte. ⇒55. Gottes Weisheit. 1995. 3-22.

1885 *Mathias, Dietmar* Das Problem der Zeit in weisheitlichen Texten des Alten Testaments. ⇒37. F_{WAGNER} S., 1995. 217-232.

1886 **Morla Asensio, Victor** Libros Sapienciales y otros escritos. ⇒10,3214. 1994. R_{Salm.} 42 (1995) 133-135 (*Pérez, Gabriel*); RET 55 (1995) 93-94 (*Barrado Fernández, P.*); EE 70 (1995) 117-118 (*Pi, Higinio*).

1887 *Murphy, Roland E.* The personification of wisdom. ⇒9. F_{EMERTON} J., 1995. 222-233.

1888 **Niccacci, Alviero** La casa della sapienza. ⇒10,3221. 1994. R_{Ang.} 72 (1995) 318-320 (*Jurič, Stipe*); LASBF 45 (1995) 611-616 (*Bottini, Giovanni Claudio*).

1889 *O'Connor, Kathleen M.* Wisdom literature and experience of the divine. ⇒6. F_{BEKER} J., 1995. 183-195 [OTA 19,493].

1890 *Pelletier, Anne-Marie* La sagesse au féminin dans la Bible: un repérage de la question. ⇒117. La sagesse biblique. 1995. 197-207.

1891 **Perdue, Leo G.** Wisdom and creation 1994. ⇒10,3224. R_{Worship} 69 (1995) 467-468 (*Nowell, Irene*); RStT 13-14/2-3 (1995) 132-133 (*Siedlicki, Armin*).

1892 **Perry, Theodore Anthony** Wisdom literature and the structure of Proverbs 1993. ⇒9,3322. R_{CritRR} 8 (1995) 142-144 (*Malchow, Bruce V.*).

1893 *Plum, Karin Friis* Den kloge kone: visdomsmetaforikken i gammeltestamentlig litteratur [The wisdom metaphor in Old Testament literature]. 1995 ⇒90. Lov og visdom. 9-21 [OTA 19,495].

1894 *Ray, J.D.* Egyptian wisdom literature. ⇒9. F_{EMERTON} J., 1995. 17-29.

1895 E_{Roccati, Alessandro} Sapienza egizia: la letteratura educativa in Egitto durante il II millennio a.C. TVOA 1/4. Brescia 1994, Paideia 151 pp. L30.000. 88-394-0505-4. R_{Anton.} 70 (1995) 688-689 (*Nobile, Marco*).

1896 *Schroer, Silvia* Wise and counselling women in ancient Israel: literary and historical ideals of the personified hokmâ 1995. ⇒69. A feminist companion to wisdom literature. 67-84.

1897 **Shupak, Nili** Where can wisdom be found? ⇒9,3328; 10,3229. OBO 130. 1993. R_{BiOr} 52 (1995) 115-116 (*Lipiński, E.*); CBQ 57

(1995) 160-162 (*Higginbotham, Carolyn R.*); VT 45 (1995) 422-423 (*Ray, J.D.*); IEJ 45 (1995) 303-304 (*Lichtheim, Miriam*).

1898 **Smend, Rudolf** The interpretation of wisdom in nineteenth-century scholarship. ⇒9. ^FEMERTON J., 1995. 257-268.

^E**Trublet, Jacques** La sagesse biblique 1995. ⇒117.

1899 **Vílchez Líndez, José** Sabiduría y sabios en Israel. El Mundo de la Biblia. Estella 1995, Verbo Divino 364 pp. 84-8169-035-X.

1900 *Vílchez-Líndez, José* Panorama des recherches actuelles sur la sagesse dans l'Ancien Testament. ⇒117. La sagesse biblique 1995. 129-137.

1901 **Weeks, Stuart** Early Israelite wisdom. ⇒10,3236. 1994. ^RJSSt 40 (1995) 329-330 (*Golka, Friedemann W.*); VT 45 (1995) 126-130 (*Dell, Katharine J.*); CBQ 57 (1995) 379-380 (*Lavoie, Jean-Jacques*).

1902 *Woude, A.S. van der* Wisdom at Qumran. ⇒9. ^FEMERTON J., 1995. 244-256.

E7.6 Proverbiorum liber, *themata, versiculi.*

Garrett, Duane A. Proverbs... ⇒1791. NAC 14. 1993.

1903 **Martin, James D.** Proverbs. OTGu. Shf 1995, Academic 105 pp. $9.95. 1-85075-752-6 [OTA 19,348].

Perry, Theodore Anthony Wisdom literature and the structure of Proverbs. ⇒1892.

1904 **Whybray, R. Norman** The book of Proverbs: a survey of modern study. History of Biblical Interpretation 1. Lei 1995, Brill x; 184 pp. $67.75. 90-04-10374-0 [OTA 19,349].

1905 ^E**Zuck, Roy B.** Learning from the sages: selected studies on the book of Proverbs.   GR 1995, Baker 438 pp. $25. 0-8010-9941-2 [RB 103,318].

1906 *Bullock, C. Hassel* The book of Proverbs. ⇒1905. Learning. 1995. 19-33.

1907 *Camp, Claudia V.* Wise and strange: an interpretation of the female imagery in Proverbs in light of trickster mythology. ⇒69. A feminist companion to wisdom literature. 1995. 131-156.

1908 *Ceresko, Anthony R.* The function "order" (ṣedeq) and "creation" in the book of Proverbs, with some implications for today. ITS 32 (1995) 208-236.

1909 *Cook, Johann* The Septuagint Proverbs as a Jewish-Hellenistic document. ⇒136. VIII Congress. SCSt 41. 1995. 349-365.

1910 *Crenshaw, James L.* Clanging symbols [1989] 371-382;

1911 Poverty and punishment in the book of Proverbs [1989] 396-405;

1912 Prohibitions in Proverbs and Qoheleth [1993] 417-425;

1913 Proverbs [1992] 355-370;

1914 The sage in Proverbs [1990] 406-416. ⇒43. Urgent advice. 1995.

1915 *Day, John* Foreign semitic influence on the wisdom of Israel and its appropriation in the book of Proverbs. ⇒9. ^FEMERTON J., 1995. 55-70 [Qoh 9,7-9].

1916 *Domeris, William R.* Shame and honour in Proverbs: wise women and foolish men. OTEs 8 (1995) 86-102.

1917 *Joosten, Jan* Doublet translations in Peshitta Proverbs. ⇒76. The Peshitta. MPIL 8. 1995. 63-72.

    Lavoie, Jean-Jacques Les livres de Job, Qohélet et Proverbes: recherche depuis 1980. ⇒1732.

1918 *Mouser, William E., Jr.* Filling in the blank: asymmetrical antithetical parallelisms. ⇒1905. Learning. 1995. 137-150.

1919 *Nobile, Marco* L'attivita dell'uomo nel libro dei Proverbi. Anton. 70 (1995) 349-365.

1920 *Parsons, Greg W.* Guidelines for understanding and proclaiming the book of Proverbs. ⇒1905. Learning. 1995. 151-168.

1921 *Ramaroson, H.* Le paresseux: une leçon de sagesse biblique. PosLuth 43 (1995) 334-337.

1922 *Robert, Pierre* La sagesse crie par les places. La Vie 53 (1995) 184-187.

1923 *Ross, Allen P.* Introduction to Proverbs. ⇒1905. Learning. 1995. 35-48.

1924 *Ruffle, John* The teaching of Amenemope and its connection with the book of Proverbs. ⇒1905. Learning. 1995. 293-331.

1925 *Scott, R.B.Y.* The proverbs of ancient Israel. ⇒1905. Learning. 1995. 67-72.

1926 **Snell, Daniel C.** Twice-told proverbs 1993 ⇒9,3358; 10,3254. RRExp 92 (1995) 384 (*Nogalski, James D.*); HebStud 36 (1995) 198-201 (*Westermann, C.*); CritRR 8 (1995) 153-157 (*Fox, Michael V.*).

1927 *Towner, W. Sibley* Proverbs and its successors. ⇒36. FTUCKER G., 1995. 157-175.

1928 *Waltke, Bruce K.* The book of Proverbs and ancient wisdom literature. ⇒1905. Learning. 1995. 49-65.

1929 **Westermann, Claus** Roots of wisdom: the oldest proverbs of Israel and other peoples. LVL/E 1995, Westminster/Clark viii; 178 pp. $20; £12.50. 0-664-25559-0/0-567-29276-2 [BoL 1996,96].

1930 **Whybray, R. Norman** The composition of the book of Proverbs. ⇒10,3255. JSOT.S 168. 1994. RJThS 46 (1995) 222-223 (*Martin, J.D.*); EThL 71 (1995) 211-212 (*Lust, J.*); VT 45 (1995) 130-133 (*Dell, Katharine J.*); JBL 114 (1995) 716-718 (*Gladson, Jerry A.*); CBQ 57 (1995) 796-797 (*Ceresko, Anthony R.*).

1931 *Williams, James G.* The power of form: a study of biblical proverbs. ⇒1905. Learning. 1995. 73-97.

1932 *Woodcock, Eldon G.* Basic terminology of wisdom, folly, righteousness, and wickedness. ⇒1905. Learning. 1995. 111-124.

1933 *Yee, Gale A.* The socio-literary production of the "foreign woman" in Proverbs. ⇒69. A feminist companion to wisdom literature. 1995. 127-130.

1934 *Zuck, Roy B.* A theology of Proverbs. ⇒1905. Learning. 1995. 99-110.

1935 *Lang, Bernhard* Figure ancienne, figure nouvelle de la sagesse en Pr 1 à 9. ⇒117. LeDiv 160. 1995. 61-97.

1936 **Maier, Christl Margarethe** Die "fremde Frau": eine exegetische und sozialgeschichtliche Studie zu Proverbien 1-9. Diss. Humboldt 1995, DWelten, P., OBO 144. Gö 1995, Vandenhoeck & Ruprecht xi; 296 pp. FS88; DM106; SCH782. 3-525-53779-4 [RB 103,477].

1937 **Baumann, Gerlinde** "Wer mich findet, hat Leben gefunden": traditionsgeschichtliche und theologische Studien zur Weiheitsgestalt in Proverbien 1-9. Diss. ^D*Janowski*, 1995, Heidelberg [ThRv 92/2,IX].

1938 **Harris, Scott L.** Proverbs 1-9: a study of inner-biblical interpretation. SBL.DS 150. Atlanta, GA 1995, Scholars xii; 193 pp. $49.95. 0-7885-0148-8.

1939 *Meynet, Roland* "Pour comprendre proverbe et énigme": analyse rhétorique de Pr 1,1-7; 10,1-5; 26,1-12. ⇒4. ^FBEAUCHAMP P., LeDiv 162. 1995. 97-118.

1940 *Ross, Allen P.* Proverbs 1:1-19. ⇒1905. Learning. 1995. 171-177.

1941 *Trible, Phyllis* Wisdom builds a poem: the architecture of Proverbs 1:20-33. ⇒1905. Learning. 1995. 179-189.

1942 *Waltke, Bruce K.* Lady Wisdom as mediatrix: an exposition of Proverbs 1:20-33. ⇒1905. Learning. 1995. 191-204.

1943 *Yee, Gale A.* "I have perfumed my bed with myrrh": the foreign woman (ʾiššâ zārâ) in Proverbs 1-9. ⇒69. A feminist companion to wisdom literature. 1995. 110-126.

1944 *Washington, Harold C.* The strange woman (אשה זרה/נכריה) of Proverbs 1-9 and post-exilic Judaean society. ⇒69. A feminist companion to wisdom literature. 1995. 157-184.

1945 *Alden, Robert L.* Advice to young men: Proverbs 3. ⇒1905. Learning. 1995. 205-212.

1946 *Aitken, Kenneth T.* Beware the seductress: Proverbs 5. ⇒1905. Learning. 1995. 213-218.

1947 *Burns, John Barclay* Proverbs 7,6-27: vignettes from the cycle of Astarte and Adonis. SJOT 9 (1995) 20-36.

1948 *McKane, William* Avoid the immoral woman: Proverbs 7. ⇒1905. Learning. 1995. 219-228.

1949 *Heijerman, Meike* Who would blame her?: the "strange" woman of Proverbs 7. ⇒69. A feminist companion to wisdom literature. 1995. 100-109.

1950 *Yee, Gale A.* An analysis of Proverbs 8:22-31 according to style and structure. ⇒1905. Learning. 1995. 229-236.

1951 *Farmer, Kathleen A.* Wisdom lists her credentials: Proverbs 8:22-31. ⇒1905. Learning. 1995. 237-240.

1952 *Hildebrandt, Ted* Motivation and antithetic parallelism in Proverbs 10-15. ⇒1905. Learning. 1995. 253-265.

1953 **Scoralick, Ruth** Einzelspruch und Sammlung: Komposition im Buch der Sprichwörter, Kapitel 10-15. Diss. St. Georgen 1993, ^D*Jüngling, Hans-Winfried*, BZAW 232. B 1995, De Gruyter ix; 285 pp. DM158. 3-11-14440-0.

1954 *Murphy, Roland E.* 'Catchwords' in Proverbs 10:1-22:13. ⇒1905. Learning. 1995. 241-248.

1955 *Whybray, R.N.* The vocabulary of wealth and poverty in the book of Proverbs (10:1-22:16 and 25-29). ⇒1905. Learning. 1995. 125-136.

1956 *Garrett, Duane A.* On order and disorder in Proverbs 10:1-24:23. ⇒1905. Learning. 1995. 249-251.

1957 *Buzzell, Sid S.* Righteous and wicked living in Proverbs 10. ⇒1905. Learning. 1995. 267-272.

1958 **Hausmann, Jutta** Studien zum Menschenbild der älteren Weisheit: (Spr 10ff.). FAT 7. Tü 1995, Mohr ix; 418 pp. DM198. 3-16-14645-2.

1959 *Krüger, Thomas* Komposition und Diskussion in Proverbia 10. ZThK 92 (1995) 413-433.

1960 *Pola, Thomas* Die Struktur von Proverbia 16,1-15. BN 80 (1995) 47-72.
1961 *Meinhold, Arndt* Zur strukturellen Eingebundenheit der JHWH-Sprüche in Prov 18. ⇒37. ^FWAGNER S., 1995. 233-245.
1962 *Hildebrandt, Ted* Proverbs 22:6a: train up a child?. ⇒1905. Learning. 1995. 277-292.
1963 *Archer, Gleason L., Jr.* Proverbs 22:6 and the training of children. ⇒1905. Learning. 1995. 273-275.
1964 *Maire, Thierry* Proverbes xxii 17ss.: enseignement à Shalishôm?. VT 45 (1995) 227-238.
1965 *Buzzell, Sid S.* Proverbs 25-26. ⇒1905. Learning. 1995. 333-338.
1966 *Hoglund, Kenneth G.* The fool and the wise in dialogue: Proverbs 26:4-5. ⇒1905. Learning. 1995. 339-352.
1967 *Malchow, Bruce V.* A manual for future monarchs: Proverbs 27:23-29:27. ⇒1905. Learning. 1995. 353-360.
1968 *Finkbeiner, Douglas* An analysis of the structure of Proverbs 28 and 29. CBTJ 11/2 (1995) 1-14.
1969 *Hubbard, David A.* Words of Agur: Proverbs 30:1-33. ⇒1905. Learning. 1995. 361-373.
1970 *Crenshaw, James L.* A mother's instruction to her son (Proverbs 31:1-9) [1988]. ⇒43. Urgent advice. 1995. 383-395.
1971 *McCreesh, Thomas P.* Wisdom as wife: Proverbs 31:10-31. ⇒1905. Learning. 1995. 391-410.
1972 **Hawkins, Tom Roger** The meaning and function of Proverbs 31:10-31 in the book of Proverbs. Diss. ^D*Zuck, Roy B.*, Dallas 1995, 276 pp. AAC 9539903; DAI-A 56,2727.
1973 *Lichtenstein, Murray H.* Chiasm and symmetry in Proverbs 31. ⇒1905. Learning. 1995. 381-390.
1974 *Farmer, Kathleen A.* The 'words' Lemuel's mother taught him: Proverbs 31. ⇒1905. Learning. 1995. 375-379.

E7.7 *Ecclesiastes* — **Qohelet;** *textus, themata, versiculi.*

1975 ^E**Bardski, Krzysztof** Hieronymus: Komentarz do Ksiegi Eklezjastesa. Kraków 1995, Wydawnictwo 173 pp. 83-86106-21-2.
1976 **Doré, Daniel** Qohélet le Siracide ou l'Ecclésiaste et l'Ecclésiastique. CEv 91. P 1995, Cerf. F30.
   Garrett, Duane A. Proverbs, Ecclesiastes... ⇒1791.
1977 ^E**Géhin, Paul** ÉVAGRE: scholies à l'Ecclésiaste. ⇒9,3385; 10,3279. SC 397. 1993. ^RJThS 46 (1995) 352-354 (*Gould, Graham*); ScEs 47 (1995) 223-224 (*Poirier, Paul-Hubert*).
1978 ^E**Jarick, John** Concordance of the Hebrew and Greek texts of Ecclesiastes. ⇒9,3388. SCSt 36. 1993. ^RCBQ 57 (1995) 347-348 (*Wright, Benjamin G.*).
1979 *Jarick, John* THEODORE of Mopsuestia and the text of Ecclesiastes. ⇒136. VIII Congress. SCSt 41. 1995. 367-385.
1980 ^E**Labate, Antonio** Catena Hauniensis. ⇒8,3539... 10,3281. CChr.SG 24. 1992. ^ROrph. 16 (1995) 197-200 (*Leanza, Sandro*); SMSR 60/1 (1994) 153-154 (*Zincone, Sergio*).
1981 **Perry, Theodore Anthony** Dialogues with Kohelet...commentary. ⇒9,3393; 10,3283. 1993. ^RJBL 114 (1995) 718-720 (*Schoors, Antoon*); Bibl.Interp. 3 (1995) 232-233 (*Salters, R.B.*).
1982 ^T**Renan, Ernest** L'Ecclésiaste: un temps pour tout. Retour aux grands textes 4. P 1995, Arléa. Traduit de l'hébreu et commenté. 2-86959-230-2.

1983 *Salters, R.B.* Observations on the peshitta of Ecclesiastes. OTEs 8 (1995) 388-397 [sum. 388].
1984 **Vílchez Líndez, José** Eclesiastés o Qohélet. ⇒10,3284. Nueva-BEsp Sap. 3. 1994. ᴿBib. 76 (1995) 565-568 (*Ravasi, Gianfranco*); Salm. 42 (1995) 135-138 (*Pérez, Gabriel*); RET 55 (1995) 91-92 (*Barrado Fernández, P.*); EE 70 (1995) 253-254 (*Morla, Victor*).

1985 *Backhaus, Franz Josef* Die Pendenskonstruktion im Buch Qohelet. ZAH 8 (1995) 1-30.
1986 *Defélix, Chantal* Qohélet dans la tradition juive. LV(L) 41 (1995) 19-31 [OTA 19,91].
1987 *Erdrich, Louise* The preacher. ⇒70. Out of the garden. 1995. 234-237.
1988 *Gire, Pierre* Qohélet: l'espérance mendiante. LV(L) 41 (1995) 41-54 [OTA 19,91].
1989 *Girlanda, A.* Qohelet: un saggio disincantato. Catechisti Parrocchiali 1 (1995) 9-11.
1990 *Jarick, John* THEODORE Mopsuestia and the interpretation of Ecclesiastes. ⇒23. ᶠROGERSON J., JSOT.S 200. 1995. 306-316.
1991 *Kaiser, Otto* Beiträge zur Kohelet-Forschung: eine Nachlese. ThR 60 (1995) 1-31, 233-253.
1992 *Kaiser, Otto* Qoheleth. ⇒9. ᶠEMERTON J., 1995. 83-93.
1993 **Kim, Hea Sun; Blakeman, Mary Lou** Ecclesiastes: the meaning of your life. NY 1995, Mission Education and Cultivation Program Department v; 137 pp.
1994 **Lange, Armin** Weisheit und Torheit bei Kohelet. ⇒7,3059; 8,3552. EHS.T 433. 1991. ᴿBiOr 52 (1995) 116-118 & ABG 38 (1995) 282-283 (*Schoors, Antoon*).
1995 **Lavoie, Jean-Jacques** La pensée du Qohélet. ⇒8,3553...10,3293. CTHP 49. 1992. ᴿRivBib 43 (1995) 278-282 (*Bianchi, Francesco*); CBQ 57 (1995) 352-353 (*Kolarcik, Michael*).
       Lavoie, Jean-Jacques Les livres de Job, Qohélet...⇒1732.
1996 **Lavoie, Jean-Jacques** Qohélet: une critique moderne de la Bible. Parole d'actualité 2. P 1995, Médiaspaul 149 pp. $19.95. 2-89420-306-3 [RB 103,477].
1997 *Lee, Archie* Death and the perception of the divine in Qohelet and Zhuang Zi. ChFe 38/1 (1995) 69-81 [ThIK 17/29].
1998 *Lohfink, Norbert* Les épilogues du livre de Qohélet et les débuts du canon. ⇒4. ᶠBEAUCHAMP P., LeDiv 162. 1995. 77-96.
1999 *Lorgunpai, Seree* The book of Ecclesiastes and Thai Buddhism. ⇒129. Voices from the margin. 1995 <1991>. 339-348 [Exod 1,8-22; 2,1-10].
2000 **Lorgunpai, Seree** World lover, worldleaver: the book of Ecclesiastes and Thai Buddhism.   Diss. E 1995, 295 pp. [RTL 27,529].
2001 *Lys, Daniel* Qohélet ou le destin de la perte de sens. LV(L) 41 (1995) 9-17 [OTA 19,92].
2002 *Machinist, Peter* Fate, miqreh, and reason: some reflections on Qohelet and biblical thought. ⇒11. ᶠGREENFIELD J., 1995. 159-175.
       Maggioni, Bruno Job y Cohélet ⇒1737.
2003 *Molina, Jean-Pierre* L'Ecclésiaste et l'Ecclésioclaste. LV(L) 41 (1995) 55-67 [OTA 19,92].

Newsom, Carol A. Job and Ecclesiastes. ⇒1741.

2004 *Ng, Eng Eng* Qohelet and the enjoyment of life. C. CTUF 103 (1995) 25-44 [ThIK 17,28].

2005 *Pury, Albert de* Qohélet, Noé et le bonheur. LV(L) 41 (1995) 33-40 [OTA 19,92].

2006 *Raurell, Frederic* Qohèlet: una visió diferent i provocadora de Déu. RCatT 20 (1995) 237-267 [sum. 267].

2007 *Schneck, R.* Qohélet y la guerra amazónica, 1995, una nota teológica. ThX(EX) 45 (1995) 321-325 [Strom. 52,345].

2008 *Schoors, Antoon* The word ʾadam in Qoheleth. ⇒18. ᶠLIPINSKI E., OLA 65. 1995. 299-304.

2009 **Schwienhorst-Schönberger, Ludger** "Nicht im Menschen gründet das Glück" (Koh 2,24): Kohelet im Spannungsfeld jüdischer Weisheit und hellenistischer Philosophie. ⇒10,3302. 1994. ᴿBib. 76 (1995) 562-565 (*Vílchez, José*).

2010 *Simian-Yofre, Horacio* Presente, speranza e memoria: una meditazione sulla temporalità a partire dal Qohelet. ⇒96. Gli anziani nella Bibbia. 1995. 141-166.

2011 **Simms, S.P.** Qoheleth: critic of post-exilic beliefs. Diss. 1995, Ox [RTL 27,531].

2012 *Tamez, Elsa* Cuando los horizontes se cierran: una reflexión sobre la razón utópica de Qohélet. CrSoc 33 (1995) 7-18 [ThIK 18,72].

2013 *Vinel, Françoise* Salomon, l'Ecclésiaste: exégèses d'un nom. ⇒13. ᶠHARL M., 1995. 499-512.

2014 **Vonach, Andreas** Weisheit aus dem Herzen: ein hörendes Herz als Quelle radikaler Verwirklichung von Weisheit bei Qohelet. Diplomarbeit, Innsbruck 1995, 90 pp.

2015 *Wallis, Gerhard* Das Zeitverständnis des Predigers Salomo. ⇒7. ᶠDONNER H., 1995. 316-323.

2016 ᴱ**Zuck, Roy B.** Reflecting with Solomon: selected studies on the book of Ecclesiastes. ⇒10,3299. 1994. ᴿOTA 18 (1995) 419-420 (*Begg, Christopher T.*).

2017 *Seow, Choon-Leong* Qohelet's autobiography. ⇒10. ᶠFREEDMAN D., 1995. 275-287 [Qoh 1,12-2,11].

2018 *Fischer, Stefan* Zur Übersetzung von Kohelet 2,25: wer isst und sorgt sich ohne mich? Fundamentum 3 (1995) 219-223 [OTA 19,92].

2019 *Maas, Jacques; Post, Jack* Qohéleth et le savoir de dieu: la modalité du croire dans Qohéleth à partir de Qo 3,1-15. SémBib 80 (1995) 34-50.

2020 *Blenkinsopp, Joseph* Ecclesiastes 3.1-15: another interpretation. JSOT 66 (1995) 55-64.

2021 *Jeppesen, Knud* Har mennesket 'evigheden' eller 'verden' i hjertet?: om praedikerens syn på mennesket og tiden, med udgangspunkt i oversaettelsen af Praed 3,11 [Does man have 'eternity' or 'the world' in his heart?: on Qoheleth's view of man and time, beginning with the translation of Qoh 3:11]. 1995 ⇒90. Lov og visdom. 22-35 [OTA 19,460].

2022 *Lavoie, Jean-Jacques* De l'inconvénient d'être né: étude de Qohélet 4,1-3. SR 24 (1995) 297-308.

2023 *Anderlini, Gianpaolo* Qohelet 5,7-8: note linguistiche ed esegetiche. BeO 37 (1995) 13-32.

2024 *Lavoie, Jean-Jacques* Vie, mort et finitude humaine en Qo 9,1-6.
      ScEs 47 (1995) 69-80.
2025 *Lohfink, Norbert* Freu dich, Jüngling—doch nicht, weil du jung
      bist: zum Formproblem im Schlußgedicht Kohelets (Koh 11,9-
      12,8). Bibl.Interp. 3 (1995) 158-189.

E7.8 *Liber Sapientiae* — Wisdom of Solomon

2026 ᴱArtz, Peter [*al. ed.*] Sprachlicher Schlüssel zur Sapientia Salomo-
      nis (Weisheit). Sprachlicher Schlüssel zu den Deuterokanonischen
      Schriften (Apokryphen) des Alten Testaments 1. Salzburg 1995,
      Institut für Neutestamentliche Bibelwissenschaft 187 pp. 3-901636-
      00-5.
2027 Gilbert, Maurice La Sapienza di Salomone. Bibbia e Preghiera 22-
      23. R 1995, ADP 2 vols; 243, 187 pp. L24.000; L24.000. 88-
      7357-148-4; -156-5.
2028 Pock, Johann Ignaz Sapientia Salomonis: Hieronymus Exegese
      des Weisheitsbuches. ⇒8,3573... 10,3315. 1992. ᴿCBQ 57 (1995)
      571-572 (*Hoppe, Leslie J.*).
2029 Vílchez Líndez, José Sabedoria. ᵀ*Rezende Costa, João*. Grande
      Comentário Bíblico. São Paulo 1995, Paulus 470 pp.

2030 *Beauchamp, Paul* Sagesse de Salomon de l'argumentation médicale
      à la resurrection. ⇒117. La sagesse biblique. LeDiv 160. 175-186.
2031 Busto Saiz, José Ramón La justicia es inmortal: una lectura del
      libro de la Sabiduría de Salomón 1992 ⇒8,3572; 9,3418. ᴿREB
      218 (1995) 479-481 (*Gruen, Wolfgang*).
2032 *Horbury, William* The christian use and the Jewish origins of the
      Wisdom of Solomon. ⇒9. ᶠEMERTON J., 1995. 182-196.
2033 *Hug, Joseph* Sagesse et condition humaine: réflexion sur le livre de
      la Sagesse. Choisir 429 (1995) 9-12.
2034 *Mazzinghi, Luca* "Non c'è regno dell'Ade sulla terra": l'inferno
      alla luce di alcuni testi del libro della Sapienza. Vivens Homo 6
      (1995) 229-255 [sum. 255].
2035 *Noel, Damien* Quelle sotériologie dans le livre de la Sagesse?
      ⇒117. La sagesse biblique. LeDiv 160. 1995. 187-196 [Wis 9]

2036 *Mazzinghi, Luca* "Dio no ha creato la morte" (Sap 1,13): il tema
      della morte nel libro della Sapienza. PSV 32 (1995) 63-75.
2037 *Scarpat, G.* Predisposizione naturale e preesistenza dell'anima
      (nota a Sap 8,19-20). RivBib 43 (1995) 93-100.
2038 *Fleteren, Frederick van* Exégesis agustiniana de Sb 9,15. Augusti-
      nus 40 (1995) 303-314.
2039 *Couto, António* A sabedoria na história de *Adam* (Sb 10,1-2).
      Did(L) 25/1-2 (1995) 169-187.
2040 *Enns, P.* A retelling of the song at the sea in Wis 10,20-21. Bib.
      76 (1995) 1-24 [Exod 15,1-21].
2041 Dumoulin, P. Entre la manne et l'eucharistie: étude de Sg 16,15-
      17,1a. ⇒10,3325. AnBib 132. 1994. ᴿVivens Homo 6 (1995) 199-
      201 (*Mazzinghi, Luca*); RevAg 36 (1995) 621-622 (*Salugal, San-
      tos*); RivBib 43 (1995) 544-546 (*Priotto, Michelangelo*).
2042 Mazzinghi, Luca Notte di paura e di luce: esegesi di Sap 17,1-
      18,4. AnBib 134. R 1995, Pont. Istituto Biblico xxxii; 357 pp.

L65.000. 88-7653-134-3 <pb>. ᴿFirmana 11 (1995) 157-160
(*Nepi, Antonio*).

E7.9 *Ecclesiasticus, Siracides;* Wisdom of Jesus Sirach.

2043 **Minissale, Antonino** La versione greca del Siracide: confronto con
il testo ebraico alla luce dell'attività midrascica e del metodo targumico. Diss. Pontificium Institutum Biblicum. ᴰ*Le Déaut, Roger,* R
1995, Biblical Institute Press x; 334 pp. L65.000. 88-7653-133-5.

2044 **Pereira, Ney Brasil** Sirácida ou Eclesiástico, a Sabedoria de Jesus,
Filho de Sirac: cosmovisão de um sábio judeu no final do AT e sua
relevância hoje. Comentário bíblico. Petrópolis 1992, Vozes viii;
252 pp. ᴿCBQ 57 (1995) 360-361 (*Lavoie, Jean-Jacques*).

2045 **Petraglio, Renzo** Il libro che contamina le mani: Ben Sira rilegge il
libro e la storia d'Israele 1993 ⇒9,3447; 10,3328. ᴿRivBib 43
(1995) 539-544 (*Prato, Gian Luigi*); CBQ 57 (1995) 781-783
(*Lavoie, Jean-Jacques*).

2046 **Samaan, Kamil W.** Sept traductions arabes de Ben Sira 1994
⇒10,3329. EHS.T 492. ᴿCBQ 57 (1995) 786-787 (*Kaltner, John*).

2047 *Alonso Schökel, Luis* Notas exegéticas al Eclesiástico (Ben Sira).
EstB 53 (1995) 433-448.

2048 *Argall, Randal A.* Reflections on 1 Enoch and Sirach: a comparative literary and conceptual analysis of the themes of revelation,
creation and judgment. SBL.SP 34. 1995. 337-351 [RB 103,633].

2049 *Crenshaw, James L.* The problem of theodicy in Sirach: on human
bondage [1975]. ⇒43. Urgent advice. 1995. 155-174.
Di Lella, A.A. Women in the Wisdom of Ben Sira and the book of
Judith. ⇒1352.
Doré, Daniel Qohélet le Siracide. ⇒1976.

2050 *Girlanda, A.* Il Siracide un saggio tradizionale e innovatore. Catechisti Parrocchiali 2 (1995) 6-9.

2051 *Goan, Seán* Creation in Ben Sira. MillSt 36 (1995) 75-85.

2052 **Kieweler, Hans Volker** Ben Sira zwischen Judentum und Hellenismus: eine Auseinandersetzung mit Th. MIDDENDORP. ⇒8,3595.
BEAT 30. 1992. ᴿBijdr. 56/1 (1995) 73-74 (*Beentjes, P.C.*).

2053 *Marböck, Johannes* Die "Geschichte Israels" als Bundesgeschichte"
nach dem Sirachbuch. ⇒55. Gottes Weisheit 1995. 103-123.
Marböck, Johannes Gottes Weisheit unter uns: zur Theologie des
Buches Sirach. 1995. ⇒55:

2054 Henoch—Adam—der Thronwagen: zur frühjüdischen pseudepigra-
phischen Tradition bei Ben Sira 133-143;

2055 Macht und Mächtige im Buch Jesus Sirach: ein Beitrag zur politischen Ethik in der Weisheitsliteratur des Alten Testaments 185-194
[5,15-26; 9,17-18; 10; 11,1-9; 13];

2056 Sündenvergebung bei Jesus Sirach: eine Notiz zur Theologie und
Frömmigkeit der deuterokanonischen Schriften 176-184.

2057 *Milani, Marcello* Pietà, moderazione e vitalità nel rituale di lutto
per il morto: Sir 38,16-23. StPat 42 (1995) 197-213.

2058 *Minissale, Antonino* Il libro del Siracide: da epigono a protagoni-
sta. Laós 2/2 (1995) 3-19.

2059 *Snaith, John G.* Ecclesiasticus: a tract for the times. ⇒9.
ᶠEMERTON J., 1995. 170-181.

2060   Thiele, Walter Sirach (Ecclesiasticus). BVLI 39 (1995) 26-29.
2061   Wischmeyer, Oda Die Kultur des Buches Jesus Sirach. BZNW 77.
       B 1995, De Gruyter vii; 318 pp. Diss.-Habil. Heidelberg 1992
       (⇒8,3598). DM158. 3-11-014564-2.

2062   Calduch Benages, Nuria Ben Sira 2 y el Nuevo Testamento. EstB
       53 (1995) 305-316.
2063   Calduch Benages, Nuria En el crisol de la prueba: estudio exegé-
       tico de Sir 2. Diss. Pontificium Institutum Biblicum. DGilbert,
       Maurice, R 1995, xi; 97 pp. [extract].
2064   Okoye, John Ifeanyichukwu Speech in Ben Sira with special refe-
       rence to 5,9-6,1. Diss. EHS.T 535. Fra 1995, Lang xix; 208 pp.
       SF56. 3-631-48923-4 [Bijdr. 57,119].
2065   Irwin, William H. Fear of God, the analogy of friendship and Ben
       Sira's theodicy. Bib. 76 (1995) 551-559 [6,16-17].
2066   Marböck, Johannes Sir 15,9f—Ansätze zu einer Theologie des Got-
       teslobes bei Jesus Sirach 167-175 [15,7-10];
2067   Gesetz und Weisheit: zum Verständnis des Gesetzes bei Jesus Ben
       Sira 52-72 [17,11-14; 24,23];
2068   Gottes Weisheit unter uns: Sir 24 als Beitrag zur biblischen Theolo-
       gie 73-87. ⇒55. Gottes Weisheit 1995.
2069   Miller, Naomi F. The Aspalathus caper. BASOR 297 (1995) 55-60
       [24,15].
2070   Faure, Patrick Comme un fleuve qui irrigue: Ben Sira 24, 30-34, I.
       critique textuelle. RB 102/ 1 (1995) 5-27.
2071   Faure, Patrick La sagesse et le sage: Ben Sira 24, 30-34, II. exégè-
       se. RB 102 (1995) 348-370.
2072   Marböck, Johannes Das Gebet um die Rettung Zions in Sir 36,1-22
       (G: 33,1-13a; 36,16b-22) im Zusammenhang der Geschichtsschau
       Ben Siras 149-166;
2073   Sir 38,24-39,11: der schriftgelehrte Weise: ein Beitrag zu Gestalt
       und Werk Ben Siras 25-51;
2074   Davids Erbe in gewandelter Zeit (Sir 47,1-11) 124-132. ⇒55. Got-
       tes Weisheit 1995.
2075   Lévêque, Jean Le portrait d'Élie dans l'éloge des Pères (Si 48, 1-
       11). ⇒22. FRenaud B., LeDiv 159. 1995. 215-229.
2076   VanderKam, James C. Simon the just: Simon I or Simon II? ⇒21.
       FMilgrom J., 1995. 303-318 [50,1-21].
2077   Wightman, G.J. Ben Sira 50:2 and the Hellenistic temple enclosure
       in Jerusalem. ⇒16. FHennessy J., 1995. 275-283.
2078   Gilbert, Maurice L'action de grâce de Ben Sira (Si 51,1-12). ⇒22.
       FRenaud B., LeDiv 159. 1995. 231-242.

Libri prophetici VT

E8.1 Prophetismus.

2079   **Abrego de Lacy, J.M.** Los libros proféticos. ⇒9,3455. 1993.
       RScrTh 27 (1995) 1056-1057 (*Ausín, S.*).

2080 *Aleixandre, Dolores* Cuando los profetas son también sabios. Sal-Ter 83 (1995) 859-875.

2081 **Amsler, Samuel** Les derniers prophètes: Aggée, Zacharie, Malachie et quelques autres. CEv 90. P 1995, Cerf. FF30.

2082 *Andersen, Francis I.* Linguistic coherence in prophetic discourse. ⇒10. FFREEDMAN D., 1995. 137-156.

2083 **Arthur, Kay** God's blueprint for bible prophecy. Eugene, OR 1995, Harvest 132 pp. 1-56507-317-7.

2084 *Auld, A. Graeme* Prophets through the looking glass: between writings and Moses. ⇒83. Israelite prophets 1995 <1983>. 289-307.

2085 *Beck, Astrid B.* An examination of the prophetic impetus in the Celtic and Norse mythical traditions in juxtaposition with the biblical corpus. ⇒10. FFREEDMAN D., 1995. 560-577.

2086 *Begg, Christopher T.* The 'classical prophets' in JOSEPHUS' Antiquities. ⇒83. Israelite prophets 1995 <1988>. 547-562.

2087 **Blenkinsopp, Joseph** Une histoire de la prophétie en Israël. ⇒9,3462. LeDiv 152. 1993. RETR 70 (1995) 114-115 (*Römer, Thomas*).

2088 *Boggio, Giovanni* I profeti del dopoesilio. ⇒97. Profeti. 1995. 157-191.

2089 *Boggio, Giovanni; Monari, Luciano; Marconcini, Benito* I profeti attorno all'esilio (sec. VII e VI). ⇒97. Profeti. 1995. 105-156.

2090 *Bony, P.* Les prophètes d'Israël: instance critique du "religieux". Chemins de Dialogue 5 (1995) 63ff [ZID 21,817].

2091 **Bosshard, Erich** Jesaja 1-39 und das "Zwölfprophetenbuch" in exilischer und frühnachexilischer Zeit: redaktionsgeschichtliche Untersuchungen zur literarischen Vernetzung der Prophetenbücher. Diss. Zürich 1995, DSteck, O.H. [RTL 26,530].

2092 **Bravo Retamal, Arturo** Y Dios perdio paciencia: estudios sobre critica profética al culto. Diss. Tü 1995, DGroß, W. [ThRv 92/2,XV].
Brenner, Athalya A feminist companion to the latter prophets 1995 ⇒68.

2093 *Bruce, F.F.* Prophetic interpretation in the Septuagint 1995 ⇒83. Israelite prophets 1995 <1979>. 539-546.

2094 **Brueggemann, Walter** A social reading of the Old Testament: prophetic approaches to Israel's communal life. Mp 1994, Fortress 328 pp. $18. RBR 11/6 (1995) 14-15 (*Gottwald, Norman K.*).

2095 *Buzzard, Anthony F.* The gospel of the kingdom in the prophets: the unfulfilled dream of messianic government. JRadRef. 4/3 (1995) 3-30 [NTA 40,84].

2096 ECagni, Luigi Le profezie di Mari. TVOA 2/2. Brescia 1995, Paideia 126 pp. L22.000. 88-394-0519-4. RAnton. 70 (1995) 686-688 (*Nobile, Marco*).

2097 *Carroll, R.P.* Ancient Israelite prophecy and dissonance theory. ⇒83. Israelite prophets 1995 <1977>. 377-391.

2098 *Carroll, Robert P.* The biblical prophets as apologists for the christian religion: reading William Robertson SMITH's The prophets of Israel today. ⇒121. William Robertson Smith 1995. JSOT.S 189. 148-157.

2099 *Carroll, Robert P.* Desire under the terebinths: on pornographic representation in the prophets—a response. ⇒68. A feminist companion to the Latter Prophets. 1995. 275-307 [Jer 2,1-37; 3; Ezek 16; 20; 23,1-49].

2100   **Cavedo, Romeo** Profeti: storia e teologia del profetismo nell'Antico Testamento. Universo Teologia 32. CinB 1995, San Paolo 264 pp. L22.000.

2101   *Childs, Brevard S.* The canonical shape of the prophetic literature 1995 < 1978 > ⇒83. Israelite prophets 513-522;

2102   The canonical shape of the prophetic literature. 1995 ⇒98. Interpreting the prophets 41-49.

2103   *Clements, Ronald E.* Prophets, editors, and tradition < 1990 > 443-452;

2104   *Clines, D.J.A.* Language as event < 1976 > 166-175. 1995 ⇒83. Israelite prophets [Isa 53].

2105   **Collins, Terence** The mantle of Elijah: the redaction criticism of the prophetical books 1993 ⇒9,3466; 10,3349. BiSe 20. ᴿCBQ 57 (1995) 343-344 (*O'Brien, Julia*).

2106   **Cook, Stephen L.** Prophecy & apocalypticism: the postexilic social setting. Mp 1995, Fortress x; 246 pp. $21. 0-8006-2839-X [OTA 19,353].

2107   *Darr, Katheryn Pfisterer* Literary perspectives on prophetic literature 1995 ⇒36. ꜰTᴜᴄᴋᴇʀ G., 127-143.

2108   *Day, John* Inner-biblical interpretation in the prophets. ⇒83. Israelite prophets 1995 < 1988 >. 230-246.

2109   **DeVries, Simon J.** From old revelation to new: a redaction-critical and tradition-historical study of temporal transitions in prophetic prediction. GR 1995, Eerdmans xxiv; 383 pp. $30. 0-8028-0683-X.

2110   *Deist, Ferdinand E.* The prophets: are we heading for a paradigm switch? ⇒83. Israelite prophets 1995 < 1989 >. 582-599.

2111   **Drwal, Tomasz Piotr** Syjon w przepowiadaniu prorockim [Sion dans la prédication prophétique]. Diss Lublin 1995, ᴰ*Homerski, J.* [RTL 27,528].

2112   *Geller, Stephen A.* Were the prophets poets? ⇒83. Israelite prophets 1995 < 1983 >. 154-165.

2113   *Gonçalves, F. J.* Isaie, Jérémie et la politique internationale de Juda. Bib. 76 (1995) 282-298.

2114   *Goodman, Allegra* Prophecy and poetry 1995 ⇒70. Out of the garden. 301-309.

2115   *Gordon, Pamela; Washington, Harold C.* Rape as a military metaphor in the Hebrew Bible 1995 ⇒68. A feminist companion to the Latter Prophets. 308-325.

     ᴱ**Gordon, Robert P.** 'The place is too small for us': the Israelite prophets in recent scholarship 1995 ⇒83.

2116   *Gordon, Robert P.* Present trends and future directions 600-605;

2117   A story of two paradigm shifts 3-26. 1995 ⇒83. Israelite prophets.

2118   *Gosse, Bernard* L'usage rédactionnel des oracles contre les nations à l'époque post-exilique. BLE 96 (1995) 219-221.

2119   *Greenberg, Moshe* Jewish conceptions of the human factor in biblical prophecy 1995 ⇒49. Studies. 405-420.

2120   *Guérard, Marie-Gabrielle* Testimonia christologiques et pédagogie monastique: la notion de prophétie chez Nɪʟ d'Ancyre 1995 ⇒13. ꜰHᴀʀʟ M., 381-391.

2121   *Homerski, J.* The message of the prophets of the Old Testament. **P.** ACra 27 (1995) 141-151.

2122 *Houston, Walter* What did the prophets think they were doing?: speech acts and prophetic discourse in the Old Testament. ⇒83. Israelite prophets 1995 <1993>. 133-153.

2123 *Huddlestun, John R.* "Who is this that rises like the Nile?": some Egyptian texts on the inundation and a prophetic trope ⇒10. FFREEDMAN D., 1995. 338-363 [Jer 46,7-8].

2124 *Hutton, Rodney R.* Magic or street-theater?: the power of the prophetic word. ZAW 107 (1995) 247-260.

2125 *Jarick, John* Prophets and losses: some themes in recent study of the prophets. ET 107 (1995) 75-77.

2126 **Jemielity, Thomas** Satire and the Hebrew prophets 1992 ⇒8,3614... 10,3359. RCritRR 7 (1994) 125-127 (*Landy, Francis*); EvQ 67 (1995) 160-161 (*Williamson, H.G.M.*); JQR 86 (1995) 222-223 (*LaCocque, André*).

2127 **Koch, Klaus** Die Profeten: assyrische Zeit. UB 280. Stu ³1995 (⇒60,4615... 3,3372), Kohlhammer 288 pp. DM34. 3-17-013678-X [NTAb 40,190].

2128 **Koenen, Klaus** Heil den Gerechten—Unheil den Sündern! ⇒10,3361. BZAW 229. 1994. RThLZ 120 (1995) 1068-1069 (*Koch, Klaus*); CBQ 57 (1995) 559-560 (*Vogels, Walter A.*).

2129 *Long, Burke O.* Social dimensions of prophetic conflict ⇒83. Israelite prophets 1995 <1981>. 308-331.

2130 *Lucas, Ernest C.* Sacrifice in the prophets 1995 ⇒61. Sacrifice. 59-74.

2131 *Magdalene, F. Rachel* Ancient Near Eastern treaty-curses and the ultimate texts of terror: a study of the language of divine sexual abuse in the prophetic corpus 1995 ⇒68. A feminist companion to the Latter Prophets. 326-352 [Isa 3,17-26; 47,1-4; Jer 13,22-26; Hos 2,4-5.11-12; Nah 2,7-8; 3,5.13; Zech 14,2].

2132 *Malamat, Abraham* Prophecy at Mari ⇒83. Israelite prophets 1995 <1984>. 50-73.

EMarconcini, Benito Profeti e apocalittici 1995 ⇒97.

2133 *Marconcini, Benito* I profeti preesilici (sec. VIII) 1995 ⇒97 Profeti. 59-104.

2134 **Marcus, David** From Balaam to Jonah: anti-prophetic satire in the Hebrew Bible. BJSt 30. Atlanta 1995, Scholars v; 214 pp. $45. 0-7885-0101-0 [OTA 18,645].

2135 *Mayoral, Juan Antonio* El uso simbólico-teológico de los animales en los profetas del exilio. EstB 53 (1995) 317-363.

EMays, James Luther (*al.*) Interpreting the prophets ⇒98.

2136 *McKane, William* Old Testament criticism and the canonical prophets 65-91, 92-113;

2137 The canonical prophets: what kind of men were they? 1995 ⇒56. A late harvest. 114-132, 133-153.

2138 *Miller, Patrick D.* The world and message of the prophets: biblical prophecy in its context 1995 ⇒FTUCKER G., 97-112.

2139 **Murphy, Richard T.A.** An introduction to the prophets of Israel. Boston 1995, Pauline xvii; 123 pp. $6. 0-8189-3672-9 [OTA 19,354].

2140 *Nicholson, Ernest W.* Prophecy and covenant <1986> 345-353;

2141 *Overholt, Thomas W.* Prophecy in history: the social reality of intermediation <1990> 354-376;

2142 The end of prophecy: no players without a program <1988> 527-538. 1995 ⇒83. Israelite prophets.

2143 **Peckham, Brian** History and prophecy 1993 ⇒9,3483. RInterp. 49 (1995) 78-80 (*Blenkinsopp, Joseph*); CBQ 57 (1995) 156-158 (*Klein, Ralph W.*).

2144 *Pesty, Monika* ORIGENE et les prophètes 1995 ⇒126. Origeniana Sexta. 411-416.

2145 *Petersen, David L.* Ecstasy and role enactment 1995 ⇒83. Israelite prophets 1995 <1981>. 279-288.

2146 **Prévost, Jean-Pierre** Pour lire les prophètes. Outremont/P 1995, Novalis/Cerf 204 pp. 2-89088-708-1/2-204-05121-7 [RSR 84,60].

2147 *Raabe, Paul R.* Why prophetic oracles against the nations? 1995 ⇒10. FFREEDMAN D., 236-257.

2148 **Raurell, Frederic** Profeta, el forjat per la paraula 1993 ⇒9,3486. RLaurentianum 36/1-2 (1995) 219-221 (*Dalbesio, Anselmo*); RCatT 20 (1995) 187-195 (*Cruells, Antoni*).

2149 *Rees, Ian* Exegesis: prophecy and Scripture. Evangel 13/2 (1995) 36-38 [2 Pet 1,16-21].

2150 *Reiser, Marius* Gericht Gottes: biblisch-theologisch 1995 ⇒122. LhTK 4. 515-516.

2151 **Rofé, Alexander** Introduzione alla letteratura profetica. EMinissale, Antonino. StBi 111. Brescia 1995, Paideia 157 pp. L23.000. 88-394-0528-3.

2152 *Sasson, Jack M.* Water beneath straw: adventures of a prophetic phrase in the Mari archives 1995 ⇒11. FGREENFIELD J., 599-608.

2153 *Sawyer, John F.A.* Prophecy and interpretation <1993> 563-575;

2154 *Schmidt, Werner H.* Contemporary <1979> 579-581. 1995 ⇒83. Israelite prophets.

2155 *Schmitt, John J.* Samaria in the books of the eighth-century prophets 1995 ⇒1. MAHLSTRÖM G., JSOT.S 190. 355-367.

2156 TESchwemer, **Anna Maria** Studien zu den frühjüdischen Prophetenlegenden: Vitae prophetarum I: die Viten der großen Propheten Jesaja, Jeremia, Ezechiel und Daniel: Einleitung, Übersetzung und Kommentar [Diss. ⇒10,3364]. TSAJ 49. Tü 1995, Mohr xiv; 448 pp. DM298. 3-16-146439-7.

2157 **Sicre, J.L.** Profetismo in Israele: il profeta—i profeti—il messaggio. R 1995, Borla 623 pp. L70.000. 88-263-1042-4.

2158 **Spreafico, Ambrogio** I profeti 1993 ⇒10,3369. RLASBF 45 (1995) 586-590 (*Cortese, Enzo*).

2159 *Stacey, W. David* The function of prophetic drama 1995 <1990> ⇒83. Israelite prophets. 112-132.

2160 **Sturm-Berger, Michael** Merkmale und Wesen von Prophetentum: eine religionsvergleichende Studie. Diss. Goethe Fra, DWeber, 1995 [ThRv 92/2,VIII].

2161 *Sweeney, Marvin A.* Formation and form in prophetic literature 1995. ⇒FTUCKER G., 113-126.

2162 **The International Commission on English in the Liturgy** The Psalter: a faithful and inclusive rendering from the Hebrew into contemporary English poetry, intended primarily for communal song and recitation. EHuck, Gabe 1995, Liturgy Training Publications xxxiv; 149 pp. $18/$12. 0-929650-77-8/-88-3. RFirst Things 58 (1995) 45-48 (*Alter, Robert*).

2163 EValerio, **Adriana** Donna potere e profezia. N 1995, D'Auria 292 pp.

2164 *VanderKam, James* Prophecy and apocalyptics in the ancient Near East 1995 ⇒127. Civilizations 3. 2083-2094.

2165 *Vigilius, N.O.* Israel, profetien og landloftet bog af Aksel VALEN-SENDSTAD [Israel, prophecy and the land promise: a book by Aksel Valen-Sendstad]. Nemalah 14 (1995) 44-64 [OTA 19,96].

2166 *Vogels, Walter* Prophètes et littérature prophétique 1995 ⇒84. De bien des manières. LeDiv 163. 79-118.

2167 **Weems, Renita J.** Battered love: marriage, sex, and violence in the Hebrew prophets. Overtures to Biblical Theology. Mp 1995, Fortress xvi; 150 pp. £11. 0-8006-2948-5.

2168 *Weinfeld, Moshe* Ancient Near Eastern patterns in prophetic literature <1977> 32-49;

2169 *Westermann, C.* Oracles of salvation <1991> 98-104. 1995 ⇒83. Israelite prophets.

2170 *Wood, Joyce Rilett* Prophecy and poetic dialogue. SR 24 (1995) 309-322.

2171 *Zimmerli, Walther* From prophetic word to prophetic book 1995 <1979> ⇒83. Israelite prophets. 419-442.

2172 *Zincone, Sergio* La funzione dell'oscurità delle profezie secondo Giovanni CRISOSTOMO. ASEs 12 (1995) 361-375 [sum. 228].

2173 **Zucker, David J.** Israel's prophets: an introduction for Christians and Jews 1994 ⇒10,3376. EeT(O) 26 (1995) 260-261 (*Vogels, Walter*).

E8.2 **Proto-Isaias,** *textus, commentarii.*

2174 **Brewster, Hoyt W.** Isaiah, plain & simple: the message of Isaiah in the book of Mormon. Salt Lake City, Utah 1995, Deseret xiv; 281 pp.

2175 **Collins, J.** Isaia. Brescia 1995, Queriniana 203 pp. L25.000 [CivCatt 147,531].

2176 **Darr, Katheryn Pfisterer** Isaiah's vision and the family of God 1994 ⇒10,3400. RThLZ 120 (1995) 990-992 (*Reventlow, Henning Graf*).

2177 EGoshen-Gottstein, Moshe H. The book of Isaiah. The Hebrew University Bible Project. J 1995, Magnes xlviii; 297 pp. $98. 965-223-905-4.

2178 EGryson, Roger Commentaires de JEROME sur le prophète Isaïe I-IV 1993 ⇒9,3505; 10,3381. AGLB 23. RREAug 41/1 (1995) 131-143 (*Milhau, Marc*).

2179 *Gryson, Roger; Auwers, Jean-Marie; Baise, Ignace* L'édition d'Isaïe. BVLI 39 (1995) 29-35.

2180 *Gryson, Roger; Somers, V.; Gabriel, C.; Bourgois, H.* Le commentaire de JEROME sur Isaïe. BVLI 39 (1995) 35-37.

2181 **Höffken, Peter** Das Buch Jesaja Kapitel 1-39 1993 ⇒9,3507. RThLZ 120 (1995) 130-132 (*Thiel, Winfried*).

2182 **MacRae, Allan A.** Studies in Isaiah. Hatfield, Pa. 1995 Interdisciplinary Biblical Research Institute vi; 358 pp. 0-944788-88-2.

2183 EManley, Johanna Isaiah through the ages. Menlo Park 1995, Monastery xxii; 1072 pp. 0-9622536-3-4.

2184 **Marconcini, Benito** Il libro di Isaia (1-39) 1993 ⇒9,3509. RCivCatt 146 (1995) 96-97 (*Scaiola, D.*).

2185 **Marconcini, Benito** El libro de Isaías (1-39). Guía espiritual del Antiguo Testamento. Barc/M 1995, Herder/Ciudad Nueva 183 pp. Ptas1.800. 84-254-1899-2.

2186 *Marconcini, Benito* Il raduno escatologico dei popoli nel libro di Isaia. PSV 31 (1995) 61-73.

2187 **Miscall, Peter D.** Isaiah 1993 ⇒9,3510; 10,3387. RProoftexts 15 (1995) 195-202 (*Sweeney, Marvin A.*); CritRR 8 (1995) 134-136 (*White, Hugh C.*).

2188 **Motyer, J. Alec** The prophecy of Isaiah 1993 ⇒9,3512; 10,3389. REvQ 67 (1995) 155-157 (*Millar, J. Gary*); CBQ 57 (1995) 566-568 (*Sweeney, Marvin A.*).

2189 **Seitz, Christopher R.** Isaiah 1-39 1993 ⇒9,3518; 10,3392. RAUSS 33 (1995) 149 (*Miller, James E.*); Horizons 22 (1995) 136-137 (*Laffey, Alice L.*); JR 75 (1995) 259-260 (*Clifford, Richard J.*); JBL 114 (1995) 503-504 (*Clements, Ronald, E.*); HebStud 36 (1995) 177-179 (*Sweeney, Marvin A.*).

2190 **Simian-Yofre, Horacio** Isaias: texto y comentario. El Mensaje del Antiguo Testamento 12. M 1995, Atenas 301 pp. 84-7020-400-9.

2191 *Virgulin, Stefano* La morte nella profezia di Isaia. PSV 32 (1995) 39-52.

2192 *Williamson, H. G. M.* Synchronic and diachronic in Isaian perspective 1995 ⇒99. Synchronic or diachronic?. OTS 34. 211-226.

2193 *Williamson, H.G.M.* Isaiah and the wise ⇒9. FEMERTON J., 1995. 133-141.

2194 *Zovkić, Mato* Religious and cultural message of the book of Isaiah. **Croatian.** Crkva u Svijetu 30 (1995) 365-379 [sum. 379].

2195 *Zurro Rodríguez, Eduardo* Siete hápax en el libro de Isaías. EstB 53 (1995) 525-535 [3,18; 9,4; 22,15; 30,24; 32,4; 34,15; 56,10].

E8.3   Proto-Isaias 1-39, themata, versiculi

2196 *Barton, John* Ethics in Isaiah of Jerusalem ⇒83. Israelite prophets 1995 <1981>. 80-97.

2197 *Büchmann, Christina* The wind of judgment and the wind of burning: the Holy One of Isaiah 1995 ⇒70. Out of the garden. 262-277.

2198 *Carroll, Robert* Revisionings: echoes and traces of Isaiah in the poetry of William BLAKE 1995 ⇒24. FSAWYER J., JSOT.S 195. 226-241.

2199 *Clampitt, Amy* The poetry of Isaiah 1995 ⇒70. Out of the garden. 252-261.

2200 **Fischer, Irmtraud** Tora für Israel—Tora für die Völker: das Konzept des Jesajabuches. SBS 164. Stu 1995, Katholisches Bibelwerk 135 pp. DM39.80 (35,80)/ÖS295 (265)/FS39.80 (35.80). 3-460-04641-4.

2201 *García Recio, Jesús* "La fauna de las ruinas", un "topos" literario de Isaías. EstB 53 (1995) 55-96.

2202 *Marconcini, Benito* Temi di teologia biblica: temi particolari: culto e giustizia in Isaia. 1995 ⇒97. Profeti. 425-433.

2203 **Pfaff, Heide-Marie** Die Entwicklung des Restgedankens in Jesaja 1-39. Diss. FrB 1995, DRuppert, L.

2204 *Sawyer, John F. A.* The ethics of comparative interpretation. CurResB 3 (1995) 153-168.

2205 *Schultz, Richard* The king in the book of Isaiah 1995 ⇒111. The Lord's anointed. 141-165 [11,6-9; 66,25].
Vegas Montaner, Luis; Seijas de los Ríos, Guadalupe A computer assisted syntactical study of poetic biblical texts 1995 ⇒1414 [Isa 1-39].

2206 *Wilson, R.R.* Interpreting Israel's religion: an anthropological perspective on the problem of false prophecy. 1995 <1984> ⇒83. Israelite prophets. 332-344.

2207 **Wong, G.C.I.** The nature of faith in Isaiah of Jerusalem. Diss. C 1995, ᴰ*Williamson, H.G.M.* [TynB 47,188].

2208 *Schibler, Daniel* Messianism and messianic prophecy in Isaiah 1-12 and 28-33 1995 ⇒111. The Lord's anointed. 87-104.

2209 *Beuken, Willem A.M.* De os en de ezel in Jesaja literair (Jes. 1:3 en 32:20) 1995 ⇒27. ꟳSᴇʀᴠᴏᴛᴛᴇ H., 161-183 [EThL 72,196*].

2210 *Koonthanam, George* Yahweh the defender of the Dalits: a reflection on Isaiah 3.12-15 1995 <1991> ⇒129. Voices from the margin. 105-116.

2211 *Gabriel, C.* Commentaires inédits d'Hᴀʏᴍᴏɴ d'Auxerre sur Isaïe 5,1-6,1. SE 35 (1995) 89-114.

2212 *Schmeller, Thomas* Der Erbe des Weinbergs: zu den Gerichtsgleichnissen Mk 12,1-12 und Jes 5,1-7. MThZ 46 (1995) 183-201.

2213 *Brueggemann, Walter* Five strong rereadings of the book of Isaiah 1995 ⇒23. ꟳRᴏɢᴇʀsᴏɴ J., JSOT.S 200. 87-104 [5,20; 55,8; 43,15-21; 49,15-16; 65,17-25].

2214 *Bartelt, Andrew H.* Isaiah 5 and 9: in- or interdependence? 1995 ⇒10. ꟳFʀᴇᴇᴅᴍᴀɴ D., 157-174.

2215 *Gosse, Bernard* Le grand prêtre et la sagesse face au livre d'Isaïe au retour de l'exil. BN 78 (1995) 11-15 [Isa 5].

2216 **Barthel, Jörg** Text und Geschichte: eine Untersuchung der Jesajaüberlieferung in Jesaja 6-8 und 28-31. Diss. Tü 1995, ᴰ*Hermisson* [ThRv 92/2,XIV].

2217 *Eslinger, Lyle* The infinite in a finite organical perception (Isaiah vi 1-5). VT 45 (1995) 145-173 [Neh 3,5].

2218 **Wagner, Renate** Textexegese als Strukturanalyse...Jes 6,1-11. 1989 ⇒5,3510... 8,3686. ATSAT 32. ᴿOLZ 90 (1995) 289-291 (*Stahl, Rainer*).

2219 *Marconcini, Benito* Saggi di esegesi: dal libro di Isaia: il racconto della vocazione (Is 6,1-13). 1995 ⇒97. Profeti. 245-264.

2220 *Osten-Sacken, Peter von der* Die altkirchlichen Belege für die synagogale Form des Sanctus (Keduscha/Jes. 6,3; Ez. 3,12) 1995 ⇒8. ꟳDᴏɴɴᴇʀ H., ÄAT 30. 172-187.

2221 **Werlitz, Jürgen** Studien...Jesaja 7,1-17 und 29,1-8. ⇒8,3691... 10,3425. BZAW 204. 1992. ᴿJBL 114 (1995) 136-138 (*Miscall, Peter D.*).

2222 *Marconcini, Benito* Saggi di esegesi: dal libro di Isaia: l'Emmanuele e il problema delle profezie messianiche [7,10-17]. 1995 ⇒97. Profeti. 265-273.

2223 *Bergey, R.* La prophétie d'Esaie 7:14-16. RRef 46/1 (1995) 9-14.

2224 *Bauckham, Richard* The messianic interpretation of Isa. 10:34 in the Dead Sea Scrolls, 2 Baruch and the preaching of John the Baptist. DSD 2 (1995) 202-216.

2225 *Williamson, H.G.M.* Isaiah xi 11-16 and the redaction of Isaiah i-xii. 1995 ⇒135. Congress Volume: Paris 1992. VT.S 61. 343-357.

2226 **Zapff, Burkard M.** Schriftgelehrte Prophetie—Jes 13 und die Komposition des Jesajabuches: ein Beitrag zur Erforschung der Redaktionsgeschichte des Jesajabuches. Diss. Wü 1993/94. ᴰ*Schreiner, Josef*, FzB 74. Wü 1995, Echter 379 pp. DM48. 3-429-01636-3.

2227 **Jones, Brian C.** Howling over Moab: irony and rhetoric in Isaiah 15-16. Diss. Emory 1995, ᴰ*Miller, J. Maxwell*, 372 pp. AAC 9605430; DAI-A 56,4006.

2228 *Schenker, A.* La fine della storia d'Israele ricapitolerà il suo inizio: esegesi d'Is 19,16-25. RivBib 43 (1995) 321-330.

2229 *Uffenheimer, Benjamin* The "desert of the sea" pronouncement (Isaiah 21:1-10) 1995 ⇒21. ᶠMɪʟɢʀᴏᴍ J., 677-688.

2230 *Amsler, Samuel* L'Apocalypse d'Ésaïe: Ésaïe 24-27. 1995 ⇒2081. Les derniers prophètes. 56-61.

2231 *Biddle, M. E.* The city of chaos and the new Jerusalem: Isaiah 24-27 in context. PRSt 22 (1995) 5-12.

2232 **Itoh, Ryo** Literary and linguistic approach to Isaiah 24-27. Diss. Trinity Evang. Div. School 1995, ᴰ*Vangemeren, Willem*, 217 pp. AAC 9608872; DAI-A 56,4429.

2233 *Miller, Glenn* Between text and sermon: Isaiah 25:6-9. Interp. 49 (1995) 175-178.

2234 *Jacob, Edmond* La pierre angulaire d'Esaie 28:16 et ses échos néotestamentaires. RHPhR 75 (1995) 3-8.

2235 *Gosse, Bernard* Isaie 28-32 et la rédaction d'ensemble du livre d'Isaie. SJOT 9 (1995) 75-82.

2236 *Beuken, Willem A.M.* Isaiah 28: is it only schismatics that drink heavily?: beyond the synchronic versus diachronic controversy 1995 ⇒99. Synchronic or diachronic? 15-38.

2237 *Römer, T.* Jugement et salut en Ésaïe 28: étude exégétique. PosLuth 43/1 (1995) 55-62.

2238 *Wong, G.C.I.* On "visits" and "visions" in Isaiah xxix 6-7. VT 45 (1995) 370-376.

2239 *Boxel, P.W. van* Isaiah 29:13 in the New Testament and early rabbinic Judaism 1995 ⇒130. Aspects of religious contact. 81-90.

2240 ᴱ**Higman, Francis M.; Parker, Thomas H.L.; Thorpe, Lewis** Sermons sur le livre d'Esaïe chapitres 30-41. Supplementa Calviniana. Sermons inédits 3. Neuk 1995, Neuk xxviii; 645 pp. 3-7887-1452-2.

2241 *Beuken, Willem A.M.* What does the vision hold: teachers or one teacher?: punning repetition in Isaiah 30:20. HeyJ 36 (1995) 451-466.

2242 *Tournaire, R.* Sur des versets ambigus d'Isaïe. BAGB (1995) 204-210 [30,20-22; EThL 72/2-3,197*].

2243 *Kaiser, Otto* Literary criticism and tendenz-criticism: methodological reflections on the exegesis of Isaiah ⇒83. Israelite prophets 1995 <1989>. 495-512 [31,1-3; 30,6-17].

2244 *Mathews, Claire R.* Apportioning desolation: contexts for interpreting Edom's fate and function in Isaiah. SBL.SP 34 (1995) 250-266 [34-35].

2245 **Mathews, Claire R.** Defending Zion: Edom's desolation and Jacob's restoration (Isaiah 34-35) in context. Diss. Yale 1994,

^D*Seitz, Christopher.* BZAW 236. B 1995, De Gruyter 190 pp. DM128/FS124/SCH999. 3-11-014665-7 [RSR 84,159].

2246 *Ackroyd, P.R.* Isaiah 36-39: structure and function ⇒83. Israelite prophets 1995 <1982>. 478-494.

2247 *Barré, Michael L.* Restoring the "lost" prayer in the psalm of Hezekiah (Isaiah 38:16-17b). JBL 114 (1995) 385-399.

E8.4 Deutero-Isaias 40-52: *commentarii, themata, versiculi*

2248 *Croatto, J. Severino* Exegesis of Second Isaiah from the perspective of the oppressed: paths for reflection 1995 ⇒113. Reading from this place 2. 219-236 [OTA 19,467].

2249 *Davies, Philip* God of Cyrus, God of Israel: some religio-historical reflections on Isaiah 40-55. 1995 ⇒24. ^FSAWYER J.,   JSOT.S 195. 207-225.

2250 *Durham, John I.* Isaiah 40-55: a new creation, a new exodus, a new messiah. 1995 ⇒12. ^FHAMRICK E., SBEC 35. 47-56.

2251 *Eaton, J.H.* Festal drama ⇒83. Israelite prophets 1995 <1979>. 247-251.

2252 **Hanson, Paul D.** Isaiah 40-66. Interpretation. LVL 1995, Westminster x; 225 pp. $23/DM198. 0-8042-3132-X.

2253 *Helberg, J.L.* The revelation of the power of God according to Isaiah 40-55. OTEs 8 (1995) 262-279 [sum. 262].

2254 *Heyns, Dalene* God and history in Deutero-Isaiah: considering theology and time. OTEs 8 (1995) 340-355 [sum. 340].

2255 **Koch, Hermann** ... mit Flügeln wie Adler: die Geschichte des Propheten, der Israel tröstet und Heil verkündet allen Völkern; Jesaja, Kapitel 40-55; eine dramatische Erzählung. Stu 1995, Junge Gemeinde 702 pp. 3-7797-0340-8 <pb>.

2256 *Kohn, Risa Levitt; Propp, William H.C.* The name of "Second Isaiah": the forgotten theory of Nehemiah RABBAN. 1995 ⇒10. ^FFREEDMAN D., 223-235.

2257 *Maggioni, Bruno* Il profeta della consolazione. RCI 76 (1995) 581-587.

2258 *Marconcini, Benito* Temi di teologia biblica: temi particolari: Dio creatore e redentore nel Secondo Isaia. 1995 ⇒97. Profeti. 443-448.

2259 **Steck, Odil Hannes** Gottesknecht und Zion: gesammelte Aufsätze zu Deuterojesaja. 1992 ⇒9,239. FAT 4. ^RJSSt 40 (1995) 117-118 (*Gelston, A.*); ThRv 91 (1995) 219-221 (*Wieringen, Archibald L.H.M. van*).

2260 *Wieringen, Archibald L.H.M. van* The application of a new kind of concordance. 1995 ⇒133. Bible et Informatique. 391-410.

2261 **Williamson, H.G.M.** The book called Isaiah: Deutero-Isaiah's role in composition and redaction. NY/Ox 1994, Clarendon xvi; 306 pp. $55/£35. 0-19-826360-0. ^RTS 56 (1995) 772-774 (*Hens-Piazza, Gina*); Reviews in Religion and Theology (1995/2) 78-80 (*Dell, Katharine*).

2262 **Hiebert, Craig Maurice** A rhetorical analysis of selections from the Masoretic Text of Isaiah 40-48. Diss. Acadia 1995, ^D*Ashley, Timothy R.*, 171 pp. MAI 34,987. 0-612-04606-0.

2263 *McLain Carr, David* Isaiah 40:1-11 in the context of the macrostructure of Second Isaiah. 1995 ⇒65. Discourse analysis. 51-74.

2264 *Wagner, Siegfried* Ruf Gottes und Aufbruch (Jes 40,1-11). 1995 ⇒8. ᶠDONNER H., ÄAT 30. 308-315.

2265 **Holter, Knut** Second Isaiah's idol-fabrication passages. BET 28. Fra 1995, Lang 286 pp. 3-631-49261-8 [40,19-46,7].

2266 **Skjoldal, Neil Oden** The election of the people of God: a rhetorical analysis of Isaiah 41:1-44:23. Diss. Trinity Evang. Div. School 1995, ᴰ*Vangemeren, Willem A.*, 251 pp. AAC 9533067; DAI-A 56,2282.

2267 **Farfán Navarro, Enrique** El desierto transformado 1992 ⇒7,3192... 10,3458. AnBib 130. ᴿJSSt 40 (1995) 114-117 (*Barstad, Hans M.*) [41,17-20].

2268 *Kiesow, K.* Wort auf dem Wege: 'seht, ich schaffe Neues—merkt ihr es nicht?'. WuA(M) 36/3 (1995) 134-135 [42,9-10; 42,16-21].

2269 *Goldingay, John* Isaiah 42.18-25. JSOT 67 (1995) 43-65.

2270 ᴱ**Gryson, Roger** Is 44,05-46,13. (Collab. *Auwers, Jean Marie; Baise, Ignace*.) Esaias VL 12/2, Fasc. 4-5. FrB 1995, Herder. 3-451-00124-1 [RBen 106,405; ThRv 91,535].

2271 *Soares-Prabhu, George M.* Laughing at idols: the dark side of biblical monotheism (an Indian reading of Isaiah 44,9-20). 1995 ⇒113. Reading from this place 2. 109-131 [OTA 19,467].

2272 *Blau, Joshua* A misunderstood medieval translation of *śered* (Isaiah 44:13) and its impact on modern scholarship 1995 ⇒21. ᶠMILGROM J., 689-695.

2273 *Spreafico, Ambrogio* Jesaja xliv 26a: ʿabdô oder ʿăbādāyw?: ein Prophet oder ein Politiker? VT 45 (1995) 561-564.

2274 *Eder, Asher* King Cyrus, anointed (Messiah) of the Lord. JBQ 23 (1995) 188-192 [45,1].

2275 *Sarna, Nahum M.* Variant scriptural readings in liturgical texts. 1995 ⇒11. ᶠGREENFIELD J., 203-206 [45,7].

2276 *Pilkington, Christine* The hidden God in Isaiah 45:15: a reflection from holocaust theology. SJTh 48 (1995) 285-300.

2277 ᴱ**Gryson, Roger** Is 46,13-50,3. (Collab. *Auwers, Jean Marie; Baise, Ignace*.) Esaias VL 12/2, Fasc. 4-5. FrB 1995, Herder. 3-451-00124-1 [RBen 106,405; ThRv 91,535].

2278 *Franzmann, Majella* The city as woman: the case of Babylon in Isaiah 47. ABR 43 (1995) 1-19.

2279 *Jacobson, Howard* A Note on Isaiah 51:6. JBL 114 (1995) 291.

E8.5 *Isaiae 53ss, Carmina Servi YHWH:* **Servant Songs.**

2280 **Bastiaens, Jean Charles** Interpretaties van Jesaja 53. 1993 ⇒10,3467. ᴿCBQ 57 (1995) 167-169 (*Olsthoorn, Martin*) [Lk 22,14-38; Acts 3,12-26; 4,23-31; 8,26-40].

2281 *Betz, Otto* The Servant tradition of Isaiah in the Dead Sea Scrolls. JSem 7/1 (1995) 40-56 [sum. 40].

2282 *Clines, D.J.A.* Language as event. ⇒83. Israelite prophets 1995 <1976>. 166-175.

2283 *Hugenberger, G.P.* The servant of the lord in the 'servant songs' of Isaiah: a second Moses figure. 1995 ⇒111. The Lord's anointed. 105-140 [Deut 18,14-23; 34,10-12].

2284 **Laato, Antti** The servant of YHWH and Cyrus...in Isaiah 40-55. 1992 ⇒8,3725... 10,3471. CB.OT 35. ᴿBiOr 52 (1995) 743-745 (*Haak, Robert D.*).

2285 *Marconcini, Benito* Saggi di esegesi: dal libro di Isaia: i canti del Servo. 1995 ⇒97. Profeti. 275-295.

2286 *Pezhumkaltil, Abraham* Psalms on the Servant of the Lord. BiBh 21/1 (1995) 22-36.

2287 **Scharbert, Josef** Deuterojesaja—der "Knecht Jahwes" ?. Hamburg 1995, Kovac 111 pp. 3-86064-319-3.

2288 *Sekine, Seizo* Identity and authorship in the fourth song of the Servant: a redactional attempt at the Second Isaianic theology of redemption I. AJBI 21 (1995) 29-56.

2289 **Varo, Francisco** Los cantos del siervo en la exégesis hispanohebrea. 1993 ⇒9,3619; 10,3476. ᴿCDios 208 (1995) 280-282; Burg. 36 (1995) 241-243 (*Otero Lazaro, T.*); Le Muséon 108/1-2 (1995) 195-196 (*Auwers, J.-M.*); RCatT 20 (1995) 411-412 (*Ferrer, Joan*).

2290 *Willey, Patricia Tull* The servant of YHWH and daughter Zion: alternating visions of YHWH's community. SBL.SP 34 (1995) 267-303.

2291 *Varo, F.* En Šĕlomoh ASTRUC y su comentario a Is 52,13-53,12. Helm. 46 (1995) 147-158 [EThL 72/2-3,198*].

2292 *Polak, Frank H.* "The restful waters of Noah": מי נח - מי מנחות. JANES 23 (1995) 69-74 [54,9].

2293 *Füssel, K.* Rettung für die Verdammten dieser Erde: Jesaja 55, 1-3b (3c-5). JK 56 (1995) 301f.

E8.6 [Trito-]Isaias 56-66.

2294 *Amsler, Samuel* Le Trito-Esaïe: Esaïe 56-66. 1995 ⇒2081. Les derniers prophètes. 41-48.

2295 *Berquist, J.L.* Reading difference in Isaiah 56-66: the interplay of literary and sociological strategies. MethT 7/1 (1995) 23ff [ZID 21,404].

2296 *Blenkinsopp, Joseph* The 'servants of the lord' in Third Isaiah: profile of a pietistic group in the Persian epoch. ⇒83. Israelite prophets 1995 <1983>. 392-412 [Ezra 9-10; Mal 3].

2297 **Lau, Wolfgang** Schriftgelehrte Prophetie in Jes 56-66. 1994 ⇒10,3481. BZAW 225. ᴿThLZ 120 (1995) 782-786 (*Steck, Odil Hannes*).

2298 **Schramm, Brooks** The opponents of Third Isaiah: reconstructing the cultic history of the restoration. Diss. Chicago 1993, ᴰ*Levenson, J.*, JSOT.S 193. Shf 1995, Academic 216 pp. $45/£30. 1-85075-538-8 [OTA 18,645].

2299 **Smith, Paul A.** Rhetoric and redaction in Trito-Isaiah: the structure, growth and authorship of Isaiah 56-66. Diss. C, ᴰ*Gordon, Robert*, VT.S 62. Lei 1995, Brill xi; 228 pp. $63. 90-04-10306-6.

2300 **Steck, Odil H.** Studien zu Tritojesaja. 1991 ⇒7,3225; 8,3752. BZAW 203. VT 45 (1995) 428-429 (*Williamson, H.G.M.*).

2301 *Ebach, Jürgen* "Hoch und heilig wohne ich—und bei dem Zermalmten und Geisterniederten": Versuch über die Schwere Gottes. 1995 ⇒46. Hiobs Post. 183-211 [57,15].

2302 *Schneider, Stanley; Berke, Joseph H.* שׁד breast, robbery or the devil? JBQ 23 (1995) 86-90 [60,16].

2303 *Aejmelaeus, Anneli* Der Prophet als Klageliedsänger: zur Funktion des Psalms Jes 63,7-64,11 in Tritojesaja. ZAW 107 (1995) 31-50.

2304 **Vanoni, Gottfried** "Du bist doch unser Vater" (Jes 63,16): zur Gottesvorstellung des Ersten Testaments. SBS 159. Stu 1995, Katholisches Bibelwerk 114 pp. DM39.80. 3-460-04591-4 [ThRv 91,535].

2305 **Wu, San-Jarn Timothy** A literary study of Isaiah 63-65 and its echo in Revelation 17-22. Diss. Trinity Evang. Div. School 1995, 312 pp. ᴰ*Vangemeren, Willem A.* AAC 9533070; DAI-A 56,2296.

E8.7 Jeremias.

2306 **Ellis, Peter** I libri di Geremia e di Baruc. ᵀ*Zoggia, R.*, La Bibbia per tutti 14. Brescia 1995, Queriniana 196 pp. L24.000. 88-399-2114-1 [CivCatt 147,532].

2307 **Fischer, Georg** Il libro di Geremia. Guide spirituali all'Antico Testamento. R 1995, Città Nuova 199 pp. 88-311-3739-5.

2308 *Hubmann, Franz* Bemerkungen zur älteren Diskussion um die Unterschiede zwischen MT und G im Jeremiabuch. 1995 ⇒86. Jeremia. BBB 98. 263-270.

2309 **Huey, F.B.** Jeremiah, Lamentations. 1993 ⇒9,3641. NAC 16. ᴿCBQ 57 (1995) 556-557 (*McConville, J. Gordon*); HebStud 36 (1995) 179-180 (*Younger, Lawson K., Jr.*).

2310 **Keown, Gerald L.; Scalise, Pamela J.; Smothers, Thomas G.** Jeremiah 26-52. WBC 27. Dallas, Texas 1995, Word xxix; 403 pp. $29. 0-8499-0226-6 [BoL 1996,61].

2311 **Wanke, Gunther** Jeremia 1,1-25,14. ZBK 20. Z 1995, Theologischer 227 pp. Teilband 1 [EThL 72/2-3,198*].

2312 *Begg, Christopher* Jeremiah under Jehoiakim according to Josephus (Ant. 10.89-95). Abr-n. 33 (1995) 1-16 [26; 36].

2313 **Bonora, Antonio** Geremia, uomo dei dolori. 1992 ⇒8,3758... 10,3490. ᴿEO 12 (1995) 465-466 (*Stadelmann, Andreas*). ᴱ**Groß, Walter** Jeremia und die 'deuteronomistische Bewegung'. 1995 ⇒86. BBB 98.

2314 *Herrmann, Siegfried* Jeremia vor Chananja: die angebliche Krise des Propheten. 1995 ⇒37. ᶠWᴀɢɴᴇʀ S., 117-122 [28].

2315 **King, Philip J.** Jeremiah: an archaeological companion. 1993 ⇒9,3643; 10,3504. ᴿJNSL 21/2 (1995) 143-144 (*Cornelius, Izak*); HebStud 36 (1995) 181-182 (*Younger, K. Lawson, Jr.*); CritRR 8 (1995) 130-132 (*Matthews, Victor H.*).

2316 *Lampe, Stephen J.* The reluctant prophet. BiTod 33 (1995) 207-211.

2317 *Lenchak, Timothy A.* Jeremiah's vocation. BiTod 33 (1995) 147-151.

2318 **Lundbom, Jack R.** The early career of the prophet Jeremiah. 1993 ⇒9,3665. ᴿCBQ 57 (1995) 150-151 (*Biddle, Mark E.*).

2319 *Marconcini, Benito* Temi de teologia biblica: temi particolari: l'uomo nuovo secondo Geremia ed Ezechiele. 1995 ⇒97. Profeti. 435-441.

2320 **Martini, Carlo Maria** Dein Wort, Herr, verschlang ich: mit Jeremia auf dem Weg der Hoffnung. FrB 1994, Herder 194 pp. DM34. 3-451-234-68-8. ᴿOrdKor 36 (1995) 239 (*Römelt, Johannes*).

2321 **Martini, Carlo Maria** Una voz profética en la ciudad: meditaciones sobre el profeta Jeremías. M 1995, PPC 179 pp. ᴿIter 6 (1995) 142-143 (*Pastore, Corrado*).

2322 **McConville, J. Gordon** Judgment and promise...Jer. 1993 ⇒9,3666; 10,3508. ᴿEvQ 67 (1995) 154-159 (*Millar, J. Gary*).

2323 *McKane, W.* Jeremiah and the wise. ⇒9. ᶠEMERTON J., 1995. 142-151.

2324 **Mesters, C.** Il profeta Geremia. 1994 ⇒10,3509. ᴿClar. 35 (1995) 537-539 (*Sánchez Bosch, Jaime*).

2325 ᵀᴱ**Mortari, Luciana** ORIGENE: omelie su Geremia. CTePa 123. R 1995, Città Nuova 353 pp. L35.000. 88-311-3123-0.

2326 **Mulzac, Kenneth Delinor** The remnant motif in the context of judgement and salvation in the book of Jeremiah. Diss. Andrews 1995. ᴰ*Storfjell, J. Bjornar*, 451 pp. DAI-A 56, 1830.

2327 *Schäfer-Lichtenberger, Christa* Überlegungen zum Hintergrund und zur Entstehung von neuen Einsichten in der Prophetie Jeremias und Ezechiels. WuD 23 (1995) 23-42.

2328 *Schreiner, Josef* Jeremia und die joschijanische Reform: Probleme—Fragen—Antworten. 1995 ⇒86. Jeremia. 11-31.

2329 **Seybold, Klaus** Der Prophet Jeremia. 1993 ⇒10,3515. ᴿRCatT 20 (1995) 197-198 (*Raurell, Frederic*).

2330 **Stipp, Hermann-Josef** Das masoretische und alexandrinische Sondergut des Jeremiabuches. 1994 ⇒10,3516. OBO 136. ᴿEThL 71 (1995) 206-208 (*Lust, J.*).

2331 *Stipp, Hermann-Josef* Probleme des redaktionsgeschichtlichen Modells der Entstehung des Jeremiabuches. 1995 ⇒86. Jeremia. 225-262.

2332 *Stipp, Hermann-Josef* The prophetic messenger formulas in Jeremiah according to the Masoretic and Alexandrian texts. Textus 18 (1995) 63-85.

2333 *Stulman, Louis* Insiders and outsiders in the book of Jeremiah: shifts in symbolic arrangements. JSOT 66 (1995) 65-85.

2334 **Vieweger, Dieter** Die literarischen Beziehungen zwischen den Büchern Jeremia und Ezechiel. 1993 ⇒9,3673; 10,3517. BEAT 26. ᴿThRv 91 (1995) 21-22 (*Stipp, Hermann-Josef*).

2335 **Wendel, Ute** Jesaja und Jeremia: Worte, Motive und Einsichten Jesajas in der Verkündigung Jeremias. Diss. Bonn 1995, ᴰ*Schmidt, W.H.*, Biblisch-theologische Studien 25. Neuk 1995, Neuk. 3-7887-1519-7 [ThRv 92/2,VII].

2336 *Willis, John T.* Dialogue between prophet and audience as a rhetorical device in the book of Jeremiah. 1995 <1985> ⇒83. Israelite prophets. 205-222 [3,21-4,4; 5,12-17; 8,13-17; 8,13-23; 14,1-10; 14,17-15,4].

2337 *Santos, B. Silva* A vocaçâo de Jeremias (Jr 1,5-10). Atualizaçâo 253 (1995) 3-25.

2338 *Bovati, Pietro* "Je ne sais pas parler" (Jr 1,6): réflexions sur la vocation prophétique. 1995 ⇒4. ᶠBEAUCHAMP P., LeDiv 162. 31-52.

2339 *Brandscheidt, Renate* "Bestellt über Völker und Königreiche" (Jer 1,10): Form und Tradition in Jeremia 1. TThZ 104 (1995) 12-37.

2340 *Craghan, John F.* A prophet for all seasons.   BiTod 33 (1995) 212-217 [1,13-19].

2341 *Matthews, Victor H.* Jeremiah 1:13-19. BiTod 33 (1995) 196-201.

2342 *Zipor, Moshe A.* "Scenes from a marriage"—according to Jeremiah. JSOT 65 (1995) 83-91 [2-3].

2343 *Brenner, Athalya* On prophetic propaganda and the politics of "love": the case of Jeremiah. 1995 ⇒68. A feminist companion to the Latter Prophets. 256-274 [2,1-37; 3,1-3; 5,7-8].

2344 *Goldman, Y. A. P.* Crispations théologiques et accidents textuels dans le TM de Jérémie 2. Bib. 76 (1995) 25-52.

2345 *Böhler, Dieter* Geschlechterdifferenz und Landbesitz: Strukturuntersuchungen zu Jer 2,2-4,2. 1995 ⇒86. Jeremia. 91-127.

2346 *Boggio, Giovanni* Saggi di esegesi: dai libri di Geremia, Ezechiele e Daniele: inviti alla conversione (Ger 3,1-4,4). 1995 ⇒97. Profeti. 299-312.

2347 *Shields, Mary E.* Circumcision of the prostitute: gender, sexuality, and the call to repentance in Jeremiah 3:1-4:4. Bibl.Interp. 3 (1995) 61-74.

2348 *Floß, Johannes P.* Methodologische Aspekte exegetischer Hypothesen am Beispiel von Theo Se ɪᴅ Lls Beitrag zur "Tempelrede" 181-185 [7; 26];

2349 *Seidl, Theodor* Jeremias Tempelrede: Polemik gegen die joschijanische Reform?: die Paralleltraditionen Jer 7 und 26 auf ihre Effizienz für das Deuteronomismusproblem in Jeremia befragt 141-179. 1995 ⇒86. Jeremia.

2350 *Boggio, Giovanni* Saggi di esegesi: dai libri di Geremia, Ezechiele e Daniele: il discorso nel tempio (Ger 7,1-15). 1995 ⇒97. Profeti. 313-323.

2351 **Jost, Renate** Frauen, Männer und die Himmelskönigin: Studien zu Jeremia 7,17-18 und Jeremia 44,15-25. Diss. Evang. Theol., ᴰ*Schottroff, W.*, Gü 1995, Gü'er 272 pp. [RTL 26,531].

2352 *Arasakumar, R.* Sin as triple alienation: Jer 9:1-10 in an ecological perspective. VJTR 59 (1995) 421-436.

2353 *Kratz, Reinhard Gregor* Die Rezeption von Jeremia 10 und 29 im Pseudepigraphen Brief des Jeremia. JSJ 26/1 (1995) 2-31.

2354 *Lundbom, Jack R.* Jeremiah 15,15-21 and the call of Jeremiah. SJOT 9 (1995) 143-155.

2355 *Gosse, Bernard* Jérémie 17,1-5aA dans la rédaction massorétique du livre de Jérémie. EstB 53 (1995) 165-180.

2356 *Kegler, J.* Ein Hochverräter im Namen Gottes: Jeremia 20,7-11a (11b,13). JK 56 (1995) 97-100.

2357 *Parajon, G.A.* One and many. ABQ 14/1 (1995) 29ff [14,1-9; ZID 21,409].

2358 *Hermisson, Hans-Jürgen* Kriterien 'wahrer' und 'falscher' Prophetie im Alten Testament: zur Auslegung von Jeremia 23,16-22 und Jeremia 28,8-9. ZThK 92 (1995) 121-139.

2359 *Carroll, Robert P.* Synchronic deconstructions of Jeremiah: diachrony to the rescue?: reflections on some reading strategies for understanding certain problems in the book of Jeremiah. 1995 ⇒99. Synchronic or diachronic?. 39-51 [23,22; 25,3-7; 25,9; 27,6; 51,34].

2360 *Coxon, Peter* Nebuchadnezzar's hermeneutical dilemma. JSOT 66 (1995) 87-97 [27-29].

2361 *Gosse, Bernard* Nabuchodonosor et les évolutions de la rédaction du livre de Jérémie. ScEs 47 (1995) 177-187.

2362 *Lee, Archie C.C.* Exile and return in the perspective of 1997. 1995 ⇒113. Reading 2. 97-108 [29].

2363 *Smelik, K.A.D.* Correspondentie in ballingschap: de literaire en theologische functie van Jeremia 29. ACEBT 14 (1995) 74-89 [EThL 72/2-3,199*].

2364 **Schmid, Konrad** Buchgestalten des Jeremiabuches: Untersuchungen zur Redaktions- und Rezeptionsgeschichte von Jer 30-33 im Kontext des Buches. Diss. Z 1995-96, ᴰ*Steck, O.H.*

2365 *Fischer, Georg* Aufnahme, Wende und Überwindung dtn/r Gedankengutes in Jer 30f. 1995 ⇒86. Jeremia. BBB 98. 129-139.

2366 *Álvarez Barredo, Miguel* Jeremías, cap. 30: fases de su formación. Carthaginensia 11 (1995) 247-262.

2367 *Gosse, Bernard* Le role de Jérémie 30,24 dans la rédaction du livre de Jérémie. BZ 39 (1995) 92-96.

2368 *Leene, Hendrik* Unripe fruit and dull teeth (Jer 31,29; Ez 18,2). 1995 ⇒26. ᶠSᴄʜɴᴇɪᴅᴇʀ W., 82-98.

2369 *Gross, W.* Neuer Bund oder erneuerter Bund: Jer 31,31-34 in der jüngsten Diskussion. 1995 ⇒25. ᶠSᴄʜɴᴇɪᴅᴇʀ T., 89-114.

2370 *Kraus, Hans-Joachim* Der erste und der neue Bund: biblisch-theologische Studie zu Jer 31,31-34: Manfred Jᴏsᴜᴛᴛɪs zum 60. Geburtstag. 1995 ⇒76. Eine Bibel. 59-69.

2371 **Marafioti, Domenico** Sant'Aɢᴏsᴛɪɴᴏ e la nuova alleanza: l'interpretazione agostiniana di Geremia 31,31-34 nell'ambito dell'esegesi patristica. Aloisiana 26. Brescia/R 1995, Morcelliana/Pont. Univ. Gregoriana 400 pp. L55.000. 88-372-1553-3/88-7652-678-1. Annales Theologici 9 (1995) 477-480 (*Tábet, Miguel Ángel*).

2372 *Bogaert, Pierre-Maurice* Les documents placés dans une jarre: texte court et texte long de Jr 32 (LXX 39). 1995 ⇒13. ᶠHᴀʀʟ M., 53-77.

2373 *Oesch, Josef M.* Zur Makrostruktur und Textintentionalität von Jer 32. 215-223;

2374 *Hardmeier, Christof* Jeremia 32,2-15 als Eröffnung der Erzählung von der Gefangenschaft und Befreiung Jeremias in Jer 34,7; 37,3-40,6. 187-214. 1995 ⇒86. Jeremia. BBB 98.

2375 *Knights, C.H.* The structure of Jeremiah 35. ET 106 (1995) 142-144.

2376 *Knights, Chris H.* The Rechabites of Jeremiah 35: forerunners of the Essenes?. 1995 ⇒72. Qumran questions. BiSe 36. 86-91.

2377 *Schart, Aaron* Combining prophetic oracles in Mari letters and Jeremiah 36. JANES 23 (1995) 75-93.

2378 **Huwyler, Beat** Untersuchungen zu den Völkersprüchen in Jeremia 46-49. Diss. Basel 1995. ᴰ*Seybold, K.* [RTL 27,529].
Huddlestun, John R. "Who is this that rises like the Nile?": some Egyptian texts on the inundation and a prophetic trope. ⇒2123 [46,7-8].

2379 **Bellis, Alice Ogden** The structure and composition of Jeremiah 50:2-51:58. Lewiston, NY 1995, Mellen iii; 238 pp. $90. 0-7734-2353-2 [OTA 19,356].

2380 *Piovanelli, P.* La condamnation de la diaspora égyptienne dans le livre de Jérémie (JrA 50,8-51,30 / JrB 43,8-44,30). Transeuphratène 9 (1995) 35-49.

2381   *McKane, William* Jeremiah's instructions to Seraiah (Jeremiah 51:59-64). 1995 ⇒21. F MILGROM J., 697-706.

2382   *Rofé, Alexander* Not exile but annihilation for Zedekiah's people: the purport of Jeremiah 52 in the Septuagint. 1995 ⇒136. VIII Congress. SCSt 41. 165-170.

E8.8   Lamentationes, *Threni;* Baruch

2383   *Assan-Dhote, Isabelle* Le texte antiochien du livre des Lamentations: tradition écrite, traditions orales. 1995 ⇒13. F HARL M., 187-206.

2384   E**Bartoli, Marco** Pietro di Giovanni OLIVI: la caduta di Gerusalemme: il commento al libro delle Lamentazioni. 1991 ⇒8,3827. R Anton. 70 (1995) 306-308 (*Alessandro, Anna d'*).

2385   **Dobbs-Allsopp, F.W.** Weep...city-lament. BibOr 44. 1993 ⇒9,3719; 10,3551. R JAOS 115 (1995) 319 (*Berlin, Adele*).

2386   **Droin, Jean-Marc** Le livre des Lamentations: une traduction et un commentaire. Essais Bibliques. Genève 1995, Labor et Fides 106 pp. FS29/FF98. 2-8309-0761-2.

       Ellis, Peter I libri di Geremia e di Baruc. ⇒2306.

2387   *Geiser, Joël E.* Une école de la prière: le livre des Lamentations. Hokhma 59 (1995) 27-40.

       Huey, F.B. Jeremiah, Lamentations. ⇒2309.

2388   Klaagliederen: de laatste strohalm. Den Bosch 1995, Katholieke Bijbelstichting 48 pp. *f*8.50. 90-6713-935-7 [Str. 64,184].

2389   *Linafelt, Tod* Surviving Lamentations. HBT 17/1 (1995) 45-61.

2390   **Neusner, Jacob** Israel after calamity: the book of Lamentations. The Bible of Judaism Library. Valley Forge 1995, Trinity xxiii; 117 pp. $13. 1-56338-105-2.

2391   *Pietersma, Albert* The acrostic poems of Lamentations in Greek translation. 1995 ⇒136. VIII Congress. SCSt 41. 183-201.

2392   *Renkema, J.* The meaning of the parallel acrostics in Lamentations. VT 45 (1995) 379-383.

2393   *Seidman, Naomi* Burning the book of Lamentations. 1995 ⇒70. Out of the garden. 278-288.

2394   **Westermann, Claus** Lamentations: issues and interpretation. T *Muenchow, Ch.* E/Mp 1995/94, Clark/Fortress xvi; 252 pp. £13/$23. 0-8006-2743-1 (Fortress).

2395   *Beentjes, P.C.* Satirical polemics against idols and idolatry in the letter of Jeremiah (Baruch ch. 6). 1995 ⇒130. Aspects of religious contact. 121-133.

2396   *Kabasele Mukenge, A.* Les citations internes en Ba. 1,15-3,8: un procédé rédactionnel et actualisant. Le Muséon 108 (1995) 211-237 [EThL 72/2-3,200*].

2397   **Lüdy, José Héctor** Daniel, Baruc, Carta de Jeremias. El mensaje del Antiguo Testamento 15. M 1995, Atenas 241 pp. 84-7020-391-6.

2398   *Otzen, Benedikt* Lov og visdom i Baruks bog [Law and wisdom in the book of Baruch]. 1995 ⇒90. Lov og visdom. 36-48 [OTA 19,473].

2399   **Steck, Odil Hannes** Das apokryphe Baruchbuch. 1993 ⇒9,3731. FRLANT 160. ThRv 91 (1995) 468-470 (*Schreiner, Josef*).

E8.9 **Ezekiel:** *textus, commentarii; themata, versiculi.*

2400 **Allen, Leslie C.** Ezekiel 20-48. 1990 ⇒6,3932... 10,3563. WBC 29. ᴿEstB 53 (1995) 406 (*Lage, F.*).
2401 *Allen, Leslie C.* Some types of textual adaption in Ezekiel. EThL 71 (1995) 5-29.
2402 **Greenhill, William** An exposition of Ezekiel in the Geneva series of commentaries. Carlisle, PA 1994, Banner of Truth 859 pp. $42.95. ᴿCTJ 30 (1995) 563-565 (*Muller, Richard A.*).
2403 **Halperin, David** Seeking Ezekiel. 1993 ⇒10,3567. ᴿJR 75 (1995) 405-406 (*Kaminsky, Joel S.*); CBQ 57 (1995) 554-555 (*Hillmer, Mark*); CritRR 8 (1995) 128-130 (*Moore, Michael S.*); Religion 25 (1995) 392-394 (*Jobling, David*).
2404 **Kessler, Stephan Ch.** GREGOR der Große als Exeget: eine theologische Interpretation der Ezechielhomilien. IThS 43. Innsbruck 1995, Tyrolia 292 pp. DM58. 3-7022-2005-4 <pb>.

2405 *Bogaert, Pierre-Maurice* Le lieu de la gloire dans le livre d'Ézéchiel et dans les Chroniques: de l'arche au char. RTL 26 (1995) 281-298.
2406 **Duguid, Iain M.** Ezekiel and the leaders of Israel. 1994 ⇒10,3576. VT.S 56. ᴿWTJ 57 (1995) 480-483 (*Ulrich, Dean R.*).
2407 **Feist, Udo** Ezechiel: das literarische Problem des Buches forschungsgeschichtlich betrachtet. BWANT 138. Stu 1995, Kohlhammer 246 pp. 3-17-013696-8 [ThRv 91,535].
2408 *Fuhs, Hans F.* Ezechiel, Ezechielschriften: biblisch. 1995 ⇒122. LThK 3. 1141-1143.
2409 *Hossfeld, Frank-Lothar* Ezechiel und die deuteronomisch-deuteronomistische Bewegung. 1995 ⇒86. Jeremia. 271-295.
2410 *Joyce, Paul M.* Synchronic and diachronic perspectives on Ezekiel. 1995 ⇒99. Synchronic or diachronic? 115-128.
      Marconcini, Benito Temi...l'uomo nuovo secondo...Ezechiele ⇒2319.
2411 *Savoca, Gaetano* La "morte" e la pienezza di "vita" in Ezechiele. PSV 32 (1995) 53-62.
      Schäfer-Lichtenberger, Christa Überlegungen...Jeremias und Ezechiels ⇒2327.
2412 *Strong, J.* Ezekiel's use of the recognition formula in his oracles against the nations. PRSt 22 (1995) 115-133.
2413 *Vianès, Laurence* Les *Gloses* sur Ezéchiel d'HESYCHIUS de Jérusalem dans le *Laurentianus Pluteus* XI 4. REAug 41 (1995) 315-323 [sum. rés. 323].
      Vieweger, Dieter Die literarischen Beziehungen zwischen den Büchern Jeremia und Ezechiel. ⇒2334.

2414 *Monari, Luciano* Saggi di esegesi: dai libri di Geremia, Ezechiele e Daniele: la visione della gloria di Dio (Ez 1,4-28). 1995 ⇒97. Profeti. 325-336.
2415 *Jensen, Robin M.* Of cherubim and gospel symbols. BArR 21/4 (1995) 42-43, 65 [1,5-10; Rev 4,6-7].
2416 *Borowski, Elie* Cherubim: God's throne?. BArR 21/4 (1995) 36-41 [1,10; 1 Kgs 6,27].
2417 **Christman, Angela Gale Russell** Ezekiel's vision of the chariot in early christian exegesis. Diss. Virginia 1995, ᴰWilken, Robert L., 270 pp. AAC 9600437; DAI-A 56,3617 [1].

2418 *Seidel, Bodo* Ezechiel und die zu vermutenden Anfänge der
      Schriftreligion im Umkreis der unmittelbaren Vorexilszeit: oder:
      die Bitternis der Schriftrolle. ZAW 107 (1995) 51-64 [2; 2 Kgs 22;
      Jer 36].

2419 *Sedlmeier, Franz* "Deine Brüder, deine Brüder...": die Beziehung
      von Ez 11,14-21 zur dtn-dtr Theologie. 1995 ⇒86. Jeremia. 297-
      312.

2420 *Bowen, Nancy R.* Can God be trusted?: confronting the deceptive
      God. 1995 ⇒68. A feminist companion to the Latter Prophets. 354-
      365 [14,1-11].

2421 **Galambush, Julie** Jerusalem in the book of Ezekiel... 1992
      ⇒8,3876; 9,3760. SBL.DS 130. ᴿCritRR 7 (1994) 539-540
      (*Strong, John T.*); CBQ 57 (1995) 133-135 (*Schmitt, John L.*);
      JSSt 40 (1995) 328-329 (*Curtis, A.H.W.*) [16; 23].

2422 *Pope, Marvin H.* Mixed marriage metaphor in Ezekiel 16. 1995
      ⇒10. ᶠFREEDMAN D., 384-399.

2423 *Swanepoel, M.G.* Esegiël 17:1-24: onopgeloste raaisels in jou lewe
      [Ezek 17:1-24: unsolved riddles in your life?]?. Acta Theologica
      15 102-110 [OTA 19,104].

2424 *Dijk-Hemmes, Fokkelien van* The metaphorization of woman in
      prophetic speech: an analysis of Ezekiel 23. 1995 ⇒68. A feminist
      companion to the Latter Prophets. 244-255.

2425 *Newsom, Carol A.* A maker of metaphors: Ezekiel's oracles against
      Tyre. 1995 <1984> ⇒83. Israelite Prophets. 191-204 [26-28].

2426 *Albrektson, Bertil* Ezekiel 30:16—a conjecture. 1995 ⇒14.
      ᶠHARTMAN L., 5-10.

2427 *Kempinski, Aharon* From death to resurrection: the early evidence.
      BArR 21/5 (1995) 56-65 [37].

2428 *Fox, Michael V.* The rhetoric of Ezekiel's vision of the valley of
      the bones. 1995 ⇒83. Israelite Prophets. 176-190 [37].

2429 *Irwin, Brian P.* Molek imagery and the slaughter of Gog in Ezekiel
      38 and 39. JSOT 65 (1995) 93-112 [Isa 30,27-33; Jer 7,30-34].

2430 *Kaltner, John* The Gog/Magog tradition in the Hebrew Bible and
      the Qur'an: points of similarity and dissimilarity. USQR 49 1/4
      (1995) 35-48 [38].

2431 **Tuell, Steven Shaun** The law of the temple in Ezekiel 40-48. 1992
      ⇒8,3893... 10,3595. HSM 49. ᴿJAOS 115 (1995) 120-121
      (*Schramm, Brooks*).

2432 *Cook, Stephen L.* Innerbiblical interpretation in Ezekiel 44 and the
      history of Israel's priesthood. JBL 114 (1995) 193-208.

2433 *Zwickel, Wolfgang* Die Tempelquelle Ezechiel 47: eine traditions-
      geschichtliche Untersuchung. EvTh 55 (1995) 140-154.

2434 *Anbar, Moshé* Deux "mots en vedette" dans une vision d'Ezéchiel
      (Ez 48,9-11). ZAW 107 (1995) 490-492.

E9.1 Apocalyptica VT.

2435 *Albrile, Ezio* Enoch e l'Iran: un'ipotesi sulle origini
      dell'apocalittica. Nicolaus 22/2 (1995) 91-136.

2436 ᴱ**Bull, Malcolm** Apocalypse theory and the end of the world.
      Wolfson College Lectures. Ox 1995, Blackwell viii; 297 pp. 0-
      631-19082-1.

2437 ^E**Cerutti, Maria Vittoria** Apocalittica e gnosticismo: atti del Colloquio Internazionale Roma, 18-19 giugno 1993. R 1995, GEI 167 pp. 88-8011-057-8. ^RComp. 40 (1995) 607-609 (*Romero-Pose, Eugenio*).

2438 **Cohn, Norman** Cosmos, chaos and the world to come. 1993 ⇒9,3782; 10,3597. ^RCBQ 57 (1995) 122-123 (*Redditt, Paul L.*).

2439 *Collins, J.J.* The origin of evil in apocalyptic literature and the Dead Sea Scrolls. 1995 ⇒135. VT.S 61. 25-38.

      Cook, Stephen L. Prophecy & apocalypticism ⇒2106.

2440 *Fusco, Vittorio* Apocalyptique et eschatologie selon Jean CARMIGNAC. 1995 ⇒4. ^FBEAUCHAMP P., LeDiv 162. 225-244.

2441 *Greenberg, Moshe* Reflections on apocalyptic. 1995 ⇒49. Studies. 163-173.

2442 *Kampen, John* The genre and function of apocalyptic literature in the African American experience. 1995 ⇒114.. Text and experience. 43-65.

2443 *Koch, Klaus* Die Bedeutung der Apokalyptik für die Interpretation der Schrift. 1995 ⇒2462 Studien. 16-45.

      ^E**Marconcini, Benito** Profeti e apocalittici. 1995 ⇒97.

2444 *Marconcini, Benito* L'apocalittica biblica. 1995 ⇒97. Profeti e apocalittici. 193-244.

2445 **Russell, David Syme** L'apocalittica giudaica. 1991 ⇒7,3338... 9,3789. ^RIrén. 68 (1995) 146-147.

2446 **Sacchi, Paolo** L'apocalittica giudaica e la sua storia. 1990 ⇒6,3984... 10,3605. ^RBZ 39 (1995) 115-116 (*Maier, Johann*).

E9.2 **Daniel:** *textus, commentarii; themata, versiculi.*

2447 **Collins, John J.** Daniel. Hermeneia. 1993 ⇒9,3794... 10,3610. ^RJThS 46 (1995) 224-225 (*Goldingay, John*); EThL 71 (1995) 208-209 (*Lust, J.*); AUSS 33 (1995) 113-115 (*Miller, James E.*); BTB 25 (1995) 144 (*Burns, John Barclay*); RB 102 (1995) 278-290 (*Grelot, Pierre*).

2448 **Di Lella, Alexander Anthony** Il libro di Daniele 1, cap. 1-6; 2, cap. 7-14. Guide spirituali all'Antico Testamento. R 1995, Città Nuova 2 vols; 158+126 pp. L18.000+14.000. 88-311-3740-9; - 42-5 [OTA 19,356].

2449 *Haag, Ernst* Daniel: Das Buch Daniel. 1995 ⇒122. LThK 3. 10-11.

2450 *Jobes, Karen H.* A comparative syntactic analysis of the Greek versions of Daniel: a test case for new methodology. BIOSCS 28 (1995) 19-41.

      Lüdy, José Héctor Daniel...⇒2397.

2451 **Miller, Stephen R.** Daniel. 1994 ⇒10,3614. NAC 18. ^RRevBib 57 (1995) 248-249 (*Croatto, J. Severino*).

2452 *Munnich, Olivier* Les versions grecques de Daniel et leurs substrats sémitiques. 1995 ⇒136. VIII Congress. SCSt 41. 291-308.

2453 ^{TE}**Parker, T.H.L.** Daniel 1 (Chapters 1-6). 1993 ⇒9,3799. Calvin's Old Testament Commentaries. ^RSBET 13/1 (1995) 90-91 (*Cook, Peter*).

2454 **Péter-Contesse, René; Ellington, John** A handbook on the book of Daniel. 1993 ⇒10,3616. ^RCBQ 57 (1995) 570 (*Aaron, Charles L.*).

Steck, O.H. (*al.*) Das Buch Baruch: zu...Daniel. ⇒1383.
2455 **Taylor, Richard A.** The Peshiṭta of Daniel. 1994 ⇒10,3620.
MPIL 7. ᴿJSSt 40 (1995) 346-347 (*Lane, D.J.*); JBL 114 (1995)
508-509 (*Collins, John J.*).

2456 **Barber, Raymond** A dozen diamonds from Daniel. Murfreesboro,
Tenn. 1995, Sword of the Lord 213 pp. 0-87398-177-4.
2457 *Bunge, Wiep van* Balthasar BEKKER on *Daniel*: an early enlightenment critique of millenarianism. History of European Ideas 21
(1995) 659-673.
2458 *Ego, Beate* Daniel und die Rabbinen: ein Beitrag zur Geschichte
des alttestamentlichen Kanons. Jud. 51/1 (1995) 18-32.
2459 *Frerichs, W.W.* How many weeks until the end? WWorld 15/2
(1995) 166-174 [NTAb 40,85].
2460 *George, J.-A.* Repentance and retribution: the use of the book of
Daniel in Old and Middle English texts. BJRL 77/3 (1995) 177-
192.
2461 *Helberg, J. L.* The determination of history according to the book
Daniel: against the background of deterministic apocalyptic. ZAW
107 (1995) 273-287.
2462 **Koch, Klaus** Die Reiche der Welt und der kommende Menschensohn: Studien zum Danielbuch. Gesammelte Aufsätze 2.
ᴱ*Rösel, Martin.* Neuk 1995, Neuk 192 pp. DM44. 3-7887-1515-4
<pb>:
2463 Ist Daniel auch unter den Profeten? <1985>, 1-15;
2464 Weltgeschichte und Gottesreich im Danielbuch und die iranischen
Parallelen <1991>, 46-65.
2465 *Mastin, B.A.* Wisdom and Daniel. ⇒9. ᶠEMERTON J., 1995. 161-
169.
2466 *Munnich, Olivier* Les nomina sacra dans les versions grecques de
Daniel et leurs suppléments deutérocanoniques. 1995 ⇒13. ᶠHARL
M., 145-167.
2467 **Otzen, B.** Daniels bog fortolket. København 1995, Danske Bibelselskab 97 pp. DKR140. 87-7523-3312 [BoL 1996,67].
Ruth-Judith-Ester-Susanna: trouw door dik en dun. ⇒1043.
2468 *Segert, Stanislav* Poetic structures in the Hebrew sections of the
book of Daniel. 1995 ⇒11. ᶠGREENFIELD J., 261-275.
2469 **Stahl, R.** Von Weltengagement...Danielbuch. 1994 ⇒10,3629.
ᴿOTEs 8 (1995) 156-158 (*Steyn, Pieter E.*).
2470 **Tomasino, Anthony James** Daniel and the revolutionaries: the use
of the Daniel tradition by Jewish resistance movements of late Second Temple Palestine. Diss. Chicago 1995, 360 pp. ᴰ*Golb, Norman*, DAI-A 56,1832.
2471 *Widengren, Geo* Les quatre âges du monde. Apocalyptique iranienne et dualisme qoumrânien. ᴱ**Widengren, Geo.** Recherches
Intertestamentaires 2. P 1995, Maisonneuve ii; 224 pp. 23-62
[OTA 19,285].
2472 ᴱ**Woude, A.S. van der** The book of Daniel in the light of new findings. 1993 ⇒9,420; 10,3633. BEThL 106. ᴿBijdr. 56/1 (1995)
74-75 (*Beentjes, P.C.*); JThS 46 (1995) 226-227 (*Casey, P.M.*);
CBQ 57 (1995) 630-631 (*Humphreys, W. Lee*).

2473 **Margain, Jean** Le livre de Daniel: commentaire philologique. 1994 ⇒10,3641. ʀREJ 154/1-2 (1995) 133-135 (*Schattner-Rieser, Ursula*).

2474 *McLay, Tim* A collation of variants from 967 to Zɪᴇɢʟᴇʀ's critical edition of Susanna, Daniel, Bel et Draco. Textus 18 (1995) 121-134.

2475 **Meadowcroft, T.J.** Aramaic Daniel and Greek Daniel: a literary comparison. Diss. (⇒10,3635) JSOT.S 198. Shf 1995, Academic 336 pp. £37.50. 1-85075-551-5. ʀEThL 71 (1995) 447-448 (*Lust, J.*).

2476 **Miegge, Mario** Il sogno del re di Babilonia: profezia e storia da Thomas Mᴜᴇɴᴛᴇʀ a Isaac Nᴇᴡᴛᴏɴ. Mi 1995, Feltrinelli 219 pp. [2].
    Brown Tkacz, Catherine The seven Maccabees, the three Hebrews and a newly discovered sermon of St. Aᴜɢᴜsᴛɪɴᴇ (Mayence 50) ⇒1394.

2477 *Husser, Jean-Marie* La fin et l'origine: conséquence inattendue de l'eschatologie en Dn 2. 1995 ⇒22. ꜰRᴇɴᴀᴜᴅ B., LeDiv 159. 243-264.

2478 *Bianchi, F.* Note in margine al libro di Daniele: Dn 3,8; 6,5 (= Gv 13,26) e Dn 8,2.3.6. RivBib 43 (1995) 521-535.

2479 *Koch, Klaus* Der "Märtyrertod" als Sühne in der aramäischen Fassung des Asarja-Gebetes Dan 3,38-40. 1995 <1992> ⇒2462. Die Reiche. 66-82.

2480 *Cowe, S. Peter* The Caucasian versions of the song of the three (Dan 3:51-90). 1995 ⇒136. VIII Congress. SCSt 41. 309-333.

2481 *Koch, Klaus* Gottes Herrschaft über das Reich des Menschen: Dan 4 im Licht neuer Funde. 1995 <1993> ⇒2462. Die Reiche. 83-124.

2482 *Hilton, Michael* Babel reversed—Daniel chapter 5. JSOT 66 (1995) 99-112.

2483 *Koch, Klaus* Dareios, der Meder. 1995 <1983> ⇒2462. Die Reiche. 125-139 [6,1].

2484 *Grelot, Pierre* Daniel VI dans la Septante. 1995 ⇒13. ꜰHᴀʀʟ M., 103-118.

2485 *Frei, Peter* Die persische Reichsautorisation: ein Überblick. ZABRG 1 (1995) 1-35 [6].

2486 *Wiesehöfer, Josef* 'Reichsgesetz' oder 'Einzelfallgerechtigkeit'? Bemerkungen zu P. Fʀᴇɪs These von der achaimenidischen 'Reichsautorisation'. ZABRG 1 (1995) 36-46 [6].

2487 *Stuckenbruck, Loren T.* "One like a son of man as the Ancient of Days" in the Old Greek recension of Daniel 7,13: scribal error or theological translation?. ZNW 86 (1995) 268-276.

2488 *Monari, Luciano* Saggi di esegesi: dai libri di Geremia, Ezechiele e Daniele: la visione del figlio dell'uomo (Dn 7). 1995 ⇒97. Profeti. 337-354.

2489 *Koch, Klaus* Das Reich der Heiligen und des Menschensohns: ein Kapitel politischer Theologie. 1995 ⇒2462. Die Reiche. 140-172 [7].

2490 **Burnier-Genton, Jean** Le rêve subversif d'un sage: Daniel 7. 1993 ⇒9,3824. MoBi 27. ʀRevSR 69 (1995) 398-399 (*Husser, Jean-Marie*); OTEs 8 (1995) 152-154 (*Steyn, Pieter. E.*).

2491 *Christie-Miller, Ian* Matfre Eʀᴍᴇɴɢᴀᴜᴅ's Breviari d'amor and Daniel 9,26. JSOT 66 (1995) 113-117.

2492 *Cáceres Guinet, Hugo* Enseñar y no pelear (Dan 12,3). RTLi 29 (1995) 379-393.
2493 *Glancy, Jennifer* The accused: Susanna and her readers. 1995 ⇒1343. A feminist companion to Esther. 288-302 [13].
2494 *Levine, Amy-Jill* "Hemmed in on every side": Jews and women in the book of Susanna. 1995 ⇒1343. A Feminist Companion to Esther. 303-323 [13].

E9.3 *Prophetae Minores*, **Dōdekaprophēton...Hosea, Joel.**

E**Bellis, Alice Ogden** Many voices: multicultural responses to the Minor Prophets. 1995 ⇒62.
2495 *Carbone, Sandro Paolo; Rizzi, Giovanni* 'Memra e paradosis': progetto di lavoro per la traduzione sinottica di TM-LXX-Tg-Profeti Minori nella collana EDB 'La Parola e la sua tradizione'. RivBib 43 (1995) 363-379.
2496 **Gordon, Robert P.** Studies in the Targum to the Twelve Prophets: from Nahum to Malachi. 1994 ⇒10,3651. VT.S 51. R JThS 46 (1995) 233-235 (*Hayward, C.T.R.*); CritRR 8 (1995) 126-128 (*Chilton, Bruce*).
2497 *Jeremias, Jörg* Die Anfänge des Dodekapropheton: Hosea und Amos. 1995 ⇒135. Congress Volume: Paris 1992. VT.S 61. 87-106.
2498 **Jones, Barry Alan** The formation of the book of the Twelve: a study in text and canon. SBL.DS 149. Atlanta, GA 1995 Scholars xii; 266 pp. $40/$25. 0-7885-0108-9/09-7.
2499 *Lescow, Theodor* Die Komposition der Bücher Nahum und Habakuk. BN 77 (1995) 59-85.
2500 E**McComiskey, T.E.** The Minor Prophets: Obadiah, Jonah, Micah, Nahum and Habakkuk. 1993 ⇒9,3838. R OTEs 8 (1995) 309-311 (*Krüger, A.J.*).
2501 **Nogalski, James** Literary precursors to the Book of the Twelve;
2502 Redactional processes in the Book of the Twelve. 1993 ⇒10,3656. BZAW 217-218. R OLZ 90 (1995) 181-184 (*Schunck, Klaus-Dietrich*); JBL 114 (1995) 720-722 (*Rogers, Jeffrey S.*).
2503 **Smith, Billy K.; Page, Frank S.** Amos, Obadiah, Jonah. NAC 19B. Nv 1995, Broadman & Holman 304 pp. 0-8054-0142-3.
2504 *Tassin, Claude* Les prophètes ont-ils disparu? 1995 ⇒2081. Les derniers prophètes 62-63.

2505 **Carbone, Sandro Paolo; Rizzi, Giovanni** Il libro di Osea...masoretico, greco, targum aramaico. 1993 ⇒8,3962... 10,3660. R LASBF 45 (1995) 633-4, 636-9 (*Bottini, Giovanni Claudio*).
2506 **Davies, Graham I.** Hosea. 1992 ⇒8,3964. NCBC. CritRR 7 (1994) 111-112 (*March, W. Eugene*).
2507 **Landy, Francis** Hosea. Readings. Shf 1995, Academic 192 pp. £30/$50. 1-85075-549-3 [BoL 1996,62].
2508 *Mulzer, Martin* Satzgrenzen im Hoseabuch im Vergleich von Hebräischer und Griechischer Texttradition. BN 79 (1995) 37-53.

2509 **Diop, A. Ganoune** The name 'Israel' and related expressions in the books of Amos and Hosea. Diss. Andrews 1995, 451 pp.

^D*Davidson, Richard*, AAC 9530651; DAI-A 56,1846.
2510 *Fontaine, Carole R.* Hosea 40-59;
2511 *Fontaine, Carole R.* A response to "Hosea" 60-69;
2512 *Graetz, Naomi* God is to Israel as husband is to wife: the metaphoric battering of Hosea's wife 126-145. 1995 ⇒68. A feminist companion to the Latter Prophets.
2513 **Holt, Else Kragelund** Prophesying the past: the use of Israel's history in the book of Hosea. Diss. JSOT.S 194. Shf 1995, Academic 160 pp. $41/£27.50. 1-85075-540-X [OTA 18,647].
2514 *Landy, Francis* In the wilderness of speech: problems of metaphor in Hosea. Bibl.Interp. 3 (1995) 35-59.
2515 *Macintosh, A.A.* Hosea and the wisdom tradition: dependence and independence. ⇒9. ^FEMERTON J., 1995. 124-132.
2516 *Ogden Bellis, Alice* The book of Hosea. 1995 ⇒62. Many voices. 19-20.
2517 *Schäfer-Lichtenberger, Christa* JHWH, Hosea und die drei Frauen im Hoseabuch. EvTh 55 (1995) 114-140.
2518 **Simian-Yofre, Horacio** El desierto de los dioses...Oseas. 1993 ⇒9,3854; 10,3664. ^RREB 55 (1995) 249-251 (*Garmus, Ludovico*); ThX 45 (1995) 105-108 (*Arango, José Roberto*); Strom. 51/1-2 (1995) 175-177 (*Albistur, F.E.*); EstB 53 (1995) 547-549 (*Estévez, Elisa*); ScrTh 27 (1995) 1057-1059 (*Ausín, S.*); Asp. 42 (1995) 591-592 (*Di Palma, G.*).
2519 *Smith, Clyde Curry* "Aha, Assyria!: rod of my fury, very staff of my sentencing-curse". 1995 ⇒24. ^FSAWYER J., JSOT.S 195. 182-206.
2520 **Šporčić, Ivan** Das untreue Volk: zum Sprachfeld der Untreue bei Hosea. Diss. Pont. Univ. Gregoriana 1995, no. 4126, Rijeka 118 pp. (excerpt), ^D*Conroy, Charles*.
2521 **Wacker, Marie-Theres** Strukturen des Weiblichen im Hoseabuch: literarische, entstehungsgeschichtliche und religionsgeschichtliche Studien unter besonderer Berücksichtigung von Hosea 1-3. Diss.-Habil. Müns 1995, ^D*Zenger, E.* [ThRv 92/2,IV] = :
2522 Figurationen des Weiblichen im Hoseabuch. Herders Biblische Studien 8. FrB 1996, Herder ix; 384 pp. 3-451-23951-5. ^RUF 27 (1995) 729-730 (*Loretz, O.*).
2523 *Wacker, Marie-Theres* Traces of the goddess in the book of Hosea. 1995 ⇒68. A feminist companion to the Latter Prophets. 219-241.

2524 *Goldingay, John* Hosea 1-3, Genesis 1-4, and masculist interpretation. HBT 17/1 (1995) 25-36.
2525 *Goldingay, John* Hosea 1-3, Genesis 1-4, and masculist interpretation 161-168;
2526 *Sherwood, Yvonne* Boxing Gomer: controlling the deviant woman in Hosea 1-3 101-125;
2527 *Keefe, Alice A.* The female body, the body politic and the land: a sociopolitical reading of Hosea 1-2 70-100. 1995 ⇒68. A feminist companion to the Latter Prophets.
2528 *Irvine, Stuart A.* The threat of Jezreel (Hosea 1:4-5). CBQ 57 (1995) 494-503.
2529 *Schmitt, John J.* Yahweh's divorce in Hosea 2—who is that woman?. SJOT 9 (1995) 119-132.

2530 *Landy, Francis* Fantasy and the displacement of pleasure: Hosea 2,4-17. 1995 ⇒68. A feminist companion to the Latter Prophets. 146-160.

2531 **Mariadass Devadass, Ambrose** New marriage in Hosea (Hos 2,18-25): a historico-critical and canonical study. Diss. Inst. Cath. de Paris 1994, I 352 pp.; II 356-663 pp. RICP 55 (1995) 213-215 (ᴰ*Briend, Jacques*).

2532 *Muraoka, Takamitsu* Hosea III in the Septuagint version. 1995 ⇒24. ᶠSᴀᴡʏᴇʀ J., JSOT.S 195. 242-252.

2533 *Gruber, Mayer I.* Marital fidelity and intimacy: a view from Hosea 4. 1995 ⇒68. A feminist companion to the Latter Prophets. 169-179.

2534 *Brueggemann, Walter* The uninflected *therefore* of Hosea 4:1-3. 1995 ⇒112. Reading 1. 231-249 [OTA 19,476].

2535 *Schuman, N.A.* Hosea 4:1-3: de schepping teruggedraaid?. ACEBT 14 (1995) 90-105 [EThL 72/2-3,202*].

2536 *Odell, Margaret S.* I will destroy your mother: the obliteration of a cultic role in Hosea 4.4-6. 1995 ⇒68. A feminist companion to the Latter Prophets. 180-193.

2537 *Gangloff, Frédéric; Haelewyck, Jean-Claude* Osée 4,17-19: un marzeah en l'honneur de la déesse Anat?. EThL 71 (1995) 370-382.

2538 *Paul, Shalom M.* Hosea 7:16: Gibberish Jabber. 1995 ⇒21. ᶠMɪʟɢʀᴏᴍ J., 707-712.

2539 *Irvine, Stuart A.* Politics and prophetic commentary in Hosea 8:8-10. JBL 114 (1995) 292-294.

2540 *Bons, Eberhard* Zwei Überlegungen zum Verständnis von Hosea xi. VT 45 (1995) 285-293.

2541 *Schüngel-Straumann, Helen* God as mother in Hosea 11. 1995 ⇒68. A feminist companion to the Latter Prophets. 194-218.

2542 *Lohfink, Norbert* "Ich komme nicht in Zornesglut" (Hos 11,9): Skizze einer synchronen Leseanweisung für das Hoseabuch. 1995 ⇒22. ᶠRᴇɴᴀᴜᴅ B., LeDiv 159. 163-190.

2543 **Ramirez, Felipe-Fruto** The Jacob typology in Hosea 12. Diss. Pont. Univ. Gregoriana 1995, no. 4134, excerpt 80 pp. ᴰ*Simian-Yofre, Horacio*.

2544 *Pennacchio, Maria Cristina* "Quasi ursa raptis catulis" Os 13,8 nell'esegesi di Gᴇʀᴏʟᴀᴍᴏ e Cɪʀɪʟʟᴏ di Alessandria. VetChr 32/1 (1995) 143-161.

2545 *Couturier, G.* Yahweh et les déesses cananéennes en Osée 14,9. 1995 ⇒35. ᶠTɪʟʟᴀʀᴅ J., BEThL 121. 245-264 [EThL 72,203*].

2546 *Amsler, Samuel* Le prophète Joël. 1995 ⇒2081. Les derniers prophètes. 49-55.

2547 *Andiñach, Pablo R.* El Día de Yavé en la profecia de Joel. RevBib 57 (1995) 1-17.

2548 **Crenshaw, James L.** Joel: a new translation with introduction and commentary. AncB 24C. NY 1995, Doubleday xiv; 251 pp. $32.50. 0-385-41205-3.

2549 *Crenshaw, James L.* Who knows what YHWH will do?: the character of God in the book of Joel. 1995 ⇒10. Fʀᴇᴇᴅᴍᴀɴ D., 185-196 [Joel 2,12-14].

2550 *Duval, Yves-Marie* Vers le Commentaire sur Joël d'Oʀɪɢᴇɴᴇ. 1995 ⇒126. Origeniana Sexta. BEThL 118. 393-410.

2551 **MacQueen, Larry R.** Joel and the spirit: the cry of a prophetic hermeneutic. JPentec Suppl. 8. Shf 1995, Academic 125 pp. £10. 1-85075-736-4 <pb>.

2552 *Ogden Bellis, Alice* The book of Joel. 1995 ⇒62. Many voices. 83.

2553 *Petit, Olivier* Bref parcours du livre de Joël. SémBib 77 (1995) 41-47.

2554 **Simkins, Ronald A.** Yahweh's activity in history and nature in the book of Joel. 1991 ⇒7,3411... 10,3688. ANETS 10. ᴿJBL 114 (1995) 140-142 (*Lowery, Richard H.*).

2555 *Simkins, Ronald A.* The day of the locusts. BiTod 33 (1995) 23-27.

2556 *Jaeggli, J. Randolph* God's wake-up call (Joel 1). BVp 29 (1995) 9-15 [OTA 19,288].

2557 *Rude, Terry* God glorifies in forgiveness (Joel 2:1-20). BVp 29 (1995) 17-22 [OTA 19,288].

2558 *Barrett, Michael P.V.* Pentecost and other blessings (Joel 2:21-28). BVp 29 (1995) 23-34 [OTA 19,288].

2559 *Boggio, Giovanni* Saggi di esegesi: dai profeti minori: il dono della spirito (Gl 3,1-5). 1995 ⇒97. Profeti. 383-389.

2560 *Wisdom, Thurman* The valley of decision (Joel 3). BVp 29 (1995) 35-41 [OTA 19,289].

E9.4 **Amos.**

2561 **Andersen, Francis I.; Freedman, David Noel** Amos. 1989 ⇒5,3827... 9,3878. AncB 24A. ᴿJNES 54 (1995) 156-157 .(*Pardee, Dennis*).

2562 *Autané, Maurice* Israël au temps d'Amos. DosB 59 (1995) 6-7.

2563 **Bovati, Pietro; Meynet, Roland** La fin d'Israël: paroles d'Amos. 1994 ⇒10,3691. LiBi 101. ᴿEeV 105 (1995) 313-314 (*Monloubou, Louis*).

2564 **Bovati, Pietro; Meynet, Roland** Il libro del profeta Amos. Retorica biblica 2. R 1995, Dehoniane 473 pp. L55.000. 88-396-0564-9. ᴿCivCatt 146 (1995) 199-200 (*Scaiola, D.*).

2565 **Carbone, Sandro Paolo; Rizzi, Giovanni** Il libro di Amos: lettura ebraica, greca e aramaica. 1993 ⇒10,3693. ᴿLASBF 45 (1995) 633-634, 639-640 (*Bottini, Giovanni Claudio*).

2566 **Jeremias, Jörg** Der Prophet Amos: übersetzt und erklärt. ATD 24/2. Gö 1995, Vandenhoeck & Ruprecht xxii; 137 pp. DM36. 3-525-51226-0.

2567 *Pigott, Susan M.* Amos: an annotated bibliography. SWJT 38/1 (1995) 29-35.

2568 **Baker, Robert G.** Amos: doing what is right: a study guide. Macon, Ga. 1995, Smyth & Helwys 137 pp. 1-57312-020-0.

2569 *Beyer, D.* Preaching from Amos. SWJT 38/1 (1995) 36-43.

2570 *Byargeon, Rick W.* Amos: the man and his times. SWJT 38/1 (1995) 4-10.

2571 *Byargeon, Rick W.* The doxologies of Amos: a study of their structure and theology. TTE 52 (1995) 47-56 [OTA 19,113].

2572 *Carroll R., M. Daniel* Reflecting on war and utopia in the book of Amos: the relevance of a literary reading of the prophetic text for

Central America. 1995 ⇒23. ^FROGERSON J., JSOT.S 200. 105-121.

2573 **Carroll Rodas, Mark Daniel** Contexts for Amos... 1992 ⇒10,3699. ^RCritRR 7 (1994) 101-103 (*Jackson, Jared J.*); JSSt 40 (1995) 118-122 (*Houston, Walter J.*); BTB 25 (1995) 48-49 (*Benjamin, Don C.*).

2574 *Clines, David J.A.* Metacommentating Amos. 1995 ⇒37. Interested parties. JSOT.S 205. 76-93 [⇒10,3700].

2575 *Davis, L.D.* The herald of God's justice. BiTod 33 (1995) 294-297.

2576 *Dell, Katharine J.* The misuse of forms in Amos. VT 45 (1995) 45-61.

      Diop, A. Ganoune The name 'Israel' and related expressions in the books of Amos and Hosea. ⇒2509.

2577 *Dubreucq, Marc* Le Dieu d'Amos. DosB 59 (1995) 24-26.

2578 *Escobar, Donoso S.* Social justice in the book of Amos. RExp 92 (1995) 169-174.

2579 *Gruson, Philippe* Paroles de prophète. DosB 59 (1995) 10-13.

2580 *House, Paul R.* Amos and literary criticism. RExp 92 (1995) 175-187.

2581 *Johnson, Rick* Prepare to meet the lion: the message of Amos. SWJT 38/1 (1995) 20-28.

2582 *Le Saux, Madeleine* Amos, un personnage. DosB 59 (1995) 3-5.

2583 *Levin, Christoph* Amos und Jerobeam I. VT 45 (1995) 307-317.

2584 *Loscalzo, Craig* Preaching themes from Amos. RExp 92 (1995) 195-206.

2585 *Moore, R. Kelvin* Amos: an introduction. TTE 52 (1995) 27-36 [OTA 19,111].

2586 *Noble, Paul* The literary structure of Amos: a thematic analysis. JBL 114 (1995) 209-226.

2587 *Nogalski, James D.* A teaching outline for Amos. RExp 92 (1995) 147-151.

2588 *Ogden Bellis, Alice* The book of Amos. 1995 ⇒62. Many voices. 1-2.

2589 *Paas, S.* De HERE als schepper en koning: de hymnen in Amos. NedThT 49/1 (1995) 124-139.

2590 **Pfeifer, Gerhard** Die Theologie des Propheten Amos. Fra 1995, Lang 147 pp. DM44. 3-631-48459-3 [TTh 36,112].

2591 **Rebič, Adalbert** Amos, Prorok pravde. Biblioteka Riječ 29. Zagreb 1993, Kršćanska sadašnjost 146 pp. ^RBogoslovska Smotra 65 (1995) 310-311 (*Hohnjec, N.*).

2592 **Reimer, Haroldo** Richtet auf das Recht! Studien zur Botschaft des Amos. 1992 ⇒8,4015; 9,3890. SBS 149. ^RITS 32 (1995) 363-366 (*Ceresko, Anthony R.*).

2593 *Richardson, Paul A.* Worship resources for Amos. RExp 92 (1995) 207-217.

2594 **Rottzoll, Dirk U.** Studien zur Redaktion und Komposition des Amosbuchs. Diss. Marburg 1995, ^D*Kaiser, O.*

2595 *Soggin, J.A.* Amos and wisdom. ⇒9. ^FEMERTON J., 1995. 119-123.

2596 *Watts, John D.W.* Amos: across fifty years of study. RExp 92 (1995) 189-193.

2597 *Zeeb, F.* Alalaḫ VII und das Amosbuch. UF 27 (1995) 641-656.

2598 *Mackiewicz, Marie-Claude* Des droits de l'homme? (Am 1-2,3). DosB 59 (1995) 20-21.

2599 *Hall, Kevin* Listen up people!: the lion has roared: a study of Amos 1-2. SWJT 38/1 (1995) 11-19.

2600 *Mosley, Harold R.* The oracles against the nations. TTE 52 (1995) 37-45 [1,3-2,16; OTA 19,112].

2601 *Noble, Paul R.* 'I will not bring "it" back' (Amos 1:3): a deliberately ambiguous oracle? ET 106 (1995) 105-109.

2602 *Gruson, Philippe* Un oracle de procès (Am 2,6-16). DosB 59 (1995) 29.

2603 *Spreafico, Ambrogio* Saggi di esegesi: dai profeti minori: la difesa dei poveri (Am 2,6-16). 1995 ⇒97. Profeti. 357-372.

2604 **Arango, José Roberto** La mujer y la familia, víctimas de la injusticia en Amós, 2,7b. ThX 45 (1995) 341-356.

2605 *Hillers, Delbert R.* Palmyrene Aramaic inscriptions and the Old Testment, especially Amos 2:8. ZAH 8/1 (1995) 55-62.

2606 *Snyman, S.D.* "Violence" in Amos 3,10 and 6,3. EThL 71 (1995) 30-47.

2607 *Dempster, Stephen G.* Amos 3: apologia of a prophet. BRT 5 (1995) 35-51 [OTA 19,112].

2608 *Ellis, R.R.* Are there any cows of Bashan on Seminary Hill? SWJT 38/1 (1995) 44-48 [4,1-3].

2609 *Brown, Walter E.* Amos 5:26: a challenge to reading and interpretation. TTE 52 (1995) 69-78 [OTA 19,113].

2610 *Cole, R. Dennis* The visions of Amos 7-9. TTE 52 (1995) 57-68 [OTA 19,113].

2611 *Soupa, Anne* Les cinq visions d'Amos. DosB 59 (1995) 22-23.

2612 *Heyns, Dalene* Teologie in beeld: oor die visioene van Amos [Image-theology: concerning the visions of Amos]. NGTT 36 (1995) 139-151 [7,1-9,4; OTA 19,113].

2613 *Weigl, Michael* Eine "unendliche Geschichte": ᵓnk (Am 7,7-8). Bib. 76 (1995) 343-387.

2614 *Jaruzelska, Izabela* ᵓAmasyah, prêtre de Béthel, fonctionnaire royal (essai socio-économique préliminaire). FolOr 31 (1995) 53-69 [7,10-17].

2615 *Williamson, H.G.M.* The prophet and the plumb-line: a redaction-critical study of Amos 7. 1995 ⇒83. Israelite prophets. 453-477.

2616 *Aulard, Stéphane* Le prêtre, le prophète et le roi (Am 7,10-17). DosB 59 (1995) 8-9.

2617 **Nägele, Sabine** Laubhütte Davids und Wolkensohn: eine auslegungsgeschichtliche Studie zu Amos 9,11 in der jüdischen und christlichen Exegese. Diss. Tü 1993, ᴰ*Betz, O.*, AGJU 24. Lei 1995, Brill xvi; 276 pp. ƒ175/$100. 90-04-10163-2. ᴿThLZ 120 (1995) 1073-1074 (*Bergmeier, Roland*).

E9.5 **Jonas.**

Craghan, John Ester...Giona. ⇒1344.

2618 **Deurloo, K.A.** Jona. Verkl. v.d. hebr. Bijbel. Baarn 1995, Callenbach 106 pp. ƒ29.90. 90-266-0365-7.

2619 ᵀ**Jundt, Pierre** Explication du prophète Jonas et du prophète Habaquq. 1993 ⇒9,3913; 10,3719. Luther: Oeuvres. BLE 96 (1995) 57 (*Monloubou, Louis*); RTL 26 (1995) 238-240 (*Gangloff, F.*).

2620 **Limburg, James** Jonah. 1993 ⇒9,3915; 10,3722. ᴿJThS 46 (1995) 230-231 (*Alexander, T.D.*); CBQ 57 (1995) 149-150 (*Berlin, Adele*); BiOr 52 (1995) 745-746 (*Haak, Robert D.*); HebStud 36 (1995) 192-193 (*Marcus, David*).

2621 **Simon, Uriel** Jonah: introduction and commentary. H. 1992 ⇒10,3726. ᴿAJS 20 (1995) 389-391 (*Grossberg, Daniel*).

2622 *Bolin, Thomas M.* "Should I not also pity Nineveh?": divine freedom in the book of Jonah. JSOT 67 (1995) 109-120.

2623 **Bolin, Thomas Michael** Jonah as subversive literature?: the book of Jonah and its biblical context. Diss. Marquette 1995, 197 pp. ᴰ*Schmitt, John J.*, DAI-A 56,3616.

   Carmody, Denise Lardner; Carmody, John Tully Corn & ivy: spiritual reading in... Jonah. ⇒1032.

2624 **Chow, Simon** The sign of Jonah reconsidered. ⇒3092.

2625 *Collins, C. John* From literary analysis to theological exposition: the book of Jonah. JTrTL 7/1 (1995) 28-44 [OTA 18,578].

2626 *Dresken-Weiland, Jutta* Ein frühchristliches Jonas-Relief in Konya (Taf. 108). MDAI.R 102 (1995) 405-412.

2627 *Flipo, Claude* Jonas à Ninive: du bon usage de la ville. Christus 42 (1995) 149-155.

2628 *Gitay, Yehoshua* Jonah: the prophecy of antirhetoric. 1995 ⇒10. ꟳFREEDMAN D., 197-206.

2629 *Hampl, Patricia* In the belly of the whale. 1995 ⇒70. Out of the garden. 289-300.

2630 *Howell, Maribeth* A prophet who pouts. BiTod 33 (1995) 75-78.

2631 **Lux, Rüdiger** Jona...eine erzählanalytische Studie. 1994 ⇒10,3732. FRLANT 162. ᴿThLZ 120 (1995) 642-644 (*Krüger, Thomas*); OTA 18, 425-426 (*Redditt, Paul L.*).

2632 *Ogden Bellis, Alice* Oracle in the style of Joel. 1995 ⇒62. Many voices. 89-90.

2633 *Payne, David F.* Jonah from the perspective of its audience. 1995 ⇒83. Israelite Prophets. 263-272.

2634 *Petit, Olivier* Jonas, un prophète travaillé par la parole. SémBib 80 (1995) 59-63.

2635 **Ratcliffe, Carolyn Ruth** The book of Jonah in the tradition of ancient Israelite wisdom.   Baylor 1995, 256 pp. AAC 9528009; DAI-A 56,1301.

   Stachowiak, Lech Der Universalismus und die Bücher Jona und Rut. ⇒1044.

2636 **Steffen, Uwe** Die Jona-Geschichte...im Judentum, Christentum und Islam. 1994 ⇒10,3739. ᴿThRv 91 (1995) 478-483 (*Pfnür, Vinzenz*).

2637 **Trible, Phyllis** Rhetorical criticism...Jonah. 1994 ⇒10,3740. ᴿJBL 114 (1995) 722-724 (*Ackerman, James S.*).

2638 *Wilcox, Lance* Staging Jonah. BiRe 11 (1995) 20-28.

2639 *Hausmann, Jutta* "Wer ist wahrhaft gottesfürchtig?": Jona 1 und sein Beitrag zur Diskussion um das Problem Israel und die Völker. 1995 ⇒37. ꟳWAGNER S., 105-116.

E9.6 *Micheas,* **Micah.**

2640 **Magary, Dennis Robert** Translation technique in the Peshitta of the book of Micah. Diss. Wisconsin 1995, 513 pp. [D]*Fox, Michael V.,* AAC 9527170; DAI-A 56,2728.

2641 **Oberforcher, Robert** Das Buch Micha. Neuer Stuttgarter Kommentar. Altes Testament 24/2. Stu 1995, Katholisches Bibelwerk 157 pp. DM32.40. 3-460-07242-3.

2642 *Bosman, J.G.* Geregtigheid in die boek Miga: 'n tradisie-historiese onderzoek na die begrip מִשְׁפָּט. Skrif en Kerk 16 (1995) 219-232 [EThL 72/2-3,204*].

2643 **Grant, George** The Micah mandate. Chicago, Ill. 1995, Moody 224 pp. 0-8024-5634-0.

2644 *Kim, Gun-Tai* The concepts of justice in Micah. **K.** The Reason and the Faith 10 (1995) 5-52 [ThIK 17,54].

2645 *Klein, Nikolaus* Die prophetische Herausforderung des Micha: zum 26. Deutschen Evangelischen Kirchentag in Hamburg. Orien. 59 (1995) 151-154 [6,8].

2646 *Lescow, Theodor* Zur Komposition des Buches Micha. SJOT 9 (1995) 200-222.

2647 Alles, was recht ist—die Botschaft des propheten Micha. Materialen zur Bibelwoche 1995/96. Stu 1995, Deutsche Bibelgesellschaft/Katholisches Bibelwerk 32 pp. Teilnehmerheft; Didaktisches Begleitheft zum Teilnehmerheft. DM1.50/3.50 [1 Thess 4,15].

2648 **Michel, Diethelm; Micheel, Rosemarie** Aufmerksam mitgehen: der Prophet Micha. Texte zur Bibel 2. Neuk 1995, Aussaat 104 pp. DM16.80.

2649 *Ogden Bellis, Alice* The book of Micah. 1995 ⇒62. Many voices. 31-32.

2650 *McKane, William* Micah 1,2-7. ZAW 107 (1995) 420-434.

2651 *Na'aman, Nadav* "The house-of-no-shade shall take away its tax from you" (Micah i 11). VT 45 (1995) 516-527 [1,8-16].

2652 **Wagenaar, Jan A.** Oordeel en heil: een onderzoek naar samenhang tussen de heils- en onheilsprofetieën in Micha 2-5 [Judgment and salvation: an investigation of the connection between the prophecies of salvation and doom in Micah 2-5]. Diss. Utrecht 1995, x; 310 pp. [D]*Leeuwen, C. van,* f45. 90-393-0747-4 [OTA 18649].

2653 *McKane, William* Micah 2:12-13. JNSL 21/2 (1995) 83-91.

2654 *Pola, T.* Micha 3: eine exegetische Besinnung zur ökumenischen Bibelwoche. ThBeitr 26 (1995) 279-284.

2655 *Crocker, P.T.* Micah 5:1: what and where is the 'city of the troops'?. BurH 31 (1995) 21-24 [OTA 18,578].

2656 *Ebach, J.* Was bei Micha "gut sein" heißt: zur Kirchentagslosung 1995. JK 56 (1995) 258f [6,1-8].

E9.7 *Abdias, Sophonias...*Obadiah, Zephaniah, Nahum.

2657 Bibliography on Obadiah. BVp 29 (1995) 57-72 [OTA 19,290].

2658 **Cogan, Mordechai** Obadiah: introduction and commentary. **H.** Miqra' le-Yisra'el. J 1993, Magnes xi; 96 pp. [R]AJS 20 (1995) 389-391 (*Grossberg, Daniel*).

2659 *Ogden Bellis, Alice* The book of Obadiah. 1995 ⇒62. Many voices. 63-64.
2660 *Steveson, Pete* Judgment of Edom (Obadiah). BVp 29 (1995) 3-8 [OTA 19,290].

2661 *Anderson, Roger W.* Zephaniah ben Cushi and Cush of Benjamin: traces of Cushite presence in Syria-Palestine. 1995 ⇒1. MAHLSTRÖM G., JSOT.S 190. 45-70 [1,1].
2662 *Berlin, Adele* Zephaniah's oracle against the nations and an Israelite cultural myth. 1995 ⇒10. FREEDMAN D., 175-184 [2,4-15].
2663 *Grayson, Byron J., Jr.* A light searching. 1995 ⇒62. Many voices. 41-46.
2664 *Haak, Robert D.* "Cush" in Zephaniah. 1995 ⇒1. MAHLSTRÖM G., JSOT.S 190. 238-251.
2665 *House, Paul R.* Dialogue in Zephaniah. 1995 ⇒83. Israelite Prophets. 252-262.
2666 *King, Greg A.* The day of the Lord in Zephaniah. BS 152 (1995) 16-32.
2667 *Ogden Bellis, Alice* The book of Zephaniah. 1995 ⇒62. Many voices. 39-40.
2668 **Ryou, Daniel Hojoon** Zephaniah's oracles against the nations: a synchronic and diachronic study of Zephaniah 2:1-3:8. Bibl.Interp. 13. Lei 1995, Brill xvii; 403 pp. ƒ173.50/$112.50. 90-04-10311-2.
2669 *Spreafico, Ambrogio* Il libro del profeta Sofonia. RCI 76 (1995) 517-527.
2670 *Spreafico, Ambrogio* Saggi di esegesi: dai profeti minori: gioisci, figlia di Sion (Sof 3,14-20). 1995 ⇒97. Profeti. 373-382.
2671 **Weigl, Michael** Zefanja und das "Israel der Armen". 1994 ⇒10,3763. ÖBS 13. RCBQ 57 (1995) 795-796 (*Dearman, J. Andrew*); LASBF 45 (1995) 590-595 (*Cortese, Enzo*).
2672 *Weigl, Michael* Zefanja und das "Israel der Armen": zu den Ursprüngen biblischer Armentheologie. BiKi 50 (1995) 6-11.

2673 *Becking, Bob* Divine wrath and the conceptual coherence of the book of Nahum. SJOT 9 (1995) 277-296.
2674 *Becking, Bob* A judge in history: notes on Nahum 3,7 and Esarhaddon's succession treaty paragraph 47:452. ZABRG 1 (1995) 111-116.
2675 *Begg, Christopher T.* JOSEPHUS and Nahum revisited. REJ 154 (1995) 5-22.
2676 *Bliese, L.F.* A cryptic chiastic acrostic: finding meaning from structure in the poetry of Nahum. JTrTL 7/3 (1995) 48-81.
2677 *Johnson, Nadankan* Oracle in the style of Nahum. 1995 ⇒62. Many voices. 48-49.
2678 *Ogden Bellis, Alice* The book of Nahum. 1995 ⇒62. Many voices. 47.
2679 *Spronk, K.* Synchronic and diachronic approaches to the book of Nahum. 1995 ⇒99. Synchronic or diachronic? 159-186.
2680 **Spronk, K.; Ridderbos, Nic H.** Wortstelen met een wrekende God: de uitleg van de profetie van Nahum. Kampen 1995, Kok 116 pp. ƒ24.50. 90-242-2218-4 [KeTh 47,252].

E9.8 Habacuc, Habakkuk.

2681 **Barsotti, Divo** Méditation sur Habaquq. P 1995, Téqui 67 pp. FF67 [EeV 106,180].

2682 *Fabry, Heinz-Josef* Habakuk, Habakukbuch. 1995 ⇒123. LThK 4. 1124-1126.

2683 **Haak, Robert D.** Habakkuk. 1991 ⇒7,3483... 10,3769. NT.S 44. ᴿBS 152 (1995) 115-116 (*Chisholm, Robert B.*); JQR 86 (1995) 259-261 (*Sweeney, Marvin A.*).

ᵀ**Jundt, Pierre** Explication...du prophète Habaquq. ⇒2619.

2684 *Ogden Bellis, Alice* The book of Habakkuk. 1995 ⇒62. Many voices. 55-56.

2685 *Trudinger, P.* Two ambiguities in Habakkuk's "unambiguous" oracle. DR 113 (1995) 282-283.

E9.9 *Aggaeus*, **Haggai** — *Zacharias*, **Zechariah** — *Malachias*, **Malachi.**

2686 *Ogden Bellis, Alice* The books of Haggai and Zechariah. 1995 ⇒62. Many voices. 71-72.

2687 **Petersen, David L.** Zechariah 9-14 and Malachi: a commentary. OTL. L/LVL 1995, SCM/Westminster xxi; 233 pp. $28. 0-334-02594-X [JBL 114,772].

2688 **Redditt, Paul L.** Haggai, Zechariah and Malachi. NCeB. GR/L 1995, Eerdmans/Marshall Pickering xxviii; 196 pp. $15. 0-8028-0748-8/0-551-02832-7.

2689 **Reventlow, Henning Graf** Die Propheten Haggai, Sacharja und Maleachi. 1993 ⇒9,3878; 10,3773. ATD 25/2. ᴿCBQ 57 (1995) 368-369 (*Landes, George M.*); CritRR 8 (1995) 144-146 (*Malchow, Bruce V.*).

2690 *Sérandour, A.* Réflexions à propos d'un livre récent sur Aggée-Zacharie 1-8. Transeuphratène 10 (1995) 75-84.

2691 **Tollington, Janet E.** Tradition and innovation in Haggai and Zechariah 1-8. 1993 ⇒9,3979; 10,3775. JSOT.S 150. ᴿCBQ 57 (1995) 375-377 (*Nash, Kathleen S.*); CritRR 8 (1995) 157-158 (*Person, Raymond F. Jr.*).

2692 *Amsler, Samuel* Le prophète Aggée. 1995 ⇒2081. Les derniers prophètes. 12-16.

2693 *Clines, David J.A.* Haggai's temple, constructed, deconstructed and reconstructed. 1995 ⇒37. Interested parties. JSOT.S 205. 46-75.

2694 *Floyd, Michael H.* The nature of the narrative and the evidence of redaction in Haggai. VT 45 (1995) 470-490.

2695 **Girard, Marc** Aggée prophète aujourd'hui. Parole d'actualité. P 1995, Médiaspaul. 2-89420-247-4.

2696 *Holbrook, David J.* Narrowing down Haggai: examining style in light of discourse and content. JTrTL 7 (1995) 1-12 [OTA 19,115].

2697 *Stiglmair, Arnold* Haggai, Haggaibuch. 1995 ⇒123. LThK 4. 1142-1143.

2698 *Amsler, Samuel* Le prophète Zacharie: Zacharie 1 à 8. 1995 ⇒2081. Les derniers prophètes. 17-29.

2699 *Bartlett, Andre Ludick* Die naggesigte van Sagaria teen die agtergrond van konflik in die vroeë-eksiliese gemeenskap in Juda

[The night visions of Zechariah against the background of conflict in the early postexilic community in Judah]. SK 16 (1995) 1-15 [1,7-6,15; OTA 19,115].

2700 **Bartlett, Andre Ludick** The night visions of Zechariah: in dialogue with P.D. HANSON [in Afrikaans]. Diss. Pretoria 1995, D*Prinsloo, W.S.*, DAI-A 56,1826.

2701 **Hanhart, Robert** Sacharja (4,1-6,8). BKAT 14/7, Fasc. 5. Neuk 1995, Neuk 321-400.

2702 *Rohrhirsch, Ferdinand* Zur Relevanz wissenschaftstheoretischer Implikationen in der Diskussion um das Qumranfragment 7Q5 und zu einem neuen Identifizierungsvorschlag von 7Q5 mit Zacharias 7,4-5. ThGl 85 (1995) 80-95.

2703 **Serandour, Arnaud** Le prophète Zacharie et la communauté de son temps d'après le livret des visions (Zacharie 1,7-6,15). Dissertation Sorbonne 1995, D*Meslin, M.* [RTL 27,531].

2704 *Amsler, Samuel* Le Deutéro-Zacharie: Zacharie 9 à 14. 1995 ⇒2081. Les derniers prophètes. 30-35.

2705 *Brzegowy, T.·* Le messianisme du Deutero-Zacharie. **P.** ACra 27 (1995) 93-109.

2706 *Dudguid, Iain* Messianic themes in Zechariah 9-14. 1995 ⇒111. The Lord's anointed. 265-280.

2707 **Larkin, Katrina J.A.** The eschatology of Second Zechariah. 1994 ⇒10,3787. RCBQ 57 (1995) 561-562 (*Person, Raymond F.*); JNSL 21 (1995) 146-147 (*Nel, Philip*).

2708 *Myers, Eric M.* The crisis of the mid-fifth century B.C.E. Second Zechariah and the "end" of prophecy. 1995 ⇒21. FMILGROM J., 713-723.

2709 **Person, Raymond F.** Second Zechariah and the Deuteronomic school. 1993 ⇒8,4097... 10,3788. JSOT.S 167. RJThS 46 (1995) 227-230 (*Mason, Rex*); JBL 114 (1995) 725-726 (*Floyd, Michael H.*); CBQ 57 (1995) 780-781 (*Cook, Stephen L.*).

2710 *Rhea, Robert* Attack on prophecy Zechariah 13,1-6. ZAW 107 (1995) 288-293.

2711 *Schaefer, Konrad R.* Zechariah 14: a study in allusion. CBQ 57 (1995) 66-91.

2712 *Amsler, Samuel* Le prophète Malachie. 1995 ⇒2081. Les derniers prophètes. 36-40.

2713 **Hugenberger, G.P.** Marriage as a covenant...Malachi. 1994 ⇒10,3795. VT.S 52. RAsp. 42 (1995) 440-441 (*Di Palma, G.*); JBL 114 (1995) 306-308 (*Collins, John J.*); CBQ 57 (1995) 557-559 (*Strong, John T.*).

2714 **Lescow, Theodor** Das Buch Maleachi: Texttheorie-Auslegung-Kanontheorie: mit einem Exkurs über Jeremiah 8:8-9. AzTh 75. 1993 ⇒9,3996. RJBL 114 (1995) 507-508 (*Redditt, Paul L.*).

2715 *O'Brien, Julia M.* Historical inquiry as liberator and master: Malachi as a post-exilic document. 1995 ⇒12. FHAMRICK E., SBEC 35. 57-79.

2716 *O'Brien, Julia M.* Malachi in recent research. CurResB 3 (1995) 81-94.

2717 *O'Brien, Julia M.* On saying "no" to a prophet. Semeia 72 (1995) 111-124.

2718 *Ogden Bellis, Alice* The book of Malachi. 1995 ⇒62. Many voices. 79.

2719 *Briend, Jacques* Malachie 1,11 et l'universalisme. 1995 ⇒22. FRENAUD B., LeDiv 159. 191-204.
2720 *Jeyaraj, Jesudason B.* Malachi and the nations—incense everywhere. VJTR 59 (1995) 41-45 [1,11].
2721 *Donner, Herbert* Ein Vorschlag zum Verständnis von Maleachi 2,10-16. 1995 ⇒37. FWAGNER S., 97-103.
2722 *Swanepoel, M.G.* Om hatende weg te stuur of egskeiding te haat: watter een wil die Here nie in Maleagi 2:13-16? [To send away in hate or to hate divorce: what is it the Lord does not want in Mal 2:13-16]. NGTT 36 (1995) 65-74 [OTA 18,581].
2723 *Gosse, Bernard* L'alliance avec Lévi et l'opposition entre les lignées royale et sacerdotale à l'époque perse. Transeuphratène 10. 29-33 [Mal 2].
2724 *Öhler, Markus* Die Gestalt des Elija und Johannes' des Täufers. PzB 4 (1995) 1-11 [3,23-24].

Evangelia

F2.6 Evangelia Synoptica; *textus, synopses, commentarii*

2725 **Barr, Allan** A diagram of synoptic relationships: with a new introduction by *James Barr*, E ²1995, Clark 18 pp. 0-567-09724-2.
2726 *Carrón Pérez, Julián* La historicidad de los evangelios. Communio 17 (1995) 271-293.
2727 EEvans, **Craig A.; Porter, Stanley E.** The synoptic gospels: a Sheffield reader. BiSe 31. Shf 1995, Academic 313 pp. 1-85075-732-1.

F2.7 *Problema synopticum:* The Synoptic Problem.

2728 *Black, Matthew* The Aramaic dimension in Q with notes on Luke 17.22 and Matthew 24.26 (Luke 17.23). 1995 ⇒103. The historical Jesus. 237-244.
2729 *Bretscher, Paul G.* When everything was "Q". ProcGLM 15 (1995) 53-64.
2730 **Catchpole, David** The quest for Q. 1993 ⇒9,4407; 10,4234. RTheology 98 (1995) 308-309 (*Telford, W.R.*).
2731 *Denaux, Adelbert* Criteria for identifying Q-passages: a critical review of a recent work by T. BERGEMANN. NT 37 (1995) 105-129.
2732 *Dungan, David Laird* "*Eppur si muove*": circumnavigating the mythical recensions of *Q*. Interview. Soundings 78 (1995) 541-570.
2733 *Evans, Craig A.* Source, form and redaction criticism: the 'traditional' methods of synoptic interpretation. 1995 ⇒106. Approaches. 17-45.

2734 *Farmer, William R.* State interesse and Markan primacy: 1870-
1914. 1995 ⇒107. Biblical studies. JSOT.S 192. 15-49.
2735 **Fleddermann, Harry T.** Mark and Q: a study of the overlap texts.
BEThL 122. Lv 1995, University Press/Peeters xi; 307 pp.
FB1800. 90-6186-710-X/90-6831-712-1. ET 107 (1995-96) 378
(*Franklin, Eric*).
2736 ᴱ**Focant, Camille** The synoptic gospels: source criticism and the
new literary criticism. 1993 ⇒9,382. BEThL 110. ᴿBZ 39 (1995)
137-139 (*Ebner, Martin*); CBQ 57 (1995) 207-208 (*Senior, Donald*); ThRv 91 (1995) 390-392 (*Söding, Thomas*); SNTU.A 20
(1995) 205-208 (*Fuchs, A.*).
2737 **Hoffmann, Paul** Tradition und Situation: Studien zur Jesusüberlieferung in der Logienquelle und den synoptischen Evangelien. TA
28. Müns 1995, Aschendorff v; 390 pp. DM93. 3-402-04776-4.
ᴿRHR 212 (1995) 479-480 (*Méhat, André*) [Matt 5,38-48; Lk
6,27-36].

ᴱ**Kloppenborg, John S.** Conflict and invention: literary, rhetorical, and social studies on the sayings gospel Q. 1995 ⇒94.
2738 *Kloppenborg, John S.* Conflict and invention: recent studies on Q.
1995 ⇒94. Conflict and invention. 1-14.
2739 *Lindsey, Robert L.* Unlocking the synoptic problem: four keys for
better understanding Jesus. Jpersp. 49 (1995) 10-17.
2740 **Linnemann, Eta** Is there a synoptic problem? 1992 ⇒8,4545…
10,4242. ᴿEvangel 13/2 (1995) 62-63 (*Bigg, Howard C.*); AUSS
33 (1995) 309-310 (*Reynolds, Edwin E.*);
2741 Gibt es ein synoptisches Problem?. Theologie für die Gemeinde 2.
Stu ²1995 <1992>, Hänssler 192 pp. DM30. 3-7751-1721-0
<pb>. ᴿJETh 9 (1995) 225-227 (*Riesner, Rainer*);
2742 Is there a gospel of Q? BiRe 11/4 (1995) 18-23, 42-43;
2743 Q—das verlorene Evangelium: Fantasie oder Faktum?. JETh 9
(1995) 43-61.
2744 **Mack, Burton L.** The lost gospel: the book of Q and Christian origins. 1993 ⇒9,4419; 10,4243. ᴿInterp. 49/1 (1995) 109-110
(*Boring, M. Eugene*); AUSS 33/1 (1995) 132-134 (*McIver, Robert
K.*); CritRR 8 (1995) 253-257 (*Jacobson, Arland D.*).
2745 *Moreland; Milton C.; Robinson, James M.* The International Q
Project: work sessions 23-27 May, 22-26 August, 17-18 November
1994. JBL 114 (1995) 475-485.
2746 **Neirynck, Frans** Q-Synopsis: the double tradition passages in
Greek. SNTA 13. Lv 1995 <1988> [⇒4,4397], University
Press/Peeters 79 pp. revised edition with appendix. FB400. 90-
6186-669-3/90-6831-662-1 [JThS 47,436].
2747 *Neirynck, Frans* The minor agreements and Q. 1995 ⇒101. The
gospel. NT.S 75. 49-72;
2748 Q: from source to gospel. EThL 71 (1995) 421-430.
2749 *Patterson, Stephen J.* Yes, Virginia, there is a Q. BiRe 11/5 (1995)
39-40.
2750 *Piper, Ronald A.* In quest of Q: the direction of Q studies. 1995
⇒101. The gospel. NT.S 75. 1-18.
2751 **Powell, E.** The myth of the lost gospel: a layman's letter to the
Jesus Seminar. Westlake Village 1995, Symposium Books 39 pp.
$6. 0-9639650-7-7 [NTAb 40,147].
2752 *Reed, Jonathan L.* The social map of Q. 1995 ⇒94. Conflict and
invention. 17-36.

ᴱRonald A. Piper The gospel behind the gospels: current studies on Q. ⇒101.

2753 Scholer, David M. Q bibliography supplement VI: 1995. SBL.SP 34 (1995) 1-5.

2754 Shellard, Barbara The relationship of Luke and John: a fresh look at an old problem. JThS 46 (1995) 71-98.

2755 ᴱStrecker, Georg Minor agreements. 1993 ⇒9,412. ᴿNeotest. 29 (1995) 135-138 (Steyn, G.J.).

2756 Thiede, C.P. Notes on P 4 = Bibliothèque Nationale Paris, Supplementum Graece 1120/5. TynB 46 (1995) 55-57.

2757 Tuckett, Christopher M. The existence of Q. 1995 ⇒101. The gospel. NT.S 75. 19-47.

2758 Tuilier, André La Didachè et le problème synoptique. The Didache in context: essays on its text, history and transmission. ᴱJefford, Clayton N. NT.S 77. Lei 1995, Brill. 90-04-10045-8. 110-130.

2759 Wenham, John W. Kan evangelierne stadig anses for troværdige til beskrivelse af den historiske Jesus? II. ᵀNissen, Michael Krogstrup. ΙΧΘΥΣ 22/2 (1995) 52-63.

F2.8 Synoptica: themata.

2760 Bailey, Kenneth E. Informal controlled oral tradition and the synoptic gospels. Themelíos 20 (1995) 4-11.

2761 Bailey, Kenneth E. Middle Eastern oral tradition and the synoptic gospels. ET 106 (1995) 363-367.

2762 Bartnicki, Roman Ewangelie synoptyczne: geneza i interpretacja. Warszawa 1993, ATK 315 pp. TK 42/1 (1995) 111-113 (Kudasiewicz, Józef).

2763 Barton, Stephen C. Discipleship and family ties in Mark and Matthew. 1994 ⇒10,4736. MSSNTS 80. ᴿReviews in Religion and Theology (1995/4) 72-74 (Carleton Paget, James; BTB 25 (1995) 194-195 (Bode, Edward L.); CritRR 8 (1995) 165-167 (Blomberg, Craig L.).

2764 Bultmann, Rudolf Geschichte der synoptischen Tradition. Afterword by G. Theissen. FRLANT 29. Gö 1995 <1931>, Vandenhoeck & Ruprecht x; 452 pp. reprint; DM115(78). 3-525-53109-5/-53110-9 [NTAb 40,335].

2765 Ennulat, Andreas Die "Minor Agreements". 1994 ⇒10,4253. WUNT 2/62. ᴿNT 37 (1995) 197-199 (Tuckett, C.M.); JETh 9 (1995) 223-225 (Riesner, Rainer).

2766 Farmer, William R. The gospel of Jesus: the pastoral relevance of the synoptic problem. 1994 ⇒10,4255. CTJ 30 (1995) 559-562 (Verbrugge, Verlyn D.); ET 106 (1994-95) 120 (Tuckett, Christopher); CritRR 8 (1995) 209-211 (Gundry, Robert H.).

2767 Ghiberti, Giuseppe La creazione, l'uomo e la donna nei sinottici. 1995 ⇒267. Dizionario di spiritualità biblico-patristica 10, 95-120.

2768 Giesen, H. Herrschaft Gottes—heute oder morgen?: zur Heilsbotschaft Jesu und der synoptischen Evangelien. BU 26. Regensburg 1995, Pustet 162 pp. DM38. 3-7917-1454-6. ᴿTGA 38 (1995) 211-222 (Weiser, Alfons); OrdKor 36 (1995) 377-378 (Porsch, Felix).

2769 Habbe, Joachim Die Landwirtschaft in Palästina zur Zeit Jesu und ihr Niederschlag im Zeugnis der synoptischen Evangelien. Diss. 1995 Erlangen-Nürnberg.

2770 *Hoffmann, Paul* The redaction of Q and the Son of Man: a preliminary sketch. 1995 ⇒101. The gospel. NT.S 75. 159-198.
2771 *Horsley, Richard* Social conflict in the synoptic sayings source Q.
1995 ⇒94. Conflict and invention. 37-52.
2772 *Jacobson, Arland D.* Divided families and christian origins. 1995
⇒94. Conflict and invention. 361-380 [Lk 12,51-53; 14,26].
2773 **Keylock, Leslie Robert** Luke and Matthew as editors: an evaluation of BULTMANN's law of increasing distinctness. Diss.
^D*McKnight, Scot*, Trinity Evang. Div. School 1995, 346 pp. AAC
9533054; DAI-A 56/6,p.2280.
2774 *Kloppenborg, John S.* Jesus and the parables of Jesus in Q. 1995
⇒101. The gospel. 275-319.
2775 ^E**Láconi, Mauro** Vangeli sinottici e Atti degli Apostoli. Logos,
Corso di studi biblici 5. T 1994, Elle Di Ci 584 pp. ^RAnnales
Theologici 9 (1995) 485-486 (*Estrada, Bernardo*).
2776 **Lang, Marijke Hélène de** De opkomst van de historische en literaire kritiek in de synoptische beschouwing van de evangelien van
CALVIJN tot GRIESBACH. 1993 ⇒9,4416. ^RThLZ 120 (1995)
903-905 (*Merk, Otto*).
2777 *Leonardi, Giovanni* "I dodici" e "gli apostoli" nei vangeli sinottici
e Atti—problemi e prospettive. StPat 42 (1995) 163-195.
2778 **Linmans, Adrianus Johannes Maria** Onderschikking in de Synoptische Evangeliën: syntaxis, discourse-functies en stilometrie
een wetenschappelijke proeve op het gebied van de godgeleerdheid
[Subordination in the synoptic gospels: syntax, discourse-function
and stylometrics]. Diss. Nijmegen 1995, xii; 320 pp. ^D*Iersel,
B.M.F. van*.
2779 **Lohmeyer, Monika** Der Apostelbegriff im Neuen Testament: eine
Untersuchung auf dem Hintergrund der synoptischen Aussendungsreden. Diss. 1994 ⇒10,4259. SBB 29. Stuttgart 1995, Katholisches Bibelwerk xi; 472 pp. 3-460-00291-3 [10].
2780 *Lührmann, Dieter* Q: sayings of Jesus or logia?. 1995 ⇒101. The
gospel. NT.S 75. 97-116.
2781 *Mattera, R.* Kingdom theology in the synoptic gospels: towards a
socio-political ethic. JRadRef. 4/3 (1995) 31-41 [NTAb 40,27—
Matthews, C.R.].
2782 *McLean, Bradley H.* On the gospel of Thomas and Q. 1995 ⇒101.
The gospel. 321-345.
2783 **Meadors, Edward P.** Jesus the messianic herald of salvation. Diss.
(⇒9,4958). WUNT 2/72. Tü 1995, Mohr xi; 387 pp. DM118. 3-
16-146251-3.
2784 **Merklein, Helmut** Die Jesusgeschichte—synoptisch gelesen. 1994
⇒10,4260. SBS 156. ^RTLZ 120 (1995) 661-662 (*Rau, Eckhard*).
2785 **Moore, Stephen D.** Literary criticism and the gospels. 1989
⇒7,3761. ^RSJTh 48 (1995) 282-284 (*Carroll, Robert P.*).
2786 **New, David S.** Old Testament quotations. 1993 ⇒9,4422;
10,4261. ^RBTB 25 (1995) 91 (*Mowery, Robert L.*); JBL 114 (1995)
516-517 (*Cope, Lamar*); NT 37 (1995) 99-101 (*Elliott, J.K.*); CBQ
57 (1995) 602-604 (*Maloney, Elliott C.*).
2787 *Neyrey, Jerome H.* Loss of wealth, loss of family and loss of honour: the cultural context of the original makarisms in Q. 1995
⇒80. Modelling early christianity. 139-158.
^E**Piper, Ronald A.** The gospel behind the gospels: current stu-
dies on Q. ⇒101.

2788 *Ramaroson, Léonard* Sur trois textes des Synoptiques. ScEs 47 (1995) 287-303 [Mark 4,3-9; 14,2; Lk 24,17].

2789 *Robinson, James M.* The incipit of the sayings gospel Q. RHPhR 75 (1995) 9-33.

2790 —The Jesus of Q as liberation theologian 259-274;

2791 *Sato, Migaku* Wisdom statements in the sphere of prophecy 139-158;

2792 *Schottroff, Luise* Itinerant prophetesses: a feminist analysis of the sayings source Q 347-360. 1995 ⇒101. The gospel. NT.S 75.

2793 **Sevenich-Bax, Elisabeth** Israels Konfrontation mit den letzten Boten der Weisheit: Form, Funktion und Interdependenz der Weisheitselemente in der Logienquelle. MThA 21. 1993 ⇒9,4437; 10,4263. RJThS 46 (1995) 255-257 (*Tuckett, C.M.*); JBL 114/3 (1995) 514-516 (*Uro, Risto*).

2794 *Sinoir, Michel* L'évêque et l'exorcisme dans les évangiles synoptiques. Sedes Sapientiae 13/4 (1995) 1-18.

2795 **Sung, Chong-Hyon** Vergebung der Sünden: Jesu Praxis der Sündenvergebung nach den Synoptikern und ihre Voraussetzungen im Alten Testament und frühen Judentum. WUNT 2/57. Tü 1994, Mohr xiv; 342 pp. DM98. 3-16-146182-7. RThLZ 120 (1995) 36-37 (*Haufe, Günter*); ThRv 91 (1995) 386-388 (*Fiedler, Peter*).

2796 **Swartley, Willard M.** Israel's scripture traditions and the synoptic gospels. 1994 ⇒10,4264. RPSB 16/1 (1995) 87-88 (*Marcus, Joel*); RTR 54/1 (1995) 34 (*Dumbrell, Bill*); CBQ 57/3 (1995) 609-610 (*Carroll, John T.*); JBL 114 (1995) 731-732 (*Stegner, William Richard*).

2797 *Tabor, James D.; Wise, Michael O.* 4Q521 "On resurrection" and the synoptic gospel tradition: a preliminary study. 1995 ⇒72. Qumran questions. BiSe 36. 151-163.

2798 **Theissen, Gerd** The gospels in context: social and political history in the synoptic tradition. 1991. ⇒7,3831... 9,4441. RCThMi 22 (1995) 146 (*Bailey, James L.*); SJTh 48 (1995) 148-150 (*Grayston, Kenneth*).

2799 *Trimaille, Michel* Jésus et la sagesse dans la "Quelle". 1995 ⇒117. La sagesse biblique. LeDiv 160. 279-319.

2800 *Tuckett, Christopher* Das Thomasevangelium und die synoptischen Evangelien. BThZ 12 (1995) 186-200.

2801 *Uro, Risto* John the Baptist and the Jesus movement: what does Q tell us? 1995 ⇒101. The gospel. NT.S 75. 231-257.

2802 **Vaage, Leif E.** Galilean upstarts: Jesus' first followers according to Q. 1994 ⇒10,4266. RRB 102 (1995) 425-428 (*Klassen, William*).

2803 *Vaage, Leif E.* Q and Cynicism: on comparison and social identity. 1995 ⇒101. The gospel. NT.S 75. 199-229.

F3.1 Matthaei evangelium: *textus, commentarii.*

2804 *Amphoux, Christian-B.* La composition de Matthieu inscrite dans dix prophéties de la Bible grecque. 1995 ⇒13. FHARL M., 333-369 [1,23; 2,15.18; 4,15-16; 8,17; 12,18-21; 13,35; 21,5; 27,9-10; 2,23].

2805 *Banning, Joop van; Mali, Franz* Opus imperfectum in Matthaeum. TRE 25 (1995) 304-307.

2806 *Bastit-Kalinowska, A.* Conception du commentaire et tradition exé-
      gétique dans les In Matthaeum d'ORIGENE et d'HILAIRE de
      Poitiers. 1995 ⇒126. Origeniana Sexta. 675-692.
2807 **Blomberg, Craig L.** Matthew. 1992 ⇒8,4569... 10,4269. NAC
      22. RCritRR 7 (1994) 142-144 (*Levine, Amy-Jill*).
2808 *Boring, M. Eugene* The gospel of Matthew: introduction, commen-
      tary, and reflections. 1995 ⇒92. NIntB 8. 87-505.
2809 **Davies, W.D.; Allison, D.C.** Matthew. ⇒4,4439... 10,4274. ICC.
      1988-1991. RBiTr 46/1 (1995) 132-133 (*Stanton, Graham N.*).
2810 **Drewermann, Eugen** Matthäusevangelium: dritter Teil. Olten
      1995, Walter 432 pp. DM64. RLM 34/10 (1995) 45 (*Jeziorowski,
      Jürgen*).
2811 *Engelbrecht, J.* Are all the commentaries on Matthew really neces-
      sary?. RelT 2/2 (1995) 206ff [ZID 21,704].
2812 **Frankemölle, Hubert** Matthäus-Kommentar 1. 1994 ⇒10,4277.
      RThLZ 120 (1995) 883-885 (*Wiefel, Wolfgang*); BiKi 50 (1995)
      248-249 (*Limbeck, Meinrad*); Entschluß 50/11 (1995) 37-38
      (*Oberforcher, Robert*).
2813 **Galizzi, Mario** Vangelo secondo Matteo: commento esegetico-
      spirituale. Commenti al Nuovo Testamento 1. Leumann 1995.
      LDC 523 pp. L25.000. 88-01-10650-5.
2814 **Garland, David E.** Reading Matthew 1993 ⇒9,4450; 10,4278.
      RCritRR 7 (1994) 189-190; (*Burnett, Fred W.*); TJT 11/1 (1995)
      95-96 (*Mino, Steven C.*).
2815 **Grasso, Santi** Il vangelo di Matteo. CBi. R 1995, Dehoniane 696
      pp. L55.000. 88-396-0646-7 [RdT 37,287].
2816 *Grelot, Pierre* Remarques sur un manuscrit de l'évangile de Matt-
      hieu. RSR 83 (1995) 403-405.
2817 **Gundry, Robert H.** Matthew: a commentary. 1994 ⇒10,4279.
      REThL 71/1 (1995) 218-221 (*Neirynck, F.*).
2818 **Hagner, Donald A.** Matthew 1-13. 1993 ⇒9,4452; 10,4280. WBC
      33A. RAnton. 70 (1995) 696-697 (*Alvarez Barredo, Miguel*); BiTr
      46/1 (1995) 134-135 (*Stanton, Graham N.*).
2819 **Hagner, Donald A.** Matthew 14-28. WBC 33B. Waco 1995,
      xxxix; 529 pp. $29. 0-8499-1096-X [NTAb 40,340].
2820 *Hagner, Donald A.* Writing a commentary on Matthew: self-
      conscious ruminations of an evangelical. Semeia 72 (1995) 51-72.
2821 **Harrington, Daniel J.** The gospel of Matthew. 1991 ⇒7,3838...
      10,4282. REvQ 67 (1995) 89-90 (*Wood, John*).
2822 *Hellholm, David* Substitutionelle Gliederungsmerkmale und die
      Komposition des Matthäusevangeliums. 1995 ⇒14. FHARTMAN
      L., 11-76.
2823 *Howard, G.* Hebrew gospel of Matthew: a report. JHiC 2/2 (1995)
      53-67.
2824 EHoward, George E. Hebrew Gospel of Matthew. TIbn Shaprut.
      Macon, GA 1995, Mercer xiv; 239 pp. $25. 0-86554-470-0.
2825 **Loski, Taduesza** Ewangelia według św. Mateusza: z komentar-
      zem. Katowice 1995, Wyd. Księgarnia św. Jacka 316 pp.
2826 **Luz, Ulrich** Matthäus. 1985-90 ⇒1,4213... 9,4459. BK.NT 1.
      RBiTr 46/1 (1995) 133-134 (*Stanton, Graham N.*).
2827 **Luz, Ulrich** Matthew 1-7. 1990 ⇒5,4333... 9,4460. EkK. RGr. 76
      (1995) 382-385 (*Farahian, Edmond*).
2828 **Mali, Franz** Das "Opus imperfectum in Matthaeum". 1991
      ⇒8,4585. RJThS 46 (1995) 359-360 (*Vaggione, R.P.*).

2829 **Mello, Alberto** Evangelo secondo Matteo: commento midrashico e narrativo. Spiritualità biblica. Magnano 1995, Qiqajon 332 pp. L65.000. 88-85227-73-2 [CivCatt 147,213].

2830 **Morris, Leon** The gospel according to Matthew. 1992 ⇒9,4464; 10,4289. RCritRR 7 (1994) 240-241 (*Garland, David E.*); EvQ 67 (1995) 90-92 (*Wood, John*).

2831 *Parker, D. C.* Was Matthew written before 50 CE?: the Magdalen papyrus of Matthew. ET 107/2 (1995) 40-43.

2832 *Pickering, Stuart R.* Controversy surrounding fragments of the gospel of Matthew in Magdalen College, Oxford. NTTRU 3 (1995) 22-25.

2833 *Stanton, G.N.* The gospel of Matthew: survey of some recent commentaries. **G.** DBM 14/1 (1995) 18-31;

2834 Matthew's gospel: a survey of some recent commentaries. BiTr 46/1 (1995) 131-140.

2835 **Swanson, Reuben J.** New Testament Greek manuscripts: variant readings arranged in horizontal lines against Codex Vaticanus 1: Matthew. Shf 1995, Academic xx; 304 pp. £20. 1-85075-772-0/-595-7.

2836 TVogt, Hermann-J. ORIGENE: der Kommentar zum Evangelium nach Matthäus 1-2. ⇒64,4205 (6,4658)... 8,4594. BGrL 18,30. 1983-90. RAsp. 42 (1995) 599-601 (*Marcheselli-Casale, C.*);

2837 ORIGENE: der Kommentar zum Evangelium nach Matthäus 3. BGrL 38. Stu 1993, Hiersemann 417 pp. DM298. 3-772-9325-3. ⇒10,4294. RSaeculum Christianum 2/1 (1995) 269-270 (*Stanula, Emil*).

2838 *Wachtel, Klaus* P64/67: Fragmente des Matthäusevangeliums aus dem 1. Jahrhundert? ZPE 107 (1995) 73-80 [26].

F3.2 **Themata** *de Matthaeo.*

2839 **Allison, Dale C.** The new Moses. 1993 ⇒9,4470; 10,4298. RJR 75 (1995) 406-408 (*Levine, Amy-Jill*); Bib. 76 (1995) 574-578 (*Roloff, Jürgen*).

2840 *Anderson, Janice Capel* Life on the Mississippi: new currents in Matthaean scholarship 1983-1993. CurResB 3 (1995) 169-218.

2841 **Attinger, D.** Evangelo secondo san Matteo: tra giudizio e misericordia. R 1995, Nuove Frontiere 210 pp. L22.000 [CivCatt 147,531].

2842 EBalch, David L. Social history of the Matthean community. 1991 ⇒7,415d... 10,4300. RSJTh 48 (1995) 394-396 (*Stanton, Graham*).

2843 **Bingham, Dwight Jeffrey** IRENAEUS' use of Matthew's gospel in 'Adversus Haereses'. Diss. Dallas Theol. Sem. 1995, 474 pp. DBlaising, Craig A., AAC 9531273; DAI-A 56/5,p.1844.

2844 *Bubar, Wallace W.* Killing two birds with one stone: the utter de(con)struction of Matthew and his church. Bibl.Interp. 3 (1995) 144-157.

2845 **Byrskog, Samuel** Jesus the only teacher: didactic authority...Matthean community. 1994 ⇒10,4301. CB.NT 24. RNRTh 177 (1995) 273-275 (*Ska, Jean Louis*); BTB 25 (1995) 91-92 (*Craghan, John F.*); Studi di Teologia 7 (1995) 195 (*Bolognesi, Pietro*); JJS 46 (1995) 296-297 (*Harvey, Graham*); CBQ 57 (1995)

383-384 (*Saldarini, Anthony J.*); JBL 114 (1995) 734-736 (*McIver, Robert K.*); Bibl.Interp. 3 (1995) 380-381 (*Taylor, N.H.*).

2846 **Carr, Dhyanchand** The prophecy-fulfillment motifs in the gospel according to Matthew and their relevance for christological reconstruction. CTC Bulletin 13-14/3-1 (1995-96) 18-23 [ThIK 18,29].

2847 **Cecni, A.M.** La parola di Dio nel vangelo di Matteo. CasM 1995, Piemme 316 pp. L30.000.

2848 **Charette, Blaine** The theme of recompense in Matthew's gospel 1992 ⇒8,4604... 10,4303. ^RCritRR 7 (1994) 158-160 (*Wainwright, Elaine M.*); EvQ 67 (1995) 268-270 (*Hingle, N.N.*).

  Dautzenberg, Gerhard Studien zur Theologie der Jesustradition ⇒44.

2849 *Dobschütz, Ernst von* Matthew as rabbi and catechist. 1995 <1928> ⇒115. The interpretation of Matthew. 27-38.

2850 *Duling, D.C.* Matthew and marginality. HTS 51 (1995) 358-387 [NTAb 40,218].

2851 *Duling, Dennis C.* The Matthean brotherhood and marginal scribal leadership. 1995 ⇒80. Modelling early christianity. 159-182.

2852 **Ekka, Martin** The ecclesial perspective of Matthew and tribal (Oraon) community life. Ranchi 1995, xi; 213 pp. master's thesis [Sevartham 21,181-183].

2853 *Engelbrecht, J.* Die rol van die dissipels in die Christologie van Matteus. HTS 51 (1995) 134-146 [NTAb 40,28—*Harrington, D.J.*].

2854 **Fusco, Vittorio** La casa sulla roccia: temi spirituali di Matteo. 1994 ⇒10,4309. ^RTer. 46 (1995) 658-659 (*Pasquetto, Virgilio*).

2855 **Grasso, Santi** Gesù e i suoi fratelli: contributo allo studio della cristologia e dell'antropologia nel vangelo di Matteo. 1993 ⇒9,4481; 10,4310. RivBib.S 29. ^RRivBib 43 (1995) 294-295 (*Vallauri, Emiliano*); CivCatt 146 (1995) 545-546 (*Grilli, M.*); Carthaginensia 11 (1995) 436-437 (*Martínez Fresneda, F.*).

2856 *Hagner, Donald A.* Imminence and parousia in the gospel of Matthew. 1995 ⇒14. ^FHARTMAN L., 77-92.

2857 **Hertig, Paul Alan** The messiah at the margins: a missiology of transformation based on the Galilee theme in Matthew. Diss. Fuller 1995, 379 pp. ^D*Van Engen, Charles*, AAC 9530354; DAI-A 56/5,p.1829.

2858 *Hill, David* The figure of Jesus in Matthew's story: a response to Professor KINGSBURY's literary-critical probe <1984> 81-96;

2859 Son and servant: an essay on Matthean christology <1980> 13-27. 1995 ⇒81. Synoptic gospels. BiSe 31.

2860 *Hoffmann, Paul* QR und der Menschensohn: eine vorläufige Skizze. 1995 ⇒51. Tradition. NTA 28. 243-278.

2861 *Hultgren, Arland J.* Liturgy and literature: the liturgical factor in Matthew's literary and communicative art. 1995 ⇒14. ^FHARTMAN L., 659-673.

2862 *Ingelaere, Jean-Claude* Universalisme et particularisme dans l'évangile de Matthieu: Matthieu et le Judaïsme. RHPhR 75 (1995) 45-59.

2863 *Ito, Akio* Matthew and the community of the Dead Sea Scrolls. 1995 <1992> ⇒81. Synoptic gospels. BiSe 31. 28-46.

2864 *Keck, Leander E.* Matthew and the Spirit. 1995 ⇒20. ^FMEEKS W., 145-155.

2865 *Kingsbury, Jack Dean* The developing conflict between Jesus and the Jewish leaders in Matthew's gospel: a literary-critical study. 1995 <1987> ⇒115. Interpretation of Matthew. 179-197.
2866 *Kingsbury, Jack Dean* The figure of Jesus in Matthew's story: a literary-critical probe <1984> 47-80;
2867 The figure of Jesus in Matthew's story: a rejoinder to David HiɪLlʟl <1985> 97-117. 1995 ⇒81. Synoptic gospels. BiSe 31.
2868 *Kingsbury, Jack Dean* The rhetoric of comprehension in the gospel of Matthew. NTS 41 (1995) 358-377.
2869 **Knowles, Michael** Jeremiah in Matthew. 1993 ⇒9,4487; 10,4313. JSNT.S 68. RBib. 76 (1995) 427-430 *Claudel, Gérard*; CritRR 8 (1995) 238-240 *(Hare, Douglas R.A.)*.
2870 **LaGrand, James** The earliest christian mission to "all nations": in the light of Matthew's gospel. University of South Florida: International Studies in Formative Christianity and Judaism 1. Atlanta, GA 1995, Scholars xi; 290 pp. 1-55540-937-7.
2871 *Lona, H.* Perdón y reconciliación en el evangelio de Mateo. ProySal 20 (1995) 37-54.
2872 **Luz, Ulrich** Die Jesusgeschichte des Matthäus. 1993 ⇒9,4490; 10,4317. RCritRR 7 (1994) 223-224 *(Linss, Wilhelm C.)*; ThLZ 120 (1995) 343-344 *(Broer, Ingo)*.
2873 *Luz, Ulrich* The disciples in the gospel according to Matthew. 1995 <1971> ⇒115. Interpretation of Matthew. 115-148.
2874 **Luz, Ulrich** The theology of the gospel of Matthew. TRobinson, J. Bradford, C/NY 1995, CUP 166 pp. £30/$45 (£9/$13). 0521-434335. RTLS 4825 (22 September 1995) 27 *(Houlden, J. Leslie)*.
2875 *Mackiewicz, Marie-Claude* Les églises de Matthieu. DosB 60 (1995) 10-11.
2876 **Madsen, Peter** Menneskesœnnen. 1995 Det Danske Bibelselskab 136 pp. DKR149. RΙΧΘΤΣ 22 (1995) 185-186 *(Herbst, Peter Kofoed)*.
2877 **Marguerat, Daniel L.** Le jugement dans l'Évangile de Matthieu. MoBi 6. Genève ²1995, Labor et Fides 624 pp. 2-8309-0755-2.
2878 **Martini, Carlo Maria** Che cosa dobbiamo fare?: meditazioni sul vangelo di Matteo. CasM 1995, Piemme 188 pp. 88-384-2292-3.
2879 *McIver, Robert K.* The sabbath in the gospel of Matthew: a paradigm for understanding the law in Matthew?. AUSS 33 (1995) 231-243.
2880 *Niclós Albarracín, J.V.* Aspectos cristólogicos y haláquicos de carácter polémico en la traducción y comentario al evangelio de San Mateo de Shem Tob Ben SHAPRUT. EscrVedat 25 (1995) 199-246 [NTAb 41,34].
2881 *Pickering, Stuart R.* Additional sayings of Jesus in some texts of the gospel of Matthew. NTTRU 3 (1995) 12-17.
2882 **Powell, Mark Allan** God with us: a pastoral theology of Matthew's gospel. Mp 1995, Fortress xi; 156 pp. $12. 0-8006-2881-0 [NTAb 40,147].
2883 *Powell, Mark Allan* A typology of worship in the gospel of Matthew. JSNT 57 (1995) 3-17.
2884 **Reilly, John** Praying Matthew. Homebush 1995, St Paul's 256 pp. AUD$18 [Pacifica 9,239].
2885 **Saldarini, Anthony J.** Matthew's Christian-Jewish community. 1994 ⇒10,4335. RBibl.Interp. 3 (1995) 375-377 *(Davies, Marga-*

ret); CrossCur 44 (1994-1995) 508-511 (*Gundry, Robert H.*); TS 56 (1995) 152-154 (*Boring, M. Eugene*); JR 75/2 (1995) 265 (*Harrington, Daniel J.*); CBQ 57 (1995) 607-609 (*Viviano, Benedict T.*); JBL 114 (1995) 732-734 (*Levine, Amy-Jill*).

2886 **Saldarini, Anthony J.** Boundaries and polemics in the gospel of Matthew. Bibl.Interp. 3 (1995) 239-265.

2887 **Scheuermann, Georg** Gemeinde im Umbruch: eine sozialgeschichtliche Studie zum Matthäusevangelium. Diss. Würzburg 1995. D*Klauck* [ThRv 92/2,XVI].

2888 *Schweizer, Eduard* Matthew's church. 1995 < 1974 > ⇒115. Interpretation of Matthew. 149-177.

2889 *Sim, David C.* The gospel of Matthew and the gentiles. JSNT 57 (1995) 19-48.

E**Stanton, Graham N.** The interpretation of Matthew ⇒115.

2890 *Stanton, Graham* Introduction: Matthew's gospel in recent scholarship. 1995 < 1994 > ⇒115. Interpretation of Matthew. 1-26.

2891 **Stanton, Graham N.** A gospel for a new people...Mt. 1992 ⇒8,313... 10,4338. R*EstB* 53 (1995) 411-413 (*Roure, D.*); NT 37 (1995) 95-97 (*Green, H. Benedict*).

2892 *Stegner, William Richard* Breaking away: the conflict with formative Judaism. BR 40 (1995) 7-36.

2893 **Stock, Augustine** The method and message of Matthew. 1994 ⇒10,4340. R*BTB* 25 (1995) 93-94 (*Bode, Edward L.*); CritRR 8 (1995) 301-303 (*Allison, Dale C.*).

2894 *Strecker, Georg* The concept of history in Matthew. 1995 < 1966 > ⇒115. Interpretation of Matthew. 81-100.

2895 *Suharyo, Ignatius* Das Matthäusevangelium und die Katechese. **Indonesian.** Umat Baru 28 (1995) 2-8 [ThIK 18,46].

2896 **Tisera, Guido** Universalism according to the gospel of Matthew. (Diss. D*Stock, Klemens*) 1993 ⇒8,4630... 10,4342. EHS.T 482. R*CBQ* 57 (1995) 832-833 (*Edwards, Richard A.*).

2897 **Trilling, W.** Il vero Israele...Mt. 1992 ⇒8,4640; 9,4506. Protest. 50 (1995) 249-250 (*Anziani, Giovanni*).

2898 *Ukpong, Justin S.* The problem of the gentile mission in Matthew's gospel. VJTR 59 (1995) 437-448.

2899 *Verseput, Donald* The Davidic messiah and Matthew's Jewish christianity. SBL.SP 34 (1995) 102-116.

2900 *Vledder, Evert-Jan; Aarde, A.G. van* The social location of the Matthean community. HTS 51 (1995) 388-408 [NTAb 40,220].

2901 **Wainwright, Elaine Mary** Towards a feminist critical reading of the gospel according to Matthew. 1991 ⇒7,3879... 10,4346. BZNW 60. R*BiKi* 50 (1995) 242-243 (*Klauck, Hans-Josef*).

2902 **Wilkins, M.J.** Discipleship in the ancient world and Matthew's gospel. GR ²1995 < 1988 ⇒4,4485 >, Baker xiii; 292 pp. $20. 0-8010-2007-7 [NTAb 40,351].

2903 **Wouters, Armin** "...wer den Willen meines Vaters tut": eine Untersuchung zum Verständnis vom Handeln im Matthäusevangelium. BU 23. 1992 ⇒8,4644; 9,4508. R*JBL* 114 (1995) 145-147 (*Weaver, Dorothy Jean*).

2904 **Yamasaki, Gary** John the Baptist in the gospel of Matthew: a narrative-critical analysis. Diss. Union Theol. Sem. 1995, 147 pp. AAC 9541705; DAI-A 56/8,p.3166.

2905 **Yang, Yong-Eui** Jesus and the sabbath in Matthew's gospel: the backgrounds, significance and implications. Diss. Coventry 1995. DAI-C 57/2,p.353.

F3.3 *Mt 1s (Lc 1s ⇒F7.5) Infantia Jesu* — **Infancy Gospels.**

2906 *Amato, Angelo* Il concepimento verginale di Gesù: introduzione a una "quaestio disputata". Theotokos 3/1 (1995) 89-103.
2907 *Bauer, David R.* The kingship of Jesus in the Matthean infancy narrative: a literary analysis. CBQ 57 (1995) 306-323.
2908 *Bolewski, Jacek* Problematyka dziewiczego poczęcia Jezusa [Problematik der jungfräulichen Empfängnis Jesu]. Bobolanum 6/1 (1995) 68-91.
2909 ᴱ**Breen, Aidan** A I L E R A N U S: interpretatio mystica et moralis progenitorum Domini Jesu Christi. Dublin 1995, Four Courts vii; 215 pp. 1-85182-193-7.
2910 **Brown, Raymond E.** The birth of the Messiah. 1993 ⇒9,4510. ScrB 25/1 (1995) 32-34 (*Swain, Lionel*); Theol. 98 (1995) 229 (*Burridge, Richard A.*); RStT 13-14 (1995) 120-121 (*Donaldson, Terence L.*).
2911 *Bucher, Anton A.* Die Kindheit Jesu im Wandel der Geschichte und in der Sicht heutiger Kinder. RPäB 35 (1995) 169-189.
2912 *Buckwalter, H.D.* The virgin birth of Jesus Christ: a union of theology and history. EvJo 13/1 (1995) 3-14 [NTAb 40,22 *Harrington, D.J.*].
2913 *Calambrogio, Leone* Storia di violenza e di salvezza in Mt 1-2. Laós 2/2 (1995) 21-33.
2914 **Ferrari d'Occhieppo, Konradin** Der Stern von Bethlehem aus der Sicht der Astronomie beschrieben und erklärt. B 1994, Ullstein. DM10. 3-548-23550-6 <pb>;
2915 Der Stern von Bethlehem in astronomischer Sicht: Legende oder Tatsache?. Studien zur Biblischen Archäologie und Zeitgeschichte 3. Gießen ²1994, Brunnen 184 pp. DM24.80. 3-7655-9803-8 <pb>. ᴿJETh 9 (1995) 230-233 (*Stenschke, Christoph*).
2916 *Kaut, Thomas* Drei Könige: biblischer Befund. 1995 ⇒122. LThK 3. 364-365.
2917 *Kremer, Jacob* "Sohn Gottes": zur Klärung des biblischen Hoheitstitels Jesu. 1995 <1973> ⇒53. Die Bibel. 339-360.
2918 *Kügler, Joachim* Die Windeln Jesu als Zeichen: religionsgeschichtliche Anmerkungen zu ΣΠΑΡΓΑΝΟΩ in Lk 2. BN 77 (1995) 20-28.
2919 *Leroy, Chantal* Arrivèrent les jours où elle devait enfanter. Vie Chrétienne 403 (1995) 1-4 [2,6].
2920 *López Fernández, Enrique* Nazoraios y sus problemas en torno a Mt 2,23. StOv 23 (1995) 17-102.
2921 **Mattison, Robin Dale** To beget or not to beget: presupposition and persuasion in Matthew chapter one. Diss. Vanderbilt 1995, 442 pp. ᴰ*Patte, Daniel*, AAC 9611808; DAI-A 56/12,p.4819.
2922 *Miles, J.* Jesus before he could talk. New York Times Magazine (24 December 1995) 28-33 [NTAb 40,220].
2923 **Parrinder, Geoffrey** Son of Joseph. 1992 ⇒8,4669... 10,4376. ᴿCritRR 7 (1994) 244-246 (*Harrison, John*); SJTh 48 (1995) 151-154 (*Bauckham, Richard*).

2924 *Picard, Gilbert* La date de naissance de Jésus du point de vue ro-
      main. CRAI (1995) 799-806.
2925 **Ranke-Heinemann, Uta** Putting away childish things. 1994
      ⇒10,4364. ᴿRExp 92 (1995) 123-124 (*Hendricks, William L.*).
2926 **Refoulé, François** Les frères et soeurs de Jésus: frères ou cousins?.
      P 1995, Desclée 124 pp. FF85. 2-220-03629-4 <pb>. ᴿÉtudes
      382 (1995) 860 (*Guillet, J.*).
2927 **Roberts, Paul William** In search of the birth of Jesus: the real
      journey of the Magi. NY 1995, Riverhead xiv; 384 pp. 1-57322-
      012-4.
2928 **Roll, Susan** Toward the origins of Christmas. Liturgia Condenda
      5. Kampen 1995, Kok Pharos 296 pp. reprint. *f*65/£25.50. 90-
      390-0531-1.
2929 **Schaberg, Jane D.** The illegitimacy of Jesus: a feminist theological
      interpretation of the infancy narratives. BiSe 28. Shf 1995 Acade-
      mic xi; 262 pp. £12.50/$18.50. 1-85075-533-7.
2930 **Stein, Edith** La crèche et la croix. Genève 1995, Ad Solem 96 pp.
      ᴿSedes Sapientiae 13/4 (1995) 61-63 (*Bazelaire, Thomas-M. de*).
2931 *Thomas, Paul W.* The virginal conception. ET 107/1 (1995) 11-14.
2932 *Valentini, Alberto* A proposito dell'Infanzia. Theotokos 3 (1995) 3-
      11.

2933 *Masini, Mario* Lectio divina su Mt 1,1-16. Theotokos 3/1 (1995)
      173-194.
2934 *Orsatti, Mauro* Gesù Cristo, Figlio di Davide, di Abramo...di
      Maria: una nota mariologica nella cristologia di Mt 1,1-17.
      Theotokos 3/1 (1995) 13-38.
2935 *Szlaga, J.* The historical truth of Jesus Christ genealogy according
      to St. Matthew. **P.** ACra 27 (1995) 303-313 [1,1-17].
2936 *Rosso, Stefano* Mt 1,1-25 nei lezionari attuali del Rito Romano.
      Theotokos 3/1 (1995) 135-158.
2937 *Hinlicky, P.R.* The presence of Jesus the Christ: readings from
      Matthew 1:18-3:17 for the Sundays from Advent IV to the baptism
      of our Lord. ProEc 4 (1995) 479-485 [ZID 22,72].
2938 *Ratzinger, Joseph* Et incarnatus est de Spiritu Sancto ex Maria Vir-
      gine... Klerusblatt 75 (1995) 107ff [ZID 21,599; 1,18-25; Lk
      1,26-38; John 1,1-18].
2939 *Toniolo, Ermanno* Mt 1,18-25: testimonianze patristiche. Theoto-
      kos 3/1 (1995) 39-87.
2940 *Stendahl, Krister* Quis et unde?: an analysis of Matthew 1-2. 1995
      <1960> ⇒115. Interpetation of Matthew. 69-80.
2941 **Mattison, Robin Dale** To beget or not to beget: presupposition
      and persuasion in Matthew chapter one. Diss. Vanderbilt 1995,
      442 pp. ᴰ*Patte, Daniel*, DAI-A 56/12,p.4819.
2942 *Bauckham, Richard* Tamar's ancestry and Rahab's marriage: two
      problems in the Matthean genealogy. NT 37 (1995) 313-329.
2943 *Bissoli, Cesare* Maria in Mt 1: prospettiva catechistica. Theotokos
      3/1 (1995) 159-171.
2944 *Schvartz, Alain* La généalogie de Jésus-Christ Tychique 118 (1995)
      27-32.
2945 **Moitel, Pierre** Des récits d'évangile: apprentissage d'une lecture. P
      1995, Cerf. CEv 93 [2,1-12; Mark 1,29-31; 6,45-53; 10,46-52; Lk
      19,1-10; John 2,1-11].

2946 *Strobel, August* Der Stern von Bethlehem (Mt 2:1-16): Bemerkungen zum zeitgeschichtlichen Rahmen des astronomischen Phänomens der conjunctio maxima des Jahres 7/6 v.Chr. 1995 ⇒31. F STROBEL A. 11-21 [RB 103,120].

2947 *Albani, Matthias* Der Stern von Bethlehem in astronomischer Sicht: Legende oder Tatsache?: eine Auseinandersetzung mit Konradin FERRARI d'Occhieppos Konjunktionstheorie. 1995 ⇒120. Mitteilungen und Beiträge 9. 26-48 [2,2].

2948 *Jenson, Philip P.* Models of prophetic prediction and Matthew's quotation of Micah 5:2. 1995 ⇒111. The Lord's anointed. 189-211 [2,6].

2949 *Kruse, Heinz* Gold und Weihrauch und Myrrhe (Mt 2,11). MThZ 46 (1995) 203-213.

2950 *Stramare, Tarcisio* Dall'Egitto ho chiamato mio figlio: un mistero della vita di Cristo. BeO 37 (1995) 193-213 [2,13-21].

2951 *Mussies, Gerard* Some astrological presuppositions of Matthew 2: oriental, classical and rabbinical parallels. 1995 ⇒130. Aspects. 25-44.

F3.4 *Mt 3...Baptismus Jesu*, Beginning of the Public Life.

2952 *Coulot, Claude* "Il vous baptisera d'esprit saint": le logion de Jean-Baptiste sur les deux baptêmes (Mc 1,7-8; Mt 3,11; Lc 3,16; Jn 1,26-27.33). 1995 ⇒22. F RENAUD B., LeDiv 159. 291-305.

2953 *Huber, Konrad* 'ΩΣ ΠΕΡΙΣΤΕΡΑ: zu einem Motiv in den Tauferzählungen der Evangelien. PzB 4 (1995) 87-101.

2954 **Kopp, Johanna** Johannes der Täufer: der Prophet zwischen den Zeiten. Aktuelle Schriften. Leutesdorf 1995, Johannes/KSM, Kath. Schr.-Mission 151 pp. 3-7794-1376-0.

2955 *Lohfink, Norbert* Vom Täufer Johannes und den Törichten Jungfrauen: das Evangelium und seine sozialen Konsequenzen. BiKi 50 (1995) 26-31 [Lk 3,10-18].

2956 *McDonnell, Killian* Jesus' baptism in the Jordan. TS 56 (1995) 209-236.

2957 *Orbe, Antonio* El Espíritu en el bautismo de Jesús. Gr. 76 (1995) 663-699.

2958 **Stegemann, Hartmut** Die Essener, Qumran, Johannes der Täufer und Jesus. 1994 ⇒10,9725. BAEO 31 (1995) 317-318 (*Sen, Felipe*).

2959 **Tilly, Michael** Johannes der Täufer. 1994 ⇒10,4392. BWANT 137. R ThGl 85/1 (1995) 132-133 (*Ernst, Josef*); ThR 60 (1995) 343 (*Lohse, Eduard*); ThLZ 120 (1995) 803-806 (*Sänger, Dieter*); SNTU.A 20 (1995) 209-210 (*Fuchs, A.*).

2960 **Vigne, Daniel** Christ au Jourdain: le baptême de Jésus dans la tradition judéo-chrétienne. 1992 ⇒8,4699... 10,4393. ÉtB 16. R JThS 46 (1995) 612-615 (*Birdsall, J. Neville*); JBL 114 (1995) 174-176 (*Stoutenburg, Dennis C.*).

2961 *Webb, Robert L.* Juan el Bautista: un profeta de su tiempo. Kairós 16 (1995) 23-38.

2962 **Yamasaki, Gary** John the Baptist in the gospel of Matthew: a narrative-critical analysis. Diss. Union Theological Seminary in Virginia 1995, 147 pp. DAI-A 56/8,p.3166.

2963 **Gibson, Jeffrey B.** The temptations of Jesus in early Christianity. Diss. Ox, ^D*Caird, G.B.*, JSNT.S 112. Shf 1995, Academic 370 pp. £37.50/$56. 1-85075-539-6 [NTAb 40,141; Mark 1,9-13; 8,1-13].

2964 *Hoffmann, Paul* Die Versuchungsgeschichte in der Logienquelle: zur Auseinandersetzung der Judenchristen mit dem politischen Messianismus. 1995 <1969> ⇒51. Tradition. NTA 28. 193-207 [4,1-11; Lk 4,1-13].

2965 *Lustiger, J.M.* Vaincre dans le Christ. NV 70/2 (1995) 7-13 [4,1-11].

F3.5   Mt 5...Sermon on the Mount [...plain, Lk 6,17]

2966 **Betz, Hans Dieter** The sermon on the mount: a commentary on the sermon on the mount, including the sermon on the plain (Matthew 5:3-7:27 and Luke 6:20-49). Hermeneia. Mp 1995, Fortress xxxvii; 695 pp. 0-8006-6031-5.

2967 *Broer, Ingo* Gesetz: Neues Testament. 1994 ⇒123. LThK 4. 584-586.

2968 **Carter, Warren** What are they saying about Matthew's sermon on the mount?. 1994 ⇒10,4400. ^RNew Theology Review 8/3 (1995) 95-96 (*Mindling, Joseph A.*).

2969 *Dautzenberg, Gerhard* Gesetzeskritik und Gesetzesgehorsam in der Jesustradition. 1995 <1986> ⇒44. Studien. SBAB 19. 106-131.

2970 **Derrett, J. Duncan M.** The sermon on the mount. 1994 ⇒10,4401. ^RTheol. 98/1 (1995) 60-61 (*Harvey, A.E.*).

2971 *Donelson, L.R.* The sermon on the mount: the stripping of ideology. Insights 110/2 (1995) 43-53 [NTAb 40,31—*Harrington, D.J.*].

2972 **Dumais, Marcel** Le sermon sur la montagne: état de la recherche: interprétation. P 1995, Letouzey et Ané 331 pp. FF199. 2-7063-0199-6 [cf. *DBS* 12,68-69, col. 699-938].

2973 **Dumais, Marcel** Le sermon sur la montagne (Matthieu 5-7). CEv 94. P 1995, Cerf.

2974 *Guillemette, N.* The sermon on the mount: feasible ethics?. Landas 9 (1995) 209ff [ZID 21,700].

2975 **Harvey, A.E.** Strenuous commands: the ethic of Jesus. 1990 ⇒6,4763... 9,4575. ^RSJTh 48 (1995) 140-142 (*Pattison, Stephen*).

2976 *Kertelge, Karl* Gesetz u. Evangelium: Biblisch-theologisch. 1995 ⇒123. LThK 4. 589-591.

2977 **Krämer, Michael** Überlieferungsgeschichte der Bergpredigt. 1994 ⇒10,4408. ^RSal. 57 (1995) 372-373 (*Wrege, Hans-Theo*); ThLZ 120 (1995) 659-661 (*Bull, Klaus-M.*).

2978 **Lambrecht, Jan**   Pero yo os digo...el sermón programático de Jesús. ^T*Ortiz García, Alfonso.* 1994 ⇒10,4409. ^RActualidad bibliográfica de filosofía y teología 63 (1995) 56-57 (*O'Callaghan, Josep*); Lumen 44 (1995) 169-171 (*Gil Ortega, Urbano*); RevBib 57 (1995) 121-123 (*Levoratti, A.J.*).

2979 **Lohfink, Gerhard** Per chi vale il discorso della montagna?. 1990 ⇒7,3935; 8,4723. ^RVivens Homo 6 (1995) 202-204 (*Cioli, Gianni*).

2980 *Robinson, G.* The sermon on the mount and eschatology. BTF 27/3-4 (1995) 30-41 [NTAb 41,36].

2981 *Stefanovic, Zdravko* "One greater than the temple": the sermon on
the mount in the early Palestinian liturgical setting. AJTh 9 (1995)
341-351.

2982 *Orbán, A.P.* JUVENCUS als Bibelexeget und als Zeuge der "Afrikanischen" Vetus-Latina-Tradition: Untersuchungen der Bergpredigt (Mt. 5,1-48) in der Vetus Latina und in der Versifikation des
Juvencus (I 452-572). VigChr 49 (1995) 334-352.

2983 *Porter, L.B.* Salt of the earth. HPR 95/10 (1995) 51-58 [5,13].

2984 *Derrett, John Duncan M.* The light and the city: Mt 5:14. 1995
<1992> ⇒45. Studies 6. 1.

2985 *Hwang, In-Chan* Exegetische Betrachtung zu Mt 5,17-20: die Identität Jesu, das Verhältnis zwischen Kirche und Christen und die
Verwirklichung von Gerechtigkeit durch Christen. K. Sinhak Jonmang 110 (1995) 2-30 [ThIK 17,58].

2986 *Theobald, Michael* Jesu Wort von der Ehescheidung: Gesetz oder
Evangelium?. ThQ 175 (1995) 109-124 [5,32; 19,9; Lk 16,18].

2987 *Dautzenberg, Gerhard* Ist das Schwurverbot Mt 5,33-37; Jak 5,12
ein Beispiel für die Torakritik Jesu? 1995 <1981> ⇒44. Studien.
SBAB 19. 38-62.

2988 *Garlington, D.* Oath-taking in the community of the New Age
(Matthew 5:33-37). Trinity Journal 16 (1995) 139-170.

2989 *Ito, Akio* The question of the authenticity of the ban on swearing
(Matthew 5.33-37). 1995 <1991> ⇒103. The historical Jesus.
BiSe 33. 140-147.

2990 *Suharyo, Ignatius* Jesus und die Gewaltlosigkeit. **Indonesian.**
Gema 50 (1995) 18-27 [5,38-42; ThIK 18,45].

2991 *Hoffmann, Paul* Tradition und Situation: zur "Verbindlichkeit" des
Gebots der Feindesliebe in der synoptischen Überlieferung und in
der gegenwärtigen Friedensdiskussion <1984> 3-61 [5,38-48; Lk
6,27-36]. 1995 ⇒51. Tradition. NTA 28.

2992 *Milavec, Aaron* The social setting of "turning the other cheek" and
"loving one's enemies" in the light of the *Didache*. BTB 25 (1995)
131-143 [5,38-48; Lk 6,27-38].

2993 *Dautzenberg, Gerhard* Mt 5,43c und die antike Tradition von der
jüdischen Misanthropie. 1995 <1988> ⇒44. Studien. SBAB 19.
156-187.

2994 *Milton, A. Edward* "Deliver us from the evil imagination": Matt.
6:13B in the light of the Jewish doctrine of the Yêṣer Hârâ. RStT
13-14 (1995) 52-67.

2995 *Derrett, John Duncan M.* The evil eye in the New Testament. 1995
⇒80. Modelling early christianity. 65-72 [6,22-23].

2996 *Hoffmann, Paul* Jesu "Verbot des Sorgens" und seine Nachgeschichte in der synoptischen Überlieferung <1989> 107-134;

2997 Der Q-Text der Sprüche vom Sorgen: Mt 6,25-33/Lk 12,22-31: ein
Rekonstruktionsversuch <1988> 62-87;

2998 Die Sprüche vom Sorgen in der vorsynoptischen Überlieferung
<1988> 88-106. 1995 ⇒51. Tradition. NTA 28.

2999 *Jones, John N.* "Think of the lilies" and Prov 6:6-11. HThR 88
(1995) 175-177 [6,28].

3000 *Theobald, Michael* Jesu Wort von der Ehescheidung: Gesetz oder
Evangelium?. ThQ 175 (1995) 109-124 [5,32; 19,9; Lk 16,18].

3001 *Suess, Gloria E.M.* Beating the (thorny) bushes. Jpersp. 48 (1995)
16-21 [7,16; Lk 6,44].

3002   *Franz, G.* The parable of the two builders. Archaeology in the Biblical World 3/1 (1995) 6-11 [7,24-27; NTAb 40,418].

F3.6   **Mt 5,3-11** (Lc 6,20-22) **Beatitudines.**

3003   *Baroffio, Bonifacio G.* Le beatitudini. Presbyteri 29 (1995) 221-227:

3004   Beati i poveri in spirito, perché di essi è il regno dei cieli. 305-310 [5,3];

3005   Beati gli afflitti, perché saranno consolati. 379-384 [5,4];
3006   Beati i miti, perché erediteranno la terra. 305-310 [5,5];
3007   Beati quelli che hanno fame e sete della giustizia, perché saranno saziati. 542-547 [5,6];
3008   Beati i misericordiosi, perché troveranno misericordia. 620-626 [5,7].

3009   *Brug, J.* Show love to your neighbor. WLQ 92 (1995) 294-295 [5,43; NTAb 40,222].

3010   ᴱ**Eigo, F.A.** New perspectives on the beatitudes. Proceedings of the Theology Institute of Villanova University 27. Villanova, PA 1995, Villanova University Press xi; 221 pp. $9. 0-87723-063-3 [NTAb 40,338].

3011   *Fracheboud, J.R.* Les béatitudes, points cardinaux de l'espérance chrétienne. NV 70 (1995) 89-90.

3012   *Frankemölle, Hubert* Die Antithesen der Bergpredigt: Glaubensbotschaft oder moralische Überforderung?. LS 46 (1995) 9-14.

3013   *Girardi, Mario* Annotazioni alla esegesi di Gregorio Nᴵꜱꜱᴇɴᴏ nel De beatitudinibus. Aug. 35/1 (1995) 161-182;

3014   Bᴀꜱɪʟɪᴏ e Gregorio Nᴵꜱꜱᴇɴᴏ sulle beatitudini. VetChr 32/1 (1995) 91-129.

3015   **Gourgues, Michel** Foi, bonheur et sens de la vie: relire aujourd'hui les béatitudes. LeBi 42. Montréal/P 1995, Médiaspaul 102 pp. $15.

3016   **Maggi, Alberto** Padre dei poveri: traduzione e commento delle beatitudini e del Padre Nostro di Matteo 1: le beatitudini. Orizzonti biblici. Assisi 1995, Cittadella 232 pp. L23.000. 88-308-0570-X. ᴿTer. 46 (1995) 664-667 (*Pasquetto, Virgilio*).

3017   *Röhser, Günter* Jesus—der wahre 'Schriftgelehrte': ein Beitrag zum Problem der 'Toraverschärfung' in den Antithesen der Bergpredigt. ZNW 86 (1995) 20-33.

3018   *Barth, Heinz-Lothar* "Wer heilig ist, trete hinzu; wer es nicht ist, tue Buße!": Texte aus Bibel und Tradition zum Sakramentenempfang wiederverheirateter Geschiedener. Una Voce-Korrespondenz 25 (1995) 140-172, 195-237.

3019   **Cornes, Andrew** Divorce and remarriage: biblical principles and pastoral practice. GR 1993, Eerdmans 528 pp. $25. 0-8028-0577-9 [5,27-32; 19,9; Mk 10,10-12; Lk 16,18]. ᴿLTJ 29/2 (1995) 82-87 (*Steicke, M.J.*)

3020   *Frankemölle, Hubert* Ehescheidung und Wiederverheiratung von Geschiedenen im Neuen Testament. 1995 ⇒128. Geschieden. QD 157. 28-50.

3021   *Heth, W.A.* Divorce and remarriage: the search for an evangelical hermeneutic. Trinity Journal 16/1 (1995) 63-64.

3022 **Keener, Craig S.** And marries another: divorce NT. 1991 ⇒
7,8354...10,4435. RTrinity Journal 16/1 (1995) 63-100 (*Heth,
W.A.*).

3023 *Kremer, Jacob* Jesu Wort zur Ehescheidung: bibeltheologische
Überlegungen zum Schreiben der Päpstlichen Glaubenskongregation vom 14.9.1994. 1995 ⇒128. Geschieden. QD 157. 51-67.

3024 **Machinek, Marian Szczepan** Gesetze oder Weisungen?: die Frage
nach der sittlichen Verbindlichkeit neutestamentlicher Aussagen
über Moral, verdeutlicht am Beispiel des Scheidungsverbotes Jesu.
Diss. Augsburg 1994. DPiegsa, MoThSt.S 21. St. Ottilien 1995,
EOS 384 pp. 3-88096-471-8 [5,32; ThRv 92/2,V].

3025 *Nolland, John* The gospel prohibition of divorce: tradition history
and meaning. JSNT 58 (1995) 19-35.

3026 *Steicke, M.J.* 'What God has joined together let no one separate': a
review essay. LTJ 29/2 (1995) 82-87.

3027 *Stramare, Tarcisio* Il "Supplément au Dictionnaire de la Bible" e le
clausole di Matteo sul divorzio. Div. 39 (1995) 269-273 [5,31-32;
19,1-9].

F3.7 *Mt 6,9-13 (Lc 11,2-4)* **Oratio Jesu,** Pater Noster, **Lord's Prayer**

3028 *Agnew, Francis H.* Almsgiving, prayer, and fasting. BiTod 33
(1995) 239-244 [6,1-18].

3029 *Carter, Warren* Recalling the Lord's Prayer: the authorial audience
and Matthew's prayer as familiar liturgical experience. CBQ 57
(1995) 514-530.

3030 *Collins, R.F.* Is the 'Our Father' Jesus' own prayer?. Living Light
31/4 (1995) 24-30 [6,9-13; NTAb 40,32—*Harrington, D.J.*].

3031 *Fattorini, Gino* "Dacci oggi il nostro pane quotidiano": la domanda
del pane nel contesto della Bibbia. Inter Fratres 45/1 (1995) 21-39
[6,11].

3032 **Hamman, Adalbert G.** Le Notre Père dans l'Église ancienne. P
1995, Franciscaines 224 pp. FF96 [EeV 107,242].

3033 **Häring, B.** Il Padre nostro: lode, preghiera, programma di vita.
Spiritualità 46. Brescia 1995, Queriniana 112 pp. L15.000 [RdT
37,143].

3034 *Jackson, St. A.* El Padrenuestro en san AGUSTIN. Augustinus 40
(1995) 125-137.

3035 **Link, Charles E.** Jesus' epilogue to the sermon on the mount: a
study of the Lord's prayer. Lima, Ohio 1995, CSS 88 pp. 0-7880-
0374-7.

3036 *Madden, Nicholas* MAXIMUS Confessor: on the Lord's prayer.
1995 ⇒82. Scriptural interpretation. 119-142.

3037 *Madden, Nicholas* A patristic salutation: the prologue to the Pater
Noster of MAXIMUS Confessor. IThQ 61 (1995) 239-249.

3038 **Maggioni, Bruno** Padre nostro. Sestante 7. Mi 1995, Vita e
Pensiero 130 pp. L27.000 [RdT 37,143].

3039 *Nos Muro, Luis* Oratorio del Padrenuestro I: pater noster; II: qui es
in caelis 147-166;

3040 III: sanctificetur nomen tuum; IV: advenit regnum tuum; V: fiat
voluntas tua, sicut in coelo, et in terra; VI: panem nostrum quoti-
dianum da nobis hodie 403-418;

3041   VII: Et dimitte nobis debita nostra, sicut et nos dimittimus debitoribus nostris 647-658. RelCult 42 (1995).
3042   **Schnackenburg, Rudolf** All things are possible to believers: reflections on the Lord's Prayer and the Sermon on the Mount. [T]*Currie, James S.*, LVL 1995, Westminster viii; 102 pp. 0-664-25517-5.
3043   **Ségalen, Jean-Marie** Prier avec Jésus. *Bourdeau, F.; Durrwell, F.-X.* <collab.>, P 1995, Droguet et Ardant 188 pp. FF98 [EeV 106,126 *Oury, G.-M.*].
3044   *Suharyo, I.* Das Vaterunser. **Indonesian**. Umat Baru 28 (1995) 26-32 [ThIK 17,51].
3045   *Sys, Jacques* La question du commencement dans l'énonciation du 'Notre Père'. Graphè 4 (1995) 105-124.
3046   *Tournay, Raymond J.* Que signifie la sixième demande du Notre-Père?. RTL 26 (1995) 299-306 [6,12; Lk 11,4].
3047   **Varro, Roger** "Notre Père": une lecture de la prière des chrétiens. Chemin d'un peuple. P 1995, L'Atelier/Ouvrières 183 pp. FF100. 2-7082-3107-3.

3048   *Crossan, John Dominic* Jesus and the leper. Forum 8 (1992) [1995] 177-190 [8,1-4].
3049   **Judge, Peter J.** Mt 8,5-13/Lk 7,1-10: the centurion from Capernaum: a history of modern interpretation. Diss. Lv 1995, [D]*Neirynck, F.*, xxxii; 223 pp. [8,5-13; Lk 7,1-10].
3050   *Grillo, Margherita* La nonna in casa. TS(I) 71 (1995) 9-13 [8,14-15].
3051   *Manns, Frédéric* La suocera guarita. TS(I) 71 (1995) 7-8 [8,14-15].
3052   *Mayhue, R.L.* For what did Christ atone in Isa 53:4-5?. MastJ 6 (1995) 121-141 [8,14-17; Isa 53,4-5; NTAb 40,223].
3053   *Fernandez Lago, José* Deja que los muertos entierren a sus muertos. Comp. 40/1 (1995) 7-27 [8,22].
3054   *Rozen, Baruch* Swine breeding in Eretz Israel after the Roman period. **H.** Cathedra 78 (1995) 25-42 [8,28-34; sum. 195].

F4.1   *Mt 9-12; Miracula Jesu* — The Gospel miracles.

3055   *Biewald, R.* Ohne Wunder geht es nicht: Skizze eine Unterrichtsreihe zum Thema Wunder in der Sekundarstufe I. CLehre 47/2 82ff [ZID 21,256].
3056   **Davies, Stevan L.** Jesus the healer: possession, trance, and the origins of christianity. L/NY 1995, SCM/Continuum 216 pp. $23. 0-334-02605-9/0-8264-0794-3 [OTA 18,667].
3057   *Evans, Craig A.* Jesus and Jewish miracle stories. 1995 ⇒47. Jesus and his contemporaries. AGJU 25. 213-243.
3058   **Fischbach, Stephanie M.** Totenerweckungen. [D]1992 ⇒8,4791..10,4463. FzB 69. [R]EstB 53 (1995) 273-275 (*Arambarri, J.*).
3059   *Habermas, Gary R.* Did Jesus perform miracles?. 1995 ⇒119. Jesus under fire. 117-140.
3060   **Houston, J.** Reported miracles: a critique of HUME. 1994 ⇒10,4465. [R]CTJ 30 (1995) 570-572 (*Brown, Colin*).

3061 **Imbach, Josef** Wunder: eine existentielle Auslegung. Wü 1995, Echter 238 pp. 3-429-01675-4.

3062 *Kirchschläger, Walter* Exorzismus: Biblisch. 1995 ⇒122. LThK 3. 1126-1127.

3063 **Kollmann, Bernd** Jesus und die Christen als Wundertäter: Studien zu Charisma, Magie und Schamanismus in Antike und Christentum. Diss.-Habil. 1995 Gö [ThRv 92/2,III].

3064 **Larmer, Robert A.H.** Water into wine?: an investigation into the concept of miracle. 1987 ⇒4,4648; 5,4553. [R]RStT 13-14 (1995) 103-105 (*Sweet, William*).

3065 **Latourelle, René** Du prodige au miracle. Montréal 1995, Bellarmin 232 pp. [SR 25,359].

3066 *Percy, Martyn* Christ the healer: modern healing movements and the imperative of praxis for the poor. Studies in World Christianity 1 (1995) 111-130.

3067 **Perrot, Charles; Souletie, Jean-Louis; Thévenot, Xavier** Les miracles. Tout simplement. P 1995, Atelier 234 pp. 2-7082-3153-7.

3068 *Saft, W.* Können wir noch an Wunder glauben?. CLehre 47/2 (1995) 59ff [ZID 21,256].

3069 **Trunk, Dieter** Der messianische Heiler: eine...Studie zu den Exorzismen im Matthäusevangelium. 1994 ⇒10,4487. [R]OrdKor 36 (1995) 499-500 (*Giesen, Heinz*); ThLZ 120 (1995) 1003-1005 (*Becker, Jürgen*).

3070 **Twelftree, Graham H.** Jesus the exorcist: a contribution to the study of the historical Jesus. 1994 ⇒9,4647. WUNT 2/54. [R]HeyJ 36 (1995) 209-210 (*Mills, Mary E.*); CBQ 57 (1995) 194-195 (*Jaquette, James L.*).

3071 **Ulonska, Herbert** Streiten mit Jesus: Konfliktgeschichten in den Evangelien. Biblisch-theologische Schwerpunkte 11. Gö 1995, Vandenhoeck & Ruprecht 208 pp. DM34. 3-525-61347-4.

3072 **Park, Eung Chun** The mission discourse in Matthew's interpretation. WUNT 2/81. Tü 1995, Mohr viii; 219 pp. DM78. 3-16-146434-6 [9,35-11,1; NTAb 41,150].

3073 *Stewart-Sykes, A.* Matthew's 'miracle chapters': from composition to narrative, and back again. ScrB 25/2 (1995) 55-65 [8-9; NTAb 40,223].

3074 *Joubert, S.* Much ado about nothing?: in discussion with the study of Evert-Jan VLEDDER: 'Conflict in the miracle stories in Matthew 8 and 9: a sociological and exegetical study'. HTS 51/1 (1995) 245-253 [NTAb 40,33—*Harrington, D.J.*].

3075 **Trummer, Peter** Die blutende Frau. 1991 ⇒7,4015... 10,4491. [R]MThZ 46 (1995) 261-262 (*Kahl, Werner*) [9,20].

3076 **Grilli, Massimo** Comunità e missione: le direttive di...Mt 9,35-11,1. 1992 ⇒8,4818... 10,4492. EHS.T 458. [R]CritRR 7 (1994) 191-192 (*Snyder, Graydon F.*); EstB 53 (1995) 140-142 (*Rubio, L.*).

3077 *Bovon, François* The life of the apostles: biblical traditions and apocryphal narratives. 1995 <1981> ⇒40. New Testament traditions. PTMS 36. 159-175, 235-241 [10,1-4; RB 103,117].

3078 *Starowieyski, Marek* Żywoty i spisy Apostołów: materiały do poznania legendy i kultu Apostołów [Les vies et les catalogues des

Apôtres: matériaux pour la légende et le culte des Apôtres
< French >]. **P.** Bobolanum 6/1 (1995) 132-154 [10,1-4].

3079 **Kaniarakath, George** The person and faith of apostle Thomas in
the gospels. Diss. extract Pont. Univ. Urbaniana, R 1995, xxxviii;
63 pp. ᴰ*Federici, Tommaso* [10,3].

3080 *Claret, B.J.* Das Phänomen der großen Schuld: von Judas Iskarioth
und einer abgründigen menschlichen Möglichkeit. LebZeug 50
(1995) 188ff [10,4; ZID 21,700].

3081 *Hoffmann, Paul* Jesus versus Menschensohn: Matthäus 10,32f und
die synoptische Menschensohn-Überlieferung. 1995 < 1991 >
⇒51. Tradition. NTA 28. 208-242.

3082 **Lohmeyer, Monika** Der Apostelbegriff im Neuen Testament: eine
Untersuchung auf dem Hintergrund der synoptischen Aussen-
dungsreden. Diss. Siegen 1994. SBB 29. Stu 1995, Katholisches
Bibelwerk xi; 472 pp. 3-460-00291-3 [10].

3083 *Bovon, François* Jesus' missionary speech as interpreted in the
patristic commentaries and the apocryphal narratives. 1995 ⇒14.
ᶠHARTMAN L., 871-886 [10].

3084 *Haldas, Georges* Question Judas. Choisir 426 (1995) 43-45.

3085 *Dennison, Charles G.* What is the gospel? Matthew 11:2-6. Kerux
10/1 (1995) 17-24 [11,2-6].

3086 *Grelot, Pierre* "Celui qui vient" (Mt 11,3 et Lc 7,19). 1995 ⇒22.
ᶠRENAUD B., LeDiv 159. 275-290.

3087 *Theißen, Gerd* Jünger als Gewalttäter (Mt 11,12f; Lk 16,16): der
Stürmerspruch als Selbststigmatisierung einer Minorität. StTh 49/1
(1995) 183-200.

3088 *Rousseau, John J.* The healing of a blind man at Bethsaida. 1995
⇒131. Bethsaida. 257-266 [11,20-24].

3089 *Choi, Hye-Yeong* Mt 11,25-27 und Lk 10,21-22: eine exegetische
Untersuchung über das Dankgebet Jesu. **K.** Sinhak Jonmang 109
(1995) 130-156 [ThIK 17,53].

3090 *Cohn-Sherbok, D.M.* An analysis of Jesus' arguments concerning
the plucking of grain on the sabbath. 1995 < 1979 > ⇒103. The
historical Jesus. BiSe 33. 131-139 [12,1-8].

3091 **Fizzotti, E.** La sfida di Beelzebul: complessità psichica o posses-
sione diabolica?. Ieri Oggi Domani 19. R 1995, LAS 117 pp.
[12,24-32; Salm. 42,488].

3092 **Chow, Simon** The sign of Jonah reconsidered: a study of its
meaning in the gospel traditions. CB.NT 27. Sto 1995, Almqvist &
Wiksell 224 pp. Diss. Uppsala. SEK182. 91-22-01695-3. ᴿThRv
91 (1995) 478-483 (*Pfnür, Vinzenz*) [12,39-41].

3093 **Reid, Barbara E.** Puzzling passages: Matt 12,43-45. BiTod 33
(1995) 49[= 228].

F4.3   Mt 13... *Parabolae Jesu*—the Parables.

3094 *Busto, J.R.* Sobre parábolas y ejemplos. Manresa 67/2 (1995) 115-
121.

3095 **Byatt, Anthony** New Testament metaphors: illustrations in word
and phrase. Durham 1995, Pentland xvii; 322 pp. £17.50. 1-
85821-239-1.

3096 **Culbertson, Philip Leroy** A word fitly spoken: context, transmission, and adoption of the parables of Jesus. SUNY Series in Reli-

gious Studies. Albany, NY 1995, State University of New York Press xvi; 390 pp. $74.50/$16. 0-7914-2312-3.

3097 **Dithmar, Reinhard** Fabeln, Parabeln und Gleichnisse. UTB.W 1892. Pd 1995, Schöningh 370 pp. 3-506-99469-7/3-8252-1892-9.

3098 **Durber, Susan** Writing and the parables: DERRIDA and parable interpretation. Diss. Manchester 1995, ^D*Tuckett, Christopher M.* [RTL 27,534].

3099 *Evans, Craig A.* Jesus and rabbinic parables, proverbs, and prayers. 1995 ⇒47. Jesus and his contemporaries. 251-297.

3100 *Evans, Craig A.* What did Jesus do? 1995 ⇒119. Jesus under fire. 101-115.

3101 *Francovic, Joseph* The power of parables. Jpersp. 48 (1995) 10-15.

3102 **Herzog, William R.** Parables as subversive speech. 1994 ⇒10,4511. ^RTheol. 98 (1995) 386-387 (*Downing, F. Gerald*); TS 56 (1995) 571-572 (*Johnson, Luke Timothy*); BTB 25 (1995) 145 (*Crossan, John Dominic*); CritRR 8 (1995) 227-229 (*Blomberg, Craig L.*).

3103 **Imbach, Josef** Und lehrte sie in Bildern: die Gleichnisse Jesu— Geschichten für unsere Zeit. Wü 1995, Echter 237 pp. 3-429-01707-6.

3104 *Irsigler, Hubert* Gleichnis: Altes Testament. 1995 ⇒123. LThK 4. 741-743.

3105 **Jones, Ivor Harold** The Matthean parables: a literary and historical commentary. NT.S 80. Lei 1995, Brill viii; 602 pp. $164.75/*f*255. 90-04-10181-0.

3106 **Kähler, Christoph** Jesu Gleichnisse als Poesie und Therapie: Versuch eines integrativen Zugangs zum kommunikativen Aspekt von den Gleichnissen Jesu. WUNT 2/78. Tü 1995, Mohr ix; 269 pp. DM168. 3-16-146233-5 [Lk 18,1-14].

3107 *Larsen, I.* The importance of context for exegesis. NotesTrans 9/4 (1995) 51-59 [11,2-19; NTAb 40,416].

3108 *McGaughy, Lane C.* A short history of parable interpretation: I. Forum 8 (1992) [1995] 229-245.

3109 *Overman, J. Andrew* Matthew's parables and Roman politics: the imperial setting of Matthew's narrative with special reference to his parables. SBL.SP 34 (1995) 425-439.

3110 **Ploeg, J.P.M. van der** Jésus nous parle: les paraboles et allégories des quatre évangiles. P 1995, Gabalda. FF210.

3111 **Sider, J.W.** Interpreting the parables: a hermeneutical guide to their meaning. GR 1995, Zondervan 283 pp. $15. 0-310-49451-6 [NTAb 40,348].

3112 *Takács, Gyula* Die existentiale Interpretation der Gleichnisse Jesu. Folia Theologica 6 (1995) 111-147.

3113 *Weiser, Alfons* Gleichnis: Neues Testament. 1995 ⇒123. LThK 4. 743-744.

3114 *McIver, Robert K.* The parable of the weeds among the wheat (Matt 13:24-30, 36-43) and the relationship between the kingdom and the church as portrayed in the gospel of Matthew. JBL 114 (1995) 643-659.

3115 *Kremer, Jacob* "Neues und Altes": Jesu Wort über den christlichen "Schriftgelehrten" (Mt 13,52). 1995 <1974> ⇒53. Die Bibel. 13-29.

3116 *Knowles, Michael P.* Abram and the birds in Jubilees 11: a subtext for the parable of the sower?. NTS 41 (1995) 145-151 [13].
3117 **Estrada-Barbier, Bernardo** El sembrador. 1994 ⇒10,4529. BSal.E 165. RThLZ 120 (1995) 439-441 (*Stenschke, Christoph*) [13].
3118 *Carter, Warren* Challenging by confirming, renewing by repeating: the parables of "the reign of the heavens" in Matthew 13 as embedded narratives. SBL.SP 34 (1995) 399-424.
3119 **Pesch, Rudolf** Über das Wunder der Brot Vermehrung, oder gibt es eine Lösung für den Hunger in der Welt?. Fra 1995 Knecht 158 pp.   DM24. 3-7820-0718-2 [14,13-21; TTh 36,112].
3120 *Fossion, A.* "Donnez-leur vous-mêmes à manger": lecture de Mt 14,13-21. LV.F 50/1 (1995) 7ff [ZID 21,394].
3121 *Langer, Wolfgang* Über Wasser gehen: Matthäus 14,22-33. CPB 108 (1995) 130-134.
3122 *Lie, Tan Giok* Analysis of Jesus' teaching episode within the framework of the seven components of teaching: conflict over the tradition of ceremonial defilement (Matt 15:1-20; Mark 7:1-23). Stulos 3/2 (1995) 83-94 [NTAb 41,38].
3123 **Baudoz, Jean-François** Les miettes de la table: étude synoptique et socio-religieuse de Mt 15,21-28 et de Mc 7,24-30. Diss. Institut Catholique 1993, DPerrot, C., EtB 27. P 1995, Gabalda 452 pp. FF340. 2-85021-076-5. REeV 105 (1995) 654-656 (*Cothenet, E.*); EThL 71 (1995) 457-459 (*Neirynck, F.*); RICP 56 (1995) 164-165 (*Quesnel, Michel*).

F4.5   Mt 16... *Primatus promissus*—The promise to Peter.

3124 **Dentin, Pierre** Les privilèges des papes devant l'Écriture et l'histoire. Parole Présente. P 1995, Cerf 296 pp.
3125 *Fornberg, Tord* The figure of Peter in Matthew and in 2 Peter. ITS 32 (1995) 237-249.
3126 **Grant, Michael** Saint Peter: a biography. NY 1995, Scribner x; 212 pp. 0-684-19354-X.
3127 **Grappe, Christian** Images de Pierre aux deux premiers siècles. EHPR 75. P 1995, PUF 349 pp. FF150. 2-13-047054-8.
3128 **Guarducci, Margherita** Le reliquie di Pietro in Vaticano. R 1995, Istituto Poligrafico e Zecca dello Stato 142 pp.
3129 EMeyendorff, John The primacy of Peter. 1992 ⇒8,407; 9,4730. ROrthFor 9 (1995) 90-91 (*Modesto, Johannes*).
3130 **Perkins, Pheme** Peter. 1994 ⇒10,4549. RCBQ 57 (1995) 822-823 (*Gillman, Florence Morgan*).
3131 **Tomić, C.** Začetki Cerkva [Church beginnings]. 1994 ⇒10,4550. RBogoslovni Vestnik 55/1 (1995) 115-117 (*Rozman, Francè*); CBQ 57 (1995) 164-165 (*Mullen, E. Theodore*).
3132 **Wehr, Lothar** Petrus und Paulus: Kontrahenten und Partner. Diss.-Habil. Mü 1995, DGnilka [ThRv 92/2,IV].

3133 **Reid, Barbara E.** The transfiguration. 1993 ⇒9,4747; 10,4554. CRB 32. RBLE 96/1 (1995) 59-61 (*Légasse, S.*); JBL 114 (1995) 526-527 (*Stegner, William Richard*) [Lk 9,28-36].
3134 *Genuyt, François* Matthieu 16,1-20. SémBib 78 (1995) 35-46.

3135 *Sieg, Franciszek* Syn Człowieczy-Mesjasz-Syn Boży i Szymon Piotr (Mt 16,13-20) [The Son of man, the messiah, the Son of God and Simon Peter (Matthew 16:13-20)]. Bobolanum 6/1 (1995) 27-48.

3136 *Derrett, John Duncan M.* "Thou art the stone and upon this stone..." 1995 <1988> ⇒45. Studies 6. 6-15 [16,16-20].

3137 *Kremer, Jacob* Viele "Kirchen"—eine "Kirche": biblische Aussagen und ihre frühchristliche Wirkungsgeschichte (unter besonderer Berücksichtigung von Mt 16,17-19). 1995 ⇒53. Die Bibel. 381-408.

3138 *Genuyt, François* Matthieu 16,21-17,9. SémBib 79 (1995) 47-50.

3139 *Mangatt, George* Jesus' predictions of his passion. BiBh 21/1 (1995) 37-52 [16,21].

3140 *Penner, James A.* Revelation and discipleship in Matthew's transfiguration account.BS 152 (1995) 201-210 [17,1-9].

3141 *Fuliga, Jose B.* The temptation on the mount of transfiguration. AJTh 9 (1995) 331-340 [17,1-9].

3142 *Fossum, Jarl E.* Ascensio, metamorphosis: the 'transfiguration' of Jesus in the synoptic gospels 71-94;

3143 Partes posteriores Dei: the 'transfiguration' of Jesus in the Acts of John. 95-108. 1995 ⇒48. The image. [17,1-9].

3144 *Genuyt, François* Matthieu 17,10-27. SémBib 80 (1995) 51-58.

3145 *Derrett, John Duncan M.* Moving mountains and uprooting trees 1995 <1988> ⇒45. Studies 6. 28-41 [17,20].

3146 *Dautzenberg, Gerhard* Jesus und der Tempel: Beobachtungen zur Exegese der Perikope von der Tempelsteuer (Mt 17,24-27). 1995 <1991> 37a. Studien. SBAB 19. 263-282.

3147 *Misiurek, Jerzy* "Zgorszenia wprawdzie przyjść musza" (Mt 18,7) ["Il est nécessaire qu'il arrive des scandales" (Mt 18,7)]. P. AtK 125 (1995) 175-185.

3148 *García Martínez, Florentino* Brotherly rebuke in Qumran and Mt 18:15-17. 1995 <1989> ⇒132. The people. 221-232 [18,15-17].

3149 *Bornkamm, Günther* The authority to "bind" and "loose" in the Church in Matthew's gospel: the problem of sources in Matthew's gospel. 1995 ⇒115. Interpretation of Matthew. 101-114 [18,15-20].

3150 *Sand, Alexander* Mt 18: Weisungen für eine Gemeinde in der Bewährung. 1995 ⇒14. ᶠHEINEMANN H., 51-57.

F4.8 Mt 20... *Regnum eschatologicum*—Kingdom eschatology.

Evans, Craig A. Excursus three: Jesus and predictions of the destruction of the Herodian temple. 1995 ⇒47. 367-380 [24,1-2].

ᴱ**Lauer, Simon** Tempelkult und Tempelzerstörung (70 n.Chr.). ⇒29 ᶠTHOMA C.

3151 *Jonge, H.J. de* De wederkomst van Christus: voortgezet overleg. 1995 ⇒91. Totdat hij komt 112-133.

3152 *Arnal, William E.* The rhetoric of marginality: apocalypticism, gnosticism, and sayings gospels. HThR 88 (1995) 471-494.

3153 **Beasley-Murray, G.R.** Jesus and the last days. 1993 ⇒9,4776. ᴿRTR 54/1 (1995) 33-34 (*Bolt, Peter*); EvQ 67 (1995) 275-276 (*Wenham, David*); JEarlyC 3 (1995) 359-361 (*Hill, Charles E.*); CritRR 8 (1995) 263-266 (*Telford, W.R.*) [Mk 13].

182   Elenchus of Biblica 11/1, 1995   [Evangelia synoptica

3154 *Noro, Harlei Antonio* Discurso escatológico e Apocalipse. Teocomunicaçâo 25 (1995) 611-625 [Strom. 52,346].
3155 **Meisinger, Hubert** Liebesgebot und Altruismusforschung: ein exegetischer Beitrag zum Dialog zwischen Theologie und Naturwissenschaft. Diss. Heidelberg 1995. DTheißen [ThRv 92/2,X].
3156 *Collins, John J.* The second coming. ChiSt 34 (1995) 262-274.
3157 *Logister, Wiel* 'Hij zal komen in macht en majesteit': de vreemde
wereld van de christelijke parousieverwachting. TTh 35 (1995)
373-395.
3158 *Kruijf, G.G. de* Die dag zal zeker komen. 1995 ⟹91. Totdat hij
komt. 69-74.
3159 **Kaylor, R.** Jesus the prophet: his vision of the kingdom on earth.
1994 ⟹10,3970. RTrinity Journal 16/1 (1995) 123-127 (*Evans,
Craig A.*); CritRR 8 (1995) 232-234 (*Sheeley, Steven M.*).
3160 **Fuellenbach, John** The kingdom of God: the message of Jesus
today. Maryknoll 1995, Orbis xi; 340 pp. $20.
3161 *Jonge, H.J. de* Jezus en de toekomst. 1995 ⟹91. Totdat hij komt
37-46.
3162 *Vogels, Walter* Justice et gratuité: analyse sémiotique de Matthieu
20;1-16. Revue de l'Institut Catholique de l'Afrique de l'Ouest
(RICAO) 10 (1995) 61-71 [ThIK 17,22].
3163 **Martens, Allan Wayne** The compositional unity of Matthew
21:12-24:2: redaction-critical, literary-rhetorical and thematic analyses. 1995 Diss. Toronto School of Theology, Wycliffe,
DLongenecker, Richard [21,12-24,2; SR 24 (1995) 521].
3164 *Marín Heredia, Francisco* Los mercaderes del templo. Carthaginensia 11 (1995) 263-271 [21,12-13].
3165 *Proverbio, Delio Vania* Osservazioni sulla *Vorlage* greca della
versione armena di *CPG* 4588 (*In parabolam de ficu*). AION 55
(1995) 176-192 [21,18-22].
3166 *Cameron, Ron* Matthew's parable of the two sons. Forum 8 (1992)
[1995] 191-209 [21,28-32].
3167 *Brooke, George J.* 4Q500 1 and the use of scripture in the parable
of the vineyard. DSD 2 (1995) 268-294 [21,33-45].
3168 **Mbena, Romanus Rocky** A call to the wedding banquet and membership of the kingdom of God: a biblical-theological study of *Mt*
22,1-14. Diss. Pontificia Universitas Urbaniana, DFederici, Tommaso, R 1995, xv; 135 pp. (extract).
3169 *Lambrecht, Jan* The great commandment pericope and Q. 1995
⟹101. The gospel. NT.S 75. 73-96 [22,34-40].
3170 *Donaldson, Terence L.* The law that hangs (Matthew 22:40): rabbinic formulation and Matthean social world. CBQ 57 (1995) 689-
709.
3171 *Powell, Mark Allan* Do and keep what Moses says (Matthew 23:2-
7). JBL 114 (1995) 419-435.
3172 *Allison, Dale C.* Matthew 23.39 = Luke 13.35b as a conditional
prophecy. 1995 <1983> ⟹103. The historical Jesus. BiSe 33.
262-270.
3173 *Pedersen, Sigfred* Israel als integrierter Teil der christlichen Hoffnung (Matthäus 23). THarbsmeier, Dietrich, StTh 49/1 (1995) 133-
149.
3174 **Newport, Kenneth G.** The sources and "Sitz im Leben" of Matthew 23. (Diss. Ox 1988 ⟹5,4686) JSNT.S 117. Shf 1995, Academic 205 pp. DM79. 1-85075-557-4 [NTAb 40,344].

3175 *Jonge, H.J. de* De oorsprong van de verwachting van Jezus'
wederkomst. 1995 ⇒91. Totdat hij komt 9-36 [24,43-44].
E**Jonge, H.J. de; Ruyter, B.W.J. de** Totdat hij komt: een discussie over de wederkomst van Jezus Christus. ⇒91.
3176 **Gibbs, Jeffrey Alan** 'Let the reader understand': the eschatological
discourse of Jesus in Matthew's gospel. Union Theol. Sem. 1995,
636 pp. AAC 9531166; DAI-A 56,1828 [24].
3177 *Gerhardsson, Birger* Mashalen om de tio bröllopstärnorna (Matt
25:1-13). SEÅ 60 (1995) 83-94.
3178 *Dipboye, Carolyn* Matthew 25:14-30: to survive or to serve?.
RExp 92 (1995) 507-512.
3179 *Fortna, Robert T.* Reading Jesus' parable of the talents through
underclass eyes: MATT 25:14-30. Forum 8 (1992) [1995] 211-
228.

F5.1 *Redemptio,* Mt 26, *Ultima coena;* **The Eucharist** [⇒H7.4].

3180 *Ahirika, Edwin* The theology of the Last Supper. BiBh 21 (1995)
272-281.
3181 **Albrecht, Rolf; Becker, Wolfgang; Hirschmüller, Martin**
Schmecket und sehet: das Abendmahl in biblischer, dogmatischer
und liturgischer Perspektive. Theologie und Gemeinde 1. Tü 1994,
Proclaim 75 pp. DM11.80. 3-931028-00-3 <pb>. RJETh 9
(1995) 375-376 (*Otto, Manfred*).
3182 **Bardet, André** Le pain du ciel dans le Christ Jésus: essai sur
l'eucharistie des premiers siècles, ses destinées historiques et son
actualité. Ouverture. Genève 1995, Labor et Fides 156 pp. [EeV
106,111].
3183 **Berquist, Jon L.** Ancient wine, new wineskins: the Lord's Supper
in Old Testament perspective. 1991 ⇒8,4950; 9,4792. RCritRR 7
(1994) 82-83 (*Smith, Dennis E.*).
3184 **Bishop, Jonathan** Some bodies: the eucharist and its implications.
1992 ⇒8,4950*... 10,4587. RCritRR 7 (1994) 487-491 (*Badham,
Roger A.*).
3185 **Canciani, Mario** Ultima cena dagli Esseni: una documentata nuova
esplorazione. Biblioteca dei misteri. R 1995, Mediterranee 122 pp.
88-272-1115-2.
3186 **Chilton, Bruce** A feast of meanings: eucharistic theologies from
Jesus through Johannine circles. NT.S 72. 1994 ⇒10,4589.
RTheology 98 (1995) 289-290 (*Morgan, Robert*); JThS 46 (1995)
634-636 (*O'Neill, J.C.*); Bib. 76 (1995) 579-582 (*O'Toole, Robert
F.*); CritRR 8 (1995) 188-191 (*Koester, Craig*).
3187 *Christie-Johnston, Hilary* The meaning and significance of the
eucharist. Discussion with *Mundin, Graeme.* CTC Bulletin 13-
14/3-1 (1995-96) 70-77 (Resp. 78-79) [ThIK 18,29].
3188 E**Dotti, G.** Vincolo di carità: la celebrazione eucaristica rinnovata
dal Vaticano II. Magnano 1995, Qiqajon 216 pp. L25.000 [CivCatt
147,431].
3189 *Head, P.M.* The date of the Magdalen papyrus of Matthew
(P.Magd.Gr. 17 = P 64): a reponse to C.P. THIEDE. TynB 46
(1995) 251-285 [26].
3190 **Jaouen, René** L'Eucharistie du mil: langages d'un peuple, expressions de la foi. P 1995, Karthala 286 pp. 2-86537-564-1.

3191 *Jaskóła, Piotr* John CALVIN's teaching on the Lord's Supper. **P.**
      Roczniki Teologiczne 42/7 87-102 [Zsfg. 101].
3192 ᵀ**Marcone, Arnaldo** Paolinus PELLAEUS: eucharisticos: discorso
      di ringraziamento. BPat 26. Fiesole 1995, Nardini 133 pp. 88-404-
      2029-0.
3193 **McAdoo, H.R.; Stevenson, Kenneth** The mystery of the Eucharist
      in the Anglican tradition. Foreword by *Williams, Rowan.* Canter-
      bury 1995, Canterbury 205 pp. £10. 1-85311-113-9. ᴿET 107
      (1995-96) 92 (*Spinks, Bryan D.*).
3194 *McGinn, Sheila E.* "Not counting [the] women...": a feminist read-
      ing of Matthew 26-28. SBL.SP 34 (1995) 168-176.
3195 *Meier, John P.* The eucharist at the last supper: did it happen?. The
      Kenrick Lecture. ThD 42 (1995) 335-351.
3196 **Moloney, Raymond** The eucharist. Problems in Theology. L
      1995, Chapman 224 pp. £16 [⇒10,4610].
3197 ᴱ**Nitti, S.** Martin LUTERO: un sermone sul Nuovo Testamento,
      cioè sulla santa messa (1520): giudizio di Martin LUTERO sulla
      necessità di abolire la messa privata (1521): la messa privata e la
      consacrazione dei preti. Opere Scelte 7. Torino 1995, Claudiana
      422 pp.
3198 *O'Neill, J.C.* Bread and wine. SJTh 48 (1995) 169-184.
3199 **Paillard, Jean** Broder Judas: en ny syn på förrädaren. Örebro
      1995, Libris 240 pp.
3200 **Paillard, Jean** Broder Judas: om en märklig upprättelse av Iskariot
      [Frère Judas: sur une curieuse réhabilitation de l'Iscariote]. Sto
      1995, Libris 240 pp. ᴿRSPhTh 79 (1995) 549-551 (*Jossua, Jean-
      Pierre*).
3201 People as exegetes: popular readings: a Nicaraguan example: the
      alabaster bottle—Matthew 26.6-13. 1995 <1991> ⇒129. Voices
      from the margin. 436-443 [26,6-13].
         ᴱ**Hilberath, Bernd J; Sattler, Dorothea** ᶠSCHNEIDER T.,
      Vorgeschmack...Eucharistie ⇒25.
3202 *Thiede, Carsten Peter* Papyrus Magdalen Greek 17 (Gregory-Aland
      P 64): a reappraisal. TynB 46 (1995) 29-42;
3203 Papyrus Magdalen Greek 17 (Gregory-Aland P⁶⁴): a reappraisal.
      ZPE 105 (1995) 13-20 [26,7-33].
3204 *Thüsing, Wilhelm* Das Opfer der Christen nach dem Neuen Testa-
      ment. 1995 <1965> ⇒60. Studien. WUNT 2/82. 171-183.
3205 *Tourón del Pie, Eliseo* Comer con Jesús (su significación
      escatológica y eucarística). RET 55 (1995) 285-329; 429-486 [sum.
      285, 429].
3206 *Trueman, Carl R.* "The Saxons be sore on the affirmative": Robert
      BARNES on the Lord's Supper. 1995 ⇒2. ᶠATKINSON J.,
      JSNT.S 105. 258-289.
3207 **Ullatt, Sebastian** The spirituality of the sacrificial and the meal
      aspects of the eucharist: an exegetical-theological-spiritual study of
      the institution narratives in the NT and the eucharistic discourse in
      John with a special reference to the institution narrative in the
      anaphora of Addai and Mari. Diss. Pont. Univ. Gregoriana, R
      1995, no. 4147, excerpt xii; 156 pp. ᴰ*Martinez, Ernest R.* [John 6;
      1 Cor 11,23-26; 10,16-17].
3208 **Vogel, Arthur A.** Radical christianity and the flesh of Jesus: the
      roots of eucharistic living. GR 1995, Eerdmans vi; 143 pp. $17
      [AThR 79,464].

3209 *Weber, Hans-Ruedi* "Ceci est...faites ceci": canevas pour une étude oecuménique de l'institution de la Cène. [T]*Le Brun, Véronique*, Hokhma 58 (1995) 51-69.

3210 *Wenham, David* How Jesus understood the Last Supper: a parable in action. Themelíos 20 (1995) 11-16.

F5.3 Mt 26,30...// Passio Christi; Passion narrative.

3211 *Bammel, Ernst* Der Prozess Jesu in der Erklärung des ORIGENES. 1995 ⇒126. Origeniana Sexta. BEThL 118. 551-558.

3212 **Barth, Gerhard** Il significato della morte di Gesù Cristo: l'interpretazione del Nuovo Testamento. PBT 38. Torino 1995, Claudiana vii; 259 pp. L32.000. 88-7016-223-0.

3213 **Bösen, Willibald** Der letzte Tag des Jesus von Nazareth. 1994 ⇒10,4632. [R]ThRv 91 (1995) 22-24 (*Dormeyer, Detlev*).

3214 **Brown, Raymond E.** The death of the Messiah. 1994 ⇒10,4634. [R]Way 35 (1995) 360-361 (*Jeffers, Ann*); JES 32 (1995) 269-270 (*Reinhartz, Adele*); HeyJ 36 (1995) 210-212 (*Ashton, John*); JR 75 (1995) 247-253 (*Crossan, John Dominic*); PSB 16 (1995) 360-363 (*Smith, D. Moody*); TLS (14 April 1995) 26 (*Goulder, Michael*); DocLife 45 (1995) 297-306 (*McConvery, B.*); CBQ 57 (1995) 797-800 (*Senior, Donald*).

3215 *Brown, Raymond E.* The narratives of Jesus' passion and anti-judaism. America 172/11 (1995) 8-12.

3216 **Carroll, John T.; Green, Joel B.** The death of Jesus in early Christianity. Peabody, MA 1995, Hendrickson xviii; 318 pp. 1-56563-151-X.

3217 **Crossan, John Dominic** Who killed Jesus?: exposing the roots of anti-semitism in the gospel story of the death of Jesus. SF 1995, Harper Collins xii; 238 pp. 0-061479-X/-80-3. [R]EThL 71 (1995) 455-457 (*Neirynck, F.*).

3218 *Dahl, Nils Alstrup* The passion narrative in Matthew. 1995 <1976> ⇒115. The interpretation of Matthew. 53-67.

3219 *Dautzenberg, Gerhard* Über die Eigenart des Konfliktes, der von jüdischer Seite im Prozeß Jesu ausgetragen wurde. 1995 <1992> ⇒44. Studien. SBAB 19. 301-333.

3220 *Delhougne, Henri* Golgotha, suprême amour de Dieu et de l'homme. La Vie 53 (1995) 133-149.

3221 *Derrett, John Duncan M.* Jesus as a seducer (ΠΛΑΝΟΣ = ΜΑΤ'ΕΗ). 1995 <1994> ⇒45. Studies 6. 202-214.

3222 *Evans, Craig A.* From public ministry to the passion: can a link be found between the (Galilean) life and the (Judean) death of Jesus? 1995 ⇒47. Jesus and his contemporaries. AGJU 25. 301-318.

3223 **Fricke, Weddig** Der Fall Jesu: eine juristische Beweisführung. Hamburg 1995, Rasch und Röhring 524 pp.

3224 *Gaboriau, Florent* Procès à Jésus. Cath(P) 47 (1995) 87-88.

3225 *Henrich, Rainer* Rationalistische Christentumskritik in essenische Gewand: der Streit um die "Enthüllungen über die wirkliche Todesart Jesu". ZKG 106 (1995) 345-362.

3226 **Imbert, Jean** Il processo di Gesù. Brescia 1994, Morcelliana 182 pp. [R]Teol. 32 (1995) 250-253 (*Hubeñák, Florencio*).

3227 *Koester, Helmut* Explaining Jesus' crucifixion. BiRe 1995 <June> 16, 48.

3228 *Koester, Helmut* Where God can be found: the radical message of Jesus' death. BiRe 11/1 (1995) 18, 46.

3229 *Krieger, Klaus-Stefan* Pontius Pilatus—ein Judenfeind?: zur Problematik einer Pilatusbiographie. BN 78 (1995) 63-83.

3230 **Légasse, Simon** Le procès de Jésus 1: l'histoire. 1994 ⇒10,4666. LeDiv 156. RCarthaginensia 11 (1995) 441-442 (*Sanz Valdivieso, R.*).

3231 **Légasse, Simon** Le procès de Jésus 2: la passion dans les quatre évangiles. LeDiv.C 3. P 1995, Cerf 632 pp. FF350. 0-8091-3302-4. REstudios Trinitarios 29 (1995) 496-497 (*Pikaza, X.*).

3232 *MacAdam, Henry Innes* Gethsemane, Gabbatha, Golgotha: the arrest, trials and execution of Jesus of Nazareth. IBSt 17 (1995) 148-176.

3233 **Maggioni, Bruno** I racconti evangelici della passione. 1994 ⇒10,4639. RCivCatt 146 (1995) 98 (*Ferrua, A.*); Ter. 46 (1995) 316-317 (*Pasquetto, Virgilio*).

3234 **Maggioni, Bruno** Los relatos evangélicos de la pasión. Salamanca 1995, Sígueme 308 pp. [Proyecció 44,321].

3235 **Myllykoski, Matti** Die letzten Tage Jesu 2. 1994 ⇒10,4644. AASF B 272. RBZ 39 (1995) 132-133 (*Schnackenburg, Rudolf*); ThLZ 120 (1995) 150-151 (*Vogler, Werner*); CBQ 57 (1995) 410-411 (*Green, Joel B.*).

3236 *Neuner, J.* Listen to the Spirit: Jesus' passion and death. VJTR 59 (1995) 265-269.

3237 **Pajardi, Piero** Il processo di Gesù. Mi 1994, Giuffré 143 pp. L20.000. 88-1405142-9. RAng. 72 (1995) 582-584 (*Jurič, Stipe*).

3238 **Reinbold, Wolfgang** Der älteste Bericht über den Tod Jesu. 1994 ⇒10,4649. BZNW 69. RBZ 39 (1995) 127-130 (*Gubler, Marie-Louise*); CBQ 57 (1995) 823-825 (*Soards, Marion L.*); ET 106 (1994-95) 270 (*Best, Ernest*).

3239 *Rizzi, Armido* La morte di Gesù come sacrificio. Servitium 29/2 (1995) 39-49.

3240 *Rothgangel, Martin* Empirische Überlegungen zur gegenwärtigen Behandlung der Passionsgeschichte im evangelischen Religionsunterricht Bayerns. Neukirchener Theologische Zeitschrift 10/1 (1995) 75-96.

3241 *Roy, Louis* ¿Tiene significación universal la muerte de Jesús?. AnáMnesis 5/2 (1995) 21-29.

3242 *Schoenborn, U.* Crucificado sob Pôncio Pilatos. EsTe (1995/1) 52-66 [Strom. 52,346].

3243 **Schwarz-Pesch, Hedwig; Pesch, Otto Hermann** Der Kreuzweg: Bilder und Meditationen. Fr/B 1995, Herder 77 pp. DM29.80 [BiKi 50,253].

3244 **Sloyan, Gerard S.** The crucifixion of Jesus: history, myth, faith. Mp 1995, Fortress x; 228 pp. $16. 0-8006-288-61.

3245 *Taylor, Joan E.* The garden of Gethsemane: not the place of Jesus' arrest. BArR 21/4 (1995) 26-35.

3246 *Thatcher, T.* PHILO on Pilate: rhetoric or reality? RestQ 37 (1995) 215-218.

3247 *Toni, Roberto* "Se il chicco di grano non muore...": la fedeltà di Gesù di fronte alla croce. Horeb 12/3 (1995) 29-34.

3248 **Walters, Muru** The perceived meanings of the sufferings of Jesus in the consciousness of the suffering and struggling peoples of Asia: a

Maori anglican perspective. Discussion with *Gray, John* (Resp. 51-53). CTC Bulletin 13-14/3-1 (1995-96) 46-51 [ThIK 18,29].

3249 **Watson, Alan** The trial of Jesus. Athens, GA 1995, University of Georgia Press xiii; 219 pp. $25. 0-8203-1717-9 [EvQ 69,370].

3250 **Zink, Jörg** Vor uns der Tag: was die Passions- und die Osterges-chichte bedeuten. Fr/B 1995, Herder 191 pp. DM15.80 [BiKi 50,253].

3251 **Dieckmann, Bernhard** Judas als Sündenbock...1991 ⇒7,4207*... 9,4854*. ᴿSJTh 48 (1995) 144-146 (*Brearley, Margaret*) [26,14].

3252 **Treichler, Rudolf** Die dreißig Silberlinge des Judas is Chariot: biblische Erzählung. Frieling Religion. B 1995, Frieling 203 pp. 3-89009-951-3 [26,15].

3253 *Choi, Hye-Yeong* Biblische Untersuchung über das Gebet Jesu in Getsemani. **K.** Sinhak Jonmang 111 (1995) 142-170 [26,36-46; ThIK 17,59].

3254 *Sutarno* Die Haltung Jesu gegenüber gewalttätigem Handeln. **Indonesian.** Gema 50 (1995) 190-197 [26,47-56; ThIK 18,45].

3255 *Kany, Roland* Die Frau des Pilatus und ihr Name: ein Kapitel aus der Geschichte neutestamentlicher Wissenschaft. ZNW 86 (1995) 104-110 [27,19].

3256 *Valauri, Emiliano* La moglie di Pilato. 1995 ⇒19. ᶠMATTIOLI A., 157-188 [27,19].

3257 *Luter, A.B.* Women disciples and the great commission. Trinity Journal 16 (1995) 171-185 [27,50-66; 28,1-20].

3258 **Minear, Paul Sevier** The Golgotha earthquake: three witnesses. Cleveland, OH 1995, Pilgrim xiv; 139 pp. $12. 0-8298-1070-6 [27,51].

F5.6 Mt 28//: Resurrectio.

3259 *Becker, Jürgen* Das Gottesbild Jesu und die älteste Auslegung von Ostern. 1995 <1975> ⇒5. ᶠBECKER J., BZNW 76. 23-47.

3260 *Berger, Klaus* Die Auferstehung Jesu Christi. 1995 ⇒66. Die Auferstehung. 31-54.

3261 **Boismard, Marie-Émile** Faut-il encore parler de "résurrection"?: les données scripturaires. Théologies. P 1995, Cerf 183 pp. FF82.

ᴱ**Bommarius, Alexander** Fand die Auferstehung wirklich statt?: eine Diskussion mit Gerd LUEDEMANN. 1995 ⇒66.

3262 *Bommarius, Alexander* "Was etwas ist": ein Nachwort, kein Schlußwort. 1995 ⇒66. Die Auferstehung. 117-123.

3263 *Broer, Ingo* Der Glaube an die Auferstehung Jesu und das ges-chichtliche Verständnis des Glaubens der Neuzeit. 1995 ⇒118. Osterglaube. QD 155. 47-64.

3264 **Bürgener, Karsten** Die Auferstehung Jesu Christi von den Toten: eine Auferstehung ist möglich. Biblia et Symbiotica 3. Bonn ⁴1993, Verlag für Kultur und Wissenschaft 160 pp. DM28. 3-926105-11-9. ᴿJETh 9 (1995) 221-222 (*Baum, Armin D.*).

3265 **Carnley, Peter** The structure of resurrection belief. Ox 1993 <1987 ⇒3,4702... 6,5103>, Clarendon 394 pp. $22.50. ᴿCTJ 30/1 (1995) 239-242 (*Brown, Colin*).

3266 *Craig, William Lane* Did Jesus rise from the dead? 1995 ⇒119. Jesus under fire. 141-176.

3267 **Davis, Stephen T.** Risen indeed. 1993 ⇒10,4687. RCritRR 8 (1995) 452-454 (*Perkins, Pheme*).

3268 *Downing, F. Gerald* The resurrection of the dead: Jesus and PHILO. 1995 <1982> ⇒103. The historical Jesus. BiSe 33. 167-175.

3269 **Essen, Georg** Historische Vernunft und Auferweckung Jesu: Theologie und Historik im Streit um den Begriff geschichtlicher Wirklichkeit. TSTP 9. Mainz 1995, Grünewald 487 pp. DM78. 3-7867-1835-0.

3270 **Gerhard, Dietlind** Osterglaube: der Stellenwert der Ostererscheinungen im Zusammenhang des Osterglaubens der Urchristen. Edition Wissenschaft: Reihe Theologie 2. Marburg 1995, Tecum 46 pp. microfiche; 3-89608-642-1.

3271 *Grelot, Pierre* La résurrection du Christ: centre du message évangélique. EeV 105 (1995) 129-137.

3272 *Hoffmann, Paul* Das Zeichen für Israel: zu einem vernachlässigten Aspekt der matthäischen Ostergeschichte <1988> 313-340;

3273 Der garstige breite Graben: zu den Anfängen der historisch-kritischen Osterdiskussion <1985> 341-372. 1995 ⇒51. Tradition. NTA 28.

3274 *Howe, Leroy T.* On the resurrection and the lordship of Jesus Christ. AJTh 9 (1995) 318-330.

3275 *Karrer, Martin* Ist Größeres nicht als Leben und Tod?: zur Auferstehung. EvErz 47 (1995) 126-141.

3276 *Larsson, Edvin* The resurrection of Jesus and the rise of christology. 1995 ⇒14. FHARTMAN L., 623-647.

3277 ELeimgruber, **J. Ernst; Leimgruber, Stephan** Surrexit Dominus vere: die Gegenwart des Auferstandenen in seiner Kirche. Festschrift für Erzbischof Dr. Johannes Joachim Degenhardt. Pd 1995, Bonifatius 576 pp. [ATG 59,341].

3278 **Lorenzen, Thorwald** Resurrection and discipleship: interpretive models, biblical reflections, theological consequences. Mkn 1995, Orbis x; 358 pp. 1-57075-042-4.

3279 **Lüdemann, Gerd** Die Auferstehung Jesu. Radius Bücher. Stu ²1994, Radius 275 pp. DM89/DM50. 3-525-53523-6/39-2. RStPat 42 (1995) 195-201 (*Segalla, Giuseppe*); RB 102 (1995) 624-626 (*Taylor, Justin*).

3280 —Die Auferstehung Jesu. 1994 ⇒10,4695. RBZ 39 (1995) 133-137 (*Roloff, Jürgen*); ETR 70 (1995) 441-443 (*Rakotoharintsifa, Andrianjatovo*); CBQ 57 (1995) 598-599 (*Morton, Russell*); SNTU.A 20 (1995) 194-198 (*Hasitschka, M.*); CritRR 8 (1995) 250-252 (*Linss, Wilhelm*).

3281 —The resurrection of Jesus. TBowden, John. 1994 ⇒10,4697. Reviews in Religion and Theology (1995/2) 38-41 (*Capper, Brian*).

3282 —What really happened to Jesus: a historical approach to the resurrection. Özen, Alf (collab.), L 1995, SCM ix; 147 pp. $13. 0-334-02607-5. RET 107 (1995-96) 194-195 (*Rodd, C.S.*).

3283 **Lüdemann, Gerd; Özen, A.** Was mit Jesus wirklich geschah: die Auferstehung historisch betrachtet. Stu 1995, Radius 139 pp. DM30. 3-87173-033-5 [NTAb 40,342].

3284 *Lüdemann, Gerd* Zwischen Karfreitag und Ostern. 1995 ⇒118. Osterglaube. QD 155. 13-46.

3285 **Malvido Miguel, Eduardo** Jesús resucitado o la perspectiva de la teología cristiana: una introducción a la teología. Textos 15. M 1993, S. Pio X 234 pp. [R]RET 55 (1995) 98-100 (*Tourón, E.*).

3286 **Martin, James** You can't be serious: resurrection: fact or fiction?. E 1995, Pentland 85 pp. £7.50. 1-85821-288-X [NTS 41,631].

3287 **Marxsen, Willi** Il terzo giorno risuscitò... 1993 ⇒9,4885; 10,4699. [R]Laur. 36/1-2 (1995) 209-210 (*Martignani, Luigi*); Lat. 61 (1995) 227-228 (*Sanna, Ignazio*); Asp. 42 (1995) 395-396 (*Cipriani, S.*).

3288 **März, Claus-Peter** Hoffnung auf Leben: die biblische Botschaft von der Auferstehung. Begegnung mit der Bibel. Stu 1995, Kath. Bibelwerk 124 pp. 3-460-33034-1.

3289 *Menke, Karl-Heinz* Das systematisch-theologische Verständnis der Auferstehung Jesu: Bemerkungen zu der von Gerd Lüdemann ausgelösten Diskussion. ThGl 85 (1995) 458-484.

3290 *Moiser, Jeremy* The resurrection: recent official pronouncements and recent exegesis. DR 113 (1995) 235-247.

3291 *Murrmann-Kahl, Michael* "Wiederkehr des Verdrängten"?: theologiegeschichtliche und systematisch-theologische Erwägungen zum Streit um die Auferstehung Jesu. 1995 ⇒66. Die Auferstehung. 83-115.

3292 *Oberlinner, Lorenz* "Gott (aber) hat ihn auferweckt"—der Anspruch eines frühchristlichen Gottesbekenntnisses. 1995 ⇒118. Osterglaube. QD 155. 65-79.

3293 *Ohlig, Karl-Heinz* Thesen zum Verständnis und zur theologischen Funktion der Auferstehungsbotschaft. 1995 ⇒118. Osterglaube. QD 155. 80-104.

3294 *Palumbo, Egidio* La vita oltre la morte. Horeb 12/3 (1995) 57-63.

3295 *Pierce, A.* Witnessing the resurrection. Search 18 (1995) 134-140 [NTAb 40,414].

3296 **Riley, Gregory John** Resurrection reconsidered: Thomas and John in controversy. Mp 1995, Fortress x; 222 pp. $15. 0-8006-2846-2 [NTAb 40,148].

3297 **Sabugal, Santos** Anástasis: resucitó y resucitaremos. BAC 536. 1993 ⇒10,4705. [R]RTLi 29/1 (1995) 172-174 (*González, Carlos Ignacio*); RTL 26 (1995) 357-358 (*Ponthot, J.*).

3298 *Smith, J.J.* Hansjürgen VERWEYEN and the ground of Easter faith. Landas 8-9 (1994-95) 147-181; 72-100; 181-208 [NTAb 40,216].

3299 *Staudinger, Hugo* Die Auferstehung Jesu im Lichte kritischer historischer Forschung. 1995 ⇒66. Die Auferstehung. 55-82.

3300 *Stoellger, Winfried* Ein protestantisches Märchen: Bemerkungen zur Medienrezeption eines Buches [⇒3280]. PTh 84 (1995) 89-96.

3301 *Stuhlmacher, Peter* Die Auferweckung Jesu und die Auferweckung der Toten. PTh 84 (1995) 72-88.

[E]**Verweyen, Hansjürgen** Osterglaube ohne Auferstehung? Diskussion mit Gerd Lüdemann. ⇒118.

3302 *Verweyen, Hansjürgen* "Auferstehung": ein Wort verstellt die Sache. 1995 ⇒118. Osterglaube. QD 155. 105-144.

Zink, Jörg Vor uns der Tag: was die Passions- und die Ostergeschichte bedeuten. ⇒3250.

3303 *Neirynck F.* Note on Mt 28,9-10. EThL 71 (1995) 161-165.

3304 *Michel, Otto* The conclusion of Matthew's gospel: a contribution to
      the history of the Easter message. 1995 <1950> ⇒115. The inter-
      pretation of Matthew. 39-51 [28,16-20].
3305 *Soares-Prabhu, George M.* Two mission commands: an interpreta-
      tion of Matthew 28.16-20 in the light of a Buddhist text. 1995
      <1991> ⇒129. Voices from the margin. 319-338 [28,16-20].

F6.1 Evangelium Marci—*Textus, commentarii.*

3306 **Brooks, James A.** Mark. 1991 ⇒9,4899. NAC 23. RCritRR 7
      (1994) 149-151 (*Black, C. Clifton*).
3307 *Criddle, A.H.* On the Mar Saba Letter attributed to CLEMENT of
      Alexandria. JEarlyC 3 (1995) 215-220 [NTAb 40,121].
3308 **Cunningham, Phillip J.** Mark: the good news preached to the
      Romans. NY 1995, Paulist x; 177 pp. $11. 0-8091-3554-X.
3309 *Dautzenberg, Gerhard* Das Markusevangelium in der Geschichte
      der urchristlichen Theologie. 1995 <1976> ⇒44. Studien. SBAB
      19. 1-15.
3310 **Grimm,   Werner** Markus: ein Arbeitsbuch zum ältesten
      Evangelium: philologische,   historische   und   theologische
      Klärungen. Calwer Studienbücher. Stu 1995, Calwer 124 pp.
      DM28. 3-7668-3316-2 [ThRv 91,534].
3311 **Gundry, Robert H.** Mark: a commentary on his apology for the
      cross. 1993 ⇒8,5144... 10,4722. RThLZ 120 (1995) 656-657
      (*Lührmann, Dieter*); CTJ 30/1 (1995) 254-258 (*Holwerda, David
      E.*); TJT 11 (1995) 242-244 (*Longenecker, Richard N.*); Bib. 76
      (1995) 107-115 (*Pesch, Rudolf*); CBQ 57 (1995) 394-395
      (*Donahue, John R.*).
3312 **Hargreaves, John** A guide to Mark's gospel. TEF.SG 2. Reading
      ²1995, SPCK. 0-281-047863.
3313 **Hervieux, Jacques** L'évangile de Marc: commentaire pastoral.
      Commentaires. P 1995, Centurion 240 pp. 2-227-366-01-X.
3314 **Hooker, Morna D.** The Gospel according to Saint Mark. 1991
      ⇒7,4268... 10,4724. REstB 53 (1995) 276-278 (*Roure, D.*).
3315 *Kaestli, Jean-Daniel* L'Evangile secret de Marc: une version
      longue de l'Evangile de Marc réservée aux chrétiens avancés dans
      l'Eglise d'Alexandrie?. Le mystère apocryphe: introduction à une
      littérature méconnue. EKaestli, Jean-Daniel; Marguerat, Daniel.
      Essais Bibliques 26. Genève 1995, Labor et Fides. 2-8309-0770-1.
      85-102.
3316 *Kalatzi, Maria* Corpus Christi College (Cambridge) 224: the miss-
      ing link. Scr. 49/2 (1995) 262-263.
3317 **Maier, Gerhard** Markus-Evangelium. Bibelkommentare 3. Stu
      1995, Hänssler 715 pp. 3-7751-2116-1.
3318 **Mateos, Juan; Camacho, Fernando** El evangelio de Marcos 1:
      analisis lingüístico y comentario exegético. 1993 ⇒9,4912. RBib.
      76 (1995) 105-106 (*Fusco, Vittorio*); EE 70 (1995) 107-110
      (*Rodríguez Carmona, A.*); CBQ 57 (1995) 405-407 (*Branick, Vin-
      cent P.*); BLE 96 (1995) 58-59 (*Dutheil, Jacques*).
3319 **Mateos, Juan; Camacho, Fernando** El Evangelio de Marcos 2:
      texto y comentario. 1994 ⇒10,4729. RPhase 35 (1995) 436-437
      (*Latorre, J.*); RTLi 29 (1995) 488-491 (*Cáceres Guinet, Hugo*);
      Isidorianum 4 (1995) 253 (*Flor Serrano, Gonzalo*).

3320 *Milgrom, Jacob* A gospel among the Scrolls? BR 11/6 (1995) 36-42.

3321 *Neirynck, F.* Urmarcus revise: la théorie synoptique de M.-E. BOISMARD nouvelle manière. EThL 71 (1995) 166-175.

3322 *Neirynck, Frans* Assessment. Mark and Q: a study of the overlap texts. **Fleddermann, Harry T.** BEThL 122. Lv 1995, Univ. Press. 90-6186-710-X/90-6831-712-1. 261-307.

3323 *Perkins, Pheme* The gospel of Mark: introduction, commentary, and reflections. 1995 ⇒93. NIntB 8. 507-733.

3324 **Robinson, Geoffrey** A change of mind and heart: the good news according to Mark. Revesby, N.S.W. 1994 Parish Ministry. 579 pp. AUD25. 1-8754-6304-6. RACR 72 (1995) 237-238 *(Mecham, F.A.)*.

3325 **Swanson, Reuben J.** New Testament Greek manuscripts: variant readings arranged in horizontal lines against Codex Vaticanus 2: Mark. Sheffield 1995, Academic xix; 271 pp. £18.50. 1-85075-773-9/-596-5.

F6.2 *Evangelium Marci,* **Themata.**

3326 EAnderson, **Janice Capel; Moore, Stephen D.** Mark and method. 1992 ⇒8,336... 10,4734. RTJT 11/1 (1995) 88-90 *(Kozar, Joseph)*; HeyJ 36 (1995) 208-209 *(Ashton, John)*.

3327 **Anthonysami, Joseph** The gentile mission in the gospel of Mark: a redaction critical study of passages with a gentile tendency. Diss. Pont. Univ. Gregoriana, excerpt, Madras 1995 <1982>, 112 pp. DRasco, *Emilio*.

3328 **Best, Ernest** Mark's preservation of the tradition. 1995 <1974> ⇒116. The interpretation of Mark. 153-168.

3329 **Black, C. Clifton** Mark: images of an apostolic interpreter. 1994 ⇒10,4738. RJThS 46 (1995) 620-625 *(Carleton Paget, James)*; AThR 77/1 (1995) 98-99 *(Graham, Holt H.)*; ThLZ 120 (1995) 436-437 *(Lührmann, Dieter)*; JR 75 (1995) 408-409 *(Grant, Robert M.)*; CritRR 8 (1995) 175-178 *(Hunt, Allen R.)*.

3330 **Boismard, Marie-Émile** L'évangile de Marc: sa préhistoire. 1994 ⇒10,4740. EtB 26. POC 45/1-2 (1995) 292-293 *(Ternant, P.)*.

3331 **Broadhead, Edwin K.** Teaching with authority: miracles and christology in the gospel of Mark. 1992 ⇒8,5125... 10,4741. JSNT.S 74. RThRv 91 (1995) 126-127 *(Scholtissek, Klaus)*.

3332 **Bryan, Christopher** A preface to Mark. 1993 ⇒9,4925; 10,4742. RCritRR 7 (1994) 151-153 *{Morton, Russell)*.

3333 *Byung-Mu, Ahn* Jesus and the minjung in the gospel of Mark. 1995 <1991> ⇒129. Voices from the margin. 85-104.

3334 **Chapman, Dean W.** The orphan gospel: Mark's perspective on Jesus. 1993 ⇒9,4928; 10,4745. BiSe 16. RInterp. 49 (1995) 107-108 *(Aageson, James W.)*.

3335 *Chapman, Dean W.* Locating the gospel of Mark: a model of agrarian biography [sic for 'geography']. BTB 25 (1995) 24-36.

3336 *Collins, Adela Yarbro* Mysteries in the gospel of Mark. StTh 49/1 (1995) 11-23.

3337 **Cook, John Granger** The structure and persuasive power of Mark: a linguistic approach. SBL Semeia Studies 28. Atlanta, GA 1995, Scholars xvii; 384 pp. Diss 1985. $45/$30. 0-7885-0027-9/28-7.

3338 *Cyen, Geert van* Het onbegrip van de leerlingen in het Mar-
      cusevangelie: een methodologisch overzicht aan de hand van Mc
      6,52 en 8,17-21. Coll. 25 (1995) 175-199.
3339 **Dannemann, Irene** "Aus dem Rahmen fallen": eine feministische
      Re-Vision von Frauen im Markusevangelium. Diss. Kassel 1995,
      ᴰ*Schottroff* [ThRv 92,XI].
3340 *Dautzenberg, Gerhard* Elija im Markusevangelium <1992> 352-
      375;
3341 "Sohn Gottes" im Evangelium nach Markus 98-105. 1995 ⇒44.
      Studien. SBAB 19.
3342 **Davidsen, Ole** The narrative Jesus: a semiotic reading of Mark's
      gospel. 1993 ⇒9,4902; 10,4750. ᴿCritRR 7 (1994) 178-180
      (*Moore, Stephen D.*); CBQ 57 (1995) 389-390 (*Cahill, P. Joseph*);
      JR 75 (1995) 550-551 (*Patte, Daniel*).
3343 *Davis, Philip G.* Mark's christological paradox. 1995 <1989>
      ⇒81. The synoptic gospels. 163-177.
3344 *Donahue, John R.* Windows and mirrors: the setting of Mark's
      gospel. CBQ 57 (1995) 1-26.
3345 *Dowd, S.E.* Reading Mark reading Isaiah. LexTQ 30/3 (1995) 133-
      143 [NTAb 41,41].
3346 **Drewermann, Eugen** Il vangelo di Marco: immagini di redenzione
      [⇒4,4956; 5,4857]. ᵀ*Laldi, Annapaola*. BTCon 78. Brescia 1994,
      Queriniana 585 pp. L70.000. 88-399-0378-X. ᴿREsp 54 (1995)
      209-211 (*Castro, Secundino*); Gr. 76 (1995) 598-599 (*Marconi,
      Gilberto*); REB 220 (1995) 1011-1012 (*Paul, Claudio*); EE 70
      (1995) 120-122 (*Castro, Secundino*); CivCatt 146 (1995) 148-156
      (*Rossi, G.*).
3347 *Dwyer, Timothy* The motif of wonder in the gospel of Mark. JSNT
      57 (1995) 49-59.
3348 **Eck, Ernest van** Galilee and Jerusalem in Mark's story of Jesus: a
      narratological and social scientific reading. HTS.S 7. Pretoria
      1995, University of Pretoria viii; 455 pp. 0-9583208-5-3.
3349 *Eck, Ernest van* Maaltye as seremonies in die Markusevangelie: 'n
      sleutel om J.H.J.A. GREYVENSTEIN en A.S. GEYSER se denke
      oor die Nederduitsch Hervormde Kerk van Afrika as volkskerk te
      evalueer [Meals as ceremonies in Mark's gospel: a key to evaluate
      the understanding of the Nederduitsch Hervormde Kerk van Afrika
      as 'people's church' by J.H.J.A. Greyvenstein and A.S. Geyser].
      HTS 51 (1995) 1114-1126 [NTA 40,420].
3350 *Ellingworth, Paul* The dog in the night: a note on Mark's non-use
      of *kai*. BiTr 46/1 (1995) 125-128.
3351 ᴱ**Elliott, J.K.** The language and style of the gospel of Mark. 1993
      <1928> ⇒9,4936; 10,4756. NT.S 71. ᴿJR 75 (1995) 266-267
      (*Brehm, H. Alan*); NT 37 (1995) 97-99 (*Heimerdinger, Jenny*).
3352 *Fowler, Robert M.* The rhetoric of direction and indirection in the
      gospel of Mark. 1995 <1989> ⇒116. The interpretation of Mark.
      207-227.
3353 *Gnanvaram, M.* Understanding of christology in Mark's gospel and
      its implication for the church's mission in Asia today. Discussion
      with *Rajkumar, Evangeline*. CTC Bulletin 13-14/3-1 (1995-96) 24-
      29 (Resp. 29-31) [ThIK 18,29].
3354 *Guarducci, Margherita* L'apostolo Pietro e l'evangelista Marco.
      RIL 9/6.1 (1995) 71-75.

3355 **Hamerton-Kelly, Robert G.** The gospel and the sacred: poetics of violence in Mark. 1994 ⇒10,4761. RCBQ 57 (1995) 809-810 (*Vaage, Leif E.*).

3356 **Hauser, Michael** Die Gottesherrschaft im Markusevangelium. Diss. Bethel 1995, DLindemann [ThRv 92/2,VI].

3357 **Huber, Konrad** Jesus in Auseinandersetzung: exegetische Untersuchungen zu den sogenannten Jerusalemer Streitgesprächen des Markusevangeliums im Blick auf ihre christologischen Implikationen. FzB 75. Wü 1995, Echter 499 pp. Diss. 1994 ⇒10,4764. ATS437. 3-429-01641-X.

3358 *Hurtado, L. W.* The gospel of Mark: evolutionary or revolutionary document?. 1995 <1990> ⇒81. The synoptic gospels. BiSe 31. 196-211.

3359 *Juel, Donald* The Markan community and the 'mighty minority'. StTh 49 (1995) 67-77.

3360 **Kampling, Rainer** Israel unter dem Anspruch des Messias... Markus. 1992 ⇒8,5148... 10,4769. SBB 25. RThRv 91 (1995) 388-390 (*Theobald, Michael*).

3361 *Kampling, Rainer* Das Gesetz im Markusevangelium. 1995 ⇒3402. Der Evangelist. SBS 163. 119-150.

3362 **Keenan, John P** The gospel of Mark: a Mahāyāna reading. Faith Meets Faith. Mkn 1995, Orbis viii; 423 pp. 1-57075-041-6.

3363 *Kertelge, Karl* The epiphany of Jesus in the gospel. 1995 <1969> ⇒116. The interpretation of Mark. 105-140.

3364 *Kertelge, Karl* Jüngerschaft und Nachfolge: Grundlegung von Kirche nach Markus. 1995 ⇒3402. Der Evangelist. SBS 163. 151-165.

3365 **Kiley, Bernadette** Jesus in Mark's gospel. Homebush, NSW 1995, St Paul's 96 pp. AUS$12 [ACR 74,372].

3366 **Kinukawa, Hisako** Women and Jesus in Mark: a Japanese feminist perspective. 1994 ⇒10,8738. RCritRR 8 (1995) 236-238 (*Ringe, Sharon*).

3367 **Kinukawa, Hisako** Frauen im Markusevangelium: eine japanische Lektüre. Luzern 1995, Exodus 189 pp. 3-905575-96-5.

3368 **Kristen, Peter** Familie, Kreuz und Leben: Nachfolge Jesu nach Q und dem Markusevangelium. Diss. Marburg 1995, DLührmann, D., Elwert 1995, Marburg 248 pp. 3-7708-1055-4 [ThRv 92/2,XII].

3369 *Kuhn, Heinz-Wolfgang* Neuere Wege in der Synoptiker-Exegese am Beispiel des Markusevangeliums. 1995 ⇒30. FSTRECKER G., BZNW 75. 30-59.

3370 *Latzoo, C.* The story of the Twelve in the gospel of Mark. Hekima Review 13 (1995) 25-33.

3371 *Malbon, Elizabeth Struthers* Galilee and Jerusalem: history and literature in Marcan interpretation. 1995 <1982> ⇒116. The interpretation of Mark. 253-268.

3372 **Marcus, Joel** The way of the Lord: christological exegesis in... Mark. 1992 ⇒8,5156... 10,4774. RCTJ 30/1 (1995) 228-230 (*Holwerda, David E.*); IBSt 17 (1995) 92-93 (*Ker, Donald P.*); Neotest. 29 (1995) 125 (*Eck, E. van*); JBL 114 (1995) 147-150 (*Juel, Donald*).

3373 **Marshall, Christopher D.** Faith as a theme in Mark's narrative. 1994 <1989 ⇒5,4920... 8,5158> ⇒10,4775. MSSNTS 94. RSJTh 48 (1995) 535-537 (*Piper, R.A.*).

3374 **Marxsen, W.** L'evangelista Marco: studi sulla storia della redazione del vangelo. *Maggioni, B.* <introd>. Theologica. CasM 1994, Piemme 196 pp. L.50.000. ᴿAsp. 42/1 (1995) 117-118 (*Di Palma, G.*).

3375 *Matera, F.J.* Ethics for the kingdom of God: the gospel according to Mark. LouvSt 20 (1995) 187-200.

3376 *Matera, Frank.J.* The crucified son of God: introducing the gospel according to Mark. ChiSt 34/1 (1995) 6-16.

3377 **May, Bonita Louise** Jesus' leadership as manifest in the gospel according to Mark: a transdisciplinary study. Diss. Gonzaga 1995, 167 pp. ᴰ*Perreault, George,* DAI-A 56,2766.

3378 **Meadors, Edward P.** Jesus the messianic herald of salvation. WUNT 2/72. Tü 1995, Mohr xi; 387 pp. Diss. ⇒9,4958. DM118. 3-16-146251-3.

3379 **Mellon, J.C.** Mark as recovery story: alcoholism and the rhetoric of gospel mystery. Chicago 1995, University of Illinois Press xiii; 310 pp. $27. 0-252-02165-7 [NTAb 40,342].

3380 *Miller, J.* The literary structure of Mark: an interpretation based on 1 Corinthians 2:1-8. ET 106 (1995) 296-299.

3381 **Moore, Stephen D.** Mark and Luke in poststructuralist perspectives. 1992 ⇒8,5164... 10,4780. ᴿJBL 114 (1995) 152-154 (*Staley, Jeffrey L.*).

3382 **Müller, Peter** 'Wer ist dieser?': Jesus im Markusevangelium: Markus als Erzähler, Verkündiger und Lehrer. Biblisch-theologische Studien 27. Neuk 1995, Neuk 192 pp. DM48. 3-7887-1538-3.

3383 *O'Grady, John F.* Evil and sin in Mark. ChiSt 34/1 (1995) 42-52.

3384 **Oyen, Geert van** De studie van de Marcusredactie in de twintigste eeuw. 1993 ⇒9,4963; 10,4785. ᴿRTL 26 (1995) 232-233 (*Focant, C.*); JThS 46 (1995) 625-628 (*De Boer, M.C.*); CBQ 57 (1995) 845-847 (*Silva, Moisés*); CritRR 8 (1995) 273-276 (*Denning-Rolle, Sara J.*).

3385 *Perrin, Norman* The christology of Mark: a study in methodology. 1995 <1971/74> ⇒116. The interpretation of Mark. 125-140.

3386 *Pickering, Stuart R.* Additional sayings of Jesus in some texts of the gospel of Mark. NTTRU 3 (1995) 26-34.

3387 **Pikaza Ibarrondo, Xabier** Para vivir el evangelio: lectura de Marcos. Estella 1995, Verbo Divino 246 pp. 84-7151-986-0.

3388 *Poetker, K.M.* Domestic domains in the gospel of Mark. Direction 24/1 (1995) 14-24 [NTAb 40,36—*Harrington, D.J.*].

3389 *Pokorny, Petr* Die Bedeutung des Markusevangeliums für die Entstehung der christlichen Bibel. 1995 ⇒14. ᶠHARTMAN L., 409-427.

3390 **Räisänen, Heikki** The 'Messianic Secret' in Mark. ᵀ*Tuckett, C.*, E 1995 <1990 ⇒6,5210>, Clark xvii; 289 pp. $25. 0-567-29253-3. [NTAb 40,345].

3391 **Reling, Hans-Otto** The composition of tripolar pronouncement stories in the gospel of Mark. Diss. Andrews 1995, 300 pp. ᴰ*Johnston, Robert M.*, AAC 9522613; DAI-A 56,591.

3392 *Rhoads, D.M.* Network for mission: the social system of the Jesus movement as depicted in the narrative of the gospel of Mark. 1995 ⇒87. Vorkonstantinisches Christentum. ANRW II,226/2. 1692-1729.

3393 —Mission in the gospel of Mark. CThMi 22 (1995) 340-355.

3394 *Rossi, G.* Interpretazione del vangelo e psicologia: osservazioni in margine a un libro di E. DREWERMANN [Vangelo di Marco ⇒3346]. CivCatt 146 (1995) 148-156.

3395 *Schlosser, Jacques* Jésus le sage et ses vues sur l'homme d'après l'évangile de Marc. 1995 ⇒117. La sagesse biblique. 321-356.

3396 **Schneck, Richard** Isaiah in the gospel of Mark, 1-8. 1994 ⇒10,4790. BIBAL.DS 1. RCritRR 8 (1995) 294-296 (*Marcus, Joel*).

3397 **Scholtissek, Klaus** Die Vollmacht Jesu. 1992. ⇒8,5179... 10,4790*. NTA 25. RJBL 114 (1995) 150-152 (*Wilson, Walter T.*).

3398 *Scholtissek, Klaus* Der Sohn Gottes für das Reich Gottes: zur Verbindung von Christologie und Eschatologie bei Markus. 1995 ⇒3402. Der Evangelist. SBS 163. 63-90.

3399 *Schulz, Siegfried* Mark's significance for the theology of early christianity. 1995 <1964> ⇒116. The interpretation of Mark. 197-206.

3400 *Schweizer, Eduard* Mark's theological achievement. 1995 <1964> ⇒116. The interpretation of Mark. 63-87.

3401 *Smith, Stephen H.* A divine tragedy: some observations on the dramatic structure of Mark's gospel. NT 37 (1995) 209-231.

3402 ESöding, Thomas Der Evangelist als Theologe: Studien zum Markusevangelium. SBS 163. Stu 1995, Katholisches Bibelwerk 195 pp. DM59. 3-460-04631-7 [ThRv 93,173].

3403 *Söding, Thomas* Der Evangelist in seiner Zeit: Voraussetzungen, Hintergründe und Schwerpunkte markinischer Theologie. 1995 ⇒3402. Der Evangelist. 11-62.

3404 *Söding, Thomas* Leben nach dem Evangelium. 1995 ⇒3402. Der Evangelist. 167-195.

3405 **Stinton, Richard Walter** A case study in application of long-term sermon preparation theory to the development and evaluation of a synthetic/homiletical message series from Mark's gospel with a preaching strategy of strengthening discipleship at Saanichton Bible Fellowship. Diss. Dallas 1995, 137 pp. DReed, John, AAC 9531283; DAI-A 56,1831.

3406 *Tannehill, Robert C.* The disciples in Mark: the function of a narrative role. 1995 <1977> ⇒116. The interpretation of Mark. 169-195.

3407 **Tate, W. Randolph** Reading Mark from the outside: Eco and Iser leave their marks. SF/Bethesda 1995, International Scholars/Christian Universities Press, x; 166 pp. $65/$45. 1-883255-83-X/-82-1 [NTAb 40,350].

3408 **Taylor, David Bruce** Mark's gospel as literature and history. 1992 ⇒8,5107; 9,4978. RSJTh 48 (1995) 116-118 (*Telford, W.R.*).
ETelford, William R. The interpretation of Mark. ⇒116.

3409 *Telford, William R.* Introduction: the interpretation of Mark: a history of developments and issues. 1995 ⇒116. 1-61.

3410 **Telford, William R.** Mark. NTGu. Shf 1995, Academic 162 pp. 1-85075-728-3.

3411 **Vogt, Thea** Angst und Identität im Markusevangelium: ein textpsychologischer und sozialgeschichtlicher Beitrag. 1993 ⇒9,4982; 10,4799. NTOA 26. RThRv 91 (1995) 127-130 (*Scholtissek, Klaus*); CritRR 8 (1995) 314-316 (*Collins, Adela Yarbro*).

3412 *Vouga, François* "Habt Glauben an Gott": der Theozentrismus der Verkündigung des Evangeliums und des christlichen Glaubens im Markusevangelium. 1995 ⇒14. [F]HARTMAN L., 93-109.
3413 *Vouga, François* Das Markusevangelium als literarisches Werk: eine Weiterentwicklung des paulinischen Evangeliums? Überlegungen zur Problematik Schriftlichkeit/Mündlichkeit. WuD 23 (1995) 109-124.
3414 **Wallis, Bascom** Mark's memory of the future: a study in the art of theology. N.Richland Hills, TX 1995, BIBAL ix; 235 pp. $15. 0-941037-34-7 [NTAb 40,151].
3415 *Weeden, T.J.* The Markan mystery and Mark's Messiah for faith. ChiSt 24/1 (1995) 17-31 [NTAb 40,37—*Harrington, D.J.*].
3416 *Weeden, Theodore J.* The heresy that necessitated Mark's gospel. 1995 <1968> ⇒116. The interpretation of Mark. 89-104.
3417 *Wefald, Eric K.* The separate gentile mission in Mark: a narrative explanation of Markan geography, the two feeding accounts and exorcisms. JSNT 60 (1995) 3-26.
3418 **Wegener, Mark I.** Cruciformed: the literary impact of Mark's story of Jesus and his disciples. Diss. 1992 ⇒8,5191. NY 1995, University Press of America vii; 277 pp. $36.50. 0-8191-9831-5 [NTAb 40,151].
3419 *Welzen, Huub* An initiation into mystical life: the gospel according to Mark. StSp 5 (1995) 86-103.
3420 **Williams, Joel F.** Other followers of Jesus... in Mark. 1994 ⇒10,4802. JSNT.S 102. [R]JThS 46 (1995) 619-620 (*Anderson, Hugh*).
3421 **Zager, Werner** Gottesherrschaft und Endgericht in der Verkündigung Jesu: eine Untersuchung zur markinischen Jesusüberlieferung einschliesslich der Q-Parallelen. Diss. Bochum 1995-96. [D]*Balz, H.*

F6.3 Evangelii Marci versiculi

3422 *Sankey, P. J.* Promise and fulfilment: reader-response to Mark 1.1-15. JSNT 58 (1995) 3-18.
3423 *Matera, Frank J.* The prologue as the interpretative key to Mark's gospel. 1995 <1988> ⇒116. Interpretation of Mark. 289-306 [1,1-15]=
3424 The prologue as the interpretative key to Mark's gospel. 1995 <1988> ⇒80. Synoptic gospels. 178-195 [1,1-15].
3425 *Adinolfi, Marco* Ἀρχή, εὐαγγέλιον, Χριστός: note filologiche a Mc 1,1. RivBib 43 (1995) 211-224.
3426 *Collins, Adela Yarbro* Establishing the text: Mark 1:1. 1995 ⇒14. [F]HARTMAN L., 111-127.
3427 *Fuchs, Albert* Exegese im elfenbeinernen Turm: das quellenkritische Problem von Mk 1,2-8 par Mt 3,1-12 par Lk 3,1-17 in der Sicht der Zweiquellentheorie und von Deuteromarkus. SNTU.A 20 (1995) 23-149.
3428 *Marcus, Joel* Jesus' baptismal vision. NTS 41 (1995) 512-521 [1,10; Lk 10,18].
3429 *Grelot, Pierre* Les tentations de Jésus. NRTh 117 (1995) 501-516 [1,12-13; Lk 4,1-13].

3430 *Iersel, B.M.F. van* Concentric structures in Mark 1:14-3:35 (4:1) with some observations on method. Bibl.Interp. 3 (1995) 75-98.

3431 *Thomas, Carolyn* A mandate for life. BiTod 33 (1995) 229-233 [1,15].

3432 *Agnew, Francis H.* Hard sayings. BiTod 33 (1995) 303-307 [1,16-18; 2,18-19; Lk 17,20-21].

3433 *Delorme, Jean* Prises de parole et parler vrai dans un récit de Marc (1,21-28). 1995 ⇒4. ᶠBEAUCHAMP P., LeDiv 162. 179-199.

3434 *Dillon, Richard J.* "As one having authority" (Mark 1:22): the controversial distinction of Jesus' teaching. CBQ 57 (1995) 92-113.

3435 *Dewey, Joanna* The literary structure of the controversy stories in Mark 2:1-3:6. 1995 <1973> ⇒116. The interpretation of Mark. 141-151.

3436 *Focant, Camille* Les implications du nouveau dans le permis (Mc 2,1-3,6). 1995 ⇒4. ᶠBEAUCHAMP P., LeDiv 162. 201-223.

3437 *Amjad-Ali, Christine* Healing and wholeness: mission in Pakistan (Mark 2:1-11). **Urdu.** Al-Mushir 37/1 (1995) 1-10 [ThIK 17,59].

3438 *Mayer, Bernhard* Beobachtungen zur Zeitangabe ἐν ἐκείνῃ τῇ ἡμέρᾳ in Mk 2,20. SNTU.A 20 (1995) 5-21.

3439 *Dillmann, Rainer* Die Bedeutung der semantischen Analyse für die Textpragmatik. BN 79 (1995) 5-9 [2,23-28].

3440 **Yoonprayong, Amnuay** Jesus and his mother according to Mk 3.20.21, 31-35. Diss. ⇒10,4816. R 1995, Pont. Univ. Gregoriana xiv; 184 pp.

3441 *Valentini, Alberto* Chi è mia madre, chi sono i miei fratelli? (Mc 3,31-35). 1995 ⇒19. ᶠMATTIOLI A., 113-156 [= Mar. 57/2 (1995) 645-684: NTAb 41,43].

3442 *Dautzenberg, Gerhard* Mk 4,1-34 als Belehrung über das Reich Gottes: Beobachtungen zum Gleichniskapitel. 1995 <1990> ⇒44. Studien. SBAB 19. 188-221.

3443 *Parente, Fausto* τὸ μυστήριον τῆς βασιλείας τοῦ θεοῦ: il 'pšr di Ḥabaqquq" (1QpHab) ed il problema del cosiddetto 'segreto messianico' (MC. 4,10-12). Aug. 35 (1995) 17-42.

3444 *Mazzucco, Clementina* 'Quelli lungo la strada' (Mc 4,15). Aug. 35 (1995) 43-59.

3445 *Marcus, Joel* Mark and Isaiah. 1995 ⇒10. ᶠFREEDMAN D., 449-466 [4,21-22; Isa 35,5-8; 29,9-10; 40,9].

3446 *Gourgues, Michel* Faire confiance à la grâce de Dieu: la parabole du blé qui pousse tout seul (Mc 4,25-29). NRTh 117 (1995) 364-375.

3447 *Derrett, John Duncan M.* Ambivalence: sowing and reaping at Mark 4:26-29. 1995 <1990> ⇒45. Studies 6. 42-63.

3448 *Peters, Friederike* 'Jesus aber schlief: warum habt ihr solche Angst?' (Mk 4,38.40). LS 46 (1995) 174-178.

3449 **Henaut, Barry W.** Oral tradition...Mk 4. 1993 ⇒9,5002; 10,4821. JSNT.S 82. ᴿJThS 46 (1995) 258-260 (*Beavis, M.A.*); JBL 114 (1995) 517-520 (*Collins, Adela Yarbro*); ScrTh 27 (1995) 671-673 (*Casciaro, J.M.*).

3450 *Krause, Mark S.* Parable, obduracy, and mystery: converging issues in Mark 4. Diss. Trinity Evang. Div. School 1995, 303 pp. ᴰ*Carson, D.A.*, AAC 9608874; DAI-A 56/11,p.4430.

3451 *Szymik, Stefan* De hodiernis methodis analyseos textus biblici in exemplo Mc 5,1-20. **P.** RBL 48 (1995) 94-100.

3452 *Masoga, M. A.* Exploring belief in "Boloi" (witchcraft) in the light of Mark 5,1-20. JBTSA 9/2 (1995) 53-69.

3453 *Wanamaker, Charles* Constructing critical and contextual readings with ordinary readers Mark 5:21-6:1. JTSA 92 (1995) 60-69 [ZID 1996/2,46].

3454 **Oppel, Dagmar** Heilsam erzählen—erzählend heilen: die Heilung der Blutflüssigen und die Erweckung der Jairustochter in Mk 5,21-43 als Beispiel markinischer Erzählfertigkeit. Diss. 1993 ⇒9,5010. BBB 102. Weinheim 1995, Beltz Athenäum 274 pp. DM68. 3-89547-092-9.

3455 *Sindt, Gérard* L'imprévu de la foi: l'histoire de Jaïre: Marc 5,21-43. Cahiers de l'Atelier 463 (1995) 51-60.

3456 *Draper, Jonathan A.* Wandering radicalism or purposeful activity?: Jesus and the sending of messengers in Mark 6:6-56. Neotest. 29 (1995) 183-202.

3457 *Bucher-Gillmayr, Susanne* "... und brachte seinen Kopf auf einem Teller...": das Schicksal des Johannes, Mk 6,14-29. PzB 4 (1995) 103-116.

3458 *Le Bars, Malou; Chamard-Bois, Pierre* Ils n'avaient rien compris à l'affaire des pains: lecture sémiotique de Mc 6,30-44. SémBib 77 (1995) 25-40.

3459 *Barrera R., Páblo* Pastoral, violencia y esperanza en el Perú de hoy: relectura de San Marcos 6,30-44. CrSoc 32 (1995) 7-35 [ThIK 17/2,71].

3460 *Stanton, Graham* A gospel among the scrolls?: scholar claims to have identified a fragment of Mark among the Dead Sea Scrolls and the oldest fragment of Matthew. BiRe 11/6 (1995) 36-42 [6,52-53].

3461 *Puech, Émile* Des fragments grecs de la Grotte 7 et le Nouveau Testament? 7Q4 et 7Q5, et le papyrus Magdalen Grec 17 = p 64. RB 102 (1995) 570-584 [6,52-53].

3462 *Grelot, Pierre* Note sur les propositions du Pr Carsten Peter Thiede. RB 102 (1995) 589-591 [6,52-53].

3463 *Chmiel, Jerzy* De aenigmate 7Q 5. **P**. RBL 48 (1995) 182-186 [6,52-53].

3464 *Boismard, M.-E.* À propos de 7Q5 et Mc 6,52-53. RB 102 (1995) 585-588.

3465 *Oyen, G. van* Het onbegrip van de leerlingen in het Marcusevangelie: een methodologisch overzicht aan de hand van Mc 6,52 en 8,17-21. Coll. 25 (1995) 175-176.

3466 *Kieffer, René* Traditions juives selon Mc 7,1-23. 1995 ⇒14. ^FHARTMAN L., 675-688.

3467 *Kinukava, Hisako* The Syrophoenician woman: Mark 7.24-30. 1995 <1991> ⇒129. Voices from the margin. 138-155.

3468 *Pokorny, P.* From a puppy to the child: some problems of contemporary biblical exegesis demonstrated from Mark 7,24-30/Matt 15,21-8. NTS 41 (1995) 199-217.

3469 *Baudoz, Jean-Francois* MC 7,31-37 et MC 8,22-26 géographie et théologie. RB 102 (1995) 560-569.

3470 *Gibson, Jeffrey* Jesus' refusal to produce a 'sign' (Mark 8.11-13). 1995 <1990> ⇒103. The historical Jesus. BiSe 33. 271-299.

3471 **Lee, Robert G.** Thinking the things of God: a literary study of Mark 8:27-9:13. Diss. Grad. Theol. Union 1995, 257 pp. ^D*Boyle, John L.*, AAC 9536759; DAI-A 56/6,p.2281.

3472 *Hoffmann, Paul* Markus 8,31: zur Herkunft und markinischen Rezeption einer alten Überlieferung. 1995 < 1973 > ⇒51. Tradition. NTA 28. 281-312.

3473 *Aichele, George* Jesus' frankness. Semeia 69/70 (1995) 261-280 [8,32].

3474 *Brower, Kent* Mark 9.1: seeing the kingdom in power. 1995 < 1980 > ⇒81. The synoptic gospels. BiSe 31. 121-142.

3475 *Clivaz, C.* La transfiguration au risque de la compréhension du disciple: Mc 9/2-10. ETR 70 (1995) 493-508.

3476 *Derrett, John Duncan M.* Peter and the tabernacles. 1995 < 1990 > ⇒45. Studies 6. 16-27 [9,5-6].

3477 **Runacher, Caroline** Croyants incrédules: la guérison de l'épileptique: Marc 9,14-29. 1994 ⇒10,4842. RCarthaginensia 11 (1995) 440-441 (*Sanz Valdivieso, R.*).

3478 *Ebach, Jürgen* Wie einer auf die eigenen Füße kam: Bibelarbeit über Markus 9,14-29, gehalten am 6.6.1991 in der Alten Synagoge in Essen (DEKT 1991). 1995 < 1992 > ⇒46. Hiobs Post. 164-182.

3479 *Hoffmann, Paul* "Dienst" als Herrschaft oder "Herrschaft" als Dienst?. BiKi 50 (1995) 146-152 [9,33-35; 10,42-45; Lk 9,46-48; 22,24-28].

3480 *Fuente Adánez, Alfonso de la* A favor o en contra de Jesús: el logion de Mc 9,40 y sus paralelos. EstB 53 (1995) 449-459.

3481 *Collier, G.D.* Rethinking Jesus on divorce.   RestQ 37 (1995) 80-96 [10,1-12; NTAb 40,39—*Matthews, C.R.*].

3482 *Green, Barbara* Jesus' teaching on divorce in the gospel of Mark. 1995 < 1990 > ⇒103. The historical Jesus. BiSe 33. 148-156 [10,1-12].

3483 *Trainor, Michael* Care for the divorced and remarried in the light of Mark's divorce text (Mk 10:1-12). ACR 72 (1995) 211-224.

3484 *Trainor, M.* The divorced and their inclusion in community (Mk 10:1-12). ACR 72 (1995) 211-212.

3485 *Baumann, Rolf* Rückfragen an die Bibel: aus Anlaß eines aktuellen Streits. BiKi 50 (1995) 49-59 [10,2-12; 1 Cor 7].

3486 *Pathrapankal, Joseph M.* The way to the kingdom of God: a semiotic reading of a Markan pericope (Mk 10:2-16). Jeevadhara 25 (1995) 105-122 [ThIK 17,36].

3487 *Beißer, Friedrich* Markus 10,13-16 (parr)—doch ein Text für die Kindertaufe. KuD 41 (1995) 244-251 [sum. 251].

3488 *Wackwitz, Heinrich* Gott die Quelle des Lebens: Auslegung zu Markus 10,17-22. 1995 ⇒88. "Ich bin der Herr". 9-11.

3489 *Soares-Prabhu, George M.* Anti-greed and anti-pride: Mark 10.17-27 and 10.35-45 in the light of tribal values. 1995 < 1991 > ⇒129. Voices from the margin. 117-137.

3490 *Schottroff, L.* Der reiche Jüngling: Bibelarbeit zu Markus 10,17-27. JK 56 (1995) 482ff [ZID 21,699].

3491 **Landgrave Gándara, Daniel R.** Los pobres y el proyecto de Jesús, en Mc 10,17-31 (notas eclesiológicas): estudio exegetico-teologico. Diss. Pont. Univ. Gregoriana, R 1995, viii; 86 pp. [abstract] DStock, Klemens.

3492 *Iersel, B.M.F. van; Nuchelmans, J.* De zoon van Timeüs en de zoon van David: Marcus 10,46-52 gelezen door een grieks-romeinse bril. TTh 35 (1995) 107-124.

3493 *Charlesworth, James H.* The son of David: Solomon and Jesus (Mark 10.47). 1995 ⇒67. The New Testament. 72-87.

3494 **Criscione, Mary** 'There were also women': the art and power of
      women characters in Mark 11-16. Diss. Grad. Theol. Union 1995,
      185 pp. [D]*Wire, Antoinette C.*, AAC 9536762; DAI-A 56/6,p.2279.
3495 *Reid, Barbara E.* Puzzling passages: Mark 11:12-14. BiTod 33
      (1995) 110.
3496 *Genton, Philippe* Marc 11,12-21: les Rameaux. Lire et Dire 24
      (1995) 3-12 [Bulletin of Biblical Bibliography 15,73].
3497 *Weir, Emmette* Fruitless fig tree—futile worship. ET 106 (1995)
      330 [11,12-21].
3498 *Ådna, Jostein* Teologisk mening bakenfor og i bibelteksten: en
      replikk til Trond Skard DOKKA. NTT 96 (1995) 117-126 [11,15-
      17].
3499 *Evans, Craig A.* Jesus and the "cave of robbers": towards a Jewish
      context for the temple action. 1995 ⇒47. Jesus and his con-
      temporaries. AGJU 25. 345-365 [11,15-17].
3500 *Evans, Craig A.* Jesus' action in the temple and evidence of corrup-
      tion in the first-century temple. 1995 ⇒47. Jesus and his con-
      temporaries. AGJU 25. 319-344 [11,15-17].
3501 **Mell, Ulrich** Die "anderen" Winzer...Markus 11,27-12,34.
      ⇒10,4850. WUNT 2/77. [R]BZ 39 (1995) 275-277 (*Scholtissek,
      Klaus*); SNTU.A 20 (1995) 212-214 (*Fuchs, A.*).
3502 *Arul Raja, A. Maria* The authority of Jesus: a Dalit reading of Mk
      11:27-33. Jeevadhara 25 (1995) 123-138 [ThIK 17,36].
3503 *Schmeller, Thomas* Der Erbe des Weinbergs: zu den
      Gerichtsgleichnissen Mk 12,1-12 und Jes 5,1-7. MThZ 46 (1995)
      183-201.
3504 *Evans, Craig A.* God's vineyard and its caretakers. 1995 ⇒47.
      Jesus and his contemporaries. AGJU 25. 381-406 [12,1-12].
3505 *Ukpong, Justin S.* Tribute to Caesar, Mark 12:13-17 (Matt 22:15-
      22; Luke 20:20-26). BiBh 21 (1995) 147-166.
3506 *Becquet, Gilles* "Sur le fil du rasoir:" les rapports ambigus du
      politique et du religieux (Marc 12,13-27). Sève 568 (1995) 38-40.
3507 *Cohn-Sherbok, D. M.* Jesus' defence of the resurrection of the dead
      <1981> 157-166 [12,18-27];
3508 **Schwankl, Otto** Die Sadduzäerfrage: Mk 12,18-27. Diss. 1987
      ⇒3,4864... 6,5284. [R]Asp. 42 (1995) 596-599 (*Marcheselli-Casale,
      C.*).
3509 *Janzen, J. Gerald* Resurrection and hermeneutics: on Exodus 3.6 in
      Mark 12.26 <1985> 176-191. ⇒103. The historical Jesus. BiSe
      33.
3510 *McIlhone, James* Not far from the kingdom: a scribe in Mark.
      ChiSt 34/1 (1995) 53-62 [12,28-34].
3511 *LaVerdiere, E.* The first of all the commandments: Jesus and the
      scribes (Mark 12:28-44). Emmanuel 101 (1995) 223-232 [NTAb
      .40,41—*Harrington, D.J.*].
3512 *Chilton, Bruce* Jesus Ben David: reflections on the
      Davidssohnfrage. 1995 <1982> ⇒103. The historical Jesus. BiSe
      33. 192-215 [12,35-37].
3513 *LaVerdiere, E.* The coming of the Son of Man: discourse on the
      Mount of Olives (Mark 13:1-37). Emmanuel 101 (1995) 283-296
      [NTAb 40,41—*Harrington, D.J.*].
3514 *Evans, Craig A.* Predictions of the destruction of the Herodian
      temple. 1995 ⇒72. Qumran questions. BiSe 36. 92-150 [13,2].

3515 *Vorster, Willem S.* Literary reflections on Mark 13:5-37: a narrated speech of Jesus. 1995 <1987> ⇒116. The interpretation of Mark. 269-288.

3516 *Dautzenberg, Gerhard* Das Wort von der weltweiten Verkündigung des Evangeliums: Mk 13,10 und seine Vorgeschichte. 1995 <1989> ⇒44. Studien. SBAB 19. 240-262.

3517 *Stowasser, Martin* Mk 13,26f und die urchristliche Rezeption des Menschensohns. BZ 39 (1995) 246-252.

3518 *Pippin, Tina* A good apocalypse is hard to find: crossing the apocalyptic borders of Mark 13. Semeia 72 (1995) 153-171.

3519 **Beasley-Murray, George R.** Jesus and the last days: the interpretation of the Olivet discourse. 1993 ⇒9,4776; 10,4856. ᴿRTR 54 (1995) 33-34 (*Bolt, Peter*); EvQ 67 (1995) 275-276 (*Wenham, David*); JEarlyC 3 (1995) 359-361 (*Hill, Charles E.*); CritRR 8 (1995) 263-266 (*Telford, W.R.*) [13].

3520 *Goulder, Michael* The phasing of the future. 1995 ⇒14. ᶠHARTMAN L., 391-408 [13].

3521 **Conyers, A.J.** The end: what Jesus *really* said about the last things. Downers Grove, Il. 1995, InterVarsity 151 pp. 0-8308-1617-8 [13; NTAb 40,336].

3522 *Bolt, Peter G.* Mark 13: an apocalyptic precursor to the passion narrative. RTR 54/1 (1995) 10-32.

F6.8 **Passio secundum Marcum, 14,1...** [⇒5.3].

3523 **Broadhead, Edwin K.** Prophet, son, messiah...Mark 14-16. 1994 ⇒10,4861. JSNT.S 97. ᴿJThS 46 (1995) 616-619 (*Anderson, Hugh*).

3524 *Broadhead, Edwin K.* In search of the gospel: research trends in Mark 14-16. ABR 43 (1995) 20-49.

3525 **Gargano, Innocenzo** "Lectio divina" sui vangeli della passione: "passione di Gesù secondo Marco". Conversazioni bibliche 54. Bo 1995, Dehoniane 140 pp. L23.000. 88-10-70954-3 [14-15].

3526 *Harrington, Daniel J.* What and why did Jesus suffer according to Mark?. ChiSt 34/1 (1995) 32-41.

3527 *LaVerdiere, E.* The passion and resurrection of Jesus Christ: introduction. Emmanuel 101 (1995) 351-361 [NTAb 40,41—*Harrington, D.J.*].

3528 **Schreiber, Johannes** Die Markuspassion. 1993 ⇒9,5407. ᴿCarthaginensia 11 (1995) 198-199 (*Sanz Valdivieso, R.*); SNTU.A 20 (1995) 215 (*Fuchs, A.*).

3529 **Sommer, Urs** Die Passionsgeschichte des Markusevangeliums. 1993 ⇒9,5048; 10,4863. WUNT 2/58. ᴿBZ 39 (1995) 131-132 (*Schnackenburg, Rudolf*); CritRR 8 (1995) 299-301 (*Marcus, Joel*).

3530 *Strecker, Georg* Die Passionsgeschichte im Markusevangelium. 1995 ⇒30. ᶠSTRECKER G., BZNW 75. 218-247.

3531 *Dennison, James T.* The unnamed woman and Jesus: Mark 14:1-11. Kerux 10/2 (1995) 41-47.

3532 *Simoens, Yves* L'onction eucharistique et la cène nuptiale selon Mc 14,1-31. 1995 ⇒4. ᶠBEAUCHAMP P., LeDiv 162. 245-266.

3533 *Cangh, J.-M. van* Le déroulement primitif de la Cène (Mc 14,18-26 et par.). RB 102 (1995) 193-225.

3534 *Madigan, Kevin* Ancient and high-medieval interpretations of Jesus in Gethsemane: some reflections on tradition and continuity in christian thought. HThR 88 (1995) 157-173 [14,32-42; Lk 22,40-46].

3535 *Vidović, Marinko* Jesus' prayer in Gethsemane Mk 14,32-42. **Croatian**. Crkva u Svijetu 30 (1995) 143-161, 243-259 [sum. 162, 259].

3536 *Pilch, John J.* Death with honor: the Mediterranean style death of Jesus in Mark. BiTod 25 (1995) 65-70 [14,39].

3537 *Hill, Richard M.* Jesus' defense in Mark 14:48: a probable historical context. ProcGLM 15 (1995) 45-51 [14,48].

3538 *Evans, Craig A.* In what sense "blasphemy"? Jesus before Caiaphas in Mark 14:61-64. 1995 ⇒47. Jesus and his contemporaries. AGJU 25. 407-434.

3539 *Schwarz, Günther* "Und er begann zu weinen"? (Markus 14,72). BN 78 (1995) 18-20.

3540 *Schmidt, T.E.* Mark 15.16-32: the crucifixion narrative and the Roman triumphal procession. NTS 41 (1995) 1-18 [15,16-32].

3541 *Klindworth, V.* Jesu Tod am Kreuz: Praxishilfe zu Mk 15,33-39. CLehre 47 (1995) 171ff [ZID 21,389].

3542 *Dautzenberg, Gerhard* Zwei unterschiedliche "Kompendien" mk Christologie: Überlegungen zum Verhältnis von Mk 15,39 zu Mk 14,61f. 1995 <1989> ⇒44. Studien. SBAB 19. 222-239.

3543 *Johnson, Earl S.* Is Mark 15.39 the key to Mark's christology?. 1995 <1987> ⇒81. The synoptic gospels. BiSe 31. 143-162.

3544 *Dagbovou, Emmanuel* De la mort selon la vie religieuse vodun à la mort-resurrection dans le Christ en référence à Mc. 15,39. RICAO 12 (1995) 65-80 [ThIK 17/2, 22].

3545 *Hester, J. David* Dramatic inconclusion: irony and the narrative rhetoric of the ending of Mark. JSNT 57 (1995) 61-86 [16,1-8].

3546 *Collins, Adela Yarbro* Apotheosis and resurrection. 1995 ⇒67. The New Testament. 88-100 [16,1-8].

3547 *Lincoln, Andrew T.* The promise and the failure: Mark 16:7,8. 1995 <1989> ⇒116. The interpretation of Mark. 229-251.

3548 *Baarda, Tjitze* An unexpected reading in the West-Saxon gospel text of Mark 16.11. NTS 41 (1995) 458-465.

3549 **Danove, Paul L.** The end of Mark: a methodological study. 1993 ⇒9,5058. [R]CritRR 8 (1995) 198-200 (*Collins, Adela Yarbro*).

3550 **Cox, Stephen Lynn** A history and critique of scholarship concerning the Markan endings. 1993 ⇒10,4868. [R]NT 37 (1995) 205 (*Elliott, J.K.*); CritRR 8 (1995) 194-195 (*Brooks, James A.*) [16].

3551 **Hanhart, Karel** The open tomb, a new approach: Mark's Passover haggada (72 C.E.). ColMn 1995, Liturgical xii; 867 pp. $60 [CBQ 59,156].

Opus Lucanum

F7.1 *Opus Lucanum* — **Luke-Acts**.

3552 **Alexander, Loveday** The preface to Luke's gospel 1.1-4 and Acts 1.1. 1993 ⇒9,5060; 10,4870. MSSNTS 78. RNT 37 (1995) 400 (*Spensley, Barbara E.*); CBQ 57 (1995) 166-167 (*Danker, Frederick W.*); JBL 114 (1995) 522-524 (*Pervo, Richard I.*).

3553 *Atkinson, W.* Pentecostal responses to DUNN's "Baptism in the Holy Spirit": Luke-Acts. JPentec 6 (1995) 87ff [ZID 21,416].

3554 **Bergholz, Thomas** Der Aufbau des lukanischen Doppelwerkes: Untersuchungen zum formalliterarischen Charakter von Lukas-Evangelium und Apostelgeschichte. Diss. Bonn 1995, ᴰ*Grässer, E.*, Fra 1995, Lang 156 pp. DM44. 3-631-49209-X [ThRv 92/2,VI].

3555 *Blomberg, Craig L.* The law in Luke-Acts. 1995 <1984> ⇒81. The synoptic gospels. BiSe 31. 240-267.

3556 **Bosetti, Elena** Luca: il cammino dell'evangelizzazione. Bibbia e catechesi NS. Bo 1995, EDB. 88-10-20209-0.

3557 *Botha, Pieter J.J.* Community and conviction in Luke-Acts. Neotest. 29 (1995) 145-165.

3558 *Bovon, François* The effect of realism and prophetic ambiguity in the works of Luke <1985> 97-104, 213-215;

3559 The God of Luke. <1981> 67-80, 202-209;

3560 The importance of mediations in Luke's theological plan <1974-5> 51-66, 196-202;

3561 Israel, the church and the gentiles in the twofold work of Luke <1983> 81-95, 209-213. ⇒40 1995. New Testament traditions. PTMS 36 [RB 103,117].

3562 *Brawley, Robert L.* For blessing all families of the earth: covenant traditions in Luke-Acts. CThMi 22 (1995) 18-26.

3563 **Brawley, Robert Lawson** Text to text pours forth speech: voices of scripture in Luke-Acts. ISBL Bloomington 1995, Indiana University Press xi; 178 pp. $28. 0-253-32939-6.

3564 *Brooke, George J.* Luke-Acts and the Qumran Scrolls: the case of MMT. 1995 ⇒3599. Luke's literary achievement. JSNT.S 116. 72-90.

3565 **Chung, Yun Lak** 'The word of God' in Luke-Acts: a study in Lukan theology. Diss. Emory 1995, 315 pp., ᴰ*Moessner, David P.*, AAC 9536679; DAI-A 56/6,p.2279.

3566 **Crump, David** Jesus the intercessor. 1992 ⇒8,5264... 10,4876. RThRev 16 (1995) 61-62 (*McCullough, J.C.*); JBL 114 (1995) 154-156 (*Landry, David*); SNTU.A 20 (1995) 221 (*Fuchs, A.*).

3567 *Cullen, P.J.* Euphoria, praise and thanksgiving: rejoicing in the spirit in Luke-Acts. JPentec 6 (1995) 13ff [ZID 21,416].

3568 *Cunningham, S.* The theology of persecution in Luke-Acts. ETSI Journal 1/1 (1995) 16-34 [NTAb 40,42—*Harrington, D.J.*].

3569 *Czachesz, I.* Narrative logic and Christology in Luke-Acts. CV 37 (1995) 93-106.

3570 **Darr, John A.** On character building Luke-Acts. 1992 ⇒8,5265... 10,4878. RCritRR 7 (1994) 176-178 (*Gowler, David B.*).

3571 *Davies, Douglas J.* Rebounding vitality: resurrection and spirit in Luke-Acts. 1995 ⇒23. ᶠRoGERSON J., JSOT.S 200. 205-224.

3572 *De Boer, Martinus C.* God-Fearers in Luke-Acts. 1995 ⇒3599. Luke's literary achievement. JSNT.S 116. 50-71.

3573 *Downing, Gerald* Theophilus's first reading of Luke-Acts. 1995 ⇒3599. Luke's literary achievement. JSNT.S 116. 91-109.

3574 **Evans, Craig A.; Sanders, James A.** Luke and scripture. 1993 ⇒9,5072. ᴿNew Theology Review 8/1 (1995) 86-88 (*McDonald, Patricia M.*); SR 24 (1995) 222-224 (*Mason, Steve*); CritRR 8 (1995) 206-208 (*Swartley, Willard M.*).

3575 **Fletcher-Louis, Crispin H.T.** Angelomorphic categories, early christology and discipleship, with special reference to Luke-Acts. Diss. Ox 1995, ᴰ*Rowland, C.C.*, [TynB 48,183-186].

3576 *Gérard, Jean-Pierre* Les riches dans la communauté lucanienne. EThL 71 (1995) 71-106.

3577 **Gerstmyer, Robert Henry Madison** The gentiles in Luke-Acts: characterization and allusion in the Lukan narrative. Diss. Duke 1995, 817 pp. ᴰ*Young, Franklin W.*, AAC 9600627; DAI-A 56/9,p.3617.

3578 **Gowler, David B.** Host...Pharisees Lk/Ac. 1991 ⇒7,4410... 10,4885. ᴿJThS 46 (1995) 269-271 (*Barton, Stephen C.*).

3579 *Kaestli, Jean-Daniel* Luke-Acts and the Pastoral Epistles: the thesis of a common authorship. 1995 ⇒3599. Luke's literary achievement. JSNT.S 116. 110-126.

3580 **Kurz, William S.** Reading Luke-Acts. 1993 ⇒9,5083; 10,4892. ᴿBib. 76 (1995) 262-265 (*Pervo, Richard I.*); CritRR 8 (1995) 240-243 (*Brawley, Robert L.*).

3581 *Larsson, Edvin* How mighty was the mighty minority? StTh 49 (1995) 93-105.

3582 **Modica, Joseph Benjamin** The function and purpose of suffering, persecution, and martyrdom in Luke-Acts: an exegetical and theological inquiry. Diss. Drew 1995, 250 pp. ᴰ*Doughty, Darrell J.*, AAC 9536139; DAI-A 56/7,p.2728.

3583 **Morgenthaler, Robert** Lukas und QuINTILIAN: Rhetorik als Erzählkunst. 1993 ⇒9,5091; 10,4897. ᴿEThL 71 (1995) 222-223 (*Neirynck, F.*); SNTU.A 20 (1995) 217-219 (*Fuchs, A.*).

3584 *Mowery, Robert L.* Lord, God, and Father: theological language in Luke-Acts. SBL.SP 34 (1995) 82-101.

3585 ᴱ**Neyrey, Jerome H.** The social world of Luke-Acts. 1991 ⇒7,450... 10,4899. ᴿEstB 53 (1995) 142-143 (*Fuente, A. de la*); Bijdr. 56 (1995) 76-78 (*Koet, Bart J.*).

3586 **Parsons, Mikeal C.; Pervo, Richard I.** Rethinking the unity of Luke and Acts. 1993 ⇒ 9,5097; 10,4902. ᴿTJT 11/1 (1995) 97-98 (*Ascough, Richard S.*); RExp 92 (1995) 243 (*Polhill, John*); JBL 114 (1995) 333-335 (*Matthews, Christopher R.*); CBQ 57 (1995) 411-413 (*Green, Joel B.*).

3587 *Rakotoharintsifa, Andrianjatovo* Luke and the internal divisions in the early church. 1995 ⇒3599. Luke's literary achievement. JSNT.S 116. 165-177.

3588 **Ravens, David** Luke and the restoration of Israel. JSNT.S 119. Shf 1995, Academic 287 pp. £39/$58.50. 0-85075-565-5.

3589 **Reinhardt, Wolfgang** Das Wachstum des Gottesvolkes: Untersuchungen zum Gemeindewachstum im lukanischen Doppelwerk auf dem Hintergrund des Alten Testaments. Gö 1995, Vandenhoeck & Ruprecht. DM89. 3-525-53632-1.

3590 **Reinmuth, Eckart** Pseudo-PHILO und Lukas: Studien zum Liber Antiquitatum Biblicarum und seiner Bedeutung für die Interpretation des lukanischen Doppelwerks. 1994 ⇒10,4907. WUNT 2/74. [R]JThS 46 (1995) 644-646 (*Alexander, Loveday*).

3591 *Segalla, Giuseppe* L'etica narrativa di Luca-Atti. Teol(Br) 20 (1995) 34-74.

3592 **Seim, Turid Karlsen** The double message: patterns of gender in Luke-Acts. 1994 ⇒10,4909. [R]RStT 13-14/2-3 (1995) 127-129 (*Carter, Philippa*).

3593 **Sheeley, Steven M.** Narrative asides in Luke-Acts. 1992 ⇒8,5290... 10,4910. JSNT.S 72. [R]EThL 71 (1995) 465-468 (*Belle, G. van*).

3594 **Squires, John T.** The plan of God in Luke-Acts. 1993 ⇒9,5107; 10,4915. MSSNTS 76. [R]EvQ 67 (1995) 92-94 (*Doble, Peter*); CBQ 57 (1995) 191-192 (*Dart, John A.*); JBL 114 (1995) 529-531 (*Hanges, James C.*); RTK 42/1 (1995) 113-115 (*Rakocy, Waldemar*); NT 37 (1995) 201-202 (*Spensley, B.E.*).

3595 **Strauss, Mark L.** The Davidic messiah in Luke-Acts: the promise and its fulfillment in Lukan christology. Diss. Aberdeen 1992 ⇒9,5110, [D]*Turner, M.*, JSNT.S 110. Shf 1995, Academic 413 pp. £35/$52.50. 1-85075-522-1 [NTAb 40,150].

3596 **Strother, William Henry, II** Rhetorical analysis of selected key sermons in Luke and Acts. Diss. South. Baptist Theol. Sem. 1995, 220 pp. [D]*Cox, James W.*, AAC 9530707; DAI-A 56/4,p.1395.

3597 *Talbert, C.H.; Hayes, J.H.* A theology of sea storms in Luke-Acts. SBL.SP 34 (1995) 321-336 [Lk 8,22-25; Acts 27].

3598 **Trainor, Michael** According to Luke: insights for contemporary pastoral practice. 1992 ⇒9,5114. [R]New Theology Review 8/1 (1995) 85-86 (*McDonald, Patricia M.*).

3599 [E]**Tuckett, Christopher M.** Luke's literary achievement: collected essays. JSNT.S 116. Shf 1995, Academic 232 pp. £27.50/$41. 1-85075-556-6 [NTAb 40,351].

3600 *Tyson, Joseph B.* Jews and Judaism in Luke-Acts: reading as a god-fearer. NTS 41 (1995) 19-38.

3601 **Weatherly, John A.** Jewish responsibility for the death of Jesus in Luke-Acts. 1994 ⇒10,4920. JSNT.S 106. [R]ThLZ 120 (1995) 1081-1082 (*Rese, Martin*).

F7.3 Evangelium Lucae — *Textus, commentarii.*

3602 [T]**Augrain, Charles** L'évangile de Luc présenté en cinq langues européennes: français, anglais, allemand, espagnol, italien. *Martini, Carlo Maria* (introd.), L'Évangile sans frontières. P 1995, Médiaspaul. FF35. 2-7122-0433-6.

3603 **Bock, Darrell L.** Luke I: 1:1-9:50. GR 1994, Baker xx; 987 pp. $45. [R]SNTU.A 20 (1995) 216-217 (*Fuchs, A.*).

3604 **Bovon, François** El evangelio según san Lucas I (Lc 1-9). [T]*Ortiz García, Alfonso*. Biblioteca de EstB 85. Sígueme 1995, Salamanca 735 pp. 84-301-1257-X [Actualidad Bibliográfica 34,46].

3605 *Cope, Lamar; Dungan, David L.; Farmer, William R.; McNicol, Allan J.; Peabody, David B.; Shuler, Philip L.* Narrative outline of the composition of Luke according to the two-gospel hypothesis. SBL.SP 34 (1995) 636-687 [Cf. SBL.SP (1992-94)].

3606 **Corsato, Celestino** La Expositio euangelii secundum Lucam di sant'AMBROGIO. 1993 ⇒9,5117; 10,4923. SEAug 43. ᴿSal. 57 (1995) 575-576 (*Dobrowolska, Katarzyna*); CivCatt 146 (1995) 511-512 (*Cremascoli, G.*).

3607 **Cousin, Hugues** Vangelo di Luca: commento pastorale. ᵀ*Gonella, A.*, Fame e sete della parola 18. CinB 1995, San Paolo 419 pp. L29.000. 88-215-3026-4.

3608 *Culpepper, R. Alan* The gospel of Luke: introduction, commentary, and reflections. 1995 ⇒92. NIntB 9. 1-490.

3609 **Ernst, Josef** Lukasevangelium: Stationen am Wege des Heils. Pd 1995, Bonifatius 198 pp. DM26.80. 3-87088-871-7 [ThRv 93,213].

3610 **Nolland, John** Luke 1-9:20. 1989. WBC 35A;
3611 Luke 9:21-18:34. 1993. WBC 35B;
3612 Luke 18:35-24:53. 1993. WBC 35C. ⇒5,5071... 10,4930. ᴿCritRR 8 (1995) 270-273 (*Talbert, Charles H.*, A-C); Themelíos 20/3 (1995) 23-24 (*Bock, Darrell L.*, C); JThS 46 (1995) 628-631 (*Franklin, Eric*, B-C).

3613 **Pate, C. Marvin** Luke. Moody Gospel Commentary. Chicago 1995, Moody 521 pp. 0-8024-5622-7.

3614 **Ringe, Sharon H.** Luke. Westminster Bible Companion. LVL 1995, Westminster xiv; 291 pp. $20. 0-664-25259-1.

3615 **Rius-Camps, Josep** O evangelho de Lucas: o êxodo do homem livre. Comentários Bíblicos. São Paulo 1995, Paulus 363 pp. 85-349-0279-8 [PerTeol 29,277].

3616 **Schürmann, Heinz** Das Lukasevangelium: 9,51-11,54. 1994 ⇒10,4933. HThKNT 3/2.1. ᴿBZ 39 (1995) 139-141 (*Kosch, Daniel*); EstAg 30 (1995) 343-344 (*Cineira, D.A.*).

3617 **Stein, Robert H.** Luke. 1992 ⇒8,5318... 10,4936. NAC. ᴿCritRR 7 (1994) 261-263 (*Chance, J. Bradley J.*.); RExp 92/1 (1995) 111-113 (*Seifrid, Mark A.*).

3618 **Tavares Zabatiero, Júlio Paulo** Evangelho de Lucas. Estudos bíblicos 47. Petrópolis 1995, Vozes 52 pp.

F7.4   *Lucae themata* — Luke's Gospel, topics.

3619 *Amphoux, Christian-Bernard* L'évangile selon les Hébreux, source de l'évangile de Luc. Apocrypha 6 (1995) 67-77.

3620 *Chang, S.* Justice of jubilee in Luke. RW 45/2 (1995) 87ff [ZID 21/8 (1995) 538].

3621 *De Virgilio, Giuseppe* εὐαγγελίζειν nel terzo vangelo. CrSt 16 (1995) 587-598 [sum. 598].

3622 **Diefenbach, Manfred** Die Komposition des Lukas-Evangeliums unter Berücksichtigung antiker Rhetorikelemente. 1993 ⇒9,5136; 10,4941. FTS 43. ᴿGuL 68 (1995) 239-240 (*Mödl, Ludwig*); ThPQ 143 (1995) 207-208 (*Niemand, Christoph*); Bib. 76 (1995) 431-433 (*Talbert, Charles H.*); JBL 114 (1995) 520-522 (*Nelson, Peter K.*).

3623 *du Plessis, I.J.* Discipleship according to Luke's gospel. RelT 2/1 58-71 [NTAb 40,42—*Matthews, C.R.*].

3624 **Franklin, Eric** Luke: interpreter of Paul, critic of Matthew. JSNT.S 92. Shf 1994, JSOT 414 pp. £42.50/$63. 1-85075-452-7. RJThS 46 (1995) 263-269 (*Nolland, John*); Theol. 98 (1995) 141-142 (*Hickling, C.J.A.*); CBQ 57 (1995) 592-594 (*Ascough, Richard S.*); JBL 114 (1995) 736-739 (*Gowler, David B.*).

3625 **García Pérez, José M.** San Lucas: evangelio y tradición: sustrato arameo en Lc 1,39; 8,26-39; 21,36; 22,28-30; 23,39-43. Studia Semitica Novi Testamenti 4. M 1995, Ciudad Nueva/Fundación San Justino 367 pp. 84-86987-91-1.

3626 **Green, Joel B.** The theology of the gospel of Luke. New Testament Theology. C 1995, CUP xiv; 170 pp. £30/$45; £10/$13. 0-521-46529-X/32-5. RExAu 11 (1995) 163-165 (*McKnight, Scot*).

3627 *Houlden, J. L.* The purpose of Luke. 1995 <1984> ⇒81. BiSe 31. The synoptic gospels. 227-239.

3628 *Kahl, Brigitte* Lukas gegen Lukas lesen: feministisch-kritische Relectura zwischen Hermeneutik des Verdachts und des Einverständnisses. BiKi 50 (1995) 222-229.

3629 *Kelley, Robert L.* Meals with Jesus in Luke's gospel. HBT 17 (1995) 123-131.

3630 **Kimball, Charles A.** Jesus' exposition of the Old Testament in Luke's gospel. 1994 ⇒10,4945. JSNT.S 94. RCBQ 57 (1995) 816-817 (*Miller, Robert J.*); CritRR 8 (1995) 234-236 (*Tyson, Joseph B.*).

3631 *Kowalski, Beate* Nachfolge Jesu Christi heute: ein Wochenendseminar auf den Spuren Jesu in der Katholischen Erwachsenenbildung. KatBl 120 (1995) 538-540.

3632 *Love, Stuart L.* Women and men at Hellenistic symposia meals in Luke. 1995 ⇒80. Modelling early christianity. 198-210.

3633 **Maynard-Reid, Pedrito Uriah** Wholistic evangelism: a Lukan paradigm. Diss. Fuller Theol. Sem. 1995, 171 pp. DVan Engen, Charles, MAI 33,1686.

3634 *Mazziotta, Richard* Luke's artistry. BiTod 33 (1995) 364-369.

3635 **Moore, Thomas S.** Luke's use of Isaiah for the gentile mission and Jewish rejection theme in the third gospel. Diss. Dallas Theol. Sem. 1995, 290 pp. AAC 9611641; DAI-A 56/12,p.4819.

3636 *Most, William G.* Did St Luke imitate the Septuagint?. 1995 <1982> ⇒81. The synoptic gospels. BiSe 31. 215-226.

3637 **Moxnes, Halvor** A economia do reino: conflito social e relações econômicas no evangelho de Lucas. Bíblia e Sociologia. São Paulo 1995, Paulus 163 pp.

3638 **Neale, David A.** None but the sinners...Lk JSNT.S 58. 1991 ⇒7,4473... 10,4951. RBijdr. 56 (1995) 457-458 (*Koet, Bart J.*).

3639 *Okorie, A.M.* The art of characterisation in the Lukan narrative: Jesus, the disciples and the populace. RelT 2/3 (1995) 274-282 [NTAb 41,48].

3640 *Okorie, A.M.* The characterization of the tax collectors in the gospel of Luke. CThMi 222 (1995) 27-32.

3641 **Paffenroth, Kim** The story of Jesus according to L. Diss. Notre Dame 1995, 309 pp. DSterling, G., DAI-A 56/7,p.2729.

3642 **Paoli, Arturo** La radice dell'uomo: meditazioni sul vangelo di Luca. Brescia 1994, Morcelliana. RFilTeo 9 (1995) 669-671 (*Fabris, Antonio*).

3643 **Perroni, Marinella** Il discepolato delle donne nel vangelo di Luca: un contributo all'ecclesiologia neotestamentaria. Thesis ad Lauream 173. R 1995, Pontificium Athenaeum S. Anselmi. 89 pp. [excerpt].

3644 *Pickering, Stuart R.* Additional sayings of Jesus in some texts of the gospel of Luke. NTTRU 3 (1995) 51-55.

3645 *Raja, R.J.* "Rich towards God": Bhakti in the gospel of Luke. VJTR 59 (1995) 233-240/307-318/389-399.

3646 *Rakotoharintsifa, Andrianjatovo* Luke and the internal divisions in the early church. 1995 ⇒3599. Luke's literary achievement. JSNT.S 116. 165-177.

3647 *Rinaldi, G.* La "lex de templo hierosolymitano" e l'atteggiamento di Luca verso Roma. Protest. 50 (1995) 269-278.

3648 *Römer, Thomas; Macchi, Jean-Daniel* Luke, disciple of the deuteronomistic school. 1995 ⇒3599. Luke's literary achievement. JSNT.S 116. 178-187.

3649 **Seland, Torrey** Establishment violence in PHILO and Luke: a study of non-conformity to the Torah and Jewish vigilante reactions. Diss. Trondheim 1991, *DBorgen, Peder* [⇒7,4692], Bibl.Interp. 15. Lei 1995, Brill xvi; 353 pp. ƒ100/$57.25. 90-04-10252-3 [NTAb 40,148].

3650 **Torres Ordoñez, Milko René** El poder y la autoridad de Jesús en Galilea: estudio desde la cristología implícita en el evangelio según san Lucas [The power and authority of Jesus in Galilee: a christological study implied in the gospel of St. Luke]. Diss. Navarra 1995, 298 pp. *DCascario, J.M.*, DAI-C 57/2,362.

3651 **Trainor, Michael** Jesus in Luke's gospel. Homebush, NSW 1995, St Paul's 112 pp. AUS$13 [ACR 74,372].

3652 *Tuckett, Christopher* The Lukan Son of Man. 1995 ⇒3599. Luke's literary achievement. JSNT.S 116. 198-217.

3653 *Wolter, Michael* "Reich Gottes" bei Lukas. NTS 41 (1995) 541-563.

F7.5 *Infantia, cantica* — **Magnificat, Benedictus: Luc. 1-3.**

3654 *Coleridge, Mark* The birth of the Lukan narrative: narrative as christology in Luke 1-2. *D*1993 ⇒9,5178; 10,4964. JSNT.S 88. RJThS 46 (1995) 260-263 (*Burridge, Richard A.*); Pacifica 8 (1995) 346-348 (*Squires, John T.*); JBL 114 (1995) 524-526 (*Brown, Raymond E.*); CBQ 57 (1995) 386-387 (*Hamm, Dennis*).

3655 **Drewermann, Eugen** Tu nombre es como el sabor de la vida: el relato de la infancia de Jesús según el evangelio de Lucas: una interpretación psicoanalítica. Barcelona 1995, Galaxia Gutenberg; Círcolo de Lectores 336 pp. 84-226-5387-7.

3656 *Fitzmyer, Joseph A.* Another query about the Lucan infancy narrative and its parallels. JBL 114 (1995) 295-296 [1,5-2,52].

3657 **Panier, Louis** La naissance du fils de Dieu...lecture de Luc 1-2. 1991 ⇒7,4489... 10,4967. CFi 164. RRB 102 (1995) 413-419 (*Nodet, Étienne*).

3658 *Panimolle, Salvatore A.* La cristologia di Luca 1-2. Aug. 35 (1995) 61-75.

3659 **Muñoz Nieto, Jesús María** Tiempo de anuncio: estudio de Lc 1,5-2,52. Taipei 1994, Facultas Theologica S. Roberti Bellarmino v; 331 pp. RMar. 57/1 (1995) 400-404 (*Valentini, Alberto*).

3660 *Reid, Barbara E.* Puzzling passages: Luke 1:26-38. BiTod 33 (1995) 346.

3661 *Sieg, Franciszek* Jezus Chrystus, Syn Boży, Syn Maryi Dziewicy (Lk 1,26-38) [Jesus Christ, the Son of God, the Son of Mary Virgin]. Bobolanum 6 (1995) 56-67 [NTAb 40,44—*Harrington, D.J.*].

3662 *Kremer, Jacob* Das Erfassen der bildsprachlichen Dimension als Hilfe für das rechte Verstehen der biblischen "Kindheitsevangelien" und ihre Vermittlung als lebendiges Wort Gottes. 1995 <1990> ⇒53. Die Bibel. 30-58 [1,26-38].

3663 *Neuner, J.* Listen to the Spirit: he was conceived by the Holy Spirit and born of the Virgin Mary. VJTR 59 (1995) 209-212 [1,26-38].

3664 *Landry, David T.* Narrative logic in the annunciation to Mary (Luke 1:26-38). JBL 114 (1995) 65-79.

3665 *Dormeyer, Detlev* Die Rolle der Imagination im Leseprozeß bei unterschiedlichen Leseweisen von Lk 1,26-38. BZ 39 (1995) 161-180.

3666 *Legrand, Lucien* The "visitation" in context. 1995 ⇒14. FHARTMAN L., 129-146 [1,26-56].

3667 **Richert, Ulrike** Magnificat und Benediktus (Lk 1,46-55 und 1,68-79). Diss. Tü 1995, 340 pp. DHengel, M. [RTL 27,537].

3668 **Laurentin, René** Il Magnificat: espressione della riconoscenza di Maria. Spiritualità 36. Brescia 1993, Queriniana 222 pp. RMar. 57 (1995) 397-400 (*Masini, Mario*).

3669 **Terrien, Samuel** The Magnificat: musicians as biblical interpreters. Mahwah 1995, Paulist xix; 89 pp. $10. 0-8091-3485-3. RVJTR 59 (1995) 549-550 (*Meagher, P.M.*).

3670 *Godzik, P.* LUTHERs Magnificatauslegung. LM 34 (1995) 38ff [1,46-55; ZID 21,294].

3671 *Kurz, Paul Konrad* Einübung und Weisung. GuL 68 (1995) 304-307 [1,46-55].

3672 *Natrup, Josef* Das Magnifikat im Bild. EvErz 47 (1995) 7-11 [1,46-55].

3673 **Nolan, Mary Catherine** The Magnificat, canticle of a liberated people: a hermeneutical study of Luke 1:46-55 investigating the world behind the text by exegesis; the world in front of the text by interpretive inquiry. Diss. University of Dayton (10) 176 pp., Dayton 1995.

3674 *Owen, Kris J.N.* The Magnificat and the empowerment of the poor: a theological reflection on Lk 1:46-55 in the context of the contemporary church social teaching on justice and peace. VJTR 59 (1995) 647-662.

3675 *Cook, Joan E.* The Magnificat: program for a new era in the spirit of the Song of Hannah. ProcGLM 15 (1995) 35-43 [1,46-55; 1 Sam 2,1-10].

3676 *Bretschneider, Wolfgang* 'Macht Lieder aus meinen Geschichten!' Notizen zu den Magnificat-Vertonungen. BiKi 50 (1995) 117-120 [1,46-55].

3677 *Rosen, Klaus* Jesu Geburtsdatum, der Census des QUIRINIUS und eine jüdische Steuererklärung aus dem Jahr 127 nC. JAC 38 (1995) 5-15 [2,1-5].

3678 *Strickert, Fred* The presentation of Jesus: the gospel of inclusion: Luke 2:22-40. CThMi 22 (1995) 33-37.

3679 *Bóid, Ruairidh (Rory)* La purification de Jésus (Luc 2:22) et la tradition dosithéenne. SJ(NY) 5. 1995 ⇒28. ^FSIXDENIER G., 19-24.

3680 **Simón Muñoz, Alfonso** El Mesías y la hija de Sión: teología de la redención en Lc 2,29-35. 1994 ⇒10,4983. ^RNatGrac 42 (1995) 136-137 (*Villamonte, Alejandro*); ScrTh 27 (1995) 999-1003 (*Aranda Pérez, G.*); Burg. 36 (1995) 558-560 (*Pérez Herrero, F.*).

3681 **Derrett, John Duncan M.** Ἀντιλεγόμενον, ῥομφαία, διαλογισμοί (Lk 2:34-35): the hidden context. 1995 <1993> ⇒45. Studies 6. 64-75.

3682 *Barkhuizen, J.H.* 'Destined for the downfall and rise of many in Israel': Luke 2,34b in patristic (and modern) exegesis. HTS 51 (1995) 891-899 [NTAb 40,426].

3683 *Laurentin, René* La foi de Marie dans l'épreuve. EtMar 52 (1995) 9-35 [2,35].

3684 *Giannarelli, Elena* Fra profezia ignorata e profezia nascosta: la storia esegetica di Anna (Lc 2,36-38). 1995 ⇒2163. Donna, potere e profezia. 61-96 [BuBbgB 20,2].

3685 *Manns, Frédéric* Gesù adolescente al Tempio. TS(I) 71 (1995) 8-11 [2,41-50].

3686 *Chang, An(n)a* Lk 2:41-52 and the family communion. C. CTUF 103 (1995) 45-54 [ThIK 17,28].

3687 *Strobel, August* Plädoyer für Lukas: zur Stimmigkeit des chronistischen Rahmens von Lk 3,1. NTS 41 (1995) 466-469.

3688 *Arnal, William* Redactional fabrication and group legitimation: the Baptist's preaching in Q 3:7-9, 16-17. 1995 ⇒94. Conflict and Invention. 165-180.

3689 *Derrett, J. Duncan M.* The Baptist's sermon: Luke 3,10-14. BeO 37 (1995) 155-165.

3690 *Lohfink, Norbert* Vom Täufer Johannes und den Törichten Jungfrauen: das Evangelium und seine sozialen Konsequenzen. BiKi 50/1-2 (1995) 26-31 [3,10-18; Mt 25,1-13].

3691 *O'Reilly, Jennifer* Exegesis and the book of Kells: the Lucan genealogy. 1995 ⇒82. Scriptural interpretation. 315-355 [3,23-38].

3692 *Vaage, Leif E.* More than a prophet, and demon-possessed: Q and the "historical" John. 1995 ⇒94. Conflict and Invention. 181-202 [3].

3693 *Cotter, Wendy* 'Yes, I tell you, and more than a Prophet': the function of John in Q. 1995 ⇒94. Conflict and Invention. 135-150 [3].

F7.6 Evangelium Lucae 4,1...

3694 *Rohrbaugh, Richard L.* Legitimating sonship—a test of honour: a social-scientific study of Luke 4:1-30. 1995 ⇒80. Modelling early christianity. 183-197.

3695 *Staley, Jeffrey L.* Narrative structure (self stricture) in Luke 4:14-9:62: the United States of Luke's story world. Semeia 72 (1995) 173-213.

3696 People as exegetes: popular readings: a South African example: Jesus' teaching at Nazareth—Luke 4.14-30. 1995 <1991> ⇒129. Voices from the margin. 447-453.

3697 O'Toole, Robert Does Luke also portray Jesus as the Christ in Luke 4,16-30?. Bib. 76 (1995) 498-522.

3698 **Prior, Michael Patrick** Jesus, the liberator: Nazareth liberation theology (Luke 4.16-30). BiSe 26. Shf 1995, Academic 228 pp. 1-85075-524-8.

3699 Reyes V., G.A. Un ejercicio de hermenéutica y contextualización basado en una lectura de Lucas 4:16-30: paradigma de misión. VoxScr 5 (1995) 163-177 [NTAb 40,233].

3700 People as exegetes: popular readings: an Indonesian example: the miraculous catch Luke 5.1-11. 1995 <1991> ⟹129. Voices from the margin. 444-446.

3701 Derrett, J. Duncan M. Luke 6:5D reexamined. NT 37 (1995) 232-248.

3702 Carruth, Shawn Strategies of authority: a rhetorical study of the character of the speaker in Q 6:20-49. 1995 ⟹94. Conflict. 98-115.

3703 Vaage, Leif E. Composite texts and oral mythology: the case of the 'Sermon' in Q (6:20-49). 1995 ⟹94. Conflict. 75-97.

3704 Hoffmann, Paul Q 6,22 in der Rezeption durch Lukas. 1995 <1994> ⟹51. Tradition. NTA 28. 162-189.

3705 Douglas, R. Conrad 'Love your enemies': rhetoric, tradents, and ethos. 1995 ⟹94. Conflict. 116-131 [6,27-36].

3706 Piper, R.A. The language of violence and the aphoristic sayings in Q. 1995 ⟹94. Conflict. 53-72 [6,27-36].

3707 Perkins, J.C. A ministry that prolongs life. ABQ 14 (1995) 48ff [ZID 21,409] [7,11-15].

3708 Sevin, Marc L'approche des textes bibliques. LV 50 (1995) 253-260 [7,11-17].

3709 Hartin, Patrick J. 'Yet wisdom is justified by her children' (Q 7:35): a rhetorical and compositional analysis of divine Sophia in Q. 1995 ⟹94. Conflict. 151-164 [7,31-35].

3710 Reid, Barbara E. 'So you see this woman?': Luke 7:36-50 as a paradigm for feminist hermeneutics. BR 40 (1995) 37-49.

3711 Vela, Raffaele Gesù, Simone e la donna peccatrice. Vita Sociale 52 (1995) 101-104 [7,36-50].

3712 **Kiedzik, Miroslaw** Ὁ λόγος τοῦ θεοῦ (Łk 8,4-21): studium z teologii św. Łukasza [Ὁ λόγος τοῦ θεοῦ (Lk 8,4-21): étude de la théologie de saint Luc]. **P.** Diss. Lublin 1995, xxiii; 238 pp. DKudasiewicz, J. [RTL 27,535].

3713 Kuhn, Heinz-Wolfgang Bethsaida in the gospels: the feeding story in Luke 9 and the Q saying in Luke 10. 1995 ⟹131. Bethsaida. 243-256 [9,10-17; 10,13-14].

3714 Pilch, John J. The transfiguration of Jesus: an experience of alternate reality. 1995 ⟹80. Modelling early christianity. 47-64 [9,28-36].

3715 **Reid, Barbara E.** The transfiguration...Luke 9:28-36. 1993 ⟹9,4747. CRB 32. RBLE 96 (1995) 59-61 (Légasse, S.); JBL 114 (1995) 526-527 (Stegner, William Richard).

3716 **Minde, Ludovick J.** True greatness in the christian community: (Luke 9:46-48 and par.). Diss. R 1995, Pont. Univ. Urbaniana xvii; 115 pp. DBiguzzi, Giancarlo.

F7.7   *Iter hierosolymitanum — Lc 9,51... —* **Jerusalem journey.**

3717   **Mayer, Edgar** Die lukanische Reiseerzählung [Lk 9,51-19,10]: Entscheidung in der Wüste. Diss. Neuendettelsau 1995, *DStegemann* [ThRv 92/2,XIII].

3718   **Marks, Edward H.** A wandering Jesus and wandering disciples: a literary/rhetorical study of Luke 9:51-10:42 as the first sub-unit of the travel narrative. Diss. Vanderbilt 1995, 298 pp. *DSegovia, F.F.*, AAC 9611807; DAI-A 56/12,p.4819.

3719   **Lane, Thomas** The anticipation of the gentile mission of the Acts of the Apostles in the gospel of Luke: the mission of the seventy (-two) (Luke 10,1-20) foreshadows the Gentile mission of Acts. Diss. R 1995, Pont. Univ. Gregoriana no. 4115, 94 pp. [excerpt], *DKilgallen, John.*

3720   *Grossi, V.* Il cristiano 'filius pacis' nell'esegesi origeniana di Luca 10,5-7. 1995 ⇒126. Origeniana Sexta. BEThL 118. 709-721.

3721   *Meier, John* "Happy the eyes that see": the tradition, message, and authenticity of Luke 10:23-24 and parallels. 1995 ⇒10. *FFREEDMAN D.*, 467-477.

3722   *Gundry, Robert H.* A rejoinder [to F. Neirynck ⇒10,5004a)] on Matthean foreign bodies in Luke 10,25-28. EThL 71 (1995) 139-150.

3723   **Wanok, Sanctus Lino** The unlimited love in Lk 10:25-37. Diss. R 1995, Pont. Univ. Urbaniana xi; 89 pp. [excerpt] *DVirgulin, Stefano.*

3724   *Phillips, Gary A.* 'What is written?: how are you reading?': gospel, intertextuality and doing Lukewise: reading Lk 10:25-42 otherwise. Semeia 69/70 (1995) 111-147.

3725   *Manns, Frédéric* Donna, libera di ascoltare. TS(I) 72 (1995) 12-13 [10,38-39].

3726   **Fornari-Carbonell, Isabel M.** La escucha del huésped (Lc 10,38-42): la hospitalidad en el horizonte de la comunicación. EMISJ 30. Estella 1995, Verbo Divino xxi; 291 pp. 84-8169-055-4.

3727   **Brutscheck, Jutta** Die Maria-Marta-Erzählung...Lk 10,38-42. 1986 ⇒2,3977... 4,5186. RRBL 48 (1995) 220-222 (*Chmiel, Jerzy*).

3728   **Constable, Giles** Three studies in medieval religious and social thought: the interpretation of Mary and Martha: the ideal of the imitation of Christ: the orders of society. NY 1995, CUP xix; 423 pp. $59 [10,38-42].

3729   *Philolenko, Marc* "Que ton Esprit-Saint vienne sur nous et qu'il nous purifie" (Luc 11,2): l'arrière-plan qoumrânien d'une variante lucanienne du "Notre Père". RHPhR 75 (1995) 61-66.

3730   *Moessner, David P.* The 'leaven of the Pharisees' and 'this generation': Israel's rejection of Jesus according to Luke. 1995 <1988> ⇒81. The synoptic gospels. BiSe 31. 268-293 [12,1].

3731   *Riley, Gregory J.* Influence of Thomas Christianity on Luke 12:14 and 5:39. HThR 88 (1995) 229-235.

3732   *Cardenas Pallares, José* Ser livres come pássaros: uma meditação ecológica de Lucas 12.22-31. Ribla 21 (1995) 235-243 [ThIK 17/2,68].

       Chow, Simon The sign of Jonah reconsidered. ⇒2624 [12,39-41].

3733 *Derrett, John Duncan M.* Christ's second baptism (Lk 12:50 etc.). 1995 <1989> ⇒45. Studies 6. 76-77.
3734 *Scholtissek, Klaus* "Könnt ihr die Zeichen der Zeit deuten?" (vgl. Lk 12,56): Christologie und Kairologie im lukanischen Doppelwerk. ThGl 85 (1995) 195-223.
3735 **Harmansa, H.-Konrad** Die Zeit der Entscheidung: Lk 13,1-9 als Beispiel für das lukanische Verständnis der Gerichtspredigt Jesu an Israel. EThSt 69. Leipzig 1995, Benno xxvi; 154 pp. 3-7462-1136-0.
3736 *Karris, Robert J.* Luke 13:10-17 and God's promises to Israel. Discussion with *Stransky, Thomas F.*, 1995 ⇒100. Divine promises. ASBF 40. 98-115.
3737 *Vinci, Gianfranco* Gesù Maestro, Salvatore e Signore: aspetti cristologici in Lc 13,10-17. Theologica & Historica 4 (1995) 9-74.
3738 *Opocenska, J.* A piece of God's intended world. RW 45 (1995) 41ff [13,10-20; ZID 21,469].
3739 *Hoffmann, Paul* PANTES ERGATAI ADIKIAS: Redaktion und Tradition in Lk 13,22-30. 1995 <1967> ⇒51. Tradition. NTA 28. 135-161.
3740 *Carey, W. Gregory* Excuses, excuses: the parable of the banquet (Luke 14:15-24) within the larger context of Luke. IBSt 17 (1995) 177-187.
3741 **Braun, Willi** Feasting and social rhetoric in Luke 14. Diss C, ⇒ᴰ*Kloppenborg, John S.*, MSSNTS 85. C 1995, University Press, £32.50/$50. 0-521-49553-9 [RB 103,475].

3742 *Schöpke, H.* Das Gleichnis vom verlorenen Schaf: schriftliche Lernkontrolle im 8. Schuljahr. ReHe 22 (1995) 120ff [15,1-7; ZID 21,602].
3743 *Lamb, Regene* Ein Licht ist angezündet: Lukas 15,8-10 aus feministisch-befreiungstheologischer Perspektive. BiKi 50 (1995) 230-234.
3744 *Geddert, T.* The parable of the Prodigal: priorities (Luke 15:11-32). Direction 24/1 (1995) 28-36 [NTAb 40,46—*Matthews, C.R.*].
3745 *Schwank, Benedikt* Der vorbildliche "Verlorene Sohn" (Lk 15,11-32). EuA 71 (1995) 419-421.
3746 *Duff, Nancy J.* Luke 15:11-32. Interp. 49 (1995) 66-69.
3747 *Linard, Hervé* Dévoilement d'une paternité: lecture, psychanalytique de la parabole des deux fils perdu(s) ou trouvé(s) (Lc 15,11-32). LV 50 (1995) 307-322.
3748 *Kremer, Jacob* Der barmherzige Vater: "die Parabel vom verlorenen Sohn" (Lk 15,11-32) als Antwort Gottes auf die Fragen der Menschen zu "Leid—Schuld—Versöhnung". 1995 <1990> ⇒53. Die Bibel. 84-107.
3749 **Nouwen, Henri** El regreso del hijo pródigo: meditaciones ante un cuadro de REMBRANDT. 1994 ⇒10,5018. ᴿRTLi 29/1 (1995) 182-184 (*Bossetti, Antonio*) [15,11-32].
3750 **Pöhlmann, Wolfgang** Der Verlorene Sohn und das Haus: Studien zu Lukas 15,11-32 im Horizont der antiken Lehre von Haus, Erziehung und Ackerbau. 1993 ⇒9,5246; 10,5017. WUNT 2/68. ᴿCBQ 57 (1995) 188-189 (*Balch, David L.*); JBL 114 (1995) 527-529 (*Wan, Sze-kar*).
3751 **De Rozario, Tapan Camillus** Joy in the parables of Luke 15. Diss. R 1995, Pont. Univ. Urbaniana xxiii; 145 pp. [excerpt].

3752 *Parsons, Mikeal C.* Hand in hand: autobiographical reflections on Luke 15. Semeia 72 (1995) 125-152.

3753 *Brodie, T.L.* Re-opening the quest for Proto-Luke: the systematic use of Judges 6-12 in Luke 16:1-18:8. JHiC 2/1 (1995) 68-101.
3754 *Hoeren, Thomas* Das Gleichnis vom ungerechten Verwalter (Lukas 16,1-8a)—zugleich ein Beitrag zur Geschichte der Restschuldbefreiung. NTS 41 (1995) 620-629.
3755 *Binder, Hermann* Mißdeutbar oder eindeutig?—Gedanken zu einem Gleichnis Jesu. ThZ 51 (1995) 41-49 [16,1-13].
3756 *Lof, L.J. van der* Abraham's bosom in the writings of IRENAEUS, TERTULLIAN and AUGUSTINE. AugSt 26 (1995) 109ff [16,17-31; ZID 21,574].
3757 *Neirynck, F.* The divorce saying in Q 16:18. LouvSt 20 (1995) 201-218 [16,18].
3758 *Kilgallen, John J.* The purpose of Luke's divorce text (16,18). Bib. 76 (1995) 229-238.
3759 *Kremer, Jacob* Der arme Lazarus: Lazarus, der Freund Jesu: Beobachtungen zur Beziehung zwischen Lk 16,19-31 und Joh 11,1-46. 1995 <1985> ⇒53. Die Bibel. 108-118.
3760 *Ball, Michael* The parables of the unjust steward and the rich man and Lazarus. ET 106 (1995) 329-330 [16].

3761 *Witherington III, Ben* Jesus the savior of the least, the last, and the lost. QR 15 (1995) 197-211 [17-19; NTAb 40,47].
3762 *Fattorini, Gino* "Siamo servi inutili": la parabola di Lc 17,7-10: dalla struttura al messaggio. Inter Fratres 45 (1995) 203-219.
3763 *Ficarra, R.* La parabola del fattore infedele in GAUDENZIO di Brescia. ASEs 12 (1995) 347-359 [19,1-8].
3764 *Terrinoni, Waldo* Zaccheo: dall'incontro alla conversione. RVS 49 (1995) 9-33 [19,1-10].
3765 *Hassold, M.J.* Eyes to see: reflections on Luke 19:1-10. LTJ 29 (1995) 68-73 [NTAb 40,47].
3766 *Raja, R.J.* Seeking God, sought by God: a Dhvani-reading of the episode of Zacchaeus (Lk 19:10). Jeevadhara 25 (1995) 139-148 [ThIK 17,36].
3767 **Kinman, Brent** Jesus' entry into Jerusalem: in the context of Lukan theology and the politics of his day. Diss. C 1993, ᴰ*Hooker, Morna*, AGJU 28. Lei 1995, Brill xvii; 223 pp. *f*115.50/$75. 90-04-10330-9 [19,28-48].
3768 *Malipuratha, Thomas* The praxis of poverty from the Lucan perspective: the example of the poor widow (Lk 21:1-4). BiBh 21 (1995) 67-183.
3769 *Buzzard, Anthony F.* Luke's prelude to the kingdom of God: the fall of Jerusalem and the end of the age—Luke 21:20-33. JRadRef. 4/4 (1995) 32-43 [NTAb 40,36].

F7.8 Passio — Lc 22....

3770 *Maniciardi, Ermenegildo* L'atteggiamento di Gesù nell'imminenza della sua morte nel vangelo secondo Luca. PSV 32 (1995) 97-119.
3771 *Brawley, Robert L.* Resistance to the carnivalization of Jesus: scripture in the Lucan passion narrative. Semeia 69/70 (1995) 33-60.

3772 *Weren, Wim; Haas, Vincent de* Oog in oog met personages uit Lucas: 1. Jezus en zijn volgelingen in Lc. 22-24. TTh 35 (1995) 125-147.

3773 **Nelson, Peter K.** Leadership and discipleship...Lk 22:24-30. 1994 ⇒10,5042. SBL.DS 138. ^RCBQ 57 (1995) 819-820 (*Hamm, Dennis*).

3774 *Heiligenthal, R.* Wehrlosigkeit oder Selbstschutz? Aspekte zum Verständnis des lukanischen Schwertwortes. NTS 41 (1995) 39-58 [22,35-38].

3775 *Mendham, P.* In the green wood: Jesus' address to the women of Jerusalem and the destiny of Israel. St Mark's Review 161 (1995) 18-22 [23,26-31; NTAb 40,48].

3776 *Ruß, Rainer* Das Vermächtnis des gekreuzigten Herrn: Jesu letzte Worte im Evangelium nach Lukas. BiKi 50 (1995) 128-135 [23].

3777 *McCole, Julie* The Emmaus journey: paradigm for mid-life. Spiritual Life 41 (1995) 131-139 [24,13-25].

3778 *Kremer, Jacob* Die Bezeugung der Auferstehung Christi in Form von Geschichten: zu Schwierigkeiten und Chancen heutigen Verstehens von Lk 24,13-53. 1995 <1988> ⇒53. Die Bibel. 119-132.

F8.1 *Actus Apostolorum*, Acts — *text, commentary, topics.*

3779 ^T**Abbolito Simonetti, Giuseppina** BEDA Venerabilis: esposizione e revisione degli Atti degli Apostoli. CTePa 121. R 1995, Città Nuova 301 pp. 88-311-3121-4.

3780 ^E**Aland, Kurt,** *al.,* Text und Textwert: Apostelgeschichte 3/1-2. 1993 ⇒9,5276; 10,5057. ANTT 20-21. ^RLe Muséon 108 (1995) 205-207 (*Coulie, B.*); NT 37 (1995) 101-104 (*Elliott, J.K.*).

3781 *Alexander, Loveday* Narrative maps: reflections on the toponymy of Acts. 1995 ⇒23. ^FROGERSON J. JSOT.S 200. 17-57.

3782 *Bammel, Ernst* Jewish activity against christians in Palestine according to Acts. 1995 ⇒3784. The book of Acts 4. 357-364.

3783 ^E**Bateman, John J.** In Acta apostolorum paraphrasis [Paraphrase on the Acts of the Apostles]. ^T*Sider, Robert D.,* Collected works of Erasmus 50. Toronto 1995, University of Toronto Press xxvi; 389 pp. £81/$125. 0-8020-0664-7.

3784 ^E**Bauckham, Richard** The book of Acts in its Palestinian setting. The book of Acts in its first century setting 4. GR/Carlisle 1995, Eerdmans/Paternoster xiv; 526 pp. $37.50. 0-8028-2436-6/0-8536-4566-3 [ZNW 87,140].

3785 *Bauckham, Richard* James and the Jerusalem church. 1995 ⇒3784. The book of Acts 4. 415-480.

3786 **Bossuyt, Philippe; Radermakers, Jean** Témoins de la parole de la grâce: Actes des Apôtres. IET 16. Bruxelles 1995, Institut d'Études Théologiques, 2 vols; 116; 782 pp. 1. Texte 2. Lecture continue. FB1680/FF280. 2-930067-15-2/-16-0. ^REeV 105 (1995) 682-684 (*Cothenet, Édouard*).

3787 *Carreira das Neves, Joaquim* História e Espírito Santo nos Actos dos Apóstolos. Did(L) 25/1-2 (1995) 195-234.

3788 *Dumais, Marcel* Les Actes des Apôtres: bilan et orientations. 1995 ⇒84. De bien des manières. LeDiv 163. 307-364.

3789 **Dupont, J.** Nouvelles études sur les Actes des Apôtres. LeDiv
       118. P 1994, Cerf 535 pp. RNeotest. 29 (1995) 424-427 (*Decock,
       Paul B.*).

3790 **Economou, Christos K.** The problem of the title "Acts of (the)
       Apostles": a new theological approach. **G.** Studies in the
       beginnings of Christianity 5. Thessaloniki 1995, 119 pp.

3791 *Falk, Daniel K.* Jewish prayer literature and the Jerusalem church
       in Acts. 1995 ⇒3784. 267-301.

3792 **Galbiati, Henri** Les Actes des Apôtres: l'église des origines dans
       les Actes des Apôtres et dans leurs écrits. P 1995, Médiaspaul.
       FF60. 2-7122-0145-0.

3793 **Geer, Thomas C.** Family 1739 in Acts. 1994 ⇒10,5063. SBL.MS
       48. RNT 37 (1995) 403-404 (*Elliott, J.K.*).

3794 *Ghiberti, Giuseppe* Questioni sul 'destinatario' della missione negli
       Atti degli Apostoli. Atti del III Simposio. 1995 ⇒138. 107-117.

3795 *Gill, David W. J.* Acts and Roman policy in Judaea. 1995 ⇒3784.
       15-26.

3796 EGill, **David W.J.**; **Gempf, Conrad** The book of Acts in its
       Graeco-Roman setting. 1994 ⇒10,5064. RThLZ 120 (1995) 1006-
       1008 (*Wolter, Michael*); Reviews in Religion and Theology
       (1995/2) 77-78 (*Capper, Brian*); CBQ 57 (1995) 840-842 (*Pervo,
       Richard I.*); JETh 9 (1995) 239-242 (*Schnabel, Eckhard J.*).

3797 *Hengel, Martin* The geography of Palestine in Acts. 1995 ⇒3784.
       27-78.

3798 *Herceg, Pál* Sermons of the book of Acts and the apocryphal Acts.
       The apocryphal Acts of John, EBremmer, **Jan N.**, SAAA 1.
       Kampen 1995, Kok. 90-390-0141-3. 153-170.

3799 **Ijatuyi, Olu** Community and self-definition in the book of Acts: a
       study of early christianity's strategic response to the world. Diss.
       Trinity Evang. Div. School 1995, 364 pp. DOsborne, G. R., AAC
       9608871; DAI-A 56/11,p.4429.

3800 *Jáuregui, José Antonio* Historiografía y teología in Hechos: estado
       de la investigación desde 1980. EstB 53 (1995) 97-123.

3801 **Johnson, Luke Timothy** The Acts of the Apostles. Sacra Pagina 5.
       1992 ⇒8,5483... 10,5070. CritRR 7 (1994) 209-211 (*Juel,
       Donald*).

3802 *Jones, F. Stanley* A Jewish christian reads Luke's Acts of the
       Apostles: the use of the canonical Acts in the ancient Jewish
       christian source behind Pseudo-CLEMENTINE *Recognitions* 1.27-
       71. SBL.SP 34 (1995) 617-635.

3803 **Kee, Howard Clark** Good news...theology of Acts. 1990
       ⇒6,5480... 8,5485. RSJTh 48 (1995) 112-114 (*Brooke, George J.*).
       ELáconi, **Mauro** Vangeli sinottici e Atti degli Apostoli. 1994
       ⇒2775.

3804 **Larkin, William J.** Acts. The IVP New Testament Commentary 5.
       Downers Grove, Il./Leicester, UK 1995, InterVarsity 422 pp. $18.
       0-8308-1805-7/0-85111-680-9.

3805 **Liefeld, W.L.** Interpreting the book of Acts. Guides to New
       Testament Exegesis 4. GR 1995, Baker 141 pp. $9. 0-8010-2015-8
       [NTAb 40,341].

3806 *Lieu, J.M.* The race of the God-fearers. JThS 46 (1995) 483-501.

3807 *Mason, Steve* Chief priests, sadducees, pharisees and sanhedrin in
       Acts. 1995 ⇒3784. 115-177.

3808 **Mbachu, Hilary** Survey and method of Acts research from 1826-1995. Deutsche Hochschulschriften 1051. Egelsbach 1995, Hänsel-Hohenhausen 70 pp. 3-8267-1051-7.

3809 *Mussies, Gerard* Variation in the book of Acts II). FgNT 8 (1995) 23-61.

3810 **Muthuraj, Joseph** The theology of God and the gentile mission in Acts. Diss. 1995, Durham [RTL 27,537].

3811 *Mworia, Thadei A.* The missionary techniques in Acts. RAT 19 (1995) 21-36.

3812 *Pervo, R. I.* A hard act to follow: the Acts of Paul and the canonical Acts. JHiC 2/2 (1995) 3-32.

3813 **Pesch, R.** Atti degli Apostoli. 1992 ⇒8,5406; 9,5300. RAsp. 42 (1995) 592-593 (*Cipriani, S.*).

3814 **Polhill, John B.** Acts. 1992 ⇒8,5497... 10,5079. NAC 26. RCritRR 7 (1994) 250-252 (*Kolasny, Judette M.*).

3815 *Rakocy, Waldemar* A contribution to the discussion on the composition of Acts of the Apostles. **P.** Roczniki Teologiczne 42/1 (1995) 103-110 [sum. 110].

3816 **Reimer, Ivoni Richter** Women in the Acts of the Apostles: a feminist liberation perspective. TMaloney, Linda M., Mp 1995, Fortress xxvi; 302 pp. $24. 0-8006-2840-3.

3817 *Reinhardt, Wolfgang* The population size of Jerusalem and the numerical growth of the Jerusalem church. 1995 ⇒3784. 237-265.

3818 **Rius-Camps, Josep** Comentari als Fets dels Apòstols I-II. 1991-3 ⇒8,5498... 10,5082. RJThS 46 (1995) 643-644 (*Chapa, Juan*).

3819 *Ruis-Camps, Josep* Cuatro paradigmas del pentateuco refundidos en los Hechos de los Apóstoles. EstB 53 (1995) 25-54.

3820 **Soards, Marion L.** The speeches in Acts. 1994 ⇒10,5085. RProEc 4 (1995) 374-375 (*Rhoads, David*); JBL 114 (1995) 741-743 (*Matthews, Christopher R.*); CBQ 57 (1995) 829-830 (*Spencer, F. Scott*).

3821 Spirit, gospel, cultures: Bible studies on the Acts of the Apostles. WCC Mission 4. Genève 1995, W.C.C. 44 pp. FS6.50. 2-8254-1167-1.

3822 *Steyn, Gert J. LXX-sitate* in die Petrus- en Paulusredes van Handelinge [LXX quotations in the Petrine and Pauline speeches in Acts]. Skrif en Kerk 16/1 (1995) 125-141 [NTAb 40,246].

3823 **Steyn, Gert J.** Septuagint quotations in the context of the Petrine and Pauline speeches in the Acta Apostolorum. Diss. ⇒10,5088. Kampen 1995, Kok xvi; 290 pp. f68.90. 90-390-0131-6 [NTAb 40,349].

3824 **Strange, W.A.** The problem of the text of Acts. 1992 ⇒8,5503... 10,5089. RSJTh 48 (1995) 410-411 (*Parker, D.C.*).

3825 *Stricher, Joseph* Les Actes des Apôtres: de l'histoire?. DosB 60 (1995) 21-22.

3826 *Taylor, J.* The book of Acts and history. ScrB 25/2 (1995) 66-76 [NTAb 40,248].

3827 **Taylor, Justin** Les Actes des deux Apôtres V: Act. 9,1-18,22. 1994 ⇒10,5092. EtB 23. RCBQ 57 (1995) 830-832 (*Rogers, Patrick*).

3828 *Varickasseril, Jose* Methods used in the Acts for strengthening the churches. IMR 17/2 (1995) 42-71 [ThIK 17,36].

3829 **Weiß, Wolfgang** "Zeichen und Wunder": eine Studie zu der Sprachtradition und ihrer Verwendung im Neuen Testament. WMANT 67. Neuk 1995, Neuk viii; 189 pp. 3-7887-1471-9.

3830 **Wendel, Ulrich** Gemeinde in Kraft: das Gemeindeverständnis in den Summarien der Apostelgeschichte: ein Beitrag zur lukanischen Ekklesiologie. Diss. Hamburg 1995-6, ^D*Schramm, G.*, 3-7720-1869-6 [RTL 27,538].

3831 *Williams, Margaret H.* Palestinian Jewish personal names in Acts. 1995 ⇒3784. The book of Acts 4. 79-113.

3832 ^E**Winter, Bruce W.; Clarke, Andrew D.** The book of Acts in its ancient literary setting. 1993 ⇒9,5310. ^RThLZ 120 (1995) 38-42 (*Wolter, Michael*); JThS 46 (1995) 275-277 (*Grayston, K.*); Kairós 16 (1995) 90-92 (*López, Gabriel*); TJT 11 (1995) 253-255 (*Matthews, Christopher*); CBQ 57 (1995) 441-442 (*Davids, Peter H.*); CTJ 30 (1995) 542-544 (*Verbrugge, Verlyn D.*).

3833 **Zedda, Silverio** Teologia della salvezza negli Atti degli Apostoli: studi sulla terminologia. 1994 ⇒10,5093. ^RGr. 76 (1995) 153-154 (*Marconi, Gilberto*); Itin. 3/4 (1995) 252-253 (*Varagona, Francesco*).

F8.3 *Ecclesia primaeva Actuum:* **Die Urgemeinde.**

3834 *Capper, Brian* The Palestinian cultural context of earliest christian community of goods. 1995 ⇒3784. The book of Acts 4. 323-356 [2,44-45].

3835 *Fiensy, David A.* The composition of the Jerusalem church. 1995 ⇒3784. The book of Acts 4. 213-236.

3836 *Franco, Ettore* La koinonia nella chiesa di Gerusalemme: archetipo di ogni comunità. PSV 31 (1995) 111-133.

3837 *Hahn, Ferdinand* Geschichte des Urchristentums als Missionsgeschichte. ZMR 79 (1995) 87-96.

3838 *Joubert, Stephan J.* The Jerusalem community as role-model for a cosmopolitan christian group: a socio-literary analysis of Luke's symbolic universe. Neotest. 29 (1995) 49-59.

3839 *Malina, Bruce J.* Early Christian groups: using small group formation theory to explain Christian organizations. 1995 ⇒80. Modelling early christianity. 96-113.

3840 *Miller, M.P.* 'Beginning from Jerusalem...': re-examining canon and consensus. JHiC 2/1 (1995) 3-30 [NTAb 40,246].

3841 *Räisänen, H.* Die "Hellenisten" der Urgemeinde 1468-1514;

3842 *Riesner, Rainer* Das Jerusalemer Essenerviertel und die Urgemeinde: JOSEPHUS, Bellum Judaicum V 145; 11 QMiqdasch 46, 13-16; Apostelgeschichte 1-6 und die Archäologie 1775-1922;

3843 *Schenk, W.* Die ältesten Selbstverständnisse christlicher Gruppen im ersten Jahrhundert 1357-1467. 1995 ⇒87. Vorkonstantinisches Christentum.

3844 **Testa, Emanuele** La fede della chiesa madre di Gerusalemme. Biblica Dehoniane. R 1995, Dehoniane 374 pp. 88-396-0555-X.

3845 **Thurston, Bonnie** Spiritual life in the early church... Acts and Ephesians. 1993 ⇒9,5327; 10,5117. ^RAThR 77/1 (1995) 96-98 (*Derrenbacker, Robert A.*); CritRR 8 (1995) 309-311 (*Mills, Watson E.*).

3846 *Vogt, Hermann J.* Bemerkungen zur frühen Amts- und Gemeindestruktur. ThQ 175 (1995) 192-198.

F8.5 Ascensio, Pentecostes; ministerium Petri — *Act 1...*

3847 *Haacker, K.* Die Stellung des Stephanus in der Geschichte des Urchristentums. 1995 ⇒87. Vorkonstantinisches Christentum. 1515-1553.
3848 *Riesner, Rainer* Synagogues in Jerusalem. 1995 ⇒3784. The book of Acts 4. 179-211.
3849 *Schwartz, Joshua* Peter and Ben Stada in Lydda. 1995 ⇒3784. The book of Acts 4. 391-414.
3850 *Rozman, Francè* Binkošti in govorjenhe v jesikih [Pentecost and speaking in tongues]. **Slovenian.** Bogoslovni Vestnik 55 (1995) 519-528 [sum. 528].
3851 *Brésard, Luc* L'Ascension pour BERNARD CCist 57 (1995) 238-248.
3852 *Pickering, Stuart R.* Can an anti-feminist tendency be found at Acts 1:14?. NTTRU 3 (1995) 17-18 [1,14].
3853 *Derrett, J.D.M.* Akeldama (Acts 1:19). Bijdr. 56 (1995) 122-132.
3854 *Kremer, Jacob* Was geschah Pfingsten?: zur Historizität des Apg 2,1-13 berichteten Pfingstereignisses. 1995 <1973> ⇒53. Die Bibel. 190-204.
3855 **Bindella, Francesco** La Pentecoste alla luce della rivelazione del nome divino: rivisitazione ermeneutica di Atti 2,1-13: il paradigma dell'Ut Unum Sint. Praesidium Assisiense 3. Assisi 1995, Porziuncola 270 pp. L40.000. 88-270-0283-9.
3856 *Rius-Camps, Josep* Las variantes de la Recensión Occidental de los Hechos de los Apóstoles (V) (Hch 2,14-40). FgNT 8 (1995) 63-78 [sum. 63].
3857 *Reid, Barbara E.* Puzzling passages: Acts 2:22. BiTod 33 (1995) 293.
3858 *Balla, Peter* Does Acts 2:36 represent an adoptionist christology?. EurJT 4/1 (1995) 137-142.
3859 *Prieur, Jean-Marc* Actes 2,42 et le culte réformé. FV 94/2 (1995) 63-72.
3860 *Murphy-O'Connor, Jerome* The cenacle—topographical setting for Acts 2:44-45. 1995 ⇒3784. The book of Acts 4. 303-321.
3861 *Theißen, Gerd* Urchristlicher Liebeskommunismus: zum "Sitz im Leben" des Topos HAPANTA KOINA in Apg 2,44 und 4,32. 1995 ⇒14. FHARTMAN L., 689-712.
3862 *Lincoln, A.T.* Theology and history in the interpretation of Luke's pentecost. ET 96 (1995) 204-209 [2].
3863 *Zerhusen, Bob* An overlooked Judean diglossia in Acts 2?. BTB 25 (1995) 118-130.
3864 *Heimerdinger, Jenny* Unintentional sins in Peter's speech: Acts 3:12-26. RCatT 20 (1995) 269-276 [sum. 276].
3865 **Carrón Pérez, Julián** Jesús, el Mesías manifestado... 3,19-26. 1993 ⇒8,5549*... 10,5139. RBib. 76 (1995) 582-587 (*Betori, Giuseppe*); ATG 58 (1995) 352-354 (*Torres, A.*); CBQ 57 (1995) 584-585 (*Witherup, Ronald D.*).
3866 *Wahlde, U.C. von* The theological assessment of the first christian persecution: the apostles' prayer and its consequences in Acts 4,24-31. Bib. 76 (1995) 523-531.

3867 Wahlde, Urban C. von The problems of Acts 4:25a: a new proposal. ZNW 86 (1995) 265-267.

3868 Dschulnigg, Peter Die Erzählung über Hananias und Saphira (Apg 5,1-11) und die Ekklesiologie der Apostelgeschichte. 1995 ⇒15. FHEINEMANN H., 59-71.

3869 O'Toole, Robert F. "You did not lie to us (human beings) but to God" (Acts 5,4c). Bib. 76 (1995) 182-209.

3870 Hill, Craig C. Hellenists and Hebrews. 1992 ⇒8,5559; 9,5345. RBibl.Interp. 3 (1995) 119-123 (Esler, Philip F.) [6,1-8,4].

3871 Pindel, R. Das Modell der Einsetzung oder Kriseüberwindung?. P. ACra 27 (1995) 263-282 [6,1-7].

3872 Brehm, H. Alan The meaning of 'Ελληνιστής in Acts in light of a diachronic analysis of 'ελληνίζειν. 1995 ⇒102. Discourse analysis. 180-199 [6,1].

3873 Barbi, Augusto Il martirio di Stefano (At 6,8-15, 7,55-8,3). PSV 32 (1995) 143-157.

3874 Shafer, Grant Raymond St. Stephen and the Samaritans: an evaluation of and a contribution to the samaritanology of the New Testament (especially Acts 7:2-53). Diss. Michigan 1995, 169 pp. DFossum, Jarl, DAI-A 56/8,p.3165.

3875 Wiens, Delbert L. Stephen's sermon and the structure of Luke-Acts. Richland Hills, TX 1995, BIBAL xii; 267 pp. 0-941037-39-8 [7].

3876 Armellini, Fernando Atti degli Apostoli/13: l'evangelista Filippo in Samaria e a Gaza. Evangelizzare 22 (1995) 173-176 [8].

3877 Czachesz, I. Socio-rhetorical exegesis of Acts 9:1-30. CV 37 (1995) 5-32.

3878 Marguerat, Daniel Saul's conversion (Acts 9,22,26) and the multiplication of narrative in Acts. 1995 ⇒3599. Luke's literary achievement. JSNT.S 116. 127-155.

3879 Kremer, Jacob "Dieser ist der Sohn Gottes" (Apg 9,20): bibeltheologische Erwägungen zur Bedeutung von "Sohn Gottes" im lukanischen Doppelwerk. 1995 <1991> ⇒53. Die Bibel. 59-83.

3880 Schlumberger, Sophie Saul renversé: Actes 9: le récit d'une identité reconstruite. FV 94 (1995) 61-74.

3881 Tassin, C. Conversion de Corneille et conversion de Pierre. Spiritus 141 (1995) 465-475 [NTAb 40,436].

3882 Łukasz, Czesław Evangelizzazione e conflitto...Atti 10,1-11,18. 1993 ⇒9,5360. EHS.T 484. RJBL 114 (1995) 531-532 (Giblin, Charles Homer).

3883 Humphrey, Edith M. Collision of modes?: vision and determining argument in Acts 10:1-11:18. Semeia 71 (1995) 65-84.

3884 Zmijewski, J. Die Aufnahme der ersten Heiden in die Kirche nach Apg 10,1-11,18: eine Interpretationsstudie. 1995 ⇒87. Vorkonstantinisches Christentum. 1554-1601.

3885 Erwin, Ed Between text and sermon: Acts 10:34-43. Interp. 49 (1995) 179-182.

3886 Cyran, Włodzimierz Die Salbung mit Heiligen Geist und mit Kraft (APG 10,38). P. Roczniki Teologiczne 42/1 (1995) 95-101 [Zsfg. 101].

3887 Kayama, Hisao The Cornelius story in the Japanese cultural context. 1995 ⇒114.. Text and experience. BiSe 35. 180-194 [10-11].

3888 *Royer, Lorraine* The God who surprises. BiTod 33 (1995) 298-302 [10].
3889 *Parry, David* Release of the captives—reflections on Acts 12. 1995 ⇒3599. Luke's literary achievement. 156-164.
3890 *Maciel del Río, C.* Pedro dormía en medio de dos soldados (análisis narrativo estilístico de Act 12,1-23). Efemérides Mexicana 37 (1995) 27-46 [NTAb 40,57].
3891 *Meester, Paul de* Juifs et chrétiens: une thélogie renouvelée: premiers repères dans un discours de Paul (Ac 13,16-41). RAT 19 (1995) 195-214.

F8.7 Act 13...*Itinera Pauli;* Paul's Journeys.

3892 *Légasse, Simon* Paul's pre-christian career according to Acts. 1995 ⇒3784. The book of Acts 4. 365-390.
3893 **Lentz, John Clayton Jr.** Luke's portrait of Paul. MSSNTS 77. 1993 ⇒9,5369; 10,5164. [R]CritRR 7 (1994) 218-220 (*Tannehill, Robert C.*).
3894 *Walker, William O.* Acts and the Pauline corpus reconsidered. 1995 <1985> ⇒105. The Pauline writings. BiSe 34. 55-74.
3895 *Di Berardino, Angelo* Viaggiando con Paolo. Atti del III Simposio. 1995 ⇒138. 27-44.
3896 *Trevijano Etcheverria, Ramón* Los primeros viajes de San Pablo a Jerusalén. Salm. 42 (1995) 173-209.
3897 **Thornton, Claus-Jürgen** Der Zeuge... WUNT 2/56. 1991 ⇒7,4711... 10,5176. RB 102 (1995) 264-278 (*Taylor, Justin*).
3898 *Alexander, Loveday* "In journeyings often": voyaging in the Acts of the Apostles and in Greek romance. 1995 ⇒3599. Luke's literary achievement. JSNT.S 116. 17-49.
3899 **Schreiber, Stefan** Paulus als Wundertäter: redaktionsgeschichtliche Untersuchungen zur Apostelgeschichte und den authentischen Paulusbriefen. Diss. 1995, Augsburg, [D]*Leroy, H.*
3900 **Rosenblatt, Marie-Eloise** Paul the accused: his portrait in the Acts of the Apostles. Zacchaeus Studies: New Testament. ColMn 1995, Liturgical Press xviii; 118 pp. $9/£7.50. 0-8146-5750-8. [R]ScrB 25/2 (1995) 85-86 (*Greenhalgh, Stephen*).
3901 *Taylor, J.* St Paul and the Roman empire: Acts of the Apostles 13-14. 1995 ⇒87. Vorkonstantinisches Christentum. 1189-1231.
3902 **Rius-Camps, Josep** "Fins als confins de la terra": primera i segona fases de la missió al paganisme (Ac 13,1-18,23). Comentari als Fets dels Apòstols 3. CStP 54. Barc 1995, Facultat de Teologia de Catalunya/Herder. 84-86065-42-9/84-254-1948-4 [RB 103,317].
3903 **Gill, D.W.** Paul's travels through Cyprus: (Acts 13:4-12). TynB 46 (1995) 219-228.
         Meester, Paul de Juifs et chrétiens (Ac 13,16-41) ⇒3891.
3904 **Pichler, Josef** Paulusrezeption und Paulusbild in Apg 13,16-52. Diss. 1995, Graz, [D]*Zeilinger* [ThRv 92/2,IX].
3905 *Martin, Luther H.* Gods or ambassadors of God? Barnabas and Paul in Lystra. NTS 41 (1995) 152-156 [14,1-7].
3906 *Detwiler, David F.* Paul's approach to the great commission in Acts 14:21-23. BS 152 (1995) 33-41.
3907 *Whitlock, D.* An exposition of Acts 15:1-29. RExp 92 (1995) 375-378.

3908   *Baasland, Ernst* Rhetorischer Kontext in Apg 15,13-21: Statuslehre und die Actareden. 1995 ⇒14. ^FHARTMAN L., 191-226.

3909   *Jervell, Jacob* Das Aposteldekret in der lukanischen Theologie. 1995 ⇒14. ^FHARTMAN L., 227-243 [15,20.29; 16,4; 21,25].

3910   *Barrett, Charles K.* The first christian moral legislation. 1995 ⇒23. ^FROGERSON J., JSOT.S 200. 58-66 [15,29].

3911   *Hilary, Mbachu* Inculturation theology of the Jerusalem council in Acts 15. Diss. Vallendar 1994, ^D*Weiser, A.*, EHS.T 520. Fra 1995, Lang 423 pp. DM98/$58. 3-631-48005-9 [NTAb 40,143].

3912   *Kremer, Jacob* Konflikte und Konfliktlösungen in der Urkirche und frühen Christenheit. 1995 <1993> ⇒53. Die Bibel. 361-380 [15].

3913   **Wehnert, Jürgen** Die Reinheit des christlichen Gottesvolkes aus Juden und Heiden: Studien zum historischen und theologischen Hintergrund des sog. Aposteldekrets. Diss.-Habil. Göttingen 1995 [15; ThRv 92/2,III].

3914   *Bockmuehl, Markus* The Noachide commandments and New Testament ethics: with special reference to Acts 15 and Pauline halakhah. RB 102 (1995) 72-101 [Gn 9].

3915   *White, L. Michael* Visualizing the "real" world of Acts 16: toward construction of a social index. 1995 ⇒^FMEEKS W., 234-261.

3916   *Rius-Camps, Josep* Pablo y el grupo "nosotros" en Filipos: dos proyectos de evangelización en conflicto (Hch 16,11-40). Laur. 36 1-2 (1995) 35-59.

3917   *Vos, C. S. de* The significance of the change from οἶκός to οἰκία in Luke's account of the Philippian gaoler (Acts 16.30-4). NTS 41 (1995) 292-296 [16,30-34].

3918   *Given, Mark D.* Not either/or but both/and in Paul's Areopagus speech. Bibl.Interp. 3 (1995) 356-372 [17,15-34].

3919   *Torrance, Thomas F.* Phusikos Kai Theologikos Logos: St Paul and ATHENAGORAS at Athens. Divine meaning: studies in patristic hermeneutics. E 1995 <1988>, Clark 439 pp. 0-567-09709-9. 40-55 [17,16-31].

3920   *Lindemann, Andreas* Die Christuspredigt des Paulus in Athen (Act 17,16-33). 1995 ⇒14. ^FHARTMAN L., 245-255 [17,16-33].

3921   *Radermakers, Jean* Rencontre de l'incroyant et inculturation: Paul à Athène (Ac 17,16-34). NRTh 117 (1995) 19-43 [17,16-34].

3922   *Penna, Romano* Paolo nell'Agorà e all'Areopago di Atene (Atti 17,16-34): un confronto tra vangelo e cultura. RdT 36 (1995) 653-677.

3923   *Charles, J.D.* Engaging the (neo)pagan mind: Paul's encounter with Athenian culture as a model for cultural apologetics (Acts 17:16-34). Trinity Journal 16/1 (1995) 47-62.

3924   *Bossuyt, Philippe; Radermakers, Jean* Rencontre de l'incroyant et inculturation: Paul à Athènes (Ac 17,16-34). NRTh 117 (1995) 19-43.

3925   *Moxnes, Halvor* "He saw that the city was full of idols" (Acts 17:16): visualizing the world of the first christians. StTh 49 (1995) 107-131.

3926   **Bartchy, S. Scott** *Agnōstos Theos*: Luke's message to the "nations" about Israel's God. SBL.SP 34 (1995) 304-320 [17,23].

3927   *Tomes, Roger* Why did Paul get his hair cut? (Acts 18.18; 21.23-24). 1995 ⇒3599. Luke's literary achievement. JSNT.S 116. 188-197.

3928 *Bovon, François* The Holy Spirit, the church and human relationships according to Acts 20:36-21:16. 1995 <1979> ⇒40. New
Testament traditions. 27-42, 186-194 [RB 103,117].

3929 *Balch, David L.* Paul in Acts: "... you teach all the Jews ... to for-
sake Moses, telling them not to ... observe the customs" (Act.
21,21). 1995 ⇒34. ᶠTHRAEDE K., JAC.E 22. 11-23.

3930 **Gineste, Bernard** *"Èsan gar proeôrakotes"* (Actes 21,29):
Trophime a-t-il été "vu" à Jérusalem? RThom 95 (1995) 251-272.

3931 *Tannehill, Robert C.* The narrator's strategy in the scenes of Paul's
defense. Forum 8 (1992) [1995] 255-269 [22-26].

3932 *Silberman, Lou H.* Paul's viper: ACTS 28:3-6. Forum 8 (1992)
[1995] 247-253 [28,3-6].

3933 *Orchard, B.* JOSEPHUS and the unnamed priests of his Roman
mission. DR 113 (1995) 248-270 [28,16-31].

3934 *Cayzer, J.* The ending of Acts: handing on the baton. St Mark's
Review 161 (1995) 23-25 [28,30-31; NTAb 40,59].

3935 *Bovon, François* 'How well the Holy Spirit spoke through the
prophet Isaiah to your ancestors' (Acts 28:35). 1995 <1984>
⇒40. New Testament traditions. 43-50, 195 [RB 103,117].

Johannes

G1 *Corpus johanneum* .1 John and his community.

3936 *Anderson, Paul N.* The cognitive origins of John's unitive and disunitive christology. HBT 17/1 (1995) 1-24.

3937 *Barrett, Charles K.* Johannine christianity. 1995 <1993> ⇒39.
Jesus and the word. 93-118.

3938 **Charlesworth, James H.** The beloved disciple: whose witness
validates the gospel of John? Valley Forge 1995, Trinity xxv; 481
pp. $30. 1-56338-135-4 [NTAb 40,336].

3939 **Culpepper, R. Alan** John, the son of Zebedee. 1994 ⇒10,5199.
ᴿJThS 46 (1995) 274-275 *(Edwards, Ruth B.)*; CritRR 8 (1995)
195-198 *(Thompson, Marianne Meye)*.

3940 *Dubreucq, Marc* Les églises de Jean. DosB 60 (1995) 12-14.

3941 *Ghiberti, Giuseppe* "Vecchio" e "nuovo" in Giovanni: per una
rilettura di Giovanni (vangelo e lettere). RivBib 43 (1995) 225-
251.

3942 *Hall, Bruce* Some thoughts about Samaritanism and the Johannine
community. SJ(NY) 5. 1995 ⇒28. ᶠSIXDENIER G., 207-215.

3943 *La Potterie, Ignace de* La morale giovannea: una morale della
verità. 1995 ⇒139. Atti V Simposio S. Giovanni. 5-17.

3944 *Logan, Alastair H. B.* John and the gnostics: the significance of the
Apocryphon of John for the debate about the origins of the Johan-
nine literature. 1995 <1991> ⇒104. The Johannine writings.
BiSe 32. 109-137.

3945 *Luzarraga, Jesús* Gesù, sistole e diastole dell'amore nella letteratura giovannea. Il cuore di Cristo luce e forza. ᴱ**Bernard, Ch.**

A., R 1995, AdP. Simposio organizzato in onore di S. Claudio la Colombière. 171-186 [AcPIB 10/1,33].

3946 **Maloney, Francis J.** Reading John: introducing the Johannine gospel and letters. North Blackburn 1995, HarperCollins 105 pp. AUS$15. 1-86371-393-X [VJTR 60,689— *Meagher, P.M.*].

3947 *Menichelli, Ernesto* Verità e libertà: annotazioni sulla tradizione giovannea. VM 49 (1995) 62-71.

3948 ᴱ**Padovese, Luigi** Atti del IV Simposio di Efeso su S. Giovanni Apostolo. 1994 ⇒10,329. POC 45 (1995) 289-290 (*Ternant, P.*).
ᴱ**Padovese, Luigi** Atti del V Simposio...S. Giovanni. 1995 ⇒139.

3949 **Painter, John** The quest for the Messiah...Johannine community. 1993 <1991> ⇒7,245... 10,5206. ᴿTheology 98/1 (1995) 61-63 (*Barton, Stephen C.*); Mid-Stream 34/1 (1995) 99-101 (*Baird, William R.*); SJTh 48 (1995) 101-102 (*Ashton, John*); CBQ 57 (1995) 604-605 (*Neufeld, Dietmar*).
ᴱ**Porter, Stanley E.; Evans, Craig A.** The Johannine writings. ⇒104.

3950 *Raabe, P.R.* A dynamic tension: God and world in John. ConJ 21 (1995) 132-147 [NTA 40,50].

3951 *Schnelle, Udo* Die johanneische Schule. 1995 ⇒30. ᶠSTRECKER G., BZNW 75. 198-217.

3952 **Smalley, Stephen S.** Thunder and love: John's Revelation and John's community. 1994 ⇒10,5210. ᴿTheol. 98/2 (1995) 142-143 (*Moyise, Steve*); CritRR 8 (1995) 296-298 (*Reddish, Mitchell G.*).

3953 **Stowasser, Martin** Johannes der Täufer im vierten Evangelium 1992 ⇒7,4735... 10,5211. ᴿJBL 114 (1995) 156-158 (*Plevnik, Joseph*).

3954 *Thüsing, Wilhelm* Die johanneische Theologie als Verkündigung der Größe Gottes. 1995 <1965> ⇒60. Studien. WUNT 2/82. 124-134.

3955 **Tuñi, Josep Oriol; Alegre, Xavier** Escritos joánicos y cartas católicas. Estella 1995, Verbo Divino 392 pp. 84-7151-909-7.

3956 *Vanni, Ugo* La figura dell'anziano della scuola giovannea. 1995 ⇒96. Gli anziani. 167-192.

3957 *Wahlde, Urban C. von* Community in conflict: the history and social context of the Johannine community. Interp. 49 (1995) 379-389.

G1.2 Evangelium Johannis: *textus, commentarii.*

3958 **Arminjon, Blaise** Nous voudrions voir Jésus: avec saint Jean découvrir son visage (Jn 1-11). Christus. Essais 82. P 1995, DDB/Bellarmin 206 pp. FF110. 2-220-03613-8/2-89007-795-0 [EeV 106,279].

3959 *Bienert, Wolfgang A.* ἈΝΑΓΩΓΉ im Johannes-Kommentar des ORIGENES. 1995 ⇒126. Origeniana Sexta. BEThL 118. 419-427 [*Gögler, R.*, 429-431].

3960 **Blanchard, Yves-Marie** Des signes pour croire?: une lecture de l'évangile de Jean. LiBi 106. P 1995, Cerf 170 pp. FF95. 2-204-05252-3. [RHPhR 75,442].

3961 **Brodie, Thomas L.** The gospel according to John: a commentary. 1993 ⇒9,5423. ᴿCrossCur 44 (1994-5) 513-515 (*Thompson,*

Marianne Meye); JThS 46 (1995) 271-273 (*Smalley, Stephen, S.*); BTB 25 (1995) 49-50 (*Wahlde, Urban C. von*); Neotest. 29 (1995) 131 (*Draper, J.A.*); CBQ 57 (1995) 172-173 (*Koester, Craig R.*); JBL 114 (1995) 340-342 (*Kysar, Robert*).

3962 **Carson, D.A.** The gospel according to John. 1991 ⇒7,4743... 9,5640. ᴿEvQ 67 (1995) 94-96 (*Edwards, Ruth B.*).

3963 *Corsini, Eugenio* Oʀɪɢᴇɴᴇ: commento al vangelo di Giovanni (libri I-II): postille a una traduzione. Aug. 35/1 (1995) 183-195.

3964 **Ehrman, Bart D.**, al., The text of the fourth gospel in the writings of Oʀɪɢᴇɴ I. 1992 ⇒8,5644... 10,5222. ᴿCritRR 7 (1994) 182-184 (*Heine, Ronald E.*).

3965 ᴱ**Elliott, W.J.; Parker, David C.** The gospel according to St. John. The New Testament in Greek IV. NTTS 20. Lei 1995, Brill xi; 420 pp. ƒ220/$142. 90-04-09940-9 [NTAb 40,140].

3966 *Heine, Ronald E.* The introduction to Oʀɪɢᴇɴ's Commentary on John compared with the introductions to the ancient philosophical commentaries on Aʀɪsᴛoᴛʟᴇ. 1995 ⇒126. Origeniana Sexta. BEThL 118. 3-12.

3967 **Iacopino, Giuliana** Il vangelo di Giovanni nei testi gnostici copti. SEAug 49. R 1995, Institutum Patristicum "Augustinianum" 264 pp. 88-7961-050-3.

3968 ᴱ**Kadan, Roland** Lᴀᴍʙᴇʀᴛs von Geldern Auslegung der Johannesbriefe: eine textkritische Edition. Dissertationen 7. Wien 1995, WUV 351 pp. ÖS348/DM50. 3-85114-208-X.

3969 *Kuyama, Michihiko* The searching spirit: the hermeneutical principle in the preface of Oʀɪɢᴇɴ's Commentary on the gospel of John. 1995 ⇒126. Origeniana Sexta. 433-439.

3970 **Léon-Dufour, Xavier** Les adieux du Seigneur (chapitres 13-17). 1993 ⇒9,5435; 10,5230. ᴿEeV 105 (1995) 169-173 (*Walter, Louis*); CivCatt 146 (1995) 543-544 (*Scaiola, D.*); ScEs 47 (1995) 338-339 (*Létourneau, Pierre*).

3971 **Manucci, V.** Giovanni: il vangelo per ogni uomo. LoB 2.4. Brescia 1995, Queriniana 227 pp. L50.000.

3972 *McGuckin, J.A.* Structural design and apologetic intent in Origen's Commentary on John. 1995 ⇒126. Origeniana Sexta. BEThL 118. 441-457.

3973 **Morris, Leon** The gospel according to John. NIC.NT. GR ²1995, Eerdmans xxii; 824 pp. $42. 0-8028-2504-4.

3974 **Nicolas, M.-J.** L'évangile bien-aimé: commentaire & méditations sur l'évangile de St. Jean. Perpignan 1995, Magnificat 298 pp. 2-910510-09-3 [ATG 59,316].

3975 *O'Day, Gail R.* The gospel of John: introduction, commentary, and reflections. NIntB 9. 1995 ⇒92. 491-865.

3976 **Paglia, Vincenzo** Rinascere: il vangelo di Giovanni in un tempo di crisi. Fame e sete della parola 20. CinB 1995, San Paolo 132 pp. 88-215-2937-1.

3977 ᵀᴱ**Rettig, John W.** Aᴜɢᴜsᴛɪɴᴇ: tractates on the gospel of John 112-24: tractates on the first epistle of John. FC 92. Wsh 1995, Catholic University of America. xvi; 301 pp. $35. 0-8132-0092-X [CBQ 57,633].

3978 **Sanford, John** Mystical christianity: a psychological commentary on the gospel of John. 1993 ⇒9,5444. ᴿCritRR 7 (1994) 254-256 (*Rollins, Wayne G.*); TJT 11 (1995) 101-102 (*Brown, Schuyler*).

3979 **Stibbe, Mark W.G.** John. Readings. 1993 ⇒9,5477; 10,5242.
      ᴿCritRR 7 (1994) 264-265 (*Koester, Craig R.*).
3980 **Stock, Klemens** Gesù, il figlio di Dio: il messaggio di Giovanni.
      1993. ⇒9,5448. ᴿCivCatt 146 (1995) 411-412 (*Scaiola, D.*).
3981 **Talbert, Charles H.** Reading John. 1992 ⇒8,5667... 10,5243.
      ᴿCritRR 7 (1994) 268-270 (*O'Day, Gail R.*).
3982 ᵀ**Vocke, Harald** Das Evangelium des Johannes aus dem Griechis-
      chen übersetzt. Insel-Bücherei 1139. Fra 1995, Insel 90 pp.
      DM17.80.
3983 *Wolinski, J.* Le recours aux 'ΕΠΙΝΟΙΑΙ du Christ dans le Com-
      mentaire sur Jean d'ORIGENE. 1995 ⇒126. Origeniana Sexta.
      BEThL 118. 465-492.
3984 **Zevini, Georges** Commentaire spirituel de l'évangile de Jean I: ch.
      1-10. ᵀ*Rayer, Madeleine*, P/Montréal 1995, Médiaspaul 259 pp.
      F120 2-7122-0543-X/2-89420-060-9.
3985 **Zevini, Giorgio** Evangelio según San Juan. ᵀ*Ortiz García,
      Alfonso*. Nueva alianza 131. S 1995, Sígueme 521 pp. 84-301-
      1248-0. ᴿREsp 54 (1995) 447-448 (*Castro, Secundino*); RET 55
      (1995) 399-400 (*Barrado Fernández, P.*).

G1.3 **Introductio** *in Evangelium Johannis.*

3986 **Ashton, John** Studying John. 1994 ⇒10,5244. ᴿTheol. 98 (1995)
      488-489 (*Burridge, Richard A.*); CrossCur 45 (1995-6) 554-555
      (*Thompson, Marianne Meye*); ET 106 (1994-5) 343 (*Stibbe, Mark
      W.G.*).
3987 **Ashton, John** Understanding the fourth gospel. 1991 ⇒7,4764...
      10,5245. ᴿStPat 42/3 (1995) 145-147 (*Segalla, Giuseppe*).
3988 **Barnhart, Bruno** The good wine: reading John from the center.
      1993 ⇒9,5455; 10,5258. ᴿCritRR 8 (1995) 161-163 (*Staley, Jef-
      frey L.*).
3989 *Barrett, Charles K.* The place of John and the synoptics within the
      early history of Christian tradition. 1995 <1992> ⇒39. Jesus and
      the word. 119-134.
3990 *Becker, Jürgen* Aus der Literatur zum Johannesevangelium (1978-
      1980) <1982>;
3991 Das Johannesevangelium im Streit der Methoden (1980-1984)
      <1986>. 1995 ⇒5. ᶠBECKER J., BZNW 76. 138-203/204-281.
3992 *Baum, Armin Daniel* PAPIAS und der Presbyter Johannes: Martin
      HENGEL und die johanneische Frage. JETh 9 (1995) 21-42.
3993 **Belle, Gilbert van** The signs source in the fourth gospel. BEThL
      116. 1994 ⇒10,5259. ᴿEThL 71 (1995) 225-226 (*Denaux, A.*).
3994 *Boer, M. C. de* Narrative criticism, historical criticism, and the
      gospel of John. 1995 <1992> ⇒104. The Johannine writings. 95-
      108.
3995 **Boismard, Marie-Émile; Lamouille, A.** Un évangile pré-
      johannique: Jean 1,1-2,12. 1993 ⇒9,5468; 10,5260. ᴿBib. 76
      (1995) 115-117 (*Amphoux, C.*).
3996 **Boismard, Marie-Émile** Un évangile pré-johannique: Jean 2,13-
      4,54. 1994 ⇒10,5261. ᴿThLZ 120 (1995) 518-520 (*Wiefel,
      Wolfgang*); POC 45 (1995) 290-292 (*Ternant, P.*).
3997 **Brodie, Thomas L.** The quest for the origin of John's gospel.
      1993 ⇒9,5469; 10,5262. ᴿCritRR 7 (1994) 146-149 (*O'Day, Gail*

R.); Neotest. 29 (1995) 129-130 (*Draper, J.A.*).

3998 *Castro, Secundino* Proyecto literario-teologico de Jn 1-12. MCom 53 (1995) 3-42, 285-322.

3999 **Chatelion Counet, P.J.E.** De sarcofaag van het woord: postmoderniteit, deconstructie en het Johannesevangelie [Le sarcophage de la parole: postmodernité, déconstruction et l'évangile de Jean]. Diss. Nimègue 1995, 420 pp. ^D*Tilborg, S. van* [RTL 27,534].

4000 *Culpepper, R. Alan* The plot of John's story of Jesus. Interp. 49 (1995) 347-358.

4001 **Dunderberg, Ismo** Johannes und die Synoptiker: Studien zu Joh 1-9. 1994 ⇒10,5249. ^RBZ 39 (1995) 141-144 (*Ludger Schenke*); ThLZ 120 (1995) 337-339 (*Bull, Klaus-M.*); ThRv 91 (1995) 311-314 (*Kowalski, Beate*); CBQ 57 (1995) 801-803 (*Koester, Craig R.*).

4002 *Gourgues, Michel* Cinquante ans de recherche johannique, de BULTMANN à la narratologie. 1995 ⇒84. De bien des manières. 229-306.

4003 **Guillerand, Augustin** San Giovanni: una lettura spirituale del quarto vangelo. Spiritualità/Maestri 24. CinB 1995, San Paolo 446 pp. L44.000. ^RTer. 46 (1995) 663-664 (*Pasquetto, Virgilio*).

4004 **Hanson, Anthony T.** The prophetic gospel. 1991 ⇒7,4725... 10,5250. ^RSJTh 48 (1995) 106-107 (*Smalley, Stephen S.*).

4005 **Harner, Philip B.** Relation analysis of the fourth gospel. 1993 ⇒9,5484; 10,5263. ^RCBQ 57 (1995) 810-812 (*Sweetland, Dennis M.*).

4006 **Hengel, Martin** Die johanneische Frage. WUNT 2/67. 1993 ⇒9,5477. ^RSvTK 71 (1995) 36-37 (*Olsson, Birger*); ThRv 91 (1995) 225-227 (*Dschulnigg, Peter*); Bib. 76 (1995) 270-273 (*Moloney, Francis J.*); SNTU.A 20 (1995) 222-223 (*Fuchs, A.*).

4007 **Kinzie, Frederick E.** John: the gospel that had to be written. Hazelwood, Mo 1995, Word Aflame 250 pp. 1-56722-037-1.

4008 **Korting, Georg** Die esoterische Struktur des Johannesevangeliums. 1994 ⇒10,5265. ^RThLZ 120 (1995) 799-801 (*Frey, Jörg*); Neotest. 29 (1995) 132-133 (*Tolmie, D.F.*); StPat 42/3 (1995) 113-117 (*Segalla, Giuseppe*).

4009 **Lee, Dorothy A.** The symbolic narratives of the fourth gospel. JSNT.S 95. 1994 ⇒10,5277. ^RJThS 46 (1995) 640-643 (*Williams, Catrin*); CBQ 57 (1995) 817-819 (*Wahlde, Urban C. von*); CritRR 8 (1995) 243-245 (*Neufeld, Dietmar*).

4010 *Lombard, Herman A.* Prolegomena to a Johannine theology: sources, method and status of a narratological model. Neotest. 29 (1995) 253-272.

4011 **Mannucci, Valerio** Giovanni: il vangelo per ogni uomo. LoB 2.4. Brescia 1995, Queriniana 227 pp. L30.000. 88-399-1580-X.

4012 **Mannucci, Valerio** Giovanni, il vangelo narrante 1993 ⇒9,5486; 10,5278. ^RRivBib 43 (1995) 283-285 (*Ghiberti, Giuseppe*); Civ-Catt 146 (1995) 89-90 (*Scaiola, D.*); Lat. 61 (1995) 201-203 (*Penna, Romano*); StPat 42/3 (1995) 151-152 (*Segalla, Giuseppe*); Vivens Homo 6 (1995) 343-357 [sum. 357] (*Giannoni, Paolo*).

4013 **Marrow, Stanley B.** The gospel of John: a reading. NY 1995, Paulist xvi; 399 pp. $20. 0-8091-3550-7.

4014 **Mills, Watson E.** Bibliographies for biblical research 4: the gospel of John. New Testament Series 4. Lewiston 1995, Mellen xxiv; 410 pp. $130. 0-7734-2357-5 [NTAb 40,343].

4015 *Morgen, Michèle* Les bulletins johanniques de Xavier LEON-DUFOUR. RSR 83 (1995) 187-191.

4016 *O'Day, Gail R.* Toward a narrative-critical study of John. Interp. 49 (1995) 341-346.

4017 **Schmithals, W.** Johannesevangelium und Johannesbriefe: Forschungsgeschichte und Analyse. BZNW 64. 1992 ⇒8,5694; 9,5480. ᴿSNTU.A 20 (1995) 223-224 *(Fuchs, A.)*.

4018 **Stibbe, Mark W.G.** John as storyteller. MSSNTS 73. 1992 ⇒ 8,5724; 10,5280. ᴿSJTh 48 (1995) 146-148 *(Stamps, Dennis)*.

4019 **Weber, George P.; Miller, Robert** Breaking open the gospel of John. Cincinnati, Ohio 1995, St. Anthony Messenger (4) 131 pp. 0-86716-219-8.

4020 **Zumstein, Jean** L'apprentissage de la foi: à la découverte de l'évangile de Jean et de ses lecteurs. 1993 ⇒9,5466; 10,5257. ᴿScrTh 27 (1995) 267-269 *(García Moreno, A.)*.

G1.4 *Themata de evangelio Johannis* — **John's Gospel, topics.**

4021 **Augenstein, Jörg** Das Liebesgebot im Johannesevangelium und in den Johannesbriefen. BWANT 134. 1993 ⇒9,5489. ᴿThLZ 120 (1995) 141-143 *(Wengst, Klaus)*; CritRR 8 (1995) 158-160 *(Rensberger, David)*.

4022 *Baker, R. O.* Pentecostal bible reading: toward a model of reading for the formation of Christian affections [Jn]. JPentec 7 (1995) 34-48.

4023 **Balfour, Glenn M.** Is John's gospel anti-Semitic?: with special reference to its use of the Old Testament. Diss. Nottingham 1995, ᴰ*Casey, P.M.* [TynB 48,369].

4024 *Bartolome, J.* Juan, un evangelio para presbíteros. Phase 205 (1995) 53-66.

4025 *Bauckham, Richard* The beloved disciple as ideal author. 1995 <1993> ⇒104. The Johannine writings. 46-68.

4026 *Brändle, F.* La fe que se hace vida: la fe en el evangelio de Juan y la experiencia del mistico. REsp 54 (1995) 523-543 [NTAb 41,53].

4027 **Burkett, Delbert** The Son of Man in the gospel of John. JSNT.S 56. 1991 ⇒7,4806... 10,5299. ABR 43 (1995) 85-87 *(Moloney, Francis J.)*.

4028 *Busse, U.* The relevance of social history to the interpretation of the gospel according to John. Skrif en Kerk 16/1 (1995) 28-38 [[NTAb 40,237].

4029 **Card, Michael** The parable of joy: reflections on the wisdom of the book of John. Nv 1995, Nelson xxii; 259 pp. 0-7852-8229-7.

4030 *Caron, Gérald* Exploring a religious dimension: the Johannine Jews. SR 24 (1995) 159-171.

4031 **Cassidy, Richard J.** John's gospel in new perspective. 1992 ⇒8,5731; 10,5300. ᴿThPh 70 (1995) 567-568 *(Beutler, J.)*.

4032 *Collins, Raymond* From John to the beloved disciple: an essay on Johannine characters. Interp. 49 (1995) 359-369.

4033 *Corona, Mary* Divinisation through grace: understanding a Johannine theme in the light of *Saiva Siddhanta*. Jeevadhara 146 (1995) 161-172 [ThIK 17,36].

4034 *Dalbesio, A.* La communione fraterna, dimensione essenziale della vita cristiana secondo il IV vangelo e la prima lettera di Giovanni.

Laur. 36 (1995) 19-33.

4035 *Destro, Adriana; Pesce, Mauro* Dialettica di riti e construzione del movimento di Gesù nel vangelo di Giovanni. Aug. 35 (1995) 77-109.

4036 *Destro, Adriana; Pesce, Mauro* I riti nel vangelo di Giovanni. 1995 ⇒139. Atti del V Simposio. 85-105.

4037 *Destro, Adriana; Pesce, Mauro* Kinship, discipleship, and movement: an anthropological study of John's gospel. Bibl.Interp. 3 (1995) 266-284.

4038 **Eguskiza, Jesús** Orar con el Evangelio según San Juan. Senderos de Oración 22. M 1995, San Pio X 173 pp. 84-7221-351-X.

4039 **Ferraro, Giuseppe** Mio-tuo: teologia del possesso reciproco del Padre e del Figlio nel vangelo di Giovanni. 1994 ⇒10,5302. RCivCatt 146 (1995) 199-200 (*Scaiola, D.*); Mar. 57/1 (1995) 429-430 (*Pasquetto, Virgilio*).

4040 **Ferraro, Giuseppe** Lo Spirito Santo nel quarto vangelo: i commenti di ORIGENE, Giovanni CRISOSTOMO, TEODORO di Mopsuestia e CIRILLO di Alessandria. OCA 246. R 1995, Pontificio Istituto Orientale 211 pp. 88-7210-306-1.

4041 *Fossum, Jarl E.* In the beginning was the name: onomanology as the key to Johannine christology. 1995 ⇒48. The image. 109-133.

4042 *Gaeta, Giancarlo* Il culto "in spirito e verità" secondo il vangelo di Giovanni. ASEs 12/1 (1995) 33-47.

4043 *García-Moreno, A.* Teología sacramentaria en el IV evangelio. Salm. 42 (1995) 5-27.

4044 **Grelot, Pierre** Les juifs dans l'évangile selon Jean: enquête historique et réflexion théologique. CRB 34. P 1995, Gabalda 211 pp. FF330. 2-85021-081-1.

4045 *Grigsby, Bruce H.* The cross as an expiatory sacrifice in the fourth gospel. 1995 < 1982 > ⇒104. The Johannine writings. 69-94.

4046 **Hendricks, Obery M.** A discourse of domination: a socio-rhetorical study of the use of ioudaios in the fourth gospel. Diss. Princeton 1995, 272 pp. DGager, John, AAC 9528906; DAI-A 56/5,p.1828.

4047 *Hengel, Martin* The kingdom of Christ in John. 1995 ⇒50. Studies. 333-357.

4048 **Hergenröder, Clemens** 'Wir schauten seine Herrlichkeit': das johanneische Sprechen vom Sehen im Horizont von Selbsterschliessung Jesu und Reaktion des Menschen. Diss. Fr/B 1995, DOberlinner, L. [RTL 27,535].

4049 **Howard-Brook, Wes** Becoming children of God: John's gospel and radical discipleship. 1994 ⇒10,5290. RTS 56 (1995) 776-777 (*Kurz, William S.*).

4050 *Infante, R.* L'Agnello nel quarto vangelo. RivBib 43 (1995) 331-361.

4051 *Ingelaere, Jean-Claude* La tradition des *logia* de Jésus dans l'évangile de Jean: introduction à la problématique. RevSR 69 (1995) 3-11.

4052 **Jerumanis, Pascal-Marie** Réaliser la communion avec Dieu: croire, vivre et demeurer dans l'évangile selon Saint Jean. Diss. Fr/S 1995, DRouiller, G. [ThRv 92/2,VIII].

4053 **Jones, Larry Paul** A study of the symbol of water in the gospel of John. Diss. Vanderbilt 1995, 393 pp. DSegovia, Fernando F., DAI-A 56/5,p.1829.

4054 *Jonge, H.J. de* Jewish arguments against Jesus at the end of the first century C.E. according to the gospel of John. 1995 ⇒130. Aspects. 45-55.

4055 **Kamara, Daniel** Incomprehension and misunderstanding in the fourth gospel as a mode of revelatory language: (a particular study of John 2,13-22; 3,1-21 and 4,1-35). Diss. R 1995, Pontificia Universitas Urbaniana xvii; 164 pp. [excerpt] D*Biguzzi, Giancarlo*.

4056 *Khoo, Kay-Heng* The Tao and the Logos: Lao Tzu and the gospel of John. ChFe 38 (1995) 271-285.

4057 **Kieschke, Hans G.** Rekonstruktion des Evangeliums nach St. Johannes: ein Versuch zur Lösung des johannëischen Problems. Fra 1995, Fischer 261 pp. DM48. 3-89501-238-6 [ThLZ 122,329].

4058 *Kobayashi, Minoru* Εγω ειμι in John's gospel. KaKe 64 (1995) 1-33 [ThIK 17,47].

4059 **Koester, Craig R.** Symbolism in the fourth gospel: meaning, mystery, community. Mp 1995, Fortress xii; 300 pp. $19. 0-8006-2893-4 [NTAb 40,144].

4060 *Koester, Craig R.* Topography and theology in the gospel of John. 1995 ⇒10. FFREEDMAN D.,   436-448.

4061 **Koottumkal, Sebastian** Words of eternal life: an exegetical-theological study on the life-giving dimension of the word of Jesus in the fourth gospel. Diss. R 1995, Pontificia Universitas Gregoriana xiv; 125 pp. [excerpt] no. 4146, D*Caba, José*.

4062 *La Potterie, Ignace de* L'emploi du verbe "demeurer" dans la mystique johannique. NRTh 117 (1995) 843-859.

4063 *La Potterie, Ignace de* La morale giovannea: una morale della verità. 1995 ⇒139. Atti del V Simposio. 5-17 [= Il Messaggio del Cuore di Gesù 18 (1995) 63-71, 143-151; AcPIB 10,36].

4064 *La Potterie, Ignace de* La moral joánea: una moral de la verdad. VE 11 (1995) 15-32 [AcPIB 10,267].

4065 *La Potterie, Ignace de* Rimanere per crescere: l'uso di "rimanere" in S. Giovanni. 30 giorni (1995/3) 10-15 [AcPIB 10,37].

4066 *La Potterie, Ignace de* San Giovanni: il vangelo antignosi. 30 giorni (1995/1) 48-53 [AcPIB 10,37].

4067 *Langkammer, Hugolin* Die Kirche im Johannesevangelium. **P.** Annals of Theology 42/1 (1995) 69-77 [Zsfg 77].

4068 *Létourneau, Pierre* La gloire de Jésus: gloire et glorification dans le IVe évangile. Laval 51 (1995) 551-572.

4069 *Lee, D. A.* Sin, self-rejection and gender: a feminist reading of John's gospel. Colloquium 27/1 (1995) 51-63.

4070 *Lindars, Barnabas* Discourse and tradition: the use of the sayings of Jesus in the discourses of the fourth gospel. 1995 <1981> ⇒104. The Johannine writings. 13-30.

4071 *Longenecker, Bruce W.* The unbroken messiah: a Johannine feature and its social functions. NTS 41 (1995) 428-441.

4072 *Lys, D.* Jamais chez Jean!: (mort et résurrection). ETR 70 (1995) 509-519.

4073 *Manns, Frédéric* Le Shema Israel, clé de lecture de quelques textes johanniques. 1995 ⇒139. Atti del V Simposio. 107-117 [Dt 6,4-5].

4074 *Mannucci, Valerio* Persone alla ricerca del senso: i discepoli nel vangelo di Giovanni. RCI 76/1 (1995) 16-28.

4075 **McGann, Diarmuid** Journeying within...gospel of John. 1988 ⇒4,5461... 7,4826. REstB 53 (1995) 143-144 (*Navarro, Mercedes*).

4076 **Morgen, Michèle** Afin que le monde soit sauvé: Jésus révèle sa mission de salut dans l'Evangile de Jean. LeDiv 154. 1993 ⇒9,5508; 10,5308. RCBQ 57 (1995) 408-409 (*Thomas, Carolyn*).

4077 *Morgen, Michèle* La venue de la lumière dans le quatrième évangile. 1995 ⇒22. FRENAUD B., LeDiv 159. 307-323.

4078 **Ndombi, Jean-Roger Pascal** La Galilée dans l'évangile de Jean: étude exégètique et théologique de l'emploi de ce terme. Diss. R 1995, Pontificia Universitas Gregoriana 362 pp. [excerpt vii; 75 pp.] DCaba, José.

4079 *Newheart, Michael Willett* Johannine symbolism. 1995 ⇒125. JUNG. 71-91.

4080 *O'Grady, John F.* Jesus the revelation of God in the fourth gospel. BTB 25 (1995) 161-165.

4081 **Obermann, Andreas** "Wir haben den gefunden, über den Mose im Gesetz geschrieben hat und die Propheten...": eine Untersuchung des christologischen Schriftverständnisses im Johannesevangelium anhand der Schriftzitate. Diss. Wu 1995, DKarrer, M. [ThRv 92/2,XVI].

4082 *Panimolle, Salvatore A.* Il creato e l'uomo nel quarto vangelo. 1995 ⇒267. Dizionario di spiritualità biblico-patristica 10, 140-161.

4083 *Pasquetto, Virgilio* La preghiera nel vangelo di Giovanni. RVS 9 (1995) 646-658.

4084 *Pesce, Mauro; Destro, Adriana* Dialettica dei riti e costruzione del movimento di Gesù nel vangelo di Giovanni. Aug. 35/1 (1995) 77-109.

4085 **Petersen, Norman R.** The gospel of John and the sociology of light. 1993 ⇒9,5532. RTJT 11 (1995) 247-248 (*Osiander, Alfons M.*).

4086 **Philippe, Marie-Dominique** Suivre l'Agneau. Versailles ²1995, Saint-Paul 273 pp. FF110 [EeV 105,125 *Tort, Fernand*].

4087 *Pickering, Stuart R.* Additional sayings of Jesus in some texts of the gospel of John. NTTRU 3 (1995) 78.

4088 **Rau, Christoph** Sakrament und Zeichentat: verborgene Motive im Johannesevangelium. Stu 1995, Urachhaus 139 pp. 3-8251-7037-3.

4089 **Reim, Günter** Jochanan: erweiterte Studien zum alttestamentlichen Hintergrund des Johannesevangeliums. Studien zum alttestamentlichen Hintergrund des Johannesevangeliums 2 [I: 1974 ⇒55,3151]. Erlangen 1995, Ev.-Luth. Mission xiii; 555 pp. DM90. 3-87214-998-9 [NTAb 40,345].

4090 *Samuel, Simon* The kairos of the Galilaioi: an Indian liberationist reading of Jn 1-7. Jeevadhara 25 (1995) 149-160 [ThIK 17,36].

4091 *Sawyer, Deborah* Water and blood: birthing images in John's gospel. JSOT.S 195. 1995 ⇒24. FSAWYER J., 300-309 [19,34].

4092 *Schlosser, Jacques* Les logia johanniques relatifs au père. RevSR 69 (1995) 87-104.

4093 **Schnelle, Udo** Antidocetic christology in the gospel of John. 1992 ⇒9,5514; 10,5310. CritRR 8 (1995) 288-291 (*Anderson, Paul N.*).

4094 **Schuchard, Bruce, G.** Scripture within Scripture. SBL.DS 133. 1992 ⇒8,5708... 10,5293. RJSSt 40 (1995) 135-136 (*Tuckett, C.M.*).

4095 *Schwank, Benedikt* Verwandtschaft als Geschenk: drei Meßansprachen zu Johannes-Texten. EuA 71 (1995) 303-315 [19,25; 21,15-17].

4096 **Schwankl, Otto** Licht und Finsternis: ein metaphorisches Paradigma in den johanneischen Schriften. Diss.-Habil. DKlauck, H.-J., Herders Biblische Studien 5. Fr/B 1995, Herder xv; 440 pp. DM88/FS86/ÖS687. 3-451-23624-9.

4097 *Segovia, Fernando F.* The significance of social location in reading John's story. Interp. 49 (1995) 370-378.

4098 **Smith, Moody D.** The theology of the gospel of John. C 1995, CUP xiv; 202 pp. £30/£9. 0-521-35776-4/514-1. RTheol. 98 (1995) 486-487 (*Smalley, Stephen S.*); RStT 13-14/2-3 (1995) 122-123 (*Litke, Wayne*).

4099 *Spielmann, K.* Participant reference and definite article in John. JTrTL 7/1 (1995) 45ff [ZID 21,309].

4100 **Staley, Jeffrey L.** Reading with a passion: rhetoric, autobiography, and the American West in the gospel of John. NY 1995, Continuum xii; 270 pp. $28. 0-8264-0859-1.

4101 **Suh, J.S.** The glory in the gospel of John: restoration of forfeited prestige. Foreword by *Kee, H.C.*, Oxford, OH 1995, M.P. xvi; 194 pp. $13. 0-932187-02-1 [NTAb 40,150].

4102 **Tilborg, Sjef van** Imaginative love in John. 1993 ⇒9,5498; 10,5327. RJThS 46 (1995) 636-639 (*Moody Smith, D.*); Bib. 76 (1995) 266-269 (*Segalla, Giuseppe*); CBQ 57 (1995) 196-197 (*Kiley, Mark*); Bibl.Interp. 3 (1995) 234-236 (*Stibbe, Mark W.G.*).

4103 *Trudinger, P.* John's gospel as testimony to the non-deity of Jesus. FaF 48 (1995) 106-110 [NTAb 40,430].

4104 *Trudinger, P.* A prophet like me (Deut. 18:15): Jesus and Moses in St John's gospel, once again. DR 113 (1995) 193-195.

4105 **Trumbower, Jeffrey A.** Born from above: anthropology of Jn. HUTh 29. 1992 ⇒8,5741... 10,5313. RRHPhR 75 (1995) 226-227 (*Grob, F.*).

4106 *Veissière, Michel* Guillaume BRICONNET et l'évangile selon saint Jean. RSPhTh 79 (1995) 431-437.

4107 **Vignolo, Roberto** Personaggi del quarto vangelo. 1994 ⇒10,5329. RGr. 76 (1995) 761-762 (*Ferraro, Giuseppe*); StPat 42/3 (1995) 147-148 (*Segalla, Giuseppe*).

4108 *Villapadierna, Carlos de* Sacramentos y práctica cristiana en el cuarto evangelio. StLeg 36 (1995) 11-34.

4109 *Wang, Hsien-Chih* The portrayal of the human one (son of man) of John: an Asian perspective. Discussion with *Chuang, Ya-Tang* [Resp. 14-17]. CTC Bulletin 13-14/3-1 (1995-6) 3-14 [ThIK 18,28].

4110 **Watson, Alan** Jesus and the Jews: the pharisaic tradition in John. Athens, GA 1995, University of Georgia Press xv; 158 pp. $25. 0-8203-1703-9 [NTAb 40,351].

4111 *Weidmann, Frederick* Intertextuality and intent: John and the apostolic mission in the Harris fragments on POLYCARP. SBL.SP 34 (1995) 394-398.

4112 **Westermann, Claus** Das Johannesevangelium aus der Sicht des Alten Testaments. AzTh 99. 1994 ⇒10,5295. RCritRR 8 (1995) 323-325 (*Schuchard, B.G.*).

4113 **Winkel, Johannes** Die Ich-bin-Worte Jesu: Texte, Kommentare, Entwürfe. Dienst am Wort 70. Gö 1995, Vandenhoeck & Ruprecht 160 pp. 3-525-59334-1.

4114 *Xavier, Aloysius* Judas Iscariot in the fourth gospel: a paradigm of lost discipleship. ITS 32 (1995) 250-258.

G1.5 Johannis Prologus 1,1...

4115 *Babinet, Robert* Au commencement était le Verbe. PenCath 278 (1995) 33-44.

4116 *Bindemann, Walther* Der Johannesprolog: ein Versuch, ihn zu verstehen. NT 37 (1995) 330-354.

4117 *Boespflug, François* Note sur l'iconographie du prologue de Jean. RSR 83 (1995) 293-303.

4118 **Cholin, M.** Le prologue et la dynamique de l'évangile de Jean. Lyon 1995, EMCC 164 pp. FF110. 2-908291-01-0.

4119 **Harris, Elizabeth** Prologue and gospel. JSNT.S 107. 1994 ⇒10,5339. ᴿTheol. 98 (1995) 487-488 (*Ashton, John*); ThLZ 120 (1995) 885-886 (*Becker, Jürgen*); CBQ 57 (1995) 812-813 (*Bruns, J. Edgar*); CritRR 8 (1995) 222-224 (*Talbert, Charles H.*).

4120 *Moingt, Joseph* La réception du prologue de Jean au IIᵉ siècle. RSR 83 (1995) 249-282.

4121 *O'Leary, Joseph S.* Le destin du Logos johannique dans la pensée d'ORIGENE. RSR 83 (1995) 283-292 [1,1-18].

4122 **Paczkowski, Mieczyslaw C.** Esegesi, teologia e mistica: il prologo di Giovanni nelle opere di S. BASILIO Magno. ASBF 39. Jerusalem 1995, Franciscan Printing Press 263 pp. $25 [CBQ 59,390].

4123 *Pazzini, Domenico* Il prologo di Giovanni in ORIGENE e CIRILLO Alessandrino: un confronto. 1995 ⇒126. Origeniana Sexta. BEThL 118. 617-625.

4124 **Reinhartz, Adele** The word...in the fourth gospel. SBL.MS 45. 1992 ⇒8,5769; 10,5345. ᴿJBL 114 (1995) 158-160 (*Segovia, Fernando F.*).

4125 *Theobald, Michael* Le prologue johannique (Jean 1,1-18) et ses "lectures implicites": remarques sur une question toujours ouverte. RSR 83 (1995) 193-216.

4126 *Watt, Jan G. van der* The composition of the prologue of John's gospel: the historical Jesus introducing divine grace. WThJ 57 (1995) 311-332.

4127 *Zumstein, Jean* Le prologue, seuil du quatrième évangile. RSR 83 (1995) 217-239.

4128 *Campbell, Charles L.* John 1:1-14. Interp. 49 (1995) 394-398.

4129 *Jeannière, Abel* "En arkhê ên o logos": note sur des problèmes de traduction. RSR 83 (1995) 241-247 [1,1].

4130 *Cohee, Peter* John 1.3-4. NTS 41 (1995) 470-477.

4131 *Downing, F. Gerald* Words as deeds and deeds as words. Bibl.Interp. 3 (1995) 129-143 [1,22].

4132 *Watt, J.G. van der* "Daar is die Lam van God...': plaasvervangende offertradisies in die Johannesevangelie ['Behold, the Lamb of God...': substitutionary sacrifice traditions in the gospel of John]. Skrif en Kerk 16/1 (1995) 142-158 [1,29; NTAb 40,241].

4133 *Scholtissek, Klaus* "Rabbi, wo wohnst du?" (Joh 1,38): die mystagogische Christologie des Johannesevangeliums (am Beispiel der Jüngerberufungen Joh 1,35-51): mit Johannes das Evangelium entdecken (3/4). BiLi 68 (1995) 223-231 [1,38.35-51].

4134 *Wegner, U.* Pode sair algo bom de Nazaré? Jo, 1,46. EsTe 1 (1995) 39-51 [Strom. 52,347].

4135   *Baarda, Tjitze* Nathanael, "the scribe of Israel": John 1,47 in
       EPHRAEM's commentary on the Diatessaron. EThL 71 (1995)
       321-336.
4136   *Fossum, Jarl E.* The son of Man's alter ego: John 1.51, targumic
       tradition and Jewish mysticism. 1995 ⇒48. The image. 135-151.

4137   *Collins, Matthew S.* The question of *doxa*: a socioliterary reading
       of the wedding at Cana. BTB 25 (1995) 100-109 [2,1-11].
4138   *Vuichard, Pierre* Marie à Cana. Choisir 425 (1995) 22-24 [2,1-11].
4139   *Vandana, Sr* Water—God's extravaganza: John 2.1-11. 1995
       <1991> ⇒129. Voices. 156-167.
4140   **Lütgehetmann, Walter** Die Hochzeit von Kana. 1990 ⇒6,5796...
       10,5354. ᴿDBM 14 (1995) 92-94 [G.] (*Léon-Dufour, Xavier Léon*)
       [2,1-11].
4141   *Carmichael, Calum* The marriage at Cana of Galilee. 1995 ⇒24.
       ᶠSAWYER J., JSOT.S 195. 310-320 [2,1-12].
4142   *Imbach, Josef* Reinen Wein einschenken!: die Hochzeit zu Kana
       (Joh 2,1-12). LS 46 (1995) 169-173.
4143   *Strandenaes, Thor* John 2:4 in a Chinese cultural context:
       unnecessary stumbling block for filial piety?. 1995 ⇒14.
       ᶠHARTMAN L., 959-978.
4144   *Reich, Ronny* Six stone water jars. Jpersp. 48 (1995) 30-33 [2,6].

G1.6   Jn 3ss...Nicodemus, Samaritana.

4145   **Létourneau, Pierre** Jésus, fils de l'homme et fils de Dieu: Jean
       2,23-3,36. 1992 ⇒8,5786; 10,5355. ᴿCBQ 57 (1995) 183-184
       (*Sloyan, Gerard S.*).
4146   *Blomberg, Craig L.* The globalization of biblical interpretation: a
       test case—John 3-4. Bulletin for Biblical Research 5 (1995) 1-15.
4147   *Munro, Winsome* The pharisee and the Samaritan in John: polar or
       parallel?. CBQ 57 (1995) 710-728 [3-4].
4148   *Benoit, Camille* Le signe à Nicodème. Sources 21 (1995) 125-128
       [3].
4149   *Bergmeier, Roland* Gottesherrschaft, Taufe und Geist: zur
       Tauftradition in Joh 3. ZNW 86 (1995) 53-73.
4150   *Morgen, Michèle* Les traditions sapientielles à l'arrière-plan de Jn
       3. 1995 ⇒117. La sagesse biblique. LeDiv 160. 385-412.
4151   *Darmawijaya, St.* Die Katechese des Johannes. **Indonesian**. Umat
       Baru 28 (1995) 9-17 [3,1-12; ThIK 18,46].
4152   *Becker, Jürgen* J 3,1-21 als Reflex johanneischer Schuldiskussion.
       1995 <1973> ⇒5. ᶠBECKER J., BZNW 76. 127-137.
4153   *Saayman, Christo* The textual strategy in John 3:12-14:
       preliminary observations. Neotest. 29 (1995) 27-48.
4154   *McDonagh, Sean* 'God loved the world so much'...John 3:13.
       South Pacific Journal of Mission Studies 15 (1995) 2-7 [ThIK
       18,66].
4155   *Trocmé, Etienne* Jean 3,29 et le thème de l'époux dans la tradition
       pré-évangélique. RevSR 69 (1995) 13-18.

4156   *Berceville, G.* l'Esprit donné aux nations: l'exégèse de Thomas
       d'AQUIN. 1995 ⇒4170. Jésus et la Samaritaine. 72-80 [4].

4157 *Berder, M.* La Samaritaine d'Edmond ROSTAND. 1995 ⇒4170.
Jésus et la Samaritaine. 115-120 [4].

4158 *Carrez, M.* Adorer en esprit et en vérité: l'exégèse de Jean
CALVIN. 1995 ⇒4170. Jésus et la Samaritaine. 81-90.

4159 *Cocchini, Francesca* La sorgente di Giacobbe (Gv 4): funzionalità
polemica ed ermeneutica di una metafora origeniana sulle scritture.
1995 ⇒139. Atti del V Simposio. 139-146.

4160 *Coloni, Marie-Jeanne* Les représentations de la Samaritaine. 1995
⇒4170. Jésus et la Samaritaine. 127 [4].

4161 *Derrett, John Duncan M.* The Samaritan woman's purity (John
4:4-52). 1995 <1988> ⇒45. Studies 6. 121-128.

4162 **Link, Andrea Hildegard** 'Was redest du mit ihr?' John 4. 1992
⇒8,5794... 10,5365. ᴿSalm. 42 (1995) 475-476 (*Ramos, Felipe
F.*).

4163 *Masson, G.H.* L'usage liturgique. 1995 ⇒4170. Jésus et la
Samaritaine. 70-71 [4].

4164 *Morgain, S.-M.* La Samaritaine et TERESA de Jesús. 1995 ⇒4170.
Jésus et la Samaritaine. 91-96 [4].

4165 *Destro, Adriana; Pesce, Mauro* Lo Spirito e il mondo "vuoto":
prospettive esegetiche e antropologiche su Gv 4,21-24. ASEs 12/1
(1995) 9-32.

4166 *Ginzburg, Lisa* L'adorazione interiore: Gv 4,23 nell'interpretazione
mistica e filosofica del Seicento. ASEs 12/1 (1995) 85-97.

4167 *Collins, C.J.* John 4:23-24, 'in spirit and truth': an idiomatic
proposal. Presbyterion 21 (1995) 118-121 [NTAb 40,432].

4168 **Kalonga, Joachim Kabatuswile** L'adoration du Père en esprit et
vérité selon Jn 4,23-24: de l'architecture du sens au contenu
dogmatico-spirituel. Diss. R 1995, Teresianum xii; 320 pp.
ᴰ*Pasquetto, Virgilio.*

4169 *Lettieri, G.* In spirito e/o verità: da ORIGENE a Tommaso
d'AQUINO. ASEs 12/1 (1995) 49-84 [4,23-24].

4170 ᴱ**Poffet, J.-M.** Jésus et la Samaritaine (Jean 4,1-42). CEv.S 93. P
1995, Cerf 132 pp. FF60. 0222-9706 [NTAb 40,345].

4171 *Poffet, J.-M.* De Moïse à Jésus: le puits, un lieu jaillissant... [4,4]
607-614;

4172 Le dossier patristique 24-69;

4173 Exégèse contemporaine 121-125;

4174 Un lecteur gnostique: HERACLEON 15-23;

4175 Le salut vient des juifs (v.22b): un verset "sensible"... 126. 1995
⇒4170. Jésus et la Samaritaine.

4176 *Rigato, Maria-Luisa* Gv 4: la mente cultuale dell'evangelista: Gesù
si rivela alla donna samaritana. 1995 ⇒139. Atti del V Simposio.
27-84.

4177 *Sheeley, Steven M.* "Lift up your eyes": John 4:4-42. RExp 92
(1995) 81-87.

4178 *Sion, D.* Sermons du grand siècle sur la Samaritaine. 1995 ⇒4170.
Jésus et la Samaritaine. 97-114.

4179 *Neirynck F.* Jean 4,46-54: une leçon de méthode. EThL 71 (1995)
176-184.

4180 *Thomas, John Christopher* "Stop sinning lest something worse
come upon you": the man at the pool in John 5. JSNT 59 (1995) 3-
20.

4181 *Manns, Frédéric* La fête des juifs de Jean 5,1. Anton. 70/1 (1995) 117-124.
4182 *Grob, Francis* "Mon père travaille toujours": Jn 5,17 et la tradition des logia de Jésus. RevSR 69 (1995) 19-27.
4183 *O'Neill, J.C.* 'Making himself equal with God' (John 5.17-18): the alleged challenge to Jewish monotheism in the fourth gospel. IBSt 17 (1995) 50-61.
4184 *Mara, Maria Grazia* L'interpretazione battesimale di Gv 5,24-25. 1995 ⇒139. Atti del V Simposio. 147-154.

G1.7 Panis Vitae — *Jn 6*...

4185 **Madden, Patrick J.** Jesus' walking on the sea: an investigation of the origin of the narrative account. Diss. Catholic University of America 1995, 284 pp. ᴰ*Fitzmyer, Joseph A.*, DAI-A 55/12,p.3880 [6,16-21].
4186 *Cuvillier, Elian* Jean 6,16-21: Pâques. Lire et Dire 24 (1995) 27-36 [Bulletin of Biblical Bibliography 15,100].
4187 *Kiley, M.* The geography of famine: John 6:22-25. RB 102 (1995) 226-230.
4188 *Derrett, John Duncan M.* Τί ἐργάζῃ (Jn 6,30): an unrecognized allusion to Is 45,9. 1995 <1989> ⇒45. Studies 6. 129-131.
4189 *Balfour, Glenn* The Jewishness of John's use of the scriptures in John 6:31 and 7:37-38. TynB 46 (1995) 357-380.
4190 *Joseph, A.* John's second discourse on the bread of life: implications for reconsideration of Eucharist theology. Prism 10 (1995) 64-70 [6,51-58; NTAb 40,52].
4191 *Scholtissek, Klaus* "Ich bin das lebendige Brot, das vom Himmel herabgekommen ist" (Joh 6,51): mit Johannes das Evangelium entdecken. BiLi 68 (1995) 45-49, 111-114 [6,51].
4192 *Broadhead, Edwin K.* Echoes of an exorcism in the fourth gospel? ZNW 86 (1995) 111-119 [6,66-71].
4193 **Caba, José** Pan de vida 1993 ⇒9,5582; 10,5371. ᴿTer. 46/1 (1995) 315-31 (*Pasquetto, Virgilio*); CivCatt 146 (1995) 96-97 (*Scaiola, D.*); EstB 53 (1995) 413-414 (*García Moreno, A.*); JBL 114 (1995) 739-740 (*Ruiz, Jean-Pierre*) [6].
4194 *Derrett, John Duncan M.* Circumcision and perfection: a Johannine equation (John 7:22-23). 1995 <1991> ⇒45. Studies 6. 97-110 [7,22-23].
4195 **Borse, Udo** Die Entscheidung...Joh 7,50.(53)-8,11. SBS 158. 1994 ⇒10,5376. ᴿZKTh 117 (1995) 236-237 (*Huber, Konrad*).
4196 *Toensing, Holly Joan* Politics of insertion: the pericope of the adulterous woman and its rhetorical context at John 7:52. Proc-GLM 15 (1995) 1-14.
4197 *Causse, Jean-Daniel; Mitrani, David* Jean 7,53-8,11: Vendredi Saint. Lire et Dire 24 (1995) 13-25 [Bulletin of Biblical Bibliography 15,101].
4198 *McDonald, J. Ian H.* The so-called pericope de adultera. NTS 41 (1995) 415-427 [7,53-8,11].
4199 *Young, Brad H.* "Save the adulteress!": ancient Jewish responsa in the gospels? NTS 41 (1995) 59-70 [7,53-8,11].
4200 *Uval, Beth* Streams of living water: the feast of Tabernacles and the Holy Spirit. Jpersp. 49 (1995) 22-23, 37 [7].

4201 *Mongillo, A. Dalmazio* Rapporto verità-libertà nella lectura in Joannem di S. TOMMASO. 1995 ⇒139. Atti del V Simposio. 215-226 [8,31-32].

4202 *Derrett, John Duncan M.* John 9:6 read with Isaiah 6:10; 29:9. Studies 6. 1995 <1994> ⇒45. 2-5.

4203 *Alison, J.* El ciego de nacimiento y la subversión del pecado: unas preguntas de moral fundamental a partir de Juan 9. Sen. 51 (1995) 9-30 [Strom. 52,346].

4204 **Rein, Matthias** Die Heilung des Blindgeborenen (Joh 9): Tradition und Redaktion. WUNT 2/73. Tü 1995, Mohr x; 401 pp. DM118. 3-16-146458-3 [NTAb 40,346].

4205 **Kowalski, Beate** Die Hirtenrede (Joh 10,1-18) im Kontext des Johannesevangeliums. Diss. Bochum 1995, 380 pp. ^D*Dschulnigg, P.*

4206 *L'Eplattenier, Charles* Jean 10,1-18. Lire et Dire 24 (1995) 25-37 [Bulletin of Biblical Bibliography 15,102].

4207 **Szamocki, Grzegorz** 'Ja jestem brama' (J 10,7.9): Podłoże hsitorycznorelijne oraz interpretacja medafory bramy y kontekście janowym ['Je suis la porte' (Jn 10,7.9): fondement historique et religieux et interprétation de la métaphore de la porte dans le contexte johannique]. Diss. Warsaw 1995, 302 pp. ^D*Mędala, S.* [RTL 27,537].

4208 **Cachia, Nicholas** 'I am the good shepherd: the good shepherd lays down his life for the sheep' (John 10,11): the image of the good shepherd as a source for the spirituality of the ministerial priesthood. Diss. R 1995, Pontificia Universitas Gregoriana. ^D*Martinez, Ernest R.*

4209 *Grassi, Joseph A.* The Bethany banquet. BiTod 33 (1995) 234-238 [11,1-12,11].

4210 **Wagner, Josef** Auferstehung und Leben: Joh. 11,1-12,19. **G.** BU 19. 1988. ⇒4,5588b... 7,4933. ^RDBM 14 (1995) 94-96 [**G.** = RSR 79 (1991) 310-313] (*Léon-Dufour, Xavier Léon*).

4211 *Barkhuizen, J.H.* Pseudo-CHRYSOSTOM, homily 'on the four-day (dead) Lazarus': an analysis. Acta Patristica et Byzantina 6 (1995) 1-14 [11,1-44; sum. 1].

4212 *Barkhuizen, J.H.* Lazarus of Bethany—suspended animation or final death?: some aspects of patristic and modern exegesis. HTS 51 (1995) 167-174 [11,1-44; NTAb 40,53].

4213 *Jensen, Robin M.* The raising of Lazarus. BiRe 11 (1995) 20-28, 45 [11,1-45].

Kremer, Jacob Der arme Lazarus: 1995 ⇒3759.

4214 *Derrett, John Duncan M.* Lazarus and his graveclothes (John 11,44). 1995 <1993> ⇒45. Studies 6. 193-201.

4215 *Tsuchido, Kiyoshi* Is there anti-semitism in the fourth gospel?: an exegetical study of John 11:45-54. AJBI 21 (1995) 57-72.

4216 **Cilia, Lucio** La morte di Gesù...soteriologia giovannea. 1992 ⇒8,5822; 9,5605. ^REeV 105 (1995) 14-16 (*Cothenet, E.*); RdT 36 (1995) 124-125 (*De Virgilio, Giuseppe*) [11,47-53; 12,32].

4217 *Albertson, Fred C.* An Isiac model for the raising of Lazarus in early Christian art. JAC 38 (1995) 123-132 [11].

4218 *Sullivan, Joseph E.* Praying for the dead in John 11. IThQ 61 (1995) 205-211.

4219 *Coakely, J.F.* Jesus' messianic entry into Jerusalem (John 12:12-19 par.). JThS 46 (1995) 461-482.

4220 *Kovacs, Judith L.* "Now shall the ruler of this world be driven out": Jesus' death as cosmic battle in John 12:20-36. JBL 114 (1995) 227-247.

4221 *Morgen, M.* "Perdre sa vie", Jn 12,25: un dit traditionnel?. RevSR 69 (1995) 29-46.

4222 *Coulot, Claude* "Si quelqu'un me sert, qu'il me suive!" (Jn 12, 26a). RevSR 69 (1995) 47-57.

4223 **Derrett, John Duncan M.** Ἄρχοντες, ἀρχαί: a wider background to the passion narratives. 1995 <1989> ⇒45. Studies 6. 132-144 [12,31].

G1.8 Jn 13...Sermo sacerdotalis et Passio.

4224 *Ford, Josephine Massyngbaerde* Jesus as sovereign in the Passion according to John. BTB 25 (1995) 110-117.

4225 **Léon-Dufour, Xavier** Lettura dell'evangelo secondo Giovanni 3: gli addii del Signore (capitoli 13-17). CinB 1995, San Paolo 414 pp.

4226 *Moloney, Francis J.* The Johannine passion and the Christian community. Sal. 57 (1995) 25-61.

4227 *Vignolo, Roberto* La morte di Gesù nel vangelo di Giovanni. PSV 32 (1995) 121-142.

4228 *La Potterie, Ignace de* Remaining in order to grow. *Valente, G.* <interviewer>, 30Days 8/3 (1995) 10-15 [NTAb 40,49].

4229 **Senior, Donald** La passione di Gesù nel vangelo di Giovanni. 1993 ⇒10,5432. RCivCatt 146 (1995) 432-433 (*Scaiola, D.*).

4230 *Kitzberger, Ingrid Rosa* Mary of Bethany and Mary of Magdala— two female characters in the Johannine passion narrative: a feminist, narrative-critical reader-response. NTS 41 (1995) 564-586 [11,1-46; 12,1-8; 20,1-18].

4231 **Léon-Dufour, Xavier** Lectura del evangelio de Juan 3: Jn 13-17. TOrtiz García, Alfonso, Biblioteca de EstB 70. S 1995, Sígueme 265 pp. 84-301-1261-8.

4232 **Winter, Martin** Das Vermächtnis Jesu...Joh. 13-17. FRLANT 161. 1994 ⇒10,5410. RLM 34/9 (1995) 44 (*Lohse, Eduard*); ThLZ 120 (1995) 1082-1085 (*Schille, Gottfried*); SNTU.A 20 (1995) 226-227 (*Fuchs, A.*).

4233 *Laufer, C.* The farewell discourse in John's gospel as a commentary on the Seder service. Colloquium 27 (1995) 147-160 [13-17].

4234 **Neugebauer, Johannes** Die eschatologischen Aussagen in den johanneischen Abschiedsreden: eine Untersuchung zu Johannes 13-17. Diss. Mainz 1994, DSchenke, Ludger, BWANT 140. Stu 1995, Kohlhammer 190 pp. DM/FS79; SCH616. 3-17-013800-6 [RB 103,316].

4235 **Tolmie, D.F.** Jesus' farewell to the disciples: John 13:1-17:26 in narratological perspective. Diss. Orange Free State, South Africa 1992, DRand, Jan A. du, Bibl.Interp. 12. Lei 1995, Brill c.272 pp. ƒ120/$68.75. 90-04-10270-1.

4236 *Zorrilla, H.* A service of sacrificial love: footwashing (John 13:1-11). Direction 24 (1995) 74-85 [NTAb 40,54].

4237 *Duke, Paul D.* John 13:1-17, 31b-35. Interp. 49 (1995) 398-402.

4238 *Neyrey, Jerome H.* The footwashing in John 13:6-11: transformation ritual or ceremony?. 1995 ⇒20. ᶠMᴇᴇᴋꜱ W., 198-213.

4239 *Schottroff, Luise* Über Herrschaftsverzicht und den Dienst der Versöhnung. BiKi 50 (1995) 153-158 [13,12-17].

4240 **Dettwiler, Andreas** Die Gegenwart des Erhöhten: eine exegetische Studie zu den johanneischen Abschiedsreden (Joh 13,31-16,33) unter besonderer Berücksichtigung ihres Relecture-Charakters. Diss. Neuchâtel 1994. FRLANT 169. Gö 1995, Vandenhoeck & Ruprecht 328 pp. DM128. 3-525-538-52-9.

4241 **Vargas, Niceta M.** 'As I have loved you...': an exegetical analysis of John 13:31-35. Diss. Leuven 1995, xcii; 595 pp. ᴰ*Bieringer, R.*

4242 *Zumstein, Jean* Le point de vue de l'école johannique sur les logia de Jésus dans le premier discours d'adieu (1). RevSR 69 (1995) 59-69 [13-14].

4243 **Niemand, Christoph** Fußwaschungserzählung. 1993 ⇒9,5612; 10,5414. ᴿCBQ 57 (1995) 184-186 (*Moloney, Francis J.*); JBL 114 (1995) 535-537 (*Thomas, John Christopher*); ThRv 91 (1995) 392-393 (*Böcher, Otto*) [13].

4244 *Lettieri, Gaetano* Oʀɪɢᴇɴᴇ, Aɢᴏꜱᴛɪɴᴏ e il mistero di Giuda: due esegesi di Ioh. XIII in conflitto. 1995 ⇒139. Atti del V Simposio. 169-213.

4245 *Parrinder, Geoffrey* Only one way? John 14:6. ET 107 (1995) 78-79.

4246 *Fernández, Victor Manuel* Hacer "obras mayores" que las de Cristo (Juan 14,12-14). RevBib 57 (1995) 65-91 [14,12-14].

4247 *Ferrando, Miguel Ángel* "El Padre es mayor que yo" (Jn 14,28). RET 55 (1995) 81-89.

4248 *Niemand, Christoph* Spuren der Täuferpredigt in Johannes 15,1-11: Motivgeschichtliches zur Weinstockrede. PzB 4 (1995) 13-28.

4249 *Zevini, Giorgio* La vita di comunione tra Gesù e is suoi: la vera vite e i tralci (Gv 15,1-17). PSV 31 (1995) 93-109.

4250 *Gourgues, Michel* La vigne du Père (Jn 15,1-17) ou le rassemblement des enfants de Dieu: les conditions d'effectuation et de durée. BEThL 121. 1995 ⇒35. ᶠTɪʟʟᴀʀᴅ J., 265-281.

4251 *De Maria, Antonio* "Sine me nihil potestis facere:" viaggio nell'opera di S. Aɢᴏꜱᴛɪɴᴏ attraverso il suo uso di GV 15,5. Laós 2/1 (1995) 21-42.

4252 *Kremer, Jacob* Jesu Verheißung des Geistes: zur Verankerung der Aussage von Joh 16,13 im Leben Jesu. 1995 <1977> ⇒53. Die Bibel. 133-160 [Mark 13,11].

4253 *Heil, John Paul* Jesus as the unique high priest in the gospel of John. CBQ 57 (1995) 729-745 [17,19].

4254 **Newton, George [1602-1681]** An exposition of John 17. E 1995, Banner of Truth viii; 403 pp. 0-85151-679-3.

4255 *Thüsing, Wilhelm* Die Bitten des johanneischen Jesus in dem Gebet Joh 17 und die Intentionen Jesu von Nazaret. WUNT 2/82 1995 <1977/78> ⇒60. Studien. 265-294.

4256 *Becker, Jürgen* Aufbau, Schichtung und theologiegeschichtliche Stellung des Gebetes in Johannes 17. 1995 <1969> ⇒5. ᶠBᴇᴄᴋᴇʀ J., BZNW 76. 99-126.

4257 **Heil, John Paul** Blood and water: the death and resurrection of Jesus in John 18-21. CBQ.MS 27. Wsh 1995, CBA xi; 196 pp. $9. 0-915170-26-4 [OTA 18,667].

4258 *Burgos Nuñez, M. de* La soberanía salvadora de Jesús en el relato del prendimiento (Juan 18,1-11). Communio 28 (1995) 349-369.

4259 *Dormeyer, Detlev* Joh 18,1-14 Par. Mk 14,43-53: methodologische Überlegungen zur Rekonstruktion einer vorsynoptischen Passionsgeschichte. NTS 41 (1995) 218-239.

4260 *Sabbe, M.* The denial of Peter in the gospel of John. LouvSt 20 (1995) 219-240 [18,13-27].

4261 **Diebold-Scheuermann, Carola** Jesus vor Pilatus: eine exegetische Untersuchung zum Verhör Jesu durch Pilatus (Joh 18,28-19,16a). Diss. Fr/B 1995, ᴰ*Oberlinner, Lorenz* [ThRv 92/2,VIII].

4262 *Marshall, B.D.* What is truth? ProEc 4 (1995) 404-430 [18,38; ZID 1996/2,72].

4263 *Weaver, Dorothy Jean* John 18:1-19:42. Interp. 49 (1995) 404-408.

4264 *Derrett, John Duncan M.* Ecce Homo Ruber (Jn 19:5 with Is 1, 18:63, 1-2). 1995 <1990> ⇒45. Studies 6. 145-159.

4265 *Böhler, Dieter* "Ecce Homo!" (Joh 19,5) ein Zitat aus dem Alten Testament. BZ 39 (1995) 104-108.

4266 *Manns, Frédéric* Encore une fois le Lithostrotos de Jn 19,13. Anton. 70/2 (1995) 187-197.

4267 *Eldred, B.G.* You're not alone. ABQ 14/1 (1995) 22ff [19,23-27; ZID 21,409].

4268 *Neirynck, F.* Short note on John 19,26-27. EThL 71 (1995) 430-434.

4269 *Grossi, Vittorino* La valenza ecclesiologica del Tr.120 in Ioannem di S. AGOSTINO. 1995 ⇒139. Atti del V Simposio. 155-168 [19,34].

4270 **Gangemi, Attilio** I racconti post-pasquali 1...Gv 20,1-18. 1989 ⇒5,5607... 10,5442. ᴿLaur. 36/1-2 (1995) 226-227 (*Martignani, Luigi*); Lat. 61 (1995) 205-207 (*Penna, Romano*).

4271 *Byrne, Brendan* The faith of the beloved disciple and the community in John 20. 1995 <1985> ⇒104. The Johannine writings. BiSe 32. 31-45.

4272 *Babinet, Robert* Une "solution extrême inutile", la correction du texte grec en Jean 20,6-7. REG 108/1 (1995) 219-222.

4273 *Vivas A., María del Socorro* El anuncio de resurrección desde María Magdalena. ThX 45 (1995) 395-406 [20,11-18].

4274 *Huprich, Amy L.* John 20:11-18: the recognition/reunion scene and its parallels in Greek romance. ProcGLM 15 (1995) 15-22.

4275 *Derrett, John Duncan M.* Miriam and the resurrection (John 20,16). 1995 <1993> ⇒45. Studies 6. 160-172.

4276 *Mohamed, A.F.; Sorg, T.* Friede sei mit euch! (Joh. 20,19-23). ThBeitr 26/3 (1995) 113-117.

4277 **Gangemi, Attilio** I racconti post-pasquali 2...Gv 20,19-31. 1990 ⇒6,5895... 10,5442. ᴿLaur. 36/1-2 (1995) 226-227 (*Martignani, Luigi*); Lat. 61 (1995) 205-207 (*Penna, Romano*).

4278 *Claudel, G.* Jean 20,23 et ses parallèles matthéens. RevSR 69 (1995) 71-86 [Mt 16,19; 18,18].

4279 *Kremer, Jacob* "Nimm deine Hand und lege sie in meine: exegetische, hermeneutische und bibeltheologische Überlegungen zu Joh 20,24-29. 1995 <1992> ⇒53. Die Bibel. 161-189.

4280 **Hollenweger, Walter J.** Wie erlebten die ersten Christen den Heiligen Geist?: und Predigt über Joh. 20.29b. Sexauer Gemeinde-preis for Theologie 12. Sexau 1995, Evang. Kirchengemeinde 27 pp. Vortrag und Predigt des Preisträgers 1995 [NThAR 1997,260].

4281 *Brownson, J. V.* John 20:31 and the purpose of the fourth gospel. RefR(H) 48 (1995) 212ff [ZID 21,559].

4282 *Lee, Dorothy A.* Partnership in Easter faith: the role of Mary Magdalene and Thomas in John 20. JSNT 58 (1995) 37-49.

4283 **Gangemi, Attilio** I racconti post-pasquali 3...Gv 21,1-14. 1993 ⇒9,5646. ᴿLaur. 36/1-2 (1995) 226-227 (*Martignani, Luigi*).

4284 *Amjad-Ali, Christine* Restoration and ministry: John 21:1-25. Al-Mushir 37/1 (1995) 1-10 [ThIK 17,59].

4285 *Derrett, J. Duncan M.* ζόννυμι, ψέρω, ἄλλος: the fate of Peter (Jn 21,18-19). FgNT 8 (1995) 79-84 [21,18-19].

4286 *Lawless, George* Habilidad exégetica de san AGUSTIN: Jn 21,19-23. Augustinus 40 (1995) 187-192.

4287 *Trudinger, P.* Subtle ironies and word-plays in John's gospel and the problems of chapter 21. St Mark's Review 162 (1995) 20-24 [NTAb 40,245].

4288 *Thyen, Hartwig* Noch einmal: Johannes 21 und "der Jünger, den Jesus liebte". 1995 ⇒14. ᶠHARTMAN L., 147-189.

G2.1   Epistulae Johannis.

4289 *Culpepper, R. Alan* 1-2-3 John. 1995 ⇒95. The general letters. 110-144.

4290 **Klauck, Hans-Josef** Die Johannesbriefe. EdF 276. Da ²1995, Da:Wiss xix; 188 pp. 3-534-10008-5.

4291 *Langkammer, Hugolin* Die Kirche in den Johannesbriefen. **P.** Annals of Theology 42/1 (1995) 79-83 [Zsfg 83].

4292 **Sloyan, Gerard Stephen** Walking in the truth: perseverers and deserters: the first, second, and third letters of John. The New Testament in context. Valley Forge, PA 1995, Trinity vii; 85 pp. 1-56338-128-1.

4293 *Thomas, John Christopher* The order of the composition of the Johannine epistles. NT 37 (1995) 68-75.

4294 *Thüsing, Wilhelm* Glaube an die Liebe: die Johannesbriefe. 1995 <1969> ⇒60. Studien. WUNT 2/82. 216-232.

4295 **Vouga, François** Die Johannesbriefe. HNT 15/3. 1990 ⇒5,5623... 10,5456. ᴿRHPhR 75 (1995) 228-229 (*Grob, F.*).

4296 **Candlish, Robert S.** A commentary on 1 John. E 1993 <1877>, Banner of Truth 577 pp. 0-85151-662-9. ᴿSBET 13 (1995) 177-178 (*Cook, Peter*).

4297 *Cassidy, Eoin* AUGUSTINE's exegesis of the first epistle of John. 1995 ⇒82. Scriptural interpretation. 201-220.

4298 *Dalbesio, Anselmo* L'imitazione di Cristo secondo la 1 Gv. 1995 ⇒19. ᶠMATTIOLI A., 341-367.

4299 *Dalbesio, Anselmo* Il riferimento a Cristo criterio ispiratore dell'etica cristiana secondo 1Gv 2,6. 1995 ⇒139. Atti del V Simposio. 119-126.

4300 **Fehlandt, Claudius** Struktur und Botschaft des 1. Johannesbriefs. Diss. Heidelberg 1995, ᴰTheißen [ThRv 92/2,X].

4301 *Maggioni, Bruno* La comunione nella prima lettera di Giovanni. PSV 31 (1995) 205-218.

4302 **Moriconi, B.** "Lectio divina" della prima Lettera di Giovanni. Leggere le Scritture 2. Padova 1995, Messaggero 208 pp. L18.000. 88-250-0222-X. RTer. 46 (1995) 667-669 (*Pasquetto, Virgilio*).

4303 *Munoz León, D.* El derás sobre Caín y Abel en 1 Jn y la situación de la comunidad joánica. EstB 53 (1995) 213-238.

4304 **Neufeld, D.** Reconceiving texts...1 John. 1994 ⇒10,5461. Bibl.Interp. 7. RNeotest. 29 (1995) 141-142 (*Botha, J. Eugene*); StPat 42 (1995) 148-150 (*Segalla, Giuseppe*); CritRR 8 (1995) 266-268 (*Rensberger, David*).

4305 *Ornellas, P. d'* L'amour mutuel: fin de la révélation: une lecture de 1 Jean 4,7-20. NV 70/3 (1995) 18-42.

4306 *Quintero, José Luis* En la cruz se explica la afirmación: "Dios es amor" (1 Jn 4,8): la pregunta por Dios. Stauros 24 (1995) 27-36.
TERettig, John W. Tractates...on the first epistle of John ⇒3977.

4307 *Sproston, Wendy E.* Witnesses to what was ἀπ' ἀρχῆς: 1 John's contribution to our knowledge of tradition in the fourth gospel. 1995 < 1992 > ⇒104. The Johannine writings. 138-160.

4308 *Ward, T.* Sin "not unto death" and sin "unto death" in 1 Joh 5:16. ChM 109 (1995) 226-237

4309 **Gentili, Antonio** L'Anticristo: attualità di una ricerca. Dominus Dixit. Rimini 1995, Cerchio 79 pp. 88-86583-05-2.

4310 **Heid, Stefan** Chiliasmus und Antichrist-Mythos 1993 ⇒9,5674. RCritRR 7 (1994) 340-342 (*Jenks, Gregory C.*) [1 Jn 2,18].

4311 *Hill, C.E.* Antichrist from the tribe of Dan. JThS 46 (1995) 99-117.

4312 **Lietaert Peerbolte, Lambertus J.** The antecedents of antichrist: a traditio-historical study of the earliest christian views on eschatological opponents. Diss. Lei 1995, 381 pp. DJonge, M. de [RTL 27,536].

4313 **McGinn, Bernard** Antichrist. 1994 ⇒10,5466. RCritRR 8 (1995) 494-496 (*Suter, David W.*).

4314 *Schoenstene, Robert* The enemy's messiah: the biblical roots of the antichrist. ChiSt 34 (1995) 236-250.

4315 **Wong, Daniel Kei Kwong** The Johannine concept of the over-comer (antichrist). Diss. Dallas Theological Seminary 1995, 360 pp. DAI-A 56/12,p.4811.

4316 **Klauck, Hans-Josef** 2-3 Joh. EKK NT 23/2. 1992 ⇒9,5654. Clar. 35 (1995) 533 (*Proietti, Bruno*).

G2.3 *Apocalypsis Johannis* — Revelation: text, introduction.

4317 **Chapman, C.T.** The message of the book of Revelation. ColMn 1995, Liturgical x; 140 pp. $12. 0-8146-2111-2 [NTAb 40,152].

4318 **Charlier, Jean-Pierre** Comprendre l'Apocalypse. 1991 ⇒7,5005... 10,5471. RRThom 95 (1995) 689-696 (*Devillers, Luc*).

4319 **Charlier, Jean-Pierre** Comprender el Apocalipsis. Bilbao 1993, Desclée 278 + 253 pp. RScrTh 27 (1995) 366-367 (*García Moreno, A.*); Studium 35/1 (1995) 155-156 (*Juan, Pedro*).

4320 **Court, John M.** The book of Revelation. 1994 ⇒10,5495. RReviews in Religion and Theology (1995/1) 52-54 (*Bryan,*

David); CritRR 8 (1995) 192-194 (*Wainwright, Arthur W.*).
4321 *De Groote, Marc* Die handschriftliche Überlieferung des OECUMENIUS-Kommentar zur Apokalypse. SE 35 (1995) 5-29.
4322 **Frank, Ewald** L'apocalypse: un livre scellé de 7 sceaux?. Krefeld 1995, Freie Volksmission 181 pp. 3-920824-08-3 [NThAR 1997,68].
4323 **Goémine, Marcel** L'évangile de Jésus-Christ selon l'Apocalypse de saint Jean. P 1995, Téqui 362 pp. FF135 [EeV 106,180].
4324 ᴱᵀ**González Echegaray, Joaquin; Campo, Alberto del; Freeman, Leslie G.** Obras completas de Beato de LIEBANA. BAC Maior 47. M 1995, BAC lxiii; 953 pp. Edición bilingüe. 84-7914-171-9. ᴿComp. 40 (1995) 393-400 (*Romero-Pose, Eugenio*).
4325 *Grosjean, Jean* A livre ouvert. MoBi 94 (1995) 26-27.
4326 **Grünberg, Karsten** Die kirchenslavische überlieferung der Johannes-Apokalypse. Diss. Heidelberg 1995 [NThAR 1997,100].
4327 **Grünzweig, Fritz** Johannes-Offenbarung. Bibelkommentare 25. Stu ⁵1995, Hänssler 315 pp. 3-7751-0643-X [NThAR 1996/3,55].
4328 **Harrington, Wilfrid J.** Revelation. 1993 ⇒9,5688; 10,5476. ᴿCritRR 7 (1994) 201-202 (*Wilson, J. Christian*); CBQ 57 (1995) 397-398 (*Thompson, Leonard L.*); Neotest. 29 (1995) 127-129 (*Long, T.*).
4329 **Newton, Isaac** Trattato sull'Apocalisse. ᵀᴱ*Mamiani, Maurizio.* T 1994, Bollati Boringhieri 258 pp. Florensia 8-9 (1994-5) 281-283 (*Zanot, Massimiliano*).
4330 **Prévost, Jean-Pierre** L'Apocalypse: commentaire pastoral. Commentaires. P 1995, Bayard 179 pp. 2-227-366-08-7.
4331 *Prévost, Jean-Pierre* L'Apocalypse (1980-1992). 1995 ⇒84. De bien des manières. 433-457.
4332 **Richard Guzman, José Pablo** Apocalypse: a people's commentary on the book of Revelation. The Bible & Liberation. Mkn 1995, Orbis vii; 184 pp. 1-57075-043-2.
4333 **Roloff, Jürgen** Revelation. 1993 ⇒9,5692; 10,5478. ᴿInterp. 49 (1995) 189-192 (*Rissi, Mathias*); CBQ 57 (1995) 189-191 (*Morton, Russell*).
4334 *Romero-Pose, Eugenio* La Biblia de ALCUINO y el perdido comentario al apocalipsis de TICONIO. REsp 55 (1995) 391-397.
4335 *Salerno, Alessandro* Chiesa e storia nel Commento all'Apocalisse di Francisco de RIBERA (1537-1591). Laós 2/2 (1995) 35-48.
4336 **Schmolinsky, Sabine** Apokalypsenkommentar...Minorita. 1991 ⇒7,5016... 10,5480. ᴿMÀ 101 (1995) 557-558 (*Overgaauw, E.A.*); AKuG 77 (1995) 479-480 (*Brincken, Anna-Dorothee von den*); ZSRG.K 81 (1995) 469-470 (*Selge, Kurt-Victor*).
4337 **Sweet, John** Revelation. 1990 ⇒6,5934; 7,5018. ᴿEstB 53 (1995) 558-559 (*Contreras, F.*).
4338 ᵀ**Tagliapietra, Andrea** Gioacchino da FIORE sull'Apocalisse: testo originale a fronte. Universale Economica Feltrinelli "I Classici". M 1994, Feltrinelli 413 pp. L20.000. ᴿCFr 65 (1995) 700-701 (*Accrocca, Felice*); Florensia 8-9 (1994-95) 257-259 (*Solvi, Daniele*).
4339 **Talbert, Charles H.** The Apocalypse. 1994 10,5484. ᴿAThR 77 (1995) 240-242 (*Laurence M. Wills*; PSB 16 (1995) 370-371 (*Minear, Paul S.*); CritRR 8 (1995) 303-305 (*Barr, David L.*).
4340 **Thomas, Robert L.** Revelation 8-22. Chicago 1995, Moody 690 pp. $29.

4341 **Wall, Robert W.** Revelation. NIBC 18. 1991 ⇒7,5022... 9,5699.
      RCritRR 7 (1994) 272-274 (*Mulholland, M. Robert Jr.*); EstB 53
      (1995) 559-560 (*Contreras, F.*).

G2.4 *Apocalypsis,* **Revelation, topics**

4342 *Adinolfi, Marco* Simbolismo teriomorfo nell'Apocalisse di
      Giovanni e nell''oneirocritica' di ARTEM IDO RO. 1995 ⇒139. Atti
      del V Simposio. 19-26.
4343 *Barker, Margaret* The Servant in the book of Revelation. HeyJ 36
      (1995) 493-511.
4344 *Barnett, Paul* Polemical parallelism: some further reflections on the
      Apocalypse. 1995 <1989> ⇒104. The Johannine writings. 223-
      231.
4345 *Barr, David L.* Using plot to discern structure in John's
      Apocalypse. ProcGLM 15 (1995) 23-33.
4346 *Barrett, Charles K.* Gnosis and the Apocalypse of John. 1995
      <1983> ⇒39. Jesus and the word. 135-148.
4347 **Bauckham, Richard** The climax of prophecy. 1993 ⇒9,5702*;
      10,5488. RReviews in Religion and Theology (1995/1) 52-56
      (*Bryan, David*); IBSt 17 (1995) 193-197 (*Campbell, Gordon*);
      AUSS 33 (1995) 288-290 (*Müller, Ekkehardt*); Neotest. 29 (1995)
      419-420 (*Hoffman, A.M.*).
4348 **Bauckham, Richard** The theology of Revelation 1993 ⇒9,5703...
      10,5489. RCritRR 7 (1994) 140-142 (*Michaels, J. Ramsey*); IBSt
      17 (1995) 193-197 (*Campbell, Gordon*); EvQ 67 (1995) 278-280
      (*Edwards, Ruth B.*); Interp. 49 (1995) 189-192 (*Rissi, Mathias*).
4349 *Bauckham, Richard* God in the book of Revelation. PIBA 18
      (1995) 40-53.
4350 *Boccaccini, Gabriele* Testi apocalittici coevi dell'Apocalisse di
      Giovanni. RStB 7/2 (1995) 151-161.
4351 *Bovon, François* Possession or enchantment: the Roman institutions
      according to the Revelation of John. 1995 <1986> ⇒40. New
      Testament traditions. PTMS 36. 133-145, 224-228 [RB 103,117].
4352 *Boyer, Frédéric* Des énigmes pour apprendre à lire. MoBi 94
      (1995) 17-18.
4353 **Bratcher, Robert G.; Hatton, Howard A.** A handbook on the
      revelation to John. 1993 ⇒9,5706. RCritRR 8 (1995) 180-181
      (*Farmer, Ronald L.*).
4354 **Brueggemann, Dale A.** The use of the psalter in John's
      Apocalypse. Diss. Westminster Theol. Sem. 1995, 288 pp.
      DLongman, Tremper III, AAC 9532737; DAI-A 56/5,p.1827.
4355 *Cahill, Michael* The horror story: a component of the book of
      Revelation. PIBA 18 (1995) 71-77.
4356 *Callahan, Allen Dwight* The language of apocalypse. HThR 88
      (1995) 453-470.
4357 *Casalegno, Alberto* A cidade entre realidade e símbolo: duas per-
      spectivas do Apocalipse. PerTeol 27/1 (1995) 7-26.
4358 *Corradino, Saverio* Note sull'Apocalisse. Quaderni di Azione
      Sociale 40/3 (1995) 75-80.
4359 *Costanzo, Giuseppe* L'Apocalisse: una luce per comprendere
      l'oggi. PresPast 65/8 (1995) 19-32.

4360 **Cothenet, Édouard** Le message de l'Apocalypse. P 1995, Mame/Plon 185 pp. FF98 [NTAb 40,54].

4361 *Daoust, J.* Patmos et l'Apocalypse. EeV 105 (1995) 664-665.

4362 *De Groote, Marc* Die Scholien aus dem OECUMENIUS-Kommentar zur Apokalypse. SE 35 (1995) 31-43.

4363 *Devillers, Luc* L'Apocalypse. RThom 95 (1995) 689-699.

4364 *Doglio, Claudio* Prima e seconda morte nell'Apocalisse. PSV 32 (1995) 219-242.

4365 *Doglio, Claudio* Quanto apocalittica è l'Apocalisse di Giovanni? RStB 7/2 (1995) 103-135.

4366 **Donegani, Isabelle** "A cause de la parole de Dieu et du témoignage de Jésus...": le témoignage comme parole de sens et d'espérance dans l'Apocalypse de Jean. Diss. Fribourg 1995, DRouiller, G. [ThRv 92/2,VIII].

4367 *Downing, F. Gerald* PLINY's prosecutions of christians: Revelation and 1 Peter. 1995 <1988> ⇒104. The Johannine writings. 232-249.

4368 EEmmerson, Richard K.; McGinn, Bernard The Apocalypse in the Middle Ages 1992 ⇒8,5949... 10,5497*. RJR 75 (1995) 275-277 (*Krey, Philip D.*).

4369 *Emmerson, Richard K.* The Apocalypse cycle in the Bedford Hours. Tr. 50 (1995) 173-198.

4370 *Etchegaray, Card. Roger* El Apocalipsis..., un nuevo Génesis. La Cuestion Social 3-4 (1995-6) 381-384.

4371 **Fekkes, Jan** Isaiah and prophetic traditions in Revelation. JSNT.S 93. 1994 ⇒10,5499. RThLZ 120 (1995) 145-147 (*Taeger, Jens-W.*); JThS 46 (1995) 293-294 (*Sweet, J.P.M.*); CBQ 57 (1995) 805-806 (*Aune, David E.*); CritRR 8 (1995) 211-213 (*Wilson, J. Christian*).

4372 *Friesen, Steven J.* Revelation, realia, and religion: archaeology in the Interpretation of the Apocalypse. HThR 88 (1995) 291-314.

4373 *Fusco, Vittorio* Gesù e l'apocalittica: i problemi e il metodo. RStB 7/2 (1995) 37-60.

4374 *Gunther, John J.* The elder John, author of Revelation. 1995 <1981> ⇒104. The Johannine writings. 163-179.

4375 *Homcy, S. L.* "To him who overcomes": a fresh look at what "victory" means for the believer according to the book of Revelation. JETS 38 (1995) 193-201.

Hübner, Hans Hebräerbrief...Offenbarung. ⇒5230.

4376 **Humphrey, Edith McEwan** The ladies and the cities: transformation and apocalyptic identity in Joseph and Aseneth, 4 Ezra, the Apocalypse and The Shepherd of Hermas. JSPE.S 17. Shf 1995, Academic 192 pp. $41/£27.50. 1-85075-535-3 [NTAb 40,175].

4377 *Infante, Renzo* L'agnello nell'Apocalisse. VetChr 32 (1995) 321-338.

4378 *Jeske, R.L.* The book of Revelation in the parish. WWorld 15 (1995) 182-194 [NTAb 40,74].

4379 **Kerner, Jürgen** Die Ethik der Johannesapokalypse im Vergleich mit der des 4. Esra: ein Beitrag zum Verhältnis von Apokalyptik und Ethik. Diss. Mainz 1995, DBöcher, O. [RTL 27,535].

4380 *Koester, C.R.* On the verge of the millennium: a history of the interpretation of Revelation. WWorld 15 (1995) 128-136 [NTAb 40,74].

4381 **Lewis, Suzanne** Reading images: narrative discourse and reception in the thirteenth-century illuminated Apocalypse. C 1995, CUP xxv; 459 pp. 252 ill. 0-521-47920-7.

4382 **Llamas Vela, Antonio** Títulos y atributos divinos que se aplican a Cristo en el libro del Apocalipsis. Diss. Comillas 1995, ᴰ*Muñoz León, D.* [Miscellanea Comillas 54/1,235].

4383 **Lorie, Peter** Revelation: St. John the Divine: prophecies for the Apocalypse and beyond. L 1995, Boxtree 224 pp. 1-85283-982-1.

4384 *Lupieri, Edmondo* Apocalisse di Giovanni e tradizione enochica. RStB 7/2 (1995) 137-150.

4385 *Magnante, A.* Líneas de espiritualidad en el Apocalipsis de San Juan. NuMu 49 (1995) 11-23 [Strom. 52,346].

4386 **Malina, Bruce J.** On the genre and message of Revelation: star visions and sky journeys. Peabody, MA 1995 Hendrickson xvii; 317 pp. $20. 1-56563-040-8.

4387 *Marchadour, Alain* Qui a écrit l'Apocalypse? MoBi 94 (1995) 11.

4388 *Martin, A.W.* The Apocalypse and the lectionary. StLi 25 (1995) 207-230.

4389 *Mentré, Mireille* L'Apocalypse dans la peinture mozarabe. MoBi 94 (1995) 32-35.

4390 *Mentré, Mireille* L'Apocalypse dans l'art médiéval. MoBi 94 (1995) 28-31.

4391 **Michaels, J. Ramsay** Interpreting the book of Revelation. 1992 ⇒8,5932… 10,5513. ᴿCritRR 7 (1994) 238-240 (*Boring, M. Eugene*).

4392 *Moore, Stephen D.* The beatific vision as a posing exhibition: Revelation's hypermasculine deity. JSNT 60 (1995) 27-55.

4393 **Moyise, Steve** The Old Testament in the book of Revelation. JSNT.S 115. Shf 1995, Academic 173 pp. £30/$45. 1-85075-554-X.

4394 *Muñoz León, Domingo* El culto imperial en el Apocalipsis. RevBib 57 (1995) 223-230.

4395 *Mwombeki, F.R.* The book of Revelation in Africa. WWorld 15 (1995) 145-150 [NTAb 40,74].

4396 *Nepi, Antonio* La scelta del libro dell'Apocalisse in preparazione al convegno di Palermo. Firmana 9-10 (1995) 275-289.

4397 *Nobile, Marco* L'Apocalisse: una lettura cristiana dell'Antico Testamento. 1995 ⇒139. Atti del V Simposio. 127-138.

4398 *Norelli, Enrico* Apocalittica: come pensarne lo sviluppo?. RStB 7/2 (1995) 163-200.

4399 **Park, Sung-Min** More than a regained Eden: the new Jerusalem as the ultimate portrayal of eschatological blessedness and its implication for the understanding of the book of Revelation. Diss. Trinity Evang. Div. School 1995, 358 pp. ᴰ*Osborne, G.*, AAC 9533062; DAI-A 56/6,p.2282.

4400 *Paulien, J.* The role of the Hebrew cultus, sanctuary and temple in the plot and structure of the book of Revelation. AUSS 33 (1995) 245-264.

4401 *Penna, Romano* introduzione: apocalittica e origini cristiane: lineamenti storici del problema. RStB 7/2 (1995) 5-17.

4402 **Pezzoli-Olgiati, Daria** Täuschung und Klarheit: zur Wechselwirkung zwischen Vision und Geschichte in der Johannesoffenbarung. Diss. Zürich 1995-6, ᴰ*Weder, H.* [RTL 27,537].

4403 *Piolanti, A.* La liturgia celeste e perennità del sacerdozio di Cristo. Div. 39 (1995) 274-281 [NTAb 40,267].

4404 **Pippin, Tina** Death and desire...Apocalypse. 1992 ⇒9,5733; 10,5519. [R]CritRR 7 (1994) 248-250 (*Linton, Gregory*).

4405 *Pistone, Rosario* Lo Spirito interpella la Chiesa: annotazioni per una lettura del rapporto Spirito-Chiesa nell'Apocalisse. Ho Theológos 13/2 (1995) 197-208.

4406 **Prévost, Jean Pierre** How to read the Apocalypse. 1993 ⇒9,5735; 10,5520. [R]BTB 25 (1995) 94 (*deSilva, David A.*).

4407 *Prévost, Jean-Pierre* La fascination de la fin des temps. MoBi 94 (1995) 15-16.

4408 *Prigent, Pierre* Qu'est-ce qu'une apocalypse? RHPhR 75 (1995) 77-84.

4409 *Ramos, Felipe Fernandez* El Apocalipsis: libro de la esperanza I. StLeg 36 (1995) 87-125.

4410 *Räisänen, Heikki* The clash between christian styles of life in the book of Revelation. StTh 49 (1995) 151-166.

4411 *Reddish, Mitchell G.* Martyr christology in the Apocalypse. 1995 <1988> ⇒104. The Johannine writings. 212-222.

4412 **Reichelt, Hansgünter** Angelus interpres—Texte in der Johannes-Apokalypse. EHS.T 507. 1994 ⇒10,5521. [R]ThLZ 120 (1995) 663-664 (*Böcher, Otto*).

4413 **Richard, Pablo** Apocalipsis: reconstrucción de la esperanza. México 1995, Dabar 278 pp.

4414 *Rowland, Christopher* 'Upon whom the ends of the ages have come': apocalyptic and the interpretation of the New Testament. Apocalypse theory and the end of the world. 1995 ⇒2436. Wolfson College Lectures. 38-57.

4415 *Russotto, Mario* Lo Spirito parla alle Chiese: l'iconia dell'Apocalisse. PresPast 65/8 (1995) 33-44.

4416 *Sacchi, Paolo* Formazione e linee portanti dall'apocalittica giudaica precristiana. RStB 7/2 (1995) 19-36.

4417 **Seel, Thomas Allen** A theology of music for worship derived from the book of Revelation. Studies in Liturgical Musicology 3. L 1995, Scarecrow xii; 209 pp. $29.50 [CBQ 57,638].

4418 [E]**Selge, Kurt-Victor** Gioacchino da Fiore: introduzione all'Apocalisse. [T]*Potestà, Gian Luca*, Opere di Gioacchino da Fiore: testi e strumenti 6. R 1995, Viella 65 pp. 88-85669-43-3.

4419 *Siniscalco, Paolo* Apocalisse: storia della salvezza e impegno del cristiano. Nuova Umanità 17/5 (1995) 39-44.

4420 *Stevenson, Gregory M.* Conceptual background to golden crown imagery in the Apocalypse of John (4:4, 10; 14:14). JBL 114 (1995) 257-272.

4421 **Stock, Klemens** L'ultima parola è di Dio: l'Apocalisse come buona notizia. Bibbia e Preghiera 21. R 1995, ADP 200 pp. L25.000. 88-7357-152-2.

4422 **Stuckenbruck, Loren T.** Angel veneration and christology: a study in early Judaism and in the christology of the Apocalypse of John. Diss. Princeton Theological Seminary 1993, [D]*Charlesworth, J.R.*, WUNT 2/70. Tü 1995, Mohr xviii; 348 pp. DM88. 3-16-146303-X [NTAb 40,159].

4423 **Sutter Rehmann, Luzia** Geh, frage die Gebärerin! Feministisch-befreiungstheologische Untersuchungen zum Gebärmotiv in der Apokalyptik. Gü 1995, Kaiser 263 pp. 3-579-00099-3.

4424 *Thiede, Werner* Drohbotschaft aus dem Wachtturm: die Johannes-Apokalypse bei den Zeugen Jehovas. EK 28 (1995) 355-357.

4425 *Thiede, Werner* Ein süßes und doch schwerverdauliches Büchlein: zur Auslegung der Johannes-Offenbarung in christlichen Sondergemeinschaften. KuD 41 (1995) 213-242 [sum. 242].

4426 *Thüsing, Wilhelm* Die theologische Mitte der Weltgerichtsvisionen in der Johannesapokalypse. 1995 <1968> ⇒60. Studien. WUNT 2/82. 135-150.

4427 *Vanni, Ugo* L'Apocalisse: una speranza che attraversa la storia. Florensia 8-9 (1994-5) 243-253.

4428 *Vanni, Ugo* L'Apocalisse: una profezia per la Chiesa in Italia. Civ-Catt 146 (1995) 17-29, 120-134.

4429 *Vanni, Ugo* L'opera creativa nell'Apocalisse. 1995 ⇒267. Dizionario di spiritualità biblico-patristica 10, 162-184.

4430 *Vetrali, Tecle* La conversione nell'Apocalisse. Dizionario di spiritualità biblico-patristica 9. ᴱPanimolle, Salvatore A., R 1995, Borla 274 pp. 88-263-1063-7. 141-154.

4431 *Vos, J.S.* Psychoanalytische uitleg van de Openbaring van Johannes. GThT 95/4 (1995) 167-181.

4432 **Wainwright, A.W.** Mysterious Apocalypse. 1993 ⇒9,5698; 10,5534. ᴿReviews in Religion and Theology (1995/1) 52-53 (*Bryan, David*); CritRR 8 (1995) 317-319 (*Bauckham, Richard*).

4433 ᴱ**Weyer-Menkhoff, Michael** Halleluja!: Wege in die 'Offenbarung'. Porta-Studien 27. Marburg 1995, SMD 287 pp. [NThAR 1997,227].

G2.5 *Apocalypsis,* **Revelation** 1,1...

4434 **Kyrtatas, Demeter** Η Αποκάλυψη του Ιωάννη και οι Επτά Εκκλησίες της Ασίας [The Apocalypse of John and the seven churches of Asia]. Athens 1994, Alexandria. DBM 14/2 (1995) 86-92 (*Agourides, S.*).

4435 **Thekkemury, Jacob** Velipadu 1-3. **Malayalam.** OIRSI 174. Vadavathoor 1995, Oriental Institute of Religious Studies 188 pp. Rs35. ᴿBiBh 21 (1995) 282-283 (*Asquith, Christie*) [1-3].

4436 **Cerquone, Anthony** Redaction and the composition of Revelation 1-4. Diss. Drew 1995, 335 pp. ᴰ*Dey, Lala Kalyan K.,* AAC 9536134; DAI-A 56/6,p.2278.

4437 *Walther, James A.* The address in Revelation 1:4,5a. HBT 17 (1995) 165-180.

4438 *Smith, Robert H.* Why John wrote the Apocalypse (Rev 1:9). CThMi 22 (1995) 356-361.

4439 *Romero-Pose, Eugenio* Los angeles de las iglesias (exegesis de Tɪᴄᴏɴɪᴏ al Apoc. 1,20-3,22). Aug. 35 (1995) 119-136.

4440 *Räisänen, H.* The Nicolaitans: Apoc. 2; Acta 6. 1995 47b. Vorkonstantinisches Christentum. 1602-1644 [2,6].

4441 **Sequeira, Jack** Laodicea: Christ's urgent cousel to a lukewarm church in the last days. Boise, Idaho 1995, Pacific 143 pp. 0-8163-1243-5 [3,14-22; NThAR 1997/3,70].

4442 *Vetrali, Tecle* "Ecco, io sto alla porta e busso" (Ap. 3,20): l'amore risveglia il fervore e sollecita l'incontro. RSE 13 (1995) 271-295 [3,14-22].

4443 **Contreras Molina, Francisco** Estoy a la puerta y llamo (Ap 3,20): estudio temático. Biblioteca EstB 84. S 1995, Sígueme 428 pp. 84-301-1254-5. ᴿCTom 122 (1995) 415-416; ATG 58 (1995) 355-359 (*Espinel, José Luis*).

4444 *Wiarda, T.* Revelation 3:20: imagery and literary context. JETS 38 (1995) 203-212.

4445 **Migliazzo, Cataldo B.** La porta del mistero: Apc 4,1. R 1995, Pontificium Athenaeum Antonianum 95 pp.

4446 *Böttrich, Christfried* Das "gläserne Meer" in Apk 4,6/15,2. BN 80 (1995) 5-15.

4447 *Ruiz, Jean-Pierre* Revelation 4:8-11; 5:9-14: hymns of the heavenly liturgy. SBL.SP 34 (1995) 216-220.

4448 *Hurtado, L. W.* Revelation 4-5 in the light of Jewish apocalyptic analogies. 1995 <1985> ⇒104. The Johannine writings. 193-211.

4449 *Bailey, James L.* Genre analysis. 1995 ⇒85. Hearing. 197-221 [5,1-14; BBB 16,57].

4450 *Smidt, J.C. de* Die oë van die gees in die boek Openbaring—'n teologiese perspektief [The eyes of the spirit in the book of Revelation—a theological perspective]. Scriptura 54 (1995) 159-176 [5,6; NTAb 40,269].

4451 *Harrington, Wilfrid* Worthy is the lamb. PIBA 18 (1995) 54-70 [5].

4452 **Stefanović, Ranko** The background and meaning of the sealed book of Revelation 5. Diss. Andrews 1995, ᴰ*Paulien, Jon* [AUSS 34/1,95].

4453 *Ruiten, Jacques van* Der alttestamentliche Hintergrund von Apokalypse 6:12-17. EstB 53 (1995) 239-260.

4454 *Smith, C. R.* The tribes of Revelation 7 and the literary competence of John the seer. JETS 38 (1995) 213-218.

4455 *Goranson, Stephen* The exclusion of Ephraim in Rev. 7:4-8 and Essene polemic against pharisees. DSD 2 (1995) 80-85.

4456 **Ulland, Harald** Die Vision als Radikalisierung der Wirklichkeit in der Apokalypse des Johannes: das Verhältnis der sieben Sendschreiben zu Apokalypse 12-13. Diss. Bethel 1995-6, ᴰ*Vouga, Fr.* [RTL 27,538].

4457 **Abir, Peter Antonysamy** The cosmic conflict of the church: an exegetico-theological study of Revelation 12,7-12. Diss. Pontificia Universitas Gregorian, ᴰ*Vanni, Ugo.* EHS.T 547. Fra 1995, Lang xxx; 365 pp. 3-631-49352-5 [NThAR 1997,162].

4458 *Schroeder, J.A.* Revelation 12: female figures and figures of evil. WWorld 15 (1995) 175-181 [NTAb 40,76].

4459 **Busch, Peter** Apokalypse 12 und die religionsgeschichtliche Exegese: ein Text und seine Auslegungsmethode. Diss. Heidelberg 1995, ᴰ*Berger* [ThRv 92/2,IX].

4460 *Riley, William* Who is the woman in Revelation 12?. PIBA 18 (1995) 15-39.

4461 *Du Rand, Jean A.* The song of the Lamb because of the victory of the Lamb. Neotest. 29 (1995) 203-210 [15,3-4].

4462 *Oberweis, Michael* Erwägungen zur apokalyptischen Ortsbezeichnung "Harmagedon". Bib. 76 (1995) 305-324 [16,16].

4463 *Holwerda, D.* Ein neuer Schlüssel zum 17. Kapitel der johanneischen Offenbarung. EstB 53 (1995) 387-396.

4464 **Rissi, Mathias** Die Hure Babylon und die Verführung der Heiligen: eine Studie zur Apokalypse des Johannes. BWANT 136.

Stu 1995, Kohlhammer 95 pp. DM89. 3-17-012988-0 [17; NTAb 40,158].

4465 *Elliott, Susan M.* Who is addressed in Revelation 18:6-7?. BR 40 (1995) 98-113.

4466 *Okorie, A.M.* Revelation 2 and 3: grammatical notes. DBM 14/2 (1995) 31-39.

G2.7 **Millenniarismus,** *Apc 20...*

4467 *Aune, David E.* The prophetic circle of John of Patmos and the exegesis of Revelation 22,16. 1995 <1989> ⇒104. The Johannine writings. 180-192.
       Bunge, Wiep van Balthasar BEKKER on *Daniel*: an early enlightenment critique of millenarianism. ⇒2457.

4468 **Delumeau, Jean** Une histoire du paradis 2: mille ans de bonheur. P 1995, Fayard 493 pp. BEF1,020.

4469 **Introvigne, Massimo** Millenarismo e nuove religioni alle soglie del duemila: mille e non più mille. M 1995, Gribaudi 253 pp. 88-7152-383-0.

4470 **Mealy, J. Webb** After the thousand years...in Revelation 20. JSNT.S 70. 1992 ⇒8,6020... 10,5561. ᴿJBL 114 (1995) 169-172 (*Hill, Charles E.*).

4471 **Meissner, William W.** Thy kingdom come: psychoanalytic perspectives on the messiah and the millennium. Kansas City MO 1995, Sheed & Ward xi; 370 pp. 1-55612-750-2.

4472 **Mickiewicz, Franciszek** Natura nowej świątyni eschatologicznej według Ap 21,1-4.22-27: studium egzegetyczno-teoliczne z uwzglednieniem innych pism nowotestamentalnych oraz apokaliptcznej literatury żydowskiej [Nature du nouveau temple eschatologique selon Ap 21,1-4.22-27: étude exégétique et théologique rendant compte des autres écrits du N.T. et de la littérature apocalyptique juive]. Diss. Warsaw 1995, 242 pp. ᴰŁach, J. [RTL 27,536].

4473 **Missler, Chuck** The Magog invasion. Palos Verdes, Calif. 1995, Western Front 311 pp. 0-9641058-6-1 [20,8; NThAR 1997/259].

4474 ᴱ**Nardi, Carlo** Il millenarismo: testi dei secoli I-II. BPat 27. Fiesole 1995, Nardini 274 pp. 88-404-2031-2.

4475 *Newport, Kenneth G.C.* Charles WESLEY's interpretation of some biblical prophecies according to a previously unpublished letter dated 25 April, 1754. BJRL 77/2 (1995) 31-52.

4476 **O'Leary, Stephen D.** Arguing the Apocalypse: a theory of millennial rhetoric. 1994 ⇒10,5562. ᴿTS 56 (1995) 154-155 (*Guinan, Michael D.*); JSSR 34 (1995) 134-135 (*Robbins, Thomas*).

4477 **Park, Sung-Min** More than a regained Eden: the new Jerusalem as the ultimate portrayal of eschatological blessedness and its implication for the understanding of the book of Revelation. Diss. Trinity Evangelical Divinity School 1995, 358 pp. ᴰOsborne, G., DAI-A 56/6,p.2282 [21].

4478 *Romero-Pose, Eugenio* El milenio en TICONIO: exegesis al Apoc. 20,1-6. ASEs 12 (1995) 327-346.

4479 **Sim, Unyong** Das himmlische Jerusalem in Apk 21,1-22,5 im Kontext biblisch-jüdischer Traditionen und antiken Städtebaus. Diss. Bochum 1995, ᴰWengst, Kl. [ThRv 92/2,VI].

4480 *Thüsing, Wilhelm* Die Vision des "Neuen Jerusalem" (Apk 21,1-22,5) als Verheißung und Gottesverkündigung. 1995 <1968> ⇒60. Studien. WUNT 2/82. 151-168.

Paulus

G3.1 Pauli biographia.

4481 [E]**Babcock, William S.** Paul and the legacies of Paul. 1990 ⇒7,5098... 9,5915. [R]JThS 46 (1995) 317-320 (*Parvis, P.M.*).

4482 **Bruce, F.F.** Paulus: von Tarsus bis Rom. Giessen 1995, Brunnen 64 pp. 3-7655-5740-4.

4483 **Bruce, F.F.** In the steps of the apostle Paul. GR 1995, Kregel 64 pp. $30. 0-8254-2254-X [NThAR 1997,260].

4484 **Cothenet, Édouard** Petite vie de saint Paul: son apostolat au miroir de ses lettres. P 1995, Desclée 173 pp. FF65. 2-220-03586-7 [NRTh 118,612].

4485 **Cremona, Carlo** St. Paul. Boston 1995, Pauline 228 pp. 0-8198-6974-0 [NThAR 1997,100].

4486 *Haacker, K.* Zum Werdegang des Apostels Paulus: biographische Daten und ihre theologische Relevanz. 1995 ⇒87. Vorkonstantinisches Christentum. 815-938.

4487 **Hengel, Martin** Il Paolo precristiano. 1992 ⇒8,6035... 10,5580. [R]EE 70 (1995) 416-417 (*Artola, A.M.*).

4488 **Hildebrandt, Dieter** Saul, Paul: une double vie. Nîmes 1994, Chambon 350 pp. FF130. 2-87711-113-X. [R]ETR 70 (1995) 278-279 (*Cuvillier, Elian*).

4489 *Hug, Joseph* A la découverte de Paul de Tarse. Choisir 431 (1995) 14-17.

4490 **Légasse, Simon** Paolo apostolo: biografia critica. R 1994, Città Nuova 312 pp. L42.000. [R]StPat 42/3 (1995) 153-154 (*Segalla, Giuseppe*).

4491 **Martin, Raymond A.** Studies in the life and ministry of Paul. 1993 ⇒9,5797; 10,5584. [R]CritRR 8 (1995) 257-259 (*Tyler, Ronald*).

4492 **Orr, Mary Cathryn** Paul as persecutor of the church: autobiography as apocalyptic paradigm. Diss. Virginia 1995, 199 pp. DAI-A 56/9,p.3618.

4493 *Pani, Giancarlo* Vocazione di Paolo o conversione?: la storia del cristianesimo dei primi secoli di fronte all'evento di Damasco. Atti del III Simposio. 1995 ⇒138. 45-62.

4494 **Riesner, Rainer** Die Frühzeit des Apostels Paulus. 1994 ⇒10,5588. [R]ET 106 (1994-95) 271 (*Best, Ernest*); ThRv 91 (1995) 227-231 (*Albert, Marcel*).

4495 **Sánchez Bosch, Jordi** Nacido a tiempo: una vida de Pablo. 1994 ⇒10,5589. [R]EE 70 (1995) 124-125 (*Pastor-Ramos, Federico*); StPat 42/3 (1995) 156-157 (*Segalla, Giuseppe*); Clar. 35 (1995) 546-551 (*Pardilla, Angel*).

4496 **Saffrey, Henri Dominique** San Paolo apostolo: una biografia
storica. Santi e sante di Dio 16. CinB 1995, San Paolo 192 pp.
L18.000 [RdT 36,384].

4497 **Storm, Hans-Martin** Die Paulusberufung nach Lukas und das
Erbe der Propheten: berufen zu Gottes Dienst. ANTJ 10. Fra 1995,
Lang 357 pp. $56. 3-631-47645-0 [NTAb 40,350].

4498 *Strecker, Georg; Nolting, Torsten* Der vorchristliche Paulus:
Überlegungen   zum   biographischen   Kontext   biblischer
Überlieferung—zugleich eine Antwort an Martin HENGEL. 1995
⇒14. F HARTMAN L.,713-741.

4499 **Tajra, Harry W.** The martyrdom of St Paul: historical and judicial
context, traditions, and legends. WUNT 2/67. Tü 1994, Mohr xii;
225 pp. DM98. 3-16-146239-4. R NT 37 (1995) 412 (*Elliott, J.K.*);
EstAg 30 (1995) 558-559 (*Cineira, D.A.*); AnBoll 113 (1995) 414-
415 (*Zanetti, U.*).

4500 **Wenham, David** Paul: follower of Jesus or founder of
Christianity?: a new look at the question of Paul and Jesus. GR
1995, Eerdmans xvi; 452 pp. $22. 0-8028-0124-2. R Trinity
Journal 16 (1995) 259-262 (*Köstenberger, Andreas J.*) [1 Cor 9; 1
Thess 4-5].

G3.2 Corpus paulinum; *generalia, technica epistularis.*

4501 E Aland, Barbara; Juckel, Andreas Das Neue Testament in syris-
cher Überlieferung II: die Paulinischen Briefe 2: Korintherbrief,
Galaterbrief, Epheserbrief, Philipperbrief und Kolosserbrief.
ANTT 23. B 1995, De Gruyter viii; 582 pp. 3-11-014613-4.

4502 *Aletti, Jean-Noel* Bulletin d'exégèse du Nouveau Testament: bulletin paulinien. RSR 83 (1995) 97-126.

4503 *Bammel, Caroline* ORIGEN'S Pauline prefaces and the chronology
of his Pauline commentaries. 1995 ⇒126. Origeniana Sexta. 495-
513.

4504 *Barr, George K.* Scale and the Pauline epistles. IBSt 17 (1995) 22-
41.

4505 *Bodjoko, L.-S.* Face to face with Saint Paul. Hekima Review 12
(1995) 3-14 [NTAb 40,250].

4506 *Boers, Hendrikus* Paul and the canon of the New Testament. 1995
⇒6. F BEKER J., 196-208 [OTA 19,493].

4507 *Boers, Hendrikus W.* A context for interpreting Paul. 1995 ⇒14.
F HARTMAN L., 429-453.

4508 *Calloud, Jean* Figure, knowledge and truth: absence and fulfillment in the scriptures. Semeia 69/70 (1995) 61-81/

4509 **Chau, Wai-Shing** The letter and the spirit: a history of interpretation from ORIGEN to LUTHER. AmUSt.TR 167. NY 1995, Lang
vii; 250 pp. 0-8204-2328-9.

4510 *Classen, Carl Joachim* Zur rhetorischen Analyse der Paulusbriefe.
ZNW 86 (1995) 120-121.

4511 *Coleridge, M.* 'The truth will set you free': the path from Egypt to
Eden. Way 35 (1995) 183-192 [NTAb 40,250].

4512 *Doty, William G.* Imaginings at the end of an era: letters as fictions. Semeia 69/70 (1995) 83-110.

4513 E Hawthorne, Gerald F.; Martin, Ralph P. Dictionary of Paul
and his letters. 1993 ⇒9,5814. R PSB 16 (1995) 251-252 (*Metzger,*

Bruce M.); AUSS 33 (1995) 122-123 (*Kubo, Sakae*); CBQ 57 (1995) 595-597 (*Danker, Frederick W.*).

4514 *Homberg, Bengt* Paul and commensality. 1995 ⇒14. F HARTMAN L., 767-780 [1 Cor 5; 10,14-22; 2 Thess 3,6-15].

4515 *Hübner, Hans* Intertextualität—die hermeneutische Strategie des Paulus?: zu einem neuen Versuch der theologischen Rezeption des Alten Testaments im Neuen. 1995 <1991> ⇒52. Biblische Theologie 252-271.

4516 **Jaquette, James L.** Discerning what counts: the function of the adiaphora topos in Paul's letters. Diss. Boston, SBL.DS 146. Atlanta, GA 1995, Scholars xiv; 282 pp. $40/$25. 0-7885-0013-9/14-7 [Rom 14,7-9; Phil 1,21-26; 1 Thess 5,9-10].

4517 **Lambrecht, Jan** Pauline studies. 1994 ⇒10,195. ThLZ 120 (1995) 886-887 (*Lohse, Eduard*).

4518 **Lapide, Pinchas** Paulus zwischen Damaskus und Qumran: Fehldeutungen und Übersetzungsfehler. 1993 ⇒9,5816. Boletin de la Asociacion Española de Orientalistas 31 (1995) 314 (*Sen, Felipe*).

4519 *Loubser, J.A.* Orality and literacy in the Pauline epistles: some new hermeneutical implications. Neotest. 29 (1995) 61-74.

4520 *Marguerat, Daniel* L'héritage de Paul en débat: Actes des Apôtres et Actes de Paul. FV 94/2 (1995) 87-97.

4521 *Mealand, D. L.* The extent of the Pauline corpus: a multivariate approach. JSNT 59 (1995) 61-92.

4522 **Moreschini, C.; Norelli, E.** Storia della letteratura cristiana antica greca e latina 1: da Paolo all'età costantiniana. Brescia 1995, Morcelliana 619 pp. L60.000. 88-372-1549-5. StPat 42/3 (1995) 160-162 (*Corsato, Celestino*).

4523 **Murphy-O'Connor, Jerome** Paul et l'art épistolaire. 1994 ⇒10,5606. R Ang. 72 (1995) 317-318 (*Jurič, Stipe*); RB 102 (1995) 626-627 (*Aletti, Jean-Noël*).

4524 **Murphy-O'Connor, Jerome** Paul the letter-writer: his world, his options, his skills. GNS 41. ColMn 1995, Liturgical viii; 152 pp. $12. 0-8146-5845-8.

4525 **Müller, Markus** Vom Schluß zum Ganzen: der Briefkorpusabschluß als Zugang zur "Texthermeneutik" des Apostelbriefes. Diss. Erlangen-Nürnberg 1995, D *Roloff* [ThRv 92/2, VII].

4526 **Neumann, Kenneth J.** The authenticity of the Pauline epistles. SBL.DS 120. 1990 ⇒6,6065... 10,5607. R RB 102 (1995) 148-149 (*Murphy-O'Connor, J.*).

4527 E **Padovese, Luigi** Atti del I Simposio di Tarso su s. Paolo apostolo. Turchia, la chiesa e la sua storia 5. R 1993, Pont. Ateneo Antonianum 157 pp. R StFr 92/3-4 (1995) 409-411 (*Giovannetti, Ottaviano*).

4528 E **Padovese, Luigi** Atti del III Simposio di Tarso su S. Paolo Apostolo [1994].Turchia, la chiesa e la sua storia 9. R 1995, Pont. Ateneo Antoniano 221 pp.

4529 E **Pastor-Ramos, Federico** San Pablo. ResB 5. Estella (Navarra) 1995, Verbo Divino 72 pp. Ptas1000.[NTAb 40,156].

4530 *Pastor-Ramos, Federico* San Pablo hoy: actualidad y utilidad. ResB 5 (1995) 27-36.

4531 *Pitta, A.* Paraenesis and kerygma in the letters of St. Paul. DBM 14/2 (1995) 65-84.

ᴱ**Porter, Stanley E.; Evans, Craig A.** The Pauline writings 1995 ⇒105.

4532 **Puskas, Charles B. Jr.** The letters of Paul 1993 ⇒9,5821; 10,5610. ᴿCritRR 7 (1994) 252-254 (*Fowl, Stephen*).

4533 **Richards, Randolph E.** The secretary. WUNT 2/42. 1991 ⇒7,5156... 10,5611. ᴿScrB 25/1 (1995) 34-37 (*Prior, Michael*).

4534 *Salles, Catherine* La lettre expression de la pensée dans le monde gréco-romain. FV 94/4 (1995) 3-14.

4535 **Sanders, Ed P.** Paulus: eine Einführung. Stu 1995, Reclam 179 pp. 3-15-009365-1.

4536 **Schmid, Ulrich** Mᴀʀᴄɪᴏɴ und sein Apostolos: Rekonstruktion und historische Einordnung der marcionitischen Paulusbriefausgabe. ANTT 25. B 1995, De Gruyter xvii; 381 pp. Diss. Müns 1994 ⇒10,5612.. DM214. 3-11-014695-9 [NT 39,394].

4537 *Stamps, Dennis L.* Interpreting the language of St. Paul: grammar, modern linguistics and translation theory. 1995 ⇒102. Discourse analysis. JSNT.S 113. 131-139.

4538 *Suhl, A.* Paulinische Chronologie im Streit der Meinungen. 1995 ⇒87. Vorkonstantinisches Christentum. 939-1188.

4539 **Thompson, Ian H.** Chiasmus in the Pauline letters. JSNT.S 111. Shf 1995, Academic 253 pp. £30/$45 [JBL 114,773].

4540 **Tomić, Celestin** Poceci crkve Pavao apostol naroda: (Dj, Rim, 1 i 2 Kor, Gal, Ef, Fil, Kol, 1 i 2 Sol, 1 i 2 Tim, Tit, Flm). Povijest spasenja 14. Zagreb 1995, Provincijalat hrvatskih franjevaca konventualaca 352 pp.

4541 **Trobisch, David** Paul's letter collection. 1994 ⇒10,5612. ᴿCritRR 8 (1995) 311-314 (*McDonald, Lee M.*).

4542 **Venable, Cornelia Michelle** 'Slave' and 'woman' in the Pauline epistles and New Testament paradigms in the slave narratives of African American women: a comparative study. Diss. Temple 1995, 234 pp. ᴰ*Limberis, Vasiliki*, AAC 9535819; DAI-A 56/6,p.2283.

4543 *Verhoef, Eduard* Numerus, Sekretär und Authentizität der paulinischen Briefe. PzB 4 (1995) 48-58.

4544 *Watson, Duane F.* Rhetorical criticism of the Pauline epistles since 1975. CurResB 3 (1995) 219-248.

4545 **Weima, Jeffrey A.D.** Neglected endings...letter closings. JSNT.S 101. 1994 ⇒10,5617. ᴿSalm. 42/1 (1995) 141-143 (*Trevijano, Ramón*).

4546 *Weima, Jeffrey A.D.* The Pauline letter closings: analysis and hermeneutical significance. Bulletin for Biblical Research 5 (1995) 177-198.

4547 **Winninge, Mikael** Sinners and the righteous: a comparative study of the Psalms of Solomon and Paul's letters. Diss. Uppsala 1994. CB.NT 26. Sto 1995, Almqvist & Wiksell 372 pp. 91-22-01638-4.

4548 **Wünsch, Hans-Michael** Der paulinische Brief als kommunikative Handlung: dargestellt an 2 Kor 1-9. Diss. Marburg 1995, ᴰ*Harnisch, W.* [ThRv 92/2,XII].

G3.3 Pauli theologia.

4549 *Aletti, Jean-Noël* Sagesse et mystère chez Paul: réflexions sur le rapprochement de deux champs lexicographiques. 1995 ⇒117. La sagesse biblique. 357-384.

4550 *Atkinson, W.* Pentecostal responses to DUNN's "baptism in the Holy Spirit": Pauline literature. JPentec 7 (1995) 49-72.

4551 **Barrett, Charles Kingsley** Paul: an introduction to his thought. 1994 ⇒10,5618. RTheol. 98 (1995) 140-141 (*Barclay, John*); Reviews in Religion and Theology (1995/2) 68-69 (*Carleton Paget, James*).

4552 *Barrett, Charles Kingsley* Paul: missionary and theologian. 1995 <1989> ⇒39. Jesus and the word. 149-162.

4553 *Becker, Jürgen* Erwägungen zur apokalyptischen Tradition in der paulinischen Theologie. 1995 <1970> ⇒5. FBECKER J., 48-64.

4554 **Bendemann, Reinhard von** Heinrich SCHLIER: eine kritische Analyse seiner Interpretation paulinischer Theologie. Diss. DSchrage, BEvTh 115. Gütersloh 1995, Kaiser 492 pp. DM168/ÖS1243. 3-579-02004-8. RSNTU.A 20 (1995) 251-252 (*Fuchs, A.*).

4555 **Capes, David B.** OT Yahweh texts in Paul's christology. 1992 ⇒8,6070... 10,5624. RThLZ 120 (1995) 880-883 (*Hübner, Hans*).

4556 **Christiansen, Ellen Juhl** The covenant in Judaism and Paul: a study of ritual boundaries as identity markers. AGJU 27. Lei 1995, Brill x; 396 pp. *f*130/$84. 90-04-10333-3 [NTAb 40,152].

4557 *Combet-Galland, Corina* Un héritage en travail: Paul et la confession de foi. FV 94/2 (1995) 15-25.

4558 **Cousar, Charles B.** A theology of the cross. 1990 ⇒6,6094... 10,5628. RCThMi 22 (1995) 218-219 (*Linss, Wilhelm C.*).

4559 **Cuvillier, E.** La tradition paulinienne: éléments bibliographiques. FV 94 (1995) 111-114.

4560 **Davis, Christopher A.** The structure of Paul's theology: "the truth which is the Gospel". Diss. ·Union Theological Seminary, DAchtemeier, P.J., Lewiston, NY 1995, Mellen vii; 437 pp. $110. 0-7734-2422-9 [NTAb 40,354].

4561 *De Lorenzi, Lorenzo* Paolo insegna la morte. PSV 32 (1995) 159-202.

4562 *Dunn, James D.G.* In quest of Paul's theology: retrospect and prospect. SBL.SP 34 (1995) 704-721.

4563 **Eastman, Bradley J.** The significance of grace in the letters of Paul. Diss. McMaster 1995, DWesterholm, Stephen [SR 24 (1995) 521].

4564 **Ettorri, Giuseppe** La liturgia dell'evangelo: annuncio, carità, culto in Paolo apostolo. Biblica. R 1995, Dehoniane 278 pp. 88-396-0554-1.

4565 **Fitzmyer, Joseph A.** According to Paul: studies in the theology of the apostle. 1993 ⇒9,196. RScrB 25/1 (1995) 37-39 (*Swain, Lionel*); Interp. 49 (1995) 212-214 (*Soards, Marion, L.*).

4566 *Guijarro Oporto, Santiago* "He sido conquistado por Cristo Jesús": la experiencia pascual como clave de la vida, de la teología y de la misión de Pablo. ResB 5 (1995) 55-63.

4567 **Hall, Sydney G.** Christian anti-Semitism and Paul's theology. 1993 ⇒9,5848; 10,10086. RCritRR 7 (1994) 194-196 (*Siker, Jeffrey S.*); Neotest. 29 (1995) 420-421 (*Miller, J.*).

4568 *Harnack, Adolf von* The Old Testament in the Pauline letters and in the Pauline churches. 1995 <1928> ⇒110. Understanding Paul's ethics. 27-49.

4569 **Horn, Friedrich-Wilhelm** Das Angeld des Geistes: Studien zur paulinischen Pneumatologie. FRLANT 154. 1992 ⇒8,6078... 10,5634. ᴿThLZ 120 (1995) 147-150 (*Vollenweider, Samuel*).

4570 *Horrell, David* The development of theological ideology in Pauline christianity: a structuration theory perspective. 1995 ⇒80. Modelling early christianity. 224-236.

4571 **Hotze, Gerharde** Paradoxien bei Paulus: Untersuchungen zu einer elementaren Denkform in seiner Theologie. Diss. Müns 1995, ᴰ*Kertelge* [ThRv 92/2,XIII].

4572 *Hübner, Hans* Pauli theologiae proprium < 1980 > 40-68;

4573 Rechtfertigung und Sühne bei Paulus: eine hermeneutische und theologische Besinnung < 1993 > 272-285. ⇒52 Biblische Theologie.

4574 **Kertelge, Karl** Grundthemen. 1991 ⇒7,217*... 10,5638. ᴿThLZ 120 (1995) 795-799 (*Hübner, Hans*).

4575 **Kim, Soo-Young David** Paul's eschatology in Acts in view of his epistles. Diss. Dallas 1995, 269 pp. AAC 9531278; DAI-A 56/5,p.1829.

4576 *Lampe, Peter* Identification with Christ: a psychological view of Pauline theology. 1995 ⇒14. ᶠHARTMAN L., 931-943.

4577 *Mainville, Odette* La justification par la foi et la loi dans les études pauliniennes contemporaines. 1995 ⇒84. De bien des manières. 365-390.

4578 **Maleparampil, Joseph** The 'Trinitarian' formulae in St. Paul: an exegetical investigation into the meaning and function of those Pauline sayings which compositely make mention of God, Christ and the Holy Spirit. Diss. Pont. Istituto Biblico 1995, ᴰ*Grech, Prosper*, EHS.T 546. Fra 1995, Lang 299 pp. 3-631-49431-9.

4579 *Meißner, Stefan* Paulinische Soteriologie und die ʾAqedat Jitzchaq. Alan Franklin Segal zum 50. Geburtstag. Jud. 51/1 (1995) 33-49 [Gen 22].

4580 *Meyer, Paul W.* Pauline theology: some thoughts for a pause in its pursuit. SBL.SP 34 (1995) 688-703.

4581 **Mijoga, Hilary Bernard P.** The Pauline notion of 'deeds of the law'. Diss. Catholic University of America 1995, 244 pp. ᴰ*Fitzmyer, Joseph A.*, DAI-A 56/4,p.1394.

4582 **Misztal, Wojciech** Dans le Christ Jésus Seigneur: les formules du type 'en Christô' chez St Paul et sa vision de la vie des chrétiens comme vie dans le Christ. Diss. R 1995, Pont. Universitas Gregoriana no. 4138, 78 pp. [excerpt], ᴰ*Martinez, Ernest R.*

4583 **Pate, C.M.** The end of the age has come: the theology of Paul. GR 1995, Zondervan 256 pp. $18. 0-310-38301-3 [NTAb 40,359].

4584 *Penna, Romano* Apocalittica enochica in s. Paolo: il concetto di peccato. RStB 7/2 (1995) 61-84.

4585 **Pitta, Antonio** Sinossi paolina. 1994 ⇒10,5644. ᴿAsp. 42 (1995) 288-290 (*Scippa, V.*); RdT 36 (1995) 501-504 (*Franco, Ettore*); RTL 26 (1995) 356 (*Ponthot, J.*); Ter. 46 (1995) 660-661 (*Pasquetto, Virgilio*); LASBF 45 (1995) 630-633 (*Busceni, Alfio Marcello*).

4586 *Reid, D.G.* Did Paul have a theology?: reconstructing the story that unites the apostle's letters. ChrTo 39/5 (1995) 18-22 [NTAb 40,60].

4587 **Reynier, Chantal** L'évangile du ressuscité: une lecture de Paul. LiBi 105. P/Saint-Laurent 1995, Cerf/Fides 304 pp. FF120/Can$33. 2-204-05209-4/2-7621-1846-8 [NTAb 40,359].

4588 **Scott, James M.** Adoption as sons of God... υἱοθεσία in the Pauline corpus. WUNT 2/48. 1992 ⇒7,5240... 10,5647. REvQ 67 (1995) 171-174 (*Proctor, John*); RB 102 (1995) 305-306 (*Murphy-O'Connor, Jerome*).

4589 *Söding, Thomas* Heilige Schriften für Israel und die Kirche: die Sicht des "Alten Testamentes" bei Paulus. MThZ 46 (1995) 159-181.

4590 *Spinetoli, Ortensio da* Il creato, l'uomo e la donna negli scritti paolini. 1995 ⇒267. Dizionario di spiritualità biblico-patristica 10, 121-139.

4591 *Tarocchi, Stefano* Il Dio longanime: la longanimità nell'epistolario paolino. 1993 ⇒9,5860; 10,7021. RAsp. 42/1 (1995) 118-119 (*Rolla, A.*); CBQ 57 (1995) 610-611 (*Fiore, Benjamin*).

4592 **Tjatra, Puspitha** Salvation according to Hindu Dharma on Bali and salvation according to Paul. **Indonesian.** Diss. Jakarta 1995, SEAGSTh [Exchange 25/1,71—*Hoekema, Alle*].

4593 *Vanni, Ugo* La creazione in Paolo: una prospettiva di teologia biblica. RdT 36 (1995) 285-325.

4594 *Vidal García, Senén* El evangelio de Pablo: aspectos de la teología paulina. ResB 5 (1995) 15-26.

4595 *Villegas M., Beltrán* Raíces pastorales de la pneumatología paulina. TyV 36/1-2 (1995) 21-30.

4596 **Witherington III, Ben** Paul's narrative thought world. 1994 ⇒10,5657. RTS 56 (1995) 358-360 (*Fiore, Benjamin*); CTJ 30 (1995) 618-623 (*DeBoer, Willis P.*).

G3.4 *Pauli stylus et modus operandi* — Paul's image.

4597 **Aageson, James W.** Written also for our sake: Paul and the art of biblical interpretation. 1993 ⇒9,5864; 10,5658. RCritRR 7 (1994) 135-138 (*Grieb, A. Katherine*); CTJ 30 (1995) 506-509 (*DeBoer, Willis P.*).

4598 **Detering, Hermann** Der gefälschte Paulus: das Urchristentum im Zwielicht. Dü 1995, Patmos 288 pp. DM32.80. 3-491-77969-3. RBiKi 50 (1995) 190 (*Beilner, Wolfgang*).

4599 *Dunn, Peter W.* L'image de Paul dans les "Actes de Paul". FV 94/2 (1995) 75-85.

4600 **Elliott, Neil** Liberating Paul: the justice of God and the politics of the Apostle. BiSe 27. Shf 1995, Academic (US: Orbis) 312 pp. £12.50/$18.50. 1-85075-529-9.

4601 EEngberg-Pedersen, Troels Paul in his Hellenistic context. E/Mp 1995, Clark/Fortress xxiv; 341 pp. $29. 0-8006-2648-6 [NTAb 40,355].

4602 **Glad, Clarence E.** Paul and Philodemus: adaptability in Epicurean and early Christian psychagogy. NT.S 81. Lei 1995, Brill xiv; 414 pp. $117.25. 90-04-10067-9 [Rom 14,1-15,14; 8-10].

4603 *Grappe, Christian* De quelques images de Paul et de la manière dont elles se déploient aux cours des deux premiers siècles. FV 94/2 (1995) 49-59.

4604 **Jewett, Robert** Saint Paul at the movies 1993 ⇒9,5871; 10,5666.
      ᴿCritRR 8 (1995) 91-92 (*Banks, Robert*).
      Lentz, John Clayton Jr. Luke's portrait of Paul ⇒3893.
4605 *Mitchell, Margaret M.* The archetypal image: John
      CHRYSOSTOM's portraits of Paul. JR 75/1 (1995) 15-43.
4606 **Orr, Mary Cathryn** Paul as persecutor of the church:
      autobiography as apocalyptic paradigm. Virginia 1995, 199 pp.
      AAC 9600426; DAI-A 56/9,p.3618.
4607 *Willert, Niels* The catalogues of hardships in the Pauline cor-
      respondence: background and function. 1995 ⇒67. The New Testa-
      ment. 217-243.

G3.5 Apostolus Gentium [⇒G4.6, Israel et Lex / Jews & Law].

4608 *Adam, A.K.* Of the Jews, to the Gentiles. AThR 77 (1995) 232-
      233.
4609 *Barclay, John M.G.* Paul among diaspora Jews: anomaly or
      apostate?. JSNT 60 (1995) 89-120.
4610 *Barrett, Charles K.* The gentile mission as an eschatological
      phenomenon. 1995 <1988> ⇒39. Jesus and the word. 185-193.
4611 **Becker, Jürgen** Paul: apostle to the gentiles. 1993 ⇒9,5881;
      10,5676. ᴿInterp. 49 (1995) 186-189 (*Roetzel, Calvin, J.*); CBQ 57
      (1995) 169-170 (*Willis, Wendell*).
4612 **Becker, Jürgen** Paul: l'apôtre des nations. ᵀ*Hoffmann, Joseph*,
      Théologies bibliques. P/Montréal 1995, Cerf/Médiaspaul 571 pp.
      FF249. 2-204-04833-X/2-89420-290-3 [RB 102,634].
4613 *Berkey, Robert F.* The New Testament and mission. Theology for
      Our Times 2 (1995) 12-16 [ThIK 17,39].
4614 *Best, Ernest* Paul's apostolic authority-? 1995 <1986> ⇒105. The
      Pauline writings. 13-34.
4615 *Boccaccini, Gabriele* Paolo l'ebreo. VM 49 (1995) 11-22.
4616 **Boyarin, Daniel** A radical Jew. 1994 ⇒10,5677. ᴿThTo 52 (1995)
      290-292 (*Gaventa, Beverly Roberts*).
4617 *Buetubela, Balembo* La notion d'apôtre selon saint Paul. RAT 19
      (1995) 5-19.
4618 **Carrillo Alday, Salvador** Pablo, apóstol de Cristo. Estudios
      Bíblicos 13. México 1995, Dabar 128 pp.
4619 ᴱ**Evans, Craig A.; Sanders, James A.** Paul and the Scriptures of
      Israel. JSNT.S 83. 1993 ⇒10,5679. ᴿThLZ 120 (1995) 999-1001
      (*Koch, Dietrich-Alex*).
4620 *Joseph, M.J.* Affirming the power of life: Pauline perspectives on
      mission in context. Theology for Our Times 2 (1995) 33-42 [ThIK
      17,39].
4621 **Niebuhr, Karl-Wilhelm** Heidenapostel. 1992. ⇒8,6142...
      10,5691. ᴿLouvSt 20 (1995) 82-83 (*Collins, Raymond F.*).
4622 **O'Brien, P.T.** Gospel and mission in the writings of Paul: an
      exegetical and theological analysis. GR/Carlisle 1995,
      Eerdmans/Paternoster xiv; 161 pp. £10. 0-85364-614-7 [EvQ
      69,284].
4623 *Reiser, Marius* Hat Paulus Heiden bekehrt? BZ 39 (1995) 76-91
      [Acts 9,15].
      Stendahl, Krister Paolo tra ebrei e pagani: e altri saggi. ⇒58.

4624 **Tomić, C.** Začetki Cerkva—Pavel, apostol narodov. Zagreb 1995, Provincijalat hrvaških frančiškanov konventualcev 352 pp.

G3.6 *Pauli fundamentum* philosophicum [⇒G4.3] *et* morale.

4625 *Barrett, Charles K.* Paul and the introspective conscience. JSNT.S 105. 1995 ⇒2. [F]ATKINSON J., 36-48.

4626 *Boyarin, Daniel* Body politic among the brides of Christ: Paul and the origins of christian sexual renunciation. Asceticism. [E]**Wimbush, Vincent L.; Valantasis, Richard.** Ox 1995, OUP xxxiii; 638 pp. 0-19-508535-3. 459-478.

4627 *Bultmann, Rudolf* The problem of ethics in Paul. 1995 <1924> ⇒110. Understanding Paul's ethics. 195-216.

4628 **Campe, Ernest R.** Measuring Paul's emphasis on ethics. Diss. Regent 1995, 100 pp. MAI 33/4,p.1100.

4629 *Grogan, Geoffrey W.* The basis of Paul's ethics in his kerygmatic theology. SBET 13 (1995) 129-147.

4630 *Jaquette, J.L.* Foundational convictions, ethical instruction and theologising in Paul. Neotest. 29 (1995) 231-252.

4631 *Judge, Edwin A.* Interpeting New Testament ideas. 1995 <1961> ⇒110. Understanding Paul's ethics. 75-84.

4632 **Keener, Craig S.** Paul, women and wives. 1992 ⇒8,9054... 10,5700. [R]CritRR 7 (1994) 541-542 (*Thurston, Bonnie*); RevBib 57 (1995) 124-125 (*Levoratti, A.J.*).

4633 *Kemdirim, Protus O.* Background influence to Paul's thought. NJT 9 (1995) 80-90 [ThIK 17,22].

4634 **Laato, Timo** Paul and Judaism: an anthropological approach. [T]*McElwain, T.*, SFSHJ 115. Atlanta, GA 1995, Scholars vii; 285 pp. $75. 0-7885-0100-3.

4635 *Liu, Ching-Qian* WANG YANG MING and St. Paul on conscience. **Chinese.** CTUF 103 (1995) 97-109 [ThIK 17,28].

4636 *Lohse, Eduard* The church in everyday life. 1995 <1980>. ⇒110. Understanding Paul's ethics. 251-265.

4637 *Lührmann, Dieter* Paul and the pharisaic tradition. 1995 <1989> ⇒105. The Pauline writings. 35-54.

4638 **Maccoby, Hyam** Paul and Hellenism. 1991 ⇒7,5132; 8,6152. [R]JQR 86/1-2 (1995) 230-232 (*Levine, Amy-Jill*).

4639 **Malherbe, Abraham J.** Paul and the popular philosophers. 1989 ⇒5,5768... 10,5701. [R]HeyJ 36 (1995) 212-213 (*Way, David*).

4640 **Neusner, Jacob** Children of the flesh, children of the promise: a rabbi talks with Paul. Cleveland 1995, Pilgrim xxvi; 119 pp. $15. 0-8298-1026-9 [NTAb 40,180].

4641 **O'Toole, Robert F.** Chi è cristiano?: saggio sull'etica paolina. Leumann 1995, LDC 134 pp. L12.000.

4642 *Odell-Scott, D.W.* Paul's skeptical critique of a primitive Christian metaphysical theology. Encounter 56 (1995) 127-146 [1 Cor 8,1-6; NTAb 40,64].

4643 *Parsons, Michael* Being precedes act: indicative and imperative in Paul's writing. 1995 <1988> ⇒110. Understanding Paul's ethics. 217-247.

4644 *Pastor-Ramos, Federico* Ética paulina y actualidad de Pablo. ResB 5 (1995) 45-53.

4645   *Pierard, Richard V.* Natural law or God's law?: a historian's perspective. ExAu 11 (1995) 129-144.
        [E]**Rosner, Brian S.** Understanding Paul's ethics. ⇒110.
4646   *Rosner, Brian S.* 'That pattern of teaching': issues and essays in Pauline ethics. 1995 ⇒110. Understanding Paul's ethics. 1-23.
4647   *Schnabel, Eckhard, J.* How Paul developed his ethics. 1995 <1992> ⇒110. Understanding Paul's ethics. 267-297.
4648   *Schrage, Wolfgang* The formal ethical interpretation of Pauline paraenesis. 1995 <1960> ⇒110. Understanding Paul's ethics. 301-335.
4649   *Seeberg, Alfred* Moral teaching: the existence and contents of 'the ways'. 1995 <1903> ⇒110. Understanding Paul's ethics. 155-175.
4650   *Taylor, Robert D.; Ricci, Ronald J.* Three biblical models of liberty and some representative laws. ExAu 11 (1995) 111-127.
4651   *Thielman, Frank* Law and liberty in the ethics of Paul. ExAu 11 (1995) 63-75.
4652   *Vanni, Ugo* La coscienza (ευνείδησις sic [συνείδησις]): una novità antropologico-teologica di Paolo? Atti del III Simposio. 1995 ⇒138. 5-25.
4653   **Warne, Graham John** Hebrew perspectives on the human person in the Hellenistic era: Philo and Paul. Mellen Biblical Press 35. Lewiston, NY 1995, Mellen xi; 291 pp. 0-7734-2420-2.
4654   *Wuellner, Wilhelm* Der vorchristliche Paulus und die Rhetorik. 1995 ⇒33. [F]Thoma C., 133-165.

G3.7 *Pauli* communitates *et* spiritualitas.

4655   *Asensio, Felix* Pablo, maestro y modelo de oración. Burg. 36 (1995) 131-158.
4656   *Astolfo, A.S.* La paternidad espiritual del apóstol según san Pablo. PaiC. 21 (1995) 28-43 [Strom. 52,346].
4657   **Bentoglio, Gabriele** Apertura e disponibilità: l'accoglienza nell'epistolario paolino. Tesi Gregoriana, Teologia 2. R 1995, Pont. Universitas Gregoriana 376 pp. L36.000. 88-7652-686-2.
4658   *Bruni, G.* "Conformi all'imagine del Figlio". Servitium 99-100 (1995) 5-9.
4659   *Cranfield, C.E.* Paul's teaching on sanctification. RefR(H) 48 (1995) 217ff [ZID 21,559].
4660   *De Lorenzi, Lorenzo* Paolo: comunione non è soltanto koinonia. PSV 31 (1995) 147-177.
4661   *Destro, Adriana; Pesce, Mauro* La ekklesía di fronte a 'quelli di fuori'. Atti del III Simposio. 1995 ⇒138. 87-105.
4662   *Fabris, Rinaldo* La koinonia in San Paolo. PSV 31 (1995) 135-145.
4663   *Fatum, Lone* Image of God and glory of man: women in the Pauline congregations. The image of God: gender models in Judaeo-christian tradition. [E]**Borresen, Kari Elisabeth**. Mp 1995, Fortress. 50-133.
4664   **Gianantoni, Luigi** La paternità apostolica di Paolo. 1993 ⇒9,5906. [R]CivCatt 146 (1995) 619-620 (*Scaiola, D.*); EThL 71 (1995) 233-234 (*Verheyden, J.*).

4665 *Gruson, Philippe* Les églises de Paul. DosB 60 (1995) 6-7.

4666 *Holtz, Traugott* The question of the content of Paul's instructions. 1995 <1981> ⇒110. Understanding Paul's ethics. 51-71.

4667 *Lincoln, Andrew T.* Liberation from the powers: supernatural spirits or societal structures? JSOT.S 200. 1995 ⇒23. FROGERSON J., 335-354.

4668 **MacDonald, Margaret** Las comunidades paulinas. 1994 ⇒10,5711. RIter 6 (1995) 143-144 (*Wyssenbach, Jean Pierre*); CTom 122 (1995) 419-421 (*Osácar, Juan Huarte*); Lumen 44 (1995) 515-517 (*Arróniz, José Manuel*).

4669 *Mourlon Beernaert, P.* Les collaboratrices de saint Paul: annonce de la parole et labeur apostolique. LV 40 (1995) 169-183 [NTAb 40,60].

4670 **Pesce, Mauro** Le due fasi della predicazione di Paolo: dall'evangelizzazione alla guida delle comunità. 1994 ⇒10,5712. RRivBib 43 (1995) 551-552 (*Penna, Romano*).

4671 *Pitta, Antonio* Paraenesis and kerygma in the letters of St. Paul. G. DBM 14 (1995) 65-84.

4672 **Polaski, Sandra Hack** Reading power relations: an assessment of Paul's authority. Diss. Duke 1995, 231 pp. D*Hays, Richard B.*, AAC 9612472; DAI-A 56/12,p.4820.

4673 *Richard, Pablo* A prática de Paulo: suas opções fundamentais. Ribla 20 (1995) 92-104 [ThIK 17,59].

4674 *Riches, John* Ni juif ni grec. 1995: Conc(F) 257,49-59; Conc(D) 31,26-32.

4675 *Salvador García, Miguel* Las comunidades paulinas y su influencia en la configuración del cristianismo primitivo. ResB 5 (1995) 37-44.

4676 **Schmeller, Thomas K.** Hierarchie und Egalität: eine sozialgeschichtliche Untersuchung paulinischer Gemeinden und griechisch-römischer Vereine. SBS 162. Stu 1995, Katholisches Bibelwerk 120 pp. DM39.80. 3-460-04621-X.

4677 *Vassiliadis, Petros* The social implications of St. Paul's theology. Atti del III Simposio. 1995 ⇒138. 63-74.

4678 **Venetz, Hermann-Josef; Bieberstein, Sabine** Im Bannkreis des Paulus: Hannah und Rufus berichten aus seinen Gemeinden. Wü 1995, Echter 368 pp. DM58. 3-429-01674-6. ROrien. 59 (1995) 225-227 (*Kosch, Daniel*).

4679 **Walter, Matthias** Gemeinde als Leib bei Paulus unter Berücksichtigung antik-paganer Vergleichstexte. Diss. Heidelberg 1994-5, D*Theißen* [ThRv 92/2,X].

G3.8 *Pauli receptio,* history of research

4680 **Beker, J. Christiaan** Heirs of Paul. 1991 ⇒7,5102... 10,5717. ABR 43 (1995) 89-90 (*Watson, Nigel M.*).

4681 **Fabris, Rinaldo** La tradizione paolina. La Bibbia nella storia 12. Bo 1995, Dehoniane 293 pp. L36.000. 88-10-40261-8.

4682 EFeld, **Helmut** Commentarii in Pauli epistolas ad Gal, Eph, Phil, Col. CALVINI opera 16. 1992 ⇒8,6187. RZKG 106 (1995) 286-287 (*Strohm, Christoph*).

4683 *Horn, Friedrich Wilhelm* Paulusforschung. BZNW 75. 1995 ⇒30. FSTRECKER G., 30-59.

4684 *Neudorfer, Heinz-Werner* Anmerkungen zur neueren Tübinger Paulusforschung. JETh 9 (1995) 62-80.

G3.9 *Themata particularia de Paulo*, details

4685 *Adams, Doug* Paul as humorist. BiTod 33 (1995) 84-87.
4686 **Andrews, Keith Stewart** How christians are to understand the Pauline phrase 'in Christ'. Diss. Regent 1995, 121 pp. MAI 33/6,p.1686.
4687 *Barrett, Charles K.* Pauline controversies in the post-Pauline period. 1995 <1974> ⇒39. Jesus and the word. 195-212.
4688 *Burke, Trevor J.* The characteristics of Paul's adoptive-sonship (HUIOTHESIA) motif. IBSt 17 (1995) 62-74.
4689 *De Lorenzi, Lorenzo* Paolo insegna la morte. PSV 32 (1995) 159-202.
4690 *Di Porto, Bruno* Il pensiero di Paolo sulla giustizia: un ebreo di oggi e Paolo di Tarso. VM 49 (1995) 23-50.
4691 **Hamerton-Kelly, Robert G.** Sacred violence: Paul's hermeneutic of the cross. 1992 ⇒9,5928. RCritRR 7 (1994) 196-198 (*Cousar, Charles B.*).
4692 **Hooker, Morna D.** From Adam to Christ: essays on Paul. 1990 ⇒6,249... 8,6200. RThLZ 120 (1995) 795-799 (*Hübner, Hans*).
4693 *Hurth, Elisabeth* Annäherungen und Verzeichnungen: der Apostel Paulus als Romanfigur. HerKorr 49 (1995) 380-385.
4694 *Jonge, M. De* Light on Paul from the Testaments of the Twelve Patriarchs? 1995 ⇒20. FMEEKS W., 100-115.
4695 *Mara, G.M.* [Maria Grazia] Note sul De laudibus S. Pauli di Giovanni CRISOSTOMO. Atti del III Simposio. 1995 ⇒138. 163-169.
4696 *Mattioli, Anselmo* La sorridente ironia di Paolo: frasi e expressioni argute negli Atti e nelle lettere. Ter. 46 (1995) 367-411.
4697 *Milazzo, V.* "Etsi imperitus sermone ...": GIROLAMO e i solecismi di Paolo nei commentari alle epistole paoline. ASEs 12 (1995) 261-277.
4698 **Mills, Kevin** Justifying language: Paul and contemporary literary theory. Studies in Literature and Religion. NY 1995, St. Martin's x; 207 pp. $50. 0-312-12989-0 [NTAb 41,160].
4699 *Penna, Romano* Le notizie di DIONE di Prusa su Tarso e il loro interesse per le lettere di S.Paolo. Atti del III Simposio. 1995 ⇒138. 119-136.
4700 *Pérez Fernández, Miguel* The Aqedah in Paul [Resp. *Taylor, Justin*]. 1995 ⇒448. The sacrifice of Isaac. 81-94.
4701 *Pérez Gordo, Angel* La cruz interpretada por S.Pablo. Burg. 36 (1995) 9-60.
4702 *Perrone, Lorenzo* Motivi paolini nell'epistolario di GEROLAMO. Atti del III Simposio. 1995 ⇒138. 171-201.
4703 **Sass, Gerhard** Leben aus den Verheißungen: traditionsgeschichtliche und biblisch-theologische Untersuchungen zur Rede von Gottes Verheißungen im Frühjudentum und beim Apostel Paulus. FRLANT 164. Gö 1995, Vandenhoeck & Ruprecht 579 pp. 3-525-53846-4.
4704 **Selvaraj, Joseph Michael** Pauline texts on slavery: ((1 Cor 7:21-24; Gal 3:28; Phlm 8-20). Diss. R 1995, Pont. Universitas

Urbaniana xii; 82 pp. [excerpt].
4705 *Thickstun, M.O.* Writing the spirit: Margaret FELL's feminist critique of Pauline theology. JAAR 63 (1995) 269-279.
4706 *Vaughan, W.* The phenomenology of time in Pauline epistles. Encounter 56 (1995) 147-173 [NTAb 40,61].
4707 *Yarbrough, O. Larry* Parents and children in the letters of Paul. 1995 ⇒20. FMEEKS W., 126-141.

G4 Ad Romanos .1 *Textus, commentarii.*

4708 *Bammel, Caroline P.* RUFINUS' translation of ORIGEN's commentary on Romans and the Pelagian controversy. 1995 ⇒38. Tradition. 131-142.
4709 **Bartlett, David Lyon** Romans. Westminster Bible Companion. LVL 1995, Westminster x; 146 pp. 0-664-25254-0.
4710 *Cocchini, Francesca* Note sul commentario di ORIGENE alla lettera ai Romani. 1995 ⇒74. Ai Romani. 11-20.
4711 *Cocchini, Francesca* ORIGENE e TEODORETO sulla lettera ai Romani: due interpretazioni a confronto. Atti del III Simposio. 1995 ⇒138. 153-161.
4712 **Edwards, James R.** Romans. 1992 ⇒7,5254... 10,5735. RCTJ 30 (1995) 224-228 (*DeBoer, Willis P.*).
4713 **Fitzmyer, Joseph A.** Romans. AncB 33. 1993 ⇒9,5945; 10,5736. RScrB 25/1 (1995) 39-41 (*Swain, Lionel*); ER 47 (1995) 232-233 (*Ziesler, John*); Gr. 76 (1995) 743-757 (*Lubomirski, Mieczysław*); Bib. 76 (1995) 434-436 (*Lambrecht, Jan*); JBL 114 (1995) 745-747 (*Jewett, Robert*); NT 37 (1995) 202-204 (*Rodgers, P.R.*); CBQ 57 (1995) 591-592 (*Stowers, Stanley K.*); VJTR 591 (1995) 766-767 (*Meagher, P.M.*); Interp. 49 (1995) 416-420 (*Morris, Leon*).
4714 **Kaiser, Bernhard** LUTHER und die Auslegung des Römerbriefes: eine theologisch-geschichtliche Beurteilung. Biblia et Symbiotica 9. Bonn 1995, Verlag für Kultur und Wissenschaft (Diss. Stellenbosch 1988) 334 pp. DM50. 3-926105-35-6 [NThAR 1996/3,55].
4715 **Leenhardt, Franz J.** L'épître de Saint Paul aux romains. Commentaires du Nouveau Testament 2. Genève ³1995, Labor et Fides 253 pp. FF180. 2-8309-0784-1 <pb> [NTAb 40,357].
4716 *Mara, Maria Grazia* [7,14-25; 9] AGOSTINO e la lettera ai Romani. 1995 ⇒74. 21-32.
4717 **Morris, Leon** The epistle to the Romans. GR 1995, Eerdmans xii; 578 pp. 0-8028-3636-4.
4718 **Mounce, Robert H.** Romans. NAC 27. Nv 1995, Broadman & Holman 301 pp. $28. 0-8054-0127-X [OTA 18,668].
4719 *Pani, Giancarlo* L'eredità di AGOSTINO nella Römerbriefvorlesung di Martin LUTERO: la Expositio quarundam propositionum ex epistola ad Romanos. SMSR 61/1 (1995) 83-97.
4720 *Pani, Giancarlo* LUTERO e la lettera ai Romani. 1995 ⇒74. Ai Romani. 33-47.
4721 **Reller, Jobst** Mose BAR KEPHA und seine Paulinenauslegung nebst Edition und Übersetzung des Kommentars zum Römerbrief. 1994 ⇒10,5739. ROS 44 (1995) 219-221 (*Tamcke, Martin*).
4722 **Rolland, Philippe** À l'écoute de l'épître aux Romains. 1991 ⇒7,5265; 8,6229. REeT(O) 26 (1995) 115-116 (*Bonneau, Normand*).

4723   *Rostagno, Sergio* Etica e dogmatica nel commentario di Karl
       BARTH. 1995 ⇒74. Ai Romani. 49-65.
4724   **Schlatter, Adolf** Romans: the righteousness of God. ᵀ*Schatzmann,*
       S.S.; Stuhlmacher, P. <introd by>. Peabody, MA 1995
       <1935>, Hendrickson xxiv; 287 pp. $20. 0-943575-89-3 [NTAb
       40,360].
4725   **Schmidt-Lauber, Gabriele** LUTHERS Vorlesung über den
       Römerbrief 1515/16: ein Vergleich zwischen Luthers Manuskript
       und den studentischen Nachschriften. 1994 ⇒10,5740. ᴿThLZ 120
       (1995) 674-677 *(Burger, Christoph)*.
4726   *Sigurdson, Ola* Den mänsklige Gudens alteritet—en alternativ läsn-
       ing av Karl BARTHs Der Römerbrief: något om alteritets prob-
       lemet i den samtida diskussionen. SvTK 71 (1995) 119-127.
4727   **Stendahl, Krister** Final account: Paul's letter to the Romans.
       Pelikan, Jaroslav <foreword by>. Mp 1995, Fortress xii; 76 pp.
       $9. 0-8006-2922-1.

G4.2 *Ad Romanos: themata,* topics

4728   *Achtemeier, Paul J.* Unsearchable judgments and inscrutable ways:
       reflections on the discussion of Romans. SBL.SP 34 (1995) 521-
       534.
4729   *Aletti, Jean-Noël* Israele in Romani: una svolta nell'esegesi. 1995
       ⇒74. Ai Romani. 107-123.
4730   **Boers, Hendrikus** The justification of the gentiles: Paul's letters to
       the Galatians and the Romans. 1994 ⇒10,5748. ᴿBib. 76 (1995)
       437-438 *(Lambrecht, Jan)*; Neotest. 29 (1995) 431-433 *(Jaquette,*
       J.L.).
4731   *Corsani, Bruno* La legge, il peccato e la grazia nella lettera ai
       Romani. 1995 ⇒74. Ai Romani. 97-105.
4732   *Davidsen, Ole* The structural typology of Adam and Christ: some
       modal-semiotic comments on the basic narrative of the letter to the
       Romans. 1995 ⇒67. The New Testament. 244-262.
4733   ᴱ**Donfried, Karl P.** The Romans debate. 1991 ⇒7,298... 9,5959.
       ᴿCThMi 22 (1995) 219-220 *(Linss, Wilhelm C.)*.
4734   *Fitzmyer, Joseph A.* The epistle to the Romans and the lectionary.
       Liturgy [Chicago] 26/7 (1995) 4-7 [NTAb 40,254].
4735   **Fitzmyer, Joseph A.** Spiritual exercises based on Paul's epistle to
       the Romans. Mahwah 1995, Paulist iv; 235 pp. $15. 0-8091-3580-
       9 [NTAb 40,356].
4736   **Guerra, Anthony J.** Romans and the apologetic tradition: the pur-
       pose, genre and audience of Paul's letter. MSSNTS 81. C 1995,
       CUP xiii; 200 pp. £32/$55. 0-521-47126-5.
4737   ᴱ**Hay, David M.; Johnson, E. Elizabeth** Pauline theology 3:
       Romans. Mp 1995, Fortress xii; 354 pp. $35. 0-8006-2929-9 [TD
       44,82].
4738   *Kertelge, Karl* La giustificazione per la fede come messaggio della
       lettera ai Romani. 1995 ⇒74. Ai Romani. 87-96.
4739   *Kraege, Jean-Denis* LUTHER lecteur de l'épître aux Romains. FV
       94/2 (1995) 99-110.
4740   *Meyer, Paul W.* AUGUSTINE's the spirit and the letter as a read-
       ing of Paul's Romans. 1995 ⇒20. ᶠMEEKS W., 366-381.

4741 **Morgan, Robert** Romans. NT Guides. Shf 1995, Academic 164 pp. £6/$10. 1-85075-739-9.

4742 *Penna, Romano* Giudaismo, paganesimo e pseudo-paolinismo nella questione dei destinatari della lettera ai Romani. 1995 ⇒74. Ai Romani. 67-85.

4743 *Porter, Stanley E.* A newer perspective on Paul: Romans 1-8 through the eyes of literary analysis. JSOT.S 200. 1995 ⇒22. [F]ROGERSON J., 366-392.

4744 *Reid, Marty L.* Paul's rhetoric of mutuality: a rhetorical reading of Romans. SBL.SP 34 (1995) 117-139.

4745 **Schirrmacher, Thomas** Der Römerbrief: für Selbststudium und Gruppengespräche I-II. Neuhausen 1994, Hänssler 331 + 323 pp. DM80. 3-7751-1930-2. [R]JETh 9 (1995) 214-217 (*Haubeck, Wilfrid*).

4746 **Walters, James C.** Ethnic issues in Romans. 1993 ⇒9,5966. [R]CBQ 57 (1995) 612-614 (*Harrill, J. Albert*); CritRR 8 (1995) 319-320 (*Jewett, Robert*).

G4.3 *Naturalis cognitio Dei...peccatum originale,* **Rom 1-5.**

4747 **Batson, Howard Keith** The relevance of Romans 1 for the nature nurture debate regarding homosexuality. Diss. Baylor 1995, 294 pp. [D]*Sloan, Robert B.*, AAC 9535459; DAI-A 56/6,p.2278.

4748 **Moores, John D.** Wrestling with rationality in Paul: Romans 1-8 in a new perspective. MSSNTS 82. C 1995, CUP xvi; 210 pp. £32.50/$55. 0-521-47223-7.

4749 *Reid, M. L.* A consideration of the function of Rom 1:8-15 in light of Greco-Roman rhetoric. JETS 38 (1995) 181-191.

4750 *Dodd, Brian* Romans 1:17—a crux interpretum for the PISTIS CHRISTOU debate? JBL 114 (1995) 470-473.

4751 *Martin, Dale B.* Heterosexism and the interpretation of Romans 1:18-32. Bibl.Interp. 3 (1995) 332-355.

4752 *Szesnat, H.* In fear of androgyny: theological reflections on masculinity and sexism, male homosexuality and homophobia, Romans 1:24-27 and hermeneutics (a response to Alexander VENTER). JTSA 93 (1995) 32-50.

4753 *Davies, Margaret* New Testament ethics and ours: homosexuality and sexuality in Romans 1:26-27. Bibl.Interp. 3 (1995) 315-331.

4754 *Miller, James E.* The practices of Romans 1:26: homosexual or heterosexual? NT 37 (1995) 1-11.

4755 **Garlington, Don B.** [1,5] "The obedience of faith". 1991 ⇒7,5304... 10,5755. [R]Asp. 42/1 (1995) 119-120 (*Pitta, A.*); FgNT 85 (1995) 98-101 (*Mateos, Juan*).

4756 *Derrett, John Duncan M.* "You abominate false gods: but do you rob shrines?" (Rom 2.22B). 1995 <1994> ⇒45. Studies 6. 215-228.

4757 *Campbell, Douglas* A rhetorical suggestion concerning Romans 2. SBL.SP 34 (1995) 140-167.

4758 *Ito, Akio* Romans 2: a deuteronomistic reading. JSNT 59 (1995) 21-37.

4759 *Moyise, Steve* The catena of Romans 3:10-18. ET 106 (1995) 367-368.

4760 **Campbell, Douglas A.** The rhetoric of righteousness in Romans 3:21-26. 1992 ⇒8,6280... 10,5769. RSJTh 48 (1995) 114-115 (*De Boer, Martinus C.*).

4761 *Piper, John* The demonstration of the righteousness of God in Romans 3.25,26. 1995 <1980> ⇒105. The Pauline writings. 175-202.

4762 *Cranford, Michael* Abraham in Romans 4: the father of all who believe. NTS 41 (1995) 71-88.

4763 **Palmer, Michael** τί οὖν; the inferential question in Paul's letter to the Romans with a proposed reading of Romans 4.1. 1995 ⇒102. Discourse analysis. JSNT.S 113. 200-218.

4764 *Pyne, Robert A.* [4; Gal 3] The "seed," the spirit, and the blessing of Abraham. BS 152 (1995) 211-222.

4765 *Tobin, Thomas H.* What shall we say that Abraham found?: the controversy behind Romans 4. HThR 88 (1995) 437-452.

G4.4 *Redemptio cosmica:* **Rom 6-8.**

4766 *Espezel, A.* San IRENEO: el nuevo Adán y la nueva Eva. Communio 28 (1995) 71-80.

4767 **Maldamé, Jean-Michel** Cristo e il cosmo: cosmologia e teologia. CinB 1995, San Paolo 271 pp.

4768 *Engberg-Pedersen, Troels* Galatians in Romans 5-8 and Paul's construction of the identity of Christ believers. 1995 ⇒14. FHARTMAN L., 477-505.

4769 *Bieringer, Reimund* Aktive Hoffnung im Leiden: Gegenstand, Grund und Praxis der Hoffnung nach Röm 5,1-5. ThZ 51 (1995) 305-325.

4770 *Maartens, P.J.* The relevance of 'context' and 'interpretation' to the semiotic relations of Romans 5:1-11. Neotest. 29 (1995) 75-108.

4771 *Greer, Rowan A.* [5,12-20] Sinned we all in Adam's fall? 1995 ⇒18 FMEEKS W., 382-393.

4772 *Kudasiewicz, J.* Libertas a lege (R 7,1-4) in luce historiae exegeseos. **P.** ACra 27 (1995) 211-217.

4773 **Díaz-Rodelas, Juan Miguel** Pablo y la ley...Rom 7,7-8,4. 1994 ⇒10,5803. RSalm. 42 (1995) 143-147 (*Trevijano, Ramón*); EE 70 (1995) 403-405 (*Pastor-Ramos, Federico*); Burg. 36 (1995) 560-562 (*Otero Lazaro, Tomas*).

4774 *Lüdemann, Gerd* [7,7-25] Psychologische Exegese oder: die Bekehrung des Paulus und die Wende des Petrus in tiefenpsychologischer Perspektive. 1995 ⇒30. FSTRECKER G., BZNW 75. 91-111.

4775 *Bruckner, James K.* The creational context of law before Sinai: law and liberty in pre-Sinai narratives and Romans 7. ExAu 11 (1995) 91-110.

4776 *Ziesler, J. A.* The role of the tenth commandment in Romans 7. 1995 <1988> ⇒105. The Pauline writings. 137-152.

4777 **Baaij, Pieter K.** Paulus over Paulus...Rom. 7. 1993 ⇒10,5783. RKeTh 46 (1995) 85 (*Vos, J.S.*).

4778 *Schlosser, Jacques* L'espérance de la création (Rm 8,18-22). 1995 ⇒22. FRENAUD B., 325-343.

4779 *Bolt, John* The relation between creation and redemption in Romans 8:18-27. CTJ 30 (1995) 34-51.
4780 *Rodgers, Peter R.* The text of Romans 8:28. JThS 46 (1995) 547-550.
4781 *Maartens, P.J.* The vindication of the righteous in Romans 8:31-39: inference and relevance. HTS 51 (1995) 1046-1087 [NTAb 40,443].
4782 *Winfield, Flora* [8,38-39] 'For nothing can separate us from the love of Christ': who does belong to the body of Christ? ER 47 (1995) 364-372.

G4.6 *Israel et Lex;* The Law and the Jews, *Rom 9-11.*

4783 *Bovon, François* The new person and the law according to the apostle Paul. 1995 <1983> ⇒40. New Testament traditions. 15-25, 183-186 [RB 103,117].
      Bruckner, James K. The creational context of law before Sinai: law and liberty in pre-Sinai narratives and Romans 7. ⇒4775.
      Díaz-Rodelas, Juan Miguel Pablo y la ley...Rom 7,7-8,4. 1994 ⇒4773.
4784 *Dunn, James D.G.* Was Paul against the law?: the law in Galatians and Romans: a test-case of text in context. 1995 ⇒13 ᶠHARTMAN L., 455-475.
4785 *Hesselink, John* John CALVIN on the law and christian freedom. ExAu 11 (1995) 77-89.
4786 *Hübner, Hans* Das ganze und das eine Gesetz: zum Problemkreis Paulus und die Stoa. 1995 <1975> ⇒52. Biblische Theologie. 9-26.
4787 **Hübner, Hans** La legge in Paolo: contributo allo sviluppo della teologia paolina. ᵀ*Favero, Roberto*, StBi 109. Brescia 1995 [<1978> ⇒65s,6800], Paideia 300 pp. L48.000. 88-394-0532-2.
4788 *Hübner, Hans* Was heißt bei Paulus "Werke des Gesetzes"? 1995 <1985> ⇒52. Biblische Theologie. 166-174.
4789 *Roetzel, Calvin J.* Paul and the law: whence and whither?. CurResB 3 (1995) 249-275.
4790 **Rothgangel, Martin** Antisemitismus als religionspädagogische Herausforderung: eine Studie unter besonderer Berücksichtigung von Röm 9-11. Lernprozeß Christen Juden 10. Fr/B 1995, Herder xv; 367 pp. Diss. DM78. 3-451-22763-0. ᴿKatBl 120 (1995) 387-388 (*Hilger, Georg*).
4791 **Sänger, Dieter** Die Verkündigung des Gekreuzigten und Israel: Studien zum Verhältnis von Kirche und Israel bei Paulus und im frühen Christentum. WUNT 2/75. 1994 10,5810. ᴿThLZ 120 (1995) 523-527 (*Wilckens, Ulrich*); JETh 9 (1995) 244-249 (*Schnabel, Eckhard J.*).
4792 **Schreiner, Thomas R.** The law...a Pauline theology of law. 1993 ⇒9,6023; 10,5811. ᴿRTR 54 (1995) 35-36 (*Peterson, David*).
4793 *Snodgrass, Klyne* Spheres of influence: a possible solution to the problem of Paul and the law. 1995 <1988> ⇒105. The Pauline writings. 154-174.
4794 **Stowers, Stanley K.** A rereading of Romans: justice, Jews and gentiles. 1994 ⇒10,5812. ᴿReviews in Religion and Theology

(1995/3) 59-61 (*Campbell, William S.*); Theol. 98 (1995) 392-394 (*Nanos, Mark D.*); JThS 46 (1995) 646-651 (*Barclay, John M.G.*); Bibl.Interp. 3 (1995) 382-384 (*Taylor, N.H.*).

4795 **Thielman, Frank** Paul and the law. 1994 ⇒10,5813. ᴿTrinity Journal 16 (1995) 101-104 (*Schreiner, Thomas R.*).

4796 **Tomson, Peter J.** Paul and the Jewish law. 1990 ⇒7,5357... 10,5815. ᴿRB 102 (1995) 150-152 (*Murphy-O'Connor, Jerome*); REJ 154 (1995) 183-184 (*Ayoun, Richard*); NT 37 (1995) 190-192 (*Uchelen, N.A. van*).

4797 **Westerholm, Stephen** Israel's law and the Church's faith. 1988 ⇒4,5981... 10,5816. ᴿRStT 13-14 (1995) 102-103 (*Gaston, Lloyd*).

4798 **Wright, N.T.** Climax of the covenant. 1991 ⇒7,5364... 10,5818. ᴿBiTr 46 (1995) 353-354 (*Hodgson, Bob*).

4799 *Aageson, James W.* Typology, correspondence, and the application of scripture in Romans 9-11. 1995 <1987> ⇒105. The Pauline writings. 76-97.

4800 **Bell, Richard H.** Provoked to jealousy: the jealousy motif in Ro 9-11. WUNT 2/63. 1994 ⇒10,5801. ᴿJThS 46 (1995) 277-279 (*Byrne, Brendan*); ThLZ 120 (1995) 434-436 (*Landmesser, Christof*); CritRR 8 (1995) 170-173 (*Jewett, Robert*).

4801 *Fernández, Victor M.* Romanos 9-11: gracia y predestinación. Teol. 65 (1995) 5-49.

4802 *Johnson, E. Elizabeth* The function of apocalyptic and wisdom traditions in Romans 9-11: rethinking the questions. SBL.SP 34 (1995) 352-361.

4803 **Kreloff, Steven A.** God's plan for Israel: a study of Romans 9-11. Neptune, NJ 1995, Loizeaux 112 pp. 0-87213-468-7 [NThAR 1997/4,100].

4804 *Räisänen, Heikki* Romans 9-11 and the "history of early christian religion". 1995 ⇒13 ᶠHARTMAN L., 743-765.

4805 **Räisänen, Heikki** Jesus, Paul and Torah. JSNT.S 43. 1992 ⇒8,294; 9,6021. ᴿThLZ 120 (1995) 795-799 (*Hübner, Hans*).

4806 *Rodríguez Plaza, Braulio* ¿Cuál fue la posición de san Pablo sobre sus hermanos judíos que no aceptaron a Jesús?: el problema de Israel en Rom 9-11. Communio 17 (1995) 229-238.

4807 **Varone, François** Inouïes les voies de la miséricorde: avec un long regard sur Israël: essai sur Rm 9-11. Théologies. P/Montréal 1995, Cerf/Médiaspaul 178 pp. FF90. 2-204-050865/2-89420-272-5. ᴿEeV 105 (1995) 316-317 (*Monloubou, Louis*) [NTAb 40,160].

4808 *Glenny, W. Edward* The "people of God" in Romans 9:25-26. BS 152 (1995) 42-59.

4809 *Refoulé, François* Du bon et du mauvais usage des parallèles et des notes en Romains IX-XI. RevSR 69 (1995) 172-193.

4810 **Lloyd-Jones, David M.** Romans...ch.9. 1991 ⇒10,5818*. ᴿStudi di teologia 7 (1995) 75-76 (*Colombo, Paolo*).

4811 *Pattee, Stephen* [10,1-13] Paul's critique of Jewish exclusivity: a sociological and anthropological perspective. Soundings 78 (1995) 589-610.

4812 *Reinbold, Wolfgang* Israel und das Evangelium: zur Exegese von Römer 10,19-21. ZNW 86 (1995) 122-129.

4813 *Bekken, Jarle* [10] Paul's use of Deut 30,12-14 in Jewish context: some observations. 1995 ⇒67. The New Testament. 183-203.

4814 **Ryan, Judith M.** The faithfulness of God: Paul's prophetic response to Israel: an exegesis of Romans 11:1-36. Diss. Fordham 1995, 220 pp., ^D*Dillon, Richard J.*, AAC 9530041; DAI-A 56/5,p.1831.

4815 *Vanlaningham, M.G.* Paul's use of Elijah's Mt. Horeb experience in Rom 11:2-6. MastJ 6 (1995) 223-232 [NTAb 40,257].

4816 *Liebscher, S.* Romans: 11:25ff. EurJT 4/1 (1995) 23ff [ZID 21,412].

4817 **Carbone, Sandro Paolo** La misericordia universale di Dio in Rom 11,30-32. 1991 ⇒8,6338. ^RRivBib 43 (1995) 296-297 (*De Virgilio, Giuseppe*).

4818 *Beauchamp, Paul* Un parallèle problématique: Rm 11 et Ez 16. 1995 ⇒20 ^FRENAUD B., LeDiv 159. 137-154.

G4.8 Rom 12....

4819 *Heither, Theresia* ORIGENES' Exegese von Römerbrief 12,1-8 als Einführung in die Spiritalis observantia. 1995 ⇒126. Origeniana Sexta. BEThL 118. 515-522.

4820 *Cipriani, Settimio* Paolo e il 'potere politico' nella lettera ai Romani (13,1-7). 1995 ⇒74. Ai Romani. 125-137.

4821 *dal Covolo, Enrico* 'Subditi estote': Romani 13,1-7 nello studio dei rapporti tra la chiesa e l'impero del I secolo. Atti del III Simposio. 1995 ⇒138. 145-151.

4822 *Bielecki, Stanisław* Kairos chrześcijanina według Rz 13,11-14 [Christian's *kairos* according to Rom 13,11-14]. **P.** CoTh 65 (1995) 85-99.

4823 **Botha, Jan** Subject to whose authority?...Ro 13. 1994 ⇒10,5831. ^RNeotest. 29 (1995) 138-139 (*Tilborg, Sjef van*); CritRR 8 (1995) 178-180 (*Hultgren, Arland J.*).

4824 *Schenk, Wolfgang* Römer 13, "Obrigkeit" und "Kirche im Sozialismus". 1995 ⇒13 ^FHARTMAN L., 979-999.

4825 *Sampley, J. Paul* The weak and the strong: Paul's careful and crafty rhetorical strategy in Romans 14:1-15:13. 1995 ⇒18 ^FMEEKS W., 40-52.

4826 *Weiss, Herold* [14,5-6] Paul and the judging of days. ZNW 86 (1995) 137-153.

4827 *Thüsing, Wilhelm* Der Gott der Hoffnung (Röm 15,13): Verheißung und Erfüllung nach dem Apostel Paulus. 1995 <1969> ⇒60. Studien. WUNT 2/82. 87-99.

4828 *Moody, Dwight A.* [16,3-5] On the road again. RExp 92 (1995) 95-101.

G5.1 Epistulae ad Corinthios I, *textus, commentarii.*

4829 ^T**Barbaglio, Giuseppe** La prima lettera ai Corinzi: introduzione, versione, commento. Scritti delle origini cristiane 7. Bo 1995, EDB 931 pp. L112.000. 88-10-20607-X.

4830 **Beardslee, William A.** First Corinthians. 1994 ⇒10,5843. ^RCritRR 8 (1995) 168-169 (*Kuck, David W.*).

4831   ᵀᴱDonnelly, John Patrick Philip MELANCHTON: annotations on
       First Corinthians. Reformation Texts with Translation (1350-
       1650): Biblical Studies 2. Milwaukee 1995, Marquette University
       Press 178 pp. 0-87462-701-X [ChH 66,351].
4832   ᴱFröhlich, Uwe Epistula ad Corinthios I: Einleitung. VL 22/1.
       Fr/B 1995, Herder 80 pp. 3-451-00161-6.
4833   Fröhlich, Uwe Der 1. Korintherbrief. BVLI 39 (1995) 13-17.
4834   Hodge, Charles 1 and 2 Corinthians I-II. Crossway Classic Com-
       mentaries. Wheaton, IL 1995, Crossway [SBET 15,81—Boyd,
       A. C.].
4835   Kistemaker, Simon J. New Testament commentary: exposition of
       the first epistle to the Corinthians. GR 1993, Baker 649 pp. $23.
       ᴿCTJ 30 (1995) 519-525 (DeBoer, Willis P.).
4836   Oster, Richard E. 1 Corinthians. College Press NIV Commentary.
       Joplin, Miss. 1995, College 426 pp. 0-89900-633-7 [NThAR
       1997,261].
4837   Schrage, Wolfgang Der erste Brief an die Korinther: 1 Kor 6/12-
       11/16. EKK 7/2. Z/Neuk 1995, Benziger/Neuk 541 pp. DM140.
       3-545-23126-7/3-7887-1491-3 [NTAb 40,158].
4838   Snyder, Graydon F. First Corinthians. 1992 ⇒8,6360. ᴿCritRR 7
       (1994) 259-260 (Fee, Gordon D.).
4839   Witherington III, Ben Conflict and community in Corinth: a
       socio-rhetorical commentary on 1 and 2 Corinthians. GR/Carlisle
       1995, Eerdmans/Paternoster $60 (cl.)/$35 (pb). 0-8028-0144-7/0-
       85364-622-8 [NTAb 40,161].

            G5.2 1 & 1-2 ad Corinthios — themata, topics.

4840   Beilner, Wolfgang Gottes Kirche in Korinth. Vermittlung 60.
       Salzburg 1995 n.p. 119 pp.
4841   Bianchi, E. (al.) L'apostolo e la sua comunità: un "dialogo" con la
       prima lettera di Paolo ai cristiani di Corinto. Strumenti per il
       lavoro pastorale 8. Mi 1995, Áncora 176 pp. L18.000. 88-7610-
       541-7.
4842   Chow Kin-mau, John K. Patronage and power: studies on social
       networks in Corinth. JSNT.S 75. 1992 ⇒8,6364; 10,5851.
       ᴿCritRR 7 (1994) 163-165 (Marshall, Peter); TJT 11 (1995) 235-
       237 (Derrenbacker, Robert A.); ABR 43 (1995) 93-94 (Watson,
       Nigel M.); EvQ 67 (1995) 163-165 (Clarke, Andrew D.).
4843   Dunn, James D.G. 1 Corinthians. NT Guides. Shf 1995,
       Academic 118 pp. £7/$10. 1-85075-742-9.
4844   ᴱHay, David M. 1 and 2 Corinthians II. 1993 ⇒9,6053; 10,5856
       [Hays] Fortress xii; 300 pp. ᴿBTB 25 (1995) 94-95 (Watson,
       Duane F.); TJT 11 (1995) 244-246 (Racine, Jean-François); CBQ
       57 (1995) 843-845 (McDonald, Patricia M.).
4845   Hyldahl, Niels Paul and Hellenistic Judaism in Corinth. 1995 ⇒67.
       The New Testament. 204-216.
4846   Joubert, Stephan J. Managing the household: Paul as paterfamilias
       of the Christian household group in Corinth. 1995 ⇒80. Modelling
       early christianity. 213-223.
4847   Legarth, Peter V. The problems of a pluralistic society illustrated
       from the church in Corinth. Evangel 13/2 (1995) 39-44.

4848 *León Azcárate, Juan Luis de* El conflicto de los idolotitos en Corinto. RTLi 29 (1995) 201-219.

4849 **Martin, Dale B.** The Corinthian body. NHv/L 1995, Yale University Press xx; 330 pp. $35. 0-300-06205-2 [NTAb 40,155].

4850 *Mearns, Christopher L.* Early eschatological development in Paul: the evidence of 1 Corinthians. 1995 <1984> ⇒105. The Pauline writings. 203-219.

4851 *Miranda, Americo* L'"uomo spirituale" (πνευματικὸς ἄνθρωπος) nella Prima ai corinzi. RivBib 43 (1995) 485-519.

4852 **Nighswander, Daniel** Shame in 1 Corinthians. Diss. Toronto School of Theology, Emmanuel 1995, ᴰ*Richardson, Peter* [SR 24,521].

4853 **Nighswander, Daniel L.** Paul's use of shame as a sanction in 1 Corinthians. Diss. Victoria 1995, 255 pp. 0-612-02630-2. ᴰ*Richardson, Peter.* DAI-A 56/12,p.4820

4854 *Reinmuth, Eckart* Narratio und argumentatio—zur Auslegung der Jesus Christus-Geschichte im ersten Korintherbrief: ein Beitrag zur mimetischen Kompetenz des Paulus. ZThK 92 (1995) 13-27.

4855 *Ruiten, Jacques van* Juifs et Grecs... Conc(F) 257 (1995) 25-34 (P22-32) [1 Co 1].

4856 *Sterling, Gregory E.* "Wisdom among the perfect:" creation traditions in Alexandrian Judaism and Corinthian christianity. NT 37 (1995) 355-384 [1 Co 15,44-49; 2,6-3,4; 11,7-12].

4857 **Terry, Ralph Bruce** A discourse analysis of First Corinthians. Summer Institute of Linguistics and The University of Texas at Arlington. Publications in Linguistics 120. Arlington 1995, The Summer Institute of Linguistics xii; 192 pp. 0-88312-707-5.

4858 *Theissen, Gerd* The strong and the weak in Corinth: a sociological analysis of a theological quarrel. 1995 <1975> ⇒110. Understanding Paul's ethics. 107-128.

4859 *Thüsing, Wilhelm* Rechtfertigungsgedanke und Christologie in den Korintherbriefen. 1995 <1974> ⇒60. Studien. WUNT 2/82. 100-123.

4860 *Winter, Bruce W.* The Achaean federal imperial cult II: the Corinthian church. TynB 46 (1995) 169-178 [1 Co 8].

G5.3 **1 Cor 1-7:** *sapientia crucis...abusus matrimonii.*

4861 **Clement, Olivier** Corps de mort et de gloire. P 1995, DDB 140 pp. [LV(L) 45/5,88].

4862 **Pöttner, Martin** Realität als Kommunikation: Ansätze zur Beschreibung der Grammatik des paulinischen Sprechens in 1 Kor 1,4-4,21 im Blick auf literarische Problematik und Situationsbezug des 1. Korintherbriefs. Diss. Marburg 1995, ᴰ*Harnisch* [ThRv 92/2,XII].

4863 *Busto Saiz, José Ramón* La sabiduría de este mundo es locura ante Dios. SalTer 83 (1995) 877-887.

4864 **Brown, Alexandra R.** The cross and human transformation: Paul's apocalyptic word in 1 Corinthians. Mp 1995, Fortress xxi; 183 pp. $16. 0-8006-2677-X [1-2; NTAb 40,353].

4865 **Clarke, Andrew D.** Secular and christian leadership in Corinth...1 Co 1-6. AGJU 18. 1993 ⇒9,6062; 10,5870. ᴿJBL 114 (1995) 344-

346 (*Furnish, Victor Paul*); CBQ 57 (1995) 384-386 (*Siken, Jeffrey S.*).

4866 **Lamp, Jeffrey S.** Christ Jesus, wisdom, and spirituality: an exegetical study of 1 Corinthians 1-4 in light of Jewish wisdom traditions. Trinity Evang. Div. School 1995, 347 pp. ᴰ*Carson, D.A.*, AAC 9608875; DAI-A 56/11,p.4430.

4867 *Rakocy, Waldemar* De arte rhetorica in 1 Cor 1-4. RBL 48 (1995) 231-242.

4868 **Litfin, Duane** St Paul's theology of proclamation: 1 Co 1-4. MSSNTS 79. 1994 ⇒10,5871. ᴿSvTK 71 (1995) 36 (*Eriksson, Anders*).

4869 **Theis, Joachim** Paulus als Weisheitslehrer...in 1 Kor 1-4. BU 22. 1991 ⇒7,5408... 9,6063. ᴿAnton. 70 (1995) 690-691 (*Nobile, Marco*).

4870 **Pogoloff, Stephen** Logos and sophia...1 Co 1-4. SBL.DS 134. 1992 ⇒8,6378. ᴿJR 75 (1995) 409-410 (*Duff, Paul B.*); Trinity Journal 16 (1995) 115-118 (*Lamp, Jeff*); JBL 114 (1995) 166-168 (*Watson, Duane F.*).

4871 *Hübner, Hans* Der vergessene Baruch: zur Baruch-Rezeption des Paulus in 1 Kor 1,18-31. 1995 <1984> ⇒52. Biblische Theologie. 155-165.

4872 *Dunn, J.* [1] In search of wisdom. EpRe 22/3 (1995) 48-53 [NTAb 40,257].

4873 **Bullmore, Michael A.** St. Paul's theology of rhetorical style: an examination of 1 Corinthians 2.1-5 in light of first century Graeco-Roman rhetorical culture. SF 1995, International Scholars 240 pp. 1-57309-019-0 [NThAR 1997/7,194].

4874 *Roukema, Riemer* La prédication du Christ crucifié (1 Corinthiens 2,2) selon Oʀɪɢᴇɴᴇ. 1995 ⇒126. Origeniana Sexta. BEThL 118. 523-529.

4875 *Gaffin, Richard B.* Some epistemological reflections on I Cor 2:6-16. WThJ 57 (1995) 103-124.

4876 **Lopes, Augustus Nicodemus G.** Paul as a charismatic interpreter of scripture: revelation and interpretation in 1 Corinthians 2:6-16. Diss. Westminster Theol. Sem. 1995, 261 pp. ᴰ*Silva, Moises*, AAC 9532740; DAI-A 56/5,p.1830.

4877 *Dubois, Jean-Daniel* L'utilisation gnostique du centon biblique cité en 1 Corinthiens 2,9. 1995 ⇒13. ꟳHᴀʀʟ M., 371-381.

4878 *Thüsing, Wilhelm* "Milch" und "feste Speise" (1 Kor 3,1f und Hebr 5,11-6,3): Elementarkatechese und theologische Vertiefung in neutestamentlicher Sicht. 1995 <1967> ⇒60. Studien. WUNT 2/82. 23-56.

4879 **Müller, Christoph G.** Gottes Pflanzung—Gottes Bau—Gottes Tempel: die metaphorische Dimension paulinischer Gemeindetheologie in 1.Kor.3,5-17. Diss. ⇒10,5876. FuSt 5. Fra 1995, Knecht xii; 209 pp. DM58/FS58/AUS453. 3-7820-0714-X [NTAb 40,358].

4880 **Kuck, David W.** Judgment and community conflict...1 Cor 3:5-4:5. NT.S 66. 1992 ⇒8,6386; 9,6070. ᴿBibl.Interp. 3 (1995) 381-382 (*Neyrey, Jerome H.*).

4881 *Vos, Johan S.* Der μετεσχημάτισμος in 1 Kor 4,6. ZNW 86 (1995) 154-172.

4882 **Rosner, Brian S.** Paul, scripture and ethics...1 Co 5-7. AGJU 22. 1994 ⇒10,5881. ᴿJETh 9 (1995) 233-236 (*Schnabel, Eckhard J.*).

4883 *Harris, Gerald* The beginnings of church discipline: 1 Corinthians 5. 1995 <1991> ⇒110. Understanding Paul's ethics. 129-151.

4884 *Winter, Bruce W.* Civil litigation in secular Corinth and the church: the forensic background to 1 Corinthians 6.1-8. 1995 <1991> ⇒110. Understanding Paul's ethics. 85-103.

4885 *Derrett, John Duncan M.* Judgment and 1 Corinthians 6. 1995 <1991> ⇒45. Studies 6. 173-187.

4886 *Hanschel, Rudolf* Alles erlaubt?—Auslegung zu 1 Korinther 6,11-12. 1995 ⇒88. "Ich bin der Herr". 13-15.

4887 **Kirchhoff, Renate** Die Sünde gegen den eigenen Leib...Porne und Porneia in 1 Kor 6,12-20. StUNT 18. 1994 ⇒10,5884. ᴿOrdKor 36 (1995) 240-241 *(Giesen, Heinz)*; ThLZ 120 (1995) 1001-1002 *(Haufe, Günther)*.

4888 *Dodd, Brian J.* Paul's paradigmatic "I" and 1 Corinthians 6.12. JSNT 59 (1995) 39-58.

4889 **Harrill, J. Albert** [7,21] The manumission of slaves in early christianity. HUTh 32. Tü 1995, Mohr xvii; 255 pp. DM148. 3-16-146285-8.

4890 *Deming, Will* A diatribe pattern in 1 Cor. 7:21-22: a new perspective on Paul's directions to slaves. NT 37 (1995) 130-137.

4891 *Ramsaran, Rollin A.* More than an opinion: Paul's rhetorical maxim in First Corinthians 7:25-26. CBQ 57 (1995) 531-541.

4892 *Geerlings, Wilhelm* 1 Kor 7 in der Interpretation des AMBROSIASTER, 1995 ⇒15. ᶠHEINEMANN H., Theologia. 459-470.

4893 **Deming, Will** Paul on marriage and celibacy: the Hellenistic background of 1 Corinthians 7. MSSNTS 83. C 1995, CUP xiv; 265 pp. £35. 0-521-47284-9.

G5.4 *Idolothyta...Eucharistia:* 1 Cor 8-11.

4894 **Heil, Christoph** Die Ablehnung der Speisegebote durch Paulus. BBB 96. 1994 ⇒10,5896. ᴿThLZ 120 (1995) 793-795 *(Horn, Friedrich Wilhelm)*.

4895 **Kaut, Thomas** Götzendienst: Neues Testament. 1995. LThK 4. ⇒123. 962.

4896 **Gooch, Peter D.** Dangerous food: 1 Co 8-10. SCJud 5. 1993 ⇒9,6085; 10,5897. ᴿJThS 46 (1995) 279-282 *(Horrell, David)*; SR 24 (1995) 224-226 *(Segal, Alan F.)*; CBQ 57 (1995) 807-809 *(Smith, Dennis E.)*.

4897 **Yeo, Khiok-khing** Rhetorical Interaction in 1 Co 8 and 10. Diss. ⇒10,5893. Bibl.Interp. 9. Lei 1995, Brill xvi; 275 pp. 90-04-10115-2. ᴿIRM 84 (1995) 309-310 *(Lee, Archie)*.

Winter, Bruce W. [8] The Achaean federal imperial cult II: the Corinthian church ⇒4860.

4898 *Yeo, Khiok-Khng* The rhetorical hermeneutic of 1 Corinthians 8 and Chinese ancestor worship. 1995 <1991> ⇒129. Voices. 349-367.

4899 *Collins, Raymond F.* "It was indeed written for our sake" (1 Cor 9,10): Paul's use of scripture in the first letter to the Corinthians. SNTU.A 20 (1995) 151-170.

4900 *Kremer, Jacob* Allen bin ich alles geworden, um jedenfalls einige zu retten (1 Kor 9,22): bibeltheologische Erwägungen zu dem

Thema "Zielgruppen im Heilsdienst der Kirche". 1995 <1977>
⇒53. Die Bibel. 223-245.
4901 **Falsini, Rinaldo** [10-11] L'eucarestia domenicale: tra teologia e
pastorale. Liturgia. Studi e Sussidi 8. CinB 1995, San Paolo 238
pp.
4902 *Sandelin, Karl-Gustav* "Do not be idolaters!" (1 Cor 10:7). 1995
⇒14. [F]HARTMAN L., 257-273.
4903 *Meeks, Wayne A.* 'And rose up to play': midrash and paraenesis in
1 Corinthians 10,1-22. 1995 <1982> ⇒105. The Pauline writings. 124-136.
4904 *Sandelin, Karl-Gustav* Does Paul argue against sacramentalism and
over-confidence in 1 Cor 10.1-14? 1995 ⇒67. The New Testament.
165-182.
4905 *Gibbs, J.A.* An exegetical case for close(d) communion: 1
Corinthians 10:14-22; 11:17-34. ConJ 21 (1995) 148-163 [NTAb
40,64].
4906 **Schirrmacher, Thomas** Paulus im Kampf...1 Kor 11,2-16. 1993
⇒10,5907. [R]JETh 9 (1995) 236-238 (*Gebauer, Roland*).
4907 *Amjad-Ali, Christine* The equality of women: form or substance (1
Corinthians 11.2-16). 1995 <1991> ⇒129. Voices. 185-193.
4908 *Kendrick, W. Gerald* Authority, women, and angels: translating 1
Corinthians 11.10. BiTr 46 (1995) 336-343.
4909 *Scippa, Vincenzo* La koinonia in 1Cor 11. PSV 31 (1995) 191-203.
4910 **Gardner, Paul Douglas** The gifts of God...1 Co 8-11:1. Diss.
⇒10,5888. 1994. [R]JThS 46 (1995) 651-654 (*Horrell, David*); CBQ
57 (1995) 806-807 (*Talbert, Charles H.*).

G5.5 1 Cor 12s... Glossolalia, charismata.

4911 **Beinert, Wolfgang** Gottes Gaben. Vermittlung 49. Salzburg 1995,
n.p. 143 pp.
4912 *Bossman, David M.* Paul's Mediterranean gospel: faith, hope,
love. BTB 25 (1995) 71-78.
4913 *Chaloner, S.W.* O dom de línguas no fim do século XX: em prol
de uma convivência paulina. VoxScr 5 (1995) 227-241 [NTAb
40,258].
4914 *Fee, Gordon D.* Toward a Pauline theology of glossolalia. Crux 31
(1995) 22-23, 26-31 [NTAb 40/1 (1996) 65].
4915 **Forbes, Christopher** Prophecy and inspired speech in early
christianity and its Hellenistic environment. Diss. Macquarie 1995,
WUNT 2/75. Tü 1995, Mohr xi; 377 pp. DM98. 3-16-146223-8
[NTAb 40,356].
4916 **Gillespie, Thomas W.** The first theologians: a study in early
Christian prophecy. 1994 ⇒10,5918. [R]PSB 16 (1995) 338-341
(*Moessner, David P.*); LASBF 45 (1995) 641-644 (*Paczkowski,
Mieczysław Celestyn*).
4917 *Kremer, Jacob* Glossolalie: Biblisch. LThK 4. 1995 ⇒123. 755-
756.
4918 *McEleney, Neil J.* Gifts serving Christ's body. BiTod 33 (1995)
134-137.
4919 *Nagel, Norman* The Spirit's gifts in the confessions and in Corinth.
Luther Digest 3 (1995) 58-59 [<ConJ 18,230-243].

4920 *Söding, Thomas* Die Trias Glaube, Hoffnung, Liebe bei Paulus. SBS 150. 1992 ⟹8,6442; 9,6131. ᴿThRv 91 (1995) 393-394 (*Häfner, Gerd*).

4921 **Terra, João Evangelista Martins** Os carismas em São Paolo. São Paulo ²1995, Loyola 79 pp. ᴿRCB 19 (1995) 158-159 (*Ribeiro, Ari Luís do Vale*).

4922 **Vadakkedom, Jose** '*πρὸς τὸ συμφέρον*': the nature and function of the manifestation of the Spirit according to 1 Cor 12,7. Excerpt diss. R 1995, Pont. Universitas Gregoriana 358 pp. ᴰ*Aletti, Jean-Noël*, no. 4174, 107 pp. [RTL 27,538].

4923 *Kremer, Jacob* "Eifert aber um die größeren Charismen!" (1 Kor 12,31a). 1995 <1980> ⟹53. Die Bibel. 246-264.

4924 *Balge, R.D.* Gift, service, and function in the New Testament church: a study of 1 Corinthians 12 and Romans 12. WLQ 92 (1995) 9-16, 83-95 [NTAb 40,64].

4925 *Frid, Bo* Structure and argumentation in 1 Cor 12. SEÅ 60 (1995) 95-113.

4926 *Caragounis, Chrys C.* "To boast" or "to be burned"?: the crux of 1 Cor 13:3. SEÅ 60 115-127.

4927 *Fisichella, Rino* [13,13] La triade fede, speranza e carità in Paolo: una riflessione teologica. Atti del III Simposio. 1995 ⟹138. 75-86.

4928 *Lambrecht, Jan* The most eminent way: a study of 1 Corinthians 13. 1995 ⟹14. ᶠHARTMAN L., 275-304.

4929 *Shepherd, J. Barrie* Aspects of love: an exploration of 1 Corinthians 13. Studies in Contemporary Interpretation. Nv 1995, Upper Room 125 pp. 0-8358-0764-9 [NThAR 1997/6,164].

4930 *Stolle, V.* I Kor 14,26-40 und die Gottesdienstreform der lutherischen Reformation: die biblische Grundlegung des Gottesdienstes als hermeneutische Frage. LuThK 19 (1995) 98-135.

4931 *Gourgues, Michel* Qui est misogyne: Paul ou certains Corinthiens?: note sur 1 Co 14,33b-36. 1995 ⟹71. Des femmes. 153-162 [RB 103,452].

4932 *Arichea, Daniel C.* The silence of women in the church: theology and translation in 1 Corinthians 14.33b-36. BiTr 46 (1995) 101-112.

4933 *Stichele, C. van der* [14,34-35] Is silence golden?: Paul and women's speech in Corinth. LouvSt 20 (1995) 241-253.

4934 *Jervis, L. Ann* 1 Corinthians 14.34-35: a reconsideration of Paul's limitation of the free speech of some Corinthian women. JSNT 58 (1995) 51-74.

4935 *Isaak, J.M.* Hearing God's word in silence: a canonical approach to 1 Corinthians 14.34-35. ᴿDirection 24 (1995) 55-64 [NTAb 40,445].

4936 *Payner, Philip B.* Fuldensis, sigla for variants in Vaticanus, and 1 Cor 14,34-5. NTS 41 (1995) 240-262.

G5.6 **Resurrectio;** *1 Cor 15...* [⟹F5.6].

4937 *Barrett, Charles K.* [15,20-22.45-49] The significance of the Adam-Christ typology for the resurrection of the dead. 1995 <1985> ⟹39. Jesus and the word. 163-184.

4938 **Boer, Martinus C. de** [15] The defeat of death. JSNT.S 22. 1988. ⇒4,6115... 8,6445*. ᴿRB 102 (1995) 149-150 (*Murphy-O'Connor, Jerome*) [Rom 5].

4939 **Boone, Richard George** Text-centered methods of interpretation as proof of the delineation and coherence of 1 Corinthians 15. Diss. Union Theol. Sem. 1995, 441 pp. ᴰ*Achtemeier, Paul J.*, AAC 9531165; DAI-A 56/5,p.1826.

4940 **Bynum, Caroline Walker** The resurrection of the body in western christianity. LHR 15. NY 1995, Columbia University Press xx; 368 pp. $30. 0-231-08126-X.

4941 *DeMaris, Richard E.* Corinthian religion and baptism for the dead (1 Corinthians 15:29): insights from archaeology and anthropology. JBL 114 (1995) 661-682.

4942 **Han, Cheon-Seol** Raised for our justification: an investigation on the significance of the resurrection of Christ within the theological structure of Paul's message. Diss. 1995, ᴰ*Baarlink, H.* [RTL 27,534].

4943 **Johnson, Clinton Andrew, Jr.** Resurrection rhetoric: a rhetorical analysis of 1 Corinthians 15. Diss. Luther Sem. 1995, 353 pp. ᴰ*Juel, Donald H.*, AAC 9535534; DAI-A 56/6,p.2280.

4944 **Lewis, Scott Martin** So that God may be all in all: the apocalyptic message of 1 Corinthians 15:12-34. Diss. R 1995, Pont. Univ. Gregoriana no.4198, 299 pp. ᴰ*Aletti, Jean-Noël.*

4945 *Meeks, Wayne A.* The temporary reign of the Son: 1 Cor 15.23-28. 1995 ⇒14. ᶠHᴀʀᴛᴍᴀɴ L., 801-811.

4946 *O'Brien, Julia M.* Between text and sermon: I Corinthians 15:19-26. Interp. 49 (1995) 182-185.

4947 *Price, R. M.* Apocryphal apparitions: 1 Corinthians 15:3-11 as a post-Pauline interpolation. JHiC 2/2 (1995) 69-99.

4948 *Rubinkiewicz, Ryszard* The resurrection of Christ—our rising from the dead. **P.** Roczniki Teologiczne 42/1 (1995) 85-93 [sum. 93].

4949 **Schneider, Sebastian** Vollendung des Auferstehens: eine exegetische Untersuchung zu 1 Kor 15,51-52. Diss. St. Georgen 1995, ᴰ*Baumert* [BZ 39,313].

4950 *Sisti, Adalberto* Morte e risurrezione in 1Cor 15. PSV 32 (1995) 203-218.

4951 **Teani, Maurizio** Corporeità e risurrezione...1 Co 15,35-49. 1994 ⇒10,5947. ᴿCritRR 8 (1995) 307-309 (*Zilonka, Paul*).

4952 *Thiselton, Anthony C.* Lᴜᴛʜᴇʀ and Bᴀʀᴛʜ on 1 Corinthians 15: six theses for theology in relation to recent interpretation. JSNT.S 105. 1995 ⇒2. ᶠAᴛᴋɪɴsᴏɴ J., 258-289.

4953 **Thomas, Pascal** Réincarnation, résurrection. P 1995, Plon 303 pp. [Telema 23,84].

4954 *Ulrichsen, Jarl Henning* [15] Die Auferstehungsleugner in Korinth: was meinten sie eigentlich? 1995 ⇒14. ᶠHᴀʀᴛᴍᴀɴ L., 781-799.

4955 **Verbrugge, Verlyn D.** [16,1-2] Paul's style of church leadership illustrated by his instructions to the Corinthians on the collection. 1992 ⇒8,6448*; 10,5951. ᴿCBQ 57 (1995) 417-418 (*Porter, Stanley E.*) [2 Cor 8-9].

4956 **Verburg, Winfried** Endzeit und Entschlafene: syntaktisch-sigmatische, semantische und pragmatische Analyse von 1 Kor 15. Diss. Regensburg 1995, 327 pp. ᴰ*Ritt, H.* [ThRv 92/2,XIV].

G5.9 Secunda epistula ad Corinthios.

4957 **Belleville, Linda** 2 Corinthians. IVP New Testament Commentary. Leicester, UK/Downers Grove, IL 1995, IVP 272 pp. $17. 0-85111-679-5/0-8308-1808-1 [NTAb 41,156].

4958 ᴱ**Feld, Helmut** Commentarii in Secundum Pauli epistolam ad Corinthios. C A L V I N I Opera exegetica 15. 1994 ⇒10,5952. ᴿGr. 76 (1995) 762-763 (*Marconi, Gilberto*); ThLZ 120 (1995) 1097-1098 (*Rogge, Joachim*).

4959 **Nielsen, Jan T.** 2 Korintiërs: een praktische bijbelverklaring. Tekst en toelichting. Kampen 1995, Kok 170 pp. 90-242-2207-9 [NThAR 1996/4,89].

4960 **Thrall, Margaret E.** ICC 2Cor 1 (1-7). 1994 ⇒10,5953. ᴿNeotest. 29 (1995) 427-428 (*Kruger, V.*).

4961 **Watson, Nigel** The second epistle to the Corinthians. 1993 ⇒9,6148. ᴿPacifica 8 (1995) 348-350 (*Campbell, Douglas A.*).

4962 **Zeilinger, Franz** Krieg und Frieden in Korinth: 2. Kor I. 1992 ⇒8,6454; 9,6149. ᴿThRv 91 (1995) 130-131 (*Oliveira, Anacleto de*).

4963 **Bosenius, Bärbel** Die Abwesenheit des Apostels als theologisches Programm: 2Kor. TANZ 11. 1994 ⇒10,5955. ᴿThLZ 120 (1995) 1074-1077 (*Aejmelaeus, Lars*).

4964 **Brendle, Albert** Im Prozeß der Konfliktüberwindung: eine exegetische Studie zur Kommunikationssituation zwischen Paulus und den Korinthern in 2 Kor 1,1-2; 13; 7,4-16. EHS.T 533. Fra 1995, Lang 365 pp. DM95. 3-631-48513-1.

4965 **Klauck, Hans-Josef** Konflikt und Versöhnung: Christsein nach dem zweiten Korintherbrief. Wü 1995, Echter 168 pp. DM29.80. 3-429-01652-5 [NTAb 40,155].

4966 *McKay, K. L.* Observations on the epistolary aorist in 2 Corinthians. NT 37 (1995) 154-158.

4967 **Pate, C. Marvin** The glory of Adam and the afflictions of the righteous: Pauline suffering. 1993 ⇒9,6158. ᴿCritRR 7 (1994) 246-248 (*Kaylor, R. David*).

4968 **Wünsch, Hans-Michael** Der paulinische Brief als kommunikative Handlung: dargestellt an 2 Kor 1-9. Diss. Marburg 1995, ᴰ*Harnisch, W.* [ThRv 92/2,XII].

4969 **Innasimuthu, Arulsamy** Comfort in affliction: an exegetical study of 2 Corinthians 1:3-11. Diss. Leuven 1995, lxv; 475 pp. 2 vols, ᴰ*Bieringer, R.*

4970 *Welborn, L. L.* The dangerous double affirmation: character and truth in 2Cor 1,17. ZNW 86 (1995) 34-52.

4971 *Derrett, John Duncan M.* Ναί (2 Cor 1:19-20). 1995 < 1991 > ⇒45. Studies 6. 188-192.

4972 *Omanson, Roger L.* Comings and goings in the Bible. BiTr 46 (1995) 112-119 [2,13; 1 Th 3,13; 4,14].

4973 *Lambrecht, Jan* The defeated Paul, aroma of Christ: an exegetical study of 2 Corinthians 2:14-16b. LouvSt 20 (1995) 170-186.

4974 **Schröter, Jens** Der versöhnte Versöhner: Paulus...2Kor 2,14-7,4. TANZ 10. 1993 ⇒9,6151; 10,5962. ᴿBZ 39 (1995) 144-146 (*Dautzenberg, Gerhard*); ThLZ 120 (1995) 242-244 (*Lohse, Eduard*).

4975 *Sloan, Robert B.* 2 Corinthians 2:14-4:6 and "New Covenant Hermeneutics" : a response to Richard HAYS. Bulletin for Biblical Research 5 (1995) 129-154.

4976 *Stimpfle, Alois* "Buchstabe und Geist": zur Geschichte eines Mißverständnisses von 2 Kor 3,6. BZ 39 (1995) 181-202.

4977 *Kremer, Jacob* "Denn der Buchstabe tötet, der Geist aber macht lebendig": methodologische und hermeneutische Erwägungen zu 2 Kor 3,6b. 1995 <1979> ⇒53. Die Bibel. 265-297.

4978 *Hanson, A. T.* The midrash in 2 Corinthians 3: a reconsideration. 1995 <1980> ⇒105. The Pauline writings. 98-123 [Exod 34].

4979 **Hafemann, Scott J.** Paul, Moses, and the history of Israel: the letter/spirit contrast and the arguments from scripture in 2 Corinthians 3. WUNT 2/81. Tü 1995, Mohr xii; 497 pp. DM228. 3-16-146270-X [RB 103,476].

4980 *Lindemann, Andreas* Die biblische Hermeneutik des Paulus: Beobachtungen zu 2Kor 3. WuD 23 (1995) 125-151.

4981 *Zanetti, Paolo Serra* Una nota su 2 Cor. 4,8b. Aug. 35 (1995) 111-117.

4982 *Kistemaker, S.J.* Temos uma habitação celestial: 2 Coríntios 5:1. VoxScr 5 (1995) 147-152 [NTAb 40,259].

4983 *Boshoff, P.B.* [5,19] Die kerk van die woord [The church proclaiming the word]. HTS 51 (1995) 581-594 [NTAb 40,446].

4984 *Reid, Barbara E.* Puzzling passages: 2 Cor 5:21. BiTod 33 (1995) 163.

4985 **Webb, William J.** Returning home...2 Co 6.14-7.1. JSNT.S 85. 1993 ⇒9,6168; 10,5974. RJThS 46 (1995) 282-285 (*Martin, Ralph P.*); CBQ 57 (1995) 199-200 (*Muller, Earl C.*); JBL 114 (1995) 347-348 (*Walker, William O.*).

4986 *Horrell, D.* [8-9] Paul's collection: resources for a materialist theology. EpRe 22/2 (1995) 74-83 [NTAb 40,66].

4987 **Betz, Hans Dieter** 2. Korinther 8 und 9. 1992 ⇒8,6476; 9,6170. RCommunio 28 (1995) 89-93 (*Burgos, M. de*).

4988 **DiCicco, Mario M.** Paul's use of ethos, pathos and logos in 2 Corinthians 10-13. Mellen 31. Lewiston 1995, Mellen xii; 303 pp. $100. 0-7734-2369-9 [NThAR 1997/2,36].

4989 **Heckel, Ulrich** Kraft in Schwachheit: Untersuchungen zu 2. Kor 10-13. WUNT 2/56. 1993 ⇒9,6173; 10,5978. RThLZ 120 (1995) 34-35 (*Vogler, Werner*); BZ 39 (1995) 147-148 (*Dautzenberg, Gerhard*); JThS 46 (1995) 285-286 (*Hickling, C.J.A.*).

4990 *Welborn, L. L.* The identification of 2 Corinthians 10-13 with the "Letter of Tears". NT 37 (1995) 138-153.

4991 **Merritt, H. Wayne** [10,11] In word and deed: moral integrity in Paul. 1993 ⇒9,6176. RETR 70 (1995) 457-459 (*Siegert, Folker*); LouvSt 20 (1995) 427-428 (*Collins, Raymond F.*); JBL 114 (1995) 743-745 (*Fitzgerald, John T.*).

4992 *Luciani, Ferdinando* 2 Cr 11,4b, testo ebraico e versioni antiche. Aevum 69 (1995) 7-13.

4993 *Andrews, Scott B.* Too weak not to lead: the form and function of 2 Cor 11,23b-33. NTS 41 (1995) 263-276.

4994 *Garrett, Susan R.* [12,7-10] Paul's thorn and cultural models of affliction. 1995 ⇒20. FMEEKS W., 82-99.

4995 *Kremer, Jacob* Worte des Herrn und Worte des Paulus als Wort Gottes: exegetische, hermeneutische und bibeltheologische

Erwägungen zu 2 Kor 12,9-10. 1995 <1989> ⇒53. Die Bibel. 298-318.

G6.1 Ad Galatas.

4996 **Barr, Philip** Teaching for renewal through an inductive bible study course on Galatians at Allensville Mennonite Church. Diss. Fuller 1995, 256 pp. ^D*Redman, Robert R. Jr.*, AAC 9521367; DAI-A 56/2,p.590.

4997 **Dunn, James D.G.** The epistle to the Galatians. 1993 ⇒9,6180. ^RCBQ 57 (1995) 175-176 (*Matera, Frank J.*).

4998 **Dunn, James D.G.** Theology of Paul's letter to the Galatians. 1993 ⇒9,6189; 10,6005. ^RPacifica 8 (1995) 350-352 (*Campbell, Douglas A.*); EvQ 67 (1995) 276-278 (*Ciampa, Roy*); JBL 114 (1995) 747-750 (*Hays, Richard B.*).

4999 **Fausti, Silvano** Verità del vangelo: libertà di figli: commentario spirituale alla lettera ai Galati. CasM 1993, Piemme 308 pp. L25.000. ^RCivCatt 146 (1995) 322-323 (*Scaiola, D.*).

5000 **George, Timothy** Galatians. NAC 30. 1994 ⇒10,5987. ^RCritRR 8 (1995) 220-222 (*Matera, Frank J.*).

5001 *Heitsch, Ernst* Glossen zum Galaterbrief. ZNW 86 (1995) 173-188.

5002 **Lührmann, Dieter** Galatians 1992 ⇒8,6505... 10,5991. ^RNew Theology Review 8/1 (1995) 90-91 (*Reid, Barbara E.*).

5003 **Matera, Frank J.** Galatians. 1992 ⇒8,6507... 10,5992. ^RCritRR 7 (1994) 235-237 (*Seifrid, Mark A.*).

5004 **McKnight, S.** Galatians. NIV Application Commentary. GR 1995, Zondervan 320 pp. $22. 3-310-48470-7 [NTAb 40,156].

5005 **Pohl, Adolf** Der Brief des Paulus an die Galater. WStB.NT. Wu 1995, Brockhaus 255 pp. DM35. 3-417-25023-4.

5006 ^E**Rosemann, Philipp W.; McEvoy, James** Opera Roberti GROSSETESTE Lincolniensis 1: expositio in epistolam sancti Pauli ad Galatas: glossarum in sancti Pauli epistolas fragmenta. CChr:CM 130. Turnhout 1995, Brepols ix; 341 pp. 2-503-04301-1.

5007 **Wachtel, Klaus; Witte, Klaus** Die paulinischen Briefe 2. ANTT 22. 1994 ⇒10,5995. ^RNT 37 (1995) 302-303 (*Elliott, J.K.*).

5008 *Barclay, John M.G.* Mirror-reading a polemical letter: Galatians as a test case. 1995 <1987> ⇒105. The Pauline writings. 247-267.

5009 **Boyarin, Daniel** Galatians and gender trouble: primal androgyny and the first-century origins of a feminist dilemma. (disc. *King, Karen L.; Wire, Antoinette; Knapp, Steven*) Protocol of the Colloquy of the Center for Hermeneutical Studies NS 1 (5 April 1992). Berkeley, CA 1995, Center for Hermeneutical Studies 70 pp. 0-89242-065-0.

5010 **Buckel, John** Free to love: Paul's defense of christian liberty in Galatians. LThPM 15. 1993 ⇒10,6000. ^RCritRR 8 (1995) 183-186 (*Calvert, Nancy L.*).

5011 *Das, A.A.* Oneness in Christ: the *nexus indivulsus* between justification and sanctification in Paul's letter to the Galatians. ConJ 21 (1995) 173-186 [NTAb 40,67].

5012 *Dunn, James D.G.* Was Paul against the law?: the law in Galatians and Romans: a test-case of text in context. 1995 ⇒14. ^FHARTMAN L., 455-475.

5013 *Hatina, Thomas R.* The perfect tense-form in recent debate: Galatians as a case study. FgNT 8 (1995) 3-22.

5014 **Hong, In-Gyu** The law in Galatians. JSNT.S 81. 1993 ⇒9,6196; 10,6009. Themelíos 20/3 (1995) 25 (*Still, Todd D.*).

5015 *Hübner, Hans* Identitätsverlust und paulinische Theologie: Anmerkungen zum Galaterbrief. 1995 <1978> ⇒52. Biblische Theologie. 27-39.

5016 **John, Thomas K.** Intentional congregational training to increase knowledge of the fruit of the spirit. Diss. Oral Roberts 1995, 286 pp. ^D*Lederle, Henry*, AAC 9603434; DAI-A 56/10,p.4009.

5017 *Kern, Philip H.* Rhetoric, scholarship and Galatians: assessing an approach to Paul's epistle. TynB 46 (1995) 201-203.

5018 *Lambrecht, J.* La voluntad universal de Dio: el verdadero evangelio de la carta a los Gálatas. RevBib 57 (1995) 131-142.

5019 *Martin, Troy* Apostasy to paganism: the rhetorical stasis of the Galatian controversy. JBL 114 (1995) 437-461.

5020 *Martyn, J. Louis* Christ, the elements of the cosmos, and the law in Galatians. 1995 ⇒20. ^FMEEKS W., 16-39.

5021 **Morland, Kjell Arne** The rhetoric of curse in Galatians: Paul confronts another gospel. Emory Studies in Early Christianity 5. Atlanta, GA 1995, Scholars xiii; 354 pp. $45. 1-55540-923-7 [NTAb 41,161].

5022 ^E**Nash, Scott** Interpreting Galatians for preaching and teaching: kerygma and church. Macon, GA 1995, Smyth & Helwys x; 182 pp.   1-880837-87-0 [NThAR 1997,132].

5023 **O'Grady, John** Pillars of Paul's gospel: Gal Rom. 1992 ⇒8,6520... 10,6011. ^REeT(O) 26 (1995) 264-265 (*Bonneau, Normand*).

5024 **Pitta, Antonio** Disposizione...Gal. AnBib 131. 1992 ⇒8,6521... 10,6014. ^RGr. 76 (1995) 153-154 (*Farahian, Edmond*); EstB 53 (1995) 279-280 (*Pastor-Ramos, F.*); JBL 114 (1995) 164-166 (*Heil, John Paul*).

5025 *Pitta, Antonio* La libertà cristiana nella lettera ai Galati. VM 49 (1995) 51-61.

5026 **Scott, James M.** Paul and the nations: the Old Testament and Jewish background of Paul's mission to the nations with special reference to the destination of Galatians. WUNT 2/84. Tü 1995, Mohr xvi; 276 pp. DM178. 3-16-146377-3 [Bijdr. 57,120].

5027 *Talbert, Charles H.* Freedom and law in Galatians. ExAu 11 (1995) 17-28.

5028 *Wan, Sze-kar* Abraham and the promise of the Spirit: Galatians and the Hellenistic-Jewish mysticism of PHILO. SBL.SP 34 (1995) 6-22.

5029 **Cummins, S.A.** Paul and the crucified Christ in Antioch: Maccabean martyrdom and Galatians 1-2. Diss. Ox 1995 [RTL 27,534].

5030 ^E**Lambrecht, Jan** The truth of the gospel (Gal 1-4). 1993 ⇒9,392; 10,6018. ^RStPat 42/3 (1995) 154-155 (*Segalla, Giuseppe*); LouvSt 20 (1995) 426-427 (*Matera, Frank J.*); CBQ 57 (1995) 625-626 (*Gignac, Francis T.*); SNTU.A 20 (1995) 235-237 (*Becker, Jürgen*).

5031 *Bovon, François* A pre-Pauline expression in the epistle to the Galatians (Gal 1:4-5). 1995 <1978> ⇒40. New Testament traditions. PTMS 36. 1-13, 177-183 [RB 103,117].

5032 *Etcheverría, Ramón Trevijano* Los primeros viajes de San Pablo a Jerusalén (Gal 1,18-20 y 2,1-10). Salm. 42 (1995) 173-209.

5033 *Penna, Romano* [2,1-10] Le collette di Paolo per la chiesa di Gerusalemme. PSV 31 (1995) 179-190.

5034 *Esler, Philip F.* Making and breaking an agreement Mediterranean style: a new reading of Galatians 2:1-14. Bibl.Interp. 3 (1995) 285-314.

5035 *Murphy-O'Connor, Jerome* Nationalism and church policy: reflections on Gal 2,1-14. BEThL 121. 1995 ⇒35. FTILLARD J., 283-291.

5036 *Legrand, Lucien* "That we should remember the poor" (Gal 2:10): the conclusion of the Jerusalem synod according to Gal 2:10. ITS 32 (1995) 161-173.

5037 *Pathrapankal, Joseph* Apostolic commitment and "remembering the poor": a study in Gal 2:10. 1995 ⇒FHARTMAN L., 1001-1018.

5038 **Hennings, Ralph** Der Briefwechsel AUGUSTINUS/HIERONYMUS...Streit um Gal. 2,11-14. SVigChr 21. 1994 ⇒10,6029. RJThS 46 (1995) 356-358 (*Bonner, Gerald*); VigChr 49 (1995) 292-294 (*Bartelink, G.J.M.*).

5039 *Fürst, Alfons* ORIGENES und EPHRAEM über Paulus' Konflikt mit Petrus (Gal. 2,11/14). JAC.E 22. 1995 ⇒34. FTHRAEDE K., 121-130.

5040 *Albright, Jack* Stand firm in freedom: summer lections from Galatians. QR 15/1 (1995) 89-105 [2,15-21; 3,23-29; 5,1.13-25; 6,1-16].

5041 *Pathrapankal, Joseph M.* "I live, not I; it is Christ who lives in me" (Gal 2:20): a Yogic interpretation of Paul's religious experience. JDh 20 (1995) 297-307.

5042 *Browne, Gerald M.* The old Nubian translation of Galatians 3:27. Muséon 108 (1995) 239-241.

5043 *Litke, Wayne* Beyond creation: Galatians 3:28, Genesis and the hermaphrodite myth. SR 24 (1995) 173-178.

5044 *Strobel, August* Astronomische Daten des sogen. Weltenjahres zum Thema 'Fülle der Zeit' (Gal 4:4). *Ahnert, Paul-Gerhard* <collab.>, 1995 ⇒31. FSTROBEL A., 26-35 [RB 103,120].

5045 *Borgen, Peder* [4,21-5,1] Some Hebrew and pagan features in Philo's and Paul's interpretation of Hagar and Ishmael. 1995 ⇒67. The New Testament. 151-164.

5046 **Gouw, Rudolf G.M.** Hagar and Isaac (Gal 4:21-31): an allegory around Jerusalem. Diss. R, Pont. Univ. Gregoriana no. 4128, DVanni, Ugo, Rotterdam 1995, CIP-Gegevens Koninklijke Bibliotheek 328 pp. 90-9008154-2.

5047 *Robscheit, Wolfgang* Durch Christus zur Freiheit berufen: Auslegung zu Galater 5,1-10. 1995 ⇒88. "Ich bin der Herr". 17-18.

5048 *Barnes, B.Z.* Called to freedom: Gal 5.1,13-26. RW 45 (1995) 187-190 [ZID 1996,72].

5049 *O'Neill, J.C.* [5,13-6,10] The Holy Spirit and the human spirit in Galatians. EThL 71 (1995) 107-120.

5050 *Mau, Rudolf* Liebe als gelebte Freiheit der Christen, LUTHERs Auslegung von G 5,13-24 im Kommentar von 1519 [Love as practiced freedom of christians, Luther's exegesis of Galatians 5:13-24 in the Commentary of 1519]. Luther Digest 3 (1995) 45-54 [< LuJ (1992) 11-37].

5051 *Russell, Walt* The apostle Paul's redemptive-historical argumentation in Galatians 5:13-26. WThJ 57 (1995) 333-357.

5052 *Rand, Thomas A.* A call to κοινωνία: a rhetorical analysis of Galatians 5:25-6:10. ProcGLM 15 (1995) 79-92.

G6.2 Ad Ephesios.

5053 **Best, Ernest** Ephesians. 1993 ⇒9,6241. RCritRR 8 (1995) 173-175 (*Patzia, Arthur G.*).

5054 **Bruce, Frederick F.** The epistles to the Colossians, to Philemon, and to the Ephesians. NIC. GR ⁵1995 [⇒65,5515...5,6269], Eerdmans xxviii; 442 pp. 0-8028-2510-9.

5055 *Engelbrecht, J.J.* Opmerkings oor vroeë katolisisme in die Nuwe Testament, met besondere verwysing na die briewe aan die Kolossense en die Efesiërs, en die Pastorale Briewe [Remarks on early catholicism in the New Testament, with special reference to the letters to the Colossians and the Ephesians, and the Pastoral letters]. HTS 51 (1995) 677-701 [NTAb 40,450].

5056 **Faust, Eberhard** Pax Christi et Pax Caesaris...Studien...Eph. NTOA 24. ⇒9,6257; 10,6070. RJThS 46 (1995) 288-293 (*Lincoln, Andrew T.*); EstB 53 (1995) 418-420 (*Huarte, J.*).

5057 **Günther, Matthias** Die Frühgeschichte des Christentums in Ephesus. Diss. Gö, DLüdemann, G., ARGU 1. Fra 1995, Lang xi; 249 pp. 3-631-49269-3.

5058 *Hoppe, Rudolf* Epheserbrief. 1995 ⇒122. LThK 3. 702-704.

5059 *Hoppe, Rudolf* Gefangenschaftsbriefe. 1995 ⇒123. LThK 4. 342-243.

5060 **Kitchen, Martin** Ephesians. 1994 ⇒10,6057. RIBSt 17 (1995) 93-95 (*Best, Ernest*).

5061 **Martin, Ralph P.** Ephesians, Colossians, and Philemon. 1991 ⇒7,5580... 9,6234. RCritRR 7 (1994) 229-231 (*Van Broekhoven, Harold*).

5062 ENeri, **Umberto** Lettera agli Efesini: versione ufficiale italiana confrontata con il greco originale, con il siriaco della Peshitta, e con il latino della Vulgata. BIBLIA NT 9. Bo 1995, EDB xcv; 191 pp. L52.000. 88-10-20581-2.

5063 **Stadelmann, Helge** Epheserbrief. Stu 1993, Hänssler 290 pp. DM35. 3-7751-1860-8. RJETh 9 (1995) 217-221 (*Moritz, Thorsten*).

5064 EUhlig, **Siegbert; Maehlum, Helge.** Novum Testamentum aethiopice: die Gefangenschaftsbriefe. AthF 33. 1993 ⇒9,6239. ROLZ 90 (1995) 402-412 (*Juckel, Andreas*); OrChr 79 (1995) 265-270 (*Weninger, Stefan*).

5065 *Baldanza, Giuseppe* Sacramentalità del matrimonio ed ecclesiologia: alcune riflessioni nella prospettiva della lettera agli Efesini. EL 109 (1995) 289-309.

5066 **Cooper, Stephen Andrew** Metaphysics and morals in Marius VICTORINUS' commentary on the letter to the Ephesians: a contribution to the history of neoplatonism and christianity. AmUSt.P 155. NY 1995, Lang xiii; 249 pp. $45. 0-8204-2330-0.

5067 *Hoppe, Rudolf* Theo-logie und Ekklesio-logie im Epheserbrief. MThZ 46 (1995) 231-245.

5068 **Lincoln, Andrew T.; Wedderburn, A.J.M.** Theology of the later Pauline letters. 1993 ⇒9,6248. RCritRR 7 (1994) 220-223 (*Wild, Robert A.*); CBQ 57 (1995) 402-403 (*Fitzgerald, John T.*).

5069 **Mouton, Aletta Elizabeth Johanna** Reading a New Testament document ethically: toward an accountable use of scripture in christian ethics, through analysing the transformation potential of the Ephesians epistle. Diss. Western Cape, Bellville 1995, 283 pp. D*Smit, D.J.* [RTL 27,574].

5070 *Reynier, Chantal* Évangile et mystère...Éph. LeDiv 149. 1992 ⇒8,6573; 9,6249. RJThS 46 (1995) 286-288 (*De Boer, Martinus C.*); MD 202 (1995) 141-142 (*Auneau, Joseph*); EeT(O) 26 (1995) 415-416 (*Laberge, Léo*).

5071 *Rosscup, J.E.* The importance of prayer in Ephesians. MastJ 6 (1995) 57-78 [NTAb 40,69].

5072 **Thiessen, Werner** Christen in Ephesus: die historische und theologische Situation in vorpaulinischer und paulinischer Zeit und zur Zeit der Apostelgeschichte und der Pastoralbriefe. Diss. Heidelberg 1990, D*Berger, Klaus*, TANZ 12. Tü 1995, Francke 410 pp. DM94. 3-7720-1863-7.

5073 *Weber, Beat* "Setzen"—"wandeln"—"stehen" im Epheserbrief. NTS 41 (1995) 478-480.

5074 *Wong, Ya-Chow T(h)eresa* Literary and theological figures in the epistle to Ephesians. C. CTUF 105 (1995) 333-352 [ThIK 17/2,30].

5075 **MacLean, Jennifer Kay Berenson** Ephesians and the problem of Colossians: interpretation of texts and traditions in Eph 1:1-2:10. Diss. Harvard 1995, 237 pp. D*Koester, Helmut*, AAC 9609158; DAI-A 56,4430.

5076 **Vigo Gutierrez, Abelardo del** [1,3-10] A solas con San Pablo. BAC Popular 104. M 1994, BAC 220 pp. RFranciscanum 37 (1995) 466-467 (*Botero P., Jorge*) [Phil 2,5-11].

5077 **Tosaus Abadía, José Pedro** Cristo y el universo: estudio lingüístico y temático de Ef 1,10b, en Efesios y en la obra de IRENEO de Lyon. Plenitudo Temporis 2. S 1995, Universidad Pontificia 341 pp. Ptas2.650. 84-7299-343-4. RRET 55 (1995) 403-404 (*Ayán, J.J.*); Salm. 42 (1995) 447-449 (*Romero Pose, Eugenio*); Burg. 36 (1995) 562-564 (*Otero Lazaro, Tomas*).

5078 *Riesenfeld, Harald* Var de kristna i Efesos fortfarande hedningar? Till Ef 2:1-3:13. SEÅ 60 (1995) 129-140.

5079 *Kuske, D.P.* Does Ephesians 2:10 teach sanctification or not? WLQ 92 (1995) 51-52 [NTAb 40,68].

5080 *Terrinoni, Waldo* "Fare la verità nella carità" (Ef 4,15). RVS 49 (1995) 659-666.

5081 **Fleckenstein, Karl-Heinz** Ordnet...die Eheperikope in Eph. 5,21-33. 1994 ⇒10,6089. REstAg 30 (1995) 345-346 (*Cineira, D.A.*); ATG 58 (1995) 391-392 (*Rodríguez Carmona, A.*).

5082 *Ádna, Jostein* Die eheliche Lebensbeziehung als Analogie zu Christi Beziehung zur Kirche: eine traditionsgeschichtliche Studie zu Epheser 5,21-33. ZThK 92 (1995) 434-465.

5083   *Volpi, Isidoro* 'Mundans lavacro aquǭ in verbo' (Ef 5,26b). 1995
       ⇒FMATTIOLI A., 305-340.
5084   *Bavel, Tarsicius Jan van* 'No one ever hated his own flesh': Eph.
       5:29 in AUGUSTINE. Aug(L) 45 (1995) 45-93.
5085   *Seim, Turid Karlsen* A superior minority?: the problem of men's
       headship in Ephesians 5. StTh 49 (1995) 167-181.
5086   *Girard, Marc* L'amour-soumission, idéal chrétien pour le mari
       comme pour la femme: étude structurelle d'Éphesiens 5. 1995 ⇒71.
       Des femmes. 163-196 [RB 103,452].
5087   *Lincoln, Andrew T.* "Stand, therefore...": Ephesians 6:10-20 as
       peroratio. Bibl.Interp. 3 (1995) 99-114.

                        G6.3 **Ad Philippenses.**

5088   **Barton, B.B.** (*al.*) Philippians, Colossians, and Philemon. Life
       Application Bible Commentary. Wheaton, IL 1995, Tyndale xv;
       275 pp. 0-8423-2974-9 [NTAb 40,353].
5089   **Fee, Gordon D.** Paul's letter to the Philippians. NIC.NT GR
       1995, Eerdmans xlvi; 497 pp. $35. 0-8028-2511-7.
5090   **Melick, Richard R. Jr.** Philippians, Colossians, Philemon. 1991
       ⇒7,5605... 10,6094. RCritRR 7 (1994) 237-238 (*DeMaris,
       Richard E.*).
5091   **Thielman, F.** Philippians. NIV Application Commentary. GR
       1995, Zondervan 256 pp. $20. 0-310-49300-5 [NTAb 40,361].

5092   **Abrahamsen, Valerie Ann** Women and worship at Philippi:
       Diana/Artemis and other cults in the early christian era. Portland,
       Me. 1995, Astarte Shell 252 pp. 1-885349-00-9.
5093   *Alexander, Loveday* Hellenistic letter-forms and the structure of
       Philippians. 1995 <1989> ⇒105. The Pauline writings. 232-246.
5094   *Black, David Alan* The discourse structure of Philippians: a study
       in textlinguistics. NT 37 (1995) 16-49.
5095   **Bloomquist, L. Gregory** The function of suffering in Philippians.
       JSNTS 78. 1993 ⇒9,6273; 10,6100. RThemelíos 20/3 (1995) 25-26
       (*Still, Todd D.*).
5096   *Bockmuehl, Markus* A commentator's approach to the "effective
       history" of Philippians. JSNT 60 (1995) 57-88.
5097   **Bormann, Lukas** Philippi: Stadt und Christengemeinde zur Zeit
       des Paulus. NT.S 78. Lei 1995, Brill xiv; 248 pp. 90-04-10232-9.
5098   *Guthrie, George H.* Cohesion shifts and stitches in Philippians.
       1995 ⇒102. Discourse analysis. JSNT.S 113. 36-59.
5099   **Keller, Marie-Noel** Choosing what is best: Paul, Roman society,
       and Philippians. Diss. Lutheran School of Theol. 1995, 208 pp.
       DKrentz, Edgar, AAC 9537825; DAI-A 56/9,p.3618.
5100   *Levinsohn, Stephen H.* A discourse study of constituent order and
       the article in Philippians. 1995 ⇒102. Discourse analysis. JSNT.S
       113. 60-74.
5101   *Llewelyn, S.R.* Sending letters in the ancient world: Paul and the
       Philippians. TynB 46 (1995) 337-356.
5102   *Luter, A. Boyd; Lee, Michelle V.* Philippians as chiasmus: key to
       the structure, unity and theme questions. NTS 41 (1995) 89-101.
5103   **Oakes, Peter** Philippians: from people to letter. Diss. Ox 1995,
       DWright, N.T. [TynB 47,371-374].

5104 **Peterlin, Davorin** Paul's letter to the Philippians in the light of disunity in the Church. Diss. Aberdeen 1992, ^{D}*Marshall, I.H.*, NT.S 79. Lei 1995, Brill xi; 272 pp. f155/$88.75. 90-04-10305-8 [NTAb 40,359].

5105 **Phillips, John** Exploring Philippians. Neptune, NJ 1995, Loizeaux 187 pp. 0-87213-580-2 [NThAR 1997,261].

5106 **Pilhofer, Peter** Philippi 1: die erste christliche Gemeinde Europas. Diss.-Habil. Mü 1994-5, ^{D}*Koch, D.-A.*, WUNT 2/87. Tü 1995, Mohr xxiii; 316 pp. DM168. 3-16-146479-6.

5107 *Pretorius, E. A. C.* New trends in reading Philippians: a literature review. Neotest. 29 (1995) 273-298.

5108 *Schlosser, Jacques* La figure de Dieu selon l'épître aux Philippiens. NTS 41 (1995) 378-399.

5109 *Segalla, Giuseppe* Salvezza cristologica universale in Filippesi e 1 Pietro. StPat 42 (1995) 215-229.

5110 *Silva, Moisés* Discourse analysis and Philippians. 1995 ⇒102. Discourse analysis. JSNT.S 113. 102-106.

5111 **Wick, Peter** Der Philipperbrief: der formale Aufbau. BWANT 135. 1994 ⇒10,6108. ^{R}ThLZ 120 (1995) 344-346 (*Schenk, Wolfgang*); JBL 114 (1995) 750-752 (*Ascough, Richard S.*).

5112 *Skeat, T. C.* Did Paul write to "bishops and deacons" at Philippi?: a note on Philippians 1:1. NT 37 (1995) 12-15.

5113 *Schlosser, Jacques* La communauté en charge de l'évangile: à propos de Ph. 1,7. RHPhR 75 (1995) 67-76.

5114 *Madison, Timothy E.* Philippians 1:21-23: hope that never ends. RExp 92 (1995) 513-517.

5115 *Trevijano Etcheverria, Ramón* Flp 2,5-11: un Λόγο' σοφία' Paulino sobre Cristo. Helm. 14 (1995) 115-145.

5116 *Bostock, Gerald* ORIGEN's exegesis of the kenosis hymn (Philippians 2:5-11). 1995 ⇒126. Origeniana Sexta. BEThL 118. 531-547.

5117 **Fields, Bruce Lester** Paul as model: the rhetoric and Old Testament background of Philippians 3:1-4:1. Diss. Marquette 1995, 386 pp. ^{D}*Stockhausen, Carol*, AAC 9600848; DAI-A 56/9,p.3617.

5118 *Doughty, Darrell J.* Citizens of heaven Philippians 3.2-21. NTS 41 (1995) 102-122.

5119 *Babinsky, Ellen L.* Philippians 3:7-15. Interp. 49 (1995) 70-72.

5120 *Otto, Randall E.* "If possible I may attain the resurrection from the dead" (Philippians 3:11). CBQ 57 (1995) 324-340.

5121 *Becker, Jürgen* Erwägungen zu Phil. 3,20-21. 1995 <1971> ⇒5. ^{F}BECKER J., BZNW 76. 65-78.

5122 *Dahl, Nils A.* [4,1-3] Euodia and Syntyche and Paul's letter to the Philippians. 1995 ⇒20. ^{F}MEEKS W., 3-15.

5123 *Carls, Peter* Wer sind Syzygos, Euodia und Syntyche in Phil 4,2F? PzB 4 (1995) 117-141.

5124 *Hertog, G.C. den* 'De here is nabij' (Filip. 4:5): een poging tot theologisch verantwoord spreken over de wederkomst van Jezus Christus. 1995 ⇒91. Totdat hij komt. 75-111.

5125 *Malherbe, Abraham J.* Paul's self-sufficiency (Philippians 4:11). 1995 ⇒14. ^{F}HARTMAN L., 813-826.

G6.4 Ad Colossenses.

5126 **Aletti, Jean-Noël** Saint Paul: épître aux Colossiens. ÉtB 20. 1993
⇒9,6299; 10,6122. ᴿJBL 114 (1995) 537-539 (*Van Broekhoven,*
Harold); Gr. 76 (1995) 155-156 (*Galot, Jean*).
　　Bruce, Frederick F. The epistles to the Colossians...⇒5054.
　　Martin, Ralph P. Ephesians, Colossians... ⇒5061.
　　Melick, Richard R. Jr. Philippians, Colossians... ⇒5090.
5127 **Thurston, Bonnie** Reading Colossians, Ephesians and 2 Thes-
salonians: a literary and theological commentary. Reading the New
Testament. NY 1995, Crossroad viii; 197 pp. $17. 0-8245-1475-0
[OTA 18,668].
5128 **Wall, Robert W.** Colossians & Philemon. 1993 ⇒9,6302. ᴿCritRR
7 (1994) 270-272 (*DeMaris, Richard E.*); BS 152 (1995) 118-119
(*Bateman, Herbert W.*).

5129 **Arnold, Clinton E.** The Colossian syncretism: the interface
between christianity and folk belief at Colossae. WUNT 2/77. Tü
1995, Mohr xii; 378 pp. DM118. 3-16-146435-4.
5130 *Betz, Hans Dieter* Paul's "second presence" in Colossians. 1995
⇒14. ᶠHARTMAN L., 507-518.
5131 *Van Broekhoven, Harold* Persuasion or praise in Colossians. Proc-
GLM 15 (1995) 65-78.
5132 **DeMaris, Richard E.** The Colossians controversy. JSNT.S 96.
1994 ⇒10,6128. ᴿThLZ 120 (1995) 240-242 (*Schweizer, Eduard*);
JBL 114 (1995) 752-754 (*Sappington, Thomas J.*); CBQ 57 (1995)
800-801 (*Wild, Robert A.*).
5133 *Detwiler, Andreas* L'épître aux Colossiens: un exemple de réception de la théologie paulinienne. FV 94 (1995) 27-40.
5134 *Drake, Alfred Edwin* The riddle of Colossians: quaerendo
invenietis. NTS 41 (1995) 123-144.
5135 *Dunn, J.D.G.* The Colossian philosophy: a confident Jewish
apologia. Bib. 76 (1995) 153-181.
　　Engelbrecht, J.J. Opmerkings oor vroeë katolisisme in die Nuwe
Testament. ⇒5055.
5136 *Goulder, Michael* Colossians and Barbelo. NTS 41 (1995) 601-
619.
5137 *Hartman, Lars* Humble and confident: on the so-called
philosophers in Colossae. StTh 49 (1995) 25-39.
5138 **Hoppe, Rudolf** Der Triumph des Kreuzes: Studien zum Verhältnis
des Kolosserbriefes zur paulinischen Kreuzestheologie. SBB 28.
Stu 1994, Katholisches Bibelwerk 313 pp. DM69. 3-460-00281.
Diss.-Habil. ᴿSNTU.A 20 (1995) 238-240 (*Giesen, H.*).
　　MacLean, Jennifer K.B. Ephesians and the problem of Colossians. ⇒5075.
5139 *Rowland, Christopher* Apocalyptic visions and the exaltation of
Christ in the letter to the Colossians. 1995 <1983> ⇒105. The
Pauline writings. 220-229.

5140 *Fossum, Jarl E.* The image of the invisible God: Colossians 1.15-
18a in the light of Jewish mysticism and gnosticism. 1995 ⇒48.
NTOA 30. 13-39.
5141 *Bottino, Adriana* Inno al primato di Cristo (Col 1,15-20). 1995
⇒19. ᶠMATTIOLI A., 189-234.

5142 *Murphy-O'Connor, J.* Tradition and redaction in Col 1:15-20. RB 102 (1995) 231-241.

5143 *Monroy Rodríguez, F.J.* Jesucristo y el universo: Colosenses 1,15-20: un himno al Señor Jesús: origen, destino, fundamento y salvación del cosmos. Mayéutica 21 (1995) 61-119 [NTAb 40,450].

5144 *Hayes, Holly Diane* Colossians 2:6-19. Interp. 49 (1995) 285-288.

5145 *Doignon, Jean* Un terme difficile de Col. 2,9 éclairé par HILAIRE de Poitiers: corporaliter. RBen 105 (1995) 5-8.

5146 *Martin, Troy* But let everyone discern the body of Christ (Colossians 2:17). JBL 114 (1995) 249-255.

5147 *Hartman, Lars* Code and context: a few reflections on the parenesis of Colossians 3:6-4:1. 1995 <1987> ⇒110. Understanding Paul's ethics. 177-191.

5148 *Martin, Troy* The Scythian perspective in Col 3:11. NT 37 (1995) 249-261.

5149 **Collins, Matthew Scott** Rhetoric, household and cosmos: a rhetorical and sociological analysis of the letter to the Colossians with particular focus on Colossians 3:18-4:1. Diss. Vanderbilt 1995, 209 pp. D*Tolbert, Mary Ann*, AAC 9528967; DAI-A 56/5,p.1827.

5150 *Lach, J.* Le code domestique dans l'épître aux Colossiens (Col 3,18-4,1). P. ACra 27 (1995) 219-231.

G6.5 Ad Philemonem

Bruce, F.F. The epistles to the Colossians...Philemon...⇒5054.

5151 *Callahan, Allen Dwight* John CHRYSOSTOM on Philemon: a response to Margaret M. MITCHELL. HThR 88 (1995) 149-156.

Donfried, K.P.; Marshall, I.H. The theology of the shorter Pauline letters [Thess Phlp Phlm]. 1993 ⇒5164.

5152 *Hock, Ronald F.* A support for his old age: Paul's plea on behalf of Onesimus. 1995 ⇒20. F*MEEKS W.*, 67-81.

5153 *Kallemeyn, H.* Philémon et son prochain. RRef 46/1 (1995) 15ff [ZID 21,153].

Martin, Ralph P. Ephesians...Philemon. 1991 ⇒5061.

Melick, Richard R. Jr. Philippians...Philemon 1991 ⇒5090.

5154 *Mitchell, Margaret M.* John CHRYSOSTOM on Philemon: a second look. HThR 88 (1995) 135-148.

Wall, Robert W. Colossians & Philemon. 1993 ⇒5128.

G6.6 Ad Thessalonicenses.

5155 *Malherbe, Abraham J.* God's new family in Thessalonica. 1995 ⇒20. F*MEEKS W.*, 116-125.

5156 **Martin, D. Michael** 1,2 Thessalonians. NAC 33. Nv 1995, Broadman & Holman 313 pp. 0-8054-0133-4.

5157 **Morris, Leon** The first and second epistles to the Thessalonians. NIC.NT. GR 1995, Eerdmans xvi; 278 pp. 0-8028-2512-5.

5158 *Okorie, A.M.* The Pauline work ethic in I and II Thessalonians. DBM 14/1 (1995) 55-64.

5159 *Varickasseril, Jose* Faith in Thessalonica. IMR 17/4 (1995) 48-60 [ThIK 17,37].

5160 **Verhoef, E.** Tessalonicenzen: een praktische bijbelverklaring. Tekst Toelichting. Kampen 1995, Kok 106 pp. *f*25. 90-242-2318-0 [TTh 36,113].

5161 *Wanamaker, Charles* "Like a father treats his own children": Paul and the conversion of the Thessalonians. JTSA 92 (1995) 46-55 [ZID 1996/2,46].

5162 **Williams, David John** 1 and 2 Thessalonians. 1992 ⇒8,6661. RCritRR 7 (1994) 274-275 (*Wanamaker, Charles A.*).

5163 **Collins, Raymond F.** The birth of the New Testament. 1993 ⇒9,6342. CritRR 7 (1994) 165-168 (*McDonald, Lee M.*); New Theology Review 8 (1995) 92-94 (*Rosenblatt, Marie-Eloise*); TJT 11/1 (1995) 4490-91 (*Jervis, L. Ann*).

5164 **Donfried, Karl P.; Marshall, I. Howard** The theology of the shorter Pauline letters [Thess Phlp Phlm]. 1993 ⇒9,6346; 10,6158. RPacifica 8 (1995) 352-354 (*Dawes, Gregory W.*); JR 75 (1995) 410-411 (*Harlow, Daniel C.*); CritRR 8 (1995) 200-203 (*Holland, Glenn*).

5165 *Becker, Jürgen* Die Erwählung der Völker durch das Evangelium: theologiegeschichtliche Erwägungen zum 1 Thess. 1995 <1986> ⇒5. FBECKER J., BZNW 76. 79-98.

5166 *Kremer, Jacob* Was heißt Parusie und Parusieerwartung heute? Überlegungen zu den Parusieaussagen von 1 Thess. 1995 <1974> ⇒53. Die Bibel. 207 -222.

5167 **Pereyra, Roberto** Paul's earliest statement concerning the christian church: a review and evaluation of research into Paul's association of the term 'ekklesia' to 'en christo' in 1 Thessalonians. Diss. Andrews 1995, 416 pp. DPaulien, Jon, AAC 9535008; DAI-A 56/6,p.2285.

5168 **Smith, Abraham** Comfort one another: reconstructing the rhetoric and audience of 1 Thessalonians. Literary Currents in Biblical Interpretation. LVL 1995, Westminster 160 pp. $16. 0-664-25178-1 [NTAb 40,159].

5169 *Walton, S.* What has ARISTOTLE to do with Paul?: rhetorical criticsm and 1 Thessalonians. TynB 46 (1995) 229-250.

5170 **Schlueter, Carol J.** Filling up the measure...1 Th 2:14-16. JSNT.S 98. 1994 ⇒10,6166. RThLZ 120 (1995) 527-529 (*Broer, Ingo*); JThS 46 (1995) 654-659 (*Griffith-Jones, Robin*); CBQ 57 (1995) 825-827 (*Jaquette, James L.*).

5171 *Wortham, Robert A.* The problem of Anti-Judaism in 1 Thess 2:14-16 and related Pauline texts. BTB 25 (1995) 37-44.

5172 *Verhoef, Eduard* Die Bedeutung des Artikels τῶν in 1 Thess 2,15. BN 80 (1995) 41-46.

5173 *Johanson, Bruce C.* 1 Thessalonians 2:15-16: prophetic woe-oracle with EPHTHASEN as prophetic aorist. 1995 ⇒14. FHARTMAN L., 519-534.

5174 *Rosner, Brian S.* Seven questions for Paul's ethics: 1 Thessalonians 4:1-12 as a case study. 1995 ⇒110. Understanding Paul's ethics. 351-360.

5175 *Hopkins, Mark* [1 Th 4,15] The dog that did nothing in the night-time: the intermediate state. TCNN Research Bulletin 28 (1995) 21-32 [ThIK 17,23].

5176 *Plevnik, Jože* Čas in trenutek Gospodovega dne 1 Tes 5,1-11 [Times and seasons of the Lord's coming 1 Thess 5,1-11]. Bogoslovni Vestnik 55 (1995) 507-517 [sum. 517].

5177 *Kahl, Werner* The structure of salvation in 2Thess and 4Q434. The Qumran Chronicle 5 (1995) 103-121.

5178 *Lubsczyk, Hans* Bibelschule: Gedanken zum 2. Thessalonicherbrief. KiHe 11 (1995) 21-23.

Thurston, Bonnie Reading Colossians, Ephesians, and 2 Thessalonians. ⇒5127.

5179 *Trudinger, Paul* The priority of 2 Thessalonians revisited: some fresh evidence. DR 113 (1995) 31-35.

G7.0 Epistulae pastorales.

5180 **Arichea, Daniel C.; Hatton, Howard A.** A handbook on Paul's letters to Timothy and to Titus. NY 1995, United Bible Societies viii; 336 pp. $14. 0-82670168-X [EvQ 69,371].

5181 **Balthasar, Hans Urs von** Le Lettere Pastorali di San Paolo: dischiuse alla preghiera contemplativa: la prima e la seconda lettera a Timoteo: la lettera a Tito. Già e non ancora 278. Mi 1995, Jaca 180 pp. 88-16-30278-X.

5182 *Dubois, Jean-Daniel* Les pastorales, la gnose et l'hérésie. FV 94/2 (1995) 41-48.

5183 *Engelbrecht, J.J.* Opmerkings oor vroeë katolisisme in die Nuwe Testament. ⇒5055.

Kaestli, Jean-Daniel Luke-Acts and the Pastoral Epistles. ⇒3579.

5184 **Marcheselli Casale, Cesare** Le Lettere Pastorali: le due lettere di Timoteo e la lettera a Tito: introduzione, versione, commento. SOCr 15. Bo 1995, EDB 876 pp. 88-10-20615-0.

5185 *Porter, Stanley E.* Pauline authorship and the Pastoral Epistles: implications for canon. DBM 5 (1995) 105-123.

5186 **Redalié, Yann** Paul après Paul: le temps, le salut, la morale selon les épîtres à Timothée et à Tite. MoBi 31. 1994 ⇒10,6185. ᴿEThR 70 (1995) 281-282 *(Cuvillier, Elian)*; Studi di Teologia 7 (1995) 202-203 *(Bolognesi, Pietro)*; EeV 105 (1995) 649-651 *(Cothenet, E.)*; ETL 71 (1995) 467-468 *(Collins, R.F.)*; BZ 39 (1995) 277-279 *(Oberlinner, Lorenz)*.

5187 *Towner, P.H.* Pauline theology or Pauline tradition in the Pastoral Epistles: the question of method. TynB 46 (1995) 287-314.

5188 **Wagener, Ulrike** Die Ordnung des "Hauses Gottes:" der Ort von Frauen in der Ekklesiologie und Ethik der Pastoralbriefe. WUNT 2/65. 1994 ⇒10,6188. ᴿBiKi 50 (1995) 243-245 *(Weiser, Alfons)*; LuThK 19 (1995) 159 *(Stolle, Volker)*.

5189 *Wall, Robert W.* Pauline authorship and the Pastoral Epistles: a response to S.E. PORTER. Bulletin for Biblical Research 5 (1995) 125-128.

5190 *Weidmann, F.* The good teacher: social identity and community purpose in the Pastoral Epistles. JHiC 2 (1995) 100-114.

5191 **Young, Frances** The theology of the Pastoral letters.1994 ⇒10,6188*. ᴿTheol. 98 (1995) 489-491 *(Prior, Michael)*; CBQ 57 (1995) 834-835 *(Fleddermann, Harry T.)*.

5192 *Young, Frances* The Pastoral Epistles and the ethics of reading.
      1995 <1992> ⇒105. The Pauline writings. 268-282.

G7.2 1-2 ad Timotheum

5193 ᵀᴱ**Di Nola, Gerardo** Giovanni CRISOSTOMO: commento alla
      prima lettera a Timoteo. CTePa 124. R 1995, Città Nuova 328 pp.
      L33.000. 88-311-3124-9 [Hum(B) 51,989—*Moreschini, Claudio*].
5194 **Martini, Carlo Maria** La via di Timoteo. CasM 1995, Piemme
      238 pp. L28.000 [CivCatt 147,531].
5195 **Oberlinner, Lorenz** Kommentar zum ersten Timotheusbrief. 1994
      ⇒10,6183. ᴿEstAg 30 (1995) 344-345 (*Cineira, D.A.*); BiLi 68
      (1995) 235-237 (*Schwarz, Roland*);
5196 Kommentar zum zweiten Timotheusbrief. HThK 11/2. Fr/B 1995,
      Herder xiii; 187 pp. DM68. 3-451-23768-7.
5197 *Redalié, Yann* "Diventa modello dei credenti": la figura pastorale
      nelle esortazioni a Timoteo. Protest. 501 (1995) 2-21.
5198 **Roloff, Jürgen** Der erste Brief an Timotheus. EKK 15. 1988
      ⇒4,6318... 6,6668. ᴿBiLi 68 (1995) 235-237 (*Schwarz, Roland*).
5199 *Green, L.C.* Universal salvation (I Timothy 2:4) according to the
      Lutheran reformers. LuthQ 9 (1995) 281-300.
5200 ᴱ**Köstenberger, Andreas J.; Schreiner, Thomas R.; Baldwin, H.
      Scott** Women in the church: a fresh analysis of 1 Timothy 2:9-15.
      GR 1995, Baker 334 pp. $22.
5201 *Köstenberger, Andreas J.* Syntactical background studies to 1
      Timothy 2.12 in the New Testament and extrabiblical Greek litera-
      ture. 1995 ⇒102. Discourse analysis. JSNT.S 113. 156-179.
5202 *Krieser, M.* 'Einer Frau gestatte ich nicht, daß sie lehre': eine
      hermeneutische Studie über I Tim 2,12. LuThK 19 (1995) 148-
      155.
5203 *North, J. Lionel* "Human speech" in Paul and the Paulines: the
      investigation and meaning of ἀνθρώπινος ὁ λόγος (1 Tim. 3:1).
      NT 37 (1995) 50-67.
5204 *Stiefel, Jennifer H.* Women deacons in 1 Timothy: a lingustic and
      literary look at "women likewise..." (1 Tim 3.11). NTS 41 (1995)
      442-457.
5205 *Campbell, R.A. καὶ μάλιστα οἰκείων*—a new look at 1 Timothy
      5.8. NTS 41 (1995) 157-160.
5206 **Mappes, David Allen** Expositional problems related to the elder-
      ship in 1 Timothy 5:17-25. Diss. Dallas 1995, 234 pp.
      ᴰ*Constable, T.L.*, AAC 9611640; DAI-A 56,4819.

5207 *Walther, F.E.* Die Zukunftsangst überwinden (2. Tim. 1,7-10).
      ThBeitr 26 (1995) 185-189.
5208 *Rodenberg, O.* Die Art unseres Kampfes (2. Tim. 2,5). ThBeitr 26
      (1995) 226-231 [1 Sam 24,1-8].
5209 *Pickering, Stuart R.* 2 Timothy 3:8-9: Jannes and Jambres.
      NTTRU 3 (1995) 35-38.

G7.3 Ad Titum.

5210 **Barra, Domenico** Le epistole di Paolo a Tito e a Filemone. Palermo 1995, Gesù vive 94 pp.
5211 *Marshall, H.* Titus 2:11-3:8. EurJT 4/1 (1995) 11ff [ZID 21,412].
5212 *Brug, J.* [3,5] A rebirth-washing and a renewal-Holy Spirit. WLQ 92 (1995) 124-128 [NTAb 40,71].

G8 Epistula ad Hebraeos.

5213 *Allen, Pauline; Mayer, Wendy* The thirty-four homilies on Hebrews: the last series delivered by CHRYSOSTOM in Constantinople? Byz. 65 (1995) 309-348.
5214 **Casalini, Nello** Agli Ebrei. 1992 ⇒8,6735... 10,6204. REstB 53 (1995) 280-281 (*Rubio, L.*); JBL 114 (1995) 168-169 (*Casurella, Anthony*).
5215 **Ellingworth, Paul** The epistle to the Hebrews. NIGTC. 1993 ⇒9,6399; 10,6207. RCritRR 7 (1994) 184-186 (*Wilson, R.McL.*); Studi di teologia 7 (1995) 77-78 (*Jones, Rod*); JETh 9 (1995) 209-211 (*Siebenthal, Heinrich von*).
5216 *Fuller, Reginald H.* Hebrews. 1995 ⇒95. The general letters. 1-23.
5217 **Gräßer, Erich** An die Hebräer 2: Hebr 7,1-10,18. 1993 ⇒10,6208. EKK 17/2. RThLZ 120 (1995) 791-793 (*März, Claus-Peter*).
5218 **Lane, William L.** Hebrews 1-8; 9-13. WBC 47AB. 1991 ⇒7,5708... 10,6210. RKerux 10/1 (1995) 32-34 (*Bergquist, Randall A.*); AUSS 33 (1995) 305-306 (*Kent, Matthew M.*).
5219 *März, Claus-Peter* Hebräerbrief. 1995 ⇒123. LThK 4. 1226-1230.
5220 **Ravasi, Gianfranco** Lettera agli Ebrei. Conversazioni bibliche. Bo 1995, EDB 132 pp. Ciclo di conferenze tenute al Centro culturale S. Fedele di Milano. L18.000. 88-10-70955-1.
5221 *Weiß, Hans-Friedrich* Ein Buch geht mit seinem Leser um: der Kommentar zum Hebräerbrief und sein Autor. BiKi 50/1-2 (1995) 32-38.

5222 **Beilner, Wolfgang** Nachpaulinische Theologie. Vermittlung 29. Salzburg 1995 n.p. 167 pp.
5223 **Blackstone, Thomas Ladd** The hermeneutics of recontextualization in the epistle to the Hebrews. Diss. Emory 1995, 367 pp. DCraddock, Fred B., AAC 9536365; DAI-A 56/7,p.2726.
5224 *Bright, Pamela* The epistle to the Hebrews in ORIGEN's christology. 1995 ⇒126. Origeniana Sexta. BEThL 118. 559-565.
5225 **deSilva, David Arthur** Despising shame: honor discourse and community maintenance in the epistle to the Hebrews. Diss. Emory 1995, DJohnson, Luke Timothy [DAI-A 56/7,2727], SBL.DS 152. Atlanta 1995, Scholars 371 pp. $40/$25. 0-7885-0200-X/-0201-8.
5226 *Dixon, R.L.* The kingdom of God in Hebrews. Stulos Theological Journal 3 (1995) 95-112 [NTAb 41,78].
5227 *Fahner, Chr.* The Greek of Hebrews. 1995 ⇒133. Bible et Informatique. 206-213.
5228 **Garuti, Paolo** Alle origini dell'omiletica cristiana: la lettera agli Ebrei: note di analisi retorica. *Boismard, M.-É.* <introd by>

ASBF 38. J 1995, Franciscan Printing Press viii; 439 pp. $35.
RVivens Homo 6 (1995) 411-413 (*Mazzinghi, Luca*); RB 102
(1995) 592-595 (*Taylor, Justin*).

5229 **Guthrie, George H.** The structure of Hebrews. NT.S 72. 1994
⇒10,6222. REE 70 (1995) 254-255 (*Ramírez Fueyo, Francisco*);
RB 102 (1995) 428-433 (*Garuti, Paolo*); Bib. 76 (1995) 587-590
(*Vanhoye, Albert*); CBQ 57 (1995) 395-397 (*deSilva, David A.*);
JBL 114 (1995) 754-755 (*Cosby, Michael R.*).

5230 **Hübner, Hans** Biblische Theologie des Neuen Testaments 3:
Hebräerbrief, Evangelien und Offenbarung: Epilegomena. Gö
1995, Vandenhoeck & Ruprecht 322 pp. DM74. 3-525-53598-8.

5231 **Isaacs, Marie E.** Sacred space...Hebrews. JSNT.S 73. 1992
⇒8,6742... 10,6227. RCritRR 7 (1994) 207-209 (*Hurst, L.D.*).

5232 **Kim, Daewon** Perseverance in Hebrews. Diss. Pretoria 1995, DDu
Toit, Andries B., DAI-A 56/11,4430.

5233 **Lindars, Barnabas** La teologia della lettera agli Ebrei. 1993
⇒9,6412. RPaVi 40/4 (1995) 55 (*Migliasso, Secondo*).

5234 **Löhr, Hermut** Umkehr und Sünde im Hebräerbrief. BZNW 73.
1994 ⇒10,6230. RThLZ 120 (1995) 1079-1080 (*Weiß, Hans-
Friedrich*).

5235 *MacLeod, David J.* The cleansing of the true tabernacle. BS 152
(1995) 60-71.

5236 *Michaud, Jean-Paul* L'épître aux Hébreux aujourd'hui. 1995 ⇒84.
"De bien des manières". LeDiv 163. 391-431.

5237 EReynier, Chantal; Sesboüé, Bernard 'Comme une ancre jetée
vers l'avenir': regards sur l'épître aux Hébreux. Atelier de
théologie du centre Sèvres. P 1995, Médiasèvres 221 pp. 2-900-
388-35-10.

5238 **Scholer, John M.** Proleptic priesthood. JSNT.S 49. 1991
⇒7,5718... 10,6236. RSvTK 71 (1995) 89-90 (*Übelacker, Walter*).

5239 *Scholtissek, Klaus* Gottesdienst: Biblisch: Neues Testament. 1995
⇒123. LThK 4. 890-891.

5240 *Siegert, Folker* Die Makrosyntax des Hebräerbriefs. 1995 ⇒14.
FHARTMAN L., 305-316.

5241 *Walton, Steve* Sacrifice and priesthood in relation to the christian
life and church in the New Testament. 1995 ⇒61. Sacrifice. 136-
156.

5242 **Wider, David** Theozentrik und Bekenntnis: Untersuchungen zur
Theologie des Reden Gottes im Hebräerbrief. Diss. Bern 1994-5,
DHasler.

5243 *Fornberg, Tord* God, the fathers, and the prophets: the use of Heb
1:1 in recent theology of religions. 1995 ⇒14. FHARTMAN L.,
887-900.

5244 *Bovon, François* The Christ, the faith and wisdom in the epistle to
the Hebrews (Hebrews 11 and 1). 1995 <1968> ⇒40. New Testament traditions. 119-131, 219-224 [RB 103,117].

5245 **Franco Martínez, César Augusto** [2,9-10] Jesucristo...en la Carta
a los Hebreos. 1992 ⇒8,6759; 9,6422. RHumTeo 16 (1995) 313-
315 (*Couto, A.*); Igreja e Missã 47 (1995) 303-304 (*Couto, A.*).

5246 *Schmidt, Thomas E.* The letter tau as the cross: ornament and content in Hebrews 2,14. Bib. 76 (1995) 75-84.
      Thüsing, Wilhelm "Milch" und "feste Speise"...Hebr 5,11-6,3).
⇒4878.

5247 *Riquelme, J.* Jesús, un laico de la tribu de Judá, Hb. 7,11-14. Test. 150 (1995) 5-8 [Strom. 52,346].
5248 *Stanley, Steven K.* A new covenant hermeneutic: the use of Scripture in Hebrews 8-10. TynB 46 (1995) 204-206.
5249 *Stanley, Steve* Hebrews 9:6-10: the "parable" of the tabernacle. NT 37 (1995) 385-399.
5250 *Álvarez Cineira, D.* Los sacrificios en la carta a los Hebreos 10,1-18. EstAg 30 (1995) 5-58, 207-237.
5251 *Vanhoye, Albert* L'ombre et l'image: discussions sur He 10,1. 1995 ⇒4. ᶠBᴇᴀᴜᴄʜᴀᴍᴘ P., LeDiv 162. 267-282.
5252 *Thüsing, Wilhelm* "Laßt uns hinzutreten..." (Hebr 10,22): zur Frage nach dem Sinn der Kulttheologie im Hebräerbrief". 1995 <1965> ⇒60. Studien. WUNT 2/82. 184-200.
5253 *Spencer, Richard A.* Hebrews 11:1-3, 8-16. Interp. 49 (1995) 288-292.
5254 **Eisenbaum, Pamela Michelle** The Jewish heroes of christian history: Hebrews 11 in literary context Diss. Columbia 1995, 307 pp. ᴰ*Scroggs, Robin,* AAC 9533545; DAI-A 56/6,2279.
5255 *Söding, Thomas* Die Antwort des Glaubens: das Vorbild Abrahams nach Hebr 11. IKaZ 24 (1995) 394-408.
5256 *Amjad-Ali, Christine* [11] Clouds of witness. **Urdu.** Al-Mushir 37 (1995) 107-117 [ThIK 18,59].
5257 **Croy, Noah Clayton** Endurance in suffering: a study of Hebrews 12:1-13 in its rhetorical, religious, and philosophical context. Diss. Emory 1995, 324 pp. ᴰ*Holladay, Carl R.,* AAC 9536374; DAI-A 56/7,p.2727.
5258 *Vigil, José María* De olhos fitos na utopia de Jesus (cf. Hb 12,2). REB 55 (1995) 147-160.
5259 *Croy, N. Clayton* A note on Hebrews 12:2. JBL 114 (1995) 117-119.
5260 *Remaud, M.* L'initiateur de la foi: Abraham et Jésus: Hébreux 12,2 à la lumière de quelques midrashim sur Abraham. RICP 54 (1995) 79-91 [NTAb 40,453].

G9.1 1 Petri.

5261 **Beck, J.T.** Petrusbriefe: ein Kommentar. Giessen 1995 <1896>, Brunnen xvi; 300 pp.   DM68. 3-7655-9226-9 [NTAb 40,353].
5262 **Brox, Norbert** La primera carta de Pedro. ᵀ*Olasagasti, Manuel.* 1994 ⇒10,6258. ᴿLumen 44 (1995) 514-515 (*Arróniz, José Manuel*).
5263 **Craddock, Fred B.** First and Second Peter and Jude. Westminster Bible companion. LVL 1995, Westminster x; 156 pp. 0-664-25265-6.
5264 **Goppelt, Leonhard** A commentary on I Peter. 1993 ⇒9,6433; 10,6259. ᴿAnton. 70 (1995) 694-695 (*Alvarez Barredo, Miguel*).
5265 **Grudem, Wayne A.** La prima epistola di Pietro: introduzione e commentario. Commentari al Nuovo Testamento. R 1995, G.B.U. 306 pp. [⇒4,6359... 10,6434].
5266 **Hillyer, Norman** 1 and 2 Peter, Jude. 1992 ⇒8,6775. ᴿCritRR 7 (1994) 206-207 (*Davids, Peter H.*).
5267 ᴱ**Hofmann, Josef†; Uhlig, Siegbert** Novum Testamentum aethiopice: die katholischen Briefe. ÄthF 29. 1993 ⇒9,6435.

ROrChr 79 (1995) 265-270 (*Weninger, Stefan*); OLZ 90 (1995) 402-412 (*Juckel, Andreas*).
5268 **Krimmer, Heiko P.; Holland, Martin** Erster und Zweiter Petrusbrief. C-Bibelkommentar 20. Neuhausen 1994, Hänssler 282 pp. DM35. 3-7751-1599-4. RJETh 9 (1995) 211-214 (*Schröder, Michael*).
5269 *Krodel, Gerhard* 1 Peter. 1995 ⇒95. The general Letters. 42-83.
5270 **Marshall, I. Howard** 1 Peter. 1991 ⇒8,6778. REvQ 67 (1995) 165-167 (*Willoughby, Robert*).
5271 **Miller, Donald C.** On this rock: a commentary on I Peter. PTMS 34. Allison Park 1993, Pickwick 390 pp. $30. 1-55435-020-1. RInterp. 49 (1995) 420-424 (*Snodgrass, Klyne*).
5272 **Perkins, Pheme** First and Second Peter, James, and Jude. Interpretation. LVL 1995, Westminster vi; 204 pp. $32. 0-8042-3145-1 [NTAb 40,156].
5273 **Wachtel, Klaus** Der byzantinische Text der Katholischen Briefe: eine Untersuchung zur Entstehung der Koine des Neuen Testaments. ANTT 24. B 1995, De Gruyter viii; 463 pp. (Diss.-Habil. Mü 1994) DM248. 3-11-014691-6 [NTAb 40,362].

Downing, F. Gerald PLINY's prosecutions of christians...1 Peter. ⇒4367.
5274 *Elliott, John H.* Disgraced yet graced: the gospel according to 1 Peter in the key of honor and shame. BTB 25 (1995) 166-178.
5275 **Elliott, John H.** Un hogar para los que no tienen patria ni hogar: estudio crítico social de la carta primera de Pedro y de su situación y estrategia. Estella 1995, Verbo Divino 400 pp. [Efemerides Mexicana 15,283].
5276 *Fabris, Rinaldo* Elementi apocalittici nelle lettere di Pietro e Giuda. RStB 7 (1995) 85-102.
5277 *Le Saux, Madeleine* Les églises de Pierre. DosB 60 (1995) 8-9.
5278 *Marconi, Gilberto* Il ruolo degli anziani nella prima lettera di Pietro e nella lettera di Giacomo. 1995 ⇒96. Gli anziani. 193-213.
5279 **Metzner, Rainer** Die Rezeption des Matthäusevangeliums im 1. Petrusbrief: Studien zum traditionsgeschichtlichen und theologischen Einfluss des 1. Evangeliums auf den 1. Petrusbrief. Diss. Humboldt, DWolff, C., WUNT 2/74. Tü 1995, Mohr x; 340 pp. DM108/FS98/SCH845. 3-16-146378-1 [NTAb 40,343].
5280 **Miller, Larry** Christianisme et société dans la première lettre de Pierre: histoire de l'interprétation, interprétation de l'histoire. Diss. Strasbourg, DTrocmé, É..
5281 *Molthagen, J.* Die Lage der Christen im römischen Reich nach dem 1. Petrusbrief: zum Problem einer domitianischen Verfolgung. Hist. 44 (1995) 422-458 [NTAb 40,453].
5282 *Olsson, Birger* A social-scientific criticism of 1 Peter. 1995 ⇒14. FHARTMAN L., 827-846.
5283 *Segalla, Giuseppe* Salvezza cristologica...1 Pietro. ⇒5109.
5284 *Slaughter, James R.* The importance of Literary argument for understanding 1 Peter. BS 152 (1995) 72-91.
5285 *Snyder, Scot* Participles and imperatives in 1 Peter: a reexamination in the light of recent scholarly trends. FgNT 8 (1995) 187-198.

5286 **Thurén, Lauri Toumas** Argument and theology in 1 Peter: the origins of Christian paraenesis. JSNT.S 114. Shf 1995, Academic 251 pp. 1-85075-546-9.

5287 *Dupont-Roc, R.* Le jeu des prépositions en 1 Pierre 1,1-12: de l'espérance finale à la joie dans les épreuves présentes. EstB 53 (1995) 201-212.

5288 *Miller, Donald G.* The resurrection as the source of living hope: an exposition of I Peter 1:3. HBT 17 (1995) 132-140.

5289 *Seland, Torrey* The "common priesthood" of PHILO and 1 Peter: a Philonic reading of 1 Peter 2.5,9. JSNT 57 (1995) 87-119.

5290 *Covolo, Enrico dal* L'interpretazione origeniana di 1 Petri 2,9. 1995 ⇒126. Origeniana Sexta. BEThL 118. 567-575.

5291 *Lovik, Eric G.* A look at the ancient house codes and their contributions to understanding 1 Pet 3:1-7. CBTJ 11 (1995) 49-63.

5292 *Erickson, Millard J.* [3,18-20; 4,6] Is there opportunity for salvation after death? BS 152 (1995) 131-144.

G9.2 2 Petri.

5293 **Bénétreau, Samuel** La deuxième épître de Pierre et l'épître de Jude. 1994 ⇒10,6272. ^RHokhma 58/1 (1995) 71-74 (*Buchhold, Jacques*).

   Craddock, Fred B. First and Second Peter...⇒5263.

5294 *Danker, Frederick W.* 2 Peter. 1995 ⇒95. The general Letters. 84-93.

   Fornberg, Tord The figure of Peter...in 2 Peter. ⇒3125.

   Hillyer, Norman 1 and 2 Peter, Jude. ⇒5266.

5295 **Knight, Jonathan** 2Peter and Jude. NTGu. Shf 1995, Academic 94 pp. 1-85075-744-5.

5296 **Neyrey, Jerome H.** 2 Peter, Jude. AncB 37C. 1993 ⇒9,6456. ^RJBL 114 (1995) 351-353 (*Pearson, Birger A.*).

5297 **Paulsen, Henning** Der zweite Petrusbrief und der Judasbrief. KEK 12/2. 1992 ⇒8,6808... 10,6273. ^RNeotest. 29 (1995) 133-135 (*Joubert, S.J.*).

   Perkins, Pheme First and Second Peter...⇒5272.

5298 **Smith, David Paul** Transforming second Peter: a historical literary rereading. Diss. Southern Baptist Theological Seminary 1995 257 pp. ^D*Dockery, David S.*, DAI-A 56/4,1395.

5299 *Lugo Rodriguez, Raul H.* Fim do mundo: destruição o recriação?: estudo sobre 2 Pd 3.5-13. Ribla 21 (1995) 244-256 [ThIK 17,68].

G9.4 Epistula Jacobi...data on both apostles James.

5300 **Frankemölle, Hubert** Der Brief des Jakobus: Kapitel 1. ÖTBK 17/1. 1994 ⇒10,6278. ^RBiKi 50/1-2 (1995) 138-139 (*Luck, Ulrich*); ThLZ 120 (1995) 650-651 (*Baasland, Ernst*); BZ 39 (1995) 279-283 (*Hoppe, Rudolf*).

5301 *Gench, Frances Taylor* James. 1995 ⇒95. The general Letters. 24-41.

5302   **Hodges, Zane C.** The epistle of James. 1994 ⇒10,6279. BS 152 (1995) 245-246 (*Constable, Thomas L.*).

5303   **Johnson, Luke Timothy** The letter of James: a new translation with introduction and commentary. AncB 37A. NY 1995, Doubleday xix; 412 pp. $35. 0-385-41360-2 [TS 58,350].

5304   **Manton, Thomas** James. ᴱ*McGrath, Alister;   Packer, J.I.*, Crossway Classic Commentaries. Wheaton 1995, Crossway x; 11-365 pp. £10. 1-85684-119-7.

       Perkins, Pheme First and Second Peter, James... ⇒5272.

5305   *Wolmarans, J.L.P.* Resente navorsing oor die Jakobusbrief. Acta Patristica et Byzantina 6 (1995) 180-191 [sum. 180].

5306   **Baker, William R.** Personal speech-ethics in the epistle of James. WUNT 2/68. Tü 1995, Mohr xvi; 364 pp. DM124. 3-16-145958-X.

5307   *Bindemann, Walther* Weisheit versus Weisheit: der Jakobusbrief als innerkirchlicher Diskurs. ZNW 86 (1995) 189-217.

5308   **Cargal, Timothy, B.** Restoring the diaspora... James. SBL.DS 144. 1993 ⇒10,6285. ᴿJBL 114 (1995) 348-351 (*Watson, Duane F.*).

5309   *Cothenet, Édouard* La sagesse dans la lettre de Jacques. 1995 ⇒117. La sagesse biblique. LeDiv 160. 413-419.

5310   *Crotty, R.* Identifying the poor in the letter of James. Colloquium 27/1 (1995) 11-21.

5311   ᴱ**Herbers, Klaus; Bauer, Dieter R.** Der Jakobskult in Süddeutschland: Kultgeschichte in regionaler und europäischer Perspektive. Jakobus-Studien 7. Tü 1995, Narr 401 pp.

5312   *Johnson, Luke Timothy* The social world of James: literary analysis and historical reconstruction. 1995 ⇒20. ᶠMᴇᴇᴋѕ W., 178-197.

5313   **Klein, Martin** "Ein vollkommenes Werk": Vollkommenheit, Gesetz und Gericht als theologische Themen des Jakobusbriefes. BWANT 139. Stu 1995, Kohlhammer 256 pp. DM89. 3-17-013697-6 [NTAb 40,154].

       Marconi, Gilberto Il ruolo degli anziani...lettera di Giacomo. ⇒5278.

5314   *Marucci, Corrado* Das Gesetz der Freiheit im Jakobusbrief. ZKTh 117 (1995) 317-331.

5315   *Popkes, Wiard* James and paraenesis, reconsidered. 1995 ⇒14. ᶠHᴀʀᴛᴍᴀɴ L., 535-561.

5316   *Terrinoni, Ubaldo* L'enigma e la portata teologica di dipsychos nell'epistola di Giacomo. 1995 ⇒19. ᶠMᴀᴛᴛɪᴏʟɪ A., 369-383.

5317   *Thurén, Lauri* Risky rhetoric in James? NT 37 (1995) 262-284.

5318   **Tsuji, Manabu** Glaube zwischen Vollkommenheit und Verweltlichung: eine Untersuchung zur literarischen Gestalt und zur inhaltlichen Kohärenz des Jakobusbrief. Diss. Bern 1995, ᴰ*Vollenweider, S.* [RTL 27,538].

5319   *Vyhmeister, Nancy Jean* [2,1-13] The rich man in James 2: does ancient patronage illumine the text? AUSS 33 (1995) 265-283.

5320   *Bauckham, Richard J.* [4,13-5,6] The relevance of extra-canonical Jewish texts to New Testament study 90-108;

5321   *Wall, Robert W.* [4,13-5,6] Reading the New Testament in canonical context 370-393. 1995 ⇒85. Hearing the New Testament.

5322 **Harrington, D.J.** [5,14-15] 'Is anyone among you sick?' New Testament foundations for anointing the sick. Emmanuel 101 (1995) 412-417 [NTAb 40,265].

G9.6 Epistula Judae.

5323 **Barra, Domenico** L'epistola di Giuda. Palermo 1995, Gesù vive 63 pp.
5324 **Charles, J. Daryl** Literary strategy in the epistle of Jude. 1993 ⇒9,6481; 10,6302. RRivBib 43 (1995) 301-302 (*Marconi, Gilberto*); JBL 114 (1995) 541-543 (*Martin, Troy W.*).
Craddock, Fred B. Comm. ⇒5263.
5325 **Dennison, James T.** What should I read on the epistle of Jude? Kerux 10/1 (1995) 25-30.
Fabris, Rinaldo Elementi apocalittici...Giuda. ⇒5276.
Hillyer, Norman Comm. ⇒5266.
5326 **Joubert, Stephan J.** Persuasion in the letter of Jude. JSNT 58 (1995) 75-87.
Knight, Jonathan Comm. ⇒5295.
5327 **Krodel, Gerhard** Jude. 1995 ⇒95. The general letters. 94-109.
Neyrey, Jerome H. Comm. ⇒5296.
Paulsen, Henning Comm. ⇒5297.
Perkins, Pheme Comm. ⇒5272.
5328 **Fossum, Jarl E.** Kyrios Jesus: angel christology in Jude 5-7. 1995 ⇒48. The image. NTOA 30. 41-69.

Index Alphabeticus

Auctores

Alcuin 4334
Alden R 1693 1945
Alegre X 3955
Alessandro A d' 2384
Aletti J 4502 4549
4729 4922 4944
5126
Alexander L 3552
3590 3781 3898
5093 Minorita 4336
T 173 219 607 687
2620
Alford J 1539
Alison J 4203
Alkier S 1221
Allen L 2400 2401 P
5213
Allison D 2809 2839
Al-Mallah Y 403
Alonso Schökel L
1010 1398 1778
1779 2047
Alsup J 4333
Alter R 1566 1781
2162
Althann R 1790
Álvarez A 349 2900
-Barredo M 2367 2818
5264
-Cineira D 5250 M
920
-Valdés A 292 304 375
Alves M 1456
Amato A 2906
Ambrose M 3606
Amjad-Ali C 3437
4284 4907 5256
Amore R 1042
Amphoux C 3619
3996
Amsler S 1841 2081
2230 2294 2546
2692 2698 2704
2712
Anbar M 536 2434
Anderlini G 2023
Andersen F 411 880
1399 2561
Anderson B 416 581 G
762 786 799 H 3420
3523 J 2840 3326 P
4093 R 2661

Andiñach P 2547
Andrés R de 595
Andrews K 4686 S
4993
Anthonysami J 3327
Antomas Oses I 1478
Antonelli J 140
Anziani G 2897
Aparicio A 1476 1540
1585
-Rodríguez Á 1596
Apponius 1795
Arambarri J 211 3058
Ararat N 668
Arasakumar R 2352
Arav R 131
Archer G 1114
Argall R 2048
Arichea D 4932 5180
Aristotle 5169
Armellini F 1432
Arminjon B 3958
Arnal W 3152 3688
Arnold C 5129
Arróniz J 5262
Arteaga Natividad R
238
Artemidorus E 4342
Arthur K 2083
Artola A 4487
Artus O 793
Artz P 2026
Arul Raja A 3502
Arzt P 1345
Aschim A 412
Ascough R 3586 3624
Asendorf U 191
Asensio F 4655
Ashby G 582
Asher ben Abraham C
1329
Ashley T 780 815
2262
Ash P 1175
Ashton J 3214 3949
3986 3987 4119
Asquith C 4435
Assan-Dhote I 2383
Astell A 1704
Asterius 1583
Astolfo A 4656
Astruc Š 2291

Asurmendi J 1269
Atkinson J 2 W 3553
4550
Attinger D 2841
Attridge H 3641
Auffret P 1072 1320
1584 1585 1598
1631 1673
Augenstein J 4021
Augrain C 3602
Augustinus 238 240
277 315 335 1478
1503 1534 1569
3034 3756 3977
4244 4251 4269
4286 4716 4719
Aulard S 2616
Auld A 799 946 1089
2084
Auneau J 146
Aune D 4371 4467
Ausín S 2079 2518
Autané M 2562
Auwers J 1013 1446
2179 2270 2277
2282
Ayán J 5077
Azria R 422

Baaij P 4777
Baarda T 3548 4135
Baarde T 1660
Baarlink H 4942
Baasland E 3908
Babcock W 4481
Babinet R 4115 4272
Babinsky E 5119
Bach A 1361
Backhaus F 1985
Bader W 1015
Badham R 3184
Bae E 494
Bailey J 2798 4449 K
2760 2761 R 220
1079
Baines J 127
Baise I 1090 2179
2270 2277
Baker R 2568 4022 W
5306
Bakon S 1085

Bengtsson P 1025
Benjamin D 2573 **W** 1722
Bennett R 1812 **S** 419
Benn G 231
Benoit C 4149
Bentoglio G 4657
Berceville G 4156
Berder M 610 1668 4157
Bergant D 1850
Bergemann T 2731
Berger 4300
Berger 4459 **K** 5072
Berges U 1707
Bergey R 2223
Bergholz T 3554
Bergmeier R 1091 2617 4150
Bergquist R 5218
Berg W 1706
Berke J 2302
Berlin A 1401 2385 2662
Berlyn P 1519
Bernabò M 435
Bernard C 3945
Bernhart W 1402
Bernos M 1820
Berquist J 2295 3183
Berry D 1403 1599
Berthoud P 694
Bertoni N J 1813
Bescond L 240
Besserman L 320
Best E 3238 3328 4614 5053 5060
Bethge E 1543
Betori G 3865
Bettenzoli G 1092
Bettocchi S 1474
Betz H 2966 4987 5130 **O** 313 2290 2617
Beuken W 134 2209 2236 2241
Beuscher B 1223
Beutel A 662
Beutler J 4031 4949
Beyer D 2569
Beyerle S 907 1224
Beyer R 1165

Beyers J 174
Bianchi E 63 192 4841 **F** 1995 2478
Biddle M 325 2318 2231
Bieberstein K 947-8 **S** 4678
Bienert W 3959
Bieringer R 4241 4769 4969
Biewald R 3055
Bigg H 2740
Biguzzi G 3716 4055
Bindella F 3855
Bindemann W 4116 5307
Binder H 3755
Bingham D 2843
Birch B 537
Birdsall J 2960
Birnbaum M 616
Bisio F 4767
Bissoli C 2943 **G** 1188
Bjorklund B 1404
Black C 3306 3329 **D** 5094
Blackstone T 5223
Blaising C 2843
Blakeman M 1993
Blake W 2198
Blanchard T 1424 **Y** 64 3960
Blancy A 873
Bland D 1791
Blau J 2272
Blaumeiser H 1458
Blecua J 1780
Blenkinsopp J 151-2 860 897 1225 1842-3 2020 2087 2144 2296
Bliese L 2676
Bloch A 1781 1838 **C** 1781
Blocher H 1625
Blomberg C 2763 2807 3102 3555 4147
Bloomquist L 5095
Blum E 159 161 475
Blumenthal E 282
Boada J 1731 4423

Boadt L 558
Boccaccini G 4350
Böcher O 3318 4243 4379 4412
Bock D 3603 3612
Bockmuehl M 695 3914 5096
Boda M 1340
Bode E 2893
Bodine W 65
Bodjoko L 4505
Boecker H 193
Boer M de 3994 4938
Boers H 4506-7 4615 4730
Boespflug F 1179
Bogaert P 538 1216 2405
Boggio G 2089 2559
Böhler D 2344 4265
Böhmisch F 934 3251
Bohren R 1483
Bóid R 3679 1093
Boismard M 3261 3321 3464 3995-6 5228
Bojorge H 1542 1565
Bolewski J 2908
Bolin T 2622-3
Bolognesi P 2845
Bolt J 4779 **P** 3153 3519 3522
Bommarius A 66
Bonato V 1782
Bonaventure St 474 656
Bonhoeffer D 1434 1543
Bonneau N 4722 5023
Bonner G 5038
Bonora A 2313
Bons E 1581 2538
Bony P 2090
Booij T 1666
Boone R 4939
Boorer S 141
Borbone P 142 2445
Borgen P 67 3649 4732 5045
Borgonovo G 1708
Boring M 2744 2808 2885 4391

Busse U 4028
Busto J 3094
Busto Saiz J 1144
    1151 4863
Buzzard A 2095
Buzzell S 1965 1957
Byargeon R 2571 2570
Byatt A 3095
Bynum C 4940
Byrne B 4271 4800
Byron W 1546
Byrskog S 2845
Byung-Mu A 3333

Caba J 4061 4078
Cabrillo F 1814
Cáceres Guinet H
    2492 4193
Caesar L 1693
Cagni L 2096
Cahill M 4355
Caird G 2963
Calambrogio L 2913
Calduch B N 2062s
Callahan A 4356 5151
Callender D J 283 314
Calloud J 4508
Calvert N 5010
Calvin J 1127 1694
    1750   2240   2453
    2776   3191   4682
    4785 4958
Camacho F 3319
Cameron R 3166
Camisani E 1815
Campbell A 161 C
    4128 D 4757 4760
    4961 4998 R 5205
    W 4794
Camp C 1907 L 1281
Campe E 4628
Campo A del 4324
Candlish R 4296
Cañellas G 1709 4555
Cangh J van 3533
Cannizzo A 1846
Capper B 3281 3834
Caquot A 583 1051
Caragounis C 4926
Carasik M 1047
Caravaggio 1669

Carbone S 2495 2505
    2565
Cardellini I 742 1094
Cardenas Pallares J
    3732
Card M 4029
Carey W 3740
Cargal T 5308
Carleton Paget J 2763
    3329
Carls P 5123
Carmichael C 698 743
    4141
Carmignac J 2440
Carmody D 1032 J
    1032 1491
Carnley P 3265
Caron G 71 4030
Carp B 1492
Carr D 159 2846
Carreira das Neves J
    3787
Carrez M 4158
Carrillo F 1788
-Alday S 4617
Carroll J 2796 3216 R
    2098-9 2198 2785 R
    M 23 109
Carrón Pérez J 2726
Carruth S 3702
Carson D 102 3450
    4763   4866   5098
    5100 5110 5201
Carter P 3592 W 2968
    3029 3118
Cartledge T 795
Casalegno A 4357
Casalini N 1191 5214
Cascario J 3650
Casciaro J 3449
Casey P 4023
Cassidy E 4297 R
    4031
Cassiodorus 1474
Castellana F 1816
Castiñeiras G M 221
Castro S 3346 3985
    3998
Catastini A 496-7
Catchpole D 2730
Cathcart K 1847
Catherwood F 1095

Catron J 1192
Causse J 4197
Cayzer J 3934
Cazelles H 584 1848
Cazier P 315
Cecni A 2847
Ceresko A 738 1673
    1908 1930 2592
Cerquone A 4436
Cerutti M 2437
Chaloner S 4913
Chamard-Bois P 1400
    3458
Chance J 3617
Chandler T 560
Chang A 3686 S 1280
    3620
Chapa J 3818
Chapalain C 561
Chapman C 4317 D
    3334-5
Charette B 2848
Charles J 3923 5324
Charlesworth J 72
    3493 3938
Charlesworth J 4422
Charlier J 4318-9
Chatelion Counet P
    3999
Chauvin D 73 J 1817
Chau W 4509
Chavalas M 145
Cheney M 1710
Childs B 526 2101-2
Chilton B 3186 3512
Chinitz J 681
Chipman J 697
Chirichigno G 744
Chisholm R 2683
Chmiel J 3463 3727
Choi A 1227 H 3089
    3253
Cholin M 4118
Chouraqui A 562 1435
Chow J 4842 S 2624
    3092
Christensen D 831 R
    895
Christiansen E 4556
Christie-Johnston H
    3187
Christie-Miller I 2491

Culbertson P 3096
Cullen P 3567
Culpepper R 3608 3939 4000 4289
Cummins S 5029
Cunningham D 585 P 3308 S 3568
Currid J 602
Currie J 3042
Curtis A 2421 J 898
Cuvillier E 4186 4488 4559 5186
Cyen G van 3338
Cyran W 3886
Cyril A 2540 4123
Czachesz I 3569 3877

Dagbovou E 3544
Dagorn R 1430
Dahl N 5122
Dailey T 1717 1776
Dalbesio A 2149 4034 4298-9
dal Covolo E 4821
Dalla Vecchia F 1119
Danker F 4513 5294
Dannemann I 3339
Danove P 3549
Daoust J 4361
Darmawijaya S 4152
Darrícal N 1148 1304 1800
Darr J 3570 K 2107 2176
Das A 5011
Dassmann E 248
Dautzenberg G 44 1663 2969 2987 2993 3146 3219 3309 3340-2 3516 3542 4974
Davey L 28
David R 153
Davidsen O 3342 4732
Davidson R 2509
Davids P 3832 5266
Davies D 3571 E 782 797 G 563 1868 2506 J 24 M 109 2572-3 2885 P 222 383 2249 S 3056 W 2809

Davila J 361
Davis B 1027 L 2575 P 3343 S 3267
Dawes G 5164
Day J 9 564 1915 2108 L 1367 1445
Dearman J 2671
De Boer M 4321 4362 4760 5070
DeBoer W 4712 4835
Déclais J 615 1437
Decock P 3789
Defélix C 1986
Deist F 714 2110
Delattre B 616 3184
Delcor M 565
Delhez C 316
Delhougne H 3220
Delkurt H 179
Dell K 1719 1870 1873 1930 2576
Dell'Orto G 566
De Lorenzi L 4561 4660 4689
Delorme J 3433
Delumeau J 317 4468
De Maria A 4251
DeMaris R 4941 5090 5128 5132
Deming W 4890 4893
Demissy C 1351
Dempster S 823 2607
Denaux A 2731 3993
Denning-Bolle S 1209 3384
Dennison C 3085 J 3531 5325
Dentin P 3124
Deproost P 2178
Derby J 1368
Derousseaux L 223
De Rozario T 3751
Derrenbacker R 3845
Derrett J 45 798 2970 2984 3136 3145 3221 3447 3476 3681 3689 3701 3733 3853 4161 4188 4194 4202 4214 4223 4264 4275 4285 4756 4885 4971
Derrida J 3098

Descoeudres J 16
deSilva D 4406 5225 5229
Destro A 4037 4084 4165 4661
Dettwiler A 3906 4240 5133
Deurloo K 170 499-501
Dever W 912 1289
Devillers L 4318 4363
De Virgilio G 3621 4817
De Vries H 1502 S 2109
Dewey J 3435
Dexinger F 718
Dey L 4436
Dhanaraj D 1495
Díaz-Rodelas J 285 4773
Di Berardino A 3895
DiCicco M 4988
Dickinson E 1399
Dicou B 473
Diebner B 999
Diebold-Scheuermann C 4261
Dieckmann B 3251
Diefenbach M 3622
Dietrich W 663 934 1052
Dietzfelbinger R 617
Di Giovambattista F 820
Dijk-Hemmes F van 2424
Dijkstra M 813-4 1634
Di Lella A 1352 2448
Dillmann R 3439
Dillon R 3434 4814
Di Marco A 213
Dines J 249 1496
Di Nola G 5193
Dion P 887
Diop A 2509
Di Palma G 2518 2713 3374
Dipboye C 3178
Di Porto B 4690
Dirksen P 76 154 1319 1321
Dittmann R 1657

Glenny W 4808
Gnanvaram M 3353
Gnilka 3132 3454
Gnuse R 156 799 922
Goan S 2051
Godden M 441
Godet J 1503
Godzik P 3670
Goémine M 4323 2524
Golb N 2470
Goldingay J 2269 2447
2525
Goldman S 503 Y
2343
Goldsworthy G 1872
Golka F 1873 1901
Gonçalves   F   2113
4324
Gonella A 3607
Goñi Gaztambide J
1699 3297
González Echegaray J
2485 4324
Gooch P 4896
Goodman A 2114
Goppelt L 5264
Goranson S 4455
Gordon P 2115 R 83
1874   2116   2299
2496
Görg M 287 620 751
1136
Goshen Gottstein A
390-1 403 M 2177
Gossai H 392
Gosse B 363 833 1341
1504   2118   2215
2235   2356   2360
2366
Gottfried R 319
Gottwald N 949 2094
Gould G 1792 1977
Goulder M 1407 1505
3214 3520 5136
Gourgues M 35 84
3015   3446   4002
4931
Gouw R 5046
Gowan D 724
Gowler D 3570 3624
Gozier A 588

Gräßer E 2663 5217
Graetz N 2512
Graf F 646
Graham M 1299 W
1750
Granild S 1301
Grant M 3126 R 3329
Grappe C 3127 4603
Grässer E 3554 4578
Grassi J 4209
Grasso S 2815 2855
Graupner A 179 3609
Gray J 3248
Gready J 294
Green B 1026 3482 E
1128 J 85 2097 3216
3235   3586   3626
4449 L 5199
Greenberg B 834 M
49 180 488 647 699
801   1726-7   2119
2441
Greene-McCreight   K
676
Greenfield J 1875 11
Greengus S 711
Greenhalgh S 3900
Greenhill W 2402
Greenspoon L 136
Greer R 4771
Gregor Z 831
Gregorius Elib. 1804
Gregorius   M   1698
2404
Gregory Nyssa 315
386 1440 1782 1785
1797 3013-4
Gregory R 1234
Greimas A 1256
Grelot P 2447 2484
2816   3086   3271
3429 3462 4044
Gremmels 3339
Grenzer M 1766
Grieb A 4597
Griesbach 2776
Grigsby B 4045
Grilli M 3076
Grillo M 3050
Grimm W 3310
Groß W 86 254 648

948 962 1537 2092
2369 4325 5006
Grob   F   4105   4182
4295
Grogan G 4629
Grossberg   D   2621
2658
Grossi V 3720 4269
Gruber M 684 2544
Grudem W 5265
Gruen W 2031
Grünbeck E 1614-5
Grünberg K 4326
Grundke C 815
Grünwaldt K 181 1219
1231-3 1439
Grünzweig F 4327
Gruson P 621-2 2602
2579 4665
Gryson   R   2178-80
2270 2277
Guarducci   M   3128
3354
Gubler M 3238
Guérard M 1792 2120
Guerra A 4736
Guest S 569
Gugler W 1157
Guijarro   Oporto   S
4566
Guillemette N 2974
Guillerand A 4003
Guinan M 4476
Gundry R 2766 2817
3311 3722
Gunther J 4374
Günther M 5057
Guthrie G 5098 5229

Haacker 4081 K 3847
4486
Haag E 1353 1613
2449 H 255 1778
Haak R 2281 2620
2664 2683
Haapiseva-Hunter J 40
Haarlem W van 290
Haase W 87 4440
4486
Haas V de 3772

Herzog W 3102
Hesichius Jerusalem 2413
Hesiod 244
Hesselink J 4785
Hess R 950
Hester J 3545
Heth W 3021-2
Heubach J 88 4886 5047
Heyns D 2254 2612
Hickling C 4989
Hiebert C 2262
Hieke T 1637
Higman F 2240
Hilarius Poit. 1670 1675 5145
Hilberath B 25
Hilbrands W 764
Hildebrandt D 1952 1962 4488
Hilger G 4790
Hill C 3153 3519 3870 4311 4470
Hillers D 2605
Hill R 3537
Hillyer N 5266
Hilten W van 1879
Hilton M 2482
Hinlicky P 2937
Hippolytus 1545
Hirschberg A 1236
Hirschmüller M 1070 3181
Hirsch S 1466
Hirth T 802
Ho C 1317 1691
Hock R 5152
Hodge C 4834
Hodges Z 5302
Hodgson B 4798
Hoeren T 3754
Höffken P 2181 3627
Hoffman A 4347 Y 924
Hoffmann J 4612 P 51 2737 2860 2964 2991 2996-8 3081 3272-3 3472 3479 3704 3739
Hoffner H 713 716
Hofmann J 5267

Hoheisel K 1060
Hohnjec N 2591
Holbrook D 2696
Holladay C 5257 W 1551 1627
Holland G 5164 M 981 5268
Hollenweger W 4280
Holloway S 1 1287
Holmes M 3964 5089
Holmgren F 89 753
Holt E 90 1237 2513
Holter K 2265
Holtz T 4666
Holwerda D 3372 4463
Homberg B 4514
Homcy S 4375
Homerski J 2111 2121
Hong I 5014
Hooker M 3314 3767 4692 4910
Hoop R De 1172
Hopkins M 5175
Hoppe L 2028 R 5058-9 5067 5138 5300
Horbury W 1526 2032
Horn F 30 4569 4683 4894 S 1337
Horrell D 4570 4896 4910
Horton F 12
Hossfeld F 649 700 2409
Hostetter E 915
Hotze G 4571
Houlden J 2874
House P 1152 2580 2665
Houston J 3060 W 754 888 1510 2122
Houten C van 701
Houtman A 885 C 157 527 563
Howard-Brook W 4049
Howard D 964 G 2823-4
Howe L 3274
Howell M 1551 2630
Hsu S 1511

Hubbard D 1969 R 1370
Hubeñák F 3226 4195
Huber K 2953 3357
Hubmann F 2308
Hübner 3155 H 52 4515 4555 4572-4 4692 4786-8 4804 4871 5015 5230
Huck G 1566 2162
Huddlestun J 2123
Huey F 2309
Huffmon H 675
Hugenberger G 2288 2713
Hug J 2033 4489
Hull E 1457
Hultgren A 2861
Human D 1633 1642
Hume D 3060
Humphrey E 3883 4376
Humphreys W 2472
Hunold G 650
Hunt A 3329
Huonder V 1552
Huprich A 4274
Hurowitz V 1197-8
Hurst L 5231
Hurtado L 3358 4448
Hurth E 4693
Hurvitz A 21 1199
Husser J 2477 2490
Hutton R 2124
Huwyler B 2378
Hvalvik R 651
Hwang I 2985
Hyldahl N 4845
Hyman R 504 1286

Iacopino G 3967
Ibn Ezra 1329 1453
Ibn Shaprut 2824
Iersel B van 2778 3492
Ijatuyi O 3799
Ilgen K 167
Illman K 1710
Imbach J 3061 3103 4142
Imbert J 3226
Infante R 4050 4377

Kautz J 1768
Kayama H 3887
Kaylor R 3159 4967
Keck L 92-3 147
Kee H 4101
Keefe A 2542
Keenan J 3362
Keener C 3022 4632
Kegler J 2357
Kellenberger E 1053
Keller M 837 5099
Kellermann U 1239
Kelley R 3629
Kelly B 1309
Kemdirim P 4633
Kempf S 322
Kempinski A 2427
Kendrick W 4908
Keown G 2310
Kerner J 4379
Kero K 803
Kertelge 4571 K 2976
   3363-4 4574 4738
Kessler D 3 R 1616 S
   2404
Keulen P van 1288
Keylock L 2773
Khoo K 4056
Kiedzik M 3712
Kieffer R 3466
Kieschke H 4057
Kiesow K 2268
Kieweler H 2052
Kiley B 3365 M 4102
   4187
Kilgallen J 3719 3758
Kille D 478
Kilpatrick G 3351 R
   604
Kimball C 3630
Kim D 5232 G 2644 H
   1993 J 1013 S 4575
   Y 891
King G 2666 K 5009 P
   2315
Kingsbury J 2868
Kinman B 3767
Kinukava H 3366-7
   3467
Kinzer M 1587
Kinzie F 4007

Kinzig W 1583
Kirchhoff R 4887
Kirchschläger W 260
   323 589 3062
Kistemaker S 4835
   4982
Kitchen K 396 M 5060
Kitzberger I 4230
Klassen W 2802
Klauck 2887 4096 H
   2901 4290 4316
   4965
Kleer M 1514
Kleiner M 1125
Kleinig J 1310
Klein L 1372 1729 M
   5313 N 2645 R 1163
   1240
Klement H 1053
Kleven T 1412
Klindworth V 3541
Klingbeil G 759 1373
   M 1601
Klopfenstein M 663
Kloppenborg J 94
   3741
Kloppers M 838
Knapp S 5009
Knauf E 1334
Knierim R 727 760
   1280 1736
Knight D 839 G 905 J
   5295
Knights C 2375-6
Knobloch F 199
Knohl I 545
Knoppers G 728 1106
   1163 1177 1201
   1210 1214
Knowles M 2869 3116
Kobayashi M 4058
Koch D 4618 5106 H
   2255 K 208 1336
   2127-8 2443 2462-4
   2479 2481 2483
   2489 T 652
Köckert M 183
Kodithuwakku N 1515
Koenen K 1018 1648
   2128
Koerrenz R 1241

Koester C 3186 3961
   3979 4001 4059-60
   4380 H 3227-8 5075
Koet B 3638
Kohn R 2256
Kolasny J 3814
König H 1795
Konkel A 1299
Koonthanam G 2210
Koopmans W 1172
Koorevaar H 1133
   1146
Koottumkal S 4061
Kopp J 2954
Korpel M 1783
Korsak M 200 324
Korting G 4008
Kosch D 3616 4678
Köstenberger A 3326
   4220 4500 5200s
Kottsieper I 1383
Kowalski B 3631 4001
   4205
Kraege J 4739
Kraftchick S 6
Krämer M 1467 2977
Kranemann B 108
Krašovec J 1535
Kratz R 1383 2353
Kraus H 1468 W 31
Krause M 3450
Krebernik M 840
Kreloff S 4803
Kremer J 53 397 3662
   3748 3759 3778
   3854 3879 3912
   4252 4279 4900
   4917 4923 4977
   4995 5166
Krentz E 5099
Kreuzer S 1075
Krey P 4369
Krieg G 1554
Krieger K 3229
Krieser M 5202
Krimmer H 5268
Kristen P 3368
Krodel G 95
Krodel G 4289 5216
   5269 5294 5301
   5327

Levison J 1357
Levy R 763
Lewis S 4381 4944
Lexutt A 1243
Lichtenstein M 1450 1973
Lichtheim M 1897
Licht J 787
Liebscher S 4816
Liefeld W 3805
Lienhard M 201
Lier J van 434
Lie T 3122
Lietaert Peerbolte L 4312
Lieu J 893 3806
Lillie B 1244
Limberis V 4542
Limburg J 2620
Lim D 1331
Linafelt T 740 2389
Linard H 3747
Lincoln A 3547 3862 4667 5056 5068
Lindars B 982 5233
Lindemann 3356 A 3920 4980
Lindsey R 2739
Lindström F 1518
Link A 4162 C 590 3035
Linmans A 2778
Linnemann E 2740-3
Linss W 2872 3280 4558 4733
Linton G 4404
Lipiński E 18 1897
Lipton D 852
Litfin D 4868
Litke W 5043
Liu C 4635
Liwak R 1077 1218
Llamas Vela A 4382
Llewelyn S 5101
Lloyd-Jones D 4810
Loader J 1769 1771 1883
Logan A 3944
Logister W 3157
Lohfink G 2979 N 54

686 841-7 872 876 884 901 926-7 1296 1998 2025 2537 2955 3690
Loh J 327
Lohmeyer M 2779 3082
Löhr H 1245 5234
Löhrer M 32 2619
Lohse E 4232 4517 4636
Lombaerts H 7
Lombard H 4010
Lona H 2871
Longacre R 229 729
Long B 1275 2129 T 92s 147 3803
Longenecker B 4071 R 3163 3311
Longman T 1528 4354
Löning 4571
Lopes A 4876
López Fernández E 2920 3756
López G 3832 4328
Lord A 1410 M 1410
Lorenzani M 96 5278
Lorenzen T 3278
Loretz O 874 2523
Lorgunpai S 1999 2000
Lorie P 4383
Lorton D 715
Loscalzo C 2584
Loski T 2825
Lou S 1690
Loubser J 4519
Louyot Y 262
Lovering E 137
Love S 3632
Lovik E 5291
Lowe M 399
Lowery R 2554
Loza J 438
Lubomirski M 4713
Lubsczyk H 5178
Lucas E 2130
Luciani F 4992 1213
Luck U 5300
Lüdemann G 66 118

3279-82 3284 3289 4774 5057
Lüders S 1246
Ludger Schenke 4001
Lugo Rodriguez R 5299
Lugt P van der 1735
Lührmann D 3311 3329 3368 4406 4637 5002
Łukasz C 591 3882
Luke K 328
Lüke U 245 3474
Lumbreras Meabe J 1442
Lund J 1422
Lundager Jensen H 90
Lundberg M 1736
Lundbom J 1836 2318 2355
Lupieri E 4384
Lustiger J 2965
Lust J 134 218 663 816 826 904 1111 1149 1308 1696 2330 2475
Luter A 1027 3257 3471 4560 5102
Lütgehetmann W 804 4140
Luther M 662 1243 1458 3197 4714 4720 4725 4739
Lux R 2631
Luzarraga J 3945
Luz U 2826s 2872 2874
Lydamore M 3281 4406
Lys D 2001 4072

Maartens P 4770 4781
Maas J 2019
Macchi J 527 702 1051 3648
MacDonald M 4668
Machetta D 952
Machinek M 3024

832 854
Nepi A 2042 4396
Neri U 203 5062
Neudorfer H 4684
Neufeld D 3949 4009
    4304 E 767
Neugebauer J 4234
Neumann H 331 K
    4526 T 284
Neuner J 3236 3663
Neusner J 509 1381
    1799 2390 4640
Neville R 1000
New D 2786
Newheart M 4079
Newport K 3174 4475
Newsom C 1362 1741
    2425
Newton G 4254 4329
Neyrey J 3585 4238
    4880 5296
Ng E 2004
Niccacci A 100 1888
Nicholson E 1700
    1742
Niclós J 332
-Albarracín J 2880
Nicolas M 3974
Nicole É 1424 J 768
Niditch S 1377-8
Niebuhr K 4620
Niehaus J 655
Niehoff M 458 509
Niehr 2092 H 1078
    1208 1291
Niekerk M van 1682
Nielsen E 824 858 J
    4959 K 1049 1301
    2643
Niemand C 4243 4248
Niemann H 1078 1165
Nighswander D 4852-
3
Nilus Ancyra 1792
    2120
Nissan E 510
Nissen M 2759
Nobile M 985 1895
    1919 2096 4397
    4787 4869
Noble P 2586 2601
Nodet É 1206 3657

Noegel S 605 1743
    1751 1762
Noel D 2035 W 1425
Nogalski J 1515 1926
    2501-2 2587
Nohrnberg J 576 852
Nolan M 3673
Nolland J 3610-2 3025
    3624
Nolting T 4498
Nordheim E von 424
    919
Norelli E 4398 4522
Noro H 3154
Norris K 1447
North J 5203 R 577
Nortjé S 449 1481
Norton G 1426 1878
Nos Muro L 3039-41
Noth M 861
Noujaim H 403 4501
Nouwen H 3749
Nowell I 1348 1557
    1891
Nuchelmans J 3430
    3492
Nützel J 870 1250

Oakes P 5103
Oberforcher R 425
    2641 2812
Oberlinner D 2203 L
    808 4048 4261 5186
    5195s
Obermann A 4081
Oberweis M 4462
O'Brien J 12 2105
    2715-7 4946 M 161
    170 596 853 930 P
    4621
O'Callaghan J 2978
Och B 266
O'Connell M 317 R
    1234
O'Connor D 1669
    1744 K 1889 M
    1211
O'Day G 3975 3981
    3997 4016
Odell M 2533
Odell-Scott D 4642

Oecumenius 4321
    4362
Oemig M 1448
Oesch J 1015 2374
Ogden G 990 1007
-Bellis A 2516 2552
    2588 2632 2649
    2659 2667 2678
    2684 2686
O'Grady J 3383 4080
    5023
Öhler M 2724
Okorie A 3639s 4466
    5158
Okoye J 2064
Olasagasti M 5262
O'Leary J 4121 S
    4476
Oliveira A de 4962
Olivi P 1803 2384
Ollenburger B 6
Olmo Lete G del 1197
Olofsson S 1579
O'Loughlin T 265 357
    1829
Olson D 854s 780 791
    1081
Olsson B 4006 5282
Olsthoorn M 2280
Omanson R 4972
O'Neill J 3198 4183
    5049
Oorschot J van 1745
Opocenska J 3738
Oppel D 3454
Orbán A 2957 2982
Orchard B 3933
O'Reilly J 1193 3691
Orel V 468 1082 1215
Origen 277 483 779
    1426 1462 1610
    1675 1797 2325
    2550 2837 3720
    3959 3966 3969
    3972 3983 4121
    4123 4169 4244
    4503 4710 4819
    4874 5116 5224
    5290
Ornellas P d' 4305
Orr M 4492 4606
Orsatti M 1074 2934

3648 4638
Rooze E 631
Rösel H 995 **M** 208s
516 3088
Rosell E 349
Rosemann P 4075
5006
Rosen K 3677
Rosenblatt M 3900
Rosenblit B 1621
Rosenkranz S 1204
Rosner B 110 4646
4882 5174
Ross A 1923 1940
Rosscup J 5071
Rossi G 3394
Rosso S 486 978 1063
2936
Rostagno S 4723
Rota Scalabrini P 690
Rothgangel M 3240
4790
Roth M 716
Rottzoli D 210 2594
Rougier S 1428
Rouiller G 4366
Roukema R 4874
Roure D 2891 3314
Rowland C 3575 4414
5139
Royer L 3888
Roy L 3241
Rozen B 3054
Rozman F 3131 3850
Rubenstein J 734
Rubinkiewicz R 4948
Rubio L 5214
Rude T 2557
Ruffle J 1924
Ruis-Camps J 3819
Ruiten J van 529 735
4453 4855
Ruiz J 4193 4447
Runacher C 3477
Ruppert L 211s 405
492 2203 4261
Ruß R 2445 3776
Russelliah C 1114
Russell W 5051
Russotto M 4415
Rüterswörden U 706
1294

Ruyter B de 91 4054
5124
Ryan J 4814
Ryou D 2668

Saadiah 1453
Sabbe M 4260
Sæbø M 665 1518
4039
Sabugal S 3297
Sacchi P 186 2446
4416
Sáenz-Badilos A 1801
Saffrey H 4496
Saft W 3068
Sailhamer J 891
Sakenfeld K 790
Sala M 163 337
Saldarini A 2845
2885s
Salerno A 4335
Salles C 4534
Salm E 492
Salmann E 32
Salters R 1983
Salvador García M
4675
Salvesen A 531
Samaan K 2046
Saßmann C 632 4703
Sampley J 4825
Samuel S 4090
Sánchez Bosch J 198
2324 4153 4495
Sandelin K 4902 4904
Sanders E 4535 **J** 3222
3574 4618
Sandevoir P 126 529
Sanford J 3978
Sänger D 2582 2959
4791
Sankey P 3422
Sanna I 238
Santos B S 1140 2337
Sanz Valdivieso R
3230 3261 3477
3528
Särkiö P 900 1163
1210
Sarna N 1450 2275
Sasson J 127 2153

Sattar S 434
Satterthwaite P 111
ˈ1118
Sattler D 25
Saux M 5277
Savoca G 213 2411
Sawyer D 4091 **J** 24
2154 2204
Scaiola D 1380 1779
2184 2564 3980
4229 4664 4999
Scalise P 2310 5017
Schaalman H 89 90
463
Schaberg J 2929
Schaefer K 2711
Schäfer-Lichtenberger
C 862 959 2327
2517
Schaper J 1205 1313
1526
Scharbert J 791 2283
Schart A 2377
Schattner-Rieser U
2473
Schatzmann S 4724
Schenk W 3843 4824
5111
Schenke L 406 4001
4234
Schenker A 218 534
677 826 2228
Schepers K 1802
Scheuermann G 2887
Schibler D 2208
Schirrmacher T 4745
4906
Schlageter J 1803
Schlatter A 4724
Schlier H 4554
Schlosser J 1668 3395
4092 4778 5108
5113
Schlueter C 5170
Schlumberger S 3880
Schmeller T 2212
3503 4676
Schmid K 2365 U
4536
Schmidt B 368 1126 **F**
1206 **L** 164s **T** 3540
5246 **W** 327 532 550

Siegert F 4991 5240
Sierra S 522
Sigurdson O 4726
Siker J 4567
Silberman L 436 3932
Silva A da 1602
-Castillo J 369 **M** 1371
   3384 4876 5110
Sim D 2889 **U** 4479
Simian-Yofre H 2010
   2190 2518 2539
Simkins R 269 1290
   2554s
Simms S 2011
Simon U 1453 2621
Simone G de 1474
Simón Muñoz A 3532
   3680
Sindt G 3455
Singgih E 370
Siniscalco P 4419
Sinoir M 2794
Sion D 4178
Sipilä S 960
Sisti A 4950
Sivan D 205 3153
Sixdenier G 28
Six J 1831
Ska J 168 187 192 580
   832 1028 1270 2845
Skeat T 5112
Skehan P 1674
Skjoldal N 2266
Slaughter J 5284
Sloan R 4747 4975
Sloyan G 1551 3244
   4146 4292
Smalley S 3952 4004
   4098
Smelik K 631 635
   2362 **W** 983
Smend R 578 1898
Smidt J de 4450
Smit D 5069
Smith A 5168 **B** 333
   2503 **C** 2519 4454 **D**
   3183 3214 4896
   5298 **J** 3298 **M** 1599
   4098 **P** 2299 **R** 4438
   S 3401 **W** 121
Smith-Christopher D
   114 1327

Smothers T 2037 2310
Snaith J 1805 2059
Snell D 1926
Snodgrass K 4793
   5271
Snyder G 3076 4838 **S**
   5285
Snyman S 2606
Soards M 3820
Soares-Prabhu G 2271
   3489
Söding T 57 60 77 77
   773 783 2736 3402-4
   4589 4920 5145
   5255
Soggin J 414 432 446
   1065 2595
Sokoloff M 11
Soll W 1443 1469
Somekh A 522
Somers V 2180
Sommer U 3529
Sonnet J 900
Sorg T 4120 4276
Souletie J 3067
Sousan A 270
Souza M de Barros
   1529
Souzenelle A de 214
Spaeth P 656
Spencer F 3820 **J** 1064
   R 5253
Spensley B 3552 3594
Speyer W 271
Speyr A von 1806
Spieckermann H 1497
   1667
Spiegel C 70 1382
Spielmann K 4099
Spier E 674
Spilly A 1391
Spinetoli O 4590
Spinks B 3193
Spinoza 186
Spiro S 205
Šporčić I 1530 2520
Spottorno V 1155
Spreafico A 533 2158
   2273 2603 2669s
Sprinkle J 692
Spronk K 2679s
Sproston W 4307

Squires J 3594
Stacey W 2159
Stachowiak L 1044
Stadelmann A 932
   1552 2313 **H** 5063 **L**
   1807s
Stagno L 1349
Stahl N 707
Stahl R 1122 2218
   2469
Staley J 3381 3695
   3988 4100
Stallman R 774
Stamps D 4018 4537
Standaert B 1564
Standhartinger A 523
Stanley S 5248s
Stanton A 1429
   Stanton G 115 2809
   2826 2833s 2842
   2891 3460
Stanula E 2837
Starke F 428
Starowieyski M 3078
Stec D 1702
Steck O 1383 2091
   2259 2297 2300
   2365 2399
Stefani P 579 1045
Stefanović R 4452 **Z**
   2981
Steffen U 2636
Stegemann 3717 **H**
   2958 **W** 4232
Stegmann F 29
Stegner W 2796 2892
Steicke M 3019 3026
Stein E 2930 **R** 3617
Steinberg N 233 1006
Steinhoff V 981 5268
Steinmann A 1761
Steins G 169 1314s
Stemberger G 599
Stendahl K 58 4623
   4727
Stenschke C 2915
   3117
Sterling G 3641 4856
Stern P 1638
Stevenson G 4420 **K**
   703 3193
Steveson P 2660

Thiede C 2756 3189
  3202s 3462 **W** 4424s
Thiele W 2060
Thielman F 4795 4651
  5091
Thiel W 1158 1261-3
  2181
Thiessen W 5072
Thiselton A 4952
Thoma C 33
Thomas A 274 **C** 3431
  4076 **J** 4180 4293 **P**
  2931 4953 **R** 4340
-Aquinas 4169 4201
  4425
Thompson I 4539 **J**
  1303 **M** 3961 **T** 170
  600 935 1116
Thomson R 275
Thordson T 464
Thornton C 3897
Thorpe L 2240
Thraede K 34
Thrall M 4960
Thurén L 3845 5286
  5317
Thurston B 4632 5127
Thüsing W 60 3204
  3954   4255   4288
  4294   4426   4480
  4827   4859   4878
  5252
Ticonius 4334 4439
Tigay J 199 894 908
Tilborg S van 3999
  4102 4823
Tillard J 35
Tillmann N 1627
Tilly M 2959
Tisera G 2896
Tjatra P 4592
Toan A van 3261
Tobias A 1531
Tobin T 4765
Toensing H 4196
Toews W 1013 1051
  1209
Tolbert M 112s 1689
  4097 5149
Tollington J 2691
Tolmie D 4235
Toloni G 1143

Tomasetto D 3287
Tomasino A 2470
Tombs D 106
Tomes R 1209 3927
Tomić C 3131 4540
  4624
Tomson P 4796
Tonder C van 158
Toni R 3247
Toniolo E 2939 ʹ
Torrance T 3919
Torres Ordoñez M
  3650
Tosaus Abadía J 5077
Tournaire R 2242
Tournay R 268 371
  637 1567 3046
Tourón del Pie E 3205
Tourón E 3285
Tov E 149 551 775
  947 1809
Towner P 5187 **W**
  1927
Trainor M 3483s 3598
  3651
Trebolle J 933
-Barrera J 132 832
Treichler R 3252
Treves M 1753
Trevijano Etcheverria
  R 3896 5115
Trevijano R 4545 4773
Trible P 1264s 1941
  2637
Trilling W 2897
Tristram H 1413
Trobisch D 4541
Trocmé E 4155 5280
Trofimova M 1643
Tromp J 1397 **N** 1416
Tronina A 1455
Troyer K De 1386
Trublet J 117 1532
Trudinger P 2685
  4103s 4287 5179
Trueman C 3206
Trumbower J 4105
Trummer P 3075
Trunk D 3069
Tsuchido K 4215
Tsuji M 5318
Tsumura D 276 1083

Tucker G 36 **W** 1533
Tuckett C 2765 2793
  2800   3390   3599
  3652 4094
Tuell S 2431
Tuñi J 2080 3955
Tuohey J 344
Turchi A 1816
Turner C 3351 **D** 1810
  M 3595 **N** 3351
Turzyński P 1534
Twelftree G 3070
Twomey V 82 362
  4297
Tyler R 4491
Tyson J 3600

Übelacker W 3355
  5238
Uchelen N van 4796
Uehlinger C 1293
Uffenheimer B 2229
Uhlig S 592 1966 5064
  5267
Ukpong J 2898 3505
Ulland H 4456
Ullatt S 3207
Ullmann D 811
Ulonska H 3071
Ulrich D 2406 **E** 1674
Ulrichsen J 4954
Uríbarri G 3261
Urvoy M 1430
Uval B 4200

Vaage L 1773 2802
  3692 3703
Vadakkedom J 4922
Vaggione R 2828
Valantasis R 4626
Valauri E 3256
Valente G 4228
Valentini A 2932 3441
  3659
Valerio A 2163
Vallauri E 2855
Vall G 1693 1759
  1774
Van Broekhoven H
  5061 5126 5131

Washington H 1944
2115 2117
Watson A 3249 4110
D 4544 4844 4870
5308 N 4680 4842
4961 W 24 1833s
Watt J van der 4126
4132
Watts J 189s 1415
2596
Watt T 524
Way D 4639
Weatherly J 3601
Weaver D 4263
Webb B 1017 R 2961
W 4985
Weber 2160 B 1452
1622 1635 5073 G
574 4019 H 3209
Wedderburn A 4070
5068
Weder H 4402
Weeden T 3415s
Weeks S 1901
Weems R 2167
Wefald E 3417
Wegener M 3418
Wegner U 4134
Wehnert J 3913
Wehr L 3132
Wehrle J 1572
Weidmann F 4111
5190
Weigl M 2613 2671s
Weiß H 5188 5221
5234 I 1573
Weima J 4545s
Weimar 1656 1692
2523 P 552 640s
Weinberg J 1316
Weinfeld M 825 840
961 2168
Weingärtler C 1246
2397
Weinreb F 1388
Weippert 281 M 8
Weir E 3497
Weiser A 3911
Weisman Z 409
Weiss H 510 3197
4826 R 1137 W
3113 3829

Welborn L 4970 4990
Weldon F 1016
Welker M 300
Welten P 1936
Welzen H 3419
Wendel U 2335 3830
Wengst K 4021 4479
Wenham D 3210 4500
G 404 642 760 827 J
2759
Wénin A 1129 1574
1623 2903
Weninger S 5267
Weren W 712 3772
Werlitz J 2221
Werman C 777
Wesley C 4475
Westbrook R 865
Westerholm S 4563
4797
Westermann C 216s
934 1926 1929 2169
2394 4112
Wetzel C 279
Wevers J 218 527 534
826
Weyer-Menkhoff M
4433
Whitekettle R 778
White L 239 445 3915
Whitelam K 935
White M 20
Whitlock D 3907
Whybray R 171s 1536
1904 1930 1955
Wiarda T 4444
Wick P 5111
Wickham L 1804
Widengren G 2471
Wider D 5242
Wieder L 1431
Wiefel W 2812 3995
Wiens D 3875
Wieringen A van 466
786 2260
Wiesehöfer J 2486
Wiesel E 373
Wiggins S 726
Wightman G 2077
Wilckens U 4791
Wilcox L 2638
Wild R 5068 5132

Wilde N de 658 2753
Wilken R 779 2417
Wilkins M 119 2902
Willert N 4607
Willey P 2286
Willi-Plein I 347 738
1130
Williams C 4009 D
5162 J 232 1931
3420 M 3831 R
3193 T 799
Williamson G 9 H 580
1340 2192s 2207
2225 2261 2300
2615
Willis J 625 2336 T
708 1325
Willoughby R 5270
Wills L 4339
Wilson I 866 J 4328
4371 L 1756 M
1020 R 1161 2206
5215 W 3397
Wimbush V 4626
Winden J van 263
Winfield F 4782
Winkel J 4113
Winklehner H 373
Winninge M 4547
Winter B 781 3832
4860 4884 M 4232
Wintermute O 194
Winther-Nielsen N 962
Wire A 3494 5009
Wischmeyer O 2061
2769 4525
Wisdom T 2560
Wiseman D 1157 W
1870
Wiskin R 301
Witherington III B
3761 4596 4839
Witherup R 3865
Witte K 2838 5007 M
1764s
Wittenberg G 164 235
693
Wodecki B 643
Wolde E van 236 472
1001 1174 1757
Wolfers D 1703
Wolff C 5279

Sacra Scriptura

18,1-15: 439s
18-19: 437
18: 436
19: 220 441s
  444s
20: 220 446
21,9: 447
21: 435
22,1-19: 451-4
  456s 459 463s
  466s
22,1-24: 4579
22,1: 511
22,12: 460
22,13: 450
22: 465
23,2-20: 468
24,63: 470
24: 469 471s
26: 220
27: 477
28,10-22: 475
  482
28,11-22: 479
28,12: 483
31: 488
32,23-33: 491
32,28: 493
34,7-10: 204
37,2-11: 501
37,36: 513
38,26: 489
38: 490 492 500
39,1: 513
39,3: 511
39,6-18: 26 505
39,8: 511
39,17: 511
39,20: 511
39: 510
44: 504
46,31-47,31: 494
47,13-26: 498
49,2-27: 522
49,8-12: 507
49: 506 515s
50,1-11: 494
50,3: 204
50,14: 494

Exodus

1-2: 563
1-15: 544
1,8-22: 554 1999
1,11: 577
2,1-10: 554 568
  1999
3,1-4,17: 556
3,1-22: 586
3,6: 3509
3,13-14: 581
3,14: 591
3: 596 600
4,22-23: 603
4,24-26: 557 582
  597
5,22-23: 587
6,14-25: 594
6: 600
7,1-10,29: 532
7,8-13: 602
9,13-19: 605
11,1-10: 613
12-14: 614-6
  618s 621s 630
12,1-14: 640s
12,12: 604
12,21-27: 608
12: 168 752
13,21-22: 536
14,11-12: 623
14,13: 639
14,19-20: 536
15,1-18: 629
15,1-21: 612
  2040
15: 637
16: 624
17,8-16: 617 620
19,1-8: 627
19,10-25: 638
20,1-17: 646 651
20,2-6: 662
20,3-6: 664
20,3: 660 663
20,5-6: 668
20,7: 675
20,8: 676
20,12: 677
20,17: 678

20,22-23,33: 689
20: 665
21,1-11: 766
21,2-11: 691
21,4-6: 684
21,23: 681
22,17: 685
23,4-5: 679
23,21: 688
24,3-8: 730
24,12-18: 735
25-30: 729
25,1-9: 727
30,11-16: 722
32,7-14: 724
32,20: 733
32: 728 1214
34: 4978
36-40: 538

Leviticus

1,1-7: 775
1,1-9: 760
3,2-4: 775
3,5-8: 775
3,16-4,6: 775
4,12-14: 775
4,23-28: 775
5,12-13: 775
7,19-26: 775
8,26-28: 775
8: 759
10,1-5: 740
10,1-20: 758
10: 770
11: 752 754
12-15: 748
12: 778
16: 751 763
17,11: 771
19,1-27: 769
19,1-37: 753
19,17-18: 679
19,18: 773
19,19: 743
19,34-37: 775
19: 869
20,1-3: 775
20,27-21,4: 775
21,9-12: 775

21,21-24: 775
22,4-6: 775
22,11-17: 775
23,40: 767
25,33: 766
25,35-43: 766
25: 739 742 747
  768

Numeri

1; 797
6,22-27: 806
6,23-27: 800
6,24-26: 796
10,31-33: 536
11,29: 810
13,1-20,13: 793
15,30-31: 794
16: 168 804
17: 168
19,1-22: 805
21,1-9: 798
21,18-19: 812
21,21-23: 896
21,4-9: 811
21,6-8: 802
24: 816
26: 797
35,4-5: 801
36,6-7: 1185

Deuteronomium

1-11: 825
1,1-5: 871
2,1: 872
4,29: 867
5,6-10: 662
5,6-21: 646 651
  665
5,7: 660
5,9-10: 668
5,11: 675
5,12-15: 676
5,16: 677
6,4-5: 4073
6,4: 873s
6,5: 875
6,17: 1296
6,20-24: 896

22: 1240

2 Regum

1: 1274
4,18-37: 1271
5: 1270
6,8-23: 1273
7,13: 1137
9: 1272
11: 1275
13,1-9: 1276
13,22-23: 1276
14,1-22: 1277
14,21-15,7: 1278
16: 1279
17,1-24: 1284
17,24-33: 1266
17: 1280
18-19: 1287
18-20: 1281
18,1-20,21: 1282
18,4: 1283
18,9-12: 1284
18,13-19,37: 1285
18,13-19,35: 1161
18,19-35: 1286
18,22: 1283
19,21-28: 1211
21,1-18: 1288
22,14-20: 1294
22: 1295
22: 2418
23,2: 1296
23: 1295 1297
24,17: 1298

1 Chronica

10,1-12: 1317
11,4-6: 1135
13-16: 1318
15,1-24: 1319
15,18: 1137
16,5: 1137
16,8-36: 1320
21,1: 1133 1146
21: 1147

22,3: 1321

2 Chronica

6,41: 1322
9,1-12: 1180
10,15: 1185
17: 1323
19-20: 1324
21,1: 1324
21,12-15: 1233
25,1-26,2: 1277
29,15-19: 1285
36,20-23: 1334

Esdras, Ezra

1,1: 1334
5,3-4: 1335
7,12-26: 1336
7: 1337
9-10: 2296

Nehemias

3,5: 2217
8,10: 1338
9,6-31: 1339
9: 1340
10,1: 1341
13,24: 1342
13,29: 1341

Tobias

13,1-14,1: 1345

Judith

1: 1358
7-13: 1354
9,1-14: 1350
16,14: 1357

Esther

1: 1360
2,8-18: 1386
2,10: 1368
2,20: 1368

3-5: 1370
8,10-14: 1373

1 Machabaeorum

15,21: 1393

2 Machabaeorum

3-4: 1395
7,28: 263
7: 1394

Psalmi

1: 1571-6
2,1-11: 1577
2,11-12: 1578
2,12: 1579
2: 1580s
3: 1571
4,5: 1582
4,6: 644
5,1: 1583
5: 1584
7: 1585
8: 1571 1585-9
9-10: 1590
9: 1585
10: 1585
13: 1591
14,4: 1592
14: 1593s
16,10: 1595
16: 1596s
18: 1598s
19: 1600
21,13: 1601
21: 1602
22: 1603
23: 1571 1604
24-26: 1605
24: 1606
26: 1607
31-55: 1477
34: 1608
35: 1585 1609
36-38: 1610
37: 1611
39: 1612

40: 1613
45: 1614s
46: 1616
47: 1586 1617
49,15: 1618
51,17: 1619
51,21: 644
51: 1620s
57,8-9: 1622
58: 1623
61: 1624
67: 1625
68: 1320 1626
69: 1627s
71,18: 1629
72: 1630
73: 1631s
74: 1633
75,9: 1634
77: 1635s
78: 1637s
82: 1639
82: 1640s
83: 1642
85,10-11: 1643
85: 1644s
87:14: 536
87: 1586
89: 1320 1646s
90-100: 1648
90: 1649s
91: 1651
95: 1652
97: 1320 1653
98: 1320 1654
99: 1320
100: 1655
102: 1320 1656-8
103: 1659
104,35: 1660
107: 1320
109: 1320 1661
110,1: 50 1662
110: 1663
113: 255
115: 1320
116,10-11: 1666
116: 1667
118,22-23: 1668

28,16: 2234
28-31: 2216
28-32: 2235
28-33: 2208
28: 2236s
29,1-8: 2221
29,6-7: 2238
29,9: 4202
29,9-10: 3445
29,13: 2239
30-41: 2240
30,6-17: 2243
30,20-22: 2242
30,24: 2195
30,27-33: 2429
30,28: 1408
31,1-3: 2243
32,4: 2195
32,7: 1408
32,20: 2209
34-35: 2244s
34,15: 2195
35,5-8: 3445
36-39: 2246
38,16-17: 2247
40-48: 2262
40,1-11: 2263s
40,9: 3445
40,19-46,7: 2265
41,1-44,23: 2266
41,17-20: 2267
42,9-10: 2268
42,16-21: 2268
42,18-25: 2269
43,15-21: 2546
44,5-46,13: 2270
44,9-20: 2271
44,13: 2272
44,26: 2273
45,1: 2274
45,7: 2275
45,9: 4188
45,15: 2276
46,13-50,3: 2277
47,1-4: 2131
47: 2278
49,15-16 2546
51,6: 2279
52,13-53,12: 2291
53,4-5: 3052

53: 2280
54,9: 2292
55,1-5: 2293
55,8: 2264 2546
56-66:　　　　2230
　　2294　　　2298
　　2546
56,10: 2195
57,15: 2301
60,16: 2302
63,1-2: 4264
63,7-64,11: 2303
63,16: 2304
65,17-25 2546
66,25: 2205

Jeremias

1,5-10: 2337
1,6: 2338
1,13-19: 2339s
1: 2341
2,1-37:　　　2099
　　2342s
2,2-4,2: 2344
2: 2345
3,1-4,4: 2347
3,1-3: 2342
3,21-4,4: 2336
3: 2099 2345
5,7-8: 2342
5,12-17 2336
6,12: 1185
7,17-18: 2349
7,30-34: 2429
8,8-9: 2714
8,13-17: 2336
8,13-23: 2336
9,1-10: 2352
10: 2353
13,22-26: 2131
14,1-9: 2354
14,1-10: 2336
14,17-15,4: 2336
15,15-21: 2355
17,1-5: 2356
20,7-13: 2357
23,16-22: 2358
26: 2312
27-29: 2360s
28,8-9: 2358

28: 2314
29,13-14: 867
29: 2353 2362
30-33: 2365
30,24: 2366
30: 2367
31,31-34:　　2369
　　2371
32: 2374
33,21: 1341
35: 2375s
36:　2312　2377
　　2418
44,15-25: 2349
46-49: 2378
46,7-8: 2123
50,8-51: 2379
50,2-51,58: 2380
51,59-64: 2381
52: 2382

Baruch

1,15-3,8: 2396
6: 2395

Ezechiel

1,1-3,15: 556
1,4-28: 2414
1,5-10: 2415
1,10: 2416
1: 2417
2: 2418
11,14-21: 2419
14,1-11: 2420
16:　2099　2421s
　　4818
17: 2423
20: 2099
23,1-49: 2099
23: 2421 2424
26-28: 2425
30,16: 2426
37: 2427s
38-39: 2429
38: 2430
40-48: 2431
44,1-31: 2432
47: 2433
48,9-11: 2434

48: 801

Daniel

1-6: 2453
2: 2476s
3,8: 2478
3,38-40: 2479
3,51-90: 2480
3: 1394
4: 2481
5: 2482
6,1: 2483
6,5: 2478
6: 2484-6
7,13: 2487
7: 2488-90
8,2-3: 2478
8,6: 2478
9,26: 2491
12,3: 2492
13: 2493s

Amos

1,1-2,3: 2598
1,1-2,16: 2599
1,3-2,16: 2600
1,3: 2601
2,6-16: 2602s
2,7: 2604
2,8: 2605
3,10: 2606
3: 2607
4,1-3: 2608
5,26: 2609
6,3: 2606
7-9: 2610s
7,1-9,4: 2612
7,7-8: 2613
7,10-17: 2614-6
9,11: 2617

Osee, **Hosea**

1-3:　2521　2523
　　2525
1,1-2,25: 2542
1,1-3,5: 2526
1,1-3: 2524
1,4-5: 2527

27,19: 3255s
27,50-66: 3257
27,51: 3258
28,1-20: 3257

Marcus

1,1-15: 3422-4
1,1: 3425s
1,2-8: 3427
1,7-8: 2952
1,9-13: 2963
1,10: 3428
1,12-13: 3429
1,14-4,1: 3430
1,15: 3431
1,16-18: 3432
1,21-28: 3433
1,22: 3434
1,29-31: 2945
2,1-3,6: 3435s
2,1-11: 3437
2,18-19: 3432
2,20: 3438
2,23-28: 3439
3,20-21: 3440
3,31-35: 3440s
4,1-34: 3442
4,3-9: 2788
4,10-12: 3443
4,15: 3444
4,21-22: 3445
4,25-29: 3446
4,26-29: 3447
4,38: 3448
4,40: 3448
4: 3450
4: 3449
5,1-20: 3451s
5,21-6,1: 3453
5,21-43: 3454s
6,6-56: 3456
6,14-29: 3457
6,30-44: 3458s
6,45-53: 2945
6,52-53:   643
   3460-4
6,52: 3338
6,52: 3465
7,1-23:   3122
   3466
7,24-30:   3123
   3467s

7,31-37: 3469
8,1-13: 2963
8,11-13: 3470
8,17-21:   3338
   3465
8,22-26: 3469
8,27-9,13: 3471
8,31: 3472
8,32: 3473
9,1: 3474
9,2-10: 3475
9,5-6: 3476
9,11-13: 1245
9,14-29: 3477s
9,33-35: 3479
9,40: 3480
10,1-12: 3481-6
10,10-12: 3019
10,13-16: 3487
10,17-22: 3488
10,17-27: 3489s
10,17-31: 3491
10,35-45: 3489
10,42-45: 3479
10,46-52:   2945
   3492
10,47: 3493
11-16: 3494
11,12-14: 3495
11,12-21: 3496s
11,15-17:   3498-
   3500
11,27-12,34:
   3501
11,27-33: 3502
12,1-12:   2212
   3503s
12,13-17: 3505s
12,18-27: 3507s
12,26: 3509
12,28-34: 3510
12,28-44: 3511
12,35-37: 3512
13,1-4: 1194
13,1-37: 3513
13,2: 3514
13,5-37: 3515
13,10: 3516
13,11: 4252
13,26-27: 3517
13:     1207   3153
   3518-22
14-15: 3525

14-16: 3523
14,1-11: 3531
14,1-31: 3532
14,2: 2788
14,18-26: 3533
14,32-42: 3534s
14,39: 3536
14,43-53: 4259
14,48: 3537
14,58: 1194
14,61-62: 3542
14,61-64: 3538
14,72: 3539
14: 3524
15,16-32: 3540
15,33-39: 3541
15,39: 3542-4
15: 3524
16,1-8: 3545s
16,7-8: 3547
16,11: 3548
16:     3524   3549-
   51

Lucas

1-2: 3654 3657s
1,1-4: 3552
1,5-2,52:   3656
   3659
1,26-38:   3660-5
   2938
1,26-56: 3666
1,39: 3625
1,46-55: 3667-76
1,68-79: 3667
2,1-5: 3677
2,6: 2919
2,7: 2918
2,12: 2918
2,22: 3679
2,22-40: 3678
2,29-35: 3680
2,34-35: 3681
2,34: 3682
2,35: 3683
2,36-38: 3684
2,41-50: 3685
2,41-52: 3686
3,1-17: 3427
3,1: 3687
3,7-9: 3688
3,10-14: 3689

3,10-18:   2955
   3690
3,16: 2952
3,16-17: 3688
3,23-38: 3691
3: 3692s
4,1-13:   2964
   3429
4,1-30: 3694
4,14-9,62: 3695
4,14-30: 3696
4,16-30: 3697-9
5,1-11: 3700
5,39: 3731
6,5: 3701
6,20-49: 3702s
6,22: 3704
6,27-36: 3705s
6,27-38: 2992
6,44: 3001
7,1-10: 3049
7,11-15: 3707
7,11-17: 3708
7,19: 3086
7,31-35: 3709
7,36-50: 3710s
8,4-21: 3712
8,22-25: 3597
8,26-39: 3625
9,10-17: 3713
9,21-18,34: 3612
9,28-36:   3714s
   3133
9,46-48: 3479
9,46-48: 3716
9,51-10,42: 3718
9,51-19,10: 3717
10,1-20: 3719
10,5-7: 3720
10,13-14: 3713
10,18: 3428
10,23-24: 3721
10,25-28: 3722
10,25-37: 3723
10,25-42: 3724
10,38-39: 3725
10,38-42: 3726-8
10:21-22: 3089
11,2: 3729
11,4: 3046
12,1: 3730
12,14: 3731
12,22-31: 2996-8

2,36: 3858
2,42: 3859
2,44-45: 3834
  3860
2,44: 3861
2: 3862s
3,12-26: 1427
  2280 3864s
4,23-31: 2280
4,24-31: 3866
4,25: 3867
4,32: 3861
5,1-11: 3868
5,4: 3869
6,1-8,4: 3870
6,1-7: 3871
6,1: 3872
6,8-15: 3873
7,2-53: 3874
7,55-8,3: 3873
7: 3875
8,26-40: 2280
8: 3876
9,1-30: 3877s
9,15: 4622
9,20: 3879
9: 3880
10,1-11,18:
  3881-4
10,34-43: 3885
10,38: 3886
10: 3887s
11: 3887
12,1-19: 3889
12,1-23: 3890
13,16-41: 3891
13,1-14,28: 3901
13,1-18,23: 3902
13,4-12: 3903
13,16-52: 3904
14,1-7: 3905
14,21-23: 3906
15,1-29: 3907
15,13-21: 3908
15,20: 3909
15,29: 3909s
15: 3911-4
16,1: 3915
16,11-40: 3916
16,30-34: 3917
16,45: 3909
17,15-34: 3918
17,16-31: 3919
17,16-33: 3920
17,16-34: 3921-4
17,16: 3925

17,23: 3926
18,18: 3927
20,36-21,16:
  3928
21,21: 3929
21,23-24: 3927
21,25: 3909
21,29: 3930
22-26: 3931
27: 3597
28,3-6: 3932
28,16-31: 3933
28,30-31: 3934
28,35: 3935

Ad Romanos

1,8-15: 4749
1,17: 4750
1,18-32: 4751
1,24-27: 4752
1,26-27: 4753
1,26: 4754
1: 4747
2,13: 4755
2,22: 4756
2-3: 4757
2: 4758
3,10-18: 4759
3,21-26: 4760
3,25-26: 4761
4,1: 4762s
4: 4764s
5-8: 4768
5,1-5: 4769
5,1-11: 4770
5,12-20: 4771
5: 4938
7,1-4: 4772
7,7-8,4: 4773
7,7-25: 4774
7,14-25: 4716
7: 4775-7
8-10: 4602
8,18-22: 4778
8,18-27: 4779
8,28: 4780
8,31-39: 4781
8,38-39: 4782
9-11: 4799-4801
  4806s
9,25-26: 4808
9: 4809s 4716
10,1-13: 4811
10,19-21: 4812
10: 4809 4813

11,1-36: 4814
11,2-6: 4815
11,25-36: 4816
11,30-32: 4817
11: 4809 4818
12,1-8: 4819
12: 4924
13,1-7: 4820s
13,11-14: 4822
13: 4823s
14,1-15,13: 4825
14,1-15,14: 4602
14,5-6: 4826
14,7-9: 4516
15,13: 4827
16,3-5: 4828

1 ad Corinthios

1-2: 4864
1-4: 4866-70
1-6: 4865
1,18-31: 4871
1: 4855 4872
2,1-5: 4873
2,1-8: 3380
2,2: 4874
2,6-16: 4876
2,6-3,4: 4856
2,9: 4877
3,1-2: 4878
3,5-4,5: 4880
3,5-17: 4879
3,7-18: 4979
4,6: 4881
5-7: 4882
5: 4514 4883
6,1-8: 4884
6,1-16: 4885
6,11-12: 4886
6,12-20: 4887
6,12-11,16: 4837
6,12: 4888
6: 4861
7,21-24: 4704
7,21-22: 4890
7,21: 4889
7,25-26: 4891
7: 3485 4892s
8-10: 4896
8,1-6: 4642
8: 4860 4897s
9,10: 4899
9,19-23: 4900
9: 4500
10-11: 4901

10,1-10: 4902
10,1-14: 4904
10,1-22: 4903
10,14-22: 4514
  4905
10,16-17: 3207
10: 4897
11,2-16: 4906s
11,7: 242
11,7-12: 4856
11,10: 4908
11,17-34: 4905
11,23-26: 3207
11: 4909
12-14: 4914
12,7: 4922
12,31: 4923
12: 4918 4924s
13,3: 4926
13,13: 4927
13: 4928s
14,26-40: 4930
14,33-36: 4931s
14,34-35: 4933-6
15,3-11: 4947
15,12-34: 4944
15,19-26: 4946
15,20-22: 4937
15,23-28: 4945
15,29: 4941
15,35-49: 4951
15,44-49: 4856
15,45-49: 4937
15,51-52: 4949
15: 4938s 4943
  4950 4952
  4954 4956
16,1-2: 4955

2 ad Corinthios

1,1-2,13: 4964
1,3-11: 4969
1,17: 4970
1,19-20: 4971
2,13: 4972
2,14-7,4: 4974
2,14-4,6: 4975
2,14-16: 4973
3,6: 4976s
3: 4978-80
4,8: 4981
5,1: 4982
5,17: 255
5,19: 4983
5,21: 4984

Finito di stampare il 2 settembre 1998
Tipografia " Giovanni Olivieri "
Via dell'Archetto, 10 - 00187 Roma

ISBN 88-7653-611-6

ROBERT NORTH S.J.

ELENCHUS OF BIBLICA

ARCHAEOLOGICA - LINGUISTICA - THEOLOGICA

1995 / 2

EDITRICE PONTIFICIO ISTITUTO BIBLICO
ROMA 1999

ROBERT NORTH S.J.

ELENCHUS OF BIBLICA

ARCHAEOLOGICA - LINGUISTICA - THEOLOGICA

1995 / 2

EDITRICE PONTIFICIO ISTITUTO BIBLICO
ROMA 1999

Amplissimae gratiae debentur iis qui adjuverunt ad productionem hujus operis, sive recurrente dono pecuniae (CBA), sive bibliothecis Romae, sive Jesuitarum communitatibus St. Louis et Milwaukee.

Cordial thanks are due to the Catholic Biblical Association of America for its annual subvention, to the rich and available collections of the French, German, and Gregorian libraries of Rome, and to the libraries and community hospitality of the St. Louis and Milwaukee Marquette universities.

NOTANDA

IATG²: *Deinceps adhibemus, debita auctoritate concessa, **abbreviationes** ex secunda editione (1995) libri SIEGFRIED SCHWERTNER maxime divulgati: praemissis tamen aliquibus titulis: vel in recognoscibiliore forma, vel periodicorum qui demum post 1992 exsistere inceperunt.*

With this 1995 volume, in place of the 90-column list of abbreviations special to the ELENCHUS and sometimes graciously followed in other periodicals, we begin using, with the publisher's authorization, the now normative *Internationales Abkürzungsverzeichnis für Theologie und Grenzgebiete* of Siegfried M. SCHWERTNER in its second edition (Berlin 1995, de Gruyter; reprinted also as a volume of the *Theologische Realenzyklopädie*). But we here give on p.6-15, in an alphabetical order ignoring the helpful fillouts in *parentheses*, some less easily recognizable acronyms, and also those relevant periodicals which either began to exist only after 1992, or deal with archeology rather than theology.

Symbola in textu vel indice: [D]: dissertatio (vel ejus director). - [E]: editor (non in sensu europaeo; potius) redactor, *'a cura di'*. - [F]: Festschrift or memorial volume. - [M]: mentio, *'de eo'*. - [R]: recensio, book-review. - †: obituary. - *Semicolon* is still used in this half-volume to separate subtitle from title.

a000 = 10,000; b = 11,000; .. c, g, k ...; q000 = 15.000.
L[m] 15 = lire 15.000. $45 or DM 35 may be rounded off for $44.95 or DM 34.90.

Resounding success is merited by the devoted work of Robert ALTHANN. S.J., compiler of the exegesis-half of Elenchus 1995 and of all foreseeably future volumes, taking into account our shared hope that these must gradually be replaced by the computer and internet, offering last-minute accessibility with 'on-line service'.

EDITRICE PONTIFICIO ISTITUTO BIBLICO
Piazza della Pilotta, 35 - 00187 Roma, Italia

Index systematicus - Contents

Index (voces; SScr.) p.844

Urbes --	Publication Cities
AA	Ann Arbor MI
Amst /At	Amsterdam / Atlanta
B / Barc	Berlin / Barcelona
Ba / BA	Basel / Buenos Aires
Bo / Bru	Bologna / Brussel
C / CM	Cambridge England / MA
CasM	Casale Monferrato
Ch / ColMin	Chicago / Collegeville MN
CinB	Cinisello Balsamo
Da: Wiss	Darmstadt. Wiss. BuchG.
DG	DownersGrove, il
D	Düsseldorf
E / F	Edinburgh / Firenze
Fra	Frankfurt am Main
FrB / FrS	Freiburg Br / Schweiz
Gö / Gü	Göttingen / Gütersloh
GR	Grand Rapids MI
Ha / Heid	Hamburg / Heidelberg
J / K	Jerusalem / København
L / LA	London / Los Angeles
Lei / Lp	Leiden / Leipzig
Lv(N)	Leuven (L. la Neuve)
LVL	Louisville
M / Mi	Madrid / Milano
Mkn	Maryknoll NY
Mp	Minneapolis
Mü / Müns	München / Münster WF
N / ND	Napoli / NotreDame
Neuk	Neukirchen (VL)-Verlag
NHv / Nv	New Haven / Nashville
NY / Ox / P	New York / Oxford / Paris
Pd / Ph	Paderborn / Philadelphia
R / Rg	Roma / Regensburg
S / Sdr	Salamanca / Santander
SF / Shf	San Francisco / Sheffield
Sto / Stu	Stockholm / Stuttgart
T / TA	Torino / Tel Aviv
Tü	Tübingen
U / W	Uppsala / Wien
WL	Winona Lake IN
Wsb	Wiesbaden
Wsh	Washington DC
Wsz	Warszawa
Wu / Wü	Wuppertal / Würzburg
Z	Zürich

Periodica, **Short Titles: as IATG**[2]
* *non / aliter* -- **not** or **otherwise** in IATG
( ) *inserta,* **fillouts** *not* alphabetized

[A] arabice, in Arabic
AALr: Lincei, rendiconti: R
A(nnales)**ASF**(ennicae):Helsinki
A(nnales)**A**(rch)**Sy**(riae):Damas
A(nzeiger)**A**(ltertums)**W**; W
A(merican)**B**(enedictine)**R**
A(rchivFür)**B**(egriffs)**G;** Bonn
***Abh** (Akad Mü..)
ABORI; Annals Bhandarkar: Bandung
ABQ: American Baptist Q: Ph
A(ustralian)**B**(iblical)**R**; Melbourne
A(nnual:)**B**(ritish)**S**(ch)**A**(thens)
A(nnuaire)**C**(oll)**F**(rance): P
A(nalecta)**C**(isterciensia); R
***Ac**(tualidad)**Bi**(**bliográfica**); M
A(cta)**CL**(assica); (Kapstad)
***ACL**(assica)Debrecen
A(ntichità)**CL**(as&)**Cr**; Brescia
***Ac**(ta)**Mdv**(alia); Lublin
A(ustralas)**C**(ath)**R**; Sydney
A(nalecta)**Cra**(coviensia); Kraków
***Ac**(ta)**Sum**(erica); Hiroshima
***ActaTheolSAf**; Bloemfontein
A(rchivo)**E**(spañolDe)**A**(rq); M
***Äg**(ypten&)**Lev**(ante); W
A(rbeiten)**GJ**(udentum&)**U**(rchr);Lei
A(usDer)**G**(esch)**L**(at)**B**(ibel);FrB
AGS(pätjudentums&)**U**(rchr); Lei
AI(st)**O**(rUniv)**N**(apoli) (*clas)
AJ(apanese)**BI**(nst); Tokyo
***A**(sn)**J**(ewish)**S**(tudiesR);CM
A(sia)**JTh**; Singapore
A(ntike)**K**(unst); Olten
***A**(ltert)**KVO**: Müns
***Aletheia** (ph.th.spir.);StJodard
***AltOrF**(orschungen); B
A(rchivFür)**L**(tg)**W**(iss); Rg
A(rch)**M**(itteilungen)**I**(ran); B
***AmNum**(ismaticSoc); NY
***AmstC**(ahiers)
***Anat**(oli)ca; Istanbul
***A**(rchaeo)naut(ica);
An(alecta)**Bib**(lica); R

Anc(hor)B(ible) - D(ictionary)
*Anc(ient)H(istory)B(ulletin)
An(nales)É(conomies)S(oc'és)C(iv's); P
*A(rchéologie du)NilM(oyen); Lille
*An(naliScuolaNormaleSup)Pisa
*An(nual)R(eview)I(nscr)Mesop; Toronto
*An(nales)T(heologici); R
*Anvil; Notttingham
(Atti/M/Rendiconti)P(ont)A(cad)RA(rch)
A(rchiv für)P(apyrus)F(orschung); B
A(cta)P(ontificii)I(nst)B(iblici); R
*Apocr(ypha); Turnhout
Arch(aeology); CM
*Archaeom(etry); L
*ArchBiblical World,Shafter CA
*Archeo; R
*Archéologia; Dijon
*Arch(aeologia)Wsz
*Arethusa; Buffalo
A(rchiv)R(eformations)G(eschichte): B
A(rchives)R(oyales de)M(ari); P
A(nalecta)S(tudii)BF(ranciscani); J
A(nnali di)S(toria dell')Es(egesi); Bo
A(rchives)S(ciences)S(ociales)R(el); P
A(nalecta)S(acra)T(arraconensia); Barc
Ath(enæum); Pavia
*Aten(e e)R(oma); F
A(rchivo)T(eol)G(ranadino)
A(nglican)ThR
At(eneum)K(aplańskie);Włocławek
A(rbeiten zu)T(ext&)S(prache)AT;Mü
A(ntike)u(nd)A(bendland); B
*AulaO(rientalis); Barc
A(ndrews)U(niv)S(em)S;BerrienSprings
A(ntike)W(elt); Feldmeilen

B(oletín)A(s)E(spañ)O(rientalistas)M
B(ulletin de l')A(ssoc)GB(udé); P
*B(u)Ang(lo)Isr(aelArchaeolog.Soc);L
*BarIl(anUniv.)An(nual); TA
B(iblical)Ar(chaeology)R(eview);Wsh
*B(erlin)B(eiträge zur)Archäom(etrie)
B(u)C(anadian)S(oc)B(ib)S;Montreal
B(eiträge zur)E(rforsch)AT(&Jud); Fra
*BeerSheva
B(u d')É(tudes)O(rientales):Beyrouth
*BFa(cultés)Cath(oliques de)L(yon)

B(ulletin d')H(umanisme&)R(en);Genève
Bi(ble)Bh(ashyam); Kottayam
*B(iblical)Interp(retation)
BIOSCS > *BSeptCog
B(ooks)I(n)P(rint)=US; + Eng,Fr,Germ.
Bi(ble)Re(view); Wsh
*B(ibel&)L(i)t(ur)g(ie); W
*B(u de)Mos(aïque)A(ntique) =AIEMA
*Bog(oslovska)Smot(ra); Zagreb
*Bog(oslovni)Vestnik; Ljubljana
Bo(ok)L(ist: Soc. OT Studies); L
Bo(nner)J(ahrbücher)
*Bor(eas)M(ünster)
B(iblical)R(esearch); Chicago
*B(u)Sept(uaginta)Cog(nate); At
B(ulletin)S(oc)L(inguistique)P
*B(u)Sum(erian)Ag(riculture);C
B(angalore)TF(orum)
B(u)Th(éologie)A(nc&)M(édv); Lv
B(erliner)Th(eologische)Z(eitsch)
B(elleten)T(ürk)T(arih)K(urumu)
*BuAnR; AA
*Bu(lletin du)Canad(a)Mésop
*BuCent(re)Preistor(ique);Camuno
*Bu(du)Cent(re)Prot(estante)
*Bu(l of)R(esearch:)B(iblical)
*Bur(ied)H(istory); Melbourne
BVAB [= Ba(nt)besch(avingen)]
By(zantinische)Z(eitschrift); Lp
Byz(antion); Bru

C(hicago)A(ssyrian)D(ictionary)
ᶜ sinice, in Chinese
Cadmo; Lisboa
Caesarod(unum); Arles
C(ambridge)A(ncient)H(istory)
*Cam(bridge)Arch(aeology)
*Canad(ian)Cath(olic);Saskatoon
*Carthag/(inensi)a; Murcia
Cath(olica:) M(ünster)
C(oniectanea)B(iblica); Malmö
C(alvary)B(aptist)TJ; Lansdale PA
CCAR (ex-'Reform Judaism '); NY
C(iviltà)C(LAS&)Cr(istiana);Genova
C(ogitatio)Fi(dei); P
C(ollectanea)Fr(anciscana); R
*C(ollectanea)ThFujen; Taipei

*C(ahiers)Glotz; P
*C(onrad)Grebel(Review); Waterloo
C(ambridge)H(istory of)Ir(an)
*C(enter)H(ermeneut.)H(ellenist.)SF
C(atholic)H(istorical)R; Wsh
*Chiron; Mü
*C(athedra:)HistEl(srael)
*ChrH
Christus; P
*ChristusM(éxico)
Ch(icago)St(udies)
*Church; NY
C(lassical)J(ournal); Greenville SC
[CalStIn]CLA(ntiquity); Berkeley
CL(assical)B(ulletin); ex-StL
*C(hristen)Lehre; B
*CL(as)Ir(eland)
C(hristianity&)Lit; GR
*Cl(as)O(utlook); Miami OH
C(lassica&)M(ediaevalia): K
Coll(ationesVlaams); Gent
Com(munio)I(talia,Mi); P; Wsh
-(deutsch=IkaZ); Rodenkirche
Com(mentary,Jewish); NY
Communio(Sevilla)
Comp(ostellanum)
Comp(uter)Bib(le); Wooster OH
*Comp(uters&)Hum(anities); Osprey
Conc(ilium: E; Brescia; P; al.)
-(deutsch=IZT; Einsiedeln)
*Confer; M
*Contacts; P
Co(llectanea)Th(eol); Wsz
C(lassical)P(hilology): Ch
C(lassical)Q(uarterly); Ox
*Cre(ation)Sp(irituality);SJosé
*Cretan (Studies); Amst
*CriswellTR; Dallas
*Crit(ical)R(eview Books in)Rel
C(hristian)Sc(holars)R; GR
C(urrents In)Th&Mi(ssion); Ch
C(alvin)TJ; GR
C(oncordia)TQ; Fort Wayne
-- J & TM; St.Louis
C(hris)t(in the)W(orld); R
*Cu(rrent)R(esearch:)B(ible)
*C(ommon)weal

*C(atholic)W(orld)Rep(ort)
D(iss)A(bstracts)I(ntntl); AA
*D(eutsches)A(rchäol.)I(nstitut)
D(ielheimer)B(lätter)AT
D(eltio)B(ib)M(eletôn); Athena
Diak(-onia,Mainz; -onie,Stu)
Did(askalion)L(isboa)
*Direction (Fresno)
*Disc(ussions in)Eg(yptology); L
Do(ctor)C(ommunis); Vatican
Do(ctrine &)Li(fe); Dublin
*Doss(iers)A(rchéol); Dijon
D(umbarton)O(aks)P(apers)Wsh
D(ownside)R(eview); Bath
D(ead)S(ea Scrolls)D(iscoveries)
D(ansk)T(eol)T(idsskrift); K
D(ivus)T(homas); Piacenza
Ea(st &)W(R)
*Ebl(aitica); R
*Ebor
*Éch(osDu)M(onde)C(lassique)
*Éch(os de)(aint)SM(aurice)
E(studios)Cl(ásicos); M
E(untes)D(ocete); R
*Ed(in)b(urgh)(Rev)T(heology)
E(studios)E(clesiásticos); M
E(sprit)e(t)V(ie); Langres
*Ef(emerides)Mex(icana);Tlalpan
É(glise)e(t)T(héologie); Ottawa
E(nglish)H(istorical)R(eview); L
E(ncyclop.of/de l')I(slam): Lei
*Eikasmos; Bo
E(vangelische)K(ommentare); Stu
E(vangelisches)K(irchen)L(exikon)
E(phemerides)L(iturgicae); Vat.
*Elenchos; N
*Elliniki; Thessaloniki
EM(erita); M
*Emm(anuel); NY
E(cclesia)O(rans); R
*Ep(igraphica)Anat(olica); Bonn
ÉPHÉR → AEPHEr
Ep(worth)Re(view); L
E(cumenical)R; Geneva
Er(anos); U / J(ahr)b(uch);Fra
Es(critos del)Ve(dat); Valencia

E(xpository)T(imes); E
E(rbe)u(nd)A(uftrag); Beuron
*Eur(opean)J(ournal of)T; Carlisle
*Eur(Soc.for)C(ath)ThBu(lletin)
*Evangel; E
Ev(angelischer)Erz(ieher); Fra
E(gitto e)V(icino)O(riente); Pisa
*EvTop
E(ast &)W(est)L
*Exch(ange); Lei
Exped(ition): Ph
*Explorations; Ph
*F(aith)&M(ission); WakeForest
*F(aith)&Ph(ilosophy); ND
F(orschungen zum)AT; Tü
F(aith)a(nd)T(hought); L
*Fav(entia); Barc
F(ontes)C(hristiani); FrB
*Fem(inist)T(heology);Shf
fg/fil: FILOLOG/FILOS → Phi-
*Fg(Filologia)Nt(-aria):Córdoba
*Fid(esEt)Hist(oria);LongviewTX
*FirstT(hings); Denville
F(rankfurter)J(üd)B(eiträge)
F(orschungen)GL(ehre)P(rot);Müns
F(orum)K(atholische)Th; Müns
F(rüh)M(ittelalterliche)St;
*Forefront
*Forum(for)B(ibelsk)Eks(egese);K
*ForumRel(igion); Stu
*Fortunatae; Tenerife
*ForumF(oundations&)F(acets)
*Fran(ciscanum)Bog(otá)
FranzSt = WissWeis < 1994
*Freik(irchen-)For(schung); Müns
Fr(eiburger)Ru(ndbrief NR)
*Fr(eiburger-)S(chweizUniv)Zt
F(rankfurterSt.Georgien)TS
*Fund(amentum)Bas(el)
F(oi et)V(ie);P

G(reece)a(nd)R(ome):Oxford
ᴳ (neo)graece, in (modern) Greek
*G(iornale)d(i)T(eol);Brescia
*GenLinguistics; PaSUniv
Geog(rafia)Ant(ica); F
*Gerión; M

G(öttinger)G(elehrte)A(nzeigen)
G(iornale)I(taliano)F(ilologia); N
Gn(omon): Mü
Gö(ttinger)Misz(ellan -- Ägypt)
Gr(egorianum); R
*Grail; Waterloo
Gr(azer)Bei(träge)
G(reek)R(oman&)B(yzantine)S; CM
*GrSinal
G(ereformeerd)ThT; Kampen
G(eist)uL(eben); Wü

H(ebrew)A(nnual)R(eview); Columbus
ᴴ (neo)hebraice; in (modern) Hebrew
H(andbuch der)A(ltertums)W(iss); Mü
H(orizons in)B(ibl)T(heol);Pittsbg
H(andbuch der)D(ogmen)G(esch): FrB
H(b der)D(ogmen&)Th(eologie)G; Gö
Heb(rew)Stud(ies); Madison WI
*Helinium; Stockholm
*Helios; TX
*Henoch; Torino
Her(mathena); Dublin
Heresis; Carcassonne
*Hethitica; Lv
He(lps for)Tr(anslators); L
Hey(throp)J(ournal); L
H(istorisches)J(ahrbuch); Mü
H(arvard)J(udaic)T(exts&)St; CM
*Hokhma; Lausanne
Ho(mo)Re(ligiosus); Lv
H(omiletic&)P(astoral)R; NY
*Horizons; Villanova PA
*HoTheol(ógos); Palermo
H(istory of)R(eligions); C
H(arvard)S(emitic)M(gs); CM
H(istory &)Th(eory); Haag
H(arvard)Th(eological)R; CM
H(ervormde)T(eologiese)S;Pret
Hyp(omnemata): Gö
I(nt)BM(ission)R(es);Ventnor NJ

I(rish)B(iblical)St(udies);Belfast
I(slamic)C(ulture): Hyderabad
*Ichthys; Aarhus
I(n)D(ie)S(kriflig);Potchefstroom
*I(nst)F(ranç)A(rchéol)O(rientale)
*IFAP(roche-)O(rient); Damas

Igl(esia)**V**(iva); Valencia
I(ndo-)**I**(ranian)**J**(ournal); Haag
I(nternat)**ka**(tholische)**Z**;Fra=Comm
I(nternationale)**k**(irchliche)**Z**; Bern
I(stanbuler)**M**(itteilungen - *DAI)
Im(ago)M(undi); Pd
*Impact
I(nd)**M**(iss)**R**; Shillong
*InB(eiträge)Spr(ach)W; Innsbruck
I(srael)**N**(umismatic)**J**; TA
IntB > *NInterp
I(sr))**O**(riental)**S**(tudies); TA
*Iran; L
Irén(ikon); Chevetogne
I(nternat)**RM**(issiology); L
*IslamoC(hristiana); R
*Isr(ael)LawR(eview); J
*IsrMus(eum)J(ournal); J
Ist(ina); P
*Iter; Caracas
I(rish)**T**(heological)**Q**; Maynooth
I(ndian)**T**(heological)**S**; Bangalore
*Ivra (Jura); N
*I(nternat)Z(ts für)T;→Conc(Mainz)

J(ournal)**A**(siatique); P
J(ahrbuch für)**A**(ntike&)**C**; Müns
*J(ournal of)AncCiv; Changchun
JA(m)**R**(es)**C**(enter)**E**(gypt); WL
J(ahrbuch des)**d**(eutschen ar)**I**; B
J(ahrbuch für)**E**(vangelische)**Th**; Wu
*J(ournal of)EarlyC(hr); Baltimore
*Jeevadhara; Kerala
J(our)**E**(cumenical)**S**(tudies); Ph
J(ournal of)**E**(mpirical)**T**; Kampen
JE(vang)**T**(heol)**S**(oc);Lynchburg VA
*J(ournal of)Field(Arch);BostonUniv.
JF(eminist)**S**(tudies in)**R**(eligion);At
*J(ournal of)**G**(lass)S(tud);Corning NY
*JGrace(EvS,Roanoke;not=GraceTJ)
J(ournal of)**H**(istory of)**I**(deas);Ph
*JHi(gher)Cr(iticism); Montclair NJ
*JHisp(anic/Latino)T(heol); ColMn
*J(ournal of)Hist(ory of)Sex; Ch
*JInd(o-)E(uropean St);Hattiesburg MS
*JInt(erreligious)D(ialogue); Kampen
*JS(oc)I(nter)discip(linary St);CM
JI(nterdenominational)**ThC**(enter): At

J(ourn)**J**(uristic)**P**(apyrology);Wsz
*J(ournal of)J(e)w(ish)Th(ought);NY
J(unge)**K**(irche); Bremen
J(ahrbuch)**L**(iturgik&)**H**(ymnologie)
JLT (now Liturgy & Theology); Ox
*J(ournal of)MdvLat(in); R
*JMedit(erranean)A(rchaeol); Shf
JM(ennonite)**S**(tudies); Winnipeg
J(ahrbuch)**N**(umism&)**G**(eldg); Rg
J(b)**Ö**(sterreich.)**B**(yzantinistik);W
*J(erusalem)Persp(ective); J
JP(re)**H**(istoric)**R**(eligion);Göteborg
J(ournal of)**R**(eligion); Ch
J(ournal of)**R**(el.in)**A**(frica);Lei
*J(ournal of)R(oman)Ar(chaeol);AA
J(ournal of)**R**(eligious)**E**(thics);ND
JR(eligious)**H**(istory); Sydney
*J(ournal of)Rit(ual St);Pittsburgh
*JRomMil(itary Equipm.St);Newcastle
JR(eligious)**St**(udies); Cleveland
*J/R(Ancient)Top(ography); F/T
J(ournal des)**S**(avants); P
*J(ournal of)Semant(ics); Oxford
J(f.)**St**(.of)**P**(seud)**E**(pigrapha);Shf
J(ournal f.)**S**(tudy of)**R**(eligion);SAf
J(f.)**S**(cientific)**S**(t.of)**R**(eligion);NHv
*JS(oc)StEg(yptianAnt); Toronto
*J(ewish)St(udies)Q(uarterly); Tü
J(ournal of)**Th**(eology);Eau Claire
*JT(ransl. &T(heory)L(ing);Dallas
JT(heology for)SA(f); Rondebosch
*J(ournal)/Tyd(skrift)Sem(itics);SAf
Jud(aica); Z
Jud(entum&)**Um**(welt); Fra
JW(arburg&)**C**(ourtauld)**I**(nst); L
*J(of)**W**(omen&)**R**(eligion);Berkeley

Kairos 1.Salzburg; 2. *Guatemala
ᴷ coreanice, in Korean
*Karthago; P
*Kernos; Liège
*Kerux; Escondido CA
*K(ristus)Jyoti; Bangalore
Koin(onia); 1. Essen; 2. * Napoli
*Kok(alos)
*Krat(ylos); Wsb
K(atolikus)**S**(zemle); Budapest
*Ktema; Strasbourg

K(irche)**u**(nd)**I**(srael); Neuk

LA = SBFLA: Jerusalem

*L(ingua)Ae(gyptia); Gö

*Landas; Manila

L(ittératures)**A**(nc.du)**P**(r)**O**; P

Lati(nitas); Vatican

*Laverna; St. Katharinen

*Letture: Mi

L(etture)**C**(hr)**P**(rimi)**M**; Mi

*Levant; London

*L(ettre)**I**(nfo)**A**(rch)**O**(r);Valbonne

Li(ving)**Li**(ght); Wsh

*Limes

*Linacre(Quarterly)

*LinceiR(endiconti ..); R

*Ling(uistics)

*Listening; St.Louis

*Lit(erary &)L(inguistic)Comput(ing)Ox

*LitTh → JLT

Liv(ing)**Wo**(rd); Kerala

L(tg)**J**(ahrbuch); Müns

L(ibrary)**J**(ewish)**L**(aw &)**E**(thics); NY

L(uth)**M**(onatshefte); Ha

L(angues)**OrA**(nc); Lv

L(ebendige)**S**(eelsorge);Wü

L(utheran)**T**(heological)**J**; Adelaide

L(aval)**T**(héologique&)**P**(hil); Québec

Lum(enVr); Vitoria

L(umière et)**V**(ie); Lyon

L(umen)**V**(itae F; also Eng.); Bru

***M**aarav; WL

ᴹ magyar, in Hungarian

*Mad(rider)Mi(tteilungen); *DAI

*M(itt.zur)A(lten)G(esch.&)A(rch);B

Man(uscripta); St. Louis

Mar(ianum); R

*Mara (voor feminisme en theologie)

*M(ari:)**A**(nnales)**R**(ech.)**I**(nterdisc);P

*Masca; Ph

*Mast(er's)J(ournal); SunValley CA

*Mayéutica; Navarra

MC(hurch)**M**(an); Ox

M(iscellanea)**Com**(illas); M

M(aison-)**D**(ieu); P

*Medit(erranean)A(rchaeology);Sydney

*MeditH(istorical)R (Univ.TA); L

M(edievalia)e(t)**H**(umanist); Boulder

M(isc)**E**(st)**A**(rabes y)**H**(ebr);Granada

Menn(onite)**Q**(uarterly)**R**; Goshen IN

Mes(opotamia ᴱTorino); Firenze

*Messorot (Language traditions); J

*Metanoia; Praha

*Métis (anthropologie grecque); P

M(iscellanea)**F**(ranciscana); R

*M(itteilungen der arch.Ges.);Graz

M(useum)**H**(elveticum);Basel

*Mid-Am(erican)JTh; Orange IA

*Mid-Stream; Indianapolis

*Midstream; NY

*Millt(own)St(udies); Dublin

*Minos; Salamanca

*Mishkan; J

Miss(iology); Scottdale PA

Miss(ionalia)**Hisp**(anica); M

*Missionalia

*MitÖ(sterrichische)Num(ismatik)

Mo(nde)**Bi**(blique) 1.P; 2.Genève

*Mondo(della)B(ibbia)

*MondeCopte

*Mod(ern)Bel(ieving)

*Moralia; M

M(ediaeval)**S**(tudies); Toronto

M(élanges de)**S**(cience)**R**(el);Lille

M(ü)**S**(tudien zur)**S**(prachwissensch)

M(elita)**Th**(eologica); Malta

*Müns(Beiträge zur)Hand(lungsgesch)

*Muz(eum)TA

M(uslim)**W**(orld); Hartford

Nat(ional)**Geog**(raphic); Wsh

Nat(uraleza y)**Grac**(ia); Salamanca

*Nature

N(achrichten)**A**(kad)**W**(issensch)**G**(ö)

N(ew)**Bl**(ackfriars); L

Ned(erlands)**Th**(eologisch)**T**(ijds.)

Neotest(amentica); Pretoria

N(eue)**E**(phemeris)**S**(emit)**E**(pig);Wsb

*N(ear)E(ast)S(chool) → **ThRev**;Beirut

*NewTh(eological)R(eview); Ch

N(ederduits)**G**(ereformeerde)**TT**(ydsk)

*Nicolaus; Bari

*Nikephoros;

*N(ew)Ox(ford)R(eview); Berkeley
N(ew)T(estament)Ab(stracts); CM
N(ouvelle)R(evue)Th(éol); Tournai
N(ovum)T(estamentum); Lei
NT (et) O(rbis)A(ntiquus); FrS
N(ew)T(estament)S(tudies);Cambridge
N(orsk)T(eologisk)T(idsskr); Oslo
*Nubica; Köln
Num(ismatic)C(hronicle); L
Numen (History of Religions); Lei
N(ova et)V(etera): 1. FrS *2. Zamora
N(eue)Z(ts)M(issionswiss);Beckenried
N(eue)Z(ts für)S(ystematische)Th;

*Obn(ovljeni)Živ(ot); Zagreb

O(rientalia)C(hr)A(nalecta); R
O(rientalia)C(hristiana)P(er); R
Ö(kumenische)R(undschau); Stu
*Offa (Frühgeschichte); Neumünster
O(ns)G(eestelijk)E(rf); Antwerpen
O(riental)I(nst)Ac(quisitions); Ch
O(riente)M(oderno); R
O(ne)i(n)C(hrist); Turvey, Bedf.
*Oikoumene; Budapest
O(rientalia)Lo(vaniensia)P(er);Lv
*Op(uscula)A(theniensia); Athens
*Op(uscula)R(omana):   } Swed. R
*Opus (stor.economica Siena); R
O(sservatore)R(omano); Vaticano
Or(ientalia); R
Or(iens)Chr(istianus); Wsb
Orien(tierung); Zürich
*Origini; R
*Origins; Wsh
Orph(eus); Catania / *Thrac;Sofiya
Or(ientalia)Suec(ana); U
Ort(odoxia)Buc(ureşti)
O(stkirchliche)S(tudien); Wü
O(ld)T(estament)A(bstracts); Wsh
O(ld)T(estament)E(ssays); Pretoria
*Ox(ford)J(ournal of)Archaeology

P(roc)A(m)A(cad)J(ewish)R(es);Ph
P polonice, in Polish
*Pacifica; Melbourne
P(roc)A(m)C(ath)P(hilos)A(sn); Wsh
*PACT; Strasbourg

*Páginas; Lima
Paid(euma); Fra
*PalaeoH(istoria); Haarlem
Pal(estra del)Cl(ero); Rovigo
*Paléor(ient); P
Pal(estinski)Sb(ornik); Petrograd
P(roc)A(mer)P(hilos)S(oc); Ph
*Parabola; NY
Par(ole de l')Or(ient); Kaslik
Par(ola del)Pass(ato); Napoli
Pa(role di)Vi(ta); Torino-Leumann
P(atristic &)B(yzantine)R(eview); NY
P(apers)B(ritish)S(chool in) Rome
P(roceedings)C(lassical)A(sn);L
P(roc)C(ambridge)P(hilological)S(oc)
P(roc)C(ambridge)Ph(ilosophical)S(oc)
P(roc)C(ath)T(h)S(oc)A(mer);Villanova
Pen(sée)Cath(olique); P
*Peritia; Dublin
*Per(spectives on)Sc(ience&)C(hr)F(aith)
*Persica
*Persp(ectives of)Ref(ormed Thought)
Per(spectiva)Teol(ógica); São Leopoldo
pg = philolog. / ph = philosoph. → fil
Ph(ilologus); B
*Pharos; Amst Athens Inst,
*Phase; Barc
P(roblèmes d')H(ist.des)R(el); Bru
Philip(piniana)Sa(cra); Manila
Phoe(nix) 1.(EOL) Lei; * 2. Toronto
*Phon(ologie)L(angues)Sém; Montréal
Phron(esis); Assen
*Ph(ilosophy &)T(heology); Milwaukee
P(roc)I(rish)B(iblical)A(sn); Dublin
P(ublications) → IFAO, Cairo
*Pneuma; Pasadena
P(roche-)O(rient)C(hrétien); J
*ProcP(hilolo)gS(oc); Cambridge
P(hilological)Q(uart); Iowa City
Prak(tische)Th(eologie); Zwolle
*Presb(yterion); St. Louis
*Presbyteri; Trento
*PresenzaP(astorale); R
*Pre-text; Arlington TX
*Priest: St. Paul
*Proc(East)G(reat Lakes&)M(idw);Buffalo
*ProDial(ogo)

*ProofT(exts); Baltimore
Protest(antesimo); R
*Protok(olle zur)B;Klosterneuburg
*Proy(ecto)C(entro)S(alesiano)E;BA
*Proyección; Granada
Pr(iest &)**Pe**(ople); L
P(erspectives)**R**(el)**St**; Danville VA
*Prudentia; Auckland
Prz(egłąd)**Pow**(szechny); Wsz
P(rinceton)S(eminary)B(ulletin)
P(erkins)S(chool of)**T**(h)**J**; Dallas
P(arola)S(pirito e)V(ita); Bo
Qad(moniot); J
Q(uarterly)**R**(ev.for Ministry); Nv
Q(iryat)S(efer); J
Q(uaderni)**Stor**(ici); Ancona
*Quad(erni Univ)Catania / Chieti
*Quad(erni di)Semant(ica); Bo
*Quaerendo (manuscripts); Amst
*QuatreF(leuves); P
Q(uaderni)U(rbinati)C(ult)C(las)
Qu(estions)**Li**(turgiques); Lv
*Qum(ran)C(hronicle); Kraków
Qu(aderni di)**Sem**(itistica); F
*Q(üestions de)VidaC(r);Montserrat
R(evue d')**A**(ssyriologie); P
ᴿ russice,in Russian / ᴿ review(er)
R(eallexikon)**A**(ntike &)**C**(hr/tum);Stu
*Rad(io)Carb(on); NHv
RA(rchéologues &)**H**(ist. d')**A**(rt);Lv
*RAMBI (ResimatMaamarim)) bibliog; J
RAM;Toulouse - **R**(iv)A(sc)**MI**(stica);F
*R(evista de)Arq(ueología); M
R(assegna di)**S**(tudi)**Et**(iopici); R
Ras(segna mensile di)**Isr**(ael);R
*Raydan
R(uch)**B**(iblijny i)**L**(iturg);Kraków
RB(elge)**N**(umismatique &)**S**(igillogr)
R(ev.de)**C**(ultura)**B**(íblica);SãoPaulo
R(iv)C(ultura)C(lass.&)**M**(edievale);R
R(ivista del)**C**(lero)**I**(taliano); Mi
R(evue)**d**(')**É**(gyptologie); P
R(assegna)**d**(i)**T**(eologia); Napoli
R(evue des)**É**(tudes)**A**(nc); Bordeaux
Ref(ormatio); Z
Ref(ormátus)**Egy**(ház); Budapest

Ref(ormed)**R**(ev);1.Holland MI; 2.Ph
Ref(ormation)**R**(eview): Amst
Re(cusant)**H**(istory); Bognor Regis
Rel(igión y)**Cult**(ura); M
Rel(igious)**Ed**(ucation); Ch
*Rel(igion &)T(heology);Pretoria
Ren(ovatio); Rg
*Rep(ort Dept.Antiq)Cyp(rus):Nicosia
*ResP(ublica)Lit(terarum); Kansas
R(azón y)**F**(e); M
*R(evue)Géor(gienne)
R(evue de l')**I**(nst.)**C**(ath)**P**(aris)
*Ric(erche)Sto(rico)B(ibliche); Bo
*RijeckiT(eološki)Č(asopis); Fiume
R(endiconti dell')I(st)L(ombardo);Mi
R(iv)I(taliana di)N(umismatica);Mi
R(iv)**I**(st)**N**(az)**A**(rte &st);R
RivA(rcheologia)**C**(ristiana):Vat
*Riv.Past(orale)Ltg(ica);Brescia
*Riv.Sc(ienze)R(elig.); Molfetta
R(eligion &)**L**(iterature); ND
R(heinisches)**M**(useum)**P**(hilologie);Fra
R(omanian)**O**(rthodox)**C**(h)**N**(ews);Buc
Ross(iyskaya)**Arkh**(eologiya): Moskva
R(endiconti)**P**(ont)**A**(ccad)**RA**(rch.)
R(ömische)**Q**(uartalschrift); FrB
*R(eviews in)Rel(igion &)T(heol); L
R(ivista)**S**(tudi)**Ec**(umenici); Verona
*RS/Ou: Ras Shamra-Ougarit
R(echerches de)**S**(cience)**R**(elig); P
R(icerche)**S**(toria)**S**(ociale &)**R**(el); R
R(elig,&)**T**(heol.)**A**(bs);Youngstown
R(echerches)**ThA**(nc.&)**M**(édiévale); Lv
R(eformed)**T**(heological)**J**; Belfast
R(oczniki)**T**(eologiczno)**K**(an.);Lublin
R(evue)**T**(héologique de)**L**(ouvain)
R(evista)**T**(eológica)**Li**(mense); Lima
R(eformed)**T**(heological)**R**; Melbourne
R(ivista di)**V**(ita)**S**(pirituale); R
*S(tate)**A**(rchiv)**A**(ssyr)**B**(u);Helsinki
Sal(esianum); R
*Sandalion; Sassari/R
*Sastuma(ltertumskunde); Saarbrücken
S(cottish)**B**(ulletin)**E**(vangelical)**T**: E
S(tudium)**B**(ib)**F**(ranciscanum(.min) → LA
S(ources)**C**(hrétiennes); P

*Sc(ientific)Am(erican)
Sc(uola)C(attolica); Varese
S(tudia)C(lassica)I(sraelitica); J
S(ixteenth)C(entury)J: Kirksville
S(tudia)C(lassica &)O(rientalia); R
Scr(iptorium); Bru
Scr(ipture)B(ulletin); L
*Scr(ittura e)Civiltà; T
ScrHie(rosolymitana); J
*Scriptura; Stellenbosch
Scr(ipta)Th(eologica); Pamplona
Scr(iptorium)Vic(toriense); Vitoria
S(acris)E(rudiri); Steenbrugge
*S(krif)enK(erk); Pretoria
Sem(itica); P
*Sém(itique et)B; Lyon
*Semiotica; Amst
*Sevartham; Ranchi
*Sève (Église aujourd'hui); P
*Sewanee (TN) Th(eological)R
SF(lorida)S(tud)H(ist)J(udaism)
SF(ormative)Sp(irituality):Pittsburgh
*SGErm(itage); St.Petersburg
S(hina)G(aku)K(enkyu); Osaka
S(tudies in)H(ist)R(el) = Numen.s
*Sic(ilia)Arch(eologica); Trapani
*Sic(ulum)Gynι(nasium); Catania
*Sidic; R
S(tudi)I(tal)F(ilologia)C(las); F
S(cot)JR(eligious)S(tudies);Stirling
S(cottish)J(ournal of)Th(eol); E
S(candinavian)JO(f)T(heol); Aarhus
*S(tudi)M(icenei)E(geo)A(natolici);R
*Spiritus; P
*Sprache; W
*StA(lt)ä(gyptischer)Kultur; Ha
*StEbl(aitici); R
*StEg(ittolog.&Ant)Pun(iche); Bo/Pisa
*St(udi)Ep(igrafici&)L(ing); Verona
*S(tudi)T(eologiciDell'IstB)Ev;Pdv
St(udia)Ir(anica); Leiden
*St(udium)Leg(ionense); León
St(udia)Li(turgica); Rotterdam
*StMark; Canberra
St(udia)Or(ientalia); Helsingfors
St(udium)Ov(etense); Ovieto
St(udia)Pat(avina); Padua

St(udia)P(ost)B(iblica); Lei
St(udia)Po(hl); R, P.Ist.Biblico
*St(udia i)Prace; Wsz
Str(even); Antwerpen
*StRefT(heolHist); Princeton
*St(udia)Rom(ana: jus); R
*St(udies in)Spir(ituality); Kampen
Studium; 1.M; 2.R
*StudosTJ
S(tudia)T(heologica)V(arsaviensia)
Sub(sidia)B(iblica Pont.Ist.B);R
Sv(ensk)T(eol)K(vartalskrift); Lund
SV(ladimir)T(heol)Q; Crestwood NY
S(tudies in)W(omen &)R(eligion); NY
Symb(olon); Basel

*Tablet; L
ᵀ translation / vertens, translator
T(exte &)A(rb)N(t)Z(eitalter); Tü
T(ransactions)A(mer)Ph(ilos)S; Ph
T(heologische)B(ücherei); Mü
*T(heolog)B(ook)R(eview); L
*T(heologica)Braga
T(eología)E(spiritual); Valencia
T(extos y)E(studios)CC(isneros); M
T(heological)Ed(ucation); Dayton
*T(heological)Ed(ucato)r;N.Orleans
*Telema; Kinshasa
*Teocom(unicação)
*Teuda
*TEv(angeli)ca; Pretoria
*Text; Haag
*TFuJen → Collectanea, Taipei
*Themelios; L
Theo(logy)L(ondon)
Theol(ogía)A(thenai)
*Théologiques; Montréal
*Th(eologika)Lima
*Thetis
TH(eologie der)G(egenwart); Müns
Th(eologie)H(istorique); P
Th(eologie)I(m)K(ontext);Aachen
Th(eologie &)Ph(ilosophie); Fra
T(ravaux d')H(umanisme&)R(en)
Th(eologische)R(undschau); Tü
Th(eologia)Ref(ormata); Woerden
ThRev(iew Near East Sch); Beirut
Th(eologische)R(e)v(ue); Müns

*Th(eology of)Sex; Shf
Th(eológiai)Sz(emle);Bud
TIC(ontext)=TeolContexto = ThIK
Ti(erra)Nu(eva); Bogotá
*T(eología)-IUSI; Caracas
T(oronto.J(ournal of)T(heology)
T(imes)L(iterary)S(upplement); L
*T(ids)M(ellan)Ö(sternstud.);Lund
*Top(oi)O(rient-Occident); Lyon
T(ransactions)P(roc)A(mer)P(g)A;NY
Tr(aditio): Fordham
Trad(ition, Jewish); NY
*Transformation: Wynnewood PA
*T(erra)S(ant)a; J
T(exte&)S(t)A(nt)Judentum); Tü
*T(heologica)Sard(egna)Cagliari
T(ijdschrift voor)Th(eologie); Nijm
T(rierer)Th(eologische)Z(eitschrift)
T(idsskrift for)T(eologi og)K; Oslo
T(exte aus der)U(mwelt)AT; Gü
*Tyche; Wien
*Tychique; Lyon

Us C(atholic)H(istorian); Baltimore

*Var(ia)Aeg(yptiaca); San Antonio
V(erkündigung &)F(orschung); Mü
*Vivarium; Catanzaro
*Viv(ens)H(omo); F
*V(icino) O(riente); R
*VoxP(atrum); Lublin
*VoxScr(ipturae); São Paulo
V(ita e)P(ensiero); Mi Univ.Catt.
V(ox)R(eformata); Geelong
V(ie)S(pirituelle); P
V(izantijskij)V(remennik);StPtburg

V(erdad)yV(ida); M

W(ege)d(er)F(orschung): Da
Wi(ssenschaft&)Wei(sheit);Mü→Franz
W(isconsin)L(utheran)Q; Mequon
W(elt des)O(rients); Gö
*WorldA(rchaeology); Henley
Wo(rld)Sp(irituality); L
W(iener)St(udien)
W(estminster)Th(eological)J; Ph
W(esleyan)TJ; Marion IN
W(ort)u(nd)A(ntwort); Mainz
W(ort)u(nd)D(ienst); Bielefeld
*W(ord+)W(orld); St.Paul
W(ege)z(um)M(enschen); Gö

Y(ale)C(lassical)S(tudies); NHv

Z(eitschrift für)A(ssyriologie); B
Z(ts)A(ltor&)B(ibl)R(echtsgeschichte)
Z(ts für)Ä(gyptische)S(prache &A); B
Z(eitschrift für)A(lt)H(ebraistik);Stu
Z(ts für)D(ialektische)T(heol); Kampen
Z(eitsch, für)E(thnologie); Braunschweig
Z(ts für)E(vangelische)E(thik); Gü
*Zeph(yrus); Salamanca
*Z(ts für)M(edizinische)Eth(ik): Salzburg
ZM(issions&)R(eligionswissenschaft)Müns
Z(eszyty)n(aukowe)K(at)U(niw)L(ublin)
*Z(ts)n(euere)T(heologie)g(eschichte); B
Z(ts für)P(apyrologie &)E(pigraphik);Bonn
*Z(eitschrift für)Semiot(ik)
Z(ts)S(avigny-Stiftung für)R(echts)G.rom
Z(ts)V(ergleichende)S(prach)F(orschung)B
Z(eit)W(ende); Gütersloh
*ŻycieD(uchowe); Kraków

I. Bibliographica

A1 *Compilationes* .1 **Festschriften & memorial volumes**

1 Collected essays: CBQ 57 (1995) 203-217 . 419-442 . 617-632 . 836-850; JQR 84 (1993s)
119-127 . 389-396; 86 (1995) 65-274; - OTA 18 (1995) 129-141 . 391-5 . 619-623. -
Collected Studies: *A(sn)JSR 19 (1994) 115-125 . 301-316; 20 (1995) 267-278 . 489-502.

-- Festschriften [= Histoire universelle!]: RHE 90 (1995) 62*-65* . 263*-265*. - JQR 86 (1995s) 265-274 . 523-533. - *Langlamet* François, Recueils et mélanges: RB 102 (1995) 132-144 . 291-302 . 438-458. - *Perdue* Leo, Collected essays: JBL 114 (1995) 363-7 . 553-561 (-569, *al.*) . 761-5.

2 Aberdeen University quincentenary, But where shall wisdom be found ?, [E]**Main** Alan. Aberdeen 1995, Univ. 115 p. £ 5. 0-904484-01-7. - [R]ET 106,12 2d-top choice (1994s) 354-6 (C.S. *Rodd*); ScotJR 16 (1995) 156-8 (J. *Drane*).

3 ACÉBAC, Actes du cinquantenaire, 'De bien de manières'; la recherche biblique aux abords du XXIe siècle. [E]**Gourgues** Michel, *Laberge* Leo. Montréal/P 1995, Fides/Cerf. 485 p. F 250. [The eleven articles are on biblical books].

4 AHLSTRÖM Gösta W. memorial: The pitcher is broken JSOT.s 190. Shf 1995, Academic. 474 p.: bibliog. 39-43. £ 45. 1-85075-525-6 [OTA 19,p321., indicating summary of each of the 19 articles].

4* ANASTOS Milton V.: Presence of Byzantium, 85th b., [E]**Dyck** Andrew R., *Takács* Sarolta A. = ByF 20 (1994) 280 p.; ill.

5 ATKINSON James: The Bible, the Reformation and the Church, 80. Gb.; [E]**Stephens** W.P.;JSNT.s 105. Shf 1995, Academic. 340 p.; portr.; bibliog. £ 40. 1-85075-502-7. 15 art.; 11 infra [NTAb 40,p.128; RStR 22,75, D.W. *Kling*]. - [R]CritRR 8 (1995) 533s (D.M. *Griswold*, tit.pp.).

6 AUMANN Jordan: Compendio di teologia spirituale, 75o anniv., [E]**DeCea** E.A. R 1992, Angelicum. 548 p. - [R]Claretianum 34 (1994) 606s (G. *Lanithottam*, Eng.)

7 BABOIN-JAUBERT Christian; De l'éthique en politique, [E]**Duffe** B.M. Lyon 1995, PROFAC. ii-279 p. 2-85317-058-6 [NTAb 40,p.542: 14 art.; *Lemonon* J.-P. sur Rom 13,1-7].

8 BAKER John P. mem. [essays from a conference he organized at Tyndale House, Cambridge, July 1987]. GR 1995, Baker. .. $ 18. 0-8010-2044-1 [< OTA 19,138, with renvoi to summaries of 6 of the 11 items].

9 BALBONI Dante, mons. dott.: 'In labore virtus', 50° di sacerdozio, [E]**Cecchelli** Marco, *Masetti Zannini* Gian Ludovico. R 1993, Ist. Beato Angelico. 485 p.; ll. - [R]CivCatt 146 (1995,2) 207s (G. *Ferlizzi*).

10 BALMAS Enea, mem., Parcours et rencontres; mélanges de langue, d'histoire et de littérature française. Langres 1993, Klincksieck. 1637 p. (2 vol.) - [R]Protest(mo) 50 (1995) 70-73, C. *Tron*, con menzione degli 11 art. del Balmas apparsi in questa rivista).

11 BALMUTH Miriam S., Sardinia in the Mediterranean; a footprint in the sea, [E]**Tykot** Robert H., *Andrews* Tamsey K. Shf 1992, Academic. 520 p.; 140 fig. $ 75. 1-85075-386-5. - [R]Jfield 22 (1995) 117-9 (Paula Kay *Lazrus*).

12 BARTH Markus 1915-1994: essays in memory of = : H(orizons)BT 17,2 (1995), phot.; 181-198 bibliog.

13 BAUMGARTNER Hans M.: Grenzbestimmungen der Vernunft; philosophische Beiträge zur Rationalitätsdebatte, [E]**Kolmar** Petra, *Korten* Harald. Mü 1994, Alber. 505 p. DM 85. 3-495-47756-X [ThRv 92,178, tit.pp].

14 BEAUCHAMP Paul: 'Ouvrir les Écritures', 70 ans, [E]**Bovati** Pietro, *Meynet* Roland: LDiv 162. P 1995, Cerf. 435 p.; bibliog. 9-20; exorde de P. *Ricœur*, 21-28. F 220. 2-204-05231-0. 21 art.: 10 infra: les autres → 11-A [NTAb 40,p.328].15 BECK Hans-Georg: 85.Gb. Byzantinische Zeitschrift 88 (1995).

16 BEKER J. Christiaan: *a*) Biblical theology, problems and perspectives. [E]**Kraftchick** Steven

J., *al.* Nv 1995, Abingdon.   336 p.; portr. $ 20 pa.   0-687-03386-1.   17 art.   [NTAb 40,p.363; ThD 43,157]. -- [R]*TBR 8,2 (1995s) 20 (L. *Houlden*). - *b)* PrincSemB 16,1 (1995) 6-35, four articles on Beker (emeritus) [by *Nichols* J.Randall, *Stiffler* Flo Guynn, *Johnson* E.Elizabeth, *Miller* Patrick D.], with his 'Farewell Remarks'.

17 BELL Roy D. = Crux 31,2 (1995) 2-54.

18 BELLAMY James A: Literary heritage of classical Islam, [E]**Mir** Mustansir, (*Fossum* Jarl E.). Princeton 1993, Darwin.   359 p. $ 35. - [R]JAOS 115 (1995) 135s (D.J. *Stewart*).

19 BERTSCH L.: Inkulturation und Kontextualität; Theologien im weltweiten Austausch: [E]**Pankoke-Schenk** M., *Evers* G. Fra 1994. Knecht. 344 p. DM 68. 3-7820-0705-0. 23 art. - [R]TTh 35 (1995) 304s (J. *Heijke*).

20 BETTI Umberto, O.F.M.: La 'Dei Verbum' trent'anni dopo, [E] **Ciola** Nicola: Lateranum 61,2s (1995) 297 p.; portr.; p. 299-373, pagine di diario 1962-5.

21 BISKUP Maria, [P] Studien zur Geschichte der Politik, Wirtschaft und Kultur des XII-XVII. Jhts, [E]**Nowak** Z.H. Toruń 1992. Naukowe. 412 p. [RHE 91,54*].

22 BOARDMAN John: The archaeology of Greek colonisation, [E]**Tsetskhladze** Gocha R., *De Angelis* Franco: Committee Arch Mg 40. Ox 1994, Oxbow. x-149 p.

23 BOEHMER Rainer M.: Beiträge zur Kulturgeschichte Vorderasiens, [E]**Finkbeiner** Uwe, *al.* Mainz 1995, von Zabern. xvi-707 p.; 257 fig.; 53 pl.; phot.; Bibliog. 699-707.   3-8053-1863-4. 67 art., 24 infra.

24 BOGACKI Henryk 1920-1993 mem., longtemps rédacteur: C(olc)Th 64,3 (1994); 5-9, fot. (J. *Charytański*).

25 BOGAERT Raymond & LOOY Herman Van: Opes atticae; miscellanea philologica, [E]**Geerard** Maurice: SEr 31, 1990 → 6,25: [R]AnCl 64 (1995) 591s (A. d'*Hautcourt*).

26 BOURRIAU Janine [< 1988 colloquia]: Middle Kingdom Studies, [E]**Quirke** Stephen. New Malden 1991, 'SIA'. 152 p.; 8 fig., 2 pl. 1-872561-02-0. - [R]JEA 81 (1995) 258-262 (Diana *Magee*).

27 BRAGANÇA Joaquim de Oliveira: = Didaskalia 25 (1995). 548 p. , portr.; bibliog. 10-13 (S. *Rodrigues*). 27 art.; 2 infra.

28 BROMBERGER Sylvain: The view from Building 20; essays in linguistics, [E]**Hale** Kenneth, *Keyser* Samuel J.: Current Studies in Linguistics 24. CM 1993, MIT. xiv-273 p. - [R]Lg 70 (1994) 802-7; 2 fig (M.A. *Covington*).

29 BUESS Eduard: Basileia, [E]**Dürr** Hans, *Ramstein* Christoph. Ba 1993, Mitenand. 515 p. 3-927534-19-6. - [R]ZKG 106 (1995) 112-4 (D. *Blaufuss*).

30 BURGER Michel: Mélanges de philologie et de littérature médiévales, [E]**Cerquiligni-Toulet** J., *Collet* O. Genève 1994. 360 p. -- [R]BSLP 90,2 (1995) 230-2 (M. *Banniard*).

31 BURNS Robert I., Iberia and the Mediterranean world of the Middle Ages. I. proceedings from Kalamazoo, [E]**Simon** Larry J.: MdvMedit 4. Lei 1995, Brill. xxvi-373 p.; 11 fig.; portr., map. 90-04-10168-3 [RHE 91, *540].

32 CARDONA Giorgio R., mem.: Ethnos lingua e cultura, [E]**Belardi** Walter, *al.*: BtRLingFg 34, Univ. Roma, Dip. Glottoantropologico. R 1993, Il Calamo. 468 p. - [R]Salesianum 57 (1995) 795s (R. *Bracchi*)

33 CARLEBACH Julius: Studien zur jüdischen Geschichte und Soziologie. Heid 1993, Winter. xx-220 p. - : [R]*A(sn)JS 20 (1995) 276, titles sans pp.

34 CESTARO Antonio: Studi di storia del Mezzogiorno, [E] **Volpe** Francesco. Venosa 1993, Osanna. 450 p. : R(ic)SS(oc)R 47 (1995) 267-271 (V. *De Marco*).

35 CHATTERJI S.K., 60th b.: Religion and Society 40,4 + 41,3 (Bangalore 1993s) 3-77, bibliog.76s / 2-74.

36 CHEVALLIER Raymond, Mélanges 2. Histoire et archéologie, 1-2, ^E**Bedon** Robert, *Martin*
Paul M. = Caesarodunum 28s (Tours 1994s). 22 + 22 art.

37 Chieti seminario, Pianum 1914-94. Chieti 1995. 119 p.; ill. 8 art.; 4 infra.

38 COLDSTREAM J.N.   Klados;   Essays in honour of J.N. Coldstream R.S.,   ^E**Morris**
Christine: Bulletin Supp. 63. London 1995. Institute of Classical Studies.   xiii-310 p.;
colour. ill.; bibliog. 285-292 (*Batten* Victoria). 0-900587-66-0. 25 art.; 2 infra.

39 COLLIARD Lin: Histoire et culture en Vallée d'Aoste. Aosta 1993, Musumeci. 405 p.;
14 fig.; 6 pl. [RHE 91,222*].

40 COLLINS Raymond F., [transferring to Washington Catholic U.], The ministry of the Word,
^E**Selling** Joseph A.: LouvSt 20,2s (1995) 101-344; portr.; bibliog. 332-340. 15 art.; 5 infra,
8 others on biblical books. [NTAb 40,p.18]. - p.134-146. *Fitzmyer* Joseph A., Problems of
the literal and spiritual [not 'scriptural' as p. 101] senses of Scripture.

41 COLOMER I POUS Eusebi, Pensar en diàleg, miscel·lània en homenatge, ^E**Rius-Camps**
Josep, *Torralba Roselló* Francesc; RCatT 19 (1994); color. portr.; biobibliog. 11-29
(Torralba), 41-50 (Ceferino *Santos-Escudero*). 29 art.; 8 infra.

42 COLPE Carsten: Tradition und Translation;   zum Problem der interkulturellen
Übersetzbarkeit religiöser Phänomene, 65. Gb., ^R**Elsas** Christoph *al.,* B 1994, de Gruyter.
xxxvi-565 p.: Bibliog. 551-6. 3-11-013930-8. 40 art.; 15 infra.

43 COQUIN Marie-Georges: (I) 1995 → 10,27: (II) = BSAC 34 (1995).

44 DAMME D. van: Peregrina curiositas; eine Reise durch den 'Orbis antiquus', ^E**Kessler** A.,
al.: NTOA 27. FrS/Gö 1994, Univ/VR. ix-318 p. - ^RRHPhR 75 (1995) 343 (D.A. *Bertrand*:
17 art., très éclectique: LATTKE M., Le débauché de Corinthe; BARTHÉLEMY D., La faillite
de la publication des textes de Qumrân).

45 DENNIS George T.: Peace and war in Byzantium, ^E**Miller** T.S., *Nesbitt* J. Wsh 1995,
Catholic University of America. xx-282 p.; 7 fig.. [RHE 90.264*; RStR 22,252].

46 DETWEILER Robert: In good company, ^E**Jasper** David, *Ledbetter* Mark. Atlanta 1994,
Scholars. xviii-415. $ 45. - ^R[J]LT(Ox) 9 (1995) 339-341 (J.S. *Fountain*).

47 DIETRICH Manfried L.G., Mitherausgeber, 60. Gb. [dedicated to., portr.] = UF 27
(1995).

48 DONNER Herbert: Meilenstein. ^E**Weippert** Manfred, *Timm* Stefan: ÄAT 30. Wsb 1995.
Harrassowitz. xviii-361 p.; Portr.; Bibliog. xi-xviii. 3-447-03713-X. 36 art.; 18 infra (+
14 über biblische Perikopen).

49 DOSTAL Walter: Studies in oriental culture and history, ^E**Gingrich** André. *al.* Fra 1993,
Lang. 287 p. 3-631-45810-X [Islam and Christian-Muslim Relations 4,233].

50 DUFT Johannes: Festschrift 80. Gb., ^E**Ochsenhein** P., *Ziegler* E. Sigmaringen 1995,
Thorbecke. xvi-215 p.; 56 fig. [RHE 90,264*]

51 DUMONT Jean-Paul (1.XII.1993) mém.: Ainsi parlaient les Anciens, ^E**Jerphagnon** Lucien,
al.: Travaux 3. Lille 1994, Univ. 379 p.; portr. - ^RREG 108 (1995) 240-2 (L. *Brisson*).

52 DUQUOC Christian: La liberté du théologien. P 1995 Cerf. 181 p. F 150. - ^RATG(ran)
58 (1995) 445 (J.A. *Estrada*); E(spr)eV 105 (1995) 673s (P. *Jay*).

53 DUSSEL Enrique: 60. Gb., ^E**Fornet-Betancourt** Rául: Concordia mg. 14. Aachen 1995,
Augustinus. 217 p. 3-86073-360-5 [ThRv 92,447. tit.pp.]. 11 art.; 2 infra.

54 ELLUL Jacques († 1994), mém: Le siècle de Jacques Ellul [ed. 1969-86]; Foi et Vie 93,5
(1994) 181 p., tout sur Ellul.

55 EMERTON John Adney: Wisdom in ancient Israel. ^E**Day** John, *Gordon* Robert P.,
Williamson H.G.M. C 1995, Univ. xiii-311 p.; portr.; bibliog. 289-294. £ 37.50. 0-521-
42013-X. 23 art. [RStR 22,238, J.L. *Crenshaw*]. 10 art. infra + 13 on Bible texts.

56 FABER Jelle: Unity in diversity, ^E**Faber** Riemer. Hamilton 1989, Canadian Ref. Theol. College. xvi-138 p. 0-88756-047-4 [< OTA 19,139, with 2 renvois].

57 FARLEY Thomas: Theology and the interhuman, ^E**Williams** Robert R. Ph 1995, Trinity. xii-271 p. 1-56338-127-3 [RStR 22,225].

58 FEHRING Günter P.: Archäologie des Mittelalters und Bauforschung im Hanseraum. ^E**Gläser** G.: Museum 1. Rostock 1993, Reich. 535 p.; ill. [RHE 91.54* < HGB 112 (1994) 267-271, R. *Hammel-Kiesow*].

FORSYTH Peter T. → 578 infra.

59 FREEDMAN David Noel; Fortunate the eyes that see, 70th b., ^E**Beck** Astrid B., *al.* GR/C 1995, Eerdmans. xix-672 p.; bibliog. to 1982, p.638-659 (M. *O;Connor*); after 1982. p. 660-9 (Kathleen J. *Beck*).. $ 45. 0-8028-0790-9. 42 art. [NTAb 40,p.510; RStR 22,250, C. *Bernas*]. ^R*TBR 8,3 (1995s) 6s (L. *Houlden*). 12 art. infra: others on Bible books

60 FRÉZOULS Edmond: Hommage [I → 10,35*] - II, Ktema 19 (1994).

61 FUHRMANN Horst, Papsttum, Kirche 1991 → 7,80: ^RE(ng)HR 110 (1995) 142 (P.N.R. *Zutshi*).

62 GALBIATI Enrico, 80° compleanno; RivB 43,1s (1995). 267 p.; portr. 14 art., infra.

63 GATTERMANN Günter: Bücher für die Wissenschaft; Bibliotheken zwischen Tradition und Fortschritt, 65. Gb., ^E**Kaiser** G., *al.* Mü 1994, Saur. 562 p.; 7 fig. - ^RDüJb 66 (1995) 431-3 (C. von *Looz-Corswarem*) [RHE 91,222*].

64 GEACH Peter & ANSCOMBE Elizabeth [Catholic philosophers]: Moral truth and moral tradition, ^E**Gormally** Luke. Dublin-Blackrock / Portland OR, Four Courts. ix-246 p. £ 35. 1-85182-158-9. - ^RTBR 8,1 (1995s) 3 (B. *Hebblethwaite*).

65 GENTILI Bruno: Tradizione e innovazione nella cultura greca da OMERO all'età ellenistica, ^E**Pretagostini** R. R 1993, Gruppo Internaz. xlviii-1260 p. (3 vol.); ill. - ^RRBPH 73 (1995) 157s (M. *Delaunois*).

66 GIGNOUX Philippe: Au carrefour des religions, ^E**Gyselen** Rika: Res Orientales 7. Bures-sur-Yvette 1995, Groupe Moyen-Orient. 311 p. 2-9508266-1-X. - ^RWZKM 85 (1995) 406s (Gisela *Procházka-Eisl*).

67 GIVERSEN Søren: Apocryphon Severini, 65th b., ^E**Bilde** P. *al.* Aarhus 1993, Univ. 258 p.; portr.; bibliog. p.9-12. Dk 158. 87-7288-101-1 [< NTAb 40,p.506].

68 GLASSER Arthur: The good news of the Kingdom; mission theology for the third millennium, ^E**Van Engen** Charles, *al.* Mkn 1993, Orbis. 320 p. $ 19 pa. - ^RIBM(iss)R 18 (1994) 86s (J.J. *Bonk*); Mid-Str 34 (1995) 101-3 (D.C. *Hoffman*).

69 GOSSMANN Klaus: Aneignung und Vermittlung; Beiträge zu Theorie und Praxis einer religionspädagogischen Hermeneutik, 65. Gb., ^E**Becker** Ulrich, *Scheilke* Christoph T.: Müns-Comenius. Gü 1995, Kaiser. 426 p. DM 78 pa. 3-579-01775-6 [ThRv 92,269, tit.pp.]: 354-363, *Schulze* Herbert, Antisemitismus .. Fremdenfeindlichkeit .. für schulische Bildung.

70 GRABAR Oleg [I. 1991s → 9.57] II, = Muqarnas 10. Leiden 1993, Brill. xiii-390 p. ƒ 110. - ^RJRAS (1994) 413-5 (G. *Goodwin*).

71 GRABOIS Aryeh; Cross-cultural convergence in the Crusader period, 65th b., ^E**Goodich** M., *al.* NY 1995, P.Lang. xxvii-334 p.; front.; map. [RHE 91,222*].

72 GREENFIELD Jonas C, mem.: Solving riddles and untying knots; biblical, epigraphic, and Semitic studies, ^E**Zevit** Ziony, *al.* WL 1993, Eisenbrauns. xxxiv-668 p.; bibliog. xiii-xxvii. $ 49.50. 0-931464-93-5 [< OTA 19,141, with renvoi to the summaries of 45 of the 54 articles].

73 GUINDON André mém. (1933-1993), ^E**Walters** Gregory J., = E(gl)eT 26,1 (1995) 1-107; portr.; bibliog. 101-8 (*Russell* K.C.). 0013-2349. 5 art., 2 infra.

74 HALL Alan S.: Studies in the history and topography of Lycia and Pisidia, ^E**French** David: Mg 19. Ankara 1994. British Institute of Archaeology. x-119 p.; ill.; portr.; ix, bibliog. 1-898249-03-2.

75 HALLENSLEBEN Horst: Studien zur byzantinischen Kunstgeschichte, 65. Gb., ^E**Borkopp** Birgitt, *al.* Amst 1995, Hakkert. 293 p.; ill.

76 HAMMOND Nicholas G.L.: Ventures into Greek history, ^E**Worthington** J. Ox 1994, Clarendon. xxvi-401 p.; 4 fig.; 23 pl. £ 45. 0-19-814928-X. 17 art. - ^RBoL (1995) 141 (M.D. *Goodman*); CLR 45 (1995) 333s (E.J. *McQueen*); RÉG 108 (1995) 603 (F. *Lefèvre*).

77 HAMRICK Emmett Willard: The Yahweh/Baal confrontation and other studies in biblical literature and archaeology, ^E**O'Brien** Julia M., *Horton* Fred L.^J: SBEC 35. Lewiston NY 1995, Mellen. xii-180 p.; bibliog. 167-9.

78 HARL Marguerite: Katà toùs O': trente études sur la Bible grecque des Septante, ^E**Dorival** Gilles, *Munnich* Olivier. P 1995, Cerf. 530 p.; color portr. F 450. 2-204-05075-X. 30 art.; 16 infra.

79 HARTMAN Lars: Texts and contexts; biblical texts in their textual and situational contexts, 65th b., ^E**Fornberg** Tord, *Hellholm* David. Oslo 1995, Scandinavian Univ. Press. xxix-1070 p.; bibliog. p. 1019-1027. Nk 700. 82-00-22446-5 [NTAb 40,p.331].

80 HAYES James (archbishop of Halifax, retired 1990): Shaping a priestly people, ^E**Gasslein** Bernadette. ... c.1995, Novalis. 200 p. $ 19. - ^R*CanadCath 13,8 (1995) 26 (D. *Donovan*).

81 HEESTERMAN J.C., Ritual, state and history in South Asia, ^E**Hoek** A. W. van den., *al.*: Kern memoir 5. Lei 1992, Brill. xi-243 p.; ill. $ 200. 90-04-09467-9. - ^R*JRit 9,2 (1995) 141-4 (B.K. *Smith*).

82 HENNESSY J. Basil; Trade, contact, and the movement of peoples in the Eastern Mediterranean, ^E**Bourke** Stephen, *Descœudres* Jean-Paul: *MeditArch.s 3. Sydney 1995, Meditarch. xix-339 p.; bibliog. xiii-s. 0-86758-944-2. 30 art., 16 infra.

83 HONDERS Casper: Ars et musica in liturgia, 70th b., ^E**Brouwer** Frans, *Leaver* Robin A. Metuchen NJ 1994. Scarecrow. 206 p. $ 19.50. - ^RLuthQ 9 (1995) 343s (Linda J. *Clark*).

84 HOUWINK TEN CATE Philo H.J.: Studio historiae ardens; Ancient Near Eastern studies, 65th b., ^E**Hout** Theo P.J.van, *Roos* Johan de: Uitgaven 74. Istanbul 1995, Nederlands HA Instituut. xxviii-344 p.; 36 pl.; bibliog xxiii-xxviii.. 90-6258-075-0. 23 art.; 10 infra.

85 HRBEK Ivan (1923-1992): Threefold wisdom; Islam, the Arab world and Africa, ^E**Hulec** Otakar, *Mendel* Miloš. Praha 1993, Czech Academy Oriental Institute. 266 p.; ill. 88-85425-13-0. - ^RJRAS (1995) 113-5 (C.F. *Beckingham*); JSSt 40 (1995) 189s (C.E. *Bosworth*).

86 JAKOBS Hermann: Papstgeschichte und Landesgeschichte, 65. Gb., ^E**Dahlhaus** Joachim, *Kohnle* Armin: AKuG.B 38. xiii-667 p. DM 138. 3-412-10894-4 [ThRv 92,79, tit.pp.].

87 JASPER Ronald C.D., mem.: Liturgy in dialogue, ^E**Bradshaw** Paul, *Spinks* Bryan: Pueblo Book. ColMn 1995, Liturgical. x-227 p. $ 20 pa. 0-8146-6149-1 [ThD 42,375].

88 JERVELL Jacob: Mighty minorities ? Minorities in early Christianity; positions and strategies, 70th b., ^E**Hellholm** David, *Moxnes* Halvor, *Seim* Turid K. = ST 49,1 (Oslo 1995; he was editor 1966-88). iv-228 p.; portr.; bibliog. p. 213-227, *Birkeflet* Svein H.; p. 1-10, *Barrett* C.K., ('almost discourteously'), What minorities ? [< NTAb 40,p.131].

89 JAZAYERY Mohammad Ali: Persian studies in North America, ^E**Marashi** Mehdi. Bethesda 1994, Iranbooks, xix-421 p.; front.; Persian text 131 p. $ 60. 30 art. - ^RJRAS (1995) 292-7 (Julie Scott *Meisami*).

90 JÜNGEL Eberhard: The possibilities of theology, 60th b, ^E**Webster** John. E 1995, Clark. 241 p. £ 20. 0-567-09720-X. - ^RE(xp)T 107 (1995s) 156 (G.W.P. *McFarlane*).

91 Kampen 140-jarige Gereformeerde Universiteit; Geloven in der minderheid ? ^E**Lange** F. de. Kampen 1994, Kok. 210 p. 90-242-2068-8. - ^RTTh 35 (1995) 398 (A. van *Harskamp*).

92 KERLOUÉGAN François: Mélanges, ^E**Conso** D., *al.*: AnnLitt Besançon 515 / Inst. Gaffiot 11. P 1994, BLettres. 701 p. [RHE 91,223*]. 49 art. - ^RBSLP 90,2 (1995) 188-195 (A. *Blanc*).

93 KIEFFER René: Svensk Exegetisk Årsbok 60 (1995); portr.; 191 bibliog.

94 KLÍMA Otakar, mem.: Iranian and Indo-European Studies, ^E**Vavroušek** Petr. Praha 1994, Enigma. ix-264 p.

95 KOROSTOVTSEV Mikhail A., mem., Ancient Egypt and Kush. Moskva 1993, Nauka Oriental. 455 p.; 25 pl.

96 KRAUSE Martin: Divitiae Aegypti; koptologische und verwandte Studien, ^E**Fluck** Cäcilia, *al.* Wsb 1995, Reichert. xxii-349 p.; Bibliog. ix-xxii. 3-88226-935-2. 39 art.; 19 infr

97 KROMMINGA John H. ('dedicated to'):: C(alvin)TJ 29,2 (1994); six articles on CALVIN.

98 KUMOR Bolesław, ^E**Makselon** Józef, *al.*: AnCracov 27 (1995). liii-791 p.; color. portr.; bibliog. xxi-liii. 0209-0864. 64 art.; 3 infra; 7 al. de locis biblicis.

99 LA BLANCHARDIÈRE Noëlle de: 'Alla Signorina', ^E**Nicolet** Claude: Coll. ÉcFrR 204. R 1995, École Française (où elle était longtemps bibliothécaire). xvi-423 p. 2-7283-0330-4. 23 art.

100 LAFONTAINE-DOSOGNE Jacqueline † 21.V.1995, mém.: Byzantion 65,2 (Bru 1995) 307-524; phot.

101 LAGORIO Valerie M.: Vox mystica; essays on medieval mysticism, ^E**Bartlett** Anne C., *al.* Rochester 1995, Boydell & B. xiv-235 p.; front. $ 71. 0-85991-439-9 [ThDi 42, 392; RHE 91,223

102 LANGELLA Vittorina mem., Oriente -- Occidente; ^E**Bencardino** Filippo: StAsiatMin 42. N 1993, Ist. Univ. Orientale. 617 p.; bibliog. 9-11. - p.81-92, *De Meo* Francesca, I missionari francescani e la riscoperta dell'Oriente.

103 LECLERCQ Jean: The joy of learning and the love of God, ^E**Elder** E.R.: CiSt 160. Kalamazoo 1995, Cistercian. xiv-503 p.; 19 fig. [RHE 91,223*].

104 LEDESMA RUBIO María Luisa: Aragón en la Edad Media X-XI s. Zaragoza 1993, Fac.Fil./Est.Árabes. ^RRP(ort)H 30 (1995) 240-6 (- *Gomes*) [RHE 91,223*].

LEHMANN Winfried P. symposium 1986/92 → 692 infra.

105 LEKAI Louis J.: Studiosorum speculum, 75th b.. ^E**Świetek** Francis R., *Sommerfeldt* John R.: CS 141. Kalamazoo 1991, Cistercian. 432 p.; 38 pl. US$ 50. 19 art. ^RE(gl)eT 26 (1995) 129s (K.C. *Russell*).

106 LÉON-DUFOUR Xavier, Autour du prologue de Jean, ^E**Moingt** J.: RechSR 83,2 (1995) 169-303. 8 art.; 4 infra.

107 LEROY Maurice (1909-1990), Mém. : Florilegium historiographiae linguisticae, ^E**Clercq** Jan De, *Desmet* Piet: BCILL 75. LvN 1994, Peeters. 512 p. Fb 1800. - ^RAnCl 64 (1995) 361s (Monique *Bile*).

108 LESSING Eckhard; Geist und Kirche, ^E**Brändle** Werner, *Stolina* Ralf. Fra 1995, Lang. → 2022 infra.

LEWICKI Tadeusz ↑ 22.XI.1992 → 727 infra.

LEWIS David: conference 1993 → 693 infra.

109 LIMA Carlos R. Cirne: Dialética e libertade, ^D**Stein** Ernildo, *Boni* Luís A. de. Petrópolis / Porto Alegre 1993, Vozes / Univ. 638 p. - REB 55 (1995) 234s (H. *Lepargneur*).

110 LIPIŃSKI Edward: Immigration and emigration within the Ancient Near East, ᴱ**Lerberghe** K. Van, *Schoors* A.: OLA 65. Lv 1995, Univ./Peeters. xxv-458 p.; portr.; bibliog. ix-xxv. 90-6831-727-X. 42 art.; 36 infra.

111 LOBATO Abelardo: S.Thomas de Aquino doctor hodiernae humanitatis, 70° compleanno, ᴱ**Ols** D.: StTom 58. Vaticano 1995. 744 p.; 2 pl. Lᵐ 70 [RHE 91,223*].

112 LOHR Charles H.: Aristotelica et Lulliana, 70th b., ᴱ**Domínguez** Fernando, *al.*: IP 26. Steenbrugge 1995, Abtei. ix-598 p.; sketch-portrait; (color.) ill.; bibliog. p.583-595. 26 art., 3 infra.

113 LORCIN Narie-Thérèse: Comprendre le XIIIᵉ siècle, ᴱ**Guichard** P., *Alexandre-Bidon* D. Lyon 1995, Univ. 313 p.; 2 fig.; map. [RHE 91,223*].

114 LOURDAUX (Guillaume/Willem) . Serta devota 1/2, Cultura mediaevalis, ᴱ**Verbeke** W., *al.* Lv 1995, Univ. xviii-494 p.; 21 fig [RHE 90.264*]

115 LUCAS Dick: When God's voice is heard; essays on preaching, ᴱ**Jackman** David, *Green* Christopher. Leicester 1995, Inter-Varsity. 187 p. £ 10. 0-85110-656-0. [*TBR 9/1,37, A. *Gilmore*]. ᴿE(xp)T 107 (1995s) 125 (G.W.S. *Knowles* prefers Kathy GALLOWAY's sermons, Getting personal, SPCK 1995).

116 LUCAS Leopold + 1943, mem.: Geschichte und Geist; fünf Essays zum Verständnis des Judentums [ev. Ringvorlesung Tübingen], ᴱ**Lucas** Franz D. B 1995, Duncker & H. 126 p. DM 28. 3-428-08168-4. - ᴿTLZ 120 (1995) 620-2 (E.-H. *Amberg*).

117 MAHDI Muhsin S.: The political aspects of Islamic philosophy, 65th b., ᴱ**Butterworth** Charles E.: ME mg 28. CM 1992, Harvard Univ. vi-406 p. $ 15 pa. 0-932885-07-1. - ᴿBiOr 52 (1995) 184s (Remke *Kruk*).

118 MANESSY-GUITTON Jacqueline: Nomina rerum, ᴱ**Kircher-Durand** Chantal: Centre Langues Médit. 13. Nice 1994, Univ. 421 p.; 5 fig. - ᴿAnCl 64 (1995) 359s Francine *Mawet*).

118* MANGO Cyril: ᵉ Bosphorus, ᴱ**Efthymiadis** S., *al.* (Oxford) = ByF 21 (1995). Amst 1995, Kakkert. 355 p. 90-256-1072-2.

119 MARA Maria Grazia: Studi sul Cristianesimo antico e moderno, ᴱ**Simonetti** M., *Siniscalco* P. = Augustinianum 35 (R 1995). 917 p.; 8 pl.; portr.<, bibliog. 9-13 [RHE 91,223*; NTAb 40,p.126]. ᴿRel(y)Cult 41 (1995) 931 (J. *Tejedor*).

120 MARLÉ René, mém.: Présence de BULTMANN: R(ech)SR 83,4 (1995) 409-637; phot.;409-513 bibliog. 5 art.; 2 infra.

121 MARSHALL I. Howard: Jesus of Nazareth, Lord and Christ, 60th b., ᴱ **Green** J.B., *Turner* M., 1994 → 10,77*: ᴿ*AnT 9 (1995) 168-171 (B. *Estrada*).

122 MASSEY James E., Sharing heaven's music; the heart of Christian preaching, ᴱ**Callem** Barry L. Nv 1995, Abingdon. 230 p. $ 19. 0-687-01108-6 [ThD 43,289]

123 MATTIOLI Anselmo, In Spiritu et veritate, 81° año. R 1995, Cappuccini. 718 p. ; biobibliog. 11-24-29 (*Volpi* Isidoro, *Cirelli* Giovanni), 33-52, autobiog. 24 art., 9 infra.- ᴿRevAg 36 (1995) 1138s (R. *Lazcano*).

124 MBITI John S.: Religious plurality in Africa, ᴱ**Olupona** Jacob K., *Nyang* Sulayman S. B/NY 1993, Mouton de Gruyter. 455 p. DM 228. 19 art.; bibliog. - Exchange 24 (1995) 279s (M. *Schoffeleers*).

125 MEEKS Wayne A.: The social world of the first Christians, ᴱ**White** Michael, *Yarbrough* O.Larry. Mp 1995, Fortress. xxix-418 p.; bibliog. xxv-xxix. 0-8006-2585-4 [RStR 22,245. Pheme *Perkins*; ThDi 43,157]. 22 art., most on Bible books; 4 infra.

126 METZGER Bruce M.: The text of the New Testament in contemporary research; [22] essays on the status quaestionis, 80th b., ᴱ**Ehrman** B.D., *Holmes* M.W.: StD 46. GR 1995,

Eerdmans. xiv-401 p. $ 40. 0-8028-2440-4 [NTAb 40,p.136; ThDi 43,189]. - [R]*CritRR 7 (1994) 579, tit.pp.; E(xp)T 107 (1995s) 61 (C.S. *Rodd:* best of six choice Festschriften); P(rinc)SB 16 (1995) 356-8 (J.A. *Brooks*).

127 MEYER Ben F. (1927 - 28.XII.1995) mem.: Ex Auditu 11 (1995).

128 MEYER Hans Bernhard: Bewahren und Erneuern; Studien zur Messliturgie, 70. Gb., [E]**Messner** Reinhard, *al.*: InTSt 42. Innsbruck 1995, Tyrolia. 416 p.; Bibliog. 386-404. Sch 540. 3-7022-1968-4 [OTA 18 (1995) p. 443; ZAW 107 (1995) 520, nur 50-76, *Braulik* G., Tora als Bahnlesung]. - [R]ZkT 117 (1995) 453-7 (E. *Renhart*).

129 MIKASA prince TAKAHITO, 80th b.: Orient 30s (1995). 3 art. infra.

130 MILGROM Jacob; Pomegranates and golden bells; studies in biblical and Near Eastern ritual, law, and literature, [E]**Wright** David, *Freedman* D.N., *Hurvitz* Avi. WL 1995, Eisenbrauns. xxxii-861 p.; bibliog. xiii-xxv. 0-931464-87-0. 62 art.; 31 infra, the other 31 on the biblical texts. [OTA 19,p.324; renvois to 35]

131 MILLER George A.: Conceptions of the human mind, [E]**Harman** Gilbert. Hillsdale NJ 1993, Erlbaum. xiii-277 p. - [R]Lg 71 (1995) 369-371 (J. *Peregrin*).

132 MITTLER Placidus, Abt: Temporibus tempora, [E]**Mittler** M., *Herborn* W.; *SiegSt 25. Siegburg 1995, Respublica. xxiii-539 p.; 32 fig.; 2 maps [RHE 91,223*].

132* MOEHRING Horst R. (1927-1986) mem.: The school of Moses; studies in Philo and Hellenistic religion, [E]**Kenney** John P.: B(rown)JS 304. At 1995, Scholars. xi-182 p. 0-7885-0162-3.

133 MÜLLER Walter W.: Arabia Felix; Beiträge zur Sprache und Kultur des vorislamischen Arabien, 60. Gb., [E]**Nebes** Norbert. Wsb 1994, Harrassowitz. xxxiv-318 p. 3-447-03603-6. - [R]WZKM 85 (1995) 401s (S. *Procházka*: tit.pp.).

134 MURRAY Robert, 70th b. [[E]1971-83]: Heythrop Journal 36,4 (1995) 381-528; portr.; bibliog. 521-8.

135 NENCI Giuseppe; *Historíē*, 70° compleanno. [E]**Alessandrì** Salvatore. Lecce 1994, Congedo. 462 p.; bibliog. 9-20. 88-80860-42-9. 27 art.; 3 infra.

136 NEVE Peter: Anatolian archaeology: BA 58,2 (1995) 62-114.

137 NEWBIGIN Lesslie: Many voices, [E]**Bellis** Alice D. Lanham MD 1995, UPA. 101 p. 0-8191-9836-6. - [R]Vidyajyoti 59 (1995) 833s (sr. *Surekha*).

138 NIEDERWIMMER Kurt: Die Kirche als historische und eschatologische Grösse, 65. Gb. [E]**Pratscher** W., *Sauer* G. Fra 1994, Lang. 355 p.; portr.; bibliog. $ 56. 3-631-56067-8. 28 art [< NTAb 40,p.511].

139 NORDHUES Paul H.: Geliebte Kirche -- gelebte Caritas, 80. Gb., [E]**Hengst** Karl, *al.:* MitDtKirchenprovinz 6. Pd 1995, Schöningh. 301 p. DM 38. 3-506-71507-0 [ThRv 92,177, tit.pp.].

140 OBERHAMMER Gerhard: Hermeneutics of encounter; essays [in philosophy of religions], 65th b., [E]**D'Sa** Francis X., *Mesquita* Roque: Pub. De Nobili 20. W/Delhi 1994, Gerrold / Motilal Banarsidass. 303 p.; portr. - [R]OLZ 90 (1995) 569-572 (K. *Klaus*).

140* OLIN John J.: Religious orders of the Catholic Reformation, [E]**De Molen** Richard. Fordham 1995, Univ. xix-290 p. $ 30. -- [R]Month 265 (1995) 174s (T. *McCoog*).

141 ORBE Antonio: *Pléroma*, salus carnis, [E]**Romero-Pose** Eugenio, *al.* Santiago de Compostela 1990, Compostellanum → 6,135 [given only as 35,1s (359 p.) & 36,1s of Compostellanum (1990s)].

142 OROZ RETA José: Thesauramata philologica, [E]**Herrera** M[a] Rosa, *al.*: Helmantica [I → 9,119: 44 (1993); bibliog 16-25; 35 art., 2 infra] -- II: 45 (1994); 36 art., 2 infra; -- III: 46 (1995).

143 OSTWALD Martin, Nomodeiktes; Greek studies, ^E**Rosen** Ralph M., *Farrell* Joseph.
AA 1993, Univ. Michigan.   xx-731 p., 22 fig.; bibliog. 643-5. $ 59.50.   0-472-10297-4.
-- ^RCLR 45 (1995) 150-2 (R. *Osborne*). 46 art.; 4 infra.

144 OWEN Dorothy M.:   Medieval ecclesiastical studies, ^E**Franklin** M.J., *Harper-Bill* C.:
SHMR 7.   Woodbridge 1995, Boydell.   xxi-310 p.; portr.   £ 39.50   [RHE 90.265*]

145 PALVA Heikki: Dialectologia arabica: StOr 75.   Helsinki 1995, Finnish Oriental Soc.
304 p.; bibliog, 295-303. 951-9380-25-6. P. 75-86, *Fischer* Wolfdietrich, Zum Verhältnis
der neuarabischen Dialekte zum Klassisch-Arabischen.

146 PATTERSON David: Jewish education and learning, 70th b., ^E**Abramson** G., *Parfitt* T.
Chur 1993, Harwood.   321 p. £ 38.   20 art., mostly modern. - ^RJS 46 (1995) 33s (L.J.
Yudkin); RasIsr 61 (1995) 180-2 (Emanuela *Trevisan Seni*).

147 PERLITT Lothar: Allein mit dem Wort; theologische Studien, 65. Gb.   Gö 1995,
Vandenhoeck & R.   370 p.

148 PETER Carl J. (1912-1991) mem.:   Church and theology, ^E**Phan** Peter C.   Wsh 1995,
Catholic University of America.   xiv-290 p. $ 60.   0-8132-0798-3 [ThD 43,61; ThRv 92,84
tit.pp.].

149 PEUKERT   [→ 10,91* 'Peuken'] Helmut: Anerkennung der Anderen; eine
theologische Grunddimension interkultureller Kommunikation, ^E**Arens** Edmund: QD 156.
FrB 1995, Herder.   208 p.; Bibliog. l93-208.   3-451-02156-0.   7 art.,infra.

150 PLANTY-BONJOUR Guy [† 1991] mém.: De saint Thomas à Hegel, ^E**Vieillard-Baron**
Jean-Louis, *al.*   P 1994, PUF.   151 p. - ^RRTPh 127 (1995) 74 (É. *Muller*).

151 PORADA Edith (1912-1994), mem.: ^E**Owen** David I., *Wilhelm* Gernot.   Studies on the
Culture and Civilization of Nuzi and the Hurrians 7.   Bethesda 1995, CDL.   x-159 p.: portr.
1-883053-07-2.   11 art., 3 infra.

152 POTTMEYER Hermann: Kirche sein [→10,95: Nachkonziliare ..] Theologie im Dienst
der Kirchenreform, ^E**Geerlings** Wilhelm, *Seckler* Max.   FrB 1994, Herder.   461 p.   DM 68.
3-451-25329-0. -- ^RThGL 85 (1995) 289s (W. *Beinert*).

153 POWER David N.: A promise of presence, ^E **Downey** Michael, *Fragomeni* Richard,
1992 → 8,148c: ^REO(rans) 11 (1994) 383-5 (P. *Lyons*).

154 PRESEDO F.: Homenaje, ^E**Sáez** P., *Ordoñez* S.   Sevilla 1994, Univ.   871 p.   84-472-
0254-2. - ^RArchEspArq 68 (1995) 317s (Adela *Cepas*).

154* RATZABY Yehuda: ^H *Meḥqarim* ... Studies in Hebrew literature and Yemenite culture,
^E**Dishon** Judith, *Hazan* Ephraim. Ramat-Gan 1991, Bar Ilan Univ. 480 p. - Hebrew Studies
15 (Madison 1994) 128-130.   28 art.

REEKMANS Louis, mem. conference 1995 → 633 infra.

155 RENAUD Bernard: Ce Dieu qui vient; études sur l'Ancien et le Nouveau Testament
65e anniv, ^E*Kuntzmann* Raymond: LDiv 159.   P 1995, Cerf. 422p.; portr; bibliog. 1961-94
p. 385-391. 2-204-05083-0.   16 art.; 7 infra. -- ^REstTrin 29 (1995) 134 (X. *Pikaza*); ZAW
107 (1995) 527 (tit.pp.). - P. 163-190, *Lohfink* N., Hos 11,9: 232-242, *Gilbert* M., Sir 51,1-
12.

156 RILEY William, 1949-1995, mem.; PI(r)BA 18 (1995) → Y8.5; p.13-39. his 1995 PIBA
paper, 'Who is the woman of Revelation 12 ?' (Daughter Zion; Mary not intended by the
author), received with spontaneous standing applause (pp. 7; 9).

157 RITSCHL Dietrich: Theologische Samenkörner. 65. Gb., ^E**Bernhardt** Reinhold, *al.*. Müns
1994, Lit.   312 p.   DM 40.   3-8258-2310-5. - S. 73-81, *Edenhofner* Helga, Was ist der
Mensch, dass du seiner gedenkst ? [ThRv 92,..172].

158 RIX Helmut, Indogermanica et italica, 65. Gb., ᴱ**Meiser** G., *al.:* I(nnsb)BSw 72. Inns 1993, Univ. vi-500 p.; 9 fig.; portr. Sch 1760. - ᴿI(nd)GF 100 (1995) 288-292 (K. H. *Schmidt*); Kratylos 40 (1995) 97-101 (R. *Gusmani*).

159 ROGERSON John: The Bible in human society. ᴱ**Carroll R.** N.Daniel, *Clines* David J.A., *Davies* Philip R.: JSOT.s 200. Shf 1995, Academic. 479 p.; portr.; bibliog. 459-461. 1-85075-568-X. 25 art.; 15 infra.

160 ROSENTHAL Leeser, 200th b.: Bibliotheca Rosenthaliana, treasures of Jewish booklore, ᴱ**Offenberg** Adri K., *al.* Amst 1994, Univ. xii-135 (54 items, each with one or more color plates). £ 25. -- ᴿJJS 46 (1995) 316-9 (D. *Frank*, also on four cognates).

161 RUBINSTEIN Eliezer, mem.: ᴴ Studies in Hebrew language, ᴱ**Dotan** Aron, *Tal* Abraham: Te'uda 9. TA 1995, Univ. 308 p. 22 art.; Eng, table of contents.

162 RUBIO Luciano: Semitica escurialensia augustiniana: CDios 208,2s (1995) 325-1187; portr. 31 art., 3 infra [RHE 91,224*].

163 RUSSELL Donald: Ethics and rhetoric; classical essays, 75th b., ᴱ**Innes** Doreen, *al.* Ox 1995, Clarendon. xvii-378 p.; bibliog. (Russell) xiv-xvii; (general) 352-368. 0-19-814962-X.

164 RUTHERFORD William E.; The current state of interlanguage, ᴱ**Eubank** Lynn, *al.* Amst 1995, Benjamins. vii-293 p.

165 SAINT-JEAN Robert: Art et histoire dans le Midi languedocien et rhodanien (Xᵉ-XIXᵉ s.). Montpellier 1993, Soc. Archéologique. 424 p. [RHE 91,55*]

166 SALESIANA Univ. Fac. Teol. 25 anni, Teologia e vita ᴱ**Ferasin** Egidio: BS 102. R 1992, LAS. 274 p. -- ᴿE(gl)eT 26 (1995) 124 (G. *Hudon*).

167 SANDERS Gabriel: Aevum inter utrumque, ᴱ**Uytfanghe** Marc van, *Demeulenaere* Roland: InstrPatrist 23, 1991 → 7,130: ᴿ*JMdvLat 4 (1994) 189-192 (W. *Goffart*).

168 SARTORI Luigi: Teologia e filosofia nella storia : StPat(av) 42 (1995) 351 p., bibliog. 15-29 (E.R.*Tura*). 7 art.; 4 infra.

169 SAUZET Robert: Foi, fidélité. amitié en Europe à la période moderne, ᴱ**Maillard** B.; I. Du Languedoc à la Touraine, les clercs, spiritualité et vie matérielle; II. Sensibilité et pratiques religieuses; amitié et fidélité. Tours 1995, Univ. xi-274 p.; p. 275-558; 1 fig.: 3 maps. [RHE 91,55*]

170 SAWYER John F.A.: Words remembered, texts renewed, ᴱ**Davies** Jon, *al.*: JSOT.s 195. Shf 1995, Academic. 533 p.; portr.; biobibliog. p. 509-513. £ 50. 1-85075-542-6 [OTA 18,619. with renvoi to the summaries of 15 OT items]. 28 art.; 15 infra.

171 SCHENKEL Wolfgang: Per aspera ad astra, 59. Gb., ᴱ**Gestermann** Louise, *Sternberg-El Hotabi* Heike. Bonn 1995, Univ. Ägyptisches Seminar. vii-237 p.

172 SCHERER Georg: Person und Sinnerfahrung; philosophische Grundlagen und interdisziplinäre Perspektiven, 65.Gb., ᴱ**Gethmann** Carl F., *Oesterreich* Peter L. Da 1993, Wiss. 280 p. DM 69 pa. 3-534-12086-8 [ThRv 92,178, tit.pp.].

173 SCHILDHAUER Johannes: Communitas et dominium. 75. Gb., ᴱ**Wernicke** H., *al.* Grossbarkau 1994, Barkau [RHE 91,55* < HGB 113 (1995) 167-9 (V. *Henn*)].

174 SCHIPPMANN K. II.: Iranica Antica 30 (1995).

175 SCHLEGELBERGER Bruno: Blicke auf das Andere [d.h. (nicht so) ungewöhnliche Themen], ᴱ**Kampling** Rainer, *Lob-Hüdepohl* Andreas. Hildesheim 1994, Morus. 141 p. 3-89543-035-8. - ᴿZkT 117 (1995) 356s (K.H. *Neufeld*).

176 SCHMITT Hatto H.: Rom und der Griechische Osten, 65. Gb., ᴱ**Schubert** C., *Brodersen* K. Stu 1995, Steiner. xiv-375 p.

177 SCHNEIDER Theodor: Vorgeschmack; ökumenische Bemühungen um die Eucharistie,

^E**Hilberath** Bernd J., *Sattler* Dorothea. Mainz 1995, Grünewald. 643 p. DM 58. 3-7867-1837-7 [TR 91,365].

178 SCHOTTROFF Luise: Für Gerechtigkeit streiten: Theologie im Alltag einer bedrohten Welt. Gü 1994, Kaiser. 224 p. DM 68. 3-579-02000-5. - ^RTTh 35 (1995) 75 (G. *Dresen*)

178* SCHOTTROFF Willy, Gott an den Rändern, ^E**Bail** U. 1996 [NTAb 40, p.506, with some tit.pp.].

179 SCHRÖDTER Hermann: Im Netz der Begriffe; religionsphilosophische Analysen, 60. Gb., ^E**Hauser** Linus, *Nordhofen* Eckhard: SRPRW 5. Wü 1994, Echter. DM 42 pa. 3-89375-095-9 [ThRv 92,179]: 97-120, *Menges* Thomas, 'Wenn ihr von ganzem Herzen nach mir fragt, lasse ich mich von euch finden' (Jer 29,13f); Gottes Absolutheit in der empirischen Kultur; -- 155-166, *Drescher* Johannes, Zum Verhältnis von Religion und Theologie.

180 SCHULTE Raphael: Variationen zur Schöpfung der Welt, ^E**Schmetterer** Eva, *al.* Innsbruck 1995, Tyrolia. 305 p. DM 42. 3-7022-2001-1 [ThRv 92,171].

181 SIEBERT Rudolf J.: The influence of the Frankfurt School on contemporary theology; critical theory and the future of religion [< Dubrovnik (since) 1977], ^E**Reimer** A.J.: T(or)ST 64. Lewiston NY 1992, Mellen. xv-342 p. 0-7734-9169-4. -- ^RTTh 35 (1995) 301 (E. *Borgman*).

182 SIMON Josef, Denken der Individualität, 65. Gb., ^E**Hoffmann** Thomas S., *Majetschak* Stefan. B 1995, de Gruyter. xi-421 p. DM 238. 3-11-014169-8. 22 art.; 4 infra [ThRv 92,534, tit.pp.].

183 SIMONSOHN Shlomo jubilee volume [8 art. Eng., 4 ital.; 6 ^H]: Univ. TA. J 1993, Graph-Chen. c.400 p.; bibliog. -- ^RRasIsr 81 (1995) 174-180 (R. *Coen, al.*).

184 SMART Ninian: Aspects of religion, ^E**Masefield** Peter, *Wiebe* Donald [→ 10,123*]: Toronto Studies in Religion 18. NY 1994, P.Lang. vii-417 p.; portr.; 391-417, biobibliog. 0-8204-2237-1 [ThD 43,55]. 17 art.; 6 infra.

185 SODEN Wolfram von: Vom Alten Orient zum Alten Testament, 85. Gb., ^E**Dietrich** Manfried, *Loretz* Oswald: AOAT 240. Kevelaer 1995. Butzon & B. viii-581 p. 3-7666-9977-6. 31 art.; 29 infra.

186 SPANNEUT Michel: Valeurs dans le stoïcisme; du Portique à nos jours. Lille 1993, Univ. 304 p. F 150. 2-85939-452-4. - ^RETRel 70 (1995) 459s (F. *Siegert*).

187 SPINDLER Marc: The changing partnership of missionary and ecumenical movements, ^E**Lagerwerf** Leny: IIMO 42. Zoetermeer c.1995, Meinema. 234 p. *f* 50. 90-211-7011-6 [Exchange 24/2 (1995) cover ad.]

188 STEERE Douglas & Dorothy: Spirituality in ecumenical perspective, ^E**Hinson** E. Glenn. LVL 1993, Westminster-Knox. 200 p. $ 15. - ^RCatholic World 238 (1995) 139 (Elizabeth *Dreyer*).

189 STEGMANN Franz Josef: Glaube in Politik und Zeitgeschichte, 65. Gb., ^E**Giegel** Georg, *al.* Pd 1995, Schöningh. 328 p. DM 98 3-506-73172-6 [TR 91,279].

190 STRAND Kenneth A.: A(ndr)USS 33,2 (1995) 164-283. 5 art.; phot.; bibliog. 171-183 (*Vyhmeister* Nancy J., *Kharbteng* Jennifer).

STRECKER Georg, 65. Gb. Symposion 1995 → 536 infra.

191 STRICKER B.H,: Hermes aegyptiacus; Egyptological studies, 85th b., ^E**DuQuesne** Terence: *DiscEg special 2. Ox 1995, DiscEg. 189 p.; portr.; bibliog. 9-17. 0-9510704-6-0. 14 art.; 7 infra.

192 SWINBURNE Richard: Reason and the Christian religion, ^E**Padgett** Alan G. Ox 1994, Clarendon. 369 p. £ 40. - ^RRelSt 31 (1995) 281 (B.R. *Clack*).

193 THAUSING Gertrud: Zwischen den beiden Ewigkeiten, ^E**Bietak** Manfred, *al.* W 1994, Univ. Inst. Ägyptologie. xx-291 p. Bibliog. xi-xiii [WZKM 85 (1995) 81].

194 THÉODORIDÈS Aristide (1911-1994), 'dédié à la mémoire': CÉg 70 (1995).

195 THOMA Clemens: Tempelkult und Tempelzerstörung (70 n.Chr.), 60. Gb., ^E**Lauer** S., *Ernst* H.: JudChr 15. Bern 1995, Lang. 256 p. $ 39 pa. 2-906753-46-8 [< NTAb 40, p.330].

196 THRAEDE K.: Panchaia, ^E**Wacht** M.: JAC Egb 22. Müns 1995, Aschendorff. 260 p. DM 100; 3-402-08106-7: ^RZkT 117 (1995) 497s (H.B. *Meyer*: tit.pp.)

197 TILLARD Jean-Marie Roger; Communion et réunion, ^E**Evans** Gillian R., *Gourgues* M.: BEThL 121. Lv/P 1995, Univ./Peeters. xii-432 p.; bibliog. 5-20 (biog./hommage 1-59). Fb 2400. 90-6186-699-5 / 2-87723-263-8. 28 art.; 7 infra (+ 3 sur livres bibliques) [EThL 72,81-205, A.*Denaux*; RHE 91,224*].

198 TOORN Karel van der: Kleine Encyclopedie van de Toorn [Zorn, divine wrath, ten studies], ^E**Jong** Ab & Aleid de: TReeks 21. Utrecht 1993, Fac. Godgeleerdheid. 127 p. 90-72235-52-5. - ^RBijdragen 56 (1995) 481 (A. *Lascaris*: Turm rather than Zorn is the origin of Toorn, so 'towers' in ancient religions would have been a more suitable theme).

199 TRAN TAM TINH Vincent: Tranquillitas, ^E**Jentel** Marie-Odile, *al.*: Hier pour aujourd'hui 7. Québec 1994, Univ. Laval. xxx-607 p.; ill.; bibliog. xxi-xxvi. 54 art.; 5 infra.

200 TROCMÉ Étienne, 70e anniv, : RHPhR 75,1 (1995); phot.

201 TUCKER Gene M.: Old Testament interpretation; past, present, and future, ^E**Mays** James L., *Petersen* David L., *Richards* Kent H. Nv/E 1995, Abingdon/Clark. 304 p. 0-567-29289-4 / 0-687-13871-X [ThD 43,282; OTA 19,p.322, with renvoi to summary of each of the 18 items]. 18 art., all on Bible books exc. 4 infra.

202 TUSA Vincenzo, Studi sulla Sicilia occidentale. Padova 1993, A. Ausilio. 379 p.; 77 pl. 28 art. - ^RCLR 45 (1995) 152s (D. *Ridgway*).

203 TYNDALE William, 500th b.: A pathway into the Holy Scripture, 1994 Tyndale Fellowship conference, ^E**Satterthwaite** P.E., *Wright* D.F. GR 1994, Eerdmans. viii-344 p. 0-8028-4078-7 [ThD 43,80].

204 UNTERMANN Jürgen: Sprachen und Schriften des antiken Mittelmeerraums, 65. Gb., ^E**Heidermanns** Frank, *al.*; I(nnsb)BSw 78. Inns 1993, Univ. ix-512 p.; portr. - ^RI(nd)GF 100 (1995) 280-4 (K.H. *Schmidt*)

205 URBACH E.E. tribute, ^E**Dan** Joseph: J(u)d(ais)m 42 (1993) 262.

205* VAN BEEK G... ZAW 107 (1995) 509: *Tsafrir* Y., The peak of settlement in Byzantine Palestine, p. 7-16 [< Michmanim 8 (1995)].

206 VAN TIL Cornelius (b. 1895): W(estm)TJ 57,1 (1995) 1-289; portr.

207 VATIN Claude: Eukrata, ^E**Amouretti** M.-C., *Villard* P. Travaux Centre Jullian 17. Univ. Provence 1994. 207 p. - ^RRPh(lgLH) 69 (1995) 360s (Françoise *Letoublon*).

208 VAVŘINEK Vladimir: Stephanos; studia byzantina et slavica, 65° nat., ^E**Dostálová** R., *al.* = Byzantinoslavica 56 (1995). xix-784 p.

209 VEISSIÈRE Michel: De l'histoire de le Brie à l'histoire des Réformes. P 1993, Fed. Soc. Hist. xi-39 p. [RHE 91,55*]

210 VERHULST Adriaan: Peasants and townsmen in medieval Europe. ^E**Duvosquel** J.-M., *Thoen* E.: CentreHistRurale 114. Gand 1995, Snoeck-Ducaju. 787 p.. 6 fig.; 24 maps [RHE 91,224*].

211 VERMES Geza, 25 years editor: JJS 46 (1995), phot.; ^E**Alexander** Philip, *Goodman* Martin.

212 VERMEULE Emily T.: The ages of HOMER, [E]Carter Jane B., *Morris* Sarah P. Austin 1995, Univ. Texas. xxi-542 p.; biobibliog. 11-18. 0-292-71169-7. 31 art.; 2 infra.

213 VIOLANTE Cinzio: Società, istituzioni, spiritualità. Spoleto 1995, Centro Alto Medioevo. xxxv-1091 p. (2 vol.) [RHE 91,224*].

214 VISENTIN Pelagio O.S.B.: Amen vestrum; miscellanea di studi liturgico-pastorali, [E]Catella Alceste: Caro salutis cardo. Padova 1994, Messaggero. xxxiv-494 p. - [R]RBén 105 (1995) 250s (D. *Misonne*); Ter(esianum) 46 (1995) 601s (J. *Castellano*).

VOGT H.-J. [→ 10,131*b*]; ORIGENES-Symposion 1995 → 539 infra.

215 VORGRIMLER Herbert: Und dennoch ist von Gott zu reden, [E]Lutz-Bachman Matthias (.. Fak. Münster). FrB 1994, Herder. 373 p. - [R]CT 121 (1994) 630s (R. de *Luis Carballada*).

216 WALSER Gerold: Historische Interpretationen, 75. Gb., [E]Weinmann-Walser Marlis: Historia Einz 100. Stu 1995, Steiner. 212 p.

217 WENZEL Siegfried: Literature and religion in the later Middle Ages: philological studies, [E]Newhauser R.G., *Alford* J.A.: MdvRen 118. Binghamton 1995, SUNY. xi-415 p. [RHE 91,224*].

218 WERNER E.: Religion und Gesellschaft im Mittelalter, [E]Scalfati S.P.P.: Collectanea 2. Spoleto 1995, Centro Alto Medioevo. xv-685 p.; 2 maps [RHE 91,224*].

218* WESTHUIZEN Jasper Petrus van der: Journal/Tydskrif vir Semitistiek 7,2 (1995) 116-250; portr. 6 art., mostly Amarna → T7.3.

219 WIESEL Élie, Telling the tale, 65th b., [E]Cargas Harry J. St.Louis 1993, Time Being. 169 p. - [R]*A(sn)JS 20 (1995) 494, titles sans pp.

220 YAVETZ Zvi, Leaders and masses in the Roman world, [E]Malkin I., *Rubinsohn* Z.W. Lei 1995, Brill. xvii-243 p. $ 63. 90-04-09917-4 [RStR 22,65, W.J. *Tatum*].

221 YELO TEMPLADO D. Antonio: Lengua e historia, 65 años, [E]González Blanco Antonino, *al.*: Antigüedad y cristianismo 12 / Scripta fulgentina 5,9s. Murcia 1995, Univ. 618 p. pt 5000. 0214-7165. 37 art.; 16 infra.

A1.2 **Miscellanea** *unius auctoris*

222 **Adinolfi** Mario, Il Verbo uscito dal silenzio; temi di cristologia biblica [1 ineditum + 8 1971-87] 1992 → 3486 infra.

223 **Alvarez Valdés** Ariel, ¿ Qué sabemos de la Biblia ? 1-3. BA 1994s, Lumen. - : [R]RevB(Arg) 57 (1995) 183s (A.J. *Levoratti*).

224 **Asad** Talal, Genealogies of religion; discipline and reasons of power in Christianity and Islam [essays 1983-1991]. Baltimore 1993, Johns Hopkins Univ. 335 p. - [R]MoTh 11 (1995) 287s (G. *Ward*).

225 **Assmann** Hugo, Crítica à lógica da exclusão (Ensaios sobre economia e teologia): Temas de Atualidade. São Paulo 1994, Paulus. 144 p. - [R]REB 55 (1995) 975-8 (J.B. *Libânio*).

226 **Aston** Margaret, Faith and fire; popular and unpopular religion 1350-1600. L 1993, Hambledon. xviii-333 p. One ineditum + 9 reprints. £ 37.50. 1-85285-073-6. - [R]JEH 46 (1995) 362 (N. *Orme*).

227 **Ayalon** David, Islam and the abode of war; military slaves and Islamic adversaries: CS 456. Brookfield VT 1994, Ashgate. xii-288 p. $ 87.50. 0-86078-217-4 [RStR 22,356, W.C. *Schultz*]. -- [R]BSOAS 58 (1995) 621s (P.M. *Holt:* 198 p.; $ 47.50).

228 **[Hammond] Bammel** Caroline P., Tradition and exegesis in early Christian writers [17 art. 1982-93 + 1]: CS 500. Aldershot/Brookfield 1995, Variorum/Ashgate. xii-312 p. 0-86078-494-0. [ThD 43,169]. -- [R]EThL 71 (1995) 465s (F. *Neirynck*).

229 **Barrett** C.K., Jesus and the Word and [16] other essays; PTMS 41. E / Allison Park PA 1995, Clark/Pickwick. xii-276 p. $ 22.50 pa. 1-55635-029-5 [< NTAb 40,507, titles only].

230 **Bethge** Eberhard, Friendship and resistance; [his own, 85th b.] essays on Dietrich BONHOEFFER. Geneva/GR 1995, WCC/Eerdmans. vii-111 p. $ 12. -- [R]*CritRR 8 (1995) 390-2 (G.B. *Kelly*: helps to remedy the much-criticised failure of his biography to distinguish what was from Bonhoeffer and what from himself).

231 La Bible au fil des jours [Oxford, Lion], [T]. tout anonyme. Méry/P 1993, Sator/Cerf. 384 p. F 160. 2-204-04675-2. -- [R]RTL 26 (1995) 395 (M. *Simon*; aucune mise en garde).

232 **Boff** Leonardo, Ecology and liberation; a new paradigm [Italian (< Portuguese)], [T]*Cumming* John: Ecology and Justice. Mkn 1995, Orbis. xii-187 p. $ 15. 0-88344-978-1 [ThD 43,58].

233 **Bovon** François, New Testament traditions and apocryphal narratives [11 reprints → 9,186], [T]*Haapiseva-Hunter* Jane: PrincTMg 26. Allison Park PA 1995, Pickwick. x-256 p. 1-55635-024-4.

234 **Boyle** John P., Church teaching authority; [9 reprinted] historical and theological studies. ND 1995, Univ. vi-241 p. $ 39. 0-265-00805-1 [< ThD 43,258].

235 **Brecht** Martin, Ausgewählte Aufsätze, I. Reformation. Stu 1995, Calwer. 576 p. DM 98 pa. 3-7668-3290-5 [ThRv 92,81].

236 **Bredero** Adriaan H., Christendom and Christianity in the Middle Ages; the relations between religion, Church, and society [11 organized reprints], [T]*Brunsma* Reinder. GR 1994, Eerdmans. xiii-402 p. $ 30. -- [R]ChH 64 (1995) 230s (C.A. *Volz*).

237 **Brilliant** Richard, Commentaries on Roman art; selected studies. L 1994, Pindar. 438p.

238 **Cancetti** Giorgio, Scritti di paleografia, [R]*Nicolaj* Giovanna. Z 1995, Urs Graf. 278 p. 3-85951-173-4.

239 **Capon** Robert F., The romance of the Word: [three books on] one man's love affair with theology. GR 1995, Eerdmans. vii-173 p. 0-8028-4084-1.

240 **Catchpole** David R., The quest for Q [10 reworked 1981-92 art.] 1993 → 9,4407; 10,4234: [R]*CritRR 8 (1995) 186-8 (S. *Carruth*).

241 **Clarke** W. Norris, [10 1952-93] Explorations in metaphysics; being -- God -- person. ND 1995, Univ. xv-228 p. £ 31.50: pa. £ 18. 0-268-00696-2; -7-0. [*TBR 9/1, 4, L.T. *Pringle*].

242 **Congar** Yves, Église et Papauté; regards historiques [12 reprints]: CFi 184. P 1994, Cerf. 317 p. F 145. 2-204-05090- . -- [R]TTh 35 (1995) 412s (N. van *Doorn*).

243 **Counelis** James S., Inheritance and change in Orthodox Christianity [14 reprints 1976-93]. Scranton 1995, Univ. xv-177 p. $ 35. 0-940866-32-3 [ThD 43,62].

244 **Crenshaw** James L., Urgent advice and probing questions; collected writings on OT wisdom [2 inedita + 36 1969-95]. Macon GA 1995, Mercer Univ. xiii-605 p. 0-86554-483-2 [< OTA 19, p.160, tit.pp.].

245 **Croke** Brian, Christian chronicles and Byzantine history, 5th-6th centuries: CS. Brookfield 1992, Ashgate. xii-336 p. $ 90. -- [R]*JEarlyC 3 (1995) 229-231 (A. *Golitzin*).

246 **Daube** David, Talmudic law [→ 10,168*d*; 31 art. 1944-86], [E]*Carmichael* Calum M.: Collected works 1, Robbins collection. Berkeley 1992, Univ. California. xli-527 p. $ 32.50. 1-882239-00-8 [ThD 43.153].

247 **Dautzenberg** Gerhard, Studien zur Theologie der Jesustradition: SBAufs NT 19. Stu 1995, KBW. xi-423 p. DM 79; sb. 71.

248 **Delebecque** Édouard, Études sur le grec du Nouveau Testament. Aix 1995, Univ. Provence. 489 p.; bibliog. 470-484. 2-85399-354-X.

249 **Derrett** J.Duncan M., [21 reprinted] Studies in the NT 6, Jesus among biblical exegetes. Lei 1995, Brill. x-251 p., with a concordance to all six volumes. $ 80.75. 90-04-10228-0 [RStR 22,66, F.W. *Burnett*]. -- [R]E(xp)T 107 (1995s) 56 (R.A.*Burridge*: interesting, idiosyncratic).

250 **Dupont** Jacques, [20 1967-82] Nouvelles études sur les Actes des Apôtres: LeDiv 118. P 1994, Cerf. 535 p. -- [R]Neotest 29 (1995) 424-7 (P.B. *Decock*: detailed summaries).

251 **Dupré** W., Patterns in meaning; reflections on meaning and truth in cultural reality, religious traditions and dialogical encounters: *StPhTh 10.. Kampen 1994, Kok Pharos. viii-288 p. *f* 70. 90-390-0203-7.- [R]G(ereformeerd)TT 95 (1995) 42 (H.M. *Vroom*); TTh 35 (1995) 316 (A. van *Harskamp*).

252 **Dupront** Alphonse (1905-1990), Puissances et latences de la religion catholique: Le Débat. P 1993, Gallimard. 118 p. -- [R]RTL 26 (1995) 370s (É. *Poulat*: substantiel, atypique; sa thèse en Sorbonne, 'Le mythe de Croisade', attendue chez Gallimard).

253 **Dussel** Enrique, Historia de la filosofía y filosofía de la liberación [20 years reprints]. Bogotá 1994, Nueva América. 322 p. -- [R]JHispLat 3,1 (1995s) 52s (E. *Mendieta*).

254 **Ebach** Jürgen, Hiobs Post; gesammelte Aufsätze zum Hiobbuch, zu Themen biblischer Theologie und zur Methodik der Exegese. Neuk 1995, Neuk.-V. 214 p. DM 68. 3-7887-1486-2 [TR 91,360].

255 **Erickson** Millard J., The evangelical mind and heart; perspectives on theological and practical issues. GR 1993, Baker. 240 p. $ 15. -- [R]A(ndr)USS 33 (1995) 118s (W. *Whidden*).

Esbroeck Michel van, Dormition [ThD 43,65] 1995 → 5121 infra.

256 **Evans** Craig A., Jesus and his contemporaries; comparative studies: AGAJU. Lei 1995, Brill. xiii-532 p. $148.50. 90-04-10279-5. -- [R]*CritRR 8 (1995) 399-401 (P.K. *Moser*).

257 **Forni** Giovanni, Scritti vari di storia, epigrafia e antichità romane, [E]*Angeli Bertinelli* Maria Gabriella: Univ. Genova StoAnt 17. R 1994, Bretschneider. 995 p. (2 vol.); 42 pl.

258 **Fouilloux** Étienne, Au cœur du XXe siècle religieux [15 réimprimés 1967-92]. P 1993, Ouvrières. 317 p. -- [R]CrSt 16 (1995) 222-231 (Maria *Paiano*).

259 **Fox** Matthew, Wrestling with the prophets; essays on creation spirituality and everyday life. SF 1995, Harper. xv-315 p. $ 14. -- [R]Creation Spirituality 11,4 (Oakland 1995) 57 (B. *Cruz*).

260 **Frieling** Rudolf † 1986. New Testament studies, [E]*Jacobs-Brown* Tony. E 1994, Floris. 255 p. 0-86315-185-X.

261 **González Faus** José Ignacio, El factor cristiano: Horizonte. Estel[l]a 1994, VDivino. 468 p. 84-7151-979-8. -- [R]E(st)E 70 (1995) 415s (M. *Matos*).

262 **Greeley** Andrew M., The sociology of ~ [46 art. 1962-92 + one ineditum]: SFla..SocialOrder 4. Atlanta 1994, Scholars. xiii-621 p. $ 100. -- [R]*CritRR 7 (1994) 590-2 (tit.pp.).

263 **Greenberg** Moshe, Studies in the Bible and Jewish thought [2 inedita + 23 edited reprints 1959-90]; JPS Scholar of Distinction series. Ph 1995, JPS. xviii-462 p. $ 40. 0-8276-0504-8 [OTA 19,139, tit.pp.; renvoi to summaries of the two inedita; ThD 43,270].

264 **Gregory** Tullio, Mundana sapientia: forme di coscienza nella cultura medievale [16 saggi 1960-90]: StT 181. R 1992, Storia & Letteratura. 481 p. -- ^RRS(to)LR 31 (1995) 355-361 (M. *Pesce*).

265 **Grelot** Pierre, La tradition apostolique, règle de foi et de vie pour l'Église [réimprimés 1979-92]. P 1995, Cerf. 337 p, -- ^RBLE 96 (1995) 317 (S. *Légasse*).

266 **Grözinger** Albrecht, Es bröckelt an den Rändern; Kirche und Theologie in einer multikulturellen Gesellschaft: Tb 120. Mü 1992, Kaiser. 160 p. -- ^RZM(iss)R 79 (1995) 247s (Astrid *Reuter*).

267 **Hauerwas** Stanley, *a)* Dispatches from the front 1994 → 10,182: ^RJRel 75 (1995) 579s (G. *Dorrien*: cantankerous, entertaining). -- *b)* [9 art. + 4 with *Willimon* W.], In good company; the church as polis. ND 1995, Univ. xv-268 p. $ 30. 0-268-01172-9 [ThD 43,368].

268 **Hengel** Martin, Studies in early Christianity [1 ineditum; 6 reprints. E/Herndon VA 1995, Clark. xix-402 p. $ 55. 0-567-09705-6 [ThD 43,368].

269 **Hodgson** Marshall G.S. † 1968, Rethinking world history; essays on Europe, Islam and world history [including 3 chapters of The venture of Islam], ^E*Burke* Edmund^{III}. C 1993, Univ. xxi-328 p. £ 35; pa. £ 13. -- ^RJRAS (1994) 399s (R.I. *Moore*: brilliant and infuriating).

270 **Hopper** Stanley R., The way of transfiguration; religious imagination as theopoiesis [essays of 40 years edited before the death in 1991 of this co-founder of the field of religion and literature], ^E*Keiser* R. Melvin, *Stoneburner* Tony. LVL 1992, W-Knox. x-337 p. ^R[J]LT(Ox) 9 (1995) 113 (D. *Jasper*).

271 **Horton** Robin, Patterns of thought in Africa and the west; essays on magic, religion and science. C 1993, Univ. 471 p. $ 60. -- ^RJR(el) 75 (1995) 310s (B.C. *Ray*).

272 **Hübner** Hans, Biblische Theologie als Hermeneutik; [16] Ges.Aufs. 65. Gb. ^E*Labahn* A. & M. Gö 1995, Vandenhoeck & R. 311 p.; Bibliog. 294-300. DM 84 pa. 3-525-53635-6 [NTAb 40, p.544].

273 **JOHANNES PAULUS II: McDermott** John M., The thought of Pope John Paul II; a collection of essays and studies. R 1993, Pont. Univ. Gregoriana. 239 p. -- ^RDoC(om) 47 (1994) 318s (D. *Composta*).

274 **Josuttis** M., Gottesliebe und Lebenslust; Beziehungsstörungen zwischen Religion und Sexualität [+ einige Inedita]. Gü 1994, Gü-V. 160 p. DM 34. 3-579-02258-X. -- ^RTTh 35 (1995) 314 (A. *Hoenkamp-Bisschops*).

275 **Jüngel** Eberhard, Theological essays [I 1989] II, ^E*Webster* J.B., ^Twith *Neufeldt-Fast* Arnold. E 1995, Clark. xxiv-272 p. $ 44. 0-567-09706-4 [ThD 43,275]. -- ^RET 106 (1994s) 345s (J. *Thompson*).

276 **Kamphaus** Franz, Bf., Auf den Punkt gebracht; biblische Anstösse. FrB 1994, Herder. 189 p. DM 26,80. -- ^RStZ 213 (1995) 357 (R. *Bleistein*).

277 **Kirchschläger** Walter, Gott spricht verbindlich: Einüben in das Hören [6 Vorträge]. Fr 1992, Paulus. 111 p. DM 22,80. -- : ^RTPQ 143 (1995) 210 (F. *Kogler*).

278 **Klauck** H.-J., Alte Welt und neuer Glaube 1994 → 10,193: ^REstAg 30 (1995) 554s (D. *Alvarez Cineira*).

279 **Kloppenborg** John S., Conflict and invention; literary art, rhetorical, and social studies on the Sayings Gospel Q. Ph 1995, Trinity. x-245 p. $ 16. 1-56338-123-0 [RStR 22,246. F.W. *Burnett*].

280 **Knierim** Rolf P., The task of Old Testament theology; substance, method, and cases. GR 1995, Eerdmans. xvi-603 p.; bibliog. 557-567. $ 40 pa. 0-8028-0715-1 [ThD 43,373].

281 **Kremer** Jacob, Die Bibel beim Wort genommen; Beiträge zu Exegese und Theologie des Neuen Testaments, [E]*Kühschelm* Roman, *Stowasser* Martin. FrB 1995, Herder. 496 p.: Kremer bibliog. 1956-94, p.489-496. DM 88. 3-451-23649-4 [ThRv 91,361; NTAb 40,p.326]. -- [R]TTh 35 (1995) 401 (H. *Berflo*).

282 **Lapsley** James N., The treasure of earthen vessels; explorations in theological anthropology. [E]*Childs* Brian H., *Waanders* David W. LVL 1994, W-Knox. xii-276 p. $ 20. 0-664-25493-4 [*TBR 8/2,29].

283 **Le Goff** Jacques, History and memory [1977-82]. [T] *Rendall* Steven, *Claman* Elizabeth. NY 1992, Columbia Univ. 265 p. $ 29.50. -- [R]JI(ntd)H 26 (1995) 80-82 (Margaret C. *Jacob*).

284 **Lévinas** Emmanuel, Difficult freedom; essays on Judaism, [T]*Hand* Seán. L 1990, Athlone. xiv-306 p. £ 35. -- [R][J]LitTOx 9 (1995) 458-460 (P. *Kemp*).

285 **Levy** Avigdor, The Sephardim of the Ottoman Empire. Princeton 1992, Darwin. xv-196 p. -- [R]*A(sn)JS 20 (1995) 222-5 (S. *Ward*).

286 **Lewis** Naphtali, On government and law in Roman Egypt [photocopies 1937-93], [E]*Hanson* Ann Ellis: ASP 33. Atlanta 1995, Scholars. xiii-383; Lewis bibliog. xi-xiii. 0-7885-0146-1 [RStR 22,346, A.T. *Kraabel*].

287 **Linehan** Peter, Past and present in medieval Spain: CS 384. Aldershot 1993, Variorum. x-347 p. £ 48.50. -- [R]JEH 46 (1995) 138 (R.B. *Tate*).

288 **Lohfink** Norbert, Studien zum Deuteronomium und zur deuteronomistischen Literatur: SBS AT 20. Stu 1995, KBW. 303 p. DM 79, sb. 71.

289 **Lord** Albert B. †, The singer resumes the tale [postuma], [E]*Lord* Mary L. Ithaca NY 1995, Cornell Univ. vii-258 p. $ 40. 0-8014-3103-4 [RStR 22,240, J.W. *Halporn*].

290 **Lubich** Clara, Alle sollen eins sein; Geistliche Schriften. Mü 1995, Neue Stadt. 293 p. DM 38. -- [R]G(eist)uL 68 (1995) 396 (F.-J. *Steinmetz*).

291 **Lukken** G., Per visibilia ad invisibilia; [19[T]] anthropological, theological and semiotic studies on the liturgy and the sacraments, [E]*Tongeren* L. van, *Caspers* C.: Liturgia condenda 2. Kampen 1994, Kok Pharos. 404 p. 90-390-0601-6. [ThD 42,375]. -- [R]TTh 35 (1995) 89 (F. *Spiertz*).

292 **McCormick** Richard A., Corrective vision; explorations in moral theology [19 1986-93]. KC 1994, Sheed & W. 256 p. $ 16 pa. 1-55612-601-8. [ThD 42,375]. -- [R]America 173,18 (1995) 27 (W.H. *Shannon*).

293 **McKane** William, A late harvest; reflections on the Old Testament. E 1995, Clark. x-182 p. 0-567-09727-7. -- [R]E(xp)T 107,5 top choice (1995) 129 (C.S.*Rodd*).

294 **Marcadé** Jean, Études de sculpture et d'iconographie antiques; scripta varia, 1941-1991. P 1993, Sorbonne. 572 p.; ill. F 330. -- [R]RBPH 73 (1995) 159s (F. *Baratte*).

295 **Mayer** Rudolf (1909-1991), Beiträge zur Geschichte von Text und Sprache des Alten Testaments, [E]*Bernhardt* W. B 1993, de Gruyter. viii-259 p.; portr. 3-11-013695-3. -- [R]Protest(antesimo) 50 (1995) 247 (J.A. *Soggin*).

296 **Minnich** Nelson H., *a)* The Catholic reformation; council, churchmen, controversies: CS. -- *b)* The fifth Lateran council .. : CS. Aldershot 1993, Variorum. x-313 p / viii-342 p. -- : [R]OCP 61 (1995) 609s (K.D. *Lewis*).

297 **Momigliano** Arnaldo D., Studies on modern scholarship, [E]*Bowersock* G.W., [T]*Cornell* T.J. Berkeley 1994, Univ. California. xxi-341 p. 0-520-07001-1.

298 **Moscati** Sabatino, Luci sul Mediterraneo; dai manoscritti del Mar Morto ai Cartaginesi in Italia; tre millenni di vicende storiche, di concezioni religiose, di creazioni artistiche alla luce dell'archeologia. R 1995, Quasar. 752 p.; 188 pl. (2 vol.).

299 **Nazir-Ali** Michael, Mission and dialogue; proclaiming the Gospel afresh in every age. L 1995, SPCK. 152 p. £ 9. 0-281-04810-X. -- [R]ET 106 (1994s) 380 (B. *Stanley*: ill-organized and paradoxically presuming exclusively Anglican readership).

300 **Neusner** Jacob, Ancient Judaism 3. ... [including 6 items with title 'Publishing too much': one on MEIER & CROSSAN]; SFSHJ 83. Atlanta 1993, Scholars. xvii-311 p. $90. -- [R]CritRR 7 (1994) 610s (19 tit.pp.).

301 **Neusner** Jacob, Åbo addresses and other recent essays on Judaism in time and eternity: SFSHJ .. Atlanta c.1994, Scholars. xi-273 p. $ 78. 1-55540-933-4 [NTAb 39, p.356; 16 art.].

302 **Newbigin** Lesslie, A word in season; perspectives on Christian world mission [17 art. since 1960], [E] *Jackson* Eleanor. GR/ .. 1994, Eerdmans/St.Andrew. 208 p. $ 15. 0-8028-0730-5 / 0-7152-0704-0. -- [R]E(xp)T 107 (1995s) 90s (K. *Cracknell*).

303 **Ong** Walter, Faith and contexts 3. Further essays, 1952-1990, [E]*Farrell* Thomas J., *Soukup* Paul A.: South Florida-Rochester-St.Louis Studies on Religion and the Social Order 3. At 1995, Scholars. xxvi-267 p. $ 85. 1-55540-976-8 [ThD 42,181]-

304 **Orbe** Antonio, [36] Estudios sobre la teología cristiana primitiva: Fuentes Patrísticas, estudios 1. M/R 1994, Ciudad Nueva / Pont. Univ. Gregoriana. viii-920 p. L[m] 120 [Greg 76 (1995) 638]. -- [R]Communio (Sev) 28 (1995) 93 (M. *Sánchez*).

305 **Overbeck** Franz, Werke und Nachlass 4, [E]*Reibnitz* Barbara von. Stu 1995, Metzler. xliv-692 p. DM 98. 3-476-00965-3 [ThRv 92,78].

306 **Papathomopoulos** M., [G] Varia philosophica et papyrologica I. Jannina 1990, Univ. 303 p. 24 art. -- [R]GitFg 47 (1995) 349-351 (E. *Dettori*).

307 **Pathrapanckal** Joseph, Text and context in biblical perspective [partly reprints]. Bangalore 1993, Dharmaram. viii-183 p. rs 90. -- [R]I(nd)TS 31 (1994) 374s (A. *Xavier*).

308 **Perlitt** Lothar. Allein mit dem Wort; [1 ineditum + 16 1962-94], [E]*Spieckermann* Hermann. Gö 1995, VR. 370 p. DM 98. 3-525-53634-8 [< OTA 19,142, tit.pp.].

309 **Pieper** Joseph, Philosophie, Kontemplation, Weisheit [5 art. 1955-90]. Einsiedeln 1991, Johannes. 96 p. -- [R]C(olc)Th 64,1 (1994) 175s (Z. *Kijas*).

310 **Pietrangeli** Carlo, [... 60 anni di] Scritti scelti, [E]*Cipriani* Angela, *al.* R 1995, Quasar. xviii-662 p.; bibliog. 647-662. 88-7140-068-2.

311 **Pietri** Charles [† 1991]. .. historien et chrétien [12 art. < QFleuves]. P 1992, Beauchesne. viii-220 p. F 120. -- [R]*JEarlyC 3 (1995) 231s (E. *Ferguson*).

312 **Pixner** Bargil, Wege des Messias und Stätten der Urkirche, [2]*Riesner* Rainer. Giessen 1994, Brunnen. 480 p. -- [R]DSD 2 (1995) 242s (B.J. *Capper*: intense praise, not only because the Austrian author 'risked all by helping to persuade the Brixen regiment *en masse* to refuse the oath of obedience to Hitler, and by openly expressing sympathy for Judaism').

313 **Puelma** Mario, Kleine Schriften und Nachträge, [E]*Fasel* Irène. Ba 1995, Schwabe. 589 p.; portr. -- MH(elv) 52 (1995) 271s (F. *Paschoud*).

314 **Rackman** Emanuel, Modern Halakhah for our time [14 art]. Hoboken 1995, KTAV. iv-195 p. $ 29.50. 0-88125-293-6 [ThD 42,383]

315 **Rao** O.M., An Asian's Christological perspective. 1994. -- [R]Vidyajyoti 59 (1995) 68s (P.M. *Meagher*).

316 **Ratzinger** Joseph Kard., Wahrheit, Werte, Macht; Prüfsteine der pluralistischen Gesellschaft. FrB 1993, Herder. 93 p. DM 22.80. -- [R]LebZeug 50 (1995) 79s (G. *Höver*).

317 **Robert** René, Quelques croix de l'exégèse néo-testamentaire: Croire et savoir. P 1993, Téqui. 264 p. -- [R]RThom 95 (1995) 313-6 (L. *Devillers*).

318 **Rose** Gillian, Judaism and modernity; philosophical essays. Ox 1993, Blackwell. xxii-297 p. £ 15 pa. -- [R]JJS 46 (1995) 345-7 (N. *Solomon*, also on her 1992 The broken middle); MoTh 11 (1995) 268-270 (Edith *Wyschogrod*).

319 **Rosén** Haiim B., [60th Gb.] Selected writings on linguistics, 3. East and West. Mü 1994, Fink. 486 p. DM 168. -- [R]Kratylos 40 (1995) 186-8 (Rüdiger *Schmitt*).

320 **Rosenzweig** Franz, La Scrittura; saggi dal 1914 al 1929, [TE]*Bonola* G. R 1991, Città Nuova. -- [R]FilTeo 8 (1994) 344-6 (Gabriella *Antinolfi*).

321 **Rudolph** Enno, Theologie -- diesseits des Dogmas; [15] Studien zur systematischen Theologie [release from BARTH-imposed isolation], Religionsphilosophie und Ethik. Tü 1994, Mohr. 232 p. DM 68. 3-16-146244-0. -- [R]E(xp)T 107 (1995s) 18 (G. *Wainwright*).

322 **Runia** D.T., Philo and the Church Fathers; a collection of [14 1991-4] papers: VigChr.s 32. Lei 1995, Brill. xii-275 p.; ill. *f* 155. 90-04-10355-4 [NTAb 40,p.384].

323 **Sass** Gerhard, Leben aus den Verheissungen; traditionsgeschichtliche und biblisch-theologische Untersuchungen zur Rede von Gottes Verheissungen im Frühjudentum und beim Apostel Paulus, [E]*Schrage* Wolfgang, *Smend* Rudolf: FRL 164. Gö 1995, Vandenhoeck & R. 579 p. DM 168. 3-525-52846-4 [TR 91,273].

324 **Schillebeeckx** Edward. The language of faith: essays on Jesus, theology, and the Church: Concilium series. Mkn/L 1995, Orbis/SCM. xv-220 p. 1-57075-017-3/ [ThD 43,62].

325 **Schilling** Heinz, Religion, political culture and the emergence of early modern society; [9 1979-88 German] essays in German and Dutch history, [T]*Burnett* Stephen G.: StMdvR 50. Lei 1992, Brill. xvi-434 p. -- [R]ChH 64 (1995) 125s (L.D. *Snyder*).

326 **Schmithals** Walter, Theologiegeschichte des Urchristentums; eine problemge-schichtliche Darstellung [16 art.] Stu 1994, Kohlhammer. 332 p. DM 50. 3-17-012965-1 [RStR 22,71, C. *Bernas*].

327 **Segal** Robert A., Explaining and interpreting religion; essays on the issue: TStR. NY 1992, P.Lang. xii-156 p. $ 36 [RStR 22,333, T. *Murphy*].-- [R]JAAR 63 (1995) 585-8(D.*Pals*).

328 **Sperber** D., Magic and folklore in rabbinic literature [25 art.]: *StNE. Ramat-Gan 1994, Bar-Ilan Univ. 256 p.; 6 fig. 965-226-1653 [NTAb 40, p.187].

329 **Speyer** Wolfgang, Religionsgeschichtliche Studien: Collectanea 15. Hildesheim 1995, Olms. xx-221 p.; bibliog. Nachweise 196-206. DM 98. 3-487-09993-4.

330 **Spini** Giorgio, Studi sull'evangelismo italiano (1950-1992) tra otto e novecento: StValdesi 14. T 1994, Claudiana. 262 p. -- [R]RS(to)LR 31 (1995) 553-9 (G.P. *Romagnani*).

331 **Stendahl** Krister, Paolo fra ebrei e pagani [Eng.1988], [T]*Ribet* Paolo: Piccola collana moderna, teologica 74. T 1995, Claudiana. 165 p. 88-7016-206-0.

332 **Strobel** August, Zurück zu den Anfängen; Beiträge und Schriftenverzeichnis, 65. Gb., [E]*Kraus* Wolfgang. Fürth 1995, Flacius. 94 p. 3-924022-364-4.

333 **Sykes** Stephen, Unashamed Anglicanism [reprints + 1 ineditum]. L 1995, Darton-LT. 233 p. £ 10. 0-232-52103-4. -- [R]*TBR 8,3 (1995s) 50 (H. *Wybrew*).

334 **Taft** Robert F., Liturgy in Byzantium and beyond: CS 494. Aldershot/Brookfield VT 1995, Ashgate/Variorum. xii-345 p. $ 95. 0-86078-483-5 [ThD 43,189].

335 **Talmon** Shemaryahu, Israels Gedankenwelt in der hebräischen Bibel: GesAufs 3 / InfJud 13. Neuk 1995. Neuk.-V. viii-280 p. 3-7887-1425-5.

336 **Thiede** Carsten P., Rekindling the word; in search of Gospel truth [19 art., 3 on Magdalen papyrus]. Ph / Leominster / Alexandria, Australia 1995, Trinity / Dwyer / Gracewing. xii-204 p. $ 25. 1-56338-136-2/../0-85244-335-8. [ThD 43,390].

337 **Thiel** Johannes H., Studies in ancient history, [E]*Wallinga* H.T. Amst 1994, Gieben. xi-174 p.; bibliog. 171-4. 90-5063-092-8. 11 art.; 2 infra.

338 **Thüsing** W., [16] Studien zur neutestamentlichen Theologie, ^E*Söding* T.: WUNT 82. Tü 1995, Mohr. viii-327 p. DM 198. 3-16-146337-4 [NTAb 40, p.166].

339 **Tracy** David, On naming the present; God, hermeneutics and Church [12 art, < Concilium 1978-95]. Mkn/L 1994, Orbis/SCM. xii-146 p. £ 11.50. 0-88344-9972-2 / 0-344-02588-5. -- ^RLexTQ 30 (1995) 122-4 (M. *Kinnamon:* dialogue with history, important not only for Catholics); Month 256 (1995) 413s (M. *Kirwan*); Tablet 249 (1995) 1413 (G. *O'Collins:* as one who learns, not out to score points); *TBR 8,1 (1995s) 28; TS 56 (1995) 817s (T.H. *Sanks*).

340 **Tuckett** Christopher M., Luke's literary achievement: collected essays: JSNT.s 116. Shf 1995, Academic. 232 p. £ 27.50. 1-85075-556-6.

341 **Ullendorff** Edward, From Emperor Haile Selassie to H.J. POLOTSKY -- an Ethiopian and Semitic miscellany: ÄthF 41. Wsb 1995, Harrassowitz. 193 p. DM 158. 3-447-03615-X. -- ^RWZKM 85 (1995) 328s (Renate *Richter*).

342 **Vajda Criado** Georges [† c.1980; 18 art.] Sages et penseurs sépharades de Baghdad à Cordoue, ^E*Jolinet* Jean, *Hayoun* M.-R.: Patrimoines Judaïsme. P 1989, Cerf. 296 p. -- ^RSefarad 55 (1995) 409-411 (Esperanza *Alfonso*).

343 **Van Inwagen** Peter, God, knowledge, and mystery; [9 reprinted] essays in philosophical theology. Ithaca 1995, Cornell Univ. 284 p. $ 42.50; pa. $ 18. 0-8014-2994-3; -8186-4 [ThD 43,293].

344 **Visotzky** Burton L., Fathers of the world; essays in rabbinic and patristic literature: WUNT 80. Tü 1995, Mohr. vi-205 p. DM 138. 3-16-146338-2 [ThRv 91,360; RStR 22,354, M.S. *Jaffee*: witty but serious].

345 **Watkins** Calvert, Selected writings, ^E*Oliver* Lisi: IB*SprW 80. In 1994, Univ. Inst. SprW. xvi-771 p. -- ^ROLZ 90 (1995) 148-152 (S. *Zimmer*)

346 **Wénin** André, L'homme biblique; anthropologie et éthique dans le Premier Testament: Théologies bibliques. P 1995, Cerf. 196 p. F 100. 2-204-05094-6. -- ^REThL 71 (1995) 439 (J. *Lust*).

347 **Wiebe** Donald, Beyond legitimation; essays on the problem of religious knowledge. NY 1994, St. Martin's. xiii-243 p. $ 65. 0-312-12084-2.

348 **Wilken** Robert L., Remembering the Christian past [1 ineditum + 7 < 1989-95]. GR 1995, Eerdmans. ix-180 p. 0-8028-0880-8 [ThD 43,195; RStR 22,255, S. *Duffy*].

349 **Wiseman** T.P., Historiography and imagination; eight [reprinted] essays on Roman culture: Hist 33. Exeter 1994, Univ. xiv-167 p.; 8 fig. £ 14 pa. -- ^RGaR 42 (1995) 241 (T. *Wiedemann*).

350 **Wittkower** Rudolf (1901-71), The impact of non-European civilizations on the art of the West; [17] selected lectures. ^E*Reynolds* Donald M. C 1989, Univ. xxx-235 p.; 271 fig. $ 49.50. -- ^RJNES 54 (1995) 144-6 (Margaret C. *Root*).

351 **Wright** Christopher J.H., Walking the ways of the Lord; the ethical theory of the OT [11 reprints edited-unified]. DG 1995, InterVarsity. 319 p. 0-8308-1867-7 [< OTA 19, p.549].

352 **Yoder** John H., The royal priesthood; essays ecclesiological and ecumenical, ^E*Cartwright* Michael G. GR 1994, Eerdmans. 400 p. $ 23. 0-8028-0707-0 [ProEccl 4 (1995) 255 adv.: ThD 43,195]. -- ^RÖ(kum)R 44 (1995) 405s (R.W. *Burkart*).

353 **Zirker** Hans, Islam; theologische und gesellschaftliche Herausforderungen [13 art.]. Dü 1993, Patmos. 368 p. DM 50. 3-491-77937-5. -- ^RNZM(iss)W 51 (1995) 148s (A. *Peter*).

354   **Zur Mühlen** Karl-Heinz,   Reformatorisches Profil; Studien zum Weg Martin
LUTHERs und der Reformation, *EBrosseder* Johannes *al.*   Gö 1995, Vandenhoeck & R. 408
p. DM 98.   3-525-58162-9 [ThRv 92,81, tit.pp.].   13-138, Luther, AUGUSTIN und das
Spätmittelalter.

A1.3   *Plurium compilationes* biblicae

355   ^E**Bauckham** Richard, Palestinian setting: [→ 10.343; ^RCBQ 57 (1995) 840 (R.J.
Pervo: 'RAMSAY updated')] The Book of Acts in its first-century setting 4. GR/Carlisle
1995, Eerdmans/Paternoster. xiv-526 p. $ 37.50. 0-85364-566-3.

356 ^E**Bianchi** Enzo, *a)* Il mistero e il ministero della koinonia; - *b)* La morte e il morire:
PSV 31s. Bo (1995) Dehoniane. 317 p. / 358 p.

357 ^E**Braaten** Carl E., *Jensen* Robert W., Reclaiming the Bible for the Church. E c.1995,
Clark. xii-137 p. 0-567-08533-3.

358 ^E**Carmilly** Moshe, *al.*, Studia Judaica II. Cluj-Napoca 1993, Sincron. 178 p. —
^R*A(sn)JS 20 (1995) 495: 21 art. suggesting Rumanian origin, without pp.

359   ^E**Castelli** Elizabeth A.: *Aichele* George and 9 others, contributions of each not
distinguished: The postmodern Bible [-research methods]. NHv 1995, Yale Univ. xiii-398
p. $ 35. 0-300-06090-4. [RStR 22,135, D.A. *Kille*].

360 ^E**Charlesworth** James H., Qumran questions [= JSPE 10, 1992]: BiSe 36. Shf 1995,
JSOT. 210 p. £ 12.50 pa. 1-85075-770-4 [< OTA 19 (1995) p.364].

361   ^E**Dohmen** Christoph, *Söding* Thomas,   Eine Bibel -- zwei Testamente; Positionen
biblischer Theologie: Uni-Tb N° 1893. Pd 1995, Schöningh. 318 p. DM 28,80. 3-8252-
1893-7 / 3-506-99471-9 [< OTA 19, p.359-361, B.A. *Asen*, with renvoi to summaries of
the 12 (out of 23) OT articles].

362 ^E**Edelman** Diana V., The triumph of Elohim; from Yahwisms to Judaisms: *CBExT 13.
Kampen 1995, Kok Pharos. 262 p. *f* 70. 90-390-0124-3 [< OTA 19, p.321, with indicated summary of the seven, apparently not reprints].-- ^RJQR 86 (1995s) 504-6 (M.S. *Smith*).

363 ^E**Esler** Philip F., Modelling early Christianity; social-scientific studies [on FREYNE,
MALINA, DERRETT, *al.*] of the NT in its context. L 1995, Routledge. xv-349 p.; 14 fig.
$ 55; pa. $ 25. 0-415-12980-X; -1-8 [NTAb 40, p.509].

364 ^E**Evans** Craig R., *Porter* Stanley E., The historical Jesus; a Sheffield reader: BiSe 33.
Shf 1995, Academic. 314 p.   £ 12. 1-85075-731-3.

365 ^E**Evans** Craig R., *Porter* Stanley E., The Synoptic Gospels; a Sheffield reader: BiSe 31.
Shf 1995, Academic. 313 p. £ 12. 1-85075-732-1. - ^REThL 71 (1995) 461s (F. *Neirynck*
on BiSe 31-34 adds usefulnesses to those cited from the book, but regrets absence of the
full original pagination, and of any explanation for the neither alphabetical nor chronological
order; but 'the two Indexes are an appreciable complement to the original texts').

366 ^E**Fitzgerald** John T., Friendship, flattery, and frankness of speech; studies on friendship
in the NT world: NT.s 82. Lei c.1995, Brill. xix-291 p. 90-04-10454-2.

367 ^E**Frank** Daniel H., Autonomy and Judaism; the individual and the community in Jewish
philosophical thought. Albany 1992, SUNY. ix-229 p. 0-7914-1209-1; pa. -10-5.

368 ^E**Frankemölle** Hubert, Die Bibel; das bekannte Buch -- das fremde Buch [13 art.]. Pd
1994, Schöningh. 250 p. 3-506-72609-9. [RStR 22,166, D.C. *Aune*].

369 ^E**Gallagher** Susan V., Postcolonial literature and the biblical call for justice. Jackson
1994, Univ. Mississippi. vii-258 p. $ 37.50. 0-87805-723-4. - ^RChrSchR 25 (1995s) 376-
9 (A. *Johnson*).

370 [E]**Geva** Hillel, Ancient Jerusalem revealed [< Qadmoniot, revised and in English] 1994 → 10.12217*: [R]JSJ 26 (1995) 360-2 (A.S. van der *Woude*: informative, captivating).

371 [E]**Goldberg** David T., *Krausz* Michael, Jewish identity. Ph 1993, Temple Univ. ix-344. $ 50; pa. $ 23 [RStR 22,215-222, S.Z. *Charmé*, also on 8 cognates].

372 [E]**Green** J.B., Hearing the New Testament; strategies for interpretation (20 ? reprints). GR/Carlisle 1995, Eerdmans/Paternoster. xvi-444 p. $ 25. 0-8028-0793-3 [NTAb 40, p.324; after this US ISBN puts only '(E)')}. -- [R]Word & World 16 [1996] 378.380.382 {J.L. *Boyce*).

374 [E]**Kaiser** O., Texte aus der Umwelt des ATs: 3/4 (*Lambert* W.G., *Hecker* K., *Müller* G.G.W., *Ünal* A.) Mythen und Epen 2. Gü 1994, Gü-V. p.561-865. DM 258. - [R]ZAW 107 (1995) 545s (M. *Köckert*)

375 [E]**Mainville** Odette, *al.*, Loi et autonomie dans la Bible et la tradition chrétienne 1994 → 10,255: [R]*CritRR 8 (1995) 531s (B.D., *Ehrman*, tit.pp.).

376 [E]**Neusner** Jacob, Judaism in late antiquity; I. The literary and archaeological sources; II. Historical syntheses: HO 16s. Lei 1995, Brill. xiv-176 p.; xiv-318 p. *f* 140 + 200. 90-04-10129-2; -30-6 [RStR 22, 257s, M.S. *Jaffee*]. - [R]JSJ(ud) 26 (1995) 207-212 (A.S. van der *Woude*).

377 [E]**Neusner** Jacob, The Torah teaches: Judaism transcends catastrophe 3. Macon 1995, Mercer Univ. x-210 p. $ 30. 0-86554-492-1 [NTAb 40,p.560].

378 [E]**Ochs** Peter, The return to Scripture in Judaism and Christianity 1993 → 10,257*a*: [R]CrossCur 45 (1995s) 253-7 (L.L. *Edwards*).

379 [E]**Parr** John, Sowers and reapers; a companion to the four Gospels and Acts [→ 10,240* '< London, Bible Reading Fellowship']. Ox/Sutherland 1994, Albatross. 446 p. £ 10. 0-7324-0905-5. - [R]*TBR 8,1 (1995s) 19 (M. *Bockmuehl*: twin to EMMERSON Grace, Prophets).

380 [E]**Piper** R.A., The gospel behind the Gospels: current studies on Q: NT.s 74. Lei 1995, Brill. xi-411 p. *f* 150. 90-04-09737-6 [NTAb 39, p.327].

381 [E]**Porter** S.E. [→ J5.1], *Tombs* D., [9] Approaches to New Testament study: JSNT.s 120. Shf 1995, Academic. £ 43. 302 p. 1-85075-567-1 [NTAb 40, p.515].

382 [E]**Porter** Stanley E., *Evans* Craig A., Sheffield Readers ['the best from 50 issues of JSNT' on Jesus, Synoptics, John, Paul]. Shf 1995, JSOT. 314, 313, 167, 300 p. £ 11 each, 1-85075-731-3; -32-1; -29-1; -30-5. - [R]E(xp)T 107 (1995s) 117 (C.S. *Rodd*).

383 [E]**Reventlow** Henning, *Farmer* William, Biblical studies and the shifting of paradigms, 1850-1914 [H.J. HOLTZMANN Two-Source influence]; JSOT.s 192 [though on NT, 9 art.]. Shf 1995, JSOT. 297 p. $ 45. 1-85075-532-9 [RStR 22,167, M.P. *Graham*].

384 [E]**Rosner** Brian S., Understanding Paul's ethics; twentieth century approaches. GR 1995, Eerdmans. 377 p. $ 22. 0-8028-0749-6 [ThRv 92,445].

385 [E]**Sandy** D. Brent, *Giese* Ronald J.[J], Cracking OT codes; a guide to interpreting the literary genres of the OT. Nv 1995, Broadman & H. vii-323 p. 0-8054-1093-7 [< OTA 19, p.150, 14 art., tit.pp. without summaries or indication of whether reprints].

386 [E]**Segovia** Fernando F., *Tolbert* Mary Jane, Reading from this place; social location and biblical interpretation, 1. in the United States [17 art.]; 2. in global perspective [19 art]. Mp 1995, Fortress. xiv-321 p.; xv-365 p. $ 18 (vol.1). 0-8006-2812-8; -949-3 [< OTA 19,p.524, with renvoi to 4 + 5 items; NTAb 40,p.135.515].

387 [E]**Shanks** Hershel, Approaches to the Bible, the best of Bible Review; I. Composition, transmission and language [27 art.]; II. A multitude of perspectives [20 art.; DE VAUX, CROSSAN ..]. Wsh 1994s, Biblical Archaeology society. 372 p.; 352 p. $ 19 each [: BArR 21,3 (1995) 75 adv.].

388 ᴱ**Sierra** Sergio J., La lettura ebraica della Scrittura [survey of 2000 years of Jewish biblical scholarship by 21 Italians and Israelis]: La Bibbia nella storia 1.   Bo 1995, Dehoniane. 464 p. Lᵐ 54 pa. 88-10-40260-X [< OTA 19, p.325, tit.pp.].

389 ᴱ**Urman** Dan, *Flesher* Paul V.M., Ancient synagogues; historical analysis and archaeological discovery, 1 (of 2): SBP 47. Leiden 1995, Brill. viii-297 p. $ 77.25. 90-04-10242-6 [< OTA 18 (1995) p. 395 with renvoi to 11 of the 18 partly reprints]. - ᴿBoL (1995) 36 (H.A. *McKay*).

390 ᴱ**Wilkins** Michael J., *Moreland* J.P., Jesus under fire [subtitle 'Modern scholarship reinvents the historical Jesus' only on reverse of title page]. ɢʀ 1995, Zondervan [now part of HarperCollins] ix-243 p $ 17. 0-310-61700-6 P.17-50, *Blomberg* Craig L., Where do we start studying Jesus ? [.. idiosyncrasies of the (ꜰᴜɴᴋ) Jesus Seminar]; - 73-99, *Bock* Darrell L., The words of Jesus: live [reported in normal human fashion], jive [freely made up to express later convictions], or [tape-recording style] memorex ? -- 6 others; 2 infra. - ᴿPerspSCF 47 (1995) 281 (R.M. *Bowman*); Presbyterion 21 (St.Louis 1995) 125s (R.W. *Yarbrough*: further 20 (1991) 8-20 (-36. *Gibbs* J.).

391 ᴱ**Zannoni** Arthur E., Jews and Christians speak of Jesus. Mp 1994, Fortress. xiv-191 p. $ 12 pa. -- ᴿ*CritRR 8 (1995) 535 (B.D, *Ehrman*, tit.pp.).

A1.4   *Plurium compilationes* **theologicae**

392 ᴱ**Alon** Ilai, *al.,* Concepts of the other in Near Eastern religions: I(sr)OS 14 (1994) entire.

393 **Amery** Carl, *Metz* J.-B. + 5 *al.,* Sind die Kirchen am Ende ? Rg 1995, Pustet. 175 p. ᴅᴍ 29,80. 3-7917-1455-4. [TPQ 143,319 adv.]

394 ᴱ**Beck** Heinrich [p.17-69.349-365], *Schmirber* Gisela. Kreativer Friede durch Begegnung der Weltkulturen: Hanns-Seidl-Stiftung STriadik 9. Fra 1995, Lang. 370 p. ᴅᴍ 95. 3-631-48934-X [ThRv 92,173]

395 ᴱ**Beinert** Wolfgang, *(Schüssler) Fiorenza* Francis, Handbook of Catholic theology [10 new NAm art. + 300 from German 1987, ᵀ*Duggan* Paul + 4] ɴʏ 1995, Crossroads. xiv-783 p. $ 70 [RStR 22,48, J.J. *Buckley*: bibliographies revised to English works, impressive but not always fitting the article; useful charts].

396 ᴱ**Beinert** Wolfgang, Kirchenbilder, Kirchenvisionen; Variationen über eine Wirklichkeit. Rg 1995, Pustet. 193 p. ᴅᴍ 29,80. 3-7917-1453-8 [ThRv 92,75, tit.pp].

397 ᴱ**Bein Ricco** Elena, Modernità politica e protestantesimo: PBT 31. T 1994, Claudiana. 264 p. Lᵐ 29. - ᴿProtest(antesimo) 50 (1995) 326s (F. *Chiarini*).

398 ᴱ**Berkey** Robert F., *Edwards* Sarah A., → 10.262: Christology in dialogue. Cleveland 1993, Pilgrim. viii-392 p. $ 25 pa. - ᴿ*CritRR 7 (1994) 559s (J.J. *Collins*, titles, pp.).

399 ᴱ**Biderman** Shlomo, *Scharfstein* Ben-Ami, *a*) Interpretation in religion; - *b*) Myths and fictions: Philosophy and religion, a comparative yearbook 2s. Lei 1992s, Brill. xi-290 p.; $ 63 / vii-397 p.; $ 106. 90-04-09519-5; -838-0. - ᴿNumen 42 (1995) 310-5 (N. *Smart*).

400 ᴱ**Birtel** Frank T., Reasoned faith: [12] essays on the interplay of faith and reason: Tulane Judeo-Christian. ɴʏ 1993, Crossroad. viii-231. $ 20. - ᴿHorizons 22 (1995) 143s (Jeanne *Evans*: Antony Fʟᴇᴡ's closing statement defends [his] unbelief).

401 ᴱ**Boulnois** Olivier, La [divine toute-] puissance et son omnbre; de Pierre ʟᴏᴍʙᴀʀᴅ à ʟᴜᴛʜᴇʀ, textes: BtPh. P 1994, Aubier. 414 p. - ᴿRTPh 127 (1995) 73s (C. *Pottier*).

402 ᴱ**Chapple** Christopher K., Ecological prospects; scientific, religious, and aesthetic perspectives. Albany 1994, ꜱᴜɴʏ. xii-236 p. $ 2 - ᴿHorizons 22 (1995) 326s (Pamela *Thimmes*: good).

403 ᴱ**Chopp** Rebecca S., *Taylor* Mark L., Reconstructing Christian theology [into politics, economics ... 16 essays]. Mp 1994, Fortress. xiii-384 p. $ 22. - ᴿP(rinc)SB 16 (1995) 249s (Leanne *Van Dyk*).

404 **Communio** 20 (1995, français):**117**, Décalogue IV, père et mère honoreras; - **118**, La sépulture; - **119**, Le Judaïsme; - **120**, Dieu et César; - **121**, La vie de foi; - **122**, La jeunesse et l'Église. F 65 chaque, c.170 p.

405 **Concilium**: **257**, La Bible, héritage culturel, ᴱ*Beuken* Wim, *Freyne* Sean; **258**, Les nombreux visages de Dieu, ᴱ*Häring* Hermann; **259**, Le corps et la sensibilité dans la liturgie, ᴱ*Chauvet* Louis-M.; **260**, La famille, ᴱ*Mieth* Dietmar, *Cahill* Lisa S.; **261**, L'écologie et la pauvreté; cri de la terre et cri des pauvres, ᴱ*Boff* Leonardo, *Elizondo* Virgil; **262**, Nationalisme et religion, ᴱ*Coleman* John, *Tomka* Miklós. P 1995, Beauchesne; c. 170 p. F 72 chaque: l'année F 310 (étranger F 390).

407 ᴱ**Delgado** Mariano, *Lob-Hüdepohl* Andreas. Markierungen; Theologie in den Zeichen der Zeit; Diöz.Berlin 11. Lp 1995, Benno. 364 p. DM 42. 3-87554-300-0 [ThRv 92,173].

408 ᴱ**Deshen** Shlomo, *al.*, The sociology of religion in Israel [18 art. 1982-1994]: Israeli Judaism, studies of Israeli society 7. New Brunswick 1995, Transaction. xii-386 p. $ 22. 1-56000-762-1 [ThD 43,89].

409 ᴱ**Devisch** R., *al.*, Le rite, source et ressources: Fac.S.Louis 69. Bru 1995. 158 p. Fb 680. 2-8028-0107-4 [NTAb 40,p.542: 4 art.; *Perrot* C., on NT ritual words and gestures].

410 ᴱ**Evans** C. Stephen, *Westphal* Merold, Christian perspectives on religious knowledge. GR 1993, Eerdmans. 288 p. $ 17 pa. 0-8028-0679-1. - ᴿCScR 25 (1995s) 197-9 (A.O. *Roberts*).

411 ᴱ**Farmer** William R., Crisis in Christology; essays in quest of resolution: Great Modern Debates 3. Dallas 1995, Truth. xxi-360. 0-9648151-3-3 [RStR 22,338, B. *Harvey* does not mention if reprints: NTAb 40, p.366 'Livonia MI 1995, Dove' with same ISBN].

412 **Fuchs** Ottmar, *al.*, Das Neue wächst; radikale Veränderungen in der Kirche. Mü 1995, Kösel. 179 p. DM 28,80. 3-466-36428-0 [ThRv 92,75, tit.pp].

413 ᴱ**Garrard-Burnett** Virginia, *Stoll* David, Rethinking Protestantism in Latin America [12 social-science art.]. Ph 1993, Temple Univ. 234 p. $ 40; pa. $ 19 - ᴿIBM(iss)R 19 (1995) 39 (G. *Cook*).

414 ᴱ**Gill** Robin, Readings in modern theology; Britain and America. Nv / L 1995, Abingdon / SCM. xi-399 p. $ 27. 0-687-04161-1 / 0-281-04819-3. - ᴿ*TBR 8,3 (1995s) 19s (I. *Markham*).

415 ᴱ**Glaz** Maxine, *Moessner* Jeanne S. [→ 7,355 'Stevenson J.'], Women in travail and transition; a new pastoral care. Mp 1991, Fortress. xii-225 p. - ᴿS(cot)JTh 48 (1995) 99-101 (Vera *Sinton*).

416 ᴿ**Grasso** Kenneth L., *al.*, Catholicism, liberalism, and communitarianism; the Catholic intellectual tradition and the moral foundatioms of democracy. Lanham MD 1995. Rowman & L. xi-271 p. $ 64.50: pa. $ 27. 0-8476-7994-2: -5-0 [ThD 43,160].

417 ᴱ**Guinness** Os, *Seel* John, No God but God. Ch 1992, Moody. 223 p. $ 17.- ᴿJETS 38 (1995) 461-3 (D. *Hall*: to expose idolatry within the evangelical camp, in light of loss of influence in the 1992 elections).

418 ᴱ**Gunton** Colin E., God and freedom; (King's College) essays in historical and systematic theology. E 1995, Clark. 137 p. £ 17. 0-567-09725-0. - ᴿE(xp)T 107 (1995s) 123 (M.D. *Chapman*); TBR 8,2 (1995s) 25 (G.R. *Jones*).

419 ᴱ**Hallman** David G., Ecotheology; voices from south and north. Geneva/Mkn 1994, WCC/Orbis. $ 18. 25 art. - ᴿModern Believing 36,2 (1995) 69-71 (Joyce *Killick*).

420 ᴱ**Hart** D.G., Reckoning with the past; [16 reprinted] historical essays on American evangelicalism. GR 1995, Baker. 429 p. $ 23. 0-8010-4397-2 [ThD 43,83].

421 ᴱ**Hawley** John S., Fundamentalism and gender. Ox 1994, UP. 220 p. -- ᴿUnSemQ 48,1 (1994) 178-182 (M. *Bagger*).

422 ᴱ**Herrera** R.A., Mystics of the Book [Jewish, Christian, Islamic]; themes, topics, and typologies. NY 1993, P. Lang. viii-415 p. 0-8204-2007-7

423 ᴿ**Idinopulos** Thomas A., *Yonan* Edward A., Religion and reductionism; essays on ELIADE, SEGAL, and the challenge of the social sciences for the study of religion 1994 → 10,278: ᴿSR 24 (1995) 213-5 (R.T. *McCutcheon*).

424 ᴱ**Johnstone** William, William Robertson SMITH; essays in reassessment: JSOT.s 189. Shf 1995, Academic. 403 p. £ 45. 1-85075-523-X.

425 ᴱ**Kerber** Walter, Religion, Grundlage oder Hindernis des Friedens ?; Fragen einer neuen Weltkultur 12. 289 p. DM 36. 3-925412-17-4 [TR 91,83].

426 ᴱ**King** Ursula [→ 5317s infra], Religion and gender. Ox 1995, Blackwell. xi-324 p. 0-631-19376-6.

427 ᴱ**Kippenberg** H.G., *Stroumsa* G.G., Secrecy and concealment: [19] studies in the history of Mediterranean and Near Eastern religion: SHR 65. Lei 1995, Brill. xxiv-406 p.; 10 fig. ƒ 175. 90-04-10235-3 [NTAb 40,p.176].

428 ᴱ**Kselman** Thomas, Belief in [the course of] history; innovative approaches to European and American religion. ND 1992, Univ. x-309 p. $ 36. 0-268-00687-3. -- ᴿJEH 46 (1995) 133s (R.W. *Scribner:* 8 art.; R. ORSI fascinating on St.Jude in 1929-65 US).

429 ᴱ**LaCocque** André, Commitment and commemoration; Jews, Christians, Muslims in dialogue [ChTheolSem]. Ch 1994, Exploration. viii-151 p. $ 26. -- ᴿZAW 107 (1995) 524 (tit.pp.).

430 ᴱ**Law** Jane Marie, Religious reflections on the human body [... also in Gnosticism, Buddhism, Islam]. Bloomington 1995, Indiana Univ. xiv-314 p. $ 35; pa. $ 15. 0-253-33263-X: -20902-1 [ThD 43,84].

431 ᴱ**Lorizio** Giuseppe, *Galantino* Nunzio, Metodologia teologica; avviamento allo studio e alla ricerca pluridisciplinare. CinB 1994, Paoline. 487 p. Lᵐ 35. 88-215-2796-4. -- ᴿCivCatt 146 (1995,2) 93-95 (G. *Marchesi*); ZkT 117 (1995) 353s (K.H. *Neufeld*)

432 ᴱ**Marc'hadour** Germain, Le lexique chrétien 2: CahLingRel 12. Angers 1993, Univ l'Ouest. 167 p. 0087-7290. -- ᴿEThL 71 (1995) 256s (J.E. *Vercruysse*).

433 ᴱ**Mattioli** Umberto, La donna nel pensiero cristiano antico: Aug(ustinianum)R 34 (1994) [12 art.]. Genova 1992, Marietti. -- ᴿAugR 34 (1994) 503-511 (Kari E. *Børresen*).

434 **Metz** Johann-Baptist, *Moltmann* Jürgen, Faith and the future; [32 Concilium-reprint] essays in theology, solidarity and modernity. Mkn/L 1995, Orbis/SCM. xvii-306 p. £ 15. 1-57075-016-5 / 0-334-02600-8. -- ᴿ*TBR 8,1 (1995s) 25 (M.H. *Creasey*).

435 ᴱ**Mieth** Dietmar, Moraltheologie im Abseits ? Antwort auf die Enzyklika 'Veritatis splendor': QDisp 153. FrB 1994, Herder. 315 p. DM 48 pa. -- ᴿTrierTZ 104 (1995) 240 (H. *Weber*).

436 ᴱ**Möller** Christian, Geschichte der Seelsorge in Einzelporträts, I (von Hiob bis Thomas von Kempen]. Gö 1994, Vandenhoeck & R. 358 p. -- ᴿTPQ 143 (1995) 197s.200 (P.*Hofer*).

437 ᴱ**Muir** Elizabeth G., *Whitely* Marian F., Changing roles of women within the Christian Church in Canada [17 art.]. Toronto 1995, Univ. xv-391 p. $ 60: pa. $ 28. 0-8020-0669-8: -7623-9 [ThD 43,60].

438 ^E**Nettler** Ronald I., Studies in Muslim-Jewish relations I. (Schweiz) 1993, Harwood. xi-205 p. 3-7186-5283-8. -- ^RJSSt 40 (1995) 181-3 (S.C. *Reif*); Sefarad 55 (1995) 402-4 (Esperanza *Alfonso*).

439 *Ottolini* Enzo V., *al.*, Cristianesimo, religioni e religioni: Sem. Bergamo Quad. 11. Mi 1993 Glossa. 152 p. L^m 18. 88-7105-026-6. -- ^RGreg 76 (1995) 195s (J. *Dupuis*: danger de faire dire trop -- mais aussi trop peu -- aux documents du Magistère)

440 ^E**Pallath** Paul, Church and its most basic element. R 1995, Herder. vii-212 p. L^m 20. 88-85876-24-2 [ThRv 92,84, tit.pp.].

441 ^E**Pfammatter** Josef, *Christen* Eduard [Chur/Luzern Fak.], Was willst du von mir, Frau ? Maria in heutiger Sicht: ThBer 21. Wü 1995, Echter. 142 p. DM 29,80. 3-7228-0357-8 [ThRv 92,84, titles, pp.].

442 ^E**Phillips** Timothy R., *Okholm* Dennis L., Christian apologetics in the postmodern world. DG 1995, InterVarsity. 138 p. $ 15 pa. 0-6308-1600-X. -- ^RChrSchR 25 (1995s) 379s (L.R. *McCormick*).

443 ^E**Pineda** Ana María, *Schreiter* Robert, Dialogue rejoined; theology and ministry in the United States Hispanic reality [< Chicago Catholic Theological Union project]. ColMn 1995, Liturgical. vii-187 p. $ 16 [RStR 22,225, J.T. *Ford*].

443* ^E**Pricoco** Salvatore, Monaci filosofi e santi [14 saggi 1974-89]: Armarium 1. Soveria Mannelli 1992, Rubbettino. 383 p. -- ^RRS(to)LR 31 (1995) 330-3 (Anna Maria *Berruto*)

444 ^E**Regan** Hilary D., *Torrance* Alan J., Christ and context; the confrontation between Gospel and culture. E 1993, Clark. 269 p. £ 14. 0-567-29235-5, -- ^R*TBR 8,1 (1995s) 39 (T. *Gorringe*, '292235'; stimulating, not of one mind; badly proofread}.

445 ^E**Riess** Richard. Abschied von der Schuld ? Zur Anthropologie und Theologie von Schuldbewusstsein, Opfer und Versöhnung: ThAkzente 1. Stu 1995, Kohlhammer. 272 p. DM 35. 3-17-013908-8 [ThRv 92,265].

446 ^E**Sedgwick** Peter, God in the city; reflections from the [Canterbury] Archbishop's urban theology group. L 1995, Mowbray. xix-218 p. £ 13. 0-264-67397-2 [*TBR 9/1,39, R.*Fernandez]*.

447 ^E**Segal** Robert A., The allure of Gnosticism; the Gnostic experience in Jungian psychology and contemporary culture [16 art., some reprinted]. Ch 1995, Open Court. xii-228 p. $ 39; pa. $ 18. 0-8126-92772; -8-0 [ThD 43,55].

448 ^E**Simon** M., Le peau de l'âme; intelligence artificielle et neurosciences; approches pluridisciplinaires. P 1994, Cerf. F 195. -- ^RRevSR 69 (1995) 411s (Marie-Jo *Thiel*).

449 ^E**Swatos** William H.^J, Religion and democracy in Latin America [10 art. < SocAn, mostly on 'base ecclesial communities']. New Brunswick 1995, Transaction. x-163 p. $ 20. 1-56000-803-9 [ThD 43,286].

450 ^E**Tang** Edmond, *Wiest* Jean-Paul, The Catholic Church in modern China; perspectives. Mkn 1993. Orbis. xvii-260 p. -- ^RHeythJ 36 (1995) 234s (E. *Ryden*; useful despite repetitions).

451 ^E**Thorogood** Bernard, Gales of changing, responding to a shifting missionary context; the story of the London missionary society 1945-1977. Geneva 1994, WCC. viii-345 p. Fs 10,50. 2-8254-1126-4. -- ^RET 106 (1994s) 283 (K. *Cracknell*).

452 ^E**Townes** Emilie M., A troubling in my soul; womanist perspectives on evil and suffering. Mkn 1993, Orbis. 257 p. -- ^RUnSemQ 48,1 (1994) 167-177 (A.A. *NcFarlane*).

453 ^E**Verbeke** Werner, *al.*, The use and abuse of eschatology in the Middle Ages: MLSt 15. Lv 1988, Univ. ix-513 p. 90-6186-259-0. -- ^REThL 70 (1994) 185s (R. *Wielockx*: tit.pp.; résumés).

454 ᴱWengert Timothy J., *Brockwell* Charles W.ᴶ, Telling the churches' stories; ecumenical perspectives on writing Christian history [14 principles, 3 test-cases: *Norris* F. on Arianism, *McKee* E.A. on Protestant Reformer Katharina Schütz ᴢᴇʟʟ, & *Hennesey* J. on Catholic theology]. ɢʀ 1995, Eerdmans. xxii-134 p. $ 15. 0-8028-0556-.. [RStR 22,339, J.T. *Ford*].

455 ᴱWillis Wesley R., *Master* John R., Issues in dispensationalism. Ch 1994, Moody. 271 p. $ 25. -- ʀBS 152 (1995) 98-100 (D.L. *Bock*).

456 ᴱWood Diana, The Church and childhood. Ox 1995, Blackwell. 530 p. £ 40; pa. £ 15. 0-631-19586-X; -7-4. -- ʀ*TBR 8,1 (1995s) 48 (L. *Houlden*).

A1.5 *Plurium compilationes* **philologicae** *vel* **archaeologicae**

457 Alvar Jaime, *al.*, Los enigmas de Tarteso. M 1993, Cátedra. 303 p., 5 fig. -- ʀSyria 72 (1995) 286-9 (H. de *Contenson*).

458 ᴱBellebaum Alfred, Vom guten Leben; Glücksvorstellungen in Hochkulturen. B 1994, Akademie. S.59-113, *Lang* Bernhard, Religion und menschliche Glückserfahrung; zur alttestamentlichen Theorie des Glücks.

459 ᴱBennett David C., *al.*. Subject, voice and ergativity; selected essays. L 1995, [B]SOAS. vi-262 p.

460 ᴱCalame Claude, Figures grecques de l'intermédiaire [malgré la logica binaria polarisée] 1992 J 9,12548: ʀEM(erita) 63 (1995) 166-9 (Ana *Iriarte*).

461 ᴱDavies W. Vivian, *Schofield* Louise, Egypt, the Aegean and the Levant; interconnections in the second millennium ʙᴄ. L 1995, British Museum. viii-156 p. 0-7141-0987-8.

462 Dettenhofer M.H., Reine Männersache ? Frauen in Männerdomänen der antiken Welt. Köln 1994, Böhlau. 266 p.; 10 fig. ᴅᴍ 58. -- ʀCLR 45 (1995) 356s (Gillian *Clark*).

463 ᴱDever William G., Preliminary excavation reports: Sardis, Bir Umm Fawakhir, Tell el-Umeiri, the combined Caesarea excavations, and Tell Dothan: ᴀᴀSOR 52. NHv 1995, ᴀSOR. [vi-] 190 p. 0-7885-0099-6

464 ᴱDillon M., *Garland* L., Ancient Greece; [translated] social and historical documents from archaic times to the death of Socrates (c. 800-399 ʙ.ᴄ.). L 1994, Routledge. xv-472 p.; 4 maps. £ 40; pa. £ 15. -- ʀCLR 45 (1995) 93s (Jane *Sherwood*).

465 Fantham Elaine, *al.*, Women in the classical world; image and text. Ox 1994, UP. xii-430 p.; 2 maps. $ 35. -- ʀCJ 91 (1995s) 76s (Susan *Treggiari*).

466 ᴱField J.V., *James* Frank A., Renaissance and revolution; humanists, scholars, craftsmen, and natural philosophers in early modern Europe. C 1993, Univ. 291 p.; ill. $ 50. 0-521-43427-0 [RStR 22,256, Laura *Stern;* 'an excellent collection of essays on the history of science, 1400-1750'].

467 ᴱFraschetti A., Roma al femminile [storia di 9 donne]. Bari 1994, Laterza. 290 p. -- ʀBSL(at) 25 (1995) 652-5 (Claudia *Neri*).

468 ᴱGallo Italo, Seconda miscellanea filologica: Univ. Salerno ant. 17. N 1995, Arte Tipografica. 302 p.

469 ᴱGippert Jost, *Vavroušek* Petr, Studia iranica mesopotamica et anatolica. Praha 1994, Enigma. I. 297 p. 978-80-90170. 17 art.; 7 infra.

470 ᴱHolliday Peter J., Narrative and event in ancient art. C 1993, Univ., .. $ 70. 0-521-43013-5. -- ʀCLB 71,1 (1995) 26-28 (Brunilde Sismondo *Ridgway*).

471 ᴱMarinatos Nanno, *Hägg* Robin, Greek sanctuaries; new approaches. L 1995, Routledge. xv-245 p.

472 ᴱ**Meyer** Marvin, *Mirecki* Paul, Ancient magic and ritual power: ÉPR 129. Lei 1995, Brill. x-477 p. 90-04-10406-2.

473 ᴱ**Morris** Ian, Classical Greece; ancient histories and modern archaeologies [→ 10,300c]: New Directions in Archaeology. C 1994, Univ. £ 40; pa. £ 15. 0-521-39279-9; -45678-9. - ᴿAntiquity 69 (1995) 182-5 (Sarah *Morris*).

474 ᴱ**Olmo Lete** G. del, Mitología y religión del Oriente Antigo II/2, Semitas occidentales (Emar, Ugarit, Hebreos, Fenicios, Arameos, Arabes): EstOr 9. Sabadell 1995, AUSA. 485 p. 84-86329-99-1; -97-4.

475 ᴱ**Rousselle** A., Frontières terrestres, frontières célestes dans l'Antiquité; Études 20. Perpignan 1995, Univ. 457 p.; 52 fig.; 7 maps. F 254 (de Boccard). 2-908912-23-6 [NTAb 40,p.562: CROUZEL on demons in Origen; DUBOIS J. on NHC 1].

476 ᴱ**Sasson** Jack, Civilizations of the Ancient Near East. NY 1995, Scribner's. I. 648 p.: II. to p. 1369; III. -1094, iv. -2791 + index -2966. 0684-19720-0; -1-9; -2-7; -3-5 (all 0-684-19279-9).

477 ᴱ**Serjeant** R.B., *al.*, New Arabian studies. Exeter 1993, Univ. xi-236 p.; ill.; maps. £ 20. - ᴿJRAS (1995) 266s (C.E. *Bosworth:* one on modern Jordan language-switching; *Healey* J.F., Sources for the study of Nabataean law 203-214 . 228-230).

478 ᴱ**Small** David B., Methods in the Mediterranean; historical and archaeological views on texts and archaeology: Mnem supp. 135. Lei 1995, Brill. 294 p.; ill. ƒ 100. - ᴿGaR 42 (1995) 242s (N. *Spivey:* thin).

479 ᴱ**Thiede** Carsten P., *Masuch* Georg, Wissenschaftstheorie und Wissenschaftspraxis; Reichweiten und Zukunftsperspektiven interdisziplinärer Forschung. Pd 1995, Bonifatius. 238 p. DM 40. 3-87088-868-7 [ThRv 92,75, tit.pp.].

480 ᴱ**Wilkins** John, Food in antiquity. Exeter 1995, Univ. xiii-459 p.

A2 *Acta congressuum* .1 **biblica** [*Notitiae*, **reports** → Y7.2]

481 ᴱ**Ajamian** S., *Stone* M.E., Text and context; studies in the Armenian New Testament, conference Univ Pennsylvania 1992: ArmenTSt 13. At 1994, Scholars. vii-124 p. 0-7885-0033-3.

482 ᴱ**Arnold** Duane W.H., *Bright* Pamela, [16 art. on 'instruction on the treatment of the Scriptures' in AUGUSTINE's] De doctrina christiana, a classic of Western culture: 1991 Notre Dame Univ. conference: Christianity and Judaism in antiquity 9. ND 1995, Univ. $ 35. 0-268-00874-4 [ThD 43,163]

483 ᴱ**Beckwith** Roger T., *Selman* Martin J., Sacrifice in the Bible [1987 conference]. Carlisle/GR 1995, Paternoster/Baker. x-186 p. £ 10, 0-85364-611-3. 11 art. - ᴿ*TBR 8,1 (1995s) 9s (M. *Bockmuehl*).

484 BIBLIA: Samuele tra politica e fede: Sorrento 17-20 febb. 1994. Settimello FI 1995, Biblia. [Gli animali, Spoleto 1993 → U25, *Stefani* P.]

485 ᴱ**Bishop** Marilyn E., Religion and disability: essays in Scripture, theology and ethics [Dayton Univ. seminar: *Senior* D., *Macquarrie* J., *Hauerwas* S.]. KC 1995, Sheed & W. x-64 p. $ 7. 1-55612-713-8 [ThD 43.184].

486 ᴱ**Borgeaud** Philippe, *al.*, Le Temple lieu de conflit: CEPOA (Centre d'Étude du Proche-Orient ancient), Univ. Genève colloque Cartigny 1991: Cahier 7. Lv 1994, Peeters. 240 p. 90-6831-682-6. 17 art.; 13 infra.

487 **EBorgen** Peder, *Giversen* Søren, The NT & Hellenistic Judaism: Aarhus, Feb. 6-10, 1992. Aarhus 1995, Univ. 293 p. Dk 230. 87-7288-458-4 [1-85075-740-2, NTAb 40,p.508: RStR 22,245, J.T. *Fitzgerald*]. 14 art.; 5 infra.

488 *EBori* P.C., *Pesce* M., Atti del XX seminario 'Studi sulla letteratura esegetica cristiana e giudaica antica', Sacrofano, 19-21 ottobre 1994; ASEs 12,2 (1995) 231-418.

489 **EBourg** Dominique, *Lion* Antoine, La Bible en philosophe [colloque Centre Thomas More, P 1990]. P 1993, Cerf. 163 p. - **RRTPh** 127 (1995) 392s (Clairette *Karąkash*).

490 **EBraulik** Georg, Bundesdokument und Gesetz; Studien zum Deuteronomium [SBL Münster 1993, with mention of 65th birthday of Norbert LOHFINK]: BibSt 4. FrB 1995, Herder. vi-198 p. DM 82 3-451-33623-0. - **ROTA** 18 (1995) p. 634, with renvoi to summary of each of the 10 art.; ZAW 107 (1995) 524 (tit.pp.)

491 **ECarroll** John T., *al.*, The death of Jesus in early Christianity [< 7 years SBL-group meetings]. Peabody MA 1995, Hendrickson. xviii-318 p. $ 25. 1-56563-151-X [< ThD 43,358].

492 **ECerutti** Maria Vittoria, Apocalittica e gnosticismo: Atti del colloquio internazionale Roma 18-19 giugno 1993. R 1995, SEI. 167 p. 88-8011-057-8.

493 **ECharlesworth** James H., *Weaver* Walter P., Earthing Christologies; from Jesus' parables to Jesus the parable: Faith and Scholarship Colloquies. Ph 1995, Trinity. xiv-111 p. 1-56338-119-2.

494 **EChrostowski** Waldemar (p.5-23; p. 129-132, Eng.), Nowy Testament a judaizm: V Sympozjum 'Kościół a Żydzi i judaizm', AkadTK Warszawa 18-19.V.1993: C(olc)Th 64,2 (1994) 132 p.

495 **ECohen** Shaye J.D., The Jewish family in antiquity [SBL Hellenistic Judaism section 1990s: BJSt 289. At 1993, Scholars. 167 p. $ 41, sb. $ 27. 1-55540-919-9. - BoL (1995) 144 (H.A. *McKay*).

496 **ECrowley** Paul, The concrete foundations of Christianity: Catholic Theological Society of America, Baltimore June 9-12, 1994: Proceedings 49. 244 p. 0069-1267. P.67-79, *Sloyan* Gerard S., presidential address, The Jesus in whom the churches of the apostolic age believed; p.90-99, *Fiorenza* Francis S., The Jesus of piety and the historical Jesus.

497 **EDan** Joseph, *Talmage* Frank, Studies in Jewish mysticism: proceedings of regional conferences UCLA and McGill, April 1978. CM 1982, Association for Jewish Studies. x-220 p. 0-915928-03-0.

498 **EDimant** Devorah, *Schiffman* Lawrence H., Time to prepare the way in the wilderness: [J Hebrew Univ. Institute for Advanced Studies endowed seminar 1989s]: STDJ 16. Lei 1995, Brill. viii-157 p. £ 90. 90-04-10225-6 [< OTA 18 (1995) p. 660, with renvoi to summary of each of the 8 all English articles); JSJ 26 (1995) 351-3 (C. *Martone*: tit.pp.; summaries).

499 **EDirksen** P.B., *Kooij* A van der, The Peshitta as a translation: 2d Symposium, Leiden 19-21 August 1993: Mg P-Inst. 8. Lei 1995, Brill. 240 p. $ 71.50. [OTA 19,p.321, with numbers of the summaries of all 16 articles].

500 **EEdelman** Diana V., You shall not abhor an Edomite for he is your brother; Edom and Seir in history and tradition [SBL-ASOR Kansas City 1991 plus religion/language invited]: Archaeology and Biblical Studies 3. At 1995, Scholars. xiv-190 p. $ 40; pa. $ 25. 0-7885-0063-5. 8 art.; 6 infra.

501 **EEmerton** J.A., [IOSOT] Congress volume, Paris 1992: VT.s 61. Lei 1995, Brill. viii-357 p. 90-04-10259-0 [RStR 22,233].

502 ᴱ**Fabiny** Tibor, Literary theory and biblical hermeneutics [international conference, Pannonhalma Benedictine monastery, July 1991]. Szeged 1992, Univ. 151 p. [J]LT(Ox) 9 (1995) 103s (D. *Jasper*).

503 ᴱ**Felici** Sergio, Esegesi e catechesi nei Padri (secc. IV-VII) [Roma Salesianum 16°, 25-27.III.1993]: BSRel 112. R 1994, LASalesiano. 287 p. Lᵐ 35. 88-213-0285-7. - ᴿEThL 71 (1995) 469s (J. *Verheyden*).

504 ᴱ**Finan** Thomas, *Twomey* Vincent, Spiritual interpretation in the Fathers; letter and spirit: 2d patristic conference, Maynooth 1993. Blackrock/Portland OR 1995, Four Courts. xi-370 p. £ 35. 1-85182-162-7. 14 art. £ 35. - ᴿ*TBR 8,2 (1995s) 50 (H. *Chadwick*: erudite and finely produced).

505 ᴱ**Fornberg** Tord, Bible, hermeneutics, mission; a contribution to the contextual study of Holy Scripture [Lund conference 1994]: MISSIO 10. U 1995, Swedish Missionary Research. v-148 p.; 2 maps. 1101-6701 [NTAb 40, p.510].

506 ᴱ**Geller** M.J., *al.* Studia aramaica; new sources and new approaches [London University College Institute of Jewish Studies conference 1991]: JSSt.s 4. Ox 1995, UP. viii-262 p.; 2 pl. $ 65. 0-19-922194-4 [NTAb 40, p.377].

507 ᴱ**Goldenberg** David M., *al.*, The Dead Sea Scrolls [Ph Center for Judaic studies colloquium May 12-13, 1993: JQR 85 (1994s) 1-271.

508 ᴱ**Greenspoon** Leonard, *Munnich* Oliver, Eighth congress of the International Organization for Septuagint and cognate studies, Paris [17s.VII] 1992: SCSt 41. Atlanta 1995, Scholars. xi-401 p.; p. 171-181, Greenspoon, The IOSCS at 25 years. 0-7885-028-5; pa. -9-3. 24 art.; 5 infra (the rest on separate biblical books). [OTA 19,p.321, with renvoi to summary of each of the 24 papers].

509 ᴱ**Gross** Walter, Jeremia und die 'deuteronomistische Bewegung' [Alttestamentler(innen) Fra St. Georgen, 30. Aug. - 3. Sept. 1993]. Weinheim 1995, Beltz Athenäum. 397 p. DM 98. 3-89547-068-6 [< OTA 18 (1995) p. 621, with renvoi to summary of each of the 14 articles]. S. 318-382, *Lohfink* Norbert, Gab es eine deuteronomistische Bewegung ?.

510 ᴱ**Janowski** Bernd, *Lohfink* Norbert, Religionsgeschichte Israels oder Theologie des Alten Testaments ? [< SBL Leuven 1994 über ALBERTZ R. 1993] = JBTh 10 (1995).

511 ᴱ**Kopf** Ulrich, Historisch-kritische Geschichtsbetrachtung; Ferdinand Christian BAUR [geb. 21.VI.17-72]: 8. Blaubeurer Symposion: TüBUW 40. Sigmaringen 1994, Thorbecke. 247 p. [RHE 91,331, R. *Reinhardt*, tit.pp.]

512 ᴱ**Lovering** Eugene H.ᴶ. SBL 1995 Seminar papers **34**, 131st annual meeting, Nov. 18-21, Philadelphia. Atlanta 1995, Georgia. ix-721 p. 0-7885-0156-9. 41 art., infra.

513 ᴱ**Manns** Frédéric, The sacrifice of Isaac [Gen. 22] in the three monotheistic religions; symposium Jerusalem March 16-17, 1995: SBF.anal 41. J 1995, Franciscan. 202 p. $ 25 [< OTA 19,p.531; NTAb 40,p.545: authors/topics sans pp.]. 19 art.; 4 infra.

514 ᴱ**Marcheselli-Casale** Cesare, (*Ska* Jean Louis, *al.*) Oltre il racconto; esegesi ed ermeneutica alla ricerca del senso: Colloquio Fac.Th. Italia merid. N 1994, D'Auria, 238 p. 13 art.; 6 infra.

515 ᴱ**Moor** J. C. de, Synchronic or diachronic ? a debate on method in Old Testament [9th joint Werkgezelschap-SOTS meeting, Kampen, August 1994]: OTS 34. Leiden 1995, Brill. viii-255 p. $ 67.75. 90-04-10342-2 [OTA 19,p.322; renvoi to the 13 art.]. - ᴿEThL 71 (1995) 435s (J. *Lust*).

516 ᴱ**Muraoka** Takamitsu, Studies in ancient Hebrew semantics: Melbourne Univ. ABR-N.s 4. Lv 1995, Peeters. vii-107 p. - Leš 59 (1995) 253-7 (J. *Blau*, ᴴ)

517 ᴱNel P.J., *Berg* D.J. van den, Concepts of textuality and religious texts [Univ. Orange 13-14 Oct. 1994]; *AcA.s 1. Bloemfontein 1995, Univ. 206 p. 0587-2405. 14 art.; 4 infra.

518 ᴱNiccacci Alviero, Divine promises to the fathers in the three monotheistic religions [symposium Jerusalem 24s.III.1993]: SBF.anal 40. J 1995, Franciscan. 220 p.; bibliog. 210-219. $ 25. 6 art. [NTAb 40, p.545: authors/topics].

519 ᴱOlivetti M.M., Religione, parola, scrittura .. spoken and written word [Castelli-Colloquium, Univ. Roma 3-6. VI. 1992]: Archivio di Filosofia 8. Padova 1992, CEDAM. 554 p. Lᵐ 70. 88-13-17925-1. - ᴿBijdragen 56 (1995) 352s (B. *Vedder*).

520 ᴱPadovese Luigi, Atti del V Simposio di Efeso su S. Giovanni Apostolo: Turchia, la Chiesa e la sua storia 8. R 1995, Antonianum. x-247 p. 12 art.; 3 infra.

521 ᴱPadovese Luigi, Atti del III Simposio di Tarso su S. Paolo Apostolo: Turchia, la Chiesa e la sua storia 9. R 1995, Antonianum. 13 art.; 3 Infra.

522 ᴱPainchaud Louis, *Pasquier* Anne, Les textes de Nag Hammadi et le problème de leur classification: Actes du Colloque, Québec 15-19 sept. 1993: BCNH.ét 3. Lv 1995, Peeters. xiv-337 p. 90-6831-749-0, 14 art.; infra.

523 ᴱPavlincová Helena, *Papoušek* Dalibor, The Bible in cultural context [Czechoslovak AsnRelSt, Brno 1992]. Brno 1994, Czech Society for the Study of Religions. 386 p. $ 52. 80-901823-0-5 44 art. deutsch/Eng. - ᴿZAW 107 (1995) 522 (M. *Köckert*, tit.pp.)

524 ᴱPenna Romano, Apocalittica e origini cristiane; Atti del V convegno di studi neotestamentari (Seiano, 15-18 sett. 1993): RicStoB 7,2 (1995).

525 ᴱPiñero Antonio, *Fernández-Galiano* Dimas, Los manuscritos del Mar Muerto; balance de hallazgos y de cuarenta años de estudios [Guadalajara 1993]. Córdoba 1994, Almendro. 205 p. 84-9005-017-9. - ᴿEstAg 30 (1995) 137s (C. *Mielgo*); EstB 53 (1995) 552 (F. *Pastor-Ramos*).

526 ᴱPrato Gian Luigi, Davide; modelli biblici e prospettive messianiche; Atti dell'VIII convegno di studi veterotestamentari (Seiano, 13-15 sett.1993): RicStoB 7,1 (1995). 203 p.

527 **Prévost** Jean-Pierre présente, Des femmes aussi faisaient route avec lui; perspectives féministes sur la Bible: congrès ACÉBAC 51 (Association catholique des études bibliques au Canada), Nicolet 29 mai - 1 juin 1994: ScB 2. Montréal/P 1995, Paulines/Médiaspaul. 230 p. 2-89420-310-1. 9 art.; 4 infra.

528 ᴱReventlow Henning, *Farmer* William R., Biblical studies and the shifting of paradigms 1850-1914 [1992 Bochum meeting]: JSOT.s 192. Shf 1995, Academic. 297 p. £ 30. 1-85075-532-9. -- ᴿE(xp)T 107 (1995s) 182 (R. *Morgan*: more academic biography than exegesis).

529 ᴱRogerson John W., *al.*, The Bible in ethics; second Sheffield colloquium 1995: JSUT.s 207. Shf 1995, Academic. 379 p. £ 49. 1-85075-573-6. p. 136-163, *Brett* Mark G., Nationalism and the Hebrew Bible.

530 ᴱRumble A.R., *(Anderson* J.J., p. 3-8) The Bible and early English literature from the beginnings to 1500; proceedings of the second G.L. Brook Symposium, Univ. Manchester 1993: BJRL 77,3 (1995). 217 p. + indexes 219-235 (Gale R. *Owen-Crocker*).

531 ᴱSegalla Giuseppe (p.307-313) , Cento anni di studi biblici (1893-1993), L'interpretazione della Bibbia nella Chiesa (Convegno di studi, Padova 17-18 febbraio 1994) : StPat(av) 41,2 (1994) 307-490.

532 ᴱShanks Hershel, Feminist approaches to the Bible [Smithsonian Sept.24,1994 panel: TRIBLE P.; FRYMER-KENSKY T.; MILNE P.; SCHABERG J.] Wsh 1995, Biblical Archaeology Soc. vii-116 p. $ 15. 1-880317-41-9 [< OTA 19,p.322; 3 OT renvois; NTAb 40,p.516].

533 ᴱ**Smith-Christopher** Daniel, Text and experience; towards a cultural exegesis of the Bible [Los Angeles Loyola-Marymount largely Third World conference 1992: BiSe 35. Shf 1995, Academic. 354 p. £ 20. 1-85075-740-2. 19 art.; 5 infra,

534 **SOTS** Bulletin for 1995; *a)* Winter meeting 3-5 Jan.1995; *Jones* Gwilym H., presidential address, Bible translation -- some second thoughts [1988 New Welsh Bible: translators are at the mercy of philological enthusiasts whose readings are beyond objective control]. -- *Thompson* bishop M.E.W., Intercession in OT. -- *Williams* Catrin H., Who may pronounce ⁿ*nî hû'* (rare in OT) ? -- *Moberly* Walter, 1 Sam 3 [does Samuel hear God or Eli ?]. -- *Davies* Eryl W., Num 1 & 26: the 600,000 a usual-type hyperbole. -- *Reif* Stefan C., [Sᴄʜᴇᴄʜᴛᴇʀ's] W.R. Sᴍɪᴛʜ on Jews. -- *Gillingham* Susan E., Exodus in Pss.

535 **SOTS** -- *b)* **Summer** meeting, Bangor 10-13 July: *Jones* Gareth L., Paul of Burgos on Jews. -- *Veijola* Timo, Dt 16,1-8 on Passover. -- *Soggin* J.Alberto, Joseph-geography. -- *Bellinger* Wm. H., Ps 61. -*O'Kane* Martin, Isaiah 'like Moses'. -- *Van Seters* John, Chronicler on Temple. -- *Paradise* Bryan J., Adam the Gardener. -- *Smith* Carol, Samson and Delilah, a parable of power ?. -*Smith-Christopher* Daniel L., Lakota reactions to Daniel. -- *Haran* Menahem, OT canon, selection or collection ?

536 ᶠSᴛʀᴇᴄᴋᴇʀ Georg 65 Gb. Symposion, Bilanz und Perspektiven gegenwärtiger Auslegung des Neuen Testaments [21.-23.III.1994; er starb 19.VI], ᴱ**Horn** Friedrich W.; ʙᴢɴᴡ 75. B 1995, de Gruyter. x-288 p.; Bibliog. (Strecker) 279-288; (allgem.) 273-8. 3-11-014595-7. 9 art. (4 infr) + 2 by Strecker and *Lüdemann* Gerd 1-6 about him.

537 ᴱ**Trublet** J., La Sagesse biblique, de l'Ancien au Nouveau Testament; Actes du XVᵉ Congrès de l'ᴀᴄꜰᴇʙ (Paris 1993): LDiv 160. P 1995, Cerf. 617 p. F 245 pa. 2-204-05153-5 [NTAb 40,p.331].

538 ᴱ**Ulrich** Eugene, *VanderKam* James, The community of the renewed covenant; the Notre Dame symposium on the Dead Sea Scrolls [April 25-27, 1993]: ChrJudAnt 10. ND 1994, Univ. xviii-290 p. $ 30. 0-268-00802-7 [< OTA 18 (1995) p. 438, with renvoi to summaries of all 14 papers]. -- ᴿJSJ 26 (1995) 388-393 (A.S. van der *Woude*).

539 ᶠVᴏɢᴛ H.-J.: Oʀɪɢᴇɴᴇs, vir ecclesiasticus; Symposion .. , ᴱ**Geerlings** Wilhelm, *König* Hildegard: Hereditas 9. Bonn 1995, Borengässer. 102 p. ᴅᴍ 32. 3-923946-27-9 [ThRv 92,78; RHE 90 (1995) 308*]. -- p. 95-100, *Ziegler* G., Der 'iubilus'.

540 ᴱ**Wise** Michael G., *al.*, Methods of investigation of the Dead Sea Scrolls and the Qumran site; present realities and future prospects [conference ɴʏ Dec. 14-17,1992]: Annals 722. NY 1994, NY Academy of Sciences. xiv-514 p. $ 125. -- ᴿCBQ 57 (1995) 848-850 (J.R. *Davila*; titles, pp.)

541 ᴱ**Wissink** J.B.M., (Dis)continuity and (de)construction; reflections on the meaning of the past in crisis situations [Cath. Univ. conference, Utrecht 1993]. Kampen 1995, Kok Pharos. v-198 p. ƒ 62. 90-390-0212-6 [NTAb 40,p.517].

A2.3 **Acta congressuum theologica** [reports → Y7.4]

542 ᴱ**Agus** Aharon R.E., *Assmann* Jan, Ocular desire / Sehnsucht des Auges [1990 Bar-Ilan Univ. colloquium, 'Apprehension of the divine; theological structuring of the sense of reality']: Yearbook for Religious Anthropology. B 1994, Akademie. 187 p. ᴅᴍ 68. 3-05-002646-4. - ᴿBoL (1995) 109 (L.L. *Grabbe*).

543 ᴱ**Aletti** M., Religione o psicoterapia ? Nuovi fenomeni e movimenti religiosi alla luce della psicologia: Atti del V convegno 'Psicologia e Religione' della Società Italiana di

Psicologia, Roma 22-23 ottobre 1994. R 1994, LAS. 402 p. L^m 50. 88-213-0294-6. - ^RAng 72 (1995) 627s (A. *Pascucci*).

544 ^EAyestarán José C., Postmodernidad, XII Semana teológica, 21-23.III.1995: Iter 6,1 (Caracas 1995). 183 p.

545 ^EBarber Malcolm, The military orders; fighting for the faith and caring for the sick [41 art. < 1992 conference org. Jonathan RILEY-SMITH]. Aldershot 1994, Variorum. xxviii-399 p.; 47 fig. $ 99.50. 0-86078-438-X [RStR 22,74, A. *Thompson*: rather specialized; not on the military or the Holy Land; ThD 43,77].

546 ^EBarot R., Religion and ethnicity; minorities and social change in the metropolis [Bristol conference 1991]. Kampen 1993. Kok Pharos. 203 p. - ^RG(ereformeerd)TT 95 (1995) 91s (H. *Mintjes*).

547 *Best* Thomas F., presentation, Papers from the meeting on 'Ecclesiology and ethics', Jerusalem, November 1994: E(cu)R 47,2 (1995) 127 (-187; 189-231, 1994 Colombo meeting on 'ethnicity and nationalism').

548 ^EBezançon Jean-Noël, Au carrefour des religions; rencontre, dialogue, annonce; ISPC [Inst. (Cath. Paris) Supérieur de Pastorale]; *ScThR 4. P 1995, Beauchesne. 162 p. 2-7010-1328-3. 11 art.; 3 infra.

549 ^EBirtel Frank T., Reasoned faith: [12 Tulane] essays on the interplay of faith and reason. NY 1993, Crossroad. viii-231 p. $ 20. - ^RCritRR 7 (1994) 563s (tit.pp.).

550 ^EBowman A.K., *Woolf* G., Literacy and power in the ancient world [13 1992 Oxford lectures] 1994 → 10,294c [not 2944 as Index]: ^RJRS 85 (1995) 264 (M. *Maas*).

551 ^EBreid Franz, Gottes Schöpfung [Linzer Sommerakademie 1994]. Steyer 1994, Ennsthaler. 376 p. 3-85068-444-X. - ^RForKT 11 (1995) 236s (M. *Hauke*).

552 ^EBremer J.M., *al.*, Hidden futures; death and immortality in ancient Egypt, Anatolia, the classical, biblical and Arabic-Islamic world [Institute for Mediterranean Studies symposium, Amsterdam Dec. 1992]. Amst 1994, Univ. 253 p.; ill. *f* 49,50. -- ^RDiscEg 33 (1995) 173s (C. *Sturtewagen*); OLZ 90 (1995) 529-532 (L. *Wächter*).

553 ^EBrittan Samuel, *Hamlin* Alan, Market capitalism and moral values: Keele 1993. Aldershot 1995, Elgar. xii-155 p. $ 64. 1-85898-080-1 [ThD 43,58].

554 ^EBrück Michael von, *Werbick* Jürgen, Traditionsabbruch -- Ende des Christentums ? [Kolloquium Siegen, Okt. 1993]. Wü 1994, Echter. 176 p. DM 34. - ^RTPQ 143 (1995) 423 (H. *Sauer*).

555 ^EBurkert Walter, *Stolz* Fritz, Hymnen der Alten Welt im Kulturvergleich [Tagung Religionsgeschichte Zürich 1991]: OBO 131. FrS/Gö 1994, Univ./VR. 124 p. 3-7278- 0229-9 / 3-525-53766-2. - ^RCBQ 57 (1995) 618s (S.A. *Wiggins*); ETRel 70 (1995) 263 (Françoise *Smyth*).

556 ^ECalvo Moralejo Gaspar, secr., La Redemptoris Mater de Juan Pablo II; análisis y perspectivas [Sigüenza 6-10.IX.1994] : EstMar 61 (1995). 302 p.; 16 art., 2 infra.

557 ^ECampbell Ted A., Sanctification in the Benedictine and Methodist traditions. World Ecumenical Conference, Rome July 4-10, 1994: AsbTJ 50,2 (1995) & 51.1 (1996). 240 p., numbered apart. 18 art.: 4 infra.

558 ^ECassio A.C., *Poccetti* P., Forme di religiosità e tradizioni sapienziali in Magna Grecia, Atti del Convegno [Ist.Univ.Or.B Napoli, 14-15 dic. 1993: AION 15. Pisa 1995, Ist. Poligrafici. 219 p.

559 Castelli Elizabeth A., ^EOcker Christopher, Visions and voyeurism; holy women and the politics of sight in early Christianity: Colloquy NS 2. Berkeley 1995, Center for Hermeneutical Studies. [iv-] 69 p. 0-89242-064-2

560 ᴱCollins J.J., *Fishbane* M., Death, ecstasy and other worldly journeys [< I. CULIANU conference Chicago 1991]. Albany 1995, SUNY. xvi-423 p. 0-7914-2345-X: -6-8 [NTAb 40, p.374]. - ᴿ*CritRR 8 (1995) 530s (Jouette *Bassler*, tit.pp.).

561 ᴱConsolino Franca E., Pagani e cristiani da Giuliano l'Apostata al sacco di Roma: Atti Rende 12-13 nov. 1993. Severia Mannelli CZ 1995, Rubbettino. [viii-] 331 p. 88-7284-380-4. 20 art.; 5 infra.

562 ᴱCornette K., *Depoortere* K., Postmoderniteit en theologie [Vliebergh aug. 1992]: Nikè 29. Lv 1993, Acco. 192 p. ƒ 42.25. 90-334-2850-4. - ᴿG(ereformeerd)TT 95 (1995) 43 (J.B.G. *Jonkers*); TTh 35 (1995) 85 (A. van *Harskamp*).

563 Cristianismo y cultura en los años 90 [a l'Europa dels anys 90, 2° simposio Maragall], ᵀ*Gabalda Irujo* Albert. M 1993, PPC. 211 p. pt 975. 84-288-1196-7. - ᴿ*ActuBbg 31 (1994) 55 (C. *Sarrias*).

564 ᴱCrowley Paul B., Evil and hope, proceedings of the [anniversary] fiftieth annual convention of the Catholic Theological Society of America, NYC June 8-11, 1995: CTS 50. [v-]338 p. 0069-1267 p.1-15 presidential address, *Haight* Roger. [ᴱCrowley, CTS 49 Baltimore June 9-12, 1994, 'Jesus and Salvation' 244 p.].

565 ᴱCrowley Paul, Ecumenism, interreligious relations, and cultural diversity: Catholic Theological Society of America, San Antonio June 10-13, 1993: Proceedings 48. v-202 p. 0069-1267. P.65-83, *Cahill* Lisa S., presidential address, Feminist ethics and the challenge of cultures.

566 ᴱDean Thomas, Religious pluralism and truth, [AAR 1970s-80s Working Group, 14] essays on cross-cultural philosophy of religion. Albany 1995, SUNY. xi-271 p. $ 59.50; pa. $ 20. 0-7914-2123-6: -4-4 [ThD 42,385].

567 ᴱDekker E., *al.*, Openbaring en werkelijkheid; systematische theologie tussen empirische werkelijkheid en christelijke zinervaring [18.IV.1994]. Zoetermeer 1994, Boeken-C. 119 p. ƒ 30. 90-239-0295-5 - ᴿTTh 35 (1995) 301s (W. *Logister*).

568 ᴱDelgado Mariano, *Lutz-Bachmann* Matthias, Theologie der Erfahrung der Gnade [K. RAHNER 10. Todestag, FU Berlin]. Hildesheim 1994, Benno. 305 p. DM 48. 3-87065-756-1.- ᴿZkT 117 (1995) 120-2 (A.*Batlogg*, auch über Freiburger Tagung 1994 ᴱRaffelt A.).

569 El diálogo entre las ciencias y la fe en el panorama actual. La Laguná Tenerife 1995, Univ. 363 p. - ᴿBurg 36 (1995) 589s (E. *Bueno*).

570 ᴱDick John A.R., *Richardson* Anne, William TYNDALE and the law [1991 Philadelphia meeting, 10 art.]: SCES 25. Kirksville MO 1994, SCJ. xi-135 p. $ 35. 0-940474-26-3. - ᴿJThS 46 (1995) 830s (P.N. *Brooks*).

571 ᴱDorival Gilles, *Le Boulluec* Alain, Origeniana sexta; ORIGÈNE et la Bible [Chantilly 30 août - 3 sept. 1993]: BETL 118. Lv 1995, Univ. xii-865 p. 90-6186-718-5.

572 ᴱEgerton George, Anglican essentials; reclaiming faith within the Anglican Church of Canada [Montreal conference June 1994]. .. 1995, Anglican Book Centre. 320 p. $ 15. 1-55126-095-3. : E(xp)T 107 (1995s) 91 (S. *Tucker:* insufficiently theological.

573 ᴱEnglish Edward D., Reading and wisdom; the De doctrina christiana of AUGUSTINE in the Middle Ages [conference 1991, 11 art.]: Conferences MdvSt 6. ND 1995, Univ. xi-188 p. $ 30. 0-268-01650-X [ThD 43,184].

574 ᴱFarina M., *Mazzarello* M.L., Gesù il Signore; la specificità di Gesù Cristo in un tempo di pluralismo religioso; Atti del Convegno di aggiornamento teologico promosso dalla Pontificia Facoltà di Scienze dell'Educazione Auxilium, Roma 29 aprile - 3 maggio 1992: Prisma 12. R 1992, Libreria Ateneo Salesiano. 243 p. Lᵐ 25. - ᴿAsprenas 42 (1995) 450-2 (A. *Russo*).

575 ^E**Fisichella** R., Noi crediamo; per una teologia dell'atto di fede [primo simposio della SIRT, Società Italiana per le Ricerca Teologica, Roma 1992]. R 1993, Dehoniane. 196 p. L^m 22.- ^RAsprenas 42 (1995) 448s (S. *Cipriani*).

576 ^E**Fisichella** Rino, [Atti: attesi], L'identità della teologia fondamentale fra fede e ragione, 20-23 sett. 1995. R, Pont. Univ. Gregoriana. - ^R*AnT 9 (1995) 465-470 (G. *Tanzella-Nitti*).

577 ^E**Fodor** A., *Shivtiel* A., Proceedings of the colloquium on popular customs and the monotheistic religions in the Middle East and North Africa, Budapest 19-25 Sept. 1993: The Arabist 9s. Budapest 1993, Univ. $ 35. - ^ROLZ 90 (1995) 187s (C.E.*Bosworth*).

578 FORSYTH Peter T. (1848-1921) mem., Aberdeen symposium 1995, Justice the true and only mercy. E 1995, Clark. $ 40. 0-567-09703-X [ThD 43,275].

579 ^E**Free** Katharine B, The formulation of Christianity by conflict through the ages [1993 Los Angeles Loyola Marymount conference chiefly on recent Eastern Europe]: Symposium 34.. Lewiston NY 1995, Mellen. viii-278 p. $ 90. 0-7734-8926-6 [< ThD 43,266].

579* **Gestrich** Christoph, *al.*, Gehirntod und Organstransplantation als Anfrage an unser Menschenbild, Symposium Berlin 26.-27. Mai 1994: BThZ 12 (1995), Beiheft 147 p.

580 ^E**Ginio** Alisa Meyuhas, Jews, Christians, and Muslims in the Mediterranean world after 1492 [16 art. < Tel Aviv Univ. conference 1991]. L 1992, F.Cass. 293 p. $ 37.50. 0-7146-3492-1 [RStR 22,172, J.*Safran*].

581 **Goldingay** John, Atonement today (St. John's College seminar). L 1995, SPCK. xiii-285 p. £ 18. 0-281-04894-0. - ^RE(xp)T 107,3 top choice (1995s) 65s (C.S. *Rodd*).

582 ^E**Greco** Carlo, Cristologia e antropologia in dialogo con Marcello BORDONI [Napoli S. Luigi 1-2.V.1992]. R 1994, A.V.E. 331 p. - ^RFilTeo 9 (1995) 671-3 (S. *Rostagno*).

583 ^E**Griffis** James E., Afro-Anglicanism: identity, integrity and impact in the decade of evangelism [2d international Powell conference, Cape Town 18-15 Jan. 1995]: A(ngl)ThR 77,4 (1995) 443-554.

584 ^E**Hanley** John C., Reform and counter-reform; dialectics of the Word in Western Christianity [14 papers from Santa Clara conference for the 450th anniversary of the founding of the Jesuits and of KNOX's Reformation. B 1994, Mouton de Gruyter. x-343 p. - ^R*TBR 8,2 (1995s) 48 (D. *Nichols*, dubious).

585 ^E**Hatem** Jad, Les Sociétés du Moyen-Orient comme lieu théologique: IIe Symposium, Harissa 11-13.XI.1988. Beyrouth 1991, St. Paul. - ^RMélSR 52 (1995) 203-6 (C. *Cannuyer*).

586 ^E**Hawley** John S., Fundamentalism and gender [< Columbia Univ. faculty seminar]. NY 1994, Oxford-UP. 220 p. - ^RUnSemQ 48,1 (1994) 178-182 (M. *Bagger*).

587 ^E**Helleman** Wendy E., Hellenization revisited, a Christian response within the Greco-Roman world [Toronto 1991 on Christianity and the classics]. Lanham 1994, UPA. 544 p.-- ^RPhoenix 49 (Tor 1995) 368-370 (N.M. *Kennell*).

588 ^E**Hille** R., *Troeger* E., Die Einzigartigkeit Jesu Christi als Grundfrage der Theologie und missionarische Herausforderung [Arbeitskreis für evangelikale Theologie 7., Aug. 1991]. Wu/Giessen 1993, Brockhaus/Brunnen. 166 p. DM 29. 3-417-29377-4 / 3-7655-9377 X. - ^RTTh 35 (1995) 305 (J. van *Lin*).

589 ^E**Hilpert** Conrad, *Werbick* Jürgen, Mit dem Anderen leben; Wege zur Toleranz. Dü 1995, Patmos. 275 p. DM 49. 3-491-77967-7 [TR 91,83].

590 ^E**Hinsdale** Mary Ann, *Kaminski* Phyllis H., Women and theology: CollThS Annual 40. Mkn 1995, Orbis. xiii-274 p. $ 20. 1-57075-035-1 [ThD 43,393].

591 ^E**Horst** Pieter W. van der, Aspects of religious contact and conflict in the ancient world [conference Utrecht 16-17 Dec. 1993]: Utrechtse ThReeks 31. Utrecht 1995, Univ. 166 p.; ill. *f* 39 pa. 90-72235-32-0 [NTAb 40,p.566]. 11 art.; 4 infra.

592 [E]**Hsiu Po-Chia** R., *Lehmann* Hartmut, In and out of the ghetto; Jewish-Gentile relations in Late Medieval and early modern Germany [17 art. < 1991 UCLA conference + 5 comments]: Wsh German Hist.Inst. C 1995, Univ. xx-330 p.; ill. $ 65. 0-521-47064-1 [RStR 22,256, H.C.E. *Midelfort*].

593 [E]**Hurtado** Larry, Goddesses in religions and in modern debate [colloquium 1988]: University of Manitoba Studies in Religion 1. At 1990, Scholars.

594 [E]**Imhof** Arthur E., *Weinknecht* Rita, Erfüllt leben -- in Gelassenheit streben; Geschichte und Gegenwart [Symposium Berlin, Freie Universität 23.-25. Nov. 1993]: BHistSt 19. B 1994, Duncker & H. 507 p. DM 148. - [R]Modern Believing [continuing the numbering of Modern Churchman] 36,1 (1995) 47s (Hanns *Engelhardt*).

595 [E]**James** Wendy, The pursuit of certainty; religious and cultural formulations; Social Anthropologists; 4th decennial, Oxford 1993. L 1995, Routledge. xii-316 p. $ 20. 0-415-10791-1 [ThD 43,382].

596 [E]**Junker-Kenny** Maureen, Christian resources of hope (1993 Dublin Trinity College lectures). Blackrock 1995, Columba. 131 p. £ 9. 1-85607-128-6. - [R]*TBR 8,1 (1995s) 31s (T. *Gray*).

597 **Kaiser** Philipp, *Peters* D. Stefan, Organismus -- Evolution -- Mensch; ein Gespräch zwischen Philosophie, Naturwissenschaft und Theologie: EichB 27. Rg 1995, Pustet. 224 p. DM 62. 3-7917-1458-9. S. 125-142, *Diedrich* Friedrich, Überlegungen zur alttestamentlichen Anthropologie; - S. 143-222. *Glässer* Alfred, Die Bestimmung des Menschen; Schöpfung, Erlösung, Vollendung [ThRv 92,171].

598 *Kapłaństwo* .. Priesthood in early Christianity [29-30.X. 1991: Vox Patrum 24-29 (Lublin 1993-5) 9-453; 499-555, bibliog, (591-637 Polish; S. *Longosz).*

599 **Kaufmann** Franz-Xaver [p.9-34], *Zingerle* Arnold [p.189-208], Vaticanum II und Modernisierung; historische, theologische und soziologische Perspektiven. Pd 1995, Schöningh. 340 p. DM 58 pa. 3-506-74252-3 [ThRv 92,175, tit.pp.].

600 [E]**Kilner** John F., *al.*, Bioethics and the future of medicine; a Christian appraisal [Center for Human Dignity, Bannockburn IL conference, 23 art.]. GR/Carlisle 1995, Eerdmans/Paternoster. xii-313 p. $ 19. 0-8028-4081-7/ [ThD 43,157].

601 [E]**Klueting** Harm, *al.*, Katholische Aufklärung; Aufklärung im katholischen Deutschland [Trier Tagung 1988]. Ha 1993, Meiner. vii-443 p. DM 138. 3-7873-1107-6. - [R]JEH 46 (1995) 160s (W.R. *Ward).*

602 [E]**Kremer** Jacob [11-45, Umkämpftes 'Ja' zur Bibelwissenschaft], Aufbruch des Zweiten Vatikanischen Konzils heute, Ringvorlesung Wien. Inns 1993, Tyrolia. 180 p. - [R]AHC 26 (1994)210-2 (M.*Hauke).*

602* [E]**Krieg** Robert A., Romano GUARDINI (1885-1968); proclaiming the faith in a modern world (Notre Dame conference 1994). Ch 1995, Liturgy Training. viii-118 p. $ 15 pa. 1-56854-106-6 [ThD 43,185].

603 **Lacunza Balda** Justo, The conference on religions in the Sudan, Khartoum, April 26-30, 1993 (review and evaluation): Encounter 201 (R 1994) 3-26.

604 [E]**Lewis** Harold, Afro-Anglicanism; identity, integrity and imapact in the decade of evangelism: 2d international conference, Cape Town West Univ., 19-25 Jan. 1995: ATR 77,4 (1995) 443-554.

605 [E]**Logan** James C., Theology and evangelism in the Wesleyan tradition [1992 international conference, Atlanta]. Nv 1994, Kingswood. 223 p. $ 15. 0-687-411395-8. - [R]*TBR 8,1 (1995s) 46 (G.S. *Wakefield).*

606 ᴱ**Lorizio** Giuseppe, Morte e sopravvivenza, in dialogo con Xavier TILLIETTE [seminario RasT, Napoli 30.IV-1.V.1993]. R 1995, A.V.E. 434 p. Lᵐ 38. - ᴿRasT 36 (1995) 629s (G. *Ancona*); RivScRel 9 (1995) 432-4 (D. *Scaramuzzi*).

607 ᴱ**Lowe** Malcolm, Orthodox Christians and Jews on continuity and renewal; the third academic meeting between Orthodoxy and Judaism [Athens March 21-24, 1993]; Immanuel 26s (1994). 195 p. 0302-8127.

608 ᴱ**Macek** Petr, Universale Kirche und Kirche in der Region (Heidelberg, 19.-21. Mai 1995); C(omm)V 37,3 (1995) 165-280.

609 ᴱ**McGregor** Bede, *Norris* Thomas, The beauty of Christ; an introduction to the theology of Hans von BALTHASAR [international conference Maynooth 1992]. E 1994, Clark. xi-277 p. £ 20. 0-567-009697-1. - ᴿET 106 (1994s) 153s (W.D. *Hudson*; 'Is this a release into ecstasy or a retreat from rationality ?' -- says as much about the reviewer as about the book).

610 *Majdańaki* abp Kazimierz, ᴾ L'Église au service de la famille [Wsz 14-17.IV.1994]: AtK(ap) 124 (1995) 166-179 (-251, *al*).

611 ᴱ**Manna** Salvatore, Atti XI colloquio, Le chiese cristiane e le sfide delle religioni, 13-14 giugno 1994: Nicolaus 22 (1995) 5-8 (-130).

612 [*Manthadam* John p.23-35] Impact of the 1844 synod of Pondicherry; seminar Bangalore 14-16 Oct. 1994 : I(nd)TS 32 (1995) 1-173.

613 ᴱ**Martin** Luther, Religious transformations and socio-political change; Eastern Europe and Latin America [26 of the 27 papers, IAHR Aug. 1991, Burlington, Univ. Vermont]: Religion and Society 33. B/NY 1993, Mouton de Gruyter. xiv-457 p. - ᴿSR 24 (1995) 215s (M. *Rumscheidt*).

614 ᴱ**Martin** Ralph, *Williamson* Peter. JOHN PAUL II and the new evangelization; how you can bring the good news to others [San Francisco conference May 1994]. SF 1995, Ignatius. 290 p. $ 13. 0-89870-536-3 [ThD 43,71].

615 ᴱ**Matthews** Clifford N., *Varghese* Roy A., Cosmic beginnings and human ends; where science and religion meet [23 art., mostly from 1993 Chicago Parliament of the World's Religions]. Ch 1995, Open Court. ix-433 p. $42: pa. $18. 0-8126-9269-1; -70-5 [ThD 42].

616 ᴱ**Ménard** Camil, *Villeneuve* Florent, Dire Dieu aujourd'hui; Actes du colloque de la Société canadienne de théologie, Montréal 1993: Héritage et projet. Montréal 1994, Fides. 352 p. $ 35. 2-7621-1734-8.- ᴿRHPhR 75 (1995) 373 (T. *Pfrimmer*).

617 La mission à la rencontre des religions; colloque intercontinental Chevilly-Larue 12-16 sept. 1994: Spiritus 36,138 (1995). 164 p.

618 ᴱ**Molette** Charles, La foi de Marie, Mère du Rédempteur [congrès Rocamadour 1994]: Études Mariales 51. P 1995, Médiaspaul. 138 p. 2-7172-0531-6.

619 **Murphy** B.J.[p.7-9], *al.*, Ecumenical symposium '95: *Hekima Review 13 (Nairobi 1995) 7-24 [NTAb 40,p.199].

620 ᴱ**Neusner** Jacob, Religion and the social order; what kinds of lessons does history teach ? [SFL conference Feb. 19-22,1994]. Atlanta 1995, Scholars. 302 p. $ 90. 0-7885-0054-6 [JBL 107,571 adv: titles]

621 ᴱ**Nichols** Francis W., Christianity and the stranger; historical essays: SFla-Rochester-St.Louis Studies on Religion and the Social Order 12. At 1995, Scholars. [viii-] 297 p. 0-7885-0125-9.

622 ᴱ**Opitz** Claudia, *al.*, Maria in der Welt; Marienverehrung im Kontext der Sozialgeschichte 10.-18. Jahrhundert [Luzern 1992]: Clio Lucernensis 2. Z 1993, Chronos. 340 p. - ᴿChH 64 (1995) 491s (W.V. *Hudon*).

623 [E]**Oroz Reta** José, San Agustín en Oxford (4.°), XI congreso internacional de estudios patrísticos [= [E]*Livingstone* E., Studia Patrística (por lo más vol. 28), 1991/3]: Aug(M) 40 (1995) 5-326.

624 PAOLO VI e la collegialità episcopale: colloquio internaz. Brescia 25-27 sett. 1992: Pubbl. 15. Brescia/R 1995, Ist. Paolo VI / Studium. xvi-389 p. L[m] 70. - [R]NRT 117 (1995) 756-8 (A. *Tourneux*).

625 [E]**Papademetriou** G., Mixed marriage; orthodox perspectives: GOTR 40,3s (1995) 376 p.

626 [E]**Papademetriou** George, (p. 1-6) Saint GREGORY [Nazianzen] the Theologian, Patriarch of Constantinople [Brookline MA Holy Cross Conference]: GOTR 39,1s & 3s (1994), 298 p. 21 art.

627 [E]**Patsavos** Lewis J.., [Brookline MA] Holy Cross Conference, The Council 'in Trullo'; basis for ecclesiastical reform ?: GOTR 40.1s (1995). 146 p. 16 art.

628 PCTSA [→ 564s above] 49 (Santa Clara 1994): 24-35, *Cooke* Bernard, Jesus of Nazareth, norm for the Church; - 65-79, *Sloyan* G.S., The Jesus in whom the churches of the Apostolic Age believed: - 100-4, *Harrington* D.J., Jesus and Wisdom; convergences and challenges [NTAb 39,p.443.442.440].

629 [E]**Peyronel** Susanna, Frontiere geografiche e religiose in Italia; fattori di conflitto e comunicazione nel XVI e XVII secolo, Atti del XXX Convegno di studi sulla Riforma e i movimenti religiosi in Italia (Torre Pellice, 29-31 agosto 1993): Bollettino della Società di Studi Valdesi 177 (1995). 183 p.. 9 art.

630 [E]**Pitassi** Maria-Cristina, Le Christ entre orthodoxie et Lumières; Actes du colloque Genève août 1993: HistId 332. Genève 1994, Droz. 214 p. 2-600-0043-7.

631 [E]**Pollet** G., Indian epic values; Rāmāyana and its impact; 8th conference, Leuven 6-8 July 1991; OLA 66. Lv 1995, Peeters. viii-248 p. 90-6831-701-6.

632 [E]**Redouille** Jean-Claude, *Roberge* René-Michel, La documentation patristique; bilan et prospective [symposium Laval 3-5 juin 1993]. P 1995, Sorbonne. -- [R]SMSR 61 (1995) 458-462 (G. *Biamonte*).

633 REEKMANS Louis mem. († 29.VI.1992; here p.31-70): Martyrium in multidisciplinary perspective, Leuven May 13-15, 1992, [E]**Lamberigts** M., *Deun* P. van: BETL 117. Lv 1995, Univ./Peeters. x-435 p.; biog. 1-8 (*IJsewijn*). 90-6186-665=0 / 90-6831-680-X.

634 [E]**Richter** Klemens, *Kranemann* Benedict, Christologie der Liturgie; der Gottesdienst der Kirche -- Christusbekenntnis und Sinaibund [Symposium]: QD 159. FrB 1995, Herder. 300 p. 3-451-02159-5 [< OTA 19,p.332; renvois to 3 of the 17; ThRv 92,177, tit.pp.]; 57-86 *Braulik* Georg, Christologisches Verständnis der Psalmen -- schon im Alten Testament ?; - 150-186, *Schulz* Hans-Joachim, Der 'Alexandrinismus' der ersten Konzilien und der byzantinischen Liturgie legitimiert durch die johanneische Christologie ?

635 *Rivas* Luis Heriberto. al., Segundo encuentro argentino de patrología [9-10 oct. 1993]: TeolBA 30 (1994) 5 (-123).

636 [E]**Roberts** Richard H., Religion and the transformations of capitalism; comparative approaches [17 art., mostly from St. Andrews conference] NY 1995, Routledge.. xi-347 p. $ 90. 0-415-11917-0 [ThD 43,286].

637 [E]**Rochat** Giorgio, La spada e la croce; I cappellani italiani nelle due guerre mondiali, Atti del XXXIV convegno di studi sulla Riforma e I movimenti religiosi in Italia (Torre Pellice, 28-30 agosto 1994): BStVald 176 (1995). 302 p, 19 art.

638 [E]**Rodríguez Rodríguez** Isacio, Agustinos en América y Filipinas; Actas dl Congreso Internacional Valladolid, 15-21 de abril de 1990. .. 1150 p. - [R]NZM(iss)W 51 (1995) 230-2 (J. *Baumgartner*).

638* ^E**Rodríguez-Souquet** Carlos A., La formación sacerdotal en la cultura actual; XIV Jornadas de Teología, Seminario Caracas 26-30 nov. 1995: T-IUSI 15 (1995) 210 p. -- p: 81-87, *Padrón Sánchez* Diego, Biblia, sin ella no hay formación posible; p. 169-210, *Magee* Peter, 'Optatam totius', psicología, madurez humana y celibato; algunos aspectos del debate conciliar.

639 *Roncolato* Angelo (p. 373-5 . 483-6), Simposio 22, Comunicazione e verità : StPat(av) 42 (1995) 373-486.

640 ^E**Rosenhäger** Ursel, *Stephens* Sarah, The ordination of women; Reformed perspectives [Geneva 1992]; Studies 18. Geneva 1993, World Alliance. Fs 15. - ^RR(ef)W 45 (1995) 44-48 ((Elizabeth *Templeton*).

641 *Rostagno* Sergio, a) Fondamento come promessa [teologia contemporanea e prospettive dell'antropologia, Roma, Facoltà Valdese (in attesa del) 24-25.XI.1995]; - b) Religione; un limite per la ricerca scientifica ? Protestantesimo 50 (1995) 99-113 [114-125, *Barth* Hans-M.] / 279-290.

642 La Sagrada Familia en el siglo XVII; 2 Congreso 1994. Barc/Begues 1995, Hijos de la Sagrada Familia. 815 p.

643 ^E**Samir** Samir Khalil, *Nielsen* Jørgen S., Christian Arabic apologetics during the Abbasid period (750-1258) [Birmingham Selly Oak symposium May 1990]: SHR 63. Lei 1994, Brill. xii-250 p. - ^ROCP 61 (1995) 259-261 (P. *Luisier*).

644 San José en el siglo XIX, Actas del Sexto Simposio internacional (Roma, 12-19 septiembre 1993); textos en español y en italiano; publicación conjunta de CahJos: EstJos 49 (1995). 705 p. 34 art.; 2 sobre el Evangelio.

645 ^E**Schmidinger** Heinrich. Die eine Welt und Europa; Salzburger Hochschulwochen 1995. Graz 1995, Styria. 309 p. DM 40. 3-222-12324-1. S. 165-206, *D'Sa* Francis X., Weltethos aus Religion -- was kann Europa dazu beitragen ? - S.249-278, *Kehl* Medard, Der Universalitätsanspruch der Kirche in einer multikulturellen Welt [ThRv 92,169].

646 ^E**Schwöbel** Christoph, Trinitarian theology today; essays on divine being and act [7 papers revised from 1990 London King's College conference]. E 1995, Clark. v-176 p. $ 35 (Herndon VA 22070, POB 605). 0-567-09731-5 [ThD 43,390].

647 (Sem.Bergamo) Cristianesimo, religione e religioni II, 1993 : ^RGreg 76 (1995) 195s (J. *Dupuis*).

648 ^E**Semerari** Giuseppe, Confronti con HEIDEGGER [Univ. Bari 1985-90]. Bari 1992, Dedalo. 256 p. L^m 28. - ^RProtest(mo) 50 (1995) 143-7 (S. *Ronchi*).

649 ^E**Siebert** H., The ethical foundations of the market economy; international workshop Univ. Kiel, Institut für Weltwirtschaft, Aug.1993. Tü 1994, Mohr. 224 p. - ^RATG(ran) 58 (1995) 425 (I.*Camacho*).

650 ^E**Siker** Jeffrey S., Homosexuality in the Church; both sides of the debate [symposium of RATZINGER with 13 North Americans of various religions]. LVL 1994, W-Knox. 211 p. $ 15. 0-664-25545-0. -- ^RET 106 (1994s) 286 (J. *Wilkinson*).

651 ^E**Silva G.** Sergio, Encuentro de facultades latinoamericanas de teología católica que editan revistas teológicas, Santiago de Chile, 20 al 24 de marzo de 1995 : TyV 36,3 (1995) 153-354.

652 ^E**Snodgrass** Klyne R., Biblical law and liberty: Chicago North Park Seminary symposium Oct. 13-15, 1995): ExAud 11 (1995). 168 p. 9 art.; 4 infra.

653 ^E**Tessin** Timothy, *Ruhr* Mario von der, Philosophy and the grammar of religious belief [14th annual conference on philosophy of religion, 14 art]. Claremont .., Univ. xi-397 p. $ 55. 0-312-12494-9 [ThD 43,81].

653* **Thompson** Thomas A., Faith, Mary, culture; 46th annual meeting of the Mariological Society of America [Dayton, May 24-26, 1995]: Marian Studies 46 (1995). 195 p. 0464-9680. -- P. 26-40, *Frizzell* Lawrence E., Mary and the biblical heritage.

654 ^E**Tijssen** Lieteke, *al.*, The search for fundamentals; the process of modernisation and the quest for meaning [15 art. revised from 1991 Zeist conference. Dordrecht 1995, Kluwer. 293 p. $ 128. 0-7923-3542-2 [ThD 43,387].

655 ^E**Tongerloo** Alois van, The Manichaean nous; proceedings of the international symposium, Lv 31 July - 3 Aug. 1991: Manichaean Studies 2. Lv 1995, Brepols. x-323 p.

656 ^E**Triacca** Achille M., Il mistero del Sangue di Cristo e la morale: atti del V convegno pastorale, R 27-30 dic. 1993: Sangue e Vita 13. R 1995, Pia Unione Prez. Sangue. 588 p.

658 ^E**Walt** B.J. van der, Windows on business ethics; a challenge to Christians [Acta], Potchefstroom 1993, Institute for Reformational Studies, 221 p. - ^RSTEv 7 (1995) 101-4 (G. *Rizza*, dettagliato).

659 ^E**Wimbush** Vincent L., *Valantasis* Richard, Asceticism [42 art. < NY Union Theol. Sem. conference 1993]. NY 1995, Oxford-UP. xxxiii-638 p. $ 125. 0-19-508535-3 [< ThD 42 (1995) 256]. - ^R*TBR 8,2 (1995s) 57 (M. *Linskill*).

660 ^E**Wood** Diana, The Church and childhood [23 art. < British Ecclesiastical 1993s]: SCH(L) 21. Ox 1994, Blackwell. $ 60; pa. $ 25. 0-631-19586-6: -7-4 [RStR 22,71, J. *Gaffney*; ThD 43,60].

A2.5 *Acta* **philologica** *et* **historica** [reports → Y7.6]

661 Actes de Colloques: Kernos 8 (1995) 323-337. -- *b)* Actes de l'Association: REG 108 (1995) ix-lxviii.

662 ^E**Alvar** Jaime, *al.*, Héroes, semidioses y daímones; primer encuentro-coloquio de [la Asociación] Arys, Jarandilla de la Vera, dic. 1989. M 1992, Clásicas. 510 p. -- ^REM(erita) 63 (1995) 165s (J. *García López*).

663 ^E**Archer** L.J., *al.*, Women in ancient societies, an illusion of the night [Oxford seminar papers 1985-8 not updated]. L 1994, Macmillan. xx-308 p. £ 45; pa. £ 16. 0-333-52396-2; -7-0. -- ^RJRS 85 (1995) 258s (Sarah B. *Pomeroy*).

664 ^E**Baggi** Giancarlo, Aspetti della poesia epica latina; Atti docenti latino e greco, Lugano 21-23 ottobre 1993. Lugano 1995, EUSI. 289 p.

665 ^E**Behrends** Okko, *Capogrossi Colognesi* Luigi, Die römische Feldmesskunst [Symposion Wolfenbüttel 1988, 14 Vorträge]: AbhGö ph/h 3/193. Gö 1992, VR. 452 p. DM 260. -- ^RHZ 260 (1995) 173s (J. *Deininger*).

666 ^E**Billault** A., LUCIEN de Samosate, colloque Lyon sept. 1993. Lyon/P 1994, Univ. Moulin / de Boccard. 220 p. F 160. -- ^RClasR 45 (1995) 26s (D. *Russell*).

667 ^E**Bodson** Liliane [→ 7,e429], Contributions à l'histoire de la domestication; Journée d'étude, 2 mars 1991: Colloq.Zool. 3. Liège 1992, Univ. vi-108 p.; maps. Fb 500. -- ^RRBPH 73 (1995) 162-4 (C. *Rommelaere*).

668 ^E**Boeft** J. den, *Hilhorst* A., Early Christian poetry [Nijmegen March 1991; 16 art.]. Lei 1993, Brill. -- ^RAt(henaeum) 83 (1995) 582s (F. *Gasti*).

669 ^E**Boegehold** Alan L., *Scafuro* Adele C., Athenian identity and civic ideology [Brown Univ. April 1990]. Baltimore 1994, Johns Hopkins Univ. -- ^RAt(henaeum) 83 (1995) 322s (Marta *Sordi*).

670 ^E**Brincat** Joseph M., Languages of the Mediterranean; substrata, the islands: InstLg 1. Malta 1994, Univ. ix-323 p.

671 ^E**Brixhe** Claude, La koinè grecque antique II. La concurrence: Nancy c. 1995. --
^RRPh(lgLH) 69 (1995) 327s (J.-L. *Perpillou*).

672 ^E**Brownrigg** Linda L., Making the medieval book; techniques of production: 4th
conference, Oxford, July 1992. Los Altos Hills CA 1994, Anderson-Lovelace. xiv-246 p.;
ill. [RHE 91,14*]. 0-9626-3722-X.

673 ^E**Bühler** Pierre, *Karakash* Clairette, Quand interpréter c'est changer; pragmatique et
lecture de la Parole [Congrès international d'herméneutique, Neuchâtel 1994]: Lieux
théologiques 28. Genève 1995, Labor et Fides. 266 p. 2-8309-0782-5.

674 ^E**Bülow-Jacobsen** Adam, Proceedings of the 20th international congress of papyrolo-
gists, Copenhagen 23-29.VIII.1992. K 1994, Museum Tusculanum. 631 p.; 37 pl. $ 88.
87-7289-264-1. 98 art., 10 infra. -- ^RCÉg 70 (1995) 336-340 (H. *Melaerts*).

675 ^E**Bulloch** Anthony, *al.*, Images and ideologies; self-definition in the Hellenistic world,
Berkeley 7-9.IV.1988; Hellenistic Culture and Society 12. Berkeley 1993, Univ. California.
viii-414 p.; ill. 0-520-07526-9. 10 art.; 5 infra.

676 ^E**Cassio** Albio C., *Poccetti* P., Forme di religiosità e tradizioni sapienziali in Magna
Grecia; Atti del Convegno, Napoli 14-15 dicembre 1993; AION-clas 16 (1994). Pisa 1995,
Editoriali / Poligrafici. 219 p. 88-8147-072-1. 11 art.; 2 infra. -- P.9-27, *Giangiulio*
Maurizio, Sapienza pitagorica e religiosità apollinea; tra cultura della città e orizzonti
panellenici.

677 Concetto di *pathos* nella cultura antica; Taormina 1-4.VI.1990: Elenchos 16,1 (1995).

678 ^E**Dąbrowa** Edward, The Roman and Byzantine army in the East: Univ. Kraków Sept.
1992. Kraków 1994, Univ. 311 p. 83-233-0750-4. 16 art.; 4 infra.

679 [*Fears* J. Rufus, organizer], *Connor* W.R., *al.*, Aspects of Athenian democracy [Boston
Univ. colloquium 18-21 June 1987]: ClasMdv diss. 11. K 1990, Univ. MusTusc. 128 p. -:
Gnomon 67 (1995) 27-33 (F. *Quass*).

680 ^E**Ferioli** Piera, *Fiandra* Enrica, Archives before writing; proceedings of the international
colloquium Oriolo Romano Oct.23-25, 1991. R 1994, Ministero Beni. 416 p.; ill. L^m 100.
88-86231-1-32 [RStR 22,55. D.I. *Owen*: T 1994, Scriptorium]. P. 13-28, *Schmandt-Besserat*
Denise, on tokens.

681 ^E**Geller** Markham J., *Maehler* Herwig, Legal documents of the Hellenistic world: Univ.
London, Warburg Inst. seminar Feb.-May 1986. L 1995, Univ. xiv-254 p. 0-85481-089-7.

682 ^E**Harris** W.V., The inscribed economy; production and distribution in the Roman Empire
in the light of the instrumentum domesticum: conference Rome 10-11.I.1992. R 1993,
American Academy.

683 ^E**Hawley** R., *Levick* B., Women in antiquity; new assessments [1993 Oxford conference].
L 1995, Routledge. xix-271 p.; 15 fig.; 8 pl. $ 55; pa. $ 18. 0-415-11368-7: -9-5 [NTAb
40,p.554].

684 ^E**Hinnells** John R., Studies in Mithraism: Mithraic Panel of 16th History of Religions
congress, Rome 1990: StRel 9. R 1994, Bretschneider. 299 p. 88-7062-834-5.

685 ^E**Hoepfner** Wolfram, *Zimmer* Gerhard, Die griechische Polis; Architektur und Politik
[Seminar, 13 art.]. Tü 1993, Wasmuth. 139 p. DM 48.- ^RHZ 261 (1995) 147 (K.-W. *Welwei*).

686 ^E**Jacquinod** Bernard, Cas et prépositions en grec ancien; Actes du colloque international
de Saint-Étienne, 3-5 juin 1993. Saint Étienne 1994, Univ. Centre Palerne. 260 p. --
^RRPh(lgLH) 69 (1995) 180-2 (Françoise *Létoublon*).

687 ^E**Jufresa** Montserrat, Saviesa I perversitat; les dones a la Grècia Antiga [< 4
conferencias en castellano, Univ. Barc. 1993]. Barc 1994, Destino. 146 p. -- ^REM(erita)
63 (1995) 375-7 (J. *Portulas*).

688 ^E**Kefer** Michael, *Auwers* Johan van der, Meaning and grammar; cross-linguistic perspectives [= 2. of conference 'BJL' 4 (1989): Empirical ALTyp 10. B 1992, Mouton de Gruyter. x-427 p. DM 200. -- ^RKratylos 40 (1995) 67-71 (F. *Serzisko*).

689 ^E**Kramer** Johannes, Die italienische Sprachwissenschaft in den deutschsprachigen Ländern; Beiträge des wissenschaftlichen Kongresses zu Ehren von Giovan Battista PELLEGRINI (Siegen, 8. März 1991): RomanistikGG 27. Ha c.1993, Buske. 160 p. -- ^RAGlot 79 (1994) 113-5 (E. *Blasco Ferrer*).

690 ^E**Kühnert** Barbara, *al.*, Prinzipat und Kultur im 1. und 2. Jh.: Wiss. Tagung Univ. Jena/Tbilissi 27.-30.X.1992. Bonn 1995, Habelt. 332 p.; 24 p. 3-7789-2674-3. 30 art.; 7 infra.

691 ^E**Laks** André, *Schofield* Malcolm, Justice and generosity; [9] studies in Hellenistic social and political philosophy: Proceedings of the Sixth Synposium Hellenisticum 1992. C 1995, Univ. ix-304 p. $ 65. 0-521-45293-7 [NTAb 40,p.178].

692 ^FLEHMANN Winfred P. symposium Austin 1986: Reconstructing languages and cultures: TrendsLing 58. B/NY 1992. x-550 p. -- : BSLP 90,2 (1995) 157-164 (C. de *Lamberterie*).

693 ^FLEWIS David: Ritual. finance, politics; Athenian democratic accounts; international conference, Oxford Christ Church 27-31.VII.1993, ^E**Osborne** Robert, *Hornblower* Simon. Ox 1994, Clarendon. xviii-408 p.; ill. 0-19-814992-1 [RelStR 22,241, R.D. *Woodard*]. 22 art.; 3 infra

694 La Magna Grecia e i grandi santuari della madrepatria: 31° convegno, Taranto 4-8 ott. 1991. Taranto 1992, Istituto per la storia e l'archeologia della Magna Grecia. 522 p.

695 ^E**Mastrocinque** Attilio, *a)* Ercole in Occidente: colloquio internaz. Trento 7 marzo 1990. Trento 1993, Univ. 123 p.; ill. -- *b)* I grandi santuari dell'Occidente [Atti del 2° Incontro, Univ.Trento 12 marzo 1991]. Trento 1993, Univ. 158 p. -- ^RAevum 49 (1995) 259-261 (Cinzia *Bearzot*).

696 ^E**Meyer** M., *Mirecki* P., Ancient magic and ritual power [Univ. Kansas conference 1992]: ÉPR 129. Lei 1995, Brill. ix-476 p.; 8 pl. *f* 230. 90-04-10406-2 [NTAb 40, p.559].

697 ^E**Moon** Warren G., Polykleitos, the doryphoros, and tradition [1989 symposium for the fine copy acquired by the Minneapolis Institute of Art]: StClas. Madison 1995, Univ. Wisconsin. xii-364 p. [RStR 22,240, R.S.*Bianchi*].

698 ^E**Olivier** Jean-Pierre, Mykenaïka 9e colloque, Athènes 2-6 octobre 1990: BCH.s 25. P 1992, Éc.Française d'Athènes / de Boccard. xx-673 p. -- ^RBSLP 90,2 (1995) 181-8 (A. *Blanc*).

699 ^E**Pagliuca** William, Perspectives on grammaticalization [Univ. Wisconsin-Milwaukee, 19th linguistic symposium, 'Explanation in Historical Linguistics', 13 art.]: *CurrentIssuesLT 109. Amst/Ph 1994, Benjamins. xx-306 p. -- ^R*AGlot 80 (1995) 249-257 (P. *Ramat*).

700 ^E**Powell** Anton, *Hodkinson* Stephen, The shadow of Sparta [Cardiff colloquium]. L 1994, Classical Press of Wales. vii-408 p. -- ^RHZ 261 (1995) 488s (K.-W, *Welwei*).

701 ^E**Reggi** Giancarlo, Aspetti della poesia epica latina: aggiornamento docenti Ticino, Lugano 21-23 ott. 1993. Lugano 1995. EUSI. 288 p. 88-7795-101-0

702 ^FRIJK L.M. de, 65th b., Leiden symposium Sept 1989: ^E**Bos** E.P., *Meijer* P.A., On PROCLUS [420-485] and his influence in medieval philosophy: PA 3. Lei 1992, Brill. vii-206 p. *f* 100. 90-04-09429-6. -- ^RJEH 46 (1995) 494-8 (Janet *Coleman*).

703 ^E**Rosen** K., Macht und Kultur im Rom der Kaiserzeit [Symposium Bonn 1989: StudUniv 16. Bonn 1994, Bouvier. 190 p.; 42 fig. DM 65. -- ^RCLR 45 (1995) 474s (B. *Campbell*).

704 ᶠSCHLERATH Bernfried, 70. Gb.: Die Indogermanen und das Pferd, ᴱHänsel Bernhard, Zimmer Stefan: int.-interdisz. Kolloquium Berlin FU 1.-3.VII.1992. Budapest 1994, Archaeolingua 4. 271 p.; 4 pl. DM 140. -- ᴿKratylos 40 (1995) 109-118 (P. Raulwing).

705 Spectacles sportifs et scéniques dans le monde étrusco-italique: Actes de la Table Ronde [CNRS UMR 126, 3-4 mai 1991]; Coll.ÉcFr 172. R 1993, École Française. 478 p.; 131 fig., 5 pl. 2-7283-0273-1. -- ᴿAJA 99 (1995) 549s (P.G. Warden).

706 ᴱStrocka Volker M., Die Regierungszeit des Kaisers Claudius [41-54 n.Chr.], Umbruch oder Episode ? FrB Univ. [Archäol. Inst. 100-Jahre] 16.-18.II.1991. Mainz 1994, von Zabern. ix-331 p. 3-8053-1503-1. 20 art.; 4 infra.

706* [Uggeri] Journal of Ancient Topography = R(ivcista)TA 4 (1993s).

707 VLASTOS Gregory mem., Virtue, love and form [Berkeley conference May 1992]. ᴱIrwin Terence, Nussbaum Martha = Apeiron 26,3s . Edmonton 1993, Academic. 224 p. - ᴿPhilipSa 30 (1995) 555-7 (N. Castillo: Vlastos tended to separate SOCRATES from PLATO).

708 ᴱVogt-Spira Gregor, Beiträge zur mündlichen Kultur der Römer: ScriptOralia 27. Tü c. 1994, Narr. x-205 p -- ᴿGnomon 67 (1995) 161-3 (G. Radke).

709 ᴱWeijers O., Vocabulary of teaching and research between Middle Ages and Renaissance: proceedings of the colloquium, London Warburg Institute 11-12 March 1994: CIVICIMA 8. Turnhout 1995, Brepols. 255 p.; 2 facsim. [RHE 91,108*].

710 ᴱWilkins John, al., Food in antiquity [conference 1992]. Exeter 1995, Univ. xiii-459 p.; ill. 0-85989-418-5. 32 art.

711 ᴱWörrle Michael, Zanker Paul, Stadtbild und Bürgerbild im Hellenismus; Kolloquium Mü 24.-26.VI.1993: Vestigia 47. Mü 1995, Beck. 273 p. 3-406-39036-6. 18 art.; 4 infra.

A2.7   Acta orientalistica

712 ᴱAbouzayd Shafiq, The Arab-Byzantine-Syriac cultural interchange during the Umayyad era in Bilad al-Sham, Oxford 27-30 September 1993: Aram 6 (1994).

713 ᴱAllen James P., Proceedings of the international conference on Egyptian grammar (Crossroads III) Yale, April 4-9, 1994: *LAe 4. Gö 1994, Univ. Sem. Äg. vii-382 p. DM 138, sb. 68.

714 ᴱBresciani Edda, Acta demotica; Acts of Fifth International Congress for Demotists, Pisa, 4th-8th September 1993 = Egitto e Vicino Oriente 17 (1994), ix-335 p.; 1-4, Haikal Fayza, Demotic documentation in the international context; 5-7, Abd-El-Halim Nur El Din, Demotic studies in Egypt: + 32 art., 6 infra.

715 ᴱBrugnatelli Vermondo, Sem Cam Iafet; Atti della 7a Giornata di Studi Camito-Semitici e Indoeuropei (Milano, 1° giugno 1993). Mi 1994, Centro Studi Camito-Semitici. ix-269 p. Lᵐ 48. -- ᴿWZKM 85 (1995) 408s (Michaela Weszeli).

716 ᴱCagni Luigi, Le profezie di Mari: Testi VOA 11/2. Brescia 1995, Paideia. 136 p. Lᵐ 22. -- ᴿAION 55 (1995) 122.4 (G. L. Prato).

717 ᴱCarruba Onofrio, Giorgieri Mauro, Mora Clelia, Atti del II Congresso Internazionale di Hittitologia: StMedit 5. Pavia 1995, Iuculano. xi-400 p. 88-7072-234-1.

718 CEPOA (Centre d'étude du Proche-Orient ancien, Cartigny): a) Histoire et conscience historique dans les civilisations du Proche-Orient ancien: Actes 1986, Cahier 5. -- b) Voyages et voyageurs au Proche-Orient ancien: Actes 1988, Cahier 6. Lv 1989/94, Peeters. 210 p.; 245 p. 90-6831-216-2; -681-8.

719 ᴱChoueiri Youssef M., State and society in Syria and Lebanon. Exeter 1993, Univ. xviii-158 p. £ 29.50. -- ᴿJRAS (1995) 284s (Ulrike Freitag).

720 [E]**Conio** Caterina, La parola creatrice in India e nel Medio Oriente [Univ. Pisa seminar 1992]. Pisa 1994, Giardini. 250 p. 88-427-0258-4. -- [R]Vidyajyoti 59 (1995) 276s (G. *Gispert-Sauch*).

721 [E]**Eyre** Christopher, Seventh international congress of Egyptologists, Cambridge, 3-9 September 1995: abstracts only of very many papers. Ox 1995, Oxbow. [vi-] 210 p. 0-946897-92-1.

722 [E]**Hawting** G.R., *Shareef* Abdul-Kader A., Approaches to the Qur'an [14 art. for SOAS, London March 1990]. L 1993, Routledge. xiv-336 p. £ 40. -- [R]JRAS (1994) 406s (W. *Madelung*).

723 [E]**Johnson** Janet H., Life in a multi-cultural society; Egypt from Cambyses to Constantine and beyond: SAOC 51, 1990/2 → 8,719: [R]Enchoria 29 (1994) 160-172 (G. *Vittmann*).

724 [E]**Joannès** Francis [139-147, L'extinction des archives cunéiformes dans la seconde partie de l'époque perse], Les phénomènes de fin d'archives en Mésopotamie [Table Ronde CNRS-UPR 193 -- Paris 9.XII.1995]: RAss 89,1 (1995) 1s (-88) & 89,2 (1995) 97-147.

725 [E]**King** G.R.D., *Cameron* Averil, The Byzantine and early Islamic Near East [1. Problems], 2. Land use and settlement patterns [2d London Univ. School of Oriental and African studies workshop, 25-27 April 1991]: Late Ant./Islam 2.. Princeton 1994, Darwin. xiv-270 p.; 56 fig. $ 35. 0-87850-106-1. 11 art.; → T46 Beth-Shan. -- [R]OCP 61 (1995) 591s (V. *Poggi*); WZKM 85 (1995) 402 (S. *Procházka*, titles sans pp.).

726 [E]**Krings** Véronique, La civilisation phénicienne et punique, manuel de recherche: HbOr 1/20. Lei 1995, Brill. vi-923 p. $ 248.75. 90-04-10068-7 [< OTA 18 (1995) p. 628 (M.S. *Smith*: 30 authors; standard)].

727 LEWICKI Tadeusz † 22.XI.1992 mem. [P] Studia orientalia, sympozjum Kraków 17-18.XI.1993. Kraków 1994, Enigma. 177 p. 83-86110-11-2. 16 art. with Eng. or French summary. -- [R]JSJ 26 (1995) 228s (Z.J. *Kapera*, mostly on S. MĘDALA MMT).

728 [E]**Lozachmeur** Hélène. Présence arabe dans le Croissant fertile avant l'Hégire; Actes de la Table ronde internationale (CNRS-1062, Paris 13 novembre 1993). P 1995, RCiv. 148 p. 2-86538-254-0. 12 art., infra.

729 [E]**Robb** Peter, Dalit movements and the meanings of labour in India [workshop Nov. 1990]: [B]SOAS Studies on South Asia. Delhi 1993, Oxford-UP. viii-354 p. £ 14. -- [R]JRAS (1995) 307-9 (A. *Copley*).

730 [E]**Teixidor** Javier, La ville, de 1200 avant J.-C. à l'Hégire ['dédié à' DELAVAULT Bernard]; Table Ronde CNRS-1062, Collège de France 14 nov. 1992: Semitica 43s (1995) 206 p.; 9 fig.

731 [E]**Vermeulen** U., *Smet* D. de, Egypt and Syria in the Fatimid, Ayyubid, and Mamluk eras; Proceedings of the 1st, 2nd, and 3rd colloquium, Kath. Univ., Leuven, May 1992/3/4: OLA 73. Lv 1995, Peeters. 371 p. 90-6831-683-4.

731* *Veselý* Rudolf, Die Reihe 'Dnešní Orient' (Der heutige Orient) und ihre Stellung im Nachlass [des berühmten Oreintforscher] Alois MUSILs: Archiv Orientální 63 (Praha 1995) 419-428.

732 **Willers** Dietrich. *al.*, Begegnung von Heidentum und Christentum im spätantiken Ägypten: Kolloquium 17.-18.V.1991. Riggisberg 1993, Abegg. 194 p.: ill. 3-905014-04-1. 11 art.; 4 infra.

732* **Wunsch** Cornelia, XXV. Orientalistentag 1991/4 → 10,454: [R]WZKM 85 (1995) 399 (S. Procházka.

A2.9 *Acta* **archaeologica**

733 ᴱ**Acquaro** E., *al.*, Biblo, una città e la sua cultura; Atti del colloquio internazionale (Roma, 5-7 dicembre 1990): *SFen.s 34. R 1994, cons. Naz. Ric. 230 p.; ill. [RStR 22,151, D.I. *Owen*].

734 ᴱ**Assmann** J., *al.*, Thebanische Beamtennekropolen, neue Perspektiven archäologischer Forschung: internationales Symposion, Heidelberg 6.-13.VI.1993: Studien zur Archäologie und Geschichte Altägyptens 12. Heid 1995, Orientverlag. xi-295 p. 3-927552-21-6.

734* ᴱ**Bietak** Manfred, Trade, power, and cultural exchange: Hyksos Egypt and the Eastern Mediterranean world 1800-1500 B.C. [New York Metropolitan Museum Nov. 3,1993]: ÄgLev 5 (1994).

735 ᴱ**Cassidy** Brendan, The [Celtic Scotland] Ruthwell Cross [1989 Princeton colloquium]. Princeton 1992, Univ. xiv-206. $ 40. -- ᴿJEarlyC 3 (1995) 363-5 (Z.P. *Thundy*).

736 ᴱ**Coulson** William D.E., The archaeology of Athens and Attica under the democracy; Athens American School 4-6.XII. 1992: Mg 37. Ox 1994, Oxbow. viii-250 p.; ill. 0-946897-67-0. 24 art.; 4 infra.

737 *Demirji**M.S., The international symposium on the looted antiquities from Iraq [during and after 1991 war]: Sumer 47 (1995) 5-17.

738 ᴱ**Dietrich** Manfred, 22. Tagung Rel.-G. Saarbrücken Okt.1992 + Symposium Tartus 1992: Mitteilungen für Anthropologie & Rel.G. 8. Münster 1994, Ugarit. viii-219 p, -- ᴿZAW 107 (1995) 165 (O. *Kaiser*).

739 Eretz-Israel in the Byzantine period -- Aspects of settlement [all ᴴ -- meeting 24-25. Feb. 1995]: Michmanim 8 (1995) 1-132; 11 art. [ZAW 107 (1995) 509, tit.pp.]

740 ᴱ**Kasher** A., *al.*, Greece and Rome in Eretz-Israel [Haifa/TA Univ. 1985]. J 1990, Yad Ben-Zvi. 172 p. 965-217-974-7. -- ᴿSyria 72 (1995) 283-6 (E. *Will*).

741 ᴱ**Kopcke** Günter, *Takumaru* Isabella, Greece between East and West, 10th-8th centuries BC: NYU Institute of Fine Arts meeting 1990. Mainz 1992, von Zabern. xviii-187 p. 3-8053-1491-4.

742 ᴱ**Liritzis** Ioannis, *Tsokas* Gregory, Archaeometry in South-Eastern Europe; second conference in Delphi, 19th-21st April 1991: PACT 45. Rivensart 1995, Pact Belgium. 541 p.; ill. Fb 5500. 0257-8727. 50 art.; 2 infra.

743 LEVI Doro, Mnemeion, giornata di studio Trieste 16.V.1992, ᴱ**Càssola Guida** Paola, *Floreano* Elisabetta: *StRicProtostMedit 3. R 1995, Quasar,

744 **Moscati** Sabatino, present., I Fenici ieri oggi domani: ricerche, scoperte, progetti (Roma, 3-5 marzo 1994, Acc. Lincei). R 1995, Ist. Fen. x-552 p.; xiv pl. -- ᴿRSO 69 (1995) 497-591 (Chiara *Peri*).

745 ᴱ**Müller** M., *Strange* J., Der Gamle testamente i jødedom og kristendom [Copenhagen Univ. Dept. Exegesis 25th anniv.]: ForumBEks 4. K 1993, Museum Tusculanum. 182 p. Dk 154. 87-7289-252-8. -- ᴿBoL (1995) 159 (K. *Jeppesen*).

746 ᴱ**O'Connor** David, *Silverman* David P., Ancient Egyptian kingship [1987 symposium in Denver]: PÄ 9. Lei 1995, Brill. xxxiii-347 p. *f* 180. 90-04-10041-5. -- ᴿBoL (1995) 135 (L.L. *Grabbe*).

747 ᴱ**Olcese** Gloria, Ceramica romana e archeometria [Montegufoni 26-27.IV.1993]: Univ. Siena Quad. 37. F 1994, Giglio. 319 p.

748 ᴱ**Orel** Sara E., Death and taxes in the Ancient Near East [Toronto University symposium, March 1991]. Lewiston NY 1992, Mellen. x-237 p.; XVII pl. -- ᴿ*JAncCiv 9 (1994) 144-9 (E. & T. *Meltzer*).

749 ᴱStruck Manuela, Römerzeitliche Gräber als Quellen zu Religion, Bevölkerungsstruktur und Sozialgeschichte; Inst. VorFGeschichte 18.-20.II.1991: ArchSchr 3. Mainz 1993, Univ. 441 p.

750 ᴱVleeming S.P., Hundred-gated Thebes; Acts of a colloquium on Thebes and the Theban area in the Graeco-Roman period (P.L.Bat. 27): PLB 27. Lei 1995, Brill. xiii-273 p. 90-04-10384-8

751 ᴱWaldren W.H., al., Ritual, rites and religion in prehistory: 3d Deya conference, Oxford 1994: BAR-Int 611. Ox 1995, Tempus Reparatum. x-353 p.; 321 p. 0-86054-791-4; -2-2. 35 art., *Frendo* Antonio, Religion in the prehistoric phases of Phoenician Malta; -- *Hoskin* Michael, *Allan* Elizabeth, Orientation of Mediterranean tombs and sanctuaries.

752 ᴱWartke Ralf B., Handwerk und Technologie im Alten Orient; ein Beitrag zur Geschichte der Technik im Altertum [Kolloquium Berlin März 1991; 19 art. + 3 Eng.]. Mainz 1994, von Zabern. 151 p. ᴅᴍ 148. -- ᴿAfO 42s (1995s) 290-2 (M.L. *Eiland*, Eng.).

753 ᴱYon Marguerite, *Sznycer* Maurice, *Bordreuil* Pierre, Le pays d'Ougarit autour de 1200 av. J.-C.; Actes du colloque international, Paris 18 juin -- 1 juillet 1993: Ras Shamra -- Ougarit 11.. P 1995, RCiv. 268 p. 2-86538-253-2.

A3 *Opera consultationis* - **Reference works** .1 *plurium* **separately** infra

754 **AnchorBD**: The Anchor Bible Dictionary, ᴱ**Freedman** D.N., *Herion* G., *al.*, 1992 → 8,741 ... 10,495: ᴿA(ustrl)BR 42 (1994) 107-9 (J. *Wright*); *CritRR 7 (1994) 1-11 (G.M. *Tucker,* OT etc.) & 13-23 (J,T, *Sanders,* NT etc.); EstB 53 (1995) 266s (A. *de la Fuente*); HebStud 36 (1995) 101-9 (P.D. *Miller*); JThS 46 (1995) 198-202 (Morna D. *Hooker*).

755 **ANRW**: Aufstieg und Niedergang der römischen Welt II. Principat [18,1; 34,1; 36,7 (1994) → 10,496]: [**37,1**, Medizin und Biologie 1993, p. 2-937, 3-11-013746-1], **37,2** (1994) Wissenschaften; Medizin und Biologie; **18,5** (1995) Heidentum; die religiösen Verhältnisse in den Provinzen 1995. xix-931 p.; 19 fig.; 61 pl.; 3 maps. ᴅᴍ 726. 3-11-014238-4 [NTAb 40,p.188, tit. topics]. - **26,2** [1. Vorkonstantinisches Christentum; NT, Sachthemen, 1992 → 8,742] 1995,p. 815-1933; 3-11-010371-0. -- ᴿAnCl 64 (1995) 302s (M.-Thérèse *Raepsaet-Charlier*, 34,1s) & 420s (S. *Byl*, 37, sciences); GaR 42 (1995) 248s (P. *Walcot*, 37.2); Gym 102 (1995) 369-373 (F. *Bömer* 34,2; 36,7; 37,2); Latomus 54 (1995) 176-9 (I. *Mazzini*, 37/1, Medizin); SNTU 19 (1994) 193-6 (A. *Fuchs*, 26,1) & 20 (1995) 179-190 (F. *Weissengruber*, 27,1).

756 -- *Schaller* B., PHILO, JOSEPHUS und das sonstige griechisch-sprachige Judentum in ANRW [2/20s] und weiteren neueren Veröffentlichungen: ThR(u) 59 (1994) 186-214 [NTAb 39,p.112].

757 **AugL**: Augustinus-Lexikon, ᴱ**Meyer** Cornelius [I (1-8) 1994 → 10,497] - Fasz. 9s, 1995: ᴿTLZ 120 (1995) 450-2 (H.-U. *Delius*, 3-10). - AnCl 64 (1995) 350s (H. *Savon*,1,5s); Greg 76 (1995) 618s (F.-A. *Pastor*, 5-8); RevAg 36 (1995) 617-620 (J. *Sepulcre*, 7s); ThZ 51 (1995) 178-180 (R. *Brändle*, 4-8).

758 **CAH**: Cambridge Ancient History² [5, 1992 → 9,583; 9. 1994 →10,498] - ᴿAJA 9 (1995) 153s (D.T. *Potts*): AnCl 64 (1995) 470-2 (M.-Thérèse *Raepsaet-Charlier*, 9); CJ 91 (1995s) 71-75 (E.S. *Gruen*); ClR 45 (1995) 91-93 (P.E. *Harding*); Gnomon 67 (1995) 36-44 (K.-E. *Petzoldt*, 8); Gym 102 (1995) 556-560 (K.W. *Welwei*, 6 & 9); REL 73 (1995) 324s (J.-C. *Richard*).

759 -- (9,1994) *Millar* Fergus, The last century of the republic; whose history ?: JRS 85 (1995) 236-243.

760 Catholicisme [XIV,64s, 1994s → 10,499; F 167,50; 169,50; /2-7063-0160-0]: XIV
entier, Sida-Timothée, 1996. 2-7063-0192-9. -- ᴿEThL 71 (1995) 264s (F. *Neirynck*, 62-
65); Greg 76 (1995) 605s (J. *Galot*, 61ss); RHE 90 (1995) 590s (R. *Aubert*): VSp 149
(1995) 477-489 (J.-M, *Fabre*, 62-64).

761 **DHGE**: Dictionnaire d'histoire et de géographie ecclésiastiques [XXV,144s, 1994 →
10,502] 146s, col. 513-1024, Hyacinthe - Inde; 248s, Inde - Iriarte 1995 [RHE 91, 251-6,
J. *Pycke*, 139-143]: ᴿE(spr)eV 105 (1995) 667-670 (G. de *Pasquier*, 146s); NRT 117 (1995)
937s (G. *Menin*, 144s).

762 **DPA** [→ 7,671*a*] Encyclopedia of the Early Church, ᴱ**di Berardino** Angelo;
ᵀᴱ*Walford* Adrian 1992 → 8,745 .. 10,506: ᴿJEarlyC 3 (1995) 357-9 (M. *Slusser*).

763 **DSp**: Dictionnaire de Spiritualité, ᴱ**Derville** A., *al.* [XVI,104-107 (fin) 1994 →
10,503] - Tables générales. P 1995, Beauchesne: 733 + 37 p. [RHE 91, 256s, R. *Aubert*].
ᴿOCP 61 (1995) 669s (V. *Poggi*). -- ᴿLavalThP 51 (1995) 690 (C. *Kannengiesser*, 106s);
Marianum 56 (1994) 558-561; VSp 149 (1995) 215-8 (J.-H. *Nicolas,* 106s*).

764 **EI**² = EncIslam², Encyclopaedia of Islam, ᴱ**Bosworth** C.E. [VIII,132 → 10,593;
Indices 1993 → 10,194*ab*]. Édition française, VIII, 133s & 135s, 1993, -Radp; 90-04-
10273-6. -- IX entier, 145s, -Salihiyya col. 1024, 1995; 90-04-10914-3.

765 **EncK**: Encyclopedia Katolicka [5, 1989 → 5,891] -- 6. Graal-Ignorancja,
ᴱ**Walkusz** Jan, *al.* Lublin 1993, KUL. viii-1456 col. - ᴿAtK(ap) 124 (1995) 149-152 (W.
Hanc): C(olc)Th 64,4 (1994) 175-7 (B. *Nadolski*).

766 **GLNT**: Grande Lessico del NT, ᵀᴱ*Montagnini* Felice, *al.*, [15,1988 → 6,845] - **16**,
Rühle O., Indici. Brescia 1992, Paideia. 1092 p. - ᴿLat 61 (1995) 199-201 (R. *Penna*).

767 **LThK**: Lexikon für Theologie und Kirche³, ᴱ**Kasper** Walter, *al.* [2. 1994 →
10,510] - 3, Dämon-Frag, 14*-1378 col. - 4. Fran-Herm. 14*-1450 col. FrB 1995, Herder
[RHE 91,12*]. - ᴿCivCatt 146 (1995,1) 575-583 (C.*Capizzi*, 1-2 dalla prima alla terza
edizione); StZ 212 (1994) 283s & 213 (1995) 427 (W. *Seibel*, 1s); ThG 85 (1995) 96-118
(K. *Baumgartner*: Pastoraltheologie und Seelsorge im Wandel seit ¹1930 ²1957).

768 **RAC**: Reallexikon für Antike und Christentum, ᴱ**Dassmann** Ernst: [17,133, 1995 →
10,512] XVII, iao-indict: 129/130, 1994; 131-5, 1995: 3-7772-5006-6; -9420-9; -9508-6; -
9513-2; -9527-2; -9529-2; -9610-4.

769 **RLA**: Reallexikon der Assyriologie, ᴱ**Edzard** Dietz O. [8,2. 1993 → 9,601; 10,514]:
VIII, Meek-Mythologie: 3s, 161-320, 1994; 5s bis 480; 8s bis 589; 3-11-014264-3; -311-0;
-512-9. -- ᴿOLZ 90 (1995) 275-8 (H. *Klengel* 8/1-4, 1993s).

770 **SDB**: Supplément au Dictionnaire de la Bible, ᴱ**Briend** J., *al.*, XII,69 (col. 769-1024,
Serm-Sex) 1994 [OTA 18 (1995) p. 397] → 10,515: ᴿRB 102 (1994) 302 (R.J. *Tournay*, 67).

771 **TDOT**: Theological dictionary of the Old Testament [TWAT, ᵀ*Green* David E..: 6,
1990 → 8,767: 9,802*] - 7. GR 1995, Eerdmans. xxiv-552 p. 0-80282331-9. - ᴿJETS 38
(1995) 253s (F.C. *Putnam* misses in 'Jubilee' a more theological-religious view)

772 **TRE**: Theologische Realenzyklopädie, ᴱ**Müller** Gerhard, *al.* [23s., 1994 → 10,517]:
25, Ochino-Parapsychologie. B 1995, de Gruyter. 787 p. 3-11-014712-2. - ᴿCDios 208
(1995) 286s (J.M. *Ozaeta*, 23); CivCatt 146 (1995,1) 519s (C. *Capizzi*, 21-23); NRT 117
(1995) 297 & 632 (A. *Harvengt*, 23s); SvTKv 70 (1994) 42-44 (B. *Hägglund*, 20-22); TPQ
143 (1995) 323s (G. *Bachl*, 22s).

773 **TUAT**: Texte aus der Umwelt des Alten Testaments, ᴱ**Kaiser** O. (→ 7,691); 2/5,
Lieder und Gebete 1, ᴱ*Römer* W., *Hecker* K. Gü 1989, Mohn. S. 641-783. DM 118. -
ᴿOrientalia 63 (1994) 136-140 (D.O. *Edzard*). -- 3/3 [/1, Mythen und Epen, ᴱ**Römer** W.],
3/3/2, 1933: ᴿBoL (1995) 140 (M.J. *Gläser*: cosmology, loosely).

774 **TWAT**: Theologisches Wörterbuch zum Alten Testament, [E]**Fabry** H.J., *Ringgren* H. [8. 1994s → 10,519]; [R]Henoch 17 (1995) 243s (J.A. *Soggin*, 7); NRT 117 (1995) 154s & 903 (J.L. *Ska*).

A3.3 *Opera consultationis* **biblica** *non excerpta infra* - **not subindexed**

775 **Augustinovich** A., Dizionario de los Evangelios: Iglesia y sociedad 43. Caracas 1995, Trípode. 669 p. 980-208-256-2.

776 [E]**Balz** Horst, *Schneider* Gerhard [**EWNT** 1980-3 → 60,880 ... 64,751; Eng. 1990 → 6,868], Dizionario esegetico del Nuovo Testamento, 1. Aaron - Kapharnaoum, [TE]*Soffritti* Omero.. Brescia 1995, Paideia. xxxviii-2024 col. 88-394-0521-6.

777 [E]**Bauer** Johannes B., *al.*, Bibeltheologisches Wörterbuch[4rev] 1994 → 10,521: [R]ThLZ 120 (1995) 432 (W. *Vogler*); TPQ 143 (1995) 91 (C. *Niemand*).

778 [E]**Bimson** John J., Illustrated encyclopedia of biblical places; towns and cities, countries and states, archaeology and topography. Leicester 1995, Inter-Varsity. 319 p. 0-85110-657-9.

779 [**Born** A. van den, [TE]*Haag* H. (*Ausejo* Serafín de, Barc 1963, [9]1987], Diccionario enciclopédico de la Biblia[rev] (Maredsous), [T]*Gallart* Miquel, [E]*Arias* Isidro 1993 → 9,606; 10,524: [R*]ActuBbg 31 (1994) 38s (J. *Boada*); *EfMex 12 (1994) 135-8 (C. *Junco*); NatGrac 41 (1994) 163s (F. *F.Ramos*); PerTeol 27 (1995) 113s (J. *Konings*): RCatT 30 (1995) 199-201 (E. *Cortès*).

780 -- Dizionario enciclopedico della Bibbia, [TE]*Penna* Romano. R 1995, Borla. 1380 p. 88-263-1050-5.

781 **Carrez** Maurice, Dictionnaire de culture biblique 1993 → 9,608; 10,525: [R]BLE 95 (1994) 245s (S. *Légasse*); FV 93,2 (1994) 80s (G. *Vahanian*); RTPh 127 (1995) 416s (P.-Y. *Ruff*).

782 **Cocagnac** Maurice, Les symboles bibliques; lexique théologique 1993 → 9,609: [R]EstTrin 29 (1995) 341s (J.M. *Arbizu*); NRT 117 (1995) 129 (A. *Toubeau*); RTPh 127 (1995) 417 (P.-Y. *Ruff*); Salesianum 57 (1995) 568 (R. *Bracchi*).

783 **Cocagnac** Maurice, I simboli biblici; lessico teologico [1993]. Bo 1994, Dehoniane. 922 p. L[m] 82. 88-10-20568-5. - [R]CivCatt 146 (1995,4) 514s (D. *Scaiola*): Ter(esianum) 46 (1995) 657s (V. *Pasquetto*).

784 **Cocagnac** Maurice de, Los símbolos bíblicos. Bilbao 1994, D-Brouwer. 456 p. - [R]Rel(y)Cult 41 (1995) 917 (E. *Martín Sanz*).

785 [E]**Coggins** R.J., *Houlden* J.L., A dictionary of [the history of] biblical interpretation 1990 → 6,865 ... 8,772: [R]Bijdragen 56 (1995) 460 (J.-J. *Suurmond*: 'meta-interpretation'); JETS 38 (1995) 465s (D.M. *Howard*: good, but evangelicals should produce their own).

786 [E]**Dohmen** Christoph, Bibel-Bilder-Lexikon. Stu 1995, KBW. 176 p.; ill. DM 68. [R]E(rbe)uA 71 (1995) 426 (B. *Schwank*).

787 [E]**Drechsel** Joachim, *al.*, Brunnen Bibel Lexikon. Giessen 1994, Brunnen. 443 p. 3-7655-5438-3.

788 [E]**Gardner** Paul, The complete Who's Who in the Bible. L 1995, Marshall Pickering. xiii-688 p. 0-551-02575-1.

789 [E]**Green** Joel B., Dictionary of Jesus and the Gospels 1992 → 8,778 ... 10,532: [R]RExp 92 (1995) 121s (W. *Hendricks*).

790 [E]**Heuer** Renate, Archiv Bibliographia Judaica: Lexikon deutsch-jüdischer Autoren 2. Bend-Bins. Mü 1993, Saur. xliii-474 p. DM 228. - [R]SNTU 19 (1994) 260s (A. *Fuchs*).

791 **Krauss** Heinrich, Geflügelte Bibelworte; das Lexikon biblischer Redensarten 1993
9,614; DM 38: RThRv 91 (1995) 307 (E. *Ribbat*).

792 **Kunduru** Joji, (in Telugu) Eternal life, a biblical dictionary (alphabetical by some 50
themes). Secundarabad 1995, Amrutavani (Catholic Mass Media). xv-294 p.

793 ELéon-Dufour Xavier, The dictionary of biblical theology, TCahill P. Joseph, *Stewart*
E.M. Montreal 1995=1968, St. Paul. 712 p. $30. - RCanadCath 13,11 (1995) 27 (G.*Davies*).

794 **Lurker** Manfred, Diccionario de imágenes y símbolos de la Biblia [²1987; ital. 1990
→ 6,875],T. Córdoba 1994, Almendro. 309 p. 84-8005-020-3. - R*Carthaginensia 11 (1995)
433s (F. *Martínez Fresneda*); Phase 35 (1995) 437s (J. *Aldazábal*); RET 55 (1995) 253s (P.
Borrado Fernández); RF 231 (1995) 659s (R. de *Andrés*).

795 EMills Watson E., The Lutterworth [= Mercer 1990 → 6,879] dictionary of the Bible.
1994, Lutterworth. 993 p. £ 30. 0-7188-2918-2. - RET 106 (1994s) 183 (C.S. *Rodd*);
JETS 38 (1995) 250s (M.R. *Fairchild*).

796 ENeusner Jacob, *Green* William S., Dictionary of Judaism in the biblical period, 450
B.C.E. to 600 C.E. [3300 items by 71 authors]. NY 1995. Macmillan Reference. xxvi-693
p. (2 vol.) $ 125. 0-02-897292-9 [ThD 43,164].

797 **Proch** Umberto, Dizionario dei termini biblico-teologici; linguaggio religioso e
linguaggio corrente²; appendici 1. termini ebraici; 2. islamici; 3. I concili ecumenici nella
vita della Chiesa; 4. Il simbolismo dei numeri nella cultura antica e nel mondo biblico; 5.
La 'strana' matematica di Dio. T 1994, Elle Di Ci. 263 p. Lᵐ 22. - RAng 72 (1995) 595s
(T. *Stancati*).

798   **Reicke** B., *Rost* L., Biblisch-historisches Handwörterbuch [1979]. Gö 1994,
Vandenhoeck & R. XL p., 2256 col.; 320 fig.; 60 pl.; 75 maps. - RSNTU 20 (1995) 191
(A. *Fuchs:* big bargain)

798*   **Retter** Hans, *Virt* Günter, Nuevo diccionario de moral cristiana. Barc 1993,
Herder. 632 p. -- RTE(spir) 39 (1995) 42 (J.A. *Heredia*).

799   **Rousseau** John J., *Arav* Rami, Jesus and his world; an archaeological and cultural
dictionary. Mp 1995, Fortress. xxiii-392 p. 0-8006-2805-5.

800 EToorn Karel van der, *al.* Dictionary of deities and demons in the Bible. Lei 1995,
Brill. xxxvi-1793 p. 90-04-10313-9.

A3.5 *Opera consultationis* **theologica** *non excerpta infra*

801 EAtkinson David J., *Field* David, New dictionary of Christian ethics and pastoral
theology. Leicester/DG 1995, Inter-Varsity. xxiii-918 p. £ 28. 0-85111-650-1 / 0-8308-
1408-6. - RET 106,10 3d-top choice (1994s) 291s (C.S. *Rodd*); *TBR 8,1 (1995s) 32s (P.
Ballard).

802 EBarratt David, *al.*, The discerning reader; Christian perspectives and theory [literary
criticism]. Leicester/GR 1995, Apollos/Baker. 320 p, 0-85111-445-8 / 0-8010-2085-9. -
R*TBR 8,3 (1995s) 17 (R.M. *Pryce*).

803 EBeinert Wolfgang, Handbook of Catholic theology [Lexikon der k. Dogmatik 1987],
TESchüssler Fiorenza Francis. NY 1995, Crossroad. $ 75. 0-8245-1423-8 [< ThD 42
(1995) 271].

804 **Bouyer** Louis, Breve dizionario di teologia [1963], T. Bo 1993, Dehoniane. 408 p. -
RFilTeo 9 (1995) 458-460 (M. *Farrugia*).

805 EByrne Peter, *Houlden* Leslie, Companion encyclopedia of theology. L 1995,
Routledge. xxiv-1092 p. 0-415-06447-3.

806 **Cameron** Nigel M., (*Wright* David F., *al.*), Dictionary of Scottish church history and theology 1993 → 9,626: [R]JETS 38 (1995) 463s (M.I. *Klauber*); ScoBuEv 12 (1994) 137-143 (M. *Noll*); W(estm)ThJ 57 (1995) 266-9 (P.G. *Ryken*).

807 [E]**Cancik** Hubert, *al.*, Handbuch religionswissenschaftlicher Grundbegriffe [1s, 1988/90 → 5,897: [R]HZ 261 (1995) 111-3 (C.J. *Classen*)] 3, 1993 → 8,627: [R]BoL (1995) 10 (L.L. *Grabbe*); ThQ 175 (1995) 72s (M. *Seckler*).

808 **Carrier** Hervé, Diccionario de cultura, para el análisis cultural y la inculturación [1992] [T]. Estella 1994, VDivino . 530 p. 84-7151-963-1. - [R]Greg 76 (1995) 790s (*ipse*).

809 **Christophe** Paul, Vocabulaire historique et culture chrétienne 1991 → 8,801: [R]FV 93,2 (1994) 81s (J.-D. *Dubois*).

[E]**Di Berardino** A., [TE]*Walford* A., Encyclopedia of the Early Church 1992 → 762 DPA supra.

811 [E]**Douglas** J.D., Twentieth-century dictionary of Christian biography. Carlisle/GR 1995, Paternoster/Baker. 439 p. $ 25. /0-8010-3031-5 [ThD 42,391]

812 [E]**Douglas** J.D., The new 20th century encyclopedia of religious knowledge [[1]1955 < *Schaff-Herzog* 1912]. GR 1991 → 7,720: [R]JETS 37 (1994) 440-2 (T.P. *Erdel*).

813 [E]**Dwyer** Judith A., The new dictionary of Catholic social thought 1994 → 10,547*: [R]CanadCath 13,6 (1995) 20 (M. *Ryan*).

814 **Ekstrom** Reynolds R., The new concise Catholic dictionary[2rev] [adding 100 items on the new Catechism]. Mystic CT / Dublin 1995, Twenty-Third / Columba. xviii-298 p. $ 10 pa. 0-89622-622-0 [< ThD 42 (1995) 267].

815 [E]**Elwell** Walter A., Concise evangelical dictionary of theology, [E]*Toon* Peter 1991 → 8,807: [R]S(co)BET 13 (1995) 180s (J. *Tallach*).

816 [E]**Encrève** André, Les Protestants: Dictionnaire du monde religieux dans la France contemporaine 5. P 1993, Beauchesne. 536 p. - [R]FV 92,6 (1993) 81-83 (P. *Grosjeanne*).

817 [E]**Floristan** Casiano, *Tamayo* Juan J., Conceptos fundamentales del cristianismo. M 1993, Trotta. 1524 p. - [R]SalTer 82 (1994) 242-4 (E. *Miret Magdalena*).

818 [E]**Glazier** Michael, *Hellwig* Monika K., The modern Catholic Encyclopedia. ColMn/L 1994, Liturgical/Gill & M. xxv-933 p. $ 70 0-8146-5495-9 / 0-7171-2192-5. - [R]CanadCath 13,8 (1995) 26s (J.M. *Samaha*); ET 106 (1994s) 188s (C.S. *Rodd* counts columns: John XXIII 23; Merton 9; Aquinas 4; -- women 9 + feminist 6; ministerial priestood 4; primacy of the Pope 1; Opus Dei factual but noteworthily; on Virgin Birth 'it is a question of whether God planted the symbol first in a historical event or only in the writings of the evangelists'; imprimatur shows 'in conformity to official Catholic teaching' as 1975 decree requires); RExp 92 (1995) 389s W.L. *Hendricks*: for Architecture and Art each more space than for Aquinas).

819 [E]**Härle** Wilfried, *Wagner* Harald, Theologenlexikon, von den Kirchenvätern bis zur Gegenwart[2rev] 1994 → 10,552: [R](Tü)TQ 175 (1995) 371s (R. *Reinhardt*).

820 [E]**Heraty** Jack. New Catholic Encyclopedia [1967] Supplement [I. 1974; II. 1979. III. 1988. (IV):] 1989-1995. Palatine IL 1995, Heraty (& Wsh Catholic U.). xiv-468 p. $ 80 (all 19 volumes $ 990) [ThD 43,78].

821 [E]**Hinnells** John R., A new dictionary of religions. Ox 1995, Blackwell. xxxvii-760 p.; bibliog. 577-676. 0-631-18139-3.

822 **Jongeneel** Jan A.B., Philosophy, science, and theology of mission in the 19th and 20th centuries, a missiological encyclopedia, I. The philosophy and science of mission. Fra/NY 1995, Lang. xxiii-403 p. $ 53. - [R]IBM(iss)R 19 (1995) 182s (G.H. *Anderson*).

823 **Kelly** Joseph F., The concise dictionary of early Christianity 1992 → 8,814; $ 25 [franç. 1994 → 10,554]: [R]ChH 64 (1995) 754 (E. *Ferguson*).

824 **McBrien** Richard, The HarperCollins encyclopedia of Catholicism. SF 1995, HarperSF. xxxviii-1349 p. $ 45. - [R]SewaneeTR 39 (1995s) 333s (D.S. *Armentrout*); Tablet 249 (1995) 1207 (M. *Walsh*: best of 5 cognates).

825 [E]**McGrath** Alister E., The Blackwell encyclopedia of modern Christian thought 1993 → 9,639: [R]A(ndr)USS 33 (1995) 137-9 (F.M. *Hasel*: best of a whole new generation of reference works); CanadCath 13,1 (1995) 30 (D. *Donovan*); Theol 97 (L 1994) 364-6 (I. *Markham*).

826 [E]**Mandziuk** Józef, [P] *Słownik polskich teologów katolickich* 1981-1993: Lexicon theologorum catholicorum Poloniae 8. Wsz 1995, Akademia Teologii Katolickiej. 693 p. 83-7072-057-9.

827 **Mondin** Battista, Dizionario enciclopedico dei Papi: storia e insegnamenti. R 1995, Città nuova. 648 p. [RHE 91.53*]. - [R]Div 40 (1995) 100-2 (D. *Composta*).

828 **O'Collins** G., *Farrugia* E.G., Dizionario sintetico di teologia [Eng. 1991 -> 7,737], [T]. Vaticano 1995, Editrice. 436 p. L[m] 32. 88-209-2049-2. - [R]Ang 72 (1995) 472s (T. *Stancati*: traduzione insoddisfacente); RasT 36 (1995) 635s (G. *Mattai*): RivScRel 9 (1995) 461s (M. *Semeraro*).

829 **Pikaza** Xabier, *Silanes* Nereo, Diccionario teológico El Dios cristiano 1992 → 9,645; 84-85376-96-X. - [R]Greg 76 (1995) 601s (F.-A. *Pastor*).

830 **Retter** Hans, *Virt* Günter, Nuevo diccionario de moral cristiana. Barc 1993, Herder. 632 p. - [R]TE(spir) 39 (1995) 42 (J.A. *Heredia*).

831 [E]**Sartori** Domenico, *Triacca* Achille M., Dictionnaire encyclopédique de la liturgie I. A-L [1984], [TE] *Delhougne* Henri. Turnhout 1992, Brepols. 2-503-50248-2. - EO(rans) 10 (1993) 111s (A. *Nocent*).

832 [E]**Smith** Jonathan Z., The HarperCollins dictionary of religion. SF 1995, HarperSF. xxx-1154 p. $ 45. 0-06-067515-2 [ThD 43,170; RStR 22,333, B.M. *Wheeler*].

833 Urbaniano, Dizionario di missiologia. Bo 1993, Dehoniane. xiv-545 p. L[m] 70. 88-10-20564-2. - [R]IBM(iss)R 19 (1995) 85 (W.R. *Burrows*).

834 **Urech** Edouard, Dizionario dei simboli cristiani: La via dei simboli. R 1995, Arkeios. 271 p.

835 [E]**Wace** Henry, *Piercy* William C., A dictionary of Christian biography and literature to the end of the sixth century A.D., with an account of the principal sects and heresies. Peabody MA 1994, Hendrickson. xi-1028 p. 1-56563-857-2.

836 **Waldenfels** Hans, Nuovo dizionario delle religioni [1987, [2]1988],[T]. Torino 1993, San Paolo. 1078 p. L[m] 85. - [R]CivCatt 146 (1995,1) 90-92 (N. *Venturini*).

837 [E]**Weller** Paul, (*Castle* Rachelle), Religions in the UK; a multi-faith directory: Inter-Faith Network, 1993 → 9,638; 0-901437-06-9: [R]ET 106 (1994s) 286 (M. *Braybrooke*).

A3.6 *Opera consultationis* **generalia**

838 **Alekseeva** O.E., *Savvonidy* N.F., English-Russian and Russian-English illustrated historical and archaeological dictionary. St. Petersburg 1993. 112 p. - [R]RossArkh (1995,2) 249s (L.S. *Klein*).

839 [E]**Apostolos-Cappadona** Diane, Dictionary of Christian art 1994 → 10,294a: [R]E(xp)T 107 (1995s) 93 (J.B. *Bates*: also Lutterworth. £ 17.50; 0-7188-2932-8); Modern Believing [continuing the numbering of Modern Churchman] 36,3 (1995) 46s (G. *Pattison*: 'Crossroad').

840 [R]**Asher** R.E., The encyclopedia of language and linguistics. Ox 1994, Pergamon. xlvii-5644 p. (10 vol.) $ 2975. --Lg 71 (1995) 146-150 (B. *Comrie*: increase over J. BRIGHT's 1992 4-vol. work well justified).

841 **Baritaud** Bernard, 50 mots-clés de la culture générale classique. P 1992, Marabout. 274 p -- [R]RÉG 108 (1995) 223 (P. *Cauderlier*).

842 [E]**Barthel** Günter, *Stock* Kristina, Lexikon Arabische Welt; Kultur, Lebensweise, Wirtschaft, Politik und Natur im Nahen Osten und Nordafrika. Wsb 1994, Reichert. xv-776 p.; 2 maps (4000 Stichwörter, 60 Mitarbeiter). DM 198. 3-88226-783-6. -- [R]WZKM 85 (1995) 303s (H. *Eisenstein*).

843 [E]**Brunel** Pierre, *a*) Dictionnaire des mythes littéraires. P 1988. --*b*) Companion to literary myths, heroes and archetypes, [E]*Allatson* W., *al.* L 1992, Routledge. xvi-1223 p. 0-415-06460-0. -: [R]Salesianum 57 (1995) 797 (R. *Bracchi*).

844 [E]**Brunner** Hellmut, *al.*, Lexikon alter Kulturen 1-3, 1990-3 → 9,666: [R]ZAW 107 (1995) 162s (M. *Köckert*).

845 [E]**Crystal** David, The Cambridge biographical encyclopedia. C 1994, Univ. 1304 p. $ 30. 0-521-43421-11. -- [R]ET 106 (1994s) 159 (C.S. *Rodd*).

846 [E]**Dinzelbacher** Peter, Sachwörterbuch der Mediävistik: Tb 477. Stu 1992, Kröner. xxii-942 p. 3-520-47701-7. -- [R]Salesianum 57 (1995) 561 (P.T. *Stella*).

847 **Kytzler** Bernhard, Frauen der Antike, von Aspasia bis Zenobia. Z 1994, Artemis. 191 p.; ill.

848 **LIMC**: Lexicon iconographicum mythologiae classicae, [E]*Kahil* Lilly [6. 1992 → 9,664; 10,571: [R]AAW 48,1s (1995) 98-100 (H. *Walter*)] -- 7. Oidipous-Theseus. Z 1994, Artemis. xxxi-1065 p., 191 fig.: vol. of 816 p. (750 pl.; 4353 phot.) 3-7608-8751-1. -- [R]AJA 99 (1995) 743s (Brunilde S. *Ridgway*); MH(elv) 52 (1995) 181 (K. *Schefold*).

849 **Liverani** Francesco, Dizionario dell'antilingua; le parole dette per non dire quello che si ha paura di dire. Mi 1993, Ares. 128 p. -- [R]VitaCons 31 (1995) 245 (G. *Poli*).

850 [E]**Maillard** J.-F., *al.*, L'Europe des humanistes (XIVe-XVIIe siècles); répertoire: Documents, Études et Répertoires. Turnhout 1995, Brepols. 543 p. 2-503-50435-3.

851 **Pastoureau** Michel, Dictionnaire des couleurs de notre temps; symbolique et société. P 1992, T. Gautier. 232 p. -- [R]MelSR 52 (1995) 115s (H. *Platelle*).

852 **Speake** G., A dictionary of ancient history. Ox 1994, Blackwell. x-758 p.; 10 maps. £ 35. -- [R]CLR 45 (1995) 149s (S.C. *Todd*).

853 [E]**Stern** Ephraim, The new encyclopedia of archaeological excavations in the Holy Land 1993 → 9,669: [R]A(ndr)USS 33 (1995) 152-4 (D. *Merling*: excellent, but lacks Arab co-editors).

854 [E]**Yarshater** Ehsan, Encyclopaedia iranica III,1-8, 1987s → 7,761: IV,1-8, Bayjú-Carpets: V. Carpets-coffee 1992; VI,1-6, Cotton-Dayerai 1993 → 9,672: [R]ArOr 62 (1994) 326-8 (M. *Shaki*, IV-V); JAOS 115 (1995) 500s (E.L. *Daniel*, V: high quality scholarship despite typos); OLZ 89 (1994) 309-313.409-413 (III-IV) & 90 (1995) 75-80 (W. *Sundermann*, V,1-8: some 50 'more notable' corrections for each); VDI 214 (1995) 206-9 (I.N. *Medvedskaya*, [R]).

A4 **Bibliographiae**, computers .1 **biblicae**

855 *a*) **Adrados** Francisco R., *Rodríguez Somolinos* Juan, The T(hesaurus)L(inguae) G(raecae) data bank, the DGE and Greek lexicography; -- *b*) *Johnson* William A., Towards an electronic Greek historical lexicon : EM(erita) 62 (1994) 241-251 / 253-261.

856 *Aletti* Jean-Noël, Bulletin paulinien: R(ech)SR 83 (1995) 97-126; 20 livres.

857 *Barnwell* K., A translation consultant's perspective on CARLA (computer-assisted related language adaptation); *NoTr 9,3 (1995) 20-28 [NTAb 40, p.402, noting 8 cognate articles there].

858 *Best* Ernest. Recent continental NT literature [GNILKA J., SCHMITHALS W., BERGER R. SCHNELLE U., RIEBERS R. ..]: : ET 106 (1994s) 247-270.

859 Bible et informatique 3, 1991/2 → 8,450*: ᴿRB 102 (1995) 470s (É. *Nodet*).

860 Bible Works for Windows: Hermeneutika, Bible Research Software. Big Fork MT (59911 POB 2200), $ 300 (if 5 or more, $ 200). -- ᴿTPQ 143 (1995) 105.107 (F. *Böhmisch*).

861 *Bloomquist* L.G., Networked pre-publication models; opportunities, possibilities. and outstanding questions in the 'University without walls': *JRTInf 2,1 (Binghamton NY) 95-114 [NTAb 39, p.302].

862 *Böhmisch* Franz, *Dandl* Christian, Mit der Bibel ins Internet-Zeitalter; --*b) Leisch-Kiesl* Monika, Mittels Computerkunst die Welt erschliessen -- ? : TPQ 143 (1995) 247-257 / 265-9, *al.*

863 **Bolognesi** Pietro, Repertorio bibliografico su Bibbia e teologia: STEv supp. Padova 1993, IFED. 102 p. --ᴿSTEv 7 (1995) 67 (L. *De Chirico*).

864 ᴱ*Camplani* Alberto, *Perrone* Lorenzo, Bibliografia generale di storia dell'interpretazione biblica 11s (1995) 171-208 . 431-480.

865 CD-ROM for PV & Macintosh, *a)* The Dead Sea Scrolls revealed. Oak Harbor WA c. 1995, Logos. $ 60. -- *b)* Exploring ancient cities. SF c.1995, Sumeria for Scientific American. $ 50. --: ᴿBArR 21,4 (1995) 6. 8 (S. *Feldman*; hot, pyrotechnics; but just an introduction).

866 Church Bytes software guide [350 programs for DOS, Windows, Macintosh & CD-ROM. Durham NC c. 1994, Church Bytes periodical. 90 p. $ 18. 1-919-490-8927 [RExp 92 (1995) 234 adv.]

867 *Daley* S.C., Seven software packages for Bible research [... Bible Word Plus ... Bible Works for Windows]: *NoTr 9,4 (1995) 1-13 [NTAb 40, p.404].

868 ᴱ*Deegan* Marilyn, *Gore* Keith. Information technology as an aid to literary research, 1: *LitLComput 10 (1995) 33-68.

869 Dissertation Abstracts 54 (1993-4) is excerpted at great length in ZAW 107 (1995) 312-9. [This Elenchus 11 (for 1995) gives relevant articles from DissA **disk** 56 (1995s), in which the single fascicles are not fully accessible, though there is varied convenient topic-indexing.]

870 Dissertationen und Habilitationsschriften: BZ 39 (1995) 312-9 [seit 34 (1990) 155-9 -- hiernach 1997, -9 usw.].

871 *Dritsas* D.,Index of authors (by subject-matter) 1971-1993: D(eltio)BM 13,2 (1993) 71-82.

872 *Gallino* Luciano, L'eco-computer planetario [non si riferisce all'ecologia. bensí al Network, 'l'insieme delle connessioni elettroniche che permettono a un qualsiasi computer di collegarsi in un paio di secondi con milioni di altri computer]: quale futuro ? : RasT 36 (1995) 327-338.

873 **Garcia** Eugenio & Rocio, Agenda bíblica 1966 [mitad de la página: lecturas y comentos para cada día]. Estella 1995, Verbo Divino.

874 *a) Glünz* Michael, Representing the text: some preliminary remarks on an important scholarly activity; --*b) Fendt* Kurt, Interactive reading; hypertext and literary studies: → 469, StIranMesopAnat 1 (Praha 1994) 179-188 / 161-6.

875 Gramcord Hebrew/Greek Macintosh 1994 [< OTA 18 (1995) p. 178s (A.A. *Di Lella*)].

876 *Harrington* Daniel, [29] Books on the Bible: America 172,12 (1995) 22-29.

877 **Holleman** Joost, An index to Vetus Testamentum, volumes 1-45 (1951-1995). Lei 1996, Brill. vii-451 p. 90-04-10605-7.

878 **Hostetter** Edwin C., Old Testament introduction: IBR bibliographies 11 (of eventually 14, to be updated every 5 years; here 500 items, almost all in English). GR 1995, Baker. 106 p. $ 8. 0-8010-2017-4 [< OTA 19,p.328; ThD 43,273].

879 **Hsu** Jeffrey, A comprehensive guide to computer study 1993 → 9,688; title differently: [R]IrBSt 16 (1994) 195s.

880 **IZBG**: Internationale Zeitschriftenschau für Bibelwissenschaft und Grenzgebiete 40 (meist 1993-4), [E]**Lang** Bernhard. Dü 1995, Patmos. xiv-405 p.; summaries English or German. 3-491-66040-8 [42, 1995s: 1997; 505 p.; 0074-9745].

881 *Lange* Armin, *Römheld* K.F.D., Dokumentation neuer Texte [Voces → 5860 infra; Grammatik → J8: ZAH(ebr) 8 (1995) 101-120 . 317-339.

882 *a) Ledger* Gerard, An exploration of differences in the Pauline Epistles using multivariant statistical analyses; --*b) Mealand* D.L., Correspondence analysis of Luke; --*c) Greenwood* H.H., Common word frequencies and authorship in Luke's Gospel and Acts: Literary and Linguistic Computing 10 (Ox 1995; 0268-1145) 35-98 / 171-182 / 183-7.

883 LÉON-DUFOUR Xavier, Publications (1937-1995). P 1995, r.Sèvres 35bis VI. 35 p. [NTAb 40,p.512].

884 **Linmans** A.J.M., Onderschikking [subordination] in de synoptische evangeliën; syntaxis, *discourse*-functies en stilometrie [diss. Nijmegen 1995, [D]*Iersel* B. van]. Lei 1995, FSW. xii-321 p.; 7 files on diskette, demarcation in ASCII, WP, SPSS: 6 p. Eng. summary.

885 Lion PC Handbook of the Bible: Lyon/Lynx computer software. £ 51. -- [R]ScotBuEv 12 (1994) 150 (B. *Akers*: hard to use).

886 Logos Bible study software. Marlton NJ 1992. 7 disks, manual. $ 129. -- A(ustrl)BR 41 (1993) 90s.

887 MARTINI Carlo M., Gli scritti; saggio bibliografico 1956-1994: S(cuol)C 123 (1995) 5-47 (A. *Orczyk, al.*) [RHE 90 (1995) 15*].

888 *Mason* Rex. Recent continental OT literature (LEVIN C., KAISER O., WÜRTHWEIN E., MATHYS H.): ET 106 (1994s) 331-4.

889 **Mills** Watson & Joyce, An Index to Novum Testamentum volumes 1-35 [1956-1990; 80 art.; reviews; themes]. Leiden 1994, Brill. ix-256 p. DM 85; sb. 65. -- [R]NT 37 (1995) 410s (J.K. *Elliott:* subject-index least likely to be used since volumes like this *Elenchus bibliographicus biblicus* are to hand).

890 **Mills** Watson E., Bibliographies for biblical research 4. The Gospel of John. Lewiston 1995, Melchior Novesianus. xxiv-410 p. 0-7734-2357-5.

891 **Minor** Mark, Literary-critical approaches to the Bible; an annotated bibliography 1992 → 8,868: [R]A(ndr)USS 33 (1995) 139s (Miary *Andriamiarisoa*).

892 New Testament Society of South Africa, list of members 1995: Neotest 29 (1995) 437-446.

893 [E]**Nogueira** Paulo A. de Souza, *al.*, Bibliografía bíblica latino-americana 6 (1993). São Paulo 1995, Vozes. 487 p. [< OTA 19, p.334s, G.A. *Klingbeil*].

894 [E]*Pesce* Mauro, Rassegna di Storia dell'esegesi, 7: ASEs 12 (1995) 145-155: 14 libri.

895 *Pilarczyk* Krzysztof, Quellen zu einer Bibliographie hebräischer Drucke des 16.-18. Jahrhunderts aus Polen -- Johannes BUXTORF's Bibliotheca Rabbinica, [T]*Schreiner* Stefan: Jud(ca) 51 (1995) 237-250.

896 *Piñero* Antonio, New Testament philology bulletin 15s: FgNt 8 (1995) 105-138 / 239-270 (*Godoy* Antonio, Libros recibidos, anotados, 141-8 . 273-281).

897 **Porter** S.E., *McDonald* L.M., New Testament introduction: IBR Bbg 12. GR 1995, Baker. 234 p. $ 14. 0-8010-2060-3 [NTAb 40,p.514].

898 ᴱ**Richler** Benjamin, Guide to Hebrew manuscript collections [50,000 items from the whole world, microfilmed in Israel]. J 1994, Israel Academy. xvi-314 p. $ 35. -- ᴿJQR 85 (1994s) 433s (R.S. *Kohn*).

899 *a) Richter* Wolfgang, Text, Sprache und Computer -- oder: Hilft der Rechner auch einem Geisteswissenschaftler [Amos and its environment -- our experiences]; -- *b) Árnason* Hróbjartur, Applying MRTs (machine-readable texts) to the PC (personal computer); the application of Biblia Hebraica Transcripta to the PC as a practical example: → 469, StIranMesopAnat 1 (Praha 1994) 237-245 [231-5] / 151-9.

900 **Riennecker** Fritz, *Maier* Gerhard, Lexikon zur Bibel auf Diskette [DOS 3.3 oder höher, ab Windows 3,1]. Giessen/Wu 1994, Brunnen/Brockhaus. 8 (3.5") Disketten. DM 148. 3-417-09000-8 [ThRv 91.360].

900* *Runia* D.T., *al.*, Philo annotated bibliography 1992 [provisional 1993-5]: StPhilo 7 (1995) 186-212 [213-22].

901 SBL annual meeting with [J]AAR [and ASOR], Philadelphia, Nov. 18-21, 1995, program (p.49-174); p. 1-47, information; 175-340, advertisers' book notices.

902 *Scholer* David M., Q bibliography supplement VI [to be included in a cumulative bibliography ᴱ**Robinson** J., *al.*, awaited 1997]: → 512, SBL Seminars 34 (1995) 1-5.

903 **Seethaler** Paula-Angelika, Register [zu]: Stu Kleiner Kommentar NT 19. Stu 1995, KBW. 192 p. 3-460-15491-8.

904 ᴱ**Shinan** Avigdor, Kiryat Sefer, Bibliography of all the publications in Israel and of Judaica from abroad 65 (1994s). 1130 p.; indexes 1131-1172.

905 Vangelo vivo su 4 floppy disc per lettura ordinata o sinottica, ricerca automatica dei paralleli e rimandi, con carte geo-topografiche e illustrazioni; pref. MARTINI C.M. CinB 1994, Paoline. 238 p. Lᵐ 85. 88-215-2889-8 : ᴿAng 72 (1995) 320-2 (T. *Stancati*: infelicemente DOS è in via di scomparire!)

906 *Velisiotis* Georgios, Computers! indefatigable contributors to the Old Testament studies nowadays: D(elt)BM 14,1 (1995) 76-79 (in English).

907 **Verheij** Adrian J.C., Grammatica digitalis 1. The morphological code in the 'Werkgroep Informatica' computer text of the entire Bible. Amst 1994, VU. 88 p. $ 20. -- ᴿCBQ 57 (1995) 794 (K.E. *Lowery* finds clues to underlying linguistic theory, but offers no comparison with the Munich project).

908 **Watson** Duane F., *Hauser* Alan J., Rhetorical criticism of the Bible: a comprehensive bibliography with notes on history and method: BInterpS 4, 1994 → 10,608: ᴿCBQ 57 (1995) 615s (Margaret M. *Mitchell*).

909 **Weisbard** Phyllis H., *Schonberg* David, Jewish law, bibliography ... : ᴿJQR 84 (1993s) 99-101 (A.M. *Fuss*, also on RAKOVER N. 1990).

910 *a) Wessely* Christian, 'Virtual reality' und christliche Theologie -- Theotechnologie; -- *b) Böhmisch* Franz, *Dandl* Christian. Mit der Bibel ins Internet-Zeitalter; *--c) Niewiadomski* Józef, Extra media nulla salus ? zum Anspruch der Medienkultur: TPQ 143 (1995) 235-245 / 247-257 [258-278, *al.*] / 227-233.

911 **Wieringen** Archibald van, Instrumentarium Oude Testament; een bibliographisch oversicht met korte annotaties. Amst 1995, VU. xiii-129 p. 90-5383-420-6 [< OTA 19, p.151].

912 *Williamson* H.G.M., Bibliographical survey; archaeology and biblical studies: JJS 46 (1995) 354-8.

913 Zeitschriftenschau : ZNW 86 (1995) 130-2 . 288-291.

914 **Zucchi** Gabriella, *al.*, Indici vol, 1-30 [1980-1994]; Parola Spirito e Vita 33 supp. (1996). 128 p.

A4.2 *Bibliographiae* **theologicae.**

915 *Alfonseca* Manuel, La religión en las autopistas de la información [... congresos; Internet] : Rel(y)Cult 41 (1995) 841-852.

916 *Allen* P., *Mayer* W., Computer and homily; accessing the everyday life of the early Christians: VigChr 47 (1993) 260-280 < RHE 90 (1995) 201*.

917 American Society of Missiology, directory of members: Missiology 22 (1994) 271-5; important / essential books, 144 . 237 . 415 . 551.

918 *Bächtold* Hans Ulrich, *Haag* Hans Jakob, Neue Literatur zur zwinglischen Reformation: Zwingliana 21 (1994) 113-135; 22 (1995) 109-128.

919 *Ballatori* Mauro, *Dell'Oro* Ferdinando, Indice 1914-1983: Rivista Liturgica 82,5s (1995) 400 p.

920 BEDNARSKI Feliks O.P., bibliog. : STV(ars) 32,1 (1994) 169-192 (J. *Wichrowicz*).

921 *Bertuletti* Angelo, *al.*, I problemi metodologici della teologia sulle riviste del 1994: TeolBr 20 (1995) 359-456.

922 BESUTTI Giuseppe M., (1919-1994), cultore di mariologia, bibliografo: Marianum 57 (1995) 439-491 (S.M. *Danieli*).

923 Bibliographia oecumenica [+ Journals table of contents]: E(cu)R 47 (1995) 121s . 242-4 . 405-7 -- [117-9 . 239-241 . 398-404 . 512-7].

924 Bibliographie 1994s: Kirchliche Zeitgeschichte 8 (1995) 674-651.

925 BÖCHER Otto, 60. Gb., Bibliographie: ThLZ 120 (1995) 382-392 (E. *Otto, al.*)..

926 Bollettino bibliografico sulla vita consacrata 1993 / 1994: Claretianum 34 (1994) 489-594 / 35 (1995) 387-493.

927 *Borasi* Carlo, Pensiero informatico, intelligenza artificiale, pensiero teologico: Anton 70,3s ('Gaudium et spes' 1995) 609-656; Eng. 609.

928 *Bouwen* Frans, *al.*, Tables générales 21-45. 1971-1995: Proche-Orient Chrétien 45,3s (1995). 176* p.

929 Catechismo della Chiesa Cattolica su sei floppy disk IBM compatibili. Vaticano/Padova 1993, Editrice/Unitelm. -- RAng 72 (1995) 115-7 (T. *Stancati*).

930 The CETEDOC library of Christian Latin texts on CD-ROM. Turnhout 1991, Brepols. $ 3800. --RCJ 90 (1994s) 90-96 (T. *Bucknall*, C.M. *McDonough*: Greek and Hebrew citations are a mess; but Latin Migne CD-ROM costs $ 50,000).

931 COLOMBO Giuseppe, 70° compleanno: TeolBrescia 19 (2994) 217-237 (*Dal Pozzo* Emma, EColombo Paolo).

932 *De Klerk* Peter, CALVIN bibliography 1992 / 1993 / 1994 / 1995: C(alvin)TJ 27 (1992) 325-352 / 28 (1993) 393-419 / 29 (1994) 451-485 / 30 (1995) 419-447.

933 DELIUS Hans-Ulrich, 65. Gb.: ThLZ 120 (1993) 727-732 (V. *Gummelt*).

934 Dissertationes doctorales 1993-4: ETL 71 (1995) 281s [those of biblical interest presumed noted here from RTLv].

935 Dissertations 1950-75, Faculté protestante de théologie: Analecta Bruxellensia 1, 191-3 (194-206 mémoires de licence).

936 Dissertations *a)* completed (some 1993, most 1994: cited in preceding Elenchus volumes); *b)* 'in progress' (about 300, rarely cited here): RStR 21 (1995) 251-7 / 162-7.

937 *Dobbeler* Stephanie von, Feministische Liturgien, eine Bibliographie : AL(tg)W 37 (1995) 1-22; Register 23s.

938 *Doré* Joseph, Bulletin de théologie fondamentale ... contemporaine: R(ech)SR 83 (1995) 73-96 . 303-323.

939 *Durand* G.-M. de, Bulletin de Patrologie: RSPT 79 (1995) 89-112.

940 Evangelical Review of Theology, Index 1997-1995 : ERT 19 (1995) 407-448.

941 Evangelical Theological Society, Directory of members [with postal address] : JETS 37 (1994) 285-317; officers 320.

942 **Fackler** P. Mark, *Lippy* Charles H., Popular religious magazines of the United States: Historical guides to the world's periodicals and newspapers. Westport CT 1995, Greenwood. xvii-595 p. $ 125, 0-313-28533-0 [ThD 43,82: 5-page article for each describes origins, policy shifts, present availability; companion to the 1986 Academic and scholarly (religious) journals].

943 **Fahey** Michael A., Ecumenism; a bibliographical overview: BbgRel 23, 1992 → 9,724: ᴿDiEc 30 (1995) 129s (J.J. *Alemany*).

944 **Flint** Kathy D., *Tacke* Margret, Index to book reviews in religion 1994. Evanston 1995, ATLA. 912 p. 0887-1574.

945 *Frei* Gunhild: Bibliographie: ZEE(thik) 38 (1994) 71 . 158-160 . 239s . 319s.

946 **Geist** Lucie, 'Ein Geschäft recht geistlicher Natur'; zum 200. Jahrestag der Gründung des J.C. Hinrichs-Verlag [TLZ seit 1876]. Lp 1991, Sachsenverlag. 83 p. DM 29.80. 3-910155-00-6. -- ᴿThLZ 120 (1995) 313 (E.-H. *Amberg*).

947 GENSICHEN Hans-Werner, Bibliographie 1980-1994: ZM(iss)R 79 (1995) 183-8 (H. *Wrogemann*); p.82 phot.; laudatio (T. *Sundermeier*).

948 *Gilliot* Claude, Islamologie: RSPT 79 (1995) 467-517

949 *Granado* Carmelo, Boletín de literatura antigua cristiana (1994): E(st)E 70(1995) 527-549.

950 *Green* Ronald M., The Journal of Religious Ethics 1973-1974: RelStR 21 (1995) 180-6

951 Habilitationen / Dissertationen im akademischen Jahr 1994/95: ThRv 92 (1996-Band!) i-xiv. Beilage Fasz. 2 nach S.136.

952 *a) Häussling* Angelus A., *Neunheuser* Burkhard, Der Gottesdienst der Kirche; Texte, Quellen, Studien : AL(tg)W 37 (1995) 93-135 (-225, *al.); -- b) Severus* Emmanuel von, Der Gottesdienst in den geistlichen Gemeinschaften und sein Fortwirken in der Spiritualität; *--c) Häussling* Angelus A., Liturgie in Arbeitsinstrumentarien und Sammelwerken : AL(tg)W 37 (1995) 367-404 / 405-441.

953 *Haquin* André, Liturgie et sacrements; quelques ouvrages récents: RTL 26 (1995) 463-483: Eng. 609.

954 **Hardcastle** Nigel, Computers for churches [his 1986-9 'Church Computer Project' updated to 1993]. L 1993, CCBI. 168 p. £ 7. 9-85169-213-3. -- ᴿS(co)BET 13 (1995) 161s (M. *Houston*).

955 **Hartley** Loyde H., Cities and churches; an international bibliography: ATLA 31. Metuchen 1992, Scarecrow. xix-2765 p. (3 vol.) -- ᴿChH 64 (1995) 544-6 (J.W. *Lewis:* valuable despite troubling omissions).

956 **Haverals** M., Bibliographie; RHE 90 (1995) 511* p., 6781 titres. Beyond praise !

957 *Hendricks* Frans, Literaturoversicht 1993: OnsGErf 68 (1994) 281-358.

958 ᴱ**Henkel** Willi, Bibliographia missionaria LVI -- 1992. R 1993, Pontifical Urban Univ. 494 p. $ 30. -- ᴿIBM(iss)R 18 (1994) 133s (J.H. *Kroeger*).

959 *Henze* Klaus-Manfred, [eingesandte] Theologische Literatur: ThRv 91 (1995) 74-90 . 179-194 . 269-282 . 357-370 . 445-8. 533-6 (Bibel 75-77 . 181-3 . 272-4 . 359-361 . 534-6).

960 Index international des dissertations doctorales en théologie et en droit canonique présentées en 1994 : RTL 26 (1995) 523-596; 924 titres surtout européens, relativement peu de duplication avec DissA. --P. 530-540, AT-Judaïsme-NT; p. 559-561 / 568-370 / 588s / 589-592, histoire/philosophie/théologie/sociologie-psychologie des religions. La plupart citée avec reconnaissance et admiration dans notre vol. 10.

961 [Innsbruck: 14] Dissertationen im Jahre 1994/5: ZkT 117 (1995) 503-512.

962 **Jones** Charles E., The charismatic movement; a guide to the study of Neo-Pentecostalism with emphasis on Anglo-American sources [11,000 items]: ATLA. Metuchen NJ, Scarecrow. xlvi-1220 p. (2 vol.) $ 120. 0-8108-2565-1 [< ThD 42 (1995) 275].

963 Journal of Psychology and Theology 21,5 (1993) 95 p.: Twenty-year Index.

964 Junge Kirche 55 (1994) Index: JK 56 (1995) 96.

965 **Kadel** Andrew, Matrology; a bibliography of writings by Christian women from the first to the fifteenth centuries. NY 1995, Continuum. 191 p. $ 29.50. 0-8264-0676-9 [RStR 22,253, Susan A. *Harvey*].

966 *Kalde* Franz, EDV [elektronische (Ordinateur-, Computer-) Datenverarbeitung] und Kirche; Aspekte eines vielschichtigen Verhältnisses: MThZ 45 (1994) 69-78.

967 *Keller* Paul, L'Église confrontée à l'espace public [trois types: proximité, télécommunication, informatica]: ETRel 70 (1995) 61-74.

968 ᴱ*Kołosowski* Tadeusz, Biuletyn patrystyzny: C(olc)Th 64,1 (1994) 87-96; 64,4 (1994) 89-94.

969 *Krüger* Klaus, Biblographische Hinweise zur ökumenischen Theologie: Cath 49 (1995) 145-162.

970 *Lamberterie* Isabelle de, Informatique, libertés et opinions religieuses; la protection des convictions individuelles et le traitement automatisé des informations nominatives: ASS(oc)R 91 (1995) 21-38; Eng.,español 39.

971 *Larkin* David, Articles on inculturation and liturgical inculturation: MilltSt 35 (1995) 89-112.

972 *Lazcano* Rafael, Bibliografía histórico-agustiniana publicada en España (1991-1994): RevAg 35 (1994) 1123-1191.

973 LEDER Hans-Günter, Bibliographie: ThLZ 120 (1995) 946-950 (V. *Gummelt*).

974 LexTQ 30 (1995) 221-297: Index 1986-1995.

975 LÖWENBERG Bruno (1907-26.X.1994) Bibliographie : AL(tg)W 37 (1995) 359-363 (F. *Schneider*).

976 ᴱ*Marcol* Alojzy, Biuletyn teologicznomoralny: C(olc)Th 64,1 (1994) 117-131 [64,3 (1994) 115-131; 64/4, 97-112, ᴱ*Graczyk* Marian].

977 *Marti* Andreas, Literaturbericht zur Hymnologie; deutschsprachige Länder (1992) 1993-1995 : JLH(ymn) 35 (1994s) 233-291.

978 *Martínez Fresneda* Francisco, Boletín de Patrística [30 escritos]: *Carthaginensia 11 (1995) 133-161.

979 Members of the American Society of Church History, September 1995: ChH 64 (1995) 762-790.

980 *Millán Romeral* Fernando, Boletín: La conciencia de Jesús: MCom(illas) 53(1995)531-64.

981 *a) Miranda* Vicente, El tema de moral en las revistas; panorama bibliografico 1994, --
b) Lobo José Antonio, Lineas y tendencias de la teología moral latinoamericana: Moralia 18 (1995) 219-317 / 343-360.

982 ᴱ*Nadolski* Bogusław, Biuletyn liturgiczny: C(olc)Th 64,1 (1994) 97-116; 64,4 (1994) 113-135.

982* Nicolaus Indici I/1973 --XX/1993: Nicolaus 21 (1994) 265-330.

983 Overzicht Tijdschriften [.. Herademing, Mara, Ter Herkenning. Speling, Theologia Reformata, Soteria, Religieuze bewegingen in Nederland > plures infra]: G(ereformeerd)TT 95 (1995) 47s . 93-95 . 150s . 205s.

984 *Painchaud* Louis, *Pasquier* Anne, *Poirier* Paul-Hubert, Ancienne littérature chrétienne et histoire de l'Église [30 livres]: LavalThP 51 (1995) 421-461.

985 *Patrylo* Isidor, Bibliographia ecclesiae ucrainae: An(alecta Ordinis S,) Bas(ilii Magni) 14 (1992) 325-439; 403 items; index 441-7. -- The articles of this volume are summarized in English on p. vi-ix.

986 Pelas revistas : REB 55 (1995) 266-270 . 507-510 . 761ss . 1027-31 [Siglas 53 (1993) 1009-12].

987 Phase 34,200 (1994) 91-160:Indices de los números 101-200.

988 ᴱ**Prebish** Charles, *CritRR,* Critical review of books in religion 8 (1995). At (1996), Scholars. v-546 p.

989 Princeton Seminary faculty publications 1994: PSB 16 (1995) 228-239.

990 *Printzipas* Y.T., Bibliographikòn deltíon : TheolA 66 (1995) 813-832 (cf. 837-9, P. *Simotas* on G. Tsananâ).

991 Pro Dialogo 87 (1994) 289-309: index 74-84.

992 Publications des professeurs de l'Institut Catholique de Toulouse (1990-1995); BLE 96 (1995) 87-126.

993 *Razzino* G., *al.*, Dai sommari delle riviste : FilTeo 8 (1994) 553-576.

994 Revista de Revistas: : RET 55 (1995) 411-7 . 269-280 . 541-553 [todos autores y periódicos incluidos en Indice 555-575 e 576].

995 **Robinson** Thomas A., The early Church; an annotated bibliography of literature in English: ATLA 33. Metuchen NJ 1993, Scarecrow. xxiii-493 p. £ 57.50. 0-8108-2763-8. - ᴿJEH 46 (1995) 351 (W.H.C. *Frend*).

996 *Roey* A. Van, Corpus Christianorum series graeca (CCSG) [vols. 12-30, 1985-94]: ETL 71 (1995) 277-280.

997 *Roll* Susan K., *al.*, Louvain theology faculty chronicle: LouvSt 20 (1995) 401-6 (-421 dissertations).

998 *Rublack* Hans-Christoph, Literaturbericht: AR(ef)G 24-Beiheft (1995) 188 p. 3-577-01718-7. 964 items; index p. 161-188.

999 ᴱ**Schäferdiek** Kurt, Bibliographia patristica internationalis 30-32 (1981-7). B 1994, de Gruyter. lvi-803 p. 3-11-012462-7.

1000 *Scholer* David M., Bibliographia Gnostica suppl. XXIII: NT 37 (1995) 159-187.

1001 Scotus: *Muñiz* Vicente, Bibliografía escotista en lengua española : NatGrac 41 (1994) 409-417.

1002 *Silanes* N., Bibliografía (boletín) trinitaria : EstTrin 28 (1994) 91-104 . 241-255 . 423-437.

1003 *Smend* Rudolf, Basels Theologische Zeitschrift [1945-1995]: ThZ 51 (1995) 95-105.

1004 *Steiner* Ruth, Cantus, a data base for Gregorian chant: AL(tg)W 37 (1995) 87s.

1005 Stott John, a comprehensive bibliography: **Dudley-Smith** Timothy. Leicester 1995, Inter-Varsity. 156 p. £ 10. 0-85111-156-4.

1006 Summaries of doctoral dissertations: HThR 87 (1994) 473-481; 88 (1995) 521-535.

1007 *Sutinen* Erkko, Computers and change in mission: IRM(iss) 83 (1994) 585-593; ill.

1008   Theologische Examensarbeiten 1993/4 zur Missionswissenschaft und Religionswissenschaft : NZM(issW) 79 (1995) 51-62.
1009 ᴱ*Thomas* Norman E., [Briefly commented] Books received on missiology : Miss(iology)
23 (1995) 109-124 . 239-254 . 367-382 . 493-511 'Books and media resources'.
1010 *Tretter* Hannelore, Bibliographie: Ostkirchliche Studien 44 (1995) 81-104 . 226-272
. 349-382.
1011 **Van Allen** Rodger, Being Catholic; Commonweal .. 1993 → 10,666: ᴿChH 64 (1995)
729-731 (Anne *Klejment*).
1012 *Walls* A.F., Bibliography on mission studies: IRM 82 (1993) 117-135 . 247-271 -- 83
(1984) 185-218 . 361-388 . 515-537 . 643-667; -- 84 (1995) 321-354 . 457-483.
1013 *Weber* E.-H., Bulletin d'histoire des doctrines médiévales : RSPT 79 (1995) 641-659.
1014 *Weder* Hans [E.-H. AMBERG als Herausgeber ersetzend: ThLZ 120 (1995) 758-760
[*al.* 753-7].
1015 **Wyckoff** D.Campbell, *Brown* Georgeᴶ, Religious education, 1960-1993; an annotated
bibliography. Westport CT 1995, Greenwood. xii-325 p. $ 75. -- ᴿP(rinc)SB 16 (1995)
348s (W.S. *Benson*).
1016 **Žitnik** Maksimilian, Sacramenta 1992 → 8,7908 ... 10,779.7827: ActuBbg 31 (1994)
76 (J. *Boada*).

A4.3 *Bibliographiae* **philologicae** *et* **generales**

1017 *Béguin* Daniel L., L'interrogation des CD-ROM du grec et du latin sur Macintosh:
RHT 25 (1995) 281-290; Eng. 303: SNS-Pise le meilleur; Pandora d'emploi plus facile.
1018 *Biber* Douglas, On the role of computational, statistical, and interpretive techniques in
multi-dimensional analysis of register variation [WATSON G.]: Text [14 (1994) 239-285]
15 (1995) 341-370 [371-8 rejoinder].
1019 *a*) Bibliographische Beilage 1-4; -- *b*) 1995 zu erwartende Neuerscheinungen des
deutschsprachigen Verlagsbuchhandels: Gnomon 67 (1995) 1-36 . 37-76 . 77-132 . 133-172
/ 180-190.
1020 **Biering** R., *Brinkmann* V., Dyabola [computer-program]; elektronische Sachkataloge
zu den Altertums- und Kunstwissenschaften 3. Gut Ahlhausen D-52856, auct. 1 Diskette;
1 CD-ROM. -- ᴿGnomon 67 (1995) 551-560 (K. *Wallat*).
1021 **Booth** Wayne C., *al.*, The craft of research: Chicago guides to writing, editing, and
publishing. Ch 1995, Univ. xii-294 p. 0-226-06584-7.
1022 **Brown** Virginia, *al.*, Catalogus ... Medieval and Renaissance Latin translations and
commentaries, 7. Wsh 1992, Catholic Univ. xxi-356 p. -- ᴿ*JEarlyC 3 (1995) 67s (M.
Vessey).
1023 *Cockshaw* Pierre, *al.*, Bulletin codicologique: ScrBru 49 (1995) 1*-82* (après p. 168)
. 83*-283* (après p. 326).
1024 Comptes-rendus, liste des membres: RÉL 73 (1995) 1-18; x-xxx.
1025 *Cupaiuolo* Giovanni, Notiziario bibliografico I. Autori [latini]; II. Materie: BSL(at) 25
(1995) 357-396 / 783-806 (Rassegna delle riviste, 283-356 . 697-752).
1026 **Fell** Martin, *al.*, Datenbanken in der Alten Geschichte: Computer und Antike 2.
St.Katharinen 1994, Scripta Mercaturae. vi-231 p. --Tyche 10 (1995) 261s (W. *Hameter*).
1027 *Horsley* G.H.R., *Lee* J.A.L., A preliminary checklist of abbreviations of Greek
epigraphic volumes: Epigraphica 56 (Faenza 1994) 129-169: aims at acronyms 'acceptable
to specialists but comprehensible in themselves' [which was the norm of P. NOBER's

admirable 30-year editing of this *Elenchus*, but which made the 'abbreviations' not very brief; and which is not at all the norm of IATG/TRE which we now follow (in some cases reluctantly or with user-aids in parentheses)].

1028 **Jacobs** Philip W., A guide to the study of Greco-Roman and Jewish and Christian history and literature. Lanham MD 1994, UPA. xi-118 p.; bibliog. 93-104. ˙0-8191-9517-0.

1029 *a) Johnson* Janet H., Computers, graphics, and papyrology; -- *b) Willis* William H., The new compact disk of documentary papyri: → 674, 20th Papyrologist 1992/4, 618-620 / 628-631.

1030 Ktema 18 (1993) 305-320: Tables des tomes 1 à 15 (1976-1990).

1031 *Lohr* Charles H., *Bodemann* Marion, Index to volumes 1-50: Traditio 50 (Fordham 1995) 347-376, authors alphabetically; 377-407, subjects by theme.

1032 *Parker* Margaret M., Research in classical studies for university degrees in Great Britain and Ireland, completed: *BuInstAr 38 (L 1991-3) 302-308 [in progress, 275-301]

1033 Periodical literature: C(ath)HR 81 (1995) 159-174 . 308-322 . 486-496 . 661-671.

1034 'Que sais-je ?' Index thématique général. P 1994, PUF. 526 p. -- ᴿRHPhR 75 (1995) 381s (T. *Pfrimmer*: ajoute peu, pas assez, au catalogue de la collection).

1035 **Rastier** François, *Cavazza* Marc, *Abeille* Anne, Sémantique pour l'analyse; de la linguistique à l'informatique: Sciences cognitives. P 1994, Masson. xii-240 p. 2-225-84537-9. -- ᴿBSLP 90,2 (1995) 121-4 (X. *Mignot*).

1036 *Schreiner* Peter, *Scholz* Cordula, Bibliographische Notizen: ByZ 88 (1995) 186-358 . 486-610.

1037 **Schuler** Peter-Johannes, Grundbibliographie mittelalterlicher Geschichte. Stu 1990, Steiner. 198 p. 3-515-04635-6. --ᴿSalesianum 57 (1995) 776 (P.T. *Stella*).

1038 *Sehlmeyer* Markus, EDV-[Computer/CD-ROM-] Einsatz in der Alten Geschichte: HZ 261 (1995) 793-811.

1039 ᴱ**Solomon** Jon, Accessing antiquity; the computerization of classical studies 1993 → 9,793: ᴿ*ClasOut 72 (1995) 72 (P. *Latpusek*): QStor 21,41 (1995) 141-7 (W.M. *Calder*).

1040 *Sverkos* Elias, Bibliography on Macedonia, 1. 1900-1945: Makedoniká 29 (1993s) 369-388.

1041 **Tischler** Johann, Linguistische Datenverarbeitung und historische Sprachwissenschaft, 1. Die Programmiersprache AWK [.. hethitische Beispiele]: BeitSprW 69, 1992 → 9,796: ᴿSalesianum 57 (1995) 800s (R. *Gottlieb*).

A4.4 *Bibliographiae* **orientalisticae**

1042 *Balconi* Carla, *al.*, Bibliografia metodica [Testi recentemente pubblicati]: Aeg 75 (1995) 339-371 [245-319].

1043 *Chappaz* Jean-Luc, *a)* Informatisierte Quellen zur Ägyptologie; Projekt eines Jahresberichts; GöMisz 145 (1995) 9-14; --*b)* Computerized Egyptological resources [not covered by Annual (or other) Egyptological Bibliography]; an annual report [projected for 1995]: DiscEg 32 (1995) 37-42

1044 *Deller* Karlheinz, *Klengel* Horst, Keilschriftbibliographie 54,1994; Orientalia 64,1 (1995) 1*-100*.

1045 **De Rossi Filibeck** Elena, Catalogue of the Tucci Tibetan Fund in the Library of IsMEO, Volume 1: Istituto Italiano per il Medio ed Estremo Oriente. R 1994. xxii-461 p.

1046 *Grützkau* Jörg, *al.* Vorstellung eines [Computer] Hieroglyphen-Schreibprogramms; GöMisz 144 (1995) 75-84 (-89, *Seliger* F., Grabungsdokumentation).

1047 **Hafez** Kai, Orientwissenschaften in der DDR; zwischen Dogma und Anpassung, 1969-1989. Ha 1995, Deutsches Orient-Institut. 548 p. -- ᴿwzkm 85 (1995) 31-40 (G. *Barthel*: gut: gleiches für Westdeutschland nötig).

1048 Hintze Fritz, Verzeichnis seiner Schriften: ZÄS 121 (1994) 159-174 (P. *Wolf*).

1048* **Hovestreydt W.**, *Zonhoven* L.M.J., Annual Egyptological bibliography (45) for 1994. Leiden 1997. x-394 p. 90-72147-10-3.

1049 *Kraus* Jürgen, Glyph und Word [-computer-program] fest im Griff: GöMiszÄg 139 (1994) 109-111.

1050 *Lesko* Leonard H., High tech projects for research and distribution: ZÄS 121 (1994) 117-122.

1050* ᴱ**Lüddeckens** Erich, Verzeichnis der orientalischen Handschriften in Deutschland, 19/4 ägypt. 4 (kleinere Museen). Stu 1994, Steiner. 255 p.; 6 pl. DM 168. 3-315-02975-3. -- ᴿWO 26 (1995) 190s (J.F. *Quack*).

1051 *Schenkel* Wolfgang, Das Tübinger Konkordanz-Programm [das frühere Darmstädter M.A.A.T. als C o m p u t e r -Programm existiert nicht mehr, aber mit seiner Erfahrung kann er voraussichtlich sein Konkordanz-Programm zu einem Standard-Computer-Programm adaptieren oder neu schaffen]: ZÄS 121 (1994) 142-153; 3 fig. (153-9; 132-142, *Plas*, D. van der). --N.B. 122 (1995) 92s richtig gibt en face die 'Darstellung am Bildschirm' S. 144, mit zwanzig neuen Zeilen meist Nummer, aber o h n e zwei Drittel der früheren S.144.

1052 **Schmitz** Barbara, Islamic manuscripts in the New York Public Library. Oxford 1992, UP. 440 p.; 298 fig.; 24 color. pl.- ᴿJRAS (1995) 285-7 (B.W. *Robinson*).

1053 *Seliger* Frank, Vorstellung von zwei Computer-Programmen; 1. Das DASS-Projekt; 2. Eine Grabungs-Dokumentation: GöMiszÄg 142 (1994) 7-25.

1054 *Vattioni* Francesco † 13.XII.1995, Saggio di bibliografia semitica 1994-1995: AION 55 (1995) 463-486.

1055 WinGlyph for Windows 1.1 (also for Macintosh. Utrecht 1994, Univ. Theol. Fac. Center for Computer Research. Manual for 1.0 (1993), 69 p. *ƒ* 350 (only price indicated, for two cognates in the series). -- ᴿ*JSStEg 21s (1991s) 104-120 (T.M. *James*: cannot word-wrap, but can print without export to a secondary word-processor).

1056 ᴱ**Wunsch** Cornelia, XXV. Orientalistentag 1991/4 → 10,454: ᴿwzkm 85 (1995) 399 (S. *Procházka*).

A4.5 *Bibliographiae* **archaeologicae**

1057 **Anastasio** Stefano, The archaeology of Upper Mesopotamia; an analytical bibliography for the pre-classical period: Subartu 1. Turnhout 1995, Brepols. vii-247 p.; map; bibliog. p. 1-190. Fb 2000. 2-503-50416-7 [RStR 22,150, D.I.*Owen*].

1058 *Arata Mantovani* Piera, L'archeologia siro-palestinese e la storia di Israele; rassegna di [9] studi archeologici -- VIII: Henoch 17 (1995) 351-369.

1059 *Bahgat* R., *Saleh* F., An image-based information system for the archaeological description of stelae: → 721, 7° Egyptol. 1995, 9s.

1060 Biblical Archaeology Review / Bible Review: 20-year index (1975-1994) [BR 1985-94]. Wsh 1995, BAr Soc. 121 p. 1-880317-40-0 [NTAb 40,p.319].

1061 *Boer* J.G. de, Models, databases and computer aided reconstruction in archaeology: → PACT 45, 1991/5, 223-234; 13 fig.

1062 *Dessel* P. van, Index to volumes 1-25 -- 1970-1994: Ancient Society 25 (Lv 1994) at end. 15 p.

1062 *Deyo* Steve, From the Good Book to the good disk: BArR 21,6 (1995) 70-77; 72, chart evaluating 8 aspects of 17 software products.

1063 *Dollfuss* Geneviève, *Lubrano di Ciccone* Christophe, Bibliographie générale annuelle: Paléorient 21,2 (1995) 157-190 .

1064 *Fortin* Michel, *Bouchard* Daniel, Le système de gestion informatisée des données de la mission archéologique canadienne en Syrie: BuCanadMesop 29 (1995) 55-65.

1065 **Hendricks** Stan, Analytical bibliography of the prehistory and the Early Dynastic period of Egypt and northern Sudan. Lv 1995, Univ. 329 p. --90-6186-683-9.

1066 **Jean** E., antérieurement *Nicolle* C., *Sauvage* M., Orient-Express 3,1-3 (1994) 112 p. Chaque numéro contient i. Chroniques de fouilles, très brèves, signées (p.3 Malatya, 35 Ebla, 38 Ougarit, 38 Doura, 68 Ghassul 1994): ii. Recherches en cours (5 ci-dessous); iii. Informations: actualités (23, Préhistoire à l'Univ.S.Joseph, Beyrouth; 54 + 101, Women's Association of NE Studies); iv. colloques, expositions, v. publications (brèvement), revues, thèses en préparation ou soutenues.

1067 *Jursa* M., *Weszeli* M., Register Assyriologie, Realien / Wörter / Texte / Mesopotamien und Nachbargebiete: AfO 42s (1995s) 390-435 / 436-459 / 460-485 / 486-502

1068 *Lubrano di Ciccone* C., Tables décennales: Paléorient 21,1 (1995) 145-160.

1069 *Marazzi* Massimiliano, (*Bolatti Guzzo* N.), Bibliographie Kleinasiens (1988-1992); AfO 42s (1995s) 340-361 (-370, thematische Listen; -389, Lexemen).

1070 *Meyers* Eric M., *al.*, Second Temple studies in the light of recent archaeology, Part II., The Roman period; a bibliography: *CuRB 3 (1995) 129-152.

1071 ᴱ**Mineo** Sergio, *Zappata* Emanuela, Bibliografia di studi dell'archeologia, scienze dell'antichità e storia dell'arte. R 1995. Bretschneider. xviii-526 p. Lᵐ 50.

1072 *Shanks* Hershel, A short history of BAR: BArR 21,2 (20th anniversary 1995) 34-41; 42-47, 'artfully'-miniatured readership-survey.

1073 *Winter* W.W., New meets old; computers in archaeology: ProcGM 14 (1994) 123-150.

1074 *Wyatt* N., *Lloyd* J.B., Ugarit in cyberspace: the Edinburgh Ras Shamra project ['digitising the alphabetic texts' which somehow includes 'a virtual flight to Damascus (and eventually to Ras Shamra)' and 'a virtual museum']: UF 27 (DIETRICH 60. Gb. 1995) 596.

1075 *Younger* John, Caught in the net; electronic opportunities in archaeology: BA 58 (1995) 179s with photo of skeleton X-rayed through mummy-case; & 243s.

II. Introductio

B1 *Introductio* .1 *tota vel VT* - **Whole Bible or OT**

1076 **Alonso Schökel** Luis, *al.*, Introduzione allo studio della Bibbia 1s. 1994 → 10,710: ᴿAnton 70 (1995) 301s (M. *Nobile*).

1077 **Alvarez Valdés** Ariel, ¿Qué sabemos de la Biblia ? 1-3. BA 1994s, Lumen. -- ᴿRevBib(Arg) 57 (1995) 183a (A.J. *Levoratti*).

1078 ᴱ**Artola** A.M., *Sánchez Caro* J.M., Bibbia e parola di Dio [1989-, → 6,370*.1502], ᵀᴱ*Zani* A., 1994 → 10,711: ᴿProtest(antesimo) 50 (1995) 219s (C. *Tron*).

1080 **Bandstra** Barry L., Reading the Old Testament; an introduction to the Hebrew Bible. NY 1995, Wadsworth. vii-576 p. 0-534-21354-5. -- ᴿOTA 18 (1995) p. 396 (R.C. *Macey*).

1081 **Barstad** Hans M., Det gamle testamente, en innføring 1993 → 9,816; 10,713: [R]NTT 94 (1993) 182s (A.S. *Kapelrud*); TT(og)K 66 (1995) 79 (A. *Tångberg*, also on TOBIASSEN T. 1994).

1082 **Barth** C., God with us 1991 → 7,919 ... 10,714: [R]JETS 38 (1995) 259s (D.J. *Evearitt*).

1083 **Bartlett** J.R., The Bible; faith and evidence 1990 → 7,921: [R]PEQ 127 (1995) 171 (T. *Axe*).

1084 *Bildenbender* Andreas, Die hebräische Bibel -- ein rabbinischer Text [produced after 90 C.E.]: Texte & Kontexte 65s (1995) 61-87 [< OTA 18 (1995) p. 457].

1085 **Blenkinsopp** Joseph, Wisdom and law in the OT; the ordering of life in Israel and early Judaism[2]. NY 1993, Oxford-UP. 197 p. [reset; 1983 158 p. text]. $ 50; pa. $ 18. 0-19-875503-1; -4-X [< OTA 19,p.168]. -- [R]*TBR 8,2 (1995s) 6 (J.C.L. *Gibson*).

1086 **Bloesch** Donald G., Holy Scripture: Christian Foundations 2. DG 1994, InterVarsity. 384 p. -- [R](Reformed) Perspectives 9,10 (1994) 20s (J.K. *Grider*: 'my kind of evangelical').

1087 **Ceresko** Anthony R., Introduction to the OT; a liberation perspective 1992 → 8,1018* ... 10,720: [R]BA 58 (1995) 173s (D.C. *Benjamin*); *CritRR 7 (1994) 103-5 (D.L. *Smith-Christopher*); RTPh 127 (1995) 195s (J.-D. *Macchi*).

1088 **Clements** R.E., Wisdom in theology 1992 → 8,3458; 10,3203: [R]TorJT 11 (1995) 229s (R. *Delsnyder*).

1089 **Collins** Terence, The mantle of Elijah; the redaction criticism of the prophetical books: BiSe 20. Shf 1993, JSOT. 197 p £ 15. -- [R]CBQ 57 (1995) 343s (Julia M. *O'Brien*).

1090 **Crüsemann** Frank, Die Tora 1992 → 8,229 ... 10,1581: [R]Protest(antesimo) 50 (1995) 154s (J.A. *Soggin*).

1091 **Dillard** Raymond B., *Longman* Tremper[III], An introduction to the OT. GR/Leicester 1994, Zondervan/Inter-Varsity. 473 p. $ 25. 0-310-43250-2. -- [R]OTA 18 (1995) p. 398s (A.E. *Steinmann*); *TBR 8,1 (1995s) 13 (R. *Coggins*).

1092 **Dinter** Paul E., Beyond naive belief; the Bible and adult Catholic faith. NY c.1995, Crossroad. 348 p. $ 30. -- *CWeal 122,5 (1995) 20-22 (D. *O'Brien*).

1093 **Dohmen** Christoph, Vom Umgang mit dem Alten Testament: NStuKomm AT 27. Stu 1995, KBW. 128 p. DM 29. -- [R]Entschluss 50,11 (1995) 40 (C. *Cebulj*).

1094 [E]**Fabris** R., *al.*, Logos, corso di studi biblici in otto volumi, 1. Introduzione generale alla Bibbia 1994 → 10,722: [R]PaVi 40,2 (1995) 60 (G. *Ghidelli*); Ter(esianum) 46 (1995) 317-9 (V. *Pasquetto*).

1095 *Fernández* S., Reflexión sapiencial en el Antiguo Testamento: NV(Zamora) 19 (1994) 195-206 [< RET 55 (1995) 420].

1096 **Fowl** Stephen, Texts don't have ideologies [Marxist, feminist, liberationist; -- ideology is a slippery word, though perhaps less so than 'meaning']: *BInterp 3 (1995) 15-34; p.31, we can focus social, political, and theological aims without claiming ideologies; though PHILO, Paul, and JUSTIN claimed Abraham for three separate and partly incompatible ideologies, which they did not uncover in the texts.

1097 **Freedman** David N., The unity of the Hebrew Bible 1993 → 7,993 ... 10,723: [R]BiOr 52 (1995) 101-3 (J. *Klener*); HebStud 36 (1995) 140-2 (L. *Boadt*).

1098 *García Cordero* Maximiliano, Sabiduría helénica y revelación bíblica: → 142, [F]OROZ RETA J., III, Helmantica 46 (1995) 81-107.

1099 *Garsiel* Moshe, Puns upon names; subtle colophons in the Bible: JBQ 23 (1995) 182-7.

1100 **Gordon** Dane R., Old Testament in its historical, cultural, and religious context. Lanham MD 1985. UPA. [viii-] 330 p.; bibliog. 311-324. 0-8191-9500-6.

1101 **Hallo** William W., The book of the people [chiefly Torah, Near East background ...]: BJSt 1991 → 7.1710: ᴿ*CritRR 7 (1994) 121-3 (M.W. *Chavalas*); JSSt 40 (1995) 105-8 (M. *Weinfeld*).

1102 **Howard** David M.ᴶ, An introduction to the OT historical books 1993 → 9,833; 10,731: ᴿCBQ 57 (1995) 555s (C.G. *Romero*); *TBR 8,2 (1995s) 10 (A. *Warren*).

1103 *Ivatte* Rafael de, La lectura del Antiguo Testamento como un todo: RLAT 12 (1995) 235-268.

1104 **Kaiser** O., Grundriss der Einleitung AT [1, 1992 → 8,1028; 9,841] -- 2. Die prophetischen Werke: 3. Die poetischen und weisheitlichen Werke 1994 →10,735: ᴿBoL (1995) 93 (R. *Mason*); ZAW 107 (1995) 355s (M. *Köckert*)

1105 ᴱ**Keck** Leander, The new Interpreter's Bible, 1. General articles [+ Gn Ex → **NInterp** 10.1575] 1994: ᴿ*JHisp/Lat 2,3 (1995) 69-71 (E. *Mendieta*, focusing GONZÁLEZ, SILVA, SEGOVIA articles); P(rinc)SB 16 (1995) 363s (J.J.M. *Roberts*); SewaneeTR 39 (1995s) 65-74; TBR 8,1 (1995s) 12 (Katrina *Larkin:*'11185 p., keenly priced').

1106 **Knauf** Ernst Axel, Die Umwelt des ATs: NStuKommAT 29, 1994 → 10,736; DM 44: Entschluss 50,9s (1995) 49 (C. *Cebulj*).

1107 *Knauf* Ernst Axel, [Tora], Die Mitte des ATs; -- b) *Willi* Thomas, *Tōrā* -- Israels Lebensprinzip nach dem Zeugnis des späteren Alten Testamentes: → 48, ᶠDONNER H., Meilenstein: ÄAT 30 (1995) 79-85 / 339-348.

1108 **Lang** Bernhard, Die Bibel; eine kritische Einführung: UTbWiss 1594: 1990 → 6.1175: 8.1031; DM 29,80 [ThRv 87,73; 91,360 '1994', 3-506-99409-3].

1109 **Lebrun** René, Sagesses d'Orient ancien et chrétien 1993 → 10.3212: ᴿE(spr)eV 105 (1995) 267s (É. *Cothenet*).

1110 *a) Loughlin* Gerard, Following to the letter; the literal use of Scripture; -- b) *Walsh* Marcus, Profession and authority; the interpretation of the Bible in the seventeenth and eighteenth centuries: LitTOx 9 (1995) 370-382 / 383-398.

1111 *Loughlin* Gerard, Using Scripture; community and literality [metaphors can pertain to the literal sense, which must be midway between historical and self-referential]: → 170, ᶠSAWYER, J., Words; JSOT.s 195 (1995) 321-339.

1112 **Mannucci** V.†, La Biblia como palabra de Dios; introducción general a la Sagrada Escritura [1981, al lugar de ᵀ1985]. Bilbao 1994, D-Brouwer. 350 p. -- ᴿEstAg 30 (1995) 551s (C. *Mielgo*).

1113 ᴱ**Metzger** Bruce M., *Coogan* Michael D., The Oxford companion to the Bible 1993 → 9,844; 10,741: ᴿFurrow 46 (1995) 601s (R. *Dunlop*); HebStud 36 (1995) 142-4 (D.N. *Freedman*); Interpretation 49 (1995) 195s (Jouette M. *Bassler*); JThS 46 (1995) 567-9 (Clare *Drury*); MeH 22 (1995) 285-8 (D. *Pearsall*); NT 37 (1995) 200s (J.K. *Elliott*); P(rinc)SB 16 (1995) 354-6 (F.W. *Danker*).

1114 **Morla Asensio** Victor, Introducción a la Biblia 5: Libros sapienciales y otros escritos 1994 → 10,3214: ᴿSalmanticensis 42 (1995) 133-5 (G. *Pérez*).

1115 **Muller** Richard A., Holy Scripture, the cognitive foundation of theology: Post-Reformation Reformed Dogmatics 2. GR 1993, Baker. 543 p. -- ᴿRefTR 54 (1995) 86s (M. *Thompson*).

1116 **Niccacci** Alviero, La casa della sapienza; voci e volti della sapienza biblica 1994 → 10.3221: ᴿAng 72 (1995) 318-320 (S. *Jurić*).

1117 *Niccacci* Alviero, Organizzazione canonica della Bibbia ebraica, tra sintassi e retorica: → 62, ᶠGALBIATI E.; RivB 43 (1995) 9-29: Eng. 29: a coherent design was given to our whole Bible much earlier than is usually held.

1118 **Nobile** Marco, Introduzione all'Antico Testamento; la letteratura veterotestamentaria: Epifania della Parola NS 5. Bo 1995, Dehoniane. 221 p. L^m 28. 88-10-40227-8 [< OTA 19, p.331].

1119 **Otto** Eckart, Gesetzesfortschreibung und Pentateuchredaktion: ZAW 107 (1995) 373-392.

1120 **Paul** André, La Bible; histoire, textes et interprétations: Repères pratiques 35. P 1995, Nathan. 160 p. F 59. 2-09-176784-0. ^{R}Cath 48 (P 1995) 115s (C. *Barthe*); E(spr)eV 105 (1995) 715 (L. *Walter*); Études 383 (1995) 284 (P. *Gibert*); PaVi 40,5 (1995) 60s (G. *Ghidelli*); Sève 572 (1995) 60s (J.P. *Lamblin*).

1121 **Paul** A., Il Giudaismo antico e la Bibbia: StRel. Bo 1991-3, Dehoniane. 358 p. L^m 40. -- ^{R}Asprenas 42 (1995) 116s (G. *Di Palma*).

1122 *Paul* A., Les diverses dénominations de [= 'names for'] la Bible: R(ech)SR 83 (1995) 373-402; Eng. 350 [NTAb 40, p.192].

1123 **Paul** M.J., Het archimedisch punt van de Pentateuchkritik [Dt 12; diss. Leiden 1988]. Haag 1988, Boeken-C. 392 p. -- ^{R}VT 45 (1995) 280 (G.I. *Davies*; useful but implausibly treats Dt & Ex as undifferentiated wholes; English version awaited).

1124 **Pilch** John J., Introducing the cultural context of the OT / NT → 7,947 ... 10,743: ^{R}BA 57 (1994) 246 (W.R. *Kotter*).

1125 **Porter** J.R., The illustrated guide to the Bible. Ox 1995, UP. 288 p. $ 35. 0-19-521159-6 [< OTA 19,p.333, Judith M. *Ryan*; ThD 43,82].

1126 ^{E}**Propp** W.H., *al.*, The Hebrew Bible and its interpreters 1986/90 → 6,550: ^{R}VT 45 (1995) 406s (J.A. *Emerton*).

1127 **Rabinowitz** Isaac †, A witness forever; ancient Israel's perception of literature and the resultant Hebrew Bible: Cornell NE/Jewish. Bethesda 1993, CDL. xvii-148 p.: bibliog. $ 20. 1-88305-302-1. -- ^{R}BoL (1995) 100s (A.H.W. *Curtis*).

1128 **Ramsay** William M., The Westminster guide to the books of the Bible. LvL 1994. W-Knox. xi-564 p. $ 30. 0-664-22061-4 [ThD 43,183].

1129 **Raurell** Frederic, 'I Déu digué ...'; la Paraula feta història. Barc 1995, Facultat de Teologia de Catalunya. ix-462 p.

1130 *Römer* Thomas, L'Ancien Testament, une littérature de crise: RTPh 127 (1995) 321-338; Eng. 423.

1131 **Roth** Martha T., Law collections from Mesopotamia and Asia Minor: SBL*W 6. Atlanta 1995, Scholars. vi-283 p. $ 40. 0-7885-0126-7 [OTA 19, p.149].

1132 **Schmidt** Werner H., Einführung in das Alte Testament^{5rev} [^{4}1988]. B 1995, de Gruyter. x-468 p.; Bibliog. 407-458. 3-11-014102-7.

1132* ^{E}**Senior** Donald, Introduzione generale allo studio della Bibbia [Oxford Catholic Study Bible 1990 → 6,2039], ^{TE}*Dalla Vecchia* Flavia, *al.* Brescia c.1995, Queriniana. 835 p.

1133 *Sevin* M., L'approche des textes bibliques; LV.F 50 (1995) 253-260 [NTAb 40, p.200].

1134 *Ska* Jean Louis, De la relative indépendance de l'écrit sacerdotal [SCHMIDT W., BZAW 214. 1993 → 9.1754; 10,1608]: Biblica 76 (1995) 396-415.

1135 **Smend** Rudolf, La formazione dell'Antico Testamento: Letture Bibliche 8, 1993; L^m 40: ^{R}Anton 70 (1995) 685s (M. *Nobile*).

1136 **Smend** Rudolf, Das Alte Testament im Protestantismus: Grundtexte zur Kirchen- und Theologiegeschichte 3. Neuk 1995. 256 p. 3-7887-1469-7.

1137 **Stahl** Nanette, Law and liminality in the Bible: JSOT.s 202. Shf 1995, Academic. 104 p. 0-85075-561-2.

1138 **Stendebach** F.J., Einleitung in das Alte Testament: LeitfadenTh 22. Dü 1994, Patmos. 306 p. DM 22,80. 0-491-77957-X.

1139 **Struppe** Ursula, Einführung in das AT: Begegnung mit der Bibel. Stu 1995, KBW. 147 p. DM 39. -- ᴱEntschluss 50,12 (1995) 36 (W. *Dettling*).

1140 **Tanazi** Paul N., The OT, an introduction; 1. historical traditions 1991 → 8,1052; 10,755: ᴿO(stk)S 42 (1993) 346 (B. *Plank*).

1141 **Trebolle Barrera** Julio, La Biblia judía y la Biblia cristiana; introducción a la historia de la Biblia 1993 → 9,851; 10,757: ᴿ*AulaO 11 (1993) 233-242 (J. *Ribera*); CritRR 7 (1994) 94s (B.M. *Metzger*: a reliable map for a broad territory); EstB 53 (1995) 539-542 (A. *García-Moreno*); ThLZ 120 (1995) 622-5 (E. S. *Gerstenberger*); VT 45 (1995) 430s (N. de *Lange*).

1142 *a) Vermeylen* Jacques, La Bible et l'héritage des cultures proche-orientales; -- *c) Sevin* Marc, L'approche des textes bibliques; -- *c) Wiame* Bernadette, L'ordre symbolique, une clef de lecture de la Bible : LV(itF) 50 (1995) 245-251; Eng. 251 / 253-260: Eng. 260 / 261-272; Eng. 272

1143 **Walton** John H., Chronological and background charts of the Old Testamentᔆʳᵉᵛ. GR 1994, Zondervan. 124 p. 0-310-48161-9.

1144 **Weeks** Stuart, Early Israelite wisdom: OTM, 1994 → 10,3236: ᴿCBQ 57 (1995) 379s (J.-J. *Lavoie*: rich orderly information, though mostly objections, disputes. and refutations); VT 45 (1995) 126-130 (Katharine J. *Dell*: not for state officials' formation).

1145 **Westermann** Claus, Books of wisdom; the oldest proverbs of Israel and other peoples, ᵀ*Charles* J. Daryl. LᴠL 1995, W-Knox. viii-178 p. $ 20. 0-664-25559-0 [ThD 43,93].

1146 **Westermann** Claus, Die Geschichtsbücher des ATs; gab es ein deuteronomistisches Geschichtswerk ? : TB 87, 1994 → 10,2465: ᴿTPQ 143 (1995) 91s.94 (F. *Böhmisch*).

1147 **Zenger** Erich, *Braulik* Georg, *Niehr* Herbert, Einleitung in das Alte Testament: StudBTh 1/1. Stu 1995, Kohlhammer. 447 p. DM 40. 3-17-012037-0 [TR 91,534]. -- ᴿBiLi 68 (1995) 238s (C. *Dohmen*).

B1.2 **'Invitations' to the Bible or OT**

1148 *a) Abrahams* Samuel, A Black theological perspective on the OT; -- *b) Adonis* J.C., How to approach the study of the OT from a church historical perspective: OTEssays 7,4 (Pretoria 1994) 244-253.

1149 **Alexander** T. Desmond, From Paradise to the Promised Land; [Singapore] inroduction to the main themes of the Pentateuch. Carlisle 1995, Paternoster. xx-227 p.; maps. £ 13. 0-85364-647-3. ᴿ*TBR 8,2 (1995s) 11 (R. *Mason*: thorny issues bypassed).

1150 **Auneau** Joseph, *al.*, Lire l'AT; une initiation I. avant l'Exil. P 1994, Service Biblique Catholique Évangile et Vie. 144 p. -- ᴿRB 102 (1995) 462s (J.-L. *Thirion*).

1151 *a) Bahnsen* Greg, Comment lire la Bible ? Affirmation Réformée sur l'interprétation de la Parole de Dieu; -- *b) Wells* Paul, Sur la contextualisation biblique: RRéf 46,1 (1995) 35-42 / 43-55.

1152 **Barton** John, What is the Bible ? 1991 → 7,962 ... 10,764*: ᴿChurchman 108 (L 1994) 82s (D. *Spanner* disapproves vignette, God on a cloud reading the Bible and saying 'I've been misquoted').

1153 **Calvocoressi** Peter, Who's who in der Bibel, ᵀ*Hausner* Angela. Stu 1993, Kreuz. 256 p.; 62 fig. + 81 color. DM 50. -- ᴿEntschluss 50,2 (1995) 43 (T.M. *Meier*).

1154 ^E**Christmann-Franck** L., *al.*, L'Antico Testamento e le culture del tempo [= vari numeri di Cahiers Évangile 1980-86] ^T*Valentini* Carlo . R 1990, Borla. 622 p. L^m 60. -- ^RAsprenas 42 (1995) 437s (V. *Scippa*).

1155 **Crenshaw** James L., Trembling at the threshold of a biblical text [sermons and prayers] 1994 → 10,167*: ^RCBQ 57 (1995) 765s (J.T. *Walsh*); -- selection in: (Reformed) Perspectives 9,6 (1994).

1156 *Crowther* Edward R., 'According to Scripture'; antebellum Southern Baptists and the use of biblical text: AmBapQ 14 (1995) 288-305.

1157 **Cunningham** P.J., Exploring Scripture; how the Bible came to be 1992 → 8,1067: ^REstB 53 (1995) 268 (A. *García Santos*).

1158 **Davies** Philip R., Whose Bible is it anyway ?: JSOT.s 204. Shf 1995, Academic. 150 p. 1-85075-569-8.

1159 **Deissler** Alfons, Con Dios paso a paso; textos clave del AT [1989], ^T*Mínguez* Dionisio: Surcos, 1992 → 8,1069*: *ActuBbg 30 (1993) 58 (J. *Ruidor*).

1160 **Eaton** John, Interpreted by love; expositions of 40 great Old Testament passages. Ox 1994, Bible Reading Fellowship. 160 p. £ 6. 0-7459-2588-X. -- ^RBoL (1995) 85 (P.M. *Joyce*: somewhat Ignatian).

1161 **Fanin** Luciano, Come leggere 'il Libro'; lineamenti di introduzione biblica: *StrumSR, 1993 → 9,827; 10,780: ^RPaVi 39.2 (1994) 60 (G. *Castello*).

1162 **Ferguson** D.S., Bible basics; mastering the content of the Bible. LVL 1995, W-Knox. vii-168 p.; 10 maps. $ 16 pa. 0-664-25570-1 [NTAb 40,p.323].

1163 **Fischer** Georg, *Hasitschka* Martin, Auf dein Wort hin; Berufung und Nachfolge in der Bibel. Innsbruck 1995, Tyrolia. 152 p. DM 29. 3-7022-1978-1. -- ^RBiLi 68 (1995) 235 (G. *Steins*); ProtokB 4,2 (1995) 143s (M. *Ernst*).

1164 *Gäde* Gerhard, 'Altes' oder [vielmehr nicht] 'Erstes' Testament ? : MThZ 45 (1994) 161-177.

1165 *George* Maurice, La Bible apprivoisée [rendue accessible]: Sève 537 (1992) 236-240.

1166 **Girardet** Giorgio, Bibbia perché ? Il linguaggio e le idee guide. T 1993, Claudiana. 211 p. L^m 20. -- ^RAsprenas 42 (1995) 115s (A. *Rolla*); FilTeo 9 (1995) 204s (Luisa *Ferrari*).

1167 **Girlanda** Antonio, Antico Testamento; iniziazione biblica 1992 → 8,1077; L^m 18: ^RPaVi 39,& 5 (1994) 52 (G. *Marocco*).

1168 *Gordon* Cyrus H., The background to Jewish studies in the Bible and in the Ancient Near East: Shofar 12 (Purdue 1994) 1-46 [< OTA 18 (1995) p. 445 (C.R. *Harrison*: anecdotally, for moderns, views the Bible as culmination of a sophisticated international civilization)].

1169 *Gottwald* Norman K., The Bible as nurturer of passive and active world-views: PerspRelSt 21 (1994) 313-327 [PRS p. 357 not in listing after p.442, presumably = PPS p. 718 in OTA 18 (1995)].

1170 **Hauerwas** Stanley, Unleashing the Scripture; freeing the Bible from captivity in America 1993 → 10,785: ^RMoTh 11 (1995) 283-5 (L.T. *Johnson*).

1171 ^E**Herrera** Robert A., Mystics of the Book: Themes, Topics, and Typologies. NY 1993, Peter Lang. viii, 415 p. 0-8204-2007-7.

1172 **Hexter** Jack H., The Judaeo-Christian tradition². NHv 1995, Yale. xvii-118 p.; bibliog. 101-114. 0-300-04572-7.

1173 **Hill** Andrew E., *Walton* John H., A survey of the OT 1991 → 7,937; 8,1025: ^RJETS 38 (1995) 256s (T.F. *Bulick*).

1174 *Hochegger* Hermann, Bible et Africanité; CEEBA -- rencontre interculturelle (1984-) 1992: Telema 81 (1995) 83-87.

1175 **Holladay** William L., Long ago God spoke; how Christians may hear the Old Testament today. Mp 1995, Fortress. x-353 p. $ 38; pa. $ 20. 0-8006-2932-9; -884-5 [ThD 43,172].

1176 **Hughes** Robert B., *Laney* J. Carl, New Bible companion. Wheaton IL 1990, Tyndale. 864 p. $20. -- [R]C(alv)BTJ 11,1 (1995) 72s (M. *Farnham*, also on 1953 MEARS H. reissue)

1177 **Josipovici** Gabriel, El libro de Dios; una respuesta a la Biblia [1988 → 4,1073; ital. → 10,734], [T]*Iglesia* Juan Andrés. Barc 1995, Herder. 516 p. -- [R]ATG(ran) 58 (1995) 363 (E. *Olivares*); Lum(Vt) 44 (1995) 524s (U. *Gil Ortega*); NatGrac 42,3 (1995) 653 (L. Vicente de *Gijón*).

1178 *Juranville* A., L'Écriture [en philosophie]: RPhil 119 (1994) 166-190.

1179 **Juster** Daniel C., The biblical world view; an apologetic. SF 1995, International Scholars. [viii-] 319 p. 1-57309-025-5.

1180 **Kevers** Paul, Op weg naar het beloofde land; Bijbelverhalen van Mozes tot David. Lv/Haag 1994, Acco/KBS. 125 p. -- [R]CVL 25 (1995) 435s (H. *Hoet*).

1181 *a) Kohler-Spiegel* H., Wege zur Bibel, ins Leben der Unbedeutenden und Namenlosen; -- *b) Hoffmann* J., De verheerende Wirkung unserer Geld-Unordnung: KatBlätt 120 (Mü 1995) 92-99 / 84-91 [< ZIT 95, p.262].

1182 *Konings* Johan, Ler a Bíblia com o povo e como povo: PerTeol 27 (1995) 27-35.
 Kwok Pui-lan, Discovering the Bible in the non-biblical world 1995 → 5034 infra.

1183 *a) Legamble* Eugène, Lire la Bible en communauté; -- *b) Cortey* M., Premiers pas dans la Bible: Sève 547 (1993) 38-41 / 545s (1993) 50-61.

1184 **McCray** Walter A., The Black presence in the Bible. Ch 1990, Black Light. 197 p.; 200 p. $ 20 each. -- [R]*JRT 50 (1994) 127-9 (Paula W. *Matabane*).

1185 **McDonnell** sr. Rea, When God comes close, a journey through Scripture. Montreal c.1995, St. Paul Books & Media. 172 p. US$ 5.25. -- [R]CanadCath 13,9 (1995) 26 (Timothy *Scott*).

1186 *McNamara* William, Biblical sensuousness: Forefront 2,3 (1995) 5-7.

1187 [E]**Madrid** Patrick, Surprised by truth ; eleven converts give the biblical and historical reasons for becoming Catholic. San Diego c.1995, Basilica. 271 p. $16. -- [R]NOxR 62,7 (1995) 25-26 (D. *Vree*).

1188 **Magonet** Jonathan, A rabbi reads the Psalms 1994 → 10,2914: [R]JBQ 23 (1995) 57s (P.J. *Berlyn*).

1189 **Magonet** Jonathan, Wie ein Rabbiner seine Bibel liest [→ 7,978], [T]*Denzel* Sieglinde, *Naumann* Susanne: GTBS 1440. Gü 1994, Gü. 238 p. DM 29,80. -- [R]Kul(sr) 10 (1995) 183s (Julie *Goldberg*).

1190 **Maiberger** Paul, Le grandi figure dell'AT, [T]: BtB 17. Brescia 1995, Queriniana. 236 p. L[m] 35. 88-399-2017-X. -- [R]PaVi 40,6 (1995) 59s (A. *Rolla*).

1191 **Mesters** Carlos, God, where are you ? Rediscovering the Bible. Mkn 1995, Orbis. vi-249 p. $ 15. 0-88344-998-5.

1192 *Metzger* Bruce, *al.*, From the Apostles to you: Christian History 13,3 (1994) (6-) 38-40.

1193 **Meynet** Roland, Lire la Bible; un exposé pour comprendre, un essai pour réfléchir: Dominos 92. P c.1995, Flammarion. 126 p. 2-08-035419-1.

1194 **Mickelsen** A. Berkeley & Alvera M., Understanding Scripture; how to read and study the Bible 1992 → 8,1037: [R]EstB 53 (1995) 537 (G. *Flor*).

1195 **Milavec** A., Exploring Scriptural sources [propaganda need no longer pass for history; 8 text-studies]. KC 1994, Sheed & W. xix-202 p. $ 20. 1-55612-706-5.

1196 *Montero* Domingo, ANTONIO de Padua y la Sagrada Escritura: NatGrac 42,3 (1995) 505-524.

1197 **Motyer** Alec, A scenic route through the Old Testament. Leicester/DG 1994, Inter-Varsity. 151 p. £ 4. 0-85111-152-1. -- [R]BoL (1995) 45 (E.B. *Mellor*).

1198 **Neri** Umberto, Leggere la Bibbia; perché e come; la Scrittura nella fede della Chiesa: TeVi 21. Bo 1995, Dehoniane. 67 p. L[m] 10. 88-10-40932-9.

1199 *a) Nodet* Étienne, La Bible et son sol; -- *b) Sevin* Marc, L'approche des textes bibliques: -- *c) Cousin* Hugues, 'Mes pensées ne sont pas vos pensées'; -- *d) Cerbelaud* Dominique, L'importance de la lecture juive; -- *e) Moitel* Pierre, Le texte liturgique trahit-il le texte biblique ? -- *f) Monsarrat* Jean-Pierre & Violaine: VSp 149 (1995) 5-12 / 13-20 / 21-33 / 35-44 / 45-55 / 57-68.

1200 **Ord** D.R., *Coote* R.B., Is the Bible true ? Understanding the Bible today. Mkn 1994, Orbis. 133 p. $ 10. -- [R]OTEs 8 (1995) 313-6 (I.J.J. *Spangenberg*).

1201 **Osborne** Grant R., Three crucial questions about the Bible [can we trust/understand it ?]. GR 1995, Baker. 192 p.; 5 fig. $ 12 pa. 0-8010-5273-4 [NTAb 40,p.513].

1202 **Panikkar** Raimon, A dwelling place for wisdom 1993 → 10,3223: [R]*CreSp 11,1 (1995) 54 (R.J. *Miller*).

1203 **Pelletier** Anne-Marie, Lectures bibliques: aux sources de la culture occidentale: Collection 'réf'. P 1995, Cerf. 384 p. 2-204-05279-5.

1203* *Pilch* John J., The Bible's sense of humor: BiTod 33,6 (1995) > [P] in R(uch)BL 49 (1996) 255-261.

1204 **Plantinga** Theodore, Christian philosophy within biblical bounds. Neerlandia 1991, Inheritance. 114 p. -- [R]JETS 38 (1995) 95s (D. *Bruce*).

1205 **Porter** Joshua R., The illustrated guide to the Bible. Ox 1995, UP. 288 p. 0-19-211660-6.

1206 **Pratt** Richard L., He gave us stories. Phillipsburg 1993, Presbyterian & R. 493 p. -- [R]STEv 7 (1995) 70s (N. *Ciniello*).

1207 **Prickett** S., *Barnes* R., The Bible: Landmarks of World Literature. C 1991, Univ. xii-141 p. £ 20; pa. £ 7. -- [R]VT 45 (1995) 282 (R.P. *Gordon*).

1208 **Ralph** N.M., Discovering prophecy and wisdom. NY 1993, Paulist. 326 p. $ 13. -- [R]OTEs 8 (1995) 301 (Y. *Gilay*).

1209 **Ramsey** William M., The Westminster [= [2]Layman's] guide to the Bible. LVL 1994, W-Knox. v-564 p. $ 30. 0-664-22061-4.

1210 **Ranke-Heinemann** Uta, Putting away childish things; the virgin birth, the empty tomb and other fairy tales 1994 → 10,4364: [R]RExp 92 (1995) 123s (W.L. *Hendricks*: childish things like this book; she was the first woman professor of Catholic theology in Germany, and also the first to be fired).

1211 **Renckens** Han, A Bible of your own; growing with the Scriptures, [T]*Forest-Flier* Nancy. Mkn 1995, Orbis. xv-140 p. $ 13 pa. 1-57075-007-6 [ThD 43,85].

1212 *a) Richards* Michael, The priority of the Word; -- *b) Boss* Sarah Jane, The Scriptures in the Mass; -- *c) Wansbrough* Henry, Some ways into the Bible; -- *d) Graffy* Adrian, How should I interpret the Bible ?: PrPe 9 (1995) 217-221 / 222-6 / 226-9 / 234-7.

1213 · *Römer* T., *al.*, Bible et jugement de Dieu: FV 91,5 (1992) 3-14 (-122).

1214 **Salas** Antonio, Un pueblo en marcha; Pentateuco y libros históricos: Biblia y Vida 3. M 1993, Paulinas. 156 p. 84-285-1515-5. -- [R]EstB 53 (1995) 275 (J. *Huarte*).

1215 ᴱSierra Sergio J., La lettura ebraica delle Scritture: La Bibbia nella storia 18. Bo 1995,
Dehoniane. 525 p. Lᵐ 58. 88-10-40260-X.

1216 Sindt Gérard, Le peuple de la Bible: 'Tout simplement'. P 1994, Ouvrières. 183
p. F 85. 2-7082-3068-9. -- ᴿE(spr)eV 105 (1995) 167 (L. Monloubou).

1217 Sloyan Gerard S., Così avete intenzione di leggere la Bibbia ? Qualche indicazione per
i principianti [1992 → 8,1102*],ᵀ. R 1994, ADP. 84 p. -- ᴿPaVi 40,1 (1995) 62 (A. Bagni).

1218 Söding Thomas, Mehr als ein Buch; die Bibel begreifen. FrB 1995, Herder. 448 p.
DM 50. 3-451-23633-8 [TR 91.360].

1219 Sorger Karlheinz, Was in der Bibel wichtig ist 1992 → 8,1103: ᴿTPQ 143 (1995) 94s
(F. Kugler).

1220 Spero Shubert (traditionalist), Zakovitz Yair (humanist, ᵀ Wolfers Aviva); Two views
of the Bible: JBQ 21 (1993) 213-7 / 218-225.

1221 Stuhlmueller Carroll, New paths through the OT 1989 → 5,1220 ... 7,987: ᴿEstB 53
(1995) 542s (J. Pérez Escobar: 'paths' not methods nor new, except for a confused
application of canonical criticism).

1222 Tilliette Xavier, I filosofi leggono la Bibbia: RasT 36 (1995) 41-52.

1223 Trible Phyllis, Exegesis for storytellers and other strangers [1 Kgs 18-21, Jezebel and
Elijah: SBL presidential address, Chicago 1994]: JBL 114 (1995) 3-19.

1224 Wachinger Lorenz, al., [11] Paare in der Bibel: KatBl 118 (1993) 370-2 (-421).

1225 Wilson Nancy L., Our tribe; queer folks, God, Jesus, and the Bible. SF 1995,
HarperCollins. xi-292 p. 0-06-069396-7.

1226 Witherup Ronald, Is there a Catholic approach to the Bible ? : Priest 51,2 (1995) 29-
35.

B1.3 *Paedagogia biblica* -- **Bible-teaching techniques**

1227 Baudler Georg, Christlicher Religionsunterricht; zur Grundlegung einer interreligiös-
dialogischen, biblisch-christologisch fundierten Symboldidaktik: KatBl 118 (1993) 298-303.

1228 Baumann Maurice, Jésus à 15 ans; didactique du catéchisme des adolescents: Pratiques
10. Geneve 1993, Labor et Fides. 262 p. -- ᴿMélSR 52 (1995) ll0 (P. Daubercies).

1229 Bettigheimer Ruth B., The Bible for children, from the age of Gutenberg to the present.
NHv c.1995, Yale Univ. xiv-338 p.; bibliog. 277-327. 0-300-06488-8

1230 Bielsford Theodore, Christian education in a pluralist environment; managing the
challenges of fostering and maintaining both identity and openness: *RelEdn 90 (1995) 172-
189.

1231 Blair C.E., Teaching the Bible to adults in the parish: *Insights 110,2 (Austin 1995)
35-41 [NTAb 40,p.2].

1232 Blasberg-Kuhnke Martina, Erwachsene glauben; Voraussetzungen und Bedingungen
des Glaubes und Glaubenlernens Erwachsener im Horizont globaler Krisen: SPTh 42. Mü
1992, St.Ottilien. 535 p. DM 58. -- ᴿBiLi 68 (1995) 51s (J. Hoeps).

1233 Boomershine Thomas E., Biblical story telling in education; JChrEd 36 (1993) 7-18
[< BS 152 (1995) 93s (J.W. Reed).

1234 Borsch Frederick H., Teaching the Bible; between seminary and congregation:
SewaneeT 38 (1994s) 351-362.

1235 ᴱBuzzetti Carlo, Cimosa M., I giovani e la lettura della Bibbia: BtScR 105, 1992 →
8,518c: ᴿScrT(Pamp) 37 (1995) 356 (J. Pujol).

1236 **Chadwick** Priscilla, Schools of reconciliation; issues in joint Roman Catholic-Anglican education. L 1994, Cassell. 229 p. £ 35; pa. £ 15. 0-304-33140-6. -- [R]ET 106 (1994s) 287 (E.B. *Mellor*).

1238 **Cully** Iris V., The Bible in Christian education. Mp 1995, Fortress. vi-154 p. $ 11 pa. 0-8006-2806-3 [NTAb 40,p.321; ThD 43,162]. -- [R]LiLi 32,3 (1995s) 78 (J.J. *Pilch*).

1239 **Drechsel** W., Pastoralpsychologische Bibelarbeit; ein Verstehens- und Praxismodell gegenwärtiger Bibel-Erfahrung. Stu 1994, Kohlhammer. 360 p. DM 50. 3-17-012847-7. -- [R]TTh 35 (1995) 433 (S. *Ypma*).

1240 *Duling* Dennis C., Small groups; social science research applied to Second Testament study: BThB 25 (1995) 179-193.

1241 *Griffin* Seán, Archbishop Murray of Dublin amd the Episcopal Church on the interdenominational school Scripture Lessons controversy: Re(cus)H 22 (1994s) 370-408.

1242 *Gross* Engelbert, Religiose Weisung in Solidarität mit der verweltlichten Welt: ThG 85 (1995) 365-383.

1243 **Hill** Robert C., Breaking the bread of the Word; principles of teaching Scriptures: SubBi(Pont) 15, 1991 → 7.992; 10,817: [R]BoL (1995) 91 (A. *Abela*).

1244 *Johnson* Luke T., The New Testament on the examined life; thoughts on teaching [not as where BARTH taught: Johnson's 150 Emory NT students possess no religious or NT background; some had never been to church in their lives; some had been told that anything they had learned about religion was wrong]: ChrCent 112 (1995) 108-111.

1245 *Kniker* Charles R., [yes], *Swomley* John M., [but ..], Should the Bible be taught in public schools ? : BiRe 11,3 (1995) 36-40.

1246 **Kohler-Spiegel** Helga, Juden und Christen -- Geschwister im Glauben: Lernprozess Christen Juden 6. FrB 1991, Herder. 398 p. -- [R]FrRu NF 1 (1993s) 294-7 (H. *Gorbauch*).

1247 *Leimgruber* Stephan, Interreligiöses Lernen. Mü 1995, Kösel. 158 p. DM 29,80. -- [R]TPQ 143 (1995) 427 (J. *Janda*).

1248 **McGehee** Michael, The Gospel according to Deborah. ColMn c.1994, Liturgical. 192 p. £ 9. -- [R]Furrow 46 (1995) 469s (Sara *Maitland:* NT stories all-in-all successfully told for ex-small-children by a fictional daughter of Luke).

1249 **Niekamp** Gabriele, Christologie nach Auschwitz; kritische Bilanz für die Religionsdidaktik aus dem christlich-jüdischen Dialog. FrB 1994, Herder, 370 p.

1250 **Oppenheimer** Helen, Finding and following; talking with children about God. L 1994, SCM. 194 p. £ 10. 0-334-02579-6. -- [R]ET 106,6 top choice (1994s) 161 (C.S. *Rodd*).

1251 *Pitta* Antonio, Bibbia e comunicazione: RivScRel 9 (1995) 171-192.

1252 *Poupard* Paul, Pédagogie chrétienne et culture moderne [i. De Juan de BONIFACIO (XVIe s., Puerilis institutio est mundi renovatio) à Vladimir YANKÉLÉVICH ('trilogie inimitable' P 1980) ...]: E(spr)eV 105 (1995) 609-616.

1253 [E]**Schlegel** Jean-Louis, La Bible illustrée [par Pierre-Olivier Leclercq; textes [T]*Osty* Émile, *Trinquet* Joseph]. P 1994, Cerf. 432 p. F 195. 2-02-020934-9. -- [R]ÉTRel 70 (1995) 610s (J. *Cottin*).

1254 *Schmauks* Susanne, Bibelarbeit in der Gemeinde: → 536, [F]STRECKER G., Bilanz 1995, 186-197.

1255 *Schori* Kurt, Die Aufgabe religiöser Erziehung auf biblische Grundlage: ThZ 51 (1995) 255-277.

1256 [E]**Steegman** P.D.D., Op zoek naar zinvol bijbels onderwijs; over levensfragen in de les; ThReeks 15. Utrecht 1992, Univ. 80 p. 90-72-23518-5. -- [R]NedThT 49 (1995) 83 (A.K. *Ploeger*).

1257 *Trublet* Jacques, La pédagogie divine selon l'Ancien Testament: Christus 42 (1994)
412-422.

1258 **Tschirsch** Reinmar, Die Kinderbibel in Kirche, Schule und Familie; eine theologisch-
kritische Untersuchung in religionspädagogischer Absicht: Diss. *DBecker*. Hannover 1995.
-- ThRv Beilage 92/2, ix.

1259 **West** Gerald O., Contextual Bible study. Pietermaritzburg 1993, Cluster. 83 p. --
RTIC(ontext) 12,2 (1995) 100 (H. *Janssen*).

B2.1 **Hermeneutica**

1260 *a) Aichele* George, *Phillips* Gary A., Exegesis, eisegesis, intergesis: -- *b) Voelz* James,
Multiple signs, aspects of meaning, and self as text; elements of intertextuality; -- *c) Mascall*
Peter, Texts, more texts, a textual reader, and a textual writer: Semeia 69s ('Intertextuality
and the Bible' 1995) 7-18 / 149-164 / 247-260.

1261 **Alonso Schökel** Luis, *Bravo Aragón* José María, Appunti di ermeneutica^T: CSB 24.
1994 → 10,831: RASEs 12 (1995) 423s (F. *Pieri*): BoL (1995) 79s (J.F. *Elwolde*, high
praise); CivCatt 146 (1995,4) 306s (D. *Scaiola*).

1262 *Amaladass* A., Dhvani [evocativeness] method of interpretation and biblical
hermeneutics: I(nd)TS 31 (1994) 199-217 [NTAb 39, p.368].

1263 *Banning* Joop Van, Systematische Überlegungen zur allegorischen Schriftauslegung:
ZkT 117 (1995) 265-295 . 416-445; Eng. 445s: defense of medieval allegorical method.

1264 **Bayer** Oswald, Autorität und Kritik; zu Hermeneutik und Wissenschaftstheorie 1991
→ 8,1140*: FilTeo 9 (1995) 198s (H.J. *Adriaanse*).

1265 **Becker** Joachim, Grundzüge einer Hermeneutik des ATs 1993 → 9,945: RCBQ 57
(1995) 542s (M.C. *Lind*).

1266 **Biderman** Shlomo, Scripture and knowledge; an essay on religious epistemology; SHR
69. Lei 1995, Brill. ix-256 p.; bibliog, 238-249. 90-04-10154-3.

1267 *Blomberg* Craig L., The globalization of hermeneutics: JETS 38 (1995) 581-593.

1268 **Blount** B.K., Cultural interpretaion [HALLIDAY M.A.K.]; reorienting NT criticism.
Mp 1995, Fortress. x-222 p.; 2 fig. $ 18. 0-8006-2859-4. [NTAb 40, p.507].

1269 *Bodendorfer-Langer* Gerhard, 'Sie ist nicht im Himmel!' Rabbinische Hermeneutik
und die Auslegung der Tora: BiNo 75 (1994) 35-47.

1270 *Brandt* Krister, 'Exegeten som visste för mycket' [where we lack genuine evidence, not
really relevant facts are brought in, which merely clutter up the problem]: SvTK 70 (1994)
57-61; Eng. 61.

1271 *Brett* Mark G., The political ethics of postmodern allegory ['The time is apparently ripe
for the return of allegory .. reading ourselves into the text']: → 159, FROGERSON, J.,
Bible/Society; JSOT.s 200 (1995) 67-86.

1272 *Brown* C., The hermeneutics of confession [word to world; 1 Cor 12,3] and accusation
[world to word; Mk 14,61]: CTJ 30 (1995) 400-471 [NTAb 40,p.194].

1273 **Caballero Cuesta** José María, Hermenéutica y Biblia. Estella 1994, VDivino. 256 p.
pt 1500. 84-7151-961-5 [NTAb 40,p.320]. -- RE(st)E 70 (1995) 567-9 (M. *Alcalá*).

1274 **Canévet** M., *al.*, Les sens spirituels [5 art. < DSp]: Coll. DSp 15. P 1993, Beauchesne.
176 p. -- RScEs 47 (1995) 226-8 (R. *Marcotte*).

1275 *Carter* Alan, Knowledge and hyperbole: HeythJ 36 (1995) 46-64.

1276 **Clines** David J.A., Interested parties; the ideology of writers and readers of the Hebrew
Bible: JSOT.s 205. Shf 1995, Academic. 296 p. £ 40; pa. £ 15. 1-85075-570-1.

1277 *a) Clines* David J.A., Varieties of indeterminacy; -- *b) Fox* Michael V., The uses of indeterminacy; -- *c) Henderson* Ian H., Rhetorical determinacy and the text; -- *d) Phillips* Gary A., 'You are either here, here, here, or here': deconstruction's troublesome interplay: Semeia 71 ('Textual determinacy II' 1995) 17-27 / 173-192 / 161-172 / 193-213.

1278 **Coulot** Claude, *al.* (CERIT), Exégèse et herméneutique; comment lire la Bible ?: LD 158, 1994 → 10,842: ᴿRevBib(Arg) 57 (1995) 182s (V.M. *Fernández:* ZUMSTEIN J., 'defensa apasionada del método histórico-crítico y de la autonomía de los exegetas'; MEYNET R., análisis retórico; BEAUCHAMP P. 'modelo valioso de lectura tipológica' ..).

1279 *Crostini* Barbara, Interpreting the interpretors [sic]; the principles and aims of the protheoria: O(stk)S 42 (1993) 51-59.

1280 *a) Dalla Mutta* Ruggero, L'allegorismo nella storia della liturgia; -- *b) Barile* Riccardo, Allegorismi oggi e discernimento pastorale; -- *c) Rocchetta* Carlo, Il linguaggio simbolico nella liturgia tra antropologia e teologia: RivPL(iturg) 33,2 (1995) 4-15 / 16-21 / 22-28.

1281 *Deist* Ferdinand E., On 'synchronic' and 'diachronic' wie es eigentlich gewesen: JNWS 31,1 (1995) 37-49.

1282 ᴱ*Di Palma* Gaetano, Oltre il racconto [→ 514, ᴱMARCHESELLI-CASALE C., colloquio N 1993/4; presentazioni 1.XII.1994:] *Penna* R., Dal racconto all''intentio auctoris', *Fisichella* R., Tra silenzio e contesto: Asprenas 42 (1995) 77-90.

1283 **Dockery** David S., Biblical interpretation then and now; contemporary hermeneutics in the light of the early Church 1992 → 8,1152 ... 10,847: ᴿC(alvin)TJ 29 (1994) 260s (R.A. *Miller*).

1284 ᴱ**Dockery** David S., *al.*, Foundations for biblical interpretation; a complete library of tools and resources. Nv 1994, Broadman & H. 614 p. $ 30. 0-8054-1039-3. -- ᴿE(xp)T 107 (1995s) 116 (K. *Grayston:* a useful updating and warning service for conservatives, but not suited to satisfy 'all moderns').

1285 *Dorman* William E., An evolving model of interpretation for Disciples [CAMPBELL A.]; a modest proposal : Encounter 56 (1995) 59-82 [NTAb 40,p.4].

1286 *Eder* Petrus, Die typologische Theologie; eine Neubesinnung aufgrund der syrisch-antiochenischen Tradition: → 10,13c, ᶠBERNHARD L., Liebe zum Wort 1993, 103-140.

1287 **Edgerton** W. Dow, The passion of interpretation 1992 → 8,1115*: ᴿCritRR 7 (1994) 69-71 (Tina *Pippin*).

1288 **Erickson** Millard J., Evangelical interpretation; perspectives on hermeneutical issues [single-meaning or reader-response; unbeliever understanding without accepting ..] 1993 → 9,965: ᴿRefR 49 (1995s) 140 (H. *Buis*); W(estm)ThJ 57 (1995) 251-3 (P. *Enns*).

1289 *Estes* Daniel J., The hermeneutics of biblical lyric poetry: BS 152 (1995) 413-439.

1289* **Evans** Jeanne, Paul RICŒUR's hermeneutic of the imagination: AmUSt 7/143. NY 1995, P.Lang. 213 p. $ 41. 0-8204-2060-3 [< ThD 43,365].

1290 **Fee** Gordon D., Gospel and Spirit in NT hermeneutics 1991 → 8,4135*: ᴿRevBib(Arg) 56 (1994) 126s (A.J. *Levoratti*).

1291 *Fitzmyer* Joseph A., Problems of the literal and spiritual [not 'scriptural' as p. 101] senses of Scripture: → 40, ᶠCOLLINS R,: LouvSt 20 (1995) 134-146 [NTAb 40, p.41].

1292 *Fowl* S., [Biblical or other] Texts don't have ideologies: *BInterp 3,1 (1995) 15-34 [NTAb 40, p.5].

1293 ᶠFROEHLICH K., Biblical hermeneutics in historical perspective, ᴱ**Burrows** M. 1991 → 7,58 ... 9,968*: ᴿJThS 46 (1995) 666-670 (J. *Milbank:* very severe).

1294 **Fruchon** Pierre, L'herméneutique de GADAMER; Platonisme et modernité: CF 182. P 1994, Cerf. 534 p. -- ᴿSR 24 (1995) 143s (Anne *Fortin-Melkevik*).

1295 **Gadamer** Hans-Georg, Truth and method[2rev] [[1]1960, Eng. [1]1979, [T]*Glen-Doepel*
William], [Trev]*Weinsheimer* Joel, *Marshall* Donald G. [< [3](GesW) 1972) with bracketed
additions from [4]19.., including Gadamer's new preface, with his reply chiefly to
HABERMAS]. L 1989, Sheed & W. xxxviii-594 p. £ 37.50. -- [R]HeythJ 36 (1995) 351s (A.
Louth).

1296 *Geffré* Claude, Les enjeux actuels de l'herméneutique chrétien: RICP 55 (1995) 131-4.

1297 **Girard** Marc, Les symboles dans la Bible 1991 → 8,1162; Montréal/P,
Bellarmine/Cerf; 1023 p.; $ 55: [R]Ang 72 (1995) 313-5 (S. *Juric*); TTh 35 (1995) 413 (V.
de *Haas*).

1298 *Godzieba* Anthony J., Method and interpretation; the New Testament's heretical
hermeneutic [seems to mean 'the heretical (i.e. literary) hermeneutic of the NT' --
'remarkably presuming that the NT is a text'] (prelude and fugue): HeythJ 36 (1995) 286-
306.

1298* **Goldingay** John, Models for interpretation of Scripture. GR/Carlisle 1995,
Eerdmans/Paternoster. x-328 p. $ 20. 0-8208-0145-5 [ThD 43,268] → 1599 below (a
different book with similar title).

1299 *a) Gresch* Jean, Elogio della filosofia ermeneutica [< RICP 45 (1993) 77-85], [T]*Ugazio*
Ugo; -- *b) Geffré* Claude, Il rischio dell'interpretazione, [T]*Bernardi* Piergiuseppe; -- *c) Ravera*
Marco, Ermeneutica 1988-1994: FilTeo 9 (1995) 9-20; Eng. 9 / 21-29; Eng, 21 [30-63,
al.] / 97-111.

1300 *Grondin* Jean, Das innere Ohr; Distanz und Selbstreflexion in der Hermeneutik: → 182,
[F]SIMON J., Denken 1995, 325-334.

1301 **Gruenler** Royce G., Meaning and interpretation 1991 → 7,1025: [R]*CritRR 6 (1993)
247s (C. *Brown*).

1302 **High** Mary Jane, A visual hermeneutic; the contribution of sign language studies to
biblical interpretation: diss. Southern Baptist Theol. Sem., [D]*Marshall* Molly, 1995. 270 p.
95-38694. -- DissA 56 (1995s) 1394.

1303 **Hodgson** Peter C., Winds of the Spirit [i. interpreting; ii. contextualizing. iii:] a
constructive Christian theology. LVL 1994, W-Knox. xv-421 p. $ 25 pa. 0-664-25443-8
[< ThD 42 (1995) 273].

1304 **Hoffmann** Manfred, Rhetoric and theology; the hermeneutic of ERASMUS. Toronto
1994, Univ. ix-303 p. $ 70. -- [R]TS 56 (1995) 164s (J. W. *O'Malley*).

1305 *a) Houtepen* Anton, Hermeneutics, mission and ecumenism; the art of understanding
a communicative God; -- *b) Steenbrink* Karel, Interactive use of Scriptures within an
interreligious network: Exchange 24 (1995) 91-110 / 111-122.

1306 *Houtepen* Anton, Ökumene und Hermeneutik: UnSa 50 (1995) 2-6 (-68, *al.*).

1307 **Jeanrond** Werner G., L'ermeneutica teologica; sviluppo e significato [1991 → 7,1027],
[T]. Brescia 1994, Queriniana. 334 p. L[m] 38. -- [R]CivCatt 146 (1995,3) 453 (G. *Pirola*).

1308 **Jeanrond** Werner G., Introduction à l'herméneutique théologique; C(og)F. P 1995,
Cerf. 270 p. F 175. -- [R]Études 382 (1995) 857 (Geneviève *Hébert*).

1309 *Jiménez* Pablo A., In search of a Hispanic model of biblical interpretation: JHispLat
3,2 (1995s) 44-64.

1310 **Kaiser** Walter C., *Silva* Moisés, An introduction to biblical hermeneutics; the search
for meaning 1994 → 10,868: [R]BoL (1995) 93s (J. *Goldingay*: sharp tension); BS 152 (1995)
367-9 (J.B. *Spikes*); RefR 49 (1995s) 61 (H. *Buis*) & 278s (M. *Van Hamersveld*).

1311 **Klein** W.W., *al.*, Introduction to biblical interpretation 1993 → 10,982: [R]ATG(ran) 58
(1995) 364s (A. *Torres*).

1312 *Kranemann* Benedikt, Die Wasser der Sintflut und das österliche Sakrament; zur Bedeutung alttestamentlicher Paradigmen .. : L(tg)J 45 (1995) 86-106.

1313 **La Matina** Marcello, Il testo antico; per una semiotica come filologia integrata. Palermo 1994, Epos. 186 p. -- [R]Orpheus 16 (1995) 449-452 (U. *Rapallo*)

1314 **Lambropoulos** Vassilis, The rise of Eurocentrism; anatomy of interpretation. Princeton 1993, Univ. 471 p. $ 30. 0-691-06949-2. -- [R]Interpretation 49 (1995) 192-4 (A. *Levenson*).

1315 *Levinas* E., The Jewish understanding of Scripture: CrossCur 44 (1994) 488-504 [NTAb 39,p.476].

1316 [E]**Loades** Ann, *McLain* Michael, Hermeneutics, the Bible and literary criticism 1992 → 8,477 ... 10,878: [R]S(cot)JTh 48 (1995) 547-9 (Francesca *Murphy*).

1317 *a) Loughlin* Gerard, Following to the letter; the literal use of Scripture; -- *b) Walsh* Marcus, Profession and authority; the interpretation of the Bible in the seventeenth and eighteenth centuries: [J]LT(Ox) 9 (1995) 370-382 / 383-398.

1318 **McCartney** Dan, *Clayton* Charles, Let the reader understand; a guide to interpreting and applying the Bible. Wheaton IL 1994, Victor. 360 p. $ 16. -- [R]BS 152 (1995) 369s (D. J. *Boyne*).

1319 *Magonet* Jonathan, How do Jews interpret the Bible today ? [Southampton Univ. 16th Montefiore Lecture 1994]: JSOT 66 (1995) 3-27.

1320 **Martin** François, Des écritures inspirées; propositions pour une théologie de la lettre: diss. [D]*Virgoulay* R. Lyon 1995. 348 p. > C(o)gF. - RTLv 27.p.526.

1321 *a) Marty* François, La lecture, un exercice des sens; -- *b) Gibert* Pierre, Au risque d'écriture [Beauchamp: 'Écrire, c'est risquer ... Y a-t-il un crime d'écrire?']; -- *c) Vasse* Denis, L'empoisonnement de la source [Beauchamp: 'La jalousie du serpent subvertit jusqu'aux racines de l'être, devient négation de soi']: → 14, [F]BEAUCHAMP P., 'Ouvrir les Écritures' 1995, 317-325 / 381-399.

1322 *Merrill* A.L., The ministry of interpretation: Prism 9,2 (St.Paul 1994) 43-49 [NTAb 39, p.375].

1323 **Meyer** Ben F., Reality and illusion in New Testament scholarship; a primer in [LONERGAN] critical realist hermeneutics. ColMn 1994, Liturgical. xi-244 p. $ 17. 0-8146-5771-0 [RStR 22,166, W.T. *Dickens*].

1324 **Noble** P.R., The canonical approach; a critical reconstruction of the hermeneutics of Brevard S. CHILDS [< diss. Cambridge, [D]*Davies* G. 1991]: BInterpS 16. Lei 1995, Brill. ix-381 p. ƒ 173.50. 90-04-10151-9 [NTAb 40,p.329].

1325 *Ochs* F., Returning to Scripture; trends in postcritical interpretation: CrossCur 44 (New Rochelle 1994s) 437-452 [NTAb 39,p.376].

1326 *Olbricht* Thomas H., Hermeneutics in the Churches of Christ : RestQ 37 (1995) 1-24.

1327 *Olmi* Antonio, Ermeneutica e senso comune: DT 97,3 (Piacenza 1994) 57-92.

1328 **Oost** R., Omstreden Bijbeluitleg; aspecten en achtergronden van de hermeneutische discussie rondom de exegese van het Oude Testament in Nederland. Kampen 1986, Kok. 125 p. -- [R]VT 45 (1995) 136-8 (J.A. *Emerton* strongly commends; a final chapter updates earlier articles).

1329 **Osborne** Grant R., The hermeneutical spiral; a comprehensive introduction to biblical interpretation 1991 → 8,1184; 9,1000: [R]BS 152 (1995) 236s (R.B. *Zuck*, K.D. *Berghuis*).

1330 *Osborne* Grant R., The many and the one; the interface between Orthodox and evangelical Protestant hermeneutics: SV(lad)TQ 39 (1995) 281-304.

1331 **Patte** Daniel, Ethics of bibical interpretation; a reevaluation. LVL 1995, W-Knox. xi-145 p.; bibliog. 113-145. $ 17. 0-664-25568-X [NTAb 40,p.132]. - [R]ChrCent 112 (1995) 723 (J.D. *Kingsbury*); *TBR 8,2 (1995s) (R.*Burridge:* raises the issues; but now we need another book to help us decide).

1332 **Petersen** David L., *Richards* Kent H.. Interpreting Hebrew poetry; GuidesBS, 1992 → 8,3121; 10,2875: [R]*CritRR 7 (1994) 130-3 (T. *Kleven*); RevB(Arg) 56 (1994) 123s (P. *Andiñach*).

1333 *Pfligersdorffer* Georg, Interpretation und Zeiterfahrung: → 10,13c, [F]BERNHARD L., Liebe zum Wort 1993, 41-53.

1334 **Powers** Philip E., Prefigurement and the hermeneutics of prophetic typology: diss. Dallas Theol. Sem., [D]*Johnson* E. 1995. 348 p. 96-11642. -- DissA 56 (1995s) 4829.

1335   **Raguse** Hartmut, Der Raum des Textes; Elemente einer transdisziplinären theologischen Hermeneutik. Stu 1994, Kohlhammer. 285 p. DM 50. 3-17-013181-8 [ThRv 91,182].

1336 *Regopoulos* G., [G] 'For a better purpose' [GREG.NYSS. B 6.31]; hermeneutical approach to a manifestation of the divine dispensation [*oikonomía*, CLEMENS A., Paid.I, viii-B7,114]: D(elt)BM 14,1 (1995) 65-75: 14/2, 40-64; 15/1, 15-37.

1337 **Ricœur** Paul, Essais d'herméneutique biblique: *a)* L'enchevêtrement de la voix et de l'écrit dans le discours biblique (1992); -- *b) Fides quaerens intellectum*: antécédents bibliques ? (1990): -- *c)* D'un Testament à l'autre (1992): → 10,220, Lectures 3 (1994) 307-326 / 327-354 / 355-366.

1338 *Rossi* Giacomo, L'ermeneutica e il problema del soggetto dell'esperienza etica [RICŒUR P., Sei come un altro 1990 [T]1993]: CivCatt 146 (1995,1) 330-341.

1339   *Rowland* Christopher, The 'interested' interpreter: → 159, [F]ROGERSON J., Bible/Society; JSOT.s 200 (1995) 429-444.

1340   *a) Russo* Adolfo, Ermeneutica della globalità e pluralismo culturale oggi; -- *b) Giustiniani* Pasquale, Esegesi ed ermeneutica; il caso Tommaso D'AQUINO: -- *c) Sarnataro* Ciro, Esegesi ed ermeneutica nella prospettiva della teologia pastorale: → 514, Oltre il racconto 1991/2, 137-158 / 167-182 / 159-166; - Eng. 158 / 182 / 166.

1341   **Sandy** D. Brent, *Giese* Ronald L.[J], Cracking Old Testament codes; a guide to interpreting the literary genres of the Old Testament. Nv 1995, Broadman & H. xii-323 p. $ 25. 0-8054-1093-7.

1342 *Scaer* David P., God the Son and hermeneutics; a brief study in the Reformation: C(oncordia)TQ 59 (1995) 49-66.

1343 **Scalise** Charles J., Hermeneutics as prolegomena; a canonical approach: Studies in biblical hermeneutics 8. Macon 1994, Mercer Univ. xiv-155 p. $17 pa. [0 or ? 1] -86554-435-2 [RStR 22,48. M.B. *Phelps*]. -- [R]*TBR 8,3 (1995s) 5s (S.W. *Need*: evangelical, ecumenical).

1344 *Schniedewind* W.M., 'Are we his people or not ? ' Biblical interpretation during crisis [FISHBANE M.; Ps 100; 79 ..]: Biblica 76 (1995) 540-550.

1345 **Schwartz** G. David, Scripture and midrash as conversation with God; how the Rabbis understood the danger of interpretation: Encounter 56 (1995) 113-126.

1345* *Schweizer* Harald, Text segmentation and levels of interpretation; reading and re-reading the biblical story of Joseph: *Semiotica 107 (1995) 273-292.

1346 *Shillington* V.G., Biblical interpretation; the state of the discipline: *Direction 24,1 (1995) 3-13 [NTAb 40,p.10, with four cognates from 1994 consultation, 'Teaching and appropriating the Bible'].

1347 **Simonetti** Manlio, Biblical interpretation in the early Church; an historical introduction to patristic exegesis, [T]*Hughes* John A. E 1994, Clark. 154 p. 0-567-09557-6; -29249-5. -- [R]*TBR 8,3 (1995s) 55s (P. *Doble*, high praise).

1348 *Standaert* Benoît, Les quatre sens de l'Écriture: VSp 149 (1995) 318-335.

1349 **Stein** Robert H., Playing by the rules. a basic guide to interpreting the Bible. GR 1994, Baker. 219 p. $ 12 pa. [JETS 39,638, R. *Erickson*]. -- [R]BS 152 (1995) 493s (R.B. *Zuck*: lively).

1350 *a) Sugirtharajah* R.S., Introduction, and some thoughts on Asian biblical hermeneutics; -- *b) Samartha* J., Religion, language and reality; towards a relational hermeneutics: BInterp 2 (1994a) 251-263 / 340 -362 [< ZAW 107 (1995) 308].

1351 **Syreeni** Kari A., Uusi Testamentti ja hermeneutiikka; tulkinnan fragmentteja: Julk. 61. Helsinki 1995, Finnish Exeg. Soc. [vi-] 346 p.; p.341-6, Hermeneutics and the NT; 1987-1994 articles revised. 951-9217-16-9.

1352 *Syreeni* Kari, Metaphorical appropriation; (post) modern biblical hermeneutic and the theory of metaphor : [J]LT(Ox) 9 (1995) 321-338 [NTAb 40,p.201].

1353 *Tábet* Miguel A., *a)* Il senso letterale ed il senso spirituale della Sacra Scrittura; un tentativo di chiarimento terminologico e concettuale; -- *b)* Ebraismo e Cristianesimo; una riflessione sul senso tipico della Sacra Scrittura: *AnT 9 (1995) 3-54 / 243-269.

1354 **Thiselton** Anthony C., New horizons in hermeneutics; the theory and practice of transforming biblical reading 1992 → 9,1020 ... 10,899: [R]C(alvin)TJ 30 (1995) 232-7 (C. *Brown*); CritRR 7 (1994) 91-94 (G. R. *Osborne*: a second masterpiece); JETS 38 (1995) 457-9 (J.S. *Reist*).

1355 **Torrance** Thomas F., Divine meaning; studies in patristic hermeneutics. E 1995, Clark. vi-439 p.; 2 fig. $ 50. 0-567-09709-9 [NTAb 40,p.517; ThD 43,292].

1356 *Tronier* Henrik, Virkeligheden som fortolknings-resultat [reality as a result of interpretation] -- om hermeneutikken hos FILON og Paulus: ForumBEks 4 (K 1993) 151-182 [< OTA 18 (1995) p. 388s (J.T. *Willis*)].

1357 **Voelz** James W., What does this mean ? Principles of biblical interpretation in the post-modern world. St. Louis 1995, Concordia. 368 p. $ 19. 0-570-04801-X [ThD 43,191].

1358 **Vogels** Walter, Interpreting Scxripture in the third millennium; author -- reader -- text. ... c.1995, Novalis. 108p. $ 12. -- [R]CanadCath 13,7 (1995) 24 (F. *Wagner*).

1359 *Vroom* H.M., Scripture read and interpreted; the development of the doctrine of Scripture and hermeneutics in gereformeerde theology in the Netherlands: C(alvin)TJ 28 ('The Dutch connection' 1993) 352-372.

1360 *a) Wall* Robert W., Toward a Wesleyan hermeneutic of Scripture; -- *b) Spina* Frank A., Wesleyan faith seeking biblical understanding; -- *c) Wright* John W., Toward a holiness hermeneutic; the OT against Israelite religion: WeslTJ 30,2 (1995) 50-67 / 26-49 / 68-90.

1361 **Wallace** Mark I., The second naiveté; Barth .. 1990 → 6,1323 ... 9,1026: [R]S(cot)JTh 48 (1995) 97-99 (K.J. *Vanhoozer*)

1362 **Watson** Francis, Text, Church and world; biblical interpretation in theological perspective. GR/E 1994, Eerdmans/Clark. viii-366 p. $ 35. 0-8028-3774-3/ [ThD 42.393]. - [R]W(estm)ThJ 57 (1995) 475-8 (V.S. *Poythress*).

1363 *a) Williamson* Peter, Actualization [a term with which 'hermeneutics' has sometimes been misleadingly equated (whole for part)]; a new emphasis in Catholic scripture study: America 172,18 (1995) 17-19; -- *b) Wurzburger* W.S., Scripture and hermeneutics; a Jewish view: Imm 26s (J 1994) 42-48 [NTAb 40,p.12; 'Traditional Jewish hermeneutics seeks not so much to ascertain the original meaning of the Torah but rather to establish its normative meaning for a given historic situation' -- i.e. actualization].

1364 *Willson* Patrick J., Interpreting Scripture for the people of God [ᴱ**Keck** L., New Interpreter's Bible (1. 1994 → 10,1575)] 8. NT general Mt Mk; Nv 1995, Abingdon; 850 p. $ 55]: 17 Roman Catholic contributors, the largest representation of any one Christian body.]

1365 *a) Wurzburger* Walter S., Scripture and hermeneutics; a Jewish view; -- *b) Oikonomou* Elias, .. an Orthodox view: → 607, Immanuel 26s (1994) 42-48 / 49-56 (-71, discussion).

1366 *a) Yates* John, How does God speak to us today ? Biblical anthropology and the witness of the Holy Spirit; -- *b) Noll* Stephen, Reading the Bible as the Word of God; -- *c) Smith* Stephen, The evangelical and redaction criticism: Churchman 107 (1993) 102-129 / 227-253 / 130-145.

1367 **Young** Frances, Virtuoso theology, the Bible and interpretation 1993 → 9,1031: ᴿ*CritRR 7 (1994) 389-2 (F.W. *Norris*).

1368 *Young* Frances, Interpretative genres and the inevitability of pluralism: JSNT 59 (1995) 93-110.

B2.2 [Post-] Structuralismus

1369 **Lescow** T., Das Stufenschema; Untersuchungen zur Struktur alttestamentlicher Texte: BZAW 211, 1992 → 8,1201; 10,917: ᴿJBL 114 (1995) 128-130 (J.K. *Kuntz*); OTEs 8 (1995) 316-8 (J.A. *Loader*, in Afrikaans).

1370 **Moore** Stephen D., Poststructuralism and the NT 1994 → 10,3851: ᴿCBQ 57 (1995) 407s (A.K.M. *Adam*); ThTo 52 (1994) 134 . 136 (R.L. *Brawley*).

1371 **Patte** Daniel, The religious dimensions of biblical texts; [A.J.] GREIMAS's structural semantics and biblical language [with COURTÉS J., Sémantique: dictionnaire raisonné de la théorie du langage 1979-86]: SBL Semeia Studies, 1990 → 7,1064 ... 9,1034: ᴿVT 45 (1995) 279s (R.P. *Gordon*).

1372 **Seeley** David, Deconstructing the New Testament. Lei 1994, Brill. xvi-201 p. - [J]LT(Ox) 9 (1995) 452s (G.W. *Dawes*, also on *Moore* S. 1994).

B2.4 Analysis narrationis

1373 *Ellenburg* B. Dale, A review of selected narrative-critical conventions in Mark's use of miracle material: JETS 38 (1995) 171-180.

1374 **Exum** J. Cheryl, Tragedy and biblical narrative 1992 → 8,1213 ... 10,909: ᴿ*A(sn)JS 20 (1995) 166-9 (Adele *Berlin*); *CritRR 7 (1994) 117s (Pamela J. *Milne*).

1375 **Fokkelman** Jan, Vertelkunst in de bijbel; een handleiding bij literair lezen. Zoetermeer 1995, Boeken-C. 222 p. 90-239-0323-4 [< OTA 19, p.526].

1376 *Frisch* Amos, Context versus criticism: the contribution of contextual circles in uncovering the biblical narrator's attitude towards a character's criticism: Dappim 9 (1993s) 175-194 [< OTA 18 (1995) p.460; Dappim not in list p. 713].

1377 *Galli* Barbara, Time, form, and content; Franz ROSENZWEIG and the secret of biblical narration: J(u)d(ais)m 44 (1995) 467-476.

1378 **Genette** Gérard, Die Erzählung, ᵀ*Knop*: UniTb Wiss. Mü 1994, Fink. 319 p. DM 58. 3-8252-8083-7. - ᴿThLZ 120 (1995) 977 (E. *Reinmuth*).

1379 **Glatt** David A., Chronological displacement in biblical and related literatures: SBLd 139, 1993 → 9,12337: [R]BoL (1995) 89 (K.W. *Whitelam*); CBQ 57 (1995) 346s (J. *Van Seters*: fine but opens out broader questions); ET 106 (1994s) 157 (C.S. *Rodd,* amid 12 SBL titles); EThL 71 (1995) 444s (J. *Lust*).

1380 *Graham* Susan L., On Scripture and authorial intent; a narratological proposal: A(ngl)ThR 77 (1995) 307-320.

1381 **Gunn** David M., *Fewell* Danna N., Narrative in the Hebrew Bible 1993 → 9,1043; 10,911: [R]*CritRR 7 (1994) 118-121 (J.G. *Williams:* attacking the Bible is 'in').

1382 **Johnson** Steven D., MOLTMANN, Yale, and the interpretation of biblical narrative: diss.Drew, [D]*Deller* Catherine. Madison NJ 1995. 295 p. 95-36137. - DissA 56 (1995s) 2292.

1383 **Licht** Jacob, La narrazione nella Bibbia [Eng. 1986], [T]: StBi 101. Brescia 1992, Paideia. 195 p. L[m] 29. 88-394-0482-1. -- [R]PaVi 39,5 (1994) 51s (S. *Migliasso*); Salesianum 57 (1995) 151 (M. *Cimosa*).

1383* **Lloyd** Genevieve, Selves and narrators in philosophy and literature: Ideas. L 1993, Routledge. viii-192 p. 0-415-07196-8. -- [R]Salesianum 57 (1995) 391s (G. *Abbà*: un prezioso contributo).

1384 *Longacre* R.E., Genesis as soap-opera; some observations about story-telling in the Hebrew Bible: *JTrTL 7 (1995) 1-5 [< OTA 18,P.506].

1384* *Margolin* Uri, Changing individuals in a narrative; science, philosophy, literature: *Semiotica 107 (1995) 5-32.

1385 **Meier** Samuel A., Speaking of speaking .. : VT.s 46, 1992 → 10,918: *A(sn)JS 19 (1994) 250-2 (F.E. *Greenspahn*); Biblica 76 (1995) 568-570 (B.L. *Bandstra*; not a dissertation); BoL (1995) 96 (D.J.A. *Clines*); JThS 46 (1995) 202-5 (A. *Millard*).

1386 **Minette de Tillesse** C., O Deus pelas costas; teologia narrativa da Bíblia = RBB 12. Fortaleza 1995, Nova Jerusalém. 495 p. -- [R]NRT 117 (1995) 901s (J.L. *Ska*); ZAW 107 (1995) 546 (J.A. *Soggin*).

1387 **Minette de Tillesse** Caetano (Gaëtan), 'Tu me verras de dos'; théologie narrative de la Bible: RBB 12, numéro spécial en français. Fortaleza 1995, Nova Jerusalém. 522 p.

1388 *a) Palache* Juda L., The nature of OT narrative [< Sinai en Paran 1959, 15ss]; - *b) Beek* M.A., Saturation points and unfinished lines in the study of OT literature [< VoxTh 39 (1968) 2-14]; -- *c) Deurloo* Karel A., The scope of the small literary unit in the OT [(Gn 4) < Kain en Abel, [D]1967, 1-23]; -- *d) Smelik* K.A.D., Narrative in the Hebrew Bible [< AmstCah 9 (1988) 8-21]; -- *e) Zuurmond* Rocius, A critical hermeneutic [< De Bijbel maakt school 1983, 15-29]: → 10,250, Voices from Amsterdam 1994, 3-22 / 23-35 / 37-51 / 53-66 / 67-80.

1389 **Polak** Frank, [H] Biblical narrative; aspects of art and design; EnşB Library 11. J 1994, Bialik. xxxi-481 p. -- [R]BetM 40,2 (141, 1995) 109-113 (Yaira *Amit*); BoL (1995) 99 (J.W. *Rogerson*: worthy of an English translation); OTA 18 (1995) p. 406.

1390 *Polak* F., [H] Epic formulae in biblical narrative and the origins of ancient Hebrew prose: Te'uda 7 (1991) 9-53 [< Jud(ca) 49,255].

1391 **Powell** Mark A., What is narrative criticism ? 1993 → 6,1349 ... 10,921: [R]EvQ 67 (1995) 167s (R. G. *Maccini*)

1392 *Reed* Jonathan, The Hebrew epic and the Didache: → 10,248, [E]*Jefford* C., Didache 1994, 213-225.

1393 [E]**Rosenblatt** Jason, *Sitterson* Joseph, 'Not in heaven'; coherence and complexity in biblical narrative 1989/91 → 7,454b; 10,923: [R]ChrLit 43 (1993s) 99-101 (W.J. *Urbrock*); VT 45 (1995) 418 (R.P. *Gordon*).

1394 **Sharon** Diane M., The literary functions of eating and drinking in Hebrew Bible narrative with reference to the literatures of the Ancient Near East: diss. Jewish Theol. Sem., ᵍGeller S. NY 1995. 374 p. 95-33462. - DissA 56 (1995s) 2282.

1395 *Ska* Jean Louis, De quelques ellipses dans les récits bibliques [conférence SBL, Leuven 9.VIII.94]: Biblica 76 (1995) 62-71.

  Swartley Willard M., Israel's Scripture traditions and the Synoptic Gospels; story shap ing story 1994 → 2272 infra; 10,926.

1397 **Tertel** Hans-Jürgen, Text and transmission; an empirical model for the literary development of Old Testament narratives: BZAW 221, 1994 → 10,926; 3-11-013921-9 [RStR 22,58: Tammi J. *Schneider*].

B2.5 *Critica reactionis lectoris* - **Reader-response criticism**

1398 *Aichele* George, *al.*, Reader-response criticism / structuralist and narratological criticism / poststructuralist criticism / rhetorical criticism / psychoanalytic criticism, *al.*: → 359, Postmodern Bible 1995, 20-69 / 70-118 / 119-148 / 149-186 / 187-224.

1399 *Noble* P.R., Hermeneutics and post-modernism; can we have a radical reader-response theory ? II: RelSt 30 (1994) 419-436; 31 (1995) 1-22 [NTAb 39,p.375].

1400 *Theobald* Michael, Le prologue johannique et ses 'lecteurs implicites': → 106, ᶠLÉON-DUFOUR X., R(ech)SR 83 (1995) 193-216: Eng. 177, 'implicit readings'.

B3 *Interpretatio ecclesiastica* .1 **Bible and Church**

1401 *Abbott* Walter M., Suggestions for the second edition of the Catechism: America 172,7 (1995) 23s.

1402 *Antall* Richard, Evangelization and the Catholic university: Listening 30,2 ('Evangelization in the modern world' 1995) 104-120.

1403 **Ariarajah** Seevaratnam W., Die Bibel und die Andersgläubigen, ᵀ*Berger* Ulrike. Fra 1994, Lembeck. 110 p. 3-87476-300-5 [TR 91.277].

1404 *Ayestarán* José C., Fundamentalismo: Iter 6,2 (1995) 43-67.

1405 **Berleur** Jacques, Des rôles et missions de l'Université. Namur 1994, Univ,: LV(itF) 50 (1995) 107-111 (P. *Maon*).

1406 *Bissoli* Cesare, La Biblia en el nuevo Catecismo: Christus 88,8 (Méx 1993) 25-28.

1407 *Blowers* P.M., *Levenson* J.D., *Wilkin* R.I., Interpreting the Bible [in the Church]; three views: *FirsT (1994) 40-42-44-46 [NTAb 39,p.2: 'vol. 45'].

1408 *Borgman* Erik, De kerk als schijnbar fondament; over het zwijgen van de theologie [after Vatican women's-ordination ukase 1994 'because theology has no clear picture of its role and function in modern culture'], en het doorbreken daarvan: TTh 35 (1995) 358-372; Eng. 372

1409 **Bourgeois** H., *al.*., La cause des Écritures 1989 → 6,1503: ᴿActuBibliog 30 (1993) 37s (X. *Alegre*).

  ᴱ**Braaten** C., *Jenson* R., Reclaiming the Bible for the Church 1994/5 → 357.

1410 *Brees* M.A., The Bible and the new Catechism: BiTod 33 (1995) 170-4 [NTAb 40, p.3].

1411 *Bronk* Andrzej, ᴾ Typy fundamentalizmu: ZNKUL 38,3s (1995) 3-14; Eng. 24s.

1412 *a) Buckley* James J., Catechism of the Catholic Church, ecumenical despite itself; -- *b) Pannenberg* Wolfhart, An evangelical viewpoint: *ProEc 4 (1995) 59-67 / 49-58.

1413 Catechism of the Catholic Church [SF 1994, Ignatius. 803 p. $ 20 pa.] [R]C(alvin)TJ 29 (1994) 561-5 (A.R. *Kayayan*, based on the French edition but with reference to the English pages).] -- [R]LiLi 32,1 (1995s) 49-57, *O'Neil* Kevin, on moral: 73s, M. *Pelzel* on [E] WALSH; 74-76, M. *Hill* on Ignatius Press compendium of texts: 76, A. *Thompson* on THOMAS-CALMAN Family style; -- 32/3, 80s, J.Martos on MARTHALER. -- [R]Theol 98 (L 1995) 44s (E. *Norman*).

1414 *Cholvy* G., L'Église et les universités de 1919 à 1960: E(spr)eV 105 (1995) 300-3.

1415 *Cipriani* Settimio, L'interpretazione della Bibbia nella Chiesa: Asp 42 (1995) 5-20.

1416 *Cole* Basil, Infallibility, breadth and depth, a possible explanation [against the view that only solemn definitions are infallible 'as if the Holy Father was not all that certain' otherwise, p.489]: Ang 72 (1995) 489-517.

1417 **Cunninggim** Merrimon [ThD 42,360 Cuninggim], Uneasy partners; the college and the church 1994 → 10,951 [Cunniggim]; 0-686-01151-1: [R]*TBR 8,1 (1995s) 65 (W. *Carr*); TS 56 (1995) 407s (T.M. *Landy*).

1418 **De Souza** Cyril, *Kalathuveettil* Thomas, Introducing the Catechism of the Catholic Church. Bangalore 1994, Kristu Jyoti. xvi-205 p. -- [R]Vidyajyoti 58 (1994) 815s (G. *Gispert-Sauch*).

1419 *Fabris* Rinaldo, Bibbia e magistero 1893-1965 : StPat(av) 41 (1994) 315-340; Eng. 340.

1420 *Falise* Michel, L'Église et l'éducation aux valeurs: NRT 117 (1995) 3-33.

1421 *Felton* Gayle C., Challenges to the teaching ministry in the contemporary Church : QR(Min) 15 (1995) 175-183.

1422 *F(ernández) Ramos* Felipe, *a)* Fundamentalismo bíblico... si pronuncia sobre él; -- *b)* El anuncio del Evangelio; la evangelización 'nueva': NatGrac 42,1 (1995) 7-101 / 41 (1994) 7-102.

1423 **Fitzmyer** Joseph A., Scripture the soul of theology 1994 → 10,959: [R]BThB 25 (1995) 92 (B.J. *Malina*: ch. 2 below his otherwise acceptable standard); ScrTP(amp)/ 27 (1995) 1054-6 (V. *Balaguer*).

1424 **Fitzmyer** Joseph A., The Biblical Commission's document 'The interpretation of the Bible in the Church', text and commentary: SubB 18. R 1994, Pontificio Istituto Biblico. xv-212 p. L[m] 30. 88-7653-605-1. -- [R]*CritRR 8 (1995) 97-99 (M. *Pesce*).

1425 *Forestell* J.T., The interpretation of the Bible in the Church: CanadCath 13,7 (1995) 11-21.

1425* *a) Fuchs* Stephen, The fundamentalists; -- *b) Valentin* F., Fudamentalists and evangelicals; -- *c) Musk* Bill A., Islamic fundamentalism: I(nd)M(iss)R 17 (1995) 5-11 / 12-19 / 33-41.

1426 **Galindo** Florencio, El Protestantismo fundamentalista 1992 → 9,1099: [R]Christus 58,7 (Méx 1993) 63 (L. del *Valle*),

1427 **García López** Félix, **Galindo García** Ángel: BtS 169. S 1995, Univ. Pontificia. 356 p.

1428 *a) García-Moreno* Antonio, La interpretación de la Biblia en la Iglesia; para comprender .., -- *b) Muñoz León* Domingo, Los sentidos de la Escritura; -- *c) Casciaro* José M., El método histórico-crítico; -- *d) Aranda-Pèrez* Gonzalo, .. canónico; -- *e) Varo* Francisco, .. psicoanalítico; -- *f) Artola* Antonio M., Inspiración : ScrT(Pamp) 37 (1995) 123-130 / 99-122 (163-177) / 131-9 / 141-8 / 149-162 / 179-185.

1429 *García Trapiello* Jesús, La misión del maestro en la Iglesia: Ang 72 (1995) 427-449.

1430　**Gil Hellín** F., Constitutio dogmatica de divina revelatione 'Dei Verbum': [schemata successiva] Concilii Vaticani II Synopsis: Athenaeum S. Crucis. Vaticano 1993, Editrice. 744 p. -- [R]*AnT 9 (1995) 171-3 (M.A. *Tábet*).

1431　*Glass* William R., From Southern Baptist to fundamentalist; the case of I.W. ROGERS and *The Faith*. 1945-57; -- *b) Mauldin* Frank L., A notion of truth among seventeenth-century Baptists in America; -- *c) Crowther* Edward R., 'According to Scripture'?; antebellum Southern Baptists and the use of biblical text: AmBapQ 14 (1995) 241-259 / 270-287 / 288-305.

1432　*González de Cardedal* Olegario, Entstehungsgeschichte und erste Auswertung des Katechismus der katholischen Kirche, [T]*Behrens* Matthias: MThZ 45(1994) 375-397 (*al.* 367-465).

1433　*Gramusset* François, Texte, parole, enseignement; lire à l'Université: → 14, [F]BEAUCHAMP P., 'Ouvrir les Écritures' 1995, 349-359.

1434　*Greinacher* Norbert, Indoktrination oder Elementarisierung ? Bemerkungen zum Weltkatechismus: (Tü)ThQ 175 (1995) 19-31.

1435　*Grimmsmann* Helmut, Elisas schwimmende Axt; das Dilemma des christlichen Fundamentalismus: LM(on) 34,2 (1995) 2-4.

1436　*Gros* Jeffrey, Reception and Roman Catholicism for the 1990s: OneInC 31 (1995) 295-328.

1437　**Hamilton** Michael S., The fundamentalist Harvard; Wheaton College and the continuing vitality of American evangelicalism, 1919-1965: diss. Notre Dame 1994, [D]*Hatch* N. 298 p. 95-16621. -- DissA 56 (1995s) p. 332.

1438　*Hattrup* Dieter, Amt und Volk in der Kirche; zum Sinn des Sensus Fidei: ThG 85 (1995) 337-364.

1439　*Heft* James, Theology in a Catholic University: Origins 25 (1995s) 243-8.

1440　*Hemrick* Eugene, The age of new intellectual enthusiasm: Priest 51,5 (1995) 30-36.

1441　*Hoppe* L.J., Premillennial dispensationalism; fundamentalism's eschatological scenario [.. DARBY J.N., in Scofield Reference Bible 1909; LINDSEY H., The late great planet earth 1970]: ChiSt 34 (1995) 222-235 [NTAb 40,p.197].

1442　*Hortal* Jesús, O uso da Bíblia na Igreja católica, antes do Concilio Vaticano II : Teocomunicação 25 (1995) 411-8.

1443　**Houlden** J. Leslie, The interpretation of the Bible in the Church; a document from the Pontifical Biblical Commission. L 1995, SCM. vii-163 p. £ 10. 0-334-02589-3. -- [R]E(xp)T 107 (1995s) 84 (A.C. *Thiselton,* comparing FITZMYER J.); TBR 8,1 (1995s) 10 (P. *Doble*: the pontifical document would make an admirable though bland introductory textbook, and seven 'responses' celebrate the large ecumenical consensus attained among biblical scholars).

1444　[*Denzinger* H.] **Hünermann** P., Enchiridion[37] ... Kompendium der Glaubensbekenntnisse 1991 → 9,15626; 10, 970: [R]Comp 38 (1993) 383s (E. *Romero Pose*).

1445　L'interprétation de la Bible dans l'Église, préf. VESCO, 1994 → [R]POrC 45 (1995) 288s (P. *Ternant*).

1446　*Jensen* M., 'Simply' reading the Geneva Bible; the Geneva Bible [1560] and its readers: JLT 9,1 (1995) 30-45 [NTAb 39,p.381].

1447　**Joh** [only, as author, in DissA *disk* 56 (1995s)], Reformed fundamentalism.

1448　Der 'Katechismus der Katholischen Kirche': [R]ThRv 91 (1995) 3-8 (H. *Vorgrimler*: in der Perspektive systematischer Theologie) & 8-11 (D. *Emeis*, in religionspädagogischer Sicht) & 11-17 (M. *Kiessig*, aus evangelischer Sicht) & 17-20 (A. *Danilov*, aus orthodoxer Sicht).

1449 **Kaucheck** Kenneth R., The infallible 'ordinary and universal magisterium'; a canonical investigation into the sources of some key expressions of Canons 749-750 of the 1983 Code of Canon Law: diss. Pontifical Gregorian University. Rome 1994. 336 p. -- DissA-C 56 (1995s) p, 891. No photocopy AA.

1450 *Kelly* George A., The battle for the Catholic campus; John Paul II vs. the American college system: *CWRep 8,1 (1995) 50-55.

1451 *Kertelge* Karl, Die Interpretation der Bibel in der Kirche 23.IV.1993: TrierTZ 104 (1995) 1-11.

1452 *a) Kinast* Robert L., Experiencing the tradition through theological reflection; -- *b) Scullion* James P., Experience encounters the sacred text; the interpretation of the Bible in the Church; -- *c) Burkhard* John J., The use of Scripture in theology and preaching; experience, interpretation, and ecclesial identity: NewThR 8,1 (1995) 6-17 / 18-29 / 30-44.

1453 *Koch* Kurt, Fundamentalismus; eine elementare Gefahr für die Zukunft: StZ 213 (1995) 521-532; > Fundamentalism [to some extent indispensable, though widely used today for 'anything (conservative) we don't like'], ᵀᴱ*Asen* B.A. : ThD 42 (1995) 239-246.

1454 ᴱ**Kochanek** Hermann, Die verdrängte Freiheit; .. Fundamentalismus 1991 → 8,1278 ... 10,975: ᴿMüTZ 45 (1994) 86s (A. *Kreiner*).

1455 ᵀ*Kocur* Miroslav, Interpretácia Biblie v Čirkvi. Spisské Podhradie 1995, Katolicke Biblické Dielo na Slovensku. 137 p.

1456 *a) Làconi* M., Biblisti e teologia; -- *b) Vanhoye* A., Esegesi e teologia. a cinquant'anni della 'Divino afflante Spirito'; -- *c) Benoît* S., L'esegesi è teologia ? : SacDo 39,6 (1994) 31-72 / 7-30 [NTAb 39, p.439] / 73-87.

1457 *Laghi* P., *al.,* Chiesa e Sacra Scrittura 1994 → 10,977: ᴿStudium 35 (M 1995) 158 (P. *Juan*).

1458 *Levoratti* A.J., La interpretación de la Biblia en la Iglesia [texto 1-64; JUAN PABLO II 179-182]: RBib(Arg) 56 (1994) 175-8.

1459 *Loza Vera* J., La interpretación de la Biblia en la Iglesia: AnáMnesis 4,2 (1994) 7 7-118 [< ZIT 95.p.281]

1460 *McGrath* Alister, Theologiae proprium subiectum; theology as the critic and servant of the Church: → **5**, ᶠATKINSON, J., Bible, Reformation, Church: JSNT.s 105 (1995) 150-165.

1461 *Maher* Michael, The catechism of the Catholic Church: MilltSt 35 (1995) 19-38.

1462 *Manns* Frédéric, Lire les Écritures en Église : RevSR 69 (1995) 436-452; Eng. 533.

1463 *Marshall* I. Howard, Review article: The interpretation of the Bible in the Church: S(co)BET 13 (1995) 72-75: all to the good but nowhere gets down to concretely how do it.

1464 **Marthaler** Bernard L., The catechism, yesterday and today; the evolution of a genre. ColMn 1995, Liturgical. 176 p. $ 16 pa. 0-8146-2151-1 [ThD 43,178]. -- ᴿ*TBR 8,3 (1995s) 27 (A. *McCoy*).

1465 ᴱ**Marthaler** B.L., Introducing the Catechism of the Catholic Church. L 1994, SPCK. 182 p. £ 10. -- ᴿ*ModBlv 36,2 (1995) 66-68 (B.P. *Harvey*: shows, though less than G. DALY in ᴱWALSH, the CCC as 'hideously regressive and question-begging', 'wilfully obscurant').

1466 **Marty** Martin E., *Appleby* R.Scott, The glory and the power; the fundamentalist challenge 1992 → 8,1292; 10,986: ᴿJAAR 63 (1995) 141-4 (M. *McMullen*).

1467 ᴱ**Marty** M., *Appleby* R., Fundamentalisms observed 1. 1992 → 8,404 [ᴿRRelRes 35 (1993s) 63-65 (H.P. *Chalfant*) & 66-68 (W.H. *Swatos*) & 68-71 (T.G. *Jelen*); 71-75, Appleby response]; -- 2 & 3, 1993 → 9,1129; 10,985: ᴿJRel 75 (1995) 287-9 (J. *Casanova*); ProEccl 4 (1995) 378-380 (D. *Sack*, 3).

1468 ^E**Marty** Martin E.,   *Appleby* R. Scott (4.) Accounting for fundamentalisms; the dynamic character of movements. Ch ...Univ. [^RRRelRes 37 (1995s) 361-8 (T.G. *Jelen, al.*, another symposium)]. -- (5.) Fundamentalisms comprehended. Ch 1995, Univ. x-522 p. $ 45. 0-226-50887-0 [ThD 42,368: the final volume].

1469   **Mouw** Richard J.,   Consulting the faithful; what intellectuals can learn from popular religion 1994 → 10,10228*: ^R(Reformed) Perspectives 10,1 (1995) 22 (M.A. *Noll*).

1470 *Moysa* Stefan ^P Le théologien catholique face au Magistère (Urząd nauczycielski) de l'Église: Bobolanum 6 (1995) 7-25; français 25-26.

1471 *Muñoz* Ronaldo, La teología del catecismo de JUAN PABLO II: Christus 58,6 (Méx 1993) 32s.

1472 **Neveu** Bruno, L'erreur et son juge; remarques sur les censures doctrinales à l'époque moderne 1993 → 10,991: ^RMélSR 52 (1995) 215-7 (G. *Dehon*).

1473 **Noll** Mark A., The scandal of the evangelical mind 1994 → 10,14912*: ^RDialog 34 (1995) 230-2 (Nancy *Koester*).

1474 **O'Brien** David, From the heart of the American church; Catholic higher education and American culture. Mkn 1994, Orbis. xxii-240 p. [RStR 22,229, J.T. *Ford* makes no mention of the Vatican's Ex corde ecclesiae]. -- ^RHorizons 22 (1995) 329-331 (R. *Van Allen*, also on HESBURGH).

1475 *a) Örsy* Ladislas, The congregation's 'response' [decree on women's ordination 'infallible']; -- *b) Sullivan* Francis A., Guideposts from Catholic tradition [not perceivably infallible]: America 173,19 (1995) 4s / 5s.

1476 *O'Ferrall* Fergus, Catholics, Protestants and the Bible today: DocLife 45 (1995) 672-680.

1477 *O'Reilly* Kevin, 'Obsequium religiosum' and dissent; the 'Instruction on the ecclesial vocation of the theologian' and the U.S. bishops: DunwoodieR 17 (1994) 25-42.

1478 *Pannenberg* Wolfhart, Eine evangelische Stellungnahme zum Weltkatechismus der katholischen Kirche: KuD 41 (1995) 2-12; Eng. 12.

1479 *a) Pannenberg* Wolfhart, Catechism of the Catholic Church; an evangelical viewpoint; -- *b) Buckley* James J., .. ecumenical despite itself: ProEccl 4 (1995) 49-57 / 59-67.

1480 *Paré* U. E., The Church and the Bible; LEO XIII, Providentissimus Deus [1893]; PIUS XII, Divino afflante Spiritu : CanadCath 13,6 (1995) 7-15.

1481 *a) Rafiński* Grzegorz, Metody i kierunki interpretacji .. [Dokument 1994]; -- *b) Chmiel* Jerzy, Hermeneutika biblijna; -- *c) M'dala* Stanisław, Charakterystyczne cechy interpretacji katolickiej; -- *d) Czajkowski* Michał, Interpretacja Biblii w życiu Kościoła: STV(ars) 33,2 (1995) 153-162 / 163-181 / 183-8.

1482   **Ratzinger** Josef, Evangelien -- Katechese -- Katechismus; Streiflichter auf dem Katechismus der katholischen Kirche. Mü 1995, Neue Stadt. 83 p. DM 17,50. 3-87996-218-2. -- ^RThGL 85 (1995) 290-2 (D. *Hattrup*).

1483 *Raurell* Frederic, El método histórico-crítico frente a las lecturas fundamentalistas integristas de la Biblia: Laur 35 (1994) 275-318.

1484 *Renker* Alwin, Der Katechismus der Katholischen Kirche [Mü 1993, Oldenbourg; 816 p.]: FrRu NF 1 (1993s) 269-275.

1485 *Roberge* René-Michel, Les centres [universitaires / évêques] de théologie et les grands débats publics: LavalThP 51 (1993) 485-496

1486 *Roche* Joseph L., Studying the new catechisms; Catechism of the Catholic Church and Catechism for Filipino Catholics: Landas 9 (Manila 1995) 101-125.

1487 *Rodríguez Carmona* A., Como leer la Biblia; un nuevo documento de la Pontificio Comisión Bíblica: Proyección 41 (1994) 219-226.

1488 **Ruh** Ulrich, Der Weltkatechismus, Anspruch und Grenzen. FrB 1993, Herder. 144 p. DM 19,80. -- [R]TPQ 143 (1995) 309s (J. *Singer*, wie S.444).

1489 [E]**Ruppert** Lothar, (*Klauck* Hans-Josef), Die Interpretation der Bibel in der Kirche, kommentiert: SBS 161. Stu 1995, KBW. 174 p. DM 44. 3-460-04511-2 [TR 91,360].

1490 *Samuel* David, The place of private judgment: Churchman 108 (L 1994) 6-21 [.. conscience vs. authority].

1491 *a) Schindler* David L., Christological aesthetics and *Evangelium vitae*: toward a definition of liberalism; -- *b) Baxter* Michael J., *Bauerschmidt* Frederick C., *Eruditio* without *religio* the dilemma of Catholics in the Academy: CommWsh 22 (1995) 193-224 / 284-302.

1492 *a) Schner* George P., Theological scholarship as a form of Church service; -- *b) Phan* Peter C., .. Roman Catholic perspective; -- *c) Kaiser* Walter C., .. Evangelical critique and plan: TEdn 32,1 (Pittsburgh 1995) 13-25 / 31-41 / 57-70 ... al. [Supplements 1-3 on Cath./Ev. seminary presidency.]

1493 **Schönborn** Christoph, Living the Catechism of the Catholic Church; a brief commentary on the Catechism for every week of the year, I. The Creed, [T]*Kipp* David. SF 1995. Ignatius. 162 p. $ 10 pa. 0-89870-560-6 [ThD 43,288].

1494 **Segundo** Juan Luis, Qu'est-ce qu'un dogme ? Vérité évangélique et vérité normative [Liberation of dogma 1992 → 8,1312 = El dogma que libera 1989 → 7,1176], [T]*Guibal* Francis: CogF 169, 1992 → 8,1310: [R]RTPh 127 (1995) 93-95 (K.*Blaser*).

1495 **Segundo** Juan Luis, The liberation of dogma; faith, revelation, and dogmatic teaching authority 1992 → 8,1312 ... 10,1011: [R]NewThR 8,2 (1995) 97s (B.P. *Stone*).

1496 **Shannon** William H., Exploring the Catechism of the Catholic Church. Cincinnati 1995, St. Anthony Messenger. 140 p. $ 9. 0-86716-234-1 [ThD 43,88].

1497 **Simon** Maurice, Un catéchisme universel pour l'Eglise catholique; du concile de Trente à nos jours; BtEThL 103, 1992 → 8,1316; 9,1161: [R]CrSt 16 (1995) 231s (L. *Sartori*); RHE 90 (1995) 544-7 (O. *Henrivaux*); TTh 35 (1995) 413 (M. *Lamberigts*).

1498 *Simonetti* Mario, La Sacra Scrittura nella Chiesa delle origini (I-III secolo): Salesianum 57 (1995) 63-74.

1499 *Sloyan* Gerard S., The use of the Bible in a new resource book: a review of the Vatican's Catechism: BThB 25 (1995) 3-13.

1500 *Stowasser* Martin, '... damit das Urteil der Kirche reife'; von 'Providentissimus Deus' zur 'Interpretation der Bibel in der Kirche': (Tü)TQ 175 (1995) 202-214.

1501 **Strozier** Charles B., Apocalypse; on the psychology of fundamentalism in America. Boston 1994, Beacon. 318 p. $ 25. 0-8070-1226-2. -- [R]JPsT 23 (1995) 139 (R. *Singelenberg*); TTod 51 (1994s) 640.2 (W.E. *Oates*).

1502 *Thiel* John E., Responsibility to the Spirit; authority in the Catholic tradition: NewThR 8,3 (1995) 53-68.

1503 **Thils** Gustave, Les doctrines théologiques et leur 'évolution': RTL Cah 28. LvN 1995, Fac.Théol. 70 p. 2-87723-177-1. -- [R]EThL 71 (1995) 252s (J. *Étienne*: d'abord hostile, le Magistère assimile ..)

1504 *a) Thornhill* John, The Gospel; the ultimate authority of life in the Church: -- *b) Arbuckle* Gerald A., Leadership for refounding; understanding contemporary tensions in the Church; -- *c) Potter* Lesley, Authority ... of popes and saints; -- *d) Glare* Paul, What is your sense of authority within the Catholic Church ? : Aus(tralas)CR 72,2 ('Authority in the Church' 1995) 131-142 / 143-150 / 157-162 / 180-2.

1505   *Van Allen* Rodger,   Law and spirit in the contemporary Catholic university: Horizons 22 (1995) 129-135.

1506   *Vanhoye* Albert,   ᴳ Past and present of the Biblical Commission [< Greg 74 (1993) 261-275], ᵀ*Maurophidis* S.: DeltBM 12.2 (1993) 35-48.

1507   *Veliath* Dominic, Youth and fundamentalism: Kristu Jyoti 10,1 (1994) 17-29.

1508   *Verbakel* Dick A.,   *Greer* Joanne M.G.,   Magisterium and psyche; interface and relative emphasis in the formation programs of Catholic seminaries in North America: JE(mp)T 7,1 (1994) 58-79.

1509   **Verweyen** Hansjürgen,   Der Weltkatechismus; Therapie oder Symptom einer kranken Kirche ? Dü 1993, Patmos. 146 p. 3-491-77938-3. -- ᴿAtK(ap) 124 (1995) 152s (C. *Rogowski*: sharper than Rᴜʜ U.. 1993); Bijdragen 56 (1995) 469s (A. *Lascaris*, Eng.).

1510   **Vitali** D., 'Sensus fidelium'; una funzione ecclesiale di intelligenza della fede. Brescia 1995, Morcelliana. 452 p. Lᵐ 50. -- ᴿVivH 6 (1995) 416s (S. *Dianich*).

1511   ᴱ**Walsh** Michael J., Commentary on the Catechism of the Catholic Church 1994 → 10,1022: ᴿET 106 (1994s) 346s (N. *Tanner*); LiLi 32,1 (1995) 73s (M. *Pelzel*) & *74-76* & 31,4 (1995) 71-73 & 32,2 (1995) 82-84 (*al.*); Tablet 249 (1995) 288 (F. *Kerr*: 'critics to make you take the catechism off the shelf').

1512   **Watson** Francis, Text, Church and world; biblical interpretation in theological perspective → 10,1023; GR/E 1994, Eerdmans/Clark. viii-366 p. $ 35. 0-8028-3774-3 / 0-567-09700-5. -- ᴿET 106 (1994s) 243 (D. *Hill*); Month 256 (1995) 159s (P. *O'Reilly*).

1513   **Werbick** Jürgen, Offenbarungsanpruch und fundamentalistische Versuchung: QDisp 129, 1991 → 7,1194; 8,1332: ᴿFrRu 2 (1995) 143s (W. *Trutwin*); MüTZ 45 (1994) 87s (A. *Kreiner*).

1514   *Whitfield* Stephen J., Separation anxiety; from founders to fundamentalists: Judaism 44 (1995) 131-145.

1515   *Witherup* R.D., Is there a Catholic approach to the Bible ? Priest 51,2 (1995) 29-35 [NTAb 39,p.379].

1516   *Zovkić* Matko, How is the Catechism interwoven with the Holy Scriptures ?: *BogSmot 65 (1995) 41-56 Croatian: Eng. 56s.

B3.2   *Homiletica* -- **The Bible in preaching**

1517   **Adams** J.E., Truth applied; application in preaching. GR 1990, Zondervan. 144 p. $ 8 pa. -- ᴿC(alvin)TJ 30 (1995) 212-4 (S. *Greidanus*).

1518   **Allen** Ronald J., *Holbert* John C.,   Holy root, holy branches; Christian preaching from the OT. Nv 1995, Abingdon. 183 p. $ 15. -- ᴿSewaneeT 38 (1994s) 386 . 388 (Lucy A. *Hogan*).

1519   **Bailey** Raymond,   Hermeneutics for preaching; approaches to contemporary interpretations of Scripture 1992 ᴾ 10,1028: ᴿRevB(arg) 56 (1994) 183-5 (A. *Ricciardi*).

1520   *Barile* Riccardo, L'omelia prima e dopo il Vaticano II : RP(ast)L 33,1 (1995) 11-25 (49-54, Riviste per preparare l'omelia).

1521   *a) Beattie* Tina, The challenge of Catholic preaching today; -- *b) O'Collins* Gerald, Making the Word come alive: PrP 9 (1995) 141-4 / 150-3.

1522   ᴱ**Blain** Susan A.,   Imaging the word; an arts and [Sunday-sermon] lectionary resource, 2. Cleveland 1995, United Church. 278 p [Word&World 16,364, Cindi B. *Johnson*).

1523 **Brienen** T., De verkondiging in het juiste spoor; de plaats van Israël in de Homiletiek en in de prediking: Verkenning en Bezinning. Kampen 1993, Kok. 76 p. ƒ 19. 90-24-28240-3. -- ᴿNedThT 49 (1995) 83s (M. den *Dulk)*.

1524 **Bristoe** D. Stuart, Fresh air in the pulpit; challenge and encouragement from a seasoned preacher. GR/Leicester 1994, Baker/Inter-Varsity. 189 p. £ 10. 0-9010-1071-3 / 0-85110-998-5.

1525 **Brueggemann** Walter, Biblical perspectives on evangelism; living in a three-storied universe [not BULTMANN's but 1. promise to the ancestors; 2. liberation from slavery: 3. gift of the Land] 1993 → 9,868: ᴿEncounter 56 (1995) 209-212 (J.G. *Linn)*.

1526 **Brueggemann** Walter, Texts under negotiation; the Bible and postmodern imagination 1993 -> 9,867: ᴿInterpretation 49 (1995) 202 . 204 (J.T. *Strong)*; RestQ 37 (1995) 61-63 (D. *Bland:* to 'give the [sermon] texts back their voice' instead of 'being managed by the Church '); TTh 34 (1994) 75 (P. *Chatelion Counet)*.

1527 *Brueggemann* Walter, Preaching as reimagination: ThTo 52 (1995s) 313-329.

1528 **Burghardt** Walter J., Speak the Word with boldness. NY 1994, Paulist. viii-230. $ 15. -- ᴿVidyajyoti 39 (1995) 66 (P.M. *Meagher)*.

1529 **Buttrick** David, A captive voice; the liberation of preaching 1994 → 10,1031: ᴿET 106 (1994s) 126 (G.W.S. *Knowles*, also on BRISTOE & EDWARDS).

1530 **Camery-Hoggatt** Jerry, Speaking of God; reading and preaching the Word of God. Peabody MA, Hendrickson. v-277 p. $ 17. 1-56563-172-2 [< ThD 43,357].

1531 *a) Cañete Castro* Carlos, La predicación de fray Diego José de Cádiz; uso preferente de la Sagrada Escritura y santos padres; -- *b) González Caballero* Alberto, La Biblia en los discursos universitarios del Beato Diego: EstFr 96,414 (centenario beatificación 1995) 289-311 / 313-343.

1532 **Chapell** Bryan, Christ-centered preaching; redeeming the expository sermon. GR 1994, Baker. 375 p. $ 25. -- : C(alvin)TJ 30 (1995) 282-5 (S. *Greidanus)*.

1533 *Chapell* Bryan, Alternative models; old friends in new clothes [< ᴱ**Duduit** Michael, Handbook of contemporary preaching (Nv 1992) Broadman] : Presbyterion 19 (St.Louis 1993) 3-16.

1534 *Charry* Ellen T., Biblical preaching as a subversive and public-spirited activity: : SewaneeT 38 (1994s) 39-53.

1535 *a)* **Cleverley Ford** D.W., Preaching what we believe. L 1995, Mowbray. 134 p. £ 9. 0-264-67363-8. -- *b)* **Brown** David, The Word to set you free. L 1995, SPCK. 193 p. £ 10. 0-281-04806-1. -- ᴿET 106 (1994s) 383 (C.S. *Rodd)*.

1536 *Colglazier* R.Scott, Great sermons are always weird: Disciple 132,7 (St. Louis 1994) 24-26.

1537 *Coogan* Donald, Spirit, Bible and preaching today, with special reference to William TYNDALE: → 5, ᶠATKINSON J., Bible,Reformation,Church: JSNT.s 105 (1995) 73-83.

1538 **Davis** Ellen F., Imagination shaped: Old Testament preaching in the Anglican tradition. Ph 1995, Trinity. ix-289 p. $ 19 pa. 1-56338-121-4 [< OTA 19,144; ThD 43,163].

1539 *Deselaers* Paul, Biblisch predigen -- ein Risiko: BiLi 68 (1995) 204-8.

1540 *Dolman* Robert E., Forgotten man of the Church of England; John Neville FIGGIS as preacher (c,1917): E(xp)T 107 (1995s) 169-172.

1541 **Edwards** Paul, The practical preacher; handy hints for hesitant homilists. Leominster 1994, Gracewing. ix-159 p. £ 8. 0-85244-241-6. -- ᴿMonth 256 (1995) 22s (M. *Ashworth)*.

1542 ᴱEslinger Richard L., Intersections; post-critical studies in preaching. GR 1994, Eerdmans. xii-156 p. $ 13. -- ᴿÉTRel 70 (1995) 609s (B. *Reymond*); P(rinc)SB 16 (1995) 384s (S. B. *Johnston*: if the historical-critical method is dead -- to some extent).

1543 *Farley* Edward, Preaching the Bible and preaching the Gospel: : TTod 51 (1994s) 90-103.

1544 *Gambarotto* Laurent, La prédication Réformée à l'épreuve de l'événement: ÉTRel 70 (1995) 241-252.

1545 **Greidanus** Stanley, The modern preacher and the ancient text 1988 → 3,1432 ... 9,1195: ᴿConcordiaTQ 59 (1995) 131-3 (C.C. *Fickenscher*).

1546 *Greidanus* Stanley, Preaching and the new literary studies of the Bible: C(alvin)TJ 28 (1993) 121-30.

1547 **Guérin** Paul, *Sutcliffe* Terence, Guide du prédicateur, à l'usage des laïcs et des prêtres. P 1994, Centurion. 211 p. F 120. 3-227-77012-7. -- ᴿAtK(ap) 125 (1995) 305-8 (A. *Dragula*); ÉTRel 70 (1995) 146s (J.-F. *Zorn*).

1548 *Hermelink* Jan, Predigt in der Werkstatt, zur Bedeutung der Predigtanalyse in der theologischen Ausbildung: BThZ 12 (1995) 50-57.

1549 *Herzog* Urs, Predigt als 'ministerium Verbi': FrSZ 42 (1995) 118-133.

1550 **Holbert** John C., Preaching Old Testament; proclamation and narrative in the Hebrew Bible. Nv 1991, Abingdon. -- ᴿRestQ 37 (1995) 250-3 (D. *Bland*)

1551 ᴱ**Holmgren** Fredrick C., *Schaalman* Herman E., Preaching biblical texts; expositions by Jewish and Christian scholars. GR 1995, Eerdmans. xvii-166 p. $ 14. 0-8028-0814-X [ThD 43,183].

1552 **Jacobson** William H., Preaching as *mimesis*; RICŒUR ..: Diss. Theol.Sem, ᴰ*Long* T. Princeton 1995 [< RStR 22, p.270].

1553 **Jamison** Renée, Christian television, 'voices of Christ'; transforming attitudes and perceptions; M.A.diss. Regent 1995. 93 p.13-76949. -- DissA (disk) 56 (1995s) MAI 34 (1996) 987.

1554 **Jenson** Richard A., Thinking in story: preaching in a post-literate age. Lima OH 1993, CSS. 145 p. 4 10.50 pa. -- ᴿC(alvin)TJ 29 (1994) 548-60 (J. *Bolt*, also on BROCKELMAN P. 1992).

1555 *a) Jones* Hywel R., La predicazione biblica, ᵀ*Piccirillo* G., *Walker* G.; -- *b) Borelli* Giovanni, .. al tempo de la Riforma: STEv 6,11 (1994) 3-25 / 26-36.

1556 *Kemp* Raymond B., The homilist's library [FALEY R. 1994; JOHNSON L., Luke 1990 ...]: Church 11,1 (NY 1995) 49-51.

1557 **Larsen** David L., Telling the old, old story; the art of narrative preaching. Wheaton IL 1995, Crossway. 320 p. $ 15 pa. -- ᴿC(alvin)TJ 30 (1995) 624s (W.M. *Van Dyk*).

1558 *a)* **Leach** Kenneth, We preach Christ crucified. .... 1994, DLT. ix-102 p. £ 7. 0-232-52085-2. -- *b)* **Phillips** Anthony, The passion of God. Norwich 1995, Canterbury. 79 p. £ 6. 1-85311-101-5. -- *c)* **Taylor** John B., Preaching on God's justice. L 1994, Mowbray. viii-119 p. £ 8. 0-264-67338-7. → 1561, ExpT infra.

1559 **Lischer** Richard, The preacher [Martin Luther] KING. NY 1995, Oxford-UP. 344 p. £ 17. 0-19-508779-8. -- ᴿE(xp)T 107 (1995s) 125 (M. *Camroux*).

1560 **Long** Thomas G., Preaching and the literary forms of the Bible 1989 → 5,1435 ... 7,1223: ᴿConcordJ 21 (1995) 111-3 (D.S. *Smith*).

1561 ᴱ**Long** Thomas G., *Plantinga* Cornelius. A chorus of witnesses; model sermons for today's preacher. GR/Leominster 1994, Eerdmans/Gracewing. xiv-306 p. $ 18/£ 13. 0-8028-0132-3. -- ᴿET 106 (1994s) 316 (G.W.S. *Knowles*); P(rinc)SB 16 (1995) 244-6

(C.J. *Campbell*); RefR 49 (1995s) 53 (T. *Bartha*); (Reformed) Perspectives 9,8 (1994) 22s (made Carol B. *Reynolds* wonder whether she was rather 'aspiring' or even 'Christian').

1562 *McClain* William B., African American preaching and the Bible; biblical authority or biblical literalism: *JRT 49,2 (1993) 72-80.

1563 **McDill** Wayne, The 12 essential skills for great preaching. Nv 1994, Broadman & H. 290 p. $ 18. -- ᴿBS 152 (1995) 381-3 (T.S. *Warren*).

1564 **McKim** Donald, The Bible in theology and preaching²ʳᵉᵛ 1994 → 10,1044: ᴿE(xp)T 107 (1995s) 26 (N. *Clark*).

1565 **Miles** Robert G., The report of good news from a far country; preparation for preaching the Old Testament in the Christian pulpit (Ex Hos): diss. ᴰ*Knierim* R. Claremont 1995. 118 p. 95-39915. -- DissA 56 (1995s) 3165.

1566 **Moeller** Pamela Ann, A kinesthetic homiletic; embodying Gospel in preaching 1993 → 9,1206; 10,1045: ᴿEncounter 56 (1995) 221s (Teresa *Stricklen*).

1567 ᴱ**Mottu** Henry, *Bettex* Pierre A. [→ 10,375c 'Dettex': textes, *Theissen* Gerd, *al.*] Le défi homilétique; l'exégèse au service de la prédication [11 art.]: Pratiques 13, Genève 1994: ᴿEeV 105 (1995) 39-44 (L. *Walter*); ETR 70 (1995) 105-110 [NTAb 39, p.369s, all 3]; ThZ 51 (1995) 180s (W. *Neidhart*).

1568 *Müller* Klaus, Homilie und Poesie; über ein enges aber nicht immer einfaches Verwandtschaftsverhältnis: ThGL 85 (1995) 64-80.

1569 **Ong** Walter [*Stevens* ...], Orality and literacy; the technologizing of the world. Bradford MA, Routledge-CA. 280 p. $ 14. 0-415-02796-9.

1570 **Parker** T.H.L., CALVIN's preaching 1992 → 8,m329 ... 10,14520: ᴿEvQ 66 (1994) 189-191 (C.R. *Trueman*).

1571 *a) Poffet* Jean-Michel, Exégèse savante et prédication naïve ? ; -- *b) Rimaud* Didier, Ouvrir les Écritures; VSp 149 (1995) 395-404 / 385-394.

1572 *Prinsloo* G.T.M., Die rol van Ou Testament teologie in die prediking: SkrifK 15 (1994) 359-376 [< OTA 18 (1995) p. 364].

1573 *Reed* Robert, *al.*, Preaching [not 'preachings' as title page] as the creation of an experience; the not-so-rational revolution of the New Homiletic [CRADDOCK, BUTTRICK ... RICŒUR]: Journal of Communication and Religion 18,1 (Azusa 1995) 1-9: trying to reach the will through the imagination rather than the reason.

1574 *Rizzo* Thomas, How to deliver effective homilies: Priest 51,11 (1995) 48-50.

1575 *Schieder* Rolf, Der 'Wirklichkeitsbezug' der Predigt; vom Nutzen einer diskurstheoretischen Predigtanalyse: EvTh 55 (1995) 322-337.

1576 *Schuringa* H. David, The vitality of Reformed preaching: C(alvin)TJ 30(1995) 184-93.

1577 *Steiger* Johann Anselm, Rhetorica sacra seu biblica; Johannes Matthäus MEYFART (1590-1642) und die Defizite der heutigen rhetorischen Homiletik: ZThK 92 (1995) 517-558.

1578 **Theissen** G., *al.*, Le défi homilétique; l'exégèse au service de la prédication: Pratiques 13. 321 p. F 132. Genève 1994, Labor et Fides. -- ᴿBLE 96 (1995) 235s (A. *Marchadour*); E(spr)eV 105 (1995) 39-44 (L. *Walter*, beaucoup sur POFFET J.-M., *al.*); Études 382 (1995) 425s (P. *Guérin*).

1579 **Theissen** Gerd, The sign language of faith; opportunities for preaching today. L 1995, SCM. xiii-177 p. 0-334-02598-2.

1580 **Van Horn** Roger, Pew rights; for people who listen to sermons 1992 → 8,1384*: ᴿC(alvin)TJ 29 (1994) 568-570 (W.M. *Van Dyk*).

1581 *Wabel* Thomas, The simplicity of Scripture in LUTHER's Christmas sermons: LuthQ 9 (1995) 241-252.

1582 ^E**Walton** Heather, *Durber* Susan, Silence in heaven; a book of women's preaching.
L 1994, SCM. xix-197. £ 10. -- ^RModern Believing [continuing the numbering of Modern
Churchman] 36,1 (1995) 51s (Ellen *Clark*).

1583 ^E**Willimon** William H., *Lischer* Richard, Concise encyclopedia of preaching [200
art. by 182 scholars]. LVL 1995, W-Knox. xxi-518 p. $ 39. 0-664-21942-X [RStR 22,336,
Mary Lin *Hudson*]. -- ^RE(xp)T 107 (1995s) 157s (J. M. *James*); *TBR 8,2 (1995s) 37 (A.
Dunstan: high praise).

1584 **Wilson** Paul S., The practice of preaching. Nv 1995, Abingdon. 329 p. $ 21.
0-687-19506-3 [ThD 43,294].

1585 **Wilson** Paul S., A concise history of preaching [mostly about 20 preachers]. Nv
1992, Abingdon. 192 p. -- ^R(NES)ThRev 16 (1995) 139-141 (J. *Derksen*).

1586 *Zorn* Jean-François, L'homilétique dans tous ses états [THEISSEN G., *al.*, Le défi
homilétique 1994]: ÉTRel 70 (1995) 105-110.

B3.3 **Inerrantia, inspiratio** [Revelatio → H1.7]

1587 **Artola Arbizu** A.M., La Escritura inspirada; estudios sobre la inspiración bíblica:
TDeusto 26. Bilbao 1994, Mensajero. 256 p. -- ^RBurg 36 (1995) 555s (F. *Pérez Herrero*).

1588 **Bloesch** Donald G. (→ 1086), Holy Scripture; revelation, inspiration and interpretation
1994 → 10,1059; ^RERT 19 (1995) 87-89 (D. *Parker*); ET 106 (1994s) 53 (R.J. *Coggins*);
S(co)BET 13 (1995) 148-150.

1589 ^E**Borsch** Frederick H., The Bible's authority in today's Church. Ph 1993, Trinity.
v-213 p.: *ProEc 4 (1995) 496-9 (Catherine *Cory*, also on three cognates).

1590 *Camroux* Martin F., Can we trust the Bible ? : ET 106 (1994s) 48s.

1591 *Canale* Fernando L., Revelation and inspiration; *a)* the liberal model; *b)* the
historical-cognitive model: A(ndr)USS 32 (1994) 169-195 / 33 (1995) 5-38 [NTAb
39,p.370; 40,p.3].

1592 *Cortes* Regino, The Bible as the *dabar* of God: PhilipSac 29 (1994) 35-53.

1593 **Countryman** L. William, Biblical authority or biblical tyranny ? 1994 -> 10,1062:
^RProEccl 4 (1995) 496-9 (Catherine *Cory*, also on 3 cognates).

1594 **Dockery** David S., Christian Scripture; an Evangelical perspective on inspiration,
authority and interpretation. Nv 1995, Broadman & H. xi-257 p.; bibliog. 217-234. $ 20.
0-8054-1040-6.

1595 **Fernhout** Rein, Canonical texts, bearers of absolute authority; Bible, Koran, Veda,
Tipiṭaka 1994 → 10358*: ^RISLCHR 21 (1995) 246s (M.L. *Fitzgerald*).

1596 **Gabel** Helmut, Inspirationsverständnis im Wandel; theologische Neuorientierung im
Umfeld des Zweiten Vatikanischen Konzils [Diss. Mainz, ^D*Schneider* T.]. Mainz 1991,
Grünewald. 351 p. -- ^R*Carthaginensia 11 (1995) 191s (R. *Sanz Valdivieso*).

1597 *George* Timothy, What we mean when we say it's true: ChrTo 89,12 ('Thw Bible
tells me so ' 1995) 16-21.

1598 *Glenny* W. Edward, The divine meaning of Scripture; explanations and limitations:
JETS 38 (1995) 481-500.

1599 **Goldingay** John, Models for Scripture [abandon the non-biblical terms 'authority',
'revelation', 'inspiration', 'inerrancy'. 'canon' -- even 'word of God'!] 1994 → 10,1303
[RStR 22,152, J. *Limburg*; OTA 18 (1995) p. 427 (J.T. *Willis*)]: ^RE(xp)T 107 (1995s) 179s
(J.F.A. *Sawyer*); *ModBlv 36,3 (1995) 53-55 (R.T. *France*); ThTo 52 (1995s) 525s . 528
(A.K.M. *Adam*). -- N.B. This is a different book from his 1995 → 1298* supra.

1600 **Hauerwas** Stanley, Dispatches from the front; theological engagements with the secular [Why choose the Bible and not some other text ? Is it enough to say simply that we prefer it ?] 1994 → 10,182: ᴿChrCent 112 (1995) 962-6 (M. L. *Stackhouse*: he hates liberalism).

1601 **Keegan** Jeffrey P., The locus of revelation in relation to text and event in light of the doctrine of inspiration; an examination in the arena of OT theology: diss. Trinity Evangelical, ᴰ*Sailhamer* J. 1995. 362 p. 95-33053. -- DissA 56 (1995s) 2292.

1602 **Lines** Dennis, Christianity is larger than fundamentalism; a series of critical studies examining the nature of biblical authority. E 1995, Pentland. xiv-181 p. 1-85821-285-5.

1603 **McKinsey** C. Dennis, The encyclopedia of biblical errancy [< journal 'Biblical Errancy']. Amherst NY 1995, Prometheus. 553 p. $ 7. 0-87975-926-7. -- ᴿ*TBR 8,2 (1995s) 7 (R. *Coggins:* tedious jokey style].

1604 *Pache* René, The inspiration and authority of Scripture, ᵀ*Needham* H.J. 'repr. Salem WI SHF publ. Co. 1969' [JSNT 54 (1994) 123 (J.T. *Reed*)]. 399 p. 1-879215-11-X.

1605 *Perrot* Charles, L'inspiration des Septante et le pouvoir scripturaire: → 78, ᶠHARL M., Katà toùs o' 1995, 169-183 [< OTA 18 (1995) p. 459].

1606 *Placher* William C., Is the Bible true ? [means 'we can trust it as a guide to faith and life ?']; ChrCent 112 (1995) 924-8.

1607 *Satinover* Jeffrey B., Divine authorship ? Computer reveals startling world patterns : BiRe 11,5 (1995) 2-31 . 44.

1608 *a) Southwick* Jay S., What to do when your neighbor says, 'The Bible says it; I believe it; that settles it!'; -- *b) Steussy* Marti J. My friend, the Bible:: Disciple 132,11 (St. Louis 1994) 10-12 / 4-8.

1609 *Speyer* Wolfgang, Das Hören einer göttlichen Stimme; zur Offenbarung und zur Heiligen Schrift im frühen Rom: → 142, ᶠOROZ RETA II, Helm 45 (1994) 7-27.

1610 **Thompson** Henry O., Authority, the Bible; who needs it ? New Delhi 1994, ISPCK. x-144 p. rs 40. 81-7214-182-3. -- ᴿVidyajyoti 59 (1995) 215s (P.M. *Meagher*).

1611 **Trobajo** A., *al.*, La palabra de Dios en lenguaje humano: Teología en diálogo 10. S 1994, Univ. Pontificia. 255 p. 84-7299-335-3.

1612 *Williams* John S., Inerrancy, inspiration, and dictation : RestQ 37 (1995) 158-177.

1613 **Wolterstorff** Nicholas, Divine discourse; philosophical reflections on the claim that God speaks [< 1993 Oxford Wilde lectures]. C 1995, Univ. viii-326 p. £ 37,50; pa. £ 19. 0-521-47539-2; -57-0.

1614 **Wright** Christopher J.H., Walking in the ways of the Lord; the ethical authority of the Old Testament. Leicester 1995, Inter-Varsity. 319 p. £ 16. 0-85111-444-X.

B3.4 **Traditio**

1615 *Barker* Margaret, The secret tradition: *JHiCr 2,1 (1995) 31-67.

1616 ᴱ**Brück** H. von, *Werbick* J., Traditionsabbruch -- Ende des Christentums ? Wü 1994, Echter. 176 p. DM 34. 3-429-01626-6. -- ᴿTTh 35 (1995) 302 P. *Valkenberg*).

1617 **Buckenmaier** Achim, Schrift und Tradition seit dem Vatikanum II. Vorgeschichte und Rezeption: kath. Diss. ᴰ*Müller* G.L. München 1995. -- ThRv Beilage 92/2, xii.

1618 *Duch* Lluís, La tradició com a fonament de la comunitat: QVidaC 176 (1995) 19-52.

1619 *Fontana* R., Senza riserve; note sulla vivente tradizione di Israele e della Chiesa: Qol 55s (1995) 2-4 [< Judaica 51,261].

1620 *Fontbona* Jaume, Conflictivitat en l'Esglesia: QVidaC 176 (1995) 68-77.

1621 **Grelot** Pierre, La tradition apostolique; règle de foi et vie pour l'Église. P 1995, Cerf. 337 p. 2-204-05133-0. -- ^RE(st)E 70 (1995) 571s (S. *Madrigal*); EstTrin 29 (1995) 132s (X. *Pikaza*).

1622 *Karlberg* Mark W., Doctrinal development in Scripture and tradition; a Reformed assessment of the Church's theological task: C(alvin)TJ 30 (1995) 401-418.

1623 *Letellier* Joël, Tradition orale et mémorisation des écritures; première auditio-lectio divina chrétienne: RSPhTh 79 (1995) 601-613; Eng. 614.

1624 *Mansfeld* Jaap, PAPIAS over traditie [KRIPP H.1994] : NedThT 49 (1995) 140-153: Eng. 155.

1625 ^E**Peeters** R.J., *al.*, De onvoltooid verleden tijd, negen bijdragen tot een bezinning op traditie [The uncompleted past: .. tradition]: TFT-Studies 19. Tilburg 1992, Univ. viii-171 p. ƒ 24,50. 90-361-9575-6. -- ^RBijdragen 56 (1995) 467s (A. van *Eijk*).

1626 *Roey* Harry F. van, The OT as tradition [*Wintle* Brian, NT; *Stamoolis* J., Orthodox; *Vandervelde* G., Catholic; *Bray* Gerald, Reformation; *Wearne* Bruce, Enlightenment: ERT 19,2 (Delhi 1995) 102-114 [115-130 / 131-143 / 144-156 / 157-166 / 167-175 < NTAb 40, p.2; OTA 18 (1995) (R.C. *Macey*)].

1627 *Sanders* Andy F., Trditionalism, fallibilism and theological relativism : NedThT 49 (1995) 194-214.

1628 **Schmucker** Robert, Sensus fidei; der Glaubenssinn in seiner vorkonziliaren Entwicklungsgeschichte und in den Dokumenten des II.Vat.; Kath. Diss. ^D*Horn*. Passau 1995. -- ThRv Beilage 92/2, xiii.

1629 *Thiel* John E., Tradition and authoritative reasoning; a nonfoundationalist perspective: TS 56 (1995) 637-651.

1630 ^E**Wertheimer** Jack, The uses of tradition; Jewish continuity in the modern era. NY/CM 1994, Jewish Theol.Sem./Harvard Univ. vii-510 p. 0-67493157-2. -- ^RKiryat Sefer 65 (1994s) p. 13s (D. *Malkiel*, ^H); RÉJ 154 (1995) 518s (Esther *Benbassa*).

1631 ^E**Wiederkehr** Dietrich, Wie geschieht Tradition ? Überlieferung im Lebensprozess der Kirche: QD 133, 1991 → 7,334: ^RTPQ 143 (1995) 313s (J. *Singer*).

1631* **Zukowsky** Mara Kelly, The concept of tradition in modern ecclesiological problems: diss. Fordham, ^D*Heaney* J. Bronx 1994 [< RStR 22,p.271].

B3.5 Canon

1632 **Blanchard** Yves-Marie, Aux sources du canon .. IRÉNÉE; CogF 175, 1993 → 9,1259; 10,1081: ^RBiblica 76 (1995) 591s (Mariette *Canévet*); CBQ 57 (1995) 171s (W.R. *Schoedel*); ETRel 70 (1995) 590s (J.-N. *Pérès*); RB 102 (1995) 419-424 (É. *Nodet*).

1633 **Bloom** Harold, The western canon; the books and school of the ages. NY 1994, Harcourt Bruce. 578 p. $ 30; pa. $ 15. 0-15-195747-9. -- ^RCithara 35,2 (1995s) 27-33 (S. *Stewart*).

1634 *Bovon* François, *Norelli* Enrico, Dal kerygma al canone; lo statuto degli scritti neotestamentari nel secondo secolo: CrSt 15 (1994) 525-540; Eng. 540 [541-557(-576) Bovon, Jesus' presence in the early Church < ThRv 91,271].

1635 *Brakke* David, Canon formation and social conflict in fourth century Egypt; ATHANASIUS of Alexandria's thirty-ninth Festal Letter: HThR 87 (1994) 205-419.

1636 **Childs** Brevard S., The NT as canon. Ph 1994, Trinity. 570 p. $ 26. -- ^RRBBras 11 (1994) 481-6 (C. *Minette de Tillesse*).

1637 *Dohmen* C., Der biblische Kanon in der Diskussion: ThRv 91 (1995) 451-460.

1638 *Ego* Beate, Daniel und die Rabbinen; ein Beitrag zur Geschichte des alttestamentlichen Kanons: Jud(ca) 51 (1995) 18-32

1639 **Ellis** E., OT in early .. canon: WUNT 54, 1991 → 7,198 ... 9,1262: [R]Bijdragen 56 (1995) 79s (M. *Parmentier*, Eng.; p.82s on HAHNEMANN); StPat(av) 41 (1994) 678-680 (A. *Moda*); TLZ 120 (1995) 143-5 (D.-A. *Koch*).

1640 *Fowler* Robert M., The fate of the notion of canon in the electronic age: ForumFF 9,1s (1993) 151-172.

1641 **Hahneman** Geoffrey M., The Muratorian fragment and the development of the canon 1992 → 8,1428 ... 10,1084 [not -nn]: [R]ChH 64 (1995) 638-640 (R.M. *Grant*); Compostellanum 38 (1993) 248s (E. *Romero Pose*); CritRR 7 (1994) 192-4 (B.M. *Metzger*); ET 106 (1994s) 48 (A. *Chester*); I(rish)BSt 17 (1995) 143s (L.S. *Kirkpatrick*); *JEarlyC 3 (1995) 89-91 (R.F. *Hull*); JEH 46 (1995) 128-130 (J.N. *Birdsall*, also on HENNINGS R. 1994 → Y25); RS(to)LR 31 (1995) 461-471 (F. *Bolgiani*); WThJ 57 (1995) 437-452 (C. E. *Hill*) [NTAb 40, p.192].

1642 *Herrmann* Wolfram, Überlegungen zu den Vorstufen der Kanonbildung: → 48, [F]DONNER, H., Meilenstein: ÄAT 30 (1995) 73-78.

1643 **Jasper** David, Readings in the canon of Scripture; written for our learning: Studies in Literature and Religion. NY 1995, St. Martin's. xx-156 p. 0-312-12687-5.

1644 *Jericó Bermejo* Ignacio, El canón de la Sagrada Escritura antes y después de Trento; dos exposiciones en la escuela de Salamanca, B. CARRANZA y P. de SOTOMAYOR: Studium 54 (M 1994) 223-278.

1645 **Jones** Barry A., The formation of the Book of the Twelve; a study in text and canon: SBL diss. 149. At 1995, Scholars. xii-266 p.; bibliog. 243-266. 0-7885-0109-7.

1646 *Kaestli* Jean-Daniel, La place du Fragment de Muratori dans l'histoire du canon: *a)* ASEs 12 (1995) 609-634; Eng. 634; -- *b)* .. à propos de la thèse de SUNDBERG et HAHNEMAN: CrSt 15 (1994) 609-634 [NTAb 39,p.367]. -- 577-607, *Penna* R., L'origine del Corpus Paulinum.

1647 *Körtner* Ulrich H.J., PAPIAS von Hierapolis: → 772, TRE 25 (1995) 641-4.

1648 *Kooij* A. van der, De canonforming van de Hebreeuwse bijbel, het Oude Testament: een overzicht van recente literatuur: NedThT 49 (1995) 42-65; Eng 70.

1649 **Lienhard** J.T., The Bible, the Church, and authority; the canon of the Christian Bible in history and theology [< Cleveland Carroll U. Tuohy lectures 1992s]. ColMn 1995, Liturgical. xi-108 p. $ 10. 0-8146-5536-X [NTAb 40,p.326; RStR 22,165, M.W. *Holmes*].

1650 **McDonald** Lee M., The formation of the Christian biblical canon[2rev]. Peabody MA 1995, Hendrickson. xxxvi-340 p. $ 20. 1-56563-052-1 [< NTAb ([1]33,p.238) 40, p.312].

1651 **Metzger** Bruce M., Der Kanon des Neuen Testaments; Entstehung, Entwicklung, Bedeutung [1987], [T]1993 → 10,1087; 3-491-71104-5: [R]ÉTRel 70 (1995) 283s (A. *Rakotoharintsifa*).

1652 **Miller** John W., The origins of the Bible; rethinking canon history 1994 → 10,1088: [R]*CGrebel 13 (1995) 227s (T. *Hiebert*); ET 106 (1994s) 341s (W. *Moberly*); TS 56 (1995) 811s (F.L. *Moriarty*); Vidyajyoti 59 (1995) 545s (G. *Gispert-Sauch*).

1653 *Miller* Merrill P., 'Beginning from Jerusalem ... ' Re-examining canon and consensus : *JHiCr 2,1 (1995) 3-29.

1654 **Müller** Mogens, Kyrkans första Bibel -- hebraica sive graeca veritas ? Frederiksberg 1994, ANIS. xvi-152 p. 87-7457-147-8. -- [R]BoL (1995) 159 (K. *Jeppesen*); OTA 18 (1995) p.151 (J.T. *Willis*); S(cand)JOT 9 (1995) 157s (N.P. *Lemche*); SvTK 70 (1994) 80-82 (B. *Johnson*).

1655 *Osborn* Eric, Literature, history and logic; the formation of the Christian Bible: A(ustrl)BR 41 (1993) 49-63.

1656 ^E**Pannenberg** W., *Schneider* T., Verbindliches Zeugnis 1. Kanon ... 1992 → 8,1435 ... 10,1090: ^RTPQ 143 (1995) 208.210 (J. *Singer*).

1657 *Penna* Romano, Il canone del NT come garanzia di unità e di pluralismo nella Chiesa: Prot(estantesimo) 49 (1994) 297-311.

1658 *Rendtorff* R., Canonical interpretation; a new approach to biblical texts: Pro Ecclesia 3 (1994) 141-151 [< ZIT 95,p.131].

1659 **Rendtorff** Rolf, Canon and theology [1991 → 9,1272], ^T*Kohl* Margaret. Mp 1993. Fortress. 235 p. $ 16. 0-8006-2665-6. -- ^RInterpretation 49 (1995) 436 . 8 (T.E. *Fretheim*); TBR 8,1 (1995s) 44 (R. *Coggins*).

1660 *Snyman* Gerrie, Intertextuality, story, and the pretense of permanence of canon [à la Salmon RUSHDIE's story-streams]: OTEs 8 (1995) 203-222 [< OTA 19,p.383].

1661 *Stewart-Sykes* Alistair: *Táxei* in PAPIAS again: *JEarlyC 3 (1995) 487-490.

1662 *Tamez* Elsa, Das Schweigen von Frauen und der Geist des Kanons : J(unge)K 56 (1995) 10-14.

1663 ^E**Tardieu** Michel, La formation des canons scripturaires 1992 → 9,415; 10,1094: ^RSalesianum 57 (1995) 171 (R. *Vicent*).

1664 *Vanhoozer* K.J., From canon to concept; 'same' and 'other' in the relation between biblical and systematic theology: SBET 12 (1994) 96-124 [NTAb 39,p.439]. -- ^RScoBuEv 12 (1994) 96-124.

1665 *a) van Rooy* Harry F., The Old Testament as tradition; -- *b) Wintle* Brian, The NT as ..; -- *c) Stamoolis* James, Scripture and tradition in the Orthodox Church; -- *d) Vandervelde* George, .. in the Roman Catholic church; -- *e) Bray* Gerald, .. in Reformation thought; -- *f) Wearne* Bruce, .. in Enlightenment thought: EvRT 19 (1995) 100-114 / 115-130 / 131-143 / 144-156 / 157-166 / 167-175.

1666 *Waltke* Bruce K., How we got the OT [canon]: Crux 30 (1994) 13-18 [< OTA 18 (1995) p. 256].

1667 *Weinberg* J.P., ^R The 'extracanonical' prophecies in the books of Chronicles: PalSb 32 (1995) 8-16 [< OTA 18 (1995) p. 535].

1668 ^E**Wiederkehr** Dietrich, Wie geschieht Tradition ? Überlieferung im Lebensprozess der Kirche: QD 133, 1991 → 7,334: ^RTPQ 143 (1995) 313s (J. *Singer*).

1669 **Zukowsky** Mara Kelly, The concept of tradition in modern ecclesiological problems: diss. Fordham, ^D*Heaney* J. Bronx 1994 [< RStR 22,p.271].

B4.1 *Interpretatio humanistica* - 1. **The Bible & man; health, toil, age**

1670 *Andrew* Joe, Cinema and youth: Kristu Jyoti 11,3 (1995) 1-20.

1671 *Apostola* Nicholas K., Labor and rest in the context of a Christian perspective on the economy: SV(lad)TQ 39 (1995) 185-194.

1672 *a) Castillo Mattasoglio* Carlos, Joven, a ti te digo, ¡levántate! Perspectivas sobre los jóvenes en el Nuevo Testamento; -- *b) Aldana Arrieta* Carmen, Fragmentación, desesperanza y humor; retos al trabajo psicológico con los adolescentes de tugurio: Páginas 20,131 ('Jóvenes entre la frustración y la audacia' 1995) 82-96 / 61-70.

1673 *Clements* R.E., Wisdom, virtue and the human condition: → 159, ^FROGERSON, J., Bible/Society, JSOT.s 200 (1995) 139-157.

1674 **Collins** Gary R., The biblical basis of Christian counseling for peoplehelpers. Colorado Springs 1993, Navpress. 285 p. $ 20. 0-89109-753-8. -- [R]JPsT 22 (1994) 230-232 (R.K. *Bufford*).

1675 *Coninck* F. de, L'homme dans l'action et ce qu'on en dit; jalons bibliques pour une éthique du travail, 2. La vérité du travail: Hokhma 58 (1995) 1-19 [NTAb 39,p.448].

1676 *Culbertson* Philip L., Men, myth, and metanoia; recent works in men's studies [[E]LEES C., [E]HALL D., MEADE M. (p.25 Mead), BOYD S., STERN G.]: *CritRR 8 (1995) 1-26.

1678 *a) Flecha* José-Ramón, 'En la vejez seguirá dando fruto' (Sal 92,15); ancianos y ancianidad en la Biblia; -- *b) Gómez Ortiz* Manuel, Sabiduría y demonios de la tercera edad; SalTer 81 (1993) 761-775 / 73-760.

1679 **Fox** Matthew, The reinvention of work; a new vision of livelihood for our time. SF 1994, Harper [*CreSp 11/1,34].

1680 **Furlanetto** Emanuela, Human work in the magisterium of JOHN PAUL II; content and interpretation for a spirituality of work (Italian): diss. Pontificia Università Gregoriana. Roma 1994. 345 p. -- DissA-C 56 (1995s) p. 345. No photocopy AA.

1681 *Harrington* D.J., Biblical contributions to a theology of aging: RfR 55 (1995) 159-170 [NTAb 40, p.465].

1682 *Hohnjec* Nikola, Inter-generation relationships in the Bible: ObŻ 50 (1995) 569-579.

1683 **Kaminsky** Joel S., Corporate responsibility in the Hebrew Bible: JSOT.s 196. Shf 1995, Academic. 211 p.; bibliog. 192-201. 1-85075-547-7

1684 [E]**Krondorfer** Bjorn, Men's bodies, men's gods; male identities in a (post-) Christian culture. NYU 1995. -- p.149-180, *Culbertson* P., Men and Christian friendship.

1685 **Leaman** Oliver, Evil and suffering in Jewish philosophy: Studies in Religious Traditions 6. C 1995, Univ. xiii-257 p. 0-521-41724-4.

1686 *Moloney* Francis J., Life, healing, and the Bible; a Christian challenge: Pacifica 8 (1995) 315-334 [NTAb 40,p.468].

1687 *Ohler* Annemarie, Mit Gott um die Würde des Menschen ringen; wie das Alte Testament vom Sterben spricht: ZMedEth 40 (1994) 223-232.

1688 **Perkins** J., The suffering self; pain and narrative representation in the early Christian era [... death/martyr complex]. L 1995, Routledge. ix-254 p. $ 60; pa. $ 19. 0-415-11363-6; -2706-8 [NTAb 40,p.561].

1689 *a) Petit* Daniel, Le travail dans la Bible; -- *b) Becquet* Gilles, Tradition et innovation dans la Bible: Sève 559 (1994) 57-61 / 556 (1994) 46-49.

1690 *Pilch* J.J., Sickness and long life: BiTod 33 (1995) 94-98 [NTAb 39,p.459].

1691 *Pleins* David J., Murderous fathers, manipulative mothers, and rivalrous siblings; rethinking the architecture of Genesis-Kings: → 59, [F]FREEDMAN D.N., Fortunate 1995, 121-136.

1692 *a) Pury* Albert de, Le bonheur est-il possible devant Dieu ? Temps, bonheur et salut dans la perspective de l'AT: -- *b) Monteil* Pierre-Olivier, Le bonheur, la forme contemporaine du salut ?: BCPÉ 47,7s (50 ans, 1995) 22-39 / 12-21.

1693 **Richard** Lucien, What are they saying about the theology of suffering ? NY 1992, Paulist. iii-163 p. -- [R]EThL 71 (1995) 492-4 (M. *Steen*, Eng.; 'ISBN 0-8091-33-4').

1694 **Rue** Loyal, By the grace of guile; the role of deception in natural history and human affairs. NY 1994, Oxford-UP. 359 p. $ 25. -- [R]JRel 75 (1995) 591s (Kelly *Bulkeley*).

1695 *Santuc* Vicente, Trabajo y ocio: Páginas 20,133 (1995) 56-69.

1696 *Silva* A. da, La conception du travail dans la Bible et dans la tradition chrétienne: *Théologiques 3,2 (Montréal 1995) 89-104 [NTAb 40, p.276].

1697 *a) Simoens* Yves, Le Sabbat, un temps d'arrêt libérateur; -- *b) Marle* Gérard, Le chômage; fonder autrement son existence; -- *c) Vallin* Pierre, Les spiritualités du travail: Christus 41 (1994) 68-79 / 47-56 / 57-67.

1698 **Stordalen** Tœrje, Stœv og livspust; mennesket I Det gamle testamente. Oslo 1994, Univ. xi-248 p. -- [R]SvTKv 70 (1994) 133s (F. *Lindström*).

1699 *Świderkówna* Anna, Hiob I tajemnica cierpienia: ŻycieD 4,2 (1995) 11-25 (-45, *Grygiel* Stanisław); Eng. 3.

1700 **Volf** Miroslav, Work in the Spirit 1991 → 8,1462; 9,1303: [R]Bijdragen 56 (1995) 107s (M. *Parmentier* Eng.: remarkable, systematic, innovative).

1701 [R]**Wagner** Silvia, *al.*, (Anti-)Rassistische Irritationen: biblische Texte und interkulturelle Zusammenarbeit. B 1994, Alektor. DM 24,80. -- [R]J(unge)K 56 (1995) 332s (G. *Reese*).

1702 *Zubero* Imanol, Etnicidad y universalismo; identidad y tolerancia : SalTer 83 (1995) 433-448 (*al*, 421-474).

B4.2 *Femina, familia* -- Women in the Bible [→H8.8s]

1703 **Ascuitto** L., Eva y sus hermanas; la Biblia en femenino. M 1993, Atenas. 298 p. -- [R]EstTrin 29 (1995) 170s (A.J.Ch.A.)

1704 **Bedini** E., *al.*, Figure femminili nella Sacra Scrittura. Bo 1994, Dehoniane. 96 p. 88-10-70944-6 [< NTAb 40, p.541].

1705 **Bellis** Alice O., Helpmates, harlots, heroes; women's stories in the Hebrew Bible 1994 → 10,1123: [R]*CritRR 8 (1995) 108-110 (Naomi *Steinberg*).

1706 **Bendrotti** Margaret L., Fundamentalism and gender, 1875 to the present. NHv 1993, Yale Univ. 179 p. $ 22.50. -- [R]JRel 75 (1995) 430-2 (D. *Frank*).

1707 **Biale** Rachel, Women and Jewish law: the essential texts, their history, and their relevance for today. NY 1995, Schocken. xvi-293 p. 0-8052-1049-0.

1708 *Blomqvist* K., Chryseïs and Clea, Eumetis and the interlocutress; PLUTARCH of Chaeronea and DIO CHRYSOSTOM on women's education [Dio enjoyed it; for Plutarch studious women would be a threat unless encouragingly channeled by males]: SEÅ 60 (1995) 173-190 [NTAb 40,p.495].

1709 [E]**Børresen** K.E., Image of God and gender models in Judaeo-Christian tradition 1991 → 7,341*a*: [R]*CritRR 7 (1994) 528-530 (Sharyn *Dowd*).

1710 **Borrowdale** Anne, Reconstructing family values. L 1994, SPCK. 221 p. £ 10. 0-281-01762-6. -- [R]ET 106,9 2d-top choice (1994s) 258-260 (C.S. *Rodd*).

1711 **Brenner** A., *Dijk-Hennes* F. van, On gendering texts 1993 → 9,1310; 10,1125; [R]A(ndr)USS 33 (1995) 154s (Leona G. *Running*, under 'Van': the biblical voices are usefully labeled M, F, 'muted F' or 'double', but the modern authors are left sexless, initials only); E(xp)T 107,1 2d-top choice (1995s) 21 (C.S. *Rodd*).

1712 **Bronner** Leila L, From Eve to Esther; rabbinic reconstructions of biblical woman 1994 → 10,1126; $ 19: [R]ET 106 (1994s) 255 (C.S. *Rodd* mentions also Sybil SHERIDAN, Hear our voice, SCM 1994).

1713 *Bronstein* G., Familia en el judaismo y en la tradición judía: RTLi 28,2s (1994) 127-145 [NTAb 40,p. 308].

1714 **Brown** Cheryl Anne, No longer be silent [D]1992 → 8,1471; 10,1311: [R]RefR 49 (1995s) 66 (D.W. *Battjes*).

1715 *Bucher-Gillmayr* Susanne, Begegnungen am Brunnen: BiNo 75 (1994) 48-66; 6 fig.

1716 ^E**Büchmann** Christina, *Spiegel* Celina, Out of the garden; [28] women writers on the Bible. NY 1994, Ballantine. 352 p. $ 23.   -- ^RCrossCur 45 (1995s) 251-3 (Carol *Ochs*).

1717 **Butting** Klara, Die Buchstaben werden sich noch wundern; innerbiblische Kritik als Wegweisung feministischer Hermeneutik 1994 → 10,1129; DM 25. -- ^RJ(unge)K 56 (1995) 397 (Ulrike *Hoffmann*).

1718   **Choe Joon Soo**, Biblical resources for pastoral care and counseling for marital conflicts in Korean immigrant families: diss. Drew. ^D*Warner* W. Madison NJ 1994. 81 p. -- DissA 56 (1995s) p.1833.

1719   *a) Coda* Piero, Familia y Trinidad; reflexión teológica. -- *b) Meis* Anneliese, Lo femenino, una vocación trinitaria. -- *c) Caire* Patrick, Trinidad y liberación, ^T*Ortiz* Alfonso : EstTrin 29 (1995) 187-219 / 221-248 / 249-286.

1720 ^E**Davidman** Lynn, *Tenenbaum* Shelly, Feminist perspectives on Jewish studies. NHv 1994, Yale Univ. vi-281 p. 0-300-06867-0.

1721   *Davies* Margaret, On prostitution [... LXX]: → 159, ^FROGERSON J., Bible/Society; JSOT.s 200 (1995) 225-248.

1722 ^E**Duby** Georges, *Perrot* Michelle, Histoire des femmes en Occident 15. 1991s → 8,d128* (1. L'Antiquité, ^E**Schmitt-Pantel** Pauline): ^RRICP 45 (1993) 143-152 (M. *Quesnel*).

1723   **Exum** J. Cheryl, Fragmented women; feminist (sub)versions of biblical narrrative: JSOT.s 163, 1993 → 9,1320; 10,1135: ^RA(ustrl)BR 43 (1995) 83 (H. *Wallace*); BiRe 11,3 (1995) 41 (D.T. *Olson*); ÉTRel 70 (1995) 116-8 (France *Beydon*); Interpretation 49 (1995) 432 . 4 (Linda *Day*); JBL 114 (1995) 489s (S. *Ackerman*); NedThT 49 (1995) 315s (A.J.O. van der *Wal*).

1724   **Fewell** Danna N., *Gunn* David M., Gender, power, and promise; the subject of the Bible's first story 1993 → 9,1322; 10,1136: ^RCBQ 57 (1995) 550s (D. *Penchansky*); Interpretation 49 (1995) 73-76 (J.S. *Ackerman*, also on Gunn-Fewell Narrative 1993; admiring, but they focus on exegetes through the ages and ignore the real world in which the story happened).

1725   **Fischer** Irmtraud, Die Erzeltern Israels; feministisch-theologische Studien zu Genesis 12-16: BZAW 222, 1994 → 10,2027: ^RZkT 117 (1995) 101 (Susanne *Bucher-Gillmayr*).

1726   **Fischer** Irmtraud, Gottesreiterinnen; biblische Erzählungen über die Anfänge Israels. Stu 1995, Kohlhammer. 200 p. DM 28. 3-17-013508-2 [< OTA 19,144].

1727   Forschungsprojekt Feministische Hermeneutik und Erstes Testament 1994, 9-25: ^ROTA 18 (1995) p.(393) 245 (Irene *Nowell*).

1728   **Frymer-Kensky** Tikva, In the wake of the goddesses; women, culture, and the biblical transformation of pagan myth 1992 → 8,1481; 9,1324: ^RCritRR 7 (1994) 65s (N. *Steinberg*); JQR 86 (1995) 213-6 (M.L. *Gruber*).

1729   **Gallares** Judette A., Images of faith; spirituality of women in the OT 1994 → 10,1138; line-drawing chapter heads: ^RBThB 25 (1995) 92s; ET 106 (1994s) 124 (C.S. *Rodd*); OTEs 8 (1995) 158-160 (M.J. *Masenya*).

1730   **Gerhart** Mary, Genre choices, gender questions ['uncritical reading rots the mind', p.224]. Norman 1992, Univ. Oklahoma. x-261 p. $ 28. -- ^RJRel 75 (1995) 165s (J.L. PRICE).

1731   *Green* Elizabeth C., Donne sagge: autorità femminile durante il regno davidico: RivB 43 (1995) 467-484.

1732   **Gruber** Mayer I., Women in the biblical world; a study guide: ATLA 38. Lanham MD 1995, Scarecrow. xxiv-272 p. I. (OT) 0-8108-3069-8.

1733 *Haas* Guenther, Patriarchy as an evil that God tolerated; analysis and implications for the authority of Scripture: JETS 38 (1995) 321-336. (No 1734)

1735 **Hammer** Margaret L., Giving birth; reclaiming biblical metaphor for pastoral practice 1994 → 10,1144: [R]SewaneeTR 39 (1995s) 208.210s (Joy E. *Rogers*); WW 15 (1995) 110 . 112 (Mary *Albeng*).

1736 **Henshaw** Richard A., Female and male, the cultic personnel; the Bible and the rest of the ancient Near East: PTMS 31. Allison Park PA 1994, Pickwick. xix-385 p. $ 52 pa.— [R]JBL 114 (1995) 711s (S.A. *Wiggins*)

1737 **Ilan** T., Jewish women in Greco-Roman Palestine; an inquiry into image and status: TSAJ 44. Tü 1995, Mohr. xiv-270 p.; bibliog. 230-244. DM 158. 3-16-146283-1. -- [R]JSJ(ud) 26 (1995) 364-6 (P.W. van der *Horst*).

1738 *Ilan* Tal, *a)* The attraction of aristocratic women to Pharisaism during the Second Temple period : HThR 88 (1995) 1-33: -- *b)* Biblical women's names in the apocryphal traditions: JSPE 11 (1993) 3-67 [NTAb 40,p.301].

1739 [*Jahnow* Hedwig (mem.), Die Frau im AT < Die Frau 1914] Feministische Hermeneutik und Erstes Testament, Analyses und Interpretationen [anonymer Marburger-Projekt]. Stu 1994, Kohlhammer. 167 p. DM 40. Auslegung 8 exemplarischer AT-Texte. -- [R]ZAW 107 (1995) 528 (tit.pp.).

1740 **Kam** Rose Sallberg, Their stories, our stories; women of the Bible. NY 1995, Continuum. 287 p. $ 19 pa. 0-8264-0804-4. -- [R]RelStR 21 (1995) 331s (Claire L. *Sahlin*).

1741 *Kraemer* Ross S., Her share of the blessings 1992 → 8,1490; 9,1331: [R]JRel 75 (1995) 269-271 (Margaret M. *Mitchell*); JThS 46 (1995) 678-680 (Frances M. *Young*).

1742 *Kraemer* Ross S., Jewish mothers and daughters in the Greco-Roman world 1994 → 10,239c, [E]**Cohen** Shaye, Jewish Family 1994, 89-112.

1743 *Kunin* Seth D., Perilous wives and (relatively) safe sisters: *JProgJ 2 (1994) 15-34 [< OTA 19, p.373].

1744 **Kytzler** B., Frauen der Antike; von Aspasia bis Zenobia. Z 1994, Artemis & W. 191 p.; 26 fig. -- [R]CLR 45 (1995) 117-9 (R. *Hawley*).

1745 *Lacelle* É.J. & 8 *al.*, → 527, Des femmes aussi faisaient route avec lui; perspectives féministes sur la Bible: ScB 2. Montréal/P 1995. Médiaspaul. 230 p. C$ 27. 2-89420-310-1 [NTAb 40,p.323].

1746 **LaCocque** André, The feminine unconventional 1990 → 6,1614 ... 10,1148: [R]HebStud 35 (1994) 171-4 (Eleanor B. *Amico*).

1747 *La Serna* Eduardo de, La familia en la Biblia : RevBib(Arg) 57 (1995) 93-110 . 143-154.

1748 *Leers* Bernardino, Sagrada família ou política ?: REB 55 (1995) 87-104.

1749 *Lilli* Betty Jane, Recovering the biblical heritage through shift of rhetorical historical paradigms [LERNER Gerda, Creation of patriarchy 1986], presidential address: ProcGM 14 (1994) 1-20.

1750 **Ljung** Inger, Silence ou suppression 1989 → 7,1325 ... 10,1151: [R]RTPh 127 (1995) 196s (J.-D. *Macchi*).

1751 **McKenna** Megan, Not counting women and children; neglected stories from the Bible 1994 → 10,1152: [R]OTEs 8 (1995) 468s (W.R. *Domens*).

1752 **Maldonado** Jorge, Even in the best of families; the family of Jesus and other biblical families like ours. Geneva 1994, WCC. x-66 p. Fs 10. 2-8254-1133-7. -- [R]I(nd)TS 32 (1995) 361s (A.R. *Ceresko*).

1753 **Manning** Christel, Coming to terms with feminism; a study of evangelical Protestant, conservative Catholic, and orthodox Jewish women; diss. California, ^D*Roof* W. Berkeley 1995. -- RStR 22,274.

1754 *Mehlman* Israel, Jephthah: JBQ 23 (1995) 73-78.

1755 ^E**Mills** Sara, Language and gender; interdisciplinary perspectives. L 1995, Longman. xiv-282 p.; bibliog. 260-275. 0-582-22631-7.

1756 **Moore** Sharon Lee, An interdisciplinary hermeneutic; Mieke BÁL's contribution to feminist biblical studies: diss. Baylor, ^D*McGee* D. 1995. 209 p. 95-39483. -- DissA 56 (1995s) 2728.

1757 *Neusner* Jacob, The feminization of Judaism; systemic reversals and their meaning in the formation of the rabbinic system: CJud 46,4 (1994) 37-52 [NTAb 39, p.110].

1758 *Neven* G.W., Het kind in het verhaal; werken met de preken van O. NOORDMANS [Verzamelte Werken 7 (1990) 145-7: Hand 4,33]: G(ereformeerd)TT 95 (1995) 99-110.

1758* *Ochs* Carol, Miriam's way : CrossCur 45 (1995s) 493-509.

1759 **Ostriker** Alice Suskin, Feminist revision and the Bible 1993 → 9,1342: ^R*TBR 8,1 (1995) 11s (Alwyn *Marriage*: essays, interviews, poems give Jewish feminist insights).

1760 **Pardes** Ilana, Countertraditions in the Bible: a feminist approach 1992 → 9,1343; 10,1158: ^RBiRe 11,2 (1995) 15s (Ilona N. *Rashkow*); BoL (1995) 98 (C.S. *Rodd*: via media between P. *Trible* and E. *Fuchs*); *PerspSCF 46 (1994) 67 (Elizabeth M. *Hairfield*). .

1761 **Plaskow** Judith, Und wieder stehen wir am Sinai; eine jüdische feministische Theologie [1990 → 6,1625],^T. Luzern 1992, Exodus. 318 p. DM 46. -- ^REntschluss 50,7s (1995) 44 (T.M. *Meier*).

1762 **Pressler** Carolyn, The view of women found in the Deuteronomic family laws [not nobler than in other biblical codes, despite WEINFELD *al.*; ^DPrinceton 1991]; BZAW 216, 1993 → 9,2536: ^RCBQ 57 (1995) 362-5 (A. *Brenner*); JBL 114 (1995) 492s (J.*Blenkinsopp*).

1763 **Rashkow** Ilona N., The phallacy of Genesis: a feminist-psychoanalytical approach [chiefly Gn 12,10-20 & 20,1-18, from FREUD via LACAN] 1993 → 9,1345: ^RBiRe 11,5 (1995) 15s . 44 (Pamela J. *Milne*); CBQ 57 (1995) 365s (J.G. *Williams*; each of the four points of her defense of her readings has a 'flip side which could be pernicious'; her assumptions contradict and undermine her own case); P(rinc)SB 16 (1995) 365s (E.L. *Greenstein*: creative but with many flaws); TorJT 11 (1995) 86s (Jacqueline R. *Isaac*).

1764 **Ruether** Rosemary R., Sexismo e religião; rumo [goal] a uma teología feminista, ^T*Altmann* Walter, *Sander* Luis M. São Leopoldo 1993, Sinodal. 239 p. 85-233-0306-5. -- ^RPerTeol 27 (1995) 123-6 (F. *Taborda*).

1765 *Salas* Antonio, La mujer en el pueblo bíblico : Rel(y)Cult 41 (1995) 773-788.

1766 **Schottroff** L., (p.175-248), *Schroer* S. (p.83-172), *Wacker* M.-T. (p.3-79), Feministische Exegese; Forschungserträge zur Bibel aus der Perspektive von Frauen. Da 1995, Wiss. xi-262 p. DM 40. 3-534-12010-1 [NTAb 40,p.329].

1767 **Schüssler Fiorenza** Elisabeth, Searching the Scriptures; a feminist introduction 1. 1993 → 9,1349; 2. commentary 1994 → 10,1166: ^RET 106 (1994s) 123s (C.S. *Rodd*: 'taken over from Crossroad'; adds 4 other books on 'Women and the Bible').

1768 *Seltzer* Sanford, Biblical women and patrilineal descent: CCAR 42,2 (1995) 17-24.

1769 **Sered** Susan Starr, Women as ritual experts; the religious lives of elderly Jewish women in Jerusalem. NY 1992, Oxford-UP. 174 p. -- ^RJQR 86 (1995) 252s (Donna *Shai*).

1770 **Shepherd** Naomi, Price below rubies; Jewish women as rebels and radicals [Europe 1920-40]. CM 1993, Harvard Univ. xii-336 p. $ 28. -- ^RJJS 46 (1995) 333 (G. *Estraikh*).

1771   *a) Silva* Aldina da, La condition féminine dans la littérature mésopotamienne et biblique; -- *b) Genest* Olivette, Théories féministes dans l'interprétation de la Bible; -- *c) Racine* Jean-François, Trois approches de la situation des femmes dans le document Q: Hal TAUSSIG, Luise SCHOTTROFF et Amy-Jill LEVINE; -- *d) Caron* Gérald, L'autorité de le Bible à l'heure de l'herméneutique féministe: → 527, Des femmes aussi 1994/5, 75-102 / 43-73 / 133-152 / 197-228.

1772   ᴿ**Soelle** Dorothee, *al.*, Great women of the Bible in art and literature. GR 1995, Eerdmans. 295 p.; 400 color. fig. $ 75. -- ᴿChrCent 112 (1995) 1090.

1773   *Stearns* Gail J., From universal caring to concrete liberation: a review of contemporary works in gender and ethics [several criticizing GILLIGAN C. 1982]: *CritRR 8 (1995) 71-90.

1774   **Steinberg** Naomi, Kinship and marriage in Genesis; a household economics perspective. Mp 1993, Fortress. 162 p. $ 12. 0-8006-2703-2. -- ᴿET 106 (1994s) 127 [C.S. *Rodd*].

1775   *Stevenson* W., The rise of eunuchs in Greco-Roman antiquity; *JHistSexuality 5 (Ch 1995) 495-511 [NTAb 40,p.285].

1776   **Teubal** Savina J., *a)* Hagar the Egyptian; the lost tradition of the matriarchs 1990 [JETS 39,294-6, JoAnn F. *Watson*]. -- *b)* Naming is creating; biblical women hold the power: BiRe 11,4 (1995) 40s . 43.

1777   **Toorn** Karel van den, From her cradle to her grave,; the role of religion in the life of the Israelite and the Babylonian woman 1994 → 10,1169: ᴿSMSR 60 (1994) 417-9 (P. *Merlo*).

1778   *a) Tremblay* Rémi, Youthanasia; breaking the souls of the young; -- *b) Parry* Robert, The rise of the right wing media machine: *CreSp 11,3 (1995) 16-21 / 22-28.

1779   *Turiot* Cécile, Femmes devant Dieu, mais jamais sans leurs hommes [Gn 12 ...]: Sève 573 (1995) 52-54.

1780   **Van Leeuwen** Mary S., *al.*, After Eden; facing the challenge of gender reconciliation. GR 1993, Eerdmans. 640 p. $ 30 pa. 0-8028-0546-5. -- ᴿInterpretation 49 (1995) 76-8 (E. *Mount*).

1781   **Vérilhac** A.-M., *Vial* C., La femme dans le monde méditerranéen: Travaux de la Maison de l'Orient 10 & 19. P 1990, de Boccard. I. Antiquité (1985) 190 p.; 6 fig.; II. Gr.-Rom. 209 p. 2-903264-39-2; -48-1.

1782   *Waltke* Bruce K., The role of women in the Bible: Crux 31,3 (1995) 29-40.

1783   *Ward* Graham, A postmodern version of Paradise [Gen 1-3 silences the woman]: JSOT 65 (1995) 3-12.

1784   **Watson** P.A., Ancient stepmothers; myth, misogyny and reality: Mnemosyne supp. 143. Leiden 1995, Brill. xii-288 p. *f* 160. -- ᴿCLR 45 (1995) 120-2 (D. *Noy*; *novercae*); GaR 42 (1995) 250 (P. *Walcot*).

1785   **Wegner** Judith R., Chattel or person ? the status of women in the Mishnah 1988 → 4,b177 ... 7,1339: ᴿJ(u)d(ais)m 44 (1995) 515-8 (Judith R. *Baskin*); JSSt 40 (1995) 145-150 (Nina L. *Collins*).

1786   **Winter** Miriam T.. The chronicles of Noah and her sisters; Genesis and Exodus according to women [her Gospel 1993 → 9,4341]. NY 1995, Crossroad. 155 p. 0-8245-1509-9.

1787   **Zimmer** Mary, Sister images; guided meditations from the stories of [22] biblical women. Nv 1993, Abingdon. 143 p. $ 9. 0-687-38556-3. -- ᴿRExp 92 (1995) 253s (Jeanette P. *Holt*).

B4.4 *Exegesis litteraria* -- **The Bible itself as literature**

1788 *a) Alford* John A., [† 1349, Richard] ROLLE's English Psalter and Lectio Divina; -- *b) Lindberg* Conrad, Literary aspects of the WYCLIF Bible: → 530, BJRL 77,3 (1995) 47-59 / 79-85.

1789 **Alonso Schökel** Luis, Antologia della poesia biblica [< bilingüe, Zaragoza 1992]. M 1995, Piemme. 589 p.

1790 **Aune** D.E., El Nuevo Testamento en su entorno literario. Bilbao 1993, D-Brouwer. 326 p. -- ᴿStudium 35 (M 1995) 155 (P. *Juan*).

1791 **Babington** Bruce, *Evans* Peter W., Biblical epics; sacred narrative in the Hollywood cinema. Manchester UK 1993, Univ. 248 p. $ 80; pa. $ 25. 0-7190-3268-7; -4030-2. -- ᴿChrSchR 25 (1995s) 209s (H.J. *Baxter*).

1792 **Berry** Donald K., An introduction to wisdom and poetry of the Old Testament. Nv 1995, Broadman & H. xvi-463. 0-8054-1547-5 [< OTA 19, p.345, K.M. *Craig*].

1793 *Brisman* Leslie, The Bible as [a coherent work of ?] literature [EXUM J.C., GUNN D., 1993, *al.*]: *ProofT 15 (1995) 263-271 [195-202, *Sweeney* Marvin A.].

1794 ᴱ**Ebach** J., *Faber* R., Bibel und Literatur. Mü 1995, Fink. 304 p. DM 48. 3-7705-2974-X [NTAb 40, p.323: 15 art., not specified whether reprints].

1795 *Exum* J. Cheryl, Michal at the movies [i.e. as treated in Zanuck's 1951 'David and Bathsheba' and Beresford's 1985 'King David' < her Sheffield course 'Bible tales and retellings in literature, art and film]: → 159, ᶠROGERSON J., Bible/Society; JSOT.s 200 (1995) 273-292.

1796 *Griffith* Michael, The religion, literature and the arts nexus in Australia in the nineties: Aus(tralas)CR 72,4 ('Creative literature and religion' 1995) 435-444.

1797 **Gros Louis** Kenneth R.R., *al.*, Literary interpretations of biblical narratives: The Bible in literature courses. Nv [I.] 1974, Abingdon. 352 p. 0-687-22131-5.

1798 **Hamilton** William, A quest [in literature, for 'anyone not doing history or theology'] for the post-historical Jesus. NY 1994, Continuum. viii-304 p. $ 27.50. 0-8264-0641-6 [RStR 22,338, B. *Harvey*].

1799 *Huizing* C., Die Bibel als literarisches Kunstwerk: EvKomm 22 (1994) 717-720 [< ZIT 95,p.145].

1800 **Humphreys** W. Lee, Joseph and his family; a literary study: StPersOT. Columbia 1988, Univ. SC. xiv-230 p. 0-87249-536-1.

1801 *Jeffrey* David L., The English cultural Bible [NORTON D.1993 → 9,1368; 10,1186]: JRel 75 (1995) 540-4.

1802 **Jossua** Jean-Pierre, Pour une histoire religieuse de l'expérience littéraire, 3. Dieu aux xixᵉ et xxᵉ siècles: Religions. P 1994, Beauchesne. 306 p. -- ᴿE(spr)eV 105 (1995) 300s-jaune [L. *Debarge*].

1803 **Kreitzer** Larry J., The NT in fiction and film; on reversing the hermeneutical flow 1993 → 9,1366: ᴿCritRR 8 (1995) 483-5 (G.E. *Forshey*).

1804 *Langenhorst* Georg, The rediscovery of Jesus as a literary figure: JLT(hOx) 9 (1995) 85-98.

1805 **Martin** Gerhard M., Sachbuch Bibliodrama; Praxis und Theorie. Stu 1995, Kohlhammer. 117 p. DM 34. 3-17-013912-6 [ThRv 92,77].

1806 *Mensch* James R., The Bible as literature: CanadCath 13,8 (1995) 14-19.

1807 **Norton** David, A history of the Bible as literature II, 1700- : 1993 → 9,1368; 10,1186: ᴿC(ath)HR 81 (1995) 600-4 (S.G. *Hornsby*); CLit 43 (1993) 95s (D.J. *McMillan*); C(alvin)TJ

30 (1995) 534-8 (Susan M. *Felch*); Interpretation 49 (1995) 410-2 (D. L. *Barr*); [J]LT(Ox) 9 (1995) 227-9 (J.R. *Watson*); P(ersp)RSt 22 (1995) 299-310 (G. *Campbell*) [NTAb 40, p.206; also JRel 75,540]; TS 56 (1995) 165s (J. *Pfordresher*); TTod 51 (1994s) 472.4 (G.T. *Sheppard*).

1808 *Pifano* Paolo, La Bibbia come letteratura e come linguaggio teologico: → 514, Oltre il racconto 1993/4, 129-136; Eng. 136.

1809 *Piselli* Francesco, Towards a biblical aesthetic; what we require of a poetic thing, [T]*Gallo* Bruno: BeOr 37 (1995) 215-250.

1810 **Reed** Walter L., Dialogues of the Word; the Bible as literature according to BAKHTIN [Mikhail 1895-1975]. Ox 1993, UP. xvi-223 p. £ 35. -- [R]CBQ 57 (1995) 367 (Beverly *Beem*); CritRR 8 (1995) 506-8 (Virginia *Wiles*); [J]LT(Ox) 9 (1995) 232s (G. *Salyer*); JThS 46 (1995) 670s (D. *Dawson*); NTT 96 (1995) 3-18; Eng. 19 (J. *Børtnes*).

1811 *Roeffaers* Hugo, Het christelijke [WITTGENSTEIN] taalspel 1in de leer bij dichters: COLLVL 25 (1995) 77-96.

1812 [E]**Ryken** Leland, *Longman* Tremper[III], A complete literary guide to the Bible 1993 → 9,1371: [R]ChrSchR 25 (1995s) 229s (B. *Jenkins*).

1813 **Scott** Bernard B., Hollywood dreams and biblical stories. Mp 1994, Fortress. xi-297 p. $ 17. 0-8006-2753-9 [ThD 43,87]. -- [R]CritRR 8 (1995) 92-94 (G.C. *Clarke*).

1814 *Telford* William R., The New Testament in fiction and film; a biblical scholar's perspective: → 170, [F]SAWYER, J., Words; JSOT.s 195 (1995) 360-394.

1815 **Wall** Joseph P., A history of literary study of the Bible: diss. Nevada, [D]*Weinstein* M. Las Vegas 1995. 376 p. 95-37103. -- DissA 56 (1995s) 2729.

B4.5 **Influxus biblicus in litteraturam profanam**, generalia

1816 *Åkerberg* Hans, Religionspsykologin och skönlitteraturen: SvTK 69 (1993) 153-160; Eng. 160, Swedish authors.

1817 **Atwan** Robert, *Wieder* Laurance, Chapters into verse; poetry in English inspired by the Bible 1993 → 9,1374; 10,1191: [R]JEH 46 (1995) 483s (P. *Hatton*); TTod 51 (1994s) 155s (T.M. *Disch*).

1818 **Axcelson** John W., The divine breath of irony; the religious consciousness of romantic literature: diss. Columbia, [D]*Kroeber* K. NY 1995. 262 p. 95-22834. -- DissA 56 (1995s) p.915.

1819 **Browne** Joy Elizabeth, The historical Word made flesh in African-American theology, literature, and biblical hermeneutics: diss. Emory, [D]*Detweiler* R. Atlanta 1995. 389 p. 95-36368. -- DissA 56 (1995s) 2726.

1820 **Castelli** Ferdinando, Volti di Gesù nella letteratura moderna 3. CinB 1995, Paoline. 777 p. L[m] 45. -- [R]RasT 36 (1995) 765-8 (F. *Marucci*).

1821 **Derosa** Edward L., The Middle English confession manual and the morality play: diss. Fordham, [D]*Erler* Mary C. NY 1995. 346 p. 95-20604. -- DissA 56 (1995s) p.544.

1822 [E]**Doglio** Federico, Il teatro e la Bibbia: Il grande codice 3. R 1995, Garamond. 262 p. 88-06180-07-1.

1823 [E]**Ebach** J., *Faber* R., Bibel und Literatur. Mü 1995, Fink. -- [ZAW 107 (1995) 521, nur 241-258, *Dietrich* W, Der Fall des Riesen Goliath (in vier modernen Davidromanen)].

1824 **Forshey** G., American religious and biblical [film-] spectaculars 1992 → 10,1194: [R]*CritRR 7 (1994) 71-73 (P. *Valenti*).

1825 **Giles** Paul, American Catholic arts and fiction; culture, ideology, aesthetics. C 1992, Univ. 547 p. $65. -- [R]JRel 75 (1995) 168s (M. *Krupnick*: partly converts; but in 'fallen-away' Catholics appears much authentic tradition).

1826 **Goedegebuure** Jaap, De Schrift herschreven; de Bijbel in de moderne literatuur. Amst 1993, Univ, 132 p. ƒ29,50. 90-5356-061-0. -- [R]Bijdragen 56 (1995) 216s (P.C. *Beentjes*).

1827 **Goergen** Peter, SeitenSprünge, Literaten als religiöse Querdenker. Solothurn 1995, Benziger. 192 p. DM 29,80. 3-545-25096-2. -- [R]THGL 85 (1995) 423 (W. *Beinert*).

1828 **Goldsmith** Steven, Upbuilding Jerusalem; apocalypse and Romantic representation [SHELLEY, PAINE ..]. Ithaca 1993, Cornell Univ. xiv-324 p. $ 47; pa. $19. -- [R]JRel 75 (1995) 167s (Meg *Armstrong*).

1829 **Gusick** Barbara Irene, Christ as a worker in the Towneley cycle (drama): diss. Loyola, [D]*Frantzen* A. Chicago c.1995. 239 p. 96-12407. -- DissA 56 (1995s) 4764.

1830 *Jasper* David, La Bible dans les arts et la littérature; source d'inspiration pour les poètes et les peintres, [T]*Divault* André: Conc.P 257 (1995) 63-78.

1831 [E]**Jeffrey** David L., A dictionary of biblical tradition in English literature 1992 → 8,1541 ... 10,1199: [R]ScotBuEv 12 (1994) 63s (S. *Prickett*); SNTU 20 (1995) 253s (A. *Fuchs*).

1832 **Kucharz** Thomas, Theologen und ihre Dichter; Literatur, Kultur und Kunst bei Karl BARTH, Rudolf BULTMANN und Paul TILLICH [Diss. Tübingen, [D]*Moltmann* J.]: Theologie und Literatur 4. Mainz 1995, Grünewald. 388 p. DM 32. 3-7867-1847-4. -- [R]THGL 85 (1995) 578s (E. *Garhammer*).

1833 *Kuschel* Karl-Josef, Christopoetik; Spurensuche in der Literatur der Gegenwart: THG 85 (1995) 499-517.

1834 **Kushelevsky** Rella, Moses and the Angel of Death; Studies on Themes and Motifs in Literature 4. NY 1995, P. Lang. xxii-325 p.; bibliog. 285-311. 0-8204-2147-2.

1835 *Longobardi* Monica, Ancora nove frammenti della 'Vulgata'; l' 'Estoire du Graal' , il 'Lancelo', la 'Queste': GIF 46 (1994) 197-228.

1836 *a) Marsden* Richard, The death of the messenger; the 'spelboda' in the Old English Exodus; -- *b) Cavill* Paul, Biblical realignment of a maxim in the Old English Phoenix, lines 355b-60; -- *c) George* J.-A., Repentance and retribution; the use of the Book of Daniel in Old and Middle English texts: → 530, BJRL 77,3 (1995) 141-164 / 193-8 / 177-192.

1836* [E]**Martin** Joel W., *Ostwalt* Conrad E.[J], Screening the sacred; religion, myth, and ideology in popular American films. Boulder 1995, Westview. x-193 p. $ 55; pa. $ 18. 0-8133-8829-5; -30-9 [ThD 43,87].

1837 **Mendl** Johann, Literatur als Spiegel christlichen Lebensvollzugs; religiöse Kinder- und Jugenderzählungen katholischer Autoren von 1750-1850: kath. Diss. [D]*Paul*. Augsburg 1995. -- ThRv Beilage 92/2, v.

1838 *a) Meredith* Peter, The direct and indirect use of the Bible in medieval English drama; -- *b) Rumble* Alexander R., The Rylands, the Bible and early English literature; an illustrated note; -- *c) Scragg* D.G., The Bible in Fontes [of authors] Anglo-Saxonici: → 530, BJRL 77,3 (1995) 61-77 / 205-217; 12 fig. / 199-203.

1839 **Muir** Lynette R., The [500 surviving items of]biblical drama of medieval Europe. C 1995, Univ. $ 60. 0-521-41291-9 [ThD 44,79].

1840 **Quinones** Ricardo J., The changes of Cain; violence and the lost brother in Cain and Abel literature 1991 → 8,2293; $ 25 [RStR 22,143, J.S. *Scott*]: [R][J]LitTOx 9 (1995) 109s (Terry *Wright*).

1841 *Shawcross* John T., The Christ figure in some literary texts; image and theme; Cithara

35,2 (1995s) 3-17.

1842 **Wicks** Katherine E., The private poetry of the (Old English) 'Exeter Book': diss. Wisconsin, [D]*Doane* A. Madison 1995. 176 p. 95-27176. -- DissA 56 (1995s) 2674.

1843 [E]**Wieder** Laurance, The poet's book of Psalms; the complete Psalter as rendered by 25 poets from the 16th to the 20th centuries. SF 1995, Harper. xxiii-311 p. $ 25. 0-06-069284-7 [ThD 42,81].

B4.6 *Singuli auctores* -- **Bible influence on individual authors**

1844 ÆLFRIC: *a) Godden* M.R., The trouble with Sodom; literary responses to biblical sexuality; -- *b) Raw* Barbara C., Verbal icons in late Old English; -- *c) Lee* Stuart, Ælfric's treatment of source material in his homily on the books of the Maccabees: → 530, BJRL 77,3 (1995) 97-121 / 123-139 / 165-176.

1845 BACHMANN: *Vliet* Jo Ann Van, Babel, Sodom und Gomorrha ... Biblische Motiven, Figuren und Sprachstrukture bei I[ngeborg] Bachmann: Orien(tierungen) 59 (1995) 127-9.

1846 BLAKE: **Ackroyd** Peter, Blake. .. c.1995, Sinclair-Stevenson. £ 20. -- [R]Tablet 249 (1995) 1382 (D.A. *Callard*).

1847 -- *Carroll* Robert, Revisionings; echoes and traces of Isaiah in the poetry of William Blake : → 170, [F]SAWYER, J., Words; JSOT.s 195 (1995) 225-241.

1848 -- **Postlethwaite** Sara Sue, William Blake's textual gnosis: diss. Pennsylvania State, [D]*Joukousky* N. University Park 1995. 284 p. 95-32010. -- DissA 56 (1995s) 1796.

1849 -- **Standish** Marc, The English roots of William Blake's radical vision; diss. Michigan, [D]*Ellison* Julie. AA 1994. 307 p. 95-13487. -- DissA 56 (1995s) p. 205.

1850 -- **Thorpe** Douglas, A new earth; the labor of language in *Pearl*, HERBERT's *Temple*, and Blake's *Jerusalem*. Wsh 1991, Catholic University of America. x-219 p. $ 40. -- [R][J]RL(itND) 26,2 (1994) 103s (B.J. *McFadden*).

1851 BOETHIUS: **Astell** Ann W., Job, Boethius and epic truth. Ithaca 1995, Cornell Univ. xv-240 p. $ 33. -- [R]Speculum 70 (1995) 869-871 (S. *Lerer*).

1852 BRECHT: *Keel* Othmar, Bertolt Brecht und das Erste Testament; Politik, Welthaftigkeit und Ideologie: BiKi 50 (1995) 13-19.

1853 BRONTË: **Thomson-Bailey** Philippa J., Neglected religious cues in nineteenth-century English novels (Charlotte & Emily Brontë, George ELIOT, Charles DICKENS): diss. Columbia. NY 1994. 313 p. 95-16194. -- DissA 56 (1995s) p. 206.

1853* --*Tkacz* Catherine B., The Bible in Jane Eyre: CLIT 44 (1994s) 3-27.

1854 BUNYAN: *Archer* Robert, Like flowers in the garden; John Bunyan and his concept of the Church: B(ap)Q 36 (1995s) 280-293.

1855 -- **Bennett** Arthur, Calvary's hill; the Cross in Pilgrim's Progress. L 1993, Avon. 134 p. £ 6. -- [R]Churchman 108 (L 1994) 93s (J. *Macnair*).

1856 -- **Luxon** Thomas H., Literal figures; Puritan allegory and the Reformation crisis in representation. Ch 1995, Univ. xii.256 p. $ 28. 0-226-49785-2 [ThD 43,177].

1857 -- **Swaim** Kathleen M., Pilgrim's progress, Puritan progress; discourses and contexts. Urbana 1993, Univ. Illinois. 368 p. $ 45. -- [R]C(alvin)TJ 30 (1995) 539-541 (D.R. *Danielson*).

1858 CAMUS: **Sutton** Robert C., Human existence and theodicy; a comparison of Jesus and Albert Camus: Contemporary Existentialism 4. NY 1992, P.Lang. x-201 p. $ 27, -- [R]TorJT 11 (1995) 137s (B.J. *Whitney*).

1859 CATHER: **Salas** Angela M.. The uses of absence in selected novels by Edith WHARTON, Willa Cather, Toni MORRISON and Anne TYLER: diss. Nebraska, [D]*Rosowski* Susan J. Lincoln 1995. 205 p. 95-36624. -- DissA 56 (1995s) 2687.

1860 CHAUCER: *Rudat* Wolfgang E.H., Gender-crossing in the Prioress' tale; Chaucer's satire on theological anti-Semitism ? : Cithara 33,2 (1993) 11-17.

1861 DANTE: **Ferrante** Joan M., Dante's Beatrice, priest of an androgynous God: MdvRenTSt, 1992 [→ 10,1222*b*: add [R]ChrLit 43 (1993) before '237s' (M. *Vander Weele*)].

1861* -- *Hawkins* Peter S., Dante; poet-theologian: P(rinc)SB 16 (1995) 327-337.

1862 -- *Manganiello* Dominic, Literature, science, and dogma; T.S. ELIOT and I.A. RICHARDS on Dante: ChrLit 43 (1993) 59-73.

1863 -- **Torrens** James, Presenting Dante's Paradise 1993 [→ 10,1222*a*: read [R]ChrLit instead of RenLit].

1864 -- **Turner** Rosine V., Breakdown in Hell; the figuration of an epistemological crisis in the 'Divina Commedia': diss. Wisconsin, [D]*Kleinhenz* C. Madison 1994. 516 p. 95-08841. -- DissA 56 (1995s) p. 187.

1865 DICKINSON: *Anderson* Francis J., What biblical scholars might learn from Emily Dickinson: → 170, [F]SAWYER, J., Words: JSOT.s 1950 (1995) 52-79.

1866 DONNE: *McIntosh* Mark A., Theology and spirituality; notes on the mystical Christology of John Donne: A(ngl)TR 77 (1995) 281-9.

1867 -- *Labriola* Albert C., Christus patiens and Christus victor; John Dunne's ultimate reality and meaning: URM 18 (1995) 92-101.

1868 -- *McIntosh* Mark A., Theology and spirituality; notes on the mystical Christology of John Donne: A(ngl)ThR 77 (1995) 281-9.

1869 ECO: *Castelli* Ferdinando, Su 'L'isola del giorno prima' di Umberto Eco; il nichilismo danza con la morte [un'opera notevole, 'l'evento letterario dell'anno']: CivCatt 146 (1995,1) 121-134.

1870 ELIOT: **Robinson** Richard D., T.S.Eliot's apprehensions of incarnation, 1927-1930; four 'Ariels' and 'Ash-Wednesday': diss. Boston Univ., 1995, [D]*Mason* H. 361 p. 95-22610. -- DissA 56 (1995s) p.947.

1871 FABBRI: *Di Sacco* Paolo, 'Processo a Gesù' e il metateatri processuale e cristologico di Diego Fabbri: VP(ens) 78 (1995) 183-196.

1872 FOSCOLI: *Bolelli* Cristina, Richiami biblici e reminiscenze classiche nel latino dell'Hypercalypsis foscoliana [1810-16]: Acme 46,2s (1993) 81-116.

1873 FROST: *a) Boogaart* Thomas A., Robert Frost and angels ascending [*Brueggemann* W. comment]; -- *b) Hutter* Charles A., Angels in the thought of C.S. LEWIS: : (Reformed) Perspectives 9,2 (1994) 8-11 [9/4, p.7] / 12-15 (-18, *Boer* Jan H.).

1874 GIDE: **Roggenkamp-Kaufmann** Antje, Der Protestant André Gide et la Bible. Gö 1993, Vandenhoeck & R. 362 p. DM 78. 3-525-87806-0. -- [R]ÉTRel 70 (1995) 470-2 (L. *Gagnebin*).

1875 GORDON: *Johnston* Eileen T., The biblical matrix of Mary Gordon's Final payments: CLit 44 (1994s) 145-167.

1876 GREEN: **Valle** Félix del, De la obsesión por el pecado al asombro por la gracia; ensayo sobre la dimensión teologal del itinerario humano en la obra de Julian Green entre 1948 y 1959: dis. Pont. Univ. Gregoriana, teol. 7194, [D]*Lafont* G. R 1994. -- *InfPUG 26,131 (1994) 32.

1877 HESSE: **Ziefle** Helmut W., Hermann Hesse und das Christentum: TVG-Orientierung. Giessen/Wu 1994, Brunnen/Brockhaus. 124 p. DM 24,80. 3-417-29064-3 [TR 91,445].

1878 HILL G. ... :   *Wakefield* Gordon S., God and some English poets, 9. Twentieth-century trends [^E**Hamilton** Ian, The Oxford companion to twentieth-century poetry 1994; RICKS C., LOWELL R., GREEN F.]: ET 106 (1994s) 138-142.

1879 HOPKINS: ^E**Allsopp** Michael E., *Downes* David A., Seeing beauty; further studies in Hopkins. NY 1994, Garland. x-351 p. $ 54. 0-8153-0834-5 . -- ^RCLIT 44 (1994s) 108s (S.C. *Walker*).

1880 -- **Marucci** Franco, The fine delight that fathers thought; rhetoric and medievalism in Gerard Manley Hopkins. Wsh 1994, Catholic University of America. xlv-267 p. $ 45. 0-8132-0778-9. -- ^RCLIT 44 (1994s) 235-7 (M.E. *Alsopp*).

1881 JABÈS: **Del Nevo** Matthew, Reading Edmond Jabès [† 1991]: [J]LitTOx 9 (1995) 399-422 (423-9, *Hutchens* B.).

1882 JAMES: **Fussell** Edwin S., The Catholic side of Henry James: StAmerLitCu 61. C 1993, Univ. xvii-168 p. $ 50. -- ^RJRel 75 (1995) 324s (Mary *Gerhart*).

1883 JOYCE: *Lindsey* William D., James Joyce's 'The Dead', eschatology and the meaning of history: TorJT 11 (1995) 7-20.

1884 KRANJČEVIĆ S.S.:   *Peterlin* Davorin, Faithfulness of Kranjčević's Moses with his Bible's ideal: *RijT 3 (1995) 139-143 Croatian; Eng. 144.

1885 LANGLAND: *Anderson* J.J., Some aspects of Scriptural quotation in Piers Plowman; Lady Holy Church: → 530, BJRL 77,3 (1995) 19-30 (31-46, *White* Hugh).

1886 -- **Kane** Paul J., Overcoming Satan; the harrowing of Hell legend in Langland, SPENSER, and MILTON: diss. Duquesne, ^D*Labriola* A. Pittsburgh 199. 426 p. 96-05369. -- DissA 56 (1995s) 3976.

1887 LAWRENCE: *Jones* Carolyn M., Male friendship and the construction of identity in D.H. Lawrence's novels [... Gen 32,22-33]: [J]LitTOx 9 (1995) 66-84.

1888 LESSING: *Schilson* Arno, 'Nathan der Weise' als poetische Predigt über die wahre Religion: ThG 85 (1995) 518-532.

1889 MCINERNY: *Labrie* Ross, Catholics, old and new; an overview of the fiction of Ralph McInerny: CanadCath 13,4 (1995) 5-10; -- 13,5 (1995) 14-19.

1890 MAURIAC: **Escallier** Claude, Mauriac et l'Évangile 1992 → 9,1409: ^RRTL 26 (1995) 84-86 (J.-F. *Grégoire*).

1891 MILTON: *Barnard* Nancy K., Beelzebub as John the Baptist in Milton's Hell: Chr&Lit 43 (1994) 301-313.

1892 -- **Carrithers** Gale H., Jr., *Hardy* James D. Jr., Milton and the hermeneutic journey. [Baton Rouge] 1994, Louisiana State Univ. xiv-256 p. $ 35. -- ^R[J]RL(itND) 27,3 (1995) 99-109 (S.M. *Fallon*, also on *Haskin* D., preferred, and two other 1994 books on Milton).

1893 -- *DuRocher* Richard J., The wounded earth in Paradise Lost:*StPg 93 (1995) 93-115.

1894 -- *Dust* Philip, Milton's Paradise lost and GROTIUS' The law of war and peace: Cithara 33,1 (1993) 17-25.

1895 -- **Esterhammer** Angela, Creating states ... Milton, BLAKE. Toronto 1994, Univ. xvii-245 p. $ 45. -- ^RCithara 35,1 (1995s) 55-57 (J.P. *Rosenblatt*).

1896 -- *a) Gay* David, Milton's Samson and the figure of the Old Testament giant; -- *b) Politi* Jina,'Is this the love' or, The origins of logomachia: [J]LitTOx 9(1995)355-369 /135-52.

1897 -- **Haskin** Dayton, Milton's burden of interpretation. Ph 1994, Univ, Pennsylvania. xxii-314 p. -- ^RHeythJ 36 (1995) 365s (E, M, *Knottenbelt*).

1898 -- **Rosenblatt** Jason P., Torah and Law in 'Paradise Lost' 1994 → 10,1239: -- ^RChr&Lit 43 (1994) 417-420 (M. *O'Connell*); Cithara 35,1 (1995s) 58s (Angela *Esterhammer*); JRel 75 (1995) 570-2 (A.C. *Labriola*, also on HASKIN D. 1994); TS 56 (1995) 193s (D. *Haskin*).

1899 -- **Shoulson** Jeffrey S.,   Interpretation in the making; the reading and creation of Genesis in the rabbis and in Milton: diss. Yale, [D]*Hartman* G. NHv 1995. 369 p, 95-37765. -- DissA 56 (1995s) p.2698.

1900 MORRISON Toni; *Taylor-Guthrie* Danielle, Who are the ['] Beloved ['] ? Old and New Testaments, old and new communities of faith: [J]RL(itND) 27,1 (1995) 119-129.

1901 O'CONNOR: **Pitts** Kathy Jean R., The influence of the Book of Revelation and medieval Catholic theology on the works of Flannery O'Connor: diss. Southern Mississippi 1994, [D]*Ryan* Maureen. 154 p. 95-21958. -- DissA 56 (1995s) p. 933.

1902 POPE *Jemielity* Thomas, A mock-biblical controversy; Sir Richard Blackmore in the Dunciad: PQ 74 (1995) 249-277.

1903 SHAKESPEARE: **Marshall** Cynthia, Last things and last plays; Shakespearean eschatology 1991 → 8,1571: [R][J]LitTOx 9 (1995) 433-5 (T. *Fabiny*).

1903* -- [E]**Battenhouse** Roy,   Shakespeare's Christian dimension; an anthology of commentary. Bloomington 1994, Indiana Univ. xii-520 p. $ 35. 0-253-31123-5. -- [R]ChrSchR 25 (1995s) 207-9 (E. Beatrice *Batson*).

1904 -- *a) Sexton* Joyce H, 'Rooted love'; metaphors for baptism in All's well that ends well; -- *b) Snyder* Susan, Theology as tragedy in Macbeth: Chr&Lit 43 (1994) 261-287 / 289-300.

1905 -- **Trotter** Jack E., Another voyage; the drama of Gnostic modernity in Shakespeare, [Christopher] MARLOWE and [John] WEBSTER: diss. Vanderbilt, [D]*Hassel* R. Nashville 1995. 318 p. 95-29012. -- DissA 56 (1995s) p.1799.

1906 SHELLEY: **Shelley** Brian, Shelley and Scripture; the intepreting angel. Ox 1994, Clarendon. xviii-212 p. $ 40. -- [R]JRel 75 (1995) 572-4 (R.M.*Ryan*: P.B. Shelley was at once a self-proclaimed atheist and an admiring reader of the Bible).

1907 SIDNEY: **Rienstra** Debra K., Aspiring to praise; the [Philip] Sidney-Pembroke psalter and the English religious lyric: diss. Rutgers, [D]*Coiro* Ann B. New Brunswick 1995. 408 p. 95-37629. -- DissA 56 (1995s) p. 2697.

1908 -- *Steinberg* Theodore L., The Sidneys and the Psalms: *StPg 92 (Chapel Hill 1995) 1s.

1909 SPENSER: **Gless** Darryl J., [Reader-response] Interpretation and theology in Spenser. C 1994, Univ. xiii-273 p. £ 32.50. 0-521-43474-2. -- [R]ET 106 (1994s) 312 (R. *Watson*: 'The Faerie Queene is so magnificent a tribute to the English Reformation, and so clearly a celebration of Protestant virtue' that it really needs these undersimplifications); *TBR 8,1 (1995s) 66 (G.S. *Wakefield*).

1910 -- **Hardin** Richard P., Civil idolatry; desacralizing and monarchy in Spenser, SHAKESPEARE & MILTON. Newark 1992, Univ. Delaware. 267 p. $ 39.50. -- [R]* CritRR 7 (1994) 73-75 (Kate G. *Frost*).

1911 SWIFT: **Craven** Kenneth, Jonathan Swift and the millennium of madness; the information age in Swift's [allegorical history of Christianity] 'The tale of a tub'. Leiden 1992, Brill. 238 p. $ 68.57. -- [R]JRel 75 (1995) 123-5 (E.W. *Rosenheim*).

1912 THOMAS Ronald S., in Welsh: *Wakefield* Gordon S., God and some English poets: ET 106 (1994s) 10-13.

1913 WIEBE: *van Toorn* Penny, Dialogizing the Scriptures; a BAKHTINian reading of the novels of [Canadian Mennonite] Rudy Wiebe: [J]LitTOx 9 (1995) 439-448.

B4.7 *Interpretatio* **psychiatrica**

1914 *Boyd* Jeffrey H., Losing soul; how and why theologians created the mental health movement: C(alvin)TJ 30 (1995) 472-482.

1915 **Bucher** Anton A., Bibelpsychologie: psychologische Zugänge zu biblischen Texten
1992 → 8,1579 ... 10,1249: [R]JE(mp)T 7,1 (1994) 109s (M. *Kassel*); PrakT 20 (1993) 312
(J.A. van *Belzen;* regrets for omitting this name → 10,1249)

1916   **Caballero Arencibia** A., Psicoanálisis y Biblia; el psicoanálisis aplicado a la
investigación de textos bíblicos: BSal 161, 1994 → 10,1250 [NTAb 40, p.128].

1917 **Corey** Michael A., Job, Jonah, and the unconscious; a psychological interpretation of
evil and spiritual growth in the OT. Lanham MD 1995, UPA. viii-150 p. 0-8191-9685-1.

1918 *Cranmer* D.J., *Eck* B.E., God said it; psychology and biblical interpretation; how text
and reader interact through the glass darkly: JPsy&T 22 (1994) 207-214 [< ZIT 95,p.260].

1919 **Dalrymple** Jock, Jack DOMINIAN: lay prophet ? L 1995, G.Chapman. xxii-154 p.
£ 12.50. 0-225-66733-9. -- [R]E(xp)T 106 (1994s) 351 (C.S. *Rodd*; best known Christian
psychiatrist today, Catholic but radical sex advocate).

DREWERMANN:

1920 *a) Ansaldi* Jean, Drewermann ou le risque de l'eclecticisme; -- *b) Schmid* Vincent,
Résonnances ECKHARTiennes chez Eugen Drewermann: BCPÉ 47,3 (1995) 7-19 / 21-38.

1921 -- **Aumont** Michèle, Qui êtes-vou, Eugen Drewermann ? P 1994, Mame. 170 p. --
[R]E(spr)eV 105 (1995) 127s (R. *Coste*); NV 70,1 (1995) 99s (G. *Bossard*).

1922 -- **Aumont** M., E. Drewermann, les 'clercs Drewermanniens' et l'Église 1993 →
9,1424: [R]FoiTe 24 (1994) 379s (H. *Thomas:* plus facile de lecture sereine que les 700 pages
de 'règlement de comptes' du 'livre bombe' souvent acerbe, à peine la vague de l'avenir);
NRT 117 (1995) 140 (A. *Toubeau). --* PeCa 263 (1993 10-15 (Y, *Daoudal:* 'Fonctionnaires'
published by A. Michel when French episcopate pressured Cerf, where seven of his works
had already been published).

1923 -- **Beyer** Uwe, Die Tragik Gottes; ein philosopischer Kommentar zur Theologie Eugen
Drewermanns. Wü 1995, Königshausen & N. 247 p. DM 40. 3-88479-984-3. -- [R]ThGL
85 (1995) 555-9 (M. *Bösch).*

1924 -- **Birnstein** Uwe, *Lehmann* Klaus-Peter, Phänomen Drewermann; Politik und Religion
einer Kultfigur. Fra 1994, Eichborn. 128 p. DM 22. -- [R]J(unge)K 56 (1995) 333s (K.
Füssel).

1925 -- *Boada* Josep, Exégesis, teología y psicología profunda; Eugen Drewermann:
*ActuBbg 30 (1993) 5-7.

1926 -- **Frey** Jörg, Eugen Drewermann und die biblische Exegese; eine methodisch-kritische
Analyse: WUNT 2/71. Tü 1995, Mohr. viii-281 p.; Bibliog. 255-271. DM 54. 3-16-
146304-8 [ThRv 92,77]. -- [R]HerKor 49 (1995) 507 (K. *Nientiedt).*

1928 -- *Gassmann* L., Von Origenes bis Drewermann; Modelle einer spirituellen Exegese und
ihre biblisch-theologische Wertung: JbEvT 8 (1994) 118 .. [< ZIT 95, p.10].

1929 -- *Genre* Ermanno, *Marcheselli Casale* Cesare, Una discussione su Eugen Drewermann:
FilTeo 9 (1995) 599-608-619.

1930 -- **Grelot** Pierre, Réponse à Eugen Drewermann 1994 → 10,1256: [R]Ang 72 (1995)
451-4 (S. *Jurić);* RICP 56 (1995) 167-174 (Y.-M. *Blanchard:* passionné plutôt que véritable
débat scientifique)

1931 -- **Haag** Herbert, *Drewermann* Eugen, No os dejéis arrebatar la libertad. Barc 1995,
Herder. 110 p. -- [R]ATG(ran) 58 (1995) 444s (J.A. *Estrada:* en ocasión del premio 'Por la
libertad en la Iglesia' a Drewermann).

1932 -- **Jarczyk** Gwendoline, Entretien avec ~, Dieu immédiat. P 1995, D-Brouwer. 290 p.
F 125. = [R]Études 383 (1995) 717 (P. *Julien).*

1933 -- *Karrer* M., Psychoanalyse und biblische Interpretation; Erwägungen nach der Studie Hartmut RAGUSEs [& DREWERMANN]: EvTh 54 (1994) 467-476. -- *b)* **Raguse** Hartmut, Psychoanalyse und biblische Interpretation ... DREWERMANN / Apokalypse 1993 → 9,1436; 10,1263: ᴿThRv 91 (1995) 24-26 (P. *Trummer*).

1934 -- **Lang** Bernhard, Drewermann, interprète de la Bible; le paradis, la naissance du Christ 1994 → 10,1257: ᴿBLE 96 (1995) 62s (L. *Monloubou*: 'est-il possible de le suivre ?'); CBQ 57 (1995) 560s (M.E. *Biddle*: clear and favoring. but not compelling); QVidaC 179 (1995) 155 (A.N. *Coll*); RTL 26 (1995) 89 (P.-M. *Bogaert* se demande en quoi donc D. serait un disciple de Jésus, mais 'tout n'est pas perdu').

1935 -- **Lang** Bernhard, Die Bibel neu entdecken; DREWERMANN als Leser der Bibel. Mü 1995, Kösel. 237 p. DM 44. 3-466-20393-7 [TR 91,360].

1936 -- *Moreira* Alberto, Eugen Drewermann e a psicanálise da Igreja clerical : REB 55 (1995) 395-405.

1937 -- *Pizzuti* Giuseppe M., In principio era l'angoscia; provocazioni KIERKEGAARDiane di E.D. alla teologia cattolica: Asprenas 42 (1995) 371-390.

1938 -- *Ritschl* Dietrich, Das Lehrverständnis der Bischöfe und die Lehre von Dr. Drewermann: ÖkRu 41 (1992) 57-65.

1939 -- *Rossi* Giacomo, Interpretazione del Vangelo e psicologia: CivCatt 146 (1995,3) 148-56.

1940 -- *Saint-Germain* Christian, Groupe et idéologie; à propos de Fonctionnaires de Dieu: L(aval)TP 51 (1995) 183-9.

1941 -- *Vergote* Antoine, Religion, pathologie, guérison: RTL 26 (1995) 3-30: Eng. 143.

1942 **Drewermann** Eugen, Dieu guérisseur .. Tobit 1993 → 10,2815: ᴿFV 93,2 (1994) 84 (G. *Vahanian*).

1942* **Drewermann**, Discovering the God-child within; a spiritual psychology of the Infancy of Jesus [Dein Name ist wie der Geschmack des Lebens 1986], ᵀ*Heinegg* P.: JSNT.s 89. Shf 1993, JSOT. 243 p. £ 35. 1

1943 **Drewermann**, Functionarissen van God; psychogramm van een ideaal [1989 → 6,8101], ᵀ. Zoetermeer 1994, Meinema. 339 p. ƒ 45. 90-211-3608-2. -- ᴿTTh 35 (1995) 434 (P. *Vandermeersch*).

1944 **Drewermann**, Giordano BRUNO al espejo del infinito. Barc 1995, Herder. 363 p. [R(az)F 232 (1995) 252].

1945 **Drewermann**, Glauben in Freiheit 1. 1993 → 10,1265: ᴿ*ActuBbg 31 (1994) 170-180 (J. *Boada*, también sobre SCHÖNBORN F., LÜDEMANN G.].

1946 **Faw** Harold W., Psychology in Christian perspective; an analysis of key issues. GR 1995, Baker. 190 p. $ 13. 0-8010-2012-3. -- ᴿJPsT 23 (1995) 317 (R.J. *Strandquist*).

1947 **Funke** D., Gott und das Unbewusste; Glaube und Tiefenpsychologie. Mü 1995, Kösel. 174 p. DM 34. 3-466-36414-0 [NTAb 40, p.129].

1948 *Gavrilovic* Zlatan, Contestation of psychoanalysis in the light of the views of Karl JASPERS and Stjepan ZIMMERMANN: ObnŽiv 49 (1994) 321-338 Croatian; 338 Eng.

1949 **Gibert** Pierre, Le récit biblique de rêve 1990 → 6,1708; 8,1613: ᴿRTPh 127 (1995) 197s (J.-D. *Macchi*).

1950 *Gnuse* Robert, Dreams in the night -- scholarly mirage or theophanic formula ? the dream report as a motif of the so-called Elohist tradition: BZ 39 (1995) 28-54.

1951 *Henking* Susan E., Rejected, reclaimed, renamed; Mary DALY on psychology and religion [both patriarchal; but her feminism has insights]: JPsT 21 (1993) 199-207 (-222, *Steichen* Donna, *al.*, responses).

1952 *a) Hunter* William F.,   Missions and mental health; a lesson from history; -- *b)*
Schubert Esther, Personality disorders and overseas missions; guidelines for the mental
health professional: JPsT 21 (1993) 9-17 / 18-25.

1953 **Husser** Jean-Marie, Le songe .. : BZAW 210, 1994 → 10,1272: ᴿCBQ 57 (1995) 771s
(A. *Gianto*).

1954 **Kähler** Christoph, Jesu Gleichnisse als Poesie und Therapie: WUNT 78. Tü 1995,
Mohr. x-264 p. 3-16-146233-5 [RStR 22,65s, F.W. *Burnett*].

1955 **Meissner** William W., Thy Kingdom come; psychoanalytic perspectives on the
Messiah and the millennium. KC 1995, Sheed & W. xi-370 p. 1-55612-750-2.

1956 **Miller** Alice, The drama of the gifted child; the search for the true self [Das Drama
1979, ᵀ1981 'Prisoners of childhood'], ᵀ*Ward* Ruth. NY 1990 ²1994, Basic. viii-150 p. $ 11
[RStR 22,191-6, Sandra L. *Dixon, al.,* also on her earlier psychological 'insightful,
inadequate critique of religion'].

1957 *a)* ᴱ**Miller** David L., JUNG and the interpretation of the Bible. NY 1995, Continuum.
143 p.; bibliog. 133-143. $ 18. 0-8264-0809-5 [ThD 43,174; OTA 18 (1995) p. 629 (D.
Penchansky)]. -- *b)* **Segal** Robert A., The Gnostic JUNG, including 'Seven sermons to the
dead ': Mythos. Princeton 1992, Univ. 259 p. -- ᴿR(ech)SR 83 (1995) 137s (Madeleine
Scopello).

1958 **Miller** Patricia C., Dreams in Late Antiquity 1994 → 10,9508*: ᴿCLR 45 (1995) 85s
(Gillian *Clark*); JThS 46 (1995) 685-9 (M. *Vessey*).

1959 *Oeming* Manfred, Altes Testament und Tiefenpsychologie; Aufklärung oder FREUDsche
Fehlleistung ?: TLZ 120 (1995) 107-120.

1960 **Ouaknin** Marc-Alain, Bibliothérapie; lire, c'est guérir 1994 → 10,1276; F 160; 2-
02-020109-7: ᴿRHPhR 75 (1995) 380s (T. *Pfrimmer*).

1961 **Porter** Stanley E., *Richter* Philip J., *al.,* The Toronto Blessing -- or is it ? L 1995,
Darton-LT. 130 p. £ 7. 0-232-52130-1. -- ᴿE(xp)T 107,3 2d-top choice (1995s) 66s (C.S.
Rodd : mainline support incredible).

1962 *a)* **Rice** Emanuel, FREUD and Moses; the long journey home 1990 → 7,1414 ...
10,1277: ᴿCCAR 42,1 (1995) 58-61 (Barbara L. *Ingram*). -- *b)* **Trincia** Francesco Saverio,
Il dio di FREUD. Mi 1992, Saggiatore. 285 p. Lᵐ 60. -- ᴿRasIsr 60,3 (1993) 140-144 (S.
Petrucciani).

1963 **Sanford** John A., Mystical Christianity; a psychological commentary on the [Fourth]
Gospel. NY 1993, Crossroad. 350 p. $ 25. 0-8245-1230-8. -- ᴿInterpretation 49 (1995)
210 . 212 (K. *Quast* admits eveything except that this is true to the character and intention
of the evangelist).

1964 *Scheffler* Eben H., Jesus from a psychological perspective: Neotest 29 (1995) 299-312.

1965 **Spero** Moshe H., Religious objects as psychological structures; a critical integration
of object flations theory, psychotherapy, and Judaism. Ch 1992, Univ. xvii-242 p. $ 27.50.
0-226-76939-9. -- ᴿJPsT 21 (1993) 249-252 (R.L. *Sorenson*: what if God is not a KLEINian
mother ?).

1966 *a) Stevens* R. Paul, Analogy or homology ? An investigation of the congruency of
systems theory and biblical theology in pastoral leadership; -- *b) Shepard* Richard G.,
Biblical progression as moral development; the analogy and its implications: JPsT 22 (1994)
173-181 / 182-6.

1967 **Symington** Neville, Emotion and spirit; questioning the claims of psychoanalysis and
[i.e. without] religion. L/NY 1994, Cassell/St. Martin's. viii-192 p. £ 15 / $ 30. 0-304-
3288-1/ [RStR 22,47, Kelley *Raab*]. -- ᴿET 106 (1994s) 317s (Stephen *Pattison*).

1968 **Thomas** Klaus, Religiöse Traüme und andere Bilderlebnisse; ärztliche Berichte über religiöse Erfahrungen bei Visionen, Träumen, Hypnosen und Erfahrungen im autogenen Training. Stu 1994, Steinkopf. xii-296 p. DM 60. 3-7984-0721-5 [ThRv 91,280].

1968* *Wulff* David M., The challenge of resurgent fundamentalism; a psychologist's reflections: SvTKv 70 (1994) 49-56.

B5 **Methodus exegetica**

1969 **Adam** A.K.M., What is postmodern biblical criticism ? *GuidesBSch NT. Mp 1995, Fortress. xiv-81 p. $ 10. 0-8006-2879-9 [RStR 22,244, G. *Aichele*]. -- [R]P(rinc)SB 16 (1995) 358s (S.*Fowl*).

1970 **Aichele** George & 9 others ('The Bible cultural collective'; no part attributed to any → 359), The postmodern Bible ['modern conscious of itself']; Bible and Culture. NHv 1995, Yale. xiii-398 p. $ 35. 0-300-06090-4. [ThD 43,82]. -- [R]*CritRR 7 (1994) 562s (7 tit.pp.: structuralism, post-s., rhetorical, psychoanalytical, feminist); *TBR 8,2 (1995s) 7 (D. *Clines*: indispensable, but really a demanding introduction to methods; we still need a 'Postmodern' like 'Women's' Bible).

1971 *Ascione* Antonio, Testo e conoscenza; alle origini del metodo della critica storica: → 514, Oltre il racconto 1993/4, 183-202; Eng. 202.

1972 *Asurmendi* Jesús, Eliseo, justicia y política [2 Re 4,1-7; 8,1-15; 9,1-13) y el relato ficticio (RICŒUR P.): EstB 53 (1995) 145-164; Eng. 145.

1973 *a) Bahnsen* Greg, Comment lire la Bible ? Affirmation réformée sur l'interprétation de la Parole de Dieu; -- *b) Courthial* Pierre, Le combat de la foi aujourd'hui; -- *c) Wells* Paul, Sur la contextualisation biblique : RRéf 46,1 (1995) 35-42 / 1-7 / 43-55.

1974 *Bailey* James L., A pattern for interpreting biblical texts: CThMi 22 (1995) 284-9.

1975 *Barr* George K., [Mathematical/graph stylometry] Scale and the Pauline epistles: I(rish)BSt 17 (1995) 22-41; 8 fig.

1976 *a) Barr* James, The synchronic, the diachronic and the historical; a triangular relationship; -- *b) Clines* D.J.A., Beyond synchronic/diachronic; -- *c) Hoftijzer* J., Holistic or compositional approach ? Linguistic remarks to the problem: → 515, Synchronic ? 1994/5, 1-14 / 52-71 / 98-114.

1977 *a) Barton* John, Historical criticism and literary interpretation; is there any common ground ? -- *b) Joyce* Paul, First among equals ? the historical-critical approach in the marketplace of methods; -- *c) Young* Frances, Typology: → 10,45, [F]GOULDER M., Crossing 1994, 3-15 / 17-27 / 29-48.

1978 *Baumann* Rolf, Rückfragen an die Bibel aus Anlass eines aktuellen Streits: BiKi 50 (1995) 49-59.

1980 [E]**Bodine** Walter R., Discourse analysis of biblical literature; what it is and what it offers [samples Ex 25-30; Isa 40; theory: 'grammar']: *SemeiaSt. Atlanta 1995, Scholars. x-264 p.; bibliog. 215-253. $ 45; pa. $ 30. 0-7885-0010-4; -1-2 [NTAb 40,p.320].

1981 *Brandt* Krister, 'Exegeten som visste för mycket' ['who knew too much': gaps filled by erudition often leave the real meaning less clear]: SvTKv 70 (1994) 57-61.

1982 **Breck** J., The shape of biblical language; chiasmus in the Scriptures and beyond. Crestwood NY 1994, St. Vladimir. x-387 p. $ 17 pa. 0-88141-139-6 [NTAb 40,p.320].

1983 **Brotzman** Ellis R., Old Testament criticism; a practical introduction. GR 1994, Baker. 208 p. $ 11. 0-8010-1065-9. -- [R]BoL (1995) 48 (R.B. *Salters*).

1984 **Brown** David, The Word to set you free; living faith and biblical criticism. L 1995, SPCK. 199 p. £ 10 pa. -- [R]Theol 98 (L 1995) 481s (R. *Davidson*).

1985 **Buchanan** George W., Introduction to intertextuality. Lewiston NY 1994, Mellen. 0-7724-2387-7 [RStR 22,239, 'ii-96 p., $59.95'].

1986 *Carroll* Robert P., An infinity of traces; on making an inventory of our ideological holdings; an introduction to *Ideologiekritik* in biblical studies: JNWSL 21,2 (1995) 25-43.

1987 *Cazelles* Henri, Sur les fondements de la recherche en théologie biblique: R(ech)SR 83 (1995) 357-371.

1988 *Crocker* Piers T., Literary 'borrowings' in the Ancient Near East [1994 lecture]: BurHist 31 (1995) 69-76.

1989 *Dangl* Oskar, Skeptische Exegese: BiNo 75 (1994) 67-81.

1990 *Dillmann* Rainer, Die Bedeutung der semantischen Analyse für die Textpragmatik: BN(otiz) 79 (1995) 5-9.

[E]**Dockery** D., Foundations .. tools, resources [l0,1296] → 1284 supra.

1991 *a) Donahue* John R., Redaction criticism; has the Hauptstrasse become a Sackgasse ?; - - *b) McKnight* Edgar V., A sheep in wolf's clothing; an option in NT hermeneutics: -- *c) Beardslee* William A., What is it about ? Reference in NT literary criticism: → 10,139, [F]WILDER A., New Lit.Crit. **New** Testament, JSNT.s 109, 1994, 27-57 / 326-347 / 367-386.

1992 [E]**Exum** J. Cheryl, *Clines* D.J.A., The new literary criticism (→ 2017) and the **Hebrew** Bible: JSOT.s 143, 1993 → 9,271; 10,1298: [R]CBQ 57 (1995) 423-5 (K.M. *Craig*: 'new' or rather 'burgeoning' means 'poststructuralism, an umbrella term for Marxist, feminist, reader-response, deconstructionist. and psychoanalytic'; refreshing withal).

1993 **Fabiny** Tibor, The lion and the lamb; figuralism and fulfilment in the Bible, art and literature 1992 → 8,3699; 10,3432: [R]JThS 46 (1995) 434-6 (J. *Barton*).

1994 [E]**Fabris** Rinaldo, Problemas e perspectivas das ciências bíblicas, [T]*Gaio* Luiz João, 1993 → 10,1299: [R]RC(u)B 19/75 (1995) 156s (A.L. do V. *Ribeiro*).

1995 *Gibert* Pierre, L'exégèse critique, témoin de l'Incarnation: → 155, [F]RENAUD B., Ce Dieu: LDIV 159 (1995) 371-384.

1995* **Goldingay** John, *a)* Models for Scripture 1994 → supra 1599 & 10,1303; -- *b)* Models for **interpretation of** Scripture 1995, also Eerdmans/Paternoster, → 1298*.

1996 **Harrisville** Roy A., *Sundberg* Walter, The Bible in modern culture; theology and historical-critical method from Spinoza to Käsemann. GR 1995, Eerdmans. xi-282 p. $ 20. 0-8028-0873-5.

1997 *Harrisville* Roy A., A critique of current biblical criticism [historical being suspiciously replaced by Anglo-American literary] : WW 15 (1995) 206-213.

1998 *Hartlich* Christian, Historical-critical method in its application to statements concerning *events* in the Holy Scriptures : *JHiCr 2,2 (1995) 129-139.

1999 [E]**House** Paul R., Beyond form criticism; [reprints since 1969] essays in OT literary criticism 1992 → 8,357; 10,1306: [R]BS 152 (1995) 237s (R.B. *Chisholm*).

2000 *a) Howard* David M.[J], Rhetorical criticism in OT studies (→ 10,1306*): -- *b) Rooker* Mark F., Diachronic analysis and the features of late biblical Hebrew: BuBR 4 (1994) 87-104 / 135-144.

2001 **Jasper** David, Rhetoric, power and community; an exercise in reserve 1993 → 9,1476: [R]CritRR 7 (1994) 75-77 (S.D. *Moore*: dense but never dull).

2002 *Jasper* David, From theology to theological thinking; the development of critical thought and its consquences for theology: [J]LitTOx 9 (1995) 293-303 [241-292, other papers from the 1993 Washington AAR symposium on literature and religion].

2003 **Jens** Walter, *Küng* Hans, Literature and religion 1991 → 8,1520: [R]JETS 38 (1995) 145s (J.S. *Reist*: bypasses cognates).

2004 *a) Kallemeyn* Harold, Drames et découvertes; pour une lecture vivifiante de l'Ancien Testament: -- *b) Berthoud* Pierre, Pour une 'apologie' biblique de la foi; -- *c) Wells* Paul, La foi 'évangélique' dans le monde contemporain : RRéf 46,2s (1995) 53-68 / 43-52 / 31-41.

2005 *Keegan* Terence J., Biblical criticism and the challenge of postmodernism: *BInterp 3.1 (1995) 1-14; of the 16 following articles, 14 deal with specific biblical books or verses [NTAb 40,p.6].

2006 *Kelber* W.H., Modalities of communication, cognition, and physiology of perception; orality, rhetoric, scribality: Semeia 65 (1994) 193-216 [NTAb 40,p.198].

2007 **Kennedy** G.A., [NT interpretation through rhetorical criticism 1984] A new history of classical rhetoric. Princeton 1994, Univ. xii-301 p. $ 55; pa. $ 18. 0-691-03443-5; - 0059-X [NTAb 40,p.557].

2008 **Kessler** Hildrun, Bibliodrama und Leiblichkeit; eine Lebhafte Textauslegung im philosophischen, therapeutischen und theologischen Diskurs: ev. Diss. [D]*Wegenast.* Bern 1995. -- ThRv Beilage 92/2, vi.

2009 *a) Kieffer* René, *Olsson* Birger, Exegetik på 90-talet; -- *b) Stenström* Hanna, Feministisk exegetik; -- *c) Übelacker* Walter, Retorisk analys och Nya testamentet; -- *d) Winninge* Mikael, Den intertestamentale litteraturen och Nya testamentet : SvTKv 70 (1994) 145-152 / 160-6 / 167-175 / 176-183: Eng. 152.166.175.183.

2010 *Kreiss* Wilbert, Que penser de la critique du Pentateuque ? : RRéf 46,4 (1995) 51-67.

2011 **Lardinois** André P., Wisdom in context; the use of gnomic statements in archaic Greek poetry: diss. Princeton, [D]*Martin* R., 1995. 397 p. 95-19143. -- DissA 56 (1995s) p. 539.

2012 *a) Lategan* Bernard, The religious text; -- *b) Nel* Philip, Text and textuality in Christian and Rabbinic traditions; -- *c) Gräbe* Ina, Poëtiese kommunikasiemiddele as leesstrategieë vir die Bybelteks; -- *d) Tolmie* Francois [not ç], Textual constraints according to Umberto ECO: → 517, Concepts 1994/5, 22-38 / 39-53 / 160-171 / 184-194.

2013 *Leroux* Neil R., Repetition, progression, and persuasion in Scripture: Neotest 29 (1995) 1-25.

2014 *Levenson* Jon D., The Hebrew Bible, the OT and historical criticism 1993 → 9,1480; 10,1311: [R]C(alvin)TJ 30 (1995) 525-530 (C.G. *Bartholomew*); JETS 38 (1995) 466s (M.A. *Harbin*); JRel 75 (1995) 260s (J.L. *Crenshaw*).

2015 *Lischer* Richard, Martin Luther King Jr., 'performing' the Scriptures: A(ngl)ThR 77 (1995) 160-172.

2016 **Mainville** Odette, La Bible au creuset de l'histoire; guide d'exégèse historico-critique: ScB 1. Montréal/P 1995, Médiaspaul. 151 p. C$ 25. 2-89420-294-6 [NTAb 40,p.327].

2017 [E]**Malbon** Elizabeth S., *McKnight* Edgar V., The new literary criticism (→ 1992) and the **New** Testament: JSNT.s 109, 1994 → 10,139: [R]A(ustrl)BR 43 (1995) 91s (F.J. *Moloney*).

2018 **Meynet** Roland, L'analyse rhétorique 1989 → 5,1642 ... 7,1440 (ital. 1992 → 8,1660): [R]EstB 53 (1995) 398-400 (A. *Rodenas*).

2019 [E]**Meynet** Roland, *al.*, Méthode rhétorique .. Bible, Hadîth 1993 → 9,1483; [R]ISLCHR 21 (1995) 255 (M. *Borrmans*).

2020 *a) Moore* Stephen D., True confessions and weird obsessions; autobiographical interventions in literary and biblical studies; - *b) Hendricks* Osayande O., Guerrilla exegesis; 'struggle' as a scholarly vocation -- a postmodern approach to African-American biblical interpretation: Semeia 72 ('Taking it personally' 1995) 19-50 / 73-90.

2020* **Moore** Stephen D., Literary criticism and the Gospels; the theoretical challenge 1989
→ 6,1359: [R]S(cot)JTh 48 (1995) 162-4 (R.P. *Carroll*).

2021 *Mueller* S., A Eucharistic model for biblical study [take. bless, break, share]: *Emm
101 (1995) 297-302 [NTAb 40, p.8].

2022 *Müller* Hans-Peter, Offene Fragen zur Entmythologisierung: → 108, [F]LESSING E., Geist
und Kirche 1995, 151-161.

2023 *Navarro* Mercedes, Tendencias actuales de la exégesis bíblica: SalTer 82 (1994) 361-
375.

2024 *Netland* John T., A modest apologia for romanticism [*Lundin* Roger, response]:
ChrSchR 25 (1995s) 297-317 . 322-5 [318-321].

2025 *a) Ochs* Peter, Returning to Scripture; trends in postcritical Scriptural interpretation;
b) Kossak Mary Phil, Eve, malignant or maligned ? ; -- *c) Harrington* Daniel J, What's
new(s) about the Dead Sea Scrolls ?; -- *d) Reid* Stephen B., Endangered reading; the
African-American scholar between text and people; -- *e) Levinas* Emmanuel, The Jewish
understanding of Scripture; -- *f) Boys* Mary C., An artist of historical criticism: R.E. BROWN,
The death of the Messiah; -- *g) Gundry* Robert H., But is it Matthew ? Anthony J.
SALDARINI, Matthew's Christian-Jewish community; -- *h) Meye Thompson* Marianne,
Mapping the journey toward God; Thomas J. BRODIE, The Gospel according to John: CCurr
44 (1944s) 44,4 (1994s) 437-452 / 453-462 / 463-475 / 476-487 / 488-504 / 505-7
/ 508-511 / 513-5.

2026 **Oeming** Manfred, Bibelkunst Altes Testament; ein Arbeitsbuch zur Information,
Repetition und Präparation: NStuKomm AT 32. Stu 1995, KBW. 112 p. 3-460-07321-7.

2027 *Osborn* E., Literature, history and logic; the formation of the Christian Bible: *ABR
41 (1993) 49-63 [NTAb 40, p.199, C.R. *Matthews* : 'Jerusalem needed Athens to be
coherent (but) the limits of literary criticism (are) illustrated by the chief weaknesses of
postmodernism'].

2028 *a) Overholt* Thomas W., Feeding the widow, raising the dead; what counts as cultural
exegesis ? -- *b) Reid* Stephen B., The role of reading in multicultural exegesis; -- *c) Pattel-
Gray* Anne, Dreaming; an aboriginal interpretation of the Bible; -- *d) Mafico* Tembel L.J.,
Were the 'Judges' of Israel like African spirit mediums ?; -- *e) Richard* Pablo, Indigenous
biblical hermeneutics; God's revelation in native religions and the Bible (after 500 years of
domination): → 534, Text & experience 1992/5, 104-121 / 210-224 / 247-259 / 330-
343 / 260-275.

2029 **Patrick** Dale, *Scult* Allen, Rhetoric and biblical interpretation: JSOT.s 82, 1990 →
6,1736 ... 10.1325; [R]VT 45 (1995) 142s (R.P. *Gordon*).

2030 *Peckham* Brian. Writing and editing: → 59, [F]FREEDMAN D.N., Fortunate 1995, 364-383

2031 *Pfeifer* Gerhard, Denkformen und Denkformenanalyse [< SBL Münster 1993]: ThZ
51 (1995) 181-195.

2033 [E]**Prickett** Stephen [[F]FROELICH K., → 10,1302, not = 7,58] Reading the text; biblical
criticism and literary theory 1991 → 7,324* : [R]JRel 75 (1995) 164s (F.B. *Brown*); JThS 46
(1995) 430-3 (J. *Barton*).

2034 *Rand* Harry, The limits of literality [... Nm 23,28; 'Speech and writing are different
worlds']: [J]LT(Ox) 9 (1995) 117-134.

2035 **Rang** Jack C., How to read the Bible aloud; oral interpretation of Scripture. NY
c.1995, Paulist. 144 p. $ 11 pa. -- [R]CanadCath 13,10 (1995) 27 (J. M. *Samaha*).

2036 *Rendtorff* Rolf, Canonical interpretation; a new approach to biblical texts: Pro Ecclesia
3,2 (1994) 141-151 [NTAb 40, p.395].

2037 ^E**Rickheit** Gert, *Habel* Christopher, Focus and coherence in discourse analysis: Research in Text Theory 22. B 1995, de Gruyter. xi-300 p. 3-11-014466-2.

2038 *Robinson* R.B., Interpretation in a new key; intrinsic criticism of the Bible [ALTER R., as against extrinsic, WESTERMANN C.]: BTF 26,1 (Bangalore 1994) 51-64 [NTAb 40,p.9].

2039 *Ruppert* Lothar, Die historisch-kritische Methode der Bibelexegese im deutschen Sprachraum; Vorgeschichte, gegenwärtige Entwickelungen, Tendenzen, Aufbrüche: → ′10,222* Studien 1994, 266-307 [OTA 18, p.395].

2040 *Sawyer* John A.F., The ethics of comparative interpretation [i.e. commendable methodology. as SCHÜSSLER FIORENZA E. 1988, YOUNG Frances 1993]: CuRB 3 (1995) 153-168.

2041 *Schweizer* Harald, Weitere Impulse zur Literarkritik: BN(otiz) 80 (1995) 73-99.

2042 **Scolnic** Benjamin E., Theme and context in biblical lists: SFSHJ 119. At 1995, Scholars. [viii-] 174 p. 0-7885-0145-3.

2043 **Selden** Raman †, ³*Widowson* Peter, A reader's guide to contemporary literary theory. Lexington 1993, Univ. Kentucky. xii-244 p. 0-8131-0816-0.

2044 ^E**Simian-Yofre** Horacio, Metodologia dell'Antico Testamento: StB 25. Bo 1994, Dehoniane. 243 p. L^m 32. 88-10-40725-3.

2045 *Small* J.P., Artificial memory and the writing habits of the [ancient, claasical] literate: *Helios 22 (1995) 159-166 [NTAb 40,p.315].

2046 ^E**Smith-Christopher** Daniel, Text and experience; towards a cultural exegesis of the Bible: BiSe 35, 1995 → 534.

2047 *Southwick* Jay S., Visual images facilitating biblical word images : Encounter 56 (1995) 49-58.

2048 **Steck** Odil H., Old Testament exegesis; a guide to the methodology [¹³1993], ^T*Nogalski* J.D.: SBL Resources 33. Atlanta 1995, Scholars. xiii-208 p. $ 40; pa. $ 25. 0-7885-0173-0; -4-7 [NTAb 40,p.516; OTA 19,p.335; ThD 43,389].

2049 ^E**Sternberg** Thomas, Neue Formen der Schriftauslegung ?: QDisp 140, 1992 → 8,495 ... 10,1335: ^RMThZ 46 (1995) 481s (T. *Böhm*); Salesianum 57 (1995) 780 (C. *Bissoli*).

2050 *Stoker* W., Een spanning tussen literair en historisch lezen ? RICŒUR over het verschil tussen spreken en schrijven: G(ereformeerd)TT 95 (1995) 156-167.

2051 **Talmon** Shemaryahu, Literary studies in the Hebrew Bible; form and content 1993 → 9,243: ^RAsprenas 42 (1995) 285-7 (G. *Di Palma*).

2052 *Talshir* Zipora, The contribution of diverging traditions preserved in the Septuagint to literary criticism of the Bible: → 508, 8th SeptCog 1992/5, 21-41.

2053 *a) Thompson* Thomas L., A Neo-Albrightean school in history and biblical scholarship ? ; -- *b) Davies* Philip R., Method and madness; some remarks on doing history with the Bible: JBL 107 (1995) [invited rejoinders to 585-606, *Provan* I.] 683-705 / 699-705.

2054 **Timm** Hermann, Sage und schreibe; Inszenierungen religiöser Lesekultur: Innen und Aussen 2. Kampen 1995, Kok Pharos. 151 p. *f* 40. 90-390-0211-8

2055 *Trautner-Kromann* Hanne, Moderne Judaistik: SvTKv 70 (1994) 106-113: Eng. 113.

2056 *Uffenheimer* Benjamin, ^H Current biblical research: BetM 40,2 (141, 1995) 97-108.

2057 *Vicente Niclós* José, Génesis 3 como relato de apropiación [a 'critical parable' concerning the monarchy, 2 Sam 12-19; 2 Re 21]: EstB 53 (1995) 181-200; Eng. 181.

2058 *Vorster* Johannes N., Why opt for a rhetorical approach ?: Neotest 29 (1995) 393-418.

2059 ^E**Warner** Martin, The Bible as rhetoric; studies in biblical persuasion and credibility 1990 → 6,561 ... 10,1337: ^RAugM 40 (1995) 411 (J. *Oroz*).

2060 **Watson** Duane F. [NT p. 101-206], *Hauser* Alan J., Rhetorical criticism of the Bible;
a comprehensive bibliography with notes on history and method: Binterp.s 4, 1994 →
10,1338: [R]BoL (1995) 106s (H.S. *Pyper*); CritRR 8 (1995) 102s (Toni *Craven*); VT 45
(1995) 575s (J.A. *Emerton*).

2061 *Wuellner* W., Rhetorical criticism in biblical studies: JianDao 4 (1995) 71-96 [NTAb
40,p.12].

2062 a) *Wuellner* Wilhelm, Death and rebirth of rhetoric in late twentieth century biblical
exegesis; -- b) *Lategan* Bernard, The function of biblical texts in a modern situational
context: → 79, [F]HARTMAN L., Texts & Contexts 1995, 917-930 / 945-958.

B6   Prophetia (... praedictio) -- miracula

2063 **Abrego de Lacy** José María, Los libros proféticos → 9,3455: Introducción al estudio
de la Biblia 4.

2064 *Aleixandre* Dolores, Cuando los profetas son también sabios: SalTer 83 (1995) 859-
875.

2065 **Alonso Schökel** Luis, *Gutiérrez* Guillermo.   [P] Mów wszystko co ci rozkaza;
aktualność proroctw Starego Testamentu [Mensajes 1991 → 7,3102; > ital. Io pongo],
[T]*Dudek* Ryszard: Duc in altum 15. Kraków c. 1995, WAM. 188 p, 83-7097-157-1.

2066 **Blenkinsopp** Joseph, Une histoire de la prophétie en Israël, depuis le temps de
l'installation en Canaan jusqu'à l'époque hellénistique [1983], [T]: LDiv 152, 1993 → 9,3462:
[R]ETRel 70 (1995) 114s (T. *Römer*).

2067 **Cavedo** Romeo, Profeti; storia e teologia del profetismo nell'Antico Testamento. CinB
1995, S. Paolo, 263 p.   88-215-2920-7.

2068 *Cruells* Antoni, Nota crítico-bibliogràfica a propòsit d'un llibre sobre el profetisme
[RAURELL Frederic, Profeta, el forjat per la Paraula 1963 !]: RCatT 30 (1995) 187-195.

2069 **Davies** Stevan L., Jesus the healer; possession, trance, and the origins of Christianity.
NY/L 1995, Continuum/SCM. $ 23. 0-8264-0794-3 / 0-334-82605-9. -- [R]*TBR 8,3 (1995s)
23s (J.I.H. *McDonald*).

2070 **Desforges** Ghislaine, Étude de la personalité de sujets qui se disent guéris par la foi:
diss. École Polytechnique. [D]*Keily* Margaret C. Montréal 1994. 139 p. NN-95750. 0-315-
95750-6. -- DissA 56 (1995s) p. 2369.

2071 **Fischbach** Stephanie M., Totenerweckungen; zur Geschichte einer Gattung [D]1992 →
8,4791 ... 10,4463: [R]EstB 53 (1995) 273-5 (J. *Arambarri*).

2072 **Forbes** Christopher, Prophecy and inspired speech in early Christianity and its
Hellenistic environment: WUNT 2/75. Tü 1995, Mohr. xi-380 p.; bibliog. 323-338. 3-16-
146223-8.

2073 *Harrison* Peter, Newtonian science, miracles, and the laws of nature: JHI(d) 56 (1995)
531-553.

2074 **Houston** Joseph, Reputed miracles; a critique of HUME 1994 → 10,4465: [R]RelSt 31
(1995) 275s (E.L. *Schoen*) [317-336, *Slupik* Chris, A new interpretation of Hume's 'Of
miracles']; RTPh 127 (1995) 380s (D. *Stauffer*)

2075 *Hutton* Rodney R., Magic or street theater ? The power of the prophetic word: ZAW
107 (1995) 247-260.

2076 *Jarick* John, Prophets and losses; some themes in recent study of the Prophets [JSOT,
AULD A.G., *al.*]: E(xp)T 107 (1995s) 75-77.

2077 **Jemielity** T., Satire and the Hebrew prophets 1992 → 8,3617; 10,1183: [R]BA 57 (1994) 179 (J. *Strong*); ChrLit 43 (1993s) 97s (D.E. *Ritchie*); CritRR 7 (1994) 125-7 (F.*Landy*); EvQ 67 (1995) 160s (H.G.M. *Williamson*); JQR 86 (1995) 223 (A. *LaCocque*).

2077* **Johnson** Douglas H., Nuer prophets; a history of prophecy from the Upper Nile in the nineteenth and twentieth centuries: Oxford Studies in Social and Cultural Anthropology. Ox 1994, Clarendon. xx-407 p. xx-407 p. £ 40. 0-19-827907-8. -- [R]BoL (1995) 41 (L.L. *Grabbe*).

2078 **Koskenniemi** Erkki, APOLLONIOS von Tyana in der neutestamentlichen Exegese: WUNT 2/61, 1994 → 10,4470: [R]ETRel 70 (1995) 447s (J.-N. *Pérès*).

2079 **Marcus** David, From Balaam to Jonah; anti-prophetic satire in the Hebrew Bible: BJSt 301. At 1995, Scholars. xiii-214 p.: bibliog. 171-198. 0-7885-0101-1.

2080 **Marín Heredia** F., La Biblia, palabra profética: MundoB. Estella 1992, VDivino. 330 p. -- [R]CiTom 121 (1994) 410-2 (E. *Rodríguez*).

2081 *Meier* John P., Miracles and modern minds: Catholic World 238 (1995) 52-58 . 92-95.

2082 **Pain** Timothy, Miracles are impossible; you decide 1994 → 10,4478: [R]Churchman 108 (L 1994) 271-4 (P. *May*: aimed to clarify the claims of M. CERULLO, whose integrity May questions).

2083 **Ralph** Margaret N., Discovering prophecy and wisdom. NY 1993, Paulist. 326 p, -; [R]VT 45 (1995) 407s (Katharine J. *Dell*).

2084 **Raurell** F. , Profeta, al forjat per la paraula; aspectes literàrio-teològics de la vocació-missió: Eines 18. Barc 1993, Claret. 200 p. -- Laur 36 (1995) 219-221 (A. *Dalbesio*).

2085 **Rofé** Alexander, Introduzione alla litteratura profetica: StB 111. Brescia 1995, Paideia. 157p. L[m] 23. 88-394-0528-3.

2086 **Schniedewind** William M., The Word of God in transition; from prophet to exegete in the Second Temple period; JSOT.s 197. 275 p. £ 27.50.

2087 *Witaszek* Gabriel W., [P] I profeti dell'VIII secolo di fronte alle deviazioni cultuali: RTK 42,1 (1995) 27-43; ital. 43.

B7 *Introductio NT* -- **New Testament Introduction**

2088 **Alberto** Stefano, Vangelo e storicità, un dibattito [O'CALLAGHAN J. 7Q4s, Mc 1Tim]. Mi 1995, Rizzoli. L[m] 15. 88-17-1112-8 -- [R]BbbOr 37 (1995) 251-4 (D. *Sardini*).

2089 **Alt** Franz, Jesús, el primer hombre nuevo, [T]. Córdoba 1994, Almendro. -- [R]Phase 35 (1995) 173 (J. *Latorre*).

2090 **Bartolomé** Juan José, El Evangelio de Jesús de Nazaret; manual para el estudio de la tradición evangélica: Claves Cristianas 3. M 1995, CCS. 233 p.; bibliog. 221-233. 84-703-830-1. -- [R]*Carthaginensia 11 (1995) 434s (R. *Sanz Valdivieso*); Phase 35 (1995) 349s (J. *Latorre*).

2091 **Bell** Albert A.[j] A guide to the New Testament world 1994 → 10,3809: [R]CritRR 8 (1995) 169s (E. *Ferguson*); (Reformed) Perspectives 10,8 (1995) 26s (Bobby *Fong*).

Berger K., *Colpe* C., Religionsgeschichtliches Textbuch zum NT 1987 → 2098 below.

2092 [E]**Black** David A., *Dockery* David S., New Testament criticism and interpretation 1991 → 7,292; 9,4347: [R]JETS 38 (1995) 275s (J.D. *Harvey*).

2093 **Blount** Brian K., Cultural interpretation: reorienting New Testament criticism. Mp 1995, Fortress. x-222 p. 0-8006-2859-4.

2094 **Bockmuehl** Markus, This Jesus; martyr, Lord, Messiah 1994 → 10,3927: [R]*ModBlv 36 (1995) 47s (R.A. *Burridge*).

2095 **Borg** Marcus J., Jesus in contemporary scholarship 1994 → 10,3929: ᴿRBBras 11 (1994) 649s (C. *Minette de Tillesse*).

2096 **Borg** Marcus J., Meeting Jesus again for the first time .. 1994 → 10,3930: ᴿHorizons 22 (1995) 201 (D. *Burton-Christie*).

2097 *a) Borg* Marcus J., The historian, the Christian, and Jesus; -- *b) Kee* Howard C., A century of quests for the culturally compatible Jesus; -- *c) Patterson* J., The end of apocalypse; rethinking the eschatological Jesus: ThTo 52 (1995s 6-16 / 17-28 / 29-48.

2098 **Boring** M. Eugene, *al.*, Hellenistic commentary to the NT [revisedᵀ of BERGER K., COLPE C., RelG Textbuch 1987; 350 texts added]; 1000 excerpts translated and annotated]. Nv 1995, Abingdon. 663 p. $ 70. 0-687-00916-2 [NTAb 30, p.373]. -- ᴿSewaneeTR 39 (1995s) 332s (J. *Dunkly*); *TBR 8,3 (1995s) 10s (F.G. *Downing*: 'should be in libraries, but with an ideological health warning ').

2099 *a) Bottini* Claudio G., Gesù dalla casa di Nazaret alla missione; gli anni oscuri della formazione di Gesù; -- *b) Corona* Raimondo, I racconti dell'infanzia di Gesù in alcune opere di arte abruzzese (sec. XII-XVIII) / Oggetti domestici di Terra Santa al tempo di Cristo e nel periodo bizantino: → Pianum (1995) 18-37 / 55-61 . 51-54.

2100 *Braaten* Carl E., The historical Jesus and the Church: *ProEc 4 (1995) 11-15.

2101 *Bretscher* Paul G., When everything was Q: ProcGM 15 (1995) 53-64.

2102 **Bro** Bernard, Peut-on éviter Jésus-Christ ? ..1995, Fallois. 310 p. -- ᴿNV 70,4 (1995) 85-87 (G. *Bossard*).

2103 **Brown** Raymond E., Death of the Messiah 1994 → 10,4634: ᴿDR 113 (1995) 74-76 (B. *Orchard*); P(rinc)SB 16 (1995) 360-3 (D.M. *Smith*).

2104 **Brown** Schuyler, The origins of Christianity² 1993 → 9,4014: ᴿBLE 96 (1995) 231s (J. des *Rochettes*).

2105 *Brown* Schuyler, Good news about what ? Hermeneutical reflections on 'gospel' and 'evangelization' : A(ustrl)BR 42 (1994) 59-68; p. 65, not 'good' news, or Torah is 'bad'; 'there is an undeniably Marcionite current in Christianity'.

2106 **Burridge** Richard A., What are the Gospels ? a comparison with Graeco-Roman biography [diss.Nottingham 1989]: SNTS.mg 70, 1992 → 8,4212 ... 10,3890: ᴿC(olc)Th 64,1 (1994) 168-170 (M. *Wojciechowski*); JRel 75 (1995) 239-246 (Adela Y. *Collins*).

2107 **Buzzetti** Carlo, 4 x 1, 1994 → 10,771: ᴿPaVi 40,1 (1995) 61 (S. *Migliasso:* meglio 1 x 4).

2108 **Byatt** Anthony, New Testament metaphors; illustrations in word and phrase. Edinburgh PB 1995. Pentland. xxvii, 322 p.; bibliography : p. 278-284. 1-85821-239-1.

2109 **Byrskog** Samuel, Jesus the only teacher; didactic authority and transmission in ancient Israel, ancient Judaism and the Matthean community: CB.o 24, 1994 → 10,3931: ᴿJJS 46 (1995) 296s (G. *Harvey*); SvTKv 70 (1994) 185-9 (H. *Kvalbein*).

2110 **Carda Pitarch** J.M., Los porqués del Evangelio; 300 dudas y preguntas: BtBásica 32. M 1995, Atenas. 224 p. -- ᴿBurg 36 (1995) 359 (F. *Pérez Herrero*).

2111 **Carmichael** J., The unriddling of Christian origins; a secular account. Amherst 1995, Prometheus. 425 p. $ 35. 0-87975-952-6 [NTAb 40,p.364].

2112 **Carson** D., *Moo* D., *Morris* L., An introduction to the NT 1992 → 8,4119 ... 10,3819: ᴿCritRR 7 (1994) 153-5 (W.M. *Dunnett*: first of its kind in 30 years).

2113 **Casciaro** J.M., Jesús de Nazaret. Murcia 1994, Alga. 593 p. -- ᴿScrT(Pamp) 37 (1995) 667-9 (L.F. *Mateo-Seco*).

2114 **Collins** Raymond F., The birth of the New Testament; the origin and development of the first Christian generation [.. really on 1 Thess] 1993: → 10,3822: ᴿ*CritRR 7 (1994)

165-8 (L. *McDonald*); CThMi 22 (1995) 59s (L.A. *Kauppi*); SWJT 37,1 (1994s) 42 (H.A. *Brehm*); TorJT 11 (1995) 90s (L. Ann *Jervis*).

2115 *Cothenet* E., Une œuvre d'envergure sur les 'Actes des Apôtres' [BOSSUYT Philippe, *Radermakers* Jean, 1995]: E(spr)eV 105 (1995) 682-4.

2116 **Countryman** L. William, Good newe of Jesus; reintroducing the Gospel 1993 → 9,4094: ᴿ*CritRR 8 (1995) 191s (D.L. *Bartlett*: for the somewhat acquainted, doubtless inadequately or wrongly).

2117 **Crossan J.D.**, The historical Jesus; the life of a Mediterranean Jewish peasant 1991 → 7,3596 ... 10,3936: ᴿ*CritRR 7 (1994) 170-6 (H. *Boers* takes seriously though with sharp critique); EvQ 67 (1995) 168-171 (R, *Shirock*).

2118 **Crossan** J.D., Jesús; vida de un campesino judío, ᵀ *Lozoya* Teófilo de. Barc 1994, Crítica. 565 p. 84-7423-655-X. pt. 4500. -- ᴿEstAg 30 (1995) 132-4 (C. *Mielgo*); EstB 53 (1995) 261-6 (R. *Aguirre* importante); Proyección 42 (1995) 320s (J.L. *Sicre*); RevAg 36 (1995) 1132-4 (L. *Estrada*).

2119 **Crossan** John D., Der historische Jesus, ᵀ*Hahlbrock* Peter. Mü 1994, Beck. 630 p. DM 68. -- ᴿE(rbe)uA 71 (1995) 70 (B. *Schwank*); KuI(sr) 10 (1995) 187s (W. *Stegemann*).

2120 **Crossan** John D., Jesus, a revolutionary biography 1994 → 10,3938: ᴿCrossCur 45 (1995s) 114-6 (J.H. *Yoder*).

2121 **Culbertson** P.L., A word fitly spoken; context, transmission, and adoption of the parables of Jesus: Series in Religious Studies. Albany 1995, SUNY. xvi-390 p. $ 64.50; pa. $ 22. 0-7914-2311-5; -2-3 [NTAb 39, p.502].

2122 *Denaux* Adelbert, Criteria for identifying Q-passages; a critical review of a recent work by T. BERGEMANN [1993 < Diss. 1992]: NT 37 (1995) 105-129.

2123 **Dirnbeck** Josef, Die Jesusfälscher [THIERING B., *al.*]; ein Originell wird entstellt. Augsburg 1995, Pattloch. 264 p. DM 32. -- ᴿG(eist)uL 68 (1995) 474s (R. *Klein*).

2124 *Dokka* Trond S., Bibelsk historie og teologisk mening [ÅDNA J., Jesu Kritik am Tempel (Mk 11,15) ᴰ1994]: NTT 95 (1994) 213-220.

2125 **Dormeyer** Detlev, Das Neue Testament im Rahmen der antiken Literaturgeschichte, eine Einführung: AW. Da 1993, Wiss. xi-314 p. DM 59. 3-534-06830-0. -- ᴿBZ 39 (1995) 265-7 (C.-P. *März*).

2126 **Downing** F. Gerald, Cynics and Christian origins 1992 → 8,4131; 9,4026: ᴿ*JEarlyC 3 (1995) 62-64 (R.L. *Pervo*).

2127 **Duquesne** Jacques, Jésus 1994 → 10,3943: ᴿDiv 39 (1995) 289 (D. *Vibrac*); Spiritus 36 (1995) 263-8 (B. *Rey*).

2128 -- *Geffroy* Christophe, Le 'Jésus' de DUQUESNE; ni nouveau ni vrai: PensCath 274 (1995) 24-27 (28-42, *Sinoir* Michel; 43s, *La Potterie* Ignace de, sur la conception virginale; 46-56, *Babinet* Robert, sur Duquesne et POTIN Jean).

2129 **Eckardt** A.Roy, Reclaiming the Jesus of history; Christology today 1992 → 8,4271 ... 10,3944: ᴿ*CritRR 7 (1994) 499s (Florence M. *Gillman*) & 501s (H.G. *Perelmuter*).

2130 **Edmonds** Peter, Three [Synoptic] portraits of Jesus and other Gospel portraits. Gweru, Zambia 1994, Mambo. 135 p. 0-86922-582.-- ᴿ*TBR 8,2 (1995s) 14s (L. *Houlden*: not easy.

2131 **Ennulat** Andreas, Die 'minor agreements': WUNT 2/62, 1993 → 10,4253: ᴿNT 37 (1995) 197-9 (C.M. *Tuckett*).

2132 **Evans** Craig A., Jesus and his contemporaries -- comparative studies: AGAJC. Lei 1995, Brill. xiii-532 p. 90-04-10279-5. -- ᴿE(xp)T 107 (1995s) 23 (I.G. *Wallis*).

2133 **Ferguson** Everett, Backgrounds of early Christianity² [¹1987]. GR 1993, Eerdmans. 610 p. -- ᴿChH 64 (1995) 636s (C.B. *Ashanin*).

2134 **Fredriksen** Paula,De Jésus aux Christs 1992 →9,4318: [R]RHR 212(1995)226-8(A.*Mehat*).
2135 [E]**Funk** Robert W., *Hoover* R., The five Gospels 1993 → 9,4098; 10,4226: [R]BZ 39 (1995) 269-271 (J. *Schlosser*: anregend; bringt Bewegung in manche festgefahrene Position); *CritRR 8 (1995) 213-7 (J.P. *Meier*: severe); JThS 46 (1995) 250-3 (C.M. *Tuckett*).
2136 *Georgi* Dieter, The early Church; internal Jewish migration or new religion ?: HThR 88 (1995) 35-66.
2137 **Goosen** Gideon, *Tomlinson* Margaret, Studying the Gospels; an introduction. Newton, Australia 1994, Dwyer. xiv-219 p. $ 13. 0-85574-389-1 [RStR 22,156: Fred W. *Burnett*; the best undergraduate text he has found in 21 years' teaching].
2138 **Goulder** M., A tale of two missions. L 1994, SCM. -- [R]TLS (June 24,1994) 31 (A.E. *Harvey*: 'Paulines v. Petrines') [NTAb 39,p.81].
2139 **Grassi** Joseph A., Rediscovering the Jesus story; a participatory guide. NY 1995, Paulist. ix-218 p. $ 13. 0-8091-3589-2.
2140 **Green** Joel B., Hearing the New Testament; strategies for interpretation. GR 1995, Eerdmans. xvi-444 p. 0-8028-0793-3.
2141 **Guillet** J., Jésus dans la foi des premières disciples. P 1995, D-Brouwer. 256 p. -- [R]RSPT 79 (1995) 688 (B. *Rey*).
2142 **Hamilton** William, A quest for the post-historical Jesus 1994 → 9,4166; 10,3959: [R]LouvSt 20 (1995) 91-93 (H.-E. *Mertens*: one of the 'death-of-God' pioneers).
2143 **Hoffmann** Paul, Tradition und Situation; Studien zur Jesusüberlieferung in der Logienquelle und den synoptischen Evangelien: NTA 28. Müns 1995, Aschendorff. 390 p.; Bibliog. 373-286. DM 93. 3-402-04776-4. -- [R]RHR 212 (1995) 479s (A. *Mehat*).
2144 *Holmberg* Bengt, En historisk vändning i forskningen om Jesus: SvTK 69 (1993) 69-76; Eng. 76: 3d quest (before end of 2d), now Jewish context.
2145 **Huber** Konrad, Jesus in Auseinandersetzung; exegetische Untersuchungen zu den sogenannten Jerusalemer Streitgesprächen des Markusevangeliums im Blick auf ihre christologischen Implikationen [< Diss. Innsbruck 1994, [D]*Hasitschka* M.]: FzB 75. Wü 1995, Echter. 499 p.; Bibliog. 449-473. 3-429-01641-X.
2146 *Johnson* Luke T., *a*) The search for (the wrong) Jesus: BiRe 11,6 (1995) 20-25 . 41. -- *b*) Who is Jesus ? The Academy vs. the Gospels: *CWeal 122,22 (1995) 12-14; Jesus called for 'a poor and giving rather than a powerful and grasping church' and is for those who desire theological integrity and honest history).
2147 **Keener** Craig S., The IVP Bible background commentary, NT. DG 1993, InterVarsity. 841 p. $ 30. -- [R]BA 58 (1995) 174s (R. *Starner*).
2148 **Kirchschläger** Walter, Le origini della Chiesa; una ricerca biblica [Rückbesinnung 1990 → 6,5221; 7,4653],[T]. R 1994, Città Nuova. 211 p. L[m] 24 [RHE 90 (1995) 267*]. -- [R]PaVi 40,1 (1995) 62s (P. *Merlo*).
2149 **Kirchschläger** Walter, Einführung in das NT: Begegnung mit der Bibel. Stu 1994, KBW. 150 p. DM 39. -- [R]Entschluss 50,12 (1995) 36 (W. *Dettling*).
2150 *Koester* Helmut, Jesus' presence in the early Church: CrSt 15 (1994) 541-557 [NTAb 39,p.444].
2151 **Koester** Helmut, Introduction to the New Testament[2rev] [no longer dependent on his Einführung c. 1982], 1. History, culture, and religion of the Hellenistic age. NY 1995, de Gruyter. xxxiv-409 p.; 15 fig.; 9 maps. $ 43; pa. $24. 3-11-014693-2; -2-4 [NTAb (25,p.79; 27,p.201) 40,p.379].
2152 *Krentz* Edgar, Epideiktik and hymnody; the New Testament and its world: BR(es) 40 (1995) 50-97.

2153 *Kurz* Paul-Konrad, Identifikations- und Projektionsgestalt Jesus; neue literarhistorische Studien [KUSCHEL K. 1980 ...] und Romane: GuL 68 (1995) 455-469.

2154 *(Conzelmann* H.) **Lindemann** A., Arbeitsbuch zum NT[11rev]: Uni-Tb 52. Tü 1995, Mohr. xix-565 p. 3-8253-0052-3. -- [R]EThL 71 (1995) 461 (F. *Neirynck*).

2155 **Linnemann** Eta, Is there a Synoptic Problem ? 1992 → 8,4545 ... 10,4242: [R]A(ndr)USS 33 (1995) 309s (E.E. *Reynolds*); ConcordiaTQ 59 (1995) 128s (D.P. *Scaer*).

2156 **Lorenzen** T., Resurrection and discipleship; interpretive models, biblical reflections, theological consequences. Mkn 1995, Orbis. x-358 p. $ 22 pa. 1-57075-042-2 [NTAb 40,p.368].

2157 **McCracken** David, The scandal of the Gospels; Jesus, story, and offense 1994 → 10,4515: [R]*CritRR 8 (1995) 260-2 (W.B. *Tatum*).

2158 *a) Mach* Michael, Verus Israel; toward the clarification of a Jewish factor in early Christian self-definition; -- *b) Stroumsa* Gedaliahu G., Early Christianity as radical religion: → 392, IOS 14 (1994) 143-172 / 173-193.

2159 **Mack** B.L., Who wrote the New Testament ? The making of the Christian myth. SF 1995, HarperCollins. ix-326 p.; 2 maps. $ 24. 0-06-065517-8 [NTAb 40,p.327].

2160 **Mack** Burton L., The lost Gospel; the book of Q and Christian origins 1993 → 9,4419; 10,4243: [R]*CritRR 8 (1995) 253-7 (A.D. *Jacobson*: high praise despite frustrations); Interpretation 49 (1995) 108-110 (M.E. *Boring*); UnSemQ 48,3 (1994) 155-8 (R. *Scroggs*).

2161 *Magne* Jean, Deux mythes et deux rites à l'origine du christianisme: CahRenan 43,190 (1995) 67-92.

2162 *Marchadour* Alain, Les Évangiles au feu de la critique. P 1995, Bayard/Centurion. 188 p. F 95. -- [R]Études 383 (1995) 570 p.(P. *Gibert*).

2163 *Mattila* Sharon Lea, A question too often neglected [in source criticism: what compositional procedures were then in use ?]: NTS 41 (1995) 199-217.

2164 **Meier** John P., A marginal Jew I, 1991 → 7,5667 ... 10,4068: [R]A(ustrl)BR 42 (1994) 100-3 (D.C. *Sim*).

2165 **Meier** J., Gesù Cristo e il cristianesimo nella tradizione giudaica antica: StB 106. Brescia 1994, Paideia. 354 p. -- [R]EstTrin 29 (1995) 497 (X. *Pikaza*).

2166 *Meynell* H., On New Testament scholarship and the integrity of faith [Hermes and Athena]: NBL 76 (1995) 127-140 [NTAb 38, p.115; 40, p.7].

2167 *Michaud* Jean-Paul, Un état de la recherche sur le Jésus de l'histoire: E(gl)eT 26 (1995) 143-163.

2168 **Migliore** Franzo, Introduzione al Nuovo Testamento [senza orientamento teologico], pref. *Corsani* B.: Armarium 3. Messina 1992, Rubbettino. 309 p. 88-7284-077-5. -- [R]RÉA(nc) 97 (1995) 653s (C. *Amphoux*); Salesianum 57 (1995) 778s (C. *Bissoli*).

2168* *Moiser* Jeremy, The Resurrection -- recent official pronouncements and recent exegesis : DR 113 (1995) 235-247.

2169 *Morris* John, Can Christology benefit from 'Life of Jesus' research ? A theological reflection on CROSSAN's The historical Jesus ['rigorous, sophisticated, successful', p. 168]: Ang 72 (1995) 161-194.

2170 **Moulton** J.J., *Milligan* G., Vocabulary of the Greek Testament illustrated from the papyri (1914-28); new Moulton and Milligan project, Lexicon of epigraphic and papyrus parallels to the NT, a joint project of Sydney, La Trobe, and Macquarie universities in Australia [data collection 1994-6, editing 1997-8]: *FgNt 7 (1994) 125s.

2171 *Moxnes* Halvor, Den historiske Jesus; mellom modernitet og postmodernitet ?: NTT 96 (1995) 139-156 (-175, *al.*).

2172 **Müller** Peter, 'Verstehest du auch, was du liest ? ' Lesen und Verstehen im Neuen Testament. Da 1994, Wiss. x-241 p. 3-534-12384-0 [RStR 22,160, Fika J. van *Rensburg*].

2173 **Nolan** Albert, Jésus avant le christianisme; l'Évangile de la libération, ^T*Dumortier* J.M. P 1995, Atelier. 190 p. -- ^RBLE 96 (1995) 230 (L. *Monloubou*).

2174 **O'Neill** John C., Who did Jesus think he was ? Lei 1995, Brill. viii-238 p.; bibliog. 191-212. 90-04-10429-1.

2175 *Orsatti* Mauro al., 1. Giovanni il Battista; 2. Maria di Nazaret; 3. Pietro; 4. I discepoli; 5. Le donne; 6. I farisei: PaVi 39,1-6 ('Uomini e donne incontro a Gesù' 1994) c.4-35 ognuno.

2176 **Paradza** Bernadette V., The four Gospels and the Acts; an introduction and short commentary. Gweru, Zimbabwe 1993, Mambo. 142 p. 0-86922-568-5. -- ^RTBR 8,1 (1995s) 19 (R.S. *Sugirtharajah*).

2177 **Patzia** Arthur G., The making of the New Testament; origins, collection, text and canon. Leicester 1995, InterVarsity/Apollos.. 205 p.; 28 fig. $ 15 pa. 0-8308-1859-6 [NTAb 40, p.132].

2178 **Pawson** David, Is the [Toronto charismatics' 'phenomenon'] blessing biblical ?. L 1995, Hodder & S. £ 6. -- ^RTablet 249 (1995) 1586s (Elaine *Sorkey*, also on cognate ^EPORTER S., RICHTER P.).

2179 *Pearson* Birger A., The Gospel according to the Jesus seminar:Religion 25(1995)317-38.

2180 *Picard* Gilbert, La date de naissance de Jésus du point de vue romain: CRAI (1995) 799-806.

2181 ^E**Piñero** Antonio, Fuentes del cristianismo 1993 → 9,4063; 10,3856; ^RBLE 96 (1995) 64s (S. *Légasse*); CDios 208 (1995) 275-7 (J. *Gutiérrez*); E(st)E 70 (1995) 123s (F. *Pastor-Ramos*); EstAg 29 (1994) 590s (D. *Alvarez Cineira*); Kiryat Sefer 65 (1994s) p.335s (Shifra *Sznol ^H*); RBBras 11 (1994) 651 (C. *Minette de Tillesse*); RevAg 35 (1994) 1202-6 (S. *Sabugal*).

2182 **Piñero** Antonio, *Peláez* Jesús, El Nuevo Testamento; introducción al estudio de los primeros escritos cristianos: *EnOrCr 8. Córdoba 1995, Almendro. 569 p. 84-8005-023-3 [NTAb 40, p.514]. -- ^RCommunio (Sev) 28 (1995) 373-5 (M. de *Burgos*).

2183 *Popkes* Wiard, Paränese NT: → 772, TRE 25 (1995) 737-742.

2184 ^E**Porter** Stanley E., *Tombs* David, Approaches to New Testament study: JSNT.s 120. Shf 1995, Academic. 392 p. 1-85075-567-1.

2185 **Potin** Jean, Jésus, l'histoire vraie 1994 → 10,4001: ^RÉtudes 382 (1995) 261-3 (J. *Guillet*, aussi sur M. QUESNEL et J. DUQUESNE); Spiritus 36 (1995) 263-8 (B. *Rey*).

2186 **Pregeant** R., Engaging the NT; an interdisciplinary introduction. Mp 1995, Fortress. xxv-581 p.; 81 fig. 0-8006-2803-9 [NTAb 40, p.133].

2187 **Pritz** Ray A., Nazarene Jewish Christianity 1988 → 4,781; 7,e999: *JHiCr 2,2 (1995) 143-7 (R.M. *Price*).

2188 **Quesnel** Michel, Jésus-Christ, un exposé: Pour comprendre: un essai pour réfléchir: Dominos 42. P 1994, Flammarion. 126 p. -- ^RE(gl)eT 26 (1995) 116s (J.P. *Michaud*).

2189 *Raguse* Hartmut, Figürlich leben -- einige Reflexionen zu neueren Ansätzen in der Gleichnistheorie: ThZ 51 (1995) 18-40 (-49, *Binder* Herrmann, zu Lk 16,1ff).

2190 **Ralph** Margaret N., Discovering the Gospels; four accounts of the Good News 1990 → 6,4249; 10,3905: ^REstB 53 (1995) 553s (Elisa *Estévez*).

2191 *Robinson* James M., The incipit of the Sayings Gospel Q [John Baptist's 'brood of vipers' with its wider context now lost]; : RHPhR 75 (1995) 9-33; franç. 9.

2192   **Rolland** Philippe, Présentation du Nouveau Testament, selon l'ordre chronologique et la structure littéraire des écrits apostoliques. P 1995, Éditions de Paris. xix-623 p. 2-85162-004-5.

2193   **Rossé** Gérard, Los evangelios; quién los ha escrito, por qué, cómo leerlos, [T] *Bellido* Juan F. M 1995. 110 p.- [R]RevAg 36 (1995) 1152s (L.A. *Sánchez Navarro*).

2194   **Sanders** E.P., The historical figure of Jesus 1993 → 9,4197; 10,4004s: [R]ChrCent 112 (1995) 23s (D.L. *Bartlett*); P(rinc)SB 16 (1995) 259s (J.T. *Carroll*).

2195   **Sawicki** Marianne, Seeing the Lord; Resurrection and early Christian practices. Mp 1994, Fortress. 375 p. 0-8006-2709-1. -- [R]E(xp)T 107 (1995s) 55s (N. *Clark*: a valuable tour-de-force, though she admits her skills are not equal to the 'alarming range of interdisciplinary competence' nowadays required).

2196   **Schnackenburg** Rudolf, Jesus in the Gospels; a biblical Christology, [T]*Dean* O.C. LVL 1995, W-Knox. 416 p. $ 35. 0-664-22059-2 [RStR 22,246, C. *Bernas*].

2197   **Schnackenburg** Rudolf, La persona di Gesù Cristo nei quattro vangeli: CommTeolNT supp.4. Brescia 1995, Paideia. 451 p. 88-394-0529-1.

2198   **Schneiders** Sandra M., The revelatory text.. NT 1991 → 7,3555 ... 10,3665: [R]JAAR 63 (1995) 903-7 (Morny *Joy*).

2199   **Schnelle** Udo. Einleitung in das Neue Testament: Uni-Tb 1830. Gö 1994, Vandenhoeck & R. 639 p. DM 49. 3-525-03286 [3-8252-1830-9, ThRv 91,182]. -- [R]EThL 71 (1995) 459-461 (F. *Neirynck*); NT 37 (1995) 409s (C. *Stenschke*); TTh 35 (1995) 187s (J. *Negenman*); ZkT 117 (1995) 230 (R. *Oberforcher*).

2200   **Schulz** Hans-Joachim. Die apostolische Herkunft der Evangelien: QD 145, 1993 → 10,3906: [R]*Carthaginensia 11 (1995) 197s (R. *Sanz Valdivieso*); CBQ 57 (1995) 414s (W.S. *Kurz* shares QD-editor SCHNACKENBURG's dissent and claim of attention deserved by this Eastern Church theologian).

2201   **Schweizer** Eduard, Jesus the parable of God; what do we really know about Jesus ? ... 1994, Pickwick. 120 p. 1-55635-025-2. -- [R]E(xp)T 107,5 3d-top choice (1995s) 130s (C.S. *Rodd*).

2202   **Schweizer** Eduard, Introduzione teologica al NT, [TE]*Soffritti* Omero 1992 → 8,4189; 9,4075: [R]RS(to)LR 31 (1995) 564s (Giuliana *Iacopino*).

2203   **Scott** J.Julius, Customs and controversies; intertestamental Jewish backgrounds of the New Testament. GR 1995, Baker. 419 p.; 6 fig.: 4 maps. $ 20 pa. 0-8010-2001-8 [NTAb 40,p.385].

2204   **Seeley** David, Deconstructing the New Testament; BInterpS 5, 1994 → 10,3868: [R]CBQ 57 (1995) 827-9 (F.F. *Segovia; historical criticism too de-constructs the text, as here); JBL 114 (1995) 729-731 (S.D. *Moore*); TTh 35 (1995) 187 (P. *Chatelion Counet*).

2205   *Shellard* Barbara, The relationship of Luke and John; a fresh look at an old problem: JThS 46 (1995) 71-98.

2206   *Sibley* Jack, Christ in Scripture, a kaleidoscope of images; even early Christians saw differences in Christ: Disciple 133,11 (St. Louis 1995) 5-7.

2207   **Sicari** Antonio. Viaggio nel Vangelo; Gesù ddi Nazareth, il 'Dio con noi ': Già e non ancora 298. Mi 1995, Jaca. 145 p. 88-16-30298-4.

2208   **Stanton** Graham, Gospel truth ? New light on the Gospels [against THIEDE C. early Mt dating]. L 1995, HarperCollins. viii-215 p. £ 15. 0-00-627963-5. -- [R]TBR 8,2 (1995s) 15 (L. *Houlden*).

2209   -- [E]*Wilkins*[E] John, Home News:] Redating the NT [THIEDE C. early dating of Mt simply on grounds of handwriting; adverse views of PARSONS P.,STANTON G.]:Tablet 249(1995)29.

2210 **Stenger** Werner, [Greekless] Introduction to New Testament exegesis [Biblische Methodenlehre], [T]*Stott* D.W. 1993 J 9,4077; 10,3871: [R]A(ndr)USS 33 (1995) 151 (H.V.A. *Kuma*).

2211 **Strecker** Georg, Literaturgeschichte des NTs: UTB 1682, 1992 → 8,4192 ... 10,3873: [R]StPat(av) 41 (1994) 680-2 (G. *Segalla*).

2212 *Strijdom* Johan, The 'unconventionality' of Jesus from the perspective of a diverse audience; an evaluation of CROSSAN's historical Jesus: Neotest 29 (1995) 313-323 [325-356, *Aarde* Andries G. van, the Third Quest; 357-392, *Venter* Rian].

2213 **Thiering** Barbara, Jesus of the Apocalypse [.. married and divorced Magdalene, continued to lead his movement until (? his) year 73] ..: [R]BurHist 31 (1995) 114-124 (C. *Forbes:* severe).

2214 **Tilliette** Xavier, Le Christ des philosophes; du Maître de sagesse au divin Témoin: Ouvertures, Namur 1993 → 10,4155: [R]EThL 71 (1995) 485-7 (E. *Brito*); L(aval)ThP 51 (1995) 210-2 (J.-L. *Vieillard-Baron*).

2215 *a) Toribio Cuadrado* J.F., 'Evangelio', obra aperta [open-ended]: *Mayéutica 20 (1994) 9-78; -- b) Price* R., The honest account of a memorable life; an apocryphal gospel [not really: a novelist's re-telling mostly of Mark]: ThTo 51,1 (1994) 38-67 [NTAb 39, p.18].

2215* *Tuckett* Christopher, Das Evangelium und die synoptischen Evangelien: BThZ 12 (1995) 186-200.

2216 **Ulonska** Herbert, Streiten mit Jesus; Konfliktgeschichten in den Evangelien. Gö 1995, Vandenhoeck & R. 208 p. DM 34. 3-525-61347-4 [RStR 22,66, F.W.*Burnett*].

2217 **Vaage** Leif, Galilean upstarts: Jesus' first followers according to Q 1994 → 10,4266: [R]RB 102 (1995) 425-8 (W. *Klassen:* clealy one of the most important of the hundreds of books now being published about Jesus).

2218 **Wallis** Ian G., The faith of Jesus Christ in early Christian traditions: SNTS.m 84. C 1995, Univ. 281 p.; bibliog. 222-246. £ 35. 0-51-47352-7. -- [R]E(xp)T 107 (1995s) 55 (D. *Hill*: high praise).

2219 *Wallis* Ian G., Jesus the believer; a fresh approach: *ModB 36,1 (MCM until 1993, Ox 1995) 10-17 [NTAb 39,p.442].

2220 *Walls* Jerry, The flight from truth in New Testament scholarship: ChrSchR 25 (1995s) 180-196.

2221 **Winter** Paul, El proceso a Jesús [1961],[TE]: Atajos 6. Barc 1995, Muchnik. 295 p. [RF 231 (1995) 447s].

2222 **Winterhalter** Robert, [E]*Fisk* George W., Jesus' parables; finding God within 1993 → 9.4708*: [R]Catholic World 238 (1995) 234s (Kathleen M. *Gaffney*).

2223 **Witherington** Ben[III.] The Jesus quest; the third search for the Jew of Nazareth [... cynic; .. BROWN R.E., MEIER J. ...]. DG 1995, InterVarsity. 404 p. $ 20. 0-8308-1861-8 [ThD 43,94].

2224 [[F]WUELLNER Wilhelm]: Rhetoric and the NT, [E]**Porter** S., *Olbricht* T., 1992/3 → 9,406: [R]TorJT 11 (1995) 250-2 (A. *Kirk*).

B7.5 *Unitas VT-NT* -- **The unity of the two Testaments**

2225 *Agua* Agustín del, El 'antiguo' Testamento, primera parte de la Biblia cristiana; lettura cr0istiana del AT: E(st)E 70 (1995) 145-189 [NTAb 40,p.77].

2226 **Allison** Dale C., The new Moses; a Matthean typology. Mp 1993, Fortress. xvi-396 p.— [R]Biblica 76 (1995) 574-8 (J. *Roloff*).

2227 *Augello* A., Gesù e la religione ebraica; tra verità e compimento: [R]*Vivarium 3 (Catanzaro 1995) 205-224 [NTAb 40, p.274].

2228 *a) Bakker* L., [P] New paradigm of the relation of Judaism to Christianity; the origin of Christianity as the actualisation of faith in the God of Israel; -- *b) Chrostowski* W., [P] The NT and Jusaism -- possibilities and challenges: CoTh 64,2 (1994) 67-78 / 11-23; NTAb 39, p.264s].

2229 [E]**Blanchetière** François, *Herr* Moshe D., Aux origines juives du christianisme: Hommes et sociétés. J c.1995, Centre de recherche français. 173 p. -- [R]ASS(oc)R 90 (1995) 74 (M. *Löwy*).

2230 **Boccara** Elio, Il peso della memoria; una lettura ebraica del Nuovo Testamento: CSB 23. Bo 1994 → 10,4031, Dehoniane. 283 p. L[m] 35. 88-10-40723-7.

2231 *Böhler* Dieter, 'Ecce homo' (Joh 19,5) ein Zitat aus dem AT ? [1Sam 9,17]: BZ 39 (1995) 104-8.

2232 [E]**Charlesworth** J.H., *Weaver* W.P., The Old and New Testaments; their relationship and the 'intertestamental' literature 1993 → 9,375*: P(rinc)SB 16 (1995) 88-90 (M. *Weinfeld*).

2233 **Chilton** Bruce D., *Neusner* Jacob, Judaism in the New Testament; practices and beliefs. L 1995, Routledge. xix-203 p. 0-415-11844-1.

2234 **Chow** Simon, The sign of Jonah reconsidered .. Gospel traditions: ConBib NT 27. Sto 1995, Almqvist & W. 224 p. Sk 182. -- [R]ThRv 91 (1995) 478-483 (V. *Pfnür*, auch über STOFFON U. 1994).

2235 *Collinson* Patrick, The coherence of the text; how it hangeth together; the Bible in Reformation England: **5**, [F]ATKINSON, J., Bible, Reformation, Church: JSNT.s 105 (1995) 84-108.

2236 *Deiana* Giovanni, Il rapporto tra Antico e Nuovo Testamento nella 'Dei Verbum': → 20, [F]BETTI U., Lateranum 61,2s (1995) 183-193; Eng. 194 [< OTA 19,p.297].

2237 **De Vries** Simon J., From old revelation to new; a tradition-historical and redaction-critical study of temporal transitions in prophetic prediction. GR 1995, Eerdmans. xxiv-383 p. 0-8028-0683-X.

2238 *Dohmen* C., Die gespaltene Seele der Theologie; zum Verhältnis von Altem und Neuem Testament: BiLi(tg) 68 (1995) 154-162 [NTAb 40, p.191; OTA 19,9.298].

2239 **Dohmen** Christoph, *Mussner* Franz, Nur die halbe Wahrheit ? Für die Einheit der ganzen Bibel 1993 → 9.4373; 10,4191: [R]KuI(sr) 104 (Julie *Kirchberg*); TPQ 143 (1995) 94 (K.M. *Woschitz*)

2240 **Doran** Robert, Birth of a worldview; early Christianity in its Jewish and pagan context. Boulder 1995, Westview. ix-183 p, $ 50; pa. $ 18. 0-8133-8745-0; -6-9 [ThD 43,63].

2241 **Ephraim** frère, Gesù ebraico praticante 1993 → 10,4044: [R]Benedictina 41 (1994) 539 (S. *de Piccoli*).

2242 *Ferrari* Pier Luigi, Abramo nel NT (*Benzi* Guido, *al.*, VT; *Perani* Mauro, Midrash; *Maritano* Mario, S. AMBROGIO): PaVi 40,1 ('Uomini e donne in cammino con Dio' 1995) 30-34 (6-9-29 / 35-37 / 21s). -- Fasc. 2, Giacobbe, 3-44; -- 3, Giuseppe, 3-47; -- 4, Giosuè, 3-40; -- 5, Rut e le altre, 3-47; -- 6, Samuele, 3-49.

2243 *Fitzmyer* Joseph A., Problems of the Semitic background of the New Testament: → 77, [F]HAMRICK E.W., Yahweh 1995. 80-93;

2244 *Gisel* Pierre, Variations sur l'accomplissement [... points de profonde consonance de ce dogmaticien-protestant avec Beauchamp exégète catholique]: → 14, [F]BEAUCHAMP P., 'Ouvrir les Écritures' 1995, 327-347.

2245 **Görg** Manfred, In Abrahams Schoss; Christsein ohne Neues Testament 1993 → 9,4378; 10,4194: [R]ZkT 117 (1995) 105s (R. *Oberforcher*).

2246 *Høgenhaven* Jesper, Kristus i Det Gamle Testamente: ForumBEks 4 (K 1994) 37-56 [< OTA 18 (1995) p. 358].

2247 **Holladay** William L., Long ago God spoke; how Christians may hear the Old Testament today. Mp 1995,Fortress. x-353 p. $ 20 pa. 0-8006-2884-5 [< OTA 18 (1995) p. 626s (R.E. *Murphy*)].

2248 *Hübner* Hans, Eine hermeneutisch unverzichtbare Unterscheidung: Vetus Testamentum und Vetus Testamentum in Novo receptum: →79, [F]HARTMAN L., Texts & Contexts 1995, 901-919.

2249 **Knowles** Michael, Jeremiah in Matthew's Gospel: jNsu 68. 1993 → 9,4487; 10,4313: Biblica 76 (1995) 427-430 (G. *Claudel*).

2250 *Leeuwen* C. van, The relation between the Old and the New Testaments: NesTR 15 (1994) 37-58 [< OTA 18 (1995) p. 587 (R.A. *Taylor*)].

2251 **Liebers** Reinhold, 'Wie geschrieben steht'; Studien zu einer besonderen Art frühchristlichen Schriftbezuges [Hab.-Diss. Kiel 1991: *deî*, 'it is necessary', not from Jesus or his earliest followers: as already PATSCH H.] 1993 → 9,4383: 10,4201: [R]CBQ 57 (1995) 587s (C.A. *Evans*: compelling, beyond DUNN and LINDARS).

2252 *Lohfink* Norbert, Eine Bibel -- zwei Testamente: → 361, Eine Bibel 1995, 71-81.

2253 **McLean** Bradley H., Citations and allusions to Jewish Scripture in early Christian and Jewish writings through 180 C.E. Lewiston NY 1992. Mellen. 138 p. $ 50. 0-7734-8430-8. -- [R]Bijdragen 56 (1995) 217-9 (J. van *Ruiten*).

2254 **Manns** Frédéric, Il Giudaismo; ambiente e memoria del Nuovo Testamento: StB 25. Bo 1995, Dehoniane. 253 p.; bibliog. 235-242. 88-10-40727-X.

2255 **Marcus** Joel, The way of the Lord; Christological exegesis of the OT in Mk 1992 → 8,5156 ... 10,4774; [R]Neotest 29 (1995) 125-7 (D.F. *Tolmie*).

2255* **Minear** Paul S., Christians and the new creation; Genesis motifs in the NT 1994 → 10,1645: [R]*TBR 8,1 (1995s) (R. *Morgan*: one of the great theologians of his generation .. ideas always sensible).

2256 *Morgan* Robert, On the unity of Scripture: → 170, [F]SAWYER, J., Words; JSOT.s 195 (1995) 395-413.

2257 *Moyise* S., Does the NT quote the OT out of context ?: *Anvil 11,2 (1994) 133-143 [NTAb 39, p.5]

2258 **New** David S., OT quotations (→ 10,4261) in the Synoptic Gospels and the Two-Document hypothesis; SBL sour 37. At 1993, Scholars, viii-140 p. $ 24; pa. $ 16.9 : [R]BThB 25 (1995) 91 (R.L. *Mowery*); CBQ 57 (1995) 602-4 (E.C. *Maloney*); JBL 114 (1995) 16s (L. *Cope*); NT 37 (1995) 99-101 (J.K. *Elliott*).

2259 a) *Nikolaus* Walter, Zur theologischen Problematik des christologischen 'Schriftbeweises' im Neuen Testament; -- b) *Lichtenberger* H., 'Älter Bund und Neuer Bund': NTS 41 (1995) 338-357 / 400-414.

2260 *a) Nobile* Marco, L'Apocalisse, una lettura cristiana dell'Antico Testamento; -- *b) Manns* Frédéric, Le Shema Israël, clé de lecture de quelques textes johanniques; -- *c) La Potterie* Ignace de, La morale giovannea; una morale della verità: → 520, Efeso 5, 1995. 127-138 / 107-117 / 5-17.

2261 **Nohrnberg** James, Like unto Moses: the constituting of an interruption: Indiana Studies in Biblical Literature. Bloomington 1995, Indiana Univ. xiv-396 p. 0-253-34090-X.

2262 **Pesce** Mauro, Il cristianesimo e la sua radice ebraica. Bo 1994, Dehoniane. 237 p. -- [R]*AnT 9 (1995) 480-2 (M.A. *Tábet*).

2263 *Rowland* Christopher, Moses and Patmos; reflections on the Jewish background of early Christianity: → 170, [F]SAWYER, J., Words; JSOT.s 195 (1995) 280-299.

2264 *Sänger* Dieter, 'Von mir hat er geschrieben' (Joh 5,46); zur Funktion und Bedeutung Mose [*sic*] im Neuen Testament: KuD 41 (1995) 112-134; Eng. 135,

2265 **Saldarini** Anthony J., Matthew's Christian-Jewish community 1994 → 10,4335: [R]JRel 75 (1995) 265 (D.J. *Harrington*).

2266 [E]**Satterthwaite** Philip E., *al.*, The Lord's anointed; interpretation of Old Testament messianic texts: Tyndale House Studies. Carlisle 1995, Paternoster. x-320 p. 0-85364-685-6.

2267 *Schmidt* Werner H., 'Das Problem des ATs in der christlichen Theologie'; ein Gespräch mit Herbert Donner [[F]TRILLHAAS W. 1968, 37-52]: → 48, [F]DONNER H., Meilenstein: ÄAT 30 (1995) 243-251.

2268 *a) Schreiner* Stefan, [P] The Bible as a document of the history of the Jewish faith -- the New Testament in the interpretation of Leo BAECK; -- *b) Safrai* Chana, [P] Culture of controversy -- applied to the Gospel tradition, [T]*Chrostowski* Waldemar: -- *c) Bakker* Leo, New paradigm of the relation of Judaism to Christianity; the origin of Christianity as the actualisation of faith in the God of Israel, [T]*Królikowski* Piotr: C(olc)Th 64,2 (1994) 25-35 / 237-42 / 67-78.

2269 **Sevenich-Bax** Elisabeth, Israels Konfrontation mit den letzten Boten der Weisheit .. Logienquelle [Q] 1993 → 9,4437; 10,4263: [R]JBL 114 (1995) 514-6 (Risto *Uro*); JThS 46 (1995) 255-7 (C.M. *Tuckett*).

2270 *Smend* Rudolf, Beziehungen zwischen alttestamentlicher und neutestamentlicher Wissenschaft: ZThK 92 (1995) 1-12.

2271 [E]**Strickland** Wayne D., The Law, the Gospel, and the modern Christian; five views [each with response from the other four] 1993 → 9,6026: [R]A(ndr)USS 33 (1995) 326-8 (R. *Badenas*: none definitive, though W. KAISER proclaims p.75 'it is time for the dispute to come to an end'); JETS 37 (1994) 447-450 (M.W. *Karlberg*).

2272 **Swartley** Willard M., Israel's Scripture traditions and the Synoptic Gospels; story shaping story 1994 → 10,926: [R]CBQ 57 (1995) 609s (J.T. *Carroll*); CGrebel 13 (1995) 113-5 (D. *Nighswander*); JBL 114 (1995) 731s (W.R. *Stegner*); P(rinc)SemBu 16 (1995) 87s (J. *Marcus*); RefTR 54 (1995) 34 (B. *Dumbrell*).

2273 *a) Theissen* Gerd, Neutestamentliche Überlegungen zu einer jüdisch-christlichen Lektüre des Alten Testaments; -- *b) Zenger* Erich, Überlegungen zu einem neuen christlichen Umgang mit dem sogenannten Alten Testament: KuI(sr) 10 (1095) 115-136 / 137-151.

2274 **Thomas** Johannes, Der jüdische PHOKYLIDES .. NT Paränese: NTO(rb)A 23, 1992 → 8,4198; 10,3874: ᴿJThS 46 (1995) 239-242 (M. *Bockmuehl*).

2275 -- **Wilson** Walter, The mysteries of righteousness; the literary composition and genre of the Sentences of Pseudo-PHOCYLIDES: TSAJ 40, 1994 → 10,3882; DM 158: ᴿJSJ(ud) 26 (1995) 231-4 (P.W. van der *Horst*).

2276 **Trevijano Etcheverría** Ramón, Orígenes del cristianismo; el trasfondo judío del cristianismo primitivo: Plenitudo Temporis 3. S 1995, Univ. 475 p. 84-7299-338-8. -- ᴿLum(Vt) 44 (1995) 512s (F. *Ortiz de Urtaran*); RET 55 (1995) 257-9 (P. *Barrado Fernández*).

2277 *Van Leeuwen* C., The relation between the Old and the New Testaments: NESThRev 15,1 (Beirut 1994) 37-58 [NTAb 39, p.439].

2278 **Wright** Christopher J.H., Knowing Jesus through the Old Testament. DG 1995, InterVarsity. xi-256 p. 0-8308-1693-3

2279 **Young** Brad H., Jesus, the Jewish theologian. Peabody MA 1995, Hendrickson. xxxvi-308 p.; bibliog. 283-295. $ 15 pa. 1-56563-060-2 [ThD 43,294].

2280 *Zenger* Erich, Die wiederentdeckte Wurzel; die Christen und ihr sogenanntes Altes Testament → 407. Markierungen 1995, 153-192.

2281 ᴱ**Zenger** Erich, Das Neue Bund im Alten; zur Bundestheologie der beiden Testamente: QD 146, 1993 → 9,421; 10,4213; ᴿMThZ 45 (1994) 219-222 (G. *Gäde*).

B8.1 **Scientia, technologia, Biblia et Ecclesia**

2282 *Adeney* Bernard T., The dark side of technology: Transformation 11,2 (1994) 21-25.

2283 *Antignani* Gerardo, GALILEO Galilei e gli Scolopi: RA(sc)M 20 (1995) 262-272.

2284 *a) Arcidiacono* Salvatore, L'evoluzionismo e le sue frontiere; -- *b) Adriani* Maurilio, La concordia degli antichi avversari: CiVi 50 (1995) 403-41o / 411-8.

2285 *Arnould* Jacques, Le 'créationisme' interroge: Études 382 (1995) 787-798

2286 *Artigas* Mariano, Ciencia y fe; nuevas perspectivas : ScrT(Pamp) 37 (1995) 285-299.

2287 **Atlan** Henri, Enlightenment to enlightenment; intercritique of science and myth. Albany 1993, SUNY. 416 p. $ 59.50. -- ᴿEncounter 56 (1995) 215s (H. *Peebles*: 'persuasive antidote to any imperialistic claim to Absolute Truth').

2288 *Aucker* W. Brian, HODGE & WARFIELD on evolution : Presbyterion 24 (St.Louis 1994) 131-142.

2289 **Aviezer** Nathan, In the beginning; biblical creation and science 1990 → 6,2193; 7,1835: ᴿJETS 38 (1995) 261-3 (R.C. *Newman*).

2290 **Aviezer** Nathan (physics prof., Univ. Bar-Ilan), In principio. Genève 1993, MJR. -- ᴿRasIsr 60,3 (1993) 135s (P.*Giniewski*, ᵀG.*Nahum*).

2291 **Barbour** Ian, Ethics in an age of technology: Gifford Lectures 1990, II: 1993 → 8,2099 ... 10,1751: ᴿ C(alvin)TJ 30 (1995) 509-512 (M. *Bolt*).

2292 **Barbour** Ian, Religion in an age of science 1990 → 6,2195 ... 10,1752 [RStR 22,36-43, Mary *Gerhart*, al.].: ᴿChurchman 108 (L 1994) 188s (D. *Spanner*).

2293 *Barrett* Cyril, Secular theologians of science [... HAWKING, DAWKINS]: MilltSt 36 (1995) 5-16.

2294 ᴱ**Bauman** Michael, Man and creation; perspectives on science and theology (seminar) 1993. 306 p.: ᴿ*PerspSCF 46 (1994) 207s (W.E. *Hamilton*).

2295 **Bayer** Klaus, Evolution -- Kultur -- Sprache; ein Einführung. Bochum 1994, Brockmeyer. 132 p. DM 45. 3-8196-0276-3. -- ᴿUniv 50 (1995) 810s (F.M. *Wucketits*).

2296 **Beretta** Francisco, Galilée devant le tribunal de l'Inquisition; une relecture des sources: diss. *DBedouelle* G. Fribourg 1995. -- RTLv 27, p.542.

2297 **Beukel** A. van den, More things in heaven and earth; God and the scientists [1990, to refute Nobel atheist S. van der MEER], *TBowden* J. 1991 → 8,2103; 10,1754: RChurchman 108 (L 1994) 274s (D. *Spanner*: 'superb').

2298 **Biagioli** Mario, GALILEO, courtier; the practice of science in the culture of absolutism 1993 → 10,1893: R*PerspSCF 47 (1995) 207 (T.T. *Chen*).

2299 **Blackwell** E.J., GALILEO, BELLARMINE .. FOSCARINI 1992 → 9,1895>; RCSt 16 (1995) 655-9 (Gigliola *Fragnito*).

2300 **Blair** Samuel W., The relationship between theology and physics with special reference to time: diss. Queen's. Belfast 1994. 373 p. No photocopy AA. -- DissA 56 (1995s) p. 577.

2301 **Bowker** John, Is God a virus ? [DAWKINS R.] L 1995. SPCK. 274 p. £ 13. 0-281-04812-6. -- RET 106 (1994s) 350 (J. *Polkinghorne*: he rambles also into religion's conflict-proneness and women's ordination).

2302 *Brancazio* Peter J., What is truth ? A course in science and religion: American Journal of Physics 62 (1994) 893-9 [< PerspSCF 47 (1995) 65].

2303 E**Breitenberg** Valentin, *Hosp* Ingo, Evolution, Entwicklung und Organisation in der Natur. Ha-Reinbek 1993, Rowohlt-Tb. 256 p. DM 16.90. 3-499-19706-5. -- RUniv 59 (1995) 1118s (A. *Bahnen*).

2304 **Brewer** Elmer W., The approaches of John POLKINGHORNE, Arthur PEACOCKE, and Ian BARBOUR for the integration of natural science and Christian theology: diss. Southern Baptist Theol. Sem. 1995, *DCunningham* R. 250 p. 95-30691. -- DissA 56 (1995s) p. 1398.

2305 **Brooke** John H., Science and religion; some historical perspectives 1991 → 8,2111 ... 10,1757: RC(alvin)TJ 29 (1994) 233-5 (M. *Bolt*); Churchman 108 (L 1994) 281 (D. *Spanner*).

2306 *Bühler* Pierre, Scienza e fede; l'apporto dell'ermeneutica [< RThP 126 (1994) 143-153]], T: Protest(antesimo) 50 (1995) 126-137; 1 fig.

2307 **Campanella** Thomas, A defense of Galileo, the mathematician from Florence, *TBlackwell* Richard J. ND c.1994,Univ. 157 p. $ 28. -- RAmerica 172,2 (1995) 27-29 (W.A. *Wallace*, also on FANTOLI A., RESTON J.).

2308 **Carles** Jules, Le premier homme. P 1994, Cerf. 124 p. -- RScrT(Pamp) 27 (1995) 1047s (A. *Pardo*).

2309 *Caudill* Edward, The bishop-eaters; the publicity campaign for DARWIN and On the origins of species: JHId 55 (1994) 441-460.

2310 **Charbonneau** Royal J., La métaphore comme passerelle entre science et théologie; vers une théopoésie pour les scientifiques: diss. *DViau* M. Laval 1995. 310 p. -- RTLv 27.p.525.

2311 **Cini** M., Un paradiso perduto; dall'universo delle leggi naturali al mondo dei processi evolutivi. Mi 1994, Feltrinelli. 109 p. L^m 32. -- RStPat(av) 41 (1994) 655-662 (N. *Dallaporta*).

2312 **Clouser** Roy A., The myth of religious neutrality; an essay on the hidden role of religious belief in theories 1991 → 7,1851; 10,1766: RRefR 49 (1995s) 64 (T.K. *Johnson*).

2313 **Conser** Walter H., God and the natural world; religion and science in antebellum America. Columbia 1993, Univ. S.Carolina. 191 p. $ 35. - RJRel 75 (1995) 285s (B.K. *Turley*).

2314 **Corey** Michael A,, Back to DARWIN; the scientific case for deistic evolution 1994 → 10,1771: RPerspSCF 47 (1995) 274s (J. *Wing*).

2315 **Craig** William L., *Smith* Quentin, Theism, atheism, and Big Bang cosmology 1993 →
10,1772: ᴿTS 56 (1995) 383-5 (F.R. *Haig*).

2316 **Creager** John A., Theodynamics; Neochristian perspectives for the modern world.
Lanham MD 1994, UPA. 452 p. $ 54.50. -- ᴿPerspSCF 47 (1995) 55s (J. de *Koning*).

2317 **Davies** Paul, The mind of God 1992 → 8,2130; 9,1910: ᴿ(Reformed) Perspectives 9,2
(1994) 22 (D.E. *Wray*: beyond the Big Bang).

2318 *Davis* Edward, Fundamentalism and folk-science [anti-evolutionism] between the wars;
R&AC(u) 5 (1995) 217-248.

2319 *Dawari* Ridā, Relationship between religion and science; conflict or conformity ? :
Hikmat 1 (Tehran 1995s) 525-533.

2320 **De Young** Donald B., Science and the Bible; 30 scientific demonstrations illustrating
scriptural truths. GR 1994, Baker. 110 p. $ 7. : PerspSCF 47 (1995) 272 (F.F. *Fleming*).

2321 *a) Dooyeweerd* Herman, La sécularisation de la science (1953); -- *b*) Bibliographie; -
c) Dengerink Jan D., Herman Dooyeweerd [1894-1977]; philosophe, chrétien, Réformé,
Œcuménique: RRéf 46,3 (1995) 19-37 / 38 / 1-18.

2322 *Drees* Willem B., Gelovend denken, denkend geloven of geschieden zaken ? Overzicht
van onderzoek over natuurwetenschap en geloof in Nederland, 1980-1994 : NedThT 49
(1995) 291-311; Eng. 312.

2323 **Drees** William B., Beyond the Big Bang 1990 → 5,2039 ... 8,2124: ᴿS(cot)JTh 48
(1995) 109s. (J.C. *Puddefoot*)

2324 **Fantoli** Annibale, GALILEO, for Copernicanism and for the Church, ᵀ*Coyne* G. 1994
→ 10,1784: ᴿTS 56 (1995) 369-371 (E *McMullin*).

2325 **Fantoli** A., GALILEO, per il copernicanismo e per la Chiesa 1993 → 10,1783:
ᴿAsprenas 42 (1995) 615-7 (M. *Caleo*).

2326 **Feldhay** Rivka, GALILEO and the Church; political inquisition or critical dialogue. C
1995, Univ. viii-303 p. $ 55. 0-521-34468-9 [RStR 22,254, D.R. *Janz*].

2327 **Ferguson** Terry A., An analysis and evaluation of Stanley JAKI's creational
apologetics; answers to science's unanswered questions: diss. Calvin GR, ᴰ*Cooper* J. -- CTJ
30 (1995) 654.

2328 **Ferré** Frederick, Hellfire and lightning rods; liberating science, technology and
religion: Ecology and Justice. Mkn 1993, Orbis. xv-223 p. $25. -- ᴿAmJTP 16 (1995)
229-232 (E.J. *Tarbox*); TorJT 11 (1995) 129s (J. *Farris*); RTPh 127 (1995) 312s (Clairette
Karakash)

2329 **Friedman** Norman, Bridging science and spirit; common elements in David BOHM's
physics, the perennial philosophy and Seth. St.Louis 1994, Living Lake. 320 p. $ 15.
0-9636-4700-8. -- ᴿJPsT 23 (1995) 60-62 (D. *Peters*).

2330 **Gascoigne** Robert M., The history of the creation; a Christian view of inorganic and
organic evolution. Sydney 1993, Fast. 326 p. -- ᴿAus(tralas)CR 72 (1995) 495 (D.
Edwards).

2331 **Gibeson** Karl, Worlds apart; the unholy war between religion and science. KC 1993,
Beacon Hill. 224 p. $ 17 pa. -- ᴿC(alvin)TJ 30 (1995) 514-517 (D.L. *Ratzsch*).

2332 **Gilkey** Langdon, Nature, reality, and the sacred 1993 → 10,1796: ᴿA(ndr)USS 33
(1995) 300-2 (M.F. *Hanna*); Dialog 34 (1995) 71s (G.L. *Murphy*); PerspSCF 47 (1995) 138s
(B.J. *Piersma*).

2333 **Gismondi** Gualberto, Fede e cultura scientifica. Bo 1993. 230 p. -- ᴿ*AnT 9 (1995)
175-8 (G. *Tanzella-Nitti*).

2334 *Gootjes* Nicolaas H., General revelation and science: C(alvin)TJ 30 (1995) 94-107.

2335 **Haught** John F., Science and religion; from conflict to conversation. NY 1995, Paulist. iii-225 p. $ 15. 0-8091-3606-6 [< ThD 43,272].

2336 *Hayes* Zachary, God & theology in an age of scientific culture: NewThR 8,3(1995) 5-18.

2337 **Hefner** Philip, The human factor; evolution, culture, and religion: Theology and the Sciences, 1993 → 9,1927; 10,1804: ᴿTBR 8,1 (1995s) 31 (D. *Atkinson*).

2338 **Herrmann** Eberhard, Scientific theory and religious belief; an essay on the rationality of views of life: Studies in Philosophical Theology 16. Kampen 1995, Kok Pharos. 127 p. *f* 70. 90-390-0222-3. -- ᴿEThL 71 (1995) 477s (V. *Neckebrouck*, Eng.).

2339 **Holton** Gerald, Science and anti-science [... LONERGAN]. CM 1994, Harvard Univ. x-203 p. -- ᴿLandas 9 (Manila 1995) 295s (V. *Marasigan*).

2340 *Hutchison* John C., DARWIN's evolutionary theory and 19th-century natural theology: BS 152 (1995) 334-354.

2341 **Jaki** Stanley J., Genesis I through the ages. L 1992, T.More. xii/317 p. 1-897713-00-2 -- ᴿGreg 76 (1995) 759s (P. *Haffner*).

2342 **Jaki** Stanley L., Is there a universe ? [Liverpool Univ. Forwood Lectures 1993] 1993 → 10,1808; 1-884530-02-8: ᴿAng 72 (1995) 329s (A. *Lobato*); DR 113 (1995) 308-311 (D. *O'Keeffe*); Faith & Reason 21 (1995) 280-7 (T.B. *Fowler*).

2343 -- *Pham* John Peter, The importance of the reality of the universe in the world of S.L.Jaki: Faith & Reason 21 (1995) 337-354.

2344 *Johansson* Sverker, Är kreationismen vetenskapligt hållbar ? : SvTK 68 (1992) 19-28 [162-171, *Görman* Ulf].

2345 **Johnson** Phillip E., Reason in the balance; the case against naturalism in science, law and education. DG 1995, InterVarsity. 245 p. $ 20 [RStR 22,137, S.M. *Heim*].

2346 *Kaiser* Christopher, Creation and the history of science: [ᴱ*Avis* P.] History of Christian Theology 3, 1991 → 8,2147 ... 10,1813: ᴿChurchman 108 (L 1994) 279s (D. *Spanner*); S(cot)JTh 48 (1995) 104-6 (P. *Murray*).

2347 **Khursheed** Anjam, The universe within; an exploration of the human spirit [while taking science seriously]. L 1995, One World. 192 p. £ 10. 1-85168-075-6. -- ᴿE(xp)T 106 (1994s) 284s (J. *Polkinghorne*).

2348 *a) King* Thomas M., An explosion of dazzling flashes; TEILHARD's unity of faith and science; -- *b) Heller* Michael, Teilhard's vision of the world and modern cosmology; -- *c) Galleni* Lodovico, How does the Teilhardian vision of evolution compare with contemporary theories: Zygon 30,1 (1995) 105-115 / 11-23 / 25-45.

2349 *a) Knapp* Andreas, 'Gut und Böse' im Spannungsfeld von Naturwissenschaft und Theologie, -- *b) Riesenhuber* Heinz, Die ethische Verantwortung der Wissenschaft: *ZMedEth 41 (1995) 9-27 / 173-184.

2350 **Kohli** Mary Ann, Cosmic Christ in a quantum universe: diss. South Carolina 1994. 281 p. 95-17285. -- DissA 56 (1995s) p. 192.

2351 **Koltermann** Rainer, Grundzüge der modernen Natur-Philosophie; ein kritischer Gesamtentwurf. Fra 1994, Knecht. 423 p. DM 49. 3-7820-068-9. -- ᴿThGL 85 (1995) 293-5 (D. *Hattrup*).

2352 *Konyndyk* Kenneth J., AQUINAS on faith and science : FAP(hil) 12 (1995) 3-21.

2353 *a) Kozhamthadam* Job, Can religion give science a heart ? -- *b) Ott* Heinrich (interview), Experience of the holy in the technological age; -- *c) Sweet* William, Technology and change in religious belief; -- *d) Malcolmson* Patrick, *Nyers* Richard, Technology and Mother Earth; the ROUSSEAUian roots of the debate: JDharma 18 (1993) 139-161 / 106-113 / 124-138 / 162-178.

2354 *Lerner* Berel D., *Omphalos* [P.J. GOSSE anti-evolution hypothesis] revisited: JBQ 23 (1995) 162-7.

2355 **Loder** James E., *Neidhardt* W. Jim, The knight's move; the relational logic of the Spirit in theology and science. Colorado Springs 1992, Helmers & H. xv-350 p. $ 25. -- RP(rinc)SB 16 (1995) 345-7 (W.Mark *Richardson*); S(cot)JTh 48 (1995) 139s (T.F. *Torrance*).

2356 *Löw* Reinhard, Evolution und System: Univ 50 (1995) 621-631.

2357 **Löw** Reinhard, Die neuen Gottebeweise. Augsburg 1994, Pattloch. 207 p., DM 34. 3-629-00651-5. -- RThGL 85 (1995) 137-9 (D. *Hattrup*).

2358 **Maldamé** Jean-Michel, Le Christ et le cosmos; incidence de la cosmologie moderne sur la théologie 1993 → 9,1951: RBLE 95 (1994) 233-8 (M.J. *Nicolas*); RTL 26 (1995) 253s (J.-M. *Counet*).

2359 EMark A. Beltrán, Galileo GALILEI: diálogo sobre los dos máximos sistemas del mundo, ptolemaico y copernicano. M 1994, Alianza. 417 p. -- RRF 232 (1995) 122 (A. *Udías*).

2360 *Mills* Gordon C., A theory of theistic evolution as an alternative to the naturalistic theory: PerspSCF 47 (1995) 112-122.

2361 **Minois** Georges, L'Église et la science; histoire d'un malentendu 1990 → 6,2241; 8,2167b: RRF 231 (1995) 215s (A. *Udías*).

2362 **Montenat** Christian, *al.*, Pour lire la Création dans l'Évolution². P c.1994, Cerf. 144 p. F 80. -- RE(spr)eV 105 (1995) 169 (L. *Monloubou*).

2363 **Moore** James, The DARWIN legend [of near-death conversion (with ? repudiation of evolution)]. GR 1994, Baker. 318 p. -- RPerspSCF 47 (1995) 267s (T.J. *Trenn*).

2364 *Morandini* Simone, Tra scienza e teologia; sul 'virtuale' [La 'realtà virtuale' (RV) sta passando dal linguaggio tecnico dell'informatica al parlare quotidiano: StPat(av) 41 (1994) 610-613.

2365 EMoreland J.P., The creation hypothesis; scientific evidence for an intelligent designer 1994 → 10,1832: RBS 152 (1995) 233s (R.A. *Pyne*); PerspSCF 47 (1995) 123-131 (H.J. *Van Till*: 'special creationism in designer clothing'); RefR 49 (1995s) 57 (D. *Wacome*).

2366 EMott Nevill, Can scientists believe ? Some examples of the attitude of scientists to religion. L c. 1991, James & James. 182 p. £ 21. 0-907383--54-8. -- RChurchman 108 (L 1994) 183-5 (D. *Spanner*).

2367 *Motta* Franco, Due copie della lettera di GALILEO a Cristina di Lorena tra sei e settecento; ASEs 12 (1995) 129-143.

2368 *Muratore* Saturnino, Futuro del cosmo, futuro dell'uomo: CivCatt 146 (1995,3) 107-121.

2369 **Murphy** Nancey, Theology in the age of scientific reasoning 1990 → 8,2170; 10,1838: RFAP(hil) 12 (1995) 277-282 (D. *Ratzsch*).

2370 **Nebelsick** Harold P., Renaissance and Reformation and the rise of science 1992 → 8,2172 ... 10,1839: Interpretation 49 (1995) 94 . 96 .98 (C. B. *Kaiser*).

2371 *Newman* Robert C., Scientific problems for scientism : Presbyterion 21 (St.Louis 1995) 73-88.

2372 *Newman* Robert C., Scientific and religious aspects of the origins debate: PerspSCF 47 (1995) 164-175 [177-186, *Lothers* John E.ʲ]

2373 **Newton** Roger G., What makes nature tick ? CM 1993, Harvard Univ. 257 p. $ 28. -- RPerspSCF 47 (1995) 55 (A.A. *Louis*).

2374 **Numbers** Ronald L., The creationists; the evolution of scientific creationism 1992 → 9,1965; 10,1843: RChH 64 (1995) 526s (W.G. *O'Neill*).

2375 **Pannenberg** Wolfhart, Towards a theology of nature; essays on science and faith 1993 → 9,228a: *ProEc 4 (1995) 251-3 (J. *Polkinghorne*).

2376 **Pannenberg** Wolfhart, Teoría de la ciencia y teología. M 1981, Europa. 462 p. 84-7057-293-8.

2377 *Pannenberg* Wolfhart, a) Theology of creation and natural science; -- b) The emergence of creatures and their succession in a developing universe: -- c) Christianity and secularism: AsbTJ 50 (1995) 5-15 / 17-25 / 27-35.

2378 *Paredes Muñoz* J.A., Fe y ciencias; dos dimensiones humanas: Isidorianum (1992,1) 51-59.

2379 **Peacocke** Arthur, Theology for a scientific age; being and becoming -- natural, divine, and human[2rev] 1993 → 9,1969; 10,1844: [R]PerspSCF 47 (1995) 58s (P.K. *Wason*).

2380 a) *Peacocke* Arthur, The challenge of science to the thinking Church; -- b) *Polkinghorne* John, Contemporary interactions between science and theology; -- c) *Knight* Christopher, A new deism? Science, religion and revelation; -- d) *Watts* Fraser, Science and eschatology: Modern Believing [continuing the numbering of Modern Churchman] 36,4 (1995) 15-26 / 33-38 / 38-47 / 48-52.

2381 **Pearcey** Nancy R., *Thaxton* Charles B., The soul of science; Christian faith and natural philosophy 1994 → 10,1845: [R]C(alvin)TJ 30 (1995) 585-9 (C. *Menninga*); PerspSCF 47 (1995) 204s (W.R. *Hearn*); RefR 49 (1995s) 149 (D.H. *Wacome*).

2382 **Peitz** Heinz-Hermann, Kriterien für den Dialog zwischen Naturwissenschaften und Theologie; Entfaltung und Operationalisierung wissenschaftlicher Implikate im Werk von Karl RAHNER: kath. Diss. [D]*Pottmeyer*. Bochum 1995. -- ThRv Beilage 92/2,vi.

2383 **Polkinghorne** John, Science and Christian belief (Gifford Lectures; SPCK) 1994 → 10,1850: [R]ChrSchR 25 (1995s) 365-7 (R. *Carlson*).

2384 **Polkinghorne** John, The faith of a physicist (Princeton) 1994 → 10,1847: [R]PerspSCF 47 (1995) 267 (W.R. *Hearn*); TTod 51 (1994s) 613s (*D. Allen*).

2385 **Polkinghorne** John C., Serious talk; science and religion in dialogue. Ph 1995, Trinity ix-117 p. $ 13.50. 1-56338-109-5 [ThD 43,81].

2386 *Polkinghorne* John, A scientist's approach to belief: SewaneeTR 39 (1995s) 11-50.

2387 *Ponterrada* G.E., ¿ Rehabilitación de Galileo ? SapDom 49 (1994) 241-272 [< ATG(ran) 58 (1995) 307s].

2388 **Predel** Gregor M., Sakrament der Gegenwart Gottes; die Interaktion von Gott und Natur in der Sicht von Arthur R. PEACOCKE; Diss. [D]*Riedlinger*. Freiburg/Br 1995. -- ThRv Beilage 92/2, viii.

2389 a) *Provine* William, Evolution and the foundation of ethics: Science 3 (Marine Biological Laboratory 1988) 27s: science imposes the view that there is no moral law, freedom, or life after death; -- b) [refutation by] *Augros* Robert M., Does science say that human existence is pointless ?: Thom 59 (1995) 577-589.

2390 *Quay* Paul M., Final causality in contemporary physics: URM 18 (1995) 3-19.

2391 RACHELS: *Dombrowski* Daniel A., On theism as the cause of agnosticism; the case of the Darwinian James Rachels: URM 18 (1995) 275-288.

2392 **Rae** Murray, al., Science and theology question at thr interface, 1993. GR 1994, Eerdmans. 0-8028-0816-6.

2393 **Reston** James [J], GALILEO, a life. NY 1994, HarperCollins. xiii-319 p. $ 25. -- [R]C(ath)HR 81 (1995) 84-86 (W.E. *Carroll*).

2394 *Rivier* Dominique, Une réflexion sur les rapports entre science et foi: RTPh 127 (1995) 55-61; Eng. 111.

2395 **Ross** Hugh, Creation and time; a biblical and scientific perspective on the creation-date controversy. Colorado Springs 1994, Navpress. 187 p. $ 10 pa. [JETS 39, 307s, P. *Copan*].

2396 *Rostagno* Sergio, La speranza cristiana interpellata dalle scienze del futuro [... TIPLER F. 1993s; ASIMOV I. 1971 ²1994: convegno ATI-Nord, Torino 14-15.IX.1994]: RasT 36 (1995) 427-445.

2397 *Schwager* Raymund, Evolution, Erbsünde und Erlösung: ZkT 117 (1995) 1-24; Eng. 24.

2398 **Seely** Paul H., Inerrant wisdom; science and inerrancy in biblical perspective. Portland OR 1989, Evangelical Reform. 216 p. $ 12 pa. -- ᴿC(alvin)TJ 29 (1994) 623 (C.P. *Venema*).

2399 **Segre** Michael, Nel segno di GALILEO (La scuola Galileiana tra storia e mito) [1991 → 10,1860], ᵀ: UnivPa 280. Bo 1993, Mulino. 224 p. Lᵐ 20. 88-15-04113-3. -- ᴿSalesianum 57 (1995) 563s (M. *Müller*); StCatt 39 (1995) 75 (R. *Cittadini*).

2400 **Selleri** Franco, Física sin dogma; el conocimiento científico a través de sus avances y retrocesos. M 1994, Aliança. 237 p. -- ᴿRF 231 (1995) 327 (A. *Udías*).

2401 *Seweryniak* Henryk, ᴾ Évolutionnismes d'aujourd'hui et foi en la création: PrzPow 891 (1995) 139-149.

2402 *Sierotowicz* Tadeusz, Le visioni del mondo come spazio del dialogo tra scienza e teologia: Vivarium 3 (1995) 425-435.

2403 **Sproul** R.C., Not a chance! The myth of chance in modern science and cosmology. GR 1994, Baker. 224 p. $ 16 pa. -- ᴿPerspSCF 47 (1995) 63 (D. *Pleticha*) & 212s (R.M. *Bowman*)

2404 *Stagliano* Antonio, Male cosmico e male morale nel dialogo tra teologia e scienza; congresso ATI/centro 26-27 settembre 1994: VivH 6 (1995) 187-198.

2405 *Tanzella-Nitti* Giuseppe, The relevance of Aristotelian-Thomistic concept of nature to the contemporary debate between science and theology: *AnT 9 (1995) 107-125.

2406 **Templeton** John M., Evidence of purpose; scientists discover the Creator. NY 1994, Continuum. 312 p. $ 34.50. -- ᴿPerspSCF 47 (1995) 205-7 (F.F. *Fleming*).

2407 **Tiffin** Lee, Creation's upside down pyramid; how science refutes fundamentalism [→ 10,1868: Amherst] NY 1994, Prometheus. 229 p. 0-87975-898-8. -- ᴿPerspSCF 47 (1995) 277-9 (J.W. *Burgeson*); TBR 8,1 (1995s) 40 (J. *Polkinghorne*).

2408 **Toumey** Christopher P., God's own scientists; creationists in a secular world 1994 → 10,1872: $ 45; pa. $ 15: ᴿPerspSCF 46 (1994) 266-8 (J.W. *Haas*).

2409 *Turnock* Jeffrey, Faith in a world of science: PrPe 9 (1995) 376-380.

2410 **Weatherly** Alan B., Christ and quarks; the spirituality of Jesus and postmodern science: diss. United Theol. Sem., ᴰ*Olson* Mary, 1994. 261 p. 95-21895. -- DissA 56 (1995s) p.976.

2411 **Weaver** John D., In the beginning God: modern science and the Christian doctrine of creation: Regent's Park College Study guides. L 1994, Smyth & H. 209 p. 1-880837-82-X. -- ᴿE(xp)T 107 (1995s) 58 (R.G. *Jones*: downplays Col 1,16; also the bloodiness and costliness of evolution).

2412 **Webb** George E., The evolution controversy in America. Lexington 1994, Univ. Kentucky. 297 p. $ 35. -- ᴿCCen 112 (1995) 59s (M.H. *Macdonald*); PerspSCF 47 (1995) 204s (C. *Wingard*).

2413 *Westhelle* Viktor, Scientific sight and embodied knowledge; social circumstances in science and theology: MoTh 11 (1995) 341-361.

2414 *Wuketits* Franz M., Evolution durch Zufall ? Zufall und Plan, Freiheit und Gesetz in der Evolution des Lebenden: Univ 47 (1992) 1153-1163.

2415 **Young** Davis A., The biblical flood; a case-study of the Church's response to [paleontologically obsolete] extrabiblical evidence. GR/.. 1995, Eerdmans/Paternoster. 327 p. $ 20. 0-8028-0719-8 / 0-85364-678-3. -- RE(xp)T 107 (1995s) 53 (C.S.*Rodd*: clear and readable warning to fellow-conservatives); PerspSCF 47 (1995) 282 (J.W. *Burgeson*); *BR 8,1 (1995s) 14 (R. *Coggins*, dismayed by arrogant evangelicals and USA creationism fantasies).

2416 **Zilles** Urbano, Criação ou evolução ? : Debates 1. Porto Alegre 1995, EDIPUCRS. 35 p. -- RTeocomunicação 25 (1995) 403-5 (R.A. *Ullmann*).

B8.5 *Sacra Scriptura et mythus* -- **The Bible and myths of origins**

2417 *Avraham* Nahum, on Gilgamesh and the Flood: BetM 40,2 (141, 1995) 156-161.

2418 *Babalola* E.O., Cosmogonic stories in the indigenous religion of the Yoruba and the Bible; a comparative investigation: Bible Bhashyam 21 (1995) 204-214.

2419 **Batto** Bernard F., Slaying the dragon; mythmaking in the biblical tradition 1992 → 9,1867; 10,1716: RA(ustrl)BR 42 (1994) 110s (D.C. *Sim*); JR(el) 75 (1995) 102 (J.J.M. *Roberts*).

2420 **Bickel** Susanne, La cosmologie égyptienne avant le Nouvel Empire: OBO 134, 1994 → 10,1718; Fs 98: RDiscEg 33 (1995) 169-171 (Rosalind *Park*); OTA 18 (1995) p. 143.

2421 **Butler** E. M., The myth of the magus [1948: Moses, Solomon .. Faust, Rasputin]. C 1993, Univ. xiv-282 p. £ 8 pa. 0-521-43777-6. -- RBoL (1995) 124s (N. *Wyatt*: high-quality and entertaining intertextuality).

2422 **Callender** Dexter E.J, The significance and use of primal man traditions in ancient Israel [Adapa; also Job 15,7s: Ezek 28,11-19]; diss.Harvard, DHackett Jo Ann. CM 1995. 276 p. 95-39073. -- DissA 56 (1995s) p.2726; HThR 88 (1995) 524s.

2423 **Carmody** Denise L., Mythological woman; contemporary reflections on ancient religious stories. NY 1992, Crossroad. 160 p. $ 12. -- RTorJT 11 (1995) 124s (Ellen M. *Leonard*, also on her Virtuous woman 1992).

2424 **Clifford** Richard J., Creation accounts .. ; CBQ mg 26, 1994 → 10,1721*: RRExp 92 (1995) 523-5 (J.F. *Drinkard*, commending also SIMKINS R. & ANDERSON B., 1994); SBF*LA 45 (1995) 580-4 (E. *Cortese*).

2425 *Davila* James R., The flood hero as king and priest: JNES 54 (1995) 199-214.

2426 **Delumeau** Jean, History of paradise; the Garden of Eden in myth and tradition (vol. 1 of 3, 1992 → 9,2004), TO'Connell Matthew. NY 1995, Continuum. x-276 p.; ill.; 25 maps. $ 19.50. 0-8264-0795-1 [< ThD 43,264; RStR 22,251, J. *Gaffney*].

2427 **Delumeau** Jean, Storia del Paradiso; il giardino delle delizie [1992], TGrasso Luciana: Le occasioni 55. Bo 1994, Mulino. 322 p. Lᵐ 36. 88-15-04685-2. -- RCiVi 50 (1995) 99 (S. *Spartà*).

2428 *Dietrich* Manfred, *ina ūmī ullûti*, 'An jenen (fernen) Tagen'; ein sumerisches kosmogonisches Mythologem in babylonischer Tradition: → 185, FSODEN W.von, Vom Alten Orient (1995) 57-72.

2429 *Dyk* P.J. van, A folkloristic approach to the OT: OTEssays 7,4 (1994? 93-98 [< OTA 18 (1995) p. 462].

2430 *Farber* Gertrud, 'Inanna and Enki' in Geneva; a Sumerian myth revisited: JNES 54 (1995) 287-292; 2 fig.

2431 *Forestell* J.T., *a)* The Church and the Bible; the interpretation of the Bible in the Church; -- *b)* Myth and biblical revelation: CanadCath 13,7 (1995) 11-21 / 13,2 (1995) 19-21.

2432 **Gibert** Pierre, Bibbia, miti e racconti dell'inizio [1986],[T]: BtBi 11. Brescia 1993, Queriniana. 247 p. L[m] 30. -- [R]NRT 117 (1995) 172 (J.-L. *Ska*); PaVi 39,5 (1994) 55s (S. *Migliasso*).

2433 *Hendel* Ronald S., The shape of Utnapishtim's ark: ZAW 107 (1995) 128s.

2434 *Huggins* Ronald V., Noah and the giants: JBL [112 (1993) 110] 114 (1995) 103-110.

2435 **Jackson** Danny P.[T], The epic of Gilgamesh 1992 → 8,2309; 10,1985: [R]*Prudentia 27,1 (1995) 79-91 (J. de *Kuyper*).

2436 *Jason* Heda, Biblical literature and epic folk tradition; some folkloristic thoughts: OTEs 8 (1995) 280-290.

2437 *Kister* M.J., Ādam; a study of some legends in Tafsīr and Ḥadīt literature: I(sr)OS 13 (1993) 113-174.

2438 **Kunin** Seth D., The logic of incest; a structuralist analysis of Hebrew mythology: JSOT.s 185. Shf 1995, Academic. 297 p. £ 32.50. 1-85075-509-4: [R]E(xp)T 107 (1995s) 56s, with seven other titles).

2439 *Kuwabara* Toshikazu, A comparison of the cosmic concept of the earth in Sumero-Akkadian literature and in the Old Testament: AnJap 20 (1994) 45-58.

2440 *a)* *Lee* A.C.C., The Chinese creation myth of Nu Kua and the narrative of Genesis 1-11; -- *b)* *Premnath* D.N., The concepts of Rta and Maat; a study in comparison: BInterp 2 (1994s) 312-324 / 325-339 [< ZAW 107 (1995) 308].

2441 **Loh** Johannes, Mythenlogik als praktisch-theologische Herausforderung biblischer Texte, dargestellt am Paradiesmythos: ev. Hab.-Diss. [D]*Schröer*. Bonn 1995. -- TR 92,iii (1996 Fasz.2, Beilage p.136).

2442 **Luginbühl** Marianne, Menschenschöpfungsmythen; ein Vergleich zwischen Griechenland und dem Alten Orient: EHS 15/58. Fra 1992, Lang. 296 p.; 10 pl. Fs 25. 3-261-04533-7. -- [R]BoL (1995) 133 (J.R. *Porter*).

2443 *Müller* H.-P., Mythos als Elementarform religiöser Rede im Alten Orient und im Alten Testament; zur Theorie der biblischen Theologie: NZSTh 37 (1995) 1-19 [NTAb 40,p.77].

2444 **Niditch** Susan, Folklore and the Hebrew Bible 1993 → 9,1879; 10,1739: [R]JRelB 75 (1995) 263s (J.J. *Collins*); (Reformed) Perspectives 9,5 (1994) 20s (Christiana *de Graaf van Houten*).

2445 *Niehoff* Marvin, The return of myth in Genesis Rabbah on the Akeda: → 211, [F]VERMES G., JJS 46 (1995) 69-87.

2446 **Penglase** Charles, Greek myths and Mesopotamia: parallels and influence in the Homeric Hymns and Hesiod 1994 → 10,1743; £ 40: [R]BoL (1995) 136 (N. *Wyatt*).

2447 **Rohl** David M., A test of time, 1. The Bible from myth to history. L 1995, Century. xiv-425 p.; bibliog. 407-412. 0-7126-5913-7.

2448 *Schmidt* W.H., Mythos und Ausschliesslichkeit des Glaubens: → 523, Bible 1992/4, 295-312.

2449 *Sellin* G., Der Mythos nach Markus; warum Glaube und Theologie auf mythische Vorstellungen angewiesen sind: EK 27 (1994) 715-7 [NTAb 39,p.379: Mark is 'myth', not that it has no historical foundation, but it gives us symbols and its narrative is an epiphany].

2450 *Stolz* Fritz, Paradies religionsgeschichtlich/biblisch: → 772, TRE 25 (1995) 705-711.

2451 **Tournay** Raymond-Jacques, *Shafter* Aaron, L'épopée de Gilgamesh; introduction, traduction et notes LAPO 15, 1994 → 10,1989 [RStR 22,148, D.I. *Owen*]: [R]ÉTRel 70 (1995)

265s (Françoise *Smyth*); OL(ov)P 26 (1995) 205 (E. *Lipiński*); POrC 45 (1995) 294s (P. *Ternant*); RevSR 69 (1995) 528s (J.-M. *Husser*).

2452 **Treumann** Rudolf, Die Elemente, Feuer, Erde, Luft und Wasser in Mythos und Wissenschaft. Mü 1994, Hanser. DM 50. 3-446-17837-6. -- [R]ThGL 85 (1995) 418s (D. *Hattrup*).

2453 *Wheeler* Stephen M., Imago mundi; another view of the creation in OVID's Metamorphoses : AJP(g) 116 (1995) 96-121.

2454 **Wright** M.R., Cosmology in antiquity; Sciences of Antiquity. L 1995, Routledge. x-201 p.; 16 fig. $ 60; pa. $ 18. 0-415-08372-9 [NTAb 40, p.567].

III. Critica Textus, Versiones

D1 **Textual criticism**

2455 *Aejmelaeus* A. [AT p.316-322], *Aland* Barbara [NT, on EPP-FEE], Methodenfragen der biblischen Textkritik: ThR(u) 60 (1995) 316-329 [NTAb 40,p.203].

2456 **Agati** Maria Luisa, La minuscola 'bouletée ' 1992 → 10,1343: [R]ByZ 88 (1995) 156s (P. *Schreiner*); Speculum 70 (1995) 106-8 (L. *Brubaker*); VizVrem 56 (1995) 365s (N.F. *Kavrus-Khoffmann*).

2457 *Álvarez Valdés* Ariel, Qui a divisé la Bible en chapitres ? La Terre Sainte (sept.1995): [R]E(spr)eV 105 (1995) 597s (J. *Daoust*).

2458 [E]**Barthélemy** Dominique, Critique textuelle 3, Ez Dan XII: OBO 50/3, 1992 → 8,1689 ... 10,1345: [R]BO 52 (1995) 112-5 (P.B. *Dirksen*); JJS 45 (1994) 299s (S. *Brock*).

2459 *Bastianini* Guido, *Biblíon elissómenon*; sull'avvolgimento dei rotoli opistografi: -> 10,42, [F]GIGANTE M., Storia 1994, 45-48.

2460 [E]**Bataillon** Louis J., *al.*, La production du livre universitaire au Moyen Age; exemplar et pecia. P 1988, CNRS. 334 p.; XIX pl. -- [R]AKuG 76 (1994) 493-5 (I. *Hlavácek*, auch über LEMAIRE J. 1989).

2461 **Blanck** Horst, Das Buch in der Antike 1992 → 9,1313; 10,1346: [R]QSt 40 (1994) 197-201 (Rosa *Otranto*).

2462 **Bologna** Giulia, Manoscritti e miniature; il libro prima di Gutenberg. Mi 1994, Fenice 2000. 197 p. 88-8017-108-9.

2463 **Borrecht** Hans-Albert, Kleine Einführung in die Papyruskunde: AltertW. Da 1994, Wiss. 274 p. 3-534-04493-2. -- [R]ActuBbg 31 (1994) 323 (J. *O'Callaghan*).

2464 **Capasso** Mario, Volumen; aspetti della tipologia del rotolo librario antico: Cultura, dall'Antico al Moderno 2. N 1995, Procaccini. 162 p.

2465 *Capasso* Mario, *Davoli* Paola, Una presunta raffigurazione di un rotolo di papiro in miniatura del Museo Archeologico Nazionale di Napoli: StEgPun 14 (1995) 7-10 + 1 fig.

2466 **Carcel Ortí** María Milagros, Vocabulaire international de la diplomatique. Valencia 1994, Consellería. 308 p. 84-370-1520-0. -- [R]RHE 90 (1995) 493s (B.-M. *Tock*).

2467 Carta azzurra, mostra di libri: Hebrew printing on blue paper. L 1995, British Library. -- [R]Raslsr 61 (1995) 201s (P. *Bernardini*).

2468 **Duft** Johannes, Die Abtei St. Gallen, I., Beiträge zur Erforschung seiner Manuskripte. Sigmaringen 1990, Thorbecke. xiv-275 p. 3-7995-7066-7. -- [R]Salesianum 57 (1995) 141s (F. *Meyer*).

2469 *Fernández-Marcos* Natalio, Recent Spanish research on the biblical texts: *BSeptC 26 (1993) 22-34 [NTAb 40, p.13].

2470 **Grafinger** Christina Maria, Die Ausleihe vatikanischer Handschriften und Druckwerke (1563-1700): StT 360. Vaticano 1993, Biblioteca apostolica. lix-724 p. 88-210-0653-0.

2471 **Haidinger** Alois, Katalog der Handschriften des Augustiner Chorherrenstiftes Klosterneuburg 2. Cod. 101-200: Denkschr ph/h 225. W 1991, Österr, Akad. xx-191 p.; Beiheft. -- ᴿRHE 90 (1995) 593s (T. *Falmagne*).

2472 *Haran* Menahem, ᴴ On archives, libraries and the order of the biblical books: → 10,63, ᶠKAMIN S., The Bible 1994, 221-234 [< OTA 18 (1995) p. 450 (J. *Corely*)].

2473 *Havas* László, La critique de textes et les humanistes: AAH 36 (1995) 359-365.

2474 *Irigoin* Jean, Pour un bon usage des abréviations; le cas du Vaticanus graecus 1611 et du Barocci 50: Scr(iptoriumBru) 48 (1994) 3-17.

2475 *Johnson* W.A., Macrocollum [Pliny NH 13,80: wide not long sheet]: CP 89 (1994) 62-64 [< NTAb 38, p.341].

2476 *Leach* Bridget,Tanning tests for 2 documents written on animal skin:JEA 81(1995)241-3.

2477 *Liberati* Anna Maria, *Pesando* Fabrizio, Libri e letture nel mondo romano: Archeo 124 (1995) 62-97 [106-8, *Pernigotti* Sergio, il papiro in Egitto].

2478 ᴱ**Manfredi** Manfredo, Dai papiri della società italiana; omaggio al XXI congresso internazionale di papirologia Berlino 13-18 agosto 1995. F 1995, Istituto Papirologico Vitelli. 131 p.; XVI pl.

2479 *Maniaci* Marilena, Ricette di costruzione della pagina nei manoscritti greci e latini: ScrBru 49 (1995) 16-41.

2480 *Matzukis* C., Observations on scribes and manuscripts (14th-16th centuries): AcPByz 6 (Pretoria 1995) 109-118.

2481 *Murphy* David J., Hyphens in Greek manuscripts: GRBS 36 (1995) 293-314; 5 pl.

2482 **Netzer** Nancy, Cultural interplay in the eighth century; the Trier Gospels and the making of a scriptorium at Echternach: StPalaeog 3. C 1994, Univ. xvi-258 p. $ 65. 0-521-41255-2 [ThD 42,282].-- ᴿRH 293 (1995) 159-162 (J. *Bousquet*).

2483 *Norton* Gerard J., Changing patterns in the study of the history of the biblical text [.... unrealistic to seek a 'final form']: Hermathena 154 (1993) 19-37 [< OTA 18 (1995) p. 459].

2484 **Parkinson** R., *Quirke* S., Papyrus [manufacture ... storage]. Austin 1995, Univ. Texas. 96 p.; ill. $ 20. 0-292-76563-0 [NTAb 40, p.381].

2485 *Paul* André, Genèse et destin du livre: Études 383 (1995) 643-652.

2486 **Richler** Benjamin, Guide to Hebrew manuscript collections 1994 → 10,1368: Sefarad 55 (1995) 219 (Emilia *Fernández Tejero*).

2487 **Rupprecht** Hans-Albert, Kleine Einführung in die Papyruskunde 1994 → 10,1371; DM 56: ᴿAnCl 64 (1995) 47 (A. *Martin*); SC(las)I(sr) 14 (1995) 173-6 (I.F. *Fikhman*).

2488 **Sautel** Jacques-Hubert, Répertoire des réglures dans les manuscrits grecs sur parchemin; base de données établie à l'aide du fichier [Julien] LEROY et des catalogues récents: Biblio[?lo]gia 13. Turnhout 1995, Brepols. 411 p. Ff 615. 2-503-50418-3. -- ᴿFgNt 8 (1995) 227s (C.-B. *Amphoux*).

2489 **Schott** Siegfried, Bücher und Bibliotheken im Alten Ägypten; Verzeichnis der Buch- und Spruchtitel und der Termini technici, Nachlass ᴱ*Schott* Erika, Index *Grimm* Alfred 1990 → 6,e591;. DM 184: ᴿWZKM 85 (1995) 281-3 (E. *Winter*).

2490 **Schubert** Ursula, Jüdische Buchkunst [I. 1938] -- II. Graz 1992, Akademische DVG. 226 p. 98 fig. DM 134. -- ᴿJud(aica) 51 (1995) 108-110 (S. *Schreiner*).

2491 *Skeat* T, C., Was papyrus regarded as 'cheap' or 'expensive' in the ancient world ?: Aeg 75 (1995) 75-94.

2492 **Stahl** Rainer, Textkritik als Erkundung von Textgeschichte [Tov E. 1992]: OLZ 90 (1995) 133-152.

2493 *Strus* A., L'isopséphie des abréviations byzantines; une solution pour une inscription de Kh. ʿAïn Fattir: RB 102 (1995) 242-254.

2494 *a) Supino Martini* Paola, Sul metodo paleografico; formulazione di problemi per una discussione; -- *b) Banti* Ottavio, Epigrafia medioevale e paleografia; specificità dell'analisi epigrafica; -- *c) Tedeschi* Carlo, Osservazioni sulla paleografia delle iscrizioni britanniche paleocristiane (V-VII secolo); -- *d) Bischoff* Frank M., *Maniaci* Marilena, Pergamentgrösse -- Handschriftenformate -- Lagenkonstruktion; Anmerkungen zur Methodik und zu den Ergebnissen der jüngeren kodikologischen Forschung [reazioni *Costamagna* Giorgio, *al.*] ; -- *e) Malavolta* Maria Edvige, Repertorio delle [186] tesi di laurea [paleografia] Univ. Roma; -- *f) Gimeno Blay* Francisco M., ʿSobre la enseñanza de las escrituras antigüasʿ [CASTRO Y VILLASANTE Alfonso de, Madrid 1749]; -- *g) Mastruzzo* Antonino, Ductus, corsività, storia della scrittura; alcune considerazioni : ScrCiv 19 (1995) 5-29 / 31-51 / 67-121; 18 pl. / 277-319; 11 fig.; 6 pl. [321-348] / 367-383; ind. 385-400 / 353-365 / 403-464.

2495 **Webber** Teresa, Scribes and scholars at Salisbury Cathedral, c.1075-c.1125: HistMg. Ox 1992, Clarendon. xii-220 p. £30. -- ᴿHeythJ 36 (1995) 87s (R.N. *Swanson*).

D2.1 *Biblia hebraica* -- **Hebrew text**

2496 *Aejmelaeus* A., Methodenfragen der biblischen Textkritik, A. Altes Testament (E. Tov, 1992): ThR 60 (1995) 316-322.

2497 *Alonso Schökel* Luis, La Bibbia poliglotta complutense: CivCatt 146 (1995,1) 366-371.

2498 *Augusto Tavares* A., *Cohen* Dov, Novos manuscritos hebraicos [.. Lev 23,10]: → 27, ᶠBRAGANÇA J., Didask 25 (1995) 189-194; 1 fig.

2499 *a) Barthélemy* Dominique, Les traditions anciennes de division du texte biblique de la Torah; -- *b) Lange* Nicholas de, La tradition des 'révisions juives' au Moyen Âge; les fragments hébraïques de la Geniza du Caire: → 78, ᶠHARL M., Katà toùs o' 1995, 27-51.

2500 *Beckwith* Roger T, The early history of the Psalter; TynB 46 (1995) 1-28.

2501 **Beit-Arié** Malachi, Hebrew manuscripts of East and West; toward a comparative codicology; The Panizzi Lectures 1992, British Library 1993 → 9,1540*; xiv-124 p.; 41 fig.; 4 colour pl. £ 16 pa. -- ᴿBoL (1995) 24 (R. *Murray*); Henoch 17 (1995) 375-7 (M. *Perani*); Manuscripta 38,1 (1994) 81 .. ; ScrBru 49 (1995) 145-8 (Sonia *Fellous*).

2502 **Beit-Arié** Malachi, ᴱ*May* E.A., Catalogue of the Hebrew manuscripts of the Bodleian library: supplement of addenda and corrigenda to [NEUBAUER A.] vol. 1. Ox 1994, Clarendon. xxxi p.; 596 col. 0-19-817386-5

2503 **Brotzman** Ellis R., OT textual criticism, a practical introduction 1994 → 10,1378; $ 11: ᴿCBQ 57 (1995) 760 (J.W. *Betlyon*).

2504 ᴱ**Cohen** Menachem, Mikraʾot gedolot ʿhaketerʿ²ʳᵉᵛ [TM & Targums with classic commentaries on same page; 1. Jos-Jg 1992 → 9,2587] -- 2. Samuel I & II. Ramat-Gan 1993, Bar-Ilan Univ. xiv-282 p. 965-266-166-4. -- ᴿRB 102 (1995) 465 (É. *Nodet*: chef-d'œuvre de composition; outil fondamental).

2505 **Davila** James R., Text-type and terminology; Genesis and Exodus as test cases: RQum 16 (1993-5) 3-38.

2506 *Díez Merino* L., Cadena de la transmisión de la Biblia hebrea según la tradición tiberiense de Ben Asher : CTom 122 (1995) 257-306 . 477-517.

2507 ᴱ**Disegni** Dario, Bibbia ebraica. F 1995-, Giuntina. I. 490 dopp. p. 88-057-012-9
2508 *Dresher* Bezalel E., The prosodic basis of the Tiberian Hebrew system of accents: Lg 70 (1994) 1-52.
2509 ᴱ**Ehrman** Bart D., HOLMES The text of the New Testament in contemporary research; essays on the status quaestionis. GR 1995, Eerdmans. xiv-401 p. $ 40.- ᴿP(rinc)SB 16 (1995) 356-8 (J.A. *Brooks*).
2510 **Fernández Tejero** Emilia, La Masora Magna del Códice de Profetas de El Cairo; transcripción alfabético-analítica: TECC(isn) 58. M 1995, Cons.Sup. Inst. Filología. 331 p. 84-00-07542-0.
2511 *Goerwitz* Richard L., Non-Judahite dialects and the diacritics of the Masoretic text: JNWS 21,1 (1995) 49-57.
2512 **Khan** Geoffrey, Karaite Bible manuscripts from the Cairo Genizah 1990 → 6,a116; 7,9929*: ᴿEstB 53 (1995) 400s (J. *Ribera*).
2513 **Metzger** Thérèse, Die Bibel von Meschullam und Joseph QALONYMOS, Ms. M 1106 der Universitätsbibliothek Breslau (Wrocław): QFWü 42. Wü 1994, Schöningh. 148 p.
2514 **Meyer** Rudolf, Beiträge zur Geschichte von Text und Sprache des ATs: BZAW 209, 1993 → 9,222: ᴿATG(ran) 97 (1994) 510-521 (A. *Torres*, muy detallado).
2515 ᶠORLINSKY Harry M., Estudios Masoréticos, ᴱ**Fernández Tejero** E., *al.*, 1992/3 → 9,400: ᴿJThS 46 (1995) 235s (C.T.R. *Hayward*).
2516 **Ortega Monasterio** María Teresa, La Masora Parva del Códice de Profetas de El Cairo, casos *lêt*: TECC(isn) 59. M 1995, Cons. Sup. Inst. Filología. 216 p
2517 **Penkower** Jordan S., ᴴ New evidence ... Aleppo codex 1993 → 10,1383: ᴿBoL (1995) 51s (G.I. *Davies*); JQR 85 (1994s) 454-6 (E.J. *Revell*).
2518 *Perani* Mauro, Un decennio di ricerca dei frammenti di manoscritti ebraici in Italia; rapporto sui rinvenimenti e bibliografia ; ASEs 12 (1995) 111-127
2519 ᴱ**Richter** Wolfgang, Biblia Hebraica transcripta [= ¹]: ATSAT 33, 16 vol. 1991-3 → 8,1757s ... 10,1387: ᴿArOr 63 (1995) 137-9 (S. *Segert* at end: what are 'the in the second column of Hexapla'?); Bijdragen 56 (1995) 210 (J. van *Ruiten*: voordeel niet geheel duidelijk).
2520 **Róth** Ernst, *Prijs* Leo, Hebräische Handschriften [Deutschland] 1-BC Fra 1990 → 7,1507: ᴿOLZ 90 (1995) 179-181 (G. *Pfeifer*).
2521 *Sirat* Colette, *al.*, Rouleaux de la Tora antérieurs à l'an mille: CRAI (1994) 861-887; IX pl. (IV moitié basse dessus dessous); X tableaux.
2522 *Steiner* R.C., ᴴ Linguistic features of the commentary on Ezekiel and the Minor Prophets in the Hebrew scrolls from Byzantium: Leš 59 (1995s) 39-56; Eng. 1,Is.
2523 ᴱ**Tal** Abraham, ᴴ The Samaritan Pentateuch 1994 → 10,1393; ᴿBSOAS 58 (1995) 52s (A.D. *Crown*); JSSt 40 (1995) 348-350 (also A.D. *Crown*); Muséon 108 (1995) 197 (J.-M. van *Cangh*); Sefarad 55 (1995) 221s (L.F. *Girón*).
2524 **Tov** Emanuel, Textual criticism of the Hebrew Bible 1992 → 8,1761 ... 10,1396: ᴿCDios 207 (1994) 879s (J. *Gutiérrez*); *CritRR 8 (1995) 107s (J.R. *Adair*); JRel 75 (1995) 111 (R.W. *Klein*); RQum 16 (1993-5) 306-8 (N. *Fernández Marcos*); UnSemQ 48,1 (1994) 183-7 (G. *Landes*).
2525 *a) Ulrich* Eugene, The Bible in the making; the Scriptures at Qumran; -- *b) Tov* Emanuel, Biblical texts as reworked in some Qumran manuscripts with special attention to 4QRP and 4QParaGen-Exod; -- *c) Trebolle Barrera* Julio, The authoritative function of Scriptural works at Qumran [.. redactional variants]: → 538, Community 1993/4, 77-93 / 111-134 / 95-110 [< OTA 18 (1995) p. 376s (P.D. *Sansone*)].

2526 *Waltke* Bruce K., OT textual criticism: → 1284, Foundations 1994, 156-186 [< OTA 18,p.393].

2527 *Weinberg* David B., 'Break in the middle of the verse'; some observations on a Masoretic feature: → 10,133, ᶠWACHOLDER B., 1994, 34-45 [< OTA 18 (1995) p. 468].

2528 *Woude* A.S. van der, Tracing the evolution of the Hebrew Bible, ᵀ*Runia* Anthony : BiRe 11,1 (1995) 42-45; the 200 Hebrew Qumran fragments have somewhat enhanced the status of the Septuagint in relation to the Masoretic Bible.

2529 **Würthwein** E., The text of the Old Testament; an introduction to the Biblia Hebraica [1979, ⁵1988], ᵀ²ʳᵉᵛ*Rhodes* Errol F. GR 1995, Eerdmans. xiv-293 p.; 40 pl. $ 20 pa. 0-8028-0788-7 [NTAb 40,p.517]. -- ᴿOTA 18 (1995) p. 630s (A.A. *Di Lella*).

2530 *Ziblin* Yael, A fifteenth-century Jewish-Christian collaboration in manuscript illumination: Viator 26 (1995) 263-282; 10 fig.

D2.2 Targum

2531 *Barc* Bernard, Du temple à la synagogue; essai d'interprétation des premiers targumismes de la Septante; → 78, ᶠHARL M., Katà toùs o' 1995, 11-26.

2532 ᴱ**Beattie** D.R.G., *McNamara* M. J., The Aramaic Bible; targums in their historical context [meeting Dublin 1992]: JSOT.s 166. Shf 1994, Academic. 470 p. £ 40. ᴿZAW 107 (1995) 519 (tit.pp.)

2533 *Becker* Hans-Jürgen, The Yerushalmi fragments in Munich, Darmstadt and Trier and their relationship to the Vatican manuscript Ebr. 133: Jewish Studies Quarterly 2 (Tü 1995) 329-335.

2534 *a) Bernstein* Moshe J., The Halakhah in the marginalia of Targum Neofiti; -- *b) Posen* Rafael B. ᴴ Rhetorical questions in Targum Onkelos: -> 10,331a, llth Jewish 1994. A-223-230 / 123-130.

2535 BÖHL F., Name und Typologie; zur Form der Namenforschung der Stammväter im Targum Pseudo-Jonathan [Gen 29,32-35]: FraJudBeit 21 (1994) 7-29 [< ZAW 107 (1995) 504].

2536 *Bombeck* Stefan, Das Partizip mit der enklitischen Subjektsform des Personalpronomens in den Targumen Onkelos, Pseudo-Jonathan und Neofiti: BN(otiz) 80 (1995) 16-19 (-22, *hwh*).

2537 **Campbell** R.M., A fragment-targum without a purpose; the raison d'être of MS. Vatican EBR 440; diss. Northwestern. Evanston 1994. 352 p. -- DissA·56 (1995s) (< ZAW 107) 502.

2538 *Carbone* Sandro P., *Rizzi* Giovanni, 'Memra e paradosis': progetto di lavoro per la traduzione sinottica di TM-LXX-TG-profeti minori della collana [Dehoniane] 'La parola e la sua tradizione': RivB 43 (1995) 363-379.

2539 *Chilton* Bruce, Reference to the Targumim in the exegesis of the New Testament; → 512, SBL Seminars 34 (1995) 77-81.

2540 ᴱ**Flesher** Paul V.M., Targum studies I. Textual and contextual studies in the Pentateuchal Targums: SFSHJ 55, 1992 → 8,1765; 10,1402: ᴿCBQ 57 (1995) 129s (Z. *Garber*).

2541 **Glessmer** U., Einleitung in die Targume zum Pentateuch; TSAJ 48. Tü 1995, Mohr. xv-274 p.; Bibliog. 233-262. DM 138. 3-16-145818-4 [NTAb 40, p.377].

2542 **Gordon** Robert, Studies in the Targum ... Nah-Mal [< diss. Cambridge, ᴰ*Emerton* J., 1973] 1994 → 10,3651: ᴿ*CritRR 8 (1995) 126-8 (B. *Chilton*).

2543 ᴱ**Kasher** Rimon, ᴴ *Toseptot targum* .. [150 fragmentary Aramaic] Targumic Toseftot to the Prophets. J c.1995, World Union of Jewish Studies. $ 28; sb. $ 18.

2544 **Kaufman** Stephen A., *Sokoloff* Michael, A key-word-in-context concordance to Targum Neofiti; a guide to the complete Palestinian Aramaic text of the Torah: AramLex Publ 2, 1993 → 9,1558; 10,1406: [R]Biblica 76 (1995) 125s (R. *Le Déaut*); CBQ 57 (1995) 348s (D.M. *Golomb*: useful access finally to the vocabulary, though involving many hard decisions; base is not DIEZ MACHO but ms. photos; sequence is 'by consonantal shape rather than by root').

2545 *Klein* Michael L., A fragment-targum of Onqelos from the Cairo Genizah: → 72, [F]GREENFIELD J., Solving 1995, 101-5.

2546 **McNamara** Martin (Neofiti I), *Clarke* Ernest G, (Pseudo-Jonathan), Targum Numbers: Aramaic Bible 4. ColMn 1995, Liturgical/Glazier. xiii-334 p. $ 80. 0-8146-5483-5 [ThD 42,356].

2547 **Margain** J., Les particules dans le Targum samaritain Gn-Ex: ÉPHÉ 29, 1993 → 10,1408: [R]RIC(ath)P 49 (1994) 85-88 (P. *Grelot*).

2548 **Moor** Johannes de, A bilingual concordance to the Targum of the Prophets. Lei 1995, Brill. x-413 p.; (II. 1997: vi-360 p.). 90-04-10277-9.

2549 **Mortensen** Beverly P., Targum Pseudo-Jonathan, a document for priests; diss. Northwestern, [D]*Flesher* P. Evanston 1994. 682 p. 95-21775. -- DissA 56 (1995s) p. 978.

2550 *Muñoz León* Domingo, [Neofiti Gen 4,1-17] El deras sobre Caín y Abel en 1 Jn y la situación de la comunidad joánica: EstB 53 (1995) 213-238; Eng. 213.

2551 [E]**Neri** Umberto, Targum Onqelos, Neofiti, Pseudo-Jonathan; versione ufficiale italiana confrontata con TM, LXX, Pes ... commenti (ORIGENE ... VON RAD). Bo 1995, Dehoniane. xxvii-662 p. L[m] 94. 88-1020580-4.

2552 **Samely** A., The interpretation of speech in the Pentateuch Targums [100 passages]: TSAJ 17,1992 → 9,1563; 10,1410; [R]JJS 45 (1994) 311-3 (P.S. *Alexander*); VT 45 (1995) 419s (R.P. *Gordon*).

2553 **Shinan** Avigdor, [H] The embroidered targum; the Aggadah in Targum Pseudo-Jonathan of the Pentateuch 1992 → 10,1411: [R]*CritRR 7 (1994) 427-9 (B.L. *Visotzky*); Tarbiz 63 (1993s) 283-290 (R. *Kasher*, [H]).

2554 **Smelik** Willem F., The Targum of Judges; OTS 36. Lei 1995, Brill. xi-681 p. 90-04-10365-1.

D31   *Textus graecus* -- **Greek New Testament**

2555 [E]**Aland** Barbara, *al.*, UBS NT[4] 1993 → 9,1564: [R]EThL 90 (1994) 154-7 (F. *Neirynck*); StVlad 39 (1995s) 199-210 (J.A. *Jillions:* now with a Greek Orthodox collaborator, J. KARAVIDOPOULOS).

2556 [E]**Aland** B., *Delobel* J., NT textual criticism 1993/4 → 10,303b: [R]*FgNt 8 (1995) 95-98 (J.K. *Elliott*).

2557 *Aland* Barbara, Neutestamentliche Textforschung; eine philologische, historische und theologische Aufgabe: → 536, [F]STRECKER G., Bilanz 1995, 7-29.

2558 **Aland** Kurt, Text und Textwert 3. Apg 1993 → 9,5276, 10,5057: [R]NT 37 (1995) 101-4 (J.K. *Elliott*).

2559 **Bover** José M., *O'Callaghan* José, Nuevo Testamento trilingüe[3] 1994 → 10,1420: [R]ActuBbg 31 (1994) 199s (A. *Borràs*, 10 eulogies of first edition).

2560 **Comfort** Philip W., The quest for the original text of the NT 1992 → 6,1852 ... 10,1421: [R]EvQ 66 (1994) 265s (I.H. *Marshall*).

2561 **Ehrman** Bart D., The orthodox corruption of Scripture .. Christological/NT 1993 →

9,1569; 10,1422: [R]CBQ 57 (1995) 391-3 (H.W. *Attridge*, unremittingly favorable); Churchman 108 (L 1994) 84-86 (G. *Bray*: a house of cards); *CritRR 8 (1995) 203-5 (G.D. *Fee*); *JEarlyC 3 (1995) 93-95 (R.F. *Collins*); TTod 51 (1994s) 614.6.8 (Virginia *Burrus*).

2562 **Elliott** J. Keith, Essays and studies in NT textual criticism 1992 → 8,239*a*; 10,1424: [R]ThRv 91 (1995) 221-5 (U. *Borse*).

2563 **Elliott** J.K., *Moir* Ian, Manuscripts and the text of the NT; an introduction for English readers. E 1995, Clark. x-111 p.; 12 pl. $ 12 pa. 0-567-29298-3   [NTAb 40, p.509].

2564 *Elliott* J.K., A comparison of two recent Greek New Testaments [NESTLE-ALAND[27] far superior to UBS[4]: E(xp)T 107 (1995s) 105s.

2565 **Epp** E., *Fee* G., Studies in the theory and method of NT textual criticism 1993 → 9,193; 10,1426: [R]EThL 70 (1994) 159s (F. *Neirynck*); TorJT 11 (1995) 92s (J.-F. *Racine*).

2566 **Funk** Robert W., *al.* The five gospels; the search for the authentic words of Jesus 1993 → 9,4098; 10,4226 : (Reformed) Perspectives 9,10 (1994) 18-20 (D.E. *Timmer*: 'an entirely congenial Jesus' despite its warning).

2567 **Greenlee** J. Harold, Introduction to New Testament textual criticism[2rev]. Peabody MA 1995, Hendrickson. xi-160 p. $ 13. 1-56563-037-8 [ThD 43,66: USB (=? UBS[4]) now base-text].

2568 **Metzger** Bruce M., A textual commentary on the (UBS[4]) Greek NT[2] 1994 → 10,1432: [R]EThL 71 (1995) 453s (F. *Neirynck* counts a 'significantly different' number of new and removed entries); P(rinc)SB 16 (1995) 252s (M.W. *Holmes*).

2569 **O'Callaghan** José, Los primeros testimonios del Nuevo Testamento; papirología neotestamentaria: En los orígenes del cristianismo. Córdoba 1995, Almendro. 149 p.; 6 pl. 84-8005-024-1 [NTAb 40, p.513]. -- [R]Communio (Sev) 28 (1995) 375-9 (M. de *Burgos*); *FgNt 8 (1995) 229-232 (J.K. *Elliott*: handsomely produced and useful; he bypasses some recent support for his 7Q5, but VERMES' two snags still hold).

2570 *Parker* D.C., Was Matthew written before 50 CE ? The Magdalen papyrus of Matthew [London Times Dec. 24 & 26, 1994 < THIEDE C.P. , ZPE 105 (1995) 13-20 = TyndB 46 (1995) 29-42]: E(xp)T 107 (1995s) 40-42: 'worthless'.

2571 **Passoni Dell'Acqua** Anna, Il testo del NT; introduzione alla critica testuale: Percorsi e Traguardi Biblici. T-Leumann 1994, Elle Di Ci. 238 p.; 16 pl. L[m] 26. 88-01-10318-2 [NTAb 40,p.513]. -- [R]ActuBbg 31 (1994) 200-2 (J. *O'Callaghan*); Asprenas 42 (1995) 287s (A. *Rolla*); CivCatt 146 (1995,4) 634 (A. *Ferrua*); Div 39 (1995) 82 (T. *Stramare*); Henoch 17 (1995) 372s (P. *Sacchi* raccomanda); RivB 43 (1995) 549s (R. *Penna*).

2572 [*Richard* Marcel], [3refaite]**Olivier** Jean-Marie, Répertoire des bibliothèques et des catalogues de manuscrits grecs: CC. Turnhout 1995, Brepols. xx-953 p. 2-503-50445-0

2573 *Rodgers* Peter R., The text of Romans 2:28: JThS 46 (1995) 547-550.

2574 **Stanton** Graham, Gospel truth ? New light on Jesus and the Gospels [dismissing THIEDE on both Magdalen and O'CALLAGHAN]. L 1995, HarperCollins. viii-215 p.; xvi pl. £ 15. 0-00-627963-5. -- [R]E(xp)T 107,4 2d-top choice (1995s) 98s (C.S. *Rodd*: solid, though downplaying the Resurrection, the Shroud, and objections to Q).

2575 [E]**Swanson** Reuben, New Testament Greek manuscripts; variant readings arranged in horizontal lines against Codex Vaticanus. Pasadena 1995, W.Carey. Mt 0-86585-051-8; Mk -2-6; Lk -3-4; Jn -4-2. $ 30 each [ThD 43,281].

2576 *a) Thiede* Carsten P., Papyrus Magdalen Greek 17 (Gregory-Aland **P**64); a reappraisal [response *Head* Peter M.] / Notes on **P**4 = Bibliothèque nationale Paris, supplementum graece 1120/5; -- *b) Comfort* Philip W., Exploring the common identification of three NT manuscripts **P**4, **P**64 and **P**67: TynB 46 (1995) 29-42 [251-276 + 9 pl.] & 55-57 / 43-54.

2577 *Wachtel* Klaus, **P**[64/67], Fragmente des Matthäusevangeliums aus dem 1. Jahrhundert ?: ZPE 107 (1995) 73-80.
2578 *a) Wallace* Daniel B., Historical revisionism and the majority text theory; the cases of F.H.A. SCRIVENER and Herman C. HOSKIER; -- *b) Lopik* T. van, Once again, floating words; their significance for textual criticism: NTS 41 (1995) 280-5 / 286-291.
2579 *Wallace* Daniel B., The majority text theory; history, methods and critique: JEvTS 37 (1994) 195-215.

2580 *Rokeah* D., The New Testament in Hebrew garb [1991 study edition < 1976]: *Mishkan 20 (J 1994) 64-72 [NTAb 39,p.10].

D3.2 *Versiones graecae* -- **VT, Septuaginta etc.**

2581 **Aejmelaeus** Anneli, On the trail of Septuagint translators 1993 → 9,176: [R]RB 102 (1994) 294 (titles, pp.).
2582 **Carbone** Sandro P., *Rizzi* Giovanni. Le scritture ai tempi di Gesù: introduzione alla LXX e alle antiche versioni aramaiche: TCom (Testi e Commenti 1. non in IATG[2]), 1992 → 8,1801; 9,1584: [R]Salesianum 57 (1995) 147 (M. *Cimosa*).
2583 **Cimosa** Mario, Guida allo studio della Bibbia Greca (LXX); storia -- lingua -- testi. R 1995 Società Biblica Britannica. 272 p.; bibliog. 215-235. 88-237-8007-1.
2584 *a) Cook* Johann, Were the persons responsible for the Septuagint translators and/or scribes and/or editors ? -- *b) Deist* Ferdinand E:, Text, textuality, and textual criticism: JNWSL 21,2 (1995) 45-58 / 59-67.
2585 **Cousin** Hugues, La Biblia griega; los Setenta, [T]1992 → 8,1803; 10,1441: [R]RevB(Arg) 56 (1994) 124-6 (J.P. *Martin*).
2586 **Dogniez** Cécile, Bibliography of the Septuagint; VTS 60. Lei 1995, Brill. xxxii-329 p. *f* 180. 90-04-10192-6. -- [R]JSJ(ud) 26 (1995) 354-7 (A. *Hilhorst*; errors 'restructed' but some 80 omissions here supplied); Sefarad 55 (1995) 398s (M.Victoria *Spottorno*).
2587 **Dorival** Gilles, Septante Nombres 1994 → 10,2350: [R]MélSR 52 (1995) 333s (M. *Spanneut*).
2588 **Fernández Marcos** Natalio, *Busto Saiz* José Ramon, El texto antioqueno de la Biblia Griega 1989-92 → 8,2819.2908: [R]Kiryat Sefer 65 (1994s) p.20-22 (Shifra *Sznol*, [H]).
2588* *Giese* Robald L.[J], Compassion for the lowly in Septuagint Proverbs: JSPE 11 (1993) 109-117.
2589 **d'Hamonville** Marc., *al.*, Autour des livres de la LXX: Proverbes, Ecclésiaste, Nombres, 1 Règnes: Le Saulchoir 4. P 1995, Cerf. 123 p. 2-204-05414-3.
2590 **Hanhart** Robert, Ein unbekannter Text zur griechischen Esra-Überlieferung [Esdras a' 5,57-59; 7,8s = Ezra 3,10s; 6,16-18]: NAWG.ph 1995/4/MSU 22 (1995) 111-132.
2591 [E]**Hengel** Martin, *Schwemer* Anna M., Die Septuaginta zwischen Judentum uns Christentum [Tü Oberseminar 1990s] WUNT 73, 1993 → 10,1446: [R]EThL 71 (1995) 195s (J. *Lust*); JRel 75 (1995) 553s (J.J. *Collins*); VigChr 49 (1995) 192-4 (M. *Harl*).
2592 *Jeppesen* K., Biblia hebraica -- et Septuaginta [MÜLLER M., Kirkens første Bibel ? 1994 → 1654 infra]: DTT 58 (1995) 256-266 [< NTAb 40,p.389].
2593 **Lowden** John, The Octateuchs; a study in Byzantine manuscript illustration 1992 → 10,1447: [R]OCP 61 (1995) 595s (V. *Ruggieri*).
2593* **Maori** Yeshayahu, The Peshitta version of the Pentateuch and early Jewish exegesis: Perry Publ. J 1995, Hebrew Univ. 403 p. Bibliog. 348-354.

Müller Mogens, Kirkens første Bibel; hebraica sive graeca veritas ? 1994 → 1654.

2594 ᴱ**Muraoka** Takamitsu, Melbourne symposium on Septuagint lexicography 1900 → 6,546*: ᴿJQR 84 (1993s) 378-380 (J.W. *Wevers*).

2595 **Muraoka** Takamitsu, Greek-English lexicon of Septuagint 12 prophets 1993 → 9,10120; 10,9308: ᴿEThL 70 (1994) 132-4 (J. *Lust*); OL(ov)P 26 (1995) 207s (E. *Eynikel*).

2596 **O'Connell** Séamus, 'How the first edition of the Greek OT was made'; the nature and text-critical use of the Greek Old Testament text of the Complutensian Polyglot Bible; kath. diss. ᴰ*Barthélemy* D. Fribourg 1995. -- ThRv Beilage 92/2, viii.

2597 **Pattie** T.S., Manuscripts of the Bible; Greek Bibles in the British Library²ʳᵉᵛ. L 1995, British Library. 48 p. 0-7123-0403-7.

2598 **Rösel** M., Übersetzung als Vollendung der Auslegung; Studien zur Genesis-Septuaginta: BZAW 223. B 1994, de Gruyter. viii-290 p. DM 139. -- ᴿZAW 107 (1995) 167s (B. *Janowski*).

2599 *Schenker* Adrian, Septuaginta und christliche Bibel: ThRv 91 (1995) 459-464.

2600 **Sollamo** Raija, Repetition of the possessive pronoun in the Septuagint: SeptCog 40. At 1995, Scholars. vi-120 p. $ 40. 0-7885-0149-6. -- ᴿE(xp)T 107 (1995s) 155,

2601 **Steyn** Gert J., Septuagint quotations in the context of the Petrine and Pauline speeches of the Acta Apostolorum. Kampen 1995, Kok Pharos. viii-290 p. *f* 70. 90-390-0131-6 [TR 91,536].

2602 **Veltri** Giuseppe, Eine Tora für den König Talmai [Diss, Berlin FU 1991]: TSAJ 41, 1994 → 10,1458: ᴿAnton 70 (1995) 302-4 (M. *Nobile*); BS 151 (1994) 171 (P.S. *Alexander*); Jud(aica) 51 (1995) 113s (D.U. *Rottzell*); *RBBras 11 (1994) 469 (C. *Minette de Tillesse*); RTL 26 (1995) 358 (P.-M. *Bogaert*: inspiré par R. LE DÉAUT & P. SCHÄFER)

D4 Versiones orientales

2603 ᴱ**Aland** Barbara, *Juckel* Andreas, Das Neue Testament in syrischer Überlieferung II. Die paulinischen Briefe [1. 1991 → 7,5249] 2. 2 Kor -- Kol: ANTT 23. B 1995, de Gruyter. viii-582 p.: Bibliog. 575-582. 3-11-014613-4.

2604 **Baarda** T., Essays on the Diatessaron: *ContriBExT 11. Kampen 1994, Kok Pharos. 320 p. *f* 80. -- ᴿNT 37 (1995) 402 (J.K. *Elliott*).

2605 **Boismard** M.-E., Le Diatessaron .. JUSTIN 1992 → 8,1919 .. 10,1460: ᴿRevBib(Arg) 55 (1993) 91-101 (J. Pablo *Martin*).

2606 **Dirksen** Piet B., La Peshitta dell'Antico Testamento, ᵀᴱ*Borbone* Pier Giorgio: StBi 103, 1993 → 9,1599; 10,1461; ᴿCrSt 16 (1995) 627-9 (Emidio *Vergani*); PaVi 40,4 (1995) 59s (Anna *Passoni dell'Acqua*); RivB 43 (1995) 537s (G. *Rizzi*).

2607 **Falla** Terry C., Key to Peshitta Gospels I. 1991 → 7,1556 ... 10,1462: ᴿAbr Nahrain 31 (1993) 136s (H.J.W. *Drijvers*); JAOS 114 (1994) 88 (J.A. *Lund*).

2608 **Kiraz** George A., Comparative Edition of the Syriac Gospels, aligning the Sinaiticus, Curetonianus, Peshitta and Harklean Versions: NTTS 21. Lei c.1995, Brill. v,1, Matthew; v.2, Mark; v.3, Luke; v.4, John. 90-04-10419-4.

2609 **Kiraz** George A., Computer generated concordance .. Syriac NT 1993 → 9,1601; 10,1465; $ 858: ᴿJBL 114 (1995) 357-9 (W.L. *Petersen*).

2610 **Maori** Yeshayahu, The Peshitta version of the Pentateuch and early Jewish exegesis [diss: Hebrew Univ. 1975]: PerryBRes. J 1995, Magnes. 403 p.; bibliog. 348-354. $ 23. 965-223-874-0.

2611 **Morrison** Craig E., The character of the Syriac version of the First Book of Samuel and its relation to other biblical versions; diss. Pontificio Istituto Biblico, ᴰ*Pisano* S. R 1995. -- Biblica 76 (1995) 443.

2612 **Petersen** William L., TATIAN's Diatessaron; its creation, dissemination, significance, and history in scholarship: VigChr.s 25. L 1994, Brill. xix-555 p. ƒ 220. 90-04-09469-5 [RStR 22,72, G.A. *Anderson*]. -- ᴿASS(oc)R 90 (1995)   113s (J.-D. *Dubois*); ET 106 (1994s) 341 (J.K. *Elliott*); NT 37 (1995) 401-3 (J.K. *Elliott*, also on McCARTHY C.); VigChr 49 (1995) 405-8 (A.F.J. *Klijn*).

2613 ᴱ**Strothmann** Werner, Konkordanz zur syrischen Bibel; die Mautbè: GOF 1/33. Wsb 1995, Harrassowitz. 6 vol.

2614 *Strothmann* Werner, Die syrische Übersetzung der Bibel: → 42, ᶠCOLPE C., Tradition (1994) 344-355.

2615 *a) Weitzmann* Michael P., Peshitta, Septuagint and Targum; -- *b) Birdsall* J. Neville, The Old Syriac gospels and the Georgian version; the question of relationship: OCA 247 → 10,451, VI Syriacum 1992/4, 51-84 / 43-50.

2616 *Bosson* Nathalie, 2 Thess 3,11, P.Mil.copti 1; GöMisz 145 (1995) 59-61.

2617 ᴱ**Diebner** B.J., *Kasser* R., Hamburger Papyrus Bil. 1 [Ct Lam Eces copt] 1989 → 5,1756; 7,1565: ᴿOrientalia 63 (1994) 299-301 (H. *Quecke*).

2618 **Gabra** Gawdat, Der Psalter im oxyrhynchitischen (mesokemischen-mittelägyptischen) Dialekt; *DAI-K, Kopt.4. Heid 1995, Orientverlag. 209 p., Bibliog. 15-22. 3-927552-11-9.

2619 *a) Hunt* Lucy-Anne, Christian manuscript production under Ottoman rule; note on an illustrated sevententh-century Copto-Arabic lectionary in Cairo; -- *b) MacCoull* Leslie S.B., Coptic Museum ms. Lit 312 revisited [.. vocation due to Scripture-reading]: Muséon 107 (1994) 299-302 + 2 pl. / 305-315 + 1 pl.

2620 *Pezin* Michel, Copta sorbonica II. NT: LOrA 4 (1993) 41-52 + 3 pl.

2621 ᴱ**Schüssler** Karlheinz, Biblia coptica; die koptischen Bibeltexte. Wsb 1995, Harrassowitz. vii-125 p.; Bibliog. 10-19. 3-447-03782-2

2622 *Schüssler* Karlheinz, Das Projekt 'Biblia coptica patristica': OrChr 79 (1995) 224-8

2623 *Zanetti* Ugo, Bohairic liturgical manuscripts: OCP 61 (1995) 65-94.

2624 **Beylot** R., *Rodinson* M., Répertoire des bibliothèques et des catalogues de manuscrits éthiopiens: CNRS-HRTextes. Turnhout 1995, Brepols. 118 p. [RHE 91,9*].

2625 **Edele** Blaine, A critical edition of Genesis in Ethiopic: diss. Duke, ᴰ*Peters* M. Durham NC 1995. -- RStR 22,272.

2626 **Hammerschmidt** E. Äthiopische Handschriften, 3. (**Six** V.) : Verzeichnis or.H. in Deutschland. Stu 1994, Steiner. 569 p. DM 368. < RHE 90 (1995)

2627 **Six** Veronika, Äthiopische Handschriften 3 (Schluss). Stu 1994, Steiner. 569 p. DM 368. -- ᴿBSOAS 58 (1995) 611-4 (E. *Ullendorff*).

2628 **Uhlig** Siegbert, *al.* NT aethiopice; die Gefangenschafts-/katholischen Briefe: ÄF 33.29. Stu 1993, Steiner. 186 p., DM 124 / 264 p., DM 168. -- ᴿOLZ 90 (1995) 402-412 (A. *Juckel*); OrChr 79 (1995) 265-270 (S. *Weninger*).

2629 *Proverbio* Delio Vania, Osservazioni sulla Vorlage greca della versione armena di CPG 4588 (In parabolam de ficu) [< diss. Napoli 1994, ᴰ*Marrassini* P.]: AION 55 (1995) 177-192.

2630 *Outtier* Bernard, Nouveaux fragments ociaux du lectionnaire géorgien ancien IV: LOrA 4 (1993) 31-34.

2631 *Moraldi* Luigi, Infanzia di Gesù; Ms arabo G 11 suo. della Biblioteca Ambrosiana: RIL 127 (1993) 79-91.

2632 *Bakker* Michael, The Slavonic version in UBS[4]: NT 37 (1995) 92-94.

D5 **Versiones latinae**

2633 **Bergren** Theodore A., A Latin- [SCHMOLLER] Greek index of the Vulgate NT 1991 → 7,1674: [R]*JEarlyC 3 (1995) 22-27 (M. *Cahill*); NT 37 (1995) 192s (J.K. *Elliott*).

2634 [E]**Colunga** Alberto [[1]1946, 1951], *Turrado* Lorenzo, Biblia sacra vulgatae editionis. CinB 1995, San Paolo. xxix-1255 p.

2635 **Coogan** Robert, ERASMUS, LEE and the correction of the Vulgate 1992 → 9,1611: [R]ChH 64 (1995) 665s (G.G. *Krodel*).

2636 [E]**Fröhlich** U., Vetus Latina; die Reste der altlateinischen Bibel 22. 1 Cor, Lfg. 1, Einleitung. FrB 1995, Herder. 80 p.

2637 [E]**Gameson** Richard, The early medieval Bible; its production, decoration and use 1994 → 10,1482: [R]JRel 75 (1995) 412s (H. L. *Kessler*); JThS 46 (1995) 387s (G.R. *Evans*); Speculum 70 (1995) 907-9 (J.J. *Contreni*).

2638 [E]**Gribomont** Jean, *Mallet* Jean, La Bibbia di San Paolo nella storia del testo della Vulgata [< Commentario della Bibbia di San Paolo fuori le mura p. 339-531]. R 1993, Poligrafico.

2639 **Gryson** Roger, Esaias 2; Fasc. 1s, Les manuscrits + Isa 40-41,20: VLat 12,2. FrB 1993s. Herder. p.801-880; 881-960. 3-451-000121-7; -2-5. -- [R]RPh(lgLH) 69 (1995) 382-4 (R. *Braun*); ZkT 117 (1995) 99 (J.M. *Oesch*). -- fasc. 5, p.1121-1200, Isa 46,13 -- 50,3: 1995.

2640   **Heinzer** Felix, *al.,* Der Landgrafenpsalter; vollständige Faksimile-Ausgabe im Originalformat der Handschrift HB II 24 der Württembergischen Landesbibliothek Stuttgart. Graz/Bielefeld 1992, Akad./Regional. x-224 p. 3-201-01558-X / 3-027085-95-2. -- [R]ScrBru 49 (1995) 148-152 (F.O. *Büttner*).

2641 **Howlett** David, The Celtic Latin tradition of biblical style. Blackrock 1995, Four Courts. ix-400 p. £ 35. 1-85182-143-0.

2642 *Jennarelli* Marco, Analisi qualitativa quantitativa computerizzata del latino del NT secondo la Biblia Vulgata [Torino 1959]: RivB 43 (1995) 381-390.

2643 **Landurant** Alain, Symboles des manuscrits médiévaux du Mont-Saint-Michel: La mémoire normande. Luneray 1993, Bertout. 130 p.   -- [R]RTPh 127 (1995) 405s (P.-Y. *Ruff*).

2644 **Leanza** Karen E.S., Biblioteca apostolica Vaticana codex Barberini latinus 711; a late tenth-century illustrated Gospel lectionary from Reichenau: diss. Rutgers, [D]*McLachlan* Elizabeth P. New Brunswick 1995. 410 p. 95-24189. -- DissA 56 (1995s) p.736.

2645 **Marsden** R., The text of the [Vulgate] Old Testament in Anglo-Saxon England: StASE 15. C 1995, Univ. xxviii-506 p.; 9 pl. 0-521-46477-3 [< NTAb 40,p.512].

2646 *Marsden* Richard, Job in his place; the Ezra miniature in the Codex Amiatinus: ScrBru 49 (1995) 3-15.

2647 *a) Mattei* Paul, Recherches sur la Bible à Rome vers le milieu du IIIe s.: NOVATIEN et la Vetus Latina -- *b) Meyvaert* Paul, BEDE's Captiula lectionum for the Old and New

Testaments; -- c) *Bogaert* Pierre-Maurice, Bulletin de la Bible latine: RBen 105 (1995) 255-279 / 348-380 / 200-236.

2648 **Orafino** Giulia, I codici decorati dell'Archivio di Montecassino.R 1994,Poligrafico.404p.

2649 *Petitmengin* Pierre, Bible latine et Europe savante; un exemple de coopération scientifique: 9,449a, ᴱ**Fontaine** J., Patristique 1991/3, 73-92.

2650 *Raurell* F., Valor teològic espicífic de 'maiestas' en la Vulgata; RCatT 20 (1995) 1-35 [NTAb 40,p.14].

2651 **Ruskin** John [† 1900], La Bibbia di Amiens, ᵀ*Quasimodo* Salvatore. ᴱ*Proust*: L'altra biblioteca 28. Mi 1988, SE. 209 p. 88-7710-092-3.

2652 **Thiele** Walter, Sirach (Ecclesiasticus) Lfg. 5, 7,30-11,35: VLat 11,2. FrB 1993, Herder. p.321-400. 3-451-00428-3. -- ᴿZkT 117 (1995) 99 (J.M. *Oesch*)

2653 ᴱ**Wetzel** Christoph, *al.*. Biblia pauperum (Armenbibel); die Bilderhandschrift des Codex Palatinus latinus 871 im Besitz der Bibliotheca Apostolica Vaticana: Kunstbuchedition. Stu 1995, Belser. 112 p. DM 98. -- ᴿE(rbe)uA 71 (1995) 510 (T.H.); ThRv 91 (1995) 480-3 (V. *Pfnür*, auch über ᴱBACKHOUSE J., *al*, 1994).

D5.5 *Citationes apud Patres* -- **the Patristic Bible**

2654 *Arranz* Miguel, Preghiere parapenitenziali di purificazione e di liberazione nella tradizione bizantina: OCP 61 (1995) 425-476.

2655 **Brooks** James A., The New Testament text of GREGORY of Nyssa 1991 → 7,1591: ᴿ*CritRR 6 (1993) 207-9 (B.D. *Ehrman*).

2656 CYRILLUS H., **Mullen ..** , Cyril of Jerusalem [sic] and the text of the New Testament in fourth-century Palestine: diss. N.Carolina, ᴰ*Ehrman* B. Chapel Hill 1995. -- RTLv 27.p.539.

2657 *Dekkers* Eligius, Les Pères grecs et orientaux dans les florilèges patristiques latins: → 10,70, ᶠLAGA C., Philohistōr 1994, 569-576.

2658 **Frede** Hermann J., Kirchenschriftsteller, Verzeichnis und Sigel⁴ʳᵉᵛ : Vlat 1/1. FrB 1995, Herder. 1049 p. 3-451-00120-9 [ThRv 92,78; RHE 90 (1995) 228*].

2659 *Heuer* Mark H., An evaluation of John W. BURGON's use of patristic evidence [c.1880; 86,589 patristic Bible citations in British Museum manuscript never published]: JETS 38 (1995) 519-530.

2660 **Joest** Christoph, Bibelstellenkonkordanz zu den wichtigsten älteren Mönchsregeln: InstrPatr 9. Steenbrugge 1994, Nijhoff. xlv-149 p. -- ᴿRHE 90 (1995) 400-501 (A. de *Vogüé*).

2661 **Labate** A., Catena hauniensis in Eces 1992 → 8,3539 ... 10,3281: ᴿOrph(eus) 16 (1995) 197-200 (Sandro *Leanza*).

2662 *Orbán* A.P., JUVENCUS als Bibelexeget und als Zeuge der 'Afrikanischen' Vetus-Latina-Tradition [Mt 5,1-48 ...] : VigChr 49 (1995) 334-352

2663 *Romero-Pose* Eugenio, La Biblia de ALCUINO y el perdido comentario al Apocalipsis de TICONIO: RET 55 (1995) 391-7.

D6 **Versiones modernae** -- .1 *romanicae*, romance

2664 **Campanale** M.I., Traduzione e tradizione della Bibbia nella letteratura dell'Occidente mediterraneo, Dai Settanta all'Alto Medioevo, 1. Africa e Spagna. Torino 1990, Giappichelli. vi-213 p.; 1 pl. -- ᴿMai 37 (1995) 129-132 (A. *Placanica*).

2665 *Colella* Pasquale, A Bíblia; séculos de estudos e de revisões críticas para oferecer um único texto a todas as comunidades : Teocomunicação 25 (1995) 581-7.

2666 *Dogniez* Cécile, Pierre GIGUET (1794-1883), premier traducteur français de la Septante; → 78, [F]HARL M., Katà toùs o' 1995, 241-252.

2667 **Alonso Schökel** Luis, Biblia del peregrino. Bilbao 1995, Mensajero, 2121 p. -- [R]BiFe 21 (1995) 460 (A. *Salas*).

2668 La Biblia de Ferrara (1553), Biblia en lengua española traduzida palabra por palabra de le verdad hebrayca por muy excelentes letrados vista y examinada por el officio de la Inquisición. M 1992, Ministero Ext. 824 p.; v-23 p. -- [R]ATG(ran) 58 (1995) 351s (G.M. *Verd*).

2669 La Biblia latinoamericana, edición pastoral[11]. M/Estella 1995, San Pablo / VDivino. 31*+1328+618 p. pt 1900.

2670 **Diego Lobejón** M.W. de, El Salterio de HERRMANN el Alemán, primera traducción castellana de la Biblia. Valladolid 1993, Univ. 174 p. -- [R]CDios 207 (1994) 241 (T. *Alonso Turienzo*).

2671 *Vilar-Mar Vilar* Juan Bautista, Juan CALDERÓN, traductor de la Biblia al español en la Inglaterra victoriana : DiEc 30 (1995) 7-30.

2672 *Plutarco Bonilla* A., Cosas olvidadas (o no sabidas) acerca de la versión de Casiodoro de REINA, luego revisada por Cipriano de VALERA ['la' Biblia protestante]: RevB(Arg) 57 (1995) 155-180.

2673 Nou Testament grec-llatí-català[27]. Barc 1995, Asociaciò Bíblica de Catalunya. 50*- 650(d) p. + 681-810. 84-7826-630-5.

2674 Bíblia, tradução ecuménica, S. Paulo 1994, Loyola, xvi-2480 p. R$ 43. -- [R]*RBBras 11 (1994) 474-6 (C. *Minette de Tillesse*).

2675 *Bertalot* Renzo, Dieci anni della traduzione della Bibbia in italiano corrente: Protest(antesimo) 50 (1995) 151-3.

2676 **Poppi** Angelico, Sinossi dei quattro vangeli; greco-italiano[10] I, 1992 → 9,4403: [R]Laur 36 (1995) 521s (L. *Martignani*).

2677 *Ramello* Laura, Le antiche versioni italiane della Bibbia; rassegna e prospettiva di ricerca [< diss. Bologna c. 1996, Gli antichi volgarizzamenti italiani della Bibbia; il Salterio toscano e il Salterio veneto: Quaderni di Filologia Romanza 9 ('Ecdotica ed esegesi ' 1992) 113-128.

D6.2 *Versiones anglicae* -- **English Bible translations**

2678 **Allen** Ward S., *Jacobs* Edward C., The coming of the King James Gospels; a collation of the translators' work-in-progress. Fayetteville 1995, Univ. Arkansas Press. x-420 p. 1-55728-327-3.

2679 **Bates** E.S., The [abbreviated King James] Bible to be read as living literature (1936). NY c. 1994, Simon & S reissue. -- [R]BR 10,4 (1994) 17 . 55 (J. *Milgrom*: amputated).

2680 *Clifford* Richard J., The bishops, the Bible, and liturgical language [.. their approval not accepted in Rome]: America 172,19 (1995) 12-16.

2681 **Duthie** Alan S., How to choose your [English] Bible wisely[2rev]. Carlisle 1995, Paternoster. 244 p. £ 9. -- 0-85364-615-5 [*TBR 9/1, 7, Maureen *Palmer*: not easy to use].

2682 **Farstad** Arthur, *Hodges* Zane, The new King James' Version Greek-English interlinear New Testament. Nv 1994, Nelson. xviii-918 p. -- [R]NT 37 (1995) 199s (J.K. *Elliott*: 'the NKJV appears as running text down the outer margins'.. 'what is new is the interlinear' English made by Farstad *al.*).

2682* *Fogarty* Gerald P., 'The English used in our country'; Bible translations for U.S. Catholics: America 172,7 (1995) 10-16.

2683 **Fox** Everett, The Schocken Bible, 1. The five books of Moses. NY 1995, Schocken. xxxii-1024 p. 0-8[7]52-4161-6 [RStR 22,234, L. *Greenspoon*: a glittering volume: perceptive translation based only partly on BUBER & ROSENZWEIG].

2684 [E]**Gold** Victor R., *al.*, The New Testament and Psalms; an inclusive version [not sponsored]. NY 1995, Oxford-UP. xxiii-535 p. 0-19-538418-6. [OTA 19,145s, A. *Di Lella*: radically flawed; patronizingly eager to leave no marginals offended or unable to understand].

2685 *Hammond* Gerald, What was the influence of the medieval English Bible upon the Renaissance Bible ?: → 530, BJRL 77,3 (1995) 87-95.

2686 **Hargreaves** Cecil, A translator's freedom; modern English Bibles and their language: BiSe 22, 1993 → 10,1544: [R]CBQ 57 (1995) 594s (F.W. *Danker*); CritRR 8 (1995) 99-102 (R.G. *Bratcher*).

2687 *Jensen* Joseph, The Oxford Inclusive Bible; politically correct or pastorally concerned ?: LiLi 32,3 (1995s) 69-77.

2688 *Jensen* Michael, 'Simply' reading the [English 1550] Geneva Bible; the Geneva Bible and its readers: [J]LitTOx 9 (1995) 30-41.

2689 **Kohlenberger** John R.[III], The precise parallel New Testament [on facing pages in eight quadrants: UBS[4], Douay, King James, Amplified, NAmStandard, NInternational, New American, NRS]. Ox 1995, UP. xli-429 p. $ 35 [RStR 22,244, M.W. *Holmes*].

2690 *Leeman* Saul, The old and the new JPS [Torah translation]: JBQ 22 (1994) 3-12.

2691 **Marsden** R., The text of the Old Testament in Anglo-Saxon England: StASax 15. C 1995, Univ. xxviii-506 p.; 10 facsim. £ 55 [RHE 91,27*].

2692 **Murphy** Conor, The African Bible, NT (OT awaited). Nairobi 1995, Pauline. 709 p. (family ed. 663 p.) ; ill. 9966-21-120-9 (-30-6). -- [R]*TBR 8,3 (1995s) 10 (H. *Marriage*).

2693 **NIRV**: New International Readers' version [English at 3d grade reading level, edition for adults], [E]**Youngblood** Ron, NT. xxvii-594 p. $ 13; pa. $ 10. 0-310-92510-X; -1-8 [ThD 43,57].

2694 **NIV**: *Stek* John H., Has the NIV 'de-catholicized' Scripture ? : (Reformed) Perspectives [8,9 (1993), *Payton* James R.] 9,4 (1994) 8-10; 10s, Payton rejoinder.

2695 **NRSV**: The Holy Bible .. with Apocryphal/Deuterocanonical, NRSV anglicized edition. Ox 1995, UP. xv-905+270+267 p.

2696 *Ohlhausen* S.K., The last [G.L.] Haydock Bible ['self-interpreting Douay', published by T. HAYDOCK 1811-4; final edition 1874-8 reprinted 1910]: ReH 22 (Durham 1995) 529-535 [NTAb 40,p.207].

2697 **Orlinsky** Harry M., *Bratcher* Robert G., A history of Bible translation and the North American connection 1991 > : *A(sn)JS 21 (1995) 169-172 (N.M. *Sarna*).

2698 'The Bible and Culture Collective', The postmodern Bible. Nhv 1995, Yale Univ. 398 p. $ 35. -- RCrossCur 45 (1995s) 638-640 (A.K.M. *Adam* leaves the ten collaborators stringently unnamed and discusses two minor limits to a 'landmark' achievement, 'subverting biblical ideologies').

2699 **Rashkow** Ilona N., Upon the dark places; anti-semitism and sexism in English Renaissance Bible translation 1990 → 8,1892: RVT 45 (1995) 409-414 (J.A. *Emerton* rejects in great detail).

2700 ESmith Craig R., The inclusive New Testament. Brentwood MD 1994, Priests for Equality. xxiv-468 p. 0-9644-2790-7.

2701 *a) Waltke* Bruce, How we got our Old Testament; -- *b) Herklots* H.G.G., Discovering the oldest New Teatments; -- *c) Galli* Marc, What the English Bible cost one man [TYNDALE: death]: ChrHist 13,43 ('How we got our Bible' 1994) 32s / 34-7 / 12-15.

2702 **White** James R., The King James only controversy. Mp 1995, Bethany. 286 p. $ 11 pa. -- RC(alv)BTJ 11,2 (1995) 86s (W. *Vanhetloo*).

2703 *Williams* J.E. Caerwyn, Welsh translations of Pseudo-Matthaei Evangelium sive de ortu beatae Mariae et infantia Salvatoris: PI(r)BA 17 (1994) 102-125.

D6.3 *Versiones germanicae* -- Deutsche Bibelübersetzungen

2704 Elberfelder Handkonkordanz; zur revidierten Elberfelder Bibel, Wort- und Zahlenkonkordanz, Wu 1995, Brockhaus. [iv-] 443 p. 3-417-25801-4.

2705 **Himmighöfer** Traudel, Die Zürcher Bibel bis zum Tode ZWINGLIS (1531); Darstellung und Bibliographie: VIEG 154. Mainz 1995, von Zabern. xiv-500 p. DM 98. 3-8053-1535-X [ThRv 92,81].

2706 **Köster** Uwe, Studien zu den katholischen deutschen Bibelübersetzungen im 16., 17. und 18, Jahrhundert: RGST 134. Müns 1995, Aschendorff. xxiii-483 p.; bibliog xi-xxiii. 3-402-03796-9.

2707 **Meiss** Klaus, Streit um die Lutherbibel; Sprachwissenschaftliche Untersuchungen zur neuhochdeutschen Standardisierung (Schwerpunkt Graphematik anhand Wittenberger und Frankfurter Drucker: EurHS 1/1437. Fra 1994, Lang. ix-220 p. 3-631-46918-7. -- RRHE 90 (1995) 598s (J.-F. *Gilmont*).

2708 **Notker** Labeo [c.1000], Der Psalter, ETax Petrus W.: Altdeutsche Textbibliothek 84.91.93 (Werke Notkers 8-10). Tü 1979-83, Niemeyer. 3-484-20097-9.

D6.4 **Versiones nordicae** *et variae*

2709 **Cromphout** Frans, *Vyvere* Peter Vande, De Bijbel in onze taal, voor elke dag [bloemlezing]. Tielt 1994, Lannoo. : CVl 25 (1995) 97-102 (W. *Weren*).

2710 **Vries** A. de, Zuiver en onvervalscht ? Een beschrijvingsmodel voor bijbelvertalingen ontwikkeld en gedemonstreerd aan de Petrus Canisius vertaling [diss.]. Amst 1994. 248 p. 90-5383-343-9. -- TTh 35 (1995) 70. RG(ereformeerd)TT 95 (1995) 87 (N.J. *Tromp*: 'toch blijft er nog veel te wensen over' .. historische gegevens).

2710* [*Rebić* Adalbert, NT *Fućak* J.] Jeruzelemska Biblia u hrvatskoj. Zagreb 1994, Kršćanska sadašnost. xxiii-1814 p. -- *BogSmot 65 (1995) 271s (Z.I. *Herman*).

2711   **Heriban** Jozef,   Sväté Pismo starého i nového Zákona.   R 1995, S. Cirillo e Metodio. 2623 p.

2712   [J] The two books of Kings: The Holy Bible, annotated critical translation from the original languages by the Studium Biblicum Franciscanum.   Tokyo 1994, San Paolo.   363 p.

2713   *Yaeko* M.,   Nineteenth-century Japanese translations of the New Testament: *JapanChrR 61 (1995) 75-90   [NTAb 40,p.404].

2714   *Tablino* Paul,   Some information about the translation of the Bible into the Borana language (dialect of Kenya Oromo): RSEt 37 (1993) 167-175: first proofs messed up in U.S. by computer-use, second proofs slowly but accurately corrected and typeset in Nairobi, printed in Korea: Brown (-bound), with deuterocanonica, and Black without.

D7 *Problemata vertentis* -- The art of translation

2715   **Askani** Hans-Christoph,   Das Problem der Übersetzung, dargestellt an Franz ROSENZWEIG, I.   Die Methoden und Prinzipien der Rosenzweigschen und BUBER-Rosenzweigschen Übersetzungen: ev. Diss. [D]*Jüngel* E.   Tübingen 1994. -- ThRv 91 (1995) 101.

2716   **Barnstone** Willis,   The poetics of translation; history, theory, practice 1993 → 9,1681: [R]CritRR 7 (1994) 77-79 (R.G. *Bratcher*: 'quirky but lucid' like LARTRAUD'S JEROME); [J]LT(Ox) 9 (1995) 230s (S. *Gillespie*).

2717   *Block* Per,   Några tankar om styrfaktorer vid tolkningsval: → 93, [F]KIEFFER R., SEÅ 60 (1995) 5-21.

2718   **Buber** Martin, *Rosenzweig* Franz,   Scripture and translation [+ Buber, The how and why of biblical translation], [T]*Rosenwald* Lawrence, (*Fox* Everett) 1994 →10,1540; $ 25: [R]OTA 18 (1995) p.144 (C.T. *Begg*).

2719   **Buzzetti** Carlo,   La Bibbia e la sua traduzione → 9,190a; studi tra esegesi, pastorale e catechesi: Strumenti per approfondire la Bibbia.   T-Leumann 1993, Elle Di Ci.   360 p. L[m] 32. -- [R]PaVi 39,4 (1994) 54 (T. *Lorenzin*); Protest(antesimo) 50 (1995) 83s (B. *Costabel*).

2720   *Callam* Daniel,   Why Rome is [apparently, in guarding against falsifications in an 'inclusive' Bible translation] obnoxious: *CanadCath 13,1 (1995) 2s.

2721 **Chouraqui** André,   Reflexion über Problematik und Methode der Übersetzung von Bible und Koran [< French lecture for Tübingen 1993 Lucas prize → 10,1541].   Tü 1994, Mohr.   66 p.   DM 39.   3-16-146202-5. -- [R]BoL (1995) 48 (G.H. *Jones*); E(xp)T 107 (1995s) 182 (R. *Mason*).

2722   *Ellington* John,   'Thus and so', 'such and such', 'so and so': [terms qualifying biblical] pseudo-quotations in translation: BTrans 45 (1994) 410-5 [< OTA 18 (1995) 255: 1 Sam 18,24; 21,2; 2 Sam 15,2; 17,15; 1 Kgs 6,1; 2 Kgs 6,8-10; 9,12; Ruth 4].

2723   **Hargreaves** Cecil,   A translator's freedom 1993 → 2686 supra.

2724   [E]**Jasper** David,   Translating religious texts 1993 → 9,1690; [R][J]LT(Ox) 9 (1995) 231s (S. *Gillespie*).

2725   *Jenkins* R.G.,   Translating the Scriptures: reflections on ancient precedent : A(ustrl)BR 41 (1993) 1-17.

2726   **Lapide** Pinchas,   Ist die Bibel richtig übersetzt ? 2; GTb 1441, 1994 → 10,1547: [R]ThLZ 120 (1995) 1077 (J. *Rohde*).

2727 *a) Lebrun* Dominique, Les traductions liturgiques; statut et enjeux; -- *b) Auneau* Joseph, AT -- NT; commentaires pastoraux: M(ais)D 202 (1995) 137-147.

2728 [E]**Marc'hadour** Germain, Le lexique chrétien; permanences et avatars. Angers 1993, Univ.Ouest. 168 p. $ 20. 0987-7290. -- [R]EThL 71 (1995) 256s (J.E. *Vercruysse*: on translation and its history); HeythJ 36 (1995) 362 (J.P. *Marmion*: of chief interest for three articles on Gregory MARTIN's 1582 real Douay version, virtually unknown since CHALLONER's drastic revision).

2729 [E]**Moreschini** C., *Menestrina* G., La traduzione dei testi religiosi [Trento 10-11.II.1993]. Brescia 1994 → 10,375*b*; L[m] 30: [R]RasT 36 (1995) 373-5 (E. *Cattaneo*).

2730 *Nida* E.A., The sociolinguistics of Bible translating: *JianD 1,2 (Hong Kong 1994) 19-34 [NTAb 39,p.10].

2731 **Orlinsky** H.M., *Bratcher* R.G., A history of Bible translation and the North American contribution 1991 → 7,1629: [R]VT 45 (1995) 238-140 (J.A. *Emerton*: biased on Isa 7,14).

2732 *Rochette* Bruno, Du grec au latin et du latin au grec; les problèmes de la traduction dans l'antiquité gréco-romaine ; Latomus 54 (1995) 245-261; p. 293, JÉRÔME.

2733 **Scanlin** Harold, The Dead Sea Scrolls and modern translations of the Old Testament. Wheaton IL 1993, Tyndale. xi-179 p.; 12 pl. 0-8423-1010-X. -- [R]OTA 18 (1995) p. 437 (P.D. *Sansone*).

2734 *Schowalter* Daniel N., Lost in translation; do we really need to read footnotes ? [yes; dangers of non-literal translation] : BiRe 11,4 (1995) 34-38.

2735 **Seele** Astrid, Römische Übersetzer -- Nöte, Freiheiten, Absichten. Da 1995, Wiss. viii-148 p. 3-534-12492-8.

2736 *Smalley* William A., Language and culture in the development of Bible Society translation theory and practice : IBM(iss)R 19 (1995) 61-71.

2737 [E]**Thiede** Carsten P., Bibelübersetzung zwischen Inkulturation und Manipulation: BeitDisk 17. Pd/W 1993, Inst. Bildung / Brockhaus. iii-207 p. 3-417-26916-4. -- [R]ActuBbg 31 (1994) 49 (J. *O'Callaghan*).

2738 La traduction; problèmes théoriques et pratiques: Cercle Ling.Travaux 10. Aix-en-Provence 1993, Univ. 286 p. 2-85399-312-4. -- [R]Salesianum 57 (1995) 801 (R. *Bracchi*).

2739 *Veltri* Giuseppe, Le traduzioni bibliche come problema testuale e storiografico nel rinascimento delle 'poliglotte ' e d'Azaria DE'ROSSI: Laur 35 (1994) 3-30.

2740 **Zeini** Nagwa Taha el-, Criteria for the evaluation of translation; a pragma-stylistic approach: diss. Cairo 1994, [D]*Gamal-Eddin* S. 527 p. 95-23614, -- DissA 56 (1995s) p. 908.

D8 *Concordantiae, lexica specialia* -- **Specialized dictionaries, synopses**

2741 **Bompois** C., Concordance du NT[2rev] [[1]1965-80]. P 1995, Mame. 610 p. F 165. 2-7289-0707-2 [< NTAb 40,p.].

2742 Concordance de la Traduction Œcuménique de la Bible [basée sur [2rev]1988, computer Maredsous] 1993 → 9,1711; 10,1554: [R]CBQ 57 (1995) 765 (A. *Cody*: first concordance of the entire Bible in which are indicated the Hebrew, Aramaic, and Greek sources of the French words); RB 102 (1995) 469 (É. *Nodet*: high praise; far superior to the Maredsous 1982 concordance)

2743 **Goodrick** Edward W., *Kohlenberger* John R.[III], *Swanson* James A., The [NIV] exhaustive concordance to the Greek New Testament. GR 1995, Zondervan. xv-1056 p. $ 50. 0-310-41030-4 [ThD 43,73, puts Kohlenberger first]. -- [R]JETS 38 (1995) 248-250

(L. I. *Hodges*, '1990').

2744 **Thompson** J. David, *Baird* J. Arthur, A critical concordance to the Gospel of Mt /
Mk / Lk / Jn: Computer Bible 39-42. Lewiston NY 1993, Jn 1994, Mellen. v-979 p. / v-641
p. / v-1071 p. / v-778 p. $ 270 each; sb. $ 200. 0-935-106-36?; -75; -83; Jn 0-7734-4094-1
[RStR 22,247, M.W. *Holmes*].

| IV. → K1 | V. Exegesis generalis VT vel cum NT |

D9 Commentaries on the whole Bible or OT

2745 **Alonso Schökel** Luis, Biblia del Peregrino II. Notas exegéticas. Bilbao 1993, Egea.
xxiv-2221 p. III. 348 p. 84-271=1834-1. -- [R]ActuBbg 31 (1994) 37s (J. *O'Callaghan*).

2746 La Biblia de estudio: Dios habla hoy. 1995, Sociedades Bíblicas Unidas. 1970 p.

2747 **Carson** D.A., *al.*, New Bible commentary[3], 21st century edition ([1]1953, [2rev]1970).
Leicester/DG 1994, Inter-Varsity. xiii-1455 p. $ 40 [JETS 39, 149s, D.M. *Howard*].

2748 Charts evaluating 14 merits: 1995 review of [52] study Bibles: BArR 21 (1995) 72 .
74 . 76.

2749 **Clare** John D.,(texto), *Wansbrough* Henry (comentario), La Biblia, historia viva. 256
p. -- [R]*Carthaginensia 11 (1995) 467 (R. *Sanz Valdivieso*, abundantes fotografías, mapas,
gráficos).

2750 [E]**Hiesberger** Jean-Marie, The Catholic Bible; personal study edition, New American
Bible. NY 1995, Oxford-UP. 0-19-528405-4.

2751 The international inductive study Bible. Eugene OR 1993, Harvest. xlviii-2214 p.
$ 40. -- [R]BS 151 (1994) 126s (C.H. *Dyer* commends above the many rivals).

2752 **Kee** Howard C., The Cambridge annotated [NRSV] study Bible[2rev.]
335 p.; maps. £ 27. 0-85384-611-2. -- : TBR 8,1 (1995s) 9 (A.*Gilmore*).

2753 **Kroeger** Catherine C., *Evans* Mary, *Storkey* Elaine, The women's study New
Testament based on the NRSV. L 1995, Marshall Pickering. [viii-] 599 p. 0-551-02908-0.

2754 [E]**Mays** James L., Harper's Bible commentary 1988 → 4,2035 ... 10,1571: [R]Vidyajyoti
59 (1995) 544s (P.M. *Meagher*).

2755 [E]**Meeks** Wayne, The HarperCollins study Bible 1992 → 10,1572: [R]Vidyajyoti 59 (1995)
64s (P.M. *Meagher*)/

2756 **Mills** Watson D., *al.*, Mercer commentary on the Bible 1994 → 10,1573: [R]OTA 18
(1995) p. 464 (R.E. *Murphy*).

2757 **NInterp**: New Interpreter's Bible, [E]**Keck** Leander E., 1 (1994) → 10,1575: [R]RExp
92 (1995) 396s (J.W. *Cox*):*RRTh 3 (1995) 9-14 (P. *Lindström*); *SewTR 39 (1995) 65-74
[both < NTAb 40,p.191]; SWJT 37,3 (19950 51s (H.B. *Hunt*). -- Vol. 8, NT general; Mt Mk
[ThD 42,379]: 9. Lk Jn. Nv 1995, Abingdon. $ 55 each. 0-687-27821-X; -2-8 [Int adv].

2758 **NJB**: The New Jerome Biblical Commentary, [E]**Brown** R.E., *al.*, 1989 → 5,384 ...
10,1526: [R]EstB 53 (1995) 125s (A. *de la Fuente*).

2759 **Sailhamer** John, The NIV compact Bible commentary. GR 1994, Zondervan, 608 p.

2758 **NJB**: The New Jerome Biblical Commentary, ᴱ**Brown** R.E., *al.*, 1989 → 5,384 ... 10,1526: ᴿEstB 53 (1995) 125s (A. *de la Fuente*).

2759 **Sailhamer** John, The NIV compact Bible commentary. GR 1994, Zondervan, 608 p. $ 15. 0-310-51460-6. -- ᴿBoL (1995) 73 (J. *Goldingay*, unfavoring).

2760 **Schüssler Fiorenza** Elisabeth, Searching the Scriptures, 2. A feminist commentary 1994 → 10,1166: ᴿDoLi 45 (1995) 387-391 (Céline *Mangan*).

2761 ᴱ**Verbrugge** Verlyn D., NRSV Harper study Bible, [1964] expanded and updated; *Lindsell* Harold, study helps. GR 1991, Zondervan. xii-1914 p. + concordance 183 p.; 6 maps. $ 36. 0-310-90203-7. -- ᴿBoL (1995) 54 (R.J. *Coggins*: 'handsome presentation volume', 'curious hybrid').

¶ *The sections E, F, G [VII-XIII] dealing with the proper exegesis of biblical books and verses, have been published already by R. ALTHANN as Elenchus of Biblica 11/1 for 1995.*

XV. Theologia biblica

H1 **Biblical theology** .1 [OT] God

2762 **Armstrong** Karen, A history of God; the 4000-year quest of Judaism, Christianity and Islam 1993 → 9,7001; 10,7000 [= 1995] :ᴿAmHR 100 (1995) 481s (H. *Mason*); Church 11,3 (NY 1995) 48-50 (Karen Sue *Smith*, also on MILES J., 'God's critics'); Encounter 56 (1995) 218s (D.A. *Pittman*): JRel 75 (1995) 293-5 (Anne *Carr*); P(ersp)Ref 9,1 (1994) 22 (J.H. *Ellens*): TTh 35 (1995) 252-270 (J. van *Laarhoven*: the God of ordinary people [who couldn't read, 900-1200 A.D.].

2763 **Armstrong** Karen, Nah ist und schwer zu fassen der Gott; 3000 Jahre Glaubensgeschichte von Abraham bis Albert EINSTEIN [A history of God 1993, ᵀ*Kornau* Doris, *al*. Mü 1993, Droemer Knaur. 608 p. DM 50. 3-426-26693-8. - ᴿActuBbg 31 (1994) 222s (J. *Boada*).

2764 **Barsotti** Divo, Il Signore é uno²: Tabor 1. Caltanisetta 1991, Seminario. 291 p. Lᵐ 32.

2765 **Beeck** Franz J. van, God encountered; a contemporary Catholic systematic theology, 2. The revelation of the glory, ii. One God, creator of all that is. ColMn 1994, Liturgical/ Glazier. xv-199 p. $ 15. 0-8146-5499-1 [< ThD 42 (1995) 257].

2766 **Benin S.,** The footprints of God 1993 → 9,7003: ᴿ*A(sn)JS 20 (1995) 414-7 (Idit *Dobbs-Weinstein*); AmHR 100 (1995) 133s (K. F. *Morrison*); Spec 40 (1995) 3393 (O. *Leaman*).

2767 **Blumenthal** David R., Facing the abusing God; a theology of protest; 208 p. $ 18 pa. 0-664-25464-0; 1993 → 8,7002: ᴿInterpretation 49 (1995) 102 (W. *Brueggemann*).

2768 **Bosetti** Elena, Yahweh, shepherd of the people 1993 → 9,7005*a*: ᴿCBQ 57 (1995) 117s (J.J. *Pilch*).

2769 **Briend** Jacques, Dieu dans l'Écriture: LD 150, 1992 → 8,7002 ... 10,7004: ᴿEstB 53 (1995) 398 (S. *Ibarzabal*); ScrT(Pamp) 37 (1995) 703s (L. F. *Mateo-Seco*).

2770 *Briend* Jacques, Le Dieu d'Israël reconnu par les étrangers, signe de l'universalisme du salut: → 14, [F]BEAUCHAMP P., 'Ouvrir les Écritures '1995, 65-76.

2771 *Daubercies* Pierre, Dieu, utile ou inutile ? ou Le paradoxe de l'utilité dans l'Écriture: E(spr)eV 105 (1995) 385-393 . 401-413.

2772 [E]**Dietrich** W., Ein Gott allein ..: OBO 139, 1994 → 10,467*: [R](Tü)TQ 175 (1995) 64-66 (W. *Gross*).

2773 *Domínguez Morano* Carlo, El Dios imaginado [3 perniciosos, 3 saludables]: RF 231 (1995) 29-40.

2774 **Friedman** Richard E., The disappearance of God; a divine mystery. Boston 1995, Little Brown. vi-335 p. 0-316-29434-9.

2775 **Garaudy** R., ¿ Tenemos necesidad de Dios ?   M 1994, PPC 200 p. -- [R]EstTrin 29 (1995) 125s (X. *Pikaza*).

2776 **Garrigues** J.-M., Ce Dieu qui passe par les hommes, I. Les alliances d'Adam à Moïse: Conférences de carême [II. Jésus; III. L'Église. P 1992 [1993s], Mame. 167 p. [168 p.   200 p.] -- [R]NRT 117 (1995) 746s (L. *Volpe*).

2777 **Geivett** Douglas, Evil and the evidence for God; the challenge of John HICK's theodicy 1994 → 10.7008: [R]NOxR 62,6 (1995) 25s (B. *Sweetman*).

2778 **Gesché** Adolphe, Dieu pour penser [1s, 1993s → 9,7235; 10,7161] -- 3s, 1994: [R]LV(itF) 50 (1995) 112s (P. *Tihon*).

2779 **Godzieba** Anthony J., Ontotheology to excess: imagining God without being [MARION, J.-Lb.,1991]: TS 56 (1995) 3-20.

2780 **Kaiser** Otto, Der Gott des ATs: ThATs 1, Uni-Tb 1747, 1993 → 9,7019: [R]CBQ 57 (1995) 143s (L. *Laberge*).

2781 **Koester** Craig R., The dwelling of God; the Tabernacle 1989 → 5,2500 ... 7,2256: [R]JQR 84 (1993s) 79s (W. *Adler*).

2782 **Labuschagne** C.J., Zin en onzin over God; een kritische beschouwing van gangbare Godsvoorstellingen. Zoetermeer 1994, Boeken-C. 187 p. 90-239-0894-5. -- [R]OTA 18 (1995) p. 428 (M. *Kessler*).

2783 **Lodahl** Michael E., Shekhina / Spirit; divine presence in Jewish and Christian religion 1992 → 8,7013 ... 10,7011: [R]EThL 71 (1995) 215s (A. *Schoors*: provocative); Greg 76 (1995) 424s (J. *Dupuis*).

2784 **Lohfink** Norbert, *al.*, Dio unico; sulla nascita del monoteismo in Israele: QD 24, 1991 → 7,7013: 8,7014: [R]PaVi 39,1 (1994) 53s (A. *Rolla*).

2785 **McFague** Sallie, Modelos de Dios; teología para una era ecológica y nuclear, [T]*López* Agustln, *Tabuyo* María: PresT 76. Sdr 1994, Sal Terrae. 309 p.   84-293-1122-X. -- [R]ActuBbg 31 (1994) 197-9 (H. *Vall*); EE 70 (1995) 126-8 (Higinio *Pi*); RF 231 (1995) 99s (R. de *Andrés*).

2786 -- *Reynolds* Terrence, Two MCFAGUEs; meaning, truth, and justification in Models of God: MoTh 11 (1995) 289-313.

2787 *Magonet* Jonathan, The names of God in biblical narratives: → 170, [F]SAWYER, J., Words; JSOT.s 195 (1995) 80-96.

2788 **Mason** Rex, Old Testament pictures of God: Regent's Study Guides 2. L 1993, Smyth & H. 210 p. 0-9518104-1-3. -- [R]ET 106 (1994s) 31 (C.S. *Rodd*).

2789 **Mettinger** Tryggve N.D., Buscando a Dios; significado y mensaje de los nombres divinos en la Biblia [1988 → 4,2477], [T]. Córdoba 1994, Almendro. 245 p. -- [R]BiFe 21 (1995) 302 (M. *Sáenz Galache*); E(st)E 70 (1995) 569-571 (E. *Pascual*); RF 232 (1995) 121 (R. de *Andrés*).

2790 **Miles** Jack, God, a biography. NY 1995, Knopf, 446 p. $ 27.50. 0-679-41833-4. --
[R]America 173,1 (1995) 24.26 (T.H. *Sanks*); Commentary 100,1 (1995) 53s (P. *Johnson*);
*CWeal 122,10 (1995) 32 -34 (L.T. *Johnson*); Midstream 41,5 (1995) 37-40 (R. *Patai*).
  Minette de Tillesse Caetano, O Deus pelas costas; teología narrativa da Bíblia: RBBras
  12,1-3 (1995) → 1386s.
2791 **Moberly** R.W.L., The OT of the OT 1992 → 8,7017 ... 10,7013: [R]Greg 76 (1995) 381s
(G.L. *Prato*).
2792 **Nicholls** David, Deity and domination; images of God and the State in the nineteenth
and twentieth centuries. L 1989, Routledge. xiv-321 p. pa.1994, $19; 0-415-01172-0.
- [R]CScR 25 (1995s) 115-8 (S.C. *Mott*).
2793 *Ohmann* H.M., Some remarks on the use of the term 'theophany' [not in LXX or NT]
in the study of the OT: → **8**, [F]BAKER J., Sacrifice 1995, 2-12 [< OTA 19,120].
2794 [E]**Philonenko** Marc, Le trône de Dieu 1990/3 → 9,404: [R]Salesianum 57 (1995) 374s (R.
Vicent).
2795 *a) Preus* J. Samuel, Anthropomorphism and SPINOZA's innovations; -- *b) Benavides*
Gustavo, Cognitive and ideological aspects of divine anthropomorphism: Religion 25
(1995) 1-8 / 9-22, → 8055a infra
2796 *Pury* Albert de, Le Dieu qui vient en adversaire; de quelques différences à propos de
la perception de Dieu dans l'AT : → 155, [F]RENAUD B., Ce Dieu: LDIV 159 (1995) 45-67.
2797 *a) Rice* G., Africans and the origins of the worship of Yahweh; -- *b) Felder* C.H.,
Afrocentrism, the Bible, and the politics of difference: JRelTht 50 (1993s) 27-44 / 45-56
[< ZAW 107 (1995) 506].
2798 **Sáenz Galache** Mercedes, El rostro oculto de Dios. M 1994, BF. 254 p. -- [R]Lum(Vt)
44 (1995) 195s (F. *Ortiz de Urtaran*).
2799 **Schillenberg** J.L., Divine hiddenness and human reason. Ithaca 1993, Cornell Univ.
217 p. $ 33.50. -- [R]JRel 75 (1995) 295s (J.D. *Kiernan-Lewis*).
2800 *Thomas* C., Der jüdische Monotheismus in christlicher Sicht -- Versuch eines neuen
Gesprächs: BuSchweizGesJudF 2 (1993) 22-32 [< ZAW 107 (1995) 134].
2801 **Trevethan** Thomas L., The beauty of God's holiness. DG/Leicester 1995, InterVarsity.
278 p. £ 10. 0-8308-1607-0.
2802 *Unterman* Jeremiah, The socio-legal origin for the image of God as redeemer *gô'el* of
Israel: → 130, [F]MILGROM J., Pomegranates 1995, 399-405.
2803 **Zeindler** Matthias, Gott und das Schöne; Studien zur Theologie der Schönheit [ev.
Diss. Bern]: ForSysÖk 68. Gö 1993, Vandenhoeck & R. 452 p. -- [R]RTPh 127 (1995) 261-
271 (J. *Cottin*; Eng. 320).

H1.3 *Immutabilitas* -- **God's suffering, process theology**

2804 **Altizer** Thomas J.J., The death of God; a theological genealogy. LvL 1993, W-Knox.
200 p. -- [R]RelStR 21 (1995) 38 (D.J. *Bryant*).
2805 *Aquino Ranhilio* C., HICK and Process Philosophy on the reality of God: PhilipSac 29
(1994) 263-279.
2806 **Barineau** R. Maurice, The theodicy of Alfred North WHITEHEAD; a logical and ethical
vindication. Lanham MD 1991, UPA. vii-195 p. $ 39.75; pa. $ 17.75. -- [R]AmJTP 16 (1995)
226-8 (H.J. *Cargas*); CritRR 6 (1993) 47s (D. *Basinger*).
2807 *Bouton-Parmentier* Suzanne, La Bible et la 'process philosophy'; perspectives sur leur
autonomie et leur complémentarité: RTL 26 (1995) 211-7; Eng. 280.

2808 **Boyd** Gregory, Trinity and process .. HARTSHORNE 1992 → 8,7030: [R]Horizons 22 (1995) 138s (J.A. *Bracken*).

2809 **Bracken** Joseph A., The divine matrix; creativity as link between East and West (in the Maryknoll series): Faith meets faith. Mkn/Herefordshire 1995, Orbis/Gracewing. xi-179 p. $ 21. 1-57075-004-1 / [ThD 43,158].

2810 *Bracken* J., Panentheism from a trinitarian perspective : Horizons 22 (1995) 7-28.

2811 **Brink** Gijsbert van den, Almighty God: a study of the doctrine of divine omnipotence [rather hedged nowadays in view of free will]: Studies in philosophical theology 7. Kampen 1992, Kok Pharos. 316 p. 90-390-0024-7. -- [R]ET 106,10 2d-top choice (1994s) 290s (C.S. *Rodd*); Bijdragen 56 (1995) 343-5 (N. *Schreurs*, Eng.).

2812 *Brom* Luco J. van den, Är det meningsfullt att tala om Guds handlande ?: SvTK 69 (1993) 16-25; Eng. 25, 'Understanding an act of God'.

2813 **Brosse** Richard, L'histoire de Dieu; historicité et devenir comme notions-clé de la théologie de Karl RAHNER: Diss. St. Georgen, [D]*Kunz* E. Frankfurt/M 1994. -- TR 91 (1995) 95.

2814 **Buckley** James J., Seeking the humanity of God 1992 → 9.7047; 10,7023: [R]RStR 21 (1995) 299-304-310 (B.E. *Hinze* & G.P. *Schner*, both also on DINOIA J., FREI H., THIEL J.: 'Postliberal theology and Roman Catholic theology').

2815 **Burrell** David B., Freedom and creation in three traditions. ND 1993, Univ. xi-225 p. -- [R]ModT 10 (1994) 419s (F. *Kerr* says the book is 'from' though not 'Acta of' the 1989 Notre Dame colloquium).

2816 *Cavalcoli* Giovanni, Il mistero dell'impassibilità divina: Div 39 (1995) 111-167.

2817 *Chisholm* Robert B.[J], Does God 'change his mind' ?: BS 152 (1995) 387-399.

2818 **Dorner** Isaak A., Divine immutability: a critical reconsideration [1858], [T]*Williams* Robert R., *Welch* Claude. Mp 1994, Fortress. 201 p. -- [R]RStR 21 (1995) 317s (M.J. *McClymond*).

2819 *Ekenberg* Anders, 'Allsmäktig' eller 'Allhärskare'? Några notiser: → 93, [F]KIEFFER R., SEÅ (1995) 165-172.

2820 *a) Esterbauer* Reinhold, Gott als physikalische Grösse; zum Zeitverständnis sowie Gottes- und Menschenbild naturwissenschaftlicher Weltanschauungen; -- *b) Cramer* Winfrid, 'Gewaltig sind die Werke Gottes'; Gedanken syrischer Christen zu Schöpfung, Erlösung und Vollendung: → 180, [F]SCHULTE R., Variationen 1995, 9-39 / 81-95 [251-284, *Kühschelm* R., Röm 8,18-22].

2821 **Franklin** Stephen T., Speaking from the depths; Alfred North WHITEHEAD's hermeneutical metaphysics of propositions, experience, symbolism, language and religion 1990 → 10,7026*: [R]JETS 38 (1995) 626-8 (J.D. *Morrison*).

2822 *Henry* Granville C., Does process thought allow personal immortality ?: RelSt 31 (1995) 311-321.

2823 *Keller* James A., The power of God and miracles in process theism: JAAR 63 (1995) 105-126.

2824 **Koltissek** Klaus, Vollmacht im AT und Judentum: PdTSt 24. Pd 1993, Schöningh. 186 p. DM 36. 3-506-76274-5. -- [R]THGL 85 (1995) 553s (C. *Dohmen*).

2825 **Korsmeyer** Jerry D., God-creature-revelation; a neoclassical framework for fundamental theology. Lanham MD 1995, UPA. xv-227 p. $ 48; pa. $29.50. 0-8191-9688-8; -9-4 [ThD 43,73: evolution and process theology for Catholics].

2826 *La Fauci* Fabio, ANSELMO rivisitato, l'argomento ontologico nella filosofia del processo di Charles HARTSHORNE: Vivarium 3 (1995) 387-404.

2827 **Leftow** Brian, Time and eternity 1991 → 8,7040: [R]JETS 38 (1995) 617-9 (W.L. *Craig*).

2827* *Lodzinski* Don, Empty time and the eternality of God: RelSt 31 (1995) 187-193.

2828 **McHenry** Leemon B., WHITEHEAD and BRADLEY -- a comparative analysis. Albany 1992, SUNY. xi-213 p. $ 57.50; pa. $ 19. -- [R]*CritRR 6 (1993) 463s (D. *Platt*).

2829 **MacKenzie** Iain, The anachronism of time; a theological study into the nature of time. Norwich 1994, Canterbury. xvi-191 p. £ 17.50. 1-85311-089-2. -- [R]ET 106 (1994s) 92 (W.D. *Hudson*).

2830 **Mesle** C. Robert, Process theology, a basic introduction. St.Louis ... Chalice. 148 p. $ 13. -- [R]Encounter 56 (1995) 101s (G. *Nordgulen*).

2831 **Moonan** Lawrence, Divine power. Ox 1994, Clarendon. xi-396. £ 40. -- [R]RelSt 31 (1995) 269-271 (G.J. *Hughes*).

2832 **Neville** Robert C., Creativity and God; a challenge to process theology[2] [= 1980 + preface and minor revisions]. Albany 1995, SUNY. xv-163 p. $ 17 pa. 0-7914-2821-4; pa. -2-2 [RStR 22,228, B.L. *Whitney*].

2833 **Nnamani** Amuluche G., *a)* The trinitarian (im)passibility of God; an inquiry into the issue of divine suffering in the classical, modern western and third world theologies: kath. Diss. [D]*Kern*. Innsbruck 1995. -- ThRv Beilage 92/2, x; ZkT 117 (1995) 507s. -- *b)* The paradox of a suffering God; on the classical, Modern-Western and Third World struggles to harmonise the incompatible attributes of the trinitarian God: SIGC 95. Fra 1995, Lang. 418 p.; bibliog. 425-428.

2834 **Padgett** Alan G., God, eternity and the nature of time 1992 → 9,9071; 10,7014: [R]EvQ 66 (1994) 337-344 (D. *Braine*)

2835 **Pinnock** Clark, *al.*, The openness of God; a biblical challenge to the traditional understanding of God [...'does not control everything that happens']. DG 1994, InterVarsity. 202 p. $ 23. -- [R]BS 152 (1995) 487-9 (G.R. *Kreider*).

2835* *Robbins* Jerry K., The wrath of God in process exposition: Dialog 33 (St. Paul 1994) 252-8 (245-251, *Paulson* Steven D., 259-262, *Lischer* Richard).

2836 **Sarot** Marcel, God, passibility and corporeality: *StPhT 6, 1992 → 9,7075b: 10,7039: [R]EThL 70 (1994) 204-7 (M. *Steen*).

2837 *Scharbau* Friedrich O., Gottes Trauer, Gottes Tränen; zur Ökumene mit der römisch-katholischen Kirche: LM 34,1 (1995) 14-20 [< NZSTh 37 (1995) 218].

2838 **Schiwy** Günther, Abschied vom allmächtigen Gott. Mü 1995, Kösel. 160 p. DM 29,80. 3-466-20396-1. -- [R]Entschluss 50,12 (1995) 33 (R. *Oberforcher*); ThGL 85 (1995) 414-6 (J.-H. *Tück*).

2839 **Scriba** Albrecht, Die Geschichte des Motivkomplexes Theophanie; seine Elemente, Einbindung in Geschehensabläufe und Verwendungsweisen in altisraelitischer, frühjüdischer und frühchristlicher Literatur [Diss. Mainz 1992, [D]*Brandenburger* E.; FRLANT 167. Gö 1995, Vandenhoeck & R. 274 p.; Bibliog. 232-250. DM 98. 3-525-53850-2 [< OTA 19, p.363, W. *Vogels*].

2840 **Sweeney** Leo, Divine infinity in Greek and medieval thought 1992 → 8,7052 ... 10,7041: [R]L(aval)TP 51 (1995) 473s (Andrius *Valevičius:* most extensive treatment available, but not as freshly down-to-earth as his 1965 Existentialism).

2841 **Whitehead** Alfred N., Dio e il mondo; L'immortalità, [E]*Bosco* Nynfa. N 1993, ESI. 62 p. -- [R]FilTeo 9 (1995) 655s (G.P. *Cammarota*).

2842 **Will** James E., The universal God; justice, love, and peace in the global village. LvL 1994, W-Knox. viii-280 p. $ 25. 0-664-25560-4. -- [R]*TBR 8,3 (1995s) 20s (I. *Markham:* process theology mediating between exclusivist and relativist Christianity).

H1.4 *Femininum in Deo* -- **God as father and mother**

2843 **Alonso Schökel** Luis, Dios padre 1994 → 10,7044*: [R]BiFe 21 (1995) 147 (M. *Sáenz Galache*); EstTrin 29 (1995) 160s (Israel *Guijarro*).

2844 *Baumann* Gerlinde, Gottes Geist und Gottes Weisheit; eine Verknüpfung: → 1739, Feministische Hermeneutik 1994, 138-148.

2845 **Bigham** Steven, The image of God the Father in Orthodox theology and iconography and other studies. Torrance CA 1995, Oakwood. xii-259 p. $ 11 pa. 1-879038-15-3 [< ThD 43,257].

2846 *Boughton* L.C., More than metaphors; masculine-gendered names and the knowability of God: Thom 58 (1994) 283-316 [NTAb 39, p.84].

2847 **Bouyer** Louis, Sophia ou le monde en Dieu: Théologies, 1994; [R]RET 55 (1995) 262s (M. *Gesteira Garza*).

2848 *Collins* Raymond F., Is the 'Our Father' Jesus' own prayer?: LiLi 31,4 (1995) 24-30.

2849 **Eilberg-Schwartz** Howard, God's phallus and other problems for men and monotheism 1994 → 10,7051: [R]BiRe 11,4 (1995) 15 (R.S. *Hendel*); JJS 46 (1995) 348 (G. *Harvey*).

2850 **Gómez Acebo** Isabel, Dios también es madre; reflexiones sobre el Antiguo Testamento. M 1995, San Pablo. 196 p. -- [R]SalTer 83 (1995) 489 (490 sobre SCHLOSSER).

Grelot Pierre, Dieu, le Père de Jésus-Christ 1994 → 3409 infra.

2851 *Harper* William, On calling God 'mother': Faith & Philosophy 11 (ND/Asbury 1994) 290-7.

2852 **Hauke** Manfred, Gott oder Göttin. 1993. [R]ForKT 11 (1995) 155s (M. *Seybold*).

2853 *Hook* Donald D., *Kimel* Alvin F., *a)* Calling God 'father', a theolinguistic analysis : FAP(hil) 12 (1995) 207-222; -- *b)* Is God a 'he' ? [yes, in grammar but not biology]: Worship 65 (1994) 145-157.

2854 **Johnson** Elizabeth A., She who is 1992 → 9,7103; 10,7058: [R]RStR 21 (1995) 19-21 (Mary Aquin *O'Neill*) & 21-25 (Mary M. *Fulkerson*).

2855 **Kimel** Alvin T., Speaking the Christian God .. feminism 1993 -> 9,7103; [R]S(cot)JTh 48 (1995) 280s (Esther *Reed*); Worship 65 (1994) 279-281 (Gail *Ramshaw*).

2856 **Mollenkott** Virginia R., Dio femminile; l'immaginario biblico di Dio come donna [The divine feminine 1984]. Padova 1993, Messaggero. 123 p. L[m] 16. 88-250-0186-X. -- [R]Greg 76 (1995) 205s (J. *Galot*).

2857 **Ramshaw** Gail, God beyond gender; feminist Christian God-language. Mp 1995, Fortress. viii-144 p. £ 9. 0-8006-2774-1. -- [R]TTh 35 (1995) 421 (Anne-Marie *Korte*).

2858 **Raschke** Carl A. & Susan D., The engendering God; male and female faces of God. LvL 1995, W-Knox. 102 p. 0-64-25502-7 [RStR 22,228, Linda A. *Mercadante*: suitable though rambling and confrontive].

2859 *Ruckstuhl* E., Abba, Vater! Überlegungen zum Stand der Frage: *FsZ 41 (1994) 515-525 (-531, *Schelbert* G. response) [NTAb 39, p.381].

2860 *Salomonsen* Jone, Er 'Gud vår Mor' avgud eller sann gud ? [Is 'God as mother' an idol or true God ?]: NTT 95 (1994) 195-212; Eng. 212 [traditional liturgy embodies a realistic magic in which God's name ('Father') and his presence are substantially connected, 'while feminists can include the female God in their worship due to a more performative magical theory'].

2861 **Sebastian** Joseph, God as feminine; Hindu and Christian visions; a dialogue [< diss. Pont. Univ. Gregoriana]: EurUnivSt 23/523. Fra/Tiruchirapalli 1995, Lang / St. Paul's Sem.

xxiv-378 p.; bibliog. 407-458. DM 118 / rs 200. 3-631-48211-6. -- RVidyajyoti 59 (1995) 548s (J. *Gispert-Sauch*).

Stienstra Nelly, YHWH is the husband of his people; analysis of a biblical metaphor with special reference to translation 1993 → 8721 infra.

2862 *Upasi* Mihir, The feminine dimension of the Holy Trinity: I(nd)TS 31 (Bangalore 1994) 140-155 [NTAb 39, p.271].

2863 **Vanoni** Gottfried, 'Du bist doch unser Vater' (Jes 63,16); zur Gottesvorstellung des Ersten Testaments; SBS 159. Stu 1995, KBW. 114p.; Bibliog. 89-102. 3-460-04591-4

2864 EWacker M.-Theres, *Zenger* E., Der eine Gott und die Göttin 1991 → 7,7065 .. 9,7120: RTLtg 66 (1993) 60-63 (C. *Frevel*).

2865 *Wagner* Walter, Divine femaleness; two second-century contributions [APULEIUS, CLEMENT A.]: JRelSt 17 (1992) 19-43.

2866 **Widdicombe** Peter, The fatherhood of God from ORIGEN to ATHANASIUS. Ox 1994, Clarendon. 220 p. £ 35. 0-19-826751-7. -- R*CanadCath 13,11 (1995) 2l (F. *Firth*); ET 106 (1994s) 124s (G. *Bostock*); RStR 21 (1995) 336 (Nonna V. *Harrison*)..

2867 EWijk-Bos Johanna W.H. van, Reimagining God; the case for Scriptural diversity [feminist meeting Minneapolis Nov. 1993]. LvL 1995, W-Knox. xii-119 p. 0-664-25569-0 [NTAb 40, p.166]. -- RSewaneeTR 39 (1995s) 87-89 (Patricia *Hunt*).

H1.7 Revelatio

2868 *Bannach* Klaus, SCHELLINGs Philosophie der Offenbarung; Gehalt und theologiegeschichtliche Bedeutung: NZSTh 37 (1995) 57-74; Eng. 74.

2869 **Dulles** Avery, Models of revelation[2] [[1]1983]. Mkn 1992, Orbis. 344 p. $ 17. 0-88344-842-4. -- REThL 70 (1994) 496s (E. *Brito*).

2870 **Fisichella** Rino, La revelación, evento y credibilidad; ensayo de teología fundamental 1989 → 7,7075: RRET 55 (1995) 96s (María A. *Navarro Girón*).

2871 **Frenschkowski** Marco, Offenbarung und Epiphanie [< ev. Diss. Mainz 1994, DBöcher O.], 1. Grundlagen des spätantiken und frühchristlichen Offenbarungsglaubens: WUNT 2/79. Tü 1995, Mohr. ix-481 p.; Bibliog. 419-481. DM 128. 3-16-146433-8 [NTAb 40, p.543].

2872 *a) Grech* Prospero, Quid est veritas ? Rivelazione e ispirazione; nuove prospettive; -- *b) Penna* Romano, In difesa della 'intentio auctoris'; -- *c) Coda* Piero, Critica illuministica ed ermeneutica romantica della rivelazione: → 20, FBETTI U., Lateranum 61,2s (1995) 147-158; Eng. 158 / 159-180; Eng. 181 / 79-120; Eng. 12l.

2873 **Guarino** Thomas G., Revelation and truth; unity and plurality in contemporary theology [→ 9,11453: 10,10404]. Scranton/Toronto 1993, Univ./Assoc.Univ. 228 p. $ 38.50. 0-940866-18-8. -- REThL 70 (1994) 497s (E. *Brito*); JRel 75 (1995) 137s (J. A. *Tetlow*); RStR 21 (1995) 38 (W.J. *Collinge*).

2874 **Gunton** Colin A., A brief theology of revelation [1993 Princeton Warfield lectures]. E 1995, Clark. 134 p. £ 17. 0-567-09726-9.-- RE(xp)T 107,2 top choice (1995s) 33s (C.S. *Rodd*); EThL 71 (1995) 478-480 (T. *Merrigan*).

2875 **Harrington** Wilfrid J., Revelation: Sacra Pagina 16. ColMn c.1995, Liturgical. 271 p. $ 30. -- RCanadCath 13,8 (1995) 28 (W. O. *McCready*).

2876 **Haught** John F.,Mystery & promise; theology of revelation: NewTSt 2, 1993 → 10, 7089*; 0-8146-5792-3:RET 106(1994s)250 (G. *Newlands*); ZkT 117(1995)117s (K. *Neufeld*).

2877   **Raurell** Frederic, 'I Déu digué'; la Paraula fata historia.   Barc 1995, Fac.Theol.Catalunya. xii-462 p. 84-920074-7-8.

2878 **Swinburne** Richard, Revelation; from metaphor to analogy 1992 → 8,7103; 10,7098: [R]Bijdragen 56 (1995) 106s (L.H. *Westra*); C(alvin)TJ 29 (1994) 565-8 (R.J. *Feenstra*); Faith & Philosophy 11 (ND 1994) 328-333 (G.B. *Spradley*).

2879 *Thunberg* Lars, Revelation in biblical and patristic thought, challenge and offer to the inter-religious dialogue: StTh 49 (1995) 287-303.

2880   *a) Torres Queiruga* Andrés, ¿ Qué significa afirmar que Dios habla ? Hacia un concepto actual de la Revelación; -- *b) Aguirre* Rafael, Reinterpretar la Palabra hoy; cómo leer de forma creyente los textos fundantes de la fe; -- *c) Aleixandre* Dolores, Usar la Palabra o escucharla: SalTer 82 (1994) 331-347 / 349-360 / 377-385.

2881 **Wolterstorff** Nicholas, Divine discourse; philosophical reflections on the claim that God speaks. C 1995, Univ. x-326 p. 0-521-47557-0. -- [R]E(xp)T 107 (1995s) 189 (W.D. *Hudson*).

H1.8   Theologia fundamentalis

2882 *Bäckström* Anders, Om stabilitet och utveckling vid religionsvetenskaplig linje: SvTK 69 (1993) 8-15; Eng. 15: students' beliefs change only marginally in the course of their theological education.

2883 **Bauman** Michael, Pilgrim theology; taking the path of theological discovery. GR 1992, Zondervan. $ 15. -- [R]JETS 38 (1995) 241s (M.J. *Sawyer*).

2884 **Berzosa Martínez** Raúl, Hacer teología hoy; retos, perspectivas, paradigmas: Teología Siglo XXI, 11. M 1994, San Pablo. 258 p. -- [R]Lum(Vr) 44 (1995) 319s (F. *Ortiz de Urtaran*).

2885 **Bonsor** Jack A., Athens and Jerusalem; the role of philosophy in theology 1993 → 10,7102: [R]*CanadCath 13,2 (1995) 23s (J.A. *Buijs*).

2886   *a) Bortolin* Valerio, La teologia fondamentale nei suoi rapporti con la filosofia; -- *b) Moda* Aldo, Dalla comprensione come evidenza alla comprensione come ermeneutica; ancora sul rapporto filosofia-teologia: → 168, [F]SARTORI L., StPatav 42 (1995) 43-66 / 85-204.

2887 *Corben* Thomas, Teaching dogmatic theology; reflections on the discipline [.. the three critiques against neoscholasticism]: I(r)ThQ 61 (1995) 44-56.

2888 **Cunningham** David S., Faithful persuasion 1991s → 8,1350 ... 10,7104: [R]JAAR 63 (1995) 404-7 (Ellen T. *Charry*; joins a number of calls for rethinking objectivity in religion studies); S(cot)JTh 48 (1995) 125s (D. *Jones*); TorJT 11 (1995) 117s (P. *Wilson*).

2889 **Döring** Heinrich, *al.*, Den Glauben denken; neue Wege der Fundamentaltheologie 1993 → 9,322*; 10,7108: ZkT 117 (1995) 108 (K.H. *Neufeld*).

2890 **Dulles** Avery, The craft of theology 1992 → 8,236d ... 10,7111: [R]Encounter 56 (1995) 86-88 (P.D. *Browning*); ThLZ 120 (1995) 161s (J. *Langer*).

2891 *Dulles* Avery, Criteria of Catholic theology .. inclusiveness plus visible mediation: Com-US 22 (1995) 303-315.

2892 **Dupré** Louis, Passage to modernity; an essay on the hermeneutics of nature and culture. NHv c.1994, Yale Univ. 300 p. $ 30. -- [R]America 172,3 (1995) 22.24 (M.P. *Gallagher*).

2893 **Erickson** Millard J., Where is theology going ? GR 1994, Baker. 230 p. -- [R]RefR 49 (1995s) 75s (R.B. *Mayers*).

2894 *Fisichella* Rino, Oportet philosophari in theologia; delineazione di un sentiero ...: Greg 76 (1995) 221-262 . 503-533 . 701-727; franç. 262 . 534 . 728.

2895   *Ford* David H.,   On being theologically hospitable to Jesus Christ; Hans FREI's achievement: JThS 46 (1995) 532-546.

2896 **Forde** Gerhard O.,   Theology is for proclamation 1990 → 7,7116: RRestQ 37 (1995) 122-4 (A. *Resner*).

2897 **Frame** John M.,   Apologetics to the glory of God. Phillipsburg 1994, Presbyterian & R. 265 p, -- RRefTR 54 (1995) 37s (A.M. *Clarke*).

2898 *González Montes* Adolfo, La serie 'Würzburger Studien zur Fundamentaltheologie' [8.-11.; KEHRBACH K. 1992 ... NNAMDI R. 1993] : Salmanticensis 42 (1995) 121-131.

2899   *a) Grey* Mary, The shaking of the foundations [P.TILLICH 1949 sermon] -- again! Culture and the liberation of theology; -- *b) Boeve* Lieven, Bearing witness to the differend; a model for theologizing in the postmodern context: LouvSt 20 (1995) 347-361 / 362-379.

2900 **Gruber** Franz, Diskurs und Konsens im Prozess theologischer Wahrheit: ITS 40, 1993 → 10,7122 [kath. Diss. Linz, DRaberger W.]: RTPQ 143 (1995) 96s (H. *Sauer*).

2902 **Haight** Roger, Dynamics of theology. NY 1990, Paulist. 274 p. -- RRTL 26 (1995) 361s (E. *Brito*: la fidélité exige une réinterprétation constante).

2903 **Jones** Gareth, Critical theology; questions of truth and method. NY 1995, Paragon. x-270 p. $ 30; pa. $ 17. 1-55778-729-8; -30-1 [ThD 43.173].

2904 **Kelsey** David H., Between Athens and Berlin; the theological education debate. GR 1993, Eerdmans. viii-235 p. $ 19 -- RP(rinc)SB 16 (1995) 387-390 (J.E. *Loder*, also on his 1992 To understand God 1992 → 9,7177; 10.7128.).

2905   **Killen** Patricia O., *de Beer* John, The art of theological reflection. NY 1994, Crossroad. 156 p. $ 15 pa. -- RRefR 49 (1995s) 50 (A. *DeGelder*: 'crude'); SewaneeT 38 (1994s) 197 . 200 (Gail C. *Jones*).

2906   **Kreeft** Peter, *Tacelli* Ronald, Handbook of Christian apologetics. DG c.1995, InterVarsity. 399 p. $ 17. -- RNOxR 62,4 (1995 22-25 (M. *Pakaluk*: it is simply not acceptable to be a Christian merely because one's parents were).

2907 **Lewis** Gordon R., Testing Christianity's truth-claims; approaches to Christian apologetics. Lanham MD 1990, UPA. 363 p. [JETS 39, 310s, J. *Crespo,* also on 3 cognates].

2908 *Lison* Jacques, La théologie est-elle déclassée ? Dix-neuf thèses sur la confrontation de la théologie avec la crise actuelle des fondements : ScEs 47 (1995) 5-11.

2909 ELorizio G., *Galantino* N., Metodologia teologica; avviamento allo studio e alla ricerca pluridisciplinari. CinB 1994, S. Paolo. 487 p. Lm 35. -- RVivH 8 (1995) 415s (S. *Dianich*).

2910 **McGrath** Alister, Christian theology; an introduction 1994 → 10,7131*; £ 45; pa. £ 13. 0-631-10678-7; -9-5. -- RET 106 (1994s) 124 (D. *Cornick*; for absolute beginners); TTh 35 (1995) 84 (F. *Peerlinck*).

2911 **McGrath** Alister, The genesis of doctrine 1990 → 7,7128 ... 10,7133: RJETS 38 (1995) 100-3 (C.F.H. *Henry*)

2912 **McGrath** Alister, Bridge-building; effective Christian apologetics 1992 → 9,7184: REvQ 67 (1995) 182-4 (R.B. *Cook*).

2913   **Malvido Miguel** E., Jesús resucitado o la perspectiva de la teología cristiana; una introducción a la teología: Textos teol. 15. M 1993, S. Pio X. 234 p. -- RRET 55 (1995) 98-100 (E. *Tourón*).

2914 *Mascord* Keith A., Apologetics as dialogue; a new way of understanding an old task: RefTR 54 (1995) 49-64.

2915   **Masetti** Nardo, Orientamenti di teologia fondamentale 1991 → 8,7131: RScrTh 26 (1994) 337s (C. *Izquierdo*).

2916 **Meynell** Hugo A., Is Christianity true ? Wsh c.1995, Catholic University of America. 145 p. $15. -- [R]CanadCath 13,9 (1995) 28 (J.M. *Miller*).

2917 **Migliore** Daniel L., Faith seeking understanding 1991 → 7,7130 ... 9,7189: [R]JETS 38 (1995) 115s (R. A. *Young*).

2918 *Müller* Gotthold, Verherrlichung Gottes, glorificatio Dei; vom Ursprung, Sinn und Ziel unserer 'Theo-logie': ThGL 85 (1995) 485-498.

2919 **Muller** Richard A., The study of theology, from biblical interpretation to contemporary formulation 1991 → 9,7192: [R]JETS 38 (1995) 134s (J.R. *Franke*).

2920 **Muller** Richard, Holy Scripture, the cognitive foundation of theology: Post-Reformation Reformed Dogmatics 2. GR 1993, Baker. 542 p. $ 25 pa. -- [R]C(alvin)TJ 30 (1995) 260-4 (W.J. *Van Asselt*).

2921 *Neuhaus* Gerd, Urvertrauen -- eine notwendige Lebenslüge ?: KatBl 118 (1993) 8-13.

2922 *Niemann* Franz-Josef, Zur Frühgeschichte des Begriffs 'Fundamentaltheologie': MThZ 46 (1995) 247-260.

2923 *Nipkow* Karl Ernst, Empirical research within practical theology; JE(mp)T 6,1 (1993) 50-63.

2924 **O'Collins** Gerald, Retrieving fundamental theology 1993 → 10,7139: [R]America 172,3 (1995) 24.26 (T.G. *Guarino*); ScrT(Pamp) 37 (1995) 696s (C. *Izquierdo*).

2925 **Placher** William C., Narratives of a vulnerable God; Christ, theology, and Scripture 1994 → 10.7036: [R]MoTh 11 (1995) 488-490 (J.W. *McClendon*: splendid 'un'-apologetics).

2926 *Richardson* John P., Need ministers be theologians?: Churchman 108 (L 1994) 306-315.

2927 [E]**Sanna** Ignazio, Il sapere teologico e il suo metodo; teologia, ermeneutica e verità 1993 → 10,7145: [R]CivCatt 146 (1995,1) 96-98 (G. *Tangorra*).

2928 *Stahel* Thomas H., Scripture, the soul of theology; an interview with Joseph A. FITZMYER ['but for Divino Afflante, Vatican II would not have occurred']: America 172,16 (1995) 8-12.

2929 [E]**Stump** E., *Flint* T., Hermes and Athena; biblical exegesis and philosophical theology. ND 1995, Univ. xxvii-325 p. 0-268-01099-4 [NTAb 38, p.115].

2930 **Thils** Gustave, Les doctrines théologiques et leur 'évolution': RTLv Cah 28. LvN 1995, Fac. Théol. 70 p. 2-87723-177-1. -- [R]EThL 71 (1995) 252s (J. *Étienne*).

2931 **Torrell** Jean-Pierre, La théologie catholique: Que sais-je ? 1269. P 1994, PUF. -- [R]Div 39 (1995) 87-89 (D. *Vibrac*).

2932 **Torres** J., Globalización y interdisciplinariedad; el currículum integrado. M 1994, Morata. 279 p. -- [R]RevAg 36 (1995) 648-650 (B. *Mateos Bermejo*).

2933 **Waldenfels** Hugo, Teología fundamental contextual: VeI(= Imagen) 125. S 1994, Sígueme. 751 p. -- [R]Lum(Vt) 44 (1995) 342-4 (U. *Gil Ortega*); RevAg [30 (1989) 287s] 36 (1995) 309s (G. *Tejerina Arias*); SalTer 83 (1995) 243s (J.J. *Alemany*); TyV(ida) 36 (1995) 357 (A. *Arteaga Manieu*).

H2.1 Anthropologia theologica -- VT & NT

2934 *Accattino* Paolo, Generazione dell'anima in ALESSANDRO di Afrodisia, De anima 2,10: 11.132: Phronesis 40 (1995) 182-201.

2935 *Alvarez Gómez* Mariano, La reconciliación en el plano antropológico : EstTrin 28 (1994) 3-19 (-61. 123-240, *al.*)

2936 **Andreas** Bernard, Odysseus; Archäologie des europäischen Menschenbildes. Fra 1994, Societäts-V. 272 p.; Bibliog. 268s. 3-7973-0397-1.

2937 *Baena* Gustavo, Antropología cristiana y sexualidad: TX 109 (1994) 267-287.

2938 **Baertschi** Bernard, Les rapports de l'âme et du corps: DESCARTES, DIDEROT, MAINE DE BIRAN: BtHistPh. P 1992, Vron. 434 p. -- ᴿRTPh 127 (1995) 75s (C. *Chiesa*).

2939 **Basti** Gianfranco, Il rapporto mente-corpo nella filosofia e nella scienza. Bo 1991, Domenicano. 298 p. -- ᴿScrT(Pamp) 27 (1995) 1048s (A. *Pardo*).

2940 *Berthoud* Pierre, La notion biblique de l'homme et les enjeux de la bioéthique [*al.*]: RRéf 46.4 (1995) 33-48 [1-81].

2941 *Berzosa Martínez* Raúl, 'Deseo natural' en santo TOMÁS según Henri de LUBAC; un capítulo básico en la renovación de la antropología teológica: Burgense 35 (1994) 505-517.

2942 *Boyd* Jeffrey H., The soul as seen through evangelical eyes, I., Mental health professionals and the soul, II., On the use of the term 'soul': JPsT 23 (1995) 151-160 . 161-10.

2943 **Braine** David, The human person; animal and spirit. ND c.1994, Univ. 555 p. $ 33; pa. $ 17. -- ᴿCanadCath 13,2 (1995) 25s (S. *Baldner*)

2944 **Capdevila** V.M., Liberación y divinización del hombre, II. Estudio sistemático: Agape. S 1994, Secr. Trinitario. 618 p. -- ᴿSalmanticensis 42 (1995) 150-2 (L. *Ruiz de la Peña*).

2945 *Castellote* S., Un manuscrito inédito suareciano, 'Controversiae de anima' (texto latino completo): AnVal 20 (1994) 251-346 [< RET 55 (1995) 411].

2946 **Chavero Blanco** F., Imago Deo .. BONAVENTURA 1993 → 9,7222; 10,7153: ᴿBurg 36 (1995) 573s (C. *García*).

2947 *Christensen* Kurt, Menneskeværdet idehistorisk og teologisk belyst: Ichthys 22 (Aarhus 1995) 100-113 . 155-164.

2948 *Colombo* Giuseppe, Sull'antropologia teologica: TeolBr 20 (1995) 223-259; Eng. 260.

2949 **Crick** Francis, Was die Seele wirklich ist; die naturwissenschaftliche Erforschung des Bewusstseins. Mü 1994, Artemis & W. 391 p. DM 64. 3-7608-1951-6 [TR 91].

2950 ᶠDEISSLER Alfons, Der Weg zum Menschen; zur philosophischen und theologischen Anthropologie, ᴱMosis R., *Ruppert* L. 1989 → 5,45; cf. 5,7183 (1,6472): ᴿBZ 38 (1994) 308s (M. *Knapp*).

2951 *Elders* L.J., La nature et l'ordre surnaturel: NV 70,1 (1995) 18-35.

2952 *Elias* Norbert, La culture des passions à l'époque du NT; une contribution théologique et psychologique: ÉTRel 70 (1995) 335-348.

2953 **Finance** Joseph de, Cittadino di due mondi: il posto dell'uomo nella creazione, ᵀ. Vaticano 1993, Editrice. 223 p. Lᵐ 32. -- ᴿDoC(om) 47 (1994) 288-310 (D. *Vibrac*).

2954 **Grabner-Heider** Anton, Kritische Anthropologie: RelWSt 29. Wü/Altenberge 1993, Echter/Oros. [vi-] 371 p. DM 65. 3-429-01523-5 / 3-89375-082-7. -- ᴿThLZ 120 (1995) 1107 (C. *Frey*: lohnt nicht); ZKTh 116 (1994) 515-7 (K.H. *Neufeld*).

2955 *Grabowski* John S., [The human] Person: substance and relation: Com(US) 22 (1995) 139-163.

2956 *Herrero* Juan L., Sobre antropología teológica (con motivo de un libro) [PANNENBERG W. 1983, Madrid 1993]: AnVal 20 (1994) 121-142.

2957 **Herrnstein** Richard J., *Murray* Charles, The Bell curve; [importance of IQ] intelligence and class structure in American life. NY 1994, Free Press. 845 p. $ 30. -- ᴿCommentary 99,1 (1995) 77-80 (C.E. *Finn*); 99.5 (1995) 23-36, *Murray*, 'The Bell Curve' and its critics; further 100,2 (1995) 15-25.

2958 *Hoffmann* Thomas S., Idee, Natur und System; das Einzelne, das Individuelle und die Frage nach der 'natürlichen Natur': → 182, ᶠSIMON J., Denken 1995, 183-208.

2959 **Hogan** M.P., The biblical vision of the human person; implications for a philosophical anthropology: EHS 23/504. xx-394 p. $ 62. 3-631-47072-X [NTAb 39,p.343].

2960 **Honderich** Ted, How free are you ? The determinism problem. Ox 1993, UP. 160 p. $ 24; pa. $ 9. -- ᴿA(ndr)USS 33 (1995) 123s (G. *Wheeler*).

2961 **Huizing** Klaas. Das erlesene Gesicht; Vorschule einer physiognomischen Theologie [... imago Christi, sola Scriptura]. Gü 1992. Mohn. 224 p.; Ill. DM 68. 3-579-00279-1. - ᴿBijdragen 56 (1995) 105 (H.G. *Adriaanse*).

2962 **Jens** Walter, *Küng* Hans, Menschwürdig sterben; ein Plädoyer für Selbstverantwortung. Mü 1995, Piper. 220 p. DM 29,80. 3-492-03791-7. -- ᴿThGL 85 (1995) 416s (D. *Hattrup*: gar nicht christlich).

2963 *Kolb* Robert, 'That I may be his own'; the anthropology of LUTHER's explanation of the Creed: ConcordJ 21 (1995) 28-41.

2964 **Kristeva** Julia, New maladies of the soul, ᵀ*Guberman* Ross: European Perspectives. NY 1995, Columbia Univ. x-242 p. 0-231-09982-7.

2965 *Kulisz* Józef, ᴾ Man is his own problem: Bobolanum 4 (1993) 43-66; Eng. 66.

2966 **Kuschel** Karl-J., Laughter -- a theological essay [cover: 'reflection'], ᵀ*Bowden* John. NY/L 1994, Continuum/SCM. 128 p. $ 16 pa. -- ᴿCrossCur 45 (1995s) 243-9 (D.R. *Blumenthal:* response to ECO's Name of the rose: high praise also for his 1992 Ich schaffe with W. GROSS); Theol 98 (L 1995) 49-51 (R. *Harries:* antithesis to BENEDICT).

2967 **Ladaria** Luis F., Antropologia teologica²ʳᵉᵛ· [¹1983, ital. 1986], ᵀ *Occhipinti* Giuseppe, *Dotolo* Carmelo. CasM/R 1995, Piemme / Pont. Univ. Gregoriana. 502 p. Lᵐ 60. 88-384-2339-3 [Greg 76 (1995) 787: interamente riscritto; inizio non ancora in spagnolo].

2968 **Ladaria** Luis F., Teología del pecado original y de la gracia; antropología teológica especial: Sapientia Fidei 10. M 1993, BAC. xix-315 p. -- ᴿNatGrac 41 (1994) 427s (A. *Villalmonte*).

2969 *La Torre Vargas* Rafael de, Nueva antropología de la imagen [de Dios] : Rel(y)Cult 41 (1995) 597-611.

2970 **López** Julián, En el Espíritu y la Verdad; introducción antropológica a la Liturgía. S 1994, Secr. Trinitario. 546 p. -- ᴿPhase 35 (1995) 167-9 (J.-M. *Ferrer*).

2970* *Lucas Lucas* Ramón, Cuerpo humano y visión integral del hombre ..

2971 *a) McNamara* William M., Biblical sensuousness; -- *b) Lickona* Lisa, Living the body; the theological anthropology of Pope JOHN PAUL II: Forefront 2,3 (1995) 5-7 / 18-22.

2972 *Magnelli* L.,Riflessioni sui problemi dell'Antropologia teologica:Vivarium 3(1995)453-8.

2973 *Mannermaa* Tuomo, Theosis as a subject of Finnish LUTHER research: ProEccl 4 (1995) 37-48.

2974 **Meis** Peter, Studien zur theologischen Anthropologie; die Impulse BONHOEFFERs für das christliche Menschenbild auf dem Hintergrund biblischer und lutherischer Tradition: Diss. ᴰ*Petzoldt*. Leipzig 1995. -- ThRv Beilage 92/2, xi.

2974* *Milano* Andrea, La persona nella novità cristiana dell'Incarnazione e della Trinità: Studium-R 91,4s (VI convegno con Enciclopedia Italiana, 1995) 549-568.

2975 **Moltmann-Wendell** Elisabeth, I am my body; new ways of embodiment, ᵀ*Bowden* John. L 1994, SCM. xv-108 p. £ 10. 0-334-02570-2. -- ᴿCrossCur 45 (1995s) 548s (Katharina von *Kellenbach*); ET 106 (1994s) 218 (Elizabeth *Stuart*); *TBR 8,3 (1995s) 28s (Carrie *Pemberton*: insights but just a sketch).

2976 **Mondin** Battista, Rifare l'uomo. R 1993, Dino. 253 p. Lᵐ 35. -- ᴿDiv 39 (1995) 183-7 (M. *Pangallo*); DoC(om) 48 (1995) 202-4 (D. *Coviello*); StPat(av) 41 (1994) 668s (C. *Scilironi*).

2977 *Mondin* Battista, Grandezza e dignità della persona umana: CiVi 50 (1995) 229-236.

2978 **Neufeld** K.-H., Der Mensch -- bewusste Nachfolge im Volk Gottes: Studienbücher Theologie 17/2. Stu 1993, Kohlhammer. -- RStPat(av) 42 (1995) 596-8 (L. *Sartori*).

2979 *O'Carroll* Noreen, What is human nature ? MilltSt 35 (1995) 51-58.

2980 **Palumbieri** S., L'uomo e il futuro, 1. È possibile un futuro dell'uomo ? 2. Germi del futuro per l'uomo: 3. atteso, R 1991-3-, Dehoniane. -- RDoC(om) 47 (1994) 285-7 (B. *Mondin*).

2981 **Panayotis** N., Voi siete dèi; antropologia dei Padri della Chiesa [1991],T; pref. *Federici* Tommaso: Collana di Teol. 24. R 1993, Città Nuova. 262 p. Lm 32. -- RAsprenas 42 (1995) 290-2 (L. *Fatica*).

2982 **Pannenberg** Wolfhart, Antropologia en perspectiva teológica; implicaciones religiosas de la teoría antropológica, TGarcía Baró Miguel: Verdad e imagen 127. S 1993, Sigueme, 700 p. 84-301-1215-4.-- RActuBbg 31 (1994) 62s (J. *Boada*); NatGrac 41 (1994) 425s (A. *Villalmonte*); RET 55 (1995) 266-8 (G. de *Pozo Abejón*).

2983 *a) Pfeiffer* Bernhard, Schlechthinnig abhängig -- radikal herkünftig; Wahlverwandtschaften anthropologischer Theologie, dargestellt an der Nähe SCHLEIERMACHERs und RAHNERs im Aufgang der Gottesfrage; -- *b) Morscher* Edgar, Die Gottesbeweise als vermeintliche Stütze von Religion und Theologie: FrSZ 42 (1995) 69-102 / 103-117.

2984 *a) Pieretti* Antonio, Oltre la razionalità scientifica; verso un umanesimo della persona: -- *b) Cirelli* Giovanni. Umanesimo e cristianesimo nella cultura della società industriale; -- *c) Bucci* Sabina, Verso una società post materialista: → 123, FMATTIOLI A., In spiritu et veritate 1995, 561-575 / 577-591 (-600) / 539-559.

2985 **Pikaza** Xabier, Antropología bíblica 1993 → 9,7255; 10,7179: RNatGrac 41 (1994) 429s (A. *Villalmonte*); RevAg 35 (1994) 741-3 (S. *Sabugal*).

2986 **Plieth** Martina, Die Seele wahrnehmen; zur Geistesgeschichte des Verhältnisses von Seelsorge und Psychologie: ArbPasT 28. Gö 1994, Vandenhoeck & R. 278 p. DM 68. 3-525-62345-3 [ThRv 91.280].

2987 **Prini** Pietro, Il corpo che siamo. T 1991, SEI. -- RFilTeo 9 (1995) 196-8 (A. *Mastantuoni*).

2988 *Reimão* Cassiano, A dimensão-fronteira do corpo na filosofia de Gabriel MARCEL: Didask 24,1 (1994) 95-117.

2989 **Rimedio** Vincenzo, vescovo, Sentieri dell'essere; progetto antropologico. Soveria Mannelli 1995, Rubbettino. 182 p. Lm 15. 88-7284-397-9.

2990 *Ruiz-Retegui* Antonio, Algunas consideraciones sobre la antropología implícita en la cristología de Hans Urs von BALTHASAR: ScrT(Pamp) 37 (1995) 459-491.

2991 **Rulla** L.M., *al.*, Antropología de la vocación cristiana, 2. Confirmaciones existenciales. M 1994, Atenas. -- RBurg 36 (1995) 243-5 (J. *Yusta Sainz*).

2992 *Sayes* José Antonio, El tema del alma y sus implicaciones teológicas en el Catecismo de la Iglesia Católica: RBurgense 35 (1994) 113-144.

2993 **Schillebeeckx** Edward, Los hombres relato de Dios 1989 → 7,7188 ... 10,7188s], T. S 1994, Sígueme. 394 p. -- REstTrin 28 (1994) 439-441 (J.M. de *Miguel*).

2994 **Schnelle** Udo, The human condition; anthropology in the teachings of Jesus, Paul, and John [Nt Anthrop.1991 → 10,7090], TDunn O.C. E c.1995, Clark. ix-123 p. 0-56708511-2.

2995 **Schulze** M., Leibhaft und unsterblich; zur Schau der Seele in der Anthropologie und Theologie des hl. Thomas von AQUIN; StFr NF 76, 1992 → 8,7201; 10,7191: RMüTZ 45 (1994) 223s (W.W. *Müller*).

2996 ᴱSimon H., La peau de l'âme. 1994. F 195. -- ᴿEeV 105 (1995) 63s (J. Milet).

2997 Söling Caspar, a) Das Gehirn-Seele-Problem; neue Einblicke in eine alte Diskussion: kath. Diss. ᴰVorgrimler H. Münster 1994. -- ThRv 91,100. -- b) Das Gehirn-Seele-Problem; Neurobiologie und theologische Anthropologie. Pd 1995, Schöningh. xiii-329 p. DM 78. 3-506-78586-9 [ThRv 91,370].

2998 Souzenelle Annick de,[aux questions de] Moutappa Jean,'La parole au cøur du corps'; l'être et le corps. P 1993, Michel. 280 p. F 98.-- ᴿE(spr)eV 105 (1995) 75s (J.Milet).

2999 Stordalen Terje, Stov og Livspust [dust and life-breath]; mennesket i Det gamle Testamente. Oslo 1994, Univ. xi-248 p. 82-00-03938-2. -- [< OTA 18 (1995) p. 421].

3000 Tappolet Christine, Les émotions sont-elles mentales ou physiques ?: RTPh 127 (1995) 251-259; Eng. 320.

3001 Vogels Walter, The human person in the image of God [< ScEs46 (1994) 189-202, ᴱAsen B.A.: ThD 43,3-7]

3002 Wénin A., L'homme biblique; anthropologie et éthique dans le premier Testament: Théologies bibliques. P 1995, Cerf. 196 p. F 100. 2-204-05094-6. -- ᴿNRT 117 (1995) 804s (J.-L. Ska).

3003 Zundel Maurice † 1975, Quale uomo e quale Dio ? Padova 1994, Messaggero. 352 p. Lᵐ 27. -- ᴿCiVi 50 (1995) 100 (Duccia Camicioni).

H2.7 Œcologia VT & NT -- saecularitas

3004 a) Adams Bill, A Christian environmentalism ?; -- b) Jarvis Gavin, Animal rights and wrongs: PaP 9 (1995) 54-57 / 74s.

3005 Alvarez Andrés S., ¿ Es la religión judeo-cristiana responsable de la crisis ecológica ?: NatGrac 42,1 (1995) 207-236.

3006 Austin Richard C., Tending the ark; the environment, a lifestyle crisis ? : Disciple 132,9 (1994) 12-16.

3007 Baranzke Heike, Lambery-Zielinski Hedwig, Lynn WHITE [Science 155 (10.III.1967] 1203-7] und das dominium terrae (Gen 1,28b); ein Beitrag zu einer doppelten Wirkungsgeschichte: BiNo 76 (1995) 32-61.

3008 Beauchamp André, Introduction a l'éthique de l'environnement: Interpellations. Montréal 1993, Paulines. 222 p. -- ᴿL(aval)TP 51 (1995) 466-8 (Dany Rondeau).

3009 Benstein Jeremy, 'One, walking and studying ...': nature vs, torah: Judaism 44 (1995) 146-168 (437-447, Schwartz Eilon).

3010 ᴱBerry Thomas, al., Befriending the earth; a theology of reconciliation between humans and the earth. Mystic CT 1991, Twenty-Third. vi-158 p. $ 8. -- ᴿNewThR 8,2 (1995) 110s (P.J. Wadell).

3011 Bertille sr. M., Religious life today; wasted or worsted ? an ecological perspective. Bangalore 1995, St. Teresa's Generalate. x-140 p. rs 55. -- ᴿI(nd)TS 32 (1995) 356 (V.M. Gnanapragasam).

3012 Bindi Stefano, Aspetti della natura e del cosmo nella Bibbia ebraica; studio lessico-semantico: diss. ᴰZatelli Ida. Firenze 1994. -- RivB 43 (1995) 443.

3013 Boff Leonardo, Ecología, política, teología y mística: Christus 60,7s (Méx 1995) 8-22.

3014 Boff Leonardo [→ 232 supra], Von der Würde der Erde; Ökologie, Politik, Mystik. Dü 1994, Patmos. 184 p. DM 35. 3-491-72308-6. -- ᴿTTh 35 (1995) 421 (J. Haers).

3015 Boff Leonard, Ecology and liberation, a new paradigm. Mkn 1995, Orbis. 187 p. $ 15. 0-88344-972-1. -- ᴿExchange 24 (1995) 278s (M. E. Brinkman).

3016 *Bolt* John, The greening of spirituality; a review article [CAMPOLO T. 1992, *al.*]: C(alvin)TJ 30 (1995) 194-211.

3017 **Bouma-Prediger** Steven, The greening of theology .. RUETHER R., SITTLER J., MOLTMANN J.: AAR 91. At 1995, Scholars. xiii-338 p. $ 36; pa. $ 24. 0-7885-0163-; - 4-X [ThD 43,356].

3018 *Bouma-Prediger* Steven, Is Christianity responsible for the ecological crisis ? : CScR 25 (1995s) 146-156.

3019 **Bradley** Ian, Dios es 'verde' 1993 → 10,7194; [T]*Rivas* Pedro J., 84-293-1098-3: [R]ActuBbg 31 (1994) 53 . 55 (H. *Vall*).

3019* **Campolo** Tony, How to rescue the earth without worshiping nature 1992 → 8,7226; 9.7288: GOTR 39 (1994) 383-7 (F. *Marangos*).

3020 *Castiello* Luigi. Etica dell'ambiente e teologia morale; un dibattito aperto: Asprenas 45 (1995) 509-522.

3021 *Champion* Françoise, Religions, approches de la nature et écologies [BOURG D. 1993, *al.*,] : ASS(oc)R 90 (1995) 39-57.

3022 *Chial* Douglas L., Creation as an ecumenical concern : R(ef)W 45 (1995) 98-112.

3023 **Coste** René, 'Dieu et l'écologie'; environnement, théologie, spiritualité. P 1994, Atelier. 271 p. F 120 -- [R]Études 383 (1995) 284 (C. *Mellon*).

3024 *a) Deffenbaugh* Daniel G., A Calvinist speaks up for the universe [MACLEAN N. ..]; -- *b) Van Till* Howard J., Retelling the creation story; -- *c) Gaál* Botond, A universe fine-tuned for intelligent life: (Reformed) Perspectives 10,10 (1995) 10-13 / 14-18 / 19-23.

3025 **de Waal** Esther, Every earthly blessing; celebrating a spirituality of creation. AA 1991, Servant. 149 p. $ 8 pa. -- [R]Weavings 10,1 (Nv 1995) 45-47 (Anne *Ramirez*).

3026 **DeWitt** Calvin B., The environment and the Christian; what can we learn from the NT? GR 1991, Baker. 156 p. -- [R]JETS 38 (1995) 473s (M. *McKenzie*).

3027 *Drane* John, Defining a biblical theology of creation [cover: 'and the New Age']: Transformation 10,2 (1993) 7-11.

3028 *Druet* Pierre-P., Éthique de la responsabilité à l'égard de l'environnement: NRT 117 (1995) 654-669; Eng. 669.

3028* *Durel* Bernard, La création tout entière gémit; une terre blessée et divisée: RÉTM (= Le Supplément) 192 (1995) 93-126.

3029 *Dwyer* Christopher, Animals and the Catholic Church [British outcry against ('Spanish ideas of entertainment'p.248) a Europe based in Catholic teaching]: Month 256 (1995) 245-8.

3030 **Easterbrook** Gregg, A moment on the earth; the coming age of environmental optimism. NY c.1995, Viking. 745 p. $ 28. -- [R]Commentary 100,2 (1995) 55s (J. *Marsh*).

3031 **Edwards** Denis, Jesus the wisdom of God; an ecological theology: Ecology and Justice. Mkn 1995, Orbis. xiv-208 p. $ 17. 1-57075-002-5 [ThD 43,64].

3032 **Elsdon** Ron, Greenhouse theology; biblical perspectives on caring for creation. .. 1992, Monarch. 253 p. 1-85424-153-2. -- [R]IrBSt 15 (1993) 186-8 (P.J. *Roche*).

3033 *a) Faggioni* Maurizio P., L'uomo é ancora signore del creato ? Tracce di etica ambientale in Gaudium et spes; -- *b) Cardellini* Innocenzo, 'Possessio' o 'dominium bonorum' ?; riflessioni sulla proprietà privata e la 'rimessa dei debiti' in Levitico 25; -- *c) Oviedo* Lluis, Secularización como contexto eclesial y de la reflexión teológica: Anton 70,3s (trentennale 'Gaudium et Spes' 1995) 429-472 / 333-348 / 401-428; Eng. 429; 333; 401.

3034 *a) Famerée* Joseph, L'Église en contexte de 'sécularisation'; - *b) Jacquemin* Dominique, La crise écologique; une chance pour l'éthique ?: FoiTe 24 (1994) 143-165 / 166-187.

3035 *Ferguson* Brian, *Roche* Patrick J., Christian attitudes to nature and the ecological crisis: IrBSt 15 (1993) 98-114.

3036 *Fox* Matthew, Creation spirituality ; 300 years from Hildegard to Julian [< his 1995 Wrestling with the prophets]: Creation Spirituality 11,3 (Oakland 1995) 10-15.

3037 *Frahier* Louis-Jean, Alliance avec Noé et écologie; la référence à Genèse 1-11 et les problèmes éthiques liés à l'écologie: RÉTM (SuppVSp) 188s (1994) 349-382.

3038 **Ganoczy** Alexandre, Dieu, l'homme et la nature: CFi 186. P 1995, Cerf. 347 p. F 240. -- ᴿEstTrin 29 (1995) 122-4 (X. *Pikaza*); NRT 117 (1995) 248 (A. *Toubeau*).

3039 **Gesché** Adolphe, Le cosmos; Dieu pour penser 4. P 1994, Cerf. 206 p. F 95. 2-204-05041-5. -- ᴿE(spr)eV 105 (1995) 207 (P. *Gire*); EThL 71 (1995) 255s (J. *Étienne*); TTh 35 (1995) 436 (B. *Vedder*).

3040 *Gilkey* Langdon,Nature as the image of God;signs of the sacred:TTod 51(1994s)127-141.

3041 **Goffi** Jean-Yves, Le philosophe et ses animaux; du statut éthique de l'animal (+ *White* Lynn, Les racines historiques de notre crise écologique). Nîmes 1994, J. Chambon. 335 p.

3042 **Gold** Ann G., Magical landscapes and moral orders; new readings in religion and ecology [SIMMONS J. 1993 and 6 on remote areas]: RStR 21 (1995) 70-77.

3043 ᴱ**Green** Elizabeth, *Grey* Mary, Ecofeminism and theology, Yearbook 2 of the European Society of Women in Theological Research. Kampen/Mainz 1994, Kok/Grünewald. 143 p. *f* 39. -- ᴿG(ereformeerd)TT 95 (1995) 201s (J. *Hopkins*); *Missionalia 23 (995) 249-251 (A. van *Schalkwyk*).

3044 ᴱ*Greisch* J., (conclusions) De la nature; de la physique classique au souci écologique [colloque mai 1991, 'Les transformations actuelles du discours sur la nature', 6 art.; + 6 thèmes reliés]: Philosophie 14. P 1992, Beauchesne. 370 p. -- ᴿScEs 47,1 (1995) 133s (J.-C. *Petit*).

3045 **Grings** Dadeus, O homem diante do universo: Filosofia 27. Porto Alegre 1995, EDIPUCRS. 119 p. -- Teocomunicação 25 (1995) 732.

3046 *Grond* A., Op zoek naar een nieuwe verhouding tussen mensen, natuur en God: Speling 46,4 (1994) 31-39 [< GTT 95,94].

3047 **Gustafson** James M., A sense of the divine; the natural environment from a theocentric perspective 1994 → 10,7216; also E 1994, Clark; 0-567-09712-9: ᴿAThR 77 (1995) 153 . 255s (D.L. *Berry*); *TBR 8,2 (1995s) 31 (I. *Markham*); TS 56 (1995) 198 (D. *Cowdin*).

3048 **Gutheinz** Luis, *Liau Yongxiang* Timothy, ᶜTheology of the earth; ecological theology in Christian perspective: Unity of Heaven and Man; Fujen Univ.Theol.37. Taipei 1994, Kuangchi. 451 p. - ᴿTIC(ontext) 12,2 (G. *Evers*) 105.

3049 ᴱ**Hallman** David, Ecotheology; voices from the north and south. Mkn 1994, Orbis. $ 19. 0-88344-993-5. -- ᴿ*ModBlv 36,2 (1995) 69-71 (J. *Killick*).

3050 **Hansson** Mats G., Human dignity and animal well-being [diss.]. U 1991, Almqvist & W. 200 p. -- ᴿRTPh 127 (1995) 87s (B. *Baertschi*).

3051 **Harj** Albert, L'écologie et la Bible; l'eau, les animaux, les humains. P 1995, Atelier. 240 p. F 110. -- ᴿE(spr)eV 105 (1995) 317 (L. *Monloubou*).

3052 **Hartlieb** Elisabeth, Natur als Schöpfung; zum Begriff der Natur in der jüngsten protestantischen Theologie: Diss. ᴰ*Ritschl* D. Heidelberg 1994. -- ThRv 91 (1995) 97.

3053 **Hattrup** Dieter, Theologie der Erde. Pd 1994, Bonifatius. 272 p. DM 40. 3-87088-826-1. -- ᴿATG(ran) 58 (1995) 399s (R. *Franco*); ThLZ 120 (1995) 1031 (W. *Beinert*); ThRv 91 (1995) 341s (G. *Kraus*).

3054 ᴱ**Hervieu-Léger** D., Religion et écologie 1993 → 10,7219: F 130: ᴿRHE 90 (1995) 230s (E. *Baratay*).

3055 *Hüttermann* A., Die ökologische Botschaft der Thora: CLehre 47 (1995) 51-58 [< ZIT 95, p.256]

3056 **Hughes** J. Donald, Pan's travail; environmental problems of the ancient Greeks and Romans. 1994. $ 40. 0-8018-4655-2. -- [R]C(las)B 71,1 (1995) 29-32 (J. *Scarborough*).

3057 *Kalbheim* B., Environmental awareness -- consciousness about creation [on 12 books]: JE(mp)T 8,2 (1995) 102-107.

3058 **Kinsley** David R., Ecology and religion; ecological spirituality in cross-cultural perspective. ENJ 1995, Prentice-Hall. xxi-248 p. $ 23.80. 0-13-138512-7 [ThD 43,72].

3059 *Kordić* Ivan, The world as the place of the divine revelation: ObŽ 50 (1995) 173-184; Eng. 184.

3060 *Kristiansen* Roald E., Worldviews and ultimate values in ecology; a further contribution to ecological anthropology: URM [8.105-122] 18 (1995) 176-191.

3061 **Ku Kyeong-Guk**, Biblisch-christliche Umweltsethik; Untersuchung zum rechten Verhältnis der Menschen zur Natur im Sinne einer lebensfreundlicher Welt: Diss. [D]*Rotter* H. Innsbruck 1995. 214 p. -- RTLv 27, p.573.

3062 *Lane* Belden C., Desert attentiveness, desert indifference; countercultural spirituality in the desert fathers and mothers: CCurr 44 (1944s) 193-206 [*al.* 147-240, ecotheology].

3063 **Linzey** Andrew, Animal theology [9 revised papers]. L/Champaign 1994, SCM / Univ. Illinois. 214 p. £ 15; pa. 14. 0-334-00005-X / 0-252-06467-4 [RStR 22,343, R.L.*Grant.* also D.K. *Johnson* on cognate PLUHAR Evelyn B. 1995]. -- [R]ET 106.1 3d-top (1994s) 3 (C.S. *Rodd*).

3064 *a) Lück* Ulrich, Verantwortung für die oder vor der Umwelt ?; -- *b) Höver* Gerhard, Umweltethik als Aufgabe der Theologie; -- *c) Kluxen* Wolfgang, Schwierigkeiten einer ökologischen Moral: LebZeug 49 (1994) 268-288 / 254-267 / 245-253.

3065 **McDonagh** Sean, Passion for the earth: Ecology and Justice. L / Mkn 1994, Chapman/Orbis. viii-164 p. £ 9 / $ 14. 0-225-66763-0 / 0-57075-021-1 [ThD 43,75]. -- [R]ET 106 (1994s) 317 (Martin *Palmer*: unlike his two prior works, a jumble of worthiness and ill-assorted data).

3066 **McFague** Sallie, The body of God; an ecological theology 1993 → 9,7328; 10,7235: [R]*FemT 8 (1995) 123-5 (Clare *Palmer*); Tod 51 (1994s) 176.8.190 (Leanne *Van Dyk*).

   McFague Sallie, Modelos de Dios; teología para una era ecológica y nuclear 1994 → 2785 supra.

3068 *Madzaridis [Mant-]* Y., [G] Orthodox views of the ecological crisis: Kler 23 (1991) 265-270.

3069 **Mante** Joseph O.Y., Towards an ecological, Christian theology of creation in an African context: diss. [Claremont 1994, [D]*Verheyden* J.]: sic RTL 27.p.573.

3070 **Marshall** Peter, Nature's web; rethinking our place on earth. NY 1994, Paragon. 513 p. $ 30. -- [R]PerspSCF 47 (1995) 213 (E,E. *Hartquist*).

3071 *Mascall* Margaret, La sacramentalidad de la creación en la teología de E. SCHILLEBEECKX, [T]*Ramos* Luis; AnáMnesis 4,1 (1994) 73-84.

3072 **Meisinger** Hubert, Liebesgebot und Altruismusforschung; ein exegetischer Beitrag zum Dialog zwischen Theologie und Naturwissenschaft: Diss. [D]*Theissen.* Heidelberg 1995. -- ThRv Beilage 92/2, x.

3073 *Moltmann* Jürgen, 'Hermana Tierra'; el rediscubrimientro de la Tierra y de la espiritualidad terrenal: *Carthaginensia 11 (1995) 1-22; Eng.iii 'society is immersed in a deadly self-destructive dynamic'.

3074 *Moltmann* Jürgen, Ökologie: → 772, TRE 25 (1995) 36-46.

3075 **Oelschlaeger** Max, Caring for creation; an ecumenical approach to the environmental crisis 1994 → 10,7242: [R]TS 56 (1995) 390c (P.Cho *Phan*); TTod 51 (1994s) 636.8 (W.P. *Jones*).

3076 *Palmer* Martin, Ecology -- prophetic or pathetic ?: ET 106 (1994s) 100-4.

3077 **Pannenberg** Wolfhart, Toward a theology of nature; essays on science and faith, [TE]*Peters* Ted, 1993 → 10,7247: [R]PerspSCF 47 (1995) 57s (R.H. *Bube*).

3078 **Panteghini** Giacomo, Il gemito della creazione; ecologia e fede cristiana 1992 → 9,7344; 10,7248; 88-250-0178-9. -- [R]Ang 72 (1995) 337s (G.M. *Salvati*).

3079 *a) Pathrapankal* Joseph, The Bible and human activity on Mother Earth; - *b) Venkatakrishna* B.V., Indian mystic approach to the earth; - *c) Vadakumchery* Johnson, The earth mother and the indigenous people of India: JDharma 18 (1993) 5-17 / 35-41 / 85-97.

3080 *a) Pearson* Anne, Aspects of Hindu women's VRAT (votive calendrical rites) tradition as constitutive for an eco-spirituality; -- *b) Chawia* Janet, Gendered representations of seed, earth, and grain; a woman centered perspective on the conflation of woman and earth; -- *c) Dietrich* Gabriele, The world as the body of God; feminist perspectives on ecology and social justice: JDharma 18 (1993) 228-236 / 237-257 / 258-284.

3081 **Perry** Luc, Vers un nouvel ordre écologique. P 1992, Grasset. - [R]FV 92,6 (1993) 86-88 (S. *Charbonneau*).

3082 **Philippe** Pierre, *Benner* Peter, Skin of the earth; a life story of environmental stewardship. Waterloo ON... Escart. 121 p. $ 10. -- [R]CanadCath 13,4 (1995) 12 (A.G. *White*).

3083 *Piacentini* Ernesto, Approccio morale al problema ecologico oggi; → 123, [F]MATTIOLI A., In spiritu et veritate 1995. 497-538.

3084 [E]**Pinches** Charles, *McDaniel* J.B., Good news for animals ? 1993 → 9,7350; 10,7251: [R]Vidyajyoti 59 (1995) 68s (J. *Kennedy*).

3085 *Pollefeyt* D., De bijbel in het ecologisch debat; hinderpaal of wegwijzer ? een lezing van de joodse traditie in het spoor van Catherine CHALIER: Ter Herkenning 22 (1994) 168-180 [< GTT 95,94].

3086 *Price* John M., Biblical foundations for justice and peace and the integrity of creation: VSVD 36 (1995) 5-27 (227-237 . 401-4 on culture and secularism).

3087 **Primavesi** Anne, From Apocalypse to Genesis; ecology, feminism 1991 → 7,7246* ... 10,7251* [R]*CritRR 6 (1993) 569-571 (Mary Rose *D'Angelo*).

3088 **Raffel** Simone, Die ökologische Krise als Folge des Christentums: Diss. [D]*Schockenhoff*. Freiburg/Br 1995. -- ThRv Beilage 92/2, viii.

3089 *Ritter* Adolf M., Natur und Landschaft als Problem von Tradition und Translation im alten Christentum: → 42, [F]COLPE C., Tradition (1994) 131-143.

3090 **Ruether** Rosemary R., Gaia and God 1992 → 9,7358; 10,7255: [R]JAAR 63 (1995) 169-171 (Paula M. *Cooey*).

3091 **Ruether** Rosemary R., Gaia e Dio; una teologia ecofemminista per la guarigione della terra. Brescia 1994, Morcelliana. -- [R](R)*StEc 13 (Venezia 1995) 539-541 (S. *Morandini*).

3092 *Ruether* Rosemary R., Ecofeminism; symbolic and social connections of the oppression of women and the domination of nature: *FemT 9 (1995) 35-50 (-62) [+ 10 (1995) 9-20].

3093 *Ruether* Rosemary R., The cycle of life and death in ecofeminist spirituality: Creation Spirituality 11,2 (Oakland 1995) 34-38.

3094 **Russell** Colin A., The earth, humanity and God [1993 Cambridge Templeton lectures] 1994 → 10,7257; also Bristol PA 1994, Taylor & F. 157 p. $ 19 pa. -- [R]PerspSCF 47 (1995) 275s (F. *Worth*).

3095 **Rüterswörden** Udo, Dominium terrae; Studien zur Genese einer alttestamentlichen Vorstellung: BZAW 215, 1993 → 9,1863; 10,1710: [R]BiOr 52 (1995) 741s (H.-J. *Zobel*); OLZ 90 (1995) 184-8 (L. *Wächter*); ZkT 117 (1995) 103 (R. *Oberforcher*)

3096 *a) Saldanha* Cecil J., Management of the earth; a responsible response; -- *b) Chethimattam* J.B., A philosophical approach to the ecological crisis: JDharma 20 (1995) 9-16 / 17-25.

3097 *Santmire* H.P., Toward a Christology of nature [Col 1,15-20]; claiming the legacy of Joseph SITTLER and Karl BARTH: Dialog 34 (Mp 1995) 270-280 [NTAb 40,p.271].

3098 **Saout** Yves, Dialogue avec la terre; l'être humain et la terre dans la Bible: Bible-Chemin d'un peuple. P 1994, Atelier. 240 p. F 110.- [#]E(spr)eV 105 (1995) 168 (L. *Monloubou*).

3099 *a) Scheinen* Richard, *Fox* Matthew, Reinventing ritual; the planetary Mass; -- *b) Mabry* John R., Uncovering the tradition; M.D. CHENU and Matthew Fox: Creation Spirituality 11,1 (Oakland 1995) 23-29 . 32-34 / 10s.

3100 **Schlette** Heinz R., Weltseele; Geschichte und Hermeneutik. Fra 1993, Knecht. 264 p. DM 76. -- [R]GuL 67 (1994) 76 (J. *Sudbrack*).

3101 **Simkins** Ronald A., Creator and creation; nature in the worldview of ancient Israel 1994 → 10.7261: [R]ET 106,5 2d-top choice (1994s) 131s (C.S. *Rodd*); OCP 61 (1995) 588-590 (E. G. *Farrugia*); OTA 18 (1995) p.171 (Katherine M. *Hayes*).

3102 **Simmons** Stephen A., The semantics of God and nature in the writings of Thomas F. TORRANCE; diss. [D]*Carr* A. Chicago 1995. -- RStR 22, p.271.

3103 *Smith* Pamela A., The ecotheology of Annie DILLARD [successful novelist 1974/7; Catholic since 1988]: CrossCur 45 (1995s) 341-358.

3104 *a) Smith* Ebbie C., Environlove; the Christian approach to ecology; - *b) Ellis* Robert R., Divine gift and human response; an OT model for stewardship; -- *c) Foster* Ruth Ann, Stewardship; sign and substance of the Christian life as taught in the NT: SWJT 37,2 (1995) 23-31 / 4-14 / 15-22.

3105 *a) Spijker* Gerard van 't, Man's kinship with nature -- African reflection on creation; - *b) Küster* Volker, Models of contextual hermeneutics; liberation and feminist theological approaches compared: Exchange 23 (1994) 89-148 / 149-171.

3106 *Tamayo* Juan-José, Secularización, religión y sociedad; RF 231 (1995 365-381.

3107 **Tosaus Abadía** José Pedro, Cristo y el universo; estudio lingüístico y temático de Ef 1,10b en Efesios y en la obra de IRENEO de Lyon [dis.]: Plenitudo Temporis 2. S 1995, Univ. Pontificia. 341 p. -- [R]RET 55 (1995) 403s (J.J. *Ayán*).

3108 *Tuin* Leo van der, Ecologische waardenoriëntaties. een filosfische und theologische benadering: Bijdragen 56 (1995) 187-427: Eng. 428.

3109 *Williams* David T., The Christian and the environment; prophet, priest and king: EvQ 66 (1994) 143-158.

3110 *Woodrum* Eric, *Hoban* Thomas, Theology and religiosity effects on environnmentalism: RRelRes 35 (1993s) 193-206.

3111 **Wright** Nancy G., *Kill* Donald, Ecological healing; a Christian vision. Mkn/NY 1993, Orbis/CODEL. ix-161 p. $ 13. -- [R]P(rinc)SB 16 (1995) 109s (Janet L. *Parker*).

3112 *a) Wright* Richard T., Tearing down the green; environmental backlash in the evangelical sub-culture; -- *b) Schafran* Philip, Is mankind the measure ? Old Testament perspectives on mankind's place in the natural world [.. Ps 104]: PerspSCF 47 (1995) 80-91 / 92-102.

3113 **Young** Richard A., Healing the earth; a theocentric perspective on environmental problems and their solutions 1994 → 10,7269: [R]CScR 25 (1995s) 87-89 (S. *Bouma-Prediger*).

3114 *Zilles* Urbano, O mundo como naturaleza, sujeito e cultura: Teocomunicação 25 (1995) 441-452.

3115 **Zuzworsky** Rose, Toward a Catholic 'theology of the environment' for a priestly and prophetic people of God: diss. Fordham, [D]*Massa* M. Bronx 1994. -- RStR 22,p.271.

H3.1 *Foedus* -- **the Covenant;** the Chosen People; Providence

3116 *Banon* David, L'alliance irrévocable; lecture juive de Jérémie 31,31-36: FV 93,1 (1994) 1-8 (9-13, *Robert* P. de; 15-18. *Jacob* E., sur LOHFINK).

3117 *Basinger* David, Can an evangelical Christian justifiably deny God's exhaustive knowledge of the future ?: ChrSchR 25 (1995s) 133-145.

3118 *Beauchamp* Paul. Élection et universalité dans la Bible: Études 382 (1995) 373-383.

3119 *Brändle* Werner, Überlegungen zur Rede vom Handeln Gottes: NZSTh 37 (1995) 96-17: Eng. 117, 'God's actions in the world' are really human actions wthin a Spirit-empowered 'field of force'.

3120 **Christiansen** Ellen Juhl, The Covenant in Judaism and Paul: a study of ritual boundaries as identity markers [diss. Durham 1993, [D]*Dunn* J.]: AGJU 27. Lei 1995, Brill. x-396 p.; bibliog. 329-360.   90-04-10333-3.

3121 **Craig** William L., Divine foreknowledge and human freedom 1991 → 9,7309: 10.7271: [R]EvQ 66 (1994) 362-4 (A.G. *Padgett*).

3122 **de Zan** Renato, La 'risposta' al dono dell'alleanza: RivLi 20 (1993) 153-167.

3123 **Dumbrell** W.J., Covenant and creation; a theology of the OT covenants. GR 1993 = 1984, Baker. -- [R]OTEs 8 (1995) 464-6 (J.J. *Borden*: no taking criticism or alternatives into account).

3124 **Elazar** Daniel J., *a)* Covenant and polity in biblical Israel; biblical foundations and Jewish expressions; -- *b)* Covenant and commonwealth; from Christian separation through the Protestant Reformation: The Covenant tradition in politics 1s. New Brunswick 1995, Transaction. xvi-477 p. / xix-389 p. $ 50 each. 1-56000-151-8; -209-5 [ThD 42,365].

3125 **Ferrier** Francis, La prédestination: QS(ais)J 2537. P 1990. PUF. 128 p. -- [R]RTL 26 (1995) 366 (E. *Brito*).

3126 *Gross* Walter, Neuer Bund oder erneuter Bund ? Jer 31,31-34 in der neuesten Diskussion; → 177, [F]SCHNEIDER T., Vorgeschmack 1995, 89-114.

3127 **Hahn** Scott W., Kingship by covenant; a biblical theological study of Covenant types and texts in the Old and New Testaments: diss. Marquette, [D]*Muller* E. Milwaukee 1995. xi-749 p.; bibliog. 673-749. -- 96-00849.

3128 **Hanson** Paul, Das berufene Volk; Entstehen und Wachsen der Gemeinde in der Bibel [1986], [T]1993 → 10,7278: [R]EvTh 55 (1995) 198-204 (H. *Bedford-Strohm*).

3129 **Helm** Paul, The providence of God 1993 → 10,7279; Contours of Christian theology; also Leicester 1993, Inter-Varsity. 246 p. £ 15. -- [R]RefR 49 (1995s) 70 (G. *Wyper*); RelSt 31 (1995) 401-3 (P. *Hebblethwaite*); RStR 21 (1995) 314 (S. *Gowler*: not a baby's sneeze nor a grain of sand falls outside it; nothing can thwart his plan).

3130 **Hoffman** Lawrence A., Covenant of blood; circumcision and gender in rabbinic Judaism. Ch c.1995, Univ. vi-258 p.

3131 **Holwerda** David E., Jesus and Israel; one covenant or two ? GR/Leicester 1995, Eerdmans/Apollos. xi-193 p. $ 13. 0-8028-0685-6/.

3132 *Kaiser* W.C., An assessment of 'replacement theology'; the relationship between the Israel of the Abrahamic-Davidic covenant and the Christian Church: *Mishkan 21 (J 1994) 9-20 [NTAb 39, p.451].

3133 **Kraemer** David, Responses to suffering in classical Rabbinic literature. NY 1994, Oxford-UP. 261 p. $ 37.50. 0-19-508900-6. -- [R]ET 106 (1994s) 287 (C.H. *Middleburgh*).

3134 **Lange** Armin, Weisheit und Prädestination; *a)* eine Untersuchung zum Zusammenhang von weisheitlicher Urordnung und prädestinatianischer Geschichtsordnung in den Texten von Qumran: ev. Diss. [D]*Lichtenberger*. Münster 1995. -- ThRv Beilage 92/2, xiii. -- *b)* Weisheitliche Urordnung und Prädestination in den Textfunden von Qumran: StTDJ 18. Lei 1995, Brill. xi-345 p.; Bibliog. 309-328

3135 *a) Lillback* Peter A., The continuing conundrum; CALVIN snd the conditionality of the Covenant; - *b) Stek* John H., 'Covenant' overload in Reformed theology; - *c) Bartholomew* Craig G., Covenant and creation; covenant overload or covenantal deconstruction: C(alvin)TJ 29 (1994) 42-74 (-101, *Muller* R.; 180-9, *King* Adrio; -208, *al.*) / 12-41 / 30 (1995) 11-33.

3136 *Lohfink* Norbert, Bund als Vertrag im Deuteronomium [Gastvorlesung Århus 1994): ZAW 107 (1995) 215-239.

3137 **Martens** Elmer A., God's design; a focus on Old Testament theology[2]. GR 1994, Baker. 320 p.

3138 **Méndez Fernández** Benito, El problema de la salvación de los 'infieles' en Francisco de VITORIA: mg.33. R 1993,Inst.Esp.Hist.Ecl. 381 p.-- [R]ZkT 117 (1995) 373s (M. *Delgado*).

3139 *Müller* Mogens, The hidden context: some observations on the concept of the New Covenant in the New Testament [the real New Testament was not a book, but the prior covenant of creed and sacraments]: → 79, [F]HARTMAN L., Texts & Contexts 1995, 649-658.

3140 *Muñoz León* Domingo, Universalidad de la salvación en la apocalíptica (Dan, 4Esd, 2 Baruch): RevB 56 (1994) 129-140.

3141 *Navarro Puerto* Mercedes, El matrimonio en el Antiguo Testamento, ¿ símbolo de la alianza ? : EstTrin 28 (1994) 283-319 (-341, en Marcos, *Pikaza* X.)

3142 **Neuhaus** Gerd, Theodizee -- Abbruch oder Anstoss des Glaubens 1993 → 9,7028: [R]ThGL 85 (1995) 547-9 (N. *Fischer*).

3143 *Nicole* Roger, Covenant, universal call and definite atonement: JETS 38 (1995) 403-411.

3144 **Niehaus** Jeffrey J., God at Sinai; covenant and theophany in the Bible and Ancient Near East: StOTBibT. Carlisle 1995, Paternoster. 426 p.; bibliog. 385-398. $ 19 pa. 0-310-49471-0 [< OTA 19, p.549].

3145 **Novak** David, The election of Israel; the idea of the Chosen People. C 1995, Univ. 285 p. £ 35. 0-521-41690-6. -- [R]E(xp)T 107 (1995s) 94s (G. *Lloyd Jones*).

3146 *Plathow* Michael, '...der alle Welt erhält allein'; Zufall -- Freiheit .. Vorsehung; zum theologischen Gespräch mit der Chaostheorie [MORFILL G.1991, BRIGGS J. 1990, EKELAND I. 1992, DAVIES P. 1988, WYSS D. 1992, *al.*]: ThZ 51 (1995) 239-254.

3147 **Rendtorff** Rolf, Die 'Bundesformel'; eine exegetisch-theologische Untersuchung: SBS 160. Stu 1995, KBW, 104 p. DM 40. 3-400-04601-5 [TR 91,534]. -- [R]Entschluss 50,9s (1995) 50s (R. *Oberforcher*).

3148 **Röhser** Günter, Prädestination und Verstockung .. ; TANZ 14. Tü 1994, Francke. xiii-279 p. DM 86. 3-7720-1865-3 (D. *Flusser*).

3149 *Rossé* Gérard, Relazione tra l'amore di Dio e l'amore del prossimo alla luce dell'Alleanza; spunti biblici per una spiritualità di comunione: NuovaUm 17,3s (1995) 101-112.

3150 **Ryrie** Charles C., Dispensationalism [= [2rev]Dispensationalism today 1965]. Ch 1995, Moody. 224 p. $ 10. [R]BS 152 (1995) 481s (R.B. *Zuck*).

3151 **Sass** Gerhard, Leben aus den Verheissungen; traditionsgeschichtliche und biblisch-theologische Untersuchungen zur Rede von Gottes Verheissungen im Frühjudentum und bei dem Apostel Paulus: FRLANT 164. Gö 1995, Vandenhoeck & R. 579 p.; Bibliog. 525-552. 3-525-53846-4.

3152 **Stalter-Fouilloy** Danielle, Histoire et violence [volonté divine en vue de responsabilité humaine]; essai sur la liberté humaine dans les premiers écrits chrétiens 1990: ÉtHPR 70 → 7,g10: [R]RTPh 127 (1995) 89s (P.-Y. *Ruff*).

3153 *Stern* Jean, À propos de l'Alliance qui n'a jamais été dénoncée par Dieu: NV 70,3 (1995) 85s.

3154 *Swetnam* James, The Old Testament and the new and eternal covenant [1 Cor 10,16s]: M(elita)Th 46,1 (1995) 65-78 [NTAb 40,p.281].

3155 *Testa* Emanuele, Il concetto di alleanza nella storia primitiva [... Ittiti; Os 6,7; Sir 17,1-4; Gen 2-11]: SBF*LA 45 (1995) 9-43: Eng. 483.

3156 *Vander Hart* Mark D., Creation and covenant: MidAmJT 6 (Orange City IA 1990) 3-18 . 105-116 [< OTA 18 (1995) p. 366s].

3157 **Walton** John H., Covenant; God's purpose, God's plan. GR 1994, Zondervan. 192 p. $ 15. 0-310-57751-9. -- [R]BoL (1995) 121 (C.H. *Knights*).

3158 **White** Peter, Predestination, policy and polemic: conflict and consensus in the English Church from the Reformation to the Civil War. C 1992, Univ. xiv-336 p.; ill. £ 35. 0-521-39433-3. -- [R]JEH 46 (1995) 110-123 (P. *Lake*, also on PENNY D.A. 1990).

3158* *Wodecki* Bernard, [P] De indole soteriologica Pacti Sinaitici: R(uch)BL 48 (1995) 1-17.

H3.3 *Fides et veritas in VT* -- **OT faith and truth**

Barr James, Biblical faith and natural theology 1991/3 → 3726 infra.

3159 *Evans* C, Stephen, Critical historical judgment and biblical faith [... FREI H.]: Faith & Philosophy 11 (ND 1994) 184-206.

3160 *Uffenheimer* Benjamin, [H] The faith of biblical Judah: BetM 40,4 (143) (1995) 302-330.

3161 *Loader* J.A., Fools can explain it, wise men never try [from the Pentateuch and Job 28, ultimate truth can not be achieved]: OTEs 8 (1995) 129-144.

H3.5 *Liturgia, spiritualitas VT* -- **OT prayer**

3162 *Ahituv* Shemuel, [H] *Esra* .. Tithe in the Bible and Hebrew epigraphic sources: BetM 40,4 (143) (1995) 331-6.

3163 **Balentine** Samuel E., Prayer in the Hebrew Bible; the dream of divine-human dialogue: *OvBT → 9,7414; 10,7292: [R]CBQ 57 (1995) 758 (J.L. *Sullivan*); JAOS 115 (1995) 320s (M. *Greenberg*).

3164 *Bekkum* W.J. van, Heiligheid en heiliging in Bijbelse en Rabbijnse traditie: Phoe 41,3 (1995) 131-142.

3165 **Blumenthal** David R., God at the center; meditations on Jewish spirituality. Northvale NJ 1994, Aronson. xxxvi-246 p. 1-56821-348-4,

3166 **Böning** Adalbert, Lebendiges Judentum; ein kurzer Überblick über jüdischen Alltag und jüdische Feste. Hagen 1992, Reiner Padligur. 52 p. DM 9,80. -- [R]GuL 67 (1994) 151s (P. *Imhof*).

3167 a) *Böttrich* Christfried, Das 'Sanctus' in der Liturgie der hellenistischen Synagoge; -
- b) *Bieritz* Karl-Heinrich, Nächstes Jahr in Jerusalem; vom Schicksal der Feste: JLH(ymn)
35 (1994s) 10-36; Eng. 36 / 17-56; Eng. 56s.

3168 **Bonora** Antonio, *al.*, Espiritualidad del Antiguo Testamento [Bo 1987], 1994 →
10,7293; [T]*Ruiz Martorell* Julián, [E]*Ortiz García* Alfonso: [R]E(st)E 70 (1995) 118-120 (J.
Alonso Díaz); Lum(Vt) 44 (1995) 174-6 (U. *Gil Ortega*).

3169 **Bradshaw** Paul F., *Hoffman* Lawrence A., The making of Jewish and Christian worship
1991 → 7,474 ... 10,7295: [R]CCAR 42,2 (1995) 86s (G.S. *Sloyan*); JSSt 40 (1995) 150-2 (A.
Gelston).

3170 **Bryan** David, Cosmos, chaos and the kosher mentality: JSPS.s 12. Shf 1995, Academic.
303 p. £ 40. 1-85075-536-1.

3171   **Cartledge** Tony W., Vows in the Hebrew Bible: JSOT.s 147, 1992 → 8.2655 ...
10,2364*: [R]*A(sn)JS 20 (1995) 391s (J. *Milgrom*).

3172 *Clément* Olivier, Convergences mystiques entre le Judaïsme et le Christianisme: FV
93,1 (1994) 19-43.

3173 **Cohen** Jeffrey M., Blessed are you; a comprehensive guide to Jewish prayer. 1993,
Aronson. 344 p. $ 30. 0-87668-465-7. [JBQ 22 (1994) 170]

3174 **Cohn-Sherbok** Dan & Lavinia, Jewish and Christian mysticism; an introduction. NY/L
1994, Continuum / Fowler Wright. 186 p. £ 15. 0-8264-0695-5 / 0-85244-259-9. : [R]ET
106 (1994s) 351 (L. *Tabick*); TS 56 (1995) 815 (M. *Rindner*).

3175 **Deiana** Giovanni, Il giorno dell'espiazione; il *kippur* nella tradizione biblica: RivBib.s
30, 1994 → 10,2338: [R]SBF*LA 45 (1995) 595-8 (E. *Cortese*).

3176 **Donin** Hayim H., To pray as a Jew; guide to the prayer book and the synagogue
service. NY 1980, Basic. 384 p. [R]CCAR 42,2 (1995) 84s (J.P. *Klein*, also on his 1972
cognate).

3177 **Douglas** Mary, In the wilderness .. defilement in Nm: JSOT.s 158, 1993 → 9,2477:
[R]BSOAS 58 (1995) 353-5 (S.C.R. *Weightman*).

3178 **Elbogen** Ismar, Jewish liturgy, a comprehensive history [German 1913], [T]*Scheindlin*
Raymond P., 1993 → 9,7429; 10.7300: [R]JSSt 40 (1995) 353s (R. *Langer*); Salesianum 57
(1995) 551s (R. *Vicent*).

3179 *Fleischer* Ezra, [H] The Shemone Esre -- its character, internal order, content and goals:
Tarbiz 62 (1992s) 179-223; Eng. VI.

3180 **Galeone** Franco, Ascolta, Israele; note di spiritualità ebraica: Religione e religioni 15.
T-Leumann 1995, Elle Di Ci. 230 p. 88-01-10619-X.

3181 [E]**Geffen** Rela M., Celebration and renewal; rites of passage in Judaism. Ph 1993,
Jewish Publ. x-277 p. -- [R]*A(sn)JS 20 (1995) 370, titles sans pp.

3182 *Glickler-Chazon* Esther, New liturgical manuscripts from Qumran: → 10,331a, 11th
Jewish 1994, A-207-215.

3183   **Gorman** Frank H.[J], The ideology of ritual; space, time and status in the Priestly
theology: JSOT.s 91, 1990 → 6,2059 ... 9,1760: [R]JNES 54 (1995) 62-64 (D. *Pardee*).

3184 [E]**Green** Arthur, Jewish spirituality [1s, 1986s → 2,5361 .. 9.7436]: World Spirituality
13s. NY 1994, Crossroad. I. From the Bible through the Middle Ages, xxv-450 p.; II. From
the 16th century revival to the present, xvii-447 p. 0-8245-0762-2; -3-0.

3185 **Grünewald** Pinchas, Licht und Stern; zum jüdischen Jahreszyklus. Bern 1994, P.Lang.
249 p. Fs 39. -- [R]Jud(aica) 51 (1995) 108 (S. *Langnas*).

3186 **Hayoun** Maurice-Ruben, La liturgie juive: Que sais-je ? N° 2883. P 1994, PUF. 128
p. 2-13-946449-1. -- [R]ZkT 117 (1995) 377 (H.B. *Meyer*).

3187 **Hill** Andrew, Enter his courts with praise; Old Testament worship for the New Testament Church. Nv 1993, Star Song. xxxi-335 p. -- [R]Presbyterion 21 (St.Louis 1995) 124s (R.W. *Yarbrough*).

Houston W.J., Purity and ... unclean animals 1993 → 3235 infra.

3188 *Hurowitz* Victor Avigdor, The form and fate of the tabernacle; reflections on a recent proposal [FRIEDMAN R.E., AnchorBD 6,292-300, modifies *paroket* < BA 43 (1981) 241-8; otherwise 'wrong in every detail']: JQR 86 (1995) 127-146 + 5 pl.

3189 *Hurowitz* Victor A., Ancient Israelite cult in history, tradition, and interpretation [MILGROM J. 1991]: *A(sn)JS 19 (1994) 213-236.

3190 *Klawans* Jonathan, Notions of Gentile impurity in ancient Judaism ; *A(sn)JS 20 (1995) 285-312.

3191 **Knohl** Israel, The sanctuary of silence; the priestly Torah and the Holiness School [Lev 16-26]. Mp 1995, Fortress. x-246 p. $ 28. 0-8006-2763-6. -- [R]OTA 18 (1995) p. 411s (R.A. *Kugler*).

3192 *Kugelmass* Harvey J., Jewish liturgy and the emergence of the synagogue as house of prayer in the post-destruction era: → 10,30, [F]COUTURIER G., Maison 1994, 289-303.

3193 **Lightstone** Jack N., *Bird* Frederick B., Ritual and ethnic identity: a comparative study of the social meaning of liturgical ritual in synagogues. Waterloo ONT 1995, Wilfrid Laurier Univ. vii- 224 p. 0-88920-247-

3194 **McKay** Heather A., Sabbath and synagogue: ÉPRO 122, 1994 → 10,7307: [R]BoL (1995) 156 (J. *Lieu*: confident, ample); ET 106,6 2d-top choice (1994s) 162s (C.S. *Rodd*): JThS 46 (1995) 610-2 (S.C. *Reif*); OTA 18 (1995) p. 433 (L.H. *Feldman*); VT 45 (1995) 569 (N. de *Lange*); Zion 60 (1995) 349-352 (S. *Safrai*,[H]).

3195 *Maher* Michael, The Psalms in Jewish worship: PI(r)BA 17 (1994) 9-36 (-54, *Zenger* Erich).

3196 *Maier* Johan, Sühne und Vergebung in der jüdischen Liturgie; JBTh 9 (1994) 145-171 [Jud(aica) 51,195].

3197 *Manns* Frédéric, The binding of Isaac in Jewish liturgy; the Targum of Gen 22: → 513, Sacrifice of Isaac 1993/5, 58-67 / 69-80.

3198 **Martin-Achard** Robert, Il dio fedele [8 feste dell'AT],[T]. Bo 1994, Dehoniane. 134 p. L[m] 16. -- [R]PaVi 40,6 (1995) 62s (L. *Melotti*).

3199 **Mathys** H.-P., Dichter und Beter .. : OBO 132, 1994 → 10,2807 ; [R]AfO 42s (1995s) 313 (A. *Kraljic*).

3200 **Miller** Patrick D., They cried to the Lord 1994 → 10,8179: [R]P(rinc)SB 16 (1995) 241-3 (J. *Limburg*); WW 15 (1995) 226 . 228 (M.A. *Throntveit*).

3201 *Moatti* Émile, Le pèlerinage de Soukkot: MoB 91 (mars 1995) [< E(spr)eV 105 (1995) 307 (J. *Daoust*)].

3202 *Neufeld* Ernest, Magical transformations; Sukkoth and the four species: JBQ 23 (1995) 27-32 . 37.

3203 **Nitzan** Bilhah, Qumran prayer and religious poetry: STDJ 12, [D]1994 → 10,7309*: [R]BetM 40,2 (141, 1995) 114-6 (G. *Brin*, [H]); CBQ 57 (1995) 779s (T.S.L. *Michael*); DSD 2 (1995) 361-5 (Esther *Chazon*); JSJ(ud) 26 (1995) 369-372 (J. *Maier* queries 'mainstream Judaism' as alternative); RB 102 (1995) 595-600 (Annette *Steudel*: incompletenesses).

3204 **Podella** Thomas, <u>Sôm</u>-Fasten; kollektive Trauer um den verborgenen Gott im AT [< Diss. Berlin, [D]*Welten* P.]; AOAT 224, 1989 → 5,7027: [R]JNES 54 (1995) 60-62 (S.W. *Holloway*).

3205 **Reif** Stefan C., Judaism and Hebrew prayer; new perspectives on Jewish liturgical history 1993 → 9,7452; 10,7312: ᴿ*A(sn)JS 20 (1995) 424-7 (L.A. *Hoffman*): BSOAS 58 (1995) 113s (I. *Jacobs*); JSSt 40 (1995) 152s (R. *Langer*); Salesianum 57 (1995) 560s (R. *Vicent*).

3206 **Rubenstein** Jeffrey L., The history of Sukkot in the Second Temple and rabbinic periods: BJSt 302. At 1995, Scholars. xiv-361 p.; Bibliog. 327-336.

3207 *Russ* Maria, Der Duft des Weihrauchs -- ein vergessenes Zeichen: BiKi 50 (1995) 20-24 + 1 fig.

3208 *Sagi* A., *Zohar* Z., The halakhic ritual of *giyyur* [irrevocable conversion of a *goy* to Judaism] : *JRit 9,1 (1995) 1-13.

3209 *Schuller* Eileen M., Prayer, hymnic and liturgical texts from Qumran: → 538, Community 1993/4, 153-171 [< OTA 18 (1995) p. 375 (P.D. *Sansone*)].

3210 **Tabory** Joseph, ᴴ Jewish festivals in the time of the Mishna and Talmud. J 1995. 446 p. -- ᴿZion 60 (1995) 473-9 (A. *Oppenheimer*).

3211 *Tabory* Joseph, ᴴ The paschal *hagiga* [extra meat] -- myth or reality ? : Tarbiz 64 (1994s) 39-49; Eng. 1,v: fell into disuse after Hillel because the lamb always sufficed for diminishing participants.

3212 **Trepp** Leo, Der judeische Gottesdienst 1992 → 9,7456: ᴿAtK(ap) 124 (1995) 458s (B. *Nadolski*).

3213 **Vicent Saera** Rafael, La fiesta judía de las Cabañas (Sukkot); interpretaciones místicas en la Biblia y en el Judaismo antiguo: BtMidrásica 17. Estella 1995, VDivino. 295 p. 84-8169-074-0.

3214 **Wolfgang** Walter, Meinen Bund habe ich mit dir geschlossen; jüdische Religion in Fest, Gebet und Brauch: Topos-Tb 236. Mainz 1993, Grünewald. 210 p. -- ᴿFrRu NF 1 (1993s) 302 (Elisabet *Plünnecke*).

H3.7 *Theologia moralis VT* -- **OT moral theology**

3215 *Bahloul* Joelle, Food practices among Sephardic·immigrants in contemporary France; dietary laws in urban society: JAAR 63,3 ('Religion and food' 1995) 485-496.

3216 *a) Barton* John, The basis of ethics in the Hebrew Bible; -- *b) Birch* Bruce C., Moral agency, community, and the character of God in the Hebrew Bible; -- *c) Davies* Eryl W., Ethics of the Hebrew Bible; the problem of methodology; -- *d) Wilson* Robert R., Sources and methods in the study of ancient Israelite ethics; -- *e) Haas* Peter J., *Otto* Eckart, *Paris* Peter J., responses: Semeia 66 (1994) 11-22 / 23-41 / 43-53 / 55-63 / 151-161 / 173-9.

3217 *Berthoud* Pierre, La Loi -- une perspective biblique: RRéf 46.1 (1995) 19-22.

3218 **Birch** Bruce C., Let justice roll down 1991 → 7.8308 ... 10,7319: ᴿJETS 38 (1995) 113s (W.C. *Williams*: hesitant); TorJT 11 (1995) 82s (J.L. *McLaughlin*).

3219 **Blenkinsopp** Joseph, Wisdom and law in the OT; the ordering of life in Israel and early Judaism. Ox 1995, UP. 197 p.

3220 *Bockmuehl* Markus, Natural law in Second Temple Judaism: VT 45 (1995) 17-44.

3221 **Brin** Gershon, Studies in biblical law: JSOT.s 176, 1994 → 10,163*: ᴿBetM 40,2 (141, 1995) 123-6 (B.J. *Shoretz*, ᴴ); JThS 46 (1995) 592-4 (A. *Phillips*).

3222 *a) Brin* G., The formula 'if he shall not (do)' and the problem of sanctions in biblical law; -- *b) Weisman* Ze'ev, The place of the people in the making of law and judgment; -- *c) Patrick* Dale, The rhetoric of collective responsibility in Deuteronomic law: → 130, ᶠMILGROM J., Pomegranates 1995, 341-362 / 407-420 / 421-436.

3223 *Cardellino* Lodovico, Occhio per occhio, guancia per guancia ['offrire l'altra guancia è paradossale applicazione e conferma']: BeO(riente) 37 (1995) 95-126.

3224 *Chinitz* Jacob, Eye for an eye --an old canard: JBQ 23 (1995) 79-85.

3225 *Clement* Carol Dorr, Bible histories on values, virtues,and vices: LiLi 32,4(1995s) 18-24.

3226 *Cohen* Jeffrey M., The nature of the Decalogue: JBQ 22 (1994) 173-7.

3227 *Cohen* Matty, [H] Biblical purity and impurity and their relation to rabbinic prohibitions and permissions: → 10,331a, 11th Jewish 1994, A-107-116.

3228 [E]**Dorff** Elliot, *Newman* Louis, Contemporary Jewish ethics; a reader. NY 1995, Oxford-UP. 468 p. £ 35; pa. £ 17.50, 0-19-509065-9; -6-7. -- [R]E(xp)T 107 (1995s) 190 (F. *Morgan*).

3229 **Droge** A., *Tabor* J., A noble death; suicide and martyrdom among Christians and Jews 1992 → 8,7423 ... 10,7323: : [R]P(rinc)SB 16 (1995) 260-2 (J.H. *Charlesworth*); SewaneeT 38 (1994s) 290s (A.Katherine *Grieb*).

3230 **Eichenstein** Zevi H., Turn aside from evil and do good; an introduction and a way to the Tree of Life. L 1995, Littman Library. xxxviii-159 p.; bibliog. 139-143. 1-874774-10-2.

3231 **Farley** Benjamin W., In praise of virtue; an exploration of the biblical [and pagan] virtues in a Christian context. GR 1995. Eerdmans. x-181 p. $ 13 pa. 0-8028-0792-3 [OTA 19,p.168s, Carol J. *Dempsey*: 'in an evangelical style of scholarship'].

3232 *Fredriksen* Paula, Did Jesus oppose the purity laws ? : BiRe 11,3 (1995) 18-25 . 42.

3233 *Gross* Walter, Wandelbares Gesetz -- unwandelbarer Dekalog ? ThQ 175 (1995) 161-170. (-178, *Hunold* Gerfried W.)

3233* *Grossberg* Daniel, Two kinds of sexual relationships in the Hebrew Bible [Ct; Prov 7]: HebStud 35 (1994) 7-25.

3234 *Harrington* Hannah E., Did the Pharisees eat ordinary food in a state of ritual purity?: JSJ(ud) 26 (1995) 42-54.

3235 **Houston** Walter J., Purity and monotheism; clean and unclean animals in biblical law. JSOT.s 140, 1993 → 9.2455; 10,2335: [R]CBQ 57 (1995) 139s (B.E. *Shafer*); *CritRR 7 (1994) 123-5 (R.A. *Simkins*); EvQ 67 (1995) 162s (G. *Wenham*): JQR 85 (1994s) 443s (J. *Milgrom*); PEQ 127 (1995) 173s (G. *Moore*).

3236 **Hugenberger** Gordon P., Marriage as a covenant .. biblical law and ethics .. Malachi: VTS 52, 1993 → 10,3795: [R]JBL 114 (1995) 306-8 (J.J. *Collins*: valuable also for social historians).

3237 *Hvalvik* Reidar, Orders from God's own mouth; the Decalogue in ancient Judaism and in the early Church: TT(og)K 66 (1995) 261-274.292: Eng. 273.

3238 **Janzen** Waldemar, OT ethics, a paradigmatic approach 1994 → 10.7324: [R]BoL (1995) 15 (J. *Barton*); CBQ 57 (1995) 772-4 (R.W. *Klein*); Interpretation 49 (1995) 310-312 (D. *Patrick*); P(rinc)SB 16 (1995) 85-87 (J.A. *Fager*).

3239 **Jaramillo Rivas** P., La injusticia y la opresión en el lenguaje figurado de los profetas [dis. Pont. Univ. Gregoriana, [D]*Conroy* C.]: Jerón 26, 1992 → 10,3357: [R]CBQ 57 (1995) 142s (H. *Gossai*); RivB 43 (1995) 430-3 (M. *Nobile*).

3240 **Kaminsky** Joel S., Corporate responsibility in the Hebrew Bible: JSOT.s 196. Shf 1995, Academic. 211 p. £ 27-50 [< OTA 19,p.169].

3240* *Klawans* Jonathan, Notions of Gentile impurity in ancient Judaism [not in all sages]: *A(sn)JS 20 (1995) 203-312.

3241 **Koch** Robert, Die Bundesmoral im Alten Testament 1994 → 10,7325: [R]BoL (1995) 115 (J.W. *Rogerson*: views of a generation ago).

3242 **Lawton** David, Blasphemy. Ph 1993, Univ. Pennsylvania [BIP:] 0-8122-1503-6. -- ^RJRel 75 (1995) 464s (E.J. *Ziolkowski*).

3243 **Leaman** Oliver, Evil and suffering in Jewish philosophy. C 1995, Univ. 257 p. £ 35. 0-521-41724-4. -- ^RE(xp)T 107 (1995s) 95 (F. *Morgan*).

3244 **Lehmann** Paul L. †, The Decalogue and a human future; the meaning of the commandments for making and keeping human life human. GR 1995, Eerdmans. 227 p. $ 18. -- ^RCCen 112 (1995) 1247-9 (J.M. *Gustafson*); *CritRR 8 (1995) 246-8 (Michelle J. *Bartel*).

3245 **Leiter** David A., The unattainable ideal; impractical and/or unenforceable rules in the ancient Israelite legal collections: diss. Drew, ^D*Huffmon* H. Madison NJ 1995. -- RStR 22,272.

3246 *Lepicard* E., L'embryon dans la Bible et la Tradition rabbinique II: Éthique (P 1992,4) 58-80 [<ZIT 95,p.178].

3247 **Levy** Leonard W,. Blasphemy; verbal offenses against the sacred from Moses to Salman Rushdie c.1994. -- ^RChrCent 112 (1995) 89 (J. *White*).

3248 *Lindemann* Andreas, 'Do not let a woman destroy the unborn babe in her belly' [Ps.-PHOCYLIDES]; abortion in ancient Judaism and Christianity: StTh 49 (1995) 253-271.

3249 **Marshall** Jay W., Israel and the Book of the Covenant: an approach to biblical law; SBL diss. 140, 1993 → 9,2364; 10,2262: ^RI(rish)BSt 17 (1995) 188-193 (T.D. *Alexander*); Interpretation 49 (1995) 196s (F.S. *Frick*).

3250 *Matić* Marko, The conception of marriage in the Old Testament: *ObnŽiv 49 (1994) 603-615 Croatian; 616 Eng.

3251 **Muffs** Yochanan, Love and joy; law, language and religion in ancient Israel 1992 → 10,208c [JQR 86,273, titles sans pages]: ^RTarbiz 64 (1994s) 309-311 (M.I. *Grubber* ^H; Eng. 2,x).

3252 **Neusner** Jacob, Judaic Law from Jesus to the Mishnah; a systematic reply to Professor E.P. SANDERS: SFSHJ 89. At 1993, Scholars. xiv-316 p. -- ^R*CritRR 8 (1995) 432-5 (A.J. *Saldarini*).

3253 **Otto** Eckart, Theologische Ethik des ATs: ThW 3/2, 1994 → 10,7238: ^RBoL (1995) 118 (G.J. *Wenham*: breathtaking, essential): EThL 71 (1995) 197 (J. *Lust*); LA 45 (1995) 599-604 (E. *Cortese*); LM(onat) 32,12 (1995) 42s (H.G. *Pöhlmann*); ThLZ 120 (1995) 992-6 (R. *Kessler*); ThQ 175 (1995) 66s (W. *Gross*); ZEE(thik) 39 (1995) 235-7 (J. von *Soosten*).

3254 *Otto* Eckart, Vom Rechtsbruch zur Sünde; priestlicher Interpretationen des Rechts: JBTh 9 (1994) 23-52.

3255 *Otto* Eckart, Biblische Rechtsgeschichte: TR 91 (1995) 283-292.

3256 ^E**Reventlow** H., *Hoffman* Y., Justice and righteousness; biblical themes and their influence 1990/2 → 9,9783; ^RVT 45 (1995) 416s (H.G.M. *Williamson*).

3257 *Rogerson* John W., Christian morality and the Old Testament: → 134, ^FMURRAY R., HeythJ 36,4 (1995) 409-421.

3258 *Rosenthal* Eliezer S. *zal,* ^H Tradition and innovation in the Halakha of the sages: Tarbiz 63 (1993s) 321-374; Eng. xix.

3259 *Sach* Avi, Models of authority and the duty of obedience in halakhic literature: *A(sn)JS 20 (1995) 1-24.

3260 *Seitz* C.R., Human sexuality, viewed from the Bible's understanding of the human condition ['all have fallen short by nature']: ThTo 52 (1995) 236-246 [NTAb 40,p.88].

3261 **Sleeper** C. Freeman, The Bible and the moral life. LVL 1992, W-Knox. x-181 p. $ 15 pa. -- ^R*CritRR 7 (1994) 89-91 (S.C. *Mott*).

3262   *Spiro* S.,   The moral vision of Saul LIEBERMAN; a historiographic approach to normative Jewish ethics: CJud 46,4 (1994) 64-84   [NTAb 39, p.113].

3263 **Stahl** Nanette, Law and liminality in the Bible; JSOT.s 202. Shf 1995, Academic. 104 p. £ 25. 0-85075-561-2.

3264   *Uchelen* N.A. van, Halacha in het Nieuwe Testament ? : NedThT 49 (1995) 177-189; Eng. 21 (190-3, weerwoord, *Tomson* P.J.).

3265   *Vanoni* Gottfried, Die Bibel Jesu und die soziale Gerechtigkeit, dargestellt am Beispiel des Themas Eigentum: Entschluss 50,3 (1995) 8-14.

3266   **Weinfeld** M.,   Social justice in ancient Israel and the Ancient Near East: Perry Foundation. J/Mp 1995, Magnes/Fortress. 300 p. $ 34, /0-8006-2596-X [NTAb 40, p.387].

3267 **Wénin** André, L'homme biblique; anthropologie et éthique dans le Premier Testament: Théologies bibliques. P 1995, Cerf. 195 p. 2-204-05094-6.

3268 **Wright** Christopher J.H., Walking in the ways of the Lord; the ethical authority of the Old Testament. Leicester 1995, Apollos. 319 p. £ 15. 0-85111-444-X. -- ᴿ*TBR 8,2 (1995s) 9 (R. *Coggins*).

H3.8 *Bellum et pax VT-NT* -- **War and peace in the whole Bible**

3269 **Baker** Anne B., The application of the criteria of the Just War theories in the resolution of medical-ethical dilemmas at the bedside: LinacreQ 62,4 (1995) 3-21.

3270   **Barbaglio** Giuseppe, Dieu est-il violent ? Une lecture des Écritures juives et chrétiennes [GIRARD R. → H7.2], ᵀ: Parole de Dieu, 1994 → 10,7748; F 160: ᴿE(spr)eV 105 (1995) 315s (L. *Monloubou*); MélSR 52 (1995) 337 (D. *Lecompte*); RHPhR 75 (1995) 217 (P. de *Robert*).

3271   **Baudler** Georg, Töten oder Lieben; Gewalt und Gewaltlosigkeit in Religion und Christentum. Mü 1994, Kösel. 432 p. DM 50. -- ᴿLebZeug 50 (1995) 295-8 (W. *Gantke*, auch über sein Stiergott 1989); TPQ 143 (1995) 303s (B. *Dieckmann*: anthropologisch Optimist, realistisch oder pessimistisch in seiner Wahrnehmung der Geschichte).

3272   **Beauchamp** Paul, *Vasse* D., La violencia en la Biblia: CuadB 76. Estella 1992. VDivino. 66 p. -- ᴿProyección 46 (1994) 63 (B.A.O.).

3273   *Belloso Martín* Nuria, De nuevo sobre la guerra y la paz : EstAg 29 (1994) 529-576.

3274   *Bishop* Peter, War, peace-keeping, and terrorism: ET 106 (1994s) 4-9.

3275   *Bivin* David, Jesus' attitude toward pacifism [not taught in his sayings if rightly interpreted]: JPersp 45 (1994) 3.6.

3276 **Cahill** Lisa S., Love your enemies; discipleship, pacifism, and the just war theory. Mp 1994, Fortress. xii-252 p. $ 17 pa. -- ᴿHorizons 22 (1995) 266-277 (Denise L. *Carmody*) & 278-281 (J.H. *Yoder*) & 281s (Moni *McIntyre*) & 282-5 (J.T. *Johnson*); Cahill response 285-290; -- RfR 54 (1995) 308s (D.P. *Reid*).

3277   *Cavanaugh* William T., 'A fire strong enough to consume the house'; the wars of religion and the rise of the state: MoTh 11 (1995) 397-420.

3278   *Clark* Mark T., The [biblical] paradox of war and pacifism: PerSCF 47 (1995) 220-232.

3279   *Cornelius* Izak, The iconography of divine war in the pre-Islamic Near East; a survey: JNWS 21,1 (1955) 15-28 + 16 fig.

3280   *Da Spinetoli* Ortensio, La violenza; riscoprire il messaggio biblico → 123, ᶠMATTIOLI A., In spiritu et veritate 1995, 97-112.

3281 **Davis** Grady S., Warcraft and the fragility of virtue. Moscow, Idaho Univ. 1992. iv-196 p. $ 15 pa. -- ᴿCCurr 44 (1944s) 117-122 (M. J. *Quirk*).

3282 **Dear** John, The God of peace; toward a theology of non-violence. Mkn 1994, Orbis. 212 p. $ 17. 0-88344-980-3. -- [R]ET 106 (1994s) 286 (K.G. *Greet*; high praise for this theological base of a Roman Catholic priest imprisoned for pouring blood on a jet fighter plane).

3283 *Enermalm* Agneta, Prayers in wartime; thematic tensions in 1 Maccabees: ST 49 (Oslo 1995) 272-286.

3284 **Faust** Eberhard, Pax Christi et pax Caesaris .. Epheserbrief: NOrb 24,1993 → 10,6070: [R]EstB 53 (1995) 418-420 (J. *Huarte*).

3285 **Görg** Manfred, Der un-heile Gott; die Bibel im Bann der Gewalt. Dü 1995, Patmos. 192 p.: 3 fig. DM 33. 3-491-77970-7 [NTAb 40, p.366].

3286 *Guillemette* Nil, *a*) Did Yahweh promote genocide ? ; -- *b*) The sermon on the mount; feasible ethics ? : Landas 9 (Manila 1995) 3-36 / 209-236.

3287 *Haese* U., Überlegungen zur Haltung der katholischen Kirche in der DDR gegenüber der Wehrdienstfrage: Kirchliche Zeitgeschichte 7 ('Kirche und Diktatur', Gö 1994) 236-263 [< ZIT 95,p.242].

3288 **Heim** François, La théologie de la victoire: THist 89, 1992 → 8,7376 ... 10,7339; [R]CrSt 16 (1995) 631s (D. De *Decker*); Gnomon 67 (1995) 48-51 (R. *Klein*); *JEarlyC 3 (1995) 87-89 (R.*Van Dam*); Latomus 54 (1995) 732-4 (S. *Deléani*).

3289 [E]**Helgeland** John, *al.*, Christians and the military: the early experience: Cath.Theol.Soc. seminar Wsh 1982. L 1987, SCM. 102 p. -- [R]Salesianum 57 (1995) 772s (Gillian *Bonney*).

3290 *Joblin* Joseph, Ingérence des États en temps de guerre; action humanitaire des organisations bénévoles chrétiennes et témoignage de l'Évangile: Greg 76 (1995) 95-122; Eng. 123.

3291 *Kemp* Kenneth W., Personal pacifism [a restricted conscientious objection]: TS 56 (1995) 21-38.

3292 *Liau* T., Theology of warfare in Deuteronomy: TaiwanJT 15 (1993) 61-81 [< ZAW 107 (1995) 513].

3293 **Longman** Tremper[III], *Reid* Daniel G., God is a warrior. GR/ 1995, Zondervan / Paternoster. 224 p. 0-85364-648-1: [R]E(xp)T 107 (1995s) 62 (C.S.*Rodd:* unwelcome*)*.

3294 **Marra** B., *Mattai* G., Dalla guerra all'ingerenza umanitaria. T 1995, SEI. 192 p. L[m] 20. -- [R]RasT 36 (1995) 381 (Antonella *Salvato*).

3295 *Mattai* Giuseppe, Dalla guerra all'ingerenza umanitaria; rassegna di recenti documenti: Asprenas 42 (1995) 249-262.

3296 **Miller** Richard B., Interpretations of conflict ethics, pacifism, and the just war tradition 1991 → 8,7396 ... 10,7350: [R]*CritRR 6 (1993) 328-330 (R.H. *Stone*).

3297 *Minois* G., L'Église et la guerre; de le Bible à l'ère atomique. P 1994, A. Fayard. -- [R]Annales 50 (1995) 1212s (M. *Lagrée*) [RHE 91,53*].

3298 *Mitchell* Gordon, War, folklore, and the mystery of a disappearing book [GUNKEL H., Israelitisches Heldentum und Kriegsfrömmigkeit im AT (Gö 1916, Vandenhoeck) 52 p.: never cited, though mentioned in the bibliographies of the 1923 Festschrift and of N. LOHFINK's 1983 Gewalt; valuable for seeking biblical origins not in the cult but in the campfire, 'a wild, warlike people fighting for survival']: JSOT 68 (1995) 113-9.

3299 **Niditch** Susan, War in the Hebrew Bible 1993 → 9,7522; 10,7352: [R]*A(sn)JS 20 (1995) 395s (S.M. *Olyan*); ChrSchR 25 (1995s) 247-9 (P.B. *Yoder*, also on VON RAD Eng. 1991); *CritRR 8 (1995) 140-2 (S.A. *Reed*); JThS 46 (1995) 206-9 (R.P. *Carroll*).

3300 *a) Niditch* Susan, War in the Hebrew Bible and contemporary parallels; - *b) Wentz* Richard E., Why do the nations rage in the name of religion ? : WW 15 (1995)

3301 *O'Connor* M., War and rebel chants in the Former Prophets: → 59, ᶠFREEDMAN D.N., Fortunate 1995, 322-337.
3302 **Panikkar** Raimon, Paz y desarme cultural. Sdr 1993, Sal Terrae. 202 p. -- ᴿSalTer 82 (1994) 237s (J.A. *García*).
3303 **Panikkar** Raimon, Cultural disarmament [religions' metanoia]; the way to peace [< Madrid Machado meeting], ᵀ*Barr* Robert R. LVL 1995, W-Knox. 142 p. 0-664-2554-3 [RStR 22,230, L.D. *Lefebure*].
3304 **Peretto** Elio, La sfida aperta; le strade della violenza e della non violenza dalla Bibbia a LATTANZIO 1993 → 9,7524; 10,7353: ᴿMélSR 52 (1995) 178s (M. *Spanneut*); NRT 117 (1995) 439s (V. *Roisel*).
3305 **Petraglio** S., Obiezione di coscienza; il NT provoca chi lo legge. Bo 1992, Dehoniane. 460 p. Lᵐ 35. -- ᴿAsprenas 42 (1995) 137s (G. *Mattai*).
3306 **Ruffino** Andreas, Jahwekrieg als Weltmetapher .. Chr 1992 → 8,3020 ... 10.2766: ᴿVT 45 (1995) 418s (H.G.M. *Williamson*); ZKT 116 (1994) 88 (G. *Fischer*).
3307 *Scippa* Vincenzo, La guerra nella Bibbia: Asprenas 42 (1995) 163-180 (-202, la pace, *Gianazza* Giorgio) [NTAb 40, p.281].
3308 *Snyman* S.D., Biblical perspectives on reconciliation and peace: ActaTheolSAf 14 (Bloemfontein 1994) 93-102 [< OTA 18 (1995) p. 366].
3309 **Wengst** Klaus, Pax romana and the peace of Jesus Christ 1987 → 3,6869 .. 5,7357 ..: ᴿLat 61 (1995) 207s (Anetta *Przybytek*).
3310 ᴱ**Wicker** Brian, Studying war -- no more ? From just war to just peace. Kampen 1993, Kok Pharos. 216 p. 90-390-0401-3. -- ᴿBijdragen 56 (1995) 470s (J. ter *Laak*).
3311 **Winn** Albert C., Ain't gonna study war no more; biblical ambiguity and the abolition of war 1993 → 9,7532: 10,7360: ᴿInterpretation 49 (1995) 322 . 4 (W.M. *Swartley*).
3312 *Wolbert* Werner, Zur 'Vermeidung des Krieges' im Weltkatechismus: THGL 85 (1995) 224-237.
3313 **Zerbe** Gordon M., Non-retaliation in early Jewish and NT texts ᴰ1993 → 9,7534; 10,7362: ᴿCBQ 57 (1995) 201s (M. *Cahill*).

H4.1 Messianismus

3314 *Bauckham* Richard, The messianic interpretation of Isa. 10:34 in the Dead Sea Scrolls, 2 Baruch and the preaching of John the Baptist: DSD 2 (1995) 202-216.
3315 *Bock* Darrell L., Current messianic activity and OT Davidic promise: ['progressive'] dispensationalism, hermeneutics, and NT fulfillment: TrinJ 15 (1994) 55-87 [< BS 152 (1995) 92s, J.A. *Witmer*); p.101s, J.L. *Burns* on cognate BLAISING-BOCK 1993].
3316 *Brzegowy* Tadeusz, ᴾ Le messianisme du Deutéro-Zacharie: → 98, ᶠKUMOR B., AnCr 27 (1995) 93-108; franç. 109.
3317 ᴱ**Charlesworth** J., The Messiah 1987/92 → 8,463 ... 10,7365: ᴿRefR 49 (1995s) 63s (C.B. *Kaiser*).
3318 **Collins** J.J., The scepter and the star; the Messiahs of the Dead Sea Scrolls and other ancient literature: AnchorB Reference. NY 1995, Doubleday. xiv-270 p. $ 30. 0-385-47457-1. -- ᴿE(xp)T 107 (1995s) 154 (J.G. *Snaith*: excellent scrolls survey).
3319 *Collins* J.J., The works of the Messiah [4Q 521]: *DSD 1 (1994) 98-112 [NTAb 39,p.464].
3320 *Collins* John J., Teacher and Messiah ? The one who will teach righteousness at the end of days: → 538, Community 1993/4, 193-210[< OTA 18 (1995) p. 369].

3321 *a) Collins* J.J., 'He shall not judge by what his eyes see'; messianic authority in the Dead Sea Scrolls; -- *b) Evans* C.A., A note on the [Davidic-messianic] 'First.Born Son' of 4Q 369; -- *c) Knibb* M.A., Messianism in the Pseudepigrapha in the light of the Scrolls; *DSD 2 (1995) 145-164 / 185-201 / 165-184 [202-216, in Isa 10,34, *Bauckham* R.].

3322 **Delgado** Mariano, Die Metamorphosen des Messianismus in den iberischen Kulturen; eine religionsgeschichtliche Studie: Schr 34. Immensee 1994, NZMW. 133 p. 3-85824-075-3. -- [R]ZkT 117 (1995) 361s (K.H. *Neufeld*).

Fredriksen Paula, De Jésus aux Christs ... dans le NT 1992 → H52.

3323 *Goldberg* A., Setting Jesus free; a response to 'The relevance of Jewish roots for our times' [WILSON M.R.]: *JRadR 4,4 (1995) 18-23: openmindedness to Judaism will cause doubt about Jesus' messianic claim; Wilson response 24-31 [NTAb 40,p.192].

3324 *Henrix* Hans-Hermann, Jüdische Messiashoffnung -- Christusglaube der Christen: FrRu NF 1 (1993s) 279-291 [< Jud(ca) 51 (1995) 58].

3325 *Hoffman* Yair, [H] The question of the Messiah in the Qumran literature: BetM 40,4 (143) (1995) 396-401.

3326 **Idel** Moshe, Messianisme et mystique [[H]], [T]*Chalier* Catherine. P 1994, Cerf. 121 p. - - [R]RTPh 127 (1995) 404s (J. *Borel*, also on his Le Golem 1993).

3327 **Kaiser** Walter C., The Messiah in the Old Testament. GR 1995, Zondervan. 256 p. 0-310-20030-X.

3328 *Kaiser* Walter C., Enheden og udviklingen i dogmet om Messias, [T]*Malmgart* Liselotte: Ichthys 22 (Århus 1995) 75-84.

3329 **Kampling** Rainer, Israel unter dem Anspruch des Messias .. Mk [Hab.-Diss. Münster 1991, [D]*Kertelge* K.]; SBB 25. Stu 1992, KBW [BZ 39,316].

3330 *Kaufmann* Yehezkel, The messianic idea; the real and the hidden Son-of-David [1961]: JBQ 22 (1994) 141-150.

3331 *Knibb* Michael A., Messianism in the Pseudepigrapha in the light of the Scrolls: DSD 2 (1995) 165-184.

3332 *Koch* Klaus, Messias und Menschensohn; die zweistufige Messianologie der jüngeren Apokalyptik (p. 73-102). und die ganze 'einzigartige und beachtenswerte Leistung', JBTh 8 (1993), [R]JSJ(ud) 26 (1995) 201-5 (A.S. van der *Woude*).

3333 **Kochan** Lionel, Jews, idols and Messiahs; the challenge from history. Ox 1990, Blackwell. 231 p. £ 35. -- [R]JJS 45 (1994) 326s C. *Alderman*).

3334 **Liebes** Yehuda, Studies in Jewish myth [... SCHOLEM mysticism] and Jewish messianism, [T]*Stein* Batya. Albany 1993, SUNY. x-226 p. $ 57.50; pa. $ 19. -- [R]*CritRR 7 (1994) 432-4 (Hava *Tirosh-Rothschild*).

3335 *Marshall* I.H., The Messiah; developments in earliest Judaism and Christianity [[E]CHARLESWORTH J.H.]: [R]*CriswellTR 7,1 (1993) 57-83 [NTAb 40, p.271].

3336 **Meissner** William W., Thy kingdom come; psychoanalytic perspectives on the Messiah and the millennium. KC 1995, Sheed & W. xi-370 p. $ 30 1-55612-750-2 [ThD 43,179].

3337 *Minear* Paul S., The Messiah forsaken ... Why ? : H(orizons)BT 17 (1995) 62-83.

3338 **Neusner** Jacob, The mother of the Messiah in Judaism ; the book of Ruth. Ph 1993, Trinity. xxi-138 p. 1-56338-061-7. -- [R]*FemT 9 (1995) 124-6 (Alice *Bach*).

3339 **Oegema** Gerbern S., Der Gesalbte und sein Volk. Untersuchungen zum Konzeptualisierungsprozess der messianischen Erwartungen von den Makkabäern bis Bar Koziba: Delitzschianum 2, 1994 → 10,7371: [R]BoL (1995) 119 (L.L. *Grabbe*: definitive, replacing KLAUSNER); JBL 114 (1995) 312-4 (J.J. *Collins*); RStR 21 (1995) 342s (F.J. *Murphy*).

3340 *O'Neill* J.C., The question of messianic expectation in Pseudo-PHILO's Biblical Antiquities; *JHiC 1 (1994) 85-93 [NTAb 39,p.293].

3341 *Ostovich* Steven T, Messianic history in BENJAMIN and METZ: PhTh 8,4 (Milwaukee 1994) 271-289.

3342 **Pomykala** Kenneth E., The Davidic dynasty tradition in early Judaism: its history and significance for messianism: SBL.EJL 7. At 1995, Scholars. 308 p. $ 40; pa. $ 25. 0-7885-0068-6; -9-4. -- ᴿE(xp)T 107 (1995s) 155 (C.S. *Rodd*); EThL 71 (1995) 442s (J. *Lust*); OTA 18 (1995) p. 429 (P.L. *Redditt*).

3343 *a) Puech* Émile, Messianism, resurrection and eschatology at Qumran and in the NT; - - *b) VanderKam* James, Messianism in the Scrolls: → 538, Community 1993/4, 235-256 / 211-234 [< OTA 18 (1995) p. 374.8].

3344 **Rowland** Christopher, Christian origins; an account of the setting and character of the most important messianic sect of Judaism. L 1993, SPCK. xx-428 p. £ 17.50. 0-281-04110-5. -- ᴿZkT 117 (1995) 235 (R. *Oberforcher*).

3345 **Sicre** José Luis, De David al Mesías; textos básicos de la esperanza mesiánica: El mundo de la Biblia. Estella 1995, VDivino. 448 p. pt 2400. 84-8169-033-3. -- ᴿOTA 18 (1995) p. 430s (C.T. *Begg*); RET 55 (1995) 256s (P. *Barrado Fernández*).

3346 **Spek** Wout van der, De Messias in de Hebreeuwse Bibel [1 Sam; diss. Amst]. Gorinchem 1992, Narratio. 168 p. ƒ 39,50. 90-5263-081-X. -- ᴿBijdragen 56 (1995) 452 (E. *Eynikel*).

3347 ᴱ**Stegemann** Ekkehard, Messiasvorstellungen 1993 → 9,7547: 10,7373*: ᴿJSJ(ud) 26 (1995) 225-8 (G.S. *Oegema*).

3348 **Thoma** Clemens, Das Messiasprojekt; Theologie jüdisch-christlicher Begegnung 1994 → 10,7374; ᴿFrRu 2 (1995) 64-67 (N. *Sonnevelt*); Jud(ca) 51 (1995) 111s (H.L. *Reichrath*).

3349 **Voigts** Manfred, Jüdischer Messianismus und Geschichte. B 1994, Agora. 127 p. -- ᴿFrRu 2 (1995) 230-2 (S. *Ben-Chorin*).

3350 *Wautier* André, À quand le vrai Messie: CahRenan 43,190 (1995) 43-59.

3351 *Wilken* Robert C., St. CYRIL of Alexandria; the mystery of Christ in the Bible: ProEccl 4 (1995) 454-478.

H4.3 *Eschatologia VT* -- **OT hope of future life**

3352 *a) Adler* Joshua J., The Bible and life after death; -- *b) Pinker* Aron, Sheol: JBQ 22 (1994) 85-90 / 23 (1995) 168-179.

3353 **Barr** James, The garden of Eden and the hope of immortality 1992 → 8,2216 ... 10,1884: ᴿ*CritRR 7 (1994) 80s (W. *Vogels*).

3354 **Barr** James, Éden et la quête de l'immortalité, ᵀ*Prignaud* J. : LiBi 107. P 1995, Cerf. 208 p. F 120. 2-204-05253-1 [< OTA 19, p.359].

3355 *Bons* Eberhard, *Elpís* comme l'espérance de la vie dans l'au-delà dans la littérature juive hellénistique [Sap, 1-2 Mcb]: → 155, ᶠRENAUD B., Ce Dieu qui viemt: LDIV 159 (1995) 345-370.

3356 **Cohn** Norman, Cosmos, chaos and the world to come; the ancient roots of apocalyptic faith [.. Zoroaster]. NHv 1993, Yale Umiv. x-271 p. $ 30. -- ᴿCBQ 57 (1995) 122s (P.L. *Redditt*).

3357 ᴱ**Cohn-Sherbok** Dan, *Lewis* Christopher, Beyond death: theological and philosophical reflections on life after death. L 1995, Macmillan. 219 p. £ 15. 0-333-63074-2. -- ᴿE(xp)T 107 (1995s) 158 (E. C. *Schofield*).

3358 *Diamond* Eliezer, Wrestling the angel of death; form and meaning in rabbinic tales of death and dying: JSJ(ud) 26 (1995) 76-92.

3359 **Kolarcik** Michael, The ambiguity of death in the Book of Wisdom 1-6: a study of literary structure and interpretation [D]1991 → 7,3090 ...10,3319: [R]BZ 39 (1995) 288-290 (W. *Schenk*); RelStR 21 (1995) 323 (J.L. *Crenshaw*).

3359* *Kyriakou* Poulheria, Katabasis and the underworld in the Argonautica of APOLLONIUS Rhodius: Philologus 134 (1995) 256-264.

3360 **Leftow** Brian, ANSELM on the necessity of the Incarnation: RelSt 31 (1995) 167-185.

3361 *Oosthuizen* R. de W., Future expectation as continuation of life *Coram Deo* in the Old Testament through generation continuity: OTEs 8 (1995) 31-47.

3362 **Puech** Émile, La croyance des esséniens en la vie future: immortalité. résurrection. vie éternelle ?: ÉtBN 21s, 1993 → 8,7427c ... 10,7383: [R]Biblica 76 (1995) 439-442 (P. *Sacchi*); JBL 114 (1995) 320-2 (J.C. *VanderKam*); RB 102 (1995) 107-116 (P. *Grelot*); RevSR 68 (1994) 350-2 (F. *Blanchetière*); RQ 16 (1993-5) 299-305 (P. *Grelot*); SBF*LA 45 (1995) 644s (M. *Pazzini*); ScrT(Pamp) 27 (1995) 1007-9 (S. *Ausín*); Sefarad 55 (1995) 404-6 (N. *Fernández Marcos*).

3363 **Schaper** Joachim, Eschatology in the Greek Psalter: WUNT 2/76. Tü 1995, Siebeck. xii-212 p. DM 78. 3-16-146434-6 [< OTA 19, p.348, L. *Greenspoon*].

3364 *Smelik* Willem F., On mystical transformation of the righteous into light in Judaism: JSJ(ud) 26 (1995) 122-144.

H4.5 *Theologia totius VT* -- **General Old Testament theology**

3365 *a) Albertz* Rainer, Religionsgeschichte Israels statt Theologie des ATs ? Plädoyer für eine forschungsgeschichtliche Umorientierung; -- *b) Müller* Hans-Peter, Fundamentalfragen jenseits der Alternative von Theologie und Religionsgeschichte: JbBT 10 (1995) 3-24 . 177-189 [*Barton* J., *Rendtorff* R., *Kalimi* I, 25-35-45-68] / 93-111 [69-78, *Crüsemann* F.; 79-82, *Lemche* M., 129-156, *Wacker* Marie-Theres; 189-206, *Sundermeier* T.; 207-230, *Lohfink* N.].

3365* *Ben Zvi* Ehud, A sense of proportion; an aspect of the theology of the Chronicler: S(cand)JOT 9 (1995) 37-51.

3366 **Brueggemann** W., OT theology 1992 → 10,7388: [R]OTEs 8 (1995) 460-4 (J.J. *Burden*).

3367 *Cazelles* Henri, Fondations de le recherche en théologie biblique: RSR 83 (1995) 357-371: Eng. 350.

3368 **Cerbelaud** Dominique, Écouter Israël! une théologie chrétienne en dialogue: Théologies. P 1995, Cerf. 188 p. 2-204-05087-3.

3369 *Clements* R.E., Wisdom and Old Testament theology; → 55, [F]EMERTON J., Wisdom 1995, 269-286.

3370 *Collins* C.J., From literary analysis to theological exposition; the book of Jonah: *JTrTL 7 (1995) 28-44 [< OTA 18,p.578].

3371 **Deissler** Alfons, Die Grundbotschaft des Alten Testaments, ein theologischer Durchblick[2rev] [[1]1972]. FrB 1995, Herder. 205 p. 3-451-23618-4.

3372 [E]**Dohmen** Christoph, *Söding* Thomas, Eine Bibel -- zwei Testamente; Positionen biblischer Theologie: Uni-Tb 1893. Pd 1995, Schöningh. 318 p. 3-8252-1893-7.

3373 **Gowan** Donald E., Theology in Exodus; a biblical theology in the form of a commentary. LVL 1994, W-Knox. xviii-297 p. $ 28 0-664-22057-6. -- [R]*TBR 8,1 (1995s) 14 (R. *Coggins*).

3374 **Green** Arthur, Seek my face, speak my name; a contemporary Jewish theology 1992 → 9,7560.

3375 **Gunneweg** Antonius H.J., Biblische Theologie des ATs 1993 → 9,7560*; 10,7393: [R]Bijdragen 56 (1995) 75 (P.C. *Beentjes*).

3376 *Holman* Jan, Het oude testament: te vatten in een 'theologie'; WESTERMANNs 'Hoofdlijnen' [1978 ²1985, [T]1981] en het bed van Procustes: TTh 35 (1995) 217-235; Eng. 235: GREIMAS approach.

3377 **Junco** Carlos, La crítica profética ante el templo; teología veterotestamentaria: diss. Pont. Univ. Mexicana. México 1994. 412 p. -- : [R]Phase 35 (1995) 435s (J. *Latorre*).

3378 *a) Kalimi* Isaac, Religionsgeschichte Israels oder Theologie des Alten Testaments ? Das jüdische Interesse an der biblischen Theologie, [T]*Beel* Rainer; -- *b) Rendtorff* Rolf, Die Hermeneutik einer kanonischen Theologie des Alten Testaments; Prolegomena; -- *c) Wacker* Marie-Theres, 'Religionsgeschichte Israels' oder 'Theologie des Alten Testaments' --(k)eine Alternative ? Anmerkungen aus feministisch-exegetischer Sicht; -- *d) Hardmeier* Christoph, Systematische Elemente der Theo-logie in der Hebräischen Bibel; das Loben Gottes -- ein Kristallisationsmoment biblischer Theo-logie: JBTh 10 (1995) 45-68 / 35-44 / 129-155 / 111-127.

3379 **Kaiser** O., Theologie des ATs 1, 1993 → 9,7019; 10,7395: [R]*CritRR 7 (1994) 127s (R.E. *Clements*).

3380 **Kaufman** Gordon D., In face of mystery; a constructive theology 1993 → 10,7396: [R]JRel 75 (1995) 135-7 (J.A. *Colombo*).

3381 **Knierim** Rolf P., The task of Old Testament theology; substance, method, and cases [< HBT 1984 < SBL 183, with 3 responses and rejoinder]. GR 1995, Eerdmans. xvi-603 p. $ 40. 0-8028-0715-1 [OTA 19, p.361]. -- [R]*TBR 8,3 (1995s) 18 (Katrina *Larkin*: mostly his new or revised essays).

3382 *a) Lemche* Niels P., Warum die Theologie des Alten Testament einen Irrweg darstellt; - -- *b) Thompson* Thomas L., Das Alte Testament als theologische Disziplin; -- *c) Barton* John, Alttestamentliche Theologie nach ALBERTZ ? [p.3-24; auch *Crüsemann* F. 69-77, *Müller* H.-P. 93-110 → M6], [T]*Hüllstrung* Wolfgang, auch *b*; -- *d) Lohfink* Norbert, Fächerpoker und Theologie: JBTh 10 (1995) 79-92 / 157-173 / 25-34 / 207-230.

3383 **Lohfink** Norbert, Studien zur biblischen Theologie: SBAufs 16, 1993 → 9,212: [R]ZkT 117 (1995) 99s (J.M. *Oesch*).

3384 **Martens** Elmer A., God's design; a focus on OT theology²ʳᵉᵛ [of 1981 Plot and purpose in the OT]. GR/Leicester 1994, Baker/Apollos. 320 p. $ 7. 0-8010-6316-7 / UK 0-85111-436-9. -- [R]*TBR 8,2 (1995s) 9 (Katrina *Larkin:* conservative but lucid and practical).

3385 **Motte** Jochen, Biblische Theologie nach Walther ZIMMERLI ... Perspektive zum NT: EurHS 23/521. Fra 1995, Lang. xv-211 p. DM 69 pa.-- [R]E(rbe)uA 71(1995)427 (B.*Schwank*).

3386 *Müller* Hans-Peter, Mythos als Elementarform religiöser Rede im Alten Orient und im Alten Testament; zur Theorie der biblischen Theologie: NZSTh 37 (1995) 1-19; Eng, 19 [beyond BULTMANN, 'pleads for a lucid scepticism' with 'a limited trust in human reason' and 'conviction of the legitimacy of religious speech'].

3387 **Neusner** Jacob, The formation of the theology of Judaism, an anthology II: SFSHJ 44. At 1992, Scholars. 148 p, 1-55540-699-8. -- [R]JSSt 39 (1994) 327s (J. *Maier*).

3388 [E]**Ollenburger** B., *al.* The flowering of OT theology (anthology) 1930-1990: 1992 → 8,363: [R]JETS 38 (1995) 260s (D.J. *Evearitt*).

3389 **Preuss** Horst D., Theologie des ATs 1991s → 7,7388 ... 10,7397: ᴿ*Carthaginensia 11 (1995) 194s (R. *Sanz Valdivieso*); ZkT 117 (1995) 98s (J.M. *Oesch*).

3390 **Preuss** Horst D., Old Testament Theology I, ᵀ*Perdue* L.: OTL. E/LVL 1995, Clark/W-Knox. xii-372 p. $ 34. 0-664-21844-X [OTA 19,p.362].

3391 *Prinsloo* G.T.M., Ou Testament teologie en/of 'Religionsgeschichte'?: SkrifK 15 (1994) 377-390 [< OTA 18 (1995) p. 364].

3392 *Pury* Albert de, *Knauf* Ernst A., La théologie de l'AT: kérygmatique ou descriptive?: ÉTRel 70 (1995) 323-334.

3393 *Sæbø* Magne, Den gammeltestamentlige teologi i nyere undersøkelser og fremstillinger: TT(og)K 66 (1995) 57-76.

3394 **Schreiner** Josef, Theologie des ATs: NEchter Egb 1. Wü 1995, Echter. 349 p. DM 44. 3-429-01669-X [TR 91,534]. ᴿEstTrin 29 (1995) 494s (X. *Pikaza*).

3395 **Smith** Ralph L., Old Testament theology; its history, method and message 1993 → 10,7570: ᴿA(ndr)USS 33 (1995) 150 (G. *Wheeler*); BoL (1995) 120 (I. *Provan*); ConcordJ 11 (1995) 115s (D.L. *Adams*); SWJT 37,2 (1995) 47s (R. *Johnson*).

3396 **Stuhlmacher** Peter, How to do biblical theology. Allison Park PA 1995, Pickwick. xli-95 p. $ 15. -- ᴿExAud 11 (1995) 161-3 (S. *McKnight*).

3397 *Wittenberg* G. H., Johann Philipp GABLER and the consequences; in search of a new paradigm for Old Testament theology: OTEs 8 (1995) 103-128.

H51   *Deus* -- **God** [as Father → H1.4]

3399 *Bauckham* Richard, God in the book of Revelation: PI(r)BA 18 (1995) 40-53 (-77, *al.*).

3400 *Bostock* Gerald, Many churches -- one God ?: E(xp)T 107 (1995s) 100-4.

3401 **Bouyer** L., Sophia ou le monde en Dieu. P 1994, Cerf. 206 p. ᴿOCP 61 (1995) 323-5 (E.G. *Farrugia*) [< RHE 90 (1995) 305*].

3402 ᴱ**Byrne** James M., The Christian understanding of God today [17 papers of the 1992 colloquium, Dublin Trinity College 400th → 9,434a]. Dublin 1993, Columba, vi=174 p. £ 10.

3403 **Carman** John E., Majesty and meekness; a comparative study of contrast and harmony in the concept of God. GR 1994, Eerdmans. 453 p. -- #WW 15 (1995) 504 -506 (P.V. *Martinson:* superbly enables Christians to think through their faith in relation to Hindu and other commitments).

3404 **Cooke** Bernard J., God's beloved; Jesus' experience of the transcendent 1992 → 8,4262 ... 10,3935: ᴿ*CritRR 7 (1994) 168-170 (Marianne *Sawicki*).

3405 **Garaudy** Roger, ¿Tenemos necesidad de Dios? M 1994, PPC. 199 p. -- ᴿSalmanticensis 42 (1995) 305s (D. *de Pablo Maroto*).

3406 **Gesché** Adolphe, Dieu pour penser [3. Dieu 1994 → 10.7406]; 4. Le cosmos. P 1994, Cerf. 206 p. F 95. 2-204-05041-5. -- ᴿEThL 70 (1994) 513s (J. *Étienne,3*); ETRel 70 (1995) 295 (A. *Gounelle*); ScrT(Pamp) 37 (1995) 707s (L.F. *Mateo-Seco*, 3).

3407 **Gesché** A., Dios para pensar, I. El mal -- el hombre: VeI 135. S 1995, Sígueme. 332 p. pt.2000. -- ᴿProyección 42 (1995) 240 (J.A. *Estrada*).

3408 *Godzieba* Anthony J., Ontotheology to excess; imagining God without being: TS 56 (1995) 3-21.

3409 **Grelot** Pierre, Dieu le Père de Jésus-Christ: JJC 60, 1994 → 10,7407: ᴿETRel 70 (1995) 396s (A. *Rakitoharintsifa*); I(nd)TS 32 (1995) 357s (L. *Legrand*); RHPR 75 (1995) 225 (É. *Trocmé*); RHR 212 (1995) 355-7 (A. *Mehat*); RivB 43 (1995) 291-3 (A. *Rolla*).

3410 *Haymes* Brian, Questions people ask [new regular ET feature], 1. Is there a God ? : ET 106 (1994s) 324-8.

3411 **Hill** William J., Search for the absent God; tradition and modernity 1992 → 8,253: ᴿTorJT 11 (1995) 131s (J. *Dool*)

3412 **Longman** Tremper, *Reid* Daniel G, God is a surprise: StOTBibT. Carlisle 1995, Paternoster. 224 p. £ 9. 0-85364-648-1. : ᴿTBR 8,1 (1995s) 10 (R. *Coggins*: mostly NT, despite series-title).

3413 **Marguerat** Daniel, Le Dieu des premiers chrétiens²: EssBib 16, 1993 → 6,7426 (1990)... 10,7409: ᴿE(spr)eV 105 (1995) 318-320 (L. *Walter*).

3414 **Newlands** George, God in Christian perspective. E 1994, Clark. 431 p. 0-567-09657-2. -- ᴿJThS 46 (1995) 418s (J. *Macquarrie*).

3415 *Pérez-Cotapos* E., El Dios de Jesús en las parábolas evangélicas: *RevCat 94 (1994) 12-19 [< RET 55 (1995) 271].

3416 **Placher** William C., Narratives of a vulnerable God; Christ, theology and Scripture 1994 → 10,7036: ᴿET 106,9 top choice (1994s) 257s (C.S. *Rodd*); (Reformed) Perspectives 10,3 (1995) 22s & 10 (D.M. *Griswold*); SewaneeT 38 (1994s) 297s (W.H. *Shepherd*).

3417 **Schall** James V., What is God like ? 1992 → 9,7583: ᴿET 106 (1994s) 30s (P. *Vardy*: from a broad spectrum of experience; p.75, 'Christianity's misfortune is that it substitutes fear for laughter' and joy).

3418 **Schlosser** Jacques, El Dios de Jesús; estudio exegético [1987 → 3,6592], ᵀ; BEB 82. S ... Sígueme. 286 p. -- ᴿ*Carthaginensia 11 (1995) 438s (R. *Sanz Valdivieso*); EstTrin 29 (1995) 122 (X. *Pikaza*).

3419 **Scott** James M., Adoption as sons of God ᴰ1992 → 8,6092: ᴿEvQ 67 (1995) 171-4 (J. *Proctor*).

3420 *Sicre* José L., L'actualité de l'idolâtrie: LV.F 48 (1993) 277-291: Eng. 291.

3421 *Splett* Jörg, Das Ärgernis der Menschlichkeit Gottes: FrSZ 42 (1995) 49-68.

3422 **Staniloae** Dumitru, The experience of God [Dogmatic Theology 1 (of 6)], ᵀ*Ioanita* Ioan, *Barringer* Robert. Brookline MA 1994, Holy Cross Orthodox. xxvii-280 p. $20. -- ᴿStVlad 39 (1995s) 425-7 (A.L. *Don*).

3423 **Swinburne** Richard, The Christian God. Ox 1994, Clarendon. 261 p. £ 14. 0-19-823512-7. -- ᴿET 106 (1994s) 381 (D.A. *Pailin*).

3424 **Taliaferro** Charles, Consciousness and the mind of God [our view of people is linked with our view of God]. C 1994, Univ. 349 p. £ 37.50. 0-521-46173-1. -- ᴿET 106 (1994s) 218 (I. *Markham*).

3425 *Turner* G., Visions of God [only in Jesus; ecstatic visions inappropriate]: NBL 75 (1994) 554-561 [NTAb 39, p.455].

3426 **Vermes** Geza, The religion of Jesus the Jew 1993 → 9,4284; 10,4102: ᴿJSJ 26 (1995) 229-231 (G.S. *Oegema*).

3427 **Wright** N.T., Christian origins and the question of God 1. (of 5) The NT and the people of God 1992 → 8,4209 .. 10,3883: ᴿJThS 46 (1995) 242-5 (J.D.G. *Dunn*).

3428 **Zeindler** Matthias, Gott und das Schöne; Studien zur Theologie der Schönheit: ForSysÖk 68. Gö 1993, VR. 452 p. DM 68. 3-525-56275-6. -- ᴿETRel 70 (1995) 300s (J. *Cottin*).

3429 **Zellner** L., Gottestherapie; Befreiung von dunklen Gottesbildern. Mü 1995, Kösel. 224 p. DM 32. 3-466-36421-3 [NTAb 40, p.138].

H5.2 Christologia ipsius NT

3430 *Anderson* Paul N., The cognitive origins of John's unitive and disunitive Christology: H(orizons)BT 17 (1995) 1-24.

3431 **Beilner** Wolfgang, Neutestamentliche Christologie als Korrektiv: Vermittlung 30. Salzburg 1995. 167 p.

3432 **Brown** Raymond E., An introduction to NT Christology 1994 → 10,7410 (Paulist; also L, Chapman): ᴿA(ngl)ThR 77 (1995) 292-4 (A. *Marmorstein*): BThB 25 (1995) 50 (T. *Callan*); *CritRR 8 (1995) 181-3 (L.W. *Hurtado*); ET 106 (1994s) 184 (E. *Franklin*: 'a shortish work' by a distinguished and influential scholar; courteous, balanced, useful 'for church rather than ultimate questions'); Horizons 22 (1995) 291 (Jane *Kopas*): NewThR 8,2 (1995) 96s (D.H, *Harrington*); ScrT(Pamp) 37 (1995) 667 (J.M. *Casciaro*); StPat(av) 42 (1995) 591s (G. *Segalla*); Studies 84 (1995) 88-90 (R. *Moloney*, also on MᴄDᴇʀᴍᴏᴛᴛ B.); TS 56 (1995) 312 (P.J. *Langsfeld*).

3433 **Brown** Raymond E., Introduzione alla Cristologia del Nuovo Testamento: BtB 19. Brescia 1995, Queriniana. 224 p. Lᵐ 35. 88-399-2019-6.

3434 **Casey** M., From Jewish prophet to Gentile God; the origin and development of NT Christology 1991 → 7,3645.7410 ... 9,7589: ᴿJJS 45 (1994) 137-140 (J. G, *Campbell*).

3435 **Coll** Niall, Some Anglican interpretations of Christ's pre-existence; a study of L.S.Tʜᴏʀɴᴛᴏɴ, E.L.Mᴀsᴄᴀʟʟ, J.A.T. Rᴏʙɪɴsᴏɴ, and J. Mᴀᴄǫᴜᴀʀʀɪᴇ: diss. Pont. Univ. Gregoriana, ᴰ*O'Collins* G. Rome 1995. 309 p.; extr. N° 4159, 260 p. : -- RTLv 27.p.562.

3436 **Doig** Kenneth F., NT Christology. Lewiston 1992, Mellen. 464 p. $ 60. 0-7334-9920-2. -- ᴿW(is)L(u)Q 91 (1994) 217-9 (J.F. *Brug*) [NTAb 39, p.92].

3437 **Dupont** Jacques, Jésus aux origines de la christologie²ʳᵉᵛ [¹1975]: ʙᴇᴛʟ 40, 1989 → Laur 36 (1995) 216-8 (A. *Dalbesio*).

3438 *Fitzmyer* Joseph A., The Palestinian background of 'Son of God' as a title for Jesus; → 79, ᶠHᴀʀᴛᴍᴀɴ L., Texts & Contexts 1995, 567-577.

3439 **Fredriksen** Paula, De Jésus aux Christs ... dans le NT 1992 → 9,4319: ᴿMélSR 52 (1995) 335s (J.C. *Matthys*).

3440 **Guillet** Jacques, Jésus dans la foi des premiers disciples. P 1995, D-Brouwer. 257 p. 2-220-03689-8.

3441 *Harrington* Daniel J., Jesus, the wisdom of God: Church 11,2 (ɴʏ 1995) 8-14.

3442 **Harris** Murray J., Jesus as God: the NT use of *theos* in reference to Jesus 1992 → 9,7592; 10,7414*: ᴿ*CritRR 7 (1994) 203-5 (L.W. *Hurtado*); EvQ 66 (1994) 263s (B.J. *Dodd*).

3443 **Kuschel** Karl-Josef, Born before all time ? The dispute over Christ's origin [ᴰ1990 → 7,7473] ᵀ1992 → 9,7595; 10,7417: ᴿ*CritRR 7 (1994) 213-5 (A. J. *Hultgren*).

3444 **Nobile** Marco, Premesse anticotestamentarie e giudaiche di cristologia: Spicilegium 31, 1993 → 9,7596: ᴿCBQ 57 (1995) 569 (C. *Bernas*); CDios 208 (1995) 277s (J. *Gutiérrez*); RivB 43 (1995) 277s (G. *Segalla*).

3445 *Panimolle* Salvatore A., La cristologia di Luca 1-2: → 119, ᶠMᴀʀᴀ M. Grazia = Aug(ustinianum)R 35 (1995) 61-73.

3446 **Rhodes** Ron, Christ before the manger; the life and times of the preincarnate Christ 1992 → 10,7419: ᴿA(ndr)USS 33 (1995) 318s (M.F. *Hanna*); ᴊᴇᴛs 37 (1994) 442-6 (J.K. *La Shell*, also on Eʀɪᴄᴋsᴏɴ, Sᴄᴀᴇʀ, Eᴠᴀɴs).

3447 **Schnackenburg** Rudolf, Jesus in the Gospels; a biblical Christology [1993 → 9,7600], ᵀ*Dean* O.C. Lᴠʟ 1995, W-Knox. xv-383 p. $ 35. 0-664-22059-2 [*TBR 9/1,26, D.

Horrell; ThD 43.288].

3448 *Schüssler Fiorenza* Elisabeth, Jesus -- messenger of divine wisdom: StTh 49 (Oslo 1995) 231-252.

3449 **Segalla** Giuseppe. A Cristologia do Novo Testamento, um ensaio, ᵀ*Prado* José L.G. do. São Paulo 1992, Loyola. 152 p. -- ᴿ*VoxScr 4 (1994) 226-8 (J. *Eber*).

3450 **Sicari** Antonio, Viaggio nel Vangelo; Gesù di Nazareth, il 'Dio con noi': Già e non ancora 288. Mi 1995, Jaca. 145 p.

3451 **Zeller** George W., *Showers* Renald [sic, also Index] E., The eternal sonship of Christ. Neptune NJ 1993, Loizeaux. 127 p. $ 9. -- ᴿBS 152 (1995) 106s (R.P. *Lightner*).

H5.3　*Christologia praemoderna* -- patristic through Reformation

3452 *Abramowski* Luise, Über die Fragmente des THEODOR von Mopsuestia in Brit.Libr.add. 12.156 und das doppelt überlieferte christologische Fragment : OrChr 79 (1995) 1-8.

3453 **Adinolfi** Marco, Il Verbo uscito dal silenzio; temi di cristologia biblica → 8,104: 9,7636: ᴿRTL 26 (1995) 234s (J. *Ponthot*: 'termi').

3454 *Bartel* T.W., Why the philosophical problems of Chalcedonian Christology have not gone away: HeythJ 36 (1995) 153-172.

3455 **Böhm** T., Die Christologie des ARIUS 1991 → 7,7421*; 8,7475; ᴿCrSt 16 (1995) 632-5 (A.M. *Ritter*).

3456 *Bok* Nico den, Totum suscepit; een christologische peiling aan de hand van AUGUSTINUS' visie op de voorbestemming van Christus en zijn menselijke willen: Bijdragen 56 (1995) 156-185; Eng. 185s.

3457 *Brock* Sebastian, ᴿ The Christology of the Church of the East, ᵀ*Muravyeva* A.B.: VDI 213 (1995) 39-52; Eng. 52s.

3458 **Carcione** F., Le eresie; Trinità e Incarnazione nella Chiesa antica. CinB 1992, Paoline. 229 p. Lᵐ 15. -- ᴿAsprenas 42 (1995) 121-3 (E. *Dovere*),

3459 **Cavadini** John C., The last Christology of the West; adoptionism 1993 → 10,7429: ᴿChH 64 (1995) 646s (J.F. *Kelly*); JRel 75 (1995) 117s (Willemien *Otten*); Speculum 70 (1995) 350-2 (J.M. *McCulloh*).

3460 *Dąbrowski* Wacław, ᴾ La christologie de saint Thomas d'AQUIN à la lumière de sa réponse sur la question concernant les raisons de l'Incarnation: STV(ars) 32,2(1994)237-264.

3461 *Daley* Brian E., Apollo as a Chalcedonian; a new fragment of a controversial work from early sixth-century Constantinople: Traditio 50 (1995) 31-54.

3462 *a) Dupuy* Bernard, La christologie de NESTORIUS; -- *b) Davids* Adelbert, *Eprem* mar, *Soro* Bawai, La théologie de l'Église d'Orient est-elle nestorienne ?: Ist(ina) 40 (1995) 56-64 / 65-72 . 73-82. 121-139.

3463 *Epalza* Mikel de, Influences islamiques dans la théologie chrétienne médiévale; l'adoptianisme espagnol (VIIIᵉ siècle), ᵀ*Zubiría* Jesús: Islamochristiana 18 (1992) 55-71. Eng. 71s.

3464 **Grillmeier** Alois, Christ in Christian tradition [2/1, 1987 → 3,7001 ...7,7435*] 2/2. L 1995, Mowbray. £ 45 0-264-67261-5. -- ᴿE(xp)T 107 (1995s) 186 (J. *McIntyre*);

3465 **Grillmeier** Aloys, L'Église de Constantinople au VIᵉ siècle; Le Christ 2/2, 1993 → 9,7613; 10,7440: ᴿETRel 70 (1995) 593s (J.-N. *Pérès*); SuppVSp 148 (1994) 136 (I.H. *Dalmais*).

3466 *Meunier* Bernard, En marge d'un nouveau classique de l'histoire des dogmes: AHC 26 (1994) 161-173 (II/1) . 364-375 (II/2).

3467 *Halleux* André de †. L'accord christologique de 433, un modèle de réconciliation ecclésiale ? : → 197, [F]TILLARD J., Communion 1995, 293-9.

3468 **Hattrup** Dieter, Ekstatik .. der christologischen Erkenntnistheorie Bonaventuras 1993 → 10,7443: [R]ActuBbg 31 (1994) 241s (J. *Boada*).

3469 **Hengel** Martin, [7] Studies in early Christology. E 1995, Clark. xix-402 p.; 2 fig. $ 55. 0-567-09705-6 [NTAb 40,p.544].

3470 **Henne** Philippe, La Christologie .. CLÉMENT R., HERMAS : Paradosis 33, 1992 → 9,7489; 10,7444: [R]*CritRR 7 (1994) 342-4 (Barbara E. *Bowe*).

3471 *Hiki* K., [J] The Christology of IGNATIUS of Antioch -- union with the prototypical Christ: KaKe 64 (Tokyo 1995) 61-84 [NTAb 40, p.122].

3472 **Kakkanatt** Antony, Christological catechesis of the liturgy; a study on the great feasts of our Lord in the Malankara church: Publ 14. R c.1995, Mar Thomas Yogam. xx-362 p.; bibliog. 341-362.

3473 *Krieg* Robert A., A fortieth-anniversary reappraisal of 'Chalcedon, end or beginning ?' [RAHNER's 1954 'breakthrough in contemporary Catholic Christology']: *PhT 9 (Milwaukee 1995) 77-116.

3474 **Lyman** J. Rebecca, Christology and cosmology .. ORIGEN ... 1993 → 9,7620; 10,7446: [R]JEH 46 (1995) 491-3 (G. *Gould*); TS 56 (1995) 190s (G.H. *Ettlinger*).

3475 **McGuckin** John A., St. CYRIL of Alexandria, the Christological controversy: VigChrS 23, 1994 → 10,7446*; *f* 225: [R]JThS 46 (1995) 729-733 (G. *Gould*); RÉByz 53 (1995) 378s (J. *Wolinski*); RS(to)LR 31 (1995) 526-531 (D. *Pazzini*).

3476 **Malingrey** Anne-Marie, Jean CHRYSOSTOME, Sur l'égalité du Père et du Fils, Contre les Anoméens VII-XII: SC 396, 1994 → 10,7447: [R]REA 97 (1995) 655s (A. *Tuilier*); RÉByz 53 (1995) 373s (J. *Wolinski*); RevSR 69 (1995) 105-7 (L. *Brottier*).

3477 *Maritz* P.J.,Logos articulation in GREGORY of Nazianzus:AcPatrByz 6 (1995) 88-108.

3478 *Mateo Seco* L.F., Adopcionismo hispánico y Concilio de Frankfurt (En la conmemoración de su XII centenario); AnVal 20 (1994) 99-120 [< RET 55 (1995) 112].

3479 **Mazzanti** Giorgio, San BASILIO Magno, Testi cristologici 1991 → 8,7301; [L][m] 20: [R]CivCatt 146 (1995,1) 306s (E. *Cattaneo*).

3480 *Need* Stephen W., Language, metaphor, and Chalcedon; a case of theological double vision : HThR 88 (1995) 237-255.

3481 **Pottier** Bernard, Dieu et le Christ selon GRÉGOIRE de Nysse [Contre Eunome]: Ouvertures 12. Namur 1994, Culture et Vérité Brepols). -- [R]RevSR 69 (1995) 529s (R. *Winling*); VigChr 49 (1995) 408-411 (A. *Meredith*).

3482 **Sesboüé** Bernard, *Meunier* Bernard, Dieu peut-il avoir un fils ? 1993 → 9,7628; 10,7455: [R]OCP 61 (1995) 642s (E.G. *Farrugia*).

3483 **Studer** Basil, Trinity and Incarnation; the faith of the early Church 1993 → 9,7631: [R]NewThR 8,3 (1995) 111s (Z. *Hayes*); TS 56 (1995) 160-2 (F.W. *Norris*).

3484 [TE]**Speer** Andreas, BONAVENTURA, Quaestiones disputatae de scientia Christi lat.-deutsch: PhBt 446, 1992 → 9,7630: [R]ThRv 91 (1995) 44 (B. *Wald*).

3485 **Zañartu** Sergio, Historia del dogma de la Encarnación, desde el siglo V al VII. Santiago 1995, Univ. Católica. -- [R]TyV 36 (1995) 458s (P. *Gutiérrez Domínguez*).

H5.4   *(Commentationes de)* **Christologia moderna**

3486 **Adinolfi** Marco, Il Verbo .. temi di cristologia biblica 1992 → 8,204; 9,7636: [R]EThL 71 (1995) 232s (J. *Verheyden*); PaVi 40,6 (1995)61s (S. *Migliasso*).

3487 *Akinade* Akintunde E., 'Who do you say that I am ?' -- an assessment of some Christological constructs in Africa : A(sia)JT 9 (1995) 181-200.

3488 *Arens* Edmund, Perspektiven und Problematik pluralistischer Christologie: MThZ 46 (1995) 329-343.

3489 *Bailey* K.E., Christology in a Middle Eastern biblical context: (NES)ThRev 16,1 (1995) 26-46 [NTAb 40, p.270].

3490 *Bamford* Christian, interview, Cosmos and incarnation; the tender strength of Celtic Christianity: Forefront 2,4 (1995) 8-11

3491 **Bessière** Gérard, Jésus, le Dieu inattendu. P 1993, Gallimard. 192 p. F 105. -- ᴿRICAO 10 (Abidjan 1995) 95s (J.-M. *Guillaume*)

3492 **Biff** Giacomo card., Approccio al Cristocentrismo; note storiche per un tema eterno. Mi 1994, Jaca. -- ᴿTer(esianum) 46 (1995) 253-7 (G. *Blandino;* 257-283, autodifesa rispettosa).

3493 *Brito* Emilio, Jésus; Christ universel; chronique de christologie: RTL 26 (1995) 326-342.

3494 *Bueno de la Fuente* Eloy,Una cristologia moderna;MALEBRANCHE: Burg 36(1995)307-31.

3495 *Callahan* James P., The convergence of narrative and Christology; Hans W. FREI on the uniqueness of Jesus Christ: JETS 38 (1995) 531-547.

3496 **Carrón** Julián, Jesús, el Mesías manifestado (Heb 3,19-26) 1993 → 10,6243* : Greg 76 (1995) 169-171 (J. *Galot*).

3497 ᴱ**Charlesworth** J.H., *Weaver* W.P., Earthing Christologies; from Jesus' parables to Jesus the parable: Faith and Scholarship colloquy [Florida Southern College 1988 = Nv 1989. Exodus]. Ph 1995, Trinity. xiv-111 p. 1-56338-119-2 [NTAb 40, p.364].

3498 **Coda** Piero, Dios entre los hombres; breve cristología [Dio tra gli uomini 1991; deutsch 1993 → 9,7648], ᵀ*Gordo Jiménez* Blas. M 1993, Ciudad Nueva. 190 p. 84-86987-52-0. -- ᴿActuBbg 31 (1994) 225 (J. *O'Callaghan*).

Crossan J.D., The historical Jesus .. peasant 1992 → 2117.

3499 **Dalferth** Ingolf U., Jenseits von Mythos und Logos; die christologishe Transformation der Theologie: QD 142, 1993 → 9,7650: ᴿThLZ 120 (1995) 67-70 (M. *Rössler*); TPQ 143 (1995) 295-7 (F. *Gruber*).

3500 **Dalferth** Ingolf U., Der auferweckte Gekreuzigte; zur Grammatik der Christologie. Tü 1994, Mohr. ix-346 p. DM 68 pa. 3-16-45296-3. -- ᴿJThS 46 (1995) 799-802 (G.M. *Newlands*).

3501 **Danz** Christian, Die philsophische Christologie im Spätwerk F.W.J. SCHILLINGs: Diss. ᴰ*Kern* U. Jena 1994. -- ThRv 91,98.

3502 **De Marchi** S., La cristologia in Italia (1930-1990). CasM 1994, Piemme. 392 p. Lᵐ 40. -- ᴿStPat(av) 42 (1995) 568-571 (E.R. *Tura*).

3503 **Dupuis** Jacques, Homme de Dieu, Dieu des hommes; introduction a la Christologie. P 1995, Cerf. 282 p -- ᴿEstTrin 29 (1995) 331s (N. *Silanes,* también sobre SESBOÜÉ-MEUNIER 1993).

3504 **Dupuis** Jacques, Who do you say I am ? Introduction to Christology 1994 → 10.7478: ᴿConcordJ 11 (1995) 452-4 (*Won Yong Ji*); EThL 71 (1995) 488s (E. *Brito*); LexTQ 30 (1995) 120s (Jane *McAvoy*: he covers the scholarly field, except BOFF & SOBRINO -- in a Maryknoll book! -- but without making perceptible an integral Christology of his own); LouvSt 20 (1995) 430s (P. De *Mey*); VSVD 36 (1995) 462s (T.A. *Krosnicki*).

3505 **Dupuis** Jacques, Introducción a la cristología. Estella 1994. VDivino. 284 p. -- ᴿ*Carthaginensia 11 (1995) 206s (J.J. *Tamayo Acosta*).

3506 **Erickson** Millard J., The Word became flesh 1991 → 8,7521: [R]RExp 92 (1995) 121 (Molly T. *Marshall*).

3507 **Espeja** Jesús, Hemos visto su gloria; introducción a la Cristología: Glosas 25. S 1994, San Esteban. 344 p. -- [R]*Carthaginensia 11 (1995) 207s (J.J. *Tamayo Acosta*); CiTom 121 (1994) 619-621 (L. *Lago Alba*).

3508 *Espeja* Jesus, Jesucristo, justicia y violencia de Dios: CiTom 121 (1994) 47-77.

3508* *Fischer* John, Wahrer Gott und wahrer Mensch; zur bleibenden Aktualität eines alten Bekenntnisses: NZSTh 37 (1995) 165-204; Eng-204, 'a revision of Christological doctrine'.

3509 *Florio* Mario, L'accesso dossologico a Gesù Cristo nella cristologia di L. BOUYER : StPat(av) 42 (1995) 713-754: Eng. 755.

3510 **Godzieba** Anthony A., Bernhard WELTE's fundamental theological approach to Christology: AmUSt 7/160. NY 1994, P.Lang. 0-8204-2218-9. -- [R]Horizons 22 (1995) 305s (T. F. *O'Meara*).

3511 **Goergen** D.J., Jesus, son of God, son of Mary: Theology of Jesus 4. ColMn 1995, Liturgical. viii-278 p. 0-8146-5520-3 [< NTAb 40,p.543].

3512 *González Faus* José Ignacio, Dogmática cristológica y lucha por la justicia: RLatAmT 12 (1995) 37-57.

3513 *a) González Faus* José Ignacio, Aportaciones, lagunas y tareas del modelo cristológico occidental: -- *b) Gispert-Sauch* Jorge, El Cristo asiático, -- *c) Porcile* Teresa, Cristología en femenino : SalTer 83 (1995) 163-171 / 173-185 / 187-204.

3514 *González Faus* José Ignacio, *Boada* Josep, Nuevos horizontes cristológicos: ActuBbg 31 (1994) 5-9-18

3515 *Gounelle* André, Recherches christologiques: FV 92,1 (1993) 19-48.

3516 *Gregersen* Niels H., Guds Visdom i person -- kristologi i forlængelse af Jesus-forskningens 'third quest': NTT 96 (1995) 203-222; Eng. 222.

3517 *Hamm* Dennis, In search of Jesus [MEIER J., CROSSAN J., BROWN R., all 1994]: Church 11,2 (NY 1995) 46-50.

3518 *Harrington* Daniel J., Jesus, the wisdom of God: : Church 11,2 (1995) 8-14.

3519 *Hart* T.A., Sinlessness and moral responsibility; a problem in Christology: S(cot)JTh 48 (1995) 37-54.

3520 **Hicks** John, The metaphor of God incarnate; Christology in a pluralistic age: SCM 1993 → 10,7485; also LVL 1994, W-Knox. 180 p. $ 17: [R]ThTo 52 (1995s) 138 . 140 (D.F. *Wells*).

3521 **Hopkins** Julie M., Towards a feminist Christology; Jesus of Nazareth, European women and the Christological crisis: --[R]*Missionalia 23 (1995) 251 (C. *Landman*).

3522 **Hünermann** Peter, Jesus Christus -- Gottes Wort in der Zeit; eine systematische Christologie 1994 → 10,7486: [R]MThZ 46 (1995) 386-8 (O. *Meuffels*); ThLZ 120 (1995) 706-8 (G. *Wenz*): ZkT 117 (1995) 85-87 (R. *Schwager*).

3523 **Iammarrone** Giovanni, Gesù di Nazaret, Messia del Regno e Figlio di Dio; lineamenti di Cristologia: Strumenti di Scienze Religiose. Padova 1995, Messaggero. 405 p. 88-250-0285-8.

3524 *Jamros* Daniel P., HEGEL on the Incarnation; unique or universal ? : TS 56 (1995) 276-300.

3525 **Kay** James F., Christus praesens, a reconsideration of Rudolf BULTMANN's Christology. GR 1994, Eerdmans. xii-187 p. $ 15. → : [R]ET 106 (1994s) 87s (R. *Morgan*); P(rinc)SB 16 (1995) 83s (R.H. *Fuller*); TS 56 (1995) 194s (M.L. *Cook*).

3526 *a) Klappert* Bertold, Israel -- Messias-Christus -- Kirche; Kriterien einer nichtantijüdischen Christologie [GODEL Erika]; -- *b) Wyschogrod* Michael, Inkarnation aus jüdischer Sicht: EvTh 55 (1995) 64-99 (-102) / 13-28.

3527 **Lee Hee-Kuk**, 'Jesus ist Sieger!' bei Christoph BLUMHARDT, Keim einer kosmischen Christologie: Diss. ^D*Lochmann* J. -- TR 91,92.

3528 *Leonardi* Leonardo, Gesù di Nazareth, il Dio-Uomo, nell'ottica di una pastorale ecumenica: Nicolaus 21 (1994) 137-156.

3529 **Lyons** Enda, Jesus, self-portrait by God 1994 → 10,7495: ^RGreg 76 (1995) 166 (J. *Galot*).

3530 **McDermott** Brian O., Word become flesh, dimensions of Christology: NewThSt 9, 1993 → 10,7496: ^RGreg 76 (1995) 606s (J. *Dupuis*: no Spirit-Christology or facing the challenge of world religions).

3531 **Maldamé** Jean-Michel, Le Christ et le cosmos; incidence de la cosmologie moderne sur la théologie 1993 > 10,7236: ^RRBPH 73 (1995) 227s (J. *Schamp*).

3532 ^FMARSHALL I.H.: Jesus .. NT Christology, ^E**Green** Joel B., *Turner* Max, 1994 → 10,77*: ^RTorJT 11 (1995) 240-2 (L.W. *Hurtado*)

3532* *a) Migliore* Daniel L., Christology in context; the doctrinal and contextual tasks of Christology today; -- *b) Erickson* Millard J., Evangelical Christology and soteriology today; -- *c) Thistlethwaite* Susan B., Christology and postmodernism; not everyone who says to me 'Lord, Lord': Interpretation 49 (1995) 242-254 / 255-266 / 267-280.

3533 **Miguez Bonino** J., Faces of Jesus 1984: ^R*JRadR 5,1 (1995) 3-11 (A.F. *Buzzard*, also on RUNIA K. 1984: no incarnate Son in the Synoptics) [NTAb 40, p.271].

3534 **Moingt** Joseph, L'homme qui venait de Dieu: CogF 170, 1993 → 9,7681; 10,3989; ^RBLE 96 (1995) 223-6 (J.-M. *Maldamé*); Christus 42 (1995) 84-87 (X. de *Chalendar*); Greg 76 (1995) 395s (J. *Galot*: déconstruction; pas une personne divine, mais un homme qui accomplit le dessin de Dieu et devient ainsi Fils de Dieu); JThS 46 (1995) 419-421 (P. *Widdicombe*): LV(itF) 50 (1995) 113-5 (J.B.); RTPh 127 (1995) 184s (B. *Hort*); ScrT(Pamp) 37 (1995) 709-711 (L.F. *Mateo-Seco*).

3535 -- *Barthe* Claude, La foi du P. Joseph Moingt mise en cause dans la revue Gregorianum [*Galot* J. '... attaque publique de jésuite à jésuite ... rarissime']: Cath 47 (P 1995) 89.

3536 **Moingt** J., El hombre que venía de Dios; Jesús en la historia del discurso cristiano [1993 → 9,7681], ^T. Bilbao 1995, D-Brouwer. 206 p., 328 p. -- ^REstTrin 29 (1995) 486s (X. *Pikaza*: 28 (1994) 451s sobre el original francés).

3537 -- *Segundo* Juan Luis, El hombre que venía de Dios [MOINGT J. 1993]: MCom(illas) 53 (1995) 43-79.

3538 **Moltmann** Jürgen, The way of Jesus Christ; Christology in messianic dimension [1989],^T*Kohl* Margaret 1991 → 7.7487 ... 10,7502: ^RA(ngl)ThR 77 (1995) 108s (J.E. *Skinner*); LuthQ 9 (1995) 89s (D. *Bielfeldt*).

3539 **Moltmann** Jürgen, Jésus le Messie de Dieu: CF 171, 1993 → ^RE(spr)eV 105 (1995) 145s (P. *Jay*); Greg 76 (1995) 168s (J. *Galot*); LV(itF) 50 (1995) 115 (P. *Mourlon Beernaert*),

3540 **Moltmann** Jürgen, El camino de Jesucristo: Verdad e Imagen 129, 1993 → 10,7503: ^RRET 55 (1995) 260s (E. *Tourón*).

3541 **Müller** Gerhard L.,Christologie im Brennpunkt;ein Lagebericht: ThRv 91 (1995) 363-79.

3542 **Murphy** Francesca Aran, Christ the form of beauty; a study in theology and literature. E 1995, Clark. 236 p. £ 20. 0-567-09708-0. -- ^RE(xp)T 107 (1995s) 87s (B.L. *Horne*: remarkable, important, difficult).

3543 *Nürnberger* K., The Son can do nothing by himself; identification and authority in modern interpretations of the doctrine of a divine and a human nature in the person of Christ: JTSA 87 (1994) 11-28 [NTAb 39, p.261].

3544 **O'Carroll** Michael, Verbum caro: an encyclopedia on Jesus, the Christ 1992 → 8,7549: [R]Worship 65 (1994) 458-460 (W.J. *Cahoy*).

3545 **O'Collins** Gerald, Christology; a biblical, historical, and systematic study of Jesus Christ. Ox 1995, UP. xi-333 p. $ 59; pa. $ 15. 0-19-87550-5; -2-3 [NTAb 40, p.369]. - - [R]CCen 112 (1995) 1138 (C.A. *Wilson*); E(xp)T 107 (1995s) 88 (J. *McIntyre*: his climax); Greg 76 (1995) 787 (*ipse*); *TBR 8,1 (1995s) 30 (L. *Houlden*).

3546 *O'Collins* Gerald, The Incarnation under fire [HICK J.]: Greg 76 (1995) 263-279; fr.28.

3547 [E]**Ohlig** Karl-Heinz, Cristologia [1989 → 5,7518*] I. [TE]*Zani* Antonio; II, *Ottolini* Enzo V. Brescia 1993, Queriniana. 275 p., 318 p. L[m] 32 + 35. -- [R]CivCatt 146 (1995,1) 525 (G. *Blandino*).

3548 **Olivera Delgadillo** Juan de Dios, Metodología cristo-lógica y reflexión personal en América Latina. Bogotá 1994, CELAM. 457 p. -- [R]Lum(Vt) 44 (1995) 171-3 (U. *Gil Ortega*).

3549 *Palma* Robert J., [Michael] POLANYI and Christological dualisms: S(cot)JTh 48 (1995) 211-224.

3550 *Parker* David, Jesus Christ; model man of faith, or saving Son of God ? : EvQ 67 (1995) 245-264.

3551 [E]**Pompei** Alfonso, *Todisco* Orlando, [Seraphicum] Cristologia 2: Il Cristo dei filosofi. R 1995, Herder. 357 p. -- [R]Ang 72 (1995) 609s (A. *Lobato*: pref. de TILLIETTE X.)

3552 **Portier** William L., Tradition and incarnation; foundations of Christian theology 1994 → 10,7512: [R]Horizons 22 (1995) 104-9 (J.L. *Buckley*) & 109-111 (Mary Anne *Mayeski*) & 112s (B. *Cooke*) & 113-5 (Sandra Y. *Mize*) & 116-120 (A.J. *Godzieba*); Portier response 120-8 + 179, missing last line.

3553 *Renwart* Léon, Jésus, le Christ de Dieu; chronique de christologie: NRT 117 (1995) 890-900.

3554 **Rieger** Michael, Inkarnation; christliches Heilsverständnis im Kontext französischsprachiger Theologie der Menschwerdung [Diss. Mü]: EurHS 23/496. 329 p. DM 89 [ThRv 91,416, K.H. *Neufeld*].

3555 *Ritter* Adolf M., Christologie im Widerstreit: ThR 60 (1995) 254-272.

3556 *Rzepkowski* Horst, Kreuz und Lotos; Bericht über die christologische Trilogie CHOAN-SENG SONGs : VSVD 36 (1995) 199-208.

3557 **Schüssler Fiorenza** Elisabeth, Jesus, Miriam's child, Sophia's prophet; critical issues in feminist Christology. NY 1994, Continuum. x-262 p. $ 23. 0-8264-0671-8. -- [R]America 172,17 (1995) 26s (Pheme *Perkins*); ET 106 (1994s) 380s (Esther D, *Reed*: fresh and readable and daringly original; a self-styled troublemaker to be taken seriously; but how far can imagination and improvisation take the place of historical reference ?); RelStR 21 (1995) 331 (Claire L. *Sahlin*: award-winning); SewaneeT 38 (1994s) 374s . 378 (Fredrica H. *Thompson*).

3558 **Sesboüé** Bernard, Pédagogie du Christ; éléments de christologie fondmentale [inédits et réimprimés]: Théologies. P 1994, Cerf. 237 p. F 120 pa. 2-204-05015-6. -- [R]E(spr)eV 105 (1995) 13s (E. *Cothenet*); SBF*LA 45 (1995) 620s (L.D *Chrupcala*); ScEs 47 (1995) 340s (G. *Langevin*); ZkT 117 (1995) 352s (K.H. *Neufeld*).

3559 *Soro* Bawai, La formule christologique de Vienne [1971] dans la perspective assyrienne: Ist(ina) 40 (1995) 7-24 (163-175 . 121-139).

3560 **Stock** Alex, Poetische Dogmatik; Christologie. Pd 1995, Schöningh. I. Namen, 205 p.; II. Schrift und Gestalt, 292 p. [III.-IV. erwartet] 3-506-78831-0.

3561 **Sturch** Richard, The Word and the Christ; an essay in analytic Christology 1991 → 7,7507 ... 9,7708: [R]A(ngl)ThR 77 (1995) 101s (C.C. *Hefling*).

3562 **Sunderman** Marilyn, Humanization in the Christology of Juan Luis SEGUNDO; diss. Fordham, [D]*Hennelly* A. Bronx 1994. -- RStR 22,p.271.

3563 **Thangarajah** M. Thomas, The crucified guru; an experiment in cross-cultural Christology. Nv 1994, Abingdon. 165 p. -- [R]Theol 98 (L 1995) 480 (R.S. *Sugirtharajah*).

3564 **Tilliette** Xavier, La cristologia idealista [1986], [T]: GdT 221, 1991 → 10,7521: [R]CivCatt 146 (1995,1) 406-8 (G. *Lorizio*).

3565 **Tilliette** Xavier, Le Christ des philosophes; du Maître de sagesse au divin Témoin [cours Paris/Rome polycopié c.1975 > Filosofi davanti a Cristo [T]*Sansonetti* G.] Namur 1993, Culture et Vérité (diffusion Brepols). 491 p. 2-87299-037-2. -- [R]EThL 71 (1995) 485-7 (E. *Brito*).

3566 *Udías Vallino* Agustín, El Cristo cósmico de TEILHARD DE CHARDIN: RF 231 (1995) 409-420.

3567 *Wallis* Ian G., Jesus the believer, a fresh approach: *ModBlv 36,1 (1995) 10-17.

3568 **Weaver** Walter P., *Charlesworth* James H., Earthing Christologies; from Jesus' parables to Jesus the parable [< Perspectives in Christology 1989]: Faith&Sch. Ph 1995, Trinity. xiv-111 p. $ 13. 1-56338-119-2 [RStR 22,245, F.W. *Burnett*].

3569 [E]**Zucal** Silvano, La figura di Cristo nella filosofia contemporanea, CinB 1993, Paoline. 598 p. L[m] 35. -- [R]ZkT 117 (1995) 480 (W. *Kern*: mit TILLIETTE X. und HENRICI P. gegen FABRO C.).

H5.5   *Spiritus Sanctus; pneumatologia* -- **The Holy Spirit**

3570 **Azzali Bernardelli** Giovanna, BASILIO di Cesarea, Lo Spirito Santo; TPatr 106, 1993 → 9,15848: [R]CivCatt 146 (1995,3) 543-5 (G. *Cremascoli*).

3571 **Brito** Emilio, La pneumatologie de SCHLEIERMACHER: BEThL 113, 1994 → 10,14696: [R]EThL 71 (1995) 185-190 (É. *Gaziaux*).

3572 **Chalassery** Joseph, The Holy Spirit and Christian initiation in the East Syrian tradition: *a)* diss. Pont.Inst.Or., [D]*Youssif* P. Rome 1995. Extr. li-250 p. -- RTLv 27.p.563. -- *b)* R 1995, Mar Thomas. 250 p. [ThRv 92,78].

3573 **Comblin** Joseph, L'Esprit Saint; économie, société, théologie: Libération. P 1994, Cerf. 206 p.- [R]L(aval)TP 51 (1995) 689 (G. *Chénard*).

3574 **Dalbesio** Anselmo, Lo Spirito Santo, nel Nuovo Testamento, nella Chiesa, nella vita del cristiano: Universo Teologia 26. T 1994, S. Paolo. 317 p.; bibliog. 299-306. 88-215-2794-8.

3575 **Doutreleau** Louis, DIDYME l'Aveugle, Traité du Saint-Esprit: SC 386, 1992 → 8,7580; 9,7725: [R]AnCl 64 (1995) 345 (H. *Savon*).

3576 *Favaro* Gaetano, Lo Spirito Santo, il cosmo e la storia nelle teologie 'inter-religiose' di CHUNG HYUNG KYUNG, Jürgen MOLTMANN e Leonardo BOFF: Nicolaus 22 (1995) 133-161.

3577 **Fee** Gordon D., God's empowering Presence: Hendrickson 1994 → 10,7529: also Paternoster: [R]ET 106 (1994s) 279 (J.A, *Ziesler*; from 795 p. of dense exegesis of every relevant Pauline passage, draws encyclopedia of NT teaching on the Spirit -- aiming rather to speak ambiguously both to the community of scholars and to the Church).

3578 *Flipo* Claude, Discerner l'action de l'Esprit: Spiritus 36 ('Esprit Saint, protagoniste de la mission' 1995) 440-451.

3579 *Galot* Jean, L'Esprit Saint et la féminité: Greg 76 (1995) 5-29, Eng. 29.

3580 *García* Lorenzo, Los símbolos del Espíritu Santo en los sermones de S. ANTONIO de Padua: VyV 53,2 (octavo centenario,1995) 285-330

3581 *Gosling* F.A., An unresolved problem of Old Testament theology ['no individualization of spirit', KOEHLER L. 1953]: ET 106 (1994s) 234-7.

3582 *Hanson* P.D., Scripture, community and spirit; biblical theology's contribution to a contextualized Christian theology: *JPent 6 (1995) 3-12 [NTAb 40, p.5].

3583 **Hilberath** Bernt J., Pneumatologie: LeitfadenTh 23. Dü 1994, Patmos. 224 p. DM 29,80. 3-491-77953-7 -- ᴿThGL 85 (1995) 137 (W. *Beinert*).

3584 **Lison** Jacques, L'Esprit répandu; la pneumatologie de Grégoire PALAMAS [† 1359]: Patrimoines Orth. 1994 → 10.7532; F 198; 2-204-04936-0: ᴿEThL 7(1995) 489s (E. *Brito*).

3585 *Marshall* Bruce D., Action and person; do PALAMAS and AQUINAS agree about the Spirit ? : StVlad 39 (1995s) 379-408.

3586 **Martínez Peque** Moisés, Lo Spirito Santo e il matrimonio nell'insegnamento della Chiesa [español], ᵀ*Zappella* Marco. R 1993, Dehoniane. 370 p. Lᵐ 35. -- ᴿTS 56 (1995) 519 (L. *Örsy*).

3587 **Moltmann** Jürgen, The Spirit of life [1991], ᵀ*Kohl* Margaret 1992 → 9,7741 (L,SCM; also Ph, Fortress): ᴿAsbTJ 49,1 (1994) 88-90 (J.C. *Cooper*).

3588 **Moltmann** Jürgen, Lo Spirito della vita; per una pneumatologia integrale [1991], ᵀ: BTCon 77. Brescia 1994, Queriniana, 370 p. Lᵐ 48. 88-399-0377-1. -- ᴿEThL 71 (1995) 490s (E. *Brito*); StPat(av) 42 (1995) 816-8 (L. *Sartori*).

3589 *a) Oro* Ari P., O Espírito Santo e o Pentecostalismo; -- *b) Comblin* José, O Espírito Santo e a história / A teologia do Espírito Santo: Teocomunicação 25 (1995) 67-101 / 55-67.273-289.

3590 ᴱ*Sieben* H.J., BASILIUS von Caesarea, De Spiritu Sancto: FC 12. FrB 1993, Herder. 368 p. DM 44. 3-431-22132-2. -- ᴿThLZ 120 (1995) 807 (G. *Haendler*).

3591 **Valle Rodríguez** Francisca J. de [1856-1930], *Diego Sánchez* Manuel [1932], Decenario al Espíritu Santo: Logos 53. M 1994, Espiritualidad. 232 p. -- ᴿTer(esianum) 46 (1995) 33s (F. *Vega Santoveña*) → p.610-2.

3592 *Vanhetloo* Warren, Timeline consideration of the works of the Holy Spirit [in chronological order]: C(alv)BTJ 11,1 (1995) 36-66.

3593 **Welker** M., Lo Spirito di Dio; teologia dello Spirito Santo. Brescia 1995, Queriniana. 339 p. 88-399-0381-X. -- ᴿE(st)E 70 (1995) 557-560 (J.R. *García-Murga* desea en castellano).

3594 **Welker** Michael, God the Spirit, ᵀ*Hoffmeyer* J.F. Mp 1994, Fortress. xvi-360 p. -- ᴿTS 56 (1995) 794-6 (Nancy A. *Dallavalle*).

3595 **Ziebritzki** Henning, Heiliger Geist und Weltseele .. bei ORIGENES, PLOTIN .. : BHTh 84. Tü 1994, Mohr. viii-286 p. DM 128. -- ᴿJThS 46 (1995) 708-710 (M.J. *Edwards*); (Tü)TQ 175 (1995) 227s (H.J. *Vogt*).

H5.6 *Spiritus et Filius* -- **Spirit-Christology**, Filioque.

3596 **Bandera** Armando, El Espíritu que ungió a Jesús. M 1995, Edibesa. 374 p. -- ᴿEstTrin 29 (1995) 500-2 (M. *Ofilada Mina*).

3597 **Del Colle** Ralph, Christ and the Spirit; Spirit-Christology in trinitarian perspective
      1993s → 9,7753; 10,7543 [RStR 22,51, M.A. *Stenger*]: [R]ET 106 (1994s) 91s (G.
      Newlands); MoTh 11 (1995) 471s (C. *Gunton*); SWJT 37,3 (1995) 59 (H.A. *Brehm*); Theol
      98 (L 1995) 52-54 (C. *Schwöbel:* discussing Australian David COFFEY, 'moves beyond Neo-
      Scholasticism'); Thom 59 (1995) 656-9 (T. *Weinandy*).
3598 *Dulles* Avery, The Filioque; what is at stake ? : ConcordiaTQ 59 (1995) 31-48.
3599 **Song Choan-Seng**, Jesus in the power of the Spirit 1994 → 10,7551: [R]A(sia)JT 9
      (1995) 205s (J.C. *England*).
3600 *Stroeher* José M., Ex Patre Filioque procedit: Teocomunicação 25 (1995) 291-304.
3601 *Weinandy* T., The case for Spirit Christology; some reflections; Thom 59 (1995) 173-
      188 [NTAb 40, p.272].

H5.7 *Ssma Trinitas* -- The Holy Trinity

3602 *Abramowski* Luise, Zur Trinitätslehre des Thomas von Aquin: ZThK 92 (1995) 466-481.
3603 *Barnes* Michel R., AUGUSTINE on contemporary Trinitarian theology: TS 56 (1995)
      237-250.
3604 *Bobrinskoy* Boris, Models of Trinitarian revelation: StVlad 39 (1995s) 115-126.
3605 [E]**Cataldo** Antonio, CIRILLO di Alessandria, Dialoghi sulla Trinità: TPatr 98, 1992 →
      8,7631; 9.7764: [R]Asprenas 42 (1995) 123s (L. *Fatica*).
3606 **Ciola** N., La crisi del teocentrismo trinitario 1993 → 9,7765; 10,7560: [R]Salesianum
      57 (1995) 574s (F. *Lambiasi*).
3607 **Courth** Franz, Der Gott der dreifältigen Liebe: N° 1 der neuen internat. Lehrbücher
      AMATECA (Associazione di Manuali di Teologia Catolica): Lehrbücher zur katholischen
      Theologie 6, Pd 1993, Bonifatius. 306 p. DM 48. 3-87088-757-5. -- [R]ZkT 117 (1995)
      368-370 (L. *Lies*).
3608 *Cowan* Tom, The sacred three; Celtic shamanism and the concept of the Trinity:
      Creation Spirituality 11,4 (Oakland 1995) 34-41
3608* *Cozzi* Alberto, L'originalità del teismo trinitario; bollettino bibliografico di teologia
      trinitaria [CODA P., O'DONNELL J., 1988, *ital.* 1989; HEMMERLE K., BREUNING W.,
      MOLTMANN J.]: S(cuola)C 123 (1995) 765-839
3609 *Dahms* John V., The subordination of the Son: JETS 37 (1994) 351-364.
3610 **Dieckmann** Elisabeth, Personalität Gottes -- Personalität des Menschen: ihre Deutung
      im theologischen Denken Wolfhart PANNENBERGS: kath. Diss. [D]*Garijo Guembe.* Münster
      1995. -- ThRv Beilage 92/2, xiii.
3611 **Erickson** Millard J., God in three persons; a contemporary interpretation of the Trinity.
      GR 1995, Baker. 356 p. $ 30. 0-8010-3229-6 [RStR 22,48, C. *Bernas:* for Evangelicals;
      not always accurate].
3612 **Farley** B., In praise of virtue; an exploration of the biblical virtues in a Christian
      context. GR 1995, Eerdmans. 181 p. -- [R]LiLi 32,4 (1995s) 75 (L. *James*).
3613 *Forschner* Franz, Der Trinitätsbegriff JOACHIMs von Fiore und seine Folgen für die
      heilsgeschichtliche Gotteserkenntnis: WissWeis 58 (1995) 117-136.
3613* **Forte** Bruno, Trinität als Geschichte 1989 → 6,7589 ... 9,7770: [R]ÖR 44 (1995) 395-8
      (D. *Ritschl*).
3614 *Galot* Jean, Vrai visage de la Trinité: E(spr)eV 105 (1995) 289-295.
3615 *Gomes* Alan W., Winds of change in the worldwide Church of God, with special
      emphasis on the doctrine of the Trinity : Presbyterion 20 (St.Louis 1994) 91-108.

3616 **Gunton** Colin E., The One, the Three, and the many 1993 → 9,7772; 10,7568: [R]JRel 75 (1995) 438s (Jo Ann *McDougall*); MoTh 11 (1995) 270-2 (P.D. *Kenneson*)

3617 *Gutenson* Chuck, Father, Son and Holy Spirit -- the one God; an exploration of the trinitarian doctrine of Wolfhart PANNENBERG: AsbTJ 49,1 (1994) 5-21.

3618 **Holzer** Vincent, Le Dieu Trinité dans l'histoire; le différend théologique BALTHASAR-RAHNER: CFi .. P 1995. Cerf. 476 p. -- [R]EstTrin 29 (1995) 484s (X. *Pikaza*).

3619 *Jenson* Robert W., Justification as a triune event: MoTh 11 (1995) 421-2.

3620 **Jones** L. Gregory, Transformed judgement: towards a trinitarian account of the moral life, ND 1990 → 8.8519; 9,8781: [R]S(cot)JTh 48 (1995) 143s (N.P. *Harvey*: 'in what sense triune?' is a question never raised until p. 98, and the answer is still postponed through seven pages of clichés).

3621 **LaCugna** Catherine M., God for us; the Trinity and Christian life 1992 → 8,7643; 9,7776: [R]CritRR 7 (1994) 513-5 (C.A. *Wilson*): LouvSt 20 (1995) 88-91 (R. *Michiels*).

3622 **Lash** Nicholas, Believing three ways in one God; a reading of the Apostles' Creed 1993 → 9,7777; 10,7574: [R]CanadCath 13,4 (1995) 14 (A.E. *Giampietro*); MoTh 11 (1995) 262-4 (Sarah *Coakley*); *ProEc 4 (1995) 370-4 (W.J. *Jennings*); S(cot)JTh 48 (1995) 135-7 (D. *Brown*); TTod 51 (1994s) 454.6 (Leanne *Van Dyk*).

3623 **Marsh** Thomas, The triune God 1994 → 10,7577: [R]AnglTR 77 (19995) 251-3 (L.G. *Patterson*); DocLife 45 (1995) 645s (T. *MacCarthy*): TS 56 (1995) 401s (P.G. *Crowley*: high praise).

3624 *Marshall* Bruce D., What is truth ? [... how does the Christian community decide that its trinitarian identification of God is true ?]: *ProEc 4 (1995) 404-430.

3625 **Merriell** D. Juvenal, To the image of the Trinity; a study in the development of AQUINAS' teaching: ST 96, 1990 → 8,7646 ... 10,7781: [R]Salesianum 57 (1995) 587 (E. *Fontana*).

3626 **Moltmann** Jürgen, History and the triune God 1991 → 8,7648; 10,7578: [R]JRel 75 (1995) 132 (Catherine M. *LaCugna*).

3627 **Moreschini** Claudio, GREGORIUS NYSS., Teologia trinitario contro Eunomio. Mi/T 1994/2, Rusconi / UTET 676 p. -- [R]FilTeo 9 (1995) 641-9 (Nynfa *Bosco*).

3628 **Obenauer** Klaus, Summa actualitas; zum Verhältnis von Einheit und Verschiedenheit in der Dreieinigkeitslehre des heiligen BONAVENTURA; Diss. [D]*Greshake*. Freiburg/Br 1995. -- ThRv Beilage 92/2, viii.

3629 *O'Donnell* John,The trinitarian panentheism of Sergej BULGAKOV:Greg 76(1995) 31-45.

3630 **Peters** Ted, God as Trinity; rationality and temporality in divine life 1993 → 9,7785; 10,7580: [R]MoTh 11 (1995) 279-281 (D.S. *Cunningham*)

3631 **Piret** P., Les athéismes et la théologie trinitaire: A.COMTE, L. FEUERBACH, K.MARX, F.NIETZSCHE: *Coll. 15. Bru 1994, Inst. Ét. Théol. 380 p. Fb 1100. 2-930067-14-4. -- [R]E(spr)eV 105 (1995) 61s (J. *Milet*); TTh 35 (1995) 303s (W. *Logister*).

3632 **Rovira Belloso** Josep M., Tratado de Dios, uno y trino. S 1993, Secr. Trinitario. 652 p. -- [R]SalTer 82 (1994) 163s (N. *Silanes*).

3633 *Santiago del Cura* Elena, Radicación trinitaria de la 'koinonia' eclesial : Salmanticensis 42 (1995) 211-234; Eng. 234.

3634 *Scheffczyk* Leo, Die Trinitätslehre des Thomas von AQUIN im Spiegel gegenwärtiger Kritik : Div 39 (1995) 211-238.

3635 *Scott* David, Speaking to form; trinitarian-performative Scripture-reading: A(ngl)ThR 77 (1995) 137-159.

3636 *a) Sesboüé* Bernard, De la confesión de fe primitiva a la fórmula del dogma trinitario; -

- *b) Rovira Belloso* J.M., La fe se hace teología refleja (S.AGUSTÍN) -- *c) Salvati* G.M., 'Cognitio divinarum Personarum .. ' La reflexión sistemática de santo Tomás sobre el Dios cristiano: EstTrin 29 (XXX simposio Salamanca oct. 1995) 387-418 / 419-441 / 443-472.

3637 **Studer** Basil, Trinity and Incarnation; the faith of the early Church, [T]*Westerhoff* M., [E]*Louth* A., 1993 → 9,7631; 10,7591 [RStR 22,72, W.M. *Wilson*; a joy to read; super-bibliography]. -- [R]ProEccl 4 (1995) 241-3 (C. *Gunton*); TS 56 (1995) 160-2 (F.W. *Norris*).

3638 **Thompson** John, Modern trinitarian perspectives. Ox 1994, UP. vi-156 p. £ 12. 0-19-508899-9. -- [R]ET 106 (1994s) 313 (C. *Gunton*); TS 56 (1995) 402 (P.D. *Molnar*).

3639 **Tobler** S., Analogia caritatis; Kirche als Geschöpf und Abbild der Trinität: Diss. [D]*Egmond* A. van. Amsterdam 1994, VU. 256 p.- : TTh 35 (1995) 71.

3640 **Torrance** Thomas F., Trinitarian perspectives; toward doctrinal agreement. E 1994, Clark. 149 p. £ 19. 0-567-09599-8. [RStR 22,49, C. *O'Regan*]. -- [R]ET 106 (1994s) 380 (J. *McIntyre*).

3641 **Weinandy** Thomas G., The Father's Spirit of Sonship; reconceiving the Trinity. E 1995, Clark. xi-148 p. £ 18. 0-567-09721-8 [ThD 43,92]. -- [R]*TBR 8,3 (1995s) 20 (T. *Williams*).

3642 *Wilks* John G.F., The trinitarian ontology of John ZIZIOULAS: VoxEv 25 (1995) 63-88.

H5.8 *Regnum messianicum, Filius Hominis* -- **Messianic Kingdom, Son of Man**

3643 *a) Amaladoss* Michaël, Le Royaume, but de la Mission; -- *b) Fuellenbach* John, Église et Royaume; -- *c) Casaldáliga* Pedro, Le Royaume est à vous: Spiritus 36 (1995) 291-304 / 305-317 / 318-325.

3644 *Bindemann* Walther, Ungerechte als Vorbilder ? Gottesreich und Gottesrecht in den Gleichnissen vom 'ungerechten Verwalter' [Lk 16,1-8] und 'ungerechten Richter' [Lk 18,1-6]: ThLZ 120 (1995) 955-970.

3645 **Burkett** Delbert, The Son of Man in the Gospel of John: JSNT.s56, [D]1991 → 7,4806 .. 10,5299: [R]JETS 38 (1995) 284-6 (M.S. *Bryan*).

3646 *a) Casey* Maurice, Idiom and translation; some aspects of the Son of Man problem; -- *b) Slater* Thomas B., One like a Son of Man in first-century CE Judaism; -- *c) Moule* C.F. D., 'The Son of Man'; some of the facts: NTS 41 (1995) 164-182 / 183-198 / 277-9.

3647 *Connors* Russell B., Jr., *Smith* Martin L., Reconciliation and the reign of God: command, call and possibility: ChSt 34 (1995) 89-104.

3648 *(Schüssler) Fiorenza* Francis, Thy kingdom come: Church 10,2 (1994) 5-9.

3649 **Fisher** Neal F., The parables of Jesus; glimpses of God's reign[2] 1990 → 6,4906 ... 8,4841: [R]JETS 38 (1995)279s (K.H. *Easley*).

3650 **Fuellenbach** John, The Kingdom of God; the message of Jesus today. Mkn 1995, Orbis. $ 20. 1-57075-028-9 [< ThD 43,365].

3651 **Gentry** K.L., Lord of the saved; getting to the heart of the Lordship. Phillipsburg NJ 1991, Presbyterian & R. 104 p. 0-87552-265-3. -- [R]ScotBuEv 12 (1994) 67s (C.R. *Trueman*).

3652 **Giesen** H., Herrschaft Gottes -- heute oder morgen ? Zur Heilsbotschaft Jesu und der synoptischen Evangelien: BU 28. Rg 1995, Pustet. 162 p. 3-7917-1454-6. -- [R]Salm 42 (1995) 138-140 (R. *Trevijano Etcheverria*).

3653 [E]**Greig** Gary S., *Springer* Kevin N., The Kingdom and the power: are healing and spiritual gifts used by Jesus and the early Church meant for the Church today ? Ventura

CA 1993, Regal. 464 p. $ 20. 0-8307-1634-3. -- [R]Crux 31,1 (1995) 43-45 (A. *Hui*).

3654 **Hare** Douglas R.A., The Son of Man tradition 1990 → 6,7625 ...10,7600: [R]A(ustrl)BR 42 (1994) 103-5 (D.C. *Sim*).

3655 **Hell** Leonhard [→ Y5], Reich Gottes als Systemidee der Theologie; historisch-systematische Untersuchungen zum theologischen Werk B. GALURAS & F. BRENNERS [Diss. Tübingen, [D]*Kasper* W.]: TSTP 6, 1993 → 9,16649; 10,7599*; DM 56; 3-7867-1690-0: [R]TTh 35 (1995) 414 (T. *Schoof*).

3656 *Homerski* Józef, [P] The Kingdom of God in the teaching of Jesus: RTK(an) 42,1 (Lublin 1995) 58-68; Eng. 68.

3657 *Humphries* Michael, The Kingdom of God in the Q version of the Beelzebul controversy [Lk] (Q 11:14-26: ForumFF 9,1s (1993) 121-150.

3658 **Kainz** Howard P., Democracy and the 'Kingdom of God': *a*) Marquette Studies in Philosophy 6. Milwaukee 1995, Marquette Univ. viii-261 p. $ 25. 0-87462-610-2 [RStR 22,338, P. *Lakeland*]. -- *b*) StPh&R 17. Dordrecht/Boston 1993, Kluwer. viii-252 p. 0-7923-2106-5. -- [R]Salesianum 57 (1995) 381s (G. *Abbà*: variations in the notion of 'Kingdom of God' among both Catholics and Lutherans; option similar to WOGAMAN's).36

3659 **Kaylor** R. David, Jesus the prophet; his vision of the Kingdom on earth. LvL 1994, W-Knox. x-227. 0-664-25505-1. -- [R]CritRR 8 (1995) 232-4 (S.M. *Sheeley*); ETRel 70 (1995) 126 (J,-P. *Gabus*); *TBR 8,3 (1995s) 23 (P. *Doble*).

3660 **Knapp** Markus; Gottesherrschaft .. HABERMAS J. 1993 → 9,7812; 10,7606: [R]MThZ 46 (1995) 265-7 (G. *Rottenwöhrer*).

3661 *Marcos* Tomás, Semilla del Reino; sobre la continuidad entre el Reino de Dios y la Iglesia: EstAg 30 (1995) 59-76.

3662 **Mateos** Juan, El Hijo del hombre; hacia la plenitud humana; En los orígines del cristianismo 9. Córdoba 1995, Almendro. xiv-360 p.; bibliog, 333-341. 84-8005-025-X.

3663 **Meadors** Edwards [sic, also p. 61] P., Jesus the messianic herald of salvation [<diss. Aberdeen]: WUNT 2/72. Tü 1995, Mohr. xi-387 p. DM 118. 3-16-146251-3. -- [R]*TBR 8,3 (1995s) 24s (R. *Morgan*, not fully convinced).

3664 *Okorie* A.M., El Reino de Dios en el ministerio de Jesús: RevB(Arg) 57 (1995) 19-28.

3665 *Robinson* James M., The Son of Man in the Sayings Gospel : → 42, [F]COLPE C., Tradition (1994) 315-335.

3666 *Rossetto* Giovanni, La tensione del Regno: tappe di un cammino di ricerca: RivB 43 (1995) 391,428; Eng. 428.

3667 **Rovira Belloso** Josep M., Sociedad y reino de Dios [Societat], [T]*Maragall Mira* Ángela. M 1992, PPC. 244 p. 84-288-1103-2. -- [R]ActuBbg 31 (1994) 65 (S. *Vergés*).

3668 *Rubinkiewicz* Ryszard, Reich Gottes im frühjüdischen Schrifttum als Hintergrund der ntl. Basileia-Verkündigung: C(olc)Th 64,spec (1994) 19-32 [NTAb 40, p.108].

3669 *Sieg* Franciszek, [P] The Son of Man, the Messiah, the Son of God and Simon Peter (Mt 16,13-20): Bobolanum 6 (1995) 27-47; Eng.47s, (56-65, Lk 1,26-28; Eng, 67).

3670 **Subilia** Vittorio, Il Regno di Dio; interpretazioni nel corso dei secoli 1993 → 9,7822; 10,7616: [R](R)*StEc 12 (Venezia 1994) 243s (S. *Morandini*).

3671 **Thiel** Gerhard, Ökumene im Kraftfeld des Reiches Gottes; Basisökumene in Brasilien unter Berücksichtigung des lateinamerkanischen Kontext: Hab.-Diss. [D]*Raiser* K. Bochum 1995. -- ThLZ 120 (1995) 1146.

3672 **Thielen** B., Befreiung; [Reich-Gottes-] Perspektiven jenseits der Moderne. Wü 1994, Echter. 192 p. DM 40. 3-429-01625-8.- [R]TTh 35 (1995) 305s (J. van *Nieuwenhove*).

3673 *Vaillancourt* Mark, The Lord of the universe; Providence and the humanity of Christ: DunwoodieR 18 (1995) 39-70.

3674 **Viviano** Benedict T., Le Royaume de Dieu dans l'histoire [1987] [T]; LiBi 96, 1992 > 9,7823; 10,7617 : Greg 76 (1995) 593s (E. *Farahian*).

3675 **Vögtle** Anton, Die 'Gretchenfrage' des Menschensohnproblems; Bilanz und Perspektive: QD 152. 1994 → 10,7618: [R]BZ 39 (1995) 274s (D. *Kosch*); ThLZ 120 (1995) 529s (T. *Schmeller*).

3676 *Wolter* Michael, 'Was heisset nu Gottes reich ? ' [LUTHER 1529]: ZNW 86 (1995) 5-19.

H6.1 *Creatio, sabbatum NT* -- **The Creation** [→ H2.8]

3677   **Arteaga Natividad** Rodolfo, La creación en los comentarios de San AGUSTÍN al Génesis: Mayéutica mg.2. Marcilla 1994. 374 p. -- [R]RevAg 36 (1995) 1124-6 (J.*Sepulcre*).

3678 **Back** Sven-Olav, Jesus of Nazareth and the sabbath commandment. Åbo 1995, Akademi. 240 p.; bibliog. 198-231. 952-9616-58-9.

3679 **Balmary** Marie, La divine origine; Dieu n'a pas créé l'homme. P 1993, Grasset. 350 p. -- [R]FV 94,1 (1995) 73s (P. de *Robert*).

3680 *Berzosa Martínez* Raúl, Teología de la creación [CatIC 282 ¿Cuál es nuestro origen ?]; implicaciones bíblico-sistemáticas : Lum(Vt) 44 (1995) 491-504.

3681 *Bezuidenhout* L.C., Die Sabbat -- irrelevante wettiese [legal] instelling of verwaarloosde Bybelse juweel ? 'n Simpatieke perspektief op die Sabbat: HTS 51 (1995) 931-941 [NTAb 40, p.463].

3682 *Bidaut* B., Le travail et le sabbat dans la Bible: L(um)V 43,220 (1994) 37-46 [NTAb 39, p.447].

3683 *Bravo* Ernesto, Jesús y el sábado: RevB 56 (1994) 149-174 253-256.

3684 *Brzegowy* Tadeusz, [P] La création du chaos par Dieu ?: Co(lc)Th 64,4 (Wsz 1994) 5-20; franç. 21.

3685 *Bultmann* Christoph, Creation at the beginning of history; Johann Gottfried HERDER's interpretation of Genesis 1: JSOT 68 (1995) 23-32.

3686 **Burrell** David B., Freedom and creation in three traditions 1993 → 9,7830: [R]JRel 75 (1995) 141s (F.X. *Clooney*).

3687 [E]**Clifford** R.J., *Collins* J.J., Creation in the biblical tradition: CBQ.mg 24, 1992 → 8.346; 9,1813: [R]Laur 36 (1995) 227-9 (L. *Martignani*).

3688 *Dan* Joseph. The language of creation and its grammar: → 42, [F]COLPE C., Tradition (1994) 42-63.

3689 *Dufay* Fernand, Sur la création du monde: CRen 190 (1995) 61-66.

3690 [E]**Eskenazi** Tamara C., *Harrington* Daniel J., *Shea* William H., The Sabbath in Jewish and Christian traditions 1991 → 7,431 ... 10,7625: [R]JQR 86 (1995) 254s (E. *Spier*: hervorragend).

3691 *Friedman* Irving, A river went out of Eden (*al.*): Parabola 20,1 ('Earth, air, fire, water' 1995) 66-72 (6-91).

3692 **Gunton** C.E., Christ and creation. Carlisle/GR 1992, Paternoster/Eerdmans. 127 p. → 8,7693; £ 6. 0-85364-527-2 / US 0-8082-0579-5: [R]S(co)BET 13 (1995) 154-5 (W.D.J. *McKay*).

3693 **Haag** Ernst, Vom Sabbat zum Sonntag; eine bibeltheologische Studie 1991 -> 7,7629; 10,7626*: [R]BZ 39 (1995) 293-5 (G. *Dautzenberg*).

3694 **Hubler** James N., Creatio ex nihilo; matter, creation, and the body in classical and Christian philosophy through AQUINAS; diss. Pennsylvania, [D]*Ross* J. Ph 1994 [< RStR 22,p.270]..

3695 *Jaki* Stanley J., The sabbath-rest of the maker of all: AsbTJ 50 (1995) 37-49.

3696 *Jensma* Jeanne L., [Heinz] KOHUT's tragic man and the imago Dei; human relational needs in creation, the fall, and redemption: JPsT 21 (1993) 288-296.

3697 *Kirchschläger* Walter, Ordnung als theologische Bewaltigung des Chaos: TPQ 143 (1995) 279-284.

3698 *Klaine* Roger, Catéchismes et sciences; la création dans les catéchismes officiels récents: NRT 117 (1995) 710-723; Eng. 723.

3699 **Kraus** Georg, Schöpfungslehre: Texte zur T: Dogmatik 3/1s, 1992 > 9,7839: [R]TR 91 (1995) 340s (R. *Schulte*); ZkT 117 (1995) 119 (L. *Lies*, auch über MULLER G., HGeist)

3700 *Lane* Dermot A., The future of creation : MilltSt 34 (1994) 94-116 (-122, responses, *O'Hanlon* Gerald, *Dromey* Francis).

3701 *Liccione* Michael, Mystery and explanation in AQUINAS's account of creation: Thom 59 (1995) 223-245 [371-8 *Dewan* Lawrence].

3702 *Lilie* Frank, Schöpfung und menschliche Freiheit in der Philosophie Gerhard KRÜGERs: NZSTh 37 (1995) 223-237; Eng. 237.

3703 **Link** Christian, Schöpfung; 1. Schöpfungstheologie in der reformatorischen Tradition; 2. Schöpfungstheologie angesichts der Herausforderung des 20. Jahrhunderts: HbSysT 7, 1991 → 10,7629: [R]TR 91 (1995) 335-340 (R. *Schulte*).

3704 *Mangan* Céline, Creation theology in the Bible: DoLi 45 (1995) 164-170 (texts 216-224).

3705 **May** Gerhard, Creatio ex nihilo; the doctrine of 'creation out of nothing' in early Christian thought [1978], [T]*Worrell* A.S. E 1994, Clark. xvi-197 p. £ 20, 0-567-09695-5 [RStR 22,72, L.J. *Swift*]. - [R]Logos 36 (Sask 1995) 425 (M. *Tataryn*, in Ukrainian); PerspSCF 47 (1995) 208s (P. *Copan*); *TBR 8,1 (1995s) 8 (T. *Bradshaw*); VigChr 49 (1995) 305s (J. van *Winden*).

3706 **Meyjes** C.B.P., Von ophouden weten, de betekenis van het sabbatsgebod voor onze tijd [diss. Amst 1993]. Zoetermeer 1993, Boeken-C. 165 p.f 29,90. 89-2391-272-1. -- [R]NedThT 49 (1995) 241s (K.A.D. *Smelik*).

3707 a) *Middleton* J. Richard, Is creation theology inherently conservative ?; - b) *Brueggemann* Walter, response: HThR 87 (1994) 257-277 / 279-289.

3708 **Morales** J., El misterio de la creación. Pamplona 1995, EUNSA. 336 p. -- [R]ScrT(Pamp) 37 (1995) 314-7 (J. *Alviar*).

3709 *Müller* Hans-Peter, Schöpfung, Zivilisation und Befreiung: → 159, [F]ROGERSON, J., Bible/Society; JSOT.s 200 (1995) 355-365.

3710 *Och* Bernard, Creation and redemption; towards a theology of creation: J(u)d(ais)m 44 (1995) 226-243.

3711 **Perdue** Leo G., Wisdom and creation; the theology of the wisdom literature 1994 → 10,3224: [R]TBR 8,1 (1995s) 15 (R. *Coggins*).

3712 *Pérez de Laborda* Alfonso, Pour une dogmatique de l'acte de la création: RTL 26 (1995) 425-449; Eng. 609.

3713 *Pozo Abejón* Gerardo del, Historia y sabiduría en la teología bíblica de la creación; la interpretación de G. VON RAD y su recepción sistemática: RET 55 (1995) 181-236.

3714 **Robbins** Guy L.[J], 'And in the seventh day?': AmUSt 7/36. NY 1995, P.Lang. xviii-198 p. 0-8204-0504-3.

3715 **Samuelson** Norbert M., The first seven days; a philosophical commentary on the Creation of Genesis; SFSHJ 61. Atlanta 1992, Scholars. 186 p. - [R]*A(sn)JS 20 (1995) 202-5.

3716 **Samuelson** Norbert M., Judaism and the doctrine of creation. C 1994, Univ. xi-362 p. £ 40. 0-521-45241-7. - [R]BoL (1995) 119 (L.L. *Grabbe*: philosophy; *TBR 8,1 (1995s) 61 (N.R.M. *de Lange*).

3717 **Spier** Erich, Der Sabbat: Judentum 1, 1989 > 5,2449 ... 8,2565*: [R]JQR 84 (1993s) 321-3 (Catherine *Hezser*).

3718 *Šporčić* Ivan, Gesù e il precetto di sabato, Mc 2,22-3,6: RijT 2 (994) 229-248 croato; ital. 248.

3719 *Strolz* Walter, Schöpfung als Urbejahung; was sich aus der jüdischen Schriftauslegung lernen lässt [.. der Sintflutmythos als Existenzprobe]: HerKor 49 (1995) 155-9.

3720 *Vaz* Armindo, A visão das origens em Gn 2,4b-3,24 como coerência temática e unidade literária: Did(ask)L 24,2 (1994) 3-118; bibliog. 123-172.

H6.3   *Fides, veritas in NT* - **Faith and truth**

3721 *Alma* Hans A., *Heitink* Gerben, Having faith in young people's world view and their life-pattern: JE(mp)T 7,2 (1994) 52-74.

3722 **Anderson** Caitlin Laura, 'How can my faith be so different ?' The emergence of religious identity in college women: diss. Indiana, [D]*Schwandt* T. Bloomington 1995. 203 p. 95-39939. - DissA 56 (1995s) p. 2622.

3723 **Ansaldi** Jean, L'articulation de la foi .. : CogF 163, 1991 → 7,7642 ... 10,7638: [R]RTL 26 (1995) 105s (E. *Brito*).

3724 *Baelz* Peter, True religion and sound learning: Theol 98 (L 1995) 19-28.

3725 *Baltar* S., ¿ Es razonable la fe ? : VyV 53 (1995) 195-228.

3726 **Barr** James, Biblical faith and natural theology 1991/3 → 10,7639: [R]BA 58 (1995) 242 (S.M. *Sheeley*);Bijdragen 56 (1995) 459s (T. de *Kruijf*); BoL (1995) 109 (R. *Davidson*); ChrSchR 25 (1995s) 122-4 (A.G. *Padgett*); CritRR 7 (1994) 485-7 (W. *Vogels*); Interpretation 49 (1995) 298-300 (T. *Hiebert*); RelSt 31 (1995) 276-8 (G. *Jones*); StPat(av) 41 (1994) 652-6 (G. *Segalla*); TTod 51 (1994s) 469s.480 (P. D. *Duerksen*); ZAW 107 (1995) 520 (C. *Bultmann*).

3727 **Bultmann** Rudolf, *Weiser* Artur, Fede nel Nuovo Testamento [< GLNT]: Letture bibliche 13. Brescia 1995, Paideia. 125 p. L[m] 18. 88-394-0524-0.

3727* *a) Codina* Víctor, Creo en la fraternidad; -- *b) Busto Saíz* José Ramón, Creo en Dios Padre: SalTer 82 (1994) 611-620 / 595-609.

3728 **Conesa** Francisco, Creer e conocer; el valor cognoscitivo de le fe en la filosofía analítica. Pamplona 1994. 351 p. -- [R]AtK(ap) 125 (1995) 300-2 (W. *Dorsz*); ScrT(Pamp) 37 (1995) 317-321 (C. *Izquierdo*).

3729 *Conesa* Francisco, *a)* ¿Qué significa conocer a Dios por la fe?: Burgense 35(1994)67-95; - *b)* ¿Qué significa *creer* ? Análisis lingüístico del verbo *creer*: CiTom 121 (1994) 113-143.

3730 **Cranfield** C. E. B., The Apostles' Creed, a faith to live by. E 1993, Clark. 58 p. £ 6. 0-567-29227-4: [R]ET 106 (1994s) 280 (J.H. *Bates*).

3731 **Dinter** P.E. (15 years Catholic chaplain at Columbia Univ.), Beyond naive belief; the Bible and adult Catholic faith. NY 1994, Crossroad, xi-348 p. $ 30. 0-8245-1421-1. - [R]*Commonweal 122,5 (1995) 20-22 (D. *O'Brien*: reserves) [NTAb 39, p.342.449]; TS 56 (1995) 771s (R.J. *Sklba*: fresh, but would require judgment from varying specialties).

3732 **Dulles** Avery, The assurance of things hoped for; a theology of Christian faith 1994 → 10,7652 [RStR 22,49, J.R. *Sachs*: nuanced 'official' Vatican II]: [R]CCen 112 (1995) 132-4 (D, *Foxgrover*); JThS 46 (1995) 802-4 (J. *Macquarrie*); *ModBlv [Modern Believing: continuing the numbering of Modern Churchman] 36,3 (1995) 52s (J. *Pridmore*: 'The fact that feelings never get in the way is a great virtue of this book but it is also the trouble with it'); Month 256 (1995) 239s (Ruth *Holgate*); NOxR 62,3 (1995) 26s (P. *O'Connell*); TS 56 (1995) 791s (G.S. *Worgul*).

3733 [E]**Eggensperger** Thomas, *Engel* Ulrich, Wahrheit; Recherchen zwischen Hochscholastik und Postmoderne: WalberbergerStPh 9. Mainz 1995, Grünewald. - [R]AnáMnesis 5,2 (1995) 134s (G. *Chico*).

3734 *García* J.A., ¿ Bajo la gracia o bajo la ley ? Cuando la fe cristiana se tiñe de moralidad [... BOLADO A. 1970] : SalTer 83 (1995) 763-776.

3735 **Gerrish** B.A., The doctrine of faith [his 5th Warfield lecture]: P(rinc)SB 16 (1995) 202-215.

3736 **González Montes** A., Fundamentación de la fe. S 1994, Segr. Trinitario. 623 p. 84-88643-14-4. - : [R]Burg 36 (1995) 565s (J. de *Sahagún L.H.*); DiEc 30 (1995) 130-4 (A. *Luengo Vicente*).

3737 *Grounds* Vernon C., The truth about truth: JETS 38 (1995) 219-229.

3738 **Hart** Trevor, Faith thinking: the dynamics of Christian theology. L 1995, SPCK. 236 p. £ 16. 0-281-04870-3. -- [R]E(xp)T 107,6 top choice with author's invited reply (1995s) 161-3 (C.S. *Rodd*).

3739 *Hellemo* Geir, Lex orandi lex credendi -- et foreldet ideal ?: NTT 96 (1995) 102-116.

3740 **Henn** W., One faith; biblical and patristic contributions toward understanding unity in faith. NY 1995, Paulist. vi-334 p. $ 23. 0-8091-3577-9 [NTAb 40, p.367].

3741 **Hoitenga** Dewey J.[J], Faith and reason from Plato to Plantinga; an introduction to Reformed epistemology. Albany 1991, SUNY. xvii-263 p. $ 19 pa.-- [R]Faith & Philosophy 11 (ND 1994) 342=8 (J. F. *Sennett*).

3742 *Jericó Bermejo* Ignacio, Symbolum fidei, determinatio fidei et sensus fidei; la problemática del artículo de fe en Domingo BÁÑEZ: ArTGran 57 (1994) 5-103.

3743 *Kaiser* Gerhard, Kann man nach der Wahrheit des Christentums fragen ?: ZThK 92 (1995) 102-122.

3744 **Küng** Hans, Credo .. for today 1993 → 9,7874: [R]TTod 51 (1994s) 618.620.624.626 (T.W. *Currie*).

3745 **Kuitert** Harry M., La fede cristiana per chi dubita; una rilettura critica [1992 → 8,7727].[T]. T 1994, Claudiana. 366 p. L[m] 39.-- [R]RivScRel 9 (1995) 459s (L. *Martella*).

3746 *a) Langevin* Gilles, La singulère unité de l'acte de foi; démarche. don mutuel et es sa ge;-- *b) Geffré* Claude, Les déplacements de la vérité dans la théologie. contemporaine: → 197, [F]TILLARD J., Communion 1995, 301-7; 1 fig. / 309-321

3747 **Leith** John ., Basic Christian doctrine; a summary of Christian doctrine. Catholic, and Reformed. LVL 1992, W-Knox. 368 p- $ 20 pa. 0-664-25192- 7.-- [R]Interpretation 49 (1995) 90 . 92 .94 (B.W. *Farley*).

3748 **McBrien** Richard R., Catholicism[2rev] 1994 → 10,7667, HarperSF: also Melbourne, Collins Dove. xlviii-1286 p. $ 50 pa. 1--86371-314-X. -- [R]Vidyajyoti 59 (1995) 827s (P.M. *Meagher*).

3749 **Macquarrie** John, Invitation to faith [1994 Oxford parish Lenten lectures, published by Copeman as 'Starting from scratch']. L 1995, SCM. 56 p. £ 5. 0-334-02587-7. [E(xp)T 107 (1995s) 63].

3750 *Mardones* José M., Una fe personal es una fe eclesial : SalTer 83 (1995) 43-53.

3751 *Marshall* Bruce D., 'We shall bear the image of the man of heaven' [1 Cor 15,49]; theology and the concept of truth: MoTh 11 (1995) 93-117.

3752 **Meynell** Hugo A., Is Christianity true ? L/Wsh c.1995, Chapman/Catholic Univ. 149 p.-- [R]*CanadCath 9,.. (1995) 28 (J.M. *Miller*); Furrow 46 (1995) 126s (D. *Carroll*).

3753 **Micks** Marianne M., Loving the questions; an exploration of the Nicene Creed. Ph 1993, Trinity. vii-134 p. 1-56101-081-2.

3754 **Middleton** J. Richard, *Walsh* Brian, Truth is stranger than it used to be; biblical faith in a postmodern age. DG 1995, InterVarsity. 250 p. C$ 22.25. 0-8308-1856-1 [RStR 22,138, S.M. *Middleton:* useful breezy approach to postmodernism]. -- [R]Crux 31,3 (1995) 45-47 (D. *Ley,* also on LYON D., Postmodernity 1994).

3755 **Mitchell** Basil, Faith and criticism. Ox 1994, Clarendon. i73 p. £ 17.50. 0-18-826758-4.-- [R]ET 106,8 top choice (1994s) 225s (C.S. *Rodd*).

3756 **Morrison** David, What do churches *really* believe ? ... c.1995, Strathmor. 234 p. $ 20.-- [R]CanadCath 13,4 (1995) 26s (M.D. *Kuemper*).

3757 **Morse** Christopher, Not every spirit [1 Jn 4,1]; a dogmatics of Christian disbelief [what Christians do not or should not believe]. Ph 1994, Trinity. xix-417 p.-- [R]MoTh 11 (1995) 387s (P. *Sherry:* some thinness).

3758 **Moser** Félix, Les croyants non pratiquants [< diss.]. P/Genève 1994, Cerf / Labor et Fides. 349 p.-- [R]FV 94,2 (1994) 87s (P. *Aubert*).

3759 **Neuhaus** Gerd, Theodizee -- Abbruch oder Anstoss des Glaubens ? 1993 → 10,7574: [R]ZkT 117 (1995) 110 (K.H. *Neufeld*).

3760 **Newbigin** Lesslie, Proper confidence; faith, doubt and certainty in Christian discipleship. GR 1995, Eerdmans. vi-105 p.-- [R]RelStR 21 (1995) 315s (S.M. *Heim*).

3761 **Penelhum** Terence, Reason and religious faith: Focus. Boulder 1995, Westview. x-166p. $ 44; pa. $ 16. 0-8133-2035-6; -6-4 [ThD 42,391]

3762 **Quay** Paul M., The mystery hidden for ages in God: AmUSt 7/161. NY 1995, P.Lang. xvi-438 p. $ 64. 0-8204-2221-5 [ThD 42,383].

3763 **Sauer** H., Erfahrung und Glaube: die Begründung des pastoralen Prinzips durch die Offenbarunskonstitution des II. Vatikanischen Konzils 1993 → 10,7682: [R]CrSt 16 (1995) 683-9 (R. *Burigana*).

3764 **Schönborn** Christoph, L'unité de la foi: Spiritualités. P 1993, Mame. 101 p. -- [R]Div 39 (1995) 195-7 (D. *Vibrac*).

3765 *Schüssler* Werner, Paul TILLICH's dynamic concpt of faith [< *FrSZ 40 (1993) 298-311], [TE]*Asen* B.A. : ThD 42 (1995) 247-252.

3766 **Sessions** William L., The concept of faith; a philosophical investigation 1994 → 10,7683; 0-8014-2873-4 [< ThD 42 (1995) 290]. -- [R]TS 56 (1995) 174-6 (A. *Dulles*).

3767 *Smith* Joseph J., Hansjürgen VERWEYEN and the ground of Easter faith 1994 → 10,7684; further Landas 9 (Manila 1995) 72-100 . 181-208.

3768 **Soelle** Dorothee, Theology for sceptics [Es muss doch mehr als alles geben], [T]. L 1995, Mowbray. 126 p. £ 9. 0-264-67333-6.-- [R]ET 106,8 2d-top choice (1994s) 226s (C.S. *Rodd*).

3769 *Stendahl* Krister, Befrielsen -- stora boken om kristen tro [Liberation -- the great book on Christian faith, 1993 updating]: SvTKv 70 (1994) 17-24; Eng. 24 [1-9, *Persson* Erik; 10-16, *Lænning* Inge; 25-34, *Selander* Sven-Åke].

3770 **Testa** Emanuele, La fede della Chiesa Madre di Gerusalemme. R 1995, Dehoniane. 374 p. 88-396-0555-X.

3771   *Wallis* J.G.,   Jesus the believer -- a fresh approach: *ModBel 36.1 (Leominster 1995) 10-17 [NTAb 39, p.442].

3772   **Wallis** J.G.,   The faith [in God!] of Jesus Christ in early Christian traditions: SNTS.mg 84.   C 1995, Univ. 281 p.   0-521-47352-7.-- [R]Neotest 29 (1995) 434s (P.J.J. *Botha*).

3773   **Wells** David F.,   God in the wasteland; the reality of truth in a world of fading dreams. GR 1994, Eerdmans. x-256 p. $ 29.-- [R]Crux 31,4 (1995) 40-43 (D. *Stewart*, also on his No place for truth*)*.

3774   **Werbick** J.,   Vom Wagnis des Christentums; wie glaubwürdig ist der Glaube ? Mü 1995, Kösel. 285 p. DM 38. 3-466-36420-5.- [R]TTh 35 (1995) 418s (P. De *Mey*).

3775   **Westphal** Merold, Suspicion and faith; the religious uses of atheism 1993 → 10,7687: [R]BS 152 (1995) 230s (S.R. *Spencer*); (Reformed) Perspectives 9,4 (1994) 22s (Caroline J. *Simon*).

3776   *Westra* Liuwe H.,   A never-tested hypothesis [KATTENBUSCH F.1894, KELLY J.N.D. 1976]: regional variants of the Apostles' Creed: Bijdragen 56 (1995) 369-385 . ... ; Eng. 386.

3777   **Young** Frances M.,   De oudste credo's van het christendom; hon ontstaan en functie. Baarn 1991, Ten Have. 179 p. *f* 25. 90-259-4477-9. -- [R]Bijdragen 56 (1995) 100 (M. *Parmentier*).

3778   **Zumstein** Jean, L'apprentissage de la foi 1993 → 10,3884: [R]ScrT(Pamp) 37 (1995) 367-9 (A. *García-Moreno*).

H6.5   **Angelologia** *biblica et apocrypha*

3779   *Abrams* J.Z.,   The reflexive relationship of the Mal'achei haSharet [ministering angels in heaven show role of rabbis on earth]: CCAR 42,2 (1995) 25-34 [NTAb 40, p.492].

3780   *a) Basset* Jean-Claude, Petite généalogie des anges; -- *b) Graesslé* Isabelle, Genèse, sources et questions des *angéliques*: BCPÉ 47,6 ('Les anges à la croisée des chemins' 1995) 4-20 / 21-23 (-41, *al.*) [NTAb 40,p.274].

3781   *Bokwa* Ignacy, [P] La querelle des anges ou une chance du christianisme [..la pratique ec-clésiale a relégué à l'ombre cet élément .. cependant]: PrzPow 891 (1995) 161-170 (-3, *al.*).

3782   *a) Borowski* Elie, Cherubim, God's throne ? .-- *b) Jensen* Robin M., Of Cherubim & Gospel symbols: BArR 21,4 (1995) 36-41 / 42s . 65.

3783   **Boyer** Mark C.,   A month by month guide to entertaining angels [three biblical mentions for each month]. Ch 1995, ACTA. xii-159 p. $ 12 pa. 0-87945-121-7 [ThD 43,158).

3784   *Cazelles* Henri, Os fundamentos da teologia dos anjos segundo o Antigo Testamento: RCB 19 (1995) 3-18 [< OTA 19,p.296].

3785   *a) Depraz* Natalie, La phénomenalité des anges -- questions de méthode; -- *b) Falque* Emmanuel,   L'altérité angélique ou l'angélologie thomiste au fil des Méditations cartésiennes de HUSSERL; -- *c) Viellart* Franck, Le statut de l'ange dans l'économie de la manifestation: L(aval)TP 51 (1995) 607-623 / 625-646 / 647-665.

3786   **Deutsch** Nathaniel P., Guardians of the gate; angelic vice regency in late antiquity: diss. [D]Fishbane M. Chicago 1995.-- RStR 22,274.

3787   *a) Elior* Rachel,   Mysticism, magic, and angelology; the perception of angels in Hekhalot literature; -- *b) Shaked* Saul, 'Peace be upon you, exalted angels'; on Hekhalot, liturgy and incantation bowls: Jewish Studies Quarterly 1 (Tü 1993s) 3-54 / 2 (1995) 197-219: 2 pl.

3788 **Galvão** António M., Os anjos existem ? Petrópolis 1994, Vozes. 101 p. -- :
  ^RTeocomunicação 25 (1995) 386.
3789 *Hoppe* L.J., Three angelic biographies: BiTod 33 (1995) 331-336 [NTAb 40,p.278].
3790 **Knapp** Gottfried, Angels, archangels and all the company of heaven. Mü 1995,
  Prestel. 96 p. 3-7913-1482-3.
3791 **Kreeft** Peter J., Angels and demons; what do we really know about them ? SF 1995,
  Ignatius. 157 p. $ 10. 0-89870-550-9 [ThD 43,275].
3792 **Lavatori** R., Gli angeli; storia e pensiero: Dabar. Genova 1991, Marietti. 294 p. L^m
  40. -- ^RAsprenas 42 (1995) 293s (P. *Pifano*).
3793 *Lee* Hindishe, On angels: JBQ 22 (1994) 51-56.
3794 **Mach** Michael, Entwicklungsstadien des jüdischen Engelglaubens in vorrabbinischer
  Zeit: TSAJ 34, ^D1992 → 8,2424 ... 10,2091: *A(sn)JS 20 (1995) 402-5 (Martha *Himmelfarb*);
  ZRGG 47 (1995) 370-2 (G. *Ahn*).
3795 *a) MAcManus* Dennis, Angels; their importance in our lives; -- *b) Riordan* Claudia,
  Reading up on angels [TAYLOR T. 1990, 1992; TYLER K. 1994]; -- *c) Moroney* James P.,
  Saints and angels, our companions on life's journey: Catholic World 238 (1995) 92-95 /
  64-67 / 59-63.
3795* *Maldamé* Jean-Michel, Les anges, les puissances, et la primauté du Christ; BLE 96
  (1995) 121-134; Eng. 134
3796 **Marconcini** B., *al.*, Angeli e demoni; il dramma della storia tra il bene e il male:
  CTSist 11. Bo 1991, Dehoniane. 42 p. L^m 49. -- ^RRA(sc)M 20 (1995) 407-410 (F.
  Sbaffoni).
3797 *Neef* Heinz-Dieter, 'Ich selber bin in ihm' (Ex 23,21); exegetische Beobachtungen zur
  Rede vom 'Engel des Herrn' in Ex 23,20-22; 32,34; 33,22; Jdc 2,1-5; 5,23: BZ 39 (1995)
  54-75 [Ähnliches CBQ 29 (1967) 419-449, *North* R.,Separated spiritual substances OT].
3798 **Olyan** Saul, A thousand thousands served him; exegesis and the naming of angels in
  ancient Judaism: TSAJ 36, 1993 → 10,2093: ^RCBQ 57 (1995) 155s (L.L. *Grabbe*; discusses
  hypóstasis bypassing PHILO and Sap.Sal.); JSJ(ud) 26 (1995) 213-5 (J. *Duhaime*); VT 45
  (1995) 135s (J.A. *Emerton*).
3799 *Romero Pose* Eugenio, Los ángeles de las Iglesias (Exégesis de TICONIO ad Apc 1,20-
  3,22 : → 119 ^FMARA M.Grazia, Aug(ustinianum)R 35 (1995) 119-136.
3800 *Terra* João E.M., Os anjos na historia da salvação [.... RAHNER]: RC(u)B 19/73s
  (Existem anjos ? 1995) 19-62 [63-131] (3-18, AT, *Cazelles* H.) -- *b)* Anjos na Biblia
  [GASTER T.J., MICHL J., GRELOT P. ...] : RC(u)B 19/75s (1995) 5-26-47-54 ... 116 [=
  ^E**Terra** J.E.Martins, Existem anjos ? / Anjos na Bíblia: RCuB 19,73s.75s. São Paulo
  1995, Loyola. 132 p.;159 p. < NTAb 40].
3801 *Welker* M., Angels in the biblical traditions; an impressive logic and the imposing
  problem of their hypercomplex reality; ThTo 51 (1994) 367-380 [NTAb 39, p.272].

H6.6 *Peccatum, diabolus* -- **Evil, Satan, demons**

3802 *Alvarez Valdés* Ariel, ¿ El diablo y el demonio son lo mismo ? : RevBib(Arg) 57 (1995)
  231-8.
3803 **Basset** Lytta, Le pardon originel; de l'abîme du mal au pouvoir de pardonner 1994 →
  10,7689: ^RATG(ran) 58 (1995) 386s (R. *Franco*); E(spr)eV 105 (1995) 167s (L. *Monloubou:*
  'l'auteure' est 'Pasteure' à Genève); ÉTRel 70 (1995) 454-6 (J.-D. *Causse*); FV 94,3 (1995)
  111 (J.-P. *Denis*).

3804 *Baudry* Gérard-Henry, À propos du péché original; approches bibliques: E(spr)eV 105 (1995) 497-511; (liturgie baptismale) 513-525 . 536-544.

3805 *Bell* R.H., Sin offerings and sinning with a high hand [= deliberately: Num 15,30s; Heb 10,26s]: *JProgJud 4 (Shf 1995) 25-59 [NTAb 40, p.275].

3806 *Bergant* Dianne, Biblical interpretation and sin in today's world: NewThR 8,2 (1995) 70-75.

3807 **Blocher** Henri, Evil and the cross; Christian thought and the problem of evil, [1982s; Eng. Churchman 1985], [T]*Preston* David G. Leicester 1994, Apollos. 154 p. £ 8. 0-85111-140-8.-- [R]*TBR 8,3 (1995s) 26 (I. *Markham*).

3808 *a)* *Boleski* Jacek, [P] Sünde als Erbsünde (*originatum*: vs. Ursünde, *originans*); -- *b)* *Pietras* Henryk, [P] La nudità perduta; il peccato originale nella 'Lettera a Gobar' di ORIGENE: C(olc)Th 64,3 (1994) 11-25; deutsch 26 / 27-37; ital. 37.

3809 **Bourrat** Marie-Michèle [psychiatre], *Soupa* Anne, Faut-il croire au diable ? : C'est-à-dire. P 1995, Bayard/Centurion. 177 p. F 69.-- [R]E(spr)eV 105 (1995) 279s (P. *Jay: équilibré:* → **5**, [F]ATKINSON, J., Bible, Reformation, Church: JSNT.s 105 (1995) .

3810 *Bray* Gerald, Original sin in patristic thought: Churchman 108 (L 1994) 37-47.

3811 **Capps** Donald, The depleted self; sin in a narcissistic age 1993 → 10,7960: [R]TorJT 11 (1995) 115s (J.A. *Loftus*).

3812 **Cervantes** Fernando, The devil in the New World; the impact of diabolism in New Spain. Nhv c.1995, Yale Univ. 182 p. $ 22.50. -- [R]*CWeal 122,9 (1995) 24s (C. L. *Bankston*, also on BERNSTEIN A.)

3813 **Claret** Bernd J., Geheimnis des Bösen; ein Beitrag zur theologischen Diskussion um die Frage nach dem Teufel: Diss. [D]*Greshake*. Freiburg/Br 1995. -- ThRv Beilage 92/2, viii.

3814 **Coate** Mary Ann, Sin, guilt, and forgiveness: the hidden dimensions of a pastoral process. L 1994, SPCK. 217 p. £ 11. 0-281-04781-2. -- [R]ET 106 (1994s) 349s (A. *McFayden*, also on PETERS T. 1994).

3815 *Cronin* Kieran, Illness, sin and metaphor: I(r)ThQ 61 (1995) 191-204.

3816 *Cunningham* Lawrence S., Satan; a theological meditation: TTod 51 (1994s) 359-366.

3817 **Delbanco** Andrew, The death of Satan; how Americans have lost the sense of evil. NY c.1995, Farrar-SG, 258 p. $ 13. -- [R]*CWeal 122,20 (1995) 26s (R. *Worth*).

3818 *Fischer* Johannes, Schuld und Sühne; über theologische, ethische und strafrechtliche Aspekte: ZEE(th) 39 (1995) 188-205.

3819 *García de la Hoz* Carmen, Totem y tabú; culpabilidad y religión: MCom(illas) 53 (1995) 459-486.

3820 **Gesché** Adolphe, Dios para pensar, I. El mal; II. El hombre [1993 → 9,7902; 10,7692*], [T]*Ortiz García* A., *Sala* Mario: Verdad e Imagen 135. S 1993, Sígueme. 332 p.

3821 *Gesché* Adolphe, L'affrontement du mal; un combat avec Dieu: Christus 42,4 ('Le mal, épreuve de la foi' 1995) 411-424.

3822 *Grbac* Josip, Okkultismus -- Spiritismus -- Satanismus: RijT 2 (1994) 207-228 kroatisch; deutsch 228.

3823 *a)* *Greco* Carlo, Per una fenomenologia biblico-teologica del male; -- *b)* *Scalera McClintock* Giuliana, L'antica natura titanica; variazioni sul mito greco della colpa: FilTeo 9 (1995) 231-249; Eng. 231 [-305, *al.*] / 307-325; Eng. 307 [-370, *al.*].

3824 **Griffin** David R., Evil revisited; responses and reconsiderations 1991 → 9,7746; 10,7694: [R]CritRR 6 (1993) 509-511 (J. K. *Robbins*).

3825 *Haas* Guenther, The effects of the fall on creational social structures; a comparison of Anabaptist and Reformed perspectives: C(alvin)TJ 30 (1995) 108-129.

3826 *Jacques* Robert, Du mal, du pardon et de Dieu: RTPh 127 (1995) 369-376; Eng. 423.
3827 **Jones** I. Gregory, Embodying forgiveness; a theological analysis. GR 1995, Eerdmans.
x-313 p. $ 28; pa. $ 18. 0-8028-3806-5; -0861-1. -- ᴿ*TBR 8,3 (1995s) 23 (A. *McCoy:*
a very good book, for a society either violent or unaware of sin; concludes with three cases
forcing the question 'are some things unforgivable ?')
3828 **Kleffmann** Tom, Die Erbsündenlehre in sprachtheologischem Horizont; eine
Interpretation AUGUSTINS, LUTHERS & HAMANNs: BHTh 86. viii-396 p. DM 168. 3-16-
146335-8 [ThRv 92,54].
3829 **Kim Jongwoo**, Das Reich des Bösen bei Albrecht RITSCHL; biblische Grundlegung und
theologiegeschiichtliches Weiterwerken; ev. Diss. ᴰ*Schwarz*. Regensburg 1995. -- ThRv
Beilage 92/2, xiv.
3830 **Ladaria** Luis F., Teología del pecado original y de la gracia. M 1993, BAC. xxix-315
p. -- ᴿBurg 36 (1995) 567s (C. *García*).
3831 **Laurentin** René, Le démon, mythe ou réalité ? enseignement et expérience du Christ
et de l'Église. P 1995, Fayard. 374 p. -- ᴿEphMar 45 (1995) 511s (P. *Largo Domínguez*).
3832 **Lifschitz** Daniel, L'inizio della storia; il peccato originale 1993: → 9,2021; Lᵐ 40:
ᴿProtest(antesimo) 50 (1995) 155s (E. *Noffke*).
3833 *Luke* K., Original sin in Jewish tradition: Bible Bhashyam 21 (1995) 219-235.
3834 *McEwen* A.R., Demonology and the occult in the OT: VoxRef 59 (1994) 1-16 [< OTA
18 (1995) p. 588].
3835 **McGinn** Bernard, Antichrist; two thousand years of the human fascination with evil
1994 → 10,5466: ᴿC(ath)HR 81 (1995) 604s (J.B. *Russell*); ChrCent 112 (1995) 1086-9 (J.
Van Engen); *CritRR 8 (1995) 494-6 (D.W. *Suter*); Horizons 22 (1995) 293 (B.L. *Whitney*).
3836 **Mattioli** Anselmo, L'inquietante mistero del male; idee e prospettive nella Bibbia. R
1994, Città Nuova. 184 p.-- ᴿTer(esianum) 46 (1995) 314s (V. *Pasquetto*).
3837 *Mauny* Michel de, Le diable dans l'histoire: PensCath 279 (1995) 77-87.
3838 **Messadie** Gérald, Histoire générale du diable. P 1993, Laffont, 490 p. F 139. --
ᴿCahRenan 43,190 (1995) 107-115 (R. *Bordes*).
3839 *a) Neugebauer* Fritz, Die biblische Rede von der Schuld; Hilfe in den Wirrnissen
unserer Tage; -- *b) Beintker* Michael. Schuld und Verstrickung in der Neuzeit: JBTh 9
(1994) 329-345 / 219-234.
3840 *Nowak* Antoni J., ᴾ Le satanisme à la lumière de le parapsychologie: AtK(ap) 125
(1995) 186-198.
3841 **Ohly** Friedrich, Metaphern für die Sündenstufen und die Gegenwirkungen der Gnade:
RhWAW.g 302. Opladen 1990, Westdeutscher. 169 p. ᴿGGA 247 (1995) 242-6 (A.
Angenendt).
3842 *O'Malley* William J., A sane sense of sin: America 172,12 (1995) 10-12.
3843 **Page** Sydney H.T., Powers of evil; a biblical study of Satan and demons. GR/Leicester
1995, Baker/Apollos. 295 p. $ 20. 0-8010-7137-2 / 0-85111-437-7 [NTAb 40,p.370].
3844 **Pagels** Elaine, The origin of Satan. NY 1995, Random. xxiii-214 p. 0-679-40140-7
ᴿCom(Jewish) 100,3 (1995) 54-57 (J. *Levenson:* Satan is other kinds of people; conflict is
the origin of this Satan, not Satan the origin of conflict; Christianity and Judaism are
disdained, gnosticism idealized): FirsT 57 (1995) 40-45 (J.B. *Russell:* Christianity has
always demonized its opponents: right; but that does not make it a dualistic religion); *New
Republic (NY July 10, 1995) 30-36 (B.D. *Shaw:* underrates the Satan of private personal
life); *New Yorker (3.IV.95) 54-60.62s (D. *Remnick*); *NYRevB 42,14 (1995) 18-20 (N.
Cohn: sound but omits Zoroastrian and other recent research); *NYTimesBR (June 18,1995)

9s (L. *Houlden:* tendentious, but depicts fairly the strengths and weaknesses of orthodoxy); RStR 22,3-9 (E. *TeSelle*) [all seven < NTAb 40, p. 18. 87 .279 .468]; further *CritRR 8 (1995) 502-6 (Mara E. *Donalson*).

3845 **Peters** Ted, Sin; radical evil in soul and society. GR 1994 → 10,7699; $ 25; $ 15: ᴿCrossCur 45 (1995s) 546s (Linda *Mercadante*); Dialog 34 (1995) 72-74 (M.C. *Mattes*); P(rinc)SB 16 (1995) 255-7 (T.D. *Parker*); RefR 49 (1995s) 73 (H. *Buis*).

3846 *Phan* Peter C., Overcoming poverty and oppression; liberation theology and the problem of evil: LouvSt 20 (1995) 3-20.

3847 ᴱ**Pizzari** Pietro, Johann WIER (1515-1588), Pseudomonarchia daemonum; organigramma dell'inferno: Piccoli saggi 43. Mi 1994, A. Mondadori. 108 p. 88-04-39042-5.

3848 **Plantinga** Corneliusᴶ, Not the way it's supposed to be; a breviary of sin 1994 → 10,7201: ᴿC(alvin)TJ 30 (1995) 627-630 (S.E. *Hoezee*); CCen 112 (1995) 1017s (W. *Wink:* 'the Powers made us do it'; the passion that drove Jesus' disciples was relief at being liberated from the powers that be); Church 11,3 (1995) 53 (F.J. McN..); RefR 49 (1995s) 145 (T. *Schwanda*}.

3849 *Porter* Jean, Virtue and sin; the connection of the virtues and the case of the flawed saint: JRel 75 (1995) 521-539.

3850 **Pricoco** Salvatore, Il demonio e i suoi complici; dottrine e credenze demonologiche nella tarda antichità: Armarium 6.. Soveria Manelli CZ 1995, Rubbettino. 371 p. 88-7284-361-8.

3851 *Ratzinger* Joseph, 'In the beginning ...' a Catholic understanding of the story of creation and the fall, ᵀ*Ramsey* Boniface: Resourcement; retrieval and renewal in Catholic thought. E 1995, Clark. xii-100 p. £ 9. 0-567-29296-7.-- ᴿ*TBR 8,3 (1995s) 7 (Elizabeth *Lord*, Munich 1981 lectures 'against today's threat to life' but tends to shape the reception of Vatican II in a way which belies its main direction; does not favour historical critical method).

3852 *Reckinger* François, Weder Hexenzauber noch Placebo, Neuerscheinungen zum Exorzismus [AMORTH G. 1990 ..]: ForKT 11 (1995) 142-6.

3853 **Richardson** James T., *al.*, The satanism scare 1991 → 7,376b̲: ᴿSvTK 69 (1993) 30-32 (C. *Dahlgren*).

3854 *Ricœur* Paul, Il male, una sfida alla filosofia e alla teologia [1986], ᵀ. Brescia 1993, Morcelliana. 77 p. -- ᴿFilTeo 9 (1995) 448-450 (G. *Razzino*).

3855 **Russell** Jeffrey B., El diablo; percepciones del mal de la antigüedad al Cristianismo primitivo [1977 → 65,1911 ... 8,2261]: Kim-Ik. Barc 1995, Laertes. 232 p. [RazF 232,127].

3856 *Saucy* Robert L.,'Sinners'who aren't forgiven or'Saints' who sin?:BS 152(1995)400-12.

3857 *Schindler* David L., Christological aesthetics and Evangelium vitae; toward a definition of liberalism; the 'structural sin' of the Pope's 'culture of death' consists in a simultaneous inclination toward arbitrary will and mechanistic reason: ComI-US 22 (1995) 193-224.

3858 **Schwarz** Hans, Im Fangnetz des Bösen; Sünde -- Übel -- Schuld: BthSchwerpunkte 10, 1993 → 9,7908*; 10,7702: ᴿActuBbg 31 (1994) 67s (J. *Boada*).

3859 **Schwarz** Hans, Evil: a historical and theological perspective, ᵀ*Worthing* Mark W. Mp 1995, Fortress. xii-226 p. -- ᴿTS 56 (1995) 813s (R.M. *Gula*).

3860 **Sentis** Laurent, Saint Thomas d'AQUIN et le mal; foi chrétienne et théodicée: THist 92. P 1993, Beauchesne. 363p.

3861 *Sill* Bernhard, Das komplexe Phänomen 'Schuld'; Bkickpunkte auf die 'Zeichen der Zeit' : LebZeug 50 (1995) 165-178.

3862 *Soossten* Joachim von, Die 'Erfindung' der Sünde; soziologische und semantische Aspekte zu der Rede von der Sünde im alttestamentlichen Sprachgebrauch: JBTh 9 (1994) 87-110 (3-24, Gn 3, *Bird* Phyllis A.; 53-85, Ps 7, *Janowski* B.; 125-142, Mk 2,5, *Hofius* O.).

3863 **Suchocki** Margaret H., The fall to violence; original sin in relational theology. NY 1994, Continuum. 168 p. $ 19. -- ᴿ*CritRR 8 (1995) 512-4 (D.R. *Bechtel*); MoTh 11 (1995) 481-3 (C. *Plantinga*).

3864 **Sung Chong-Hyon**, Vergebung der Sünden: Jesu Praxis der Sündenvergebung nach den Synoptikern und ihre Voraussetzungen im AT und frühen Judentum: WUNT 2/57. Tü 1994, Mohr. xiv-342 p. DM 98. 3-16-146182-7. -- ᴿThLZ 120 (1995) 36 (G. *Haufe*).

3865 **Thome** Gabriele, Vorstellungen vom Bösen in der lateinischen Literatur; Begriffe, Motive, Gestalten. Stu 1993, Steiner. 469 p. DM 128.-- ᴿJbAC 37 (1994) 174-7 (C. *Schulte*).

3866 *Tracy* David, Evil, suffering, hope; [p.15] the search for new forms of contemporary theodicy / [p.iii] foundational systematic perspectives: → 564, CTS 50 (1995) 15-36; responses 37-40, M.S. *Copeland,* 41-45, D.N. *Power.*

3867 *Trevijano* Pedro, Pecado, conversión y perdón en el Nuevo Testamento: ScripV 41 (1994) 127-170.

3868 **Ulmer** Rivka, The Evil Eye in the Bible and in rabbinic literature. Hoboken 1994, KTAV. x-214 p. $ 29.50. 0-88125-463-0 [NTAb 39,p.363]. -- ᴿSefarad 55 (1995) 406 (E.*Fernández Tejero*).

3869 *Vermeylen* J.E., Le méchant dans le discours des amis de Job → 483*, BtETL 1995, 101-127 [< OTA 18, p.549, P. *Redditt*].

3870 *Viallaneix* Paul. Le défi du mal: dialogue avec Albert CAMUS; FV 94,1 (1995) 25-34.

3871 **Victor** Jeffrey S., Satanic panic; the creation of a contemporary legend. Ch 1993, Open Court. xiv-408 p. $ 17. -- ᴿLexTQ 30 (1995) 49-54 (R.A. *Baker*, also on RICHARDSON J., *al.*, The Satanism scare 1991)

3872 *Voorwinde* S., Demons and the occult in the New Testament: VR 39 (1994) 17-38 [NTAb 39, p.271].

3873 **West** Angela, Deadly innocence; feminist theology and the mythology of sin. L 1995, Cassell. xviii-218 p. 0-264-67341-7.

3874 **Wink** Walter, Engaging the powers; discernment and resistance in a world of domination 1992 → 8,6642 ... 10,6132: ᴿJHisp/Lat 2,2 (1994) 79s (T.M. *Matovina*); (Reformed) Perspectives 9,6 (1994) 13-15 (Marchiene V. *Rienstra).*

H7 **Soteriologia Novi Testamenti**

3875 **Ani** Ikechukwu, Die befreiende Versöhnung; die christliche Heilsbotschaft der Sündenvergebung in ihrem heilsgeschichtlich-politischen Zusammenhang bei Ernst MICHEL: Diss. ᴰ*Rotter* H. Innsbruck 1995. -- ZkT 117 (1995) 506.

3876 **Auer** Johan, Cristologia / Soteriologia e mariologia: Gesù il Salvatore, piccola dogmatica cattolica 4/1s, ᵀᴱ *Molari* C. Assisi 1993, Cittadella. 624 p.; 712 p. Lᵐ 70 + 80. -- ᴿAsprenas 42 (1995) 605 (P. *Pifano:* co-responsabile RATZINGER ha collaborato solo per l'escatologia).

3877 ᴱ**Carson** D.A., Justification in the Bible and the world [14 art.]. Carlisle 1992, Paternoster. 309 p. 0-85364-516-7.

3878 *Collins* Kenneth J., The soteriological orientation of John WESLEY's ministry to the poor: AsbTJ 50 (1995) 75-91

3879   *Dianich* Severino,   La Chiesa nella storia fra santità e peccato: dottrina della giustificazione ed ecclesiologia: VivH 6 (1995) 257-278; Eng. 278.

3880   *Erickson* Millard J., The destiny of the unevangelized / Is there opportunity for salvation after death / Is Hell forever ? : The fate of those who never hear 1-3: BS 152 (1995) 3-15 / 131-144 / 259-272.

3881   **Farris** T.V., Mighty to save; a study in Old Testament soteriology 1993 → 9,7921: [R]A(ndr)USS 33 (1995) 119s (J.E. *Miller*).

3882   **Gäde** Gerhard, Eine andere Barmherzigkeit; zum Verständnis der Erlösungslehre ANSELMs 1989 → 6,7719: [R]MüTZ 45 (1994) 232-5 (M. *Enders*).

3883   *García Cordero* Maximiliano, La correlación de la fe y las obras en la justificación del creyente según los escritos del Nuevo Testamento: CTom 122 (1995) 219-255 . 439-476 [NTAb 40,p.465].

3884   **Garrison** Roman, Redemptive almsgiving in early Christianity [diss. Toronto, [D]*Richardson* P.]; JSNT.s 77, 1993 →̲ 9.7925; 10,7711: [R]*CritRR 8 (1995) 407-9 (J.S. *Jeffers*).

3885   **Grant** Colin, A salvation audit. Scranton 1994, Univ. 397p. £ 14.50. 0-940866-34-X. -- [R]E(xp)T 107 (1995s) 188 (G. *Slater*).

3886   *Henry* Carl F.H., Justification; a doctrine in crisis: JETS 38 (1995) 57-65.

3887   *Hryniewicz* Wacław, [P] Hope of universal salvation and the drama of human freedom [on the 'animated debate' about his 1989 Hope of salvation for all; from an eschatology of fear to an eschatology of hope (Wsz, Verbinum)] : STV(ars) 33,2 (1995) 91-110; Eng. 110

3888   **Hunt** Boyd, Redeemed! eschatological redemption and the Kingdom of God 1993 → 9.7809; [R]RExp 92 (1995) 114s (W.J. *Hendricks*); SWJT 37,2 (1995) 46 (A.F. *Johnson*).

3889   *Jurčević* Marijan, Anthropology and salvation today: RijT 2 (1994) 275-286 Croatian; Eng. 286.

3890   **Kaiser** Thomas, Versöhnung und Gerechtigkeit; das Konzept der Versöhnung und seine Kritik im Kontext Südafrika : Diss. [D]*Huber* W. Heidelberg 1994. -- TR 91 (1995) 97.

3891   **Kettler** Christian D., The vicarious humanity of Christ and the reality of salvation 1991 → 8,7771 ... 10,7719: [R]RefR 49 (1995s) 74s (B.L. *Wynveen*).

3892   *Kinnear* Malcolm A., Marcus DODS, John McLeod CAMPBELL and the Atonement: SBET 13,1 (1995) 4-14 [NTAb 40,p.17].

3893   *Lewis* Gordon R., *Demarest* Bruce K., Our primary need; Christ's atoning provisions: Integrative Theology 2. GR 1990, Zondervan. 574 p. $ 35. 0-310-39240-3. -- [R]S(co)BET 13 (1995) 76 (Roy *Kearsley*: courageous assault on an impossibly ambitious programme).

3894   *Lies* Lothar, *Heil* Silvia, Heilsmysterium, eine Hinführung zu Christus. Graz 1992, Styria. 351 p. -- [R]HeythJ 36 (1995) 67s (B, R. *Brinkman*, also on NICHOLS A,)

3895   **McDonald** H.D., The New Testament concept of atonement; the gospel of the Calvary event 1994 → 10.7722: [R]ET 106 (1994s) 27 (E. *Franklin*); RefR 49 (1995s) 66 (G. *Wyper*).

3896   *McIntyre* John. The shape of soteriology 1992 → 9,7937; 10,7724: [R]EvQ 67 (1995) 284s (D.A.S. *Fergusson*); S(cot)JTh 48 (1995) 541-3 (G. *McFarlane*).

3897   **Martens** Gottfried, Rechtfertigung .. Interpretament ? 1992 → 9,7939; 10,7725: [R]TR 91 (1995) 150-2 (G.*Wenz*).

3898   **Meadors** Edward P., Jesus the messianic herald of salvation [diss. Aberdeen 1993. [D]*Marshall* I.]; WUNT 2/72. Tü 1995, Mohr. xi-387 p. 3-16-146251.

3899   **Méndez Fernández** Benito, El problema de la salvación de los 'infieles' en Francisco de VITORIA [→ 10,7283*]; desafíos humanos y respuestas teológicas en el contexto del descubrimiento de América. R 1993, Iglesia Nacional Española. 381 p. -- ^RBurg 36 (1995) 250s (E. *Bueno*); CTom 122 (1995) 426s (R. *Hernández*): Lum(Vt) 44 (1995) 331s (U. *Gil Ortega*); RasT 36 (1995) 379-381 (U. *Parente*).

3900 *Mordecai* Huw, The problem of co-inherence; can R.C. MOBERLY [Atonement and personality, '1901'!] bear the burdens of Charles WILLIAMS [He came down from heaven 1938; Descent into Hell 1937]: Theol 98 (L 1995) 456-461.

3901 ^E**Morrone** Fortunato, NEWMAN John H., Che cosa ci salva ? Corso sulla dottrina della giustificazione [Lectures on the doctrine .. 1837]: Già e non ancora 263. Mi 1994, Jaca. 375 p. ^RTer(esianum) 46 (1995) 313 (P. *Boyce*).

3902 *Müller* Wolfgang W., Gotteskindschaft als Paradigma neutestamentlicher Rede vom Heil des Menschen unter den Bedingungen der Neuzeit: ZkT 117 (1995) 59-67; Eng. 67.

3903 **Richard** Ramesh P., The population of Heaven [only explicit believers]. Ch 1994, Moody. 170 p. $ 10. -- ^RBS 152 (1995) 107s (R.A. *Pyne*); p.108s, Richard's critique of C. PINNOCK.

3904 **Sattler** Dorothea, Gelebte Busse; das menschliche Busswerk (satisfactio) im ökumenischen Gespräch 1992 → 8,7290 ... 10,7730: ^RThRv 91 (1995) 342-4 (H. *Vorgrimler*).

3905 *Sayes* José Antonio, El tema de la redención en el Catecismo de la Iglesia Católica: Burgense 35 (1994) 321-348.

3906 *Schreurs* Nico, Eén voor alle anderen; plaatsbekleding als metafoor in de soteriologie: TTh 35 (1995) 3-23; Eng. 23.

3907 *Seidler* Elisabeth, Versöhnung; Prolegomena einer künftigen Soteriologie: FrSZ 42 (1995) 5-45.

3908 **Seifrid** Mark A., Justification by faith .. : NT supp 68, 1992 → 9,7954: ^RJBL 114 (1995) 160-3 (K.P. *Donfried*).

3909 **Seiger** Bernhard, Versöhnung -- Gabe und Aufgabe; eine Untersuchung zur neueren Bedeutungsentwicklung eines theologischen Begriffs: ev. Diss. ^D*Sauter.* Bonn 1995.-- ThRv Beilage 92/2, vii; TLZ 120 (1995) 1146.

3910 **Sesboüé** Bernard, Gesù Cristo l'unico mediatore: saggio sulla redenzione e la salvezza, 2. I racconti della salvezza; soteriologia narrativa [1991 → 9,7794],^T: Prospettive teologiche 12. CinB 1994, Paoline. 424 p.-- ^RLat 61 (1995) 237-9 (I. *Sanna*).

3911 **Sesboüé** Bernard, *Wolinski* Joseph, Le Dieu du salut: Histoire des dogmes 1. P 1994, Desclée. 544 p. F 250. -- ^RÉtudes 382 (1005) 279 (M. *Fédou*).

3912 **Tamez** Elsa, The amnesty of grace; justification by faith from a Latin American perspective, ^T*Ringe* Sharon H., 1993 → 10,7734: ^RProEccl 4 (1995) 243-6 (K.A. *Pasewark*: despite reserves, makes a political interpretation of justification unavoidable).

3913 **Vandevelde** G., Expression de la cohérence du mystère de Dieu et du Salut; la réciprocité dans la 'théologie' et 'l'économie' [diss. Pont. Univ. Gregoriana, ^D*Pelland* G.]; AnGreg 88. R 1993, Univ. Greg. 176 p. -- ^REstTrin 29 (1995) 124 (X. *Pikaza*).

3914 *Vitoria Cormenzana* F. Javier, La soteriología histórica; un modelo a partir de la teología salvadoreña: RLatAmT 11 (1994) 285-305; 12 (1995) 59-78.

3915 **Winter** Michael, The Atonement: Problems in theology. L/ColMn 1995, G.Chapman/Liturgical (Glazier). viii-136 p. £ 12. 0-225-66759-2. -- ^RET 106 (1994s) 344 (M. *Bockmuehl*: how it actually works: purely by intercession, even in the Crucifixion); MilltSt 36 (1995) 131-4 (R. *Moloney*); Tablet 249 (1995) 1584s (E. *Yarnold*: with R. MOLONEY's Eucharist, inaugurates this new series with great promise).

H7.2 *Crux, sacrificium* -- **The Cross, the nature of sacrifice**

3916 *a) Alison* James, El retorno de Abel: la teología como elaboración de historias de vida;-
- *b) Roy* Louis, ¿ Tiene significación universal la muerte de Jesús ? [T]*Loza* José: AnáMnesis
5,2 (1995) 5-18 (18s, bibliografía de René GIRARD] / 21-29.

3917 *Alvarez Cineira* D., Los sacrificios en la Carta a los Hebreos 10,1-18 [tesina del Pont.
Ist. Biblico, [D]*Vanhoye* A.; 'prescinde' del problema de GIRARD R./violencia]: EstAg 30
(1995) 5-59 . 207-237.

3918 **Bailie** Gil, Violence unveiled; humanity at the crossroads [pref. *Girard* René: my ideas
'have never looked better than they do here']. NY 1995, Crossroad. xvii-293 p. 0-8245-
1464-5.

3919 **Barth** Gerhard, Il significato della morte di Gesù Cristo; l'interpretazione del Nuovo
Testamento: PiccBtT 38. T 1995, Claudiana. vii-259 p. L[m] 32. 88-7016-223-0.

3920 *Baudry* P., La violence ritualisée une dynamique tensionnelle: Religiologiques 10
(1994) 247-254 [< ZIT 95,p.69].

3921 *Bekker* C.J., *Nortjé* S., Die gebruik van die 'offer' van Isak as 'n motief vir die
verkondiging van Jesus as die lydende Christus: HTS 51 (1995) 454-464 [NTAb 40, p.270].

3922 *Berquist* J.L., What does the Lord require ? OT child sacrifice and NT Christology:
Encounter 55,2 (1994) 107-128 [NTAb 39, p.77].

3923 *Boys* Mary C., The Cross: should a symbol betrayed be redeemed?: CCurr 44 (1944s)
5-27.

3924 *Bradbury* Scott, Julian's pagan revival and the decline of blood sacrifice: Phoenix 49
(Tor 1995) 331-356.

3925 **Bradley** Ian, The power of sacrifice [basically liturgical, but unguardedly merging
senses like 'self-sacrificingly']. L 1995, Darton-LT. 328 P. £ 12. 0-232-52057-7.-- [R]ET
106,10 top choice (1994s) 289 (C.S. *Rodd*).

3926 **Brown** Raymond E., Death of the Messiah 1994 → 2103 above; 10,4634: [R]BZ 39
(1995) 125-7 (H.-J. *Klauck*); CBQ 57 (1995) 797-800 (D. *Senior*).

3927 **Chilton** Bruce, The temple of Jesus; his sacrificial program 1992 → 8,4361 ... 10,7755:
[R]CritRR 7 (1994) 160-3 (R. *Hamerton-Kelly:* reinforces without accepting GIRARD).

3928 *Chilton* Bruce, The hungry knife [.. Gen 22]; towards a sense of sacrifice : → 159,
[F]ROGERSON, J., Bible/Society; JSOT.s 200 (1995) 122-138.

3929 *Dinkler-von Schubert* Erika, Nomen ipsum crucis absit (CICERO Rab. 5,16); zur
Abschaffung der Kreuzigungsstrafe in der Antike: Gym 102 (1995) 225-241; pl. XXIV.

3930 *Duff* Paul B., René GIRARD in Corinth; an early Christian social crisis and a biblical
text of persecution [1 Cor 5,1-6]: Helios 22,1 (Lubbock TX 1995) 79-99 [< NTAb 39,
p.427].

3931 *García Martínez* Francisco, La salvación como revelación del mecanismo victimal de
la cultura de la violencia; en torno a la soteriología de R. GIRARD : EstTrin 28 (1994) 63-86.

3932 *Genest* Olivette, Le Temple de Jérusalem et ses rites dans le discours des épîtres et de
l'Apocalypse sur la mort de Jésus; → 10,30,[F]COUTURIER G., Maison 1994, 365-387.

3933 *Gerlitz* Peter, Opfer, religionsgeschichtlich: → 772, TRE 25 (1995) 253-8 (-267,
Seebass H.,AT; 270,*Stemberger* G.,Judentum; 271-8,*Young* Frances M., NT,[T]*Schäferdiek* K).

3934 **Girard** René, 'Quand ces choses commencent ...'. P 1994, Arlet. 149 p. F 100. --
[R]NRT 117 (1995) 426-432 (P. *Gardeil*).

3935 *Gorgulho* Gilberto, La religión de la violencia y el evangelio: Revista de interpretación bíblica latinoamericana 10 (1991) 21-26 [favors GIRARD]: CBQ 57 (1995) 510].

3936 *Greer* Rowan A., Christ the victor and the victim: ConcordiaTQ 59 (1995) 1-30.

3937 **Hamerton-Kelly** R.G., Sacred violence 1992 → 8,7824 ... 10,7750: [R]*CritRR 7 (1994) 196-8 (C.B. *Cousar*: he has to make Rom 9-11 a 'myth of scapegoating' which Paul clings to out of nostalgia).

3938 **Hamerton-Kelly** Robert G., The Gospel and the Sacred; poetics of violence in Mark 1994 → 10,4761: [R]CBQ 57 (1995) 809s (L.E. *Vaage*; stands or, perhaps chiefly, falls with GIRARD).

3939 **Heesterman** J.C., The broken world of [ancient India] sacrifice. Ch 1993, Univ. x-296 p. $ 60; pa. $ 25. -- [R]JRel 75 (1995) 159-161 (F.X. *Clooney*).

3940 *a) Hicks* John M., What did Christ accomplish on the Cross ? Atonement in CAMPBELL [A.], STONE [B.] & SCOTT [W., all c. 1830];-- *b) Burns-Watson* Roger, The role of women; a study of Stone-Campbell movement journals : LexTQ 30 (1995) 145-170 / 171-192 [29,2 (1994) 75-139, *al.*, 'The Stone-Campbell movement in Kentucky']

3941 *Holoubek* Joe E, & Alice B., both M.D., A study of death by crucifixion with attempted explanation of the death of Jesus Christ: LinacreQ 61,1 (1994) 10-19.

3942 **Hooker** Morna D., Not ashamed .. NT death of Christ 1988/94 → 10,7761: [R]ET 106,3, 2d-top choice (1994s) 66s (C.S. *Rodd*).

3943 *Kittel* Gisela, Die biblische Rede vom Sühnopfer Christi und ihre unsere Wirklichkeit erschliessende Kraft: JBTh 9 (1994) 285-313.

3944 **Krupp** Michael, Den Sohn opfern ? Die Isaak-Überlieferung bei Juden, Christen und Muslimen. Gü 1995, Kaiser. 91 p. DM 38. 3-579-00289-9 [< OTA 19, p.170].

3945 **Levenson** Jon D., The death and resurrection of the beloved son .. child-sacrifice 1993 → 9,7998; 10,7766 [RStR 22,10-20, I. *Strenski*, also on 6 cognates]: [R]BiRe 11,1 (1995) 14s (R.S. *Hendel*); *CritRR 8 (1995) 103-7 (J.G. *Williams*: GIRARD better); CrossCur 45 (1995s) 132.4.6.8 (J. *Cunneen*); Dialog 34,1 (St. Paul 1995) 52-66 (T. *Peters* .. R. *Girard, al.*) [NTAb 39, p.441]; JRel 75 (1995) 262s (W. *Moberly*); *ProEc 4 (1995) 492-4 (R.J. *Daly*); TTod 51 (1994s) 295-7 (W. *Brueggemann*).

3946 *Luke* K., Sacrifice in the Old Testament: LivWo 100 (1994) 258-268 [< OTA 19].

3947 *Meissner* Stefan, Paulinische Soteriologie und die 'Aqedat Jitzchaq': Jud(aica) 51 (1995) 33-49.

3948 **Menke** Karl-Heinz, Stellvertretung 1991 → 8.7777: [R]TR 91 (1995) 240-4, R. *Schulte*].

Moore Stephen D., Poststructuralism .. DERRIDA & FOUCAULT at the foot of the Cross → 1370 supra.

3949 [E]**Niewiadomski** Józef, *Palaver* Wolfgang, Dramatische Erlösungslehre [SCHWAGER R., GIRARD R.] 1991/2 → 9,602; 10,7773: [R]ActuBbg 31 (1994) 241s (J. *Boada*); AugR 34 (1994) 248s (B. *Studer*); TPQ 143 (1995) 432s.435 (R. *Siebenrock*); ZkT 117 (1995) 218-220 (M. *Reus Canals*).

3950 *Niewiadomski* Józef. Das Jesus-Drama und der Teufelskreis der Gewalt; zur Theologie von Raymund SCHWAGER [.. GIRARD R.]: → 407, Markierungen 1995, 119-157.

3951 **Palaver** Wolfgang, Politik und Religion bei Thomas HOBBES .. aus der Sicht R. GIRARDs 1991 → 7,7765; 8,7836: [R]MilltSt 36 (1995) 153-7 (P. *Riordan*).

3952 *Pötscher* Walter, *Ostea leuka*; zur Formation und Struktur des olympischen Opfers: GrazB 11 (1995) 19-46; Eng, vi.

3953 [E]**Quaegebeur** Jan, Ritual and sacrifice in the Ancient Near East 1991/3 → 9,949: [R](Tü)TQ 175 (1995) 226s (H. *Niehr*).

3954 **Rosivach** Vincent J., The system of public sacrifice in fourth-century Athens: AmCSt 34. Atlanta 1994, Scholars. X-171 p. $ 30; pa. $ 20. 1-55540-942-3; 943-1. -- [R]AnCL 64 (1995) 393s (J. *Labarbe*).

3955 *Sandnes* Karl Olaf, The death of Jesus for human sins; the historical basis for a theological concept: Theology and Life 15s (Hong Kong 1993) 45-52.

3956 [E]**Schenk** Richard, Zur Theorie des Opfers: ein interdisziplinäres Gespräch [Hannover, Collegium Philosophicum 6.XI.1993]. Stu 1995, Frommann-Holzboog. -- [R]AnáMnesis 5,2 (1995s) 136s (G. *Chico*).

3957 [E]**Schenker** Adrian, Studien zu Opfer und Kult im AT 1990/2 → 8,491: [R]VT 45 (1995) 420 (P.P. *Jenson*).

3958 *Selman* Martin J., Sacrifice in the Ancient Near East → **8**, [F]BAKER J., Sacrifice 1995, 88-104 [< OTA 19, p.9 & 138].

3959 *Sequeri* Pierangelo, Il tragico nell'esistenza e la teologia crucis: Teol(Br) 19 (1994) 311-339.

3960 Sobre idolos y sacrificios; René GIRARD con teólogos de la liberación. San José CR, 1991, Dep. Ecuménico [favorable: CBQ 57 (1995) 810].

3961 *Sobrino* Jon, *a)* La pascua de Jesús y la revelación de Dios desde la perspectiva de las victimas [= SalTer 83 (1995) 205-219]; -- *b)* La teología y el 'principio liberación': RLatAmT 12 (1995) 79-91 / 115-1.

3962 *Sonderegger* Katherine, Must Christ suffer to redeem ? The doctrine of vicarious atonement in SCHLEIERMACHER & BAECK: *ZnTg 2 (1995) 175-192; deutsch 175

3963 *a) Stegemann* Wolfgang, Der Tod Jesu als Opfer ? Anthropologische Aspekte seiner Deutung im NT;-- *b) Track* Joachim, Das Opfer am Ende; eine kritische Analyse zum Opferverständnis in der christlichen Theologie: → 445, Abschied ? 1995. 120-139 / 140-167 [96-119, *Utzschneider* Helmut, Lev 4s *ḥaṭṭa]*

3964 *Stubenrauch* Bertram, Die Menschheit Jesu als Schlüssel zur Heilsbedeutsamkeit des Kreuzes; ein Brückenschlag vom Dogma zum Kerygma: MThZ 46 (1995) 345-54.

3965 [E]**Sykes** S.W., Sacrifice and redemption 1991 → 7,384 ... 10,7780: [R]EvQ 67 (1995) 374s (R.T. *Beckwith*).

3966 **Torrance** Thomas F., The mediation of Christ [1983 + new Atonement and Trinity] 1992 → 9,7964: [R]EvQ 66 (1994) 361s (T. *Hart*).

3967 *Trout* Dennis, Christianizing the [PAULINUS Carmen 20] Nolan countryside] animal sacrifice at the tomb of St. Felix: JEarlyC 3 (1995) 281-298.

3968 *Van Dam* C., The origin and character of sacrifice in Scripture: MidAmJT 7 (1991) 3-16 [< OTA 18 (1995) p. 366].

3969 *a) Wenham* Gordon J., The Akedah, a paradigm of sacrifice [Gen 22]; -- *b) Meyers* Carol, An ethnoarchaeological analysis of Hannah's sacrifice [1 Sam 1,24];-- *c) Hendel* Ronald S., Prophets, priests, and the efficacy of ritual: → 130, [F]MILGROM J., Pomegranates 1995, 93-102 / 77-91 / 185-198.

3970 **Williams** James G., The Bible, violence, and the sacred; liberation from the myth of sanctioned violence → 8,7847; 9,8008 [RStR 22,240, J.M. *Hallman*].-- [R]*CritRR 7 (1994) 95-97 (M.J. *Desjardins*); JAAR 63 (1995) 186-190 (N. *Elliott*); S(cot)JTh 48 (1995) 408s (G. *Pattison*); TorJT 11 (1995) 232-4 (L.E. *Vaage*: no viable answers).

3971 *a) Williams* James G., Sacrifice and the beginning of kingship (response *Krondorfer* Björn); -- *b) McNutt* Paula M., The Kenites, the Midianites, and the Rechabites (response *Benjamin* Don C.): Semeia 67 ('Transformations, passages, and processes; ritual approaches to biblical texts'1994)73-92(93-107)/109-132(-45).

H7.4 **Sacramenta**, *Gratia*

3972 **Adam** Adolf, The eucharistic celebration; the source and summit of faith, [T]*Schultz* Robert C. ColMn 1994, Liturgical. xvi-135 p. $13. 0-8146-6123-8 [< ThD 42 (1995) 255].

3973 **Arnau** Ramónë, Tratado general de los sacramentos: SapFidei 4. M 1994, BAC. 372 p. -- [R]Ter(esianum) 46 (1995) 279 (J. *Castellano*).

3974 *a) Bajorski* Adam, [P] The Eucharistic liturgy of Lima, The Feast of Life with special reference to the Epiclesis; -- *b) Jaskóla* Piotr, [P] John CALVIN's teaching on the Lord's Supper: R(ocz)T(Lub) 42,7 (1995) 151-163; deutsch 163s / 87-101; deutsch 101s.

3975 **Bishop** Jonathan, Some bodies; the Eucharist 1992 → 10.4587: [R]CritRR 7 (1994) 487-491 (R.A. *Badham*: elegant prose, not for specialists).

3976 **Bourgeois** Henri, *al.*, Les signes du salut: Histoire des dogmes 3. P 1995, Desclée. 666 p. F 250. -- [R]Études 383 (1995) 426 (P. *Vallin*).

3977 *a) Burgaleta* Jesús, Celebrar la comunión excluyendo a 'algunos' ? -- *b) Díaz Marcos* Cipriano & *Saborido* José Luis, Uso y abuso de la palabra en la Eucaristía: SalTer 83 (1995) 367-376 / 377-396.

3978 *Butler* Sara, In persona Christi: a reponse to Dennis M. FERRARA: TS 56 (1995) 61-80: 81-91 rejoinder.

3979 **Caba** José, Cristo, pan de vida: BAC 531, 1993 → 9,5582: [R]Ter(esianum) 46 (1995) 35s (V. *Pasquetto*).

3980 **Capdevila y Montaner** Vicenç-María, Liberación y divinización del hombre; teología de la gracia, 2. estudio sistemático. S 1994, Secr. Trin. 618 p. -- [R]Burg 36 (1995) 568-570 (C. *García*).

3981 **Chauvet** Louis-Marie, Symbol and sacrament; a sacramental reinterpretation of Christian experience, [T]*Madigan* Patrick, *Beaumont* Madeleine: Pueblo. ColMn 1995, Liturgical. xvii-568 p. $ 40. 0-8146-6124-6 [ThD 42,359].

3982 **Chilton** Bruce, A feast of meanings; Eucharistic theologies: NT supp. 72, 1994 → 10,4589: [R]Biblica 76 (1995) 579-582 (R.F. *O'Toole*); *CritRR 8 (1995) 188-191 (C. *Koester*); JThS 46 (1995) 634-6 (J.C. *O'Neill*); StPat(av) 42 (1995) 558-562 (G. *Segalla*).

3983 *Clendenin* Daniel B., Partakers of divinity; the Orthodox doctrine of *théōsis*: JETS 37 (1994) 365-379.

3984 **Cocksworth** Christopher J., Evangelical eucharistic thought in the Church of England [downplayed by Evangelicals since Tractarianism]. C 1993, Univ. xiv-383 p. -- [R]S(cot)JTh 48 (1995) 265s (B.D. *Spinks*).

3985 *Colombo* Giuseppe, La transustanziazione: TeolBr 20 (1995) 8-32; Eng. 33.

3986 *a) Cuvillier* Elian, Le baptême chrétien dans le NT; -- *b) Gounelle* Rémi, Le baptême aux temps patristiques; le cas de la Tradition apostolique; -- *c) Gounelle* André, Pédobaptisme; le débat au XVIe siècle: ETRel 70 (1995) 161-177 / 179-189 / 191-206 (259-262 sur P. GISEL 1994).

3987 **David** Kenith A., Sacrament and struggle. L 1994, WCC. 142 p. £ 7.25. 2-8254-1143-4. -- [R]E(xp)T 107 (1995s) 93 (G.W.S. *Knowles*: warns of too narrowly ecclesiastical framework).

3988 *Ferguson* E., Early Church penance: RestQ 26 (1994) 81-100 [NTAb 39, p.118].

3989 *Freyer* Thomas, 'Transsubstantiation' versus 'Transfinalisation/Transsignifikation' ? Bemerkungen zu einer aktuellen Debatte: Cath 49 (1995) 174-195.

3990 **Greshake** Gisbert, Geschenkte Freiheit ... Gnadenlehre[2] 1991 → 8,7872*b: [R]MüTZ 45 (1994) 94s (G.L. *Müller*).

3991 *Hahn* Ferdinand, Das Herrenmahl im NT; sein Verständnis in Geschichte und Gegenwart der Kirche: Entschluss 50,2 (1995) 4-8.

3992 **Henson** John, Other communions of Jesus [beside the Last Supper which we focus too exclusively]. Cardiff c. 1994, Stantonbury Parish. 85 p. £ 5. -- ᴿE(xp)T 107 (1995s) 92s (G.W.S. *Knowles*).

3992* *a) Jeanes* Gordon, Baptism portrayed as martyrdom in the early Church: -- *b) Vellian* Jacob, The development of the baptismal font in the Syro-Malabar church: StLi(turgica) 23 (1993) 158-176 / 24 (1994) 145-9.

3993 **Légasse** Simon, Naissance du baptême; LDiv 153, 1993 → 9,8047; 10,7809: ᴿPOrC 45 (1995) 287 (B.T. *Viviano*: neither from mystery-initiation rites nor from Jewish proselyte-baptism, but from John's influence); RB 102 (1995) 600-811 (É. *Nodet*).

3994 *a) Légasse* Simon, L'eau du baptême d'après le NT; -- *b) Beaude* Pierre-M., Les eaux qui tuent et qui sauvent: VS.s 148 (1994) 447-459 / 437-445

3995 **Levesque** Paul J., Symbol as the primary religious category in the thought of Louis DUPRÉ; foundations for contemporary sacramentology: diss. Leuven 1995, ᴰ*Leijssen* L. cxlv-377 p. -- LouvSt 20 (1995) 417.

3996 **Lies** Lothar, Sakramententheologie 1990 → 6,7833 ... 9,8048: ᴿThRv 91 (1995) 418 (R. *Schulte*, auch über TABORDA F. 1988].

3997 **McAdoo** H.R., *Stevenson* Kenneth, The mystery of the Eucharist in the Anglican tradition. .. 1995, Canterbury. 205 p. £ 10. 1-85311-113-9. -- ᴿE(xp)T 107 (1995s) 92 (B.D. *Spinks*).

3998 *McGowan* Andrew, 'First regarding the cup ...'; PAPIAS and the diversity of early Eucharistic practice: JThS 46 (1995) 551-5.

3999 **McPartlan** Paul, The Eucharist .. DE LUBAC/ZIZIOULAS 1993 → 9,4824: 10,4607: ᴿAmerica 173,27 (1995) 27-29 (K.B. *Osborne*, also on SOKOLOWSKI R.); Greg 76 (1995) 172-4 (A. *Antón*); JThS 46 (1995) 423-6 (A. *Louth*); MilltSt 34 (1994) 151-3 (C. *O'Donnell*); MoTh 11 (1995) 475s (J.L. *Mangina*); StVlad 39 (1995s) 107-112 (A. *Smith*).

4000 **Macy** Gary, The banquet's wisdom 1992 → 8,4981; 9,4825: ᴿChH 64(1995) 291s (R.L. *Harrison*: exceptionally successful).

4001 *Magne* Jean, Deux mythes [création → baptême, eucharistie] et deux rites à l'origine du christianisme: CRen 190 (1995) 67-92.

4002 *Martínez Cavero* M., Matrimonio-sacramento, bautismo y matrimonio creacional: RET 55 (1995) 487-531.

4003 *Martos* Joseph, A new conceptual context for the sacramentality of marriage: Horizons 22 (1995) 215-236.

4004 *Meier* John P., The Eucharist at the Last Supper; did it happen ? [Kenrick Lecture, St. Louis Seminary, March 31, 1995]: ThD 42 (1995) 335-351.

4005 *Navarra Girón* María Ángeles, La eucaristía, memorial del sacrificio de Cristo en la primera controversia eucarística (s.ix): RET 55 (1995) 29-63 . 135-179.

4006 **Oden** Thomas C., The transforming power of grace 1993 → 9,8054: ᴿ*ProEc 4 (1995) 494-6 (R. *Cessario*).

4007 *a) O'Neill* J.C., Bread and wine [not of Passover origin]; -- *b) Ford* David F., What happens in the Eucharist: S(cot)JTh 48 (1995) 169-184 / 359-381.

4008 **Paprocki** Henryk, Le mystère de l'Eucharistie; genèse et interprétation de la liturgie eucharistique byzantine. P 1993, Cerf. iii-555 p. -- ᴿOrChr 79 (1995) 233-6 (R.J. *Taft*).

4009 **Perham** Michael, Lively sacrifice -- the Eucharist in the Church of England today. L 1992, SPCK. xii-208 p. £ 10. -- ᴿS(cot)JTh 48 (1995) 402-4 (K. *Stevenson*).

4010 **Power** David N., The Eucharistic mystery; revitalizing the tradition 1992 → 8,4996 ... 10,4611: ᴿWW 15 (1995) 236 . 238s.

4011 **Prades** Javier, 'Deus .. per gratiam ': AnGreg 261, 1993 → 10,7818: ᴿBurg 36 (1995) 570-2 (C. *García*).

4012 *Roux G.* Rodolfo E. de, La mesa del resucitado y exaltado; manifestación del Señor presente y actuante en su Iglesia: TX 109 (1994) 7-33.

4013 **Sayes** J.A., La gracia de Cristo 1993 → 10,7820: ᴿBurgense 35 (1994) 296s (*Garrudo*); NRT 117 (1995) 749s (L. *Renwart*).

4014 ᴱ**Schreiner** Thomas R., *Ware* Bruce A., John CALVIN, Grace of God, the bondage of the will. GR 1995, Baker. 248 p. 0-8010-2002-6.

4015 *Schulz* Frieder, Ministerium reconciliationis; evangelische Marginalien zu einer katholischen Darstellung der Feiern der Umkehr und Versöhnung: AL(tg)W 37 (1995) 68-86.

4016 *Schwank* Benedikt, Die neutestamentlichen Wurzeln unserer heutigen Sakramentenpastoral: E(rbe)uA 71 (1995) 41-53.

4017 *Seidl* Horst, Zum Substanzbegriff der katholischen Transsubstantiationslehre: ForKT 11 (1995) 1-16.

4018 **Slenczka** Notger, Realpräsenz und Ontologie; Untersuchung der ontologischen Grundlagen der Transsignifikationslehre: ForSysÖT 66, 1993 → 9,4832; 10, 4616: ᴿThLZ 120 (1995) 1117-20 (A. *Schilson*).

4019 *a) Sloyan* Gerard S., Do Catholics understand the Sacraments ? ; -- *b) Ciangio* Donna L., Small Christian communities ? : Church 11,3 (NY 1995) 12-17 / 5-10.

4020 *a) Söding* Thomas, Das Mahl des Herrn; zur Gestalt und Theologie der ältesten nachösterlichen Tradition; -- *b) Reiser* Marius, Eucharistische Wissenschaft; eine exegetische Betrachtung zu Joh 6,26-59: → 177, ᶠSCHNEIDER T., Vorgeschmack 1995, 134-163 / 164-177 [ThRv 91,365].

4021 **Sokolowski** Robert, Eucharistic presence; a study in the theology of disclosure 1994 → 10,4618; pa. $ 15: ᴿ*CWeal 122, (1995) 26-28 (J. *Garvey*); TS 56 (1995) 801s (J.F. *Baldovin*).

4022 *Spinks* Bryan D., CALVIN's baptismal theology and the making of the Strasbourgh and Genevan baptismal liturgies 1540 and 1542: S(cot)JTh 48 (1995) 55-78.

4023 *Splett* Jörg, Gnade; zu einem Grundbegriff -- philosophisch: ZkT 117 (1995) 152-166; Eng. 166.

4024 **Stevenson** Kenneth, [Eucharistic] Covenant of grace renewed 1994 → 10,4619: ᴿE(xp)T 107 (1995s) 92 (C. *Irvine*).

4025 *Tavard* George H., For a dialogue on sacraments: OneInC 31 (1995) 122-145.

4026 *Triacca* A.M., Tradiciones sacramentarias occidental y oriental; originalidad y reciprocidad: Phase 34 (1994) 265-296.

4027 ᴱ**Turner** Paul, Sources of Confirmation, from the Fathers through the Reformers. ColMn 1993, Liturgical. 96 p. $ 7. 0-8146-2006-X. -- ᴿ*JEarlyC 3 (1995) 61s (Joanne M. *Pierce*).

4028 **Vogel** Arthur A. (Episcopal bishop), Radical Christianity and the flesh of Jesus; the roots of Eucharistic living. GR 1995, Eerdmans. vi-143 p. $ 17 pa. 0-8028-0881-6 [NTAb 40, p.548; *TBR 9/1,27, P. *Doble*].

4029 **Vorgrimler** H., Teologia dei sacramenti [1987 ³1992], ᵀ *Della Mutta* R.: GdT 212. Brescia 1992, Queriniana. 442 p. Lᵐ 38. -- ᴿAsprenas 42 (1995) 127s (G. *Di Napoli*).

4030 *Wollbold* Andreas, Sakrament des Anfangs: eine Zwischenbilanz zur Taufpastoral: TrierTZ 104 (1995) 256-271.

4031   *Wolterstorff* Nicholas, Not presence but action; CALVIN on sacraments: (Reformed) Perspectives 9,3 (1994) 16-22.
4032   *Zilles* Urbano, O sacramento da Ordem: Teocomunicação 25 (1995) 233-271.
4033   **Žitnik** Maksimilian, Sacramenta, bibliographia internationalis 1992 → 8,7908 ... 10,7827: ᴿTR 91 (1995) 346s (B. *Kranemann*).

H7.6   *Ecclesiologia, theologia missionis, laici* -- **The Church**

4034   **Ackley** John R., The Church of the Word; a comparative study of Word, Church, and office in the thought of Karl RAHNER and Gerhard EBELING: AmUSt7/81. NY ᴰ1993, P. Lang. 500 p. $ 65. 0-8204-1389-5. -- ᴿConcordJ 11 (1995) 113s (D.A. *Lumpp*).
4035   *a) Alvarez Bolado* Alfonso, Nuevos horizontes de la misión; -- *b) Fernández Martos* José M., Retratos con paisaje; ventana abierta al mundo: Manresa 67 (1995) 237-248 / 219-226.
4036   *Barilier* Roger, 'Sacerdoce universel' ou 'sacerdoce commun' ? : RRéf 46.4 (1995) 39-50.
4037   **Barnes** Elizabeth B., The story of discipleship; Christ, humanity, and Church in narrative perspective. Nv 1995, Abingdon. 176 p. 0-687-39657-3.
4038   **Beilner** Wolfgang, Kirche nach dem Neuen Testament: Vermittlung 31. Salzburg 1995.
4039   *a) Bennett* John, Small churches; insignificant you are not; *b) (8 pastors)*, Small is beautiful: Disciple 132,2 (St. Louis 1994) 4-7 / 8-11.
4040   ᴱ**Berentsen** Jan-Martin, *al.*, Missiologi i dag. Oslo 1994, Univ. 486 p. Nk 447. -- ᴿIchthys 22 (1995) 143s (L.M. *Christensen*),
4041   ᴱ**Bianchi** Eugene C., *Ruether* Rosemary R., A democratic Catholic Church 1993 → 9,8080; 10,7835: ᴿ*ProEccl 4 (1995) 238-240 (W.T *Cavanaugh*: would not serve the desired goal).
4042   **Blei** Karel, On being the Church across frontiers; a vision of Europe today. Geneva 1992, WCC. 81 p. -- ᴿ(NES)ThRev 16 (1995) 62-67 (C. *Chimelli*).
4043   *Bleyenberg* Ursula, 'Im einen Leib seiner Kirche'; zum Verhältnis von Eucharistie und Kirche bei IGNATIUS von Antiochien: T(rier)ThZ 104 (1995) 106-124.
4044   **Bosch** David J., Transforming mission 1992 → 7,7851 ... 10,7836: ᴿEvQ 67 (1995) 186-190 (J.H. *Marshall*); RestQ 37 (1995) 184-6 (R. *Oltmanns*).
4045   *a) Bovon* François, The Church in the New Testament, servant and victorious; -- *b) Carlson* R.W., The transfiguration of power: ExAu 10 (1994) 43-54 / 87-103.
4046   **Brown** Raymond E., Le chiese degli Apostoli; indagine esegetica sulle origini dell'ecclesiologia. CasM 1992, Piemme. 189 p. Lᵐ 30. -- ᴿSBF*LA 45 (1995) 621-5 (A.M. *Buscemi*).
4047   *Bueno* Eloy, La misión hoy; aspectos teológicos: Burgense 35 (1994) 349-379.
4048   **Calvez** J.-Y., *Tincq* H., L'Église pour la démocratie. P 1992, Centurion. 219 p. -- ᴿTelema 20 (1994) 93s (J.-C. *Djerke*).
4049   *Cavanaugh* William T., The ecclesiologies of Medellín and the lessons of the base communities: CCurr 44 (1944s) 67-84.
4050   **Conigliaro** Francesco, Un gioco senza regole; chiesa-eschaton, potere-persona. Palermo 1992, Augustinus. 237 p. -- ᴿRTPh 127 (1995) 191 (J.-N. *Aletti*: examine avec respect et courage le fonctionnement de l'autorité dans l'Église catholique romaine).

4051 *Cornwall* Robert D., The ministry of reconciliation; toward a balanced understanding of the global mission of the Christian Church (Disciples of Christ) : LexTQ 30 (1995) 1-28.

4052 **Cornwall** Robert D., Visible and apostolic 1993 → 10,7844: ᴿSewaneeT 38 (1994s) 192-4 (W.S. *Stafford*).

4053 *Decker* Rodney J., The Church's relationship to the New Covenant: : BS 152 (1995) 290-305 . 431-456.

4054 **Delpero** Claudio, La credibilità de la Iglesia ieri, oggi, domani. R 1994, Glossa. 160 p. -- ᴿTer(esianum) 46 (1995) 302s (A. *Alvarez Suárez:* no el sin fin de problemas estancos, sino nuevos horizontes).

4055 *Denaux* Adelbert, Heeft Jezus de kerk gesticht ? : CVl 25 (1995) 341-360.

4056 **Dentin** Pierre, Peuple de prêtres 1992 → 8,7929*: ᴿTéléma 19 (1993) 90s (M. *Kayisiré*).

4057 *a) DeSiano* Frank P., The legacy of the 'non-Catholic' missions [special 'revival' sermon-occasions]; -- *b) Sirico* Robert A., Reflections on marketplace ministry: Journal of Paulist Studies 1 (1992) 19-39 / 62-69 . 72s (70s, reply, *Cary* Robert M.).

4058 **Dharmaraj** Jacob S., Colonialism and Christian mission; post-colonial reflections. Delhi 1993, ISPCK. 149 p. rs 75. -- ᴿA(sia)JT 9 (1995) 412-4 (F.J. *Balasundaram*).

4059 **Dianich** Severino, Ecclesiologia; questioni di metodo e una proposta. Mi 1993, Paoline. 262 p. Lᵐ 25. : ᴿTS 56 (1995) 178s (J.A, *Komonchak*).

4060 *Donneaud* Henry, Note sur l'Église [pour, par, et] comme communion dans le Catéchisme de l'Église catholique: RThom 95 (1995) 665-671

4061 **Esquerda Bifet** Juan, Teología de la evangelización; curso de misionología. M 1995, BAC. xviii-491 p. 84-7914-161-1. -- ᴿVSVD 36 (1995) 308-310 (H. *Rzepkowski*).

4062 **Faber** Eva-Maria, Kirche -- Gottes Weg und die Träume der Menschen. Wü 1994, Echter. 168 p. DM 28. 3-429-01607-X. -- ᴿThGL 85 (1995) 559s (J. *Meyer zu Schlochtern*).

4063 *Fabris* Rinaldo, La Chiesa di Cristo e il suo rapporto con la storia; confronto con I testi del NT: (R)*StEc 12 (Venezia 1994) 99-105.

4064 **Faivre** Alexandre, Os leigos nas origens da Igreja, ᵀ*Reis* Orlando dos. Petrópolis 1992, Vozes. 247 p. -- ᴿREB 55 (1995) 983-5 (H. *Lepargneur*).

4065 **Famerée** J., L'ecclesiologie de Yves CONGAR: BEThL 107, 1992 → 8,7939 ... 10,7855: ᴿGreg 76 (1995) 172s (A. *Antón*); LavalThP 51 (1995) 691-3 (G. *Routhier*).

4066 *Feilzer* Heinz, Leben in der Kirche; Erinnerungen -- Wandlungen -- Hoffnungen: TrierTZ 104 (1995) 241-255.

4067 **Forte** Bruno, La Chiesa della Trinità; saggio sul mistero della Chiesa, comunione e missione. CinB 1995, S. Paolo. 386 p. Lᵐ 34. ᴿCivCatt 146 (1995,4) 200s (A. *Barruffo*); VivH 6 (1995) 201s (S. *Dianich*).

4068 **Garijo-Guembe** Miguel M., Communion of the saints; foundation, nature, and structure of the Church, [German] ᵀ*Madigan* Patrick, 1994 → 10,7858: ᴿTS 56 (1995) 797-9 (Judith A. *Merkle:* ecumenical).

4069 **George** Carl F., Prepare your church for the future ['meta-church' stressing lay-led small groups]. GR 1991, Baker/Revell. -- ᴿConcordiaTQ 59 (1995) 219-224 (Fort Wayne 'faculty statement': menaces mission, evangelism, and worship; reflects unhappy *ecclesiolae* of Pietism).

4070 **Giles** Kevin, What on earth is the Church ? A biblical and theological inquiry. L 1995, SPCK. x-310 p.; bibliog, 388-399. 0-281-04842-7.

4071 **Gomes Barbosa** M.J., I Igreja como comunhão, à luz das noções de 'mistério / sacramento' e de 'povo de Deus' no Concilio Vaticano II e no Sínodo extraordinario dos Bispos de 1985. Porto 1990, Univ. Católica Portuguesa. 173 p. -- [R]Salmanticensis 42 (1995) 155-8 (F. *Rodríguez Garrapucho*).

4072 **Grandjean** M., Laïcs dans l'Église. P 1994, Beauchesne. 434 p. -- [R]ATG(ran) 58 (1995) 443 (J.A. *Estrada*).

4073 *Grappe* Christian, Cène, baptême et ecclésiologie du Nouveau Temple: RHPhR 75 (1995) 35-43; Eng. 149.

4074 *Grings* Dadeus, bispo, A Romanidade da Igreja: Teocomunicação 25 (1995) 589-610.

4075 **Gromada** Conrad T., The theology of mission in the 'Lima Document': a Roman Catholic critique. SF 1995, International Scholars. xv-525. $ 65; pa. $ 45. 1-883255-97-X; -6-1 [< ThD 43,270].

4076 *Hahn* Ferdinand, Geschichte des Urchristentums als Missionsgeschichte: ZM(iss)R 79 (1995) 87-96.

4077 **Hall** Douglas J., The Church and its ministry; responding to the changing context in worship, preaching, education, outreach: CThMi 22 (1995) (405-) 426-433 (-450, responses).

4078 *Hauerwas* Stanley, What could it mean for the Church to be Christ's body ?: S(cot)JTh 48 (1995) 1-22.

4079 a) *Hauser Borel* Silvie, Alcune riflessioni sulla storia, la memoria, la dimenticanza, il perdono e la Chiesa nella Bibbia; -- b) *Hauser* Martin, Koinonia e memoria ecclesiale; alcuni punti sistematici di riferimento: (R)*StEc 13 (Venezia 1995) 227-242; Eng. 242 / 159-165; Eng. 165s.

4080 [E]**Hauser** Martin, *al.*, Unsichtbare oder sichtbare Kirche (FrB Univ 1990-1 Gastvor-lesungen): FbZ ÖB 20. FrS 1992, Univ. 100 p. -- [R]ThZ 51 (1995) 90s (K. *Hummer*).

4081 a) *Hearne* Brian, Mission, ecumenism and fundamentalism; -- b) *Kealy* Sean P., Christ's mission; hope to a broken world: AfER 37 (1995) 105-113 / 123-132.

4082 **Hebblethwaite** Margaret, Base communities; an introduction 1994 → 10,7863; 0-8091-3409-8: [R]TBR 8,1 (1995s) 37 (J.A. *Kirk*).

4083 **Hemphill** Kenneth, The Antioch effect; eight characteristics of highly effective churches [growth]. Nv 1994, Broadman & H. 217 p. $ 18. -- [R]SWJT 37,3 (1995) 48s (Ebbie C. *Smith*).

4084 **Hinton** Jeanne, Walking in the same direction; a new way of being Church: Risk book 67. Geneva 1995, WCC. x-106 p. $ 9.50 pa. 2-8254-1160-4 [ThD 43,171].

4085 *Hünermann* Peter, Volk Gottes -- katholische Kirche -- Gemeinde; Dreiheit und Einheit in der Ekklesiologie des Zweiten Vatikanischen Konzils: ThQ 175 (1995) 32-43.

4086 **Icenogle** Gareth W., Biblical foundations for small group ministry; an integrational approach. DG 1994, InterVarsity. 396 p. $ 13 pa. -- [R]RefR 49 (1995s) 52 (S. *Van Dop*).

4087 **Jeon Kwang-Jin**. Die Kirche bei Joseph RATZINGER; kath. Diss. [D]Lies. Innsbruck 1995. -- ThRv Beilage 92/2, x.

4088 *Jericó Bermejo* Ignacio, Una ecclesia Christi; el nacimiento del moderno tratado sobre la Iglesia y la escuela de Salamanca (1559-1584): RET 55 (1995) 331-389.

4089 *Jericó Bermejo* Ignacio, El moderno tratado de 'De ecclesia' y sus inicios en la Escuela de Salamanca: Communio (Sev) 28 (1995) 3-46 (185-260).

4090 **Jongeneel** J.A.B., Missiologie. I. Zendingswetenschap; II. Missionaire theologie. Haag 1991, Boeken-C. 108 p.; 401 p. ƒ 100. -- [R]Miss(iology) 23 (1995) 479 (F.J. *Verstraelen*).

4091 **Jongeneel** J.A.B., Philosophy, science, and theology of mission in the 19th and 20th centuries: a missiological encyclopedia I; StIntercultHC 92. Fra 1995, Lang. xxiii-402 p. [ThD 43,372; RHE 90, 414*].

4092 **Karotemprel** Sebastian, Following Christ in mission; a foundation course in missiology. Nairobi 1995, Pauline. 336 p. £ 3.50. 9966-21-166-7 [*TBR 9/2, 50, F. *King*].

4093 **Kee** Howard C., Who are the people of God ? Early Christian models of community. NHv 1995, Yale. vii-280 p. £ 22.50. 0-300-05952-3. -- ^R*TBR 8,1 (1995s) 49 (L. *Houlden*: '3000'; original, efficient).

4094 **Kehl** Medard, Die Kirche 1992 → 8.7961 ... 10,7868: ^RTPQ 143 (1995) 311s (J.*Singer*).

4095 **Keller** Erwin, Vom grossen Geheimnis der Kirche; Betrachtungen zu 'Lumen gentium'. Graz 1993, Styria. 253 p. DM 40. -- ^RTPQ 143 (1995) 205s (H. *Sauer*).

4096 **Kirchschläger** Walter, Le origini della Chiesa [Anfänge 1990], ^T*Pulcinelli* G. R 1994, Città Nuova. 211 p.: bibliog. 197-207.

4097 **Kirkpatrick** Frank G., Together bound; God, history and the [Church as] religious community. NY 1994, Oxford-UP. xiii-195 p. £ 27.50. 0-19-508342-3. -- ^RET 106 (1994s) 30 (W.D. *Hudson*).

4098 *Krieg* Gustav A., Pragmatismus als nota ecclesiae ? Zum Identitätsproblem gemeindlicher Praxis: TLZ 120 (1995) 595-612.

4099 *Kroeger* James H., Mission, conversion and the Paschal mystery : VSVD 36 (1995) 167-187.

4100 **Kuhnke** Ulrich, Koinonia; zur theologischen Rekonstruktion der Identität christlicher Gemeinde [Diss. Paderborn 1990, ^D*Mette* N.]: ThemThes. Dü 1992, Patmos. 344 p. DM 45. 3-491-71094-4 [NTAb 38, p.476]. -- ^RRTL 26 (1995) 387s (P. *Weber*).

4101 **Lawler** Michael G., *Shanahan* Thomas J., Church, a spirited communion. ColMn 1995, Liturgical. xvii-171 p. $ 13. 0-8146-5821-0. -- ^R*CritRR 8 (1995) 411-3 (Margaret M. *Watzek*); *TBR 8,2 (1995s) 44 (Elizabeth *Lord*).

4102 *Lera* José M., Espíritu e Iglesia; la eclesiología de IGNACIO como 'ecclesiologia crucis' (apuntes para una pneumatología de los Ejercicios): Manresa 67 (1995) 373-389

4103 **Lindner** Herbert, Kirche am Ort; eine Gemeindetheorie; PTHe 16. Stu 1994, Kohlhammer. 375 p. DM 50. -- ^RTPQ 143 (1995) 200s (M. *Lehner*).

4104 *a) Loonbeek* Raymond, La Communion de Jérusalem [petite communauté à Paris dès 1975]; des moines dans la ville: -- *b) Deneken* Michel, Vos fils et vos filles prophétiseront; réflexions sur le prophétisme dans l'Église d'aujourd'hui: FoiTe 24 (1994) 101-119 / 120-35.

4105 *Lorscheider* Aloisius, card., Uma possivel conferência nacional de cristãos leigos : REB 55 (1995) 515-524.

4106 **Maccarrone** Michele † 1.V.1993, Romana ecclesia [varia]. 1991. ^RRHE 90 (1995) 496-9 (R. *Aubert*).

4107 **McPartlan** Paul, The Eucharist makes the Church 1993: SV(lad)TQ 39 (1995) 107-112 (Allyne *Smith*).

4108 *Madrid* Teodoro C., La Iglesia misionera de san Agustín: RevAg 36 (1995) 1005-1052.

4109 **Marriage** Alwyn, The people of God; a royal priesthood. L 1995, Darwin-LT. 215 p. £ 10. 0-232-57989-7. -- ^R*TBR 8,3 (1995s) 39s (P. *Doble*).

4110 *Martins* António M. Alves, A sacramentalidade da Igreja na teologia actual: Eborensia 6 (Évora 1993) 3-29.

4111 **Martos** Ana, Los pecados de la Iglesia: Grupo Libre 80. M 1994. 151 p. -- ^RR(az)F 231 (1995) 556s (J.M. *Vallarino*),

4112 *Marucci* Corrado, Immagini e problemi della Chiesa nel NT [ROLOFF J. 1993]: CivCatt 146 (1995,3) 399-412.

4113 **Maurier** Henri, Les missions; religions et civilisations confrontées à l'universalisme: L'histoire à vif. P 1993, Cerf. 209 p. -- [R]NZM 50 (1994) 327s (J. *Baumgartner*).

4114 *Mawhinney* Allen, The family of God; one model for the Church of the 90s: Presbyterion 19 (St.Louis 1993) 77-96.

4115 *Mazzillo* Giovanni, 'Popolo di Dio'; categoria teologica o metafora?: RasT 36 (1995) 553-587.

4116 *Möde* Erwin, Der ekklesiologische Ansatz in E. BISERS hermeneutischer Fundamentaltheologie [1975]: MThZ 46 (1995) 375-380.

4117 *Molina* Jean-Pierre, Bible, théologie et entreprise: FV 91,4 ('L'entreprise, une nouvelle Église ?' 1992) 5-17.

4118 **Neuner** Peter, Ekklesiologie I. Von den Anfängen bis zum Mittelalter: TzT 5/1. Graz 1994, Styria. 150 p. DM 40. 3-222-12105-2. -- [R]Ang 72 (1995) 118s (T. *Stancati*).

4119 *Oñate* Juan Angel, En torno al sacerdocio común de los fieles [ELBERTI A.]: *AnVal 20 (1994) 229-231.

4120 *Pelser* G.M.M., Die kerk in die Nuwe Testament: HTS 51 (1995) 645-676 [NTAb 40, p.461].

4121 *a) Pfeiffer* Antoine, De la Bible à la théologie, l'Église; -- *b) Lienhard* Marc, Théologie et sacerdoce universel: FV 91,6 (1992) 12-15 / 16-21.

4122 **Puthivedath** Jose, Catechesis of an evangelizing church; a study on the nature of catechesis. Alwaye 1994, St. Thomas Academy for Research. x-185 p. rs 40. -- [R]Kristu Jyoti 11,2 (1995) 83-85 (M. *Puthumana*).

4123 *Rees* sr. Elizabeth, Is the Church in mid-life crisis ? : *FemT 7 (1995) 29-33.

4124 **Richards** Michael, A people of priests. L 1995,Darton-LT. xii-148 p. £ 9. -- [R]O(ne)iC 31 (1995) 188-190 (D. *Carter*).

4125 **Rigal** Jean, Le mystère de l'Église. fondements théologiques et perspectives pastorales 1992 → 8,8006; 9,8171: [R]LV(itF) 50 (1995) 116 (P. *Tihon*); RevSR 68 (1994) 386s (P. *Minnerath*).

4126 **Roloff** Jürgen, Die Kirche im NT 1993 → 9,8174; 10,7895: [R]JBL 114 (1995) 510-512 (J. C. *Hanges*).

4127 *Rusecki* Marian, [P] L'ecclésiogenèse contemporaine [Act 2,42 .. : testimonium, koinonia, liturgia, diakonia]: AtK(ap) 125 (1995) 226-234.

4128 *Russell* John F., 'The people of God' in Vatican II's Lumen Gentium; an essay on text and context: Anton 70 (1995) 199-216; ital. 177.

4129 *Rzepkowski* Horst, Professor Dr. Josef SCHMIDLIN, Begründer der katholischen Missionswissenschaft: VSVD 35 (1994) 147-170.

4130 *a) Sánchez Chamoso* Román, Pueblo de Dios; herencia y programa; -- *b) Gutiérrez* Alfonso, Algunas de las preguntas suscitadas en las XXXI Jornadas de Estudio de Teología: T-IUSI 13 ('Lumen gentium 1964-' 1994) 7-51 / 113-8.

4131 **Sánchez Monge** M., Eclesiología; la Iglesia, misterio de comunión y de misión: Síntesis. M 1994, Atenas. 500 p. 84-7020-376-2. -- [R]Burg 36 (1995) 252s (E. *Bueno*); E(st)E 70 (1995) 130 (S. *Madrigal*).

4132 *Sanneh* Lamin, Christian missions and the western guilt complex: [R]ERT 19 (1995) 393-400 [< CCcn 1987],

4133 *Schelbert* Georg, Vom traditionellen zum heutigen Missionsverständnis, am Beispiel der Dokumente der SMB-Generalkapitel: NZM 50 (1994) 163-175.

4134 **Schillebeeckx** Edward, Los hombres relatos de Dios [1989]. S 1994, Sígueme. 394 p. -- [R]Communio (Sev) 28 (1995) 94-96 (V.J. *Anselde*).

4135 **Schroeter** Harald, Kirchen [p.iv; p. 78 Kirchentag] als vor-läufige Kirche; der Kirchentag als eine besondere Gestalt des Christseins zwischen Kirche und Welt: PrakThH 13. Su 1993. -- [R]ZEE(th) 39 (1995) 78-80 (P. *Bubman*).

4136 *a) Senior* Donald, Correlating images of Church and images of mission in the New Testament; -- *b) Thomas* Norman E., Images of Church and mission in African Independent churches [5000 groups in 34 nations (250 tribes) with 7 million adherents]; -- *c) Grant* Robert [Duquesne], Trauma in missionary life: Miss(iology) 23 (1995) 3-16 / 17-29 / 71-83.

4137 **Seumois** André, Teologia missionaria [1973-91]. Bo 1993, Dehoniane. -- [R]Greg 76 (1995) 590-2 (J. *Dupuis*: le livre semble regretter ou plutôt ignorer que l'évangélisation n'est plus seul la prédication de l'évangile mais s'étend au dialogue religieux et la libération intégrale de l'homme).

4138 **Sicre** José Luis. *al*.., La Chiesa e i profeti [1989], [T]*Sorsaja* Anita: Orizzonti biblici. Assisi 1993, Cittadella. 134 p. 88-308-0536-X.

4139 *Siegwalt* Gérard, La vocation de l'Église dans notre société: FV 94,1 (1995) 35-50.

4140 *Smith* David, A theology of mission or a missionary theology ? A burning question for today's Church: S(co)BET 13 (1995) 15-25.

4141 *Soares-Prabhu* George, The Church as mission; reflection on Mt 5:13-16: Jeevadhara 24 (1994) 271-281.

4142 *Sonnberger* Klaus, *Ven* Johannes A. van der, The structure of the Church: JE(mp)T 8,1 (1995) 24-45.

4143 *a) Stegmann* Franz Josef, Subsidiarität in der Kirche; Anmerkungen zu einem gravissimum principium; -- *b) Heinemann* Heribert, Demokratisierung oder Synodalisierung ? Ein Beitrag zur Diskussion: → 10,95, [F]POTTMEYER H., Kirche sein, [E]**Geerlings** W. 1994, 361-371 / 349-360 [TR 91,75].

4144 *a) Steinacker* Peter, La Chiesa alla ricerca di un modello; -- *b) Redalié* Yann, 'Diventa modello dei credenti'; la figura pastorale nelle esortazioni a Timoteo: Protest(antesimo) 50 (1995) 23-36 / 2-21.

4145 *Stevens* R. Paul, On the abolition of the laity: toward a trinitarian theology of the people of God: Crux 31,2 (1995) 5-14.

4146 *Stuhlmacher* P., Kirche nach dem Neuen Testament: ThBeitr 26 (1995) 301-325 [NTAb 40,p.462].

4147 *Szabó* István, Die Kirche -- sündig und gerecht zugleich ? Einige Bemerkungen zur Problematik der Übertragung der Rechtfertigungslehre auf die Ekklesiologie: EvTh 55 (1995) 256-9.

4148 **Tavard** George H., The Church, community of salvation. ColMn 1992, Liturgical. 264 p. -- [R]GOTR 39 (1994) 376s (J. *Gros*, p. vi); Thom 59 (1995) 140-5 (L.B. *Porter*, also on AUER J., [T]*Waldstein* M. 1993).

4149 **Terry** John M., Evangelism ['missions', largely, though more recently 'youth', 'media', 'revivalist'], a concise history. Nv 1994, Broadman & H. 210 p. [JETS 39, 304s, P. *Copan*].

4150 *Theodorou* Evangelos D., Die Orthodoxe ekklesiologische Dimension im Hymnos Akathistos: TheolA 66 (1995) 7-18 (cf. 193-211; 385-413, 577-602).

4151 [E]**Thomas** Norman E., Classic texts in mission and world Christianity. Mkn 1995, Orbis. xviii-346 p. $ 25. 1-57075-005-8. -- [R]Vidyajyoti 59 (1995) 830s (P.M. *Meagher*).

4152 **Tillard** Jean-Marie R., L'Église locale; ecclésiologie de communion et catholicité: CF .. P 1995, Cerf. 578 p. -- ᴿEstTrin 29 (1995) 499 (X. *Pikaza*).

4153 *Towner* Philip H., Paradigms lost; mission to the Kosmos in John and in David BOSCH's Models of Mission [Orbis 1991]: EvQ 67 (1995) 99-119.

4154 *Tzscheetzsch* Werner, Auswege aus der Kirchenverdrossenheit junger Menschen ? Eine Anfrage -- zuerst an die Erwachsenen: KatBl 118 (1993) 241-250.

4155 **Üffing** Martin, Die deutsche Kirche und Mission: StSVD 60. Nettetal 1994, Steyler. 285 p. DM 40. 3-8050-0346-3. -- ᴿTLZ 120 (1995) 848s (T. *Ahrens*).

4156 *a) Ugeux* Bernard, Inculturation through small Christian communities: -- *b) Healey* Joseph, The need for an effective Bible reflection method in SSCs in Africa; -- *c) Kwame* George Kumi, Basic ecclesial communities as communion: AfER 37 (1995) 134-141 / 156-9 / 160-179.

4157 **Van Vlieth** Cornelis, Communio sacramentalis: das Kirchenverständnis von Yves CONGAR O.P., genetisch und systematisch betrachtet: kath. Diss. ᴰ*Hünermann*. Tübingen 1994. -- ThRv 91,102.

4158 ᴱ**Verstraelen** F.J., Missiology; an ecumenical introduction [28 art. < Oecumenische inleiding in de Missiologie]; texts and contexts of global Christianity. GR 1995, Eerdmans. vii-498 p. $ 25. 0-8028-0487-X [ThD 43,179].

4159 *a) Walters* Stanley, The voice of God's people in exile; -- *b) Carlson* Richard W., The transfiguration of power; -- *c) Graff* Ann O'Hara, The practice of compassion and the discipleship of equals; ExAud 10 ('The Church' 1994) 73-86 / 87-103 / 105-112.

4160 **Walton** M., Marginal communities; the ethical enterprise of the followers of Jesus. Kampen 1994, Kok. 294 p. *f* 70. 90-390-0116-2. -- ᴿTTh 35 (1995) 309 (G. *Manenschijn*).

4161 **Warren** Robert, Building missionary congregations; towards a postmodern way of being Church. L 1995, Church House. 54 p. £ 4. 0-7151-5532-6. -- ᴿ*Missionalia 23 (1995) 253-5 (M. *McCoy*) & 255s (Janet *Hodgson*).

4162 **Wiedenhofer** Siegfried, Das katholische Kirchenverständnis; ein Lehrbuch der Ekklesiologie. Graz 1992, Styria. 384 p. DM 54. -- ᴿWisWei 57 (this 1994 volume and henceforth is united with FranzSt & FranzAugTheol) 155-7 (B. *Mierzwa*).

4163 *Williams* Stephen N., The pilgrim people of God: I(rish)BSt 17 (1995) 129-137.

4164 *Winter* Bruce W., The public place for the People of God (1995 Laing lecture): VoxEv 25 (1995) 7-16.

4165 *Witte* Henk, Das Erneuerungspotential von Metaphern von Kirche; zur innerkatholischen Rezeption von 'Volk Gottes' und 'Kirche der Armen': Bijdragen 56 (1995) 187-210; Eng. 210s.

4166 **Yates** Timothy, Christian mission in the twentieth century 1994 → 10,7916: ᴿC(ath)HR 81 (1995) 620s (L. *Nemer*); *CWeal 122,1 (1995) 25 (L.S. *Cunningham*): PhilipSa 30 (1995) 363s (N.M. *Castillo*); TS 56 (1995) 196 (S. *Bevans*); VSVD 36 (1995) 301s (L. *Nemer*); ZM(iss)R 79 (1995) 191s (H.-W. *Gensichen*).

H7.7 *Oecumenismus* -- -- **The ecumenical movement**

4167 ARCIC II, Life in Christ; morals, communion and the Church; agreed statement Anglican-RC-2. 1994. -- ᴿR(ocz)T(Lub) 42,7 (1995) 242-7 (S. *Nowosad* ᴾ).

4168 *Aubert* Roger, Rome et les Églises d'Orient dans 'Orientalis varietas' de Vittorio PERI [1994]: OCP 61 (1995) 37-46.

4169 *Bandera* Armando, Vita eclesial; la Iglesia cuerpo di Cristo según el P. Juan G. ARINTERO O.P.: ScrT(Pamp) 37 (1995) 13-67.

4170 *Bavaud* Georges, Le fruit d'un dialogue entre luthériens et catholiques; le mystère de l'Église et celui de la justification: NV 70,1 (1995) 50-65.

4171 *Bavinck* Herman, The Catholicity of Christianity and the Church [1888 classic, but critique of Immaculata and Neo-Thomism to be reviewed in light of Vatican II], ᵀ*Bolt* John: C(alvin)TJ 27 (1992) (217-) 220-251.

4172 **Beaupère** R., L'ecumenismo. Brescia 1993, Morcelliana. 138 p. -- ᴿ(R)*StEc 12 (Venezia 1994) 124-8 (T. *Sguazzero*).

4173 ᴱ**Bergmann** Sigurd, *Frostin* Per. Ekumeniken och forskningen .. teorier och metoder [föreläsningar Lund 1991]. U 1992, Nordiska Ekumeniska Rådet. 251 p. -- ᴿNTT 94 (1993) 184s (N.E. *Bloch-Hoell*).

4174 **Bichelberger** Roger, L'unité maintenant; le cri d'un chrétien. P 1993, Michel. 214 p. F 85. -- ᴿFV 94,1 (1995) 74s (S. *Dujancourt*).

4175 *Birmelé* André, Status quaestionis de le théologie de la communion à travers les dialogues oecuméniques et l'évolution des différentes théologies confessionnelles; CrSt 16 (1995) 245-284 [307-319 *Marloni* Albero; 321-340, *Komonchak* Joseph A.; 361-381, *Dupuis* Jacques; 407-430, *Alberigo* Giuseppe].

4176 *a) Birmelé* André, La réception comme exigence œcuménique; -- *b) Chadwick* Henry, Reception: → 197, ᶠTILLARD J., Communion 1995, 75-94 / 95-107.

4177 *Blancy* Alain, Langage des identités et nécessaire conversion des églises: FV 92,1 (1993) 49-65.

4178 **Blaser** Klauspeter, Le confessioni cristiane; le dottrine e la prassi, tavole sinottiche [Une Église 1990], ᵀ*Rebuffo* Monica, ᴱ*Collo* Carlo. CinB 1995, Paoline. 143 p. Lᵐ 42. - -- ᴿRasT 36 (1995) 763-5 (J.E. *Vercruysse*).

4179 **Borges de Pinto** José E., A recepção como realidade eclesiale e tarefa ecuménica = Did(ask)L 23 (1993). 389 p.; bibliog. 335-385.

4180 **Brosseder** Johannes, *Link* Hans-Georg, Gemeinschaft der Kirchen, Traum oder Wahrheit ? Z/Neuk 1992, Benziger / Neuk. 208 p. DM 34. -- ᴿWiWei 58 (1995) 324s (H. von der *Bey*).

4181 *a) Cassidy* Edward I., Il nuovo 'Direttorio ecumenico della Chiesa cattolica'; un passo in avanti nel cammino dell'Ecumenismo : (R)*StEc 12 (Venezia 1994) 9-28; Eng. 28.

4182 *a) Chadwick* Henry, Anglican ecclesiology and its challenges; -- *b) Tavard* George H., Considerations on an ecclesiology of *koinonia*: O(ne)iC 31 (1995) 32-41 / 42-51.

4183 **Clendenin** Daniel B., Eastern Orthodox Christianity; a western perspective. GR 1994, Baker. 176 p. $ 15. 0-8010-2588-5 [ThD 42 (1995) 262].

4184 *Cobb* John B.ᴶ, The unity of the Church and the unity of humanity: 13th Ainslie Lecture: *Mid-Str 34 (1995) 1-19: phot.

4185 *a) Coenen* Lothar, Gelingt ein neuer ökumenischer Aufbruch ? Reflexionen über den 'Konziliaren Prozess'; -- *b) Klaiber* Walter, Wie verwirklicht die Evangelisch-methodistische Kirche ihre missionarische Aufgabe in ihren ökumenischen, gesellschaftlichen und politischen Beziehungen ?: Ö(kum)R 44 (1995) 207-215 / 57-73.

4186 ᴱ**Colson** Charles, *Neuhaus* Richard J., Evangelicals and Catholics together; toward a common mission. Dallas 1995, Word. xxxv-236 p. $ 15 pa. 0-8499-3860-0 [ThD 43,65; JETS 39,303s, C.F.H. *Henry*].

4187 **Constantelos** Demetrios J., Understanding the Greek Orthodox Church; its faith, history and practice. Brookline MA 1990, Hellenic. xiv-220 p. - KL(eronomia) 26 (1994)

350s (V.T. *Stavridis*).

4188 *Cornwell* Peter, Real priests ? [1896 rejection of Anglican Orders; 'Prejudice unmasked' 5]: Tablet 249 (1995) 417-9.

4189 **Cragg** Kenneth, Troubled by truth; [13 biographical] life-studies in inter-faith concern [= ? 10,7947]. Durham UK 1992, Pentland. 320 p. £ 14.50. -- [R]Miss(iology) 23 (1995) 93 (C. *Bennett*).

4190 *Crow* Paul A.[J], The quest for unity between the Disciples of Christ and the United Church of Christ; history's lessons for tomorrow's Church: Discipliana 53 (1993) 67-83.

4191 **Cullmann** Oscar, Le vie dell'unità cristiana: GDT 224. Brescia 1994, Queriniana. 100 p. L[m] 15. -- [R]StPat(av) 41 (1994) 719s (L. *Sartori*: reazioni, ma non ancora alle sue GDT 191).

4192 **Curran** Neil, Biblical Christianity for Catholics [enmeshed (like him for 20 years) in a system which hides the simple truth of the Gospel]. Dallas 1994, Biblical Communications. 28 p. $ 3. -- [R]BS 152 (1995) 105 (J.A. *Witmer* praises, adding 'the same indictment can be made of many Protestant groups').

4193 **Dentin** Pierre, Les privilèges des Papes devant l'Écriture et l'histoire: Parole présente. P 1995, Cerf. 282 p F 100. -- [R]E(spr)eV 105 (1995) 465s (P. *Jay*).

4194 Der 'andere Katholizismus' in Deutschland -- -- Vermächtnis und Verpflichtung; ThQ 175 (1995) 187-191.

4195 **Descy** Serge F., The Melkite church; an historical and ecclesiological approach [Lebanon, French], [T]. Newton MA 1993, Sophia. 106 p. -- [R]E(cu)R 47 (1995) 233s (A. *Nichols*).

4196 *a) de Souza* Cyril, History of catechesis in India; -- *b) Kochuparampil* Xavier, The St. Thomas Christians of Kerala; evolution of a catechesis; -- *c) Kattianimattathil* Jose, The journey towards interreligious dialogue -- -- a historical sketch; -- *d) Balasundaram* Franklyn J.. The Dalits and the London Missionary Society -- -- a historical study: Kristu Jyoti 11,4 (1995) 1-26 / 27-52 / 53-66 / 90-109.

4197 *Devčić* Ivan, Das Problem Gottes als Ausgangspunkt des interreligiösen Dialogs: RijT 2 (1994) 177-206 kroatisch; deutsch 206.

4198 *a) Dhavamony* Mariasusai, The Christian theology of interreligious dialogue; -- *b) Borrmans* Maurice, Le dialogue islamo-chrétien des trente dernières années ; *c) Coward* Harold, Hindu-Christian dialogue as 'mutual conversation'; -- *d) Starkloff* Carl F., Dialogue, evangelization and church growth among aboriginal North Americans; -- *e) Give* Bernard de, Une entreprise féconde; le dialogue interreligieux monastique [Inde, Japon ...]: StMiss 43 (1994) 61-93 / 115-137 [-176, *al.*] / 177-192 [-244, *al.*] / 279-294 / 95-113.

4199 **Döring** Heinrich, *al.*, Ist die Ökumene am Ende ? Rg 1994, Pustet. 129 p. 3-7917-1407-4. -- [R]ZkT 117 (1995) 238 (L. *Lies*).

4200 Dombes, groupe [→ 4177, BLANCY A.], For the conversion of the churches. 1993. -- [R]*ProEccl 4 (1995) 119-122 (M.*Root*); R(ocz)T(Lub) 42,7 (1995) 227-231 (L.*Górka*, [P]).

4201 *a) Dumas* Francine & André, Marie dans la tradition protestante; -- *b) Touron* Eliseo, El Magnificat de LUTERO; -- *c) Blanco* Severiano, Sola Scriptura o hermenéutica bíblica ?; -- *d) Fernández García* Domiciano, Diálogos ecuménicos en los congresos mariológicos: EphMar 44 (1994) 365-9; español Eng. 370 / 371-390; franç. Eng. 391 [& 453-465, *Díez Presa* Macario] / 393-410; franç. Eng. 411 / 413-433; franç. Eng. 434.

4202 **Edwards** David L., What is Catholicism ? An Anglican responds to the official teaching of the Roman Catholic Church. L 1994, Mowbray. xii-179 p. £ 13. -- [R]Month

256 (1995) 158s (A. *Meredith*: a critique of the Catechism).

4203 **Evans** Gillian R., The Church and the churches; toward an ecumenical ecclesiology. C 1994, Univ. xvi-p. £ 37.50. 0-521-46286-X. -- ^RE(xp)T 107 (1995s) 124s (J. *Begbie*): *ModBlv 36,3 (1995) 56s (Flora *Winfield*); OiC 30 (1994) 388-394 (D. *Carter*); TS 56 (1995) 799s (G.H. *Tavard*).

4204 **Fackre** Gabriel, Ecumenical faith in evangelical perspective 1993 → 9,8269; 10,7953*: ^RInterpretation 49 (1995) 218 . 220 (D.G. *Bloesch*).

4205 *a) Falardeau* Ernest, Religious formation and ecumenical formation; -- *b) Weisenbeck* Jude D., Ecumenism a Scripture mandate for religious: RfR 53 (1994) 724-7 / 54 (1995) 675-680.

4206 *Famerée* Joseph, La communion ecclésiale dans l'histoire [TILLARD 1992 ...]; bulletin d'ecclésiologie : RTL 26 (1995) 62-74.

4207 *Feldmann* Felix, Das [Russland-]Altgläubigentum, seine Struktur und sein Zustand heute: ZM(iss)R 79 (1995) 226-239; Eng. 239.

4208 **Fitzgerald** Thomas E., The Orthodox Church: Denominations in America 7. Westport CT 1995. Greenwood. xiii-240 p. $ 18 pa. 0-313-36281-0 [ThD 43,265].

4209 **Fournier** Keith A., *(Watkins* William D.), A house united ? Evangelicals and Catholics together, a winning alliance for the 21st century. CO Springs 1994, Navpress. 365 p. $ 18. -- ^RBS 152 (1995) 228s (J.R. *Blue*: back to the drawing-board).

4210 *Frankemölle* H., Biblische Grundlagen einer Ökumene der Weltreligionen ?: Diak(-a) 25,2 (1994) 79-91 [NTAb 39,p.262].

4211 *Franquesa* Adalbert, El ecumenismo en el Vaticano II, y en particular en la reforma litúrgica : Phase 35 (1995) 11-25.

4212 *Frieling* Reinhard, Ökumene: → 772, TRE 25 (1995) 46-77 [-80-86, Ökumenismus, *Petri* Heinrich, *Raem* Heinz-A.].

4213 *Garijo-Guembe* Miguel M., Unidad en una diversidad reconciliada; reflexiones sobre modelos de unidad a la luz de recientes acuerdos ecuménicos : DiEc 30 (1995) 67-81.

4214 *Garvey* John, Orthodox / Roman Catholic relations today: DocLife 45 (1995) 140-7.

4215 *Gaudemet* Jean, Note sur [les vicissitudes historiques de] l'excommunication; CrSt 16 (1995) 285-306; Eng. 306.

4216 *a) Geernaert* Donna, *Koinonia*; integrating issues of faith and justice in ecumenical dialogue; -- *b) Greatrex* Joan, *Koinonia* as the key to the Church's self-understanding and to ecumenical rapprochement: → 197, ^FTILLARD J., Communion 1995, 139-147 / 149-156.

4217 **Gerland** Manfred, Wesentliche Vereinigung; Untersuchungen zum Abendmahlsver-ständnis ZINZENDORFs: ThTSt 2. Hildesheim 1992, Olms. xii-186 p. DM 40. 3-487-09664-1. -- ^RZkT 117 (1995) 239s (L. *Lies*).

4218 **Glaeser** Zygfryd, ^P Pneumatologiczna eklezjologia Nikosa A. NISSIOTIS: diss. ^D*Hryniewicz* W. Lublin 1995. 288 p. -- RTLv 27.p.558.

4219 **Goosen** Gideon, Bringing churches together 1993 → 9,8284; 10,7966: ^RNRT 117 (1995) 308 (A. *Harvengt*: clair, serein).

4220 *a) Górka* Leonard, ^P Morphologie der Christenheit .. Ut unum sint; -- *b) Hryniewicz* Wacław, Reconciliation and ecclesiology of sister churches; -- *c) Gebhardt* Günther, Bekehrung zur Toleranz, eine Aufgabe für die Religionen: R(ocz)T(Lub) 42,7 (1995) 31-40; deutsch 40 / 41-55; ^P 55s / 57-67; ^P 67s.

4221 **Górka** Leonard, *Napiórkowski* Stanisław, ^P *Kościoły ?* Churches or Church: select dilemmas of ecumenism. Wsz 1995, Verbinum. 268 p. -- ^RR(ocz)T(Lub) 42,7 (1995)

231s (P. *Jaskóla*, [P]).

4222 *Gounelle* André, Catholicisme et Protestantisme selon TILLICH; FV 94,2 (1995) 23-34.

4223 *Gros* Jeffrey, [*al.*,], Protestants in the American Christian community: Catholic World 238 (1995) 244-252 [-281: 5 groups]

4224 *Harrison* Richard J.,[J] Holding back the tide; J.W. McGARVEY and division in the Christian Church: Discipliana 53 (1993) 17-26: portr.

4225 **Haudel** Matthias, Die Bibel und die Einheit der Kirchen [D]1993 → 9,8292; 10,7973: [R]ÖR 43 (1994) 483-5 (W.A. *Beinert*).

4226 *Haudel* Matthias, Vergessene Kriterien; hermeneutische Kriterien für die Weiterentwicklung des Koinonia-Konzepts: ÖR 43 (1994) 292-304.

4227 *Healy* Nicholas M., Communion ecclesiology [TILLARD, L.BOFF]; a cautionary note: ProEccl 4 (1995) 442-453.

4228 *Helleman* Adrian, The contribution of John CALVIN to an ecumenical dialogue on papal primacy: OiC 30 (1994) 328-343

4229 *Hocken* Peter, Ecumenical issues in evangelization O(ne)iC 31 (1995) 3-19.

4230 *Houtepen* Anton, *a)* Wachsende Gemeinschaft, abwartende Kirchen ?: ÖR 43 ('Santiago 1993', 1994) 2-13 (-59, *al.*); -- *b)* Superare la storia con la storia; verso una revisione degli anatemi del passato : (R)*StEc 13 (Venezia 1995) 185-193; Eng. 193.

4231 *a) Hryniewicz* Wacław, [P] Should Russia be converted ? Ecumenical lessons from the past and the dialogue with Orthodoxy: -- *b) Teklak* Czesław, [P] New evangelization in post-communist countries: ZNKUL 37,1s (1994) 3-19; Eng. 19s / 65-96; Eng. 96s.

4232 **Hugon** Édouard [†1929], Hors de l'Église point de salut ? Bitche 1995 = [3]1927 * '?', Bitche. 216 p. F 90.- [R]E(spr)eV 105 (1995) 678s (P. *Jay*: réimpression injustifiée).

4233 **Imbach** Josef, ¿ De quién es Jesús ? Su significación para judíos, cristianos y musulmanes. Barc 1991, Herder. 270 p. -- [R]TeolBA 30 (1993) 247-250 (F. *Hubeñák*).

4234 **Irvin** Dale T., Hearing many voices; dialogue and diversity in the ecumenical movement. Lanham MD 1994, UPA. 208 p. $ 26.50 [RStR 22,52, J.Y. *Ford*]. -- [R]E(cu)R 47 (1995) 109-112 (M. *Conway*: respectful, infuriated) [490-502, *Irvin* on 'hermeneutics of difference'].

4235 *Jenson* Robert W., The Church as communion; a Catholic-Lutheran-dialogue-consensus-statement dreamed in the night: ProEccl 4 (1995) 68-78.

4236 *Jenson* Robert W., al,, A symposium on Ut unum sint [chiefly on the infrequent sections that cannot be so well documented from Vatican II]: ProEccl 4 (1995) 389-397.

4237 *Kelly* Gerard, The recognition of ministries; a shift in ecumenical thinking: O(ne)iC 30 (1994) 10-21.

4238 **Keshishian** Aram, Conciliar fellowship, a common goal [< diss. Fordham 1980] 1992 → 8,8107 ... 10,7982: [R]Bijdragen 56 (1995) 345 (A. van *Eijk*).

4239 *Kessler* Diane C., The new Catholic Ecumenical Directory, a Protestant reading: E(cu)R 47 (1995) 419-425 (-429 *al.*, Orthodox ..).

4240 *Knitter* Paul F., Toward a liberative interreligious dialogue: CrossCur 45 (1995s)451-68.

4241 *Knowles* Peter, A renaissance in the study of Byzantine liturgy ?: Worship 65 (1994) 232-241.

4242 **Köhler** Wiebke, Rezeption, eine ökumenische Begriffsgeschichte: Rudolph SOHM, Nikolaj AFANASEV, Hans DOMBOIS, Yves CONGAR: ev. Diss. [D]*Lesinng* (sic) E. Münster/Wf 1995.

4243 **Koivisto** Rex A., One Lord, one faith; a theology for cross-denominational renewal, Wheaton IL 1993, Victor. 498 p. $ 20. -- [R]BS 152 (1995) 362s (G.L. *Nebeker*).

4244 *Kunrath* Pedro, Ecumenismo; problemas teológicos fundamentais: Teocomunicação 24 (1994) 649-664.

4245 **Kuschel** Karl-Joseph, Abraham. a symbol of hope for Jews, Christians and Muslims, ᵀ*Bowden* John. L 1995, SCM. xxix-286 p. £ 15.-- ᴿ*TBR 8,1 (1995s) 13 (R. *Coggins:* KÜNG associate).

4246 **Kuttianimattathil** Jose, Practice and theology of interreltigious dialogue; a critical study of Indian Christian attempts since Vatican II [< diss. Pontifical Gregorian University, Rome]. Bangalore 1995, Kristu Jyoti. xxiv-757 p. rs 175. -- ᴿKristu Jyoti 11,3 (1995) 96-100 (D. *Veliath*).

4247 *a) Kuttianimattathil* Jose, From tolerance to harmony; -- *b) Anchukandam* Thomas, Gandhian satyagraha and tolerance -- a Christian perspective; -- *c) Thuruthiyil* Scaria, Jiddu KRISHNAMURTI's answer to the problem of religious fundamentalism and intolerance; -- *d*) Indian Theological Association 1994 statement, A Christian response to religious tensions in our country: Kristu Jyoti 11,2 (1995) 1-10 / 11-38 / 39-64 / 65-75.

4248 *Labbé* Yves, Communication de la foi et co-référence des doctrines: ETRel 70 (1995) 31-45.

4249 *Lehmann* Karl, Eine Lebensfrage für die Kirche; zum Dialog als Form der Wahrheitsfindung: HerKor 49 (1995) 29-35.

4250 *Lilienfeld* Fairy von, Orthodoxe Kirchen: → 772, TRE 25 (1995) 423-464.

4251 *Limouris* Gennadios, 'Foi et constitution' [WCC]; de la grandeur d'un mouvement à l'étroitesse d'une commission: Kler 24 (1992) 77-98.

4252 ᴱ**Littel** F.H., A half-century of religious dialogue (Amsterdam Christian Youth testimonies), 1939-1989; making the circles larger: Toronto StT 46. Lewiston 1989, Mellen. 335 p. $ 70. -- ᴿRHE 90 (1995) 341 (J. *Famerée*).

4253 ᴱ**Lossky** N., *al,*, Dizionario del movimento ecumenicoᵀ 1994 → 8,8121* ... 10,7997: Lᵐ 148. -- ᴿCivCatt 146 (1995,3) 311s (J. *Vercruysse* : 'Per l'edizione italiana .. P. RICCA sul valdismo'); (R)*StEc 13 (Venezia 1995) 251s (S. *Morandini*).

4254 *Maas* A.G.J. van der, Het oecumenisch leesrooster: G(ereformeerd)TT 94 (1994) 99-112.

4255 *McCoy* Michael J., Anglican; *Prior* Anselm, Catholic: Equipping the People of God for Christian witness: IRM(iss) 83 (1994) 45-55 / 57-65.

4256 *McDonnell* Kilian, *a*) Improbable conversations / Five defining issues; the international classical Pentecostal / Roman Catholic dialogue: Pneuma 17 (1995) 163-174 / 175-188 (189-201 *Gros* Jeffrey); -- *b*) The death of mythologies; the classical Pentecostal / Roman Catholic dialogue: America 172,10 (1995) 14-19.

4257 *Maffeis* Angelo, Modelli di unità della Chiesa nella storia del movimento ecumenico e nel dibattito attuale: Teol(Br) 19 (1994) 62-93 . 109-150; Eng. 150

4258 *Majdansky* bp. Vsevolod, Orthodox-Catholic reconciliation and the Ukrainian church: Logos 36 (Ottawa 1995) 199-216.

4259 *Manna* Salvatore, The presence of the Byzantines in Puglia: Kler 24 (1992) 99-139.

4260 ᴱ**Marty** Martin E., Missions and ecumenical expressions. Mü 1993, Saur. xiii-208. DM 178. -- ᴿMiss(iology) 23 (1995) 98s (D.L. *Robert*: except for Marty, paternalistically outdated and needless).

4261 **Meyendorff** John, Unité de l'Empire et division des Chrétiens; l'Église de 450 à 680, ᵀ*Lhoest* Françoise 1993 → 10,8000: ᴿOrChr 79 (1995) 243s (M. van *Esbroeck*).

4262 ᴱ**Mojzes** Paul, *Swidler* Leonard, Christian mission and interreligious dialogue: Religions in Dialogue 4, 1990 → 8,409a: ᴿE(st)E 70 (1995) 284 (J.J. *Alemany*).

4263 *Moltmann* Jürgen, Hat das Papsttum eine ökumenische Zukunft ? [zu 'Ut unum sint' 1995: 'Die katholische Gemeinschaftseinheit ist viel weiter und kräftiger als die zentralische Papsteinheit']: EvTh 55 (1995) 578-580.

4264 *a) Napiórkowski* Stanisław C., P An introduction to the Roman Catholic -- Pentecostal/Anglican dialogue; -- *b) Cupiał* Darius, P Evangelism and ecumenism in the experience of the [BŁACNICKI F., 'Oasis' or] 'Light-Life' movement: RTK 41,7 (Teologia ekumeniczna, 1994) 105s . 121s / 37-46; Eng. 46.

4265 *a) Neumann* Burkhard, Überlegungen zu der Frage 'Was ist kirchentrennend?'; -- *b) Sattler* Dorothea, Neue Urteile zu den alten Lehrverurteilungen; die evangelischen Kirchen in Deutschland und die Studie des ökumenischen Arbeitskreises:Cath49(1995)32-43/98-113

4266 *Newbigin* Lesslie, Ecumenical amnesia [on RAISER K., Ecumenism in transition 1991 → 7,8066*] : IBM(iss)R 18 (1994) 2-5 (50, response; 51s, rejoinder).

4267 **Nichols** Aidan, Rome and the Eastern Churches 1992 → 9,8131; 9,8340: R*CritRR 7 (1994) 354-6 (T. *Pulcini*).

4268 ENickle Keith F., *Lull* Timothy F., A common calling; the witness of our [Ev.Luth. -- Presb. -- Ref. -- United Church of Christ] Reformation Churches in North America today. Mp 1993, Augsburg. 88 p. $ 5. -- RP(rinc)SB 16 (1995) 96s (D.W.A. *Taylor*).

4269 *Nilson* Jon, Must disagreements divide ? The achievements and challenges of ARCIC-II's Life in Christ: OneInC 31 (1995) 222-236.

4270 **Nilson** Jon, Nothing beyond the necessary [as RAHNER-FRIES 1985]; Roman Catholicism and the ecumenical future. NY 1995, Paulist. ix-105 p. $ 8. 0-8091-3576-0 [RStR 22,53, J.T. *Ford*].

4271 **Oakham** Ronald A., *al.*, One at the table; the reception of baptized Christians: Font and Table. Ch 1995, Liturgical Training. xii-159 p. $ 11 pa. 1-56854-070-1 [ThD 40,379].

4272 *Olson* Roger E., Whales and elephants; both God's creatures but can they meet ? Evangelicals and liberals in dialogue: *ProEccl 4 (1995) 165-189.

4273 Orthodox-Reformed theological dialogue, Limassol, Cyprus, January 13, 1994: KL(eronomia) 25 (1993 !) 334-9.

4274 **Osburn** Carroll D., The peaceable kingdom; [six] essays favoring non-sectarian ['fellowship'] Christianity. Abilene TX 1993, Restoration Perspectives. $ 11. -- RRestQ 37 (1995) 120-2 (S. *Casey*).

4275 EPannenberg Wolfhart, *Schneider* Theodor, Lehrverurteilungen -- kirchentrennend? IV. Antworte auf kirchliche Stellungnahmen: Dialog der Kirchen 8. 152 p. DM 30. FrB/Gö 1994, Herder/VR. 3-525-56929-7 / 3-451-23559-5 [ThRv 91,365].

4276 *a) Parré* Pierre, Multiplication des liens entre Églises; liens interconfessionels, jumelages ...; -- *b) Gaziaux* Éric, La foi dans le temps de risque: FoiTe 24 (1994) 312-330 / 348-354.

4277 *Patsavos* Lewis J., The synodal structure of the Orthodox Church: SV(lad)TQ 39 (1995s) 71-94.

4278 **Peri** Vittorio, Lo scambio fraterno fra le Chiese; componenti storiche della comunione; Storia e attualità 13. Vaticano 1993, Editrice. 493 p. -- RRS(to)LR 31 (1995) 340-5 (P.A. *Gramaglia*).

4279 **Peri** Vittorio, Orientalis varietas [ristampe]. Vaticano 1994s, Editrice. 500 p. -- RCrSt 16 (1995) 689s (J.M.R. *Tillard*) / 690-3 (M. *Velati*).

4280 **Preston** Ronald H., Confusions in Christian social ethics; problems for Geneva and Rome. L 1994, SCM. xiii-202 p. £ 13. 0-334-02573-7. -- R*TBR 8,2 (1995s) 40s (I.

Rome. L 1994, SCM. xiii-202 p. £ 13. 0-334-02573-7. -- ᴿ*TBR 8,2 (1995s) 40s (I. *Markham:* 'angry young man' 'with delightful lucidity').

4281 **Raiser** Konrad, Ecumenism in transition 1991 →7,8066*: ᴿC(alvin)TJ 30 (1995) 214-221 (P.C. *Schrotenboer*).

4282 *a) Reumann* J., Koinonia en las Escrituras; vista panorámica de los textos bíblicos; -- *b) Zizioulas* J., La Iglesia como comunión; exposición sobre el tema de la Conferencia; -- *c) Pannenberg* W., La comunión de la fe; -- *d) Tillard* J.-M. R., El futuro de Fe y Constitución: Quinta Conferencia Mundial de Fe y Constitución, Santiago de Compostela 1993: DiEc 29 (1994) 239-286 / 305-318 / 319-326 / 373-381 [< RET 55 (1995) 415].

4283 **Reuver** M., *al.*, The ecumenical movement tomorrow; suggestions for approaches and alternatives. Kampen/Genève 1993, Kok/WCC. 410 p. *f* 62,50. 90-242-6201-1 / 2-8254-1122-1. -- ᴿTTh 35 (1995) 198 (T. *Brattinga*).

4284 *Rhem* Richard A., Interreligious dialogue; what is required of us ?: P(ersp)Ref 10,5 (1995) 10-15.

4285 *Ricca* Paolo, *Ferrario* Fulvio, Il papato e l'ecumenismo [Ut unum sint 1995]: Protest(antesimo) 50 (1995) 241-5.

4286 *Saffrey* Henri Dominique, Florence, 1492; réapparaît PLOTIN [< Eng RenQ]: FrSZ 42 (1995) 134-151.

4287 *Sartori* Luigi, *a)* Ecumenismo del terzo millennio; considerazioni sull'Enciclica 'Ut unum sint' : StPat(av) 42 (1995) 527-650; Eng. 650; -- *b)* Battesimo e unità della Chiesa; un unico battesimo, un'unica Chiesa : (R)*StEc 13 (Venezia 1995) (5-7) 59-71; Eng. 72.

4288 **Schönborn** Christoph, L'unité de la foi. 1993. -- ᴿDiv 39 (1995) 195-7 (D. *Vibrac*).

4289 *Schon* Dietmar, Der ökumenische Charakter des Gesetzbuches für die katholischen Ostkirchen: OS(tk) 44 (1995) 135-170.

4290 **Schütte** Heinz, Kirche im ökumenischen Verständnis [1991 → 7,8078 ... 9,8363]. Pd/Fra 1993, Bonifatius/Lembeck. 216 p. DM 19,80. 3-87088-758-3 / 3-87476-289-0. -- ᴿForKT 11 (1995) 76-78 (M. *Lochbrunner*); ThLZ 120 (1995) 588 (H.-G. *Link*).

4291 **Schwain** Barbara, Die Arbeit des Ökumenischen Arbeitskreises evangelischer und katholischer Theologen von 1946 bis 1975: ev. Diss. ᴰ*Pannenberg* W. München 1994. -- ThRv 91,99.

4292 *Segal* Charles, Classics, ecumenicism, and Greek tragedy: ΤΡΑΡΑ 125 (1995) 1-26.

4293 *a) Sgarbossa* Rino, Koinonia/comunione; nozione ecclesiologica centrale nei dialoghi bilaterali fra le comunioni cristiane mondiali d'Occidente; -- *b) Reumann* John, La 'koinonia' nelle Scritture; esame dei testi biblici, ᵀ*Cantimiri* Luca: (R)*StEc 12 (Venezia 1994) 343-377; Eng. 377 / 391-428; Eng. 428 [*al.* 261-341 . 379-389].

4294 **Shortz** Joianne L.. Interfaith relationship development; a proposed model: diss. Virginia Commonwealth Univ. 1995, ᴰ*Worthington* E. 95-28110. -- D(iss)AI 56 (1995) p. 1544.

4295 *Sidorak* Stephen J.,ᴶ Ten truths and consequences for the ecumenical movement today: Mid-Str 34 (1995) 177-185.

4296 *Sorokowski* Andrew, Vatican diplomacy and the Ukrainian Greco-Catholic Church: Logos 36 (Sask 1995) 47-66: 66, Ukrainian summary.

4297 **Spiteris** Yannis, La teologia ortodossa neo-greca 1992 → 9,8369; 10,8021: ᴿLaur 36 (1995) 212-4 (A. *Dalbesio*).

4298 *Staples* Peter, Ultimates as paradoxical limits in Christian ecumenical science: URM 18 (1995) 139-150 (-154 comment, *Jesson* Nicholas).

4299 *a) Stavridis* Basile, L'autorité du patriarche œcuménique dans la vie de l'Église orthodoxe; -- *b) Papathomas* Grigorios D., Les différentes modalités d'exercice de la juridiction du Patriarche de Constantinople: Ist(ina) 40 (1995) 357-368 / 369-385.

4300 *Stefani* Piero, 'Se qualcuno ascolta la mia voce e apre la porta, entrerò .. (Ap 3,20): l'accoglienza nella tradizione biblica e nella tradizione cristiana : (R)*StEc 13 ('Ecco, io busso alla porta' gen. 1995) 331-9; Eng. 340 (*al.* 265-330 .

4301 *Stricker* Gerd, Die orthodoxen Kirchen CVIII / CIX: IK(i)Z 85 (1995) 73-113 / 201-242.

4302 **Stubenrauch** Bertram, Die Kenosis Gottes und das Pleroma des Menschen; zur dogmatischen Begründung des interreligiösen Dialogs: kath. Hab-Diss. ᴰ*Beinert*. Regensburg 1995. -- ThRv Beilage 92/2, iv.

4303 *Sullivan* Francis A., Lessons we have learned from the participation of Rome in ecumenism: MilltSt 34 (1994) 13-30.

4304 **Swidler** Leonard, After the absolute 1990 (→ 10,8023): RMiss(iology) 23 (1995) 101s (S.T. *Franklin:* his intellectual and moral presuppositions urgently need rethinking).

4305 *Taylor* David W.A., *al.*, What is covenant communion ?: Mid-Str 34 (1995) 1-12 (-112).

4306 *Teasdale* Wayne, The Church in an age of pluralism; report on the Parliament of the World's Religions: *CanadCath 13,9 (1995) 12-18.

4307 *a) Tesfai* Yacob, Ecumenism, culture and syncretism; -- *b) Kretschmar* Georg, The early Church and Hellenistic culture; -- *c) Geffré* Claude, Christianity and culture; -- *d) Sanneh* Lamin, The gospel, language and culture; the theological method in cultural analysis: IRM(iss) 84 (1995) 7-16 / 33-46 / 17-31 / 47-64.

4308 *Tillard* J.M.R., The Gospel of God and the Church of God: O(ne)iC 31 (1995) 211-221.

4309 **Tillard** J.-M. R., Chair de l'Église .. : C(og)Fi 168, 1992 → 8,8165 ... 10,8028: ᴿETL 70 (1994) 191-3 (J.E. *Vercruysse.* Eng.); StVlad 39 (1995s) 315-7 (J. *Gros*).

4310 **Tillard** J.-M.R., Carne de la Iglesia, carne de Cristo; en las fuentes de la eclesiología de comunión, ᵀ*Ortiz García* Alfonso: VeI 111.. S 1994, Sígueme. 147 p. 84-301-1240-5. -- ᴿE(st)E 70 (1995) 128-130 (A. *Madrigal*); EstTrin 28 (1994) 261s (J.M. de *Miguel*); Lum(Vt) 44 (1995) 180-2 (U. *Gil Ortega*); RET 55 (1995) 102-4 (María Ángeles *Navarro Girón*).

4311 *Tillard* J.M.R., Église catholique ou église universelle ?: CrSt 16 (1995) 341-358; Eng. 358s.

4312 *a) Tillard* Jean-Marie R., Faith; the believer and the Church; -- *b) Thompson* David M., Faith; the individual and the Church [RC-Disciples dialog 1994]: *Mid-Str 34 (1995) 43-60 / 61-73 (77-86. 'agreed account').

4313 **Tillard** Jean-Marie R., Church of Churches 1992 → 8,8163 ... 10,8026: ᴿThLZ 120 (1995) 274-6 (G. *Gassmann*).

4314 ᴱ**Torrance** Thomas F., Theological dialogue between Orthodox and Reformed Churches [I. 1985] II [of 1988 & 1990] 1993 → 9,8383: ᴿChurchman 108 (L 1994) 87-89 (G. *Bray*); EvQ 67 (1995) 285s (D.A.S. *Fergusson*).

4315 *Tovey* Phillip, [Significant variations within] West Syrian marriage rites: StLi(turgica) 25 (ND 1995) 192-206.

4316 *Tsirpanlis* Constantine, Theological development and consensus in post-Vatican II ecumenism: P(atr)BR 14 (1995) 19-34.

4317 *Valdrini* Patrick, L'*Æqualis dignitas* des Églises d'Orient et d'Occident: RICP 56 (1995) 109-126.

4318 **Valognes** Jean-Pierre, Vie et mort des chrétiens d'Orient, des origines à nos jours. P

1994, Fayard. 974 p. -- [R]RHPhR 75 (1995) 229s (J.-C. *Larchet*).

4319 **Vanhoye** Albert, Lo spirito dell'unità: I triangoli 20. CasM 1995, Piemme. 95 p. 88-384-2304-0.

4320 **Vilar** Juan B., Intolerancia y libertad en la España contemporanea; los orígenes del Protestantismo español actual. M 1994, Itsmo. 452 p. 84-7090-284-9. -- [R]E(st)E 70 (1995) 244-8 (M. *Revuelta González*).

4321 *a) Vineeth* V.F., Interreligious dialogue, past and present; a critical appraisal: -- *b) Koenig* Otto, Intrerreligious dialogue in the present world context; -- *c) Samartha* Stanley J., The future of interreligious dialogue; threats and promises: JDh 19 (1994) 36-58 / 59-67 / 74-83.

4322 *Wainwright* Geoffrey, Towards an ecumenical hermeneutic; how can all Christians read the Scriptures together ? [McCarthy Lecture 1995]: Greg 76 (1995) 639-662

4323 *Wendebourg* Dorothea, Chalkedon in der ökumenischen Diskussion: ZThK 92 (1995) 207-238.

4324 *a) Werblowski* R.J. Zvi, Faithfulness to the roots and commitment toward the future; a Jewish view; -- *b) Stylianopoulos* Theodore, .. an Orthodox view; -- *c) Halpérin* Jean, Memory and responsibility; a Jewish view; -- *d) Irineos* bp., .. an Orthodox vie: → 607, Immanuel 26s (1994) 136-141 / 142-159 (-170, discussion) / 74-79 / 8=-86 (-98, discussion).

4325 *a) Westerwelt* Benjamin W., Confessionalism, ecumenism and the Christian churches; -- *b) Neuner* Joseph, What is religious freedom ?: Way 35 (1995) 237-245 / 215-225.

4326 *Wever* Adam, 'Wir verwerfen die falsche Lehre'; über den Umgang mit Anders-Glaubenden oder die 'Lerngeschichte einer Religion': → 589, Mit den Anderen 1995, 57-88.

4327 *Williams* Stuart, Sharing communion; a common inheritance: O(ne)iC 31 (1995) 347-64.

4328 *Wood* Susan, Ecclesial koinonia in ecumenical dialogue: OiC 30 (1994) 124-145.

H7.8   **Amt** -- *Ministerium ecclesiasticum*

4329 *Abe* G.O., Yahwism and priesthood in the OT: AsiaJT 8 (1994) 251-260 [< OTA 18 (1995) p. 355].

4330 *Anderson* Leith, Christian ministry in the 21st century 1-4: BS 151 (1994) 3-11..

4331 *a) Armentrout* Don S., Ministry in the history of the Episcopal Church; -- *b) Lytle* Guy F.[III], The recovery of priestly identity and the revival of the Church: SewaneeT 38 (1994s) 241-266 / 227-240.

4332 **Barnett** James M., The diaconate[2] [[1]1981]. Ph 1995, Trinity. xviii-253 p. $ 16. 1-56338-093-5 [RStR 22,250, J.T. *Fitzgerald*].

4333 **Bartlett** David L., Ministry in the NT: OvBT 1993 → 9,8412: [R]CBQ 57 (1995) 580-2 (S. *Kealy*); *CritRR 8 (1995) 163-5 (J. *Reumann*); TS 56 (1995) 189 (Karen A. *Barta*).

4334 *Bayerlein* Walter (interview), Ein Gegenüber zum kirchlichen Amt; Fragen zue Lage des verfassten Laienkatholizismus: HerKor 49 (1995) 587-594.

4335 *Bleunven* Pierre, Prêtre pour l'éternité selon l'ordre de Melchisédech: PensCath 274 (1995) 12-23.

4336 **Bowden** Andrew, Ministry in the countryside; a model for the future. L 1994, Mowbray. xii-244 p. £ 13. -- [R]JE(mp)T 8,1 (1995) 96s (L.J. *Francis*); *ModBlv 36,1 (1995) 37-39 (J. *King*); Theol 98 (L 1995) 153-5 (P. *Avis*).

4337 **Breuning** Wilhelm, *Hemmerle* Klaus, Prêtres; vivre plutôt que survivre, 10 priorités pour aujourd'hui: Racines. Montrouge 1994, Nouvelle Cité. 69 p. F 40. -- ᴿE(spr)eV 105 (1995) 139 (P. *Jay*).

4338 *Brug* J.F., Ordination and installation in the Scriptures: WLQ 92 (Milwaukee 1995) 263-270 [NTAb 40, p.272: 'there is no scriptural statement that commands the ordination of pastors and other ministers as a rite through which they receive special gifts'].

4339 **Bühlmann** Walbert, A Igreja no limiar do terceiro milênio. São Paulo 1994. -- ᴿREB 55 (1995) 475-8 (H. *Lepargneur*).

4340 **Burtchaell** James T., From synagogue to Church; public services and offices 1992 → 8.8192.8306 ... 10,8059: ᴿChH 64 (1995) 335s (E.G. *Hinson*); *CritRR 7 (1994) 319-321 (J.C. *Hanges*); CrSt 16 (1995) 165-9 (A. *Di Berardino*); EvQ 66 (1994) 187s (B.J. *Dodd*); *JEarlyC 3 (1995) 499s (L.D. *Franklin*): S(cot)JTh 48 (1995) 142s (A. *Stewart-Sykes*).

4341 *Butler* Sara, In persona Christi: representation of Christ or servant of Christ's presence ? : → 564, CTS 50 (1995) 138-155.

4342 **Campbell** R. Alastair. The Elders; seniority within earliest Christianity. E 1994, Clark. 309 p. £ 22. -- ᴿET 106 (1994s) 377 (N. *Clark*).

4343 *Campbell* R.A., Leaders and fathers; Church government in earliest Christianity [classic threefold ministry scarcely before 3d century]:I(rish)BSt 17,1 (1995) 2-21 [NTAb 39,443].

4344 *Chang* Aloysius B., ᶜ Classifying the People of God; a reconsideration: CollFujen 101 (1994) 25 [< TIC 12/2, 25: laity's ministry is fundamental, clergy's specific].

4345 *Clifford* Alan C., Bishop or presbyter ? French Reformed ecclesiology in 1559: EvQ 67 (1995) 211-7.

4346 *Coleman* Gerald, El seminarista actual y el papel del sacerdote [< America], ᵀ *Tabuyo* María: SalTer 82 (1994) 811-820.

4347 *Colijn* H. J., A biblical and contemporary model of ministry: AThJ 27 (1995) 1-14 [NTAb 40, p.460].

4348 **Collins** John N., Are all Christians ministers ? 1992 → 9,8531*; 10,8064: ᴿNewThR 8,1 (1995) 193-5 (M. *Trainor*).

4349 *Collins* Raymond F., Ministry and the Christian scriptures → 40, ꟳCOLLINS: LouvSt 20 (1995) 112-125.

4350 **Congar** Yves, Église et papauté, regards historiques: C(og)Fi 84. P 1994, Cerf. 318 p. F 145. 2-204-05090-3 -- ᴿRET 55 (1995) 100-2 (M. *Gesteira Garza*); RevSR 69 (1995) 135s (M. *Metzger*); ZkT 117 (1995) 447-452 (K.H. *Neufeld*).

4351 **Dassmann** Ernst, Ämter und Dienste in den frühchristlichen Gemeinden: Hereditas 8. Alfter 1994, Borengässer. 244 p. DM 42. 3-923946-26-0. -- ᴿThGL 85 (1995) 412s (K. *Backhaus*).

4352 **Deming** Willoughby H.,, Paul on marriage and celibacy; the Hellenistic background of 1 Corinthians: SNTS.m 83. C 1995, Univ. xiv-265 p.; bibliog. 232-258. 0-521-47284-9.

4353 *Domagalski* Bernhard, Der Diakon -- 'Sinnbild der ganzen Kirche '; zur Ausformung des Diakonenamtes in patristischer Zeit: LebZeug 50 ('Diakonat -- wie werd es weitergehen ?' 1995) 15-24.

4354 **Drewermann** Eugen (→ 1943 supra; deutsch 1989 → 9,8442s), Clérigos; psicograma de un ideal. M 1995, Trotta. 788 p. 84-8164-038-7. -- ᴿE(st)E 70 (1995) 579s (M. *Alcalá*: errores metodológicos pero no sin valor); RF 232 (1995) 113-6 (también M. *Alcalá*: psicocaricatura, con gran dosis de razón); EstAg 30 (1995) 566s (T. *Marcos*: despersonalización a que pueden conducir las instituciones eclesiales).

4355 **Garuti** Adriano, S. Pietro unico titolare del primato 1993 → 9,4723; 10,4544: ᴿDiv 39 (1995) 68-71 (B. *Gherardini*); TeolBA 30 (1994) 253-6 (A.H. *Zecca*).

4356 *Garuti* Adriano, Ancora a proposito del Papa patriarca d'Occidente: Anton 70 (1995) 31-45: Eng. 31: answers to criticisms of his 1993 book.

4357 **González Faus** J.I., 'Ningún obispo impuesto' 1992 → 10,8080: ᴿActuBbg 31 (1994) 101s (J. *Vives*).

4358 *González Faus* José Ignacio, ¿ Hacia un clero analfabeto ? ; SalTer 82 (1994) 735-8.

4359 *Gramaglia* Pier Angelo, Episcopato monarchico e primato romano [Maccarrone M. 1989/91]: RSLR 31 (1995) 73-99.

4360 **Greenwood** Robin, Transforming priesthood; a new theology of ministry. L 1994, SPCK. xi-238 p. £ 15. -- ᴿModern Believing [continuing the numbering of Modern Churchman] 36,1 (1995) 42-44 (A. *Billings*).

4361 **Greshake** G., Ser sacerdote; teología y espiritualidad del ministerio sacerdotal. S 1995, Sígueme. 247 p. -- ᴿEstTrin 29 (1995) 136s (J.M. de *Miguel*); RevAg 36 (1995) 1139s (M. *Boyano*).

4362 *a) Griswold* Frank T., The bishop as presider, teacher, and person of prayer; -- *b) Borsch* Frederick H., The ministry and authority of bishops in a changing world and church; -- *c) Anderson* Craig B., Theological method and episcopal vocation: A(ngl)ThR 77,1 ('Bishops and the Church' 1995) 5-13 / 14-30 / 31-46 (-75, *al.*).

4363 **Häring** Bernhard, Preti di oggi, preti der domani; quale prete per la Chiesa ? [1955 (per 1995, 'subito tradotto' ?], ᵀ*Danna* Carlo. Brescia 1995, Queriniana. 186 p. -- ᴿTer(esianum) 46 (1995) 616 (M. *Caprioli*).

4364 **Hammann** G., L'amour retrouvé; le ministère du diacre, du christianisme primitif aux Réformés protestants du XVIᵉ siècle: Univ. Neuchâtel 13, 1994 → 10,8086; F 140. -- ᴿTTh 35 (1995) 411s (Angela *Berlis*).

4365 *Haquin* André, Un colloque consacré au diaconat permanent (LvN 15-17 sept. 1994): RTL 26 (1995) 418-423.

4366 *Hauser-Borel* S., Algunos testimonios neotestamentarios sobre la diaconia: AnáMnesis 4,1 (Méx 1994) 85-94.

4367 *Heim* S. Mark, Improving our gifts; ordination in Baptist perspective: AmBapQ 14 (1995) 190-206.

4368 **Helm** A. van der, Un clergé parallèle ? Étude socio-juridique de l'activité des laïcs dans l'Église catholique en France et aux Pays-Bas. Strasbourg 1993. CERDIC. -- ᴿThRv 91 (1995) 429s (W. *Rüfner*).

4369 **Herbert** Alphonso, Priestly vocation and consecrated life. Anand-SP 1994. 84 p. rs 27. -- ᴿI(nd)TS 32 (1995) 186s (C.G. *Pushparaj*).

4370 *a) Hoffmann* Paul, 'Dienst' als Herrschaft oder 'Herrschaft' als Dienst; -- *b) Schottroff* Luise, Über Herrschaftsverzicht und den Dienst der Versöhnung: BiKi 50,3 ('Diakonie -- biblischer Anspruch und heutige Praxis' 1995) 146-152 / 153-9.

4371 *Hohmann* Joachim, Der immerwährende Streitfall; Standpunkte über die priesterlichen Zölibat seit den sechsiger Jahren: KZg 8 (1995) 143-158.

4372 **Icenogle** Gareth W., Biblical foundations for small group ministry: an integrational approach. DG 1994, InterVarsity. 396 p. $ 13 (M. Christine *Sullivan*).

4373 **Jäger** Alfred, Konzepte der Kirchenleitung (→10,8092); wissenschaftliche Analysen und theologische Perspektiven. Gü 1993, Kaiser. 477 p. DM 138. 3-579-00196-5. -- ᴿTHGL 85 (1995) 561s (D. *Hattrup*).

4374 *Jenson* Philip P., Ordination AT, ᵀ*Kirsch* Tilman: → 772, TRE 25 (1995) 334-7 (340-3, *Lips* Hermann von, NT).

4375 **John Paul II** (18 1993 weekly audiences), ^E*Socias* James P., Priesthood in the third millennium. ... c.1995, Scepter. 158 p. $ 10. -- ^RCanadCath 13,5 (1995) 20 (J. A. *Ihnatowicz*).

4376 *Johnson* John E., The Old Testament offices as paradigm for pastoral identity: BS 152 (1995) 182-200.

4377 **Josuttis** M., Petrus, die Kirche und die verdammte Macht. Stu 1993, Kreuz. 216 p. DM 26,80. 3-7831-1233-8. -- ^RTTh 35 (1995) 312 (P. *Haarsma*).

4378 **King** Eugene F.A., Church and ministry; the role of church, pastor, and people from Luther to Walther. St,Louis 1993, Concordia. -- : ^RConcordiaTQ 59 (Fort Wayne 1995) 134-7 (C.A. *MacKenzie*: good but really only on LUTHER's views).

4379 *Knauer* Peter, El 'celibato por el Reino' y la ley del celibato: RF 232 (1995) 393-405.

4380 *a) Krasiński* Józef, ^P Collegiality of authority in the Church before Vatican Council II and the conciliar breakthrough; -- *b) Nosowski* Zbigbniew, ^P Collegiality of the Church and the challenges of modern democracy : STV(ars) 33,2 (1995) 5-29; Eng. 29s / 47-61: Eng. 62.

4381 *Lamoureaux* John, Episcopal courts in late Antiquity: JEarlyC 3 (1995) 143-167.

4382 **Lane** Thomas, A priesthood in tune; theological reflections on ministry. 1993 → 9,8476; 10,9097: ^RI(r)ThQ 61 (1995) 313s (D. *O'Callaghan*: a masterpiece): MilltSt 35 (1995) 138-145 (F. *Clancy:* clear except on the complexities of current debates on celibacy and women's ordination).

4383 *Lehtio* Pirkko, The Lutheran understanding of diakonia: Thwology and Life 15s (Hong Kong 1993) 40-44.

4384 **Loretan** Adrian, Laien im pastoralen Dienst; ein Amt in der kirchlichen Gesetzgebung; Pastoralassistent/-assistentin -- Pastoralreferent/-referentin: PrakTDialog 9. FrS 1994, Univ. 405 p. DM 74. -- ^RThRv 91 (1995) 430-2 (B. *Studer*).

4385 *MacLeod* Donald, Deacons and elders: *a)* (Tü)TQ 175 (1995) 26-50; -- *b)* SBET 13,1 (1995) 26-50 [NTAb 40, p.82].

4386 **Manaranche** André, Vouloir et former des prêtres 1994 → 10,8103: ^RE(spr)eV 105 (1995) 206s (C. *Bouchard*).

4387 **Mateo-Seco** Lucas F., *Rodríguez-Ocaña* Rafael, Sacerdotes en el Opus Dei. Pamplona 1994, EUNSA. 329 p. -- ^RScrT(Pamp) 37 (1995) 309-313 (J. *Alviar*).

4388 ^E**Meyendorff** John, The primacy of Peter; essays in ecclesiology and the early Church 1992 → 8,407: 9,4720: ^RRHE 90 (1995) 239s (J. *Famerée*).

4389 **Miller** J. Michael, The shepherd and the rock; origins, development, and mission of the Papacy. Huntington IN 1995, Our Sunday Visitor. 384 p. $ 20. -- ^R*CritRR 8 (1995) 414s (P.E. *Yevics*): Priest 51,9 (1995) 56 (C. *Dollen*).

4390 *Minnerath* R., De Jérusalem à Rome; Pierre et l'unité de l'Église apostolique. P 1994, Beauchesne. 616 p. F 150. 2-7010-1321-6 [NTAb 40,p.545].

4391 **Müller** Wunibald, Liebe und Zölibat; wie eheloses Leben gelingen kann. Mainz 1994, Grünewald. 160 p. DM 24,80. -- ^REntschluss 50,1 (1995) 41s (C. *Schwaiger*).

4392 **Nelson** Richard D., Raising up a faithful priest; community and priesthood in [OT] biblical theology 1993 → 9,8498: 10.8108: ^RBoL (1995) 147s (D.J. *Reimer*: Jesus 'obliterates, annihilates, demolishes', p.170s); Interpretation 49 (1995) 200 (J. *Milgrom*; superb, and sorely needed); RefR 49 (1995s) 71 (Sylvio J. *Scorza*).

4393 *Neuner* Peter (*al.*), Die Kirche entwickelt heute neue Ämter: HerKor 49 (1995) 128-133.

4394 *Nichols* Terence L., Hierarchy and the Church: ProEccl 4 (1995) 261-300.

4395 *Niewiadomski* Józef, 'Menschen, Christen, Priester ...'; dogmatische Überlegungen zur

Amtstheologie auf dem Hintergrund der Diskussion über 'kooperative Seelsorgemodelle': TPQ 143 (1995) 159-169.

4396 **Olson** Jeannine E., One ministry, many roles; deacons anD deaconesses through the centuries. St.Louis 1992, Concordia. 461 p. $ 22. -- [R]A(ndr)USS 33 (1995) 313s (R.L. *Dudley*).

4397 **Pallath** Paul, The synod of bishops of Catholic Oriental Churches. R 1994, Mar Thomas. 234 p. -- [R]OCP 61 (1995) 275-8 (D. *Salachas*).

4398 **Poma** Gianfranco, *al.*, La formazione del presbitero diocesano: S(cuol)C 123,3s intero (1995) 261-587.

4399 **Powers** William F., Free priests; the movement for ministerial reform in the Roman Catholic Church [...(organizations of U.S.) married priests] 1992 → 8,8257: 9.8506: [R]NewThR 8,2 (1995) 106s (J.A. *Coriden*).

4400 *Ratzinger* J., *Cochini* C., *al.*, Celibato e magistero; interventi dei Padri nel Concilio Vaticano II e nei Sinodi dei Vescovi del 1971 e del 1990. CinB 1994, Paoline. -- [R]Ter(esianum) 46 (1995) 626s (M. *Caprioli*).

4401 *Rousseau* Mary, The ministry of the laity: NOxR 62,5 (1995) 8-13.

4402 *a) Russell* John M., [John] MACQUARRIE on ministry; a critical analysis; -- *b) Flemming* Dean, The clergy/laity dichotomy; a New Testament exegetical and theological analysis : A(sia)JT 8 (1994) 210-231 / 232-250.

4403 *Schwaiger* Georg, Papsttum: → 772, TRE 25 (1995) 647-676 (-695, *Leipold* Heinrich, neueres).

4404 **Seagraves** Richard, Pascentes cum disciplina; a lexical survey of the clergy in the Cyprianic correspondence [*sacerdos* always means bishop]: Paradosis, 1993 → 8,8269; 9,8519; Fs 66: [R]TS 56 (1995) 360s (R.R. *Noll*).

4405 **Špehar** Milan, Die priesterliche Spiritualität: RijT 2 (1994) 41-61 . 287-304 kroatisch; deutsch 62; 304.

4406 **Stickler** Alfons Maria, card., Il celibato ecclesiastico; la sua storia e i suoi fondamenti teologici; Cultura Religiosa 3. Vaticano 1994, Editrice. -- [R]Div 39 (1995) 78-81 (D. *Vibrac*).

4407 **Strauch** Alexander, Biblical eldership. Littleton CO 1988 reprint,, Leis & R. 288 p. A$ 19. -- [R]RefTR 54 (1995) 91s (B. *Secombe*)

4408 **Thiede** Christian, Bischöfe-kollegial für Europa; der Rat der Europäischen Bischofskonferenzen im Dienst einer sozialethisch konkretisierten Evangelisierung [Diss. Müns, [D]*Furger*]: ICS 22. Müns 1991. 268 p. -- [R]AtK(ap) 125 (1995) 288-291 (T. *Fitych*).

4409 **Thurian** Max, Le prêtre configuré au Christ. P 1993, Mame. 107 p. 3-2780-0502-2. -- [R]RTL 26 (1995) 372 (G. *Thils*: meilleur A. de HALLEUX, RTL 18,281.425).

4410 *Torelló* Juan Bautista, Las ciencias humanas ante el celibato sacerdotal: ScrT(Pamp) 37 (1995) 269-284.

4411 **Unworth** Tim, The last priests in America; conversations with remarkable men. NY 1993, Crossroad. -- [R]CCurr 44 (1944s) 136 (W. F. *Powers*, echoing H. KÜNG's 1972 Why priests? a proposal for a new Church ministry).

4412 *Vogt* Hermann J., Bemerkungen zur frühen Amts- und Gemeindestruktur: (Tü) ThQ 175 (1995) 192-8.

4413 *Weitlauff* Manfred, Priesterbild und Priesterbildung bei Johann Michael SAILER: MThZ 46 (1995) 69-97.

4414 **Ysebaert** Joseph, Die Amtsterminologie im Neuen Testament und in der Alten Kirche; eine lexikographische Untersuchung 1994 → 10,8139: [R]EThL 71 (1995) 234-7 (J.

Verheyden); E(rbe)uA 71 (1995) 165 (B. *Schwank*); FgNt 8 (1995) 229s (A. *Piñero*).
4415 *Zemek* G.J., The modeling of ministers: MastJ 4,2 (1993) 165-185 [< NTAb 38, p.236].
4416 **Zizola** Giancarlo, Il conclave -- storia e segreti; l'elezione papale da San Pietro a Giovanni Paolo II. R 1993, Newton Compton. 415 p. -- [R]TS 56 (1995) 377s (F.X. *Murphy*).

H8.0 **Oratio,** *spiritualitas personalis*

4417 **Allen** Joseph A., Inner way; toward a rebirth of Eastern Christian spiritual direction. GR c.1994, Eerdmans.-- 141 p. US$ 16. -- [R]CanadCath 13,3 (1995) 26 (T. Allan *Smith*).
4418 **Alonso Schökel** Luis, Piantata in terra, toccava il cielo; meditazioni bibliche 1993 → 9,8540; 10,8140: [R]CivCatt 146 (1995,1) 98s (D. *Scaiola*).
4419 **Ashley** Benedict M., Spiritual direction in the Dominican tradition: Integration books. NY 1995, Paulist. vii-168 p. $ 13. 0-8091-3567-1 [ThD 43,156]
4420 *Asti* Francesco, Per una lettura critica dell'esperienza mistica: Asprenas 42 (1995) 523-538.
4421 **Backus** Iréna, Ainsi priaient les Luthériens; la vie religieuse, la pratique et lá foi des luthériens de Paris au XVIIIe siècle. P 1992, Cerf. 240 p. -- DissA 56 (1995s) 305s.
4422 [E]**Barbaglio** Giuseppe, Espiritualidad del Nuevo Testamento. S 1994, Sígueme. 352 p. 84-301-1244-4. - [R]E(st)E 70 (1995) 409s (J. *Alonso Dïaz*); RET 55 (1995) 94-96 (P. *Barrado Fernández*); RevAg 36 (1995) 630s J. *Domínguez Sanabria*).
4423 **Barth** Hans-M., Spiritualität: Bensheimer Hefte 74. Gö 1993, Vandenhoeck & R. 191 p. 3-525-87162-7. - [R]ZkT 117 (1995) 489s (H. *Rotter*: besonders lesenswert).
4424 *a) Beauchamp* Paul, Sagesse biblique et expérience mystique: -- *b) Léon-Dufour* Xavier, Ouvertures johanniques sur la mystique; -- *c) Bastian* Bernard, Jésus dans la religiosité contemporaine: Christus 41 (1994) 157-166 / 180-8 / 236-245.
4425 *Bulhof* Ilse N., Towards a 'postmodern' spirituality ?: JIntRD 5 (1995) 5-30.
4426 *Brownson* William C., The biblical background of prayer: RefR 49 ('Prayer in the Post-Modern world' 1995s) 85-98 [-125, *al.*].
4427 *Chmielewski* Marek, [P] Zagadnienie .. Il problema di spiritualità nel Catechismo CC: R(ocz)T(Lub) 42,5 (1995) 5-25; ital. 25.
4428 *Corneanu* Nicolae, The Jesus prayer and deification: SV(lad)TQ 39 (1995s) 3-24.
4429 **Cullmann** Oscar, Das Gebet im NT 1994 → 10,168: [R]Presbyterion 21 (St.Louis 1995) 49-56 (R.W. *Yarbrough*); Protest(antesimo) 50 (1995) 325s (A. *Comba*); Ter(esianum) 46 (1995) 284s (A. *Borell*); ThZ 51 (1995) 370-2 (G. *Müller*).
4430 **Cullmann** Oscar, Prayer in the NT, with answers from the NT to today's questions. L 1995, SCM. xvii-190 p. £ 10. 0-334-02590-7. -- [R]ET 107 (1995s) 86s (J. *Law*).
4431 **Cullmann** Oscar, La prière dans le Nouveau Testament; essai de réponse à des questions contemporaines [Das Gebet 1994], [T]*Arnold* M.; Théologies Bibliques. P 1995, Cerf. 260 p. F 149. 2-204-05284-1 [NTAb 40,p. 365].
4432 **Cullmann** O., La preghiera nel NT; una risposta alle domande odierne: PiccBtTh 39. T 1995, Claudiana 251 p. L[m] 29. 88-7016-225-7.
4433 **Deville** Raymond, The French [BERULLE (CONDREN, OLIER, EUDES)] school of spirituality; an introduction and reader, [T]*Cunningham* Agnes. Pittsburgh 1994, Duquesne Univ. xii-289 p. $ 22.50. 0-8207-0258-7 [< ThD 42 (1995) 265].

4434 **Doohan** Helen & Leonard, Prayer in the NT. ColMn ... Liturgical/Glazier. 143 p. £ 8.50. - [R]DoLi 45 (1995) 455 (E. *Griffin*).

4435 **Dossetti** Giuseppe, L'esegesi spirituale secondo d. Divo BARSOTTI: Sussidi biblici 67. Reggio Emilia 1995, S. Lorenzo. xiv-117 p. 88-8071-049-4.

4436 [E]**Downey** Michael, The new dictionary of Catholic spirituality 1993 > 9,8562; 10,8157: [R]*CritRR 7 (1994) 327-9 (R. *Penaskovic*: first-rate).

4437 [E]**Dupré** Louis, *Saliers* Don E., Christian spirituality 3. Post Reformation and modern 1991 > 5,8151 ... 9,8563: [R]NewThR 8,1 (1995) 112-4 (Elizabeth *Dryer*).

4438 **Dwyer** E.J., Living stones. Dublin 1994, Columba. 180 p. £ 8. 0-85574-373-5. - [R]ET 106 (1994s) 254 (R. *Howe*: author a Sydney Marist).

4439 *Fee* Gordon D., Exegesis and spirituality; reflections on completing the exegetical circle: Crux 31,4 (1995) 29-35.

4440 **Fisher** Kathleen, Women at the well; feminist perspectives on spiritual direction. L 1989, SPCK. 215p. £ 8. 0-281-04426-0. -- [R]S(co)BET 13 (1995) 174-6 (Ruth B. *Edwards*).

4441 *Francis* Leslie J., *Evans* Thomas F., The psychology of Christian prayer; a review of empirical research: Religion 25 (1995) 371-388.

4442 **Gamarra** Saturnino, Teología espiritual: Sapientia Fidei 7. M 1994, BAC. 312 p. 84-7914-144-1. -- [R]RET 55 (1995) 538 (M. *Gesteira*).

4443 *García Hirschfeld* Carlos, La parábola del Rey temporal (Fidelidad al texto o esfuerzo de traducción): Manresa 67 (1995) 123-138.

4444 **George** K.M., The silent roots; Orthodox perspectives on Christian spirituality: Risk Book. Geneva 1994, WCC. 91 p. Fs 10. 2-8254-1147-7. -- [R]ET 106 (1994s) 283 (Ann *Shukman*).

4445 *Grimm* Veronika, Fasting women in Judaism and Christianity in late antiquity: → 710, Food 1992/5, 225-240.

4446 **Guinan** M.D., To be human before God; insights from biblical spirituality. ColMn 1994, Liturgical. ix-92 p. $ 8 pa. 0-8146-2207-0 [NTAb 39,p.343].

4447 **Hamman** Adalbert G., La preghiera nella Chiesa antica. T 1994, SEI. xlvi-234 p. L[m] 40. -- [R]CivCatt 146 (1995,1) 622s (A. *Ferrua*).

4448 [E]**Hinson** E. Glenn, Spirituality in ecumenical perspective. LvL 1993, W-Knox. 160 p. $ 15. 0-664-25385-7. -- [R]Mid-Str 34 (1995) 106-9 (W.O. *Paulsell*).

4449 *Horst* Pieter W. van der, MAXIMUS van Tyrus over het gebed: een geannoteerde vertaling van *Ei deî eúchesthai*: NedThT 49 (1995) 12-23.

4450 *Iammarrone* Giovanni, L'uomo immagine di Dio -- riflessioni per una spiritualità dell'immagine: Ter(esianum) 46 (1995) 583-592.

4451 *Jaspard* Jean-Marie, Paramètres pour une compréhension psychologique des apparitions: FoiTe 24 (1994) 217-245.

4452 **Kern** Kathleen, We are the Pharisees. Scottdale PA 1995, Herald. 160 p. $ 10 pa. 0-8361-3071-3.

4453 *a) Klaiber* Walter F., bp. (Methodist), Sanctification in the New Testament [*Theisen* Jerome, abbot: response]; -- *b) Bondì* Roberta C., Sanctification in the tradition of the desert fathers; a Methodist perspective; -- *c) Dodaro* Robert, Sacramentum caritatis as the foundation of AUGUSTINE's spirituality: → 557, AsbTJ 50s (1995s) 11-21 23-25 / 27-33 / 45-55.

4454 **Klinger** Elmar, Das absolute Geheimnis im Alltag entdecken; zur spirituellen Theologie Karl RAHNERs [nicht unverständlich wie allgemein behauptet]. Wü 1994, Echter.

60 p. DM 12,80. 3-429-01614-2. -- [R]ZkT 117 (1995) 375s (A. *Batlogg*).

4455 *Korpel* M.C.A., Troost in bijbels perspectief: G(ereformeerd)TT 94 (1994) 51-59 [-76].

4456 **La Potterie** Ignace de, La preghiera di Gesù 1992 → 10.8168; [T]*Berényi* Gabriella: [R]RA(sc)M 20 (1995) 223s (G. *Podio*).

4457 **López Melús** Francisco María, Desierto; una experiencia de gracia 1994 → 9,8586; 8171: [R]Ang 72 (1995) 119s (J. *Salguero*);RevAg 36 (1995) 317-9 (J. *Domínguez Sanabria*).

4458 **Luibl** Hans Jürgen, Des Fremden Sprachgestalt; Beobachtungen zum Bedeutungswandel des Gebets in der Geschichte de Neuzeit: HUTh 30, [D]1993 > 10,8172: [R]ThR(u) 60 (1995) 330-4 (T, *Koch*: Theologie als kritische 'Nach-Lese' des Gebets).

4459 **McDannell** Colleen, Material Christianity [images and objects used to foster piety; also the (Victorian) Bible; cemeteries]: religion and popular culture in America. NHv 1995, Yale Univ. x-312 p. $ 35- 0-300-06440-3 [ThD 43,177].

4460 [E]**McGinn** Bernard, *al.*, Christian spirituality 1-3: World Spirituality 16ss, 1986-90: [R]E(st)E 70 (1995) 248-250 (P. *Cebollada*).

4461 [E]**McGinn** Bernard, *al.*, Geschichte der christlichen Spiritualität, I. Von den Anfängen bis zum 12. Jahrhundert [1985-91], [T][*Sudbrack* Josef, present.] 1993 → 10,8174; DM 78; 3-429-01500-6: [R]ZkT 117 (1995) 457-460 (R. *Messner*).

4462 **McGrath** Alister, Spirituality in an age of change: rediscovering the spirit of the Reformation. GR 1994, Zondervan. 206 p. $ 17. 0-310-42921-8 [< ThD 42 (1995) 278].

4463 **Madigan** Patrick, Penance, contemplation and service; pivotal experiences of Christian spirituality. ColMn 1994, Liturgical. xvii-210 p. £ 13.50. 0-8146-5911-X. -- [R]*TBR 8,1 (1995s) 34s (P. *Sheldrake*).

4464 **Martini** Carlo M., Im Zweifel nicht unterbrechen; Christus und der Weg des Christen. FrB 1994, Herder. 203 p. DM 19,80. 3-451-23349-5.-- [R]ThGL 85 (1995) 143s (W. *Beinert*).

4465 **Martini** Carlo M., Weil ihr Zeugen Christi seid, [T]*Berz* August. FrS 1994, Paulus. 160 p. Fs 24. 3-7228-0308-X [GuL 67,161 adv.].

4466 **Martini** Carlo M., Promise fulfilled; meditations on the Passion narratives, [T]*Neame* Alan. .. Mediaspaul. 175 p. $ 11. -- [R]CanadCath 13,10 (1995) 27 (Madeleine *Grace*).

4467 *Martini* Carlo Maria, Une parole née dans le silence : LV(itF) 50,4 ('Silence' 1995) 365s.

4468 **Martini** Carlo M., Vie de Moïse, vie de Jésus et expërience pascale [retraite 1978, italien 1992], [T]*Ispérian* Gabriel. Saint-Maurice (Suisse) 1994, S. Augustin. 125 p -- [R]E(spr)eV 105 (1995) 450 (G.-M. *Oury*, aussi sur leur Abraham 1994).

4469 **Mathys** Hans-Peter, Dichter und Beter .. : OBO 132, 1994 → 10,2807: [R]CBQ 57 (1995) 777s (R. *Gnuse*).

4470 **Miller** Patrick, They cried to the Lord; the forms and theology of biblical prayer 1994 → 10,8179; $ 40; pa. $ 24: [R]ChrCent 112 (1995) 341s (K.H. *Carter*); P(rinc)SB 16 (1995) 241-3 (J. *Limburg*).

4471 **Oropeza** B.J., A time to laugh; the ['Toronto Blessing'] holy laughter phenomenon. Peabody MA 1995, Hendrickson. vi-194 p. 1-56563-183-8 [*TBR 9/2,51, Una *Kroll*].

4472 *Palmer* Martin E., The Spiritual Exercises and the Bible; CIS 26,2 (Center of Ignatian Spirituality review 1995) 28-39 = Les Exercices Spirituels et la Bible (éd. française) 29-42.

4473 **Panikkar** Raimun, Action and contemplation as categories of human understanding: Forefront 1,3 (1994) 15 . 18-21.

4474 **Park Young-Mann,** Thomas MERTON's prayer from an Asian Christian perspective: Diss. *GTheologicalU, [D]*Martin* H. Berkeley 1995 [< RStR 22,p.269].

4475 *Perrar* H.J., 'Ihr sollt heilige werden ... ' (Lev 19,2): Annäherungen an Leviticus

19,1-27: RU(ökZ: Religionsunterricht) 25 (Stu/Mü 1995) 17-20 [< ZIT 95,p.191].

4476 **Peterson** David, Possessed by God, a NT theology of sanctification and holiness: NStBT. GR/Leicester 1995, Eerdmans/Apollos. 191 p.; 10 fig. $ 18 pa. 0-8028-4173-2 [NTAb 40, p.546].

4477 **Powell** John, A life-giving vision. Allen TX c.1995, T.More/Tabor. 342 p. $ 18 pa. -- ᴿPriest 51,11 (1995) (C.*Dollen*)

4478 *Prakash* P. Surya, The Bible and Christian practices: Kristu Jyoti 10,4 (1994) 19-38.

4479 ᴱ**Rakoczy** Susan, Common journey, different paths; spiritual direction in cross-cultural perspective 1992; 0-88344-789-4. -- ᴿETL 70 (1994) 510s (V. *Neckebrouck* : utile; il n'existe pas de meilleur de ce genre).

4480 **Renzi** Angelo, La scala di Giacobbe [... la preghiera]; introduzione alla lectio divina. Assisi 1992, Cittadella. 246 p. Lᵐ 18. -- ᴿParVi 39,3 (1994) 61 (L. *Melotti*).

4481 *a) Rienstra* Marchiene V., Reforming spirituality; -- *b) Old* Hughes O., What is Reformed spirituality ?: (Reformed) Perspectives 9,1 (1994) 6s / 8-10.

4482 *a) Romaniuk* bp. Kazimierz, ᴾ Necessity of openness to God (1 Sm 3,9); -- *b) Bolewski* Jacek, ᴾ The open space of confidence: *ŻycieD 3,2 (1995) 11-25 / 51-66; Eng.3s

4483 **Schnackenburg** Rudolf, Gesù verso Gerusalemme; meditazioni sulla Quaresima e la Pasqua: I triangoli 1. CasM 1995, Piemme. 94 p. 88-384-2293-1.

4484 *Smith* A.C. & L.K.R., 'Shadowlands' [C.S. LEWIS film: against cancer 'prayer doesn't work']; reflections on prayers for people who are seriously ill: ET 106 (1994s) 265.

4485 *Smith* Steven G., Piety's problems: ScotJR 16 (1995) 5-24.

4486 **Stefani** Piero, Davanti a Dio; il cammino spirituale di Mosè, di Elia e di Gesù: Quad Camaldoli Ric 3. Bo 1995, Dehoniane. 59 p. 88-10-41105-6.

4487 **Stibbe** Mark, A kingdom of priests; deeper into God in prayer. L 1994, Darton-LT. xiv-146 p. £ 9. 0-232-52064-X. -- ᴿET 106 (1994s) 155 (A. *Dunstan*).

4487* *Suurmond* J.J.(→ 10,5931), Charismatisch pastoraat: PrakT 19 (19920 32-21.

4488 *Teasdale* Wayne, Entering the interspiritual age; the possibility of a global spirituality: Vidyajyoti 59 (1995) 290-306.

4489 **Thomas** Carolyn, Gift and response; a biblical spirituality for contemporary Christians. NY 1994, Paulist. vii-167 p. $ 10 pa. 0-8091-3510-8 [ThD 43,92].

4490 *Timm* Hermann, Formation des Geistes: ThLZ 120 (1995) 859-866.

4491 *Tracy* David [interview], Why theologians should pray: CCurr 44 (1944s) 293-315.

4492 **Trevethan** Thomas L., The beauty of God's holiness. DG/Leicester 1995, InterVarsity. 278 p. £ 10. 0-8038-1607-0.

4493 **Vanhoye** Albert, Vivere nella nuova alleanza; meditazioni bibliche: Bibbia e Preghiera 25. R 1995, Apost.Preghiera. 250 p. 88-7357-160-3.

4494 *Wallis* Ian G., Jesus, human being and the praxis of intercession; towards a biblical perspective: S(cot)JTh 48 (1995) 225-250.

4495 *Zekiyan* Boghos L., Riflessioni preliminari sulla spritualità armena, una cristianità di 'frontiera'; martyria ed apertura all'oikumene: OCP 61 (1995) 333-365.

H8.1 *Spiritualitas publica*: **Liturgia, vita communitatis, Sancti**

4496 *Babcock* Robert, The Luxeuil Prophets and the Gallican liturgy: Scr 47 (1993) 52-55.

4497 *a) Becker* Hansjörg, Die Bibel Jesu und das Evangelium Jesu; ein konkreter Vorschlag zur Weiterführung des Wortgottesdienstes; -- *b) Braulik* Georg, Kanon und liturgische Schriftlesung; -- *c) Monshouwer* Dirk, Überraschende Erfahrungen; der dreijährige Torazyklus im christlichen Gottesdienst; -- *d) Kranemann* Benedikt, Abwertung des Alten Testaments in der Liturgie ?: BiLi 68 (1995) 186-194 / 181-5 / 172-180 / 191-8.

4498 **Berg** Karl, CÄSARIUS von Arles; ein Bischof des sechsten Jahrhunderts erschliesst das liturgische Leben seiner Zeit [Diss. Pont. Univ. Gregoriana, R 1935/44/46]. als Festgabe für ihn jetzt Alterzbischof von Salzburg, 85. Gb., [E]*Paarhammer* Hans. *Hofrichter* Peter: Frühes Christentum 1. Thaur 1994. Kultur. 390 p.; Portr. Sch 298, 3-85395-185-6. -- [R]ZkT 117 (1995) 379s (H.B. *Meyer*).

4499 **Bradshaw** Paul F., The search for the origins of Christian worship; sources and methods for the study of early liturgy 1992 → 8,8303 ... 10,8198: [R]*CritRR 7 (1994) 316-9 (R.P. *Martin*); NewThR 8,1 (1995) 95s (M.D. *Whalen*): P(atr)BR 14 (1995) 110-2 (T. *Maschke*).

4500 **Bradshaw** Paul, La liturgie chrétienne et ses origines. P 1995, Cerf. 250 p. -- [R]Phase 35 (1995) 528s (J. *Llopis*).

4501 **Bradshaw** Paul F., Two ways of praying ['cathedral', 'monastic']. Nv/L 1995, Abingdon/SPCK. 140 p. 0-687-42667-7 [ThD 43,158]. -- [R]ET 106,12 top choice (1994s) 353s (C.S. *Rodd*).

4502 *Braulik* Georg, Die Tora als Bahnlesung; zur Hermeneutik einer zukünftigen Auswahl der Sonntagsperikopen: → 128, [F]MEYER H., Bewahren 1995, 51-76.

4503 *Bux* Nicola, Le liturgie pasquali della croce e del fuoco, da Gerusalemme a Roma: Nicolaus 21 (1994) 5-12.

4504 *Daschner* Dominik, Vom Diözesanmessbuch zum Missale Romanum Pius' V (1570); die Übernahme des Missale Romanum in den Diözesen des südlichen deutschen Sprachgebietes: AL(tg)W 37 (1995) 304-346.

4505 **Egbulem** Nwaka Chris, The power of Afrocentric celebrations; inspirations from the [now Congo] Zairean liturgy. NY 1995, Crossroad. 167 p. $ 15. 0-8245-1489-0.

4506 *Gerl-Falkovitz* Hanna-Barbara, Zur Anti-Ekstase im christlichen Gottesdienst: FrRu NF 1 (1993s) 138-142.

4507 *Gorman* F.H., Ritual studies and biblical studies; assessment of the past, prospects for the future: Semeia 67 (1994) 13-36; response 37-42, *Pilch* J.J.; 209-225, afterword, *Alexander* Bobby C.: bibliog. 227-232. *McVann* M. [NTAb 40, p.196].

4508 *Hahn* Ferdinand, Le culte dans l'Église primitive, [T]*Sabourin* Léopold : ScEs 45 (1994) 309-332; 47 (1995) 189-213.

4509 *Hofius* Otfried, [G] The communion of the heavenly and the earthly world in the divine liturgy of the Church, [T]*Karakolis* Christos: D(elt)BM 14,1 (1995) 32-54.

4510 *Iwanowski* Thomas B., Qualities of a good presider: Priest 51,9 (1995) 18-24.

4511 **Johnston** Michael N., Natalis vocis in honore verbi; an examination of the way the Church prays the Scriptures in the ancient Mass formularies for the Natale S. Iohannis Baptistae with the help of other related sources: diss. 209. R 1995, Pont. Athenaeum S. Anselmi. xxxvii-539 p

4512 *Jones* W. Paul, Pastures of the wilderness; worship as historical and cosmic gesture: Weavings 10,4 (Nv 1995) 6-15.

4513 *Kleinig* John W., The biblical view of worship: ConcordTQ 58 (1994) 245-254.

4514 *Kranemann* Benedikt, Geschichte des katholischen Gottesdienstes in den Kirchen des deutschen Sprachgebietes, ein Forschungsbericht (1980-1995 : AL(tg)W 37 (1995) 227-303.

4515 *Lara Polaina* Antonio, La celebración litúrgica es también 'fuente' de la vida cristiana: RET 55 (1995) 65-80.

4516 *a) Lathrop* Gordon W., La Koinonia et la forme de la liturgie; -- *b) Gerhards* Albert, La Koinonia et le développement de la litrugie: MaisD 204 (1995) 83-106 / 107-116.

4517 *Laurance* John D., The power of ritual: Church 11,2 (NY 1995) 5-7.

4518 **López Martínez** Julián, La liturgía de la Iglesia; teología, historia, espiritualidad. M 1994, BAC. 367 p. -- ᴿNatGrac 42 (1995) 142s (A. *Villalmonte*).

4519 **McBrien** Richard P., *al.*, Inside Catholicism; rituals and symbols revealed [with color photos]: Signs of the Sacred 2. SF 1995, Collins. 112 p. $ 20. 0-00-640052-2 [ThD 43.177].

4520 ᴱ**Mark** Arlene M, [Mennonite] Words for worship. Scottdale PA c.1995, Herald. 240 p. $ 16 spiral-bound. 0-8361-9037-8.

4521 **Merras** Marja, The origins of the celebration of the Christian feast of the Epiphany: Humanities 16. Joensu 1995, Univ. x-218 p.; bibliog. 193-218. 952-9800-09-6.

4522 **Metzger** Marcel, Storia della liturgia; le grandi tappe, ᵀ. CinB 1995, S. Paolo. -- ᴿRivLi 82 (1995) 333-340 (E. *Mazza*).

4523 ᴱ**Neuheuser** Hanns P., Wort und Buch in der Liturgie; interdisziplinäre Beiträge zur Wirkmächtigkeit des Wortes und Zeichenhaftigkeit des Buches. Mü St. Ottilien 1995, EOS. viii-520 p. 3-88096-787-3.

4524 **Peterson** David, Engaging with God; a biblical theology of worship 1993 → 9,8651; 10,8214: ᴿA(ndr)USS 33 (1995) 142-4 (S.P. *Vitrano*: a 'must' book but with some edges of inconsistency); EvQ 67 (1995) 287s (E.O. *Meadors*).

4525 *Reese* Thomas J., In the Catholic Church, a kiss is never just a kiss [on the proposal to remove the giving of peace to the end of the Liturgy of the Word]: America 172,13 (1995) 12-19.

4526 *a) Renaud-Chamska* Isabelle, Le statut linguistique de la citation biblique dans le discours liturgique; -- *b) Chauvet* Louis-Marie, La fonction du prêtre dans le récit de l'institution à la lumière de la linguistique: RICP 56 (1995) 11-39 / 41-61.

4527 *Richardson* J.P., Is 'worship' biblical ? [NT not much, because Jesus fulfilled the cultus]: ChM 109 (1995) 197-218 [NTAb 40,p.280].

4528 *a) Robert* Michel, La liturgie, voix de l'Écriture: -- *b) Nissim* Gabriel M., Les psaumes, pour notre prière: VSp149 (1995) 265-278 / 257-264.

4529 **Roca-Puig** Ramón, Anàfora de Barcelona i altres pregàries (Missa del segle IV. Barc 1994, Grafos. 151 p. 84-605-1851-5.

4530 **Rossi de Gasperis** Francesco, E videro la sua gloria (Lc 9,32); una scuola della fede secondo la liturgia dell'anno C: Bibbia e preghiera 24. R 1995, Apost. Preghiera. 420 p. 88-7357-158-1.

4531 **Salzmann** Jorg C., Lehren und Ermahnen; zur Geschichte des christlichen Wortgottesdienstes in den ersten drei Jahrhunderten: WUNT 2/59, 1994 → 10,8216; DM 128: ᴿ*CritRR 8 (1995) 416s (R.L. *Mullen*); JThS 46 (1995) 676-8 (P. *Bradshaw*); VigChr 49 (1995) 393-6 (G. *Rouwhorst*).

4532 *Scheinen* Richard, *Fox* Matthew, Reinventing ritual; the planetary Mass, ... techno-liturgical event of the year: *CreSp 11,1 (1995) 21-34.

4533 ᴱ**Schmidt-Lauber** Hans-Christoph, *Bieritz* Karl-Heinrich, Handbuch der Liturgik; Liturgiewissenschaft in Theologie und Praxis der Kirche. Gö/Lp 1995, Vandenhoeck & R / Ev.-VA. 1023 p. DM 128. 3-525-57191-7 / 3-374-01524-7 [ThRv 91,278]

4534 *Vagaggini* Cipriano, La preghiera cristiana dei Salmi... che inveiscono contro i 'nemici' o affermano il primevo concetto dell'AT sullo *sheol* (gli 'inferi'): RivLi 82 (1995) 282-332.

4535 *Weakland* R., El canto y los símbolos en la liturgía: Phase 34 (1994) 45-58.

4536 **Wegman** Herman A,J,. Liturgie in der Geschichte des Christentums [Ned. 1971; Fortschreibung von 1977 ²1983; deutsch mangelhaft 1979], [T] besser aber nicht genug. Rg 1994. Pustet. 402 p. DM 68. 3-7917-1427-9 -- [R]ZkT 117 (1995) 377-9 (H.B. *Meyer*).

4537 **White** James F., Documents of Christian worship; descriptive and interpretive sources. E 1995, Clark = W-Knox 1992. 267 p. £ 14. 0-567-29218-5. -- [R]*TBR 8,2 (1995s) 45 (V.*de Waal*).

4538 *Bissoni* Angelo, Integrare 'divino' e 'umano': VitaCons 31 (1995) 134-149.

4539 *Blough* N., Les églises de professants; un monachisme de substitution ? : FV 93,2 (1994) 29-44.

4540 **Böhler** Heidi, I consigli evangelici in prospettiva trinitaria; sintesi dottrinale. CinB 1993, Paoline. 245 p. -- [R]Claretianum 35 (1995) 510s (J. *Rovira*).

4541 **Boni** Andrea, Vangelo e vita religiosa (Rilettura teologica e storico-giuridica delle fonti: Spicilegium 32. R 1994, Pont. Athenaeum Antonianum. 444 p. L[m] 50. -- [R]Anton 70 (1995) 140-4 (G. *Bourdeau)* & 144-8 (G. *Rocca)* & 148-153; replica 153-5; ThRv 91 (1995) 509s (R. *Sebott*).

4542 *Boswell* John, Homosexuality and religious life; a historical approach: → 10,283, Sexuality 1994, 361-373.

4543 **Brown** Peter, The body and society 1988 → 4,9307 ... 9,8662: [R]ChH 63 (1994) 256-9 (R.M. *Grant*).

4544 **Brown** Peter. El cuerpo y la sociedad; los hombres, las mujeres y la renuncia sexual en el cristianismo primitivo [1988 → 4,9307], [T]. Barc 1993, Muchnik. 673 p. 84-7669-178-5. -- → 221, [F]YELO TEMPLADO A., Lengua 1995, 603-6 (J.A. *Molina Gómez*).

4545 **Brown** Peter, Le renoncement à la chair; virginité, célibat et continence dans le christianisme primitif [1988], [T]*Dauzat* Pierre-Emmanuel, *Jacob* Christian: BtHistoires. P 1995, Gallimard. 598 p. F 230. -- [R]Études 383 (19995) 281s (A. *Demoustier*).

4546 **Burton-Christie** Douglas, The Word in the desert; Scripture and the quest for holiness in early Christian monasticism 1993 → 9,8664; 10,8228: [R]ChH 64 (1995) 87s (F.W. *Norris*); *CritRR 7 (1994) 321-3 (G. *Weekman*); *JEarlyC 3 (1995) 99s (J.E. *Goeltring*): JRel 75 (1995) 114s (S.H. *Griffith*); RfR 53 (1994) 310s (A.J. *Curley*; RHPhR 75 (1995) 348s (F. *Vinel*); VigChr 49 (1995) 86-88 (G.J.M. *Bartelink*); Worship 65 (1994) 269s (D.R. *Dumm*).

4547 *Carbo* R.A., *Gartner* J., Can religious communities become dysfunctional families ? Sources of countertransference for the religiously committed psychotherapist: JPsy&T 22 (1994) 264-271; 275s to comment of *Narramore* B. [< ZIT 95,p.260s]

4548 **Dalbesio** Anselmo, E lasciato tutto lo seguirono; i fondamenti biblici della vita consecrata; Problemi di vita religiosa 2. Bo 1994, Dehoniane. 350 p. L[m] 27. -- [R]ParVi 39,4 (1994) 53s (Y. *Spiteris*).

4549 **Dilanni** Albert, [3 inedita + 5] Religious life as adventure; renewal, refounding, or reform ? NY 1994, Alba. xix-155 p. $ 10. 0-8189-0716-9 [< ThD 42 (1995) 266].

4550 **Elm** Susanna, 'Virgins of God'; the making of asceticism in late antiquity: OxClasMg 1994 → 10,8233; $ 70; 0-19-814920-4. -- [R]VigChr 49 (1995) 294-7 (G.J.M. *Bartelink*).

4551 *Espinel* José Luis, Sobre el origen bíblico de la vida religiosa:: CiTom 121 (1994) 433-450 . 99-618.

4552 **Frank** Karl Suso, With great liberty; a short history of Christian monasticism and

religious orders, [T]*Lienhard* Joseph T.: C(ist)CS 104. Kalamazoo 1993, Cistercian. 269 p. -
- [R]C(ath)HR 81 (1995) 410s (T. *Sullivan*).

4553 **Germain** Élisabeth, La vie consacrée dans l'Église; approche historique. P 1994,
Médiaspaul. 200 p. F 115. -- [R]MélSR 51 (1994) 463-5 (L. *Debarge*).

4554 **Gould** Graham, The desert fathers on monastic community 1993 → 9,8675;
10,8237: [R]GOTR 39 (1994) 381-3 (C. B. *Christakis*); JEH 46 (1995) 310-2 (G. *Bonner*,
also on [E]LEBRUN R. 1991-3); JThS 46 (1995) 733s (Benedicta *Ward*).

4555 **Hardy** Gilbert, Monastic quest and interreligious dialogue 1990 → 7,a975:
[R]*CritRR 6 (1993) 309-311 (W G. *Paulsell*).

4556 **Harpham** Geoffrey G., The ascetic imperative in culture and tradition [pervades the
West, also pre-Christian and non-religious). Ch 1987, Univ. UnSemQ 48,3 (1994) 170-3
(A.J. *Dell'Olio*).

4557 *a) Harrison* Nonna V., The feminine man in late antique ascetic piety; -- *b) Gundry-
Volf* Judith M., Pneumatism and celibacy in Corinth in light of history of religions
parallels; -- *c) Diamond* Eliezer, Hunger artists and householders; the tension between
asceticism and family responsibility among Jewish pietists in late antiquity: UnSemQ 48,3s
('The sexual politics of the ascetic life' 1994) 49-71 / 105-126 / 29-47.

4558 **Hawel** Peter, Das Mönchtum im Abendland; Geschichte -- Kultur -- Lebensform 1993
→ 10,8239:[R]Communio(Sev) 28(1995)389s (M.*Sánchez*);ThGL 85(1995)287s (K.*Zacharias*).

4559 **Kinberger** Mary Kay, [B.] LONERGAN on conversion; applications for religious
formation 1992 → 9,8678: [R]RfR 52 (1993) 937 (E.L. *Donahue*).

4560 *a) Lienhard* M., LUTHER et le monachisme; -- *b) Blough* N., Les églises de
professants; un monachisme de substitution ? -- *c) Fleinert-Jensen* Flemming, Pertinence
de la vie monastique dans la société d'aujourd'hui: FV 93,2 ('Monachisme / Protestantisme'
1994) 9-28 / 29-44 / 45-55.

4561 **Martini** Carlo Maria, Bible et vocation; de la vocation baptismale à la vocation
sacerdotale [conférences Pont. Univ. Gregoriana], [T]*Haussière* M.-A. P 1995, Médiaspaul.
130 p. F 85. -- [R]E(spr)eV 105 (1995) 254-*jaune* (M. de *Paillerets*).

4562 **Murphy** Desmond, The death and rebirth of religious life. Alexandria NSW 1995,
Dwyer. xi-243 . A$ 25. 0-85574-126-0. -- [R]*TBR 8,1 (1995s) 38 (G. *Jeff*: claims not
revitalization but transformation is needed).

4563 *Oesterle* Hans J., Antonius von Koma und die Ursprünge des Mönchtums: AKuG
75 (1993) 1-18.

4564 **Patrich** Joseph, SABAS, leader of Palestinian monasticism; a comparative study in
eastern monasticism, fourth to seventh centuries; DO Studies. Wsh 1995, Dumbarton Oaks.
xv-419 p. 0-99402-221-8 [ThD 42,82].

4565 **Poirot** Éliane sr., Élie, archétype du moine; pour un ressourcement prophétique de
la vie monastique: Spiritualité orientale 65. Bellefontaine 1995, Abbaye. 275 p. --
[R]Ter(esianum) 46 (1995) 602-4 (J. *Castellano*).

4566 *Rodríguez Briz* Pilar, Siguiendo a Jesús, pero ¿ cómo ? algunas reflexiones sobre la
vida religiosa actual: REsp 53,213 (1994) 451-481.

4567 *a) Russell* Kenneth C., The desert and the cell (c. 300 A.D.) -- *b) Stoudt* Robert S.,
The midlife crisis; God's second call: RfR 54 (1995) 100-113 / 131-132.

4568 *Schenker* Adrian, Y a-t-il une dimension ministérielle de la vie consacrée dans
l'Église ? : RevSR 69 (1995) 239-153; Eng. 272.

4569 *Teilhard de Chardin* Pierre, Die Evolution der Keuschheit, [TE]*Sudbrack* Josef :
GuL 67 (1994) 243-263.

4570 *Velasco* Juan Martín, Los monjes; identidad y misión en nuestro tiempo: RET 55 (1995) 5-27.

4571 *Viefhues* Ludger, Dem kreuztragenden Christus folgen; Gedanken zu einer Theologie der Gelübden: OrdKor 36 (1995) 157-170 → Following Christ: toward a theology of religious life, [TE]*Asen* B.A.: ThD 42 (1995) 109-116.

4572 *Vigil* José María, ¿Parábola o hipérbole ? Para una reinterpretación teológica e histórica de la Vida Religiosa como signo escatológico: Claretianum 34 (1994) 447-466.

4573 **Vogüé** A, de, Histoire littéraire du mouvement monastique [1. 1991 >] ; 2. De l'Itinéraire d'Egérie à l'éloge funéraire de Népotien (384-396): Patrimoines Christianisme. P 1993, Cerf. 448 p. 2-204-04586-1. [R]RHE 90 (1995) 119s (P.-A. *Deproost*).

4574 **Wenzelmann** Gottfried, Nachfolge und Gemeinschaft: eine theologische Grundlegung des kommunitären Lebens → 10,8258 [Diss. Erlangen 1991, [D]*Peters* A.]: CThM 21. Stu 1994, Calwer. 304 p. DM 78. 3-7668-3286-7 [NTAb 39, p.329].

4575 [E]**Wimbush** Vincent L., *Valantasis* Richard, Asceticism. NY 1995, Oxford-UP. xxxiii-638 p.; bibliog. 607-621.

4576 **Angenendt** Arnold, Heilige und Reliquien; die Geschichte ihres Kultes vom frühen Christentum bis zur Gegenwart 1994 → 10,9262; 3-406-38096-4: [R]GuL 68 (1995) 72s (J. *Sudbrack*); R(öm)Q 90 (1995) 266-8 (H. *Moll*); ZkT 117 (1995) 215-8 (H.B. *Meyer*).

4577 [E]**Dinzelbacher** Peter, *Bauer* Dieter R., Heiligenverehrung in Geschichte und Gegenwart [Tagung Weingarten 8.-12, April 1987] 1990 → 6,403: ThRv 91 (1995) 244 (M. *Gerwing*).

4578 *Sanders* Theresa, Seeking a minor sun: saints after the death of God [WYSCHOGROD Edith, Saints (defined as 'devoted to the alleviation of pain') and postmodernism (Ch 1990), Univ]: Horizons 22 (1995) 183-197.

4579 *Thompson* William M., The saints, justification and sanctification; an ecumenical thought experiment: ProEccl 4 (1995) 16-36.

H8.2 Theologia moralis NT

4580 *a) Adeney* Bernard, Polygamy; how many wives in the Kingdom of God ?; -- *b) Bediako* Kwame, De-sacralization and democratization; some theological reflections on the role of Christianity in nation-building in modern Africa: Transformation 12,1 (1995) 1-4 / 5-11.

4581 **Adeney** Bernard T., Strange virtues; ethics in a multicultural world. Leicester 1995, Apollos. 286 p. £ 13. 0-85111-442-3. -- [R]E(xp)T 107,1 top choice (1995s) 1s (C.S. *Rodd*).

4582 [E]**Allsopp** Michael E., *O'Keefe* John J., Veritatis splendor; American responses. KC 1995, Sheed & W. x-313 p. $ 20 pa. 1-55612-760-X [ThD 43,191].

4583 **Arens** Edmund, Christopraxis: a theology of action [1992 → 9,8709], [T]*Hoffmeyer* John F. Mp 1995, Fortress. viii-205 p. $ 17 pa. 0-8006-2746-6 [ThD 43,156].

4584 **Bachmann** Christina, Religion und Sexualität; die Sehnsucht nach Transzendenz. Stu 1994, Kohlhammer. 252 p. DM 40. 3-17-012555-9. -- [R]ThLZ 120 (1995) 121s M. *Josuttis*).

4585 **Bahnsen** Greg L., No other standard; theonomy and its critics [Westminster 'Reformed Critique']. Tyler 1991, Institute for Christian Economics. 345 p. $ 10 pa.- [R]JETS 38 (1995) 460s (A. *Paetz*).

4586 **Barone-Adesi** Giorgio. L'età della Lex Dei: Univ. Roma Ist. Diritto 71. N 1992, Jovene. xiii-230 p.; bibliog. 197-221. 88-243-0998-4.

4587 **Barry** Robert L., Breaking the thread of life; on [against] rational suicide. New Brunswick 1994, Transaction. xxii-353 p. $ 35. -- ᴿTS 56 (1995) 406s (M.N. *Sheehan*: gives good arguments, but not enough on why they leave many unconvinced).

4588 *Barton* S.C., Is the Bible good news for human sexuality ? Reflections on method is biblical interpretation: *ThSex 1,1 (Shf 1994) 42-54 [NTAb 39, p.369].

4589 *Barton* Stephen C., Marriage and family life as Christian concerns: ET 106 (1994s) 69-74.

4590 **Beach** Waldo, L'etica cristiana nella tradizione protestante. T 1993, Claudiana. 208 p. -- ᴿFilTeo 9 (1995) 199S (A. *Mastrantoni*); (R)*StEc 12 (Venezia 1994) 251s (S. *Morandini*, p.432).

4591 *a) Berthoud* Pierre, La notion biblique de l'homme et les enjeux de la bioéthique; - *b) Ceccaldi* Joël, Le comencement de la vie; le statut de l'embryon : RRéf 46.5s (1995) 33-47 / 49-60.

4592 **Birch** B.C., *Rasmussen* L., Bibel und Ethik im christlichen Leben [1989 → 5,8259], ᵀ*Goldmann* M.: Öffentliche Theol.1. Gü 1993, Kaiser. 259 p. ᴅᴍ 78. 3-579-02011-0 [NTAb 38, p.311].

4593 *Blancy* Alain, Aquinati[s] (alias Aristotelis) splendor, ou la morale du Pape: FV 94,2 (1995) 35-55 [84, **Fuchs** Éric 1994, ᴿ*Dujancourt* S.).

4594 *Bockmuehl* Markus, The Noachide commandments and New Testament ethics, with special reference to Acts 15 and Pauline Halakhah: RB 102 (1995) 72-101.

4595 *a) Bordeyne* Philippe, Le problème posé par les transgressions des adolescents; contribution des aumoniers scolaires à une éthique de l'éducation; - *b) Gire* Pierre, Morale et éthique; le problème du fondement et du pluralisme: RICP 55 (1995) 49-80 / 81-87 [erreur p. 85 → 56 (1995) 128].

4596 *Brajičic* Rudolf, Freedom, anthropological views, situationalism in Christian ethics: ObnŽiv 49 (1994) 9-23 Croatian; 23 Eng.

4597 *Breck* John, Procreation and 'the beginning of life': StVlad 39 (1995s) 215-232.

4598 **Breitsching** Konrad, Verantwortungsübertragung im NT -- Formen und Voraussetzungen; ein Deutungsversuch an Hand der Ergebnisse der modernen Exegese unter Berücksichtigung der rechtlichen Aspekte; kath. Diss. ᴰ*Mühlsteiger*. Innsbruck 1995.

4599 *Bretzke* J.T., Scripture, the 'soul' of moral theology ? -- The second stage: I(rish)ThQ 60 (1994) 249-271 [NTAb 39, p.448].

4600 **Breuer** Clemens, Person vom Anfang an ? Der Mensch aus der Retorte und die Frage nach dem Beginn des menschlichen Lebens: kath. Diss. ᴰ*Piegsa* J. Augsburg 1994. - - ThRv 91 (1995) 92.

4600* *Brown* Neil, Experience as a moral source; a literary commentary on official Catholic ethics: I(r)ThQ 61 (1995) 182-190.

4601 ᴱ**Carey** John J., The sexuality debate in [five Presbyterian-related] North American churches, 1988-1995; controversy, unresolved issues, future prospects: Symposium 36. Lewiston ɴʏ, Mellen. xxiv-389 p. $ 100. 0-7734-9111-2 [< ThD 43,358].

4601* *Cavalcoli* Giovanni, La castità nel Nuovo Catechismo: SacDo 40,5 (1995) 24-72.

4602 ᴱ**Chirban** John T., Clergy sexual misconduct; Orthodox Christian perspectives. Brookline ᴍᴀ 1994, Hellenic. 101 p. -- ᴿStVlad 39 (1995s) 317-9 (G. *Morelli*).

4602* **Cole-Turner** Ronald, The new Genesis; theology and the genetic revolution. Lvl - 1993, W-Knox. 127 p. $13 pa. -- sᴡᴊᴛ 37,1 (1994s) 47s (R.E. *Higgins*).

4603   *Collier* Gary D., Rethinking Jesus on divorce: RestQ 37 (1995) 80-96.

4603*   **Collins** Raymond F., Divorce in the NT 1992 → 8.4751: ^RTorJT 11 (1995) 91s (R.L. *Webb*).

4604   **Cornes** Andrew, Divorce and remarriage; biblical principles and pastoral practice 1993 → 9,8729; 10,8289: ^RChurchman 108 (L 1994) 283s (R. *Combes*); LTJ 29 (Adelaide 1995) 82-87 (M.J. *Steicke*) [NTAb 37,p.543; 40,p.84].

4604*   *Countryman* L.W., NT sexual ethics and today's world: → 10.283, Sexuality 1994, 28-53.

4605   **Curran** Charles E., The Church and morality; an ecumenical and Catholic approach. Mp 1993, Fortress. $ 10. 0-8006-2756-3. -- ^RHeythJ 36 (1995) 105s (J.R. *Williams*) & 231s (J.H. *McKenna*); MoTh 11 (1995) 243-258 (M.J. *Baxter*, also on HIMES M. & K.; 'The non-Catholic character of the "public Church" ').

4605*   *DeFerrari* Patricia, Seeking full dignity; Catholic social teaching and women in the Third World: Horizons 22 (1995) 237-259.

4606   *Dierken* Jörg, Religion und Sittlichkeit; Erwägungen zur Aufgabe moderner systematischer Theologie im Anschluss an Wilhelm HERRMANN: ZThK 92 (1995) 376-395.

4606*   *Dillon* Michele, Religion and cultures in tension; the abortion discourses of the U.S. Catholic bishops and the Southern Baptist convention: R&AC(u) 5 (1995) 139-180.

4607   *Downing* F. Gerald, Words as deeds and deeds as words [querying E.P. SANDERS' stinction between 'sayings' and 'facts']: *BInterp 3 (1995) 129-144.

4607*   **Dunn** James D.G., Christian liberty; a NT perspective. GR 1993, Eerdmans. 115 p. -- ^RRefR 49 (1995s) 54 (G.P. *Timberlake*)

4608   **Eenigenburg** Elton M., Biblical foundations and a method for doing Christian ethics. Lanham MD 1994, UPA. xii-166 p. $ 36.50. -- ^{R*}CritRR 8 (1995) 355s (W.B. *Barclay*).

4608*   *Eibach* Ulrich, Der Wandel moralischer Werte -- eine Herausforderung für die Kirchen: KuD 40 (1994) 80-100 [< NZSTh 37 (1995) 121].

4609   *Eid* V., '...dann erhebt ihre Häupter' (Lk 21,28); die sittlichen Weisungen Jesu als Evangelium: LebSeels 46 (1995) 4-8 [< ZIT 95,p.263].

4609*   **Ewald** George R., Jesus and divorce.   ... Herald. $ 10. -- ^RCThMi 22 (1995) 221 (J.L. *Bailey:* urges compassion, but with not-updated exegesis).

4610   **Farley** Benjamin W., In praise of virtue; an exploration of the biblical virtues in a Christian context. GR 1995, Eerdmans. x-181 p. $ 13 pa. 0-8028-0792-5. -- ^{R*}TBR 8,3 (1995s) 30s (S. *Plant:* unoriginal, too rapid, overextends definition of virtue: 'kindness' maybe, 'repentance' hardly).

4610*   *a) Ferrari* Valentino, La 'Veritatis splendor' a confronto con l'odierno teologismo e con S. Tommaso d'AQUINO; -- *b) Meyer* J.R., Veritatis splendor; intellect, will and freedom in human acts: Ang 72 (1995) 3-21 (23-39, *Seidl* Horst) / 217-242.

4611   *Fischer* Johannes, Theologische Ethik und Christologie: ZThK 92 (1995) 481-516.

4611*   *Fisher* Anthony, *a)* The brave new world of reproductive technologies: -- *b)* The human genome project; hopes and fears : PhilipSa 30 (1995) 277-291 / 483-498.

4612   *Flusser* David, Die beiden wichtigsten Gebote bei den Griechen: FrRu NF 2 (1995) 27-30 [< Jud(aica) 51 (1995) 58].

4612*   **Frigato** Sabino, Vita in Cristo e agire morale: saggio di teologia morale fondamentale: CorsoStT. T 1995, LDC. 264 p. -- ^RSalesianum 57 (1995) 577s (G. *Gatti*).

4613   *Fuchs* Éric, *Dermange* François, Une nouvelle casuistique menace-t-elle l'éthique ?: ÉTRel 70 (1995) 377-389.

4613* **Fuchs** Éric, Comment faire pour bien faire ? Introduction à l'éthique: Le champ éthique 28. Genève 1995, Labor et Fides. 196 p. -- [R]RÉTM = Le Supplément 195 (1995) 197-200 (P. *Gire*); RTPh 127 (1995) 309 (A. *Peter*)

4614 **Fuchs** Josef, Moral demands and personal obligations. Wsh 1993, Georgetown Univ. xii-218 p. $ 35. -- [R]HeythJ 36 (1995) 217s (T.R. *Kopfensteiner*: articles all published before Veritatis splendor).

4614* **Gardner** Edward C., Justice and Christian ethics. C 1995, Univ. xiv-179 p. £ 30. 0-521-49639-X. -- [R]*TBR 8,3 (1995s) 31 (Kate *Partridge:* ARISTOTLE-AQUINAS updated, but without reference to non-Western traditions).

4615 *Gaziaux* É., Éthique de la foi et morale autonome à la lumière de la révélation: Didask 24,2 (1994) 229-251.

4615* **Gaziaux** Éric, Morale de la foi et morale autonome; confrontation entre P. DELHAYE [Philippe, 33 ans d'écrits EeV, † 1990] et J. FUCHS [< diss. LvN 1994, [D]*Wattiaux* H.]: BEThL 119. Lv 1995, Univ. (Paris: Procure). 545 p. Fb 3000. 90-6831-665-6. -- [R]E(spr)eV 105 (1995) 559s (H. *Wattiaux:* 'Fuchs met en évidence un aspect connu de son contradicteur mais non exploité'); EThL 71 (1995) 498-500 (J. *Étienne*).

4616 [3] German bishops' response to the Vatican letter [14.!X.1994] 'Holy Communion for Catholics who have divorced and remarried': DoLi 45 (1995) 185-190.

4616* **Getz** Gene A., A biblical theology of material possessions. Ch 1990, Moody, 438 p. $25. -- [R]JETS 38 (1995) 252s (J.R. *Master*)

4617 **Gil Delgado** Francisco, Divorcio en la Iglesia; historia y futuro; BtBAsica Dcan 21. M 1993, Atenas. 140 p. 84-7020-266-9. -- : [R]ActuBbg 31 (1994) 253 (I. *Salvat*).

4617* *Gleixner* Hans, Sittliche Erkenntnis im Horizont des Gottesglaubens: THGL 85 (1995) 161-180.

4618 **Goody** Jack, La evolución de la familia y del matrimonio en Europa. Barc 1986, Herder. 418 p. -- [R]TEspir 38 (1994) 367s (A. *Esponera*).

4618* *Grabowski* John S., NEWTON, HUME and the ethics of the closed system: I(r)ThQ 61 (1995) 138-158.

4619 **Grenz** Stanley J., Sexual ethics; a biblical perspective 1990 → 10,8315: [R]JETS 37 (1994) 627s (D.K. *Clark*).

4619* **Grisez** Germain, Living a Christian life: The Way of the Lord Jesus 2, 1993 → 9,8760; 10,8316: [R]Anthropotes (1993,2) 245-9 (W.E. *May*); Aus(tralas)CR 72 (1995) 481-9 (T. *Kennedy:* expert casuistry of a pessimist-probabiliorist): FaR 21 (1995) 151-167 (P.F. *Ryan*: remarkably clear); HeythJ 36 (1995) 216s (B. *Hoose*); HPR 95,8 (1995) 72-77 (J.F. *Harvey*); LinacreQ 62,3 (91-95 (J. *Hartley*); NOxR 62,3 (1995) 27 (J.R. *Popiden*: in the blink of an eye moral manuals ceased to be used because Vatican II decreed that moral should draw more fully on Scripture); Salesianum 57 (1995) 156-8 (G. *Abbà*).

4620 *Gründel* Johannes, Katholische Kirche und Homosexualität: MThZ 45,1 ('Moral-theologie und Sozialethik' 1994) (473-6) 509-520.

4620* **Gudorf** Christine E., Body, sex, and pleasure; reconstructing Christian sexual ethics. Cleveland 1994, Pilgrim. 276 p. $ 20. -- [R]CrossCur 45 (1995s) 557s (G.D. *Randels*).

4621 *Gudorf* Chris, Women and Catholic Church politics in eastern Europe: JF(em)StR 11,2 ('State and Church resistance to women's reproductive choices and well-being' 1995) 101-116.

4621* **Häring** Bernhard, Ausweglos ? Zur Pastoral bei Scheidung und Wiederverheiratung 1990 → 6,8337: [R]C(olc)Th 64,1 (1994) 177-9 (P. *Góralczyk*).

4622 *Hallebeek* Jan, Omnis jurisdictionis fons ecclesia; an eighteenth-century debate on the origin of jurisdiction: IK(i)Z 85 (1995) 114-133.

4622* **Harvey** A.E., Strenuous commands; the ethic of Jesus 1990 → 7,8374 ... 10,8322: [R]S(cot)JTh 48 (1995) 140-2 (S. *Pattison*).

4623 **Harvey** Anthony, Promise or pretence ? A Christian's guide to sexual morals. L 1994, SCM. viii-136 p. £ 8. 0-334-01283-X. -- : [R]ET 106 (1994s) 94 (D.G. *Deeks*; an experienced exegete who writes like an angel).

4623* *Hiebert* Paul G., Are we our others' keepers ? [and anthropologically how has the 'other' been regarded through the centuries]: CThMi 22 (1995) 325-337 (-339, *Akrong* Abraham, response).

4624 *Höver* Gerhard, Gewissen und Gewissensbildung in moraltheologischer Sicht: LebZeug 50 (1995) 179-187.

4624* *Hoffmann* Thomas S., *Metallage* [Röm 1,25s]. gleichgeschechtliche Ersatzhandlungen und Eheimitate als theologisch-ethisches Sprach- und Sachproblem: KuD 41 (1995) 176-194; Eng. 195: not 'another kind of love' but violation of the double divine commandent of love.

4625 *Honings* Bonifacio, 'Veritatis splendor,' dialogo religioso circa l'agire morale: Ter(esianum) 46 (1995) 23-49.

4625* **Hoose** Bernard, Received wisdom ? Reviewing the role of tradition in Christian ethics. L/Ridgefield CT 1994, Chapman/Morehouse. vi-186 p. $ 20 pa. 0-225-66739-8 [ThD 42,370].

4626 *Horn* Friedrich W., Ethik des Neuen Testaments 1982-1992 : ThR 60 (1995) 32-

4626* *a) Jaki* Stanley L., The ethical foundations of bioethics; -- *b) Howard* Joseph, vitro fertilization; destroyer of Christian marriage; -- *c) Sutton* Agnete, The new genetics; facts, fictions and fears: LinacreQ 62,4 (1995) 74-85 / 62/3, 37-41 / 76-88.

4627 **John Paul II,** Encyclical Evangelium Vitae: Origins 24 (1994s) 689-727.

4628 **Jones** L. Gregory, Transformed judgment, towards a trinitarian account of the moral life 1990 → 8,8519; 9,8781: [R]CThMi 22 (1995) 215 (R. *Hütter*).

4628* *Jurčević* Marijan, Biblical and dogmatic teaching about marriage and family: RijT 3 (1995) 1-18 Hrvatski; Eng. 19.

4629 **Keeling** Michael, The foundations of Christian ethics 1990 → 9,8784: [R]A(ustrl)BR 41 (1993) 83s (N.M. *Pritchard*).

4629* **Keener** Craig S., And marries another .. NT 1991 → 7,8354; 8.8523: [R]JETS 38 (1995) 277s (R. *Fuller*)

4630 *Kraft* Martin, 'Wer glaubt denn heute noch an die sieben [!] Gebote ?'; kritische Auseinandersetzung mit der Studie von Heiner BARZ, Jugend und Religion: KatBl 118 (1993) 66-68.

4630* *Kramer* Hans, Sexus, Eros und die Gesellschaft; Heutiges aus der Moraltheologie: KatBl 118 (1993)154-163

4631 *Krasevac* Edward L., AQUINAS, *Veritatis splendor,* and contemporary moral theology [p.61, 'most areas of human activity lie outside the (few, rightly claimed absolute) negative precepts']: Listening 30,1 'Aquinas; some reflections for our times' 1995) 50-63.

4631* *a) Kremer* Jacob, Jesu Wort zur Ehescheidung; bibeltheologische Überlegungen zum Schreiben der Glaubenskongregation [14.IX.1994]; -- *b) Fuchs* Josef, Die Last moraltheologischer Lehrautorität: StZ 213 (1995) 89-105 / 219-232.

4632 [E]**Küng** Hans, *Kuschel* K.-J., A global ethic; the [1893] declaration of the parliament of the world's religions 1993 → 10,8337; 0-334-02561-3: [R]TTh 35 (1995) 91 (H. *Spee*).

4632*   EKüng H., *Küschel* K.-J.,   Per un'etica mondiale; la dichiarazione del Parlamento delle religioni mondiali [1893 poi 1993], T: I Torchi. Mi 1995, Rizzoli. 136 p. Lᵐ 20. - -- RStPat(av) 42 (1995) 819 (G. *Segalla*).

4633   **Lacroix** Xavier,   Il corpo di carne; la dimensione etica, estetica e spirituale dell'amore [P 1992, Cerf], TZaccherini Giovanni: Persona e psiche 7.   Bo c.1995, Dehoniane. 336 p. Lᵐ 42. 66-10-80775-8.

4633*   **Lange** Dietz,   Ethik in evangelischer Perspektive; Grundfragen christlicher Lebenspraxis 1992 → 9,8791; 10,8339: RActuBbg 31 (1994) 253s (J. *Boada*).

4634 *a*) *Langhorst* Peter, Das Handeln Jesu als Modell praxisorientierter Sozialethik; -- *b*) *Berg* Werner, Arbeit und Soziales im Buch Ijob: → 189, FSTEGMANN F.J., Glaube 1495, 31-44 / 151-168.

4634* *Lazcano* Rafael, *al.*,   Sobre los valores: RevAg 36 (1995) 345-359 (-596), bibliog. 597-611.

4635 *Lindemann* Andreas, 'Do not let a woman destroy the unborn babe in her belly'; abortion in ancient Judaism and Christianity: ST 49 (Oslo 1995) 253-271,

4635* *Liss* Bernhard, Die Gemeinde und ihre wiederverheirateten Geschiedenen: BiLi 68 (1995) 38-42.

4636 **Lohfink** Gerhard. Per chi vale il discorso della Montagna ? Contributi per una etica cristiana 1990 → 7,3935: RViVH 6 (1995) 202-4 (G. *Cioli*).

4636* **Lohse** Eduard, Theological ethics of the NT 1991: → 4,9394 ...10,8343: HeythJ 36 (1995) 215s (J.J. *Kotva*).

4637 *Lowery* Mark, A new proposal for the proportionalist/traditionalist discussion [not far from CONNERY's response to MCCORMICK]: I(r)ThQ 61 (1995) 115-124 [319-334, *Connors* Russell B.]

4637* **McCloughry** Roy, Population growth and Christian ethics: Grove ethical series 98. 24 p. £ 2.25. 1-85174-295-6. -- [*TBR 8,3 (1995s) 27s with many titles only 93-100 (and p. 37, pastoral series 57-65; p. 40, worship series 128-135)].

4638 *a*) *McCormick* Richard A., Birth regulation, 'Veritatis splendor', and other ways of viewing things; -- *b*) *Curran* Charles E., The theory and practice of academic freedom in Catholic higher education in the United States: → 73, Mém. GUINDON A.,: E(gl)eT 26,1 (1995) 31-42 / 79-100.

4638*   **McDonald** J.J.H., Biblical interpretation and Christian ethics 1993 → 10,8350: RSalesianum 57 (1995) 151s (G. *Abbà*); TTh 35 (1995) 92 (G. *Manenschijn*).

4639 **MacIntyre** Alasdair, Enciclopedia, genealogia e tradizione; tre versioni rivali di ricerca morale [1990 → 6,8354]: *SciUmFilos 34. Mi 1993, Massimo. 336 p. Lᵐ 40. - ViVH 6 (1995) 423s (G. *Cioli*).

4639* TMcVeigh Terrence A., John WYCLIF, On simony. NY 1992, Fordham Univ. 179 . $ 27. -- RJETS 38 (1995) 452s (R.R. *Heiser*).

4640 **Maguire** Daniel C., The moral core of Judaism and Christianity; reclaiming the [social justice] revolution 1993 → 9,8804: RTTod 51 (1994s) 465.8s (S. *Schimmel*)

4641 *Majorano* Sabatino, 'Evangelium vitae'; per una strategia globale a favore della vita: RasT 36 (1995) 389-405.

4642 **Markham** Ian, Plurality and Christian ethics 1994 → 10,8354: RHeythJ 36 (1995) 218s (Linda *Hogan*); MoTh 11 (1995) 478-480 (B. *Harvey* .. now that Reinhold NIEBUHR's grip has loosened); Salesianum 57 (1995) 383-5 (G. *Abbà*); S(cot)JTh 48 (1995) 383-391 (B. *Sedgwick*); TS 56 (1995) 805-7 (J.T. *Bretzke*).

4643 *a*) *Martínez Cortés* Javier,   Sociología y psicología de una fragilidad; la del matrimonio; -- *b) Moreno* Alicia, Cuando la pareja no marcha ... ¿ Qué hacer ? : SalTer 82 (1994) 99-111 / 125-134.

4644 **Marxsen** Willi, NT foundations for Christian ethics 1993 → 9,8808; 10,8356; £ 15: [R]CBQ 57 (1995) 403-5 (L.T. *Johnson*); *TBR 8,1 (1995s) 18 (L. *Houlden*); TS 56 (1995) 157s (J. *Topel*).

4645 *a) Mathonnet-Vanderwell* Stephen, Virtue in the covenant community; can virtue ethics revive Reformed church discipline ? ; -- *b) Japinga* Lynn Winkels, Gender and virtue: RefR 49 ('Virtue; its loss and recovery' 1995s) 195-207 / 179-194.

4646 **Meeks** Wayne A., Los orígenes de la moralidad cristiana. Barc 1994, Ariel. 294 p. -- [R]RF 231 (1995) 666s (J.M. *Vallarino*).

4647 **Meeks** Wayne A., The origins of Christian morality; the first two centuries 1993 → 9,8809; 10,8360: [R]BiRe 11,3 (1995) 13s (F.J. *Matera*); ChH 64 (1995) 84-86 (Elizabeth *Clark*); Churchman 108 (L 1994) 369s (R. S. *Ascough*); ETRel 70 (1995) 592s (J.-N. *Pérès*); Interpretation 49 (1995) 412 . 4 . 6 (J.G. *Gager*); JAAR 63 (1995) 907-910 (J.S. *Siker*); JRel 75 (1995) 561-3 (A.J. *Droge*); JRS 85 (1995) 318 (M.J. *Edwards*); JThS 46 (1995) 299-301 (A.E. *Harvey*); MoTh 11 (1995) 161s (J.M.G. *Barclay*); ThTo 52 (1995s) 269s (B.J. *Malina*).

4648 **Meeks** Wayne A., El mundo moral de los primeros cristianos. Bilbao 1992, D-Brouwer. 184 p. 84-330-09331-1. -- [R]E(st)E 70 (1995) 270 (L. *Vela*).

4649 *Meilaender* Gilbert, *Veritatis splendor*; reopening some questions of the Reformation: JRE(thics) 23 (1995) 225-238.

4650 [E]**Mieth** Dietmar, Moraltheologie im Abseits ? Antwort auf die Enzyklika 'Veritatis Splendor': QDisp 153. FrB 1994, Herder. 315 p. DM 48. 3-451-02153-6. -- [R]ÖR 44 (1995) 404s (M. *Kneib*); ZkT 117 (1995) 248s (H. *Rotter*).

4651 **Mieth** Dietmar, Geburtenregelung, ein Konflikt in der katholischen Kirche. Mainz 1990, Grünewald. DM 16,80. -- [R]MThZ 45 (1994) 601s (J. *Grundel*).

4652 **Mommsen** Wolfgang, Christliche Ethik und Teleologie; eine Untersuchung der ethischen Normierungstheorien von Germain GRISEZ, John FINNIS und Alan DONAGAN [Diss. München]. Altenberge 1993, Oros. 228 p. 3-89375-079-7. -- [R]ZkT 117 (1995) 245s (H. *Rotter*).

4653 **Mortensen** Viggo, Life and death. moral implications of biotechnology. Geneva 1995, WCC. x-109 p. 2-8254-1170-1. -- [R]*TBR 8,3 (1995s) 3 (P. *Ballard*).

4654 *Muguiro* I., La buena fama y la privacidad en la Iglesia: RTLi(ma) 28 (1994) 50-77.

4655 *Murphy* Séamus, The myths of divorce; a survey of some recent literature / Divorce and public policy: MilltSt 35 (1995) 69-88 / 36 (1995) 17-41.

4656 [E]**Nelson** James B., *Longfellow* Sandra P., Sexuality and the sacred; sources for theological reflection. LvL 1994, W-Knox. xviii-406 p. $ 25. -- [R]Horizons 22 (1995) 147s (Elizabeth A. *Dreyer*).

4657 *Neuhaus* Richard J., [1980 Homosexuality arguments] in the case of John BOSWELL: *FirsT 41 (1994) 56-59; -- reprinted in E(v)RT 19 (Delhi 1995) 64-70 [NTAb 39, p.453]

4658 *Neuner* J., Second marriage; separation from the community?: Month 256 (1995) 182-6.

4659 *Nientiedt* Klaus, Die Diskusssion geht weiter; zur jüngsten Debatte über den Kommunionempfang wiederverheirateter Geschiedener: HerKor 49 (1995) 322-7.

4660 *Noichl* F., Das 'Projekt Weltethos' aus moraltheologischer Sicht: JbRwTR 2 (1994) 7-43 [ThRv 91,281].

4661 *Nolland* John, The Gospel prohibition of divorce; tradition history and meaning: JSNT 58 (1995) 19-35.

4662 *Nowosad* Sławomir, P 'Veritatis splendor' in 'The Tablet': STV(ars) 32,1 (1994) 101-6: Eng. 106s (5-100 *al.*).

4663 EO'Brien William J., Riding time like a river; the Catholic moral tradition since Vatican II, 1993 → 9,471: RHorizons 22 (1995) 157s (C.E. *Curran*); JRel 75 (1995) 444s (M.J. *Schuck*).

4664 O'Connell Timothy K., Principles for a Catholic morality2rev (11978). SF 1990, Harper. xvi-303 p. $ 15 pa. -- RLinacreQ 94,1 (1994) 89-92 (W.E. *May*: the new edition acknowledges as at least one moral absolute the probibition of direct intentional killing of innocent humans, and seemingly repudiates his former proportionalism).

4665 **Odozor** Paulinus Ikechukwu, Richard A. MCCORMICK and the renewal of moral theology. ND c. 1995, Univ. 270 p. $ 35. -- RAmerica 173,18 (1995) 26 (B.F.*Linnane*).

4666 *Otowizicz* Ryszard, P Problematyka moralna w Katechizmie Kościoła Katolickiego: Bobolanum 6 (1995) 120-130; 130s français (eklezjologia *Ludwisiak* Tomasz, 49-55; français 55).

4668 *a) Papademetriou* George C., Mixed marriages and the Orthodox Church;-- *b) Patsavos* Lewis J., A canonical response to intra-Christian and inter-religious marriage: GOTR 40,3s ('Mixed Marriage' 1995) xi-xiii / 287-298.

4669 *Pellauer* Mary D., Pornography; an agenda for the churches; → 10,283. Sexuality 1994, 345-353.

4670 *a) Perón* Juan Pablo, ¿ Moral sin Dios ? Una lectura bíblica del primer capítulo del Veritatis Splendor; -- *b) Godey* José R., ¿ Una moral sin pecado ?; -- *c) Martínez Díez* Felicísimo, Presupuestos antropológicos en la Veritatis Splendor; algunas anotaciones: Iter 5,2 (Caracas 1994) 23-27 / 7-21 / 29-43.

4671 *Pinckaers* S., The use of Scripture and the renewal of moral theology; the Catechism and Veritatis splendor: Thom 59 (1995) 1-19 [NTAb 39, p.454].

4672 **Pinckaers** Servais, The sources of Christian ethics3, TNoble sr. M. Thomas. Wsh 1995, Catholic Univ. xxi-489 p. $ 45; pa. $ 25. 0-9132-0834-3; -18-1 [ThD 43,182].

4673 *Pinckaers* Servais, *a)* L'usage de l'Écriture en théologie morale; -- *b)* 'L'Évangile de la vie' face à une culture de la mort; -- *c)* La Bible et l'élaboration d'une morale chrétienne: NV 70,2 (1995) 23-36 / 70,3 (1995) 5-17 / 70,4 (1995) 16-27 [NTAb 40, p.88].

4675 *Piñero y Piñero* Francisco de Paula, El protestantismo ante la moral: Isidorianum 4 (1993) 7-42 [< RET 55 (1995) 122].

4676 *Porter* Jean, Delayed hominization; reflections on some recent Catholic claims [after AAS 80 (1988) 70-102]: TS 56 (1995) 743-770.

4677 **Porter** Jean, [AQUINAS on] Moral action and Christian ethics: New Studies in Christian Ethics. C 1995, Univ. xvi-235 p. £ 35. 0-521-44329-6. -- R*TBR 8,3 (1995s) 29 (I. *Markham*).

4678 **Porter** Jean, The recovery of virtue; the relevance of AQUINAS for Christian ethics. L 1994, SPCK (= US 1990 → 7,8385; 8,8553). 298 p. $ 15. -- R*ModBlv 36,1 (1995) 50s (S. *Matthews*).

4679 *a) Potter* Harry, The special relationship; Anglo-American attitudes to the death penalty; -- *b) Gillingham* Susan. The ethics of love; doing the right thing in the Christian tradition : ET 106 (1994s) 228-231 / 231-4.

4680 *Puza* Richard, Französische Beiträge zum Thema Ehe und Ehescheidung: ThQ 175 (1995) 142-6.

4681 **Rehg** William, Insight and solidarity. a study in the discourse ethics of Jürgen HABERMAS: Philosophy, social theory, and the rule of law. Berkeley 1994, Univ. California. xvi-273 p. -- ᴿTS 56 (1995) 180-2 (T.R. *Kopfensteiner*).

4682 *Ross* Susan A., Evil and hope; foundational moral perspectives: → 564, CTS 50 (1995) 46-63: response 64-70, *Hollenbach* David.

4683 *Rubio* Miguel, Hermenéutica moral del fin de siglo: Moralia 18 (1995) 3-46.

4684 *Sanford* Keith, Toward a masturbation ethic: JPsT 22 (1994) 21-28.

4685 **Schenk-Ziegler** Alois, Correctio fraterna im NT; die 'brüderliche Zurechtweisung' in biblischen, frühjüdischen und hellenistischen Schriften; kath. Diss. ᴰ*Theobald*. Tübingen 1995. -- ThRv Beilage 92/2, xv.

4686 *Schmidt* W.R., Kirche in der sexualisierten Gesellschaft: EvKomm 28 (1994) 721-4 [< ZIT 95,p.145].

4687 **Schubeck** Thomas L., Liberation ethics; sources, models, and norms. Mp 1993, Fortress. 266 p. $17 pa. ᴿCrossCur 45 (1995s) 123-5 (J.H. *McKenna*).

4688 **Schweiker** William, Responsibility [.. postmodernism] and Christian ethics. C 1995, Univ. xiv-255 p. $ 55. 0-521-47527-9. £ 35. 0-521-47527-9. -- ᴿ*TBR 8,3 (1995s) 30 (S. *Robinson*).

4689 *Selling* Joseph A., Evangelium Vitae and the question of infallibility: DoLi 45 (1995) 330-9.

4690 ᴱ**Selling** J., *Jans* J., The splendor of accuracy 1994 → 10,8385: ᴿSalmanticensis 42 (1995) 284s (J.-R. *Flecha-Andrés*).

4691 -- *May* William E., The splendor of accuracy--how accurate?: Thom 59 (1995) 465-483.

4692 **Servais** Paul, Histoire de la famille et de la sexualité occidentale (XVIᵉ-XXᵉ siècle): Pedasup 26. LvN 1993, Academia. 232 p. Fb 880. 2-87209-292-7 [RHE 91.280s, H. *Wattiaux*].

4693 **Sevegrand** Martine, Les enfants du bon Dieu; les catholiques français et la procréation. P 1995, A. Michel. 486 p. F 150. -- ᴿÉtudes 382 (1995) 639s (P. *Vallin*).

4694 *Shepard* R.G., Biblical progression as moral development; the analogy and its implications: JPsy&T 22 (1994) 182-6 [< ZIT 95,p.260].

4695 *Simons* Robert G., Is the Gospel good news for homo economicus ? : ᴿAus(tralas)CR 72,3 ('Evangelization' 1995) 280-294.

4696 **Soards** Marion L., Scripture and homosexuality; biblical authority and the Church today. LVL 1995, W-Knox. x-84 p. $ 10. 0-664-25595-7 [*TBR 9/1,33, P.E. *Coleman*].

4697 **Spohn** W.C., What are they saying about Scripture and ethics?²ʳᵉᵛ [¹1984]. NY 1995, Paulist. iii-142 p. $ 9 pa. 0-8091-3609-0 [NTAb 40, p.546].

4698 *a) Spohn* William C., Jesus and Christian ethics; -- *b) Schubeck* Thomas L., Ethics and liberation theology; -- *c) Longan* John F., Nationalism, ethnic conflict, and religion; -- *d) Keveny* M.C., *Keenan* James F., Ethical issues in health-care restructuring: TS 56 (1995) 92-107-122-136-150.

4699 *Stramare* Tarcisio, Il **SDB** [69,843-851; Mt 5,32: *Dumais* M.] e le clausole die Matteo sul divorzio; Div 39 (1995) 269-273.

4700 **Stuart** Eileen F., Dissolution and annulment of marriage by the Catholic Church [diss. Monash 1991]. .. 1994, Federation. xx-244 p. $ 35. -- ᴿAus(tralas)CR 72 (1995) 238-240 (J. *Doherty* cannot recommend).

4701 *Sutton* Agneta A., Ten years after the [British government 1984] Warnock report: is the human neo-conceptus a person ? [says only rather 'embryonic' not 'personal' life begins at fertilisation]: LinacreQ 62,2 (1995) 63-74 (75-87, *Puca* Antonio, < Medicina e Morale).

4702　Szostek Andrzej, Natur -- Vernunft -- Freiheit; philosophische Analyse der Konzeption 'schöpferischer Vernunft' in der zeitgenössischen Moraltheologie [Hab.-Diss. Lublin 1989], ᵀ 1992 → 10,8390: 3!-631-43861-3. -- ᴿMThZ 45 (1994) 559-592 (Barbara *Gollwitzer*).

4703　Tanner Klaus, Der lange Schatten des Naturrechts; eine fundamentalethische Untersuchung. Stu 1993, Kohlhammer. 248s. Fs 80. -- ᴿThZ 51 (1995) 91-93 (N. *Peter*: ist das nicht katholische Domäne ?)

4704　*Theobald* Christoph, La règle d'or [Lc 6,31; Mt 7,12] chez Paul RICŒUR; une interrogation théologique: R(ech)SR 83 (1995) 43-59; Eng. 10.

4705　*Theobald* Michael, Jesu Wort von der Ehescheidung; Gesetz oder Evangelium ?: (Tü)TQ 175 ('Wiederheiratete Geschiedene' 1995) 109-124 (142-6, *Puza* Richard, 4 französische Beiträge zum Thema Ehe und Ehescheidung).

4706　*Trentin* Giuseppe, 'Veritatis splendor'; sui fondamenti teologici della morale : StPat(av) 42 (1995) 355-371; Eng. 371.

4707　*Tuohey* John F., The gender distinctions of [Gen 1-3] primeval history and a Christian sexual ethic: HeythJ 36 (1995) 173-189.

4708　*Twiss* Sumner B., Alternative approaches to patient and family medical ethics; review and assessment (MAY W.; KLIEVER L.): RStR 21 (1995) 263-6.

4709　*Ullrich* Anneliese, Hilfen zur verantworteten Entscheidung; Erfahrungen mit der Schwangerschaftskonfliktberatung: HerKor 49 (1995) 25-29.

4710　Uniacke Suzanne, Permissible killing; the self-defence justification of homicide. C 1994, Univ. ix-244 p. $ 50. -- ᴿTS 56 (1995) 809s (R.A. *Araujo*: touches the question of abortion; not really two unintentional aggressors).

4711　Valadier Paul, Éloge de la conscience; Esprit. P 1994, Seuil. 280 p. -- ᴿBLE 96 (1995) 162-5 (J.-M. *Maldamé*).

4712　*a) Verney* Allen D., The Holy Bible and sanctified sexuality; an evangelical approach to Scripture and sexual ethics; -- *b) Scroggs* Robin, The Bible as foundational document; -- *c) Fulkerson* Mary M., Church documents on human sexuality and the authority of Scripture, -- *d) Cahill* Lisa S., Sexual ethics; a feminist biblical perspective : Interpretation 49 (1995) 31-45 / 17-30 / 46-58 / 5-16.

4713　*Vives* Josep, Ni esclavos de la ley ni flotando en la anarquía; 'libres en el Espíritu': SalTer 82 (1994) 171-180.

4714　Walters J.R., [*teleiosis*] Perfection in NT theology: ethics and eschatology in relational dynamic: BibS 25. Lewiston NY 1995, Mellen. vii-304 p. $ 100. 0-7734-2355-9 [NTAb 40, p.371].

4715　*Ward* R.B., The use of the Bible in the abortion debate: StL Univ Public Law Review 13,1 (1993) 391-408 [NTAb 39, p.91: invalid].

4716　*Weber* Helmut, Kirchliches Lehramt, Glaube und Moral; Geschichtlich-Systematisches zu einem katholischen Problem der Neuzeit: TrierTZ 104 (1995) 223-238.

4717　Wegan Martha, Ehescheidung möglich ? Auswege mit der Kirche, mit praktischen Hinweisen. Graz 1993, Styria. 309 p. Sch 298. 3-2221-2198-2. -- ᴿAnton 70 (1995) 135-8 (N. *Schöck*: hervorragend!)

4718　*a) Welker* Michael, Auf der theologischen Suche nach einem 'Weltethos' in einer Zeit kurzlebiger moralischer Märkte; KÜNG, TRACY und die Bedeutung der neueren Biblischen Theologie; -- *b) Moltmann* Jürgen, Theologie im Projekt der Moderne: EvTh 55 (1995) 436-456 / 402-415.

4719 **Wheeler** Sondra Ely, Wealth as peril and obligation: the New Testament on possessions. GR 1995, Eerdmans. 158 p. $ 15. 0-8028-0733-X. -- [R]E(xp)T 107 (1995s) 185 (M. J. *Townsend*).

4720 *White* Leland J., Does the Bible speak about gays or same-sex orientation ? A test case in biblical ethics, Part I: BThB 25 (1995) 14-23.

4721 [E]**Wilkins** John, Considering Veritatis splendor [the eleven brief articles from The Tablet which he edits]. Cleveland 1994, Pilgrim. xv-182 p. $ 13. 0-8298-1007-2 [ThD 43,62]. -- [R]ScrT(Pamp) 37 (1995) 650-3 (E. *Molina*).

4722 *Williams* M., Quest for an evangelical ethics [reply to BRIDGER F. on Rom 1,26s]: *Anvil 11,1 (1994) 25-28 [NTAb 39, p.57].

4723 **Wogaman** J. Philip, Christian ethics; a historical introduction 1993 → 9,8846; 10,8397: [R]MoTh 11 (1995) 285s (J.H. *Yoder*); Salesianum 57 (1995) 162-4 (G. *Abbà*); SewaneeT 38 (1994s) 76s (T.F. *Sedgwick*); ThTo 52 (1995s) 158 . 160 (D.F. *Ottati*); TS 56 (1995) 404s (J.F. *Keenan*).

4724 *Woods* Constance, [BOSWELL J. 1994, Pre-Modern Europe] Same-sex unions or semantic illusions ? : ComI-US 22 (1995) 316-342.

4725 *a) Yanes* E., Moral cristiana en una sociedad democrática; -- *b) Gil de Muro* E.T., Corrupción y moralización en la sociedad española: 'Corintios XIII' 69 (1994) 25-98 / 97-118 [RET 55,117].

4726 *Yates* John C., Towards a theology of homosexuality: EvQ 67 (1995) 71-87.

H8.4 *NT ipsum de reformatione sociali* -- **Political action in Scripture**

4727 *Albertz* Rainer, Die Tora Gottes gegen die wirtschaftlichen Sachzwänge; die Sabbat- und Jobeljahrgesetzgebung Lev 25 in ihrer Geschichte: Ö(kum)R 44 (1995) 290-310 [311-327, *Dörrfuss* Ernst M., Da Jobeljahr in Verkündigung und Theologie der Kirche; systematisch-theologische Implikationen].

4728 *Amstutz* Mark R., Religion and politics in South African Christian churches during the apartheid era: ChrSchR 25 (1995s) 8-29.

4729 [E]**Arjomand** Said Amir, The political dimensions of religion. Albany 1993, SUNY. 293 p. $ 19. -- [R]JRel 75 (1995) 303s (B.M. *Wheeler*).

4730 **Assmann** Hugo, *Hinkelammert* Franz, Götze Markt: BThB, 1992 → 10,8400: [R]TPQ 143 (1995) 306s (F. *Gruber*).

4731 **Atherton** John, Christianity and the market; Christian social thought for our times 1992 → 9,8853: [R]JRel 75 (1995) 149-152 (D.A. *Krueger*); S(cot)JTh 48 (1995) 132-4 (R. *Higginson*).

4732 *a) Barreiro Valera* Edmundo, The [U.S., Protestant, 1890-19l0] social gospel as imperialism [no advertence to any Latin American contrasts or similarities]; -- *b) Carney* Martin F., Liberation theology and the social gospel; can the Gospel reform the structures of the world ?: Listening 30,3 ('Half-finished heaven; the social gospel and an American agenda' 1995) 162-177 / 178-192.

4733 **Bellet** Maurice, La seconde humanité; de l'impasse majeure de ce que nous appelons l'économie. P 1993, D-Brouwer. 222 p. F 125. -- [R]FoiTe 24 (1994) 88 (H. *Thomas*); R(öm)Q 90 (1995) 266-8 (H. *Moll*).

4734 **Boer** Jan H., Missions; heralds of capitalism or Christ ? Ibadan 1984, Day Star. -- [R]IRM(iss) 84 (1995) 173s (A. *Howell*: adds to defense of his 1979 Missionary Messengers).

4735 **Booth** William J., Households; on the moral architecture of the economy. Ithaca 1993, Cornell Univ. xiv-305 p. $33.50. 0-8014-2791-6. -- [R]RStR 21 (1995) 49 (D.E. *Oakman*).

4736 **Braungart** Karl, Heiliger Geist und politischer Herrschaft bei den Neopfingstlern in Honduras: Diss. [D]*Sundermeier* T. Heidelberg 1994. -- ThRv 91 (1995) 96.

4737 **Budde** Michael L., The two churches; communism and capitalism in the world system. Durham NC c.1994, Duke Univ. 172 p. US$ 32. : [R]*CanadCath 13,1 (1995) 23 (A. *McKee*).

4738 *Burggraeve* R., The ethical meaning of money in the thought of Emmanuel LEVINAS: Ethical Perspectives 2,2 (1995) 85-90 [< Judaica 51,259].

4739 *Calvez* Jean-Yves, Experiencia cristiana y experiencia política según San IGNACIO, [T]*Iglesias* I.: Manresa 67 (1995) 21-26.

4740 *Camroux* M. F., When the Holy Spirit comes [from the history of opposition to Church involvement in social issues]: E(xp)T 106 (1994s) 240s.

4741 *Chelliah* Raja, The impact of the market economy on the poor: Transformation 12,3 (1995) 1-4 (-29).

4742 **Cheneaux** Philippe, Une Europe vaticane ? Entre le plan Marshall et les traités de Rome. .. 1990, Ciaco. -- [R]RICAO 12 (1995) 89s (A. *Quenum*).

4743 **Christians** Clifford G., *Ferré* John P., *Fackler* P. Mark, Good News, social ethics and the Press. NY 1993, Oxford-UP. xvi-265 p. $ 50; pa. $18. 0-19-508432-2. -- [R]CScR 25 (1995s) 83-85 (R.A. *Atwood*: good media critique, but his Good News is not The Gospel).

4744 **Claringhall** Denis, Front line mission; ministry in the market place [Christian values no longer assumed]. Norwich 1994, Canterbury, 206 p. £ 8. 1-85311-081-7. -- [R]ET 106 (1994s) 253 (P. *Sedgwick*: the real sense of 'God is dead').

4745 **Cobb** John B.[J], Sustaining the common good; a Christian perspective on the global economy. Cleveland 1995, Pilgrim. xii-148 p. $ 13. 0-8298-1010-2 [ThD 43,61].

4746 **Cobo Suero** J.M., Contribución a la crítica de la política social. M 1993, UPCO. 188 p. -- [R]Salmanticensis 42 (1995) 295s (A. *Galindo García*).

4747 **Copeland** Warren R., And the poor get welfare. Nv 1994, Abingdon. 210 p. $ 14. -- [R]TS 56 (1995) 406 (W.J. *Byron*: excellent except for segregating experts).

4748 **Crüsemann** Frank, Bewahrung der Freiheit; das Thema des Dekalogs in sozialge-schichtlicher Perspektive: Tb 128. Gü 1993, Kaiser. 99 p. DM 16,80. 3-570-05128. -- [R]TTh 35 (1995) 93s (T. *Veerkamp*).

4749 **Dal Covolo** Enrico, Chiesa, società, politica; aree di 'laicità' nel cristianesimo delle origini: Ieri oggi domani 14. R 1994, LAS. 192 p. L[m] 18. 88-213-0278-4. -- [R]Ang 72 (1995) 584-6 (B. *Degórski*); Salesianum 57 (1995) 576s (R. *Iacoangeli*).

4750 **Davis** Charles, Religion and the making of society [3 inedita incorporating 9 reprints]. C 1994, Univ. xiv-208 p. £ 32.50. -- [R]HeythJ 36 (1995) 226s (J. *Sullivan*).

4751 **Dawes** Stuart W., Toward a biblical and pneumatic theology of social concerns for the Pentecostal movement: diss. Laval, [D]*Richard* J. Montreal 1994. 359 p. NN97829 (ISBN 0-315-97829-5). -- DissA 56 (1995s) p. 2735.

4752 **Dölken** Clemens, Katholische Soziallehre und liberale Ökonomik 1992 →10,8419: [R]Anton 69 (1994) 129-131 (L. *Oviedo*).

4753 **Dorrien** Gary J., Reconstructing the common good; theology and the social order 1990 → 6,8426; 8,8601: [R]CritRR 6 (1993) 486s (D.C. *Maguire*).

4754 *a) Dorrien* Gary, Beyond state and market; Christianity and the future of economic democracy; -- *b) Brown* Robert M., Toward a just and compassionate society; a Christian view; -- c) Sherwin Byron L., ... a Jewish view: CrossCur 45 (1995s) 184-204 / 164-174 / 149-163.

4755 EDuchini Francesca, al., La dottrina sociale della Chiesa nella 'Rivista internazionale di scienze sociali' (1943-1967): Quaderno 2, 'non periodico'. Mi 1995, Univ. cattolica centro dottrina sociale. 61 p, bibliografia brevemente commentata; 1-8 articoli; 9-31 recensioni: 32-61, notiziario, congressi; ind. 52-64

4756 Duchrow Ulrich, Alternativen zur kapitalistischen Weltwirtschaft: biblische Erinnerung .. 1994 → 10,8420: RCiTom 121 (1994) 626-8 (R. de Luis Carballada); E(cu)R 47 (1995) 112-4 (H.M. de Lange); ThRv 91 (1995) 61-63 (F. Furger); ThLZ 120 (1995) 167-9 (T. Jähnichen).

4757 Dünnbier Wernher, Was ist mit unserer Wirtschaft los ? Die Wirtschaft und ihre Störenfriede. Fra 1994, Haag & H. 197 p. DM 29,80. 3-86137-219-3.

4758 Ellingsen Mark, The cutting edge, how churches speak on social issues. Geneva/GR 1993. 370 p. Fs 39,50. -- RÖR 44 (1995) 138 (R.M. Burkart).

4759 Ellul Jacques, Anarchy and Christianity [in the Bible, all government is necessarily evil], TBromiley Geoffrey W. GR1991. Eerdmans. 109 p. -- RRefR 49 (1995s) 210 (T.K. Johnson).

4760 Elsbernd Mary, Whatever happened to Octogesima adveniens [Paul VI 1971 broaching historical methodology in Papal teaching]: TS 56 (1995) 39-60.

4761 EEnderle Georges, al., Lexikon der Wirtschaftsethik 1993 → 10,8423; DM 158. -- RThRv 91 (1995) 436-8 (R. Marx).

4762 Ernst W., Gerechtigkeit in Gesellschaft, Wirtschaft und Politik 1992 → 9,8882: Anton 89 (1994) 131-3 (L. Oviedo.)

4763 Etzion Amitai, The moral dimension (Toward a new economics). NY 1990, Free Press. 314 p. -- RScrT(Pamp) 37 (1995) 306-9 (A. Carol i Hostench).

4764 Foitzik Alexander, Menschengerecht und sachgemäss; ein Literaturbericht zur theologischen Wirtschaftsethik: HerKor 49 (1995) 150-155.

4765 a) Fuchs Ottmar, Fluch und Klage als biblische Herausforderung; zur spirituellen und sozialen Praxis der Christen; -- b) Hengsbach Friedhelm, Eine 'biblische Revolution' jenseits katholischer Soziallehre; der Ort biblischer UEberlieferungen in einer gesellschaftlichen Reflexion: BiKi 50 (1995) 64-75 / 77-82.

4766 Furger Franz, Moral oder Kapital ? 1992 → 8,8887; DM 38; 3-545-34102-5: RThLZ 120 (1995) 169-171 (A. Jäger).

4767 García Roca Joaquín, Público y privado en la acción social; del estado de bienestar al estado social. M 1992, Popular. 175 p. -- RSalTer 82 (1994) 74s (F. Herrero).

4768 Gatti G., Solidarietà o mercato ? T 1955, sei. 141 p. Lm 19. -- RAsprenas 42 (1995) 457s (G. Mattai: 'funzione del mercato per l'ottimale allocazione delle risorse' insostituibile malgrado i suoi limiti e distorsioni).

4769 Gay Craig M., With liberty and justice for whom ? The recent evangelical debate over capitalism 1992 → 8,8610: R*CritRR 6 (1993) 367-9 (D. Sturm).

4770 a) González Carvajal Luis, El fracaso del colectivismo; -- b) Camacho Ildefonso, La apoteosis del capitalismo; -- c) Mardones José M., Funciones y tareas para un mesianismo de resistencia y creatividad: SalTer 82 (1994) 3-17 / 19-30 / 43-51.

4771 González-Carvajal Santabárbara L., a) La distribución de le riqueza; - b) La empresa: 'Corintios XIII' 71 (1994) 91-102 / 103-120 (149-192).

4772 Gorringe Timothy J., Capital and the Kingdom; theological ethics and the economic order. Mkn/L 1994, Orbis/SPCK. 200 p. £ 15. 0-88344-944-7 / 0-281-04773-1. -- RET

106,3 top choice (1994s) 65 (C.S. *Rodd*; angry, passionate; NT competence and India experience fine, economics less reassuring; Manasseh/Deuteronomists outset off-putting); Theol 98 (L 1995) 150s (J. *Reader*).

4773 **Goudzwaard** Bob, *Lange* Harry de, Beyond poverty and affluence; towad an economy of care. Geneva/GR 1994, WCC/Eerdmans. 176 p. Fs 20. 2-8254-1138-8 / 0-8028-0827-1. -- ^RE(xp)T 107 (1995s) 94 (W. *Storrar*).

4774 **Haas** Richard C., We all have a share; a Catholic vision of prosperity through productivity. Ch 1995, ACTA. 188 p. $ 15 pa. 0-87946-103-9 [ThD 42,370].

4775 a) *Hausmanninger* Thomas, 'Neue Armut' -- die Rückseite der Wohlstandsgesellschaft; -- b) *Wils* Jean Pierre, Die disziplinierte Ökonomie [KOSLOWSKI P. 1985]: MThZ 45 (1994) 543-561 / 563-575

4776 *Hiebert* Paul G. & Barbara (-Crape), The role of religion in international development: CGrebel 13,3 ('the religious relief' 1995) ...

4777 **Higginson** Edward,. Called to account [aim: 'to bring together Christian theology and business practice in an exciting way']. Guildford 1993, Eagle. 266 p. £ 8. 0-86347-07-2. -- ^RS(co)BET 13 (1995) 89s (F.V. *Waddleton*).

4778 *Hinze* Christine F., John A. RYAN [† 1945], theological ethics and political engagement: → 564, CTS 50 (1995) 174-191.

4779 *Honecker* Martin, a) Wirtschaftsethik und Soziallehre: ThR(u) 60 (1995) 152-162; -- b) Perspektiven der Wirtschaftsethik: ThLZ 120 (1995) 395-410.

4780 **Jong Mo Sung**, Teologia e economia (Repensando a teologia da libertação e Utopias). Petrópolis 1994, Vozes. 271 p. -- ^RREB 55 (1995) 971-5 (J.B. *Libânio*).

4781 a) *Josaphat* Lebulu L., The Church's social teaching on development; -- b) *Mpundu* Telesphore, The Church's life style in the context of Africa's poverty: AfER 37 (1995) 316-327 / 170-7.

4782 *Kaiser* Helmut, Provecho proprio, bien común y solidaridad; hacia la fundamentación antropológica de la economia [< ZEE 37 (1993) 189-204], ^{TE}*Sala* Mario: SalT 33 (1994) 107-219.

4783 *Kealy* Seán P., The political Jesus: I(r)ThQ 61 (1995) 89-98.

4784 **Kroeker** P. Travis, Christian ethics and political economy in North America; a critical analysis. Montreal 1995, McGill-Queen's Univ. xv-201 p. $ 45; pa. $ 19. 0-7735-1267-5; -8-3 [ThD 42,373].

4785 a) *Kwak Pui-Lan,* Business ethics in the economic development of Asia; a feminist analysis; -- b) *Joseph* M.P., An ethical critique of the concepts of wealth and poverty in the Bible: A(sia)JT 9 (1995) 133-145 / 123-132.

4786 **Lawrence** William D., (*Turpin* Jack A.), Beyond the bottom line; where faith and business meet. Ch 1994, Moody. 189 p. $ 10. -- ^RBS 152 (1995) 247 (S.L. *Canine*).

4787 *Lindsey* William D., Telling it slant; American Catholic public theology and prophetic discourse: Horizons 22 (1995) 88-103.

4788 **McCarthy** George E., *Rhodes* Royal W., Eclipse of justice [bishops on economics] 1992 → 8,8636; 9,8915: ^R*CritRR 7 (1994) 348-350 (T.R. *Rourke*).

4789 *McDonagh* William, Can social ethics be public and Christian at the same time ? ; a review essay [HIMES M. & K. 1993; SANKS T. & COLEMAN J. 1993; THIEMANN R. 1991; OKIN Susan 1989]: NewThR 8,1 (1995) 75-83.

4790 *McKenzie* Michael, Christian norms in the ethical square; an impossible dream ? : JETS 38 (1995) 413-427.

4791 **Mackey** James P., Power and Christian ethics. C 1994, Univ. x-241 p. $ 55. --

[R]JRel 75 (1995) 594-6 (R.B. *Miller*); MoTh 11 (1995) 485s (L. *Rasmussen*).

4792 *Marty* Martin E.,Religion, a private affair, in public affairs: R&AC(u) 3 (1993) 115-27

4790 *Mattai* Giuseppe, Gli eventi 'rivoluzionari' del biennio 1989-91 e il revival neocapitalistico [NEUHAUS R., NOVAK M., WEIGEL G., tutti [T]ital. 1994]: RasT 36 (1995) 233-241.

4794 *a) Melchin* Kenneth R., Ecologies, economies, and communities; the alternative of community economic development; -- *b) Pushparajan* A., Eco-harmony and economic equality; a vindication of Gandhian economics: JDharma 18 (1993) 322-332 / 340-363 [*al*.301-321; 333-9].

4795 **Milbank** John, Theology and social theory 1991 → 8,8641 ... 10,8450: [R]Greg 76 (1995) 770 (T. *Kennedy*).

4796 -- *Murphy* Debra D., Power, politics, and difference; a feminist response to John MILBANK: MoTh 10 (1994) 131-142.

4797 *a) Mora Lomelí* Raúl, Reflexión crítico ética sobre los proyectos de los partidos políticos (*al.*): Xipe-Totek 3,2 ('Chiapas y el futuro de México' 1994) 139-143 (86-171); -- *b) Ruiz García* Samuel, Carta pastoral: Xipe-Totek 3,3 (1994) 257-292 (219-222, La redacción, Campaña contra los Jesuitas, contra Don Samuel y contra los que tienen la opción por los pobres).

4798 **Mott** Stephen C., A Christian perspective on political thought 1993 → 10,8453: [R]JRel 75 (1995) 148s (M.L. *Stackhouse*); TTod 51 (1994s) 308.310.312 (G. *Tinder*).

4799 **Mott** Stephen C., Ética bíblica y cambio social [Ox 1992], [T] BA 1995, Nueva creación. xv-259 p. 0-8028-0923-5.

4800 **Nelson** Robert H., Reaching for heaven on earth; the theological meaning of economics 1993 → 10,8456: [R]*CritRR 6 (1993) 492 (C.A. *Kucheman*: theologizing economists are either in the Catholic tradition of ARISTOTLE, AQUINAS, & SAINT-SIMON, or in the Protestant tradition of PLATO, AUGUSTINE, CALVIN & KEYNES).

4801 **Nitecki** Piotr, [P] Socjalizm, komunizm i ewangelizacja I [dysertacja]. Suwałki 1994, Blachnicki. 171 p. -- [R]AtK(ap) 125 (1995) 291-5 (M. *Marczewski*).

4802 **Novak** David, Jewish social ethics 1992 → 9,8935; [R]Jud(aism) 43 (1994) 325-8 (A.J. *Yuter*).

4803 *a) Otto* E., Wirtschaftsethik im Alten Testament; -- *b) Hengstbach* F., Gerechtigkeit in der Marktwirtschaft; -- *c) O'Collins* G., University of the nations: Informationes theologiae Europae 3 (Fra 1994) 379-290 / 267-278 / 261-6 [< ZIT 95,p.81]

4804 *Oviedo Torró* L., La fe cristiana en el contexto de los sistemas sociales avanzados; cuestiones en torno a la economía y la política: *Carthaginensia 11 (1995) 273-303.

4805 *Panthanmackel* George, The roots of economic disparity and poverty: JDh 20 (1995) 89-93 (94-103 response, *Manimala* Varghese).

4806 *a) Perry* Michael J., Religion, politics and human rights [query, *Boland* Vivian]; -- *b) Keogh* Dermot, Church, state and pressure groups: DoLi 45 (1995) 16-41 [62-67] / 42-61.

4807 *a) Petit* Daniel, Le pouvoir au risque de l'Évangile; -- *b) Becquet* Gilles, 'Sur le fil du rasoir'; les rapports ambigus du politique et du religieux (Mc 1,13-17): Sève 568 (1995) 33-37 / 38-40.

4808 *Pieris* Aloysius, Les pauvres et le Règne de Dieu; -- *b) Guitton* Gérard, Pauvretè et mission: Spiritus 36 (1995) 339-347 / 364-370.

4809 **Preston** Ronald H., Confusion in Christian social ethics; problems for Geneva and Rome. GR/L 1994, Eerdmans/SCM. xiii-195 p. £ 13. -- [R]*CritRR 8 (1995) 362s (J.W. *de Gruchy*: ... and for Preston); E(cu)R 47 (1995) 503s (P. *Lodberg*).

4810 **Prien** Hans-Jürgen, LUTHERs Wirtschaftsethik 1992 → 9,8947; 10,8456; 3-525-55338-2: ᴿRHPhR 75 (1995) 356s (M. *Lienhard*).

4811 *a) Pröpper* Thomas, Autonomie und Solidarität; Begründungsprobleme sozialethischer Verpflichtung; -- *b) Suess* Paulo, Über die Unfähigkeit der Einen, sich der Andern zu erinnern; -- *c) Dussel* Enrique, Die Priorität der Befreiungsethik gegenüber der Diskursethik, ᵀ*Proske* Matthias: → 149, ᶠPEUKERT H., Anerkennung 1995, 95-112 / 64-94 / 113-127.

4812 **Randels** George D.ᴶ, Caveat procurator; virtues and business ethics: diss. Virginia 1995, ᴰ*Childress* James. 289 p. 95-25067. -- DissA 56 (1996s) p.1393.

4813 **Rasmussen** Arne, The Church as polis ... MOLTMANN. HAUERWAS 1994 → 10,8466: ᴿE(xp)T 107 (1995s) 187 (D. *Cornick*); *ModBlv 36,3 (1995) 67s (A. *Shanks*).

4814 ᴱ**Rauscher** Anton, Die gesellschaftliche Verantwortung der Kirche: Theologie interdisziplinär 8. Donauwörth 1992, Auer. 254 p. DM 16,80 [ThRv 91,249-252, G. *Wilhelms*].

4815 *Razafiarison* Emilien, The evangelicals and politics in Africa; Transformation 11,4 (1994) 19s (*al.* 1-31).

4816 **Rich** Arthur, Etica economica, ᵀ*Danna* Carlos: BtTContemp 73, 1993 → 9,8950; 88-399-0373-9: ᴿActuBbg 31 (1994) 256s (J. *Boada*).

4817 *Rizza* Giuseppe, La dichiarazione di Oxford [1987] su cristianesimo ed economia [... SCHLOSSENBERG H., *al.* 1994]: STEv 7,14 ('Dio e Cesare' 1995) 166-177.

4818 **Robra** Martin, Ökumenische Sozialethik. Gü 1994, Gü-V. 255 p. DM 78. 3-579-00296-1.-- ᴿE(cu)R 47 (1995) 112 (L. *Rasmussen*: a jargon-free Part I on paradigm-shifts); THGL 85 (1995) 573-5 (R. *Geisen*).

4819 ᴱ**Royon** Claude, *Philibert* Robert, Les pauvres, un défi pour l'Église [dossier 1 (des 4), biblique]. P 1994, Ouvrières. 553 p. F 290. 3-7082-3071-9. -- ᴿRTL 26 (1995) 396s (R. *Guelluy*).

4820 *Salvatierra* Angel, Neoliberalismo; ¿qué has hecho de los excluidos del sistema ? : Lum(Vr) 44 (1995) 285-314.

4821 **Salzman** Todd A., Deontology and teleology; an investiagtion of the normative debate in Roman Catholic moral theology: BtETL 120. Lv 1995. Univ./Peeters. xvii-555 p. Fb 2900. /90-6186-709-6 [ThD 43.185].

4822 ᴱ**Schlossberg** Herbert, *Samuel* V., *Sider* R., Christianity and economics in the post-cold war era; the Oxford Declaration and beyond. GR 1994, Eerdmans. viii-186 p £ 9. 0-8028-0798-4. -- ᴿ*TBR 8,2 (1995s) 42 (C. *Elliott*: not much praise except for KILLEN J.)

4823 **Schneider** John, Godly materialism; rethinking money and possessions .. Intervarsity; 213 p. US$ 19. -- ᴿ*CanadCath 13,3 (1995) 25 (A. *McKee*).

4824 **Schweickart** David, Against capitalism. C 1993, Univ. xiii-387 p. £ 40. -- ᴿMonth 56 (1995) 190s (P. *Burns*).

4825 **Sedgwick** Peter, The enterprise culture. L 1992, SPCK. 197 p. £ 15. -- ᴿS(cot)JTh 48 (1995) 134s (R. *Higginson*)

4826 *Selling* Joseph A., Values, goods and priorities: can law determine the pattern ?: LouvSt 20 (1995) 58-64.

4827 *Seurin* J.L., Religion et politique à la lumière de la Bible selon Jacques ELLUL: FoiVie 93,4s ('Le siècle de Jacques Ellul', 1994) 95-198 [< ZIT 95,p.78

4828 *a) Simons* Robert G., Is the Gospel good news for *homo economicus* ? , -- *b) Wilcken* John, The Gospel and evangelization: A(usAs)CR 72 (1995) 280-294 / 259-268.

4829 **Simons** Robert G., Competing Gospels: public theology and economic theory.

Alexandria NSW / Ridgefield CT 1995, Dwyer / Morehouse distrib. xxii-231 p. $ 15 pa.
0-85574-142-2 [ThD 43,289].

4830 *Sobrino* Jon, ¿ Es Jesús una buena noticia ?: SalTer 81 (1993) 595-608.

4831 *Štuhec* Ivan, The meaning of Jesus' redemption for socio-political engagement of
Christians: BogVest 53 (1993) 107-122, Slovene; 123 Eng.

4832 **Sung Jung Mo**, Teología e economia; repensando a Teologia da Libertação e utopias.
Petrópolis 1994, Vozes. 271 p. 85-326-1168-0. -- [R]PerTeol 27 (1995) 119-23 (J.B.
Libanio).

4833 **Tanner** Kathryn, The politics of God; Christian theologies and social justice 1992 →
9,8966; 10,8477: [R]JRel 75 (1995) 147s (W. *Schweiker*); MoTh 10 (1994) 291-3 (S. *Davis*).

4834 **Taylor** Charles, *al.*, Multikulturalismus und die Politik der Anerkennung [... Quebec!],
[T]*Kaiser* Reinhard. Fra 1993. S.Fischer. 198 p. DM 36. -- [R]ThRv 91 (1995) 149s (E. *Arens*:
brillantes Plädoyer).

4835 **Tosato** A., Economia di mercato e cristianesimo: QuadScSoc 11. R 1994, Borla. 180
p. L[m] 30. 88-263-1086-4 [NTAb 40, p.547].

4836 *Vaillancourt* Mark, [M.] NOVAK, [G.] WEIGEL & [R.] NEUHAUS; a critique of Pope
John Paul II and western capitalism: DunwoodieR 17 (1994) 43-55.

4837 *Vidović* Pero, Dignity of the poor in the Bible: ObŽ 50 (1995) 135-150; Eng. 151.

Wheeler Sondra Ely, Wealth as peril and obligation; the New Testament on possessions
1995 → 4719 supra.

4839 [E]**Wilkie** George, *al.* (E Univ. Centre for theology and public issues: one woman amid
10 bankers and 5 academics), Capital; a moral instrument ? E 1992, St. Andrew Press.
xi-79 p. £ 5.50. -- [R]S(cot)JTh 48 (1995) 525s (P. *Sedgwick*).

4840 *a) Vives* Josep. M. NOVAK, ¿ una teología del capitalismo ? -- *b) Robles* Ricardo,
Elementos básicos en la consideración de las autonomías de los pueblos indígenas:
Christus 60,l (Méx 1995) 19-23 / 60,4s (1995) 22-29.

4841 **Wink** Walter, Engaging the powers; discernment and resistance in a world of
domination 1992 → 8,6624; 10,6132: [R]S(co)BET 13 (1995) 77s (R. *Calvert* says that for
Wink the powers are 'foreign policy, nationalism, militarism, the media, comics and cartoon
shows', but he premises or summarizes 'multinationals, banks').

4842 **Zamagni** S., Economia ed etica; saggi sul fondamento etico del discorso economico.
R 1994, A.V.E. 223 p. L[m] 25. -- [R]CivCatt 146 (1995,3) 542s (F. *Cultrera*); RasT 36
(1995) 633s (G. *Mattai*).

4843 *a) Zauner* W., Religion und Geld; -- *b) Gubler* M.A., Jesus und das Geld; -- *c)*
Hoffmann J., Das Mammondilemma des Sozialstaates und die Involviertheit der Kirche; --
d) Siegwart J., Die Kirche und das Geld in der Geschichte: Diakonia 26 (1995) 73-78 / 79-
89 / 90-104 / 105-110 [< ZIT 95,p.328].

4844 **Ziesche** Frank, Evangelische Wirtschaftsethik; eine Untersuchung zu Georg WÜNSCHs
wirtschaftsethischem Werk: Diss. [D]*Brakelmann* G. Bochum 1995. -- ThLZ 120 (1995)
1146.

4845 **Zsifkovits** V., Wirtschaft ohne Moral ? Innsbruck 1994, Tyrolia. 138 p. DM 28.
3-7022-1929-3. -- [R]TTh 35 (1995) 310s (G. *Manenschijn*).

H8.5 Theologia liberationis latino-americana

4846 *Arens* Edmund, Der Ort der Religion [Diskursethik, Befreiungsphilosophie:
Or(ientierung) 58 (1994) 113-8.

4847 ᴱ**Bañuelas** Arturo J., Mestizo Christianity; theology from a Latin perspective [14 reprints]. Mkn 1995, Orbis. vi-278 p. $ 17 pa. 1-57075-032-7.

4848 **Batstone** David, From conquest to struggle 1991 → 7,8494 ... 10,8489: ᴿ*CritRR 6 (1993) 495-7 (J.R. *Sibley*).

4849 *Baumgartner* Jacob, Gottes Wohlgefallen an den Armen; Las Casas-Rezeption heute: NZM(iss) 50 (1994) 207-222.

4850 **Bedford-Strohm** Heinrich,   Vorrang für die Armen; auf dem Weg zu einer theologischen Theorie der Gerechtigkeit: Öffentliche Theologie 4. Gü 1993, Kaiser. 352 p. DM 78. -- ᴿTPQ 142 (1994) 403-6 (J. *Schwabeneder*).

4851 **Belli** Humberto, *Nash* Ronald, Beyond liberation theology 1992 → 8,8690: ᴿJETS 38 (1995) 93s (T. N. *Brown*).

4852 **Bidegain** Ana María, História dos Cristãos na América Latina. Petrópolis 1994, Vozes. 324 p. -- ᴿREB 55 (1995) 712-4 (R. *Azzi*).

4853 **Borges** Pedro, Historia de la Iglesia en Hispanoamérica y Filipinas 1992 → 9,8994; 10,8495: ᴿForKT 10 (1994) 237 (J. *Grohe*).

4854 *Bourque* L.Nicole, Priests and saints; syncretism and power in the Ecuadorian Andes: ScotJR 16 (1995) 25-36.

4855 *Caldecott* Stratford, Theological dimensions of human liberation; ... starts not from abstract notions of 'the people' and 'their oppressors' but from a personal encounter with Christ in prayer and sacraments: ComI-US 22 (1995) 225-241.

4856 *Cardoza-Orlandi* Carlos F., Drum beats of resistance and liberation; Afro-Caribbean religions, the struggle for life, and the Christian theologian: JHispLat 3,1 (1995s) 50-61.

4857 **Casaldáliga** Pedro, *Vigil* José M., The spirituality of liberation [1992 → 10,8498], ᵀ*Burns* Paul, *McDonagh* Frances. L 1994, Burns & O. 244 p. £ 12. 0-86012-215-8. -- ᴿET 106 (1994s) 154 (D.D. *Wilson*: the translators have captured wonderfully the freshness of the Nicaraguan Claretians).

4858 **Caturelli** Alberto, El Nuevo Mundo; el descubrimiento, la conquista y la evangelización de América y la cultura occidental. Puebla 1991, Univ./Adamex. 455 p. -- ᴿAng 71 (1994) 615-7 (A. *Lobato*).

4859 ᴱ**Cook** Guillermo, New face of the Church in Latin America. Mkn 1994, Orbis. -- ᴿMid-Str 34 (1995) 97-99 (C.E. *Álvarez*).

4860 *Corkery* James, The social dimensions of grace and 'dis-grace' in the theology of Leonard BOFF: Bobolanum 6 (1995) 92-118; ᴾ 118s.

4862 **Dussel** Enrique, Historia liberationis (500 anos de história da Igreja na América Latina, ᵀ*Costa* Rezende. São Paulo 1993, Paulinas, 712 p. -- ᴿREB 52 (1993) 987-993 (E. *Hoornaert*).

4863 **Dussel** Enrique, The Church in Latin America 1992 → 9,9007: 10,8502: ᴿ*CritRR 7 (1994) 329s (P.J. *Williams*).

4864 *Dussel* Enrique, Ética de la liberación; hacia el 'punto de partida' como ejercicio de la 'razón exegética *originaria*': *Carthaginensia 11 (1995) 327-353; Eng. 246.

4865 ᴱ**Dussel** Enrique, Historia general de la Iglesia en América Latina IX. Cono Sur (Argentina, Chile, Uruguay, Paraguay): CEHILA. S 1994, Sígueme. -- ᴿNatGrac 42,3 (1995) 662s (E. *Rivera*).

4866 *a)* **Dussel** Enrique, Historia de la filiosofía y filosofía de la liberación. Bogotá 1994, Nueva América. 322 p. -- ᴿ*JHispT 3 (1995s) 62s (Eduardo *Mendieta*). -- *b)* **Scheelkshorn** Hans, Ethik der Befreiung: Einführung in die Philosophie Enrique DUSSELS. W 1992, Herder. 172 p. -- ᴿ*JHispT 3,1 (1995s) 71-75 (E. *Mendieta*).

4867 *a) Echarren* R., La Iglesia y los pobres; -- *b) Vicente Eguiguren* J., Nueva evangelización, liberación cristiana y opción por los pobres: 'Corintios XIII' 70 (1994) 11-80 / 81-110 [RET 55,117].

4868 *Eckholt* Margit, Präsenz des Weiblichen; die Rolle der Frau in Kultur und Theologie Lateinamerikas: HerKor 49 (1995) 141-6.

4869 **Eidsmoe** John, Columbus and Cortez, conquerors for Christ. Green Forest AR 1992, New Leaf. 304 p. $ 10. -- [R]BS 151 (1994) 375 (J.A. *Witmer*: they wanted to help peoples who were often exploiting and slaughtering one another; both died penniless).

4870 [E]**Ellacuria** Ignacio, *Sobrino* Jon, Mysterium liberationis 1993 → 10,8503s: [R]S(co)BET 13 (1995) 172-4 (D.D. *Morgan*: important reading as either transition or epitaph).

4871 *Equiza* Jesús, Teología de la liberación; revalorización de la dimensión social de la persona: Lum(Vr) 44 (1995) 449-489.

4872 *Estermann* Josef, Die Armen haben Namen und Gesichter; Anmerkungen zu einer hermeneutischen Verschiebung in der Befreiungstheologie: NZM(iss) 50 (1994) 307-320.

4873 **Fabris** Rinaldo, La opción por los pobres en la Biblia, [T]*Ortiz* A, Estella 1992, VDivino. 329 p. -- [R]RelCult 40 (1994) 879 (A. *Moral*).

4874 *Fawcett* Bruce G., A critical analysis of some hermeneutical principles found in Latin American theologies of liberation: JETS 37 (1994) 569-581.

4875 *Forrester* Duncan B., Can liberation theology survive 1989 ? [communist collapse]: S(cot)JTh 47 (1994) 245-253.

4876 [E]**García Antezana** Jorge, Liberation theology and sociopolitical transformation, a reader. ... Simon Fraser Univ. 432 p. $ 20. -- [R]*CanadCath 13,7 (1995) 23 (D. *McLeod*).

4877 [E]**Getz** Lorine M., *Costa* Ruy O., Struggles for solidarity; liberation theologies in tension. Mp 1992, Fortress. 171 p. $ 11 pa. -- [R]*CritRR 7 (1994) 504-6 (Priscilla *Pope-Levison*).

4878 **Gonzalez** Justo L., Out of every tribe and nation; Christian theology at the ethnic roundtable. Nv 1992, Abingdon. 244 p. -- [R]*JHispT 3,2 (1995s) 78 (Eliseo *Pérez-Álvarez*).

4879 *a) González* Antonio, La vigencia del 'método teológico' de la teología de la liberación; -- *b) González Faus* José Ignacio, Una tarea historica; de la liberación a la apocalíptica: SalTer 83 (1995) 667-675 / 717-728.

4880 **Gossen** Gary H., *León-Portilla* Miguel, South and Meso-American native spirituality; WSp 4, 1993 → 10,8510: [R]C(ath)HR 81 (1995) 550-2 (Leslie Ellen *Straub*); NewThR 8,3 (1995) 112s (G. *Riebe-Estrella*).

4881 **Gutiérrez** Gustavo, The God of life 1991 → 8,8722 ... 10,8512: [R]JE(mp)T 6,1 (1993) 102 (L.J. *Francis*); Pacifica 6 (1993) 347-9 (A. *Hamilton*: unction which L. BOFF lacks).

4882 *a) Gutiérrez* Gustavo, Option for the poor; review and challenges; -- *b) Cullinan* Thomas, The politics of ownership : Month 256 (1995) 5-10 / 11-15.

4883 **Gutiérrez** Lucio, Historia de la Iglesia Católica en Filipinas; Iglesia Católica en el Nuevo Mundo 6/4. M 1992, Mapfre. -- [R]ScrTh(Pamp) 26 (1994) 333s (J.G. *Martín de la Hoz*).

4884 *a) Guzmán* Anibal, 'Martyrdom and hope'; five hundred years of Christian presence in Latin America and the Caribbean; -- *b) Richard* Pablo, 1492; God's violence and the future of Christianity: IRM(iss) 82 (1993) 11-17 / 87-93.

4885 **Hennelly** Alfred T., *a)* Liberation theologies; the global pursuit of justice. Mystic CT 1995, Twenty-Third. 382 p. $ 20. 0-89622-647-6 [< ThD 43,272]. -- *b)* Liberation theology; a documentary history 1990 → 6,8544 ... 9,9019: [R]NZM(iss) 51 (1995) 157s (S. *Herbst*).

4886 **Hoornaert** Eduardo, História do Cristianismo na América Latina e no Caribe. São Paulo 1994, Paulus. 443 p. -- [R]RBBras 11 (1994) 703 (C. *Minette de Tillesse*).

4887 **Howard-Brook** Wes, Becoming children of God; John's Gospel and radical discipleship: Bible & Liberation. Mkn 1994, Orbis. xviii-510 p. $ 22. -- [R]TS 56 (1995) 776s (W.S. *Kurz*).

4888 **Iraburu** J.M., Hechos de los Apóstoles de América. Pamplona 1992, Gratis date. 621 p. -- [R]Burgense 35 (1994) 392s (N. *López Martínez*).

4889 *a) Jiménez* Pablo A., In search of a Hispanic model of biblical interpretation; -- *b) Espín* Orlando O., Pentecostalism and popular Catholicism; the poor and tradition: *JHispT 3,2 (1995s) 44-64 / 14-43.

4890 **Knolle** Helmut, 500 Jahre Verirrung; Voraussetzungen und Folgen der Entdeckung Amerikas. Olten 1992, Walter. 154 p. -- [R]ZNM(iss) 50 (1994) 77-79 (J. *Baumgartner*).

4891 *Lugo Rodríguez* Raúl, La Biblia en manos del pueblo; retos y perspectivas: VSVD 35 (1994) 323-332.

4892 *McCarthy* Katherine G., Liberation in a religiously plural world; the problem of normative Christological claims in Latin American theology: T(oronto)JT 10 (1994) 197-213.

4893 *MacCormack* Sabine, Ubi Ecclesia ? Perceptions of medieval Europe in Spanish America: Speculum 69 (1994) 74 ..

4894 **Mannu** Maria, I Francescani sulle orme di Cristoforo Colombo. R 1992. -- [R]SMSR 55 (1993) 166-175 (Anna *Unali*: riuscita).

4895 **Manzone** Gianni, La libertà cristiana e le sue mediazioni sociali nel pensiero di Jacques ELLUL [diss.Fac.It.Sett.]. Mi 1993, Glossa. L[m] 45. -- [R]StPat(av) 41 (1994) 643-6 (G. *Trentin*).

4896 **Marlé** René, Introduzione alla teologia della liberazione [1988 → 4,9603], [T]*Canobbio* G. (con bibliografia). Brescia 1991, Morcelliana.154 p. -- [R]Lat 50 (1994) 194-6 (N. *Ciola*).

4897 *Martínez Gordo* Jesús, Compromiso, espiritualidad y razón teológica; la perpectiva teológica de Gustavo GUTIÉRREZ: *a)* Lum(Vr) 44 (1995) 97-120; -- *b)* RLatAmT 12 (1995) 163-201 [Gutiérrez art. p.259-280].

4898 *Medina* Ignacio, Los derechos humanos en América Latina; el caso de El Salvador: Xipe-Totek 4,2 (Guadalajara Méx. 1995) 115-131 (*al.* 184-233).

4899 *Moltmann* Jürgen, Die Zukunft der Befreiungstheologie: Orien(tierung) 59 (1995) 207-210.

4900 **Mullo Sandoval** Mario, *al.*, Cristianos [católicos en Ecuador] hoy; testimonios de liberación. Quito 1993, FEPP. 119 p. -- [R]RStR 19 (1993) 337 (J.T. *Ford*).

4901 **Murad** Afonso, Este Cristianismo inquieto; a Fé cristã encarnada em J. L. SEGUNDO [dis. Roma, Pont. Univ. Gregoriana]: Fé e Realidade 33. São Paulo 1994, Loyola. 207 p. - - [R]REB 55 (1995) 979s (A.Alves de *Melo*).

4902 **Núñez C.** Emilio A., *Taylor* William D., Crisis in Latin America; an evangelical perspective. Ch 1989, Moody. 439 p. $ 20 pa. -- [R]JETS 38 (1995) 94s (M. *Carroll R.*)

4903 **Panikkar** Raimundo, The Vedic experience Mantramanjari; an anthology of the Vedas for modern man and contemporary celebration. 1994. xxxvii-937 p. rs 375 [JDh 20,313].

4904 **Pelton** Robert S., (*Calero* Luis), From power to communion; toward a new way of being Church based on the Latin American experience. ND c.1995, Univ. 95 p. $12 pa. - - [R]*CanadCath 13,6 (1995) 24 (R.J. *Seguin*).

4905 **Persaud** Winston D., The theology of the Cross and MARX's anthropology; a view from the Caribbean [D]1991 → 9,9043; 10,8534: [R]S(cot)JT 47 (1994) 535s (P. *Scott*).

4906 *Peterson* Anna L., Religion in Latin America; new methods and approaches [LEVINE D. 1992 & 3 Brazil, 2 Nicaragua]: RStR 21 (1995) 3-8.

4907 *Phan* Peter C., *a)* Cultural diversity; a blessing or a curse for theology and spirituality: LvSt 19 (1994) 195-211: -- *b)* Peacemaking in Latin American theology [.. not advocating (Marxist) violence]; < ÉgT 24 (1993) 25-41], [E]*Asen* B.A. : ThD 42 (1995) 225-8.

4908 **Piar** Carlos R., Jesus and liberation; a critical analysis of the Christology of Latin American liberation theology: AmUSt 7/148. NY 1994, P. Lang. 178 p. $ 33. 0-8204-2098-0 [ThD 43,81].

4909 *Pottmeyer* Hermann J., Das Evangelium der Freiheit und der freiheitliche, säkulare Staat: StZ 213 (1995) 759-767.

4910 **Preiswerk** Matthias, Apprendre la libération; exemple d'éducation populaire en Bolivie [expérience de dix ans]. Genève 1994, Labor et Fides. 448 p. F 178. 2-8309-0705-1. -- [R]ETRel 70 (1995) 149s (M. *Muller*).

4911 **Prior** Michael, Jesus, the liberator; Nazareth liberation theology (Luke 4.16-30): Biblical Seminar 16. Shf 1995, Academic. 228 p.; bibliog. 203-216. 1-85075-524-8

4912 *Rivera de Ventosa* Enrique, Lo vivo y lo muerto del pensamiento hispánico ante el problema de América: NatGrac 41 (1994) 103-124.

4913 **Rivera** Luis N., A violent evangelism 1992 → 9,9050: 10,8538: [R]*CritRR 7 (1994) 360-2 (R.C. *Goode*); Horizons 22 (1995) 153-5 (J.B. *Nickoloff*: useful but with several cautions); Interpretation 48 (1994) 326 (H.M. *Goodpasture*).

4914 **Rivera** Roberto, The oppositional nature of liberation discourses (GUTIÉRREZ G., FREIRE P.): diss. California, Santa Cruz 1994. 236 p. 95-00546. -- DissA 55 (1954s) p. 2430.

4915 **Rowland** Christopher, *Corner* Mark, The liberating exegesis; the challenge of liberation theology to biblical studies 1990 → 7,8573; 8,8762: [R]EvQ 66 (1994) 183-6 (M. *Turner*: lucid, enjoyable -- and unacceptable).

4916 *Sastre Santos* E., ¿ Por qué fue posible construir la Iglesia en Hispanoamérica y en las Islas Filipinas ?: Commentarium pro Religiosis 74 (1993) 171-163 [< ArTGran 57 (1994) 385s, E. *Moore*].

4917 **Sawyer** Frank, The poor are many; political ethics in the social encyclicals, Christian democracy, and liberation theology in Latin America. Kampen 1992, Kok. 202 p. -- [R]ScEs 46 (1994) 263-7 (J.-L. *D'Aragon*).

4918 **Schelkshorn** Hans, Ethik der Befreiung; Einführung in die Philosophie Enrique DUSSELs. W 1992, Herder. 172 p. -- [R]JHispLat 3,1 (1995s) 71-75 (E. *Mendieta*).

4919 [E]**Schlegelberger** Bruno, *Delgado* Mariano, Die Armut macht uns reich; zur Geschichte und Gegenwart des Christentums in Lateinamerika. B/Hildesheim 1992, Morus/Bernward. 264 p. DM 48. -- [R]WiWei 58 (1995) 160s (H. von der *Bey*).

4920 **Schmeller** Thomas, Das Recht der Anderen; Befreiungstheologische Lektüre des NTs in Lateinamerika [GADAMER: 'The possibility that the other is right is the heart of hermeneutics']: NTAbh 27, 1994 → 10,8541: [R]JThS 46 (1995) 671-3 (T. *Gorringe*); RBBras 11 (1994) 702s (C. *Minette de Tillesse*).

4921 *Schoelles* Patricia A., Discipleship and liberation theology; the critical and reforming tendencies of basic Christian identity: LouvSt 19 (1994) 46-64.

4922 **Schubeck** Thomas, Liberation ethics; sources, models, and norms 1993 → 10,8542;

$ 17; 0-8006-2755-5: ᴿET 106 (1994s) 252s (D.*Brown*: gives chief critics' views often more clearly than they, and adds his own wholly constructive critique); TS 56 (1995) 162-4 (R. *Betsworth*).

4923 **Schutte** Ofelia, Cultural identity and social liberation in Latin American thought. Albany 1993, SUNY. x-313 p. $ 54.50; pa. $ 18. -- ᴿ*CritRR 7 (1994) 517s (S. *Bevans*).

4924 **Scott** Peter, Theology, ideology and liberation; towards a liberation theology: C Studies in Ideology and Religion 6. C 1994, Univ. xiv-272 p. $ 60. -- ᴿET 106 (1994s) 346s (J. *Parr*); TS 56 (1995) 804s (A.F. *McGovern*: he holds it must still begin with MARX's fundamentally correct analysis of society).

4925 **Segundo** J.L., Quel homme, quel monde, quel Dieu ? [1993 → 9,9062], ᵀ: Théologies. P 1993, Cerf. 142 p. F 100. 2-204-04892-5. -- ᴿE(spr)eV 105 (1995) 75 (J. *Milet*); TTh 35 (1995) 200s (J. Van *Nieuwenhove*).

4926 **Shariati** Mendi S., From modernization theory to liberation theology: diss. Missouri, KC 1994. 299 p. 94-28736. -- DissA 55 (1994s) p. 1658.

4927 **Smith** Christian, The emergence of liberation theology; radical religion and social movement theory 1991 → 8,8771; 9,9071: ᴿ*CanadCath 13,5 (1995) 19 (Lee *Cormie*); *CritRR 7 (1994) 370-4 (L. *Cormie*, R. *McKeon*).

4928 *Sobrino* Jon, Evil and hope; a reflection from the victims: → 564, CTS 50 (1995) 71-84, response 85-92, *Aquino* María Pilar.

4929 *Sobrino* Jon, al., La teología de la liberación y el levantamiento indiano de Chiapas: Christus 59,2 (Méx 1994) 34-38.

4930 **Sobrino** Jon, Jesus the liberator; a historical theological reading [1991 → 8,8772], ᵀ*Burns* Paul, *McDonagh* Francis, Mkn 1993 → 10,8550; also LibT: Tunbridge Wells 1994, Burns & O. viii-308 p. £ 13. 0-86012-200-X. -- ᴿ*TBR 8,1 (1995s) 30 (D. *Lehmann*)

4931 *Stålset* Sturla, Når de fattige blir pinsevenner [Pentecostals]: frigjørensteologien og protestantismens vekst i Latin-Amerika; NTT 96 (1995) 223-240; Eng. 240.

4932 **Stefano** Frances, † 1992, The absolute value of human action in the theology of Juan Luis SEGUNDO. Lanham MD 1992, UPA. xx-298 p. $ 42.50. -- ᴿ*CritRR 6 (1993) 393s (R. *Haight*: high praise).

4933 *Storrar* William, The underprivileged and the oppressed: ET 106 (1994s) 197-202.

4934 *Talbot* John K., Who evangelizes whom ? The poor evangelizers: RfR 52 (1993) 893-6.

4935 *Tamayo-Acosta* Juan José, Teología de la liberación; revolución metodológica y desafíos: Communio (Sev) 28 (1995) 47-71.

4936 **Tamez** Elsa, The amnesty of grace; justification by faith from a Latin American perspective, ᵀ*Ringe* Sharon H. Nv 1993, Abingdon. 208 p. -- ᴿMoTh 10 (1994) 937-9 (B. *Harvey*).

4937 **Taylor** Mark K., Remembering Esperanza 1990 → 9,8781; 10,8554: ᴿInterpretation 48 (1994) 222-4 (J.L. *Gonzalez*).

4938 *Vigo* Abelardo del, Economía y moral en el Siglo de Oro; el tráfico de esclavos de España a las Indias: ScripV 41 (1994) 221-245.

4939 **Wind** Renate, Befreiung buchstabieren: Basislektüre Bibel / Tb 137. Gü 1995, Kaiser. 96 p. 3-579-05137-7.

4941 **Zubero** Imanol, Las nuevas condiciones de la solidaridad. Bilbao 1994, Desclée. 167 p. -- ᴿRLatAmT 12 (1995) 223-230 (J.I. *González Faus*: '¿ Rehacer la Solidaridad o seguir "bailando sobre el Titanic" ? ')

H8.6 *Theologiae emergentes* -- 'Theologies of' emergent groups

4942 *Aarde* A. van, Kultuurimperialisme as 'n hermeneutiese dilemma; eerste-wêreldse en deerde-wêreldse perspektiewe op Jesus as die Seun van God: H(erv)TS 50 (1994) 345-367 [NTAb 39,p.261].

4943 *a) Aldazábal* José, Lecciones de la historia sobre la inculturación: -- *b) Canals* Joan M., Realizaciones de inculturación en la liturgia romana : Phase 35 (1995) 93-112 / 113-126.

4944 **Aleaz** K.P., The Gospel and Indian culture. Calcutta 1994, Punti Pustak. xiii-344 p. -- ᴿA(sia)JT 9 (1995) 201-4 (S. *Samartha*).

4945 *Anthony* Francis-Vincent, Naming an evolving process; toward a theory of inculturation praxis: Salesianum 57 (1995) 283-304 . 503-526.

4946 *a) Avotri* Solomon K., Globalization in theological education; reflections from an African perspective; -- *b) Habito* Robert, *Poitros* Edward W., Globalization and its ironies; -- *c) Inbody* Tyson, Melting pot or mosaic; what difference does difference make ? : QR(Min) 15 (1995) 389-397 / 375-387 / 399-414.

4947 *Ayrookuzhiel* A.M.Abraham, Dalit identity and the religio-cultural situation; a working paper: Kristu Jyoti 10,3 (1994) 27-34.

4948 *Azevedo* Marcelo, Cristianismo, uma experiência multicultural; como viver e anunciar a fé cristã nas diferentes culturas: REB 55 (1995) 771-787.

4949 *a) Balquierda* Luis, The liturgical principles used by the missionaries and the missionary background to the Christianization of the Philippines: -- *b) Gutiérrez* Lucio, The evangelization of the Philippines and the formative years of the Archdiocese of Manila (1565-1700); -- *c) Piryns* Ernest D., A new approach to mission and evangelization : PhilipSa 30 (1995) 5-79 / 373-424 / 81-98.

4950 *a) Bao Jiayuan*, Co-workers in the China Christian Council; -- *b) Carino* Theresa & Feliciano, Cosmic Christ and ecumenical fellowship. -- *c) Potter* Philip, The Student Christian Movement and the Chinese Church: ChineseThR 10 (Holland MI 1995) 37-45 / 46-51 / 75-88 [175-190, index 1985-1995].

4951 *Bate* Stuart C., Inculturation; the local church emerges: Missionalia 22,2 (1994) 93-117 [< TIC(ontext) 12,2 (1995) 87].

4952 ᴱ**Baumann** Peter, Kosmos der Anden: Weltbild und Symbolik indianischer Tradition in Südamerika. Mü 1994, Diederichs. 588 p. DM 58. 3-424-01202-5. -- ᴿZkT 117 (1995) 113-5 (K.H. *Neufeld*).

4953 **Baur** John, 2000 years of Christianity in Africa, 62-[1500-1792-] 1992. Nairobi 1995, Pauline. 560 p.; ill. £ 8. 9966-21-110-1. -- ᴿ*TBR 8,3 (1995s) 46s (F. *King*).

4954 **Bediako** Kwame, Christianity in Africa; the renewal of a non-Western religion. E/Mkn 1995, Univ./Orbis. xii-278 p. £ 17. 0-7486-0625-4 / US 1-57075-048-3. -- ᴿ*TBR 8,2 (1995s) 52 (A. *Anderson*).

4955 *Bediako* Kwame, De-sacralization and democratization; some theological reflections on the role of Christianity in nation-building in modern Africa: Transformation 12,1 (Wynnewood PA 1995) 5-11.

4956 **Bevans** Stephen B., Models of contextual theology 1992 → 9,9102; 10,8566: ᴿE(cu)R 47 (1995) 395s (C.H. *Moon*); NewTR 7,3 (1994) 92-94 (R. *Haight*); Spiritus 36 (1995) 493s (B. *Ugeux*).

4957 **Beyer** Peter, Religion and globalization. L / New Delhi, Newbury Park / Sage. 250 p. -- ᴿASS(oc)R 92 1995) 95-97 (Y. *Lambert*).

4958 Biernatzki William, Roots of acceptance; the intercultural communication of religious meanings: [^E*Roest Crollius* Arij A.] Interculturation 13. R 1991, Pontifical Gregorian University. 186 p. -- ^RRStR 21 (1995) 100 (C. *Arthur*).

4959 Blaser Klauspeter, Les théologies nord-américaines. Genève 1995, Labor et Fides. 168 p. F 130. -- ^RÉtudes 382 (1995) 857s [J.-Y. *Calvez*, avec renvoi à 375 (1991) 89-100, RICHARD L., Géographie théologique des États-Unis].

4960 *a) Bowman* Thea, Being a black Catholic; -- *b) Richardson* Janet D., A sense of the Church in the USA; a modern mosaic from the perspective of a woman religious; -- *c) Earaplackal* V., Christian mission in liberalized India : I(nd)M(iss)R 17 (1995) 39-45 / 47-56 / 70-82.

4961 *Breivik* N.O., Religious ['prairie'] dialogue between North American Indians and Catholics [STARKLOFF C., STOLZMANN W.]: TT(og)K 66 (1995) Norwegian 293-303.

4962 *Bria* Ion, A new typology for gospel and culture syntax, from an Eastern European Orthodox perspective: IRM(iss) 84 (1995) 273-293.

4963 ^E**Budick** Sanford, *Iser* Wolfgang, The translatability of cultures; figurations of the space between: Irvine studies in the humanities. Stanford c. 1995, Univ. xvi-348 p. 0-8047-2561-6.

4964 Bujo Bénézet, Africa e morale cristiana [Eng. 1990], ^T. R 1994, Cittá Nuova. 180 p. L^m 20. -- ^RRasT 36 (1995) 122-4 (Antonietta *Marini Mansi*).

4965 *Bujo* Bénézet, Anamnetische Solidarität und afrikanisches Ahnendenken, ^T*Arens* E.: → 149, ^FPEUKERT H., Anerkennung 1995, 31-63.

Cardoza-Orlandi Carlos F., Drum-beats of resistance and liberation; Afro-Caribbean religions, the struggle for life, and the Christian theologian 1995s → 4856 supra.

4966 *Carr* Dhyanchand, An understanding of the suffering and glorified human one (Son of Man) from the perspective of suffering and struggling peoples of Asia : VSVD 36 (1995) 317-348.

4967 Carrier Hervé, Evangelizing the culture of modernity 1993 → 10,8571, Orbis. viii-168 p. $ 17 pa. -- ^RMiss(iology) 23 (1995) 213s (A.J. *Gittins*).

4968 Chung Song-Tae, The God of Minjung: diss. Southern Baptist Theol. Sem., ^DStiver D. 1995. 95-30693. -- [D(iss)AI] MAI 33 (1995) 1682.

4969 *Chupungco* Anscar J., *a)* Remarks on 'The Roman liturgy and inculturation' [Vatican 1994]: ^REO(rans) 11 (1994) 269-277; -- *b)* Inculturazione e liturgia; i termini del problema, ^T*Pelizza* Giuseppe: RivLi 82 (1995) 361-385.

4970 *a) Co* Maria Anicia, Inculturation and the Bible; - *b) Chupungco* Anscar J., Liturgical inculturation; - *c) Miranda* Dionisio M., Outlines of a method of inculturation: EAPR 30 (1993) 202-217 / 108-119 / 145-197.

4971 Coakley J.F., The Church of the East and .. Canterbury 1992 -→ 8,8067 ... 10,8577: ^RChH 64 (1995) 710s (W.L. *Sachs*); S(cot)JTh 48 (1995) 269-271 (B.D. *Spinks*).

4972 ^E**Cone** James H., *Wilmore* Gayraud S., Black Theology, a documentary history, 1980-1992: 1² [¹1979 → 9,9115]; 2. Mkn 1993, Orbis. ix-462 p.; ix-450 p. $ 19 each, pa. -- ^RJRel 75 (1995) 433-5 (Diana L. *Hayes*).

4973 *a) Copeland* M. Shawn, The exercise of black theology in the United States; -- *b) Phelps* Jamie T., African American culture; source and content of black theology and mission: *JHispT 3,2 (1995s) 5-15 / 43-58

4974 Costen Melva W., African American Christian worship. Nv 1993, Abingdon. 160 p. $ 13 pa. 0-88344-923-4. -- ^RWorship 65 (1994) 281-3 (J. *Gros*).

4975 Covell Ralph R., The liberating Gospel in China; the Christian faith among China's minority peoples. GR 1995, Baker. 318 p. $ 18. 0-8010-2595-8 [ThD 43,162].

4976 *Daneel* M.L., African Independent Church pneumatology and the salvation of all creation: IRM(iss) 82 (1993) 143-166.

4977 *Davis* Cyprian, A place to call home; a (U.S.) parish for all races: Church 11,l (NY 1955) 21-24.

4978 *Davis* Kenneth, U.S. Hispanic Catholics; trends and works 1992: RfR 52 (1993) 283-295.

4979 [E][Figueroa] Deck Allan, Frontiers of Hispanic theology in the U,S, 1992 → 8,289 ... 10,8582: [R]EThL 70 (1994) 195s (V. *Neckebrouck*); RfR 52 (1993) 298s (K. *Davis*)

4980 [E]De Gruchy John W., *Villa-Vincencio* Charles, Doing theology in context; South African perspectives: Theology and praxis 1. Mkn / Cape Town 1994, Orbis/Philip. $ 19. 0-88344-989-7 [ThD 42,363].

4981 *Derroitte* Henri, Lieux et outils d'approfondissement théologique en Afrique francophone: NZM(iss)W 51 (1995) 81-116.

4982 *a) Dhavamony* Mariasusai, The Christian theology of inculturation; -- *b) Kilgallen* John J., The Christian Bible and culture; -- *c) Osborn* Eric, Christianity and classical thought; -- *d) McDermott* John J., Christ and culture; - *e) D'Costa* Gavin, Inculturation, India and other religions: StMiss 44 (1995) 1-43 / 45-67 / 69-90 / 91-119 / 121-147.

4983 [E]Dolan J.P., *Deck* Allan F., Hispanic Catholic culture in the U.S. ND 1994, Univ, 447 p. -- [R]*JHispT 3,2 (1995s) 59-62 (Teresa *Maya Sotomayor*).

4984 *Domínguez Sánchez* Benito, Algunas exigencias culturales de la Nueva Evangelización: EstAg 30 (1995) 239-280.

4985 **Downs** Frederick S., History of Christianity in India 5/5, North East India in the nineteenth and twentieth centuries. Bangalore 1992, Church History Asn. xvi-236 p. -- [R]OCP 61 (1995) 282-4 (P. *Pallath*).

4986 *a) Dulles* Avery, interview, Christ and culture; -- *b) Neuhaus* Richard J., Dual citizenship; religion and public life (interviews, *Denny* D.): Forefront 2,2 (1995) 8-11 / 20-24.

4987 **Dyrness** William, Learning about theology from the Third World 1992 → 7,8614 ... 10,8587: [R]JETS 37 (1994) 591-3 (D.B. *Clendenin*).

4988 **Echeme** Austin, Corporate personality in traditional Igbo society and the sacrament of reconciliation: EHS 23/538. NY 1995, P.Lang. xxiv-334 p.

4989 [E]Espeja Jesús, Inculturación y teología indígena [II Encuentro, 19-24.I.1992, Cochabamba, Bolivia]: Glosas 21. S 1993, San Esteban. 240 p. -- [R]AnáMnesis 5,1 (1995) 107-9 (F. *Garcia*).

4990 **Evans** James H.[J]. We have been believers; an African-American systematic theology 1992 → 9,9135; 10,8590: [R]MoTh 10 (1994) 110-2 (W.J. *Jennings*).

4991 *Fang* Mark, Faire de la théologie en chinois: → 14, [F]BEAUCHAMP P., 'Ouvrir les Écritures' 1995, 307-316.

4992 **Federschmidt** Karl H., Theologie aus asiatischen Quellen; der theologische Weg CHOAN-SENG SONGs vor dem Hintergrund der asiatischen ökumenischen Diskussion: Beiträge zur Missionswissenschaft und interkultureller Theologie 7. Müns 1994, LIT. xiv-304 p. [RStR 22,340, J.A. *Bracken*].

4993 *Felder* Cain H., Afrocentrism, the Bible, and the politics of difference: *JRT 50 (1994) 45-56.

4994 **Fernandez** E.S., Toward a [Philippines Protestant] theology of struggle. Mkn 1994, Orbis. vi-193 p. $ 19. 0-88344-982-X.- [R]TTh 35 (1995) 425 (J. van *Nieuwenhove*).

4995 *a) Fiedler* Klaus, Post-classical missions and churches in Africa; identity and challenge to missiological research; -- *b)* *Saayman* Willem, Christian mission history in South Africa; re-thinking the concept; -- *c)* *Hale* Frederick, 'The Mission' as the cinema of liberation theology: *Missionalia 23 (1995) 92-107 / 184-200 / 72-91.

4996 **Forslund** Eskil, The Word of God in Ethiopian tongues; rhetorical features in the preaching of the Ethiopian evangelical church Mekane Yesus: StMiss 58.   U 1993, Swedish Institute for Missionary Research.   269 p. --   ᴿNZM(iss) 51 (1995) 151s (G. *Schelbert*).

4997 **Foster** Anne L., Alienation and cooperation: European, southeast Asian, and American perceptions of anti-colonial rebellion, 1919-1937: diss. Cornell, ᴰ*Lafeber* Walter.   Ithaca NY 1995.   386 p.   95-11954. -- DissA 55 (1994s) p.3957.

4998 **Fujita** Neil S., Japan's encounter with Christianity 1991 → 10,8594: ᴿ*CritRR 6 (1993) 363-5 (T.M. *Ludwig*),

4999 ᴱ**Furniss** Graham, *Gunner* Liz, Power. marginality, and African oral literature. C 1995, Univ. xiv-285 p.; bibliog, 260-276. 0-521-48061-2.

5000 *Geffré* Claude, La rencontre du christianisme et des cultures; fondements théologiques de l'inculturation: RÉTM = Le Supplément 192 (1995) 69-91.

5001 *Gelabert Ballester* Martín, Cristianismo y cultura; una relación ambivalente: RF 231 (1995) 283-297.

5002 **Gibbs** Philip, *Akali andake;* reflections on Engan Christology: Catalyst 24,1 (Papua 1994) 27-42 [< TIC(ontext) 12,2 (1995) 84].

5003 **Gibellini** Rosino, [Between inculturation and liberation;] Paths of African theology. L 1994, SCM. 202 p. £ 13. 0-334-02568-0. -- ᴿET 106 (1994s) 313s (A.C. *Ross*; the Christian Church became Greek to win the Greeks, but Africa was another story); Month 256 (1995) 192s (A. *Egan*); *TBR 8,2 (1995s) 53 (C. *Lee*).

5004 ᴱ**Gibellini** Rosino, Percorsi di teología africana: *GdT 226. Brescia 1994, Queriniana. 332 p. Lᵐ 35. 88-399-0726-2. -- ᴿGreg 76 (1995) 163-5 (A. *Wolanin*)

5005 **Gill** Kenneth D., Toward a contextualized theology for the Third World. Fra 1994, Lang. xi-311 p. 3-631-47096-7. -- ᴿAsbTJ 50 (1995) 98-100 (D. *Bundy*).

5006 ᴱ**Goizueta** Roberto S., We are a people! 1990/2 → 8,564b; 10,8596: ᴿRfR 53 (1993) 296-8 (Jeanette *Rodriguez*).

5007 **González** Justo L., Out of every tribe and nation; Christian theology at the ethnic roundtable. Nv 1992, Abingdon. 244 p, $ 11 pa.- ᴿ*CritRR 7 (1994) 506-8 (Marilyn J. *Legge*); JHispLat 3,2 (1995s) 78 (E. *Pérez-Álvarez*).

5008   ᴱ**Gordan** Paulus,   Evangelium   und   Inkulturation   (1492-1992),   Salzburger Hochschulwochen 1992. Graz 1992, Styria. 231 p. --   ᴿNZM(iss) 51 (1995) 223s (F. *Frei*).

5009   *a)* *Gründer* Horst, Rückwirkungen der deutschen Kolonialinaugurierung auf die Stellung der christlichen Mission in Kirche, Staat und Gesellschaft; -- *b)* *Koschorke* Klaus, Kirchengeschichte, Missionsgeschichte, transkontinentale Christentumsgeschichte; -- *c)* *Okalla* Joseph Ndi, Kirchengeschichte und Missionsgeschichte; afrikanische Perspektiven: ZM(iss)R 79 (1995) 120-132 / 133-144 / 145-160 (-182, Kunst, *Rzepkowski* Horst).

5010 *Gwembe* Pedro E., La piété envers les ancêtres dans la religion africaine: Telema 82 (1995) 53-60 (-78

5011   *Haar* Gerrie ter, Strangers in the promised land; African Christians in Europe: Exchange 14 (Utrecht 1995) 1-33.

5012 *Hardawiryana* Robert, Theological perspectives on mission in Asia : VSVD 36 (1995) 51-89 . 115-156

5013 **Hastings** Adrian, The Church in Africa 1450-1950. Ox 1994, Clarendon. xiv-706 p.; 8 maps. £ 65. 0-19-826921-8. -- ᴿET 106 (1994s) 379 (M. Louise *Pirouet*; a magnificent first); ÉTRel 70 (1995) 615s (J.-F. *Zorn*); RHE 90 (1995) 607s (J. *Pirotte*).

5014 *Heideman* Eugene P., Following the Holy Spirit through Africa: RefR 49 (1995s) 5-18.

5015 ᴱ**Hillman** Eugene, Toward an African Christianity; inculturation applied 1993 → 9,9151: 10,8601* ᴿMid-Str 34 (1995) 110-121 (J.D. *May*).

5016 **Hunter** Alan, *Chan Kim-Kwong*, Protestantism in contemporary China: Cambridge Studies in Ideology and Religion. C 1993, Univ. xix-291 p. $ 35. -- ᴿTS 56 (1995) 172-4 (P. *Fleming*).

5017 *Hwa Yung*, Critical issues facing theological education in Asia: Transformation 12,4 (1995) 1-6.

5018 **Isasi Díaz** Ada María, *Tarango* Yolanda, Hispanic women, prophetic voices of the Church. Mp 1992, Fortress. 144 p. $ 10 pa. 0-8006-2617-7 -- ᴿT(or)JT 10 (1994) 281s (Barbara *Paleczny*).

5019 *a) Ishida* Manabu, Doing theology in Japan; the alternative way of reading the Scriptures as the book of sacred drama in dialogue with Minjung theology; -- *b) Brouer* G, Thompson [*Underwood* Horace G.], Why has Christianity grown faster in Korea than in China ?: Miss(iology) 22 (Scottdale PA 1994) 55-63 / 77-88 [65-76].

5020 **Isichei** Elizabeth Allo, A history of Christianity in Africa from antiquity to the present. GR / Lawrenceville NJ 1995, Eerdmans / Africa World. xi-420 p. £ 25. pa. $ 20. 0-8028-0843-3 / 0-281-0474-2. -- ᴿE(xp)T 107 (1995s) 29s (T.J. *Thompson*).

5021 *(Kä) Mana*, L'Église africaine et la théologie de la reconstruction; réflexions sur les nouveaux appels de la mission en Afrique: BCPÉ: 46,4 (1994) 5-42.

5022 ᴱ**Kaplan** Steven, Indigenous responses to western Christianity. NYU 1995, x-183 p. $ 40. [RStR 22,87. Anna L. *Peterson*].

5023 ᴱ**Karunkal** Jacob, *Krangkhuma* F., Bible and Mission in India today. Bombay-Bandra 1993, St. Pauls. 336 p. rs 96 pa. -- ᴿMiss(iology) 23 (1995) 105s (T.A. *Lenchak*).

5024 **Kasukuti** Ngoy M., [seit 1992 ev. Bischof Kongos], Recht und Grenze der Inkulturation; Heilserfahrungen im Christentum Afrikas am Beispiel der Kimbanguistenkirche [Diss. Neuendettelsau 1990]: MgMissÖk 13. Erlangen 1991, Ev.-Luth. Mission. 165 p. 3-87214-313-1. -- ᴿVSVD 36 (1995) 208-211 (J. *Ndi-Okalla*).

5025 *a) Kawale* W.R., Divergent interpretations of the relationship between some concepts of God in the Old Testament and in African traditional religions -- a theological critique; -- *b) Le Roux* J.H., No theology, no relevance, no new South Africa [really seems to mean, p.181, that there *will* be a theology for a *new* South Africa, but it must be life-related and diverge from the standard theologies: OTEs 8 (1995) 7-30 / 167-190.

5026 **Killoren** John J., Come, Blackrobe; De SMET and the Indian tragedy. Norman 1994, Univ. Oklahoma. xv-448 p. $ 30. -- ᴿAmHR 100 (1995) 1298 (C. *Vecsey*: following PRUCHA, prolongs two myths); TS 56 (1995) 401 (C.J. *Starkloff*).

5027 **Kim Kyoung Jae**, Christianity and the encounter of Asian religions; method of correlation, fusion of horizons, and paradigm shifts in the Korean grafting process: diss. Utrecht, ᴰ*Jongeneel* J. Zoetermeer 1995, Boeken-C. 213 p. 90-239-0831-7.

5028 **King** N., Setting the Gospel free [< 1993 S.Africa lectures]. Pietermaritzburg 1995, Cluster. 142 p. R 30. 1-87053-03-4 [NTAb 40, p.325].

5029 *Kirby* Jon P., Language and culture-learning IS conversion ... IS ministry : Miss(iology) 23 (1995) 131-143.

5030 **Kitagawa** Joseph M., The Christian tradition, beyond its European captivity 1992 →
9,9166; [R]NewTR 7,4 (1994)105s (R. *Schreiter*).

5031 **Kochuparampil** Xavier, Evangelization in India; a theological analysis of the
missionary role of the Syro-Malabar Church in the light of Vatican II and post-conciliar
documents. Kottayam 1992, Oriental Institute of religious studies India. 556 p. rs 150. -
- [R]Exchange 14 (1995) 81s (K. *Steenbrink*).

5032 **Kochuthara** Thomas, Theology of liberation and ideology critique. New Delhi 1993,
Intercultural. xiv-283 p. rs 200. 81-85574-08-1. -- [R]Vidyajyoti 59 (1995) 624s (Poulose
Mangal).

5033 **Kubo** Sakae, The God of relationships; how the Gospel helps us to reach across
barriers such as race, culture, and gender. Hagerstown MD 1993, Review & H. 159 p.
$ 10. -- [R]A(ndr)USS 33 (1995) 217 (Leona G. *Running*: high praise).

5034 **Kwok Pui-lan**, [feminist Boston theologian] Discovering the Bible in the non-biblical
world: Bible & Liberation.. Mkn 1995, Orbis. xvi-136 p. $ 17. 0-88344-997-8 [NTAb
40, p.326; E(xp)T 107 (1995s) 127].

5035 *Langevin* Gilles, L'inculturation selon le magistère de l'Église catholique romaine
[conférence Bossey 20.VIII.1993]: ScEs 46 (1994) 179-188.

5036 *a) Lanzetti* Raúl, L'inculturazione della fede e il Catechismo della Chiesa Cattolica; --
b) Berlingieri Giovanni, Rivelazione, mistero di Cristo, acculturazione; dall'agire di Dio
all'agire della Chiesa; -- *c) De Simone* Giuseppe, Lo studio dei Padri e l'inculturazione
della fede: Vivarium 3 (1995) 97-107 / 19-49 / 51-72.

5037 **Larson** Gerald J., India's agony over religion. Albany 1995, SUNY. xiv-393 p.
$ 39.50; pa. $ 20. 0-7914-2411/-1: -2-X [ThD 43,73]

5038 *Lee Sook Jong*, A study of the relationship of the Korea Church to the indigenous
culture of Korea: A(sia)JT 9 (1995) 230-247.

5039 **Leung** Beatrice, Sino-Vatican relations; problems in conflicting authority 1976-1986:
London School of Economics mg. C 1992, Univ. 415 p. $ 80. -- [R]*CritRR 6 (1993) 275-8
(M.L. *Budde*).

5040 *Levison* John & Priscilla P., Toward an ecumenical Christology for Asia: Miss(iology)
22 (1994) 3-17.

5041 *López de la Osa* José R., El pecado capital de ignorar la pluralidad cultural: SalT 81
(1993) 555-565.

5042 *McGarry* Cecil, The implications of the (April 1994) synod discussions for the Church
in Africa: AfER 37 (1995) 15-34.

5043 *Madangi Sengi* Jean de Dieu, La teología africana: E(st)E 70 (1995) 85-100.

5044 *Madey* Johannes, India's 'Syriac' churches 1990-1994: Logos 36 (Sask 1995) 277-
313. 314 Ukrainian.

5045 **Martey** Emmanuel, African theology; inculturation and liberation 1993 → 9,9179:
[R]EThL 70 (1994) 200s (V. *Neckebrouck*); EvQ 67 (1995) 375-7 (M.O. *Fape*); JAAR 63
(1995) 878-881 (J. *Kunnie*); NewThR 8,3 (1995) 112s (R.J. *Schreiter*).

5046 *Mendoza Ríos* Mario, Principios agustinianos para una praxis de inculturación; una
visión para América Latina: EstAg 30 (1995) 77-97.

5047 *Metz* Johann-Baptist, Perspectivas de un cristianismo multicultural: *Carthaginensia 11
(1995) 23-33; Eng. ii

5048 *a) Michael* S.M., The emerging Dalit consciousness; -- *b) Mubgekar* B.L., The socioeconomic conditions of the Dalits: I(nd)M(iss)R 17 (1995) 5-13 / 14-18.

5049 **Moffett** Samuel H., A history of Christianity in Asia, 1. Beginnings to 1500. SF

1992, Harper. xxvi-560 p. $ 45. -- ᴿC(ath)HR 81 (1995) 474s (G. *Kottuppallil*); C(alvin)TJ 29 (1994) 264-8 (E.A. *Van Bask*).

5050 **Mungello** D.E., The forgotten Christians of Hangzhou. Honolulu 1994, Univ. Hawaii. 248 p. $ 36. -- ᴿJRel 75 (1995) 609-611 (P.V. *Martinson*).

5051 **Murphy** Joseph M., Working the spirit; ceremonies of the African diaspora [Brazil, Haiti, Cuba, Jamaica, US]. Boston 1994, Beacon. xii-263 p. $ 25; pa. $ 14. 0-8070-1220-3; *l.* -- ᴿJRel 75 (1995) 306-8 (P.C. *Johnson*, also on Brown K., Mama Lola): Numen 42 (1995) 326s (S.D. *Glazier*).

5052 **Musopole** Augustine C., Being human in Africa; toward an African Christian anthropology: AmUSt 11/65. NY 1994, P. Lang. 261 p.$ 35. 0-8204-2304-1 [< ThD 42 (1995) 282].

5053 **Neckebrouck** V., De Derde Kerk: cultuur en geloof. Lv 1993, Acco, 168 p. -- ᴿCVL 25 (1995) 197s (W. Van *Soom*).

5054 **Neckebrouck** Valeer, Paradoxes de l'inculturation; les nouveaux habits des Yanomami. Lv 1994, Univ. 214 p. 90-8186-611-1. -- ᴿVSVD 36 (1995) 97s (H. *Hochegger*).

5055 **Nkabahona** Alex, Towards an African reception of Jürgen Moltmann's theology of suffering and resurrection: diss. Leuven Flemish-English faculty, ᴰ*Schrijver* G. de, 1994. xxxv-210 p. -- ᴿEThL 71 (1995) 281.

5056 *Nothomb* Dominique, Langue locale africaine -- lieu théologique: RICAO 11 (1995) 63-72 ; 12 (1995) 81-87.

5057 *a) Okorocha* Cyril C., African social history and the Christian mission in Africa; implications and challenges for the Afro-Anglican movement [response *Battle* Michael J.]: -- *b) Goodrich* Sehon S., The integrity of Anglicanism; myth or mission ? → 604, Afro-Anglicanism 1995, AnglTR 77 (1995) 480-496 [497-501] / 471-9.

5058 ᴱ**Olupona** Jacob K., Religion and peace in multi-faith Nigeria. Nigeria 1992, O.Awelowe Univ . 203 p. £ 7.50. -- ᴿ*TBR 8,1 (1995s) 57 (M. *Conway*).

5059 **Oosthuizen** G.C., *al.*, Afro-Christiaity at the grassroots; its dynamics and strategies: Studies of religion in Africa 9. Lei 1994, Brill. -: TT(og)K 66 (1995) 216 (N.O. *Breivik*, Norwegian).

5060 **Padinjarekuttu** Isaac, The missionary movement of the 19th and 20th centuries and its encounter with India [on Vath A., Schmidlin J., Ohm T.; diss. Fra 1993, ᴰ *Schatz* K.]: EurUSt 23/527. Fra 1995, Lang. 305 p. 3-631-47415-6. -- ᴿVSVD 36 (1995) 453s (K. *Müller*).

5061 **Paris** Peter J., The spirituality of African peoples; the search for a common moral discourse. Mp 1995, Fortress. xii-194 p. $ 13. -- ᴿ*CritRR 8 (1995) 359-361 (D.R.*Bechtel*); P(rin)cSB 16 (1995) 240 (D.N. *Hopkins*).

5062 ᴱ**Parratt** J., Cristo in Africa; teologi africani oggi [antologia]. T 1994, Claudiana. 200 p.; 16 fig. Lᵐ 25. -- ᴿStPat(av) 42 (1995) 832s (L. *Sartori*).

5063 **Pathil** Kuncheria, Indian churches at the crossroads (Rome Placid Lecture 16): Centre for Indian and Interreligious Studies. Bangalore 1994, Dharmaram. x-143 p. -- ᴿKristu Jyoti 11,4 (1995) 133s (D. *Veliath*).

5064 **Peelman** Achiel, L'inculturazione: *GdT 216. Brescia ᵀ1993, Queriniana. 204 p. Lᵐ 22. 88-399-0736-5. -- ᴿ*ActuBbg 31 (1994) 63 (I. *Salvat*).

5065 **Perniola** V., The Catholic Church in Sri Lanka, the British period, I. 1795-1844: the Colombo vicariate: Ceylon HistJ mg 17. Dehiwala 1992, Tisara Prakasakayo. 512 p. -- ᴿNZM(iss) 50 (1994) 146s (F. *Frei*, also on Bercatta B., Colombo).

5066 *a) Phelps* Jamie T., The theology and process of inculturation; a theology of hope for

African American Catholics in the U.S.; -- *b) Henderson* Leon, The sacraments and American rites of passage; -- *c) Haight* Roger, Responding to fundamentalism in Africa; three questions for the mainline churches: NewTR 7,1 (1994) 5-13 / 27-36 / 59-67.

5067 *a) Philip* T.V., Christian conference of Asia; a historical overview; -- *b) Roxborough* John, Context and continuity; regional patterns in the history of Southeast Asian Christianity : A(sia)JT 9 (1995) 2-29 / 30-46 (-122, *al.*).

5068 *a) Piepel* Klaus, Lerngemeinschaft Weltkirche; zur pädagogischen Konzeption von Lernprozesses in Partnerschaften zwischen Christen in der Ersten und der Dritten Welt; -- *b) Ahrens* Theodor, Christentum im Dialog der Kulturen; eine westeuropäische Perspektive: NZM(issW) 79 (1995) 3-26; Eng. 26 / 27-42; Eng. 42.

5069 *a) Puthanangady* Paul, Which culture for inculturation; the dominant or the popular ?: - *b) Pattery* George, Inculturation and/or liberation: EAPR 30 (1993) 295-310 / 317-345.

5070 **Raboteau** Albert J., A fire in the heart; reflections on African-American religious history [4 inedita + 7]. Boston 1995, Beacon. xi-224 p. $ 23. 0-8070-0932-0 [ThD 43,183].

5071 **Reid** David, New wine; the changing shape of Japanese Christianity: Nanzan Studies in Asian religions 2. Berkeley 1991, Asian Humanities. iv-199 p. $ 45; pa. $ 15. -- R*CritRR 6 (1993) 384s (Neil S. *Fujita*).

5072 *Ro Bong Rin,* The Korean church; growing or declining ? : Ev)RT 19 (1995) 336-353.

5073 E**Rodríguez-Díaz** Daniel R., *Cortés-Fuentes* David, Hidden stories; unveiling the history of the [U.S.] Latino church. Decatur GA 1994, Asoc.Educ.Teol.Hispana. xviii-165 p. $ 10 pa. [ThD 43,171].

5074 E**Rotzetter** Anton, *al.*, Von der Conquista zur Theologie der Befreiung; der franziskanische Traum einer indianischen Kirche. Z 1993, Benziger. -- RNZM(iss) 51 (1995) 158s (J. *Baumgartner*).

5075 *Rücker* Heribert, Lernen statt 'Kontextualisieren' [Kongo-Messritus]: ÖR 43 (1994) 72-81.

5076 *Rzepkowski* Horst, Anmerkungen zu einem Versuch einer systematischen Grundlegung der kontextuellen Theologie : VSVD 36 (1995) 419-452.

5077 *Sanders* Cheryl J., Afrocentric social ethics; more power to the people [WALKER T. 1991]: *JRT(ht) 49,2 (1992s) 97-102.

5078 *Sang Hyun Lee*, (inaugural) Pilgrimage and home in the wilderness of marginality; symbols and context in Asian American theology: P(rinc)SB 16 (1995) 49-64.

5079 **Sanneh** Lamin, Encountering the West; Christianity and the global cultural process; the African dimension 1993 → 10,8639: RP(rinc)SB 16 (1995) 100s (C.C. *West*).

5080 **Schaaf** Ype, L'histoire et le rôle de la Bible en Afrique. Lavigny/Nairobi 1994, Groupes Missionnaires / Défi Africain. 287 p. F 100. 2-88050-051-6 / 9966-886-72-9. -- RÉTRel 70 (1995) 618s (J.-F. *Zorn*).

5081 **Schaaf** Ype, On their way rejoicing; the history and role of the Bible in Africa, T*Ellingworth* Paul: African Challenge 5. Carlisle/Nairobi 1994, Paternoster / All Africa Conference of Churches. xii- 254 p. 0-85364-561-2 / 9966-886-84-2. -- RExchange 24 (1995) 85s (L.*Lagerwerf,* also on the French).

5082 E**Schreiter** Robert J., Faces of Jesus in Africa 1991 → 8.8891 ... 10,8641: R*JRT(ht) 49,1 (1992s) 98-101 (H.J. *Sindima*).

5083 *Segovia* Fernando E., Theological education and scholarship as struggle; the life of racial/ethnic minorities in the profession: JHispLat 2/2 (1994) 5-25.

5084 *Shelke* Christopher, Dalit theology; emergence and emergency: NZM(iss) 50 (1994) 257-273.

5085 **Shorter** Aylward, Evangelization and culture. L 1994, Chapman. 160 p. £ 15. 0-225-66723-1. -- [R]ET 106 (1994s) 61s (K. *Cracknell*: the Gospel does not say 'go into all the world and teach them Latin' -- nor English, as already G. WARNECK 1900).

5086 **Shorter** A., Toward a theology of inculturation 1988 → 4,9753 ... 10,8644*: [R]BogVest 53 (1993) 374-7 (J. *Plut*).

5087 *Slobodian* Samuel P., Off the street and into the kitchen; contextualizing the Gospel for Russians: C(alv)BTJ 10,2 (1994) 1-31.

5088 **Smith** Donald K., Creating understanding; a handbook for Christian communication across cultural landscapes. GR 1992, Zondervan. 382 p. $ 18.- : [R]RefR(H) 49 (1995s) 56s (Joyce E. *Carroll*).

5089 **Smith** Theophus H., Conjuring culture; biblical formations in black America 1994 → 10,8645: [R]JRel 75 (1995) 435s (D. N. *Hopkins*); TS 56 (1995) 280s (V.L. *Wimbush*).

5090 *Sommer* J.H., 'Waar de Nil uitmondt in de Nordzee ...' Koptisch en Ethiopisch orthodoxe Christenen in Nederland: *RelBewegN 28 (1994) 37-78, met reactie: [< G(ereformeerd)TT 95 (1995) 48].

5091 **Song Choan-Seng**, La teologia del terzo occhio; teologia in formazione nel contesto asiatico. Padova 1993, Messaggero. 412 p. L[m] 35. -- [R](R)*StEc 12 (Venezia 1994) 253s (S. *Morandini*): StPat(av) 42 (1995) 831s (L. *Sartori*).

5092 **Stockton** Eugene D.. The aboriginal gift [to (Catholic) theology]; spirituality for a nation, Alexandria NSW 1995, Dwyer. vii-208 p. A$ 20. 1-86429-026-9. -- [R]*TBR 8,1 (1995s) 56 (J. *Capper*).

5093 [E]**Tang** Edmond, *Wiest* Jean-Paul. The Catholic Church in modern China; perspectives. Mkn 1993, Orbis. xvii-260 p. $ 19 - [R]TS 56 (1995) 172-4 (P. *Fleming*'s review adds issues overlooked also by HUNTER/CHAN).

5094 **Thangaranj** Melchizedec T., The crucified guru; an experiment in cross-cultural Christology. Nv 1994, Abingdon. 165 p. $ 7. 0-687-10008-9. -- [R]*TBR 8,3 (1995s) 22 (A. *Race*).

5095 *Thomas* M.M., Europe and Asia at the end of the Vasco da Gama era -- VISSER 'T HOOFT's theology of radical cultural renewal: A(sia)JT 8 (1994) 13-30.

5096 **Tinker** George E., Missionary conquest, the Gospel and native American cultural genocide. Mp 1993, Fortress. ix-182 p. -- : [R]C(ath)HR 81 (1995) 98s (F.F. *Guest* : SERRA, DE SMET, and Protestants ELIOT, WHIPPLE; strangely, he suspects the breakdown of their good intentions); JAAR 63 (1995) 858-860 (Vine *Deloria*); JRel 75 (1995) 601s (Inez *Talamantez*).

5097 [E]**Verstraelen** Franz J., *al.* 'Rewriting' the Bible; the real issues [... BANANA C. S.]; perspectives from within biblical and religious studies in Zimbabwe. Gwerl 1993, Mambo. xiv-309 p. -- [R]NZM(iss)W 51 (1995) 145 (G. *Schelbert*).

5098 *Vroom* H.M., Evangelie en cultuur; hun onderlinge verhouding: G(ereformeerd)TT 95 (1995) 3-12.

5099 **Webster** John C., A history of the Dalit Christians in India. SF 1992, Mellen Univ. iv-243 p. $ 70. -= [R]IBM(iss)R 18 (1994) 85s (R.E. *Frykenberg*).

5100 *Wilson* H.S., Gospel and cultures; a perennial challenge: [R]R(ef)W 45 (1995) 177-186.

5101 **Woga** Edmund, Der parentale Gott; zum Dialog zwischen der Religion der indonesischen Völker und dem Christentum [Diss. Mü 1993]: StSVD 59. Nettetal 1994, Steyler. 439 p. -- TIC(context) 12,2 (1995) 96 (G. *Evers*).

5102 ^E**Anderson** H. George, *al.*, The one mediator, the Saints, and Mary: LuthCathDialogue 8, 1992 → 8,8926; 9,9236: ^RThRv 91 (1995) 245 (F. *Courth*).

5103 *Aoanan* M. LaGuardia (m.), Does the Blessed Virgin Mary have a place among the Protestant churches ?: A(sia)JT 8 (1994) 271-280.

5104 *Aparicio* A., *Mihalovici* I., El Corán y los Judíos hablan de María: EphMar 44 (1994) 149-159 (135-145, *Sahioni* M.) [NTAb 39, p.83].

5105 ^E**Bäumer** Remigius, *Scheffczyk* Leo, Marienlexikon [3.-5. → 10,8668]; 6. Scherer-Zypresse. Mü-S.Ottilien 1994, EOS. 872 p.; ill. DM 168 [RHE 91,12*]. 3-88096-896-9 [TR 91,277].

5106 *Bandera* Armando, Cristología y Mariología: TE 38 (1994) 31-51.

5107 **Beattie** Tina, Rediscovering Mary; insights from the Gospels. Tunbridge Wells / Northburn, Victoria 1995, Burns & O., / Dove.   125 p. 1-86371-609-2 [*TBR 9/1,28, Ruth B. *Edwards*: imaginative rather than exegetical].

5108 **Benko** Stephen, The virgin goddess; studies in the pagan and Christian roots of Mariology: Numen book 59. Lei 1993, Brill. viii-293 p.; 8 pl. *f* 160. -- ^RChH 63 (1994) 259-261 (F.W. *Norris*); *CritRR 7 (1994) 311-3 (Wendy *Cotter*).

5109 *Billet* Bernard, La 52e session de la Société française d'études mariales, Josselin, 28-31 août 1995: E(spr)eV 105 (1995) 639s.

5110 **Binder** Tulja, Maria in Finnland -- vom Missale Aboense zu den Schriften Mikael AGRICOLAS: Diss. ^D*Martikainen*. Göttingen 1995. -- ThRv Beilage 92/2, ix.

5111 *Bolewski* Jacek, ^P Problematik der jungfräulichen Empfängnis Jesu: Bobolanum 6 (1995) 68-90; deutsch 90s.

5112 *Breck* John, *a)* Mary in the NT: Pro Ecclesia 2 (Northfield MN 1993) 460-472 [NTAb 40, p.464]; -- *b)* Mary, mother of believers, mother of God [SCHILLEBEECKX Edward, HALKES Catharina: important for Christology]: *ProEc 4 (1995) 105-111.

5113 *Brennan* Walter, Rethinking Marian theology; the new creation: MilltSt ₃₅ (1995) 113-129.

5114 **Brock** Sebastian P., Bride of light; hymns on Mary from the Syriac churches: Moran Eth'o 6. Kerala 1994, St. Ephrem. 171 p. [RStR 22,252, Susan A. *Harvey*].

5115 **Buby** Bertrand, Mary of Galilee, I. Mary in the NT [2s awaited: in the Hebrew Scriptures / Apocrypha] 1994 → 10,8671: ^RMarianum 57 (1995) 404s (W. *Brennan*).

5116 **Buby** Bertrand, Mary of Galilee 2. Woman of Israel, Daughter of Zion; a biblical, liturgical, and catechetical celebration of the Mother of Jesus. NY 1995, Alba. viii-338 p. $ 18. 0-8189-0697-9 [< ThD 43,357].

5117 **Carroll** Michael P., Madonnas that maim 1992 → 8,8936 ... 10,8673: ^R*JRit 9,1 (1995) 133s (A.E. *Barnes*).

5118 *Cerbelaud* Dominique, Y a-t-il un 'dogme d'Ephèse' [*theotókos*] ? ; BLE 96 (1995) 171-183.

5119 *a) Díez Merino* Luis, Fundamentación bíblica de ...: -- *b) Muñoz Iglesias* Salvador, Apostillas al entramado bíblico de la Encíclica 'Redemptoris mater': → 556, EstMar 61 (1995) 3-56 / 57-73.

5120 *Dupuy* Bernard, The Mariology of CALVIN [< Istina 5 (1958) 479-490], ^T*Pearson* Lennart: SewaneeT 38 (1994s) 114-126.

5121 **Esbroeck** Michel Van, Aux origines de la Dormition de la Vierge: [15] études historiques sur les traditions orientales: CS 472. Aldershot 1995, Variorum. viii-325 p. £ 50.50. 0-86078-454-1. -- [R]NT 37 (1995) 415 (J.K. *Elliott*).

5122 **Folgado** S., María de Nazaret: Nuevos Horizontes 37. M 1994. 128 p. -- [R]Claretianum 34 (1994) 608s (A. *Pardilla*).

5123 **García de Paredes** J.C.R., Mariología. M 1995, BAC. xv-418 p. -- [R]ATG(ran) 58 (1995) 395-8 (C. *Pozo*).

5124 **Gaventa** Beverly R., Mary; glimpses of the Mother of Jesus: Studies on personalities of the NT. Columbia 1995, Univ. S.Carolina. xiv-164 p. $ 35. 1-57003-072-3 [ThD 43,267].

5125 *Gaventa* Beverly R., A place for Mary in Protestant ministry: WW 12 (1993) 273-8 [< NTAb 33, p.187]

5126 **González** Carlos Ignacio, María en los Padres Griegos; estudio introductorio y textos. México 1993, Episcopado. 823 p. -- [R]Marianum 57 (1995) 405-9 (L. *Gambero*).

5127 **Grass** Hans, Traktat über Mariologie: MTSt 30. Marburg 1991, Elwert. vii-116 p. -- [R]Marianum 57 (1995) 416-8 (A. *Escudero*).

5128 **Gruber** Mayer I., The motherhood of God and other studies: SFSJ 37, 1992 → 8,247d̲: [R]C(olc)Th 64,3 (1994) 183-5 (W. *Chrostowski*).

5129 *Guarducci* Margherita, La più antica icone di Maria 1989 → 5,8730; 7,8756: *JEarlyC 1 (1993) 204s (P.C. *Finney*: a theory).

5130 **Hagemann** Ludwig, *Pulsfort* Ernst, Maria, die Mutter Jesu, in Bibel und Koran: FMRW 19. Würzburg 1992, Echter. 138 p. -- [R]Marianum 57 (1995) 422 (Ortensio da *Spinetoli*).

5131 **Haile** Getatchew, The [Ge'ez + English] mariology of the emperor Zär'a Ya'aqob; OCA 242, 1992 → 8,8962; 9,9170: [R]JRAS (1994) 85s (R. *Pankhurst*): JThS 46 (1995) 389s (M.A. *Knibb*); ZKG 106 (1995) 427s (M. *Vinzent*).

5132 [TE]**Huille** Marie-Imolde, *Regnard* Joël, BERNARD de Clairvaux, À l'image de la vierge Marie: SC 390, 1993 → 9,9273: [R]REAug 40 (1994) 369-271 (L. *Bréard*); ScEs 45 (1994) 371s (C. *Barry*).

5133 **Jost** Renate, Frauen, Männer und die Himmelskönigin; exegetische Studien. Gü 1995, Gü-V. 268p.; Bibliog. 253-268. 3-579-00098-5.

5134 *Langella* Alfonso, La verginità di Maria tra storia e teologia; un convegno di studi mariologici a Capua [19-24 maggio 1992; Atti 1993, [E]LICCARDO G., *al.*]: Asprenas 42 (1995) 263-8.

5135 **La Potterie** Ignace De, Mary in the mystery of the Covenant, [T]*Buby* Bertrand, 1992 → 9,9070: [R]Bobolanum 6 (1995) 171-180 (S. *Moysa, P*).

5136 **La Potterie** Ignace de, María en el misterio de la alianza, [T]*Parera Galmés* Bartolomé: BAC 533, 1993 → 10,8691; xii-316 p. 84-7914-094-1. -- [R]*ActuBbg 31 (1994) 246 (J. *O'Callaghan*); ATG(ran) 58 (1995) 368-371 (C. *Pozo*); BiFe 20,59 (1994) 193 (M. *Saenz Galache*); CiTom 121 (1994) 413s (A. *Bandera*); EstTrin 28 (1994) 257s (J.M. de *Miguel*)

5137 **Laurentin** René, Marie, clé du mystère chrétien; la plus proche des hommes parce que la plus proche de Dieu. P 1994, Fayard. 139 + 121 p. -- [R]Marianum 57 (1995) 412-6 (F. *Lambiasi*).

5138 **Limberis** Vasiliki, Divine heiress; the Virgin Mary and the creation of Christian Constantinople [< Harvard diss.]. L 1994, Routledge. xi-199 p.: map £ 30. 0-415-09677-4. -- [R]GaR 42 (1995) 259s (P. *Walcot*, dubious); JEH 46 (1995) 697-9 (J. *Elsner*); RStR 21 (1995) 333 (N. *Costas*).

5139 **Macquarrie** J., Mary for all Christians 1990: 7,8767 ... 9,9279: [R]ChrSchR 25 (1995s) 201-2 (D.H. *Shantz*); EvQ 66 (1994) 357s (D.F. *Wright*).

5140 **Maeckelberghe** Els, Desperately seeking Mary [D]1991 → 7,8768 ... 9,9280: [R]*CritRR

6 (1993) 563-5 (Debra *Campbell*); ETL 70 (1994) 515s (T. *Merrigan*).

5141 **Miller** Elliot, *Samples* Kenneth R., The cult of the virgin; Catholic Mariology and the apparitions of Mary. GR 1992, Baker. 188 p. $ 9 pa. -- [R]CScR 25 (1995s) 202s (D.H. *Shantz*: not adequately ecumenical, despite final chapter by Catholic M. PACWA).

5142 **Mimouni** S.C., Dormition et assomption de Marie; histoire des traditions anciennes [diss. ÉPHÉR 1991. [D]*Geoltrain* P.]: ThH 98. P 1995, Beauchesne. 716 p. F 300. 2-7010-1320-8 [NTAb 40, p.559].

5143 *Mimouni* S.C. *a)* Controverse ancienne et récente autour d'une apparition du Christ ressuscité à la Vierge Marie: Marianum 57 (1995) 239-268; -- *b)* Les Vies de le Vierge; état de la question: *Apocrypha 5 (Turnhout 1994) 211-248 [NTAb 40, p.123].

5144 **Muser** Ivo, Das mariologische Prinzip 'gottesbräutliche Mutterschaft' und das Verständnis der Kirche bei M.J. SCHEEBEN: Diss. Pont. Univ. Gregoriana, [D]*Antón* A. Rom 1995. 351 p. -- RTLv 27, p.558.

5145 **Mussner** Franz, Maria, die Mutter Jesu im NT 1993 → 10,8699: [R]BZ 39 (1995) 283-5 (R. *Schnackenburg*).

5146 [E]**Pfammatter** J., *Christen* E., Was willst du von mir, Frau? Maria in heutiger Sicht: TBer 21. FrS 1995, Paulus. 142 p. DM 29,80. 2-7228-0357-8. -- [R]TTh 35 (1995) 423s (H.-E. *Mertens*).

5147 *Pikaza Ibarrondo* X., María; de la historia al símbolo en el Nuevo Testamento: EphMar 45,1 (1995) 9-41 [NTAb 40, p.87: risk of her being demoted to a timeless type, the domain of myth; Mariology is symbolic (believing) expression, not myth of the eternal feminine].

5148 **Pons** Guillermo, Textos marianos de los primeros siglos; antología patrística. M 1994, Ciudad Nueva. 287 p.- [R]Ter(esianum) 46 (1995) 283s (J. *Castellano*).

5149 *Rossetto* G., A proposito di 'Maria terra vergine' [1985] di Emanuele TESTA: Mar 55 (1993) 555-578 [NTAb 39, p.270].

5150 **Schillebeeckx** E., *Halkes* C., Mary yesterday, today, tomorrow 1993 → 9,9291b: 10,8706: [R]ProEccl 4 (1995) 105-111 (J. *Breck*).

5151 *Serra* A.M., Alle origini della letteratura assunzionista; uno studio di Frédéric MANNS [Le récit de la Dormition 1989]: Mar 56 (1994) 291-309 [NTAb 40, p.317].

5152 **Stravinskas** Peter M.J. The psychology and methods of proselytizing [ch.4 of diss. Dayton 1995, 'The place of Mary in the proselytizing efforts of fundamentalists' (among Catholics)]: Faith & Reason 21 (1995) 173-220.

5153 *Thomas* Paul W., The virginal conception: E(xp)T 107 (1995s) 11-14.

5154 *White* Susan, The Church in the pattern of Mary: E(xp)T 107 (1995s) 147s.

5155 *Wilckens* Ulrich, Maria im Neuen Testament: TR 91 (1995) 215-220.

5156 **Yoonprayong** Amnuay, Jesus and his mother according to Mk. 3,20.21.31-35: diss. Pont. Univ. Gregoriana, [D]*Agius* J. R 1995. xiv-194 p.; bibliog. 1-11.

5157 **Zeliko** Ivan, Theologische und psychologische Problematik von Privatoffenbarungen in Form von Marienerscheinungen, dargestellt am Beispiel der Erscheinungen der Muttergottes in Medjugorje; kath. Diss. [D]*Greshake* G. Freiburg/B 1994.--ThRv 91(1995)95.

5158 **Zimdars-Swartz** Sandra L., Encountering Mary 1991 → 7,3795 ... 9,9303: [R]ChH 64 (1995) 551s (J.P. *Gaffey*: the devotees tend to bind all others to often secret 'messages').

H8.8 *Feminae NT* -- **Women in the NT and church history**

5159 **Abrahamsen** V.A., Women and worship at Philippi; Diana/ Artemis and other cults in the early Christian era. Portland ME 1995, Astarte Shell. vii-252 p.; 20 fig.; map. $ 17.

1-885349-00-9 [NTAb 40, p.167].

5160 **Achard** Guy, La femme à Rome; Que sais-je? P 1995, PUF. 128 p. -- [R]BSL(at) 25 (1995) 651s (Antonella *Borgo*).

5161 **Aspegren** Kerstin, The male woman, a feminine ideal in the early Church 1990 → 6,8827 ... 9,9308: [R]TT(Og)K 65 (1994) 145s (Fredrik *Saxegaard*).

5162 **Atwood** Richard, Mary Magdalene in the NT gospels and early tradition: EHS 23/457. Fra 1993, Lang. 235 p.; bibliog. 221-235. 3-261-04519-1.

5163 **Bainton** R.H., Donne delle Riforma. T 1993, Claudiana. 423 p. -- [R]STEv 7 (1995) 81s (Katia *Bonucchi-Lamorte*: tre parti, Germania-Italia-Francia).

5164 *Bandera* Armando, Cooperación salvífica femenina y misterio de la redención: CiTom 121 (1994) 3-46.

5165 **Bartlett** Anne Clark, Male authors, female readers; representation and subjectivity in Middle English devotional literature. Ithaca 1995, Cornell Univ. xii-212 p. $ 32.50. 0-8014-3039-0 [ThD 43,157].

5166 **Bautista** Esperanza, La mujer en la Iglesia primitiva 1993 → 10,8714: [R]ScrT(Pamp) 37 (1995) 675 (D. *Ramos-Lissón*).

5167 **Bernabé Ubieta** C., María Magdalena; tradiciones en el cristianismo primitivo: EMISJ(erón) 27, 1994 → 10,8716: [R]Salmanticensis 42 (1995) 147-152 (R. *Trevijano*). → 5313 infra.

5168 **Blevins** Carolyn D., Women in Christian history; a bibliography. Macon GA 1995, Mercer Univ. viii-114 p. $ 30. 0-86554-493-X [< ThD 43,258].

5169 **Boomsma** Clarence, Male and female, one in Christ; NT teaching on [not against] women in office. GR 1993, Baker. 105 p. $ 7. -- [R]BS 151 (1994) 247s (M. Christine *Sullivan*); C(alvin)TJ 29 (1994) 278-285 (A. *Wolters*: no other Reformed leader has ever dared to suggest that the scriptural argumentation of an apostle is clearly mistaken and unacceptable); RefTR 53 (1994) 46s (G.N. *Davies*).

5170 **Børresen** Kari E., Image of God and gender models in Judaeo-Christian tradition 1991 → 7,341a ... 10,8717: [R]ThRv 91 (1995) 28s (Anne *Jensen*).

5171 **Boyarin** Daniel, Galatians and gender trouble; primal androgyny and the first-century origins of a feminist dilemma, [E]*Ocker* Christopher: Protocol NS 1. Berkeley 1995, Center for hermeneutical studies. [iv-] 70 p. 0-89242-065-0.

5172 **Brereton** Virginia, From sin to salvation; stories of women's conversions, 1800 to the present. Bloomington 1991, Indiana Univ. xvi-175 p. $ 11. -- [R]*CritRR 6 (1993) 549-551 (L.D. *Lagerquist*: 'feminism is salvific'; her own book is here reviewed p.562).

5173 *a) Bührig* Martha, Elizabeth Cody STANTON (1815-1902) und die Woman's Bible; -- *b) Wacker* Marie-Theres, 'Gottgewollte Emanzipation'; 150 Jahre Frauen und Bibel im deutschsprachigen Raum; -- *c) Schüssler Fiorenza* Elisabeth, Das zwiespältige Erbe der Woman's Bible: BiKi 50,4 ('100 Jahre Woman's Bible' 1995) 198-202 / 203-210 / 211-9.

5174 **Burrus** Virginia, The making of a heretic; gender, authority, and the Priscillianist controversy: Transformation of the Classical Heritage 24. Berkeley 1995, Univ. California. xi-252p. $ 45. 0-520-08997-9 [< ThD 43,259].

5175 **Caine** Barbara, Victorian feminists. Ox 1992, UP. xii-284 p. $ 20. -- [R]Cithara 33,1 (1993) 39s (G. *Robb*).

5176 **Carr** Anne E., Transforming grace; Christian tradition and women's experience 1990 → 5,5997: [R]S(cot)JTh 48 (1995) 393 (Esther *Reed*).

5177 **Carr** Anne, La femme dans l'Église: CF 173, 1993 → 9,9320; 10,8722: [R]NRT 117 (1995) 140s (A. *Toubeau*).

5178 *Castelli* E.A., Heteroglossia, hermeneutics and history; a review essay of recent feminist studies in early Christianity: JFemR 10,2 (1994) 73-98 [< ZIT 95].

5179 *Castelli* E.A., Visions and voyeurism; holy women and the politics of sight in early Christianity; *CHHP 2 (Berkeley 1995) 1-20 [NTAb 39, p.487].

5180 *Cheung* L., ᶜ Women in the Gospel of John: *CGST 18 (1995) 89-124 [NTAb 39,p.412].

5181 *Cholvy* Gérard, Église et apostolat féminin au XIXᵉ siècle: E(spr)eV 105 (1995) 110-2.

5182 *Clark* Elizabeth A., Ideology, history, and the construction of 'woman' in late ancient Christianity: *JEarlyC 2 (1994) 155-184 (137-153, *Miller*, 'the body').

5183 **Clark** Gillian, Women in late antiquity; pagan and Christian life-styles 1993 → 9,9323: ᴿBoL (1995) 126 (A. *Jeffers*: fascinating); RHE 90 (1995) 628 (Alice *Dermience*); VigChr 49 (1995) 90-93 (Heleen *Sancisi-Weerdenburg*).

5184 *a) Clark* M.S., The role of women in the early Church; indications from the New Testament for the practice of a modern Spirit movement; -- *b) Sansaridou-Hendrickx* T., Attitudes of 'feminism' and 'anti-feminism'; examples of gender-power relations in the Chronicle of Morea: AcPByz 6 (Pretoria 1995) 27-35 / 119-129.

5185 **Cloke** Gillian, 'The female man of God'; women and spiritual power in the patristic age, AD 350-450. L 1995, Routledge. xi-243 p. £ 35; pa. £ 12. 0-415-09469-0; -70-4. -- ᴿET 106 (1994s) 347 (G. *Huelin*); GaR 42 (1995) 230 (P. *Walcot*, also on ELM S. 1994); *TBR 8,1 (1995s) 49 (G. *Gould*); Theol 98 (L 1995) 491s (Christine *Trevitt*).

5186 **Coll** Regina A., Christianity and feminism in conversation. Mystic CT c.1994, Twenty-third. 197 p. $ 15. -- ᴿCanadCath 13,1 (1995) 23s (Carol *Kavanagh*).

5187 **Corley** Kathleen E., Private women, public meals; social conflict in the Synoptic tradition 1993 → 9,9324; 10,8724: ᴿCBQ 57 (1995) 173-5 (R.J. *Miller*); JBL 114 (1995) 327-9 (D.E.*Smith*); JThS 46 (1995) 631-4 (G. *Theissen*); RevBib(Arg) 57 (1995) 181s (A.J. *Levoratti*); TorJT 11 (1995) 237-9 (Margaret Y. *MacDonald*).

5188 **Corrington** Gail P., Her image of salvation; female saviors and formative Christianity 1992 → 9,9405; 10,8725: ᴿTorJT 11 (1995) 239s (R.S. *Ascough*).

5189 **DeBerg** Betty A., Ungodly women; gender and the first wave of American fundamentalism 1990 → 7,8808 ... 9,9326: ᴿ*CritRR 6 (1993) 555s (D. *Watt*).

5190 **Demers** Patricia, Women as interpreters of the Bible 1991 → 8,9030 ... 10,8727: ᴿ*CritRR 6 (1993) 556-8 (Marie-Eloise *Rosenblatt*).

5191 *a) Dermience* Alice, Femmes et ministères dans l'Église primitive; -- *b) Hébrard* Monique, Les ministères; possibilités actuelles: Spiritus 35,137 (1994) 382-395 / 371-381

5192 *Dewey* Joanna, Jesus' healings of women; clues for historical reconstruction: BibTB 24 (1994) 122-131.

5193 **Dimino** Ignazio, Gesù Cristo e le donne del Vangelo; studio storico-esegetico per gli studiosi di Sacra Scrittura e di storia della Chiesa, per atenei e seminary. Sciacca AG 1994, Domus mea. 408 p.; bibliog. 387-405.

5194 *Dooley* Kate, Women confessors in the Middle Ages ?: → 40, ᶠCOLLINS R.: LouvSt 20 (1995) 271-281.

5195 *Fernández* Domiciano, Ministerios de la mujer en el Nuevo Testamento : Proyecciòn 42 (1995) 247-302.

5196 *a) Fox* Ruth, Où sont les femmes-clés de l'Écriture dans le Lectionnaire d'aujourd'hui ?: -- *b) Gombault* Alice, Femmes et hommes en Église; -- *c) Bacq* Philippe, Vers des ministères apostoliques féminins ? : LV(itF) 50 (1995) 185-194 / 155-168 / 145-154.

5197 **García Estebanez** Emilio, ¿Es cristiano ser mujer ? La condición servil de la mujer según la BIblia y la Iglesia (Desigualdades y diferencias). M 1992, Siglo XXI. xvi-178 -- ^RCiTom 121 (1994) 205s (E.G. *Álvarez*).

5198 *Geis* Sally B., Church perceptions of power [Cross/feminist, PURVIS S.; ambition in ministry, SCHNASE R.; pastorpower, STORTZ M., all 1993]: QR(Min) 15 (1995) 213-223.

5199 **Grelot** Pierre, La condition de la femme d'après le Nouveau Testament. P 1995, D-Brouwer. 168 p. F 110. 2-220-03574-3. -- ^RBLE 96 (1995) 316s (L. *Monloubou*); ThLZ 120 (1995) 1002s (W. *Rebell*).

5200 **Grenz** Stanley [→ 5309], (*Kjesbo* Denise M.), Women in the Church; a biblical theology of women in ministry. DG 1995, InterVarsity. 284 p. $ 16. 0-8308-1862-6 [< ThD 43,270].

5201 *Harrison* N.V., The feminine man in late antique ascetic piety: USQR 48,3 (1994) 49-71 [NTAb 40, p.473: (not 'effeminate' but) males should have some qualities thought distinctively feminine; also, basically, Plato's 'spiritual childbearing'].

5202 **Hartel** Joseph F., Femina ut imago Dei in the integral feminism of St. Thomas AQUINAS; AnGr 260, 1993 → 9,9338: ^RAng 72 (1995) 138-141 (Margherita Maria *Rossi*).

5203 **Haskins** Susan, Mary Magdalen, myth and metaphor 1993 → 9,9339; 10,8734; $ 28: ^RC(ath)HR 81 (1995) 413-6 (Katherine L. *Jansen*); *CritRR 8 (1995) 224-6 (Marjorie *Brown*).

5204 *Heijst* Annelies van, Voorbij het scheidende denken; het Salomonsordeel [1 Kon 3,16-28] en wijsheidstradities van vrouwen: CVL (1995) 5-24.

5205 *a) Henderson* Frank, Feminizing the rule of Benedict in medieval England: -- *b) Spreckelmeyer* Antha, Feminine exerience in the northern metrical version of the Benedictine rule: Magistra, a journal of women's spirituality in history 1,1 (Dunwoody GA 1995) 9-38 / 1/2, 267-280.

5206 **Hewitt** Marsha A., Critical theory of religion; a feminist analysis. Mp 1995, Fortress. xiv-234 p. $ 17, -- ^R*CritRR 8 (1995) 524-7 (L.A. *Golemon*).

5207 **Hoffman** Donald F., The status of women and Gnosticism in IRENAEUS & TERTULLIAN [diss. critical of E. PAGELS]. Lewiston 1995, Mellen. x-239 p. 0-7734-8996-7 [RStR 22,165, B.A. *Pearson*]. -- ^RE(xp)T 107 (1995s) 27 (G. *Huelin* does not fear for Pagels).

5208 **Ibarra Benlloch** Martín, Mulier fortis; la mujer en las fuentes cristianas (280-313): MgHistAnt 6, 1990 → 7,8816; 8,9048: ^RRS(tor)A 25 (1995) 242-8 (U. *Mattioli*).

5209 **Jacobs-Malina** Diane, Beyond patriarchy; images of the family in Jesus 1993 → 9,4172: ^RBTB 24 (1994) 143s (T.R. *Hobbs*); TorJT 11 (1995) 220-3 (Alicia *Batten*, also on Cheryl BROWN and Luise SCHOTTROFF).

5210 **Jantzen** Grace M., Power, gender and Christian mysticism: Ideology & Religion 8. C 1995, Univ. xvii-384 p. £ 40: pa. £ 14. 0-521-47376-4; -926-6. -- *TBR 8,3 (1995s) 32s (Jane *Charman*).

5211 **Jensen** Anne, Gottes selbstbewusste Töchter 1992 → 9,9342; 10,8737: ^RRS(to)LR 31 (1995) 326-330 (Anna Maria *Berruto*); RTL 26 (1995) 225-8 (A. *Dermience*); Salesianum 57 (1995) 555-7 (O. *Pasquato*); ThLZ 120 (1995) 564-6 (Hedwig *Meyr-Wilmes*).

5212 ^{TE}**Jensen** Anne. Thekla, die Apostolin: ein apokrypher Text neu entdeckt; Frauen -- Kultur -- Geschichte 3. FrB 1995, Herder. 134 p.; Bibliog. 121-132. 3-451-23674-5.

5213 **Kadel** Andrew, A bibliography of writings by Christian women from the first to the fifteenth centuries. NY 1995, Continuum. 200 p. $ 30. 0-8264-0676-9. -- ^RMagistra 1/2 (1995) 374s (Deborah *Vess*).

5214 **Keener** C.S., Paul, women, wives: marriage and women's ministry in the letters of

Paul 1992 → 8,9054: ᴿRevBib(Arg) 57 (1995) 124s (A.J. *Levoratti*).

5215 *a) Keller* Rosemary S., *al.*, Female experience in American religion; -- *b) Hackett* David G., Gender and religion in American culture, 1870-1930: R&AC(u) 5 (1995) 1-21 / 127-157.

5216 **Kinukawa** Hisako, Women and Jesus in Mark 1994 → 10,8738: ᴿET 106 (1994s) 184s (Ruth B. *Edwards*).

5217 **Koivunen** Hannele S.M., The woman who understood completely; a semiotic analysis of the Mary Magdalene myth in the Gnostic Gospel of Mary; diss. Helsinki 1994, 318 p. 951-96306-4-3. -- DissA-C 56 (1995s) p, 39.

5218 *Kremer* J., Die Frauen in der Bibel und in der Kirche: StZ 213 (1995) 377-386 [NTAb 40, p.86].

5219 *Lamoureux* Patricia A., Deadly vices and redeeming virtues; a feminist perspective: NewThR 8,2 (1995) 6-20.

5220 *Love* S.L., Gender status and roles in the Church; some social considerations [agrarian society; Lk/Acts, 1 Cor 14; industrialization finds no parallel in history]: RestQ 36 (1994) 251-266 [NTAb 39, p.445].

5221 *Masenya* M., The Bible and women; black feminist hermeneutics: *Scriptura 54 (1995) 189-201 [NTAb 40, p.199].

5222 **Mazzucco** Clementina, 'E fui fatta maschio'; la donna nel cristianesimo primitivo 1989 → 6,8870: ᴿSalesianum 57 (1995) 144s (S. Kyalondawa *Kazamwali*).

5223 **Miller** Monica M., Sexuality and authority in the Catholic Church ['authority has little to do with holding visible office or power over others']. Cranbury NJ 1995, Univ. Scranton Press. xvi-286 p. $ 45. 0-940866-24-2 [ThD 42,377].

5224 **Nolan** Michael, Defective tales; the story of three myths [Macon bishops' denial that women have souls; AQUINAS, 'woman is an imperfect man'; ARISTOTLE, 'woman is a deformed man']. .. New Blackfriars [sans data]. -- ᴿAng 72 (1995) 600 (Margherita Maria *Rossi*).

5225 ᴱ**Ogden** Amy, In her words: women's writing in the history of Christian thought, Nv c. 1994, Abingdon. 347 p. $ 19. -- ᴿ*CWeal 122,1 (1995) 28 (L.S. *Cunningham*).

5226 **Petersen-Szemerédy** Griet, Zwischen Weltstadt und Wüste; römische Asketinnen in der Spätantike; eine Studie zu Motivation und Gestaltung der Askese christlicher Frauen Roms auf dem Hintergrund der Zeit: FKDG 54. Gö 1993, Vandenhoeck & R. 239 p. 3-525-55162-2. -- ᴿRHPhR 75 (1995) 349s (P. *Maraval*).

5227 **Pikaza** Xabier, La mujer en las grandes religiones: Cristianismo y sociedad 22, 1991 → 8,9069: ᴿMarianum 56 (1994) 527-9 (M. *Semeraro*).

5228   **Praetorius** Ina, Anthropologie und Frauenbild in der deutschsprachigen protestantischen Ethik seit 1949 [Diss.] Gü 1993, Mohn. 264 p. Fs 58. -- ᴿOrien(tierung) 58 (1994) 9-11 (Marga *Bührig*).

5229 *Rees-Hanley* Amanda,Un féminisme biblique: Certitudes (août 1994) 13s [<Telema 86,17-20].

5230 **Ricci** Carla, Mary Magdalene and many others; women who followed Jesus [→ 10,8749; < diss.→ 9,9358], ᵀ*Burns* Paul. Tunbridge Wells/Mp 1994, Burns & O./Fortress. 237 p. £ 13. 0-86012-208-5/. -- ᴿ*TBR 8,3 (1995s) 22 (P. *Doble:* scholarly, interesting, popular); TS 56 (1995) 357s (Sonya A. *Quitslund*).

5231 *Ricci* Carla, La donna nel cristianesimo del I secolo a Roma nel Paolo della lettera ai Romani: Studi Romani 43 (1995) 12-25.

5232 *a) Ricci* Carla, Maria di Magdala; -- *b) Perroni* Marinella, Le molte altre ...; -- *c) Martini* Carlo M., Un'opera bella: PaVi 39,5 (1994) 10-13 / 14-16 / 16-21.

5233 **Ruf** Sieglinde M., Maria aus Magdala [*nicht* Maria Magdalena, S. 5]: → b117 infra]; eine Studie der neutestamentlichen Zeugnisse und archäologischen Befunde: BibNot Beih 9. Mü 1995, Biblische Notizen. 116 p.: Bibliog. 105-116 DM 10.

5234 **Sandblom** Alice, La tradition de la Bible chez la femme de la C[omunità]E[vangelica]Z[airese] 1993 → 9,9360: [R]CivCatt 146 (1995,4) 413s (D. *Scaiola*).

5235 **Sands** Kathleen M., Escape from Paradise; evil and tragedy in feminist theology. Mp 1994, Fortress. xii-212 p. $ 15. -- [R]*CritRR 8 (1995) 527-530 (Millicent C. *Feske*).

5236 **Salisbury** Joyce E., Church fathers. independent virgins 1991 → 7,8839; 8,9073: [R]ChH 63 (1994) 431-3 (Susan A. *Harvey*).

5237 *Sansaridou-Hendrickx* T., Attitudes of 'feminism' and 'anti-feminism'; examples of gender-power relations in the Chronicle of Morea: AcPatrByz 6 (Pretoria 1995) 119-129.

5238 *Schlatter* Fredric W. The two women in the mosaic of Santa Pudenziana: *JEarlyC 3 (1995) 1-22.

5239 **Schottroff** Luise, Lydias ungeduldige Schwestern; feministische Sozialgeschichte des frühen Christentums 1994 → 10,8751: [R]BiKi 50 (1995) 240-2 (J. *Beutler*); J(unge)K 56 (1995) 187 (Silvia *Wagner*): ThRv 91 (1995) 27s (R. *Pesch*); TTh 35 (1995) 402s (Caroline Vander *Stichele*).

5240 **Schottroff** Luise, Lydia's impatient sisters; a feminist social history of early Christianity, [T]*Rumscheidt* Barbara & Martin. L 1995, SCM. xvi-298 p. £ 20. 0-334-02610-5. -- [R]*TBR 8,3 (1995s) 44 (Bridget *Upton*).

5241 **Schottroff** Luise, Let the oppressed go free 1993 → 10.8752: [R]P(rinc)SB 16 (1995) 92-4 (Kathleen E. *Corley*: feminist essays on Paul and the Gospels}.

5242 **Schüssler Fiorenza** Elisabeth, [Elizabeth STANTON centenary] Searching the Scriptures, 2. a feminist commentary [on whole NT and some other texts] 1994 → 10,1166: [R]America 173,26 (1995) 26 (R. *Scroggs*: why search where you don't find ?); *TBR 8,3 (1995s) 6 (Ruth B. *Edwards*).

5243 **Selvidge** M.J., Notorious voices; feminist biblical interpretation, 1500-1920. NY 1995, Continuum. x-246 p. $ 30. 0-8264-0913-X [NTAb 40, p.515].

5244 *Smeeton* Donald, Marriage, motherhood and ministry; women in the dispute between Thomas MORE and William TYNDALE: Churchman 108 (L 1994) 197-212.

5245 *Soskice* J.M., Blood and defilement; Jesus, gender and the universality of Christ: *EurTBu 5 (1994) 230-.. [<ZIT 95,p.173.

5246 *Spain* Sidney J., How Phoebe regained her rank, and all those 'shes' got written back into the Bible: Disciple 133-8 (1995) 15s.

5247 *Stearns* Gail J., From universal caring to concrete liberation; a review of contemporary works in gender and ethics: *CritRR 8 (1995) 71-90.

5248 **Synek** Eva Maria, Heilige Frauen der frühen Christenheit [kath. Diss. Wien 1990, [D]*Suttner* E.]: ÖC 43. Wü 1994, Augustinus. 239 p. -- [R]OCP 61 (1995) 605-7 (E.G. *Farrugia*).

5249 *Synek* Eva M., *a)* Aufgehobene Frauentraditionen: IK(i)Z 85 (1995) 137-164; -- *b)* 'Die andere Maria': zum Bild der Maria von Magdala in den östlichen Kirchentraditionen: OrChr 79 (1995) 181-196.

5250 *Thickstun* Margaret O., Writing the Spirit; Margaret FELL's [1667] critique of Pauline theology: JAAR 63 (1995) 269-279.

5251 *Thompson* David L., Women, men, slaves and the Bible; hermeneutical inquiries: CSchR 25 (1995s) 326-349.

5252 **Thompson** Mary R., Mary of Magdala, apostle and leader. NY 1995, Paulist. v-145 p.; bibliog. 138-143. $ 13. 0-8091-35736 [RStR 22,161, Claire L. *Sahlin*].

5253 *Thompson* William M., Women and 'conformity to Christ's image'; the challenge of avoiding docetism and affirming inclusivism [scholastic 'sex is an "accident"' true but inadequate]: S(cot)JTh 48 (1995) 23-35.

5254 *Todd* A., [STANTON E.C., 1895/8] The Woman's Bible; 100 years ahead of its time ?: Daughters of Sarah 21,4 (Evanston 1995) 47-51 [NTAb 40, p.397].

5255 **Torjesen** Karen Jo, When women were priests ..scandal of their subordination 1993 → 10,8759: [R]BiRe 11,4 (1995) 14s (Carolyn *Osiek*); *CritRR 8 (1995) 420-2 (D. *Good*); MoTh 11 (1995) 265-8 (Anne *McGuire*); TTod 51 (1994s) 446.8.450 (Gail *Corrington Streete*).

5256 **Wagener** Ulrike, Die Ordnung des 'Hauses Gottes'; der Ort von Frauen in der Ekklesiologie und Ethik der Pastoralbriefe 1994 → 10,6188: [R]BiKi 50 (1995) 243-5 (A. *Weiser*).

5257 **Wagener-Rau** Ulrike, Zwischen Vaterwelt und Feminismus; eine Studie zur pastoralen Identität von Frauen. Gü 1992, Gü.-V. 222 p. DM 68, 3-579-00252-X. -- [R]TLZ 120 (1995) 1040-2 (Christine *Globig*).

5258 **Weems** Renita J., Battered love; marriage, sex, and violence in the Hebrew prophets: *OvBT. Mp 1995, Fortress. xvi-150 p. 0-8006-2948-5.

H8.9   *Theologia feminae* -- **Feminist theology**

5259 **Alcalá** Manuel, Mujer, Iglesia, sacerdocio [= [2]La mujer y los ministerios 1982]: La barca de Pedro 1. Bilbao 1995, Mensajero. 469 p. -- [R]RF 232 (1995) 363.

5260 **Amîn** Qâsim, Die Befreiung der Frau, [E]*Balić* Smail: RelWSt 20.   Wü/Altenberge 1992, Echter/Oros. 129 p. -- [R]ZM(iss)R 79 (1995) 245s (G. *Swietlik*).

5261 **Anatrella** Tony, El sexo olvidado 1994 → 10,8765: [R]SalTer 82 (1994) 497s (J.A. *García*).

5262 **Aquino** María Pilar, La teología, la Iglesia y la mujer en América Latina. Bogotá 1994, Indo-American. 132 p. -- [R]JHispLat 3,1 (1995s) 67s (Sally T. *Gómez-Kelley*).

5263   **Aquino** María Pilar, Our cry for life; feminist theology from Latin America, [T]*Livingston* Dinah. Mkn 1993, Orbis. $ 17. 0-88344-373-2. -- [R]Horizons 22 (1995) 314s (Phyllis H. *Kaminski*); RStR 21 (1995) 213 (Teresa *Berger*).

5264 *Armstrong* Karen, The end of silence; women and priesthood. L 1993, 4th Estate. 247 p. £ 9. 1-85702-145-2. -- [R]*FemT 9 (1995) 126 (J. *Clague*).

5265 **Aumont** Michèle, Homme et femme dans le dessein de Dieu; deux sacerdoces en un. P 1994, Édigraphie. 164 p. F 110. -- [R]Études 383 (1995) 140 (J.-Y. *Calvez*).

5266 *Bacq* P., Vers des ministères apostoliques féminins ?: LV.f 50,2 (1995) 158-168 [NTAb 40, p.78].

5267 *Baker* Harriet, Feminism and Christian ethics: A(ngl)TR 77 (1995) 335-354.

5268 *a) Bartolomei* Maria Cristina, Donne presbitere; sono proprio ragioni quelle del 'no' ?; - *b) Dupré* Annemarie, Il nuovo ruolo delle donne nel Sud del mondo: Protest(antesimo) 50 (1995) 37-52 / 53-64.

5269 *Berger* T., A female Christ child in the manger and a woman on the Cross, or: The historicity of the Jesus event and the inculturation of the Gospel [StZ 213 (1995) 251-260]: *FemT 11,32-45 [NTAb 40, p.458].

5270 *Blenkinsopp* Joseph, Sacrifice and social maintenance; what's at stake in the (non-) ordination of Roman Catholic women : CrossCur 45 (1995s) 359-367.

5271 *Blyskal* Lucy, The question of ordaining deaconesses in the Church: NewThR 8,2 (1995) 59-69.

5272 *Börsig-Hover* Lina, Die heilsgeschichtliche Bedeutung der Frau; Edith STEINS Beitrag zum Verhältnis von Frau and Kirche: ForKT 11 (1995) 193-202.

5273 **Brusco** Elizabeth E., The reformation of machismo; evangelical conversion and gender in Columbia. Austin 1995, Univ. Texas. -- [R]*JHispT 3,3 (1995s) 55-69 (R. *Urrabazo*).

5274 **Bührig** Marga, Woman invisible; a personal odyssey in Christian feminism. Kent 1993, Burns & O. 126 p. 0-86012-202-6. -- [R]Vidyajyoti 59 (1995) 410-4 (Marianne *Katoppo*, also on Delores WILLIAMS).

5275 **Byrne** Lavinia, Woman at the altar; the ordination of women in the Catholic Church [completed before Pope's decree printed as an appendix]. L 1994, Mowbray. 132 p. £ 9. 0-264-67335-2. -- [R]ET 106 (1994s) 252 (Ruth B. *Edwards*; a kind of answer; commended); Modern Believing [continuing the numbering of Modern Churchman] 36,3 (1995) 48-50 (Natalie *Knödel*: 'Rome seems to be reconsidering the role and place of women in the Church'); PrPe 9 (1995) 295s (M. *Evans*).

5276 *Cahill* Lisa S., Sex and gender; Catholic teaching and the signs of our times : MilltSt 34 (1994) 31-52.

5277 *Cahoy* William J., One species or two ? KIERKEGAARD's anthropology and the feminist critique of the concept of sin: MoTh 11 (1995) 429-454.

5278 **Coll** Regina A., Christianity and feminism in conversation. ... Twenty-Third. 197 p. US$ 15. -- [R]*CanadCath 13,1 (1995) 23s (Carol *Kavanagh*).

5279 **Cooey** Paula M., Religious imagination and the body; a feminist analysis. NY 1994, Oxford-UP. vii-184 p. $ 25. -- [R]TS 56 (1995) 810s (Marilyn *Martone*).

5280 **Couture** Pamela, Blessed are the poor ? Women's poverty, family policy, and practical theology 1991 → 9,9406: [R]*CritRR 6 (1993) 553s (Mary Ellen *Ross*: based on LUTHER & CALVIN).

5281 *Crysdale* Cynthia, Horizons that differ; women and men and the flight from understanding: CrossCur 44 (1994s) 345-361.

5282 [E]**Daly** Lois K., Feminist theological ethics; a reader [1972-92 reprints]. LvL 1994, W-Knox. 325 p. $ 35. 0-664-25327-X. -- [R]TBR 8,2 (1995s) 32 (Alison *Pryce*).

5283 **Darling** Pamela W., New wine; women transforming leadership and power in the Episcopal Church. Boston 1994, Cowley. 258 p. $ 17 pa. -- [R]A(ngl)ThR 77 (1995) 111-3 (A.M. *Cheek*).

5284 **Denfeld** René, New Victorians; a young woman's challenge to the old feminist order. L 1995, Simon & S. £ 17. -- [R]Tablet 249 (1995) 842s (Monica *Furlong*).

5285 *Douglas* Mary, The gender of the beloved [1976 Vatican declaration implies 'Israel was feminine and the Church is feminine, therefore the priest representing Christ has to be masculine']: → 134, [F]MURRAY R., HeythJ 36,4 (1995) 397-408.

5286 **Eller** Cynthia, Living in the lap of the goddess: the feminist spirituality movement in America 1993 → 9,9416: [R]JAAR 63 (1995) 875-8 (Mary Z. *Stange*).

5287 **Evdokimov** Paul, Women and the salvation of the world; a Christian anthropology on the charisms of women [1958], [T]*Gythiel* Anthony P. Crestwood NY 1977. 285 p. -- [R]OCP 61 (1995) 676s (E.G. *Farrugia*: timely -- 1977 ?).

5288 **Fasoli** M. Grazia, Gli specchi delle donne: per una teologia al femminile: Transizione 15.. Liscate MI 1994, Cens. 138 p. L[m] 20.-- [R]Asprenas 42 (1995) 128s (P. *Pifano*); (R)*StEc 13 (Venezia 1995) 529s (T. *Vetrali*).

5289 *Fernández* Domiciano, La ordenación sacerdotal de la mujer en la comunión anglicana y su repercusión en las demás iglesias cristianas [< dis. La mujer y los ministerios en la historia de la Iglesia]: NatGrac 42,1 (1995) 103-128.

5290 **France** R.T., Women in the Church's ministry; a test case for biblical hermeneutics. Carlisle 1995, Paternoster. £ 7. 0-85364-675-9. -- [R]*TBR 8,1 (1995s) 43s (P. *Doble*).

5291 *France* R.T. vs. *Tinker* M. on ordaining women: Churchman 108 (L 1994) 234-242-7.

5292 **Fulkerson** Mary McClintock, Changing the subject; women's discourses and feminist theology 1994 → 10,8779: [R]ET 106 (1994s) 190s (Mary *Barr*: claims to surmount feminism's exclusive 'white Euro-American heterosexual privileged middle class' origins - - precisely the group in which are those who feel themselves 'not represented' by demand of asexual God-reference and anti-sexist exegesis); MoTh 11 (1995) 477s (G. *Ward*); RefR 49 (1995s) 210s (D.W. *Battjes*); TTh 35 (1995) 419s (Els *Maeckelberghe*).

5293 **Gebara** I., Teología a ritmo de mujer. M 1995, San Pablo. 166 p. pt. 1300. -- [R]Proyecciòn 42 (1995) 321s (J.A. *Estrada*).

5294 *Gil* Josep, Una proposta de teologia feminística (I) [[D]1993, MISSEGUE Marie-Geneviève, Trinité de Dieu et Trinité de l'homme]: RCatT 30 (1995) 307-342; Eng. 343.

5295 **Goldenberg** Naomi R., Resurrecting the body; feminism, religion and psychoanalysis [= Returning words to flesh, Beacon 1990]. NY 1993, Crossroad. vii-255 p. $ 15. -- [R]*CritRR 7 (1994) 588s (tit.pp.).

5296 *Goldingay* John, Hosea 1-3, Genesis 1-4, and masculist interpretation : H(orizons)BT 17 (1995) 37-43.

5297 *Graham* Elaine L.; Gender, personhood and theology: S(cot)JTh 48 (1995) 341-358.

5298 *Green* Chris, Gender and ministry: : Churchman 108 (L 1994) 329-352.

5299 [E]**Green** E., *Grey* M., Ecofeminism and theology: Yearbook of the European Society of Women in Theological Research 2. Kampen/Mainz 1994, Kok/Grünewald. 145 p. *f* 39. 90-390-0204-5 / 3-7867-1784-2. -- [R]TTh 35 (1995) 307s (Els *Maeckelberghe*).

5300 *a) Green* Elizabeth E., Indirizzi di cristologia femminista; -- *b) Tomassone* Erike, 'Gesù Sophia'; tracce di un concetto negletto di Dio: Prot(estantesimo) 49 (1994) 354-366 / 367-371.

5301 **Grenz** S. (*Kjesbo* D.M.), Women in the Church; a biblical theology of women in ministry. DG 1995, InterVarsity. 284 p. $ 16. 0-8308-1862-6 [→ 5200; NTAb 40, p.544].

5302 *Grenz* Stanley J., Anticipating God's new community; theological foundations for women in ministry: JETS 38 (1995) 595-611.

5303 *a) Groot* Meck, On being working class and educated; -- *b) Yeskel* Felice, Caught between two cultures : *JWm&R 12 ('Hearing the voices of working-class women; the ethical challenge of class in the U.S.' 1993) 11-15 / 16-20.

5304 **Groothuis** Rebecca M., Women caught in the conflict; the culture war between traditionalism and feminism. GR 1994, Baker. 249 p. -- [R]BS 151 (1994) 493s (R.A. *Pyne*); ERT 19 (1995) 86s (D. *Parker*).

5305 **Hampson** Daphne, Theology and feminism 1990 → 6,8760 ... 10,8787: [R]CritRR 6 (1993) 558-560 (Pamela D. *Young*).

5306 **Harper** Michael, Equal and different; male and female in church and family. L 1994, Hodder & S. xiv-242 p. £ 9. 0-340-61230-4. -- [R]TBR 8,1 (1995s) (Alison *Gelder*: hysterical).

5307 **Hauke** Manfred, Gott oder Göttin; feministische Theologie auf dem Prüfstein. Aachen 1993. 265 p. -- [R]AtK(ap) 125 (1995) 138-140 (A.J. *Nowak*).

5308 **Hauke** Manfred, God or goddess ? Feminist theology; what is it ? where does it lead ?, [T]*Kipp* David. SF 1995, Ignatius. 343 p. $ 18. 0-80870-559-2 [< ThD 43,272].

5309 **Hogan** Linda, From women's experience to feminist theology. Shf 1995, Academic. 192 p. £ 15. -- [R]DoLi 45 (1995) 641s (Mary *Condren*).

5310 **Hopkins** J.M., Towards a feminist Christology; Jesus of Nazareth, European women, and the Christological crisis. GR 1995, Eerdmans. 134 p. $ 15 pa. 0-8028-4074-4 [NTAb 40, p.367].

5311 **Isherwood** Lisa, **McEwen** Dorothea, Introducing feminist theology 1993 → 9,9450: [R]S(cot)JTh 48 (1995) 401s (Isabel *Wollaston*).

5312 *Jantzen* Grace M., Feminism and flourishing; gender and metaphor in feminist theology: *FemT 10 (1995) 81-101.

5313 *Jáuregui* J. Antonio, Exégesis feminista; a propósito de una obra reciente [BERNABÉ UBIETA C. 1994 → 5167 supra]: E(st)E 70 (1995) 55-84.

5314 **Jay** Nancy, Throughout your generations forever [sociology on male dominance of religion]. Ch 1992, Univ. xxvii-194 p. -- [R]JAAR 63 (1995) 144-6 (Janet *Hoskins*).

5315 *Jobes* Serene, 'Women's experience'; between a rock and a hard place; feminist, womanist, and *mujerista* theologies in North America [JOHNSON Elizabeth; MCFAGUE Sallie; and 7 others]; RStR 21 (1995) 171-8.

5316 **Kim** C.W.Maggie, *al.*, Transfigurations; theology and the French feminists. Mp 1993, Fortress. $ 15. 0-8006-2697-4. -- [R]TorJT 11 (1995) 277-9 (Marsha A. *Hewitt*)

5317 [E]**King** U., Religion and gender. Ox 1995, Blackwell. xi-324 p. £ 14. 0-631-19376-6; pa. -7-4. -- [R]TTh 35 (1995) 308 (M. de *Haardt*).

5318 [E]**King** Ursula, Feminist theology from the Third World; a reader 1994 → 10,9796: [R]JHispLat 3,1 (1995s) 65-77 (Rose Mary *Chavarria*);LiLi 32,1 (1995) 80s (Mary *Collins*); Modern Believing [continuing the numbering of Modern Churchman] 36,2 (1995) 59-62 (Abina *Prasad-Griffin*).

5319 *a) Kirk* Pamela, Women and God in the Church; critique and construction; -- *b) Moody* Linda A., Constructive theological understandings of God; methodological and epistemological contributions of Sallie MCFAGUE : NewThR 8,3 (1995) 19-28 / 29-39.

5320 *Kleinig* John H., Scripture and [= supports] the exclusion of women from the pastorate: LTJ 29 (1995) 74-81 . 123-129.

5321 *Körner* Barbara, Patterns of conflict and consensus in feminist politics; a potential for social change ?: *FemT 7 (1995) 8-14.

5322 [E]**LaCugna** Catherine M., Freeing theology; the essentials of theology in feminist perspective. SF 1993, HarperCollins. 266 p. $ 18 pa. -- [R]JRel 75 (1995) 173 (Barbara *Pitkin*).

5323 *Link-Wieczorek* Ulrike, Mehr Vaterkirche als Mutter Kirche ?: Ö(kum)R 44 (1995) 352-364.

5324 *Lobato* Abelardo, La mujer y el varón cara a cara; el problema de la diferencia: Ang 72 (1995) 541-577.

5325 *Magesa* Laurenti, Christology, African women and ministry: EAPR 31 (1994) 119-140.

5326 *Marsden* George M., Women's ordination for conservative biblicists: P(ersp)Ref 10,5 (1995) 3-5: NT allows for adjustment at local levels.

5327 **Martin** Francis, The feminist question; feminist theology in the light of Christian tradition. E 1995, Clark. 461 p. £ 17. -- [R]Month 256 (1995) 410s (Sheila *Birtchnell:* thorough and thoroughly against); ScotJR 16 (1995) 159s (Mary M. *Maaga*); Thom 59 (1995) 674-8 (R.D. *Young*).

5328 [E]**May** Melanie A., Women and church; the challenge of ecumenical solidarity in an age of alienation. NY 1991, Faith & Order US. 197 p. $ 18. -- RCThMi 22 (1995) 56s (May Lou *Geer*).

5329 **Miller** Bonnie F., Also a mother; work and family as theological dilemma. Nv 1994, Abingdon. 215 p. 0-687-11020-3. -- RRStR 21 (1995) 212 (Linell E. *Cady*).

5330 *Morgan* Sue, Race and the appeal to experience in feminist theology; the challenge of the womanist perspective: *ModBlv 36,2 (1995) 18-26.

5331 **Nixson** Rosie, Liberating the Gospel for women: Evangelism sries, 28, Nottingham 1994, Grove, 24 p. £ 2. 1-85174-281-6. -- R*TBR 8,2 (1995s) 47,'listing only' with 7 other titles.

5332 **Öchsner** Iris, Arbeit am Mythos der Weiblichkeit; Kritik und Konstruktion feministischer Weisheitstheologie: ev. Diss. DTimm. München 1995. -- ThRv Beilage 92/2, xii.

5333 *O'Neill* Mary Agnes, The nature of women and the method of theology: TS 56 (1995) 730-742.

5334 *Parmentier* Élisabeth, Les femmes auraient-elles besoin d'être sauvées ? Les concepts de péché et de salut dans les théologies féministes: ÉTRel 70 (1995) 521-533.

5335 *Pears* Angela, Women's experience and authority in the work of Elisabeth SCHÜSSLER FIORENZA: *ModBlv 36,3 (1995) 16-21.

5336 *a) Peña* Milagros, Feminist Christian women in Latin America; other voices, other visions; -- *b) Gallagher* Nancy E., Compañeras in the Peruvian feminist movement; a conversation with Rosa Dominga and Timotea, Maryknoll Sisters: JF(em)StR 11,1 (1995) 81-94 / 95-109.

5337 **Rae** Eleanor, Women, the earth, the divine. Mkn 1994, Orbis. 160 p. $ 15. -- RL(ex)TQ 30 (1995) 216s (Anne E. *Gregory*).

5338 *Reid* Barbara E., 'Do you see this woman ?' Luke 7:36-50 as a paradigm for feminist hermeneutics: BR(es) 40 (1995) 37-49.

5339 *Reynolds* Philip L., Scholastic theology and the case against women's ordination [AQUINAS clearly based on women's inferiority; BONAVENTURE-SCOTUS less; in none any appeal to existing tradition]: HeythJ 36 (1995) 249-285.

5340 *Ross* Susan A., *Hilkert* Mary Catherine, Feminist theology; a review of literature: TS 56 (1995) 327-341-352.

5341 **Russell** Letty M., Church in the round; feminist interpretation of the Church 1993 → 9,9497; 10,8816: RE(cu)R 47 (1995) 107s (Flora *Winfield*); Interpretation 49 (1995) 103 (Elizabeth *Barnes*); MoTh 11 (1995) 390-2 (Susan K. *Wood*).

5342 **Salas** María, De la promoción de la mujer a la teología feminista; cuarenta años de historia: servidores y testigos 55. Sdr 1993, Sal Terrae. 194 p. 84-293-1091-6. -- R*ActuBbg 31 (1994) 105s (I. *Salvat*).

5343 **Sands** Kathleen M., Escape from Paradise; evil and tragedy in feminist theology 1994 → 10.8819; $ 14: RP(rinc)SB 16 (1995) 257s (Wendy *Farley*).

5344 *Saussure* Thierry de, Questions psychoanalytiques sur la prévalence masculine dans la religion chrétienne: ÉTRel 70 (1995) 405-417.

5345 *Scherzberg* Lucia, Sünde und Gnade in der feministischen Theologie: JBTh 9 (1994) 261-283 (315-328, *Müller* Wunibald).

5346 **Schmetterer** Eva, 'Was ist die Frau, dass du ihrer gedenkst D1989 →6,9011: RTLZ 120 (1995) 162-5 (J. Christine *Janowski*).

5347 E**Schmidt** Eva R., *al.*, [27 delle 60 1988s] Riletture bibliche al femminile, TE*Gandolfo* Giuliana, 1994 → 10,8821; Lm 20: RAng 72 (1995) 315-7 (S. *Jurić*); Protest(antesimo) 50

(1995) 291-3 (J.A. *Soggin*: riflette l'esegesi degli anni nemmeno '80 bensí '60).

5348 *Schöne* Jobst, (German Lutheran) bishop, Pastoral on [against] the ordination of women (1994), [T]*Moellering* Armin: C(oncordia)TQ 59 (1995) 301-316.

5350 **Schüssler Fiorenza** Elisabeth, Discipleship of equals 1993 → 10,8827: [R]A(ngl)ThR 77 (1995) 109-111 (Ellen K. *Wondra*, also on WILLIAMS Delores 1993, p.113-5); MoTh 11 (1995) 281s (Susan K. *Wood*); NewThR 8,2 (1995) 113-5 (Carolyn *Osiek*); TorJT 11 (1995) 134s (Theresa *O'Donovan*).

5351 **Schüssler Fiorenza** Elisabeth, Jesus, Miriam's son, Sophia's prophet; critical issues in feminist Christology. NY 1994, Continuum. x-262 p. $ 23. 0-8264-0671-8. -- [R]Commonweal 122,5 (1995) 18 . 20 (D.M. *Doyle*: intentionally unsettling; jettisons the most classic Christian formulations, clearing the decks for fertile imaginations) [NTAb 39, p.442]; CrossCur 45 (1995s) 406-9 (Mary *Collins*).

5352 **Schüssler Fiorenza** Elisabeth, But she said 1992 → 8,8173 ... 10,8825: [R]CCurr 44 (1994s) 267-9 (Kathleen M. *O'Connor*); *FemT 7 (1995) 136-9 (Asphodel F. *Long*).

5353 **Schüssler Fiorenza** Elisabeth, Bread not stone 1984 → 1,8622 ... 8,9172: [R]ThLZ 120 (1995) 628-631 (J. Christine *Janowski*).

5354 *Shannon* Thomas A., A SCOTISTIC aside to the [FERRARA-BUTLER] ordination-of-women debate: TS 56 (1995) 353s.

5355 *Shepherd* Lorain M., The deceptive monolith of women's experience; struggling for common feminist visions amidst diversity: TorJT 11 (1995) 151-164 (-216, *al.*).

5356 *Soédé Nathanaël Y.*, Théologie féministe et théologie africaine: RICAO 11 (Abidjan 1995) 37-61.

5357 **Sommers** Christina H., Who stole feminism ? neurotic self-indulgent exaggeratresses / how women have betrayed women. NY 1994, Simon & S. 320 p. $ 23. -- [R]*CanadCath 13,2 (1995) 4s (M. *Coren*: contemporary myths); SewaneeT 38 (1994s) 200-2 (Susan *Bear*: praise).

5358 **Steichen** Donna, Ungodly rage 1991 → 7,8930; 9,9521: [R]DunwoodieR 17 (1994) 174-6 (T. *Kreser*).

5359 *Strohl* Jane E., Twenty-five years ago, twenty-five years from now; the ministry of women: WW 15 ('The ministry of women' 1995) 251-7.

5360 *a) Sullivan* Francis A., Room for doubt [< America; here headlining: the statement of the Vatican congregation declaring the decree infallible is itself not infallible, even if published with papal approval]; -- *b) Dulles* Avery, Tradition says no: Women's ordination and infallibility [articles 4 & 2 of a series]: Tablet 249 (1995) l646 / 1572s.

5361 *Talbert-Wettler* Betty, Secular feminist religious metaphor and Christianity: JETS 38 (1995) 77-92.

5362 *Tekippe* Terry J., A Catholic looks at the feminist movement: DunwoodieR 18 (1995) 23-37.

5363 **Thurston** Anne, Because of her testimony; the Word in female experience. Dublin 1995, Gill & M. 128 p £ 9. -- [R]DocLife 45 (1995) 582s (Marian *Shanley*); MilltSt 36 (1995) 163-5 (Bernadette *Flanagan*).

5364 [E]**Townes** Emilie M., A troubling in my soul; womanist perspectives on evil and suffering. Mkn 1993, Orbis. -- [R]USQR 8,1 (1994) 167-177 (A.A. *McFarlane*).

5365 *Tunc* Suzanne, L'ordination des femmes; un débat clos ? : L(umière)V 224 (1995) 7-21 (-106).

5366 **Valls Lobet** Carme [endocrinóloga], Mujeres y hombres; salud y diferencias. Barc 1994, Folio. 249 p. -- [R]EstFr 96 (1995) 177-9 (J. *Llimona*).

5367 **Williams** Delores S., Sisters in the wilderness 1993 → 9.9535; 10,8834: [R]Horizons 22 (1995) 145s (June *O'Connor*): LouvSt 20 (1995) 93s (Susan K. *Roll*); MoTh 10 (1994) 314-6 (Josiah *Young*).

5368 **Winter** Miriam T., *al.*, Defecting in place [not leaving their church but staying in though with their own terms and agenda, as ascertained from 16-page questionnaire]; women claiming responsibility for their own spiritual lives. NY 1994, Crossroad. 312 p. $ 23. -- [R]CrossCur 45 (1995s) 422-4 (Joann W. *Conn*).

5369 **Wondra** Ellen K., Humanity has been a holy thing; toward a contemporary feminist Christianity. Lanham MD 1994, upa. 382 p. $ 28.50 pa. -- [R]A(ngl)ThR 77 (1995) 410.422s (Flora A. *Keshgegian*).

5370 *Wootton* Janet, The ministry of women in the free churches: *FemT 8 (1995) 55-74.

5371 *a) Wright* Wendy M., Woman-body, man-body; knowing God; -- *b) Buckingham* Jane, 'Yet in my flesh shall I see God'; culture and embodiment: Way 35 (1995) 133-143 / 122-132.

5372 [E]**Young** Serinity, An anthology of sacred texts by and about women 1993 → 9,1357: [R]TorJT 11 (1995) 81s (Patricia *McLean*).

5373 *Younger* Doris Anne, Margaret N. WENGER; from mutual ministry to merger [(1800-) 1995]: AB(aptist)Q 14 (1995) 381-391; portr.

5374 **Zwank** Rudolf, Phänomenologie des Geschlechtlichen in theologischer Perspektive ? Zur Geschlechteranthropologie in Hans Urs von BALTHASARs 'Theodramatik': kath. Diss. [D]*Beinert*. Regensburg 1995. -- ThRv Beilage 92/2, xiv.

H9 Eschatologia NT, *spes*, hope

5375 *Adriaanse* H.J., *al.*, [E]*Jonge* H. de, Totdat hij komt; een discussie over de wederkomst van Jezus Christus. Baarn 1995, Ten Have. 138 p. 90-259-4575-0.

5376 *Aichinger* Herbert, Würde des Lebens -- Würde des Sterbens: ThPQ 143 (1995) 21-29.

5377 **Aliti** Angelika, Die Sucht, unsterblich zu sein; warum der Mensch den Tod fürchtet und darüber das Leben versäumt. Stu 1991, Kreuz. 240 p. DM 25,80. -- [R]BiKi 49 (1994) 66 (Verena *Lenzen*).

5378 **Almond** Philip C., Heaven and Hell in Enlightenment England 1994 → 10,8837: [R]ChH 64 (1995) 126s (N.C. *Gillespie*); ET 106 (1994s) 153 (H.D. *Rack*); JEH 46 (1995) 530-2 (B.W. *Young*): JThS 46 (1995) 772-5 (G. *Reedy*); RHE 90 (1995) 658 (J.-L. *Quantin*).

5379 **Anbeek** C.W., Denken over de dood; de boeddhist Nishatani en de christen PANNENBERG vergeleken: diss. Amsterdam VU, [D]*Vetter* T. Kampen 1994, Kok. 278 p. 90-242-8401-5. -- [R]TTh 35 (1995) 70.

5380 **Ancona** G., La morte; teologia e catechesi: Universo Teologia 16. CinB 1993, Paoline. 122 p. L[m] 18. -- [R]*RicScR 8 (1994) 237s (M. *Semeraro*).

5381 **Anderson** Ray S., La fede, la morte e il morire: PiccBT 29. T 1993, Claudiana. 205 p. L[m] 24. -- [R]CivCatt 146 (1995,1) 525s (F. *Cultrera*); *RicScR 8 (1994) 238-260 (G. *Ancona*); StPat(av) 41 (1994) 735-7 (E.R. *Tura*).

5382 *Bandstra* Andrew J., 'A kingship and priests'; inaugurated eschatology in the Apocalypse: C(alvin)TJ 27 (1992) 10-25.

5383 **Barr** James, The garden of Eden and the hope of immortality 1992 → 9,1990: 10,1884: [R]NewThR 8,2 (1995) 93s (Barbara *Reid*).

5384 *Baschet* Jérôme, Jugement de l'âme, jugement dernier; contradiction, complémentarité, chevauchement: RMab 67 (1995) 159-203.

5385 *Baudry* Gérard-Henry, Le Tartare; de la mythologie grecque à la liturgie chrétienne: MélSR 52 (1995) 87-103; Eng. 104 [NTAb 39, p.456].

5386 **Beasley-Murray** George R., Jesus and the last days [Mk 13 (1954) 1962]. Peabody MA 1993, Hendrickson. x-518 p. $ 30. -- [R]*CritRR 8 (1995) 263-6 (W.R. *Telford*); *JEarlyC 3 (1995) 359-361 (C.E. *Hill*).

5387 **Behrenberg** Peter, Endliche Unsterblichkeit; Studien zur Theologiekritik Hans BLUMENBERGs [Diss. [D]*Metz* J.-B.]. Wü 1994, Königshausen & N. 228 p. DM 48. 3-88479-895-2. -- [R]ThGL 85 (1995) 551s (M. *Bösch*); ThLZ 120 (1995) 825-8 (P. *Stoellger*).

5388 *a) Beinert* Wolfgang, Rechenschaft über den Grund der christlichen Hoffnung; Unsterblichkeit und christlicher Glaube; -- *b) Lüllsdorff* Raimund, Eschatologie und Ökumene: Cath 49 (1995) 44-57 / 195-204.

5389 *Beisser* Friedrich, Aufgaben heutiger Eschatologie -- Probleme und Lösungsmöglichkeiten: ThLZ 120 (1995) 495-510.

5390 **Bernstein** Alan E., The formation of hell; death and retribution in the ancient and early Christian worlds 1993 → 9,9545; 10.8843: [R]CBQ 57 (1995) 382s (W. *Adler*; masterfully organized, though more as 'warehouse for the dead' than his claimed 'place of eternal torment'): *CritRR 7 (1994) 313s (H. *Collins*): ET 106 (1994s) 28 (J.M. *Court*); JRS 85 (1995) 267s (T. *Gray*); Speculum 70 (1995) 119-121 (R.A. *Markus*); *TBR 8,1 (1995s) 58 (also T. *Gray*).

5391 **Bischofberger** Norbert, Werden wir wiederkommen ? Der Reinkarnationsgedanke im Westen und die Sicht der christlichen Eschatologie: kath. Diss. [D]*Koch*. Luzern 1995. -- ThRv Beilage 92/2, xi.

5392 **Boer** Martinus C. de, The defeat of death: apocalyptic eschatology in 1 Corinthians 15 and Romans 5 [diss. NY Union]: JSNT.s 22, 1988: [R]RB 102 (1995) 149s (J. *Murphy-O'Connor*).

5393 **Boismard** Marie-Émile, Faut-il encore parler de 'Résurrection'? Les données scripturaires: Théologiques. P 1995, Cerf. 180 p. F 82. 2-204-05204-3 [NTAb 40, p.364]. -- [R]E(spr)eV 105 (1995) 577-583 (P. *Grelot*) & couverture jaune du même numéro 42, p.293s (L. *Debarge*).

5394 *Bonino* Serge-Thomas, Résurrection de la chair ou immortalité de l'âme ? ; NV 70,4 (1995) 4-15 [= EeV 106,59-64: NTAb 40,p.463].

5395 **Bowker** John, The meanings of death 1991 → 7,8943 ... 10,9547: [R]CritRR 6 (1993) 304s (D. *Merkur*); S(cot)JTh 48 (1995) 102-4 (D. *Atkinson*).

5396 **Bremer** Jan M., Hidden futures; death and immortality in ancient Egypt, Anatolia, the classical, biblical, and Arabic-Islamic world. Amst 1994, Univ. 253 p.

5397 [E]**Bull** Malcolm, Apocalypse theory and the ends [cessation? fulfilment? eschaton-transformation?] of the world [Oxford Wolfson College lectures 1993, Zoroaster to Derrida]. Ox 1995, Blackwell. 297 p. £ 50; pa. £ 16. 0-631-19081-3; -2-1. -- [R*]TBR 8,2 (1995s) 3 (J. *Polkinghorne*).

5398 **Bynum** Caroline W. The resurrection of the body in Western Christianity, 200-1336: Lectures on the history of religion 15. NY 1995, Columbia Univ. ix-368 p. $ 32.50. 0-231-8126-2. -- [R]*CritRR 8 (1995) 473s (Catherine F. *O'Callaghan*); JThS 46 (1995) 740-2 (G.R. *Evans*); *TBR 8,1 (1995s) 32 (G. *Gould*).

5399 [E]**Cameron** Nigel M., Universalism and the doctrine of Hell 1991/2 → 9,434c; 10,8851: [R]JETS 38 (1995) 624-6 (R.A.*Peterson*); Presbyterion 21 (St.Louis 1995) 57-59 (also R.A. *Peterson*).

5400 **Camporesi** Piero, The fear of Hell; images of damnation in early modern Europe 1991

→ 8,9212; 9,9551; [R]*CritRR 6 (1993) 354s (C. *Garrett*).

5401 **Carozzi** Claude, Le voyage de l'âme dans l'au-delà d'après la littérature latine (Ve-XIIIe siècle: ÉcFrR 189. R 1994, École Française. vi-711 p.; bibliog. 651-675. 2-7283-0289-8.

5402 *Castillo* Dennis, The Parousia and discipleship: Priest 51,12 (1995) 17-19

5403 **Cohn** Norman, Cosmos, chaos and the world to come; the ancient [... Zoroastrian] roots of apocalyptic faith. NHv 1994, Yale Univ. x-271 p. $ 30. 0-300-05598-6.-- [R]CCurr 44 (1944s) 420-2 (A.W, *Wainwright*); ChH 64 (1995) 452s (E.R. *Daniel*).

5404 *Colwell* John E., The glory of God's justice and the glory of God's grace; contemporary reflections on the doctrine of Hell in the teaching of Jonathan EDWARDS: EvQ 67 (1995) 291-308.

5405 **Connelly** D., After life; what the Bible really says. DG 1995, InterVarsity. 140 p. $ 10. 0-8308-1648-6 [NTAb 40, p.365].

5406 *Conus* H.T., Notre vie après la mort: NV 70,1 (1995) 36-49.

5407 *Cook* R.R., Is universalism an implication of the [C. PINNOCK] notion of post-mortem evangelism ?: TynB 45 (1994) 395-409.

5408 *Court* John M., A future for eschatology ? : → 159, [F]ROGERSON, J., Bible/Society; JSOT.s 200 (1995) 186-204.

5409 **Couture** André, (*Saidon* Marcelle), La réincarnation; théorie, science ou croyance ? Étude de 45 livres qui plaident en faveur de la réincarnation 1992 → 8,9218 ... 10,8855: [R]MelSR 52 (1995) ll2s (L. *Debarge*); RThPh 127 (1995) 201 (C.A. *Keller*).

5410 [E]**Crockett** William, Four views on Hell 1992 → 9,9557: [R]EvQ 66 (1994) 287s (J. *Wenham*).

5411 **Cullmann** Oscar, [G] Immortality of the dead or resurrection ?, [T]*Koumantos* Antony. Athēna 1994, Artos Zōês. -- [R]DeltioVM 13 (1994) 104-7 (S. *Agourides*).

5412 **Daley** Brian E., The hope of the early Church 1991 → 7,8950 ... 10,8856: [R]ChH 64 (1995) 91s (Antonía *Tripolitis*); JThS 46 (1995) 304-6 (Frances M. *Young*).

5413 *Davidson* Bruce W., Reasonable damnation; how Jonathan EDWARDS argued for the rationality of Hell: JETS 38 (1995) 47-56.

5414 [E]**Davies** Jon, Ritual and remembrance; responses to death in human societies 1994 → 10,8857; £ 22.50: [R]ScotJR 16 (1995) 154-150 (P. *Badham*).

5415 **Deardorff** James W., Jesus in India; a reexamination of Jesus' Asian traditions in the light of evidence supporting reincarnation. SF 1994, International Scholars. x-315 p. $ 65; pa. $ 45. 1-883255-37-6; -6-8 [ThD 42,362].

5416 *Dekker* G., [questionnaire] Over het geloof in een eeuwig leven [increases slightly with age, but diminishes between 1966 and 1979]: G(ereformeerd)TT 94 (1994) 5-13 (-18).

5417 **Delumeau** Jean, History of Paradise; the garden of Eden in myth and tradition [1992 → 9,9562], [T]. NY 1995, Continuum. 276 p. $ 29.50 -- [R]RRelRes 37 (1995s) 188 (Kathryn *Jarrett*).

5418 **di Noia** Alfonso, La nera signora; antropologia della morte: Magia e religioni 32. R 1995, Newton Compton. 416 p.; bibliog. 389-400. 88-8183-114-7.

5419 **Dixon** Larry, The other side of the good news ... Hell 1992 → 9,8563; 10,8860: [R]JETS 37 (1994) 624-6 (E. *Fudge*).

5420 *Downing* F. Gerald, *a)* Common strands in pagan, Jewish and Christian eschatologies in the first century: ThZ 51 (1995) 196-211; -- *b)* Cosmic eschatology in the first century; 'pagan', Jewish and Christian: AnCL 64 (1995) 99-109.

5421 **Dumbrell** William J., The search for order; biblical eschatology in focus. GR 1994,

Baker. 381 p. 0-8010-3011-0. [RStR 22,167, A. *Scott*: focus it is not, nor order either].

5422 **Durrwell** F.X., Cristo, l'uomo e la morte [1991 → 10,8862], [T]. Mi 1993, Ancora. 94 p. L[m] 12. -- [R]CiVi 48 (1993) 399 (F. *Pecci*).

5423 **Eicher** Peter, ¿ Hay una vida antes de la muerte? 1993 → 10,8864: [R]SalT 82 (1994) 75.

5424 *Elders* Leo J., L'escatologia de San Tommaso d'AQUINO: DoCom 46 (1993) 207-220.

5425 **Elluin** Jean (†, pseudonyme), Quel enfer ? : Théologies. P 1994, Cerf. 198 p. F 120. -- [R]E(spr)eV 105 (1995) 140-2 (P. *Jay*: holds with AMBROSE that every individual will be *'partly* saved and *partly* condemned'!).

5426 **Erlemann** Kurt, Naherwartung und Parusieverzögerung im Neuen Testament; ein Beitrag zur Frage religiöser Zeiterfahrung [Diss.1993 → 9,9567*]; TANZ 17. Tü [D]1995, Francke. xv-511 p. DM 120. 3-7720-1868-8.

5427 **Feuerbach** Ludwig, Pensées sur le mort et l'immortalité, [TE]*Berner* Christian: Passages. P 1991, Cerf. 250 p. -- [R]RThPh 127 (1995) 172-4 (L. *Freuler*).

5428 *Flynn* Johnny P., *Laderman* Gary, Purgatory and the powerful dead; a case study of native American repatriation [Chumash 'Hammond's Meadow' 1973 views compared with LE GOFF J.]: R&AC(u) 4 (1994) 51-75.

5429 **Frosini** Giordano, Aspettando l'aurora; saggio di escatologia cristiana. Bo 1994, Dehoniane. 247 p. -- [R]Asprenas 42 (1995) 129s (B. *Forte*).

5430 -- *Giannoni* Paolo, Problemi di escatologia [FROSINI G., Aspettando l'aurora 1994]: VivH 6 (1995) 375-386 (-394 risposta); Eng. 394.

5431 *Fusco* Vittorio, Apocalyptique et eschatologie selon Jean CARMIGNAC: → 14, [F]BEAUCHAMP P., 'Ouvrir les Écritures' 1995, 225-244.

5432 [E]**Galvin** John P., Faith and the future [not 'facts' as 10,8868]; studies in Christian eschatology [BROWN R.E., KASPER W., O'COLLINS G.]. NY 1992/4, Paulist. iv-75 p. $ 7. 0-8091-3455-1. -- [R]Greg 76 (1995) 213 (G. *O'Collins*); Landas 9 (Manila 1995) 286-290 (V. *Marasigan*).

5433 *García-Murga Vázquez* José R.,¿Dios de amor e infierno eterno?: E(st)E 70 (1995) 3-30.

5434 *Giardini* Fabio,La liberazione cristiana dalla paura della morte:SacDo 40,5(1995)73-146.

5435 **Gil i Ribas** Josep, Escatología cristiana: Col·l. S. Pacià. Barc 1994, Herder. -- [R]*QVidCr 174 (1994) 126 (E. *Vilanova*).

5436 *a) Gil i Ribas* Josep, La problemàtica de la resurrecció dels morts, avui: -- *b) Aguilar i Matas* Enric, La problemàtica de la reencarnació: *QVidCr 173 ('Immortalitat' 1994) 2336 / 53-70.

5437 **Girard** Jean-Michel, La mort chez saint AUGUSTIN; grandes lignes de l'évolution de sa pensée, telle qu'elle apparaît dans ses traités: Paradosis 34, 1992 → 8,9235 ... 10,8869:[R]RThPh 127 (1995) 91 (J. *Borel*).

5438 **González de Cardedal** Olegario, Raiz de le esperanza: Verdad e Imagen 132. S 1995, Sígueme. 541 p. -- [R]Communio (Sev) 28 (1995) 382-4 (M. *Sánchez*); Lum(Vr) 44 (1995) 518-520 (U. *Gil Ortega*).

5439 **Gozzelino** Giorgio, Nell'attesa della beata speranza; saggio di escatologia cristiana: CorsStT 1995 → 10,8870: [R]Salesianum 57 (1995) 578s (B. *Amata*).

5440 *Gray* Tony, Post-mortem evangelism; a response to R.R. COOK [upholding C. PINNOCK]: TynB [45 (1994) 395-409] 46 (1995) 141-150.

5441 **Greshake** Gisbert, Tod -- und dann ? Ende -- Reinkarnation-- Auferstehung ? der Streit der Hoffnungen[2]: BüchereiTb 1504. FrB 1990. Herder. 93 p. DM 8. -- [R]BiKi 49 (1994) 67 (R. *Russ*).

5442 **Haardt** Maria de, Dichter bij de dood: feministisch-theologische aanzetten tot een theologie van de dood [diss. Tilburg, ᴰ*Schreurs* N.]. Zoetermeer 1993, Boeken-C. 384 p. 90-239-0443-5 -- ᴿRTL 26 (1995) 385 (H. *Wattiaux*: le féminisme avec ostentation risque de se déprécier).

5443 *Hartman* Lars, Att tolka eskatologiska texter: → 93, ᶠKɪᴇꜰꜰᴇʀR., SEÅ (1995) 23-38

5444 **Hellamo** Geir, Adventus Domini; eschatological thought in 4th-century apses and catecheses [Kristus på Keisertronen, diss. Oslo 1985], ᵀ*Wooler* E.R.; VigChr.s 5, Lei 1989, Brill.

5445 **Hill** Charles E., Regnum caelorum; patterns of future hope 1992 → 9,9581; 10,8872: ᴿ*CritRR 6 (1993) 372-4 (A. *Marmorstein*).

5446 ᴱ**Hornung** Erik, *Schabert* Tilo, Auferstehung und Unsterblichkeit: Eranos NF 1. Mü 1993, Fink. -- ᴿFilTeo 8 (1994) 541-3 (S. *Sorrentino*).

5447 **Hubaut** M., La vie au-delà de la vie. P 1994, Desclée. -- ᴿNRT 117 (1995) 292 (A. *Toubeau*).

5448 **Hummel** Reinhart, Reinkarnation; Weltbilder des Reinkarnationsglaubens und das Christentum: Unterscheidung. Mainz/Stu 1988, Grünewald/Quell. 129 p. DM 19,80. -- ThRv 91 (1995) 176s (H. *Waldenfels*).

5449 **Jens** Walter (→ 5461 infra), KüNG Hans, Menschenwürdig sterben; ein Plädoyer für Selbstverantwortung. Mü 1995, Piper. 220 p. DM 29,80. 3-491-03791-7.-- ᴿEntschluss 50,7s (1995) 44s (H. *Brandt*); ᵀʜGʟ 85 (1995) 416s (D. *Hattrup*).

5450 **Jüngling** Elke, Die Hölle -- veralteter Glaubensartikel oder unverzichtbares Element im Gottesbild ? ; Diss. ᴰ*Grewel*. Dortmund 1995. -- ThRv Beilage 92/2, vii.

5451 **Kaimakos** Dimitris, ᴳ The resurrection of the dead in the Old Testament. Thessaloniki 1994. -- ᴿDeltioVM 13 (1994) 102-4 (S. *Agourides*).

5452 **Kamm** F.M., Morality, mortality, 1. Death and whom to save from it. NY 1993, Oxford-UP. 344 p. £ 35. 0-19-507789-X. -- ᴿET 106 (1994s) 60s (G.J. *Warnock*: glittering, difficult; first 'discern whether, and exactly why, death is usually a Bad Thing').

5453 **Kaufmann** Rolf, Die Hölle; eine neue Reise in unsere Unterwelt. Solothurn 1994, Benziger. 207 p. DM 37. 3-545-25094-6 [ThRv 91].

5454 *a) Kennedy* Emmanuel, Unsterblichkeit; das Selbst als die post-mortale Belohnung; -- *b) Betz* Otto, Die Jenseitsfahrt und ihre Spuren im Volksmärchen; -- *c) Beck* Heinrich, Die Lebensetappen als Trinitätssymbol; -- *d) Clarus* Ingeborg, Des Menschen und der Sonne Weg durch Nacht und Tod, dargestellt an dem ägyptischen Buch 'Amduat': Symb 11 (Fra 1993) 11-34 / 35-45 / 53-74 / 89-120; 12 fig.

5455 *Kenny* John, On the fringe of eternal life ['Limbo' unfounded, though a reaction against Aᴜɢᴜsᴛɪɴᴇ's severity]: Month 256 (1995) 27-31.

5456 *Kerkhofs* Jan, Western European attitudes to death and the hereafter: → 40, ᶠCᴏʟʟɪɴs R., LouvSt 20 (1995) 282-293.

5457 *Klaghofer* Wolfgang, Der Hoffnungslogos des Glaubens; seine Erprobung an der Endgültigkeit der Höllenstrafen: MThZ 46 (1995) 355-378.

5458 ᴱ**Kochanek** Hermann, Reinkarnation oder Auferstehung ? Konsequenzen für das Leben. FrB 1992 ²1994, Herder. 288 p. DM 46. 3-451-22866-1. -- ᴿ*ActuBbg 31 (1994) 60s (J. *Boada*).

5459 **Kolarcik** Michael, The ambiguity of death in the book of Wisdom: AnB 127, 1991 → 5,3381; 7,3080: ᴿBoL (1995) 152 (L.L. *Grabbe*).

5460 **Kortner** Ulrich H.J., The end of the world; a theological interpretation [1988], ᵀ*Stott* Douglas W. Lvʟ 1995, W-Knox. xii-367 p. $ 30. 0-664-25631-7. -- ᴿ*TBR 8.3 (1995s) 26 (J. *Polkinghorne*).

5461 **Küng** Hans, *Jens* Walter, A dignified dying (^{T} → 5449 supra). L 1995, SCM. £ 10. --
^{R}Tablet 249 (1995) 1412 (R. *McCormick*).

5462 **Kvanvig** Jonathan L., The problem of Hell 1993 → 10,8884: ^{R}FAP(hil) 12 (1995) 441-
450 (Frances *Howard-Snyder*).

5463 **Laansma** John, (dissertation summary. Aberdeen 1995, ^{D}*Marshall* I.) 'I will give you
rest'; the background and significance of the rest motif in the NT (Mt 11,28-30; Heb 3,7-
4,11): TynB 46 (1995) 385-8.

5464 *Lebourlier* Jean, Note sur la résurrection des morts: LumièreV 43,219 ('L'espérance'
1994) 77s.

5465 **Lester** Andrew L., Hope in pastoral care and counselling. LVL 1995, W-Knox. 168
p. $ 17. 0-664-25588-4. -- ^{R}*TBR 8,3 (1995s) 35 (J. *Woodward*).

5466 ^{E}**Leuba** J.-L., Temps et eschatologie [22 art.]: Académie internationale des sciences
religieuses. P 1994, Cerf. 371 p. F 150. -- ^{R}E(spr)eV 105 (1995) 415s (P. *Gire: riche,
féconde*).

5467 *a) Lodahl* Michael, Wesleyan reservations about eschatological 'enthusiasm'; -- *b)
Hoskins* Steven T., Eucharist and eschatology in the writings of the Wesleys; -- *c)
Underwood* Grant, Millenarianism and popular Methodism in early nineteenth century
England and Canada; -- *d) Blaising* Craig A., Changing patterns in American
dispensational theology; -- *e) McCant* Jerry W., Competing Pauline eschatologies .. 1 Cor
15 / 2 Cor 5: : W(esl)TJ 29 (1994) 50-63 / 64-80 / 81-91 / 149-164 / 23-49.

5468 *Logister* Wiel, 'Hij zal komen in macht en majesteit'; de vreemde wereld van de
christelijke parousieverwachting: TTh 35 (1995) 373-394; Eng. 394s

5469 **Lohner** Alexander, Der Tod im Existenzialismus; eine Analyse unter besonderer
Berücksichtigung des philosophiegeschichtlichen Hintergrundes und paralleler theologischer
Bemühungen in der heutigen Eschatologie; kath. Diss. ^{D}*Döring*. München 1995. -- ThRv
Beilage 92/2, xii.

5470 **Maier** G., Er wird kommen; was die Bibel über die Wiederkunft Jesu sagt: Tb 522.
Wu 1995, Brockhaus. 124 p. DM 13. 3-417-20522-0 [NTAb 40, p.369].

5471 *Markham* Ian S., Life after death: E(xp)T 107 (1995s) 164-9.

5472 **Marquardt** Friedrich W., Was dürfen wir hoffen ? 1993 → 9,9601: 10,8889: ^{R}Judaica
50 (1994) 162s (H.L. *Reichrath*); Protest(antesimo) 50 (1995) 87s (B. *Rostagno*); ThGl 85
(1995) 292s (D. *Hattrup*); TTh 35 (1995) 304 (W. *Logister*).

5473 **Martensen** Hans L., Reincarnazione e dottrina cattolica; la Chiesa di fronte alla
dottrina della reincarnazione, ^{T}*Adner* Daniel, al. Piacenza 1993, Cristianità. 52 p. L^m 6.
-- ^{R}VP 77 (1994) 308-310 (Claudia *Navarrini*).

5474 ^{TE}**Martini** Mario, Il Giudizio universale di Giovanni SULPIZIO Verolano. Sora 1994,
Centro Vincenzo. 157 p.

5475 *Mazzinghi* Luca, 'Non c'é regno dell'Ade sulla terra'; l'inferno alla luce di alcuni testi
del libro della Sapienza: VivH 6 (1995) 229-255; Eng. 255.

5476 **Minois** Georges, Histoire [des enfers, Fayard 1991 → 9,9606] de l'Enfer: Que sais-je?
2823. P 1994, PUF. 128 p. 2-13-046021-6. -- ^{R}ÉTRel 70 (1995) 130 (A. *Gounelle*); NRT
117 (1995) 470s (L.J. *Renard*).

5477 **Moltmann** Jürgen, Das Kommen Gottes: christliche Eschatologie. Gü 1995, Kaiser.
389 p. -- ^{R}*CritRR 8 (1995) 496-8 (R.T. *Cornelison*).

5478 *Mondin* Battista, Il senso cristiano della morte: CiVi 50 (1995) 5-14; 1 fig.

5479 **Moore** David G., The battle for Hell; a survey and evaluation of Evangelicals' growing
attraction to the doctrine of annihilationism. Lanham MD 1995, UPA.   xiii-102 p. --

[R]Presbyterion 21 (St.Louis 1995) 126s (R.A. *Peterson*).

5480   *Moore* Stephen D., The beatific vision as a posing exhibition; Revelation's hypermasculine deity: JSNT 60 (1995) 27-55.

5481 **Müller** Denis, Réincarnation et foi chrétienne: Entrée libre 26. Genève 1991, Labor et Fides. -- [R]*QVidCr 173 (1994) 133s (A. *Ros*).

5482 **Ngayihembako** Samuel, Les temps de la fin; approche exégétique de l'eschatologie du NT: MondeB 29. Genève 1994, Labor et Fides. 430 p.; bibliog. 395-424. F 135. 2-8309-0702-7. -- [R]*CritRR 8 (1995) 268-270 (J.T. *Carroll*); ÉTRel 70 (1995) 443s (P. *Genton*); FV 94,2 (1995) 88s (D. *Halter*); VSp 149 (1995) 221 (H. *Cousin*).

5483   *Noro* Harlei A., Discurso escatológico e apocalipse : Teocomunicação 25 (1995) 611-625.

5484   *Noske* M. Rainer, Zu KANTs Vorstellung von Unsterblichkeit: NZSTh 37 (1995) 238-241; Eng. 241.

5485   *a) O'Malley* J. Steven, Pietist influences in the eschatological thought of John Wesley and Jürgen MOLTMANN; -- *b) Dabney* D. Lyle, Jürgen Moltmann and John Wesley's third article theology; -- *c) Lennox* Stephen J., The eschatology of Geroge D. WATSON; -- *d) Whidden* Woodrow W., Eschatology, soteriology, and social activism in four mid-nineteenth century holiness Methodists: WeslTJ 29 (1994) 127-139 / 140-8 / 111-126 / 92-110.

5486 **Ott** Ludwig († 1985), Eschatologie in der Scholastik, [E]*Naab* Erich: HDG 4/7b, 1990 → 6,9096 ... 8,9280: [R]TPQ 143 (1995) 210s (R. *Schulte*).

5487 **Owusu** Vincent Kwame, The Roman funeral liturgy; history, celebration and theology [diss. S. Anselmo, [D] *Chupungco* A., Roma 1992]: VSAug 41. Nettetal 1993, Steyler. -- [R]NZM(iss)W 51 (1995) 147s (J. *Baumgartner*).

5488   *Pannenberg* Wolfhart, Die Aufgabe christlicher Eschatologie: ZThK 92 (1995) 71-82.

5489 **Pate** C.M., *Haines* C.B., Doomsday delusions; what's wrong with predictions about the end of the world. DG 1995, InterVarsity. 180 p. $ 10 pa. 0-8308-1621-6 [NTAb 40, p.370].

5490   *Pellegrino* U., *al.*, Siamo immortali ? La riforma rosminiana della teologia, Atti del XXVI Corso della Cattedra Rosmini, 1992. Stesa-Milazzo 1993, Sodalitas Spes. 338 p. - - [R]DoC(om) 47 (1994) 208 (A. *Pedrini*).

5491   *a) Peters* Friederike, Gemeinde vor Tod und Auferstehung; -- *b) Frede* Britta, Der Tod -- das Ende ? -- *c) Namyslo* Mechtilde, Auferstehung vor dem Tod; -- *d) Benkowitz* Jörg, Bilder der Auferstehung: KatBL 119 (1994) 154-8 / 159-164 / 165-7 / 168-171 [< ZIT 94,244].

5492   *Peterson* Robert A., The hermeneutics of annihilationism; the theological method of Edward FUDGE (The fire that consumes; the biblical case for conditional immortality [2]1982 → 10,8867).

5493 [E]**Pfammatter** Josef, *Christen* Eduard, Hoffnung über den Tod hinaus; Antworten und Fragen der Eschatologie: ThBer 19. Z 1990. Benziger. 225 p. -- [R]TPQ 143 (1995) 87s (R. *Schulte*: Faszikel 'In Würde sterben').

5494 **Pluta** Olaf, Kritiker der Unsterblichkeitsdoktrin im Mittelalter und Renaissance: Bochumer StPh 7. Amst 1986, Grüner/Benjamins. 137 p. ƒ 50. 90-6032-276-2. -- [R]Bijdragen 56 (1995) 229s (P. van *Veldhuijsen*. ook over POMPONAZZI P. 1516, [T]*Mojsisch* B. 1990).

5495 **Pokorn**ỳ Petr, Die Zukunft des Glaubens; sechs Kapitel über Eschatologie: ArbT 72. Stu 1992, Calwer. 108 p. DM 34. 3-7668-3114-3. -- [R]*CritRR 7 (1994) 87-89 (A.

Marmorstein: refreshing but brief); RStR 21 (1995) 332 (G. *Holland*).

5496 **Pozo** Cándido, La venida del Señor en la gloria: AMATECA 22. Bari 1994, EDICEP [per la Associazione (internazionale) Manualistica di Teologia Cattolica] 1994 → 10,8895: ᴿArTGran 57 (1994) 261-8 (J.A. *Goenaga*).

5497 *a) Pylak* abp Bolesław, ᴾ Reinkarnacja -- prawda czy mistyfikacja ? ; -- *b) Herbut* Józef, ᴾ On two conceptions of 'mystery' employed in theology: ZNKUL 38,3 (1995) 121-4 / 109-119; Eng. 119s.

5498 *a) Ravasi* Gianfranco, La morte del vecchio sazio di giorni: -- *b) Cortese* Enzo, La morte che viene dalla colpa; -- *c) Bergamelli* Ferdinando, Morte e vita in IGNAZIO di Antiochia; -- *d) Noce* Celestino, La morte in ORIGENE: ᴱ**Bianchi** Enzo, La morte e il morire: PSV 32 (1995) 27-38 / 77-93 / 273-288 / 289-303.

5499 **Rebillard** E., In hora mortis; évolution de la pastorale chrétienne de la mort aux IVᵉ et Vᵉ siècles dans l'Occident latin: BtÉcFr 283. R 1994, École Française. 269 p. -- VetChr 32 (1995) 217s (C. *Colafemmina*).

5500 *Reid* Daniel R., LUTHER, MÜNTZER, and the last day; eschatological hope, apocalyptic expectations: MennQR 69 (1995) 53-74.   [There is no -- N° 5501-5600 -- *deest*]

5601 ! **Richards** Jeffrey J., The promise of dawn; the eschatology of Lewis S. CHAFER. Lanham MD 1991, UPA. 359 p. $ 27.50. -- ᴿ*CritRR 6 (1993) 386-8 (W.C. *Johnson*: founder of 'dispensationalist' Dallas seminary).

5602 **Riley** Gregory J., Resurrection reconsidered; Thomas [Gospel/Acts/Book] and John in controversy. Mp 1995, Fortress. x-222 p. $ 15 pa. 0-8006-2846-2 [ThD 43,85].

5603 *Rordorf* Bernard, Comment parler du jugement dernier ? : ÉTRel 70 (1995) 367-375.

5604   **Rosenau** Hartmut,   Allversöhnung;   ein   transzendentaltheologischer Grundlegungsversuch: ThBt 57. B 1993, de Gruyter. x-544 p. DM 212. 3-11-013738-0. - - ᴿBijdragen 56 (1995) 469 (H.J. *Adriaanse*).

5605 *a) Rota Scalabrini* Patrizio, La 'beata speranza' nel Nuovo Testamento; -- *b) Donghi* Antonio, Il significato escatologico della celebrazione eucaristica : RivPL(iturgica) 33,3 (1995) 10-17 / 18-11.

5606 ᴱ**Ruggieri** G., La cattura della fine [→ 9.9616]; variazioni dell'escatologia in regime di cristianità [< seminari Bologna 1899-91 (?Ist. Medio Evo, Roma 15 genn. 1993)]. Genova 1992. -- ᴿCrSt 15 (1994) 393-402 (P. *Siniscalco*) & 403-414 (O. *Capitani*); Eng. 415s.

5607 *Sabugal* Santos, Anastasis; la recensión superficial y tendenciosa de C. MIELGO [EstAg 29,2 (1994) 377-9]; RevAg 36 (1995) 283-5 (298s aquí, ᴿ*Vargas-Machuca* A.: '*Scmitt* debe ser *Scmid*').

5608 *Sachs* John R., ¿ Cómo se entiende la doctrina del Purgatorio ? [< ¿ Resurrección o reincarnación ? Concilium 29 (M 1993) 883-890], ᴱ*Castillero* Jordi: SalTer 33 (1994) 238-240.

5609 *Sahagún Lucas* Juan de, Muerte, inmortalidad, resurrección; perspectiva filosófica: Burgense 35 (1994) 97-111.

5610 **Saucy** Robert L., The case for progressive dispensationalism; the interface between dispensational and non-dispensational theology [diss. 1961]. GR 1993, Zondervan. 336 p. - - ᴿJETS 38 (1995) 116-8 (J.D. *Morrison*; 118s, K.R. *Pulliam* on GERSTNER J.).

5611 **Sauter** Gerhard, Einführung in die Eschatologie: Die Theologie.. Da 1995, Wiss. xiv-232 p. DM 38. 3-534-07044-5.

5612 **Schaper** Joachim, Eschatology in the Greek Psalter: WUNT 2/76. Tü 1995, Mohr. xii-212 p.; bibliog. 177-193. 3-16-146434-6.

5613 **Schmidt** Thomas, Das Ende der Zeit; Mythos und Metaphorik als Fundamente einer Hermeneutik biblischer Eschatologie: Diss. ^{D}*Ohlig.* Saarbrücken 1995.-- ThRv Beilage 92/2, xiv.

5614 *Silke* John J., The afterlife; a historical enquiry: I(r)ThQ 61 (1995 99-114 [NTAb 40, p.281].

5615 *Slocum* Robert B., *a)* Christian assurance in the face of death; Anglican witnesses: SewaneeT 38 (1994s) 126-136; -- *b)* William STRINGFELLOW [1928-1985] and the Christian witness against death: A(ngl)ThR 77 (1995) 173-186.

5616 *Spellman* William M., Between death and judgment; conflicting images of the afterlife in late seventeenth-century English eulogies: HThR 87 (1994) 49-65

5617 *Sullivan* Joseph E., Praying for the dead in John 11: I(r)ThQ 61 (1995) 205-212.

5618 **Tamayo-Acosta** Juan-José, Para comprender la escatología cristiana 1993: → 10,8913: ^{R}TX 109 (1994) 297-9 (M. *Gutiérrez J.*).

5619 **Teani** Maurizio, Corporeità e risurrezione .. 1 Cor 15,35-49 nel novecento [diss. Gregoriana, R 1992]: Aloisiana 24, 1994 → 10,5947: ^{R}*CritRR 8 (1995) 307-9 (P. *Zilonka*).

5620 *Thodberg* C., Eskatologien i den liturgiske tradition [MARXSEN W. 1963; GRUNDTVIG N. † 1872]: D(ansk)TT 58 (1995) 67-69 [NTAb 40, p.89].

5621 **Thomas** Pascal, La réincarnation: C'est-à-dire. P 1994, Centurion. 101 p. F 89. -- ^{R}E(spr)eV 105 (1995) 139s (P. *Jay*).

5622 **Tilliette** Xavier, ^{E}*Lorizio* G., in dialogo, Morte e sopravvivenza: Saggi 32. R 1995, A.V.E. 434 p. L^m 38. -- ^{R}NRT 117 (1995) 773 (A. *Pighin*).

5623 *Tinker* Melvin, Does the Christian view of death need reviving ? : Churchman 107 (1993) 215-226.

5624 **Tipler** Frank J., The physics of immortality. NY c.1994, Doubleday. 528 p. $ 33. -- ^{R}*CanadCath 13,2 (1995) 29s (D. *Lococo*).

5625 -- *Pannenberg* Wolfhart, Breaking a taboo [dealing as a physicist with the theological themes of God and immortality]; The physics of immortality by Frank TIPLER [(Doubleday 1994) < Rheinischer Merkur (15.VII.1994)]: Zygon 30 (1995) 309-314 (315-327 . 477-490, 3 other reviews of Tipler).

5626 **Tornos** Andrés, Escatología II 1991 → 8,9310; 9,9626: ^{R}RTL 26 (1995) 106s (E. *Brito*).

5627 *Tourón del Pie* Eliseo, Comer con Jesús; su significación escatológica y eucarística: RET 55 (1995) 285-329 . 429-486; Eng. 285.

5628 **Turner** Alice K., The history of hell. L 1995, R.Hale. £ 20. -- ^{R}Tablet 249 (1995) 1142 (P.*Stanford*).

5629 **Van Kampen** Robert, The sign [.. the pre-wrath rapture of the Church]. Wheaton IL 1992, Crossway. 528 p. $ 16 pa. -- ^{R}BS 151 (1994) 113-6 (J.A. *Witmer*).

5630 **Varone** François, Ce Dieu Juge qui nous attend 1993 → 10,8915: ^{R}E(spr)eV 105 (1995) 152 (P. *Jay*); ScEs 47,1 (1995) *first* 127s (R. *Marcotte*. -- N.B. The pagination 117-137 is repeated at the beginning of the second issue.)

5631 *Volf* Miroslav, Eschaton, creation, and social ethics [response *Schuurman* Douglas J.]: C(alvin)TJ 30 (1995) 130-143 [-158].

5632 *Vorgrimler* H., Wiederkehr der Hölle ? : KatBL 120 (Mü 1995) 156-9 [< ZIT 95,p.331].

5633 **Vorgrimler** Herbert, Geschichte der Hölle 1992 → 9.9631: 10,8915; ^{R}Numen 42 (1995) 319-321 (P. W. van der *Horst*, also on BERNSTEIN A. 1993).

5634 **Walbrunn** Peter, Der Gerichtsgedanke in der Verkündigung -- eine Untersuchung zur Wirkungsgeschichte des biblischen Gerichtsgedankens am Beispiel der Zeitschrift 'Der Prediger und der Katechet' sowie ausgewählter Evangelienperikopen der erneuerten Leseordnung: kath. Diss. [D]*Mödl*. Eichstätt 1995.

5635 **Walls** Jerry L., Hell; the logic of damnation 1992 → 8,9313; 10,8917: [R]FAP(hil) 12 (1995) 143-8 (T. *Talbott:* on NT less convincing than J. HICKS); RelSt 31 (1995) 271s (K. E. *Yandell*: a gem; convincing).

5636 **Walther** Christian, Eschatologie als Theorie der Freiheit; Einführung in neuzeitliche Gestalten eschatologischen Denkens:ThBt Töpelmann 48. B 1991,de Gruyter. xii-307 p.DM 12.

5637 *Ward* Graham, A postmodern version of Paradise [Gen 2 ...]: JSOT 65 (1995) 3-12.

5638 [E]**Xella** Paolo, Arqueología del infierno; el más allá en el mundo antiguo Próximo-Oriental y Clásico [1987]: EstOr 6. Sabadell 1991, AUSA. 270 p. 84-88810-04-0. -- [R]RET 55 (1995) 251-3 (P. *Barrado Fernández*).

5639 **Zander** Helmut, Reinkarnation und Christentum; *a)* Dialog im europäischen Kontext, Rudolf STEINERs Reinkarnationsmodell: kath. Diss [D]*Waldenfels* H. Bonn 1994. -- ThRv 91,94. -- *b)* Rudolf STEINERs Theorie der Wiederverkörperung im Dialog mit der Theologie. Pd 1995, Schöningh. 347 p. DM 88. 3-506-78789-7 [ThRv 91,370].

H9.5 *Theologia totius [V-] NT* -- **General [O-] NT theology**

5640 **Adam** Andrew K.M., Making sense of New Testament theology; 'modern' problems and prospects: Studies in American biblical hermeneutics 11. Macon GA 1995, Mercer Univ. x-238 p.; bibliog. 215-234. 0-86554-459-X.

5641 **Bayer** Oswald, Handbuch systematischer Theologie I. Gü 1994. 548 p. -- [R]ThZ 51 (1995) 174-8 (U.H.J. *Körtner*).

5642 **Beeck** Frans van. God encountered [→ 5,9067 ... 10.8921] 2/1, The revelation of the glory 1993: [R]ET 106 (1994s) 189 (R. *Butterworth*).

5643 **Beilner** Wolfgang, *Ernst* Michael, Unter dem Wort Gottes; Theologie aus dem NT. Thaur 1993, Kultur-V. 903 p. -- [R]CBQ 57 (1995) 582-4 (C. *Bernas*: encyclopedic, though not as folksy as claimed); RivB 43 (1995) 553-5 (G. *Segalla*); TPQ 143 (1995) 300.302 (K.M. *Woschitz*).

5644 **Berger** Klaus, Theologiegeschichte des Urchristentums [1994,746 p. →10.8922], Auflage[2]: Theologie des NTs; UTB.Wiss. Tü 1995, Francke. xxvi-808 p. DM 78. 3-8252-8082-9. -- [R]StPat(av) 42 (1995) 541-7 (G. *Segalla*).

5645 **Caird** George B., NT Theology. [E]*Hurst* Lincoln D. 1994 → 10.8923: [R]ET 106 (1994s) 119s (D. *Hill*; theology that burns with passion); JThS 46 (1995) 245-250 (C.F.D. *Moule*); P(rinc)SB 16 (1995) 366-8 (B.M.*Metzger*);RStR 21 (1995) 141 (C. *Bernas*); TS 56 (1995) 774-6 (J. A. *Fitzmyer*: adequate, innovative; some queries).

5646 **Casalini** Nello, I misteri della fede; teologia del NT; SBF Anal 32, 1991 → 7,9027 ... 9,9637: [R]EstB 53 (1995) 276 (Tessa *Calders*).

5647 **Childs** Brevard S., Biblical theology of the Old and New Testaments 1992 → 8,9322 ... 10.8924: [R]*BInterp 2 (1994) 246-250 (R. *Bauckham*); BS 151 (1994) 121s (E.H. *Merrill*); BTB 24 (1994) 92 (A.K.M. *Adam*); *CritRR 7 (1994) 83-85 (J. *Reumann*); JBTh 9 (1994) 359-369 (R. *Rendtorff*); Pro Ecclesia 2,4 (Northfield MN 1993) 485-492 (P.C. *McGlasson*: 'the single most important work in church scholarship since CALVIN' < NTAb 40, p.457]: Protest(antesimo) 50 (1995) 321s (J.A. *Soggin*); RStR 21 (1995) 90-96 (M. *O'Connor*).

5648 **Childs** Brevard, Die Theologie der einen Bibel, I. Grundstrukturen (), [T]*Oeming* Christiane. FrB 1994, Herder. 411 p. DM 88. 3-451-23291-X [ThRv 91,95]. -- [R]E(rbe)uA 71 (1995) 164 (B. *Schwank*).

5649 [E]**(Schüssler) Fiorenza** F., *Galvin* J.P., Systematic theology; Roman Catholic perspectives 1991 → 7,379 ... 10,8927: [R]EThL 71 (1995) 253-5 (A. *Vanneste*: son 'tout premier mérite est incontestablement celui d'exister').

5650 **Garrett** James L., Systematic theology; biblical, historical, and evangelical [1, 1990 → 9,9644], 2. GR 1995, Eerdmans. xi-872 p. $ 45. 0-8028-2426-9 [< ThD 43,267].

5651 **Genderen** J. van, *Velema* W.H., Beknopte gereformeerde dogmatiek. Kampen 1992, Kok. 829 p. -- [R]RefTR 54 (1995) 90s (R. B. *Gaffin*).

5652 **Gnilka** J. Teologia del Nuovo Testamento 1992 → 8,9329 ... 10,8930: [R]RivBib 43 (1995) 290s (G. *De Virgilio*).

5653 **Gnilka** Joachim, Theologie des NTs: HTK.s 5, 1994 → 10,8929: [R]Biblica 76 (1995) 571-4 (E. *Lohse*); BZ 39 (1995) 267-0 (A. *Welser*): CiTom 121 (1994) 628s (de *Luis Carballada*); Entschluss 50,6 (1995) 34s (R. *Oberforcher*); StPat(av) 42 (1995) 553-8 (G. *Segalla*); ThLZ 120 (1995) 651-6 (A. *Lindemann*).

5654 **Grenz** Stanley J., Theology for the community of God. Nv 1994, Broadman & H. 900 p. $ 40. -- [R]BS 152 (1995) 232s (R.P. *Lightner*: his own positions unclear or 'bothersome').

5655 **Grudem** Wayne, Systematic theology; an introduction to biblical doctrine. Leicester/GR 1994, Inter-Varsity/Zondervan. 1264 p. £ 20. 0-85110-652-8 / 0-310-28670-0. -- [R]ET 106 (1994s) 243 (I.H. *Marshall*); *TBR 8,2 (1995s) 25 (M. *Elliott*).

5656 **Haacker** Klaus, Biblische Theologie als engagierte Exegese; theologische Grundfragen und thematische Studien: TVG 384. Wu 1993, Brockhaus. 216 p. 3-417-29384-7.

5657 *Hasel* Gerhard F., Recent models of biblical theology; three major perspectives [COLLINS J.; CHILDS B., HÜBNER H.]: A(ndr)USS 33 (1995) 55-75.

5658 **Hoch** C.B., All things new; the significance of newness for biblical theology. GR 1995, Baker. 365 p. $ 20. 0-8010-2048-4 [NTAb 40, p.367].

5659 **Hodgson** Peter C., Winds of the Spirit; a constructive Christian theology. LvL 1994, W-Knox. xx-421 p- $ 25. -- [R]MoTh 11 (1995) 473s (W.C. *Placher*); TS 56 (1995) 387s (P. *Lakeland*).

5660 *Holtz* Traugott, Neutestamentliche Theologie im Horizont der ganzen Schrift [STUHLMACHER P., I 1992]: JBTh 10 (1995) 2

5661 **Hübner** H., Biblische Theologie des Neuen Testaments, 3. Hebräerbrief, Evangelien und Offenbarung; Epilegomena. Gö 1995. Vandenhoeck & R. 322 p. DM 74. 3-525-53598-8 [NTAb 40, p.367; RStR 22,156, C. *Bernas*].

5662 **Hübner** Hans, Biblische Theologie des NTs 1993 → 9,9650; 10,8935: [R]NT 37 (1995) 188-190 (J.S. *Vos*); StPat(av) 41 (1994) 627-632 (G. *Segalla*); ZKTh 116 (1994) 215-7 (R. *Oberforcher*, auch über STUHLMACHER P.).

5663 **Ingraffia** Brian D., Postmodern theory and biblical theology; vanquishing God's shadow. C 1995, Univ. xvi-284 p.; bibliog. 270-280. 0-521-56840-4.

5664 **Kaufman** Gordon D., In face of mystery; a constructive theology 1993 → 10,8937: [R]Horizons 22 (1995) 308s (P.F. *Knitter*)

5665 **Keefe** Donald, Covenantal theology; the Eucharistic order of history 1991 → 7,4163; 9,4819: [R]HeythJ 36 (1995) 69s (R.R. *Brinkman*: a powerful new Loci Theologici; not really on Covenant or Eucharist; not always serene).

5666 **Ladd** George E.[1974], [2rev]*Hagner* Donald A., A theology of the NT 1993 → 9,9651*

[NTAb 38, p.313] -- [R]RefR 49 (1995s) 151s (S.W. *Van Dop*).

5667 **Langkammer** Hugolin, [P] Teologia Nowego Testamentu, I. 1985. -- [R]BZ 38 (1994) 304s (J. *Scharbert*).

5668 *Lyons* George, Biblical theology and Wesleyan theology: Wesleyan Theological Journal 30,2 (1995) 7-25.

5669 *Macquarrie* John, A revival of systematic theology ? [DULLES A., HODGSON P. both 1994]: ET 106 (1994s) 210s.

5670 *Mauser* Ulrich, Eine existentiale Interpretation der biblischen Theologie des Neuen Testaments: JBTh 9 (1994) 349-358.

5671 **Mildenberger F.,** Biblische Dogmatik 1991 → 7,9042 ... 10,8940s: [R]*CritRR 7 (1994) 86s (W. C. *Linss*: a difficult book).

5672 *a) Merk* Otto, Theologie des NTs und biblische Theologie; -- *b) Müller* Ulrich B., Apokaluptik im NT: → 536, [F]STRECKER G., Bilanz 1995, 112-143 / 144-169.

5673 **Mondin** Battista, Corso di teologia dogmatica. Bo 1992s, Studio Domenicano. 2000 p. (5 vol.) -- [R]DoC(om) 48 (1995) 181-192 (D. *Composta*).

5674 **Murrmann-Kahl** M., Strukturprobleme moderner Exegese: eine Analyse von Rudolf BULTMANNs und Leonhard GOPPELTs 'Theologie des NTs': *BeitRatT 4. Fra 1995, Lang. iv-127 p. Fs 40. 3-631-48342-2 [NTAb 40, p.165].

5675 **Oden** Thomas C., Life in the Spirit: SysT 3. 1992 → 9,9654; 10,8942: [R]C(alvin)TJ 30 (1995) 230-2 (H.I. *Lederle*).

5676 **Pannenberg** W., Systematische Theologie 1988-93 → 7,9655; 9,8943: [R]ActuBbg 31 (1994) 244-6 (J. *Boada*); Protest(antesimo) 50 (1995) 138-141 (F. *Ferrario*); SvTKv 70 (1994) 137-9 (P.E.*Persson*, 1-3).

5677 -- *Oviedo* Lluis, La teología de Wolfhart PANNENBERG: Antonianum 69 (Roma 1994) 370-9.

5678 **Pannenberg** Wolfhart, Systematic theology 2, [T]*Bromiley* G.W., 1994 → 10,9656: [R]C(alvin)TJ 27 (1992) 307-312-318-325 (symposium, S. *Grenz*, R. *Hinton*, J. *Olthuis*) [167s, C. *Pinnock* on his Introduction 1991]; NewTR 7,3 (1994) 91s (J. *Gros*); ProEccl 4 (1995) 364=9 (J.J.*Buckley*); TS 56 (1995) 385-7 (R. *Viladesau*).

5679 **Penchansky** David, The politics of biblical theology [BARR, GILKEY, CHILDS VS. T.BOMAN, G.E. WRIGHT]; a postmodern reading: SABH 10. Macon 1995, Mercer Univ. ix-109 p. $ 18. 0-86554-462-X [RStR 22,251, D.E. *Callender*].

5680 **Peterson** David, Possessed by God: a New Testament theology of sanctification and holiness. Leicester 1995, Apollos. 191 p. 0-85111-510-1.

5681 **Pinnock** Clark H., *Brown* Robert C., Unbounded love; a Good News theology for the 21st century. DG/Carlisle 1994, InterVarsity/Paternoster. 189 p. 0-85364-634-1 / 0-8308-1853-7. -- [R]TBR 8,1 (1995s) 27 (T. *Gorringe*: understandable evangelical but without some Calvinist key-points, and against socialism).

5682 **Quay** Paul M., The mystery hidden for ages in God: AmUSt 7/161. NY 1995, Lang. xvi-438 p. 0-8204-2221-5.

5683 *Räisänen* H., Nytestamentlig teologi: SvTK 71,2 (1995) 58-65 [NTAb 40, p.77: 'should be replaced by accounts of early Christian religion that analyze .. the interplay between tradition, experience, and interpretation'].

5684 *Ratzinger* Joseph card., La Nuova Alleanza; sulla teologia dell'Alleanza nel Nuovo Testamento: RasT 36 (1995) 9-22.

5685 [E]**Reumann** John, The promise and practice of biblical theology 1991 → 7,326; 8,9343: [R]RExp 91 (1994) 272 (Molly T. *Marshall* commends highly).

5686   **Siegwalt** Gérard,   Dogmatique pour la catholicité évangélique; système mystagogique de la foi chrétienne. II. La réalisation de la foi, 1. L'Église chrétienne dans la société moderne; 2. Les médiations; l'Église et les moyens de grâce. Genève/P 1991, Labor et Fides / Cerf.   F 220 + F 240. -- ᴿE(spr)eV 105 (1995) 620 -2 (P. *Jay*); RevSR 68 (1994) 114-6 (C. *Wackenheim*, 2/2); RTL 26 (1995) 221s (E. *Brito*, 2/1).

5687   **Stuhlmacher** Peter, Biblische Theologie des NTs I. Grundlegung von Jesus zu Paulus 1992 → 8,9346 ... 10,8952: ᴿJThS 46 (1995) 659-662 (R. *Morgan*); StPat(av) 41 (1994) 620-6 (G. *Segalla*); SvTKv 70 (1994) 189-192 (D. *Mitternacht*); ThRv 91 (1995) 381-4 (T. *Söding*).

5688   **Stuhlmacher** Peter,   Wie treibt man Biblische Theologie ?: BThSt 24. Neuk 1995, Neuk.-V. 96 p. 3-7887-1518-9.

5689   **Stuhlmacher** Peter,   How to do biblical theology: Princeton ThMg 38. Allison Park PA 1995, Pickwick.   xli-95 p. $ 15 pa. 1-55635-026-0 [NTAb 40,p.371]. -- ᴿE(xp)T 107 (1995s) 150 (L. *Houlden*: unremarkable and contentious).

5690   *Vanhoozer* Kevin J.,   From canon to concept; 'same' and 'other' in the relation between biblical and systematic theology [Edinburgh Finlayson lecture]: ScotBuEv 12 (1994) 96-124.

5691   *a) Vignolo* Roberto,   La forma teandrica della Sacra Scrittura; elementi biblici per una teologia della Scrittura e loro rilevanza ermeneutica; -- *b) Colombo* Giuseppe, Bibbia e teologia, dalla Providentissimus Deus alla Dei Verbum : StPat(av) 41 (1994) 413-437; Eng. 437 / 439-455; Eng, 456.

5692   **Weiser** Alfons,   Theologie des Neuen Testaments II. Die Theologie der Evangelien: StudBüT 8, 1993 → 10,8953: ᴿBurg 36 (1995) 557 (F. *Pérez Herrero*); BZ 39 (1995) 153-5 (Maria *Trautmann*); *CritRR 8 (1995) 320-3 (W.E. *Pilgrim*); ThLZ 120 (1995) 889-893 (O. *Merk*); ThRv 91 (1995) 131-5 (J. *Roloff*).

5693   ᴱ**Zuck** R.B., [Dallas Theol.Sem.] A biblical theology of the NT. Ch 1994, Moody. 487 p. $ 30. 0-8024-0735-8 [NTAb 40, p.548].

XVI. Philologia biblica

J1 **Hebraica** .1 *grammatica*

5694   *Aslanoff* Cyrille,   Pour une révision des modèles grecs dans l'analyse des parties du discours de l'hébreu; le statut du participe: RÉJ 154 (1995) 77-88.

5695   *Backhaus* Franz J.,   Die Pendenskonstruktion im Buch Qohelet: ZAH(ebr) 8 (1995) 1-30.

5696   *Bat-El* Outi.   On the apparent ambiguity of the schwa symbol in Tiberian Hebrew: LOrA 5s (1995) 79-96

5697   *Beal* T.K.,   The system and the speaking subject in the Hebrew Bible [Mi 1,8]; reading for divine abjection: BInterp 2 (1994) 171-189 [< ZAW 107 (1995) 308].

5698   ᴱ**Bergen** Robert D.,   Biblical Hebrew and discourse linguistics 1993/4 → 10,8959: ZAW 107 (1995) 346 (tit.pp.)

5699   *a) Blau* Joshua, ᴴ Elimination of final yod, dropping of final vowels and the formation of biblical syllables; -- *b) Florentin* Moshe, ᴴ Distinctions between various meanings and their phonological notation in Samaritan Hebrew: → 161, ᶠRUBINSTEIN E., Te`uda 9 (1995) 1-6 / 107-116.

5700 **Blokland** A.F. den Exter, In search of text syntax; towards a syntactic text-segmentation model for biblical Hebrew: diss. [D]*Talstra* E. Amsterdam V.U. 318 p.-- TTh 35 (1995) 277; RTLv 27.p.526.

5701 [E]**Bodine** Walter R., Linguistics and biblical Hebrew 1992 → 8,343: [R]JAOS 114 (1994) 88-90 (A.S. *Kaye*).

5702 **Bose** Timothy R., A strategy for teaching biblical Hebrew to native speakers of Hiligaynon (Philippines): diss. Fuller Theol. Sem., [D]*Redman* R. Pasadena 1995. 357 p. 95-33480. -- DissA 56 (1995s) p. 1826.

5703 **Ciprotti** Pio, Introduzione pratica allo studio dell'ebraico 1993 → 9,9673; 10,8962: [R]SBF*LA 44 (1994) 692s (M. *Pazzini*).

5704 *Collins* C.John, The *wayyiqtol* as 'pluperfect'; when and why: TynB 46 (1995) 117-140.

5705 **Creason** Stuart A., Semantic classes of Hebrew verbs; a study of *Aktionsart* in the Hebrew verbal system: diss. [D]*Pardee* D. Chicago 1995. 423 p. 95-42717. -- DissA 56 (1995s) p. 3102.

5706 DAVIDSON's introductory Hebrew grammar[4] [**Martin** James, grammar → infra] **Gibson** J.C.L., syntax. E 1994, Clark. xii-229 p. 0-567-09713-7 [RStR 22,144, F.E. *Greenspahn*]. -- [R]BoL (1995) 175 (J.F.A. *Sawyer*).

5707 **Dawson** David A., Text-linguistics and biblical Hebrew [< diss. Edinburgh 1993, [D]*Gibson* J.→ 9,9675]: JSOT.s 177. Shf 1994,Academic. 241 p. £ 37.50. 1-85075-400-X. [< OTA 18 (1995) p. 398 (W. *Vogels*)]. -- [R]SBF*LA 45 (1995) 543-580! (A. *Niccacci*).

5708 **Decaen** Vincent J.J., On the placement and interpretation of the verb in standard biblical Hebrew prose; diss. [D]*Revell* E. Toronto 1995. 363 p. NN02741 (ISBN 0-612-02741-4). -- DissA 56 (1995s) p. 4818.

5709 *Dohmen* Ulrich, Der infinitivus absolutus als Imperativ -- ein redaktionskritisches Kriterium ?: BiNo 76 (1995) 62-81.

5710 **Donnet-Guez** Brigitte, Grammaire de l'hébreu, simple et pratique. Montpellier 1993. Vera Pax. -- [R]FV 93,2 (1994) 83 (B. *Keller*: cite comme 1991 l'ouvrage important de FABRE D'OLIVET 1816).

5711 **Doukhan** Jacques B., Hebrew for theologians; a textbook for the study of biblical Hebrew in relation to Hebrew thinking. Lanham MD 1993, UPA. xxxii-243 p. $ 28.50 pa. 0-8191-9269-4. -- [R]A(ndr)USS 33 (1995) 197-9 (Beatrice S. *Neall*: user-friendly); CBQ 57 (1995) 344s (G.J. *Hamilton*); EvQ 67 (1995) 377s (P.E. *Satterthwaite*).

5712 **Eskhult** Mats, Studies in verbal aspect [D]1990 → 6,9158 ... 8,9352: [R]JNES 54 (1995) 64-66 (D. *Pardee*).

5713 *Fellman* Jack, Biblical Hebrew; a socio-linguistic history: JBQ 23 (1995) 24-26.

5714 *a) Fontinoy* Charles, La langue lien social; ombres et incertitudes concernant les origines de l'hébreu biblique; -- *b) Gibson* John C.L., The Vav consecutive; -- *c) Millard* Alan, Strangers from Egypt and Greece -- the signs for numbers in early Hebrew: →110, [F]LIPIŃSKI, E., Immigration: OLA 65 (1995) 65-77 / 93-100 / 189-94.

5715 **Freedman** David N., *al.* Studies in Hebrew and Aramaic orthography 1986/92 → 8,9354; 10,8955: [R]*A(sn)JS 20 (1995) 393-5 (S. *Levin*); ZAW 107 (1995) 271s (I. *Kottsieper*).

5716 *Gibson* John, Coordination by *vav* in biblical Hebrew : → 170, [F]SAWYER, J., Words; JSOT.s 195 (1995) 272-9.

5717 *Goerwitz* Richard L., How do you say *debar* [and the whole class of apparent enclitic with shortened vowels] ?: JSSt 40 (1995) 31-38

5718   **EGossmann** Hans-Christoph, *Schneider* Wolfgang, Alles Qatal -- oder was? Beiträge zur Didaktik des Hebräischunterrichts. Müns 1994, Waxmann. viii-122 p. DM 38. 3-89325-201-0. -- RThLZ 120 (1995) 128-130 (R. *Bartelmus*).

5719   *a) Hillers* Delbert R., Some performative utterances [PARDEE D., MAYER Werner ..] in the Bible; -- *b) Hallo* William W., Scurrilous [i.e. unflattering, p.769] etymologies: → 130, FMILGROM J., Pomegranates 1995, 757-766 / 767-776.

5720   *Johnson* Robert M.J., *Goerwitz* Richard, A simple, practical system for transliterating Tiberian Hebrew vowels: HebStud 36 (1995) 13-24,

5721   **Johnstone** William, *al.*, Computerized introductory Hebrew grammar. E 1993, Clark. In three editions: full ($ 70. 4 disks), some, or no sound pronunciation. -- RA(ndr)USS 33 (1995) 303s; 1 fig. (Miary *Andriamiarisoa*: innovative, unique, but offering access to numerous printed resources).

5722   *Joosten* Jan, Textlinguïstiek en het Bijbels-Hebreeuw- se werkwoord: een kritische uiteenzetting : NedThT 49 (1995) 265-272; Eng. 311.

5723   *a) Kaufman* Stephen A., Paragogic *nun* in biblical Hebrew; hypercorrection as a clue to lost scribal practice: -- *b) Blau* Joshua, The monophthongization of diphthongs as reflected in the use of vowel letters in the Pentateuch: → 72, FGREENFIELD J., Solving 1995, 95-99 / 7-11.

5724   **Kelley** Page H., *al.*, A handbook to [his 1992 → 8,9363] Biblical Hebrew. GR 1994, Eerdmans. v-223 p. $ 18. 0-8028-0828-X [OTA 18,149]. -- RRExp 92 (1995) 521 (H.W. *Ballard*).

5725   *Khan* Geoffrey, The pronunciation of *reš* in the Tiberian tradition of biblical Hebrew: AHUC (= HUCA) 66 (1995) 67-80.

5726   *Klein* J.L., The prophetic perfect [only Isa 5,13; 9,1-5; 10,28; 43,14; Jer 48,41; 51,30; Dan 7,27; Gn 17,20; Nm 24,17 admitted]: JNSWL 16 (1990) 45-60 [< OTA 19, p.207].

5727   **Kogut** Simcha, H Correlations between biblical accentuation and traditional Jewish exegesis; linguistic and contextual studies 1994 → 10,8978: RCBQ 57 (1995) 776s (H.W. *Basser*: good on cantillation in exegesis, but 'will not help those seeking to trace the history of biblical interpretation through the ancient versions').

5728   **Lambdin** T.O., Lehrbuch Bibelhebräisch, TESiebenthal H. von, 1990 → 10,8980: RBZ 39 (1995) 116s (J. *Maier*, 'Lamdin', auch Index).

5729   **Malone** Joseph L., Tiberian Hebrew phonology 1993 → 10,8983: RJAOS 115 (1995) 726-9 (Alice *Faber*); JBL 114 (1995) 355-7 (R. *Fuller*).

5730   **Manuel** Paul W., Tiberian reflexes of proto-Semitic /a/: diss. Wisconsin, DFox M. Madison 1995. 288 p. 95-27109. -- DissA 56 (1995s) p. 1754.

5731   *Marks* Herbert, Biblical naming and poetic etymology [80 explicit name-etymologies]: JBL 114 (1995) 21-42.

5732   **Martin** James D., DAVIDSON's introductory Hebrew grammar[27], 1993 → 9,9689: RBSOAS 58 (1995) 217s (L. *Glinert*). → 5706, DAVIDSON-GIBSON supra.

5733   *Morag* Shelomo, H The double letters *bgd-kpt* + *r*: Tarbiz [61 (1991s) 237-248, LIEBES Y.] 63 (1993s) 133-142 (143s rejoinder).

5734   **Niccacci** Alviero, The syntax of the verb in classical Hebrew prose: JSNT.s 86, 1990: RArOr 63 (1995) 376s (S. *Segert*); BZ 38 (1994) 312s (J. *Scharbert*).

5735   **Parker** Don, Using biblical Hebrew in ministry; a practical guide for pastors, seminarians, and Bible students. Lanham MD 1995, UPA. viii-289 p.; bibliog. 257-265. 0-7618-0124-3,

5736 **Pérez Fernández** M., La lengua [rabínica] de los sabios 1. Morfosintaxis: BtMidrásica 13. 1992. -- ᴿArTGran 57 (1994) 527-531 (A. *Torres*).

5737 *Qimron* Elisha, *Sivan* Daniel, ᴴ Interchanges of *pataḥ* and *ḥiriq* in the attenuation law: Leš 59 (1995s) 7-38; Eng 1,I.

5738 **Rechenmacher** Hans, Der Attributsatz; Beobachtungen zu Syntax und Redetypik: ATSAT 46. Mü St-Ottilien 1995, EOS. DM 24. 3-88096-546-3 [< OTA 19, p.333, T. *Hieke*].

5739 RICHTER Wolfgang, Biblia Hebraica transcripta 1991-3 → 8,1757s; 9,1550: ᴿJSSt 40 (1995) 97-103 (H.J. *Bosman*, 10.12s) & 103-5 (A.J.C. *Verlieij*, 6s.15).

5740 *Rooker* Mark E., Diachronic analysis and the features of late biblical Hebrew; *BuBR 4 (1994) 135-144.

5741 **Sáenz-Badillos** A., A history of the Hebrew language, ᵀ*Elwolde* John, 1993 → 10,8990: ᴿJJS 46 (1995) 283-292 (E. *Ullendorff*: immense praise), citing The (London) Times (23 Dec. 1993, Enoch *Powell*); OTEs 8 (1995) 318-320 (J.A. *Naudé*: Hebrew spent half its life in a bilingual setting).

5742 *Schindele* Martin, Darstellung morphologischer Zerlegungen hebräischer Wörter: BiNo 75 (1994) 22-25.

5743 **Seow Choon-Leong,** A grammar for biblical Hebrew²ʳᵉᵛ. Nv 1995, Abingdon. xii-366 p. $ 30. 0-687-15786-2 [ThD 43,289].

5744 **Siebesma** P., Function of niph'al 1991 → 7,9079 ... 10,8991: ᴿBiOr 52 (1995) 97-100 (C. van der *Merwe*); HebStud 35 (1994) 217-9 (P.H. *Kelley*); OTEs 8 (1995) 149-152 (J.H. *Kropeze*).

5745 **Volgger** David, Notizen der Phonologie des Bibelhebräischen [< Diss. Salzburg]: ATSAT 36, 1992 → 9,9707; 10,8999: ᴿCBQ 57 (1995) 378s (F.E. *Greenspahn*); EstB 53 (1995) 126s (J. *Arambarri*).

5746 **Weinberg** Werner, Studies on Hebrew, ᴱ*Citrin* P.: SFSHJ 46. Atlanta 1993, Scholars xx-373 p. -- ᴿ*A(sn)JS 20 (1995) 277: 10 titles sans pp.

5747 *Yaron* Reuven, Stylistic conceits [I. ᶠMUFFI, JANES 22 (1993) 141-8] II. The absolute infinitive in biblical law: → 130, ᶠMilgrom J., Pomegranates 1995, 448-460.

5748 **Young** Ian, Diversity in pre-exilic Hebrew: FAT 5, 1993; DM 158: ᴿArTGran 57 (1994) 536-542 (A. *Torres*); BiOr 52 (1995) 751-6 (T. *Muraoka*): CBQ 57 (1995) 380s (P.C. *Schmitz*: unsystematic); HebStud 36 (1995) 135-140 (G.A. *Rendsburg*); OTEs 8 (1995) 302 (C.A.P. van *Tonder*: a splendid new model; but title gives the date as 1933); ThLZ 120 (1995) 998-990 (Arafa *Mustafa*).

J1.2 Lexica et inscriptiones hebraicae; later Hebrew

5749 **Alonso Schökel** Luis, Diccionario bíblico hebreo-español [1990s → 6,9182 ... 10,9004], ᴱ*Morla* Víctor [pero sin su Glosario esp-hebr], *Collado* Vicente. M 1994, Trotta. 908 p. pt 25,000. 84-8164-026-3. -- ᴿE(st)E 70 (1995) 129-242 (E. *Zurro*); Kiryat Sefer 65 (1994s) p. 1098-1110 (Shifra *Sznol*, ᴴ); RasT 36 (1995) 504-7 (E. *Franco*).

5750 **Andersen** Francis I., *Forbes* A Dean, The vocabulary of the OT 1989 → 5,9120 ... 9,9711: ᴿBoL (1995) 172s (J.C.L. *Gibson*).

5751 **Babut** Jean-Marc, Les expressions idiomatiques de l'hébreu biblique, signification et traduction; un essai d'analyse componentielle [diss. prot. ᴰ*Waard* J. de, Strasbourg 1993 → 9,9713]: C(ah)RB 33. P 1995, Gabalda. 282 p.; bibliog. < 248-264. 2-85021-080-3.

5752 *Ben-Hayyim* Ze'ev, [H] The Academy of the Hebrew Language -- its role and the historical dictionary project: Leš 59 (1995) 185-202 (93-97).

5753 **Ben Zvi** Ehud, *Hancock* Maxine, *Beinert* Richard, Readings in biblical Hebrew; an intermediate textbook 1993 → 9,9716: [R]BoL (1995) 173 (J.C.L. *Gibson* hopes that it is not too detailed to attain the laudable aim of replacing a teacher's explanations); JAOS 115 (1995) 522s (G.M. *Landes*).

5754 *Broshi* Magen, *Qimron* Elisha, A Hebrew I.O.U. note from the second year of the Bar Kokhba revolt: JJS 45 (1994) 286-284; 2 fig.

5755 [E]**Clines** David J.A., I. [E]*Elwolde* J., The dictionary of classical Hebrew 1993 → 9,9718; 10,9006: [R]A(ustrl)BR 43 (1995) 50-71 . 74s (F.I. *Andersen*; response 72-74): Biblica 76 (1995) 416-8 (R. *Althann*); *DSD 2 (1995) 355-7 (S.E. *Fassberg*); ETRel 70 (1995) 118s (J.-D. *Macchi*): JThS 46 (1995) 569-572 (J.C.L. *Gibson*); RExp 92 (1995) 108s (J.F. *Drinkard*): STEv 7 (1995) 69 (P. *Bolognesi*); TLZ 120 (1995) 21-24 (Jutta *Körner*); WZKM 85 (1995) 292-5 (S. *Segert*): ZAW 107 (1995) 525s (M. *Köckert*).

5756 *Corell* Josep, La llamada inscripción de Adoniram y el cementerio judío de Sagunto; nuevas fuentes manuscritas y revisión de las conocidas; Sefarad 55 (1995) 239-252; 3 fig.; Eng. 256 [273-283, *Hinojoso Montalvo* José, demografía de Sagunto; Eng. 284].

5757 **Davies** G.J., Ancient Hebrew inscriptions 1991 → 7,9097 .. 10,9007: [R]RA 57 (1994) 247 (J. R. *Adair*): R(uch)BL 47 (1994) 132s (M. *Wodziński*, P); Syria 71 (1994) 456 (A. *Caquot*: 'on peut douter que beaucoup d'hébraïsants trouvent un réel intérêt à ce pur produit de l'ordinateur').

5758 **Deutsch** Robert, *Heltzer* Michael, *a)* Forty new ancient West Semitic inscriptions [1994→ 10,9008]: -- *b)* New epigraphic evidence from the biblical period [39 items, from ostraca or other small objects mostly in private collections] -- TA 1994/5, Archaeological Center. 100 p., DM 88 / 116 p. 965-222-511-8; -612-2 [< OTA 19, p.326].

5759 Dictionnaire des racines hébraïques[4]. Rochefort 1994, N.-D.S.Rémy. vii-631 p.

5760 **Fowler** Jeaneane D., Theophoric personal names in ancient Hebrew: JSOT.s 49, 1988 → 4,a221 ... 9.9722: [R]Syria 72 (1995) 449s (F. *Israel*).

5761 *Galil* Gershon, A new look at the 'Azekah inscription' [G. SMITH 1875 + H. WINKLER 1901: relates to 712 BCE, not 701]: RB 102 (1995) 321-9; franç. 321.

5762 (*Gesenius*[18]) **Donner** Herbert, Hebräisches und aramäisches Handwörterbuch [1. 1987 → 3,9253] 2. Dalet-Yod. B 1995, Springer. p.235-517. DM 348. 3-540 [-18206-3] -58048-4. -- [R]ThQ 175 (1995) 365s (W. *Gross*).

5763 **John** Lloyd C.[II]. A study of predicate *liqtol* in the Hebrew Bible, with examples from the Qumran writings: diss. Catholic Univ. of America, [D]*Fitzgerald* A. Washington DC 1995. 185 p. 95-28883. -- DissA 56 (1995s) p. 1754.

5764 *Kampen* John, A fresh look at the masculine plural suffix in CD IV,21: RQum 16 (1993-5) 91-97.

5765 (**Koehler-Baumgartner**) [3]*Stamm* Johann J., *Hartmann* Benedikt, Hebräisches und aramäisches Lexikon zum AT [4.1990 → 7.9095; 8,9419; [R]WZKM 83 (1993) 297-9 (S. *Segert*)] Lfg. 5, Aramäisches Lexikon. Lei 1995, Brill. xxv + p. 1661-1801. ƒ 131,50.

5766 (**Koehler-Baumgartner**, *al.*) [T]*Richardson* M.E.J., *al.*, The Hebrew and Aramaic lexicon of the OT 1994 → 10,9012: [R]BS 152 (1995) 370-2 (R.B. *Chisholm*): ET 106 (1994s) 67s (C.S. *Rodd*).

5767 *Lemaire* André, Épigraphie palestinienne; nouveaux documents II -- décennie 1985-1995: Henoch 17 (1995) 209-242 ...

5768 *Merlini* Carola Giovanna, Analisi lessico-semantica dell'onomastica femminile ebraico-biblica: RivB 43 (1995) 449-465; Eng. 466; theophoric less frequent and do not refer to God as ruler; the others emphasize feminine beauty as important to others, hinting 'to bring pleasure and offspring'.

5769 *Muraoka* Takamitsu, *Shavitsky* Ziva, A biblical Hebrew lexicon of Abraham Ibn Ezra. Daniel: Abr Nahrain 31 (1993) 106-9.

5770 *Na'aman* Nadav, Hazael of `Amqi and Hadadezer of Beth-rehob [Semitic inscriptions to Hazael of Damascus found in Euboea and Samos]: UF 27 (DIETRICH 60. Gb. 1995) 381-394.

5771 *Probstle* Martin T, The advantages of W. RICHTER's approach for a lexical description of biblical Hebrew: JNWS 21,1 (1995) 95-110.

5772 *Qimron* Elisha, The biblical lexicon in light of the Dead Sea Scrolls: *DSD 2 (1995) 295-329.

5773 *Rendsburg* Gary A., Linguistic variation and the 'foreign' factor in the Hebrew Bible: I(sr)OS 15 (1995) 177-190 [[E]Izreel S., *Drory* R., Language and culture in the Near East, 279 p.].

5774 **Renz** Johannes [[D] → 18,9018], Die althebräischen Inschriften 1-3:(*Röllig* Wolfgang), Handbuch der althebräischen Epigraphik 1. Da 1995, Wiss. xiii-465; viii-236 p.; vii-35 p.; 58 pl. DM 270 [EstAg 31,125, C. *Mielgo*]. -- [R](Tü)ThQ 175 (1995) 367s (W. *Gross*); UF 27 (DIETRICH 60. Gb. 1995) 722-5 (M. *Heltzer*).

5775 **Reymond** Philippe, *a)* Dictionnaire d'hébreu et d'araméen bibliques 1991 → 7,9120 ... 9,9735; [R]*TransEuph 8 (1994) 175 (A. *Lemaire*). -- *b)* Dizionario di ebraico e di aramaico biblici. R 1995, Soc. Biblica Britannica. 497 p. 88-237-8040-3.

5776 **Rosén** Haiim B., Hebrew at the crossroads of cultures; from outgoing antiquity to the Middle Ages: Orbis supp. Lv 1995, Peeters. [iv-] 86 p. 90-6831-685-0.

5777 *Schwartz* S., Language [Hebrew dwindling], power and identity in ancient Palestine: PaP 148 (Ox 1995) 3-47 [NTAb 40, p.306].

5778 **Simon** Ethelyn, *al.* Tall tales [Cinderella etc.] told in biblical Hebrew [a virtual third edition of 1983 Tall tales told and retold in BH, [2]incorporated into First Hebrew Primer]. Oakland 1994, EKS. 144 p. $ 15 pa. -- [R]JETS 38 (1995) 257s (D.M. *Howard*).

5779 *a) Stern* Naphtali, [H] The component *yeš* in Mishnaic Hebrew; -- *b) Sharvit* Shimon, [H] The cardinal number in rabbinic Hebrew; the weakening of gender correlation → 161, [F]RUBINSTEIN E., Te'uda 9 (1995) 33-48 / 49-63.

5780 **Testa** Emanuele, Nomi personali semitici; biblici, angelici, profani. Assisi 1994, Porziuncola. xxvi-581 p.; bibliog. xix-xxiv. 88-270-0261-8.

5781 **Wagner** Andreas M.A., Sprechakte und Sprechaktanalyse im AT: Untersuchungen im biblischen Hebräisch and der Nahtstelle zwischen Handlungsebene und Grammatik: ev. Diss. [D]*Michel*. Mainz 1995. -- ThRv Beilage 92/2, xii.

5782 *Yifrach* Esther, [H] The construct infinitive in the language of Ben Sira: Leš 59 (1995) 273-294; Eng. 4,I.

5783 *Young* Jon, The 'Northernisms' of the Israelite narratives in Kings [BURNEY C.1903, uncritically followed by RENDSBURG G. 1990]: ZAH(ebr) 8 (1995) 63-70.

5784 **Zadok** Ran, The pre-Hellenistic Israelite anthroponomy and prosopography 1988 → 5,9160: [R]BoL (1995) 181 (L.L. *Grabbe*).

5785 *Allan* Nigel, Catalogue of Hebrew printed books (1491-1900) in the Wellcome Institute, London: JSS 39 (1994) 183-206.

5786 **Alter** Robert, Hebrew and modernity [11 art. 1981-93 on modern Hebrew literature]. Bloomington 1994, Indiana Univ. xi-192 p. $ 11 pa. -- [R]HebStud 36 (1995) 239-242 (W. *Bargad*).

5787 *Azar* Moshe, [H] Functional words viewed in a synchronic and diachronic perspective [**Kaddari** Menahem Z., [H] Post-biblical Hebrew syntax and semantics (Ramat-Gan 1991-5)]: Leš 59 (1995s) 151-174; Eng. 2.IIIs.

5788 **Bahat** Shoshana, *Mishor* Mordechay, [H] Dictionary of contemporary Hebrew; a practical dictionary of normative Hebrew usage. J 1995, Ma'ariv-Eitav. 815 p. 21,000 entries. -- [R]Leš 59 (1995) 259-266 (Y. *Shlesinger*, [H]; Eng, 3.Vs).

5789 **Blohm** Dieter, *Stillmann* Rachel, Modernes Hebräisch, Lehrgang für Fortgeschrittene I, 1992 → 9,9745; DM 38; Kassette DM 34: [R]Judaica 50 (1994) 161s (F. *Werner*).

5790 **Coffin** Edna A., Encounters in modern Hebrew, Level I. AA 1992, Univ. Michigan. xii-270 p. 0-472-10124-2. -- [R]BiOr 52 (1995) 101s (W.J. van *Bekkum*).

5791 **Glinert** L. The grammar of modern Hebrew 1989 → 5,9132: [R]JSSt 40 (1995) 361-9 (T. *Muraoka*).

5792 [E]**Glinert** Lewis, Hebrew in Ashkenaz; a language in exile. NY 1993, Oxford-UP. x-254 p. £ 30 [JQR 86,269, titles sans pp.]. -- [R]BSOAS 58 (1995) 355s (B. *Spolsky*).

5793 **Wexler** Paul, The schizoid nature of modern Hebrew, a Slavic language in search of a Semitic past; MeditLg 4, 1990 → 8.9424: [R]JQR 85 (1994s) 451s (H.H. *Paper*).

5794 *Baumgarten* Jean, Les études Yiddish; jalons historiques et perspectives: RÉJ 154 (1995) 247-265.

5795 **Fishman** Joshua A., Yiddish; turning to life. Amst 1991, Benjamins. xii-522 p. $ 110; pa. $ 38. -- [R]BSOAS 58 (1995) 547s (L. *Glinert*).

5796 *Fuks-Mansfeld* R., [Yiddish] De taal die niet sterven wil; Jiddisj in de joodse wereld van vroeger en thans: Ter Herkenning 22,2 (1994) 77-83 [< G(ereformeerd)TT 95 (1995) 48].

J1.3 Voces ordine alphabetico *consonantium* hebraicarum

† *aramaica* ‡ *ugaritica/phoenicia* *akkadica °*arabica*

5797 *abal*: Leš 59 (1995) 313-335 (Hana B. *Sagi*, [H]; Eng. 4,III).

5798 *adraba*: Leš 59 (1995) 337-351 (Adina *Abadi*, [H]; Eng. 4,IIIs).

5799 *Eloah*: **Schaupp** Joan P., Elohim; a search of a symbol for human fulfillment. SF 1995, Catholic Scholars. xv-122 p.

5800 *anōki*: *Revell* E.J., The two forms of first person singular pronoun in biblical Hebrew; redundancy or expressive contrast ?: JSSt 40 (1995) 199-219.

5801 *et*: *Elwolde* John, The use of *'et* in non-biblical Hebrew texts: VT 44 (1994) 170-183.

5802 *b°-*: **Jenni** Ernst, The preposition beth 1992 → 8,9435: [R]JSSt 40 (1995) 123-5 (O. *Loretz*)

5803 -- *Müller* Hans-Peter, Das Beth existentiae im Althebräischen: → 185, [F]SODEN W. von, Vom Alten Orient zum AT 1995, 361-378.

5804 *bāṭin* (Arabic `esoteric' opp, *ẓāhir* `evident'): *Smet* D. de, Au-delà de l'apparent; les notions de *ẓāhir* et *bāṭin* dans l'ésotérisme musulman: OL(ov)P 25 (1994) 197-220.

5805 *bākā'*: **Anderson** Gary A., A time to mourn, a time to dance 1991 → 7,a725: [R]JQR 86 (1995) 217-221 (V.A. *Hurowitz*).

5806 *b't* `(partly incapacitating) fright':→ 130, [F]MILGROM J., Pomegranates 1995, 777-783 (J. +*Hoftijzer*).

5807 *b'rît*: *Human* Dirk, Die begrip `berit': Nduits 35 (1994) 459-468 [< OTA 18 (1995) p. 359].

5808 -- *Rupčić*; J., Is `berît' an alliance ?: ObŽ 50 (1995) 81-90; Eng. 91: *diathēkē* rather `last (irrevocable) will'.

5809 *bārak*: *MitJudLp 9 (1995) 49-54 (T. *Arndt*) [< OTA 39, p.34].

5810 -- *Barben-Müller* Christoph, Segen und Fluch; Überlegungen zu theologisch wenig beachteten Weisen religiöser Interaktion: EvTh 55 (1995) 351-273.

5811 -- *Dawes* Stephen B., `Bless the Lord'; an invitation to affirm the living God: ET 106 (1994s) 293-6.

5812 -- *b'rākâ*: *Dahl* Nils A., Benediction and congratulation [OT/NT]; à 79, [F]HARTMAN L., Texts & Contexts 1995, 319-332.

5813 **gamertum*: göttliche Beschlussfassung [wie VON SODEN 1973, nicht 'total destruction' wie [E]LAMBERT-MILLARD] im Atram-ḥasis Epos: UF 27 (DIETRICH 60 Gb. 1995) 355-369 (K.A. *Metzler*).

5814 *gešem, al*: *Kernulmer* Brigitte (Rivka), Consistency and change in rabbinic literature as reflected in the terms Rain and Dew: JSJ 26 (1995) 55-75.

5815 DLG: *Görg* Manfred, Die basis DLG und ihre Herkunft: BN(otiz) 77 (1995) 13-16.

5816 *dam*: *Werman* Cana, [H] Consumption of the blood and its covering in the priestly and rabbinic traditions: Tarbiz 63 (1993s) 173-183; Eng. xii.

5817 *w'-*; *Gibson* J.C.L., Coordination by *vav* in biblical Hebrew [many different implications]; → 170, [F]SAWYER J., Words 1995, 272-9 [< OTA 18 (1995) p. 492 & 619].

5818 *zhr*: *Tropper* Josef, Hebräisch *zhr₂* `kundtun, warnen': ZAH(ebr) 8 (1995) 144-8.

5819 *ḥābar*: *Dirksen* Piet, What are the *m'ḥabb'rōt* in 1 Chron.22:37 ?: BN(otiz) 80 (1995) 23s: dubious that the same term can mean `connecting' small iron clamps as well as voluminous wooden beams.

5820 *ḥālaq, ābad*; *Levine* Baruch A., The semantics of loss; two exercises in biblical Hebrew lexicography: → 72, [F]GREENFIELD J., Solving 1995, 157-158.

5821 *ḥesed* : **Clark** Gordon J., ... JSOT.s 157, 1993 à 9,9766: [R]*CritRR 7 (1994) 105s (Alice L. *Laffey*).

5822 -- *Görg* Manfred, Das Nomen *ḥæsæd* -- ein Klärungsversuch: BN(otiz) 79 (1995) 10-14.

5823 -- *Routledge* Robin, *Ḥesed* as obligation; a re-examination; TynB 46 (1995) 179-196.

5824 *ḥerem* : *Suzuki* Yoshihide, A new aspect of *ḥerem* in Deuteronomy in view of an assimilation policy of King Josiah [exilic editors set aside any notion of Canaanite annihilation and took *ḥerem* to imply 'holy, eligible to live in the Promised Land': AJBI 21 (1995) 3-27.

5825 *ḥaṭṭa*: *Renz* Johannes, Terror und Erosion; ein Beitrag zur Klärung der Bedeutungs-breite der Wurzel *ḥṭṭ* : → 48, [F]DONNER H., Meilenstein: ÄAT 30 (1995) 204-224.

5826 *yad* : *Friedman* Mordechai A., [H] The `hand-writing' (*k'yad*) of the Almighty on the tablets of the Decalogue according to a new passage in the Mekhilta: → 161, [F]RUBINSTEIN E., Te'uda 9 (1995) 65-73.

5827 *yādā'*: *Trublet* Jacques, Admiration et louange dans la Bible: Christus 42,3 (`L'admi-ration' 1995) 291-9.

5828 *y'sad*: *Azar* Moshe, [H] *Kîsad* -- explanation or limitation ? →161, [F]RUBINSTEIN E., Te'uda 9 (1995) 19-32.

5829 *y'šūrūn*. *Toloni* Giancarlo, Il significato di Y'šurun nei profeti e negli agiografi; TM e versioni greche: BeO(riente) 37 (1995) 65-92; Eng. 93 [NTAb 40, p.206].

5830 *y'tôm* `fatherless' ?: VT 45 (1995) 121-4 (J. *Renkema*) on RINGGREN H., TWAT 3,1075.

5831 *k*ᵉ :   **Jenni** Ernst, Die hebräischen Präpositionen 2, 1994 → 10,9043*: ᴿ(Tü)ThQ 175 (1995) 147s (W. *Gross*).

5832 *kipper*: *a) Schwartz* Baruch J., The bearing of sin in the priestly literature; - *b) Koch* Klaus, Some considerations on the translation of *kappōret* in the Septuagint: → 130, ᶠMILGROM J., Pomegranates 1995, 3-21 / 65-75.

5833 *lᵉ'ûm*: *Malamat* Abraham, A recently discovered word for `clan' [*lîmum*] at Mari and its Hebrew cognate: → 72, ᶠGREENFIELD J., Solving 1995, 177-9.

5834 *lēb* (*libb* drittes nach *sadr, kabîd): **Seidensticker** Tilman, Altarabisch `Herz' und sein Wortfeld. Wsb 1992, Harrassowitz. ix-286 p. DM 128. -- ᴿWZKM 85 (1995) 298-301 (A.A. *Ambros*).

5835 °*lawn, ḥumrà*: SBAW.ph/h 1993/4, Beitr. Arab. 11, Mü (M. *Ullmann*) -- ᴿWZKM 85 (1995) 302s (A.A. *Ambros*).

5836 *malṣar*: Leš 59 (1995) 207-215 (H. *Mack,* ᴴ).

5837 *nāgiru*: *Sassmannshausen* Leonhard, Funktion und Stellung der Herolde (*nigir/nāgiru*) im Alten Orient: BaghM 16 (1995) 85-194.

5838 *nādab*: *Weinberg* J.P., The word *ndb* in the Bible; a study in historical semantics and biblical thought: → 72, ᶠGREENFIELD J., Solving 1995, 365-375.

5839 *niddâ*: *Greenberg* Moshe. The eytmology of *niddâ*, `(menstrual) impurity': → 72, ᶠGREENFIELD J., Solving 1995, 69-77.

5840 *neder*: *Benovitz* Moshe, ᴴ The prohibitive vow in Second Temple and Tannaitic lite-

5841 *nwḥ*: *Polak* Frank H., The restful waters of Noah [Isa 54,9]: JANES 23 (1995) 69-74.

5842 *nākâh, rapāsu*: *Fox* Nili S., Clapping hands as a gesture of anguish and anger in Mesopotamia and in Israel: JANES 23 (1995) 49-60; 2 fig.

5843 *nāśâ'* (*awen, peša', ḥaṭṭa'*), `term' or metaphor ?: Tarbiz 63 (1993s) 149-171; Eng. xi (B.J. *Schwartz*, ᴴ).

5844 *nāśâ' yad* (17 times): *Seely* David R., The raised hand of God as an oath gesture: → 59, ᶠFREEDMAN D.N., Fortunate 1995, 411-421.

5845 *nāqam*: **Peels** Hendrik G.M., The vengeance of God [De wraak, diss. 1992 - *AcTSAf 15 (1995) 27-45], ᵀ*Koopmans* W.: OTS 31. Lei 1995, Brill. xvi-321 p. ƒ135. 90-04-10164-0 [OTA 18 (1995) p. 429]. - ᴿTTh 35 (1995) 401 (P. van *Hecke*); VT 45 (1995) 143 . 404 (J.A. *Emerton*).

5846 *sûp*: *Vervenne* Marc, The lexeme *sûph* and the phrase *yam sûph*: → 110, ᶠLIPIŃSKI, E., Immigration: OLA 65 (1995) 403-429: neither 'Reed' nor 'Red'.

5847 *salal, mᵉsillâ*: *Tidwell* N.L., No highway! The outline of a semantic description of *mᵉsillâ*: VT 45 (1995) 251-269.

5848 *sārîs*: *Tadmor* Hayim, Was the biblical *sārîs* a eunuch ?: → 72, ᶠGREENFIELD J., Solving 1995, 317-325.

5849 '*Azʻazel*: *Görg* Manfred, `Asaselogen' unter sich -- eine neue Runde ? : BN(otiz) 80 (1995) 25-31.

5850 '*ēqeb*: *Abrams* Judith Z., Eikev [`consequence' > Jacob]; the consequence of God's judgment: JBQ 22 (1994) 47-50.

5851 '*itti*:   JBQ 22 (1994) 110-114 (H. *Rand*: `ad hoc').

5852 *pānîm*: *Brin* Gershon, ᴴ The expressions *lᵉpânîm, bârîšônâ et al.* as descriptions of the distant past in the Bible: → 161, ᶠRUBINSTEIN E., Te'uda 9 (1995) 7-17.

5853 *pāra'* `shave', not 'let run wild': *Goerwitz* Richard L., What does the priestly source mean by *para' et ha-ro'* [Lv 10,6 + 3 t.] ?: JQR 86 (1995) 377-394.

5854 *ṣedeq*: **Ho** J., ᴿ HebStud 36 (1995) 132 (*Mitchell*).

5855 *ṣwr*: **Olofsson** Steffan, God is my rock 1990 → 6,9279 ... 9,9784: ᴿBTB 23 (1993) 179s (R.L. *Mowery*, also on his LXX).

5856 *ṣāḥaq, ʰdahika*: **Müller** Kathrin, `Und der Kalif lachte ..'; ein Beitrag zur Phraseologie und Stilkunde des klassischen Arabisch: SBAW.ph 2. Mü 1992, Beck. 360 p. - [R]JRAS (1995) 407s (C. *Holes*).

5857 *ṣinnor* -- ein Versuch zur Wortdeutung: BiNo 76 (1995) 7-13 (M. *Görg*).

5858 *ṣāpōn*: **Wyatt** Nicholas, The significance of s³PN in West-Semitic thought: Ugarit 1993, 213-237 [239-266, *Xella*, Ugarit et les Phéniciens].

5859 *ṣrq / ḥšb / šwt*. **Puech** Émile, Note de lexicographie hébraïque qumrânienne: → 72, [F]GREENFIELD J., Solving 1995, 181-9.

5860 *ṣārāp*: **Hirth** Thomas, Überlegungen zu den Serafim: BN(otiz) 77 (1995) 17-19.

→ Q: Here should be included the words *q't - rtq* [and after them *a-t*] from *Härtling* P. *al.*, in Bibliographische Dokumentation; lexikalisches und grammatisches Material: ZAH(ebr) 8 (1995) 82-100 [149-221] (for Grammatisches → 222-245; further 300-316, Phonologie - Wortbildung - Morphologie → J82 infra).

5861 *qādēš*. **Burns** John B., *qādēš* and *qᵉdēšâ*; did they live off immoral earnings ?: ProcGM 15 (1995) 157-160.

5862 *qûm*: **Dobbs-Alsopp** F.W., Ingressive *qwm* in biblical Hebrew: ZAH(ebr) 8 (1995) 31-54.

5863 -- **Hiragi** Akeo, *hēqîm bᵉrît/dābār*: AnJap 20 (1994) 3-44.

5864 *qāṭar*. **Heger** Paul, *qṭr: nsq / šlq* ? A study of two different verbs used by Onkelos to translate the term *qṭr* of the Masoretic Text: ZAW 107 (1995) 466-481.

5865 *qārōb*. **Schweizer** Harald, Sprachkritik als Ideologiekritik; zur Grammatikrevision am Beispiel von QRB: Textw/Inf 1, 1991 → 7,9188 : BZ 39 (1995) 118s (T. *Seidl*).

5866 *rebaʿ, arbaʿîm*: **Pinker** Aron, The number 40 in the Bible : JBQ 22 (1994) 163-172.

5867 *rᵉgîʿa*, `agreement': Leš 59 (1995) 295-8 (N.M. *Bronznick*, [H] ; Eng. 4,I).

5868 *rûaḥ*: **Dreytza** [D]1969/1993: [R]HebStud 25 (1994) 130 (C. *Begg*).

5869 *rûm*: **Seidl** Theodor, *Trûma*-- die `Priesterhebe' ? Ein angeblicher Kultterminus -- syntaktisch und semantisch untersucht: BN(otiz) 79 (1995) 30-36.

5870 *rîb*: **Bovati** Pietro, Re-establishing justice [AnBib 110, à 2,7458 ... 10,2276], [T]*Smyth* M.: JOTS.s 105, 1994 → 10,9055: [R]ETRel 70 (1995) 430s (Françoise *Smyth*); OTA 18 (1995) p. 171 (C.T. *Begg*).

5871 *raq*: **Kogut** Simcha, [H] The excluding biblical *raq* -- its syntactical usages as reflected in its accentuation: Leš 59 (1995) 203-6; Eng, 3,Is.

5872 *šad*: **Schneider** Stanley, **Berke** Joseph H.. *šad*: breast, robbery [*šod* Isa 60,16] or the devil ?: JBQ 23 (1995) 86-90.

5873 *šadday* : **Lipiński** Édouard, Shadday, Shadrapha [Punic god of healing, *rp'*] et le dieu Satrape [PAUSANIAS; Aramaic and Greek inscriptions]: ZAH(ebr) 8 (1995) 247-274.

5874 *šāw*. **Reiterer** Friedrich V., Die Bedeutsamkeit von 54, Stil und Paralleltermini zur Erfassung des Inhaltes von *šāw*: → 10,13c, [F]BERNHARD H., Liebe zum Wort 1993, 173-213.

5875 *šuah* (hapax Gen 24,63): Eikasmos 6 (1995) 175-181 (P. Serra *Zanetti*).

5876 *šākab `im / et*: BetM 40,3 (142, 1995) 276-8 (A. *Ahuvia*, [H])

5877 *šᵉkînâ*: **Ernst** Hanspeter, Die Schekîna in rabbi-nischen Gleichnissen [< Diss. 1993]: JudChr 14. Bern 1994, P.Lang. 399 p. - [R]FrRu 2 (1995)276s (M. *Köferli*).

5878 *šālōm*. **Zoughbie** Anton E., Shalom in the Hebrew Bible; semantic study and theo-logical implications: diss. Golden Gate Baptist Theol. Sem., [D]*Tang* S., 1994. 228 p. 95-24523. - DissA 56 (1995s) p. 979.

5879 *šᵉmayim*: **Houtman** Cornelis. Der Himmel im AT: OTS 30, 1993 → 9,9813; 10,9069: [R]BiOr (1995) 103s (M.J. *Mulder*).

5880 *šāmaʿ*: **Arambarri** Jesús, Der Wortstamm `hören' im AT: SBB 20, 1990 → 6,9362; 7,9200: [R]EstB 53 (1995) 544-7 (A. *Torres*).

5881 *tmk*: *Heltzer* Michael. The root *tmk* in Ammonite, Phoenician and Hebrew: ZAH(ebr) 8 (1995) 140-3.

5882 *torma*: *Borger* Rykle. Hebr. *tormâ, mirmâ* und die grosse IahÇdum-Lim-Inschrift [Mari: DOSSIN 1995. 'tromperie' wie hapax Ri 9,31; aber *TUR-*mi-im* kann nicht Dossins *tur-mi-im* sein] : ZAH(ebr) 8 (1995) 293-8.

J1.5 *Phoenicia, ugaritica* -- North-West Semitic [→ T5.4]

5883 **Aartun** K., Studien zur ugaritischen Lexikographie, mit kultur- und religionsgeschichtlichen Parallelen, I. Bäume, Tiere, Gerüche, Götterepitheta, Götternamen, Verbalbegriffe 1991 → 7,9202; 9,9819: ^RJNWSL 21,1 (1995) 125s (L. M. *Muntingh*); ZDMG 144 (1994) 151s (L. *Delekat*).

5884 *a) Beyer* Klaus, The Ammonite Tell Siran bottle inscription reconsidered; -- *b) Cross* Frank M., Paleography and the date of the Tell Faḥariyeh bilingual inscription; - - *c) Lipiński* E., The inscribed marble vessels from Kition; -- *d) Naveh* Joseph, Phoenician ostraca from Tel Dor: → 72, ^FGREENFIELD J., Solving 1995, 389-391 / 393-409 / 433-441; 2 fig. / 459-464; 5 fig.

5885 *Bonnet* Corinne, Phénicien *šm* = accadien *šurinnu* ? À propos de l'inscription de Bodashtart CIS I 4; Orientalia 64 (1995) 214-222; pl. II.

5886 **Caquot** A., *al.,* Textes ougaritiques 2: LAPO 14,1989 → 5,9253 ... 8,9538: ^RBZ 38 (1994) 307s (H. *Niehr*).

5887 *Colless* Brian E, The syllabic inscriptions of Byblos, text D: Abr Nahrain 31 (1993) 7-11.

5888 **Cunchillos** J.-L., La trouvaille épigraphique de l'Ougarit 2, Bibliog. 1990 → 9,9822: ^RAbr Nahrain 31 (1993) 126 (W.G.E. *Watson*).

5889 **Cunchillos** Jesús-Luis, *Vita* Juan Pablo, Concordancia de palabras ugaríticas en morfología desplegada: Banco de datos [→ 8,9542] 2. M 1995, Cons Sup. Inv. 3 vol.

5890 *Cunchillos* Jesús-Luis, *Vita* Juan Pablo, El sello de Ilṣrp; nota filológica sobre TU 00-6.69 (RS 17.25); Sefarad 55 (1995) 389-392; Eng. 392.

5891 ^E**Dietrich** Manfried, *al.,* The cuneiform alphabetic texts from Ugarit, Ras ibn Hani and other places (KTU^{2rev}) [¹1976]: *AbhAltSyr 8. Müns 1995, Ugarit. xvi-666 p. 3-927120-24-3 [RStR 22.232. S.B. *Parker*: (short of definitive because) differs sometimes from BORDREUIL & PARDEE]. -- ^RAfO 42s (1995s) 264-274 (J. *Tropper*); UF 26 (1994) 598-600 (P. *Xella*) & 27 (DIETRICH 60. Gb. 1995) 707-8 (G. del *Olmo Lete*).

5892 *a) Ferjaoui* Ahmed, À propos de la formule *bym n'm wbym brk* dans les inscriptions néopuniques; -- *b) Vattioni* Francesco, Appunti africani: → 10,73, Mém. LE GLAY M., L'Afrique 1994, 9-12 / 34-45.

5893 **Fuentes Estañol** María Josep, Manual de gramática fenícia: Textos docents 28. Barc 1995, Univ. vii-76 p. 84-475-0990-7.

5894 *Garbini* Giovanni, Ugaritico *ġzr* 'circoncidere': → 10.31, [F]BELARDI W., Studi linguistici 1994, 483-494.

5895 **Hoftijzer** J., *Jongeling* K., *al.*, Dictionary of the North-West Semitic inscriptions: HO 1/21. Lei 1995, Brill. x-1266 p.(2 vol.) $ 343. 90-04-09821-6 [RStR 22,144, D.I. *Owen*]. -- [R]BoL (1995) 177 (M.E.J. *Richardson*): Leš 59 (1995s) 75-78 (J. *Blau*); OTA 18 (1995) p. 400 (M.S. *Smith*: massively surpasses JEAN-Hoftijzer 1960-5); RSO 69 (1995) 501-4 (G. *Garbini*).

5896 *Margalit* Baruch, Studies in NWSemitic inscriptions .. Samal; Ammon: UF 26 (1994) 271-320 / 27 (DIETRICH 60. Gb. 1995) 177-214 (215-315, K-R-T studies).

5897 *Noegel* Scott B., A Janus parallelism in the Baal and Anat story: JNWSL 21,1 (1995) 91-94.

5898 *Olmo Lete* Gregorio del, The sacrificial vocabulary at Ugarit: StEpL 12 (1995) 37-49.

5899 *Pardee* Dennis, RS 1.009 (*CTA* 36, *KTU* 1.46); reconstructing a Ugaritic ritual [DIJKSTRA M. 1984]: BSOAS 58 (1995) 229-242.

5900 *Pucciarini* Mario, Iscrizioni funerarie fenice e puniche a carattere privato [diss. 1985]: *ConvA 1 (1993) 167-177: genealogy without death date/age or regrets/hope [< OTA 19, p.33].

5901 **Pummer** R., Samaritan marriage contracts and deeds of divorce I [Firkovitch collection, St. Petersburg]. Wsb 1993. xi-380 p.; 37 pl. -- [R]AION 55 (1995) 489s (S. Noja *Noseda*).

5902 **Rin** Svi & Shifra, Acts of the gods; the Ugaritic epic poetry. Ph (^{2rev}1996), Inbal. lxxxi-881 p.; bibliog. 865-881.

5903 *Schmitz* Philip C., Prepositions with pronominal suffixes in Phoenician and Punic: → 59, [F]FREEDMAN D.N., Fortunate 1995, 400-5.

5904 *Schmitz* Philip C., *a*) A problem of Punic morphology; the third person singular feminine of the suffixing conjugation with affixed object pronoun: JSSt 40 (1995) 219-225; -- *b*) The Phoenician text from the Etruscan sanctuary at Pyrgi: JAOS 115 (1995) 559-575.

5905 *Schmitz* P.-C., The Deir`Alla plaster text; combination one, line two : OL(ov)P 25 (1994) 81-87.

5906 **Sivan** Daniel, [H] Ugaritic Grammar: EnşBL 8, 1993: [R]CBQ 57 (1995) 369-371 (S.D. *Sperling*).

5907 **Smith** Mark S., The Ugaritic Baal cycle I [KTU 1.1-1.2: VTS 55, 1994: OTA 18 (1995) p. 407], 1994 → 10,9107: [R]BoL (1995) 138 (N. *Wyatt*); UF 27 (DIETRICH 60. Gb. 1995) 726s (O. *Loretz*).

5908 *Smith* Mark S., The *qatala* form in Ugaritic narrative poetry: → 130, [F]MILGROM J., Pomegranates 1995, 789-803.

5909 *a) Smith* Mark S., The god Athtar in the Ancient Near East and his place in KTU 1.6 I; -- *b) Amadasi Guzzo* Maria Giulia, More on the Latin personal names ending with -*us* and -*ius* in Punic): → 72, [F]GREENFIELD J., Solving 1995, 627-640 / 495-504.

5910 **Tropper** Josef, Der Ugaritische Kausativstamm und die Kausativbildungen im Semitischen 1990 → 7,9229: [R]ZDMG 145 (1995) 435-7 (D. *Blohm*).

5911 *Tropper* Josef, Die phönizisch-punischen Kausativbildungen im Lichte von Präjotierung und Dejotierung im Semitischen: ZDMG 145 (1995) 28-37.

5912 *Tropper* Josef, *a*) Das letzte Zeichen des ugaritischen Alphabets [Nr 30, *s'* für samech; Lautwert '*s* vorgeschlagen]; - *b*) Die sieben Frauen des Königs Keret: UF 27 (DIETRICH 60.

Gb. 1995) 505-528 / 529-532.

5913 *Vance* Donald R., Phoenician inscriptions: BA 57 (1994) 2-19. 110-120; ill.

5914 *Vattioni* Francesco †, *a)* Il dio mauro Iocolon [nome punico; → sue p.34s, ᶠLE GLAY M. 1994 → 10.73]: SMSR 61 (1995) 423-5;-- *b)* Varia semitica IX: AION 55 (1995) 109-15.

5915 *Watson* Wilfred G.E., *a)* Comments on Ugaritic *wn*: AulaO 12 (1994) 229-232; -- *b)* Non-Semitic words in the Ugaritic lexicon: UF 27 (DIETRICH 60. Gb. 1995) 533-558.

5916 *Xella* Paolo, *a)* Lexicographie phénico-punique; le projet international Thesaurus der phönizisch-punischen Sprache: StEpL 12 (1995) 229-240; -- *b)* *P'L en Phénicien et Punique; matériaux pour le Lexique Phénicien-II: → 185, ᶠSODEN W.von, Vom Alten Orient (1995) 529-540.

J1.6 Aramaica

5917 *Aggoula* Basile, *a)* Les mots *blw* et *blwy'* dans une inscription palmyrénienne; -- *b)* Remarques sur les inscriptions hatréennes XX-XXIII: Syria 71 (1994) 415-7 / 397-414.

5918 **Arnold** Werner, Das Neuwestaramäische 3. Volkskundliche Texte aus Maʻlūla: Semitica Viva 4, 1991 → 7,9232: ᴿJAOS 115 (1995) 176 (G. *Krotkoff*); ZDMG 144 (1994) 174s (C. *Correll*).

5919 **Ballaban** Steven, The reemergence of lost Hebrew and Aramaic literature in the Middle Ages: diss. HUC, ᴰ*Wacholder* B.-Z. Cincinnati 1995. -- RStR 22,274.

5920 **Beyer** Klaus, Die aramäischen Texten vom Toten Meer .. [1984] Ergänzungsband. Gö 1994, Vandenhoeck & R. 450 p. 3-525-53599-6. -- ᴿ*CritRR 7 (1994) 393s (J.J. *Collins*); *DSD 2 (1995) 217-227 (M. *Sokoloff* with high praise and mild regret lists the 106 items as now divided between the two volumes; both volumes begin with same (?/updated) 'History of the Aramaic language', which appeared separately in J.F. *Healey*'s English in 1986); E(rbe)uA 71 (1995) 335 (B. *Schwank*); Jud(aica) 51 (1995) 110s (S. *Schreiner*);RQum 16,64 (1995) 665-7 (F. *García Martínez*); WZKM 85 (1995) 290-2 (S. *Segert*).

5921 *Beyer* Klaus, Die Aussprache des christlich-palästinischen Aramäisch; zur neuen Grammatik von Christa MÜLLER-KESSLER [1991]: JSSt 40 (1995) 241-257.

5922 *Bohas* Georges, *Ghazali* Salem, Le prétendu synharmonisme dans les parlers araméens modernes: *LOrA 5s (1995) 153-160 + 5 sonagrams.

5923 *Brugnatelli* Vermondo, The 'chickens' of Sefire: Henoch 17 (1995) 259-266; ital. 266.

5924 *Bunnens* Guy, Hittites and Aramaeans at Til Barsib; a reappraisal : → 110, ᶠLIPIŃSKI, E., Immigration: OLA 65 (1995) 19-27.

5925 *Contini* Riccardo, Epistolary evidence of address phenomena in official and biblical Aramaic: → 72, ᶠGREENFIELD J., Solving 1995, 57-67.

5926 *Cook* J.M., 4Q 246 [Aramaic 'Son of God' text]: *BuRB 5 (1995) 43-66 [NTAb 40, p.291].

5927 *Correll* Christoph, Zur Geschichte des *I*-Infixes im Neuwestaramäischen : ZDMG 143 (1993) 255-264.

5928 *Díez Merino* J., Historia [*i.e.* bibliografía] de la lexicografía aramea: AulaO 12 (1994) 211-224.

5929 *Emerton* J.A., New evidence for the use of *waw* conversive in Aramaic: VT 44 (1994) 255-8.

5930 *Eshel* E., *Kloner* A., ᴴ An Aramaic ostracon of an Edomite marriage document, Maresha 176 B.C.E.; Tarbiz 63 (1994) 485-502 [NTAb 40, p.286].

5931   *Fales* F.M., Riflessioni sull'Aḥiqar di Elefantina: OrAnt 33 (1993) 38-60 [< ZAW 107 (1995) 328].

5932   **Fassberg** Steven E., A grammar of the Palestinian Targum fragments from the Cairo Genizah: HSM 38, 1990 → 6,9397 ... 9,9843: [R]BoL (1994) 160 (M.J. *Geller*); JJS 46 (1995) 302 (Alison *Salvesen*); Orientalia 64 (1995) 146-150 (K. *Beyer*).

5933   **Fitzmyer** Joseph A., *Kaufman* Stephen A., An Aramaic bibliography, I. Old, official, and biblical Aramaic 1992 → 8,7573: [R]Greg 76 (1995) 375-7 (G.L. *Prato*); JSSt 40 (1995) 125s (J.E. *Healey*): LouvSt 20 (1995) 81s (M. *Vervenne*).

5934   **Fitzmyer** Joseph A., The Aramaic inscriptions of Sefire[2rev] [[1]1967]: BibOr 19A. R 1995, Pontificio Istituto Biblico. 251 p.; bibliog. 21-38. 88-7653-347-8.

5935   **Folmer** M.L., The Aramaic language in the Achaemenid period; a study in linguistic variation: OLA 68. Lv 1995, Peeters. xviii-849 p.; bibliog. 801-824. 90-6831-740-7.

5936   *Fox* Samuel E., The relationships of the eastern Neo-Aramaic dialects: JAOS 14 (1994) 154-162.

5937   **Frank** Yitzhak, Grammar for Gemara; an introduction to Babylonian Aramaic[2rev]. J 1995, Ariel. [viii-] 143 p. 0-87306-612-X.

5938   **Garbini** Giovanni. Aramaica [Eng., franç., ital. reprints]: SS 10. R 1993, Univ. 230 p.; ill. [RStR 22,56, D.I. *Owen*].

5939   **García Martínez** Florentino, Qumran and apocalyptic; [7 1980-7] studies on the Aramaic texts from Qumran: STDJ 9, 1992 → 10,9738: [R]DSD 2 (1995) 235-8 (G.W.E. *Nickelsburg*: working from such fragmentary materials risks continuing to misconstrue as 'apocalyptic' texts bearing no relation to 'revelation').

5940   *Gianto* Agustinus, A new edition of Aramaic texts from Egypt [PORTEN B., YARDENI A. 1993] (Ahiqar, Bar Punesh, Bisitun, accounts and lists): Biblica 76 (1995) 85-92.

5941   **Healey** John F., The Nabataean tomb inscriptions of Mad'in Salih [Hijaz]: JSS.s 1. Ox 1993, UP. xiv-298 p.; 19 fig.; 13 + 35 pl; 3 maps + A summary 55 p. -- [R]BASOR 299s (1995) 130-2 (D.F. *Graf*); BoL (1995) 27 (M.J. *Geller*).

5942   *Hillers* Delbert R., Palmyrene Aramaic inscriptions and the Old Testament, especially Amos 2:8: ZAH(ebr) 8 (1995) 55-62.

5943   **Hug** Volker, Altaramäische Grammatik der Texte des 7. und 6. Jh.v.Chr. [< Diss. 1990, [D]*Beyer* K.]: HEIDSAO 4. Heid 1993, Orientverlag. xiv-162 p. DM 128. -- [R]JAOS 115 (1995) 125s (S.A. *Kaufman*).

5944   *Jastrow* Otto, Der neuaramäische Dialekt von Hertevin 1988 → 4,a369 ... 10,9120: [R]BoL (1995) 177 (M.J. *Geller*); JSSt 38 (1993) 295-308 (G. *Goldenberg*).

5945   *Jastrow* Otto, Die 'Sprache Jesu' lebt; in drei syrischen Dörfern wird Aramäisch gesprochen; HLL 125,1 (1993) 8-11.

   Kaufman S., *Sokoloff* M., Concordance to Neofiti ... to complete Palestinian / Aramaic text of the Torah 1993 → 2544 supra.

5946   *Klingbeil* Gerald A., The Aramaic ostracon from Lachish; a new reading and interpretation: A(ndr)USS 33 (1995) 77-84; 1 fig.: called illegible by O. TUFNELL 1953; from a reading '20 donkeys .. barley 10 qabs' concludes to economic and administrative activity more important than had been admitted for the Ezra period.

5947   **Kottsieper** Ingo, Die Sprache der Aḥiqar-Sprüche: BZAW 194, 1990 → 6,3563; 7.2991; AfO 42s (1995s) 278s (M. *Jursa*).

5948   *Kottsieper* Ingo, Das aramäische Wörterbuch [als Band 9 geplant] im Rahmen des ThWAT: ZAH(ebr) 8 (1995) 80s.

5949   *Lacerenza* Giancarlo, I sela' di Areta; a proposito del lessico monetario nabateo:

AION 55 (1995) 353-7; 1 pl

5950 *Lehmann* Reinhard G., Vom Hebraicum zum Aramaicum; Uüberlegungen zur Didaktik des Biblisch-Aramäischen im Kontext des Reichsaramäischen: BN(otiz) 77 (1995) 41-58.

5951 *Lemaire* André, The Xanthos trilingual [Greek, Lycian; here chiefly Aramaic] revisited: → 72, ᶠGREENFIELD J., Solving 1995, 423-432.

5952 *Lemaire* André, Les inscriptions araméennes anciennes de Teima: → 728, Présence 1993/5, 59-72.

5953 *Leonhard* Clemens, Die literarische Struktur der Bilingue von Tell Fakhariyeh: WZKM 85 (1995) 157-179.

5954 **Lindenberger** James M., [70] Ancient Aramaic and Hebrew letters, ᴱ*Richards* Kent H.: SBL Writings 4. Atlanta 1994, Scholars. xv-155 p. $ 45; sb./ pa. $ 30. 1-55540-839-7; -40-0 [BArR 21,1 (1995) 8; RStR 22,144, M.A. *Sweeney*]. -- ᴿOTA 18 (1995) p. 403 (J. *Kaltner*).

5955 **Lipiński** Edward, Studies in Aramaic inscriptions and onomastics: OLA 57. Lv 1994, Peeters / Univ. 90-6831-510-9.

5956 **Moriya** Akio, Aramaic epistolography: the Hermopolis letters and related material in the Persian period: diss. Hebrew Union College -- Jewish Institute of Religion, ᴰ*Kaufman* S. Cincinnati 1995. 407 p. 95-19177. -- DissA 56 (1995s) p. 530; RStR 22,272.

5957 *Müller* Hans-Peter, Die aramäische Inschrift von Tel Dan: ZAH(ebr) 8 (1995) 121-139.

5958 **Müller-Kessler** Christa, Grammatik des Christlich-Palästinisch-Aramäischen 1991 → 9,9857 [NTAb 40,p.285]; ᴿArTGran 57 (1994) 523-6 (A. *Torres*): BSOAS 58 (1995) 434 (S.E. *Brock*); JSSt 40 (1995) 241-257 (K. *Beyer*); Syria 72 (1995) 275-8 (Ursula *Schattner-Rieser*).

5959 *Müller-Kessler* Christa, Eine aramäische Zauberschale im Museum für Vor- und Frühgeschichte zu Berlin: Orientalia 63 (1994) 5-9.

5960 **Mutius** Hans-Georg von, Jüdische Urkundenformulare aus Marseille in babylonisch-aramäischer Sprache: JudUm 50. Fra 1994, Lang. 98 p. -- ᴿRÉJ 154 (1995) 186s (J. *Shatzmiller*).

5961 *Naudé* J.A., The verbless clause with pleonastic pronoun in biblical Aramaic: J/TydSem 6 (1994) 74-93 [< OTA 19, p.208].

5962 **Naveh** Joseph, *Shaked* Shaul, Magic spells and formulae; Aramaic incantations of late antiquity 1993 → 9,9860; 10,9129: ᴿJAOS 115 (1995) 525s (M.E. *Stone*); JRAS (1995) 262-4 (S. *Brock*); Muséon 108 (1995) 193s (J.-M. *Auwers*).

5963 *Naveh* Joseph, The inscriptions from Failaka and the lapidary Aramaic script: BASOR 297 (1995) 1-4; 1 fig. [NTAb 40, p.478].

5964 *Naveh* Joseph, ᴴ [(5+) 7] Aramaic tombstones from Zoar: Tarbiz 64 (1994s) 477-497; 12 fig.; 12 pl.; Eng. 4,v.

5965 **Negev** A., Personal names in the Nabataean realm: Qedem 32, 1991 → 8,9551: ᴿPEQ 127 (1995) 79s (E.A. *Knauf*).

5966 *Piersimoni* Palmira, *a)* New Palmyrene inscriptions; onomastics and prsospography: AION 54 (1994) 298-316; -- *b)* Who's who at Palmyra; an overview [< Venice 1989 M.A., Arabs and Aramaeans at Palmyra; & awaited Ph.D. The Palmyrene prosopography]: OL(ov)P 25 (1994) 89-98.

5967 **Porten** Bezalel, *Yardeni* Ada, Textbook of Aramaic documents from ancient Egypt [1. Letters 1986 → 2,7529 ; 2. Contracts 1989 → 7,9248] 3. Literature, accounts, lists: new copies, Heb./Eng.ᵀ, 1993 → 9,9866; 10,9131: ᴿCBQ 57 (1995) 361-3 (D.R. *Hillers*: Ahiqar and other values for exegetes); JAOS 115 (1995) 710s (J.A. *Fitzmyer*); OL(ov)P 25 (1994)

61-68 (E. *Lipiński*).

5968 *Porten* Bezalel, *Szubin* H.Z., An Aramaic joint venture agreement (a new interpretation of the Bauer-Meissner papyrus): → 10.443, Grund/Boden im Altägypten 1990/4, 65-95.

5969 **Qimron** Elisha, [H] Biblical Aramaic: EnṣM Library 10, 1993 → 10.9868: [R]CBQ 57 (1995) 158s (E.M. *Cook*, unfavoring).

5970 *Sabar* Yona, The Christian neo-Aramaic dialects of Zakho and Dihok; two text samples: JAOS 115 (1995) 33-51.

5971 *Sasson* Victor, The Old Aramaic inscription from Tell Dan; philological, literary, and historical Aspects: JSSt 40 (1995) 11-30. → 5957 supra; b095-b109 infra.

5972 **Schiffman** Lawrence H., *Swartz* Michael D., Hebrew and Aramaic incantation texts from the Cairo Genizah 1992 → 9,9868*; 10,9134: [R]AfO 42s (1995s) 322s (C. *Müller-Kessler*) *A(sn)JS 19 (1994) 411-4 & 20 (1995) 199-202 (S.M. *Wasserstrom*).

5973 *Segert* Stanislav, Ägypten und Biblisch-Aramäisch: → 48, [F]DONNER, H., Meilenstein: ÄAT 30 (1995) 252-8.

5974 *Segert* Stanislav, *a)* Bileam, der Sohn Beors [from Aramaic]: ZAH(ebr) 8 (1995) 71-77; -- *b)* Recent editions of Imperial Aramaic texts: ArOr 63 (1995) 217-232.

5975 **Shinan** Avigdor, The biblical story as reflected in its Aramaic translations. TA 1993, Meuchad. 191 p.

5976 *Sperling* S. David, [Babylonian/Palestinian] Aramaic spousal misunderstandings: JAOS 115 (1995) 205-9.

5977 **Stefanovic** Zdravko, The Aramaic of Daniel in the light of Old Aramaic: JSOT.s 129, 1992 → 9,9870: [R]JETS 38 (1995) 469s (*Jongtae Choi*); *TBR 8,1 (1995) 17s (A. *Warren*).

5978 *Tal* Abraham, [H] Concerning the formation of nouns in Samaritan Aramaic; the pattern qtwl: → 161, [F]RUBINSTEIN E., Te'uda 9 (1995) 93-105.

5979 **Tropper** Josef, Die Inschriften von Zincirli .. phön./aramäisch 1993 → 9,9833: 10,911o; [R]AfO 42s (1995s) 277s (J. *Naveh*); Orientalia 64 (1995) 140-4 (A. *Gianto*).

5980 *Tsereteli* K., Grammatica generale dell'aramaico, [T]*Noseda* Sergio N.: *Henoch 17,1s (1995) 3-101 [NTAb 40, p.285].

5981 *Vittmann* Günther, Ägyptisch-Aramäische Kleinigkeiten [aram. *wprt:* äg. Stele KAI 267 mit aram. Inschrift (phot.)]: WZKM 83 (1993) 233-246.

5982 *Willis* John T., The newly discovered fragmentary Aramaic inscription from Tel Dan: RestQ 37 (1995) 219-226. → T4.6.

5983 *Yamada* Shigeo, Aram-Israel relations as reflected in the Aramaic inscription from Tel Dan: UF 27 (DIETRICH 60. Gb. 1995) 611-625.

5984 *Zuckerman* Bruce, On being 'damned certain' [i.e. sans evidence]; the story of a curse in the Sefire inscription and its interpretation: → 59, [F]FREEDMAN D.N., Fortunate 1995, 422-435; 3 fig.

J1.7 Syriaca

5985 *Altheim-Stiehl* Ruth, Zu einem Datum [617s] der frühchristlichen Geschichte; → 96, [F]KRAUSE M., Divitiae Aegypti 1995, 1-8.

5986 *Brock* Sebasian P., Notulae syriacae; some miscellaneous identifications: Muséon 108 (1995) 69-78.

5987 *Brock* Sebastian P., Two Syriac papyrus fragments from the Schøyen collection: OrChr 79 (1995) 9-17: facsimiles.

5988 *Desreumaux* A., Un manuscrit syriaque de Téhéran contenant des apocryphes: *Apocrypha 5 (1994) 137-164 [NTAb 40,p.121].

5989 **Forkel** Fritz, Die heutige traditionelle Aussprache des klassischen Westsyrisch bei den syrisch-orthodoxen Christen in Tur 'Abdin und in Syrien. Bad Homburg 1995. 45 p.

5990 **González Nuñez** Jacinto, La leyenda del rey Abgar y Jesús; orígenes del cristianismo en Edesa; Enseñanza del apóstol Addai, texto siríaco[TE]: Apócrifos cristianos 1. M 1995, Ciudad Nueva. 236 pp.; bibliog.203-7. 84-86987-86-5.

5991 **Kiraz** George A., Lexical tools to the Syriac New Testament: JSOT Manualss 7. Shf 1994, JSOT. v-137 p. £ 25.

5992 *Harrak* Amir, Notes on Syriac inscriptions, I. The inscription of Ma'ar-zaytā (Syria); Orientalia 64 (1995) 110-9. 2 fig.; pl. I.

5993 *Healey* John F., Lexical loans in early Syriac; a comparison with Nabataean Aramaic: StEpL 12 (1995) 75-84.

5994 *Nouro* Abrohom, Terminologie syriaque; les néologismes: *LOrA 4 (1993) 191-7.

5995 *Perrier* Pierre, *Qnoma* et *Shelia;* deux thèmes-clés de. la spiritualité de l'Église syriaque: Ist(ina) 40 (1995) 182-190.

5996 **Ritter** Hellmut †1971, [E]*Sellheim* Rudolf, Tūrōyo, die Volkssprache der syrischen Christen des Tūr ' Abdīn, C.: Univ. Fra Geistesw. 6. Stu 1990. 810 p. DM 150. -- [R]WZKM 85 (1995) 338-343 (O. *Jastrow*).

5997 **Selb** Walter, Sententiae syriacae 1990 → 7,9265: [R]JRAS (1994) 255 (S.P. *Brock*); JSSt 39 (1994) 300-2 (also S. *Brock*).

5998 *Tubach* Jürgen, Syr. Haudā = Diadem oder Tiara ? : Syria 72 (1995) 381-5.

5999 *Watt* John, Grammar, rhetoric, and the enkyklios paideia in Syriac: ZDMG 143 (1993) 45-71.

J2.1 **Akkadica** (sumerica)

6000 *Alster* Bendt, The Sumerian love song SRT 31: → 469, StIranMesopAnat 1 (Praha 1994) 1-11.

6001 **Attinger** Pascal, Éléments de linguistique sumérienne; la construction de ... 'dire': OBO.s, 1993 → 9,9886; 10,9145: [R]AfO 42s (1995s) 214-7 (J.A. *Black*).

6002 **CAD** 17 'Š' [l. 1989 *ša - šapūlu* > 65-758 ... 10,9146: [R]Orientalia 63 (1994) 111-120] -- 2. *šakālu - šilūtu* 1992, xxviii-452 p.; DM 187. -- 3. *šimāgu - šuzuta* 1992, published 1994, xxiv-420 p.; DM 179. 0-918986-79-6. -- [R]ZA(ssyr) 85 (1995) 302-6 (D.O. *Edzard*).

6003 **Cifola** Barbara, Analysis of variants in the Assyrian royal titulary from the origins to Tiglath-Pileser III: StAsiat minor 47. N 1995, Ist.Univ.Or. xvi-221 p.

6004 **De Odorico** Marco, The use of numbers and quantifications in the Assyrian royal inscriptions: SAA.s 3. Helsinki 1995, Univ. xxxi-206 p.; bibliog. xvi-xxxi. 951-45-7125-8.

6005 **De Vito** Robert A., Studies in third millennium Sumerian and Akkadian personal names; the designation and conception of the personal God: StPohl 16,1993 → 9,9890: [R]BoL (1995) 127 (D.J. *Wiseman*).

6006 *Edel* Elmar, *a) allu,* eine keilschriftliche Umschreibung in den Assurbanipal-Annalen für ägyptisches *inr,* 'Kopftuch mit Uräus': BiNo 76 (1995) 5s (14s, Eponymen); -- *b)* Neues zum ägyptisch-akkadischen Keilschriftvokabular Ashmolean Museum 1921.1145:

BiMo 71 (1994) 53-64.

6007 **Englund** Robert K., *Nissen* Hans J., Die lexikalischen Listen der archaischen Texte aus Uruk: ADFGUW 13, 1993 → 9,9891: [R]AfO 42s (1995s) 211-4 (P. *Steinkeller*); BiOr 52 (1995) 433-440 (N. *Veldhuis*).

6008 *Ferrara* A.J., Topoi and stock-strophes in Sumerian literary tradition; some observations: JNES 54 (1995) 81-117; 1 fig.

6009 **Foster** Benjamin R., Before the Muses; an anthology of Akkadian literature 1993 → 9,9892: [R]BiOr 52 (1995) 83-87 (Stephanie *Dalley-Page*).

6010 **Foster** Benjamin R., From distant days; myths, tales, and poetry of ancient Mesopotamia [= [2]Before the Muses, abridged]. Bethesda 1995, CDL. vii-438 p. $ 20. 1-883053-09-9 [RStR 22,149, D.I.*Owen*; OTA 18, p.625].

6011 *a) Galter* Hannes D., Cuneiform bilingual royal inscriptions: -- *b) Porter* Barbara N., Language, audience and impact in imperial Assyria: IOS 15 (1995) 25-50 / 51-72; 1 fig.

6012 *Gianto* Agustinus, Amarna lexicography; the glosses in the Byblos letters: StEpL 12 (1995) 65-73.

6013 *Götzelt* Thomas, Zur sumerischen und akkadischen Verwandtschaftsterminologie: → 23, [F]BOEHMER R.M., Beiträge 1995, 177-182.

6014 **Gong** Yushu, Studien zur Bildung und Entwicklung der Keilschriftzeichen [Diss. München 1991]: Antiquitates 7. Ha 1993, Kovac. iii-154 p. 3-86064-144-1 [OIAc 11 (1995) 24].

6015 **Hayes** John L., A manual of Sumerian grammar and texts 1990 → 8,9615 ... 10,9150: [R]RA 88 (1994) 180s (D. *Charpin*: 'manuel', aussi p.192; 'sa méthode me laisse sceptique').

6016 *Heimpel* W., Towards an understanding of the term *sikkum* [equids' equipment or stopover for royal messengers]: RA 88 (1994) 5-31: map.

6017 **Hess** Richard S., Amarna personal names 1993 → 9,14392; 10,12732: [R]BoL (1995) 175 (W.G. *Lambert*).

6018 *a) Hirsch* Hans, [*lā balṭāta*] Leben oder nicht leben; -- *b) Knudsen* Ebbe E., The Ashmolean Museum incantation in Greek orthography [since SOLLBERGER E. 1962]; -- *c) Voigt* Rainer, Akkadisch *šumma* 'wenn' und die Konditionalpartikeln des Westsemitischen: → 185, [F]SODEN W.von, Vom Alten Orient (1995) 99-104 / 135-140 / 517-528.

6019 **Hübner** Barbara. Inim Kiengi; deutsch-sumerisches Glossar, l. A-G; 1993; viii-455 p.→ 9,9896. -- 2. H-R, p. 457-879. Marktredwitz 1994, Reizammer.

6020 **Izre'el** Shlomo, Amurru Akkadian [Amarna letters] 1991 → 9,9897: [R]BoL (1995) 177 (W.G. *Lambert*: masterly).

6021 **Jacobsen** Thorkild, The harp .. Sumerian poetry in translation 1987 → 3,9580; 10.9151*: [R]JNES 54 (1995) 148-150 (B. *Alster*).

6022 *Kaplan* G.Kh., [R] The use of the perfect in the Akkadian language: VDI 213 (1995) 136-146; Eng. 146.

6023 *Kaswalder* Pietro A., Due tavolette cuneiformi ritrovate a Hazor e decifrate: *TSa 71,1 (1995) 38-43 (44, il David-Orfeo di Gaza).

6024 **Kienast** B., *Sommerfeld* W., Glossar zu den altakkadischen Königsinchriften: FAOS 8. Stu 1994, Steiner. ix-406 p. DM 116. 3-515-04249-0 [RStR 22,57, D.I. *Owen:* to accompany GELB-KIENAST 1990].

6025 **Kienast** Burkhart, *Volk* Konrad, Die sumerischen und akkadischen Briefe des III. Jahrtausends aus der Zeit der III. Dynastie von Ur (SAB): FAOS 19. Stu 1995, Steiner. xxiii-295 p. 3-515-06546-6.

6026 *Kogan* L.E., [R] On irregular reflexes of proto-Semitic laryngeals in Akkadian: VDI 213

(1995) 156-162; Eng. 162.

6027 a) *Krebernik* Manfred, M. WEINFELDs Deuteronomiumkommentar aus assyriologischer Sicht; -- b) *Levinson* Bernard M., The text-critical and Neo-Assyrian evidence for MT Dt 13:10; -- c) *Steymans* Hans-Ulrich, Eine assyrische Vorlage für Dt 38,20-24: → 490, Bundesdokument 1995, 27-36 / 37-63 / 119-141.

6028 *Krecher* Joachim, Die *marû*-Formen des sumerischen Verbums: → 185, ᶠSODEN W.von, Vom Alten Orient (1995) 141-200.

6029 *Lambert* W.G., The language of ARET V 6 and 7: → 8,e731, ᴱ**Fronzaroli** P.,Literature 1992, 41-62

6030 *Lambert* W.G., Some new Babylonian wisdom literature: → 55, ᶠEMERTON J., Wisdom 1995, 30-42.

6031 **Leick** Gwendolyn, Sex and eroticism in Mesopotamian literature. L 1994, Routledge. xvi-320 p.; bibliog. 299-310. 0-415-06534-8. -- ᴿAntiquity 69 (1995) 632s (T. *Taylor*); BoL (1995) 132 (M.J. *Geller*: a serious treatment of cuneiform myths and songs).

6032 **Longman** Tremperᴵᴵᴵ, Fictional Akkadian autobiography 1991 > 7,9284: 8,9621*: ᴿOrientalia 64 (1995) 138-140 (D.O. *Edzard*).

6033 **Malbran-Labat** Florence, La version akkadienne de l'inscription trilingue de Darius à Behistun: Documenta Asiana 1. R 1994, Gruppo Internaz. 174 p. 88-8011-034-9.

6034 *Mayer* Werner R., Zum Terminativ-Adverbiales im Akkadischen; die Modaladverben auf -*iš*; Orientalia 64 (1995) 151-186.

6035 **Molina** Manuel, Tablillas administrativas neosumerias de la Abadía de Montserrat (Barcelona): Coptas Cuneiformes: Materiali per il vocabolario neosumerico 18. R 1993, Bonsignori. 43 p.

6036 *Paul* Shalom M., Euphemistically 'speaking' [= sex] and a covetous eye: HAR 14 (1994) 193-204 [< OTA 19,39].

6037 *Römer* Willem H.P., Die Sumerologie; Versuch einer Einführung in den Forschungsstand nebst einer Bibliographie im Auswahl: AOAT 238 / Nimwegener Sumerologische Studien 2. Kevelaer 1994, Butzon & B. ix-208 p. 3-7666-9931-8.

6038 **Saporetti** Claudio, Arad mitanguranni; dialogo fra schiavo e padrone nell'antica Mesopotamia². Pisa 1995, Univ. viii-253 p.

6039 **Saporetti** Claudio, Nergal ed Ereškigal; una storia d'amore e di morte. Pisa 1995, Univ. vii-141 p.

6040 a) *Sigrist* Marcel, Some d i - t i l - l a tablets in the British Museum; -- b) *Paul* Shalom M., The 'plural of ecstasy' in Mesopotamian and biblical love poetry: → 72, ᶠGREENFIELD J., Solving 1995, 609-618 / 585-597.

6041 *Silva* Aldina da, L'élément E *(bît/bayit)* dans les anthroponymes du Proche-Orient ancien; l'apport des noms théophores; → 10,30.ᶠCOUTURIER G., Maison 1994, 17-30.

6042 **Sjöberg** Åke W., Sumerian dictionary A/1, 1992 > 10,9162: ᴿJAOS 115 (1995) 293-7 (J. *Bauer*); ZA(ssyr) 85 (1995) 127-141 (P. *Attinger*).

6043 **Soden** Wolfram von, The ancient Orient; an introduction to the study of the Ancient Near East [Einführung 1985 → 1,9116], ᵀ*Schley* Donald G. → 10,9163: GR/Leominster 1994, Eerdmans/Gracewing. xx-262 p. $ 15. 0-8028-0142-0 / 0-85244-252-1. -- ᴿBArR 21,3 (1995) 6 (R.S. *Hendel*); JAOS 115 (1995) 531-3 (J. *Cooper*); *TBR 8,2 (1995s) 64 (A. *Warren*)

6044 **Soden** Wolfram von, Grundriss der akkadischen Grammatik³ʳᵉᵛ: AnOr 33. R 1995, Pontificio Istituto Biblico. xxxi-328 + 55 p. $ 60. 88-7653-258-7. -- ᴿWZKM 85 (1995) 396s (M. *Jursa*).

6045 **Soden** Wolfram von, Introduzione all'orientalistica antica 1989 → 5,9857 ... 9,9908: [R]Athenaeum 82 (1994) 239-242 (M. *Giorgieri*).

6046 **Soldt** W.H. van, Letters in the British Museum, transliterated and translated, 1-2: ABBU 12. Lei 1990/4, Brill. v-155 p.; x-163 p. *f* 62 / 85. 90-04-09208-0; -948-4. -- [R]BoL (1995) 139 (M.E.J. *Richardson*).

6047 *a) Soldt* Wilfred H. van, The Akkadian of Ugarit: lexicographical aspects: -- *b) Watson* Wilfred G.E., Ugaritic lexical studies in perspective: StEpL 12 (1995) 205-215 / 217-228.

6048 *a) Stol* Marten, Old Babylonian corvée (*tupšikkum*); -- *b) Veenhof* Klaas R., Old Assyrian *isurtum*, Akkadian *esērum* and Hittite GIŠ.HUR ['sketch, drawing', in some relation to the much more frequent *tuppum*, 'clay tablet']: → 84, [F]HOUWINK TEN CATE, H., Studio (1995) 293-308 + pl. 35 / 311-332.

6049 **Streck** Michael P., Zahl und Zeit; Grammatik der Numeralia und des Verbalsystems im Spätbabylonischen: CunMg 5. Groningen 1995, Styx. xxix-293 p.; Bibliog. 259-269. 90-72371-85-2.

6050 *Streck* Michael P., *ittašab ibakki*, 'weinend setzte er sich'; *iparras* für die Vergangenheit in der akkadischen Epik; Orientalia 64 (1995) 33-91.

6051 *Tinney* Steve, On the poetry for King Išme-Dagan [LUDWIG Marie-Christine 1990]: OLZ 90 (1995) 5-26.

6052 **Tournay** Raymond-J., *Shafter* Aaron, L'Épopée de Gilgamesh: LAPO 15, 1994 > 10,9189: [R]ETRel 70 (1995) 265s (Françoise *Smyth*).

6053 *Tropper* Josef, Akkadisch *nuhhutu* und die Repräsentation des Phonems /h/ im Akkadischen: ZA(ssyr) 85 (1995) 58-66.

6054 *Vanstiphout* H.L.J., *Veldhuis* N., *Tuppi ilāni* [= 'liver' =] *takālta* .. [to LAMBERT W.G., JCS 21 (1967) 126-139]: AION 55 (1995) 30-32.

6055 *Wilhelm* Gernot, *a) Bit papāhi* in Nuzi; *b)* (with others) Nuzi joins, etc.: → 51, PORADA, E., mem., [E]**Owen** David L., StNuzi 7 (1995) 129-155 . 37-55.

6056 *Wu Yuhong*, The treaty between Shadlash (Sumu-Numhim) and Neribtum (Hammi-Dushur [Greengus no. 326]: *JAncCiv 9 (1994) 124-136.

6057 **Yoshikawa** Mamoru, Studies in the Sumerian verbal system [reprints]: AcSum.s 1. Tokyo 1993, Middle E. Center. iv-374 p. [OIAc 11 (1995) 46].

6058 *Zewi* Tamar, Subject-predicate word order of nominal clauses in El-Amarna letters: UF 27 (DIETRICH 60. Gb. 1995) 657-693.

J2.7 Arabica

6059 **Abu-Haidar** Farida, Christian Arabic of Baghdad: Semitica Viva 7. Wsb 1991, Harrassowitz. xi-203 p. DM 78. -- [R]BSOAS 58 (1995) 140s (C. *Holes*); OLZ 89 (1994) 164-6 (H.R. *Singer*: sequel to her [D]1979).

6060 *Ambros* Arne A., Eine Konkordanz zum Spätwerk (Post-Sayfiyāt) von al-Mutanabbī: WZKM 85 (1995) 9-29.

6061 *a) Atallah* Nabil, Inscriptions inédites du Hawran (Raodat al-Roye'y); -- *b) Khraysheh* Fawwaz H., New Safaitic inscriptions from Jordan [Rwayšid]: Syria 72 (1995) 387-399; 11 fig. (map) / 401-4; 4 fig.

6062 *Baalbaki* Ramzi, Reclassification in Arab grammatical theory: JNES 54 (1995) 1-14.

6063 *Bar-Asher* Meir M., *Kopsky* Aryeh, An early Nusayri theological dialogue on the relation between the *ma'nā* and the *ism*: Muséon 108 (1995) 169-172; Arabic text 173-180.

6064 **Behnstedt** Peter, Der arabische Dialekt von Soukhne (Syrien): Semitica viva 15. Wsb 1994, Harrassowitz. xvii-423 + xxii-406 p. DM 396. 3-447-03486-6: -8-2. -- ᴿWZKM 85 (1995) 317-321 (S. *Procházka*: un des parlers sédentaires les plus aberrants que CANTINEAU connaisse).

6065 **Bohas** Georges, *Guillaume* Jean-Patrick. Études des théories des grammairiens arabes, I. Morphologie et phonologie. Damas 1984, IFAD. xviii-502 p. -- ᴿBiOr 52 (1995) 850-3 (Nadia *Anghelescu*, 'dix ans après').

6066 *Brett* Michael, The way of the nomad [IBN KHALDUN]: BSOAS 58 (1995) 251-269.

6067 *Brinner* William M., Some problems in the Arabic transmission of biblical names: → 72, ᶠGREENFIELD J., Solving 1995,19-27.

6068 **Cadora** F.J., Bedouin, village, and urban Arabic; an ecolinguistic study: SStLL 18. Lei 1992, Brill. xv-168 p. *f* 80. -- ᴿBSOAS 58 (1995) 142-4 (C. *Holes*); OLZ 90 (1995) 188-191 (W. *Diem*).

6069 **Cannon** Garland, (*Kaye* Alan S.), The Arabic contribution to the English language; an historical dictionary. Wsb 1994, Harrassowitz. xi-345 p. DM 98. -- ᴿWZKM 85 (1995) 296-8 (A.A. *Ambros*).

6070 *Chmiel* J., ᴾ Les études arabes et l'exégèse biblique d'aujourd'hui: → 727, LEWICKI T. mem. 1993/4, 57-63.

6071 **Durand** Olivier, Introduzione ai dialetti arabi: Sussidi Didattici 1. Mi 1995, Centro Studi Camito-Semitici. ix-165 p. Lᵐ 24. -- ᴿWZKM 85 (1995) 321-3 (S. *Procházka*).

6072 ᴱ**Eid** Mushira, *al.*, Perspectives on Arabic linguistics [1s. 1989s → 8,686; 5, 1993 → 9,543] 3s, 1989/90 / 1990/2: ᴿJAOS 114 (1994) 107-9 (K. *Versteegh*).

6073 *Gelder* G.J.van, Pointed and well-rounded; Arabic encomiastic and elegiac epigrams [numerous, though there is no Arabic word for 'epigram']: OL(ov)P 26 (1995) 101-140.

6074 **Gramlich** Richard, Die Nahrung der Herzen, ABŪ ṬĀLIB AL-MAKKĪS .. I/1-3: FrIslamSt 15. Stu 1992, Steiner. 556 p. DM 228. -- ᴿOrientalia 64 (1995) 373-5 (G. *Bowering*).

6075 [**Grohmann** Adolf, I. Praha 1954], II. ᴱ**Khoury** Raif G., Chrestomathie de papyrologie arabe: HO 1e/2, 1993 > 9,9921*: ᴿJRAS (1994) 87-92 (G.R. *Smith:* plenty of improvements for the 'massive forward step' also of KHAN G.1992).

6076 **Gruendler** Beatrice, The development of the Arabic scripts 1993 > 9,9922; 10,9177: ᴿJAOS 115 (1995) 487s (J.A. *Bellamy*); JSSt 40 (1995) 176-9 (J.F. *Healey* & G. R. *Smith*).

6077 **Hameen-Anttila** Jaakko M., Lexical *Ibdal*, part I, introduction, source studies, with a reconstruction of ABU TURAB's *K. al-I'tiqab'*: diss. Helsingin Yliopisto (Finland). 1994. 245 p. 951-9300-20-5 (No AA photocopy.) -- D(iss)AI-C 56 (1995s) p. 20.

6078 **Hary** Benjamin H., Multiglossia in Judeo-Arabic .. Purim scroll [< diss. Berkeley 1987, ᴰ*Brinner* W.]; ÉJM 14, 1992 → 9,9923*; 10,9178: *A(sn)JS 20 (1995) 216-9 (A.S. *Kaye*, defending his 1972 Diglossia; 'Arabic colloquial dialects are all native tongues, whereas Modern Standard Arabic is not anyone's native tongue').

6079 **Humbert** Geneviève. Les voies de transmission du Kitab de Sībawayhi [DERENBOURG H. c.1899]: SStLL 20. Lei 1995, Brill. xvi-374 p.; XIX pl. 90-04-09918-2.

6080 **Hunwick** John O., Arabic literature of Africa, 2. The writings of Central Sudan; HO 13/2. Lei 1995, Brill. xxvi-732 p. 90-04-10494-1.

6081 **Jastrow** Otto, Der arabische Dialekt der Juden von 'Agra und Arbil. 1990. -- ᴿOLZ 89 (1994) 66 (H.-R. *Singer*).

6082 **Jongeling** K., North African names from Latin sources: Publ. 21. Leiden 1994, Research School CNWS. xxxviii-216 p. 90-73782-25-2.

6083 **Kaplan** Robert D., The Arabists; the romance of an American elite 1993 → 9,9926:

[R]AmHR 100 (1995) 261s (J.F. *Goode*).

6084 **Kharusi** Nafilah S., The linguistic analysis of Arabic loan-words in Swahili: diss. Georgetown, [D]*Sara* S.I. Wsh 1995. 380 p. 95-26151. -- DissA 56 (1995s) p. 1338.

6085 **Langhade** Jacques, Du Coran à la philosophie; la langue arabe et la formation du vocabulaire philosophique de FARABI: PIFD 149. Damas 1994, Inst. Français. 430 p.; bibliog. 399-415. 2-901315-16-X.

6086 **Mitchell** T.F., Pronouncing Arabic, 2., 1993 → 9,9929; £ 37.50. -- [R]BSOAS 58 (1995) 360s (Y. *Suleiman*).

6087 **Mitchell** Terence F., *Hassan* S.A. al-, Modality, mood and aspect in spoken Arabic, with special reference to Egypt and the Levant: Arabic LingMg 11. L 1994, Kegan Paul. 0-7103-0406-6.

6088 **Nebes** Norbert, Die Konstruktionen mit /fa-/ im Altsüdarabischen; syntaktische und epigraphische Untersuchungen: Mainz-VOK 40. Wsb 1995, Harrassowitz. 302 p. 3-447-03576-5.

6089 **Paajanen** Timo, Scribal treatment of the literary and vernacular proverbs of AL-MUSTAṬRAF in 15th-17th century manuscripts, with special reference to diglossic variation: StOr 77. Helsinki 1995, Finnish Oriental Soc. 250 p.; bibliog, 234-245.

6090 **Procházka** Stephan, Die Präpositionen in den neuarabischen Dialekten [Diss. Wien 238]. W 1993, *vwGO. ix-312 p.; 4 pl. Sch 383. -- [R]OLZ 90 (1995) 58-65 (M. *Woidich*).

6091 *a) Procházka* Stephan, Semantische Funktionen der reduplizierten Wurzeln im Arabischen; -- *b) Borg* Alexander, *Kressel* Gideon M., Personal names, surnames and nicknames among the 'Azazmeh bedouin in the Negev highlands; anthropological and linguistic aspects: ArOr 63 (1995) 39-70 / 478-487.

6092 *Saguer* Abderrahim, A propos des formes dites rares en arabe: LOrA 5s (1995) 21-52.

6093 **Schregle** Götz, (*Rizk* Sayed M.), Arabisch-deutsches Wörterbuch, II/1s. Stu 1992. -- [R]JSSt 39 (1994) 402-4 (A. *Shivtiel*: more overloaded with combinations than unrivalled rival WEHR).

6094 *Snir* Reuven, The inscription of 'En 'Abdat, an early evolutionary stage of ancient Arabic poetry: Abr Nahrain 31 (1993) 110-125.

6095 **Sowayan** Saad A., The Arabian oral historical narrative: Semitica viva 6. Wsb 1992, Harrassowitz. xii-323 p. DM 88. -- [R]OLZ 89 (1994) 293-6 (H. *Fahndrick*).

6096 *Snir* Reuven, Asseverative *la*- in Arabic and related Semitic particles: diss. [D]*Gragg* G. Chicago 1995. 294 p. 95-23533. -- DissA 56 (1995s) p. 913.

6097 **Thackston** Wheeler M., An introduction to Koranic and classical Arabic; an elementary grammar of the language. Bethesda 1994, Iranbooks. xxv-327 p. $ 30. 0-936347-40-6. -- [R]JRAS (1995) 405-7 (O. *Wright*); WZKM 85 (1995) 301s (A.A. *Ambros*).

6098 **Ullmann** Manfred, Wörterbuch der klassischen arabischen Sprache 2/1s, L bis laka. Wsb 1983, 1991, Harrassowitz. xii-673 + xviii, 675-1267 + dritter Band noch. -- [R]ZDMG 145 (1995) 157s (H.R. *Singer*: Lam already has three times as much as for Kaf in the current dictionaries (BELOT 39 p., WAHRMUND 63, WEHR 57; for Lam less ! 38, 57, 46).

6099 **Urvoy** Marie-Thérèse, Le Psautier mozarabe de HAFI le Goth: Textes. Toulouse 1994, Mirail. xxii-236 p. (226 doubles). -- [R]BLE 96 (1995) 227s (R. *Dagorn*); RThom 95 (1995) 701s (J. *Jomier*).

6100 [E]**Versteegh** Kees, *Carter* Michael G., Studies in the history of Arabic grammar [Kolloquium Nijmegen Univ., 23 art.]: *StHistLangSc 56. Amst/Ph 1990, Benjamins. 322 p. -- [R]ZDMG 145 (1995) 158-160 (D. *Blohm*).

6101 **Wilmsen** David W., The word play's the thing: educated spoken Arabic in a theatrical

community in Cairo: diss. Michigan, ᴾ*McCarus* E. AA 1995. 297 p. 96-10267. -- DissA
56 (1995s) p. 4754.

6102 **Mifsud** Manwel. Loan verbs in Maltese; a descriptive and comparative study: StSLL
21. Lei 1995, Brill. xvii-339 p. 90-04-10091-1.

₃ **Aegyptia**

6103 *Beckerath* Jürgen von, *Hpr / hpr(w) / hpr(w)w* in den Königsnamen des Neuen
Reiches nach griechischer Überlieferung; → 96, ᶠKRAUSE M., Divitiae Aegypti 1995, 15-18.
6104 *Bolshakov* Andrey O., *mw.t.f n(j).t d̲.t.f* --'his own mother': GöMiszÄg 141 (1994) 39-42.
6105 **Borghouts** J.F., Egyptisch; een inleiding in taal en schrift van het Middenrijk, I.
Grammatica en syntaxis. Lei/Lv 1993, Ex Oriente Lux / Peeters. x-366 p. 90-72690-07-9
[*OIAc 11 (1995) 15].
6106 *Borla* Matilde, Alcuni aspetti dell'autobiografia di Ineni: StEgPun 14 (1995) 13-30 +
1 fig.
6107 **Bradshaw** Joseph, Imperishable stars .. Pyramid texts 1990 → 8,9686: ᴿBiOr 52
(1995) 576-8 (P. De *Smet*).
6108 **Buchberger** Hannes, [*heper*] Transformation und Transformat; Supertextstudien 1:
ÄgAbh 52. Wsb 1993, Harrassowitz. xviii-708 p. DM 148. 3-447-03078-X. -- ᴿBiOr 52
(1995) 578-581 (P. *Derchain*).
6109 *Buongarzone* Roberto, La *rw(y).t* e il *rw(i).t*: EVO 18 (1995) 45-63.
6110 *Crevatin* Franco, Questioni di lingua e cultura egiziana: Aeg 75 (1995) 3-15.
6111 *Depuydt* Leo, *a)* On a late Egyptian and demotic idiom: -- *b)* Condition and premise
in Egyptian: RdÉ 45 (1994) 49-72: franç. 72s / 46 (1995) 81-88.
6112 *Depuydt* Leo, On the empirical distinctness of certain adverbial clauses in Old and
Middle Egyptian: CÉg 70 (1995) 18-33.
6113 *Depuydt* Leo, Sentence pattern and verb form; Egyptian grammar since POLOTSKY:
Muséon 108 (1995) 39-48.
6114   *Depuydt* Leo, [Jean-François] CHAMPOLLION's ideogram and SAUSSURE's *signe
linguistique*; Orientalia 64 (1995) 1-11.
6115 *a) Depuydt* L., On the stative ending *tj.tj.t* in Middle Egyptian; -- *b) Coenen* M.,
Books of breathings [tending to replace the Book of the Dead at Thebes]; more than a
terminological question ? -- *c) Depauw* M., A demotic business letter (O.Brux. E 354):
OL(ov)P 26 (1995) 21-26 / 27-38 / 39-49; 4 fig.
6116 *Derchain-Urtel* Maria-Theresia, Das *snd̲*-Zeichen und seine Verwendung in griechisch-
romischer Zeit: → 10,145, ᶠWINTER E., Aspekte 1994, 77-80.
6117 *Devauchelle* Didier, Le [conte hiératique av. XIII Dynastie] Paysan déraciné: CÉg 70
(1995) 34-40.
6118 *Dochniak* Craig C. A note on Shipwrecked Sailor 135-38: GöMiszÄg 142 (1994) 69-71
6119 *Dodson* Aidan. Amenmesse in Kent, Liverpool, and Thebes: JEA 81 (1995) 115-128;
7 fig.
6120 **Doret** Eric, The narrative verbal system of Old and Middle Egyptian: COr 12, 1986
→ 2,7603: ᴿOL(ov)P 25 (1994) 278-280 (L. *Pantalacci*).
6121 *a) Eyre* Christopher J., Word order hierarchies and word order change in the history of
Egyptian; -- *b) Foster* John L., Thought couplets and the standard theory; a brief overview;
-- *c) Sweeney* Deborah. Idiolects in the Late Ramesside letters: → 713, LAe 4 (1994) 117-

138 / 139-163 / 275-324.

6122 **Farid** Adel, Die demotischen Inschriften der Strategen. San Antonio 1992, Van Siclen. v-82 p., 31 fig.; vol. of 20 pl. 0-933175-334-5 [OIAc 11,22].

6123 *Felber* Hans, Demotischer Literaturübersicht XXII: Enchoria 22 (1995) 182-217.

6124 *Ferrari* Daniela, L'occhio w*d̲3t* nel mondo punico; importazione ed imitazione: StEgPun 14 (1995) 53-62.

6125 *Fischer-Elfert* Hans-W., *a)* Vermischtes III [.. iii. Härfnerlied]: GöMiszÄg 143 (1994) 41-49; -- *b)* P.demot. Rylands 50: Enchoria 22 (1995) 1-15; 1 pl.

6126 **Foster** John L., Thought couplets in the tale of Sinuhe: MüÄgU 3. Fra 1993, Lang. v-128 p. 3-631-40005-8. -- [R]JA(m)RCE(g) 32 (1995) 271-3 (E.S. *Meltzer*).

6127 [T]**Foster** John L, Hymns, prayers, and songs; anthology of ancient Egyptian lyric poetry: SBL Writings 8. Atlanta 1995, Scholars. xvii-211 p. $ 50; pa. $ 30. 9-7885-0157-7; -8-5 [< OTA 19, p.126].

6128 *Fox* Michael V., World order and *ma'at*; a crooked parallel: JANES 23 (1995) 37-45.

6129 *Goebs* Katja, Untersuchungen zu Funktionen und Symbolgehalt des *nms* [tägliche Wiedergeburt der Sonne]: ZÄS 122 (1995) 155-183.

6130 *Goedicke* Hans, The teaching of Amenemope, chapter XX (20,20 -- 21,20): RdÉ 46 (1995) 99-106; franç. 106.

6131 *Görg* Manfred, Zu einem semitischen Personennamen [*mngbt*] in der Erzählung des Wenamun: BiNo 74 (1994) 24-26.

6132 **Goldwasser** Orly, From icon to metaphor; studies in the semiotics of the hieroglyphs: OBO 142. Gö 1995, Vandenhoeck. x-185 p.; bibliog. 159-174. 3-7278-1015-7.

6133 *Goldwasser* Orly, On the conception of the poetic form -- a love letter to a departed wife, Ostracon Louvre 698: IOS 15 (1995) 191-205.

6134 *a) Graefe* Erhart, Zur Struktur der Thronnamen der ägyptischen Könige und zur Lesung des Thronnamens der Königin Hatschepsut; -- *b) Shisha-Halevy* Ariel, Some reflections on the Eguptian conjunctive: → 96, [F]KRAUSE M., Divitiae Aegypti 1995, 119-127 / 300-314.

6135 **Hannig** Rainer, Grosses Handwörterbuch Ägyptisch-Deutsch: die Sprache der Pharaonen (2800-950 v.Chr.): KuGaW 64. Mainz 1995, von Zabern. lix-1414 p.; 20 maps. 3-8053-1771-9.

6136 *Hannig* Rainer, Die erste Parabel des 'Lebensmüden' (LM 68-80): *JAncCiv 6 (Changchun 1991) 23-31.

6137 *a) Heerma van Voss* Matthieu, Eine dunkle mythische Episode im Totenbuch: -- *b) Hollis* Susan T., Anubis's mortuary functions in The tale of two brothers: → 191, [F]STRICKER, B., Hermes: DISCEg.sp.2 (1995) 69-722 / 87-99 + 4 fig.

6138 **Helck** Wolfgang, Die 'Admonitions' Pap. Leiden I 344 recto: KÄT 11. Wsb 1995, Harrassowitz. viii-79 p. 3-447-03439-4.

6139 **Helck** Wolfgang, Historisch-biographische Texte der 2. Zwischenzeit und neue Texte der 18. Dynastie, Nachträge: KÄT 6/2. Wsb 1995, Harrassowitz. x-72 p. 3-447-03440-8.

6140 *a) Hoch* James E., The teaching of Dua-Kheti; a new look at the Satire of the trades. -- *b) Ali* Mahrous A., Ushabtis of priestess *3w t ḥ'w* Tentamun from Tell el-Maskhuta: *(J)SStEg 21s (1991s) 88-100 / 41-43 [< OTA 19,p.7.22].

6141 **Hoch** James E., [595] Semitic words in Egyptian texts of the New Kingdom and Third Intermediate Period [diss. Toronto 1991 → 8,9702] 1994 → 10,9205; $ 65 [RStR 22,144, D.I. *Owen*]. -- [R]CBQ 57 (1995) 770s (C.H. *Gordon*: high praise; 10 mild proposals).

6142 **Hornung** Erik, Idea into image; essays on ancient Egyptian thought [Geist der

Pharaonenzeit 1989 minus three chapters], [T]. NY 1992, Tinken. 210 p., 36 fig. -- [R]*JSStEg
21s (1991s) 102 (Carolyn *Routledge*).

6143 **Hornung** Erik, Gesänge vom Nil; Dichtung am Hofe der Pharaonen [= [2]Meisterwerke
1978 verdoppelt]. Z 1990, Artemis. 204 p. DM 42. 3-7608-1040-3. -- [R]BiOr 52 (1995)
318-321 (Irene *Shirun-Grumach*).

6144 *Hussein* Mahmoud I., Notes on some hieroglyphic signs [*s3*, bolt not quiver; *nd̠*, not
thread-winder or porridge-stirrer but cross-shaped field-measuring pole].: DiscEg 30 (1994)
47-54; 4 fig.

6145 *Iversen* E., *Sd̠m.f* and *sd̠mn.f* and the Egyptian conception of time: DiscEg 31 (1995)
69-79.

6146 *Jackson* Howard M., 'The shadow of Pharaoh, your lord, falls upon you'; once again
Wenamun 2,46: JNES 54 (1995) 273-286

6147 *Jansen-Winkeln* Karl, a) Der Schreiber Butehamun; -- b) Finalsatz und Subjunktiv:
GöMiszÄg 139 (1994) 35-40 / 146 (1995) 37-60.

6148 *Jansen-Winkeln* Karl, Diglossie und Zweisprachigkeit im alten Ägypten: WZKM 85
(1995) 85-115.

6149 a) *Jansen-Winkeln* Karl, Exozentrische Komposita als Relativphrasen im älteren Ägyp-
tisch .. *nfr ḥr* 'mit schönem Gesicht'; -- b) *Kaplony-Heckel* Ursula, Demotische Verwal-
tungsakten aus Gebelein; der grosse Berliner Papyrus 13608: ZÄS 121 (1994) 51-75 /75-91.

6150 **Jürgens** Peter, Grundlinien einer Überlieferungsgeschichte der altägyptischen Sargtexte;
Stemmata und Archetypen der Spruchgruppen 30-32 + 33-37, 75(-83), 162 + 164, 225 +
226 und 343 * 345: GOF 4/31. Wsb 1995, Harrassowitz. xiii-480 p.; Bibliog. 465-480.
3-447-03696-6.

6151 **Kahl** Jochem, *al.*, Die Inschriften der 3. Dynastie: eine Bestandsaufnahme: ÄA 56.
Wsb 1995, Harrassowitz. vii-262 p. 3-447-03733-4.

6152 a) *Kammerzell* Frank, Zur Etymologie des ägyptischen Zahlworts '4'; -- b) *Allen*
James P., Colloquial Middle Egyptian; some observations on the language of Heka-Nakht;
-- c) *Loprieno* Antonio, As a summary; new tendencies in Egyptological languistics: → 713,
LAe 4 (1994) 165-189 / 1-12 / 369-382.

6153 *Kitchen* Kenneth A., Sinuhe's foreign friends, and Papyri (Coptic) Greenhill 1-4: →
10,118, [F]SHORE A.F., The unbroken reed 1994, 161-9.

6154 [E]**Klengel** Horst, *Sundermann* Werner, Ägypten .. Probleme der Edition 1987/91 →
7,619: [R]WO 24 (1993) 146s (J.P. *Laut*).

6155 **Koch** Roland, Die Erzählung des Sinuhe: BAeg 17, 1990 > 6,9534; 8,9710: [R]JEA 81
(1995) 255 (R.B. *Parkinson*).

6156 *Kügler* Joachim, Propaganda oder performativer Sprechakt ? Zur Pragmatik von
Demotischer Chronik und Töpferorakel: GöMiszÄg 142 (1994) 83-92.

6157 [E]**Kurth** Dieter, Edfu; Studien zu Vokabular, Ikonographie und Grammatik: Inschr. Edfu,Begleitheft 4. Wsb 1994, Harrassowitz. viii-102 p.;ill.--[R]OLZ 90 (1995) 152-4 (J. *Hallof*).

6158 **Loprieno** Antonio, Ancient Egyptian; a linguistic introduction. C 1995, Univ. xv-322
p.; bibliog. 279-292. 0-521-44849-2.

6159 a) *Loprieno* Antonio, Zu einigen Phänomenen ägyptischer Phonologie; -- b) *Fehlig*
Albrecht, Die ägyptischen Hieroglyphen und ihr Informationsgehalt -- eine quantitative
Betrachtung: → 10,137*, [F]WESTENDORF W. 1994, 115-131 / 27-39.

6160 **Lüddeckens** Erich, Ägyptische Handschriften 4 [1. 1971]: VOHD 19. Stu 1994, Steiner.
255p.; ill. 3-515-02975-3.

6161 **Luft** Ulrich, Das Archiv von Illahun: Hieratische Papyri. B 1992, Akademie. vi-94

p. DM 248. 3-05-001854-2. -- ᴿBiOr 52 (1995) 323-7 (W.K. *Simpson*).

6162 **MacDowell** A.G., Hieratic ostraca 1993 → 9.9973; ᴿOrientalia 64 (1995) 356s (Renate *Müller-Wollermann* gives a concordance to ČERNY and/or KITCHEN, where all but one of these Glasgow items were already published).

6163 *Meltzer* Edmund S., *a)* A note on the employment of the dedication formula *ir.n.f m mnw.f* for non-royal individuals; -- *b)* An observation on nominal sentences with *n*-demonstratives in classical Egyptian: *JAncCiv 9 (1994) 95-98 / 10 (1995) 83s.

6164 *Morenz* Ludwig, Gottes Unmittelbarkeit und ein skandalöses Suffixpronomen -- zum 13. Kapitel des Schiffbrüchigen: GöMiszÄg 141 (1994) 77-80.

6165 **Murnane** William J., Texts from the Amarna period in Egypt: SBL.Writings 5. At 1995, Scholars. xix-289 p.; bibliog. 264-277. 1-55540-965-2.

6166 *Naguib* Saphinaz-Amal, Interpreting abstract concepts; towards an attempt to classify the ancient Egyptian notion of person: *DiscEg 29 (1994) 99-124; 2 fig.

6167 *Ndigi* Oum, L'expression des cardinaux et des ordinaux en Égyptien et en Basaa: *DiscEg 33 (1995) 57-72.

6168 **Obenga** Théophile, Origine commune de l'égyptien ancien, du copte et des langues négro-africaines modernes; introduction à la linguistique historique africaine. P 1993, L'Harmattan. 402 p. 2-7384-1347-1 [OIAc 11.35].

6169 *Patané* Massimo, A propos de quelques valeurs du perfectif: DiscEg 30 (1994) 143-6.

6170 **Pestman** P.W., Il processo di Hermias e altri documenti dell'archivio dei Choachiti: catalogo 6. T 1992, Museo egizio. xxx-280 p.; 62 pl. Lᵐ 60. 3-87490-563-2. -- ᴿBiOr 52 (1995) 69-73 (M. *Chauveau*).

6171 *a) Peust* C., Möglichkeiten einer Rekonstruktion ägyptischer Vortonvokale aus dem Befund der koptischen Dialekte; -- *b) Reintges* Chris, Verbal tenses in older Egyptian -- a Reichenbachian approach; GöMisz 149 (1995) 67-82 / 83-97

6172 *a) Plas* Dirk van der, Wörterbuch und Textcorpus; Bemerkungen, Vorschläge und Angebote; -- *b) Schenkel* Wolfgang, Das Tübinger Konkordanz-Programm: ZÄS 121 (194) 132-142 / 142-144(-159).

6173 **Polotsky** H.J.,Ausgewählte Briefe 1992 → 8,291a: ᴿJSSt 38 (1993) 327-330 (P. *Frankl*).

6174 *Quack* Joachim F.,Notes en marge du papyrus Vandier:RdÉ 46 (1995) 163-170;Eng. 170.

6175 *Ray* J.D., Egyptian wisdom literature; → 55, ᶠEMERTON J., Wisdom 1995, 17-29.

6176 *Reintges* C.H., A mentalist view on Egyptian grammar [SCHENKEL W. 1991]: BiOr 52 (1995) 525-544.

6177 **Renaud** Odette, Le dialogue du Désespéré avec son âme, une interprétation littéraire: SocÉg Cah 1. Genève 1991, Challande. 74 p. Fs 36. -- ᴿJNES 54 (1995) 305s (J.L. *Foster*); WO 26 (1995) 184-6 (J.F. *Quack*).

6178 **Ritter** Thomas, Das Verbalsystem der königlichen und privaten Inschriften, XVIII. Dynastie bis einschliesslich Amenophis III: GOF 4/30. Wsb 1995, Harrassowitz. 389 p.; Bibliog. 359-368. 3-447-03600-1.

6179 *a) Ritter* Thomas, On cleft sentences in Late Egyptian; -- *b) Neveu* François, Vraie et pseudo Cleft Sentences en Néo-Égyptien; -- *c) Cassonet* Patricia, Modalités énonciatives et temps second en Néo-Égyptien: → 713, LAe 4 (1994) 245-269 / 191-212 / 35-56.

6180 **Roccati** Alessandro, Sapientia egizia; la letteratura educativa in Egitto durante il II millennio a.C.: *TVOA 1/4: ᴿAnton 70 (1995) 688 (M. *Nobile*).

6181 *Roeder* H., 'Mit dem Auge des Horus' [Sinnhorizonte: ... ; weisse Krone]: GöMisz 138 (1994) 37-69.

6182 *Rydström* Kjell T., _Hry sst3_, 'in charge of secrets'; the 3000-year evolution of a title:

*DiscEg 28 (1994) 53-94.

6183 *Satzinger* Helmut, 'Emphase' oder die Rhematisierung eines adverbialen Komplements im Ägyptischen [JUNE F. 1989; DEPUYDT L. 1991]: WZKM 83 (1993) 189-206.

6184 **Schenkel** Wolfgang, Einführung in die altägyptische Sprachwissenschaft 1990 → 8,9731 [1994: Tübinger Einführung in die klassisch-ägyptische Sprache und Schrift, 351 p.]: ᴿBiOr 52 (1995) 307-316 (J. *Winand*).

6185 *Schenkel* Wolfgang, Zur Formenbildung des Verbs im Neuägyptischen [WINAND J. 1992]: Orien(talia) 63 (1994) 11-15.

6186 **Schneider** Thomas, Asiatische Personennamen in ägyptischen Quellen des Neuen Reiches: OBO 114, 1992 → 8,9734; 10,9228: ᴿBiOr 52 (1995) 317s (K.A. *Kitchen*).

6187 **Shupak** Nili, Where can wisdom be found ? The sage's language in the Bible and in ancient Egyptian literature: OBO 130,1993 → 9.3334; 10,3229: ᴿCBQ 57 (1995) 160-2 (Carolyn R. *Higginbotham*: very useful); IEJ 45 (1995) 303s (Miriam *Lichtheim*).

6188 *Smith* H.S., Sunt lacrimae rerum [three short demotic letters c, 300 B.C.]: → 10,118, ᶠSHORE A.F., The unbroken reed 1994, 281-293.

6189 *Takács* Gábor, *a*) The Afrasian origin of Egyptian new 'gold'; AAH 36 (1995) 1-3; *b*) Egyptian *m3ṯ*, 'to think out': ArOr 63 (1995) 159-161.

6190 *Thirion* Michelle, Notes d'onomastique; contribution à une révision du RANKE PN (neuvième/dixième série): RdÉ 45 (1994) 175-188 / 46 (1995) 171-186.

6191 *Tobin* Vincent A., The secret of Sinuhe: JA(m)RCE(g) 32 (1995) 161-178.

6192 **Verhoeven** Ursula, Das saitische Totenbuch der Iachtesnacht: PapTA 41. Bonn 1993, Habelt. ix-318 p.; v-191 p.; iv-32 pl. 3-7749-2564-X. -- ᴿEnchoria 22 (1995) 229-238 (H. van *Voss*).

6193 **Vleeming** S.P., The gooseherds of Hou [13 documents studied together for the first time] 1991 → 10,9232: ᴿBiOr 52 (1995) 353s (M. *Smith*: good).

6194 **Vycichl** Werner, La vocalisation de la langue égyptienne 1990 → 6.9556; 10,9233: ᴿBiOr 52 (1995) 317s (L. *Depuydt*).

6195 **Watterson** Barbara, Introducing Egyptian hieroglyphs². E 1993, Scottish Academic. xi-152 p. 0-7073-0738-4 [*OIAc 11,44].

6196 **Wilson** Hilary, Understanding hieroglyphs; a quick and simple guide. L 1993, O'Mara. 192 p.; ill. 1-85479-164-8 [*OIAc 11,45].

6197 *Winand* Jean, *a*) La grammaire au secours de la datation des textes: RdÉ 46 (1995) 187-202; -- *b*) Derechef *Ounamon* 2,13-14; GöMisz 139 (1994) 95-108.

6198 **Zauzich** Karl-Theodor, Papyri [13535-15695] von der Insel Elephantine: Demotische Papyri 3. B 1993, Akademie. ix + brief descriptions of each, then all plates at end.

6199 **Browne** Gerald M., Introduction to Old Nubian 1989 > 5,9462; 7,9380; ᴿOrientalia 64 (1995) 156-8 (H. *Satzinger*).

6200 **Browne** Gerald M., (1 with *Plumley* J. Martin), Old Nubian texts from Qaşr Ibrim, 1-3, 1988s → 5,9463 ... 10,9236: ᴿBiOr 52 (1995) 421-3 (H. *Satzinger*); *JSStEg 21s (1991s) 181s (P.L. *Shinnie*).

J3.4 Coptica

6201 **Brunsch** W., Kleine Chrestomathie nichtliterarischer koptischer Texte 1987 > 3,9709 ... 7,9384: ᴿWZKM 83 (1993)259-261 (S. *Pernigotti*).

6202 **Depuydt** Leo, Catalogue of Coptic manuscripts in the [NY] Pierpont Morgan Library

[→ 9,10011; diss. Yale, ᴰ*Layton* B.]: Corpus of illuminated manuscripts 4s. Lv 1993, Peeters. cxvii-709 p. + Album, xxxix-468 (color.) pl. Fb 3600 each. -- ᴿOLZ 90 (1995) 154-162 (H.-M. *Schenke:* some misplacements in the Plates).

6203 **Elanskaya** Alla I., The literary Coptic manuscripts in the A.S. Pushkin State Fine Arts Museum in Moscow: VigChr.s 18 → 10,9240; Lei 1994, Brill. vii-527 p.; 192 pl. -- ᴿMuséon 108 (1995) 425s (L. *Depuydt*); Orientalia 64 (1995) 368-373 (H. *Quecke*).

6204 *Ernst* Ralf, NP-Koordination im Koptischen und Neu-Ägyptischen: → 713, LAe 4 (1994) 89-115.

6205 **Hasitzka** Monika R.M., Neue Texte .. zum Koptisch-Unterricht 1990 → 7,9389*: ᴿBASP 30 (1993) 7678 (G. *Wilfong*); JNES 54 (1995) 306-8 (D. *Monserrat*).

6206 ᴱ**Hasitzka** Monika R.M., Koptisches Sammelbuch I, 1993 → 9,10017; 10,9243: ᴿBiOr 52 (1995) 668-674 (W. *Brunsch*: Lob, Bemerkungen).

6207 *Kasser* Rodolphe, Les sonantes portant l'accent tonique et les sonantes entièrement atones en usage ou non-usage dans l'orthographie spécifique des langues et (sub)dialectes coptes; → 96, ᶠKRAUSE M., Divitiae Aegypti 1995, 181-199; 2 fig.

6208 *Kasser* Rodolphe, *a)* Le *tfê* punisseur des Kellia (Basse-Égypte et langue bohaïrique; -- *b)* La conjonction de coordination copulative *awō* en langue copte saïdique; proclitique ?; -- *c)* L'Histoire de l'âme (ou Exégèse de l'âme. NH II,6) en langue copte saïdique; passage controversé (132,27-35) soumis à un nouvel examen; GöMisz 139 (1994) 43-51 / 144 (1995) 51-62 / 147 (1995) 71-78.

6209 *Kasser* Rodolphe, *a)* Ef'*sōtm* ou *ef'sōtp* de l'apodose; nouveaux exemples en dialecte copte *P* (dit 'Paléo-Thébain'); *b)* Ma n st ho, apostrophé ou anach*ō̱*rēsis, 'lieu de refuge, de retraite' en langue copte saïdique [sur PEZIN R., Mélanges COQUIN R. 1994,10]: DiscEg 30 (1994) 65-72 / 32 (1995) 63-66.

6210 *MacCoull* L.S.B., *a)* The Bawit [Apa Apollo monastery] contracts [833-839 A.D.]; texts and translations: BASP 31 (1994) 141-158; pl. 36-53; -- *b)* Further notes on interrelated Greek and Coptic documents of the sixth and seventh centuries: CÉg 70 (1995) 341-353.

6211 *Mirecki* Paul, The Coptic wizard's hoard [4-7 c., at Michigan Univ. since 1921; preview of his critical edition]: HThR 87 (1994) 435-460.

6212 *Nessim Youssef* Youhanna, Quelques titres des congrégations des moines coptes: GöMiszÄg 139 (1994) 61-67.

6213 *Proverbio* D.V., Coptica Aquilana; di un codice copto-arabo del convento di S. Giuliano: SeEgPun 11 (1992) 47-59

6214 *Schenkel* Wolfgang, Die Lexikographie des altägyptisch-koptischen: StEpL 12 (1995) 191-203.

6215 *Tov* Emanuel, Letters of the 'Cryptic A script' [PFANN S., JQR 85 (1994) 203-235] and paleo-Hebrew letters used as scribal marks in some Qumran scrolls: DSD 2 (1995) 330-7; table indicating (paleo-) Hebrew equivalent, p. 338s.

6216 *a) Vliet* Jacques van der, Spätantikes Heidentum in Ägypten im Spiegel der koptischen Literatur; -- *b) Nauerth* Claudia, Mythologische Themen in der koptischen Kunst -- neue Bestandsaufnahme 1991/92: → 732, Begegnung 1991/3, 99-138 / 67-98.

J3.8 **Aethiopica**

6217 **Bernand** E., *al.*, Recueil des inscriptions de l'Éthiopie des périodes pré-axoumites et axoumites 1991 → 7,9400* ... 10,9251: ᴿRSÉt 37 (1993) 187-197 (L. *Ricci*).

6218 *Denais* Michel, Alternances vocaliques en Tigrigna: *LOrA 5s (1995) 193-209.

6219 **Ellero** G., Antropologia e storia dell'Etiopia [scritti sparsi], [E]*Luzini* Gianfranco. Udine 1995, Campanotto. xxi-146 p.; XV fig. -- RSEt 37 (1993 !) 198s (L. *Ricci*).

6220 *Halefom* Girma, Head movement triggered by weak functional heads [in Amharic]: LOrA 4 (1993) 125-138.

6221 **Kane** Thomas L., Amharic-English dictionary, I *ha-no*, II *ña-pa* 1990 → 8,9764*: [R]RSEt 36 (1992) 161-4 (L. *Ricci*, cominciando con lunga analisi ammirante di tre computer-stampati 'supplementi' di nuovo materiale già forniti dall'autore, ma concludendo che la traslitterazione con [e] capovolta 'trasforma ogni entità rappresentata in una forma metafisica, inarticolabile').

6222 **Kapeliuk** Olga, Syntax of the noun in Amharic: ÄthF 37. Wsb 1994, Harrassowitz. 129 p. -- [R]WZKM 85 (1995) 327 (Renate *Richter*).

6223 *Lamberti* Marcello, Some phonetic laws of the Gonga languages [West-Cushite akin to provincial Ethiopian Yemsa, Ometo ..]: RSEt 36 (1992) 57-76 / 37 (1993) 89-114.

6224 *Ricci* Lanfranco, XII congresso internazionale di studi etiopici (5-10 settembre 1994) [East Lansing MI]; RSEt 36 (1992 !) 135-141.

6225 *Richter* Renate, Einige Aspekte der modernen Lexikentwicklung im Amharischen: WXKM 83 (1993) 167-187.

6226 *Rose* Sharon, Ethio-Semitic inflectional affix oder; a phonological solution: *LOrA 5s (1995) 259-291.

6227 **Uhlig** Siegbert, Äthiopische Paläographie 1988 → 4,a550 ... 7,9408; Eng. (introd.) 1990 → 9,10038: [R]WZKM 83 (1993) 332-5 (U. *Pietruschka*).

J4 Anatolica

6228 *a) Archi* Alfonso, 'Pensavano' gli Ittiti ? ; -- *b) Polvani* Anna Maria, Contributo alla lessicografia ittita: StEpL 12 (1995) 13-18 / 149-158.

6229 *Archi* Alfonso, The 'Kleine Schriften' of Annelies KAMMENHUBER (→ 6236 infra; a way to Anatolian studies; Orientalia 64(1995) 460-4

6230 *Bernabé* Alberto, *Rodríguez Somolinos* Helena, Hittite *munnai-*, grec *munámenos, múnē, amúnō*: Glotta 71 (1993) 121-9.

6231 *a) Carruba* Onofrio, Der Stamm für 'Frau' im Hethitischen; -- *b) Puhvel* Jaan, Ash and soap in Hittite; -- *c) Hout* Theo P.J. van den, Hethitisch *ḫadduli-* 'gesund'; -- *d) Neu* Erich, Zur mittelhethitischen Sprachform der hurritisch-hethitischen Bilingue aus Hattuša: → 94, Mem. KLÍMA O., Iranian 1994, 13-25 / 215-8 / 109-114 / 189-202.

6232 a) *Chen Xu*, Hittite *ker/kart-* 'heart'; functional and ritual aspects; -- *b) Bayun* Lilia, Remarks on Hittite 'traditional literature' (cannibals in Northern Syria): *JAncCiv 10 (Changchun 1995) 33-40 / 21-32.

6233 **Güterbock** Hans G., *Hoffner* Harry A., The Hittite Dictionary of the Oriental Institute of the University of Chicago [vol. 1, L-N] vol.2, the letter P, fasc. 1 *pa-para*. Ch 1994, Univ. xvi-112 p. -- [R]OLZ 90 (1995) 514-7 (V. *Haas*).

6234 *Hamp* Eric P., Hittite *meju-, miju-* '4': → 469, StIranMesopAnat 1 (Praha 1994) 61s.

6235 *a) Hoffner* Harry A.[J], The stem of the Hittite word for 'house': -- *b) Güterbock* Hans G., The Hittite word for 'woman' again: -- *c) Ofitsch* Michael, Zu den anlautenden Laryngalen im Hethitischen; -- *d) Neu* Erich, Zu einem vermutlichen Impersonale des Hethitischen: HSF 108 (1995) 192-4 / 12-15 / 16-29 / 6-11.

6236 **Kammenhuber** Annelies, Kleine Schriften [→ 6229 supra] zum Altanatolischen und

Indogermanischen, 1. 1955-68; 2. 1969-90. Heid 1993, Winter. vii-857 p. DM 258. 3-8253-0142-7. -- ᴿBiOr 52 (1995) 735-7 (H.C. *Melchert*).

6237 *a) Kimball* Sara E., The IE short diphthongs *oi. *ai, *ou and *au in Hittite; -- *b) Boley* Jacqueline, Further thoughts on language change, as evidenced by Hittite: *Sprache 36 (Wsb 1994) 1-28 / 129-174.

6238 *Kimball* Sara E., The phonological pre-history of some Hittite *mi*-conjugation verbs: MüSSW 53 (1992) 75-97.

6239 *a) Kimball* Sara E., Loss and retention of voiced velars in Luvian; another look; -- *b) Oshiro* Terumasa, The mediopassive endings in hieroglyphic Luvian: I(ndo)GF 99 (1994) 75-85 / 95-100.

6240 *a) Marazzi* Massimiliano, Ma gli Hittiti scrivevano veramente in 'legno'?; -- *b) Di Giovine* Paolo, Le lingue anatoliche e il perfetto indoeuropeo; una 'petitio principii'?: → 10,31, ᶠBELARDI W., Studi linguistici 1994, 131-160 / 113-130.

6241 **Melchert** H. Craig, Anatolian historical phonology: Leiden Studies in Indo-European 3. Amst 1994, Rodopi. x-457 p.; bibliog. 419-457. 90-5183-697-X.

6241* *a) Müller* G.G. W., Zur Bedeutung von hurro-akkadisch *hasahusennu*; -- *b) Neu* Erich, Hethitisch *zapzagi-*: UF 27 (DIETRICH 60. Gb. 1995) 271-280 / 395-402.

6242 **Puhvel** Jaan, Hittite etymological dictionary 1-3, 1984-91 → 65.8133 ... 8,9788: ᴿHSF 106 (1993) 307-312 (G. *Neumann*).

6243 **Rüster** Christel, *Neu* Erich, Konträr-index der hethitischen Keilschriftzeichen: StBT 40, 1993 → 9,10059: 10,9268; DM 89: ᴿOLZ 90 (1995) 173-5 (Jana *Siegelová*).

6244 **Rüster** Christel, *Neu* Erich, Hethitisches Zeichenlexikon 1989 → 5,9510 ... 10,9789: ᴿIGF 99 (1994) 301-335 (J. *Catsanicos*: 'la mise au jour du système de transcription des textes hittites'); WZKM 83 (1993) 266-276 (H.A. *Hoffner*).

6245 *Singer* Itamar, Some thoughts on translated and original Hittite literature: IOS 15 (1995) 123-8.

6246 *Starostin* S.A., ᴿ [28] New Hurrian etymologies: VDI 213 (1995) 133-6; Eng. 136.

J4.4 Phrygia, Lydia, Lycia

6247 *Garrett* Andrew, *a)* A note on the syntax of Lycian and Anatolian possession; -- *b)* Relative clause syntax in Lycian and Hittite: *Sprache 35 (1991-3) 155-161 / 36 (1994) 29-69.

6248 *Hout* Theo van den, Lycian consonantal orthography and some of its consequences for Lycian phonology: → 84, ᶠHOUWINK TEN CATE, H., Studio (1995) 105-141.

6249 *Hout* Theo P.J. van der, Lycian *telezi(je)*: Kadmos 34 (1995) 155-162: 2 pl.

6250 *Innocente* Lucia, The Oxford paracarian inscription: Kadmos 34 (1995) 149-154; 3 fig.; 1 pl.

6251 **Kammerzell** Frank, Studien zu ... Karer in Ägyptem 1993 → 9,90071: ᴿKratylos 40 (1995) 172-7 (O. *Masson*).

6252 *a) Kearns* John M., The Lydian consonant system; -- *b) Orel* Vladimir, Two dialects in New Phrygian ?: Kadmos 33 (1994) 38-59 / 60-64.

6253 *Kearns* John M., A Greek genitive from Lydia: Glotta 72 (1994/5) 5-14.

6254 *a) Melchert* H. Craig, The middle voice in Lycian; -- *b) Garrett* Andrew, Topics in Lydian syntax: HSF 105 (1992) 189-199 / 200-211.

6255 *Oettinger* Norbert, Anatolische Etymologien: HSF 108 (1995) 39-49.

6256   *Tzanavari* Katreina, *Christidis* Anastasios-P., A Carian graffito from the Lebet table, Thessaloniki; -- *b) Adiego* Ignacio-J., Contribuciones al desciframiento del Cario: Kadmos 34 (1995) 13-17; 2 pl. / 18-34.

J4.8   Armena, georgica

6257   *Aleksidze* Zaza, *Mahé* Jean-Pierre, Manuscrits géorgiens découverts à Sainte-Catherine du Sinaï: CRAI (1995) 487-494.

6258   **Dankoff** Robert, Armenian loanwords in Turkish: Turcologica 21. Wsb 1995, Harrassowitz. 216 p. -- ᴿWZKM 85 (1995) 355-7 (A. *Hetzer*).

6259   **Fähnreich** Heinz, *Sardschweladse* Surab, Etymologisches Wörterbuch der Kartwel-Sprachen: HO 1/24. Leiden 1995, Brill. 682 p. 90-04-10444-5.

J5   Graeca   .1 *grammatica, onomastica*

6260   ᴱ**Adrados** Francisco R., Diccionario griego-español [→ 2,7689 ... 10,9279] 4. *basileutós-daímōn* 1994: ᴿCÉg 70 (1995) 309 (G. *Nachtergael*).

6261   *Alonge* Antonietta, Sulla classificazione verbale cosiddetta 'aspettuale'; discussione di alcuni problemi: AGlot 79 (1994) 160-199.

6262   **Baldwin** Henry S., Improper prepositions in the New Testament; their classification, meaning, and use, and their exegetical significance in selected passages: diss. Trinity Evangelical, ᴰ*Harris M.*, 1994. 278 p. 95-20982. -- Dissertation Abstracts 56 (1995s) p. 589.

6263   **Biville** Frédérique, Les emprunts du latin au grec 1990 → 7,9542 ... 10,9281: ᴿArctos 27 (1993) 163s (Hanna *Paunonen*).

6264   **Black** David A., Learn to read NT Greek 1993 → 10,9282: ᴿRevB 57 (1995) 186 (J.P. *Martín*).

6265   *Böhlig* Alexander, Die Form der griechischen Verben in den [koptischen] Texten von Nag Hammadi; → 96, ꟻKRAUSE M., Divitiae Aegypti 1995, 19-28.

6266   **Bouttier** Michel, Mots de passe; tentatives pour saisir quelques terms insaisissables du NT 1993 → 9,10094; 10,9283: ᴿEstB 53 (1995) 422-4 (A. *Urbán*).

6267   **Calame** Claude, Figures grecques de l'intermédiaire. Lausanne 1992, Études de Lettres. 146 p. -- ᴿEM(erita) 63 (1995) 166-8 (Ana *Iriarte*).

6268   *Campanile* Enrico, Riflessioni sulla koiné;: → 10,440, ᴱ*Virgilio* B., Aspetti e problemi dell'ellenismo (Pisa 1992/4) 23-35.

6269   *Caragounis* Chrys C., The error of ERASMUS [tricked by LORITUS of Glarus] and un-Greek pronunciations of Greek: FgNt 8 (1995) 151-184; español 185.

6270   **Carson** D.A., Greek accents; a student's manual. GR/Carlisle 1995, Baker/Paternoster. 167 p. $ 12 pa. 0-8010-2494-3 / 0-85364-715-1 [NTAb 40, p.509].

6271 *Chadwick* John, The Thessalian accent: Glotta 70 (1992) 2-14.

6272 *Cignelli* Lino, Concordanza del pronome *autós* nel greco biblico: SBF*LA 45 (1995) 143-164; Eng. 484.

6273 **Cimosa** Mario, Guida allo studio della Bibbia greca (LXX); storia -- lingua -- testi. R 1995, Soc.Biblica Britannica. 272 p.

6274 **Conybeare** F.C., *Stock* St. George, Grammar of Septuagint Greek with selected readings [1905], vocabularies, and updated indexes. Peabody MA 1995, Hendrickson. x-382 p. $ 17. 1-56563-150-1 [RStR 22,143, L. *Greenspoon*].

6275 **Corsani** Bruno, Guida allo studio del greco del Nuovo Testamento. R 1994, Soc. Biblica Britannica. 427 p.

6276 *a) Cristofaro* Sonia, Lo sviluppo dei complementatori come modello di grammaticalizzazione; il caso del greco antico; - *b) Mancini* Marco, Dalle 'origini della grammatica' alla 'grammaticalizzazione': CONDILLAC ... HUMBOLDT: *AGlot 80 (1995) 101-121 / 1-38.

6277 *Devine* A.M., *Stephens* Laurence D., Ancient Greek and the typology of tone in pitch accent languages:*Sprache 35 (1991-3) 221-5, with musical notation for *écheis trípoda, al.*

6278 **Dihle** Albrecht, Greek and Latin literature of the Roman Empire [1989],[T]. NY 1994, Routledge. 0-415-06367-1. -- [R]GaR 42 (1995) 76-78 (G. *Anderson*).

6279 **Dik** Helma, Word order in ancient Greek; a pragmatic account of word order variations in HERODOTUS: AmStClasPg 5. Amst 1995, Gieben. xii-294 p. 90-5063-457-5.

6280 *Donderer* Michael, Merkwürdigkeiten im Umgang mit griechischer und lateinischer Schrift in der Antike: Gym 102 (1995) 97-172 + 434, pl. I-VIII.

6281 *Doriani* Paul M., A pastor's advice on maintaining original language skills [Greek, Hebrew; 3 'laws' or rather obstacles]: Presbyterion 19 (St.Louis 1993) 103-115.

6282 **Duhoux** Yves, Le verbe grec ancien 1992 → 8,9827 ...10,9291: [R]AnCl 64 (1995) 364-6 (P. *Wathelet*).

6283 *Duhoux* Yves, Études sur l'apect verbal en grec ancien; présentation d'une méthode : BSLP 90,1(1995) 241-298; Eng. 298; español 299.

6284 *Dupont-Roc* Roselyne, Le jeu des prépositions en 1 Pierre 1,1-12 ... : EstB 53 (1995) 201-212: Eng. 201.

6285 **Easley** Kendell H., User-friendly Greek: a common sense approach to the Greek New Testament. Nv 1994, Broadman & H. viii-167 p. $ 15 pa. 0-8045-1043-0 [JETS 39.681, W.A. *Brindle*]. -- [R]RStR 21 (1995) 232 (D.L. *Alexander*).

6286 **Giannecchini** Giulio, Il controllo infinitivo in greco antico: Univ. Perugia Ist. Linguistica 1. Perugia 1995, Ed. scientifiche. xv-281 p.; bibliog. 249-267. 88-8114-242-2.

6287 **Haubeck** Wilfrid, *Siebenthal* Heinrich von, Neuer sprachlicher Schlüssel zum griechischen Neuen Testament [1. erwartet] 2. Römer bis Offenbarung. Giessen 1994, Brunnen. xxxiv-507 p. DM 49. 3-7655-9392-3 [NTAb 39,p.335: updating of RIENECKER F.]. -- [R]NT 37 (1995) 404s (C. *Stenschke*)

6288 *Horrocks* Geoffrey, On condition ...; aspect and modakity in the history of Greek: PCP(g)S 41 (1995) 153-173.

6289 *Kitchell* Kenneth F., *al.,* Greek 2000: CJ 91 (1995s) 393-420.

6290 **Ko** Mireille, *Delmas-Massouline* Marie-Françoise, *Boehrer* Paul, Lire le grec; textes et civilisation. P 1995, Hachette. 272 p. -- [R]RÉG 108 (1995) 601s (Véronique *Boudon*, aussi sur leur Lire le latin).

6291 *Lange* N.R.M. de, Judaeo-Greek studies: achievements [1600-1920 Jewish writings in (*sic*) Greek] and prospects: *BuJudaeoGSt 17 (C 1995) 27-26 [NTAb 40, p.485].

6292 ᴱ**Létoublon** Françoise, La langue et les textes en grec ancien; colloque P. CHANTRAINE 1989/92 → 8,663*: ᴿSalesianum 57 (1995) 401s (R. *Bracchi*).

6293 **Leukart** Alex. Die frühgriechischen Nomina auf -tas und -as; Untersuchingen zu ihrer Herkunft und Ausbreitung (unter Vergleich mit den Nomina auf -eús): Szb ph/h 558, Myken. Komm. 12. W 1994, Akademie. 354 p. 3-7001-2075-3.

6294 *Levin* Saul, Greek as the superstrate written language of Jews and other Semitic populations: IOS 15 (1995) 265-279.

6295 **López Eire** Antonio, Atico, koiné y aticismo; estudios sobre ARISTOFANES & LIBANIO: Cuad 2. Murcia 1991, Univ. 103 p. -- ᴿIGF 99 (1994) 357s (H. *Schmoll*).

6296 **Lust** J., *al.*, Greek-English lexicon of the Septuagint 1, A-I. 1992 → 8,9839 ... 10,9503: ᴿVT 44 (1994) 133s (J.A. *Emerton*).

6297 **McKay** Kenneth L., A new syntax of the verb in New Testament Greek: Studies in Biblical Greek 5. NY 1994, P. Lang. 205 p. $ 30. 0-8024-2123-5. -- ᴿRelStR 21 (1995) 232 (J. *Herzog*).

6298 **Marc'hadour** Germain, Le lexique chrétien; permanences et avatars 2: CahLingLittRel 12. Angers 1993, Univ. Cath. de l'Ouest. 162 p.

6299 **Massaro** Laura Tusa, Sintassi del greco antico e tradizione grammaticale 1: SubsPg 2. Palermo 1993, Epos. 253 p. Lᵐ 43. -- ᴿAnCl 64 (1995) 366s (Monique *Bile*); CLR 45 (1995) 469s (J. *Clackson*); REA 97 (1995) 646s (L. *Basset*).

6300 *Masson* Olivier, Sur la notation occasionelle du *digamma* grec par d'autres consonnes et la glose macédonienne *abroûtes* (eyebrows): BSLP 90,1(1995) 232-238; Eng. deutsch 239.

6301 **Mastronarde** Donald J., Introduction to Attic Greek 1993 → 10,9305: ᴿCJ 90 (1994s) 183-193 (J.C. *Gibert*).

6302 *Méndez Dosuna* Julián, Contactos silábicos y procesos de geminación en griego antiguo; a propósito de las variantes dialectales *orros* (át. *óros*) y *Korra* (át. *Kórē*): *Sprache 36 (1994) 103-127.

6303 **Montanari** Franco, *al.*, Vocabolario della lingua greca. T 1995, Loescher. 2304 p. Lᵐ 148. -- ᴿAt(henaeum) 83 (1995) 574-6 (E. *Gabba*).

6304 *Morpurgo Davies* Anna, Il significato della linguistica storica nell'indagine delle lingue classiche: → 10,414*, Atti Convegni Lincei 94 (1991/2) ..

6305 **Morrice** William G., The Durham NT Greek course; a three-month introduction [but supposing the students will have done the first half for themselves] 1993 → 9,10118: ᴿRTL 26 (1995) 230s (A. *Wénin*).

6306 **Mounce** William D., The morphology of biblical Greek; a companion to [his] Basics of biblical Greek and [→9,10119] The analytical lexicon to the Greek NT. GR 1994, Zondervan. xxii-362 p. $ 40. 0-310-41040-1 [ThD 42,378].

6307 **Muraoka** T., Greek-English lexicon to the Septuagint (Twelve Prophets) 1993 → 9,10120; 10,9308: ᴿBiblica 76 (1995) 250-4 (M. *Harl*); JSSt 40 (1995) 139-141 (J.M. *Wevers*).

6308 *Opelt* Ilona, Schimpfwörter bei den attischen Rednern [alphabetische Liste]: Glotta 70 (1992) 226-238.

6309 **Palmer** M.W., Levels of constituent structure in NT Greek: *StBGk 4. NY 1995, Lang. xi-145 p. $ 20. 0-8204-2113-4 [NTAb 40,p.132]. -- ᴿRelStR 21 (1995) 329 (J. *Herzog*).

6310 **Paul** A., *Ruhbach* A., *Eklogaí*, Einführung in das neutestamentliche Griechisch [1-2], 3, Begleitgrammatik. Neuk xxi-298. DM 50. 3-7887-1497-2 [NTAb (18,p.239) 40,p.514].

6311 *Pernée* Lucien, Cas et prépositions en grec ancien: ÉtCL 63 (1995) 155-160.

6312 *Petersmann* H., Zur Entstehung der hellenistischen Koine: Ph(g) 139 (1995) 3-14 [NTAb 40, p.205].

6313 *Piñero* Antonio, New Testament philology bulletin 15s: FgNt 8 (1995) 105-137 . 239-270 [141-7 . 273-281, *Godoy* Rufino, Libros recibidos, with 80-word Spanish comment on each].

6314 **Popowski** Remigiusz, Wielki słownik grecko-polski Nowego Testamentu; wydania z pełną lokalizacją haseł, kluczem polsko-greckim oraz indeksem form czasownikowych. Wsz 1995, Vocatio. xix-939 p. 83-85435-53-0.

6315 **Porter** Stanley L., Idioms of the Greek NT 1992 → 9,10125; 10,9311: ᴿEvQ 66 (1994) 182s (D.I. *Brewer*).

6316 ᴱ**Porter** S.E., *Carson* D.A., Biblical Greek ... open questions 1993 → 1,10123; 10,9310: ᴿEvQ 67 (1995) 280s (I.H. *Marshall*).

6317 ᴱ**Porter** Stanley E., *Carson* D.A., Discourse analysis and other topics in biblical Greek. Shf 1995, Academic. 227 p. £ 35. 1-85075-545-0. -- ᴿE(xp)T 107 (1995s) 152 (N. *Richardson*).

6318 *Rochette* Bruno, Grecs et Latins face aux langues étrangères; contribution à l'étude de la diversité linguistique dans l'antiquité classique: RBPH 73 (1995) 5-16.

6319 *Ruiz Yamuza* Emilia, Verbos modales en griego antiguo, 1, *échō* + infinitivo en PLATÓN: EM(erita) 62 (1994) 1-22.

6320 **Scott** Bernard B., *al.*, Reading NT Greek; complete word lists and reader's guide 1993 → 9,10130: ᴿRevBib(Arg) 56 (1994) 251s (A.J. *Levoratti*).

6321 **Sharp** Granville, Remarks on the uses of the definitive article in the Greek text of the NT [1778, ³1803], ᴱ*McBrayer* W.D. Atlanta 1995, Original Word. viii-115 p. $ 18. 0-9826-5444-2 [NTAb 40,p.516].

6322 *Sollamo* Raija, The pleonastic use of the pronoun in connection with the relative pronoun in the LXX of Leviticus, Numbers and Deuteronomy : → 508, 8th Septuagint 1992/5, 43-62.

6323 *Souza* Draiton Gonzaga de, O grego neotestamentário: Teocomunicaçâo 24 (1994) 329-341.

6324 **Spicq** Ceslas, Theological Lexicon of the NT, ᵀ*Ernest* James D., 1994 → 10,9318 : ᴿBThB 25 (1995) 144s (J.F. *Craghan*); ET 106 (1994s) 340s (D. *Horrell*); EThL 71 (1995) 216s (F. *Neirynck*).

6325 *Spielmann* K., Participant reference and definite article in John: *JTrTL 7,1 (1995) 45-85 [NTAb 39,p.413].

6326 **Stevens** Gerald L., NT Greek & Workbook. Lanham MD 1994, UPA. [²1997: xxviii-491 p. 0-7618-0892-2.] -- ᴿE(xp)T 107 (1995s) 63 (C.S. *Rodd*, also on SCOTT B. 1995).

6327 **Summers** R., Essentials of NT Greek [1950], ²ʳᵉᵛ*Sawyer* T. [**Cox** S.L., student's guide]. Nv 1995, Broadman & H. viii-200 p. $ 25 [ix-269 p., $ 15]. 0-8054-1001-5 [-96-1: NTAb 40, p.330.321].

6328 **Swetnam** James, An introduction to the study of NT Greek 1992   → 8,9861 ...
10,8321: [R]*CritRR 7 (1994) 265-8 (S.E. *Porter*: several useful characteristics, plus others).

6329 **Swetnam** James, Il greco del Nuovo Testamento, [T]*Rusconi* Carlo. Bo 1995,
Dehoniane. xxix-451 p.; xvi-383 p. L[m] 76. 88-10-20582-0.

6330 **Swetnam** James, Wstup do grieckoi mowy nowogo zawitu; morfologija. Lwiw 1995,
Bogoslovska Akadiemija. 400 p. 5-7707-8797-X.

6331 **Trenchard** Warren C., The student's complete vocabulary guide to the Greek NT 1992
→ 10.9322: [R]JETS 38 (1995) 274s (R. *Minton*).

6332 **Wachtel** Klaus, Der byzantinische Text der katholischen Briefe; eine Untersuchung zur
Entstehung der Koine des Neuen Testament [Diss. Münster 1994, [D]*Baltes* M.]: ANTT 24.
B 1995, de Gruyter. viii-463 p.; Bibliog. 420-441.

6333 **Wakker** Gerry, Conditions and conditionals; an investigation of ancient Greek;
A(mst)StCP 3. Amst 1994, Gieben. xii-450 p. *f* 170. 90-563-196-7. -- [R]AnCL 64 (1995)
367s (Monique *Bile*).

6334 **Wallace** Daniel B., The article with multiple substantives connected by *kaì* in the New
Testament; semantics and significance: diss. Dallas Theol. Sem., [D]*Fanning* B., 1995. 350
p. 95-31285. -- DissA 56 (1995s) p. 350.

6335 *Zemek* George J, Awesome analogies; *kathōs* constructs in the NT: JETS 38 (1995)
337-348.

6336 **Zuntz** Günther, Greek; a course in classical and post-classical Greek grammar from
original texts, [TE]*Porter* Stanley E.: BLang, Greek 4. Shf 1994, Academic. 704 p.; 433 p.
$ 80. 1-85075-341-5. -- [R]RStR 21 (1995) 232 (M.W. *Holmes*).

J5.2 **Voces** *ordine alphabetico consonantium* **graecarum**

6337   *aidōs* : Cairns D. 1993 → 9,10145; 10,9334; [R]CJ 90 (1994s) 451-5 (A.W.H. *Adkins*,
also on FISHER N., WILLIAMS B.*)*.

6338 *akeideíē*: *Toohey* Peter, *Akeideíē* and *Erōs* in APOLLONIUS of Rhodes (Arg. 3,260-
298): Glotta 70 (1992) 239-247.

6339 *állos*: *Tzamali* Ekaterini, Das komparativische *állos* bei HERODOT: MüSSW 55 (1994s)
125-130.

6340 *anazōgráphēma*: SCI 14 (1995) 33-41 (P.*Lautner*).

6341 *anápausis*: *Holze* Heinrich, Anápausis im anachoretischen Mönchtum und in der Gnosis:
ZKG 106 (1995) 1-17

6342 *áneu*: *Fritz* Matthias, Griechisch *áneu* -- ein adver-biales Privativkompositum: HSF 108
(1995) 195-204.

6343   *apóstolos*:   Lohmeyer Monika, Der Apostelbegriff im Neuen Testament; eine
Untersuchung auf dem Hinter-grund der synoptischen Aussendungsreden: SBS 29. Stu 1995,
KBW. xii-472 p.; Bibliog. 445-472. DM 89.

6344 *archē* `rudiments, examples, totality': *Adinolfi* Marco, *Archē, euangélion, Christós;* note
filologiche a Mc 1,1 → 62, [F]GALBIATI E.; RivB 43 (1995) 211-4 (-222. Eng. 222).

6345 *aristo-* Masson Olivier, Une inscription chypriote syllabique de Dora (Tel Dor) et les avatars des noms grecs en Aristo- : Kadmos 33 (1994) 87-92; 1 pl.

6346 **arrabōn**: *Nikopoulos* B.E. [G] The legal sense of *arrabōn* in the letters of Paul; DBM 21,2 (1992) 28-40 [NTAb 39, p.241: down-payment].

6347 *árti*: *Mateos* Juan, *Peláez* Jesús, El adverbio *árti* en el NT: *FgNt 8,15 (1995) 85-94 [NTAb 40, p.205].

6348 **authentéō**: *Barnett* Paul W., *Authenteîn* once more: EvQ [61 (1989) 225; 65 (1993) 43 (*Wilshire* L. E.)] 66 (1994) 159-162.

6349 **aphtharsía** in Sap.; analisi letteraria e semantica: → 514, Oltre il raccon-to 1993/4, 69-92; Eng. 92 (E. *Della Corte*).

6350 **bathýs**: *Hummel* Pascale, Archilexique épique et formulaire lyrique; les emplois des composés *bathy-* dans la poésie épique et la poésie lyrique grecques: Glotta 72 (1994/5) 168-171.

6351 *basileía*;   **Barceló** Pedro, Basileia, monarchia, tyrannis ... Alleinherrschaft im vorhellenistischen Griechenland 1993 → 10,9363: [R]HZ 261 (1995) 141-3 (E. *Wirbelauer*: negativ); Klio 77 (1995) 453s (Loretana *de Libero*) [NTAb 40, p.205].

6352 **basileús**: *Lévy* Edmond, *Basileús* et *túrannos* chez HÉRODOTE: Ktema 18 (`Le pouvoir dans l'Antiquité' 1993) 7-18 [19-27, *Jacquemin* Anne, Oikiste et tyran].

6353 *gê*: *Meier-Brügger* Michael, Zu griechisch *gê* und *gaîa*: MüSSW 53 (1992/4) 113-6.

6354 -- *Peters* Martin, Griech. *gê*, *gaîa*, armen. *erkir*, `Erde' : → 94, Mem. KLÍMA O., Iranian 1994, 203-213.

6355 **diakonía**: **Collins** John N., Diakonía; reinterpreting the ancient sources 1990 → 8,9729 ... 9,10153: [R]RB 102 (1995) 152s (J. *Murphy-O'Connor*).

6356 **dikaíōma**: *Cadell* Hélène, Vocabulaire de la législation ptolémaïque; problème du sens de ~ dans le Pentateuque: →   78, [F]HARL M., Katà toùs o' 1995, 207-221.

6357 **dóxa**: *Raurell* Frederic, Anthropological meaning of `doxa' [not `doxas' as Index p.537] in Job-LXX: EstFr 96 (1995) 197-227: against TWNT, an internal and not merely social trait.

6358 **dôron**: *O'Loughlin* Thomas, The meaning of gift in Latin and English theological usage: MilltSt 35 (1995) 134-137.

6359 **éthnos**: *Takahashi* Yoshimoto, The NT view of 'people' or 'race' as presented in the letters of Paul and the Gospel of Mark, [T]*Brannen* Noah S.: AJBI 21 (1995) 73-91: p. 87, in Mk more aptly *basileía (toû theoû)*.

6360 **eirōn**: *Cotter* Joseph, The etymology and earliest significance of *eirōn*: Glotta 70 (1992) 31-34; neither *eíromai* `ask' nor *eírō* `say (without thinking so)' but Spartan *eírēn* (< *arsēn*) `sly aggressive young male'.

6361 **ekklēsía**: *Bolognesi* P., L'uso biblico del termine Ekklesia: BeO 36 (1994) 181-4 [NTAb 39, p.443].

6362 **eleuthería**: **Vollenweider** Samuel, Freiheit als neue Schöpfung ... Paulus: FRL 147, 1989 → 5,5880 ... 7,5246: [R]ZkT 117 (1995) 232s (R. *Oberforcher*).

6363 **exousía**: *Kudlien* Fridolf, *exousiastikós*, ein Nachtrag zu *authéntēs*: Glotta 72 (1994/5) 219-221.

6364 **epangéllō**: *Nickau* Klaus, *epangéllesthai* als Metapher für `bedeuten': Glotta 72 (1994/5) 206-218.

6365 **epioúsios**: *Peirone* Luigi, La traduzione di *epioúsios* nella `Vulgata': GIF 46 (1994) 71-78.

6366 *érchesthai*: **Toribio Cuadrado** J.F., `El viniente'1993 → 9,10158; 10.9344: [R]CBQ 57 (1995) 415-7 (Barbara E. *Reid*); EstB 53 (1995) 560-2 (A. *García-Moreno*); NT 37 (1995) 303-5 (M. *Silva*).

6367 *euanglízein* nel terzo vangelo: CrSt 16 (1995) 587-598; Eng. 598 (Giuseppe *De Virgilio*).

6368 *eurískō*: *Beckwith* Miles C., Greek *ēûron*, laryngeal loss and the Greek reduplicated aorist [relation to Celtic *fuar* denied by PETERS M. 1980]: Glotta 72 (1994/5) 24-32

6369 *euschēmōn*: *Lewis* Naphtali, Euschemonos in Roman Egypt: BASP 30 (1993) 106-113.

6370 *záō*: *Hagen* Hansludwig. Die Diskussion von der Schreibweise von *zên*[']? im homerischen Epos: Glotta 72 (1994/5) 98-104 (82-97, *Erbse* Hartmut).

6371 *ēchē*: *Cusset* Christophe, Exercices rhétoriques d'ARATUS autour du terme *ēchē*: : RPh(lgLH) 69 (1995) 245-8; Eng. 427.

6372 *thállos, -ion*: *Perpillou-Thomas* Françoise, Sur les emplois de *thállos, tháallion* à l'époque romaine et byzantine : REG 108 (1995) 1-6.

6373 *theología*   *Berzosa Martínez* Raúl, Apuntes para una historia de la palabra `teología': Lum(Vt) 44 (1995) 75-93,

6374 *thymós*   *Sullivan* Shirley D., The relationship of person and *thymós* in the Greek lyric poets (excluding PINDAR and BACCHYLIDES): SIF(g)C 12 (1994) 12-57 . 149-174.

6375 *ilingos* `dizziness': *Bosch i Veciana Antoni*,  Els `rodaments de cap' en PLATÓ; l'ús de *(e)ilingiân* en el Corpus Platonicum: → 41, [F]COLOMER E., RCatT 19 (1994) 53-64; Eng. 65.

6376 *hína*: *Sluiter* Ineke, Causal *hína* -- sound Greek: Glotta 70 (1992) 39-53.

6377 *katallássō*: **Porter** Stanley E., *Katalássō* in ancient Greek literature, with reference to the Pauline writings 1994 → 10,9348: [R]ET 106 (1994s) 280s (I.H. *Marshall*); LouvSt 20 (1995) 85s (J. *Lambrecht*).

6378 *kidnón*: *Prósper* Blanca, Über die Etymologie von griechisch *kidnón*: HSF 108 (1995) 75-83.

6379 *krábatos*   *Kramer* Johannes, *krábatos, krabátion* und Verwandtes in den Papyri: APF 41 (1995) 205-216.

6380 *kradíē*:   *Sullivan* Shirley D., Kradíē, ētor, and kēr in poetry after HOMER: RBPH 73 (1995) 17-38.

6381 *kybernáō*: HSF 105 (1992) 188 (G. *Neumann*).

6382 *lithoboléō*: *Casevitz* Michel, Le mots [grecs] de la lapidation dans la Bible: → 78, [F]HARL M., Katà toùs o' 1995, 223-239.

6383 *makrothymía*: **Tarocchi** Stefano, Il Dio longanime 1993 → 10,7021 (9349*): [R]Asprenas 42 (1995) 118s (A. *Rolla*); CBQ 57 (1995) 610s (B. *Fiore*); RS(to)LR 31 (1995) 565 (Gabriella *Dogliani Saladini*); SBF*LA 44 (1994) 705-7 (A.M. *Buscemi*).

6384 *ménō*:   *La Potterie* Ignace de, L'emploi du verbe demeurer dans la mystique johannique [*ménein* 67 fois, Paul 17, Synoptiques 12]: NRT 117 (1995) 843-859.

6385 *mesēmbría*: *Maraval* Pierre, `Midi', variations sur un symbole [région / lumière]: → 78, [F]HARL M., Katà toùs o' 1995, 463-471.

6386 *mímēsis*: *Ong* Walter J., Mimesis [*akolouthéō* preferred in NT except Paul]: RL(it) 26,2 (ND 1994) 73-77 [NTAb 39, p.269].

6387 *misthophóros*: *Foulon* Éric, *Misthophóroi* et *xénoi* hellénistiques: RÉG 108 (1995) 211-8.

6388 *mógis*: *Meier-Brugger* Michael, Zu griechisch *mogéō* und Familie: Glotta 70 (1992) 134s.

6389 *néktar* [< Eg. *neṯer* `divine'] and nitron [post-`ambrosia' use of same root for metallurgy and mummification] : Glotta 72 (1994/5) 10-23 (R.D. *Griffith*).

6390 *nêsos*: HSF 106 (1993) 302 (M. *Meier-Brügger*).

6391 *obelós*: *Plath* Robert, Zur Etymologie von homerisch *obelós*: HSF 105 (1992) 243-259.

6392 *ónoma*: *Adorno* Francesco. Riflessioni su *ónoma-rhêma-lógos* nel `Peri hermeneias' di ARISTOTELE: → 10,42, [F]GIGANTE M., Storia 1994, 1-14.

6393 *opêtion*: *Vine* Brent, Greek *ópeas/ópear* `awl': Glotta 72 (1994/5) 31-40.

6394 *óchlos*: *Karpyuk* S.G., [R] *Ochlos* from Aeschylus to Aristotle; history of the word in the context of history of Athenian democracy: VDI 214 (1995,4) 35-50; Eng. 50.

6395 -- **Park Tae-Sik**, Ochlos im NT: Diss. [D]*Hübner*. Göttingen 1995. - ThRv Beilage 92/2, ix.

6396 *parabolē*: **Cuvillier** Élian. Le concept de *parabolē* [Mc]: ÉtBN 19, 1993 → 9,4676; 10,4748: [R]Biblica 76 (1995) 118-121 (A. *Puig*).

6397 *parádosis*: *Viljamaa* Toivo, *Parádosis* and *synétheía;* language study in classical antiquity: AAH 36 (1995) 169-176,

6398 *periphrasē*: *Hoffmann* Roland, `Periphrase' (`periphrastisch'); zu Herkunft und Geschichte eines sprachwissenschaftlichen Begriffs: Glotta 71 (1993) 223-242.

6399 *pístis, pistós*: *Haraguchi* Takaaki, *pistòs ho theós / pístis toû theoû* in Paul: AnJap 20 (1994 59-77.

6400 *pólemos*: *Dunkel* G.E., Two old problems in Greek; *ptólemos* and *terpsímbrotos*; [relatable via Vedic]: Glotta 70 (1992) 197-225.

6401 *sikários*: *Kramer* Johannes, Sica, sicilis, sicarius, e papirologiche: → 10,42, [F]GIGANTE M., Storia 1994, 321-6.

6402 *skándalon*: **McCracken** David M., The scandal of the Gospels; Jesus, story, and offense. NY 1994, Oxford-UP. xii-204 p. $ 30. - [R]CBQ 57 (1995) 599s (F.W. *Burnett*: `the Gospel's basic offensiveness -- i.e. whatever violates rules and norms -- forced readers and institutions to domesticate and nullify it': disconcertingly unproved except as support for KIERKEGAARD).

6403 *sparganóō* *Kügler* Joachim, Die Windeln Jesu als Zeichen; religionsgeschichtliche Anmerkungen zu sparganóō: BN(otiz) 77 (1995) 20-28.

6404 *splánchna*: *Montevecchi* Orsolina, 'Viscere di misericordia' → 62, [F]GALBIATI E.; RivB 43 (1995) 125-133.

6406 *táxis* in the Vita Antonii and in some martyr-acts: JThS 46 (1995) 556-8 (C.P. *Jones*; wrongly *práxis* in excellent BARTELINK 1994).

6407 -- *Stewart-Sykes* Alistair, Taxei in PAPIAS, again: *JEarlyC 3 (1995) 487-492.

6408 *tēle*: *Harðarson* Jón A., Griechisch *tēle*: HSF 108 (1995) 205s.

6409 *tryphē* (inscriptions Triphiodore par iotacisme): *Husson* Geneviève, La graphie Tryphiodore a-t-elle pu être influencée par la Bible des Septante [Gen 3,23s] ?: → 78, [F]HARL M., Katà toùs o' 1995, 433-440.

6410 *hýbris*, **Fisher** N.R.E., Hybris, a study in the values of honour and ahame in ancient Greece 1992 → 9,15283; 10,13599: [R]RÉG 108 (1995) 242 (Jacqueline *Assaël*).

6411 *hygiēs*. *Weiss* Michael, Life everlasting; Latin *iūgis* `overflowing', Greek *hygiēs* `healthy'. Gothic *ajukdūps* `eternity' and Avestan *yauuaējī* (j = !) `living forever': MüSSW 55 (1994s) 131-156.

6412 *hypakoúō*: *Mateos* Juan, *Hypakoúō* y términos afines en el NT [< dicc.]: FgNt 8 (1995) 209-226.

6413 *hypó*: **Villey** Lucile, Soumission 1992 → [R]VigChr 49 (1995) 411-3 (G.J.M. *Bartelink*).

6414 *phi ...*: *Blank* D.L., Stop or spirant; a note on the division of semivocal alements: Glotta 72 (1994/5) 200-5: the fact that *ph, ch, ps* were sometimes classed with spirants does not justify including in that class also the aspirants, `whose addition to a stop would result in a "semivocal" element'.

6415 *phásis*: **Naddaf** Gérard, L'origine et évolution du concept grec de phasis. Lewiston NY 1992, Mellen. 603 p. - [R]RTPh 127 (1995) 164s (A. *Étienne*).

6416 *phílos*: **Puthenkandathil** Eldho, *Phílos*, a [Jn] designation for the Jesus-disciple relationship: EurUnivSt 23/475. Fra/NY 1993, Lang. xxiv-379 p. $ 60.80 pa. - [R]CBQ 57 (1995) 413s (J.E. *Bruns*: `deadening', banal, though claiming Jn 'took shape as the *Sitz im Leben* of Qumran'; ignores the highly relevant 'beloved disciple').

6417 *phrátēr*: *Morani* Moreno, Il fratello, la casa, il villaggio; sull'etimologia di *phrátēr* in greco: Aevum 49 (1995) 3-6.

6418 *cháris*: **MacLachlan** Bonnie, The age of grace 1993 → 10,9368: [R]Phoenix 49 (Tor 1995) 260s (Sylvia *Barnard*).

6419 -- **Zeller** Dieter, *Charis* bei Philon und Paulus: SBS 190, 1990 →6,6174 ... 9,10194: [R]TR 91 (1995) 314-5 (K.G. *Sandelin*).

6420 *psychē*: *Rankin* David, *Psychē* and *lógos* in HERACLITUS B45 and B115 (DIELS-KRANZ) : EM(erita) 62 (1994) 289-294.

J5.4 *Papyri et inscriptiones graecae* -- **Greek epigraphy**

6421 *Arzt* Peter, The 'epistolary introductory thanksgiving' in the papyri and in Paul: NT 36 (1994) 29-46.

6422 *Bagnall* Roger S., [Hermopolis] Charite's Christianity [c. 300; at least her long-deceased husband had a name likelier to be Christian]: BASPAP 32 (1995) 37-40.

6423 *Bagnall* Roger S., *Sheridan* Jennifer A., Greek and Latin documents from Abu Sha'ar [Delaware Univ. Red Sea excavation]: BASPAP 31 (1994) 109-120; pl. 22-23.

6424 *Barag* Dan, The dated Jewish inscription from Binyamina reconsidered [540 c.e. instead of 408 as L. DI SEGNI]: Atiqot [22 (1993) 133-6] 25 (1994) 179-181; 1 fig.; 183-6, reply.

6425 **Bernand** André, De Thèbes à Syène 1989 → 6,9637: [R]BiOr 52 (1995) 398-404 (H. *Heinen*).

6426 **Bertrand** Jean-Marie, Inscriptions historiques grecques 1992 → 10.9374: [R]Gnomon 67 (1995) 269-271 (P, *Herrmann*).

6427 **Bingen** Jean, *al.*, Mons Claudianus ostraca 1992 → 8,9964 ... 10,9377: [R]Latomus 54 (1995) 461-3 (H. *Melaerts*).

6428 **Boffo** Laura, Iscrizioni greche e latine per lo studio della Bibbia: BSSTB 9, 1994 → 9,9379; L[m] 79: [R]Anton 70 (1995) 692-4 (M. *Nobile*); Did(ask)L 24 (1994) 141a (A. *Vaz*); PaVi 40,5 (1995) 61s (Anna *Passoni dell'Acqua*).

6429 *Boffo* Laura. Ancora una volta sugli 'archivi' nel mondo greco; conservazione e 'pubblicazione' epigrafica: At(henaeum) 83 (1995) 91-130.

6430 *Bousquet* J., *Gauthier* P., Inscriptions du Létôon de Xanthos: RÉG 107 (1994) 319-331; 3 fig.

6431 **Brashear** William M., Magica varia 1991 → 9,10202: [R]BASPAP 30 (1993) 73-75 (T.G. *Wilfong*).

6432 *Brice* William C., *Neumann* Günter, Epigraphische Mitteilungen: Kadmos 33 (1994) 163-7.

6433 *Cassio* Albio C., La più antica iscrizione greca di Cuma e *tin(n)umai* in Omero: *Sprache 35 (1991-3) 187-207; 2 fig.

6434 **Cervenka-Ehrenstrasser** Irene-Maria, Lexikon der lateinischen Lehnwörter in den griechischsprachigen dokumentarischen Texten Ägyptens mit Berücksichtigung koptischer

Quellen, I (Alpha): MPER27. W 1996, Hollinek. 132 p. -- ^{R}Aeg 75 (1995) 331-3 (G. *Geraci*).

6435 **Chastagnol** A., *al.*, L'année épigraphique 1990, P 1993, PUF. 378 p. -- ^{R}RÉL 73 (1995) 360s (J.-P. *Martin*, aussi sur CORBIER M. 1991, 595 p.)

6436 **Clarysse** W., The Petrie papyri[2] I. The wills 1991 → 9,10206; 10,9385: ^{R}Aeg 75 (1995) 323-5 (Orsolina *Montevecchi*).

6437 **Clarysse** Willy, Zénon, un homme d'affaires à l'ombre des Pyramides: ANCORAE 14. Lv 1995, Univ. 112 p. 90-6186-674-X.

6438 *Crocker* Piers, Papyri from Petra [1993: parish benefactors ? covering 22 years under Justinian]: BurHist 31 (1995) 101-5.

6439 **Cuvigny** Hélène, Papyrus Graux II (P.Graux 9 à 29): AEPHE.h 3. Genève 1995, Droz. 93 p. 2-600-00041-0.

6440 **Cuvigny** H., *Wagner* G., Les ostraca grecs de Douch 3 (184-355): Fouilles 24/3. Le Caire 1992, IFAO. xi-92 p.; XXIII pl. 2-7247-0118-6. -- ^{R}BiOr 52 (1995) 394-8 (M. Lauretta *Moioli*).

6441 **Cuvigny** H., *al.*, Les ostraca grecs d'Aïn Waqfa (Oasis de Kharga): DFIFAO 30. La Caire 1993, IFAO. 91 * 125 p. 2-7247-0143-7 [OIAc 11,19, 'Cuvu-']-

6442 **Daris** Sergio, Papiri documentari greci del fondo Palau-Ribes: EstPapirFg 4. Barc 1995, Institut de Teología Fonamental. 148 p; VII pl. 84-87843-03-4. -- ^{R}Aeg 75 (1995) 329s (Orsolina *Montevecchi*); AulaO 12 (1994) 240s (J. *O'Callaghan*); BASPAP 32 (1995) 89s (J.G. *Keenan*).

6443 **Derda** Tomasz, Deir el-Naqlun, The Greek papyri. Wsz 1995, Univ. 196 p.; XVI loose pl. -- ^{R}Aeg 75 (1995) 333-5 (Orsolina *Montevecchi*).

6444 *Dubois* Laurent, Une tablette de malédiction de Pella; s'agit-il du premier texte macédonien ?: RÉG 108 (1995) 190-7.

6445 **Effenterre** Henri van, *Ruzé* Françoise, Nomima; recueil d'inscriptions politiques et juridiques de l'archaïsme grec: Coll. ÉcF 188. R 1994, École Française. xx-404 p. 2-7283-0304-5.

6446 *a) Errington* R. Malcolm, *Ekklēsías kyrías genoménēs* [technical terms vary in meaning in places] ; - *b) Rhodes* P.J., Ekklesia kyria and the schedule of assemblies in Athens: Chiron 25 (1995) 19-42 / 187-198.

6447 *Feissel* Denis, Notes d'épigraphie chrétienne (X): BCH 119 (1995) 375-389; 4 fig.

6448 **Gagos** T., *al.*, The Oxyrhynchus papyri **61**: Memoir 81. L 1995, Egypt Expl. Soc. 163 p.; XII pl. 0-85698-126-5.

6449 *Galvao-Sobrinho* Carlos R., Funerary epigraphy and the spread of Christianity in the west: At(h-Pavia) 83 (1995) 431-462 + 8 fig.

6450 *Gauthier* P., *al.*, Bulletin épigraphique: RÉG 108 (1995) 430-574.

6451 **Guarducci** Margherita, Epigrafia greca. R 1989-95 [= 1967], Poligrafico. I. bibliog. 507-532; II. 703-705 [III.-IV: 88-240-..].

6452 **Handley** E.W., *al.*, The Oxyrhynchus papyri **59**: Memoir 79, 1992 → 9,10212: ^{R}VDI 212 (1995) 222-9 (V.N. *Yarkho*).

6453 *Harrauer* Hermann, *Taeuber* Hans, Inschriften aus Syrien: Tyche 6 (1993) 31-34.

6454 **Haslam** M.W., *al.*, Oxyrhynchus papyri **57** (3876-3914), Mem. 77, 1990 → 7.9565 ... 10,9392: ^{R}Tyche 9 (1994) 244s (B. *Palme*; auch über REA S. 58).

6455 *Hengstl* Joachim, Juristische Literaturübersicht 1990-1992 (mit Nachträgen) I.: Muséon 108 (1995) 93-165.

6456 ^{E}**Henten** J. Van, *Horst* P. van der, Studies in early Jewish epigraphy [Utrecht conference]: ArbGJU 21, 1994 → 10,323*b*: ^RBiOr 52 (1995) 120s (E. *Lipiński*).

6457 **Hoogendijk** Francisca A.J., *al.*, [^E**Pestman** P., *al.]* Berichtigungsliste 9, 1995 → 10,9393: ^RBASPAP 32 (1995) 204-6 (J.F. *Oates*).

6458 **Horbury** William, *Noy* David, Jewish inscriptions of Graeco-Roman Egypt 1992 → 8.9982 ... 10,9395: ^RBiOr 52 (1995) 774-8 (G. *Mussies*); *CritRR 7 (1994) 404s (J.J. *Collins*); Gnomon 67 (1995) 276-8 (A. *Kasher*); JAOS 115 (1995) 324s (R.S. *Bagnall*: some mild warnings); JRS 83 (1993) 248s (C. *Roueché*).

6459 -- *Horsley* G.H.R., Towards a new Corpus inscriptionum iudaicarum ? [HORBURY W., NOY D., 1992]: *JSQ 2 (Tü 1995) 77-97.

6460 **Horst** Pieter W. van der, Ancient Jewish epitaphs 1991 → 8,9402 ... 10.9396: ^RStPhilo 7 (1995) 239-241 (G.E. *Sterling*); TorJT 10 (1994) 247s (J.S. *Kloppenborg*).

6461 ^E**Huttenhöfer** Ruth, [25] Ptolemäische Urkunden aus der Heidelberger Papyrus-Sammlung (P.Heid. VI). Heid 1994, Winter. xxi-199 p.; 32 pl. DM 130. 3-8253-0143-5. -- ^RBoL (1995) 29 (L.L. *Grabbe*: three references to Samareios; a city of Fayûm perhaps with settlers from Palestine; also Dositheos two or three times).

6462 **Johnson** Gary J., Early-Christian epitaphs from Anatolia: SBL.TT 35. At 1995, Scholars. xiii-181 p. $ 40. 0-7885-0120-8.

6463 **Kayser** François, Recueil des inscriptions grecques et latines (non funéraires) d'Alexandrie impériale (I^e-IIIe s. ap. J.-C.): IFAO BEt 108, 1994; 60 pl.; 2 maps: CÉg 70 (1995) 330-2 (A. *Martin*).

6464 *Kramer* Bärbel, Urkundenreferat: APF 41 (1995) 273-333 [86-92 . 263-272, *Poethke* G., *al.*, Darstellungen und Hilfsmittel].

6465 **Lewis** Naphtali, *Yadin* Yigael, *al.*, The documents from the Bar Kokhba period in the Cave of Letters 1989 → 6.9678 ... 9,10224: ^RJAOS 115 (1995) 523s (J.J. *Farber*); JQR 84 (1993s) 373-7 (A. *Wasserstein*).

6466 **LiDonnici** Lynn R., The Epidaurian miracle inscriptions: SBL.TT 36. At 1995. Scholars. iv-155 p. $ 35. 0-7885-0104-6.

6467 **Llewelyn** S.R., (*Kearsley* R.A.), New documents illustrating early Christianity, 6. A review of the Greek inscriptions and papyri published in 1980-81: 1992 → 9,10225; 10, 9401; vii-227 p. A$ 30: ^RGnomon 67 (1995) 563-6 (W. *Wischmeyer*).

6468 **McGing** Brian C., Greek papyri from Dublin: PTA 142. Bonn 1995, Habelt. xxviii-203 p.; 25 pl.; bibliog. xi-xxviii. 3-7749-2656-5.

6469 **Meimaris** Yiannis E., *al.*, Chronological ssystems -- Roman-Byzantine Palestine and Arabia; the evidence of the dated Greek inscriptions: Meletemata 17. Athena 1992, National Hellenic. 432 p.; 3 maps. -- ^RPEQ 127 (1995) 77s (N. *Kokkinos*).

6470 *Méndez Dosuna* Julián, On (Z) for (A) in Greek dialectal inscriptions: *Sprache 35 (1991-3) 82-114.

6471 ^E**Miranda** Elena, Inscriptiones graecae d'Italia. N 1990. Quasar. 176 p. L^m 60. 88-7140-083-6.

6472 *Montserrat* Dominic, *Fantoni* Georgina, *Robinson* Patrick, Varia descripta Oxyrhynchita: BASPAP 31 (1994) 11-80; pl. 1-18.

6473 **O'Callaghan** José, Papiros literarios griegos del Fondo Palau-Ribes 1993 → 9,10230: ^RAeg 75 (1995) 327-9 (Orsolina *Montevecchi*); RCatT 30 (1995) 198 (F. *Nicolau*).

6474 **Pintaudi** Rosario, *al.*, Papyri graecae Wessely Pragenses (PPrag II): Papyrologica florentina 26. F 1995, Gonnelli. xviii-219 p.

6475 ^E**Rupprecht** Hans-Albert, *Jordens* Andrea, Wörterbuch der griechischen

Papyrusurkunden, Supp. 2 (1967-1976): AkMainz. Wsb 1991, Harrassowitz. xi-335 p. DM 168. -- ᴿCÉg 70 (1995) 317s (G. *Nachtergael*, aussi sur leur Sammelbuch 15, Index zu 14, 1994).

6476 *Rydbeck* Lars, *Eusébeian édeixen toîs anthrópois*; the significance of the lingual Asoka [Kandahar, found 1957] inscription for NT philology and for research into the nature of Hellenism; → 79, ᶠHARTMAN L., Texts & Contexts 1995, 591-6; 1 fig.

6477 **SEG:** Supplementum epigraphicum graecum 40 for 1990 / 41 for 1991, ᴱ**Pleket** H.W., *Stroud* R.S. Amst 1993s, Gieben. xxxv-668 p. *f* 195. -- ᴿCLR 45 (1995) 397s (P.J. *Rhodes*, 40).

6478 **Tréheux** Jacques, Inscriptions de Délos, Index; 1, Les étrangers [exc. Athéniens .. Romains]: AIBL. P 1992, de Boccard. 113 p. -- ᴿGnom 67 (1995) 369s (P. *Herrmann*),

6479 **Treu** Kurt †, *Diethart* Johannes, Griechische literarische Papyri christlichen Inhaltes 2, 1993 → 9,10243; 141 p.; vol. of 55 pl.; 3-85119-250-8: ᴿBASPAP 30 (1993) 155-164 (C.A. *Kuehn*); BiOr 52 (1995) 73-75 (J. *O'Callaghan*).

6480 **Vleeming** S.P., Ostraka varia; tax receipts and legal documents on Demotic, Greek, and Greek-Demotic ostraka, chiefly of the early Ptolemaic period, from various collections (P.L.Bat. 26). Lei 1994, Brill. xiii-173 p.; 62 pl. *f* 185. 90-04-10132-2. -- ᴿBoL (1995) 36 (L.L. *Grabbe*).

6481 ᵀ**Wente** Edward F., ᴱ*Meltzer* Edmund S., Letters from ancient Egypt 1990 → 6,9559; 7,9377: ᴿRB 102 (1995) 128-131 (T. *Axe*).

6482 *Wörrle* Michael, *a)* Neue Inschriftenfunde aus Aizanoi II., Das Problem der Ära von Aizanoi; - *b)* Epigraphische Forschungen zur Geschichte Lykiens V. Die griechischen Inschriften de Nekropolen von Limyra: Chiron 25 (1995) 63-76; 6 pl. / 387-412 + 26 fig.

6483 **Worp** Klaas, XVII-A → 9,10245: 10,9419; **Sijpesteijn** P.,XVII-B; **Kramer** B., XVIII: Corpus papyrorum Raineri 1991: ᴿGnomon 67 (1995) 431-8 (A. *Jördens*).

6484 **Worp** K.A., Greek papyri from Kellis (P.Kell.G), Nᵒˢ 1-90: Dakhleh mg. 3. Ox 1995, Oxbow. xi-281 p. 0-946897-97-2.

J5.5 **Cypro-Minoa** [→ T9.1-4]

6485 **Aura Jorro** Francisco, Diccionario micénico 2. M 1993, CSIC. 473 p. -- ᴿRÉA 96 (1994) 582 (J.-L. *Perpillou*).

6486 *Egetmeyer* Markus, Zur kyprischen Bronze von Idalion: Glotta 71 (1993) 39-59.

6487 *Evely* Doniert, *al.*, New fragments of Linear B tablets from Knossos: Kadmos 33 (1994) 10-21.

6488 *Floyd* Cheryl R., Fragments from two pithoi with Linear A inscriptions from Pseira: Kadmos 34 (1995) 39-48; 3 fig.; 2 pl.

6489 **Godart** Louis, Il disco di Festo; l'enigma di una scrittura 1994 → 10.9427: 35 fig.: ᴿArcheo 9,111 (1994) 106 (S. *Moscati*).

6490 **Hajnal** Ivo, Studien zum mykenischen Kasussystem: UIGSK 7. B 1995, de Gruyter. xvii-377 p.; Bibliog. 343-366. 3-11-013986-3.

6491 *a) Lebessi* Angeliki, *al.*, An inscription in the hieroglyphic script from the Yme sanctuary, Crete (SY Hf 01); -- *b) Schoep* Ilse, A new Cretan hieroglyphic inscription from Malia (MA/V Yb 03): Kadmos 34 (1995) 63-77; 7 fig. / 78-80; 1 fig.; 1 pl.

6492   a) *Lejeune* M., *Godart* L., Le syllabogramme *56 dans le Linéaire B thébain; - b) *Sacconi* Anna, Riflessioni sull'economia micenea, economia de baratto o economia monetaria ?: RFIC 122 (1995) 272-7 / 257-271.

6493   *Manganaro* Giacomo, Rilettura di tre iscrizioni archaiche greche : Kadmos 34 (1995) 141-8.

6494   a) *Marazzi* Massimiliano, Appunti per un dossier sulla circolazione del vino attraverso le testimonianze in Lineare B; -- b) *Parise* Nicola F., Misure di capacità e distribuzione del vino nei testi 'micenei': → 10,480, Drinking ANE. 1990/4, 139-150 / 151-4.

6495   *Masson* Olivier, Une nouvelle épitaphe syllabique de l'Ancienne-Paphos: Kadmos 34 (1995) 137-140; 4 fig.

6496   *Meier-Brügger* Michael, a) Mykenisch *te-u-to* = *stéût*$_o$*r* ?; - b) Zu kyprisch *e-tu-wa-no-í-nu* und *e-to-ko-í-nu*: Glotta 70 (1992) 1 nur / 129s.

6497   **Melena** José L., *Olivier* Jean-Pierre, Tithemy; the tablets and nodules in Linear B from Tiryns, Thebes and Mycenae: Minos sup. 12. S 1991, Univ. 97 p. -- [R]EM(erita) 62 (1994) 187s (F. *Aura Jorro*).

6498   *Méndez Dosuna* Julián, A note on Myc. *a-ze-ti-ri-ja*, Att. *sbénnumi*, and palatalization: *Sprache 35 (1991-3) 208-220.

6500   **Negri** Mario, Le tavolette delle classi A, C, E, F, G di Pilo; saggio di traduzione: Univ. Macerata QuadLingFg 6. R 1993, Il Calamo. xv-87 p. -- [R]Salesianum 57 (1995) 799s (R. *Gottlieb*).

6502   *Nicolaou* Ino, Inscriptiones Cypriae alphabeticae [in English] xxxiv, 1994 : RDACyp (1995) 221-7.

6503   *Orel* Vladimir, Notes on Eteo-Cretan [two pre-Greek Cretan spells preserved in Egyptian medical sources]: *JAncCiv 9 (1994) 99-103.

6504   *Panagl* Oswald, Etymologie und philologische Deutung in den Linear-B-Tafeln: → 10,13c, [F]BERNHARD L., Liebe zum Wort 1993, 33-40.

6505   *Shelmerdine* Cynthia W., *Bennet* John, Two new Linear B documents from Bronze Age Pylos: Kadmos 34 (1995) 123-136; 2 fig.

6506   *Slavkova* Irene, Some aspects of the palace organization; the Knossos E and F tablets: Thetis 2 (Mannheim 1995) 15-20.

6507   **Varias García** Carlos, Los documentos en Lineal B de Micenas; ensayo de interpretación global: dis. Univ. Autónoma. Barcelona 1993. 525 p. 84-7929-938-X. (No AA photocopy.) -- DissA-C 56 (1995s) p. 21.

6508   *Varias García* Carlos, El dativo singular atemático en las inscripciones en lineal B de Micenas: Fav 16,2 (1994) 7-21.

6509   *Vokotopoulou* Ioulia, *Christidis* Anastasios-Phoebus, A Cypriote graffito on an SOS amphora from Mende, Chalcidice: Kadmos 34 (1995) 5-12; 2 fig.; 3 pl.

J6   Indo-Iranica

6510   a) *Bielmeier* Roland, Zur Konzeption des avestischen Kalenders; -- b) *Schmitt* Rüdiger, Zu einigen avestischen Gebirgsnamen; -- c) *Kellens* Jean, Retour à l'infinitif avestique: MüSSW 53 (1992) 15-74 / 175-8 / 55.

6511   *de Blois* François, 'Place' and 'throne' in Persian: Iran 33 (1995) 61-65.

6512   *Duchesne-Guillemin* Jacques,   Coups d'œil sur la linguistique iranienne →
10,414*. Lincei Convegni 94 (1991-2) 131-145.

6513   **Emmerick** Ronald E., *Voror'éva-Desjatovskaya* Margarita J.,   Saka
St.Petersburg: Corpus inscriptionum iranicarum 2/5/7. L 1993, [B]SOAS. 24 p.; 159 pl.
£ 47. -- ᴿJRAS (1995) 119s (A. *Degener*).

6514   *Fussman* Gérard,   L'Indo-Grec Ménandre, ou Paul DEMIÉVILLE revisité: JA
281 (1993) 61-138

6515   **Gignoux** Philippe,   Noms perses sassanides en moyen-perse épigraphique,
[ᴱ*Mayrhofer* R.] Iranisches Personennamenbuch 2/2. W 1986, Akademie. 227 p. -- ᴿ StIr
22 (1993) 127-133 (P. *Lecoq*: de qualité inestimable; nombreuses remarques).

6516   *Giovinazzo* Grazia, I '*puhu*' nei testi di Persepoli; nuove interpretazioni: AION
55 (1995) 141-157: 'boys' but in (training for) valet-service.

6517   *Grillot-Susini* Françoise, *al.*,   La version élamite de la trilingue de Béhistun;
une nouvelle lecture: JA 281 (1993) 19-59

6518   *a) Grillot-Susini* Françoise, Une nouvelle approche de la morphologie élamite;
racines, bases et familles de mots; -- *b) Kellens* Jean, Interrogation [Avestan *mainiiu*]; --
c) Pirart Eric, Les noms des Perses [HÉRODOTE 7,61]: JA 282 (1994) 1-17; Eng. 17 /
283 (1995) 271-4 / 57-68; Eng. 68.

6519   **Hammond** N.G.L.   The language of the Macedonians and other peoples in
early times. Oxford 1979.--   ᴿMaia 37 (1995) 423-5 (G. *Bonfante:* non fa onore a 'la
Cabridge ancient History', *sic*).

6520   *Maciuszak* Kinga.   Some remarks on the northern Iranian dialect of the Alamut
region: Iran 33 (1995) 111-4.

6521   **Schmitt** Rüdiger,   The Bisitun inscription 1991 → 9,10274; 10,9446: *Sprache
35 (1991-3) 140-5 (Chlodwig H. *Werba*).

6522   *Swennen* Philippe,   Les participes présents féminins actifs dans l'Avesta:
AION 55 (1995) 207-216.

6523   *Zadok* Ran, On the current state of Elamite lexicography: StEpL 12 (1995)
241-252.

J6.5 Latina

6524   *Arascal Palazón* Juan Manuel,   Epigrafía latina e historia antigua: → 221,
ᶠYELO TEMPLADO A., Lengua 1995, 437-447.

6525   *Banniard* Michel,   Latin tardif et latin mérovingien; communication et
modèles langagiers: RÉL 73 (1995) 213-230.

6526   *Beikircher* Hugo,   Zur Etymologie und Bedeutungsentwicklung von *praestare*:
Glotta 70 (1992) 88-95.

6527   *Bodelot* Colette,   Propositions complétives et construction appositionnelle en
latin; ébauche de synthèse : RPh(lgLH) 69 (1995) 36-71; Eng. 242.

6528   *Castillo* Carmen,   El progreso de la epigrafía romana en 'Hispania
[Epigráfica]' (1988-1992) : EM(erita) 63 (1995) 187-223; Eng. 187.

6529   *Cavazza* Franco,   Gli aggettivi in -*i-timus* e il rapporto fra *aedituus* ed
aeditumus: Latomus 54 (1995) 576-591 . 784-792.

6530 **Dangel** Jacqueline,   Histoire de la langue latine: Que sais-je ? 1281. P 1995,

PUF. 128 p. 2-13-046848-9. -- ᴿBSL(at) 25 (1995) 635s (I. *Lana*): RÉL 73 (1995) 244s (F. *Biville*).

6531 **D'Elia** S., Letteratura latina cristiana: Guide allo studio della civiltà romana 4/3. R 1982, Jouvence. 206 p.; bibliog. 167-204.

6532 **De Prisco** A., Il latino tardoantico e altomedievale: Guide 23. R 1991, Jouvence. 269 p.; bibliog. 227-267. 88-7801-202-5.

6533 **Eckert** Günter, Thema, rhema und fokus: eine Studie zur Klassifizierung von indirekten Fragensätzen und Relativsätzen im Lateinischen [Diss. Münster 1992]: StSprW.b 20. Müns 1992, Nodus. 283 p. DM 75. 3-89323-120-X. -- : ᴿAnCL 64 (1995) 372-4 (Dominique *Longrée*).

6534 ᴱ**Egger** Carolus, Lexicon recentioris latinitatis A-L 1992 → 8,a49: ᴿSalesianum 57 (1995) 398s (R. *Bracchi*).

6535 *a)* *Ehrenfellner* Ulrike, Etymologie von ai. *yáth_* and lat. *ut*; -- *b)* *García-Hernández* Benjamín, Die Evolution des lat. *sub* und die Urbedeutung des idg. **(s)upo; -* *- c)* *Rosén* Haiim B., Lat. *rete*: I(nd)GF 100 (1995) 129-124 / 163-171 / 210s.

6536 **Evans** Michael, Basic [Latin] grammar for medieval and Renaissance studies. L 1995, Warburg. 108 p. 0-85481-093-5.

6537 *Felle* Antonio E., Loci scritturistici nella produzione epigrafica romana: VetChr 32 (1995) 61-89.

6538 *García-Hernández* Benjamín, Polysémie et signification fondamental du préverbe *sub-* : BSLP 90,1 (1995) 301-311; Eng, español 312.

6539 *a)* *García-Jurado* F., Die Syntax der uerba uestiendi im archaischen Latein; -- *b)* *Wenskus* Otta, Triggering und Einschaltung griechischer Formen in lateinischer Prosa: I(nd)GF 100 (1995) 193-209 / 172-192.

6540 ᴱ**Iliescu** Maria, *Marxgut* Werner, Latin vulgaire, latin tardif .. III colloque 1991/2 → 8,656c: ᴿSalesianum 57 (1995) 181s (R. *Bracchi*).

6541 **Keller** Madeleine, Les verbes latin à infectum en *-sc-*; étude morphologique à partir des formations attestées dès l'époque préclassique [< diss. Sorbonne 1987]: Latomus.c 216, 1992 → 10,9454: Fb 2750; 2-87031-156-7. -- ᴿAnCL 64 (1995) 371s (Dominique *Longrée*).

6542 ᴱ**Krömer** Dietfried, Wie die Blätter am Baum, so wechseln die Wörter; 100 Jahre Thesaurus Linguae Latinae, Veranstaltungen (1994 München). Stu 1995, Teubner. x-238 p. 3-8154-7100-1.

6543 **Maltby** Robert, A lexicon of ancient Latin etymologies: Arca 25, 1991 → 9,10281; 0-905205-74-X. -- ᴿLatomus 54 (1995) 156s (J.-C. *Fredouille*).

6544 ᴱ**Moussy** Claude, Les problèmes de la synonymie en latin. P 1994, Sorbonne Centre Ernout. 222 p. -- ᴿRÉL 73 (1995) 245s (M. *Baratin*).

6545 *Panchón* Federico, Relativas sin verbo y la función del relativo en latín : EM(erita) 62 (1994) 125-139.

6546 *Pavanetto* Cleto, Le latin, le grec ancien et leurs littératures; patrimoine commun des Européens: Salesianum 57 (1995) 131-5.

6547 ᴱ**Poole** Adrian, *Maule* Jeremy, The Oxford book of classical verse in translation. Ox 1995, UP. xlix-606 p.; bibliog. 547-580. 0-19-214209-7.

6548 **Reichler-Béguelin** Marie-José, Les noms latins du type mens .. : Coll. Latomus 195, 1986. -- ᴿGnomon 67 (1995) 63 (D. *Langslow*).

6549 **Sblendorio Cugusi** Maria Teresa, I sostantivi latini in *-tudo*: TManUnivLat 34, 1991; Lᵐ 48: ᴿSalesianum 57 (1995) 405s (R. *Bracchi*).

6550   *Schindel* Ulrich,   Energia, metathesis, metastasis; Figurendefinitionen bei ISIDOR und QUINTILIAN: Glotta 71 (1993) 112-119.

6551   **Sidwell** Keith C.,   Reading medieval Latin.   C 1995, Univ.   xviii-398 p. 0-521-44239-7; -747-X pa.

6552   **Solin** Heikki,   Namenpaare; eine Studie zur römischen Namengebung 1990 → 10,9457: [R]EM(erita) 63 (1995) 151-3 (Gloria *Sedeño Mombiedro*).

6553   **Stelten** Leo F.,   Dictionary of ecclesiastical Latin.   Peabody MA 1995, Hendrickson. xiv-330 p. 1-56563-131-5 [RStR 22,251, D.R. *Janz*: ThD 43,188]. -- [R]OCP 61 (1995) 646 (R.M. *Mackowski*).

6554   *Stempel* Reinhard,   Das lateinische Gerundium und Gerundivum in historischer und typologischer Perspektive: Glotta 72 (1994/5) 235-251.

6555   *Vaahtera* Jyri, The origin of Latin *suffragium*: Glotta 71 (1993) 66-80.

6556   **Vine** Brent,   Studies in archaic Latin inscriptions: IBS 75.   Inns 1993, Univ. 419 p. -- [R]BSLP 90,2 (1995) 198-207 (Madeleine *Keller*); RPh(lgLH) 69 (1995) 227-9 (P. *Flobert*).

J8.1   **Philologia generalis**

6557   *Andersen* Paul K.,   Zur Diathese: HSF 106 (1993) 177-231.

6558   *Angoujard* Jean-Pierre,   Quelques 'éléments' pour la représentation des gutturales: LOrA 5s (1995) 107-126.

6559   **Bartoněk** Antonín,   Grundzüge der altgriechischen mundartlichen Frühgeschichte: IBS. Inn 1991, Inst. SprW. 33 p. -- [R]AAW 46 (1993) 157s (F. *Lochner von Hüttenbach*).

6560   *Borochovsky* Esther,   [H] The difference between 'verbs of expression' [information] and 'verbs of announcement' [message]: Leš 59 (1995) 243-252; Eng. 3,IV.

6561   **Bybee** Joan L., *al.*. The evolution of grammar; tense, aspect and modality in the languages of the world. Ch 1994, Univ. xxii-398 p. 0-226-08665-8.

6562   **Campbell** George L.,   Compendium of the world's [5000] languages. L 1991, Routledge. xxiv-1574 p. (2 vol.). -- [R]Salesianum 57 (1995) 179 (R. *Bracchi*).

6563   *Eco* Umberto, *a*)   Die Suche nach der vollkommenen Sprache [R 1993, Laterza], [T]*Kroeber* Burkhart. Mü 1994, Beck. 388 p. DM 48. -- [R]Kratylos 40 (1995) 49-53 (M. *Mayrhofer*). -- *b*) The search for the perfect language, [T]*Fentress* James: The Making of Europe. Ox 1994, Blackwell. xii-385 p.; bibliog. 355-371. 0-631-17465-6.

6564   **Hagège** Claude,   Le souffle de la langue; voies et destins des parlers d'Europe. P 1992, Odile Jacob. 280 p.; 4 maps. -- [R]BSLP 90,2 (1995) 50-53 (Jack *Feuillet*).

6565   *Hagège* Claude,   La rôle des médiaphoriques [not (news-) media but innovation for testimonials, evidentials]: BSLP 90,1(1995) 1-17; Eng.Gk. 18; Sv. 19.

6566   **Heine** Bernd,   Auxiliaries, cognitive forces and grammaticalization.   Ox 1993, UP. 161 p[. *AGlot 80 (1995) 241-9 (Grazia *Crocco Galèas*).

6567   *Kleiber* Georges,   Sur les (in)définis en général et les SN (in)définis en particulier : BSLP 90,1(1995) 21-50; Eng. 50 : 'NPs'.

6568   **La Stella** T.Enzo,   Uomini dietro le parole; 500 personaggi divenuti vocaboli di tutti i giorni: Bivio. Mi 1992, Mursia. 180 p. -- [R]Salesianum 57 (1995) 400s (R. *Bracchi*; piacevole, informativo).

6569   **Lightfoot** David,   How to set parameters; arguments from language change. CM 1993, MIT. xi-214 p.; bibliog. 199-210. 0-262-62090-1.

6570   *Livnat* Zohar, *Sela* Meir, [H] Apposition -- the third relation ? [linguistic elements neither coordinate nor subordinate]: Leš 59 (1995s) 57-70.

6571   [E]**Lutzeier** Peter R., Studien zur Wortfeldtheorie / [20] Studies in lexical field theory: *LingArb 288. Tü 1993, Niemeyer. vii-282 p. DM 124. -- [R]Kratylos 40 (1995) 71-77 (C.-P. *Herbermann*).

6572   **Olsen** Mari Jean B., A semantic and pragmatic model of lexical and grammatical aspect: diss. Northwestern, [D]*Levin* Beth. Evanston 1994. 368 p. 95-21784. -- DissA 56 (1995s) p. 911.

6573   *Peters* Martin, Indogermanische Chronik 35: *Sprache 36,3 (1994), c. 400 p. numbered by section through Altslavisch and to be continued.

6574   *Radici Colace* Paola, Per un lessico didattico-pedagogico nelle lingue classiche; metafore spazio-temporali nei processi di apprendimento e di insegnamento: GIF 46 (1994) 169-182.

6575   **Rosén** Haiim B., Die Periphrase; Wesen und Entstehung: VorträgeKS 57. Inn 1992, Univ. Inst. SprW. 100 p. Sch 280. -- [R]Kratylos 40 (1995) 77-80 (K.-H. *Schmidt*).

6576   **Schwall** Ulrike, Aspektualität; eine semantisch-funktionelle Kategorie: BBeit-Ling 344. Tü 1991, Narr. xv-449 p. DM 124. -- [R]Kratylos 40 (1995) 152-161 (N. *Nübler*).

6577   **Silva** M., Biblical words and their meaning; an introduction to lexical semantics[2rev] [[1]1983]. 224 p. $ 20. 0-310-47981-9 [NTAb 40,p.329].

6578   **Silvestri** Domenico, La forbice e il ventaglio; descrivere, interpretare, operare da un punto di vista linguistico; lezioni di glottologia. N 1994, Arte Tipografica. 295 p.

6579   **Watkins** Calvert, How to kill a dragon; aspects of Indo-European poetics. NY 1995, Oxford-UP. xv-613 p.; bibliog. 550-576. 0-19-508595-7.

J8.2 Grammatica comparata

6580   *Andreyev* N.D., Early Indo-European typology: IGF 99 (1994) 1-20.

6581   *Angoujard* Jean-Pierre, Syncope et voyelles accentuées (parler du Hedjaz, Bani Hasan et Hébreu biblique: LOrA 4 (1993) 103-123.

6582   *Aslanoff* C., Pour une révision des modèles grecs dans l'analyse des parties du discours en hébreu; le statut du participe: RÉJ 154 (1995) 77-88 [NTAb 40, p.204].

6583   **Beekes** Robert S.P., Comparative Indo-European linguistics; an introduction. Amst 1995, Benjamins. xxii-376 p.; bibliog. 284-300. 90-272-2151-0.

6584   **Benveniste** Émile, Indoeuropäische Institutionen; Wortschatz, Geschichte, Funktionen [1969 franç. (Eng. 1973; ital. 1976)], [T]*Beyer* Wolfgang, [E]*Zimmer* Stefan. Fra/P 1993, Campus/Maison des Sciences de l'Homme. 537 p. DM 128. 3-593-34453-X. -- [R]Numen 41 (1994) 195s (C. *Auffarth*).

6585   *Bohas* Georges, 'OCP' et la persistance des représentations sous-jacentes: LOrA 4 (1993) 35-40.

6586   *Calame* Claude, La Grèce archaïque entre analyse sémantique et comparatisme indo-européen: une étude de G. NAGY [Greek muthology and poetics, Cornell 1990]: Quaderni Urbinati 77 (1994) 151-7.

6587   **Cohen** David, Dictionnaire des racines sémitiques ou attestées dans les langues sémitiques 3 (*gld -- dhml/r*) -- 4 (*dhmm -- drr*). Lv 1993, Peeters. p. 119-227 / 228-342. -- [R]RSO 69 (1995) 231-3 (G. *Garbini*).

6588 *Gal* Amikam, The category 'adjective'in Semitic languages: JSSt 40 (1995) 1-9.

6589   **Gamkrelidze** Thomas V., *Ivanov* Vyačeslav V., Indo-European and the Indo-

Europeans; a reconstruction and historical analysis of a proto-language and proto-culture; I. The text, [T]Nichols Johanna.: Trends in Linguistics 80. B 1995, Mouton de Gruyter. cvi-864 p. 3-11-009646-3.

6590   **Garbini** Giovanni, *Durand* Olivier,   Introduzione alle lingue semitiche. Brescia 1994, Paideia. 191 p. -- [R]BSLP 90,2 (1995)332-6 (Dominique *Caubet*); WZKM 85 (1995) 343-350 (A. *Zaborski*, Eng.)

6591   **Gimbutas** Marijo,   Die Ethnogenese der europäischen Indogermanen [Remarks 1986]: InBeitSprW K 54. Inns 1992, Univ. 29 p. -- [R]BNF 29s (1994s) 313-6 (J. *Udolphi*).

6592   *Goldenberg* Gideon, Attribution in Semitic languages: LOrA 5s (1995) 1-20.

6593   *Hackstein* Olav, On the prehistory of dual inflection in the Tocharian verb: *Sprache 35 (1991-3) 47-70 [176-186, initial labiovelars, *Hilmarsson* Jörundur].

6594   *Hamp* Eric P.,   Indo-European bases of the form *$g^w el$- in Greek: Glotta 72 (1994/5) 16s (14, *blépharon*: 18s. *kérdo : kérdos*).

6595   **Haudry** Jean,   L'Indo-Européen[3]: Que sais-je ? N° 1798.   P 1994.   128 p. -- [R]BSLP 90,2 (1995) 169-173 (C. de *Lamberterie*).

6596   *a) Kienast* Burkhart,   Gedanken zur Geschichte der semitischen 'Tempora' -- *b) Sanmartín* Joaquín, Über Regeln und Ausnahmen; Verhalten des vorkonsonantischen /n/ im 'Altsemitischen'; -- *c) Tropper* Josef, Die semitische 'Suffixkonjugation' im Wandel -- von der Prädikativform zum Perfekt: → 185, [F]SODEN W. von, Vom Alten Orient (1995) 119-133 / 433-466 / 491-516.

6597   *Knauf* Ernst A.,   Die Höchstzahl möglicher zweiradikaler Wurzeln des Ursemitischen: BiNo 75 (1994) 20s.

6598   **Levin** Saul,   Semitic and Indo-European; the principal etymologies, with emphasis on Afro-Asiatic: Current Issues in Linguistic Theory 129. Amst/Ph 1995, Benjamins. xxii-514 p. 90-272-3632-1 / US 1-55619-583-4.

6599   *Loewenstamm* Jean, *Alaoui ElMhammedi* Saïda, On the correctness of the biliteral analysis of mediae geminatae verbs: *LOrA 5s (1995) 127-132.

6600   **Masica** Colin P., The Indo-Aryan languages 1993 → 9.10310; £ 65:   [R]JRAS (1994) 284s (R. *Snell*); Salesianum 57 (1995) 799 (R. *Bracchi*).

6601   *Minissi* Nullo, Il presunto carattere consonantico delle protolingue e la teoria delle laringali: AION 54 (1994) 257-274.

6602   *Müller* Hans-Peter, Ergative constructions in early Semitic languages: JNES 54 (1995) 261-271.

6603   **Nerlich** Brigitte, Semantic theories in Europe 1830-1930: from etymology to contextuality: AsTHoLS 3/59. Amst/Ph 1992, Benjamins. xi-359 p. *f* 125. -- [R]Kratylos 40 (1995) 61-67 (C. *Hassler*).

6604   **Orel** Vladimir E., *Stolbova* Olga V.,   Hamito-Semitic etymological dictionary; materials for a reconstruction [2672 roots]: HO 1/18. Lei 1995, Brill. xxxviii-578 p. $ 200. 90-04-10051-2 [RStR 22,144, D.I. *Owen*]. -- [R]BoL (1995) 179 (A.E. *Millard*).

6605   *Prósper* Blanca,   Estudios sobre la estructura del adverbio pronominal indo-europeo; EM(erita) 62 (1994) 75-107.

6606   [E]**Ramat** A. Giacalone & P., Le lingue indoeuropee. Bo 1993, [2]1994, Mulino. 548 p. -- [R]*AGlot 79 (1994) 104-113 (P. *Di Giovine*).

6607   **Shields** Kenneth C.,   A history of Indo-European verb morphology: AsTHoLS 4/88. Amst/Ph 1992, Benjamins. x-160 p. *f* 80. -- [R]Kratylos 40 (1995) 101-5 (A. *Erhart*).

6608   *a) Shields* Kenneth[J],   On the origin of the Indo-European feminine gender category; -- *b) Wolf* George, Derivation and morpho-syntactic change; the Indo-European attributive genitive: I(nd)GF 100 (1995) 101-9 / 110-5.

6609   **Sihler** Andrew L.,   New [beyond C.D. BUCK 1933] comparative grammar of Greek and Latin. NY 1995, Oxford-UP. viii-686 p. 0-19-508345-8 [RStR 22,61, F.W. *Danker*]. -- ᴿMH(elv) 52 (1995) 260s (J.-P. *Borle*).

6610   *Soden* Wolfram von,   Entsprechungen von deutsch 'zu' in Ausdrücken wie 'zu viel, zu wenig' in einigen indogermanischen Sprachen, aber nicht in den semitischen Sprachen: UF 27 (DIETRICH 60. Gb. 1995) 481-6.

6611   *Woodhouse* Robert,   Proto Indo-European injective asperes: I(nd)GF 100 (1995) 92-100.

J8.3   Linguistica generalis

6612   *Auroux* S., *al.,* on the four new encyclopedias of linguistics published 1990-4: BSLP 90,2 (1995) 34-49.

6613   *Becerra* Anissia, *Usage* et *raison* nella riflessione filosofico-linguistica di Bernard LAMY (1640-1715; Rhétorique 1675 ⁵1715): Acme 48,3 (1995) 85-109.

6614   **Berruto** Gaetano,   Fondamenti di sociolinguistica: Manuali 59.   R 1995, Laterza. vii-315 p.: bibliog. 269-298.   88-420-4571-3.

6615   ᴱ**Black** David A.,   Linguistics and New Testament interpretation.   Nv 1992. Broadman.   319 p --   ᴿRevBib(Arg) 57 (1995) 185s (J.P. *Martín,* también sobre su Learn to read NT Greek 1993).

6616   **Blake** Barry,   Case: Textbooks in Linguistics.   C 1994, Univ. --   ᴿBSLP 90,2 (1995) 95-102 (J. *François*).

6617   *Blasco Ferrer* Eduardo,   Across linguistics; towards a functional theory of variation and linguistic change: I(nd)GF 100 (1995) 77-91.

6618   ᴱ**Brogyányi** Béla,   Prehistory, history, and historiography of language, speech, and linguistic theory: Current Issues 64, 1992 → 10,9492: ᴿRBPH 72 (1994) 643s (J. *Goes*).

6619   **Bybee** Joan L.,   Morphology; a study of the relation between meaning and form: Typological Studies in Language 9.   Amst 1985, Benjamins.   xii-234 p.   90-272-2877-9.

6620   ᴱ**Bybee** Joan, *Fleischman* Suzanne,   Modality in grammar and discourse: Typological Studies in Language 32.   Amst 1995, Benjamins. viii-575 p.   90-272-2926-0.

6621   **Croft** William,   Typology and universals: Textbooks in Linguistics.   C 1993, Univ. xiv-311 p.; bibliog. 278-292.   0-521-36755-4.

6622   *Croft* William, Autonomy and functionalist linguistics: Lg 71 (1995) 490-532.

6623   **Crystal** David,   The Cambridge encyclopedia of language 1991 → 7,747; 8,830c: ᴿSalesianum 57 (1995) 179s (R. *Bracchi*).

6624   **Dauses** August,   Theorien der Linguistik; Grundprobleme der Theoriebildung. Stu 1994, Steiner. 95 p. --   ᴿBSLP 90,2 (1995) 57-60 (Jack *Feuillet*).

6625   ᴱ**De Mauro** Tullio, *Sugeta* Shigeaki,   SAUSSURE and linguistics today.   R 1995, Bulzoni. 352 p.   88-7119-829-8.

6626   **Dinneen** Francis P.,   General linguistics. Wsh 1995, Georgetown Univ. xvii-646 p.   0-87840-278-0.

6627   **Dixon** R.M.W.,   Ergativity: StLing 69.   C 1994, Univ. xxii-271 p.   -- ᴿBSLP 90,2 (1995) 89-94 (G. *Lazard*).

6628 ᴱ**Downing** Pamela, *Noonan* Michael, Word order in discourse: Typological Studies in Language 30. ix-595 p. 90-272-2922-8.

6629 **Fine** Jonathan, How language works; cohesion in normal and nonstandard communication: Advances in Discourse Processes 51. Norwood NJ 1994, Ablex. xxiii-286 p.; ill. 1-56750-044-7.

6630 **Geis** Michael L., Speech acts and conversational interaction. C 1995, Univ. xiv-248 p. 0-521-46499-4.

6631 **Guasti** Maria Teresa, Causative and perceptive verbs; a comparative study. T 1993, Rosenberg & S. 194 p. -- ᴿBSLP 90,2 (1995) 102s (J. *Feuillet*: riche).

6632 **Hall** Christopher, Morphology and mind; a unified approach to explanation in linguistics. NY 1992, Routledge. xx-224 p. $ 69.50. -- ᴿLg 70 (1994) 178-181 (R. *Hamilton*: why suffixing gets preferred to prefixing).

6633 **Hipkiss** Robert A., Semantics; defining the discipline. Mahwah NJ 1995, L.Erlbaum. xvii-123 p. 0-8058-1593-7.

6634 **Hirsh-Pasek** Kathy, *Golinkoff* Roberta M., The origins of grammar; evidence from early language comprehension: Language, Speech & Communication. CM c.1995, MIT. x-230 p.; bibliog. 205-222. 0-262-08242-X.

6635 **Huck** Geoffrey J., *Goldsmith* John A., Ideology and linguistic theory; Noam CHOMSKY and the deep structure debates: History of linguistic thought. L 1885, Routledge. x-186 p.; bibliog. 165-177. 0-415-11735-6.

6636 **Jackendorff** Ray, Patterns in the mind; language and human nature. NY 1994, Basic. ix-246 p. $ 25. -- ᴿLg 71 (1995) 592-5 (T. *Wasow*: unduly overshadowed by more entertaining S. PINKER).

6637 ᴱ**Jorna** René J., *al.*, Signs, search and communication; semiotic aspects of artificial intelligence: Grundlagen der Kommunikation und Kognition. B 1993, de Gruyter. viii-378 p.; ill.

6638 *Kaplan* Roger J., Derivational processes: underlying forms and analogies in [990 Yehuda] H̲AYYUJ's linguistic works [c. 980]: *A(sn)JS 20 (1995) 313-332.

6639 **Klein** Wolfpeter, Am Anfang war das Wort; theorie- und wissenschaftge-schichtliche Elemente frühneuzeitlichen Sprachbewusstseins. B 1992, Akademie. x-382 p.; 10 fig. -- ᴿBHR 56 (1994) 585-7 (Irena *Backus*); Laur 35 (1994) 180-2 (G. *Veltri*).

6640 *Kniffka* Hannes, Hearsay vs. autoptic evidence in linguistics: some 'eastern' and 'western' perspectives and perspectives of perspectives [some linguistic 'truths' never made it across the Atlantic (either way) or were 'changed'] : ZDMG 14 (1994) 345-376.

6641 ᴱ**Lapschy** Giulio, History of linguistics [Storia 1990 → 10338], ᵀ. L 1994, Longman. xx-203 p.; xx-380 p. 0-582-0949189-5; -91-7.

6642 **Laurier** Daniel, Introduction à la philosophie du langage: ᴿBSLP 90,2 (1995) 53-57 (A. *Lemaréchal*).

6643 **McMahon** April M.S., Understanding language change, 1994 → 10,9506; $ 60; pa. $ 18. -- ᴿLg 71 (1995) 600-3 (W.N. *Francis*).

6644 **Malmberg** Bertil, Histoire de la linguistique, de Sumer à Saussure 1991 → 9,10339; 2-13-043357-X.

6645 **Masterson** Karen Jean, An information-theoretic approach to the analysis of Semitic texts: diss. UCLA 1994, ᴰ*Segert* S. 577 p. 95-18999. -- D(iss)A 56,p.530.

6646 **Matthews** Peter H.,Grammatical theory in the U.S.. Bloomfield to Chomsky: StLing 67, 1993 → 9,10340; 10, 9508: ᴿLg 71 (1995) 595-600 (D.T. *Langendoen*).

6647 **Meillet** Antoine, Pour un manuel de linguistique générale: Lincei Mem. mor.

1/6/1. R 1995, Accademia Lincei. 245 p.

6648 **Pinker** Steven, The language instinct; how the mind creates language. NY 1994, Morrow. 494 p. 0-688-12141-1. -- [R]Lg 71 (1995) 610-4 (R.P. *Meier*).

6649 *Plank* Frans, Professor [August F. 1802-1887] POTT und die Lehre der Allgemeinen Sprachwissenschaft : ZDMG 145 (1995) 328-364.

6650 **Pottier** Bernard, Sémantique générale. P 1993, PUF. 227 p. -- [R]BSLP 90,2 (1995) 111-121 (J.-P. *Desclés*).

6651 [E]**Quasthoff** Uta M., Aspects of oral communication; Research in Text Theory 21. Berlin 1995, de Gruyter. v-493 p. 3-11-014465-4.

6652 **Reis** Marga, Wortstellung und Informationsstruktur: Linguistische Arbeiten 306. Tü 1993, Niemeyer. vii-356 p. 3-484-30305-9.

6653 *Richter* Wolfgang, Zum Verhältnis von Literaturwissenschaft, Linguistik und Theologie : → 159, [F]ROGERSON, J., Bible/Society; JSOT.s 200 (1995) 422-8.

6654 *Santulli* Francesca, Sprachwissenschaft und Sprachgeschichte nella concezione epistemologica di Hermann PAUL: *AGlot 79 (1994) 1-22.

6655 [E]**Simone** Raffaele, Iconicity in language; Current Issues 110. Amst 1995, Benjamins. xi-317 p. 90-272-3613-5.

6656 **Tejera** Victorino, Literature, criticism, and the theory of signs: Semiotic crossroads 7. Amst 1995, Benjamins. x-158 p. 90-272-1948-6.

6657 **Todesco** Orlando, Parola e verità; AGOSTINO e la filosofia del linguaggio: Filosofia e società 6. R 1993, Anicia. -- [R]Angelicum 71 (1994) 625s (A. *Lobato*).

6658 *Washburn* David I., CHOMSKY's separation of syntax and semantics: HebSt 35 (Madison WI 1994) 27-46 [< OTA 18 (1995) p. 496].

6659 *Willems* Klaas, Sprache und Sprachgemeinschaft:Überlegungen zu den Voraussetzungen des'Sprachapriori'in Linguistik und Philosophie:I(nd)GF 100(1995)1-76

6660 **Williams** Glyn, Sociolinguistics; a sociological critique [conflict model; linguists tend to approve mobility away from a minor language]. L 1992, Routledge. xv-278 p. $ 17. -- [R]Lg 70 (1994) 340-4 (Nancy C. *Dorian*).

J8.4 *Origines artis scribendi* -- **The origin of writing**

6661 **Assmann** Jan, Das kulturelle Gedächtnis; Schrift, Erinnerung und politische Identität in frühen Hochkulturen. Mü 1992, Beck. 344 p. DM 68. 3-406-36088-2. -- [R]Numen 41 (1994) 196s (Gerdien *Jonker*).

6662 **Bernal** Martin, Cadmean letters 1990 → 6,9859; 8,a144: [R]WO 26 (1995) 209s (W. *Röllig*, auch über SASS B. 1991).

6663 *Briquel-Chatonnet* Françoise, Étude comparée de l'évolution des alphabets judéen, israélite et phénicien: LOrA 4 (1993) 1-8; 9-30, charts.

6664 **Brookfield** Karen, La scrittura. Novara 1994, De Agostini. 64 p.; 300 color. ill. L[m] 26. -- [R]Archeo 9,113 (1994) 121 (S. *Moscati*),

6665 *Frankfurter* D., The magic of writing & the writing of magic; the power of the word in Egyptian & Greek traditions: *Helios 21 (1994) 189-221 [NTAb 39,273] 6666 **Gasparri** Françoise, Introduction à l'histoire de l'écriture. Turnhout 1994, Brepols. 240 p.; 70 pl. -- [R]RÉL 73 (1995) 367s (V. *Zarini*).

6667 **Godart** Louis, L'invenzione della scrittura; dal Nilo alla Grecia 1992 → 9,10362: [R]QuadUrb 75 (1994) 155-163 (C. *Brillante*).

6668 **Goody** Jack, Entre l'oralité et l'Écriture, [T]*Paulme* Denise: Ethnologies. P

1994, PUF. 326 p. F 198. -- [R]Études 382 (1995) 134 (C. *Pairault*).

6669 **Green** Margaret W., *Nissen* Hans J., Zeichenliste der archaischen Texte aus Uruk 1987 → 3,a49 ... 10,9525: [R]BiOr 52 (1995) 689-713 (P. *Steinkeller*).

6670 *Hoz* Javier de, Las sociedades paleohispánicas de l'area no indoeuropea y la escritura: AEAr 66 (1993) 3-29; Eng.3.

6671 *Justeson* John J., *Stephens* Laurence D., The evolution of syllabaries from alphabets; transmission, language contrast, and script typology: *Sprache 35 (1991-3) 2-40; bibliog. 41-46.

6672 *Klotchkoff* J.S., [R] Signs on a potsherd from Gonur (What kind of script did ancient Margianians have ?) [Elamite]: VDI 213 (1995) 54-60; 4 fig.; Eng. 60.

6673 *Mastruzzo* Antonino, Ductus, corsività, storia della scrittura; alcune considerazioni: *ScrCiv 19 (1993) 403-454.

6674 *Millard* Alan, The knowledge of writing in Iron Age Palestine: TynB 46 (1995) 207-217 [< OTA 19, p.392].

6675 **Nissen** Hans J., *al.*, Archaic bookkeeping; early writing and techniques of the economic administration of the Ancient Near East, [T]*Larsen* Paul. Ch 1993, Univ. 224 p. $ 30. 0-226-58659-6. -- [R]JAOS 115 (1995) 533s (M.A. *Powell*).

6676 **Parpola** Asko, Deciphering the Indus script. C 1994, Univ. xxii-374 p.; 225 fig. £ 60. -- [R]JRAS (1995) 428-430 (D.K. *Chakrabarti*: the few chapters sticking to the facts are useful).

6677 **Sass** Benjamin, Studia alphabetica: OBO 102, 1991 → 7,9688 ... 9.10373: [R]ArTGran 57 (1994) 531-4 (A. *Torres*): WZKM 83 (1993) 300-2 (S. *Segert*).

6678 **Schmandt-Besserat** Denise, Before writing 1992 → 8.a162: 9,10374: [R]JAOS 114 (1994) 96s (M.A. *Powers*); Syria 71 (1994) 455s (H. de *Contenson*).

6679 **Silvestri** D., *al.*, The earliest script of Uruk (syntactic analysis): Annali MeditA 2. N 1990. Ist. Univ. Orientale. 234 p.; 553 p.

J9.1 *Analysis linguistica loquelae de Deo* -- **God-talk**

6680 **Alston** William P., Divine nature and human language; essays in philosophical theology 1989 → 6.196*, Cornell Univ. xiv-281 p. -- ZNKUL 38,3 (1995) 143-150 (T. *Szubka*, [P]).

6681 *a) Aróstegui* Luis, La palabra filosófica de las religiones; -- *b) Guerra* Santiago, El reto del discurso cristiano, decir hoy 'Dios' significativamente; -- *c) Polo* Teodoro, Decir 'lo otro' que todavía habla; el lenguaje herido de los místicos: REsp 53,212 (1994) 233-253 / 255-315 / 317-347

6682 *a) Beck* Mordechai, Speaking in tongues. the meaning of Babel; -- *b) Harris* Tod, The word made flesh; the roots of written language: Parabola 20,3 ('Language and meaning' 1995) 13-15 / 16-20 (*al.*).

6683 **Boeve** Lieven, Spreken over God in 'open verhalen'; de theologie uitgedaagd ['challenged'] door het postmoderne denken: diss. Leuven 1995, [R]*Schrijver* G. de. lxxii-696 p. -- [R]LouvSt 20 (1995) 409s.

6684 *Clarkson* Shannon, God as a second language? Learning from the Pacific rim: *JWm&R 13 ('Mapping a Pan-Pacific Feminist Theology' 1995) 26-28 [14 (1996) 'Bringing Beijing home'].

6685 **Cupitt** Don, The last philosophy. L 1995, SCM. viii-149 p. £ 10 pa. -- [R]Theol 98 (L 1995) 477s (G. *Ward*).

6686   *DePater* Wim A.,   Analogie en disclosures; over religieuze taal: Bijdragen 56 (1995) 242-256: Eng. 256.

6687   **Fodor** James,   Christian hermeneutics; Paul RICŒUR and the refiguring of theology. Ox 1995, Clarendon. xiv-370 p. $ 65. 0-19-826349-X [< ThD 43,265].

6688   *Gilbert* Paul,   Paul RICŒUR; réflexion, ontologie et action: NRT 117 (1995) 339-362 , 552-562 [461-4, ses revues de CHIODI M., ᴱGREISCH J.]

6689   **Grosshans** Hans-Peter,   Theologischer Realismus; ein sprachphilosophischer Beitrag zu einer theologischen Sprachenlehre: ev. Diss. ᴰ*Jüngel.* Tübingen 1995. -- ThRv Beilage 92/2, xv.

6690   *Häring* Hermann, Opnieuw leren wat wij zijn vergeten; de vele kanten van het spreken over God in een seculaire samenleving: TTh 35 (1995) 148-170; Eng. 170.

6691   **Humphreys** Frank,   Sensory language and the divine-human relationship in the Tenak: diss. McGill, ᴰ*Runnalls* D. -- RStR 22,272.

6692   *Lange* F. de,   Transformerend evangelie; christelijke verkondiging als taalhandeling: G(ereformeerd)TT 95 (1995) 12-23.

6693   *McMinn* Mark R. + 4 *al.,* The effects of God language on perceived attributes of God: JPsT 21 (1993) 309-314.

6694   *Masiá Clavel* Juan,   Paul RICŒUR, en la frontera de filosofía y teología: MCom(illas) 53 (1995) 115-133 (1994s) 45-59.

6695   *Meyr-Blanck* Michael,   Vom Symbol zum Zeichen; Plädoyer für eine semiotische Revision der Symboldidaktik [p.344 'Unterricht als Aufdecken von theologischen Codierungen']: EvTh 55 (1995) 337-351.

6696   *Miccoli* Paolo,   Dire Dio, possibilità e limiti dell'umano intendere: *RivScRel 9 (1995) 259-306.

6697   *Nicolson* Ronald B.,   Real evil needs a real God ? Non-realist theology in a third world: HeythJ 36 (1995) 140-152.

6698   **Nuechterlein** John D.,   The conceptual theory of meaning; God, the world, and everything [WITTGENSTEIN L., HEIDEGGER M.]: diss. Univ. Miami, ᴰ*Haack* Susan, 1995. 425 p. 95-37951. -- DissA 56 (1995s) p. 2719.

6699   **Pandikattu** Kuruvilla,   Idol must die so that Symbols might live; towards an ontological understanding of religious language with special reference to RICŒURian symbols: kath. Diss. ᴰ*Coreth.* Innsbruck 1995.--ThRv Beilage 92/2, xi.

6700   **Ricœur** Paul,   Figuring the sacred; religion, narrative, and imagination. Mp 1995, Fortress. x-340 p. 0-8006-2894-2.

6701   *Russo* Adolfo,   Pensare Dio; percorsi della teologia oggi: Asprenas 42 (1995) 483-508.

6702   *Samartha* S.,   Religion, language and reality: *BInterp 2 (1994) 340-362.

6703   **Scharfstein** Ben-Ami,   Ineffability; the failure of words in philosophy and religion. Albany 1993, SUNY. 291 p. -- ᴿJAAR 63 (1995) 900-3 (B.L. *Whitney*).

6704   *Schouwey* Jacques,   De la possibilité d'une herméneutique philosophique de la religion [RICŒUR J., Lectures 3, Aux frontières de la philosophie, Seuil 1994]: RTPh 127 (1995) 357-367; Eng. 423.

6705   *a) Schreiter* Robert J.,   Theorie und Praxis interkultureller Kommunikations-kompetenz in der Theologie; -- *b) Lamb* Matthew L.,   Kommunikative Praxis, die Offenheit der Geschichte und die Dialektik von Gemeinschaft und Herrschaft; (beides) ᵀ*Arens* E. → 149, ᶠPEUKERT H., Anerkennung 1995, 9-30 / 167-192.

6706   *Schröer* Christian,   Der Beitrag der sprachanalytischen Philosophie zur historischen Forschung der christlichen Philosophie: Sprache und Seinsbegriff bei PARMENIDES, PLATON & ARISTOTELES: MThZ 46 (1995) 409-423.

6707   *Sedmak* Clemens,   WITTGENSTEINs Sprachspielmodell und die pluralistische Religionstheorie: ZkT 117 (1995) 383-415

6708   **Sells** Michael A.,   Mystical languages of unsaying.   Ch 1994, Univ.   x-316 p. -- [R]MoTh 11 (1995) 486-8 (A. *Louth*).

6709   [E]**Sicking** Thom, [A]   *Ma huwa ilahuka* ?   Quel est ton Dieu   [nos images de Dieu et manières de parler de lui; 8 art.].   Beyrouth 1994, Univ.S.J. Institut Supérieur de Sciences Religieuses.   250 p. -- [R]POrC 45 (1995) 327-330 (P. *Ternant*).

6710   **Silva** Moisés,   God, language, and Scripture; reading the Bible in the light of general linguistics: Foundations of contemporary interpretation 4.   GR 1990, Zondervan. -- [R]SBF*LA 45 (1995) 537-9 (L.D. *Chrupcala*).

6711   *Smalbrugge* Matthias A.,   La prédestination entre subjectivité et langage; le premier dogme moderne: RTPh 127 (1995) 43-54; Eng. 111.

6712   *Sommerville* C. John,   Is religion a language-game ?   A real-world critique of the cultural-linguistic theory: TTod 51 (1994s) 594=9.

6713   **Stiver** Dan R.,   The philosophy of religious language; sign, symbol and story. Ox 1995, Blackwell.   xiii-258 p.   £ 40; pa. £ 14.   1-55786-581-7; -2-5. --   [R]*TBR 8,3 (1995s) 4s (B. *Clark*).

6714   **Templeton** Elizabeth,   The strangeness of God 1993 → 10,9563: [R]ScoBuEv ë 12 (1994) 145-7 (C.M. *Cameron*).

6715   **Thiselton** Anthony C.,   Interpreting God and the postmodern self; on meaning, manipulation and promise: S(cot)JTh series.   E 1995, Clark.   xi-180 p.; bibliog. 165-172. 0-567-29302-5.

6716   **Timm** Hermann,Wahr-Zeichen; Angebote zur Erneuerung religiöser Symbolkultur. Stu 1993,Kohlhammer.159 p.DM 29,80.--[R]LebZeug 50(1995) 150s (W. *Gantke*)

6717   *Willi-Plein* Ina,.   Sprache als Schlüssel zur Schöpfung: Überlegungen zur sogenanten Sündenfallgeschichte in Gen 3: ThZ 31 (1995) 1-17.

6718   *Wittig* Joseph   (1879-1949),   Der Geburtstag der christlichen Sprache [Pfingstfest]: GuL 68 (1995) 161-5.

J9.2 *Hermeneutica paratheologica* -- **wider linguistic analysis**

6719   **Dicenso** James,   Hermeneutics and the disclosure of truth ... HEIDEGGER, GADAMER, RICŒUR ...   1990 → 7,1015*; 10,9567:   [R]JETS 37 (1994) 597s (J. *Morrison*).

6720   **Evans** Jeanne,   Paul RICŒUR's hermeneutics of the imagination: AmUSt 2/143.   NY 1995, Lang.   xi-213 p.   0-8204-2060-3.

6721   **Hintikka** Jaakko,   La Vérité est-elle ineffable ?, [T]*Soulez* A., *Schmitz* F. Combas 1994, Éclat.   126 p. --   [R]RTPh 127 (1995) 81 (Nathalie *Janz*).

6722   *McCagney* Nancy,   Language as liberation: → 184, [F]SMART N., Aspects of religion 1994, 193-206.

6723   **Moore** Robert C., Logic and representation: Studies 39.   Stanford 1995, CSLI. xiv-196 p.   1-881526-16-X.

6724   **Simon** Joseph,   Philosophy of the sign, [T]*Heffernan* George: Contemporary continental philosophy.   Albany 1995, SUNY.   ix-291 p.   0-7914-2453-7.

J9.6   **Analysis et theologia narrationis**

Minette de Tillesse Caetano,   O Deus pelas costas; teologia narrativa da
Bíblia: RBBras 12, 1995   → 1386 supra; français 1387.]: RBBras 12,1-3.
6726   *Økland* Nils A.,   Narrativ teologi [KEMP P., BJERG S., SLØK J.]: NTT 96
(1995) 35-42; Eng. 42.
6727   **Stegner** William R.,   Narrative theology in early Jewish Christianity.   LVL
1989, W-Knox. x-141 p. $ 12. -- ᴿJETS 37 (1994) 429s (D.T. *Williams*).

(IV.)   **Postbiblica**

K1 **Pseudepigrapha [= catholicis 'Apocrypha '] .1** *VT. generalia*

6728   **Amsler** F., *al.*, Le mystère apocryphe: introduction à une littérature méconnue:
EssBib 26. Genève 1995, Labor et Fides. 152 p. Fs 32. 6729 *Bar-Ilan* M., The discovery
of the [Cochin] Words of Gad the Seer: JSPE 11 (1993) 93-107 [NTAb 40, p.297].
6730   **Bryan** David. Cosmos, chaos and the Kosher mentality: JSPE.s 12.   Shf 1995,
Academic. 303 p.; bibliog. p. 273-285. 1-85075-536-1
6731   ᴱ**Charlesworth** James H., *Evans* Craig A., The Pseudepigrapha and early biblical
interpretation JSPE.s 14, 1993: ᴿSalesianum 57 (1995) 375s (R. *Vicent*).
6732   **Cimosa** Mario, La letteratura intertestamentaria: La Bibbia nella storia 1992 →
8,a239; 9,10434: ᴿSales 57 (1995) 567s (E. *Dal Covolo*).
6733   **Denis** Albert-Marie, Concordance latine des pseudépigraphes AT [grecque 1987 →
3,a212; 9,10435]: CCLat sup, 1993 → 10,9588: ᴿJSJ(ud) 26 (1995) 350s (A. *Hilhorst*);
RBén 104 (1994) 424 (P.-M. *Bogaert*).
6734   **Ehrmann** Michael G., Klagephänomene in zwischentestamentlicher Literatur: Diss.
ᴰ*Welten* B.   Berlin 1994. - ThRv 91 (1995) 92.
6735   **Evans** Craig A., Noncanonical writings & NT 1992 → 9,10436: ᴿJAAR 63 (1995)
190-2 (T.S.L. *Michael*).
6736   *Jonge* Marinus de, The so-called Pseudepigrapha of the OT and early Christianity:
→ 487, NT & Hellenistic [on Mk: 72-87, *Charlesworth* James H., The Son of David;
Solomon and Jesus; 88-100, *Collins* Adela Y., Apotheosis and resurrection].
6737   **Kee** Howard C., The Cambridge annotated study [deuterocanonical] Apocrypha
NRSV. C 1994, Univ. 363 p.; maps £ 11. 0-521-50875-4. -- ᴿTBR 8,1 (1995s) 24 (A.
Gilmore).
6738   *Klener* J., The throne and reign of David in the Apocrypha and Pseudepigrapha: →
10,81, ᶠMEYER L. de, 52 Réflexions 1994, 455-475.
6739   ᵀ**Meyer** Johann F. von, Das Buch Jezira: Jüdische Quellen 1. B 1993, Akademie.
xvii-64 p. 3-05-002313-9.
6740   **Montero Carrión** Domingo, Literatura apocalíptica e intertestamental: Cursos
bíblicos a distancia 14. M 1992, PCC / Casa de la Biblia. 122 p. -- ᴿCiTom 121 (1994)
200s (J.L. *Espinel*).
6741   *a) Otzen* Benedikt. Himmelrejser og himmelvisioner i jødisk apokalyptik; - *b)*
Nielsen Kirsten, 'Gud Herren kaldte på elden til dom' [fire for judgment];

dommedagsmotivet og dets forskydninger [variations]: DanTT 58 (1995) 16-26 / 3-15 [< OTA 18 (1995) p. 570.590 'ilden'].

6742 ^E**Reeves** John C., Tracing the threads; studies in the vitality of Jewish pseudepigrapha 1994 → 10,257d: ^RJRel 75 (1995) 551-3 (G.A. *Anderson*); ZAW 107 (1995) 172s (J. *Herzer*).

6743 **Sacchi** Paolo, L'apocalittica giudaica e la sua storia 1990 → 6,3984 ... 8,3913: ^RBZ 39 (1995) 115s (J. *Maier*).

6744 *a) Sappington* Thomas J., The factor of function in defining Jewish apocalyptic literature; -- *b) Sim* David C., The social setting of ancient apocalypticism; a question of method: JSPE 12 (1994) 93-123 / 13 (1995) 5-16.

6745 **Satran** David, Biblical prophets in Byzantine Palestine; reassessing the Lives of the Prophets [origin not first-century Judaic but 4th-5th Christian]; SVTP 11. Lei 1995, Brill. 150 p.; bibliog. 129-144. 90-04-10234-5. - [< OTA 18 (1995) p. 437]. -- ^RThLZ 120 (1995) 1017s (H.-J. *Stipp*).

6746 **Schwemer** Anna Maria, Studien zu den frühjüdischen Prophetenlegenden Vitae Prophetarum; I. Die Vitae der grossen Propheten; Einleitung, Übersetzung und Kommentar: TSAJ 49. Tü 1995, Mohr. xiv-448 p.; Bibliog. 374-448. 3-16-146439-7.

6747 -- **Tilly** Michael, Johannes der Täufer und die Biographie der Propheten: BWANT 137, 1994 → 9,4556: SNTU 20 (1995) 209s (A. *Fuchs*).

6748 *Verheyden* J., Les pseudépigraphes d'Ancien Testament, textes latins: à propos d'une concordance [DENIS A.M. (1987) 1993]: EThL 71 (1995) 382-420.

κ1.2 Henoch

6749 *Albrile* Ezio, Enoch e l'Iran; un'ipotesi sulle origini dell'apocalittica: Nicolaus 22,2 (1995) 91-136.

6750 **Argall** R.A., 1 Enoch and Sirach; a comparative literary analysis of the themes of revelation, creation and judgment [diss. Iowa 1992, ^D*Nickelsburg* G.]; SBL EJud 8. Atlanta 1995, Scholars. xiii-304 p. $ 35. 0-7885-0175-5; pa. -6-3 [NTAb 40,p.548].

6751 *Argall* Randall A., Reflections on 1 Enoch and Sirach; a comparative literary and conceptual analysis of the themes of revelation, creation and judgment: → 512, SBL Seminars 34 (1995) 337-351.

6752 **Böttrich** Christfried, 'Die Vögel des Himmels haben ihn begraben' [as jackdaws in Slavic Enoch]; Überlieferungen zu Abels Bestattung und zur Ätiologie des Grabes; SIJD 3. Gö 1995, Vandenhoeck & R. 157 p. DM 78. 3-525-54203-8 [< OTA 19,p.364, L.H. *Feldman*].

6753 **Böttrich** Christfried, Das slavische Henochbuch; *a)* Einleitung -- Übersetzung -- Kommentierung: Diss. ^D*Kähler*. Leipzig 1995. - ThRv Beilage 92/2, xi. - *b)* Apokalypsen: JSHRZ 5/7. Gü 1995, Gü-V. p.702-1040; Bibliog. 821-8. 3-579-03957-1.

6754 **Böttrich** C., Weltweisheit, Menschheitsethik, Urkult; Studien zum slavischen Henochbuch: WUNT 2/50, 1992 → 9,10443: ^RBoL (1994) 132 (L. *Grabbe*).

6755 **Davidson** Maxwell J., Angels at Qumran; a comparative study of 1 Enoch 1-36, 72-108 and sectarian writings from Qumran [diss. Queensland 1988]: JSP.s 11,1992 → 9,10444: ^RJQR 86 (1995) 186-9 (G.J. *Brooke*).

6756 **Larson** Erik W., The translation of Enoch; from Aramaic into Greek: diss. NYU, ^D*Schiffman* L., 1995. 372 p. 96-09218. - DissA 56 (1995s) p. 4376.

6757 *a) Nickelsburg* George W.E., Scripture in 1 Enoch and 1 Enoch as Scripture; - *b)*

Pearson Birger A., 1 Enoch in the Apocryphon of John: → 79, [F]HARTMAN L., Texts & Contexts 1995, 333-354 / 355-367.

6758 *Olson* D.C., Recovering the original sequence of 1 Enoch 91-93: JSPE 11 (1993) 69-94 [NTAb 40,p.304].

6759 *Sacchi* Paolo, Die Macht der Sünde in der Apokalyptik: JBTh 9 (1994) 111-124.

6760 *a) Sacchi* Paolo, Formazione e linee portanti dell'apocalittica giudaica precristiana; - *b) Penna* Romano, Apocalittica enochica in s.Paolo; il concetto di peccato: → 524, Apocalittica, RicStoB 7,2 (1993/5) 19-36 / 61-84.

6761 **Tiller** Patrick A., A commentary on the animal apocalypse of 1 Enoch [84-90] 1992 → 9,10446*: [R]CBQ 57 (1995) 192-4 (T.A. *Bergren*); EThL 71 (1995) 451 (J. *Lust*); JBL 114 (1995) 726-9 (Devorah *Dimant*); JRel 75 (1995) 106s (J.J. *Collins*).

6762 **VanderKam** J.C., Enoch, a man for all generations: *StPersOT. Columbia 1995, Univ. S. Carolina. ix-207 p. $ 35. 1-57003-060-X [NTAb 40, p.387; ThD 43,391].

K1.3 **Testamenta**

6763 *a) Hollander* H.W., Israel and God's eschatological agent in the Testaments of the Twelve Patriarchs; - *b) Horst* P.W. van der, Jewish self-definition by way of contrast in Oracula Sibyllina III 218-247: → 591, Aspects 1993/5, 91-104 / 147-166.

6764 *Stone* Michael E., The textual affinities of the Epitome of the Testaments of the Twelve Patriarchs in Matenadaran No. 2679 : Muséon 108 (1995) 265-276 + 1 fig.

6765 *Kugel* James, Reuben's sin with Bilhah in the Testament of Reuben: → 130, [F]MILGROM J., Pomegranates 1995, 525-554.

6766 **Colafemmina** Cesare, Il testamento di Abramo, apocrifo giudeo-cristiano: TPatr 118. R 1995, Città Nuova. 105 p.; bibliog. 38-41. 88-311-3118-4. -- [R]Nicolaus 22 (1995) 249s (S. *Manna*).

6767 **Schenderling**[TE] J.G., Het Testament van Job; een document van joodse vroomheid uit het begin van onze jaartelling -- & *Cozijnsen* L., Het Testament van Salomo; een document van joodse magie uit de eerste eeuwen van onze jaartelling: Na de Schriften. Kampen 1990, Kok. 132 p. *f* 29,50. 90-242-2030-0. -- [R]Bijdragen 56 (1995) 86s (M. *Parmentier*).

K1.4 **Apocryphi Esdras, Baruch, Maccabei**

6768 *Canessa* André, De l'originalité d'Esdras A': → 78, [F]HARL M., Katà toùs o' 1995, 79-101.

6769 **Longenecker** Bruce W., 2 Esdras [= 4 Esdras about Uriel + Christian 5 & 6 Esdras]: GuidesBS. Shf 1995, Academic. 127 p. $ 12.50 pa. 1-85075-726-7 [< OTA 19,p.171].

6770 **Bergren** Theodore A., Fifth Ezra 1990 → 6,3167; 7,2659: [R]JQR 85 (1994s) 449s (J.R. *Mueller*).

6771 *Bergren* Theodore A., Assessing the two recensions of 6 Ezra: → 508, 8th Septuagint 1992/5, 387-401.

6772 *Stone* Michael E., A new edition and translation of the [Armenian] Questions of Ezra: → 72, [F]GREENFIELD J., Solving 1995, 293-316.

6773 *Tromp* Johannes, The formation of the Third Book of Maccabees: Henoch 17

(1995) 311-328; deutsch 328.

6774 *Passoni Dell'Acqua* Anna, Le preghiere del III libro dei Maccabei [2,2-20; 6.1-15]; genere letterario e tematica → 62, FGALBIATI E.; RivB 43 (1995) 125-179; Eng, 179.

6775 *a) Williams* David S., 3 Maccabees; a defense of diaspora Judaism ?; -- *b) deSilva* David A., The noble contest; honor, shame, and the rhetorical strategy of 4 Maccabees: JSPE 13 (1995) 17-29 / 31-57.

6776 *Kabasele Mukenge* Andrè, Les citations internes en Baruch 1,15 - 3,8; un procédé redactionnel et actualisant: Muséon 108 (1995) 211-237.

6777 **Steck** Odil Hannes, Das apokryphe Baruchbuch ..: FRLANT 160, 1993 → 9,3731: RBoL (1995) 168s (J. *Snaith*); RTL 26 (1995) 218-220 (A. *Kabasele Mukenge*); TLZ 120 (1995) 632 (J. *Hetzer*).

6778 *Ulfgard* Håkan, ['Now we have nothing but the Almighty and his Law'; crisis ..] Kris. kontinuiteit och apokalyptik i 2 Baruch: ForumBEks 4 (K 1993) 79-121 [< OTA 18 (1995) p. 389 (J.T. *Willis*)].

к15 **Salomonis Psalmi** *et odae*

6779 *Trafton* Joseph L., The Psalms of Solomon in recent research: JSPE 12 (1994) 3-19.

6780 *Tronina* Antoni. P Die Psalmen Salomos und ihr Nachklang im NT: RTK 41,1 (Lublin 1994) 65-78 [NTAb 40,p.108]; 42,1 (1995) 45-58; deutsch 58.

6781 **Winninge** Mikael. Sinners and the righteous; a comparative study of the Psalms of Solomon and Paul's letters: CBNT 26. Sto 1995, Almqvist & W. [x-] 372 p.; bibliog. 338-360.   91-22-01638-4.

6782 **Franzmann** Majella, The odes of Solomon: NTOA 20, 1991 → 9,10457; 10,9599: R*CritRR 7 (1994) 396s (J.H. *Charlesworth*); OrChr 78 (1994) 260-2 (J. *Wehrle*).

6783 **Pierre** Marie-Joseph, Les Odes de Salomon: AELAC Apocryphes 4, 1994 → 10,9600: ROCP 61 (1995) 583s (V. *Poggi*); RThom 95 (1995) 699s (D. *Cerbelaud*).

к1.6 **Jubilaea, Adam, Aḥiqar, Asenet**

6784 **Halpern-Amaru** Betsy, Rewriting the Bible; land covenant in postbiblical Jewish literature [Jubilees ...]. Ph 1994, Trinity. xi-189 p. $ 15. 1-56338-091-9. -- RBoL (1995) 150 (H.A. *McKay*).

6785 *Knowles* Michael P., Abram and the birds in Jubilees 11 [?< Gen 15.11]; a subtext for the parable of the sower ?: NTS 41 (1995) 145-151.

6786 *Milgrom* Jacob, The concept of impurity in Jubilees and [i.e.'written *during* the composition of'] the Temple Scroll: RQum 16 (1993-5) 277-284.

6787 *Ruijten* Jacques van, The rewriting of Exodus 24:12-18 in Jubilees 1:1-4: BN(otiz) 79 (1995) 25-29.

6788 *VanderKam* J.C., *Milik* J.T., 4Q Jubᶜ (4Q 218) and 4Q Jubᵉ (4Q 220), a preliminary edition: Textus 17 (1994) 43-56; 2 pl. [NTAb 39,p.469].

6789 *a) VanderKam* James C., Das chronologische Konzept des Jubiläenbuches; - *b) Steck* Odil H., Die getöteten 'Zeugen' und die verfolgten 'Tora-Sucher' in Jub 1,12; ein Beitrag zur Zeugnis-Terminologie des Jubiläenbuches: ZAW 107 (1995) 80-100 / 445-465.

6790 *Werman* Cana, [H] The story of the flood in the book of Jubilees: Tarbiz 64 (1994s) 183-202; Eng. 2,v.

6791 **Anderson** Gary A., *Stone* Michael E., A synopsis of the Books of Adam and Eve: SBL EJudL 5. At 1994, Scholars. xi-76 p. $ 25; pa.$ 15. 1-55540-963-6; -4-4. -- [R]BoL (1995) 141 (G.J. *Brooke*).

6792 **Stone** Nichael E., History of the literature of Adam and Eve 1992 → 8,a258: [R]JBL 114 (1995) 509s (J.J.*Collins*: rather 'materials' for such a history).

6793 *Cazelles* Henri, A̲ḥiqar, *ummân* and *amun*, and biblical wisdom texts [Prov 8,30]: → 72, [F]GREENFIELD J., Solving 1995,45-55.

6794 *Greenfield* Jonas C. †, The wisdom of A̲ḥiqar: → 55, [F]EMERTON J., Wisdom 1995, 43-52.

6795 *Luzzatto* Maria J., Ancora sulla 'storia di Ahiqar: QSt [36 (1992) 5-84] 39 (1994) 253-277.

6796 *Bohak* Gideon, Asenath's honeycomb and Onias' temple; the key to Joseph and Asenath: -> 10,331a, 11th Jewish 1994. A-163.

6797 **Chesnutt** R.D., From death to life; conversion in Joseph and Aseneth [diss. Duke 1986, [D]*Charlesworth* J.]: JSPE.s 16. Shf 1995, Academic. 308 p. £ 37.50. 1-85075-516-7 [NTAb 40,p.551].

6798 **Humphrey** Edith M., The ladies and the cities; transformation and apocalyptic identity in Joseph and Aseneth, 4 Ezra, the Apocalypse and the Shepherd of Hermas [< diss. McGill 1991 [D]*Wright* N.]: JSPE.S 17. Shf 1995, Academic. 192 p. £ 27.50. 1-85075-525-3 [NTAb 40,p.175].

6799 *O'Neill* J.C., What is Joseph and Aseneth about ? [apostate Israel won back by Messiah Joseph]: Henoch 16 (1994) 189-198 [NTAb 40,p.304].

6800 **Standhartinger** Angela, Das Frauenbild im Judentum der hellenistischen Zeit; ein Beitrag anhand von 'Joseph und Aseneth ': AGJU 26. Lei 1995, Brill. xi-289 p. 90-04-10350-3.

6801 **Wills** Lawrence M., The Jewish novel in the ancient world [Aseneth, Test.Abr.; but also Judith, Tobit; and Gk Dan Esth]: Myth and poetics. Ithaca NY 1995, Cornell Univ. xi-279 p. $ 37.50. 0-8014-3075-5 [ThD 43,294]

K1.7 Apocalypses, ascensiones

6802 *Bauckham* Richard, Visiting the places of the dead in the extra-canonical apocalypses: PI(r)BA 18 (1995) 78-93.

6803 **Himmelfarb** Martha, Ascent to heaven in Jewish and Christian apocalypses [Henoch ..] 1993 → 10,8873: [R]JBL 114 (1995) 323s (J.C. *VanderKam*); JRel 75 (1995) 108s (D.C. *Harlow*).

6804 **O'Leary** Stephen, Arguing the Apocalypse; a theory of millennial rhetoric [→ 10,5562; apocalyptic in general was a mythical and theoretical solution to the problem of evil]. NY 1994, Oxford Univ. x-314 p. $ 35. -- [R]CBQ 57 (1995) 186s (L.J. *Hoppe*).

6805 *Kugel* James, The ladder of Jacob [Slavonic *Tolkovaya Paleya* on Gen 28,11-22]: HThR 88 (1995) 209-227.

6806 **Schalit** Abraham, Untersuchungen zur Assumptio Mosis: ALGHJ 17, 1989 → : JQR 84 (1993s) 293-7 (H.-J. *Becker*).

6807 **Tromp**[TE] Johannes, The Assumption of Moses, [E]*Denis* A.M., *Jonge* M.D.: SVTP 10, 1993 → 9,10465; 10,9609: [R]JBL 114 (1995) 143s (A. *LaCocque*); JJS 46 (1995) 303s (A. *Kamesar*); VT 45 (1995) 398-403 (W. *Horbury*).

6808 **Frankfurter** David, [Apocalypse of] Elijah in Upper Egypt 1993 → 9,10466: [R]JEarlyC 3 (1995) 237-9 (J.O. *Gooch*); JEH 46 (1995) 488-490 (R. *Bauckham*); RS(to)LR 31 (1995) 519-522 (C. *Gianotto*).

6809 **Acerbi** Antonio, L'Ascensione di Isaia 1988 → 5,9929; 6,9984: [R]ZKG 105 (1994) 99-101 (Luise *Abramowski*).

6810 **Bettiolo** Paolo, *al.*, Ascensio Isaiae; textus, commentarius [italiano]: CCApocr 7s. Turnhout 1995, Brepols. 1. Text, xxxi-444 p., bibliog. xvii-xxxi; 2. Comm. 722 p. 2-503-41071-5; -81-2.

6811 **Knight** Jonathan, The Ascension of Isaiah: Guides to Apocrypha and Pseudepigrapha. Shf 1995, Academic. 105 p. £ 8. 1-85075-543-4.

6812 **Norelli** Enrico, Ascension du prophète Isaïe: CCApocrypha 1993 → 8,a264; 9,10467: [R]ETRel 70 (1995) 128s (J.-M. *Prieur*, aussi sur KAESTLI, Barthélemy).

6813 **Norelli** E., L'Ascensione di Isaia; studi su un apocrifo al crocevia dei cristianesimi: Origini NS 1, 1994 → 10,9612: [R]EThL 71 (1995) 230s (J. *Verheyden*); RivB 43 (1995) 302-6 (M. *Pesce*).

K2.1 Philo judaeus alexandrinus

6815 *Borgen* Peter, Man's sovereignty over animals and nature according to Philo of Alexandria; → 79, [F]HARTMAN L., Texts & Contexts 1995, 369-389.

6816 *Borgen* Peder, Some Hebrew and pagan features in Philo's and Paul's interpretation of Hagar and Ishmael: → 487, NT & Hellenistic 1992/5. 151-164 (-262 *al.* on Paul).

6817 *Cazeaux* Jacques, 'Nul n'est prophète en son pays' -- contribution à l'étude de Joseph [Gn 37] d'après PHILON: →132*,Mem. MOEHRING H.,School of Moses 1995,41-81.

6818 **Cohen** Naomi G., Philo Judaeus; his universe of discourse: BEAT 24. Fra 1995, Lang. xx-381 p.; Bibliog. 321-348. Fs 80. 3-820-41650-1. [NTAb 40, p.171]. -- [R]JQR 86 (1995s) 510-5 (D. *Winston*).

6819 *a) Cohen* Naomi G., Philo's 'literal meaning' and rabbinic *peshat*; - *b) Kahn* Jean-Georges, [H] Libido sciendi; the lust for knowledge according to Philo Alexandrinus: -→ 10,331a, 11th Jewish 1994. A-171-8 / 103-6.

6820 *Cook* John B., Females and the feminine in Pseudo-Philo: ProcGM 13 (1993) 151-9.

6821 [T]**Daniel-Nataf** Suzanne, [H] Philo, Exposition of the Laws 1: Writings 2. J 1991, Bialik / Israel Academy. xi-307 p. -- [R]StPhilo 7 (1995) 225s (D. *Satran*).

6822 *Daubercies* P., La vertu chez Philon d'Alexandrie: RTL 26 (1995) 185-210; Eng. 279s.

6823 **Dawson** David, Allegorical readers and cultural revision in ancient Alexandria [< diss. Yale 1988] 1992 → 9,10471; 10,9614: [R]Kiryat Sefer 65 (1994s) p.331s (Shifra *Sznol*, [H])

6824 *a) Dillon* John, Reclaiming the heritage of Moses; Philo's confrontation with Greek philosophy; -- *b) Winston* David, Philo and the Hellenistic Jewish encounter; -- *c) Runia* David T., Philo of Alexandria and the beginnings of Christian thought: StPhilo 7 (15-17

Nov. 1994 conference at Notre Dame; 1995) 108-123 / 124-142 / 143-160.

6825 **Goodman** Lenn E., Neoplatonism and Jewish thought 1992 → 8,433*b*: [R]*CritRR 7 (1994) 387s (M. *Verman*).

6826 **Grabbe** Lester L., Etymology in early Jewish interpretation; the Hebrew names in Philo: BJSt 115, 1988 → 5,9938 .. 7,9814: [R]JQR 84 (1993s) 386s (D. *Winston*).

6827 **Hay** David M., Both literal and allegorical .. Philo QGnEx 1992 → 9,10478: [R]BoL (1994) 139s (N. de *Lange*).

6828 *a) Hilgaert* Earle, Philo Judaeus et Alexandrinus; the state of the question; -- *b) Mack* Burton, Moses on the mountaintop; a Philonic view; -- *c) Winston* David, Philo's doctrine of repentance; -- *d) Moehring* Horst R., Arithmology as an exegetical tool in the writings of Philo of Alexandria: → 132*. Mem. MOEHRING, School of Moses 1995, 1-15 / 16-28 / 29-40 / 141-176.

6829 **Jacobson** Howard, A commentary on Pseudo-Philo's Liber Antiquitatum Biblicarum, with Latin text and English translation: AGJU 31. Lei 1996, Brill. xvi-1208 p. -- [R]JQR 86 (1995s) 456-9 (D.J. *Harrington*).

6830 *a) Jastram* Daniel N., The 'Praeparatio evangelica' and 'Spoliatio' motifs as patterns of Hellenistic Judaism in Philo of Alexandria; - *b) Frizzell* Lawrence E., 'Spoils from Egypt' between Jews and Gnostics; - *c) Wolters* Albert M., Creatio ex nihilo in Philo; - *d) Booth* Peter, The voice of the serpent; Philo's Epicureanism; - *e) Aune* David C., Mastery of the passions; Philo, 4 Maccabees and earliest Christianity: -→ 10,322, Hellenization 1991/4, 189-203 / 383-394 / 159-172 / 159-172 / 125-158.

6831 *Kamesar* Adam, San BASILIO, Filone, e la tradizione ebraica: Henoch 17 (1995) 129-139; Eng.140.

6832 *a) Kamesar* Adam, Philo and the literary quality of the Bible; a theoretical aspect of the problem; - *b) Hayward* Robert, Pseudo-Philo and the priestly oracle: → 211, [F]VERMES G., JJS 46 (1995) 55-68 / 43-54.

6833 [E]**Kenney** John P., Studies in Philo and Hellenistic religion: BJSt 304. At 1995, Scholars. xi-182 p.

6834 **La Porte** Jean, Eucharistia in Philo [1972, [T] not updated, but the reviews cited p.187 show its importance]: SBEC 3. Lewiston 1893, Mellen. 261 p. $ 90. 0-88946-601-7. -- [R]BoL (1995) 153 (M. *Barker*).

6835 **Laporte** J., Théologie liturgique de Philon d'Alexandrie et d'ORIGÈNE: Liturgie 6. P 1995, Cerf. 278 p. F 150. 2-204-05130-6 [NTAb 40,p.380].

6836 **Leloup** Jean-Yves, Prendre soin de l'être; Philon et les Thérapeutes d'Alexandrie. P 1993, Michel. 143 p. 2-226-06314-5. -- [R]StPhilo 7 (1995) 226-9 (J. *Riaud*, aussi sur GRAFFIGNA P. 1992).

6837 *Levison* John R., *a)* Inspiration and the divine spirit in the writings of Philo Judaeus: JSJ 26 (1995) 271-3231 -- *b)* The prophetic spirit as an angel according to Philo: HThR 88 (1995) 189-207; -- *c)* Prophetic inspiration in Pseudo-Philo's Liber Antiquitatum Biblicarum: JQR 85 (1994s) 297-329.

6838 *Mach* Michael, PHILO's 'philosophical' turn to 'religion': → 10,344*a*, Notion of religion 1990/4, 403-413.

6839 **Murphy** Frederick J., Pseudo-Philo, re-writing the Bible 1993 → 9,10486; 10,9620: [R]BiRe 10,4 (1994) 54 (R. *Doran*).JEH 46 (1995) 484-6 (G.J. *Brooke*); JRel 75 (1995) 411s (J.J. *Collins*); JSJ(ud) 26 (1995) 206s (J. *Tromp*); JThS 46 (1995) 239s (L.L. *Grabbe*).

6840 *Murphy* Frederick J., The martial option [at the Red Sea: not (as OLYAN S. 1991) favored in (Ex) 10.3] in Pseudo-Philo: CBQ 57 (1995) 676-688.

6841 *a) Niehoff* Maren R., What's in a name ? Philo's mystical philosophy of language; - *b) Veltri* Giuseppe, The humanist sense of history and the Jewish idea of tradition; Azaria DE' ROSSI's critique of Philo Alexandrinus: Jewish Studies Quarterly 2 (Tü 1995) 220-252 / 372-393.

6842 *Phaneuf* J.P., Philon d'Alexandrie: Revue Scriptura [not Stellenbosch: and neither is in IATG] 17 (été 1994) 79-87 [< JSJ(ud) 26 (1995) 264].

6843 ^{TE}**Radice** Roberto, Filone di Alessandria; tutti i trattati del Commentario Allegorico alla Bibbia: Classsici del pensiero. Mi 1994, Rusconi. clvii-1342 p. L^m 65. 88-18-22029-2. -- ^RStPhilo 7 (1995) 223-5 (D.T. *Runia* also on his 1994 reprise of his 1981 Erede with debatable Greek text).

6844 **Royse** James R., The spurious texts of Philo 1991 → 7,9822 ... 9,10491: ^RJQR 85 (1994s) 479-481 (D. *Winston*).

6845 **Runia** David T.[→ 322], Philo in early Christian literature: CRI 3/3. 1993 → 9,10494; 10,9523: ^RElenchos 16 (1995) 410-5 (R. *Radice*); JAOS 115 (1995) 713s (H.W. *Attridge*)]; JRel 75 (1995) 274s (R.M. *Grant*); JThS 46 (1995) 691-4 (C. *Riedweg*).

6846 *Runia* David T., Why does CLEMENT of Alexandria call Philo 'the Pythagorean'?: VigChr 49 (1995) 1-22.

6847 *a) Scott* James M., Philo and the restoration of Israel; - *b) Sterling* Gregory E., Recluse or representative ? Philo and Greek-speaking Judaism beyond Alexandria; - *c) Birnbaum* Ellen, What does Philo mean by 'seeing God'?; some methodological considerations; *d) Wan Sze-kar*, Abraham and the promise of the Spirit; Galatians and the Hellenistic-Jewish mysticism of Philo: → 512, SBL Seminars 34 (1995) 553-575 / 595-616 / 535-552 / 6-22.

6848 **Seland** Torrey, Establishment violence in Philo and Luke; a study of non-conformity to the Torah and Jewish vigilante reaction: *BInterpS 15. Lei 1995, Brill. xvi-353 p.; bibliog. 305-326. 90-04-10252-3.

6849 *Seland* Torrey, The 'common priesthood' of Philo and 1 Peter; a Philonic reading of 1 Peter 2.5,9: JSNT 57 (1995) 87-119.

6850 *a) Sterling* Gregory E., 'Thus are Israel'; Jewish self-definition in Alexandria; -- *b) Zeller* D., The life and death of the soul in Philo of Alexandria; the use and origin of a metaphor; -- *c) Terian* Abraham, Inspiration and originality; Philo's distinctive exclamations; -- *d) Reydams-Schils* Gretchen, Stoicized readings of PLATO's Timaeus in Philo of Alexandria; -- *e) Srigley* Ronald D., Albert CAMUS on Philo and Gnosticism: StPhilo 7 (1995) 1-18 / 19-55 / 56-84 / 85-102 / 103-6.

6851 *Terian* Abraham, Had the works of Philo been newly discovered [they would have got headlines rivaling Qumran and Nag' Hammadi]: BA 57 (1994) 86-97; ill.

6852 *Thatcher* Tom, Philo [LGai 300s] on Pilate; rhetoric or reality: RestQ 37 (1995) 215-8 [NTAb 40, p.306].

6853 **Warne** Graham J., Hebrew perspectives on the human person in the Hellenistic era; Philo and Paul: Mellen Biblical 35. Lewiston NY 1995, Mellen. xi-291 p. $ 100. 0-7734-2420-2 [ThD 43,293].

6854 *Winston* David, Sage and super-sage in Philo of Alexandria: → 130, ^FMILGROM J., Pomegranates 1995, 815-824.

6855 **Yonge** C.D., The works of Philo 1993 → 9,10504; 10,9627: ^RA(ndr)USS 33 (1995) 157s (M. *Veloso*: everything but A. TERIAN's 1981 On Animals from Armenian); VigChr 49 (1995) 194-8 (D.T. *Runia*).

K2.4   *Evangelia apocrypha* -- **Apocryphal Gospels**

6856 *Barker* Margaret, The secret tradition : *JHiCr 2,1 (1995) 31-67.
6857 BARNABAS: **Linges** S.M., Das Barnabas-Evangelium, wahres Evangelium Jesu ... Bonndorf/Schwarzwald 1994, Turban. 319 p.; ill. DM 42. < RHE 90 (1995) 230*.
6858 -- **Schirrmacher** Christine, Mit den Waffen des Gegners; christlich-muslimische Kontroversen im 19. und 20. Jh. ... K.G. PFANDER ..Diskussion über das Barnabasevangelium: IKU 162. B 1992, Schwarz. xvi-437 p. -- ᴿOLZ 90 (1995) 417-421 (Isabel *Stümpel*).
6859 **Bovon** François, New Testament tradltions and apocryphal narratives: PTMS 36. Allison Park PA 1995, Pickwick. x-256 p. 1-55635-024-4
6860 *Bovon* François, Jesus' missionary speech [Mt 10 ‖] as interpreted in the patristic commentaries and the apocryphal narratives: → 79, ᶠHARTMAN L., Texts & Contexts 1995, 871-886.
6861 **Bovon** François, Révélations .. NT/apocryphe 1993 → 9,186: ᴿFV 93,2 (1994) 78s (J.-P. *Monsarrat*).
6863 **Elliott** J.K., The apocryphal NT 1993 → 10505: ᴿBiRe 11,6 (1995) 15s (A. *Callahan*); Churchman 108 (L 1994) 372-4 (Jenny *Heimerdinger*); Neotest 29 (1995) 142s (P.J.J. *Botha*); NT 37 (1995) 193s (D.R. *MacDonald*).
6864 **Evans** Craig A., Noncanonical writings and NT interpretation 1992 → 99,10436: ᴱBiblica 76 (1995) 121-5 (J.A. *Fitzmyer*, severe); Churchman 108 (L 1994) 84 (G. *Bray*: very useful); *CritRR 7 (1994) 186s (Deirdre *Good*); EstB 53 (1995) 425-9 (A. *Urbán*); EvQ 67 (1995) 281s (I.H. *Marshall*); JAAR 63 (1995) 190-2 (T.S.L. *Michael*).
6865 *Hermansen* Søren, Some thoughts on The book of resurrection of Jesus Christ -- by Bartholomey, the apostle [ᴱ*Wallis Budge* E. 1913]: → 67, ᶠGIVERSEN H., Apocryphon 1993, 60-67.
6866 *Howard* George, Hebrew Gospel of Matthew; a report : *JHiCr 2,2 (1995) 53-67.
6867 *Izydorczyk* Zbigniew, The Latin source of an Old French Gospel of Nicodemus: RHT 15 (1995) 265-279; Eng. 303
6868 JACOBUS (→ 6883): ᴱ**Di Noia** Alfonso M., Vangeli apocrifi; natività e infanzia: Religioni e miti 182. Mi c.1995, TEA. 222 p. Lᵐ 16. 88-7819-958-3.
6869 ᴱ**Kaestli** J.-D., *Marguerat* D., Le mystère apocryphe; introduction à une littérature méconnue [chrétienne: 9 Lausanne lectures 1994]: EssBib 26. Genève 1995, Labor et Fides. 152 p.; ill. F 125. 2-8309-0770-1 [NTAb 40, p.176]. -- ᴿE(spr)eV 105 (1995) 651-3 (É. *Cothenet*); RHPhR 75 (1995) 344 (D.A. *Bertrand*).
6870 **Moraldi** Luigi, Apocrifi del NT. CasM 1994, Piemme. I. Vangeli, 910 p.; II. Atti, 750 p.; III. 557 p. Lᵐ 330. -- ᴿCivCatt 146 (1995,4) 619-621 (G.L. *Prato*); CiVi 50 (1995) 191 (S. *Spartà*).
6871 PETRUS: *Dewey* Arthur J., Four visions and a funeral; resurrection in the Gospel of Peter: *JHiCr 2,2 (1995) 33-51.
6872 PHILIPPUS: *Thiering* Barbara, The date [not after 70 A.D. by a group derived from Qumran] and unity of the Gospel of Philip: *JHiCr 2,1 (1995) 102-111 [NTAb 40, p.318].
6873 **Piñero** Antonio, El otro Jesús; vida de Jesús según los Evangelios Apócrifos. Córdoba 1993, Almendro. 184 p. 84-8005-009-8. -- ᴿEstTrin 28 (1994) 443 (X. *Pikaza*).
6874 **Piñero** Antonio, L'altro Gesù; vita di Gesù secondo i Vangeli apocrifi: Teologia viva 24. Bo 1995, Dehoniane. 197 p. 88-10-40934-5.
6875 **Prieur** J.-M., Apocryphes chrétiens; un regard inattendu sur le christianisme

ancien. Poliez 1995, Moulin. 89 p. -- [R]RHPhR 75 (1995) 344 (D.A. *Bertrand*).

6876 [E]**Schneemelcher** Wilhelm, [TE]*Wilson* R.M.,   NT Apocrypha I[2], 1991 → 9,10511; 10,9631: [R]BA 57 (1994) 180s (C.W. *Hedrick*); *CritRR 7 (1994) 256-8 (R.L. *Pervo*); S(cot)JTh 48 (1995) 530s (A.H.B. *Logan*).

6877 **Aranda Pérez** Gonzalo, Dormición de la Virgen; relatos de la tradición copta; introducción, traducción y notas: Apócrifos cristianos 2. m 1995, Ciudad Nueva. 324 p. 84-86987-87-3.

K2.7 *Alia apocrypha NT* -- **Apocryphal Acts of apostles**

6878 *Dolbeau* François, Nouvelles recherches sur le De ortu et obitu prophetarum et apostolorum: AugR 34 (1994) 91-103; texte 104-7.

6879 ANDREAS: **McDonald** Dennis R., Christianizing HOMER; the Odyssey, PLATO, and the Acts of Andrew. Ox 1994, UP. xv-352 p. -- [R]JRel 75 (1995) 557s (R.I. *Pervo*); NT 37 (1995) 307s (J.K. *Elliott*).

6880 -- *Pao* D.W., The genre of The Acts of Andrew: *Apocrypha 6 (1995) 179-202 [NTAb 40, p.502].

6881 -- *Bovon* François, *a)* The Words of Life in the Acts of the Apostle Andrew: HThR 87 (1994) 139-154; -- *b)* Miracles, magie et guérison dans les Actes apocryphes des apôtres: *JEarlyC 3 (1995) 245-259.

6882 **Desreumaux** Alain, Histoire du roi Abgar et de Jésus; collection de poche de l'AELAC (Association pour l'étude de la littérature apocryphe chrétienne) 1993 → 9,10542; 10,9642*; Fb 354: [R]RHE 90 (1995) 622s (J.-M. *Auwers*).

6883 JACOBUS: *Canal* J.M., Versión latina A[rundel 404 14th c., British Library, named after commentator M.R.] 'JAMES' del Protoevangelio de Santiago: Mar 36 (1994) 17-69 [NTAb 40, p.315].

6884 -- *Backus* I., Guillaume POSTEL, Théodore BIBLIANDER et le 'Protévangile de Jacques' [British ms Sloane 1411. 260-7l]: *Apocrypha 6 (1995) 7-65 [NTAb 40, p.499].

6885 -- **Van Voorst** Robert E., The ascents of James; history and theology of a Jewish-Christian community: SBL diss.112, 1989 → 5,9976 ... 7,9841: [R]Bijdragen 56 (1995) 83s (M. *Parmentier*. Eng.); *JHiCr 2,2 (1995) 140-2 (R.M. *Price*).

6886 JOHANNES: **Bremmer** Jan N., The apocryphal Acts of John: Studies on the apocryphal Acts of the Apostles. Kampen 1995, Kok Pharos. v-243 p.; bibliog 231-5. *f* 60. 90-390-0141-3 [NTAb 40, p.550].

6887 -- *Schneider* Paul G., The Acts of John; the Gnostic transformation of a Christian community: -→ 10,322, Hellenization 1991/4, 241-269.

6888 -- *Waldstein* Michael, The Providence monologue in the Apocryphon of John and the Johannine Prologue: *JEarlyC 3 (1995) 369-402.

6889 **Pastis** Jacqueline Z., Representations of Jews and Judaism in 'The dialogue of Timothy and Aquila'; construct or social reality ?: diss. Pennsylvania, [D]*Kraft* R. Ph 1994. 301 p. 95-21099. - DissA 56 (1995s) p. 975; RStR 22,273.

6890 PAULUS: **Carozzi** Claude, Eschatologie et au-delà; recherches sur l'Apocalypse de Paul. Aix 1994, Univ. Provence. 137 p. 2-8539-348-5.

6891 -- *Pippin* Tina, [Apocalypses: Paul, Peter, John ..] Peering into the abyss: a postmodern reading of the biblical bottomless pit: → 2017, New Lit.Crit.NT 1994, 251-267.

6892 -- *a) Bovon* F., Une nouvelle citation des Actes de Paul chez ORIGÈNE; -- *b) Brock* A.G., Genre of the Acts of Paul; one genre enhancing another: *Apocrypha 5 (Turnhout 1994) 113-7 / 119-136 [NTAb 40, p.120].

6893 -- *Dunn* Peter W., L'image de Paul dans les 'Actes de Paul': FV 94,4 ('Trajectoires pauliniennes' 1995) 75-85 (87-97, *Marguerat* Daniel).

6894 -- *Pervo* Richard R., A hard Acts to follow: the Acts of Paul and the canonical Acts: *JHiCr 2,2 (1995) 3-32.

6895 -- **Tajra** Harry W., The martyrdom of St. Paul; historical and judicial contexts, traditions and legends [... Acta Pauli]: WUNT 2/67. Tü 1994, Mohr. 225 p. DM 98. 3-16-146239-4. -- ᴿ*TBR 8,1 (1995s) 48 (Judith *Lieu*).

6896 **Pérès** Jacques-Noël, L'Épître des Apôtres: Apocryphes 5, 1994 → 10,9641*: ᴿOCP 61 (1995) 582s (P. *Luisier*).

6897 PETRUS: **Bauckham** R., The Apocalypse of Peter, a Jewish Christian apocalypse from the time of Bar Kokhba: *Apocrypha 5 (1994) 7-111 [NTAb 40,p.119].

6898 -- *Karavidopoulou* Ioannis A., ᴳ The metamorphosis of the just in the apocryphal Apocalypse of Peter: Kler 24 (1992) 35-46.

6899 -- **Thomas** Christine Marie, The Acts of Peter, the ancient novel, and early Christian history: diss. Harvard, ᴰ*Koester* Helmut. CM 1995. 208 p. 95-39435. - DissA 56 (1995s) p. 2729; HThR 88 (1995) 534.

6900 PHILIPPUS: **Leloir** Louis, Écrits apocryphes sur les Apôtres 2, 1992 → 8,a302 ... 10,9636: ᴿCBQ 57 (1995) 401s (R.J. *Pervo*); RevBib(Arg) 56 (1994) 127s (J.P. *Martín*); R(ech)SR 83 (1995) 150-2 (Madeleine *Scopello*).

6901 -- *Esbroeck* Michel van, Les Actes syriaques de Philippe à Carthagène en version arabe: OrChr 79 (1995) 120-3; 124-143 texte avec français en face; 2 phot.

6902 **Pietersma** Albert, The apocryphon of Jannes and Jambres the magicians .. : ÉPR 119, 1994 → 10,9643*: ᴿJBL 114 (1995) 548-550 (T.H. *Tobin*).

6903 **Prieur** J.-M., Apocryphes chrétiens; un regard inattendu sur le christianisme ancien. Poliez 1995, Moulin. 89 p. [NTAb 40,p.382].

6904 *Starowieyski* M., ᴾ Les vies et les catalogues des Apôtres; matériaux pour la légende et le culte des Apôtres: *Bobolanum 6 (Wsz 1995) 132-154; français 154. [NTAb 40,p.124].

6905 *Szepessy* Tibor, Les actes d'apôtres apocryphes et le roman antique: AAH 36 (1995) 133-167.

6906 **Beylot** Robert, Martyre de Pilate éthiope & T: PatrOr 45. Turnhout 1993. Brepols. p.617-686. -- ᴿOCP 61 (1995) 249-252 (P. *Luisier*).

6907 **Majercik** Ruth, The Chaldaean oracles 1989 → 7,a561; 9,10544*: ᴿThLZ 120 (1995) 228-231 (H.-M. *Schenke*).

6908 *Nieto Ibáñez* J.B., A metrical peculiarity of the Sibylline Oracles: Museum Philologum Londiniense 9 (1992) 33-36 [< JSJ 26 (1995) 260: 36 lines lack one short syllable at the same point].

к3 **Qumran** -- .1 *generalia*

6909 **Baigent** M., *Leigh* R., *a)* DSS deception 1991 → 7,9854 ... 9,10548: ᴿ*JHiCr 2,2 (1995) 148-151 (R.M. *Price*, mostly on the views drawn from EISENMAN). -- *b)*

Verschlusssache Jesus 1991 → 7,9855* ... 10,9645: ᴿHLand 124,1 (1992) 4-6 (A. *Fuchs*: absolut unwissenschaftlich .. ein Skandal).

6910 ᶠCARMIGNAC J,, Mogilany 1989 papers on the Dead Sea Scrolls I. 1993 → 9,375; II. 1991 → 7,420: ᴿBArR 20,1 (1994) 78s (L.H. *Schiffman*).

6911 **Charlesworth** J.H., Graphic concordance to the DSS 1991 → 7,9857 ... 10,9647: ᴿA(ustrl)BR 41 (1993) 88-90 (G. *Jenkins*); NRT 117 (195) 116s (J.L. *Ska*); VigChr 49 (1995) 290-2 (A.S. van der *Woude*).

6912 ᴱ**Charlesworth** James H., *al.*, The Dead Sea Scrolls; Hebrew, Aramaic, and Greek texts with English translations, 1. Rule of the Community and related documents: Princeton DSS project. Tü/LᴠL 1994. Mohr / W-Knox. xxiii-185 p. DM 168. 3-16-148199-1 [TR 91,182]. -- ᴿAJA 99 (1995) 749s B.B. *Schmidt*); ATG(ran) 58 (1995) 470-2 (A. *Torres*); BASOR 298 (1995) 82-94 (R. *Fuller*) CBQ 57 (1995) 762s (D.J. *Harrington*; some things new; but too much for students, too little for experts); *DSD 2 (1995) 227-232 (D. *Falk*); ET 106 (1994s) 152s (C.S. *Rodd*); JThS 46 (1995) 601-5 (G.J. *Brooke*); Muséon 108 (1995) 425 (P.-M. *Bogaert*); NT 37 (1995) 413s (J.K. *Elliott*, also on GARCÍA MARTÍNEZ 1994).

6913 ᴱ**Charlesworth** James H., Qumran questions: BiSe 36. Shf 1995, Academic. 210 p. 1-85075-770-4.

6914 **Cook** Edward M., Solving the mysteries of the DSS 1994 → 10,9650: ᴿBoL (1995) 145 (G.J. *Brooke*: not enthusiastic); *CritRR 7 (1994) 394s (J.J. *Collins*); *DSD 2 (1995) 108s (Sidnie W. *Crawford*).

6915 *Cook* Johann, Madrid, a watershed in Qumran research [18-21.III.1991, ᴱ**Trebolle Barrera** J.]: BiOr 52 (1995) 25-36.

6916 *Cothenet* E., Polémiques autour des documents de Qumran [EISENMAN-WISE, BAIGENT-LEIGH]: E(spr)eV 105 (1995) 525-8.

6917 **Cross** Frank M., The ancient library at Qumran³ [¹1958; ²1961]: BiSe 27. Shf 1995, Academic. 204 p. £ 27.50. 1-85075-511-6.

6918 *Davies* Philip R., Khirbet Qumran revisited: → 10,67, ᶠKING P., Scripture 1994, 126-142.

6919 [*Davies* Philip ... *Murphy-O'Connor* Jerome, *al.*] CD-ROM (Macintosh or Windows), The Dead Sea Scrolls revealed. .... Logos. $ 60. -- ᴿCThMi 22 (1995) 142s (R.W. *Klein*; p.144 unfavorably on American Bible Society's CD-ROM Bibles with Hebrew-Greek in keyboard transliteration).

6920 **Dimant** Devorah, *Rappaport* Uriel, The Dead Sea Scrolls; forty years of research [Haifa/TA symposium 1988] 1992 → 8,460*; 10,9652: ᴿBiOr 52 (1995) 778-782 (Lena *Cansdale*); JSSt 40 (1995) 130-5 (M.J. *Bernstein*).

6921 *Dimant* Devorah, Apocalyptic texts at Qumran: → 538, Community 1993/4, 175-191 [< OTA 18 (1995) p. 370].

6922 *Di Palma* Gaetano, I manoscritti del Mar Morto [MORALDI L., EISENMAN R. ...]: Asprenas 42 (1995) 401-412.

6923 *Dohmen* Ulrich, Weitere Nachträge zur Qumran [Text- und Wort-Konkordanz: ZAH(ebr) [4 (1991) 213-235] 8 (1995) 340-357.

6924 *Donceel-Voûte* Pauline, Les ruines de Qumrân réinterprétées: Archéologia 298 (1994) 24-35; ill.

6925 **Eisenman** Robert H., *Wise* Michael, The Dead Sea Scrolls uncovered 1992 → 8,a326 ... 10,9653: ᴿJHiCr 2,1 (1995) 142-9 (R.M. *Price*); JRelH 19 (1995) 111-3 (M. *Harding*); RQum 16 (1993-5) 123-145 (F. *García-Martínez*) [-150, 1992s (Ph Annenberg, 22 signers) ethically-condemnatory statement; and counter-statement of 8 of the signers

(NY Academy of Sciences meeting; after) regret-clarification statement of Wise 1992 (Eisenman silent)].

6926 **Eisenman** R.H., *Wise* M., Manoscritti segreti di Qumran, ᵀ. CasM 1994, Piemme. 290 p. Lᵐ 38. -- ᴿAsprenas 42 (1995) 438-440 (A. *Rolla*, sfavorevole).

6927 **Eisenman** Robert, *Wise* Michael, Les manuscrits de la Mer morte révélés, ᵀ*Attias* Jean-C. P 1995, Fayard. 366 p. F 150. -- ᴿÉtudes 382 (1995) 715s (P. *Gibert*).

6928 **Eisenman** R., *Wise* M., De Dode-zeerollen onthuld. 1993. -- ᴿNedThT 49 (1995) 240s (P.W. van der *Horst*).

6929 **Fitzmyer** Joseph A., Responses to 101 questions on the DSS 1992 → 8,a328 ... 10,9655: ᴿOTEs 8 (1995) 466-8 (J.F.J. van *Rensburg*).

6930 **Fitzmyer** J.A., Qumran, le [101] domande e le risposte essenziali sui manoscritti del Mar Mortoᵀ: *GdT 230. Brescia 1994, Queriniana. 288 p. Lᵐ 33. -- ᴿ*AnT 9 (1995) 165-8 (B. *Estrada*); CivCatt 146 (1995,4) 633s (A. *Ferrua*); PaVi 40,1 (1995) 61s (A. *Rolla*).

6931 **Fitzmyer** Joseph A., Qumran, die Antwort, 101 Fragen: sᴛʙ 18, 1993 → 10,9656: ᴿFrRu NF 1 (1993s) 209-212 (M. *Kreuzer*).

6932 *Flusser* David, ᴴ The second benediction of the *Amida* and a text from Qumran [4Q 521, Puech E., RQ 15 (1992) 485]: Tarbiz 64 (1994s) 331-4; Eng. 3,v.

6933 **García Martínez** Florentino, The Dead Sea Scrolls translated; the Qumran texts in English 1994 → 10,9661; ᵀ*Watson* Wilfred G.E., adding 70 recently available texts; $ 80: pa. $ 30: ᴿ*DSD 2 (1995) 357-9 (J.M. *Baumgarten*); JBL 114 (1995) 359s (J.J. *Collins*: the best; also on S.Reed catalogue); NT 37 (1995) 413s (J.K. *Elliott*, also on Charlesworth).

6934 *García Martínez* F., De handschriften van de Dode Zee: *Hermeneus 67 (1995) 139-150 [< JSJ(ud) 26 (1995) 406].

6935 **Golb** Norman, Who wrote the Dead Sea Scrolls ? The search for the secret of Qumran. ɴʏ 1995, Scribner's. xvi-446 p. $ 25. 0-02-544395-X. -- ᴿChH 64 (1995) 635s (G.T. *Armstrong*).

6936 *Harrington* D.J., *a)* What's new(s) about the Dead Sea Scrolls: CCurr 44 (1944s) 463-474; -- *b)* News from the Dead Sea Scrolls: CathDig 59,8 (St.Paul 1995) 39-45 [NTAb 40, p.99].

6937 *Hendel* Ronald S., *al.,* The Dead Sea Scrolls, 6 video tapes. Wsh 1993, Biblical Archaeology Society. -- ᴿ*DSD 2 (1995) 238-240 (L.H. *Schifmann*).

6938 *Hombergen* Daniel, Jakobus de Rechtvaardige: een anti-Romeinse rebel ? De 'Dead Sea Scrollsì en de 'deception' [Baigent M., Leigh R. 1991, ned. 1994]: NedThT 49 (1995) 215-230; Eng. 231.

6939 *Humbert* J.-B., *al.,* Fouilles de Khirbet Qumran et de Aïn Feshkha: ɴᴛᴏᴀ. arch. 1, 1994 → 10,9663: ᴿBArR 21 (1995) 6. 8 (H. *Shanks:* R. Donceel's assigned part-authorship is tardy and infelicitous); E(rbe)uA 71 (1995) 251 (B. *Schwank*); JSJ(ud) 26 (1995) 199s (A.S. van der *Woude*); RB 102 (1995) 460 (J.-M. de *Tarragon*); RBBras 11 (1994) 666s (C. *Minette de Tillesse*).

6940 *a) Jull* A.J. Timothy, *al.,* Radiocarbon dating of scrolls and linen fragments from the Judean Desert; - *b) Caldararo* Niccolo, Storage conditions and physical treatments relating to the dating of the Dead Sea Scrolls: Radiocarbon 37,1 (1995) 11-19; 2 fig. / 21-32.

6941 *Kapera* Zdzisław J., ᴾ First Polish translation of the Judean desert texts: Filomata 429s (Kraków 1995) 67 . 96; 437s (1996) 239-246.

6942 *Klingbeil* Gerald, Los rollos del Mar Muerto; su arqueología, historia e importancia: *Theologika 10,1 (Lima 1995) 48-96 [< OTA 19,128].

6943 *Laperrousaz* Ernest-Marie, *Nahon* Gérard, La position des bras des squelettes dans les tombes de Qoumran et [sépharades] d'Ennezat (Puy de Dôme): RÉJ 154 (1995) 227-238.

6944 **Maass** Hans, Qumran; Texte contra Phantasien 1994 → 10,9669: [R]FrRu 2 (1995) 136-141 (A. *Renker*); ZAW 107 (1995) 359s (A.-C. *Wegner*).

6945 *Magness* Jodi, A villa at Khirbet Qumran ?: RQum 16 (1993-5) 397-419; 10 fig.

6946 **Mossek** Eugene, 58-min. filmstrip, script *Cohen* Daniel, The enigma of the Dead Sea Scrolls. J 1991, Biblical Productions. -- [R]*DSD 2 (1995) 112-4 (G.J. *Brooke*: high praise, informative critique).

6947 *Patrich* Joseph, [H] Khirbet Qumran in light of new archaeological explorations in Qumran caves: -> 10,331a, llth Jewish 1994. A-95-102.

6948 *Puech* Émile, La 'forteresse des pieux' et Kh. Qumrân, à propos du papyrus Murabba'ât 45: RQum 16 (1993-5) 463-9.

6949 **Reed** Stephen A., The Dead Sea Scrolls catalogue; documents, photographs and museum inventory numbers 1994 → 10,9673 = [2rev]*Lundberg* Marilyn J. [[1]1988]: [R]BoL (1995) 33 (G.J. *Brooke*: most comprehensive yet); EThL 71 (1995) 212s (J. *Lust*); RQum 16,64 (1995) 668-673 (F. *García Martínez*).

6950 **Schiffman** Lawrence H., Reclaiming the Dead Sea Scrolls 1994 → 10,9676: [R]BArR 21,2 (1995) 6 . 8. 10 (G. *Vermes*; careless and complacent; from the start scholars have recognized that their importance for Christianity is secondary in relation to Judaism) [21,4 (1995) 20s, further Schiffman-Vermes exchange]; JJS 46 (1995) 294s (M.A. *Knibb*).

6951 *Schiffman* Lawrence H., New tools for the study of the Dead Sea Scrolls: RStR 20 (Valparaiso IN 1994) 112-6 [< OTA 18 (1995) p. 130].

6952 *Segert* Stanislav, Answers and questions concerning publications on the Dead Sea Scrolls: *Metanoia 4 (Praha 1994) 57-65 [& 1 (1991) 256-261].

6953 *Shanks* Hershel, The honor due Dead Sea Scroll scholar Józef MILIK ... he's published more than anyone: BArR 21,1 (1995) 24. - 21,3 (1995) 11 . 13, respectful rectification of an oral citation from Milik on E. TOV.

6954 [E]**Shanks** Hershel, Understanding the Dead Sea Scrolls [22 art. < BArR] 1992 → 8,367b: [R]WZKM 83 (1993) 346s (J. *Maier*).

6955 **Silberman** Neil A., The hidden scrolls; Christianity, Judaism and the war for the Dead Sea Scrolls. NY 1994, Grosset/Putnam. xii-306 p. $ 25. 0-399-13982-6 [NTAb 39,p.362]. -- [R]BArR 21,2 (1995) 10 . 12 (J.N. *Wilford*).

6956 [E]**Skehan** P. *al.*, Cave 4.DSD 9,1991: → 8,a367 ... 10,9678: [R]Abr Nahrain 31 (1993) 133-5 (T. *Muraoka*).

6957 **Soggin** J. Alberto, I manoscritti del Mar Morto[2rev] [[1]1978]. R 1995, Newton Compton. 208 p. L[m] 4.9. -- [R]*Archeo 15 (1995) 109 (S. *Moscati*).

6958 **Stegemann** Hartmut, Die Essener, Qumran, Johannes der Täufer und Jesus; ein Sachbuch: Spektrum 4249, 1993 → 9,10653; 10,9725: [R]DSD 2 (1995) 114-8 (E.M. *Cook*: a needed but not definitive 'fresh start' against BAIGENT-LEIGH & THIERING].

6959 *a) Talmon* Shemaryahu, Qumran studies; past, present and future; -- *b) Baumgarten* Joseph M., Liquids and susceptibility to defilement in new 4Q texts: JQR 85 (1994s) 1-31 / 91-102; 103-8, response *Knohl* Isaac -- [*Baumgarten*, Liquids and susceptibility to defilement in 4Q fragments: → 10,331a, llth Jewish 1994. A-193-7].

6960 **Tov** Emanuel, *al.*, The Dead Sea Scrolls on microfiche 1993 → 9,10583; 10,9681:

[R]VT 44 (1994) 279-284 (E.D. *Herbert*; K.D. *Falk*).

6961 [E]**Trebolle Barrera** J., *Vegas Montaner* L., The Qumran congress, Madrid 18-21.III.1991: 1992 → 8,498 ... 10,9682: [R]Communio (Sev) 28 (1995) 85-88 (M. de *Burgos*).

6962 **VanderKam** James C., The Dead Sea Scrolls today 1994 → 10,9683: [R]CBQ 57 (1995) 377s (E.M. *Cook*): *CWeal 122,7 (1995) 27 (L.S. *Cunningham*); ETRel 70 (1995) 590 (J.-D. *Macchi*); *TBR 8,2 (1995s) 60 (A. *Warren*, sub 'Kam'); Theol 98 (L 1995) 137s (Meg *Davies*); TorJT 11 (1995) 217-9 (M. *Knowles*, also on BETZ-RIESNER Eng.)

6963 **Vermes** Geza, The Dead Sea Scrolls in English[4rev]. Shf 1995, Acadenic. lvii-392 p. £ 25 1-85075-563-9 [NTAb 40, p.566].

6964 [E]**Wise** Michael G., *al.*, Methods of investigation of the Dead Sea Scrolls: NY Academy of Sciences 722, 1994 → 540.

6965 **Yadin** Yigael, The message of the Scrolls, [E]*Charlesworth* J.
1992 = 1957, → 8,a350: [R]BS 151 (1994) 237s (R.A. *Taylor*: still fine).

K3.4 *Qumran*, **libri biblici et parabiblici**

6966 *a)* [E]**Ulrich** Eugene, *al.*, Qumran Cave 4, VII, Genesis to Numbers; - *b)* [E]**Attridge** Harold, *al.*, VIII. Parabiblical texts 1 [→ 10,9687]: DJD 12s. Ox 1994, Clarendon. 272 p.; 48 pl, + 1 colour. / 470 p.; 43 pl. $ 120. $ 130. -- [R]BArR 21,5 (1995) 6.8 (H. *Shanks*).

6967 [E]**Ulrich** Eugene, *Cross* Frank M., *al.*, Qumran Cave 4, IX: Dt Jos Jg Kgs: DJD 14. Ox 1995, Clarendon. xv-188 p. 0-19-826366-X.

6968 **Qimron** Elisha, *Strugnell* John, Qumran Cave 4, V. *Miqsat ma 'aśe ha-torah*: DJD 10, 1994 → 10,9693; [R]DSD 2 (1995) 365-377 (D. *Talshir*: some 50 -- 'hardly any' -- corrections); ET 106 (1994s) 152s (P.R. *Davies*); JJS 46 (1995) 295s (T.H. *Lim*); JRel 75 (1995) 548-550 (J.C. *VanderKam*); JSSt 40 (1995) 334-342 (G. *Brin*); JThS 46 (1995) 597-601 (G.J. *Brooke*); VT 45 (1995) 283s (J.A. *Emerton*).

6969 [E]**Broshi** Magen, *al.* Qumran Cave 4, XIV; parabiblical texts 2: DJD 19. Ox 1995, Clarendon. xi-267 p; XXIX pl. $ 125. 0-19-826389-9 [< OTA 19,p., J.A. *Fitzmyer*, listing 13 titles with editors and plates but not pages].

Beyer Klaus, Die aramäischen Texte vom Toten Meer usw. 1994 → 5920.

6971 **Meier** Johann, Die Qumran-Essener; die Texte vom Toten Meer: I. Die Texte der Höhlen 1-3 und 5-11; II. Die Texte der Höhle 4: UTBWiss N° 1862s. Mü 1995, Reinhardt. xxvi-441 p.: viii-741 p. DM 50. [III. (UTBW N° 1916, year 1996) xv (plans)-477 p.; bibliog. 381-477]. 3-8252-1862-7; -863-5 [-916-X].

6972 *Aschim* Anders, The oldest Bible commentary ? The Melchizedek document from Qumran: TT(og)K 66 (1995) Norwegian 85-102, Verdens eldste bibelkommentar ?: Eng. 103 [NTAb 40,p.98].

6973 *Bateman* Herbert W.[IV], Two first-century messianic uses of the OT; Heb 1:5-13 and 4QFlor 1,1-19: JETS 38 (1995) 11-27.

6974 *Baumgarten* Joseph M., A fragment on fetal life and pregnancy in 4Q 270: → 130, [F]MILGROM J., Pomegranates 1995, 445-8.

6975 **Berger** Klaus, Psalmen aus Qumran. Stu 1994, Quell. 164 p. DM 40. -- [R]Entschluss 50,1 (1995) 43 (R. *Oberforcher*); FrRu 2 (1995) 213-7 (H. A. *Rapp*).

6976 **Berger** Klaus, I salmi di Qumran, [TE]*Bianchi* Francesco. CasM 1995, Piemme. 309 p. 88-384-2405-5.

6977 *Bergmeier* R., 4Q 521 f II, 1-13 [eschatological psalm]: ZDMG 145 (1995) 38-48 [NTAb 40, p.98].

6978 *Bernstein* Moshe J., 4Q252 i 2 [Gen 6,3], *lô y^{e}dôr rûḥî bā'ādām:* biblical text or biblical interpretation ? : RQum 16 (1993-5) 421-7.

6979 **Brooke** George J., The thematic content of 4Q252 [Genesis passages probably without Exodus]: → 507. JQR 85 (1994s) 33-57 + 6 fig,; responses 61-79, *Bernstein* Moshe J.; 81-90, *Fröhlich* Ida [NTAb 40,p.479].

6980 *a) Broshi* Magen, *Yardeni* Ada, On *netinim* and false prophets [4Q 340 & 339]; -- *b) Caquot* André, Grandeur et pureté du sacerdoce; remarques sur le Testament de Qahat (4Q 542): → 72, [F]GREENFIELD J., Solving 1995,29-37; 2 fig. / 39-44.

6981 *Chyutin* Michael, The redaction of the Qumranic and the traditional Book of Psalms as a calendar: RQum 16 (1994) 367-395 [< OTA 18 (1995) p. 595 (P.D. *Sansone*)].

6982 *Dimant* Devorah, *a)* 4Q 127, an unknown Jewish apocryphal work ?: → 130, [F]MILGROM J., Pomegranates 1995, 805-813; -- *b)* Apocrypha and pseudepigrapha at Qumran [808 texts are neither fully biblical nor community-related]: *DSD 1 (1994) 151-9 [NTAb 39, p.465].

6984 *Duncan* Julie A., New readings for the 'Blessings of Moses' from Qumran: JBL 114 (1995) 273-290.

6985 *Elgvin* Torleif, *a)* Wisdom, revelation, and eschatology in an early Essene writing ['Sapiential Work A', = 1Q 26 & 6 portions from Cave 4]: → 512, SBL Seminars 34 (1995) 440-463. -- *b)* The reconstruction of sapiential work A: RQum 16,64 (1995) 559-580.

6986 *Glessmer* Uwe, Liste der biblischen Texte aus Qumran: RQum 16 (1993-5) 153-192 [193-202, *Fuller* Russell, 4QMicah 5,1s].

6987 *Milgrom* Jacob, On the purification offering in the Temple scroll: RQum 16 (1993-5) 99-101.

6988 *Goldberg* I., [H] Variant readings in Pesher Habakkuk: Textus 17 (1994) 9-24, Eng. 134 [NTAb 39, p.465].

6989 *Grelot* Pierre, Les œuvres de la Loi (à propos de 4Q394-398): RQum 16 (1993-5) 441-8.

6990 *Harrington* Daniel J., Wisdom at Qumran: → 538, Community 1993/4, 137-152 [< OTA 18 (1995) p. 371].

6991 *Hendel* Ronald S., 4Q 252 and the Flood chronology of Genesis 7-8; a text-critical solution: DSD 2 (1995) 72-79.

6992 **Kapera** Z.J., Qumran Cave 4 and MMT, special report *Zagenberg* J.[→ 7,7893*; 10,9693*]: *QumC 4,1 (1994) 67-72 [41-52. *Kapera,* How not to publish MMT, & 114-124 bibliog.: NTAb 36,p.448: 39,p.99].

6993 **Molin** Georg, [Lob Gottes 1957] [2rev]*Betz* Otto, *Riesner* Rainer, Das Geheimnis von Qumran, wiederentdeckte Lieder und Gebete. FrB 1994, Herder. 128 p. DM 19,80. 3-451-23324-X. -- [R]*DSD 2 (1995) 359s (D.K. *Falk*).

6994 **Nitzan** Bilhah, Qumran prayer and religious poetry: STDJ 12, 1994 → 10,7309*: [R]JBL 114 (1995) 316-9 (J.J. *Collins*).

6995 *Nitzan* Bilhah, *a)* Benedictions and instructions for the eschatological community (11QBer; 4Q285): RQum 16 (1993-5) 77-90; -- *b)* [H] The Merkabah descriptions in 4Q Berakhot: -> 10,331a, 11th Jewish 1994, A-87-94.

6996 *Nodet* Étienne, La Loi à Qumrân et SCHIFFMAN: RB 102 (1995) 38-71.

6997 *Palumbo* Arthur E., A new interpretation of the [4Qp] Nahum commentary: FolOr 29 (1992s) 153-162 [< OTA 18 (1995) p.127].

6998 **Pouilly** Jean, Qumrã (textos escolhidos). São Paulo 1992. Paulinas, 141 p. -- [R]RBBras 11 (1994) 673s (C. *Minette de Tillesse*).

6999 *Puech* Émile, *a)* Restauration d'un texte hymnique à partir de trois manuscrits fragmentaires: *4* xv 37 - xvi 4 (vii 34 - viii 3), *1Q35 (H^b)* 1, 9-14, *4,428 (H^b)* 7; -- *b)* Un autre manuscrit de la Genèse récemment identifié dans les fragments de la Grotte 4 *(4QGn^n)*: RQum 16,64 (1995) 637-640; 8 fig. / 543-555; 3 fig.

7000 *Qimron* Elisha, [H] Concerning 'Joshua cycles' from Qumran [4Q 522, not as PUECH E., RB 99 (1992) 676-696]: Tarbiz 63 (1993s) 503-8; 1 pl.; Eng.xxvii.

7001 *Rooy* H.F. van, Psalm 155; one, two, or three texts ? : RQum 16 (1993-5) 109-122: three, not juxtaposed *texts* but 11QPs^a, BAARS 12t4, and Syriac *traditions* throughout.

7002 *Schuller* Eileen M., *a)* A thanksgiving hymn from 4Q Hodayot (4Q428 7): RQum 16,64 (1995) 527-540 + 1 fig.; -- *b)* The Cave 4 Hodayot manuscripts; a preliminary description: → 507, JQR 85 (1994s) 137-149; response 151-5, *Collins* J.J.; 157-161, *Dimant* Devorah.

7003 *Skehan* P.W., *Ulrich* E., *Flint* P.W., Two manuscripts of Psalm 119 from Qumran Cave 4: RQum 16,64 (1995) 477-484; 2 fig.

7004 *Steiner* Richard C., The heading of the Book of the words of Noah on a fragment of the Genesis Apocryphon; new light on a 'lost' work: *DSD 2 (1995) 66-71 [< JSJ(ud) 26 (1995) 403].

7005 **Steudel** Annette, Der Midrasch zur Eschatologie [[D]1990]: STDJ 13, 1994 → 10,9694: [R]CBQ 57 (1995) 576s (J.C. *VanderKam*); JBL 114 (1995) 314-6 (J.J. *Collins*); JSJ 26 (1995) 380-4 (G.J. *Brooke*); JThS 46 (1995) 235-9 (P.R. *Davies*); TLZ 120 (1995) 137-9 (R. *Bergmeier*); VetChr 32 (1995) 481s (C.*Colafemmina*); VT 45 (1995) 429s (M. *Bockmuehl*).

7006 *Steudel* Annette, *a)* aḥerît ha-yāmim [14 times in MT - page-heads 'The end of the days'] in the Qumran texts; -- *b)* 4Q 408, a liturgy on morning and evening prayer -- preliminary edition: RQum 16 (1993-5) 225-246 / 313-334; 1 pl.

7007 *Strugnell* John, MMT; second thoughts on a forthcoming edition [DJD 10 by QIMRON and him]: → 538, Community 1993/4, 57-73 [< OTA 18 (1995) p. 370 (P.D. *Sansone*)].

7008 *Talmon* Shemaryahu, Was the book of Esther known at Qumran ? [only in 8 citations, not as a canonical text]: *DSD 2 (1995) 249-267 [< OTA 19,p.313].

7009 **Tantlevskij** Igor R., The two wicked priests in the Qumran commentary on Habakkuk: *QumC supp. C. Kraków 1995, Enigma. 39 p. $ 10. 83-86110-14-7 [NTAb 40, p.187]. -- [R]JSJ(ud) 26 (1995) 387s (A.S. van der *Woude* is impressed but not convinced).

7010 *Tov* Emanuel, *a)* The Exodus section of 4Q 422: *DSD 1 (1994) 197-209; - *b)* 4Q Jer^a -- a preliminary edition: Textus 17 (1994) 1-41; 7 pl. [NTAb 39,p.468]. -- *c)* 4Q Reworked Pentateuch; a synopsis of its contents: RQum 16,64 (1995) 649-653.

7011 *Ulrich* Eugene, An index of the passages in the biblical manuscripts from the Judean Desert: *DSD 2 (1995) 86-88 [errata for 1 (1994) 113-129] 2. Is-Chr, 88-107.

7012 *VanderKam* James C., [1QapGen XII,1-27, QIMRON E.] The granddaughters and grandsons of Noah: RQum 16 (1993-5) 457-461.

7013 *Wacholder* Ben-Zion & Sholom, Patterns of biblical dates and Qumran's calendar: the fallacy of JAUBERT's hypothesis: AHUC 66 (IATG for HUCA, 1995) 1-40.

K3.5 *Qumran --* **varii rotuli et fragmenta**

7014 *Bergmeier* Roland, Beobachtungen zu [Messias] 4 Q 521f 2,II,1-13 : ZDMG 145 (1995) 38-48.

7015 *a) Brin* Gershon, [H] Qumran D[e,f] [WACHOLDER-ABEGG 1 (1991) 23; 37; 51]; -- *b) Nitzan* Bilhah, [H] Qumran 4Q471, 286, 280 & M xvi,9-xvii,9: BetM 40,3 (142, 1995) 224-231 / 232-248.

7016 *Brooke* George J., *a)* 4Q 253, a preliminary edition: JSSt 40 (1995) 227-239; -- *b)* 4Q-254 fragments 1 and 4, and 4Q 254a; some preliminary comments: -> 10,331a, 11th Jewish 1994, A-185-192.

7017 *Cansdale* Lena, Women members of the *Yaḥad* according to the Qumran scrolls: - → 10,331a, 11th Jewish 1994, A-215-223.

7018 [E]**Charlesworth** James H., *Rietz* Henry W.L., *al.*, The Dead Sea Scrolls, Rule of the Community [modern Hebrew ..] Photographic multi-language edition. Ph c.1995, American Interfaith. 148 p. 0-8264-0911-3.

7019 *Collins* John J., Asking for the meaning [Hartman echo] of a fragmentary Qumran text; the referential background of 4QAaronA: → 79, [F]HARTMAN L., Texts & Contexts 1995, 579-590.

7020 *Dombrowski* Bruno W.W., 4Q MMT in English: *QumC 4 (1994) 28-36 (correcting QumC Dec.1990); 39s answers 37-39, *Muchowski* Piotr on non-use of ms. photos; -- 1-27, *Mędala* Stanisław, MMT setting; (41-) 53, *Kapera* Z.J., MMT bibliography [< OTA 18 (1995), p. 121-6].

7021 *Duhaime* Jean, *a)* Le Messie et les saints dans un fragment apocalyptique de Qumran (4Q 521 2): → 155, [F]RENAUD, B., Ce Dieu: LDiv 159 (1995) 265-273; -- *b)* Stratégies de persuasion dans le Rouleau du Temple; → 10,30, [F]COUTURIER G., Maison 1994, 245-261.

7022 *Eshel* Esther, 4QLev[d], a possible source for the Temple Scroll and MMT: *DSD 2 (1995) 1-13; 1 pl. [summary in JSJ(ud) 26 (1995) 402s]

7023 *Evans* Craig A., A note on the 'first-born Son' [of God ? messianic *pace* FITZMYER] of 4Q 369: *DSD 2 (1995) 185-201.

7024 *Finkel* Asher, The oracular interpretation of the Torah and Prophets as reflected in the Temple Scroll and the Pesharim of Qumran:→ 10,331a,11th Jewish 1994, A-179-184.

7025 *Gagnon* Robert A.J., How did the rule of the community obtain its final form ? A review of scholarly research [GUIBERT P., MURPHY-O'CONNOR J.]: JPseud 10 (1992) 61-76 [< OTA 18 (1995) p. 598].

7026 *García Martínez* Florentino, Dos notas sobre 4QMMT ['calendaric' and 'two separate letters' added by EISENMAN-WISE to STRUGNELL]: RQum 16 (1993-5) 295-7.

7027 *Greenfield* J.C. *zal,, Sokoloff* M., An astrological text from Qumran (4Q 318 and reflections on some zodiacal names: RQum 16,64 (1995) 508-517 (-519, *Pingree* D.; 520-3, *Yardeni* Ada); 2 fig.

7028 *Hempel* Charlotte, Who rebukes in *4Q 477* ? : RQum 16,64 (1995) 655s on ESHEL Esther, JJS 45 (1994) 111.

7029 *Larson* Erik, *Schiffman* L.H., *Strugnell* John, 4Q 470, preliminary publication of a fragment mentioning Zedekiah: RQum 16 (1993-5) 335-349;1 fig.

7030 *Mandel* Paul, On the 'duplicate copy' of the Copper Scroll (3Q15): RQum 16 (1993-5) 69-78.

7031 **Martone** Corrado, La 'Regola della Comunità', ed. critica: Henoch Quad 8. T 1995, Zamorani. x-234 p.; bibliog. 217-234. 88-7158-043-5.

7032 *Martone* Corrado, [4Q 265] La Regola di Damasco; una regola qumranica sui generis: Henoch 17 (1995) 103-115.

7033 *Mędala* Stanisław, [P] A letter to the High Priest from Qumran (4QMMT) and 'snake's venom' of the Pharisees: Co(lc)Th 64,3 (1994) 47-71; Eng. 72 [NTAb 40, p.100].

7034 *Mędala* Stanisław, *a)* The character and original setting of 4QMMT: *QChr 4 (1994) 1-27: - *b)* [P] Attempts to establish the nature and the circumstances of origin of .. 4QMMT: → 727, LEWICKI T. mem. 1993/4, 141-165; - *c)* [P] The letter to the High Priest from the Fourth Cave of Qumran (4QMMT): Szczecińskie Studia Koscielne 4 (1993) 29-45 [< JSJ(ud) 26 (1995) 267].

7035 *Nickelsburg* George W.E., Dealing with challenges and limitations; a response [in five mostly approving points on *Elgvin* R., *Brooke* G., *Larson* E., *Dimant* D. here]: *DSD 1 (1994) 229-237 [< OTA 18 (1995) p.128: 122, 118, 125, 120].

7036 *Nitzan* Bilhah, *a)* 4Q Berakhot[a-e] 4Q 286-290; a covenantal ceremony in the light of related texts: RQum 16,64 (1995) 487-506; 5 fig. -- *b)* Harmonic and mystical characteristics in poetic and liturgical writings from Qumran: → 507, JQR 85 (1994s) 163-183; response 185-202, *Wolfson* Elliot R.

7037 *a)* *Pfann* Stephen, 4Q 98; the Maskil's address to all sons of dawn; -- *b)* *Crawford* Sidnie W., Three fragments from Qumran Cave 4 and their relationship to the Temple Scroll; -- *c)* *Kister* Menahem, Commentary to 4Q 298 [a poetic form of the sect's self-definition formula: JQR 85 (1994s) 203-235; 4 pl. / 259-273 / 237-249.

7038 *Puech* Émile, *a)* Préséance sacerdotale et Messie-Roi dans la Règle de la Congrégation (1QSa ii 11-22): RQum 16 (1993-5) 351-365; 3 pl.; -- *b)* À propos de la Jérusalem nouvelle d'après les mauscrits de la Mer morte: 730, Semitica 43s (1992/5) 87-102.

7039 **Qimron** Elisha, The Temple Scroll; a critical edition with extensive reconstructions. Beer Sheva c.1995, Ben-Gurion Univ. vii-124 p.; bibliog. 95-122. 965-21-030-7.

7040 *a)* *Qimron* Elisha, A work concerning Divine Providence, 4Q 413; -- *b)* *Schiffman* Lawrence H., 4Q Mysteries, a preliminary edition and translation; -- *c)* *Talmon* Shemaryahu, A calendrical document from Qumran Cave 4 (mišmarot D, 4Q 325: → 72, [F]GREENFIELD J., Solving 1995, 181-189 / 207-260 / 327-344.

7041 *Qimron* Elisha, [H] Note on the list of false prophets from Qumran: Tarbiz [62 (1992s) 45] 63 (1993s) 273-8.

7042 *Scheepstra* S.E., True and righteous are all the works of God; a proposal for reconstruction of *1QS 1,26*: RQum 16,64 (1995) 643-646.

7043 *Schiffman* Lawrence H., *a)* 4qMysteries[b] [creation, history, in wisdom-view], a preliminary edition: RQum 16 (1993-5) 203-223; -- *b)* 4Q Mysteries, a preliminary translation: → 10,331a, llth Jewish 1994, A-199-206.

7044 *Schiffman* Lawrence H., The theology of the Temple Scroll: JQR 85 (1994s) 109-123; responses 125-8, *Milgrom* J.; 129-135, *VanderKam* J.

7045 *a) Schiffman* Lawrence, *'ôlâ* and *ḥaṭṭā't* in the Temple Scroll; - *b) Zevit* Ziony, Philology. archeology, and a terminus a quo for P's *ḥaṭṭā'i* legislation; - *c) Anderson* Gary A., Intentional and unintentional sin in the Dead Sea Scrolls: → 130, [F]MILGROM J., Pomegranates 1995, 39-48 / 29-38 / 49-64.

7046 **Swanson** Dwight D., The Temple Scroll and the Bible; the methodology of 11QT [diss. Manchester 1990, [D]*Brooke* G.]: STDJ 14. Lei 1995, Brill. xi-268 p. *f* 125. 90-04-09849-6 [< OTA 18 (1995) p. 437]. -- [R]BoL (1995) 170 (L.L. *Grabbe*); *DSD 2 (1995) 377-381 (G. *Brin*); JSJ(ud) 26 (1995) 384-7 (J. *Maier*).

7047 *Tov* Emanuel, Excerpted and abbreviated biblical texts from Qumran: RQum 16,64 (1995) 581-600.

7048 *a) Wise* Michael O., The copper scroll. - *b) Schwartz* Howard, Spirit possession in Judaism; the secret powers of *dybbuk* and *ibur*: Parabola 19,4 ('Hidden treasure' 1994) 44-54 / 72-76.

K3.6 Qumran et Novum Testamentum

7049 *Alberto* S., Unexpected confirmation [O'CALLAGHAN J., 7Q5 = Mk 6,52 as reported in 30 Days and Il Sabato 1991-4]: 30 Days 7,11 (R 1994) 56-61 [NTAb 39, p.380].

7050 **Allegro** John, [G] The men of Qumran and the Christian myth. Athena 1986, Divris. 298 p. -- [R]D(elt)BM 14,1 (1995) 98-99 (S. *Agourides*, [G]).

7051 *Arens* Eduardo, ¿El manuscrito más antiguo de Marcos ?: Páginas 20,135 (1995) 57-61: Q7 cueva de cristianos 'carece del más mínimo fundamento'

7052 **Berger** Klaus, The truth under lock and key ? Jesus and the Dead Sea scrolls [BAIGENT → 6909] [5]1993 → 9,10616; 10,9710*b*], [T]*Currie* J.S. LVL 1995, W-Knox. xi-113 p. $ 13 pa. 0-664-25547-7 [NTAb 40, p.170]. -- [R]E(xp)T 107 (1995s) 153s (J.G. *Snaith*: careless); *TBR 8,2 (1995s) 59s (M. *Bockmuehl*).

7053 **Betz** O. *Riesner* R., Jesus, Qumran und der Vatikan [BAIGENT] 1993 → 9,10617; 10,9711; [3rev]1995: [R]SNTU 20 (1995) 244s (A. *Fuchs*).

7054 **Betz** O., *Riesner* R., Jesus, Qumran and the Vatican 1993 → 10,9711s: [R]CBQ 57 (1995) 543s (D.J. *Harrrington*); NewThR 8,3 (1995) 98s (Patricia *Macdonald*); OTEs 8 (1995) 458s (W.R. *Domeris*); Proyecciòn 42 (1995) 239 (J.L. *Sicre*); RExp 92 (1995) 241-3 (D.E. *Garland*: a check to the lies and innuendo); SewaneeT 38 (1994s) 302 (C. *Bryan*); TS 56 (1995) 396s (V.R. *Gold*). -- N.B. Interpretation 49 (1995) 300-2 (J.A. *Sanders* demands and sets forth the greater complexity of how Elizabeth Bechtel until her death kept the corpus not at the [Claremont] Manuscript Center as the Jerusalem contract had stipulated, but at the San Marino Huntington library, where she also hid away an unauthorized copy made for herself).

7055 **Betz** Otto, *Riesner* Rainer, Jesús, Qumrán y el Vaticano; puntualizaciones, ^T*Gancho* Claudio. Barc 1994, Herder. 228 p. -- ^RATG(ran) 58 (1995) 350s (J.L. *Sicre*); Lum(Vt) 44 (1995) 522s (F. *Ortiz de Urtaran*).

7056 **Betz** O., *Riesner* R., Gesù, Qumran e il Vaticano; chiarimenti. Vaticano 1995, Libreria. 269 p.; bibliog. 243-9. 88-209-2137-5

7057 *a) Betz* O., Peschermethode und Jesusroman; - *b) Chmiel* J., Christianity and Qumran: *QChr 5,1 (1995) 23-30 / 46-54 [NTAb 40,p.289s].

7058 *Brooke* George J., 4Q 500 I and the use of Scripture in the parable of the vineyard [Mt 21,13-45‖]: *DSD 2 (1995) 268-294.

7059 **Charlesworth** J.H., Gesù nel giudaismo del suo tempo alla luce delle più recenti scoperte [... exciting archeological discoveries 1988], TE *Tomasetto* D.: PiccBT 30. T 1994, Claudiana. 392 p.; 21 fig.; 5 maps. L^m 36. -- ^RStPat(av) 41 (1994) 684s (G. *Leonardi*).

7060 ^E**Charlesworth** James H., Jesus and the DSS 1992 → 8,345.a387; 9,10618: ^RCBQ 57 (1995) 422s (J.J. *Collins*: editor's three claims mildly exaggerated, and SACCHI falls far short of proving 'Jesus' formative background was of an Essene type').

7061 *Chmiel* Jerzy, ^P *a)* The enigma of a manuscript of Mark's Gospel from Qumran Cave 7; -- *b)* Sesja kumranologiczna (Kraków 1994: KŁAWEK A. †1969): R(uch)BL 48 (1995) 182-6 / 214.

7062 *DeSilva* David A., The Dead Sea Scrolls and early Christianity: SewaneeTR 39 (1995s) 285-302.

7063 **Finger** Joachim, Jesus -- Essener, Guru, Esoteriker ? 1993 → 9,10620: ^RActuBbg 31 (1994) 225s (J. *Boada*).

7064 *Fitzmyer* Joseph A., The Dead Sea Scrolls and early Christianity [St. Louis University Bellarmine Lecture, Oct. 25, 1995]: ThD 42,4 (1995) 303-319.

7065 **Flusser** David, Das essenische Abenteuer; die jüdische Gemeinde vom Toten Meer; Auffälligkeiten bei Jesus, Paulus, Didache und Martin BUBER. Winterthur 1994, Cardun. 161 p. -- ^RFrRu NF 2 (1995) 48-49 (M. *Iten*).

7066 -- *Giniewski* P., La secte de Qumran, chaînon manquant entre judaïsme et christianisme [FLUSSER D., Das essenische Abenteuer ..]: FoiVie 94,5 (1995, 83-88 [NTAb 40, p.480].

7067 *Johnson* Alan F., Are there New Testament fragments among the Dead Sea Scrolls? [THIEDE C.]: *ABW 3,1 (1995) 16-25: not impossible.

7068 **Krupp** Michael, Qumran-Texte zum Streit um Jesus und das Urchristentum 1993 → 9,10622*: ^RRelStR 21 (1995) 332 (S. *Goranson*).

7069 ^E**Mayer** Bernhard, Christen und Christliches in Qumran ? 1992 → 9,396: ^RRBBras 11 (1994) 674s (C. *Minette de Tillesse*).

7070 *Most* W., Threat to Christianity ? [disproved by EISENMAN-WISE]: H(om)PR 95,5 (1995) 50-53 [NTAb 39, p.467].

7071 ^E**Murphy-O'Connor** Jerome, *Charlesworth* James H., Paul and the Dead Sea Scrolls 1990 = 1968: ^RJETS 38 (1995) 290s (J.A.D. *Weima*).

7072 *Norton* G.J., Qumran and Christian origins: PIBA 16 (1993) 99-113 [NTAb 39, p.283].

7073 *Palumbo* A.E., 1QpHab 5:8-12, the 'Pillars' [Gal 2,1s], and Paul [the 'Man of Lies']: FolOr 30 (Kraków 1994) 125-137 [NTAb 40, p.101].

7074 *a) Puech* Émile, Des fragments grecs de la grotte 7 et le NT? 7Q4 et 7Q5 et le papyrus Magdalen grec 17 = P^{64} ['ne confirme en rien l'hypothèse de THIEDE à propos de Marc qu'on ne peut nullement identifier en 7Q5']; -- *b) Boismard* M.-É., À propos de 7Q5 et Mc 6,52-53 [insoutenables les solutions des trois anomalies dans la seule ligne 3]: RB 102 (1995) 570-584; Eng. 570 / 585-8; Eng. 585 [589-591, *Grelot* Pierre, contre les vulgarisations des médias sur Thiede].

7075 *Rabuske* Irineu J., Qumran e o Novo Testamento: Teocomunicação 25 (1995) 306-316.

7076 *Rohrhirsch* Ferdinand, Zur Relevanz wissenschaftstheoretischer Implikationen in der Diskussion um das Qumranfragment 7Q5 und zu einer neuen [SPOTTORNO M. 1992] Identifizierungsvorschlag von 7Q5 mit Zacharias 7,4.5: ThG 85 (1995) 80-95: O'CALLAGHAN'S Mk 6,52 ist erklärungsstärker.

7077 **Rosenberg** Roy A., The veneration of divine justice; the Dead Sea Scrolls and Christianity: CSRel 40. L 1995, Greenwood. xiii-145 p. $ 45. 0-313-29655-3 [NTAb 40,p.185; OTA 19,p.172; ThD 43,287.

7078 **Rudolf** Paul F., Jesus und Qumran; war der Nazarener ein Essener ? 1993 → 10,9722*: ^{R}ActuBbg 31 (1994) 66s (J. *Boada*).

7079 *Stanton* Graham, A Gospel among the scrolls ? Scholar [THIEDE championing O'CALLAGHAN, (+) 3 Oxford Magdalen papyri] claims to have identified a fragment of Mark among the Dead Sea Scrolls and the earliest fragment of Matthew: BiRe 11,6 (1995) 36-42.

7080 ^{E}**Strus** Andrzej, Tra giudaismo e cristianesimo; Qumran -- Giudeocristiani: Ieri oggi domani 17. R 1995, LAS(alesianum). 181 p. 88-213-0315-2.

7081 **Thiede** C.P., The earliest Gospel manuscript ? 1992 → 8,a399: ^{R}BS 151 (1994) 350-4, also in WThJ 56 (1994) 173-180 (D. B. *Wallace*) [NTAb 39, p.8].

7082 **Thiering** Barbara, Jesus von Qumran; sein Leben -- neu geschrieben, ^{T}1993 → 9,10632: ^{R}ThZ 51 (1995) 281s (W. *Neidhart*: phantastische Spekulationen).

7083 **Thiering** Barbara, Jesus and the riddle of the DSS; unlocking the secrets of his life story 1992 → 8,a400; 10,9731: *JHiCr 2,1 (1995) 149-153 (R.M. *Price* defends); NewTR 7,1 (1994) 106s (Barbara E. *Bowe*).

7084 *a) Thiering* Barbara, Pesher and Gospel; - *b) Kapera* Z.J., Thiering bibliography: *QumC 5,1 (Kraków 1995) 13-22 / 10-12 [NTAb 40,p.296].

7085 *Ulfgard* Håkan, Nya hypotheser om gamla texter och gamla hypotheser om nya texter; ny debattbok kring Qumranrörelsen och urkristendomen [EISENMAN-WISE 1992, ^{T} *Krantz* Eva S., Rösterna ur Dödahavsrullarna 1993]: SvTK 69 (1993) 161-172; Eng. 172.

7086 *Wallace* Daniel B., 7Q5 the earliest NT papyrus?: W(estm)TJ 46 (1994) 153-18): no.

7087 *Weber* Kathleen, Is there a Qumran parallel to Matthew 24,51 ‖ Luke 12,46 ? : RQum 16,64 (1995) 657-663.

7088 *Yamauchi* Edwin M., Jesus outside the New Testament [.. Qumran]; what is the evidence ?: → 390, Jesus under fire 1995, 207-229.

K3.8 **Historia et doctrinae Qumran**

7089 *a) Abegg* M.G.,   The Messiah at Qumran;   are we still seeing double ?; - *b)*
Bauckham R., The messianic interpretation of Isa. 10:34 in the Dead Sea scrolls, 2 Baruch
and the preaching of John the Baptist: *DSD 2 (1995) 125-144 / 202-216 [NTAb 40,
p.288].

7090 **Batzner** D.,   Die Qumran-Gemeinde; Lebensform und Grundlagen ihrer Theologie:
*Theorie und Forschung 287/20. Rg 1994, Roderer. iv-78 p. DM 28, 3-89073-713-7
[NTAb 40, p.373].

7091 *Baumgarten* Albert I.,   *a)* Crisis in the scrollery; a dying consensus [Essene rebellion
against Maccabee priesthood]: Judaism 44 (1995) 399-413; 4 fig.; -- *b)* Rabbinic literature
as a source for the history of Jewish sectarianism in the Second Temple period: *DSD 2
(1995) 14-57; -- *c)* The rule of the Martian [hostility is greatest between two groups which
a non-Earthan would judge practically identical] as applied to Qumran: → 392, IOS 14
(1994) 121-143.

7092 **Besch** Bernt,   Der Dualismus in den Kernschriften von Qumran; ein Beitrag zur
Diskussion über Wesen und Herleitung des Qumranischen Dualismus. R c. 1995, Univ.
S.Thomae. xiv-247 p.; Bibliog. 243-247.

7093 **Brin** G., [H] *Sugiyyot* .... Pairs in Bible and scrolls. TA 1994, Univ. 287 p. - BetM
40,2 (141, 1995) 117-122 (Bilhah *Nitzan*, [H]).

7094 *a) Campbell* Jonathan G.,   Essene-Qumran origins in the Exile; a scriptural basis ?; -
b) Reich Ronny,   A note on the function of Room 30 (the 'Scriptorium') at Khirbet
Qumran; - *c) Goodman* Martin,   A note on the Qumran sectarians, the Essenes and
JOSEPHUS: → 211, [F]VERMES G.,JJS 46 (1995) 143-156 / 157-160 / 161-6.

7095 *Collins* John J.,   'He shall not judge by what his eyes see'; messianic authority in
the Dead Sea Scrolls: *DSD 2 (1995) 145-164.

7096 *Davies* Philip R.,   *a)* Was there really a Qumran community ?: *CuRB 3 (1995) 9-
35; -- *b)* Communities in the Qumran scrolls: PI(r)BA 17 (1994) 55-68: not an Essene
community, but neither as GOLB '*no* communities'; -- *c)* Communities in the Qumran
scrolls [unproved]: PIBA 17 (1994) 55-68 [< NTAb 40, p.99 & 479; OTA 19, p.126].

7097 *Deines* Roland,   Die Abwehr der Fremden in den Texten aus Qumran; zum Verständnis der Fremdenfeindlichkeit in der Qumrangemeinde: → Feld, Die Heiden 1994, 59-
91.

7098 **Dombrowski** Bruno W.W.,   Ideological and socio-structural developments of the
Qumran association I: QMogil 2. Kraków 1994, Enigma. 184 p. $ 28; pa. $ 18. 63-
86110-12-0. -- [R]JSJ(ud) 26 (1995) 187-9 (A.S. van der *Woude:* unsatisfactory).

7099 *Fitzmyer* Joseph A., The Qumran community: Essene or Sadducean ? : → 134,
[F]MURRAY R., HeythJ 36,4 (1995) 467-476.

7100 *Flusser* David,   Qumran und die Hungersnot unter König Herodes [< IsrMusJ 6
(1987) 7-16], [T]*Mach* Dafna: FrRu 2 (1995) 93-118;1 phot.

7101 *Gagnon* Robert A.J.,   How did the Rule of the Community obtain its final shape ? A
review of scholarly research: JSPE 10 (1992) 61-79.

7102 **García Martínez** Florentino, *Trebolle Barrera* Julio,   Los homnbres de Qumran
1993 → 9,10642; 10,9738*: *DSD 2 (1995) 233-5 (G.S. *Brooke:* most has already

appeared in print, and the unification is sometimes imperfect; anyway the primary intention was not to bring together everything in a single English volume; 'rather, the most valuable contribution is to shift the general reader's attention away from predominantly Christian concerns towards the importance of the interpretation of the Law,' even for NT studies).

7103 **García Martínez** F., *Trebolle Barrera* J., The people of the Dead Sea Scrolls, [T]*Watson* W.G.E. Lei 1995, Brill. ix-269 p. *f* 65. 90-04-10085-7 [NTAb (39,p.168) 40, p.376].

7104 **Golb** Norman, Who wrote the Dead Sea Scrolls ? NY 1994, Scribner. 446 p. $ 25. -- [R]BArR 21,2 (1995) 10 . 86 (H. *Shanks*).

7105 **Harrington** Hannah, The impurity systems of Qumran and the rabbis: SBL.d 143 [California 1992], 1993 → 10,9739: [R]CBQ 57 (1995) 136s (J. *Duhaime*); CritRR 7 (1994) 402-4 (R.A. *Kugler*); RB 102 (1995) 116-128 (É. *Nodet*).

7106 *a) Jucci* Elio, Davide a Qumran; -- *b) Boccaccini* Gabriele, La figura di Davide nei giudaismi di età ellenistico-romana: → 526, Davide: RicStoB 7,1 (1993/5) 157-173 / 175-185.

7107 **Lange** A., Weisheit und Prädestination; weisheitliche Urordnung und Prädestination in den Textfunden von Qumran [ev. Diss. Münster 1994, [D]*Lichtenberger* H.]: StTDJ 18. Lei 1995, Brill. xi-349 p.; 7 fig. *f* 170. 90-04-10432-1 [NTAb 40, p.380].

7108 *Lange* Armin, Wisdom and predestination in the Dead Sea Scrolls: *DSD 2 (1995) 340-354.

7109 *Larson* Erik, 4Q 470 and the angelic rehabilitation of King Zedekiah: *DSD 1 (1994) 210-118 [< OTA 18 (1995) p. 125].

7110 *Lichtenberger* H., Alter Bund und [Qumran; Jer 31; NT] Neuer Bund: NTS 41 (1995) 400-414.

7111 *Loader* B., The new [EISENMAN-WISE] Dead Sea Scrolls, new light on [a very militaristic Davidic] messianism and the history of the community: *Colloquium 25,2 (Brisbane 1993) 65-87 [NTAb 39, p.99; JSJ(ud) 26,402].

7112 *Magness* Jodi, The chronology of the settlement at Qumran in the Herodian period: *DSD 2 (1995) 58-65.

7113 *Milgrom* Jacob, Qumran's biblical hermeneutics; the case of the wood offering [11QT LI,19-LII,3 (Dt 16,,21s; Lv 26,1; VERMES G.]: RQum 16 (1993-5) 449-456.

7114 *Nodet* Étienne, La loi à Qumrân et SCHIFFMAN: RB 102 (1995) 38-71. Eng. 38.

7115 *Pfitzner* Victor C., Worshipping with the angels (... 1Q Hod 11,11): L(ex)TQ 29 (1995) 50-60.

7116 **Ringgren** Helmer, The faith of Qumran; theology of the Dead Sea Scrolls[2rev] [svensk 1961, [T]*Sander* Emilie T. 1963]: Christian Origins Library. NY 1995, Crossroad. xxxvii-330 p.; bibliog. 255-305. 0-8245-1258-8.

7117 *Ruderman* Abraham, The Qumran settlement; scriptorium, villa or fortress: JBQ 23 (1995) 131s.

7118 **Schiffman** Lawrence H., The eschatological community of the Dead Sea Scrolls 1989 → 5,130 ... 10,9744*: [R]Kiryat Sefer 65 (1994s) p.43s (Devorah *Dimant*, [H]).

7119 **Schiffman** Lawrence H., Reclaiming the Dead Sea Scrolls [with running polemic against exaggerating affinities with Christianity]; the history of Judaism, the background of Christianity, the lost library of Qumran. Ph 1994, Jewish Publ.Soc. xxvii-529 p. - 0-8276-0530-7. -- [R]*DSD 2 (1995) 241-7 (J.J. *Collins*: the polemic is justified but not its lack of nuances or citation).

7120 **Schiffman** Yehudah [= Lawrence; his 1975, 1983, and 1989 books updated in one, → 9,10645; ^T*Ilan* Tal], ^H Law, custom and messianism in the Dead Sea Sect. J 1993, Shazar. 391 p. $ 30. 965-227-074-1. -- ^R*DSD 2 (1995) 120-3 (J.C. *VanderKam*: exhaustive compendium of Qumran law); JSJ(ud) 26 (1995) 374-8 (D. *Dimant*: rich, but with some traces of his now superseded views).

7121 *Schiffman* Lawrence H., Origin and early history of the Qumran sect; BA 58 (1995) 37-48; ill.

7122 **Schmidt** F., La pensée du Temple, de Jérusalem à Qoumran 1994 → 10,9745: ^RÉTRel 70 (1995) 120 (Françoise *Smyth*); RB 102 (1995) 257-262 (E. *Nodet*).

7123 *Shaked* Shaul, Qumran; some Iranian connections: → 72, ^FGREENFIELD J., Solving 1995, 277-281.

7124 **Sheres** Ita, *Blau* Anne Kohn, The truth about the virgin; sex and ritual defilement [one ritual for males' 'angelic' perfection; another for virgins' immaculate conception]. NY 1995, Continuum. xiii-236 p. $ 27.50. 0-8264-0816-8 [< OTA 19, p.172].

7125 *a) Talmon* Shemaryahu, The community of the renewed covenant; between Judaism and Christianity [.. not to be identified with any known group in Judaism]; - *b) Baumgarten* Joseph M., Sadducean elements in Qumran law: → 538. Community 1993/4, 3-24 / 27-36 [< OTA 18 (1995) p. 377.368 (P.D. *Sansone*)].

7126 ^E**Ulrich** E., *VanderKam* J., The community of the renewed covenant, ND 1993: Christianity and Judaism in Antiquity 10. ND 1993, Univ. xviii-290 p, 0-268-0082-7. -- ^RSefarad 55 (1995) 406-9 (N. *Fernández Marcos*).

7127 **Widengren** Geo, *al.*, Apocalyptique iranienne et dualisme qoumrânien: *RechIntT 2. P 1995, A. Maisonneuve. ii-224 p. F 240. 2-7200-1098-7 [< OTA 19, p.324, 3 renvois].

7128 *Witaszek* Gabriel, ^P Particularist tendencies in the Qumran community: R(uch)BL 48 (1995) 169-181.

7129 *Woude* A.S. van der, Wisdom at Qumran: → 55,^FEMERTON J.,Wisdom 1995, 244-56.

K4.1 **Sectae jam extra Qumran notae: Esseni, Zelotae**

7130 **Bergmeier** Roland, Die Essener-Berichte des Flavius JOSEPHUS 1993 → 9,10659; 10,9749: ^RBijdragen 56 (1995) 219s (L.H. *Westra*).

7131 *Bojesen* S., Essæerne. Dodehavsskrifterne og Khirbet Qumran [not Essene]: *Nemelah 13 (1994) 21-29 [< JSJ 26 (1995) 411].

7132 **Campserveux** Max, Méditation sur les Esséniens exclus: CahRenan 43,190 bis (1995). 42 p.

7133 **Canciani** Maria, Ultima cena dagli Esseni; una documentata nuova esplorazione. BtMisteri. R 1995, Mediterranee. 122 p. 88-272-1115-2.

7134 *Goranson* Stephen, The exclusion of Ephraim in Rev. 7:4-8 and Essene polemic against Pharisees: *DSD 2 (1995) 80-85.

7135 *Henrich* Rainer, Rationalistische Christentumskritik in essenischem Gewand; der Streit um die 'Enthüllungen' über die wirkliche Todesart Jesu [KLENCKE Philipp 1849]: ZKG 106 (1995) 345-362.

7136 *Puech* Émile, Les Esséniens et le Temple de Jérusalem; → 10,30, ^FCOUTURIER G., Maison 1994, 263-287.

7137 *Rabuske* Irineu J., A questão dos saduceos : Teocomunicação 24 (1994) 257-277.

7138 **Schonfield** Hugh J., The Essene odyssey. Rockport MA 1993, Element. 180 p. $ 13. -- ^R*JHiCr 2,2 (1995) 151-5 (R.M. *Price*: defensive praise).

7139 *Söding* Thomas, Feindhass und Bruderliebe: Beobachtungen zur essenischen Ethik: RQum 16,64 (1995) 601-619.

7140 **Stemberger** G., Farisei, Sadducei, Esseni: SBPaid 105, 1993 → 10,9753: [R]Anton 70 (1995) 691 (M. *Nobile*); Henoch 17 (1995) 248-252 (P. *Sacchi*); RivB 43 (1995) 546-8 (G. *Jossa*).

7141 **Stemberger** Günter, Jewish contemporaries of Jesus; Pharisees, Sadducees, Essenes, [T]*Mahnke* Alan W. Mp 1995, Fortress. ix-161 p. $ 15 pa. 0-8006-2624-9 [ThD 44,89; OTA 19, p.555, R.D. *Witherup*].

7142 **Welburn** A., Aan de wortels van het Christendom; het mysterie der Essenen, de gnostische openbaring en de christelijke visie. Zeist 1994, Christofoor. 332 p. *f* 60. -- [R]G(ereformeerd)TT 95 (1995) 88 (R. *Roukema*: curieus, voor antroposofen).

K4.2 **Samaritani**

7143 **Bójd** I.R.M., Principles of Samaritan Halachah 1989 → 5,a65; 7,9918: [R]RQum 16,64 (1995) 673s (J.*Margain*).

7144 **Crown** Alan D., A bibliography of the Samaritans2 (= 11984 + 1000 items): ATLA 32, 1993 → 9,10656: [R]JAOS 115 (1995) 724-6 (L.H.*Feldman* adds some 60 more).

7145 [E]**Crown** Alan D., *al.*, A companion to Samaritan studies 1992 → 9,10655; 10,9756: [R]ÉTRel 70 (1995) 121 (J.-D. *Macchi*); Salesianum 57 (1995) 767 (R. *Vicent*).

7146 *Diebner* B.J., Die antisamaritanische Polemik im TNK als konfessionelles Problem: → 523, Bible 1992/4, 95-110.

7147 *Florentin* Moshe, [H] Studies in the morphology of Samaritan Hebrew: Les 59 (1995) 217-241; Eng. 3,III.

7148 *Giles* Terry, The Chamberlain-Warren Samaritan inscription CW 2472 [Ex 15,3.11]: JBL 114 (1995) 111-6; 2 fig.

7149 *Goussikindey* E., Jesus and the Samaritans; paradigm for dialogue [< Pentecôte d'Afrique 14 (1993) 64-73], [TE]: ThD 41 (1994) 37-40 [NTAb 39, p.81].

7150 *Harviainen* Tapani, *Shehadeh* Haseeb, How did Abraham FIRKOVICH acquire the great collection of Samaritan manuscripts; in Nablus in 1864 ?: StOr 73 (1994) 167-187 + 4 phot.

7151 *Lindemann* A., Samaria und Samaritaner im NT: WuD 22 (1993) 51-76 [NTAb 39, p.93].

7152 **Macchi** Jean-Daniel, Les Samaritains, histoire d'une légende; Israël et la province de Samarie: MondeB 30. Genève 1994. Labor et Fides. 191 p. Fs 35. 3-8309-0712-4 [< OTA 18 (1995) p. 432]. -- [R]HebStud 36 (1995) 212-5 (R. *Pummer*); RB(elg)PH 73 (1995) 225s (J. *Schamp*); RevSR 69 (1995) 527s (J.-M. *Husser*); VS.s 148 (1994) 533 (H. *Cousin*); VT 45 (1995) 568s (H.G.M. *Williamson*).

7153 **Zangenberg** Jürgen. SAMAREIA; antike Quellen zur Geschichte und Kultur der Samaritaner in deutscher Übersetzung: TANZ 15, 1994 → 10,9764; DM 94: [R]JSJ(ud) 26 (1995) 393s (G. *Sixdenier*); ThZ 51 (1995) 280s (B. *Weber*).

K4.5 *Sadoqitae, Qaraitae* -- **Cairo Genizah; Zadokites, Karaites**

7154 [E]**Broshi** Magen, The Damascus document reconsidered 1992 → 8,a440 ... 10,9766:

^{R}Syria 71 (1994) 460 (A. *Caquot*).

7155 **Campbell** Jonathan, The use of Scripture in the Damascus Document 1-8, 19-20. B 1995, de Gruyter. 218 p. DM 124. 3-11-014240-6. -- ^{R}E(xp)T 107 (1995s) 56 (P.R. *Davies* welcomes).

7156 *Caquot* André, Nouveaux´fragments de l'écrit de Damas: RHPhR 74 (1994) 369-394; Eng. 475

7157 *Davies* Philip R., Who can join the 'Damascus Covenant' ? : → 211, ^{F}VERMES G.,JJS 46 (1995) 134-142.

7158 *Erder* Yoram, The Karaites' Sadducee dilemma: → 392, IOS 14 (1994) 195-226.

7159 **Freund** Roman, Karaites and dejudaization; a historical review of an endogenous and exogenous paradigm [diss.Stockholm]. Sto 1991, Almqvist & W. v-133 p. - ^{R}JQR 86 (1995) 241s (L. *Nemoy*).

7160 **Genot-Bismuth** Jacqueline, Le scénario de Damas [document Zadokite], Jérusalem hellénistique et les origines de l'Essénisme. P 1992, OEIL. 478 p. F 210. -- ^{R}RasIsr 60,3 (1993) 121-6 (Francesca *Calabi*).

7161 *McCready* W.O., Sadducees and ancient sectarianism: RStT 12,2s (1992) 79-97 [NTAb 40, p.303].

7162 *Martone* C., La Regola di Damasco [^{H} + ital.; ‖, comm.]; una regola qumranica sui generis: Henoch 17 (1995) 103-113.

7163 *Nebe* G. Wilhelm, *a*) Noch einmal zu Text und Übersetzung von CD VI, 11-14 [4QD^a (266) Fr.3,III,4-7: covenanters reject current Jerusalem sacrifices]; - *b*) Das Sprachvermögen des mebaqqer in Damaskusschrift XIV,10: RQum [7 (1971) 553, *Murphy-O'Connor* J.]]16 (1993-5) 285-7 / 289-291.

7164 *Qimron* E., Further observations on tbe laws of oaths in the Damascus Document 15: JQR 85 (1994s) 251-7.

7165 **Rubinstein** Jeffrey, The Sadducees and the water libation: JQR 84 (1993s) 417-444.

7166 *Steudel* Annette, The houses of prostration, CD XI,21 - XII,1 -- duplicates of the Temple: RQum 16 (1993-5) 49-66.

K5 **Judaismus prior vel totus**

7167 *Aaron* David H., Early rabbinic exegesis on Noah's son Ham and the so-called 'Hamitic myth': JAAR 63 (1995) 721-759.

7168 *Alexander* Philip, 'A sixtieth part of prophecy'; the problem of continuing revelation in Judaism: → 170, ^{F}SAWYER, J., Words; JSOT.s 195 (1995) 414-433.

7169 **Avemarie** Friedrich, Tora und Leben; Untersuchungen zur Heilsbedeutung der Tora in der frühen rabbinischen Literatur: TSAJ 55. Tü c. 1995, Mohr. xiv-664 p. Bibliog. 597-620. 3-16-146532-6.

7170 ^{E}**Baarda** T., *al.*, Jodemdom en vroeg christendom, continuiteit en discontinueit: StNT Conventus 1991 → 7,415*a*: ^{R}EThL 70 (1994) 479s (A. *Denaux*).

7171 *Baumgarten* A.I., Rabbinic literature as a source for the history of Jewish sectarianism in the Second Temple period: *DSD 2 (1995) 14-57.

7172 **Berquist** Jon L., Judaism in Persia's shadow; a social and historical approach. Mp 1995, Fortress. vi-287 p.; bibliog, 257-273. 0-8006-2845-4,

7173 **Boccaccini** G., Il Medio Giudaismo 1993 → 9,10670*; 10,9774: ᴿRivBib 43 (1995) 285-7 (R. *Penna*).

7174 **Boccaccini** Gabriele, Middle Judaism 1991 → 8,a450; 10,9773: ᴿNewTR 7,2 (1994) 105-7 (H.G. *Perelmuter*); S(cot)JTh 48 (1995) 281s (G. *Stanton*).

7175 *Boccaccini* Gabriele, *a)* Multiple Judaisms; a new understanding of the context of earliest Christianity : BiRe 11,1 (1995) 38-41 . 46; -- *b)* The preexistence of the Torah; a commonplace in Second Temple Judaism [no], or a later rabbinic development ? [yes; 150 C.E., applying the Wisdom-myth as in Christianity]: Henoch 17 (1995) 329-350; ital. 350.

7176 **Bonfil** Robert, Jewish life in Renaissance Italy [1991], ᵀ*Oldcorn* Anthony. Berkeley 1994, Univ. California. xiii-320 p. -- ᴿJQR 85 (1994s) 437-440 (G. *Mazzotta*).

7177 **Brewer** David I., Techniques and assumptions in Jewish exegesis before 70 CE, 1992 → 8,a451 ... 10,9775: ᴿHebStud 35 (1994) 107-9 (R. *Goldenberg*); RB 102 (1995) 262 (É. *Nodet*).

Chilton B., *Neusner* J., Judaism in the New Testament; practices and beliefs 1995 → 2223 supra [NTAb 40, p.551].

7178 *Cohen* Mathy, 'Torah' dans les Pirqey Abot: MélSR 52 (1995) 317 . 322-332.

7179 **Cohen** Shaye J.D., From the Maccabees to the Mishnah 1987 → 3,a413 ... 7,9938*: ᴿCCAR 42,1 (1995) 71-75 (Tzvee *Zahavy*)

7180 **Danzig** Neil, ᴴ Introduction to Halakhot Pesuqot [Geonic period up to 900]. NY/J 1993, Jewish Theol. Sem. 708 p. -- ᴿTarbiz 64 (1994s) 139-152 (R. *Brody*, ᴴ, Eng, 1,ix).

7181 *Davies* William D., Reflections on the nature of Judaism : RHPhR 75 (1995) 85-11; franç. 85.

7182 *Dunn* J.D.G., What did Christianity lose when it parted from Judaism ?: *Explorations 8,2 (Ph 1994) 2s [NTAb 39,p.266].

7183 *a) Evans* Craig A., Early Rabbinic sources and Jesus research; - *b) Neusner* Jacob, The Gospels and the Mishnah; the Church Fathers and the Talmud; if Christianity were written down by rabbis: → 512, SBL Seminars 34 (1995) 53-76 / 37-52.

7184 **Goodman** Martin, Mission and conversion; proselytizing in the religious history of the Roman Empire [invented by Christianity: < 1992 Oxford Wilde lectures]. Ox 1994, Clarendon. xiv-194 p. 0-19-814941-7 [NTAb 39,p.535; 40,p.91; ThD 43,66]. -- ᴿBoL (1995) 149 (J.L. *North*); Reviews in Religion and Theology 2,2 (L 1995) 13-19 (J.C. *Paget*: challenging the assumptions).

7185 ᴱ**Goodman-Thau** Eveline, *Schulte* Christoph, Das Buch Yezira / Sefer Yesîrâ, ᵀMAYER Johann F. von: Jüdische Quellen 1. B 1994, Akademie. iv-64 p. DM 48. 3-05-002313-9. - - ᴿBoL (1995) 149 (A.P. *Hayman*: useless reprint of an 1830 classic).

7186 **Grabbe** Lester L., Judaism from Cyrus to Hadrian, 1. Persian and Greek periods;. 2. The Roman period 1992 → 9,10681; 10,9782: ᴿ*CritRR 7 (1994) 400-2 (R.D. *Chesnutt*); JAOS 115 (1995) 463-472 (S. *Mason*: 'dialogue', i.e. some few 'marring' weaknesses); StPhilo 7 (1995) 231-6 (C.R. *Holladay*). -- Now paperback, both volumes in one, L 1994, SCM; xxv-722 p.; £ 35; 0-334-03578-8: ᴿBoL (1995) 149s (Tessa *Rajak*: lyric praise).

7187 *Gruber* Mayer I., Matrilineal determination of Jewishness; biblical [against FRANCUS I. 1988] and Near Eastern roots: → 130, ᶠMILGROM J., Pomegranates 1995, 437-443

7188 *Hayes* C(hristine) E., Amoraic interpretation and halakhic development; the case of the prohibited basilica: JSJ(ud) 26 (1995) 156-168.

7189 *Hayward* Robert, Some ancient Jewish reflections on Isarel's imminent redemption: → 159, [F]ROGERSON, J., Bible/Society; JSOT.s 200 (1995) 293-305.

7190 *Heide* A. van der, Verzoening in het klassieke rabbijnse Jodendom: G(ereformeerd)TT 94 (1994) 26-23.

7191 *a) Hengel* Martin, 'Schriftauslegung' und 'Schrift-werdung' in der Zeit des Zweiten Tempels; - *b) Avemarie* Friedrich, Schriftgebrauch in der haggadischen Exegese der Amoräer, am Beispiel der Peticha WuR 27,3: → 10.322*, Schriftauslegung (1994) 1-71 / 133-152.

7192 *Hengel* Martin, *Deines* Roland, E.P. SANDERS, 'Common Judaism ', Jesus, and the Pharisees [Jewish law 1992, Judaism practice 1992], [T]*Bailey* Daniel P.: JThS 46 (1995) 1-70.

7193 *Hezser* Catherine, Social fragmentation, plurality of opinion, and nonobservance of halakhah; Rabbis and community in Late Roman Palestine: Jewish Studies Quarterly 1 (Tü 1993s) 234-251.

7194 **Hirshman** Marc G., A rivalry of genius; Jewish and Christian biblical interpretation in late antiquity, [T]*Stein* Batya. Albany 1995, SUNY. ix-179 p. $ 50: pa- $ 17. 0-7914-2727-7; -8-5 [< ThD 43,273].

7195 *Höffken* Peter, Gleichnisse in der rabbinischen Tradition: ThZ 51 (1995) 326-339.

7196 **Holladay** Carl R., ARISTOBULUS: Fragments from Hellenistic Jewish authors 3 / SBL TTr 20. Atlanta 1995, Scholars. x-255 p. $ 45. 0-7885-0119-4 [< ThD 43,266].

7197 *Horst* P.W. van der, De Joden van Napels in de Romeinse keizertijd: Ter Herkenning 23 (1995) 55-64 [< GTT 95,205].

7198 *a) Ilan* Tal, The attraction of aristocratic women to Pharisaism during the Second Temple period; -- *b) Georgi* Dieter, The early Church; internal Jewish migration or new religion ? [Harvard lecture 1988 > 1984]: HThR 88 (1995) 1-33 / 35-68.

7199 **Jacobs** Martin, Die Institution des jüdischen Patriarchen [*nasî*'; .. Judah]; eine quellen- und traditionskritische Studie zur Geschichte der Juden in der Spätantike [< Diss. Berlin FU 1994, [D]*Schäfer* P.]: TSAJ 52. Tü 1995, Mohr. xiv-401 p. 3-16-146503-2 [< OTA 19,p.365s, L.H. *Feldman*].

7200 *a) Kalmin* Richard, Christians and heretics in rabbinic literature of late antiquity; -- *b) Goshen Gottstein* Alon, The body as image of God in rabbinic literature: HThR 87 (1994) 155-169 / 171-195.

7201 *Kee* Howard C., Defining the first-century CE synagogue; problems and progress: NTS 41 (1995) 481-500.

7202 **Kraemer** David C., Responses to suffering in classical rabbinic literature. Ox 1995, Univ. xv-261 p.; bibliog. 249-254. $ 50. 0-10-508900-6. -- [R]BoL (1995) 153 (S.C. *Reif*).

7203 **Kushelevsky** Rella, Moses and the angel of death: *StThemesLit 4. NY 1995, Lang. xxii-325 p. $ 58. 0-8204-2147-2 [< OTA 19, p.366s, L.H. *Feldman*].

7204 **Levinson** Pnina N., Einführung in die rabbinische Theologie[3rev]. Da 1993, Wiss. xii-169 p. DM 39. 3-534-08558-2. -- [R]BoL (1995) 154 (L.L. *Grabbe*: traditional, Orthodox, frustrating).

7205 *Levison* John R., The angelic spirit in early Judaism: → 512, SBL Seminars 34 (1995) 464-493.

7206 *Lieu* Judith M., The race of the God-fearers: JThS 46 (1995) 483-501.

7207 *Maccoby* H., BEN ZOMA's trance: *JProgJ 1 (Shf 1993) 103-8 [NTAb 40, p.111].

7208 **Maier** Johann, Gesù Cristo e il cristianesimo nella tradizione giudaica antica: SB 106. Brescia 1994, Paideia. 354 p. L^m 48. 88-394-0512-7.
Manns Frédéric, Il giudaismo, ambiente e memoria del NT 1995 → 2254 supra.

7209 *a) Manns* Frédéric, Littérature rabbinique et exégèse; -- *b) Lourenço* João Duarte, Sofrimento e glorificação em Is 52,13-53,12; sua interpretação na exegese judaica e cristã Did(ask)L 22,2 (1992) 3-18 / 22,1 (1992) 17-38 [23,1 (1994) 3-47.

7210 **Mattioli** Anselmo, Quel no del giudaismo a Gesù; i motivi e le cause di un gran fatto storico. R c. 1995, Città Nuova. 263 p.

7211 **Mayer** Günter, Das Judentum [124-158, Die Bibel und ihre Geschichte; 17-72 mit *Trepp* Leo, Geschichte des nachbiblischen Judentums in Grundzugen: *al.*]. Stu 1994, Kohlhammer.

7212 **Mélèze-Modrzejewski** Joseph, The Jews of Egypt, from Ramesses II to Emperor Hadrian, ^T*Cornman* Robert.. E 1995, Clark. xxii-279 p.; bibliog. 247-255. 0-567-09739-0.

7213 **Mello** Alberto, Detti di rabbini, 'Pirqê avot' con i loro commenti tradizionali. Magnano vc 1993, Qiqajon. 231 p. L^m 26. -- ^RCivCatt 146 (1995,1) 99s (D. *Scaiola*).

7214 *Millard* Matthias, Die rabbinischen noachidischen Gebote und das biblische Gebot Gottes an Noah; ein Beitrag zur Methodendiskussion: WuD(ienst) 23 (1995) 71-90.

7215 **Neusner** Jacob, Die Gestaltwerdung des Judentums; die jüdische Religion als Antwort auf die kritischen Herausforderungen der ersten sechs Jahrhunderte der christlichen Ära: JudUm 51. Fra 1994, Lang. 277 p. DM 72. -- ^RSNTU 20 (1995) 246-8 (H. *Giesen*).

7216 **Neusner** Jacob, Introduction to rabbinic literature ['my favorite and definitive closure of 500 books ... ']: AnchorRef, 1994 → 10,9803; $ 40: ^RBiRe 11,3 (1995) 12s (S. *Stern*).
^E**Neusner** Jacob, Judaism in Late Antiquity, 1. The literary and archaeological sources; 2. Historical syntheses: HO 1/17, 1995 → 376.

7217 **Neusner** Jacob, Purity in rabbinic Judaism; a systematic account: SFSHJ 95. At 1994, Scholars. xiv-217 p. 1-55540-929-6.

7218 **Neusner** Jacob, Rabbinic Judaism, structure and system. Mp 1995, Fortress. xi-241 p. $ 24 pa. 0-8006-2909-4 [NTAb 40, p.560].

7219 **Neusner** Jacob, Rabbinic Judaism; the documentary history of its formative age 70-600 CE. Bethesda 1994, CDL. xiv-408 p. 1-883053-06-4.

7220 **Neusner** Jacob, Rabbinic literature and the NT. 1994. $ 17 pa. 1-56338-074-9. -- ^RNeotest 29 (1995) 421-3 (H.R. *Lemmer*).

7221 **Neusner** Jacob, Symbol and theology in early Judaism 1991 → 7,9961* ... 10,9805: ^RGreg 76 (1995) 373-5 (G.L. *Prato*).

7222 *Neusner* Jacob, *a)* Evaluating the attributions of sayings to named sages in the rabbinic literature: JSJ(ud) 26 (1995) 93-111; -- *b)* Was rabbinic Judaism really 'ethnic' [about what Christianity reshaped in universal terms] ?: CBQ 57 (1995) 281-305.

7223 *Norman* R.V., Why Odysseus wept [lack of intergenerational continuity in interpretion, starting from Rabbis' radical reinterpretation of Torah]: Soundings 77 (1994) 239-252 [< ZAW 107 (1995) 513].

7224 **Ognibeni** B., Index biblique à la 'Ochlah w^eochlah' de S. FRENSDORFF [1864 = Ktav 1972]: Henoch quad. 5, 1992 → 8,a474: ^RRB 102 (1995) 465 (É. *Nodet*).

7225 **Ognibeni** Bruno, La seconda parte del Sefer 'oklah w^e 'oklah; edizione del ms. Halle Universitätsbibliothek Y b 4 10 ff. 68-24: TECC(isn) 57. M/FrS 1995, CSIC Inst. Fg. / Univ.

LIII p. (bibliog.)-556 p. 84-00-04525-0.

7226 **Otzen** Benedikt, Judaism in antiquity [1986], [T]1990 → 6,a155; b,73*b* ... 10,9810*:
[R]RestQ 37 (1995) 182s (R.D. *Chesnutt*); VT 45 (1995) 142 (W. *Horbury*: some comments
outstanding, others queried).

7227 **Paul** André, Il giudaismo antico e la Bibbia [1987], [T]*Cestari* Giuseppe, *Cantoni* Anna
M., 1991 → 10,9811; 88-10-40791-1.

7228 **Porton** Gary G., The stranger within your gates; converts and conversion in rabbinic
literature 1994 → 10,9812: [R]JJS 46 (1995) 300s (Caroline *Wickens*).

7229 **Sacchi** Paolo, Storia del secondo tempio 1994 → 10,9813; [R]StCatt 39 (1995) 747 (C.
Morganti).

7230 *Sagi* Avi, [Eruvin 13b: where HILLEL and SHAMMAI differ]: 'Both are the words of
the living God'; a typological analysis of halakhic pluralism: AHUC (= HUCA) 65 (1994)
105-136.

7231 **Sanders** E.P., Judaism .. 63 B.C.E. - 66 C.E. 1992 → 8,a480 .... 10,9814: [R]*A(sn)JSR
20 (1994) 252-4 (S. *Isser*); Interpretation 49 (1995) 86 . 88 (L.E. *Frizzell*).

7232 *Satlow* Michael [→ 9,10704], Reconsidering the rabbinic *ketubah* payment [first-
century C.E. innovation]: → 495, Jewish family 1994, 133-141.

7233 **Schiffman** Lawrence H., From text to tradition; a history of second temple and
rabbinic Judaism 1991 → 7,9970 ... 10,9813: [R]CCAR 42,2 (1995) 88-91 (Tzvi *Zahavy*);
JEvTS 38 (1995) 470s (J. M. *Sprinkle*).

7234 **Schwartz** Daniel R... Studies in the Jewish background of Christianity: WUNT 60, 1992
→ 8,4405; 10,4092: [R]FrRu NF 1 (1993s) 21-24 (C. *Thoma*).

7235 **Schwartzfuchs** Simon, A concise history of the rabbinate 1993 → 9,10707: [R]*A(sn)JS
20 (1995) 422-4 (C.A. *Waxman*: good except for the sketchy modern period).

7236 **Setzer** Claudia J., Jewish responses to early Christians; history and polemics, 30-150
C.E. Mp 1994, Fortress. viii-154 p. $ 17. 0-8006-2680-X [RStR 22,72, C.T. *McCollough*;
ThD 42 (1995) 290].

7237 [E]**Shanks** Hershel, Christianity and Judaism; a parallel history of their origins and early
development 1992 → 8,367*a* ... 10,4094; also L 1993, SPCK: [R]JRel 75 (1995) 112s (A.
Saldarini: overall views of the contents by VERMES unduly critical, by CHARLESWORTH
hasty); S(cot)JTh 48 (1995) 278s (Isabel *Wollason*: everything is just fine, even the
SANDERS-LEE disaccord).

7238 *Siegert* Folker, La naissance de l'identité juive dans le monde antique, [T]*Aubert* Jacques:
FV 92,5 (1993) 3-39.

7239 *Stachowiak* Lech, [P] The problem of proselytism in Judaism BCE: RT 41,1 (Lublin
1994) 55-64 [NTAb 40, p.108].

7240 **Stemberger** Günter, Die Juden: ein historisches Lesebuch: Becksche Reihe 410, 1990
→ 6,a166; 7,9973: [R]Salesianum 57 (1995) 143 (G. *Gentileschi*).

7241 *Sznol* Shifra, Addenda a Sifre-Números: EM 63 (1995) 117-128; Eng. 117.

7242 *Verman* M., *Adler* S.H., Path jumping in the Jewish magical tradition [*qepîṣat ha-
derek*, a kind of bilocation attributed to many sages]: *JStQ 1,2 (Tü 1993s) 131-148 [NTAb
39, p.296].

7243 **Wander** Bernd, Trennungsprozesse zwischen frühem Christentum und Judentum im
1 Jh. n. Chr: TANZ 16. Tü 1994, Francke. x-315 p. DM 94. 3-7220-1876-X [RStR 22,69,

F.W. *Burnett*].

7244 **Will** E., *Orrieux* C., 'Prosélytisme' ... erreur 1992 → 8,2486 ... 10,9823: [R]JQR 86 (1995s) 429-434 (Shaye *Cohen);* *TopO 3 (1993) 299-304 (F. *Millar*).

7245 *Wischmeyer* Oda, Das heilige Buch im Judentum des Zweiten Tempels: ZNW 86 (1995) 218-242.

7246 **Zohar** Zvi, *Sagui* Avraham, [H] Conversion to Judaism and the meaning of Jewish identity. J 1995, Hartman/Bialik. 259 p. -- [R]Tarbiz 64 (1994s) 461-6 (M. *Lorberbaum,* [H]; Eng. 3,ix).

к6 **Mišna**, tosepta; Tannaim.

7247 **Álvarez Pereyre** Frank, La transmission orale de la Mishnah; une méthode d'analyse appliquée à la tradition d'Alep: Ethnomusicology 5, Yuval 8 → 9,16711 [giving publisher as Peeters, Paris]. J 1990, Magnes [Eng. Yuval 6 (1994) 225-233]. -- [R]JQR 85 (1994s) 474s (D.M. *Weil*).

7248 **Bornhäuser** Hans, *Mayer* Günter, Die Tosefta, Seder II. Moēd, 1. Sukka -- Jom tob -- Rosch ha-Schana: RT 1. Stu 1993, Kohlhammer. viii-196 p. DM 280. 3-17-012694-6. -- [R]BoL (1995) 142 (P.S. *Alexander*).

7249 **Bronner** Leila Leah, From Eve to Esther; rabbinic reconstructions of biblical women. LVL 1994, W-Knox. xxiii-199 p. $ 19. 0-664-25542-6. -- [R]RelStR 21 (1995) 223s (W. L. *Humphreys*).

7250 *a) Caquot* André, Le témoignage de la Mishna sur la ville dans l'ancien Judaïsme; -- *b) Margain* Jean, Les termes relatifs à la ville dans le Targoum samaritain (ms J): → 730, Semitica 43s (1992/5) 79-86 (177-9) / 169-175.

7251 **Correns** D., Gittin, Scheidebriefe: Mischna 3/5, 1991 → 7,9975: [R]ZAW 107 (1995) 154s (I.*Kottsieper*).

7252 **Elman** Yaakov, Authority and tradition; Toseftan *baraitot* in talmudic Babylonia 1994 → 10,9843: [R]BoL (1995) 147s (S.C. *Reif*).

7253 **Fishbane** Simcha, The method and meaning of the Mishnah Berurah 1991 → 10,9844: [R]*A(sn)JSR 20 (1994) 106-8 (M. *Washofsky*); JJS 45 (1994) 145 (L. *Jacobs*).

7254 **Houtman** Alberdina, *Ezer kenegedo* ... A synoptic inquiry into the relationship between Mishna and Tosefta: diss. [D]*Horst* P.W. van der. Utrecht Rijksuniv. 1995. 255+95 p. > Mohr. -- TvTh 36,82; RTLv 27.p.532.

7255 *Jaffee* M.S., Writing and rabbinic oral tradition; on Mishnaic narrative lists and mnemonics; *JJwTht 4,1 (NY 1994) 123-146 [NTAb 40, p.309].

7256 **Kaufman** Asher S., [H] The Temple of Jerusalem, Tractate Middot, an ancient version. J 1991, Har Yera'eh. 96 p. -- [R]JQR 85 (1994s) 453 (J. *Patrich*).

7257 *Milikowski* Chaim, On editing rabbinic texts [KIRSCHNER R., Baraita 1992]: JQR 86 (1995s) 409-417.

7258 *Naeh* Shlomo, [H] 'Creates the fruit of lips'; a phenomenological study of prayer according to Mishnah Berakhot 4:3, 5:5: Tarbiz 63 (1993s) 185-218; Eng. xiii.

7259 **Neusner** Jacob, Uniting the dual Torah; Sifra and the problem of the Mishnah 1990 → 6,a182: [R]S(cot)JTh 48 (1995) 412-4 (N. *Solomon*).

7260 **Neusner** Jacob, The Tosefta ... :SFSHJ 47, 1992 → 9,10721: [R]Salesianum 57 (1995)

159s (R. *Vicent*).

7261 **Neusner** Jacob, The transformation of Judaism; from philosophy [Mishnah] to religion [Talmud]. Urbana 1992, Univ. Illinois. $ 35. 0-252-01805-2. -- [R]Religion 25 (1995) 395-7 (A.J. *Saldarini*).

7262 **Neusner** Jacob, Classical Judaism; Torah [vol.1], learning [2], virtue [3]; an anthology of the Mishnah, Talmud and Midrash: Jud/Realms 36-38. Fra 1993, Lang. 260 p.; 254 p.; 256 p. 3-631-45061-3; -2-1.

7263 **Neusner** Jacob, The documentary foundation of rabbinic culture; mopping up after debates with Gerald L. BRUNS et al.:SFSHJ 113. At 1995, Scholars. xxvi-213 p. xxvi-213 p. 0-7885-0092-9.

7264 **Neusner** Jacob, Il Giudaismo nella testimonianza della Mishnah, [T]*Volpe* G., [E]*Perani* Mauro: StRel. Bo 1995, Dehoniane. 744 p., bibliog. 705-731. 88-10-40792-8.

7265 **Neusner** Jacob, The Judaism the Rabbis take for granted: *SFlaJud 102. Atlanta 1994, Scholars. xviii-257 p. $ 75. 1-55540-954-7 [NTAb 39, p.357].

7266 **Neusner** Jacob, The Judaism behind the texts; the generative premises of rabbinic literature [1A, 1993 → 10,9830] 1B-C / 2.-5: *SFlaJ [89.] 90.97 / 98-101. Atlanta 1993s, Scholars. xviii-243 p. + xix-213 p. / xx-246; xxix-270; xxvii-223; xiii-325 p. All 6 $ 75 each. 1-55540-916-4; -34-2;- 34-5; -47-4; -48-2; -48-0 [NTAb 40,p.181].

7267 *Perani* M., *Stemberger* G., Nuova luce sulla tradizione manoscritta della Tosefta; i frammenti rinvenuti a Bologna: *Henoch 16 (1994) 227-252 [NTAb 40,p.310].

7268 *Poorthuis* Marcel J.H.M., Tradition and religious authority: on a neglected Christian parallel [MG 10,701s; LAGARDE P. de] to the Mishna Abot 1-10: AHUC (= HUCA) 66 (1995) 169-201.

7269 *Rottzoll* Dirk U., [Mischna Schabbat VI,4] Wird es in den Tagen des Messias Waffen geben ?: Jud(aica) 50 (1994) 103-112.

7270 **Schlüter** Margarete, Auf welche Weise wurde die Mishna geschrieben ? Das Antwortschreiben des Rav SHERIRA Gaon [9.Jh.] 1993 → 10,9837: [R]*A(sn)JSR 20 (1995) 180-6 (Y. *Elman*); FrRu 2 (1995) 153-6 (H.A. *Rapp*); JAOS 115 (1995) 552 (J.M. *Baumgarten*); Salesianum 57 (1995) 377s (R. *Vicent*).

7271 *Schremer* Adiel, [H] Kinship terminology and endogamous marriage in the Mishnaic and Talmudic periods: Zion 60 (1995) 5-35, Eng. IV.

K6.5 Talmud; midraš

7272 **Apophthaker** Howard, An analysis of Sifra, Dibbura Desinai: diss. HUC, [D]*Sarason* R. Cincinnati 1995. -- RStR 22,274.

7273 **Astor** Carl N., The *petihta'ot* of Eicha Rabba [Lam]: diss. Jewish Theol. Sem., [D]*Visotzky* B. NY 1995. 227 p. 95-43160. - DissA 56 (1995s) p. 3616; RStR 22,274.

7274 **Avemarie** F., Yoma -- Versöhnungstag: ÜTY 2/4. Tü 1995, Mohr. xxi-249 p. DM 168. 3-15-146379-X [NTAb 40, p.168].

7275 **Banon** David, Le Midrach: QSJ 3019. P 1995, PUF. 128 p. 2-13-047211-7.

7276 **Becker** Hans-Jürgen, Der Jerusalemer Talmud; sieben ausgewählte Kapitel: UnivBt 1733. Stu 1995, Reclam. 352 p. DM 14 7277 **Bergler** Siegfried, Talmud für Anfänger, [→ 9,10727] Talmud für Fortgeschrittene[2], Hannover 1992s, Luther. 145 p.; 171 p.[je] DM

16,80. -- [R]Entschluss 50,11 (1995) 36 (R. *Oberforcher*).

7278 **Boyarin** Daniel, Intertextuality & .. midrash 1990 → 7,9988 ... 10,9841: [R]CCAR 42,2 (1995) 81-83 (D.R. *Blumenthal*)

7279 *Boyarin* D., The eye in the Torah; ocular desire in Midrashic hermeneutic: Yearbook for Religious Anthropology (B 1994) 30-48 [< Judaica 51,125].

7280 **Boyarin** Daniel, Carnal Israel; reading sex in Talmudic culture 1993 → 9,10730: [R]RStR 21 (1995) 285-290 (Miriam *Peskowitz*).

7281 [E]**Chernick** Michael, Essential papers on the Talmud. NYU 1994. ix-484 p. [JQR 86,267, titles sans pp.].

7282 **Cohen** Abraham, Everyman's Talmud; the major teachings of the rabbinic sages. NY 1995, Schocken. lv-405 p. $ 18 pa. 0-8052-1032-6 [thd 42,360].

7283 **Cohen** Menachem, Mikra'ot gedolot Jos-Jg 1992 → 9,2687: [R]FrRu NF 1 (1993s) 55-57 (D. *Flusser*); HebStud 36 (1995) 230-5 (B. *Walfish*).

7284 *Diamond* E., Hunger artists and householders; the tension between asceticism and family responsibility among Jewish pietists in late antiquity [bTa'anit 23s shows three *hasidim* shoving off the burden on their wives and children]: US(em)QR 48,3 (1994) 29-47 [NTAb 40, p.492].

7285 *Fitzmyer* Joseph A., Another query about the Lucan infancy narrative and its parallels [piyyut in Amidah Meg 3.5]: JBL [113 (1994) 491-3. *Silberman* L.] 114 (1995) 295s.

7286 *Friedman* Shamma, An ancient scroll fragment (b.Ḥullin 101a-105a) and the rediscovery of the Babylonian branch of Tannaitic Hebrew: JQR 86 (1995s) 9-50; 1 pl.

7287 [E]**Goldwurm** Hersh, Talmud Bavli, the Schottenstein edition, 1. Bava Metzia: Artscroll. Brooklyn 1992, Mesorah.. -- [R]BSOAS 58 (1995) 114s (L. *Glinert* takes off from ONG W. 1985; the English is highly appropriate, but the Steinsaltz edition is far better for taking account of modern archeology and philology).

7288 **Harris** Jay M., How do we know this ? Midrash and the fragmentation of modern Judaism; Judaic Hermeneutics. Albany 1995, SUNY. xii-377 p. $ 25. 0-7914-2144-9. -- [R]JSJ(ud) 26 (1995) 362s (W.J. van *Bekkum*; a real eye-opener).

7289 [E]**Hasida** Yishaq, [H] Encyclopedia of biblical peronalities as seen by the sages of the Talmud and Midrash. J 1995, Ludwig Mayer. 408 p.

7290 **Hayes** Christine E., Between the Babylonian and Palestinian Talmuds; accounting for halakhic difference in selected sugyot from Tractate Avodah Zarah [diss.] 1993 → 9,10733: [R]JSJ(ud) 26 (1995) 194-9 (J. *Neusner*: 'without a theory of the whole, there is no comparing of parts').

7291 **Hezser** Catherine, Form, function, and historical significance of the rabbinic story in Yerushalmi Neziqin: TSAJ 37' 1993 → 10,9850: [R]*CritRR 8 (1995) 429-431 (J. *Neusner*); JSJ(ud) 26 (1995) 364 (W.J. van *Bekkum*: solid application of BOKSER-NEUSNER-SCHÄFER approach); ThLZ 120 (1995) 426-8 (W. *Herrmann*).

7292 **Jacobs** Irving, The midrashic process; tradition and interpretation in rabbinic Judaism. C 1995, Univ. xiii-218 p. £ 35. 0-521-46174-X. -- [R]E(xp)T 107 (1995s) 31 (F. *Morgan*); JSJ(ud) 26 (1995) 366s (W.J. van *Bekkum*).

7293 **Jacobs** Louis, Structure and form in the Babylonian Talmud 1991 → 9,10736; 10,9851: *A(sn)JS 20 (1995) 186-8 (R. *Goldenberg*).

7294 **Kalmin** Richard, Sages, stories, authors, and editors in rabbinic Babylonia: BJSt 300.

Atlanta 1994, Scholars. xvi-340 p. $ 60. 0-7885-0045-7 [NTAb 39, p.354]. -- [R]HebStud 36 (1995) 218-221 (D. *Boyarin:* first effective challenge to NEUSNER's skepticism); JSJ(ud) 26 (1995) 367s (W.J. van *Bekkum*).

7295 *Kalmin* Richard, Rabbinic attitudes toward rabbis as a key to the dating of Talmudic sources: JQR 84 (1993s) 1-27.

7296 **Kalmin** Richard, The redaction of the Babylonian Talmud: Amoraic or Saboraic ? : HUC mg 12, 1989 → 6,a205; 8,a513: [R]JQR 84 (1993s) 283-8 (N. *Aminoah*).

7297 *Kosmann* Admiel, [H] Note; more on associative thinking in the Midrash: Tarbiz [62 (1992s) 339-359, NIEHOFF M.] 63 (1993s) 443-450; Eng.xxii.

7298 **Kraemer** David, The mind of the Talmud 1990 → 7,9996; 8,a514: [R]JQR 84 (1993s) 261-282 (Y. *Elman*).

7299 **Krupp** Michael, Der Talmud; eine Einleitung in die Grundschrift des Judentums mit ausgewählten Texten: Tb 772. Gü 1995, Gü-V. 224 p. DM 34. 3-579-00772-6. -- [R]Entschluss 50,11 (1995) 36s (T.M. *Meier*).

7300 *La Maisonneuve* Dominique de, Le Midrash, une re-lecture de l'Écriture: VSp 149 (1995) 545-561.

7301 **Lightstone** Jack N., The rhetoric of the Babylonian Talmud 1994 → 10,9859: [R]BoL (1995) 155 (N. *de Lange*).

7302 **Minissale** Antonino. La versione greca del Siracide; confronto con il testo ebraico alla luce dell'attività midrascica e del metodo targumico: AnBib 133. R 1995, Pontificio Istituto Biblico. 332 p. L[m] 65. 88-7653-133-5 [< OTA 19: A.A. *Di Lella*, 'Minisalle'].

7303 *Moskovitz* Leib, [H] On the Aggadic 'foreign bodies' in the Yerushalmi: Tarbiz 64 (1994s) 237-258; Eng.2,vii.

7304 *Nádor* Georg, Sophismus und seine Beurteilung im Talmud; Sef 55 (1995) 327-33.

7305 **Neusner** Jacob, Why there never was a 'Talmud of Caesarea'; [Tarbiz supp. 4, 1931] Saul LIEBERMAN's mistakes: SFSHJ 108. Atlanta 1994, Scholars. xii-178 p. $ 70. 0-7885-0047-3 [NTAb 39, p.358].

7306 *Neusner* Jacob, Das Problem des babylonischen Talmud als Literatur; der Bavli und seine Quellen: Kairos 34s (Salzburg 1992s) 64-74 [NTAb 39, p.110].

7307 **Neusner** Jacob, The canonical history of ideas .. Mekhilta Ishmael, Sifra. Sifré Nm/Dt: SFSHJ 4, 1990 → 6,a218; 9,10749: *A(sn)JSR 20 (1995) 191-3 (L.M. *Barth*).

7308 **Neusner** Jacob, Scripture and Midrash in Judaism: JudUm 47s. Fra 1994s, Lang. 387 p.; 318 p.; 413 p.; bibliog. 3,385-415. 3-631-46461-4; -2-2; -3-0.

7309 *Neusner* Jacob, The Torah in the Talmud: SFSHJ 61. At 1993, Scholars. xvi-194 p. $ 60. -- [R]*CritRR 7 (1994) 419-422 (A.J. *Avery-Peck*) [409-411, E. *Goldman*, & 412-9, S. *Levey*, on his Bavli 1992].

7310 **Neusner** Jacob, The Talmudic anthology in three volumes: JudUm 52-54. Fra 1995, Lang. 299 p.; 325 p.; 296 p. 3-631-47131-9; -2-7; -3-5.

7311 **Neusner** Jacob, Talmudic thinking; language, logic, law 1992 → 9,10757: *A(sn)JS 20 (1995) 188-191 (D. *Kraemer*, disappointed).

7312 **Neusner** Jacob, The Bavli, an inroduction / The Bavli's massive miscellanies: SFSHJ 42s, 1992 → 9,10746s: [R]*CritRR 7 (1994) 409-411 (E. A. *Goldman*).

7313 *Ostmeyer* Karl-Heinrich, Die Sexualethik des antiken Judentums im Licht des babylonischen Talmuds: BThZ 12 (1995) 167-185.

7314 [TE]**Rottzoll** Dirk U., Rabbinischer Kommentar zum Buch Genesis; Darstellung der Rezeption des Buches Genesis in Mischna und Talmud unter Angabe targumischer und midrasischer Paralleltexte: StJud 14. B 1994, de Gruyter. x-539 p. DM 198. -- [R]ZAW 107 (1995) 167 (M. *Köckert*),

7315 *Samely* Alexander, Justifying midrash; or an 'intertextual' interpretation of rabbinic interpretation: JSSt 39 (1994) 19-32.

7316 [E]**Schäfer** Peter, *Becker* Hans-Jürgen, Synopse zu Talmud Yerushalmi Band IV, Ordnung Neziqin; Ordnung Toharot, Nidda: TSAJ 477. Tü 1995, Mohr. xiii-321 p. 3-16-146380-3 [[R]Bijd 55 (1994) 305s, J. van *Ruiten* over 1/1s 1991].

7317 **Segal** Eliezer, The Babylonian Esther midrash: BJSt 291-3, 1994 → 10,2829: [R]JSJ(ud) 26 (1995) 219-225 (J. *Neusner*).

7318 **Sperber** Daniel, A commentary on *Derech Ereṣ Zuta 5-8*. Ramat-Gan 1990, Bar-Ilan Univ. -- [R]JQR 85 (1994s) 445-8 (S. *Morell*).

7319 **Stemberger** Günter, Introduzione al Talmud e al Midrash, [TE]*Cattani* Daniela: Tradizione d'Israele 10. R 1995, Città Nuova. 519 p. 88-311-4916-4.

7320 **Stern** David, Parables in Midrash; narrative and exegesis in rabbinic literature. CM 1991, Harvard Univ. xvi-347 p. -- *A(sn)JS 20 (1995) 123-138 (D. *Boyarin*).

7321 *a) Stern* Sacha, The concept of authorship in the Babylonian Talmud [no midway position: veers dramatically from an extreme (our, Western) individualism to an (anonymous) collectivism -- and back]; -- *b) Samely* Alexander, Stressing Scripture's words; semantic contrast as a midrashic technique in the Mishnah; -= *c) Alexander* Philip S., Bavli Berakhot 551-57b; the talmudic dreambook in context: → 211, [F]VERMES G., JJS 46 (1995) 183-195 / 196-229 / 230-248.

7322 **Teugels** Godelieve M., Midrasj in de Bijbel of midrasj op de Bijbel? Een exemplarische studie van 'De verloving van Rebekka' (Gn 24) in de Bijbel en de rabbijnse midrasj [Midrash in the Bible or midrash on the Bible? An exemplary study of the 'Wooing of Rebekah']; diss. Leuven 1994. 275 p. [No AA N°] - D(iss)AI-C 56 (1995s) p. 576.

7323 *Teugels* Lieve, Midrasj in, en, op de Bijbel? Kritische kanttekeningen bij ontkritische gebruik van een term: NedThT 49 (1995) 273-290.

7324 [T]**Tilly**, Qiddushin-Antrauung: Tj 3/7. Tü 1995, Mohr. xx-286 p. DM 178. 3-16-146437-0 [NTAb 40,p. 565].

7325 **Tilly** Heinz-Peter, Zur Redaktion des Traktates Moed Qatan des Talmud Yerushalmi; Versuch einer formanalytische Diskusbeschreibung: FJS 9. Fra 1995, Förderung Jud. St. [viii-]482 p.; Bibliog. 468-474. 3-922056-06-7.

7326 *Valler* Shulamit, The number fourteen as a literary device in the Babylonian Talmud: JSJ(ud) 26 (1995) 169-184.

7327 *Vázquez* R., El midrash en la historia de la exégesis hebrea: Kairós 16 (Guat 1995) 39-60 [NTAb 40, p.494].

7328 *Veltri* Giuseppe, Rassegna di studi sul giudaismo antico (I) il Talmud Yerushalmi: RCatT 30 (1995) 177-186.

7329 *Wajsberg* Eljakim, [H] Form and meaning in Talmudic sugyot: Leš 59 (1995s) 119-149;

7330 **Weinstein** Sara E.. Rabbinic criticism of self-imposed religious stringency: diss. [D]*Schiffman* L. NYU 1994. 362 p. 95-28544. -- DAI 56 (1995) p.1842.

7331 *Werman* Cana, The rules of consuming and covering the blood in priestly and rabbinic law: RQum 16,64 (1995) 621-636.

7332 **Wewers** Gerd A., *Huttenmeister* Frowald G., Demai (Zweifelhaftes) [about tithes, Num 18,20-29]: ÜTY 1/3. Tü 1995, Mohr. xviii-209 p. DM 158. 3-16-146436-2 [NTAb 40, p.388].

7333 **Wiesel** Elie, Die Weisheit des Talmuds; Geschichten und Portraits, [T]*Bücker* Hanns: Spektrum 4384. FrB 1992-5, Herder. 360 p. DM 20. 3-451-21019-3 (-04354-X). -- [R]ZkT 117 (1995) 107 (R. *Oberforcher*, auch über sein Chassidische Feier 1988).

K7.1 **Judaismus mediaevalis**, *generalia*

7334 *a)* **Abulafia** Anna S., Christians and Jews in the twelfth-century renaissance. L 1995, Routledge. x-196 p. £ 37.50. 0-415-00012-2. -- *b)* **Hood** John Y.B., AQUINAS and the Jews. Ph 1995, Univ. Pennsylvania. xiv-145 p. 0-8122-3305-0; pa. -1523-0. -- [R]TBR 8,2 (1995s) 39 (J. *Lowerson*, both).

7335 **Adang** Camilla P.W.M., Muslim writers on Judaism and the Hebrew Bible from IBN RABBAN to İBN HAZM. Nijmegen 1993. 337 p. -- [R]Zion 60 (1995) 353-6 (S. *Stober*, [H]).

7336 **Alexy** Trudi, The mezuzah in the Madonna's foot; oral histories exploring five hundred years in the paradoxical relationship of Spain and the Jews. NY 1993, Simon & S. 316 p. $ 20. -- [R]C(ath)HR 81 (1995) 134 (J.M. *Sánchez*); RfR 53 (1994) 311s (J. *Gros*).

7337 *Baker* Colin F., Judaeo-Arabic material in the Cambridge Genizah collections: BSOAS 58 (1995) 445-454.

7338 [E]**Barkaï** Ron, Chrétiens, musulmans et juifs dans l'Espagne médiévale 1994 → 10,261: [R]Speculum 70 (1995) 976 (titres, pp.)

7339 *Bedos-Rezak* Brigitte, Les juifs et l'écrit dans la mentalité eschatologique du Moyen-Âge chrétien occidental (France 1000-1200): Annales(ESC) 49 ('Histoire juive, histoire de juifs' 1994) 1049-1063 [1019-1240].

7340 *a)* *Bezler* Francis, Pénitence chrétienne et or musulman dans l'Espagne médiévale; -- *b)* *Nirenberg* David, Les juifs, la violence et le sacré: Annales(ESC) 50,1 (1995) 93-108 / 109-131.

7341 **Bonfil** Robert, Jewish life in Renaissance Italy, [T]*Oldcorn* Anthony. Berkeley 1994, Univ. California. xiii-320 p.; ill. -- [R]MeH 22 (1995) 202-4 (W.C. *Jordan*).

7342 *Brann* Ross, Power in the portrayal representations of Muslims and Jews in Judah al Ḥariẓi's *Tahkemoni*: P(rinceton)PNE 1 (1992) .. [< BSOAS 58 (1995) 436].

7343 *Brinner* William M., The image of the Jew as other in medieval Arabic texts: → 392, I(sr)OS 14 (1994) 227-240.

7344 *Burns* R.J., The Guidaticum safe-conduct in medieval Arago-Catalonia; a mini-institution for Muslims, Christians and Jews: Medieval Encounters 1,1 (1995) 51-113 [< Judaica 51,261].

7345 **Cohen** Mark R., Under Crescent and Cross; the Jews in the Middle Ages 1994 → 10,9886: [R]BSOAS 58 (1995) 545s (A. *Gross*); TS 56 (1995) 398 (W.V. *Hudon*).

7346 **Dahan** Gilbert, Les intellectuels chrétiens et les juifs au Moyen Âge 1990 → 6,k430: [R]Salesianum 57 (1995) 140s (P.T. *Stella*).

7347 *Dahan* Gilbert, La prière juive au regard des chrétiens au Moyen Âge: RÉJ 154 (1995) 437-448.

7348 [E]**Díaz Esteban** Fernando, Los judaizantes en Europa y la literatura castellana del Siglo de Oro [< congreso internacional Madrid 14-19.XII.1992]. M 1994, Letrúmero. 396 p. -

- [R]Sefarad 55 (1995) 395-8 (Esperanza *Alfonso*).

7349 **Díaz-Mas** Paloma, Sephardim, the Jews from Spain, [T]*Zucker* George K. Ch 1992, Univ. xiv-235 p. -- [R]RÉJ 154 (1995) 147s (R. *Ayoun:* ch. 5 adapté aux relations diplomatiques Espagne-Israël).

7350 [E]**Ebenbauer** Alfred, Die Juden in ihrer mittelalterlichen Umwelt 1991 → 7,350c: [R]Speculum 69 (1994) 1304s (titles, pp.)

7351 [T]**Edwards** John, The Jews in Western Europe, 1400-1600 [49 documents]. Manchester UK 1995, Univ. xvi-159 p. $ 60; pa. $ 20 (St. Martin's NY). 0-7190-3508-2; -9-0 [ThD 42,372].

7352 *Faingold* Reuven, Los Judíos en las cortes reales portuguesas: Sefarad 55 (1995) 77-104; Eng. 104.

7353 **Fintz Menascé** Esther, L'Ebreo errante; metamorfosi di un mito ['favola' nata c, 1300 nel monastero S. Albano di Inghilterra]. Mi 1993, Cisalpino / Univ. Ist, Anglistica. 410 p. L[m] 62. 88-205-0745-5. -- [R]Anton 70 (1995) 305s (M. *Nobile*).

7354 **Gerber** Jane S., The Jews of Spain; a history of the Sephardic experience 1992 → 9,10786: [R]*AsnJS 20 (1995) 219-222 (Renée L. *Melammed*).

7355 **Ginzberg** Louis, Le leggende degli Ebrei, I. Dalla creazione al diluvio [1925, 1953]. Mi 1995, Adelphi. 454 p. 88-459-1168-5.

7356 **Graboïs** Arieh, Les sources hébraïques médiévales, 2. Les commentateurs exégétiques: TSMAO 66, 1993 → 10,9892: [R]Speculum 70 (1995) 149s (J. *Cohen*).

7357 **Guttmann** Julius, Histoire des philosophies juives, de l'époque biblique à Franz Rosenzweig [1993], [T]*Courtine-Denamy* Sylvie. P 1994, Gallimard. 580 p. F 220. -- [R]Études 382 (1995) 278 (J. *Petitdemange*); RÉJ 154 (1995) 125-9 (G. *Freudenthal*) & 129-133 (M.-R. *Hayoun*).

7358 **Hallevi** Juda, Le Kuzari, apologie de le religion méprisée [arabe + hébreu][T.E]*Touati* Charles: Les Dix Paroles. Lagrasse 1994, Verdier. 254 p. -- [R]RTPh 127 (1995) 296 (P.-Y. *Ruff*).

7359 **Iancu** Danièle et Carole, Les Juifs du midi; une histoire millénaire. Avignon 1995. 347 p. -- [R]RH 294 (1995) 156-8 (P. *Guiral*).

7360 *Kirschenbaum* A., Continuity and change in Jewish law during the 5th to 8th centuries: La giustizia nell'alto medioevo, 7-13 aprile 1994 (Spoleto 1995, Centro medioevo) I, 337-369 [< RHE 90 (1995) 300*s].

7361 *Kriegel* Maurice, La definitiva soppressione del pluralismo religioso nella Spagna dei re cattolici [? in rapporto con l'espulsione degi ebrei da Inghilterra e da Francia due secoli prima]; limiti e efficacia dell'approccio 'intenzionalista', [T]*Marinucci* Andrea: RasIsr 58,1s (1992) 1-12.

7362 **Lazarus-Yafeh** Hava, Intertwined worlds; medieval Islam and Bible criticism. Princeton 1992, Univ. xiv-178 p. -- [R]JSSt 40 (1995) 179-181 (Jane D. *McAuliffe*); [J]LitTOx 9 (1995) 107s (N. *Robinson*); VT 44 (1994) 129 (J.A. *Emerton*).

7363 *Liss* Hanna, Copyright im Mittelalter ? Die esoterischen Schriften von R. EL'AZAR von Worms zwischen Traditions- und Autorenliteratur: FJB 21 (1994) 81-108 [< Jud(aica) 51 (1995) 58].

7364 **Méchoulan** Henri, Les Juifs de España, historia de una diaspora (1482-)[1992],[T]. M 1993, Trotta. 668 p. -- [R]BoL (1995) 157 (J.F. *Elwolde*); Hispania Sacra 47 (1995) 379s (*López Aparicio*).

7365 *Melzi* Robert C., Ebrei e Marrani in Italia in una commedia rinascimentale; Sefarad 55

(1995) 313-324; español & Eng. 325

7366 *Meyuhas Ginio* Alisa, [H] An appeal in favour of the Judeoconversos; [1450 Dominican Cardinal] Juan de TORQUEMADA and his Tractatus contra Madianitas et Ismaelitas: Zion 60 (1995) 301-333, Eng. XX [does not make clear the relevance of the title; it was really *contra* rebel Toledo 'Old Christians' claiming that the conversos were still anti-Christian Jews and should be prohibited from holding authority, like unbaptized Jews].

7367 **Minervini** Laura, Testi giudeospagnoli medievali (Castiglio e Aragona) [inediti 2 dei 26]. N 1992, Liguori. -- [R]RasIsr 60,3 (1993) 126-9 (Lea *Sestieri*).

7368 [E]**Mopsik** Charles, Lettre sur la sainteté; la relation de l'homme avec sa femme (*Iggeret ha-Qodeš*): Les Dix Paroles. Lagrasse 1993, Verdier. 96 p. -- [R]RTPh 127 (1995) 403 (P.-Y. *Ruff*).

7369 [E]**Mutius** Hans-Georg von, Jüdische Urkundenformulare aus Marseille in babylonisch-arabischer Sprache: JudUm 50. Fra 1994, Lang. xiv-99 p. Fs 29. 3-631-46900-4. -- [R]BoL (1995) 160 (W.G.E. *Watson*).

7370 **Netanyahu** B., The origins of the Inquisition in fifteenth-century Spain. NY c. 1955, Random. 1384 p. $ 50. -- [R]Commentary 100,4 (1995) 55-57 (D. *Berger*).

7371 [TE]**Noy** David, Jewish inscriptions of western Europe [1. 1993: Spain, Gaul]; 2. The city of Rome. C 1995, Univ. xi-573 p; xx pl.; 6 maps. $ 130. 0-521-44202-8 [ThD 44.71].

7372 **Pérez** Joseph, Historia de una tragedia; la expulsión de los judíos de España. Barc 1993, Crítica. 174 p. -- [R]ScrT(Pamp) 37 (1995) 679s (J.C. *Martín de la Hoz*).

7373 **Reilly** Bernard F., *Lynch* John, The context of Christian and Muslim Spain. 1031-1156. Ox 1992, Blackwell. 300 p. $ 50. 0-631-16913-X. -- [R]HeythJ 36 (1995) 84s (A. *Hamilton*).

7374 *Romano* David, *a)* Coesistenza/convivenza tra ebrei e cristiani ispanici; -- *b)* ¿ Ascendencia judía de Fernando el Católico ? [unproved]; Sefarad 55 (1995) 359-380; español & Eng. 381 / 163-170; Eng. 171.

7375 **Romero Castelló** Elena, *Macías Kapón* Uriel, Los judíos de Europa; un legado de 2000 años. M 1994, Anaya. 240 p. -- [R]Sefarad 55 (1995) 219-221 (J. *Vándor*).

7376 *Romero* Elena, Una versión española del relato hebreo Ma'asé Yerušalmí [siglo xiii; texto Istanbul 1823]; Sefarad 55 (1995) 173-193; Eng. 194; 'The story of the Jerusalemite' -- it nowhere even mentions Jerusalem.

7377 **Sachar** Howard M., Farewell España; the world of the Sephardim remembered. NY 1994, Knopf. xii-439 p.; map. $ 30. 0-679-40960-2 [< ThD 42 (1995) 289].

7378 [E]**Santiago-Otero** H., Diálogo filosófico-religioso entre cristianismo, judaismo e islamismo durante la Edad Media en la península ibérica: *SIEPM 3. Turnhout 1994. xi-507 p. -- [R]RasIsr 61 (1995) 167s (P. *Morpurgo*).

7379 *Seror* Simon, Les noms des femmes juives en Angleterre au Moyen Âge: RÉJ 154 (1995) 295-325.

7380 *Shmeruk* Ḥone', [H] *Mayufes* [humiliating dance with Sabbath song *ma yapît*] -- a key concept in Polish-Jewish relations: Tarbiz 63 (1993s) 119-133; Eng. vii.

7381 *Simha* Goldin, The synagogue in medieval Jewish community as an integral institution: *JRit 9,1 (1995) 15-40.

7382 *Soloff* Rav A., Proof texts [... Spain; no need for such bitter disputes to continue]: JBQ 23 (1995) 17-23.

7383 **Taitz** E., The Jews of medieval France; the community of Champagne. Westport CT 1994, Greenwood. viii-341 p., 3 maps [< RHE 90 (1995) 385*].

7384 **Varo** Francisco, Los cantos del Siervo en la exégesis hispano-hebrea 1993 → 9,3619:

^RBurg 36 (1995) 241-3 (T. *Otero Lazaro*).

7385 **Yerushalmi** Yosef H.,   Ein Feld in Anatot; Versuche über jüdische Geschichte [Wanderungen ... Spanien]. B 1993, Wagenbach. 96 p. -- ^EFrRu NF 1 (1993s) 303s (Eva *Auf der Maur*).

'386 **Zonta** Mauro, La filosofia antica nel Medioevo ebraico; le traduzioni ebraiche medievali dei testi filosofici antichi: Philosophica 2. Brescia c.1995, Paideia. 301 p. 88-394-0533-X.

387 *Zuckerman* Constantine, On the date of the Khazars' conversion to Judaism and the chronology of the kings of the Rus Oleg and Igor; a study of the anonymous Khazar letter from the Genizah of Cairo: RÉByz 53 (1995) 237-270.

K7.2 **Maimonides**

88 **Benor** Ehud, Worship of the heart; a study of Maimonides' philosophy of religion. Albany 1995, SUNY. ix-282 p.

89 *Benor* Ehud Z., Meaning and reference in Maimonides' negative theology: HThR 88 (1995) 339-360 [87 (1994) 461-472, *Kasher* Hannah].

90 *Bos* Gerrit, Maimonides on the preservation of health: JRAS (1994) 213-235.

91 ^E**Debenedetti Stow** S., Jehudàh BEN MOŠÈH ben Dani'èl Romano, La chiarificazione in volgare delle 'espressioni difficili' ricorrenti del Mišnèh Toràh di Mosè Maimonide; glossario inedito del XIV secolo: Giudaismo italiano 1s, 1990 → 9,9914*: ^RRivB 43 (1995) 555-7 (A. *Passoni dell'Acqua*).

92 **Dobbs-Weinstein** Idit, Maimonides and St. THOMAS on the limits of reason. Albany 1995, SUNY. x-278 p. $ 64.50; pa. $ 22. 0-7914-2415-4; -6-2 [ThD 43,164].

393 **Fox** Marvin, Interpreting Maimonides; studies in methodology, metaphysics, and moral philosophy: *ChStHJ, 1990 → 6,a259 ... 10,9915: *A(sn)JS 20 (1995) 207-210 (R. *Jospe*).

394 **Green** Kenneth H., Jew and philosopher; the return to Maimonides in the Jewish thought of Leo STRAUSS. Albany 1993, SUNY. 278 p. $ 19. -- ^R*A(sn)JS 20 (1995) 470-2 (A. *Arkush*); JRel 75 (1995) 299s (J.L. *Kraemer*).

'395 *Halbertal* Moshe, ^H Mena<u>h</u>em HA-ME'IRI -- [sole continuer of Maimonides as both] talmudist and philosopher: Tarbiz 63 (1993s) 63-118; Eng. vi.

7396 *Harvey* W. Zeev, Les sacrifices, la prière, et l'étude chez Maímonide: RÉJ 154 (1995) 97-108.

7397 *Kasher* Hanna,   ^H Maimonides' explanation of the equivocality of the term 'son': Tarbiz 63 (1993s) 235-248; Eng.xiv.

7398 *Kreisel* Howard. Imitatio Dei in Maimonides' Guide of the Perplexed: *A(sn)JSR 19 (1994) 169-211.

7399 *Lahey* Stephen E.,   Maimonides and analogy [Judaica 50,183, attributing to AmerCathPhQ without date].

7400 *Nehorai* Michael Z.,   ^H How a righteous Gentile can merit the world to come [Maimonides]: Tarbiz 64 (1994s) 307s in answer to *Kasher* Hannah 301-6 on his 61 (1992) 465-487.

7401 *a) Schwartz* Dov, The debate over the Maimonidean theory of Providence in thirteenth-century philosophy: -- *b) Gordon* Peter E., The erotics of negative theology; Maimonides on apprehension: Jewish Studies Quarterly 2 (Tü 1995): 185-196 / 1-38.

7402 **Seeskin** Kenneth, Maimonides, a guide for today's perplexed 1991 → 10,9928: ^RJAAR 63 (1995) 153-5 (A.L. *Ivry*).

7403 *Shifman* Yair, ᴴ On AVICENNA and [= influencing, as FALAQUERA saw] Maimonides: Tarbiz 64 (1994s) 523-534; Eng.4,v.

7404 **Wohlman** Avital, Maimonide et Thomas d'AQUIN; un dialogue [comme le sien de 1988!] impossible: Dokimion 16. FrS 1995, Univ. vi-202 p. -- ᴿRThom 95 (1995) 518-520 (S.-T. *Bonino*).

K7.3 **Alii magistri Judaismi mediaevalis**

7405 SAADYA: *Brody* Robert, ᴴ The conclusion of Se'adya Gaon's prayerbook: Tarbiz 63 (1993s) 393-401; Eng. xxi.

7406 *Dana* Joseph, The *piyyut* on the Ten Commandments ascribed to Saadiah Gaon: JQR 86 (1995s) 323-375.

7407 *Dotan* Aron, Particularism and universalism in the linguistic theory of Saadia Gaon: Sefarad 55 (1995) 61-75; español 76.

7408 *Drory* Rino, Bilingualism and cultural images; the Hebrew and the Arabic introductions of Saadia Gaon's *Sefer ha-Egron*: I(sr)OS 15 (1995) 11-23.

7409 *a) Kaplan* Roger J., More on Sa'adia Gaon's perspective on the grammatical root [< NYU diss. 1992]; -- *b) Tobi* Yosef, The reaction of rav Sa'adia Gaon to Arabic poetry and poetics: HebStud 36 (1995) 25-33 / 35-53.

7410 RASHI; **Kamin** Sarah, Jews and Christians interpret the Bible. J 1991, Magnes. viii-168 p. (also on other exegetes). -- ᴿSefarad 55 (1995) 214-6 (M. *Orfali*).

7411 *Sed-Rajna* Gabrielle, Some further data on Rashi's diagrams to his commentary on the Bible: Jewish Studies Quarterly 1 (Tü 1993s) 149-157. 12 pl.

7412 NACHMANIDES: **Novak** David, The theology of Nahmanides systematically presented, ᴱ*Goodman* Lenn E.: BJSt 271, 1992 → 9,10825; 10,9935*; ᴿ*A(sn)JS 20 (1995) 417-9 (D.H. *Frank*); RÉJ 154 (1995) 187s (R. *Ayoun*).

7413 *Gottlieb* Isaac B., ᴴ 'There is no before/after' (chronology in the Bible; cited ten times) in Ramban's commentary on the Torah: Tarbiz 63 (1993s) 41-62; Eng.vi.

7414 *Idel* Moshe, ᴴ Nahmanides; Kabbala, Halakha and spiritual leadership: Tarbiz 64 (1994s) 535-580; Eng.4,vi.

7415 *Saperstein* Marc, Jewish typological exegesis after Nahmanides: Jewish Studies Quarterly 1 (Tü 1993s) 158-170.

7416 IBN BAL'AM (c.1070): **Goshen-Gottstein** Moshe *zal.*, (*Perez* Ma'aravi), ᴴ R. Judah ibn Bal'am's commentary on Isaiah; the Arabic original according to MS Firkovitch (Ebr-arab I 1377): Meqorot 5. Ramat-Gan 1992, Bar-Ilan Univ. vii-267 p. -- ᴿJQR 86 (1995) 468-476 (A. *Maman*).

7417 IBN EZRA: ᴱ**Díaz Esteban** F., Abraham ibn Ezra y su tiempo 1989/90 → 7,427*: ᴿBiOr 52 (1995) 213-6 (A. *Schippers*).

7418 *Gärtig* William C., The attribution of the Ben Ezra supercommentary *Avvat Nefesh* to Asher ben Abraham CRESCAS reconsidered: AHUC (= HUCA) 66 (1995) 239-257.

7419 *Gómez Aranda* Mariano, Teorías astronómicas y astrológicas en el Comentario de Abraham Ibn Ezra al libro del Eclesiastés: Sefarad 55 (1995) 257-272; Eng. 272.

7420 ᴱ**Twersky** Isadore, *Harris* Jay M., Rabbi Abraham Ibn Ezra; studies in the writings of a twelfth-century Jewish polymath [< Harvard conference]: HJTS 10. CM 1993. v-170

p. + [H] 48. $ 30; pa. $ 15. 0-674-74554-X; -5-8. -- [R]BoL (1995) 171 (S.C. *Reif*),

7421 IBN JANAH 1050: *Becker* Dan, Linguistic rules and definitions in ibn Janāh's *Kitāb al-Luma' (Sefer ha-Riqmah)* copied from the Arab grammarians> JQR 86 (1995s) 278-298.

7422 ḤAYYŪJ: *a) Dotan* Aron, [H] Linguistics and comparative linguistics in the Middle Ages; an analysis of one verbal pattern in Judah Ḥayyūj's grammar; -- *b) Basal* Nasir, [H] *Kitāb al-nutaf* and the supplementation of Judah Ḥayyūj's grammar : → 161, [F]RUBINSTEIN E., Te'uda 9 (1995) 117-130 / 131-142.

7423 *Ben Menachem* David, [H] *Sefer ha-Eshel* [Ashkenazi biblical-Hebrew grammar] by R. Yizḥak BEN YEHUDA: Leš 59 (1995) 299-312; Eng. 4,II.

7424 **Pulcini** Theodore, Exegesis as polemical discourse; IBN HAZM on Jewish and Christian scriptures: Diss. Univ. Pittsburgh 1994. 426 p. 95-21454. -- DissA 56 (1995s) p. 232.

7425 QIMḤI: *Niclós* José Vicente, Un tratado de polémica judeocristiana de raíces sefardíes, Yosef Qimḥi y su Libro de la Alianza, introducción, traducción y notas: Hispania Sacra 47 (1995) 251-298.

к7.4 *Qabbalâ, Zohar, Merkabâ* -- Jewish mysticism

7426 **Benamozegh** Elia [1823-1900], [TE]*Luria* Maxwell [< 1961 French abridgment], Israel and humanity; *Idel* Moshe. appendix on relevance of Kabbalah. NY 1995, Paulist. xxiii-436 p. $ 30; pa. $ 23. 0-8091-o468-7; -3541-8 [ThD 43,57].

7427 [E]**Busi** Giulio, *Loewenthal* Elena, Mistica ebraica; testi della tradizione segreta del giudaismo dal III al XVIII secolo. T 1995, Einaudi. lxxiv-723 p. 88-06-13712-3.

7428 *Dan* Joseph, [H] The mystical 'descenders to the chariot' in historical context: Zion 60 (1995) 179-199, Eng. XI.

7429 *Elior* Rachel, [H] From earthly temple to heavenly shrines; prayer and sacred liturgy in the *Hekhalot* literature and its relation to Temple traditions: Tarbiz 64 (1994s) 341-280; Eng,3,v..

7430 [E]**Fine** Lawrence, Essential papers on Kabbalah. NYU 1995. ix, 551 p. 0-8147-2623-2.

7431 **Fishbane** Michael, The kiss of God; spiritual and mystical death in Judaism: Stroum Lectures. Seattle 1994, Univ. Washington. xii-156 p. $ 25. -- [R]JRel 75 (1995) 597-9 (T. *Gruenwald*).

7432 **Fossum** J.E., The image of the invisible God; essays on the influence of Jewish mysticism on early Christology [Col 1,15-18; Jude 5-7; Jn 1,51; Acts of John]: NTOA 30. FrS/Gö 1995, Univ./VR. ix-181 p. Fs 58. 3-7278-1002-5 / 3-525-53933-0 [< NTAb 40, p.543].

7433 *Galas* Michał, Die Mystik der polnischen Juden in Gershom SCHOLEMs Arbeiten -- ein forschungsgeschichtlicher Überblick: Jud(aica) 51 (1995) 97-101.

7435 *Ginsburg* Elliot K., Tha many faces of Kabbalah [IDEL M. 1988]: HebStud 36 (1995) 111-122.

7436 *Goshen Gottstein* Alon, Four entered Paradise revisited: HThR 88 (1995) 69-133.

7437 HA-LEVI Y.: **Lobel** Diana N., Between mysticism and philosophy; Arabic terms for mystical experience in r. Yehudah ha-Levi's Kuzari: diss. Harvard, [P]*Twersky* I. CM 1995. 504 p. 95-39086. -- D(iss)AI 56 (1995s) p. 2734.

7438 **Herrmann** Klaus, *Massekhet hekhalot*, Traktat von den himmlischen Palästen: TStAJud 19, 1994 → 10,9948: [R]BoL (1995) 150s (A.P. *Hayman*); Salesianum 57 (1995) 559s (R. *Vicent*).

7439 **Idel** Moshe, Golem; Jewish magical and mystical traditions on the artificial anthropoid. Albany 1990, SUNY. xxi-323 p. -- [R]JQR 85 (1994s) 459-461 (M. A. *Sells*).

7440 **Idel** Moshe, Le Golem [antropoide fabricado y luego destruido por el Maharal de Praga (1512-1608)], [T]*Aslanoff* Cyrille: Patrimoines Judaïsme. [°]P 1992, Cerf. 426 p. 2-204=04583-7. -- [R]Salesianum 57 (1995) 150s (R. *Vicent*).

7441 -- [TE]**Gourévitch** Édouard, Yehudah LOEW, dit le Maharal de Prague, Les hauts faits de l'Éternel [1582] 1994.-- [R]ETRel 70 (1995) 122 (Jeanne Marie *Léonard*).

7442 *a) Klein* Alessandro, Cabbala ebraica, 'pia filosofia' e modernità. -- *b) Stefani* Piero, Esegesi ebraica e pensiero moderno: FilTeo 8 (1994) 207-216 / 217-229.

7443 **Kuyt** A., The 'Descent' to the chariot; towards a description of the terminology, place, function, and nature of the *yeridah* in Hekhalot literature [< diss. Amsterdam 1991, [D]*Uchelen* N. van]: TSAJ 45. Tü 1995, Mohr. xi-412 p. DM 248. 3-16-146284-X [NTAb 40, p.177].

7444 **Leeses** Rebecca, Ritual practices to gain power; adjurations in the Hekalot literature, Jewish amulets, and Greek revelatory adjurations: diss. Harvard, [D]*Brooten* B. CM 1995. 457 p. 95-39085. -- DAI 56 (1995s) p. 2732; RStR 22,274.

7445 *Lerner* D.G., *Hekhalot Rabbati*; the mystical text and its liturgical elements: CJud 47,1 (1994) 74-83 [NTAb 39, p. 476].

7446 **Liebes** Yehuda, Studies in the Zohar, [T]*Schwartz* A., *al.* 1993 → 9,10838: [R]BoL (1994) 144 (J.F. *Elwolde*); R(uch)BL 47 (1994) 292s (M. *Galas*, [P]. also on his Jewish myth 1993 → 10,9949).

7447 [E]**Maier** Johann, Die Kabbalah; Einführung, klassische Texte, Erläuterungen. Mü 1995, Beck. 416 p. DM 78. 3-406-39659-3 [ThRv 92,87].

7448 **Mathieu** Jean-Marie, Le nom de la gloire; essai sur la Qabale 1992 → 9,10839: [R]RevSR 68 (1994) 121 (R. *Goetschel*).

7449 *Reuchlin* Johann [1455-1522], L'arte cabbalistica, [T]*Busi* Giulio, *Campanini* Saverio: Eurasiatica 38. F 1995, Opus Libri. lxx-292 p.; bibliog. 239-270. 88-8116-029-3/

7450 *Rotenberg* Mordechai, Cabalic sexuality and creativity: *IntJPsyR 5 (1995) 225-244 . 255-8; comment 245-9, *Witztum* Eliezer; 251s, *Bakan* D.

7451 **Schäfer** Peter, The hidden and manifest God 1992 → 8,a602 ... 10,9956: [R]*A(sn)JR 19 (1994) 255-7 (D.J. *Halperin*).

7452 **Schäfer** Peter, Le Dieu caché et révélé, [T]*Aslanoff* C. 1993 → 9,10845; 10,9957: [R]Salesianum 57 (1995) 376s (R. *Vicent*).

7453 [E]**Schäfer** Peter, Übersetzung der Hekhalot-Literatur 1987s/95 → 7,a65 ... 9,10842: [R]ThLZ 120 (1995) 134-6 (S. *Schreiner*).

7454 [E]**Schäfer** Peter, *Dan* Joseph, G. SCHOLEM's Major trends in Jewish mysticism 50 years after, 1992/3 → 9,483*: [R]Salesianum 57 (1995) 553s (R. *Vicent*).

7455 **Scholem** Gershom, Alchimia e kabbalah, [T]*Sartorio* Marina: Saggi 800. T 1995, Einaudi. 96 p. 88-06-13681-X.

7456 **Swartz** Michael, Mystical prayer in ancient Judaism; an analysis of Ma'aseh Merkavah: TSAJ 28, 1992 → 8,a605 ... 10,9960: [R]HebStud 35 (1994) 227-230 (Naomi *Janowitz*); JQR 86 (1995s) 616-8 (E.R. *Wolfson*).

7457 **Ta-Shma** Israel M., [H] The halachic residue in the Zohar. TA 1995, Meuhad. 126 p. -- [R]Tarbiz 64 (1994s) 581-605 (Y. *Liebes*, [H], Eng, 4,vii).

7458 **Tolan** John, PETRUS ALFONSI [Christian from 1106; b. Moses the Jew of Huesca] and his medieval readers. Gainesville 1993, Univ.Press of Florida. xv-288 p. $ 35. [RStR 22,354, S.D. *Benin*].

7459 *a) Vigée* Claude, [(Argentin) Jorge Luis] BORGES devant la Kabbale juive; de l'écriture de Dieu au silence de l'aleph; -- *b) Safran* Alexandre (Grand Rabbin), *al.*, À la découverte de la Kabbale: BCPÉ 47,1 (1995) 4-23 / 46,1 (1994) 4-11 (-24).

7460 **Wolfson** Elliot R., Through a speculum that shines; vision and imagination in medieval Jewish mysticism. Princeton 1995, Univ. x-452 p. $ 49.40. 0-691-07343-0 [ThD 42,394].

7461 *Wolfson* Elliot R., The mystical significance of Torah study in German pietism: JQR 84 (1993s) 43-77.

7462 *Wolfson* Elliot R., The doctrine of *sefirot* in the prophetic Kabbalah of Abraham ABULAFIA: Jewish Studies Quarterly 2 (Tü 1995) 337-371

K7.5 Judaismus saec. 14-18

7463 *Ortega Monasterio* María Teresa, *Fernández Tejero* Emilia, El Sefer 'oklâ we'oklâ [c. 900 C.E.] y la masora magna del códice de profetas de El Cairo; Sefarad 55 (1995) 147-160; Eng. 161.

7464 **Howard** George, *a) [Even Bohan* c.1300] Hebrew Gospel of Matthew[2rev] [[1]1987]. Macon 1995, Mercer Univ.; -- *b) ..* , a report: *JHiCrit 2,2 (1995) 53-67.

7465 *Rigo* Caterina, Yehuda ben Mosheh ROMANO [c.1320] traduttore degli scolastici latini: Henoch 17 (1995) 141-169; Eng. 170.

7466 GERSONIDES Levi, 1288-1344; [E]**Freudenthal** Gad, Studies on Gersonides, a fourteenth-century Jewish philosopher-scientist [meeting at Peyresq June 1988 for his 700th birthday]: Acad. Internat. Hist Sciences 36, 1992 → 9,10856: [R]Sefarad 55 (1995) 212-4 (M. *Gómez Aranda*).

7467 [E]**Dahan** Gilbert, Gersonide en son temps 1991 → 8,a618: [R]Speculum 69 (1994) 598 (titres, pp.).

7468 *Kellner* Menachem, Gersonides on imitatio Dei and the dissemination of scientific knowledge: JQR 85 (1994s) 275-296.

7469 *Touati* Charles, Le problème du *Kol Nidrey* et le responsum inédit de Gersonide (Lévi ben Gershom): RÉJ 154 (1995) 327-342.

7470 *Glasner* Ruth, Levi BEN GERSHOM and the study of Ibn Rushd [1125-1198] in the fourteenth century: JQR 86 (1995s) 51-82; tables 83-90.

7471 COMTINO 1402-1482: **Attias** Jean-Christophe, Le commentaire biblique; Mordekhai Komtino ou l'herméneutique du dialogue 1991 → 8,a610; 9,10863: *A(sn)JS 20 (1995) 210-3 (K.P. *Bland*: scholarly, persuasive).

7472 ABRAVANEL 1437-1508: *Genot-Bismuth* Jacqueline, La replica ideologica degli Ebrei della penisola iberica all'antisemitismo dei re cattolici; la tesi di Isaac Abravanel sulle origini del cristianesimo e del cattolicesimo romano, [T]*Voicu* Sever J.: RasIsr 58,1s (1992) 23-46.

7473 *Lawee* Eric, On the threshold of the Renaissance; new methods and sensibilities in the biblical commentaries of Isaac Abarbanel: Viator 26 (1995) 281-319.

7474 **Gaon** Solomon, The influence of the Catholic theologian Alfonso TOSTADO on the Pentateuch commentary of Isaac Abravanel: Library of Sephardic history and thought 2, 1993: → 10,9968: [R]FrRu NF 2 (1995) 49s (C. *Thoma*); Speculum 70 (1995) 909s (O. *Leaman*).

7475 **Attias** Jean-Christophe, Isaac Abravanel; La mémoire et l'espérance, textes choisis[TE]: Toledot, 1992 → 8,a586; 10,9968: [R]Salesianum 57 (1995) 146 (R. *Vicent*).

7476 LEÓN 1470-1515: **Tirosh-Rothschild** Hava, Between worlds ... David ben Messer León 1991 → 9,10870; 10,9977: [R]JAAR 63 (1995) 387-391 (L.A. *Segal*); JQR 85 (1994s) 62s (H. *Sukenic*).

7477 QARA; **Brin** Gershon, [H] Studies in the biblical exegesis of r. Joseph Qara 1990 → 6,a298; 8,a609: [R]JQR 85 (1994s) 469-473 (B. *Walfish*).

7478 *Mak* Hananel, [H] New fragments from the biblical commentary of r. Joseph Kara: Tarbiz 63 (1993s) 533-553; Eng.xxvii.

7479 **Stow** Kenneth R., The Jews in Rome, I. 1536-1551: A documentary history of the Jews in Italy 11; SPB 48. Lei 1995/7, Brill. I. lxxx-411 p., bibliog. lxxi-lxxviii; II. p.413-951. 90-04-10463-1; -806-8.

7480 *Stow* Kenneth R., Prossimità o distanza; etnicità, sefarditi e assenza di conflitti etnici nella Roma del sedicesimo secolo, [T]*Ranzato* Irene: RasIsr 58,1s (1992) 61-74.

7481 IBN LEV 16th c.: **Morell** Samuel, Precedent and judicial discretion; the case of Joseph ibn Lev: SFSHJ 26. Atlanta 1991, Scholars. xii-213 p. -: *A(sn)JS 20 (1995) 213-6 (E. *Kanarfogel*).

LOEW Y., 1582, 'Maharal of Prague' → 7440s supra; 9,10865.

7482 DA COSTA 1583-1640: **Salomon** H.P., *Sassoon* S.D., Uriel da Costa, Examination of pharisaic traditions [irreconcilable with Pentateuch] 1993 [NTAb 38, p.486].

7483 [E]**Luzzati** M., L'Inquisizione e gli ebrei in Italia: BCM 1066. R 1994, Laterza. -- [R]ASEs 12 (1995) 424-8 (F. *Motta*).

7484 *Barnai* Jakob, La diaspora sefardita nell'impero ottomano (dal quindicesimo al diciottesimo secolo), [T]*Portaleone* Andrea: RasIsr 58,1s (1992) 203-241.

7485 KATZ Joshua (ha-Kohen Soper) d.1673: **Hoeschke** Reuben, [H] Yalkut Reuveni ha-shalem, [E]*Lindau* Besalel, *al*. J 1994, Vagshai. I.Gn-Ex, 203 p.;II.Lv-Jg, 40 p.;III.suppl.31p.

7486 **Benbassa** Esther, *Rodrigue* Aron, Juifs des Balkans -- espaces judéo-ibériques, XIVe-XXe siècles. P 1993, Découverte. 415 p. F 220. -- [R]RasIsr 60,3 (1993) 129-131 (G. *Saban*).

7487 *Baskin* Judith R., From separation to displacement; the problem of women [c. 1300] in Sefer Hasidim: *A(sn)JS 19 (1994) 1-18.

7488 *Breuer* Edward, Rabbinic law and spirituality in [1780, Moses] MENDELSSOHN's *Jerusalem:* JQR 86 (1995s) 299-321.

7489 *Etkes* Emanuel, [H] The role of magic and *ba'alei-šem* in Ashkenazic society in the late seventeenth and early eighteenth centuries: Zion 60 (1995) 69-104, Eng. VI.

7490 **Katz** David S., The Jews in the history of England 1485-1850. Ox 1994, Clarendon. xv-447 p. £ 40. 0-19-822912-7 [RHE 91,281s, F.-J. *Ruggiu*]. -- [R]JEH 46 (1995) 722-4 (G. *Lloyd Jones*).

7491 **Levy** Avigdor, The Sephardim of the Ottoman Empire. xv-196 p. [< his preface to conference, The Jews of the Ottoman Empire]. both Princeton 1992, Darwin. -- [R*]A(sn)JS 20 (1995) 222-5 (S. *Ward*); JQR 86 (1995s) 426-8 (M.R. *Cohen*).

7492 [E]**Levy** Avigdor, The Jews of the Ottoman Empire. Princeton/Wsh 1994. Darwin / Inst. Turkish Studies. xvi-783 p.; ill. $ 50. 0-87850-090-1 [RStR 22,354, M. *Haddad*].

7493 MAIMON 1753-1800: **Pfaff** Konrad, Salomon Maimon; Hiob der Aufklärung; Mosaiksteine zu seinem Bildnis: PhTSt 41. Hildesheim 1995, Olms. viii-320 p. 3-487-10068-1.

7494 **Rozen** Minna, Jewish identity and society in the 17th c.; reflections on the life and work of Rafael Mordekai MALKI, [T]*Wachsmann* Goldie. Tü 1992, Mohr. x=190 p. -- [R]*AJSR 19 (1994) 265-8 (D.B. *Ruderman*).

7495 **Ruderman** D.B., Jewish thought and scientific discovery in early modern Europe. NHv 1995. xi-392 p.; ill. -- [R]JQR 86 (1995) 208-210 (M. *Goldish*); RasIsr 61,1 (1995) 169s (P. *Morpurgo*).

K7.7 Hasidismus et Judaismus saeculi XIX

7496 **Ayoun** Richard, Typologie d'une carrière rabbinique; l'exemple de Mahir CHARLEVILLE [1814-88]. Nancy 1993, Presses Univ. 1003 p. (2 vol.) -- [R]RevSR 68 (1994) 511-3 (P. *Chaunu*).

7497 *a)* **Benbassa** Esther, Une diaspora sépharade en transition (Istanbul, XIXe-XXe siècle). P 1993, Cerf. 300 p. 2-204-04668-X. -- *b)* **Nahon** Gérard, Métropoles et périphéries séfarades d'Occident [.. Tunis; Jérusalem: 12 déjà imprimés, ici en français]: Passages. P 1993, Cerf. 494 p. 2-204-04597-7. -- [R]Salesianum 57 (1995) 270s . 373 (R. *Vicent* tous deux).

7498 **Berg** Roger, Histoire du rabbinat français (XVIe-XXe s.) 1992 → 8,a638: [R]RÉJ 154 (1995) 151-4 (Eliane *Roos Schuhl*).

7499 *Berkovitz* Jay R., The French Revolution and the Jews; assessing the cultural impact: *A(sn)JS 20 (1995) 25-86.

7500 [E]**Birnbaum** Pierre, *Katznelson* Ira, Paths of emancipation; Jews, states, and citizenship. Princeton 1995, Univ. 308 p. $ 17. 0-691-03461-3. -- [R]*TBR 8,3 (1995) 58s (A. *Race*)

7501 *Deshen* Shlomo, Baghdad Jewry in late Ottoman times; the emergence of social classes and of secularization: *A(sn)JS 19 (1994) 19-44.

7502 **Etkes** Immanuel, Rabbi Israel SALANTER and the [late 19th c.] Mussar movement; seeking the Torah of truth [[H] 1981]. Ph 1993, Jewish Publication. x-389 p. $ 40. -- [R]JRel 75 (1995) 447s (Tamar *Ross*).

7503 **Feldman** David, Englishmen and Jews; social relations and political culture, 1840-1914. NHv 1994, Yale Univ. xii-401 p. $ 45. -- [R]A(mer)HR 100 (1995) 524 (R.W. *Davis*).

7504 **Green** Arthur, Tormented master; a life and spiritual quest of Rabbi Nahman of Bratslav [1772-1810]. Woodstock VT 1992, Jewish Lights (= Univ. Alabama 1979). x-395 p.; bibliog. 381-8. 1-87905-11-7.

7505 **Hagy** James W., This happy land .. Charleston: 1993 → 10,9979: [R]*A(sn)JS 20 (1995) 440s (S.M. *Blumin*).

7506 **Harris** Jay M., Nachman KROCHMAL; guiding the perplexed of the modern age. NYU 1991. xxi-366p. -- [R]JQR 85 (1994s) 419-421 (E. *Breuer*).

7507 [E]**Hayoun** M.-R,. Heinrich GRÄTZ, La construction de l'histoire juive + Gnosticisme et judaïsme: Passages. P 1992, Cerf. 176 p.-- [R]RTPh 127 (1995) 297s (Esther *Starobinski-Safran*).

7508 **Idel** Moshe, Hasidim, between ecstasy and magic. Albany 1995, SUNY. x-438 p.; bibliog. 393-402

7509 **Katz** Jacob, Juifs et francs-maçons en Europe, 1723-1939. P 1995, Cerf. F 250, -- [R]RH 294 (1995) 154s (Esther *Benbassa*).

7510 **Klorman** Bat-Zion E., The Jews of Yemen in the nineteenth century; a portrait of a messianic community: *JewishSt 6. L 1993, Brill. viii-209 p. -- [R]*A(sn)JS 20 (1995)

477-481 (R. *Ahroni*).

7511 **Kushner** Tony, The Jewish heritage in British history, Englishness and Jewishness. L 1992, Cass. 234 p. -- ᴿJQR 86 (1995s) 483-7 (Meri-Jane *Rochelson*).

7512 ᴱ**Lifschitz** Daniel, I Chassidim commentano la Scrittura; 300 omelie e racconti inediti: Ascolta Israele. R 1995, Dehoniane. 198 p. 88-396-0622-X.

7513 **Marcus** Jacob R., United States Jewry, 1776-1985. Detroit 1993, Wayne State Univ. 3. (from 1860) 925 p.; 4. 952 p. -- ᴿ*A(sn)JSR 20 (1995) 441-7 (G. *Sorin*).

7514 **Menasce** Jean de, Quand Israël aime Dieu. introduction au hassidisme [1931] 1992 → 8,a665: ᴿSalesianum 57 (1995) 148s (R. *Vicent*).

7515 *Polonovski* Max, Un aventurier mythomane sous l'Empire, Samson CERFBERR [né juif 1777, musulman 1801, suicide 1826]: RÉJ 154 (1995) 43-76.

7516 **Rodrigue** Aron, Images of Sephardi and Eastern Jewries in transition; the teachers of the Alliance Israélite Universelle 1860-1939 [1989]ᵀᴱ. Seattle 1993, Univ. Washington. 319 p.; ill., map. $ 40. -- ᴿRelStR 21 (1995) 58 (M.M. *Laskier*).

7517 **Shapiro** Marc B., Between East and West; the life and works of Rabbi Jehiel Jacob WEINBERG: diss. Harvard, ᴰ*Twersky* Isadore. CM 1995. 373 p. 95-39431. -- DissA 56 (1995s) p. 2737.

7518 **Shaw** Stanford J., The Jews of the Ottoman Empire and the Turkish Republic. NYU 1991. 380 p. $ 60. -- ᴿWZKM 85 (1995) 358-360 (Gyula *Káldy-Nagy*).

7519 **Steinsaltz** Adin, In the beginning; discourse on Chasidic thought, ᵀᴱ*Hanegbi* Yehuda. Northvale NJ 1995, Aronson. xvi-300 p. 1-56821-741-2.

7520 **Sussman** Lance J., Isaac LEESER and the making of American Judaism. Detroit 1995, Wayne State Univ. 311 p. [RStR 22,262, Dianne *Ashton*].

κ7.8 **Judaismus contemporaneus**

7521 **Alderman** Geoffrey, Modern British Jewry. Ox 1992, Clarendon. ix-397 p. £ 40. -- ᴿHZ 261 (1995) 135 (P. *Alter*).

7522 **Ariel** David S., What do Jews believe; the spiritual foundations of Judaism. NY 1995, Schocken. xi-290 p. $ 25. 0-8052-4119-1 [ThD 42,354].

7523 **Artson** Bradley, It's a mitzvah ! step-by-step to Jewish living. West Orange NJ 1995, Behrman. ix-244 p. $ 18. 0-87441-585-3 [< ThD 42 (1995) 255].

7524 **Ashton** Diane, Recent scholarship on American Jewry [7 books + DINNERSTEIN L. & JAHER F., both 1994 on antisemitism]: RStR 21 (1995) 78-85.

7525 *Baker* Zachary M., Die Amerikanisierung der jüdischen Wissenschaft; Gedanken zur 70. Jahresfeier des YIVO [Akronym irgendwie (p.209) aus dem Yiddish 'Jidisher Wisnshaftlecher (sic) Institut']-Institutes für Jüdische Forschung, ᵀ*Rubeli-Guthauser* Nico: Jud(aica) 51 (1995) 222-236

7526 **Ben Chlomo** Josef, Introduction à la pensée de Rav Kook, ᵀ*Chalier* Catherine, 1992 → 8,a664; 10,10009: ᴿSalesianum 57 (1995) 153s (R. *Vicent*).

7527 **Bernstein** Michael A., Foregone conclusions; against apocalyptic [Shoah] history. Berkeley 1994, Univ. California. xiii-181 p. -- ᴿ*ProofT 15 (1995) 282-291 (J.E. *Young*).

7528 **Biale** David, Eros and the Jews; from biblical Israel to contemporary America. NY 1992, Basic. 288 p. $ 24. -- ᴿCCurr 44 (1944s) 114-7 (S. D. *Breslauer*).

7529 **Borowitz** Eugene B., Renewing the Covenant; a theology for the postmodern Jew 1991 → 8,a665: ᴿJJS 46 (1995) 342-5 (N. *Solomon*, also on his Exploring Jewish ethics; Wayne State 1990; 498 p., $ 50; pa. $ 20).

7530 **Borowitz** Eugene B., Choices in modern Jewish thought; a partisan guide[2] [[1]1983; 7 20th-century Jewish thinkers; now adding *Umansky* Ellen M., on Jewish feminism]. West Orange NJ 1995, Behrman. xii-372 p. $ 15. 0-87441-581-0 [ThD 43,158].

7531 **Brauer** E., [E]*Patai* Raphael, The Jews of Kurdistan. Detroit 1993, Wayne State Univ. $ 45. -- [R]BuCanadMesop 30 (1995) 43s (S.C. *Brown*).

7532 *Caron* Vicki, French-Jewish assimilation reassessed; a review of the recent literature: Judaism 42 (1993) 134-159.

7533 **Cohen** Hermann, Religione della ragione dalle fonti dell'ebraismo [[2]1929, [E]*Strauss* Bruno], [T]*Fiorato* P., [E]*Poma* A.: Classici del Pensiero 3. CinB 1994, Paoline. -- [R]RasT 36 (1995) 97-105 (G. *Lorizio*; 'ragione e rivelazione tra ebraismo e modernità').

7534 **Cohn-Sherbok** Dan, The future of Judaism 1994 → 10,10014: [R]Religion 25 (1995) 193s (J. *Neusner,* 'a lightweight and silly book').

7535 *Cohn-Sherbok* Dan, Dog-rabbis [friendly, osculative] and cat rabbis: CCAR 42,1 (1995) 21-24 (-32, three responses).

7536 **Cohn-Sherbok** Dan & Lavinia, The American Jew; voices from an American Jewish community. L 1994, Collins Fount. 357 p. £ 10. -- 0-00-627687-3. -- [R]ET 106 (1994s) 223 (C.S. *Rodd*); Furrow 46 (1995) 55 (T. *Waldron*).

7537 *Ellenson* David, A sociologist's view of contemporary Jewish orthodoxy; the work of Samuel HEILMAN [Defenders 1992 ...]: RelStR 21 (1995) 14-18.

7538 [E]**Feingold** Henry L., The Jewish people in America. 5 vol., of which he edited vol. 4, A time for searching; entering the mainstream, 1920-1945. Baltimore 1992, Johns Hopkins Univ. xvii-338 p. -- : *A(sn)JS 20 (1995) 139-151 (G.C. *Altschuler,* 'shver zu zein a yid', on all five volumes).

7539 *a) Finestein* Israel, Judaism in the modern world; -- *b) Borovoy* Vitaly, Christian Orthodoxy in the modern world: → 607, Immanuel 26s (1994) 100-106 / 107-119 (-134, discussion).

7540 **Fishman** Aryeh, Judaism and modernization on the religious kibbutz 1992 → 10,10020: [R]*CritRR 7 (1994) 441-3 (Debra R. *Kaufman*).

7541 *Fishman* Aryeh, Modern Orthodox Judaism, a study in ambivalence: Social Compass 42 (1995) 89-95.

7542 *Funkenstein* Amos, [H] Jewish history among thorns: Zion 60 (1995) 335-347, Eng. XXII: forgetting the historico-evolutionary *Wissenschaft des Judentums* of ZUNZ, GEIGER and even KROCHMAL, the acrimonious disputes of the current *hokmat Yiśrā'ēl* (midrash + kabbala + responsa) against LIEBES, IDEL, & NEUSNER imply that 'some recent historians had good reasons to *lose* the faith we all once shared in the existence of one coherent and harmonious master narrative that is capable of representing a reality not of its own making'.

7542* *Galas* Michael, The state of Jewish studies in Poland: FraJudBei 22 (1995) 105-119.

7543 *Galchinsky* Michael, The new Anglo-Jewish literary criticism:*ProofT 15 (1995) 272-82.

7544 *Goldberg* Jacob, *a)* Majer BALABAN -- der führende Historiker der polnischen Juden; -
- *b)* Moses SCHORR, Pionier der Erforschung der Geschichte der polnischen Juden: Jud(ca) 51 (1995) 3-17 / 83-96.

7545 **Gressel** Josh, The Jew as chosen / the Jew as victim: diss. California Institute of Integral Studies, [D]*Rosenbaum* Robert, 1995. 300 p. 95-40697.--D(iss)AI 56 (1995s) p.4060.

7546 **Herweg** Rachel M., La yidishe meme; storia di un matriarcato occulto ma non troppo, da Isacco a Philip Roth: Judaica. Geneva c.1995, ECIO. 237 p.; bibliog. 213-234. 88-7545-683-6.

7547 **Ish-Shalom** Benjamin, Rav Avraham I.H.KOOK [1865-1935]; between rationalism and mysticism. Albany 1993, SUNY . xiv-357 p. $ 22. -- [R]JRel 75 (1995) 446s (D. *Shatz*).

7548 **Jacobs** Louis, We have reason to believe; some aspects of Jewish theology examined in the light of modern thought[4rev] [[1]1957]. L 1995, V.Mitchell. 157 p. £ 15 pa. $ 10. 0-85303-310-2; -4-5. -- [R]*TBR 8,1 (1995s) 60 (R. *Coggins*).

7549 **Jacobs** Louis, The Jewish religion; a companion. Ox 1995, UP. [vi-] 641 p. 0-19-826463-1.

7550 **Katz** Nathan, *Goldberg* Ellen S., The last Jews of Cochin; Jewish identity in Hindu India. Columbia 1993, Univ. S.Carolina. 352 p. -- *A(sn)JS 20 (1995) 473s (D. *Gold*).

7551 *Katz* Nathan, The Judaisms of Kaifeng and Cochin; parallel and divergent styles of religious acculturation: Numen 42 (1995) 118-140.

7552 **Kazzaz** Nissim, [H] The Jews in Iraq in the twentieth century. J 1991, Ben-Zvi. 367 p. -- [R]JQR 84 (1993s) 495-500 (R. *Snir*).

7553 **Laskier** Michael M., The Jews of Egypt, 1920-1970; in the midst of Zionism, anti-Semitism and the Middle East conflict 1992 → 8,k522: [R]*A(sn)JS 20 (1995) 245-8 (Rachel *Simon*, also on his 1992 [H] Maghrib).

7554 **Lerner** Michael, Jewish renewal; a path to healng and transformation. NY 1994, Putnam. xxviii-436 p. $ 26. -- [R]CritRR 8 (1995) 427-9 (L.L. *Rasmussen*).

7555 **Lipman** Vivian D., A history of the Jews in Britain since 1858. Leicester 1990, Univ. xvi-274 p. -- [R]Zion 60 (1995) 357-363 (D. *Gutwein*, [H]).

7556 **MacDonald** Kevin, A people that shall dwell alone; Judaism as a group evolutionary strategy. Westport CT 1994. xi-202 p. -- [R]JQR 86 (1995) 198-201 (S.L. *Gilman*).

7557 **Marcus** Jacob R., United States Jewry, 1776-1985, vol. 1s (of 4). Detroit 1989-91, Wayne State Univ. 820 p., 419 p. -- [R]*A(sn)JS 20 (1995) 229-234 (G. *Sorin*, 'with almost as much awe as to the five books of Moses'; p. 441-7 on vol.3, 1993).

7558 [E]**Mendes-Flohr** Paul, Gershom SCHOLEM, the man and his work [1982 'month's mind ' eulogies]. Albany 1994, SUNY. xi-127 p. $ 39.50; pa. $ 13. 0-7914-2125-2; pa. -6-0. -- [R]BoL (1995) 157 (A.F. *Hayman*: 'slight ', but mentions some points of interest).

7559 **Morgan** Michael L., Dilemmas in modern Jewish thought; the dialectics of revelation and history. Bloomington 1992, Indiana Univ. xxi-121 p. -- [R]*A(sn)JS 20 (1995) 237-240 (Z. *Garber:* irenically, is Judaism perpetual ?).

7560 *Neusner* Jacob, The foundations of Jewish existence: CJud 47,3 (1995) 42-52 [NTAb 40, p.82].

7561 **Prager** Dennis, *Telushkin* Joseph, Judentum heute; neun Fragen an eine Weltreligion [The nine questions people ask about Judaism 1986], [T]*Kesten* E., Essen U. von: Gü Tb 766, 1993 → 9,10933 [NTAb 38,p.325].

7562 **Ritterband** Paul, *Wechsler* Harold S., Jewish learning in American universities; the first century [since 1950]. Bloomington c.1995, Indiana Univ. 384 p. $ 35. 0-253-35039-5 [*A(sn)JS 20 (1995) 266 adv.].

7563 *Rozenberg* Danielle, Les Juifs dans l'Espagne contemporaine: RÉJ 154 (1995) 267-275.

7564 **Sacks** Jonathan, One people ? Tradition, modernity and Jewish unity: Littman Library. L 1993. -- [R]ZRGG 47 (1995) 372-4 (J. *Neusner:* England's Chief Rabbi, a first-rate mind on urgent theological issues).

7565 **Schwartz** Shuly R., The emergence of .. the Jewish Encyclopedia: HUC mg 13. Cincinnati 1991. -- *A(sn)JS 19 (1994) 112-4 (H.D. *Shapiro*).

7566 **Shmueli** Efraim, Seven Jewish cultures 1990 → 6,a163 ... 10,10042: [R]EstB 53 (1995) 420-2 (Esperança *Bariau*).

7567 **Stemberger** Günter, Jüdische Religion: Beck'sche Reihe 2003. 114 p. DM 14,80. 3-

406-39003-X [TR 91].

7568 **Stillman** Norman A., The Jews of Arab lands in modern times 1991 → 7,e954 ... 9,15604: [R]JQR 84 (1993s) 107s (Vera B, *Moreen*).

7569 **Tagliacozzo** Franco, *Migliau* Bice, Gli ebrei nella storia e nella società contemporanea. Scandicci FI 1993, La nuova Italia. 581 p. L[m] 49. -- [R]CivCatt 146 (1995,1) 196-8 (S. *Mazzolini*).

7570 **Uzzel** Robert L., The Kabbalistic thought of Eliphaz LEVI and its influence of modern occultism in America: diss. Baylor, [D]*Jonsson* J., 1995. 217 p. 95-28010. -- DissA 56 (1995s) p. 1394.

7571 **Vital** David, *a*) The future of the Jews 1990 → 8,a699: [R]A(sn)JS 17 (1992) 369-371 (E. *Tabory*); -- *b*) Il futuro degli ebrei, [T]*Bemporad Servi* Silvia. F 1992, Giuntina. 155 p. L[m] 23.-- [R]RasIsr 59(1,=58,)3 (1992) 167-9 (Lea *Sestieri*).

7572 WIENER: **Scine** Robert S., Jewish thought adrift; Max Wiener, 1881-1950 [last pre-Nazi heir to GEIGER and BAECK]: BJSt 259. Atlanta 1992, Scholars. xii-211 p. -- [R]*A(sn)JS 20 (1995) 234-6 (Susannah *Heschel*).

7573 **Wilkes** Paul, And they shall be my people; an American rabbi and his congregation [.. *any* case, though researched in Worcester, by a Catholic]. c.1995, Atlantic Monthly Press. 348 p. $ 23. -- [R]America 172,20 (1995) 26s (A.J. *Avery-Peck*).

7574 *Zelizer* Gerald L., Conservative rabbis, their movement, and American Judaism: Judaism 44 (1995) 242-303 (-313 responses).

7575 **Zipperstein** Steven J., Elusive prophet, AHAD HA'AM (Asher GINZBERG) 1993 → 9,15610: [R]*A(sn)JS 20 (1995) 438-440 (A.S. *Zuckerman*: 'still offers the hope of a Judaism that is not encompassed by religion and controlled by rabbis'); JJS 45 (1994) 317-326 (G. *Mandel*).

7576 *Zucker* David J., Rabbitzens and women rabbis; portrayals in contemporary American Jewish fiction: CCAR 42,1 (1995) 1-12.

K8 *Philosemitismus* -- Judeo-Christian rapprochement

7577 *Adams* Robert, Chaucer's 'new Rachel' and the theological roots of medieval anti-Semitism: → 530, BJRL 77,3 (1995) 9-18.

7578 **Amersfoort** J. van, *Oort* J. van, Juden und Christen in der Antike 1990 → 6,506* ... 9,10946: [R]JQR 85 (1994s) 457s (L.V. *Rutgers*).

7579 **Barth** Markus, The people of God; JSNT.s 5, 1983 → 64,8996: [R]RB(elg)PH 73 (1995) 209s (J. *Klener*: full of critical good will, though with some outdated moralizing).

7580 *Beaude* Pierre-Marie, Judaïsme rabbinique et christianisme; deux modèles d'accomplissement: → 14, [F]BEAUCHAMP P., 'Ouvrir les Écritures' 1995, 285-305.

7581 **Beck** Norman A., Mature Christianity in the 21st century; the recognition and repudiation of the anti-Jewish polemic of the NT[2rev]. NY 1994, Crossroad. 372 p. $ 25. -- [R]*NewThR 8,1 (1995) 91-93 (D. J, *Harrington*).

7582 **Berding** Helmut, Histoire de l'antisémitisme en Allemagne. P 1991, Sciences de l'Homme. 282 p. -- [R]RHR 212 (1995) 370s (S. *Schwarzfuchs*).

7583 *Bidussa* David, Razzismo e antisemitismo in Italia; ontologia e fenomenologia del 'bravo Italiano': RasIsr 59,3 (cioè fasc. unico del volume inspiegatamente cambiata da 58 dell'annata 1992) 1-36.

7584 **Blanchetière** François, Aux sources de l'antisémitisme chrétien, IIe-IIIe siècles: Centre de recherche français de Jérusalem, Hommes et sociétés. Lv 1995, Peeters. 191 p. Ff 160.

2-910343-02-2.

7586 *Borowitz* Eugene B., *al.*, Symposium on [WYSCHOGROD Michael ... whose friend insisted like LUSTIGER that in being baptized a Christian he did not cease being a Jew] 'Jewish-Christians and the Torah': MoTh 11 (1995) 165-241.

7587 ᴱ**Brändle** R., ᵀ*Jegher-Bucher* V., Johannes CHRYSOSTOMUS, Acht Reden gegen Juden: BGrL 41. Stu 1995, Hiersemann. xi-316 p. [RHE 91,31*].

7588 **Braybrooke** Marcus, Children of one God; a history of the Council of Christians and Jews. L 1991, Vallentine Mitchell. 168 p. £ 9.50. -- ᴿJJS 46 (1995) 334s (N. *Solomon*).

7589 *Bregman* Marc, The riddle of the ram in Genesis chapter 22: Jewish-Christian contacts in late antiquity: → 513, Sacrifice of Isaac 127-146 [81-98, *Pérez Fernández* Miguel, *Taylor* Justin, on possible comparisons of Aqeda to Jesus in NT outside Paul].

7590 *Brown* Raymond, The narratives of Jesus' Passion and anti-Judaism: America 172,11 (1995) 8-12.

7591 **Bunte** Wolfgang, Anonymus, Tractatus adversus Judaeum (1122): JudUmw 40, 1993 → 9,10961: ᴿRHE 90 (1995) 646s (Bat-Sheva *Albert*).

7592 *Callahan* Daniel F., ADEMAR of Chabannes, millennial fears and the development of western anti-Judaism: JEH 46 (1995) 19-35.

7593 *a) Campion* Owen F., Catholic-Jewish dialogue (1965-1995); -- *b) Fisher* Eugene J., Jews, Catholics and the holocaust: Priest 51,8 (1995) 16-20 / 10-15 & 51/9, 34-38.

7594 *Cerbelaud* D., Le regard de l'Église sur le Judaïsme comme clé de son dialogue avec les autres religions: Sens 47,4 (1995) 139-147 [< Judaica 51.196].

7595 ᴱ**Charlesworth** James H., Jews and Christians 1990 → 6,396 ... 8,a714: ᴿA(ustrl)BR 41 (1993) 65-71 (R. *Anderson*).

7596 **Chazan** Robert, Barcelona and beyond 1992 → 8,a715; 10,10058: ᴿ*A(sn)JSR 20 (1995) 379-388 (D. *Berger*); ChH 64 (1995) 652-4 (R.S. *Armour* Sr.); RÉJ 154 (1995) 500-2 (R. *Ayoun*).

7597 **Cheyette** Brian, Constructions of 'the Jew' in English literature and society; racial representations, 1875-1945. C 1993, Univ. xx-30l p. -- : *A(sn)JS 20 (1995) 433-7 (D.R. *Schwartz*: he discounts the teleological significance of the holocaust).

7598 *Chrostowski* Waldemar, Auschwitz; polnisches und jüdisches Empfinden: FrRu 2 (1995) 174-182

7599 *Chrostowski* Waldemar, Towards a new Christian perception of Jesus as a Jew: C(olc)Th 64,spec (1994) 41-54 [75-99, *Królikowski* Piotr; 55-61 . 63-73 . 101-9 *al.*, Schoah].

7600 *Chrostowski* Waldemar, *a)* (entretien avec *Oszajca* Wacław), ᴾ La Bible, les Juifs et les Polonais à l'heure du dialogue: -- *b)* ᴾ Judaism and Christianity as agents of redemption, symposium Auburn ɴʏ Theol. Sem. 4-16.III.1994: PrzPow 882 (1995) 139-152 / 221-5 [& 890 (1995) 26-35 (92s, *Żurek* S., sympozjum Wsz 18.V.1995)].

7601 *Colomer* Eusebio, La controversia islamo-judeo-cristiana en la obra apologética de Ramon MARTÍ: Diálogo filosofico-religioso entre cristianismo, judaísmo y islamismo durante le Edad Media en la península ibérica (Turnhout 1994, Brepols) 229-257 [< StLul 34 (1994) 119 . 131 (J. *Gayà*)].

7602 **Crossan** John D., Who killed Jesus ? Exposing the roots of antisemitism in the gospel story of the death of Jesus. SF 1995, HarperCollins. xii-238 p. 0-06-061479-X / -80-3.-- ᴿAmerica 173,6 (1995) 24.26 (Linda M. *Maloney*); ChrCent 112 (1995) 1222-4 (J. Christian *Wilson*); EThL 71 (1995) 455s (F. *Neirynck*: Crossan is here frankly anti-BROWN; p. 90 'the repentant Jewish people and the Jewish authorities who had lied, deceived, and misled them' in the Gospel of Peter may have grown out of Mt).

7602 **Cunningham** Philip A., Education for shalom; religion textbooks and the enhancement of the Catholic and Jewish relationship. Ph/ColMn 1995, American Interfaith / Liturgical. xviii-169 p. $ 12. /0-8146-2248-8 [ThD 43,62]. -- R*CritRR 8 (1995) 343-5 (P.L. *Culbertson*).

7603 EDavies Alan, Antisemitism in Canada; history and interpretation. Waterloo 1992, W.Laurier Univ. viii-304 p. A$ 35. -- RTorJT 11 (1995) 255s (D. *Marmur*).

7604 **Declerck** José H., Anonymus dialogus cum Iudaeis saec. 6: CCG 30. Turnhout/Lv 1994, Brepols/Univ. cxli-134 p. -- RRS(to)LR 31 (1995)

7605 *Dehullu* Joanie, L'affaire des billettes, une accusation de profanation d'hosties portée contre les Juifs à Paris, 1290: Bijdragen 56 (1995) 133-154; Eng. 155.

7606 *Delmaire* Danielle, Les impacts de l'affaire DREYFUS dans le nord de la France: RÉJ 154 (1995) 463-474 (-488, *Goetschel* Roland).

7607 *Derousseaux* L., *Bernard* Jacques, Bilan de l'équipe de recherche sur 'Judaïsme et christianisme des origines'; méthodologie pour l'analyse d'une rupture: MélSR 52 (1995) 301-321; 320s, *Henne*, JUSTIN, la Loi et les Juifs; 321, *Verhaeghe* Régis, La cessation de la Bat Qol.

7608 **Dinnerstein** Leonard, Antisemitism in America. NY 1994, Oxford-UP. xxvii-369 p. $ 25. 0-19-503780-4 [< ThD 42 (1995) 266]. -- RA(mer)HR 100 (1995) 1286s (O.B. *Pollak*).

7609 RDunn J.D.G., Jews and Christians .. parting: WUNT 66, 1989/92 → 8,467; 10,10071: RJS(Jud) 26 (1995) 190-3 (A.S. van der *Woude*); NT 36 (1994) 412-4 (C.C. *Newman*); ZRGG 47 (1995) 368s (F.W. *Horn*).

7610 **Eder** [→ 10,10074, not 'Egger '] Manfred, Die 'Deggendorfer Gnad' 1992: Jud(ca) 51 (1995) 55s (H.L. *Reichrath*); MüTZ 45 (1994) 349s (G. *Schwaiger*).

7611 EEfroymson David P., Within context; essays on Jews and Judaism in the NT 1993 → 9,10978: RNewThR 7,3 (1994) 85-87 (G.M. *Smiga*).

7612 *Ehrlich* Ernst L., Christen und Juden in neuen Gesprächen: FrRu NF 1 (1993s) 276-84.

7614 **Elderen** Reinier J. van, Toekomst voor Israël; een theologie-historisch onderzoek naar de visie op de bekering der joden en de toekomst van Israël bij Engelse protestanten in de periode 1547-1670, tegen de achtergrond van hun eschatologie [diss. Kampen]. Kampen 1992, Mondiss. 324 p. f 40. 90-53370-13-7. -- RNedThT 49 (1995) 76s (T. *Brienen*).

7615 **Ellis** Marc H., Ending Auschwitz [its lesson has gone awry, for Israel is no more humble or compassionate than that intolerance]; the future of Jewish and Christian life. LVL 1994, W-Knox. 126 p. $ 17 pa. -- RC(alvin)TJ 30 (1995) 638s (E. *Rubingh*).

7616 *Ephraïm* frère, Gesù ebreo praticante [1987], T. Mi 1993, Ancora. 315 p. Lm 35. - - RAsprenas 42 (1995) 594s (V. *Scippa*: 'é sorprendente il poco entusiasmo per gli studi storico-critici della Bibbia').

7617 EEvans Craig A., *Hagner* Donald A., Anti-Semitism and early Christianity; issues of polemic and faith [inner-Jewish, not anti-Jewish] 1993 → 9,10982: RCBQ 57 (1995) 620s (R.F. *O'Toole*); *CritRR 7 (1994) 582 (tit. pp.); JAOS 115 (1995) 115s (L.H. *Feldman*).

7618 EFisher Eugene J., *Klenicki* Leon, JOHN PAUL II, Spiritual pilgrimage; texts on Jews and Judaism. NY 1995, Crossroad Herder. xxxix-208 p. $ 20. 0-8245-1544-7 [ThD 43,172].

7619 *Flusser* David, LESSINGs Ringparabel und die jüdisch-christliche Begegnung: FrRu NF 1 (1993s) 177-182.

7620 **Foss** Øyvind, Antijudaisme, kirke og misjon. Oslo 1994, Gyldendal. 263 p. --

[R]SvTKv 70 (1994) 134-6 (J. *Åberg*).

7621 *Fredriksen* Paula, Excaecati occulta justitia Dei; AUGUSTINE on Jews and Judaism: *JEarlyC 3 (1995) 299-324.

7622 **Freudmann** Lillian C., Antisemitism in the NT 1994 → 10,10081 [-isms]; $47.50; pa. $ 28; 0-8191=9294-5; -5-3: [R]CritRR 7 (1994) 187-9 (D.J. *Harrington:* many errors of fact and in asssuming unvaried continuity of 'Judaism'); ET 106 (1994s) 57 (G. *Lloyd Jones*).

7623 *Friedmann* Friedrich G., Christians and Jews [postscript to a correspondence with Karl RAHNER, StZ 178 (1966) 81-97] 213 (1995) 30-36, [T]*Asen* B.A.: ThD 42 (1995) 203-8.

7624 [T]**Gandillac** M. de, Pierre ABELARD, Conférences: dialogue d'un philosophe avec un juif et un chrétien [1125s &] Connais-toi toi-même: éthique [1138]: Sagesses chrétiennes. P 1993, Cerf. 295 p. F 150. 2-204-04760-0. -- [R]Bijdragen 56 (1995) 221s (A. van de *Pavert*).

7625 *Gollinger* H., Katholische Theologie und Judentum: EurTBu 5,2 (1994) 175-181 [< ZIT 95,p.173].

7626 **Grelot** Pierre, Les Juifs dans l'Évangile selon Jean; enquête historique et rèflexion théologique: RB.cah 34. P 1995, Gabalda. 211 p. 2-85021-081-1.

7627 **Hall** S.G.[III], Christian anti-Semitism and Paul's theology 1993 → 9,11000; 10,10086: [R]Neotest 29 (1995) 420s (J. *Miller*).

7628 **Harrowitz** Nancy A., Tainted greatness; antisemitism and cultural heroes. Ph 1994, Temple Univ. 314p. $ 50; pa. $ 25. 1-56639-153-9; -61-X. -- [R]Religion 25 (1995) 285-8 (I. *Strenski*).

7629 *Harvey* Graham, Jewish Christians, Jesus and now [privileged; unlike (never so-called) 'pagan Christians', who have been expected to deny and denigrate their former background]: Theol 98 (L 1995) 461-6.

7630 *Hauerwas* Stanley, Jews and the Eucharist : (Reformed) Perspectives 9,2 (1994) 14s.

7631 **Haynes** Stephen R., Reluctant witnesses; Jews and the Christian imagination. LvL 1995, W-Knox. xi-221 p. $ 19. 0-664-25579-5 [ThD 43,170].

7632 *Heldt* Petra, A brief history of dialogue between Orthodox Christians and Jews: Immanuel 26s (1994) 211-224; bibliog. 240-9.

7633 **Hilton** Michael, The Christian effect on Jewish life. L 1994, SCM. 309 p. £ 15. 0-334-02582-6. -- [R]ET 106 (1994s) 318 (C.H. *Middleburgh*).

7634 *a) Hoeckman* Remi, Jewish-Christian dialogue; promise and possibility; -- *b) Hilton* Michael, rabbi, How far dare we go ? [Cardinal Bea Lectures 1 & 2] : Month 256 (1995) 214-221 / 222-7.

7635 *Holmberg* Bengt, Judisk contra kristen identitet i urkyrkan ?: → 93, [F]KIEFFERR., SEÅ (1995) 49-67.

7636 **Holwerda** David E., Jesus and Israel; one covenant or two? GR/Leicester 1995, Eerdmans/Apollos. xi-193 p. $ 13 pa. -- [R]IBM(iss)R 19 (1995) 181s (A.F. *Glasser*).

7637 **Hood** J.Y.B., Aquinas and the Jews. Ph 1995. Univ. Pennsylvania. xiv-145 p. £ 28.50; pa. £ 14. 0-8122-3305-0; -1523-0. -- [R]E(xp)T 107 (1995s) 121s (F. *Selman*).

7638 *Horbury* William, Judah BRIEL and seventeenth-century Jewish anti-Christian polemic in Italy: Jewish Studies Quarterly 1 (Tü 1993s) 171-192.

7639 *Horowitz* Nisan, Gespräch mit Kardinal Jean-Marie LUSTIGER ['Ich habe keine Antwort'], [T]*Lauer* Simon: FrRu 2 (1995) 257-266.

7640 **Hsia Po-Chia** A., Trent 1475; stories of a ritual murder trial 1992 → 8,a747; 9,11007: [R]*A(sn)JS 20 (1995) 427-9 (Judith R. *Baskin*).

7641 *Huizing* Klaas, Das jüdische Apriori; die Bedeutung der Religionsphilosophie

[Hermann] COHENs für den jüdisch-christlichen Dialog: NZSTh 37 (1995) 75-95; Eng. 95.

7642 **Isser** Natalie, Antisemitism during the French Second Empire 1991 → 9,10091: R*A(sn)JSR 19 (1994) 96-99 (Vicki *Caron*); JQR 85 (1994s) 435s (F. *Malino*).

7643 *Jacob* E., L'alliance toujours valable, selon Norbert LOHFINK: FV 93,1 (1994) 15-18.

7644 **Jaher** Frederic C., A scapegoat in the new wilderness; the origins and rise of anti-Semitism in America. C 1994, Harvard Univ. viii-229 p. -- R*A(sn)JS 20 (1995) 449-451 (S.E. *Knee*).

7645 *Joly* Bertrand, Les antidreyfusards considéraient Dreyfus coupable ?: RH 291 (1994) 401-457.

7646 **Katunarich** Sergio M., Ebrei e cristiani 1993 → 10,10094: RAsprenas 42 (1995) 134c (G. *Di Palma*).

7647 **Katz** Steven T., The holocaust in historical context, 1. the holocaust and mass death before the modern age. NY 1994, Oxford-UP. 702 p. -- R*A(sn)JS 20 (1995) 454-8 (J. *Neusner*: an academic masterpiece, not ideology but rigorous philosophical research).

7648 **Kaufmann** Philip S., The beloved disciple, witness against anti-Semitism 1991 → 7,4820; 8,5755: RRB 102 (1995) 623 (J. *Taylor*).

7649 **Kellenbach** Katharina von, Anti-Judaism in feminist religious writings [diss. Temple Univ.]: AAR Cultural Criticism 1. Atlanta 1994, Scholars. x-173 p. $ 30; pa. $ 18. 0-7885-0043-0; -4-9 [ThD 42,373].

7650 *Kenney* J.T., Enemies near and far; the image of the Jews in Islamist discourse in Egypt: Religion 24 (L 1994) 253-270 [< ZIT 95, p.69]

7651 *Kluback* William, Juifs et chrétiens au-delà du dialogue; en mémoire de Jacob FLEISCHMANN, TKlopfenstein Caroline: FV 94,5 (1995) 35-53.

7652 **Kohler-Spiegel** Helga, Juden und Christen, Geschwister im Glaube 1991 → 9,11017: RBiLi(turg) 66 (1993) 55s (K. *Schubert*).

7653 **Küng** Hans, Das Judentum 1991 → 8,a757 ... 10,10101; DM 68; 3-492-03496-9: RZkT 117 (1995) 106s (R. *Oberforcher*).

7654 **Küng** Hans, Judaism, between yesterday and tomorrow 1992 → 8,a758 ... 10,10102: *CritRR 7 (1994) 388-390 (J.K. *Roth*); Midstream 41,7 (1995) 41s (M.R. *Lehmann;* from a limited perspective); RefR 49 (1995s) 220s (E. *Heideman*, also on his 1995 Christianity).

7655 **Küng** Hans, El Judaismo; pasado, presente y futuro, TMartlnez de Lapera Victor A., *Canal Marcos* Gilberto: Estructuras y procesos 1993 10,10103; 84-87699-84-7: RActuBbg 31 (1994) 111s (J. *Boada*).

7656 **Küng** Hans, Le judaïsme, TFesthauer Joseph. P 1995, Seuil. 959 p. 2-02-020189-5.

7657 *Küng* Hans, Jewish Christianity and its significance for ecumenism today: → 59, FFREEDMAN D.N., Fortunate 1995, 584-606.

7658 **Kuschel** Karl-Josef, Abraham, a symbol of hope for Jews, Christians and Muslims. NY/L 1995, Continuum/SCM. xxix-286 p. $ 25. 0-8264-0808-7 [< OTA 19, p.361s, J.W. *Hilber*].

7659 **Langer** Michael, Zwischen Vorurteil und Aggression; zum Judenbild in der deutschsprachigen katholischen Volksbildung des 19. Jahrhunderts [Hab.-Diss. München; RHE 90 (1995) 384*]: Lernprozess Christen Juden 9. FrB 1994, Herder. xiii-587 p. DM 78. 3-451-23443-2. -- RFrRu 2 (1995) 52-55 (S. *Ben-Chorin*); Jud(aica) 51 (1995) 117s (S. *Leimgruber*); THGL 85 (1995) 127 (also S. *Leimgruber*); ZkT 117 (1995) 468-470 (M. *Rothgangel*).

7660 **Langmuir** Gavin I., History / Toward a definition 1990 → 8,a760s: RJQR 84 (1993s) 114.6 (K.R. *Stow*).

7661 *Lavajo* Joachim Chorão, A controvérsia judio-cristã: Eborensia 7 (Évora 1994) 1-44.

7662 **Lazare** Bernard [1865-1903], Antisemitism; its history and causes, [T]*Wistrich* Robert S. Lincoln 1995, Univ. Nebraska. xxv-208 p. 0-8032-7954-X

7663 *Lenzen* Verena, Zu J.J. PETUCHOWSKIs Buch 'Mein Judesein' [1992]: BiKi 50 (1995) 83-91.

7664 **Levine** Hillel, Economic origins of antisemitism; Poland and its Jews in the early modern period. NHv 1991, Yale Univ. xiii-271 p. -- [R]*A(sn)JS 19 (1994) 90-93 (D. *Engel*).

7665 *Lewis* Jonathan, PIUS XII and the Jews; the myths and the facts: Tablet 249 (1995) 248 . 250-2; p.320s & 320, letters of R.*Graham* from Rome; p.359 & 390s, from others..

7666 *a)* *Ley* Michael, Der Antichrist in der Moderne; -- *b)* *Frey* Winfried, Zacharias BLETZ [1549 → Y43, Heimann] und die neue Zeit; zum Luzerner Antichristspiel: -- *c)* *Bärsch* Claus-E., Der Jude als Antichrist in der NS [Nazi] -Ideologie: ZRGG 47 (1995) 145-159 / 126-144 / 160-188.

7667 **Limor** Ora, Die Disputationen zu Ceuta (1179) und Mallorca (1286); zwei antijüdische Schriften aus dem mittelalterlichen Genua [< Diss.1985]: QGGMA 15. Mü 1994, MGH. DM 84. [her Contra Iudaeos is awaited Tü 1996, Mohr]. -- [R]JJS 46 (1995) 311-4 (Anna *Sapir Abulafia*; much more up-to-date than DAHAN G., CONTARDO 1993, really 1983, which however includes a translation).

7668 **Lohfink** Norbert, L'alleanza mai revocata; riflessioni esegetiche per il dialogo tra cristiani ed ebrei [→ 8,7321; 9,11033]: GdT 201, 1991 → 8,7322: [R]Greg 76 (1995) 196-8 (E. *Farahian*).

7669 *López Martínez* N., Teología de controversia sobre judíos y judaizantes españoles del siglo XV; ambientación y principales escritos: Anuario de Historia de la Iglesia 1 (1992) 39-70 [< RHE 90 (1995) 648].

7670 *Luzzati* Michele, Quod non fecerunt barbari: Amicizia ebraico-cristiana 29 (F 1994) 118-123 [< Jud(aica) 51 (1995) 57].

7671 [E]**Luzzati** M., L'Inquisizione e gli Ebrei in Italia; Atti del convegno Livorno-Pisa 1992. Bari 1994, Laterza. xvi-340 p. < RHE 90 (1995) 298*.

7672 **Maccoby** Hyam, Judas Iscariot and the myth of Jewish evil 1992 → 8,5031: [R]*A(sn)JS 20 (1995) 178-180 (J.T. *Townsend:* useful despite assumptions and overspeculation).

7673 [E]**McInnes** Val A., New visions; historical and theological perspectives on the Jewish-Christian dialogue [Tulane lectures 1992s] 1993 → 9,334*a*: [R]JAAR 63 (1995) 857s (D.E.*Timmer*).

7674 **McMichael** Steven M., Was Jesus of Nazareth the Messiah ? Alphonso de ESPINA and the [his, 1464] 'Fortalitium fidei' (c.1464): SFSHJ 77. Atlanta 1994, Scholars. xxi-677 p. $ 135. 1-55540-930-X. -- [R]*CritRR 8 (1995) 413 (M. *Pesce*); RelStR 21 (1995) 337 (D.R. *Janz*).

7675 *Magonet* Jonathan, Guests and hosts [... diaspora]: → 134, [F]MURRAY R., HeythJ 36,4 (1995) 409-421.

7676 *Maidl* Lydia, *Bendel* Rainer, Das Drama Synagoge -- Ecclesia in der Seele des Gott suchenden Menschen; eine Interpretation der Sermones 14 und 15 in Canticum Canticorum des BERNHARD von Clairvaux: MüTZ 45 (1994) 271-287 (289-300, *Krichbaumer* Maria).

7677 [E]**Maier** Johann, *al.*, Polémica judeo-cristiana; estudios [parte Medina del Campo 1991]. M 1992, Aben Ezra. 132 p. -- [R]Sefarad 55 (1995) 216-8 (J.V. *Niclós*).

7678 *Marcus* Ivan G., Jews and Christians imagining the other in medieval Europe: *ProofT 15 (1995) 209-226.

7679 **Martin** Tony, The Jewish onslaught [on him as professor, tolerating the book The secret relationship between blacks and Jews]; despatches from the Wellesley battlefront. Dover MA 1994, Majority. -- [R]JB(lack)St 25 (1994) 118s (Molefi Kete *Asante*).

7680 **Martin** Vincent, A house divided; the parting of the ways between synagogue and Church: SJC. NY 1995, Paulist. 194 p. $ 12 pa. 0-8091-3569-8 [NTAb 40, p.369]. -- [R]Li(ving)Li 32,4 (1995s) 80s (J. *Leibig*).

7681 *Mędala* S., Funkcja Żydów .. Jews in the Gospel of John: CoTh 64,2 (1994) 79-101 [NTAb 39, p.233].

7682 [E]**Medina** João, Judaismo, Inquisição e Sebastianismo: História de Portugal 6. Amadora 1993, Ediclube. 388 p.; (color.) ill. 972-719-058-8. -- [R]Kiryat Sefer 65 (1994s) p.706-8 (F. Moreno *Carvalho*, [H]).

7683 *Menze* Ernest A., HERDERS 'deutsche Art von "Humanität" ' und die jüdische Frage; geschichtliches Umfeld und moderne Kritik [ROSE L., Revolutionary Antisemitism in Germany p. 108s]: Jud(aica) 49 (1993) 156-169.

7684 *Meuhas Ginio* Alisa, El concepto de 'perfidia judaica' de la época visigoda en la perspectiva castellana del siglo XV: → 142, [F]OROZ RETA III, Helmantica 46 (1995) 299-311.

7685 *Mikolajczyk* Mirosław, Bibliografia dialogu chrześcijańsko-judaistycznego, publikacje polskie 5 (1990-1991): C(olc)Th 64,1 (1994) 145-139.

7686 **Modras** Ronald, The Catholic Church and Antisemitism, Poland 1933-9. Langhorne PA 1994, Academic. -- [R]TS 56 (1995) 816 (J.T. *Pawlikowski*: ultimately on Catholicism's struggle with modernity).

7687 *a) Moltmann* Jürgen, Zeit der Hoffnung; das Exil in christlicher und jüdischer Sicht; -- *b) Bubis* Ignatz, (Gespräch) Bleiben die Juden ewig Fremde ?: E(v)K 27 (1994) 688-690 / 404-7.

7688 *Mussner* Franz, Was haben die Juden mit der christlichen Ökumene zu tun ?: UnSa 50 (1995) 331-9.

7689 *Neudecker* R., Sprache und Sprachlosigkeit im jüdisch-christlichen Dialog: Dialog der Religionen 5,1 (1995) 32-41 [< Judaica 51.259].

7690 **Neusner** Jacob, Telling tales ... Judeo-Christian dialogue 1993 → 9,11082; 10,10127: [R]E(cu)R 47 (1995) 108s (H. *Ucko*).

7691 **Neusner** Jacob, Children of the flesh, children of the promise; a rabbi talks with Paul [and J.D.G.DUNN]. Cleveland 1995, Pilgrim. xxv-119 p. $ 15 pa. 0-8298-1026-9 [NTAb 40, p.180].

7692 **Neusner** Jacob, A rabbi talks with Jesus 1993 → 9,11051: [R]LexTQ 30 (1995) 118-120 (r. J.F. *Adland*).

7693 *Neusner* Jacob, Blacks and Jews; new views on an old relation: Midstream 41,2 (1995) 25-28.

7694 **Neusner** Jacob, *Chilton* Bruce D., Revelation, the Torah and the Bible: Christianity and Judaism -- the formative categories. Ph 1995, Trinity. xv-175 p. $ 17. 1-56338-124-9 [ThD 43,378]

7695 *a) Nicholls* William, Against Jewish-Christian dialogue; -- *b) Ash* James K., The confusion about the historical Jesus; -- *c) Breitbart* Sidney, Thoughts for 'Jews for Jesus': Midstream 31,6 (1995) 27s / 29s / 31.

7696 *Nickelsburg* G.W.E., The first century; a time to rejoice and a time to weep. ...

7697 **Olster** Davie M., Roman defeat, Christian response amd the literary construction of the Jew. Ph 1994, Univ. Pennsylvania. x-203 p. £ 30. 0-8122-3152-X. -- [R]ET 106

(1994s) 222 (S.N.C. Lieu).

7698 **Opalski** Magdalena, *Bartal* Israel, Poles and Jews; a failed brotherhood. Hanover NH 1992, Brandeis Univ. 191 p. -- [R]*A(sn)JS 20 (1995) 430-3 (M.C. *Steinlauf*).

7699 **Paul** André, Il giudaismo antico e la Bibbia [1987 → 3,b893], [T]: StRel. Bo 1991, Dehoniane. 358 p. L[m] 40. -- [R]Asprenas 42 (1995) 116s (G. *Di Palma*).

7700 *Pedersen* Sigfred, Israel als integrierter Teil der christlichen Hoffnung: → 88, [F]JERVELL J.: ST 49 (Oslo 1995) 133-149.

7701 **Pesce** M., Il cristianesimo e la sua radice ebraica, con una raccolta di test sul dialogo ebraico-cristiano 1994 → 10,10133; L[m] 30. -- [R]Asprenas 42 (1995) 299s (G. *Di Palma*).

7702 **Peterse** Hans, Jacobus HOOGSTRAETEN gegen Johannes REUCHLIN; ein Beitrag zur Geschichte des Antijudaismus im 16. Jahrhundert; VIEG 165. viii-194 p. DM 68. 3-8053-1794-8 [ThRv 92,81].

7703 **Petuchowski** Jacob J., *Thoma* Clemens, *a)* Lessico del'incontro cristiano-ebraico 1992 → 9,10061; [T]*Gatti* Enzo, [E]*Stefani* Piero: [R]Prot(estantesimo) 49 (1994) 413s (M. *Abbà*); RasIsr 59 (1, = 58,) 3 (1992) 164-6 (Lea *Sestieri*). -- *b)* Leksykon dialogu chrześcijańskiego-żydowskiego: Kościół a Żydzi i Judaizm 5. Wsz 1995, Akademia Teologii Katolickiej. 295 p. 83-7072-059-5.

7704 **Petzel** Paul, Was uns an Gott fehlt, wenn uns die Juden fehlen; eine erkenntnistheologische Studie. Mainz 1994, Grünewald. 274 p. DM 48. -- [R]KuI(sr) 10 (1995) 185s (Julie *Goldberg*); FrRu 2 (1995) 227-230 (G. *Bubolz*).

7705 *Petzel* P., Das neue Verhältnis der Kirchen zum Judentum; die jüdische Bibel und die Christen, 1. -- 2. Das bleibende Zeugnis des Judentums; Orien(tierung) 59 (1995) 219-222 . 237-240

7706 *Phayer* Michael, The postwar German Catholic debate over holocaust guilt [historian K. REPGEN: bishops' 1965 statement overlooked some facts; 92% of Dachau clergy were Catholic]: ZKG 8 (1995) 426-439.

7707 **Poliakov** Léon, Vom Antizionismus zum Antisemitismus [1969], [T]*Sick* Franziska. Fr 1992, Ça Ira. 159 p. DM 18. -- [R]Jud(aica) 50 (1994) 172s (A. *Pfahl-Traughber*).

7708 *Rendtorff* Rolf, Christliche Identität in Israels Gegenwart [*Lindemann* Andreas, *Moltmann* Jürgen ..]: EvTh 55 (1995) 3-12 [28-49-63.

7709 **Robinson** Jack H., John CALVIN and the Jews: A(mer)US 8/123. NY 1992, Lang. 152 p. $ 36. -- [R]*CritRR 7 (1994) 362-4 (D.C. *Nugent*).

7710 *Rokéah* David, TACITUS and ancient antisemitism: RÉJ 154 (1995) 281-294.

7711 *Rossi de Gasperis* Francesco, A new Jewish Christianity [< Études June 1993]: Month 256 (1995) 305-9.

7712 *Rubinkiewicz* Ryszard, [P] Religious and human contents of the Jewish-Christian dialogue; → 98, [F]KUMOR B., AnCr 27 (1995) 283-295; Eng. 295.

7713 *a) Rufeisen* P. Daniel, Das Pascha unter den Juden gefeiert; -- *b) Hemker* Elisheva, Die Wiederbegegnung der Christen mit dem Hebräischen in der Kirche: BiLi(turg) 66 (1993) 229-233 / 233-6.

7714 **Sanders** Jack T., Schismatics .. the first one hundred years of Jewish-Christian relations 1993 → 9,11073: [R]A(ndr)USS 33 (1995) 324-6 (J.E. *Miller*); BoL (1994) 150 (J.L. *North*); JBL 114 (1995) 755-7 (D.P. *Efroymson*); JSJ(ud) 26 (1995) 216-9 (J. *Duhaime*).

7715 **Santaniello** Weaver, NIETZSCHE, God, and the Jews; his critique of Judeo-Christianity in relation to the Nazi myth. Albany 1994, SUNY. xvi-232 p. $ 54.50; pa. $ 18. 0-7914-2135-X; -6-8 [ThD 42,386].

7716 *Scaramuzzi* Domenico, Il dialogo interreligioso a trent'anni dalla 'Nostra aetate ': *RivScRel 9 (1995) 409-425.

7717 **Schöppner** Lothar, Begegnungsmodell jüdisch-christlicher Dialog; empirische Analyse des Würzburger Lernprojektes: Lernprozess Christen -- Juden 7. FrB 1993, Herder. 480 p. -- ᴿFrRu 2 (1995) 61s (Hildegard *Gollinger*).

7718 **Schreckenberg** Heinz, Die christlichen Adversus Judaeos-Texte und ihr literarisches und historisches Umfeld (13.-20. Jh.) 1994 → 10,10145: DM 126: ᴿWissWeis 58 (1995) 317-9 (Rotraud *Ries*).

7719 *Schwager* Raymund, Messianische Logik; eine neue Dimension für das jüdisch-christliche Gespräch: StZ 213 (1995) 545-554.

7720 *Schwartz* Dov, ᴴ Rabbi Jehuda HA-LEVI on Christianity: *A(sn)JS 19 (1994) 1*-24*.

7721 **Schwartz** G. David, A Jewish appraisal of dialogue. Lanham MD 1994, UPA. 148 p. $ 24.50. -- ᴿEncounter 56 (1995) 418-420 (D.C. *Sasso*: intense).

7722 **Schweitzer** Wolfgang, Der Jude Jesus und die Völker der Welt; ein Gespräch mit Paul M. VAN BUREN 1993 → 9,341*: ᴿ*CritRR 8 (1995) 510-2 (J. *Siker*); J(unge)K 56 (1995) 58s (Hanna *Lehming*).

7723 *Schweitzer* Wolfgang, Das Hinzutreten von Heiden -- Anlass für Erhöhungschristologien im Neuen Testament ? ein Versuch im Kontext des christlich-jüdischen Gesprächs: WuD(ienst) 23 (1995) 153-165.

7724 **Segel** Binjamin W., A lie and a libel; the history of the Protocols of the Elders of Zion [1926], ᵀ*Levy* Richard S. Lincoln 1995, Univ. Nebraska. xv-148 p. 0-8032-4243-3.

7725 ᴱ**Siegele-Wenschkewitz** Leonore, Christlicher Antijudaismus und Antisemitismus; theologische und kirchliche Programme; ArTe 85. Fra 1994, Haag & H. 320 p. DM 50. - - ᴿKuI(sr) 10 (1995) 107s (Julie *Kirchberg*).

7726 **Smiga** George M., Pain and polemic; anti-Judaism in the Gospels 1992 → 8,a788 ... 10,10146: ᴿ*CritRR 7 (1994) 258s (L. *Gaston*).

7727 **Sonderegger** Katherine, That Jesus Christ was born a Jew ..BARTH: 1992 → 8,a789: ᴿP(rinc)SB 16 (1995) 103-5 (Ellen T. *Charry*).

7728 ᴱ**Staffa** Christian, Vom protestantischen Antijudaismus und seinen Lügen; Versuche einer Standort- und Gehwegbestimmung des christlich-jüdischen Gesprächs. Magdeburg 1993 ²1994, Ev. Akad. 150 p. DM 4. -- ᴿJud(aica) 51 (1995) 116s (F. von *Hammerstein*).

7729 *Stegner* William R., Breaking away; the conflict with formative Judaism: BR(es) 40 (1995) 7-37.

7730 *Stow* Kenneth R., The pitfalls of writing papal documentary history; SIMONSOHN's Apostolic See and the Jews [1988-91]: JQR 85 (1994s) 397-412.

7731 **Stravinskas** Peter, *Klenicki* Leon, A Catholic-Jewish encounter. Huntington IN 1994, Our Sunday Visitor. 156 p. $ 20. 0-87973-619-4 [< ThD 42 (1995) 293].

7732 **Taylor** Miriam S., Anti-Judaism and early Christian identity; a critique pf the scholarly consensus: StPB 46. Lei 1995, Brill. x-207 p. $ 56. 90-04-10186-1 [RStR 22,72, F.W. *Burnett*].

7733 *Thoma* Clemens, Die Affäre DREYFUS in neuer Sicht; FrRu 2 (1995) 81-86; phot.; p. 317-9, Briefe *Flusser* D., *Licharz* W.

7734 **Thoma** Clemens, Das Messiasprojekt Theologie jüdisch-christlicher Begegnung 1994 → 10,10150*; DM 42: ᴿBiKi 50 (1995) 189 (R. *Baumann*); ThGL 85 (1995) 130s (S. *Leimgruber*).

7735 *Thoma* Clemens, Vcrschaukeltes Judentum [US Messianic-Jewish alliance 'expects the end of the world and conversion of the Jews too soon, thereby offending the Jewish people and their faith' p.250]; FrRu 2 (1995) 241-250; 244, 12 magazine-covers etc.

7736 **Tolan** J., Petrus ALFONSI and his medieval readers. Gainesville 1993, Univ. Florida. xv-288. -- ᴿRasIsr 61,1 (199%) 163-6 (P. *Morpurgo*).

7737 **Trautner-Kromann** Hanne, Shield and sword; [17] Jewish polemics against Christianity and the Christians in France and Spain from 1100-1500: TSMJ 8, 1993 → 9,11086 [RStR 22,259, S.D. *Benin*]: ᴿHeythJ 36 (1995) 85s (L. *Jacobs*).

7738 *Tyson* Joseph B., Jews and Judaism in Luke-Acts; reading as a Godfearer; NTS 41 (1995) 19-38.

7739 **Ucko** Hans, Common roots; new horizons 1994 → 10,10151: ᴿET 106 (1994s) 126 (M. *Braybrooke*).

7740 **Ucko** Hans, Vom Judentum lernen, gemeinsame Wurzeln -- neue Wege [ORK 1994], ᵀ*Voigt* H. Fra 1995, Lembeck. 149 p. 3-87476-302-1. -- ᴿThLZ 120 (1995) 1029s (B. *Schröder*).

7741 *Utterback* Christine T., 'Conversi' revert; voluntary and forced return to Judaism in the early fourteenth century: ChH 64 (1995) 17-28.

7742 **Valerio** Karolina de, Altes Testament und Judentum im Frühwerk Rudolf BULTMANNs [ev. Diss. Erlangen 1991]: BZNW 71. B 1994, de Gruyter. xix-454 p. DM 172. 3-11-014201-5. -- ᴿThGL 85 (1995) 131s (B. *Dieckmann*).

7743 *Vogler* W., Antijudaismus im Neuen Testament ? ZdZ 5,3 (1995) 109-.. [< Jud(aica) 51,259].

7744 *Von Waldow* H. Eberhard, The Christian-Jewish dialogue; in the footsteps of Markus BARTH: H(orizons)BT 17 (1995)

7745 *Walz* Rainer, Der vormoderne Antisemitismus; religiöser Fanatismus oder Rassenwahn ? : HZ 260 (1995) 719-748.

7746 *Walzer* Michael, The public impact of the Christian-Jewish dialogue: *NewThR 8,2 (1995) 79-83.

7747 **Wander** Bernd, Trennungsprozesse zwischen frühem Christentum und Judentum im 1. Jahrhundert n. Chr.; datierbare Abfolgen zwischen der Hinrichtung Jesu und der Zerstörung des Jerusalemer Tempels [< Diss. ᴰ*Berger* K., Heidelberg 1992]: TANZ 16. Tü 1994, Francke. ix-315 p.; Bibliog. 290-307. DM 94. 3-7720-1867-X. -- ᴿKuI(sr) 10 (1995) 105s (Julie *Kirchberg*).

7748 *a) Wander* Bernd, Auseinandersetzungen, Ablösungsvorgänge und 'Trennungsprozesse' zwischen frühem Christentum und Judentum im 1. Jh. d.C.; -- *b) Stegemann* Ekkehard E., Judenfeindschaft zwischen Xenophobie und Antisemitismus: KuI(sr) 10 (1995) 152-166 / 167-179.

7749 *Weismann* Francisco J., Diálogo entre el judaismo y el cristianismo: Rel(y)Cult 41 (1995) 281-303.

7750 **Willebrands** Johannes card., Church and Jewish people; new considerations (24, 1974-90) 1992 → 8,a797; $ 15 [RStR 22,54, E.J. *Fisher*]: ᴿ*NewThR 7,2 (1994) 110-2 (R.C. *Lux*).

7751 **Williamson** Clark M., A guest in the house of Israel; post-holocaust [revision of covenant, Christology, and] Church theology 1993; $ 20 pa. [RStR 22,197, Beverley A. *Asbury* & M.C. *Hawk*, also on BLUMENTHAL D., PLANK K., GUSHEE D.]. -- ᴿJRel 75 (1995) 292s (M.H. *Vogel*); RExp 92 (1995) 117-9 (D.P. *Gushee*).

7752 **Wilson** Stephen G., Related strangers; Jews and Christians 70-170 C.E. Mp 1995, Fortress. xvi-416 p. $ 26 pa. 0-8006-2950-7 [ThD 44,94].

7753 **Wistrich** Robert S., Antisemitism; the longest hatred 1992 → 8,a798; 9,11093: [R]CCAR 42,1 (1995) 61-64 (R. *Melson*).

7754 [E]**Wood** Diana, Christianity and Judaism 1991/2 → 8,502: [R]Speculum 69 (1994) 1311 (some titles & p.).

7755 *Wyschogrod* M., Letter to a friend [a baptized Jew, about continuing to be (also) Jewish, as in Acts 15]: MoTh 11 (1995) 165-171 (229-241 to 7 respondents, 173-227) [NTAb 39, p.446].

XVII,3 Religiones parabiblicae

M1.1 **Gnosticismus classicus**

7756 **Bouyer** Louis, [Mysterion, Gnosis,] Sophia ou le monde en Dieu. P 1994, Cerf. 212 p. -- [R]OCP 61 (1995) 323-5 (E.G. *Farrugia*).

7757 *a) Brown* Schuyler, Gnosis, theology and historical method; -- *b) Carroll* Scott T., Gnosticism and the classical tradition; -- *c) Desjardins* Michel, Judaism and Gnosticism; -- *d) Tiessen* Terrance, Gnosticism as heresy; the response of IRENAEUS; -- *e) O'Cleirigh* Padraig, Symbol and science in early Christian Gnosis: → 10,322, Hellenization 1991/4, 279-291 / 293-307 / 309-321 / 339-359 / 409-427.

7758 **Copenhaver** Brian P., Hermetica; the Greek Corpus hermeticum and the Latin Asclepius in a new English translation. C 1995, Univ. lxxxiii-320 p.; now pa. $ 18. 0-521-42543-3 [NTAb 38, p.142; 40, p.375]. -- [R]BoL (1995) 126 (L.L. *Grabbe*).

7759 *Dan* Joseph, Jewish Gnosticism ? : Jewish Studies Quarterly 2 (Tü 1995) 309-329.

7760 *DeConick* April, Becoming God's body; the KAVOD in Valentinianism: → 512, SBL Seminars 34 (1995) 23-56.

7761 **Desjardins** Michel R., Sin in Valentinianism: SBL.d 108, 1990 → 6,a496; 8,a818: [R]A(ustrl)BR 43 (1995) 94s (A.H. *Cadwallader*).

7762 *Edwards* M.J., The Epistle to Rheginus; Valentinianism in the fourth century: NT 37 (1995) 76-91.

7763 **Faivre** A., The eternal Hermes; from Greek god to alchemical magus [6 art. now all Eng.], [T]*Godwin* J. GR 1995, Phanes. 210 p. 39 pl. $ 35; pa. $ 19. 0-933999-53-4; -2-6 [NTAb 40, p.172].

7764 **Filoramo** Giovanni, A history of Gnosticism [L'attesa della fine 1983 → 64,9102], [T]*Alcock* Anthony, 1990 → 6,a474 ... 10,10160: [R]ChrCent 112 (1995) 1053-6 (R.A. *Segal*: rather a survey of themes; review includes also SINGER June and COULIANO J. but has more to say on JONAS H.; 'Gnostic' as a term often used to describe the modern world is unclear).

7765 **Flory** W.S., The Gnostic concept of authority and the Nag Hammadi documents: Mellen Biblical 33. Lewiston NY 1995, Mellen. viii-176 p. $ 80. 0-7734-2391-5 [NTAb 40,p.553].

7766 [E]**Foerster** Werner, *al.*, Die Gnosis [slightly revised anthology of 1969/76/80]. Mü 1995, Artemis & W. 1. Zeugnisse der Kirchenväter, 493 p. -- 2. Koptische und Mandäische Quellen, 499 p. -- 3. Der Manichäismus, 464 p. DM 198 alle 3. 3-7608-1105-1; -6-X.-7-8 [RStR 22,B.A. *Pearson*].

7767 **Fowden** G., The Egyptian Hermes; a historical approach to the late pagan mind. Princeton 1993 (= 1986 = pref.), Univ. xxv-334 p. $ 18. 0-691-02498-7. -- [R]BoL (1995)

129 (W.G.E. *Watson*: limpid).

7768 **Geisen** Richard, Antroposophie und Gnostizismus; Darstellung, Vergleich und theologische Kritik. Pd 1992, Schöningh. -- ^RThGL 85 (1995) 119-123 (M. *Kriele*).

7769 *Gignoux* Philippe, La doctrine du macrocosme-microcosme et ses origines gréco-gnostiques: → 94, Mem. KLÍMA O., Iranian 1994, 27-5.

7770 *Görg* Manfred, Bythos und Nun; zur ägyptischen Basis einer altchristlich-gnostischen Gottesidee: → 48, ^FDONNER, H., Meilenstein: ÄAT 30 (1995) 52-59; 2 fig.

7771 *Grech* Prosper, Lo gnosticismo; un'eresia cristiana : → 119, ^FMARA M.Grazia = Aug(ustinianum)R 35 (1995) 587-596.

7772 *Griffiths* J. Gwyn, Possible Egyptian elements in Tractate XIII of the Corpus Hermeticum: → 10,145, ^FWINTER E., Aspekte 1994, 97-102.

7773 *Griffiths* J. Gwyn, Divine judgement in the Hermetic writings: → 10,118, ^FSHORE A.F., The unbroken reed 1994, 125-137.

7774 *a) Hellholm* David, The mighty minority of Gnostic Christians; -- *b) Larsson* Edvin, How mighty was the mighty minority ? [*Juel* Donald. on Mark]: → 88, ^FJERVELL J., Mighty minorities ? ST 49 (1995) 41-66 / 93-105 [67-77].

7775 **Iwersen** Julia, Gnosis und Geschichte; gnostisches ich- und Weltverständnis im Spiegel der Geschichte des östlichen Mittelmeerraumes von Alexander dem Grossen bis ins zweite nachchristliche Jahrhundert. Ha 1994, Kovac. ix-163 p. 3-86064-235-9 [RStR 22,168, B.A. *Pearson*].

7776 **Janssens** Yvonne, Évangiles gnostiques: Homo Religiosus 15, 1991 → 7,a293; Fb 1000: ^RMelSR 52 (1995) 180-3 (C. *Cannuyer*).

7777 **Jonas** Hans (d.1993), Gnosis und spätantiker Geist [I. Die mythologische Gnosis = ³1964 (¹1934): II/1 = ²1966 (¹1954); von der Mythologie zur mystischen Philosophie]; II/2 never finished, here, ^E*Rudolph* Kurt, partly working with Jonas 1990-3, partly from published pieces (on PLOTINUS): FRLANT 159. Gö 1993, Vandenhoeck & R. xvi-410 p. DM 128. 3-525-53841-3 [RStR 22, 168, B.A. *Pearson*]. -- ^RRBBras 11 (1994) 678s (C. *Minette de Tillesse*); R(ech)SR 83 (1995) 135s (Madeleine *Scopello*).

7778 **Jonas** Hans, Lo gnosticismo, ^{TE}*Farina* Raffaele: Religione. T 1995, Soc. ed, internazionale. 438 p. 88-05-05503-4.

7779 *Kotansky* Roy, *Spier* Jeffrey, The 'horned hunter' on a lost Gnostic gem: HThR 88 (1995) 315-337.

7780 *Lampe* Peter, An early (Valentinian) Christian inscription in the Musei Capitolini: → 88, ^FJERVELL J.,: ST 49 (Oslo 1995) 79-92; 2 fig.

7781 **Löhr** Winrich Alfried, BASILIDES und seine Schule; eine Studie zur Theologie und Kirchengeschichte des zweiten Jahrhunderts [ev. Diss. Bonn 1993, ^D*Schäferdiek* K.: WUNT 83. Tü c. 1995, Mohr. x-414 p.; Bibliog. 338-382. 3-16-146300-5.

7782 *Lüdemann* Gerd, Concerning the history of earliest Christianity in Rome, l. VALENTINUS & MARCION; 2. PTOLEMAEUS & JUSTIN [< ZNW]: *JHiCr 2,1 (1995) 112-141 [NTAb 40,p.317].

7783 **McBride** Daniel, The Egyptian foundations of Gnostic thought: diss.^D*Redford* D. Toronto 1994. -- RTLv 27.p.556.

7784 *Magris* Aldo, Trasformazioni del modello biblico di Dio nello gnosticismo; → 488, ASEs 12 (1995) 233-51.

7785 **Markschies** Christoph, VALENTINUS gnosticus ?: WUNT 65, 1992 → 8,a820; 10,10177: ^RBiOr 52 (1995) 765-7 (J. *Helderman*); *CritRR 7 (1994) 301-3 (J. D. *Turner*); JAC 38 (1995) 173-7 (H.-M. *Schenke*); NedThT 49 (1995) 244s (G.P. *Luttikhuizen*); SNTU 19

(1994) 252-4 (F. *Weissengruber*).

7786 **Masaracchia** Agostino, Orfeo e l'Orfismo, Atti del seminario nazionale (Roma-Perugia 1985-1991): QuadUrb Atti 4, 1993 → 9,531: [R]RÉG 108 (1995) 231s (F. *Vian*).

7787 *a) Pearson* Birger A., Is Gnosticism a religion ? -- *b) Ries* Julien, La notion de religion dans les textes manichéens: -> 10,344*a*, Notion of religion 1990/4, 105-114 / 123-129

7788 **Perkins** Pheme, Gnosticism and the New Testament 1993 → 9,11121; 10,10169: [R]BiRe 11,5 (1995) 14s (S. *Davies*); CBQ 57 (1995) 820-2 (W.R. *Schoedel*); *CritRR 8 (1995) 276-8 (Deirdre *Good*); C(alvin)TJ 29 (1994) 602-4 (Verlyn D. *Verbrugge*); JAOS 115 (1995) 306s (Michel *Desjardins*); JRel 75 (1995) 555-7 (M.A. *Williams*); L(ex)TJ 29 (1995) 134s (V.C. *Pfitzner*); TS 56 (1995) 155-7 (J.D. *Turner*).

7789 **Procter** Everett, Christian controversy in Alexandria; CLEMENT's polemic against the Basilideans and Valentinians [diss. Santa Barbara, [D]*Pearson* B.]; AmUSt 7/172. NY 1995, Lang. xi-121 p. $ 38. 0-8204-2378-5 [NTAb 40, p.383; RStR 22,165, Ruth *Majercik*].

7790 **Quispel** Gilles, Gnosis als Weltreligion; die Bedeutung der Gnosis in der Antike[3] [Auflage; [1]1951, [2]1971]. Bern 1995, Origo. 144 p. 3-282-00037-5.

7791 *a) Rudolph* Kurt, 'Christlich' und 'Christentum' in der Auseinandesetzung zwischen 'Kirche' und 'Gnosis'; -- *b) Thomassen* Einar, The Platonic and the Gnostic 'demiurge'; -- *c) Sørensen* Jørgen P., The Egyptian background of the *hieròs lógos* (Corpus Hermeticum III): → 67, [F]GIVERSEN H., Apocryphon 1993, 192-214 / 226-244 / 215-225.

7792 *Scholer* David M., Bibliographia gnostica supplementum XXII / XXIII: NT 36 (1994) 58-96 / 37 (1995) 159-187.

7793 [E]**Scholer** David M., Gnosticism in the Early Church; a collection of [21 1964-88] scholarly essays: Studies in Early Christianity 5, 1993 → 9,11125; $ 66 [RStR 22,165, B.A. *Pearson*].

7794 **Scopello** Maddalena, Gli Gnostici [1991 → 8,a813]. 1993. -- [R]StCatt 39 (1995) 74s (S. *Tognoli*).

7795 *Scopello* Madeleine, Bulletin sur la Gnose [... iv. Manichaïka; vi. Coptica]: R(ech)SR 83 (1995) 127-163.

7796 *Scott* Alan B., Churches or books ? Sethian social organization: *JEarlyC 3 (1995) 109-122.

7797 **Scott** Thomas M., Egyptian elements in Hermetic literature: diss. Harvard Divinity, [D]*Brooten* Bernadette. CM 1987. 262 p. -- OIAc 10 (1994) 40.

7798 *Segal* R.A., Gnosticism, ancient and modern: CCen 112 (1995) 1053-6 [NTAb 40,p.318: J. SINGER, G. FILORAMO, & I.P. COULIANO: by selected aspects of both Gnosticism and modernity evaluated through modern eyes 'project onto gnosticism their own hopes, anxieties, and convictions'].

7799 **Segal** Robert A., The Gnostic [citations and influence in Carl Gustav] JUNG. Princeton / L 1992, Univ. / Routledge. $ 39.50; pa. $ 15. 0-691-09975-8; -1923-1 / 0-415-08038-X. -- Religion 25 (1995) 97s (M. *Howard*).

7800 *Smagina* Ye. B., 'The Gospel of the Egyptians', a monument to mythological Gnosticism, intr. tr. comm.: VDI 213 (1995) 230-251.

7801 **Smith** David B., Nativitos; an oratorio based on writings from the Gnostic Gospels: diss. Cincinnati 1995. 147 p. 95-38328. -- DissA 56 (1995s) p. 2479.

7802 **Sorel** Reynal, Orphée et l'Orphisme: QS(ais)J 3018. P 1995, Presses Univ. 128 p. 2-13-047210-9.

7803 **Stroumsa** Gedaliahu G., Savoir et salut; Gnoses de l'antiquité tardive 1992 → 8,316 ... 10,10172: [R]JQR 86 (1995) 195-7 (Paula *Fredriksen;* not 'Savior' as title).

7804 *a*) *Stroumsa* Gedaliahu G., Gnostic secret myths; -- *b*) *King* Karen L., Translating history; reframing Gnosticism in postmodernity [JONAS H.]: → 42, FCOLPE C., Tradition (1994) 26-41 / 264-277.

7805 **Wink** Walter, Cracking the Gnostic code; the powers in Gnosticism 1993 → 9,11121: RCBQ 57 (1995) 200s (Janet *Timbie*); *CritRR 7 (1994) 306-8 (Jorunn J. *Buckley*); JRel 75 (1995) 267s (H.W. *Attridge*).

7806 *a*) *Yamauchi* Edwin M., Gnosticism and early Christianity [response *Desjardins* Michel]; -- *b*) *Bos* Abraham P., Cosmic and meta-cosmic theology in Greek philosophy and Gnosticism [response *Arnal* William E., Aristotle and the Jewish God: → 10,322, Hellenization 1991/4, 29-61 [63-67] / 1-21 [23-28].

M1.5 **Mani**, *dualismus*; **Mandaei**

7807 *Albrile* Ezio, Iran e Gnosticismo; riflessioni sul retroterra iranico del Manicheismo: Salesianum 57 (1995) 691-713 [NTAb 40,p.503].

7808 EBauer J.R., AUGUSTINUS, De moribus .. Manichaeorum: CSEL 90. W 1992, Hoelder-PT. xxx-224 p. 3-209-0122-9 [ThLZ 119 (1994) 328].

7809 *a*) *Bianchi* Ugo, Sur la théologie et l'anthropologie de Mani; -- *b*) *Kasser* Rodolphe, Le manichéisme triomphant, rêve enflammé d'une communauté écrasée et souffrante (ManiH 22,3-23,12 en version française); -- *c*) *Pedersen* Nils A., Some comments on the relationships between Marcionism and Manichaeism: -- *d*) *Ries* Julien, L'âme du monde et la rédemption de la lumière dans le manichéisme: → 67, FGIVERSEN H., Apocryphon 1993, 19-28 / 83-94 / 166-177 / 178-191.

7810 **Böhlig** Alexander, *Markschies* Christoph, Gnosis und Manichäismus; Forschungen und Studien zu Texten von VALENTIN und MANI sowie zu den Bibliotheken von Nag Hammadi und Medinet Madi: BZNW 72. Berlin 1994, de Gruyter. xi-316 p. DM 148. 3-11-014294-5, -- RRStR 21 (1995) 330s (B.A. *Pearson*); VigChr 49 (1995) 95s (J. van *Oort*).

7811 **Bosson** Nathalie, Des deux royaumes du 'premier temps' (Kephalaia VI, VII, XXI, XXV, XXVII, LXIII & LXXIII de Mani en version française): Muséon 108 (1995) 1-38.

7812 **Buckley** Jorunn J., The scroll of exalted kingship [Oxford Drower Mandean 14). NHv 1993, AOS. xix-106 p., 4 pl. $ 22. -- RJAOS 115 (1995) 526s (E.M. *Yamauchi*).

7813 *Decret* François, Le manichéisme présentait-11 en Afrique et à Rome des particularismes régionaux distinctifs ?: Aug(ustinianum)R 34 (1994) 5-40.

7814 **Deutsch** Nathaniel, The Gnostic imagination; Gnosticism, Mandaeism, and Merkabah mysticism: *JeSt 13. Lei 1995, Brill. x-163 p. 90-04-10264-7.

7815 **Gardner** Iain, The Kephalaia of the teacher; the edited Coptic Manichaean texts in translation with commentary: NHManich 37. Lei 1995, Brill. xli-307 p. *f* 170. 90-04-10248-5 [NTAb 40, p.376].

7816 *Gardner* Iain, Glory be to Mani! : → 96, FKRAUSE M., Divitiae Aegypti 1995, 105-112.

7817 **Hutter** Manfred, Manis kosmogonische Šābuhragān-Texte 1992 → 8,a833; 10,10186: RNumen 41 (1994) 204s (W. *Klein*).

7818 **Klein** W.W., Die Argumentation in den griechisch-christlichen antimanichaica: StOR 19, D1991: RJRAS (1994) 258s (S.N.C. *Lieu*); Kler 23 (1991) 346-8 (N. *Matsoukas* G).

7819 *Lieu* Samuel N.C., From Parthian into Chinese; the transmission of Manichaean texts in Central Asia: OLZ 90 (1995) 357-372.

7820 **Lindt** Paul Van, The names of Manichaean mythological figures; a comparative study on terminology in the Coptic sources: StOR 26. Wsb 1992, Harrassowitz. 247 p. DM 138.

3-447-03312-6. -- ᴿBiOr 52 (1995) 678s (G.G. *Stroumsa*); JRAS (1994) 259-261 (S.N.C. *Lieu*); Numen 42 (1995) 93s (W. *Klein*).

7821 **Lupieri** Edmondo, I Mandei, gli ultimi gnostici: *BtCuR 61, 1993: → 9,11157: ᴿEstTrin 29 (1995) 497s (X. *Pikaza*); Lat 61 (1995) 204s (R. *Penna*); SNTU 19 (1994) 254-6 (F. *Weissengruber*).

7822 **Macuch** Rudolf, Neumandäische Texte im Dialekt von Ahwaz; SV 12. Wsb 1993, Harrassowitz. xxxviii-444 p.; 1 pl.; 2 maps. DM 194. 3-447-03382-7. -- ᴿThLZ 120 (1995) 124-6 (K. *Rudolph*).

7823 *Malone* Joseph L., La circonscription prosodique en Mandéen classique: *LOrA 5s (1995) 233-257.

7824 *Mancini* Marco, A proposito di prestiti partici in mandaico: *hambaga* [con] index iranicus a T. NÖLDEKE: AION 55 (1995) 82-95.

7825 *Quispel* Gilles, Transformation through vision in Jewish gnosticism and the Cologne Mani Codex: VigChr 49 (1995) 189-191.

7826 **Reeves** John C., Jewish lore in Manichaean cosmogony; studies in The Book of the Giants traditions; HUC 1992 → 8,a842 ... 10,10192: ᴿ*A(sn)JS 20 (1995) 396-9 (M.E. *Stone*); *CritRR 7 (1994) 423s (A.F. *Segal*: an astoundingly learned detective story); JSSt 40 (1995) 161-3 (S.N.C. *Lieu*).

7827 **Richter** S., Exegetisch-literarkritische Untersuchungen von Herakleidespsalmen des koptisch-manichäischen Psalmenbuches: *ArbSpÄ 5, 1994 → 10,10193: ᴿOCP 61 (1995) 623-5 (P. *Luisier*) [RHE 91,34*].

7828 *a) Ries* Julien, L'eschatologie manichéenne selon les textes occidentaux et orientaux; - - *b) Rudolph* Kurt, Zweierlei Jenseitsreisen; die altägyptische Nachtfahrt der Sonne und die gnostisch-mandäische Himmelsreise der Seele: → 96, ᶠKRAUSE M., Divitiae Aegypti 1995, 264-270 / 271-8.

7829 *a) Ries* Julien, Notes de lecture du Contra epistulam fundamenti d'AUGUSTIN à la lumière de quelques documents manichéens; -- *b) Decret* François, La christologie manichéenne dans la controverse d'Augustin avec Fortunatus : → 119, ᶠMARA M.Grazia = Aug(ustinianum)R 35 (1995) 537-548 / 443-455.

7830 *a) Ries* Julien, Manichéens, Pauliciens, Bogomiles, Cathares; transmission et fonctionnement des systèmes dualistes dans l'Europe médiévale; -- *b) Sundermann* Werner, Eine Liste manichäischer Götter in soghdischer Sprache: → 42, ᶠCOLPE C., Tradition (1994) 154-164 / 452-462; 1 pl.

7831 *Scopello* M., Vérités et contre-vérités; la vie de Mani selon les Acta Archelai [episcopi, chap. 61]: Apocrypha 6 (1995) 209-234 [NTAb 40, p.502].

7832 *Sundermann* Werner, Iranische Personennamen der Manichäer [Symposion Iranistik, Wien 4.-5. Nov. 1994]: *Sprache 36 (1994) 244-270.

7833 *Tongerloo* Alois van,Reflections on the Manichean *noûs:*→655,Symposium1991/5,302-15

7834 **Villey** André, Psaumes des errants; écrits manichéens du Fayyûm: SGM 4, 1994 → 10,10198: ᴿGreg 76 (1995) 622s (G. *Pelland*); VigChr 49 (1995) 97-99 (J. van *Oort*).

7835 **Wurst** Gregor, Das Bêmafest der ägyptischen Manichäer: *ArbSpätant&KoptÄg 8. Altenberge 1995, Oros. viii-258 p.; Bibliog. 237-248. 2-503-50526-0.

M2.1 **Nag' Hammadi**, *generalia*

7836 **Charron** Régine, Concordance des textes de Nag Hammadi, le Codex III: BCNH.conc 3. Sainte-Foy 1995, Univ. Laval. xxx11-600 p. 2-7637-7401-6 (Peeters 90-6881-674-5).

7837 **Charron** Régine, Concordance NHC-7, 1992 → 8,a849; 10,10205: [R]BiOr 52 (1995) 419-421 (H.G. *Bethge*).

7838 **Cherix** Pierre, Concordance des textes de Nag Hammadi, le Codex I: BCNH. conc 4. Sainte-Foy 1995, Univ. Laval. ix-989 p. 2-7637-7429-6 (Peeters 90-6831-675-3).

7839 [E]**Evans** Craig A., *Webb* R.L., *Wiebe* R.A., Nag Hammadi texts and the Bible; a synopsis and index: NTTSt 18, 1993 → 10,10205*: [R]BoL (1994) 135s (L.L. *Grabbe*); JAOS 115 (1995) 305s (Michel *Desjardins*); JETS 38 (1995) 112s (R. *Youngblood*); RS(to)LR 31 (1995) 321-3 (C. *Gianotto*).

7840 **Flory** Wayne S., The Gnostic concept of authority and the Nag Hammadi documents: Biblical Press 33. Lewiston NY 1995, Mellen. xvii-176 p.; bibliog. 161-171. 0-7734-2391-5.

7841 **Khosroyev** A., Die Bibliothek von Nag Hammadi; einige Probleme des Christentums in Ägypten während der ersten Jahrhunderte: ASKÄ 7. Altenberge 1995, Oros. x-195 p. DM 60. 3-89375-107-6 [RHE 90 (1995) 368*; RStR 22,168, B.A. *Pearson*]. -- [R]OCP 61 (1995) 201-213 (P. *Luisier*, sur l'appendice, Lettres de s. Antoine).

7842 *Khosroyev* Alexandr L., Bemerkungen über die vermutlichen Besitzer der Nag-Hammadi-Texte: → 96, [F]KRAUSE M., Divitiae Aegypti 1995, 200-5.

7843 *a) Painchaud* Louis, La classification des textes de Nag Hammadi et le phénomène des réécritures: - *b) Pasquier* Anne, La 'bibliothèque' de Nag Hammadi; traces d'un enseignement gnostique cohérent; - *c) Williams* Michael A., Interpreting the Nag Hammadi Library as 'Collection(s) in the history of Gnosticism(s)'; *d) Funk* Wolf-Peter, The linguistic aspect of classifying the Nag Hammadi codices: → 522, Textes 1993/5, 51-86 / 85-105 / 3-50 / 107-147.

7844 *Robinson* James M., The significance of the Nag Hammadi library for contemporary theology and early Christianity: Metanoia 4 (Praha 1994) 120-133; franç. 133.

7845 [E]**Robinson** James M., The Nag Hammadi library in English[3rev] 1988 → 4,b460 ... 10,10208: [R]JETS 37 (1994) 438s (M.R. *Fairchild*).

7846 **Slavenburg** J., *Gaudemans* W.G., Nag Hammadi geschriften, I. Een integrale vertaling van alle teksten uit de Nag Hammadi-vondst en de Berlijnse Codex, 1. Jezus van Nazareth en Hermes Trismegistos. Deventer 1994, Ankh-Hermes. 459 p. *f* 99. -- [R]G(ereformeerd)TT 94 (1994) 195s (R. *Roukema*).

M2.2 *Evangelium etc. Thomae* -- **The Gospel of Thomas**

7847 *Arnal* William E., The rhetoric of marginality; apocalypticism, Gnosticism, and Sayings Gospels: HThR 88 (1995) 471-494.

7848 *Baarda* T., 'The cornerstone' an Aramaism in the Diatessaron and the Gospel of Thomas ?: NT 37 (1995) 285-300.

7849 *a) Diebner* Bernd Jörg, Bemerkungen zur 'Mitte' [core, Leitfaden: aber genau Nr 125 der 249 bei KASSER] des Thomas-Evangeliums; -- *b) Wilson* Robert M., The Gospel of Thomas reconsidered ['must preserve some genuine Jesus-traditions' (PATTERSON S. 1993)]: → 96, [F]KRAUSE M., Divitiae Aegypti 1995, 77-84.

7850 **Eccles** Lance, Introductory Coptic reader [40 out of 114 Thomas-Logia] 1991 → 8,a860; 0-931-74582-9: [R]JEA 81 (1995) 274s (A. *Alcock*).

7851 **Fieger** Michael, Das Thomasevangelium [Diss. [D]*Gnilka* J. München 1989 -- BZ 39 (1995) 315] 1991 → 7,a302; 8,a862: [R]TorJT 11 (1995) 94 (S. *Brown*).

7852 *Frenschkowski* M., The enigma of the three words of Jesus in Gospel of Thomas logion

13 [perhaps gnostic *egō sú eimi*]: *JHiCr 1 (1994) 73-84 [NTAb 39, p.307].

7853 **Patterson** Stephen J., The Gospel of Thomas and Jesus 1993 → 9,11183; 10,10214: [R]JBL 114 (1995) 329-331 (C.W. *Hedrick*); TJT 10 (1994) 264s (W.E. *Arnal*).

7854 *Riley* Gregory J., *a)* A note on the text of Gospel of Thomas 37; -- *b)* Influence of Thomas Christianity on Luke 12:14 and 5:39: HThR 88 (1995) 179-181 / 229-235.

7855 **Ruysbeek** Erik van [= André van *Eyck*], *Messing* Marcel, Das Thomas-Evangelium; seine östliche Spiritualität. Dü 1993, Walter. 164 p. DM 29,80.-- [R]RBBras 11 (1994) 681s (*C. Minette de Tillesse*).

7856 *Schüngel* Paul, Ein Vorschlag, EvTho 114 neu zu übersetzen [Jesus said, 'Who shall drag her in order that I may make her male ?']: NT 36 (1994) 394-401.

7857 *a) Sevrin* Jean-Marie, Remarques sur le genre littéraire de l'Évangile selon Thomas (II,2); - *b) Kuntzmann* Raymond, Le Livre de Thomas (NH II,7) et la tradition de Thomas: → 522, Textes 1993/5, 263-278 / 295-309.

7858 *Valantasis* Richard, The nuptial chamber revisited; the *Acts of Thomas* and cultural intertextuality: → 512, SBL Seminars 34 (1955) 380-393.

7859 *Zur* Yiphtah, Parallels between Acts of Thomas 6-7 and 4Q184: RdQ 16 (1993-5) 103-7.

M2.3 *Singula scripta* -- **Apocryphon of John and other titles**

7860 *Funk* Wolf-Peter, Die ersten Seiten des Codex III von Nag Hammadi [ApocrJoh]; → 96, [F]KRAUSE M., Divitiae Aegypti 1995, 99-104.

7861 *a) Gilhus* Ingvild Sælid, The perception of spiritual reality; Apocryphon of John (NHC II,1) and the problem of knowledge; -- *b) Pearson* Birger, Apocryphon Johannis revisited; -- *c) Lindt* Paul van, Adamas, the belligerent hero; -- *d) Otzen* Benedikt, The paradise trees [NHC II,69-72] in Jewish apocalyptic: → 67, [F]GIVERSEN H., Apocryphon 1993, 50-59 / 155-165 / 95-105 / 140-154.

7862 -- *King* Karen L., The body and society in PHILO and the Apocryphon of John: → 132*, Mem. MOEHRING H., School of Moses 1995, 82-97.

7863 *Quack* Joachim F., Dekane und Gliedervergottung; altägyptische Traditionen im Apokryphon Johannis [NHC II und IV]: JAC 38 (1995) 97-122.

7864 *Śiśmanian* A.A., Sémiologie et ontologie; quelques observations méthodologiques à partir d'une 'spectroscopie' de l'Apocryphon de Jean (NHC II.1.2.25-9.24) : OL(ov)P 25 (1994) 143-167; 26 (1995) 51-76.

7865 **Waldstein** Michael [→ K2.5], *Wisse* Frederik, The Apocryphon of John; synopsis of Nag Hammadi Codices II,1; III,1; and IV,1 with BG 8502,2: *NHManich 33. Lei 1995, Brill. xii-244 p. *f* 150. 90-04-10395-3 [NTAb 40, p.387]. → 6886-8 supra.

7866 *a) Dubois* Jean Daniel, La sotériologie valentinienne du Traité tripartite (NH 1,5): - *b) Mahé* Jean-Pierre, Le témoignage véritable et quelques écrits valentiniens de Nag Hammadi; - *c) Thomassen* Einar, Notes pour la délimitation d'un corpus valentinien à Nag Hammadi; - *d) Morard* Françoise, Les apocalypses du Codex V de Nag Hammadi:→ 522, Textes 1993/5: 221-232 / 233-242 / 243-259 / 341-357.

7867 *Emmel* Stephen, On the restoration of two passages in A Valentinian Exposition (NHC XI,2): BASPap 31 (1994) 5-10.

7868 *García Bazán* Francisco, Ricos y pobres, las gratificaciones del injusto mammón; el Testimonio de la Verdad (CNH IX 3, 68, 3-4): RevBib(Arg) 57 (1995) 29-39.

7869 *Halford* Rosemary, Trimorphic Protennoia and the wisdom tradition: → 10,322,

Hellenization 1991/4, 271-8.

7870 **Painchaud** Louis, L'écrit sans titre; traité sur l'origine du monde [NH II,5 et XIII,2 et Brit.Lib.Or. 4926[1]): BCNH.t 21. Lv 1995, Peeters. xvi-622 p. 90-6831-702-4

7871 *Painchaud* Louis, The literary contacts between the writing without title On the origin of the world (CG II,5 and XIII,2) and Eugnostos the Blessed (CG III.3 and V.1): JBL 114 (1995) 81-101.

7872 ᴱ**Parrot** Douglas M., NH Codices III,3-4 and V,1 .. [Eugnostos and very similar Sophia]: NHSt 7, 1991 → 7,a287 ... 10,10207: ᴿBiOr 52 (1995) 675s (G.G. *Stroumsa*); JAC 38 (1995) 177-181 (H.-M. *Schenke*).

7873 ᵀᴱ**Plisch** Uwe-Karsten, Die Auslegung der Erkenntnis (NHC XI,1): Diss. ᴰ*Schenke* H.M. Berlin 1994. -- ThRv 91 (1995) 93.

7874 **Poirier** Paul-Hubert, La tonnerre, intellect parfait [NH VI,2]: BCNH.t 22. Lv 1995, Peeters. xix-372 p.; bibliog. ix-xviii. 90-6831-738-5

7875 *Poirier* Paul-Hubert, [Tonnerre] *a)* Traits isiaques dans un triaté de Nag Hammadi; à propos de NH VI,2: → 199, ᶠTRAN TAM TINH V., Tranquillitas 1995, 475-481; -- *b)* Juifs et Grecs; la médiation barbare: ScEs 46 (1994) 293-307 [NTAb 39, p.459].

7876 *a) Poirier* Paul-Hubert, Interprétation et situation du traité Le tonnerre, intellect parfait (NH VI,2); -- *b) Barry* Catherine, Un exemple de réécriture à Nag Hammadi, La sagesse de Jésus-Christ (BG,3; NH III,4): -- *c) Roberge* Michel, La Paraphrase de Sem (NH VII,1) et le problème des trois natures; -- *d) Turner* John D., Typologies of the Sethian Gnostic treatises from Nag Hammadi: → 522, Textes 1993/5, 311-340 / 131-168 / 279-293 / 169-217.

7877 **Schoenborn** U., Diverbium salutis; Studien zur Interdependenz von literarischer Struktur und theologischer Intention des gnostischen Dialogs, ausgeführt an der koptischen 'Apokalypse des Petrus' aus Nag Hammadi (NHC VII,3) [ev. Hab.-Diss. Marburg 1993, ᴰ*Horbury* W.]: StUNT 19. Gö 1995, Vandenhoeck & R. 260 p.; Bibliog. 241-260. DM 84. 3-525-53374-8 [NTAb 40, p.384].

7878 **Zandee** J., The teaching of Silvanus (NHC VII,4) 1991 → 7,a324 ... 10,10219: ᴿRechSR 33 (1995) 139-171 (Madeleine *Scopello*).

7879 -- *Sumney* Jerry L., The teaching of Silvanus as a Gnostic work: JRelSt 19 (1995)145-61

M3.1 *Quid est religio ?* -- **What is religion ?**

7880 *Amiet* Pierre, La naissance des dieux: approche iconographique: RB 102 (1995) 481-505; Eng. 481.

7881 *Ammermann* Norbert, Religiosity -- indefinable feeling or specific theory of knowledge ?: JE(mp)T 8,2 (1995) 82-101; 6 fig.

7882 ᴱ**Bianchi** Ugo [p.xix-xxi, Perspectives; 919-121, concluding remarks], *al.*, The notion of 'religion' in comparative research, 16th Congress 1990/4 → 10,344*a* [ZkT 117 (1995) 357s (K.H. *Neufeld*)]; p. 63-73, *Irmscher* Johannes, Der Terminus *religio* und seine antiken Entsprechungen im philologischen und religionsgeschichtlichen Vergleich; p. 131-9, *Rudolph* Kurt, Inwieweit ist der Begriff 'Religion' eurozentrisch ?

7883 **Capps** Walter H., Religious studies; the making of a discipline. Mp 1995, Fortress. xxiii-368 p. $ 29 pa. 0-8006-2535-8 [ThD 42.359].

7885 *Coste* René, La religion .. objet d'entente ou de division entre les peuples ? : E(spr)eV 105 (1995) 684-8.

7886 **Emmerson** Richard K., *Herzman* Ronald B., The apocalyptic imagination in medieval literature: Middle Ages. Ph 1992, Univ. Pennsylvania. xi-244 p. $ 28, -- ᴿChH 64 (1995)

466-8 (K. *Madigan*).

7887 **Hatzfeld** Henri, Les racines de la religion; tradition, rituel, valeurs: Esprit. P 1993, Seuil. 270 p. -- [R]RevSR 69 (1995) 266s (E. *Boespflug*).

7888 *Karavanić I.*, The origins of symbolics and religious rites in prehistoric hunters and gatherers: ObŹ 50 (1995) 25-44; Eng. 45.

7889 [E]**Kerber** Walter, Der Begriff der Religion: Fragen einer neuen Weltkultur 9. Mü 1992, Kindt. 220 p. DM 29,80. 3-925412-14-X. -- [R]Bijdragen 56 (1995) 234 (L. *Minnema*).

7890 **Laube** Martin, Im Bann der Sprache; das Problem der religiösen Eigenständigkeit in der analytischen Religionsphilosophie: ev. Diss. [D]*Rohls*. München 1995. -- ThRv Beilage 92/2, xi.

7891 **Lee Seong-Woo**, Das Wesen der Religion und ihr Verhältnis zu Wissenschaft und Sittlichkeit bei Wilhelm HERRMANN; kath. Diss.[D]*Greshake* G. Freiburg/B 1994. -- ThRv 91,95.

7892 *McCutcheon* Russell T., The category 'religion' in recent publications; a critical survey: Numen 42 (1995) 284-309.

7893 **Masuzawa** Tomoko [f.], In search of dreamtime; the quest for the origin of religion. Ch 1993, Univ. vii-223 p. $ 45; pa. $ 15. -- [R]CrossCur 45 (1995s) 426 .428 (F.A. *Salamone*); JRel 75 (1995) 301s (R.A. *Segal*).

7894 *Moore* Peter, Religions as systems: → 184, [F]SMART N., Aspects of religion 1994, 39-57.

7895 *Pailin* D.A., The confused and confusing story of natural religion: Religion 24 (L 1994) 199-212 [< ZIT 95, p.69]

7896 **Reynolds** Vernon, *Tanner* Ralph, The social ecology of religion [=[2]The biology of religion 1983]. Oxford 1995, UP. vii-322 p. £ 30; pa. £ 13. 0-19-506973-0; -4-9. [ThD 43,85] -- [R]*TBR 8,2 (1995s) 61 (M. *Conway*).

7897 -- *Arranz Rodrigo* Marceliano, La sonrisa de la dama de Elche; en torno a los intentos de explicar el fenómeno religioso desde la Biología : Rel(y)Cult 41 (1995) 745-772.

7898 **Saler** Benson, Conceptualizing religion; immanent anthropologists, transcendent natives, and unbounded categories: Numen.s 56, 1993 → 9,11362: [R]Numen 42 (1995) 78-82 (D. *Wiebe*); ScrT(Pamp) 37 (1995) 379s (F. *Conesa*).

7899 **Strenski** Ivan, Religion in relation; method, application. and moral location 1993, Univ → 9,11370; 10,10330: [R]JRel 75 (1995) 154s (Laurie L. *Patton*); Numen 41 (1994) 98-101 (D. *Wiebe*).

7900 **Yandell** Keith, The epistemology of religious experience. C 1993, Univ. viii-371 p. $ 55. 0-521-37426-X. -- [R]C(hr)ScR 25 (1995s) 214-6 (A.J. *Dell'Olio*); FAP(hil) 12 (1995) 133-9 (R.M. *Gale*); JRel 75 (1995) 297-9 (Carol *Zaleski*).

7901 **Young** Dudley, Origins of the sacred; the ecstasies of love and war. NY 1995, Harper Perennial. xiii-493 p.; bibliog. 463-8. 0-06-097511-3.

7902 *Zondag* Hessel J., Religion in modern society: JE(mp)T 5,2 (1992) 63-73. --

M3.2 **Historia** *comparationis religionum,* **centra, scholae**

7903 *Baccarini* Emilio, A.J. HESCHEL, Il pluralismo religioso come volontà di Dio: NuovaUm 17,5 (1995) 109-120.

7904 BARTH: *Green* Garrett, Challenging the religious studies canon; Karl Barth's theory of religion: JRel 75 (1995) 473-486.

7905 *Belier* Wouter W., Arnold VAN GENNEP and the rise of French sociology of religion: Numen 41 (1994) 141-162.

7906 BRADLEY's [1846-1924] philosophy of religion: RelSt 31 (1995) 285-301 (W. J. *Mander*).

7907 **Broadribb** Donald, The mystical chorus; JUNG and the religious dimension. Alexandria NSW 1995, Dwyer. 276 p. 1-86439-019-6. -- R*TBR 8,3 (1995s) 4 (Margaret *Yee*).

7908 **Cain** Seymour, Gabriel MARCEL's theory of religious experience: AmUSt 7/182. NY P.Lang. xv-205 p. $ 41. 0-8204-2595-8 [< ThD 43,357].

7909 *Cave* Eric, A LEIBNIZian account of why belief in the Christian mysteries is justified: RelSt 31 (1995) 463-473.

7910 **Demange** Pierre, L'essence dela religion selon SCHLEIERMACHER: BtAPh 53. P 1991, Beauchesne. -- RFilTeo 8 (1994) 524-7 (S. *Sorrentino*).

7911 DUMÉZIL: **Belier** Wouter W., Decayed gods .. Dumézil 1991 → 7,a390 ... 9,11712*: JAAR 63 (1995) 370-3 (B. *Erling*).

7912 -- *Schlerath* Bernfried, Georges Dumézil und die Rekonstruktion der indogermanischen Kultur I: Kratylos 40 (1995) 1-48.

7913 DURKHEIM: *Hawkins* M.J., Durkheim on occupational corporations; an exegesis and interpretation: JHId 55 (1994) 461-481.

7914 -- *Sánchez Capdequí* Celso, Reactualización del pensamiento religioso de E. DURKHEIM: EDeusto 43,2 (1995) 191-210.

7915 **Durkheim** Émile, Las formas elementales de la vida religiosa [1912], T. M 1993, Alianza. 696 p. -- RScrT(Pamp) 37 (1995) 383s (F. *Conesa*).

7916 ELIADE: *Montanari* Enrico, Eliade e GUÉNON: SMSR 61 (1995) 131-149.

7917 -- **Keshavjee** Shafique. Mircea ELIADE et la coïncidence des opposés ou L'existence en duel [diss.]. Bern 1993, Lang. [xxi-] 477 p. Fs 49. 3-906750-83-3. -- RFV 94,2 (1995) 84-86 (G. *Vahanian*); RTL 26 (1995) 502-4 (J. *Scheuer*).

7918 -- **Wachtmann** Christian, Der Religionsbegriff bei Mircea ELIADE; ev. Diss. DTrowitzsch. Münster 1995. -- ThRv Beilage 92/2, xiii.

7919 EMERSON: *Wilson* P. Eddy, Emerson and DEWEY on natural piety: JRel 75 (1995) 329-346.

7920 E**Fraijo** M., Filosofía de la religión; estudios y textos. M 1994, Trotta. 774 p. -- RCommunio (Sev) 28 (1995) 98-100 (M. *Sánchez*).

7921 FREUD: **Elder** Charles R., The Freudian critique of religion; remarks on its meaning and conditions: JRel 75 (1995) 347-370.

7922 HABERMAS: **Meyer** William J., Private faith or public religion? An assessment of [Jürgen] Habermas's changing view of religion: JRel 75 (1995) 371-391.

7923 **Hall** David L., Richard RORTY, prophet and poet of the new pragmatism. Albany 1994, SUNY. 290 p. -- RAmJTP 16 (1995) 217-221 (J.W. *Robbins*).

7924 **Hall** Gerald V., Raimon PANIKKAR's hermeneutics of religious pluralism: diss. Catholic Univ, DHappel S. Wsh 1994. 354 p. 94-18584. - D(iss)AI 55 (1994s) p.301.

7925 HEGEL: **Jamros** Daniel P., The human shape of God; religion in Hegel's Phenomenology of Spirit. NY 1994, Paragon. x-289 p. $ 30. 1-55778-703-4 [ThD 42,372].

7926 -- E**Kolb** David, New perspectives on Hegel's philosophy of religion. Albany 1992, SUNY. 224 p. $ 44.50; pa. $ 15. -- RJRel 75 (1995) 127s (A. *Kyongsuk Min*).

7927 -- **Kruck** Gunter, HEGELs Religionsphilosophie der absoluten Subjektivität und die Grundzüge des spekulativen Theismus Christian Hermann WEISSes [Diss. 1993]: Philosophische Theologie 4. W 1994, Passagen. 252 p. -- RFilTeo 9 (1995) 662s (H.J. *Adriaanse*).

7928 -- **Schlitt** Dale M., Divine subjectivity; understanding HEGEL's philosophy of religion.

Toronto 1990, Assoc. Univ. 344 p. -- ^RRTL 26 (1995) 364 (E. *Brito*).

7929 HICK: *Begley* John, Philosophy of the world religions; the views of John Hick: Aus(tralas)CR 72 (1995) 306-315.

7930 **Hick** John, The metaphor of God incarnate; Christology in a pluralist age. LvL 1993, W-Knox. x-180 p. $ 17 pa. -- ^RC(alvin)TJ 29 (1994) 578-580 (C.H. *Pinnock*: high-level, important, doubly wrong).

7931 *Hick* John, Religious pluralism and the divine; a response to Paul EDDY]: RelSt [30 (1994) ..] 31 (1995) 31 (1995) 417-420.

7932 **Hick** John, *a)* A Christian theology of religion; the rainbow of faiths [underlying all is 'the Real']. LvL 1995, W-Knox. x-160. $ 15. 0-664-25596-5 [RStR 22,137, B. *Stetson*]. [= ?] *b)* The rainbow of faiths; critical dialogues on religious pluralism. L 1995, SCM. x-160 p. 0-334-02608-3.

7933 **Hick** John, Disputed questions in theology and philosophy of religion 1993 → 9,11240; 10,10254: ^RRelSt 31 (1995) 399s (P. *Byrne*).

7934 ^FHICK John, God, truth and reality, ^E**Sharma** Arvind 1993 → 9,65*:   ^RHeythJ 36 (1995) 232s (G. *Loughlin*: the new paganism, sometimes called pluralism).

7935 HUME: *Herdt* Jennifer, Opposite sentiments; Hume's fear of faction and the philosophy of religion: AmJTP 16 (1995) 245-259.

7936 -- *Segal* R.A., Hume's 'Natural history of religion' and the beginning of the social scientific study of religion: Religion 24 (L 1994) 225-234 [< ZIT 95,p.69]

7937 **James** George A., Interpreting religion; the phenomenological approaches of Pierre Daniël CHANTEPIE DE LA SAUSSAYE, W.Brede KRISTENSEN, and Gerardus VAN DER LEEUW. Wsh 1995, Catholic University of America. xiii-304 p. $ 60. 0-8132-0831-9 [ThD 43,371],
-----

7939 JAMES W.: *a) Cooper* Wesley E., JAMES's God: -- *b) Hallberg* Fred W., Neo-Kantian constraints on legitimate religious beliefs: AmJTP 16 (1995) 261-277 / 279-298.

7940 -- **Croce** Paul J., Science and religion in the era of William James, 1. Eclipse of certainty, 1820-1880. Chapel Hill 1995, Univ. N. Carolina. xxi-350 p. $ 42.50; pa. $ 18. 0-8078-2200-0; -4506-X [ThD 43,62].

7941 -- *Cosgrove* Brian, 'We cannot do without any view' -- J.J. NEWMAN, William JAMES and the case against scepticism: I(r)ThQ 61 (1995) 32-41.

7942 -- *Funkenstein* Amos, The polytheism of William JAMES: JHId 55 (1994) 99-111.

7943 -- **Graham** George P., William JAMES and the affirmation of God. NY 1992, P.Lang. 237 p. $ 40 [RStR 22,51, R.F. *Scharlemann*].

7944 -- **Hadley** Mark, Religious thinking in an age of disillusionment; William JAMES and Ernst TROELTSCH on the possibilities of a science of religion: diss. Brown, ^D*Twiss* S. Providence 1995 [< RStR 22, p.270].

7945 -- *Kather* Regine, Die Vielfalt menschlicher Erfahrung; der Psychologe und Philosoph William James: GuL 67 (1994) 329-345.

7946 -- **Lamberth** David C., Squaring logic and life; metaphysics, experience, and religion in William James's philosophical worldview; diss. Harvard, ^D*Niebuhr* R.R. CM 1994. 317 p. 95-14854. -- HThR 88 (1995) 532; DissA 56 (1995s) p. 220; RStR 22,p.270.

7947 -- **Ramsey** Bennett, Submitting to freedom; the religious vision of William James 1993 → 9,11264; 10,10268: ^RJRel 75 (1995) 326s (J.F. *Byrnes*); RRelRes 35 (1993s) 283 (Susan F. *Greenwood*).

7948 -- *Spohn* W.C., William JAMES on religious experience; an elitist account ? : AmJTP 15 (1994) 27-42 [< ZIT 95, p.113].

7949 -- **James** William, Was ist Pragmatismus ? [1907], [T]*Jerusalem* W. Weinheim1994, Beltz. 108 p. DM 24. 3-89547-060-0. -- [R]*ZnTg 2 (1995) 319s (M. *Heesch*).

7950 *Jaspard* Bernd, Theologische Mystikforschung vor der Aufklärung: ThLZ 120 (1995) 203-218.

7951 KANT: **Odero** José Miguel, La fe en Kant. Pamplona 1992, Univ. Navarra. 626 p. $ 22.40. -- [R]JRel 75 (1995) 133s (A. *Lopez)*

7952 -- (= 7939*b*) *Hallberg* Fred W., Neo-Kantian constraints on legitimate religious belief: AmJTP 16 (1995) 279-298.

7953 [E]**Kreck** Volkhard, *Tyrell* Hartmann, Religionssoziologie um 1900: Religion in der Gesellschaft 1.. Wü 1995, Ergon. 377 p. DM 44. 3-028034-57-X [ThRv 92,86, tit.pp.].

7954 *Lange* Dietz, Religionsphilosophische Entwürfe: ThR 60 (1995) 300-315.

7955 *Lasić* Hrvoye, Phenomenology of religion -- origins and historical development: ObnŽiv 49 (1994) 25-40 Croatian; 41 Eng. (339-348).

7956 **Lehmkühler** Karsten. Kultus und Theologie: Dogmatik und Exegese in der religionsgeschichtichen Schule: Diss. [D]*Slenczka* R. Erlangen 1995. 327 p. -- RTLv 27, p.526.

7957 *Lerner* Berel D., Understanding a (secular) primitive society [Mary DOUGLAS, Heathen Darkness 1975, on 'the myth of primitive piety']: RelSt 31 (1995) 303-9.

7958 *Mason* David R., [Langdon] GILKEY on 'God and the world'; an appraisal: AmJTP 16 (1995) 315-334.

7960 *a)* **Neville** Robert, Highroad around modernism. Albany 1992, SUNY . -- *b)* *Wyschogrod* Edith, Taking the low road; postmodernism and interreligious conversation; -- *c) Gulick* Walter, Neville's projects of reconstruction and recovery; how firm a foundation ? -- *d) Cobb* John B.[J], Creation ex nihilo and a theology of religions: AmJTP 16 (' R. Neville's theology: basis for interfaith dialogue ?' 1995) [189] / 189-197 / 199-208 / 209-212.

7961 [E]**Niewöhner** Friedrich, Klassiker der Religionsphilosophie, von Platon bis Kierkegaard. Mü 1995, Beck. 396 p.; ill. DM 88. 3-406-39912-6 [ThRv 92,180].

7962 *O'Neill* J.C., GUNKEL versus WELLHAUSEN; the unfinished task of the Religionsgeschichtliche Schule: *JHiCr 2,2 (1995) 115-121.

7963 OTTO: *Almond* Philip C., Rudolf Otto and Buddhism: → 184, [F]SMART N., Aspects of religion 1994, 59-71.

7964 -- **Sequeri** P.A., Estetica e teologia; l'indicibile emozione del Sacro: R. OTTO, A. SCHÖNBERG, M. HEIDEGGER. Mi 1993, Glossa. 229 p. L[m] 25. -- [R]Asprenas 42 (1995) 131s (F. *Asti)*; StPat(av) 42 (1995) 751s (V. *Bortolin)*.

7965 -- *Paden* William E., Before 'The Sacred' became theological; DURKHEIM and reductionism: →10,278, Eliade/Segal 1990/4, 198-210.

7966 -- *Williams* Jay G., The idea of the Holy. a study of the development of Rudolf OTTO's thought: JRelSt 18 (1993) 50-66.

7967 *Pintor-Ramos* Antonio. ZUBIRI; una filosofía de la religión cristiana : Salmanticensis 42 (1995) 369-399; Eng. 399.

7968 **Ries** Julien, Les religions, leurs origines: BtOrigines 3, 1993 → 3,11270 [Eng.; ital. → 10,10273(*)]: [R]MélSR 51 (1994) 331 (G.-H. *Baudry)*.

7969 [E]**Ries** J., *al.*, Les origines et le problème de l'Homo Religiosus 1992 → 9,11279; 10,10272: [R]E(gl)eT 26 (1995) 290s (L. *Laberge)*.

7970 **Rudolph** Kurt, Geschichte und Probleme der Religionswissenschaft 1992 → 9,11276;

10,10275: ᴿJRel 75 (1995) 156s (G. D. *Alles*).

7971 RUSSELL: **Andersson** Stefan, *a)* In quest of certainty; Bertrand Russell's search for certainty in religion and mathematics in 'The principles of mathematics': StPhRel 18. Sto 1994, Almqvist & W. xiv-192 p Sk 182. -- ᴿJRel 75 (1995) 583s (P.J. *Griffiths*). -- *b)* Bertrand Russells sökande efter visshet i religion og matematik: SvTK 70 (1994) 62-70; Eng 70.

7972 -- *Wood* Joanne A., Lighthouse bodies; the neutral monism of Virginia WOOLF and Bertrand Russell: JHId 55 (1994) 483-502.

7973 *a) Séguy* Jean, La religion dans la modernité ou relire les classiques; -- *b) Colliot-Thélène* Catherine, Rationalisation et désenchantement du monde; problèmes d'interprétation de la sociologie des religions de Max WEBER; -- *c) Gisel* Pierre, Ernst TROELTSCH; un dépassement des 'lumières': ASS(oc)R 89 (1995) 5-7 / 61-80; Eng. esp. 81 / 83-94; Eng., esp. 94.

7974 SMITH W.C.: **Grünschloss** Andreas, Religionswissenschaft als Welt-Theologie; Wilfred Cantwell Smith's interreligiöse Hermeneutik; FSÖT 71. Gö 1994, Vandenhoeck & R. 360 p. -- ᴿZM(iss)R 79 (1995) 315s (H. *Waldenfels*).

7975 SMITH W.R: Essays in reassessment, ᴱ**Johnstone** William: JSOT.s 189. Shf 1995, Academic. 403 p. 1-85075-523-X.

7976 **Sumner** George R., PANNENBERG and the religions: conflictuality and the demonstration of power in a Christian theology of the religions: diss. Yale, ᴰ*Lindbeck* G. New Haven 1994. 407 p. 95-23238. -- D(iss)AI 56 (1995s) p. 987.

7977 **Torno** Armando, [*a)* Pro o contro Dio 1993; -- *b)*] Senza Dio ['due secoli di riflessioni tra speranza e negazione']. Mi 1995, Mondadori. 261 p. Lᵐ 30. -- ᴿRasT 36 (1995) 377-9 (F. *Morandi*).

7978 **Zirker** Hans, Critica della religione, ᵀᴱ*Camera* Franco. Brescia 1989, Queriniana. 286 p. Lᵐ 24. -- ᴿCivCatt 146 (1995,4) 105s (B. *Groth*).

M3.3 Investigationes particulares religionum

7979 *Ahern* Annette, Re-enchanting the world; BERGER's sacramental approach to religion: TorJT 11 (1995) 21-38.

7980 **Alston** William P. Perceiving God; the epistemology of religious experience 1991 → 10,10287: ᴿFaith & Philosophy 11 (ND 1994) 311-321 (J. L. *Kvanvig*).

7981 **Arens** Edmund, Religion und Ritual [GENNEP A. van, Übergangsriten, *al.*]: ThRv 91 (1995) 105-114.

7982 *Arens* Edmund, Konturen einer praktischen Religionstheorie: → 149, ᶠPEUKERT H., Anerkennung 1995, 138-167.

7983 *Arens* Edmund, Der Sinn für Zugehörigkeit; Religion und Gesellschaft in kommunitarischer Sicht: Orien(tierung) 59 (1995) 154-9.

7984 **Bahm** Archie J., The world's living religions. Berkeley 1992, Asian Humanities. 384 p. 0-87573-000-0. -- ᴿActuBbg 31 (1994) 108s (A. *Borràs*).

7985 **Barthe** Claude, La fusion des langues; dialogue entre les religions et croissance du dogme. P 1993, Catholica. 128 p. -- ᴿRThom 95 (1995) 343s (S.-T. *Bonino*).

7986 **Bateson** Gregory & Catherine, Wo Engel zögern; Unterwegs zu einer Epistemologie des Heiligen [1987], ᵀMöhring Hans-Ulrich. Fra 1993, Suhrkamp. 312 p. -- ᴿZRGG 47 (1995) 364s (V. *Krech*).

7987 *Berger* Peter L., Rückkehr der Engel [about church, not angels]: EK 27 (19940 93-96.

7988 **Bhattacharyya** Haridas † 1956, The foundations of living faiths; an introduction to comparative religion[2] [[1]1938; there is a second volume unpublished]. Delhi 1994, Motilal Banarsidass. xvii-557 p.   rs 425 [RStR 22,45, G.R. *Thursby:* highly readable but not updated].

7989 *Bocquet* Étienne, La psychologie de le religion; repères historiques et enjeux épistémologiques: MélSR 52 (1995) 263-279; Eng. 279.

7990 *Bœspflug* François, Chronique d'histoire des religions: RevSR 69 (1995) 259-270: 5 ouvrages infra + 1.

7991 **Burke** Thomas P.,   The major religions; an introduction with texts.   Ox 1995, Blackwell. xxiii-348 p. £ 50; pa. £ 14. 1-55786-714-3; -5-1. -- [R]*TBR 8,3 (1995s) 53s (L.T. *Pringle*).

7992 **Burkhardt** Helmut, Ein Gott in allen Religionen ? Wiederkehr der Religiosität -- Chance und Gefahr. Giessen 1993, Brunnen. 112 p. DM 16,80. 3-7655-9435?-9. -- [R]ThLZ 120 (1995) 317s (H. *Wagner*).

7993 *Carrasco* David, Cosmic jaws; we eat the gods and the gods eat us [Aztec ritual cannibalism]: JAAR 63,3 ('Religion and food' 1995) 429-453.

7994 **Casanova** José, Public religions in the modern world [religion is being deprivatized ...]. Ch 1994, Univ. x-320 p. $ 50; pa. $ 18. -- [R]C(ath)HR 81 (1995) 407s (J.A, *Varacalli*); JRel 75 (1995) 469s (S.M. *Tipton*).

7995 [E]**Champion** Françoise, *Hervieu-Léger* Danièle, De l'émotion en religion; renoveau et traditions 1990 → 7,342*: [R]ScEs 46 (1994) 136-8 (J.-P. *Rouleau*).

7996 **Clouser** Roy A., The myth of religions; neutrality [impossible]; an essay on the hidden role of religious belief in theories 1991 → 7,1851: [R]RelSt 31 (1995) 142s.

7997 [E]**Díaz Salazar** R., *Giner* S., *Velasco* F., Formas modernas de religión. M 1994, Alianza. 311 p. -- [R]RF 231 (1995) 439s (R. *Muñoz Palacios*).

7998 *Elford* R.J., Questions people ask, 2. Why bother about religion ? [Isn't helping other people more important than singing hymns .. ?]: ET 106 (1994s) 357-362.

7999 [E]**Filoramo** Giovanni, Dizionario delle religioni. T 1993, Einaudi. 824 p. L[m] 85. -- [R]CivCatt 146 (1995,3) 549-551 (N. *Venturini*).

8000 **Friedman** Maurice, A heart of wisdom; religion and human wholeness. Albany 1992, SUNY. 254 p [RStR 22,49, T.C. *Muck:* dialogue not diatribe is the way].

8001 **Gellner** Ernst, Ragione e religione, [T]*Fedegari* A. Mi 1993, Saggiatore. -- [R]FilTeo 9 (1995) 202s (G. *Ventrone*).

8002 **Geyer** Carl-Friedrich, Religion und Diskurs; die Hellenisierung des Christentums aus der Perspektive der Religionsphilosophie [D]1990 → 6,k140; 7,g107;   3-515-05626-2: [R]Bijdragen 56 (1995) 232 (H.J. *Adriaanse*).

8003 **Gilkey** Langdon, God and the world .. : [R]AmJTP 16 (1995) 315-334 (D.R. *Mason*).

8004 *a) Gold* Daniel, Making UFO's [unidentified flying objects]; aesthetics and argument in writing on religion; -- *b) Sutherland* Stewart R., The role of religion in international conflicts; the task of religious studies; -- *c) Cheetham* David, Religious surveying; commonality between traditions: ScotJR 16 (1995) 75-88 / 89-102 / 103-114.

8005   **Greeley** Andrew M.,   Religion as poetry [... the Church is 'a story-telling community']. New Brunswick 1995, Transaction. xix-281 p. $ 33. 1-56000-183-6 [ThD 43,66]. -- [R]Furrow 46 (1995) 532-4 (M.P. *Gallagher*).

8006 **Grom** Bernhard, Psicología de la religión [1992 → 9,11323], [T]*Villanueva* Marciano. Barc 1994, Herder. 476 p. -- [R]Rel(y)Cult 41 (1995) 913-6 (I. *Diez del Rio*); Lum(Vt) 44 (1995) 334-6 (U. *Gil Ortega*); RevAg 36 (1995) 1161s (B. *Mateos Bermejo*).

8007 *Grube* Dirk-Martin, Religious experience after the demise of foundationalism: : RelSt 31 (1995) 37-52.

8008 **Guthrie** Stewart E., Faces in the clouds: a new theory of religion. Ox 1993, UP. v-290 p.; ill. £ 25. 0-19-506901-3. -- ᴿBijdragen 56 (1995) 112s (L. *Minnema*, Eng.: a persuasive approach, which could accommodate even some areas he excludes); JRel 75 (1995) 392s (B.C. *Ray*).

8009 **Haas** Germaine, Symbolik und Magie in der Urgeschichte -- ihre Bedeutung für den heutigen Menschen. Bern 1992, Haupt. 238 p.; 211 fig. + 22 color. -- ᴿA(nz)AW 46 (1993) 38s (W. *Pötscher*).

8010 **Hans** James S., The origins of the gods 1991 → 8,b260 'origin': ᴿJAAR 63 (1995) 412-4 (R.D. *Shofner*).

8011 ᴱ**Harris** Ian, *al.*, Longman guide to living religions. L 1994, Longman. 278 p. £ 14. 0-582-25297-0. -- ᴿET 106 (1994s) 382 (P. *Bishop*).

8012 **Hefner** Philip. The human factor; evolution, culture and religion 1993 → 10,10311: ᴿTS 56 (1995) 176-8 (J.H. *Wright*).

8013 *Heim* S. Mark, Salvations; a more pluralistic hypothesis: MoTh 10 (1994) 341-360.

8014 **Hijmans** E.J.S., Je moet er het beste van maken; een empirisch onderzoek naar hedendaagse zingevingssystemen. Nijmegen 1994, ITS. 247 p. *f* 52. -- ᴿG(ereformeerd)TT 95 (1995) 89s (H.C. *Stoffels:* LUCKMANNs 'onzichtbare religie').

8015 **Höhn** Hans-Joachim. Gegen- [moderne und sogar postmoderne] Mythen; religionsproduktive Tendenzen der Gegenwart: QD 154. FrB 1994, Herder. 150 p. DM 38. 3-451-03154-4. -- ᴿMThZ 46 (1995) 388s (W.W. *Müller*); ZkT 117 (1995) 358s (K.H. *Neufeld*).

8016 **Hoyle** Fred, The origin of the universe and the origin of religion. Wakefield RI 1993, Meyer Bell. 91 p. $ 10. -- ᴿPerspSCF 47 (1995) 210s (P.*Copan*).

8017 *Kelly* Sean M., The Great Mother/Goddess and the psychogenesis of patriarchy: JDharma 18 (1993) 114-123.

8018 **Kirkpatrick** Frank G., Together bound; God, history, and the religious community. NY 1994, Oxford-UP. xiii-195 p. $35. -- ᴿRStR 21 (1995) 39 (Mary Ann *Stenger*).

8019 **Klass** Morton, Ordered universes; approaches to the anthropology of religion. Boulder 1995, Westview. xiv-177 p. 4 50; pa. $ 17. 0-8133-12132; -4-0 [ThD 43,72].

8020 **Krejčí** Jaroslav, The human predicament; its changing image; a study in comparative religious history. Basingstoke/NY 1993,Macmillan / St.Martin's. xii-194 p. £ 35. 0-333-55081-1 / US 0-312-09101-X. -- ᴿJEH 46 (1995) 484s (J.J. *Lipner*); TBR 8,1 (1995s) 54s (K.M. *Gaseltine*).

8021 **LaMothe** Ryan W., Messengers of hate; a psychoanalytic and theological analysis of intransigence in religion: diss. Vanderbilt, ᴰMills L. Nashville 1994. 488 p. 95-14958. -- D(iss)AI 56 (1995s) p. 557.

8022 *Laperrousaz* E.-M., La religion est-elle, comme l'a souligné le cardinal Jean DANIÉLOU dans ses mémoires, 'création de la religiosité humaine'? : → 10,344a, Notion of 'religion' 1990/4, 675-682.

8023 **Lewis** James F., *Travis* William G., Religious traditions of the world. GR 1991, Zondervan. ix-422 p. $ 25. -- ᴿIBM(iss)R 18 (1994) 43 (E. *Rommen*).

8024 **Macquarrie** John, The mediators [founders of religions]; nine stars in the human sky. L 1995, SCM. 171 p. £ 13. 0-334-02621-0 [*TBR 9/1, 8, I. *Markham*: high praise]. -- ᴿE(xp)T 107 (1995s) 191 (G. *Parrinder*).

8025 **Malherbe** Michel, Les religions de l'humanité. P 1990 ²1992, Criterion. 650 p. --

^RRevSR 69 (1995) 262-5 (F. *Bæspflug*).

8026 ^E**Markham** Ian S., A world religions reader. Ox 1995, Blackwell. xvi-368 p.; maps. £ 45; pa. £ 14. 0-631-18239-X; -42-X. -- ^R*TBR 8,3 (1995s) 54 (L.T. *Pringle*).

8027 *Mooren* Thomas, Das weite Land der Religionen; eine Entdeckungsfahrt. Dü 1995, Patmos. 192 p. DM 29,80. - ^RGuL 68 (1995) 397s (Karin *Frammelsberger*).

8028 ^E**Mugambi** Jesse N.K., A comparative study of religions. Nairobi 1993 = 1990, Univ. 311 p. £ 12. 9966-846-03-8, -- ^R*TBR 8,1 (1995s) 55s (M. *Conway*).

8029 **Oksanen** Antti, Religious conversion; a meta-analytical study: PsRel 2. Lund 1994, Univ. 175 p. 91-7966-266-8. -- ^RThLZ 120 (1995) 180s (H.J. *Frans*).

8030 **Paden** William E., Interpreting the sacred; ways of viewing religion 1992 → 8,a984; 9,11347: ^R*CritRR 7 (1994) 282s (B.L. *Whitney*).

8031 **Panikkar** R., La experiencia de Dios [Silos 1992, profesores de religión]. M 1994, PPC. 95 p. -- ^RSalmanticensis 42 (1995) 302s (D. *de Pablo Maroto*).

8032 **Panikkar** Raimon, The cosmotheandric experience 1993 → 9,11348; 10,10323: ^RHorizons 22 (1995) 325s (C.K. *Chapple*).

8033 *Panikkar* Raimon, Are there 'anonymous religions' ? The name and the thing: -> 10,344a, Notion of 'religion' 1990/4, 889-894.

8034 **Peterson** Michael, *al.*, Reason and religious belief; an introduction to the philosophy of religion 1991 → 9,11351; 10.10324: ^RJETS 37 (1994) 593-5 (B. *Stetson*).

8035 **Rambo** Lewis R., Understanding religious conversion. NHv 1993, Yale Univ. xix-240 p. $ 25. -- ^RJRel 75 (1995) 169-171 (H.N. *Malony*).

8036 ^E**Reynolds** Frank E., *Tracy* David, Religion and practical reason; new essays in the comparative philosophy of [largely Eastern] religion. Albany 1994, SUNY. ix-444. $ 22 [RStR 22,48, J.V. *Apczynski*].

8037 **Rizzi** Armido, Il Sacro e il Senso; lineamenti di filosofia della religione. T-Leumann 1995, Elle Di Ci. 251 p. L^m 25. -- ^RRasT 36 (1995) 369-372 (C. *Greco*); VivH 6 (1995) 423 (A. *Fabris*).

8038 **Roson Galache** Luis, La filosofía de la religión en Jean GUITTON; posibilidad y fundamento: Burgense 35 (1994) 469-501.

8039 **St. Clair** Michael, Human relationships and the experience of God; object relations and religion: StPastPsy. NY 1994, Paulist. x-93 p. $ 9. 0-8091-3530-2 [RStR 22,46, Sheila *Redmond*; ThD 43,86 'Integration books '].

8040 **Schuon** Frithjof, Stations of wisdom [Les stations de la sagesse], ^T. Bloomington IN, World Wisdom. xii-163 p. $ 13. 0-941532-18-6 [RStR 22,46, G.R. *Thursby*: 'newly revised ^T(ranslation)', no name or earlier date; 'La Stations', 'Schuom' in title only].

8041 *a)* **Segal** Robert A., Reductionism in the study of religion; -- *b)* *Ryba* Thomas, Are religious theories susceptible to reduction ? -- *c)* *Yonan* Edward A., Clarifying the strengths and limits of reductionism in the discipline of religion; -- *d)* *Godlove* Terry E.^J, The instability of religious belief; some reductionistic and eliminative pressures: →10,278, Eliade/Segal 1990/4, 4-14 / 15-42 / 43-48 / 49-64.

8042 ^E**Sharma** Arvind, Our religions; the seven world religions introduced by prominent scholars from each religion. SF 1993, Harper. xi-536 p. $ 30. -- ^RP(rinc)SB 16 (1995) 101-3 (A. *Neely*).

8043 **Smart** Ninian, Choosing a faith. .. c.1995, Boyars/Bowerdean. £ 10. -- ^RTablet 249 (1995) 543s (M. *Barnes*).

8044 **Templeton** John M., The humble approach [a scientist's: religion not based on the past or on any one tradition]^{2rev}. NY 1996, Continuum. 172p. $ 15. -- ^RJETS 38 (1995!) 619-621

(C.F.H. *Henry*).

8045 *Terrin* Aldo N., L'esperienza religiosa parametro per la storia comparata delle religioni e per l'esercizio del dialogo ecumenico: → 168, [F]SARTORI L., StPat(av) 42 (1995) 137-161.

8046 **Thiel** John E., Nonfoundationalism [religion cannot be based on a claim of absolutely certain first principles]. Mp 1994, Fortress. xii-123 p. -- [R]RelStR 21 (1995) 209 (M.S. *Cladis*).

8047 *Tuwere* Ilaitia S., Mana and the Fijian sense of place; a theological reflection: SoPacJMiss 11 (1994) 3-15 [< TIC(context) 12,2 (1995) 83].

8048 **Vergote** Antoine, Explorations de l'espace théologique: BEThL 110, 1990 → 6,215*; 8,a999: [R]RThom 54 (1994) 667-670 (G. *Narcisse*).

8049 **Verkamp** Bernard J., The evolution of religion; a re-examination. Fordham/Scranton 1995, Universities. xv-227 p.; biog. 197-213. $ 30; pa. $ 20. 0-940866-49-8

8050 **Waardenburg** Jacques, Des dieux qui se rapprochent; introduction systématique à la science des religions, [TE] avec *Welscher* Claude, 1993 → 10,10338: [R]RevSR 68 (1994) 248s (F. *Boespflug*); RTPh 127 (1995) 199 (A. *Nayak*).

8051 **Waldenfels** Hans, Auf der Suche nach dem Lebensgrund. Hildesheim 1995, Benno-BW. 119 p. DM 14,80. -- [R]G(eist)uL 68 (1995) 395 (J. *Sudbrack*).

8052 **Watts M.,** *Williams* M., The psychology of religious knowing. L 1994, Chapman. 169 p. £ 12 pa. -- [R]Month 256 (1995) 105s (J. *Campbell*).

8053 *a) Wiebe* Donald, A new era of promise for religious studies ?; -- *b) Gates* Brian, Secular education and the logic of religion; shall we re-invent the wheel: → 184, SMART N., Aspects 1994, 93-112 / 115-129.

8054 **Wuthnow** Robert, Rediscovering the sacred; perspectives on religion in contemporary society 1992 → 8,b6; 9, 11381: [R]*CritRR 7 (1994) 481s (L.D. *Kliever*).

8055 *a) Yonan* Edward A., Religion as anthropomorphism; a new theory that invites defintitional and epistemic scrutiny; -- *b) Segal* Robert A., TYLOR's anthropomorphic theory of religion: Religion 25 (1995) 21-35 (35.40, *Guthrie* Stewart, response) / 23-30. → H11, PREUS.

M3.4 **Aspectus particulares religionum mundi**

8056 [E]**Balsley** Anandita N., *Mohanty* J.N., Religion and time: StHR 54, 1993 → 9,309 ('Balslev'); $ 63: [R]Numen 42 (1995) 91-93 (S. *Biderman*).

8057 **Beers** William, Women and sacrifice; male narcissism and the psychology of religion. Detroit 1992, Wayne State Univ. 205 p. $ 29. -- [R]*CritRR 7 (1994) 526-8 (J'nan M. *Sellery*).

8058 **Bent** Ann Joachim van der, Historical dictionary of ecumenical Christianity: Movements 3. Meuchen NJ 2994, Scarecrow. xxiii-599 p. $ 70. 0-8108-3853-7 [ThD 43,92].

8059 *Bergeron* Richard, Les religions sont-elles des demeures de Dieu; → 10,30,[F]COUTURIER G., Maison 1994, 461-485.

8060 **Beversluis** Joel B., A source book for earth's community of religions. NY 1995, Global Education. x-366 p. $27 [JDh 20,395].

8061 *Bishop* Peter D., How do we actually use religious texts [three books plus Bede GRIFFITHS' 1993 Universal Wisdom]: ET 106 (1994s) 254s.

8062 *Brueggemann* Walter, 'In the image of God ' .. pluralism: MoTh 11 (1995) 455-469.

8063 **Bulkeley** Kelly, The wilderness of dreams; exploring the religious meanings of dreams in modern western culture. Albany 1994, SUNY. 308 p. $ 20. -- [R]JRel 75 (1995) 466s (A. *Argüelles*).

8064 **Carmody** Denise L. & John T., Peace and justice in the scriptures of the world religions 1988 → 4,8361: [R]EstB 53 (1995) 307 (F. *Lage*).

8065 *Champion* Françoise, Religions, approches de la nature et écologies: ASSR 90 (1995) 39-55.

8066 *Clare* Anthony, Psychiatry, psychotherapy and religion; reflections and observations: MilltSt 34 (1994) 53-73.

8067 **Coleman** Simon, *Elsner* John, Pilgriamge; past and present in the world religions. CM 1995, Harvard Univ. 240 p. $ 30. 0-674-66765-4

8068 *Cowan* Tom, The sacred three; Celtic shamanism and the concept of the Trinity: *CreSp 11,4 (1995) 34-41.

8069 *D'Costa* Gavin, Revelation and revelations; discerning God in other religions, beyond a static evaluation: MoTh 10 (1994) 165-183.

8070 **Dalai Lama**, *Drewermann* Eugen, Les voies du cœur; non-violence et dialogue entre religions. P 1993, Cerf. 124 p. F 70. -- [R]FoiTe 24 (1994) 87 (H. *Thomas*).

8071 [E]**Detienne** Marcel, *Hamonic* Gilbert, La déesse Parole; quatre figures de la langue des dieux [5 intervenants, 8 questions]: Idées et recherches. P 1995, Flammarion. 120 p. F 110. 2-08-012628-8. -- [R]ÉTRel 70 (1995) 421 (J. *Argaud*).

8072 **Fetscher** Irving [Frankfurt], La tolerancia, una pequeña virtud imprescindible para la democracía; panorama histórico y problemas actuales. Barc 1994, Gedisa. 167 p. : E(st)E 70 (1995) 435s (A. *Matos*).

8073 *Flanagan* James W., Finding the arrow of time; constructs of ancient history and religion: *CuRB 3 (1995) 37-80.

8074 *Fornberg* Tord, Bibeln och de många religionerna; harmoni eller konflikt ?: → 93, [F]KIEFFER R., SEÅ 60 (1995) 39-48.

8075 *Fredericks* James L., A universal religious experience ? Comparative theology as an alternative to a theology of religion: Horizons 22 (1995) 67-87.

8076 *a) Fuller* Robert C., Wine, symbolic boundary setting, and American religious communities; -- *b) Dodson* Jualynne E., *Gilkes* Cheryl T., 'There's nothing like church food'; food and the U.S. Afro-Christian tradition; re-membering community and feeding the embodied S/spirit(s): JAAR 63,3 ('Religion and food' 1995) 519-538.

8077 **Golan** Ariel, Myth and symbol; symbolism in prehistoric religions [... Daghestan] 1991 → 7,a509; 965-222-245-3. -- [R]AKuG 76 (1994) 231-3 (K. J. *Narr*).

8078 *a) Grabar* Oleg, Le temple, lieu de conflit; le monde de l'Islam; - *b) Chamay* Jacques, Le temple, lieu du sacrilège; - *c) Grossmann* Peter, Tempel als Ort des Konflikts in christlicher Zeit: → 486, Temple lieu de conflit 1991/4, 213-225 / 103-5; 2 fig. / 181-201; 6 fig.

8079 **Graham** William A., Beyond the written word: oral aspects of Scripture in the history of religion. C pa.1993, Univ. xiv-306 p. 0-521-44820-4. -- [R]Salesianum 57 (1995) 771s (R. *Vicent*).

8080 [E]**Griffiths** Bede, Universal wisdom; a journey through the sacred wisdom of the world. L c.1994, HarperCollins. £ 17. -- [R]Tablet 249 (1995) 21s (M. *Barnes* 'the man and the myth'; a massive anthology).

8081 *Haussig* Hans-Michael, Heilige Texte und heilige Schriften; einige Bemerkungen zu religiösen Überlieferungen: -> 10,322*, Schriftauslegung 1994, 72-90.

8082 **Hayes** Michael, The infinite harmony; musical structures [the octave .. I Ching] in science and theology. L 1994, Weidenfeld & N. 256 p. £ 20. 0-297-81450-8. -- R*TBR 8,1 (1995s) 62 (N. *Adams*).

8083 EHolm Jean, (*Bowker* John), Sacred Writings. L 1994, Pinter. xii-201 p. £ 30; pa. £ 10. -- RScotJR 16 (1995) 161-4 (Jennifer *Caswell*, also on Attitudes to Nature 1994 [→ 10,277.10361] in the series); Theol 98 (L 1995) 329 (P. *Weller*).

8084 *a) Idinopulos* Thomas A., Must professors of religion be religious ? On Eliade's method of inquiry and Segal's defense of reductionism; -- *b) Elzey* Wayne, Mircea ELIADE and the battle against reductionism; -- *c) Wiebe* Donald, Beyond the sceptic and the devotee; reductionism in the scientific study of religion: →10,278, Eliade/Segal 1990/4, 65-81 / 82-94 / 108-126.

8085 EKerber W., Die Wahrheit der Religionen [Symposion]: Fragen einer neuen Weltkultur. Mü 1994, Kindt. 248 p. DM 32. 3-925412-15-8. -- RAnton 70 (1995) 697-9 (Ll. *Oviedo*); ZkT 117 (1995) 111s (K.H. *Neufeld*).

8086 EKloppenborg Ria, *Hanegraaff* Wouter J., Female stereotypes in religious traditions: SHR 66. Lei 1995. xii-261 p. 90-04-10290-6.

8087 *Knitter* Paul F., Toward a liberative interreligious dialogue: CrossCur 45 (1995s) 451-68.

8088 *Knohl* Israel, H Biblical attitudes to Gentile idolatry : Tarbiz 64 (1994s) 5-12; Eng, 1,v.

8089 **Kurtz** Lester R., Gods in the global village; the world's religions in sociological perspective: Sociology for a new century. Thousand Oaks CA 1995, Pine Forge. vi-279 p. £ 16. 0-8039-9037-5. -- R*TBR 8,3 (1995s) 55 (A. *Wilson*).

8090 **Lambert** Jean, Le Dieu distribué; une anthropologie comparée des monothéismes: Patrimoines. P 1995, Cerf. 406 p. -- REstTrin 29 (1995) 485s (X. *Pikaza*).

8091 *Legrand* Lucien, The Bible and the religions of the nations: I(nd)TS 32 (1995) 193-207.

8092 **McClenon** James, Wondrous events. Ph 1995, Univ. Pennsylvania. 281 p. $ 38; pa. $ 20. 0-8122-3074-4; -1355-6. -- RET 106 (1994s) 319 (A. *Ford*).

8093 EMalony H. Newton, *Southard* Samuel, Handbook of religious conversion [within the context of comparative religions]. Birmingham AL 1992, Religious Education. 314 p. $24. -- RSWJT 37,1 (1994s) 40s (M. *McDow*).

8094 **Manninezhath** Thomas, Harmony of religions. Delhi 1993, Motilal Banarsidass. xvii-193 p. rs 175. -- RJDharma 19 (1994) 93-96 (S.N. *Rao*).

8095 **Ma'súmián** Farnás, Life after death; a study of the afterlife in world religions. L 1995, One World. 153 p. £ 10. 1-85168-074-8.-- RE(xp)T 107 (1995s) 158 (E.C. *Schofield*).

8096 **Minnema** L., Bespiegelung aan het venster; anthropologische bouwstenen voor een vergelijkend godsdienstwetenschappelijke verheldering van interreligieuze dialoog ... NISHITANI K., RAHNER K. [diss.]. Kampen 1990, Mondiss. 329 p. 90-5337-007-2. -- RBijdragen 56 (1995) 234s (J. van *Litt*).

8097 *Mion* Renato, Domanda di valori di religione nei giovani dell'Europa dell'est e dell'ovest: Salesianum 57 (1995) 305-357.

8098 *Morgan* Peggy, The study of religions and interfaith encounter: Numen 42 (1995) 156-71

8099 *Oommen* T.K., Globalisation and structural change; historicity and implications: Religion & Society 41 (Bangalore 1994) 216-222 [< TIC(ontext) 12,2 (1995) 89].

8100 EPathrapankal Joseph, Text and context in biblical interpretation 1993 → 292c: RCBQ 57 (1995) 187s (G.T. *Montague:* on Christianity amid world religions, with focus on India).

8101 EPlatvoet Jan, *Toorn* Karel van der, Pluralism and identity; studies in ritual behaviour: SHR 67. Lei 1995, Brill. vi-376 p. 90-04-10373-2.

8102 **Rausch** D.A., *Voss* C.H., World religions; a simple guide. Mp/L 1994, Fortress/SCM.

212 p. £ 9. /0-334-01820-X. -- [R]ET 106 (1994s) 95 (P.D. *Bishop*).

8103 *Rennstich* Karl, Heil und Unheil in der Sicht der Religionen: ThZ 50 (Basel 1994) 220-251.

8104 *Sanz* Víctor, Los radicales de la religión: ScrT(Pamp) 37 (1995) 567-582.

8105 *Schilson* Arno, Fest und Feier in anthropologischer und theologischer Sicht, ein Literaturbericht: L(tg)J 44 (1994) 5-32.

8106 **Schimmel** Annemarie, The mystery of numbers. NY 1993, Oxford-UP. 314 p. $22. -- [R]JRel 75 (1995) 162s (S. H. *Nasr*: intended as a comparative religionist's symbolism survey, but became rather an updating of F.C.ENDRES, 1984).

8107 **Schöll** Albrecht, Zwischen religiöser Revolte und frommer Anpassung, die Rolle der Religion in der Adoleszenzkrise. Gü 1992, Mohn. 3-579-01771-3. -- [R]JE(mp)T 8,2 (1995) 120s (B. *Porzelt*).

8108 *a) Sfameni Gasparro* Giulia, 'Religione' e 'teologia', due 'quantità' della ricerca storico-religiosa; -- *b) Haussig* Hans-Michael, Some observations on the idea 'religion' in the various religions: -> 10,344a, Notion of 'religion' 1990/4, 733-740 / 797-802.

8109 **Shenk** David, Global gods; exploring the role of religions in modern societies. Scottdale PA 1995, Herald. 403 p. $ 17. 0-8361-9006-8 [ThD 43,289].

8110 *Shepherd* John J., Social justice in world religions a modern ideal in comparative perspective: → 184, [F]SMART N., Aspects 1894. 313-329.

8111 *Siegwalt* G., L'universalité du thème baptismal de la mort et de la résurrection: FV 91.1 (1992) 53-60.

8112 *Slik* Frans van der, Measuring Christian beliefs [HUNT R. 1972: FELLING A. ..] : JE(mp)T 7,1 (1994) 5-34.

8113 **Smith** Wilfred Cantwell, What is Scripture ? [not texts ! p. 223; but interaction between texts and communities]; a comparative approach, 1993 → 9,11418; 10,10279: [R]Encounter 56 (1995) 427-9 (R.B. *Williams*); JBL 114 (1995) 487-9 (Sandra M. *Schneiders*); JThS 46 (1995) 794-7 (J. *Barton*).

8114 **Smith** W.C., Towards a world theology. 1981. -- [R]I(nd)TS 32 (1995) 375s (A. *Kolencherry*).

8115 [E]**Stevens-Arroyo** Anthony M., Program for the analysis of religion among Latinos. NY 1994s, Bildner. 4 vol.; $ 30 each. 0-929972-07-4; 09-0; -11-2; -13-9 [ThD 43,83: vol.4 is a summary and bibliography].

8116 *Stock* Alex, Tempel der Toleranz; zur Musealisierung der Religion: → 589, Mit den Anderen 1995, 86-92.

8117 **Sudbrack** Josef, Meditative Erfahrung Quellgrund der Religionen ? Mainz/Stu 1994, Grünewald/ Quell. 183 p. DM 29,80. -- [R]GuL 67 (1994) 395s (H. *Gasper*).

8118 *Tilley* Terrence W., The institutional element in religious experience: MoTh 10 (1994) 185-212.

8119 **Timm** Hermann, Sage und Schreibe; Inszenierungen religiöser Lesekultur: Innen & Aussen 2. Kampen 1995, Pharos. 141 p. 90-390-0211-8.

8120 *Ven* Johannes A. van der, Death, a central theme in religious socialization [not 'education' as page-headings]: JE(mp)T 7,1 (1994) 35-57.

8121 *Waldenfels* Hans, Pluralität der Religionen; Folgen für Mission und kirchliche Entwicklungsarbeit: StZ 213 (1995) 593-603 [677-690, *Sievernich* Michael].

8122 **Ward** Keith, Religion and revelation; a theology of revelation in the world's religions 1994 → 10,10386: [R]Churchman 108 (L 1994) 377-9 (B. *Cook*); Month 256 (1995) 240s (R. *Schniertshauer*); MoTh 11 (1995) 483-5 (S.M. *Heim*); S(cot)JTh 48 (1995) 251-8 (S.

Williams; reply 258-262); ThTo 52 (1995s) 398s (A. *Dulles*).

8123 **Ward** Keith, Images of eternity. Chatham NY pa. 1993, Oneworld (= 1987, Darton-LT) 197 p. $ 17. -- [R]JRel 75 (1995) 140 (D. Burrell).

8124 *Wiessner* Gernot, Offenbarung, Religionsphänomenologie: → 772, TRE 25 (1995) 117-117 [-128, AT, *Preuss* Horst D. †; 135-146, NT, *Balz* Horst; -210, *Herms* Eilert, Theologiegeschichte und Dogmatik]

8125 **Young** William A., The world's religions: worldviews and contemporary issues. ENJ 1995, Prentice-Hall. xiv-400 p. $ 46. 0-13-032806-5 [< ThD 42 (1995) 296].

M3.5 Religiones mundi cum christianismo comparatae

8126 *Adrian* V., Jesus and the religions of the world: *Direction 23,1 (1994) 29-43 [NTAb 39, p.83].

8127 *Altemeyer* Fernando[J], Théologie des religions non-chrétiennes ['croire posséder le monopole de la vérité' est le cinquième des 10 'fruits défendus de l'arbre de la vie religieuse']: FoiTe 24 (1994) 517-531.

8128 **Arregui** José, URS VON BALTHASAR, dos propuestas de diálogo con las religiones: ScrVic 42 (1995) 5-81.

8129 **Arts** H., Wereldgodsdiensten; allemal gelijkwaardig ? Lv 1993, Davidfonds. 160 p. Fb 545. -- [R]Coll 24 (Gent 1994) 103 (J. de *Kesel*).

8130 **Barnes** M., Christian identity and religious pluralism; religions in conversation. Nv 1989, Abingdon. -- [R]*BogVest 53 (1993) 282-6 (J. *Plut*).

8131 *a) Baum* Gregory, The Church's response to the challenge of pluralism; *b) Audinet* Jacques, Position du christianisme dans la société; critères pour un repérage: LavalThP 51 (1995) 35-47 / 7-15.

8132 *Bell* James L., Extolling the virtues of pluralism: Modern Believing [continuing the numbering of Modern Churchman] 36,2 (1995) 33-41.

8133 *Bellah* Robert N., At home and not at home; religious pluralism and religious truth: CCen 112 (1995) 423-8.

8134 *Bellis* Alice O., Objective biblical truth versus the value of various viewpoints : H(orizons)BT 17 (1995) 25-36

8135 **Berger** Peter L., Una gloria remota; aver fede nell'epoca del pluralismo,[T]. Bo 1994, Mulino. 216 p. l[m] 20. -- [R]*StEc 13 (1995) 119s (S. *Morandini*).

8136 **Bernhardt** R., Zwischen Grössenwahn, Fanatismus und Bekennermut; für ein Christentum ohne Absolutheitsanspruch. Stu 1994, Kreuz. 235 p. DM 32. 3-7831-1299-0. -- [R]ThLZ 120 (1995) 66 (J. *Werbick*); TTh 35 (1995) 202s (A. van *Harskamp*).

8137 **Bernhardt** Reinhold, Christianity without absolutes, [T]*Bowden* John. L 1994, SCM. 162 p. $ 10. 0-334-02566-4. -- [R]ET 106,5 top choice (1994s) 139s (C.S. *Rodd*: merits pondering despite some weaknesses); *TBR 8,1 (1995s) 7s (M.D. *Chapman*).

8138 *Bernhardt* Reinhold, Zur Diskussion um die pluralistische Theologie der Religionen: ÖR 43 (1994) 172-189.

8139 *a) Bertuletti* Angelo, Il sacro e la fede, la pertinenza teologica di una categoria religiosa; -- *b) Ubbiale* Sergio, Il sacro, la religione, la salvezza; l'evento cristologico e le forme del cristianesimo: S(cuol)C 123,5 ('La questione teologica del "sacro" ' 1995) 665-688 / 689-720.

8140 *Borrmans* Maurice, Pluralism and its limits in the Qur'an and the Bible: Islamochristiana 17 (1991) 1-14. franç. 114.

8141 **Brueggemann** Walter, Biblical perspectives on evangelism; living in a three-storied universe. NVL 1993, Abingdon. 139 p. $ 13. -- [R]P(rinc)SB 16 (1995) 114-6 (J. W. *Stewart*).

8142 *Bürkle* Horst, Die Pluralität der Religionen und die Sendung der Kirche: VSVD 36 (1995) 215-226.

8143 [E]**Cantone** Carlo, La svolta planetaria di Dio; dall''esperienza religiosa' all''esperienza secolare' [Vielfalt der Religionen .. Gebetstreffen des Papstes]. R 1992, Borla. 307 p. L[m] 35. 88-263-0965-5. -- [R]ZkT 117 (1995) 108s (K.H. *Neufeld*).

8144 *a) Chenu* Bruno, Histoire et typologie de la théologie catholique face au pluralisme religieux; - *b) Geffré* Claude, Le fondement théologique du dialogue interreligieux: → 548, Au carrefour 1993/5, 17-41 / 83-106.

8145 **Clouser** Roy A., The myth of religious neutrality 1991 → 7,1851: [R]C(alvin)TJ 30 (1995) 494-9 (J. *Cooper*: important).

8146 **Cox** Harvey, Many mansions; a Christian's encounter with other faiths 1989 → 5,248; 8,b31 (Boston 1992, Beacon): [R]WW 15 (1995) 112 .116 (G. *Stevensen*).

8147 **Cracknell** Kenneth, Justice, courtesy and love; [Protestant] theologians and missionaries encountering world religions, 1846-1914. L 1995, Epworth. xviii-459 p. £ 20. 0-7162-0501-7. -- [R]E(xp)T 107 (1995s) 90 (P.D. *Bishop*); *TBR 8,3 (1995s) 42 (A. *Race*).

8148 [E]**Crockett** William V., *Sigountos* James G., Through no fault of their own 1991 → 8,7759: [R]ERT 18 (1994) 79-81.

8149 *Curry* Thomas J., Pluralism; worth the price; the Catholic contribution: Church 11,4 (NY 1995) 5-10.

8150 [E]**Dean** Thomas, Religious pluralism and truth; essays on cross-cultural philosophy of religion. Albany 1995, SUNY. 282 p. $ 20. -- [R]RelSt 31 (1995) 544-6 (P. *Donovan*).

8151 *D'Costa* G., Revelation and revelations; the role and value of different religious traditions: Pro Dialogo 85s (Pune colloquium 24-28.VIII.1993: 1994) 145-164 (1-96. *al.*).

8152 *Delorme* Christian, Chrétiens et musulmans en France: Études 382 (1995) 649-660.

8153 **DiNoia** Joseph A., The diversity of religions; a Christian perspective 1992 → 8,b37 ... 10,10398: [R]ChrSchR 25 (1995s) 104-6 (S.Mark *Heim*); EThL 71 (1995) 476s (V. *Neckebrouck*); JETS 38 (1995) 136s (B. *Stetson*: valuable, not fully biblical); MoTh 10 (1994) 107-9 (D.C. *Burrell*); ScrT(Pamp) 37 (1995) 691s (J.M. *Odero*).

8154 *Doré* Joseph, La présence du Christ dans les religions non-chrétiennes: Salmanticensis 42 ('VII.[as] Jornadas' 1995) 315-340: español 340.

8155 **Dupuis** Jacques, Jesucristo al encuentro de las religiones 1991 → 9,11141; 10.10400*: [R]Burgense 35 (1994) 298 (E. *Bueno*),

8156 *Dupuis* Jacques, Il cristianesimo di fronte alla sfida del pluralismo religioso; la proposta di R. PANIKKAR e H. LE SAUX: StPat(av) 42 (1995) 487-496; Eng. 497.

8157 [E]**Farina** Marcella, *Mazzarella* Maria Luisa, Gesù è il Signore; la specificità di Gesù Cristo in tempo di pluralismo religioso 1992 → 9,448: [R]Benedictina 41 (1994) 556s (S. *De Piccoli*).

8158 *Fitzgerald* Michael L., Other religions in the Catechism of the Catholic Church: Islamochristiana 19 (1993) 29-41; Eng, 41 (41-54, *Arkoun* Mohammed, Réflexions d'un Musulman).

8159 **Fornberg** Tord, The problem of Christianity in multi-religious societies today; the Bible in a world of many faiths: T(oronto)ST 70. Lewiston NY 1995, Mellen. [iv-] 304 p.; bibliog. 263-286. 0-7734-8877-4.

8160 **Gaede** S.D., When tolerance is no virtue; political correctness, multiculturalism, and the future of truth and justice. DG 1993, InterVarsity. 119 p. $ 10. -- ᴿBS 152 (1995) 235 (R.A. *Pyne*: superb).

8161 *a) Gäde* Gerhard, Offenbarung in den Religionen ?; -- *b) Knoch* Wendelin, 'Toleranz und Gleichgültigkeit'; -- *c) Splett* Jörg, Gtotteserfahrung im Antlitz des Anderen ? [LEVINAS E. ohne Akzent wie bei ihm selbst, p.49,n.2)]: MThZ 45,1 ('Christlicher Wahrheitsanspruch und postmoderner Liberalismus' 1994) 11-24 / 25-33 / 49-62 [1-10 → Y68, *Knapp* über LINDBECK].

8162 **Galli** Carlos M., El pueblo de Dios en los pueblos del mundo; catolicidad, encarnación e intercambio en la eclesiología actual: diss. ᴰ*Gera* L., Buenos Aires 1993. - TeolBA 30 (1993) 240.

8163 *a) Geffré* Claude, Les religions dans le plan du salut; -- *b) Legrand* Lucien, Jésus et l'Église primitive; un éclairage biblique; -- *c) Kovac* Eduard, La rencontre de l'autre; -- *d) Machado* Félix, La mission en crise ? → 617, Mission, Spiritus 36 (1995) 78-97 / 64-77 / 52-63 / 98-114.

8164 *Geivett* R. Douglas, Is Jesus the only way ?: → 390, Jesus under fire 1995, 177-205.

8165 *Genre* Ermanno, Pluralismo nella pastorale contemporanea [ZULEHNER P., .. PACOMIO L., VANZANᴱ P.]: Protest(antesimo) 50 (1995) 225-231.

8166 *Gerry* Joseph A., The commitment of the Catholic Church to interreligious relations: LiLi 32,2 (1995s) 6-12.

8167 *a) Geyer* Alan, Pluralism and religious freedom; -- *b) West* Charles C., Nationalism and ethnicity: Religion in Eastern Europe 15,6 (Princeton 1995) 8-21 / 1-7.

8168 *Gire* Pierre, Le Christianisme dans son rapport aux traditions religieuses: E(spr)eV 105 (1995) 353-361.

8169 **Giussani** Luigi, Warum Jesus Christus ? Am Ursprung des christlichen Anspruchs: TheolRomanica 19. Fr 1994, Johannes. 171 p. 3-89411-322-7 [TR 91,277].

8170 ᶠGRAEVE Frank de: A universal faith, ᴱ**Cornille** Catherine, *Neckebrouck* V. 1992 → 8,67 (also GR, Eerdmans; Peeters 90-6831-425-7): ᴿVidyajyoti 59 (1995) 828s (A. *Sebastian*).

8171 *Grenz* Stanley J., Toward an evangelical theology of the religions: JE(cu)S 31 (1994) 49-65.

8172 *Grundmann* Christoffer, The Gospel in our pluralist culture; what the healing mandate of the Gospel calls a pluralist society for: VSVD 36 (1995) 389-400.

8173 *Hagemann* L., Der Katechismus der katholischen Kirche und das Heil der anderen: JbRwTR 2 (1994) 129-137 [ThRv 91,281].

8174 *Hagemann* Ludwig, Zur Diskussion um eine 'Theologie der Religionen': TrierTZ 104 (1995) 317-9.

8175 **Heim** S. Mark, Salvations; truth and difference in religion [a 'pluralist inclusiveness', against HICK, KNITTTER, & W.C.SMITH, who conceal their own inclusivist assumptions]: Faith Meets Faith. Mkn 1995, Orbis. x-242 p. [RStR 22,228, L.D. *Lefebure*].

Hick John A., Christian theology of religion; the rainbow of faiths 1994 → 7932b above.

8176 *a) *ᴱ**Hick** John, *Knitter* Paul F., L'unicità cristiana, un mito ? Per una teologia pluralista delle religioni [1987], ᵀ. Assisi 1994, Cittadella. 378 p. Lᵐ 55. 88-308-0566-1: ᴿGreg 76 (1995) 782 (J. *Galot*, riserve). -- *b)* ᴱ**D'Costa** Gavin, La teologia pluralista delle religioni, un mito? [1990]. Assisi 1994, Cittadella. 368 p. Lᵐ 55. 88-308-0567-X. -- ᴿ*StEc 13 (Venezia 1995) 234-6 (S. *Morandini*).

8177 **Hjelde** Sigurd, Die Religionswissenschaft und das Christentum; eine historische Untersuchung über das Verhältnis von Religionswissenschaft und Theologie: StHistRel 61,

1994: → 10,10407: ᴿNedThT 49 (1995) 158s (H.J. *Adriaanse*); RStR 21 (1995) 316 (L.D. *Lefebure*).

8178 *Hoogerwerf* Steven D., Culture wars; Christian convictions in a pluralistic public square: RefR 49 (1995s) 165-178.

8179 **Hummel** Reinhart, Religiöser Pluralismus oder christliches Abendland ? Herausforderung an Kirche und Gesellschaft. Da 1994, Wiss. 223 p. DM 40. 3-534-11717-4. -- ᴿThLZ 120 (1995) 511-3 (H. *Obst*); TPQ 143 (1995) 422 (F. *Gruber*).

8180 ᴱ**Jeanrond** W., *Rike* Jennifer, Radical pluralism and truth .. TRACY 1991 → 8,183*; 10,10408: ᴿLouvSt 20 (1995) 86-88 (T. *Merrigan*).

8181 *a)* Keller Carl-Albert, Religion; Ursache von Toleranz oder Intoleranz ? -- *b) Waldenfels* Hans, Die Heilsbedeutung nichtchristlicher Religionen nach katholischem Glaubensverständnis: → 425, Religion (c.1994) 13-77 / 217-266.

8182 *Kettner* Edward G., Jr., Christian dialogue with the world's religions; is it possible: L(ex)TJ 28 (1994) 98-105.

8183 *Kilgallen* J.J., Jesus, savior [NT: no other person or thing can perform the salvific role ascribed to Jesus]: StMiss 42 (1993) 41-65 [< NTAb 40, p.459].

8184 **Knitter** Paul, One earth, many religions; multi-faith dialogue and global responsibility. Mkn 1995, Orbis. xiv-218 p. 1-57075-037-8 [RStR 22,228, S.M. *Heim*: partly autobiographical & favoring India; ThD 43,373].

8185 **Koshy** Ninan, Religious freedom in a changing world. Geneva 1992, WCC. 115 p. Fs 12,50. -- ᴿProtest(antesimo) 50 (1995) 91s (V. *Bernardi*).

8186 **Küng** Hans, *al.*, Christianity and the world religions 1986 → 3,a936; 4,b555: ᴿMid-Str 34 (1995) 108-110 (Diane *Willey*).

8187 *Küng* Hans, Christ, our light, and world religions [< LV(ie)L(yon) 44.2 (1995) 33-43], ᵀᴱ*Jermann* Rosemary: ThD 42 (1995) 215-9.

8188 *a) Lange* F. de, Pluralisme en christelijke traditie [NEUHAUS R.J., The naked public square (1984): 'Pluralism is a jealous god. When pluralism is established as a dogma, there is no room for other dogmas.']; -- *b) Stoker* W., Religies en (on)gelijkheid; het Christendom en gelijkheid [8 juni 1995 Amst VU, ᴱKRANENBORG R.]: G(ereformeerd)TT 95 (1995) 110-124 / 136-141.

8189 *Legrand* L., The Bible and the religions of the nations: ITS 32 (Bangalore 1995) 193-207 [NTAb 40, p.467].

8190 **Little** Christopher R., The role of general and special revelation in relation to the unevangelized among the nations: diss. Fuller Theol. Sem. Pasadena 1995. 224 p. 13-76875. DᴿissòAI-disk 56 (1995s) MAI 34, p.548.

8191 *McVey* Chris, The challenge of other religions; from the problematic to the possible: Encounter 206 (R 1994) 3-12.

8192 *Miranda* Mário de França, O pluralismo religioso como desafio e chance : REB 55 (1995) 323-337.

8193 *Misiaszek* Kazimierz, ᴾ La catechesi di fronte al pluralismo contemporaneo in Polonia: Bobolanum 4 (1993) 91-102; ital. 102; 111-120, small groups, Eng 120s.

8194 *Murphy* Nancey, Christianity and theories of truth: Dialog 34 (1995) 99-105.

8195 **Nash** Ronald H., Is Jesus the only savior ? GR 1994, Zondervan. 188 p. $ 12. 0-310-44391-3. -- ᴿRExp 92 (1995) 529s (M. *Terry*; yes, against HICK. PINNOCK, J.SANDERS).

8196 **Netland** Harold A., Dissonant voices; religious pluralism and the question of truth 1991 → 7,a447 ...10,10414: ᴿJETS 37 (1994) 593 (B. *Stetson*).

8197 *Newbigin* Lesslie, Confessing Christ in a multi-religion society: ScotBuEv 12 (1994) 125-136.

8198 *a) Ocáriz* Fernando, Delimitación del concepto de tolerancia y su relación con el principio de libertad; -- *b) Ollero* Andrés, Tolerancia y verdad: ScrT(Pamp) 37 (1995) 865-883 / 885-920.

8199 **O'Leary** Joseph S., La vérité chrétienne à l'âge du pluralisme religieux; CogFi 181. P 1994, Cerf. 330 p. F 170. 2-204-04900-X. -- RCath 47 (P 1995) 106s (C. *Barthe*); FilTeo 9 (1995) 192-4 (F.S. *Festa*); Furrow 46 (1995) 124s (T. *O'Connor*); L(aval)TP 51 (1995) 212-6 (F. *Nault*: apories); MélSR 52 (1995) 213-5 (J.-M. *Breuvart*); NZM(iss)W 51 (1995) 224-6 (A. *Peter*); TTh 35 (1995) 202 (M. Van *Tente*).

8200 *Palacio* Carlos (p.311-329), Repensar a Cristianismo num mundo plural, 2ª Semana Teológica, Belo Horizonte 1-4 agosto: PerTeol 26 (1994) 307-402: *Sung Jung Mo; Vázquez* Ulpiano; *Miranda* Mario de F.; *Pastor* F.A.

8201 **Pan Chiu-Lai,** Towards a Trinitarian theology of religions; a study of Paul TILLICH's thought. Kampen 1994, Kok Pharos. 181 p. 90-390-0025-5. -- RETRel 70 (1995) 29s (A. *Gounelle*: sur la Trinité bon mais pas Tillich); JThS 46 (1995) 421-3 (T.S.M. *Williams*).

8202 **Park** Kitae, A missiological study on the image of God in humankind from a redemptive and eschatological perspective: diss. Fuller Theol. Sem., DGilliland D. Pasadena 1995. 190 p. 13-76876. D(iss)AI-disk 56 (1995s) MAI 34, p.548.

8203 *Phan* Peter C., The claim of uniqueness and universality in interreligious dialogue : I(nd)TS 31 (1994) 44-66.

8204 *Phillips* W. Gary, Evangelical pluralism; a singular problem: BS 151 (1994) 140-154.

8205 **Pinnock** Clark H., A wideness in God's mercy 1992 → 9,11174; 10,10419: RAUSS 33 (1995) 315-8 (S. *Kuranteng-Pipim*); EvQ 67 (1995) 181s (L. *McCurdy*).

8206 *Prakash* P, Surya, Mission of the Church in a pluralistic society biblical and theological perspectives: Kristu Jyoti 11,1 (1995) 32-49.

8207 *a) Rieger* Reinhold, Reflexion oder Spekulation; Prinzipien zur Deutung des Konfessionspluralismus bei Johann Adam MÖHLER und Ferdinand Christian BAUR; *b) Hick* John, Eine Philosophie des religiösen Pluralismus [angesichts der Auseinandersetzung Freising 26.-20.IX.1994; *Müller* G.L. p.301s], TSchmidt-Leukel Perry: MThZ 45 (1994) 247-270 / 301-318.

8208 **Rodriguez Panizo** Pedro, El encuentro entre el cristianismo y las grandes religiones en la obra de R.C. ZAEHNER; estudio fenomenológico y teológico; diss. Pont. Univ. Gregoriana. Roma 1994. 679 p. D(iss)AI-C 56 (1995s) p. 860.

8209 *Ruggieri* Giuseppe, La verità crocifissa fra Trinità e storia; per una determinazione del rapporto tra verità e comunione; CrSt 16 (1995) 383-405; Eng. 405.

8210 **Ruokanen** Miika, The Catholic doctrine of non-Christian religions according to the Second Vatican Council 1993 → 9,11477: RAHC(onc) 26 (1994) 423s (L.J. *Elders,* deutsch).

8211 **Sanders** John, No other name ? Can only Christians be saved ? : C.S. Lewis Centre. L 1994, SPCK. 315 p. £ 13. 0-281-04774-8. -- RET 106 (1994s) 190 (W.D. *Hudson*).

8212 **Sanders** John, No other name; an investigation into the destiny of the unevangelized 1992 → 9,11478; 10,10421: RBS 151 (1994) 254-6 (R.P. *Richard*: reductionist); JETS 37 (1994) 615s (E. *Fudge*).

8213 **Schaeffer** Frank, Dancing alone; the quest for Orthodox faith in the age of false religions. ... c.1995, Holy Cross Orthodox. 327 p. $ 20 pa. -- RCCen 112 (1995) 608-610 (Vigen *Guroian*).

8214 *Schillebeeckx* E., Universalité unique d'une figure religieuse historique nommée Jésus de Nazareth: L(aval)TP 50 (1994) 265-281 [NTAb 39, p.79].

8215 *Seckler* Max, Religionsfreiheit und Toleranz; die 'Erklärung über die Religionsfreiheit' des Zweiten Vatikanischen Konzils im Kontext der kirchlichen Toleranz- und Intoleranzdoktrinen; ThQ 175 (1995) 1-18.

8216 *Siegwalt* Gérard, Le christianisme et le discours inter-religieux; vérité et tolérance: L(umière)V 222 (1995) 45-60 (2-78).

8217 **Smith** Jonathan Z., Drudgery divine; on the comparison of early Christianity and the religions of late antiquity 1990 → 6,a706 ... 10,10424: ᴿJAAR 63 (1995) 574-7 (R.L. *Wilken*); SvTK 70 (1994) 77-80 (J.P. *Södergård*).

8218 **Song** C.S., Jesus in the power of the spirit 1994 → 10,7551: ᴿTS 56 (1995) 796s (J.L. *Fredericks*: sermonic anti-Barth theology of also non-Christian religions).

8219 **Straelen** Henri van, L'Église et les religions non chrétiennes au seuil du XXIᵉ siècle; étude historique et théologique. P 1994, Beauchesne. 324 p. F 150. 2-7010-1314-3. -- ᴿATG(ran) 58 (1995) 409-413 (J.L. *Sánchez Nogales*); Études 382 (1995) 280s (M. *Fédou*); Greg 76 (1995) 585-9 (J. *Dupuis*: dur, sévère, d'une lecture pènible); PenCath 279 (1995) 92s (Andrée *Perrachon*); ZkT 117 (1995) 90-93 (K.H. *Neufeld*).

8220 *Sudbrack* Josef, Dialog der Religionen und pluralistische Religionstheologie : GuL 67 (1994) 435-459.

8222 **Swidler** Leonard, After the absolute 1990 → 8,a487: ᴿNewThR 8,3 (1995) 114s (P. *Knitter*).

8223 *Tamayo* Juan-José, El retorno de los dioses y de las diosas:RF 232 (1995) 197-214.

8224 *Teixeiro* Faustino L.C., O cristianismo entre a identidade singular e o desafio plural: PerTeol 27 (1995) 83-101; 8 errata.

8225 **Thiemann** Ronald F., Constructing a public theology; the Church in a pluralistic culture. LVL 1991, W-Knox. 176 p. $ 15. -- ᴿRefR 49 (1995s) 55 (F.S. *Petersen*).

8225* *Thomas* M.M., Mission of the Church in the pluralistic context of India; -- *b)* *Mathew* John, The mission of the Church in a pluralist context; a Pauline perspective: Bible Bhashyam 21 (1995) 81-88 / 121-130.

8226 *Valen-Sendstad* Aksel, Areopagus og vi; om kristendom og religion i teologihistorisk og bibelteologisk lys: Ichthys 22 (Aarhus 1995) 64-74 . 114-126.

8227 *a) Velasco* Fernando, La religión a prueba; tolerancia versus fanatismo; -- *b) González* Ignacio, La tolerancia, razones y sinrazones; -- *c) Moya* José, *Cilleruelo* Ana I., Raíces psicosociales de le intolerancia: Moralia 18 (1995) 189-202 / 143-172 / 173-188.

8228 *Vergauwen* Guido, Jesus Christus Universalität einer historischen Person: KatBlätt 118 (1993) 80-97.

8229 ᴱ**Viladesau** Richard, *Massa* Mark, World religions; a sourcebook for students of Christian theology. NY 1994, Paulist. ix-276 p. $ 24. 0-8091-3461-6 [< ThD 42 (1995) 296].

8230 *Vives* Josep, Los Padres de le Iglesia ante las religiones non cristianas: E(st)E 70 (1995) 289-316.

8231 *Waldenfels* Hans, Pluralità delle religioni; consequenze e sfide per la missione della Chiesa in Europa: CivCatt 146 (1995,4) 537-550.

8232 **Wells** David F., No place for truth; or, whatever happened to evangelical theology ? 1993 → 9,11493; 10,10430: ᴿBS 152 (1995) 360s (R.A. *Pyne*); ConcordJ 11 (1995) 187-193 (D.O. *Berger*, also on his 1994 God in the wasteland); *ProEc 4 (1995) 112s (C.H. *Pinnock*: well received, partly because vague; also on GRENZ S. 1993); RestQ 37 (1995) 59s (J.S. *Williams*); STEv 6 (1994) 99s (P. *Bolognesi*); TTod 51 (1994s) 180 . 2 (J. *Gros*).

M3.6 *Sectae* -- **Cults**

8233 **Ahonen** Lauri K., Suomen Helluntaiherätyksen historia (Pentecostalism in Finland). Hämeenlinna 1994, Päivä Osakeyhtiö. 432 p. -- ᴿPneuma 17 (1995) 291-4 (-304, D. *Bundy,* also on 7 cognates).

8234 **Blandre** B., I testimoni di Geova: Interlogos. Vaticano 1994. 240 p. -- ᴿ(R)*StEc 13 (Venezia 1995) 123s (G. *Dal Ferro*).

8235 *Blough* N., Secte et modernité: BuHProt 140 (1994) 581-602 [< ᴢɪᴛ 95,p.106].

8236 **Bochinger** Christoph, 'New Age' und moderne Religion [ᴰMünchen 1993 → 9,11508]; religionswissenchaftliche Analysen. Gü 1994, Kaiser. 695 p. ᴅᴍ 168. 3-579-00299-6. -- ᴿRTPh 127 (1995) 315s (C.-A. *Keller*); ᴛʟᴢ 120 (1995) 865 (H. *Obst*).

8237 **Bouman** D., New Age; op weg naar een nieuwe wereld ? Nijkerk 1993, Callenbach. 136 p. -- ᴿCVI 25 (1995) 105s (W. Van *Soom*).

8238 *a) Cartledge* M.J., Charismatic prophecy; -- *b) Fuchs* Ottmar, ... and innovation: JE(mp)T 8,1 (1995) 71-88 / 89-95.

8239 *Champion* Françoise, La nébuleuse New Age: Études 382 (1995) 233-242.

8240 **Collins** John J., The cult experience; their traditions and why people join them. Springfield ɪʟ 1991. 133 p. $ 29.75. -- ᴿPerspSCF 47 (1995) 145s (M. *Epstein*).

8241 **Cox** Harvey, Fire from heaven; the rise of Pentecostal spirituality and the reshaping of religion in the twenty-first century. Reading ᴍᴀ 1995, Addison-Wesley. 321 p. $ 24. -- ᴿCrossCur 45 (1995s) 257-161 (Carol *LeMasters*).

8242 **Cox** Harvey, Le retour de Dieu; voyage en pays pentecostiste. P 1995, D-Brouwer. 300 p. -- ᴿÉtudes 383 (1995) 284 (C. *Flipo*).

8243 **Deignan** Kathleen, Christ spirit; the eschatology of Shaker Christianity. Metuchen ɴᴊ 1992, ATLA/Scarecrow. -- ᴿCCurr 44 (1994s) 122s (Linda A. *Mercadante*).

8244 *DePillis* Mario S., This is the place; The Encyclopedia of Mormonism as a presentation of faith: *CritRR 7 (1994) 43-55.

8245 **Dericquebourg** Régis, Les Antoinistes [schisme catholique de Louis ᴀɴᴛᴏɪɴᴇ 1846-1993]: Fils d'Abraham. Maredsous 1993, Brepols. 200 F 149. -- ᴿMélSR 52 (1995) 201s (L. *Debarge*).

8246 *Dintaman* Stephen F., Reading the reactions to [his] 'The spiritual poverty of the Anabaptist vision': CGrebel [10 (1992) 205-8] 1 (1995) 2-9 [10-14-18-22, other reactions, *Peachey* J,Lorne; *Showalter* Richard; *Brown* Mitchell; further *Kraus* C,Norman, An Anabaptist spirituality for the 21st century 23-32 (-86, *al.*)].

8247 *Drane* John W., Christians, New Agers, and changing cultural paradigms: ET 106 (1994s) 172-6.

8248 *a) D'Souza* Corinne Kumar, The South Wind; towards new cosmologies; -- *b) Keck* L. Robert, The next step in humanity's evolutionary journey; the prodigal comes home; -- *c) Panikkar* Raimundo, A new vision of reality (a tribute to Fr. Bede ɢʀɪꜰꜰɪᴛʜs): JDharma 18 ('Mother Earth and New Age Spirituality' 1993) 196-210 / 211-227 / 285-293.

8249 *Duhaime* Jean, Relative deprivation in new religious movements and the Qumran community: RQum 16 (1993-5) 265-276.

8250 ᴱ**Dunde** S.P., Wörterbuch der Religionssoziologie [.. Sekten]. Gü 1994. Vg. 378 p. ᴅᴍ 128. 3-579-00287-2. -- ᴿTTh 35 (1995) 313 (J. *Sloot*).

8251 *Espín* Orlando O., Pentecostalism and popular Catholicism; the poor and tradition: JHispLat 3,2 (1995s) 14-43.

8252 **Faivre** Antoine, *Needleman* Jacob, Modern exoteric spirituality: EncQuest 21. NY 1992, Crossroad. xxx-413 p. $ 49.50. -- RT(oronto)JT 289-291 (Kate P.C. *Galen*).

8253 *Faivre* Antoine, *Voss* Karen-Claire, Western esotericism and the science of religions: Numen 42 (1995) 48-77.

8254 *Fernández Bañuelos* Vicente A., La ambigüedad de las sectas: Burg 36 (1995) 509-44.

8255 **Friesen** Abraham, History and renewal in the Anabaptist/Mennonite tradition. North Newton KA 1994, Bethel College. -- RCGrebel 13 (1995) 107-9 (W.O. *Packull*).

8256 **Garbe** Detlef, Zwischen Widerstand und Martyrium; die Zeugen Jeovas im 'Dritten Reich'; StZg 22. Mü 1993, Oldenbourg. 557 p. 3-486-55992-3. -- R*ActuBbg 31 (1994) 186s (A. *Borràs*).

8257 *Gil B.* Juan C., Trets individualistes en l'espiritualitat de la 'New Age': QVidaC 177 (1995) 31-40.

8258 **Gil** Juan Carlos, *Nistal* J.A., 'New Age', una religiosidad desconcertante. Barc 1994, Herder. 280 p. pt. 2200. 84-254-1863-1. -- RAng 72 (1995) 460s (A. *Lobato*); Burg 36 (1995) 245s (R. *Berzosa Martínez*); EstTrin 29 (1995) 175 (J.M. *Arbizu*); Lum(Vt) 44 (1995) 333s (U. *Gil Ortega*); Rel(y)Cult 41 (1995) 167-9 (J.D. *Jiménez*); R(az)F 231 (1995) 554s (J.M. *Vallarino*: 'el último engaño ').

8259 *Gil* Juan Carlos, Lo religioso y espiritual en la New Age: Rel(y)Cult 41 (1995) 93-112.

8260 **Gomes** Michael, Theosophy in the nineteenth century; an annotated bibliography: Religious Information Systems 15. NY 1994, Garland. vi-582 p. $ 88. -- RRelStR 21 (1995) 249 (S. *Prothero*).

8261 *a) González* Ignacio, La tolerancia, razones y sinrazones; -- *b) Moya* José, *Cilleruelo* Ana I., Raíces psicosociales de la intolerancia: Moralia 18 (1995)143-172 / 173-188.

8262 *Hauerwas* Stanley, Storytelling; a response to 'Mennonites on Hauerwas' ['theie are few people to whom I owe more tthan the Mennonites']: CGrebel 13 (1995) 166-173; 136-141, *Kroeker* P.Travis, The peaceable creation; Hauerwas and the Mennonites; *al.* 142-65, from 1993 Duke Divinity colloquium].

8263 **Hillstrom** Elizabeth L., Testing the spirits. DG 1995, InterVarsity. 240 p. $ 13. 0-8308-1604-6 [ThD 43,68: the 'new mysticisms ' in today's media].

8264 *Hortal* Jesús, Um caso singular de Pentecostalismo autônomo, a Igreja Universal do Reino de Deus: Teocomunicação 24 (1994) 547-559.

8265 EHughes Richard T., The primitive Church in the modern world. Urbana 1995, Univ. Illinois. xviii-229 p. 0-252-02194-0; pa. -2-5. -- R*TBR 8,3 (1995s) 45s (D. *Martin*: valuable on and beyond how Mormons, Mennonites, Pentecostals kept trying to recapture the original forms of Christianity).

8266 **Introvigne** Massimo, La Magie, les nouveaux mouvements magiques [... dallo spiritismo al satanismo 500 p. 1990 allégé].T. P 1993, Droguet & A. 312 p. 88-7152-383-0. -- RMélSR 52 (1995) 199-201 (R.*Dericquebourg*).

8267 **Introvigne** Massimo, Idee che uccidono; Jonestown, Waco, el Tempio Solare. Pessano MI 1995, Mimep-nocete. 123 p. -- RBurg 36 (1995) 584s (M.*Guerra*).

8268 **Introvigne** Massimo, Millenarismo e nuove religioni alle soglie del Duemila: Mille e non più mille. Mi 1995, Gribaudi. 253 p.

8269 *Johns* Cheryl B., The adolescence of Pentecostalism; in search of a legitimate sectarian identity [23d presidential address 1993]: Pneuma 17 (1995) 3-17 (19-87 *al.* Women in Pentecostalism; further 229-278).

8270 *Kranenborg* R., De verwachting van de nieuwe tijd binnen de New Age-beweging; Herademing 3 (1994) 4-11 [GTT 94,141].

8271 *Kriele* Martin, Anthroposophie und Glaube: THGL 85 (1995) 119-126.

8272 **Kyle** Richard, The religious fringe; a history of alternative religions in America. DG 1993, InterVarsity, 467 p. $ 18 pa. -- RA(ndr)USS 33 (1995) 127-9 (W.W. *Whidden*); BS 152 (1995) 488 (R.A. *Pyne*).

8273 **Lacroix** Michel, La spiritualité totalitaire; le New Age et les sectes. P 1995, Plon. 212 p. F 125. -- RÉtudes 383 (1995) 428 (C. *Flipo*).

8274 **Lane** David C., Exposing cults; when the skeptical mind confronts the mystical: *RelInfSys 10. NY 1994, Garland. xiv-285 p. $ 45. 0-8153-1275-X [< ThD 42 (1995) 276].

8275 **Lederberger** Karl, *Bieri* Peter, Nouvel Âge et christianisme; passerelle pour une compréhension réciproque, TFranck Bernard. P 1992, Droguet & A. 190 p. F 69. -- RE(spr)eV 105 (1995) 107s (M. *Delahoutre*: ambiguïtés).

8276 *Lenaers* Roger, New Age; appel aan de Kerken: Streven 61 (1994) 114-126.

8277 a) *Macchia* Frank, The Spirit and the Kingdom; implications in the message of the Blumhardts for a Pentecostal social spirituality; -- b) *Villafañe* Eldin, The contours of a Pentecostal social ethic; a North American Hispanic perspective; -- c) *Johns* Cheryl B., Pentecostals and the praxis of liberation; a proposal for subversive theological education: Transformation 11,1 (1994) 1-5 + inside back cover / 6-10 / 11-15 (-32, *al.*).

8278 **Mardones** J.M., Para comprender las nuevas formas de la religión. Estella 1994, VDivino. 193 p. -- REstTrin 29 (1995) 175s (J.M. *Arbizu*); SalTer 83 (1995) 155s (J.A. *García*).

8279 *Martin* Bernice, New mutations of the Protestant ethic among Latin American Pentecostals: Religion 25 (1995) 101-117 (119-135-145, in Brazil, *Freston* Paul, *Ireland* Rowan).

8280 **Martín Estalayo** Cándido, A nuestra imagen ... en torno a la religiosidad sectaria 1993 → 10,10459: RBurgense 35 (1994) 295s (M. *Guerra Gómez*); Div 39 (1995) 82s (T. *Stramare*).

8281 EMarty Martin E., New and intense movements; Modern American Protestantism and its world 11. Mü 1993, Saur. xiv-390 p. -- RChH 64 (1995) 746s (A.G. *Schneider*).

8282 *Maser* P., Die Freikirchen und kleineren Religionsgemeinschaften in der Politik des SED-Staates: Freikirchenforschung 4 (Münster 1994) 1-14 [< ZIT 95,p.241].

8283 **Mather** George A., *Nichols* Larry A., Dictionary of cults, sects, religions, and the occult 1993 → 10,10458*: RA(ndr)USS 33 (1995) 136s (R. *Bruinsma*: 'Black Muslims' under 'World Community of Ali Islam in the West'; no article on Adventists or Roman Catholics, but several on 'Catholic orders').

8284 a) *Mayer* Jean-François, L'évolution des nouveaux mouvements religieux, quelques observations sur le cas de la Suisse; -- b) *Introvigne* Massimo, L'évolution du 'mouvement contre les sectes' chrétien 1978-1993: Social Compass 42 (1995) 181-192 / 337-347.

8285 **Mayer** Jean-François, Les nouvelles voies spirituelles; enquête sur le religiosité parallèle en Suisse. Lausanne 1993, Âge d'Homme. 428 p. -- RRTPh 127 (1995) 204 (F. *Frigerio*, inquiet).

8286 EMiller Timothy, America's alternative religions [43 art.]. Albany 1995, SUNY. ix-474 p. $ 74.50; pa. $ 25. 0-7914-2397-2; -8-0 [ThD 43,55].

8287 EMiller Timothy, When prophets die 1991 → 8,b126 ... 10,10460: RChH 64 (1995) 536-8 (R. *Kyle:* a challenge to the view that new religions then degenerate); RExp 92 (1995) 247s (B.J. *Leonard*).

8288 **Mirbach** Wolfram, Universelles Leben [früher 'Heimholungswerk ', dynamischkirchenkritische Sondergruppe]; Originalität und Christlichkeit einer Neureligion [Diss. Erlangen]: MgMissÖk 19. Erlangen 1994, Ev.-Luth. viii-338 p. DM 45. 3-87214-319-0. - - ᴿThLZ 120 (1995) 126-8 (H. *Obst*); VSVD 36 (1995) 302-4 (J. *Salmen*).

8289 *Morganti* Camillo, Inchiesta sul New Age: StCatt 39 (1995) 615-620.

8290 **Moriarty** Michael, The new charismatics; a concerned voice responds to dangerous new trends. GR 1992, Zondervan. 384 p. $ 18. -- ᴿPneuma 17 (1995) 283-7 (W.L. *de Arteaga*).

8291 *Napiórkowski* Stanisław C., Nouveaux mouvements religieux en Pologne; pour comprendre le phénomène polonais: R(ocz)T(Lub) 42,7 (1995) 183-193; ᴾ 193s.

8292 *Ocvirk* Drago, New Age ?: *BogVest 53 (1993) 265-272, Slovene only.

8293 **Oropeza** B.J., A time to laugh ['Toronto blessing' Holy Laughter renewal movement]. Peabody MA 1995, Hendrickson. vi-194 p. $ 13 pa. 1-56563-183-8 [ThD 43,380].

8294 **Palmer** Susan Jean, Moon sisters, Krishna mothers, Rajneesh lovers; women's roles in new religions. Syracuse NY 1995, Univ. xx-287 p. $ 25. 0-8156-0297-9 [ThD 43,80].

8295 *Pawlowicz* bp. Zygmunt, Kościół i sekty w Polsce ... 'wyjaśniene' przeciw recenzji *Fic* L.: AtK(ap) [123 (1994) 600-3] 124 (1995) 146-9.

8296 **Piette** Albert, Les religiosités séculières [activités 'imprégnées d'une certaine religiosité': sport, écologie, politique ..]: QSJ 2764, 1993 → 10,10466: ᴿRevSR 69 (1995) 265s (F. *Bœspflug*).

8297 ᴱ**Poewe** Carla, Charismatic Christianity as a global culture. Columbia c.1994, Univ. S. Carolina Press. 300 p. $ 35. -- ᴿ*CWeal 122,1 (1995) 26 (L. S. *Cunningham*).

8298 **Pousson** Edward K., Spreading the flame; charismatic churches and missions today 1992 → 9,11554: ᴿRefR 49 (1995s) 228s (P.R. *Meyerink*).

8299 **Quillo** Ronald, Companions in consciousness; the Bible and the New Age movement 1994 → 10,10468: ᴿHorizons 22 (1995) 137s (J. *Martos*).

8300 **Raj** A.S.Victor, The Hindu connection; roots of the New Age. St. Louis 1995, Concordia. 240 p. $ 13 pa. -- ᴿRefR 49 (1995s) l4l (D.J. *Adams*).

8301 *Richardson* James T., Clinical and personality assessment of participants in new religions: *IntJPsyR 5 (1995) 145-170 . 181-5; comment 171-6, *Hutch* R.A., 177-180, *Latkin* C.A.

8302 **Saliba** John A., Perspectives on new religious movements. L 1995, Chapman. x-240 p. £ 35; pa. £ 15. 0-225-66786-X; -7-8. -- ᴿ*TBR 8,3 (1995s) 53 (G. *Stone*).

8303 *Sánchez Nogales* José Luis, De le religión a la espiritualidad (La religiosidad sin Dios): Proyección 42 (1995) 51-69.

8304 *Scherrer* Monique, Grain de soleil [Bayard Presse 1988 ...] et les autres religions: → 548, Au carrefour 1993/5, 43-51.

8305 **Singer** Margaret T., (*Lalich* Janja), Cults in our midst. SF 1995, Jossey-Bass. xxiv-379 p. $ 25. 0-7879-0051-6 [ThD 43,88].

8306 **Smith** John E., Quasi-religions: humanism, marxism and nationalism. L 1994, Macmillan. viii-154 p. £ 12. 0-333-53982-6. -- ᴿET 106 (1994s) 218s (D.A. *Pailin*).

8307 *Stronstad* Roger, Affirming diversity; God's people as a community of prophets [24th Pentecostal meeting 1994 presidential address]: Pneuma 17 (1995) 145-157.

8308 **Sudbrack** Josef, Meditative Erfahrung Quellgrund der Religionen ? : Unterscheidung. Mainz/Stu 1994, Grünewald/ Quell. 183 p. Sch 233. 3-7867-1741-9 / 3-7918-2287-X. -- ᴿZkT 117 (1995) 491s (H. *Rotter*: New-Age-Phänomene).

8309 **Tabor** James D., *Gallagher* Eugene V., Why Waco ? Cults and the battle for religious freedom in America. Berkeley 1995, Univ. California. xiv-252 p. $ 27.50. 0-520-20186-8

[ThD 43.91].

8310 **Taylor** Clarence, The black churches of Brooklyn: History of urban life. NY 1994, Columbia Univ. xix-297 p. $ 27.50. 0-231-09980-0 [ThD 43.91]. → H8.6.

8311 **Terrin** Aldo N., New Age, la religiosità del postmoderno. Bo 1993, Dehoniane. 260 p. L^m 25. -- ^{R}E(spr)eV 105 (1995) 107 (M. *Delahoutre*).

8312 **Underwood** Grant, The millenarian world of early Mormonism. Urbana 1993, Univ. Illinois. vi-213 p. $ 25. -- ^{R}A(ndr)USS 33 (1995) 328-330 (G.R. *Knight*).

8313 **Urquhart** Gordon, The Pope's armada; unlocking the secrets of mysterious and powerful new sects in the Church [Focolari, Communion and liberation, Neocatechumenate] .. 1995, Bantam. 419 p. -- ^{R}*CreSp 11 (1995) 59 (-: the Pope himself has claimed them as 'sect[s] of our own ').

8315 *Valevičius* Andrius, Le Nouvel Âge ou l'eternel retour du même: NRT 117 (1995) 694-8; Eng. 699.

8314 *a) Vergote* Antoon, Religion, pathologie, guérison; RTLv 26 (1995) 3-30; -- *b)* ^{T}*Berghe* E. Vanden, Kan religie genezing brengen ?: Coll 25 (Gent 1995) 361-386.

8316 **Vernette** Jean, *Moncelon* Claire, Dictionnaire des groupes religieux aujourd'hui: Politique d'aujourd'hui. P 1995, PUF. 288 p. F 148. E(spr)eV 105 (1995) 255-*jaune*, adv.

8317 **Vernette** Jean, Sectes; que dire ? que faire ? Mulhouse 1994, Salvator. 199 p. F 95. 2-7067-0164-1. -- ^{R}NRT 117 (1995) 294s (A. *Toubeau*); RTL 26 (1995) 377s (J. *Scheuer*: un peu rapide).

8318 *Vernette* Jean, Sectes, nouvelles mouvements religieux et nouvelles croyances: E(spr)eV 105 (1995) 481-491.

8319 **Walton** M., Marginal communities; the ethical enterprise of the Followers of Jesus. Kampen 1994, Kok Pharos. 294 p. -- ^{R}Salmanticensis 42 (1995) 283s (J.-R. *Flecha Andrés*).

8320 ^{E}**Wessinger** Catherine, Women's leadership in marginal religions; explorations outside the mainstream 1993 → 10,10476 (subtitle first):^{R}*TBR 8,1 (1995s) 59 (Georgiana *Heskins*).

8321 **Wijnkoop** Marc van, 'La secte c'est l'autre' ? Rückblicke und Vorschläge zum Sektenbegriff: Diss. ^{D}*Dellsperger* R. Bern 1995. 370 p. -- RTLv 27.p.551.

8322 *a) Williamson* Clark M., Confusions in Disciples' talk and practice; theology in the life of the Church; -- *b) Stroup* Karen Leigh, The 'unacceptable face' of Disciples history; the mass suicides at Jonestown, Guyana [Jim Jones was a minister in good standing of a Disciples congregation]: Discipliana 55 (1995) 3-13 / 14-24.

8323 **Winker** Eldon K., The New Age is lying to you. St.Louis 1994, Concordia, 223 p. $ 11. -- ^{R}ConcordiaTQ 59 (Fort Wayne 1995) 317-9 (W.M. *Cwirla*: informative, journalistic).

8324 *a) Woods* Richard, What is New Age spirituality ? -- *b) Saliba* John A., A Christian response to the New Age: Way 33 (1993) 176-188 / 222-232 [*al.*].

8325 ^{E}**Wuthnow** Robert, 'I come away stronger'; how small groups are shaping American religion. GR 1994, Eerdmans. viii-401 p. $ 15. 0-8028-0737-2 [ThD 42,371].

8326 *Zinser* Hartmut, Ist das New Age eine religion ? oder brauchen wir einen neuen Religionsbegriff ?: → 10,344a, Notion of 'religion' 1990/4, 633-640.

M3.8 **Mythologia**

8327 **Bietenholz** Peter G., Historia and fabula; myths and legends in historical thought from antiquity to the modern age: StIntelH 59. Lei 1994, Brill. xii-434 p.; ill. 90-04-10063-6.-- ^{R}RStR 21 (1995) 311 (R.A. *Swanson*).

8328   **Blok** Josine H.,   The early Amazons; modern and ancient perspectives on a persistent myth [< diss.]; EPR 120. Lei 1995, Brill. xxi-473 p.; 9 fig.; bibliog. 443-460. *f* 228. 90-04-10077-6. -- ᴿGaR 42 (1995) 247 (P. *Walcot*: a blockbuster).

8329   **Campbell** Joseph,   Mythen der Menschheit. Mü 1992, Kösel. 254 p. DM 50. 3-466-34297-X. -- ᴿ*ActuBbg 31 (1994) 110.

8330   **Cook** Erwin F.,   The Odyssey in Athens; myths of cultural origins: Myth and Poetics. Ithaca NY 1995, Cornell. xiv-216 p.; bibliog. 195-208. 0-8014-3121-2.

8331   **Dubuisson** Daniel,   Mythologies du XXᵉ siècle (DUMÉZIL, LÉVY-STRAUSS, ELIADE): Racines et modèles. Lille 1993, Univ. 348 p.

8332   **Duchemin** Jacqueline,   Mythes grecs et sources orientales: Vérité des Mythes. P 1995, BLettres. xv-349 p. 2-251-32422-4.

8333   **Evers** John D.,   Myth and narrative; narrative and meaning in some Ancient Near Eastern texts: AOAT 241. Neuk/Kevelaer 1995, Neuk/Buxton & B. vii-133 p. 3-7666-9978-4.

8334   **Frank** Manfred,   Il dio a venire; lezioni sulla Nuova Mitologia, ᵀ*Cuniberto* Flavio. T 1994, Einaudi. xii-344 p. -- ᴿFilTeo 9 (1995) 203s (E. *Guglielminetti*).

8335   *Gagliuardo* Francesca,   Discussione del modello di V.PROPP applicato alla storia della mitologia scandinava; riduzione delle funzioni ad unità primarie: RIL(omb) 127 (1993) 285-296.

8336   **Giani** Leo Maria,   In heiliger Leidenschaft; Mythen, Kulte und Mysterien.   Mü 1994, Kösel. 264 p. DM 40. 3-466-36398-5. -- ᴿ*ActuBbg 31 (1994) 273s (J. *Boada*): TPQ 143 (1995) 428s (J. *Janda:* informierend und anregend).

8337   ᴱ**Graf** Fritz,   Mythos in mythenloser Gesellschaft; das Paradigma Roms: Colloquia Raurica 3.   Stu 1993, Teubner.   x-335 p.; 26 fig.; 4 pl. DM 110.   3-519-07413-3. -- ᴿGnomon 67 (1995) 385-9 (G. *Radke*); JRS 85 (1995) 265s (A. *Bendlin*).

8338   **Hammel** Jean-Pierre, *al.*, L'homme et ses mythes: Héritages. P 1994, Hatier. 336 p. - - ᴿRevSR 69 (1995) 259s (F. *Bœspflug*).

8339   *Jacob* Christian,   Le savoir des mythographes [CARRIÈRE Jean-Claude, MASSONNE Bertrand, La bibliothèque d'Apollodore: Ann.Besançon 443, 1991] → Annales(ESC).

8340   **Lee Hong-Jung,**   The Minjung behind the folktale; an example of narrative hermeneutics: A(sia)JT 8 (1994) 89-94.

8341   **Leeming** David A., *Page* Jake, The goddess; myths of the female divine. Ox 1994, UP. xiv-189 p.; bibliog. 179-183. 0-19-508639-2.

8342   **MacDonald** K.R.   The gods. Modgantown 1993, auct, xii-293 p.; ill. [OIAc 11,32].

8343   **Mambella** Raffaele,   Antinoo, l'ultimo mito dell'antichità nella storia e nell'arte: Saggistica. Mi 1995, Nuovi Autori. 303 p. Lᵐ 28. 88-7230-353-2.

8344   **Ribichini** Sergio,   Nel mondo dei miti: Archeo mg. 4/4. Mi 1995, De Agostini. 98 p. Lᵐ 9.

8345   *Strenski* Ivan, 'We have met these "dead men" and they are us ! '; theory of myth, theory of religion and history: → 184, ᶠSMART N., Aspects of religion 1994, 73-92.

8346   **Walker** Steven F.,   JUNG and the Jungians on myth; an introduction: Theorists of Myth 4 / Ref.Libr.1163. NY 1995, Garland. xiii-198 p.; bibliog. 167-198. 0-8240-3443-0.

8347   **Watson** Patricia A.,   Ancient stepmothers; myth, misogyny and reality. Mnem.s 143, 1995 → 1784 supra.

8348   *Wessels* Anton,   Von der Wahrheit der Entmythologisierung zur Wahrheit des Mythos: VSVD 36 (1995) 349-367.

8349 *a) Wunenberger* J. J., Mytho-phories; formes et transformations du mythe; -- *b) Lacourse* J., Les incursions de la mythologie dans la vie d'un ethnographe; -- *c) Côté* A., Qu'est-ce qu'une transformation mythique ? remarques sur une notion fondamentale de l'analyse structurale des mythes: Religiologiques 10 (Montréal 1994) 49-70 / 71-82 / 183-210 [< ZIT 95,p.68].

M4 Religio romana

8350 *a) Anderson* Graham, *Ut ornatius et uberius dici posset*; morals into epigram in the elder SENECA; - *b) Hine* Harry, Seneca, Stoicism, and the problem of moral evil; - *c) Pelling* Christopher, The moralism of PLUTARCH's *Lives*; - *d) Stadter* Philip, 'Subject to the erotic'; male sexual behaviour in Plutarch: → 163, ^FRUSSELL Donald, Ethics 1995, 75-91 / 93-106 / 205-220 / 221-236.

8351 *Armisen-Marchetti* Mireille, Sénèque et l'appropriation du temps: Latomus 54 (1995) 545-567.

8352 *Arnaud* Annie & Pascal, De la toponymie à l'histoire des religions; réflexion sur Mercure africain: → 10,73, Mém. LE GLAY M., L'Afrique 1994, 142-153.

8353 **Bergemann** Claudia, Politik und Religion im spätrepublikanischen Rom: Palingenesia 38, 1992 → 9,11545; 10.10498*: ^RCJ 90 (1994s) 332-4 (W.J. *Tatum*); Labeo 39 (1993) 279s (F. *Amarelli*); ZSRG.r 111 (1994) 692-7 (J.M. *Rainer*).

8354 *Berry* Ingrid E., Whether goddess, priestess or worshipper; considerations of female divinities and cults in Roman religion: Opus Mixtum (OpRom 21, 1994) 25-33.

8355 *Bilde* Pia Guldager, The sanctuary of Diana Nemorensis (Albano); the Late Republican acrolithic cult statues: AcAr 66 (K 1995) 191-217; 26 fig.

8356 **Biró** M.T., The unknown goddess of Late Roman popular religious belief: AArH 46 (1994) 195-229; 20 fig (2 maps).

8357 *Blaive* Frédéric, *Rex sacrorum;* recherches sur la fonction religieuse de la royauté romaine: RIDA 42 (1995) 125-154.

8358 *a) Cancik* Hubert & Hildegard -*Lindemaier*, Universalistische Tendenzen in der römischen Religion; -- *b) Lefèvre* Eckard, Götter, Schicksal und Handlungsfreiheit in SENECAs Tragödien: → 690, Prinzipat 1992/5, 100-2 / 164-185.

8359 *Cancik* Hubert & Hildegard -*Lindemaier*, Patria -- peregrina -- universa; Versuch einer Typologie der universalistischen Tendenzen in der Geschichte der römischen Religion: → 42, ^FCOLPE C., Tradition (1994) 64-74.

8360 **Canfora** Luciano, Vita di LUCREZIO. Palermo 1994, Sellerio. 123 p. L^m 20. -- ^RArcheo 9,112 (1994) 109 (Giovanna *Quatrocchi*).

8361 **Cantarella** Eva, Bisexuality in the ancient world. NHv 1992, Yale Univ. xii-284 p. 0-300-04844-0. -- ^RCJ 90 (1994s) 204s (J.F. *Makowski*).

8362 **Champeaux** Jacqueline, Fortuna: ÉcFrR 64, 1982-7 → 5,a760 ... 7,a539: ^RAnCl 64 (1995) 396-9 (J. *Poucet*).

8363 *Chastagnol* André, L'expression épigraphique du culte impérial dans les provinces gauloises: REA(nc) 97 (1995) 593-612 + 8 fig.; Eng. 593.

8364 **Citroni Marchetti** Sandra, PLINIO il Vecchio e la tradizione del moralismo romano: BtMatCL 9, 1991 → 8,b177; 9,11624: ^RÉtCL 63 (1995) 86s (O. *Devillers*).

8365 *Collas-Heddeland* Emmanuelle, Le culte impérial dans la compétition des titres sous le Haut-Empire; une lettre d'Antonin aux Éphésiens: REG 108 (1995) 410-429.

8366 **Conte** Gian Biagio, Genres and readers; LUCRETIUS, love elegy, PLINY's encyclopedia, [T]*Most* Glenn W. Baltimore 1993, Johns Hopkins Univ. xxiii-185 p. $32.50. 0-9018-4679-X. - [R]RStR 21 (1995) 229 (W.J. *Tatum*).

8367 *Cook* Albert, The angling of poetry to philosophy; the nature of LUCRETIUS: Arethusa 27 (1994) 193-222.

8368 **Costa** C.D.N., SENECA, four dialogues. Wmr 1994, Aris & P. £ 35; pa. £ 15. 0-85668560-7; -1-5. -- [R]*Prudentia 27,1 (1995) 68-71 (M. *Wilson*).

8369 *Cucchiarelli* Andrea, LUCREZIO, d rer. nat. IV 984, voluntas o voluptas ? Una difficoltà testuale e l'interpretazione epicuro-lucreziano del fenomeno onirico: SIF(g)C 12 (1994) 50-102 . 208-253.

8370 **Del Ponte** Renato, Dèi e miti italici; archetipi e forme della sacralità[2rev]: Nuova Atlantide Polimetis. Genova 1988, ECIG. 250 p. 88-7545-262-8.

8371 **Dorcey** Peter F., The cult of Silvanus; a study in Roman folk religion: ColumbiaStClas 20, 1993 → 8,b182 ... 10,10507: [R]AnCL 64 (1995) 400s (D. *Toulec*); Gnomon 67 (1995) 167-9 (H. *Brandt*); Latomus 54 (1995) 730 (G. *Moitrieux*).

8372 **Downing** F. Gerald, Cynics and Christian origins 1992 → 8,4131: [R]HeythJ 36 (1995) 73s (L.W, *Barnard*).

8373 *Fau* Guy, La religion dans la Rome des Césars: CahRenan 43,190 (Garches 1995) 5-35.

8374 **Fauth** Wolfgang, Helios megistos; zur synkretistischen Theologie der Spätantike: ÉPR 125. Lei 1995, Brill. xxxiii-268 p. $ 83. 90-04-10194-2 [RStR 22,346, B.A. *Pearson*].

8375 *Fishwick* Duncan, The inscription of Mamia again; the cult of the Genius Augusti and the temple of the imperial cult on the forum of Pompeii: Epigraphica 57 (Faenza 1995) 17-38.

8376 *Flory* Marleen B., The deification of Roman women: *AncHB 9 (1995) 127-134.

8377 [E]**Focardi** Gabriella, Lucius Annaeus SENECA, Apokolokyntosis, la deificazione della zucca (lat.-ital.). F 1995, Giunti. xxxvii-69 p.; bibliog. 57-65. 88-09-20710-6.

8378 **Francis** James A., Subversive virtue; asceticism and authority in the second-century pagan world. Univ.Park 1995, Penn State Univ. xviii-222 p. $ 32.50. 0-271-01304-4 [RStR 22,155, W.G. *Rusch*].

8379 **Gager** John G., Curse tablets and binding spells from the ancient world 1992 → 8,b188; 9,11637: [R]*CritRR 7 (1994) 299s (H.C.*Kee*).

8380 -- *Bravo* Benedetto, Magia tra virgolette ? [GAGER J., defixiones 1992]: At(henaeum) 83 (1995) 517-525; p. 525, la magia delle defixiones é 'sempre stata un fenomeno patologico e non una forma di cultura' (*koinè* mediterranea come Gager).

8381 **Gale** Monica R., Myth and poetry in LUCRETIUS 1994 → 10,10515b; £ 35: [R]C(las)R 45 (1995) 28-30 (C.D.N. *Costa*); GaR 42 (1995) 105s (R. *Wallace*); RStR 21 (1995) 51 (J. D. *Hague*).

8382 **García Sánchez** Justo, Las vestales romanas [1562, tratado de *Gómez de Castro* Alvar]. Oviedo 1993, Univ. 353 p.; ill. [R]AugR 34 (1994) 501 (A. *Di Berardino*).

8383 [TE]**Giancotti** F., Tito LUCREZIO Caro, La natura: I grandi libri 522, 1994 → 10,10517; L[m] 19: [R]C(las)R 45 (1995) 255s (Monica R. *Gale*); REA 97 (1995) 657s (Mireille *Armisen-Marchetti*).

8384 -- *Giannantoni* Gabriele, LUCREZIO [la sua edizione 1994 riepiloga GIANCOTTI F.]: Elenchos 15 (1994) 288-298.

8385 **Gleason** M.W., Making men; sophists and self-presentation in ancient Rome. Princeton 1995, Univ. xxxii-193 p. $ 30. -- [R]CLR 45 (1995) 115s (J. *Walters*).

8386 **Green** Miranda, The sun-gods of ancient Europe 1991 → 9,11643: [R]*ArEspArq 99

(1993) 331s (Concepción *Neira Faleiro*).

8387 *Grilli* Alberto, LUCREZIO ed EPICURO; la storia dell'uomo: ParPass 230 (1995) 16-45.

8388 **Hadot** Pierre, La citadelle intérieure; introduction aux Pensées de MARC-AURÈLE 1992 → 10,10524; F 150: ^RANCL 64 (1995) 381s (O. *Balériaux*).

8389 **Heim** François, Virtus .. croyances religieuses 1991 → 7,a550: ^RRÉAug 40 (1994) 227s (J. *Fontaine*).

8390 **Hickson** F.V., Roman prayer-language: LIVY and the Aeneid of VERGIL : BeitAK 30, 1993 → 9,11645: ^RCLR 45 (1995) 458s (Christina S. *Kraus*).

8391 *a) Holzhausen* Jens, Von Gott besessen ? ; -- *b) Bernard* Wolfgang, Zur Dämonologie des APULEIUS von Madaura: RMP 137 (1994) 53-65 / 358-373.

8392 *a) Ioppolo* Anna Maria, L'*hormē pleonázousa* nella dottrina stoica della passione: -- *b) Donini* Pierluigi, Pathos nello Stoicismo romano: Elenchos 16 (1995) 23-55.

8393 **Isnardi Parente** Margherita, Introduzione allo stoicismo ellenistico: I Filosofi 59. Bari 1993, Laterza. 196 p. 88-420-4312-5. -- ^RSalesianum 57 (1995) 589s (M. *Müller*).

8394 **Jones** Prudence, *Pennick* Nigel, A history of pagan Europe. L 1995, Routledge. xv-262 p.; bibliog. 232-242. 0-415-09136-5.

Kah Marianne, ' Die Welt der Römer mit der Seele suchend ...' ... PRUDENTIUS 1990 → 6,k259 ... 8,k969 → g577 infra.

8395 **Kirste** Reinhard, *al.*, Die Feste der Religionen; ein interreligiöser Kalender mit einer synoptischen Übersicht: Tb 771. Gü 1995, Gü-Vg. 127 p. 3-579-00771-8.

8396   **Klauck** Hans-Josef, Die religöse Umwelt des Urchristentums; I. Stadt- und Hausreligion, Mysterienkulte, Volksglaube; II. Herrscher- und Kaiserkulte, Philosophie, Gnosis: StBü 9.   Stu 1995, Kohlhammer.   207 p.; 206 p. je DM 34.   3-17-010312-1; -378-6.

8397 *La Penna* Antonio, Un' altra eco di LUCREZIO in SENECA ?: Maia 46 (19940 319-322.

8398 *Laroche* Roland A., Popular symbolic/mystic numbers in antiquity: Latomus 54 (1995) 568-576.

8399 **Lembke** Katja, Das Iseum Campense in Rom; Studie über den Isiskult unter Domitian. Heid 1994, Archäologie und Geschichte (3). 271 p. 3-9801863-2-6. -- → 8786, **Leclant** J., Isiaca bibliog.

8400 *Le Roux* Patrick, Cultes indigènes et religion romaine en Hispanie sous l'Empire: → 10,73, Mém. LE GLAY M., L'Afrique 1994, 560-7.

8401 **Levene** D.S., Religion in LIVY; Mn.s 127, 1993 → 9,11650: ^RANCL 64 (1995) 399s (J. *Poucet*); ÉtCL 63 (1995) 386s (G. *Freyburger*); JRS 85 (1995) 314s (W. *Liebeschuetz*); Latomus 54 (1995) 730-2 (J. *Champeaux*).

8402 **Liverani** M., Prestige and interest; international relations in the Near East c. 1600-1100 B.C. 1990 → 7,d296*: ^RAt(h-Pavia) 83 (1995) 277-282 (Clelia *Mora*).

8403 LUCREZIO, l'uomo e la parola. Bo 1990, CLUEB. 199 p. -- ^RA(nz)AW 46 (1993) 23-27 (K. *Sallmann*).

8404 *Marlasca* Olga, Aspectos jurídicos en la obra de SENECA: EDeusto 43,2 (1995) 125-153.

8405 ^E**Mastrocinque** Attilio, Culti pagani nell'Italia settentrionale: Labirinti 6. Trento 1994. -- ^RREL 73 (1995) 339-341 (C. *Guittard*).

8406 *Meier-Brügger* Michael, Zu lateinisch *ōmen*: Glotta 70 (1992) 248s.

8407 *Michel* Alain, A propos de LUCRÈCE et de l'épicurisme; la poésie peut-elle être didactique ?: → 10,42, ^FGIGANTE M., Storia 1994, 459-473.

8408 **Montero** Santiago, Política y adivinación en el Bajo Impero romano; emperadores y harúspices (193-408 d.C.): Latomus.c 211, 1991 → 8,b200; 9,11660: ^REM(erita) 62 (1994)

217s (J.M. *Blázquez*).

8409 **Mora** Fabio, Prosopografia isiaca ... : ÉPR 113, 1990 → 8,b201 ... 10,10534: ᴿNumen 41 (1994) 198-202 (J. *Rüpke*).

8410 ᴱ**Moreau** Alain, L'initiation 1991/2 → 8,670: ᴿCLR 45 (1995) 113-5 (K. *Dowden*).

8411 ᴱ**Mueller** Konrad, PETRONIUS, Satyricon reliquiae IV. Stu 1995, Teubner. xlviii-195 p. 3-519-01580-3.

8412 *Mutschler* Fritz-Heiner, *Dialogi* and *epistulae*; observations on SENECA's development as a philosophical writer: *JAncCiv 10 (Changchun 1995) 85-100.

8413 *Otón Sobrino* Enrique, El culto impetratorio en LUCRECIO: → 142, ᶠOROZ RETA J., I, Helm 44 (1993) 194-8.

8414 **Reiser** R., Götter und Kaiser; antike Vorbilder Jesu. Mü 1995, Kösel. 240 p. DM 40. 3-466-36419-1 [NTAb 40, p.384].

8415 **Rives** J.M., Religion and authority in Roman Carthage from Augustus to Constantine. Ox 1995, Clarendon. xvii-334 p.; bibliog. 311-326. 0-19-814083-5.

8416 *Rives* J., Venus genetrix outside Rome: *Phoenix 48 (Toronto 1994) 294-306 [NTAb 40, p.116].

8417 **Rozelaar** Marc, LUCREZ -- Versuch einer Deutung (Amst 1943). Hildesheim 1989, Olms. 267 p. -- ᴿTyche 9 (1994) 248-250 (G. *Dobesch*).

8418 **Rüpke** Jörg, Kalender und Öffentlichkeit; die Geschichte der Repräsentation und religiösen Qualifikation von Zeit in Rom: RVV 40. B 1995, de Gruyter. 740 p.; Bibliog. 629-700. 3-11-014514-6.

8419 **Salem** Jean, La mort n'est rien pour nous; LUCRÈCE et l'éthique. P 1990, Vrin. 302 p. -- ᴿRTPh 127 (1995) 378s (S. *Imhoof*).

8420 **Santi** Claudia, I libri Sibyllini e i decemviri sacris faciundis. R 1985, Il Bagatto. iii-77p

8421 *Sayar* Mustafa H., *al.*, Asylie-Erklärungen für das Isis- und Sarapisheiligtum von Mopsuhestia (Ostkilikien): Tyche 9 (1994) 113-130: pl. 20-24.

8422 **Scheid** J., Le collège des Frères Arvales 1990 → 8,b211 ... 10545: ᴿAt(henaeum) 83 (1995) 290-3 (C. *Letta*).

8423 *Scheid* John, Le *desmós* de Gaionas: observations sur une plaque inscrite du sanctuaire des dieux syriens à Rome (*IGUR* 109) : MÉFRA 107 (1995) 301-314.

8424 *a) Schiesaro* Alessandro, The palingenesis of [LUCRETIUS] *De rerum natura* -- *b) Gale* Monica, Lucretius 4.1-25 and the proems of the *De rerum natura*: PCP(g)S 40 (1994) 81-107 / 1-17.

8425 **Schowalter** Daniel N., The emperor and the gods; images from the time of Trajan [diss. Harvard, ᴰ*Mitten* D.]: HDR 28, 1993 → 9,11677; 10,10548: ᴿ*CritRR 7 (1994) 303-6 (D.L. *Jones:* important, though with limitations); EThL 70 (1994) 180s (J. *Verheyden*); T(oronto)JT 11 (1995) 102-4 (E.P. *Janzen*).

8426 *Siat* Jeannine, La pensée philosophique dans les inscriptions funéraires païennes d'Italie au début de l'ère chrétienne [< diss. Strasbourg 1992]: RevSR 68 (1994) 427-446 [NTAb 40,p.314].

8427 *a) Spawforth* Antony J.S., The Achaean federal cult [Corinth emperor-worship], part I, Pseudo-Julian, Letters 198 [< Hesperia 63 (1994) 211-232]; -- *b) Winter* Bruce W., II. The Corinthian ...

8428 *Stewart* R., Domitian and Roman religion; JUVENAL, Satires 2 & 4; TPAPA 124 (1994) 309-332 [NTAb 40,p.315].

8429 *Stone* G.R., The son of Caesar and the Son of God: BurHist 31 (1995) 105-114; 2 fig.

8430 *Stoop* Ben, The sins of their fathers; *si pater filium ter venum duit* [obscure Lex duodecim Tabularum exempts from *patria potestas* a son whom he has three times prostituted]: RIDA 42 (1995) 331-392.

8431 *Strunk* Klaus, Lateinisch *sacerdos* und damit verglichene Komposita: Glotta 72 (1994/5) 222-234.

8432 *Styka* Jerzy, De Titi LUCRETII Cari doctrina aesthetica: Mea(nder) 50 (1995) 15-22: lat.22

8433 **Takács** Sarolta A,. Isis and Sarapis in the Roman world [< diss. Los Angeles 1992]: ÉPR 124. Leiden 1995, Brill. xiv-235 p. $ 57.25. 90-04-10121-7. -- [R]REL 73 (1995) 341-3 (R. *Turcan*); RStR 21 (1995) 328 (R.S. *Ascough*).

8434 *Turcan* Robert, Les dieux de l'Orient dans l'Histoire Auguste: JS(avants) 93(1993)20-62.

8435 **Versnel** H., Inconsistencies 2: 1993 → 9,11773; 10,10556: [R]AnCl 64 (1995) 386-8 (Vinciane *Pirenne-Delforge*); Numen 41 (1994) 101s (C. *Auffarth*).

8436 **Watson** Alan, International law in archaic Rome; war and religion 1993 → 9,11688; 10,10558: [R]A(mer)HR 100 (1995) 141s (R.E. *Mitchell*); ÉtCL 63 (1995) 93s (R. *Roberge*).

8437 **Watson** Alan, The state, law and religion; pagan Rome 1992 → 9,11689; 10,10559: [R]AnCl 64 (1995) 401s (J.-P. *Martin*); ZSRG.r 111 (1994) 488-498 (R. *Gamauf*).

8438 **Watson** Lindsay, *Arae*, the curse poetry of antiquity 1991 → 8,b291 ... 10,10560: [R]JRS 85 (1995) 270s (M. *Fantuzzi*).

8439 **Wright** Richard E., Vesta; a study on the origin of a goddess and her cultus; diss. Washington, [D]*Harmon* D. Seattle 1995. 248 p 96-09814. - D(iss)AI 56 (1995s) p. 4744.

8440 *Zanzarri* R., CICERONE, PLUTARCO, APULEIO sul 'divino'; tre trattati quasi analoghi; E(untes)D 48 (1995) 233-230 [NTAb 40,p.315].

8441 **Zeller** Dieter, Christus unter den Göttern; zum antiken Umfeld des Christusglaubens: Sachbücher zur Bibel. Stu 1993, *KBW. 143 p. DM 44. 3-460-33021-X [RStR 22,245, D.C. *Aune*; Christianity unique, but other religions duly appreciated]. -- [R]BiLi 68 (1995) 50s (K. *Scholtissek*).

8442 **Ziolkowski** A., The temples of mid-republican Rome and their historical and topographical context: Saggi Storia Antica 4, 1992 → 10,10562; L[m] 200. -- [R]CLR 45 (1995) 380-2 (E. *Thomas*); Gnomon 67 (1995) 715-9 (J.-C. *Richard*)

8443 **Zuntz** G., Aiōn 1990 → 8,9887; 9,11695: [R]Latomus 54 (1995) 913s (L. *Foucher*).

M4.5 Mithraismus

8444 *Bianchi* Ugo †, Novità mitriache: *StRom 43 (1995) 135-143.

8445 **Brashear** William M., A Mithraic catechism from Egypt 1992 → 8,b226 ... 10,10565: [R]Numen 41 (1994) 325s (L.H. *Martin*).

8446 *Brashear* William M., Ein mithraischer Katechismus aus Ägypten in Berlin: AW 24 (1993) 2-20.

8447 *Cargal* Timothy B., Seated in the heavenlies; cosmic mediators in the mysteries of Mithras and the letter to the Ephesians: → 10,325.6069*, SBL Sem. 33 (1994) 804-821; 2 fig.

8448 **Clauss** Manfred, Cultores Mithrae 1992 → 8,b228 ... 10,10566: [R]Gnomon 67 (1995) 140-7 (R. *Turcan*); Klio 77 (1995) 523s (R. *Vollkommer*).

8449 *Clauss* Manfred, Die Verbreitung des Mithras-Kultes in den nordafrikanischen Provinzen: -> 10,73, Mém. LE GLAY M, L'Afrique 1994, 165-173.

8450 **Hinnells** John R., Studies in Mithraism [< 16th History of Religions congress, Rome 1990]: Storia delle religioni 9. R 1994, Bretschneider. 299 p.; 30 pl. L[m] 300. -- [R]SMSR

61 (1995) 252-5 (A. *Panaino*).

8451 *Merkelbach* Reinhold, Das Mainzer Mithrasgefäss [HORN H. 1994]: ZPE 108 (1995) 1-6; 5 fig.

8452 *Schofield* A., The search for iconographic variation in Roman Mithraism: Religion 25,1 (L 1995) 51-66 [NTAb 40, p.117].

8453 *Schofield* Alan, The search for iconographic variation in Roman Mithraism: Religion 25 (1995) 51-66.

8454 **Ulansey** David, The origins of the Mithraic mysteries; cosmology and salvation in the ancient world 1989 →5,808 ... 9,11708: ᴿAnCL 64 (1995) 402s (A. *Deman, aussi sur la* réfutation par TURCAN R., Mithra² 1993).

8455 *Ulansey* David, Solving the [bull-slaying, Christianity-rivaling] Mithraic mysteries: BAAr 20,5 (1994) 40-53 . 79.

M5.1 *Divinitates Graeciae* -- **Greek gods and goddesses**

8456 **Antonaccio** Carla M., An archaeology of ancestors; tomb cult and hero cult in early Greece: Greek studies, interdisciplinary approaches. Lanham MD 1995, Rowman & L. xiv-295 p.; bibliog. 269-292. 0-8746-7941-1.

8457 **Antonetti** Claudia, Les Étoliens, image et religion [diss. Lyon II, ᴰ*Pouilloux* J.]: Ann. Besançon 405, 1990 → 10,10570*: ᴿREA(nc) 96 (1994) 628s (P. *Cabanès*).

8458 *Avram* A., *Lefèvre* P., Les cultes de Callatis et l'oracle de Delphes: REG 108 (1995) 7-23; 2 fig.

8459 **Boitani** Piero, The shadow of Ulysses; figures of a myth, ᵀ*Weston* Anita. Ox 1994, Clarendon. xii-195 p. $ 40. 0-19-912268-3. -- ᴿRStR 21 (1995) 132 (R.A. *Swanson*).

8460 **Brandão** Junito de Souza, Mitologia grega. Petrópolis 1985-7, Vozes. I. ⁸1993, 404 p. II. 323 p.; 64 pl. III. ⁵1993, 407 p. [+ Dicionário I. A-I, 1993) -- : ᴿRBBras 11 (1994) 675s (C. *Minette de Tillesse*).

8461 **Bremmer** Jan N., Greek religion: GaR New Surveys 24. Ox 1994, UP. x-111 p.; ill. $ 12. 0-19-922073-5 [RStR 22,63. A.T. *Kraabel*].

8462 *Burkert* Walter, MENTOR. eine Datenbank zur griechischen Religion: MH(elv) 51 (1994) 226-8.

8463 **Buxton** Richard, Imaginary Greece: the contexts of mythology. C 1994, Univ. 250 p. - ᴿRPh(lgLH) 69 (1995) 209 (Françoise *Letoublon*).

8464 *Byrne* Michael, The pomegranate in modern Greek folklore and ancient Greek religion: RAHAL 26 (1993) 165-9.

8465 *Calame* Claude, Variations énonciatives, relations avec les dieux et fonctions poétiques dans les Hymnes Homériques: MH(elv) 52 (1995) 2-19.

8466 **Caldwell** Richard, The origin of the gods; a psychoanlytic study of [HESIOD] Greek theogonic myth. Ox 1989, UP. xiv-206 p. $ 15. - ᴿCLJ 91 (1995s) 199-202 (C.M. *McDonough*).

8467 **Capdeville** Gérard, Volcanus; recherches comparatives sur les origines du culte de Vulcain: BEFAR 288. R 1995, École Française. [viii-] 521 p.; bibliog. 425-475; 30 pl. 2-7283-0272-3. -- ᴿRÉG 108 (1995) 611s (P. *Faure*).

8468 *Casadio* Giovanni, Storia del culto di Dionisio in Argolide 1994 → 10,10582: ᴿEikasmos 6 (1995) 357-361 (G. Aurelio *Privitera*); Gerión 13 (1995) 361-3 (J.M. *Casillas*).

8469 *Chaniotis* G., Epigraphic bulletin for Greek religion 1991: Kernos 8 (1995) 205-266.

8470 **Dawson** Doyne, Cities of the gods 1992 → 9,11722; 10, 10587: [R]Bijdragen 56 (1995) 110 (M. *Parmentier*. Eng.)

8471 **Dowden** Ken, The uses of Greek mythology 1992 → 9,11727; 10,10589: [R]AnCl 64 (1995) 389-391 (Vinciane *Pirenne-Delforge*).

8472 **Dräger** P., Argo Pasimelousa; der Argonautenmythos in der griechischen und römischen Literatur [< Diss. Trier]: Palingenesia 43. Stu 1993, Steiner. x-400 p. DM 136. - - [R]CLR 45 (1995) 47-49 (R. *Hunter*).

8473 *Dubois* Laurent, Une nouvelle inscription archaïque [... lex sacra] de Sélinonte : RPh(lgLH) 69 (1995) 127-144.

8474 *Ducat* Jean, Un rituel samien: BCH 119 (1995) 339-368.

8476 **Faraone** C.A., Talismans and Trojan horses; guardian statues in ancient Greek myth and ritual 1992 → 8,b251; 9,11752: Tyche 10 (1995) 259ss (W. *Brashear*).

8477 [E]**Foley** Helene P., The Homeric hymn to Demeter 1994 → 10,10592: [R]AnCL 64 (1995) 263s (Madeleine *Jost*); CLR 45 (1995) 222-4 (S. *Instone*).

8478 *Frangeskou* Vassiliki, The Homeric Hymn to Aphrodite; a new interpretation: *StClasIsr 14 (1995) 1-16.

8479 **Gantz** Timothy, Early Greek myth; a guide to literary and artistic sources 1993 → 8,11736; 10,10595: [R]Phoenix 49 (Tor 1995) 176s (S.M. *Honea*).

8480 **Garland** Robert, Religion and the Greeks; ClasW. L 1994, Bristol Classical. xii-109 p.; 19 fig. £ 7. -- [R]CLR 45 (1995) 466s (H. *Bowden*); GaR 42 (1995) 247 (P. *Walcot*: one of the best in a fine series).

8481 **Garland** Robert, Introducing new gods; the politics of Athenian religion 1992 → 8,b257 ... 10,10596: [R]HZ 260 (1995) 517s (C. *Auffarth*).

8482 **Graf** Fritz, Greek mythology, an introduction [1987], [T]*Marier* Thomas. Baltimore 1993, Johns Hopkins Univ. 240 p.; 17 fig. 0-8018-4657-9. -- [R]CLB 71 (19955) 55-57 (T.F. *Winters*); Kernos 8 (1995) 306s (Vinciane *Pirenne-Delforge*).

8483 **Hägg** Robin, The iconography of Greek cult in the archaic and classical periods [conference at Delphi. Nov 16-18, 1990]: Kernos supp. 2 [1? → 10,423*=470], 1992; 230 p. -- [R]AnCL 64 (1995) 391-3 (Madeleine *Jost*); RÉG 108 (1995) 227-9 (Hélène *Cassimatis*).

8484 **Hatzopoulos** M.B., Cultes et rites de passage en Macédoine: Meletemata 19. Athènes/P 1994, de Boccard. 169 p.; 36 pl.; 2 maps. -- [R]RPh(lgLH) 69 (1995) 210-2 (É. *Will*).

8485 *Jouanna* Jacques, Espaces sacrés, rites et oracles dans l'Œdipe à Colone de Sophocle: RÉG 108 (1995) 38-58.

8486 *Kelly* David M., Satyrs [Lev 17,7; 2 Chr 11,15; Is 13,21]; CanadCath 13,5 (1995) 40.

8487 *Leduc* Claudine, Une théologie du signe en pays grec; l'hymne homérique à Hermès (I), commentaire des vers 1-181: RHR 212 (1995) 5-49.

8488 **Lonsdale** Steven H., Dance and ritual play in Greek religion 1993 → 10,10606: [R]CLR 45 (1995) 182s (H. *Bowden*); ÉtCL 63 (1995) 192s (D. *Gengler*); *JRit 9,1 (1995) 138-140 (M. *Gumpert*).

8489 **Marinatos** Nanno, [Greek sanctuaries 1995 → 471 supra]; Minoan religion 1993 → 9,11755; 10,10609: [R]GaR 42 (1995) 245 (P. *Walcot*).

8490 [E]**Marinatos** N., *Hägg* R., Greek sanctuaries 1993 → 10,12076: [R]AnCL 64 (1995) 520s (Madeleine *Jost*).

8491 *Mora* Fabio, L'interpretazione delle collettività divine in STRABONE (X,3) e la fenomenologia religiosa di POSIDONIO: SMSR 59 (1993) 7-19.

8492 *Müller* Hans-Peter, Ein griechisches Handerhebungsgebet ? Zu SAPPHO 1 D (= 1 L.P.) [als Parallele zu nicht-zitierten Psalmen]: → 48, ᶠDONNER H., Meilenstein 1995, 134-142.

8493 **Neils** Jennifer, Goddess and polis; Panathenaic 1992 → 8,b268 ... 10,10612: ᴿÉtCL 63 (1995) 393 (J. *Vanschoonwinkel*).

8494 *Nuttall* Geoffrey F., Cassandra and the language of prophecy: → 134, ᶠMURRAY R., HeythJ 36,4 (1995) 512-520.0

8495 **Parada** Carlos, Genealogical guide to Greek mythology: SIMA 107, 1993 ᴴ 9,11786: ᴿPhoenix 49 (Tor 1995) 175s (Sion M. *Honea*).

8496 *Peatfield* Alan, Water, fertility, and purification in Minoan religion: → 38, ᶠCOLDSTREAM J., Klados 1995, 217-227; 5 fig.

8497 **Petterson** Michael, Cults of Apollo at Sparta: ActaAth 12. Sto ᴰ1992. 170 p.; 10 fig. 91-7916-027-1. -- ᴿOpAth 20 (1994) 281-4 (Brin-Mari *Näsström*) & 284-7 (J. *Blomqvist*) & 287-290 (P. *Cartledge*).

8498 **Pirenne-Delforge** Vinciane, L'Aphrodite grecque; contribution à l'étude de ses cultes et de sa personnalité dans le panthéon archaïque et classique: Kernos supp.4. Athènes/Liège 1994, Centre Religion Grecque. xiii-527 p. -- ᴿÉtCL 63 (1995) 394 (M. *Mund-Dopchie*); RÉG 108 (1995) 233s (Christine *Mauduit*); SMSR 61 (1995) 249-252 (Corinne *Bonnet*).

8499 **Rehm** Rush, Marriage to death; the conflation of wedding and funeral rituals in Greek tragedy. Princeton 1994, Univ. 246 p.; 11 fig. $ 30. 0-691-03369-2. -- ᴿRStR 21 (1995) 228s (A. Tatiana *Summers*).

8500 *Roller* Lynn E., Attis on Greek votive monuments; Greek god or Phrygian ?: Hesp 63 (1994) 245-262; pl. 55-56.

8501 *Rutherford* Ian, Theoric crisis; the dangers of pilgrimage in Greek religion and society: SMSR 61 (1995) 274-293.

8502 *Scheffer* Charlotte, Female deities, horses and death (?) in archaic Greek religion: Opus Mixtum (OpRom 21,1994) 111-133.

8503 *Schmidt* Jens-Uwe, Menschenopfer bei Euripides; 'Lichtblicke' einer zerfallenen Polis-Ordnung oder Symptome einer Krise ?: WuD(ienst) 23 (1995) 91-108.

8504 ᴱ**Solomon** Jon, Apollo; origins and influences [Univ. conference, 9 art.]. Tucson 1994, Univ. Arizona. xii-196 p.; 8 fig. -- ᴿCLR 45 (1995) 83s (Jennifer R.*Marks*); RStR 21 (1995) 138 (H.F. *Mueller*).

8505 *(Mašlanka) Soro* Maria, La legge del *páthei máthos* nel Prometeo incatenato di ESCHILO: Sandalion 12s (1989s) 5-25.

8506 *Specht* Edith, Prometheus und Zeus [Hesiod]; zum Ursprung des Tieropferrituals: Tyche 10 (1995) 211-7.

8507 *Stowers* Stanley K., Greeks who sacrifice and those who do not; an anthropology of Greek religion: → 125, ᶠMEEKS W., social world 1995, 292-333 [334-350, *Layton* Bentley, Gnosticism; 274-292, *Segal* Alan F., magic].

8508 **Straten** Folkert T. van, *Hierà kalá*; images of animal sacrifice in archaic and classical Greece: ÉPR 127. Lei 1995, Brill. viii-374 p.; ill. 90-04-10292-2.

8509 **Tochtermann** Sibylle, Die allegorisch gedeutete Kirke-Mythos [HOMER's Circe]; Studien zur Entwicklungs- und Rezeptionsgeschichte: StKlasPg 24. Fra 1993, Lang. 288 p. DM 79 pa. -- ᴿJbAC 37 (1994) 181s (G.J.M. *Bartelink*).

   Versnel H.S., Inconsistencies in Greek and Roman religion 1993 → 8435 supra.

8510 **West** David R., Some cults of Greek goddesses and female daemons of oriental origin:

AOAT 233. Kevelaer/Neuk 1995, Buxton & B./Neuk-V. xvi-373 p. 3-7666-9843-5 / 3-7887-1456-5.

8511 **Yamagata** Naoko, Homeric morality. Leiden 1994, Brill. vii-261 p. $ 71.50. -- ᴿRelStR 21 (1995) 227 (L.J. *Alderink*)

8512 **(Bruit) Zaidman** Louise, *Schmitt Pantel* Pauline, Religion in the ancient Greek city [1989], ᵀ *Cartledge* Paul 1992 → 10,10579: £ 13: ᴿHZ 260 (1995) 165-7 (M. *Zimmermann*).

M52 *Philosophorum critica religionis* -- Greek philosopher-religion

8513 *Adrados* Francisco R., Human vocabulary and naturalist vocabulary in the Presocratics: Glotta 72 (1994/5) 182-195.

8514 **Alt** K., Weltflucht und Weltbejahung; zur Frage des Dualismus bei PLUTARCH. NUMEINIOS, PLOTIN: MainzAbh g/soz 1993/8. Stu 1993, Steiner. 277 p. DM 98. -- ᴿCLR 45 (1995) 64s (M.J. *Edwards*).

8515 *Amorós* Pedro, Lengua e historia en Platón; oralidad y escritura, *mythologeîn* y *mythología* en el Timeo y en el Critias; → 221, ᶠYELO TEMPLADO A., Lengua 1995, 125-142.

8516 ᵀ**Annas** Julia, *Barnes* Jonathan, Sextus EMPIRICUS, Outlines of scepticism. C 1994, Univ. xviii-249 p. £ 32; pa. £ 11. 0-521-30950-6 [RStR 22,154. T. *Brauch*]. -- ᴿCLR 45 (1995) 252s (C. *Kirwan*).

8517 *Athanassiadi* Polymnia, The œcumenism of Iamblichus; latent knowledge and its awakening (BLUMENTHAL-CLARK 1993): JRS 85 (1995) 244-250.

8518 ᴱ**Baldwin** Anna, *Hutton* Sarah, Platonism and the English imagination [28 essays starting with its influence on Christianity]. C 1994, Univ. xv-357 p. £ 40. -- ᴿGaR 42 (1995) 103 (R. *Wallace*: high standard).

8519 *Bassi* Karen, Male nudity and disguise in the discourse of Greek histrionics: Helios 22 (1995) 3-22.

8520 ᴱ**Billerbeck** Margarethe, Die Kyniker in der modernen Forschung 1991 → 8,b301: ᴿA(nz)AW 46 (1993) 34s (Malte *Hossenfelder*).

8521 **Bormann** K., PLATON. Mü 1993, Alber. 192 p. -- ᴿColl 25 (Gent 1995) 105 (L. *Anckaert*).

8522 **Brachet** Robert, L'âme religieuse du jeune Aristote 1990 → 8,b304: ᴿRTPh 127 (1995) 166s (P.-Y. *Ruff*).

8523 **Brickhouse** Thomas C., *Smith* Nicholas D., PLATO's Socrates. NY 1994, Oxford-UP. xiv-240 p. $ 35. 0-19-508175-7 [RStR 22,62, A.T. *Kraabel*, also on P. VANDER WAERDT's (non-Platonic) Socratic Movement 1994].

8524 *a) Casadio* Giovanni, The [PLATO] Politicus myth (268 D - 274 E) and the history of religions; -- *b) Eggers Lan* Conrado, Body and soul in Plato's anthropology: Kernos 8 (1995) 85-95 / 107-112.

8525 **Cropsey** Joseph, Plato's world; man's place in the cosmos. Ch 1995, Univ. x-227 p. $ 30. 0-226-12121-6 [RStR 22,253, C.W. *Conrad*].

8526 *deSilva* David, Paul and the Stoa, a comparison: JETS 38 (1995) 549-564.

8527 *Delle Donne* Vittorio, Sulla nuova edizione della Ethikē stoicheiōsis di IEROCLE stoico [BASTIANINI Guido,LONG Anthony A., Corpus Olschki, F 1992]: SIF(g)C 13 (1995) 29-99.

8528 **Dörrie** Heinrich, Der Platonismus in der Antike [1s 1987-90]; 3 mit *Balter* Matthias. Stu 1993, Frommann-Holzboog. xx-440 p. -- ᴿJA(nt)C 37 (1994) 171-3 & 173s (J. *Dillon*)

8529   *Dudley* J.E.J.,   Das betrachtende Leben (bios theoretikos) bei PLATON und ARISTOTELES; ein kritischer Ansatz: NZSTh 37 (1995) 20-40; Eng. 40.

8530   [E]**Duke** E.A., *al.*, PLATO, Opera omnia: SCBO. Ox 1995, Clarendon. xxvi-572 p. 0-19-814569-1.

8531 *Enders* Marcus, Zur Frage nach dem Tod in PLATONs Apologie: FrSZ 42 (1995) 237-66.

8532   [E]**Erbse** Hartmut, Theosophorum graecorum fragmenta[2]. Stu 1995, Teubner. lviii-144 p. 3-519-0184-3.

8533   *Fago* Angelica,   Il mito di Er; il mondo come 'caverna' e l'Ade come 'regno luminoso' di Ananke: SMSR 60 (1994) 183-218.

8534   **Ferraro** Giuseppe,   I greci e il trascendente: Oxenford 66. F 1995, Atheneum.   55 p. 88-7255-083-7,

8535   *Flückiger* Hansueli,   Der Weg zum Glück in der pyrrhonischen Skepsis und im griechischen Roman; die Beobachtung des *bíos* gegen die Erkenntnis der Philosophen: MH(elv) 51 (1994) 198-205.

8536 *Flusser* David, Die beiden wichtigen Gebote bei den Griechen: FrRuNF 2 (1995) 27-30.

8537 *Gianquinto* Antonino, 'Tenero' o 'folle'? ancora su *malakós/mantikós* (PLAT. Symp. 173 d8): SIF(g)C 12 (1994) 178-186.

8538   **Gigante** M.,   Nomos basileus [1956: ...   PINDARO] + POxy 2450.   N 1993, Bibliopolis. 357 p.; 3 pl. -- [R]RivB 43 (1995) 297-290 (R. *Penna*: alta lode).

8539   **Gigante** Marcello,   La bibliothèque de Philodème et l'épicurisme romain.   P 1987, BLettres.   128 p. -- [R]GGA 247 (1995) 190-206 (T.A. *Szlezák*, auch über K. GAISERs Herculanensia).

8540   **Gill** Christopher,   Greek thought: Greece & Rome 25. Ox 1995, UP. [vi-] 103 p. 0-19-922074-3.

8541   **Görgemanns** H.,   Platon. Heid 1994, Winter.   186 p.   DM 26. -- [R]Gym 102 (1995) 444s (H. *Steinthal*).

8542   [E]**Goulet-Cazé** Marie-Odile,   *Goulet* Richard,   Le cynisme ancien et ses prolongements 1991/3 → 9,510:   [R]AnCL 64 (1995) 378-380 (O. *Ballériaux*); RÉA(nc) 97 (1995) 675s (Susanne *Husson*).

8543   [E]**Gower** Barry S., *Stokes* Michael C., Socratic questions; the philosophy of Socrates and its significance [6 Univ. Durham lectures 1992 → 10,10637; 0-415-06931-9 [RStR 22,62, J. G. *DeFilippo* greatly prefers to L. NAVIA 1993].

8544   **Hankinson** R.J., The Sceptics. L 1995, Routledge. viii-376 p. £ 50. 0-415-04772-2. -- [R]CLR 45 (1995) 75s (Julia *Annas*).

8545   **Harris** Stephen L.,   *Platzner* Gloria,   Classical mythology; images and insights. Mountain View CA 1995, Mayfield. xxi-1065 p.; ill.; maps. $ 38 X [RStR 22,65, R.A. *Swanson*: fine massive anthology, including DANTE & AUDEN].

8546   **Heitsch** E., PLATON, Phaidros: Werke 3/1. Gö 1993, Vandenhoeck & R. 267 p. DM 68. -- [R]CLR 45 (1995) 17s (D. *Rankin*).

8547   **Hulse** James W.,   The reputations of Socrates; the afterlife of a gadfly: Reviewing philosophy 23. NY 1995, Lang.   220 p. $ 49.   0-8204-2008-3 [RStR 22,153, C.W. *Conrad*].

8548   [TE]**Inwood** Brad, *Gerson* L. P., The EPICURUS reader; selected writings and testimonia. Indianapolis 1994, Hackett. xvi-111 p. $ 22; pa. $ 6. -- [R]RStR 21 (1995) 137 (D. E. *Oakman*).

8549   **Irwin** Terence, PLATO's ethics. Ox 1995, UP. xx-436 p. $ 22.   0-19-508645-7. - [R]RStR 21 (1995) 229 (A. *Marmorstein*).

8550 **Kingsley** Peter, Ancient philosophy, mystery and magic; EMPEDOCLES and Pythagorean tradition. Ox 1995, Clarendon. ix-422 p.; bibliog. 403-416. 0-19-814988-3.

8551 [E]**Kraut** Richard, The Cambridge companion to Plato [a collection of articles]. C 1992, Univ. xiv-560 p. $ 55; pa. $ 18. 0-521-43018-6; -6310-9. -- [R]RelStR 21 (1995) 326 (M. *Slusser*).

8552 [E]**Lachenaud** G., PLUTARQUE, Œuvres morales 12/2, Opinions des philosophes: Coll. Budé. P 1993, BLettres. 352 (d.) p. F 335. -- [R]CLR 45 (1995) 21s (M. *Trapp*).

8553 **McCabe** M.M., PLATO's individuals. Princeton 1994, Univ. xiv-339 p. $ 45. 0-691-07351-1. -- [R]*Prudentia 2,27 (1995) 86-91 (D. *Blyth*).

8554 **Menn** Stephen, Plato on God as *noûs*. Carbondale 1995, S.Illinois Univ. xiii-86 p. $ 25. 0-8093-1970-5 [RStR 22,154, S.D. *Carter*].

8555 **Mourelatos** Alexander P.D., The Pre-Socratics[2] [[1]1974]. Princeton 1993, Univ. 550 p. -- [R]RTPh 127 (1995) 377s (S. *Imhoof*: actuel).

8556 *a) Németh* György, The words of Socrates; -- *b) Hegy* Dolores, Die Vorläufer des Hellenismus im Alten Orient: → 10,48, Mem. HAHN I., 1993, 33-39 / 41-52.

8557 *North* Helen F., The acropolis of the soul: → 143, [F]OSTWALD M., Nomodeiktes (1993) 423-433 (369-422 . 435-445 *al.*, also on Plato).

8558 **Nunes Carreira** José, Filosofia antes dos Gregos: BtUniv 71. Mem-Martins 1994, Europa-América. 282 p. 972-1-03890-3.

8559 *Places* É. des, Chronique de la philosophie religieuse des Grecs: BAGB 52 (1993) 408-423 / 53 (1994) 461-476 [NTAb 39, p.115: also 40, p.115].

8560 [F]PLACES Édouard des: Platonism in late antiquity, [E]**Gersh** S. 1992 → 8,147: [R]CLR 45 (1995) 68-70 (J. *Dillon*).

8561 PORPHYRE: [E]**Patillon** Michel, *Segonds* Alain P., De l'abstinence, tome III, livre IV: coll. Budé. P 1995, BLettres. lxiv-177 (doubles) p. -- [R]RPh(lgLH) 69 (1995) 192s (É. *des Places*).

8562 **Poulakis** John, Sophistical rhetoric in classical Greece. Columbia 1995, Univ. S. Carolina. xiv-220 p. $ 40 [RStR 22,242].

8563 [E]**Press** Gerald, Plato's dialogues; new studies and interpretations [as dramatic readings rather than systematic philosophy]. Lanham MD 1993, Rowman & L. vii-275 p. $ 23.50. 0-8476-7836-9. - [R]RStR 21 (1995) 326 (G.E. *Kessler*.)

8564 **Price** A.W., Mental conflict: Issues in ancient philosophy. L 1995, Routledge. xiv-218 p. £ 35; pa. £ 13. -- [R]CLR 45 (1995) 78s (Sabina *Lovibond*).

8565 **Reale** Giovanni, Zu einer neuen [1989] Interpretation PLATONs .. im Lichte der 'ungeschriebenen Lehren', [T]*Holscher* L., [E]*Seifert* J. Pd 1993, Schöningh. 640 p. DM 128. 3-506-77050-0. -- [R]Gym 102 (1995) 446s (F.F. *Schwarz*); THGL 85 (1995) 543-7 (N. *Fischer*).

8566 **Rowe** C.J., PLATO, Phaedo. C 1993, Univ. xi-301 p. £ 37.50; pa. £ 15. 0-521-30796-1: -1318-X. -- [R]AnCl 64 (1995) 288 (B. *Vancamp*).

8567 **Sánchez Manzano** María A., *Rus Rufino* S., Introducción al movimiento sofístico griego. León 1995, Univ. 194 p. -- [R]EM(erita) 62 (1994) 203-5 (E.A. *Ramos Jurado*).

8568 *Schall* James V., On the uniqueness of Socrates; political philosophy and the rediscovery of the human body: Greg 76 (1995) 343-362; franç.362

8569 [E]**Smith** Martin F., DIOGENES of Oinoanda; the Epicurean inscription 1993 → 10,10657: [R]CLR 45 (1995) 22-24 (M. *Erler*); CP(g) 89 (1994) 379-384 (T. *Dorandi*, ital.); MH(elv) 51 (1994) 237s (T. *Kappeler*).

8570 **Stern** Paul, Socratic rationalism and political philosophy. an interpretation of Plato's

'Phaedo'. Albany 1993, SUNY. x-225. $ 15. 0-7914-1574-0. - ᴿRStR 21 (1995) 326 (G.T. *Smith*, also on HARRISON R.).

8571 **Strycker** Émile de, ᴱ*Slings* S.R., Plato's Apology of Socrates, a literary and philosophical study with a running commentary: Mnemosyne supp. 137, 1994 → 10,10658; £ 90: ᴿClasR 45 (1995) 244-6 (R. *Waterfield*); RStR 21 (1995) 326 (C.W. *Conrad*).

8572 **Sullivan** Shirley Darcus, Psychological and ethical ideas; what early Greeks say: Mnem.s 144. Lei 1995, Brill. xiii-252 p.; bibliog. 243-8. 90-04-10185-3.

8573 **Thom** Johan C., The Pythagorean Golden Verses, with introduction and commentary: ÉPR 123. Lei 1995, Brill. xv-277 p.; bibliog. 230-244. 90-04-10105-5.

8574 ᵀ**Waterfield** R., PLATO, Symposium. Ox 1994. Univ. xlv-104 p. £ 5. -- ᴿCLR 45 (1995) 437 (Elizabeth *Pender*).

8575 **Williams** Bernard, Shame and necessity [Greek moral philosophy: Sather Classical Lectures 57]. Berkeley 1993, Univ. California. xii-254 p. $ 25. -- ᴿAJP(g) 116 (1995) 137-140 (C. *Segal*).

8576 **Zanker** P., The mask of Socrates [and cognates, including Jesus]; the image of the intellectual in antiquity [< 1991 Berkeley Sather lectures]. Berkeley 1995, Univ. California. x-426 p.; 179 fig. $ 45. 0-520-20105-1 [NTAb 40, p.568].

M53 *Mysteria Eleusinia; Hellenistica* -- **Mysteries; Hellenistic cults**

8577 *Agosti* Gianfranco, La cosmogonia di Strasburgo 'comunemente' per HEITSCH Ernst, Die griechischen Dichterfragmente der römischen Kaiserzeit I-II, Gö 1963²-4]: AtenR 39 (1994) 27-40.

8578 **Anderson** Graham, The Second Sophistic; a cultural phenomenon in the Roman Empire 1993 → 9,11831; 10,10494: ᴿAnCL 64 (1995) 382s (O. *Ballériaux*); CLR 45 (1995) 44s (J.R, *Morgan*); GGA 247 (1995) 217-33 (H.-G. *Nesselrath*); StClasIsr 14 (1995) 163s (J. *Geiger*).

8579 -- **Pernot** L., La rhétorique de l'éloge dans le monde gréco-romaine, 1. Histoire et technique; 2. Les valeurs: Coll. ÉtAug 137s. P 1993, Inst. EtAug. 490 p.; 391 p. -- ᴿCLR 45 (1995) 50-52 (S. *Usher*: fine; on the Second Sophistic, AELIUS ARISTIDES ...)

8580 *Ballèriaux* Omer, Le dernier chapitre d'une longue histoire; la religion grecque dans l'Empire chrétien [TROMBLEY F. ÉPR 115, 1993s]: Kernos 8 (1995) 299-303.

8581 *a) Baudy* Gerhard, Cereal diet and the origins of man; myths of the Eleusinia in the context of ancient Mediterranean harvest festivals; -- *b) Zaidman* Louise B., Ritual eating in archaic Greece; parasites and paredroi: → 727, Food 1992/5, 177-195 / 196-203.

8582 ᴱ**Bilde** Per, Religion and religious practice in the Seleucid kingdom 1990 → 6,325* ... 9,11839: ᴿJQR 85 (1994s) 441s (D. *Mendels*).

8583 **Burkert** Walter, Les cultes à mystères 1992 → 10,10665: ᴿ*TopO 3 (1993) 293-8 (Madeleine *Jost*).

8584 **Burkert** Walter, Antike Mysterien; Funktionen und Gehalt [Harvard 1992; Eng. 1987; ital. 1989] 1990 → 6,a934; 8,b365: ᴿA(nz)AW 48,1s (1995) 17-22 (R. *Muth*); Gnomon 67 (1995) 1-5 (U. *Bianchi*, franç.); Salesianum 57 (1995) 360s (F. *Canaccini*).

8585 *a) Cain* Hans-Ulrich, Hellenistische Kultbilder, religiöse Präsenz und museale Präsentation der Götter im Heiligtum und beim Fest; -- *b) Chaniotis* Angelos, Sich selbst feiern ? Städtische Feste des Hellenismus im Spannungsfeld von Religion und Politik: → 711, Stadtbild 1993/5, 115-122 + 19 fig. / 147-172.

8586 **Chuvin** Pierre, Mythologie et géographie dionysiaques; recherches sur l'œuvre de

NONNOS de Panopolis. Clermont-Ferrand 1992, Adosa. 366 p.; 4 pl.;2 maps. -- ᴿRÉG 108 (1995) 264s (Hélène *Cassimatis*).

8587 *a) Clinton* Kevin, The Eleusinian mysteries and panhellenism in democratic Athens; - - *b) Shapiro* H. Alan, Religion and politics in democratic Athens: → 736, Archaeology of Athens 1992/4, 161-172; 10 fig. / 123-9; 8 fig.

8588 *Couloubaritsis* Lambros, La religion chrétienne a-t-elle influencé la philosophie grecque ?: Kernos 8 (1995) 97-106.

8589 *Craven* Toni, Judith prays for help (9,1-14); a critical anthology of prayer from Alexander to Constantine: → 512, SBL Seminars 34 (1995) 208-212.

8590 **Dacosta** Yves, Initiations et sociétés secrètes dans l'antiquité gréco-romaine: L'île verte. P 1991, Berg. -- ᴿRÉA(nc) 96 (1994) 621 (P. *Lévêque*).

8591 *Delaygue* M.-P., Les Grecs connaissaient-ils les religions de l'Inde à l'époque hellénistique ?; BAGB 54 (1995) 152-172 [NTAb 40,p.312: no, except for Brahmanism imperfectly].

8592 *DeMaris* Richard E., a) Demeter in Roman Corinth; local development in a Mediterranean religion: Numen 42 (1995) 105-117 [NTAb 40,p.114].; -- *b)* Corinthian religion and baptism for the dead (1 Cor 15:29); insights from archaeology and anthropology: JBL 114 (1995) 661-682.

8593 ᵀᴱ**Dillon** John, *Hershbell* Jackson, IAMBLICHUS, On the PYTHAGOREAN way of life: SBL TTr 20 / GrRRel 11, 1991 → 8,b171 ... 10,668: ᴿZAW 107 (1995) 176-8 (G. *Shaw*).

8594 **Downing** F. Gerald, Cynics and Christian origins 1992 → 8,4131: ᴿCLR 45 (1995) 67s (C. *Forbes*); *JEarlyC 3 (1995) 62-64 (R.I. *Pervo*).

8595 *Goff* Barbara, Aithra at Eleusis: Helios 22,1 (1995) 65-78.

8596 **Graf** Fritz, La magie dans l'antiquité gréco-romaine; idéologie et pratique: Histoire 28, 1994 → 10,10671*: ᴿMH(elv) 51 (1994) 251 (T. *Gelzer*).

8597 ᴱ**Hägg** Robin, Ancient Greek cult practice from the epigraphic evidence, 2d int. Seminar, Athens Swedish Insitute 22-24.XI,1991: Skrifter 13. Sto 1994, Åström. 184 p,

8598 ᴱ**Holladay** Carl R., ARISTOBULUS: Fragments from Hellenistic Jewish authors 3: SBL.ttr 39. At 1995, Scholars. x-255 p. 0-7885-0119-4.

8599 ᴱ**Hopkinson** Neil, Les Dionysiaques III, chants XX-XXIV, ᵀ*Vian* Francis. P 1994, B Lettres. 306 (d.) p. -- ᴿRÉG 108 (1995) 265-7 (B. *Gerlaud*).

8600 **Isnardi Parente** M., Filosofia e scienza nel pensiero ellenistico: Collana di Filosofia NS 17. N 1992, Morano. 338 p. -- ᴿElenchos 15 (1994) 325-330 (Francesca *Alesse*).

8601 **Klauck** H.-J., Die religiöse Umwelt des Urchristentums, 1. Stadt- und Hausreligion, Mysterienkulte, Volksglaube: StBTh 9. Stu 1995, Kohlhammer. 207 p. DM 34 pa. 3-17-010312-1; -3781-6 vol.2 [NTAb 40, p.379].

8602 *Kloos* John, The phallus-bearing winnow and initiation into the Dionysiac mysteries: JR(el)St 16 (1990) 63-75.

8603 ᴱ**Koniaris** George L., MAXIMUS TYRIUS, *Philosophoumena-Dialexeis:* Texte &K 17. B 1995, de Gruyter. lxxxiii-527 p. -- ᴿRPh(lgLH) 69 (1995) 332-4 (J. *Bouffartigue*).

8604 *Manakidou* Flora, Die Seher in den Argonautika des Apollonios Rhodios: SIF(g)C 13 (1995) 190-208.

8605 *Mora* F., ARNOBIO e il culto del mistero; analisi storico-religiosa dell'Adversus nationes: StRel 10. R 1994, Bretschneider. 217 p. 88-7062-058-2. -- ᴿVetChr 32 (1995) 465-8 (N. *Biffi*).

8606 **Nussbaum** Martha C., The therapy of desire; theory and practice in Hellenistic ethics. Princeton 1994, Univ. ix-558 p. [RStR 21,135, R. *Ylvisaker*]. -- ᴿUnSemQ 48,1 (1994)

194-9 (P. H. *Van Ness*).
8607 *a) Parker* Robert, Athenian religion abroad; -- *b) Aleshire* Sara B., The demos and the priests; the selection of sacred officials at Athens from Cleisthenes to Augustus: → 693, ᶠLEWIS D., Ritual, finance 1993/4, 339-346 / 325-337.
8608 ᴱ**Raffaelli** Renato, Il mistero nel racconto classico; convegno del XIII Mystfest Cattolica, 29 giugno 1992: Letteratura e antropologia 5. Urbino 1995, Quattroventi. 67 p. 88-392-0341-9.
8609 ᴱ**Schröder** Stephan, PLUTARCHs Schrift De Pythiae oraculis 1990 → 6,a945*: ᴿGnomon 67 (1995) 108-111 (S.-T. *Teodorsson*).
8610 **Spek** R.J. van der, '... en hun machthebbers worden weldoeners genoemd'; religieuze [bijna geheel] en economische politiek in het Seleucidische Rijk. Amst 1994, VU inaugural. 51 p. 90-5383-316-1. -- ᴿAfO 42s (1995s) 263s (T. *Boiy*).
8611 *Suárez de la Torre* Emilio, Gli oracoli relativi alla colonizzazione della Sicilia e della Magna Grecia: QUCC 77 (1994) 7-37.
8612 *a) Tortorelli Ghidini* Marisa, Visioni eschatologiche in Magna Grecia; - *b) Giangiulio* Maurizio, Sapienza pitagorica e religiosità apollinea; tra cultura della città e orizzonti panellenici: → 676, Forme 1993/5, 207-217 / 9-27.
8613 **Trombley** Frank R., Hellenic religion and Christianisation, c,370-529: ÉPRO 115 [/1 to 325 → 9,11862] /2 to 529. Lei 1994, Brill. : ZRGG 47 (1995) 366s (W. *Beltz*).
8614 **Voelke** André-Jean, La philosophie comme thérapie de l'âme: Vestigia 12, 1993 → 9,11864: ᴿRevSR 68 (1994) 358-360 (L. *Bouttier*).
8615 *Williams* C.A., Greek love at Rome [VEYNE P. 1978, 1985]: CQ 45 (1995) 517-539.
8616 *Williams* Hector, Secret rites of Lesbos: Archaeology 47,4 (1994) 34-41.
8617 **Wright** Richard A., Christians, Epicureans and the critique of Greco-Roman religion; diss. Brown, ᴰ*Stowers* S. Providence 1994. - RTLv 27. p.557.

M5.5 Religiones anatolicae

8618 *Anastasiadis* Aristodimos, ᴳ Cybele and Sabazios, two Phrygian deities on Cyprus: RDACyp (1995) 229-235: pl. XXVII.
8619 **Arnold** Clinton E. (→ b822 infra) The Colossian syncretism; the interface between Christianity and folk belief at Colossae: WUNT 2/77. Tü 1995, Mohr. xii-378 p.; bibliog. 313-335. 3-16-146435-4.
8620 *Collins* Billie Jean, Greek *ololýzō* and Hittite *palwai*-; exultation in the ritual slaughter of animals: grbs 36 (1995) 319-325.
8621 **Haas** Volkert, Geschichte der hethitischen Religion: HO 1/15. Lei 1994, Brill. xxi-1031 p.; ill. $ 263. 90-04-09799-6 [RStR 22,148, D.I. *Owen*]. -- ᴿBoL (1995) 129 (L.L. *Grabbe*); OTA 18 (1995) p. 636 (M.S. *Smith*).
8622   **Kippenberg** Hans G., Die vorderasiatischen Erlösungsreligionen in ihrem Zusammenhang mit der antiken Stadtherrschaft 1988/91 → 9,11869: ᴿHZ 260 (1995) 164s (J. *Deininger*).
8623 **McMahon** Gregory, The Hittite state cult of the tutelary deities: AS 25, 1991 → 7,a716 ... 9,11872: ᴿJNES 54 (1995) 158s (C. *Melchert*).
8624 **Popko** Maciej, Religions of Asia Minor, ᵀ*Zych* Iwona. Wsz 1995, Academic. 230 p.; bibliog. 195-217. 83-86483-18-0.
8625 *Popko* Maciej, Towards a history of Hittite religion: OLZ 90 (1995) 469-483.

8626 *a) Rey-Coquais* Jean-Paul, Du sanctuaire de Pan à la 'Guirlande' de Méléagre; cultes et culture dans la Syrie hellénistique: - *b) Letta* Cesare, Il dossier di Opramoas e le liste Idei legati e degli archiereis di Licia; - *c) Gigante Lanzara* Valeria, 'Da Zeus i re'; poesia e0000 potere nell'Alessandria dei Tolemei [sic]: → 10,440, Aspetti/Ellenismo 1992/4, 47-90 / 203-246 / 91-118.

8627 *Scheer* Tanja S., Res gestae divi Augusti 24; die Restituierung göttlichen Eigentums in Kleinasien durch Augustus; → 176 [F]SCHMITT H., Rom & Osten 1995, 209-223.

8628 *Singer* Itamar, 'The thousand gods of Hatti'; the limits of an expanding pantheon: → 392, I(sr)OS 14 (1994) 81-102.

8629 **Wegner** Ilse, Hurritische Opferlisten aus hethitischen Festbeschreibungen: Corpus der hurritischen Sprachdenkmäler 3/1 Boğazköy. R 1995, Bonsignori. xvi-231 p. 88-7597-264-8.

8630 **Wilhelm** Gernot, Ein Ritual des AZU-Priesters: Corpus hurrit. Boğazköy 3/1 Ergänzungsheft, R 1995, Bonsignori. x-37 p,

8631 **Yoshida** Daisuke, Untersuchungen zu den Sonnengottheiten bei den Hethiter; Schwurgötterlisten, helfende Gottheit, Feste: Texte der Hethiter 22. Heid c. 1995, Winter. xviii-391 p. 3-8253-0402-7.

8632 *Zinko* Christian, Hethitische und vedische Geburtsrituale im sprach- und kulturgechichtlichen Vergleich; ein Arbeitsbericht: → 469, StIranMesopAnat 1 (Praha 1994) 110-148.

M6 **Religio canaanaea, syra**

8633 **Ackerman** Susan, Under every green tree; popular religion 1992 → 8,b411 ... 10,10687: [R]JAOS 115 (1995) 315-7 (M. *Cogan*).

8634 *Agourides* S., [G] The religion of the Hebrew patriarchs: D(elt)BM 14,1 (1995) 5-17.

8635 **Albertz** Rainer, A history of Israelite religion in the Old Testament period, 1. From the beginning; 2. From the Exile to the Maccabees [1992 → 8,b412], [T]*Bowden* J. 1994: [R]BS 152 (1995) 494s (E.H. *Merrill*); C(alvin)TJ 30 (1995) 544-8 (G.N. *Knoppers*, 2); ET [104 (1992s) 300s, R. *Coggins* on German original] 106 (1994s) 34s & 278s (C.S. *Rodd*); I(rish)BSt 17 (1995) 42-45 (G. *McConville*); JRel 75 (1995) 547s (J.J. *Collins*); OTA 18 (1995) p. 396 (R.E. *Murphy*: scant interest in Sapientials, but important: note J. BARTON, 'OT theology after Albertz ? ' in Louvain 1994 SBL); WW 15 (1995) 500 . 502; ZkT 117 (1995) 80-82 (R. *Oberforcher:* deutsch).

8636 *Archi* Alfonso, Šalaš [Ebla Šalaša] consort of Dagan and Kumarbi: → 84, [F]HOUWINK TEN CATE, H., Studio (1995) 1-6.

8637 *Barc* Bernard, Du Temple à la synagogue; essai d'interprétation des premiers targumismes de la Septante: → 78, [F]HARL M., Selon la Septante 1995, 11-26 [< OTA 18 (1995) p. 456].

8638 **Barker** Margaret, The great angel; a study of Israel's second God 1991 → 8,414 ... 10,10692: [R]IrBSt 15 (1993) 188-191 (Clare *Amos*).

8639 **Barker** Margaret, On earth as it is in heaven; Temple symbolism in the New Testament. E 1995, Clark. xv-96 p. 0-567-29278-9.

8640 **Bergmann** M.S., In the shadow of Moloch; the sacrifice of children and its impact on Western religions 1992 → 8,7809; 9,7973: [R]RSFen 23 (1995) 120-3 (S. *Ribichini*).

8641 *Berlinerblau* Jacques, Some sociological observations on Moshe GREENBERG's Biblical prose prayer as a window on the popular religion of ancient Israel: JNWS 21,1 (1995) 1-14.

8642 *a) Binger* Tilde, Ashera in Israel; -- *b) Burns* John B., Proverbs 7,5-27; vignettes from
the cycle of Astarte and Adonis; -- *c) Schmitt* John J., Yahweh's divorce in Hosea 2 --
who is that woman ?; -- *d) Smelik* Klaas A.D., Moloch, Molech or Molk-sacrifice ? A
reassessment of the evidence concerning the Hebrew term Molekh: S(cand)JOT 9 (1995)
3-18 / 20-36 / 119-132 / 133-142.

8643 **Blázquez** José M., *al.*, Historia de las religiones antiguas 1993 → 9,11619: ᴿBiOr 52
(1995) 764s (J.A. *Soggin*: conservative on Israel).

8644 **Blenkinsopp** Joseph, Sage, priest, prophet: religious and intellectual leadership in
ancient Israel: Library of Ancient Israel. LᵛL 1995, W-Knox. xi-191 p. $ 19. 0-664-
21954-3 [RStR 22,235].

8645 *a) Blum* Erhard, Volk oder Kultgemeinde ? Zum Bild des nachexilischen Judentums
in der alttestamentlichen Wissenschaft; -- *b) Seim* Jürgen, Der Gott Israels und der
dreieinige Gott, oder: Wie sprechen Christen angemessen vom Gott Abrahams, Isaaks und
Jacobs ? KuI(sr) 10 (1995) 24-42 / 43-57.

8646 *Bonnet* Corinne, Melqart est-il vraiment le Baal de Tyr: UF 27 (DIETRICH 60. Gb.
1995) 695-701.

8647 *Caquot* André, L'honneur du groupe et la religion; le cas de l'ancien Israël: → 10,344*a*,
Notion of religion 1990/4, 11-17.

8648 **Cartledge** Tony W., Vows in the Hebrew Bible and the Ancient Near East: JSOT.s 147,
1992 → 8,2655 (Nm 6; 15; 30): ᴿJBL 114 (1995) 130s (Z. *Garber*).

8649 *Cazelles* Henri, Yahwisme ou Yahwé en son peuple: →155, ᶠRENAUD, B., Ce Dieu,
LD 159 (1995) 13-29.

8650 **Cornelius** Izak, The iconography of the Canaanite gods Reshef and Ba'al; Late
Bronze and Iron Age I periods (ca. 1500-1000 BCE): OBO 140, 1994 → 10,10699; Fs 120
[RStR 22,232, S.B. *Parker*]: -- ᴿÉTRel 70 (1995) 420s (Françoise *Smyth*); OTA 18 (1995)
p. 397; R(uch)BL 48 (1995) 152 (J. *Śliwa*).

8651 **Cosand** James R., The theology of remembrance in the cultus of Israel; diss. Trinity
Evangelical Divinity School, ᴰ*McGary* D., 1995. 336 p. 95-33047. -- D(iss)AI 56 (1995s)
p. 2279.

8652 **Cryer** F.H., Divination in ancient Israel .. : JSOT.s 142, 1994 → 10,10700: ᴿEThL 71
(1995) 438s (J. *Lust*: dreams of the patriarchs, but nothing on Daniel).

8653 *Davies* Philip R., Abraham and Yahweh -- a case of male bonding: BiRe 11,4 (1995)
24-33 . 44.

8654 **Day** John, Molech, a god of human sacrifice in the Old Testament 1989 → 5,a948 ...
10,10702*: ᴿS(cot)JTh 48 (1995) 130s (G.C. *Heider*).

8655 **Dearman** J. Andrew, Religion and culture in ancient Israel 1992 → 8,b424 ...
10,10703: ᴿBA 57 (1994) 64 (D.C. *Benjamin*); BThB 25 (1995) 46 (R.A. *Simkins*);
*CritRR 7 (1994) 115s (J.B. *Burns*); É(gl)eT 26 (1995) 113-5 (L. *Laberge*); EstFr 96
(1995) 268 (F. *Raurell*); Interpretation 49 (1995) 434 (E.W. *Nicholson*); JAOS 115 (1995)
518-520 (L.K. *Handy*); JNWS 21,1 (1995) 126s (W. *Boshoff*); JRel 75 (1995) 109s (G.N.
Knoppers); RB 102 (1995) 463s (J.M. de *Tarragon*).

8656 *Dearman* J. Andrew, Edomite religion; a survey and examination of some recent
contributions: → 500, Edom 1990/5, 119-136.

8657 *Dever* William C., 'Will the real Israel please stand up ?' Part II: [post-ALBRIGHT]
Archaeology and the religions of ancient Israel: BASOR 298 (1995) 37-58.

8658 *Dietrich* Manfred, Altsyrische Götter und Rituale aus Emar [FLEMING D. 1992 →
8,b421 ...10,10707]: Biblica 76 (1995) 239-249.

8659 **Dietrich** Manfred, *Loretz* Oswald, 'Jahwe und seine Aschera' 1992 → 8,b426; 9,11893: ᴿJAOS 115 (1995) 301-3 (D. *Pardee*: views too hastily shifting).

8660 **Dietrich** Manfried, *Loretz* Oswald, *al.*, Mantik in Ugarit; Keilalphabetische Texte der Opferschau -- Omensammlungen -- Nekromantie: AbhLitAltsyrPal 3. Müns 1990, Ugarit-V. 3-927120-05-7. -- ᴿUF 27 (DIETRICH 60. Gb. 1995) 704-6 (A.F. *Rainey*).

8661 ᴱ**Dietrich** Walter, *Klopfenstein* M., Ein Gott allein ?: OBO 139, 1993/4 → 10,467*: ᴿEThL 71 (1995) 436s (J. *Lust*); ÉTRel 70 (1995) 274s (Françoise *Smyth*); ThQ 175 (1995) 64-66 (W. *Gross*).

8662 *Dion* Paul-Eugène, 'Voici! Yahvé n'a pas de maison comme les dieux, ni de cour comme les fils d'Ashérah'; pourquoi les Israélites jugèrent nécessaire d'élever un Temple à leur Dieu: → 10,30, ᶠCOUTURIER G., Maison 1994, 139-151.

ᴱ**Edelman** Diana V., The triumph of Elohim; from Yahwisms to Judaisms 1995→ 362.

8663 **Feldtkeller** Andreas, Im Reich der syrischen Göttin; eine religiös plurale Kultur als Umwelt des frühen Christentums [< Diss.]: SVFR 8. Gü 1994, Gü-V. 332p.; maps. DM 148. 3-579-01790-X. -- ᴿBoL (1995) 112 (S.P. *Brock*).

8664 *Flanagan* James W., Finding the arrow of time; constructs of ancient history and religion: *CuRB 3 (1995) 37-80.

8665 *a) Fleming* Daniel E., New Moon celebration once a year; Emar's ḥidašu of Dagan; -- *b) Homès-Fredericq* Denyse, Deux témoignages des cultes astraux [... Harran] : → 110, ᶠLIPIŃSKI, E., Immigration: OLA 65 (1995) 57-64 / 107-115 + 6 fig.

8666 **Fleming** Daniel E., The installation of Baal's high priestess at Emar 1992 → 8,b421 ... 10,10707: ᴿBiOr 52 (1995) 87-90 (W.G. *Lambert*: the improved text is an achievement, but the translation meant for PhD examiners is almost unusable for non-Assyriologists); JAOS 115 (1995) 129s W.D. *Whitt*).

8667 **Frevel** Christian, Aschera und der Aussschliesslichkeitsanspruch YHWHs; Beiträge zu literarischen, religionsgeschichtlichen und ikonographischen Aspekten der Ascheradiskussion [kath. Diss. ᴰ*Hossfeld* F. Bonn 1994. -- TR 91,94]: BBB 94. Weinheim 1995, Beltz Athenäum. xxix-1023 p. (2 vol.) DM 198. 3-89547-061-9. -- ᴿUF 27 (DIETRICH 60. Gb. 1995) 709-712 (O. *Loretz*).

8668 *Gangloff* Frédéric, *Haelewyck* Jean-Claude, Osée 4,17-19, un marzeah en l'honneur de la déesse ꜥAnat ? [à partir de 80 corrections pour les interprétations données à ces 18 mots que WELLHAUSEN 1892 déclara incompréhensibles]: EThL 71 (1995) 370-382.

8669 **Garbini** Giovanni, La religione dei Fenici in Occidente: SS(emitici NS) 12. R 1994, Univ. 122 p.; 11 p.

8670 *Garbini* Giovanni, Culti fenici a Pyrgi: *StEgP 11 (1992) 77-85.

8671 **Grabbe** Lester L., Priests, prophets, diviners, sages; a socio-historical study of religious specialists in ancient Israel. Ph 1995, Trinity. xviii-261 p.; bibliog. 222-243. 1-56338-132-X [OTA 19, p.127, M. *Hillmer*].

8672 **Grünwald** Klaus, Exil und Identität; Beschneidung, Passa und Sabbat in der Priesterschrift: BoBB 85, ᴰ1992 → 10,2211: ᴿJBL 114 (1995) 493-5 (J,C. *VanderKam*: queries subtle stratification).

8673 *a) Hadas-Lebel* Mireille, Le second Temple, lieu de conflits: -- *b) Smyth-Florentin* Françoise, 'Entre le sanctuaire et l'autel', un espace de violence traversé[e]; -- *c) Destro* Adriana, *Pesce* Mauro, Conflits et rites dans le Temple de Jérusalem d'après la Mishna; le rite de *Yom Kippur* (traité *Yoma*) et l'ordalie des eaux amères (traité *Sota*); -- *d) Starobinski-Safran* Esther, Moriyya [Gn 22,1; 2 Chr 3,1]: → 486, Temple lieu de conflit 1991/4, 115-125 / 109-114 / 127-137 / 171-9.

8674 *a) Hadley* Judith M., Wisdom and the goddess; -- *b) Murphy* Roland E., The personification of Wisdom → 55, ᶠEMERTON J., Wisdom 1995, 244-256 / 222-233.

8675 **Handy** Lowell K., Among the host of heaven; the Syro-Palestinian pantheon as bureaucracy 1994 → 10,10712: ᴿBASOR 297 (1995) 94s (S.A. *Wiggins*); BoL (1995) 130 (L.L. *Grabbe*); CBQ 57 (1995) 769s (S.B. *Parker*: good on Ugarit, inadequate on 'relationship between divine power relations and contemporary society').

8676 *Hartenstein* Friedhelm, Der Beitrag der Ikonographie zu einer Religionsgeschchte Kanaans und Israels: VF 40 (1995) 74-85; 1 fig.

8677 **Henshaw** Richard A., Female and male, the cultic personnel; the Bible and the rest of the Ancient Near East: PTMS 31. Allison Park PA 1994, Pickwick. 385 p. $ 52. 1-55635-015-5 [RStR 22,58, D.I. *Owen*]. -- ᴿBoL (1995) 114 (A. *Gelston*).

8678 *Herr* Bertram, Die Vorgeschichte des Baal-Mythos; ein Vorschlag zu KTU 1.1-1.6 [SMITH M.S. 1994 ...]: UF 27 (DIETRICH 60. Gb. 1995) 41-58.

8679 *Hoffman* Yair, The conception of 'other gods' in Deuteronomistic literature: → 392, IOS 14 (1994) 103-118.

8680 **Husser** Jean-Marie, Le songe et la parole .. 1994 → 10,10714 (should be BZAW 210): ᴿZAW 107 (1995) 160s (G. *Metzner*).

8681 *Hutton* Rodney R., Magic or street-theater ? The power of the prophetic word: ZAW 107 (1995) 247-260.

8682 *a) Hvidberg-Hansen* Finn O., De quelques symboles religieux dans trois tombeaux puniques datant de la période punico-romaine; -- *b) Lipiński* E., Apollon/Eshmun en Afrique proconsulaire:→ 10,73, Mém. LE GLAY M., L'Afrique 1994, 13-16; pl.I-II / 19-26

8683 *Janowski* B., YHWH und der Sonnengott; Aspekte der Solarisierung YHWHs in vorexilischer Zeit: ᴱ**Mehlhauser** J., Pluralismus und Identität (Gü 12995, Kaiser) 214-241 [< ZAW 107,539].

8684 ᴱ**Janowski** Bernd, al., Religionsgeschichtliche Beziehungen zwischen Kleinasien, Syrien und dem AT: OBO 129, 1990/3 → 9,567; 10,10718: ᴿAfO 42s (1995s) 311s (G. *Sauer*); JNWSL 21,2 (1995) 144s (G. *Klingbeil*); Mes(op-T/F) 29 (1994) 305-9 (A.M. *Jasink*); OLZ 90 (1995) 399-402 (W. *Thiel*).

8685 **Junco Garza** Carlos, La crítica profética ante el Templo 1994 → 10,2669: ᴿOTA 18 (1995) p. 427.

8686 **Keel** O., *Uehlinger* C., Göttinnen, Götter und Gottessymbole 1992 → 8,b439 ... 10,10719: ᴿSvTKv 70 (1994) 39-41 (T.N.D. *Mettinger*); TLtg 66 (1993) 117s (C. *Dohmen*).

8687 *Keel* O., Eine Kurzbiographie der Frühzeit des Gottes Israels -- im Ausgang von Ausgrabungsbefunden im syro-palästinischen Raum: EST (European Society for Catholic Theology Bulletin) 5 (Tü 1994) 158-174 [< ZIT 95, p.173].

8688 ᴱ**Klauck** Hans-Josef, Monotheismus und Christologie; zur Gottesfrage im hellenistischen Judentum und im Urchristentum: QD 138, 1991/2 → 8,573: ᴿBiLi 68 (1995) 52s (K. *Scholtissek*).

8689 *Klingbeil* Gerald A., Ritual space in the ordination ritual of Leviticus 8: JNWSL 21,1 (1995) 59-83.

8690 *Knights* Chris S., Towards a critical introduction to 'The History of the Rechabites' [= The story of Zosimus. but properly only ch. 8-10 as a later insertion]: JSJ(ud) 26 (1995) 324-342.

8691 *Kotansky* Roy, Remnants of a liturgical exorcism on a gem [in Greek: Cherubim, Iaō]: Muséon 108 (1995) 143-156; 1 fig.

8692 **Kunin** Seth D., The logic of incest; a structuralist analysis of Hebrew mythology: JSOT.s 185. Shf 1995, Academic. 297 p.; bibliog. 282-291. 1-85075-509-4.

8693 **LaRocca-Pitts** Elizabeth C., 'Of wood and stone'; a source critical analysis and study of early biblical interpretation concerning bāmôt, maṣṣēbôt, 'ašērîm, & mizbᵉḥôt: diss. Harvard, ᴰHackett Jo Ann. CM 1994. 441 p. 95-14853. -- D(iss)AI 56 (1995s) p. 229; HThR 88 (1995) 523s.

8694 **Lipiński** Édouard, Dieux et déesses de l'univers phénicien et punique: OLA 64. Lv 1995, Peeters. 536 p. 90-6831-690-7. -- ᴿUF 27 (DIETRICH 60. Gb. 1995) 716-8 (M. Heltzer).

8695 Loretz Oswald, Die Einzigkeit Jahwes (Dtn 6,4) im Licht des ugaritischen Baal-Mythos; das Argumentationsmodell des altassyrisch-kanaanäischen und biblischen 'Monotheismus': → 185, ᶠSODEN W.von, Vom Alten Orient (1995) 215-304.

8696 Margalit Baruch, **H** The couple 'YHWH and Ashera': BetM 40,4 (1995) 376-391; 2 fig.

8697 Merklein Helmut, Dušara-Ídole in den Heiligtümern vom Bāb es-Sīq und von al-Medras [Petra]: → 48, ᶠDONNER, H., Meilenstein: ÄAT 30 (1995) 109-120.

8698 **Mettinger** Tryggve N.D., No graven image ? Israelite aniconism in the Ancient Near Eastern context: CB.OT 42. Sto 1995, Almqvist & W. 252 p. 91-22-01664-3.

8699 **Moenikes** Ansgar, Die grundsätzliche Ablehnung des Königtums in der Hebräischen Bibel; ein Beitrag zur Religionsgeschichte des Alten Israel [Diss. Bonn 1994, ᴰHoheisel K.]: BBB 99. Weinheim 1995, Beltz Athenäum. 256 p. DM 88. 3-89547-073-2. -- ᴿEThL 71 (1995) 439s (J. Lust); (Tü)ThQ 175 (1995) 366s (W. Gross).

8700 **Moor** Johannes C. de, The rise of Yahwism; the roots of Israelite monotheism: BETL 91, 1990 → 6,7022 ... 8,b442: ᴿ*HebSt 35 (1994) 125-8 (S.B. Parker).

8701 a) Moor Johannes C. de, Standing stones and ancestor worship; -- b) Husser Jean-Marie, Culte des ancêtres ou rites funéraires ? à propos du 'catalogue' des devoirs du fils (KTU 1.17:I-II): UF 27 (ᶠDIETRICH 60. Gb. 1995) 1-30 / 115-127.

8702 **Neef** H.D., Gottes himmlischer Thronrat .. sôd 1994 → 10,9046: ᴿEThL 71 (1995) 445 (J. Lust).

8703 a) Oliva Juan, El sacerdote de Ishtar en la sociedad de Alalah: un texto relativo, ⌣ Alalakh-T. *378; -- b) Hidalgo Moreno Mᵃ Dolores, Nuevas categorías de oficiantes em el Corpus de rituales de Emar: → 221, ᶠYELO TEMPLADO A., Lengua 1995, 81-85 / 87-92.

8704 **Olmo Lete** Gregorio del, La religión cananea según la liturgia de Ugarit 1992 → 9,11918. 10,10729: ᴿAfO 42s (1995s) 274-7 (D. Pardee compares to the less-detailed but more objective and overall-serviceable TARRAGON J. 1989); Orientalia 64 (1995) 144-6 (A. Gianto); RB 102 (1995) 102-5 (J.M. de Tarragon).

8705 Pitard Wayne T., The 'libation installations' of the tombs at Ugarit: BA 57 (1994) 20-37; ill.

8706 Ramafuthula L.F., The involvement of the Assyrian religion in the religious syncretism in the capital city of Samaria (Sebastye) after 722/721 B.C. (II Kings 17): NduitsG 36 (1995) [< OTA 18 (1995) p. 99-106].

8707 Rey-Coquais Jean-Paul, Du sanctuaire de Pan [Banyas] à la 'Guirlande' de Méléagre; cultes et culture dans la Syrie hellénistique: → 9,440, ᴱVirgilio B., Aspetti e problemi dell'ellenismo (Pisa 1992/4) 47-90.

8708 **Ribichini** Sergio, Xella Paolo, La religione fenicia e punica in Italia: Itinerari fenici 14. R 1994, Ministero Beni. 141 p.; ill.

8709 Rice Gene, Africans and the origin of the worship of Yahweh: *JRT 50 (1994) 27-44.

8710 *Rota Scalabrini* Patrizio, L'originalità della religione di Israele: Ambrosius 71 (1995) 9-47.

8711 *Sasson* Jack M., Water beneath straw; adventures of a prophetic [Dagon] phrase in the Mari archives: → 72, ᶠGREENFIELD J., Solving 1995, 599-609.

8712 ᴱ**Schenker** Adrian, Studien zu Opfer und Kult im AT: ForAT 3, 1992 → 9,297: ᴿBiOr 52 (1995) 756-760 (C. *Houtman*, W. *Hilbrands*).

8713 **Schmidt** Francis, La pensée du Temple .. 1994 → 19,2668: ᴿCBQ 57 (1995) 788s (Corrine *Patton*).

8714 **Schniedewind** William M., The Word of God in transition; from prophet to exegete in the Second Temple period: JSOT.s 197. Shf 1995, Academic. 275 p.; bibliog. 253-9. 1-05075-550-7.

8715 *a) Schoville* Keith M., W.F. ALBRIGHT's Archaeology and the religion of Israel in retrospect; -- *b) Long* Burker, W. F. ALBRIGHT, G.E. WRIGHT, and the legacies of Christian Hebraism: → 10,331a, 11th Jewish 1994. A-231-8 / 239-246.

8716 **Seebass** Horst, Herrscherverheissungen im AT 1992 → 8,b839: ᴿ*CritRR 7 (1994) 133-5 (W.H. *Irwin*; alternative to the Davidic monarch expected in the Psalms -- and at Christmas).

8717 **Simian-Yofre** Horacio, El desierto de los dioses 1993 → 8,3975 ... 10,3664 (-6): ᴿEborensia 7 (1994) 153s (M.P.)

8718 *Smelik* Klaas A.D., Moloch, Molekh, or Molk-sacrifice: a reassessment of the evidence concerning the Hebrew term Molekh: ScandJOT 9 (1995) 133-142 [< OTA 18 (1995) p.591s: Persian-period invention to obscure the fact of child-sacrifice in earlier Judah].

8719 **Smith** Mark S., The early history of God 1990 → 6,b11 ... 10,10731: ᴿ*NewTR 7,1 (1994) 97s (L. *Boadt*).

8720 **Smith** William R. [1846-1894], Lectures on the religion of the Semites, series 2s, ᴱ*Day* John: JSOT.s 183. Shf 1995, Academic. 149 p.   £ 27. 1-85075-500-0.

8721 **Stienstra** Nelly, YHWH is the husband of his people; analysis of a biblical metaphor [ᴰUtrecht 1991]1993 9,9760 (< 7034): ᴿBoL (1995) 105 (G.H. *Jones*); CBQ 57 (1995) 577-9 (M.S. *Moore*: clear and user-friendly, but with four undebated assumptions and too much reliance on David MACE, Hebrew marriage 1953).

8722 *Stoebe* Hans Joachim, Überlegungen zum Synkretismus der jüdischen Tempelgemeinde in Elephantine: →23, ᶠBOEHMER R.M., Beiträge 1995, 619-626.

8723 **Synowiec** Juliusz S., Patriarchowie Izraela i ich religia. Kraków 1995, Bratni Zew. 178 p. 83-903571-3-5.

8724 **Taylor** J. Glen, Yahweh and the sun: biblical and archaeological evidence for sun worship in ancient Israel: JSOT.s 111, 1993 → 9,11925: ᴿBoL (1995) 120s (N. *Wyatt*); ÉTRel 70 (1995) 270s (J.-D. *Macchi*); JAOS 115 (1995) 719s (Carol *Meyers*).

8725 *Taylor* Joan E., The Asherah, the Menorah and the Sacred Tree: JSOT 66 (1995) 29-54

8726 *Thompson* Thomas L., How Yahweh became God: Genesis 3 and 6 and the heart of the Pentateuch [< DTT 57 (1994) 1-19]: JSOT 68 (1995) 57-74.

8727 **Toews** Wesley I., Monarchy and religious institution in Israel under Jeroboam I, 1993 → 9,2806; At 1993, Scholars: ᴿCBQ 57 (1995) 164-6 (E.T. *Mullen*); EThL 71 (1995) 443s (J. *Lust*); JBL 114 (1995) 133s (Sara J.*Denning-Bolle*).

8728 *Toombs* Lawrence E., When religions collide, the Yahweh/Baal confrontation: → 77, ᶠHAMRICK E.W., Yahweh 1995, 13-46

8729 ᴱ**Toorn** Karel van der, *Horst* Pieter van der, *Becking* Bob, Dictionary of deities and demons in the Bible. Lei 1995, Brill. c.960 p. *f* 225. 90-04-10313-9 [BArR 21,5 (1995)

10 adv.]
8730 **Voss** Jens, Die Menora: OBO 128, 1993 → 9,13685: [R]BiOr 52 (1995) 769s (Trudy *Labuschagne*).
8731 **Wiggins** Steve A., A reassessment of 'Asherah'; a study according to the textual sources of the first two millennia B.C.E., 1993 → 9,11930: [R]BiOr 52 (1995) 762-4 (K. *Spronk*: 'consort to the chief deity'); VT 45 (1995) 574-6 (Judith M. *Hadley*).
8732 *Wyatt* N., The liturgical context of Psalm 19 and its mythical and ritual origin: UF 27 ([F]DIETRICH 60. Gb. 1995) 359-596 [429-453, Ps 137,5, *Rabe* Norbert].
8733 *Xella* Paolo, *a)* Baal Hammon nel Pantheon punico: SMSR 60 (1994) 165-181; -- *b)* Le dieu et 'sa' déesse; l'utilisation des suffixes pronominaux avec des théonymes d'Ebla à Ugarit et à Kuntillet 'Ajrud: UF 27 ([F]DIETRICH 60. Gb. 1995) 599-610.
8734 **Zwickel** Wolfgang, Der Tempelkult in Kanaan und Israel; Studien zur Kultgeschichte Palästinas von der Mittelbronzezeit bis zum Untergang Judas: ForAT 10. xvi-424 p. DM 228. 3-16-146218-1 [ThRv 91,535]. -- [R]SBF*LA 45 (1995) 607-611 (E. *Cortese*); (Tü)TQ 175 (1995) 269s (H. *Niehr*).

M6.5 Religio aegyptia

8735 **Abitz** Friedrich, Pharao als Gott in den Unterweltsbüchern des Neuen Reiches: OBO 146. Gö 1995, Vandenhoeck & R. vii-219 p. 3-525-53781-6.
8736 **Assmann** Jan, Egyptian solar religion in the New Kingdom; Re, Amun and the crisis of polytheism, [T]*Alcock* Anthony: *StEg. L 1995, Kegan Paul. xiii-233 p.; bibliog. 211-219. 0-7103-0465-X.
8737 *Assmann* Jan, *a)* Der Amunshymnus des Papyrus Leiden I 344, verso; -- *b)* Maat und die gespaltene Welt, oder, Ägyptertum und Pessimismus [some answers to critics of his 1993 Maat]; -- *c)* Das göttliche Richtertum und die Lesbarkeit der Geschichte [GRIFFITHS J.G., The divine verdict 1991]: Orientalia 63 (1994) 98-110 / GöMisz 140 (1994) 93-100 / DiscEg 30 (1994) 5-16.
8738 *a) Assmann* Jan, Le temple égyptien et la distinction entre le *dedans* et le *dehors*; -- *b) Roccati* Alessandro, Le temple égyptien en tant que centre de la civilisation pharaonique au cours des trois millénaires de son histoire: → 486, Temple lieu de conflit 1991/4, 13-25 + 9 fig. / 73-75.
8739 **Bagnall** R.S., Egypt in Late Antiquity. Princeton 1993, Univ. xii-370 p. 0-691-06986-7: [R]*NYRBooks 42,11 (1995) 55-58 (A. *Cameron*: 'Before the Fall ') ['demolishes the notion of a local Coptic culture easily separable from the Greek culture' as F. MILLAR denies 'any "Arab" or "Semitic" ethnic identity in the Roman Near East ': [NTAb 40,p.90s; 38,p.315.323].
8740 **Barta** Winfried, Komparative Untersuchungen zu vier Unterweltsbüchern 1990 → 9,11937: [R]BiOr 52 (1995) 351-3 (W. *Waitkus*).
8741 *Beckerath* J. von, Osorkon IV = Herakles: GöMiszÄg 139 (1994) 7s.
8742 **Bedier** Shafia, Die Rolle des Gottes Geb in den ägyptischen Tempelinschriften der griechisch-römischen Zeit [Diss. Trier 1984]: Pelizäus-Museum HÄgB 41. Hildesheim 1995, Gerstenberg. xxiv-223 p.; ill.; Bibliog. ix-xxiv. 3-8067-8134-6.
8743 *Beinlich* Horst, Zwei Osirishymnen in Dendera: ZÄS 122 (1995) 5-31; 2 fig.
8744 *Belluccio* Adriana, Le nombre caché dans l'Œil d'Horus: DiscEg 32 (1995) 7s.
8745 *Berlandini* Jocelyne, Ptah-Démiurge et l'exaltation du ciel: RdÉ 46 (1995) 9-40: 5 fig.; pl. II-IV; Eng. 41

8746 **Bomann** Ann, The private tomb chapel in ancient Egypt 1990 → 7,a776; [R]GöMisz 140 (1994) 107-110 (Dagmar *Winzer*).

8747 *a) Borghouts* J.F., Rethinking the Papremis ritual (HERODOTUS II 63); -- *b) Quaegebeur* Jan, DIODORE I,20 et les mystères d'Osiris: → 191, [F]STRICKER, B., Hermes: DISCEG.sp.2 (1995) 43-52 / 157-181.

8748 **Buchberger** Hannes, Transformation und Transformat: Sargtextstudien I; ÄA 52. Wsb 1993, Harrassowitz. 707 p. DM 148. 3-447-03078-X. -- [R]DiscEg 32 (1995) 117-120 (T. *DuQuesne*: on divine fission).

8749 *Cauville* Sylvie, Un inventaire de temple; les Papyrus Berlin 10.472A et 14.400: ZÄS 122 (1995) 38-61; 4 fig.; pl. I-II; 3 tables de signes avec équivalent hiéroglyphique et nombre de MÖLLER N.

8750 **Chiodi** Silvia M., La religione dell'antico Egitto. Mi 1995, Rusconi. 208 p. L[m] 33. -- [R]Archeo 123 (1995) 110 (S. *Pernigotti*).

8751 *Collombert* Philippe, Hout-Sekhem et le septième nome de Haute-Égypte, I. La divine Oudjarenes: RdÉ 46 (1995) 55-79; pl. V-VIII; 2 fig.; Eng. 79.

8752 *Cribiore* Raffaella, A hymn to the Nile [Greek c. 300. A.D.]: ZPE 106 (1995) 97-106.

8753 **Darnell** John C., The enigmatic netherworld books of the solar-Osirian unity; cryptographic compositions in the tombs of Tutankhamun, Ramesses VI, and Ramesses IX: diss. [D]*Wente*. Chicago 1995. 877 p. 96-09965. -- DissA 56 (1995s) p. 4744.

8754 *DuQuesne* Terence, Openers of the paths; canid psychopomps in ancient Egypt and India: *JAncCiv 10 (Changchun 1995) 41-53.

8755 *DuQuesne* Terence, *a)* Guide to the ways of Ro-Setawe [HERMSEN E., Die zwei Wege des Jenseits ... ; -- *b)* [I know Ma'et ...] Semen of the bull; reflexions on the symbolism of Ma'et with reference to recent studies [LICHTHEIM M. ...]; -- *c)* Squaring the Ouroboros; a discussion of two new studies of Egyptian religion [KOCH K., MEEKS D. & C., both 1993]: OBO 112, 1991]: DiscEg 31 (1995) 99-112; 2 fig. / 32 (195) 107-116 / 33 (1995) 141-155; 2 fig.

8756 *DuQuesne* Terence, The raw and the half-baked; approaches to Egyptian religion [< Marburg lecture 1993: 'Before Islam or Christianity can propose that either is tailor-fitted for the nude body of African spirituality, it should first take a spiritual journey through ancient Egypt, ancient Greece and the Far East of Hinduism', SOYINKA W.]: DiscEg 30 (1994) 29-35; 1 fig.

8757 **Egberts** A., In quest of meaning; a study of the ancient Eguptian rites of consecrating the Meret-chests and driving the calves: EgUitg 8. Lei 1995, Ned. Instituut Nabije Oosten. .. bibliog. xiii-xxxvii. 90-6258-208-7.

8758 *Emmel* Stephen, Ithyphallic gods and undetected ligatures; Pan is not 'ours': he is Min (rectification of a misreading in a work of Shenute): GöMiszÄg 141 (1994) 43-46.

8759 **Eschweiler** Peter, Bildzauber im alten Ägypten; die Verwendung von Bildern und Gegenständen in magischen Handlungen nach den Texten des Mittleren und Neuen Reiches; OBO 137. FrS/Gö 1994, Univ./VR. x-371 p.; XXVI pl. 3-7278-0958-7 / 3-525-53772-7.-- [R]DiscEg 32 (1995) 121-3 (C. *Sturtewagen*: fine); ÉTRel 70 (1995) 264 (Françoise *Smyth*).

8760 **Fazzini** Richard A., Egypt dynasty XXII-XXV: I(conography)oR 16/10, 1988 → 4,b901; 5,b3: WZKM 83 (1993) 263s (E. *Winter*).

8761 *Fitzenreiter* Martin, Zum Ahnenkult in Ägypten: GöMiszÄg 143 (1994) 51-72.

8762 *Fox* Michael V., World order and *ma'at*; a crooked parallel: JANES 23 (1995) 37-48.

8763 *Galan* J.M., Religious beliefs in the early history of ancient Egypt: AulaO 12 (1994) 147-157. .

8764 **Gallorini** Carla, Formule magiche dell'antico Egitto. Brescia 1994, Edis. 106 p. L^m 25. -- ^R*ArVi 14,53 (1995) 96 (Edda *Bresciani*).

8765 *Galpaz-Feller* Pnina, The stela of King Piye; a brief consideration of 'clean' and 'unclean' in ancient Egypt and the Bible: RB 102 (1995) 506-521; franç. 506.

8766 **Gasse** Annie, Données nouvelles administratives et sacerdotales sur l'organisation du domaine d'Amon XXe-XXIe dynasties ... papyrus: IFAO BEt 104, 1988; F 468. -- ^RCÉg 70 (1995) 138-140 (S. *Allam*).

8767 *Gillam* Robyn A., Priestesses of Hathor; their function, decline and disappearance: JA(m)RCE(g) 32 (1995) 211-237.

8768 *Godron* Gérard, Études sur le Horus Den 1990 → 8,b942; 9,11953: ^ROL(ov)P 25 (1994) 277s (P. *Dils*).

8769 *Gordon* Andrew H., *Schwabe* Calvin W., The Egyptian *w3s*-scepter and its modern analogues; uses as symbol of divine power or authority: JA(m)RCE(g) 32 (1995) 185-196.

8770 *Gosline* Sheldon L., The *mnjt* as an instrument of divine assimilation: DiscEg 30 (1994) 37-46.

8771 **Grof** Stanislav, Books of the dead; manuals for living and dying. L 1994, Thames & H. 96 p.; ill. 0-500-81041-9 [*OIAc 11 (1994) 24].

8772 **Guglielmi** W., Die Göttin Mr.t; Entstehung und Verehrung einer Personification: PÄ 7, 1991 → 7,a789 ... 10,10757: ^ROLZ 90 (1995) 28-31 (J. *Hallof*).

8773 *a) Guglielmi* Waltraud, Die Funktion von Tempeleingang und Gegentempel als Gebetsort; zu Deutung einiger Widder- und Gansstelen des Amun; -- *b) Kurth* Dieter. Die Reise der Hathor von Dendera nach Edfu: → 10,470, Äg. Tempel 1990/2/4, 55-66 + 3 fig. / 211-6.

8774 *Hegedus* Tim, The theme of initiation into the cult of Isis in Book 11 of APULEIUS' Metamorphoses: *JSStEg 21s (1991s) 48-87.

8775 -- *a) Holzhausen* Jens, Von Gott besessen? ; -- *b) Bernard* Wolfgang, Zur Dämonologie des APULEIUS von Madaura: RMP 137 (1994) 53-65 / 358-373.

8776 *a) Helmis* Andréas, La terre, les hommes et les dieux; un dufférend de bornage dans l'Égypte ptolémaïque; -- *b) Manning* J.G., Land and status in Ptolemaic Egypt; the status designation 'occupation title + *b3k* + divine name'; -- *c) Kessler* Dieter, Die Gottes-Diener in den Nekropolen-Bezirken: → 10.443, Grund/Boden im Altägypten 1990/4, 327-340 / 147-175.

8777 *Hönig* Werner, Die 9 Götter von Heliopolis in der Cheopspyramide: *DiscEg 33 (1995) 33-39; 3 fig.

8778 **Hornung** Erik, Echnaton; die Religion des Lichtes. Z 1995, Artemis. 159 p.; Bibliog. 138-151. 3-7608-1111-6.

8779 *Hull* Robert F.,^J, A prayer to Serapis: → 512, SBL Seminars 34 (1995) 213-5

8780 *a) Junge* Friedrich, Mythos und Literärizität; die Geschichte vom Streit der Götter Horus und Seth; -- *b) Leitz* Christian, Auseinandersetzung zwischen Thoth und Baba: → 10,137*, ^FWESTENDORF W., Quaerentes 1994, 83-101 / 103-117.

8781 *Kakovkine* Alexandre, Les autels en bronze de l'Égypte dans la collection de l'Ermitage (Saint-Pétersbourg): GöMiszÄg 141 (1994) 55-65; 3 fig. [two of the altars have four horns like the several found in Palestine-Sinai excavation].

8782 **Koch** Klaus, Geschichte der ägyptischen Religion von den Pyramiden bis zu den Mysterien der Isis 1993 → 9,11967; DM 129. 3-17-009808-X: ^RBoL (1995) 132 (L.L. *Grabbe*: useful synthesis of Egyptologists by an admittedly non-Egyptologist); DiscEg 33 (1995) 144-7 (T. *DuQuesne*: masterly, the best).

8783 *Kügler* Joachim, Priestersynoden im hellenistischen Ägypten; ein Vorschlag zu ihrer sozio-historischen Deutung: GöMiszÄg 139 (1994) 53-60.

8784 *Kurhan* Mürüvvet, ^T *a*) Dieu Rê tout le long des siècles; -- *b*) Ptah, le dieu de l'ancien royaume égyptien; -- *c*) Amon dieu de l'empire: B(elleten)TTK 58 (1994) 1-27; 16 fig. / 265-278; 4 fig. / 59 (1995) 499-582.

8785 **Kurth** Dieter, Treffpunkt der Götter; Inschriften aus dem Tempel des Horus von Idfu. Z 1994, Artemis. 419 p.; 11 pl. DM 78. 3-7608-1097-7. -- ^ROL(ov)P 26 (1995) 210-2 (O.E. *Kaper*).

8786 **Leclant** J., *Clerc* G., Inventaire bibliographique des Isiaca: ÉPR 18, 1991 → 8,b492; 9,11969*: ^RAulaO 11 (1993) 263s (J. *Padró*); RÉA(nc) 96 (1994) 633 (J. *Desanges*); WZKM 83 (1993) 261-3 (E. *Winter*).

8787 **Lichtheim** Miriam, Maat in Egyptian autobiographies and related studies: OBO 120, 1992 → 9,11971: ^RBiOr 52 (1995) 39-42 (Gertie *Englund*); CÉg 70 (1995) 135-7 (H. De *Meulenaere*, aussi sur son OBO 84,1988).

8788 **López** Jesús, *Sanmartín* Joaquín, Mitología y religión del Oriente Antiguo, I. Egipto - - Mesopotamia; EstOr 7. Sabadell 1993, AUSA. 563 p.; 44 fig.: map. -- ^ROrientalia 64 (1995) 120-3 (Gabriella *Scandone Matthiae*).

8789 *Lorton* David, God; transcendent, dead, or everything ? [i. Amun-Re versus Aquinas ..]: GöMiszÄg 140 (1994) 53-68.

8790 **Luckert** Karl W., Egyptian light and Hebrew fire 1991 → 8,a806; 10,10765: ^RRTPh 127 (1995) 202 (M. *Patané*).

8791 **Meeks** Dimitri, *Fayard-Meeks* Christine, *a*) La vie quotidienne des dieux égyptiens. P 1995, Hachette. 364 p. F 125. -- ^RRHR 212 (1995) 99-103 (Y. *Volokhine*). -- *b*) Les dieux égyptiens [La vie quotidienne des .. 1993, réimprimé dans la série]: La Vie Quotidienne. P 1995, Hachette. 324 p.; 16 pl. F 95. 2-01-235175-1 [DiscEg 33 (1995) 140].

8792 **Merkelbach** Reinhold, Isis regina -- Zeus Sarapis; die griechisch-ägyptische Religion nach den Quellen dargestellt. Stu 1995, Teubner. xxviii-722 p. 3-519-07427-3.

8793 **Morschauser** Scott, Threat-formulae in ancient Egypt 1991 → 8,b498: ^ROLZ 90 (1995) 25-28 (R. *Grieshammer*).

8794 *Mostafa* Doha, Lieux saints populaires dans l'Égypte ancienne: *DiscEg 29 (1994) 97s.

8795 *Nardoni* Enrique, *a*) La justicia en Egipto antico -- *b*) El Éxodo como acontecimiento de justicia liberadora: RevB 56 (1994) 193-217 / 57 (1995) 193-222.

8796 *Parkinson* R.B., 'Homosexual' desire and Middle Kingdom literature: JEA 81 (1995) 57-76 [< OTA 19, p.380].

8797 **Perpillou-Thomas** Françoise, Fêtes d'Égypte ptolemaïque .. : StHell 31, 1993 → 10,10771; Fb 1600: ^RHZ 261 (1995) 497s (Holger *Sonnabend*).

8798 **Places** Édouard des, JAMBLIQUE; les mystères d'Égypte [^T 1966]: Aux sources de la tradition. P 1993, Blettres. xxx-237 p. F 135. 2-251-47001-8. -- ^RAnCL 64 (1995) 308s (F. *Colin*).

8799 **Poo** Mu-Chou, Wine and wine-offering in the religion of ancient Egypt [diss. Johns Hopkins 1984]. L 1995, Kegan Paul. xvii-187 p.; bibliog. 171-185. 0-7103-0501-X.

8800 *Prunet* Jean-François, *Chamora* Berhann, A history of the thunder-god cult in central Ethiopia, with text and analysis: LOrA 5s (1995) 53-77.

8801 **Quack** Joachim F., Die Lehre des Ani; ein neuägyptischer Weisheitstext in seinem kulturellen Umfeld: OBO 141. Gö 1994, Vandenhoeck & R. x-338 p. 3-7278-0984-1. -- ^RÉTRel 70 (1995) 419s (Françoise *Smyth*).

8802 *Quaegebeur* Jan, La table d'offrandes grande et pure d'Amon: RdÉ 45 (1994) 155-172: 6 fig.; Eng. 173.

8803 *Quaegebeur* Jan, Le papyrus Denon à La Haye et une famille de prophètes de Min-Amon: → 10,145, ᶠWINTER E., Aspekte 1994, 213-223 + 4 fig.

8804 **Ritner** Robert K., The mechanics of ancient Egyptian magical practice: SAOC 54, 1993 → 9,11983 [RStR 22,55, S.B. *Noegel*]. -- ᴿRdÉ 46 (1995) 247s (J. *Vercoutter*).

8805 *a) Roccati* Alessandro, Liste alimentari nella tradizione di testi religiosi egizi; -- *b) Sist* Loredana, Le bevande nei Testi delle Piramidi: → 10,480, Drinking ANE. 1990/4, 440-457 + 12 fig. / 129-137 + 1 fig.; pl.XI.

8806 *a) Rochette* Bruno, La traduction de textes religieux dans l'Égypte gréco-romaine; -- *b) Zographou G.,* L'argumentation d'HÉRODOTE concernant les emprunts faits par les Grecs à la religion égyptienne: Kernos 8 (1995) 151-166 / 187-203.

8807 **Sadek** Ashraf I., Popular religion in Egypt during the New Kingdom: HÄB 27. Hildesheim 1988, Gerstenberg. xxx-311 p.; 28 pl. DM 59. -- ᴿJNES 54 (1995) 56s (L.H. *Leszko*).

8808 *Schmidt* Heike C., Ein Fall von Amtsanmassung ? Die Gottesgemahlin Nefertari-Meritenmut: GöMiszÄg 140 (1994) 81-92.

8809 **Schweizer** Andreas, Seelenführer durch den verborgenen Raum; das ägyptische Unterweltsbuch Amduat; Vorwort *Hornung* Erik. Mü 1994, Kösel. 240 p. DM 40. 3-466-36411-6. -- ᴿBoL (1995) 138 (K.A. *Kitchen*: elegantly produced JUNG-psychologizing curio).

8810 ᴱ**Shafer** Byron E., Religion in ancient Egypt; gods, myths, and personal practice 1987/91 → 7,625 ... 10,10778: ᴿJNES 54 (1995) 57s (H. *Goedicke*); RdÉ 46 (1995) 245-7 (Y. *Volokhine*); VT 45 (1995) 422 (J.D. *Ray*).

8811 **Smith** M., The liturgy of opening the mouth for breathing 1993 → 10,10780: ᴿOLZ 90 (1995) 267-9 (J.F. *Quack*).

8812 *Sørensen* Jørgen P., Religion in context and isolation; the transition from pharaonic to Hellenistic Egypt: → 10,344a, Notion of 'religion' 1990/4, 277-282.

8813 **Spalinger** Anthony, Three studies on Egyptian feasts and their chronological implications. Baltimore 1992, Halgo. xi-64 p.; 4 pl. 0-9613-8056-X [*OIAc 11 (1994) 42].

8814 *Spalinger* Anthony, A religious calendar year in the Mut temple at Karnak: RdÉ 44 (1993) 161-183; franç. 184.

8815 **Spiegelberg** Wilhelm, Der ägyptische Mythus vom Sonnenauge, nach dem Leidener demotischen Papyrus I 384. Hildesheim 1994 = 1917, Olms. viii-383 p. 3-487-09844-X.

8816 *Stadnikow* S., Gottkönig und Fremdländer; universalistische Ausdrücke der Könige des Alten Reichs in Ägypten nach offiziellen Texten: MittAnthropRelG 9 (Münster 1994) 291-310 [< ZIT 95, p.276].

8817 **Sternberg-El Hotabi** Heike, Ein Hymnus an die Göttin Hathor 1992 → 8,b507: ᴿBiOr 52 (1995) 593-6 (Chantal *Sambin*).

8818 *Stricker* B.H., The enemies of Re II. The textual tradition: *DiscEg [23 (1992) 5-76] 28 (1994) 97-122; fig. 17-21

8819 *Teeter* Emily, Amunhotep son of Hapu at Medinet Habu [statue of seated scribe holding papyrus was used as intermediary to god Amun]: JEA 81 (1995) 232-6.

8820 **Thissen** H.J., Die demotischen Graffiti von Medinet Habu; Zeugnisse zu Tempel und Kult im ptolemäischen Ägypten. Sommerhausen 1989, Zauzich. viii-264 p. -- ᴿRdÉ 46 (1995) 250-5 (M. *Chauveau*).

8821 *Zivie-Coche* Christiane, Dieux autres, dieux des autres; identité culturelle et altérité dans l'Égypte ancienne: → 392, IOS 14 (1994) 39-80.

8822 **Willers** Dietrich, *al.*, Begegnung von Heidentum und Christentum im spätantiken Ägypten: Bericht 1. Riggisberg 1993, Abegg. 194 p. [RHE 90,66*]. 3-905014-04-1.. -- ᴿZKG 106 (1995) 122-4 (R. *Klein*).

M7 **Religio mesopotamica**

8823 *Abusch* Tzvi, The socio-religious framework of the Babylonian witchcraft ceremony *maglû*: some observations on the introductory section of the text (I awaited), II: → 72, ꟳGʀᴇᴇɴꜰɪᴇʟᴅ J., Solving 1995, 467-494.

8824 *Beaulieu* Paul-Alain, Theological and philological speculations on the [Seleucid Uruk] names of the goddess Antu; Orientalia 64 (1995) 187-213.

8825 **Black** Jeremy, *Green* Anthony, Gods, demons and symbols of ancient Mesopotamia: an illustrated dictionary 1992 → 9,12004: ᴿʙꜱᴏᴀꜱ 58 (1995) 543s (W.G. *Lambert:* the competent authors fail their intended readers).

8826 *Bottéro* Jean, Les étrangers et leurs dieux, vus de Mésopotamie: → 392, IOS 14 (1994) 23-38.

8827 **Bottéro** Jean, Mesopotamia; writing, reasoning, and the gods [1987; 15 art.], ᵀ*Bahrani* Zeinab, *Mieroop* Marc Van De, 1992 → 8,b525; 9,12006: ᴿNumen 42 (1995) 83-90 (K. van der *Toorn*).

8828 **Braun-Holzinger** Eva Andrea, Mesopotamische Weihgaben 1991 → 7,a820; 10,10792: ᴿJAOS 115 (1995) 298-300 (Sally *Dunham*).

8829 *Cavigneaux* Antoine, *Rawi* Farouk N.H. al-, Textes magiques de Tell Haddad : ZA(ssyr) 83 (1993) 179-203; 85 (1995) 19-46 . 169-220.

8830 *Chiodi* Silvia Maria, Il g i d i m [Gilgames]; un problema storico-religioso: ᴀɪᴏɴ 54 (1994) 438-454.

8831 **Cohen** Mark E., The cultic calendars of the ancient Near East 1993 → 9,12008: ᴿArOr 63 (1995) 233-7 (B. *Hruška*); A(ndr)USS 33 (1995) 295-7 (R. *Gane*).

8832 *a) Dandamayev* Muhammad, The confrontation between state and temple in Babylonia in the sixth century ʙ.ᴄ.; -- *b) Kellens* Jean, Formules d'exécration et mimes de combat dans le rituel mazdéen ancien: → 486, Temple lieu de conflit 1991/4, 77-88 / 89-94.

8833 *Di Gennaro* Teodolinda, Lo *šApiru* nell'Ebabbara [tempio (p.es. Sippar)] neo-babilonese e achemenide: ᴀɪᴏɴ 55 (1995) 381-405: soprintendente dei cibi destinati al dio.

8834 **Dijkstra** Klaas, Life and loyalty; a study in the socio-religious culture of Syria and Mesopotamia in the Graeco-Roman period based on epigraphical evidence: ÉPR 128. Lei 1995, Brill. xii-375 p.; bibliog. 351-366. 90-04-09996-4

8835 **Di Vito** Robert A., Studies in third millennium Sumerian and Akkadian personal names; the designation and conception of the personal God [< diss. 1986]: SP(ohl) 16, 1993 → : ᴿAfO 42s (1995s) 217-222 (A. *Westenholz* admires the 'personal god' concerns, but doubts that the 'resource for biblical students' goal is reliably attained); ᴊᴀᴏꜱ 115 (1995) 537-9 (B.R. *Foster:* good on the god, but a viable catalogue of the personal names would have required a few months more time); Orientalia 64 (1995) 131-6 (W.G. *Lambert*).

8836 *Finkel* Irving L., In black and white; remarks on the Assur psephomancy ritual : ZA(ssyr) 85 (1995) 271-6.

8837 *a) Fronzaroli* Pelio, The ritual texts of Ebla; -- *b) Michalowski* Piotr, The early

Mesopotamian incantation tradition: → 8,e731, ^E**Fronzaroli** P.,Literature 1992, 163-185 / 305-326.

8838 **Green** Tamara M., The city of the moon god: the religious traditions of Harran: ÉPR 114, 1992 → 10,10795: ^RNumen 41 (1994) 197s (K. *Dijkstra*; OLZ 90 (1995) 259-267 (J. *Tubach*).

8839 *a) Hunger* Hermann, Ein Kommentar zu Mond-Omina; -- *b) Kryszat* Guido, Ilu-šuma und der Gott aus dem Brunnen; -- *c) Sack* Ronald H., Royal and temple officials in Eanna and Uruk in the Chaldean period: → 185, ^FSODEN W.von, Vom Alten Orient (1995) 105-118 / 201-8 (+) 9 fig. / 425 ..

8840 *Jacobsen* Thorkild [† 2.V.1993], The historian and the Sumerian gods [presidential address, Chapel Hill NC 20.IV.1993], with presentation by *Abusch* Zvi and note by *Sasson* Jack M.: JAOS 114 (1994) 145-153.

8841 **Jonker** Gerdien, The topography of remembrance; the dead, tradition and collective memory in Mesopotamia [diss. Groningen 1993, ^D*Bremmer* I.]: (Numen)SHR 68. Lei 1995, Brill. xiii-284 p.; bibliog. 255-276. 90-04-10162-4

8842 *Katz* Dina, Inanna's descent and undressing the dead as a divine law : ZA(ssyr) 85 (1995) 221-233.

8843 *Lee* Thomas G., A table for Ištar [BM 38770]: *JAncCiv 10 (Changchun 1995) 65-69.

8844 *Michalowski* Piotr, The drinking gods; alcohol in Mesopotamian ritual and mythology: → 10,480, Drinking ANE. 1990/4, 27-44.

8845 **Oberhuber** Karl, Linguistisch-philologische Prolegomena zur altorientalischen Religionsgeschichte: *InBSprW 53, 1991: ^RA(nz)AW 96 (1993) 291-3 (W. *Pötscher*).

8846 *a) Paul* Shalom M., 'Emigration' from the netherworld in the Ancient Near East; -- *b) Toorn* Karel van der, Migration and the spread of local cults : → 110. ^FLIPIŃSKI, E., Immigration: OLA 65 (1995) 221-7 / 365-377.

8847 **Reiner** Erica, Astral magic in Babylonia: TAPhS 85/4. Ph 1995, Amer. Ph. xiii-150 p. $ 20. 0-87169-854-4 [< OTA 19, p.334, S.A. *Wiggins*: 'Transcriptions APhS'].

8848 **Sallaberger** Walther, Der kultische Kalender der Ur III-Zeit 1993 → 9,12027: ^RBiOr 52 (1995) 716-8 (M. Van De *Mieroop*).

8849 *Saporetti* C., Appunti sul poemetto 'Nergal ed Ereškigal'; OrAnt 33 (1993) 35-38 ZAW 107 (1995) 328].

8850 *Simonetti* Cristina, *Torti* Rita, Le porte aperte del cielo; il motivo della notte nelle preghiere mesopotamiche: BbbOr 37 (1995) 129-141 [OTA 19, p.380].

8851 **Soldt** Wilfred H. Van, Solar omens of Enuma Anu Enlil; tablets 23 (24) - 25 (30): Uitg 73. Lei 1995, Ned.Inst.Istanbul. xi-151 p. 90-6258-074-2.

8852 **Suter** Claudia E., Gudea's temple building; a comparison of written and pictorial accounts: diss. Pennsylvania, ^D*Zettler* R. Ph 1995. 480 p. 95-32289. -- DissA 56 (1995s) p. 1564.

8853 *Vanstiphout* H.L.J., Another attempt at the 'Spell of Nudimmud ': RA(ssyr) 88 (1994) 135-154.

8854 **Veldhuis** Niek, A cow of Sîn: *LibrOrT 1/2, 1991 → 7,9294: ^EOLZ 90 (1995) 508-510 (Beate *Pongratz-Leisten*).

8855 *Veldhuis* Niek, On interpreting Mesopotamian Namburbi rituals [MAUL S. 1994]: AfO 42s (1995s) 145-154.

8856 *Villard* Pierre, Les derniers rapports des devins néo-assyriens: RAss 89 (1995) 97-107.

8857 *Westenholz* Joan G., Heilige Hochzeit und kultische Prostitution im alten Mesopotamien -- sexuelle Vereinigung im sakralen Raum ?: WuD(ienst) 23 (1995) 43-62

(63-70, *Ulshöfer* Andrea gegen WILHELM G. über HERODOT)

8858 **Wilson** E. Jan, 'Holiness' and 'purity' in Mesopotamia: AOAT 237, 1994 → 10,10807 [RStR 22,148, Tammi J. *Schneider*].

8859 *Wilson* E. Jan, A note on the use of *erinnu* [not staff but 'tree (-representation)'] in *bārû*-rituals: JANES 23 (1995) 95-98.

8860 *Zawadzki* Stefan, Another Babylonian 'prebend text' from the British Museum; AfO 42s (1995s) 210.

M7.5 *Religio persiana* -- Iran

8861 **Boyce** Mary, Zoroastrianism, its antiquity and constant vigour 1992 → 9,12034; 10,10810: [R]BSOAS 58 (1995) 375-9 (S. *Shaked*); ZDMG 145 (1995) 447-9 (W. *Sundermann*).

8862 **Boyce** Mary, *Grenet* Frantz, A history of Zoroastrianism 3. under Macedonian and Roman rule: HO 1/8/1 1991 → 7,a842* ... 10,10811: [R]Numen 41 (1994) 202-4 (M. *Hutter*).

8863 *a) Boyce* Mary, Zoroaster's theology; translation as an obstacle to understanding; -- *b) Shaked* Saul, The Zoroastrian demon of wrath: : → 42, [F]COLPE C., Tradition (1994) 278-284 / 285-291.

8864 **Breuil** P. du, Lo Zoroastrismo. Genova 1993, Melangolo. 124 p. [R] .... (1995) 837s (C. *Saccone*).

8865 *Briant* Pierre, L'eau du Grand Roi [perse: HÉRODOTE 1,188]: → 10,480, Drinking ANE. 1990/4, 45-65.

8866 *Cereti* Carlo G., La figura del redentore futuro nei testi zoroastriani; aspetti dell'evoluzione di un mito: AION 55,1 (1995) 33-81.

8867 *Colpe* Carsten, Priesterschrift und Videvdad; ritualistische Gesetzgebung für Israeliten und Iranier: → 48, [F]DONNER, H., Meilenstein: ÄAT 30 (1995) 9-18.

8868 *Gershevitch* Ilya, Approaches to ZOROASTER's Gathas: Iran 33 (1995) 1-29.

8869 *a) Gnoli* Gherardo, Tendenze attuali negli studi zoroastriani; -- *b) Waldmann* Helmut, Theology and ideology in ancient Iran: → 10,344a, Notion of 'religion' 1990/4, 55-62 / 271-6.

8870 [E]**Kellens** Jean, La religion iranienne àl'époque achéménide: actes du colloque, Liège 11 déc. 1987: IrAnt.s 5. Lv 1993, Peeters/Univ. vii-135 p. Fb 900. 90-6831-329-0. -- [R]BoL (1995) 131 (L.L. *Grabbe*).

8871 *Kellens* Jean, L'âme entre le cadavre et le paradis: JA 283 (1995) 19-56; Eng. 56.

8872 *Kingsley* Peter. Greeks, shamans and magi: StIr 33 (1994) 187-197.

8873 *Koshelenko* G.A., *al.*, [R] Two (Parthian) goddesses ?: VDI 213 (1995) 194-202; 3 fig.; Eng. 202s.

8874 **Neusner** Jacob, Judaism and Zoroastrianism at the dusk of late antiquity; how the two ancient faiths wrote down their great traditions: SFLJ 87, 1993 → 9,12037: [R]Numen 42 (1995) 209s (M. *Stausberg*).

8875 **Nigosian** S.A., The Zoroastrian faith; tradition and modern research 1993 → 9,12038; 10,10815: [R]ET 106 (1994s) 31 (C.S. *Rodd*); Numen 42 (1995) 207-9 (M. *Hutter*: flaws).

8876 *Panaino* Antonio, Philologia avestica IV: av. *yaštay-* / *yešti-; yašta-;* phl. *yašt;* quelques réflexions sur les titres des hymnes de l'Avesta: StIr 23 (1994) 162-185;Eng.184s.

8877 **Shaked** Shaul, Dualism in transformation; varieties of religion in Sasanian Iran [16th Jordan Lectures 1991] -- [R]AION 55 (1995) 124-7 (C.G. *Cereti*).

8878 **Shaked** Shaul, From Zoroastrian Iran to Islam; studies in religious history and intercultural contacts: CS 505. Aldershot 1995, Variorum. x-321 p. 0-06078-539-4.

8879 **Waldmann** Helmut, Heilsgeschichtlich verfasste Theologie und Männerbünde; die Grundlagen des gnostischen Weltbildes [Zarathustra, Zurvanismus; < kath. Diss.Innsbruck 1985]: WissR 4. Tü 1994, Tü Ges. xxix-183 p. 3-928096-05-2 [RStR 22,66, B.A. *Pearson*]. -- ᴿOLZ 90 (1995) 548-554 (M. *Hutter*).

M8.1 *Religio proto-arabica* -- **Early Arabic religious graffiti**

8880 *Avanzini* Alessandra, Brevi osservazioni sul lessico delle lingue epigrafiche dell'Arabia meridionale preislamica: StEpL 12 (1995) 27-36.

8881 *Garbini* Giovanni, Sulla più antica scrittura sudarabica: RSO 69 (1995) 275-289 + 4 pl.

8882 *Gawlikowski* Michał, Les Arabes de Syrie dans l'antiquité: → 110, ᶠLIPIŃSKI, E., Immigration: OLA 65 (1995) 83-92.

8883 *Grouchevoy* A.G., Trois 'niveaux' de phylarques; étude terminologique sur les relations de Rome et de Byzance avec les arabes avant l'Islam; Syria 72 (1995) 105-131.

8884 *Hayes* John,Traces of BARTH's law in epigraphic South Arabic:ZDMG 143(1993)250-8

8885 **Krone** Susanne, Die altarabische Gottheit al-Lât [< Diss. Erlangen]: H(eid)OrSt 23, 1992 → 8,b580; 10,10822; DM 128: ᴿNumen 42 (1995) 94-96 (H.J.W. *Drijvers*).

8886 **Nevon** Yehuda D., *al.*, Ancient Arabic inscriptions from the Negev. Beersheba 1993, Ben-Gurion Univ. 144 p.; 34 pl. 965-435-001-7 [*OIAc 11 (1994) 35

8887 **Robin** Christian, Inventaire des inscriptions sudarabiques 1. (2. **Gnoli** Gherardo): AIBL. P/R 1992(s). de Boccard / Herder. 221 p. + 60 pl. (128 p., 18 pl.) -- ᴿAION 54 (1994) 416-422 (Alessandra *Avanzini*)JRAS (1995) 95-97 (A. *Korotayev*); JSSt 40 (1995) 170-6 (A.F.L. *Beeston*).

8888 **Ryckmans** Jacques, *al,*, Textes du Yémen antique inscrits sur bois 1994 → 10,10825: ᴿAfO 42s (1995s) 313-5 (M. *Patzelt*); AION 55 (1995) 379s (S. *Noja Noseda*).

8889 **Said** Said F, al-, Die Personanenamen in den minäischen Inschriften; eine etymologische und lexikalische Studie im Bereich der semitischen Sprache: MainzAkad.OrKomm Veröff 41. Wsb 1995, Harrassowitz. [iv-] 277 p. 3-447-03638-9.

8890 *Swiggers* Pierre, A Minaean sarcophagus inscription from Egypt: → 110, ᶠLIPIŃSKI, E., Immigration: OLA 65 (1995) 335-342 [343 adding ROBIN C., ᶠLECLANT 4 (1994) 285-301].

8891 **Tairan** Salem A., Die Personennamen in den altsabäischen Inschriften; ein Beitrag zur altsüdarabischen Namengebung: TStOr 3. Hildesheim 1992, Olms. → 9,12054; 3-487-09665-X: ᴿWZKM 83 (1994) 302-6 (A.F.L. *Beeston*).

8892 *Toll* C., Eine kurze Bemerkung zu den nabatäischen Graffiti [*šlm, btb, bryk, dkyr*: craving for power]: ZDMG 145 (1995) 7s [NTAb 40, p.98].

8893 **Zein** Amira el-, The evolution of the concept of 'Jinn' [spirit-beings] from pre-Islam to Islam; diss. Georgetown, ᴰ*Shahi* I. Washington DC 1995. 408 p. 96-08818. -- D(iss)AI 56 (1995s) p. 4416.

M8.2 *Muhammad et asseclae* - **Qur'an and early diffusion of Islam**

8894 **Ayoub** Mahmoud M., The house of Imran: The Qur'an and its interpreters 2, 1992 → 10,10827; $ 19: ᴿBiOr 52 (1995) 174-6 (J. *Burton*: for those, chiefly Muslims, not knowing Arabic).

8895 **Bell** Richard, A commentary on the Qur'ān 1991 → 10,10828: [R]BSOAS 58 (1995) 119-121 (J. *Burton*).

8896 **Calder** Norman, Studies in early Muslim jurisprudence. Ox 1993, Clarendon. x-257 p. $ 35. -- [R]JRel 75 (1995) 604-6 (Irene *Schneider*).

8897 [E]**Cameron** Averil, *Conrad* Lawrence I., The Byzantine and Early Islamic Near East, I. Problems in the literary source material [first of the workshops held in London since 1989] 1992 → 8,682: [R]HeythJ 36 (1995) 81-83 (A. *Louth*).

8898 [E]**Canivet** Pierre, *Rey-Coquais* Jean-Paul, La Syrie de Byzance à l'Islam, VIIᵉ-VIIIᵉ siècles 1990/2 → 8,682*: [R]RHE 90 (1995) 129-134 (C. *Cannuyer*).

8899 **Clifford** Winslow W., State formation and the structure of politics in Mamluk Syro-Egypt, 648-741 AH/1250-1340 CE: diss. [D]*Woods* J. Chicago 1995. 356 p. 96-09979. -- D(iss)AI 56 (1995s) p. 4911.

8900 **Dabashi** Hamid, Authority in Islam: from the rise of Muhammad to the establishment of the Umayyads 1989 (1992) → 7,a854/ 9,12066; £ 17; 1-56000-586-6: [R]BiOr 52 (1995) 846-8 (R.G. *Hoyland*).

8901 **Daiber** Hans, The Islamic concept of belief in the 4th/10th century [**Samarqandī** 'Abu-Lait, on ABU HANĪFA]: Studia Culturae Islamicae 52. Tokyo 1995, Inst. Asia-Africa. v-299 p.

8902 **Déclais** Jean-Louis, Les premiers musulmans face à la tradition biblique; trois récits sur Job. P c.1995, L'Harmattan. 318 p. 2-7384-4136-X.

8903 **Ess** Josef van, Theologie und Gesellschaft im 2. und 3. Jahrhundert Hidschra; eine Geschichte des religiösen Denkens im frühen Islam. V. [Arabische (zu I-III. 1992 → 10,10830) Beweis-] Texte I-XXI. B 1993, de Gruyter. x-457 p. DM 310. [RStR 22,80. G. *Bowering*].

8904 **Ess** Jozef van, Theologie und Gesellschaft im 2. und 3. Jahrhundert Hidschra: Geschichte des religiösen Denkens im frühen Islam [1s 1992 → 10,10830] 3. B 1992. de Gruyter. xii-508 p. DM 344. 3-11-013161-7. -- [R]BiOr 52 (1995) 179s (M. *Cook*).

8905 *Figueras* Pau, The impact of the Islamic conquest on the Christian communities of South Palestine: → 712, Aram 6 (1993/4) 279-293.

8906 **Freeman-Grenville** G..P., The Islamic and Christian calendars, AD 622-2222 (AH 1-1650); a complete guide for converting Christian and Islamic dates and dates of festivals. Reading UK 1995, Garnet. v-113 p. 1-85964-066-4.

8907 **Gil** Moshe, A history of Palestine, 634-1099: 1992 → 8,b591 ... 10,10831: [R]JQR 86 (1995) 190s (M.R. *Cohen*); Speculum 69 (1994) 1172s (S. *Bowman*).

8908 *Gilliot* Claude, Mythe, récit, histoire du salut dans le commentaire coranique de TABARI: JA 282 (1994) 237-270; Eng. 270.

8909 *Griffith* Sidney H., Muḥammad and the monk Baḥîrâ; reflections on a Syriac and Arabic text from early Abbasid times: OrChr 79 (1995) 146-174.

8910 **Guzzetti** C., Bibbia e Corano; confronto sinottico. Mi 1995, San Paolo. 350 p. -- [R]EstTrin 29 (1995) 133s (X. *Pikaza*).

8911 **Halm** Heimz, The empire of the Mahdi; the rise of the Fatimids: HO 1/26/1. Lei c. 1995, Brill. xiii-452 p; bibliog, 429-434. 90-04-10056-3.

8912 *Halperin* David J., The hidden made manifest; Muslim [Tabari ...] traditions and the 'latent content' of biblical and rabbinic stories: → 130, [F]MILGROM J., Pomegranates 1995, 581-594.

8913 **Humphreys** R. Stephen, Islamic history; a framework for inquiry[2rev] [[1]1988]. Princeton 1991, Univ, xiv-401 p. $40; pa. $ 13, -- [R]JRAS (1994) 403s (Isabel *Miller* concludes 'let he who is without sin'); Speculum 69 (1994) 504-6 (C.F. *Petry*).

8914 **Ibrahim** Aiman, Der Herausbildungsprozess des arabisch-islamischen Staates; eine quellenkritische Untersuchung des Zusammenhangs zwischen den staatlichen Zentralisierungstendenzen und der Stammesorganisation in der frühislamischen Geschichte 1-60 H. / 622-680 [< Diss. Halle]; IKU 177. B 1994, Schwarz. xvii-265 p. -- [R]JRAS (1995) 272s (W. *Madelung*).

8915 *Juynboll Gautier* H.A., Early Islamic society as reflected in its use of isnads [a variant of hadith not notably defined]: Muséon 107 (1994) 151-194; 5 very complex diagrams.

8916 **Khoury** Adel T., Der Koran arabisch-deutsch, Sure 4,1-176, Übersetzung und wissenschaftlicher Kommentar. Gü 1994, Gü-V. 304 p. DM 250. 3-579-00340-2 [TR 91,281].

8917 *Khurramshāhi* Baha al-Din, The Qur'an as its own interpreter: Hikmat 1 (Tehran 1995s) 3-25.

8918 **Lassner** Jacob, Demonizing the Queen of Sheba [1 Kgs 10] 1993 → 9,2798; 10,2675: [R]BSOAS 58 (1995) 357s (A. *Rippin*); *CritRR 8 (1995) 345-7 (A. *Cooper*).

8919 *Lassner* Jacob, 'Doing' early Islamic history; Brooklyn baseball, Arabic historiography and historical memory [presidential address CM, March 31, 1992]: JAOS 114 (1994) 1-10

8920 **Lecker** Michael, Muslims, Jews and pagans; studies in early Islamic Medina. Lei 1993, Brill. xvi-180 p.: AION 55 (1995) 245s (R. *Tottoli*).

8921 *Lecker* Michael, *a)* WĀQIDĪ's account on the status of the Jews of Medina [strongest element in the population during the Hegira]: JNES 54 (1995) 15-29; [A] 29-32; — *b)* Conversion of Himyar to Judaism: WO 26 (1995) 129-136.

8922 **Lüling** Günter, Über den Urkoran; Ansätze zur Rekonstruktion der vorislamischen christlichen Strophenlieder im Koran[2] [[1]1973]. Erlangen 1993, auct. xvii-542 p. -- [R]Islamochristiana 20 (1994) 310-2 (J. *Stamer*).

8923 **Noth** Albrecht, The early Arabic historical tradition; a source-critical study [1973], [2]*Conrad* Lawrence I., [T]*Bonner* Michael: Studies in Late Antiquity and Early Islam 2. Princeton 1994, Darwin. -- [R]At(henaeum) 83 (1995) 577 (B. *Chiesa*); POrC 45 (1995) 309s (P. *Ternant*).

8924 **Pentz** Peter, The invisible conquest; the ontogenesis of sixth and seventh century Syria. K 1992. National Museum. -- [R]Ber 41 (1993/4) 225s (Nadia M. *el-Cheikh*).

8925 *Pereira* José , The portrait of Christ in the Koran: CanadCath 13,3 (1995) 6-12.

8926 **Perho** Irmeli, The Prophet's medicine; a creation of the Muslim traditionalist scholars: StOr 74. Helsinki 1995, Finnish Oriental Soc. 158 p.; bibliog. 149-154. 951-9380-24-8

8927 **Peters** F.E., Muhammad and the origins of Islam 1994 → 10,10837; $ 60, pa. $ 20: [R]JRAS (1995) 269-272 (Patricia *Crone:* takes the WATT-RODINSON-LINGS 'common ? sense' easy way out instead of struggling to supply some context as KISTER & HAWTING); JRel 75 (1995) 602-4 (T. *Lawson*).

8928 **Peters** F.E., A reader on classical Islam 1994 → 10,10838; $ 35; pa. $ 20: [R]BSOAS 58 (1995) 436 (A. *Rippin:* good classroom equivalent of his Judaism, Christianity and Islam).

8929 *Premaire* A.-L. de, Violence et sacré dans les premières traditions islamiques; Umm Qirfa et Salma et le mythe des peuples anéantis: JA 282 (1994) 19-36; Eng. 36: focuses women's opposition to the new Islamic power.

8930 **Qadi 'Iyad**, I miracoli del Profeta [= Muhammad messenger of Allah 1991], [T]*Zilio Grandi* Ida. T 1995, Einaudi. xxi-127 p. L[m] 32. -- [R]RasT 36 (1995) 375-7 (Ornella *Marra:* the translation is from the Arabic, clear and with abundant explanatory notes).

8931 **Rippin** Andrew, Muslims; their religious beliefs and practices, I. The formative period 1990 → 6,b153 ... 9,12083: [R]JAAR 63 (1995) 359-361 (D. *Beaumont*). II. 1993 → M8.3.

8932 **Rubin** Uri, The eye of the beholder; the life of Muhammad as viewed by the early
Muslims. Princeton 1995, Darwin. ix-288 p. -- [R]AION 55 (1995) 248s (R. *Tottoli*); POrC
45 (1995) 318s (P. *Ternant*).

8933 **Schöck** Cornelia, Adam in Islam: IKU 168. B 1993, K.Schwarz. 232 p. -- [R]AION 55
(1995) 437-445 (R. *Tottoli*).

8934 **Stowasser** Barbara F., Women in the Qur'an, traditions and interpretation. NY 1994,
Oxford-UP. $ 30. 0-19-508480-2 [ThD 42 (1995) 293].

8935 [T]**Tottoli** Roberto, AL-AZRAQĪ, La Ka'bah, tempio al centro del mondo. Trieste 1992,
Soc. Ital. Testi Islamici. 117 p. -- [R]AION 55 (1995) 131s (C. *Lo Jacono*).

8936 **Waines** David, An introduction to Islam. C 1995, Univ. 332 p. £ 32.50; pa. £ 11.
0-521-41880-1; -2929-3. -- [R]ET 106 (1994s) 351 (O. *Leaman*).

8937 **Wasserstrom** Steven M., Between Muslim and Jew; the problem of symbiosis under
early Islam. Princeton 1995, Univ. 300 p. $ 45. 0-691-03455-9. -- [R]*TBR 8,3 (1995s)
56s (D. *Thomas:* an important uninvestigated area).

8938 *Wiegers* G.A., Muhammad as the Messiah; a comparison of the polemical works of
Juan ALONSO with the Gospel of Barnabas: BiOr 52 (1995) 245-291.

8939 [E]**Wild** Stefan, The Qur'an as text: Islamic philosophy 27. Lei c.1995, Brill. xi-298
p. 90-04-10344-9.

M8.3 **Islam,** *evolutio recentior* -- **later theory and practice**

8940 **Abedin** Syed Z. † 5.VI.1993, Islamic fundamentalism, Islamic Ummah and the World
Conference on Muslim Minorities: Encounter 204 (R 1994) 3-27.

8941 [E]**Abedin** Syed Z., *Ziauddin* Sardar, Muslim minorities in the west. L 1995, Grey Seal.
212 p. -- [R]ISLCHR 21 (1995) 227 (J. *Lacunza Balda*).

8942 **Abu-Sahlieh** Sami A., Les Musulmans face aux droits de l'homme (religion, droit et
politique; études et documents). Bochum 1994, Winkler. 610 p. -- [R]Islamochristiana 20
(1994) 293-5 (M. *Borrmans*),

8943 **Ahmed** Akbar S., Postmodernism and Islam; predicament and promise. L 1992,
Routledge. x-294. -- [R]JRAS (1994) 83-85 (V. *Choueiri* with GELLNER 1992, its intended
introduction).

8944 **Antes** Peter, *Durán* Khalid, *al.,* Der Islam; Religion -- Ethik -- Politik 1991 → 8,b669:
[R]ThLZ 120 (1995) 119-121 (H. *Preissler*).

8945 *Ayoub* Mahmoud, Religious freedom and the law of apostasy in Islam;
Islamochristiana 20 (1994) 75-91. Eng. 91 (83-116, *Abu-Sahlieh* S., en français).

8946 **Baldick** Julian, Mystical Islam, an introduction to Sufism. L 1989, Tauris. 208 p.
£ 25; pa. £ 8. -- [R]JSSt 39 (1994) 354s (I.R. *Netton*).

8947 [E]**Barthel** Günter, *Stock* Kristina, Lexikon arabische Welt 1994 →842.

8948 **Bork-Qaysieh** Waltraud, Die Geschichte von Kain und Abel (Hābīl wa-Qābīl) in der
sunnitisch-islamischen Überlieferung; Untersuchung von Beispielen aus verschiedenen
Literaturwerken unter Berücksichtigung ihres Einflusses auf den Volksglauben [Diss.
Mainz]: IKU 169. B 1993, Schwarz. 181 p.; 19 fig. -- [R]OLZ 90 (1995) 65-69 (Cornelia
Schöck).

8949 **Brosh** Na'ama, (*Milstein* Rachel), Biblical stories in Islamic painting. J 1991, Israel
Museum. 132 p.; bibliog. 126-131. 965-278-113-9.

8950 [E]**Buitelaer** Marjo, *Motzki* Harald, De Koran; ontstaan, interpretatie en praktijk.
Muiderberg 1993, Coutinho. 128 p. *f*22,50. 90-6283-887-1. -- [R]Bijdragen 56 (1995) 114

(K. *Verduijn*).

8951 [T]**Burrell** David B, *Dahir* Nazih, AL-GHAZĀLI, The ninety-nine beautiful names of God. C 1992, Islamic Texts Soc. x-205 p. £ 30; pa. £ 12. -- [R]JRAS (1994) 407s (I.R. *Netton*: first complete English).

8952 **Chittick** William C., Imaginal worlds; IBN AL-'ARABI and the problem of religious divesity. Albany 1994, SUNY. vii-208 p. $ 57.50; PA. $ 19. 0-7914-2249-6; -50-X [ThD 42 (1995) 262].

8953 **Corbin** Henry, Trilogie ismaélienne [trois traductions longtemps introuvables], [E]*Jambet* Christian: Islam spirituel. Lagrasse 1994, Verdier. 460 p. F 250. -- [R]ÉTRel 70 (1995) 422s (S. *Guilmin*).

8954 **Corbin** Henry, History of Islamic philosophy [1964 (only part I)], [T]*Sherrard* Liadain & P. 1993 → 10,10853: [R]JRAS (1994) 262s (I.R. *Netton*); Numen 41 (1994) 212s (P. *Antes*).

8955 **Daftary** Farhad, The Assassin legends; myths of the Isma'ilis. L 1994. viii-213 p. -- [R]WO 26 (1995) 223s (J. van *Ess*: 'in German the word has no implication of *Meuchelmörder* ').

8956 **Douglas-Klotz** Neil, Desert wisdom; sacred Middle Eastern writings from the goddess through the Sufis; translations, commentaries, and body prayers. SF 1995, Harper. xxxvii-266 p. 0-06-061996-1.

8957 *Ebert* Hans-Georg, Kontinuität und Wandel im Verständnis des *ğihād*: → 10,453, Mem. REUSCHEL, Kolloquium Leipzig 1991/4, 39-47.

8958 **Effendy** Bahtiar, Islam and the State; the transformation of Islamic political ideas and practices in Indonesia: diss. Ohio State, [D]*Liddle* R., 1994. 414 p. 95-16989 -- DissA 56 (1995s) p. 338.

8959 **Faroqhi** Suraya, Herrscher über Mekka; die Geschichte der Pilgerfahrt [logistics, politics]. Mü 1990, Artemis. 351 p. DM 48. -- [R]WZKM 83 (1993) 308s (H. *Eisenstein*).

8960 **Garcin** Jean-Claude, *al.*, États, sociétés et cultures du monde médiéval, X[e]-XVe siècle: Nouvelle Clio. P 1995, PUF. I. clxxii + 35 maps + 466 p.; bibliog. xi-cxx. 2-13-046696-6.

8961 *Gezels* John, Le culte des saints dans l'Islam: MélSR 52 (1995) 139-153; Eng.153.

8962 **Goodman** Lenn E., AVICENNA; Arabic Thought and Culture. L 1992, Routledge. £ 13. -- [R]JRAS (1994) 263s (I.R. *Netton*).

8964 **Jolivet** Jean, *Monnot* Guy, SHAHRASTANI, Livre des religions et des sectes[T], 2. ['the followers of arbitrary doctrines']. Lv 1993, Peeters/Unesco. 578 p. Fb 4300. 90-6831-488-2. -- [R]BSOAS 58 (1995) 124s (Tamima Bayhom *Daou*); Muséon 107 (1994) 411s (J. *Grand'Henry*).

8965 **Jomier** Jacques, L'Islam vécu en Égypte: EtMus 35. P 1994, Vrin. 268 p. -- [R]RThom 95 (1995) 536-8 (D. *Urvoy*).

8966 [→u6 KRO] *Krikavová* Adéla, Some aspects of the man-nature relationship in the Islamic world: ArOr 63 (1995) 251-285.

8967 **Mernissi** Fatema, Die vergessene Macht; Frauen im Wandel der islamischen Welt [franç./Eng.], [T]*Peinelt* Edgart. B 1993, Orlanda Frauenverlag. 190 p. 3-929823-01-2. -- [R]WZKM 85 (1995) 311s (Renate *Malina*).

8968 **Modarressi** Hossein, Crisis and consolidation in the formative period of Shi'ite Islam. Princeton 1993, Darwin. 280 p. $ 35. -- [R]JRel 75 (1995) 314s (S.A. *Arjomand*).

8969 *Mortel* Richard T., The mercantile community of Mecca during the late Mamlūk period: JRAS (1994) 15-35.

8970   **Nagel** Tilman, Geschichte der islamischen Theologie, von Mohammed bis zur Gegenwart. Mü 1994, Beck. 314 p. DM 58. -- [R]ArOr 63 (1995) 242s (L. *Kropáček*); ThRv 91 (1995) 256 (W. *Beinert*).

8971   **Nasr** Seyyed Hossain, Islamic art and spirituality. C 1987, Golgonooza. x-213 p. 0-903880-35-0.

8972   **Pitzer-Reyl** Renate, Gemäss den Bedürfnissen der Zeit; Türkische Muslime im Prozess religiösen Wandels: Diss. [D]*Greschat* H.-J. Marburg 1995. -- RTLv 27.p.557.

8973   **Radtke** Bernd, Weltgeschichte und Weltbeschreibung im mittelalterlichen Islam: Beiruter TSt 51. Stu 1992, Steiner. 344 p. DM 160. -- [R]JAOS 115 (1995) 133-5 (U. *Haarmann*).

8974   **Rippin** Andrew, Muslims, their religious beliefs and practices [I. 1990 → M8.2 supra] - - 2. The contemporary period 1993 → 10,10863; £ 13. -- [R]BSOAS 58 (1995) 127s (Kate *Zebiri*); JRAS (1995) 277s (Moojan *Momen* doubts that the intellectuals here portrayed have affected more than a small fraction of the world's Muslims).

8975   [E]**Robbe** Martin, Welt des Islam; Geschichte und Alltag einer Religion[2rev] [[1]1988]. Lp 1991, Urania. 304 p. DM 40. -- [R]WO 26 (1995) 220-2 (J. *Danecki*, Eng.).

8976   **Scarcia Amoretti** Biancamaria, Sciiti nel mondo: Storia 32, R 1994, Jouvence. 350 p.; 8 fot. -- [R]OCP 61 (1995) 303-5 (V. *Poggi*).

8977   **Schimmel** Annemarie, Islamic names. E 1989, Univ. xii-137 p. $ 17.50. 0-614-21514-5. -- [R]JAOS 114 (1994) 109s (Fedwa *Malti-Douglas*).

8978   **Schubel** Vernon J., Religious performance in contemporary [South Asian] Islam; Shi'i devotional rituals in South Asia. 1993. -- [R]JRel 75 (1995) 459s (Aditya *Behl*)

8979   **Smet** D. De, La quiétude de l'intellect; néoplatonisme et gnose ismaélienne dans l'œuvre de Hamīd ad-Din AL-KIRMĀNI (X[e]-XIe s.): OL(ov)A 67. Lv 1995, Peeters. xi-429 p.; bibliog. 399-414. 90-6831-692-3.

8980   **Tibi** Bassam, Im Schatten Allahs; der Islam und die Menschenrechte. Mü 1994, Piper. 406 p. DM 44. 3-492-03642-2 [ThRv 91,282].

8981   *Urvoy* Marie-Thérèse, Aspects de l'hagiographie musulmane: BLE 96 (1995) 97-120.

8982   *Walker* Paul E., Succession to rule in the Shiite caliphate: JA(m)RCE(g) 32 (1995) 239-264.

8983   [T]**Watt** W.Montgomery, Islamic creeds; a selection [background for his *'akida,* EI[2] 332-6]: Islamic Surveys. E 1994, Univ. vi-107 p. £ 30; pa. £ 14.($ 25 NY Columbia Univ.). 0-7846-0513-4 [ThD 43,70]. -- [R]JRAS (1995) 408s (Simonetta *Calderini*).

8984   *Weibel* Nadine, L'Europe, berceau d'une *umma* reconstituée ou l'émergence d'une nouvelle utopie religieuse: ASSR 92 (1995) 25-33; Eng. 34.

8985   **Weintritt** Otfried, Formen spätmittelalterlicher Geschichtsdasrtellung; Untersuchungen zu an-Nuwairî al-Iskandarânîs Kitâb al-Ilmâm und verwandten zeitgenössischen Texten [Diss. Freiburg 1988]. Beirut (Stu 1992, Steiner). viii-224 p + [A] 2 p. -- [R]AION 54 (1994) 414s (Carmela *Baffioni*).

8986   **Yeoh Siok Cheng**, Umara-Ulama-Ummah relations and pesantrens in Aceh province, Indonesia; a study of the challenges to the authority of a traditional Kiyi (Muslim): diss. Washington, [D]*Van den Berghe* P. Seattle 1994. 449 p. 95-23778. -- DissA 56 (1995s) p. 1550.

8987   *Yocum* Glenn, Islam and gender in Turkey [DELANEY Carol; MARCUS Julie]: RStR 21 (1995) 189-190.

8988   [E]**Young** M.J.L., al., Religion, learning and science in the 'Abbasid period: History of Arabic Literature. C 1990, Univ. xxiii-587 p.; bibliog. 524-548. 0-521-32763-6.

8989 *Zaman* Muhammad K., A venture in critical Islamic historiography and the significance of its failure: Numen 4l (1994) 26-50,

M8.4 *Alter philosemitismus* -- **Islamic-Christian rapprochement**

8990 **Adang** Camilla, Muslim writers on Judaism and the Hebrew Bible, from IBN RABBAN to IBN HAZM: Islamic Philosophy 22. Lei c.1995, Brill. [viii-] 321 p.; bibliog. 279-306. 90-04-10034-2.

8991 **Anawati** G.C., Islam e cristianesimo; l'incontro tra due culture nell'Occidente moderno. Mi 1995, VP. 106 p. L^m 20. -- ^RAsprenas 42 (1995) 619-621 (G. *Ragazzino*).

8992 *Arinze* Francis, card., Christians and Muslims: interreligious relations in a pluralistic world (Baltimore Aug.9): Origins 25 (1995s) 217 . 219-22.

8993 **Asad** Talal, Genealogies of religion; discipline and reasons of power in Christianity and Islam 1992 → 9,12141; $ 42,50; pa. $ 16 [RStR 22,183-190, Catherine *Bell*].

8994 **Basetti Sani** Giulio, L'Islam nel piano della salvezza: Uomo planetario 9, 1992 → 9,12143; 88-09-00667-4. -- ^RGreg 76 (1995) 776-8 (E. *Farahian* n'accepte pas).

8995 **Bayly** Susan, Saints, goddesses and kings; Muslims and Christians in South Indian society 1700-1900^2 [^11989 → 6,b211]. C 1992, Univ. 502 p. 0-521-37201-1. -- ^RNZM(issW) 79 (1995) 63s (H.-W. *Gensichen*).

8996 **Becht** Dieter, Offenbarungsschrift und Offenbarungsträger; der Beitrag indischer Christen in der Auseinandersetzung mit dem Islam: ev. Diss. ^DBeyerhaus F. Tübingen 1994. -- ThRv 91 (1995) 101.

8997 **Bennett** Clinton, Victorian images of Islam. L 1992, Grey Seal.xii-204 p. £ 25. -- ^RBSOAS 58 (1995) 150s (H.T. *Norris*).

8998 *Berisha* Anton K., Islamization -- seed of discord or the only way of salvation for Albanians ? [70% Muslim, 20% Orthodox, 10% Catholic]: Religion in Eastern Europe 15,5 (Princeton 1995) 1-7.

8999 **Bonanate** Ugo, Bibbia e Corano; I testi sacri confrontati: Nuova vultura 45. M 1995, Bollati Boringhieri. 265 p. 88-339-0891-7.-- ^RISLCHR 21 (1995) 231 (M. *Borrmans*); ZAW 107 (1995) 523 (J.A. *Soggin*: wichtig, aber Parallelen/Antithesen und Register fehlen).

9000 **Boumann** J., Il Corano e gli Ebrei; la storia di una tragedia. Brescia 1992, Queriniana. 136 p. L^m 18. -- ^RStPat(av) 42 (1995) 844s (C.*Saccone*).

9001 **Bowker** John, Voices of Islam. 1995, Oneworld. 188 p. £ 9. 1-85168-095-0. -- ^RE(xp)T 107 (1995s) 191 (O. *Leaman*).

9003 **Brown** Stuart, The nearest in affection; towards a Christian understanding of Islam: Risk Book. Geneva 1994, WCC / Ph 1995, Trinity. x-124 p. Fs 13.50. 2-8254-0970-7 / 1-56338-114-1 [ThD 42 (1995) 259]. -- ^RC(alvin)TJ 30 (1995) 551-4 (B.M. *Madany*); ET 106 (1994s) 254 (W.M. *Watt*); ISLCHR 21 (1995) 232s (M.L. *Fitzgerald*).

9004 *Bruinessen* Martin van, Muslim fundamentalism; something to be understood or to be explained away: Islam and Christian-Muslim Relations 6 (1995) 157-171.

9005 ^EBsteh Andreas, Hören auf sein Wort .. chr./islam. 1977/92 → 9,12152: ^RZkT 117 (1995) 362s (K.H. *Neufeld*).

9006 ^EBsteh Andreas, Friede für die Menschheit; Grundlagen, Probleme und Zukunftsperspektiven aus islamischer und christlicher Sicht (Wien 30.III-2,IV.1993): BeitRelT 8, 1994: → 10,10872: ^RZkT 117 (1995) 363s (K.H. *Neufeld*).

9007 ^EBsteh Andreas, Der Islam als Anfrage an christliche Theologie und Philosophie [Mödling 1993]: StRelTh 1, 1994; DM 43: ^REntschluss 50,7s (1995) 43s (T.M. *Meier*);

FrRu 2 (1995) 183s (C. *Thoma*); ISLCHR 21 (1995) 233-5 (J. *Stamer,* auch über sein Friede 1994 & Hören 1992); OCP 61 (1995) 610-2 (C.W. *Troll*); ZkT 117 (1995) 364-6 (K.H. *Neufeld*).

9008 *Bustros* Cyrille S., Relations entre christianisme et Islam; histoire -- actualité -- perspectives d'avenir: POrC 45 (1995) 79-110; Eng. 110.

9009 **Chapman** Colin, Cross and Crescent; responding to the challenge of Islam. Leicester 1995, Inter-Varsity. 346 p. 0-85110-992-6. -- R*TBR 8,2 (1995s) 56 (J. *Nielsen*).

9010 **Combs-Schilling** M.E., Sacred performances; Islam, sexuality, and sacrifice. NY 1990, Columbia Univ. xx-177 p. $ 15.50 [RStR 22,209-213. T. *Bremer,* also on YOUNG W., HAMMOUDI A.].

9011 **Cragg** Kenneth, Faith and life negotiate; a Christian story-study book. Norwich 1994, Canterbury. 336 p. £ 15. 1-85311-088-4. -- RET 106 (1994s) 127 (O. *Leaman*; Anglican Islamist, dubious project).

9012 **Daniel** Norman, Islam et l'Occident [1930, ⁴1980] ᵀ*Spiess* Alain: Patrimoines, 1993: RIslamochristiana 19 (1993) 323-5 (M. *Borrmans*); SuppVSp 148 (1994) 1382 (S. de *Beaurecueil*).

9013 *Déclais* Jean-Louis, Les ouvriers de la onzième heure ou la parabole du salaire contesté (De l'évangile au midrash et au hadîth): ISLCHR 21 (1995) 43-63.

9014 **DeWeese** Devin, Islamization and native religion in the golden horde; Baba Tükles and the conversion to Islam in historical and epic traditions. Univ. Park 1994, Penn State. xvii-638 p. $ 85; pa. $ 25. 0-271-01072-X; -3-8. -- RET 106 (1994s) 318s (W.M. *Watt*).

9015 **Esposito** John, Islamic threat; myth or reality [on HUNTINGTON S.]. Ox 1993, UP. 243 p. £ 16. 0-19-507184-0. -- RIslam and Christian-Muslim Relations 5 (1994) 2ll (J.S. *Nielsen*).

9016 *Forward* Martin, Understanding Islam: ET 106 (1994s)299-302: Christians and Muslims alike put top value on love of fellow-man, and express that love ultimately in forcible conversion.

9017 *Geffré* Claude, La portée théologique du dialogue islamo-chrétien: Islamochristiana 18 (1992) 1-23. Eng. 23.

9018 **Geisler** N.L., *Saleeb* A. {reared as a Muslim], Answering Islam; the crescent in the light of the Cross. GR 1993, Baker. 336 p. -- RRefTR 54 (1955) 41 (Len *Pearce*)

9019 **Ghadbian** Najib, Democratization and the Islamist challenge in the Arab world: diss. City University, ᴰ*Rustow* D. NY 1995. 289 p. 95-21271. -- D(iss)AI 56 (1995s) p. 1102.

9020 **Goddard** Hugh, Christians and Muslims; from double standards to mutual understanding. L 1995, Curzon. [RStR 22,340, J. *Renard*].

9021 **Guzzetti Cherubini** Mario, Bibbia e Corano; confronto sinottico. Mi 1995, San Paolo. 350 p. -- RISLCHR 21 (1995) 248 (M. *Borrmans*).

9022 ᴱ**Haddad** Yvonne Y. & Wadi Z., Christian-Muslim encounters [Hartford Sem. 3-day meeting 1990; 28 art.]. Gainesville FL 1995, Univ. xi-508 p. $ 50; pa. $ 30. 0-8130-1356-9; -9-3 [ThD 43,261].

9023 *Hagemann* Ludwig, Der Islam als Anfrage; Schritte auf dem Weg, Raimundus LULLUS und Nicolaus CUSANUS: → 589, Mit den Anderen 1995, 70-85. [cf. T(rier)ThZ 103 (1994) 131-151]

9024 *a)* *Iyer* V.R. Krishna, Religious fundamentalism and the present crisis; -- *b) Engineer* Ashgar A., The Islamic outlook on interreligious dialogue; -- *c) Samartha* S., The future of interreligious dialogue; threats and promises: JDharma 19 (1994) 13-19 / 20-25 / 74-83.

9025 *Jacob* Xavier, Les relations islamo-chrétiennes en Turquie: ISLCHR 21 (1995) 95-119.

9026 **Jaoudi** Maria, Christian and Islamic spirituality; sharing a journey 1993 → 10,10888: ᴿHorizons 22 (1995) 316s (J.A. *Wiseman*).

9027 **Jomier** Jacques, Islamismo, história e doutrina, ᵀ*Baraúna* Luis J., 1993 → 10,10899: ᴿREB 55 (1995) 468-471 (J.B. *Libanio*).

9028 **Jones** Catherine, Women in Muslim-Christian dialogue: Encounter 207s (R 1994) 3-32.

9029 **Kelsay** John, Islam and war; a study in comparative ethics. LᵥL 1993, W-Knox. ix-149 p. $ 14. -- ᴿHorizons 22 (1995) 166s (D.R. *Burrell*).

9030 **Kepel** Gilles, Revenge of God; resurgence of Islam [franç. esp. 1991],ᵀ. L 1993, Polity. ii-215 p. £ 39.50; pa. £ 12. 0-7456-099-6; -1269-5. -- ᴿET 106 (1994s) 63 (W.M. *Watt*).

9031 ᴱ**Kerber** Walter, Wie tolerant ist der Islam ? 1991 → 9,12175: ᴿIslamochristiana 18 (1992) 336-8 (J. *Stamer*).

9032 *Khoury* Adel T., Christen unter Halbmond; religiöse Minderheiten unter der Herrschaft des Islam. FrB 1994, Herder. 155 p. DM 24,80. -- ᴿNRT 117 (1995) 404s (J. *Scheuer*).

9033 **Khoury** Paul, L'Islam critique de l'Occident dans la pensée arabe actuelle: Islam et sécularité 1 / RwSt 35/1. Wü/Altenberge 1995, Echter/Oros. 322 p. DM 75. 3-429-01682-7 / 3-89375-109-2 [ThRv 91].

9034 ᵀᴱ**Khoury** Paul, PAUL D'ANTIOCHE, Traités théologiques: Corpus Islamo-Christianum 1. Wü/Altenberge 1994, Echter/Oros. iv-345 p. DM 90. 3-429-01593-6 / 3-89375-088-6.— ᴿThLZ 120 (1995) 317-320 (W. *Kinzig*).

9035 **Kropáček** Luboš, Duchovní cesty islámu (Les chemins spirituels de l'Islam). Praha 1992. 292 p. -- ᴿArOr 63 (1995) 129s (Zdenka *Veselá-Přenosilová*, aussi sur MENDEL M. 1994).

9036 **Kuschel** Karl-Josef, Streit um Abraham; was Juden, Christen und Muslime trennt -- und was sie eint. Mü 1994, Piper. 334 p. DM 40. 3-492-03739-9. -- ᴿThLZ 120 (1995) 514 (T. *Sundermeier*).

9037 *Leaman* Oliver, Christian ethics in the light of Muslim ethics: ET 106 (1994s) 164-8.

9038 **Leuze** Reinhard, Christentum und Islam. Tü 1994, Mohr. 371 p. DM 78. 3-16-146281-5; -67-X. -- ᴿ*TBR 8,1 (1995s) 56 (R. *Coggins:* exception to TBR policy of no German books); ThLZ 120 (1995) 515s (A.T. *Khoury*); TTh 35 (1995) 315 (J. *Peters*, ook over BSTEH A. 1994).

9039 **Lewis** Bernard, *a)* Islam and the West 1993 → 9,12181; 10,10897: ᴿA(mer)HR 100 (1995) 1234 (C.E. *Farah*). -- *b)* Der Atem Allahs; die islamische Welt und der Westen; Kampf der Kulturen ? ᵀ*Möhring* Hans-Ulrich. W 1994, Europaverlag. 264 p. DM 40. 3-203-51229-7.

9040 *Madigan* Daniel A., Reflections on some current directions in Islamic studies: Mus(lim)W 85 (1995) 345-362.

9041 *Martini* Carlo Maria, Wij en de Islam; van gastvrijheid tot dialoog ! [(Gen 21,13-20) 1990], ᵀ*Lembrechts* Pieter-P.: CVl 25 (1995) 115-128 [129-150, *Goorden* Constant, Boeddhisme].

9042 *Michel* Thomas, Presenting one's faith to another as a witness: IslChr 21 (1995) 15-21.

9043 **Mitri** Tarek, Religion, law and society; a Christian-Muslim discussion [1992s]. Geneva 1995, WCC. 154 p. £ 10. 2-8254-1148-5. -- ᴿE(xp)T 107 (1995s) 95 (W.M. *Watt*).

9044 *a) Narithookil* James, Islam's encounter with Christianity: -- *b) Ali Khan* Mumtaz, Islam's encounter with Hinduism in secular India; -- *c) Sho'ala* Abdulnabi al-, Islam and the concept of tolerance and co-existence; -- *d) Koovackal* George, Inherent problems in Islam's encounter with other religions: JDh 19 (1994) 358-369 / 370-383 / 350-7 / 384-396.

9045   *Niclós* José Vicente,   *a)* La familia en el mundo hebreo e islámico; -- *b)* Fundamentalismo religioso e Islam: TE(spir) 38 (1994) 205-287 / 461-495.

9046   *Peroncel-Hugoz* Jean-Pierre, De l'irresponsabilité à la haine de soi [... critique des gouvernants plutôt que de l'Islam]: Cath 47 (P 1995) 60-67.

9047   **Rocalve** Pierre, Louis MASSIGNON et l'Islam 1993 → 9,12196: [R]RHR 212 (1995) 228s (G. *Monnot*).

9048   [E]**Samir** Khalil Samir, *Nielsen* Jorgen S.,   Christian Arabic apologetics during the Abbasid period (750-1258) [Birmingham Selly Oak conference 1990] 1994 → 10,10911: [R]ISLCHR 21 (1995) 261s (M.L. *Fitzgerald*).

9049   *Savage* Elizabeth, Iraqi Christian links with an early Islamic sect: → 712, Aram 6 (1993/4) 170-192.

9050   **Schimmel** A., L'Islam. Bo 1992, Dehoniane. 141 p. L[m] 16. -- [R]StPat(av) 42 (1995) 841s (C. *Saccone*).

9051   **Schimmel** Annemarie, Deciphering the signs of God: a phenomenological approach to Islam. Albany 1994, *SUNY. xvii-302 p. $ 59.50; pa. 17. 0-7914-1982-7 [ThD 42 (1995) 290].

9052   [E]**Schwartländer** Johannes, Freiheit der Religion; Christentum und Islam unter dem Anspruch der Menschenrechte: Forum Weltkirche, Entwicklung und Frieden 2, 1993 → 9,12204: [R]ISLCHR 21 (1995) 263-8 (J. *Stamer*); ThLZ 120 (1995) 320-2 (G. *Krusche*).

9053   **Sha'ban** Fuad, Islam and the Arabs in early American thought; the roots of Orientalism in America. Durham NC 1991, Acorn / Duke Univ. xxi-244 p. $ 38,50. -- [R]A(mer)HR 99 (1994) 1421s (K.E. *Barbir*).

9054   **Stoll** Georg, Muslimische Migranten in Deutschland; eine neue Situation für Kirchen, Islam und säkulare Gesellschaft, beleuchtet aus der Perspektive fiktionaler Migrantenliteratur und katholischer kirchlicher Stellungnahmen: Diss. Pont. Univ. Gregoriana, [D]*Roest Crollius* A. Rom 1995. 479 p.; Extr. N° 4197, 166 p. -- RTLv 27.p.550.

9055   *Suermann* H., Muhammad in Christian and Jewish apocalyptic expectations: Islam and Christian-Muslim Relations 5 (1994) 15-21.

9056   **Tartar** Georges, Jésus-Christ dans le Coran.   Combes-la-Ville 1995, Centre Évangélique. 280 p. -- [R]ISLCHR 21 (1995) 270 (M. *Borrmans*).

9057   **Tessitore** Fulvio, Schizzi e schegge di storiografia arabo-islamica italiana. Bari 1995, Palomar. 254 p. -- [R]AION 55 (1995) 243-6 (G. *Gnoli*).

9058   **Thomsen** Mark W., The Word and the Way of the Cross; Christian witness among Muslim and Buddhist people. Ch 1993, ELCA. -- [R]CThMi 22 (1995) 60s (C.A. *Nessan*).

9059   *Thurston* Bonnie, Thomas MERTON's interest in Islam; the example of *dhikr* ['the means whereby God can be known experientially and realized inwardly']: ABenR 45 (1994) 131-141.

9060   *a) Tröger* Karl-Wolfgang, Bibel und Koran; historische und theologische Geschichtspunkte für den christlich-muslimischen Dialog: -- *b) Berner* Ulrich, Zur Geschichte und Problematik des interreligiösen Dialoges [page-headings 'Dialogs']: → 42, [F]COLPE C., Tradition (1994) 422-434 / 391-404.

9061   *Tröger* Karl-Wolfgang, The Bible and the Koran [< [F]COLPE C., Tradition 1994], [TE]*Asen* B.A.: ThD 42 (1995) 209-214.

9062   [E]**Waardenburg** Jacques, Scholarly approaches to religion, interreligious perceptions, and Islam: StRelHelv 1. Fra 1995, Lang. xv-464 p. DM 95 pa. 3-906752-93-4 [ThRv 92,88].

9063 **Watt** W.M., Muslim-Christian encounters 1991 → 7,a939* ... 10,10920: [R]S(cot)JTh 48 (1995) 533-5 (S. von *Sicard*).

9064 **Watt** Wm. Montgomery [lifelong Islamologist], Religious truth for our time. ... 1995, Oneworld. 109 p. £ 6, 1-85168-102-7. -- [R]E(xp)T 107,5 2d-top choice (1995s) 130 (C.S. *Rodd*).

9065 [E]**Zaborski** Andrzej, Islam i Chrześcijaństwo; materiały sympozjum Kraków, 12-14 IV 1994. Kraków 1995, Pap. Akad. Teol. xv-336 p. 83-85245-28-6.

9066 *Zakas* Grigorios D., The reality of education in Greece; the picture of the Muslim in school textbooks and the mass media: ISLCHR 21 (1995) 65-74.

9067 *a) Zarzour* Mahmoud, La contribució de le religió islàmica a la cultura de la pau; -- *b) Dajani* Ahmed S. al-, Les causes de l'extremisme religiós (fonamentalisme) als països àrabs: QvidaC 178 (1995) 78-85 / 86-94.

9068 **Zirker** Hans, Islam; theologische und gesellschaftliche Herusaforderungen. Dü 1993, Patmos. -- [R]OCP 61 (1995) 571-580 (C.W. *Troll*: mutual challenges); TPQ 143 (1995) 427s (F. *Böhmisch*).

M8.5 **Religiones Indiae** et Extremi Orientis

9069 *a) Arapura* J.G., Buddhist encounter with other world religions; -- *b) Padmanabh* S. Jaini, Salvation, civilization and social ethos; an issue in historic Buddhism-Jainism vis-à-vis Brahmanism; -- *c) Kochumuttom* Thomas, Buddhism; its rise and fall in India in confrontation with Hinduism: JDharma 20 (1995) 109-121 / 137-153 / 178-189.

9070 **Bautze** Joachim K., Early Indian terracottas: Iconography of Religions 11/17. Lei 1995, Brill. xii-45 p. 90-04-09924-7.

9071 **Beck** Guy, Sonic theology; Hinduism and sacred sound. Columbia 1993, Univ. S, Carolina. xvi-290 p. $ 40. -- [R]JRel 75 (1995) 449s (Laurie L. *Patton*).

9072 **Bronkhorst** Johannes, The two traditions of meditations in ancient India. Delhi 1993, Motilal Banarsidass. xviii-153 p. rs 150. -- [R]JDharma 19 (1994) 99.

9073 **Cabezón** José Ignacio, Buddhism and language; a study of Indo-Tibetan scholasticism. Albany 1991, SUNY. 299 p. $ 20. -- [R]JRel 75 (1995) 453-5 (M.D. *Eckel*).

9074 **Chackalackal** Saju, Ramayama amd the Indian ideal; a search into the prevailing humanistic values in the Ramayana of Valmiki. Bangalore 1992, Dharmaram. xvii-122 p. rs.40 -- [R]JDharma 19 (1994) 199 (reviewer's name uncertain).

9075 *Coward* Harold, The role of Scripture in the self-definition of Hinduism and Buddhism in India: → 10,344*a*, Notion of 'religion' 1990/4. 19-32.

9076 **Dean** Kenneth, Taoist ritual and popular cults of south-east China. Princeton 1993, Univ. 290 p. $ 35. -- [R]JRel 75 (1995) 316-8 (J. *DeBernard*).

9077 *Doniger* Wendy, Rationality and authority in the Laws of Manu [India; her edition 1994: 'an elaborate web which if followed would paralyze human life entirely', p. 53]: → 10,344*a*, Notion of 'religion' 1990/4, 43-53.

9078 **Erndl** Kathleen M., Victory to the mother; the Hindu goddess of Northwest India in myth, ritual, and symbol. Ox 1993, UP. viii-208 p. £ 27.50; pa. £ 12. 0-19-505014-3; -705-1. -- [R]Bijdragen 56 (1995) 480s (J.P. *Schouten*).

9079 **Feuerstein** George, *Kak* Subhash, *Frawley* David, In search of the cradle of civilization; new light on ancient India. Wheaton IL 1995, Quest Theosophical. xx-341 p.; 47 fig.; 5 maps. $ 25. 0-8356-0720-8 [ThD 43,167].

9080 **Frawley** David, Hinduism, the eternal tradition. New Delhi 1995, Voice of India. x-

262 p. rs. 100 [JDh 20,308].

9081 **Frédéric** Louis, Les dieux du Bouddhisme; guide iconographique. P 1992, Flammarion. 359 p.; bibliog. 344-350. 2-08-011741-6

9082 *Hiltebeitel* Alf, Religious studies and [India] Indian epic texts: RStR 21 (1995) 26-32 (42 books + 2 of his awaited).

9083 *Kister* Daniel, Korean Shamanism: Landas 9 (Manila 1995) 53-71.

9084 **Krishnamurthy** V., The ten commandments of Hinduism. New Delhi 1994, Wiley Eastern. xvi-344 p. rs 150. -- ^RJDh 19 (1994) 405-7 (M. *Kareethara*).

9085 *a) Kullu* Paulus, Tribal religion and culture; -- *b) Meneses* Rui de, The tribes of Israel; -- *c) Soares-Prabhu* George, Anti-greed and anti-pride: Jeevadhara 24 (1994) 89-109 / 110-129 / 129-150.

9086 *Lin Zhichun*, Huangdi, Gonghe, Confucius and Chen Wang; on the classical tradition of the periodization of ancient Chinese classical civilization: *JAncCiv 10 (Changchun 1995) 71-81.

9087 ^R**Lopez** Donald S., Buddhism in practice: Readings in religions. Princeton 1995, Univ. xvi-608 p. 0-691-04442-2; pa. -14. -- ^R*TBR 8,2 (1995s) 58 (Susan *Hamilton*).

9088 ^R**Lopez** Donald S., Religions of India in practice. Princeton 1995, Univ. xvi-655 p. $ 59.50; pa. $ 20. 0-691-04325-6; -41-8. -- ^R*TBR 8,1 (1995s) 59 (S.T. *Ruparell*).

9089 **Morris** Stephen R., Beyond religion; transcendentalism and Zen answers for today: diss. California Institute of Integral Studies. ^D*Wu Yi*, 1994. 286 p. 95-18325. -- DissA 56 (1995s) p. 226.

9090 **Narayanan** Vasudha, The vernacular Veda; revelation, recitation, and ritual: StCompRel. Columbia 1994, Univ. S. Carolina. xvi-265 p. $43. 0-87249-965-0 [ThD 43,78].

9091 **Olivelle** Patrick, The Āśrama system; the history and hermeneutics of a religious institution [the four vocations open in upper-class India: student, householder, hermit, renouncer]. NY 1993, Oxford-UP. xiii-274 p. $ 20. -- ^RJRel 75 (1995) 311s (F.X. *Clooney*); TS 56 (1995) 159s (W. *Cenkner*); UnSemQ 48,3 (1994) 161-5 (T. *Lubin*).

9092 **Panikkar** Raimon, A dwelling place for wisdom 1993 → 9,12250: ^RJRel 75 (1995) 312-4 (M.N. *Schmalz*: all his writings are essential).

9093 *a) Panikkar* Raimon, El espíritu del hinduismo; -- *b) Jiménez* José Demetrio, Cristo y Krishna; similitudes y diferencias : Rel(y)Cult 41 (1995) 21-32 / 33-55.

9094 **Peters** Ulrike, Wie der biblische Prophet Henoch zum Buddha wurde; die jüdische Henochtradition als Beispiel interkultureller Vermittlung zwischen Ost und West 1987: ^RNumen 42 (1995) 296s (R.J.Z. *Werblowsky*).

9095 **Powers** John, Introduction to Tibetan Buddhism. Ithaca NY 1995, Snow Lion. 501 p. $ 17. 1-55939-026-3 [ThD 43,82].

9096 **Pyysiainen** Ilkka E., Beyond language and reason; mysticism in Indian Buddhism: diss. Helsingin Yliopisto 1993. 106 p. 951-41-0709-8. -- DissA-C 56 (1995s) p.39.

9097 **Rambachan** Anantanand, The limits of Scripture; VIVEKANANDA's reinterpretations of the Vedas. Honolulu 1994, Univ. Hawaii. 170 p. -- ^RJDh 19 (1994) 40-45 (M. *Kareethara*).

9098 *a) Ravindra* Ravi, Yoga and the quintessential search for holiness; -- *b) Kadankavil* Thomas, Holiness as culmination of yoga; -- *c) Pathrapankal* Joseph, 'I live, not I; it is Christ who lives in me ' (Gal 2:20); a yogic interpretation of Paul's religious experience: JDharma 20 (1995) 245-253 / 254-269 / 297-307.

9099 **Ray** Reginald A., Buddhist saints in India; a study in Buddhist values and orientations. NY 1994, Oxford-UP. xviii-508 p. $ 50. -- ^R*CritRR 8 (1995) 45-70 (D. *Keown*).

9100 *Scott* David, Buddhism and Islam; past to present encounters and interfaith lessons: Numen 42 (1995) 141-155.

9101 **Sharma** Arvind, Hinduism, an encyclopedic survey of its encyclopedic surveys [ELIADE and 28 others]: RStR 21 (1995) 106-9.

9102 **Shaw** Miranda, Passionate enlightenment; women in Tantric Buddhism. Princeton 1994, Univ. xiii-291 p.; 18 fig. $ 30. -- ^RJRel 75 (1995) 455-7 (J.N. *Kinnard*).

9103 ^E**Sommer** Deborah, Chinese religion; an anthology of sources. Ox 1995, UP. xxiii-375 p. $ 24 pa. 0-19-508895-6 [ThD 44,61].

9104 **Swarup** Ram, Hindu view of Christianity and Islam. New Delhi 1992, Voice of India. 131 p. -- ^RScotJR 16 (1995) 153s (J. *Brockington*)

9105 **Theertha** Swami Dharma, History of Hindu [brahman] imperialism⁵ [¹1941, The menace of Hindu imperialism]. Madras 1992, Dalit centre. x-280 p. rs.100. -- ^RJDh 18 (1994) 397-402 (D.C. *Scott*).

9106 **Thundy** Zacharias P., Buddha and Christ; Nativity stories and Indian traditions: Numen book 60. Lei 1993, Brill. x-294 p. *f* 135. -- ^R*CritRR 7 (1994) 286-8 (M. *Lattke*), preferring ^FKLAUSER T., JAC Egb 11 (1984) 57-81 (C. *Colpe*) & JR(el?)H 14 (1987) 235-245 (P.C. *Almond*); NRT 117 (1995) 423-5 (J. *Scheuer*).

9108 **Vyas** C.S., Buddhist theory of perception. New Delhi 1991, Navrang, viii-180 p. rs 180. -- ^RJDharma 18 (1993) 367-371 (B. V. *Vankatakrishna*).

9109 *Werblowsky* R.J.Z., Recent studies on Chinese religions: Numen 42 (1995) 197-203 [172-196, *Poo Mu-Chou*].

9110 ^E**Yoshinori** Takeuchi, Buddhist spirituality: World Spirituality [12th to appear]. L 1994, SCM. 428 p. £ 35. -- 0-334-02543-5. -- ^RET 106 (1994s) 63 (D. *Keown*).

M8.7 *Interactio cum religione orientali* -- **Christian dialogue with the East**

9111 ABE Masao, 'conversation', Divine emptiness and historical fullness; a Buddhist-Jewish-Christian conversation, ^E**Ives** Christopher. Ph 1995, Trinity. xii-272 p. $ 18 pa. 1-56338-122-2 [ThD 43.164].

9112 **Anandam** Lourdu, Jesus Christ, the Purusha; Christology of Bede GRIFFITHS: Diss. ^D*Walter*. Freiburg/B 1995. -- ThRv Beilage 92/2, viii.

9113 *Bastow* David, Levels of self-awareness in Pali Buddhism: ScotR 15 (1994) 5-20.

9114 *Baumann* Martin, Analytische Rationalisten und romantische Sucher; Motive der Konversion zum Buddhismus in Deutschland: ZM(iss)R 79 (1995) 207-224; Eng. 224s.

9115 **Brockington** John, Hinduism and Christianity 1993 → 9,12261: ^RScotJR 16 (1995) 62s (S.D.B. *Picken*).

9116 **Brück** Michael von, The unity of reality; God, God-experience, and meditation in the Hindu-Christian dialogue, ^T*Zeitz* J.V. 1991: ^RJDharma 18 (1993) 175-8 (S. *Athappilly*: good except for putting on a par advaitic/trinitarian experience).

9117 **Carman** John B., Majesty and meekness; a comparative [Hindu] study of contrasts and harmony in the concept of God 1994 → 10,10940: ^RTS 56 (1995) 393s (F.X. *Clooney*).

9118 **Carpenter** Edward (David), Revelation, history, and the dialogue of religions; a study of Bhartrari and BONAVENTURE. Mkn 1995, Orbis. xi-208 p. 1-57075-039-4 [RStR 22,229, W. *Cenkner*].

9119 **Clooney** Francis X., Theology after Vedānta; an experiment in comparative theology. Albany 1993, SUNY. xviii-265 p. $ 49,50; pa. $ 17. 0-7914-1365-9 [ThD 42,360]. -- ^RMoTh 10 (1994) 431s (G. *D'Costa*: secondary reserves).

9120 **Cole** W. Owen, *Sambhi* P.S., Sikhism and Christianity; a comparative study 1993 →
10,10945: [R]ScotJR 16 (1995) 63-65 (S.D.B.*Picken*).

9121 **Conio** Caterina, Abhis³iktananda [Henri LE SAUX]; sulle frontiere dell'incontro
cristiano-indù. Assisi 1994, Cittadella. 319 p. L[m] 25. 88-308-0541-6. -- [R]Greg 76
(1995) 198 (J. *Dupuis*; in testo 'Cunio').

9122 *Dean* Thomas, Enlightenment or liberation; two models of Christ in contemporary
Japanese theology: Japan Christian Review 61 (1995) 91-105 [< TIC 13/2,86].

9123 *Dehn* Ulrich, Christlicher Zen; Auseinandersetzungen mit neueren Konzepten eines
Phänomens im buddhistisch-christlichen Gespräch: NZM(iss)W 51 (1995) 19-29.

9124 *Derrett* J.D.M., Diffusion; Korah and Devadatta [Buddhism-Judaism both-way
borrowings]: ArOr 63 (1995) 330-3.

9125 *Doniger* Wendy, Hindu pluralism and Hindu intolerance of the other: → 392, I(sr)OS
14 (1994) 369-386.

9126 **Dumoulin** Heinrich, Spiritualität des Buddhismus -- Einheit in lebendiger Vielfalt.
Mainz 1995, Grünewald. DM 42. -- [R]G(eist)uL 68 (1995) 395s (S. *Brunner*).

9127 *a) Gittins* Anthony J., Beyond hospitality; the missionary status and role revisited; --
b) Brownson James V., Speaking the truth in love; elements of a missional hermeneutic:
IRM(iss) 83 (1994) 397-416 / 479-504.

9128 *Goffi* Tullo, Spirito Santo, anima dell'Induismo : (R)*StEc 12 (Venezia 1994) 199-206.

9129 **Hardy** Friedhelm, The religious culture of India; power, love and wisdom: StRelTrad
4. C 1994, Univ. xiii-613 p.: 3 fig.; 19 phot. £ 55. -- [R]JRAS (1995) 440-2 (K. *Werner*).

9130 **Heyman** Derek K., Two versions of the non-substantial self; SARTRE and Yogacara
Buddhism compared: diss. SUNY, [D]*Lawler* J. Buffalo 1995. 298 p. 95-38086 -- DissA
56 (1995s) p. 2717.

9131 **Holdrege** Barbara A., Veda and Torah; transcending the textuality of Scripture.
Albany 1995, SUNY. xiii-765 p. 4 60; pa. $ 20. 0-7914-1639-9; -40-2 [ThD 44,70].

9132 *Janda* Josef, Fasziniert von fernöstlicher Religiösität: TPQ 143 (1995) 382-391(-403).

9133 *Keown* Damien, Christian ethics in the light of Buddhist ethics: ET 106 (1994s) 132-7.

9134 **Kern** Iso, Buddhistische Kritik am Christentum im China des 17. Jahrhunderts:
Schweizer Asiatische Studien mg 11. Bern 1982, Lang. 418 p. -- [R]ThPh 69 (1994) 601s
(K. *Schatz*).

9135 **Kim Young-Dong**, Der Schamanismus und das Christentum in Korea: Diss. [D]*Balz* H.
Berlin 1994. -- ThRv 91 (1995) 92.

9136 **Küng** Hans, *Ching* Julia, Christianity and Chinese religions 1993 → 10,8609: [R]HeythJ
36 (1995) 234 (E. *Ryden*: how not to do it; Küng knows little of China and resorts to red
herrings; Ching's 1993 Chinese religions corrects her part).

9137 **Lang** Max, Die Tür zur Erfüllung des Lebens; die Weisheit Asiens und die christliche
Botschaft. Mü 1993, Don Bosco. 147 p. DM 19,80. -- [R]G(eist)uL 68 (1995) 396s (J.
Mayer).

9138 **Laycock** Steven W., Mind as mirror and the mirroring of mind; Buddhist reflections
on Western phenomenology. Albany 1994, SUNY. xvi-337 p. $ 22. 0-7914-1997-5; pa.
8-3. -- [R]J(ap)JRS 22 (1995) 227-9 (J. *O'Leary*).

9139 **Lee Jung Young**, Embracing change; postmodern interpretations of the 'I Ching'[→
8082 supra] from a Christian perspective. Scranton / Cranbury NJ 1994, Univ. /
Asssoc.Univ. 351 p. £ 30. 0-940866-23-4. -- [R]TBR 8,1 (1995s) 62 (L. *Houlden*).

9140 **Lefebure** Leo D., The Buddha and the Christ; explorations in Buddhist and Christian
dialogue: Faith Meets Faith, 1993 → 9,12285; 10,10962: [R]Greg 76 (1995) 425s (J..

Dupuis); RStR 21 (1995) 33 (R.L.F. *Habito*: excellent); RTL 26 (1995) 376s (J. *Scheuer*: mais 'la Compagnie de Jésus n'a pas l'honneur de compter Raimundo PANIKKAR parmi ses membres, p.47').

9141 **Leong** Kenneth S., The Zen teachings of Jesus. NY 1995, Crossroad. 204 p. $ 15 pa. 0-8245-1481-5 [ThD 43,176].

9142 **Liang Chin-Hsien** Joshua, A missiological study on the ethical teachings of Jesus and of Confucius; deriving elenctic implications from comparative ethics: diss. Reformed Theol. Sem. 1995. 265 p. 95-22044. -- DissA 56 (1995s) p. 984.

9143 **Lipner** Julius, Hindus; their religious beliefs and practices. L 1994, Routledge. xiii-375 p. £ 45. -- ^RJRAS (1995) 442-4 (D. *Killingley*).

9144 *Löhr* Gebhard, Das indische Gleichnis vom Elephanten und den Blinden und seine verschiedenen Deutungen; zum Problem interreligiöser Toleranz und des interreligiösen Dialoges: ZM(iss)R 79 (1995) 290-303; Eng. 304.

9145 **Mabry** John R., God as nature sees God; a Christian reading of the Tao Te Ching. ... 1994, Element. -- ^RCreation Spirituality 11,1 (Oakland 1995) 55s (J. *Provost*).

9146 ^E**Mataji** Vandana, Christian ashrams, a movement with a future. Delhi 1993, ISPCK. 160 p. $ 8. -- ^RTBR 8,1 (1995s) 18 (D.R.*Forrester*: excellent).

9147 **Moran** J.F., The Japanese and the Jesuits; Alessandro VALIGNANO in sixteenth-century Japan. L 1993, Routledge. 238 p. $ 70. -- ^RIBM(iss)R 19 (1995) 32 (A.C. *Ross*).

9148 **Nelson** Ethel R., *Broadberry* Richard E., Genesis and the mystery Confucius couldn't solve. St.Louis 1994, Concordia. 174 p. $ 10. -- ^RConcordia J 11 (1995) 248s (H.*Rowold*: implausible).

9149 **Panikkar** Raimon, The cosmotheandric experience; an emerging religious consciousness, ^E *Eastham* Scott. Mkn 1993, Orbis. xv-160 p. $ 25. -- ^R*CritRR 7 (1994) 284s (A. *Sung Park*: what is awaited from Orbis as his 1989 Gifford Lectures, The rhythm of being).

9150 *Parratt* John, Recent writing on Dalit theology; a bibliographical essay: IRM(iss) 83 (1994) 329-337.

9151 **Powell** Andrew, Living Buddhism. Berkeley 1995, Univ. California (= British Museum 1989). 200 p.; 150 color. pl. (G. Harrison). $ 25. 0-520-20410-7 [ThD 42,383].

9152 *a) Pushparajan* A., Christian response to Indian religions. -- *b) Grant* Sara, Jesus Christ as locus for the meeting of world religions; -- *c) Ward* J.S.K., The question of truth in religion; -- *d) Brück* Michael von, Interreligious communication and the future of religions: JDharma 19 (1994) 275-299 / 300-313 / 209-223 / 224-234.

9153 *a) Pye* Michael, [... Japanese] Religion; shape and shadow: -- *b) Cen Linshu*, Studies on religion in modern China: Numen 41 (1994) 51-75 / 76-87.

9154 *a) Rao* S.N., Encounter of Hindus with the ancient Thomas Christians in India; -- *b) Raman* N.S.S., Encounter of Hinduism with Islam in Islamic countries: JDharma 19 (1994) 138-159 / 166-174.

9155 **Roetz** Heiner, Confucian ethics of the axial age; a reconstruction under the aspect of the breakthrough toward postconventional thinking. Albany 1993, SUNY. 373 p. $ 22. -- ^RJRel 75 (1995) 607s (Francisca Cho *Bantly*).

9156 **Seager** Richard H., The World's Parliament of Religions, the East/West encounter, Chicago 1893. Bloomington 1995, Indiana Univ. xxxi-208 p. $ 35. 0-253-35137-5 [ThD 43,87].

9157 ^E**Sharma** Arvind, Our religions; the seven [4 Far East] world religions, introduced by prominent scholars from each tradition. SF 1993, Harper. xi-536. $ 30. -- ^RP(rinc)SB

16 (1995) 101-3 (A. *Neely*).

9158 **Sharma** Arvind, The Philosophy of Religion [J. HICK] and Advaita Vedānta [SANKARA 9th c.]; a comparative study in religion and reason: Hermeneutics. Univ.Park 1995, Penn State. viii-232 p. $ 32,50. 0-271-01032-0 [ThD 43,88].

9159 **Shaw** Stephen J., The dynamic interplay between silence and language in HEIDEGGER and Taoism: diss. SUNY, ^D*Cho Kah Kyung*. Buffalo 1995. 199 p. 95-38130. -- DissA 56 (1995s) p. 2720.

9160 **Staffner** Hans, Dialogue; stimulating contacts with Hindus. Anand 1993, GJPrakash. 167 p. $ 6. -- ^RGreg 76 (1995) 199 (J. *Dupuis*); I(nd)TS 32 (1995) 373s (Sr. *Namita*).

9161 **Stoeber** Michael, Theo-monistic mysticism; a Hindu-Christian comparison. NY 1994, St.Martin's. x-135 p. $ 50. -- ^RRelSt 31 (1995) 140s (J. *Lipner*); RStR 21 (1995) 311 (M.P. *Samartha*).

9162 **Stoneman** Richard, Who are the Brahmans ? Indian lore and Cynic doctrine in PALLADIUS' De Bragmanibus and its models: CQ 44 (1994) 500-510.

9163 **Suwanbubbha** Parichart, Grace and Kamma: a case study of religio-cultural encounters in Protestant and Buddhist communities in Bangkok and its relevant environs: diss. Lutheran School of Theology, ^D*Hefner* P., 1994. 317 p. 95-21177. -- D(iss)AI 56 (1995s) p. 238.

9164 **Talbott** Rick F.,Sacred sacrifice; ritual paradigms in Vedic religion and early Christianity: AmUSt 9/150. NY 1995, P.Lang. vii-356 p.; bibliog. 325-346. 0-8204-2322-X.

9165 **Teshima** Jacob Y., Zen Buddhism and Hasidism, a comparative study. Lanham MD 1995, UPA. xviii-188 p.; bibliog. 169-176. 0-7618-0003-4.

9167 **Thurman** Robert A.F., The holy teaching of Vimalakurthi, a Mahayana scripture. Delhi 1991, Motilal Banaarsidass. x-166 p. rs.125. -- ^RJDh 19 (1994) 185s (B.V. *Venketa Krishna*).

9168 ^E**Vandana** (Mataji), SWAMI ABHISHIKTANANDA [Henri LE SAUX, Benedictine who came to India in 1947 and died in 1973], the man and his message^{2·} Delhi 1994, ISPCK. 82 p. $6. 81-7214-120-3. -- ^RTBR 8,1 (1995s) 36 (R.S. *Sugirtharajah*).

9169 **Versluis** Arthur, American transcendentalism and Asian religions. NY 1993, Oxford-UP. 355p. $ 48. -- ^RJRel 75 (1995) 322s (T. A. *Tweed*).

9170 **Vineeth** V. Francis, Yoga of spirituality; Christian initiation into Indian spiritual traditions. Bangalore 1995, Dharmaram College. 227 p. $ 15 pa. [ThD 43,92].

9171 **Vroom** H.M., Geen andere Goden; christelijk geloof in gesprek met boeddhisme, hindoeïsme en islam: Interacties. Kampen 1993, Kok. 155 p. *f* 35. 90-242-8085-0. -- ^RTTh 35 (1995) 203 (P. *Valkenberg*).

9172 **Werner** Karel, A popular dictionary of Hinduism. Richmond, Surrey 1994, Curzon. v-185 p. £ 10. -- ^RJRAS (1995) 450s (P. *Marett*).

9173 **Woga** Edmund, Der parentale Gott; zum Dialog zwischen den Religionen der indonesischen Völker Sumbas und dem Christentum: StSVD 59. Nettetal 1994, Steyler. 439 p DM 58. 3-8050-0344-7. -- ^RZkT 117 (1995) 360s (K.H. *Neufeld*).

9174 **Wong** Joseph H., Some affinities between Taoism and Christianity; toward a dialogue: LivLight 32,2 (Wsh 1995) 31-40.

9175 *Yao Xinzhong*, Jesus and Confucius; a comparison: ScotJR 16 (1995) 37-50 [< ZIT 95, p.277].

M8.9   **Religiones Africae et Amerindiae** [→ H8.6]

9176 **Deloria** Vine, God is red; a native view of religion² [¹1973]. Golden 1992, North American. 313 p. $ 23. -- ^RJRel 75 (1995) 161s (T.D. *Swanson*).

9177 **Killoren** John J., 'Come, Blackrobe'; De SMET and the Indian tragedy 1994 → 5026 above; add ᴿC(ath)HR 81 (1995) 461-3 (D.M. *Brumbach*).

9178 *Platvoet* J.G., God als vijand; de genezingsdansen van de ! [Zuidelijk Afrika volk] Kung: NedThT 49 (1995) 89-107; Eng. 154.

9179 **Sered** Susan S., Priestess, mother, sacred sister; religions dominated by women. Ox c.1994, UP. 330 p. $ 27,50. -- ᴿCCen 112 (1995) 59s (Mary Louise *Bringle*).

9180 **Stamm** Anne, Les religions africaines: QS(ais)J? 632. P 1995, PUF. 128 p. 2-13-047212-5.

9181 **Steltenkamp** Michael F., BLACK ELK, holy man of the Oglala. Norman 1993, Univ. Oklahoma. 211 p. $ 20. -- ᴿJRel 75 (1995) 304-6 (W. K. *Powers*).

9182 **Swain** Tony, A place for strangers; towards a history of aboriginal being. C 1993, Univ. xi-303 p. $ 60. -- ᴿJRel 75 (1995) 463s (G.L. *Ebersoll*).

9183 **Swain** Tony, *Trompf* Garry, The religions of Oceania. L 1995, Routledge. 244 p. $ 18. 0-415-06019-2 [ThD 43,91].

9184 **Vachon** Robert, Guswenta or the [Mohawk-US] cultural imperative: Interculture 28,2-4 (1995) 73 p.; 41 p.; 46 p.

| **XVII. Historia Medii Orientis Biblici** |

Q1 *Syria prae-islamica, Canaan,* **Israel Veteris Testamenti**

9185 *Adler* Jonathan, Dating the Exodus [under Horemheb]; a new perspective: JBQ 23 (1995) 44-51.

9186 **Ahlström** Gösta W., The history of ancient Palestine: JSOT.s 146, 1993 → 9,12326; 10,10979: ᴿBA 57 (1994) 245s (P.S. *Ash*); *Carthaginensia 11 (1995) 192-4 (R. *Sanz Valdivieso*); *CritRR 7 (1994) 62-64 (W.C. *Dever*); Interpretation 49 (1995) 80 . 82 . 84 (J.M. *Miller*); JRel 75 (1995) 401s (J.A. *Dearman*); PEQ 127 (1995) 70s (J.R. *Bartlett*: stimulating; alternative inevitable); PrP 9 (1995) 128 (B. *Robinson*); RB 102 (1995) 146s (J.-M. de *Tarragon*); Salesianum 57 (1995) 369 (R. *Vicent*); ThLZ 120 (1995) 873-6 (H.M. *Niemann*).

9187 **Assmann** Jan, Politische Theologie zwischen Ägypten und Israel [< Vortrag 1991]: Themen 52. Mü 1992, C. von Siemens Stiftung. 120 p. [*OIAc 11 (1994) 12].

9188 **Barnes** William H., Studies in the chronology of the Divided Monarchy of Israel: HSM 1991 → 7,2557; 8,2944: ᴿBZ 39 (1995) 290-3 (W. *Thiel*); JAOS 115 (1995) 122 (J.E. *Reade*); JNES 54 (1995) 157s (Diana *Edelman*).

9189 **Becking** B., The fall of Samaria 1992 → 8,2991 ... 10,10982: ᴿZAW 107 (1995) 345s (M. *Köckert*).

9190 **Berquist** J.L., Judaism in Persia's shadow [539-333 BCE]; a social and historical approach. Mp 1995, Fortress. vi-282 p. $ 21 pa. 0-8006-2845-4 [NTAb 40,p.550].

9191 **Bianchi** Francesco, Ricerche storico-bibliche sulla Giudea in età neobabilonese e achemenide (586 a.C. - 442 a.C) [... iii. L'economia]: 'I superstiti della deportazione sono là nella provincia' (Neemia 1,3), 2: AION 55. supp. 82 (1995). 97 p.

9192 **Blázquez** José M., *al.*, Historia de Oriente antiguo. M 1992. Cátedra. 648 p., ill. 84-376-1044-3. -- ᴿBiOr 52 (1995) 37-39 (J. *Padró*).

9193 **Bock** Sebastian, Breve storia del popolo d'Israele [1989] ,[T]. Bo 1992, Dehoniane. 183 p. L[m] 18. -- [R]PaVi 39,5 (1994) 50s (G. *Marocco*).

9194 *Borowski* Oded, Hezekiah's reforms and the revolt against Assyria: BA 58 (1995) 148-155; ill.

9195 *Botta* Alejandro Félix, Problemas históricos en torno a los orígenes de Israel: Boletín Teológico 57 (BA 1995) 61-70 [< OTA 18 (1995) p. 497].

9196 **Bright** John, [P] Historia Izraela [[3]1981], [T]*Radoszycki* Jan, Wsz 1994, PAX. 440 p. -- [R]R(uch)BL 47 (1994) 285-8 (J. *Warzecha*, [P]).

9197 **Brown** John Pairman, Israel and Hellas: BZAW 231. B 1995, de Gruyter. xxii-407 p. 3-11-014233-3.

9198 *Coggins* Richard, What does 'deuteronomistic' mean ?: → 170, [F]SAWYER, J., Words; JSOT.s 195 (1995) 135-148.

9199 *Davies* G.J., Were there schools in ancient Israel ?: → 55, [F]EMERTON J., Wisdom 1995, 199-211.

9200 **Davies** Philip R., In search of 'Ancient Israel': JSOT.s 148, 1992 → 8,b818 ... 10,10986: [R]*A(sn)JS 20 (1995) 153-6 (Z. *Zevit*); *CritRR 7 (1994) 112-4 (C.D. *Evans*).

9201 *Dion* Paul E., Syro-Palestinian resistance to Shalmaneser III in the light of new documents: ZAW 107 (1995) 482-9

9202 *Duckworth* Robin, Exodus; the myth and the reality: Scripture Bulletin 25 (Hertford UK 1995) 15-23 [< OTA 18 (1995) p. 408 (P.L. *Redditt*)].

9203 **Edelman** Diana, King Saul in the historiography of Israel: jOsu 121, 1991 → 7,2482 ... 10,2570: [R]JBL 114 (1995) 131-3 (G.N. *Knoppers*).

9204 *Frolov* Serge, 'Days of Shiloh' in the Kingdom of Israel [HALPERN B., CROSS F.; 1Kgs 12,26-28]: Biblica 76 (1995) 210-218.

9205 *Galil* Gershon, The last years of the Kingdom of Israel and the fall of Samaria: CBQ 57 (1995) 52-65.

9206 *Gelinas* Margaret M., United monarchy -- divided monarchy; fact or fiction ?: → 4, [F]AHLSTRÖM, G., Pitcher; JSOT.s 190 (1995) 227-237.

9207 *Geus* Cornelis H.J. de, Reflections on the continuity of Egyptian influence in the administration and material culture of pre-exilic Israel: → 48, [F]DONNER, H., Meilenstein: ÄAT 30 (1995) 44-51; 1 fig.

9208 *Gonçalves* Francolino J., Isaïe, Jérémie et la politique internationale de Juda [Pont. Biblical Inst. McCarthy Lecture 10.III.1995]: Biblica 76 (1995) 282-298.

9209 **González-Lamadrid** Antonio, Las tradiciones históricas de Israel: El mundo de la Biblia 6, 1993 → 9,12338; 10,10989: [R]Ang 71 (1994) 445s (J. *García Trapiello*); EstB 53 (1995) 129 (J.A. *Mayoral*); ScrT(Pamp) 37 (1995) 370 (P. *Varo*).

9210 *Goulder* Michael, Asaph's *History of Israel* (Elohist Press, Bethel, 725 BCE) [Ps 53 & 73-83]: JSOT 65 (1995) 71-81.

9211 *Hadidi* Adnan, Hyksos influence in Jordan and Palestine: → 82, [F]HENNESSY J.B., Trade 1995, 133-6.

9212 [E]**Halpern** Baruch, **Hobson** Deborah W., Biblical law and ideology in monarchic Israel: JSOT.S 124, 1991 → 7,436; 8,2852: [R]BZ 39 (1995) 297s (H. *Seebass*: Lob für P. DION).

9213 *Harrison* Robert, Hellenization in Syria-Palestine; the case of Judea in the third century B.C.: BA 57 (1994) 98-108; ill.

9214 **Hayes** J.H., **Hooker** P.K., A new chronology for the Kings 1988 → 4,2931 ... 7,2558: [R]JQR 84 (1993s) 298-300 (M. *Cogan*).

9215 *Hendel* Ronald S., Finding historical memories in the patriarchal narratives: BArR

21,4 (1995) 52-59 . 70.

9216 **Hoglund** Kenneth G., Achaemenid imperial administration in Syria-Palestine and the missions of Ezra and Nehemiah: SBL diss. 125, 1992 → 8,3044: ᴿCBQ 57 (1995) 137-9 (A. *Cody*); RB 102 (1995) 612-4 (É. *Nodet*).

9217 **Hostetter** Edwin C., [pre-Israel] Nations mightier and more numerous; the biblical view of Palestine's pre-Israelite peoples: BIBAL diss. 3. New Richland 1995, BIBAL. xiii-172 p.; bibliog. 155-172 [< 1991 Johns Hopkins diss: OTA 19,p.328, S.L. *McKenzie*].

9218 **Jagersma** H., A history of Israel to Bar Kochba [I. 1982; II. 1985; unrevised in one volume] 1994 → 10,10993: ᴿBoL (1995) 40 (L.L. *Grabbe*).

9219 **Kessler** Rainer, Staat und Gesellschaft im vorexilischen Juda 1993 → 8,b824 ... 10,10995: ᴿEstFr 96 (1995) 263 (F.*Raurell:* 'Kessler' rightly in text; title and index have 'Kesster').

9220 *Kitchen* Kenneth A., The patriarchal age; myth or history?: BArR 21,2 (1995) 48-57.88.

9221 **Land** J.G. van der, Van Abraham tot David; de oudste geschiedenis van het volk Israël; archeologische, chronologische en historische aspecten. Amst 1993, Buijten & S. 128 p. f 22,50. 90-6064-810-3. -- ᴿTTh 35 (1995) 100 (J. *Negenman:* Abraham c. 1850, Exodus nearer 1400 than 1200).

9222 *Lassner* Jacob, Ritual purity and political exile; Solomon, the queen of Sheba, and the events of 586 B.C.E. in a Yemenite folktale: → 72, ᶠGREENFIELD J., Solving 1995, 117-136.

9223 **Le Roux** Magdel, Identiteit, 'n vlietende entiteit; die politieke invloed op die israelitiese stamme gedurende die tyd <van> die Rigters: *R&T 1 (Pretoria 1994) 308-338 [< OTA 18 (1995) p. 282].

9224 **Levin** Christoph, Der Jahwist: FRLANT 157, 1993: → 9,1747; 10,1591 (not 1991 as Index): ᴿThLZ 120 (1995) 786-790 (E. *Blum*).

9225 *Levy* Thomas E., *al.*, New light on King Narmer and the protodynastic Egyptian presence in Canaan: BA 58 (1995) 26-35; ill.

9226 *Liwak* Rüdiger, Omri: → 772, TRE 25 (1995) 242-4.

9227 *Lovik* Eric, Moses' preparation for ministry; the significance of his Egyptian background: C(alv)BTJ 10,2 (1994) 43-63.

Macchi J., Les Samaritains 1994 → 7152 supra.

9228 *Macchi* Jean-Daniel, Histoire d'Israël ou histoire de la Palestine [AHLSTRÖM G. 1993, monumental; THOMPSON T. 1992, plus cohérent méthodologiquement]: ÉTRel 70 (1995) 85-97.

9229 **Meimaris** Y. E., *al.*, Chronological systems, Roman-Byzantine Palestine and Arabia; the evidence of the dated Greek inscriptions: Meletemata 17, 1992 → 8,9993: ᴿPEQ 127 (1995) 77s (N. *Kokkinos*).

9230 *Mielgo* Constantino, La enseñanza escolar en el antiguo Israel: EstAg 29 (1994) 419-453.

9231 *Na'aman* Nadav, Tiglath-Pileser III's campaign against Tyre and Israel (734-732 B.C.E.) [TADMOR H. 1994]: *TAJ 22 (1995) 268-278.

9232 **Niemann** Hermann M., Herrschaft, Königtum und Staat: FAT 6, 1993 → 9,15351: ᴿThQ 175 (1995) 150s (H. *Niehr*).

9233 *Pienaar* D.N., Aram and Israel during the reigns of Omri and Ahab reconsidered: *J/TydSem 6 (1994) 34-45 [< OTA 19,p.214].

9234 **Pixley** Jorge, Biblical Israel, a people's history 1992 → 8,b835; 9,12351: ᴿT(oronto)JT 10 (1994) 246 (J.L. *McLaughlin*).

9235 **Redford** D.B., Egypt, Canaan, and Israel in ancient times 1992 → 8,b836 ... 10,11005: ᴿVT 45 (1995) 415 (J.D. *Ray*).

9236 *Reventlow* Henning, Computing times, ages and the millennium; an astroomer defends the Bible, William WHISTON (1667-1752) and biblical chronology: → 159, [F]ROGERSON, J., Bible/Society; JSOT.s 200 (1995) 411-421.

9237 **Sacchi** Paolo, Storia del Secondo Tempio; Israele tra VI. secolo a.C. e I. secolo d,C. T 1994, SEI. xxii-529 p. L[m] 60. -- [R]CivCatt 146 (1995,3) 322-5 (G.-L. *Prato*); RivB 43 (1995) 269-276 (B.G. *Boschi*).

9238 **Sader** Hélène S., Les états araméens en Syrie. 1987. -- [R]Syria 72 (1995) 446-9 (A. *Millard*).

9239 **Schäfer** Peter, The history of the Jews in antiquity; the Jews of Palestine from Alexander the Great to the Arab conquest [1983], [T]*Chowcat* David. Luxembourg 1995, Harwood. xxi-231 p., without the illustrations. $ 18. 3-7186-5794-5 [< OTA 19,p.334].

9240 *Schneider* Tammi, Did King Jehu kill his own family ? New interpretation reconciles biblical text with famous Assyrian inscription: BArR 21,1 (1995) 23-33 . 80.

9241 **Schubert** Kurt, Jüdische Geschichte: B-Reihe 2018. Mü 1995, Beck. 144 p. 3-406-39175-3

9242 [E]**Shanks** Hershel, *al.*, The rise of ancient Israel, Smithsonian symposium 1991/2 → 9,408: [R]CBQ 57 (1995) 438s (J.K. *Kuntz*: includes overly technical sent-in replies by GOTTWALD, FINKELSTEIN, ZERTAL to *Dever*, who rightly reminds that 'archaeological data, *once interpreted,* lose their unbiased status').

9243 [E]**Shanks** Hershel, A short history 1988 → 4,326 ... 8,b840: [R]JNES 54 (1995) 66-68 (E.A. *Knauf*: essays; not a history).

9244 *Skov* Knud W., Hvor historisk troværdigt er Det gamle Testamente ? [there is no archeological evidence for an exodus to Canaan (VAN SETERS J., THOMPSON T.L., nor ? for David), but that is no less than for Anglo-Saxon or Norman invasions of England 5th cent. & 1066, or Arab invasion of Palestine 7th cent.]: *Nemalah 14 (K 1995) 90-95 [< OTA 19, p.217].

9245 *Smend* Rudolf, Mose als geschichtliche Gestalt: HZ 260 (1995) 1-19.

9246 **Soggin** J. Alberto, An introduction to the history of Israel and Judah[2] 1993 → 10,11007: [R]Bijd 56 (1995) 73 (P.C. *Beentjes*); VT 45 (1995) 425-7 (J.A. *Emerton* shows in detail the complexities of the revision).

9247 **Stow** Kenneth R., The Jews; a Mediterranean culture. Fasano 1994, Schena (Comunità delle Università Mediterranee). 151 p.; 36 pl. 88-7514-720-5.

9248 *Sweeney* Marvin A., The critique of Solomon in the Josianic edition of the deuteronomistic history: JBL 114 (1995) 607-622.

9249 ȚABARI [earlier SUNY volumes listed → 7,b34; 8,b846]: **29.** [T]**Kennedy** Hugh, Al-Manṣûr and al-Mahdî, A.D. 763-786 / A.H. 146-169. Albany 1990, SUNY. xvi-282 p. $ 44.50; pa. $ 17. 0-7914-0142-1; -3-X. -- [R]BiOr 52 (1995) 479s (J.A. *Nawas*).

9250 -- **36.** [T]**Waines** David, The revolt of the Zanj [870-880 CE]. Albany 1991, SUNY. xxii-229 p. $ 49.50. 0-7914-0763-2; -4-0. -- [R]BiOr 52 (1995) 848s (J.A. *Nawas*).

9251 *Talmon* Shemaryahu, [H] The reckoning of the day in the biblical and early post-biblical periods, [power-struggle between parties favoring respectively] from morning or from evening: → 10,63 Mem. KAMIN S., 1994, 109-129 [< OTA 18 (1995) p. 449 (J. *Corely*)].

9252 **Talshir** Zipora, The alternative story of the division of the Kingdom [3 Kdms 12,24; < [H] 1989]: JBiSt 6. J 1993, Simor. 318 [-xii] p.; insert. $ 27. -- [R]CBQ 57 (1995) 792s (L.L. *Grabbe*).

9253 *Thompson* Thomas L., Gosta Ahlström's History of Palestine: → 4, [F]AHLSTRÖM, G., Pitcher; JSOT.s 190 (1995) 420-434: would have been our first real history of *Palestine* (four pages of previous Palestine-Israel confusion premised) but the obligatory debate with FINKELSTEIN at the LB ending undesirably shifted the focus back toward 'Israel'.

9254 **Thompson** Thomas L., Early history of the Israelite people from the written and archaeological sources 1994 → 8,b848 ... 10,11009: [R]*A(sn)JS 20 (1995) 156-160 (A.F. *Rainey*: detailed, severe; Morton SMITH preferable); ScrT(Pamp) 37 (1995) 635-641 (D. *Varo*).

9255 **Van Seters** John, Prologue to history .. Yahwist 1992 → 8,1977; 10,1611: [R]A(ustrl)BR 43 (1995) 78-81 (M. A. *O'Brien*); BiOr 52 (1995) 105-7 (K. *Deurloo*); CBQ 57 (1995) 579s (T.L. *Thompson*: very fine, his best); JBL 114 (1995) 127s (J.S. *Kaminsky*); RestQ 37 (1995) 126s (R.R. *Marrs*).

9256 **Van Seters** John. The life of Moses; the Yahwist as historian 1994 → 10,2177: [R]Biblica 76 (1995) 419-422 (J. L. *Ska*); BThB 25 (1995) 47s (R. *Gnuse*); JRel 75 (1995) 545-7 (T.B. *Dozeman*); VT 45 (1995) 431s (H.G.M. *Williamson*).

9257 *Varo* Francisco, El marco histórico del Antiguo Testamento; perspectivas actuales [KITTEL R. 1888 to THOMPSON T., then an archeological-sans-biblical summary of Palestine history 1300-200 B.C.]: ScrTh 27 (Pamplona 1995) 751-788 [< OTA 19, p.218].

9258 **Warzecha** Julian, [P] Dawny Izrael od Abrahama do Salomona. Wsz 1995. Akad. Teol.Katol. 214 p. 83-7072-055-2.

9259 **Weinberg** Joel, The citizen-temple community: JSOT.s 151, 1992 → 8,329*b*; [R]VT 45 (1995) 574 (H.G.M. *Williamson*).

9260 **Weinfeld** Moshe, [H] From Joshua to Josiah, turning points in the history of Israel. J 1992, Magnes. 299 p. -- [R]JQR 86 (1995) 205-7 (D.A. *Glatt-Gilad*: a master-synthesis).

9261 *Wesselius* J.W., HERODOTUS [of Halicarnassus, 490-430, imitated in Gen-Kgs], vader van de bibjbelse geschiedenis ?: A(mst)CEBT 14 (1995) 9-6l; Eng. 142 [< OTA 19, p.180].

9262 *Whitelam* Keith W., New Deuteronomistic heroes and villains; a response to T.L. THOMPSON: S(cand)JOT 9 (1995) 97-118.

9263 **Willi** Thomas, Juda -- Jehud -- Israel; Studien zum Selbstverständnis des Judentums in persischer Zeit: FAT 12. Tü 1995, Mohr. x-209 p.; bibliog. 183-193. 3-16-146478-8.

9264 **Zwickel** Wolfgang, Geschichte Palästinas von der Mittelbronzezeit bis zum Untergang Judas: FAT 10. Tü 1994, Mohr. xvi-424 p.; ill. DM 228. 3-16-146218-1 [RStR 22,58, M.S.*Smith*: a standard reference].

Q2 **Historiographia** -- *theologia historiae*

9265 *André* Jean-Marie, SÉNÈQUE et la philosophie de l'histoire: Fav 17,1 (1995) 27-37.

9266 *Armisen-Marchetti* Mireille, Pourquoi SÉNÈQUE n'a-t-il pas écrit l'histoire ? [il juge les historiens malhonnêtes ...]: RÉL 73 (1995) 151-167.

9267 **Assmann** Jan, Das kulturelle Gedächtnis; Schrift, Erinnerung und politische Identität in frühen Hochkulturen 1992 → 8,b854; DM 68: [R]VT 44 (1994) 416s (J.D. *Ray*).

9268 **Bagnall** R.S., Reading papyri, writing ancient history: Approaching the Ancient World. L 1995, Routledge. xvi-145 p.; 8 pl. $ 55; pa. $ 16. 0-415-09376-7; -7-5 [NTAb 40, p.549].

9269 **Bauman** Michael, *Klauber* Martin I., Historians of the Christian tradition; their methodology and influence on western thought. Nv 1995, Broadman & H. vi-631 p. $ 50. 0-8054-1160-7 [ThD 43,369].

9270 **Bearzot** Cinzia, Storia e storiografia ellenistica in PAUSANIA il Periegeta: Unov. Venezia. Venezia 1992, Cardo. 312 p. L[m] 42. -- [R]AnCL 64 (1995) 305s (Véronique

Krings); Klio 77 (1995) 529 (K.M. *Errington*).

9271 *a) Beierwaltes* Werner, Distanz und Nähe der Geschichte; HEGEL & PLATON; -- *b)*
Beister Hartmut, Pragmatische Geschichtsschreibung und zeitliche Dimension: → 176,
F SCHMITT H., Rom & Osten 1995, 9-21 / 329-349.

9272 **Bietenholz** Peter G., Historia and fabula; myths and legends in historical thought from
antiquity to the modern age: StIntelH 59. Lei 1994, Brill. xii-434 p.; 9 fig. *f* 160. 90-04-
10063-6 [VT 45, after 284. adv.].

9273 *Bost* Hubert, Résurrection et histoire: RHPhR 75 (1995) 419-437, Eng. 439,

9274 **Bowersock** G.W., Fiction as history, Nero to Julian. 1995. -- R RÉG 108 (1995) 254-6
(A. *Billault*).

9275 **Brauer** Markus, Theologie im Horizont der Geschichte; Fortgang und Schwerpunkt
geschichtstheologischen Denkens ... : kath. Diss. D *Pottmeyer* H. Bochum 1992. - ThRv
91,93.

9276 **Brettler** Marc Zvi, The creation of history in ancient Israel. L 1995, Routledge. xv-
254 p.; bibliog. 223-9. 0-415-11860-3.

9277 **Canfora** L., [26] Studi di storia della storiografia romana 1993 → 10,164*d*; L^m 50; 88-
7228-114-4: R JRS 85 (1995) 268 (T.J. *Luce*).

9278 *a)* **Cantillo** Giuseppe, L'eccedenza del passato; per uno storicismo esistenziale. N
1993, Morano. 410 p. L^m 45. - *b)* **Cacciatore** Giuseppe, Storicismo problematico e
metodo critico. N 1993, Guida. 426 p. L^m 50. -- R CivCatt 146 (1995,1) 620s (G. *Pirola*).

9279 *a) Cavalcanti* Elena, 'Solacium miseriae', l'imperfezione della storia (AUG. Civ.Dei
XIX,21-27); -- *b) Piccaluga* Giulia, Fondazione della realtà e uscita dalla storia nel Sermo
[AUG.] 'De Urbis excidio' : → 119, F MARA M.Grazia = Aug(ustinianum)R 35 (1995) 413-
428 / 497-510.

9280 *Chavalas* Mark W., Recent trends in the study of Israelite historiography: JETS 38
(1995) 161-9.

9281 *Chazan* R., The time-bound and the timeless; medieval Jewish narration of events;
History and memory 6,1 (TA 1994) 5-34 [RHE 90 (1995) 7*].

9282 *Chédozeau* Bernard, L'Histoire sainte, un genre injustement oubli ?: vSp 149 (1995)
562-573.

9283 *Cholvy* Gérard, 'Religion populaire' et 'intériorisation du christianisme'; les pesanteurs
de l'historiographie (XIXe-XXe siècle): E(spr)eV 105 (1995) 700-703.

9284 **Clagett** Marshall, Ancient Egyptian science, a source book, 2. Calendars, clocks, and
astronomy. Ph 1995, AmPh. vii-575 p.; 150 pl. 0-87169-214-7. -- R OTA 18 (1995) p.
625 (A. *Fitzgerald*).

9285 **Cottier** Georges, Histoire et connaissance de Dieu: StFrSN 79. FrS 1993, Uni. 255
p. -- R ScrT(Pamp) 27 (1995) 1012-8 (M. *Lluch Baixauli*).

9286 *D'Ambrosio* Rocco, La rappresentazione politica tra pensiero classico ed eredità
cristiana in Eric VOEGELIN: RivScRel 9 (1995) 365-379.

9287 *Deist* Ferdinand, The nature of historical understanding: OTEssays 6 (1993) 384-398.

9288 *De Rosa* Gabriele, Verso quale storiografia di fine millennio ? Bilancio e prospettive
del nostro lavoro : R(ic)SS(oc)R 47 (1995) 7-22.

9289 **Dobesch** Gerhard, Das europäische 'Barbaricum' und die Zone der Mediterrankultur;
ihre historische Wechselwirkung und das Geschichtbild des POSEIDONIOS: Tyche Supp. 2.
W 1995, Holzhausen. 118 p.

9290 *Ego* Beate, ^H The concept of history in the Targum Sheni to Esther: → 10,331a, llth
Jewish 1994. A-131-4.

9291   *Elath* Moshe, [H] Saul at the apex of his success and the beginning of his decline (the historiographical significance of 1 Samuel 13-14): Tarbiz 63 (1993s) 5-25; Eng.v.

9292   *Ellacuría* Ignacio, Escatología e historia: RLatAmT 11 (1994) 113-129 [-161 & 215-244, *Sobrino* J. sobre Ellacuría).

9293   *Flanagan* J.W. [→ 8664], Finding the arrow of time; constructs of ancient history and religion: CuRB 3 (1995) 37-80 [< NTAb 40, p.392].

9294   **Forte** Bruno, Teología de la historia [1991 → 7,b61], [T]*Ortiz García* Alfonso. S 1995, Sígueme. 410 p. -- [R]EstTrin 29 (1995) 502s (M. *Ofilada Mina*).

9295   *Gagey* Henri-Jérôme,   *Souletie* Jean-Louis,   La théologie aux prises avec l'historiographie: → 120, Mém. MARLÉ R.,   RSR 83,4 (1995) 557-583 [595-606, *Gisel* P. sur Marlé sur BULTMANN: NTAb 40, p.392].

9296   *a) Georgiadou* A., *Larmour* D.H.J. [*al.*], LUCIAN and historiography; -- *b) Strobel* K., Zeitgeschichte unter den Antoninen: → 755, ANRW 2,34,2 (1994) [1362-] 1448-1509 / 1315-60.

9297   **Goertz** H.J., Umgang mit Geschichte; eine Einführung in die Geschichtstheorie: Enz 555.   Ha-Reinbek 1005. Rowohlt. 194 p.   DM 18,90 [RHE 91,6*]

9298   *González Faus* José I., Una tarea histórica; de la liberación a la apocalíptica [= Sal Terrae (oct.1995) 717-728]: RLatAmT 12 (1995) 281-290.

9299   **Grant** M., Greek and Roman historians; information and misinformation.   L 1995, Routledge. xii-172 p.; 6 maps. $ 60; pa. $ 17. 0-415-11769-0; -70-4 [NTAb 40, p.553].

9300   **Hall** Robert G., Revealed histories 1991 → 7,b68 ... 10,11037*; [R]VT 45 (1995) 567s (M.P. *Wadsworth*).

9301   *Hammond* David M.,   Hayden WHITE; meaning and truth in history: *PhTh 8,4 (Milwaukee 1994) 289-307.

9302   *Hanges* James C., The Greek [city-] foundation-legend; its form and relation to history: → 512, SBL Seminars 34 (1995) 494-520.

9303   *Heehs* Peter, Myth, history, and theory: HTh 33 (1994) 1-19.

9304   **Heinzelmann** Martin,   GREGOR von Tours (538-594), 'Zehn Bücher Geschichte'; Historiographie und Gesellschaftskonzept im 6. Jahrhundert. Da 1994, Wiss. x-275 p. DM 69. 3-534-08348-2 [ThRv 91].

9305   *Helberg* J.L., The determination of history according to the book Daniel: ZAW 107 (1995) 273-287.

9306   *Hinchliff* Peter, God and history 1992 → 8,b877 ... 10,11039: [R]HeyJ 35 (1994) 211-3 (M.D. *Chapman*); S(cot)JTh 48 (1995) 271s (I. *Bradley*).

9307   [E]**Hornblower** Simon, Greek historiography. Ox 1994, UP. xii-286 p. £ 35. -- [R]GaR 42 (1995) 236 (H. van *Wees*).

9308   **Jacobs** Wilhelm G.. Gottebegriff und Geschichtsphilosophie in der Sicht SCHELLINGs. Stu - Bad Cannstadt 1993, Frommann-Holzboog. 291 p. DM 105. -- [R]Bijdragen 56 (1995) 349s (B. *Vedder*).

9309   *a) Klein* Richard, Zum Kultur- und Geschichtsverständnis in der Romrede des Aelius ARISTIDES; -- *b) Schmidt* Ernst G.,   PLUTARCH's Athenerbiographien: → 690, Prinzipat 1992/5, 283-292 / 251-266.

9310   **Laato** Antti, History and ideology in the Old Testament prophetic literature; a semiotic approach to the reconstruction of the proclamation of the historical prophets: CBOT 41. Sto 1995, Almqvist & W. x-435 p. 91-22-01701-1.

9311   **Lami** Gian Franco, Introduzione a Eric VOEGELIN: Univ. Roma Teoria dello Stato 3. Mi 1993, Giuffré. xxxvi-316 p. 88-14-04417-1. -- [R]Salesianum 57 (1995) 191 (G. *Abbà* non commenda; gergo).

9312 *Lepenies* Wolf,Von der Geschichte zur Politik der Mentalitäten: HZ 261 (1995) 673-94.

9313 *Levoratti* A.J., Apocalipsis y filosofía de la historia : RevBib(Arg) 57 (1995) 41-57.

9314 **Long** V. Philips, The art of biblical history: Foundations of contemporary interpretation 5 (last of the 7 to appear). → 10,11045: GR/Leicester 1994, Zondervan/Apollos.. 247 p. $ 18. 0-310-43180-8 [ThD 42 (1995) 277]. -- [R]ET 106 (1994s) 308 (J.R. *Bartlett*); JSOT 66 (1995) 119; OTA 18 (1995) p. 407 (W. *Vogels*); RefR 49 (1995s) 135 (Sylvio J. *Scorza*); SBF*LA 45 (1995) 539-543 (L.D. *Chrupcala*); *TBR 8,1 (1995s) 33s (M. *Elliott*).

9315 *Loretz* O., Geschichte und Geschichtsschreibung im Alten Testament; biblische Historik und jüdische Identität: Mitteilungen für Anthropologie und Religionsgeschichte 9 (1994) 181-221 [< ZIT 95, p.276].

9316 **Mandell** Sara, *Friedman* David N., The relationship between HERODOTUS' history and primary history: SFLJud 60, 1993 → 9,12411: [R] 61 (1994) 94 (K.W. *Whitelam*); JBL 114 (1995) 123-6 (T.S.L. *Michael*).

9317 **Mause M.,** Die Darstellung des Kaisers in der lateinischen Panegyrik: Palingenesia 50. Stu 1994. 317 p. -- [R]RÉL 73 (1995) 306s (J.- P. *Callu*).

9318 *Mazo Martín* Hernando, Fe e historia en la teología de Emil BRUNNER: ScripV 41 (1994) 5-73

9319 *a) Millard* A.R. (also [E]) Story, history, and theology; -- *b) Yamauchi* Edwin, The current state of OT historiography; -- *c) Martens* Elmer A., The oscillating fortunes of 'history ' within OT theology; -- *d) McMahon* Gregory, History and legend in early Hittite historiography; -- *e) Wolf* Herbert M., The historical reliability of the Hittite annals; -- *f) Baker* David W., Scribes as transmitters of tradition: → 10,326*, Faith 1990/4, 37-64 / 1-326 / 313-340 / 149-157 /159-164 / 65-77.

9320 **Momigliano** A., The classical foundations of modern historiography 1990 → 8,386 ... 10,11050: [R]EM(erita) 62 (1994) 218s (J.M. *Candau*).

9321 *a) Montoya Sáenz* José, Lenguaje, conocimiento y historia; -- *b) Sánchez Ferra* Anselmo, La historia y la tradición; razón y sentimiento abordan el tiempo; -- *c) Sanmartín Ascaso* Joaquín, Macrohistoria, microhistoria o historia; -- *d) Navarro Suárez* Francisco J., *al.*, Informática e historia antigua; el uso del P[ersonal]C[omputer] en el estudio de los textos clásicos; -- *e) Marín Conesa* Rita, Determinismo y contingencia en la obra historiográfica de PROCOPIO Cesariense; la significación de *Tyche* y Zeos; → 221, [F]YELO TEMPLADO A., Lengua 1995, 15-24 / 25-28 / 219-36 / 37-43 / 143-162.

9322 *Moreno G.* Jaime, El pensamiento historiográfico en la antigua Mesopotamia: TyV 35 (1994) 289-296.

9323 **Morgan** Michael L., Dilemmas in modern Jewish thought; the dialectics of revelation and history. Bloomington 1992, Indiana Univ. xxi-121 p. -- [R]*A(sn)JS 20 (1995) 237-240 (Z. *Garber*).

9324 **Morrissey** Michael P., Consciousness and transcendence; the theology of Eric VOEGELIN 1994 → 10,11051 [RStR 22,50, M. *Franz*]. -- [R]AmJTP 16 (1995) 233-6 (G. *Mann*); JRel 75 (1995) 484-6 (E. *Webb*).

9325 **Müller** Christof, Geschichtsbewusstsein bei A. AUGUSTINUS ...: Cassiciacum 39/2, 1993 → 9,12415; 10,11053: [R]Greg 76 (1995) 421s (F.-A. *Pastor*).

9326 **Muhlack** Ulrich, Geschichtswissenschaft im Humanismus und in der Aufklärung; die Vorgeschichte des Historismus 1991 → 11055: [R]E(ng)HR 110 (1995) 205s (Fania *Oz-Salzberger*).

9327 **Murrmann-Kahl** Michael, Der entzauberte Heilsgeschichte 1992 → 8.B895 ...

10,11056: [R]FilTeo 9 (1995) 188-191 (H. J. *Adriaanse* come p. 199); NedTTh 49 (1995) 173-5 (ook H.-J. *Adriaanse*).

9328 **Nicolai** Roberto, La storiografia nell'educazione antica: BtMatClas 10, 1992 → 9,12417; 10,11058: [R]CLR 45 (1995) 49s (I. *Rutherford*: excellent); RÉG 108 (1995) 602s (L. *Pernot*).

9329 [E]**Nippel** Wilfried, [25 Texte] Über das Studium der Alten Geschichte 1993 → 10,11059; DM 26,90 -- [R]HZ 261 (1995) 136s (R. *Bichler*).

9330 **Nunes Carreira** José, História antes de Heródoto; historiografia e ideia de história na antiguidade oriental. Lisboa 1993, Cosmos. 257 p. 972-8081-03-0.

9331 *a) Padberg* Lutz E. von, Gechichtsschreibung und kulturelles Gedächtnis; -- *b) Grosse* Sven, Zum Verhältnis von Mentalitäts- und Theologiegeschiichtsschreibung: ZKG 105 (1994) 156-177 / 178-190.

9332 **Peckham** Brian, History and prophecy; the development of late Judaean literary traditions: AncBRef, 1993 → 9,12419: [R]CBQ 57 (1995) 156-8 (R.W. *Klein*: basic insight intriguing, dating-authenticity decisions scary); Interpretation 49 (1995) 78-80 (J. *Blenkinsopp*).

9333 **Perdue** Leo G., The collapse of history; reconstructing Old Testament theology: *OvBT. Mp 1994, Fortress. xvi-317 p. 0-8006-1563-8 [< OTA 19, p.169].

9334 **Pernot** Laurent, La rhétorique d'éloge dans le monde gréco-romain; Antiquité 138. P 1993, Inst. Et. Augustiniennes. 881 p. (2 vol.) 2-85121-135-8. -- [R]REL 73 (1995) 303-6 (G. *Sabbah*: magistral).

9335 *a) Porciani* Leone, Oralità, scrittura, storiografia; -- *b) Moreschini* Donatella, STRABONE e PAUSANIA sull'Ionia; due prospettive storiografiche: → 135, [F] NENCI G., *Historíē* 1994, 377-397 / 333-344.

9336 *Provan* Iain W., Ideologies, literary and critical; reflections on recent writing on the history of Israel: JBL 114 (1995) 585-606.

9337 *Rafferty* Oliver P., Memory in history: Way 35 (1995) 23-33.

9338 **Schillebeeckx** Edward, História humana revelação de Deus. São Paulo 1995, Paulus. 340 p. 85-349-0106-6. -- [R]PerTeol 27 (1995) 395-8 (Vera *Bombonatto*).

9339 **Schreckenberg** Heinz, *Schubert* Kurt, Jewish historiography and iconography in early and medieval Christianity: CRINT 3/2, 1992 → 8,9195: [R]*CritRR 7 (1994) 424-7 (P.C. *Finney* : only half the monuments illustrated; Schubert resembles GOODENOUGH).

9340 **Shute** Michael, The origins of LONERGAN's notion of the dialectic of history 1993 → 10,11071: [R]TS 56 (1995) 404 (J. *Dool*).

9341 *Small* Jocelyn P., *Tatum* James, Memory and the study of classical antiquity; Helios 22 (1995) 149 -173.

9342 **Smelik** Klaas A.D., Converting the past; studies in ancient Israelite and Moabite historiography: OTS 28, 1992→ 8,110; 10,11072: [R]*A(sn)JS 20 (1995) 163-6 (B. *Halpern*: an adept practitioner of what he rejects in theory).

9343 *Sommer* Andreas A., Gott als Knecht der Geschichte [JONAS H. 1984]: ThZ 51 (1995) 340-356.

9344 **Stanford** Michael, A companion to the study of history. Ox/CM 1994, Blackwell. viii-310 p. 0-631-18159-8. -- [R]Salesianum 57 (1995) 793 (G. *Abbà*).

9345 **Swanstrom** Roy, History in the making; an introduction to the study of the past. Lanham MD 1994, UPA. 137 p. £ 9.75. -- [R]EvQ 67 (1995) 174 (D.W. *Bebbington*)

9346 *Thiel* Johannes, *a)* Ancient history and historical criticism, past and present [< MKNAW 15/6, 1952]; -- *b)* The role of personality in the history of the Roman republic [Groningen inaugural 1930] → 337, Studies 1994, 151-170 / 111-127.

9347 **Voegelin** Eric, Das Volk Gottes; Sektenbewegungen und der Geist der Moderne [< History of political ideas 1952], [T]*Kaltschmidt* Heike, [E]*Opitz* Peter J.: Periagoge. Mü 1994, Fink. 160 p. -- [R]RHE 90 (1995) 612 (G. *Hendrix*).

9348 **Weinstein** Fred, History and theory after the Fall. an essay of interpretation. Ch 1990, Univ. x-205 p. $ 35. -- [R]RStR 21 (1995) 10-12 (W. *Beers*).

9349 **Weintritt** Otfried [→ 8985], Formen spätmittelalterlicher islamischer Geschichtsdarstellung [NUWAIRĪ ...< Diss. Freiburg 1988]: BeiruterTSt 45. Stu 1992, Steiner. viii-226 p. 3-515-05587-8. -- [R]WZKM 85 (1995) 307s (H. *Eisenstein*).

9350 *Wilkens* W., Geschichtlich denken; gegen die Angst vor der historisch-kritischen Forschung: DPfarrB 94 (1994) 585-... [< ZIT 95,p.119].

9351 *Witte* Henk, Katholieke theologen over waarheid en historiciteit [Haag 17 feb. 1995]: TTh 35 (1995) 171s.

9352 *Wolsza* Janina, [P] De POLYBII historiae colore oratorio: Mea(nder) 50 (1995) 95-106; lat. 106.

9353 **Woudenberg** A.S.L., Kairos en het eeuwige nu; een onderzoek naar de verhouding tussen het presentische en het futurische in TILLICHs theologie van de geschiedenis. Bolsward 1993, Het Witte Boekhuis. 276 p. *f* 45. 90-70365-79-0. -- [R]TTh 35 (1995) 299s (W. *Stoker*).

9354 *Zecchini* Giuseppe, POLYBIOS zwischen *metus hostilis* und *nova sapientia:* Tyche 10 (1995) 219-232.

Q3 *Historia Ægypti* -- **Egypt**

9355 *Allam* S., *Quenebete* et administration autonome en Égypte pharaonique: RIDA 42 (1995) 11-69.

9356 **Anagnostou-Canas** Barbara, Juge et sentence dans l'Égypte romaine 1991 → 8,b919; 10,11077: [R]BiOr 52 (1995) 659-661 (J. *Whitehorne*); RÉAnc 96 (1994) 632s (J.A. *Straus*).

9357 *Bard* Kathryn A., State collapse in Egypt in the late third millennium B.C.: AION 54 (1994) 275-281.

9358 *Beckerath* Jürgen von, *a)* Nochmals zur Chronologie der XII. Dynastie [SIMPSON W. 1972] Orientalia 64 (1995) 445-9; -- *b)* Die Thronbesteigungsdaten Ramses' V. und VII.: ZÄS 122 (1995) 97-100.

9359 *Bennett* Chris, *a)* Thutmosis I and Ahmes-Sapaïr; -- *b)* The first three Sekhemre kings of the seventeenth dynasty: GöMiszÄg 141 (1994) 35-37 / 143 (1994) 21-28.

9360 **Bonhême** Marie-Ange, Le Livre des Rois de la troisième période intermédiaire, I: XXIe dynastie: BÉt 94, 1987 → 3,b659: [R]CÉg 70 (1995) 142-4 (J.-C. *Degardin*).

9361 **Boorn** G.P.F. Van den, The duties of the vizier; civil administration in the early New Kingdom 1988 → 4,d177 ... 7,b109: [R]CÉg 70 (1995) 123-132 (D. *Lorton*).

9362 [E]**Bowman** Alan K., *Woolf* Greg., Literacy and power in the ancient world 1994 → 10,294d: [R]AnCL 64 (1995) 257s (Marie-Christine *Leclerc*).

9363 *Brueggemann* Walter, Pharaoh as [YHWH's] vassal; a study of a political metaphor: CBQ 57 (1995) 27-51.

9364 **Bryan** Betsy M., The reign of Thutmosis 4 [D]1991 → 7,b112 ... 10,11079: [R]BIOr 52 (1995) 334-6 (C. *Vandersleyen*).

9365 *a) Buchberger* Hennes, Aus der Arbeit am Semantem ['Transformation'] -- Supplenda zu 'Transformation und Transformat [I]'; -- *b) Ritter* Thomas, Semantische

Diskursstrukturen. erläutert am Beispiel des narrativen Texttyps: → 171, ᶠSCHENKEL W., Per aspera 1995, 1-29 / 123-162.

9366 *Burkard* Günter, Literarische Tradition und historische Realität; die persische Eroberung Ägyptens am Beispiel Elephantine: ZÄS 121 (1994) 93-105; 122 (1995) 31-37 (183, Zusatz).

9367 **Cimmino** Franco, Ramesses II il Grande. Mi c.1994, Rusconi. 427 p. L^m 16. -- ᴿArcheo 10,119 (1995) 119s (S. *Pernigotti*).

9368 **Clayton** Peter A., Chronicle of the Pharaohs; the reign-by-reign record of the rulers and dynasties of ancient Egypt. NY c.1994, Thames & H. 224 p.$30 [BArR 21,3 (1995) 8]

9369 *Cozi* Massimo, Khefethernebes et la stèle de Hatshepsut: GöMiszÄg 143 (1994) 31-35.

9370 *Dautzenberg* N., Neferhotep III und Sebekhotep VIII; Datierungsüberlegungen anhand der Königstitulaturen in der 13. Dynastie: GöMiszÄg 140 (1994) 19-25.

9371 *Davies* Benedict G., Two or three 'chiefs of Medjay'; a conundrum of Nebsmens: GöMiszÄg 143 (1994) 37-38.

9372 *Depuydt* Leo, *a)* On the consistency of the wandering year as backbone of Egyptian chronology: JA(m)RCE(g) 32 (1995) 43-58; -- *b)* Regnal years and civil calendar in Achaemenid Egypt: JEA 81 (1995) 151-173.

9373 **Der Manuelian** Peter, Living in the past: studies in archaism of the Egyptian twenty-sixth dynasty: *StEg; 1994 → 10,11094; £ 85: ᴿOLZ 90 (1995) 483-5 (J. *Hallof*).

9374 **Dodson** Aidan, Monarchs of the Nile. L 1995, Rubicon. xviii-238 p. -- ᴿOCP 61 (1995) 581s (R.M. *Mackowski*).

9375 **Doxey** Denise M., A social and historical analysis of Egyptian non-royal epithets in the Middle Kingdom: diss. Pennsylvania, ᴰ*Silverman* D. Ph 1995. 516 p. 95-32167. - D(iss)AI 56 (1995s) p. 1930.

9376 **Eide** Tormod, *al.,* Fontes historiae Nubiorum; textual sources for the history of the Middle Nile region between the eighth century BC and the sixth century AD, 1. From the eighth to the mid-fifth century BC, 1994 → 10,11088; Nk 180: ᴿOrientalia 64 (1995) 473s (Inge *Hofmann*).

9377 *Elias* J.P.. A northern member of the 'Theban' Twenty-Third Dynasty [Osorkon of Teudjoi, 500 k N Thebes: < Diss. Chicago 1993]: DiscEg 31 (1995) 57-67.

9378 **Ellis** Walter M., Ptolemy of Egypt. L 1994, Routledge. xix-104 p.; 24 pl. 0-415-10020-8. -- ᴿDiscEg 30 (1994) 201-4 (J.D. *Ray*).

9379 *Endesfelder* Erika, Götter. Herrscher, König -- zur Rolle der Ideologie bei der Formierungs des ägyptischen Königtums: → 10,470, Äg. Tempel 1990/2/4, 47-54.

9380 *Eyre* Christopher J., Weni's career and Old Kingdom historiography: → 10,118, ᶠSHORE A.F., The unbroken reed 1994, 107-124.

9381 **Galán** José N., Victory and border; terminology related to Egyptian imperialism in the XVIIIth dynasty [diss. Johns Hopkins 1994 → 10,11091]: HäB 40. Hildesheim 1995, Gerstenberg. xiii-192 p.; bibliog. 161-180. ë-8067-81ëë-8

9382 *Galán Allué* José M., Aspectos de la diplomacía del antiguo Egipto hasta ca, 1320 a.C.; Sefarad 55 (1995) 105-126; 8 fig.; Eng. 126.

9383 *Gestermann* Louise, Der politische und kulturelle Wandel unter Sesostris III. -- ein Entwurf: → 171, ᶠSCHENKEL W., Per aspera 1995, 31-50.

9384 *Goedicke* Hans, 'Narmer' [WINTER Erich, Wer steht hinter Narmer ? → 193, ᶠTHAUSING G. 1994, 279-290]: WZKM 85 (1995) 81-84.

9385 *a) Goedicke* Hans, Administrative notions in the First Intermediate period; - *b) Menu* Bernadette, Principes fondamentaux du droit égyptien; - *c) Saldarini* Anthony, Month

representations: CÉg 70 (1995) 41-51 / 99-109 / 110-122.

9386 *Goldberg* J., The 23rd dynasty problem revisited; where, when and who ?: *DiscEg 29 (1994) 55-85.

9387 **Grandet** Pierre, Ramsès III, histoire d'un règne. P 1993, Pygmalion. 420 p.; 8 pl. F 130. 2-85704-408-9. -- ᴿBiOr 52 (1995) 600s (A. *Spalinger*).

9388 *Greenberg* Gary, MANETHO rehabilitated; a new analysis of his Second Intermediate period: → 721, 7° Egyptol. 1995, 73.

9389 *Grimm* Alfred, Zur kalendarischen Fixierung des *jhhj*-(Freuden-) Festes nach derm Festkalender des Königs Amenophis I. aus Karnak: GöMiszÄg 143 (1994) 73s + 2 fig.

9390 **Guksch** Heike, Königsdienst; zur Selbstdarstellung der Beamten in der 18. Dynastie [Diss. Heidelberg 1986]: *StArchGAltäg 11. Heid 1994, Orientverlag. ix-277 p. 3-927552-20-8 [*OIAc 11 (1994) 24].

9391 **Gundlach** Rolf, Die Zwangsumsiedlung auswärtiger Bevölkerung als Mittel ägyptischer Politik bis zum Ende des Mittleren Reiches: FASk 26. Stu 1994, Steiner. viii-238 p. 3-515-06664-0.

9392 *Gundlach* Rolf, Das Königtum des Herihor; zum Umbruch in der ägyptischen Königsideologie am Beginn der 3. Zwischenzeit: → 10,145, ᶠWINTER E., Aspekte 1994, 133-8.

9393 *Helck* W., Die Männer hinter dem König und die Königswahl: ZäS 121 (1994) 36-51.

9394 *Hoch* James E., Egyptian hieratic writing in the Byblos pseudo-hieroglyphic Stele L: JA(m)RCE(g) 32 (1995) 59-85, 1 fig.

9395 **Hölbl** Günther, Geschichte des Ptolemäerreiches; Politik, Ideologie und religiöse Kultur von Alexander dem Grossen bis zur römischen Eroberung. Da 1994, Wiss. xxxii-402 p; 3 maps. DM 78. 3-534-10422-6. -- ᴿBoL (1995) 130 (L.L. *Grabbe*).

9396 **Husson** Geneviève, *Valbelle* Dominique, L'État et les institutions en Égypte des premiers pharaons aux empereurs romains 1992: → BASPAP 32 (1995) 195-201 (J.G. *Manning*).

9397 *Jánosi* Peter, Bemerkungen zur Regierung des Schepseskaf [4. Dynastie]: GöMiszÄg 141 (1994) 49-54; 1 fig.

9398 *Jansen-Winkeln* Karl, Historische Probleme der 3. Zwischenzeit [Bes statue in Durham museum]: JEA 81 (1995) 129-149; 5 fig.

9399 *a) Kákosy* László, PLATO and Egypt; the Egyptian tradition; -- *b) Luft* Ulrich, Thw date of the *w3g.i*-feast; considerations for the chronology of the Egyptian Old and Middle Kingdom: → 10,48, Mem. HAHN I. 1993, 25-28 / 19-23.

9400 *Kelley* A.L., Foreign domination and cultural absorption; a comparison of Egypt's African Pharaohs (dynasty 25) and China's Mongol overlords (Yuan dynasty): *JAncCiv 9 (Changchun 1994) 62-74.

9401 **Kozloff** Arielle P., *Bryan* Betsy M., Egypt's dazzling sun; Amenhotep III 1992 → 9,12453; 10,11099: ᴿBiOr 52 (1995) 336-340 (M. *Schade-Busch*); JEA 81 (1995) 265s (Maya *Müller*).

9402 *Krauss* Rolf, *a)* Nur ein kurioser Irrtum oder ein Beleg für die Jahre 26 und 27 von Haremhab ?: DiscEg 30 (1994) 73-85; -- *b)* Fällt im Illahun-Archiv [LUFT U. 1992] der 15. Mondmonatstag auf den 16. Mondmonatstag ? : GöMiszÄg 138 (1994) 81-92 [141 (1994) 109-111, Luft, Antwort]; -- *c)* Zur Chronologie des Neuen Reiches: OLZ 90 (1995) 237-252.

9403 **Mélèze-Modrzejewski** Joseph, The Jews in Egypt from Rameses II to Emperor Hadrian, ᵀ . E 1995, Clark. xxii-279 p. £ 25. 0-567-09739-0. -- ᴿE(xp)T 107 (1995s) 153 (J. *Ray*).

9404 **Montet** Pierre † 1966, L'Égypte aux temps des Ramsès 1300-1100 av. J.-C.: La vie quotidienne. P 1995, Hachette. 707 p; bibliog. 397-404 (*Guillemette* Andreu update). 2-01-235134-4.

9405 *a) Müller-Wollermann* Renate, Ägyptische und chinesische Charakter; zur Entzifferungsgeschichte der Hieroglyphen im 17. und 18. Jahrhundert: -- *b) Quack* Joachim F., Das Monumental-Demotische: → 171, ᶠSCHENKEL W., Per aspera 1995, 91-105 / 107-121.

9406 **Naguib** Saphinaz-Amal, Miroirs du passé [échos pharaoniques dans l'Égypte d'aujourd'hui]: Cah 2. Genève 1993, Soc. d'Égyptologie. 72 p.; ill. -- ᴿOLZ 90 (1995) 493-7 (M. *Fitzenreiter:* systematisch, utile).

9407 *Nardoni* Enrique, La justicia en el Egipto antiguo: RevBib(Arg) 56 (1994) 193-217.

9408 **Obsomer** Claude, Sesostris Iᵉʳ: études chronologique et historique du règne: Ét.5 Bru 1995, Connaissance de l'Égypte ancienne. 740 p.; bibliog. 435-469. 2-87268-004-7.

9409 ᴱO'**Connor** David, *Silverman* David P., Ancient Egyptian kingship [< Denver Museum exhibit lectures]: P(roblems)Ä 9. Lei 1995, Brill. viii-347 p.; bibliog. 301-338. $ 130. 90-04-10041-5 [RStR 22,151. D.I. *Owen*]. -- ᴿOTA 18 (1995) p. 405s (M.S. *Smith*).

9410 *Patanè* Massimo, Quelques considérations sur l'origine de la civilisation [GIRARD]: DiscEg 32 (1995) 85-89.

9411 **Peden** A.J., The reign of Ramesses IV: 1994 → 10,11107: ᴿBoL (1995) 136 (K.A. *Kitchen*).

9412 *Pérez Largacha* Antonio, Chiefs and chiefdoms in protodynastic Egypt: *JAncCiv 10 (Changchun 1995) 101-110.

9413 **Pfeifer** Gerhard, Ägypten im Alten Testament: BN.b 8. Mü 1995, BN. 112 p. [< OTA 19, p.332].

9414 **Piacentini** Patrizia, L'autobiografia di Uni, principe e governatore dell'Alto Egitto: SEAP min. mg 1. Pisa 1990, Giardini. iv-108 p.; ill. -- ᴿBiOr 52 (1995) 321s (Renate *Müller-Wollermann*, kritisch).

9415 *Premnath* D.M., Rta, Maat: *BInterp 2 (1994) 325-339.

9416 **Quirke** Stephen, The administration of Egypt in the late Middle Kingdom; the hieratic documents 1990 → 6,b450; 10,11110; 1-872561-01-2. -- ᴿBiOr 52 (1995) 328-334 (Louise *Gestermann*).

9417 **Robins** Gay, Women in ancient Egypt 1993 → 9,12464: ᴿDiscEg 31 (1995) 123-9 (Deborah *Sweeney*).

9418 **Schade-Busch** Mechtild, Zur Königsideologie Amenophis' III [Diss. Mainz 1989]. Hildesheim 1992, Gerstenberg. xx-392 p. 3-8067-8128-1. -- ᴿBiOr 52 (1995) 340s (W.J. *Murnane*).

9419 *Schloz* Sabine, Das Königtum der Ptolemäer -- Grenzgänge der Ideologie: → 10,145, ᶠWINTER E., Aspekte 1994, 227-234.

9420 **Schmidt** Heike C., *Wileituer* Joachim, Nefertari, Gemählin Ramses' II: Bildband Arch. 10. Mainz 1994, von Zabern. iv-144 p.; 117 fig. + 108 color. DM 50. -- ᴿE(rbe)uA 71 (1995) 78 (H. *Herden*).

9421 *Schwarz* Stephanie, Ausgegrenzt ? Frauen in der Ägyptologie des 19. und 20. Jahrhunderts: GöMiszÄg 138 (1994) 93-111.

9422 **Serrano Delgado** José M., Textos para la historia antigua de Egipto. M 1993, Cátedra. 283 p.; 30 fig. -- ᴿMemHAnt 15s (Oviedo 1994s) 345s (Mercedes *García Martínez*).

9423 *Spalinger* Anthony, *a)* Notes on the ancient Egyptian calendars; Orientalia 64 (1995) 17-32; -- *b)* Some remarks on the epagomenal days in ancient Egypt: JNES 54 (1995) 33-47.

9424 ᶠTHÉODORIDÈS Aristide, Individu, société et spiritualité dans l'Égypte pharonique et copte, [E]**Cannuyer** C., *al.*, 1993 → 9,151: [R]MélSR 51 (1994) 93s (L. *Debarge*).

9425 **Troy** Lana, Patterns of queenship in ancient Egyptian myth and history 1986: [R]RB(elg)PH 73 (1995) 239s (C. *Vandersleyen*).

9426 **Valbelle** Dominique, Les neuf arcs 1990 → 7,b149; 10,11120: [R]BiOr 52 (1995) 42-46 (P.W. *Haider*).

9427 **Vandersleyen** C., L'Égypte et la vallée du Nil, 2. De la fin de l;ancien Empire à la fin du Nouvel Empire: NClio. P 1995, PUF. 658 p..; 5 maps. F 298. 2-13-046552-8 [*JSStEg 21s (1991s) 113]. -- [R]DiscEg 32 (1995) 101-6 (J. *Malek*).

9428 **Vercoutter** Jean, L'Égypte et la vallée du Nil, 1. Des origines à la fin de l'Ancien Empire: Nouvelle Clio [remplaçant DRIOTON-VANDIER c.1960] 1992 → 8,b975: [R]BiOr 52 (1995) 327s (W. *Kaiser*).

9429 **Vernus** Pascal, Affaires et scandales sous les Ramsès. P 1993, Pygmalion. 274 p. 2-85704-393-7 [*OIAc 11 (1994) 44].

9430 **Walker** Edward J., Aspects of the primaeval nature of Egyptian kingship: diss. [D]*Wente* E. Chicago 1991. iv-313 p. [*OIAc 11 (1994) 44].

9431 **Way** Thomas von der, Untersuchungen zur Spätvor- und Frühgeschichte Altägyptens: StArchGÄg. Heid 1993. xxviii-140 p.; ill. DM 78. -- [R]Orientalia 64 (1995) 465-7 (J. von *Beckerath*).

9432 **Way** Thomas von der, Göttergericht und 'heiliger' Krieg im alten Ägypten .. Merenptah, Libyerkrieg [D]1992 → 8,b977: [R]BiOr 52 (1995) 347-350 (A. *Spalinger*).

9433 **Weber** Gregor, Dichtung und höfische Gesellschaft [unter Ptolemäi I.-III.: < Diss. 1991, [D]*Gehrke* H.-J.]: Hermes Einz 62, 1993 → 10,11123: [R]BiOr 52 (1995) 657-9 (M. *Huys*).

9434 **Whitehorne** John, Cleopatras. L 1994, Routledge. x-243 p., 21 fig. £ 35. -- [R]GaR 42 (1995) 95 (H. van *Wees*: not even up to the author's modest aims).

9435 *Wilkinson* Toby A.H., A new king in the Western Desert [.. reading of the (predynastic Naqada IIIb) name]: JEA 81 (1995) 205-210.

9436 **Bagnall** Roger S., Egypt in late antiquity 1993 → 9.12437; 10,11125: [R]A(mer)HR 100 (1995) 884s (J.A.S.*Evans*: Egypt became ½ Christian between 300 and 325); BiOr 52 (1995) 75-79 (Ewa *Wipszycka*); CLR 45 (1995) 108-110 (D.W. *Rathbone*); *CritRR 7 (1994) 296-8 (D. *Brakke*).

Q4 Historia Mesopotamiae

9437 **Bustenay** Oded, War, peace and empire; justifications for war in Assyrian royal inscriptions. Wsb 1992, Reichert. 199 p. -- [R]AfO 42s (1995s) 238-244 (E. *Frahm* recommends despite some 120 corrections).

9437* *a) Cancik-Kirschbaum* Eva, Konzeption und Legitimation von Herrschaft in neuassyrischer Zeit; -- *b) MacGinnis* John, The Šatammu of Sippar: WO 26 (1995) 5-20 / 21-26; facsim.

9438 **Charvát** Petr, Ancient Mesopotamia; humankind's long journey into civilization. Praha 1993, Oriental Institute. 368 p. -- [R]OLZ 90 (1995) 499-508 (R. *Bernbeck*).

9439 **Crawford** Harriet, Sumer and the Sumerians 1991 → 7,b156; 8,b989: [R]BiOr 52 (1995) 683-9 (L. *Bachelot*).

9440 [E]**Curtis** John, Early Mesopotamia and Iran: contact and conflict 3500-1600 BC: 1991/3 → 9,571; 10,11129: [R]BiOr 52 (1995) 137-140 (J.-L. *Huot*).

9441 *D'Agostino* Franco, *a)* Nabonedo e il deserto (a proposito delle cause della caduta di Babilonia): EVO 18 (1995) 193-209 + 2 maps. -- *b)* Nabonidus and the 'cylinder of Cyrus': VDI 213 (1995) 169-175 (in Russian); Eng. 175.

9442 *a) Dandamayev* M.A., Babylonian popular assemblies in the first millennium B,C,; -- *b) Gerardi* Pamela, Cartoons, captions, and war; Neo-Assyrian palace reliefs: BuCanadMesop 30 (1995) 23-29 / 31-36.

9443 *Dandamayeva* M.M., ᴿ The legend about three Assyrian rulers (the early Greek tradition about Nonus, Semiramis and Sardanapalus): VDI (1995,4) 14-34; Eng.34

9444 *Dion* Paul E., Syro-Palestinian resistance to Shalmaneser III in the light of new documents [Aramaic on harness published 1988]: ZAW 107 (1995) 482-9.

9445 **Fales** J.M., *Postgate* J.N., Imperial administrative records, 1. Palace and temple administration: *SAA 7. Helsinki 1992, Univ. xiii-211 p. 951-570-249-6; pa. -8-8. -- ᴿZA(ssyr) 85 (1995) 145-8 (S. *Zawadzki*).

9446 **Frame** Grant, Babylonia 689-627: 1992 → 8,b992 ... 10,11132: ᴿBiOr 52 (1995) 447-9 (A. *Livingstone*); JAOS 114 (1994) 495-7 (M.A. *Dandamayev*).

9447 **Frame** Grant, Rulers of Babylonia from the second sealand dynasty of Babylonia to the end of Assyrian domination (1157-612 BC): Royal Inscr.Bab.2. Toronto 1995, Univ. xxvi-350 p.: microfiche. $ 150. 0-8020-0724-4.

9448 **Franke** Sabina, Königsinschriften und Königsideologie; die Könige von Akkade zwischen Tradition und Neuerung [Diss. Hamburg 1992, ᴰ*Wilhelm* D.]: Altorientalistik 1. Müns 1995, *LIT. xvi-275 p.; Bibliog. 252-268. 3-38473-109-5.

9449 *García Recio* J., Fragmento de una inscripción de Nabucodonosor II: AulaO 12 (1994) 225-7.

9450 *a) Garelli* Paul, Les déplacements de personnes dans l'empire assyrien; -- *b) Oded* Bustenay, Observations on the Israelite/Judaean exiles in Mesopotamia during the eighth/sixth centuries BCE: -- *c) Zadok* Ran, Foreigners and foreign linguistic material in Mesopotamia and Egypt: → 110, ᶠLIPIŃSKI, E., Immigration: OLA 65 (1995) 79-82 / 205-212 / 431-447.

9451 *a) Grayson* A. Kirk, Eunuchs in power; their role in the Assyrian bureaucracy; -- *b) Parpola* Simo, The Assyrian cabinet; -- *c) Mayer* Walter, Sanherib und Babylonien; der Staatsmann und Feldherr im Spiegel seiner Babylonienpolitik; -- *d) Sommerfeld* Walter, Der babylonische 'Feudalismus': → 185, ᶠSODEN W. von, Vom Alten Orient (1995) 85-98 / 379-401; 4 fig. / 305-332 / 467-490.

9452 *Hirsch* Hans, (unter Anderem) Hammurabi von Babylon, König, stellt Bedingungen, schriftlich; AfO 42s (1995s) (122-) 137-9.

9453 *Horowitz* Wayne, An astronomical fragment from Columbia University and the Babylonian revolts against Xerxes: JANES 23 (1995) 61-67.

9454 ᴱ**Hunger** Hermann, Astrological reports to Assyrian kings [567 texts reediting R.C. THOMPSON's 1900 Reports of the magicians]; *SAA 8. Helsinki 1992, Univ. xxix-384 p,; XV pl. -- ᴿAfO 42s (1995s) 244s (A. *Livingstone*); BoL (1995) 131 (M.J. *Geller*).

9455 *Karstens* Karsten, Die erste Dynastie von Ur; Überlegungen zur relativen Datierungen: → 10,55, ᶠHROUDA B., Beiträge 1994, 133-142.

9456 *Klengel* Horst, Richter Sippars in der Zeit des Ammişaduqa; ein neuer Text: → 10,81, ᶠMEYER L. de, 52 Réflexions 1994, 169-174; 6 phot.

9457 **Kuhrt** Amélie, The Ancient Near East, c. 3000-300 BC: History of the ancient world. L 1995, Routledge. I. xxviii-381 -415 p.; II. xix-383-782. 0-415-01352-6.

9458 *Laato* Antti, Assyrian propaganda and the falsification of history in the royal inscriptions of Sennacherib; VT 45 (1995) 198-226.

9459 *Lambert* W.G., The fall of the Cassite dynasty to the Elamites; an historical epic: →
10,81, ᶠMEYER L. de, 52 Réflexions 1994, 67-72.

9460 **Lamprichs** Roland, Die Westexpansion des neuassyrischen Reiches; eine
Strukturanalyse: AOAT 239. Kevelaer 1995, Butzon & B. xii-457 p.; Bibliog. 409-439.
3-766-9976-8.

9461 **Lerberghe** K. van, The ladies Amat-Aja and S̲at-Aja, business associates under
Hammurabi : OL(ov)P 25 (1994) 5-25.

9462 **Liverani** Mario, Prestige and interest; international relations in the Near East ca. 1600-
1100 B.C., 1990 → 6,b506: ᴿJNES 54 (1995) 54s (N. *Yoffee*).

9463 **Longman** T., Fictional Akkadian autobiography 1991 → 7,9284; 8,9621*: ᴿBiOr 52
(1995) 92-97 (W. *Schramm*: genre existiert nicht).

9464 **MacGinnis** John, Letter orders from Sippar and the administration of the Ebabbara in
the Late Babylonian period. Poznań 1995, Bonami. ciii-228 p.; bibliog. 207-228. 83-
85274-07-3.

9465 **Mansfied** [*sic*] P., Storia del Medio Oriente. T 1993, SEI. 413 p. -- ᴿAION 54 (1994)
534s (V. *Strika*).

9466 **Mayer** Walter, Politik und Kriegskunst der Assyrer: *ALASP 9 Müns 1995, Ugarit-V.
xvii-545 p.; Bibliog. 525-545. 3-927120-26-X. -- ᴿUF 27 (ᶠDIETRICH 60. Gb. 1995) 718s
(A. *Malamat*: only few oversights).

9467 *Militarev* A.Yu., ᴿ Sumerians and Afrasians: VDI 213 (1995) 113-126; Eng. 126s.

9468 **Millard** Alan, (*Whiting* Robert, 'extra-canonical'), The eponyms of the Assyrian Empire
910-612 B.C.: SAA.s 2. Helsinki 1994, Univ. Neo-Assyrian. xvi-153 p.; 1ll. $ 36.50. 951-
45-6715-3 [RStR 22,150, D.I.*Owen*]. -- ᴿBoL (1995) 135 (W.O. *Lambert*); OLZ 90 (1995)
511-4 (H. *Freydank*).

9469 *Molina* Manuel, Las 'reformas' de Urukagina: → 221, ᶠYELO TEMPLADO A., Lengua
1995, 47-57.

9470 **Msetti** Maria-Gracia, Pouvoir assyrien et pouvoirs locaux; idéologie, conceptions
religieuses et politiques au Moyen-Euphrate à l'âge du fer: diss. Sorbonne, ᴰ*Meslin* M.
Paris 1995. -- RTLv 27.p.556.

9471 *Neumann* Heinz, Die Berichte der Astrologen an die assyrischen Könige, ihr
astronomischer Inhalt und ihre zeitliche Einordnung [HUNGER H., SAA 8, Helsinki 1992]:
WZKM 85 (1995) 239-264; zahlreiche Beobachtungen.

9472 **Porter** Barbara Nevling, Images, power, and politics; figurative aspects of
Asarhaddon's Babylonian policy: AmPhMem 208. Ph 1993. viii-230 p. $ 30. 0-87169-
208-2. -- ᴿOTA 18 (1995) p. 150s (M.S. *Smith*); RStR 21 (1995) 42 (D.I. *Owen*: peace-
loving; overturning common view).

9473 **Rollinger** Robert, HERODOTs Babylonischer Logos 1993 → 10,11146, Sch 640:
ᴿAAW 48,13 (1995) 75-77 (M. *Ehrhardt*); Or 52 (1995) 79-83 (E. *Klengel-Brandt*);
Orientalia 64 (1995) 474-7 (R.J. van der *Spek*).

9474 **Roth** Martha T., Law collections from Mesopotamia and Asia Minor: SBL.wr 6. At
1995, Scholars. xviii-283 p.; bibliog. 255-266. $ 60; pa. $ 40. 0-7885-0126-7.

9475 **Sack** Ronald H., Neriglissar -- king of Babylon: AOAT 236. Neuk/Kevelaer 1994,
Neuk/Butzon & B. xiii-270 p.: ill. DM 106. 3-7887-1480-8 / 3-7666-9894-X [RStR
22,151, D.I. *Owen*].

9476 **Saggs** H.W.F., Babylonians: People of the Past. Norman 1995, Univ. Oklahoma. 192
p. $ 29. 0-8061-27651 [ThD 42,385].

9477 **Sassoon** John, From Sumer to Jerusalem; the forbidden hypothesis 1993 → 9,14189: ᴿBoL (1995) 137s (T.C. *Mitchell*: unconvincing).

9478 **Sigrist** Marcel, Neo-Sumerian texts from the Royal Ontario Museum, 1. The administration at Drehem. Bethesda MD 1995, CDL. [vi-] 125 p. 1-883053-16-1.

9479 *Smith* Clyde C., 'Aha! Assyria! Rod of my fury, very staff of my sentencing-curse ': → 170, ᶠSAWYER, J., Words; JSOT.s 195 (1995) 182-206.

9480 **Stolper** Matthew W., Late Achaemenid, Early Macedonian, and Early Seleucid records of deposit and related texts: AION supp. 77 to 53,4 (1993). N, Univ. 99 p. [< OTA 19, p.150].

9481 *Vanstiphout* H.L.J., The matter of Aratta [its ruler's conflict with Uruk's Enmmerkar 4 times peacefully resolved]: OL(ov)P 26 (1995) 5-20.

9482 *Vera Chamaza* Galo W., Der VIII. Feldzug Sargons II.; eine Untersuchung zu Politik und historischer Geographie des späten 8. Jhs. v. Chr: AMI(ran) 27 (1994) 91-118; 28 (1995s) 215-267.

9483 *Vermaak* P. Stefanus, Abu-simti, a Semitic matriarch in Sumer: JNWSL 21,2 (1995) 105-122.

9484 *Vincente* Claudine-Adrienne, The Tell Leilan recension of the Sumerian king list: ZA(ssyr) 85 (1995) 234-270.

9485 **Volk** Konrad, Inanna and Sukaletuda; zur historisch-politischen Deutung eines sumerischen Literaturwerkes: SANTAG 3. Wsb 1995, Harrassowitz. xv-227 p. 3-447-03635-4.

9486 **Wu Yuhong,** A political history of Eshnunna, Mari and Assyria during the Old Babylonian period (from the end of Ur III to the death of Šamši-Adad): *JAncC.s 1. Changchun 1994, NE Normal Univ. vii-344 p,

9487 *Wu Yuhong*, High-ranking 'scribes' and intellectual governors during the Akkadian and Ur III periods: *JAncCiv 10 (Changchun 1995) 127-145.

9488 **Wunsch** Cornelia, Die Frauen der [neubabylonischen] Familie Egibi; AfO 42s (1995s) 33-63; 3 phot.; facsimiles.

9489 *Zawadzki* Stefan, A contribution to the chronology of the last days of the Assyrian empire : ZA(ssyr) 85 (1995) 67-73.

Q4.5 *Historia Persiae* -- **Iran**

9490 **Berquist** Jon L., Judaism in Persia's shadow; a social and historical approach. Mp 1995, Fortress. vi-282 p. $ 21. 0-8006-2845-4 [< OTA 19, p.324, his own summary].

9491 **Briant** Pierre, Darius, les Perses et l'Empire 1992 → 9,12508: ᴿGnomon 67 (1995) 271-3 (Heidemarie *Koch*).

9492 *Briant* P., L'histoire achéménide; sources, méthodes, raisonnements et modèles: *TopO 4 (1994) 109-130.

9493 *Briant* Pierre, La date des révoltes babyloniennes contre Xerxès: StIr 21 (1992) 7-20; Eng. 20: 481 and 479.

9495 *a) Depuydt* Leo, The date of death of Artaxerxes I [Feb. 424]; -- *b) Tubach* Jürgen, Seleukos' Sieg über den medischen Satrapen Nikanor: WO 26 (1995) 86-96 / 97-128.

9496 *Feldman* L.H., JOSEPHUS' portrait of Ahasuerus [whitewashed in A 11]: ABR 42 (1994) 17-38 [NTAb 40, p.299].

9497 *a) Frei* Peter, Die persische Reichsautorisation [Esra 7,12-26; Neh 11,23s. 13,30s]; ein Überblick; -- *b) Wiesehöfer* Josef, 'Reichsgesetz' oder 'Einzelfallgerechtigkeit' ?

Bemerkungen zu Peter Freis These von der achämenidischen 'Reichsautorisation'; -- c)
Rüterswörden Udo, Die persische Reichsautorisation der Thora; fact or fiction ?: *ZtsAlt-
orBiblRechtsgeschichte 1 (1995) 1-35 / 36-46 / 47-61 [< OTA 19, p.212.219.215].

9498 Glassner Jean-Jacques, Ruhušak -- mār ahatim; la transmission du pouvoir en Elam:
JA 282 (1994) 219-236; Eng. 236.

9499 Grantovsky E.A., Ivanchik A.J., 'Heralds' at the courts of Iranian kings: VDI 213
(1995) 162-8; Eng. 168.

9500 Hamilton Mark W., Who was a Jew ? Jewish ethnicity during the Achaemenid period:
RestQ 37 (1995) 102-117.

9501 Heltzer Michael, The flogging and plucking of beards in the Achaemenid empire and
the chronology of Nehemia: AMI(ran) 28 (1995s) 305-7.

9502 Kingsley Peter, Meetings with Magi; Iranian themes among the Greeks, from Xanthus
of Lydia to Plato's Academy: JRAS (1995) 173-209.

9503 Koch Heidemarie, Zu den Frauen im Achämenidenreich: → 94, Mem. KLÍMA O.,
Iranian 1994, 125-141.

9504 Koch Heidemarie, Achämeniden-Studien. Wsb 1993, Harrassowitz. iv-150 p. DN
88. 3-447-03328-2. -- ᴿBiOr 52 (1995) 733-5 (M.A. Dandamayev).

9505 a) Lambton A.K.S., Major General Sir John MALCOLM (1769-1833) and The history
of Persia; -- b) Morgan D.O., Edward GIBBON and the East: Iran 33 (1995) 97- 109 /
85-92.

9506 Littman Robert J., Athens, Persia and the Book of Ezra: TPAPA 125 (1995) 251-9.

9507 Lloyd Alan B., Cambyses in late tradition [HERODOTUS: Egypt]: → 10,118, ᶠSHORE
A.F., The unbroken reed 1994, 195-204.

9508 Petit Thierry, Satrapes et satrapies ᴰ1990 → 7,b196 ... 10,11155: ᴿTopO 3 (1993) 255-
266 (R. Descat).

9509 Petit Thierry, Synchronie et diachronie chez les historiens de l'empire achéménide
[DANDAMAYEV M. 1980, Eng. 1989; 1985,Eng. 1989]: *TopO 3 (1993) 39-71.

9510 Schmitt Rüdiger, Eine Goldtafel mit angeblicher Dareios-Inschrift : AMI(ran) 28
(1995s) 269-273: pl. 16,1.

9511 Shahbazi A.S., The 'King's eyes' in classical and Iranian literature: *AJAH 13,2 (1997
for 1988) 170-189.

9512 Vogelsang W.J., The rise and organisation of the Achaemenid empire 1992 → 8,d47
... 10,11156*: ᴿZAW 107 (1995) 547s (M. Köckert).

9513 Wiesehöfer Josef, Das antike Persien, von 550 v.Chr. bis 650 n.Chr. Mü/Z 1994,
Artemis/Winkler. 426 p.; 6 fig.; 32 pl.; 4 maps. DM 79. 3-7608-1080-2. -- ᴿA(nz)AW
48,1s (1995) 78-83 (R. Klein); HZ 260 (1995) 829s (E. Kettenhofen).

9514 Wiesehöfer Josef, Die 'dunklen Zeitalter' der Persis; Untersuchungen zu Geschichte
und Kultur von Fārs in frühhellenistischer Zeit (330-140 v.Chr.): Zetemata 90. Mü 1994,
Beck. 187 p. 3-406-37619-3 [*OIAc 11,45]

9515 Wolski Józef, L'empire des Arsacides: Acta Iranica 3/18/32, 1993 → 9,12519: Mes
29 (T/F 1994) 339-342 (A. Invernizzi).

9516 Zawadzki Stefan, Bardiya, Darius and Babylonian usurpers in the light of the Bisitun
inscription and Babylonian sources: AMI(ran) 27 (1994) 127-145.

Q5 *Historia Anatoliae* --**Asia Minor, Hittites [→T8.2]**, Armenia [T8.9]

9517 **Cornelius** Friedrich † 1976, Geschichte der Hethiter, mit besonderer Berücksichtigung der geographischen Verhältnisse und der Rechtsgeschichte. Da 1992, Wiss. xiv-378 p.; 48 pl.; 2 maps. DM 79. 3-534-06190-X. -- ᴿBoL (1995) 126s (L.L. *Grabbe*).

9518 **Del Monte** Giuseppe F., L'annalistica ittita; *TVOA 4/2. Brescia 1993, Paideia. 153 p. Lᵐ 30. 88-394-0500-3. -- ᴿAnton 70 (1995) 689 (M. *Nobile*).

9519 a) *Hasse* Richard, Der Vertrag im Privatrecht der Hethiter; Versuch eines Überblicks; -- b) *Starke* Franz, Zur urkundlichen Charakterisierung neuassyrischer Treueide anhand einschlägiger hethitischer Texte des 13. Jh.: *ZABR 1 (1995) 62-69 / 70-82 [< OTA 19, p.182.184].

9520 **Jasink** Anna Margherita, Gli stati neo-ittiti; analisi delle fonti scritte e sintesi storica: *StMedit 10. Pavia 1995, Tuculano. 246 p.; bibliog. 207-224. 88-7072-226-0.

9521 **Leschhorn** W., Antike Ären; Zeitrechnung, Politik und Geschichte im Schwarzmeerraum und in Kleinasien nördlich des Taurus: HistEinz 81. Stu 1993, Steiner. ix-576 p.; 10 pl. DM 168. 3-515-06018-9. -- ᴿHZ 261 (1995) 836-8 (W. *Orth*); JRS 85 (1995) 304 (J.G.F. *Hind*).

9522 *Masson* Emilia, La ville hittite: → 730, Semitica 43s (1992/5) 63-66.

9523 *Memiş* Ekrem, ᵀ Le rôle des reines dans le palais hittite: Belleten 58,222 (1994) 279-93.

9524 **Murrmann-Kahl** M., Die entzauberte Heilsgeschichte; der Historismus erobert die Theologie, 1880-1920 [Diss. München 1990]. Gü 1992, Mohn. -- ᴿCrSt 16 (1995) 443-7 (A. *Russo*)

9525 *Roos* Johan de, The Hittites and their history [Changchun lecture 1993]: *JAncCiv 9 (1994) 104-114.

9526 *Roszkowska-Mutschler* Hanna, '... and on its site I sowed cress '; some remarks on the execration of defeated enemy cities by the Hittite kings: *JAncCiv 7 (1992) 1-11.

9527 **Scheer** Tanja S., Mythische Vorväter; zur Bedeutung griechischer Heroenmythen im Selbstverständnis kleinasiatischer Städte: ArbAG 7. Mü 1993, Maris. 369 p.; 6 pl. DM 88. -- ᴿHZ 61 (1995) 835s (P. *Herrmann*).

9528 **Strobel** Karl, Das Imperium Romanum im '3.Jh.' Modell einer historischen Krise ? Zur Frage mentaler Strukturen breiterer Bevölkerungsschichten in der Zeit von Marc Aurel bis zum Ausgang des 3. Jhs.: HistEinz 75. Stu 1993, Steiner. 408 p. -- ᴿBo(nn)J 195 (1995) 706-9 (A.R. *Birley*, Eng.).

9529 **Galletti** Mirella, I Curdi nella storia. Chieti 1990, Vecchio Faggio. 352 p. -- ᴿOCP 61 (1995) 646-8 (V. *Poggi*).

9530 **Wilhelm** Gernot, The Hurrians [1982, Russian 1992], ᵀ*Barnes* Jennifer, with revisions by the author and a chapter by *Stein* Diana, Wmr 1989, Aris & P. ix-132 p.; 31 pl. -- ᴿAulaO 12 (1994) 247-9 (G.B. *Gragg*).

Q6.1 **Historiae Graeciae classicae**

9531 **Banek** Kazimierz, ᴾ Amfiktionie starożytne. Kraków 1993, Univ. 148 p. -- ᴿCLB 71,1 (1995) 37 (Krystyna *Stebnicka*).

9532 *Baslez* Marie-Françoise, Histoire politique du monde grec antique: FAC-Hist, 1994 → 10,11967; F 139: ᴿCLR 45 (1995) 331-3 (P. *Cartledge*); RÉA(nc) 96 (1994) 622 (P. *Brun*).

9533 *Berger* Philippe, La xénophobie de Polybe : RÉA(nc) 97 (1995) 517-525

9534 *Bernabé* Alberto, Influences orientales sur la littérature grecque; quelques réflexions de méthode: Kernos 8 (1995) 9-22.

9535 **Bernal** Martin, Atena nera 2. Documenti e testimonianze archeologiche [1991 → 7,b214*]. R c. 1995, Pratiche. 815 p. L^m 88. -- ^R*Archeo 10,122 (1995) 110 (S. *Moscati*)

9536 *Beye* Charles R., [Five] New studies in the Argonautica: CJ 90 (1994s) 305- 313.

9537 *Blaise* Fabienne, Solon, fragment 36 W, pratique et fondation des normes politiques: RÉG 108 (1995) 24-37.

9538 *Bleicken* Jochen, Wann begann die athenische Demokratie ? : HZ 260 (1995) 337-364.

9539 **Bodéüs** Richard, Politique et philosophie chez ARISTOTE: Coll. ÉtCL. Namur 1991, Soc.Ét.Clas. x-185 p. Fb 2000. -- ^RGnomon 67 (1995) 662-671 (C. *Pietsch*).

9540 **Boegehold** Alan L., The lawcourts at Athens; sites, buildings, equipment, procedure, and testimonia: Athenian Agora 28. Princeton 1995, American School Athens. xxviii-256 p.; bibliog. xvi-xxi. 0-87661-228-1.

9541 **Boulogne** Jacques, PLUTARQUE, un aristocrate grec sous l'occupation romaine: Racines et Modèles. Lille 1994, Univ. 221 p. -- ^RRÉL 73 (1995) 301s (L. *Pernot*).

9542 *Bowersock* G,W., Nonnos rising [CHUVIN P. 1991s]: *TopO 4 (1994) 385-399.

9543 **Bruyn** Odile de, La compétence de l'Aréopage en matière de procès publics; des origines de la Polis athénienne à la conquête romaine de la Grèce (vers 700-146 av. J.-C.): HistEinz 90. Stu 1995, Steiner. 226 p. 3-515-06654-3.

9544 *a) Carruba* Onofrio, L'arrivo dei Greci; le migrazioni indoeuropee e il 'ritorno' degli Eraclidi [DREWS R. 1988]; -- *b) Pesely* George E., ARISTOTLE's source for the tyranny of Peisistratos: At(henaeum) 83 (1995) 5-44; 12 maps. / 45-66.

9545 **Cartledge** Paul, The Greeks; a portrait of self and others 1993 → 10,11174: ^RMH(elv) 51 (1994) 256 (L. *Burckhardt*).

9546 **Cohen** David J., Law, violence, and community in classical Athens: Key themes in ancient history. C 1995, Univ. xii-214 p.; bibliog. 199-211. 0-521-38837-6.

9547 **Dahlheim** W., Die Antike; Griechenland und Rom von den Anfängen bis zur Expansion des Islam^4rev [^11994 !]. Pd 1995, Schöningh. 814 p.; 47 maps. 3-506-71980-7 [NTAb 40, p.551: 814 p. ^11994 ^41995, but price not shown]. -- ^RHZ 260 (1995) 819-822 (U. *Gotter*).

9548 **Develin** Robert, Athenian officials. 1989. -- *AJAH 3,2 (1997 for 1988) 139-153 (H. *Mattingly*).

9549 **Diano** Carlo, Forme et événement; principes pour une interpretation du monde grec [1952 + appendices 61-124], ^TGrenet P., *Valensi* M. Combas 1994, Éclat. 126 p.-- ^RRTPh 127 (1995) 163s (S. *Imhoof*).

9550 **Dihle** Albrecht, Die Griechen und die Fremden. Mü 1994, Beck. 173 p.; 6 fig.; 5 maps. 3-406-38168-5. -- ^RA(nz)AW 48,1s (1995) 25-28 (G. *Dobesch*).

9551 **Erbse** Hartmut, Studien zum Verständnis HERODOTs: UALG 38. B 1992, de Gruyter. xiv-199 p. DM 120. 3-11-013621-X. -- ^RAnCL 64 (1995) 283s (J. *Labarbe*).

9552 **Fuchs** Elfriede, Pseudologia; Formen und Funktionen fiktionaler Trugrede in de griechischen Literatur der Antike [Diss. Düsseldorf 1992): *BtKlasAltW 2/91. Heid 1993, Winter. v-295 p. 3-8253-0115-X.

9553 **Georges** P., Barbarian Asia and the Greek experience, from the archaic period to the age of Xenophon: Ancient Society and History. Baltimore 1994, Johns Hopkins Univ. xx-358 p. £ 35. -- ^RCLR 45 (1995) 102s (Gocha R. *Tsetskhladze*).

9554 *Georges* Pericles, Darius in Scythia; the formation of HERODOTUS' sources and the nature of Darius' campaign: *AJAH 12,1 (1987/95) 97-147.

9555 *Gil* Luis, La mentalidad democrática ateniense: →142, FOROZ RETA III, Helmantica 46 (1995) 5-21.

9556 **Gould** J., Give and take in HERODOTUS [Oxford Myres Lecture 1989]. Ox 1991, Leopard's Head. 19 p. [*OIAc 11 (1994) 24].

9557 *a) Hedrick* Charles W.[J,] The meaning of material culture; HERODOTUS, THUCYDIDES, and their sources; -- *b) Fornara* Charles W., Thucydides' birth date [c. 471]: → 143, FOSTWALD M., Nomodeiktes 1993, 17-37 / 71-80.

9558 *a) Hedrick* Charles B.[J], Writing, reading, and democracy; -- *b) Davies* John, Accounts and accountability in classical Athens: → 693, FLEWIS D., Ritual, finance 1993/4, 157-174 / 201-212.

9559 **Hunter** Virginia J., Policing Athens; social control in the Attic lawsuits, 420-320 B.C. Princeton 1994, Univ. xv-303. $ 30. -- R*Prudentia 27,2 (1995) 77-81.

9560 *Kallet-Marx* Lisa, Institutions, ideology and political consciousness in ancient Greece; some recent books on Athenian democracy [STOCKTON D., 1990; HANSEN M., FORNARA C. 1991, *al.*]: JHI(d) 55 (1994) 307-335.

9561 *Kapparis* K., When were the Athenian adultery laws introduced?: RIDA 42(1995) 97-122.

9562 **Karavites** Peter (Panayiotis), (*Wren* Thomas), Promise-giving and treaty-making; HOMER and the Near East: Mnemosyne supp. 119, 1992 → 8,d92: RGnomon 67 (1995) 389-393 (V. *Parker*).

9563 **Keaney** John J., The composition of ARISTOTLE's Athenaion politeia; observation and explanation. NY 1992, Oxford-UP. xii-191 p. £ 12.50. -- RGnomon 67 (1995) 400-4 (M. *Chambers*).

9564 *Kuch* Heinrich, Narrative Strategie bei HERODOT : Eikasmos 6 (1995) 57-65.

9565 **Kullmann** W., *Althoff* J., Vermittlung und Tradierung von Wissen in der griechischen Kultur: ScriptOralia 61. Tü 1993, Narr. 390 p. -- RCLR 45 (1995) 364-6 (R.I. *Winton*).

9566 **Kwintner** Michelle, Interpretation in HERODOTUS: diss. Cornell, DRusten S. Ithaca NY, 1995. 95-28239. -- D(iss)AI 56 (1995s) p. 1242.

9567 *Langin* Hartmut, Entzauberung des griechischen Mirakels ? Zur Kritik des Autarkiekonzepts (COOLSAET W., Autarkeia; rivaliteit en zelfgenoegzaamheid in de Griekse cultuur: Kampen/Kapellen 1993): Gym 102 (1995) 157-9.

9568 *Lapini* Walter, TUCIDIDE rimpatriato (esilio di vent'anni?): SIF(g)C 9 (1991) 9-51.

9569 **Lendle** Otto, Einfuhrung in die griechische Geschichtschreibung von Hekataios bis Zosimos. Da 1992, Wiss. viii-311 p. DM 59. -- RHZ 260 (1995) 159-161 (B. *Meissner*).

9570 **Lévêque** Pierre, Ancient Greece, Utopia and reality[T]. L 1994, Thames & H. 175 p.; ill. £ 7. -- RGaR 42 (1995) 108 (P. *Walcot*; price and illustrations splendid; text not).

9571 ELevi Giovanni, *Schmitt* Jean-Claude, Storia dei giovani, l. Dall'antichità all'età moderna. R c.1994, Laterza. 430 p. L[m] 45. -- R*Archeo 9,118 (1994) 128s (Giovanna *Quattrocchi*).

9572 **Lo Magro** Raffaele, *a)* Dal mito di Minosse all'impero di Alessandro il Grande; -- *b)* L'origine della civiltà ellenica Eracle: Turris Babylonia 8/-. Pioltello MI 1995, Rangoni. 127 p. / 143 p. 88-86513-18-6 / 02-X.

9573 **McGlew** J.F., Tyranny and political culture in ancient Greece. Ithaca 1993, Cornell Univ. viii-234 p. $ 34.65. -- RCLR 45 (1995) 95s (C. *Tuplin*).

9574 **McGregor** Malcolm F., The Athenians and their empire. Vancouver 1987, Univ. British Columbia. xx-215 p. 0-7748-0269-3.

9575 **Malkin** Irad, Myth and territory in the Spartan Mediterranean. C 1994, Univ. xvii-

235 p; maps. $ 60. -- ᴿRStR 21 (1995) 226 (B.P. *Nystrom*).

9576 **Maurer** Karl, Interpolation in THUCYDIDES: MNEM.s 150. Lei 1995, Brill. xxiv-243 p. -- ᴿRPh(lgLH) 69 (1995) 344-6 (P. *Payen*).

9577 *Meadows* A.R., PAUSANIAS and the historiography of classical Sparta: CQ 45 (1995) 92-113.

9578 **Meier** Christian, Athen, ein Neubeginn der Weltgeschichte. B 1993, Siedler. 703 p. DM 56. -- ᴿHZ 261 (1995) 148-151 (W, *Dahlheim*).

9579 **Mikroyiannakis** E., ᴳ *Pathología politeumáton* ...Disorders of ancient governments. Athena 1990, Kardomitsa. 236 p -- ᴿAtenR 49 (1995) 120s (F. *Sartori*).

9580 **Mondrain** Brigitte, Le nouveau manuscrit d'HÉRODOTE; le modèle de l'impression Aldine: ScrBru 49 (1995) 263-273.

9581 *Nesselrath* Heinz-Günther, HERODOT und die Enden der Erde: MH(elv) 52 (1995) 20-44.

9582 **Ober** Josiah, Mass and elite in democratic Athens; rhetoric, ideology, and the power of the people 1989 → 6,b607; 7,b248: ᴿ*TopO 3 (1993) 271-283 (I. *Morris*).

9583 **Orwin** Clifford, The humanity of THUCYDIDES. Princeton 1994, Univ. xiii-235 p. $ 35. 0-691-03449-4. -- ᴿHZ 261 (1995) 840-2 (H. *Erbse* ist nicht ganz einverstanden); *Prudentia 27,1 (1995) 84-91 (K. *Adshead*).

9584 *Oswald* Renate, Gedankliche und thematische Linien in HERODOTs Werk: GrazB 21 (1995) 47-58; Eng. vi.

9585 *Payen* Pascal, Comment résister à la conquête ? Temps, espace et récit chez HÉRODOTE [< diss. à paraître]: RÉG 108 (1995) 308-338.

9586 *Podes* Stephan, *Ekklēsiastikón* and participation in public service in classical Athens: *AJAH 12,1 (1987/95) 167-188.

9587 **Pritchett** W. Kendrick, The liar school of HERODOTUS. Amst 1993, Gieben. v-353 p. -- ᴿAnCL 64 (1995) 284s (Véronique *Krings*); CLR 45 (1995) 15-17 (H. *Bowden*); GaR 42 (1995) 90 (H. van *Wees*; feeble defense against FEHLING D., *al.*).

9588 **Ridgway** David, The first Western Greeks 1992 → 8,g480: ᴿAJA 99 (1995) 159s (Mary E. *Moser*); HZ 260 (1995) 163 (W. *Leschhorn*).

9589 **Ridgway** David, Les premiers Grecs d'Occident; l'aube de la Grande Grèce [L'alba della Magna Grecia 1984], ᵀ*Cassimatis* Hélène. P 1992, de Boccard. 105 p.; ill. -- ᴿRÉA(nc) 96 (1994) 645 (J.-L. *Lamboley*).

9590 **Robb** Kevin, Literacy and paideia in ancient Greece 1994 → 10,11205: ᴿA(mer)HR 100 (1995) 1539 (B.R. *Powell*); AJP(g) 116 (1995) 635-7 (W.C. *West*); CJ 91 (1995s) 338-40 (A. *Ford*, also on BOWMAN A. & WOOLF W. 1994*).

9591 **Roberts** Jennifer T., Athens on trial: the antidemocratic tradition in Western thought. Princeton 1994, Univ. xix-405 p. 0-691-05697-8. -- ᴿRStR 21 (1995) 236 (A.C. *Daly*).

9592 **Romilly** Jacqueline de, La costruzione della verità in TUCIDIDE [1990], ᵀᴱ*Ferrari* Maria Luisa. F 1995, Nuova Italia. xv-92 p. Lᵐ 16. -- ᴿEikasmos 6 (1995) 362s (R. *Tosi*).

9593 *a) Rosén* Haiim B., *Historíēs apódeixis*; zum Problem der herodotischen Textkritik -- *b) Hagen* Hansludwig, Zu *éōtha* bei HERODOT: Glotta 71 (1993) 146-153 / 154-7.

9594 **Rouillard** Pierre, Les Grecs et la péninsule ibérique du VIIIe au IVe siècle 1991 → 10,11206: ᴿBo(nn)J 195 (1995) 630-2 (H. G. *Niemeyer*).

9595 **Samuel** Alan E., The Greeks in history 1992 → 9,12586: ᴿPhoenix 49 (Tor 1995) 78s (L.A. *Losada*).

9596 **Schuller** Wolfgang, Einführung in die Geschichte des Altertums: UTB.wiss N° 1794. Stu 1994, Ulmer. 207 p. DM 24,80. -- ᴿGym 102 (1995) 364s (R. *Klein*); MH(elv) 51 (1994) 255 (T. *Gelzer*: sehr originell).

9597 **Sealey** Raphael, DEMOSTHENES and his time; a study in defeat, Ox 1993, UP. x-340 p. £ 40. -- [R]HZ 261 (1995) 489-491 (J. *Engels*).

9598 **Shapiro** Harvey A., Art and cult under the tyrants in Athens. Mainz 1989, von Zabern. xiii-195 p. 3-8053-1038-2.

9599 **Steiner** Deborah T., The tyrant's writ; myths and images of writing in ancient Greece 1994 → 10,11215; £30. -- [R]GaR 42 (1995) 109 (P. *Walcot*: remarkable; writing as oppression).

9600 **Tausend** K., Amphiktyonie und Symmachie 1992 → 10,11217: [R]Klio 77 (1995) 454s (W. *Ehrhardt*).

9601 **Thomas** Rosalind, Literacy and orality in ancient Greece 1992 → 8,d138 ... 10,11218: [R]Arctos 27 (1993) 161s (J. *Aronen*).

9602 *Tsakimakis* Antonis, THUCYDIDES & HERODOTUS; remarks on the attitude of the historian regarding literature: SCI(sr) 14 (1995) 17-32.

9603 *Tzipopoulos* Yannis Z., Thucydidean rhetoric and the propaganda of the Persian Wars topoi: ParPass 281 (1995) 91-115.

9604 **Vandiver** Elisabeth, Heroes in HERODOTUS; the interaction of myth and history 1991 → 7,b271; 10,11219: [R]AnCL 64 (1995) 285s (D. *Viviers*).

9605 *Vanschoonwinkel* Jacques, Des Héraclides du mythe aux Doriens de l'archéologie: RB(elg)PH 73 (1995) 127-148.

9606 *Wallace* Robert W., Frammentarietà e trasformazione; evoluzioni nei modi della comunicazione nella cultura ateniese fra V e IV secolo: QU(rb)CC 46 (1994) 7-20.

9607 **Wenskus** Otta, Astronomische Zeitangaben von Homer bis Theophrast 1990 → 8,d145: [R]Salesianum 57 (1995) 168s (P. *Canaccini*).

9608 **Wickersham** John, Hegemony and Greek historians. Lanham 1994, Rowman & L. 195 p. -- [R]RÉA(nc) 96 (1994) 622s (P. *Brun*).

9609 **Wirth** Gerhard (I-III), *Veh* Otto (IV-X), *Nothers* Thomas (Komm.), DIODOROS, Griechische Weltgeschichte: BtGL34s. Stu 1992s, Hiersemann. viii-330 p.; p. 331-660. -- [R]Tyche 9 (1994) 230s (G. *Dobesch*).

9610 *Zagdoun* Mary-Anne, PLUTARQUE à Delphes: REG 108 (1995) 586-592.

Q6.5 **Alexander, Seleucidae; historia Hellenismi**

9611 **Bearzot** Cinzia, Storia e storiografia ellenistica in PAUSANIA 1992 → 10,11224: [R]RÉA(nc) 96 (1994) 593-5 (E. *Will*); Klio 77 (1995) 529 (K.M. *Errington*).

9612 *Beyer-Rotthoff* B., Untersuchungen zur Aussenpolitik Ptolemaios' III: Diss AltG 37. Bonn 1993, Habelt. 342 p. DM 48. -- [R]CLR 45 (1995) 328s (E. *Erskine*).

9613 *Biffi* Nicola, L'excursus Liviano [9,16s] su Alessandro Magno: BSL(at) 25(1995)461-76.

9614 **Billows** Richard A., Kings and colonists; aspects of Macedonian imperialism: C(olumbia)SCT 22. Lei 1995, Brill. xv-240 p.; 10 pl.; bibliog. 221-230. 90-04-10177-2.

9615 **Billows** R.A., Antigonos 1990 → 7,b277; 9,12603: [R]HZ 260 (1995) 841s (E. *Olshausen*).

9616 a) *Bloedow* Edmund F., 'That great puzzle in the history of Alexander'; back into 'the primal pit of historical murk' [BADIAN E. against BOSWORTH A.]; -- b) *Gauger* Jörg-Dieter, Orakel und Brief; zu zwei hellenistischen Formen geistiger Auseinandersetzung mit Rom: → 176, [F]SCHMITT H., Rom & Osten 1995, 23-41 / 51-67.

[*Berger* K., *Colpe* C.] **Boring** M. Eugene, *al.*, Hellenistic commentary to the NT 1995 → 2098 above.

9617 *a) Braccesi* Lorenzo, Alessandro, Siracusa e l'Occidente; -- *b) Gabba* Emilio, Roma nel mondo ellenistico: → 9,440, ^E*Virgilio* B., Aspetti e problemi dell'ellenismo (Pisa 1992/4) 9-22 / 37-45.

9618 *Brentjes* B., Der Alexanderzug durch Mittelasien und seine Folgen; Gedanken zum Hellenismus in Zentralasien: OL(ov)P 25 (1994) 107-124; 6 fig. (map).

9619 *a) Bringmann* Klaus, The king as benefactor; some remarks on ideal kingship in the age of Hellenism; -- *b) Koenen* Ludwig, The Ptolemaic king as a religious figure; *c) Smith* R.R.R., Kings and philosophers; -- *d) Straten* Volkert van, Images of gods and men in a changing society; -- *e) Giovannini* Alberto, Greek cities and the Greek commonwealth: → 674, K Pap 1994, 7-24 / 25-115 / 202-211 + 6 pl. / 248-264 + 32 pl. / 265-286.

9620 ^E**Carlsen** J. *al.,* Alexander the Great, reality and myth. R 1993, Danish Inst. 207 p. 88-7062-817-5. -- ^RAnCL 64 (1995) 463s (J.-M. *Bertrand*).

9621 **Caven** Brian, Dionysius I, war-lord of Sicily. NHv 1990, Yale Univ. 284 p., 15 fig.; 6 maps. -- ^RA(nz)AW 46 (1993) 48-50 (G. *Dobesch*).

9622 *Crowther* Charles, Foreign judges in Seleucid cities: *JAncCiv 8 (1993) 40-77.

9623 *Demandt* Alexander, MOMMSEN zum Niedergang Roms: HZ 261 (1995) 23-49.

9624 **Faraguna** Michele, Atene nell'età di Alessandro; problemi politici, economici, finanziari: Lincei Atti sto/fg mem.9/2/2. R 1992; p.165-447. -- ^RGnomon 67 (1995) 33-36 (C. *Habicht*).

9625 **Flower** Michael A., Theopompus of Chios; history and rhetoric in the fourth century B.C. Ox 1994, Clarendon. xii-252 p. 0-19-814079-7.

9626 **Fouyas** Méthodios G., ^G *a)* The Greek base of Islam; -- *b)* Hellenism and Judaism. Athena 1994s, Nea Synora. 267 p.; 239 p. -- ^RPOrC 45 (1995) 310s (P. *Ternant*).

9627 **Ginouvès** René, *al.,* La Macédoine de Philippe à la conquête romaine. P 1993, CNRS. 254 p.; 200 fig. -- ^RRÉA(nc) 96 (1994) 626-8 (J. *Marcadé*).

9628 *Goldstein* J.A., Alexander and the Jews [JOSEPHUS A 11,302-345 false]: PAAJR 59 (1993) 59-101 [NTAb 39, p.289].

9629 **Grainger** John D., Seleukos Nikator; constructing a Hellenistic kingdom 1990: ^RHZ 260 (1995) 522 (W. *Orth*).

9630 ^E**Green** Peter, Hellenistic history and culture 1988/93 → 10,11236: ^RT(imes)LS (27.I.1995) 24 (S. *Schwartz*: brilliant; BILDE P. and WHITTAKER C. disappointing) [NTAb 38, p.489; 39, p.460.530.550].

9631 **Green** Peter, Alexander to Actium; the Hellenistic age 1990 → 6,653; 7,b290: ^RTyche 9 (1994) 232-4 (I. *Kertész*).

9632 *Hammond* N.G.L., Did Alexander use one or two seals ?: Chiron [17 (1987) 395-449: two after 330] 25 (1995) 199-203 contra.

9633 **Hammond** N.G.L., Philip of Macedon. Baltimore 1994, Johns Hopkins Univ. xvii-235 p. $ 45. -- ^RA(mer)HR 100 (1995) 1541 (E.A. *Fredricksmeyer*; HZ 261 (1995) 843-5 (R.M. *Errington*).

9634 **Hammond** N.G.L., Sources for Alexander ... PLUTARCH, ARRIAN 1993 → 9,12619; 10,11240: ^RAJP(g) 116 (1995) 490-4 (W.J. *McCoy*).

9635 *a) Hartman* Lars, 'Guiding the knowing vessel of your heart' ['Orpheus' *hieros logos*]; on Bible usage and Jewish identity in Alexandrian Judaism; -- *b) Giversen* Søren, The Covenant -- theirs or ours ?: → 487, NT & Hellenistic 1992/5 19-36 / 14-18.

9636 **Hengel** Martin, L''ellenizzazione' della Giudea nel I. sec. d.C. [1989 → 6,b673],^T: *StBPaid 104, 1993 → 9,12713: ^RAnton 70 (1995) 692 (M. *Nobile*).

9637 *Horsley* G.H.R., The politarchs in Macedonia and beyond: →10,416, MeditAch 7 (1991/4) 99-126; pl. 9-14.

9638 **Huss** Werner, Der makedonische König und die ägyptischen Priester; Hist.e 85, 1994 → 10,11246; DM 80: [R]HZ 261 (1995) 845s (R.M. *Errington*).

9639 *Jouanno* Corinne, Un épisode embarrassant dans l'histoire d'Alexandre, la prise de Thèbes [Béoc]: Ktema 18 (1993) 245-258.

9640 **Leontis** Artemis, Topographies of Hellenism; mapping the homeland: Myth and Poetics. Ithaca NY 1995, Cornell Univ. xiii-257 p.; bibliog. 227-247. 0-8014-3057=7.

9641 *Marcos Marín* Francisco A., La variante, le choix électronique, le Libro de Alexandre [13e s.] et une hypothèse sur son auteur: RBPH 72 (1994) 609-615.

9642 *Martin* Luther H., The anti-individualistic ideology of Hellenistic culture: Numen 41 (1994) 117-140.

9643 *Molinier* Agnès, Philippe [II de Macédoine] le bon roi de Cicéron à Sénèque: RÉL 73 (1995) 60-79.

9644 *Muccioli* F., Considerazioni generali sull'epiteto *philádelphos* nella titolatura degli ultimi Seleucidi: Hist 43 (Wsb 1994) 402-422 [JSJ(ud) 26 (1995) 255].

9645 **O'Brien** John M., Alexander .. the invisible enemy 1992 → 8,d169 ... 10,11252: [R]Gnomon 67 (1995) 137-141 (G. *Wirth*); HZ 260 (1995) 837s (J. *Seibert*).

9646 **Pokorný** Petr, Řecké ...(Helénismus v Egypte — a Syrii). Praha 1993, Oikoumene. 378 p.; 8 pl. -- [R]ArOr 63 (1995) 236s (S. *Segert*).

9647 [E]**Roisman** Joseph, Alexander the Great; ancient and modern perspectives. Lexington MA 1995, Heath. xxv-241 p. [RStR 22,63, D.M. *Hooley*, also on R. STONEMAN's Legends 1994].

9648 *Rostovtzeff* Michael, L'Asia ellenistica all'epoca dei Seleucidi [BOUCHÉ-LECLERCQ 1913]: QSt 40 (1994) 9-32 ([T]*Marcone* Arnaldo, con presentazione).

9649 **Schmitt** Hatto H., Rom und die griechische Welt von der Frühzeit bis 133 v. Chr.: Auditorium 1. -- [R]Gnom 67 (1995) 170s (J. *Delorme*).

9650 [E]**Schmitt** Hatto H., *Vogt* Ernst, Kleines Lexikon des Hellenismus[2rev] [[1]1988, 'k. Wörterbuch']. Wsb 1993, Harrassowitz. xiv-885 p.: 6 fig.; 30 pl. -- [R]CLR 45 (1995) 148 (R. *Osborne*, lyric praise); Gnomon 67 (1995) 583-7 (J. *Werner*).

9651 *Shavit* Yaacov, [H] Judaism and Hellenism -- scientific criticism as opposed to critical journalism: Tarbiz [53 (1993s) 451-480; Eng.xxiii, BAR-KOCHVA B. on Shavit 1992] 64 (1994s) 115-129; Eng. 1,vii: rejoinder 131-8; Eng. viii..

9652 **Sherwin-White** Susan, *Kuhrt* Amélie, From Samarkhand .. Seleucid empire 1993 → 9,12634; 10,11255: [R]JRAS (1995) 426s (S.N.C. *Lieu*); · PEQ 127 (1995) 81-83 (S. *Simpson*).

9653 **Sirinelli** Jean, Les enfants d'Alexandre; la littérature et la pensée grecques (334 av. J.-C. -- 519 ap. J.-C.) 1993 → 9,12635; 10,11257: [R]AnCL 64 (1995) 294s (A. *Martin*).

9654 **Stewart** Andrew, Faces of power; Alexander's image and Hellenistic politics: HellenCuSoc 11, 1993 → 9,12636; $ 80: [R]CJ 91 (1995s) 210s (I. *Worthington*); CLR 45 (1995) 377-9 (A.M. *Devine*).

9655 **Tabacco** Raffaella, Per una nuova edizione critica dell'Itinerarium Alexandri [sostituendo HAUSMANN H. [D]1970]. Bo 1992, Pàtron. 214 p. -- [R]BStL(at) 24 (1994) 277-9 (D. *Nardo*).

9656 *VanElderen* B., Hellenistic influence in first-century Palestine and Transjordan: Ref(d)R 47 (1994) 207-220 [NTAb 39, p.275].

9657 *Whitehorne* J.E.G., A reassessment of Cleopatra III's Syrian campaign [Akko 103 B.C.:

DACK E. Van 't, *al.*, 1989]: CÉg 70 (1995) 197-205.
9658 **Wirth** Gerhard, Der Brand von Persepolis; Folgerungen zur Geschichte Alexanders des Grossen. Amst 1993, Hakkert. vii-394 p. *f* 140. -- [R]HZ 261 (1995) 842s (J, *Wiesehöfer*).

Q7   Josephus Flavius

9659 **Begg** Christopher, Josephus' account of the early divided monarchy (AJ 8,212-420); rewriting the Bible [1 Kgs 12-22]: BEThL 108, 1993 → 9,12640; 10,11261: [R]Biblica 76 (1995) 273-7 L.H. *Feldman*); CBQ 57 (1995) 341-3 (P.W. *Flint*); EThL 70 (1994) 151-4 (J. *Verheyden*); JSJ 26 (1995) 343s (L.L. *Grabbe*); JThS 46 (1995) 590s (P. *Spilsbury*); RTL 26 (1995) 235s (J. *Ponthot*).

9660 *Begg* Christopher, *a)* Ahaziah's fall (2 Kings 1); the version of Josephus; -- *b)* Jehoahaz, king of Israel according to Josephus; Sefarad 55 (1995) 25-39 / 227-236; español 40 / 237.

9661 *Begg* C.T., Amaziah of Judah according to Josephus (Ant. 9, 186-204): Anton 70 (1995) 3-30 [NTAb 40, p.103].

9662 *Begg* Christopher T., *a)* Hezekiah's illness and visit according to Josephus [A 10,24-35 ‖ 2 Kgs 20,1-19; Isa 38s]: EstB 53 (1995) 365-385; -- *b)* The Gedaliah episode and its sequels in Josephus [A 10,155-175 ‖ Jer 40s; 2 Kgs 25,22s]: JSPE 12 (1994) 21-46 [NTAb 40, p.298].

9663 *Begg* Christopher T., *a)* Jehoshaphat at mid-career according to AJ 9,1-17: RB 102 (1995) 379-402; -- *b)* Josephus' portrait of Jehoshaphat compared with the biblical and rabbinic portrayals; BN 78 (1995) 39-48 [NTAb 40, p.298s, also on his REJ Nahum and Henoch David's census].

9664 *Begg* Christopher, Josephus and Nahum [2,9-12] revisited: RÉJ [76 (1923) 96-98] 154 (1995) 5-22.

9665 *Begg* Christopher T., Uzziah (Azariah) of Judah according to Josephus: EstB 53 (1995) 5-24; esp. 5.

9666 **Ben-Yehuda** Nachman, The Masada myth; collective memory and mythmaking in Israel. Madison 1995, Univ. Wisconsin. xxi-401 p.; bibliog. 350-374. 0-299-14830-0.

9667 *Bohak* Gideon, CPJ III,520 [VITELLI 1927 c, 116 C.E.]: the Egyptian reaction to Onias' temple [B1.33; 7,422 ..]: : JSJ(ud) 26 (1995) 32-41.

9668 **Bohrmann** Monette, Flavius Josephus; the Zealots and Yavne; towards a rereading of 'The war of the Jews' [Bern 1989], [T]Lloyd Janet. NY 1989, Lang. 392 p. $ 41 pa. 3-906752-10-0. -- [R]JRS 85 (1995) 307s (J.J. *Price*); OTA 18 (1995) p. 431 (L.H. *Feldman*).

9669 *Botha* P.J.J., Herodes -- die Grote ?: HTS 51 (1995) 996-1028 [NTAb 40, p.485].

9670 *Broer* Ingo, Die Konversion des Königshauses von Adiabene nach Josephus (Ant XX): → 10,31*, [F]DAUTZENBERG G., Nach 1994, 133-162.

9671 *Brottier* Laurence, Flavius Josèphe en Galilée; les ambiguïtés d'une image : RPh(lgLH) 69 (1995) 75-93; Eng. 243.

9672 **Buckwalter** H. Douglas, *Shaaff* Mary Keil, Guide to the reference systems for the works of Flavius Josephus: JETS.mg 3. WL 1995, Eisenbrauns. [x-] 41 p. 0-932055-01-X.

9673 [TE]**Calabi** Francesca, In difesa degli Ebrei (Contra Apionem). Venezia 1993, Marsilio.— [R]At(h-Pavia) 83 (1995) 542-4 (L. *Troiani*).

9674 *Catastini* Alessandro, Le testimonianze di Manetone [Ap 1,73-105.228-252] e la 'storia di Giuseppe' (Genesi 37-50): Henoch 17 (1995) 279-299; Eng. 299s.

9675 *Day* John, The pharaoh of the Exodus; Josephus [Ant 2,224] and Jubilees [47,5; both inconclusive, *pace* WITHERINGTON B., BAR 15,3 (1989) 18s]; VT 45 (1995) 377s.

9676 *Evans* Katherine G., [JW 5,206; Ant 18,159] Alexander the alabarch, Roman and Jew: → 512, SBL Seminars 34 (1995) 576-594.

9677 *Feldman* L.H., Josephus' portraits of the Pharaohs: *Syllecta Classica 4 (1993) 49-63 [NTAb 39, p.473].

9678 *Feldman* Louis H., Josephus' portrait of Ahasuerus: A(ustrl)BR 42 (1994) 17-38.

9679 **Fenn** Richard, Death of Herod 1992 : *A(sn)JS 20 (1995) 176-9 (Shaye J.D. *Cohen*: salvageable failure due to Christian perspective and three cognate oversights); *CritRR 7 (1994) 470s (J.C. *VanderKam*); EstB 53 (1995) 281-5 (A. *Urbán*).

9680 *Flusser* David, *Amorai-Stark* Shua, The goddess Thermuthis [Ant 2,224 name of Moses' foster-mother, unnamed in Exodus], Moses, and Artapanus [before 100 B.C.E. left the longest list of Jewish contributions to culture]: Jewish Studies Quarterly 1 (Tü 1993s) 217-233; 1 pl.

9681 *Gager* J.G., Moses the magician; hero of an ancient counter-culture: *Helios 21 (1994) 179-198 [NTAb 39, p.289: regard for the magic (Ex 7) is shown while disproved in Josephus and PHILO].

9682 *Gerber* Christine, Die Heiligen Schriften des Judentums nach Flavius Josephus: → 10,322*, Schriftauslegung 1994, 91-113.

9683 *Goldberg* Gary J., The coincidences of the Emmaus narrative of Luke [24,18-27] and the Testimonium of Josephus [A 18,63s]: JSPE 13 (1995) 59-77.

9684 *a) Goodblatt* David, Suicide [JW 7; YADIN Masada] in the sanctuary; traditions on priestly martyrdom; -- *b) Pearce* Sarah, Josephus as interpreter of biblical law [A 4,218 on Dt 17,8-12]: JJS 46 (1995) 10-29 / 30-42

9685 *Grabbe* L.L., Who was the Bagoses of Josephus (Ant.II.7.1. § 297-301) ?: *TEuph 5 (1992) 49-55; franç. 49 (celui d'Éléphantine).

9686 **Gray** Rebecca, Prophetic figures in Late Second Temple Jewish Palestine; the evidence from Josephus [< diss. Oxford 1990, ^D*Sanders* E.] 1993 → 9,12648; 10,11269; $ 45: ^RCBQ 57 (1995) 179s (C.G. *Newman* regards as pejorative the term *Spätjudentum*, but not apparently the title's 'Late Jewish'; there was a genuine Second Temple prophecy, legitimately including dream interpretation, and 'not to be read through the filter of the Hebrew Bible'); *DSD 2 (1995) 109-111 (R. *Bergmeier*); HebStud 35 (1994) 146-8 (L.H. *Feldman*); Interpretation 49 (1995) 202 . 204 (J.T. *Strong*); JAOS 115 (1995) 117s (D. *Mendels*); JBL 114 (1995) 308-312 (S. *Mason*).

9687 **Hadas-Lebel** Mireille, Flavio Josefo, el Judío de Roma [1989 → 5,b635], ^T *Colom de Llops* María, 1994 → 10,11270; pt. 2600: ^RATG(ran) 58 (1995) 363s (J.L. *Sicre*); Proyección 426 (1995) 158s (también J.L. *Sicre*); RevAg 36 (1995) 1134s (S. *Sabugal*).

9688 **Hadas-Lebel** Mireille, Flavius Josephus eyewitness, ^T*Miller* Richard 1993 → 9,12650: Midstream 41,7 (1995) 43z (J.M. *Rosenberg*).

9689 *a) Hadas-Lebel* Mireille, Flavius Josèphe apologète; à propos des récits de la Genèse et de l'Exode dans les Antiquités, livres I à III; -- *b) Houdu* Laurence, La translittération des mots hébreux et leurs équivalents grecs dans les Antiquités juives de Flavius Josèphe; *korbán / dôron* en AJ IV,73: → 78, ^FHARL M., Katà toùs o' 1995, 409-422 / 423-431.

9690 **Halpern-Amaru** Betsy, Rewriting the Bible; land and covenant in post-biblical Jewish literature [Jub., Test.Mos., Ps-Philo, Josephus]. Ph 1994, Trinity. xi-189 p. $ 15. 1-56338-091-9 [< ThD 42 (1995) 271].

9691 *Harl* Marguerite, *a)* L'originalité lexicale de la version grecque du Deutéronome (LXX) et la 'paraphrase' de Flavius Josèphe (A.J. IV, 176-331); -- *b) Spottorno* María Victoria, Josephus' text for 1-2 Kings (3-4 Kingdoms): → 508, 8th SeptCog 1992/5, 1-20 / 145-152.

9692 **Hartingsfeld** J. van [† 1993], Moses als Wetgever naar de beschrijving van Flavius Josephus in de Antiquitates boek II-IV. Kampen 1994, Kok. 259 p. *f* 47.50. 90-242-6940-7 [< OTA 18 (1995) p. 175].

9693 *Hirschmüller* M., Der Zensus des Quirinius bei Josephus: JbEvT 8 (1994) 33-68.

9694 **Krieger** Klaus-Stephan, Geschichtsschreibung als Apologetik bei Flavius Josephus [< kath. Diss. Regensburg 1990, ᴰ*Hoffmann* P.]: TANZ 9. Tü 1994, Francke. 306 p. DM 120. 3-7720-1888-2 [OTA 18 (1995) p. 171; RHE 90 (1995) 201*].

9695 *Levison* John R., The debut of the Divine Spirit in Josephus's Antiquities: HThR 87 (1994) 123-138.

9696 **Lindsay** Dennis R., Josephus and faith [diss. Tü 1990] 1993 → 9,10182: ᴿ* CritRR 8 (1995) 248-250 (H.W. *Attridge*).

9697 **Mason** Steve, Flavius Josephus on the Pharisees 1991 → 7,b314 ... 10,11273*: ᴿ*A(sn)JS 19 (1994) 83-88 (S. *Schwartz*: naive; overinterprets) [< JSJ(ud) 26 (1995) 242, G. *Stemberger*, very negative].

9698 **Mason** S., Josephus & NT 1992 → 8,d187 .. 10,11274: ᴿBijdragen 56 (1995) 456 (B.J. *Koet*); BS 151 (1994) 370 (H.W. *Hoehner*); *CritRR 7 (1994) 231-5 (Honora H. *Chapman*) EstB 53 (1995) 137-9 (F. *González García*), repeated 286s; EvQ 67 (1995) 267s (D. *de Lacey*); RevBib(Arg) 57 (1995) 186-9 (J.P. *Martín*).

9699 **Mayer-Schärtel** Bärbel, 'Die Frau ist in jeder Hinsicht schwächer als der Mann'; eine sozialgeschichtliche und kulturanthropologische Untersuchung zum Frauenbild des Josephus: *a)* ev.Diss. ᴰ*Stegemann* W. Neuendettelsau 1994. viii-415 p.; ThRv 91,100. - - *b)* Stu 1995, Kohlhammer. 400 p. DM 98. 3-17-013913-4 [< OTA 19,p.553, L.H. *Feldman*; NTAb 40, p.559].

9700 **Meijer** F.J.A.M. [ᵀVita, B1-3], *Wes* M.A. [ᵀB,4-7], Flavius Josephus, De Joodse Oorlog & Uit mijn leven. Baarn 1992, Ambo. 646 p. *f* 95. 90-263-1152-4. -- ᴿBijdragen 56 (1995) 87s (M. *Parmentier*); JSJ(ud) 26 (1995) 358-360 (J.W. van *Henten*).

9701 *Mor* Menahem, ᴴ The second Samaritan temple; Josephus and archeological finds: BetM 40,1 (140,1994) 43-64.

9702 **Mussies**ᵀᴱ G., De autobiografie van de joodse historicus Flavius Josephus: Na de Schriften 8. Kampen 1991, Kok. 80 p. *f* 22,30. 90-242-6531-2. -- ᴿBijdragen 56 (1995) 86s (M. *Parmentier*).

9703 ᴱ**Nodet** Étienne, *al.*, Flavius Josèphe, Les Antiquités juives [I. 1990 → 6,b692], II: livres iv & v. P 1995, Cerf. xxi-202 p. F 200. 2-204-05257-4 [NTAb (34,p.412) 40,p.381; OTA 19,p.367].-- ᴿEstB 53 (1995) 265s (Esperança *Bariau*, 1); RÉJ 154 (1995) 511s (Madeleine *Petit*).

9704 *Orchard* Bernard, Josephus and the unnamed priests of his Roman mission [Vita 13s: = Paul and companions! Acts 28,17s]: DR 113 (1995) 248-270 [NTAb 40, p.304].

9705 *Parente* Fausto, Le témoignage de *Théodore* de Mopsueste sur le sort d'Onias III [B 1,31; 7,420; A 13,383; 2 Mcb 3s] et la fondation du temple de Léontopolis: RÉJ 154 (1995) 429-436.

9706 *Parmentier* Edith, Rois et tyrans chez NICOLAS de Damas: Ktema 16 (1991) 229-244.

9707 *Pucci ben Zeev* Miriam, *a)* Josephus, bronze tablets and Greek inscriptions : AnCL 64 (1995) 211-5; -- *b)* Seleukos of Rhosos [inscription find-site in Syria, SHERK K. 1969] and Hyrcanus II [Ant 14,90 ..]: JSJ(ud) 26 (1995) 113-121.

9708 **Schreckenberg** Heinz [Josephus], *Schubert* Kurt, Jewish historiography and iconography: CRI 3, 1992 → 8,d195; 10,11277: [R]RÉJ 154 (1995) 136-140 (Gabrielle *Sed-Rajna*); TorJT 11 (1995) 104s (A.F. *Segal*).

9709 **Schröder** Bernd, Die 'väterlichen Gesetze'; Flavius Josephus als Vermittler von Halachah an Griechen und Römer: TSAJ 53. Tü c.1995, Mohr. xi-216 p., Bibliog. 271-299. 3-16-146481-8.

9710 **Schwartz** Seth, Josephus and Judaean politics 1990 → 6,b695 ... 10,11278: [R]Gnomon 67 (1995) 443-6 (P. *Bilde*).

9711 *Sela* Shulamit, [H] From Joseph son of Matthias to Joseph son of Gorion (on the origin and development of the Josippon narrative) [< pseudo-Hegesippus]: Tarbiz 64 (1994s) 51-63; Eng. 1,vi.

9712 *Semenchenko* L.V., [R] The concept of divine interference in the course of hostilities in 'The Jewish Antiquities': VDI 213 (1995) 173-180; Eng. 180s.

9713 **Setzer** Claudia, Jewish responses to early Christian history and polemics,30-350 C.E. Mp 1994, Fortress. 254 p. 0-006-2680-X. -- [R]ET 106 (1994s) 318 (C.S. *Rodd*).

9714 *Shaw* Brent D., Josephus; Roman power and responses to it: At(henaeum) 83 (1995) 357-390.

9715 **Sterling** G.E., Historiography and self-definition: Josephus, Luke-Acts and apologetic historiography: NT.s 64, 1992 → 9,5109: [R]JQR 86 (1995s) 452-5 (Rebecca *Gray*); JSPE 13 (1995) 108-110 (R.I. *Pervo*).

9716 *Tal* Ilan, *Price* Jonathan J., Seven onomastic problems in Josephus' Bellum Judaicum: JQR 84 (1993s) 189-208.

9717 *VanderKam* James C., Simon the Just: Simon I [c.250 BCE: so Ant 12,43, rightly] or Simon II [a century later; so most moderns; no evidence]: → 130, [F]MILGROM J., Pomegranates 1995, 303-318.

9718 *Walbank* Frank W., 'Treason' and Roman domination; two case-studies, POLYBIUS and Josephus: → 176, [F]SCHMITT H., Rom & Osten 1995, 273-285.

9719 *Whealey* Alice, Josephus on Jesus; evidence from the first millennium: ThZ 51 (1995) 285-304.

9720 *Williams* David S., Morton SMITH on the Pharisees in Josephus: JQR 84 (1993s) 29-42.

Q8.1 *Roma Pompeii et Caesaris* -- **Hyrcanus to Herod**

9721 **Baar** Manfred, Das Bild des Kaisers Tiberius bei TACITUS, SUETON & CASSIUS DIO: Beiträge zur Altertmskunde 7, 1990 → 8,d237: [R]Bo(nn)J 195 (1995) 685s (P. *Schrömbges*); HZ 260 (1995) 181s (M. *Vielberg*).

9722 *Baldwin* Barry, PLINY the elder and MUCIANUS : EM(erita) 63 (1995) 291-301.

9723 **Bellen** Heinz, Grundzüge der römischen Geschichte, I. Von der Königszeit bis zum Übergang der Republik in den Prinzipat. Da 1994, Wiss. viii-245 p. DM 38. -- [R]HZ 261 (1995) 159s (R. *Rilinger*).

9724 **Bergemann** C., Politik und Religion im spätrepublikanischen Rom 1992 → 9,11616; 10,11287*: [R]Gym 102 (1995) 376s (U. *Lambrecht*).

9725 *Bilde* Per, The Jews in the diaspora of the Roman Empire: *NordJud 14 (1993) 103-124 [< Jud(aica) 51 (1995) 60].

9726 **Bleicken** Jochen, Zwischen Republik und Prinzipat 1990 → 7,b324 ... 9,12670*: [R]Gnomon 67 (1995) 141-4 (M. *Pani*).

9727 *Cairns* Francis, M. [Vipsanius] Agrippa in HORACE 'Odes' 1-6: Hermes 128 (1995) 211-7: he had proposed that all works of art be nationalized (*Pliny* NH 35,26) but Horace here is not refusing to praise him (as NISBET-HUBBARD still 1970), only chuckling.

9728 **Christ** K., Caesar; Annäherung an einen Diktator. Mü 1994, Beck. 398 p; 16 fig., 5 maps. DM 58. -- ^{R}CLR 45 (1995) 109-111 (L.G.H. *Hall*).

9729 **Dettenhofer** Maria H., Perdita iuventus; zwischen den Generationen von Caesar und Augustus: Vestigia 44, 1992 → 10,11299: ^{R}HZ 260 (1995) 527-9 (K.M. *Girardet*).

Grabbe Lester L., Judaism from Cyrus to Hadrian 1992 → 7186.

9731 **Gruen** Erich S., Culture and national identity in republican Rome 1993 → 9,12679; 10,11309; 0-8014-2759-2: ^{R}HZ 260 (1995) 171-3 (D. *Kienast*); Latomus 54 (1995) 702s (J. *Poucet*); RÉA(nc) 96 (1994) 636s (P. *Cordier*).

9731* **Gruen** Erich S., Criminal trials and Roman politics 149-78 B.C.: American Doctoral Dissertations: D(iss)AI 56 (1995s) p.1931.

9732 *Hanhart* Robert, Der status confessionis Israels in hellenistischer Zeit: ZThK 92 (1995) 314-328.

9733 *Harrison* George W.M., The semiotics of PLUTARCH's *synkriseis*: the Hellenistic lives of Demetrius-Antony and Agesilaus-Pompey [BRENK & HAMILTON in ANRW 233/6]: RB(elg)PH 73 (1995) 91-104.

9734 *Inglebert* Hervé, Les causes de l'existence de l'Empire romain selon les auteurs chrétiens des IIIe-IVe siècles: Latomus 54 (1995) 18-50.

9735 **Kallet-Marx** R.M., Hegemony to empire; the development of the Roman imperium in the East from 148 to 62 B.C. [< diss. Berkeley 1988, ^{D}*Gruen* E.]: *HelCuS 15. Berkeley 1995, Univ. California. xiv-428 p. $ 55. 0-520-08075-0 [NTAb 40,p.556].

9736 **Kasher** Aryeh, Jews and Hellenistic cities in Eretz-Israel 1990 → 6,b717; 8,d219*: ^{R}Gnomon 67 (1995) 274-6 (N. *Walter*).

9737 *Konrad* C.F., A new chronology of the Sertorian war [Iberia, time of Pompey 77 BC]: At(henaeum) 83 (1995) 143-187.

9738 *Kushner-Stein* Alla, Another look at JOSEPHUS' evidence for the date of Herod's death: *IsrClas 14 (1995) 73-86 [winter 4/3 B.C. preferable to SCHÜRER's date].

9739 **Le Bohec** Yves, César: QS 1049. P 1994, PUF. 128 p., 7 fig. 2-13-046142-5. -- ^{R}Latomus 54 (1995) 905-7 (R. *Bedon*).

9740 **Lee** B.J., The future church of 140 BCE; a hidden revolution [parallel to U.S. Church today]. NY 1995, Crossroad. vii-218 p. $ 18 pa. 0-8245-1529-3 [NTAb 40,p.368].

9741 **Levi** Mario A., Augusto e il suo tempo. Mi 1994, Rusconi. 577 p. L^m 18. ^{R}Archeo 9,113 (1994) 123s (S. *Moscati*).

9742 **Lindsay** Hugh, A fertile marriage; Agrippina and the chronology of her children by Germanicus: Latomus 54 (1995) 3-17.

9743 **Lott** John B., The earliest use of the divine epithet Augustus, 17 BCE -- 37 CE; dynastic names and religion in the Augustan principate; diss. Pennsylvania, ^{D}*Palmer* R. Ph 1995. 297 p. 95-32238. -- DissA 56 (1995s) p. 1930.

9744 **McLaren** James S., Power and politics in Palestine [< diss. Oxford 1990. 'Jewish involvement in the administration of Palestine] 1991 → 7,b339 ... 10,11214*: ^{R}JJS 46 (1995) 306-8 (J. *Schwartz*).

9745 *Maleuvre* J.-Y., Octave-Auguste, fils plus qu'adoptif de son grand-oncle ?: RB(elg)PH 73 (1995) 73s.

9746 **Martin** P.M., L'idée de royauté à Rome, II. Haine de la royauté et séductions monarchiques (du IV siècle av. J.-C. au principat augustéen: Miroir des civilisations antiques 2. Clermont-Ferrand 1994, Adosa. xxiii-511 p. F 480. -- ᴿCLR 45 (1995) 107-9 (M. *Fox*)

9747 **Mendels** Doron, The rise [Hasmonean] and fall [Herodian] of Jewish nationalism: AnchorBRef. NY 1991, Doubleday. -- ᴿ*A(sn)JS 20 (1995) 409-411 (S. *Schwartz*).

9748 *Nicholson* John, The delivery and confidentiality of CICERO'S letters [HERODOTUS' famed 8,98 refers to post-republican Rome]: CJ 90 (1994s) 33-63.

9749 *a) Pelletier* André, [Drusus] Le 1ᵉʳ août de l'an 12 av. J.-C. -- *b) Raepsaet-Charlier* M.-T., *Raepsaet* G., Drusus et les origines augustéennes de Namur: -→ 10,73, Mém. LE GLAY M., L'Afrique 1994, 441-6 / 449-457.

9750 **Philipp-Stephan** G. Freber, Der hellenistische Osten und das Illyricum unter Caesar: Palingenesis 42. Stu 1993, Steiner. 226 p. -- ᴿBo(nn)J 195 (1995) 682-5 (M. *Jehne*).

9751 ᴱ**Raaflaub** Kurt, *Toher* Mark, Between Republic and Empire 1987/90 → 6,764 ... 10,11317: ᴿAnCL 64 (1995) 480s (J.-P. *Martin*); Latomus 54 (1995) 907-9 (J.-M. *André*); RÉA(mv) 96 (1994) 640s (J.-M. *Roddaz*).

9752 **Ruebel** J.S., Caesar and the crisis of the Roman aristocracy: ClasCu 18. Norman 1994, Univ. Oklahoma. xx-189 p., 4 maps. $ 19. -- ᴿCLR 45 (1995) 343s (J. *Carter*).

9753 *Rutgers* Leonard V., Attitudes to Judaism in the Greco-Roman period [FELDMAN L. 1993]: JQR 85 (1994s) 361-395.

9754 **Scardigli** Barbara, I trattati romano cartaginesi, Pisa 1991, Scuola sup. xxi-373 p. — ᴿGnom 67 (1995) 336-351 (K.-E. *Petzold*).

9755 **Schmitt** Tassilo, Hannibals Siegeszug; historiographische und historische Studien, vor allem zu POLYBIUS und LIVIUS: QFAW 10. Mü 1991, tuduv. ix-388 p. -- ᴿGnom 67 (1995) 79-81 (J, *Seibert*).

9756 ᴱ**(Sena) Chiesa** Gemma, Augusto in Cisalpina; ritratti augustei e giulio-claudi in Italia Settentrionale: Acme quad. 22. Bo 1995, Cisalpino. x-280 p.; bibliog. 1-31. 88-205-0764-1.

9757 **Unnik** W.C. van, Das Selbstverständnis der jüdischen Diaspora (1967), ᴱ*Horst* P.W. van der: AGJU 17, 1993 → 9.12706: ᴿ*A(sn)JS 20 (1995) 399-402 (D. *Winston*); CBQ 57 (1995) 197s (T.H. *Tobin*); JThS 46 (1995) 605-9 (K.-W. *Niebuhr*); ZAH(ebr) 8 (1995) 399-402 (D. *Winston*).

9758 **Williams** Margaret H., Tiberius and the disobliging [? Jewish] grammarian of Rhodes; SUETONIUS, Vita Tiberi XXXII,2 re-considered: Latomus 54 (1995) 624-633.

9759 *Yakobson* Alexander, Secret ballot and its effects in the Late Roman republic: Hermes 128 (1995) 426-442.

Q8.4 **Zeitalter Jesu Christi**: particular/general

9760 **Deviller** Olivier, L'art de la persuasion dans les Annales de TACITE: coll. Latomus 223. Bru 1994. 390 p. Fb 1950. -- ᴿRÉL 73 (1995) 297s (J. *Hellegouarc'h*).

9761 *Dunn* James D.G., Historical text as historical text; some basic hermeneutical reflections in relation to the New Testament: → 170, ᶠSAWYER, J., Words; JSOT.s 195 (1995) 340-359.

9762 *Eck* Werner, Augustus und Claudius in Perusia: At(henaeum) 83 (1995) 83-90; 1 fig.

9763 **Grabbe** L.L., Sects and violence; Judaism in the time of Hillel and Jesus. Hull 1995, Univ. inaugural. iii-17 p. 0-85958-641-3 [NTAb 40, p.377].

9764 **Horsley** Richard A., *Hanson* John S., Banditi, profeti e messia; movimenti popolari al tempo di Gesù: StB 110. Brescia 1995, Paideia. 324 p. Lᵐ 40. 88-944-0526-7.

9765 *Krieger* Klaus-Stefan, Pontius Pilatus -- ein Judenfeind ? Zur Problematik einer Pilatusbiographie: BN(otiz) 78 (1995) 63-83.

9766 *Macdonald* M.C.A., Herodian echoes in the Syrian desert; → 82, [F]HENNESSY J.B., Trade 1995, 285-290.

9767 [E]**Pedersen** S., Den nytestamentlige tids historie; Dansk KomNT 2. Aarhus 1994, Univ. 489 p.; 14 fig.; 5 maps. Dk 298 ($40). 87-7288-498-3 [NTAb 40, p.561].

9768 **Phillips** Darryl A., Elections in the principate of Augustus; diss. Duke, [D]*Boatwright* M. Durham NC 1995. 213 p. 96-12471. -- DissA 56 (1995s) p. 4898.

9769 *Rosen* Klaus, Jesu Geburtsdatum, der Census des Quirinius und eine jüdische Steuererklärung aus dem Jahr 127 nC [Babatha]: JAC 38 (1995) 5-15.

9770 *Ruiz Arzalluz* Iñigo, Augusto, Nerón y el *puer* de la cuarta égloga: Aevum 49 (1995) 115-145.

9771 **Schwartz** Daniel R., Agrippa I : TStAJ 23, 1990 → 8,d259: [R]JQR 84(1993s) 329-333 (A. *Kasher*).

9772 **Sinclair** Patrick, TACITUS, the sententious historian; a sociology of rhetoric in Annales 1-6. Univ. Park 1995, Pennsylvania State. x-262 p. -- [R]RÉL 73 (1995) 298s (J. *Hellegouarc'h*).

9773 *Troiani* Lucio, Giudaismo ellenistico e cristianesimo: → 9,440, [E]*Virgilio* B., Aspetti e problemi dell'ellenismo (Pisa 1992/4) 187-201.

9774 *Vallauri* Emiliano, La moglie di Pilato → 123, [F]MATTIOLI A., In spiritu et veritate 1995. 157-188.

9775 **Vidal Manzanares** C., El judeo-cristianismo palestino en el siglo I, de Pentecostés a Jamnia [< dis. Univ.Dist. 1993, [D]*Fernández Uriel* P.]: Paradigmas 5. Madrid 1995, Trotta. 414 p. pt 3000. 84-8164-037-9 [NTAb 40, p.188].

9776 **Wallace-Hadrill** Andrew, Augustan Rome: Classical World. L 1993, Bristol Classical. xii-105 p. £ 7. 1-85399-138-4. -- [R]BoL (1995) 140 (M.D. *Goodman*)

9777 *Weiss* Zev, [H] Roman leisure culture and its influence upon the Jewish population in the land of Israel: Qadm 28 (1995) 2-19; ill.

Q8.7 *Roma et Oriens*, **prima decennia post Christum**

9778 *Abramenko* Andrik, Zeitkritik bei SUETON; zur Datierung der 'Vitae Caesarum': Hermes 122 (1994) 80-94 [before his 'Titus'; critical of Hadrian].

9779 *André* Jean-Marie, La peregrinatio achaica et le philhellénisme de Néron: RÉL 73 (1995) 168-182.

9780 *a) Bonnefond-Coudry* Marianne, Princeps et sénat sous les Julio-Claudiens; des relations à inventer; -- *b) Mourgues* Jean-Louis, Les formules 'rescripsi' 'recognovi' et les étapes de la rédaction des souscriptions impériales sous le Haut-Empire romain: MÉFRA 107 (1995) 225-254 / 255-300.

9781 **Cesaretti** Maria Pia, Nerone e l'Egitto; messaggio politico e continuità culturale: StudiStoAnt 12. Bo 1989, Coop.Libraria Univ. 124 p. -- [R]BiOr 52 (1995) 404-6 (H.J. *Thissen*: Realismus fehlt; so schon GRENIER)[CdÉ 65 (1990) 360].

9782 *Chastagnol* André, L'empereur Hadrien et la destinée du droit latin provincial au second siècle ap. J.-C.: RH 292 (1994) 217-227 [RHE 91,79*]..

9783 *a)* **Croisille** Jean-Michel, 59, Néron a tué Agrippine [sa mère. P 1994, Complexe. 229 p. F 69. 2-87027-506-4. -- [R]Latomus 54 (1995) 169-171 (P. *Grimal*). -- *b) Devillers* Olivier, TACITE, les sources et les impératifs de la narration; le récit de la mort d'Agrippine (Annales XIV,1-13); Latomus 54 (1995) 324-345.

9784 *a) Demougin* Ségolène, Claude et la société de son temps; -- *b) Trillmich* Walter, Aspekte der 'Augustus-Nachfolge' des Kaisers Claudius; -- *c) Torelli* Mario, Per un'eziologia del cambiamento in epoca claudia; vicende vicine e vicende lontane; -- *d) Hesberg* Henner von, Bogenmonumente und Stadttore in claudischer Zeit: →706, Umbruch ? 1991/4, 11-22 / 69-89; 14 fig. / 177-190 / 245-260; 15 fig.

9785 **Edmondson** Jonathan, [Cassius] DIO, the Julio-Claudians 1992 → 10,11343: ᴿRÉA(nc) 96 (1994) 643s (J.-M. *Roddaz*).

9786 ᴱ**Elsner** Jás, *Masters* Jamie, Reflections of Nero; culture, history and representation. L / Chapel Hill 1994, Duckworth / Univ. N Carolina. viii-239 p.; 11 fig. £ 35. -- ᴿCLR 45 (1995) 345-7 (D. *Wardle*); HZ 261 (1995) 501-3 (R. *Urban*).

9788 **Fell** Martin, Optimus princeps ? Anspruch und Wirklichkeit der imperialen Programmatik Kaiser Traians: QFAW 7. Mü 1992, tuduv. 199 p. DM 40. -- ᴿAAW 48,1s (1995) 86-89 (R. *Klein*); HZ 261 (1995) 515-520 (K. *Strobel*).

9789 **Fini** M., Nerone; duemila anni di calunnie 1993 → 9,12742: ᴿAtenR 39 (1994) 211s (L. *Bessone*).

9790 ᴱ**Frassinetti** Paolo, ²*Di Salvo* Lucia, SALLUSTIO, Opere 1991 → 8,d275: ᴿAt(henaeum) 83 (1995) 563-7 (R. *Funari*).

9791 **Galli** Francesco, SUETONIO, Vita di Domiziano: TComm 11, 1991→ 9,12743: ᴿGnomon 67 (1995) 418-421 (B.W. *Jones*).

9792 **Geckle** Richard P., The rhetoric of morality in SALLUST's speeches and letters: diss. Columbia, ᴰ*Zetzel* J. NY 1955. 173 p. 95-33560. -- DissA 56 (1995s) p. 2225.

9793 **Gillieron** Bernard, Cette Église qui vient de naître; histoire et vie quotidienne des premiers chrétiens. Aubonne 1993, Moulin. 108 p. -- ᴿFV 92.6 (1993) 96s (G. *Vahanian*); Protest(antesimo) 50 (1995) 248 (R. *Subilia*).

9794 **Guastella** Gianni, Gaio SVETONIO Tranquillo, La vita di Caligola: Nis 126. R 1992. 307 p. -- ᴿA(ten)eR 39 (1994) 49s (L. *Bessone*).

9795 **Hadas-Lebel** Mireille, Jérusalem contre Rome 1990 → 6,b792 ... 10,11346; ᴿRasIsr 59 (,1 = 58,) 3 (1992) 147-151 (Francesca *Calabi*).

9796 *a) Heck* Eberhard, Zu Hadrians Christenrescript an Minicius Fundanus (Euseb. hist. eccl. 4,9,1-3); -- *b) Dolidse* Tina, Die Christos-Logos-Lehre in der grosskirchlichen Theologie des 2. Jahrhunderts: → 690, Prinzipat 1992/5, 103-117 / 118-130.

9797 **Hurley** Donna W., An historical and historiographical commentary on SUETONIUS' Life of C. Caligula: ACSt 32, 1993 →9,13745*; 10,11348: ᴿCJ 90 (1994s) 328s (S. *Cerutti*); CLR 45 (1995) 171s (D. *Wardle*); Phoenix 49 (Tor 1995) 270-2 (A.A. *Barrett*).

9798 **Jones** Brian W., The emperor Domitian 1992 → 9,12727; 10,11349: ᴿAtenR 39 (1994) 212 (L. *Bessone*).

9799 ᴱ**Kaster** Robert A., SUETONIUS Tranquillus, De grammaticis et rhetoribus. Ox 1995, Clarendon. lx-370 p. 0-19-814091-6.

9800 **Kierdorf** Wilhelm, Leben des Claudius und Nero; UniTb 1715. Pd 1992, Schöningh. 238 p. 3-8252-1715-9. -- ᴿAt(h-Pavia) 83 (1995) 309s (Lucia *Di Salvo*) Gnomon 67 (1995) 597-9 (J. *Gascou*); Latomus 54 (1995) 677s (E. *Cizek*).

9801 **Kuhoff** Wolfgang, Felicior Augusto melior Traiano; Aspekte der Selbstdarstellung der römischen Kaiser während der Prinzipatszeit [< Hab.-Diss. Augsburg 1988]. Fra 1993, Lang. 373 p.; 15 pl. DM 98. -- ᴿCLR 45 (1995) 347s (P. *Matyszak*); HZ 261 (1995) 854-6 (P. *Kneissl*).

9802 *Lambrecht* Ulrich, SUETONs Domitian-Vita: Gym 102 (1995) 508-536.

9803 **Levi** Mario A., Adriano Augusto; studi e ricerche. R 1994, Bretschneider. 148 p. Lᵐ

100. -- R*Archeo 9,111 (1994) 106 [S. M(oscati].

9804 **Lilley** John M., The narrative presentation of ethical paradigms in DIONYSIUS's Roman Antiquities and Luke-Acts: diss. Marquette. Milwaukee 1994. 281 p. 95-17934. -- DissA 56 (1995s) p. 229.

9805 ᴱ**Luce** T.J., *Woodman* A.J., TACITUS and the Tacitean tradition 1990/3 → 10,430c: RGym 102 (1995) 173-5 (S. *Borzsa'k*).

9806 ᴱ**McGushin** Patrick, SALLUST, The Histories I (1-2) 1992 → 8,d283 [II (3-4) 1994 → 10,11354]: RCJ 90 (1994s) 96-101 (S.P. *Schierling*, also on L. REYNOLDS' Jugurtha).

9807 **Marks** Richard G., The image of Bar Kokhba in traditional Jewish literature: false messiah and national hero [IBN DAUD, MAIMONIDES, Kabbala] 1994 → 10,11355: RDSD 2 (1995) 111s (M.O. *Wise*); JJS 46 (1995) 308s (J. *Schwartz*); Midstream 41,3 (1995) 40-422 (J.M. *Rosenberg*).

9808 **Martin** Régis F., Les douze Césars [< SUÉTONE]; du mythe à la réalité. P 1991, Blettres. 441 p. -- RRÉL 73 (1995) 327s (E. *Cizek*).

9809 **Mellor** Ronald, Tacitus 1992 → 10,11356: RGnomon 67 (1995) 265-7 (J. *Hellegouarc'h*).

9810 **Mendels** Doron, The rise and fall of Jewish nationalism 1992 → 8,d287*: R*A(sn)JSR 20 (1995) 409-411 (S. *Schwartz*: 'a stern warning'; credulous, chaotic); BArR 21,1 (1995) 8 . 10 (L.H. *Feldman*); *CritRR 7 (1994) 406-8 (L.L. *Grabbe*); JQR 86 (1995) 237s (J. *Marcus*).

9811 *Meulder* Marcel, Bons et mauvais généraux chez TACITE: RB(elg)PH 73 (1995) 75-89.

9812 *Motto* Anna L., *Clark* John R.. SENECA gives thanks to Nero: SIF(g)C 12(1994)110-7.

9813 *Muñoz León* Domingo, El culto imperial en el Apocalipsis: RevB(Arg) 57 (1995) 223-230.

9814 **Murison** Charles I., Galba, Otho and Vitellius; careers and controversies: Spudasmata 52. Hildesheim 1993, Olms. xvi-180 p.; 1 fig.; 4 maps. DM 40. 3-487-09756-7. -- RLatomus 54 (1995) 911s (J. *Gascou*).

9815 *Murison* Charles L., The death of Titus; a reconsideration: *AncHB 9 (1995) 135-142.

9816 **Pani** Mario, Potere e valori a Roma fra Augusto e Traiano² 1993: RRÉL 73 (1995) 328s (F. *Bérard*).

9817 ᵀ**Pierron** J. Alexis, ᴱ*Frazier* Françoise, PLUTARQUE, Vies parallèles, I. P 1995, Flammarion. 458 p. 2-0807-0820-1.

9818 **Price** J., Jerusalem under siege; the collapse of the Jewish state 66-70, 1992 → 8,d292 ... 10,11361: R*A(sn)JS 20 (1995) 405-9 (S.S. *Miller*); JBL 114 (1995) 143-5 (D. *Rhoads*); JQR 86 (1995s) 496s (S. *Schwartz*).

9819 **Pritz** Ray A., Nazarene Jewish Christianity 1988 → 4,e781; 6,e156: RJHiCr 2,2 (1995) 143-7 (R.M. *Price*).

9820 **Rapsch** Jürgen, *Najock* Dietmar, Concordantia in corpus SALLUSTIANUM. Hildesheim 1991, Olms-Weidemann. xii-1472 p. -- RA(nz)AW 46 (1993) 154-6 (G. *Dobesch*).

9821 *Ricci* Cecilia, L'affranchi impérial T. Flavius Euschemon et le *fiscus judaicus* [Frey, CII 352 ensuite disparu]: RÉJ 154 (1995) 89-95.

9822 **Rudich** Vasily, Political dissidence under Nero; the price of dissimulation 1993 → 10,11363: RBoL (1995) 137 (J. *Lieu*); Latomus 54 (1995) 909s (E. *Cizek*); VDI 213 (1995) 239 (I. *Cogitore*, R).

9823 **Sanders** Jack A., Schismatics .. the first one hundred years of Jewish-Christian relations 1993 → 9,12756*: R*BInterp 3 (1995) 378s (J.D.G. *Dunn*: still unremittingly hostile to Acts); JRel 75 (1995) 554s (W.L. *Petersen*); TorJT 11 (1995) 99-101 (S.G. *Wilson*).

9824 ᴱScardigli Barbara, [12] Essays on PLUTARCH's 'Lives'. Ox 1995, Clarendon. iv-403 p. $ 72 [RStR 22,64, E. *Krentz*: every NT student needs to read Plutarch].

9825 Schmid W., Frühschriften SALLUSTs im Horizont des Gesamtwerkes. Neustadt/Aisch 1993, P.Schmidt. ix-379 p. -- ᴿCLR 45 (1995) 39s (J.G.F. *Powell*).

9826 Shotter David C.A., SUETONIUS, The lives of Galba, Otho, and Vitellius 1993 → 10,11366; 5 maps; £ 35; pa. £ 13.50. 0-85668-537-2; -8-0: ᴿAnCL 64 (1995) 333s (J. *Wankenne*).

9827 *Siat* J., La persécution des chrétiens au début du IIᵉ s. d'après la lettre de PLINE le Jeune et la réponse de Trajan en 112: ÉtCL 63 (1995) 161-170

9828 Späth Tomas, Männlichkeit und Weiblichkeit bei TACITUS; zur Konstruktion der Geschlechter in der römischen Kaiserzeit: Geschichte und Geschlechter 8. Fra 1994, Campus. 380 p. -- ᴿMH(elv) 52 (1995) 252 (B. *Näf*).

9829 ᴱStrocka V.M., Die Regierungszeit des Kaisers Claudius (41-54 n.Chr.): Umbruch oder Episode ?) [Symposion für seinen 2000. Gb. und 100 des Inst,Arch. Freiburg/Br 1991]. Mainz 1994, von Zabern. 331 p. -- ᴿRÉL 73 (1995) 330 (Y. *Le Bohec*).

9830 Vacher Marie-Claude, SUÉTONE, Grammairiens et rhéteurs: Coll. Budé, 1993; F 310: ᴿAnCL 64 (1995) 334-6 (P. *Desy*, aussi sur KASTER R. 1992); Latomus 54 (1995) 145-7 (G. *Achard*).

9831 *Vigourt* Anne, Les présages impériaux et le temps dans le De fine Caesarum de SUÉTONE: Ktema 18 ('La chronologie dans les sociétés antiques' 1993) 131-145.

9832 Wander Berndt, Trennungsprozess zwischen Frühem Christentum und Judentum im I. Jahrhundert n.Chr.; datierbare Abfolgen zwischen der Hinrichtung Jesu und der Zerstörung des Jerusalemer Tempels: TANZ 19. Tü 1994, Francke. ix-315 p. 3-7720-1867-X. [< OTA 18 (1995) p. 438 (L.H. *Feldman*)].

9833 Wardle D., SUETONIUS' Life of Caligula; a commentary. Bru 223, coll. Latomus 225. Bru 1994. 395 p. 2-87031-165-6. -- ᴿRÉL 73 (1995) 269s (R. *Poignault*); RPh(lgLH) 69 (1995) 399-401 (I. *Cogitore*).

9834 *Weiss* Peter, Hadrian in Lydien: Chiron 25 (1995) 213-223; 9 fig. (coins).

9835 *Wilson* S.G., Related strangers, Jews and Christians, 70-170 C.E. Mp 1995, Fortress. xvi-416 p. $ 26. 0-8006-2950-7 [NTAb 40, p.567].

Q9.1 *Historia Romae generalis et* post-christiana

9836 Adam Anne-Marie, TITE-LIVE, Histoire romaine, tome XXIX, livre XXXIX: Coll. Budé. P 1994, BLettres. cxlii-205 p. (86 doubles), maps. -- ᴿRÉA(nc) 97 (1995) 660s (É. *Will*); RÉL 73 (1995) 253-6 (C. *Guittard*).

9837 Albrecht M. von, Geschichte der römischen Literatur von Andronicus bis Boethius mit Berücksichtigung ihrer Bedeutung für die Neuzeit. Bern 1992,Francke. xviii-704 p.; xiv-762 p. -- ᴿCLR 45 (1995) 57-59 (P. *Hardie*).

9838 Anderson Graham, Sage, saint and sophist; holy men and their associates in the early Roman empire. L 1994, Routledge. xii-188 p.-- ᴿET 106 (1994s) 56s (Ruth B. *Edwards*).

9839 ᴱArnaud-Lindet Marie P., [Rutilius] Rufus FESTUS [→ 10,11302], Abrégé des hauts faits du peuple romain: Coll. Budé. P 1994, BLettres. xliv-83 p. 2-251-01380-6.

9840 Bauman Richard A., Women and politics in ancient Rome. L 1992, Routledge. xvi-294 p. £ 37.50. 0-415-00932-4 (0-415-05777-9). -- ᴿLatomus 54 (1995) 668-671 (T. *Späth*).

9841 *Bellandi* Franco, L'immagine di Mecenate protettore delle lettere nella poesia fra I e II sec. d.C.: AtenR 40 (1995) 78-101.

9842 *Blomqvist* Karin, Chryseis and Clea, Eumetis and the interlocutress; PLUTARCH of Chaeronea and DIO CHRYSOSTOM on women's education: → 93, ᶠKIEFFERR., SEÅ (1995) 173-190.

9843 **Boeft** J. den, Philological .. on AMMIANUS 20. 1987. -- ᴿByZ(ts) 87 (1994) 493s (A. *Demandt*).

9844 *Bollansée* Jan, P.*Fay*, 19, HADRIAN's memoirs, and imperial epistolary autobiography: AncSoc 25 (1994) 279-392.

9845 ᴱ**Bompaire** J., LUCIEN, Œuvres I, Introduction générale; Opuscules 1-10: Coll. Budé. P 1993, BLettres. clxiv-188 (d) p. -- ᴿCLR 45 (1995) 24-26 (G. *Anderson*).

9846 *Boscherini* Silvano, La cultura generale dei Romani: → 10,92, Mem. PIERACCIONI D. 1993, 89-101.

9847 **Bowersock** Glen W., Martyrdom and Rome [Belfast Wiles lectures]. C 1995, Univ. xii-106 p. 0-521-46539-7.

9848 **Bowersock** G.W., Fiction as history, Nero to Julian (Sather Lectures 58). SF 1995. xiv-181 p.; bibliog. 161-7. 0-520-08824-7. -- ᴿPh(lgLH) 69 (1995) 207-9 (L. *Pernot*).

9849 **Braund** David, Georgia in antiquity; a history of Colchis and transcaucasian Iberia, 550 BC-AD 562. Ox 1994, UP. xvi-359 p.; 21 pl.; 8 maps. £ 40. -- ᴿGaR 42 (1995) 231 p. (P. *Walcot*).

9850 **Bringmann** Klaus, Römische Geschichte; von den Anfängen bis zur Spätantike: BR 2012. Mü 1995, Beck. 128 p. 4 maps. -- ᴿAAW 48,1s (1995) 30-33 (R. *Klein*); Gr(az)B 21 (1995) 251s (G. *Doblhofer*); RÉL 73 (1995) 314s (R. *Poignault*).

9851 **Brugnoli** Giorgio, *Santini* Carlo, L'Additamentum Aldinum di SILIO Italico: BCL.s 14. R 1995, Accad. Lincei. 111 p.

9852 *Canfora* Luciano, Roma, città greca: QSt 39 (1994) 5-42.

9853 ᴱ**Chamoux** François, *Bertrac* Pierre, DIODORE de Sicile, Bibliothèque historique livre I, 1993 → 10,11381: ᴿAnCL 64 (1995) 300s (F. *Colin*); RÉA(nc) 46 (1994) 590s (M. *Casevitz*).

9855 **Chastagnol** André, Le Sénat romain à l'époque impériale 1992 → 8,d309: ᴿLatomus 54 (1995) 713-5 (J. *Gascou*).

9856 *Chausson* Françoise, L'autobiographie [perdue] de Septime Sévère: RÉL 73 (1995) 183-198.

9857 *Cizek* Eugen, La poétique de l'histoire chez Ammien MARCELLIN:BSL(at)25(1995)550-64

9858 ᵀ**Combes-Dounous** Jean-Isaac, *al.*, APPIEN, Les guerres civiles à Rome I: La Roue à Livres. P 1993, BLettres. 218 p. F 130. 2-251-33921-3. -- ᴿLatomus 54 (1995) 903s (Estelle *Bertrand*).

9859 **Cornell** Tim J., The beginnings of Rome: Italy and Rome from the Bronze Age to the Punic Wars (c. 1000-264 BC: History of the ancient world. L 1995, Routledge. xx-507 p.; bibliog. 472-491. 0-415-01595-2.

9860 **Crook** J.A., Legal advocacy in the Roman world. L 1995, Duckworth. v-225 p.; bibliog. 204-219. 0-7156-2650-7.

9861 *Dal Covolo* Enrico, I Severi precursori di Costantino ? Per una 'messa a punto' delle riceerche sui Severi e il cristianesimo : → 119, ᶠMARA M.Grazia = Aug(ustinianum)R 35 (1995) 505-622.

9862 **Dal Covolo** Enrico, I Severi 1989 → 5,b659 ... 7,b416: ᴿETL 70 (1994) 484 (J. *Verheyden*).

9863 **Doukellis** P.N., LIBANIOS et la terre; discours et idéologie politique: BAH 145. Beyrouth 1995, IFAPO. 280 p.; bibliog. 248-268. 2-7053-0561-0.

9864 **Edwards** Catharine, The politics of immorality in ancient Rome 1993 → 9,12784; 10,11389: [R]BSL(at) 25 (1995) 260-3 (R. *Perrelli*); CP(g) 89 (1994) 391-4 (B.D. *Shaw*); Latomus 54 (1995) 703s (J. *Walters*).

9865 **Evans** J.D., The art of persuasion: political propaganda from Brutus to Aeneas. AA 1992, Univ. Michigan xii-176 p.; 56 fig.; 32 pl. $ 39.50. 0-472-10282-6. -- [R]JRS 85 (1995) 275 (Catharine *Edwards*).

9866 **Famerie** Étienne, Concordance d'Appien. Hildesheim 1993, Olms-Weidmann. xxxii-2149 p, (3 vol.). -- [R]Gnomon 67 (1995) 60s (K. *Brodersen*).

9867 [T]**Faranda Villa** Giovanna, [E]*Affortunati* Monica, PLUTARCHUS, Vitae parallelae, intr. *Ruschenbusch* Eberhard; (8 vol., greco di fronte) I. Solon: I classici della BUR. Mi [1987-] 1994, Rizzoli. vii-411 p. 88-17-17008-7.

9868 *a) Fedeli* Paolo, [R] Man and his environment in the Roman world, [T]*Stratonovsky* G.A.; - - *b) Sallares* Robert, The ecology of the ancient world; problems and approaches, [T]*Litvenenko* Yu. H.: VDI 213 (1995) 103-9; Eng. 109s / 80-102; Eng. 102s.

9869 **Feldman** Louis H., Jew and Gentile in the ancient world 1993 → 9,12785; 10,11454: [R]AnCL 64 (1995) 395s (J.A. *Straus*); Biblica 76 (1995) 277-281 (J. *Sievers:* an optimistic presentation); BiRe 11,5 (1995) 12s (Amy-Jill *Levine*); CLR 45 (1995) 117-9 (F. *Millar*); SCI(sr) 14 (1995) 192s (J.J. *Price*).

9870 *Feldman* Louis H., Reflections on RUTGERS's 'Attitudes to Judaism in the Greco-Roman period' [on his 'Jew and Gentile']: JQR [85 (1994s) 361-395] 86 (1995s)ر153-170.

9871 *Fishwick* Duncan, DIO [Cassius 53,12.4-7] and the provinces: → 10,73. Mém. LE GLAY M., L'Afrique 1994, 116-128.

9872 **Flaig** Egon, Den Kaiser herausfordern; die Usurpation im römischen Reich 1992 → 10,11392: [R]Bo(nn)J 195 (1995) 691-700 (R. *Urban*).

9873 [T]**Flobert** Annette, TITE-LIVE, La seconde guerre punique II.´ Histoire romaine, livres XXVI à XXX. P 1994, Flammarion.-- [R]RÉL 73 (1995) 265-8 (P. *Jal*).

9874 *Frakes* R.M., Cross-references to the lost books of AMMIANUS Marcellinus: Phoenix 49 (Tor 1995) 232-246.

9875 **Fraschetti** Augusto, Rome et le Prince [1990], [T]*Jolivet* V. P 1994, Belin. -- [R]RPh(lgLH) 69 (1995) 412-4 (Annie *Dubourdieu*).

9876 [E]**Fraschetti** Augusto, Roma al femminile. R c.1995, Laterza. 290 p. L[m] 30. -- [R]*Archeo 10,121 (1995) 125s (S. *Moscati*).

9877 **Freyburger** Marie-Laure, *Roddaz* Jean-Michel, DION CASSIUS, Histoire romaine 48s, 1994 → 10,11394: [R]MH(elv) 52 (1995) 336s (B.W. *Häuptli*).

9878 **Fuhrmann** Manfred, Rom in der Spätantike; Porträt einer Epoche 1994 → 10,11457: [R]Latomus 54 (1995) 424-6 (J. *Fontaine*); Tyche 10 (1995) 265s (G. *Dobesch*).

9879 **Gabba** E., DIONYSIUS and The History of archaic Rome (Sather Classical Lectures 56). 1991 → 8,d322; 9,12791; $ 35: [R] CLR 45 (1995) 340-2 (C.E. *Schultze*).

9880 *a) Gabba* Emilio, Roma nel mondo ellenistico; -- *b) Troiani* Lucio, Giudaismo ellenistico e cristianesimo: → 10,440, Aspetti/ Ellenismo 1992/4, 37-45 / 187-201.

9881 *Geider* Marie-Blanche, Les communautés des provinces romaines de Syrie et d'Arabie, de la fin de l'époque hellénistique à la conquête arabe: RÉJ 154 (1995) 219-225.

9882 [E]**Gerlaud** B.. NONNOS de Panopolis, Les Dionysiaques 6, chants 14-17: Coll Budé. P 1994, BLettres. xviii-271 (d.) p. -- [R]CLR 45 (1995) 14 (N. *Hopkinson*).

9883 **Goodman** Martin, Mission and conversion; proselytizing in the religious history of the Roman Empire. Ox 1994, Clarendon. 194 p. £ 25. 0-19-814941-7. -- [R]ChH 64 (1995) 252s (E. *Ferguson*); ET 106 (1994s) 89 (C.H. *Middleburgh*); JJS 46 (1995) 297-300 (Shaye *Cohen*); JRS 85 (1995) 316s (Catherine *Hezser*).

9884 **Gottlieb** Gunther, Christentum und Kirche in den ersten drei Jahrhunderten 1991 → 9,12795: [R]*CritRR 7 (1994) 336s (D.N. *Schowalter*); G(raz)B 21 (1995) 266s (J.-B. *Bauer*); HZ 261 (1995) 858s (Elisabeth *Herrmann-Otto*).

9885 [E]**Gottlieb** Günther, *Barceló* Pedro, Christen und Heiden in Staat und Gesellschaft des zweiten bis vierten Jahrhunderts; Gedanken und Thesen zu einem schwierigen Verhältnis; Augsburg Univ. ph. Fak. Mü 1992, Vögel. vi-212 p.; 5 pl. DM 48. 3-925355-44-8. -- [R]Latomus 54 (1995) 171-3 (F. *Ruggiero*); ZKG 105 (1994) 106s (R.M. *Hübner*)

9886 **Grant** Michael, The Antonines; the Roman Empire in transition 1994 → 10,11401: [R]GaR 42 (1995) 239 (T. *Wiedemann*: most welcome); RÉA(nc) 96 (1994) 645 (J.-M. *Roddaz*).

9887 **Gras** Michel, La Méditerranée archaïque: Cursus Histoire. P 1995, A. Colin. 189 p. 2-200-21674-2.

9888 [E]**Guyot** P., *Klein* R., Das frühe Christentum bis zum Ende der Verfolgungen; eine Dokumentation, 1, Die Christen im heidnischen Staat; 2. Die Christen in der heidnischen Gesellschaft; TF 60.62. Da 1993s, Wiss. xii-516 p. DM 112. [RHE 90 (1995) 266*].

9889 [E]**Haase** Wolfgang, *Meyer* Reinhold, The classical tradition and the Americas, I. European images of the Americas and the classical tradition 1. B/NY 1994, de Gruyter. xxxviii-681 p. DM 498. -- [R]HZ 261 (1995) 113s (J. *Heideking*).

9890 **Hägg** T., Eros und Tyche [Den antike Romanen 1986] 1987. -- [R]*AulaO 12 (1994) 139s (M. *Camps-Gaset*).

9891 **Hahn** Ulrike, Die Frauen des römischen Kaiserhauses und ihre Ehrungen im griechischen Osten anhand epigraphischen und numismatischen Zeugnisse von Livia bis Sabina [Diss. 1992]: StArchAG 8. Saarbrücken 1994, Druckerei. 447 p.

9892 *Irshai* Oded, [H] Constantine and the Jews; the prohibition against entering Jerusalem, history and hagiography: Zion 60 (1995) 129-178, Eng. X.

9893 **Jacks** Philips, The antiquarian and the myth of antiquity; the origins of Rome in Renaissance thought 1993 → 10,11403: [R]At(henaeum) 83 (1995) 530s (Claudia *Maccabruni*).

9894 [E]**Jenkyns** R., El legado de Roma; una nueva valoración [1992 → 8,656d]: Mayor. Barc 1995, Crítica. 424 p. -- [R]Communio (Sev) 28 (1995) 387-9 (M. *Sánchez*: a ZUBIRI, 'los griegos somos nosotros').

9895 **Jerphagnon** Lucien, Le divin César; étude sur le pouvoir impérial à Rome. P 1991, Tallandier → 9,12714; F 158; 2-235-02053-4: [R]Latomus 54 (1995) 441-3 (H. *Inglebert*).

9896 *Junod* E., L'Église des premiers siècles fut-elle une 'minorité religieuse' ?: Suppl 194 (1995) 74-93 [NTAb 40, p.316].

9897 **Kamm** A., The Romans; an introduction. L 1995, Routledge. xiv-24 p.; 41 fig.; 2 maps. $ 50; pa. $ 16. 0-415-12039-X: -40-3 [NTAb 40, p.557].

9898 **Kerr** William G., A chronological study of the Marcomannic wars of Marcus Aurelius: diss. Princeton 1995. 295 p. 95-41180. -- DissA 56 (1995s) p. 3260.

9899 **Kneppe** Alfred, Metus temporum; zur Bedeutung von Angst in Politik und Gesellschaft der römischen Kaiserzeit des 1. und 2. Jts. n. Chr. [Diss. Münster]. Stu 1994, Steiner. 410 p. DM 128. -- [R]GaR 42 (1995) 238 (T. *Wiedemann*).

9900 **Kraus** Christina S., LIVY, Ab urbe condita, book VI. C 1994, Univ. x-356 p. --

^{R}RÉL 73 (1995) 260s (J.-C. *Richard*).

9901 **Kruta** Venceslas, Die Anfänge Europas von 6000 bis 500 v.Chr. [franç.], ^{T}*Weippert* Helga. Mü 1993, Beck. 410 p. -- ^{R}Tyche 9 (1994) 238s (G. *Dobesch*).

9903 ^{E}**La Garanderie** Marie-Madeleine, *Penham* Daniel F., Guillaume BUDÉ, Le passage de l'hellénisme au christianisme [1535], lat./fr.: Les classiques de l'humanisme 9. P 1993, Blettres. lxxii-294 p. 2-251-34441-1. -- ^{R}RHPhR 75 (1995) 354 (P. *Maraval*).

9904 **Lane Fox** Robin, Pagani e cristiani [1986 → 3,d87]. R 1991, Laterza. 872 p. -- ^{R}RSLR30 (1994) 365-9 (Anna Maria *Berruto*).

9905 **Laqueur** Richard †, DIODOR's Geschichtswerk -- die Überlieferung von Buch I-V, ^{E}*Brodersen* Kai: StKP 71, 1992 → 9,12802; DM 42: ^{R}HZ 260 (1995) 822s (K. *Rosen*); Klio 77 (1995) 496s (J. *Wiesehöfer*).

9906 **Leon** Harry J. [1896-1967], The Jews of ancient Rome ^{2rev} [^{1}1960]. Peabody MA 1995, Hendrickson. xxiii-394 p. 1-56563-076-7.

9907 ^{E}**Lieu** Judith, *al.*, The Jews among pagans and Christians 1992 → 8,476: ^{R}ChH 64 (1995) 642s (J.S. *Kaminsky*).

9908 **Lim** Richard, Public disputation, power, and social order in late antiquity: *TransfCLH 23. Berkeley 1995, Univ. California. xvii-278 p.; bibliog. 241-265. 0-520-08577-9.

9909 **Lintott** A., Imperium romanum: politics and administration 1993 → 10,11413: ^{R}JRS 85 (1995) 253s (K. *Buraselis*).

9910 **Lomas** K., Rome and the western Greeks 1993 → 10,11414: ^{R}JRS 85 (1995) 263s (Susan E. *Alcock*).

9911 *Matthews* J.F., The origin of AMMIANUS: CQ 44 (1994) 230-269.

9912 *Mattioli* Marina, Roma e la Sicilia nel III sec. a.C.; Morgantina ed Entella: Acme 48,2 (1995) 5-22.

9913 **Matzerath** Josef, Albert SCHWEGLER (1819-1957; römische Geschichte) [Diss. Bonn 1990]: Contubernium 37. Sigmaringen 1993, Thorbecke. 345 p. -- ^{R}RÉA(nc) 96 (1994) 574-6 (J. *Deininger*).

9914 **Millar** Fergus, The Roman Near East, 31 B.C. -- A.D. 337. CM 1993, Harvard Univ. xxix-587 p.; 12 maps. $ 54. -- ^{R}A(mer)HR 100 (1995) 123-5 (G.M. *Rogers*); A(ndr)USS 33 (1995) 312s (H.P. *Krug*); C(ath)HR 81 (1995) 251s (Irfan *Shahîd*); CLR 45 (1995) 104-6 (M. *Whitby*); TorJT 11 (1995) 113s (P. *Richardson*); VDI (1995,4: fasc. numbered 215 but next after 213) p.212-6 (G.A. *Koshelenko*, G.M. *Bongard-Levin*) & 217-9 (A.L. *Smyshlyaev*).

9915 *Moles* John, LIVY's preface: PCP(g)S 39 (1993) 141-168.

9916 ^{E}**Müller** Carl W., Zum Umgang mit fremden Sprachen in der griechisch-römischen Antike [Saarbrücken 21.-22. XI. 1989]: Palingenesia 36, 1992 → 10,11419: ^{R}Gnomon 67 (1995) 396-400 (Ruzena *Dosta'lova'*).

9917 **Mustakallio** K., Death and disgrace 1994 → 10,11420: ^{R}BSL(at) 25 (1995) 249-252 (G. *Comerci*).

9918 **Nippel** Wilfried. Public order in ancient Rome: Key Themes in Ancient History. C 1995, Univ. x-163 p.; bibliog. 126-157. 0-521-38327-7.

9919 **Ogilvie** Robert M., Le origini di Roma. Bo 1995, Mulino. 233 p. L^m 24. -- ^{R}Archeo 126 (1995) 110 (S. *Moscati*, anche su CRAWFORD M., età repubblicana).

9920 *Ortiz de Urbina* Esíbaliz, Die römische municipale Ordnung; Realität und Virtualität [< Diss. 1992]: B(onn)Jb 195 (1995) 39-66.

9921 **Perelli** L., La corruzione politica nell'antica Roma 1994 → 10,11423: ^{R}CivCatt 146 (1995,1) 55-60 (F.P. *Rizzo*); Labeo 40 (1994) 405s (A. *Guarino*).

9922　*Pucci Ben Zeev* Miriam, Did the Jews enjoy a privileged position in the Roman world ? [JUSTER J. 1914, unchallenged until RAJAK T. 1984]: RÉJ 154 (1995) 23-42: 'rights' not = privileges.

9923　*Pucci Ben Zeev* Miriam, Caesar and Jewish law: RB 102 (1995) 28-37; franç. 28.

9924　**Raskolnikoff** Mouza, Histoire romaine et critique historique dans l'Europe des Lumières: CEFR 163. R 1993, École Française. xiii-886 p. -- ᴿRÉA(nc) 96 (1994) 624s (J.-M. *Roddaz*).

9925　**Rawson** Elizabeth † 1988, Roman culture and society, ᴱMillar F,. 1991 → 7,251*; 10,11426: ᴿJRS 84 (1994) 209-211 (T.H. *Tawer*).

9926　*Ricci* Cecilia, Africani a Roma; testimonianze epigrafiche di età imperiale di personaggi provenienti dal Nordafrica: AntAfr 30 (1994) 189-207.

9927　**Richardson** John, Roman provincial administration: Inside the Ancient World. L 1994 = 1976, Duckworth. 88 p. £ 7. 0-86292-128-7. -- ᴿBoL (1995) 137 (L.L. *Grabbe*).

9928　**Rostovtzeff** M., Per la storia del colonato romano [1910], ᵀMarcone Arnaldo. Brescia 1994, Paideia. 423 p. -- ᴿAeg 75 (1995) 330s (G. *Geraci*, anche su Scripta varia 1995 ᵀᴱMarcone).

9929　*Sautel* Jacques-Hubert, La tradition manuscrit du livre III des Antiquités romaines de DENYS d'Halicarnasse (témoins grecs): RHT 25 (1995) 61-79; stemata 80; Eng. 301.

9930　*Schmidt* Victor, LUKIAN über die Auferstehung der Toten : VigChr 49 (1995) 388-392.

9931　*Schubert* Charlotte, Mischverfassung [Rom] und Gleichgewichtssystem; POLYBIOS und seine Vorläufer → 176, ᶠSCHMITT H., Rom & Osten 1995, 225-235.

9932　*Schultze* C.E., DIONYSIUS of Halicarnassus and Roman chronology: PCP(g)S 41 (1995) 192-214.

9933　**Schwarz** Ludwig, Il concetto di *romanitas* in rapporto ad alcuni valori etici: Salesianum 57 (1995) 527-548.

9934　*Solin* Heikki, Namensgebung und Politik; zu Namenswechsel und besonderen Vornamen römischer Senatoren: Tyche 10 (1995) 185-210.

9935　**Stoffel** Pascal, Über die Staatspost, die Ochsengespanne und die requirierten Ochsengespanne: eine Darstellung des römischen Postwesens auf Grund der Gesetze des Codex Theodosianus und des Codex Iustinianus [Diss. Zürich]: EHS 3/595. Fra 1994, Lang. xi-192 p. DM 57. -- ᴿHZ 261 (1995) 520-2 (R. *Klein*).

9936　**Strobel** K., Das Imperium romanum im '3. Jahrhundert' [A.D.; ... Palmyra]; Modell einer historischen Krise ? : Hist.Einz 75. Stuttgart 1993, Steiner. -- ᴿAt(henaeum) 83 (1995) 552s (A. *Marcone*).

9937　**Sullivan** J.P. †, MARTIAL, the unexpected classic 1991 → 9,12838: ᴿCP 89 (1994) 194-9 (J. *Tatum*).

9938　**Vidén** Gunhild, Women in Roman literature. 1993. -- ᴿRÉA(nc) 96 (1994) 602 (Lucienne *Deschamps*).

9939　*Wasserstein* Abraham, Non-Hellenized Jews in the semi-Hellenized East: IsrClas 14 (1995) 111-137.

9940　**Wellesley** K., Cornelius TACITUS 11,1, Historiae: BSGL. Lp 1988, Teubner. 222 p. M 64. 3-222-00671-8. -- ᴿArctos 27 (1993) 156s (Heikki *Solin*).

9941　**Wells** Colin, The Roman Empire². CM 1995, Harvard Univ. xiii-266 p. $ 14. 0-674-77770. [RStR 22,242, A.T. *Kraabel*].

9942　**Wes** Marinus A., M. ROSTOVTZEFF. 1990. -- ᴿ*TopO 4 (1994) 281-3 (J. *Andreau*).

9943　*Woolf* Greg, Becoming Roman, staying Greek; culture, identity and the civilizing process in the Roman East: PCP(g)S 40 (1994) 116-143.

Q9.5   Constantinus, Julianus -- Imperium Byzantinum

9944 **Angold** Michael, Church and society in Byzantium under the Comneni, 1081-1261.
C 1995, Univ. xvi-604 p. $ 90. 0-521-26432-4 [< ThD 43,354].

9945 *Bammel* Ernst, Heidentum und Judentum in Rom nach einer christlichen Darstellung
des fünften Jahrhunderts: AugR 34 (1994) 437-446.

9946 **Barnes** Timothy D., Athanasius and Constantius; theology and politics in the
Constantinian empire 1993 → 9,12850 (not 'Constantine '!); 10,11142: [R]Aevum 49 (1995)
265s (G. *Zecchini*); At(henaeum) 83 (1995) 551s (A. *Marcone*); HeythJ 36 (1995) 360
(A. *Louth*); HZ 261 (1995) 863s (K.M. *Girardet*); RÉA(nc) 97 (1995) 667-671 (Annik
Marin); Theol 97 (L 1994) 209s (M. *Fraser*).

9947 *Beatrice* Pier Franco, Pagan wisdom and Christian theology according to the
[Byzantine c.500] Tübingen Theosophy: *JEarlyC 3 (1995) 403-418.

9948 **Beaucamp** Joëlle, Le statut de la femme à Byzance (IVe-VIIe siècle); I. Le droit
impérial; II. Les pratiques sociales 1990-2 → 9,12852: [R]BASPAP 32 (1995) 65-86 (R.S.
Bagnall); RH 293(1995) 389-393 (M. *Kaplan*).

9949 *Bellen* Heinz, Christianissimus imperator; zur Christianisierung der römischen
Kaiserideologie von Constantin bis Theodosius: → 10,22c, [F]CHANTRAINE H., E fontibus
1994 [3-506-79038-7] 3-19.

9950 [TE]**Bird** H.W., The Breviarium ab urbe condita: Translated texts for historians 14.
Liverpool 1993, Univ. lvii-186 p. $ 16. -- [R]JEarlyC 3 (1995) 500s (C.C. *Smith*).

9951 *Bleckmann* Bruno, Constantin und die Donaubarbaren; ideologische
Auseinandersetzungen um die Sieghaftigkeit Constantins: JAC 38 (1995) 38-66.

9952 **Bleicken** Jochen, Constantin der Grosse und die Christen 1992 → 9,12854; 10,11443:
[R]Gnom 67 (1995) 341-8 (F. *Paschoud*); ZKG 105 (1994) 107-9 (E. *Bammel*).

9953 **Blockley** R.C., East Roman foreign policy from Diocletian to Anastasius: ARCA 30.
Leeds 1992, Cairns. viii-283 p.

9954 *Boeft* Jan den, Knowledge of the gods is the essence of human happiness [JULIAN]: →
591, Aspects 1993/5, 17-24.

9955 *Bosinis* Konstantinos, Die Artikulation des Volkswillen in den Städten der Spätantike
(Ostreich): Kler 24,1s (1992) 9-21.

9956 **Bouffartigue** Jean, L'empereur Julien 1992 → 9,12855; 10,11445: [R]Byzantion 64
(1994) 513-5 (O. *Ballériaux*).

9957 *Bradbury* Scott, Constantine and the problem of anti-pagan legislation in the fourth
century: CP 89 (1994) 120-139.

9958 *Brauch* Thomas, *a)* The prefect of Constantinople for 362 A.D., Themistius; -- *b)*
Themistius and the emperor Julian: Byzantion 63 (1993) 37-78 / 79-115.

9959 *Brennan* Brian, BURCKHARDT & RANKE on the age of Constantine the Great: QStor
21,41 (1995) 53-65.

9960 *Bringmann* Klaus, Die konstantinische Wende; zum Verhältnis von politischer und
religiöser Motivation: HZ 260 (1995) 21-47.

9961 *a) Brock* Sebastian, L'Église d'Orient dans l'Empire sassanide jusqu'au VIe siècle et son
absence aux conciles de l'Empire romain; -- *b) Abramowski* Luise, Histoire de la recherche
sur NESTORIUS et le Nestorianisme: Ist(ina) 40 (1995) 25-43 / 44-55.

9962 *Brodd* Jeffrey, JULIAN the Apostate and his plan to rebuild the Jerusalem Temple:
BiRe(v) 11,5 (1995) 32-38 . 48.

9963 **Brown** Peter, Power and persuasion 1988/92 → 9.12856; 10.11446: [R]At(henaeum) 83 (1995) 289s (A. *Marcone*); ChH 64 (1995) 254-6 (E. *TeSelle*); CLR 45 (1995) 110s (M. *Whitby*); JRel 75 (1995) 273s (J.C. *Cavadini*).

9964 **Brown** Peter, Authority and the sacred; aspects of the Christianisation of the Roman world [4th c.; 1993 lectures]. C 1995, Univ. xiii-91 p. £ 28: pa. £ 10. 0-521-49557-1; -904-6. -- [R]E(xp)T 107 (1995s) 185 (G. *Huelin*).

9965 **Cameron** Averil, The Mediterranean world in late antiquity, A.D. 395-600. L 1993, Routledge. xvii-251 p.; 5 fig.; 12 pl. £ 35; pa. £ 11. 0-415-01420-4; -1-2. -- [R]JRS 85 (1995) 331-4 (I.N. *Wood*, also on her Later Roman Empire 284-430).

9966 **Cameron** Averil, The later Roman Empire 1993 → 9,12859; 10,11449: [R]CLR 45 (1995) 191s (J.G.F. *Hind*); Phoenix 49 (Tor 1995) 81-83 (T.D.*Barnes*, also on her 1993 Mediterranean World).

9967 **Cameron** A., Das späte Rom, 284-430 n.Chr. [1993][T]: dtv 4621. Mü 1994, Dts. Taschenbuch. 264 p. < RHE 90 (1995) 269*.

9968   **Clark** Gillian, Women in late antiquity; pagan and Christian life styles 1993 → 10.11451: [R]A(mer)HR 100 (1995) 502 (Natalie B. *Kampen*).

9969 *Claussen* M.A., Pagan rebellion and Christian apologetics in fourth-century Rome; the Consultationes Zacchaei et Apollonii : JEH 46 (1995) 589-614.

9970 **Croke** Brian, Christian chronicles and Byzantine history, 5th-6th centuries [19 reprints]: CS 386. Ashgate 1992, Variorum. 352 p. $ 88. 0-86078-343-X. -- [R]*JEarlyC 3 (1995) 229-231 (A. *Golitzzin*).

9971 *Curta* Florin, Atticism, Homer, Neoplatonism, and Fürstenspiegel; Julian's second panegyric on Constantius: GRBS 36 (1995) 177-211.

9972   **Dagron** Gilbert, *al.*, Évêques, moines et empereurs (610-1054): Histoire du christianisme 4, 1993 → 10,14294 [R]RÉByz 53 (1995) 346s (A. *Failler*).

9973 *Drake* H.A., Constantine and consensus: ChH 64 (1995) 1-15.

9974 **Dreher** Martin, A Igreja no Império Romano. São Leopoldo 1994, Sinodal. -- [R]REB 55 (1995) 347-9 (E. *Hoornaert*).

9975 **Eleuteri** Paolo, *Bigo* Antonio, Eretici, dissidenti, Musulmani ed Ebrei a Bizanzio. Venezia 1993, Cardo. 168 p. L[m] 30. -- [R]RÉByz 52 (1994) 303s (Marie-Hélène *Congourdeau*); Speculum 70 (1995) 362 (J.W. *Barker*).

9976 *Failler* Albert, Le centenaire de l'Institut Byzantin des Assomptionistes: RÉByz 53 (1995) 5-40.

9977 [E]**Feldmeier** Reinhard, *Heckel* Ulrich, Die Heiden; Juden Christen und das Problem des Fremden: WUNT 70. Tü 1994, Mohr. 449 p. -- [R]ThR(und) 60 (1995) 227s (E. *Lohse*).

9978   **Fowden** Garth, Empire to commonwealth; consequences of monotheism in late antiquity 1993 → 9,12865; 10,11455: [R]A(mer)HR 100 (1995) 885s (D.A. *Miller*); CLR 45 (1995) 111s (Jill *Harries*); Horizons 22 (1995) 194s (J.C. *Cavadini*); HZ 260 (1995) 541-3 (R. *Klein*); *JEarlyC 3 (1995) 507-9 (J.P. *Amar*); JRel 75 (1995) 271s (R.J. *Wilken*); JThS 46 (1995) 737-740 (A. *Louth*).

9979 *Freund* Richard A., Which Christians, pagans and Jews ? Varying reponses to Julian's attempt to rebuild the Temple in Jerusalem in the fourth century CE: JRelSt 18 (1993) 67-93.

9980 *Gillett* Andrew, The date and circumstances of OLYMPIODORUS of Thebes [History, c.440, on the western half of the empire from 407 to 425]: Traditio 48 (1993) 1-29.

9981 *Gliściński* Jan, [P] Cristianità e decadenza nell'Impero Romano: C(olc)Th 64,1 (1994) 63-69; ital. 69.

9982 ^E**González Blanco** Antonino, *Blázquez Martínez* José M., Cristianismo y aculturación en tiempos del Imperio Romano: Antigüedad y Cristianismo 7. Murcia 1990, Univ. 667 p. pt 5000. -- ^RJbAC 37 (1994) 177-181 (A. *Viciano*).

9983 **Grant** M., The Emperor Constantine. 1991. -- ^RGym 102 (1995) 379-381 (J. *Rist*).

9984 **Grant** Michael, Constantine the Great 1994 → 10,11459: ^RChH 64 (1995) 253s (R.M. *Grant*); C(ath)HR 81 (1995) 631s (C.M. *Odahl*); CJ 90 (1994s) 330s (H.A. *Pohlsander*).

9985 **Grubbs** Judith E., Law and family in late antiquity; the emperor Constantine's marriage legislation. Ox 1995, Clarendon. x-390 p. 0-19-814768-6.

9986 **Haase** Richard, Untersuchungen zur Verwaltung des spätrömischen Reiches unter Kaiser Justinian I (527 bis 585). Wsb 1994, Reichert. xi-162 p.; bibliog. 139-159. 3-88226-750-5.

9987 **Haldon** John P., Byzantium in the seventh century; the transformation of a culture 1990 → 8,d396: ^RJNES 54 (1995) 302s (P.M. *Cobb*).

9988 **Heather** Peter J., Goths and Romans 332-459 [< diss.]. Ox 1991, Clarendon. xvi-378 p. $ 81. -- ^R*JEarlyC 3 (1995) 79-81 (A. *Ferreiro*).

9989 **Heim** F., Virtus; idéologie politique et croyances religieuses au IVe siécle. Bern 1991, P.Lang. -- ^RCrSt 16 (1995) 630s (M. *Maas*).

9990 **Hinson** E. Glen, The early Church; origins to the dawn of the Middle Ages. Nv 1995, Abingdon. 365 p. $ 16. 0-687-00603-1. -- ^R*TBR 8,3 (1995s) 43s (Jill D. *Harries*).

9991 *Irmscher* Johannes, Der Demokratismus der frühbyzantinischen Zirkusparteien: *JAncCiv 9 (Changchun 1994) 56-61.

9992 **Keil** Volkmar, Quellensammlung zur Religionspolitik Konstantins des Grossen; TF 54. Da 1989, Wiss, 244 p. -- ^RA(nz)AW 48,1s (1995) 22-25 (R. *Muth*).

9993 **Kuhnke** .. Koinonia, zur theologischen Rekonstruktion der Identität christlicher Gemeinde [Diss. 1991]. .. 1992, Patmos. 393 p. DM 45. 3-491-71094-4 [NTAb 38, p. 476].

9994 **Lee** A.D., Information and frontiers; Roman foreign relations in late antiquity 1993 → 10,11466: At(h-Pavia) 83 (1995) 560s (A. *Marcone*); CLR 45 (1995) 113s (B. *Rankov*); Latomus 54 (1995) 912s (R. *Delmaire*).

9995 **Leeb** Rudolf, Konstantin und Christus: AKG 58, 1992 → 8,d408; 10,1146: ^RC(L)B 71,2 (1995) 159-161 (H. *Pohlsander*); ChH 64 (1995) 637s (E.G. *Hinson*); Gnomon 67 (1995) 281-3 (T.G. *Elliott*, Eng.); HZ 261 (1995) 859-863 (W. *Kuhoff*); ZKG 105 (1994) 109s (R. *Klein*).

9996 **Liebeschuetz** J., Barbarians and bishops 1990 → 6.b882; 7,b456*: ^RGnom 67 (1995) 173s (A. *Demandt*).

9997 *a) Lizzi* Rita, Discordia in Urbe; pagani e cristiani in rivolta; -- *b) Burgarelli* Filippo, Pagani e cristiani tra IV e V secolo a Costantinopoli: → 561, Pagani 1993/5, 115-140 / 181-191.

9998 **Lorenz** Rudolf, Das vierte Jahrhundert (Osten); die Kirche in ihrer Geschichte 1. Lfg. C2 (2-4 erwartet). Gö 1992, Vandenhoeck & R. 158 p. DM 38. 3-5525-2300-4. -- NedThT 49 (1995) 79s (J. van *Amersfoort*).

9999 **Maas** M., J.Lydus 1992 → 8,12880; 9,11468: ^RGnomon 67 (1995) 468-470 (A. *Lippold*).

a000 **McMullen** Ramsay, *a)* Le déclin de Rome et la corruption du pouvoir [1988 → 4,d609],^T 1991; 474 p.; 17 fig. 2-251-38013-5. -- ^RLatomus 54 (1995) 720-2 (R. *Chevallier*). -- *b)* La corruzione e il declino di Roma 1991 → d3444; 17 fig. L^m 50. -- ^R*Archeo 9,113 (1994) 124s (E. *Gizzi*).

a001 *Malosse* P.-L., Les alternances de l'amitié; Julien et Libanios (349-363 et au-delà : RPh(lgLH) 69 (1995) 249-262; Eng. 427.

a002 **Meyendorff** John, Unité de l'Empire et divisions des Chrétiens; l'Église de 450 à 680 [1989 → 6,b887], ᵀ*Lhoest* Françoise: Théologies. P 1993, Cerf. 427 p. F 238. 2-204-04646-9. -- ᴿRBBras 11 (1994) 690-2 (C. *Minette de Tillesse*); RHPhR 75 (1995) 341s (P. *Maraval*); ScEs 47 (1995) 350-2 (G. *Novotny*).

a003 **Moorhead** John, Justinian; the medieval world. L 1994, Longman. ix-202 p.; map. £ . -- ᴿGaR 42 (1995) 240 (T. *Wiedemann*).

a004 **Näf** Beat, Senatorisches Standesbewusstsein in spatrömischer Zeit: Paradosis 40. FrS 1995, Univ. ix-344 p. 3-7278-0930-0.

a005 *Näsström* Britt-Mari, 'Jag tillber fortfarande Abrahams, Isaks och Jakobs Gud'; Kejsar Julianus och religionen: SvTK 69 (1993) 76-83; Eng, 83: he disliked Christians but tried to prevent their persecution, until his ban on Christian teachers in 363 just before his death.

a006 **Neri** Valerio, Medius princeps, Costantino 1992 → 9,12886; ,11473: ᴿA(nz)AW 45 (1993) 219-223 (R. *Klein*).

a007 ᴱ**Norman** A.Frank, LIBANIUS {314-393), Autobiography and selected letters: Loeb. CM 1992, Harvard Unic. 529 p., 486 p. $ 15.50 each. -- ᴿJEarlyC 3 (1995) 70-72 (T.M. *Banchich*).

a008 *Odahl* Charles, God and Constantine, divine sanction for imperial rule in the first Christian emperor's early letters and art: C(ath)HR 81 (1995) 327-352.

a009 **Olster** David M., Roman defeat, Christian response, and the literary construction of the Jew. Ph 1994, Univ. Pennsylvania. xii-203 p. $ 33. 0-8122-3162-X. -- ᴿChr&Lit 43 (1944) 416s (G. C. *Roti*).

a010 ᴱ**Piétri** Charles & Luce, Naissance d'une chrétienté (250-430): Histoire du Christianisme 2. P 1995, Desclée. 94 p. F 430. -- ᴿÉtudes 393 (1995) 426s (P. *Vallin*).

a011 **Potter** David, Prophets [Delphi, Sibylline] and emperors; human and divine authority from Augustine to Theodosius: Revealing Antiquity. CM 1994, Harvard Univ. x-281 p. $ 45. -- ᴿTS 56 (1995) 814 (G.T. *Dennis*).

a012 **Praet** D., De God der goden; de christianisiering van het Romeinse Rijk: Mens en Tid. Kapellen/Kampen 1995, Pelckmans/Kok. 232 p. [RHE 90,65*].

a013 **Robins** R.H., The Byzantine grammarians; their place in history; ᴛʟsᴍ 70, 1993 → 9,12892; ᴅᴍ 168: ᴿAnCʟ 64 (1995) 362-4 (J. *Schamp*).

a014 **Rutgers** Leonard V., The Jews in late ancient Rome; evidence of cultural interactions in the Roman diaspora [< diss. Duke 1993 → 9,12894]. Lei 1995, Brill. xx-283 p. -- ᴿJQR 86 (1995s) 439-443 (L.H. *Feldman*: from 594 catacomb-epitaphs; clearly supersedes LEON H. 1960).

a015 *Salzman* Michèle R., On Roman time ... 354: 1990 → 9.15365: ᴿHZ 260 (1995) 853s (A. *Demandt*); Klio 77 (1995) 537s (D. *Schlinkert*); Numen 42 (1995) 2-7 (J. *Rüpke*).

a016 *Santos Yanguas* Narciso, Juliano y Teodosio; ¿ la antítesis de dos emperadores ?: *MemHAnt 15s (Oviedo 1994s) 183-213,

a017 *Shanks* Hershel, Ferment in Byzantine studies: BArR 21,5 (1995) 66 . 68.

a018 **Sordi** Marta, The Christians and the Roman Empire [1991 → ,11478], ᵀ*Bedini* Annabel. Norman 1994, Univ. Oklahoma, vi-215 p. $ 15 pa. -- ᴿC(ath)HR 81 (1995) 409-411 (H.A. *Drake*); RRelRes 37 (1995s) 181s (P. *Staples*).

a019 **(Di Mauro) Todini** Antonella, Aspetti della legislazione religiosa del IV secolo: Pubbl. 67. R 1990, Ist Diritto Romano. 288 p. -- ᴿLabeo 40 (1994) 2-111 (L. *De Giovanni*).

a020 **Trombley** F.R., Hellenic religion and Christianisation I, c.370-529: ÉPRO 115, 1993 → 9,12899; ,11480; *f* 375: ᴿGym 2 (1995) 189-3 (R. *Klein*); *JEarlyC 3 (1995) 220-2 (K.P. *Wesche*).

a021 **Ugenti** Valerio, GIULIANO. Alla madre degli dèi 1992 → 9,12900; ,11481: ᴿAevum 49 (1995) 266-9 (C.M. *Mazzucchi*); EM(erita) 63 (1995) 359s (S. *Montero*); CLR 45 (1995) 160s (M.B. *Trapp*); RB(elg)PH 73 (1995) 179s (J. *Declerck*).

a022 **Vacca** S., Prima sedes a nemine iudicatur; genesi e sviluppo storico dell'assioma fino al Decreto di Graziano: MHP(ont) 61. R 1993, Pont. Univ. Gregoriana. 269 p. -- ᴿLaur 36 (1995) 221-5 (Y. *Spiteris*).

a023 *Varella* Evangelia A., SYNESIOS von Ptolemais und die Christianisierung der griechischen Alchemie: Kler 24 (1992) 311-321.

a024 **Watts** Dorothy, Christians and pagans in Roman Britain 1991 → 9,12903: ᴿChH 64 (1995) 256-8 (F.W. *Norris*).

a025 **Williams** Stephen, *Friell* Gerard, Theodosius; the Empire at bay. L 1994, Batsford. 238 p.; 19 pl.; 4 maps. $ 30. -- ᴿGaR 42 (1995) 239s (T. *Wiedemann*).

a026 **Wipszycka** Ewa, ᴾ *Kościół* .. The Church in the late antique world (4th-5th c.). Wsz 1994, PIW. 414 p., 44 pl. -- ᴿCLB 71,1 (1995) 37 (K. *Stebnicka*).

a027 **Wischmeyer** W., Von Golgatha zum Ponte Molle [= Milvio]. Gö 1992. Vandenhoeck & R. 258 p. -- ᴿR(ech)SR 83 (1995) 639s (P. *Vallin*).

XVIII. Archaeologia terrae biblicae

T1.1 **General biblical-area archeologies**

a028 *Anderson* Bernhard W. and 13 other experts on 'What is biblical archaeology's greatest achievement / failure / challenge ?': BArR 21,3 (20th anniversary 1995) 24-35 [49-53, selection from letters of readers and volunteers on 'How BAR chsnged my life'].

a029 ᴱ**Ben-Tor** Amnon, The archaeology of ancient Israel 1993 → 9,12910: ᴿA(ndr)USS 33 (1995) 290-2 (M.G. *Hasel*).

a030 **Biran** Avraham, *Aviram* Joseph, Biblical archaeology today 1990/3 → 9.555; 10,11485*: ᴿOLZ 90 (1995) 522-9 (Gunnar *Lehmann*); RB 102 (1995) 132-5 (tit.pp.).

a031 *Bunimovitz* Shlomo, How mute stones speak; interpreting what we dig up: BArR 21,2 (1995) 58-67 . 96.

a032 ᴱ**Charlesworth** J.H., *Weaver* W.P., What has archaeology to do with faith ? 1990/2 → 8.705; 10,11488*: ᴿBA 57 (1994) 181s (G.L. *Johnson*).

a033 *Conrad* Diethelm, Biblische Archäologie heute: VF 40 (1995) 51-74 [NTAb 40, p.93].

a034 *a) Coogan* Michael D., Ten great[est] finds [1. Gilgamesh; 2. Beni Hasan; 3. Gezer High Place; 4. Megiddo ivory Canaanites; . . 6. Gibeon pit; .. 9. Masada; 10. Madaba map]: BArR 21,3 (20th anniversary 1995) 36-47. *b) Lehmann* Manfred R., in a reader's letter cogently proposes ten entirely different except for the silver scroll of Num 6,24s (his N° 10; the others:) 1. Rosetta stone; 2, Hammurabi Code; 3. Mesha Stele. 4. Amarna Tablets; 5. Elephantine papyri; 6. Ras Shamra tablets; 7. Cairo Genizah; 8. Dead Sea Scrolls; 9. Dan 'house of David' [mostly long inscriptional material as distinct from the mostly 'realia' of Coogan: BArR 21 (1995) 16 . 18.

a035 *Cullen* Tracey , Women in archaeology; perils and progress [ᴱCLAASSEN Cheryl 1994; NELSON Margaret C., *al.,* Equity issues 1994]: Antiquity 69 (1995) 1042-5.

a036 **Deichmann** F.W.,, Archeologia cristiana [Einführung 1983, updated and illustrated],ᵀ: StArch 63. R 1993, Bretschneider. 355 p.; 194 fig. -- ᴿAevum 49 (1995) 288s (M. *Sannazaro*); CLR 45 (1995) 392s (N. *Christie*).

a037 *Dever* William G., The death of a discipline [U.S. scientific archeology; his very successful Arizona Univ. department will not be continued at his retirement]: BArR 21,5 (1995) 50-55 . 70.

a038 **Dever** William G., Recent archaeological discoveries and biblical research 1990 → 6,b908 ... 8,d438: ᴿJQR 85 (1994s) 464-6 (Lynn *Tatum*).

a039 **Diakonoff** I.M, Early antiquity, ᵀ*Kirjanov* Alexander. Ch 1991, Univ. $ 50. 0-226-14465-8. -- ᴿAJA 99 (1995) 360s (B.R. *Foster*).

a040 **Elsner** John, *Cardinal* Roger. The cultures of collecting. L 1994, Reaktion. viii-312 p.; 50 pl. £ 11. 0-048462-51-5. -- ᴿAntiquity 69 (1995) 624s (P. *Brears*).

a041 Excavation opportunities for volunteers: BArR 21,1 (1995) 34-49 . 56s . chart 46-49.

a042 **Finegan** Jack, The archaeology of the NT² 1992 → 9,12916*; 10,11495: ᴿBA 58 (1995) 55s (J. *McRay*)

a043 **Free** Joseph P., ᴱ*Vos* Howard, Archaeology and Bible history 1992 → 8.d443: ᴿBA 57 (1994) 182s (G. D. *Pratico*).

a044 *Friesen* Steven J., Revelation, realia, and religion; archaeology in the interpretation of the Apocalypse: HThR 88 (1995) 291-314.

a045 **Fritz** Volkmar, An introduction to biblical archaeology [1985], ᵀ with updated bibliographies 1994 → 10,11496: ᴿBArR 21,4 (1995) 10 (K.N. *Schoville*, also on RAST W.E. 1992); ET 106 (1994s) 22 (C.S. *Rodd*, amid 20 other Sheffield titles).

a046 *Gill* David W,J., Archaeology on the world wide web [Internet]: Antiquity 69 (1995) 626-630.

a047 **González Echegaray** Joaquín, Arqueología y evangelios 1994 → 10,11500: ᴿCTom 122 (1995) 417s (J.L. *Espinel*); EstTrin 28 (1994) 441s (X. *Pikaza*).

a048 **Greene** Kevin, Archaeology, an introduction; the history, principles and methods of modern archaeology²ʳᵉᵛ ['1983]. L 1993, Batsford. 190 p. 96 fig. £ 15. 0-7134-3646-8. -- ᴿAnCL 64 (1995) 504s (P. *Leman*).

a049 **Harris** Roberta L., The [excavated] world of the Bible. L 1995, Thames & H. 192 p., ill. 0-500-05073-2 [NTAb 40, p.378; ThD 42,272].

a050 **Henke** Winfried, *Rothe* Hartmut, Paläoanthropologie. B 1994, Springer. 699 p.; 327 fig. -- ᴿBo(nn)J 195 (1995) 621-5 (A. *Czarnetzki*).

a051 **Hodder** Ian, Theory and practice in archaeology [7 inedita + 12 reprints]. NY 1992, Routledge. xii-285 p.; 24 fig. $ 53. 0-415-065208. -- ᴿAJA 99 (1995) 151 (M. *Fotiadis*).

a052 *Hodder* Ian, Symbolic and cognitive studies in archaeology [GARDIN J. & PEEBLES C, 1992]: Semiotica 107 (1995) 81-88

a053 **Kokkinidou** Dimitra, *Nikolaidou* Marianna, ᴳ Archeology and the social identity of gender (*koinōnikē tautotēta tou phylou*); approaches to Aegean prehistory, Thessaloniki 1993, Banias. 163 p.; 27 fig. -- ᴿAJA 99 (1995) 738s (D.C. *Haggis*).

a054 ᴱ**Levy** Thomas E., The archaeology of society in the Holy Land. L 1995, Leicester Univ. xvi-224 p. £ 60. 0-7185-1388-6

a055 *Levy* Thomas E., From camels to computers; a short history of archaeological method: BArR 21,4 (1995) 44-51 . 64.

a056 *McGlade* James, Archaeology and the ecodynamics of human-modified landscapes: Antiquity 69 (1995) 113-132; 6 fig.

a057 *Mann* Alan, Modern human origins; evidence from the Near East: Paléor 21,2 (1995) 35-46; franç, 35s.

a058 *Miller* J. Maxwell, The Ancient Near East and archaeology: → 201, ᶠTUCKER G., OT Interpretation 1995, 245-260.

a059 **Moorey** P.R.S., A century of biblical archaeology 1991 → 9,12928; 10,11507: ᴿJAOS 115 (1995) 720s (J.D. *Seger*); PerspSCF 47 (1995) 136s (E.O. *Bowser*).

a060 **Moscati** Sabatino, Dove va l'archeologia ? T 1995, SEI. 278 p. Lᵐ 40 [parte in Archeo 129 (1995) 38-41]. 88-05-05449-6.

a061 **Moscati** Sabatino (→ 298), Luci sul Mediterraneo; dai manoscritti del Mar Morto ai Cartaginesi in Italia; tre millenni di vicende storiche, di concezioni religiose, di creazioni artistiche alla luce dell'archeologia. R 1995, Quasar. I. xvi-408 p.; 112 pl.; II. p. 409-752.; pl. 113-188. 88-7140-075-5 (entrambi).

a062 **Muensterberger** Werner, Collecting; an unruly passion; psychological perspectives. Princeton 1994, Univ. xii-295 p.; 12 pl. $25. 0-691-03361-7. -- ᴿAntiquity 69 (1995) 625s (P. *Brears*).

a063 *a) Olivier* J.P.J., The dawn of biblical archaeology; -- *b) Pienaar* D.N., A critical evaluation of certain leading concepts in biblical archaeology: JNWSL 16 (1990) 131-140 / 141-151 [< OTA 19, p.198s].

a064 **Rast** Walter E., Through the ages in Palestinian archaeology 1992 → 8,d471; 10,11508*: ᴿBA 57 (1994) 60 (J.C. *Moyer*).

a065 **Renfrew** Colin, The roots of ethnicity; archaeology, genetics, and the origins of Europe. R 1993, Unione/Arte. 68 p., 3 fig. Lᵐ 16. -- ᴿAJA 99 (1995) 359s (P. *Bogucki*).

a066 ᴱ**Renfrew** Colin, *Zubrow* Ezra B.W., The ancient mind; elements of cognitive archaeology: NewDir, 1994; £35; pa. £15: ᴿAntiquity 69 (1995) 614-7 (S. *Shennan*).

a067 *Routledge* Bruce, 'For the sake of argument'; reflections on the structure of argumentation in Syro-Palestinian archaeology: PEQ 127 (1995) 41-49.

a068 **Schnapp** Alain, La conquête du passé; aux origines de l'archéologie 1993 → 10,11511: ᴿAntiquity 69 (1995) 1031 (C. *Broodbank:* wonderful; English awaited); *TopO 4 (1994) 223-230 (A. *Farnoux*).

a069 *Schwank* Benedikt, Wenn Steine zu reden beginnen; Archäologie zum Verständnis des Neuen Testaments: BiKi 50 (1995) 40-47; 3 fig. [NTAb 40,p.97].

a070 ᴱ**Small** David B., Methods in the Mediterranean; historical and archaeological views on texts and archaeology: MNEM.s 135. Lei 1995, Brill. [vi-] 294 p.; bibliog. 274-292. 90-04-09581-0.

a071 ᴱ**Stern** Ephraim, The new encyclopedia of archaeological excavations in the Holy Land [¹1975-8] 1993 → 9,12937: ᴿBA 57 (1994) 177-9 (D.H. *Wimmer*); *CritRR 7 (1994) 25-41 (P.J. *King*); JRAS (1994) 325-331 (G.S.P. *Freeman-Grenville*); RestQ 37 (1995) 118s (D.W. *Manor*).

a072 *Sweek* Joel, The monuments, the *Babel-Bibel-Streit* and responses to historical criticism: → 4, ᶠAHLSTRÖM G., Pitcher; JSOT.s 190 (1995) 401-419.

a073 **Tilley** Christopher, A phenomenology of landscape; places, paths and monuments. Ox/Providence 1994, Berg. vii-221 p.; 73 fig. £ 30. 0-85496-919-5. -- ᴿAntiquity 69 (1995) 1040-2 (A. *Fleming*, also on his collection Interpretative archaeology 1993).

a074 **Wilham** Larry, The Negev project [a novel about violence, sale of antiquities, and 'H.S.']: ᴿBArR 21,3 (1995) 6 . 8 (Linda *Bayer:* world-roaming; good].

a075 ᴱYoffee Norman, *Sherratt* Andrew, Archaeological theory; who sets the agenda ?; NewDir. C 1995, Univ. ix-139 p. 0-521-44958-8.

a076 **Zanini** Enrico, Introduzione all'archeologia bizantina. R 1994, Nuova Italia Scientifica. 274 p.; 82 fig.; 43 fot. Lᵐ 38. -- ᴿArcheo 10,121 (1995) 126s (D. *Mazzoleni*);VetChr 32 (1995) 233s (Filomena *d'Aloia*).

т1.2 **Musea, organismi, exploratores**

a077 AIA: The 96th annual meeting of the Archaeological Institute of America [Atlanta, 27-30 December 1994: some 250 summaries): AJA 99 (1995) 303-356; index 356-8.

a078 Anniversary meeting (etc.): JRAS (1995) 477-482 (-499).

a079 *Bianchi* Robert S., Splendors of ancient Egypt, from the Egyptian museum, Cairo. L c. 1995, Booth-Clibborn. 224 p. 1-873968-91-4.

a080 Bible lands museum, Jerusalem; guide to the collections. J 1992, Sirkis. 128 p. 965-387-031-9 [*OIAc 11,14].

a081 **Bongioanni** Alessandro, *Grazzi* Riccardo, Torino, l'Egitto e l'Oriente fra storia e leggenda; Le Radici. T 1994, Manzoni. xii-173 p.; ill. 88-86142-08-0 [*OIAc 11,15].

a082 ᴱ**Brier** Bob, Egyptomania; Hillwood Art Museum exposition 1994. Brookville NY, Long Island Univ. 56 p,l 24 fig.; 8 color. pl. 0-933699-26-0 [*OIAc 11,1994].

a083 *Buranelli* Francesco, Gli Etruschi in Vaticano: Archeo 124 (1995) 98-105.

a084 **Buschhausen** Helmut, *al.*, Der Lebenskreis der Kopten; Dokumente, Textilien, Funde, Ausgrabungen; Katalog der Ausstellung Wien Nationalbibliothek: Papyr.Rainer NF 28. W 1995. Hollinek. xx-308 p.; ill.

a085 **Crowfoot-Payne** C.R. Joan, Catalogue of the predynastic Egyptian collection in the Ashmolean museum. Ox 1990, Clarendon. -- ᴿDiscEg 33 (1995) 157-9 (Béatrix *Midant-Reynes*).

a086 *Cuomo Di Caprio* Ninina [... il suo libro simpatico 'La galleria dei falsi; dal vasaio al mercato di antiquariato' (R 1992 → 10,12959 ha fatto piangere tante persone] Vero o falso ? ArVi 14,54 (1995) 60-67.

a087 ᴱ**Curtis** J.E., *Reade* J.E., Art and empire; treasures from Assyria in the British Museum. NY 1995, Metropolitan Museum of Art. 224 p. 0-87099-738-6.

a088 **Dondin-Payre** Monique. *a)* La Commission d'exploration scientifique d'Algérie, une héritière méconnue de la Commission d'Égypte; *b)* La réussite de l'archéologie romaine au sein de la Commission d'exploration scientifique d'Algérie: AIBL.m 14s. P 1995, de Boccard. 142 p. / 166 p.

a089 From the lands of the Scythians; ancient treaures from the museums of the U.S.S.R. 3000 BC - 100 BC. NY c.1990, Met. 160 p., 32 color. pl.

a090 **Fuchs** Michaela, Römische Idealplastik; Glyptothek München, Katalog der Skulpturen. Mü 1992, Beck. viii-258 p.; 230 fig. -- ᴿBo(nn)J 195 (1995) 712-9 (A. *Linfert*).

a091 *a) Geoffroy* Bérénice, Égyptomania; -- *b) Pasquier* Alain, La sculpture cycladique: Archéologia 299 (1994) 32-37 / 44-51.

a092 *a) Gewertz* Ken, Giza exhibit opens; -- *b)* [ᴱ*Greene* J.A.] Cypriot collection added to Museum's holdings: Harvard Semitic Museum News 1,1 (1995) 1.3.7 / 2.

a093 [*a) Gibson* -., *McMahon* -., fasc. 1] *b) Baker* H.D., *al.*, fasc.2, Lost heritage; antiquities stolen from Iraq's regional museums. L 1993, British School of Archaeology in Iraq, viii-153 p.; ill. 0-903472-14-7 [*OIAc 11,12].

a094 ᴱ*Gitin* Seymour, Project descriptions of [forty Jerusalem Albright Institute] appointees 1994-5: BASOR 298 (1995) 69-78.

a095 **Guidotti** Maria Cristina,, Museo egizio di Firenze; vasi dall'epoca predinastica al nuovo regno: Ministero beni culturali, R 1991, Ist. Poligrafico. x-361 p.; ill.; foldout. 88-240-0177-7 [*OIAc 11,24].

a096 [E]**Guidotti** Maria Cristina, *Leospo* Enrichetta, La collezione egizia. Como 1994, Civico Museo Archeologico. 119 p. 88-85680-03-8.

a097 *Gyselen* Rika, Quelques manifestations autour de la culture iranienne [expositions 1993, Bruxelles & Hamburg; symposium numismatique, Tübingen 1994]: StIr 23 (1994) 141-4.

a098 [E]**Harper** Prudence O., *al.*, Assyrian origins; discoveries at Ashur on the Tigris; antiquities in the Vorderasiatisches Museum, Berlin. NY 1995, Metropolitan Musuem of Art. 142 p.; bibliog. 130-140. 0-87099-743-2.

a099 **Haynes** Joyce L., Nubia; ancient kingdoms of Africa: permanent exhibition. Boston 1992, Museum of Fine Arts. 64 p.; 61 fig. 0-87846-362-3. -- [R]BiOr 52 (1995) 390s (F.W. *Hinkel*).

a100 **Humbert** Jean-Marcel, *Pantazzi* Michael, *Ziegler* Christiane, Egyptomania; Egypt in western art 1730-1930 [Canada National Museum and Louvre exhibition]. P/Ottawa 1994. 607 p.; 74l (colour.) fig. $ 50 pa. 0-88884-636-3. -- [R]Antiquity 69 (1995) 172 (C. *Broodbank*).

a101 **Hutchinson** T.P., Version 2 (history and archaeology) of Essentials of statistical methods. Adelaide 1993, Rumsby. xii-152 p. 0-646-15653-5. -- [R]AnCL 64 (1995) 505 (J.-L. *Slachmuylder*).

a102 *Isman* Fabio, I tesori restituiti ... nuova legislazione internazionale [auspicata]: Archeo 10,119 (1995) 108-113.

a103 Jüdische Kultur in Museen und Ausstellungen bis 1938: Wiener Jahrbuch für Jüdische Geschichte, Kultur und Museumswesen 1 (1994s). W 1995, Brandstätter. 200 p. -- [R]FrRu 2 (1995) 296s (H.I. *Schmelzer*).

a104 **King** Laurence, The Israel Museum, Jerusalem. L 1995, King. 240 p. 1-85669-063-6.

a105 [E]**Langdon** Susan, From pasture to polis; art in the age of Homer; exhibition Columbia MO 1993, Berkeley & CM 1994. Columbia 1993, Univ. Missouri. xiii-250 p.; ill.

a106 *Le Rider* Georges / *Mollat de Jourdin* Michel / *Caquot* André, Rapport sur l'École d'Athènes / Rome / Jérusalem: CRAI (1995) 635-8 / 831-852 / 873s.

a107 [E]**Lewin** Irene, The Israel Museum, Jerusalem. NY 1995, Vendôme. 240 p. $ 65. 0-86565-960-5 [ThD 42,371].

a108 **Maass** Michael, *Fabricius* Johanna, Antike Kulturen ... Führer. Karlsruhe 1995, Badisches Landesmuseum. 171 p.

a109 **Manzella** Ivan D., Index inscriptionum Musei Vaticani I. Ambulacrum iulianum sive 'galleria lapidaria': Inscriptiones Sanctae Sedis 1. Vaticano 1995, Libreria. 272 p.

a110 [E]**Mattila** Toimittaja R., Nineveh, 612 BC; the glory and fall of the Assyrian Empire; catalogue of the 10th anniversary exhibition of the Neo-Assyrian text corpus project. Helsinki 1995, Univ. 215 p. 951-570-257-7.

a111 *Mura Sommella* Anna, *al.*, I musei capitolini: Archeo 123 (1995) 48-99.

a112 *Nista* Lelia, I Dioscuri a Roma [mostra museo Massimo-Terme]: Archeo 10,119 (1995) 8-17.

a113 Paris, Petit Palais: À l'ombre de Vésuve, exposition nov. 1995: MoBi 95 (1995) 49-55; → 92,53-59, Carthage.

a114 *Pelletier-Hornby* Paulette, A l'ombre du Vésuve [Pompée, Herculanum ... 80 objets, Exposition du Musée du Petit Palais]: Archéologia 319 (1995) 28-37 (-47).

a115 **Ploug** Gunhild, Catalogue of the Palmyrene sculptures. K 1995, Ny Carlsberg

Glyptotek. 269 p.; ill.

a116 ᴱ**Renda** Günsel, Woman in Anatolia; 9000 years of the Anatolian woman [Topkapì exposition 1993s]. İstanbul 1993, Ministry of Culture. 303 p.; ill. 978-17-1186-X [*OIAc 11,38].

a117 ᴱ**Rimon** Ofra, 'Purity broke out in Israel' (Tractate Shabbat 13b); stone vessels in the late Second Temple period: Hecht Museum Catalog 9. Haifa 1994, Univ. 63* p. Eng.; ᴴ 36 [*OIAc 11,39]

a118 **Roccati** Alessandro, Museo egizio Torino (⁴ristampa): Itinerari NS 1. R 1995, Ist. Poligrafico. 109 p. 88-240-3935-9.

a119 *Schmaltz* Bernhard, 'Aspectus' und 'effectus' -- Hermogenes und VITRUV [foldout fig. 1, 'Computergestützte Rekonstruktion des Artemisions in Magnesia' mit 13 Statuen]: MDAI-R 102 (1995) 133-140.

a120 ᴱ**Shanks** Hershel, In the Temple of Solomon and the Tomb of Caiaphas [exhibit for ASOR & SBL 1993]. Wsh 1993, Biblical Archaeology Soc. 47 p.; ill. 1-880317-11-7 [*OIAc 11,41].

a121 **Török** László, Coptic antiquities, Budapest Museum of Fine Arts. R 1993, Bretschneider. I. Sculpture, 74 p., cvi pl.; III. Textiles. 91 p., xcvi (color.) pl. 88-7062-805-1.

a122 **Toker** Ayse, ᴱ*Öztürk* Jean, Metal vessels, Museum of ancient civilizations. Ankara 1992, Directorate of Monuments. 225 p.; ill.

a123 *Vassilika* Eleni, Egyptian antiquities accessioned in 1993 by museums in the United Kingdom: JEA 81 (1995) 201-3.

a124 **Williams** Dyfri, *Ogden* Jack, Greek gold, jewellery of the classical world; exhibition. L 1994, British Museum. 256 p.; ill.

a125 *Zanini* Enrico, Byzantium, in mostra a Londra [British Museum; 250 opere]: Archeo 10,122 (1995) 96-105.

T1.3 *Methodi* -- **Science in archeology**

a126 *Aczel* Amir D., Improved radiocarbon age estimation using the bootstrap [non-parametric computer-intensive technique]: Radiocarbon 37,3 (1995) 845-9; 2 fig.

a127 **Bel** James A., Reconstructing prehistory; scientific method in archaeology. Ph 1994, Temple Univ. xii-327 p. 1-56639-160-1. -- ᴿAJA 99 (1995) 756s (P.N. *Kardulias*).

a128 **Biers** William R., *al.*, Lost scents; investigation of Corinthian 'plastic' vases by gas chromatography -- mass spectrometry: Masca 11. Ph 1994, Univ. Museum. 1x-59 p.; 17 fig. 1048-5325.

a129 *Bildgen* Pierre, *Gilg* Jean-Paul, L'apport de l'imagerie satellitaire à l'étude des paysages antiques, perspectives et méthodes; le cas de la Syrie du nord; Syria 72 (1995) 1-21; 9 (color.) fig.

a130 *Bossière* Gérard, *Moguedet* Gérard, Étude chimico-minéralogique de céramiques étrusco-corinthiennes d'Étrurie méridionale: RÉA 97 (1995) 5-26; IV pl., Eng. 5.

a131 *Evin* Jacques, Possibilité et nécessité de la calibration des datations C-14 de l'archéologie du Proche-Orient: Paléor 21,1 (1995) 5-16; 8 fig.; Eng. 5

a132 *Heinemann* Olliver, Die 'Lade' aus Akazienholz -- ägyptische Wurzeln eines israelitischen Kultobjekts ? : BN(otiz) 80 (1995) 32-40.

a133 *Leach* Jeff D., *Mauldin* Raymond P., Additional comments on blood residue analysis in archaeology: Antiquity 69 (1995) 1020-2.

a134   *McGovern* Patrick E., *al.*, Science in archaeology; a review [... remote sensing, accelerator mass spectrometry, xeroradiographic imaging, immunochemistry, palaeo-DNA ..]: AJA 99 (1995) 79-142; 55 fig.

a135 *Shanks* Hershel, *a)* New Carbon-14 results leave room for debate; -- *b)* Did a letter to BAR end a Cornell graduate student's [Greg DOUDNA's] career?: BArR 21,4 (1995) 61 / 60s.

T1.4   *Exploratores* -- **Excavators, pioneers**

a136 *Amandry* Pierre, Notice sur la vie et travaux de Georges DAUX: CRAI (1995) 886-904; portr.

a137 ASHMOLE Bernard, 1894-1988, an autobiography. Ox 1994, Oxbow. xvii-236 p.

a138 **Baruffa** Antonio, G.B. DE ROSSI, l'archeologo esploratore delle Catacombe 1994 → 10,11549; L^m 18: ^RArcheo 10,119 (1995)124s (D. *Mazzoleni*); SMSR 60 (1994) 157s (Myla *Perraymond*).

a139 *a) Bečka Jiři*, Alois MUSIL und die Gründung des Orientalischen Institutes in Prag: ArOr 63 (1995) 431-4; -- *b) Segert* Stanislav, Alois Musil -- Bible scholar: ArOr 63 (1995) 401-9 / 393-400.

a140 *Bosworth* C. Edmund, *a)* E[dward] G. BROWNE's A year amongst the Persians: Iran 33 (1995) 115-122; -- *b)* The Hon. George Nathaniel CURZON's Travels in Russian Central Asia and Persia: Iran 31 (1993) 127-137.

a141 **Bowden** Mark, H.L.F. PITT-RIVERS, life and archaeological work 1991 → 10,11550*: ^RJField 21 (1994) 249-251 (N. *Hammond*).

a143 CROSS Frank M.: [^EShanks Hershel], Conversations with a Bible scholar [< BiRe]. Wsh 1994, Biblical Archaeology Soc. 186 p. 1-880317-18-4 [ThD 43,162].

a144 *Davis* Thomas W., ALBRIGHT & archaeology; the search for realia: *ABW 3,1 (1995) 42-50.

a145 **Drower** M.S., Flinders PETRIE; a life in archaeology². 1995. -- ^EBuCanadMesop 30 (1995) 41s (S. C. *Brown*).

a146 ^EHarris David R., The archaeology of V. Gordon CHILDE: contemporary perspectives. Ch 1994, Univ. xii-148 p.; 11 pl. $ 41. 0-226-31759-5. -- ^RJField 22 (1995) 497-9 (C. *Runnels*).

a147 -- **Peace** William J., The enigmatic career of Vere Gordon CHILDE, a peculiar and individual manifestation of the human spirit: diss. Columbia, ^DNewman Katherine. NY 1992. 348 p. 94-21386. -- DissA 56 (1995s) p. 621.

a148 **James** T., H.CARTER .. Tutankhamun [→ b550 infra] 1992 → 8,d546: ^RBiOr 52 (1995) 306s (H.A. *Schlögl*).

a149 *Kettel* Jeannot, Un portrait de CHAMPOLLION par Carl Vogel VON VOGELSTEIN: → 10,145, ^FWINTER E., Aspekte 1994, 183-9.

a150 **Kettel** Jeannot, Jean-François CHAMPOLLION le jeune 1990 → 6,d37; 8,d548: ^RCÉg 70 (1995) 133s (J.-C. *Degardin*).

a151 ^EKytzler Bernhard. *al.*, Eduard NORDEN [1868-1941], ein deutscher Gelehrter jüdischer Herkunft: Palingenesia 49. Stu 1994, Steiner. 239 p.; 8 pl.

a152 *MacEnroe* John, Sir Arthur EVANS and Edwardian archaeology: CLB 71,1 (1995) 3-18.

a153 ^EMacGregor Arthur, Sir Hans SLOANE; collector, scientist, antiquary; founding father of the British Musuem. L 1994, British Museum. 308; 115 fig.; 40 colour.pl. £ 50. 0-7141-2085-5. -- ^RAntiquity 69 (1995) 174 (C. *Broodbank*).

a154 **Männchen** Julia, Gustaf DALMAN als Palästinawissenschaftler [Diss. 1992]: AbhDPV

9/2. Wsb 1993, Harrassowitz. 3-447-03425-4 → 9,13015: ᴿThLZ 120 (1995) 227s (C.G. den *Hertog*).

a155 **Marchand** Suzanne L., Archaeology and cultural politics in Germany, 1800-1965 [diss. Chicago 1992]. 608 p. - *OIAc 11,32.

a156 *Mattingly* Gerald L., Searching for benchmarks in the biblical world; the development of Joseph A. CALLAWAY as field archaeologist: BA 58 (1995) 14-25; ill.

a157 *Mattingly* Gerald, Père LAGRANGE and the role of archaeology in the establishment of the École Biblique in 1890: *ABW 1,1 (Shafter CA 1991) 38-45.

a158 *Metzger* Henri, Notice sur la vie et les travaux d'Emmanuel LAROCHE (1914-1991): CRAI (1995) 362-371: portr.

a159 ᴱNaff Thomas, Paths to the Middle East; ten scholars look back. Albany 1993, SUNY. xix-360 p. $ 17. -- ᴿJRAS (1995) 93s (C.E. *Bosworth*).

NORDEN F.L. → **Buhl** M. b494 infra.

a160 **Parslow** Christopher C., Rediscovering antiquity; Karl WEBER [1712-1784] and the excavation of Herculaneum, Pompeii, and Stabiae. C 1995, Univ. xx-394 p.; bibliog. 374-382. 0-521-47150-8

a161 *Pernigotti* Sergio, I Faraoni a colori; BELZONI Giovanni Battista, splendide tavole riedite: Archeo 9.116 (1994) 8-19.

a162 *a) Pisini* Maurus, Ioannes Baptista DE ROSSI archaeologiae christianae conditor; - *b) Ippolito* Antoniola, De antiquae Syracusarum urbis situ ac conformazione: Latinitas 43 (Vaticanum 1995) 17-20 / 11-16.

a163 *Preissler* Hölger, Die Anfänge der Deutschen Morgenländischen Gesellschaft: ZDMG 145 (1995) 241-327.

a164 *Quaegebeur* Jan,*Rammant-Peeters* Agnes, Un relief memphite d'époque ptolemaïque de l'héritage de William Fox TALBOT [pionier photographe c.1846]; GöMisz 148 (1995)71-88.

a165 ᴱSaint-Roch Patrick, Correspondance de Giovanni Battista DE ROSSI et de Louis DUCHESNE, 1873-1874: CEFR 205. R 1995, École Française. 729 p.

a166 *Schwarz* Stephanie. Ausgegrenzt ? Frauen in der Ägyptologie des 19. und 20. Jahrhunderts; GöMisz 138 (1994) 93-111.

a167 SEETZEN; *a) Olivier* Johannes J.P., Ulrich Jasper Seetzen, a pioneer in need of recognition; -- *b) Weippert* Helga, Unterwegs nach Afrika, U.J. Seetzen (1767-1811) : → 48, ᶠDONNER, H., Meilenstein: ÄAT 30 (1995) 164-171 / 324-332.

a168 **Silberman** Neil A., A prophet from amongst you ... YADIN → 9,13025; 10,11567*: ᴿArch 47,2 (CM 1994) 59-61 (W.G. *Dever*).

a169 **Traill** David A., SCHLIEMANN of Troy; treasure and deceit. L 1995, J. Murray. xiv-365 p. 0-7195-5082-3.

a170 -- *Masson* Olivier, Recherches récentes sur Heinrich SCHLIEMANN: RÉG 108 (1995) 593-600: severe critique of D. TRAILL, who however in the end has to admit 'thanks to his astonishing success, likely to remain the emblematic archaeologist of all time'.

a171 **Tutsch** Claudia, 'Man muss ... ' Zum Bildnis Johann J. WINCKELMANNs [→ a546 infra, POTTS] von Anton von MARON [Diss. Köln 1990]: Winckelmann-Ges, 13. Mainz 1995, von Zabern. 213 p.; 29 pl.

T1.5 *Materiae primae* -- **metals, glass**

a172 *Bartel* Hans-Georg. *Hallof* Jochen, Über den 'oberägyptischen Grünstein' *w'3d-šm'* und die Eigenschaft šm': GöMisz 148 (1995) 23-27.

a173 **Giardino** Claudio, Il Mediterraneo occidentale fra XIV ed VIII secolo a.C.; cerchie minerarie e metallurgiche: BAR-Int 612. Ox 1995, Tempus Reparatum. v-410 p.; bibliog. 345-368. 0-86054-793-0.

a174 *Kurke* Leslie, HERODOTUS and the language of metals: Helios 22,1 (1995) 36-64.

---

a175 *Aes,* BRONZE: *Jacobson* D.M., *Weitzman* M.P., Black bronze and the 'Corinthian alloy': CQ 45 (1995) 580-3.

a176 -- [E]**Pirzio Biroli Stefanelli** Lucia, Il bronzo dei Romani 1990 → 7,b688 ... 10,11573: [R]Bo(nn)J 195 (1995) 725-7 (Ulla *Kreilinger*).

a177 AMBER: *Beck* Kurt W. & Lily Y., Analysis and provenience of Minoan and Mycenaean amber, V. Pylos and Messenia: GRBS 36 (1995) 119-136; 5 fig.

a178 *Argentum,* SILVER: *Sturm* T., *kaspum ammurum,* ein Begriff der Silbermetallurgie in den Kültepe-Texten: UF 27 ([F]DIETRICH 60. Gb. 1995) 487-503.

a179 -- *Pierre* Geneviève, *Menu* Michel, À propos de la composition de l'argent du trésor de Tod: BSFE 130 (1994) 18-45.

a180 *Aurum,* GOLD: *Camporeale* Giovannangelo, Gli Etruschi e l'oro secondo gli scrittori antichi: AtenR 39 (1994) 16-25.

a181 BASALT: *Harrell* James A., *Bown* Thomas M., An Old Kingdom basalt quarry at Widan al-Faras and the quarry road to Lake Moeris: JA(m)RCE(g) 32 (1995) 71-91; 22 fig.; maps.

a182 *Ebur,* IVORY: **Muscarella** Oscar W., The catalogue of ivories from Hasanlu, Iran: Mg 40. Ph 1980, Univ. Museum. xi=231 p.

a183 *Saxum,* STONE: *Puttert* T. de, *Karlshausen* C., Provenance du calcaire de l'architecture thoutmoside à Thèbes: GöMisz(Äg) 142 (1994) 103-7: Gebelein.

a184 *Vitrum,* GLASS: *Brill* Robert H., Laboratory stdies of some glasses from Vergina: JGS 36 (1994) 11-23; 11 fig.

a185 -- *Lightfoot* C.S., Some examples of ancient [50 BC - 50 AD] cast and ribbed bowls in Turkey [15 in Antalya museum]: JGS 35 (1993) 22-38; 56 fig.

a186 -- *Lierke* Rosemarie, Vasa diatreta; ein kritischer Exkurs über die Glasschneidekunst der Römer: AW(elt) 26 (1995) 42-59; 44 fig.; -- 251-269; 35 fig.

a187 -- *Lilyquist* C., *Brill* R.H., Studies in early Egyptian glass 1993 → 9,13042; 10,11582; 21 fig.; 32 pl. + 7 color; [R]AfO 42s (1995s) 302s (Irmgard *Hein*) & 303s (B. *Rasch*); OLZ 90 (1995) 488-493 (Birgit *Schlick-Nolte*).

a188 -- **Nicholson** Paul T., Egyptian faience and glass: Eg. 19. Princes Risborough 1993, Shire. 80 p.; 58 fig. 0-7478-0197-5 [*OIAc 11,35].

a189 -- *Wight* Carol B., Mythological beakers [first-century A.D. mold-blown type; 24 objects studied by G. WEINBERG in 1972, plus 17 more]: JGS 36 (1994) 24-55; 29 fig. (some show Hercules, Mercury, Fortuna, 'Winter ').

T1.6 *Silex, os* -- 'Prehistory' flint and bone industries

a190 *Bailey* Geoff, The Balkans in prehistory; the palaeolithic archaeology of Greece and adjacent areas: Antiquity 69 (1995) 19-34; map.

a191 *Barsotti* Gianfranco, Preistoria Giordana: ArVi 14,49 (1995) 42-55.

a192 **Bar-Yosef** Ofer, *Valla* François R., The Natufian culture in the Levant. AA 1992, IntMgPreh. 644 p.; 281 fig. $ 75. 1-879621-03-7. -- [R]*JField 21 (1994) 376s (D.E. *Lieberman*).

a193   *a) Belfer-Cohen* Anna, *Goren-Inbar* Naama, Cognition and communication in the Levantine Lower Palaeolithic; -- *b) Graves* Paul, Flakes and ladders; what the archaeological record cannot tell us about the origins of language: *WorldA 26 ('Communication and language' 1994) 144-157; 3 fig.; map / 158-171.

a194   *Castaldi* Editta, Esegesi d'arte preistorica: SU(rb)SF 65 (1992) 207-226; 7 fig.

a195   **Debénath** A., *Dibble* H.I., Handbook of paleolithic typology, I. Lower and middle paleolithic of Europe. Ph 1994, Univ. Museum. -- [R]BuCanadMesop 29 (1995) 67s (M. *Fortin*).

a196   *Eisele* J.A., *al.*, Survival and detection of blood residue on stone tools: Antiquity 69 (1995) 3646; 1 fig.

a197   **Gopher** A., Arrowheads of the neolithic Levant 1994 → 10,11669: [R]BASOR 297 (1995) 81s (A.H. *Simmons*); BoL (1995) 26 (A.R. *Millard*).

a198   **Held** Steve O., Pleistocene fauna and human remains .. on Cyprus: SIMA 95. Jonsered 1992. Åström. 172 p.; 3 maps. 91-9081-025-7.

a199   **Megarry** Tim, Society in prehistory; the origins of human culture. L 1995, Macmillan. ix-400 p.; bibliog. 356-386. 0-333-31117-5.

a200   **Morell** Virginia, Ancestral passions; the LEAKEY family and the quest for humankind's beginnings. NY 1995, Simon & S. 618 p.; bibliog. 605-617. 0-684-80192-2.

a201   **Olszewski** D.I., *Dibble* H.I., The paleolithic prehistory of the Zagros-Taurus: Museum Mg 83. Ph 1993, Univ. Pennsylvania. -- [R]BuCanadMesop 29 (1995) 67 (M. *Fortin*).

a202   *Quintero* Leslie A., *Wilke* Philip J., Evolution and economic significance of naviform core-and-blade technology in the Southern Levant [... Ghazal]: Paléor 21,1 (1995) 17-33; 9 fig.

a203   **Stringer** Christopher, *Gamble* Clive, In search of the Neanderthals 1993 → 10,11593: [R]*JField 21 (1994) 526-530 (J.J. *Shea*).

a204   **Talaley** Lauren B., Deities. dolls, and devices; neolithic figurines from Franchthi Cave: 9. Bloomington 1993, Indiana Univ. 149 p.; 29 pl. $ 40. 0-253-31981-1. -- [R]*JField 21 (1994) 279-284 (C. *Renfrew*, also on the preceding 8 volumes).

T1.7   **Technologia antiqua**

a205   **Amouretti** Marie-Claire, *Comet* Georges, Hommes et techniques 1993 → 10,11594*: [R]*TopO 4 (1994) 219-222 (P. *Bruneau*).

a206   **Aberbach** Moshe, Labor, crafts and commerce in ancient Israel. J 1994, Magnes. xii-294 p. $ 30. -- [R]CBQ 57 (1995) 755s (P. *Doron*); OTA 18 (1995) p.143 (J.J. *Pilch*); Zion 60 (1995) 105-7 (Z. *Safrai*,[H]).

a207   *Bergamasco* Marco, Le *didaskalikaí* nella ricerca attuale [... gli apprendisti]: Aeg 75 (1995) 95-161 (-167, prospetto dei documenti).

a208   **Bernbeck** Reinhard, Auflösung der häuslichen Produktionsweise; das Beispiel Mesopotamiens [Diss. 1991]: *BBVO 14. B 1994, Reimer. [xii-] 392 p.; Bibliog. 351-386. 3-496-02525-5.

a209   *a) Chernykh* Y.N.,   [R] Ancient mining and smelting and anthropogenic ecological disasters; -- *b) Sallares* Robert,   [R] The ecology of the ancient world; problems and approaches, [T]*Litvinenko* Y.N.; -- *c) Fedeli* Paolo, Man and the environment in the Roman world, [T] *Lyapustinoi* E.V.:   VDI 213 (1995) 110-121: Eng. 121 / 80-102; Eng. 102s / 103-9; Eng. 109s.

a210 **Chevallier** Raymond, Sciences et techniques à Rome; Que sais-je? 2763. P 1993, PUF. 128 p.; ill. 2-13-045538-7. -- ᴿLatomus 54 (1995) 724-7 (J.-M. *Delire*).

a211 ᴱ**Curtis** John, Bronzeworking centers of Western Asia c. 1000-538 B.C. L 1988, Kegan Paul. 342 p. 0-7103-0274-6.

a212 *Dvorjetski* Esti, ᴴ 'Šᵉrifa in Askalon' [not Serapis but 'metal-work', ✓ *ṣārap*], a Talmudic reality in the art of fine metal work in Eretz-Israel in the Roman and Byzantine periods: Tarbiz 63 (1993s) 27-40; Eng. v.

a213 **Fleury** Philippe, La mécanique de VITRUVE. Caen 1993, Univ. 380 p.; 87 fig. F 240. -- ᴿCLR 45 (1995) 141-3 (J.F. *Healy*); RB(elg)PH 73 (1995) 218s (R. *Chevallier*).

a214 *Foxvog* Daniel A., Sumerian brands and branding-irons: ZA(ssyr) 85 (1995) 1-7.

a215 **Hägermann** Dieter, *Schneider* Helmuth, Landbau und Handwerk, 750 v.Chr. bis 1000 n.Chr.: Propyläen Technikgeschichte 1. Fra 1991. 544 p.; 238 fig.; 32 color.pl. -- ᴿTyche 9 (1994) 234 (W. *Scheidel*).

a215* **Hassan** Ahmad Y. al-, *Hill* Donald R., Islamic technology; an illustrated history: Unesco, Paris. C 1993, Univ. xvi-304 p.; ill. £ 15. -- ᴿBiOr 483s (J.D. *North*).

a216 *Krejčí* Jaromír. Eine Lehmziegelwerkstatt aus dem Alten Reich in Abusir: GöMisz 148 (1995) 63s + 3 fig.

a217 *Krischer* Tilman, Die Rolle der Magna Graecia in der Geschichte der Mechanik: AntAb 41 (1995) 60-71.

a218 *Landels* J.G., Engineering in the ancient world. Berkeley 1978, Univ. California. 224 p. 0-520-03429-5.

a219 ᴱ**Masters** Robert G., The artisans of ancient Egypt and their tools; exposition 1991. Fullerton 1991, California State Univ. Museum of Anthropology. 44 p.; ill. [*OIAc 11,32]

a220 **Moorey** P.R.S., Ancient Mesopotamian materials and industries; the archaeological evidence. Ox 1994, UP. xxiii-414 p.; ill. $ 105. 0-19-814921-2 [RStR 22,190, D.I. *Owen*].

a221 **Müller-Karpe** Andreas, Altorientalisches Metallhandwerk: OffaB 75. Neumünster 1994, Wachholtz. 264 p.; 108 fig.; 98 pl. -- ᴿRA(ssyr) 89,1 (1995) 90s (P. *Amiet*).

a222 *Nenna* Marie-Dominique, La verrerie d'époque hellénistique à Delos: JGS 35 (1993) 11-21; 11 fig.; Eng. 21.

a223 *Northover* P., *Evely* D., Towards an appreciation of Minoan metallurgical techniques; information provided by copper alloy tools from the Ashmolean museum, Oxford: AB(rit)SA 90 (1995) 83-105; 4 fig.; pl. 10-13.

a224 *Rehder* J.E., Blowpipes versus bellows in ancient metallurgy: *JField 21 (1994) 345-50.

a225 *Riggans* Walter, Not a blacksmith could be found [1 Sam 13,19]: JBQ 22 (1994) 32-37.

a226 *Sanmartín* Joaquín, Das Handwerk in Ugarit; eine lexikalische Studie: SEpL 12 (1995) 169-190.

a227 **Schürman** Astrid, Griechische Mechanik und antike Gesellschaft; Studien zur staatlichen Förderung einer technischen Wissenschaft: Boethius 17. Stu 1991, Steiner. 348 p. DM 88. -- ᴿHZ 260 (1995) 520 (H. *Schneider*).

a228 **Shepherd** Robert, Ancient mining 1993 → 10,11607: ᴿCLR 45 (1995) 143-5 (D.W. *Gill*).

a229 *Traina* Giusto, La tecnica in Grecia e a Roma: Laterza 'niv ' 749, 1994: ᴿ*QStor 21,41 (1995) 149-156 (C. *Franco*).

a230 **Vickers** M., *Gill* D., Artful crafts; ancient Greek silverware and pottery 1994 → 10,11817: ᴿAntiquity 69 (1995) 619-621 (B. A. *Sparkes*); CLR 45 (1995) 123-6 (J. *Bordman*).

a231 [E]**Wanderer** Jochen, Archäometallurgie; Geschichte der Metallherstellung. Heere 1995, auct. 100 p. 3-927726-31-1.

a232 [E]**Wartke** Rolf-B., Handwerk und Technologie im Alten Orient 1991/4 → 10.11608*: [R]AJA 99 (1995) 753 (J.D. *Muhly*).

a233 *White* K.D., The base mechanic arts → 9,520, Hellenistic 1988/93, 211-220.

T1.8   **Architectura**

a234 **Adam** Jean-Pierre, Roman building materials and techniques [La construction romaine 1984 [2]1989 → 65,a200 ...7,b649], [T]. L/Bloomington 1994, Batsford/Univ. Indiana. 360 p.; 755 fig. £ 50. 0-7134-7167-0 / 0-253-30124-6. -- [R]Antiquity 69 (1995) 174 (C. *Broodbank*); JField 22 (1995) 400-501 (R.B. *Ulrich*); GaR 42 (1995) 244 (N. *Spivey*).

a235 **Arnold** Dieter, Lexikon der ägyptischen Baukunst. Z 1994, Artemis & W. 303 p.; 290 fig.; 48 color. pl. DM 98. -- [R]WZKM 85 (1995) 268-272.

a236 **Arnold** Dieter, Building in Egypt; pharaonic stone masonry 1991 → 7,b651; 8,d632: [R]JEA 81 (1995) 245-9 (J. *Jacquet*, franç.); JRS 85 (1995) 295s (E. *Thomas*).

a237 **Balty** J. C., Curia ordinis; recherches d'architecture et d'urbanisme antiques sur les curies provinciales du monde romain. Bru 1991, Académie. xxi-656 p., 287 fig. Fb 3000. -- [R]RB(elg)PH 73 (1995) 252-4 (Claire De *Ruyt*: modèle du genre; tant attendu depuis le doctorat 1968).

a238 *a*) *Bietak* Manfred, 'Götterwohnung und Menschenwohnung' -- die Entstehung eines Tempeltyps des Mittleren Reiches aus der zeitgenössischen Wohnarchitektur; ein Vorbericht; -- *b*) *Plas* Dirk van der, Tempel in Ägypten; einige religionsphänomenologische Bemerkungen: → 10,470, Äg. Tempel 1990/2/4, 13-16 + 7 fig. / 239-253.

a239 *Bourgeois* Daniel, Voûtes, coupules et colonnades: Pierre d'Angle 1 (Aix-en-Provence c.1995) [< E(spr)eV 105 (1995) 529 (J. *Daoust*)].

a240 **Bouyer** Louis, Liturgie et architecture [1967 → 8,636], [T]*Gisi* Martha 1993 → 9,13087: [R]RTPh 127 (1995) 191s (B. *Reymond*).

a241 *Brandenburg* Hugo, Kirchenbau und Liturgie; Überlegungen zum Verhältnis von architektonischer Gestalt und Zweckbestimmung des frühchristlichen Kultbaues im 4. und 5. Jh.; → 96, [F]KRAUSE M., Divitiae Aegypti 1995, 36-61 + 8 fig.

a242 *Briend* Jacques, La maison aux temps bibliques: MoBi 91 (1995) 43-5.

a243 *Broshi* Magen, Visionary architecture and town planning in the Dead Sea Scrolls: → 498, Time to prepare 1989/95, 9-22.

a244 **Castel** Corinne, Habitat urbain néo-assyrien et babylonien; IFAPO-BAH 143, 1992 → 9,13090: [R]RA{ssyr} 89,1 (1995) 92s (F. *Braemer*).

a245 **Clarke** John R., The houses of Roman Italy, 100 BC - AD 250; ritual, space and decoration 1991 → 8,d640 ... 10,11613: [R]*ABW 3,1 (1995) 52s (J. *McRay*).

a246 [F]DUNAYEVSKY I., The architecture of ancient Israel, [E]**Kempinski** A., *Reich* R. 1992 → 8,48; 9,13095: [R]BA 57 (1994) 176s (J. *Zorn*); BO 52 (1995) 153-7 (G.R.H. *Wright*).

a247 **Endruweit** Albrecht, Städtischer Wohnbau in Ägypten -- klimagerechte Lehmarchitektur in Amarna 1994 → 10,12730 (T73 infra): [R]WZKM 85 (1995) 265-8 (D. *Eigner*).

a248 **Förtsch** Reinhard, Archäologischer Kommentar zu den Villabriefen des Jüngeren PLINIUS: BeitrHellenSkArchit 12. Mainz 1993, von Zabern. xii-202 p.; 86 pl. -- [R]RB(elg)PH 73 (1995) 255s (P. *Gros*).

a249 *Fritz* V., Eine neue Bauform der Frühbronzezeit in Palästina: →10,80, [F]MAYER-OPIFICIUS R., Beschreiben 1994, 85-89ñ 3 fig.

a250   *Gautier di Confiengo* E., Nota sul valore di alcune dimensioni dell'architettura paleocristiana [il numero 300 (cubiti dell'Anastasis; piedi del Vaticano/Laterano) in greco é T, simbolo anche della Croce]: SBF*LA 45 (1995) 451-479; Eng. 488.

a251 **Green** Richard, *Handley* Eric, Images of the Greek theatre: Classical bookshelf. L 1995, British Museum. 127 p. 0-7141-2207-6.

a252 *Halm-Tisserant* Monique, *Éxō--entòs* -- de l'ambiguïté des portes et des fenêtres dans la peinture de vases grecques: RÉA 97 (1995) 473-490 + XIII pl.; Eng. 473.

a253 *Harrison* Steven, Domestic architecture in Early Helladic II; some observations on the form of non-monumental houses: AB(rit)SA 90 (1995) 23-40; 11 fig.

a254 **Heisel** Joachim P., Antike Bauzeichnungen. Da 1993, Wiss. 279 p., 105 fig.; 16 pl. — ᴿBo(nn)J 195 (1995) 710-2 (H. *Knell*).

a255 *a) Hellmann* Marie Christine, La maison grecque; les sources épigraphiques; -- *b) Husson* Geneviève, Les constructions isolées dans la campagne égyptienne d'après les papyrus grecs: *TopO 4 (1994) 131-146 / 147-152.

a256 **Hillenbrand** Robert, Islamic architecture; form, function and meaning. E 1994, Univ. xxvi-; 645 p.;1246 fig.; 1246 fig.; 324 pl. [+] 32 colour. £ 49.50. 0-7486-0470-0. -- ᴿAntiquity 69 (1995) 174 (C. *Broodbank*).

a257 **Hirschfeld** Yizhar, The Palestinian dwelling in the Roman-Byzantine period [ᴴ1987 → 8.d661]: SBF.m 34. J 1995, Franciscan. 318 p.; bibliog. 286-310. 965-472-000-0.

a258 **Hostetter** Eric, Lydian architectural terracottas; a study in tile replication, display and technique: Sardis/ILCL.s 5. Atlanta 1994, Scholars. xxii-108 p.; 110 fig. $ 50. 1-55540-746-3. -- ᴿLatomus 54 (1995) 215s (R. *Bouloumié*).

a259 **Hurowitz** V., I have built you an exalted house; temple building in the light of Mesopotamian and Northwest Semitic writings: JSOT.s 113, 1992 → 9,2778: ᴿJAOS 115 (1995) 119s (J. *Van Seters*).

a260 ᴱ**Kempinski** Aharon [d.1994], *Reich* Ronny, The architecture of ancient Israel [= Ha-Adrikhalut, ᴱ*Katzenstein* H., al. 1987], ᵀ. J 1992, Israel Exploration. xiv-332 p. -- ᴿJJS 46 (1995) 352s (J. *Schwartz*).

a261 **Kleinbauer** W. Eugene, Early Christian and Byzantine architecture; an annotated bibliography and historiography. Boston 1992, Hall. cxxiii-779 p. $125. -- ᴿRStR 21 (1995) 57 (Ann *Terry*: impressive).

a262 **Kolb** Anne, Die kaiserzeitliche Bauverwaltung in der Stadt Rom; Geschichte und Aufbau der cura operum publicorum unter dem Prinzipat: HABES 13. Stu 1993, Steiner. 367 p. — ᴿGerión 13 (1995) 382-4 (Rona *Sanz*); Tyche 9 (1994) 236s (E. *Weber*).

a263 **Krafeld-Daugherty** Maria, Wohnen im Alten Orient; eine Untersuchung zur Verwendung von Rä[u]men in altorientalischen Wohnhäuse[r]n [< Diss. Münster 1992. ᴰ*Mayer-Opificius* R.]: *AKVO 3. Müns 1994, Ugarit. x-401 p. DM 146. 3-927120-16-2 [RStR 22,232s, D.I. *Owen*: in title 'Rämen','Wohnhäusen'].

a264 *Malamat* A., Is there a word for the royal harem in the Bible ? The *inside* [*pᵉnîmâ* Ps 45,14s, as Mari *tubqum*] story: → 130, ᶠMILGROM J., Pomegranates 1995, 785-7.

a265 *Maselli* Giorgio, Moduli descrittivi nelle ville PLINIANE; percezione, animazione, concezione dello spazio: BSL(at) 25 (1995) 90-104; Eng. 104.

a266 **McEwen** Indra K., Socrates' ancestor; an essay on architectural beginnings. CM 1993, MIT. x-194 p.; ill. $15. 0-262-63148-2. -- ᴿRStR 21 (1995) 50 (J.M. *Balcer*: expressions of Greek harmony).

a267 **Meinecke** Michael, Die mamlukische Architektur in Ägypten und Syrien (648/1250 bis 923/1517): *DAI.K Abh.Islam 5. xiv-243 p.; x-576 p. 3-870030-071-X; -6-0. -- ᴿZDMG

145 (1995) 171-4 (C. *Ewert*).

a268 *Monelli* Alma & Nanni, L'architettura cristiana delle origini; i primi trecento anni: BeO(riente) 37 (1995) 49-59   [NTAb 40, p.95].

a269 *Montserrat* Dominic, Early Byzantine church lighting; a new [Greek] text; Orientalia 64 (1995) 430-444; pl. XLVIs.

a270 *Moret* Pierre, Les maisons fortes de la Bétique et de la Lusitanie romaines : REA 97 (1995) 527-554 + 7 fig. (maps); Eng. 527.

a271 *Moretti* Jean-Charles, Les débuts de l'architecture théâtrale en Sicile et en Italie méridionale (Vᵉ-IIIᵉ s.):   *TopO 3 (1993) 72-100.

a272 *Mosca* Annapaola, I ponti romani della VII regio (Etruria); JAT/RTA 5 (1995) 31-86; 27 fig.; Eng. 211.

a273 **Nielsen** Inge, Hellenistic palaces; tradition and renewaL: Studies iN Hellenistic civilization 5. Aarhus 1994, Univ. 341 p.; bibliog. 306-319.   87-7288-445-2.

a274 **Nigro** Lorenzo, Ricerche sull'architettura palaziale della Palestina nelle età del Bronzo e del Ferro: Contributi Arch.5. R 1995. Univ. (ScStor). xi-493 p.; Ill. Lᵐ 90. 1120-9631 [RStR 22,231, D.I. *Owen*].

a275 **Nunnerich-Asmus** Annette, Basilika und Portikus; die Architektur der Säulenhallen als Ausdruck gewandelter Urbanität in später Republik und früher Kaiserzeit [Diss. Köln 1991]. Köln 1994, Böhlau. xii-147 p.; 242 fig. 3-412-09590-1.

a276 **O'Connor** Colin, Roman bridges 1993 → 10,11634*: ᴿJRS 85 (1995) 296s (N. *Holbrook*); Latomus 54 (1995) 211 (J. *Debergh*).

a277 *Otto* Eckart, Zivile Funktionen des Stadttores in Palästina und Mesopotamien: → 48, ᶠDONNER, H., Meilenstein: ÄAT 30 (1995) 188-197.

  Pensabene P., Elementi architettonici di Alessandria 1993 →b642 infra.

a279 ᴱ**Piras** Susanne, Latrines, antike toiletten -- modern onderzoek. Meppel 1994, Edu Actief. 40 p.

a280 *Reymond* Bernard, Le paradoxe de l'architecture religieuse; remarques en marge de Paul TILLICH: RTPh 127 (1995) 143-153; Eng. 208.

a281 **Rodley** Lyn, Byzantine art and architecture; an introduction. C 1994, Univ. xiv-380 p.; 285 fig. $ 80. -- ᴿRÉByz 63 (1995) 389s (C. *Walter*).

a282 **Ruggieri** Vincenzo, Byzantine religious architecture (582-867); its history and structural elements 1991 → 7,b679 ... 9,13121: ᴿKler 23 (1991) 363s (K.P. *Karalabidis*).

a283 *Saidel* Benjamin A., Round house or square ? architectural form and socioeconomic organization in the pre-pottery neolihic B: *JMeditA 6 (19930 109-117; responses *Flannery* Kenet V., *Belfer-Cohen* A., 109-118-124.

a284 **Saliou** Catherine, Les lois des bâtiments; voisinage et habitat urbain dans l'Empire romain; recherches sur les rapports entre le droit et la construction privée du siècle d'Auguste au siècle de Justinien: BAH 116. Beyrouth 1994, IFAPO. viii-340 p.; 68 fig. 2-7953-0560-2. -- ᴿLatomus 54 (1995) 443-8 (Y. *Janvier*).

a285 *Sauvage* Martin, La brique et sa mise en œuvre en Mésopotamie, des origines à l'époque achéménide [< diss. Paris I, 1994]: *OrExp 3 (1994) 94-96.

a286 **Schaaf** Hildegard, Untersuchungen zu Gebäudestiftungen in hellenistischer Zeit. Köln 1992, Böhlau. 148 p.; 32 fig. -- ᴿBo(nn)J 195 (1995) 671-6 (H.-J. *Schalles*).

a287 **Segal** Arthur, Theatres in Roman Palestine and Provincia Arabia: MNEM.s 140. 1x-117 p.; bibliog. 103-111. ƒ 125. 90-04-10145-4. -- ᴿBoL (1995) 35 (L.L. *Grabbe*).

a288 **Sevín** Velf, ᵀ Yeni Assur sanatì, 1. Mimarlik [art: architecture]; TTKY 6/38. Ankara 1991, Türk tarih kurumu. ix-190 p. 975-16-0255-6.

a289 *Smart* David H., Christopher Wren and the architectural context of Anglican liturgy: A(ngl)ThR 77 (1995) 290-306.

a290 *Sonia Mollá* M.A., *Llanos* José M., Prohibición de demolición de edificaciones; aspectos legales y procesales: RIDA 42 (1995) 235-287.

a291 *Soren* David, *Aylward* William, Dazzling spaces; indulging in architectural fantasies was one way for a rich Roman to keep up with the Julio-Claudii: Archaeology 47,4 (CM 1994) 24-28.

a292 *Stupperich* Reinhard, Überlegungen zum Fussmass mykenischer Bauten: Thetis 2 (1995) 21-30; 5 fig.

a293 *Walthew* C.V., Roman basilicas; a progress report: *Classics Ireland 2 (1995) 133-149 [NTAb 40, p.287].

a294 **White** L. Michael, Building God's house 1990 → 6,d189 ... 8,d684: ᴿC(ath)HR 81 (1995) 627-9 (G. *Montanari*).

a295 **Winter** N,A., Greek architectural terracottas, from the prehistoric to the end of the archaic period. Ox 1995, Clarendon. xxxvii-360 p.; 27 fig., 3 maps. £ 55. -- ᴿCLR 45 (1995) 132-4 (B.A. *Sparkes*).

T1.9 *Supellex* -- furniture; objects of daily life

a296 *Briend* Jacques, Le mobilier aux temps bibliques: MoBi 92 (1995) 48-50 (l'éclairage, 94,51s; 52s NT, cuisine, M. *Quesnel*. encore 95,42-44).

a297 **Cholidis** Nadja, Möbel in Ton 1992 → 8,d689; 10,11643: ᴿOLZ 90 (1995) 394-8 (R.-B. *Wartke*); Syria 72 (1995) 271-3 (E. *Gubel*).

a298 **Daviau** P,M. Michèle, Houses and their furnishings in Bronze Age Palestine; domestic activity areas and artefact distribution in the Middle and Late Bronze Ages; JSOT/ASOR mg 8. Shf 1993, JSOT. 489 p.; 86 fig. £ 45. 1-8507-5355-5 [RStR 22,231, J. *Monson*]. -- ᴿBiOr 52 (1995) 157-9 (Helga *Weippert*).

a299 **Dupont** Florence, Daily life in ancient Rome [1939], ᵀ *Woodall* Christopher. Ox 1992, Blackwell. xi-314 p. £ 20. -- ᴿHZ 260 (1995) 170s (Marieluise *Deissmann*).

a300 *Eaton-Krauss* Marianne, Notes on some New Kingdom stools with bulls' legs and Tutankhamun's 'feeding chair'; → 96, ꟳKRAUSE M., Divitiae Aegypti 1995, 85-89 * 6 fig.; pl. 5-6.

a301 **Killen** G., Ancient Egyptian furniture II: Modern Egyptology. Wmr 1995, Aris & P. 91 p.; 86 fig.: 72 pl. $ 30. 0-85668-511-9 [*JSStEg 21s (1991s) 113]

a302 ᴱ**Philonenko** Marco, Le trône de Dieu 1990/3 → 9,404: ᴿThLZ 120 (1995) 520 (A.M. *Schwemer*).

a303 *Pischilova* E.V., 'Mistakes' in the representation of objects in Saite reliefs of daily life; GöMisz 139 (1994) 69-87 + 5 pl.

a304 **Strouhal** Eugen, Life in ancient Egypt [1989], ᵀ. L 1992, Opus. 279 p., 70 phot. + 219 colour. DM 74. -- ᴿArOr 63 (1995) 131s (M. *Bárta*).

T2.1 *Res militaris* -- weapons, army activities

a305 **Baatz** Dietwulf, Bauten und Katapulte des römischen Heeres: Mavors 11. Stu 1994, Steiner. 312 p. DM 164. -- ᴿHZ 261 (1995) 857 (H. *Freis*).

a306 **Breeze** David J., *Dobson* Brian, Roman officers and frontiers [38 (of their own) art.]: Mavors 10. Stu 1993, Steiner. 631 p.; ill.; maps. DM 288. 3-515-06181-9. -- ᴿCLR 45

(1995) 335s (N.J.E. *Austin*); HZ 261 (1995) 509-511 (R. *Haensch*); Klio 77 (1995) 509s (M. *Clauss*); Latomus 54 (1995) 706s (P. *Le Roux*).

a307 *Brentjes* Burchard, Waffen der Steppenvölker (II): Kompositbogen, Goryt und Pfeil -- ein Waffenkomplex der Steppenvölker: AMI(ran) 28 (1995s) 179-210; 43 fig.; pl. 5,3 -- 7,2.

a308 **Campbell** Brian, The Roman army, 31 B.C.-A.D. 337; a sourcebook 1994 → 10,11656; 5 fig.; 18 pl. £ 35; pa. £ 13. -- ^RCLR 45 (1995) 337s (R. *Alston*).

a309 *Ceccherelli* Ignazio M., La fionda di Davide; una riflessione sul Cristo storico ['tutto s'incentra nella scoperta del P. O'CALLAGHAN', p.176; → p.251-4, *Sardini* Davide]: BeO(riente) 37 (1995) 167-192.

a310 **Dąbrowa** Edward, Legio X Fretensis, a prosopographical study 1993 → 9,13155; 10,11661: ^RSCI(sr) 14 (1995) 169-171 (B. *Isaac*).

a311 *a) Daris* Sergio, Esercito romano e società civile d'Egitto; -- *b) Keenan* James G., Soldier and civilian in Byzantine Hermopolis: → 674, 20th Papyrologist 1992/4, 437-443 / 444-451.

a312 **Devijver** Hubert, The equestrian officers of the Roman imperial army 2, 1992 → 9,13156: ^RGnomon 67 (1995) 279-281 (G. *Wesch-Klein*).

a313 **Dixon** Karen R., *Southern* Pat, The Roman cavalry; from the first to the third century A.D. 1992 → 9,13157; 10,11663: ^RAnCL 64 (1995) 488 (P. *Leman*); RÉL 73 (1995) 331s (F. *Bérard*); Klio 77 (1995) 508s (Margot *Klee*).

a314 **Dodge** Theodore A., Alexander; a history of the origin and growth of the art of war from the earliest times. L / Mechanicsburg PA 1994, Greenhill / Stackpole. xxv-694p.; Iii.; map. 1-85367-178-9.

a315 **Feugère** Michel, Les casques antiques; visages de la guerre de Mycènes à l'antiquité tardive: Hesperides. P 1994, Errance. 173 p.; ill.

a316 **Franke** Thomas, Die Legionslegaten der römischen Armee in der Zeit von Augustus bis Traian 1991 → 10.11667*: ^RHZ 260 (1995) 536-9 (K. *Strobel*).

a317 **Gagsteiger** Gerti, Die ptolemäischen Waffenmodelle aus Memphis [Magisterarbeit Erlangen] 1993 → 9,13160; 10,11668: ^RBiOr 52 (1995) 663-5 (M. *Pfrommer*).

a318 *a) Graf* David F., The Nabatean army and the *cohortes ulpiae Petraeorum;* -- *b) Barański* Marek, The Roman army in Palmyra; a case of adaptation of a pre-existing city; - *c) Kennedy* D.L., The *cohors XX Palmyrenorum* at Dura Europos; -- *d) Gawlikowski* Michał, A fortress in Mesopotamia, Hatra: → 678, Roman/Byz Army 1992/4, 265-311; 7 fig. / 9-17 / 89-98 / 47-56.

a319 **Hill** D.F., An archer looks at the Bible; a study of the [120] literal and figurative allusions to the bow and arrow. E 1994, Pentland. xii-108 p.; ill.: 3 maps. £ 11. 1-85821-167-0 [NTAb 40, p.175].

a320 **Horsmann** Gerhard, Untersuchungen zur militärischen Ausbildung im republikanischen und kaiserzeitlichen Rom: Wehrwissenschaftliche Forschungen, milit.35, 1991 → 8,d725*; 9,13154: ^RTyche 9 (1994) 234-6 (B. *Palme*).

a321 *Hrouda* Barthel, Der elamitische Streitwagen: → 10,81, ^FMEYER L. de, 52 Réflexions, 53-57; 9 fig.

a322 **Isaac** B., The limits of empire; the Roman army^{2rev} [¹1990 → 8,d726; 10,11672]. Ox 1992, Clarendon. -- ^R*TopO 4 (1994) 371-6 (M. *Gawlikowski*).

a323 **Jarvo** Eero, Archaiologia on archaic Greek body armour. Rovaniemi 1995, Soc. Historica Finlandiae Septentrionalis. 176 p.

a324 **Junkelmann** Marcus, Die Reiter Roms, 1. Reise, Jagd, Triumph und Circusrennen; 2. Der militarische Einsatz; 3. Zubehör. Reitweise, Bewaffnung: KGAW 53. Mainz 1990-2, von Zabern. 293 p. / 222 p. /277 p. DM 50. -- [R]HZ 260 (1995) 533-5 (K. *Strobel*, 3); Labeo 40 (1994) 118s (F. *Mercogliano*).

a325 *Knauer* Elfriede R., *Knemides* in the East ? Some observations on the impact of Greek body armor on 'barbarian' tribes: → 143,[F]OSTWALD M.,Nomodeiktes 1993,235-254; 12 fig.

a326 **Le Bohec** Yann, *a)* The imperial Roman army [1989 → 8,d729], [T]1994. £ 30. -- [R]CLR 45 (1995) 125s (R. *Alston*: needed, but too conservative on the social-economic). -- *b)* Die römische Armée, [T]1993. -- [R]Klio 77 (1995) 507s (M. *Speidel*).

a327 [E]**Leriche** Pierre, *Tréziny* Henry, La fortification dans l'histoire du monde grec. 1982/6, -- [R]BiOr 52 (1995) 167-173 (S.C. *Bakhuizen*).

a328 **Lissarague** François, L'autre guerrier; archers, peltastes, cavaliers dans l'image antique 1990 → 7,b722 ... 9,13173: [R]RB(elg)PH 73 (1995) 246 (H. *Devijver*).

a329 **Milner** N.P., VEGETIUS, Epitome of military science: Translated texts for historians 16. Liverpool 1993, Univ. xxx-152 p. £ 8.50. 0-85323-228-8. -- [R]Bijdragen 56 (1995) 90 (M. *Parmentier*. Eng.).

a330 -- [E]**Önnerfors** Alf, Flavius VEGETIUS Renatus, Epitoma rei militaris: BSGR. Stu 1995, Teubner. lxi-268 p.

a331 **Munn** M.H., The defense of Attica 1993 → 9,13176; 10,11684: [R]RossArkh (1995,4) 197-202 (G.A. *Koshelenko*).

a332 **Negahban** Ezat O., Weapons from Marlik: AMI Egb 16. B 1995, Reimer. 124 p.; 97 fig.; 18 pl. + 3 color. -- [R]RA(ssyr) 89,1 (1995) 95s (P. *Amiet*).

a333 *Németh* György, Der Preis einer Panoplie: AAH 36 (1995) 5-13.

a334 *Noè* Eralda, Cedat forum castris; esercito e ascesa politica nella riflessione ciceroniana: At(henaeum) 83 (1995) 67-82.

a335 **Peddie** John, The Roman war machine. Stroud 1994, Sutton. xv-169 p.; 59 fig.; £ 19. -- [R]GaR 42 (1995) 218s (Catherine *Gilliver*).

a336 **Plath** Robert, Der Streitwagen und seine Teile im frühen Griechischen; sprachliche Untersuchungen zu den mykenischen Texten und zum homerischen Epos [Diss. Erlangen/N]: EBSLK 74. Nürnberg 1994, H. Carl. ix-450 p. DM 39. 3-418-00076-2. -- [R]I(nd)GF 100 (1995) 284-7 (Rüdiger *Schmitt*).

a337 *Prestiani* Giallombardo, Il bronzo e la pietra; strumenti di guerra e tecniche di combattimento nell'Anabasi di SENOFONTE: Pallas 43 (1995) 21-40; franç. Eng. 40.

a338 *Raulwing* Peter, Ein indoarischer Streitwagenterminus im Ägyptischen ? : GöMiszÄg 140 (1994) 71-79

a339 *Ricci* Cecilia, Soldati delle milizie urbane fuori di Roma; la documentazione epigrafica: Opuscula Epigraphica 5. 57 p.

a340 [E]**Rich** John, *Shipley* Graham, War and society *a)* in the Greek world [Leicester-Nottingham 1988, [2]1990 → 9,13181]; -- *b)* in the Roman world. L 1993, Routledge. xiii-263 p. xi-315 p. 0-415-06644-1. -- [R]BoL (1995) 137 (M. *Goodman*); CLR 45 (1995) 122s (N.V. *Sekunda*) / 124s (B. *Rankov*).

a341 *Rossoni* G., Le catapulte di Uzzia re di Giuda [2 Cr 16,15]: EVO 18 (1995) 213-9.

a342 **Roth** Jonathan, The logistics of the Roman army in the Jewish War: diss. Columbia. NY 1991. 509 p. -- MBAH 14,1 (1995) 109-116 (T. *Kissel*).

a343 **Selkirk** Raymond, On the trail of the legions. Ipswich 1995, Anglia. [x-] 410 p.

a344 *Shatzman* Israel, Stone-balls from Tel Dor and the artillery of the Hellenistic world [Rhodes, Pergamum]: SCI(sr) 14 (1995) 52-87 + 6 fig. (maps).

a345 **Speidel** M.P., Riding for Caesar; the Roman Emperor's horse guards [L, Batsford → 10,11689]. CM 1994, Harvard Univ. 223 p.; 6 fig.; 20 pl.; 4 maps. $ 28. 0-674-76897-3

[NTAb 40, p.186].

a346 **Speidel** M.P., Roman army studies II [59 art. since I. 1984]: Mavors 8, 1992 → 8,d745; 10,11690; DM 158: ᴿArctos 27 (1993) 193-6 (C. *Bruun*).

a347 *Speidel* Michael P., The fustis as a soldier's weapon: AntAfr 29 (1993) 137-149; 9 fig.

a348 *Tokmakov* V.N., The structure and battle formation of the Roman troops of the early republic; VDI (1995,4) 138-160; Eng. 160.

a349 **Vita** Juan-Pablo. El ejército de Ugarit: Banco de datos filológicos semíticos noroccidentales, mg.1. M 1995, Cons. Sup. Inv. xiii-235 p.; bibliog. 189-205

a350 **Wees** Hans van, Status warriors 1987 → d,746*: ᴿR(Belg)PH 73 (1995) 240s (J.A. *Straus*).

a351 **Worley** Leslie J., Hippeis; the cavalry of ancient Greece [→ 10,11692*]: History and Ancient Warfare. Boulder 1994, Westview. xii-241 p. $ 25. -- ᴿA(mer)HR 100 (1995) 498 (G.R. *Bugh*).

a352 *Yener* K. Ashhan, Swords, armor, and figurines; a metaliferous view from the central Taurus: → 136, ᶠNEVE P., BA 58 (1995) 101-7; ill. [Göltepe and Kültepe switched on map; corrected p. 178, with author's name now spelled once Yenner, once Yener].

T2.2   *Vehicula*, **transportation**

a353 *Anthony* D.W., *Vinogradov* N.B., Birth of the chariot [W Ural, 2000 B.C.]: Archaeology 48,.. (1995) 36-41 [< ZAW 107 (1995) 496].

a354 **Crouwel** J.H., Chariots and other wheeled vehicles in Iron Age Greece 1993 → 9,13194: ᴿCLR 45 (1995) 193s (J.N. *Coldstream*).

a355 *Muzzolini* Alfred, Les chars [... au 'galop volant'] au Sahara et en Égypte; les chars des 'peuples de la mer' et la 'vague orientalisante' en Afrique: RdÉ 45 (1994) 208-234; 15 fig.; Eng. deutsch 252

a356 *Lacocque* André, La Shulamite et les chars d'Aminadab [1 Sm 6]; un essai herméneutique sur Cantique 6,12-7,1: RB 102 (1995) 330-347; Eng. 330.

a357 *Pilch* John J., Travel in the ancient world: BiTod 12 (1994) 100-107; 6 fig.

a358 *Woytowitsch* Eugen, Die Wagen der Schweiz in der europäischen Bronzezeit: *HelvArch 26,103s (1995) 83-149; 341 fig.

T2.3   **Nautica**

a359 *Bakr* Mohammed I., *Nibbi* Alessandra, A stone anchor workshop at Marsa Matruh (250 k W Alexandria]: *DiscEg 29 (1994) 5-22; 14 fig. (map).

a360 **Baudoin** Catherine, *Liou* Bernard, *Long* Luc, Une cargaison de bronzes hellénistiques; l'épave Fourmigue C à Golfe-Juan [Cannes]: Archéonautica 12 (1994) 9-143; 93 fig.; IV col.pl.

a361 *Campatella* Moreno, Gli epigrammi per I morti in mare dell'Antologia Greca; il realismo, l'etica e la moira: Annali Macerata 28 (1995) 47-86.

a362 **Casson** Lionel, The ancient mariners; seafarers and sea fighters of the Mediterranean in ancient times²ʳᵉᵛ [¹1959]. Princeton 1991, Univ. xviii-246 p. $ 52.50; pa. $ 18. 0-691-06836-4; -1477-9. -- ᴿBoL (1995) 125 (J.R. *Bartlett*).

a363 **Casson** Lionel, Ships and seafaring in ancient times. Austin 1994, Univ. Texas. 160 p.

a364 *Degas* Jacques, Don Joam de CASTRO sur l'itinéraire de Pount (1541): RdÉ 46 (1995) 215-237; 5 fig.; 6 maps; Eng. 237.

a365 **De Salvo** Lietta, Economia privata e pubblici servizi nell'Impero Romano; i corpora naviculariorum: Kleio 5. Messina 1992, Sampero. 797 p. -- ᴿBSL(at) 25 (1995) 263-6 (G. *Bonamente*); HZ 261 (1995) 515s (L. *Wierschowski*: mustergültig).

a366 *a) Dijk* F.H. van, Scheepvaart in de Perzische Golf; maritieme contacten in het derde millennium voor Christus: -- *b) Wachsmann* S., Zeevaarders in het Oude Nabije Oosten; -- *c) Meijer* F., Van monoreme naar trireme .. 1500-500: -- *d) Wegener Sleeswijk* A., Oude scheepvaartkanalen in Egypte: Phoe 41,2 (1995) 64-71; 4 fig. / 72-80; 3 fig. / 82-96; 6 (color.) fig. / 41,3 (1995) 97-118; 19 fig. (map).

a367 *Dvorjetski* E., Nautical symbols on the Gadara coins and their link to the thermae of the three graces at Hammat-Gader: *MeditHR 9,1 (TA 1994) 100-115 [NTAb 39, p.461].

a368 **Gabrielsen** V., Financing the Athenian fleet; public taxation and social relations. Baltimore 1994, Johns Hopkins Univ. xvii-306 p. £ 37. 0-8018-4692-7. -- ᴿCLR 45 (1995) 96-98 (P. *Harding*).

a369 *Geominy* Wilfred, Il relitto di Mahdia [Tunis, 120 a.C., scoperta 1907: mostra Bonn]: Archeo 10,119 (1995) 48-57.

a370 *Grassi* Vincenza, Inchiesta sulla terminologia marinaresca in uso nelle acque del Nilo in Sudan (Khartum e Gebel Aulia): AION 55 (1995) 269-295 ...

a371 *Harris* J., BESSARION on shipbuilding; a reinterpretation: BYSL 55 (1994) 291-303 [RHE 91,113*].

a372 *Hase* Friedrich W. von, Navigare con gli antichi [nuovo Museum für antike Schiffahrt, Mainz]: Archeo 125 (1995) 48-55 [96-99, *al.*, archeologia subacquea a San Vito lo Capo, Trapani].

a373 *Jannot* Jean-René, Les navires étrusques, instruments d'une thalassocratie ?: CRAI (1995) 743-778: 27 fig.

a374 **Jones** Dilwyn, Boats: Egyptian Bookshelf. L 1995, British Museum. 96 p.

a375 *Karlshausen* Christina, L'évolution de la barque processionnelle d'Amon à la 18ᵉ dynastie: RdÉ 46 (1995) 119-133 + 9 fig.

a376 **Kettenbach** Günter, Einführung in die Schiffahrtsmetaphorik der Bibel: E(ur)HS 23/512. Fra 1994, Lang. 538 p. DM 128 / 72. 3-631-46950-0 [RStR 22,160, C. *Bernas*]. -- ᴿE(rbe)uA 71 (1995) 164 (SP); SNTU 20 (1995) 252s (A. *Fuchs*).

a377 *Kramer* Willi, *Schlichtherle* Helmut, Unterwasser-Archäologie in Deutschland: Antike Welt 26 (1995) 3-14; 31 fig.

a378 *Long* Luc, *Domergue* Claude, Le 'véritable plomb de L. Flavivs Vervcla' [titres; texte 'Flauius Verucla'] et autres lingots; l'Épave I des Saintes-Maries-de-la-Mer : MÉFRA 107 (1995) 801-867; 15 fig.

a379 *a) Maarleveld* Thijs J., Type or technique; some thoughts on boat and ship finds as indicative of cultural traditions; -- *b) Cederlund* Carl O., Marine archaeology in society and science; -- *c) Crumlin-Pedersen* Ole, Experimental archaeology and ships -- bridging the arts and the sciences: IJNaut 24 (1995) 3-7 / 9-13 / (293-) 303-6; 1 fig.

a380 *Marc* J.-Y., Recherches récentes au Pirée [GARLAND R. 1987; KLAUS-VALTIN VON EICKSTEDT 1991]: *TopO 3 (1993) 100-8.

a381 *Murgatroyd* P., The sea of love [marine and nautical references]: CQ 45 (1995) 9-25.

a382 *Nibbi* Akessandra, An Early Dynastic hide-covered model papyrus boat: RdÉ 44 (1993) 81-100; 15 fig.; pl. 4-7; franç. 101.

a383 **Pohl** H., Die römische Politik und die Piraterie im östlichen Mittelmeer vom 3. bis zum 1. Jh. v. Chr.: UALG 42. B 1993, de Gruyter. x-310 p. DM 172. -- ᴿAAH 36 (1995) 367-374 (E. *Maróti); CLR 45 (1995) 99-101 (P. de *Souza*); JRS 85 (1995) 277s (A. *Avidov*);

Klio 77 (1995) 494s (Loretana de *Libero*).

a384 *Potts* Daniel T., Watercraft of the Lower Sea: → 23, ^FBOEHMER R.M., Beiträge 1995, 559-568 + 14 fig.

a385 **Rival** Michel, La charpenterie navale romaine; matériaux, méthodes, moyens; Centre Jullian 4. P 1991, CNRS. 333 p-; 123 fig.; 8 maps. F 190. 2-222-04391-3. -- ^RAJA 99 (1995) 165s (M.A. *Fitzgerald*); TopO 3 (1993) 355-361 (Suzanne *Amigues*).

a386 **Santamaria** Claude, L'épave Dramont 'E' à Saint-Raphaël [N. Afrique] (Ve siècle ap. J.-C.): Archaeonautica 13 (1995). 198 p.; 161 fig. 2-271-05357-9.

a387 *(Santillo) Frizell* Barbro, 'I am a ship'; the iconography of a water temple: Opus Mixtum (OpRom 21,1994) 97-109; 10 fig.

a388 *Shear* Julia L., Fragments of naval inventories from the Athenian Agora: Hesp 64 (1995) 179-224; pl. 42-44.

a389 **Steffy** J. Richard, Wooden ship building and the interpretation of shipwrecks. College 1994, TX A&M. 314 p.; 250 fig. $ 75. 0-89096-52-8. -- ^RJField 22 (1995) 245-8 (R.A. *Gould*).

a390 *Stern* Ephraim, Priestly blessing of a voyage: recovery of a harbor scene at Dor [on cow-collarbone, c. 600 B.C.E.]: BArR 21,1 (1995) 50-55 . 82 [IEJ 44,1 (1994)].

a391 **Tramonti** Stefano, 'Hostes communes omnium'; la pirateria e la fine della Repubblica Romana (145-33 a.C.): Annali 7/1. Ferrara 1994, Univ. -- ^REpigraphica 57 (Faenza 1995) 331-4 (G. *Frassinetti*).

a392 *Tramonti* Stefano, La pirateria ligure e sardo-corsa nel Tirreno nel II sec. a.C.: AtenR 40 (1995) 197-212.

a393 **Vinson** Steve, Egyptian boats and ships. Shire 1994. £ 4. 0-7478-0223-X. -- ^RIJNaut 24 (1995) 170s (M. *Horton*).

a394 **Wallinga** H.T., Ships and sea-power 1993 → 9,13225; 10,11714: ^RAt(henaeum) 83 (1995) 533-6 (Laura *Boffo*); JAOS 115 (1995) 314 (T.C. *Young*).

a395 **Wachsman** Shelley, The Sea of Galilee boat; an extraordinary 2000 year old discovery. NY 1995, Plenum. xviii-420 p.; bibliog. 385-392.

a396 **Westerdahl** Christian, Crossroads in ancient shipbuilding. 1994.

a397 *Wilkinson* John, The inscription on the Jerusalem ship drawing: PEQ 127 (1995) 159s.

T2.4 *Athletica* -- **sport, games**

a398 **Auguet** Roland, Cruelty and civilization; the Roman games [1970], ^T. L 1994 = 1972, Routledge. 222 p. 42 fig. 0-415-10452-1. -- ^RAnCL 64 (1995) 413 (P. Van *Langhoven*); MBAH 14,2 (1995) 118-120 (Julia S. *Thompson*, deutsch).

a399 **Bernstein** Frank, Ludi publici; Untersuchungen zur Entstehung und Entwicklung der öffentlichen Spiele im republikanischen Rom: Diss. Duisburg 1994.- Chiron 25 (1995) 419.

a400 **Davis** Whitney, Masking the blow ... in Egyptian art 1992 → 8,d788; 10,11724: ^RBiOr 52 (1995) 626-631 (K.M. *Ciałowicz*); *JSStEg 23 (1993) 77-79 (Robyn *Gillam*).

a401 **Decker** Wolfgang, *Herr* Michael, Atlas zum Sport im alten Ägypten 1993 → 9,13235; *f* 650: ^RBoL (1995) 127 (K.A. *Kitchen*).

a402 *Gauthier* Philippe, Du nouveau sur les courses aux flambeaux d'après deux inscriptions de Kos: RÉG 108 (1995) 576-585.

a403 *a) Gauthier* Philippe, Notes sur le rôle du gymnase dans les cités hellénistiques; -- *b) Hesberg* Henner von, Das griechische Gymnasium im 2. Jh. v. Chr.; → 711, Stadtbild 1993/5, 1-11 + 2 fig. / 13-21 + 19 fig.

a404 **Hübner** U., Spiele und Spielzeug im antiken Palästina: OBO 121, 1992 → 8.d797: ᴿBiOr 52 (1995) 807-812 (B. *Becking*, K. *Vriezen*); RB 102 (1995) 460s (J.M. de *Tarragon*).

a405 *Jordan* David R., [Five] Inscribed lead tablets from the games in the [Corinth] sanctuary of Poseidon: Hesp 63 (1994) 111-126; 5 fig. [p.1-104, Frankish-Hellenistic Corinth].

a406 **Kamper** Robert, Spiel und Transzendenz; eine Untersuchung über den Transzendenzbezug des Phänomens Spiel; kath. Diss. ᴰ*Figl*. Wien 1994. -- ThRv 91 (1995) 102.

a407 *Khanoussi* Mustapha, Sports inédits; Tunisie, une mosaïque inédite dans le monde romain: Archéologia 297 (1994) 10-15; ill.

a408 **Mabrouk** Mahmoud, Sport in Pharaonic Egypt. Cairo c. 1994, State Information Service. 40 p.; ill [*OIAc 11,32].

a409 **Maniscalco** Fabio, Il nuoto nel mondo greco-romano; pref. *Camodeca* Giuseppe. N 1995, Graphotronic.

a410 ᴱ**Mazza** Carlo, Fede e sport; fondamenti, contesti, proposte pastorali [Seminario naz. 1992]. CasM 1994, Piemme. 240 p. Lᵐ 30. -- ᴿCivCatt 146 (1995,3) 451 (I.M. *Ganzi*).

a411 *Moore* Timothy J., Seats and social status in the Plautine theatre: CJ 90 (1994s) 113-123.

a412 *Pennitz* Martin, Zur Postulationsfähigkeit der Athleten im klassischen römischen Recht: ZS(av)RG.r 112 (1995) 91-108.

a413 **Plass** Paul, The game of death in ancient Rome; arena sport and political suicide [as punishment; both served as crime-deterrent]: StClas. Madison 1995, Univ. Wisconsin. xi-283 p.; bibliog. 262-271. $ 48.75 [NTAb 40, p.500; RStR 22,346, B.P. *Nystrom*]. -- TLS (Dec.22,1995) 22 (C. *Kelly*; also on BOWERSOCK G., Martyrdom and Rome 1995, 'Christian martydom had no Jewish or classical antecedents').

a414 ᴱ**Prebish** Charles C., Religion and sport; the meeting of sacred and profane [reprints since SLUSHER H. 1967] 1993 → 9,13258; 10,11741: ᴿ*CritRR 7 (1994) 474s (S.K. *Wertz*).

a415 *Purcell* N., Literate games; Roman urban society and the game of *alea:* PaP 147 (Ox 1995) 3-37 [NTAb 40, p.116].

a416 **Reis** Martin, Sport bei Horaz: *Nikephoros Beih.2. Hildesheim 1994, Weidmann. 120 p. -- ᴿA(nz)AW 48,1s (1995) 10-12 (E. *Dohlhofer*); RÉL 73 (1995) 292s (H. *Zehnacker*).

a417 **Romano** D.G., Athletics and mathematics .. stadion. 1993. -- ᴿCLR 45 (1995) 372 (R.A. *Tomlinson*: fascinating).

a418 *Schwartz* Joshua, Ishmael at play (Gn 21,9 ṣāḥēq); on exegesis and Jewish society: AHUC (IATG for HUCA) 66 (1995) 203-221: the Rabbis commended play of the right kinds.

a419 *Schwartz* Joshua, a) ᴴ Ball play in Jewish society in the Second Temple [apart from gymnasium], Mishnah and Talmud periods: Zion 60 (1995) 247-276, Eng. XIX; -- b) ᴴglh šl qtn', a child's wagon (Besa 2,10): Tarbiz 63 (1994) 375-392; 10 fig.; Eng. xxi [NTAb 40, p.112].

a420 Spectacles sportifs et scéniques dans le monde étrusco-italique: Table Ronde CNRS:UMR 126, Rome 3-4 mai 1991: Coll. ÉcF 172. 478 p. 140 fig. -- ᴿCLR 45 (1995) 98s (C. *Smith*).

a421 *Thuillier* Jean-Paul, Pretium victoribus; l'exemple des vases étrusques: RÉA 97 (1995) 153-161 + 11 fig.; Eng. 153: metal vessels were a frequent prize,also in Iliad 23;Aeneid 5

a422 *Triantaphyllopoulos* Giovanni, I giochi olimpici ieri e oggi; somiglianze e dissomiglianze: A(ten)eR 39 (1994) 182-191.

a423 *Vermaak* P.S., The mother goddess and her games/gaming connection; an iconographic study: *J/Tyd Sem 7 (1995) 16-30; bibliog. 31-34; 19 fig.

a424 **Villalba i Varneda** Pere, Olimpia; origens dels jocs olimpics. Barc 1994, Univ. 663 p.

a425 **Weeber** Karl W., Panem et circenses; Massenunterhaltung als Politik im antiken Rom: Bildbandarch 15. Mainz 1994, von Zabern. 180 p.; 262 pl. DM 58. 3-8053-1580-5. -- ᴿAnCl 64 (1995) 413s (P. Van *Langhoven*).

a426 **Weeber** Karl-Wilhelm, Die unheiligen Spiele: das antike Olympia zwischen Legende und Wirklichkeit 1991 → 8,d826: ᴿAnCL 64 (1995) 409s (Véronique *Suys*).

a427 **Wistrand** Magnus, Entertainment and violence in ancient Rome, the attitudes of Roman writers of the first century A.D. Göteborg 1992, Acta Univ. 133 p. -- ᴿEM(erita) 63 (1995) 170s (G. *Carrasco Serrano*); RB(elg)PH 73 (1995) 242s (J,A. *Straus*).

T2.5 **Musica**, dance

a428 **Adler** Israel, The study of Jewish music; a bibliographical guide: Yuval mg. 10. J 1995, Magnes. [viii-] 87 p.; bibliog. 43-87.

a429 *Barker* Andrew, An Oxyrhynchus fragment on harmonic theory: CQ 44 (1994) 75-84.

a430 *Boisjoly* Richard, Le syrinx, attribut du Bon Pasteur ?; → 29, ᶠTRAN TAM TINH V., Tranquillitas 1994, 75=80; 3 fig.

a431 *Černý* M.K., Some musicological remarks on the Old Mesopotamian music and its terminology [KILMER A.D., Musical practice in Nippur 1992]: ArOr 62 (1994) 17-26.

a432 *De Giorgi* Maria Carla, Sul discorso intorno alla musica del P. Hibeh I 13: → 574, 20th Papyrologist 1992/4, 295-8.

a433 *Delavaud-Roux* Marie-Hélène, L'énigme des danseurs barbus au parasol et les vases [attiques c. 450] 'des Lénéennes': RAr (1995) 227-263; 42 fig.

a434 *Dicen* Dean P., Dancing with tribes; the relationship of the Church with indigenous religions in the Philippine context : A(sia)JT 8 (1994) 77-88.

a435 *Draheim* Joachim, Das Notenarchiv zur musikalischen Rezeption der Antike in der Bibliothek für klassische Philologie der Universität Heidelberg: Gym 102 (1955) 160-2.

a436 **Fubini** Enrico, La musica nella tradizione ebraica: Saggi 791. T 1994, Einaudi. 155 p. Lᵐ 28. -- ᴿPaVi 40,6 (1995) 52s (A. *Piovano*).

a437 *Garelli-François* M.-H., Le danseur dans la cité, quelques remarques sur la danse à Rome: RÉL 73 (1995) 29-43.

a438 *Green* Lyn, The origins of the giant lyre and Asiatic influences on the cult of the Aten: *JSStEg 23 (1993) 56-62.

a439 **Güterbock** Hans G., Reflections on the musical instruments *arkammi, galgalturi,* and *huhupal* in Hittite : → 84, ᶠHOUWINK TEN CATE, H., Studio (1995) 57-72; pl. 18.

a440 **Guicharrousse** Hubert, Les musiques de LUTHER: Histoire et Société 31. Genève 1995, Labor et Fides. 326 p.; ill. Fs 42. 2-8309-0747-7. -- ᴿRHE 90 (1995) 663s (J.-F. *Gilmont*).

a441 **Guidobaldi** Maria Paola, La musica e la danza nell'antica Roma: *Archeo 129 (1995) 59-97.

a442 *Hentschel* Frank, Sinnlichkeit und Vernunft in AUGUSTIN's 'De musica': WiWei 57 (1994) 189-200.

a443 *Hofreiter* Paul, Johann S. BACH and Scripture: ConcordiaTQ 59 (1995) 67-92.

a444 *Huglo* Michel, Les diagrammes d'harmonique interpolés dans les manuscrits hispaniques de la Musica ISIDORI: Scr 48 (Bru 1994) 171-186.

a445 *Jian Liu*,Hittite women singers: *munus_{zintuhi}* and *munus_{KI.SIKIL}*:*JAncCiv 9 (1994) 82-94.

a446 **Keller** Adalbert, Aurelius AUGUSTINŪS und die Musik; Untersuchungen zu 'De musica' im Kontext seines Schrifttums: Cassiciacum 44, 1993 → 9,13285: ᴿEstAg 30 (1995) 160s (P. de *Luis*); ForKT 11 (1995) 158s (W. *Geerlings*); RHE 90 (1995) 124s (P.-A. *Deproost*).

a447 *Levinson* Nathan P., Jüdische liturgische Musik zwischen Tradition und Anpassung [< Symposium 1994 Hannover]: FrRu 2 (1995) 267-273.

a448 **Lonsdale** S.H., Dance and ritual play in Greek religion 1993 → 10,11758: ᴿCLR 45 (1995) 182s (H. *Bowden*).

a449 **Manniche** Lise, Music and musicians in ancient Egypt 1991 → 8.d844; £ 10: ᴿDiscEg 30 (1994) 187-192 (M. *Megally*).

a450 *Mühlbauer* Karl R., *Miller* Theresa, Spielzeug und Kult; zur religiösen und kultischen Bedeutung von Kinderspielzeug in der griechischen Antike: *AJAH 13,2 (1997 for 1988) 154-169; 20 pl.

a451 *Phillips* D., Musical instruments in the Peshitta to Chronicles [not favored] and contacts with the Peshitta to Ben Sira: Muséon 108 (1995) 49-67 [NTAb 40, p.107].

a452 *Piguet* J.-Claude, Esthétique musicale et éthique humaine: RTPh 127 (1995) 63-70; Eng. 112.

a453 *Rashid* Subhi A., Untersuchungen zum Musikinstrumentarium Assyriens: → 23, ᶠBOEHMER R.M., Beiträge 1995, 573-585 + 18 fig.; Bibliog. p. 591-5.

a454 *Rystedt* Eva, Women, music and a white-ground lecythus in the Medelhavsmuseet: Opus Mixtum (OpRom 21, 1994) 73-91; 11 fig.

a455 *Schwalbe* Johanna, Musik in der Mystik; zur Sprache der Musik in den Schriften der heiligen Gertrud von Helfta: E(rbe)uA 71 (1995) 108-124.

a456 **Terrien** Samuel, The Magnificat; musicians as biblical interpreters. NY 1995, Paulist. xxii-89 p. $ 10. 0-8091-3485-3. -- ᴿE(xp)T 107 (1995s) 87 (J. *Eaton*).

a457 *Tobias* Alexander, On the musical instruments in Psalms: JBQ 23 (1995) 53-55, querying POLLACK A. psalms commentary *Al ha-setumot ba-mizmor* 1991, reviewed here 22 (1994) 124-8 (S. *Spero*).

a458 *Watts* J.W., Song and the ancient reader: P(ersp)RSt 22 (1995) 135-147 [< OTA 19, p.385].

a459 **Weil** Daniel M., The Masoretic Chant of the Bible. J 1995, Rubin Mass. [x-] 397 [-39] p.; bibliog. 383-397.

a460 **Wilson-Dickson** Andrew, Histoire de la musique chrétienne [... liturgique, 1992], ᵀ. Turnhout 1992, Brepols. -- ᴿFoiTe 24 (1994) 471s (P. *Robert*).

a461 **Wright** O., A preliminary version of the Kitāb al-Adwār [omitted in H.G. FARMER, Sources of Arabic music 1940,though in his JRAS 1929,639-654]:BSOAS 58(1995)455-78.

a462 *Zyl* Daniel C. van, In Africa theology is not thought out but danced out -- on the theological significance of Old Testament symbolism and rituals in African Zionist churches: OTEs 8 (1995) 425-438.

T2.6 **Textilia**, *vestis*, clothing

a463 *Boissonneault* Jeanne d'Arc, Les textiles de l'antiquité classique: → 199, ᶠTRAN TAM TINH 1995, 83-90.

a464 **Bruhn** Jutta-Annette, Coins and costume in late antiquity: ByzPub 9. Wsh 1993, Dumbarton Oaks Library. iii-68 p. $ 12 pa.-- ᴿJbAC 37 (1994) 207-210 (M. *Schmauder*).

a465 *Husson* Geneviève, *al.*, Papyrus Sorb., inv. 2980-2081; un modèle de tisserand ou de mosaïste sur papyrus ?: RAr(1995) 365-373 (-386),

a466 *Kakovkine* A.J., Le tissu copte de la Galerie Nationale à Érévan (Arménie): GöMisz 145 (1995) 71-77.

a467 **Losfeld** Georges, L'art grec et le vêtement 1994 → 10,11774; bibliog. 447-507: ᴿRÉG 108 (1995) 223s (A. *Wartelle*).

a468 *Mandolfo* Carmela, L'influsso GERONIMIANO sulla terminologia del 'De vestibus' (Instr.II) di EUCHERIO di Lione: Orpheus 16 (1995) 441-8.

a469 *Matthews* Victor H., The anthropology of clothing in the Joseph narrative: JSOT 65 (1995) 25-36.

a470 *Patch* Diana C., A 'Lower Egyptian' costume; its origin, development and meaning: JA(m)RCE(g) 32 (1995) 93-118; 16 fig.

a471 **Potthoff** Anne, Lateinische Kleidungsbezeichnungen 1992 → 9,13318; 10,11778: ᴿKratylos 40 (1995) 138-143 (A. *Hintze*).

a472 **Sebasta** Judith L., *Bonfante* Larissa, The world of Roman costume. Madison 1995, Univ. Wisconsin. 292 p.: ill. $ 47.50 [BArR 21,5 (1995) 8].

a473 *Shamir* Orit,*al.*,Early Islamic textiles .. Shaḥaq, Omer: "Atiqot 26 (1995) 21-56.113s.

a474 *Sheffer* Avigail, Needlework and sewing in Israel from prehistoric times to the Roman period:→ 59, ᶠFREEDMAN D.N., Fortunate 1995, 527-559; 23 fig.

a475 **Stauffer** Annemarie, Spätantike und koptische Wirkereien; Untersuchungen zur ikonographischen Tradition in spätantiken und frühmittelalterlichen Textilwerkstätten 1992 → 9,13323; DM 70 pa.: JbAC 37 (1994) 210-3 (Claudia *Nauerth*).

a476 *Stauffer* Annemarie, Textilgeschichtliche Bemerkungen zu einer Kleiderliste des 7. Jahrhunderts aus Ägypten;→ 96,ᶠKRAUSE M.,Divitiae Aegypti 1995, 315-320; pl. 22-24.

a477 *Stone* R., Grasping the fringe [1 Sam 15,27; 24,4s]; *BurHist 31 (1995) 4-20 . 36-47; 13 fig. [< OTA 18 (1995) p. 530 (Kathleen S. *Nash*)].

a478 **Török** László, [Budapest] Coptic antiquities [→ a121 infra], II. Textiles. 1993. -- ᴿBiOr 52 (1995) 679-682 (P. *Cauderlier*).

a479 *Toorn* Karel van der, The significance of the veil in the Ancient Near East: → 130, ᶠMILGROM J., Pomegranates 1995, 327-339.

a480 **Vogelsang-Eastwood** Gillian, Pharaonic Egyptian clothing 1993 → 9,13325; 10,11786; ᴿVT 45 (1995) 572s (J.D.*Ray*).

Willers Dietrich, *al.*, [Textilien] Begegnung von Heidentum und Christentum im spätantiken Ägypten 1993 → 8822 supra.

T2.7 *Ornamenta corporis*, **jewelry, mirrors**

a481 *Asher-Grève* Julia M., Reading the horned crown [FURLONG Iris, Divine headdresses 1987 ... not the needed iconological study; superficial]; AfO 42s (1995s) 181-8 + 1 pl.

a482 *Gutzwiller* Kathryn J., Cleopatra's ring: GRBS 36 (1995) 383-398: amethyst (believed antidote against inebriation) described in Greek Anthology as bearing an image of goddess Methē (drunkenness).

a483 **Henig** Martin, *al.*, Classical gems; ancient and modern intaglios and cameos in the Fitzwilliam Museum. C 1994, Univ. xx-537 p.; ill, a484 *Henkelman* Wouter, The royal Achaemenid crown : AMI(ran) 28 (1995s) 275-293; 3 fig.; pl.16-19.

a485 *Homès-Fredericq* Denyse, A cosmetic palette from Lehun, Jordan; → 82, [F]HENNESSY J.B., Trade 1995, 265-270; 1 fig.; pl. 17,2.

a486 *Horak* Ulrike, Amulett mit fünf Anhängern und perlenverziertes Haarband: Tyche 10 (1995) 27-35; 14 fig.

a487 *Merhav* Rivka, Gold and silver pins from Urartu; typology and methods of manufacture: TAJ 21 (1994) 129-143 [< OTA 19, p.198].

a488 **Musche** Brigitte, Vorderasiatische Schmuck 1992 → 8,d896 ... 10,11795: [R]ArOr 63 (1995) 133s (B. *Hruška*); JAOS 115 (1995) 309s (O.W. *Muscarella*).

a489 *Pisano* Giovanna, Considerazioni sui gioelli fenici alla luce dlle nuove scoperte: StEgPun 14 (1995) 63-70 + 3 pl.

a490 **Rehm** Ellen, Der Schmuck der Achämeniden 1992 → 10,11796*: [R]JAOS 115 (1995) 307-9 (O.W. *Muscarella*).

a491 *Russmann* Edna R., Kushite headdresses and 'Kushite' style: JEA 81 (1995) 227-232.

a492 *Sannibale* Maurizio, Cinturoni [buckles ...] italici della collezione Gorga [< diss. Univ. Roma 1985]: MÉFRA 107 (1995) 937-1020; 85 pezzi, molti con fig.

a493 *Schick* Tamar, al., A 10,000 year old comb from Wadi Murabba''at in the Judean desert: "Atiqot 27 (1995) 199-206.

a494 *Stutzinger* Dagmar, Römische Haarnadeln mit Frauenbüste: B(onn)Jb 195 (1995) 135-108: 56 fig.

a495 *Tietz* Stefanie, Die männlichen Haartrachten in der Rundplastik: GöMisz 148 (1995) 95-103; 16 fig.

T2.8 Utensilia

a496 *Acquaro* E., I rasoi punici, 1971-1995: RSFen 23 (1995) 207-211; 5 fig.

a497 *Archi* Alfonso, Lists of tools [Ebla]: → 185, [F]SODEN W.von, Vom Alten Orient (1995) 7-10.

a498 **Aston** Barbara G., Ancient Egyptian stone vessels; materials and forms: StArchGAÄg 5. Heid 1994, Orientverlag. xix-196 p.; 16 pl.

a499 *Belletti* Vincenzo, 'Anomalie pompeiane' [bronze utensils]: Prospettiva 77 (1995) 2-15; 16 fig.

a500 **Bemmann K.,** Füllhörner [cornucopias] in klassischer und hellenistischer Zeit: EurHS 38/51. Fra 1994, Lang. 333 p.; 59 fig. -- [R]CLR 45 (1995) 478 (A. *Johnston*).

a501 *a) Caneva* Isabella, Recipienti per liquidi nelle culture pastorali dell'alto Nilo: -- *b) Mazzoni* Stefania, Drinking vessels in Syria; Ebla and the early Bronze Age; -- *c) Baffi Guardata* Francesca, Recipienti per bevande in Siria; la documentazione ceramica nel Bronzo Medio: → 10,480, Drinking ANE. 1990/4, 209-219 + 7 fig.(map) / 245-255 + 7+11 fig. / 277-286 + 9 fig.

a502 *Curtis* J.E., al., A silver bowl of Artaxerxes I: Iran 33 (1995) 149-153: pl. XXVIab.

a503 **Deines** Roland, Jüdische Steingefässe und pharisäische Frömmigkeit .. Joh 2,5: WUNT 2/52, 1993 → 9,5561: [R]CBQ 57 (1995) (L.J. *Hoppe* here discovers and glorifies a completely new use of archeology); JBL 114 (1995) 533-5 (W. *Braun*).

a504 *a) Frangipane* Marcella, Repertorio ceramico e consumo di liquidi alimentari in alcune società pre- e protourbane del Vicino Oriente; -- *b) Dolce* Rita, Luoghi e sistemi di conservazione di liquidi nel Vicino Oriente Antico; alcuni casi significativi; -- *c) del*

Monte Giuseppe F., Recipienti enigmatici: → 10,480, Drinking ANE. 1990/4, 227-235 + 9 fig. / 295-307 + 11 fig. / 187-198; testi 199-208.

a505 *Germer* Renatem *al.,* Untersuchung der altägyptischen Mumien [in] Leipzig: ZÄS 122 (1995) 137-154; 13 X-rays.

a506 *Goldman* Bernard, Persian domed turibula: StIr 20 (1991) 179-188: pl- XVII-XX.

a507 *Gouchani* A., *Adle* C., A sphero-conical vesel as .. a gourd for 'beer': Muqarnas 9 (1992) 72-92 [< StIr 33 (1994) 148s (J. *Dumarçay*).

a508 *a) Greenhut* Zvi, EB IV tombs and burials in Palestine; -- *b) Tal* Oren, Roman-Byzantine cemeteries and tombs around Apollonia [Arsuf/Herzliya]: *TAJ 22 (1995) 3-46; 21 fig. / 107-120; 10 fig.

a509 *Jannot* Jean-René, Les vases métalliques dans les représentations picturales étrusques : REA 97 (1995) 167-182; Eng. 167.

a510 ᴱ**Lalou** Élisabeth, Les tablettes à écrire 1991/2 → 9,527: ᴿBiOr 52 (1995) 654-7 (W. *Clarysse*).

a511 **Müller-Karpe** Michael, Metalgefässe im Iraq I (von den Anfängen bis zur Akkad-Zeit: PrähBr 2/14, 1993; DM 248. 3-515-05864-8: ᴿLevant 25 (1995) 256s (P.R.S. *Moorey*); Syria 72 (1995) 444-6 (P. *Amiet*).

a512 **Muscarella** Oscar W., Bronze and iron .. artifacts 1988 → 5.d281*; 6,d444 : ZA(ssyr) 85 (1995) 155-162 (P. *Calmeyer*).

a513 *Reich* R., Six stone water jars [Jn 2,6 like one found in the 'Burnt House' of Jerusalem: *JPersp 48 (1995) 30-33 [NTAb 40, p.96].

a514 *Tadmor* Miriam, *al.,* The Naḥal Mishmar hoard [28 metal objects] from the Judean Desert; technology, composition, and provenance: "Atiqot 27 (1995) 95-148; 34 fig.

T2.9 *Pondera et mensurae* -- **weights and measures**

a515 *Jankowska* N.B., *Jankowski* A.J., ᴿ Confrontation and unity in Mesopotamian and Egyptian weights for balance payments [Hermitage Museum from Kültepe]: VDI 213 (1995) 127-132; Eng. 132s.

a516 *Krauss* Rolf, Zur stilgeschichtlichen Einordnung der Gefässfragmente Berlin AGM 15084/15693 und des Messers vom Gebel el-Arak: MDOG 127 (1995) 151-171; 14 fig.

a517 *Kushnir-Stein* A., Two inscribed weights from Banias: IEJ 45 (1995) 48-51 [NTAb 40, p.95].

a518 *a) Lambert* Wilfred G., An inscribed weight; -- *b) Fales* Frederick M., Assyro-aramaica; the [16 BM] Assyrian lion-weights : → 110, ᶠLIPIŃSKI, E., Immigration: OLA 65 (1995) 135-8; 1 fig, / 33-55; 17 fig.

a519 *Legon* John A.R., Measurement in ancient Egypt [ROIK Elke, Das Längenmass-system 1993]: DiscEg 30 (1994) 87-100; 1 fig. [32 (1995) 91s, G. ROBINS demurs 'grid-square never represented any metrological unit' (IVERSEN E. 'fist'); further 33 (1995), 105-121; 2 fig., *Rousseau* Jean. Métrologie et coudée].

a520 **Leitz** Christian, Altägyptische Sternuhren: OLA 62. Lv 1995, Peeters. xi-317 p.; foldout star-map.

a521 **Roik** Elke, Das Längenmasssystem im alten Ägypten. Ha 1993, Rosenkreutz. 497 p.; 106 fig. DM 129 [DiscEg 30,87].

T3.0 **Ars antiqua**, *motiva, picturae* [icones → T3.1 infra]

a522 **Belting** Hans, Likeness and presence; a history of the image before the era of art, [T]*Jephcott* Edmund, 1994 → [R]CLR 45 (1995) 373-5 (J. *Elsner*); TS 56 (1995) 363s (J. *Dillenberger*).

a523 **Boardman** John, The diffusion of classical art in antiquity (1993 Mellon Lectures). Wsh/L 1994, National Gallery/Thames & H, 352 p.; 422 fig.; 9 maps. £ 34, 0-500-23696-8. -- [R]Antiquity 69 (1995) 621-3 (J. *Elsner*).

a524 [E]**Boardman** John, The Oxford history of classical art. 1993. £ 35: [R]HZ 261 (1995) 138s (P. *Zanker*).

a525 **Brahms** Tatjana, Archaismus: Diss. FrB 1993: EurHS 38/53. Fra 1994.

a526 **Cohn-Wiener** Ernst, Die jüdische Kunst; ihre Geschichte von den Anfängen bis zur Gegenwart; Nachwort zur Neuausgabe, *Künzl* Hannelore. B 1995, Mann. [vi-] 283 p. 3-7861-1556-7.

a527 **Collon** Dominique, Ancient Near Eastern art. L 1995, British Museum. 247 p.; 194 fig. £ 18. 0-7141-1135-X.-- [R]AfO 42s (1995s) 292s (Erika *Bleibtreu*).

a528 **Dominicus** Brigitte, Gesten und Gebärden in Darstellungen des Alten und Mittleren Reiches: StAltäg 10. Heid 1994, Orient-V. xiv-191 p.; 64 fig. DM 98. -- [R]Orientalia 64 (1995) 470-2 (Gabriella *Scandone Matthiae*).

a529 *Dziobek* E. [Diss. 1980]., *al.*, Eine ikonographische Datierungsmethode für thebanische Wandmalereien der 18. Dynastie: *StArGAä 3. 1992. -- [R]DiscEg 30 (1994) 181 (Lise *Manniche*).

a530 *Evans* Carl D., Cult images, royal policies and the origins of aniconism : → **4**, [F]AHLSTRÖM, G., Pitcher; JSOT.s 190 (1995) 192-212.

a531 **Frontisi-Ducroux** F., Du masque au visage; [*prósōpon*, frontality]; aspects de l'identité en Grèce ancienne: Idées et recherches. 192 p.; 106 fig. P 1995, Flammarion. F 180. — [R]CLR 45 (1995) 111-3 (S. *Goldhill*).

a532 **Goldhill** Simon, *Osborne* Robin, Art and text in ancient Greek culture 1994 → 10,11839: [R]CLR 45 (1995) 375-7 (Jennifer R. *March*).

a533 **Grant** M., Art in the Roman Empire. L 1995, Routledge. xxii-146 p.; ill.; 5 maps. 0-415-12031-4 [NTAb 40, p.553].

a534 [E]**Gubel** E., In de schaduw van Babel; de kunst van het Oude Nabije Oosten in belgische verzamelinge. Lv 1995, Peeters. 183 p. 90-6831-654-0

a535 **Haussperger** Martha. Die Einführungsszene [D]1991 → 7,b922; 9,13393: [R]BiOr 52 (1995) 460-4 (R.H. *Mayr*).

a536 [E]**Holliday** Peter J., Narrative and event in ancient art 1994 → 10,11842*; CJ 91 (1995s) 421-5 (Eleanor *Leach*, also on GOLDHILL S. & OSBORNE R. 1994*).*

a537 *a) Invernizzi* Antonio, Die hellenistischen Grundlagen der frühparthischen Kunst: -- *b) Brentjes* Burchard, Ortband, Rolltier und Vielfrass; Beobachtungen zur ' skythischen' Akinakes-Zier: AMI(ran) 27 (1994) 191-203; pl. 33-38 / 147-164; 36 fig.; pl. 24.

a538 **Jacobson** Esther, The art of the Scythians; the interpenetration of cultures at the edge of the Hellenic world: HO 8/2. Lei 1995, Brill. xviii-305 p.; bibliog. 275-293. 90-04-09856-9.

a539 *Kakovkine* Alexandre, La scène unique de la peinture murale dans une chapelle à Baouit: GöMiszÄg 138 (1994) 27-36.

a540 **Mackintosh** Marjorie, The divine rider in the art of the Western Roman Empire: BAR-Int 607. Ox 1995, Tempus Reparatum. [vi-] 115 p.; bibliog. 85-89. 0-86054-786-8 a541 **Mettinger** Tryggve N.D., No graven image ? Israelite aniconism in its Ancient Near East context: CBOT 42. Sto 1995, Almqvist & W. 250 p.; ill. Sk 192. 91-22-01664-3. - -[R]ThLZ 120 (1995) 986s (W. *Zwickel*).

a542 **Metwally** Edmad (p.150; Emad richtig iii), Entwicklung der Grabdekoration in den altägyptischen Privatgräbern: GÖF 4/24. Wsb 1992. 251 p.; 183 fig. DM 98. 3-447-03270-7. -- [R]ZDMG 145 (1995) 150s.

a543 *Parrish* David, A mythological theme in the decoration of Late Roman dining rooms: Dionysos and his circle: RAr(1995) 307-332; 16 (color.) fig.

a544 **Patrich** Joseph, The formation of Nabataean art 1990 → 6,2666, 7,b948: [R]JAOS 114 (1994) 665s (H. *Liebowitz*).

a545 [E]**Pointon** Marcia, The image in the ancient [Dura, Ara Pacis] and early Christian worlds [Peter-Paul; Sinai apse]: *Art History 17,1 (Ox 1994) viii-142 p. $ 20 pa. 0-631-19474-6 [NTAb 39, p.359]. -- [R]BoL (1995) 164 (L.L. *Grabbe*: debate arising out of the passing of *Kunstgeschichte* with the death of Kurt WEITZMANN.

a546 **Potts** Alex, Flesh and the ideal; WINCKELMANN and the origins of art history 1994 → 10,11849*: [R]CJ 91 (1995s) 433 (P. *Barolsky*); E(spr)eV 105 (1995) 185s (H. *Platelle*); RStR 21 (1995) 209 (Sally *Schulz*).

a547 *Robert* Renaud, Immensa potentia artis; prestige et statut des œuvres d'art à Rome à la fin de la République et au début de l'Empire: RAr (1995) 291-305.

a548 **Rozenberg** S., Enchanted landscapes; wall paintings from the Roman era. L 1994, Thames & H. 176 p.; ill. £ 28. CLR 45 (1995) 379s (Janet *Huskinson*).

a549 **Schefold** Karl, Gods and heroes in late archaic Greek art 1992 → 9,13410, xiii-361 fig.; $ 125. 0-5213-2718-0: [R]CLB 71 (1995) 44s (Judith L. *Sebesta*).

a550 **Shapiro** Harvey A., Myth into art; poet and painter in classical Greece 1994 → 10,11857; 130 fig.; £ 35; pa. £ 13: [R]CTom 122 (1995) 455s (Jennifer R. *March*).

Sommer Rainer, Marc CHAGALL als Maler der Bibel 1995 → a614 infra.

a552 **Turcan** Robert, L'art romain dans l'histoire, six siècles d'expressions de la romanité. P 1995, Flammarion. 383 p.; 495 (color.) fig. 2-08-010187-0.

a553 *Vincent* Jacques, Aux origines de l'individualisation des images historiques dans la production grecque: RH 293 (1995) 3-2l.

T3.1 *Theologia iconis* -- **ars postbiblica**

a554 *Bernabò* Massimo, Agar e Ismaele: varianti non conosciute di Genesi 16 e 2l nella illustrazione bizantina dei Settanta: OCP 61 (1995) 215-222; 8 pl.

a555 La Bibbia dell'amore commentata dai Padri della Chiesa; miniature del XV-XVI seeolo. Mi 1994, Paoline. 318 p.; 65 color. fig. L^m 55. -- [R]CivCatt 146 (1995,2) 437s (A. *Ferrua*).

a556 *Boespflug* François, *Zaluska* Violanta, Note sur l'iconogaphie du Prologue de Jean: → 106, [F]LÉON-DUFOUR X.,R(ech)SR 83,2 (1995) 293-303; Eng. 180.

Brosh Na`ama, Biblical stories in Islamic painting 1991 → 9002 supra.

a557 **Butzkamm** Aloys, Moderne Kunst. Pd 1992, Bonifatius. 7O p. DM 19,80. -- [R]BLtg 67 (1994) 52s (Martina *Blasberg-Kuhnke*).

a558 *a)* *Butzkamm* Aloys, Kirche und Kunst, Kunst in der Kirche; -- *b)* *Romhold* Günter, Religiöse Aspekte in der modernen Kunst: BLtg 67 (1994) 3-10 / 10-l8 + 6 fig.

a559 *Calabi* Francesca, Simbolo dell'assenza; le immagini nel Giudaismo [Dura Europos ...]: QStor 21,41 (1995) 5-32.

a560 *a) Cassimatis* Hélène, Fenêtre de l'au-delà dans l'iconographie italiote; -- *b) Guillaume-Coirier* Germaine, Images du *coronarius* dans la littérature et l'art de Rome: MÉFRA 107 (1995) 1061-1092; 19 fig. / 1093-151; 29 fig.

a561 **Cavarnos** Constantine, Guide to Byzantine iconography I. Boston 1993, Holy Transfiguration. 263 p. -- ᴿGOTR 39 (1994) 387s (G.C. *Papademetriou*).

a562 **Charalampidis** Constantine P., The dendrites in pre-Christian and Christian historical-literary tradition and iconography: StArch 73. R 1995, Bretschneider. 99 p. 88-7062-867-1.

a563 **Cherchi Chiarini** Gavina, Il cervo e il dragone, simboli cristiani e immagini cosmiche sulla facciata della Pieve di San Casciano di Cascina. Pisa 1995, ETS. 120 p. 88-7741-876-1.

a564 *Clendenin* Daniel B., From the verbal to the visual; Orthodox icons and the sanctification of sight: CScR 25 (1995s) 30-46.

a565 **Corrigan** Kathleen, Visual polemics in the ninth-century Byzantine psalters. C 1992, Univ. xv-325 p.; 113 fig. -- ᴿOCP 61 (1995) 266-8 (V. *Ruggieri*).

a566 **Cottin** Jérôme, Le regard et la Parole; une théologie protestante de l'image: LieuxTh 25, 1994 → 10,11864*: ᴿE(xp)T 107 (1995s) 17 (G. *Wainwright*); ÉTRel 70 (1995) 144s (J.L. *Klein*).

a567 *Dael* Peter van, Aniconic decoration in early Christian and medieval churches: → 134, ᶠMURRAY R., HeythJ 36,4 (1995) 382-396.

a568 **Der Nersessian** Sirarpie, Miniature painting in the Armenian kingdom of Cilicia from the twelfth to the fourteenth century: DOSt 31. Wsh 1993. xvi-198 p. $ 165. 0-88402-202-1. -- ᴿScr 49 (Bru 1995) 154-159 (Jacqueline *Lafontaine-Dosogne*).

a569 *Dulaey* Martine, La grâce faite à Isaac; Gn 22,1-19 à l'époque paléochrétienne: RechAug 27 (1994) 3-40.

a570 ᴱ(**Dupuigrenet) Desroussilles** François, La symbolique du livre dans l'art occidental du Haut Moyen Âge à Rembrandt. Bordeaux 1995, Société des Bibliophiles de Guyenne. 229 p. 2-904532-25-0.

a571 ᴱ**Duval** Noël, Naissance des arts paléochrétiens 1991 → 8,e2 ... 10,11867: ᴿAJA 99 (1995) 748s (Caroline J. *Hemann*).

a572 **D'Antiga** R., L'icona nella chiesa ortodossa. Padova 1994, EMP. 100 p. Lᵐ 13. -- ᴿStPat(av) 41 (1994) 701 (Augusta *Lena*).

a573 *Efthymiadis* Stephanos, Notes on the correspondence of Theodore the Studite [.. iconoclasm second phase]: RÉByz 53 (1995) 141-163.

a574 **Finney** Paul C., The invisible God; the earliest Christians on art 1994: ᴿ*CritRR 8 (1995) 40-43 (R. *Jensen*); RStR 21 (1995) 243 (J.C. *Anderson*); TS 56 (1995) 190 (B. *Ramsey*).

a575 *Fontana* Maria Vittoria, The influence of Islamic art in Italy: AION 55 (1995) 296-319.

a576 **Gauer** Heinz, Texte zum byzantinischen Bilderstreit; der Synodalbrief der drei Patriarchen des Ostens von 836 und seine Verwandlung in sieben Jahrhunderten: StTByz 1. Fra 1994, Lang. lxxxiv-198 p. - ᴿAHC 26 (1994) 182-5 (H.G. *Thümmel*).

a577 *Gharib* Georges, Le icone della Madre di Dio: EphMar 44 (1994) 241-268; español Eng. 269.

a578 **Giakalis** Ambrosios, Images of the divine; the theology of icons at the seventh ecumenical council [843]: SHCT 14. Leiden 1994, Brill. 151 p. *f* 100. 90-04-00946-8. − ᴿJThS 46 (1995) 372s (A. *Louth*).

a579 *Gilles* René,Il simbolismo nell'arte religiosa: La via dei simboli. R 1995, Arkeios. 369p

a580 *Gitay* Zefira, The portrayal of Job's wife [only 2,9] and her representation in the visual arts: → 59, ᶠFREEDMAN D.N., Fortunate 1995, 516-526; 4 fig.

a581   **Goecke-Seischab** Margarete L.,   Von Klee bis Chagall; kreativ arbeiten mit zeitgenössischen Graphiken zur Bibel. Mü/Stu 1994, Kösel/Calwer. 247 p. DM 38. 3-466-36495-1 / 3-7668-3299-9. -- ᴿ*ActuBbg 31 (1994) 320s (A. *Borràs*).

a582   *Gorringe* Tim, Rembrandt's religious art: Theol 98 (L 1995) 15-19.

a583   **Grabar** André, Les voies de la création en iconographie chrétienne, Antiquité et Moyen Âge: Champs 615. P reprint 1994, Flammarion. 442p. 2-08-081615-2. -- ᴿÉTRel 70 (1995) 595s (J. *Cottin*).

a584   **Grappe** Christian, Images de Pierre aux deux premiers siècles: ÉHPR 75. P 1995, PUF. 349 p. 2-13-047054-8.

a585   **Grossman** Grace C., Jewish art. China 1995, Levin. 320 p. 0-88363-695-6.

a586   **Heimann** Nora M., 'What honor for the feminine sex'; a cultural study of Joan of Arc and the representation of gender, religion, and nationalism in French nineteenth-century painting, prints, and sculpture: diss. City Univ., ᴰ*Mainardi* Patricia. NY 1994. 581 p. 95-10671. -- DissA 56 (1995s) p. 6.

a587   **Hirst** Michael, The Sistine Chapel; a glorious restoration... c.1994, Abrams, 271 p. $ 75. -- ᴿAmerica 172,13 (1995) 36s (J. *Howett*).

a588   *a) Hohmann* Friedhelm, Kunst und Kirche; Spannungsfekd in der theologischen Aus- und Fortbildung. -- *b) Dohmen* Christoph, Vom Gottesbild zum Menschenbild; Aspekte der innerbiblischen Dynamik des Bilderverbots: LebZeug 50 (1995) 287-293 / 245-252.

a589   *Jensen* Robin M., Integrating art history and the history of Christianity[MATHEWS T., FINNEY P., MALBON E., SNYDER G., MILES M.]: *CritRR 8 (1995) 27-43.

a590   **Kemp** Wolfgang, Christliche Kunst; ihre Anfänge, ihre Strukturen. Mü 1994, Schirmer-Mosel. 307 p.; 76 fig.; 16 color. pl. DM 48. 3-88814-737-9. -- ᴿZkT 117 (1995) 463-5 (H.B. *Meyer*).

a591   *Kinney* Dale, The iconography of the ivory diptych Nicomachorum-Symmachorum: JbAC 37 (1994) 64-96. pl. 3-10.

a592   *Krivak* Andrew J., (interview with *McNichols* William H.), Prayer and iconography: America 173/14 (1995) 18-20.

a593   **Lafontaine-Dosogne** Jacqueline, Histoire de l'art byzantin et chrétien d'Orient²ʳᵉᵛ [¹1987 → 4,e384 ... 10,11876*]: Publ 45. Lv 1995, Univ. Inst.Orientaliste. xxvi-295 p.; bibliog. ix-xxvi. 90-6831-719-9.

a594   **Mathews** Thomas F., The clash of the gods; a reinterpretation of early Christian art 1993 → 9.13453; 10,11879: ᴿAmerica 173,4 (1995) 35s (M. *Morris*); ChH 64 (1995) 251s (F. W. *Norris*); *CritRR 8 (1995) 36-39 (R.M. *Jensen*); RÉByz 53 (1995) 377s (A. *Failler*); *TBR 8,1 (1995s) 34 (L. *Houlden*).

a595   ᴱ**Mathews** Thomas F., *Wieck* Roger S., Treasures in heaven; Armenian illustrated manuscripts: exhibition Morgan NY & Baltimore Walters. NY 1994, Pierpont Morgan Library. xv-220 p., 48 pl,

a596   *Mazurczak* Urszula, Das Sechstagewerk in der Ikonographie des Mittelalters; Forschungsstand und Forschungsperspektiven: Acta Mediaevalia 8 (Lublin 1995) 117-135.

a597   **Nichols** John E., Seeable signs; the iconography of the seven sacraments, 1350-1544. Woodbridge 1994, Boydell. xvii-412 p, -- ᴿJRelH 19 (1995) 251-5 (F. *Brooks*).

a598   *Nientiedt* Klaus, Religion und Kunst; Fremdheit trotz verwndter Anliegen: HerKor 49 (1995) 121-3.

a599   **Pellegrini** Giancarlo, 'Il tuo volto, Signore, io cerco'; l'icona, il rinvenimento della presenza: Sussidi Biblici 48s. Reggio Emilia 1995, San Lorenzo. xiv-225p. Lᵐ 28.

88-8071-056-7.

a600 **Pillinger** Renate, Der Apostel Andreas; ein Heiliger von Ost und West im Bild der frühen Kirche (ikonographisch-ikonologische Studie): Szb 612. W 1994, Österr. Akad. 40 p. 3-7001-2147-4.

a601 ᵀᴱ**Pizzo** Paolo, Teodoro ABU QURRAH, La difesa delle icone (Trattato sulla venerazione delle immagini). Mi 1995, Jaca. 187 p. -- ᴿ ISLCHR 21 (1995) 228 (M. *Borrmans*).

a602 **Prigent** Pierre, L'art des premiers chrétiens; l'héritage culturel et la foi nouvelle. P 1995, D-Brouwer. 277 p., bibliog. 251-267. 2-220-03726-6.

a603 *Quacquarelli* Antonio, Lettere e segni nella iconografia cristiana antica dei secoli III e IV: VetChr 32 (1995) 255-268.

a604 **Quenot** Michael, The icon, window on the Kingdom 1991 → 9,13465: ᴿCanadCath 13,1 (1995) 28 (R. *Eady*).

a605 *Rachaman* Yosefa, ᴴ Midrashic literature as a starting point toward an artistic illumination of Scripture: → 10,331a, 11th Jewish 1994. A-115-122.

a606 **Riess** Jonathan B., The Renaissance Antichrist; Luca Signorelli's Orvieto frescoes. Princeton 1995, Univ. xv-191 p.; 38 pl. $ 59.50. 0-691-04086-9 [ThD 43,384].

a607 **Robinson** Edward, Icons of the present; some reflections on art, the sacred and the holy. L 1993, SCM. 146 p. £ 12.50 pa. -- ᴿTheol 98 (L 1995) 247s (H. *Wybrew*, also on HARRIES R.).

a608 **Sáenz** Alfredo, El icono, esplendor de lo sagrado 1991 → 9,13473: ᴿTeolBA 30 (1993) 89s (L. *Glinka*).

a609 *Sauser* Ekkart, Klemens von Rom und Petros von Alexandrien auf einer russischen Ikone: E(rbe)uA 71 (1995) 413-7: color.pl.

a610 **Schönborn** Christoph, God's human face; the Christ-icon [French 1976, ²1978; German (revised) 1984], ᵀ*Krauth* Lothar. SF 1994, Ignatius. xvi-254 p. $ 17. 0-89870-514-2. -- ᴿThD 42 (1995) 386 (W.C. *Heiser:* Archbishop Schönborn was principal editor of The Catechism of the Catholic Church).

a611 **Schrenk** S., Typos und Antitypos in der frühchristlichen Kunst: JAC.e 21. Müns 1995, Aschendorff. 217 p.; 3 fig.; 45 pl. DM 98. 3-402-08105-9 [NTAb 40, p.563].

a612 **Schwebel** H., Die Bibel in der Kunst, I. 19. Jh.; II. 20. Jh. Stu 1993s, Bibelges. 144 p.; 143 p. je DM 78. 3-438-04461-7; -2-5. -- ᴿÉTRel 70 (1995) 466s (B. *Reymond*).

a613 **Sepière** Marie-Christine, L'image d'un Dieu souffrant. P 1994, Cerf. 2-204-04606-X. -- ᴿBLE 96 (1995) 149s (J. *Rocacher*); E(xp)T 107 (1995s) 17 (G. *Wainwright*).

a614 **Sommer** Rainer, Marc CHAGALL als Maler der Bibel. Rg 1995, Pustet. 144 p. 3-7917-1474-0.

a615 **Staps** Heinz D., Speculum Passionis; ikonographische Untersuchungen zum Bild des Gekreuzigten in der mittelalterlichen Kunst des Abendlands anhand der Leidensspuren: Diss. Pont. Univ. Gregoriana. Rom 1994. 392 p. -- D(iss)AI-C 56 (1995s) p. 836. (No AA photocopy.)

a616 *Thijs* L., Geloven voorbij de beeldenstorm; gedachten over geloofsverbeelding: G(ereformeerd)TT 95 (1995) 24-36; 1 fig.

a617 **Thümmel** H.G., Die Frühgeschichte der ostkirchlichen Bilderlehre 1991 → 8,e35; 10,11899: ᴿVDI 213 (1995) 215-7 (D.E. *Afinogenov*, ᴿ).

a618 *Turchini* Angelo, Iconografia e vita religiosa in età moderna; committenza e commercio: RS(tor)SR 23,46 (1994) 95-111; 4 pl.

a619 *Valenziano* Crispino, *a)* Riflessi antropologici dell'iconografia e dell'iconologia teologica; - *b*) Il mare 'tema' nella liturgia: EO(rans) 10 (1993) 79-103 / 253-268.

a620 *Vogt* Hermann J., Das Bild als Ausdruck des Glaubens in der frühen Kirche: (Tü)TQ 175 ('Die Theologie und die Bilder der Kunst' 1995) 306-329; fig. 16-27; color. phot. 7-16 (andere und die meisten Artikel von Künstlern HAJEK O., FALKEN H., *al.*).

a621 *Walter* Christopher, The origins of the cult of Saint George [< 4th Symposium on Georgian art, Tbilissi May 1993, not included in the two volumes of Acta 1989]: RÉByz 53 (1995) 295-326; 3 pl.

a622 **Wolf** Gerhard, Salus populi romani; die Geschichte römischer Kultbilder im Mittelalter [Diss. *PReith* R., Heidelberg 1989] Weinheim 1990. 469 p.; 129 fig.-- *R*EO(rans) 12 (1995) 457-463 (H.P. *Neuheuser*).

a623 **Wolohojian** Stephan S., Closed encounters; female piety, art, and visual experience in the church of Santa Maria Donna Regina in Naples: diss. Harvard. CM 1994. 315 p. 95-14848. -- DissA 56 (1995s) p. 9.

a625 **Zibawi** Mahmoud, The icon, its meaning and history, *TMadigan* Patrick. ColMn 1993, Liturgical. 176 p.; ill. $90. -- *R*Furrow 46 (1995) 530-2 (P. *Pye*); RStR 21 (1995) 57 (J.J. *Yiannis*: high praise).

T3.2 Sculptura

a626 *Amedick* Rita, Unwürdige [nicht schöne] Greisinnen: MDAI-R 102 (1995) 141-170; 4 fig.; pl. 27-36.

a627 *E*Andreae Bernard, DAI-R Bildkatalog der Skulpturen des Vatikanischen Museums, 1. Museo Chiaramonti, *EStadler.* B 1995, de Gruyter. I. xiii-401 p.; II. p. 402-801; III. p. 802-1106, Bibliog. 146* p. 3-11-013899-9.

a628 *Andreae* Bernard, Il messaggio politico di gruppi scultorei ellenistici, *TBaroni* Anselmo, *EVirgilio* Biagio: → 10,440, Aspetti/Ellenismo 1992/4, 119-136; 5 fig.

a629 **Andreae** Bernhard, Laokoon und die Gründung Roms 1988 → 4.e254*; 7,d9: *R*RB(elg)PH 73 (1995) ...; RAr (1995) 264-6 (F. *Baratte:* particulièrement brillant).

a630 **Auerbach** Elise, Terra cotta plaques from the Diyala and their archaeological and cultural contexts; Diss. Chicago 1994. xi-551 p.; 15 fig.; 86 pl. -- *OIAc 11 (1994) 12.

a631 **Basile** John Joseph, Mediterranean and continental European stone warriors statuary of the 7th to 5th centuries B.C.; diss. Brown Univ. Providence 1992. xiv-254 p.; 48 pl. 93-08783. -- *OIAc 11 (1994) 12.

a632 *Basile* Joseph J., The Capestrano Warrior and related monuments of the seventh to fifth centuries B.C. : RAHAL 26 (1993) 9-31; 14 fig.

a633 **Begg** Patrick, Late Cypriot terracotta figurines: SIMA pocket 10, Jonsered 1991, Åström. vi-109 p. 91-7081-036-2. -- *R*BiOr 52 (1995) 794-8 (Brita *Alroth*); Gnomon 67 (1995) 177s (H. *Matthäus*).

a634 *Bienkowski* Piotr, A servant in the land of Egypt [pitifully bent and burdened, carved in wood; in Liverpool museum]: → 10,118, *F*SHORE A.F., The unbroken reed 1994, 54-64; 4 photos; 3 drawings.

a635 **Böhm** Stephanie, Die 'nackte Göttin'. Mainz 1990, von Zabern. xv-192 p.; 42 fig. DM 98. 3-8053-1085-4. -- *R*AJA 99 (1995) 741s (Larissa *Bonfante*); ClR 45 (1995) 371s (J.N. *Coldstream*).

a636 *Blomé* Borje, *Åström* Paul, The Laocoon group; a tentative reconstruction: Opus Mixtum, essays on ancient art and society (OpRom 21, 1994) 7-24.

a637 **Boschung** Dietrich, Die Bildnisse des Augustus: Das römische Herrscherbild 1/2. B 1993, Mann. xv-237 p.; 239 pl.; 8 maps; 9 diagrams. DM 290. -- ᴿArch 46 (Wsz 1995) 113s (Z. *Kiss*); CLR 45 (1995) 479s (J. *Elsner*).

a638 *Cornelius* I., on bronze figurines of Reshef and Baal: Michmanim 7 (Haifa 1994) [mentioned among other English (and Hebrew) articles of that issue in BoL (1995) 34 (L.L. *Grabbe*)].

a639 *Croissant* F., La sculpture grecque est-elle un art abstrait ?: *TopO 4 (1994) 95-107

a640 **Czichon** Rainer M., Die Gestaltungsprinzipien der neuassyrischen Flachbildkunst und ihre Entwicklung vom 9. zum 7.Jahrhundert 1992 → 8,e56;10,11915: ᴿBiOr 52 (1995)448-50 (Pauline *Albenda*: 'carving','surface modeling'); ZA(ssyr) 85 (1995) 162s (U. *Seidl*).

a641 *Davoli* P., Il gruppo statuario di Senuaset (Cairo J.E. 46600 + Monaco AS 6296: *StEgPun 12 (1993) 17-28 + 4 pl.; 5 fig.

a642 **D'Ercole** Maria-Cecilia, Observations sur quelques ambres sculptés archaïques d'Italie méridionale: RAr (1995) 265-289; 29 fig.

a643 **Fleischer** Robert, Studien zur seleukidischen Kunst, I. Herrscherbildnisse 1991 → 8,d849.e63; 9,13502: ᴿAJA 99 (1995) 363 (Beryl *Barr-Sharrar*).

a644 *Gasparri* Carlo, L'officina dei calchi di Baia; sulla produzione copistica [da bronzo in gesso] di età romana in area flegrea: MDAI-R 102 (1995) 173-187; pl. 39-47.

a645 **Haynes** Denys, The technique of Greek bronze statuary 1992 → 9,13508; 10,11925: ᴿAnCL 64 (1995) 506s (Sophie *Descamps*); Bo(nn)J 195 (1995) 661-3 (Carol C. *Mattusch*).

a646 **Hein** Irmgard, *Satzinger* Helmut, Stelen des Mittleren Reiches [II. 1993 → 9,13509] I, 1989 → 5,d408: ᴿBiOr 52 (1995) 639-642 (O.D. *Berlev*).

a647 **Hintzen-Bohlen** Brigitte, Herrscherrepräsentation im Hellenismus; Untersuchungen zu Weihgeschenken, Stiftungen und Ehrenmonumenten in den mütterländischen Heiligtümern von Delphi, Olympia, Delos und Dodona 1992 → 8,e68: ᴿBo(nn)J 195 (1995) 666-671 (H.-J. *Schalles*).

a648 **Höcker** Christoph, *Schneider* Lambert, Phidias. Ha 1993, Rowohlt. 160 p, -- ᴿRAr (1995) 421s (B. *Holtzmann*).

a649 **Hoff** Rolf von den, Philsophenporträts des Früh- und Hochhellenismus: Diss. Bonn 1992. Mü 1994, Biering & B. 209 p.; 58 pl.

a650 *a) Isager* Jacob, The lack of evidence for a Rhodian school [Samothrace Nike! Laocoon!!]; -- *b) Salanitro* Maria, Il sacrificium di Laocoonte in VIRGILIO e in PETRONIO: MDAI-R 102 (1995) 115-131 / 291-4.

a651 **Krierer** Karl R., Sieg und Niederlage; Untersuchung physiognomischer und mimischer Phänomene in Kampfdarstellungen der römischen Plastik, ᴱ*Borchardt* Jürgen, *Krinzinger* Fritz: ForAr 1. W 1994, Phoibos. 448 p.; 510 fig. DM 107 pa. 3-901232-02-8.

a652 **Lawton** Carol L., Attic document reliefs; art and politics in ancient Athens: MgClasAr. Ox 1995, Clarendon. xxi-169 p. 0-19-814955-7.

a653 *a) Le Dinahet Couilloud* M.-Th., *Mouret* N., Stèles funéraires grecques, études stylistiques et iconographiques 1980-92; -- *b) Montchamp* J.-P., .. du Bosphore et de la Chersonèse: ᴿ*TopO 3 (1993) 109-166 / 167-209 = 2 maps.

a654 **Leprohon** Ronald J., Boston museum of fine arts stelae; CorpusÄg 3/2 [3/1, 1985 → 9,13519] Mainz 1991, von Zabern. 24 p. + 124 loose fig. DM 78.-- ᴿOLZ 90 (1995) 31-35 (H. *Felber*).

a655 **Lewerentz** Annette, Stehende männliche Gewandstatuen im Hellenismus; ein Beitrag zur Stilgeschichte und Ikonologie hellenistischer Plastik [Diss. Heidelberg 1992]:

Antiquitates 5. Hamburg 1993, Kovač. 313 p.; ill. 3-86064-116-6.

a656   *Lulof* Patricia S., Terracotta statues from Olympia [MOUSTAKA Aliki 1993]: BVAB(abesch) 70 (1995) 225-232.

a657 **Mojsov** Bojana, The sculpture and relief of Ramesses III: diss. Institute of Fine Arts, ᴰ*Bothmer* B. NYU 1992. 325 p.; 81 pl. 93-33659. -- *OIAc 11 (1994) 34.

a658 *MacGinnis* John, Statue manufacture in Sippar [BM 62602]: WZKM 85 (1995) 181-4; facsimiles 105.

a659 **Mangold** Meret, Athenatypen auf antiken Weihreliefs: ArchSemBeih 2. Bern 1993, Univ. 77 p.; 10 pl.. -- ᴿGnomon 67 (1995) 710-5 (Marion *Meyer*).

a660 **Manzelli** V., La policromia nella statuaria greca antica: StArch 69. R 1994, Bretschneider. 340 p. -- ᴿCLR 45 (1995) 126-8 (Liz *James*).

a661 **Mattusch** Carol C., Greek bronze statuary 1988 → 5,d424; 7,d44: ᴿAJA 99 (1995) 161s (Frances *Van Keuren*).

a662 *Mayer-Opificius* Ruth, Das Relief des Šamaš-rēš-uṣur aus Babylon: → 185, ᶠSODEN W. von, Vom Alten Orient (1995) 333-344 + 7 fig.

a663 **Moreno** Paolo, Scultura ellenistica 1994 10,11938; (2 vol.) Lᵐ 195. -- ᴿArVi 14,51 (1995) 92.

a664 *Nachtergael* Georges, Terres cuites de l'Égypte gréco-romaine [BAYER-NIEMEIER E. 1988; SCHÜRMANN W. 1989; DURAND F. 1990; BESQUES S. 1992]: CÉg 70 (1995) 254-294.

a665   *a) Osborne* Robin, Democracy and imperialism in the panathenaic procession; the Parthenon frieze in its context; -- *b) Palagia* Olga, No Demokratia [doubtful name of a female statue]: → 736, Archaeology of Athens 1992/4, 143-150; 5 fig. / 113-122; 11 fig.

a666 **Pons Melladoa** Esther, Terracotas egipcias de época greco-romana, del Museo del Oriente Bíblico del Monasterio de Montserrat: *AulaO.s 9. Barc-Sabadell 1995, AUSA. 117 p.; bibliog. 109-113. 84-88810-10-5.

a667 **Reiser-Haslauer** Elfriede, Uschebti I-II, Wien Lfg 5s: CAÆg. Mainz 1990/2, von Zabern. xvi-147 p., Text; xvi-147 fig., 5 color.pl. 3-8053-1155-9; -290-3. -- ᴿBiOr 52 (1995) 62-65 (J.-L. *Chappaz*).

a668 **Ridgway** Brunilde S., *al.*, Greek sculpture in the Art Museum; Greek originals, Roman copies and variants. Princeton 1994, Univ. 131 p.; ill. -- ᴿRÉG 108 (1995) 229s (Mary-Anne *Zagdoun*).

a669   **Rogge** Eva, [28] Statuen der Spätzeit (750 -ca.300 v.Chr: Corpus Antiquitatum Ægyptiacarum, Katalog Wien Æg 9. Mainz 1992, von Zabern. xix-118 lose Blätter, 76 p. Text, 151 fig. 3-8053-1306-3. -- ᴿBiOr 52 (1995) 58-61 (E. *Graefe*).

a670 *Rolley* C., Bronzes: RAr (1995) 387-414; 5 fig.

a671 *Saady* Hassan El-, Two Heliopolitan stelae of the New Kingdom: ZÄS 122 (1995) 101-4; 2 fig.

a672 *Schäfer* Jörg, Die Lügen der Musen in der frühgriechischen Bildkunst: Thetis 2 (1995)47-54; 4 fig.

a673 **Schlögl** Hermann A. & Christa *Meyes*-, Uschebti [24]; Arbeiter im ägyptischen Totenreich. Wsb 1993, Harrassowitz. 72 fig. DM 108. 3-447-03357-6. -- ᴿBiOr 52 (1995) 62s (W.M. van *Haarlem* adds 1977 H.D. SCHNEIDER classification).

a674 **Schulz** Regine, Die Entwicklung und Bedeutung des kuboiden Statuentypus; HÄB 332, 1992 → 8,e92; 10,11948: ᴿJEA 81 (1995) 250-4 (J.F. *Romano*).

a675   *a) Smith* Federica, Apoteosi di Tolemeo III quale Ermete in un bronzetto di Vienna [esposizione Lisippo di Roma]: -- *b) Cittadini* Rita, La Prassilla di Lisippo ['danzatrice di Berlino']: MÉFRA 107 (1995) 1153-63; 12 fig. / 1165-80: 15 fig.

a676 **Speidel** M.P., Die Denkmäler der Kaiserreiter: BonnJb.b 50. Köln/Bonn 1994, Rheinland/Habelt. 460 p.; ill. -- ᴿMBAH 14,1 (1995) 117-126 (O. *Stoll*).

a677 *Sternberg-El Hotabi* Heike, Ein vorläufiger Katalog der sog. Horusstelen: GöMiszÄg 142 (1994) 27-54.

a678 **Tefnin** Roland, Art .. 'de remplacement' 1991 → 9.13533: ᴿBiOr 52 (1995) 377-383 (Eva *Martin-Pardey*).

a679 *Tefnin* Roland, Amenophis III sur son traîneau; mise en abîme et/ou cryptogramme ?: GöMiszÄg 138 (1994) 71-80.

a680 *Tooley* Angela M.J., Notes on wooden models [...boatmen] and the 'Gebelein style': → 10,118, ꟳSHORE A.F., The unbroken reed 1994, 343-353; 1 fig.; pl. XLI-XLIV.

a681 *Varner* Eric R., Domitia Longina [wife of Domitian) and the politics of portraiture: AJA 99 (1995) 187-206; 15 fig.

a682 **Viviers** Didier, Recherches sur les ateliers de sculpteurs et la Cité d'Athènes à l'époque archaïque; Endoios, Philergos, Aristoklès. Bru 1992, Acad. 263 p.; 59 fig. Fb 950. -- ᴿCJ 90 (1994s) 326s (Mary *Stieber*).

a683 *Zagdoun* Mary-Anne, Bulletin archéologique; la sculpture hellénistique: REG 108 (1995) 150-189.

a684 **Zanker** Paul, Die Maske des Sokrates; das Bild des Intellektuellen in der antiken Kunst. Mü 1993, Beck. 383 p.; 179 fig. -- ᴿBo(nn)J 195 (1995) 653-661 (N. *Himmelmann*).

a685 *Zhuravlev* D.V., ᴿ The Late Hellenistic Pergamenian skyphos with appliqué [lovemaking] reliefs from Chrysaliskos estate: VDI 213 (1995) 72-79; Eng. 79.

T3.3 *Glyptica;* **stamp and cylinder seals**, scarabs, amulets

a686 *a) Amiet* P., Quelques sceaux élamites; -- *b) Collon* Dominique, Some thoughts on Kassite seals: -→ 10,81, ꟳMEYER L. de, 52 Réflexions 1994, 59-66; 7 fig, / 293-7.

a687 *Aufrecht* Walter E., A Phoenician seal [showing two roosters and *hrs* 'gold']: -→72, ꟳGREENFIELD J., Solving 1995, 385-7; 2 fig.

a688 *Barkay* Gabriel, *Vaughn* Andrew C., An official seal impression from Lachish reconsidered [hitherto illegible because with blurring re-stamp]: *TAJ 22 (1995) 94-97: 4 fig. [p.98-106. *Zorn* Jeffrey R. on 3 Nasbeh *tet* (+ or x shaped stamps].

a689 **Basmachi** Faraj, Cylinder seals in the Iraq Museum, Uruk and Jamdat Nasr periods: EDUBBA 3. L 1994, NABU. 1-897750-03-6.

a690 *Ben-Tor* Daphne, The relations between Egypt and Palestine during the Middle Kingdom as reflected by contemporary Canaanite scarabs: → 721, 7° Egyptol. 1995, 16s.

a691 *a) Bleibtreu* E., Festungsanlagen auf neuassyrischen Rollsiegeln und Siegelabrollungen; -- *b) Klengel-Brandt* E., Einige Siegelabdrücke wohl nachassyrischer Zeit aus Assur; → 10,80, ꟳMAYER-OPIFICIUS R., Beschreiben 1994, 7-12 + 7 fig. / 111-7 +8 fig. [*al.* 163; 177; 191; 269; 327].

a692 **Blocher** Felix, Siegelabrollungen BM / Yale 1992 → 9,13545: ᴿZA(ssyr) 85 (1995) 307-311 (Eva A. *Braun-Holzinger*).

a693 *Callieri* P., La glittica greco-persiana nelle regioni orientali dell'impero achemenide: *StEgPun 11 (1992) 63-72 + 4 pl.

a694 **Colbow** Gudrun, Die spätaltbabylonische Glyptik Südbabyloniens: Univ. Vorderas 17. Mü 1995, Profil. 220 p. 3-89019-361-7.

a695   *Colbow* Gudrun, Samsu'iluna-zeitliche Abrollungen aus nordbabylonischen Archiven ausserhalb Sippars: RA(ssyr) 89 (1995) 149-189.

a696 **Doumet** Mme Claude, Sceaux et cylindres orientaux .. Chiha: OBO.a 9, 1992 → 8,e122; 19,13554: ᴿAfO 42s (1995s) 280-2 (D.M. *Matthews*); RB 102 (1995) 461 (J.M. de *Tarragon*).

a697 **Eder** Christian, Die ägyptischen Motive in der Glyptik des östlichen Mittelmeerraumes zu Anfang des 2. Jts. v. Chr.: OLA 171. Lv 1995, Peeters, ix-324 p.; Bibliog. 287-310. 90-6831-775-X.

a698   *Gignoux* Philippe, *Gyselen* Rika, Une collection d'empreintes de sceaux sassanides: StIr 21 (1992) 49-56; pl. X-XXI [95-102, pl.XX].

a699 **Gyselen** Rika, Catalogue des sceaux ... BN/Louvre 1, 1993 [2. by GIGNOUX P. was 1973]: ᴿBSOAS 58 (1995) 566s (A.D.H. *Bivar*).

a700   *Grünbart* Michael, Stempel in Mondsichelform; ein Beitrag zur frühbyzantinischen Stempelkunde: Tyche 9 (1994) 41-49; pl. 8-9.

a701 **Hammade** Hamido, Cylinder seals of the Aleppo Museum [1, of unknown provenance, 1987], 2. Seals of known provenance: BAR-Int 597. Ox 1994. Tempus Reparatum. 201 p. 0-86054-772-8. ᴿ*BuCanadMesop 29 (1995) 70 (M. *Fortin*).

a702 **Herbordt** Suzanne, Neuassyrische Glyptik: *SAA.s 1, 1992 → 8,e131; 9,13561: ᴿBoL (1995) 28 (W.G. *Lambert*).

a703   **Herrmann** Christian, Ägyptische Amulette aus Palästina/Israel: OBO 138, ᴰ1994 → 10,11978: ᴿBoL (1995) 28 (K.L. *Kitchen*: expensive and unwieldy, but provisionally useful); ÉTRel 70 (1995) 264s (Françoise *Smyth*); (Tü)ThQ 175 (1995) 368 (W. *Gross*); UF 26 (1994) 601 (O. *Loretz*).

a704   *Invernizzi* Antonio, Seal impressions of Achaemenid and Graeco-Persian style from Seleucia on the Tigris: Mesop-T 30 (1995) 39-50; 16 fig.

a705 **Jaeger** Bertrand, Les scarabées à noms royaux du Museo Civico Archeologico de Bologna [592; 94 ici + 32 sceaux]. ... -- *DiscEg 31 (1995) 47-56 (P. *Davoli*).

a706   **Keel** Othmar, Corpus der Stempelsiegel-Amulette aus Palästina/Israel von den Anfängen bis zur Perserzeit; Einleitung: OBO.a 10. FrS/Gö 1995, Univ./VR. x-366 p. DM 148. 3-7278-1013-0 / VR 3-525-53891-X   [OTA 19,p.329, A. *Fitzgerald*]. -- ᴿUF 27 (DIETRICH 60. Gb. 1995) 713 (O. *Loretz*).

a707 **Keel** Othmar, Stempelsiegeln IV.: OBO 135, 1994 → 10,11981: ᴿÉTRel 70 (1995) 273s (Françoise *Smyth*).

a708 **Keel-Leu** Hildi, Vorderasiatische Stempelsiegel: OBO 110, 1991 → 7.d94 ... 10,11983: ᴿBlOr 52 (1995) 146-8 (A. von *Wickede*); PEQ 127 (1995) 76s (D.M. *Matthews*).

a709   *Kühne* Hartmut,Der mittelassyrische 'Cut Style':ZA(ssyr) 85(1995)277-301;19 fig.;2 pl

a710   *Lapp* Nancy, Some Early Bronze Age seal impressions from the Dead Sea plain and their implications for contacts in the Eastern Mediterranesn; → 82, ᶠHENNESSY J.B., Trade 1995, 43-51; pl. 2-5.

a711   *Lemaire* André, Name of Israel's last king surfaces in a private collection [Hoshea stamp-seal sold at Sotheby auction 1993 for $80,000]; BArR 21,6 (1995) 48-52.

a712   *Lucchesi-Palli* Elisabetta, Die römische Bulla [Amulett] und ihre Verbreitung in Ägypten; → 96, ᶠKRAUSE M., Divitiae Aegypti 1995, 206-213; pl. 10-11.

a713 **McDowell** A.G., Hieratic ostraca in the Hunterian Museum Glasgow 1993 → 9,13568: ᴿBiOr 52 (1995) 574-6 (J. *López*); DiscEg 31 (1995) 113-7 (B. *Haring*).

a713* **Matthews** Donald M., The Kassite glyptic of Nippur: OBO 116, 1992 → 8,e143 ... 10,11986: ᴿWO 26 (1995) 206-8 (Beate *Salje*); ZA(ssyr) 85 (1995) 148-155 (Eva A.

Braun-Holzinger auch über sein Principles, OBO.A 8,1990); ZAW 107 (1995) 535 (M. *Köckert*).

a714 *a) Matthews* Donald, A twist in the tale ['Brak (room 18) style' dockets, of Akkadian period though never with Akkadian seal impression]; -- *b) Matthews* Roger J., Offerings to the gods; seal impressions on archaic tablets; -- *c) Maul* Stefan M., Das 'dreifache Königtum'; Überlegungen zu einer Sonderform des neuassyrischen Königssiegels; -- *d) Vértesalji* Peter P., Zum ältesten [mesopotamischen] Glyptikfund in Ägypten: → 23, ᶠBOEHMER R.M., Beiträge 1995, 385-8; 4 fig.; pl. 31 d-k / 389-394; 12 fig. / 395-402; p. 33 a-c / 643-657; 3 fig.

a715 **Matthews** Roger J., Cities, seals, and writing .. Jemdet Nasr, Ur 1993 → 10.11987: ᴿOLZ 90 (1995) 391-4 (W. *Nagel*, Eva *Strommenger*).

a716 **Møller** Eva, Ancient NE seals ..1992 → 8,e146 ... 10,11989; ᴿOrientalia 64 (1995) 365s (Edith *Porada* †).

a717 *Moret* Jean-Marc, Un groupe de scarabées italiques: JS(av 1995) 31-50 + 27 fig.

a718 *Nagel* Wolfgang, *Strommenger* Eva, Sechzig Jahre Bildkunstbund; ein neues Denkmal des Urdynastikums [Goldblech; sonst meist Rollsiegel]: → 23, ᶠBOEHMER R.M., Beiträge 1995, 455-468; pl. 34s.

a719 **Otten** Heinrich, Die hethitischen Königssiegel der frühen Grossreichszeit: Abh g/soz 1995/7. Mainz 1995, Akademie Wiss./Lit. 43 p. 3-515-06855-4.

a720 *Perna* Massimo, The roundels of Haghia Triada: Kadmos 33 (1994) 93-141; 10 plus facsimiles; 14 pl.

a721 **Pittman** Holly, The glazed steatite glyptic style; the structure and function of an image system in the administration of protoliterate Mesopotamia: BBV 16. B 1994, Reimer. xxii-393 p. 3-496-02527-4 [RStR 22,233, title (BB) 'zum Vorderen Orient' not in IATG].

a722 **Regner** Christina, Skarabäen und Skaraboide: Bonner Sammlung von Aegyptiaca 1. Wsb 1995, Harrassowitz. [iv-] 160 p.; Bibliog. 143-150. 3-447-03613-3.

a723 *Rehak* Paul, The Aegean 'priest' on CMS 1.223: Kadmos 33 (1994) 78-84;4 fig.;1 pl

a724 **Richards** Fiona V., Scarab seals from a Middle to Late Bronze Age tomb at Pella in Jordan: OBO 117, 1992 → 8,e151; 9,13584: ᴿRB 102 (1995) 461 (J.M. de *Tarragon*); ZDMG 145 (1995) 149s (W. *Zwickel*).

a725 **Salje** Beate, Der 'Common Style' der Mitanni-Glyptik 1990 → 7,d108; 8,e152: ᴿBiOr 52 (1995) 464-7 (D.L. *Stein*).

a726 *Sanmartín* J., Zur Schreibpraxis der ugaritischen Siegelschneider; die Siegellegende KTU 6,66: UF 27 (DIETRICH 60. Gb. 1995) 455-465.

a727 ᴱ**Sass** B., *Uehlinger* C., Studies in the iconography of Northwest Semitic inscribed seals: OBO 125, 1991/3 → 10,11996: ᴿCBQ 57 (1995) 436-8 (W.E. *Aufrecht*).

a728 **Schlick-Nolte** Birgit, *Droste zu Hülshoff* Vera, Skarabäen, Amulette und Schmuck: Museum Liebighaus 1. Melsungen 1990, Gutenberg. 454 p.; Ill. 3-87280-053-1. -- ᴿBiOr 52 (1995) 383-5 (G. *Clerc*).

a729 *Selman* Ṣelāḥ, *Muhsen* Riyā, ᴬ Shishin site seals: Sumer 47 (1995) 14-20.

a730 **Śliwa** Joachim, Egyptian scarabs [150 in 1985; now 50 more] and magical gems from the collection of Constantine Schmidt-Ciazyński: Zeszyt 917, 1989 → 6,d695; 8,e156: ᴿBiOr 52 (1995) 385s (Birgit *Schlick-Nolte*).

a731 **Smith** Joanna S., Seals for sealing in the Late Cypriot period: diss. ᴰ*Magness-Gardiner* Bonnie S. Bryn Mawr 1994. 407 p. 95-16576. -- DissA 56 (1995s) p. 245.

a732 **Stein** Diana, The seal impressions, 1. text; 2. catalogue: Nuzi Archiv des Šilwa-teššup

8s. → 10,11999;   Wsb 1993, Harrassowitz [RStR 22,55, M.P. *Maidman*; 'superb' successor to 'masterful' PORADA 1947].

a733 *Steinkeller* Piotr, Early Semitic literature and third millennium seals with mythological motifs: → 8,e731, **ᴱFronzaroli** P., Literature 1992, 243-272 + 8 pl.

a734 **Stoof** Magdalena, Ägyptische Siegelamulette 1992 → 9,13587: ᴿBiOr 52 (1995) 651s (J. *Śliwa*).

a735 *Tadmor* Hayim & Myriam, The seal of Bel-Asharedu -- a case of 'migration' : → 110, ᶠLIPIŃSKI, E., Immigration: OLA 65 (1995) 345-355; 2 fig.; 3 pl.

a736 **Teissier** Beatrice, Sealing and seals on texts from Kültepe 'Karum' level 2: InstNedIst 70. L 1994, Brill. xi-278 p.; 1ll. ƒ75 pa. 90-6258-070-X [RStR 22,56 (D.I. *Owen*). - - ᴿBoL (1995) 139 (W.G. *Lambert*).

a737 **Wiese** André, Zum Bild des Königs auf ägyptischen Siegelamuletten: OBO 96, 1990 → 7,d116; 8,e166: ᴿCÉg 70 (1995) 154-7 (W.A. *Ward*); WO 26 (1995) 187-190 (J.F. *Quack*).

a738 **Younger** J.G., Bronze Age Aegean seals 1700-1500: SIMA 102, 1993; 81-7081-049-4: ᴿBiOr 52 (1995) 470-4 (Judith *Weingarten*).

a739 *Zhang Qjang*, The origins of seals and sealing in China [known after 770 B.C., but claimed earlier under Mesopotamian influence]: *JAncCiv 9 (1994) 137-141 + 4 fig.

a740 *Zuin* Alessandra, Interpretazione del sigillo cilindrico Delaporte, Louvre I, T 88: AION 54 (1994) 282-8.

T3.4 **Mosaica**

a741 *Avner* R., ᴴ *Pesîpus* ... A Roman mosaic on Mt. Zion, Jerusalem: 'Atiqot 25 (1994) 21*- 25* . 188s [NTAb 40, p.91].

a742 **Donceel-Voûte** Pauline, Les pavements des églises byzantines de Syrie et du Liban 1988/91 → 9,13668: ᴿAnCL 64 (1995) 578-580 (Catherine *Balmelle*).

a743 **Kondoleon** Christine, Domestic and divine; Roman mosaics in the [Paphos] House of Dionysos. Ithaca NY 1995, Cornell. xii-361 p. $ 65. 0-8014-3058-5 [RStR 22,64, W.F. *Bunge*].

a744 **Meyboom** Paul G.P., The Nile mosaic of Palestrina; early evidence of Egyptian religion in Italy: ÉPR 121. Lei 1995, Brill. ix-409 p.; 78 pl.;bibliog. 383-8.   90-04-10137-3. -- ᴿRÉL 73 (1995) 350s (R.*Turcan*).

a745 **Piccirillo** Michele, The mosaics of Jordan: *ACOR 1 → 10,12016; Amman 1993, American Center of Oriental Research; $ 150:   ᴿArch 46 (Wsz 1995) 124s (T. *Waliszewski*); JRAS (1995) 287-9 (G.S.P. *Freeman-Grenville:* 'superbly illustrated book by our Honorary Fellow').

a746 *Schlatter* Fredric W. *a)* The two women in the mosaic of Santa Pudenziana [OT prophecy vs. Rome challenger]: *JEarlyC 3 (1995) 1-24; 5 fig.; -- *b)* A [Rome S. Pudenziana] mosaic interpretation of Jerome,*In Hiezechielem*: VigChr 49 (1995) 64-81;3pl

a747 **Wattel-De Croizant** Odile, Les mosaïques représentant le mythe d'Europe (Iᵉʳ-VIᵉ siècles); évolution et interprétation des modèles grecques au milieu romain: De l'archéologie à l'histoire. P 1995, de Boccard. [iv-] 313 p.; bibliog. 277-303. 2-7018-0091-9.

T3.5 *Ceramica,* **pottery** [→ *singuli situs,* infra]

a748 **Adan-Bayevitz** David, Common pottery in Roman Galilee 1993 → 9,13610; 10,12021: ^RBiOr 52 (1995) 812s (H.J. *Franken*).

a749 *Alexandre* Yardenna, The 'hippo' jar [4 samples shown in fig. 2 have rounded sides and bottom but no animal characteristics, and are somewhat dumpier than the Iron-II cognates (or the shorter Qumran jar)] and other storage jars at Hurvat Rosh Zayit: *TAJ 22 (1995) 77-88; 3 fig. (map) [p.89-93, *Gal* Zvi on Phoenician influence there].

a750 *Argyropoulos* Vasilike, Sorting through ceramic assemblages using a material characterization approach; applying scientific analysis to the study of Mesopotamian pottery: *BuCanadMesop 29 (1995) 47-53.

a751 *Arias* Paolo E., Ceramica greca e metallotecnica; un rapporto dialettico: Prospettiva 79 (1995) 18-23; 4 fig.

a752 ^E**Barnett** William K., *Hoopes* John W., The emergence of pottery: technology and innovation in ancient societies. Wsh 1995, Smithsonian. xviii-285 p. 1-56098-516-X.

a753 *Bartoloni* P., *Moscati* S., La ceramica e la storia: RSFen 23 (1995) 37-45; pl. I.

a754 *Bémont* Colette, Chronique de céramologie de la Gaule : RÉA(nc) 97 (1995) 633-643.

a755 *a) Buchholz* Hans-Günter, Keramik mit Schnurabdrücken aus Tamassos; -- *b) Gomez* Basil, *al.*, Clays related to the production of white slip ware : RDACyp (1995) 119-136: 6 fig.; pl. X / 113-8; 2 fig. (map).

a756 **Buitron-Oliver** Diana, Douris, a master-painter of Athenian red-figure vases: Kerameus 9. Mainz 1995, von Zabern. xi-115 p.; 150 fig. 3-8053-1357-8.

a757 **Campenon** C., La céramique attique à figures rouges autour de 400 av, J.-C. P 1994, de Boccard. 162 p.; 17 pl. -- ^RCLR 45 (1995) 475 (Lucilla *Burn*).

a758 **Cavagnera** Luisa, Ceramica protocorinzia dall'Incoronata presso Metaponto (scavi 1971-1993): MÉFRA 107 (1995) 869-936; 111 pezzi, molti con fig.

a759 **Cohen** Getzel M.,The Hellenistic settlement in Europe, the Islands, and Asia Minor: Hellenistic Culture and Society 17. Berkeley 1995, Univ. California. xiii-481 p.; bibliog. 459-465. 0-520-08329-6.

a760 *Davoli* P., Ricerche aull'orientamento dei templi nel Fayyum: *StEgPun 13 (1994) 43-62 + 6 fig.

a761 *a) Dever* William G., Ceramics, ethnicity, and the question of Israel's origins; -- *b) Franken* H.J., *London* Gloria, Why painted pottery disappeared at the end of the second millennium B.C.: BA 58 (1995) 200-213 / 214-222; ill.

a762 **Eriksson** Kathryn O., Red lustrous wheel-made ware: SIMA 103, 1993 → 9,13624; 10,12028: ^RBiOr 52 (1995) 824s (Diane L. *Bolger*).

a763 *Frankel* David, Color variation on prehistoric Cypriot red polished pottery: JField 21 (1994) 221-233.

a764 *Jamieson* Andrew S., The Euphrates valley and Early Bronze Age ceramic traditions: Abr Nahrain 31 (1993) 36-78; bibliog. 78-87; figures and concordance 88-92.

a765 **Killet** Heike, Die Ikonographie der Frau auf attischen Vasen archaischer und klassischer Zeit [Diss. Giessen 1993]: WissSchrArch 1. B 1994, Köster. 139 + 144 p. 3-929937-63-8.

a766 *Kluiver* Jersen, Early 'Tyrrhenians'; Prometheus painter, Timiades painter, Goityr painter: BVAB(eschav) 70 (1995) 55-103.

a767 **Magness** Jodi, Jerusalem ceramic chronology, circa 200-800 CE: JSOT/ASOR mg 9, 1993 → 9,13643: ^RAJA 99 (1995) 555s (Andrea *Berlin*); BASOR 298 (1995) 85s (M. *Rautman*).

a768 **Manning** Sturt W., The absolute chronology of the Aegean Early Bronze Age; archaeology, radiocarbon and history: *MgMeditArch 1. Shf 1995, Academic. 370 p.; bibliog. 328-366. 1-85075-336-9.

a769 *Marro* Cathérine, *Helwing* Barbara, Vers une chronologie des cultures du Haut-Euphrate au troisième millénaire / Untersuchungen zur bemalten Keramik des 3 Jt. am oberen und mittleren Euphrat → 23, ᶠBOEHMER R.M., Beiträge 1995, 341-384; 9 fig.

a770 *Meinardus* Otto F.A., The [1300 A.D.] Damascus unicorn bowl; Orientalia 64 (1995) 223s; pl. III.

a771 **Orton** Clive, *al.*, Pottery in archaeology 1993 → 9,13648; 10,12044: ᴿAJA 99 (1995) 535s (J.T. *Peña*); ClasB 71 (1995) 40-44 (J.G. *Younger*).

a772 **Pfälzner** Peter, Mittanische [sic] und mittelassyrische Keramik; eine chronologische, funktionale und produktionsökonomische Analyse: Berichte Hamad/Katlimmu 3. B 1995, Reimer. I. / Bibliog. 265-276; II. 3-496-02505-0.

a773 **Pilides** Despina, Handmade burnished wares of the Late Bronze Age in Cyprus: SIMA 105. Jonsered 1994, Åström. xiv-159 p. 91-7081-074-5.

a774 **Robertson** Martin, The art of vase-painting in classical Athens 1992 → 9,13650; 10,12047: ᴿGnom 67 (1995) 348-352 (M. *Prange*).

a775 *Silvano* Flora, Vasetti a staffa in faïence nel Mediterraneo orientale: EVO 18 (1995) 31-38; 12 fig. p. 39; 2 pl. p.42s.

a775 *Tsetlin* J.B., ᴿ Problems of the scientific experiment in ancient pottery studies: *RossA (1995,2) 59-68; Eng. 68.

a776 **Whitley** James, Style and society in Dark Age Greece [... vase painting]; the changing face of a pre-literate society 1991 l0,11223; 0-521-37383-2: ᴿAJA 99 (1995) 157-9 (I. *Morris*).

a777 **Wood** Bryant G., The sociology of pottery in ancient Palestine 1990 → 6.d777 ... 10,12059: ᴿA(ndr)USS 33 (1995) 155-7 (D. *Merling*); BA 58 (1995) 176s (B.M. *Gittlen*).

T3.6 **Lampas**

a778 **Amante Sánchez** Manuel, Lucernas romanas de la región de Murcia, Hispania citerior: Antigüedad y cristianismo, Anejos 1. Murcia 1993, Univ. 341 p. 84-7684-395-X.

a779 *Bunimovitz* Shlomo, *Zimhoni* Orna, 'Lamp and bowl' foundation deposits in Canaan [... an Egyptian tradition]: IsrEJ 43 (1993) 99-125 [< OTA 18 (1995) p. 471].

a780 *Jordan* David, Inscribed lamps from a cult at Corinth in late antiquity: HThR 87 (1994) 223-9; corrected drawing p.483.

a781 *Kakovkin* Alexander, Eine [fischförmige] Tonlampe des 4.-5. Jh. aus Ägypten in der Sammlung der Ermitage: GöMiszÄg 143 (1994) 85s + 2 fig

a782 *Lapp* Eric C., Byzantine and early Islamic oil-lamp fragments from house 119 at Umm al-Jimāl [1993]: ADAJ 39 (1995) 437-445; 7 fig.

a783 **Loffreda** Stanislao, Luce e vita, nelle antiche lucerne cristiane della Terra Santa: SBF Museum 13. J 1995, Franciscan. 53 p.

a784 *Lynch* Kathleen M., Desperately seeking Faustus [lamp-maker]: BA 58 (1995) 115.

a785 **Oziol** T., Les lampes au Musée de la Fondation Piéridès, Larnaca (Chypre). Nicosia 1993, Leventis. 80 p.; 19 fig. -- ᴿCLR 45 (1995) 470 (D.M. *Bailey*).

a786 **Paleani** M. Teresa, Le lucerne paleocristiane [72 nell'Antiquarium romanum del Museo Vaticano]: Catalogo 1, 1993; 88-7062-815-9 -- ᴿCLR 45 (1995) 202s (D.M. *Bailey*); Salesianum 57 (1995) 560 (B. *Amata*).

a787 *Yannai* Eli, A group of Early Iron Age lamps from the northern Sharon valley: *TAJ 22 (1995) 279-281; 1 fig.

т3.7 Cultica [→ м4-7 et singuli situs]

a788 **Anati** Emanuel, La religione delle origini: *StCamuni 14. Capo di Ponte 1995, Centro. 139 p.; bibliog. 133-9.

a789 *Baines* John, King, temple and cosmos; an earlier model for framing columns in temple scenes of the Graeco-Roman period [Egypt]: -→ 10,145, ^FWINTER E., Aspekte 1994, 23-33; pl. 4-5.

a790 *Bargen* Friederieke van, Žur Materialkunde und Form spätantiker Elfenbeinpyxiden: JbAC 37 (1994) 45-58, 8 fig., pl. 1-2.

a791 **Barker** Margaret, On earth as it is in heaven; Temple symbolism in the New Testament [from extracanonica; light, life, blood, robe]. E 1995, Clark. xv-86 p. $ 15. 0-567-29278-9 [OTA 19,p.363, R.D. *Witherup*; NTAb 40, p.541].

a792 **Binns** John, Ascetics and ambassadors of Christ; the monasteries of Palestine 314-631: EarlyChrSt. Ox 1994, Clarendon. xi-276 p.; bibliog. 254-269. 0-19-826465-8.

a793 *Bissoli* Giovanni, Il tempio nella letteratura giudaica e neotestamentaria; studio sulla corrispondenza fra tempio celeste e tempio terrestre [< diss. Roma, Pont. Ist. Biblico 1993, ^D*Le Déaut* R.]: ASBF 37. J 1994, Franciscan. xiv-239 p. $ 25 [OTA 19, p.363, A. *Niccacci*].

a794 **Brech-Neldner** Ruth, *Budde* Dagmar, Der Mumiensarkophag des Nes-pa-kai-schuti; Monographie zu einem altägyptischen Mumiensarkophag der Völkerkunde-Abteilung. Detmold 1994, Lippisches Landesmuseum. 132 p.; ill. [*OIAc 11,15].

a795 **Carmichael** David L., *al*,, Sacred sites, sacred places: One world 23. L 1994, Routledge. xiv-300 p. £ 45. 0-415-09603-0. -- ^RAntiquity 69 (1995) 642-4 (A.A.D. *Peatfield*).

a796 *Chiat* M.J., Form and function in the early synagogue and church: Worship 69 (1995) 406-426 [NTAb 40, p.286].

a797 **Dräger** Olaf, Religionem significare; Studien zu reich verzierten römischen Altären und Basen aus Marmor: *DAI.R Egh 33. Mianz 1994, von Zabern. 297 p. 3-8053-1659-3. **George** T.A., House most high: the temples of ancient Mesopotamia 1993 → b377.

a798 *a) Grabbe* L.L., Synagogues in pre-70 Palestine; a re-assessment [no firm evidence]; -- *b) Griffiths* J.G., Egypt and the rise of the synagogue: → a812 below, *Urman/Flesher*, Ancient synagogues 1 (1995) 17-26 / 3-16 [< OTA 18 (1995) 263 (Jodi *Magness*) → p.394 there].

a799 **Hastings** Arthur, In His honor; a pictorial journal through the early years of the Church. Muskego WI 1994, H.H.P. 288 p. $ 85 [BArR 21,1 (1995) 8]. **Hurowitz** V., I have built .. temple building 1992 → a259 supra.

a800 **Jacoby** Ruth, Ancient synagogues; plans and illustrations. J 1993,Hebrew Univ. 113 p.

a801 *Kee* Howard C., Defining the first-century CE synagogue; problems and progress [.. LEVINE Lee J., 1981 & 1987]: NTS 41 (1995) 481-500.

a802 **Kletter** Raz, The Judean pillar-figurines and the archaeology of Asherah: BAR-Int 636. Ox c.1995, Tempus Reparatum. 232 p.; bibliog. 115-134. 0-86054-810-X.

a803 *Mack* H., ^H The seat of Moses: *CHistEl 72 (1994) 3-12 [<JSJud 26 (1995) 247].

a804 *Margalit* S., The binated churches and the hybrid binated church complexes in Palestine: SBF*LA 45 (1995) 357-400.

a805 **Marinatos** N., *Hägg* R., Greek sanctuaries 1993 → 10,12076 [cf. 1995 → 471 supra]:
ᴿRAr (1995) 417s (C. *Rolley*).

a806 **Meek** H.A., The synagogue. L/SF 1995, Phaidon/Chronicle. 240 p. $ 60. 0-7148-
2932-3 [BArR 21,6 (1995) 10].

a807 *Merhav* R., Two limestone stelae depicting Canaanite deities in the [Haifa Univ.] Hecht
Museum: Michmanim 7 (Haifa 1994) 7-24, c. 1400 B.C. from near Tell Beit Mirsim [<
ZAW 107 (1995) 327, with excerpts also from 1 (1985), 2 (1985), 3 (1986), 4 (1989), 5
(1991), and 6 (1992)].

a808 *Meskell* Lynn, Goddesses, [Marija] GIMBUTAS and 'New Age' archaeology: Antiquity
69 (1995) 74-86; 6 fig.[87-100, *Hurcombe* Linda].

a809 **Pinch** Geraldine, Votive offerings to Hathor. Ox 1993, Ashmolean Museum. xxvii-
408 p.; 18 fig.; 64 pl.; 6 plans. 0-900416-55-6 [*OIAc 11,37].

a810 **Thierry** Michel, Répertoire des monastères arméniens [600 en Turquie + 400]: CC.
Turnhout 1993, Brepols. xvi-250 p. 3-503-50329-2; pa. -30-6. -- ᴿSyria 72 (1995) 458s
(R.H. *Kevorkian*).

a811 ᴱ**Tsafrir** Yoram, Ancient churches revealed 1993 → 9.13683; 10,12081: ᴿBASOR 298
(1995) 94s (R. *Schick*); OCP 61 (1995) 632-8 (P.L. *Gatier*); ThLZ 120 (1995) 231-4
(Gisela *Jeremias-Büttner*).

a812 ᴱ**Urman** Dan, *Flesher* Paul V.M., Ancient synagogues; historical analysis and
archaeological discovery: StPB 47. Lei 1995, Brill. I. xxxvii-297 p.; II. xii-299-677 p;
53 pl. 90-04-19242-9; -3-4.

a813 **Vazhuthanapally** Joseph, The biblical and archaeological foundations of the Mar
Thoma Sliba [diss. Jerusalem, Antonianum 1988]: Publ. 129. Kerala 1990, Oriental
Institute of Religious Studies. xvi-144 p.

a814 *Vitto* Fanny, The interior decoration of Palestinian churches and synagogues: → 118*,
ᶠMANGO C., ByF 21 (1995) 283-300.

a815 **Voss** Jens, Die Menorah .. : OBO 128, 1993 → 9,13685: ᴿZAW 107 (1995) 368 (M.
Köckert)

a816 *Vriezen* Karel J.H., Churches built over pagan sanctuaries; a frequent phenomenon in
Byzantine Palaestina/Arabia ? On churches, temples and theatres: → 591, Aspects 1993/5,
69-79: 1 plan (Umm Qeis).

a817 **Zwickel** Wolfgang, Räucherkult und Räuchergeräte: OBO 97, 1990 → 6,2721 ... 8,2517:
ᴿWO 26 (1995) 211-4 (Kjeld *Nielsen*).

T3.8 **Funeraria**; *Sindon*, **the Shroud**

a818 *Alföldy* Géza, Bricht der Schweigsame sein Schweigen ? Eine Grabinschrift aus Rom:
MDAI-R 102 (1995) 351-268; 2 fig.

a819 *a) Ali* Mohamed S., *Sternberg-El Hotabi* Heike, Ein Sargfragment des T3.k3p(.t)-
h3.Hnsw; -- *b) Depuydt* Leo, Apis burials in the twenty-fifth dynasty: GöMiszÄg 138
(1994) 11-18 + 3 fig. / 23-25.

a820 **Antonaccio** Carla M., An archaeology of ancestors; tomb cult and hero cult in early
Greece. Lanham MD 1995, Rowman & L. xiv-297 p.; 24 fig. $ 39.50; pa. $ 18. 0-
8476-7941-1; pa. -2-X. -- ᴿAJA 99 (1995) 740s (J. *Whitley*); GaR 42 (1995) 246 (P.
Walcot).

a821 **Bloch-Smith** Elizabeth, Judahite burial practices 1992 → 8,e275 ... 10,12086: ᴿBA 58
(1995) 172s (J-P. *Dessel*).

a822 [E]**Campbell** Stuart, *Green* Anthony, The archaeology of death in the Ancient Near East: Mg 51. Ox 1995, Oxbow. x-297 p.; bibliog. 253-297. 0-946897-93-X.

a823 **Clairmont** Christoph W., Classical Attic tombstones. Kilchberg 1993, Akanthus. xxi-343 p.; 6l fig., intr. Catalogue 5 vol.: 520 . 836 . 523 . 193 . 196 p, Indexes 374-LXVI p. -- [R]Gnomon 67 (1995) 532-541 (J. *Bergemann*).

a824 **Combi** Nenod, The Salone Good Shepherd sarcophagus and its group [Eng. & Croatian]. Split 1994, Museum. 131 p.; ill.

a825 *Cooper* Alan, *Goldstein* Bernard R., The cult of the dead and the theme of entry into the land: BInterp 1 (1993) 285-303 [OTA 18 (1995) p. 355s (Chris *Franke*)].

a826 *a)* **Corcoran** Lorelei H., Portrait mummies from Roman Egypt (I-IV centuries A.D.), with a catalog or portrait mummies in Egyptian museums: SAOC 56. Ch 1995. Univ. Or. Inst. xxxii-223 p; bibliog. xix-xxxii. 0-918986-99-0.-- *b)* **Doxiadis** E., The mysterious Fayum portraits: faces from ancient Egypt. 1995. -- *c)* **Borg** B., Mummienporträts. 1995. -- [R]Archaeology 48,6 (Boston 1995) 60-66 (R.S. *Bianchi*) [NTAb 40, p.286: Corcoran more originally interprets pharaonically; the others routinely Hellenistic].

a827 **Cremer** Marie-Louise, Hellenistisch-römische Grabstelen, NW Kleinasien, 1. Mysien; 2. Bithynien. Bonn 1991s, Habelt. xviii-204 p.; 14 fig. / xvi-199 p.; 9 fig. 3-7749-2521-6; -2-4. -- [R]*TopO 3 (1993) 305-320 (T. *Corsten*).

a828 *D'Ambra* E., Mourning and the making of ancestors in the [Rome Capitoline Trajanic] Testamentum relief: AJA 99 (1995) 667-681 [NTAb 40, p.286].

a829 **Dodson** Aidan, *al.*, The Canopic equipment of the king of Egypt 1994 → 10,12094; £ 65; [R]Orientalia 64 (1995) 467-470 (K. *Martin*).

a830 **Egner** Roswitha, *Haslauer* Elfriede, Särge der dritten Zwischenzeit I: Lose-Blatt-Katalog ägyptischer Altertümer, Wien 10. Mainz 1994, von Zabern. xvi p.; 206 cards. 3-8053-1498-1 [*OIAc 11,21].

a831 *Frisone* Flavia, Tra linguaggio rituale e vita materiale; le leggi sul rituale funerario nel mondo greco: → 135, [F]NENCI G., Historíē 1994, 183-210.

a831* *a)* *Greenhut* Zvi, EB IV tombs and burials in Palestine; -- *b)* *Tal* Oren, Roman-Byzantine cemeteries and tombs around Apollonia [Arsuf/Herzliya]: *TAJ 22 (1995) 3-46; 21 fig. / 107-120; 10 fig.

a832 *Hachlili* Rachel, Burial practices at Qumran: RQum 16 (1993-5) 247-264; 10 fig.

a833 **Hesberg** Henner von, Römische Grabbauten 1992 → 10,12098; DM 76: [R]HZ 260 (1995) 526s (Brigitte *Galsterer*).

a834 **Hewitt** Sonia, A study of Mycenaean and Minoan warrior burials in the Aegean from the period of the shaft graves to the fall of the palace at Knossos: diss. Queen's Univ., [D]*Simpson* R. Kingston 1993. viii-128 p. 0-315-80615-X.

a835 *Hoskin* Michael, *Allan* Elizabeth, Orientation of Mediterranean tombs and sanctuaries: → 751, Ritual 1984/95, BAR-Int 611.

a836 *Jansen-Winkeln* Carl, *a)* Ein Anruf an den Sarg: *DiscEg 30 (1994) 55-63 (long facsimile); -- *b)* Bezeichnung und Funktion einer Situla: *DiscEg 32 (1995) 57-62.

a837 [E]**Koch** Guntram, Grabeskunst der römischen Kaiserzeit; 4. Symposium des Sarkophag-Corpus, Marburg 23.-27.VII.1990, zu Ehren von Bernard ANDREAE. Mainz 1993, von Zabern. 267 p.; 100 pl. 3-8053-1484-1.

a838 **Kockel** Valentin, Porträtreliefs stadtrömischer Grabbauten; ein Beitrag zur Geschichte und zum Verständnis des spätrepublikanish-frühkaiserzeitlichen Prvatporträts, [E]*Fittschen* Klaus, *Zanker* Paul. Mainz 1993, von Zabern. xi-264 p.; 41 fig.; 70 pl. + foldout. DM 198. 3-8053-0480-3. -- [R]Latomus 54 (1995) 914s (L. *Foucher*).

a839 **Koortbojian** Michael, Myth, meaning, and memory on Roman sarcophagi. Berkeley 1995, Univ. California. ix-172 p. $ 40. 0-520-08518-3 [RStR 22,242, R.S. *Ascough*].

a840 **Lapp** Günther, Typologie der Särge und Sargkammern von der 6. bis 13. Dynastie: *SAGA 7, 1993 →9,13701: DiscEg 33 (1995) 161-8 (L.D. *Morenz*).

a841 **Lilliu** Giovanni, Betili e betilini nelle tombe di giganti della Sardegna: Mem. 9/6/4. R 1995, Acc. Naz. Lincei. P. 421-507.

a842 *McRay* J., Tomb typology and the tomb of Jesus: *ArchBW 2,2 (Shafter CA 1994) 34-44 [NTAb 39, p.209].

a843 **Metwally** Emad El-, Entwickung der Grabdekoration in den altägyptischen Privatgräbern; ikonographische Analyse der Totendarstellungen von der Vorgeschichte bis zum Ende der 4.Dynastie: GOF.A 24, 1992 → 8,g33; DM 98: ᴿArOr 63 (1995) 132s (M. *Bárta*).

a844 **Morris** Ian, Death-ritual and social structure in classical antiquity 1992 → 8,e293 ... 10,12106: ᴿ*TopO 4 (1994) 277-280 (R. *Étienne*).

a845 *Pelon* Olivier, Les tombes circulaires dans l'Égée de l'Âge du Bronze; état des questions: *TopO 4 (1994) 153-189 + 23 fig.

a846 *a) Petrosillo* Orazio, La Sindone e l'Eucaristia; - *b) Fossati* Luigi, Sindonologia; non insistere con le monete: StCatt 39 (1995) 33-38 / 207-213.

a847 *Petrosillo* Orazio, La sindone, simbolo della Risurrezione: StCatt 38 (1994) 202-8.

a848 *Ramafuthula* L.F., Clay sarcophagi from ancient Palestine; a neo-Assyrian influence: Nduits 35 (1994) 475-9 [< OTA 18 (1995) p. 265].

a849 *Reinssberg* Carola, Senatorensarkophage: MDAI-R 102 (1995) 353-370: pl. 85-93.

a850 *Saidah* Roger, ᴱ*Seeden* Helga, Beirut in the Bronze Age; The Kharji tombs: Ber 41 (1993/4) 137-210; ill.

a851 *Sauser* Ekkart, Die Tunika Christi in der Exegese der Kirchenväter: TrierTZ 104 (1995) 81-105.

a852 *Seigne* Jacques, *Morin* Thierry, Preliminary report on a mausoleum at the turn of the BC/AD century at Jerash: ADAJ 39 (1995) 175-19l; 12 fig, + 13, proposed restoration.

a853 **Sichtermann** Hellmut, Die mythologischen Sarkophage 2; DAI Sark. 12/2. B 1992, Mann. 196 p., 128 pl. DM 198. 3-7861-1563-X. -- ᴿLatomus 54 (1995) 181-3 (F. *Baratte*).

a854 **Stewart** Harry M., Egyptian shabtis: Eg 23. Princes Risborough 1995, Shire. 64 p. 0-7478-0901-9.

a855 *Tappy* Ron, Did the dead ever die in biblical Judah ? [BLOCH-SMITH E. 1992]: BASOR 298 (1995) 59-68.

a856 *Tillier* Anne-Marie, Paléoanthropologie et archéologie funéraire au Levant méditerranéen durant le paléolithique moyen; le cas des sujets non adultes: Paléor 21,2 (1995) 63-76; 7 fig.; Eng. 63.

a857 **Toynbee** J.M.C., Morte e sepoltura nel mondo romano [Death and burial 1971], ᵀ*Strazzulla* M.J.; pref. *Bacchielli* L.: SocCuGR 2. R 1993, Bretschneider. xv-285 p.; 30 fig.; 90 pl. 88-7062-728-4. -- ᴿSalesianum 57 (1995) 564s (B. *Amata*).

a858 *Valloggia* Michel, Le complexe funéraire de Radjedef à Abu Roasch: BSFÉ 130 (1994) 5-17.

a859 *Weber-Lehmann* Cornelia, Polyphem in der Unterwelt ? Zur Tomba dell'Orco II in Tarquinia: MDAI-R 102 (1995) 71-100; 11 (foldout) fig.; color.pl. 21-24.

a860 **Wesch-Klein** G., Funus publicum; eine Studie zur öffentlichen Beisetzung und Gewäährung von Ehrengräbern in Rom und den Westprovinzen; HeidAltHB 14. Stu 1993, Steiner. 238 p. DM 78. 3-515-06363-3. -- ᴿJRS 85 (1995) 256-8 (Susan *Treggiari*, also on three cognates in German).

a861 **Wilson** Ian, Holy faces, secret places; an amazing quest for the face of Jesus. NY 1991, Doubleday. xvii-238 p.; ill. $26. 0-385-26105-5. -- ᴿRStR 21 (1995) 41 (C. *Bernas*: no longer defends the Shroud, but seeks its antecedents).

a862 *Zeidler* Jürgen, Strukturanalyse spätägyptischer Grabarchitektur; ein Beitrag zum Vergleich ägyptischer und hellenistischer Sepulkralarchitektur: -→ 10,145, ᶠWINTER E., Aspekte 1994, 269-283 + 5 fig.

T3.9 *Numismatica*, coins

a863 *Acquaro* Enrico, *Manfredi* L.I., Rassegna di numismatica punica 1989-1991: *StEgPun 10 (1992) 7-70.

a864 **Arslan** Melih, ᴱ*Öztürk* Jean. *Lightfoot* Chris, Roman coins. Ankara 1993, Museum Direction. 170 p.; 292 fig.; map. 975-17-1127-4.

a865 *a) Barkay* R., The Marisa hoard of [25] Seleucid tetradrachms minted in Ascalon; -- *b) Barag* D., New evidence on the foreign policy of John Hyrcanus I: INJ 12 (1992s) 21-26; pl. 3-5 / 1-12 [NTAb 40, p.92].

a866 **Bastien** Pierre, Le buste monétaire des empereurs romains 1992 → 10,12126: ᴿLatomus 54 (1995) 746-8 (H. *Zehnacker*).

a867 **Belloni** Gian Guido, La moneta romana; società, politica, cultura: StSup 148. R 1993, Nuova Italia Scientifica. 284 p.

a868 *Bruijn* Erik de, *Dudley* Dennine, The [80 k N 'Aqaba] Humeima hoard; Byzantine and Sasanian coins and jewelry: AJA 99 (1995) 683-697; 6 fig.

a869 **Caccamo Caltabiano** Maria, *Radici Colace* Paola, Dalla premoneta alla moneta; lessico monetale greco tra semantica e ideologia. Pisa 1992, ETS. xix-217 p.; 6 pl. Lᵐ 28. -- ᴿCLR 45 (1995) 398-400 (K.R.T. *Butcher*); HZ 260 (1995) 823-5 (Maria R.-*Alföldi*).

a870 **Callatay** François de, *al.*, L'argent monnayé d'Alexandre le Grand à Auguste 1993 → 10,12131*: ᴿAnCL 64 (1995) 442s (Véronique Van *Driessche*).

a871 *Davesne* Alain, *Yenisoğanci* Veli, Les Ptolémées en Seleucide; le trésor de Hüseyinli: RNum 34 (1992) 23-36; pl. II-V.

a872 *Deutsch* R., A unique prutah from the first year of the Jewish war against Rome: INJ 12 (1992s) 71s; pl. 16 [NTAb 40, p.93].

a873 **Duncan-Jones** Richard, Money and government in the Roman Empire. C 1994, Univ. xix-300 p.; bibliog. 269-283. 0-521-44192-7.

a874 **Elayi** J. & A.G., Trésors de monnaies phéniciennes et circulation monétaire: TEuph supp.1, 1993 -→ 9,13723; 10,12133; F 345: ᴿRB 102 (1995) 106-7 (G. *Le Rider*)

a875 *Evans* Jane D., Ancient coins [2300] from the Drew excavations of Caesarea Maritima, 1971-1984: BA 58 (1995) 156-166; ill. [NTAb 40, p.287].

a876 *Foraboschi* Daniele, Civiltà della moneta e politica monetaria nell'ellenismo: → 10,440, Aspetti/Ellenismo 1992/4, 173-186; 1 fig.

a877 *Gjongecaj* Shpresa, *Nicolet-Pierre* Hélène, Le monnayage d'argent d'Égine et le trésor de Hollm (Albanie): BCH 119 (1995) 283-331; 6 fig.; VI pl. [761-781, *al.*, rapport sur Apollonia d'Illyrie 1994].

a878 **Göbl** Robert, Die Münzprägung des Kaisers Aurelianus: Denks, 233. W 1993. Österr. Akad. 282 p.; 165 pl. Sch 770. -- ᴿGnomon 67 (1995) 446-451 (D. *Kienast*).

a879 *Golenko* Vladimir K., Notes on the coinage and currency of the early Seleucid state II-IV: Mesop-T 30 (1995) 51-203 + 18 fig.

a880 *Grandjean* Catherine, Les comptes de Pompidas (IG VII 2426); drachmes d'argent symmachique et drachmes de bronze : BCH 119 (1995) 1-26.

a881 **Hars** Peter, Der Dareikos; Schicksale um eine Geldmünze. Stu 1992, Theiss. 337 p. 3-8062-1047-0 [*OIAc 11,25].

a882 *Hazzard* R.A., Theos epiphanes; crisis and response [coin of Ptolemy V 199 B.C., not VI after 180]: HThR 88 (1995) 415-433 + 4 pl.

a883 **Hazzard** R.A., Ptolemaic coins; an introduction for collectors. Toronto 1995, Kirk & B. 132 p.; 153 fig. -- ᴿ*JSStEg 23 (1993) 75-77 (T.M. *James*).

a884 **Heipp-Tamer** Christine, Die Münzprägung der lykischen Stadt Phaselis in griechischer Zeit 1993 → 10,12138: ᴿJNG(eld) 44 (1994) 215-8 (D.O.A. *Klose*).

a885 *Hollstein* Wilhelm, Apollo und Libertas in der Münzprägung des Brutus und Cassius: JNG(eld) 44 (1994) 113-133; 2 pl.

a886   *a)* *Hollstein* Wilhelm, *Jarman* Francis, Isis und Sarapis in Ionopolis; -- *b)* *Nollé* Johannes, *Zellner* Herbert, Von Anazarbos nach Mopsuhestia .... Stadtprägungen der römischen Kaiserzeit aus Kilikien; -- *c)* *Nollé*, Athen in der Schmiede des Hephaistos: ZN(Geldg) 45 (1995) 29-37 / 39-49 / 51-77.

a887 **Howgego** C., Ancient history from coins: *ApprAW. L 1995, Routledge. xvi-176 p.; 3 fig.; 23 pl. $ 55; pa. $ 17. 0-415-08992-1; -3-X [NTAb 40, p.556].

a888 *Hübner* U., Die Münzprägung Palästinas in alttestamentlicher Zeit: *Trumah 4 (Heid 1994) 119-145 [< ZAW 107 (1995) 336; OTA 18 (1995) p. 268].

a889 **Ilisch** Lutz, Palästina IV-A, Bilād aš-Šam: Sylloge numorum arabicorum Univ. Tübingen (Westphal-Sammlung). Tü 1993, Wasmuth. 51 p.; 18 pl. DM 80. -- ᴿBSOAS 58 (1995) 551s (A.D.H. *Bivar*); JRAS (1995) 413s (N.D. *Nicol*); WZKM 85 (1995) 315-7 (S. *Nebehay*).

a890 **Ingoglia** Robert T., Popes and coins; the ceremonial distribution of money by the papacy during the Middle Ages: diss. City Univ.; ᴰ*Adelson* H. NY 1995. 276 p. 95-21280. -- D(iss)AI 56 (1995s) p. 1078.

a891 **Karola** Margret, *Nollé* Johannes, Götter, Städte. Feste; kleinasiatische Münzen der römischen Kaiserzeit; Ausstellung, Pfalzer Privatsammlungen. Mü 1994, Staatliche Münzensammlung. 120 p.; ill. 3-922840-06-X.

a892 *Kindler* A., A Bar Kokhba coin used as a charity token: INJ 12 (1992s) 73-75; pl. 16 [NTAb 40, p.94].

a893 **Koch** H., A hoard of [266] coins from Eastern Parthia: NumMg 165. NY/Malibu 1990, Am.Num.Soc./Getty Museum. 64 p.; 12 pl. -- ᴿStIr 22 (1993) 140s (Rika *Gyselen*).

a894 **Kroll** John H., The Greek coins; Athenian Agora 26. Princeton 1993, Amer. Sch. Athens. xxvi-376 p. $ 150. -- ᴿAnCL 64 (1995) 437-9 (F. de *Callatay*); CLR 45 (1995) 400s (K. *Rutter*); JNG(eld) 44 (1994) 212-4 (B. *Overbeck*).

a895 *Le Rider* Georges, *a)* La politique monétaire des Séleucides en Coelesyrie et en Phénicie après 200 [av.J.-C., victoire d'Antiochos III à Banyas]: BCH 119 (1995) 391-404; -- *b)* Séleucos IV à Ptolemaïs; le trésor du Liban 1989; ᴿNum 34 (1992) 37-45; pl. VI-VII.

a896 **Llorens Forcada** M. del Mar, La ciudad de Carthago nova; las emisiones romanas: CN 6. Murcia 1994, Univ. 345 p.; LVII pl. -- ᴿAcNum 24 (Barc 1994) 236-8 (L. *Villaronga*).

a897 *Lönnqvist* K.K.A., New vistas on the countermarked coins of the Roman prefects of Judaea: I(sr)NJ 12 (1992s) 13-20; pl. 1s [NTAb 40, p.95].

a898 *Lusnia* Susann S., Julia Domna's coinage and Severan dynastic propaganda; Latomus 54 (1995) 119-139; pl. II-V.

a899 *Malek* Hodge M., A fifth century hoard of Sasanian drachms (A.D. 399-460): Iran 33 (1995) 67-84; 6 fig.; pl. IV-XIII [31 (1993) 77-93, 7th cent.]

a900 *a) Mattingly* Harold B., The Mesagne hoard and the coinage of the late Republic; -- *b) Duncan-Jones* R.P., Change in the Late-Republican denarius: NumC 155 (1995) 101-8 ; pl. 19-21 / 109-117; 5 fig.

a901 *Meyer-Zwiffelhofer* Eckhard, Die Münzprägung von Paltos in Syrien: JNG(eld) 44 (1994) 91-111; 3 pl.

a902 **Mørkholm** Otto, Early Hellenistic coinage 1991 → 7,d265 ... 10,12153: ᴿAnCL 64 (1995) 439-331 (F. de *Callatay*).

a903 *Munzi* Massimiliano, Un nummus inedito di Valentiniano III : MÉFRA 107 (1995) 1021-5.

a904 *Nicolet-Pierre* Hélène, Xerxès et le trésor de l'Athos (ICGH 362): RNum 34 (1992) 7-22; 1 pl.

a905 Numismatic literature 134. NY 1995, American Numismatic Soc. 241 p. 0-89722-258-X. -- 143 items plus reviews, obituaries, indices.

a906 *Pilch* John J., Coins of the Bible: BiTod 32 (1994) 172-6.

a907 *Pincock* Richard, Nero's large bronze coinage for Egypt: NumC 155 (1995) 266-271; pl. 48.

a908 *Sarfatti* Gad B., ᴴ The inscriptions on the Hebrew coins of the Second Temple period -- linguistic comments → 161, ᶠRUBINSTEIN E., *Te'uda 9 (1995) 75-87.

a909 *Syon* D., The [82 out of 6200] coins from Gamala; interim report: I(sr)NJ 12 (1992s) 34-55; pl. 8-13 [NTAb 40, p.98].

a910 *Todesca* J.J., Means of exchange; Islamic coinage in Christian Spain, 1000-1200; → 31, ᶠBURNS R., Iberia 1995. 232-258; 10 fig.

a911 **Welser** Wolfram, Katalog Ptolemäischer Bronzemünzen Univ. Köln: PapyCol 23. Köln 1995, Westdeutscher. 127 p.

a912 **Williams** Roderick T., The silver coinage of Velia [near Paestum]: Royal Numismatic special 25 → 10,12168. L 1992, Spink. xii-152 p.; XLVII pl. -- ᴿRÉG 108 (1995) 230s (O. *Masson*).

a913 **Ziegler** Ruprecht, Kaiser, Herr und städtisches Geld; Untersuchungen zur Münzprägung von Anazarbo und anderer ostkilikischer Städte: Tituli Asiae Minoris Egb 16 / Denks p/h 234. W 1993, ÖsAkW. 374 p.; 36 pl.; map. Sch 770. 3-7001-2001-X. -- ᴿLatomus 54 (1995) 915-9 (J.-P. *Callu*).

T4 *Situs,* **excavation-sites** 1. *Chronica,* **bulletins**

a914 *Bikai* Patricia M., *Kooring* Deborah, Archaeology in Jordan: AJA 99 (1995) 507-533; 22 fig.

a915 ᴱ**Eroğlu** Ismail, *al.,* XVII. Kazi sonuçlari toplantisi I-II. Ankara 1995, Kultur Bakanliği Basimevi. 485 p.; 512 p,; ill. 30 + 33 reports. 975-17-1615-2.

a916 *Maqdissi* Michel Al-, Chronique des activités archéologiques en Syrie (II); Syria 72 (1995) 159-266; 72 fig.; maps, bibliographie.

a917 ᴱ*Piccirillo* Michele, Ricerca storico-archeologica in Giordania I. Relazioni delle spedizioni archeologiche: SBF*LA 45 (1995) 491-529; map 490; 491-9, The Madaba National Park. 529-531, P. *Kaswalder* summary of ADAJ 38 (1994) & Studies/Jordan 5 (1995).

T4.2   *Situs effossi*, **syntheses.**

a918 ^E**Bienkowski** P., Early Edom and Moab .. Iron Age 1992 → 8,340; ^RSyria 72 (1995)
274s (F. *Braemer*).

a919 **Bierling** Neal, Giving Goliath his due; ... Philistines 1992 → 8,e365 ... 10,12178:
^RAndrUnSem 32 (1994) 115-7 (R.E. *Hendrix*); BA 57 (1994) 63s (P. *Schreiber*).
Chang-ho J., Iron Age ... Transjordan 1995 → *Ji*, a934 below.

a921 *Cifola* B., The role of the Sea Peoples at the end of the Late Bronze Age: OrAnt 33
(1993) 1-23 [< ZAW 107 (1995) 328].

a922 *David* Robert, La maison à piliers dans l'argumentation concernant l'émergence d'Israël
en Palestine à l'époque du Fer I → 10,30, ^FCOUTURIER G., Maison 1994, 53-69.

a923 **Dickinson** Oliver, The Aegean Bronze Age: WArch. C 1994, Univ. 342 p. $ 28 pa.
0-521-45664-9. -- ^RAJA 99 (1995) 732-5 (J.L. *Davis*).

a924 **Dothan** Trude & Moshe, People of the sea; the search for the Philistines 1992 →
8,a368* ... 10,12182: ^RAndrUSs 32 (1994) 126-8 (D. *Merling*); BA 58 (1995) 58 (P.
Warnock); *CritRR 7 (1994) 97-99 (Carol *Meyers*); *DiscEg 29 (1994) 147-151 (C.
Vandersleyen: the Philistines arrived overland and had nothing to do with the sea!).

a925 **Drews** Robert, The end of the Bronze Age ... catastrophe in 1200: 1993 → 9,13755;
10,12183: ^RA(mer)HR 100 (1993) 141 (Carol G. *Thomas*); AJP(g) 116 (1995) 321-4 (D.C.
Haggis); Arch 46 (Wsz 1995) 107-9 (P. *Taracha*); BiOr 52 (1995) 825-9 (P. van
Dommelen); CBQ 57 (1995) 126-8 (T.R. *Hobbs*); CLR 45 (1995) 119-121 (N.V.
Sekunda); JAOS 115 (1995) 312-4 (T.C. *Young*); JSSt 40 (1995) 86-90 (K.A. *Kitchen*).

a926 **Finkelstein** Israel, The archaeology of the Israelite settlement 1988 → 4,e629 ...
10,12184*: RevBib(Arg) 56 (1994) 119-122 (P. *Andiñach*).

a927 *Finkelstein* Israel, The date of the settlement of the Philistines in Canaan [after 1100
BCE, not under Ramses III 1130 as T. DOTHAN]: *TAJ 22 (1995) 213-239; map.

a928 **Fitten** J. Lesley, The discovery of the Greek Bronze Age. L 1995, British Museum.
212 p. 0-7141-1298-4.

a929 **Forsberg** Stig, Near Eastern destruction datings as sources for Greek and Near Eastern
Iron Age chronology; archaeological and historical studies, the cases of Samaria (722 B.C.)
and Tarsus (696 B.C.): Boreas 19. U 1995, Acta Univ. 106 p. 91-554-3592-0.

a930 **Gal** Zvi, Lower Galilee during the Iron Age [diss. Tel Aviv], ^T*Josephy* Marcia R. →
7,d290*]: ASOR.D 8, 1992 → 10,12185; $ 20. 0-931464-69-2 [RStR 22,230, W.
Schniedewind].

a931 *Galgounis* George J., The role of the Philistines in the Hebrew Bible: Bible Bhashyam
21 (1995) 236-249.

a932 *Goldberg* J., Centuries of darkness [JAMES P. 1991 → 7,d283 ... 10,12187] and
Egyptian chronology; another look: DiscEg 33 (1995) 1-32.

a933 *Hoglund* Kenneth G., The archaeology of silence; recent treatments of the Persian
period: *ABW 3,1 (1995) 35-41.

a934 *Ji* Chang-Ho C., Iron Age I in central and northern Transjordan; an interim summary
of archaeological data: PEQ 127 (1995) 122-140; map.

a935 **Joffe** Alexander H., Settlement and society in the Early Bronze Age I and II, southern
Levant [... Decapolis environs]; complementarity and contradiction in a small-scale
complex society: MgMeditArch 4. Shf 1993, Academic. vii-129 p.; 23 fig.; 5 maps. $
27.50. 1-85075-437-3. -- ^RAJA 99 (1995) 154s (S.F. *Falconer*); BASOR 298 (1995) 81-
83 (W. E. *Rost*).

a936 **Kuri** Sami, Monumenta [i.e 43 documents 1582-1624] Proximi-Orientis III. Palestine -
- Liban -- Syrie -- Mésopotamie: MHSJ. R 1994, Curia S.J. 373 p. -- [R]OCP 61 (1995)
654s (V. *Poggi*); POrC 45 (1995) 312s (P. *Ternant*).

a937 [E]**Laperrousaz** E.M., *Lemaire* A., La Palestine à l'époque perse 1994 → 10,12193:
[R]AulaO 12 (1994) 342-4 (G. del *Olmo Lete*); EThL 71 (1995) 198 (J. *Lust*); RB 102
(1995) 614s (É. *Nodet*); RevBib(Arg) 57 (1995) 250s (A.J. *Levoratti*).

a938 **Lehmann** G., Untersuchungsforschungen zur späten Eisenzeit in Syrien und Lebanon;
Stratigraphie und Keramikformen zwischen ca. 720 bis 300 v.Chr. *AVO 5. Münster c.
1995, Ugarit-V. x-548-p.; 113 pl.; 3 maps. 3-927120-33-2. -- [R]UF 27 (DIETRICH 60. Gb.
1995) 714s (W. *Zwickel*).

a939 *Margalith* Othniel, Where did the Philistines come from ? [Pylos]: ZAW 107 (1995)
101-9.

a940 **Mathers** Clay, *Stoddart* Simon, Development and decline in the Mediterranean Bronze
Age: ArchMg 8. Shf 1994, Collis. viii-367 p. 0-906090-49-0.

a941 *Merrill* Eugene H., The Late Bronze / Early Iron Age transition and the emergence of
Israel: BS 152 (1995) 145-162.

a942 **Noort** Ed, Die Seevölker in Palästina: Palestina antiqua 8, 1994 → 10,12196; 90-390-
0012-3 [JSOT 67,122]. -- [R]OTA 18 (1995) p. 405 (S.L. *McKenzie*); ThLZ 120 (1995)
987-9 (W, *Zwickel*).

a943 *Noort* Ed, Text und Archäologie; die Küstenregion Palästinas in der Frühen Eisenzeit:
UF 27 (DIETRICH 60. Gb. 1995) 403-428.

a944 *Rainey* Anson F., Unruly elements in Late Bronze Canaanite society ['*apîrû* ..]: →
130, [F]MILGROM J., Pomegranates 1995, 481-496.

a945 *Routledge* Bruce, 'For the sake of argument'; reflections on the structure of
argumentation in Syro-Palestinian archaeology [DEVER vs. ALBRIGHT ...]: PEQ 127 (1995)
41-49.

a946 **Schmitt** Götz, Siedlungen Palästinas in griechisch-römischer Zei; Ostjordanland,
Negeb und (in Auswahl) Westjordanland: TAVO B-93. Wsb 1995, Reichert. 371 p.;
foldout map. 3-88226-820-4.

a947 *Stone* Bryan J., The Philistines and acculturation;; culture change and ethnic continuity
in the Iron Age: BASOR 298 (1995) 7-32; 6 fig.

a948 [F]TESTA E., Early Christianity in context; monuments and documents [E]**Manns** F., *Alliata*
E.: SBF Publ.38, 1993 → 9,150; 10,12198: [R]Arch 46 (Wsz 1995) 122-4 (T. *Waliszewski*).

a949 **Thomas** Homer L., The transitional age; a handbook of archaeology, cultures and sites,
North Africa, Egypt, Southwest Asia: 1/3: SIMA 106. Jonsered 1994, Åström. iii-262 p.
91-7081-078-8.

a950 *Tsafrir* Y., [H] The peak of settlement in Byzantine Palestine; the archaeological
evidence and the literary sources: Eretz/Byz, Michmanim 8 (1995) 7-16 [Eng. → 205*,
[F]VAN BEEK G.; < ZAW 107 (1995) 509].

T4.3 Jerusalem, *archaeologia et historia*

a951 *Abells* Zvi, *Arbit* Asher, Some new thoughts on Jerusalem's ancient water
systems: PEQ 127 (1995) 2-7; 2 plans.

a952 *Alliata* Eugenio, *Kaswalder* Pietro, La Settima Stazione della Via Crucis e le mura di
Gerusalemme [Aelia 135 p.C.]: SBF*LA 45 (1995) 217-246; pl. 1-4; Eng. 485.

a953 *Alvarez Valdés* Ariel, La nueva Jerusalén del Apocalipsis y sus raíces en el AT; el período de la 'Jerusalén nueva': RevB 56 (1994) 103-113 . 231-236.

a954 **Ariel** T., Excavations at the City of David 1978-85 .. Y. SHILOH, 2., Imported stamped amphora handles .. : Qedem 30, 1990 → 8,e395 ... 10,12203: ᴿRB 102 (1995) 631-3 (J. *Murphy-O'Connor*, also on 3, Qedem 33 → a976 below).

a955 **Averincev** Sergei S., Atene e Gerusalemme; contraposizione e incontro di due principi creativi. R 1994, Donzelli. 63 p. -- ᴿQStor 21,42 (1995) 233-8 (Francesca *Calabi*).

a956 *Bahat* Dan, Jerusalem down under; traveling along Herod's Temple Mount wall [the 'Tunnel']: BArR 21,6 (1995) 30-47.

a957 **Bieberstein** Klaus, *Bloedhorn* Hanswulf, Jerusalem, Grundzüge der Baugeschichte vom Chalkolithikum bis zur Frühzeit der osmanischen Herrschaft: TAVO B-100, 1994 → 10,12209; DM 158: ᴿJAC 38 (1995) 206-8 (E. *Dassmann*); Levant 25 (1995) 255s (Kay *Prag*).

a958 *Busse* Heribert, Jerusalem im Kreis der heiligen Städte des Islams in der Auslegung von Sure 95,1-3: → 48, ᶠDONNER H., Meilenstein: ÄAT 30 (1995) 1-8.

a959 *Casalini* Nello, Il Tempio nella letteratura giudaica e intertestamentaria [BISSOLI G., diss. PIB 1994]: → 62, ᶠGALBIATI E.; RivB 43 (1995) 181-209; Eng. 210.

a960 *a) Catron* Janice E., Temple and *bāmāh*; some considerations; -- *b) Bedford* Peter R., Discerning the time; Haggai, Zechariah and the 'delay' in the rebuilding of the Jerusalem Temple: → 4, ᶠAHLSTRÖM G., Pitcher; JSOT.s 190 (1995) 150-165 / 71-94.

a961 **Chyutin** Michael, The New Jerusalem, ideal city [BibOrPont 34 (1978) 54]: *DSD 1 (1994) 71-97 [OTA 18. p.119; NTAb 39, p.464].

a962 *a) De Benedetti* Paolo, Gerusalemme, città di comunione ? -- *b) Boschi* Bernardo G., Fattori di comunione; legge, tempio, Gerusalemme; -- *c) Franco* Ettore, La koinonia nella Chiesa di Gerusalemme, archetipo di ogni comunità: P(arola)SV 31 (1995) 83-89 / 75-82 / 111-133.

a963 **Döpp** Heinz-Martin, Die Deutung der Zerstörung Jerusalems und des Zweiten Tempels im Jahre 70 in den ersten drei Jahrhunderten n.Chr.: Diss. ᴰ*Berger*. Heidelberg 1995. - - ThRv Beilage 92/2, x.

a964 *Domeris* W.R., *Long* S.M., The recently excavated tomb of Joseph Bar Caipha and the biblical Caiaphas: JTSAf 89 (1994) 50-58 [< ZIT 95, p.219].

a965 **Drijvers** Jan W., Helena Augusta 1992 → 8.e389 ... 10,12213: ᴿGnomon 67 (1995) 51-56 (T. *Grünewald*).

a966 ᴱ**Eshel** I., *Prag* K., Excavations by K.M. KENYON in Jerusalem 1961-1967, I. The Iron Age cave deposits on the south-east hill and isolated burials and cemeteries elsewhere: British Academy Monographs in Archaeology 6. [x-] 278 p. £ 40. 0-19-727005-0.

a967 **Flusin** Bernard, Saint ANASTASE le Perse et l'histoire de la Palestine au début du VIIᵉ siècle, I. Les textes; II. Commentaire; les moines de Jérusalem et l'invasion perse: Le monde byzantin, 1992 → 10,12215; 2-222-04554-1: ᴿRHPhR 75 (1995) 351s (P. *Maraval*).

a968 *a) Franken* H.J., [K. KENYON's] Cave I at Jerusalem -- an interpretation; -- *b) Wightman* G.J., Ben Sira 50:2 and the Hellenistic Temple enclosure in Jerusalem; → 82, ᶠHENNESSY J.B., Trade 1995, 233-240 / 275-283; plan.

a969 *Gelio* Roberto, Davide conquista la 'Rocca di Sion': Lat 61 (1995) 11-76; Eng. 77.

a970 ᴱ**Geva** Hillel, Ancient Jerusalem revealed 1994 → 10,12217*; 965-221-021-8: ᴿBASOR 298 (1995) 89s (Carol *Meyers*); OTA 18 (1995) p.145 (Diana V. *Edelman*: 39 Qadmoniot Hebrew articlesᵀ, continuing 1976 Jerusalem revealed).

a971 **Gibson** S., *Taylor* Joan E., Beneath the church of the Holy Sepulchre, Jerusalem; the archaeology and early history of traditional Golgotha: PEF mg.1, 1994 → 12218*: ᴿJJS 46 (1995) 310s (Vired *Shalev*); PEQ 127 (1995) 173 (J. *Wilkinson*).

a972 *Gibson* Shimon, *Jacobson* David M., The oldest datable chambers on the Temple Mount in Jerusalem: BA 57 (1994) 150-160; ill.

a973 **Goldsmith** Steven, Unbuilding Jerusalem; apocalypse and romantic representation. Ithaca NY 1993, Cornell. xvi-324 p. 0-8014-9999-2.

a974 *Goren* Haim, An imaginary European concept of Jerusalem in a late sixteenth-century model: PEQ 127 (1995) 106-121; 7 fig.

a975 *Grego* Igino, 'Tutti là sono nati'; Gerusalemme nella Bibbia e nei Padri: Asprenas 42 (1995) 203-220.

a976 **Groot** Alon D., *Ariel* Donald T., Excavations in the City of David 1978-1985, [II. a954 above] III. Stratigraphical, environmental and other reports: Qedem 33. J 1992, Israel Exploration Soc. xiv-278 p. $ 45. 0333-5884. -- ᴿBiOr 52 (1995) 800-803 (C.H.J. de *Geus*).

a977 *Grossberg* Asher, ᴴ The façade of the Temple depicted on ossuaries in Jerusalem 27,1 (1994) 38-42; ill.; reply to query, 142 [NTAb 39, p.96].

a978 *Gruson* Philippe, *al.*, Jérusalem; itinéraires, héritages: MoBi 91 (1995) 2-30.

a979 *Hiestand* Rudolf, Melisende von Jerusalem und Prémontré; einige Nachträge zum Thema: Die Prämonstratenser und das Hl. Land: APraem 71 (1995) 77-95.

a980 *Jack* Sybil M., No heavenly Jerusalem; the Anglican bishopric, 1841-83: JRH 19 (1995) 181-203.

a981 *Jospe* Raphael, Jerusalem's significance to world Jewry: JDharma 18 (1993) 18-34.

a982 *Jursa* Michael, *Radner* Karen, Keilschrifttexte aus Jerusalem [meist École Biblique]; AfO 42s (1995s) 89-108; facsimiles.

a983 *Kochav* Sarah, The search for a Protestant Holy Sepulchre; the Garden Tomb in nineteenth-century Jerusalem: JEH 46 (1995) 278-301.

a984 **Konzelmann** G., *a*) Jerusalem, 4000 Jahre Kampf um eine heilige Stadt. Ha 1993, Hoffmann & C. -- *b*) Gerusalemme, 4000 anni di guerra per la [!] Città Santa. CasM 1993, Piemme. 535 p. Lᵐ 45. -- ᴿStPat(av) 41 (1994) 676-8 (G. *Leonardi*).

a985 **Kroyanker** David, Die Architektur Jerusalems; 3000 Jahre Heilige Stadt [*Adrikalut* 1993 → 9,13796],ᵀ.. Stu 1994, Kohlhammer. 210 p.; 125 fig. + 317 color. DM 98. -- ᴿThR(und) 60 (1995) 473s (L.*Perlitt*); ThLZ 120 (1995) 918-920 (K.M. *Beyse*); ZAW 107 (1995) 533s (M. *Köckert*).

a986 **Kroyanker** David, Jerusalem architecture → 10,12224; also L 1994, Tauris Parke. 210 p. 1-85043-873-0.

a987 **Krüger** Jürgen, Rom und Jerusalem: Kirchenbauvorstellungen der Hohenzollern im 19. Jahrhundert [kunsthistorische Hab/Diss Karlsruhe]: Acta Humaniora. B 1995, Akademie. 320 p. 3-05-002427-5. -- ᴿR(öm)Q 90 (1995) 274 (E. *Gatz*).

a988 *Küchler* M., Ein jüdischer Jerusalem-Führer aus der Kairoer Geniza 1: Bulletin der Schweizerischen Gesellschaft für judaistische Forschung 1 (1992) 10-25 [< ZAW 107,134].

a989 **Lückhoff** Martin, Das protestantische Bistum in Jerusalem (1841-1886): ev. Diss. ᴰ*Schneider* H. Marburg 1994. -- ThRv 91,99.

Männchen Julia, G. DALMAN als Palästinawissenschaftler 1993 → a154 supra.

a990 *Manns* Frédéric, Encore une fois le Lithostrotos de Jn 19,13: Anton 70 (1995) 187-197; Eng. 187: a place on the hills *outside* Jerusalem, where Jesus as New Temple of Jn 2,21 could look on the Old Temple.

a991 *Martin-Achard* Robert, Remarques sur la bénédiction sacerdotale (Nm 6/22-27) [lamelles de Ketef Hinnom, BARKAY G, TAJ 19 (1992) 139-194]: ÉTRel 70 (1995) 75-84 . 253-8.

a992 **Mazar** Eilat & Benjamin, Excavations in the south of the Temple Mount: Qedem 29, 1989 → 6,d962: [R]JQR 84 (1993s) 109-111 (A.F. *Rainey*).

a993 *Mendecki* Norbert, Palestyna i Jerozolima w okresie przedisraelskim [pre-Israelite period]: R(uch)BL 48 (1995) 81-94 [< OTA 19, p.213].

a994 **Naredi-Rainer** Paul von, Salomos Tempel und das Abendland: monumentale Folgen historischer Irrtümer [... *Limpricht* Cornelia, à Venise]. Köln 1994, Dumont.

a995 *Niniże* Davit, Aus der Geschichte des Kampfes um die Befreiung des Kreuzklosters zu Jerusalem: Georgica 18 (1995) 5-13.

a996 *Paczkowski* M.C., Gerusalemme negli scrittori cristiani del II-III secolo [.. dimensione spirituale]: SBF*LA 45 (1995) 165-202; Eng. 484s.

a997 *Parente* F., *Toùs* ... (II Macc. IV,9), Gerusalemme è mai stata una *pólis:* RSLR 30,1 (1994) 3-38 [NTAb 40, p.107].

a998 **Pellistrandi** Christine, Jérusalem, épouse et mère: Lire la Bible 87, 1989 → 5,d766; 6,d964: [R]MélSR 51 (1994) 445-7 (Christine *Cannuyer*).

a999 *Pennacchini* Bruno, Gerusalemme e [=] l'Eden: *ConvA 2 (1994) 93-120 [< OTA 19,43].

b000 *Perrone* Lorenzo, *a)* Monasticism in the Holy Land; from the beginnings to the Crusaders [[T]< DizIstPerf]: POrC 45 (1995) 31-63; franç. 61; bibliog. 62-63. -- *b)* I monaci e gli 'altri'; il monachesimo come fattore d'interazione religiosa nella Terra Santa di epoca bizantina : → 119, [F]MARA M.Grazia = Aug(ustinianum)R 35 (1995) 729-761.

b001 [E]**Poorthuis** M., *Safrai* J., The centrality of Jerusalem; historical perspectives. Kampen c. 1995, Kok. v-244 p. 90-390-0151-0.

b002 **Purvis** James D., Jerusalem .. bibliography 2: ATLA 20, 1991 → 9,13803: [R]RB 102 (1995) 629 (J. *Murphy-O'Connor*: opens windows we did not know existed).

b003 *Robert* Philippe D., Jérusalem et Bethléem: → 155, [F]RENAUD B., Ce Dieu: LEDIV 159 (1995) 155-161.

b004 *Runje* Petar, Sacerdoti 'glagoljasi' nel 15. secolo [FABBRI F., Gerusalemme 1484] in Terra Santa: *RijT 3 (1995) 261-6 Croatian; 267 ital.

b005 *Rupprecht* Arthur, The house of Annas-Caiaphas: *ABW 1,1 (1991) 4-17.

b006 *Sauser* Ekkart, CYRILL von Jerusalem - Helena - und das Kreuz des Erlösers : E(rbe)uA 71 (1995) 222-230.

b007 *Schaper* Joachim L.W., The Jerusalem Temple as an instrument of the Achaemenid fiscal administration; VT 45 (1995) 529-539.

b008 **Schmidt** Francis, La pensée du Temple; de Jérusalem à Qoumran 1994 → 10,9745: [R]ASS(oc)R 90 (1995) 117s (J. *Lambert*).

b009 *Shalem* Avinoam, Bi'r al-Waraqa [Aqsa well fancifully linked with Gihon], legend and truth; a note on medieval sacred geography: PEQ 127 (1995) 50-61; 3 fig. (plans).

b010 *Shanks* Hershel, *a)* Sprucing up for Jerusalem's 3,000th anniversary; -- *b)* Is this [WEILL R. 1913 east of Siloam (tunnel)] King David's tomb ?: BArR 21.1 (1995) 59-61 / 62-67; ill.

b011 *Shanks* Hershel, Jerusalem 3000, a yearlong celebration: BArR 21,6 (1995) 24-28, stressing excavators' failure to publish.

b012 **Shanks** Hershel, Jerusalem, an archaeological biography. Wsh 1995, Biblical Archaeology Society. 272 p.; 9 fig. + 189 color.; 58 maps. $ 45. 0-879-44528-9 [BArR 21,5 (1995) 26s adv.; ThD 43,88].

b013 **Strohmeier** Martin, *Al-kulliya aṣ-Ṣalāḥīya* in Jerusalem; Arabismus, Osmanismus und Panislamismus im ersten Weltkrieg: AKM 49/4. Stu 1991, Steiner. -- [R]ZDMG 145 (1995) 180s (W. *Schmucker*).

b014 *Taylor* Joan F., The garden of Gethsemane, *not* the place of Jesus' arrest; BArR 21,4 (1995) 26-35 . 62.

b015 **Thorau** Peter, The lion of Egypt, Baybars [Jerusalem East Gate] 1992 → 10,12242: [R]JRAS (1994) 94s (P. *Jackson*).

b016 **Wightman** G.J., The walls of Jerusalem, from the Canaanites to the Mamluks: MeditArch supp. 4, 1993 → 9,13812; 10,12245; A$ 170: [R]BA 57 (1994) 236-8 (*ipse*) & 58 (1995) 58s (Jodi *Magness*); BArR 21.6 (1995) 6 (J. *Murphy-O'Connor*); RB 102 (1995) 433-7 (also J. *Murphy-O'Connor*).

b017 *Wilkinson* John, The inscription on the Jerusalem ship drawing: PEQ 127 (1995) 159s; 1 fig.

b017* *Wit* J.H. de, De afdaling van het nieuwe Jeruzalem; bevrijding en hermeneutik [RICHARD P., TAMEZ E., CROATTO J.S.]: G(ereformeerd)TT 95 (1995) 181-194.

-----

b018 *Gib'a*: **Arnold** P.M., Gibeah [Jg 19-21], the search for a biblical city [diss. Emory]: JSOT.s 79, 1990 → 6,d988 ... 9,13918: [R]JNES 54 (1995) 160s (N. *Na'aman*); PEQ 127 (1995) 71s (T.C. *Mitchell*).

b019 *Silwan:* **Ussishkin** David, The village of Silwan.. necropolis 1993 → 9,13809; 10,12243: [R]BiOr 52 (1995) 803-7 (C.H.J. de *Geus*); PEQ 127 (1995) 83s (Kay *Prag*); RB 102 (1995) 629s (J. *Murphy-O'Connor*: magnificently produced); Syria 72 (1995) 281-3 (Jacqueline *Dentzer-Feydy*).

b020 *Suweinit:* **Wyatt** N., Jonathan's adventure [1 Sam 14,4] and a philological conundrum: PEQ 127 (1995) 62-69; 5 fig.

T4.4 *Situs alphabetice:* **Judaea, Negeb**

b021 *'Ajjul:* **Daly** Richard L., Kings of the Hyksos; Tell el-'Ajjul in the bichrome ware period; a comparative stratigraphic analysis: diss. Utah, [D]*Daly* R., 1994. 551 p. 95-22048. -- D(iss)AI 56 (1995s) p. 991.

b022 *'Ajrud:* **Ayalon** Etan, (*al.*), The Iron Age II pottery assemblage from Horvat Teiman (Kuntillet 'Ajrud): *TAJ 22 (1995) 141-205 (-212); 30 fig.

b023 *Ascalon:* **Carmi** I., *al.*, The dating of ancient water-wells by archaeological and 14C methods: comparative study of ceramics and wood [2 wells re-dug 1987 dated 200 B.C.E - - 100 C.E]: IsrEJ 44 (1994) 184-200.

b024 *Beersheba-Saba:* **Chapman** Rupert L., The defences of Tell as-Saba (Beersheba); a stratigraphic analysis: Levant 25 (1995) 127-143; 14 fig.

b025 *Beit Jimal:* **Piccirillo** Michele, Interessanti scavi dei PP. Salesiani ne La chiesa di Khirbet Fattir: : *TSa 71,6 (1995) 31s

b026 *Beth Guvrin:* **Arnould** Caroline, **Hübsch** Alain, Israël; l'antique Beth-Guvrin [amphithéâtre]: *Archéologia 305 (1994) 50-57.

b027 *Bethlehem:* **Sered** Susan S., Rachel's tomb; the development of a cult: Jewish Studies Quarterly 2 (Tü 1995) 103-148.

b028 *'En-Gedi:* **Hadas** Gideon, Nine tombs of the Second Temple period at 'En-Gedi: 'Atiqot 24. J 1994, Israel Antiquities Authority. 75 p. [H] (Eng. 14); 79 fig.; 12 color. pl.; 8 plans. 0792-8424 [*OIAc 11,25].

b029 *Gaza*: *Quaegebeur* Jan, À propos de l'identification de la 'Kadytis' d'HÉRODOTE avec la ville de Gaza : → 110, [F]LIPIŃSKI, E., Immigration: OLA 65 (1995) 245-270.

b030 *Ḥalif* 30 k SW Lachish: *Alon* David, *Yekutieli* Yuval, The Tell Halif terrace 'silo site' and its implications for Early Bronze Age I: "Atiqot 27 (1995) 149-189; 31 fig, (maps).

b031 *Ḥaṣeva* (40 k W Edom-Buṣeira): *Cohen* Rudolph, *Yisrael* Yigal, The Iron Age fortresses at 'En Haseva: BA 58 (1995) 223-235; ill.

b032 *Hatoula*: [E]**Lechevallier** M., *Ronen* A., Le gisement de Hatoula en Judée occidentale, Israël; rapport de fouilles 1980-88: Mémoires et Travaux du Centre de Recherche Français de Jérusalem 8. P 1994, Association Paléorient. 315 p.; 100 fig.; XXV pl. -- [R]Paléor 21,2 (1995) 148-151 (T. *Watkins*).

b033 **Hebron**: *Orel* Vladimir, The deal of Machpelah [Gen 23,2-20]: BbbOr 37 (1995) 3-11.

b034 *Ḥeṣi:* *Blakely* Jeffrey A., *Horton* Fred L., Tell El-Hesi; what's in a name ?: → 77, [F]HAMRICK E.W., Yahweh 1995. 94-133; 134-149, Ḥeṣi bibliography.

b035 *Hever*: a) *Puech* Émile, Présence arabe dans les manuscrits de 'la grotte aux lettres' du wadi Khabra; -- b) *Israel* Felice, L'onomastique arabe dans les inscriptions de Syrie et de Palestine; -- c) *Gatier* Pierre-Louis, La présence arabe à Gérasa et la Décapole: → 728, Présence 1993/5, 37-46 / 47-57 / 109-118.

b036 *Jericho*: *Colbi* S., Jéricho, la cité des palmes; La Terre Sainte (mars 1995): E(spr)eV 105 (1995) 438s (J. *Daoust*).

b037 -- *Rosen* Baruch, A note on the Middle Bronze Age cemetery at Jericho: *TAJ 22 (1995) 70-76.

b038 -- **Hirschfeld** Yizhar, The Judean Desert monasteries in the Byzantine period 1992 → 9,13841; 10,12265: [R]BiOr 52 (1995) 813-6 (K. *Vriezen*); *JEarlyC 3 (1995) 505.7 (D. *Burton-Christie*).

b039 -- *Goldfus* H., *Arubas* B., *Alliata* E., The monastery of St. Theoctistus (Deir Muqallik): SBF*LA 45 (1995) 247-292; pl. 5-24; Eng. 485s.

b040 *Judeida*: *Crocker* Piers T., Micah 5,1 [H4,14 *bat*(sic)-*gedud*]; what and where is the 'city of troops' ?: BurHist 31 (1995) 21-24.

b041 *Ma'ale Adummim*: **Magen** Yitzhak, The monastery of Martyrius at Ma'ale Adummim; a guide. J 1993, Israel Antiquities authority. 72 p.; ill. 965-406-013-2 [*OIAc 11,32].

b042 -- a) *Hirschfeld* Yizhar, Spirituality in the desert; Judean wilderness monasteries: -- b) *Magen* Yitzhak, Martyrius; lavish living for monks: BArR 21,5 (1995) 28-37 . 70 / 38-49.

b043 *Ma'on*: *Chen* D., *Milson* D., The design of the ancient synagogues in Judaea; Horvat Ma'on and Horvat 'Anim: SBF*LA 45 (1995) 351-6.

b044 *Maresha*: MoBi 92 (1995) 42-47 (G. *Finkielsztejn*).

b045 *Masada:* **Hadas-Lebel** Mireille, Massada, histoire et symbole. P 1995, A.Michel. 163 p. -- [R]QStor 21,42 (1995) 239-242 (Francesca *Calabi*).

b046 -- **Cotton** H., *Geiger* J., Masada II (inscriptions) 1989 → 5.9552; 10,12273: [R]JRS 83 (1993) 241s (H.B. *Jones*).

b047 -- **Foerster** Gideon, Masada V; art and architecture. J 1995, Israel Exploration Society. xxvi-238 p. $ 80. 965-221-028-5

b048 -- *Roth* Jonathan, The length of the siege of Masada [47 days; not the alleged 7-36 months]: SCI(sr) 14 (1995) 87-110; 1 fig.

b049 *Miqne*: *Dothan* Trude, *Gittin* Seymour, [H] Tel Miqne/Ekron -- the rise and fall of a

Philistine city: Qadmoniot 27 (1994) 2-28; ill.

b050 **Negeb**: *Finkelstein* Israel, *Zilberman* Yitzhak, Site-planning and subsistence economy; Negev settlements [Arad EB2] as a case-study : → **4**, [F]AHLSTRÖM G., Pitcher; JSOT.s 190 (1995) 213-226.

b051 -- *Hess* Richard S., The southern desert [Negev, Sinai]: *ABW 2,2 (1994) 21-33.

b052 **Nessana**: *Figueras* P., Monks and monasteries in the Negev desert: SBF*LA 45 (1995) 401-450; pl. 53-58.

b053 **Qadeš-Barnea'**: *Goring-Morris* A. Nigel, *al.*, Upper paleolithic / neolithic occupation of the "Ein Qadis region on the Sinai/Negev border: "Atiqot 27 (1995) 1-36.

b054 **Qitmit**: **Beit-Arieh** Itzhaq, Ḥorvat Qitmit, an Edomite shrine in the biblical Negev: Mg 11. TA 1995, Univ. Inst. Arch. xvi-319 p. 965-440-004-9.

b055 **Timna**: **Kelm** George, *Mazar* Amihai, Timnah A biblical city in the Sorek Valley. WL 1995, Eisenbrauns. xix-186 p. 0-931464-97-8.

b056 **Ṭin**, 5 k SSE Bethlehem: *Mirazón Lahr* María, *Haydenblit* Rebecca, The human remains from the site of Et-Tin, Israel: Paléor 21,1 (1995) 97-111; 5 fig.; franç.97.

T4.5 Samaria, Sharon

b057 **Goodblatt** D. [H] The coastal district [of Israel is *medînat ha-yam* in Gittin 1/1, not the Hellenistic diaspora as usually held]: Tarbiz 64,1 (1994) 13-37 [NTAb 40, p.493].

b058 **Apollonia**: *Tal* O., Roman-Byzantine cemeteries and tombs around Apollonia: *TAJ 22 (1995) 107-120 [NTAb 40, p.478].

b059 **Caesarea M.;** *Horton* Fred L., Bathing in the face of the enemy; a Late Byzantine bath complex in Field E: → 77, [F]HAMRICK E.W., Yahweh 1995. 150-166.

b060 -- [E]**Oleson** John P., The finds and the ship: Harbours of Caesarea 2. Ox 1994, BAR-Int (594).

b061 -- *Porath* Y., [H] Herod's amphitheater [JOSEPHUS A 15,341]: 'Atiqot 25 (1994) 11*-19*.188 [NTAb 40, p.96].

b062 **Carmelus**: [E]**Giordano** Silvano. El Carmelo en Tierra Santa, desde los orígenes hasta nuestros días. Arenzano 1995, Messaggero. 224 p.

b063 **Dor**: **Stern** Ephraim, Dor, ruler of the seas. J 1994, Israel Exploration Soc. 348 p.; 479 fig.; 24 color. pl. $ 35. [= ? Dor, ha-mošelet ba-yamim, 193 p.; 242 ill. 965-342588-9. -- [R]BASOR 298 (1995) 84s (P.J. *King*: rich and complex site).

b064 -- **Stern** Ephraim, [H] A Cypro-Phoenician dedicatory offering from Tel Dor depicting a maritime scene [tip of a boat]: Qadmoniot 27 (1994) 34-38; ill.

b065 -- **Gitin** Seymour, Recent excavations in Israel; a view to the west; reports on Kabri, Nami, Miqne-Ekron, Dor, and Ashkelon; AIA 1. Dubuque 1995, Kendall/Hunt. xiii-122 p. 0-7872-0486-2.[On Kabri 1982/3 further IEJ 43 (1993) 181-4 . 256-9 (A. *Kempinski*, W. *Niemeier*)].

b066 **Gezer**: **Seger** Joe D., Gezer V, The Field 1 caves 1988 → 5,d812; 8,e445: [R]BASOR 297 (1995) 86-88 (P.E. *McGovern*).

b067 -- *Brett* M., The battles of Ramla (1099-1105): → 731, Egypt and Syria 1995, 17-39.

b068 **Samaria-Sebaste**: **Tappy** Ron E., The archaeology of Israelite Samaria I, 1992 → 8,e500 ... 10,12302: [R]BiOr 52 (1995) 798-800 (M. *Steiner*); JThS 46 (1995) 205 (G.I. *Davies*).

b069 -- *Albenda* Pauline, Some remarks on the Samaria ivories and other iconographic resources [.. *marzeah*, BEACH F.]: BA 57 (1994) 60; ill.

b070 -- *Schmitt* John J., Samaria in the books of the eighth-century prophets: → **4**, [F]AHL-STRÖM G., Pitcher; JSOT.s 190 (1995) 355-367.

b071 *Šekem*: **Campbell** Edward F., Shechem II: ASOR rep.2, 1991 → 7,d423; 10,12303: [R]JNES 54 (1995) 299-302 (A.H. *Yoffe,* comparing MILLER I., Kerak 1991) Orientalia 64 (1995) 479-481 (A.J. *Frendo*).

b072 -- Gerizim: *Magen* Yitzhak, Un tempio come il Tempio: Archeo 128 (1995) 30-37.

b073 *Šiloh*: **Schley** Donald G., Shiloh: JSOT.s 63, 1989 → 5,d886; 7,d425: [R]PEQ 127 (1995) 81 (T. *Mitchell*).

b074 -- [E]**Finkelstein** Israel, Shiloh: the archaeology of a biblical site 1992 → 9,13881; $ 50: [R]BArR 21,6 (1995) 6 . 8 . 10 (W.G. *Dever*).

b075 *Yarmuth*: Qadm 28 (1995) 27-38 (P. de *Miroschedji,* [H]).

T4.6 **Galilaea;** pro tempore *Golan*

b076 *Freyne* S., The ethos of first century Galilee: PIBA 17 (1994) 69-80 [NTAb 40, p.105].

b077 **Horsley** Richard A., Galilee; history, politics, people. Ph 1995, Trinity. vii-357 p. $ 30. 1-56338-133-8 [NTAb 40, p.379; ThD 43,369].

b078 *Horsley* Richard A., *a)* Archaeology and the villages of Upper Galilee; response *Meyers* Eric M.: BASOR 297 (1995) 5-16, 27s / 17-26; -- *b)* Archaeology of Galilee and the historical context of Jesus: Neotest 29 (1995) 211-229.

b079 [E]**Levine L.I.,** The Galilee in late antiquity 1992 → 8,e511; 10,12308: [R]JAOS 115 (1995) 123-5 (Daniel R. *Schwartz*); JRS 85 (1995) 308s (S. *Schwartz*).

b080 a) *Tsafrir* Y., On the source of the architectural design of the ancient synagogues in the Galilee; a new appraisal; -- *b)* *Urman* D., The house of assembly [*keneset*] and the house of study [*midraš*]; are they one and the same ? : → 389, Ancient synagogues 1 (1995) 70-86 / 232-255 [< OTA 18 (1995) p. 267 (Jodi *Magness*)].

b081 *Achzib*: *Mazar* Eilat, [H] Phoenician ashlar-built Iron Age tombs at Achzib: Qadmoniot 27 (1994) 29-34; ill.

b082 *Amirim*: *Zwickel* Wolfgang, Ein perserzeitlich-hellenistischer Tempel in der Nähe von Sefad: BiKi 50 (1995) 235s.

b083 *Bethsaida*: *Arav* Rami, Diminutive deity [Pataekos]: Egyptian amuulet [discovered 1994 in Omaha Nebraska Univ. excavations]: BArR 21,1 (1995) 44 & imposing cover photo.

b084 -- *Rousseau* John J., The impact of the Bethsaida finds on our knowledge of the historical Jesus; → 512, SBL Seminars 34 (1995) 187-207.

b085 *Beth-Shan* 1980-94: Qadmoniot 27 (1994) 93-116; ill. (*Tsafrir* Y., *Foerster* G. [H]); 87-92 . 117-137 Scythopolis (*Mazor* G., *al.*)

b086 -- **James** Frances W., *McGovern* Patrick E., The Late Bronze Egyptian garrison at Beth-Shan; a study of Levels VII and VIII: Museum Mg 85, 1993 → 10,12311; $ 115: [R]BASOR 297 (1995) 88s (A. *Leonard*).

b087 -- Beth-Shan, Hellenistic period: Qad 27,3 (1994) 87-92 (R. *Bar-Nathan*, G. *Mazor* [H]) [NTAb 40, p.92].

b088 -- *Kaswalder* Pietro, [< La Terre Sainte mai 1994]: E(spr)eV 105 (1995) 182-4 (J. *Daoust*).

b089 -- *Lattanzi* Giovanni, Beth Shean, la Pompei d'Israele : ArVi 14,54 (1995) 32-45.

b090 -- *Mazar* Amihai, [H] Four thousand years of history at Tel Beth-Shean: Qadmoniot 27 (1994) 66-83; ill. (84-86, *Horowitz* W.).

b091 -- **Ovadiah** A., *Turnheim* Y., 'Peopled' scrolls in Roman architectural decoration in Israel: RivAr.s 12. R 1994, Bretschneider. 184 p.; 283 phot. + 4 col. -- [R]RPh(lgLH) 69 (1995) 419s (H. *Lavagne*).

b092 -- *Tsafrir* Yoram, *Foerster* Gideon, From Scythopolis to Baysān -- changing concepts of urbanism [= [H] 10,12313] → 688*, [E]*King*, Land use 1991/2, 95-115 (117-170, *al.*, Jordan).

b093 ***Capharnaum;*** **Bloedhorn** Hanswulf, Die Kapitelle der Synagoge von Kapernaum; ihre zeitliche und stilistische Einordnung im Rahmen der Kapitellenenwicklung in der Dekapolis und in Palästina: AbhDPV 11. Wsb 1993, Harrassowitz. xiii-111 p. 3-447-02787-8.

b094 -- *Kühnel* Gustav, Gemeinsame [Bau-] Kunstsprache und rivalisierende Ikonographie; jüdische und christliche Kunst in Galiläa vom 4.-7.Jahrhundert: OrChr 79 (1995) 197-223: 17 fig.

----

b095 ***Dan*** *a) Barstad* Hans M., *Becking* Bob, Does the stele from Tel-Dan refer to a deity Dod ? ; -- *b) Lehmann* Reinhard G., *Reichel* Marcus, *Dod* und *asima* in Tell Dan; -- *c) Na'aman* Nadav, Beth-David in the Aramaic stela from Tel Dan: BN(otiz) 77 (1995) 5-11 / 29-33 / 79 (1995) 17-24.

b096 -- *Becking* Bob, Het 'huis van David' in een pre-exilische inscriptie uit Tel Dan: NedThT 49 (1995) 108-123; Eng.154.

b097 -- *Biran* A., *Naveh* J., [H] The Dan inscription, the maṣṣebot and the marketplaces: Qadm 28 (1995) 39-47.

b098 -- **Biran** A., Biblical Dan [1982], [T]*Shadur* Joseph, 1994 → 10,12319, Isr.Expl. / HUC. 280 p.; 228 fig.; 44 colour. pl. $ 32. 965-221-020-X. -- [R]BoL (1995) 24 (G.I. *Davies*); PEQ 127 (1995) 171s (R.M. *Porter*).

b099 -- *a) Biran* Avraham, Dan, la cité biblique au nord d'Israël; -- *b) Puech* Émile, Surprenante révélation, la stèle de Dan: MoBi 90 (1995) 32-37 / 38s.

b100 -- *a) Cryer* Frederick H., A 'Betdawd' miscellany: *dwd, dwd', or dwdh* ?; (further on King Hadad); -- *b) Thompson* Thomas L., 'House of David', an eponymic reference to Yahweh as godfather (further: Dissonance and disconnections; notes on the *bytdwd* and *hmlkhdd* fragments from Tel Dan: S(cand)JOT 9 (1995) 52-58 (223-235) / 59-74 (236-40).

b101 -- *Demsky* Aaron, On reading ancient inscriptions; the monumental Aramaic stele fragment from Tel Dan: JANES 23 (1995) 29-35 (postscript finds support in the two new fragments; approves their joining to each other only).

b102 -- *Hoffmeier* James K., The recently discovered Tell Dan inscription; controversy & confirmation: *ABW 3,1 (1995) 12-15.

b103 -- *Lemche* Niels P., Bemerkungen über einen Paradigmenwechsel aus Anlass einer neu-entdeckten Inschrift [*betdavid*] : → 48, [F]DONNER H., Meilenstein: ÄAT 30 (1995) 99-108.

b104 -- *Willis* John T., The newly discovered fragmentary Aramaic inscription from Tel Dan: RestQ 37 (1995) 219-226.

b105 -- stele: Phoe 41,3 (1995) 119-130; 3 fig. (C.H.J. de *Geus*).

b106 -- *Ahituv* Shmuel, Suzerain or vassal ? Notes on the Aramaic inscription from Tel Dan: IsrEJ 43 (1993) 246s [81-98. *Biran* A.].

b107 -- *Freedman* David N., *Geoghegan* Jeffrey C., 'House of David' is there [P. DAVIES' rejection is his only out for continuing his anti-maximizing exegesis]: BArR [20,4 (1994)]

21.2 (1995) 78s.

b108 -- *Noll* K.J., The city of Dan in the pre-Assyrian Iron Age: ProcGM 15 (1995) 145-154.

b109 -- *a) Smelik* K.A.D., Nieuwe ontwikkelingen rond de inscriptie uit Tel Dan: A(mst)CEBT 14 (1995) 131-141 [< OTA 19, p.203: further-discovered fragments show that *bytdwd* was not a sanctuary but a country (Judah); Hazael (not Jehu as 2 Kgs 9) killed Jehoram and Ahaziah]; -- *b) Willis* John T., The newly [i.e. earlier] discovered fragmentary Aramaic inscription from Tel Dan: RestQ 37 (1995) 219-226.

----

b110 **Golan**: *Epstein* Claire, Before history; the Golan's chalcolithic heritage: BArR 21.6 (1995) 54-58 . 66. 68.

b111 -- **Dar** S., Settlements and cult sites on Mt. Hermon: BAR-Int 589, 1993 → 9,13907: ᴿSCI(sr) 14 (1995) 184s (I. *Shatzman*).

b112 -- *Dauphine* Claudine, Sedentaires juifs et nomades arabes chrétiens; Golan, villages déserts: Archéologia 297 (1994) 52-64.

b113 **Hazor** 1994:   *Rubiato Díaz* María Teresa, Hatsor salomónica y Hatsor cananea; V campaña de excavaciones arqueológicas en Tell Hatsor: Sefarad 55 (1995) 195-201 + 6 fig.; Eng. 206.

b114 -- **Yadin** Yigael, ᴱ*Ben-Tor* A., *Geva* S., Hazor III-IV (3d-4th 1957-8) 1989 → 5,d915 ... 9,13913: ᴿBiOr 52 (1995) 151-3 (G.I. *Davies*).

b115 -- *Daviau* P.M. Michèle, Traces of cultic behaviour in the Bronze Age orthostat temple at Hazor; → 10,30, ᶠCOUTURIER G., Maison 1994, 71-90; 4 fig.

b116 **Kefar Horeš** 1991:   *a)* "Atiqot 27 (1995) 45-62; 14 fig. (A.N. *Goring-Morris, al.*).; -- *b)* Kfar Horeš   pre-pottery Neolithic daily and cultic life: Qadm 28 (1995) 20-26 (A.N. *Goring-Morris,* ᴴ)

b117 **Magdala**: **Ruf** Sieglinde M., [→ 5233 supra] Maria aus Magdala: eine Studie der neutestamentlichen Zeugnisse und archäologischen Befunde; BibNot Beih 9. Mü 1995. 116 p. DM 10. Editor Manfred GÖRG kindly informs us that this research should be classed under Archeology: either 'Magdala' or 'Early Synagogues', before (?) Second Temple destruction.

b118 **Megiddo**: *Nigro* Lorenzo, Nota sulla trasformazione planimetrica dell'ala sudoccidentale del Palazzo 2041 di Megiddo nei livelli VIIB-VIIA: *OrExp 3 (1994) 22-24; 3 fig.

b119 -- *Singer* Itamar, A Hittite seal from Megiddo → 136, ᶠNEVE P.,BA 58 (1995) 91-93;ill.

b120 -- *Ussishkin* David, The destruction of Megiddo at the end of the Late Bronze Age and its historical significance: *TAJ 22 (1995) 240-267; 15 fig.

b121 -- *Oberweis* Michael, Erwägungen zur apokalyptischen Ortsbezeichnung 'Harmagedon' [(Apk 16,16); the tell is too small for a 'mountain' unlocalized in OT; gematria for Nod + Gomorrah]: Biblica 76 (1995) 305-324; franç. 324.

b122 **Meiron, Gischala**: *Horsley* R.A., (*Meyers* E.M.), Archaeology and the villages of Upper Galilee: BASOR 297 (1995) 5-16 . 27s (17-26) [NTAb 40, p.476].

b123 **Nazareth**: *Hoško* Franjo E., L'historia loretana di Bartol KAŠIĆ alla luce della storiografia di Loreto e di Trsat (Tersatto): RijT 2 (1994) 79-84 croato: ital. 84.

b124 -- *Sánchez Bourdin* Anita, La 'Santa Casa' de Lorette: Famille chrétienne 921 (7 sept.1995): E(spr)eV 105 (1995) 600s (J.*Daoust*, converti!).

b125 -- *Santarelli* Giuseppe, La tradizione lauretana nelle indagini degli ultimi tre decenni: Marianum 57 (1995) 321-334 (-368, bibliog.).

b126 -- *Daoust* J., La grotte et les sanctuaires de l'Annonciation: E(spr)eV 105 (1995) 243s [< *Díez Fernández* M., MoB 90 (janv.1995)].

b127 -- MoBi 90 (1995) 3-30 (S. *Loffreda, al.)*

b128 -- **Testa** E., The faith of the mother church; an essay on the theology of the Judeo-Christians, [T]*Rotondi* P.; SBF min 22, 1992 → 9,13923: [R]BiOr 52 (1995) 122s (P.W. van der *Horst*: strange).

b129 *Qedeš*: Roman Temple: IsrEJ 40 (1990) 171-181 (J. *Magness*); 43 (1993) 60-63 (A. *Ovadiah, al.*, reply).

b130 **Sepphoris** 1993: IsrEJ 44 (1994) 247-40 (E. *Meyers, al.*).; 1994: BA 58 (1995) 117-9 (Carol *Meyers*).

b131 -- **Batey** R.A., Jesus and the forgotten city 1991 → 7,d456 ... 10,12350: PEQ 127 (1995) 72s (Joan E. *Taylor*).

b132 -- **Goranson** Stephen C., The Joseph of Tiberias [perhaps donor of the first church known at Sepphoris] episode in EPIPHANIUS: diss. [place and date not given, only AA photocopy 1992: SBF*LA 45 (1995) 654-7 (M.C. *Paczkowski*)].

b133 -- *Strange* J.F., *al.*, The location and identification of Shikhin ['rabbinic', 1 k N]: IEJ 44 (1994) 216-227 [NTAb 40, p.97].

b134 *Tiberias*: *Hirschfeld* Yizhar, The anchor church at the summit of Mt. Berenice, Tiberias: BA 57 (1994) 122-133; ill (134-7, *Ben-Arieh* Roni, A wall-painting of a saint's face).

T4.8 *Transjordania;* (East-) Jordan

b135 *'Abāṭa* 1994: ADAJ 39 (1995) 477-491; 22 fig. (K:D. *Politis*).

b136 *Abila: Mare* W. Harold, The Christian church of Abila of the Decapolis of the Yarmouk Valley system in the Umayyad period: → 712, Aram 6 (1993/4) 359-379.

b137 -- *Muheisin* Zeidoun al-, *Tarrier* Dominique, La période omeyyade dans le nord de la Jordanie; continuité et rupture: → 712, Aram 6 (1993/4) 333-341.

b138 *'Amman* nymphaeum: ADAJ 39 (1995) 229-240; 5 fig. (M. *Waheeb*, Z. *Zu'bi*).

b139 -- **Kanellopoulos** Chrysantos, The great temple of Amman; the architecture: *ACOR 2. Amman 1994. 123 p.; 13 pl. -- SBF*LA 45 (1995) 531s.

b140 -- *Hankey* Vronwy, A Late Bronze Age temple at Amman airport; small finds and pottery discovered in 1955: → 82, [F]HENNESSY J.B., Trade 1995, 169-185; 14 fig.; pl. 10-14.

b141 -- **Northedge** Alastair, Studies on Roman and Islamic 'Amman .. C.-M. BENNETT, 1, 1992 → 9,13942; 10,12366: [R]BSOAS 58 (1995) 552s (M. *Shokoohy*).

b142 *'Aqaba* 1992: ADAJ 39 (1995) 499-507; 6 fig. (D. *Whitcomb*; p. 507 *Whitecomb*).

b143 -- Roman Aila rediscovered: BA 57 (1994) 172 (S.T. *Parker*).

b144 -- **Portico** Gary D., Nelson GLUECK's 1938-1940 excavations at Tell el-Kheleifeh; a reappraisal 1993 → 10,12367: [R]BASOR 298 (1995) 94s (W. G. *Dever*); OLZ 90 (1995) 293-5 (G. *Pfeifer*).

b145 -- *a) Whitcomb* Donald, The *Misr* of Ayla; settlement at al-'Aqaba in the early Islamic period; -- *b) Schick* Robert, The settlement patterns of southern Jordan; the nature of the evidence [further *Zeyadeh* Ali]: → 725, *King*. Land use 1994 ...

b146 *'Aqaba-Magaṣṣ* 2d 1990: ADAJ 39 (1995) 65-79; 11 fig. (L.A. *Khalil*).

b147 **Bet Ras** (Capitolias), N.Jordan: *Lenzen* C.J., Continuity or discontinuity; urban change or demise ? : → 82, ᶠHENNESSY J.B., Trade 1995, 325-331.

b148 **Buṣeira**, S wadi Hasa: *Hart* Stephen, Area D at Buseira and Edomite chronology: → 82, ᶠHENNESSY J.B., Trade 1995, 241-264; 13 fig. (plans).

b149 **Callirhoe**: ᵀᴱGould G.P., CHARITON APHRODISIENSIS, *De Chaerea et Callirhoe*: Loeb. L/CM 1995, Heinemann/ Harvard Univ. x-425 p., bibliog. 20-26. 0-674-99530-9.

b150 **Deir''Alla**: Balaam inscription: Qadm 28 (1995) 90-96 (B. *Levine* ᴴ).

b151 **Edom**: *a) Knauf-Belleri* Ernst-Axel, Edom, The social and economic history: - *b) Vanderhooft* David S., The Edomite dialect and script; a review of the evidence: → 500, Edomite 1991/5, 93-117 / 137-157; 1 fig.

b152 -- **Dicou** Bert, Edom, Israel's brother and antagonist; the role of Edom in biblical prophecy and story: jOsu 169. Shf 1994, JSOT. 227 p. £ 30. -- ᴿJBL 114 (1995) 713 (J.M. *Miller*).

b153 *a) Edelman* Diana V., Edom; a historical geography; - *b) Bienkowski* Piotr, The Edomites; the archaeological evidence from Transjordan; - *c) Beit Arieh* Itzhaq, The Edomites in Cisjordan: → 500, Edom 1990/5, 1-11 / 41-62 + 31 fig. / 33-38 + 2 fig.

b154 -- ᴱ**Bienkowski** Piotr, *a)* Early Edom and Moab; the beginning of the Iron Age in southern Jordan [*pace* GLUECK N.] 1992 → 8,340: ᴿBArR 21,5 (1995) 8-10 (L. *Herr*); BASOR 297 (1995) 91s (W.G. *Dever*); -- *b)* Treasures from ... Jordan 1991 → 7,b513: ᴿJNES 54 (1995) 146s (K.L. *Wilson*).

b155 **Fahil**: *a) Bourke* Stephen J., *Sparks* Rachael T., The DAJ [Jordan Antiquities Dept.] excavations at Pella in Jordan 1963/64; -- *b) Edwards* P.C., *Macumber* P.G., The last half million years at Pella; -- *c) Walmsley* Alan G., Christians and Christianity at early Islamic Pella (Fihl): → 82, ᶠHENNESSY J.B., Trade 1995, 149-167; 7 fig. (plan) / 1-14; 4 fig. (map): pl. I / 321-4.

b156 -- **Knapp** A. Bernard, Society and polity at Bronze Age Pella; an Annales perspective, JSOT/ASOR 6, 1993 → 10,12402: ᴿAJA 99 (1995) 155s (M.W.*Chavalas*); JAOS 115 (1995) 131s (J. M. *Weinstein*).

b157 -- **Falconer** Steven E., Rural response to early urbanism; Bronze Age household and village economy at Tell el-Hayyat, Jordan: *JField 22 (1995) 399-419; 11 fig.

b158 **Feinan**: *Adams* Russell, *Genz* Hermann, Excavations at Wadi Fidan [western extension of w.Feinan/Ghwair] 4; a chalcolithic village complex in the copper ore district of Feinan, southern Jordan: PEQ 127 (1995) 8-20; 8 fig.

b159 **Ghassul**, Sydney-renewed 1st 1994: ADAJ 39 (1995) 31-63; 9 fig. (Stephen J. *Bourke*, al.)

b160 -- **Seaton** Peta, A note on possible chemical industries at Teleilat Ghassul: → 82, ᶠHENNESSY J.B., Trade 1995, 27-30; plan.

b161 **Ghazal** 8th, 1994: ADAJ 39 (1995) 13-29; 7 fig. (Zeidan *Kafafi*, G.O. *Rollefson*); Qadm 28 (1995) 67-76 (G.A. *Rollefson*, ᴴ)

b162 **Hayyan al-Mushrif** 8 km SE Mafraq: → a917, SBF*LA 45 (1995) 519-522 (Zeidoun *al-Muheisin*, Dominique *Tarrier*); 523s, pl. 79, iscrizione aramaica (M. *Pazzini*).

b163 **Heshbon**: *Merling* David, A lost city of the Bible: *ABW 1,2 (1991) 10-17.

b164 **Ḥumayma** 1993 : ADAJ 39 (1995) 317-354; 29 fig. (J.P. *Oleson, al.*).

b165 -- **Schick** R., Christianity at Ḥumayma, [S] Jordan: SBF*LA 45 (1995) 319-342; pl.43-50.

b166 **'Iraq al-Amîr:** **Will** Ernest, *Larché* François, I., le château du Tobiade Hyrcan: BAH

132, 1991 → 9,13971: [R]Latomus 54 (1995) 740s (M. *Rassart-Debergh*).

b167 *Irbid/Marū* 1994: ADAJ 39 (1995) [A] 5-16; 20 fig. (Hikmat *Ta'ani*).

b168 *Iskandar* (w. Wala) 5th 1994: ADAJ 39 (1995) 81-92; 10 fig. (Suzanne *Richard*, J.C.*Long*).

b169 *Jawa-E*: *Philip* Graham, Jawa [BETTS A. 1991] and Tell Um Hammad [1990], two Early Bronze Age sites in Jordan: PEQ 127 (1995) 161-170.

b170 *Jerash* (sub-)'Cathedral' 2d 1993: ADAJ 39 (1995) 211-220; 7 fig. (B. *Brenk,al.*) → a852 & c555 infra.

b171 *Kharaneh*, 30 k SE "Amman: *Muheisen* Mujahed, *Wada* Hisahiko, An analysis of the microliths at Kharaneh IV phase D, square A20/37: Paléor 21,1 (1995) 75-95; 9 fig.; 11 graphs; franç. 75.

b172 *Kharaz* (N w. Yābis; 4 k S Fahil) 4th, 1993: ADAJ 39 (1995) 93-119; 12 fig. (P. *Fischer*).

b173 -- *Fischer* Peter M., *Herrmann* Georgina, A carved bone object from Tell Abu al-Kharaz in Jordan [c. 800 B.C.]; a Palestinian workshop for bone and ivory ?: Levant 25 (1995) 145-163; 19 fig.

b174 *Lehun*: *Homès-Fredericq* D., Le site archéologique de Lehun en Jordanie au 2e millénaire avant J.-C.: → 10,81, [F]Meyer L. de, 52 Réflexions 1994, 427-430 + 4 fig.

b175 *Machaerus*: *Piccirillo* Michele, Le antichità cristiane del villaggio di Mekawer: SBF*LA 45 (1995) 293-318; pl. 25-42; Eng. 486.

b176 *Madaba*: *Hübner* Ulrich, [Madaba-Mosaikkarte] Baaras und Zeus Beelbaaros: BZ 39 (1995) 252-5.

b177 -- Faysaliyah church: SBF*LA 45 (1995) 512s; pl.72 (M. *Piccirillo*).

b178 *Mafraq w.'Ajib* 1st-2d 1992s: ADAJ 39 (1995) 149-168; 10 fig. (A.*Betts, al.*).

b179 *Mahoz(a)*: *Cotton* H.M., *Greenfield* J.C., Babatha's patria; Mahoza, [=] Mahoz 'Eglatain and Zo'ar: ZPE 107 (1995) 126-132: Ghor Safi near wadi Hasa.

b180 *Nebo* Theotokos chapel: ADAJ 39 (1995) 409-420; 13 fig. (M. *Piccirillo*).

b181 -- *Daoust* J., Avec les Franciscains au Mont Nébo: E(spr)eV 105 (1995) 244-6 [< *Piccirillo* Michele, La Terre Sainte, janv. 1995].

b182 -- *Piccirillo* Michele, [H] Nebo, sixty years of archaeological research: Qadm 28 (1995) 113-8.

b183 *Nebo*-Siyagha 1995 → 517, SBF*LA 45 (1995) 499-511; pl. 66s (Alessandra *Acconci*).

-----

b184 *Petra*: Southern temple 1994 : ADAJ 39 (1995) 241-266; 28 fig. (Martha S. *Joukowsky*, Erika *Schluntz*) [267-280, Slaysil, *Lindner* M.; 281-295, archaeo-geology, *Pflüger* F.).

b185 -- *Joukowsky* Martha S., Archaeological survey of the southern temple at Petra; Syria 72 (1995) 133-142; 3 fig.

b186 -- *Fiema* Zbigniew T., Une église byzantine à Pétra [... mosaïques, rouleaux de papyrus]: Archéologia 302 (1994) 26-35.

b187 -- *Nehmé* Laïla, L'espace urbain de Pétra (Jordanie) de l'époque nabatéenne à l'époque byzantine à travers les sources archéologiques et épigraphiques: *OrExp 3 (1994) 87-89.

b188 -- *Matthiae* K., Ein Opferplatz [Zibb 'Atûf] der Karawanenstadt Petra: Altertum 40,2 (B 1994) 99-114 [NTAb 39, p.462].

b189 -- a) *Teixidor* Javier, Le campement; ville des Nabatéens; -- b) *Bron* François, La ville dans les inscriptions qatabanites: → 730, Semitica 43s (1992/5) 111-121 / 135-139 [141-161, *Robin* Christian, Jawf; 163-8, *Aggoula* Basile, Hatra].

b190 -- Petra-Zantur 6th 1994: ADAJ 39 (1995) 297-315; 16 fig. (R.A. *Stucky, al.*).

b191 -- *Peterman* Glen L., Discovery of papyri in Petra: BA 57 (1994) 55-57 . 242s.

b192 -- *Briend* Jacques, *Puech* Émile, Pétra dans la Bible et les manuscrits: MoB 88 (1994) < E(spr)eV 105 (1995) 51s (J. *Daoust*).

b193 -- **Taylor** J., Petra. L 1993, Aurum. 80 p.; 76 pl. £ 20. -- [R]PEQ 127 (1995) 176 (P. *Dorrell*).

b194 -- *Vattioni* Francesco, Petra e le città caravaniere [[E]ZAYADINE F. 1990]: AION 54 (1994) 527-530.

-----

b195 *Ramm* inscription revised: ADAJ [27 (1983) 558 (D. *Graf*)] 39 (1995) 493-7; 3 fig. (Saba *Farès-Drappeau*).

b196 *Sa'ad* kh. 27 k W Mafraq, mosaic church: → a917, SBF*LA 45 (1995) 526-9 (S. *Sari*).

b197 *Sapsafas* [*p* for *f* or *b* ?], w. Kharrar N Ghassul: SBF*LA 45 (1995) 515-8 (M. *Piccirillo*).

b198 *Sukhne-N*, Zerqa basin NE 'Amman, EB-II: Paléor 21,1 (1995) 113-123; 4 fig. (map); 2 pl. (M. *Chesson*, G. *Palumbo, al.*).

b199 *Thamāyil*, E Karak, 1992: ADAJ 39 (1995) 127-147; 10 fig. (B. *Routledge*).

b200 *'Umeiri*: Qadm 28 (1995) 83-89 (L.G. *Herr*, [H]).

b201 -- *Clark* Douglas R., The Iron 1 western defense system at Tell el-' Umeiri, Jordan: BA 57 (1994) 138-148; ill.

b202 *Um Hammad:* **Betts** A.V.G. [HELMS ... highlighted as source only in review text], Excavations at Tell Um Hammad, the early assemblages (EB I-II). E 1992, Univ. xiv-425 p. -- [R]PEQ 127 (1995) 165-170 (G. *Philip*).

b203 *Umm Jimāl* 1993s: ADAJ 39 (1995) 421-435; 11 fig. (B. *de Vries*); 447-455, Melissa *Cheynet*; 457-668, Janet *Brashler*; 469-476, A. *al-Momani*, M. *Horstmanshof*. -- 1994: BA 57 (1994) 171 . 215-9 (B. *de Vries*).

b204 *Umm Rasās*: SBF*LA 45 (1995) 513s; pl. 70s (M. *Piccirillo*).

b205 -- **Piccirillo** Michele, *Alliata* Eugenio, Umm al-Rasas -- Mayfa''ah I: SBF 28, 1994: Syria 72 (1995) 427-9 (M. *Sartre*) & 430-3 (T. *Waliszewski*).

b206 *Ziqlab*: *Banning* E.B., Herders or homesteaders ? A neolithic farm in wadi Ziqlab, Jordan: BA 58 (1995) 2-13; ill.

T5.1 **Phoenicia** -- *Libanus*, **Lebanon**

b207 **Briquel-Chatonnet** Françoise, Les relations entre les cités de la côte phénicienne et les royaumes d'Israël et de Juda: OLA(nalecta) 46, 1992 → 8,e636 ... 10,12420: [R]BiOr 52 (1995) 127-134 (S. *Timm*); RÉA(nc) 97 (1995) 666s (A. *Lemaire*); RHR 212 (1995) 193-6 (S. *Ribichini*).

b208 *Carreira* J.N., Hermopolitan traditions in PHILO BYBLIUS' Phoenician History: Cadmo 1 (Lisboa 1991) 31-44 [< ZAW 107 (1995) 135].

b209 **Cors i Meya** J., A concordance of the Phoenician History of PHILO of Byblos: *AulaO.s 10. Barc-Sabadell 1995, AUSA. 120 p. 84-88810-17-2.

b210 **Grainger** John D., Hellenistic Phoenicia 1991 → 7,d533 ... 9,14103: [R]HZ 260 (1995) 168s (K. *Brodersen*); *TopO 3 (1993) 321-344 (H.J. *MacAdam*).

b211 ^E**Lipiński** E., Phoenicia and the Bible: OLA 44, 1990/1 → 7,445; 10,12420*: ^RAulaO 12 (1994) 244-6 (G. del *Olmo Lete*); BASOR 299s (1995) 127s (S.R. *Wolff*).

b212 *Tochtermann* Wolfgang, *al.*, Le Liban: MoBi 93 (1995) 1-55.

b213 *Ward* William A., Archaeology in Lebanon in the twentieth century: BA 57 (1994) 66-85; ill.

b214 **Beqa':** *Vandersleyen* C., La localisation du Naharina: OLo(v)P 25 (1994) 27-35.

b215 **Berytus:** *Lefèvre* Alain-Charles, Beyrouth, le plus grand chantier d'archéologie urbaine au monde: Archéologia 316 (1995) 14-33: 318 (1995) 4-9 [317 (1995) 4-11, *Lauffray* Jean, Ce qui n'a pas été dit ... les photos que la presse n'a pas pu prendre].

b216 **Byblos:** *Nibbi* Alessandra, The Byblos question again: DiscEg 30 (1994) 117-141; 5 fig. (maps).

b217 -- ^E**Acquaro** F., Biblo, colloquio 1990/4 → 733 supra; 10,12422.

b218 -- *Dandamayev* Muhammad, A governor of Byblos in Sippar: → 110. ^FLIPIŃSKI, E., Immigration: OLA 65 (1995) 29-31.

b219 **Kamid/Loz:** **Metzger** M., *al.*, Die spätbronzezeitlichen Tempelanlagen: Kāmid el-Lōz 7. 1991 → 8,e645; 10,12424: ^RPEQ 127 (1995) 175s (H.J. *Franken*).

b220 -- **Metzger** M., *al.*, 8. Die spätbronzezeitlichen Tempelanlagen; die Kleinfunde im 1993: K/Loz 8. Bonn 1993. Habelt. -- ^RAfO 42s (1995s) 289s (Ö. *Tunca*); ZAW 107 (1995) 360s (O. *Kaiser*).

b221 -- **Adler** W., Kāmid el-Loz 11, Schatzhaus 1994 → 10,12423*: ^RZAW 107 (1995) 342s.

b222 **Sidon:** **Stucky** Rolf A., Die Skulpturen aus dem Eschmun-Heiligtum: AK.b 17, 1993 → 10,12424*; 115 p.; 11 fig.; 64 pl.; 3-909064-15-5: ^RA(nz)AW 48,1s (1995) 104-6 (E.M. *Ruprechtsberger*); AnCL 64 (1995) 562s (F. *Baratte*); Bo(nn)J 195 (1995) 663-7; 1 fig. (A. *Linfert*).

b223 **Tyrus:** *Işık* Fahri, Ein Sarkophagfragment aus Tivoli und seine Lokalisierung in Tyros: MDAI-R 102 (1995) 381-386; pl.98-100.

b224 -- **Aubet** Maria Eugenia, The Phoenicians and the West; politics, colonies and trade [Tiro 1987], ^T*Turton* Mary. C 1993, Univ. xviii-348 p.; 70 fig. £ 37.50. 0-521-41141-6. -- ^RAntiquity 69 (1995) 189-192 (A.T. *Reyes*, also on LIPIŃSKI's Dictionnaire 1992); GaR 42 (1995) 108s (P. *Walcot*: but what about craftsmen reaching Crete?).

T5.2 *Situs mediterranei* **phoenicei et punici**

b225 *Acquaro* E., *al.*, Bibliografia 23 (1994): RSFen 23 (1995) 217-239.

b226 **Baurain** C., *Bonnet* C. Les Phéniciens marins de trois continents 1992 → 8.e655; 10.12428*: ^R*TopO 4 (1994) 236-243 (T. *Petit*).

b227 ^E**González Blanco** A., *al.*, El mundo púnico; historia, sociedad y cultura: BtBásicaM extra 4. Murcia 1994, Regional. 516 p. -- ^R*AulaO 12 (1994) 241s (G. *Matilla Séiquer*).

b228 ^E**Krings** Veronique, → 726 supra: La civilisation phénicienne et punique; manuel de recherche: HO 1/20. Lei 1995, Brill. xx-923 p. $ 248.75. 90-04-10068-7 [RStR 22,148, D.I. *Owen*]. -- ^RBoL (1995) 132 (A.R. *Millard*); (Tü)TQ 175 (1995) 368s (H. *Niehr*).

b229 **Lipiński** E., Dictionnaire de la civilisation phénicienne et punique 1992 → 8.e664; 10.12431: ^R*AulaO 12 (1994) 233s (G. del *Olmo Lete*); A(ndr)USS 32 (1994) 286-8 (W. E. *Aufrecht*); RAHAL(ouv) 27 (1994) 160s (P.-H. *Tilmant*).

b230 *Moscati* Sabatino, Formalizzazione e deformalizzazione nelle stele puniche: *StEgPun 12 (1993) 89-91.

b231 *Sznycer* Maurice, La cité punique d'après les sources épigraphiques: → 730, Semitica 43s (1992/5) (5s) 103-9.

b232 *Hamat*: a) *Heltzer* Michael, Phoenician trade and Phoenicians in Hamath; -- b) *Stern* Ephraim, Four Phoenician finds from Israel: → 110, ᶠLIPIŃSKI, E., Immigration: OLA 65 (1995) 101-5 / 319-334; 10 fig.

b233 *Hammanim*: *Cazelles* Henri, *Hammanim-hamon/humun* et l'expansion phénicienne; → 10,30, ᶠCOUTURIER G., Maison 1994, 99-107

b234 *Ibiza*: **Fernández** Jordi H., Excavaciones en la necrópolis del Puig des Molins (Eivissa); las campañas de D. Carlos ROMÁN FERRER 1921-1929: Museo 28s. Eivissa 1992. -- ᴿAt(henaeum) 83 (1995) 283-5 (Maria P. *Lavizzari Pedrazzini*).

b235 *Lipari*: **Bernabò Brea** Luigi, *Cavalier* Madeleine, Scavi nella necropoli greca di Lipari: Meligunìs Lipára 5. R 1991, Bretschneider. xxxvi-199 p.; 187 pl. + 6 color. -- ᴿAt(henaeum) 83 (1995) 285s (Elena *Calandra*).

b236 *Melita:* **Freeden** Joachim von, Malta und die Baukunst seiner Megalith-Tempel. Da 1993, Wiss. 305 p.; 179 (color.) fig. -- ᴿBo(nn)J 195 (1995) 625-8 (O. *Höckmann*).

b237 -- a) *Frendo* Antonio, Religion in the prehistoric phases of Phoenician Malta; -- b) *Hoskin* Michael, *Allan* Elizabeth, Orientation of Mediterranean tombs and sanctuaries: → 751, Ritual 1994/5, 114-121 / 38-67.

b238 *Mozia*: **Moscati** Sabatino, Le officine di Mozia: Lincei Mem.mor. 9/7/1. R 1995. 128 p.; 24 fig.; 24 pl. -- ᴿEpigraphica 57 (Faenza 1995) 319-322 (G. *Susini*).

b239 *Pozo Moro*: *Kempinski* Aharon, From death to resurrection: the early [Phoenician] evidence: BArR 21,5 (1995) 56-65 . 83.

b240 *Sardinia*: *Moscati* Sabatino, Appunti sulle stele sarde: StEgPun 14 (1995) 91-98: IV pl.; 1 fig.

b241 -- **Moscati** Sabatino, Le stele a 'specchio '; artigianato popolare nel Sassarese: Unione Accad.Naz., corpus fen/pun. R 1992, Bonsignori. 111 p. 88-7597-231-1.

b242 *Tharros:* *Vighi* Sara, *Kóssai* [merli, pinnacoli] da Tharros: StEgPun 14 (1995) 75-81 + 8 fig.; 1 pl.

T5.3 Carthago

b243 **Ameling** Walter, Karthago; Studien zu Militär, Staat und Gesellschaft: Vestigia 45. Mü 1993, Beck. → 10,12455*; DM 140. 3-406-37490-5: ᴿHZ 261 (1995) 850-2 (K.-H. *Schwarte*); MBAH 14,2 (1995) 108-113 (M. *Fell*).

b244 **Blázquez** J.M., Fenicios, Griegos y Cartagineses en Occidente. M 1992, Cátedra. 546 p.; 59 fig.; 5 mapas. -- ᴿEM(erita) 63 (1995) 169s (J. *Cabréro*).

b245 *Bonnet* Corinne, Réflexions historiques sur le culte d'Astarté à Carthage: → 10,73, Mém. LE GLAY M., L'Afrique 1994, 3-8.

b246 Carthage, exposition au Petit Palais: MoBi 92 (1995) 53-59.

b247 *Chiera* G., Artigiani a Cartagine: RSFen 23 (1995) 47-54; pl. II-V.

b248 *Docter* R., Karthago; de Phœnicische stad onder het romeinse Carthago: Phoe 41,1 (1995) 43-57.

b249 *Ennabli* Abdelmajid, *al.*, Cartagine, civiltà risorta: ArVi 14,52 (1995) 42-55.

b250 **Huss** W., Los cartagineses [Mü 1990, Bock],ᵀ. M 1993, Gredos. 431 p. -- ᴿMemHAnt 15s (Oviedo 1994s) 353s (N. *Santos Yanguas*, también sobre LANCEL S., Barc 1994).

b251 **Lancel** Serge, Carthage 1992 → 9,14067. 10,12467: ᴿRAHAL(ov) 27 (1994) 161-3 (P.-H. *Tilmant*); RB(elg)PH 73 (1995) 222-5 (J. *Debergh*).

b252 *Lund* J., A synagogue at Carthage ? menorah-lamps from the Danish excavations: *JRAr 8 (1995) 245-262 [NTAb 40, p.287].

b253 *a) Niemeyer* Hans-Georg, *al.*, Die Grabung unter dem Decumanus Maximus; -- *b) Rakob* Friedrich *al.*, Forschungen im Stadtzentrum: Karthago, Zweiter Vorbericht: MDAI-R 102 (1995) 475-502; 12 (foldout) fig.; pl.125-8 / 413-474; 19 (color) fig.; pl. 109-114.

b254 *Pisano* Giovanna, L'oro di Cartagine: Archeo 130 (1995) 60-86.

b255 ᴱ**Rakob** Friedrich, Die deutschen Ausgrabungen in Karthago. Mainz 1991, von Zabern. xx-282 p., iv-22 p., 52 fig., 70 pl., 41 plans. DM 198. 3-8053-0985-6. -- ᴿLatomus 54 (1995) 180s (J. *Desanges*).

b256 *Rakob* Friedrich, Karthago -- 1500 Jahre Stadtgeschichte: Aarchäologie in Deutschland (1995,2) 12-19; color.ill.

b257 *Visonà* Paolo, Carthage; a numismatic bibliography: *StEgPun 13 (1994) 117-220; indices 220-231.

-----

b258 *Amante Sánchez* Manuel, *Pérez Bonet* Mᵃ Angeles, Cerámicas tardías de producción egipcia en Carthago Nova; → 221, ᶠYELO TEMPLADO A., Lengua 1995, 521-532; 8 fig. [533-562, *al.*, sacellum en Cartagena]

T5.4 **Ugarit** -- *Ras Šamra*

b259 **Aboud** J., Die Rolle des Königs und seiner Familie nach den Texten von Ugarit: ForAnthropRG 27, 1994; DM 38,50: ᴿZAW 107 (1995) 152 (O. *Kaiser*).

b260 **Callot** Olivier, La tranchée 'ville sud'; études d'architecture domestique: RS-Ou 10, 1994 → 10,12480; F 373 [RStR 22,232, D.I. *Owen*].

b261 *Cunchillos Ilarri* Jesús Luis, *Vita Barro* Juan Pablo, Historia de una carta [Ugarítica Puduhepa] y de su lectura; → 221, ᶠYELO TEMPLADO A., Lengua 1995, 93-110.

b262 ᴱ**Dietrich** Manfried, *Loretz* Oswald, Ugarit, ein ostmediterranes Kulturzentrum im Alten Orient; Ergebnisse und Perspektiven der Forschung, I. Ugarit und seine altorientalische Umwelt [Kolloquium Münster 11.-12. Feb. 1993]: *ALASP 7. Müns 1995, Ugarit-Vg. xii-287 p. 3-927120-17-0.

b263 *Kruger* Paul A., Rank symbolism in the Baal epic; some further indicators: UF 27 (DIETRICH 60. Gb. 1995) 169-173.

b264 *Lackenbacher* Sylvie, La correspondance internationale dans les archives d'Ugarit: → 724, RA(ssyr) 89 (1995) 67-76.

b265 *Margueron* Jean, *a)* Feu le four à tablettes de l'ex 'Cour V' du palais d'Ugarit; -- *b)* Tessons et architecture de terre; Syria 72 (1995) 55-69; 6 fig. / 70-103; 11 fig.

b266 *Mayer* Walter, *a)* Die historische Einordnung der 'Autobiographie' des Idrimi von Alalah [... KLENGEL H. 1981]; -- *b)* Anmerkungen zu den Zincirli-Inschriften: UF 27 (DIETRICH 60. Gb. 1995) 333-350 / 351-4.

b267 *Petersen* Allan R., Where did SCHAEFFER find the clay tablets of the Ugaritis Baal-cycle ?: S(cand)JOT 8 (1994) 45-58 + 2 fig.

b268 *Smith* Mark S., Anat's warfare cannibalism and the West Semitic ban:→ 4, ᶠAHLSTRÖM G., Pitcher; JSOT.s 190 (1995) 368-386.

b269 *Vargyas* Peter, Immigration into Ugarit: → 110, ᶠLIPIŃSKI, E., Immigration: OLA 65 (1995) 395-402.

(1995) 395-402.

b270 **Whitt** William D., Archives and administration in the royal palace of Ugarit: diss. Duke, ᴰ*Wintermute* O. Durham NC 1993. -- RTLv 27.

b271 *Wyatt* Nicolas, Le centre du monde dans les littératures d'Ougarit et d'Israël: JNWSL 21,2 (1995) 123-142.

b272 **Yon** M., Arts et industries de la pierre, RS/O 6, 1991: → 7,d605 ... 10,12485: ᴿAbr Nahrain 31 (1993) 127s (Alison *Betts*); AfO 42s (1995s) 293s (R.T. *Sparks*. Eng.).

b273 *Yon* Marguerite, La maison d'Ourtenou dans le quartier sud d'Ougarit (fouilles 1994): CRAI (1995) 427-449: 9 fig. [855-860, *Bordreuil* Pierre, *Pardee* Dennis, abécédaire sud-sémitique].

T5.5 Ebla

b274 **Archi** Alfonso, Five tablets from the southern wing of Palace G, Ebla: SNS 5/2. Malibu 1993, Undena. 39 p.; 16 pl.; 2 fig. $ 12 pa. -- ᴿJAOS 115 (1995) 297s (Maria Giovanna *Biga*).

b275 *Archi* Alfonso, Transmission of the Mesopotamian lexical and literary texts from Ebla; -- *b) Krebernik* Manfred, Mesopotamian myths at Ebla; ARET 5,6 and ARET 5,7; -- *c) Matthiae* Paolo, Figurative themes and literary texts [...Mardikh Palace G]: → 8,e731, ᴱ**Fronzaroli** Pelio, Literature and literary language at Ebla 1992, 1-29 + 10 pl. / 63-149 / 219-241.

b276 *Astour* Michael C., An outline of the history of Ebla: Eblaitica 3 (1992) 1-82 [noted with tit.pp. of the five other articles in BASOR 298 (1995) 83s].

b277 *Çeçen* Sālih, *Hecker* Karl, *ina mātika eblum* [Ebla, not On-Ebla], zu einem neuen Text zum Wegerecht in der Kültepe-Zeit: → 185, ᶠSODEN W.von, Vom Alten Orient (1995) 31-41; 6 fig.; 3 facsim.

b278 **Conti** Giovanni, Index of Eblaic texts: QuSem Mat.1. F 1992, Univ. xxii-202 p. -- ᴿWO 26 (1995) 191-3 (F. *Pomponio*).

b279 *Dolce* Rita, Un arredo di lusso del Palazzo Reale G di Ebla; note in margine: RSO 69 (1995) 1-9; 6 fig.; Eng. 10.

b280 *Dombrowski* Bruno W.W., Das System der eblaitischen Zahlen im Vergleich zu anderen, vornehmlich in den semitischen und hamitischen Sprachbereichen: FolOr 30 (1994) 39-76 [< OTA 19, p.181].

b281 *Erkanal* Armağan, Gedanken zu einem Kultgefäss [Ebla, Byblos, besonders Kültepe: Rollsiegel]: B(elleten)TTK 59 (1995) 60-63; 6 fig.

b282 *a) Fronzaroli* Pelio, Fonti di lessico nei testi di Ebla; -- *b) Milano* Lucio, Lessicografia e storia sociale; gli 'schiavi' di Ebla: StEpL 12 (1985) 51-64 / 121-134.

b283 *Fronzaroli* Pelio, Osservazioni sul lessico delle bevande dei testi di Ebla: → 10.480, Drinking ANE. 1990/4, 121-7,

b284 ᴱ**Fronzaroli** Pelio, Literature and literary language at Ebla: Univ.F QuadSemit 18. R 1992, Herder. x-330 p.; 8 pl. Lᵐ 80. -- ᴿBiOr 52 (1995) 713-6 (B.R. *Foster*. also on Misc 1s, Quad 16s).

b285 ᴱ**Gordon** C.H., *Rendsburg* G.A., Eblaitica 3, 1992 → 8,433c: BSOAS 58 (1995) 348-350; JSSt 40 (1995) 319-321 (M.J. *Geller*).

b286 *Mander* Pietro, Designs on the Fara, Abu-Salabikh and Ebla tablets: AION 55,1 (1995) 18-28 + 9 fig.

b287 **Matthiae** Paolo. Ebla, la città rivelata: Universale Electa/Gallimard 56. [Trieste] 1995.

b288 *Matthiae* Paolo, *a)* Trent'anni di Ebla : ArVi 14,50 (1995) 36-45; -- *b)* Ebla; alle origini della civiltà urbana ... mostra Roma: Archeo 10,121 (1995) 50-63.

b289 *Matthiae* Paolo, Fouilles d'Ébla en 1993-1994; les palais de la ville basse nord: CRAI (1995) 651-681; 21 fig.

b290 *a) Matthiae* Paolo, The lions of the great goddess of Ebla; a hypothesis about some archaic Old Syrian cylinders; -- *b) Archi* Alfonso, Udua (*LAK*-777) and Uzu (*LAK*-350) in the Ebla texts: → 10,81, [F]Meyer L. de, 52 RÉFLEXIONS 1994, 329--338; 8 fig. / 321-6; 327, table of signs.

b291 **Pettinato** G., Ebla, a new look at history [1986 → 2,a841], [T]*Richardson* C.Faith, 1991 → 7.d621; 8,e741: [R]PEQ 127 (1995) 80s (Harriet *Crawford*).

b292 *a) Pettinato* Giovanni, Il regno Mar-tu[ki] nella documentazione di Ebla; -- *b) Klengel* Horst, Tunip und andere Probleme der historischen Geographie Mittelsyriens [ARCHI A. *al.*1993; BONECHI M. 1993 ...]: → 110, [F]LIPIŃSKI, E., Immigration: OLA 65 (1995) 229-243 / 125-134.

b293 **Pinnock** Frances, Le perle del palazzo reale G: Materiali e studi archeologici di Ebla 2. R 1993, Univ. lxxii-172 p. L[m] 90. -- [R]RStR 21 (1995) 222 (D.I. *Owen*, also on 1. MAZZONI S., Impronte).

b294 *Rebić* Adalbert, Archäologische Funde, Ebla und Ugarit: *BogSmot 65 (Zagreb 1995) 256-266 croat.; deutsch 266.

b295 *Simonetti* Cristina, Three Eblaite officers, *Ra-i-zú, i-ti-[d]NI-lam,* and *na-am[6]-i-giš*; AfO 42s (1995s) 176-180.

b296 **Tångberg** Arvid, Der geographische Horizont der Texte aus Ebla [→ c149]; Untersuchungen zur eblaitischen Toponymie: Mü Univ ATSAT 42. St.Ottilien 1994, EOS. 94 p. DM 24. 3-88096-542-0 [RStR 22,56, D.I. *Owen*: too little and too late].

b297 **Toueir** Kassem, Allah und seine quranischen Attribute im Archiv von Ebla ['davon ausgehend, dass El/Il, Eloh, Allah identisch sind']: → 23, [F]BOEHMER R.M., Beiträge 1995, 639-641.

b298 *Viganò* Lorenzo, *a)* Rituals at Ebla : JNES 54 (1995) 215-222; -- *b)* The use of the Sumerian word *níg-ba,* 'gift', in the Ebla administrative reports: SBF*LA 45 (1995) 203-215; Eng. 485.

T5.8 **Situs effossi Syriae in ordine alphabetico**

b299 [E]**Chavalas** Mark W., *Hayes* John L., New horizons in the study of ancient Syria 1991/2 → 8,705* ... 10,12494: [R]AfO 42s (1995s) 232s (D. *Charpin*, unenthusiastic); OLZ 90 (1995) 170-3 (H. *Klengel*).

b300 **Elayi** Josette, *Sapin* Jean, Nouveaux regards sur la Transeuphratène 1991 → 8,e,747; 9,14110*: *TopO 4 (1994) 244-250 (T. *Petit*)

b301 *Kennedy* David, The [BUTLER] publications of the Princeton University archaeological expeditions to Syria in 1904-05 and 1909 relating to southern Syria [complexity of photonumberings noted but scarcely improved by H. MACADAM BAR 295, 1986]: PEQ 127 (1995) 21-32.

b302 **Klengel** Horst, Syria 1992 → 8,b825: [R]Gnomon 67 (1995) 519-522 (P. *Hegemann*).

b303 *Afis* (Idlib) 1994: EVO 18 (1995) 243-282 + XXIV pl. (Stefania *Mazzoni. al.*).

b304 *Aḥmar*: [E]**Bunnens** Guy, Tell Aḥmar 1988 season: 1990 → 7,d632 ... 10,12503: BiOr 52 (1995) 140-6 (J,-W. *Meyer*).

b305 **Aḥmar** -- Barsip: *Zaccagnini* Carlo, Sulla collina rossa: Archeo 127 (1995) 24-32.

b306 **Aleppo**: *Malamat* Abraham, [H] A new prophecy from Aleppo and its biblical parallels: Qadmoniot 27 (1994) 44-46.

b307 -- (W.Idlib/Aleppo): *Besançon* Jacques, *Geyer* Bernard, La cuvette du Ruǧ (Syrie du Nord); les conditions naturelles et les étapes de la mise en valeur; Syria 72 (1995) 307-354; 18 fig.; 3 dépliants.

b308 **Apameia**: *Balty* Janine & Jean-Charles, Promenade dans les ruines d'Apamée: MoBi 91 (1995) 36-41; color.il.

b309 **'Atij** 5th, Gudeda 4th, 1993; Syria 72 (1995) 23-53; 25 fig. (M. *Fortin*).

b310 -- **Bernbeck** Reinhard, Steppe als Kulturlandgebiet: das "Aǧiǧ-Gebiet Ostsyriens [→ 10,12504] .. : BBVO.A-1 1993; xii-210 p., 155 fig.; 8 pl. DM 98. 3-496-02511-5. -- [R]Mesop-T 30 (1995) 265-277 (D. *Morandi Bonacossi*).

b311 **Balikh**: **Akkermans** Peter M., Villages in the steppe; late neolithic settlement and subsistence in the Balikh Valley, northern Syria [diss. Amst 1990 → 9,14124]. AA 1993, International Monographs in Prehistory. 351 p.; 60 fig. 1-879621-10-X. -- [R]BuCanadMesop 29 (1995) 68 (M. *Fortin*); JField 22 (1995) 363-5 (A. *Sherratt*).

b312 **Bassit**: **Courbin** P., Fouilles de Bassit; [47] tombes du Fer. P 1993, RCiv. 178 p.; 35 pl. -- [R]PEQ 127 (1995) 73s (W.P. *Ridley*).

b313 **Beydar**: Phoe 41,1 (1995) 27-42; 9 fig. (K. van *Lerberghe* & G. *Voet*).

b314 **Bi"a** 1994s: MDOG 127 (1995) 43-55; 9 fig. (K. *Kohlmeyer*, E. *Strommenger*).

b315 **Boṣra**: *Habas* Ephrat, [H] The halachic status of Bostra, metropolis Arabiae [the city itself was beyond Israel's northeast border, but some of its terrritory was within]: Zion 60 (1995) 375-391, Eng. XXVI.

b316 **Damascus** SE to Suweida: *Echallier* Jean-Claude, *Braemer* Frank, Nature et fonction des 'desert kites'; données et hypothèses nouvelles: Paléor 21,1 (1995) 35-63; 28 fig.; Eng. 35: not gazelle 'traps' but to 'capture and corral' semi-domesticated animals.

b317 -- **Contenson** Henri de, Aswad et Ghoraifé, sites néolithiques en Damascène (Syrie) au IXème et VIIIème millénaires avant l'ère chrétienne: BAH 137. Beyrouth 1995, IFAPO. 393 p.; bibliog. 377-385. 2-7053-0673-0.

b318 -- **Miura** Toru, The Ṣaliḥiyya quarter of Damascus; its formation, structure, and transformation in the Ayyubid and Mamluk periods: BEO(r) 47(1995)129-177;4 fig.

b319 **Dara** ['ain → 10,12501] 40 k NW Aleppo: **Abu 'Assaf** 'Ali, Der Tempel von 'Ain Dara 1990 → 6,e358; 7,d651: [R]AulaO 12 (1994) 234-9 (A. *González Blanco*); Syria 72 (1995) 441-4 (J.-C. *Margueron*).

b320 **Derkuš**: *Peña* I., Un puerto fluvial romano en el Orontes: SBF*LA 45 (1995) 343-350; pl. 51s; Eng. 486s.

b321 **Dura**: *Wharton* A.J., Good and bad images from the synagogue of Dura Europos; contexts, subtexts, intertexts: *Art History 17,1 (Ox 1994) 1-25 [NTAb 39, p.277].

b322 -- Dura-Europos 1994, Zeus temple: Mesop-T 30 (1995) 241-250; 10 fig. (Susan B. *Downey*).

b323 **Emar**: *Dietrich* Manfried, Altsyrische Götter und Rituale aus Emar [FLEMING D. 1992]: Biblica 76 (1995) 239-249.

b324 -- *a*) *Margueron* Jean-Claude, Emar, capital of Aštata in the fourteenth century BCE; -- *b*) *Fleming* Daniel E., More help from Syria: introducing Emar to biblical study: BA 58 (1995) 126-138 / 139-147; ill.

b325 -- *Seminara* S., Un dilemma della topografia di Emar: *kirṣitu* o *ki[erṣe]tu* ? : UF 27 (DIETRICH 60. Gb. 1995) 467-480; Eng. 467.

b326 -- *Zaccagnini* Carlo, War and famine at Emar; Orientalia 64 (1995) 92-109.

b327 *Hamman/Turkman*: **Loon** Maurits N. van, Report 1s, 1988 → 6,e370 ... 9,14144: [R]JNES 54 (1995) 152-4 (A.H. *Joffe*).

b328 *Hamrin*: **Yaseen** Ghassan T., Old Babylonian pottery from the Hamrin Tell Halawa: EDUBBA 4. L 1995, NABU. [viii-] 107 p. 1-897750-04-4.

b329 *Haradum* 90 k SE Mari: [E]**Képinski-Lecomte** Christine, Haradum I, 1992 → 8,e799; 10,12521; [R]AfO 42s (1995s) 287 (Ö. *Tunca*).

b330 *Jerablus-Tahtani* 1992-4: Levant 27 (1995) 1-28; 29 fig. (E. *Peltenburg, al.*).

b331 *Khabur*: *a) Blackburn* Michel, Environnement géomorphologique du centre de la moyenne vallée du Khabour, Syrie; -- *b) Zeder* Melinda A., The archaeology of the Khabur basin; -- *c) McCorriston* Joy, Preliminary archaeobotanical analysis in the Middle Habur valley, Syria; and studies of socioeconomic change in the early third millennium B.C.: BuCanadMesop 29 (1995) 5-20; 16 fig. / 21-32; 4 fig.: / 33-46.

b332 *Magara* 50 k SE Carchemish: *Matilla Séiquer* Gonzalo, *González Blanco* Antonino, El conjunto funerario bizantino de Tell Magara; → 221, [F]YELO TEMPLADO A., Lengua 1995, 579-593: 9 fig. (2 mapas; inscripción siríaca)

-----

b333 *Mari* **Cagni** Luigi, Le profezie di Mari; TestiVOA 11/2. Brescia 1995, Paideia. 126 p. L[m] 22. 88-394-0519-4 [< OTA 19, p.325s, C.T. *Begg*].-- [R]AION 55 (1995) 122-4 (G.L. *Prato*); Anton 70 (1995) 686-8 (M. *Nobile*); Mesop-T 30 (1995) 295s (A. *Lombardi*).

b334 -- *Charpin* Dominique, 'Lies natürlich ...'; à propos des erreurs de scribes dans les lettres de Mari: → 185, [F]SODEN W. von, Vom Alten Orient (1995) 43-55; 6 facsim.

b335 -- *Charpin* Dominique, La fin des archives dans le palais de Mari: → 724, RA(ssyr) 89 (1995) 29-40; 3 fig.

b336-- [F]FINET André. Reflets des deux fleuves, [E]**Lebeau M.,** *Talon* T.: Akkadica supp. 6. Lv 1989, Peeters. viii-193 p. Fb 1850. -- [R]JAOS 115 (1995) 544-6 (J.F. *Robertson*).

b337 -- *Heintz* Jean-Georges, 'Dans la plénitude du cœur'; à propos d'une formule d'alliance à Mari et Assyrie et dans la Bible: → 155. [F]RENAUD B., Ce Dieu .. : LD(iv) 159 (1995) 31-44 [< OTA 18 (1995) p. 451].

b338 -- *Nakata* Ichiro, A study of women's theophoric personal names in the Old Babylonian texts from Mari: → 129, [F]MIKASA T., Orient 30s (1995) 234-253; color. portr.; biobibliog. vii-ix (N. *Egami*).

b339 -- **Anbar** Moshe, Les tribus amurrites de Mari; OBO 108, 1991 → 7,d669 ... 10,12529; [R]AfO 42s (1995s) 233s (G. *Buccellati*).

b340 -- *Avner* Moshe, *a)* [H] *Sugiyyot* ... SEELIGMAN's pairs in the light of Mari documents; *b)* [H] Mari and Ex 19: BetM 40,3 (142,1995) 205-211 / 40,1 (140,1994) 65-70.

b341 -- *a) Bonneterre* Daniel, The structure of violence in the Kingdom of Mari; -- *b) Dion* Paul E., The Syro-Mesopotamian border in the VIIIth century b,c.; the Aramaeans and the Establishment: BuCanadMesop 30 (1995) 11-22 / 5-10.

b342 -- *a) Michalowski* Piotr, The men from Mari; -- *b) Sasson* Jack M., Mari apocalypticism revisited; -- *c) Anbar* Moshe, Les milieux de vie de deux motifs dans le récit de l'Exode illustrés par ARM; -- *d) Owen* David I., Amorites and the location of Bàd[ki] [between Mari and Kiš]: → 110. [F]LIPIŃSKI, E., Immigration: OLA 65 (1995) 181-8 / 285-298 / 11-17 / 213-9; 1 facsim.

b343 -- *Schart* Aaron, Combining prophetic oracles in Mari letters and Jeremiah 36: JANES 23 (1995) 75-93.

-----

b344 *Melebiya*: **Lebeau** M., Tell Melebiya; cinq campagnes .. (1994-8): Akkadica supp.9. Lv 1993, Peeters. -- ^RBuCanadMesop 29 (1995) 71s (M. *Fortin*).

b345 *Mozan*; *Buccellati* Giorgio, *Kelly-Buccellati* Marilyn, The royal storehouse of Urkesh; the glyptic evidence from the southwest wing; AfO 42s (1995s) 1-32; 10 fig.; (map, complete sign-list).

b346 *Nabk*-Qalamun 80 k N Damaskus: *Kaufhold* Hubert, Notizen über das Moseskloster bei Nabk und das Julianskloster bei Qaryatein in Syrien [Strasse Damaskus-Palmyra]: OrChr 79 (1995) 48-119; 2 fig.

b347 *Neirab* 7 k S Aleppo: *Timm* Stefan, Die Bedeutung der spätbabylonischen Texte aus Nērab für die Rückkehr der Judäer aus dem Exil): → 48, ^FDONNER H., Meilenstein: ÄAT 30 (1995) 276-289.

-----

b348 *Palmyra:* **Sadurska** Anna, *Bounni* Adnan, Les sculptures funéraires de Palmyre. R 1994, Bretschneider. 213 p.; ill.; 14 plans. -- ParPass 286 (1996) 78-80 (Raffaella *Pierobon Benoit*).

b349 -- **Schmidt-Colinet** Andreas, Das Tempelgrab Nr 36, 1992 → 10.12539: ^RGnomon 67 (1995) 284-6 (Anna *Sadurska*); Syria 72 (1995) 453-6 (M. *Griesheimer*).

b350 -- *Gawlikowski* Michel, Les oreilles de cheval ou un souvenir de la Décapole à Palmyre: → 199, ^FTRAN TAM TINH V., Tranquillitas 1995, 199-205; 4 fig.

b351 -- *a) Gawlikowski* Michel, Les Arabes en Palmyrène; -- *b) Bron* François, Vestiges de l'écriture sud-sémitique dans le Croissant fertile; -- *c) Briquel-Chatonnet* Françoise, La pénétration de la culture du Croissant fertile en Arabie; à propos des inscriptions nabatéennes: → 728, Présence 1993/5, 103-8 / 81-91; 12 fig. / 133-141.

b352 -- *Arnaud* Daniel, Les traces des 'Arabes' dans les textes syriens du début du IIe millénaire à l'époque néo-assyrienne; esquisse de quelques thèmes [...*ta 'tamum*; pluriels brisés] → 728, Présence 1993/5, 19-22.

b353 -- *Simiot* B., *Degeorge* G., Zenobia di Palmira 1993 → 10.12541: ^RArVi 14,49 (1995) 92 [P. *Pruneti*].

b354 -- **Stoneman** Richard, Palmyra and its empire; Zenobia's revolt against Rome 1992 → 9.14163*; 10,12540: ^RBiOr 52 (1995) 781-4 (J.W. *Drijvers*: remarkable though not by or for a professional).

b355 -- **Will** Ernst, Les Palmyréniens; la Venise des sables (Ier s. avant - IIIe s. après J.-C.): Civilisations-U. P 1992, A. Colin. 208 p. 2-200-21224-0. -- ^RTopO 4 (1994) 363-370 (A. *Gawlikowski*).

-----

b356 *Qadeš*: **Giles** F.J., The relative chronology of the Hittite conquest of Syria and Aitakama of Qadesh; → 82, ^FHENNESSY J.B., Trade 1995, 137-148.

b357 *Qaṣṭūn* W.Ebla: *Fourdrin* Jean-Pascal, Qaṣṭūn et Chastel de Ruge: Syria 72 (1995) 415-426; 8 fig.

b358 *Rešafa*: **Fowden** Elizabeth K., Sergius of Rušafa; sacred defense in late antique Syria-Mesopotamia: diss. ^D*Brown* P. Princeton 1995. 195 p. 96-11553. -- D(iss)AI 56 (1995s) p. 4897.

b359 *Sabi Abyad* Late Neo: AJA 99 (1995) 5-32; 17 fig. (P. *Akkermans*, M. *Verhoeven*).

b360 **Tabqa** MB-LB; *Müller* Béatrice, Deux nouvelles 'maquettes architecturales' en terre cuite du Moyen-Euphrate syrien: Syria 72 (1995) 357-380: 13 fig.

b361 **Tuneinir**: *Fuller* Michael & Neathery, A medieval church in Mesopotamia: BA 57 (1994) 38-45; ill.

T6.1 **Mesopotamia,** *generalia*

b362 **Algaze** Guillermo, The Uruk world system 1993 → 9,14174; 10,12551: ^RBASOR 297 (1995) 84s (T.C. *Young*).

b363 **Amiet** Pierre J., L'antiquité orientale: Q(ue)SJ? 185. P 1995, PUF. 128 p. 2-13-046453-X.

b364 *Antonova* Ye. V., ^R Symbols of cosmic forces and social reality of Mesopotamia at the end of the 4th-3rd millennoum B.C.: VDI 214 (1995) 3-13; Eng. 13.

b365 **Bottéro** Jean, interview de *Monsacré* Hélène, Babylone et la Bible 1994 → 10,12554: ^RRICAO 11 (1995) 85-90 (J.-M. *Guillaume*).

b366 **Bottéro** Jean, *Stève* Marie-Joseph, La Mesopotamia, dalla scrittura all'archeologia. Mi 1995, Electa/Gallimard. 192 p.; 172 fig. L^m 20. -- ^RArcheo 124 (1995) 109 (S.P. *Bondì*).

b367 *a) Bottéro* Jean, Boisson, banquet et vie sociale en Mésopotamie; -- *b) Pinnock* Frances, Considerations on the 'Banquet theme' in the figurative art of Mesopotamia and Syria: → 10,480, Drinking ANE. 1990/4, 3-13 / 15-26; pl. I-IX.

b368 *Buccellati* Giorgio, The kudurrus as monuments: → 10,81, ^FMEYER L. de, 52 Réflexions 1994, 283-291. 3 fig.

b369 *Castel* Corinne, Contexte archéologique et statut des documents; les textes retrouvés dans les maisons mésopotamiennes du Ier millénaire av. J,.C.: → 724, RA(ssyr) 89 (1995) 109-137; 20 fig.

b370 ^E**Charpin** D,M., *Joannès* F., La circulation des biens, 38e Rencontre 1991/2 → 8,683: ^RBiOr 52 (1995) 90-92 (D.C. *Snell*: speed of 'the Mari boys').

b371 ^E**Curtis** John, Later Mesopotamia and Iran; tribes and empires 1600-539 BC. L 1995, British Museum. 96 p. 0-7141-1138-4.

b372 ^E**Dolce** Rita, *(Nota) Santi* Maresita, Dai palazzi assiri; immagini di potere da Assurnasirpal II ad Assurbanipal: *StArch 76. R 1995, Bretschneider. 339 p.; bibliog. 324-333. 88-7062-893-0.

b373 **Dolukhanov** Pavel, Environment and ethnicity in the ancient Middle East [Jemdet Nasr & Uruk periods enriched from areas unfamiliar to western scholarship]: *WorldAr 7. Brookfield 1994, Ashgate. x-406 p.: Ill. $ 77. 1-85628-706-8 [RStR 22,150, D.I. *Owen*].

b374 **Emberling** Geoff, Ethnicity and the State in early third millennium Mesopotamia: diss. Michigan, ^D*Wright* H. Ann Arbor.

b375 *Faivre* Xavier, Le recyclage des tablettes cunéiformes; → 724, RA(ssyr) 89 (1995) 57-66.

b376 *Forest* J.-D., L'apparition de l'État en Mésopotamie: *OrExp 3 (1994) 48.

b377 **George** A.R., House most high; the temples of ancient Babylonia [→ a259 above]: *MesopCiv 5, 1993 → 9,14178: ^RBiOr 52 (1995) 451 (R. *Livingstone*); OLZ 90 (1995) 175s (J. *Black*).

b378 *Gordon* Cyrus H., Diffusion of Near East culture in antiquity and in Byzantine times: → 129, ^FMIKASA T., Orient 30s (1995) 69-81.

b379 **Huot** Jean-Louis, Les premiers villageois de Mésopotamie; du village à la ville. P 1994, Colin. 223 p. 2-200-21493-6. -- ^RMesop-T 30 (1995) 263-5 (P. *Brusasco*).

1994, Colin. 223 p. 2-200-21493-6. -- ᴿMesop-T 30 (1995) 263-5 (P. *Brusasco*).

b380 **Invernizzi** Antonio, Dal Tigri all'Eufrate 1s, 1992 → 8,e845: ᴿ*TopO 4 (1994) 233-6 (Y. *Calvet*).

b381 ᴱ**Kataja** L., *Whiting* R., Grants, decrees and gifts of the Neo Assyrian period: SAA 12. Helsinki 1995, Univ. xlv-174 p. 951-370-283-4; pa. -34-2.

b382 **Koch-Westenholz** Ulla, Mesopotamian astrology; an introduction to Babylonian and Assyrian celestial divination: Niebuhr 19. K 1995, C.Niebuhr Inst, 223 p.; bibliog. 209-219. 87-7289-287-0.

b383 *Kuhrt* Amelia,The Assyrian heartland in the Achaemenid period: Pallas 43 (1995) 239-53

b384 *Lange* Judith, Passaggio in Iraq [stato pericoloso dei monumenti ... archeological jackals] : ArVi 14,51 (1995) 19-33.

b385 **Nemat-Nejat** Karen R., Cuneiform mathematical texts: Amer.Or.Series 75. NHv 1993, American Oriental Soc. xii-335 p. $ 42. 0-940590-75-7. -- ᴿBiOr 52 (1995) 424-432 (Eleanor *Robson*).

b386 *Nemat-Nejat* Karen R., Systems for learning mathematics in Mesopotamian scribal schools: JNES 54 (1995) 241-260; 9 fig.

b387 **Neumann** Heinz, Die Berichte der Astrologen an die assyrischen Könige, ihr astronomischer Inhalt und ihre zeitliche Einordnung: WZKM 85 (1995) 239-264.

b388 *Nissen* Hans J., Kulturelle und politische Vernetzungen im Vorderen Orient des 4. und 3. vorchristlichen Jahrtausends: → 23, ᶠBOEHMER R.M., Beiträge 1995, 473-490.

b389 **Postgate** J.H., Early Mesopotamia 1992 → 9,14188: ᴿBoL (1995) 32s (M.J. *Geller*).

b390 **Reiner** Erica, Astral magic in Babylonia: TAPhS 85/4. Ph 1995, Amer.Philosophical. xiii-159 p. 0-87169-854-4.

b391 **Roth** Martha T., Law collections from Mesopotamia and Asia Minor: SBL.w 6. At 1995, Scholars. xviii-283 p. $ 60; pa. 40. 0-7885-0104-6; -26-7 [ThD 43,185].

b392 *Sauren* Herbert, Zum Beweis des Eigentums an Grund und Boden in Mesopotamien: → 10.443, Grund/Boden im Altägypten 1990/4, 45-64.

b393 ᴱ**Vivante** Anna, Assiri; l'arte, la guerra, il potere. Mi 1995 , Guerini. 145 p. 88-7802-577-1.

b394 *a) Walker* Christopher B.F., The Dalbanna text; a Mesopotamian star-list; -- *b) Koch* Johannes, Der Dalbanna-Sternenkatalog: WO 26 (1995) 27-42 / 43-85.

> T6.3 on publications of excavated cuneiform texts is being
> abandoned because such data are better available elsewhere;
> but texts of specifically biblical pertinence will be found in
> the **relevant** sections: B8.5 Creation, Gilgameš; J2.1 Semitics;
> M7 religion; Q4 history; U5s, socioeconomics

b395 **Wilkinson** T.J., *Tucker* D,J., Settlement development in the North Jazira, Iraq; a study of the archaeological landscape: Iraq Archaeological Reports 3. Baghdad 1995, British School / Antiquities Dept. xv-246 p.; bibliog. 135-144. 0-85668-658-1.

b396 ᴱ**Yoffee** N., *Clark* J., Early stages in the evolution of Mesopotamian civilization; Soviet excavations in northern Iraq [Sinjar plain 1969-80] 1993 → 9,14190; $ 50 [RStR 22,57, D.I. *Owen*]: ᴿArOr 63 (1995) 135s (P. *Charvát*); Paléor 21,1 (1995) 133s (J.-L. *Huot*); RossArkh (1995,4) 192-6 (S.N. *Amirov*).

T6.5 **Situs effossi 'Iraq** *in ordine alphabetico*

b397 *Abu-Thor* 1981: Sumer 47 (1995) 35-45; 26 fig. (H. *Fujii*, Y. *Okada*).

b398 *Ahmed/Hattu*: **Eickhoff** Tilman, Grab und Beigabe ... Mesopotamien, Luristan: MüVorderas 14. Mü 1993, Profil. xviii-212 p., XLIV pl. 3-89019-343-9. -- [R]BiOr 52 (1995) 787-793 (J.D. *Forest*, franç.).

b399 *Assur*: **Haller** Arndt, Die [1140 W. ANDRAE] Gräber und Grüfte von Assur: WVDOG 65. B 1995 = 1952, Mann. viii-201 p.; ill. DM 380. 2-7861-2003-X [< OTA 19,p.527].

b400 *Babylon* 1987: Sumer 47 (1995) 30-34; 4 fig. (G. *Bergamini*).

b401 -- **Karstens** Karsten, Überlegungen zur Rekonstruktion der Fassade am Thronsaal Nebukadnezars II. in Babylon: MDOG 127 (1995) 57-81: pocket-foldout.

b402 -- **Saggs** Henry W.F., Babylonians: Peoples of the Past. L 1995, British Museum. 192 p. 0-7141-2094-4.

b403 -- **Schmid** Hansjürg, Der Tempelturm Etemenanki in Babylon: BaghFor 17. Mainz 1995, von Zabern. xix-155 p. 3-8053-1610-o.

b404 *Basrah* 2d 1979: [A] Sumer 48 (1995s) 44-62 (K. *Aziz*, 63-88, M. *Lutfi*).

b405 *Bismayah*: Sumer 45 (1987s; English of excavation reports only, 1986) 1-8 (Sumer Arabic p. 9-30, A. *Khairi*, I. *Ahmed*), [T]*Al-Jazairi* Kawther.

b406 *Diniyé*-Harâdum: *Sauvage* Martin, Le contexte archéologique et la fin des archives à Khirbet ed-Diniyé -- Harâdum: → 724, RA(ssyr) 89 (1995) 41-55; 10 fig.

b407 -- **Kepinski-Lecomte** C., *al.*, Haradum I, 1992 → 9.e779; 9,14239: [R]CLR 45 (1995) 295s (Catherine *Breniquet*).

b408 *Drehem*: **Sigrist** Marcel, Drehem 1992 → 9,14237: [R]BiOr 52 (1995) 440-6 (W. *Sallaberger*).

b409 *Duwari* 14 k N Nippur, 1987: Sumer 47 (1995) 19-27; 12 fig. (Elizabeth C. *Stone*).

b410 *Fara*: **Visicato** Giuseppe, The bureaucracy of Šuruppak; administrative centers,central offices, intermediate structures and hierarchies in the economic documentation of Fara; *AbhAltS 10.Müns 1995, Ug.-V. xix-165 p. DM 120. 3-927120-35-9 [RStR 22,149,D. *Owen*].

b411 -- *Schachner* Şenay & Andreas, Eine 'syrische' Flasche aus Fara [Museum Istanbul]: MDOG 127 (1995) 83-96.

b412 *Ginnig* & Garsour, N. Jazira 1987s: Sumer 48 (1995s) 6-10 (S. *Campbell*); 11-25, Jazira survey (W. *Ball*, T.J. *Wilkinson*).

b413 *Hatra*: **Aggoula** Basile, Inventaire des inscriptions hatréennes: IFAPO-BAH 139. P 1991, Geuthner. xxxv-195 p.; XXXVII pl. -- [R]AfO 42s (1995s) 316-322 (A. *Sims*: störende Mängel).

b414 -- **Bertolino** Roberto, La cronologia di Hatra; interazione di archeologia e di epigrafia: AION.s 83. N 1995, Ist. Univ. Orientale. xi-77 p.

b415 -- **Vattioni** Francesco, Hatra: AION.s 81. N 1995, Ist.Univ. Orientale. 127 p.

b416 *Isin*: **Hrouda** B., Isin 4 (1986-9), BayerAkad Abh ph/h 105. Mü 1992, Bayerische Akademie. 211 p.; 67 pl.; 18 plans. DM 150. 3-7696-0100-9. -- [R]BiOr 52 (1995) 134-7 (Ö. *Tunca*).

b417 *Khorsabad:* **Durand** Jean-Marie, *Charpin* Dominique, *al.*, Khorsabad, capitale de Sargon II: Dossiers d'Archéologie hors-série 4 (1994). 72 p. F 4.

b418 *Lagaš*: **Mander** Pietro, An archive of kennelmen and other workers in Ur III Lagash: AION.s 80. N 1994, Ist. Univ. Orientale. xi-105 p.

b419 *Larsa*: *Calvet* Y., Les grandes résidences paléo-babyloniennes de Larsa: → 10,81,

[F]MEYER L. de, 52 Réflexions 1994, 215-228; 9 fig.

b420 -- (Goodnick-)Westenholz Joan M., Eight days in the Temples of Larsa; celebrations in the month of Shevat in the time of Abraham. J 1994, Sirkis. 31 .. p.

b421 *Mashkan-Shapir*: Pellegrino Charles, Return to Sodom and Gomorrah; Bible stories from archaeologists. NY 1994, Random. 386 p. $ 25. -- [R]BArR 21,4 (1995) 9s (M.T. *Shoemaker*).

b422 -- *Stone* Elizabeth C., *Zimansky* P., Maškan-Sapir; the Tell Abu Duwari project. 1988-90: [R]*JField 21 (1994) 437-455; 13 fig.

b423 *Ninive:* *Hamel* Gildas, Taking the Argo to Nineveh; Jonah and Jason in a Mediterranean context: J(u)d(ais)m 44 (1995) 341-359 (362-8, *Zucker* David, on Jonah).

b424 -- *Gut* Renate V., Das prähistorische Ninive; zur relativ Chronologie der frühen Perioden Nordmesopotamiens: BaghFo 19. Mainz 1995, von Zabern. I. xxi-357 p.; II. 124 p. (figures with explanation facing) + p. 125-140, (color.) pl.; 141 maps. 3-8053-1751-4.

b425 -- *Calvi* Gabriele, Ninive, una città immensa: Ambrosius 71 (1995) 107-124 (-139, *Fausto* Silvano).

b426 *Nippur:* Zettler Richard L., Nippur III; Kassite buildings in Area WC-1: OIP 111. Ch 1993, Univ. Oriental Inst. xxxvii-347 p.; bibliog. xix-xxxi. 0-918986-91-5.

b427 *Nuzi;* *Lion* Brigitte, La fin du site de Nuzi et la distribution chronologique des archives: → 724, RA(ssyr) 89 (1995) 77-88.

b428 -- *a) Fincke* Jeanette, *a)* Beiträge zum Lexikon des Hurritischen von Nuzi; -- *b)* Einige Joins von Nuzi-Texten des British Museum: → 151, PORADA E., mem.,[E]Owen David L., *Wilhelm* Gernot, StNuzi 7 (1995) 5-21 / 22-36.

b429 -- [E]Owen David I., *Morrison* Martha A., The eastern archives of Nuzu and excavation at Nuzi 9/2 (4). WL 1993, Eisenbrauns. xii-430 p. $ 65, -- [R]WO 26 (1995) 198-201 (Jeanette *Fincke*).

b430 -- [E]Owen David I., General studies; excavations at Nuzi 9/3: Studies Nuzi/Hurrians 5. WL 1995, Eisenbrauns. viii-357 p. $ 65. 0-931464-67-6 [< OTA 19,p.332, V.H. *Matthews*].

b431 *Salabîkh*: [E]Green Anthony, The 6G ash-tip and its contents; cultic and administrative discard from the Temple? 1993 → 9.14254; 10,12629: [R]AfO 42s (1995s) 282-4 (J.D. *Forest*, français); BuCanadMesop 29 (1995) 69 (M. *Fortin*); Orientalia 64 (1995) 357-360 (Enrica *Flandra*).

b432 *Seleucia:* *Invernizzi* Antonio, Seleucia und Uruk; cities of Seleucid Babylonia → 23, [F]BOEHMER R.M., Beiträge 1995, 273-280.

b433 *Sippar:* *Di Gennaro* Teodolinda, Famiglie e professioni nella Sippar achemenide; il caso di Taqîš-Gula: AION 54 (1994) 289-297.

-----

b434 *Ur:* Tombes royales, British Museum: MoBi 91 (1995) 49-55 (Dominique *Collon*).

b435 -- *Lafont* Bertrand, La chute des rois d'Ur et la fin des archives dans les grands centres administratifs de leur empire: → 724, [R]RA(ssyr) 89 (1995) 3-13.

b436 -- Pinnock Frances, Ur la città del dio-luna: Quadrante 79. R 1995, Laterza. vii-244 p. 88-420-4757-0.

-----

b437 *Uruk*: Becker Andrea, Kleinfunde I. Stein: Endb 6, 1993 → 9,14265; 10,12634: [R]OLZ 90 (1995) 176-9 (L. *Martin*); RA(ssyr) 89,1 (1995) 89s (P. *Amiet*, aussi sur Endb 9).

b438 -- Boehmer Rainer M., *Pedde* F., *Salje* B., Uruk, die Gräber: Endb 10. Mainz 1995, von Zabern. xx-239 p. 3-8053-1590-2.

b439 -- **Ess** Margarete van, *Pedde* Friedhelm, Kleinfunde II: Endbericht 7, 1992 → 8,e963 ... 10,12635: [R]JAOS 115 (1995) 716-8 (Sally *Dunham*).

b440 -- **Finkbeiner** Uwe, Uruk, Kampagne 35-37, 1982-4: Endb 4,1991 → 9,14269; 10,12636: [R]BiOr 52 (1995) 784-7 (Ö. *Tunca*).

b441 -- *Okada* Akiko, Die Entstehung des frühesten Palastes bzw. der Residenz für die sumerischen Herrscher in den archaischen Schichten in Uruk: → 129, [F] MIKASA T., Orient 30s (1995) 270-287 + 6 fig.

b442 -- *Schmandt-Besserat* D., Tokens, seals and administration in Uruk in the fourth millennium B.C.: → 10,80, [F]MAYER-OPIFICIUS Ruth, Beschreiben 1994, 283-293 + 3 fig.

b443 -- **Weiher** Egbert von, Uruk -- spätbabylonische Texte .. : Endb12, 1993 → 9,1224; [R]Orientalia 64 (1995) 137s (R.D. *Biggs*).

T6.7 Arabia

b444 *Abu Duruk* Hamid, Archaeology thriving in Saudi Arabia: BArR 21,2 (1995) 68-73.

b445 *a) Aggoula* Basile, Arabie et Arabes en Mésopotamie; -- *b) Macdonald* M.C.A., Quelques réflexions sur les Saracènes; l'inscription de Rawwāfa et l'armée romaine, [T]*Fauveaud* C.; -- *c) Scagliarini* Fiorella, La chronologie dédanite et lihyanite; mise au point: → 728, Présence 1993/5, 73-79 / 93-101 / 118-132.

b446 *Avanzini* Alessandra, Profumi d'Arabia: Archeo 119 (1995) 67-107.

b447 **Breton** Jean-François, *Bāfaqīh* Muhammad A., Trésors du Wadi Dura .. Yémen Hajar ad-Dhaybiyya: IFAPO-BAH 141. P 1993, Geuthner. 109 p. + [A] 31; 41 pl. 2-7053-0559-9. - - [R]AfO 42s (1995s) 296-8 (W.W. *Müller*: materials stolen in 1994 Gulf War); Syria 72 (1995) 279-281 (F. *Bron*).

b448 *Grainger* John D., Village government in Roman Syria and Arabia: Levant 25 (1995)170-195; 3 fig. (maps).

b449 **Høylund** Flemming, *Andersen* H. Hellmuth, *al.,* [P-V. GLOB excavation begun 1995], Qala'at al-Bahrain I. Aarhus 1994, Jutland Archaeological Soc. 510 p.; 2105 fig.; 35 (foldout) plans. Dk 360. -; AfO 42s (1995s) 299s (D.T. *Potts*, Eng.)

b450 **Kitchen** K.A., Documentation for ancient Arabia I. Chronological framework and historical sources. Liverpool 1994, Univ. 0-85323-359-4.

b451 *Kitchen* K.A., Ancient Arabia and the Bible: *ABW 3,1 (1995) 26-34; ill.; map.

b452 *Korotayev* Andrey, Middle Sabaean cultural-political area; material sources of Qayite political power: Abr Nahrain 31 (1993) 91-105.

b453 *Lundin* A.G., [R] Archives of ancient Yemen: VDI 213 (1995) 3-13; Eng.13.

b454 *Müller* Walter W., Südarabien im Altertum .. kommentierte Bibliographie 1992s; AfO 42s (1995s) 503-511.

b455 **Rice** Michael, The archaeology of the Arabian Gulf, c.5000-323 B.C.: 1994 → 10,12640: [R]AfO 42s (1995s) 295s (P. *Yule*, Eng.); BoL (1995) 34 (T.C. *Mitchell*).

b456 [E]**Robin** C., L'Arabie antique de Karib'il à Mahomet; nouvelles données sur l'histoire des Arabes grâce aux inscriptions. Aix/P 1992, Edisud. 168 p.; 43 fig.; 10 maps, F 120. 2-85774-584-9. -- [R]Syria 72 (1995) 450s (J.-F. *Breton*).

b457 **Shahid** Irfan, Byzantium and the Arabs in the sixth century. Wsh 1995, Dumbarton Oaks. xxx-995 p. ; ill.; maps. $ 75. -- [R]SV(lad)TQ 39 (1995) 313-5 (A. *Papadakis*: completes the trilogy).

b458 *Khayma, Ḥulayla* island: JRAS (1994) 163-213; 16 fig.(D. *Kennett*).

b459 **Oman:** *Méry* Sophie, Archaeology of the borderlands; 4th millennium BC Mesopotamian pottery at Ra's al-Hamra RH-5 (Sultanate of Oman): AION 55 (1995) 193-203; 2 fig. (map); color. pl.

b460 *Qaṭar*: **Inizian** Marie-Louise, Préhistoire à Qaṭar: Mission J. TIXIER, 1976-82: 2. P 1988, RCiv. 234 p., ill., + ᴬ 52 p. 2-86538-168-4.

b461 *Saba* et Salomon: MoBi 95 (1995) 2-30 (C. *Robin, al.*).

b462 *Sawda'*: **Avanzini** Alessandra, As-Sawda': Inventario delle iscrizioni sudarabiche 4. P 1995, de Boccard. [iv-] 229 p.; 42 pl. bibliog. 211-220. Lᵐ ⁶⁰·

b463 *Yemen*: **Glanzman** William D., Toward a classification and chronology of pottery from HR3 (Hajar al-Rayhani, wadi Jubah): diss. Pennsylvania, ᴰ*Zettler* R. Ph 1994. 1073 p. 95-21036. -- D(iss)AI 56 (1995s) p. 991.

T6.9 **Iran,** *Persia,* Asia centralis

b464 *a) Calmeyer* Peter, Metamorphosen iranischer Denkmäler; -- *b) Seidl* Ursula, Der Thron von [Van-] Toprakkale, ein neuer Rekonstruktionsversuch: AMI(ran) 27 (1994) 1-27; 17 fig.; pl. 1-5 / 67-84; 12 (foldout) fig.; pl. 6-23.

b465 **Finster** Barbara, Frühe iranische Moscheen vom Beginn des Islam bis zur Zeit salǧūqidischer Herrschaft: AMI.e 19. B 1994, Reimer. 321 p.;48 pl.3-496-02521-2 [OIAc 11,22].

b466 **Horne** L., Village spaces; settlement and society in northeastern Iran. Wsh 1994, Smithsonian. xvi-246 p. -- ᴿBuCanadMesop 29 (1995) 68 (M. *Fortin*); Paléor 21,2 (1995) 154-6 (C. *Bromberger*).

b467 ᶠPERROT Jean, Contribution à l'histoire de l'Iran, ᴱ**Vallat** François 1990 → 6,138; 10,12647: .. 148-150 (M. van *Loon*).

b468 **Yamauchi** Edwin M., Persia and the Bible 1990 → 6,b553 ... 9,14285: ᴿC(oncordia)TQ 59 (1995) 130s (W.A. *Maier*); JETS 38 (1995) 254-6 (G.N. *Knoppers*).

b469 *Zadok* Ron, Elamites and other peoples from Iran and the Persian Gulf region in early Mesopotamian sources: Iran 32 (1994) 31-51.

b470 *Bukan*: *Mousavi* Ali, Une brique à décor polychrome [taureau ailé androcéphale, Bukan-Qalâyči 1985, Azerbaidjan] de l'Iran occidentale (VIIIᵉ - VIIᵉ s. av. J.-C): StIr 23 (1994) 7-18; 4 fig. (map); Eng. 18s; ᴬ 19.

b471 *Ecbatana*: *Medvedskaya* I.N., ᴿ Have the Assyrians been in Ecbatana ?: VDI 213 (1995) 147-155; Eng. 155.

b472 *Gonur*: Iran 31 (1993) 25-37; 11 fig. (V. *Sarianidi,* ᵀ*Judelson* K.)

b473 *Haft*: **Negahban** Ezat O., Excavations at Haft Tepe, Iran, 1991 → 7,d807; 8,e989: ᴿJNES 54 (1995) 2936 (A. *Alizadeh*).

b474 *Hajiabad*: **Azarnoush** Massoud, The Sassanian manor house. F 1994, Le Lettere. xii-251 p. xii-251 p.; 190 fig.; 35 (color.) pl. = 6 loose. 88-7166-177-X [*OIAc 11,12].

b475 *Khorasan*: **Gropp** Gerd, Archäologische Forschungen in Khorasan, Iran: TAVO.b 84. Wsb 1995, Reichert. ix-306 p. 3-88226-775-5.

b476 *Luristan*: [*Schmidt* Erich F. †] **Loon** Maurits H. van, *al.*, The Holmes expedition to Luristan: OIP 108, 1989: → 5,e282 ... 10,12653: ᴿTopO 3 (1993) 213-5 (D.T. *Potts*).

b477 *Marlik*: *Löw* Ulrike, Der Friedhof von Marlik -- ein Datierungsvorschlag (I) : AMI(ran) 28 (1995s) 119-16l: 45 Gräber (fig.)

b479 **Persepolis:** *Callieri* Pierfrancesco, Une borne routière grecque de la région de Persépolis: CRAI (1995) 65-73; 2 fig (73-95, *Bernard* Paul).

b480 -- [Naqš-i Rustam] *Jamzadeh* Parivash. Darius' thrones, temporal and eternal; → 174, [F]SCHIPPMANN K., II: IrAnt 30 (1995) 1-21; 4 fig.

b481 **Susa**: *a) Amiet* P., Un Étage au palais de Darius à Suse; -- *b) Strommenger* E., Elamier, Perser und Babylonier; → 10,80, [F]MAYER-OPIFICIUS R., Beschreiben 1994, 1-3 + 3 fig. / 313-323 + 6 fig.

b482 -- *Biggs* R.D., *Šušan* in Babylonia [in Murašu texts, not Susa but not necessarily near Nippur as DANDAMAYEV A, 1986]: → 10,81, [F]MEYER L. de, 52 Réflexions 1994, 299-304.

b483 -- **Malbran-Labat** Florence, Briques de l'époque paléo-élamite à l'Empire néo-élamite: [Louvre] Inscriptions royales de Suse. P 1995, Réunion des musées nationaux. 272 p. 2-7118-2868-9.

b484 -- **Spycket** Agnès, Les figurines de Suse I, 1992 → 8,e96; 9,14290; [R]AfO 42s (1995s) 285s (Irene J. *Winter*); Orientalia 64 (1995) 361-5 (Eva A. *Braun-Holzinger*); Syria 72 (1995) 302-5 (Françoise *Tallon*).

b485 **Tehran:** *Kleiss* Wolfram, Fundplätze in der Umgebung von Teheran : AMI(ran) 28 (1995s) 29-83; 84 fig.; pl. 1-5 (p. 85-117; 56 fig., West-Iran). : AMI(ran) 28 (1995s).

------

b486 [E]**Gardin** J.-C. (p. 17), L'Asie centrale et ses rapports avec les civilisations orientales, des origines à l'Âge du Fer; Actes du colloque franco-soviétique, Paris 19-26 nov. 1985. P 1988, de Boccard. 290 p. 2-907431-90-5.

b487 *Lala Comneno* Marie Adelaide, Cristianesimo nestoriano in Asia centrale nel primo millennio; testimonianze archeologiche: OCP 61 (1995) 495-535; 32 fig. (map, plans ..).

T7.1 **Aegyptus,** *generalia*

b488 *Bahgat* Reem, Towards the standardization of scenes' description: GöMiszÄg 141 (1994) 19-34; 2 fig.

b489 *Bard* Kathryn A., The Egyptian predynastic; a review of the evidence: *JField 21 (1994) 265-283; bibliog. 283-8.

b490 **Beaumont** Olivier de, Meraviglioso Egitto. Novara c.1994, De Agostini. 116 p.; fotografie di *Sloen* Gérard. L[m] 57. - [R]*Archeo 9,117 (1994) 124 (S. *Pernigotti*).

b491 [E]**Bernard** Giovanna G., L'Egitto nei libri e nelle immagini della biblioteca reale di Torino. T 1991, Ministero beni. 261 p.; ill. [*OIAc 11,13].

b492 *Bolshakov* Andrey O., Hinting as a method of Old Kingdom tomb decoration: the offering-stone and the false door of the dwarf Snb; GöMisz 139 (1994) 9-33; 12 pl. [addendum 143 (1994) 29s].

b493 **Bongioanni** Alessandro, *Grazzi* Riccardo. Torino, l'Egitto e l'Oriente fra storia e leggenda. T 1994, Manzoni. xiii-173 p.; ill.

b494 **Buhl** Marie-Louise, Dessins .. Égypte, F.L. NORDEN. K 1993, Vidensk. Selskab. 148 p.; 107 pl. Dk 750. 87-7304-239-2. -- [R]AfO 42s (1995s) 304s (K. *Antonicek*); BiOr 62 (1995) 573s (P. A. *Clayton*).

b495 *Casarico* Loisa, La metropoli dell'Arsinoite in epoca romana: Aevum 49 (1995) 69-94.

b496 **Clagett** Marshall, Ancient Egyptian science [1. 1989], 2. Calendars, clocks, and astronomy; a source book: Mem 214. Ph 1995, American Philosophical. xvi-577 p.; bibliog. 507-519. 0-87169-214-7.

b497 **Clère** Jacques J., Les chauves d'Hathor: OLA 63. Lv 1995, Peeters. xx-257 p.; bibliog. vii-xvii. 90-6831-695-8.

b498 **Dawson** Warren R., *Uphill* Eric P., *³Bierbrier* M.L., Who was who in Egyptology ? L 1995, Egypt Exploration. xiv-458 p.; ill. 0-85098-125-7. -- ᴿAntiquity 69 (1995) 1033 (C. *Broodbank*).

b499 **Der Manuelian** Peter, Living in the past; studies in the archaism of the Egyptian twenty-sixth dynasty [< diss. ᴰ*Baer* K., Chicago 1990]. L 1994, Kegan Paul. xliii-466 p.; 20 pl. 0-7103-0461-7 [*OIAc 11,32].

b500 *Dobrev* Vassil, *Baud* Michel, Les annales royales de la VIᵉ dynastie égyptienne, récemment identifiées au Musée du Caire: CRAI (1995) 415-426; 8 fig.

b501 *Fay* Biri,More Old Kingdom sphinxes with human hands; GöMisz 146 (1995) 29s,6 pl.

b502 *Fiore-Marochetti* Elisa, On the design, symbolism, and dating of some XIIth dynasty tomb superstructure; GöMisz 144 (1995) 43-42; 3 fig.

b503 **Gamer-Wallert** Ingrid, *Grieshammer* Reinhard, Ägyptische Kunst. Karlsruhe 1992, Badisches Landesmuseum. 132 p.; ill. 3-923-132-20-4 [*OIAc 11,23].

b504 *Goedicke* Hans, 'Narmer' [on WINTER E. in ᶠTHAUSING (above → 193) 279-290]: WZKM 85 (1995) 81-84.

b505 **Halthoer** Rotislav, *al., Muinainen Egypti* ... Ancient Egypt, a monument of eternity, exposition 1993s: Publ. 51. Tampere 1993, Art Museum. 224 p.; ill. [*OIAc 11,25].

b506 **Harlé** Diane, *Lefebvre* Jean, Sur le Nil avec CHAMPOLLION; lettres, journaux, et dessins inédits de Nestor L'HÔTE, premier voyage en Égypte, 1828-1830. Orléans-Caen 1993, Paradigme. 334 p.; ill. 2-86878-114-4 [*OIAc 11,25].

b508 **Helck** (Hans) Wolfgang. Die Beziehungen Ägyptens und Vorderasiens zur Ägäis bis ins 7. Jahrhundert²ʳᵉᵛ [²1971]: EdF 120. Da 1995, Wiss. xiii-355 p. 3-534-07509-9.

b509 **Humbert** Jean-Marcel, *al..*, Egyptomania; Egypt in western art, 1730-1930: catalogue Louvre/Ottawa 1994, Vienna 1995. Ottawa 1994, National Gallery. 607 p. 0-88884-636-3 [*OIAc] 11,27].

b510 *Iversen* E., Two suggestions concerning obelisks: DiscEg 33 (1995) 41-44.

b511 ᴱ**Johnson** Janet H., Life in a multi-cultural society; Egypt from Cambyses to Constantine: SAOC 51; symposium 1990/2 → 8,719: ᴿEnchoria 21 (1994) 160-172 (G. *Vittman*, alle 44 art., detailliert).

b512 *Leclant* Jean, *Clerc* Gisèle, Fouilles et travaux en Égypte et au Soudan, 1993-4; Orientalia 64 (1995) 225-355; pl. IV-XLV.

b513 **Levallois** Nicole, Les déserts d'Égypte. Courbevoie 1992, ACR. 356 p.; (color.) ill. 2-86770-050-7 [*OIAc 11,31].

b514 ᴱ**Malek** Jaromir, Egypt, ancient culture, modern land: Cradles of civilization. Sydney 1993, Russell → 9,14335; also Norman 1993, Univ.; 1-875202-47-1: ᴿDiscEg 29 (1994) 153-6 (J. *Vercoutter*).

b515 *Pelsmaekers* Johnny, *a*) Christelijke symboliek op een schaal uit Egypte; -- *b*) Studies on the funerary stelae from Kom Abou Billou: BIHBR 65 (1995) 13-22; Eng. 22s / 59 (1989) 3-29; 65 (1995) 5.12; 2 pl.

b516 *Roberts* David, Egypt's Old Kingdom: National Geographic 187,1 (1995) 2-43; color.ill.; 32s, bread-baking technology.

b517 **Robins** Gay, Proportion and style in ancient Egyptian art. Austin 1994, Univ. Texas. xii-283 p; bibliog. 173-8. 0-292-77064-2.

b518 **Rosellini** Ippolito, Bilderwelten und Weltbilder der Pharaonen; das alte Ägypten in den Tafeln der 'Documenti dell'Egitto e della Nubia', ᴱ*Bresciani* Edda, *al.* Mainz 1995, von Zabern. 224 p. 3-8053-1755-7.

b519 **Rothe** Russell D., Human activity in the southern Eastern Desert of Egypt during the pharaonic period; an interdisciplinary research project: diss. Minnesota, [D]*Rapp* G. Mp 1995. 230 p. 96-10388. -- D(iss)AI 56 (1995s) p. 4831.

b520 *Russmann* Edna R., A [6th dynasty] Second Style in Egyptian art of the Old Kingdom: MIDAI-K 51 (1995) 269-279; pl. 53-56.

b521 **Seidlmayer** Stephan J., Gräberfelder aus dem Übergang vom Alten zum Mittleren Reich. Studien zur Archäologie der Ersten Zwischenzeit. Heid 1990m Orient-V. xiv-465 p. -- [R]BiOr 52 (1995) 616-623 (H. *Willems*).

b522 **Shaw** Ian, *Nicholson* Paul, British Museum dictionary of ancient Egypt. L 1995, British Museum. 328 p. 0-7141-0982-7.

b523 **Stierlin** Henri, Tesori d'arte in Egitto. Novara 1995, De Agostini. 278 p.; 200 color.fig. L[m] 200. -- [R]*Archeo 124 (1995) 109 (S. *Pernigotti*).

b524 **Taylor** John H., Unwrapping a mummy; the life, death, and embalming of Horemkenesi: Egyptian Bookshelf. L 1995, British Museum. 111 p. 0-7141-0978-9.

b525 [F]THÉODORIDÈS Aristide, Individu, société et spiritualité dans l'Égypte pharaonique et copte, [E]**Cannuyer** C., *Krüchten* J., 1993 → 9,151: [R]BiOr 52 (1995) 293-9 (Annie *Gasse*) [292s, *Roccati* A. sur [F]IVERSEN E. 1992 → 8,894; -- 299-306, H. *Satzinger* sur Mém. BEHRENS P. 1991 → 7,20c].

b526 **Tooley** Angela M.J., Egyptian models and scenes: Eg.22. Princes Risborough 1995, Shire. 72 p. 0-7478-0285-8.

b527 **Trigger** Bruce G., Ancient Egypt in context 1993 → 9,14349: [R]*JField 21 (1994) 360-2 (Kathryn A. *Bard*).

b528 **Vassilika** E., Egyptian art. 1995. -- [R]*EgA 7 (1995) 38 (G. *Hart*).

b529 **Vandersleyen** Claude, L'Égypte et la vallée du Nil, 2. De la fin de l'Ancien Empire à la fin du Nouvel Empire: NClio. P 1995, PUF. cxvii-710 p.; bibliog. v-cxiii. 2-13-046552-8.

b530 **Vatin** Jean-Claude, Images d'Égypte, de la fresque à la bande dessinée: CEDEJ-IFAO, Le Caire mai 1987. Le Caire 1991, *CEDEJ. 312 p. 2-905838-24-8 [*OIAc 11,44].

b531 **Vercoutter** Jean, L'Égypte et la vallée du Nil, 1. Des origines à la fin de l'Ancien Empire, 12000-2000 av.J.-C.: NClio. P 1992, PUF. li-382 p. F 220. 2-13-044157-2. -- [R]ÉTRel 69 (1994) 565 (Françoise *Smyth*); HZ 260 (1995) 817-9 (H. *Heinen*); JAOS 115 (1995) 528s W.L. *Murnane*); RAHAL 27 (1994) 159 (T. *De Putter*).

b532 **Wace** Rupert, Ancient Egyptian art: Daedalus ancient art. L 1992, Wace/Daedalus. 18 p. [*OIAc 11.44].

T7.2 **Luxor**, *Karnak* [East Bank] -- **Thebae** [West Bank]

b533 **Saghir** Mohammed El-, Der Statuenversteck im Luxortempel [1989]; BildbandArch 6, 1992 → 8,g58; DM 40: [R]BiOr 52 (1995) 623-5 (Ingegerd *Lindblad*).

b534 *Karnak-Khonsu*: Derchain Philippe, Allusion, citation, intertextualité: → 10,145, [F]WINTER E., Aspekte 1994, 69-73 + 2 facsimiles.

b535 *Eissa* Ahmed, Zur Etymologie des modernen Namens vom grossen Amuntempel in Theben,'Karnak' [k3r 'shrine'+ ngg 'goose(-egg)']: GöMisz 144 (1995) 31-37; 6 fig.; 2 pl.

b536 **Lauffray** Jean, La chapelle d'Achôris à Karnak, 1. Les fouilles, l'architecture, le mobilier et l'anastylose. P 1995, RCiv. 189 p. 2-86538-246-X.

b537 Cahiers de Karnak 16.   P 1995, RCiv. xxxii-572 p.

b538 *Leclant* J., *Clerc* G., Karnak, Louqsor rive gauche; Orientalia 64 (1995) 282-304; pl. XXVII-XXXI.

b539 *Hamza* Usama R., Some remarks concerning Chapel XII of Hatshepsut at Karnak Temple: *JSStEg 21s (1991s) 37-40; 2 fig.

b540 **Sternberg-El Hotabi** Heike, Der Propylon des Montu-Tempels in Karnak-Nord; zum Dekorationsprinzip des Tores; Übersetzung und Kommentierung der Urkunden VIII, Texte Nr. 1 Nr. 50: GOF 4/25, 1993 →9,14359; 10,12703: ᴿBiOr 52 (1995) 596-600 (M.T. *Derchain-Urtel*); *DiscEg 28 (1994) 141-5 (G. *Harrison*).

----

b541 **Gohary** Jocelyn, Akhenaten's Sed-Festival at Karnak 1992 → 8,g66; 10,12700: ᴿBiOr 52 (1995) 342-7 (J.-L. *Chappaz:* assemblages faux; non-respect de la 'grille', non-respect de la continuité iconographique); *DiscEg 28 (1994) 153s (A. *Dodson:* Amarna-period *talatât*); Orientalia 64 (1995) 123-8 (K. *Martin*).

----

b542 *Pernigotti* Sergio, I figli di Ramesse [subito dietro la tomba di Ramesse II; tomba collettiva, già conosciuta 1820, riscoperta]: Archeo 125 (1995) 8-13.

b543 *Crocker* Piers T., Tomb of the sons of Ramesses II [recent find in newspaper claims]; how much do we know ? : BurHist 31 (1995) 89-92.

b544 *Bolshakov* Andrey O., Princes who became kings; where are their tombs? [every tomb prepared for a prince from his infancy was destroyed (mutilated) after he became pharaoh]; GöMisz 146 (1995) 11-22.

b545 **Hornung** Erik, Zwei ramessidische Königsgräber, Ramses IV und Ramses VII: Theben 11, 1990 → 6,e619; 9,14364: ᴿBiOr 52 (1995) 645-650 (T. *Podgórski*); JEA 81 (1995) 267s (N. *Strudwick*).

b546 *Jansen-Winkeln* Karl, Die Plünderung der Königsgräber des Neuen Reiches: ZÄS 122 (1995) 62-78.

b547 **Reeves** Carl N., Valley of the Kings; the decline of a royal necropolis 1990 → 10,12708: ᴿ*DiscEg 28 (1994) 167-171 (O.J. *Schaden*).

b548 **Roccati** Alessandro, *al.*, Tomba tebana 27 di Sheshonq all'Asasif [1978-93+; III rapporto preliminare = VO 9 (1993). 149 p.; XXXV pl.

b549 ᴱ**Baines** John, Stone vessels, pottery and sealings from the tomb of Tut'ankhamûn 1993 → 9,14363; £ 60: ᴿDiscEg 32 (1995) 125-9 (F. *Welsh*).

b550 *Carter* Howard, Personal diaries of the first excavation season in the tomb of Tutankhamun, 1922-3 [at Oxford Ashmolean only two small appointment-books and notes compiled somewhat later; it seems there never was a real day-by-day diary]: DiscEg 32 (1995) 9-36 [but note p.129. *Welsh* F., 'the meticulous records kept by Carter'].

b551 **Eaton-Krauss** Marianne, The sarcophagus in the tomb of Tutankhamun 1993 → 9,14362; £ 6: ᴿBiOr 52 (1995) 642-5 (M.J. *Raven*); DiscEg 31 (1995) 131-7 (J. *Taylor*); OLZ 90 (1995) 378-381 (G.T. *Martin*).

b552 *Goedicke* Hans, Tutankhamun's shields [7 wooden plaques, rather political posters]; GöMisz 140 (1994) 27-37.

b553 ᴱ**Reeves** C.R., After Tutankhamun ... Thebes [Carnarvon 1990, 14 art.] 1992 → 10,12707: ᴿBiOr 52 (1995) 361-372 (O.J. *Schaden*: Eng., in great detail).

b554 *Alfano* Carlo, Nefertari, luce d'Egitto; in mostra a Roma [Palazzo Ruspoli] la tomba restaurata della celebre regina egiziana: Archeo 9,118 (1994) 46-59 (-61, *Luzi* Adriano).

b555 **Barthelmess** Petra, Der Übergang ins Jenseits in den thebanischen Beamtengräbern der Ramessidenzeit: *StAGAä 2. 1992 → 10,12716; DM 98; 3-927552-04-6: ᴿAfO 42s (1995s) 301s (Elfriede *Haslauer*); *DiscEg 28 (1994) 155-8 (T. *DuQuesne*).

b556 **Dziobek** Eberhard, Das Grab des Ineni -- Theben Nr. 81: ArchVeröff 68, 1992 → 8,g87; 10,12713: ᴿRdÉ 45 (1994) 235-7 (Annie *Gasse*).

b557 **Feucht** Erika, Das Grab des Nefersecheru (TT 296): Theben 2. Mainz 1985, von Zabern. ix-163 p. 3-8053-0825-6.

b558 **Guksch** Heike, Die Gräber des Nacht-Min und des Men-Cheper-Ra-Seneb;,Theben Nr. 87 und 79: ArchVeröff 34. Mainz 1995, von Zabern. 181 p. 3-8053-0497-8,

b559 *Kampp* Friederike, *Seyfried* Karl Joachim, Eine Rückkehr nach Theben das Grab des Pa-en-nefer Hoherpriester des Amun zur Zeit Tutanchamuns: AW(elt) 26 (1995) 325-342; 33 fig.

b560 *Strudwick* Nigel, Change and continuity at Thebes; the private tomb after Akhenaten: → 10,118, ᶠSHORE A.F., The unbroken reed 1994, 321-336.

-----

b561 Mnemonia; bulletin édité par l'Association pour la sauvegarde du Ramesseum, 1 (1990s) 142 p., 3 pl.; 2 (1991) 79 p., 11 pl.; 3 (1992) 16 p., 29 pl. -- ᴿ*DiscEg 28 (1994) 159-163 (J. *Malek*); 163-6, 30 19th c. photos of Ramesseum in Ashmolean.

b562 *Pirelli* Rosanna, Some considerations on the temple of Queen Hatshepsut al Deir al-Bahari: AION 54 (1994) 455-463.

b563 *Donohue* V.A., Hatshepsut and Nebhetre' Mentuhotpe: *DiscEg 29 (1994) 37-44; 3 fig. [reprinted by error in 30 (1994) 22-28].

b564 ᴱ**Vleeming** S.P., Hundred-gated Thebes; Acts of a colloquium on Thebes and the Theban area in the Graeco-Roman period [Leiden 1992; 15 art.]: PLB 27. Lei 1995, Brill. xiii-283 p.; 7 pl. *f* 170. 90-04-10384-8 [NTAb 40, p.566].

-----

b565 ᴱ**Lesko** Leonard H., Pharaoh's workers; the villagers of Deir el Medina 1994 → 10,12719; $ 14 pa: ᴿAJA 99 (1995) 541 (J.M. *Weinstein*); Antiquity 69 (1995) 636s (R.B. *Parkinson*).

b566 ᴱ**Demarée** R.J., *Egberts* A., Village voices; proceedings of the symposium 'Texts from Deir el-Medina and their interpretation', Leiden, May 31 June 1, 1991. Lei 1992, CNWS. 147 p. *f* 40. 90-73872-16-3. -- ᴿ*DiscEg 30 (1994) 205-210 (Deborah *Sweeney*).

b567 *Wilfong* Terry G., Mummy labels from the [Chicago Univ.] Oriental Institute's excavations at Medinet Habu: BASPAP 32 (1995) 157-181.

b568 **Dra' Abu Naga** 4th-5th 1992.4: MDAI-K 51 (1995) 207-225; 6 fig.; pl. 45-47 (Daniel *Polz, al.*).

b569 *Jaritz* Horst, *al.*, Der Totentempel des Merenptah in Qurna; 2. Grabungsbericht (7. und 9. Kampagne: MDAI-k 51 (1995) 57-83; 15 (foldout) fig.;18-23.

b570 *Hornung* Erik, Frühe Besucher und frühe Zerstörungen im Sethos-Grab: → 96, ᶠKRAUSE M., Divitiae Aegypti 1995, 162-7.

т7.3 **Amarna**

b571 *Allen* James P., *a)* Nefertiti and Smenkh-ka-re [updating of still-unpublished 1987 Chicago Univ. ASOR symposium]: GöMisz 141 (1994) 7-17; -- *b)* Further evidence for the coregency of Amenhotep III and IV ? (Dahshur graffito, NY-Met 1992]; GöMisz 140 (1994) 7-12; 3 fig.; 2 pl.

b572 **Bomann** Ann H., The private tomb chapel in ancient Egypt; a study of the chapel in the workmen's village at El Amarna with special reference to Deir el Medina and other sites 1990 → 7,a776; 10,12727: ᴿGöMiszÄg 140 (1994) 107-110 (Dagmar *Winzer*).

b573 *Capriotti Vittozzi* Giuseppina, *Ciampini* Emanuele M., Note sulle rappresentazione del defunto in abiti da vivente [Amarna non mummiforme]: RSO 69 (1995) 267-273; Eng 274.

Endruweit Albrecht, ...Klimagerechte Architektur in Amarna 1994 → a247 supra.

b574 *Ertman* Earl L., Tut-Tut: newly identified images of the boy king: → 721, 7° Egyptol. 1995, 53.

Gohary Jocelyn, Akhenaten's Sed-Festival at Karnak 1992 → b541 supra.

b575 **Heintz** Jean-Georges. Index documentaire d'El-Amarna -- I.D.E.A. [1. 1982], 2. bibliographie des textes babyloniens d'El Amarna [1888 à 1993] et concordance des sigles EA: GRESA 4 (Groupe de Recherches et d'Études Sémitiques Anciennes, Univ. Strasbourg). Wsb 1995, Harrassowitz. viii-223 p. 3-447-[01990-5]..348-0.

b576 *Heintz* Jean-Georges, *Millot* Lison, Bibliographie d'El-Amarna, supplément 1 (1994-1995): UF 27 (DIETRICH 60. Gb. 1995) 21-40.

b577 **Hess** Richard S., Amarna personal names 1993 → 9,14392; 10,12732: ᴿOrientalia 64 (1995) 477-9 (R.A. *Di Vito*); UF 26 (1994) 601s (O. *Loretz*).

b578 *Hornung* Erik, Thomas MANN, Akhenaten, and the Egyptologists : → 191, ᶠSTRICKER,, Hermes: DISCEG.sp.2 (1995) 101-113.

b579 *Izre'el* Shlomo, The Amarna glosses; who wrote what for whom ? some sociolinguistic considerations: I(sr)OS 15 (1995) 101-122; 4 fig.

b580 *Kahl* Jochem, Der Gebrauch morphologischer und phonologischer Stilmittel im grossen Atonhymnus: → i7i, ᶠSCHENKEL W., Per aspera 1995, 51-89.

b581 ᴱ**Kemp** Barry J., Amarna reports [5,1989 → 7,d895*b*] 6: OccasP 10. L 1995, Egypt Exploration Soc. vii-462 p. 0-85698-123-0.

b582 **Kemp** B.J., *Garfi* S., A survey of the ancient city of Al-'Amarna: OccasP 9. L 1993, Egypt Expl. Soc. 112 p., 14 fig.; 9 plans. £ 70. -- ᴿWZKM 85 (1995) 272 (P. *Jánosi*).

b583 *a) Krauss* Rolf, (*Ullrich* Detlef), Piktograamme des jüngeren Goldhorusnamens von Achenaten; - *b) Pflüger* Kurt, Beiträge zur Amarnazeit: ZÄS 121 (1994) 105-117; 4 fig. / 123-132.

b584 *Leclant* J., *Clerc* G., Tell el-Amarna; Orientalia 64 (1995) 273s.

b585 **Moran** W.L., The Amarna letters 1993 → 8,9627 ... 10,12724: ᴿPEQ 127 (1995) 78s (D.M. *Rohl*).

b586 -- *Rainey* Anson F., A new English translation [MORAN W., 1992] of the Amarna Letters; AfO 42s (1995s) 109-121 [his review of the French forerunner was in AfO 36s (1989s) 56-75].

b587 *Moran* William L., Some reflections on Amarna politics: → 72, ᶠGREENFIELD J., Solving 1995, 559-572.

b588 **Murnane** William J., Texts from the Amarna period in Egypt, ᴱ*Meltzer* Edmund S.: *WritAW 3. Atlanta 1995, Scholars. xviii-289 p. $ 50; pa. $ 35. 1-55540-965-2; -6-0 [RStR 22,232, Tammi J. *Schneider*].

b589 **Murnane** William J., *Van Siclen* Charles C., The boundary stelae of Akhenaten 1993
→ 10.12735: ᴿBiOr 52 (1995) 52-54 (Marianne *Eaton-Krauss*); *DiscEg 29 (1994) 131-4
(A. *Dodson*).

b590 *Nicholson* Paul, Industrial archaeology at Amarna: *EgA 7 (1995) 14-16.

b591 *Shaw* Ian, The simulation of artifact diversity at el-Amarna, Egypt: *JField 22 (1995)
223-238.

b592 *a) Tobin* Vincent A., Akhenaten as a tragedy of history; a critique of the Amarna
period; -- *b) Burridge* Alwyn L., Akhenaten, a new perspective; evidence of a genetic
disorder in the royal family of 18th Dynasty Egypt -- *c) Ertman* Earl L., From two to
many: the symbolism of additional Uraei worn by Nefertity and Akhenaten; -- *d) Robins*
Guy, The representation of sexual characteristics in Amarna art: *JSStEg 23 (1993) 5-28
/ 63-74; 4 fig.; XI pl. / 42-50 (-55) / 29-41; 7 fig.

b593 *Warburton* D.A., The Egyptian response to the Hittite threat as seen from the Amarna
letters: → 10,81, ᶠMEYER L. de 52 Réflexions 1994, 433-8.

b594 *Weatherhead* Fran, Wall-paintings from the King's house at Amarna: JEA 81 (1995)
95113; 8 fig.

b595 **Welsh** Frances, Tutankhamun's Egypt: Shire 19. Princes Risborough 1993. $ 14. 0-
7478-0196-7. -- ᴿ*BurHist 31 (1995) 93-95 (H.S.S.)

b596 *a) Westhuizen* Jasper P. van der, The situation in Syro-Palestine prior to the Exodus/
conquest as reflected in the Amarna letters (also in preceding fascicle: Word order variation
of verbal sentences in selected Gezer Amarna letters); -- *b) Artzi* Pinhas, A Canaanite-
Babylonian caravan venture; a note on EA 255 and 256; -- *c) Izre 'el* Shlomo, Amarna
tablets in the collection of the Pushkin Museum of Fine Arts, Moscow; -- *d) Muntingh*
L.M., An Amarna letter (EA 162) from a pharaoh to Aziru of Amurru in light of recent
research: → 218*, ᶠWESTHUIZEN, *J/TydSem 7,2 (1995) 196-231 (1-15) / 118-124 / 125-
161 / 162-195.

T7.4 **Memphis**, *Saqqara* -- **Pyramides**, *Giza* (Cairo)

b597 **Maystre** Charles, Les grands prêtres de Ptah de Memphis [< diss. Sorbonne 1948 !
→ 9,13083]; OBO 113, 1992. -- ᴿJEA 81 (1995) 245 (K.A *Kitchen*).

b598 **Munro** Peter, Der Unas-Friedhof Nord-West 1. Topographisch-historische
Einleitung; das Doppelgrab der Königinnen Nebet und Khenut. Mainz 1993, von Zabern.
xvi-146 p.; 2 fig.; 2 pl. DM 200. -- ᴿOLZ 90 (1995) 372-8 (P. *Jánosi*).

b599 *Saqqarah, Memphis*: Orientalia 64 (1995) 256-263; fig. 19-29 (J. *Leclant*, G. *Clerc*).

b600 *Schneider* H.D., Pay en Raia, Haremdirecteuren van de Heer der Beide Landen ...
Memphis begraafplats: Phoe(nixEOL) 41,1 (1995) 4-25; 12 fig.

b601 **Simpson** William K., The offering chapel of Kayem-nofret (Şaqqara, Mariette;
after 1904] in the Museum of Fine Arts, Boston. Boston 1992. x-32 p-; vol. of 26 pl.
$50. 0-87846-361-5. -- ᴿBiOr 52 (1995) 46-48 (Hartwig *Altenmüller*).

b602 **Wietheger** Cäcilia, Der Jeremias-Kloster zu Saqqara 1992 → 9,14407: OCP 61
(1995) 586s (V. *Ruggieri*).

b603 **Ziegler** Christiane, Le mastaba d'Akhethetep; une chambre funéraire de l'Ancien
Empire. P 1993, Réunion Musées Nat. 238 p.; ill. F 295. 2-7118-2469- 1. -- ᴿBiOr 52
(1995) 635-8 (Rosemarie *Drenkhahn*).

b604 *Daoud* K.A., The tomb of Kairer [Memphis mastaba], 1993 field-work: GöMisz
147 (1995) 35-47 + 1 fig.; 4 pl.

b605 *a) Depuydt* Leo, Murder in Memphis; the story of Cambyses's mortal wounding of the Apis Bull (ca, 523 B.C.E.): JNES 54 (1995) 119-126. -- *b) Quack* J.F., Zwei Handbücher zur MumIfizierung .. des Apisstieres: Enchoria 22 (1995) 123-9.

b606 **Giddy** Lisa L., The Anubieion at Saqqàra 1992 → 9.1405; 10,12745*; [R]Orientalia 64 (1995) 130s (Loredana *Sist*).

b607 *Friedman* Florence D., The underground relief panels of King Djoser at the Step Pyramid complex: JA(m)RCE(g) 32 (1995) 1-42; 25 fig.

b608 **Labrousse** Audran, *Moussa* Ahmed M., Le temple d'accueil du complexe funéraire du roi Ounas: BtÉt 111. Le Caire c. 1995, IFAO. [iv-] 113 p. 2-7247-0168-2.

b609 **Munro** Peter, Der Unas-Friedhof Nord-West I. topographisch-historische Einleitung; das Doppelgrab der Königinnen Nebet und Khenut. Mainz 1993, von Zabern. xvi-146 p.; 43 pl.; 2 foldout plans. 3-8053-1353-5 [*OIAc 11,35].

b610 **Abusir:** *Verner* Miroslav, An early Old Kingdom cemetery at Abusir [south; Memphis]: ZÄS 122 (1995) 78-90; 12 fig.

b611 *Smoláriková* K., Chios-Keramik in Abusir: GöMiszÄg 141 (1994) 81-87 + 1 fig.

------

b612 **Bauval** Robert [→ 10,12759* wrongly Dauval], *Gilbert* Adrian, The Orion mystery; unlocking the secrets of the pyramids. L 1994, Heinemann. 325 p.; ill. £ 17. -- [R]*DiscEg 30 (1994) 101-114; 1 fig.(J. *Malek*).

b613 *a) Bauval* R.G., *Gilbert* A.G., The adze of Upuaut; the opening of the mouth ceremony and the northern shafts in Cheops's pyramid; -- *b) Hellestam* Sigvard, The pyramid of Cheops as calendar; -- *c) Legon* John A.R., Air-shaft alignments in the Great Pyramid: *DiscEg 28 (1994) 5-10 + 7 fig. / 21.-27 / 29-34

b614 *a) Bauval* Robert G., The star-shafts of Cheops' pyramid; -- *b) Cook* R.J., The stellar geometry of the Great Pyramid: *DiscEg 29 (1994) 25-28; 3 fig. / 29-36; 3 fig.

b615 *a) Bauval* Robert G., *a)* The horizon of Khufu; a 'stellar' name for Cheops's pyramid; -- *b)* Logistics of the shafts in Cheops' pyramid; a religious 'function' expressed with geometrical astronomy and built in architecture: DiscEg 30 (1995) 17s + 4 fig. / 31 (1995) 5-9 + 4 fig.

b616 *Cook* R.J., The elaboration of the Giza site plan: DiscEg 31 (1995) 35-45; 7 fig.

b617 **Steindorff** Georg [1903], *Hölscher* Uvo, Die Mastabas westlich der Cheopspyramide, [E]*Grimm* A.: MüÄgUnt 2. Fra 1991. 121 p.; 21 pl. -- [R]WZKM 83 (1993) 255-9 (P. *Jánosi*).

b618 [TE]**Haarmann** Ulrich, Pyramidenbuch .. IDRISI: BeiruterTSt 38, 1991 → 8,g149; 9,14410*; DM 98. 3-515-05116-3. -- [R]JSSt 39 (1994) 359s (O. *Kahl*).

b619 **Jánosi** Peter, Die Pyramidenanlagen der Königinnen; Untersuchungen zu einem Grabtyp des Alten und Mittleren Reiches: Denks.13. W c.1995, Österr. Akad, xvi-195 p. 3-7001-2207-1.

b620 *Porter* Robert M. An easy way to build a pyramid [a 3-ton stone block can be dragged up the side by 100 men with 63-mm diameter papyrus rope such as have been found in the Tura quarries]: GöMiszÄg 139 (1994) 93s; 1 fig.

b621 *a) Legon* John A.R., The [BAUVAL R.] Orion correlation and air-shaft theories; *b) O'Mara* Patrick F., Can the Gizeh pyramids be dated astronomically ? Logical foundations for an Old Kingdom astronomical chronology: DiscEg 33 (1995) 45-56; 2 fig. / 73-85.

b622 **Zivie-Coche** Christiane M., Giza au premier millénaire; autour du temple d'Isis, dame des Pyramides. Boston 1991, Museum of Fine Arts. xx-331 p.; 47 pl. $ 45. 0-87846-343-7. -- [R]BiOr 52 (1995) 372-5 (J. *Malek*).

b623 *Reeth* J.M.F. van, Caliph al-Ma'mūn and the treasure of the pyramids : OL(ov)P 25 (1994) 221-236.

b624 **Dahshûr**: *Testa* Pietro, Il complesso funerario regale del re Snefru in Dahshûr Sud; ricerca del progetto architettonico originario: *DiscEg 28 (1994) 123-142 + 9 plans.

b625 *Edwards* I.E.S., Chephren's place among the kings of the fourth dynasty: → 10,118, [F]SHORE A.F., The unbroken reed 1994, 97-l05; 8 fig. (pyramids).

b626 **Lišt**: **Arnold** Felix, *al.*, Control marks: South cemeteries 2, 1990 → 7,d960: [R]JEA 81 (1995) 256s (M. *Verner*).

b627 **Matariyâ**: *Alfi* Mostafa El- †, Miscellanea Heliopolitana: *DiscEg 29 (1994) 45-54; 1 fig.

b628 *Read* John G., Placement of El-Lahun lunar dates and resulting chronology: DiscEg 33 (1995) 87-113.

---

b629 *Scanlon* George T., Al-Fustāt; the riddle of the earliest settlement: → 725, Land use 1994 ...

b630 [E]**Lambert** Phyllis, Fortifications and the synagogue; the fortress of Babylon and the Ben Ezra synagogue, Cairo. L 1995, Weidenfeld & N. 282 p. $ 65 [BArR 21,5 (1995) 8].

T7.5 **Delta Nili**

b631 **Alexandria**: Orientalia 64 (1995) 229-235; p. IV-V (J. *Leclant*, G. *Clerc*).

b632 *De Martino* Francesco, Il Faro di Alessandria e GIUSEPPE FLAVIO → 10,42, [F]GIGANTE M., Storia 1994, 191-195.

b633 **Dzielska** M., Hypatia of Alexandria: Revealing Antiquity 8. CM 1995, Harvard Univ. xii-157 p. $ 30. -- [R]CLR 45 (1995) 119s (R. *Hawley*).

b634 **Blum** Rudolf, Kallimachos, the Alexandrian library and the origins of bibliography [1977], [T]*Wellisch* H.H., 1991 → 10,12780: [R]CJ 90 (1994s) 87-89 (Mary *Depew*).

b635 *Barrois* Emmeline, L'antique bibliothèque [Revue de l'Amopa (Association des membres de l'Ordre des Palmes académiques) 129 (juin 1995)]: E(spr)eV 105 (1995) 531s (J. *Daoust*).

Schott Siegfried, Bücher aus Bibliotheken im antiken Ägypten 1990 → 1489 supra.

b636 *Chauveau* Catherine, L'Alexandrie antique retrouvée: Science et Vie 931 (avril 1995) [< E(spr)eV 105 (1995) 310s (J. *Daoust*)].

b637 *Erskine* Andrew, Culture and power in Ptolemaic Egypt; the museum and library of Alexandria: GaR 42 (1995) 38-48.

b638 *Gigante Lanzara* Valeria, 'Da Zeus i re'; poesia e potere nell'Alessandria dei Tolemei: → 9,440, [E]*Virgilio* B., Aspetti e problemi dell'ellenismo (Pisa 1992/4) 91-118.

b639 *Saïd* Dorreya, Les mosaïques de la bibliothèque d'Alexandrie: MoBi 90 (1995) 32s; 2 color. phot.

b640 **Kolataj** Wojciech, Imperial baths at Kom el-Dikka: Alexandrie 6. Wsz 1992, Univ. 218 p.; 137 pl., 33 fig. + 30 foldout plans. 83-900096-2-5. -- [R]Latomus 54 (1995) 495 (M. *Rassart-Debergh*).

b641   *Daszewski* Wiktor A., The origins of Hellenistic hypogea in Alexandria: → 10,145, ᶠWINTER E., Aspekte 1994, 51-63 + 6 fig.

b642   **Pensabene** Patrizio, Elementi architettonici di Alessandria e di altri siti egiziani. R 1993, Bretschneider. xx-662 p.; 229 fig.; 137 pl.; map [→ 9,13118]: Lᵐ 800. 88-7062-810-8. -- ᴿA(nz)AW 48,1s (1995) 106-110 (T. *Schäfer*); JRS 85 (1995) 272s (M.W. *Jones*); Latomus 54 (1995) 496s (M. *Rassart-Debergh*).

b643   ᴱ**Steen** Gareth L., Alexandria, the site and its history. NYU 1993. 126 p.; ill. 0-8147-7986-7.

b644   **Fernández Sangrador** Jorge J., Los orígenes de la comunidad cristiana de Alejandría; *Plenitudo Temporis 1, 1994 → 10,12777: ᴿAng 72 (1995) 147-9 (B. *Degórski*); *CritRR 8 (1995) 418-420 (Maureen A. *Tilley*); EstAg 30 (1995) 145s (D. *Alvarez Cineira*); JThS 46 (1995) 694-6 (S.E. *Hall*); StPat(av) 41 (1994) 639-541 (C. *Corsato*); RB 102 (1995) 403-412 (J. *Taylor*); Ter(esianum) 46 (1995) 291s (M. *Diego Sánchez*).

b645   **Müller-Wiener** Martina, Eine Stadtgeschichte Alexandrias von 564/1169 bis in die Mitte des 9./15. Jahrhunderts: IKU 159. B 1992, K. Schwarz. 331 p.; map. -- ᴿJAOS 114 (1994) 114-6 (Doris *Behrens-Abouseif*: good on biography; oversights on institutions); WO 26 (1995) 224s (H. *Holm*).

b646   *Maṣkhuta*: *Abdalla Ali* Mahrous, Ushabtis of priestess *3w.t ḥ'w* Tentamun from Tell el-Maṣkhuta: *JSStEg 21s (1991s) 41-43; 3 fig.

b647   *Redmount* Carol A., Ethnicity, pottery, and the Hyksos at Tell el-Maṣkhuta in the Egyptian delta: BA 58 (1995) 181-190 [191-9, on Mexico, *Arnold* Philip J.].

b648   *Mendes*-Rub'a, 1992 : *JSStEg 21s (1991s) 1-12, 5 fig. (D.B. *Redford*); 14-19; 5 fig., ceramic (Rexine *Hummel, S.B. Shubert*): 20-26; 9 fig., Kom/Adhem (Nancy C. *Lovell*).

b649   *Pelusium*-Farama: → 10,491, Sociétés urbaines (1994) 95-103 (M. *el-Maksoud, al.*); 109-121 (K. *Grzymski, al.*); 123-166 (H. *Jaritz, al.*).

b650   *Pithom*: *Minas* Martina, Die Pithom-Stele; chronologische Bemerkungen zur frühen Ptolemäerzeit: → 10,145, ᶠWINTER E., Aspekte 1994, 203-211 + 1 fig.

b651 *Qanṭîr, Dab'a; Tanis*: Orientalia 64 (1995) 241-5 (J. *Leclant*, G. *Clerc*).

b652   **Bietak** Manfred, Avaris, the capital of the Hyksos; recent excavations at [Qanṭir] Tell el-Dab'a. L 1995, British Musuem. ix-98 p.; bibliog. 90-98. 0-7141-0968-1.

b653   **Bietak** Manfred, Tell el Dab'a V/1, Friedhofsbezirk 1991 → 7,d940: ᴿBiOr 52 (1995) 607-615 (S. *Seidlmayer*).

b654   a) *Shaw* Maria C., Bull leaping frescoes at Knossos and their influence on the Tell el-Dab'a murals; -- b) *Bietak* M., *Marinatos* N., The Minoan wall paintings from Avaris: → 734*, ÄgLev 5 (Trade 1993/5) 91-120; 11 fig.; 16 color. pl. / 49-62; 16 (color.) fig. [also on Dab'a: 63-71 *Jánosi* P.; 81-84 *MacGillivray* J.A.]. Further on the Dab'a bull-paintings, ÄgLev 4 (1994) 89-94; 22 (color.) fig. (*Marinatos*); 81-85; 17 fig. (*Collon* D.)

b655   *North* Robert, State of the published proof that Qanṭir is Raamses; → 82, ᶠHENNESSY J.B., Trade 1995, 207-217; map.

b656   ᴱ**Davies** W. Vivian, *Schofield* Louise, Egypt, the Aegean and the Levant; interconnections in the second millennium B.C. L 1995, British Museum. viii-188 p.; 53 fig.; 55 pl. + 27 colour. -- ᴿAntiquity 69 (1995) 1033 (C. *Broodbank*).

b657   *Suez*: *Mayerson* Philip, Aelius GALLUS at Cleopatris (Suez) and on the Red Sea [26 B.C., information on Arabian sites]: GRBS 36 (1995) 17-24.

T7.6 *Alii situs Aegypti* **alphabetice**

b658 **Abu Fano** 30 k S Minya: *Buschhausen* Helmut, Die Peregrinatio nach Jerusalem in der Einsiedelei zu Abu Fano in Mittelägypten; → 96, [F]KRAUSE M., Divitiae Aegypti 1995, 70-76; pl. 2-4.

b659 **Abydos**; Orientalia 64 (1995) 276-8; fig. 31-35 (J. *Leclant*, G. *Clerc*).

b660 *Park* Rosalind, The raising of the *djed* [temple-pillars as measuring poles for equinoxes]: DiscEg 32 (1995) 75-84; 6 fig.

b661 **Akhmim**: **Kanawati** Naguib, Akhmim in the Old Kingdom [excavations 1979-92], I. Chronology and administration: Studies 2. Sydney 1992, Australian Centre for Egyptology. ix-325 p. 0-83837-791-8. -- [R]DiscEg 30 (1994) 183-5 (G.T. *Martin*).

b662 **Armant**: **Ginter** Bolesław, *Kozlowski* Janusz K., Predynastic settlement near Armant: *StArGAltäg 6. Heid 1994, Orient-Vg. viii-195p. 3-927552-15-1.

b663 **Aswan-Elephantine:** *Bommas* Martin, Ramessidische Graffiti aus Elephantine: MDAI-K 51 (1995) 1-9; 2 fig,: pl. 1 (p. 99-187, pl. 26-41 (p.99-187, Kampagne 1992, *Kaiser* Walter, *al.*).

b664 **Franke** Detlef, Das Heiligtum des Heqaib auf Elephantine; Geschichte eines Provinzheiligtums im Mittleren Reich: *StArGAltäg 9. Heid 1994, Orient-Vg. xvi-289 p.; Bibliog. 252-269. 3-927552-17-8.

b665 **Gempeler** R.D., Elephantine X. Die Keramik römischer bis frühharabischer Zeit: ArchVeröff 43, 1992 → 9,14442: [R]RossArkh (1995,2) 236-241 (A.V. *Sazanov*).

b666 *Martin* Cary J., The [oracle-giving] child born in Elephantine; Papyrus Dodgson revisited; → 714, E(g)VO 17 (1994) 199-212.

b667 **Zauzich** Karl T., Papyri von der Insel Elephantine 1993 → 9,14447; DM 228: [R]OLZ 90 (1995) 269-273.

b668 **Ziermann** Martin, Elephantine XVI; Befestigungsanlagen und Stadtentwicklung in der Frühzeit und im frühen Alten Reich: DAI-K ArchVeröff 87, 1993 → 9,14444; DM 198: [R]BiOr 52 (1995) 601-7 (M. *Atzler*).

b669 **Pilgrim** Cornelius von, Elephantine XVIII; Untersuchungen in der Stadt des Mittleren Reiches und der Zweiten Zwischenzeit: ArchVeröff 91. Mainz c. 1995, von Zabern. 364 p. 3-8053-1746-8.

b670 -- *Porten* Bezalel, Did the Ark stop at Elephantine ? [en route to its present abode in Axum, Ethiopia; HANCOCK Graham, The sign and the seal; the quest for the lost Ark of the Covenant, NY 1992, Crown (p.438-482); the Italian [T]*Massarotti* Maria, Il mistero del sacro Graal, CasM 1995, Piemme, is also a best-seller]: [R]BArR 21.3 (1995) 54-67 . 76, with notable citations from the Aramaic letters.

b671 **Balamun:** *Spencer* Jeffrey, Work of the British Museum at Tell el-Balamun: *EgA 7 (1995) 9-11.

b672 **Bawît**: *Rutschowscaya* Marie-Hélène, Le monastère de Baouit -- état des publications; → 96, [F]KRAUSE M., Divitiae Aegypti 1995, 279-288.

b673 **Beni Hasan**: *Baines* Alice V., The function of iconography as autobiographical narration in the tomb of Khnemhotep at Beni Hasan (Tomb 3): JNWSL 21,2 (1995) 1-21 + 5 fig.

b674 *Guo Dantong*, The inscription of Khnumhotpe II; a new study: *JAncCiv 10 (Changchun 1995) 55-63.

b675 **Berša**: [E]**Silverman** David P., *al.*, Bersheh reports I 1990: 1992 →9,14452; 10,12798; $ 35: [R]BiOr 52 (1995) 49-52 (S. *Seidlmayer*).

b676 **Dakhleh**; **Kapwe** Olaf E., The astronomical ceiling of Deir el-Haggar in the Dakhleh oasis: JEA 81 (1995) 175-195; 4 fig.

b677 -- **Balat**: **Minault-Gout** Anne, *al.*, Balat 2. Le Mastaba (II) d'Ina-Pepi, fin de l'Ancien Empire: IFAO Fouilles 33, 1992 → 8,g210: [R]BiOr 52 (1995) 358-361 (N. *Kanawati*).

b678 **Dendera**: *Eldamaty* Mamdouh M., Isis-Hathor im Tempel von Dendera: → 10,145, [F]WINTER E., Aspekte 1994, 81-87.

b679 **Dûš**: **Dunand** Françoise, *al.*, La nécropole, tombes 1-72: Douch 1, 1992 → 8,g215: [R]OLZ 90 (1995) 35-38 (K. *Parlasca*).

b680 **Reddé** Michel, Douch IV, le trésor 1992 → 9,14461; 10,12800: [R]BiOr 52 (1995) 665-8 (K. *Parlasca*).

b681 **Elkab**: **Hartmann** Hartwig, Nechb und Nechbet, Untersuchungen zur Geschichte des Kultortes Elkab: Diss. Mainz: Hochschulschriften 822. Egelsbach 1993, Hänsel-H. xx-404 p.; 36 fig. [*OIAc 11,25].

b682 **Esna**: *Broze* Michèle, La création du monde et l'opposition *sḏm.f . sḏm.n.f* dans le temple d'Esna: RdÉ 44 (1993) 3-9; Eng. 10.

b683 **Fayûm: Bakchias**: **Pernigotti** Sergio, *Capasso* Mario, Bakchias, una città del deserto egiziano che torna a vivere; prima campagna .. Bologna/Lecce: 1994 → 10,12797*: [R]CÉg 70 (1995) 327s (G. *Nachtergael*).

b684 *Pernigotti* Sergio, Per le strade di Bakchias [scavi delle Università di Bologna e Lecce]: Archeo 130 (1995) 96-101.

b685 **Hagarsa** opposite Ahmim → 10,12802: **Kanawati** Naguib, The tombs. 1993. -- [R]DiscEg 31 (1995) 119-121 (G.T. *Martin*).

b686 **Hermopolis** (Tuna el-Gebel), Tierfriedhof 1993: AW(elt) 25 (1994) 252-285; 23 fig. (D. *Kessler*, A. *Nureddin*).

b687 **Idfu: Chassinat** Émile, [2rev]*Cauville* Sylvie, *Devauchelle* Didier, Le temple d'Edfou 2. Le Caire 1987-90, IFAO. xii-206 p. 3-2547-0054-6. -- [R]BiOr 52 (1995) 56-58 (A. *Egberts*: more accurate than vol. 1).

b688 **Kurth** Dieter, Treffpunkt der Götter; Inschriften auf dem Tempel des Horus von Edfu. Z c.1994, Artemis & W. 432 p.; 94 fig.-- [R]AW(elt) 26 (1995) 159 (jowi).

b689 [E]**Kurth** Dieter, Edfu; Studien zu Vokabular, Ikonographie und Grammatik: Inschriften Begleithefte 4. Wsb 1994, Harrassowitz. viii-102 p. 3-447-03478-5 [*OIAc 11,30].

b690 *Kurth* D., *a)* Edfu-Inschriften-Projekt 2; -- *b)* Zur Lage von Behedet, dem heiligen Bezirk von Edfu: GöMiszÄg 140 (1994) 105s / 142 (1994) 93-99; map 100.

b691 **Kerma**: *Bonnet* Charles, Palais et temples dans la topographie urbaine; les exemples du bassin de Kerma: RdÉ 45 (1994)41-48; 5 fig.

b692 **Koptos**: **Traunecker** C., Coptos: hommes et dieux sur le parvis de Geb: OrLovAnal 43, 1992 → 8,g231; Fb 3900: [R]BiOr 52 (1995) 589-593 (P. *Germond*).

b693 **Merimde-Benisalâme**: **Eiwanger** J., 2 & 3. Die Funde der mittleren / jüngeren Merimdekultur: DAI-K 51 & 59, 1988/92 → 8,g234; DM 149 + 185; 3-8053-0606-7; -14-8: [R]BiOr 52 (1995) 357s (W.M. van *Haarlem*).

b694 **Mons Claudianus**: *Castiglioni* Angela & Alfredo, Mons Claudianus, la madre delle colonne [*umm dikal*]: ArVi 14,53 (1995) 46-57.

b695 **Philae**: **Vassilika** Eleni, Ptolemaic Philae: OLA 34, 1989 → 5,e483 ... 10,12811: [R]CÉg 70 (1995) 147-9 (P. *Derchain*).

b696 *Desroches-Noblecourt* Christiane, Égypte, le reveil des temples de la Nubie ... Philae, Abou Simbel: Archéologia 300 (1994) 16-25.

b697 **Tebtynis** (Fayûm): *Gallazzi* Claudio, La ripresa degli scavi a Umm-el-Breigât (Tebtynis): Acme 48.3 (1995) 3-24; 10 (color.) fig.

b698 **Zawyet Sultan**: **Osing** Jürgen, Das Grab des Nefersecheru 1992 → 8,g244: [R]BiOr 52 (1995) 54s (M. *Patanè*).

T7.7 *Antiquitates Nubiae et alibi;* Egypt outside Egypt

b699 *Bontty* Mónica M., The Haunebu [... expanded borders, for the maintenance of (world-) order; GöMisz 145 (1995) 45-58.

b700 **Zaoual** Hassan, The economy and the symbolic sites of Africa: Interculture 27,1 (1994) 1-44.

b701 **Abruzzi**: *Staffa* Andrea R., *al.*, Dall'Egitto copto all'Abruzzo bizantino : ArVi 14.54 (1995) 18-31.

b702 **Berytus**: *Ward* William A., Egyptian objects from the Beirut tombs: Ber 41 (1993/4) 211-220 + 2 pl.

b703 **Cyprus**: **Jacobsson** Inga, Aegyptiaca from Late Bronze Age Cyprus: SIMA 112, 1994 → 10,12680: [R]BASOR 299s (1995) 126s (J.M. *Weinstein*).

b704 **Cyrene**: [E]**Fulford** M., *Tomber* R., Excavations at Sabratha 1948-1951, 2/2. The finds .. lamps. L 1994, Soc. Libyan Studies. xiii-210 p.; 56 fig.; 1 pl. £ 45. -- [R]JRS 85 (1995) 273-5 (P. *Arthur*).

b705 -- **Mattingly** David J., Tripolitania. L c.1994, Batsford. xx-265 p., 89 fig.; 61 pl. £ 55. 0-7134-5742-2. -- [R]Antiquity 69 (1995) 1067s (D.P.S. *Peacock*).

b706 -- *Nibbi* Alessandra, Some 'Libyans' in the Thera frescoes ?: DiscEg 31 (1995) 81-98; 15 fig.

b707 -- **Thiry** Jacques, Le Sahara Libyen dans l'Afrique du Nord médiévale: OLA 72. Lv 1995. Peeters. xiii-604 p.; bibliog. 553-576. 90-6831-739-3.

b708 -- **White** Donald, The extramural sanctuary of Demeter and Persephone 1993 → 10,12829: [R]AnCL 64 (1995) 531-3 (F. *Colin*).

b709 -- *Yamauchi* Edwin, Cyrene in Libya; the archaeology of biblical Africa: *ABW 2,1 (1992) 6-18.

b710 **Kharga**: *Sternberg-el Hotabi* Heike, Die 'Götterliste' des Sanktuars im Hibis-Tempel von El-Chargeh: → 10,145, [F]WINTER E., Aspekte 1994, 239-251 + 3 fig.

b711 **Leptis Magna**: *Marzano* Annalisa, *Soren* David, Splendors of Lepcis; a Roman emperor's dream city emerges from the sands: Arch 48,5 (Boston 1995) 30-41 [NTAb 40, p.287].

b712 -- *Salza Prina Ricotti* Eugenia, Leptis Magna, la città delle ombre bianche: *Archeo 127 (1995) 50-91.

b713 -- **Ward-Perkins** John B., The Severan buildings of Lepcis Magna, an architectural survey, [E]*Kenrick* P., *al.* L 1993, Soc. for Libyan Studies. 109 p., 45 fig.; 48 pl.; 8 p.[A] -- [R]Bo(nn)J 195 (1995) 745-751 (Anette *Nüunnerich-Asmus*).

b714 **Meroe**: **Török** László, Meroe; six studies on the cultural identity of an ancient African site: *StAeg 16. Budapest 1995, Univ. 242 p.; bibliog. 215-232. 96-3463015-4.

b715 **Nubia**: Gratien Brigitte, La Basse Nubie à l'Ancien Empire; Égyptiens et autochtones: JEA 81 (1995) 43-56.

b716 -- **Heidorn** Lisa Ann, The fortress of Dorginarti and Lower Nubia during the seventh to fifth centuries B.C.: diss. ᴰKantor H. Chicago 1992. xi-240 p.; 36 fig. -- *OIAc 11,26.

b717 -- a) Nobles Vera L., Nubia and Egypt; is it Ella or a copy ? -- b) Tibebu Teshale, Ethiopia, the 'anomaly' and 'paradox' of Africa: JB(lack)St 26 (1995s) 431-446 / 414-430.

b718 -- **Otto** Karl-Heinz [→9,14503], Buschendorf-Otto Gisela, Felsbilder aus dem sudanesischen Nubien [1961-3] 1993; DM 420: ᴿOLZ 90 (1995) 274s (Angelika Jakobi).

b719 -- **Shinnie** Peter L., Ancient Nubia. L 1995, Kegan Paul. xvii-145 p.; bibliog. 135-140. 0-7103-0517-6.

b720 -- Vercoutter Jean, The Unesco 'campaign of Nubia' in the Sudan; success or failure ?: DiscEg 33 (1995) 133-140; 2 fig.

b721 -- Wegner Josef W., Regional control in Middle Kingdom Lower Nubia; the function and history of the State of Areika: JA(m)RCE(g) 32 (1995) 127-160; 14 fig. (maps).

b722 **Numidia:** **Duval** Yvette, Lambèse chrétienne, la gloire et l'oubli; de la Numidie romaine à l'Ifriqiya; ÉAug.Ant 144. P 1995, Inst. Ét. Aug. 215 p.

b723 **Qarara** opp. Mağağa 1993: GöMisz 144 (1995) 63-68; * 2 fig.; 4 pl. (F. Gomaa, S. Farid).

b724 **Qeili**: 100 k E Khartoum: Zach Michael H., Die Höhlenmalerei vom Jebel Qeili; GöMisz 145 (1995) 105-12.

b725 **Roma**: Grimm Günter, Antinous renatus et felix ? Überlegungen zur Statue des Antinous-Jonas in Santa Maria del Popolo: → 10,145, ᶠWINTER E., Aspekte 1994, 104-112; pl. 7-10.

b726 Curran Brian, Grafton Anthony, A fifteenth-century site report on the Vatican obelisk: JW(arb)CI 58 (1995) 234.248; fig. 81s.

b727 **(Lollio) Barberi** O., al., Le antichità egiziane di Roma imperiale. R 1995, Poligrafico. 329 p.; bibliog. 277-304. 88-240-3894-8.

b728 Pernigotti Sergio, Quilici Lorenzo, I pilastri del dio-sole; archeologia e storia degli obelischi, dall'antico Egitto a Roma imperiale: Archeo 128 (1995) 38-93.

b729 **Somalia**: Fattovich Rodolfo, L'archeologia del Mar Rosso; problemi e prospettive: AION 55 (1995) 158-176.

b730 **Stoffregen-Pedersen** Kirsten → 7,e955 (wrongly 8,k539), Les Éthiopiens: Fils d'Abraham 1990; Fb 750: ᴿCÉg 70 (1995) 356-9 (M. Megally).

b731 **Sudan**: Leclant J., Clerc G., Soudan / hors d'Égypte; Orientalia 64 (1995) 324-347-355; pl. XLIII-XLV.

b732 **Thuburbo**: Jashemski Wilhelmina E., Roman gardens in Tunisia: AJA 99 (1995) 559-576; 16 fig.

T7.9 **Sinai**

b733 Faiman David, From Horeb to Kadesh Barnea in eleven days [Dt 1,2; Nm 33,18-36]: JBQ 22 (1994) 91-102 (map).

b734 **Hobbs** Joseph J., Mount Sinai [monks and bedouin]. Austin 1995, Univ. Texas. vi-631 p. $ 50; pa. $ 20. 0-202-73091-8: -4-2 [ThD 43,369].

b735 *Lane* Belden C., The Sinai image in the apophatic tradition: SVlad 39(1995s)47-69.

b736 **Schultz** Joseph P., *Spatz* Lois, Sinai and Olympus; a comparative study. Lanham MD 1995, upa. xxv-790 p.; bibliog. 759-778. 0-7618-0032-8.

b737 *Tengström* Mose, Sinai och Horeb; Bilden av Mose i Dt (Presesföreläsning Söderblom-S. 1993): Religion och Bibel 53 (1994) 3-24 [< ZAW 107 (1995) 511].

b738 *Karkom:* Anati Emmanuel, Har Karkom, la montagna di Dio: ArVi 14,50 (1995) 60-73.

b739 *Serabit al-Khadem:* Beit-Arieh I., on ROTHENBERG B., GLASS J.: Levant [24 (1994) 141-157] 25 (1995) 125s.

b740 -- *Bonnet* Charles, Le temple d'Hathor à Sérabit el-Khadim (troisième campagne): CRAI (1995) 917-941: 11 fig.

T8 **Anatolia** *1. generalia*

b741 **Arens** E., Asia Menor en tiempos de Pablo, Lucas y Juan; aspectos sociales y económicos para la comprensión del Nuevo Testamento. Córdoba 1995, Almendro. 234 p. -- [R]BiFe 21 (1995) 461s (A. *Salas*).

b742 **Borchhardt** J., Lykien-Symposion 1990/3 → 10,460: [R]Aevum 49 (1995) 271-3 (Cinzia *Bearzot*).

b743 **Braund** D., Georgia in antiquity; a history of Colchis and transcaucasian Iberia, 350 B.C.- A.D. 362. Ox 1994, Clarendon. xviii-360 p. £ 40. -- [R]CLR 45 (1955) 358-360 (Gocha R. *Tsetskhladze*).

b744 **Brewster** Harry, Classical Anatolia, the glory of Hellenism. L 1993, Tauris. 192 p.; 46 color. phot. 1-85043-773-4.

b745 **Desideri** Paolo, *Jasink* Anna Margherita, Cilicia, dall'età di Kizzuwatna alla conquista macedone 1990 → 9,14525: [R]Gnomon 67 (1995) 74-76 (M. *Zimmermann*).

b746 *Edens* Christopher, Transcaucasia at the end of the Early Bronze Age: BASOR 299s (1995) 53-64.

b747 *Gates* Marie H., Archaeology in Turkey: AJA 99 (1995) 207-255; 41 fig. (map); Pergamon 240-3.

b748 **Heper** Metin, Historical dictionary of Turkey: European Historical Dictionaries 2. Metuchen 1995, Scarecrow. xv-593 p. $ 72.50. -- [R]WZKM 85 (1995) 363-5 (K. *Kreiser*: usable despite errors and omissions; more than half a loose-jointed bibliography).

b749 *Johnson* Gary J., Early-Christian epitaphs from Anatolia: SBL.tt 35. At 1995, Scholars. xiii-161 p. $ 40. 0-7885-0120-8 [ThD 43,172].

b750 *Kirkland* Alastair, The beginnings of Christianity in the Lycus valley [Rev 1-3, Phlm, Col]; an exercise in historical reconstruction: Neotest 29 (1995) 109-124 [121s, earthquakes].

b751 **Kolb** Frank, *Kupke* Barbara, Lykien; Geschichte Lykiens im Altertum: Bildband 2. Mainz 1992, von Zabern. 84 p.; ill. DM 35. 3-8053-1415-9. -- [R]BiOr 52 (1995) 166s, repeated 831s (J.M. *Hemelrijk*); HZ 260 (1995) 827s (J. *Nollé*); ZAW 107 (1995) 161 (M. *Köckert*).

b752 **Lindner** Ruth, Mythos und Identität; Studien zur Selbstdarstellung kleinasiatischer Städte in der römischen Kaiserzeit [Hab.-Diss. Würzburg 1991]: Fra Univ. Geistesw. 9.

Stu 1994, Steiner. 212 p.; 24 pl. 3-515-06529-6.

b753 MAMA (Monumenta Asiae Minoris Antiqua: vol. 9. 1988 after 25-year break), 10, ᴱLevick B., al.: JRS.m 7, 1993. xlv-201 p.; 56 pl.; 2 maps. £ 40. 0-907764-18-5. -- ᴿJRS 85 (1995) 302-4 (G. Petzl).

b754 Marek Christian, Stadt, Ära und Territorium in Pontus-Bithynia und Nord-Galatia: IstF 39. Tü 1993, Wasmuth. xviii-260 p.; 56 (color.) pl. -- ᴿTyche 10 (1995) 271s (K. Belke).

b755 Mitchell Stephen, Anatolia; land, men, and gods 1993 → 9,14537: ᴿHZ 261 (1995) 494-6 (P.Herrmann); JEH 46 (1995) 485-8 (G. Bonner, 2); JRS 85 (1995) 301s (C. Foss); JThS 46 (1995) 323-6 (J.Liebeschuetz); RB 102 (1995) 616s (J. Murphy-O'Connor); RStR 21 (1995) 54 (A.T. Kraabel).

b756 Rose Mark, Cruising Turkey's southern coast: Arch(aeology) 48,4 (Boston 1995) 54-63.

b757 Rostowzeff Michael J., Skythien und der Bosporus, II. Wiederentdeckte Kapitel auf der Grundlage der russischen Edition, Zuev V.J., al.: HistEinz 83. Stu 1993, Steiner. viii-263 p.; 36 p.; 4 foldout maps. -- ᴿBo(nn)J 195 (1995) 651-3 (P. Herz).

b758 Rumscheid Frank, Untersuchungen zur kleinasiatischen Bauornamentik des Hellenismus; BeitrHellenSkArchit 14. Mainz 1994, von Zabern. xiv-352 p., iv-112 p.; 204 pl.; 6 foldouts. DM 360. -- ᴿRBPH 73 (1995) 257-9 (P. Gros).

b759 Schütte Anke, Studien zur antiken Kleinasien II [ᴱSchwertheim Elmar, Münster 16.-18.III.1992]: Asia Minor Studien 8. Bonn 1992, Habelt. vii-183 p. 3-7749-2591-7.

b760 Steadman Sharon R., Prehistoric interregional interaction in Anatolia and the Balkans; an overview: BASOR 299s (1995) 13-32; 6 fig.

b761 Trebilco Paul R., Jewish communities in Asia Minor: SNTS.m 69, 1991 → 7,e24 ... 10,12876: ᴿ*CritRR 8 (1995) 440-4 (R.S. Kraemer); JRAS (1994) 256-8 (G. Khan).

b762 Yener K. Aslihan, The archaeology of empire in Anatolia; comments: BASOR 299s (1995) 117-121 [3-11, Sinopoli Carla A.].

b763 Zimmermann M., Untersuchungen zur historischen Landeskunde Zentrallykiens: Antiquitas 1/42, 1992 → 10,12880: ᴿCLR 45 (1995) 103-5 (S. Mitchell).

т8.2 Boğazköy -- Hethaei, the Hittites

b764 Bayun Lilia. [OTTEN H. 1973] The legend about the queen of Kanis; a historical source ?: *JAncCiv 9 (Changchun 1994) 1-13.

b765 Edel Elmar, Die ägyptisch-hethitische Korrespondenz aus Boğazköi in babylonischer und hethitischer Sprache, I. Umschriften und Übersetzungen; II. Kommentar: Rh/Wf Akad Abh 77, 1994 → 10,12882; DM 98 + 128. 3-531-95111-3; -2-1 [RStR 22,55. D.J. Owen].

b766 González Salazar J. M., Tiliura, un ejemplo de la política fronteriza durante el imperio hitita (CTH 89): AulaO 12 (1994) 159-176.

b767 Hawkins John D., The hieroglyphic inscription of the Sacred Pool complex at Ḫattuša (Südburg); intr. Neve P.; StBT.b3. Wsb 1995, Harrassowitz. 139 p. 3-447-03438-6.

b768 a) Henrickson Robert C., Hittite pottery and potters; -- b) Hoffner Harry J., Oil in Hittite texts: → 136, ᶠNEVE P., BA 58 (1995) 82-90 / 108-114.

b769 Hout Theo F.J. van den, Tudḫalia IV. und die Ikonographie hethitischer Grosskönige des 13. Jhrs. [Neve P. 1992]: BiOr 52 (1995) 549-574; 4 fig.

b770 *Klinger* J., Das Corpus der Maşat-Briefe und seine Beziehung zu den Texten aus Hattuša: ZA(ssyr) 85 (1995) 74-108.

b771 **Koşak** Silvin, Konkordanz der [Boğazköy] Keilschrifttafeln [1. 1931 → 9,14553]: 2. 1932: StBT [34] 39. Wsb 199[2/]5, Harrassowitz. xi-276 p. -- [R]BiOr 52 (1995) 737-9 (P. *Taracha*, 1); OLZ 90 (1995) 278-282 (O. *Pedersén*, 1).

b772 *a) Košak* Silvin, The palace library 'Building A' on Büyükkale; -- *b) Otten* Heinrich, Das Siegel B 229 von Hattušili III Puduhepa: → 84, [F]HOUWINK TEN CATE, H., Studio (1995) 173-9 / 245-9 + pl. 27-29.

b773 *Lebrun* René, Réflexions sur le Lukka [SW Anatolie en rapport avec Ḫattuša] et environs au 13ème s. av. J.-C.: → 110 [F]LIPIŃSKI, E., Immigration: OLA 65 (1995) 139-152.

b774 **Neve** P., Hattuša -- Stadt der Götter und Tempel 1991 → 10,12886: [R]ZAW 107 (1995) 166s (M. *Köckert*).

b775 *a) Neve* Peter, Ein hethitisches Relieffragment von Büyükkaya (Boğazköy); -- *b) Parzinger* Hermann, Bemalte Keramik aus Boğazköy-Ḫattuša und die frühe Eisenzeit im westlichen Ostanatolien; -- *c) Otten* Heinrich, *Rüster* Christel, Ein Siegel des hethitischen Grosskönigs Muršili II. und der Tawananna; -- *d) Haas* Volkert, *Wegener* Ilse, Stadtverfluchungen aus den Texten in Boğazköy sowie die hurritischen Termini für 'Oberstadt' 'Unterstadt' und 'Herd': → 23, [F]BOEHMER R.M., Beiträge 1995, 469-472; 2 fig.; pl. 36c / 527-531 + 5 fig. / 507-512; 8 fig; Zeichenliste; pl.36 d-f / 187-194; pl.19c.

b776 **Otten** Heinrich, *Rüster* Christel, Hethitische Texte vorwiegend von Büyükkale Gebäude A: K(aus)Bo 39. B 1995, Mann. xviii-50 p. 3-7861-1887-6.

b777 *Seeher* Jürgen, Boğazköy-Hattuša 1994: → a915, Kazi 1 (1995) 249-253; 15 fig.

b778 *Seeher* Jürgen [successor]: Forty years in the capital of the Hittites: → 136, [F]NEVE P., BA 58 (1995) 63-67; ill.

b779 **Starke** Frank, Ausbildung und Training von Streitwagenpferden; eine hippologisch orientierte Interpretation des Kikkuli-Textes: StBT 41. Wsb 1995, Harrassowitz. xiii-172 p. 3-447-03501-3.

b780 **Wilhelm** Gernot, Ein Ritual des AZU-Priesters: Corpus der hurritischen Sprachdenkmäler, 1. Texte aus Boğazköy, Egheft 1. R 1995, Bonsignori. x-37 p.

b781 *Alaca*: *Baltacıoğlu* Hatçe, [T] L'ébauche de lion à double tête d'Alaca Höyük: Belleten 59.225 (1995) 285-295; color.pl.2.

b782 -- *a) Kolbus* S., *Vértesalji* P.P., Wächter oder Atlasfiguren ? Zu den Stierdämonen zwischen den Schriftzeichen für Himmel und Erde in Yazıhkaya; -- *b) Neve* P., Zur Datierung des Sphinxtores in Alaca Höyük: →10,80, [F]MAYER-OPIFICIUS R., Beschreiben 1994, 121-129 + 10 fig. / 213-9 + 16 fig.

T8.3 Ephesus

b783 **Elliger** Winfried, Ephesos, Geschichte einer antiken Weltstadt[2] (Auflage): Urban-Tb 375. 224 p. 3-17-012383-1. -- [R]BiOr 52 (1995) 173s (J.M. *Hemelrijk*: all it lacks is 150 pictures).

b784 *Engelmann* Helmut, Philostrat und Ephesos: ZPE 108 (1995) 77-87.

b785 **Günther** Matthias, Die Frühgeschichte des Christentums in Ephesus: *ArbRGUrc 1. Fra 1995, Lang. xi-249 p.; Bibliog. 212-237. 3-631-49269-3.

b786 *Guerber* E., Cité libre ou stipendiaire ? À propos du statut juridique d'Éphèse à l'époque du haut empire romain: RÉG 108 (1995) 388-409.

b787 *Jastrzębowska* Elisabeth, [P] De B. Mariae Virginis Ephesi cultus origine: Mea(nder) 50 (1995) 469-481; lat. 481.

b788 **Karwiese** Stefan, Gross ist die Artemis von Ephesos; die Geschichte einer der grossen Städte der Antike. W 1995, Phoibos. 184 p.; ill.; 6 maps.; bibliog. 154-161. 3-901232-05-2.

b789 [E]**Koester** Helmut, Ephesos, metropolis of Asia; an interdisciplinary approach to its archaeology, religion, and culture [Harvard symposium 1994]: HThS 41. Ph 1995, Trinity. xix-357 p.; foldout map. $ 25 pa. 1-56338-156-7 [NTAb 40, p.557].

b790 [E]**Padovese** L., Efeso 3 1992/3 → 8,845; 10,12895: [R]Laur 36 (1995) 211s (L. *Martignani*); OrChr 79 (1995) 241s (W. *Gessel*).

b791 [E]**Padovese** Ludovico, Efeso 4, 1993/4 → 10.329: [R]Greg 76 (1995) 599-601 (G. *Ferraro*); PaVi 40.4 (1995) 56; POrC 45 (1995) 289s (P. *Ternant*).

b792 **Rogers** Guy M., The sacred identity of Ephesus 1991 → 7,e44 ... 10,12896: [R]JRS 83 (1993) 145s (R. *van Bremen*).

b793 *Rogers* G.M., The constructions of women [benefactors or otherwise in inscriptions] at Ephesos: VDI (1995,4) 132-8; Eng. 138.

b794 **Schulte** Claudia, Die Grammateis von Ephesos; Schreiberamt und Sozialstruktur in einer Provinzhauptstadt des römischen Kaiserreiches; HeidAltHB 15, 1994 → 10,12897; DM 74: [R]HZ 261 (1995) 508s (B. *Meissner*).

b795 **Thiessen** Werner, Christen in Ephesus; die historische und theologische Situation in vorpaulinischer und paulinischer Zeit und zur Zeit der Apostelgeschichte und der Pastoralbriefe: TANZ 12. Tü 1995, Franke. 410 p.; Bibliog. 354-395. 3-7720-1863-7.

b796 **Thür** Hilke, Das Hadrianstor in Ephesus 1989 → 6,e843; 7,e46: [R]GGA 247 (1995) 207-216 (K.S. *Freyberger*).

b797 **Wohlers-Scharf** Traute, Die Forschungsgeschichte von Ephesus (→ 10,12900); Entdeckungen, Grabungen und Persönlichkeiten: Diss. Wien 1994: EHS 38/54. Fra 1995, Lang. x-337 p. 3-631-47964-6.

T8.4 Pergamum

b798 **Coarelli** Filippo, Da Pergamo a Roma; i Galati nella città degli Attalidi: Univ. Roma, mostra 20/3. R 1995,Quasar. 84 p.; ill.

b799 *Kertész* István, Die Darstellung von Attalos I in der antiken Geschichtsschreibung: → 10,4, Mem. HAHN I. 1993, 53-58

b800 *Koester* Helmut, The red hall in Pergamon: → 125, [F]MEEKS W., Social world 1995, 265-274.

b801 *Kunze* Max, Pergamon im Jahre 1750; Reisetagebücher und Zeichnungen von Giovanni Battista BORRA: AW(elt) 26 (1995) 177-186: 14 fig.

b802 *Radt* Wolfgang, Pergamon, Bericht über die Kampagne 1994 / 1994 kampanyasi raporu: → a915, Kazı 2 (1995) 63-68 / 57-61; 10 fig.

b803 *a) Virgilio* Biagio, Fama, eredità e memoria degli Attalidi di Pergamo; -- *b) Letta* Cesare, Il dossier di Opramoas e la serie dei legati e degli *archiereis* di Lici: → 9,440, [E]*Virgilio* B., Aspetti e problemi dell'ellenismo (Pisa 1992/4) 137-171 / 203-246.

b804 **Voegtli** Hans, al., Die Fundmünzen aus der Stadtgrabung von Pergamon. B 1993. 106 p.; 14 pl. -- [R]JNG(eld) 44 (1994) 214s (D.O.A. *Klose*).

T8.6 *Situs Anatoliae* -- **Turkey sites in alphabetical order**

b805 **Akdamat**: Öney Gönül, The church of Akdamat: Introducing monuments 31. Ankara 1990. Ministry of Culture. v-73 p.; ill.

b806 **Alalaḫ**: Zeeb Frank, Alalah VII und das Amosbuch: UF 27 (DIETRICH 60. Gb. 1995) 641-656.

b807 **Ališar**: *Gorny* Ronald L., Hittite imperialism and anti-imperial resistance as viewed from Ališar Höyük: BASOR 299s (1995) 65-89; 13 fig.

b808 **Altın**: **Masson** Vadim M., Altyn-Depe, [T]*Michel* Henry N,: Mg 5. Ph 1988, Univ. Museum. xx-153 p.; bibliog. 138-146. 0-934718-54-7.

b809 **Anamur**: *Russell* James, A Roman military diploma from Rough Cilicia: B(onn)Jb 195 (1995) 67-133; 5 fig. (map).

b810 **Ancyra**: *Özaktürk* Mehmet, [T] Ankara aniti (Monumentum ancyranum)...: B(el-leten)TTK 59,224 (1995) 17-54.

b811 **Antiochia syr.** *Esbroeck* Michel van, La légende des apôtres Pierre, Jean et Paul à Antioche: OrChr 78 (1994) 64-73. 74-85, texte arabe en face.

b812 -- **Dauer** Anton, Paulus und die christliche Gemeinde im syrischen Antiochia; kritische Bestandaufnahme der modernen Forschung mit einigen weiterführenden Überlegungen: BBB 106. Weinheim c. 1995, Beltz. 299 p. DM 98. 3-89547-106-2.

b813 **Antiochia pisid.**: *Taşlialan* Mehmet, *Granella* Oriano, *al.*, Antiochia di Pisidia una nuova Efeso ? i recenti scavi lasciano intravvedere reperti molto significativi: Eteria 1 (1995) 24s . 25-27 (-29); color. ill.

b814 **Aphrodisias** 1993: AJA 99 (1995) 33-59; 35 fig.; foldout plan (R.R.R. *Smith*, C. *Ratté*).

b815 -- **Campbell** Sheila, The mosaics of Aphrodisias in Caria 1991 → 8.g355: [R]Gnomon 67 (1995) 638-642 (W. *Jobst*).

b816 -- *Edwards* Douglas R., Religion, politics and entertainment in the Graeco-Roman world; Chariton and his city Aphrodisias: → 10,344a, Notion of 'religion' 1990/4, 283-7 (289-294, *Mierse* William E.).

b817 -- *Johnston* Ann, Aphrodisias reconsidered: NumC 155 (1995) 43--101; pl. 17-18.

b818 -- **MacDonald** David, The coinage of Aphrodisias 1992 → 10,12923: [R]JNG(eld) 44 (1994) 218-223 (D.O.A. *Klose*).

b819 -- **Roueché** Charlotte, Performers and partisans at Aphrodisias 1993 → 10,12922: [R]*TopO 4 (1994) 351-361 (J.-C. *Moretti*: 'Showbizz à Aphrodise ').

b820 -- **Smith** R.R.R., The monument of C. Julius Zollos. Mainz 1993, von Zabern. 68 p.; 33 pl. DM 98. 3-8053-1448-5. -- [R]AnCL 64 (1995) 542-4 (A. *Hermary*).

b821 **Claros**, sanctuaire d'Apollon, fouilles de 1994: → a915, Kazì 2 (1995) 47-51; plan; 5 fig. (Juliette de *La Genière*).

b822 **Colossae**: **Arnold** Clinton E.(→ 8619 supra), The Colossian syncretism; the interface between Christianity and folk-belief at Colossae; WUNT 2/77. Tü 1995, Mohr. xii-378 p. DM 118. 3-16-146435-4 [*TBR 9/2,20, A. *Chester*].

b823 **Daskyleion**: *Vassileva* Maya, Thracian-Phrygian cultural zone; the Daskyleion evidence: OrpheusT 5 (1995)27-34.

b824 -- (**Erğili**): **Nollé** Margret, Denkmäler vom Satrapensitz Daskyleion; Studien zur graeco-persischen Kunst: Antike in der Moderne. B 1992, Akademie, xvi-179 p. DM 148. -- [R]WO 26 (1995) 229-233 (Heidemarie *Koch*).

b825 **Eflatun Pinar, Fasıllar:** *Masson* Emilia, Turquie, deux monuments hittites: Archéologia 301 (1994) 30-35; ill.

b826 **Gaziantep:** *Kennedy* David, *al.,* Mining the mosaics of Roman Zeugma: Arch(aeology) 48,2 (1995) 34s (44-56 *al.,* Turkey's war on the illicit antiquities trade).

b827 **Göreme:** *Bejor* Giorgio, Millenni di storia ... panoramici selvaggi: ArVi 14,50 (1995) 46-58.

b828 **Gordion:** *Muscarella* Oscar W., The Iron Age background to the formation of the Phrygian state: BASOR 299s (1995) 91-101.

b829 -- **Kohler** Ellen L., The Gordion excavations (1950-1973), final reports II, The lesser Phrygian tumuli, 1. the inhumations: mg 88. Ph 1995, Univ. Museum. xxxvi-262 p. 0-934718-39-3.

b830 -- **Romano** Irene B., Gordion special studies, II. The terracotta figurines and related vessels: mg. 86. Ph 1995, Univ. Museum. xxvii-91 p.; bibliog. xvii-xxvii. 0-92417-129-4.

b831 -- **Sams** G. Kenneth, The early Phrygian pottery: Gordion 4. Ph 1994, Univ. Museum. 346 p., vol. of 65 fig., 170 pl., + 3 color., 4 plans. $ 120. 0-924171-18-9. — ᴿAJA 99 (1995) 544s (A. *Ramage*).

b832 **Hierapolis**-Pamukkale, excavations and restorations during 1994: → a915, Kazì 2 (1995) 95-100; 101-5 (Daria di Bernardi *Ferrero*).

b833 -- *d'Andria* Francesco, La signora delle ninfe .. scavi italiani: *Archeo 129 (1995) 100-105.

b834 **Höyücek** (Antalya) 1991-2: Belleten 59,225 (1995) 479-490; 57 pl. (R. *Duru*).

b835 **Iasos:** **Tomasello** F., Missione italiana 2. L'acquedotto .. ; Archaeologica 95, 1991 → 9,14603*: ᴿCLR 45 (1995) 130s (R. *Ling*).

b836 -- *Mastrocinque* Attilio, Iaso e i Seleucidi: At(henaeum) 83 (1995) 131-141 + 11 fig.

b837 **Iconium:** *Dresken-Weiland* Jutta, Ein frühchristliches Jonasrelief in Konya: MDAI-R 102 (1995) 405-412; pl. 108.

b838 **İstanbul:** *Ciggaar* Krijnie N., Une description de Constantinople [c. 1200] dans le Tarragonensis 55: RÉByz 53 (1995) 117-140.

b839 -- *Donceel-Voûte* Pauline, *al.,* Byzance; histoire, hauts-lieux; manuscrits, collections: MoBi 92 (1995) 2-37.

b840 -- **Harrison** Martin, A temple for Byzantium 1989 → 6.e878; 9,14605: ᴿJAAR 63 (1995) 623-6 (Ann *Terry*).

b841 -- **Lewis** Bernard, Istanbul et la civilisation ottomane, ᵀ*Thoraval* Yves. P 1990, Lattke. 200 p. -- ᴿRThom 95 (1995) 531s (J. *Jomier*).

b842 -- **Mango** Cyril, [22] Studies on Constantinople: CS 394. Aldershot 1993, Variorum. xii-274 p. -- ᴿRÉByz 53 (1995) 374-6 (C. *Walter*).

b843 **Karataş:** **Warner** Jayne L., Elmali-Karataş II, the Early Bronze age village. Ph 1994, Bryn Mawr College. xxxii-219 p.; 21 fig.; 206 pl. $ 40. 0-929524-80-2. -- ᴿAJA 99 (1995) 739s (D.J. *Pullen*).

b844 **Karatepe** Aslantaş-Domuztepe 1993s: → a915, Kazì I (1995) 229-237; 15 fig. (Halet *Çambel, al.*)

b845 **Kilise** tepe 1994; a summary of the principal results: → a915, Kazì 1 (1995) 419-423; 12 fig. (J.N. *Postgate*).

b846 **Kültepe**: *a) Özgüç* Tahsin, Two eagle-shaped cult vessels discovered at Kanish; -- *b) Özgüç* Nimet, Silver and copper ingots from Acemhöyük: → 23, ^FBOEHMER R.M., Beiträge 1995, 521-5; 3 fig.; pl. 41 / 513-9; pl. 40.

b847 -- *Özgüç* Tahsin, A boat-shaped cult-vessel from the Karum of Kanish: → 10,81, ^FMEYER L. de, 52 Réflexions 1994, 369-375; 2 fig.; 2 pl.

b848 -- **Veenhof** Klaas R., *Klengel-Brandt* Evelyn, Altassyrische Tontafeln aus Kültepe; Texte und Siegelabrollungen 1992 → 9,14221: ^RBiOr 52 (1995) 721-8 (Cécile *Michel*).

b849 **Kuşakli** 750 k SE Boğazköy 1992-4: MDOG 127 (1995) 5-36; 29 fig. (A. *Müller-Karpe*); 37-42 (G.*Wilhelm*, Tontafelfunde).

b850 **Kyaneai**: ^E**Kolb** F.(→ b751), Lykische Studien, 2. Forschungen auf dem Gebiet der Polis Kyaneai in Zentrallykien; Bericht über die Kampagne 1991: Asia-Minor-Studien 18. Bonn 1995, Habelt. x-243 p.; 58 pl.; 10 foldout plans. 3-7749-2640-9.

b851 **Latmos**: *Peschlow-Bindokat* Anneliese, Ziegenjagd und Kulttanz; die ältesten prähistorischen Felsmalereien in Westkleinasien: AW(elt) 26 (1995) 114-7; 8 fig. [118s, 215-9 *Ehringhaus* Horst, hethitisches Felsrelief].

b852 **Malatya-Arslan**: *Trufeldi* Franca, Standardisation, mass production and potters' marks in the Late Chalcolithic pottery of Arslan Tepe (Malatya): Origini 18 (R 1994) 245-288; 19 fig. [391-409, *Persiani* Carlo, Eng.].

b853 **Maşat**: *Özgüç* Tahsin, A votive foundation-nail in the temple of Maşathöyük; → 10,80, ^FMAYER-OPIFICIUS Ruth, Beschreiben 1994. 227-230 + 9 fig.

b854 **Miletus** 1899!: **Kossatz** Anne-Ulrike, Die [753] megarischen Becher: Milet 5/1. B 1990, de Gruyter. ix-154 p,: 46 fig.; 55 pl. DM 320. -- ^RJNES 54 (1995) 59s (Eleanor *Guralnick*).

b855 -- *Delorme* Jean, Athènes et Milet au milieu du Ve s. av. J.-C.: JS(av) (1995) 209-281.

b856 -- *a) Ehrhardt* Norbert, *Weiss* Peter, Trajan, Didyma und Milet; -- *b) Günther* Wolfgang, Zwei neue Temenitenverzeichnisse aus Milet: Chiron 25 (1995) 315-353 / 43-52; 2 fig.

b857 **Nemrut Dağ**: *Zaffanella* Gian Carlo, Nemrut Dağ, il trono degli dèi: ArVi 14,51 (1995) 42-54.

b858 **Nicaea**: 1994 Iznik Roma tiyatrosu kazisi: → a915, Kazı 2 (1995) 337-346; 25 fig. (Bedri *Yalman*).[*al.* 411-5].

b859 **Perge** acropolis 1994: → a915, Kazı 2 (1995) 121-4; 7 fig. (Haluk *Abbasoğlu*, Wolfram *Martini*).

b860 -- *Jones* Christopher P., A decree from Perge in Pamphylia: *EpAnat 23 (1995) 29-33; ^T 34.

b861 -- *Ruggieri* Vincenzo, Appunti sulla continuità urbana di Side, in Panfilia: OCP 61 (1995) 95-116; 12 fig.; 54 fot.

b862 -- **Nollé** J., Side im Altertum, Geschichte und Zeugnisse, I. Geographie, Geschichte, Testimonia, griechische und lateinische Inschriften (1-4): IGSK 43. Bonn 1993, Habelt. xxiii-355 p. -- ^RCLR 45 (1995) 393-5 (K. *Hopwood*); JNG(eld) 44 (1994) 226 (Mechtild *Overbeck*).

b863 **Sagalassos,** 20 k E Burdur: *Waelkens* Marc, Rise and fall of Sagalassos: Arch(aeology) 48,3 (1995) 28-34; ill.

b864 *Sardis* archaeological research in 1994: → a915, Kazì 1 (1995) 409-412; 10 fig,

b865 -- *Greenewalt* Crawford H.¹, Sardis in the age of XENOPHON: Pallas 43 (1995) 123-9 + fig. 5-10.

b866 -- *Le Rider* Georges, Les trouvailles monétaires dans le temple d'Artémis à Sardes (IGCH 1299 et 1300): RNum 33 (1991) 71-88; 1 fig.; pl. VIII.

b867 *Smyrna:* *French* David H., Milestones from the Izmir region 1994: *EpAnat 23 (1995) 85-102: ᵀ 102.

b868 *Tarsus*: *Zoroğlu* Levent, Ritrovata un'antica strada a Tarso: Eteria, viaggi di cultura nell'Oriente cristiano 1 (Modena 1995) 8s [9-22, altro su Tarso; 13, incontro Antonio-Cleopatra].

b869 *Tille*: **Sunners** G.D., Tille Höyük 4, the Late Bronze Age and Iron Age transition: Mg 15. L 1993, British Institute of Archaeology at Ankara. xxiii-205 p.; 75 fig.; 8 pl. [*OIAc 11,43].

b870 *Titriş:* *Matney* Timothy, *Algaze* Guillermo, Urban development at mid-late Early Bronze Age Titriş Höyük in southeastern Anatolia: BASOR 299s (1995) 33-52; 17 fig.

----

b871 *Troia* 1994: → a915, Kazi i (1995) 283-293; 20 fig. (M. *Korfmann*).

b872 -- *Allen* Susan H., 'Finding the walls of Troy'; Frank CALVERT, excavator: AJA 99 (1995) 379-407; 13 pl.

b873 -- *Arias* P.E., L'Ilioupersis nella ceramica a figura rossa di Spina: SIF(g)C 12 (1994) 3-11; 2 fig.

b874 -- **Austin** Norman, Helen of Troy and her shameless phantom: Myth and Poetics. Ithaca c.1994, Cornell Univ. xiv-223 p.; ill. $ 30. -- ᴿRelStR 21 (1995) 228 (S. *Levin*: erudite, enjoyable, unconvincing).

b875 -- *Bonfante* G., La nazionalità dei Troiani e dei loro alleati [illyrica]: I(nd)GF 100 (1995) 135s.

b876 -- *Easton* D.F., The Troy treasures in Russia: Antiquity 69 (1995) 11-14.

b877 -- *Amandry* Pierre, *al.*, SCHLIEMANN, le trésor de Priam retrouvé: Dossiers d'Archéologie 206 (1995) 2-15 . 42-83.

b878 -- *Meyer* Karl E., Who owns the spoils of war ? : Arch(aeology) 48,4 (1995) 46-52.

b879 -- **Moorehead** Caroline, The lost treasures of Troy 1994 → 10,12972;, £ 20: ᴿGaR 42 (1995) 253 (P. *Walcot*).

b880 -- **Fehling** Detlev, Die ursprüngliche Geschichte vom Fall Trojas 1991 → 8,g419*: ᴿGnomon 67 (1995) 189-198 (Ø. *Andersen*).

b881 -- *Gindin* L.A., *Tsymbursky* V.L., ᴿ Troy and Proto-Ahhijawa: VDI 213 (1995) 14-36; Eng. 36s.

b882 -- a) *Hood* Sinclair, The Bronze Age context of Homer; -- b) *Burkert* Walter, Lydia between East and West, or how to date the Trojan War: → 212, ᶠVERMEULE E., The ages of Homer 1995, 25-32 / 139-148.

b883 -- a) *Mannsperger* Brigitte, Das Stadtbild von Troia in VERGILs Aeneis; -- b) *Siebler* Ichael, Hatte die Ilias doch recht ? Zum ersten Mal Schriftfunde in Troia: AW(elt) 26 (1995) 463-471; 11 fig. / 472s.

b884 -- de Vos Mariette, Eracle e Priamo, trasmissione di potere; mitologia e ideologia imperiale: → 695, Ercole 1990/3, 81-89.

b885 -- **Siehler** Michael, Troia; Gechichte, Grabungen, Kontroversen: Bildband Arch 17. Mainz 1994, von Zabern. iv-120 p.; 177 fig. DM 50. -- ᴿE(rbe)uA 71 (1995) 78s.

b885* -- **Woodford** Susan, The Trojan War in ancient art. L 1993, Duckworth. 129 p.; 113 fig. £ 10. 0-7156-2468-7. -- [R]BVAB(abesch) 70 (1995) 243-5 (J.M. *Hemelrijk*).

b886 -- **Zangger** Eberhard, Ein neuer Kampf von Troia; Archäologie in der Krise [Trojans are Akhijawa and Sea-Peoples]. Mü 1994, Knaur. 352 p.; ill. 3-426-26682-2. -- [R]*JField 21 (1994) 522-5 (D. *Pullen*, also on his Flood/Atlantis).

----

b887 *Trysa*: *Oberleiner* Wolfgang, Das Heroon von Trysa, ein lykisches Fürstengrab des 4. Jh. n. Chr.: AW(elt) 25 Sond. (1994) 67 p.; 132 fig.

b888 *Urfa*: **Green** Tamara M., The city of the moon-god; religious traditions of Harran 1992 → 8,g426: [R]BiOr 52 (1995) 505s (R.M. *Frank*).

b889 *Uşak*: *Acar* Özgen, Come ho ritrovato il tesoro di Creso [poi rubato, finalmente restituito dal Museo Metropolitano NY]: Archeo 120 (1995) 70-75 (*al. 60-89*).

b890 *Xanthus*: **Slatter** Enid, Xanthus; [Charles FELLOWS, 1838-44, whence British Museum marbles] travels of discovery in Turkey. L 1994, Rubicon. v-362 p. -RelStR 21 (1995) 132 (W.M. *Calder*).

b891 -- *Bourgarel* André, *al.*, Fouilles de Xanthos IX. P 1992. x-208 p.; xii-82 pl.; 8 plans.- MH(elv) 52 (1995) 184s (P. *Frei*).

T8.9 Armenia, Urarṭu

b892 [E]**Burchard** Christoph, Armenia and the Bible 1990/3 → 9,374: [R]ThLZ 120 (1995) 720-2 (A. *Meissner*).

b893 **Mouradian** Claire, L'Arménie: QSJ? 851. P 1995, PUF. 127 p. 2-13-847327-X.

b894 **Nersessian** Vrej Nerses, Armenia: World Bibliog. 163. Ox 1993, Clio. xxiii-304 p.; 2 maps. £ 49.50. : JRAS (1995) 122-4 (C.J. *Walker*).

b895 **Salvini** Mirjo, Geschichte und Kultur der Urartäer. Da 1995, Wiss. x-257 p.; bibliog. 211-238. 3-534-01870-2.

b896 *Salvini* Mirjo, Il lessico delle lingue hurrica e urartea; progressi di interpretazione e problemi particolari: StEpL 12 (1995) 159-167

b897 *a)* Schottky Martin, Dunkle Punkte in der armenischen Königsliste; -- *b)* Sarkisjan Gagik, Eine Ergänzung zur Rekonstruktion der Artasesidendynastie Armeniens nach dem seleukidischen astronomischen Tagebuch BM 34791: AMI(ran) 27 (1994) 223-235; 4 fig.; pl. 41,5 / 237-240.

b898 *Thierry* Michel, Le lieu d'échouage de l'arche de Noé dans la tradition arménienne: Syria 72 (1995) 143-158; 5 fig. (maps).

b899 **Wartke** R.-B., Urarṭu, das Reich am Ararat: *KuGaW 58, 1993 → 9,14641: [R]ZAW 107 (1995) 369 (M. *Köckert*).

b900 *Zimansky* Paul, *a)* Urartian material culture as state assemblage; an anomaly in the archaeology of empire: BASOR 299s (1995) 103-115; -- *b)* An Urartian Ozymandias: → 136, [F]NEVE P., BA 58 (1995) 94-100; ill. -- *c)* XENOPHON and the Urartian legacy: Pallas 43 (1995) 255-268; franç. 268.

b901 *Horom*: 1st-2d, 1992s: Iran 31 (1993) 1-24; 19 fig.; 32 (1994) 1-29; 20 fig. (R.S. *2 Badaljan, al.*)

b902 *Işik* Fahri, Das Felsgrab von Koseoğlu und Totentempel Urartus: AMI(ran) 28 (1995s) 211-234; 7 fig.; pl. 8-15.

b903　*Velikent* 1994: Iran 33 (1995) 139-147; 5 fig.; pl XXIII-XXV (M.G. *Gadzhiev, al.*).

T9.1　Cyprus

b904　*Herscher* Ellen, Archaeology in Cyprus: AJA 99 (1995) 257-294; 35 fig.

b905　*Iakōvou* Maria, [G] Early history of Cyprus before kingship: RDACyp (1995) 95-110; 3 fig.

b906　**Jennings** Ronald C., Christians and Muslims in Ottoman Cyprus and the Mediterranean world 1571-1670: 1993 → 10,12996; $ 60: [R]WZKM 85 (1995) 384s (Elizabth A. *Zachariadou*, franç.).

b907　*Karageorghis* Vassos, *Hermary* Antoine, *al.*, Chypre au cœur des civilisations méditerranéennes: Les Dossiers d'Archéologie 205 (1995). 136 p. F 68.

b908　**Karageorghis** Vassos, The coroplastic art of ancient Cyprus [1. 1991 → 9,13513] 2. Late Cypriote II Cypro-Geometric III. Nicosia 1993, Levantis. xii-112 p.M 7 fig.; 65 pl.; map. 9963-560-18-0. -- [R]RÉG 108 (1995) 609-611 (Hélène *Cassimatis*, also on his Tombs at Palaepaphos 1990); Syria 72 (1995) 298-302 (H. de *Contenson*).

b909　**Kehrberg** Ira, Northern Cyprus in the transition from the early to the middle Cypriot period... tombs: SIMA.p 108. Jonsered 1995, Åström. 351 p.; 24 fig.; 26 pl. $ 63.20. 91-7081-089-3. -- [R]BASOR 299s (1995) 124-6 (Jane A. *Barlow*).

b910　*Webb* Jennifer M., *Frankel* David, Making an impression; storage and surplus finance in Late Bronze Age Cyprus: JMeditA 7,1 (1994) 5-26; 6 fig.

b911　[E]**Yon** Marguerite, Kinyras, l'archéologie française à Chypre 1991/3 → 10,494: [R]PEQ 127 (1995) 84 (Louise *Steel*); RÉA(nc) 97 (1995) 676s (P. *Aupert*, P.-Y. *Péchoux*); Syria 72 (1995) 440s (H. de *Contenson*).

b912　*Amathus:* *Coldstream* J.N.; *a)* Greek Geometric and Archaic imports from the tombs of Amathus; -- *b)* Amathus tomb NW 194; the Greek pottery imports [*Tytgat* Christiane, La tombe NW 194]: RDACyp (1995) 199-214: 8 fig.; pl. XVI-XIX / 187-198; 3 fig.; pl. XIV-XV [137-185: 5 fig.; pl. XI-XIII].

b913　**Karageorghis** V., *al.* La nécropole 5, 1991 → 8,g455: [R]Gnomon 67 (1995) 731-4 (A. *Hermary*).

b914　**Karageorghis** V., *al.*, Amathonte VI. 1992. -- [R]PEQ 127 (1995) 76s (Louise *Steel*).

b915　*Idalion*; **Senff** Bernard, Das Apollonheiligtum von Idalion; Architektur und Statuenaussattung eines zyprischen Heiligtums; SIMA 94. Jonsered 1993, Åström. 99 p.; 64 pl. -- [R]RÉG 108 (1995) 226s (O. *Masson*); [*Schmitt* Rüdiger, Eine ketzerische Bemerkung ...]

b916　*Kamares:* *Vavouranakis* Georgios, *Manginis* Georgis, [G] Middle Cypriote tombs at the site Avdimo-Kamarès: RDACyp (1995) 67-94: 10 fig.

b917　*Kissonerga*: *Peltenburg* Edgar, Kissonerga in Cyprus and the appearance of faience in the Eastern Mediterranean; → 82, [F]HENNESSY J.B., Trade 1995, 31-41; map; pl. 2,1.

b918　*Kition-Bamboula*: **Salles** J.-F., Les niveaux hellénistiques 1993 → 10,13016: [R]BO 52 (1995) 840-4 (G.R.H. *Wright*); RÉA 97 (1995) 677s (P. *Aupert*).

b919　*Kourion*: **Sinos** S., *al.*, The temple of Apollo Hylates at Kourion and the restoration of its southwest corner. Athenae 1990, Leventis. 301 p.; 363 fig. -- [R]Syria 72 (1995) 456-8 (E. *Will*).

b920　*Paphos*, cave of the amphoras: BA 58 (1995) 49-51 (R.L. *Hohlfelder*).

(1995) 456-8 (E. *Will*).

b920 *Paphos*, cave of the amphoras: BA 58 (1995) 49-51 (R.L. *Hohlfelder*).

b921 -- *Leonard* J.R., *al.*, Evidence for a lighthouse at Nea Paphos ?: RDACyp (1995) 237-248; 7 fig.

b922 *Pyrgos*: a) *Belgiorno* Maria Rosaria, Pyrgos in the Early Bronze Age; -- b) *Mali-szewski* Dariusz, Polis-Pyrgos archaeological project; second preliminary report on the 1994 survey season in northwestern Cyprus: RDACyp (1995) 61-65; 3 fig.; pl. V / 311-6; map; pl.XXXVI-XXXVIII.

b923 *Salamis*: **Cesnola** Alexander Palma di, Salaminia; the history, treasures, and antiquities of Salamis in the island of Cyprus. Nicosia 1993 = 1882, Star. xlviii-329 p. 9963-579-61-2 [*OIAc 11.17].

b924 *Toumba*: **Vermeule** Emily D.T., *Wolsky* Florence Z., Toumba tou Skourou, a Bronze Age potters' quarter 1990 → 8,g473*: [R]JNES 54 (1995) 296-9 (C.M. *Adelman* with lengthy citations).

т9.3 *Graecia*, **Greece** -- mainland sites in alphabetical order

b925 **Burkert** Walter, The orientalizing revolution: Near Eastern influence on Greek culture in the early archaic age 1992 → 8,g477: *JMeditA 6 (1993) 231-7 (R. *Osborne*) & 239-245 (P. *Zimansky*), both also on MORRIS S.P. 1992.

b926 [E]**Lauffer** Siegfried, Griechenland; Lexikon der historischen Stätten, von den Anfängen bis zur Gegenwart. Mü 1989, Beck. 775 p.; 14 maps. -- [R]Gnomon 67 (1995) 522-8 (S.C. *Bakhuizen*, Eng.)

b927 *Loucas-Durie* Éveline, Chronique des fouilles: Kernos 8 (1995) 267-285.

b928 [E]**Morris** Ian, Classical Greece; ancient histories and modern archaeologies: New Directions in Archaeology. C 1994, Univ. xiv-244 p.; bibliog, 201-238. 0-521-45678-9.

b929 *Petrachou* Vasilios C., *al.*, [G] Excavation reports / essays: PraktikaAth (1994) xiii-xxi, 1-230 / 231-252.

b930 *Argos*: **Bommelaer** Jean-Francois, *Courtils* Jacques des, La salle hypostyle d'Argos: Études péloponnésiens 10. P 1994, de Boccard. 72 p.; 26 fig. + dépliant. 2-86958-07-1.

b931 -- **Dietz** Søren, The Argolid at the transition to the Mycenaean age 1991 → 7,e149 ... 10,13050: [R]ÉtCL 63 (1995) 389s (J. *Vanschoonwinkel*).

b932 -- **James** M.H., *al.*, A Greek countryside ... Argolid 1994 → : ... (1995) 128-130 (D.W.J. *Gill*).

b933 -- *Marchetti* Patrick, *Rizakis* Yvonne, Recherches sur les mythes et la topographie d'Argos IV. L'agora revisitée: BCH 119 (1995) 437-472 (-477, *Piérart* Marcel).

----

b934 *Athenae*: *Andreae* Bernard, Per la libertà dei Greci; rivelati I segreti del donario di Attalo [PAUSANIA]; un'affascinante sperimentazione sull'Acropoli di Atene: Archeo 9,116 (1994) 38-47.

b935 -- *Fagerström* Kåre, All the Virgin's horses and all the Virgin's men; on the choice of moment in the Parthenon frieze: Opus Mixtum (OpRom 21, 1994) 35-46, 3 fig.

b936 -- **Habicht** Christian, Athen; die Geschichte der Stadt in hellenistischer Zeit. Mü 1995, Beck. 379 p. 28 reprints. 3-406-38164-2.

b937 -- *Harrington* Spencer P.M., Rebuilding the monuments of Pericles [Propylaia,

(1995) 171-186; 7 fig.

b939 -- *Jenkins* Ian, The south frieze of the Parthenon; problems in arrangement: AJA 99 (1995) 445-456; 10 fig.

b940 -- **Keesling** Catherine M., Monumental private votive dedications on the Athenian acropolis, ca. 600-400 B.C.: diss. Michigan, ᴰ*Pedley* J. Ann Arbor 1995. 550 p. 95-27660. -- D(iss)AI 56 (1995s) p. 1484.

b941 -- *Moore* Mary B., The central group in the gigantomachy of the old Athena temple on the Acropolis: AJA 99 (1995) 633-9; 7 fig.

b942 -- *Nicholls* Richard V., The stele-goddess workshop; terracottas from Well U 13:1 in the Athenian agora: Hesp 64 (1995) 405-492; pl. 101-113.

b943 -- **Oakley** John H., *Sinos* Rebecca, The wedding in ancient Athens. Madison 1993, Univ. Wisconsin. 153 p.; 130 fig. $ 40. 0-299-13720-1. -- ᴿAJA 99 (1995) 160 (Mary B. *Moore*).

b944 -- **Palagia** Olga, The pediments of the Parthenon: MonumGR 7, 1993 → 9,14689: ᴿAJA 99 (1995) 162s (Katherine A. *Schwab*).

b945 -- *Papadopoulos* John K., To kill a cemetery; the Athenian Kerameikos and the Early Iron Age in the Aegean: *JMeditA 6 (1993) 175-206; responses *Morris* Ian 207-221; *Whitley* James 222-9.

b946 -- **Rhodes** Robin F., Architecture and meaning on the Athenian acropolis. C 1995, Univ. xvi-218 p.; ill. 0-521-47024-2; -6981-3 [RStR 22,345, O.J. *Storvick*].

b947 -- *Surikov* I.E., ᴿ The Athenian acropolis in the first half of the Vth century B.C.: VDI 212 (1995) 23-40; Eng. 40.

b948 -- **Tölle-Kastenbein** Renate, Das Olympieion in Athen: ArbArch. Köln 1994, Böhlau. 238 p.; 32 pl. 3-412-02794-4.

b949 -- **Willers** Dietrich, Hadrians panhellenisches Programm ... Athen 1990 → 7.e163; 8,g501: ᴿA(nz)AW 48,1s (1995) 114-6 (Florens *Felten*); *JRomAr 7 (1994) 426-431 (Mary T. *Boatwright*).

---

b950   **Cargill** Jack, Athenian settlements of the fourth century B.C.: Mnem.s 145. Lei 1995, Brill. xxvii-489 p.; bibliog. 442-462. 90-04-09991-3.

----

b951 *Chimera*: *Ruggieri* V., *Giordano* F., *Furnari* A., Il sito bizantino di Chimera: OCP 60 (1994) 471-502 / 61 (1995) 367-380. 15 fot.; foldout plan.

b952 *Corinthus*: *Gregory* Timothy E., The Roman bath at Isthmia; preliminary report 1972-1992: Hesp 64 (1995) 279-313; 13 fig.; pl. 53-62 [1-60, *Williams* C., *Zervos* O., Frankish Corinth].

b953 -- *Spawforth* Anthony J.S., The Achaean federal imperial cult I; pseudo-Julian letters 198 [II. *Winter* Bruce W., The Corinthian church]: TynB 46 (1995) 151-168 [169-178].

b954 *Delphi*: *Jacquemin* Anne al., Delphes, le roi Persée et les Romains : BCH 119 (1995) 125-136; 3 fig. (137-208 . 565-573 . 645-654 al.)

b955 -- *Makarov* J.A., ᴿ Tyranny and Delphi within the framework of the political history of Greece of the second half of the 7th-6th c.B.C.: VDI (1995,4) 117-131: Eng.131.

b956 *Dion*: *Harrington* Spencer P.M., Sanctuary of the gods, Macedonian Dion: Arch 49,2 (1996) 28=35.

b957 -- *Ginouvès* René, La scoperta dei Macedoni, ᵀ*Rohr* Francesca: ArVi 14,49 (1995) 18-33.

b958 *Marathon*: *Albersmeier* Sabine, Ägyptisierende Statuen aus Marathon: → 10,145, [F]WINTER E., Aspekte 1994, 9-21; 3 pl.

b959 *Messenia*: *Kelly* Nancy, The archaic temple of Apollo at Bassai; correspondences to the classical temple: Hesp 64 (1995) 227-277; 20 fig.; pl. 45-52.

----

b960 *Mycenae*:   **Albers** Gabriele,   Spätmykenische 'Stadtheiligtümer';   systematische Analyse und vergleichende Auswertung der archäologischen Befunde: BAR-Int 596. Ox 1994, Tempus reparatum. xi-234 p.; 53 pl. 0-86054-770-1.

b961 -- **Bowkett** L.C.,   The Hellenistic dye-works: Well-built Mycenae (excavations 1959-69). 36 p.; 3 microfiches. 0-85668-196-2.

b962 -- **Lutz** Norbert,   Der Einfluss Ägyptens, Vorderasiens und Kretas auf den mykenischen Fresken; Studien zum Ursprung der frühgriechischen Wandmalerei: Diss. FrB 1993, EurHS 38/48. Fra 1994, Lang. 284 p.; 31 pl. 3-631-46766-4.

b963 -- [E]**Olivier** J.-P., Mykenaïka [Colloque Éc.Ér. Athènes, 2-6.oct, 1990]: BCH.s 25. P 1992. de Boccard. xx-678 p. F 1000. 2-86958-057-6. --[R]AnCL 64 (1995) 421-3 (Ilse *Schoep*).

b964 -- **Tournavitou** Iphiyenia, The 'ivory houses' at Mycenae: supp.24. L 1995, British School at Athens. xx-341 p.; 39 pl.; map. 0-904887-12-X.

----

b965 *Olbia*: *Leypunskaya* Nina A., Olbia Pontica and the 'Olbian Muse ': Expedition 36,3s (1994) 7-17; 13 fig. [+ 40-p.: The ancient Greek world in the Philadelphia museum].

b966 *Olympia*: *Arafat* K.W.,   PAUSANIAS   and the temple of Hera at Olympia : AB(rit)SA 90 (1995) 461-473.

b967 -- **Heiden** Joachim, Die Tondächer von Olympia: OLFor 24. B 1995, de Gruyter. xiii-241 p.: 120 pl. 3-1101-4374-7.

b968 *Philippi*: **Abrahamsen** Valeria Ann, Women and worship at Philippi; Diana/Artemis and other cults in the early Christian era. Portland ME 1995, Astarte Shell. [viii-] 252 p.; bibliog. 223-247.   1-885349-00-9

b969 -- **Bormann** Lukas, Philippi -- Stadt und Christusgemeinde zur Zeit des Paulus: NT.s 28. Lei 1995, Brill.   xiii-248 p.; Bibliog. 225-237.   90-04-10232-9.

b970 -- *Penna* Charalambos, Early Christian burials at Philippi: → 118*. [F]MANGO C., ByF 21 (1995) 215-227 + XII pl.

b971 -- *Picard* Olivier, Les Thasiens du continent et la fondation de Philippes: → 199, [F]TRAN TAM TINH V., Tranquillitas 1995, 459-473; map 474.

b972 -- **Pilhofer** Peter, Philippi, I. Die erste christliche Gemeinde Europas: WUNT 87. Tü 1995, Mohr. xxiii-316 p.; Bibliog. 259-295.   3-16-146479-6.

b973 *Sparta*: *Waywell* G.B., *Wilkes* J.J., Excavations at the ancient theatre of Sparta 1992-4; preliminary report: AB(rit)SA 90 (1995) 434-460; 6 fig. (foldout plan); pl. 44-49.

b974 -- **Falkner** Caroline, Sparta and the sea; a history of Spartan sea power, c. 706 - c.373 B.C.: diss. Univ. Alberta, [D]*Buck* R. Edmonton 1992. 0-315-77374-X. - *OIAc 11,22.

b975 *Thebae*: *Aravantinos* Vassilis, *Godart* Louis, Nel palazzo di Cadmo ...archivio di tavolette micenee: Archeo 125 (1995) 40-47.

T9.4   Creta

b976 *Andreev* Yu. V., [R] Between Eurasia and Europe (on historical specificity of the Minoan civilization): VDI 213 (1995) 94-112; Eng. 112.

b977 **Godart** Louis, *Tzédakis* Yannis, Témoignages archéologiques et épigraphiques en Crète occidentale, du Néolithique au Minoen Récent III B: Incunabula Graeca 93.. R 1992, Gruppo Int. 356 p.; CLXXIII pl. -- ᴿRÉG 108 (1995) 224s (P. *Faure*).

b978 **Kreuter** Sylvia, Aussenbeziehungen kretischer Gemeinden zu den hellenistischen Staaten .. : ArbAG 6. Mü 1992, Maris. 140 p., 2 maps. DM 49. -- ᴿHZ 261 (1995) 496s (Chrissoula *Veligianni*).

b979 **Link** Stefan, Das griechische Kreta; Untersuchungen zu seinen staatlichen und gesellschaftlichen Entwicklung vom 6. bis 4. Jh. v. Chr. Stu 1994, Steiner. 149 p. 3-515-06554-7.

b980 *Aptera*: *Capdeville* Gérard, Mythes et cultes de la cité d'Aptera (Crète occidentale): Kernos 8 (1995) 41-84; 2 fig.

b981 *Kavousi* 1989s: Hesp 64 (1995) 67-120; 22 fig.; pl. 17-34 (Geraldine C. *Gesell, al.*).

b982 -- *Haggis* Donald C., Intensive survey, traditional patterns, and Dark Age Crete; the case of Early Iron Age Kavousi: JMeditA 6 (1993) 131-174; 9 fig.

b983 *Knossos*: *Broodbank* Cyprian, The neolithic labyrinth; social change at Knossos before the Bronze Age: JMeditA 5 (1992) 39-75.

b984 -- *Godart* Louis, *Tzédakis* Yannis, La chute de Cnossos; le royaume de Kydonia et le scribe 115: BCH 119 (1995) 27-33; 1 fig.

b985 -- **Popham** Mervyn R., *Gill* Margaret A.V., The latest sealings from the palace and houses at Knossos. L 1995, British School at Athens. x-65 p. 0-904887-24-3.

b986 -- **Sjöquist** Karl-Erik, *Åström* Paul, Knossos, keepers and needers; SIMA pocket 82. Göteborg 1991, Åström.   128 p.; 36 fig. -- ᴿGnomon 67 (1995) 470s (I. *Pini*).

b987 *Pyrgos*: *a) Rehak* Paul, *Younger* John G., A Minoan roundel from Pyrgos, southeastern Crete; -- *b) Perna* Massimo, The roundels of Phaistos: Kadmos 34 (1995) 81-102; 16 fig.; 4 pl. / 103-122; 7 fig., 17 pl.

T9.5 Insulae graecae

b988 **Alram-Stern** Eva, Die ägäische Frühzeit (2. Serie); Forschungsbericht 1973-1993. W c. 1995, Österr. Akad. 627 p.; Bibliog. 19-80.   3-7001-2280-2.   '1

b989 **Schallin** Anne-Louise, Islands under influence; the Cyclades in the Late Bronze Age and the nature of Mycenaean presence: SIMA 111. Jonsered 1993, Åström. 210 p.; 57 fig. 91-7081-098-2. -- ᴿThetis 2 (1995) 301s (P. *Misch*).

b990 **Vanschoonwinkel** Jacques, L'Égee et la Méditerranée orientale 1991 → 7,a215; 9,14773: ᴿÉtCL 62 (1994) 405s (O. *Gengler*).

b991 *Wąsowicz* Aleksandra, Deux modèles d'aménagement de l'espace dans les colonies grecques: Arch 46 (Wsz 1995) 7-18.

b992 *Chios*: **Lemos** A.A., Archaic pottery of Chios; the decorated styles. Ox 1991, Comm. Arch. xiv-335 p.; vol. of 245 pl. + 5 colour. £ 75. -- ᴿCLR 45 (1995) 369s (Elizabeth *Moignard*).

b993 *Claros:* *Étienne* Roland, *Varène* Pierre, VITRUVE et Claros: CRAI (1995) 495-513; 5 fig. [519-524 *Bourbon* Michel].

b994 *Delos:* *Tréheux* Jacques, Archéologie délienne -- L'Artémision *en nēsōi*, localisation et histoire: JS(av 1995) 199-207; 19 fig.

b995 -- *Étienne* Roland, *Braun* Jean-Pierre, L'autel monumental du théâtre à Délos: BCH 119 (1995) 63-87; 35 fig. (35-62 . 89-123 . 479-563 . 697-701, *al.*).

b996 -- *Bruneau* Philippe, L'autel de cornes à Délos: CRAI (1995) 321-334: 2 fig.

b997 **Euboea**: *Crielard* Jan P., *Driessen* Jan, The hero's home; some reflections on the building at Toumba, Lefkandi (Euboea) [POPHAM M.R., *al.* 1990-2]: *TopO 4 (1992) 251-270.

b998 **Kalymna**: *Crowther* Charles, Foreign courts on Kalymna in the third century B.C.: *JAncCiv 9 (Changchun 1994) 33-55.

b999 **Keos**: **Cherry** John F., *al.*, Landscape archaeology ...Keos 1991: → 9,14780; 10,13137: *JField 20 (1993) 367-372 (A.J. *Ammermann*).

c000 **Mochlos** 1990s: Hesp 63 (1994) 391-436; 22 fig.; pl. 89-107 (J.E. *Soles*, C. *Davaras*).

c001 **Patmos**; *Carrez* Maurice, *al.*, Patmos et l'Apocalypse: MoBi 94 (1995): E(spr)eV 105 (1995) 664s (J. *Daoust*).

c002 -- *Granella* Oriano, Patmos, l'isola dell'Apocalisse: Eteria 1 (1995) 3o-42; color. ill.

c003 **Rhodus:** *Irmscher* Johannes, ᴳ The beginnings of Christianity on Rhodes: P(atr)BR 14 (1995) 35-44.

c004 **Syros**: Chalendriani Cycladic cemetery 1991: NedInstAth 4 (1991) 17-32 + 12 fig.; 6 pl. (J.J. *Hekman*).

c005 **Thasos** 1994: BCH 119 (1995) 661-696; 47 fig. (R. *Dalongeville, al.*)

c006 **Thera**: *Negbi* Ora, The 'Libyan landscape' from Thera; a review of Aegean enterprises overseas in the Late Minoan IA period: JMeditA 7,1 (1994) 73-111.

c007 -- *Foster* Karen P., A flight of swallows [courting ? painted on three Akrotiri walls]: AJA 99 (1995) 409-425; 14 fig.

T9.6 Urbs Roma

c008 *Balensiefen* Lilian, Überlegungen zu Aufbau und Lage der Danaidenhalle auf dem Palatin: MDAI-R 102 (1995) 189-209; 4 fig., pl. 48-53.

c009 ᴱ**Blázquez Martínez** J.M., *al.*, Excavaciones arqueológicas en el Monte Testaccio, Memoria campaña 1989. M 1994, Inst. Bienes Culturales. 220 p. -- ᴿEpigraphica 57 (Faenza 1995) 341-4 (Valeria *Righini*).

c010 *Broise* Henri, *Jolivet* Vincent, Leonardo BUFALINI, Pirro LIGORIO et les antiquités du Pincio: CRAI (1995) 7-29; 11 fig,

c011 **Castriota** D., The Ara Pacis Augustae and the imagery of abundance in later Greek and early Roman Imperial art. Princeton 1995, Univ. xviii-326 p.; 91 fig. $ 45. 0-691-03715-9 [NTAb 40, p.550].

c012 *Chevallier* Raymond, Ostia antica; la città e il suo porto: *Archeo 9,118 (1994) 64-108.

c013 *Courtright* Nicola, The transformation of ancient landscape through the ideology of Christian reform in Gregory XIII's [1580 Vatican] Tower of the Winds: ZfK(unst)G 58 (1995) 526-541; 15 fig.

c014 *D'Ambra* Eve, Mourning and the making of ancestors in the [Capitoline Trajanic] Testamentum relief: AJA 99 (1995) 667-681; 14 fig.

c015 *Donderer* Michael, Zu den Häusern des Kaisers Augustus : MÉFRA 107 (1995) 621-660.

c016   *Esch* Arnold, Die Via Flaminia in der Landschaft .. Soracte, Otricoli: AW(elt) 26 (1995) 85-113; 43 fig.

c017   *Felici* Enrico, Anzio, un porto per [il luogo di nascita di] Nerone : ArVi 14,52 (1995) 56-62.

c018   **Hesberg** Henner von, *Panciera* Silvio, Das Mausoleum des Augustus; der Bau und seine Inschriften; AbhBayer ph/h 108, 1994 → 10,13160: ᴿA(nz)AW 48,1s (1995) 36-39 (T. *Lorenz*); CLR 45 (1995)

c019   **Holloway** H. Ross, The archaeology of early Rome and Latium 1994 → 10,13162: ᴿÉtCL 63 (19950 92s (J. *Poucet*).

c020   *Kazakov* M.M., ᴿ Rome on the way from paganism to Christianity; the altar of victory: VDI (1995,4) 161-174; Eng. 174.

c021   *Kellum* B.A., What we see and what we don't see; narrative structure and the Ara Pacis Augustae: *Art History 17,1 (Ox 1994) 26-45 [NTAb 39, p.276].

c022   *Lancaster* Lynne, The date of Trajan's Markets: an assessment in the light of some unpublished brick stamps: PBSR 63 (1995) 25-44;

c023   *Liberati* Anna M., *al.*, Così rivive la più antica Roma; il plastico della città arcaica al museo della civiltà romana: *Archeo 126 (1995) 24.27 (-33).

c024   **Menichetti** Mauro, Archeologia del potere; re, immagini e miti a Roma e in Etruria in età arcaica: BtArch 21. Mi 1994, Longrassi. 172 p.; ill.

c025   *Pavia* Carlo, *Pietrangeli* Carlo, Sotto il Palazzo della Cancelleria [... canale antico; tomba di console]: *ArVi 14, 52 (1995) 18-25.

c026   *Pavia* Carlo, *Ramieri* Anna Maria, Una caserma in Trastevere: *ArVi 14,49 (1995) 34-41.

c027   **Philipp** Hanna, Der grosse trajanische Fries 1991 → 9,14800*: ᴿGnom 67 (1995) 356-9 (T. *Schäfer*).

c028   a) *Pomponi* Massimo, La Colonna Traiana nelle incisioni di P.S. BARTOLI; contributi allo studio del monumento nel XVII secolo; -- b) *De Caprariis* Francesca, Due note di topografia romana: *RINASA 14s (1991s) 347-378; 23 fig. / 153-191; 21 fig.

c029   **Richardson** L.ᴶ, A new topographical dictionary of ancient Rome 1992 → 9,14801; 10,13170: ᴿJRS 85 (1995) 251-3 (R.J.A. *Wilson*, also on Steinby 1992); HZ 260 (1995) 173-5 (J. *Bleichen*).

c030   *Rizzo* Giorgio, *al.*, Le Palatin; vigna Barberini : MÉFRA 107 (1995) 459-496; 16 fig. [661-765, *Chausson* François].

Robinson O.F., Ancient Rome; city planning and administration 1992 → c902 infra.

c032   ᴱ**Steinby** Eva M., Lexicon topographicum urbis Romae I, A-C 1993 → 9,14803: ᴿAJA 99 (1995) 147-150 (R.B. *Ulrich*); At(h-Pavia) 83 (1995) 529s (S. *Maggi*); CLR 45 (1995) 135-7 (Catharine *Edwards*); RÉL 73 (1995) 343s (J.-C. *Richard*); Latomus 54 (1995) 198s (J. *Debergh*).

c033   *Tomei* Maria Antonietta, *Domus* oppure *lupanar* ? I materiali dallo scavo [1898, Giacomo] BONI della 'Casa Repubblicana' a ovest dell'Arco di Tito : MÉFRA 107 (1995) 549-619; 22 fig.; VIII fig.

Ziolkowski Adam, The temples of mid-Republican Rome 1992 → 8442 supra.

T9.7   Catacumbae

c034   **Bavoillot-Laussade** Colette, Une tombe sur la colline vaticane: Des chrétiens/Lieux saints. P 1995, Fayard. 150 p. F 98.-- ᴿE(spr)eV 105 (1995) 185s (H. *Platelle*).

c035 **Fiocchi Nicolai** Vincenzo, Santa Teodora di Rignano Flaminio: Catacombe di Roma e d'Italia 5. Vaticano 1995, Pontificia Commissione di Archeologia Sacra. 70 p.; 35 (color.) fig. -- [R]SMSR 61 (1995) 463s (Myla *Perraymond*).

c036 *Fiocchi Nicolai* Vincenzo, Una nuova catacomba presso 'Visentium' sul lago di Bolsena: APARA.R 65 (1992s) 23-40; 18 (foldout) fig.

c037 **Guarducci** Margherita, Le chiavi sulla pietra; studi, ricordi e documenti inediti intorno alla tomba di Pietro in Vaticano. CasM 1995, Piemme. 156 p. L[m] 26. -- [R]CivCatt 146 (1995,2) 528s (A. *Ferrua*, molto severo; un suo documento e delle foto pubblicati senza autorizzazione ..).

c038 **Guarducci** Margherita, Le reliquie di Pietro in Vaticano. R 1995, Poligrafico. 142 p.; bibliog. 135-9.

c039 **Nestori** Aldo, Repertorio delle pitture delle catacombe romane[2] [[1]1975]. Vaticano 1993, Pont. Ist. Arch. Cr. xii-220 p.; 36 pl. L[m] 145. -- [R]CivCatt 146 (1995,1) 205 (A. *Ferrua*).

c040 **Rutgers** L.V., The Jews in Late Ancient Rome [catacomb inscriptions]; evidence of cultural interaction in the Roman diaspora [< diss. Duke 1993, [D]*Meyers* E.]: ÉPR 126. Lei 1995, Brill. xx-283 p. *f* 135. 90-04-10269-8 [NTAb 40, p.185].

T9.8 *Roma*, ars palaeocristiana

c041 *Felle* Antonio E., Loci scritturistici nella produzione epigrafica romana: VetChr 32 (1995) 61-89

c042 [E]**Gauthier** Nancy, *Picard* Jean-Charles, Topographie chrétienne des cités de la Gaule des origines au milieu du VIIIe s., 8. Sens. P 1992, de Boccard. 157 p.; 14 maps. -- [R]Bo(nn)J 195 (1995) 842s (R. *Kaiser*).

c043 *Liverani* Paolo, Le colonne e il capitello in bronzo d'età romana dell'altare del SS.Sacramento in Laterano; analisi archeologica e problematica storica; APARA.R 65 (1992s) 75-125; 19 (foldout/color.) fig.

c044 *Sgarlata* Mariarita, Frühchristliche Archäologie in Sizilien; neue Forschungen und Entdeckungen: R(öm)Q 90 (1995) 147-182; 10 fig. (maps).

T9.9 *(Roma); imperium occidentale,* **Europa**

c045 *Hispania*: *Moret* Pierre, *al.*, Histoire et archéologie de la péninsule ibérique antique, Chronique V : REA 97 (1995) 253-443; index géographique 444-453.

c046 *Melita: Bondì* Sandro F., Malta: *Archeo 122 (1995) 52-95.

c047 *Paestum*: **Mertens** Dieter, Der alte Heratempel in Paestum und die archaische Baukunst in Unteritalien: DAI. Mainz 1993, von Zabern. xviii-193 p.; 92 fig.; 92 pl. + 4 color.; 17 foldouts. -- [R]RossArkh (1995,4) 187-191 (J.E. *Tchistjakov*).

c048 *Pompeii*: [E]**Eschenbach** Liselotte, Gebäudeverzeichnis und Stadtplan der antiken Stadt Pompeji. Köln 1993, Böhlau. xii-500 p., 3 foldouts. 3-412-03791-5. -- [R]Bo(nn)J 195 (1995) 740-3 (V. *Kockel*).

c049 -- **Iappolo** Giovanni, Le terme del Sarno a Pompei: 1992 → 10,13200: [R]At(henaeum) 83 (1995) 288s (Elena *Calandra*).

c050 -- **La Rocca** Eugenio, *al.*, [E]*Coarelli* Filippo, Pompeii; guida[2rev]. Mi 1994, Mondadori. 368 p.; ill.

c051 -- **Laurence** Ray, Roman Pompeii; space and society 1994 → 10,13199: [R*]CLOutlook 72 (1995) 108 (R.I. *Curtis*); GaR 42 (1995) 244 (N. *Spivey*).

c052 -- **Ohr** Karlfriedrich, Die Basilika in Pompeji 1991 → 10,13201: [R]A(nz)AW 48,1s (1995) 117-124 (W. *Wohlmayr*).

c053 -- *Strocka* Völker M., Das Bildprogramm des Epigrammzimmers in Pompeji: MDAI-R 102 (1995) 269-290; 9 (foldout) fig.; (color.) pl. 62-65.

   Wallace-Hadrill A., Houses and society in Pompeii and Herculaneum 1994 → c773.

c055 -- **Zanker** Paul, Pompei. T 1993, Einaudi. At(henaeum) 83 (1995) 282s (S. *Maggi* anche e soprattutto su CLARKE J. 1991).

c056 -- **Berry** Paul, The Christian inscription at Pompeii. Lewiston NY 1995, Mellen. xiv-60 p. 0-7734-8899-5.

c057 *Praeneste*: *Gatti* Sandra, *al.*, Alla riscoperta dell'antica Praeneste [mosaico del Nilo ...]: *Archeo 123 (1995) 100-5.

c058 *Syracusae*: *Lange* Judith, Siracusa, la città che ha vinto il tempo: *ArVi 14.,50 (1995) 18-35.

c059 *Tibur-Tivoli*: **MacDonald** William L., *Pinto* John A., Hadrian's villa and its legacy. NHv 1995, Yale Univ. 392 p. $ 55. 0-300-05381-9 [Arch-Boston 49/2, 68-73, A. *Wallace*].

c060 -- *Salza Prina Ricotti* Eugenia, *a)* Villa Adriana, un sogno fatto pietra: *Archeo 9.,117 (1994) 64-109 (→ 10,13213); -- *b)* Nascita e sviluppo di Villa Adriana: APARA-R 65 (1992s) 41-73; 29 (foldout) fig...

c061 *Vivaro*, archipelagus flegraeum: *Marazzi* Massimiliano, Un'isola nel golfo .. età micenea: *Archeo 127 (1995) 92-99.

XIX. Geographia biblica

U1   Geographica

c062 **Alcock** Susan E., Graecia capta; the landscapes of Roman Greece 1993 → 9,14839; 10,13214: [R]Antiquity 68 (1994) 162-5 (D.J. *Mattingly*); HZ 260 (1995) 179-181 (J. *Deininger*).

c063 *Alexander* Loveday, Narrative maps; reflections on the toponymy of Acts : → 159, [F]ROGERSON, J., Bible/Society; JSOT.s 200 (1995) 17-45; 46-48, toponym list; 49-55, 8 maps.

c064 [E]**Barker** Graeme, *Lloyd* John. Roman landscapes 1988/91 → 7,629; 10,13226: *JField 20 (1993) 109 (Susan E. *Alcock*).

c065 *Bartelmus* Rüdiger, Begegnung in der Fremde; Anmerkungen zur theologischen Relevanz der Berufungsvisionen .. Ex 3s Ezech 1ss: BN(otiz) 78 (1995) 21-38.

c066 [E]**Bimson** John J., Illustrated encyclopedia of Bible places; towns and cities, countries and states, archaeology and topography. Leicester 1995, Inter-Varsity. 319 p. 0-85110-657-9.

c067 *Carroué* F., Études de géographie et de topographie sumériennes III. L'Iturungal et le Sud sumérien: *AcSum 15 (1993) 11-69.

c068 *Elitzur* Yoel, [H] After all [as 1987], *gab** and not *geba'* [MAZAR B. 1940]: Tarbiz [61 (1991) 1-13 (*Galil* G.)] 63 (1993s) 267-272.

c069 *Gershevitch* Ilya, Linguistic geography and historical linguistics: Atti convegno Lincei 1994 (R 1994/2) 165-181.

c070 *Godart* Louis, Mediterraneo: *ArVi 14,51 (1995) 56-64.

c071 **Gomaà** Farouk, *al.*, Mittelägypten .. Topographie: TAVO B-69, 1991 → 8,g681; 9,14842*: [R]BiOr 52 (1995) 354-7 (D. *Kessler*).

c072 **González Echegaray** Joaquín, El Creciente Fértil y la Biblia 1991 → 7,e302 ... 10,13219: [R]EstB 53 (1995) 128 (J. *Mayoral*).

c073 *Goodblatt* David, [H] *Medinat hayam* - the coastal district [in Gittin 1,1 the Hellenistic diaspora, not foreign territory in general: Tarbiz 64 (1994s) 13-37; Eng. 1,v.

c074 **Gyselen** Rika, La géographie administrative de l'Empire sassanide; les témoignages sigillographiques. P 1989, Groupe Moyen-Orient. xx-166 p.; 4 pl. Fb 1200. -- [R]JNES 54 (1995) 305-7 (A.G. *Morony*).

c075 **Hennessy** Anne, The Galilee of Jesus. R 1994, Pont. Univ. Gregoriana. x-77 p. $ 12. -- [R]BThB 25 (1995) 45s (J.J. *Pilch*).

c076 *Holum* Kenneth, Palästina, [T]*Schäferdiek* Kurt: → 772, TRE 25 (1995) 591-9.

c077 **Jenkins** Simon, Nelson's 3-D Bible mapbook. Nv 1995, Nelson. 128 p.; 100+ colored maps. $ 10. 0-8407-1964-7 [ThD 43,274]

c078 *Kervran* Monique, Le Delta de l'Indus au temps d'Alexandre: CRAI (1995) 259-311; 14 fig.

c079 *a) Legras* Bernard, L'horizon géographique de la jeunesse grecque d'Égypte (IIIème siècle av. n.è. - VIème siècle de n.è.; -- *b) Worp* K.A., The Notitia Dignitatum and the geography of Egypt: → 674, 20th Papyrologist 1992/4, 165-176 / 463-8 + map.

c080 *Levy* Thomas E., *al.*, Denizens of the desert; geophysical imaging maps subterranean settlements in the hard hillsides of Israel's Negev desert: Archaeology 49,2 (Boston 1996) 36-40.

c081 [E]**Liverani** Mario, Neo-Assyrian geography: QuadGeogStor 5. R 1995, Univ. x-282 p.

c082 **Mackowski** Richard M., Cities of Jesus; a study of the 'Three Degrees of Importance' in the Holy Land. R 1995, Pontifical Oriental Institute. 114 p.; ill.

c083 *Marangio* Cesare, L'epigrafia nella ricerca topografica; edifici di culto ed aree sacre nella Regio Secunda (Apulia, Calabria): → 706*, JAT/RTA 4 (1993/4) 35-58; Eng. 213s.

c084 *Mayerson* Philip, A note on Iotabê and several other islands in the Red Sea: BASOR 298 (1995) 33-35.

c085 **Monmonier** Mark, Mapping it out; expository cartography for the humanities and social sciences. Ch 1993, Univ. 260 p.; 111 maps. $ 16 pa. 0-226-53417-0. -- [R]*JField 21 (1994) 516-520 (Eliza *McClennen*).

c086 **Müller** Gerfrid G.W., Studien zur Siedlungsgeographie und Bevölkerung des mittleren Osttigrisgebietes [Diss. Heidelberg 1990]: StAOr 7. Heid 1994, Orientverlag. xvi-323 p.; foldout map. 3-927552-19-3 [*OIAc 11,34].

c087 **Orth** Wolfgang, Die Diadochenzeit im Spiegel der historischen Geographie; Kommentar zu Karte B V 2: TAVO.b 80, 1993 → 9,12631: [R]HZ 261 (1995) 847s (J. *Wiesehöfer*).

c088 **Page** Charles R., *Volz* Carl A., The land and the book; an introduction to the world of the Bible 1993 → 9,14850; 10,13225 [RStR 22,151, W.M. *Schniedewind*]: [R]CThMi 22 (1995) 61 (S.A. *Knapp*: unsuccessful mixture).

c089 **Page** Charles R., Jesus and the land. Nv 1995, Abingdon. 201 p. £ 15. 0-687-00544-2. -- [R]*TBR 8,2 (1995s) 16 (L. *Houlden*: informative, uncritical).

c090 *Popko* Maciej, Zur Geographie des nördlichen Zentralanatoliens in der Hethiterzeit :
→ 84, ᶠHOUWINK TEN CATE, H., Studio (1995) 253-9.

c091 **Svensson** Jon, Towns and toponyms in the Old Testament, with special emphasis on
Joshua 14-21: CBOT 38. Sto 1994, Almqvist & W. 156 p.; map. 91-22-01581-7. --
ᴿProtest(antesimo) 50 (1995) 247 (J.A. *Soggin*).

c092 *Uval* Beth, Reading the landscape; Neot Kedumim -- the biblical landscape reserve in
Israel: *JPersp 49 (1995) 18-21 (-23, Streams of living water; the feast of Tabernacles and
the Holy Spirit).

c093 *Vandersleyen* C., L'Asie des Égyptiens et les îles de la Méditerranée orientale sous le
Nouvel Empire : OL(ov)P 25 (1994) 37-47.

U1.2 Historia geographiae

c094 **Aujac** Germaine, Claude PTOLÉMÉE, astronome, astrologue, géographe; connaissance
et représentation du monde habité. P 1993, 'CTHS'. 427 p.; ill.; maps. -- ᴿRÉA(nc) 97
(1995) 654s (P. *Arnaud*).

c095 **Barton** Tamsyn, Ancient astrology: Sciences of antiquity. L 1994, Routledge. 245
p. -- ᴿEikasmos 6 (1995) 349-351 (Anna *Maranini*).

c096 *Beitzel* B.J., Exegesis, dogmatics and cartography: a strange alchemy in earlier Church
traditions: *ArchBW 2,2 (1994) 8-21 [NTAb 39, p.272].

c097 *Blau* Joyce, Le Cagani: lori ou kurde ? [*Lor* est le nom pour un vaste territoire du
Zagros au Golfe, la plupart de parlers persans]: StIr 22 (1993) 93-119; Eng. 119.

c098 *Brodersen* Kai, Die geographischen Schriften des 'Nikephoros Blemmydes' [c.1200,
zitierend]; → 176, ᶠSCHMITT H., Rom & Osten 1995, 43-50; 2 fig.

c099 *Carroccia* Michele, Questioni di metodo nella lettura della Tabula Peutingeriana e
problemi della viabilità romana nel territorio abruzzese-molisano: JAT(opog) 5 (1995) 111-
130; 15 fig.; Eng. 211s.

c100 *Ceccherelli* Ignazio M., Le mappe del mondo antico : BeO(riente) 37 (1995) 33-48;
3 fig.

c101 **[Gautier] Dalché** Patrick G., La 'descriptio mappe mundi ' de HUGUES de Saint-Victor
1988 → 5,e821 ... 7,e320*: ᴿOrpheus 16 (1995) 233s (B. *Clausi*).

c102 ᴱ**Desreumaux** Alain, *Schmidt* Francis, Moïse géographe; recherches sur les
représentations juives et chrétiens de l'espace 1988 → 5.e823; 6,329: ᴿRTPh 127 (1995)
410s (C.-A. *Keller*),

c103 **Donner** H., The mosaic map of Madaba, an introductory guide 1992 → 8,g712 ...
9,13243: ᴿOS(tk) 44 (1995) 66s (O.F.A. *Meinardus*).

c104 **Harvey** P.D.A., Medieval maps. Toronto 1993. Univ. 96 p.; 77 fig. -- ᴿ*JMdvLat 5
(1995) 276-8 (M. *Lafferty*) [RHE 91,18*].

c105 **Hutton** William E., The topographical methods of PAUSANIAS: diss. Texas, ᴰ*Perlman
Paula J. Austin 1995. 349 p. 95-34814. - D(iss)AI 56 (1995s) p. 2225.

c106 *Lecoq* Danielle, Gog et Magog sur les mappemondes: MoBi 94 (1995) 36s

c107 *Panaino* Antonio, Uranographica iranica II; Avestan *hapta.srū* and *mₑrₑzu*-: Ursa Minor
and the North Pole ?; AfO 42s (1995s) 190-207; 3 star-maps.

c108 *Puskás* Ildikó, STRABO and his sources on India: → 10,48, Mem. HAHN I. 1993, 59-73.

c109 *Riley* Mark T., PTOLEMY's use of his predecessors' data: TPAPA 125 (1995) 221-250.

c110 ᴱ**Röllig** Wolfgang, Von der Quelle zur Karte; Abschlussbuch des Sonderfor-
schungbereich TAVO 1991 → 7,e346; DM 98: ᴿHZ 260 (1995) 514s (A. *Mehl*).

c111 **Romm** J.S., The edges of the earth in ancient thought; geography, exploration and fiction 1992 → 9,14887; 10,13260; £ 22.50; 0-691-06933-6: [R]JRS 85 (1995) 266s (Katherine *Clarke,* also on BEAGON M. 1992).

c112 [TE]**Silberman** Alain, ARRIANUS Flavius, Périple du Pont-Euxin: CBudé. P 1995, BLettres. xlvi-75 p.; bibliog. xxxvi-xlv. 2-251-00446-7.

c113 *Sturm* Dieter, Äusserungen arabischer Geographen des Mittelalters zur Verwendung von Termini: ZDMG 144 (1994) 15-26.

c114 **Syme** Ronald, Anatolica; studies in STRABO. Ox 1995, Clarendon. xxiii-396 p. 0-19-814943-3.

c115 *Tardieu* Michel, Lexicographie historique des deux mers [*baḥrayn,* marais de l'Euphrate quelques fois jusqu'à Mésène; une seule fois pour l'île actuelle]: RÉJ 154 (1995)

c116 *Thornton* John, Al di qua e al di là del Tauro; una nozione geografico di Alessandro Magno alla tarda antichità: RCCM 37 (1995) 97-126

c117 *Weippert* Manfred, [Peutinger IX 5 = Rabba 90 k S 'Amman] Rababatora: → 48, [F]DONNER, H., Meilenstein: ÄAT 30 (1995) 333-8.

c118 **Wöhrle** Georg, ANAXIMENES aus Milet; die Fragmente zu seiner Lehre. Stu 1993, Steiner. 88 p. -- [R]RTPh 127 (1995) 273 (S. *Imhoof*).

c119 *Zubarov* V.G., Distortions and the whole picture of the northern Pontic area in 'Guide to geography' by PTOLEMY: RossArkh (1995,3) 47-59; Eng. 59.

U1.4 Atlas -- maps

c120 **Aharoni** Yohanan, *Avi-Yonah* Michael, [3rev]*Rainey* A., Macmillan Bible Atlas 1993 → 9,14900; 10,13265: [R]BA 58 (1995) 239s (B.J. *Beitzel*).

c121 **Baladier** Charles, Atlante delle religioni. Mi c.1995, Garzanti. viii-610 p.; bibliog. 576-588. 88-11-34024-1.

c122 [E]**Fatás Cabeza** G., *al.*, Tabula imperii romani K-30 Madrid (Caesaraugusta-Clunia). M 1993, Cons. Sup. Inv. 339 p.; map. 84-7819-047-3. -- [R]AJA 99 (1995) 744s (R.E. *Knapp*).

c123 **Freeman-Grenville** G.S.P., Historical atlas of the Middle East 1993 → 9,14903; Simon & S (UK Kuperard): [R]BoL (1994) 35s (J.W. *Rogerson:* Allenby's Sinai command was only from 1917); JRAS (1995) 265s (D.O. *Morgan*); PEQ 127 (1995) 172s (P. *Dorrell*).

c124 **Grant** Michael, Atlas of classical history[5]. Ox 1994, UP. Unpaginated uncoloured maps. $ 17. 0-19-521074 [RStR 22,61, A.T. *Kraabel:* not for research, but a handy teaching tool].

c125 **Harpur** James, The atlas of [33 worldwide] sacred places; meeting points of heaven and earth. NY 1994, Holt. 140 p. $ 45 [BArR 21,5 (1995) 8].

c126 [TE]**Keel** Othmar, *Küchler* Max, Herders grosser Bibel-Atlas. FrB c.1995, Herder. 255 p. 3-451-26138-3.

c127 **Kopp** Horst, *Röllig* Wolfgang, Tübinger Atlas des Vorderen Orients; Register zu den Karten; General Index. Wsb 1994. Reichert. I. A-G, L-626 p; II. H-P, p. 627-1265; III. Q-Z + Sachindex, p. 1267-1894. 3-88226-800-X.

c128 **Pritchard** James B., [E]*White* L. Michael, The Harper concise atlas of the Bible [1987 → 3,e869, abridged] 1991 → 7,e362: [R]BA 57 (1994) 175s (B.J. *Beitzel*).

c129 [E]**Stezycki** Zenon, Atlas hierarchicus .. Ecclesiae Catholicae[5.]. W-Mödling 1992, Sankt-Gabriel. 118 + 122 p.; xii-63 maps. Sch 1880. -- [R]ThQ 175 (1995) 70s (R. *Reinhardt*).

c130 ^E**Strange** John, Bijbelatlas; historische kaarten van de bijbelse wereld [→ 5,e878],^T.
Kampen 1992, Kok. 63 p. *f* 35. -- ^RG(ereformeerd)TT 94 (1994) 42 (W. van der *Meer*).

c131 **Tsafrir** Y., *al.*, Tabula imperii romani, Iudaea - Palaestina 1994 → 10,13231: ^RPEQ
127 (1995) 176s (J. *Wilkinson*).

c132 **Wajntraub** Eva & Gimpel, Hebrew maps of the Holy Land 1992 → 10,13280: ^RBiRe
11,1 (1995) 15s (H. *Brodsky*).

U1.5 **Photographiae**

c133 *Cleave* Richard, Satellite revelations; new views of the Holy Land [computer-imaging]:
National Geographic 187,6 (1995) 88-105.

c134 **Kennedy** David, *Riley* Derrick, Rome's desert frontier from the air 1990 → 6,g164 ...
8,g769: ^RJNES 54 (1995) 55s (R. *Schick*).

c135 **Kochav** Sarah, Israel; splendors of the Holy Land. L 1995, Thames & H [NY Norton
$ 50]. 292 p.; 37 fig.; 400 color.ill. 0-500-01668-2 [ThD 42,373].

c136 **Milner** Moshe, *Salomon* Yehuda, Jerusalem of the heavens; the eternal city in bird's
eye view. J 1993, Alfa. 192 p.; color. ill. 965-474-000-1 [*OIAc 11,34].

c137 **Myers** J.W. & Eleanor E., *al.*, The aerial atlas of ancient Crete 1992 → 10,13284:
^R*JField 20 (1993) 392-4 (C. *Broodbank*).

c138 **Piccirillo** Michele, With Jesus in the Holy Land. R 1994, Arti Grafiche Garroni. 70 p.

c139 ^E**Schiller** Ely, The first photographs of Jerusalem and the Holy Land. J 1980, Ariel.
238 p.

c140 ^E**Tarragon** Jean-Michel de, Itinéraires bibliques; photographies de la collection de
l'École Biblique et Archéologique Française de Jérusalem début du XXe siècle. J 1995,
École Biblique. 92 p. 2-90-606275-8.

U1.6 **Guide-books,** *Führer*

c141 **Ball** Warwick, Syria; a historical and architectural guide → 10,13290: Buckhurst Hill
1994, Scorpion. £ 15: ^RBoL (1995) 37 (N. *Wyatt*: competently fills a distressing lacuna).

c142 **Burns** Ross, Monuments of Syria, an historical guide. NYU 1992. xvii-297 p.; 14
fig.; 79 maps. $ 95. -- ^RBuCanadMesop (c.1995) 38 (M. *Fortin*); JNES 54 (1995) 231s
(F.M. *Donner*: 'a wonderful and most useful book').

c143 **Buzzi** Giancarlo, Magna Graecia e Sicilia: Guide Archeologiche. Mi 1995, Mondadori.
240 p. 88-04-39705-5.

c144 **Damiano-Appia** Maurizio, Egitto e Nubia: Guide Archeologiche. Mi 1995.
Mondadori. 384 p. 88-04-39704-7.

c145 **Darke** Diana, Discovery guide to Jordan and the Holy Land. L 1993, Immel. 231 p.;
(colour.) fig. £ 13. -- ^RPEQ 127 (1995) 74s (W. *Ball*: one of the best among many
guides).

c145* **Duchet-Suchaux** Gaston, *Pastoureau* Michel, La Bible et les saints; guide iconographique [surtout pour la visite des églises et musées]. P 1990, Flammarion. 319 p.; 258
fig.: 32 color. pl. F 195. 2-08-011725-4. -- ^RRHE 90 (1995) 247s (J.-P. H.).

c146 Israele: Guide del Mondo. Mi 1993, Touring Club Italiano. 220 p. -- ^RRasIsr 60,3
(1993) 152s (Anna *Colombo*: spiacevoli errori di trascrizione).

c147 **Kinet** Dirk, Jordanien: Kunst- und Reiseführer. Stu 1992, Kohlhammer. 249 p; 20
phot.; 46 maps. DM 79. -- ^RAfO 42s (1995s) 323-5 (S. *Procházka*).

c148 **Röwekamp** Georg, Israel: ein Reisebegleiter zu den heiligen Stätten von Judentum, Christentum und Islam. FrB 1994, Herder. 250 p. DM 40. - [R]KuI(sr) 10 (1995) 186s (Julie *Goldberg*).

U1.7 Onomastica

c149 **Bonechi** Marco, I nomi geografici dei testi di Ebla: RépGéogCun 12/1, TAVO B-7/12. Wsb 1993.Reichert. xxli-423 p.; map. DM 92. 3-88226-587-6 [RStR 22,56, D.I. *Owen*: partly overlaps or reinterprets ARCHI-POMPONIO 1993 (→ 9,14932) which however includes some unpublished data].

c150 *a) Carruba* Onofrio, *Aḫḫiya* e *Aḫḫiyawā*, la Grecia e l'Egeo; -- *b) Singer* Itamar, The toponyms Tiwa and Tawa: → 84, [F]HOUWINK TEN CATE, H., Studio (1995) 7-21 / 271-4.

c151 *Dobbs-Allsopp* F.W., The syntagma of *bat* followed by a geographical name in the Hebrew Bible; a reconsideration of its meaning and grammar: CBQ 57 (1995) 451-470.

c152 *Elitzur* Yoel, Ruman in Judah [not Duman Jos 15,52; perhaps near Hebron]: IsrEJ 44 (1994) 123-8.

c153 **Frayne** Douglas R., The [(Salabikh-) Ebla] Early Dynastic list of geographical names: AOS 74, 1992 → 9,14939*: [R]AfO 42s (1995s) 222 (J.N. *Postgate*); OLZ 90 (1995) 162-9; map (R. *Englund*).

c154 **George** A.R., Babylonian topographical texts [< diss. Birmingham]: OLA 40, 1992 → 8,g790; 9,14940: [R]AfO 42s (1995s) 248-250 (M.J. *Geller*); BiOr 52 (1995) 449-451 (A. *Livingstone*); BSOAS 58 (1995) 540s (J.A. *Black*); WZKM 85 (1995) 284s (H. *Hunger*).

c155 *Görg* Manfred, Zu zwei asiatischen Ländernamen im Tempel von Soleb/Sudan [*Nulluaju, Arrapḫe*]: BN(otiz) 78 (1995) 5-8 (-10, sumerisches Fragment).

c156 *Görg* Manfred, Das Land Ta'idu in hieroglyphischer Schreibung: GöMiszÄg 141 (1994) 47s.

c157 **Hakkert** Adolf M., Lexicon of the Greek and Roman cities and place-names in antiquity 1s, 1992s → 8,14942: [R]Latomus 54 (1995) 435-7 (J. *Debergh*).

c158 **Liverani** Mario, Studies [1st = VO 5 (1982) 13-73, *Badalì* E., *al.*] on the Annals of Ashurnasirpal II: 2. Topographical analysis; *QGeogSto 4, 1992 →9,14943: L[m] 35: [R]AfO 42s (1995s) 235s (G. *Frame*: highly favorable); JAOS 115 (1995) 126s (H.D. *Galter*).

c159 *a) Pellegrini* Giovan Battista, Il contributo della toponomastica alle ricerche topografiche ed archeologiche; -- *b) Alfieri* Nereo, Le fonti letterarie antiche; -- *c) Nicolet* Claude, Les 'mégapoles' méditerranéennes: → 706*, JAT/RTA 4 (1993/4) 23-34 9-22 / 7s; all Eng. 212s.

c160 **Schmitt** Götz, Siedlungen Palästinas in griechisch-römischer Zeit; Ostjordanland, Negeb und (in Auswahl) Westjordanland: TAVO B-93. Wsb 1995, Reichert. 171 p.; Bibliog. 358-370. 3-920153-62-6.

c161 *Shtober* Shimon, [H] Geographic and topographic aspects in Japhet BEN ALI's translation and commentary to the Bible: → 10,331a, 11th Jewish 1994. A-151-8.

c162 *Thissen* Heinz J., Varia onomastica: GöMiszÄg 141 (1994) 89-95.

c163 **Thompson** T.I., *al.*, Toponymie palestinienne Acre/J. 1988. -- [R]AulaO 12 (1994) 246s (G. del *Olmo Lete*).

c164 **Vallat** François, (*Groneberg* B.), Les noms géographiques des sources suso-élamites: TAVO B-7/11, 1993, Reichert → 9,14948; 10,13301; DM 88 [RStR 22,58, D.I. *Owen*]. -- [R]WO 26 (1995) 202-5 (Florence *Malbran-Labat*).

c165   *Van Minnen* Peter,   Deserted villages [Soknopaiou Nesos and later Karanis, in Fayûm Arsinoite nome]: BASPAP 32 (1995) 41-55; map 56.

c166   *Zadok* Ran,   Notes on Syro-Palestinian toponymy and anthroponymy: UF 27 (DIETRICH 60. Gb. 1995) 627-640.

U2.1 Geologia: soils, mountains, volcanoes, earthquakes

c167   *Amiran* D., *al.*,   Earthquakes in Israel and adjacent areas; macroseismic observations since 100 B.C.E.: IEJ 44 (1994) 260-205, updating 1950s [NTAb 40, p.91].

c168   *a) Dall'Aglio* Pier Luigi, Topografia antica e geomorfologia; - *b) Belvedere* Oscar, La ricognizione sul terreno: → 706*, JAT/RTA 4 (1993/4) 59-68 / 69-75; bibliog. 77-84; Eng. 214.

c169   *Ito* Agnès Yoshié, Les sept montagnes de Jésus dans saint Matthieu: LV(itae).F 49 (1994) 413-423; Eng. 423.

c170   *Lapini* Walter,   SENECA e il terremoto di Delo; alcuni esempi di confusione tra assestamento geografico e movimento tellurico: Maia 37 (1995) 183-200.

c171   **Minear** Paul S.,   The Golgotha earthquake; three witnesses.   Cleveland 1995, Pilgrim. xiv-139 p. 0-8298-1070-6.

c172   **Neev** David, *Emery* K.O.,   The destruction of Sodom, Gomorrah, and Jericho. NY 1995, Oxford-UP. xii-175 p.; bibliog. 151-163. $ 30. 0-19-509094-2 [ThD 43,378].

c173   *Papazachos* B.C.,   Historical earthquakes in Greece: PACT 45, 1991/5, 481-6; 2 fig.

c174   *Willemsen* Mick,   L'île d'Ischia et les vagues de Cumes; essai de volcanologie appliquée à l'histoire de la Campanie: RAHAL(ov) 27 (1994) 9-19.

U2.2 *Hydrographia*; rivers, seas, salt

c175   **Aicher** Peter J.,   Guide to the aqueducts of ancient Rome.   Wauconda IL 1995, Bolchazy-Carducci. xiii-183 p. 0-86516-271-9.

c176   *Baslez* Marie-Françoise,   Fleuves et voies d'eau dans l'Anabase: Pallas 43 (1995) 79-88; Eng. 88.

c177   *Belli* Oktay,   Neue Funde urartäischer Bewässerungsanlagen in Ostanatolien [c. 100 k N & S Van]: → 23, [F]BOEHMER R.M., Beiträge 1995, 19-48; 32 fig. (maps); pl. 2-10.

c178   **Blottière** Alain,   L'oasis, Siwa.   P 1992, Quai Voltaire.   177 p. 2-87653-118-6.

c179   **Bodan** Giulia, *al.*,   Utilitas necessaria; sistemi idraulici nell'Italia romana, [E]*Riera* I. -- Il sottosuolo nel mondo antico.   Mi 1994, Quarta Dimensione. xxxi-565 p.; ill.

c180   *Boëdec* François, Les guerres de l'eau au Moyen-Orient: Études 382 (1995) 5-14; maps.

c181   **Bonneau** Danielle,   Le régime administratif de l'eau du Nil 1993 → 9.14959; 10,13309: [R]BiOr 52 (1995) 661-3 (D. *Rathbone*).

c182   *Bonneau* Danielle † ,   Le régime administratif de l'eau du Nil dans l'Égypte grecque, romaine et byzantine; but recherché et problèmes posés: → 674, 20th Papyrologist 1992/4, 474-7.

c183   [E]**Brink** E. van den, The Nile Delta in transition 1990/2 → 8,703: [R]JAOS 115 (1995) 303s (Elizabeth *Finkenstaedt*).

c184   **Bruun** Christer,   The water supply of ancient Rome 1991 → 8,g814; 10,13310: [R]Latomus 54 (1995) 715s (M. *Cebeillac Gervasoni*); RB(elg)PH 73 (1995) 211 (H. *Devijver*: excellent).

c185 *Corbett* John H., Muddying the water; metaphors for exegesis [taken from various aspects of water]: → 10,322, Hellenization 1991/4, 205-221.

c186 **Crouch D.P.**, Water management in ancient Greek cities 1993 → 9,14961; 10,13313; xx-380 p., 126 fig. £ 60. 0-19-507280-4. -- [R]CLB 71,1 (1995) 48s (A.J. *Papalas*); CLR 45 (1995) 128-130 (E.J. *Owens*).

c187 **Evans** Harry N., Water distribution in ancient Rome; the evidence of FRONTINUS 1994 → 10,13315; $39.50: [R]CLB 71,1 (1995) 47s (M.K. *Thornton*); Phoenix 49 (Tor 1995) 279-282 (C. *Bruun*).

c188 *Garbrecht* Günter, *Peleg* Yehuda, The water supply of the desert fortresses in the Jordan valley: BA 57 (1994) 161-171; ill.

c189 *Grewe* Klaus, *al.*, Die antiken Flussüberbauungen von Pergamon und Nysa (Türkei): AW(elt) 25 (1994) 348-352; 11 fig.

c190 *Harverson* Michael, Watermills in Iran ['horizontal' from as early as the more complicated 'Vitruvian']: Iran 31 (1993) 149-177; 8 fig. (map).

c191 **Hehmeyer** I., *Schmidt* J., Irrigation at Ma'rib: Antike Technologie, Sabäische Wasserwirtschaft 1; Yemen. Mainz c.1993, von Zabern. ... 3-8053-1215-6. -- [R]BiOr 52 (1995) 820-3 (A.Y. *al-Hassan*).

c192 **Hemker** Christiane, Altorientalische Kanalisation; Untersuchungen zu Be- und Entwässerungsanlagen im mesopotamisch-syrisch-anatolischen Raum: A(bh)DOG 22, 1993 → 9,14697: [R]BiOr 52 (1995) 475-8 (G.R.H. *Wright*); OLZ 90 (1995) 517-522 (P. *Werner*).

c193 **Hodge** A. Trevor, Roman aqueducts and water supply. L 1992, Duckworth. viii-504 p. -- [R]Phoenix 49 (Tor 1995) 91-9 (C. *O'Connor*).

c194 *Huddleston* John R., 'Who is this that rises like the Nile ?' [Jer 46,7]; some Egyptian texts on the inundation and a prophetic trope: → 59, [F]FREEDMAN D.N., Fortunate 1995, 338-363.

c195 *Kennedy* David, Water supply and use in the southern Hauran, Jordan: *JField 22 (1995) 275-290: 12 fig.

c196 **Kleiss** Wolfram, Brücken und Dämme in Südwest-. Nordost- und Südiran: AMI(ran) 28 (1995s) 347-366: 27 fig.; pl. 29-46.

c197 **Knörnschild** Lutz, Zur Geschichte der Nilwassernutzung in der ägyptischen Landwirtschaft von den Anfängen bis zur Gegenwart [Diss. Leipzig 1993]: *LpBeitOrF 1. Fra 1993, Lang. 284 p. 3-631-44755-8 [*OIAc 11,29].

c198 *Plazenet* L., Le Nil et son delta dans les romans grecs: Phoenix 49 (Tor 1995) 5-22.

c199 **Rattue** James, The living stream; holy wells in historical context. Woodbridge 1995, Beydell. viii-138 p.; bibliog. 150-177. 0-85115-601-0.

c200 *Redmount* Carola A., The Wadi Tumilat and the 'canal of the Pharaohs': JAOS 54 (1995) 127-135.

c201 **Said** Rushim, The river Nile; geology, hydrology and utilization. Ox 1993, Pergamon. £ 75.

c202 **Schnitter** Nicholas J., A history of dams; the useful pyramids. Rotterdam 1994, Balkema. xvi-266 p.; 203 fig. 90-5410-149-0 [*OIAc 11,40].

c203 *Taylor* Rabun, A citeriore ripa aquae; aqueduct river crossings in the ancient city of Rome: PBSR 63 (1995) 75-103: 9 fig.

c204 **Tölle-Kastenbein** Renate, Das archaische Wasserleitungsnetz für Athen und seine späteren Bauphasen; Bildband Archäologie 19. Mainz 1994, von Zabern. 120 p.; ill.; foldouts. 2-8053-1619-4.

c205 *Ussishkin* David, The water-systems of Jerusalem during Hezekiah's reign: → 48, [F]DONNER, H., Meilenstein: ÄAT 30 (1995) 289-303 + 4 fig.

c206 *Van Lepp* Jonathan, Evidence for artificial irrigation in Amratian art: JA(m)RCE(g) 32 (1995) 197-209; 20 fig.

U2.3 Clima, pluvia

c207 ᴱ**Bar-Yosef** O., *Kra* R.S., Late Quaternary chronology and palaeoclimates of the Eastern Mediterranean [< Tucson radiocarbon conference 1991]. Tucson 1994, Univ. Arizona. 371p. -- ᴿPaléor 21,2 (1995) 143-6 (P. *Sanlaville*).

c208 *Bonneau* Danielle †, La sécheresse en Égypte ancienne et ses conséquences institutionnelles (la terre *chérsos* et la terre *ábrochos*): → 10.443, Grund/Boden im Altägypten 1990/4, 15-29.

c209 **Dehon** P.J., Hiems latina; études sur l'hiver dans la poésie latine, des origines á l'époque de Néron: Coll. Latomus 219. Bru 1993, RÉL. -- ᴿCLR 45 (1995) 33s (Alison *Sharrock*).

c210 ᴱ**Meijer** D. (ᶠVAN LOON M.), Natural phenomena 1992 → 8,727*: ᴿSyria 72 (1995) 273s (J.-L. *Huot*).

U2.5 *Fauna,* animalia

c211 ᴱ**Aafke** M., ARISTOTLE De animalibus; Michael SCOT's Arabic-Latin translation 3, books XV-XIX: Aristoteles Semitico-Latinus 5. Lei 1992, Brill. xxviii-504 p. 90-04-09603-5. -- ᴿZDMG 145 (1995) 175 (H. *Eisenstein*).

c212 *Asmussen* Jes P., Some bird names in the Judeo-Persian translations of the Hebrew Bible: → 72, ᶠGREENFIELD J., Solving 1995, 3-5.

c213 *Baum* Nathalie, *Sntr*; une révision [encens de Boswellia plutôt que résine de pistache/térébinthe]: RdÉ 45 (1994) 17-39; 1 fig.; Eng. 39.

c214 *Behrmann* Almuth, Überlegungen zur Darstellung von Nilpferden im Papyrus-dickicht in den Gräbern des Alten Reiches: GöMisz 147 (1995) 15-18.

c215 *Belluccio* Adriana, Les poissons célestes: → 721, 7° Egyptol. 1995, 15.

c216 ᵀᴱ**Bertier** Janine, ARISTOTE, Histoire des animaux: Folio-Essais 241. P 1994, Gallimard. 590 p. 2-07-03877-8. -- ᴿANCL 64 (1995) 290s (S. *Byl*).

ᴱ**Bodson** Liliane, Histoire de la domestication 1991/2 → 667 supra.

c217 *Bona* Isabella, Alcune osservazioni sul simbolismo antropologico degli animali in AMBROGIO: → 142, ᶠOROZ RETA J., I, Helm 44 (1993) 489-496.

c218 *Borsje* J., *ó Cróinín* D., [Augustine in Irish on Leviathan Job 40s] A monster in the Indian ocean: NedThT 49 (1995) 1-11.

c219 **Bosetti** Elena, La tenda e il bastone; figure e simboli della pastorale biblica: Narrare la Bibbia 1. 1992 → 8,1145: ᴿSBF*LA 45 (1995) 611-6 (G.C. *Bottini*, anche su 2, NICCACCI A., Sapienza).

c220 *Bresciani* Edda, Nuovi statuti demotici di 'Confraternite' dalla necropoli di Coccodrilli a Tebtynis (P.Vogl[iano] demot. Inv. 77 e Inv. 78); → 714, E(g)VO 17 (1994) 49-69; foldout photo.

c221 *Briquel* Dominique, Des comparaisons animales homériques aux guerriers-fauves indo-européens: Kernos 8 (1995) 21-39.

c222 *Celle* Caroline, La femme et l'oiseau dans la céramique grecque: Pallas 42 (1995) 113-128.

c223 **Charbonneau-Lassay** Louis, Il bestiario di Cristo, [T]*Paluzzi* Maria Rita, *Marinese* Luciana, 1994 → 10,13352; 1157 fig.; L[m] 300: [R]CiVi 50 (1995) 102 (S. *Spartá*); VP(ens) 78 (1995) 233-6 (I.M. *Somma di Galesano*.

c224 *a) Charvát* P., Pig, or, On ethnicity in archaeology; -- *b) Hruška* B., Die Zugtiere in den altsumerischen Wirtschaftsurkunden: ArOr 62 (1994) 1-6 / 7-16

c225 *Ciccarese* Maria Pia, Il parto della donnola [weasel: through the mouth; conception through the ear (*Conceptio per aurem* 1992 → 8,e40 ... 10,1190); hence unclean in Lev 11,29]; da Aristotele al Fisiologo: ASEs 12 (1995) 377-392 [NTAb 40, p.472].

c226 *Courtils* Jacques de, Un nouveau bas-relief archaïque [de lion] de Xanthos: RAr (1995) 337-364; 4 fig.

c227 **Cowen** Jill Sanchia, *Kalila wa dimna*; an [Iranian] animal allegory of the Mongol court: Istanbul Univ. album. Ox 1989, UP. xiii-176 p.; 60 fig.; 26 pl. -- [R]JNES 54 (1995) 72-74 (Priscilla P. *Soucek*, also on SWIETOCHOWSKI M. 1989).

c228 [E]**Delvaux** Luc, *Warmanbol* Eugène, Les divins chats d'Égypte [art. de conférence d'exposition] 1991 → 7,a781: [R]DiscEg 30 (1994) 197-9 (Geraldine *Pinch*).

c229 *Depew* David J., Humans and other political animals in ARISTOTLE's History of Animals: Phronesis 40 (1995) 156-181.

c230 *Dor* Menahem, [H] Falconiformes (raptors): BetM 40,1 (140, 1994) 71-75.

c231 *Dubielzig* Uwe, *kynámuia/kynómuia*, Varianten eines Wortes oder zwei Wörter ?: Glotta 72 (1994/5) 44-57: both mean 'dog-fly', but the *-a-* form was of independent 'skoptisch' origin.

c232 *DuQuesne* Terence, Raising the serpent power; some parallels between Egyptian religion and Indian Tantra : → 191, [F]STRICKER, B., Hermes: DiscEg.sp.2 (1995) 53-63 + 9 fig.

c233 **Eaton** John, The circle of creation; animals in the light of the Bible. L 1995, SCM. 116 p. £ 7. 0-334-02619-9. -- [R]E(xp)T 107 (1995s) 159 (C.S. *Rodd*: charming).

c234 *Englund* Robert K., Late Uruk pigs and other herded animals → 23, [F]BOEH-MER R.M., Beiträge 1995, 121-122; 8 fig.

c235 *García Recio* Jesús, 'La fauna de las ruinas', un tópos literario de Isaías: EstB 53 (1995) 53-96; Eng. 55.

c236 *Goodfriend* Elaine A., Could *keleb* in Dt 23:19 actually refer to a canine ? [and not a male cult prostitute]: → 130, [F]MILGROM J., Pomegranates 1995, 381-397.

c237 **Gundel** Hans G., Zodiakos, Tierbilder 1992 → 9,15004; 10,13362: [R]AnCL 64 (1995) 404-6 (A. *Deman*).

c238 *a) Gurshtein* A.A., [R] Zodiac and the sources of European culture; -- *b) Kurtik* G.Ye., [R] History of Zodiac according to cuneiform sources: VDI 212 (1995) 153-161 / 175-188 [-199, *al.*; 200 Eng.].

c239 *Haarmann* Ulrich, Krokodile aus Holz und Krokodile aus Marmor; altägyptisches in einem marokkanischen Pilgerbericht des vierzehnten Jahrhunderts: → 48, [F]DONNER, H., Meilenstein: ÄAT 30 (1995) 60-72.

c240 *Heinen* Heinz, Ägyptische Tierkulte und ihre hellenischen Protektoren: → 10,145, [F]WINTER E., Aspekte 1994, 157-168.

c241 *Hengstl* Joachim, Zur Boden-Nutzung im römischen Ägypten; Fischerei-Pacht-Verträge: → 10.443, Grund/Boden im Altägypten 1990/4, 275-284.

c242 *Hillard* Kent, niga sá.u[11] [sheep-] fattening grade in Ur III texts: ZA(ss) 85 (1995) 8-18.

c243 *Huot* J.-L., De leonibus [franç.]: → 10,81, [F]MEYER L. de, 52 Réflexions 1994, 277-282; 2 fig.

c244 EJanowski Bernd, al., Gefährten und Feinde des Menschen, das Tier 1993 → 9,287
      (15013, 5 items); 10,13368: RZkT 117 (1995) 104 (R, Oberforcher).

c245 Kantorovitch A.R., One of the hoofed animals images in the Scythian animal style:
      RossArkh (1995,4) 45-55; Eng. 55 'elk-goat'.

c246   Keith A.J. & Massey-Gillespie Kevin,   Semitic quadriliteral animal terms; an
      explanation: JNWS 21,1 (1995) 83-91.

c247 Koenen Klaus, 'Süsses geht vom Starken aus' (Ri 14,14); Vergleiche zwischen Gott
      und Tier im Alten Testament: EvTh 55 (1995) 174-197.

c248 EKozloff Arielle P., a) Animals in ancient art from the Leo Mildenberg collection.
      Cleveland 1981, Museum of art.   ix-207 p. 0-910386-65-X. -- b) , with Mitten D.,
      Sguaitamatti M.; More animals .. [c) Walker A., Part III. 1996]. Mainz 1986, von Zabern.
      [vi-] 58 p. 3-8053-0927-9.

c249 Kürzdörfer Klaus, Das Harren der Kreatur, das biblische Mensch-Tier-Verhält-nis:
      LM(on) 32,3 (1995) 23-27.

c250 Kusatman Berrin, The origins of pig domestication with particular reference to the
      Near East: diss. Univ. College Inst.Arch. L 1992. vi-454 p. -- *OIAc 11,30.

c251 La Penna Antonio, Gli animali come strumenti di guerra (LUCREZIO V,1297-1349): →
      10,42, FGIGANTE M., Storia 1994, 333-345.

c252 Lockwood W.B., Lynx; the motivation of the name [lux 'light' for color of body; eyes
      no brighter than cat's; intense vision a myth]: Glotta 72 (1994/5) 41-42.

c253 Mayoral Juan Antonio, El uso simbólico-teológico de los animales en los profetas del
      exilio: EstB 53 (1995) 317-363; Eng. 317.

c254 Melville Charles, The Chinese Uighur animal calendar in Persian historiography of the
      Mongol period: Iran 232 (1994) 83-98.

c255 Michel Simone,   Der Fisch in der skythischen Kunst; zur Deutung skythischer
      Bildnisinhalte [Diss. Hamburg 1994 → 10,13380]: EurHS 38/52. Fra 1995, Lang. 274 p.;
      71 fig. 3-631-48081-4.

c256 Müller Hans-Peter,   Das Problem der Tierbezeichnungen in der althebräischen
      Lexikographie: StEpL 12 (1995) 135-147.

c257 Munier Charles, Pour une relecture de l'Ecbasis [cujusdam] captivi [per tropologiam;
      renard d'Ésope 72; Eng. 1964, TZeydel E.]: RevSR 69 (1995) 202-215 . 463-480; Eng. 271
      . 534.

c258 Nightingale Tom, Hill Mike, Birds of Bahrain. L 1993, Immel. 283 p.; 175 pl.; 5
      maps. £ 45. -- RJRAS (1995) 116s (G.R. Smith).

c259 Osten-Sacken E. von der, Wild als Opfertier: → 10,80, FMAYER-OPIFICIUS Ruth,
      Beschreiben 1994, 235-254 + 18 fig. (Rollsiegel).

c260   Pastor de Arozena Barbara, Metaxa 'raw silk' -- an exotical word ? [rather ma
      'moth'+ < Lat. texere (Gk. téktōn, Sansk.*tekh); only mulberry-worms spin cultivated silk,
      but others too spin cocoons]: Hermes 122 (1994) 505s.

c261 Paton David, Animals of ancient Egypt: Materials for a 'sign list', E. San Antonio
      1994, Van Siclen [= Princeton 1925]. 37 p. 0-933175-37-X [*OIAc 11,36].

c262 Perpillou Jean-Louis, Quelle sorte de therion fut DÉMOSTHÈNE ? [dans l'invective, non
      'monstre' mais petit parasite nuisible, aussi cancer]: RPh(lgLH) 69 (1995) 263-8; Eng .
      428, 'vermin'.

c263 a) Pintus Maria Giovanna, Il bestiario del diavolo; l'esegesi biblica nelle Formulae spi-
      ritalis intellegentiae di EUCHERIO di Lione; -- b) Curletto Silvio,Temi e trasformazioni nella
      favola del leone malato e del lupo scorticato: Sandalion 12s (1989s) 99-114 / 115-138.

c264 ^E**Postgate** N., *Powell* M., Domestic animals of Mesopotamia: *BSumAg 7 (c. 1993). vi-258p. -- ^RArOr 62 (1994) c.343 (B. *Hruška*); JAOS 115 (1995) 729s (B.R. *Foster*).

c265 **Pury** Albert de, Homme et animal Dieu les créa; l'AT et les animaux [= 1983, deutsch 1992]; Essais Bibliques 25, 1993 → 9,15035; 10,13383: ^RFV 93,2 (1994) 91s (B. *Keller*); RB(elg)PH 73 (1995) 164s (H. *Limet*); RTPh 127 (1995) 98s (D. *Faivre*).

c266 *Qimron* Elisha, ^H Chickens in the Temple Scroll (11QT^c): Tarbiz 64 (1994s) 473-6; 4,v: prohibited in Jerusalem. -- [Birds: Leš 58 (1994s) 389.]

c267 *Riede* Peter, *a)* David und der Floh [flea]; Tiere und Tiervergleiche in den Samuelbüchern: BN(otiz) 77 (1995) 86-115 + 6 fig. -- *b)* Forschungsprojekt zu Tier- und Pflanzenwelt der Bibel: ZNW 86 (1995) 286.

c268 *Roitman* Adolfo D., ^H 'Crawl upon your belly' (Gen.3:14) -- the physical aspect of the serpent in early Jewish exegesis: Tarbiz 64 (1994s) 157-173 + 12 fig.; Eng.2,v.

c269 *Römer* W.H.P., Eine Beschwörung in sumerischer Sprache gegen die Folgen von Schlangen- und Hundebiss, sowie Skorpionenstich: → 185, ^FSODEN W.von, Vom Alten Orient (1995) 413-423.

c270 *Schlichting* Robert, Vom Entenvogel zum Entenvogelboot: → 10,137, ^FWESTENDORF W. 1994, 183-7 + 5 fig.

c271 *Shaheen* Alaael-din M., Royal hunting scenes on scarabs: DiscEg 30 (1994) 147-163 + 6 fig.

c272 *Simpson* St.John, Mouse traps in Mesopotamia: *OrExp 2 (1993) 18-20; 2 fig.

c273 **Sorabji** Richard, Animal minds and human morals; the origins of the western debate. Ithaca 1993, Cornell Univ. 267 p. -- ^RC(las)B 71,1 (1995) 62-64 (O. *Goldin*).

c274 *a) Sparkes* Brian, A pretty kettle of fish [vase-paintings]; -- *b) Purcell* Nicholas, Eating fish; the paradoxes of seafood: → 710, Food 1992/5, 150-161; 9 fig, / 132-149. ^FSCHLERATH B., ^E*Hänsel* B., Die Indogermanen und das Pferd 1992/4 → 704.

c275 ^E**Stefani** Piero (p.117-130; 125s su Giobbe), Gli animali e la Bibbia; i nostri fratelli minori [Biblia, Spoleto 23-25 aprile 1993] 1994 → 10,306: ^RPaVi 39,6 (1994) 57s (A. *Rolla*). **Tiller** Patricia A., Commentary on the animal apocalypse of 1 Enoch 1993 → 6761

c276 *Torre* Chiara, Il cavallo immagine del Sapiens in SENECA: Maia 37 (1995) (349-) 371-8.

c277 **Voisenet** Jacques, Bestiaire chrétien ..(V^e-XIe siècle. 1994. -- ^RMélSR 52 (1995) 337-9 (H. *Platelle*).

c278 *West* M.I., Elephant: Glotta 70 (1992) 125-8.

c279 *Westendorf* Wolfhart, Schlange und Schlangenkraut: → 10,145, ^FWINTER E., Aspekte 1994, 265-7.

c280 *Witakowski* W., The miracles of Jesus [notably on animals and plants, 9-13; 20s; 23s; 26s]; an Ethiopian apocryphal gospel: *Apocrypha 6 (1995) 27-298 [NTAb 40, p.503].

c281 *Witczak* Krzysztof T., New findings in Thracian etymology I-II. Terms for 'goat' and 'mouse': OrpheusT 5 (1995) 35-38.

c282 *a)* **Wright** Robert, The moral animal, why we are the way we are; the new science of evolutionary psychology. ... Pantheon. 467 p. $ 27.50. - *b)* **Midgley** Mary, The ethical primate; humans, freedom, and morality. NY c. 1995 Routledge. 193 p. $ 23. -- ^R*CWeal 122,11 (1995) 26s (D. *O'Brien*, both).

U2.7   *Flora*;   **plantae biblicae et antiquae**

c283 *Amadasi Guzzo* Maria Giulia, Note su un 'venditore di canna pura' in CIS 1,3889:
       StEpL 12 (1995) 3-11.
c284 *Amigues* Susanne, Végétation et cultures du Proche-Orient dans l'Anabase: Pallas 43
       (1995) 61-78; Eng. 78.
c285 ᴱ**Amouretti*** M.-C., *Comet* G., Des hommes et des plantes; plantes méditerranéennes,
       vocabulaire et usages anciens; Table-ronde Aix-en-Provence, mai 1992/3 → 10,486; F 120;
       2-85399-316-7:   ᴿLatomus 54 (1995) 201 (R. *Chevallier*); RÉA(nc) 97 (1995) 663s
       (Claudine *Leduc*).
c286 **Barakat** Haya N., *Baum* Nathalie, La végétation antique de Douch (oasis de Kharga),
       une approche microbotanique: IFAO-DF 27, 1992 → 8,g931; 10,13393; 107 fig.; F 200. --
       ᴿCÉg 70 (1995) 163-5 (P.P. *Koemoth*).
c287 *Baruch* Uri, ᴴ Palynological evidence for human impact upon the flora of the land of
       Israel: Qadmoniot 27 (1994) 47-63.
c288 **Baum** Nathalie, Arbres et arbustes de l'Égypte ancienne; la liste de la tombe thébaine
       d'Inéni (N° 81): OLA 31. xix-384 p.
c289 *Belluccio* Adriana, La pianta del dio Min [silphium, lattuga afrodisiaca]; la sua
       funzione sul piano mitico-rituale: DiscEg 31 (1995) 15-34; 7 fig.
c290 **Berlin** Brent, Ethnobiological classification; principles of categorization of plants and
       animals in traditional [illiterate] society. Princeton 1992, Univ. xvii-335 p- $ 45. -- ᴿLg
       71 (1995) 160-3 (R. *Sokal*).
c291 *Betrò* Maria Carmela, Il demotico, la lessicografia botanica e gli incensi: → 714,
       E(g)VO 17 (1994) 39-48.
c292 *Betz* Otto, Der Garten und der Traum von Paradies; oder, Die Spuren des nie ganz
       verlorenen Paradieses: Symb 12 (Fra 1995) 13-25.
c293 *Bloch* Ariel A., The cedar and the palm tree; a paired male/female symbol in Hebrew
       and Aramaic: → 72, ᶠGREENFIELD J., Solving 1995,13-17.
c294 **Blunt** Wilfrid, *Stearn* William T., The art of botanical illustration[2rev]. Woodbridge
       1994, Antique Collectors. 348 p.; ill.
c295 **Brewer** Douglas J., *Redford* Donald & Susan, Domestic plants and animals; the
       Egyptian origins: The Natural History of Egypt. Wmr 1994, Aris & P. 149 p.; 94 fig. £ 40;
       pa. £ 30. 0-85668-584-4; -5-2 [*JSStEg 21s (1991s) 113]. -- ᴿCÉg 70 (1995) 160-2 (P.P.
       Koemoth, aussi sur GERMER R. 1989.
c296 ᴱ**Carroll-Spillecke** Maureen, Der Garten von der Antike bis zum Mittelalter: KuGaW
       57, 1992 → 9,15054; DM 78. -- ᴿAnCL 64 (1995) 406-8 (Janine *Balty*); ZAW 107 (1995) 157
       (M. *Köckert*).
c297 *Cathcart* Kevin J., The trees, the beasts and the birds; fables, parables, and allegories
       in the Old Testament; → 55, ᶠEMERTON J., Wisdom 1995, 212-221.
c298 *Feliks* Yehuda, The incense of the tabernacle, ᵀ*Wright* David B.: → 130, ᶠMILGROM
       J., Pomegranates 1995, 125-149: 12 different Hebrew words (rabbinic *aparsemôn*) all refer
       to Commifora opobalsamum.
c299 **French** R., Ancient natural history; histories of nature: Sciences of Antiquity 1. L
       1994, Routledge. xxii-355 p.; 33 pl £ 16. -- ᴿCLR 45 (1995) 403s (J.F. *Healy*).
c300 **Hepper** F. Nigel, (Baker → 9,15060) Illustrated encyclopedia of Bible plants; flowers
       and trees -- fruits and vegetables -- ecology. Leicester 1992, Inter-Varsity. 192 p. £ 18. -
       - ᴿPEQ 127 (1995) 75 (D. *Samuel*).

c301 **Hepper** F.Nigel, *Friis* I., The plants of Per FORSSKÅL's 'Flora aegyptiaco-arabica' collected on the Royal Danish expedition to Egypt and the Yemen 1761-1763: K Botanical Museum. L 1994, Kew Royal Botanic Gardens. xii-400 p.; 29 fig. £ 15. -- ᴿJRAS (1995) 289s (G.R. *Smith:* also important but complex for Arabic studies).

c302 **Hughes** Donald J., Pan's travail; environmental problems of the ancient Greeks and Romans. Baltimore 1994, Johns Hopkins Univ. xii-277 p. -- ᴿPhoenix 49 (Tor 1995) 187s (A.T. *Hodge*).

c303 *Hugonot* Jean-Claude, Le liseron et le lierre [bindweed/ivy] dans l'Égypte ancienne: GöMiszÄg 142 (1994) 73-81; 16 fig.

c304 *Kelso* Gerald K., *Good* Irene L., Quseir al-Qadim, Egypt, and the potential of archaeological pollen analysis in the Near East: JField 22 (1995) 191-202; 3 fig.

c305 *Kobak* Cantius, *Gutiérrez* Lucio, ALCINA, Historia l,1 .. 12. Various delicious fruits: 13. oranges / 14s. palms / 17ss, palms *buri, bonga, bejuco* : PhilipSa 30 (1995) 135-171 / 312-361 / 499-549 [Eng. facing Spanish].

c306 *Kramer* Bärbel, Arborikultur und Holzwirtschaft im griechischen, römischen und byzantinischen Ägypten: AP(ap)F 41 (1995) 217-231.

c307 *Küster* Hansjörg, Weizen, Pfeffer, Tannenholz; botanische Unteruchungen zur Verbreitung von Handelsgütern in römischer Zeit: MBAH 14,2 (1995) 1-25; Eng. franç. 26

c308 *a) Liphschitz* Nili, *Biger* Gideon, The timber trade in ancient Palestine; -- *b) Lev-Yadun* S., *al.*, Conifer beans of *juniperus phoenica* found in the well of Tel Beer-Sheba: *TAJ 22 (1995) 121-7 / 128-135 [NTAb 40,p.477: 'phoenica' twice, but 'Phoenician juniper'].

c309 *Malaise* Michel, Le perséa, l'olivier, le lierre et le palme dans la religion égyptienne tardive: → 191. ᶠSTRICKER, B., Hermes: DiscEg.sp.2 (1995) 131-144.

c310 *Miller* Naomi F., The Aspalathus caper [Sir 24,15; PLINY, THEOPHRASTUS; maybe Akkadian *supālu*]: BASOR 297 (1995) 55-60; 2 fig. [NTAb 40, p.474].

c311 *Nesbitt* Mark, Plants and people in ancient Anatolia: → 136, ᶠNEVE P., BA 58 (1995) 68-81.

c312 *Nibbi* Alessandra, *a)* Some remarks on papyrus and lily in Egypt and in the Aegean: RdÉ 46 (1995) 139-147: 8 fig.; pl. XII; franç. 147; -- *b)* Some remarks on the Cedar of Lebanon [cannot be distinguished even by microscope from other cedars; Egyptian 's was not cedar and so did not need to be sought in Lebanon]: DiscEg 28 (1994) 35-52; 4 fig.; 3 maps.

c313 **Parkinson** Richard, *Quirke* Stephen, Papyrus: Egyptian bookshelf. L 1995, British Museum. 96 p. 0-7141-0979-7.

c314 *Patera* Maria, Les rites d'extraction des plantes dans l'Antiquité; magie, botanique et religion; l'exemple de la mandragore: RAHAL(ov) 27 (1994) 21-34.

c315 *Puech* Émile, L'image de l'arbre en 4QDeutéro-Ézéchiel (4Q385 2,9-10) [Éz 37,1-10; 17,24]: RQum 16 (1993-5) 429-440.

c316 *Rosen* Arlene M., *a)* Analytical techniques in Near Eastern archaeology; phytolith analysis: BA 58 (1995) 170; ill. [237, *Mason* R., scanning microscope]; -- *b)* Levant cereals [→ 9,15067, ᴱ**Pearsall** Deborah M., *Piperno* Dolores R.], Current research in phytolith analysis; applications in archaeology and paleoecology: Masca 10 {1993) 160-171.

c317 *Russman* Edna R., The motif of bound papyrus plants and the decorative program in Mentuemhat's First Court (further remarks on the decoration of the tomb of Mentuemhat, 1): JA(m)RCE(g) 32 (1995) 117-126; 5 fig.

c318 **Sallares** Robert, The ecology of the ancient Greek world 1991 → 8,k27; 10,13416: [R]VDI 313 (1995) 221-9 (Yu.N. *Litvinenko*, [R]).

c319 *Salvador* Jesús A., El fitónimo *satýrion;* un estudio sobre la denominación de plantas, el mundo vegetal y la religión griega: Fav 16,2 (1994) 33-49.

c320 *Schneider* M., Un rapport en arabe sur un pétiole de palme originaire du Yemen: AulaO 12 (1994) 193-210.

c321 **Schoske** Sylvia, *al.*, Ankh ... Pflanzen im alten Ägypten 1992 → 9,15070; DM 30: [R]BiOr 52 (1995) 68.

c322 *Shinoff* Sandra R., Gardens; from Eden to Jerusalem : JSJ(ud) 26 (1995) 145-155.

c323 *Suess* G.E.M., Beating the [70 species of] (thorny) bushes: JPersp 48 (1995) 16-21 [NTAb 40, p.91; chiefly caper, hawthorn, holy raspberry, Christ-thorn].

c324 *Tanner* William F., How many trees did Noah take on the ark ?: PerspSCF 47 (1995) 260-3.

c325 *a)* [E]**Tjon Sie Fat**, *Jong* E. de, The authentic garden; a symposium on gardens [Leiden Univ. Clusius Foundation 1990]. Lei 1991. - *b)* [E]**Carroll-Spillecke** M., Der Garten → c296 supra: [R]*KuGaW 57, Mainz 1992 [< JNES 54 (1995) 52 (R.D.*Biggs* on GYSELEN R.1991].

c326 *Tomei* Paolo E., *Maccioni* Simonetta, *a)* Flora faraonica; schede botaniche (1-2); - *b)* Primi appunti sull'uso di alcune droghe vegetali in Egitto attraverso i secoli: EVO 18 (1995) 167-170; 2 pl. / 155-164; 2 pl.

c327 *Wall* Peter, The cedar and the date palm: BurHist 31 (1995) 77-80.

c328 *Western* A.C., *McLeod* W., Woods used in Egyptian bows and arrows: JEA 81 (1995) 77-94.

c329 *Zeist* W. van, Some notes on second millennium B.C. plant cultivation in the Syrian Jazira: → 10,81, [F]MEYER L. de, 52 Réflexions 1994, 541-3.

c330 **Zohary** Daniel, *Hopf* Maria, Domestication of plants in the Old World; the origin and spread of cultivated plants in West Asia, Europe, and the Nile Valley[2] [[1]1988]. Ox 1994, Clarendon. x-279 p.; bibliog. 245-272.   0-19-854795-1.

U2.8 Agricultura, alimentatio

c331 *Ahituv* Shmuel, Flour and dough; gleanings from tha Arad letters: → 72, [F]GREENFIELD J., Solving 1995, 379-383.

c332 *Auberger* Janick, Dis-moi ce que tu manges, je te dirai qui tu es: RÉA(nc) 97 (1995) 461-471; Eng. 461.

c333 *Aviam* M., [H] Large scale production of olive oil in Galilee: *CHistEI 73 (1994) 26-33 [< JSJ(ud) 26 (1995) 246].

c334 *Baumgarten* Joseph M., A Qumran text with agrarian halakhah: JQR 86 (1995s) 1-8.

c335 **Berger** Klaus, Manna, Mehl und Sauerteig; Korn und Brot im Alltag der frühen Christen 1993 → 9,15080: [R]GuL 67 (1994) 153s (H. *Brandt*).

c336 *Bielefeld* Doris, Zur Ikonographie attischer Sarkophage mit Eroten-Weinlese-Darstellungen: MDAI-R 102 (1995) 397-404; 1 fig.; pl. 104-107.

c337 **Bottéro** Jean, Textes culinaires mésopotamiens: MesopC 6. WL 1995, Eisenbrauns. x-252 p.; ill. $ 39.50. 0-931464-92-7 [OTA 19, p.325. A. *Fitzgerald*; RStR 22,150, D.I. *Owen*].

c338 *Breckwoldt* Tina, Management of grain storage in Old-Babylonian Larsa; AfO 42s (1995s) 64-88; 10 fig., mostly tables; + facsimiles.

c339 *Campbell* J.B., Sharing out land; two passages in the Corpus agrimensorum romanorum: CQ 45 (1995) 540-6.

c340 **Cauvin** Jacques, Naissance des divinités, naissance de l'agriculture 1994 → 10,10696: [R]Syria 72 (1995) 435-440 (H. de *Contenson*).

c341 **Civil** Miguel, The farmer's instructions; a Sumerian agricultural manual [Nippur c.1800 B.C.]: *AulaO.s 5, 1994 → 10.13427: [R]BoL (1995) 126 (W.G.E. *Watson*).

c342 **Cowan** C. Wesley, *Watson* Patty Jo, The origins of agriculture, an international perspective 1992 → 9,15086; 10,14329*: [R*]JField 21 (1994) 374-6 (B. *Fagan*).

c343 **Criniti** N., La tabula alimentaria di Veleia → 10,13430; Parma 1991, Storia Patria. 345 p.; 13 pl. -- [R]JRS 85 (1995) 290s (W.M. *Jongman*).

c344 *Crocker* Piers T., Wine in the biblical world: BurHist 31 (1995) 81-88.

c345 *Del Monte* Giuseppe F., Bier und Wein bei den Hethitern: → 84, [F]HOUWINK TEN CATE, H., Studio (1995) 211-224.

c346 *a) Dor* Shimon, Food and archaeology in Romano-Byzantine Palestine; -- *b) Bottéro* Jean, The most ancient recipes of all; -- *c) Thompson* Dorothy J., Food for Ptolemaic temple-workers; -- *d) Sancisi-Weerdenburg* Heleen, Persian food; stereotypes and political identity: → 710, Food 1992/5, 326-335 / 148-255 / 316-325 / 286-302.

c347 *Englund* Robert K., Regulating dairy productivity in the Ur III period; Orientalia 64 (1995) 377-429.

c348 **Faiz** Mohammed El-, L'agronomie de la Mésopotamie antique; analyse du 'Livre de l'agriculture nabatéenne ' de QÛTÂMÂ: *StHistANE 5. Lei 1995, Brill. xx-332 p. 90-04-10199-3.

c349 *Faltings* Dina, *bš3* und *zwt* -- zwei ungeklärte Begriffe der Getreidewirtschaft im Alten Reich; GöMisz 148 (1995) 35-44.

c350 **Flach** Dieter, Römische Agrargeschichte: HbAw 3/9, 1990 → 7,a517 ...10,13436: [R]Salesianum 57 (1995) 770 (D. *Verri*).

c351 **Frankel** Rafael, *al.*, History and technology of olive oil in the Holy Land. Arlington VA 1994, Olearius. 208 p. $ 40 [BArR 21,5 (1995) 8].

c352 *a) Frayne* Joan, The Roman meat table; -- *b) Solomon* Jon, The Apician sauce: → 710, Food 1992/5, 107-114 / 115-131.

c353 **Gallant** Thomas W., Risk and survival in ancient Greece; reconstructing the rural domestic economy 1991 → 8,g993: [R]Phoenix 48 (Toronto 1994) 79-81 (R. *Develin*).

c354 [E]**Geyer** Bernard, Techniques et pratiques hydro-agricoles traditionnelles en domaine irrigué; approche pluridisciplinaire des modes de culture avant la motorisation en Syrie; Actes du Colloque de Damas 27 juin - 1 juillet 1987: IFAPO-BAH 136. P 1990, Geuthner. xv-521 p.; ill. F 280. -- [R]AfO 42s (1995s) 225s (M.A. *Powell*: 'pre-motorized' here is a synonym of ancient, extended with adaptations far into the 20th century, but with goals and achievements which today's experts will have to aim chiefly to avoid).

c355 *Ghaleb* Barbara, Choice cuts; butchery practices at New Kingdom Memphis: *EgA 7 (1995) 23-25.

c356 *Gharib* Badri, Persan *kešāvarz* 'agriculteur': StIR 23 (1994) 131-5.

c357 *Giacomelli* Roberto, Appunti sul lessico latino della cucina: → 10,31, [F]BELARDI W., Studi linguistici 1994, 215-252.

c358 *Gilula* Dwora, Food, an effective tool of amatory persuasion; a commentary on MNESIMACHUS, fr. 4 K-A: At(henaeum) 83 (1995) 143-156.

c359 [E]**Giovannini** Adalberto, Nourrir la plèbe 1989/91 → 8,645; 9,15101: [R]HZ 260 (1995) 183s (H. *Schneider*).

c360 *Glassner* Jean-Jacques, La gestion de la terre en Mésopotamie selon le témoignage des kudurrus anciens [GELB I., *al.* 1991]: BiOr 52 (1995) 5-24.

c361 *a) Grottanelli* Cristiano, Aspetti simbolici del latte nella Bibbia: -- *b) Biga* Maria Giovanna, Il latte nella documentzione cuneiforme del III e II millennio; -- *c) Zaccagnini* Carlo. Breath of life and water to drink: → 10,480, Drinking ANE. 1990/4, 381-397 / 333-345 / 347-360.

c362 *Guerrero* V.M., La vaijilla púnica de usos culinarios: RSFen 23 (1995) 61-69; pl. VIII-X.

c363 *Guglielmi* Waltraud, Die Biergöttin Menket: → 10,145, ᶠWINTER E., Aspekte 1994, 113-132.

c364 ᴱ**Gyselen** Rika, Banquets d'Orient 1992 →10,13441: ᴿAION 55 (1995) 117-121 (Simonetta *Graziani*); StIr 22 (1993) 313-7 (P. *Gignoux*).

c365 **Habbe** Joachim, Die Landwirtschaft in Palästina zur Zeit Jesu und ihr Niederschlag im Zeugnis der synoptischen Evangelien; Diss. ᴰ*Merk.* Erlangen 1995. - ThRv Beilage 92/2, vii.

c366 *a) Halstead* Paul, Late Bronze Age grain crops and Linear B ideograms *65, *120, and *121: -- *b) Jones* Glynn, Charred grain from Late Bronze Age Gla, Boiotia; -- *c) Foxhall* Lyn, Bronze to iron; agricultural systems and political structures in Late Bronze Age and Early Iron Age Greece: AB(rit)SA 90 (1995) 229-234 / 235-8; 1 fig. / 239-250.

c367 *Herr* Larry G., Wine production in the hills of southern Ammon and the founding of Tall al-'Umayri in the sixth century B.C.: ADAJ 39 (1995) 121-5.

c368 **Hruška** Blahoslav, Sumerian agriculture; new findings. B 1995, Planck. 110 p.; bibliog. 98-110.

c369 **Ikram** Salima, Choice cuts; meat production in ancient Egypt: OLA 69. Lv 1995, Peeters. xvii-326 p.; bibliog. 307-326. 90-6831-745-8.

c370 **Jursa** Michael. Die Landwirtschaft in Sippar in neubabylonischer Zeit: AfO Beih 25. Horn 1995, Berger. ix-264 p., Bibliog. iii-ix. 3-900345-03-1.

c371 *Konen* Heinrich, Die Kürbisgewächse (Cucurbitaceen) als Kulturpflanzen im römischen Ägypten (1.-3. Jh. n. Chr.): MBAH 14,1 (1995) 43-81; Eng. fr. 81.

c372 *Kranz* Peter, Ein ungewöhnlicher Musen- oder zweiter Annona-Sarkophag [Roma Tre Fontane]: MDAI-R 102 (1995) 391-6; pl. 102s.

c373 **Kunisch** Norbert, Griechische Fischteller; Natur und Bild. B 1989, Mann. → 6,d440; 150 p.; 23 fig.; 17 pl.: ᴿGnom 67 (1995) 352-6 (Simone *Wolf*).

c374 **Lavrencic** Monika, Spartanische Küche 1993 → 10,13449: ᴿHZ 260 (1995) 834s (M. *Clauss*).

c375 **Lewit** Tamara, Agricultural production in the Roman economy A.D. 200-400: BAR-Int 568. Ox 1991, Tempus Reparatum. vi-261 p.; 8 fig. £ 25. 0-86054-717-5. -- ᴿBo(nn)J 195 (1995) 777s (W.H. *Manning*, Eng.); JRS 85 (1995) 289 (Joan M. *Frayn*).

c376 *Maekawa* K., The agricultural texts of Ur III Lagash of the British Museum (IX): *AcSum 15 (1993) 107-129.

c377 *Martin* René, Ars an qvid alivd ? La conception varronienne de l'agriculture: RÉL 73 (1995) 80-91.

c378 *a) Milano* Lucio, Vino e birra in Oriente; confini geografici e confini culturali; -- *b) Fales* Frederick M., A fresh look at the Nimrud wine lists: → 10,480, Drinking ANE. 1990/4, 421-440 / 360-380.

c379 ᴱ**Milano** Lucio, Drinking in ancient societies 1990/4 → 10,480: ᴿUF 27 (DIETRICH 60. Gb. 1995) 720-2 (M. *Heltzer*).

c380 NEEVE Peter Willem de (1945-1990) mem.: De agricultura, ^EMeijer F.J., *Pleket* H.W.: DutchMgAr 10, 1993 → 9,111: ^RGaR 42 (1995) 112 (P. *Walcot*: high standard).

c381 **Palmer** Ruth, Wine in the Mycenaean palace economy: Aegaeum 10. Liège/Austin 1994, Univ. xxx-209 p.; 7 pl. -- ^RAnCL 64 (1995) 423s (Y. *Duhoux*).

c382 *Pavlovskaya* A.I., ^R Land degradation in the Fayûm in the 4th-5th centuries A.D.: VDI 213 (1995) 28-37; Eng. 38.

c383 *Pons Pons* Guillermo, La naturaleza y la agricultura en los sermones de San AGUSTÍN: RevAg 36 (1995) 975-1003.

c384 *Porée* Brigitte, L'exploitation des ressources agricoles dans le Royaume Croisé de Jérusalem (12e-13e siècles): *OrExp 3 (1994) 87.

c385 *a) Powell* Marvin A., Metron ariston; measure as a tool for studying beer in ancient Mesopotamia; -- *b) Stol* Marten, Beer in Neo-Babylonian times; -- *c) Neumann* Hans, Beer as a means of compensation for work in Mesopotamia during the Ur III period: → 10,480, Drinking ANE. 1990/4, 91-119 / 155-183 / 321-331.

c386 *Quattrocchi* Giovanna, A tavola nel medioevo: *Archeo 10,119 (1995) 58-65.

c387 *Ruffing* Kai, *Kinapa* [artichoke]; Anbau und Vertrieb im römischen Ägypten; MBAH 14,2 (1995) 61-69; Eng. fr. 69.

c388 **Salza Prina Ricotti** Eugenia, L'arte del convito nella Roma antica, con 90 ricette: StAr 35. R 1983, 2ª ristampa 1993, Bretschneider. 313 p.; 121 fig. 88-7062-535-4. -- ^RAnCL 64 (1995) 414-6 (Christiane *Delplace*).

c389 *a) Sasson* Jack M., The blood of grapes; agriculture and intoxication in the Hebrew Bible; -- *b) Belisario* M.V., *al.*, Nuovi dati archeobotanici sulla cultivazione di *Vitis vinifera L.* ad Arslantepe (Malatya, Turchia); -- *c) Zito* Romano, Biochimica nutrizionale degli alimenti liquidi: → 10.480, Drinking ANE. 1990/4, 399-419 / 77-90; pl.X / 60-75.

c390 **Schmitt** E., Das Essen in der Bibel; literaturethnologische Aspekte des Alltäglichen [Diss. Mainz 1991, ^D*Müller* E.]: *StKuAnthrop 2. Müns 1994, Lit. ix-204 p. DM 49. 3-88660-524-4 [NTAb 40, p.186].

c391 **Sharon** Diane, The literary function of eating and drinking events in the Hebrew Bible with reference to the literature of the Ancient Near East: diss. Jewish Theol.Sem., ^D*Geller* S. - RStR 22,272.

c392 **Sirks** Boudewijn, Food for Rome 1991 → 7,e545 ... 10,13466; ^RLatomus 54 (1995) 167s (S. *Mrozek*).

c393 *Subtelny* M.E., A medieval Persian agricultural manual in context; the *Irshād al-Zirā'a* in Late Timurid and Early Safavid Khorasan: StIr 22 (1993) 167-217; franç. 217.

c394 *Tripodi* Bruno, Il cibo dell'altro; regimi e codici alimentari nell'Anabasi di SENOFONTE: Pallas 43 (1995) 41-57; franç.Eng. 58.

c395 *Vachala* Bretislav, *Faltings* Dina, Töpferei und Brauerei im Alten Reich -- einige Relieffragmente aus der Mastaba des Ptahschepses in Abusir: MIDAI-K 51 (1995) 282-6; foldout; pl. 57-59.

c396 *a) Valencia Hernández* Manuela, CICERÓN y las leyes agrarias: un exemplum de divina eloquentia; -- *b) Salanitro* Maria, Il vino e i pesci di Trimalchione (Satyr. 39,2): RÉA(nc) 97 (1995) 575-587 / 589-592.

c397 **Vandermeersch** Christian, Vins et amphores de Grande Grèce et de Sicile, IVe-IIIe s. av. J.-C.: Ét 1. N 1994, Centre Bérard (P, de Boccard). 279 p.; bibliog. 255-279. 2-903189-45-5.

c398 **Varisco** Daniel M., Medieval agriculture and Islamic science; the almanac of a Yemeni sultan [MALIK AŠRAF 1296, ch. 12 of the astronomical Tabsirâ]: NearEast 5. Seattle 1994, Univ. Washington. xv-149 p. $ 40. -- ᴿJRAS (1995) 415-7 (G.R. *Smith*).

c399 *Vera* Domenico, Dalla 'villa perfecta' alla villa di Palladio; sulle trasformazioni del sistema agrario in Italia fra principato e dominato: At(henaeum) 83 (1995) 189-211 . 331-356.

c400 **Virlouvet** Catherine, Tessera frumentaria; les procédures de distribution du blé public à Rome à la fin de la République et au début de l'Empire: BEFAR 286. R 1994, Éc. Française. [iv-] 424 p.; bibliog. 381-403. 2-7283-0331-2.

c401 **Wagner** Christoph, Alles was Gott erlaubt hat; die kulinarische Bibel; Essen und Trinken im Alten und Neuen Testament. W 1994, Brandstetter. 240 p.; ill. -- ᴿThR(und) 60 (1995) 230s (L. *Perlitt*).

c402 **Weeber** Karl-W., Die Weinkultur der Römer. Z 1993, Artemis. 188 p.; 37 fig.; map. Fs 58. 3-7608-1093-4. -- ᴿAnCL 64 (1995) 411s (P. Van *Langenhoven*); RB(elg)PH 73 (1995) 21s (R. *Chevallier*).

c403 *a)* *White* K.D., Cereals, bread and milling in the Roman world; -- *b) Cabberley* Anthony, Bread-baking in ancient Italy; *clibanus* and *sub testu* in the Roman world: → 710, Food 1992/5, 38-43 / 55-68.

c404 **Wunsch** Cornelia, Die Urkunden des babylonischen Geschaftsmannes Iddin-Marduk; zum Handeln mit Naturalien [onions, dates, barley; financing cattle-operations] im 6. Jh. v.Chr.: *CunMg 3. Groningen 1993, Styx. xviii-163 p., xi-323 p. *f* 185. -- ᴿOLZ 90 (1995) 282-4 (S. *Zawadzki*).

U2.9 **Medicina** biblica et antiqua

c405 **Adams** James N., PELAGONIUS and Latin veterinary terminology in the Roman Empire: StAncMed 11. Lei 1995, Brill. viii-695 p. 90-04-10291-7.

c406 *Amitai* Pinchas, Scorpion ash saves woman's eyesight : BiRe(v) 11,2 (1995) 36s.

c407 *Andouche* Iris, *Simelon* Paul, STACE et la mortalité masculine [65 ans normal]; Latomus 54 (1995) 319-323.

c408 **Avalos** Hector, Illness and health care in the Ancient Near East; the role of the temple in Greece, Mesopotamia, and Israel: HSM 54. At 1995, Scholars. xxv-463 p.; bibliog. 427-448. $ 50. 0-7885-0098-8.

c409 *Avalos* Hector, Ancient medicine: BiRe(v) 11,2 (1995) 26-32 . 33s . 48.

c410 **Bardinet** Thierry, Dents et mâchoires dans les représentations religieuses et la pratique médicale de l'Égypte acienne: StPohl 15. R 1990, Pontificio Istituto Biblico. xxii-280 p.; 11 fig. Lᵐ 31,5. 88-7653-591-8. -- ᴿBiOr 52 (1995) 65-68 (W. *Westendorf*: viele neue Ergebnisse).

c411 **Barrett-Lennard** R.J.S., Christian healing after the New Testament; some approaches to illness in the second, third and fourth centuries [< diss. Macquarie 1988, ᴰ*Judge* E.] Lanham MD 1994, UPA. xi-419 p. $ 46.50. 0-8191-9129-9 [NTAb 40, p.549].

c412 **Batton** Tamsyn S., Power and knowledge; astrology, physiognomics, and medicine under the Roman Empire: The Body in Theory. AA 1994, Univ. Michigan. xiv-254 p. 0-472-10425-X.

c413 *Bauer* Axel W., Der Hippokratische Eid; medizinhistorische Neuinterpretation eines (un)bekannten Textes im Kontext der Professionalisierung des griechischen Arztes: *ZMedEth 41 (1995) 141-5.

c414 **Beckmann-Hueber** Dorothee, Hippokratisches Ethos und ärztliche Verantwortung; zur Genese eines anthropologischen Selbstverständnisses griechischer Heilkunst ... : kath. Diss. ᴰ*Hunold*. Tübingen 1994. - ThRv 91 (1995) 101.

c415 *Béguin* Daniel, Le problème de la connaissance dans le De optima doctrina de GALIEN: RÉG 108 (1995) 107-127.

c416 **Bliquez** Lawrence J., Roman surgical instruments ... Napoli (Pompeii, *Jackson* R.). Mainz 1994, von Zabern. xvi-238 p.; 27 pl. 3-8053-1667-1.

c417 **Bono** James J., The word of God and the languages of men; interpreting nature in early modern science and medicine, 1. Ficino to Descartes: Science and Literature. Madison 1995, Univ. Wisconsin. xi-317 p. 0-299-14790-8

c418 ᴱ**Bowman** Sheridan, Science and the past. L 1991, British Museum. 192 p.; ill. 0-7141-2071-5 [*OIAc 11,15].

c419 **Brown** Michael L., Israel's divine healer: StOTbT. GR 1995, Zondervan. 462 p.; bibliog. 423-441. 0-310-20029-6.

c420 *Byl* Simon, MOLIÈRE et la médecine antique: ÉtCl 63 (1995) 55-66.

c421 **Cameron** Nigel M., Life and death after [medicine's abandonment of the Oath of] Hippocrates. Wheaton IL 1991, Crossway. 187 p. $ 12 pa. [JETS 39, 306, M. *McKenzie*].

c422 **Capasso** Luigi, Le origini della chirurgia italiana: mostra Roma 1993. R 1993, Ministero Cultura, 135 p.; ill.

c423 *a) Carroll* John T., Sickness and healing in the New Testament Gospels; -- *b) Wind* James F., A case for theology in the ministry of healing; -- *c) Evans* Abigail Rian, The Church as an institution of health; making it happen: Interpretation 49 (1995) 130-142 / 143-157 / 158-171.

c424 **Chevallier** Raymond, Sciences et techniques à Rome: Que sais-je? 2763. P 1993, PUF. 128 p. -- ᴿRB(elg)PH 73 (1995) 212s (R. *Lambrechts*).

c425 **Clagett** M., Ancient Egyptian science; a source book, I/1s.. Ph 1989, American Philosophical. xv-863. $ 60. -- ᴿAeg 75 (1995) 321s (Patrizia *Piacentini*).

c426 **Cordes** Peter, Iatros; das Bild des Arztes in der griechischen Literatur von Homer bis Aristoteles: Palingenesia 39. Stu 1994, Steiner. 208 p. DM 78. 3-515-06191-6. -- ᴿCLR 45 (1995) 205 (S. *Instone*).

c427 *a) Craik* Elizabeth, Hipppokratic diaita; -- b) *Nutton* Vivian, GALEN and the traveller's fare: → 710, Food in antiquity 1992/5, 343-350 / 359-370.

c428 **Dasen** V., Dwarfs in ancient Egypt and Greece: MgClasAr, 1993 → 9,15153; £ 60. -- ᴿCLR 45 (1995) 116s (Kate *Bosse-Griffiths*); Klio 77 (1995) 448s (N. *Himmelmann*).

c429 ᴱ**David** A.R., *Tapp* E., The mummy's tale; the scientific and medical investigation of Natsef-Amun, priest in the temple of Karnak 1992 → 8,g68; £ 16: ᴿDiscEg 30 (1994) 177-180 (J.-C. *Goyon*).

c430 **Davies** Stevan L., Jesus the healer; possession, trance, and the origins of Christianity. L 1995, SCM. 216 p. £ 13. 0-334-02605-9. -- ᴿE(xp)T 107 (1995s) 118 (I.G. *Wallis*: somewhat parallel to social-science tools).

c431 ᴱ**Davies** W. Vivian, *Walker* Roxie, Biological anthropology and the study of ancient Egypt 1993 → 9,15153*: ᴿJA(m)RCE(g) 32 (1995) 269s (W.B. *Harer*).

c432 **Davis** Eli, *Frenkel* David A., ᴴ The Hebrew amulet; biblical-medical-general [from Jerusalem Medical School collections ...]. J 1995, Inst. Jewish St. 212 p. $ 30. [NTAb 40, p.552].

c433 **Dean-Jones** L.A., Women's bodies in classical Greek science 1994 → 10,13487; £ 30: ᴿCLR 45 (1995) 137-9 (Helen *King*).

c434 **De Filippis Cappai** C., Medici e medicina in Roma antica 1993 → 9,15155: [R]JRS 85 (1995) 261s (Helen *King*).

c435 **Durling** R.J., A dictionary of medical terms in GALEN: StAncMed 5, 1993 → 9,15159; 10,13487*d*: [R]CLR 45 (1995) 139s (Helen *King*).

c436 *Durling* Richard J., A guide to the medical manuscripts mentioned in [1990 Paul O.] KRISTELLER's Iter italicum V-VI: Traditio 48 (1993) 253-316.

c437 *Durling* Richard J., The language of Galenic pharmacy: Glotta 70 (1992) 62-70.

c438 **Eijk** P.J. van der, *al.*, Ancient medicine in its socio-cultural context: Clio Medica. Amst/Atlanta 1995, Rodopi. 637 p. (2 vol.) -- [R]RÉG 108 (1995) 607s (Véronique *Boudon*).

c439 *Engelmann* Heinz, *Hallof* Jochen, Zur medizinischen Nothilfe und Unfallversorgung auf staatlichen Arbeitsplätzen im Alten Ägypten: ZÄS 122 (1995) 104-136; 2 fig.

c440 **Estes** J. Worth, The medical skills of ancient Egypt 1989 → 5,g161 ... 8,k52: [R]CÉg 70 (1995) 157-160 (E. *Strouhal*).

c441 **Filer** Joyce, Disease: Egyptian Bookshelf. L 1995, British Museum. 112 p.; 68 fig.; VIII colour. pl. £ 10. 0-7141-0930-0.

c442 **Finkel** Avraham Y., In my flesh I see God; a treasury of rabbinic insights about the human anatomy. Northvale NJ 1995, Aronson. xxviii-356 p.; bibliog. 329-332. 1-56821-425-1.

c443 *Fischer* Klaus-Dietrich, Ein neuer Textzeuge der altlateinischen Übersetzung der hippokratischen Schrift Über die Umwelt: Latomus 54 (1995) 50-57; 1 pl.

c444 **Garofalo** Ivan, GALENO, Procedimenti anatomici, testo greco a fronte. Mi 1991, Rizzoli. 1145 p. (3 vol.). -- [R]EM(erita) 62 (1994) 195s (J.A. *López Férez*).

c445 *Gasti* Fabio, I pupilli senza occhi; una noterella ISIDORiana (Etym. 11,2,12): At(henaeum) 83 (1995) 264-270.

c446 *Germer* Renate, *al.*, Die Wiederentdeckung der Lübecker Apotheken-Mumie: AW(elt) 26 (1995) 17-40; 38 fig.

c447 **Ginouvès** R., *al.*, L'eau, la santé et la maladie dans le monde grec; Actes du colloque de Paris (25-27 nov. 1992); BCH.s 28. P 1994, de Boccard. 339 p. -- [R]RÉG 108 (1995) 606s (P. *Nautin*).

c448 *Gourévitch* Danielle, Correction d'une correction [among skin-diseases in ISIDORE 4,8,9, *satyriasis* is not redundant, and W. SHARPE's tolerable *pityriasis* is wrongly copied *phthiriasis* in J. OROZ RETA 1982 edition]: Traditio 49 (1994) 317-9.

c449 *Guilhou* Nadine, Un texte de guérison [BM 10059, 38]: CÉg 70 (1995) 52-64.

c450 *Harer* W. Benson[J], Implications of molecular biology for Egyptology: JA(m)RCE(g) 32 (1995) 67-70.

c451 **Hauerwas** Stanley, Naming the silences; God, medicine, and the problem of suffering. E 1993, Clark [= Eerdmans 1990]. xiv-154 p. 0-567-29234-7. -- [R]*TBR 8,3 (1995s) 37s (I. *Markham*: 'This is Hauerwas' finest book ...our attitudes to medicine and death are all linked up with our perception of the problem of evil. Medicine has become so noisy that it has hidden the gaping silences created by the experiences of childhood illness and death').

c452 *Herzog* Markwart, Christus medicus, apothecarius, samaritanus, balneator; Motive einer medizinisch-pharmazeutischen Soteriologie: GuL 67 (1994) 414-434: 2 pl.

c453 *Holoubek* Joe E. M.D. & Alice B. M.D., A study of death by crucifixion with attempted explanation of the death of Jesus Christ: LinacreQ (1994) 10-19.

c454 *Horsfall* Nicholas, Rome without spectacles [eye-glasses]: GaR 42 (1995) 49-56.

c455 ^E**Huss-Ashmore** Rebecca, *al.*, Health and lifestyle change: Masca 9. Ph 1992, Univ. Museum. 144 p. 1048-5325. -- 14 art.; none on Mid-East; p. 83-89, *Leatherman* Thomas L., Illness as lifestyle change.

c456 *Irarrázaval* Diego, Con-vocación evangélica a la salud: Páginas 20,132 (1995) 51-58.

c457 **Isaacs** Haskell D., (*Baker* Colin F.), [1616 Judeo-Arabic] Medical and para-medical manuscripts in the Cambridge Genizah collections: Genizah series 11. C 1994, Univ. xxi-144 p.; 20 pl. £ 70. 0-521-47050-1. -- ^RBoL (1995) 29 (J.F. *Elwolde*).

c458 ^E**Jacob** Irene & Walter, The healing past; pharmaceuticals in the biblical and rabbinic world [1989 symposium] 1993 → 9,283: ^RBiOr 52 (1995) 768s (M. *Stol*: sources mostly secondary, and I. Löw's 1934 Flora unpardonably overlooked); JAOS 115 (1995) 326s (M.J. *Geller*); JSSt 40 (1995) 144s (O. *Kahl*).

c459 *Jansen* Gerard, Christian ministry of healing on its way to the year 2000; an archaeology of medical missions: Miss(iology) 23 (1995) 295-308.

c460 *Jekel* James F., Biblical foundations for health and healing: PerspSCF 47 (1995) 150-8.

c461 ^{TE}**Jones** W.H.S., *al.*, HIPPOCRATES, The works, with an English translation: Loeb Classical Library (104 ..) 182. CM 1994s Harvard Univ. -- 7. Epidemics, ^T*Smith* Wesley D., 424 p.; -- 8. Glands, varia. ^T*Potter* Paul, 418 p. 0-674-89526-0; -31-7.

c462 **Jouanna** Jacques, HIPPOCRATE. P 1992, Fayard. 652 p. -- ^RAt(h-Pavia) 83 (1995) 301-4 (Daniela *Manetti*).

c463 *Jouanna* Jacques, L'HIPPOCRATE de Modène: ScrBru 49 (1995) 273-283.

c464 *a) Kákosy* László, Ouroboros on magical healing statues; -- *b) Meeks* Dimitri, Le foie, Maat et la nature humaine: → 191, ^FSTRICKER B., Hermes: DiscEg.sp.2 (1995) 123-6 + 5 fig.; 2 pl. / 145-157.

c465 *Kammerer* T., Die erste Pockendiagnose stammt aus Babylonien: UF 27 (DIETRICH 60. Gb. 1995) 129-168.

c466 **Kee** Howard C., Medicina, miracolo e magia nei tempi del NT [1986, ²1990], ^T: StB 102. Brescia 1993, Paideia. 245 p. L^m 35. -- ^RDidask 14,2 (1994) 285s (A. *Couto*); Protest(antesimo) 50 (1995) 324 (P. *Ribet*).

c467 **Kee** Howard C., Medicina, milagro y magía en tiempos del Nuevo Testamento 1992 → 9,15171: ^RRevBib(Arg) 57 (1995) 252 (J.P. *Martín*).

c468 ^E**Kollesch** J., *Nickel* D., GALEN und das hellenistische Erbe: Symposium Berlin Univ. 18.-20. Sept. 1989: Sudhoff 32. Tü 1993, Steiner. 214 p. DM 74. -- ^RCLR 45 (1995) 405-7 (P.J. van der *Eijk*).

c469 **Kottek** Samuel S., Medicine .. in JOSEPHUS 1994 → 10.13500 [NTAb 39, p.171]: ^RJAOS 115 (1995) 325s (M.J. *Geller*).

c470 *Kronholm* Tryggve, Abraham, the physician; the image of Abraham the Patriarch in the genuine hymns of EPHRAEM Syrus: → 72, ^FGREENFIELD J., Solving 1995, 107-115.

c471 *Langermann* Y. Tzvi, MAIMONIDES on the synochous fever ['continuous'; he wrote abridgments of some twenty works of GALEN]: I(sr)OS 13 (1993) 175-198.

c472 **Larchet** Jean-Claude, Thérapeutique des maladies mentales; l'expérience de l'Orient chrétien des premiers siècles: Théologies, 1992 → 8,k74: ^RMélSR 51 (1994) 94-96 (L. *Debarge*).

c473 **Leavesley** J.H., Potions and panaceas, physicians and prophets; medicine in the Bible, the Talmud, the Koran and the Vedas. Crows Nest NSW 1990, Australian Broadcasting Co. viii-103 p. 0-7333-0034-0 [*OIAc 11,30].

c474 **Lloyd** Geoffrey E.R., The revolutions of wisdom; studies in the claims and practice of ancient Greek science: Sather Classical Lectures 52, 1987 → 5,g196; 6,g519; xii-468 p.; 0-520-06742-8.

c475 *Lloyd* Geoffrey, Adversaries and authorities [Greek versus Chinese origins of science]: PCP(g)S 40 (1994) 27-48.

c476 **Longrigg** J., Greek rational medicine; philosophy and medicine from Alcmaeon to the Alexandrians 1993 → 9,15183*; 0-415-02594-X. -- ᴿAnCʟ 64 (1995) 417 (S. *Byl*); CLR 45 (1995) 140s (Helen *King*).

c477 **López Férez*** J.A., Tratados hipocráticos 1990/2 → 10,13507: ᴿAnCʟ 64 (1995) 418s (Marie-Hélène *Marganne*).

c478   **Marganne** Marie-Hélène, L'ophtalmologie dans l'Égypte gréco-romaine d'après les papyrus littéraires grecs: StAMed 8, 1994 → 10,13508: ᴿAnCʟ 64 (1995) 419s (B. *Vancamp*); CÉg 70 (1995) 310-5 (Isabella *Andorlini*).

c479 *Margel* Serge, Les nourritures de l'âme; essai sur la fonction nutritive et séminale dans la biologie d'Aʀɪsᴛᴏᴛᴇ: RÉG 108 (1995) 91-106.

c480 *a) Marty* Martin E., The tradition of the Church in health and healing; -- *b) Mògedal* Sigrun, *Bergh* Mirjam, Challenges, issues and trends in health care and the Church's mission; -- *c) Crawley* Gwen, A new paradigm for medical mission -- a North American perspective: IRM(iss) 83 (1994) 227-245 / 257-276 / 303-313.

c481 **Milanesi** Claudio, Mort apparente, mort imparfaite; médecine et mentalités au XVIIIᵉ siècle: BtScientifique. P 1991, Payot. 268 p. -- ᴿRTPh 127 (1995) 382 (P.-Y. *Ruff*).

c482 *Miller* Robert L., *Ritner* Robert K., *Rwy.t*; 'radiating' symptoms of gallstone disease in ancient Egypt: GöMisz 141 (1994) 71-76.

c483 *Moore* Stephen D., How Jesus' risen body became a cadaver [exegesis uses techniques like dissection, earlier abhorred by society and church]: → 139, New Lit.Crit.NT 1994, 268-282.

c484 *Muir* Steven C., Touched by a god; Aelius Aʀɪsᴛɪᴅᴇs, religious healing, and Asclepius cults: → 512, SBL Seminars 34 (1995) 362-379.

c485 *Newmeyer* Stephen T., Pʟᴜᴛᴀʀᴄʜ on the moral grounds for vegetarianism: *ClasOut 32 (1995) 41-43.

c486 *North* Robert, Did ancient Israelites have a heart ?: BiRe(v) 11,3 (1995) 33; ill.; 11,5 (1995) 10, reply to objections.

c487   **Panikkar** Raimon, Medicine and religion: Interculture 27,4. Montréal 1994, Intercultural Institute. 40 p. 0828-797X (English; 0172-1571 français).

c488 *Park* Rosalind, Kidneys in ancient Egypt: *DiscEg 29 (1994) 125-9; 1 fig.

c489 *Paxton* Frederick S., Liturgy and healing in an early medieval saint's cult; the Mass in honore sancti Sigismundi for the cure of fevers: Traditio 49 (1994) 23-43.

c490 **Penn** R.G., Medicine on ancient Greek and Roman coins. L 1994, Seaby Batsford. vi-186 p. 1-85264-07(0)-1.

c491 **Perho** Irmeli (→ 8926 supra), The Prophet's medicine; a creation of the Muslim traditionalist scholars: StOr 74. Helsinki 1995, Univ. 158 p. 951-9380-24-8.

c492   **Rechenauer** Georg, Tʜᴜᴄʏᴅɪᴅᴇs und die hippokratische Medizin; naturwissenschaftliche Methodik als Modell für Geschichtsdeutung: Spudasmata 47, 1991 → 9,15197: ᴿÉtCL 63 (1995) 77s (B. *Vancamp*).

c493 *Reiner* Erica, At the fuller's [.. scorn for medicos]: → 185, ᶠSᴏᴅᴇɴ W.von, Vom Alten Orient (1995) 407-411.

c494 **Schipperges** Heinrich,   Die Kranken im Mittelalter.   Mü 1990, Beck. 250 p. 3-406-33603-5. -- [R]Salesianum 57 (1995) 365s (E. *Fontana*).

c495 [TE]**Serbat** Guy, CELSE, De la médecine: Coll. Budé. P 1995, BLettres. 2-251-01384-9.

c496 **Smutny** Robert J., Latin readings in the history of medicine. Lanham MD 1995, UPA. xii-453 p. 0-8191-9766-1.

c497 **Stol** M., Epilepsy in Babylonia: *CunMg 2, 1991 → 9,15206: [R]AfO 42s (1995s) 250-4 (Jo Ann *Scurlock*: amid high praise and some 'quibbles': 'the right side is male' not universal as p.36; not in China, the then majority of world-population); BiOr 52 (1995) 728-730 (R. *Biggs*: fine but no list of passages cited); *TopO 4 (1994) 231s (B.R. *Foster*).

c498 *Stolz* Fritz, Gott, Kaiser, Arzt; Konfigurationen religiöser Symbolsysteme: → 42, [F]COLPE C., Tradition (1994) 113-130.

c499 **Stuckelberger** Alfred, Bild und Wort; das illustrierte Fachbuch in der antiken Naturwissenschaft, Medizin und Technik: KuGaW 62. Mainz 1994, von Zabern. 139 p.; 39 pl. 3-8053-1698-4.

c500 *Svenbro* Jesper, Notes sur le calendrier hippocratique: Ktema 18 (1993) 69-78.

c501 *Swain* Simon, Man and medicine in THUCYDIDES: Arethusa 27 (1994) 303-327.

c502 **Temkin** Owsei, HIPPOCRATES in a world of pagans and Christians 1991 → 7,e59 ... 10,13526: [R]*JEarlyC 3 (1995) 495-9 (M.R. *Barnes*, also on [E]*Kudlien* F., 1982/91 GALEN).

c503 *Testa* Emanuele, Le malattie e il medico secondo la Bibbia [Esodo 15,26 ...Mt 8.1-16; - Sir 38,1-15] → 62, [F]GALBIATI E.; RivB 43 (1995) 253-267; Eng. 267.

c504 *Thivel* Antoine, Theorie und Empirie in der römischen Medizin und bei GALEN: → 690, Prinzipat 1992/5, 90-99.

c505 *Tigay* J.H., Examination of the accused bride in 4Q 159; forensic medicine at Qumran: JANES 22 (1993) 129-134 [NTAb 40, p.296].

c506 *Vegetti* Mario, Tra passioni e malattia; pathos nel pensiero medico antico: Elenchos 16 (1995) 217-230.

c507 [E]**Weber** Giorgio, Antonio BENEVIENI, De abditis nonnullis ac mirandis morborum et sanationum causis: Acc. Toscana St.142. F 1994, Olschki. 291 p.

c508 **Westendorf** Wolfhart, Erwachen der Heilkunst; die Medizin im Alten Ägypten 1992 → 8,k110; 3-7608-1072-1: [R]BiOr 52 (1995) 387-390 (C. *Couchoud*).

c509 **Wilhelm** Gernot, Medizinische Omina aus Hattuša in akkadischer Sprache: StBT 36, 1994 → 10,13528; DM 42 [RStR 22,145, D.I. *Owen*].

c510 *Wöhrle* Georg, CATO und die griechischen Ärzte: Eranos 90 (1992) 112-5.

c511 *Ziegler* Ruprecht, Aigeai, der Asklepioskult, das Kaiserhaus der Decier und das Christentum: Tyche 9 (1994) 187-212.

U3 *Duodecim tribus;* **Israel tribes;** land-ideology

c512 *Ben-Zvi* Ehud, Inclusion in and exclusion from Israel as conveyed by the use of the term 'Israel' in post-monarchic biblical texts: → 4, [F]AHLSTRÖM G., Pitcher; JSOT.s 190 (1995) 95-149.

c513 **Boorer** Suzanne, The promise of the Land as oath: BZAW 205, 1992 → 9,1729: [R]CBQ 57 (1995) 544-6 (T.B. *Dozeman*).

c514 **Davies** William D., The terrritorial dimension of Judaism [1982, continuing The Gospel and the Land; early Christianity and Jewish territorial doctrine 1974] with a symposium and further reflections 1991 → 8,13533: [R]RB 102 (1995) 467s (É. *Nodet*: amid useful data could not indicate symposium date/place).

c515 **Habel** N.C., The land is mine; six biblical land ideologies: *OvBT. Mp 1995, Fortress. xv-190 p. $ 12 pa. 0-8006-2664-8 [NTAb 40, p.366].

c516 **Halpern-Amaru** Betsy, Rewriting the Bible; [Jubilees, PS.-PHILO, JOSEPHUS on] land and covenant in post-biblical Jewish literature. Ph 1994, Trinity. x-189 p.; bibliog. 171-180. $ 15. 1-56338-091-9. -- [R]JBL 114 (1995) 319s (J.J. *Collins*); OTA 18 (1995) p. 174 (L.H. *Feldman*).

c517 *Milgrom* Jacob, The land redeemer and the jubilee [Lev 25] : → 59, [F]FREEDMAN D.N., Fortunate 1995, 66-69.

c518 **Neef** Heinz-Dieter, Ephraim; Studien zur Geschichte des Stammes Ephraim von der Landnahme bis zur frühen Königszeit [Diss. Tübingen 1993, [D]*Mittmann* S. → 10,13540: BZAW 238. B 1995, de Gruyter. xvi-389 p.; Bibliog. 339-377. 3-11-014756-4.

c519 **Page** Charles R., Jesus and the land. Nv 1995, Abingdon. 201 p.; 87 fig. $ 15. 0-687-00544-2 [ThD 43,283].

c520 *Robinson* D, Biblical understandings of Israel -- the geographical entity; some prolegomena: *StMk 159 (Canberra 1994) 24-29 [NTAb 39, p.269].

c521 **Weinfeld** Moshe, The promise of the land; the inheritance of the land of Canaan by the Israelites (Taubman Lectures 3) 1993 → 9,15229: [R]BSOAS 58 (1995) 351s (A.G. *Auld*); JBL 114 (1995) 122s (Diana *Edelmann*).

c522 **Willi** Thomas, Juda -- Jehud -- Israel: FAT 12. Tü 1995, Mohr. ix-209 p.; Bibliog. 183-193. 3-16-146478-8. DM 168.

U4 *Limitrophi,* **adjacent lands**

c523 *a) Anderson* Robert W.[J], Zephaniah ben Cushi and Cush of Benjamin; traces of Cushite presence in Syria-Palestine; -- *b) Haak* Robert D., 'Cush' in Zephaniah : → 4, [F]AHLSTRÖM G., Pitcher; JSOT.s 190 (1995) 45-70 / 238-251.

c524 **André** Jean-Marie, *Baslez* Marie-Françoise, Voyager dans l'Antiquité. P 1993, Fayard. 594 p.; maps. -- [R]RÉA 97 (1995) 665s (P. *Arnaud*).

c525 **Bock** Susan. Los Hunos; tradición e historia; Antigüedad y cristianismo 9. Murcia 1992, Univ. 503 p. pt.5.000

c526 **Braund** David, Georgia in antiquity; a history of Colchis and transcaucasian Iberia 550 BC -- AD 562. Ox 1994, Clarendon. xvii-359 p.; maps. $ 50. -- [R]RStR 21 (1995) 133 (R. S. *MacLennan*).

c527 **Dicou** Bert, Edom, Israel's brother and antagonist: JSOT.S 169. Shf 1994, Academic. -- [R]CBQ 57 (1995) 547s (J.T. *Walsh*); EThL 71 (1995) 205s (J. *Lust*); JThS 46 (1995) 209s (R. *Mason*).

[E]**Edelman** Diana V., You shall not abhor an Edomite for he is your brother 1995 → 500.

c528 *Erlich* V.R.,[R] On the Black Sea origin of Cimmerians: VDI 210 (1994)168-175;Eng.176.

c529 *Görg* Manfred, Nochmals zu Amalek: BN(otiz) 79 (1995) 15s.

c530 *Haider* Peter W., Ura -- eine hethitische Handelsstadt: MBAH 14,2 (1995) 70-106; Eng. franç. 107.

c531 *Hallbäck* Geert, *Strange* John, Sem, Kam og Jafet; en studie i bibelsk geografi: F(orum)BE 4 (K 1993) 9-36 [< OTA 18 (1995) p. 277 (J.T. *Willis*)].

c532 [E]**Hoerth** A.J., *al.*, Peoples of the OT world 1994 → 10,246*: [R]BA 58 (1995) 175s (T.W. *Eddinger*).

c533 **Hübner** Ulrich, Die Ammoniter 1992 → 9,13945: [R]AfO 42s (1995s) 306-8 (S. *Kreuzer*).

c534 **Ivantchik** Askold I., Les Cimmeriens au Proche-Orient: OBO 127, 1993 → 9,15236; 10,13548; [R]AfO 42s (1995s) 236-8 (W.R. *Gallagher*).

c535 *Ivantchik* A.J., [R] On the question of the ethnic origin and archaeological culture of the Cimmerians, 2. Early Scythian finds in Asia Minor: VDI 212 (1995) 3-22; Eng. 22.

c536 *Knauf* Ernst A., Supplementa Ismaelitica 5. 1 Makk 9,15-41 oder eine transjordanische Art der Konfliktbewaltigung: BiNo 75 (1994) 18-20.

c537 *Kurochkin* G.N. †, [R] The chronology of the [Scythian] Near East war expeditions according to written sources and archaeological data [MEDVEDSKAYA I.]: RossArkh (1994,1) 117-122.

c538 **Lemche** Niels P., The Canaanites and their land: JSOT.S 110, 1990 → 7,b17: [R]BZ 39 (1995) 109-112 (R. *Albertz*); NedThT 49 (1995) 72s (K.A.D. *Smelik*).

c539 *Marcaccini* Carlo, Il ruolo dei Traci nell'immaginario greco di V-IV sec. a.C., tra storiografia e iconografia: RS(tor)A 25 (1995) 7-53.

c540 *Margalith* Othniel, Where did the Philistines come from ? ZAW 107 (1995) 101-9.

c541 *Parker* Victor, Bemerkungen zu den Zügen der Kimmerier und der Skythen durch Vorderasien: Klio 77 (1995) 7-34.

c542 **Pogrebova** M.N., *Raevsky* D.S., Early Scythians and the Ancient East. Moskva 1992. - - [R]RossArkh (1994,3) 230-5 (S.V. *Makhortykh*).

c543 *Rouillard-Bonraisin* Hedwige, Presence et représentations des arabes dans les écrits bibliques: → 728, Présence 1993/5, 23-35; p.34, liste d'une vingtaine de noms.

c544 **Samsaris** Dimitrios C., Les Thraces dans l'Empire romain d'Orient (le territoire de la Grèce actuelle); étude ethnographique, sociale, prosopograpique et anthroponymique. Janina 1993, Univ. 371 p. -- [R]RB(elg)PH 73 (1995) 232-4 (B. *Rochette*).

c545 **Schiltz** Véronique, Gli Sciti, dalla Siberia al Mar Nero. T 1995, Electa Gallimard. 176 p. L^m 20. -- [R]Archeo 128 (1995) 110 (Giovanna *Quattrocchi*).

c546 *Węcowski* Marek, [P] De excursu Scythico (HERODOTI Hist. IV,1-144) eiusque compositione: Mea(nder) 50 (1995) 305-319; lat. 319.

u4.5 *Viae* -- **Roads, routes**

c547 **Casson** Lionel, Travel in the ancient world^2 1994 → 10,13803: [R]BA 58 (1995) 123s (W.D. *Glanzmann*).

c548 *Chevallier* Raymond, Les textes littéraires latins et grecs concernant la voirie romaine: *JAT/RTA 5 (1995) 7-30; Eng. 211.

c549 **Desanges** Jehan, *Stern* E. Marianne, *Ballet* Pascale, Sur les routes antiques del'Azanie et del'Inde: Fonds Révoil (Somalie) / Mémoire 13. P 1993, AIBL. 80 p. -- [R]Gnomon 67 (1995) 73 (A. *Dihle*).

c550 **Dorsey** David D., The roads and highways of ancient Israel [< [D]1981, Dropsie] 1991 → 8,k136; 9,15242: [R]JNES 54 (1995) 232-4 (A.H. *Joffe*); JQR 86 (1995s) 179-181 (S. *Aḥituv*).

c551 *Habas(-Rubin)* Ephrat, The [Damascus] Nawa-Dur'a road: SCI(sr) 14 (1995) 138-42.

c552 *Hauser* Stefan R., Zu den mesopotamischen Handelswegen nach der Tabula Peutingeriana → 23, [F]BOEHMER R.M., Beiträge 1995, 225-234 + map; pl. 20.

c553 *Joannès* Francis, L'itinéraire des Dix-Mille en Mésopotamie et l'apport des sources cunéiformes: Pallas 43 (1995) 171-199; Eng. 199 [89-97 routes royales, *Debord* P.].

c554   *Ledo Cballero* Antonio C.,   Itinera loquuntur; los contenidos históricos de los antiguos caminos; → 221, [F]YELO TEMPLADO A., Lengua 1995, 451 [459-467. *López Campuzano* Manuel, Via,, iter, actus y limes .. en Murcia].

c555   *a) Rasson-Seigne* Anne-Michel, *Seigne* Jacques,   Notes préliminaires à l'étude de la voie rommaine Gerasa / Philadelphia: -- *b) Kennedy* David, The Via nova traiana in northern Jordan; a cultural resource under threat: ADAJ 39 (1995) 193-210; 8 fig. / 221-7; 5 fig. [365-408, *Uscatescu* Alexandra, Jerash macellum bowls].

c556   *a) Salles* J.-F.,   The Periplus of the Erythraean Sea and the Arab-Persian Gulf; -- *b) Ray* Himanshu Prabha,   A resurvey of Roman contacts with the East [page-headings 'with India ']: *TopO 3 (1993) 493-523 / 479-491.

c557   *Sidebotham* Steven E.,   Routes through the Eastern Desert of Egypt: Expedition 17,2 (1995) 39-52; 21 fig.

c558   *a) Uggeri* Giovanni,   Metodologia della ricostruzione della viabilità romana; -- *b) Bonora Mazzoli* Giovanni, La centurazione; osservazioni di metodo: → 706*, *JAT/RTA 4 (1993/4) 91-100; 1 fig. / 101-8; Eng. 215.

c559   *Yamauchi* Edwin M.,   On the road with Paul; the ease -- and dangers -- of travel in the ancient world: ChrHist 14,47 (1995) 16-19.

U5   *Ethnographia,* **sociologia;** servitus

c560   **Abraham** Gary A.,   Max WEBER and the Jewish question; a study of the social outlook of his sociology 1992 → 9,15249; 10, 13563: [R]*A(sn)JS 19 (1994) 281-4 (Christa *Schäfer-Lichtenberger*).

c561   *a) Adam* Anne-Marie,   *Rouveret* Agnès,   Cavaleries et aristocraties cavalières en Italie entre la fin du VIe siècle et le premier tiers du IIIe siècle avant notre ère: MEFRA 107 (1995) 7-12 [71-96; *al. 12-31*]; -- *b) Massa-Pairault* Françoise-Hélène,   'Eques romanus -- eques latinus' (V[e]-VIe siècle): MEFRA 107 (1995) 33-70.

c562   **Aguirre** Rafael,   La mesa compartida; estudios del Nuevo Testamento desde las ciencias sociales: PresTeol 77. Sdr 1994, Sal Terrae.   242 p.   84-293-1127-3. -- [R]*Carthaginensia 11 (1995) 203 (J.J. *Tamayo Acosta*); EstB 53 (1995) 429-431 (S. *Guijarro*); RF 231 (1995)n441s (R. de *Andrés*); SalTer 83 (1995) 413s (A. *Macuñana*).

c563   **Alföldy** Geza,   Histoire sociale de Rome [[3]1984], [T]*Evrard* Etienne 1991 → 8,k148; 9,15249*; F 250;   3-7084-0402-4: [R]Latomus 54 (1995) 199 (P. *Salmon*).

c564   **Alston** R.,   Soldier and society in Roman Egypt; a social history [diss. London 1990, [D]*Rathbone* D.]. L 1995, Routledge. viii-263 p.; 21 fig. 0-415-12270-8 [NTAb 40, p.548].

c565   **Antoniazzi** Alberto, *al.,*   Nem anjos nem demônios (interpretações sociológicas do Pentecostalismo). Petrópolis 1994, Vozes.   270 p. -- [R]REB 55 (1995) 716-9 (A.P. *Oro*) & 985-9 (F.C. *Rolim*).

c566   **Arens** E.,   Asia Menor en tiempos de Pablo, Lucas y Juan; aspectos sociales y económicos para la comprensión del Nuevo Testamento. Córdoba 1995, Almendro.   234 p.; bibliog. 225-234. pt. 1600. 84-8005-022-5. -- [R]BiFe 21 (1995) (A. *Salas*); Proyección 42 (1995) 319 (J.L. *Sicre*); RevAg 36 (1995) 1131s (J. Manuel *Paniagua*).

c567   *Arnaoutoglou* Ilias,   Associations and patronage in ancient Athens: AncSoc 25 (1994) 5-17.

c568   *a) Audinet* Jacques,   Position du christianisme dans la société, critères pour un repérage; -- *b) Baum* Gregory, The Church's response to the challenge of pluralism: L(aval)TP 51 (1995) 7-15; Eng. 7 / 35-47; franç. 35.

c569 *Ay* Karl-Ludwig, Geography and mentality; some aspects of Max WEBER's Protestantism thesis, [T]*Dolphin* Amy C.: Numen 41 (1994) 163-194.

c570 *Bar-Eilan* Meir, [H] Childhood and its status in biblical and talmudic society [... ARIES P., Eng. 1962]: BetM 40,1 (140, 1994) 19-32 [32-42, *Wolfenson* A., Democracy in Torah].

c571 **Barrett** John C., Fragments from antiquity; an archaeology of social life in Britain, 2900-120 B.C.: Social Archaeology. Ox 1994, Blackwell. x-190 p.; 34 fig. £ 35; pa. £ 15. 0-632-18953-X; -4-8. -- [R]*Antiquity* 69 (1995) 179-182 (Barbara *Bender*; also on GOSDEN C. in the series.)

c572 *Bell* Brenda M., The contribution of Julius Caesar to the vocabulary of ethnography: Latomus 54 (1995) 753-767.

c573 **Berlinerblau** Jacques, The vow and the 'popular religious groups' of ancient Israel; a philological and sociological inquiry: JSOT.s 210. Shf c.1995, Academic. £ 39. 1-85075-578-7.

c574 **Bernbeck** Reinhard, Die Auflösung der häuslichen Produktionsweise: BBV(Orient) 14. B 1994, Reimer. 387 p. DM 80. 3-496-02525-5. -- [R]BoL (1995) 123 (M.J. *Geller*: really a dissertation on the early evolution of society in Mesopotamia).

c575 **Bettini** Maurizio, Familie und Verwandtschaft im antiken Rom [Antropologia e cultura romana; parentela, tempo, immagini dell'anima 1986], [T]*Zittel* Diemut: HistSt 8. Fra 1992, Campus. 256 p. DM 68. -- [R]HZ 260 (1995) 523s (Beate *Wagner-Hasel*).

c576 **Bianchi** Ugo, *al.*, Crisi, rotture e cambiamenti: Trattato di antropologia del sacro 4. Mi 1995, Jaca. 415 p.; bibliog. 387-409. 88-16-40363-2.

c577 **Bindemann** W., Gemeinde und Gesellschaft im Neuen Testament; ZeichZt 48 (Lp 1994) 226-231 [< ZIT 95, p.96].

c578 *a) Blasi* Anthony J, The more basic method in the sociology of early Christianity; -- *b) Hanson* K.C., Greco-Roman studies and the social-scientific study of the Bible; a classified periodical bibliography: ForumFF 9,1s (1993) 7-18 / 63-119.

c579 **Blenkinsopp** Joseph. Sage, priest, prophet; religious and intellectual leadership in ancient Israel: Library of Ancient Israel. LVL 1995, W-Knox. xi-191 p. 0-664-21954-3.

c580 *Bouzon* E., O alcance social da *şimdat šarrim* nos contratos paleobabilónicos de Larsa: Cadmo 2 (Lisboa 1992) 77-100 [< ZAW 107 (1995) 135].

c581 *Bouzon* Emanuel, Die soziale Bedeutung des *simdat-šarrim*-Aktes nach den Kaufverträgen der Rim-Sin-Zeit: → 185, [F]SODEN W.von,Vom Alten Orient (1995) 11-30.

c582 **Bradley** K., Slavery and rebellion in the Roman world 1989 → 5,6293 ... 8,k159a: [R]EM(erita) 62 (1994) 220-2 (J.J. *Caerols Pérez*).

c583 **Bradley** Keith, Slavery and society at Rome: Key Themes in Ancient History. C 1994, Univ. 1x-202 p. $ 55; pa. $ 18. [RStR 22,155, E. *Krentz*].

c584 **Bradley** Keith R., Discovering the Roman family; studies in Roman social history 1991 → 8,217a: [R]HZ 260 (1995) 169s (Marieluise *Deissmann*).

c585 **Brashear** William M., Vereine im griechisch-römischen Ägypten: Xenia 34. Konstanz 1993, Univ. 49 p. 3-87940-432-1. -- [R]Klio 77 (1995) 498 (R. *Scholl*).

c586 [E]**Brett** Mark G., Ethnicity and the Bible: Biblical interpretation 9. Lei c.1995, Brill. x-509 p. 90-04-10317-1.

c587 *a) Breuer* Stefan, Herrschaftsstruktur und städtischer Raum, Überlegungen in Anschluss an Max WEBER; -- *b) Lehmann* Gustav A., Eduard MEYER, Oswald SPENG- LER und die Epoche des Hellenismus in universalhistorischer Perspektive: AKuG 77 (1995) 135-164 / 165-196.

c588 **Brueggemann** Walter, A social reading of the Old Testament; prophetic approaches to Israel's communal life. Mp 1994, Fortress. viii-328 p. $ 18. 0-8006-2734-2.-- [R]BiRe(v) 11,6 (1995) 14s (N.K. *Gottwald*).

c589 *Bush* Joseph E., The vanua [land] is the Lord's: *PacJT 2,13 (1995) 75-87 [< TIC 13/1,81].

c590 **Butler** Lee H.[J], African American identity formation; an ERIKSONIAN approach: diss. Drew, [D]*Pressley* A. Madison NJ 1994. 270 p. 95-23580.-- D(iss)AI 56 (1995s) p.972.

c591 **Cantarella** Eva, Bisexuality in the ancient world [1988], [T]*Ó Cuilleanáin* Cormac. NHv 1994 = 1992. xii-284 p. £ 9 pa. 0-300-04844-0. -- [R]BoL (1995) 125 (M.D. *Goodman*).

c592 **Cassidy** Richard J., Society and politics in the Acts 1987 → 3,5088 ... 6,5471: [R]MélSR 52 (1995) 336s (J.C. *Matthys*).

c593 *Caulley* Thomas R., Sociological methods in the study of the New Testament; a review and assessment: RestQ 37,1 (1995) 36-44 [NTAb 39, p.371].

c594 *Cavazzani* Guido, Metodo e carisma nell'analisi di Max WEBER: SU(rb)SF 65 (1992) 363-379.

c595 **Cazora Russo** Gaetana, [ricerca statistica sociologica dei 4322 sacerdoti incluso stranieri residenti nella diocesi di Roma: 440 risposte di 1100 interrogati] Essere sacerdote in un mondo che cambia. Mi 1994, F. Angeli. 278 p. L[m] 35. -- [R]RasT 36 (1995) 112-6 (Cloe *Taddei Ferretti*).

c598 *a) Chance* John K., The anthropology of honor and shame; culture, values, and practice; -- *b) Kressel* Gideon M., An anthropologist's response to the use of social science models in biblical studies: Semeia 68 ('Honor and shame in the world of the Bible' 1994) 139-151 / 153-161

c599 **Chirichigno** Gregory C., Debt slavery in Israel and the Ancient Near East: JSOT.s 141, 1993 → 9,2466: [R]Biblica 76 (1995) 254-261 (E. *Otto*); CBQ 57 (1995) 546s (D.E. *Fleming*).

c600 **Chow** John K., Patronage and power; a study of social networks in Corinth: JSNT.s 75, 1992 → 8,6364: [R]A(ustrl)BR 43 (1995) 93s (N.M. *Watson*); *CritRR 7 (1994) 163-5 (P. *Marshall*); EvQ 67 (1995) 163-5 (A.D. *Clarke*); TorJT 11 (1995) 235-7 (R.A. *Derrenbacker*).

c601 **Clarke** Andrew D., Secular and Christian leadership in Corinth .. AGJU 18, 1993 → 9,6062: [R]JBL 114 (1995) 344-6 (V.P. *Furnish*).

c602 [E]**Cohen** Shaye J.D., The Jewish family in antiquity; BJS 289, 1993 → 9,376: [R]CBQ 57 (1995) 836s (C. *Osiek*).

c603 **Cook** S.L., Prophecy and apocalypticism; the postexilic social setting. Mp 1995, Fortress.x-246 p.; bibliog. 223-239; 3 charts.$ 21 pa. 0-8006-2839-X [NTAb 40, p. 551].

c604 *Copher* C.B., Blacks/Negroes, participants in the development of civilization in the ancient world and their presence in the Bible: JI(ntdenom)TC 23,1 (1995) 3-47 [NTAb 40, p.472].

c605 **Corley** Kathleen E., Private women, public meals; social conflict ... 1933 → 9,9324; 10,8724: [R]BiRe(v) 11,1 (1995) 16s (Judith K. *Applegate*); RevB(Arg) 57 (1995) 181s (A.J. *Levoratti*).

c606 [E]**Cornell** T.J., *Lomas* Kathryn, Urban society in Roman Italy {London Inst.Clas.

July 1991]. L 1995, UCL. xii-221 p. 1-85728-033-4. -- 11 art.

c607 *Craffert* P.F., Is the emic-etic distinction a useful tool for cross-cultural interpretation of the New Testament ? ; *RelT 2,1 (Pretoria 1995) 14-37.

c608 *Craffert* Peter F., The anthropological turn in New Testament intepretation; dialogue as negotiation and cultural critique: Neotest 29 (1995) 167-182.

c609 *Crocker* Piers T., Voluntary slavery for food ? Was Joseph's treatment of the Egyptians politically corect ? [Gen 47,13]: BurHist 31 (1995) 56-62.

c610 *Crocker* Piers. It's all happening ... down at the city gate: BurHist 31 (1995) 48-56.

Crossan John D., The historical Jesus .. Mediterranean Jewish peasant 1991 → 2117.

c611 **Davis** Charles, Religion and the making of society; essays in social theology 1994 → 10,10300: ᴿMoTh 11 (1995) 392-4 (Linda *Woodhead*: modest aim, not really achieved; NTT 95 (1994) 231-5 (Ingun *Montgomery*).

c612 **Demand** Nancy, Birth, death, and motherhood in classical Greece: Ancient Society and History. Baltimore 1994, Johns Hopkins Univ. xx-276 p. £ 33. -- ᴿGaR 42 (1995) 246s (P. *Walcot*).

c613 **Demandt** Alexander, Antike Staatsformen; eine vergleichende Verfassungsge-schichte der Alten Welt. B 1995, Akademie. 672 p. 3-05-002794-0.

c614 **Deniaux** É., Clientèles et pouvoir à l'époque de Cicéron: ÉcFrR 182, 1993 → 10,13589: ᴿCLR 45 (1995) 342s (J, *Carter*); ÉtCL 63 (1995) 94 (V. *Marin*).

c615 **Destro** Adriana, *Pesce* Mauro, Antropologia delle origini cristiane: Quadrante 78. R 1995, Laterza. xv-243 p.; bibliog. 185-217. Lᵐ 29. 88-420-4728-7 [NTAb 40, p.322].

c616 *Di Marco* Angelico, I codici familiari ['conduct-codes, Haustafeln' not '(textcritical) codex'] nel Nuovo Testamento; sociologia o teologia ?: → 123, ᶠMATTIOLI A., In spiritu et veritate 1995, 235-304.

c617 **Dixon** Susanne, The Roman family 1991 → 8,k171 ... 10,13590: ᴿGnomon 67 (1995) 619-622 (Hinnerk *Bruhns*).

c618 **Dolukhanov** Pavel, Environment and ethnicity in the Ancient Middle East: Worldwide Archaeology 7. Aldershot 1994, Avebury. x-406 p. 1-85628-706-8 [*OIAc 11,20].

c619 *a) Domeris* W.R., Sociological studies and the interpretation of the Bible [NTAb 40, p.195]; -- *b) Snyman* Gerrie, Towards an aesthetic reading of the Bible: *Scriptura 54 (SAf 1995) 203-213. / 147-157.

c620 **Douglas** Mary, In the wilderness [Num] 1993 → 10,2357: ᴿTorJT 11 (1995) 230s (T.F. *Williams*).

c621 **Dyson** Stephen L., Community and society in Roman Italy 1992 → 9,15275; 10.13592: ᴿHZ 260 (1995) 524-6 (H. *Galsterer*).

c622 ᴱ**Eck** Werner, *Heinrichs* Johannes, Sklaven und Freigelassene in der Gesellschaft der Kaiserzeit [zweisprachig]: TFo 61, 1993 → 9,6326 [NTAb 40, p.375]: ᴿHZ 261 (1995) 505s (C. *Schäfer*); Klio 77 (1995) 522s (L. *Schumacher*).

c623 **Edersheim** Alfred, Sketches of Jewish social lifeʳᵉᵛ [1876]. Peabody MA 1995, Hendrickson. viii-307 p. 1-56563-138-2.

c624 *Ehrlich* Carl S., Sklavenauslieferung in der Bibel [1 Kön 2,39s] und in dem Alten Orient: Trumah 4 (Wsb 1994) 111-8 [< OTA 18 (1995) p. 277].

c625 **Elliott** John H., What is social-scientific criticism ? 1993 → 9,15276: ᴿCBQ 57 (1995) 177 (D.J. *Harrington*: an enormous amount of information, perhaps too strong on theory for the intended users); *CritRR 8 (1995) 95-97 D.M. *May*); CThMi 22 (1995) 216 (E. *Krentz*); LTJ 29 (1995) 42s (V.C. *Pfitzner*); NewThR 8,4 (1995) 110s (Carolyn *Osiek*).

c626 **Elliott** John, Social-scientific criticism of the NT. L 1995, SPCK. ix-174 p. £ 10 pa. -- [R]Theol 98 (L 1995) 485s (P.F. *Esler*).

c627 **Esler** P-F., The first Christians in their social worlds; social-scientific approaches to NT interpretation [1992 Scotland lectures] 1994 → 10,13595; £ 11: [R]TTh 35 (1995) 402 (J. *Negenman*).

c628 **Eyben** Emiel, Restless youth in ancient Rome 1993 → 9,15279; 10,12597: [R]HZ 261 (1995) 499-501 (E. *Meyer-Zwiffelhoffer*); *JEarlyC 3 (1995) 91-93 (B. *Leyerle*); JRS 85 (1995) 259 (D. *Montserrat*).

c629 *Eyre* Christopher, Feudal tenure and absentee landlords: → 10.443, Grund/Boden im Altägypten 1990/4, 107-134.

c630 **Fager** Jeffrey A., Land tenure and the biblical Jubilee ... sociology of knowledge 1993 → 9,2467: [R]BiOr 52 (1995) 771-3 (E.*Otto*); JAOS 115 (1995) 166s (N.P. *Lemche*).

c631 **Fayer** Carla, La familia romana; aspetti giuridici ed antiquari I; ProbRicStoAnt 16, 1994 → 10,13598: [R]RÉL 73 (1995) 316-8 (P. *Moreau*).

c632 **Feldmeier** R., *Heckel* U., Die Heiden; Juden, Christen und das Problem des Fremden: WUNT 70, 1994 → 10,241c: [R]VigChr 49 (1995) 93-95 (P.W. van der *Horst*).

c633 **Feldmeier** Reinhard, Die Christen als Fremde [1 Pt 2,11] 1994 → 10,6270: [R]NT 37 (1995) 406-8 (E.J. *Schnabel*).

c634 *Fernández Uriel* Pilar, *Vidal Manzanares* César, Familia y *oikos*, un estudio puntual sobre la composición socio-económica de las primitivas comunidades cristianas; → 221, [F]YELO TEMPLADO A., Lengua 1995, 165-180.

c635 **Fiensy** David A., The social history of Palestine in the Herodian period; the land is mine: StBEarlyC 20, 1991 → 8,k181 ... 10,13598*: [R]ProcGM 14 (1994) 205-210 (J. *Kampen*).

c636 **Fisher** N.R.E., Slavery in classical Greece 1993 → 9,6327; 10,6147: [R]CLR 45 (1995) 190 (J. *Roy*).

c637 **Fournier** Marcel, Marcel MAUSS. P 1994, Fayard. 846 p. F 240. -- [R]Études 382 (1995) 134 (P. *Valadier*: neveu de DURKHEIM, trop à son ombre).

c638 **Fraser** David A., *Campolo* Tony, Sociology through the eyes of faith 1992 → 8,k182; 9,15287; $11 pa. 0-06-061315-7: [R]CScR 25 (1995s) 367-370 (R.A. *Clark*: ambitious, largely successful).

c639 **Gardner** Jane, Being a Roman citizen 1993 → 9,15289: [R]AJP(g) 116 (1995) 671-3 (Susan D. *Martin*); BoL (1995) 129 (M. *Goodman*: the book profits by researches of JOHN GOODMAN); JRS 85 (1995) 254-6 (K. *Buraselis*).

c640 **Ginestet** Pierre, Les organisations de la jeunesse dans l'Occident romain [dissertation de 1951 mise à jour] 1991 → 9,15293. 10,13602: [R]RB(elg)PH 73 (1995) 219s (H. *Devijver*).

c641 *Gingrich* André, *Haas* Sylvia, Vom Orientalismus zur Sozialanthropologie; ein Überblick zu österreichischen Beiträgen für die Ethnologie der islamischen Welt; MitAntW 125s (1995s) 115-134.

c642 **Gottwald** Norman K., The Hebrew Bible in its social world and in ours: SemeiaSt 1993 → 9,201: [R]Interpretation 49 (1995) 302-4 (J.A. *Dearman*, a bit probingly; also, more briefly, on MATTHEWS & BENJAMIN).

c643 **Grabbe** Lester L., Priests, prophets, diviners, sages; a socio-historical study of religious specialists in ancient Israel. Ph 1995, Trinity. xviii-261 p. $ 20. 1-56338-132-X [RStR 22,234: '26 p.'].

c644 **Greek** Cecil E., The religious roots of American sociology. NY 1992, Garland.

282 p. $ 42. -- [R]AmJTP 16 (1995) 111-5 (J.A. *Denton*).

c645 **Greenspahn** Frederick E., When brothers dwell together; the preeminence of younger siblings in the Hebrew Bible. Ox 1994, UP. xi-193 p. £ 22.50. 0-19-508253-2. - - [R]BoL (1995) 89 (W.J. *Houston*); CBQ 57 (1995) 767-9 (H. *Gossai*); JThS 46 (1995) 572-5 (Eryl W. *Davies*).

c646 *Guijarro Oporto* Santiago, La familia en la Galilea del siglo primero: EstB 53 (1995) 461-488; Eng.461: no information beyond title.

c647 *Gustafson* James M., Explaining and valuing: an exchange between theology and the human sciences / tracing a trajectory: Zygon 30,2 (1995) 159-175 / 177-190 (responses 191-220; rejoinder 221-6).

c648 *Haas* Guenther, The Kingdom and slavery; a test case for social ethics: C(alvin)TJ 28 (1993) 74-89 [90-109, *Weima* Jeffrey A.D., Gal 6,11-18].

c649 *Haase* Richard, Dienstleistungsverträge in der hethitischen Rechtssammlung: ZA(ssyr) 85 (1995) 109-115.

c650 *Hachmann* Rolf, Die Völkerschaften auf den Bildwerken von Persepolis → 23, [F]BOEHMER R.M., Beiträge 1995, 195-213 + 10 fig.

c651 *Hall* Jonathan M., The role of language in Greek ethnicities: PCP(g)S 41 (1995) 83-100; 2 fig.

c652 [E]**Halpern** Baruch, *Hobson* Deborah W., Laws, politics and society 1988/93 → 9,522: [R]AnCL 64 (1995) 446-8 (Monique *Dondin-Payre*).

c653 **Hamel** Gildas, Poverty and charity in Roman Palestine 1990 → 6,g407 ... 10,13607: [R]CThMi 22 (1995) 145s (E. *Krentz*); JJS 46 (1995) 304-6 (J. *Schwartz*).

c654 *Hallo* William W., Slave release [*andurarum, derôr*] in the biblical world in light of a new text: → 72, [F]GREENFIELD J., Solving 1995, 79-93.

c655 **Hallote** Rachel S., Mortuary practices and their implications for social organization in the Middle Bronze southern Levant: diss. [D]*Gibson* M. Chicago 1994. 305 p. 95-13979. -- D(iss)AI 55 (1994s) p.3894.

c656 **Harrill** J. Albert, The manumission of slaves in early Christianity: HUTh 32. Tu 1995, Mohr. xvii-255 p. DM 148. 3-16-146285-8. -- [R]E(xp)T 107,2 2d-top choice (1995s) 34 (C.S. *Rodd*); R(öm)Q 90 (1995) 262-6 (R. *Klein*); *TBR 8,2 (1995s) 48.

c657 *Helve* Helena, The formation of a world view and the religious socialization of young people: JE(mp)T 8,2 (1995) 39-57.

c658 *Henking* Susan E., Sociological Christianity and Christian sociology; the paradox of early American sociology: R&AC(u) 3 (1993) 49-67.

c659 **Herrmann-Otto** Elisabeth, Ex ancilla natus; Untersuchungen zu den 'Hausgeborenen' Sklaven und Sklavinnen im Wesen des römischen Kaiserreichs [Hab.-Diss Mainz]; FASk 24. Stu 1994, Steiner. viii.512 p. DM 168. -- [R]AnCL 64 (1995) 497s (Huguette *Jones*); CLR 45 (1995) 349-351 (Jane F. *Gardner*); HZ 261 (1995) 503-5 (F. *Bern-stein*); JRS 85 (1995) 291s (J.A. *Crook*).

c660 **Höghammar** Kerstin, Sculpture and society; a study of the connection between the freestanding sculpture and society on Kos in the Hellenistic and Augustan periods: Boreas 23. U 1993, Acta Univ. 228 p.; 28 fig. Sk 206. -- [R]RB(elg)PH 73 (1995) 267-9 (F. *Baratte*).

c661 **Hoffmann** Paul, Studien zur Frühgeschichte der Jesus-Bewegung; SBAufs 17, 1994 → 10,185: [R]BiKi 50 (1995) 190 (R. *Hoppe*); BZ 39 (1995) 271-4 (D. *Dormeyer*).

c662 **Holmberg** Bengt V., Historia social del cristianismo primitivo; la sociología y el NT [1990],[T]: EnOrCr 6. Córdoba 1995, Almendro. 220 p. pt. 2700. 84-8005-021-7. --

^{R}BiFe 21 (1995) 464 (A. *Salas*); Communio (Sev) 28 (1995) 379-381 (M. de *Burgos*); EstAg 30 (1995) 556 (D. *Alvarez Cineira*); Proyección 42 (1995) 322 (J.L. *Sicre*).

c663 **Hoornaert** Eduardo, O movimento de Jesus [< 1991]: Uma História do Cristianismo na perpectiva do Pobre 1994 → 10,13610: ^{R}REB 55 (1995) 710-2 (J.B. *Libânio*).

c664 **Horsley** Richard A., Sociology and the Jesus movement 1989 → 7,e673 ... 10,13611: ^{R}JETS 37 (1994) 427-9 (M.R. *Fairchild*).

c665 **Houten** Christiana van, The alien in Israelite law: JSOT.s 107, 1991 → 8,2584: ^{R}JAOS 115 (1995)722-4 (V.H. *Matthews*).

c666 **How** Alan, The HABERMAS-GADAMER debate and the nature of the social; back to bedrock. Aldershot 1995, Avebury. xi-215 p.; bibliog. 229-244. 1-85628-179-5.

c667 *Hubert* Bernard, Approche d'une définition de la culture: NV 70,4 (1995) 41-65.

c668 **Jackson** Alvin A., Examining the record; an exegetical and homiletical study of Blacks in the Bible: King Mem. 4. NY 1994, P. Lang. ix-112 p. 0-8204-2389-0.

c669 **Jamieson-Drake** D.W., Scribes and schools in monarchic Juda; a socio-archeological approach: JSOT.S 109, 1991 → 7,e676 ... 10,13613: ^{R}BZ 39 (1995) 122-4 (H. *Niehr*).

c670 *Jördens* Andrea, Sozialstrukturen im Arbeitshandel des kaiserzeitlichen Ägypten: Tyche 10 (1995) 37-100.

c671 *Johnson* Willa M., Ethnicity in Persian Yehud [Ezra 9s]; between anthropological analysis and ideological criticism; → 512, SBL Seminars 34 (1995) 177-186.

c672 *Joncheray* Jean, Comment peuvent travailler ensemble des sociologues, des théologiens, des pasteurs ?: RevSR 69,3 ('Théologie pratique et/ou pastorale' francophone cath/prot, germanophone, anglo-saxonne 1995) 322-333; Eng.415.

c673 **Joshel** Sandra R., Work, identity, and legal status at Rome; a study of the occupational inscriptions 1992 → 9,15510; 10,13615; $ 28: ^{R}CJ 90 (1994s) 445-450 (K. *Bradley*, also on GIARDINA A., EDWARDS C.).

c674 *Joubert* Stephan J., The Jerusalem community as role-model for a cosmopolitan Christian group; a socio-literary analysis of Luke's symbolic universe: Neotest 29 (1995) 49-59.

c675 **Kalberg** Stephen, Max WEBER's comparative-historical sociology. Ch 1994, Univ. xi-221 p. $ 19. 0-226-42303-4. -- ^{R}BoL (1995) 41 (L.L. *Grabbe*).

c676 **Kee** Howard C., Who are the people of God ? Early Christian models of community. NHv 1995, Yale Univ. viii-280 p. £ 22.50. 0-300-05952-3. -- ^{R}E(xp)T 107 (1995s) 26 (M. *Bockmuehl*).

c677 **Koffi** Ettien N., Language and society in biblical times. SF .. International Scholars. xvi-254 p.; bibliog. 233-244.

c678 **Kontoulis** Georg, Zum Problem der Sklaverei (*douleia*) bei den kappadokischen Kirchenvätern und J. CHRYSOSTOMUS: Diss. AltG 38, 1993 → 9,6331: ^{R}CLR 45 (1995) 122s (I.G. *Tompkins*); HZ 261 (1995) 506-8 (R.*Klein*: mangelhaft).

c679 **Krause** Jens-Uwe, Die Familie und weitere anthropologische Grundlagen; Bibliographie der römischen Sozialgeschichte 1, HABES 11. Stu 1992, Steiner. xii-260 p. - - ^{R}Tyche 9 (1994) 237s (W. *Scheidel*).

c680 *Kruger* Paul, Rites of passage relating to marriage and divorce in the Hebrew Bible: JNWSL 21,2 (1995) 69-81.

c681 **Kudlien** Fridolf, Sklaven-Mentalität 1991 → 8.k209*: ^{R}Latomus 54 (1995) 465s (J.P. *Brisson*).

c682 *a) Kügler* Joachim, Priestersynoden im hellenistischen Ägypten; ein Vorschlag zu ihrer sozio-historischen Deutung; -- *b) Youssef* Y. Nessim, Quelques titres des congrégations des moines coptes: GöMisz 139 (1994) 53-60 / 61-68.

c683 **Laato** Timo, Paul and Judaism; an anthropological approach [German 1991], ^T*McElwain* T.: SFSHJ 115. At 1995, Scholars. vii-285 p.; bibliog. 215-261. 0-7885-0100-3.

c684 ^E**Lehmann** Harmut, *Roth* Guenther, Max WEBER's Protestant Ethic; origins; evidence, contexts 1990/3 → 9,464*e*: ^RJEH 46 (1995) 164s (R.W. *Scribner*); JRel 75 (1995) 467s (M. *Riesebrodt*).

c685 *a) Lemche* Neils P., Kings and clients; on loyalty between the ruler and the ruled in ancient 'Israel'; -- *b) Knight* Douglas A., Political rights and powers in monarchic Israel: Semeia 66 ('Ethics and politics in the Hebrew Bible' 1994) 119-132 / 93-117.

c686 *a) Lerberghe* Karel van, Kassites and Old Babylonian society; a reappraisal; -- *b) Zawadzki* Stefan, Hostages in Assyrian royal inscriptions: → 110, ^FLIPIŃSKI, E., Immigration: OLA 65 (1995) 379-390; 3 facsim. / 449-458.

c687 ^E**Levy** Thomas E., The archaeology of society in the Holy Land [Univ. Calif. in San Diego, 29-31 Jan. 1993]. London 1995, Leicester Univ. xvi-624 p.; bibliog. 549-604. £ 60. 0-7185-1388-6.

c688 **Lewis** Bernard, Race and slavery in the Middle East; an historical inquiry. NY 1990, Oxford-UP. vii-184 p.; 24 pl. $ 25. -- ^RJNES 54 (1995) 69-71 (M.G. *Morony*).

c689 *Lincoln* Andrew T., Liberation from the powers; supernatural spirits or societal structures ?: → 159, ^FROGERSON, J., Bible/Society; JSOT.s 200 (1995) 335-354.

c690 **Link** Stefan, Landverteilung und sozialer Frieden im archaischen Griechenland; Hist.e 69, 1991 → 10,13626: ^RHZ 260 (1995) 515-7 (P. *Spahn*).

c691 *Liverani* Paolo, 'Nationes' et 'civitates' nella propaganda imperiale: MDAI-R 102 (1995) 219-249; 7 fig.; pl. 55-61.

c692 **Lo Magro** Raffaele, L'origine della civiltà nei popoli: Turris Babylonia. Pioltello MI 1995, Rangoni. 159 p. 88-86513-02-X.

c693 *Luke* Helen M., Jacob and Esau; what we must learn from the biblical story of rivalry and reconciliation: Parabola 19,2 ('Twins' 1994) 22-24 (*al,*)

c694 **Lustig** Judith, Ideologies of social relations in Middle Kingdom Egypt; gender, kinship, ancestors: diss. Temple, ^D*Miller* E. Ph 1993. x-273 p. 94-08801. -- *OIAc 11,32.

c695 *Ma* John, Black hunter variations [mythe composite de l'éphébie d'après P. VIDAL-NAQUET], I. Damon le chasseur noir (PLUTARQUE, Cimon 1-2); II. (in English) Damon of Chaironeia, a historical commentary (Kim.1-2): PCP(g)S 40 (1994) 49-51 / 60-80.

c696 *Machinist* Peter, The transfer of kingship; a divine turning: → 59, ^FFREEDMAN D.N., Fortunate 1995, 105-120.

c697 **McLaren** James S., Power and politics in Palestine. 1991. -- ^RA(ustrl)BR 41 (1993) 78s (J.S. *Levi*).

c698 **Maisels** Charles K. [→ c862 infra; 9,15155], The Near East; archaeology in the 'cradle of civilization' 1993 → 9,12923 [RStR 22,57, D.I. *Owen:* sociology of knowledge frame].

c699 **Malina** B., *Rohrbaugh* R., Social-science commentary on the synoptic gospels 1992 → 8,k220 ... 10,13633: ^RChurchman 108 (L 1994) 81s (R. *Ascough*); *CritRR 7 (1994) 227-9 (J.J. *Pilch*); Metanoia 3 (Praha 1993) 255s.

c700 **Malina** Bruce J., The NT world; insights from cultural anthropology^{2rev} [¹1981] 1993 → 9,15338; 10.13634: ^RNewThR 8,3 (1995) 93s (C. *Osiek*).

c701 **Malina** Bruce J., Windows on the world of Jesus 1993 → 9,15340; 10,13632: ᴿBA 58 (1995) 242 (S.M. *Sheeley*); BThB 25 (1995) 45 (K.C. *Hanson*); *CritRR 7 (1994) 225-7 (C.S. *Keener;* useful and delightful reading); Neotest 29 (1995) 430s (W.R. *Domeris*).

c702 *Malina* Bruce, *a)* Religion in the imagined New Testament world; more social science lenses; -- *b)* Establishment violence in the NT world: *Scriptura 51 (Stellenbosch 1994 1-26 / 51-78 [NTAb 39, p.459].

c703 *Malkin* Irad W., Land ownership, territorial possession, hero cults, and scholarly theory: → 143, ᶠOsᴛwᴀʟᴅ M., Nomodeiktes 1993, 225-234.

c704 *Marin* Maurizio, 'Anomeomerie' [parti non omogenee di un vivente] e potenza: il concetto aristotelico di specie animale: Salesianum 57 (1995) 657-689

c705 **Marinović** I.P., *al.,* Die Sklaverei in den ostlichen Provinzen des römischen Reiches im 1.-2. Jh. [1987], ᵀ*Kriz* J., *al.* Stu 1992, Steiner. 283 p. -- ᴿBo(nn)J 195 (1995) 700-706 (P. *Herz*).

c706 **Marshall** Jay W., Israel and the Book of the Covenant [Ex 21s], an anthropological approach to biblical law: SBL diss. 140, 1993 → 9,2364: ᴿCBQ 57 (1995) 564s (D.C. *Benjamin*).

c707 *Martin* Dale B., Slavery and the ancient Jewish family: → 495, Jewish family 1994, 113-129 [< OTA 18 (1995) p.249].

c708 *a) Martin* David, Sociology, religion and secularization: an orientation; -- *b) Waldmann* Helmut, Religion in the service of an elite; a sociologically defined imposture, the case of ancient Sparta: Religion 25 (1995) 295-303 / 305-316.

c709 *a) Martínez Cortés* Javier, Pertenencia grupal y necesidades humanas; confianza -- autonomía -- creatividad; -- *b) García-Monge* José Antonio, Comunicación y relaciones interpersonales en el interior del grupo; -- *c) Domínguez* Carlos, Ideales e idealismo del grupo: SalTer 83 (1995) 83-100 / 101-113 / 115-127.

c710 **Martínez Sastre** Pedro, Carisma e Institución. Murcia 1994, Espigas. -- *Carthaginensia 11 (1995) 237s (F.G.O.).

c711 *Matthews* Victor H., The anthropology of clothing in the Joseph narrative [Gen 37,3; 39,12 ..]: ᴊꜱoᴛ 65 (1995) 25-36.

c712 **Matthews** Victor H., *Benjamin* Don C., Social world of ancient İsrael 1250-687 BCE 1993 → 9,15342; 10,13637: BA 58 (1995) 238s (F.S. *Frick*); *BInterp 2 (1995) 373-5 (H. *Gossai*); CBQ 57 (1995) 355-7 (K.C. *Henson*); CScR 25 (1995s) 96-98 (R.K. *Buckinshaw*); JBL 114 (1995) 490-2 (D.L. *Smith-Christopher*); LexTQ 30 (1995) 55s (F.H. *Gorman*); NRT 117 (1995) 117 (J.-L. *Ska*); RevBib(Arg) 57 (1995) 126s (A.J. *Levoratti*); RExp 92 (1995) 383 (J.F. *Drinkard*); TorJT 11 (1995) 231s (J.L. *McLaugh-lin*).

c713 **Meeks** Wayne A., I cristiani dei primi secoli; il mondo sociale dell'apostolo Paolo 1993 → 9,15344; 10,13640: ᴿRivB 43 (1995) 297-301 (J. *De Virgilio*).

c714 **Meeks** W.A., El mundo moral de los primeros cristianos [1992 → 9,8809], ᵀ*Avalos Cadena* Blanca: Cristianismo y sociedad. 1992. -- ᴿCDios 207 (1994) 516s (J. *Gutiérrez*).

c715 **Meeks** Wayne A., Urchristentum und Stadtkultur; die soziale Welt der paulinischen Gemeinde 1993 → 10,13639: ᴿBiKi 50 (1995) 187 (M. *Helsper*); ZkT 117 (1995) 234s (R. *Oberforcher*).

c716 **Miller** Jon, The social control of religious zeal; a study of [Ghana Swiss missioners'] organizational contradictions; ᴀꜱᴀ Rose mg. New Brunswick 1994, Rutgers Univ. 248 p. $48. 0-8135-2060-6. -- ᴿJRel 75 (1995) 613-6 (J.D. *Carter*); VSVD 36 (1995) 104s (R. *Schroeder*).

c717 **Mödritzer** Helmut, Stigma und Charisma im NT und seiner Umwelt: zur Soziologie des Urchristentums [Diss. Heidelberg 1993, ^D*Theissen* G.]: NTOA 28, 1994 → 10,13643; DM 115: ^RBZ 39 (1995) 150-3 (T. *Schmeller*); Entschluss 50,9s (1995) 49 (C. *Cebulj*); ThLZ 120 (1995) 441 (M. *Karrer*); TTh 35 (1995) 77 (J. *Negenman*).

c718 *Mommsen* Wolfgang J., Max WEBER -- ein politischer Intellektueller der Jahrhundertwende: Univ 47 (1992) 671-683, 4 fotos.

c719 **Morris** Ian, Death-ritual and social structure in classical antiquity 1991 → 8,e293 ... 10,13644: ^RÉtCL 63 (1995) 387-9 (P. *Bonnechère*).

c720 *Moxnes* Halvor, Sosialantropologi I bibeltolkningen; det Nye Testamente I lys av middelhavskulturen: SvTKv 70 (1994) 153-9; Eng. 159.

c721 **Mratschek-Halfmann** Sigrid, Divites et praepotentes ... Prinzipatszeit 1993 → 9,15349; 10,13645: ^RBo(nn)J 195 (1995) 686-691 (K. *Vössing*); GrazB 21 (1995) 261s (G. *Doblhofer*); HZ 261 (1995) 166s (R. *Rilinger*).

c722 **Müller** Peter, In der Mitte der Gemeinde; Kinder im NT. Neuk-Verlag 1992. 447 p. DM 58. -- ^R*CritRR 7 (1994) 242-4 (J. A. *Harrill*).

c723 **Nakanose** Shigeyuki, Josiah's Passover [2 Kgs 23,21s]; sociology and the liberating Bible [diss. NY theol. sem.], pref. GOTTWALD N.: Bible & Liberation. Mkn 1993, Orbis. xvi-192 p. $ 20 pa. -- ^RCBQ 57 (1995) 359s (R.A. *Simkins*: his aim is to furnish base-communities a hermeneutic for replacing their inadequate or oppressive exegesis: not clear whether really in function of Josiah's own dynamic).

c724 **Nathan** Geoffrey S., The Roman family in late antiquity; the endurance of tradition and the rise of Christianity: diss. UCLA, ^D*Mellor* R., 1995. 522 p. 96-10533. -- D(iss)AI 56 (1995s) p. 4898.

c725 ^E**Neyrey** J., The social world of Luke-Acts 1991 → 7,450 ... 9,5093: ^RBA 57 (1994) 61s (Catherine C. *Kroeger*); Bijdragen 56 (1995) 76-78 (B.J. *Koet*); C(alvin)TJ 29 (1994) 253-6 (D.E. *Holwerda*).

c726 ^E**Nichols** Francis W., & St. Louis University faculty, Christianity and the stranger. Atlanta 1995, Scholars. 297 p. $ 95. 0-7885-0125-9. -- ^RE(xp)T 107 (1995s) 155 (C.S. *Rodd:* most interesting essays).

c727 **Niemann** Hermann M., Herrschaft, Königtum und Staat; Skizzen zur soziokulturellen Entwicklung im monarchischen Israel: FAT 6, 1993 → 9,15351: ^RBiOr 52 (1995) 109-111 (M.J. *Mulder* †); CBQ 57 (1995) 153 (T.L. *Burden*: the theme is whether changing social structures led to social cultural changes); E(xp)T 107 (1995s) 181 (R. *Mason*); JBL 114 (1995) 715s (L.K.*Handy*); ThQ 175 (1995) 150s (H. *Niehr*).

c728 **Nighswander** Daniel L., Paul's use of shame as a sanction in 1 Corinthians: diss. ^D*Richardson* P. Victoria, Canada 1995. 255 p. NN02630 -- 0-612-02630-2. -- DissA 56 (1995s) p. 4820.

c729 **Oakley** John H., *Sinos* Rebecca H, The wedding in ancient Athens. Madison 1993, Univ. Wisconsin. xiv-153 p.; 130 fig. $ 40. 0-299-13720-1. -- ^RCLR 45 (1995) 470s (Karen *Stears*); Kernos 8 (1995) 318-321 (Vinciane *Pirenne-Delforge*); RStR 21 (1995) 49s (Sally P. *Schultz*).

c730 *a) Olkhovsky* B.S., ^R Funeral ceremonies and the sociological reconstructions; -- *b)* *Kyzlasov* I.L., ^R The funeral ceremony and the standard of a society development: RossA (1995,2) 85-98; Eng. 98 / 9-103; 3 fig.; Eng. 103.

c731 *Olsen* Glenn W., Marriage, feminism, theology and the new social history: Dyan ELLIOTT's Spiritual marriage [his 'fantasy' or 'ethereal' corresponds to what AUGUSTINE said defies explanatory categories]: ComI-US 22 (1995) 342-356.

c732   **Osiek** Carolyn,   What are they saying about the social setting of the New

Testament?[2rev] [[1]1984] 1992 → 8,k236; 10,13651: [R]RefTR 54 (1955) 40s (M. *Harding*).

c733 *Oviedo* Lluis, Legitimidad sociológica del Cristianismo como religión en el ambiente contemporáneo: Salmanticensis 42 (1995) 341-367; Eng. 367.

c734 *Papageorgiou* Nikis, [G] Max WEBER's lay religion: Kler 24 (1992) 163-172.

c735 *Pedroni* Luigi, Censo, moneta e 'rivoluzione della plebe': MEFRA 107 (1995) 197-223.

c736 *Pilch* J.J., Illuminating the world of Jesus through cultural anthropology: LiLi 31,1 (Wsh 1994) 20-31 [NTAb 39, p.191].

c737 [E]**Pilch** John J., *Malina* Bruce J., Biblical social values and their meaning 1993 → 9,15357; 10,13654: [R]BA 57 (1994) 249 (V. H. *Matthews*); CBQ 57 (1995) 606s (S. *McKnight*); Neotest 29 (1995) 139s (J.E. *Botha*); NRT 117 (1995) 118s (J.-L. *Ska*); RevBib(Arg) 56 (1994) 188s (A.J. *Levoratti*); TorJT 11 (1995) 249s (W. *Braun*).

c738   *a) Pitschl* Florian, 'Unless you become like children'; Ferdinand ULRICH's philosophical anthropology of childhood, [T]*Dorin* R., *Walker* A.; -- *b) Sales* Michel, The honor of becoming children; what it means to honor one's father and mother, [T]*Schindler* D.: ComI-US 22 (1995) 56-64 / 5-27.

c739 **Reviv** Henoch [*zal* 1990]. The society in the kingdoms of Israel and Judah: EnşBL 8, 1993 → 9,15361: [R]CBQ 57 (1995) 573s (E. *Ben Zvi*); ZAW 107 (1995) 364 (E. *Blum*).

c740 [E]**Rich** John, *Shipley* Graham, War and society in the Roman world 1993 → 9,535; £ 35: [R]AnCL 64 (1995) 472s (J.-P. *Martin*); JRS 85 (1995) 260s (Phyllis *Culham*, also on WATSON A. 1993); Latomus 54 (1995) 705s (P. *Le Roux*).

c741 **Rilinger** Rolf, Humiliores -- honestiores .. im Strafrecht 1988 → 6,g676 ... 8,k247: [R]HZ 260 (1995) 847s (W. *Waldstein*).

c742 **Rizzo** Francesco P., La menzione del lavoro nelle epigrafi della Sicilia antica (per una storia della mentalità): SEIA 6. Palermo 1993, Univ. 169 p. -- [R]Epigraphica 57 (Faenza 1995) 344s (Francesca *Cenerini*).

c743 *Rochettes* Jacqueline des, Famiglia, tribù, popolo; tre modi di comunione: PSV 31 (1995) 11-24.

c744 *Rokeah* David, [H] *Giyyur* ... Alien [.. proselytizing] in ancient Judah; the halaka and the facts: BetM 40,2 (141, 1995) 135-152.

c745 *Saavedra Guerrero* M.D., La cooptatio patroni o el elogio de la virtus en el patronato colegial: At(henaeum) 83 (1995) 497-507.

c746 **Saller** Richard P., Patriarchy, property and death in the Roman family; Population, economy, society in past time. C 1994, Univ. xiv-250 p.; ill. £ 35. 0-521-32603-6, -- [R]A(mer)HR 100 (1995) 1231s (K. *Bradley*); CLR 45 (1995) 106s (Jane F. *Gardner*).

c747 *Salmen* Josef, Historischer Materialismus als heuristisches Prinzip ethnologischer Forschung: VSVD 36 (1995) 289-300.

c748 *a) Samuel* Vinay, Strangers and exiles in the Bible; -- *b) Sugden* Christopher, The right to be human in the OT [Isa 5]: Transformation 12,2 (1995) 28s / 3-33.

c749 *Schäfer-Lichtenberger* Christa, La génesis de las nuevas ideas de la profecía; lectura de Max WEBER, [T]*Trebolle Barrera* Julio: RevAg 36 (1995) 117-157.

c750 *Scheidel* Walter, The most silent women of Greece and Rome; rural labour and women's life in the ancient world: GaR 42 (1995) 202-217 ...

c751 **Schmeller** Thomas, Hierarchie und Egalität; eine sozialgeschichtliche Untersuchung paulinischer Gemeinden und griechisch-römischer Vereine: SBS 162. Stu 1995, KBW. 120 p.; Bibliog. 113-120 DM 40. 3-460-04621-X.

c752 **Serrano Gómez** E., Legitimación y racionalización; WEBER y HABERMAS: la dimensión normativa de un orden secularizado. Barc 1994, Anthropos. 302 p. -- RCommunio (Sev) 28 (1995) 145 (J. *Duque*).

c753 **Singer** Karl H., Alttestamentliche Blutrachepraxis [Jud 8,18; 2 Sam 2,18; 2 Reg 14,5] im Vergleich mit der Ausübung der Blutrache in der Türkei; ein kultur- und rechtshistorischer Vergleich [Diss. Paderborn, *DLang* B.]: EHS 23/509. Fra 1994, Lang. 183 p. Fs 32. 3-361-47301-X. -- RBoL (1995) 119s (R.E. *Clements*).

c754 *Slater* W.J., Pantomime riots: CLAn 25,1 (1994) 120-144.

c755 **Stambaugh** John, *Balch* David, Het Nieuwe Testament in zijn sociale omgeving; schets van de historische en sociale achtergronden van het NT [c.1987], *THeyer* C.J. den, 1992 → 10,13670: RG(ereformeerd)TT 95 (1995) 45 (J.S. *Vos*).

c756 **Stegemann** Ekkehard W. & Wolfgang, Urchristliche Sozialgeschichte; die Anfänge im Judentum und die Christusgemeinden in der mediterranen Welt. Stu 1995, Kohlhammer. 416 p.; 6 fig.; 2 maps DM 45. 3-17-011316-X [NTAb 40, p.386; ThRv 92,77].

c757 **EStein** Gil, *Rothman* Mitchell S., Chiefdoms and early states in the Near East; the organizational dynamics of complexity: *WArch mg 18. Madison 1994, Prehistory. 236 p. 1-881094-07-3 [RStR 22,57, D.I. *Owen:* Madison WI (? or NJ or ?)].

c758 *Stieglitz* Robert R., The Minoan origin of Tyrian purple: BA 57 (1994) 46-54; ill.

c759 **Stone** Elizabeth C., *Owen* David I., Adoption in Old Babylonian Nippur 1991 → 8,k255: RZA(ssyr) 85 (1995) 163-6 (E. *Otto*).

c760 **Stone** Kenneth A., Sex. honor and power in the Deuteronomistic history; a narratological and anthropological analysis: diss. Vanderbilt, *DKnight* D. Nashville 1995. 294 p. 95-29005. -- DissA 56 (1995s) p. 1832.

c761 *Suder* Wiesław, *Sexagenarios de ponte*; statut juridique des vieillards dans la famille et dans la société romaine; quelques remarques et opinions:RIDA 42(1995)393-413.

c762 **Sullivan** Charles R., The education of Auguste COMTE: social science, political economy, and secular religion in early nineteenth-century France: diss. Columbia, *DWoloch* I. NY 1992. 338 p. 95-16072. -- DissA 56 (1995s) p. 327.

c763 **Svenbro** Jesper, Phrasikleia; an anthropology of reading in ancient Greece → 10,13672*: Myth and poetics. Ithaca 1993, Cornell Univ. xxiv-333 p. $ 41.75; pa. $ 14.75. -- RCLR 45 (1995) 54s (J. *Whitley*).

c764 **Theissen** Gerd, Social reality and the early Christians; theology, ethics, and the world of the New Testament, *TKohl* M. → 8,k258 ... 10,13674: RRHPhR 75 (1995) 222s (P. *Prigent*).

c765 **Theissen** Gerd, The Gospels in context; social and political history in the Synoptic tradition,T. E 1992, Clark. xvi-320 p.; bibliog. 294-310.-- RA(ustrl)BR 42 (1994) 79s (D.C. *Sim*).

c766 *Tornos* A., Del giro antropológico al giro textual; hombres y textos [< Cuando hoy vivimos la fe, próximamente Paulinas; → su Los planteamientos antropológicos de la teología (in Pintos y Tornos 1977) 139-148]: EE 70 (1995) 191-210.

c767 **Touraine** Alain, Crítica da modernidade, *TEdel* Elia Ferreira. Petrópolis 1994, Vozes. 431 p. -- RREB 55 (1995) 998-1000 (J.B. *Libânio*).

c768 **Treggiari** Susan, Roman marriage 1991 → 7,e734; 9,15389: RAJP(g) 116 (1995) 154-6 (J. *Linderski*).

c769 **Valbelle** Dominique, Les neuf arcs; l'Égyptien et les étrangers de la préhistoire à la conquête d'Alexandre 1990 → 7,b149: RCÉg 70 (1995) 140-2 (B. Van *Rinsveld*).

c770 *Valle* Rogerio, Tecnoestruturas e exclusão social: PerTeol 27 (1995)

c771 **Venable** Cornelia M., 'Slave' and 'woman' in the Pauline epistles and New Testament paradigms in the slave narratives of African American women; a comparative tudy: diss. Temple, ᴰ*Limberis* Vasiliki. Ph 1995. 234 p. 95-35819. -- D(iss)AI 56 (1995s) p. 2283.

c772 *Vogels* Walter, L'immigrant dans la maison d'Israël: → 10,30, ᶠCOUTURIER G., Maison 1994, 227-244.

c773 **Wallace-Hadrill** Andrew, Houses and society in Pompeii and Herculaneum 1994 → 10,13681; 0-691-06087-5: ᴿJRS 85 (1995) 299s (R. *Ling*).

c774 **Wason** Paul K., The archaeology of rank: NewStA. C 1994, Univ. xiv-208 p. 0-521-38072-3. -- ᴿAJA 99 (1995) 737s (T.S. *Strasser*).

c775 **Wees** Hans von, Status warriors; war, violence and society in HOMER and history: DutchMgHA 9, 1992 → 8,d746*; 9,13190: ᴿGnomon 67 (1995) 97-99 (Barbara *Patzek*).

c776 **Weinberg** Joel, The [Achaemenid-era] citizen-temple community 1992 → 8,2916: ᴿBiOr 52 (1995) 760s (E. *Eynikel*).

c777 **Weinfeld** Moshe, Social justice in ancient Israel and in the Ancient Near East: Perry Foundation. J/Mp 1995, Magnes/Fortress. 300 p.; bibliog. 252-272. 0-8006-2596-X. -- ᴿUF 27 (DIETRICH 60. Gb. 1995) 730-3 (M. *Heltzer*).

c778 *Weisman* Ze'ev, Societal divergences in the patriarchal narratives [< ᴴ , source and translator not indicated in note p.117]: Henoch 17 (1995) 117126; ital. 126s.

c779 *Weiss* Z., ᴴ Roman leisure culture and its influence upon the Jewish population in the Land of Israel: Qad 28,1 (1995) 2-19 [NTAb 40, p.287].

c780 *Whitelam* Keith, Sociology or history; towards a (human) history of ancient Palestine: → 170, ᶠSAWYER, J., Words; JSOT.s 195 (1995) 149-166.

c781 **Williams** Bernard, Shame and necessity (Sather Lectures 57) 1993 → 9,15387: ᴿCLB 71,1 (1995) 39s (J.E. *Rexine* †).

c782 ᴱ**Witaszek** Gabriel, Biblia o rodzinie [family; 9 art.]. Lublin 1995, KUL. 135 p. 83-228-0442-3.

c783 *Witschen* Dieter, Menschenrechte der dritten Generation als Leitprinzipien eines internationalen Ethos: ZkT 117 (1995) 129-151; Eng. 151.

c784 *Wuketits* Franz M., Entwurzelte Seele; biologische und anthropologische Aspekte des Heimatgedenkens: Univ 50 (1995) 11-24.

c785 *Yarbrough* O. Larry, Parents and children in the Jewish family of antiquity [Prov Sir, PHILO]: → 495, Jewish family 1994, 39-59.

c786 *Zaev* Y.Yu. ᴿ On the question of Scythians' blinding slaves (HERODOTUS 4,2): VDI 213 (1995) 175-182; Eng. 182.

U5.3 Commercium, oeconomica

c787 *Abraham* Kathleen, The end of Marduk-Nasir-Apli's career as business man and scribe [BM 30591]: → 110, ᶠLIPIŃSKI, E. Immigration: OLA 65 (1995) 1-8; 1 fig.

c788 **Alfonso Troncoso** Víctor, El comercio griego arcaico; historiografía de las cuatro últimas décadas, 1954-1993. La Coruña 1994. 157 p. -- ᴿGerión 13 (1995) 356s (Mirella *Romero Recio*).

c789 **Alpers** Michael, Die nachrepublikanische Finanzsystem; Fiscus und Fisci in der frühen Kaiserzeit [Diss. Hamburg 1993]: UALG 45. B 1995, de Gruyter. viii-349 p. 3-11-014562-6.

c790 *a) Andreau* Jean, Vingt ans après L'économie antique de Moses I. FINLEY; -- *b) Descat* Raymond, L'économie antique et la cité grecque; un modèle en question; -- *c) Tchernia* André, Moussons et monnaies; les voies du commerce entre le monde grèco-romaine et l'Inde; -- *d) Loś* Andrzej, La condition sociale des affranchis privés au 1er siècle après J.-C., -- *e) Récensions:* *AnESC 50,5 (1995) 947-960 / 961-989 / 991-1009 / 1011-1043 / 1079-1133.

c791 **Andrews** Steven, The *supe' 'ultu* exchange transaction at Nuzi: diss. HUC, ᴰ*Greengus* S. Cincinnati 1995. -- RStR 22, p.272.

c792 **Aubert** Jean-Jacques, Business managers in ancient Rome; a social and economic study of *institores*, 200 BC -- AD 250 [diss. Columbia, ᴰ*Harris* W.]: Columbia ClasTrad 21. Lei 1994, Brill. xv-520 p. *f* 220. -- ᴿGaR 42 (1995) 237s (T, *Wiedemann*).

c793 **Baloglou** Christos P., *Constantinidis* Anestis, Die Wirtschaft in der Gedankenwelt der Griechen 1993 → 10,1368*: ᴿAnCL 64 (1995) 458s (L. *Migeotte*); HZ 260 (1995) 825s (L. *Wierschowski*).

c794 *Beach* Eleanor F., *Pryor* Frederic L., How did Adam and Eve make a living ? : BiRe 11,2 (1995) 38-42; in Eden, gatherers; outside, farmers.

c795 ᴱ**Begley** Vimala. *de Puma* Richard D., Rome and India. the ancient sea trade 1986/91: ᴿ*JIntdis 25 (1994s) 103-7 (J.-F. *Salles*); *JRomA 7 (1994) 457s (D.P.S. *Peacock*).

c796 *a) Beyer* Frank, Gab es eine systematische Geldpolitik in der römischen Kaiserzeit (I.-3. Jh.) ?; -- *b) Ruffing* Kai, Einige Überlegungen zu Koptos; ein Handelsplatz Ober-ägyptens in römischer Zeit: MBAH 14,1 (1995) 1-16: Eng., fr. 16 / 17-42; Eng. fr. 38.

c797 *Boochs* Wolfgang, Deliktsobligationen: CÉg 70 (1995) 9-12.

c798 **Brandt** Hartwin, Gesellschaft und Wirtschaft Pamphyliens und Pisidiens im Altertum: AsiaMSt 7, 1992 (Univ.Münster; Bonn, Habelt); 3-7749-2554-2: ᴿCLR 45 (1995) 114-6 (Barbara M. *Levick*): Gnomon 67 (1995) 273s (B. *Rémy*) Latomus 54 (1995) 704s (H. *Devijver*).

c799 *a) Cadell* Héléne, Le prix de vente des terres dans l'Égypte ptolémaïque d'après les papyrus grecs: -- *b) Nur-el-Din* M.A., Terms of 'payment' in demotic; -- *c) Menu* Bernadette, Questions relatives à la détention des terres au premier millénaire av. J.-C.: → 10.443, Grund/Boden im Altägypten 1990/4, 289-305 / 285-8 / 135-145.

c800 *Cattaneo* E., Il sostentamento nella Chiesa dei primi secoli: RdT 34,6 (1993) 674-691 [NTAb 40,p. 500].

c801 **Clarysse** Willy, *Vandorpe* Katelijn, Zénon, un homme d'affaires grec à l'ombre des pyramides: Ancorae 14. Lv 1995, Univ. 112 p.; 11 maps; 7 pl. + 3 color. Fb 550. 90-6186-674-X. -- ᴿBASPAP 32 (1995) 87s (J.G. *Keenan*).

c802 **Cline** Eric W., Sailing the wine-dark sea 1994 → 10,13696: ᴿBASOR 299s (1995) 89-91 (J.M. *Weinstein*).

c803 **Cohen** Edward E., Athenian economy and society. a banking perspective 1992 → 9,15396; 10,16397: ᴿAnCL 64 (1995) 461s (L. *Migeotte*); Gnomon 67 (1995) 604-9 (R. *Bogaert*); HZ 261 (1995) 491-3 (J. *Engels*).

c804 *a) Dandamayev* M.A., The Neo-Babylonian *tamkāru* ['merchant' operating for temple or palace before 1000, independently after]; -- *b) Skaist* Aaron, *šimu gamru* ['as its full price']: its function and history: → 72 ᶠGREENFIELD J., Solving 1995, 523-530 / 619-626.

c805 *Doumet-Serhal* Claude, La cruche à 'arête sur le col'; à propos de l'expansion phénicienne en Méditerranée au 9ème et 8ème siècles avant J.C.: Ber 41 (1993/4) 99-136; XV fig.

c806 **Duncan-Jones** Richard, Money and government in the Roman Empire. C 1994, Univ. xix-300 p.; 59 fig.; 11 pl. £ 45. 0-521-44192-7. -- [R]BoL (1995) 127s (M.D. *Goodman*); GaR 42 (1995) 238 (T. *Wiedemann*).

c807 *Foraboschi* Daniele, Civiltà della moneta e politica monetaria nell'ellenismo: → 9,440, [E]*Virgilio* B., Aspetti e problemi dell'ellenismo (Pisa 1992/4) 173-186; 1 fig.

c808 *Golovina* V.A., [R] *kdb*, a special type of the lease of land in Egypt of the early Middle Kingdom: VDI 213 (1995) 4-26; Eng. 27.

c809 *Gilat* Yizhak D., [H] Does the jubilee year cancel debts ? [for Tannaites no, only shemitta does]: Tarbiz 64 (1994s) 229-236; Eng,2,vii.

c810 *a) Helck* Wolfgang †, Wege zum Eigentum an Grund und Boden im Alten Reich; -- *b) Grunert* Stefan, Zur Definition 'Eigentum'; -- *c) Andrassy* Petra, Überlegungen zum Boden-Eigentum und zur Acker-Verwaltung im Alten Reich: → 10.443, Grund/Boden im Altägypten 1990/4, 9-13 / 389-396 / 341-9.

c811 *Hernández* M. Valencia, Agricultura comercio y ética; ideología económica y economía en Roma (II a.e -- I d.e.): MgHist 7. Zaragoza 1991, Univ. 245 p. -- [R]BSL(at) 25 (1995) 646-651 (Lietta *Di Salvo*).

c812 *Isaac* B., Tax collection in Roman Arabia; a new interpretation of the evidence from the Babatha Archive: *MeditHR 9 (TA 1994) 256-266 [NTAb 40, p.292].

c813 **Johne** K.P., Gesellschaft und Wirtschaft des römischen Reiches im 3. Jh. B 1993, Akademie. 403 p. DM 194. 3-05-001991-3. -- [R]JRS 85 (1995) 289s (W. *Scheidel*).

c814 **Kallet-Marx** Lisa, Money, expense, and naval power in THUCYDIDES 1993 → 9, 15414*: [R]A(mer)HR 100 (1995) 500s (T. *Kelly*).

c815 **Katary** Sally L.D., Land tenure in the Ramesside period 1989 → 5,g112; 7,e776: [R]CÉg 70 (1995) 144s (B. *Menu*).

c816 **Kehoe** Dennis P., Management and investment on estates in Roman Egypt during the Early Empire: PapyrTAbh 40, 1982 → 8,k303; 9,15416; 10,13717*: [R]BiOr 52 (1995) 406-410 (A.E. *Hanson*).

c817 *Kehoe* Dennis, Legal institutions and the bargaining power of the tenant in Roman Egypt: APF 41 (1995) 232-252.

c818 **Kloft** Hans, Die Wirtschaft der griechisch-römischen Welt; eine Einführung 1992 → 8,k303: [R]HZ 261 (1995) 144 (W. *Nippel*).

c819 *Koshelenko* G.A., *Shakova* N.A., The new literature on the problem of the economic ties betwen India and the Mediterranean region in the ancient times: RossArkh (1995,2) 217-229.

c820 **Kramer** Bärbel, Das Vertragsregister von Theogenis (P.Vindob. G 40618); PRainer 18, gr. 13. W 1991. -- [R]BASPAP 32 (1995) 209-212 (J.K. *Winnicki*).

c821 **Langholm** Odd, Economics in the medieval schools: wealth, exchange, value, money and usury according to the Paris theological tradition 1200-1350: STGgMa 29. Lei 1992, Brill. ix-633 p. *f* 265. 90-04-09422-9. -- [R]JEH 46 (1995) 325s (I.P. *Wei*).

c822 **Ligt** L. de, Fairs and markets in the Roman Empire; economic and social aspects of periodic trade in a pre-industrial society. Amst 1993, Gieben. -- [R]At(henaeum) 83 (1995) 556-8 (A. *Marcone*).

c823 **Love** John R., Antiquity and capitalism; Max WEBER and the sociological foundations of Roman civilization 1991 → 7,e688: [R]Gnomon 67 (1995) 283s (W. *Nippel*).

c824 *Maidman* M.P., A unique Tehip-Tilla family [property division] document from the British Museum: → 151, PORADA E., mem., [E]**Owen** David L., *Wilhelm* Gernot, StNuzi 7 (1995) 57-63.

c825 *Márquez Rowe* I., More evidence of the grazing tax in Ugarit: UF 27 (DIETRICH 60. Gb. 1995) 317-331.

c826 *a) Mehl* Andreas, Zyperns Wirtschaft in hellenistischer Zeit; -- *b) Kracht* Peter, Adria und Spina; zwei bedeutende antike Handelszentren: MBAH 14,2 (1995) 27-49 / 51-59; Eng. fr. 50/60.

c827 *Meikle* Scott, Modernism, economics, and the ancient economy: PCP(g)S 41 (1995) 174-191.

c828 **Meyer** Carol, Glass from [Egypt Red Sea port Leukos Limen] Quseir al-Qadim and the Indian Ocean trade; SAOC 53, 1992 → 8,d581; 10,13727: [R]BiOr 52 (1995) 833-840 (E. Marianne *Stern*).

c829 *Michel* Cécile, Validité et durée de vie des contrats et reconnaissances de dettes paléo-assyriennes: → 724, RAss 89 (1995) 15-27.

c830 *Mieroop* Marc van de, Old Babylonian interest rates; were they annual ? : → 110, [F]LIPIŃSKI, E., Immigration: OLA 65 (1995) 357-364.

c831 **Millett** Paul, Lending and borrowing in ancient Athens 1991 → 7,e784 ... 10,13729: [R]Phoenix 49 (Tor 1995) 79-81 (Virginia *Hunter*); *TopO 3 (1993) 285-291 (L. *Migeotte*).

c832 *Müller* Gerfrid G.W., Die Teuerung in Babylon im 6. Jh. v. Chr: AfO 42s (1995s) 163-7 + 8 graphs.

c833 *O'Callaghan* José, Lettre concernant un prêt d'argent: CÉg 70 (1995) 189-192; 1 fig.

c834 **Ohrenstein** Roman A., *Gordon* Barry, Economic analysis in Talmudic literature; rabbinic thought in the light of modern economics: StPB 40, 1992 → 8,k319: [R]*A(sn)JS 20 (1995) 197-9 (M. *Silver*: excellent).

c835 *Olivier* J.P.J., Kantaantekeninge ten opsigte van die sosioekonomiese opset tydens die regering van koning Manasse van Juda: N(duits)G(ereformeerd)TT 35 (1994) 174-185 [< OTA 18 (1995) p. 281].

c836 *Pečírková* Jana, Property of Assyrian officials: ArOr 63 (1995) 1-13.

c837 *Pérez Largacha* Antonio, Some reflections on trade relations between Egypt and Palestine (IV-III millenia): GöMisz 145 (1995) 3-94.

c838 *a) Postgate* J.N., Some latter-day merchants of Aššur; -- *b) Zeeb* Frank, Das *teqnītu* in den Immobilienkaufurkunden aus Alalah VII: → 185, [F]SODEN W.von, Vom Alten Orient (1995) 403-6 / 541-9.

c839 **Rathbone** Dominic, Economic rationalism and rural society in third-century A.D. Egypt ... Heroninos 1991 → 8,k324 ... 10,13737: [R]BiOr 52 (1995) 410-9 (Andrea *Kordens*); CÉg 70 (1995) 323-7 (J. *Bingen*).

c840 **Rauh** Nicholas K., The sacred bonds of commerce ... Delos 1993 → 9,15436: [R]JRS 85 (1995) 278s (G.M. *Rogers*).

c841 *Reekmans* T., The behaviour of consumers in the Zenon papyri [primary needs not purchased but provided by institutions]: AncSoc 25 (1994) 119-140 [-8, *al.*]

c842 **Reger** G., Regionalism and change in the economy of independent Delos, 314-167 B.C. Berkeley 1994, Univ. California. xviii-396 p. $ 55. -- [R]CLR 45 (1995) 100-102 (A. *Erskine*).

c843 **Reynolds** Paul, Trade in the western Mediterranean AD 399-700; the ceramic evidence: BAR S604. Ox 1995. -- [R]Antiquity 69 (1995) 639-641 (R. *Dennell*, with seven other similarly peripheral titles).

c844 *Rico* Christian, La diffusion par mer des matériaux de construction en terre cuite; un aspect mal connu du commerce antique en Méditerranée occidentale: MÉFRA 107 (1995) 767-800.

c845 **Safrai** Ze'ev, The economy of Roman Palestine 1994 → 10,13739; £ 35: [R]BoL (1995) 167 (L.L. *Grabbe*); GaR 42 (1995) 98s (T. *Wiedemann*).

c846 **Silver** M., Taking ancient mythology economically 1992 → 8,k329 ... 10,13742: [R]VT 45 (1995) 423 (J.N.*Postgate*; football without a mine-detector; his plea for experts' tolerance will be unheard).

c847 **Skaist** Aaron, The Old Babylonian loan contract; its history and geography: StNELang. Ramat-Gan 1994, Bar Ilan Univ. 292 p.; bibliog. 246-257. 965-226-161-0.

c848 **Smith** Stuart T., Askut in Nubia; the economics and ideology of Egyptian imperialism in the second millennium B.C. L 1995, Kegan Paul. xviii-242 p.; bibliog. 218-234. 0-7103-0500-1.

c849 *Stary* Peter F., Rohstoffe im früheisenzeitlichen Nord-Süd-Handel [Europas]: MBAH 14,1 (1995) 82-106: Eng. 107; franç. 108.

c850 *Strydom* J.G., Redistribution of land; the eighth century in Israel, the twentieth century in South Africa: OTEs 8 (1995) 398-413.

c851 **Tenger** Bernhard, Die Verschuldung im römischen Ägypten (1.-2. Jh. n. Chr.) [Diss.Münster 1994]: Pharos 3. Müns .. Scripta Mercaturae. -- Chiron 25 (1995) 410.

c852 *Vinson* Steve, In defense of an ancient reputation [Turin Taxation scribe against A.H. GARDINER 1941]; GöMisz 146 (1995) 93-102.

c853 *a) Vitelli* Karen D.; Power to the potters [on]: *b) Perlès* Catherine, Systems of exchange and organization of production in neolithic Greece: *JMeditA 6 (1993) 247-257 / 5 (1992) 115-164.

c854 *Warburton* David, The economy of ancient Egypt revisited yet again [... POLANYI]; GöMisz 146 (1995) 103-111.

c855 **Wartenberg** Ute, After Marathon; war, society and money in fifth-century Greece. L 1995, British Museum. 84 p. 0-7141-0882-0.

c856 **Whittaker** C.R., Frontiers of the Roman Empire; a social and economic study: AncSocH, 1994 → 10,13744; $ 33: [R]CLR 45 (1995) 338s (M. *Whitby*); GaR 42 (1995) 98 (T. *Wiedemann*); JRS 85 (1995) 292-4 (B. *Isaac*).

c857 **Wunsch** Cornelia, Die Urkunden des babylonischen Geschäftsmannes Iddin-Marduk; zum Handel mit Naturalien im 6. Jh.v.Chr.: *CunMg 3, 1993 → 9,15454: [R]AfO 42s (1995s) 255-262 (M. *Jursa*).

U5.7 **Nomadismus**, ecology

c858 *Forbes* Hamish, The identification of pastoralist sites within the context of estate-based architecture in ancient Greece beyond the 'transhumance versus agro-pastoralism' debate: AB(rit)SA 90 (1995) 325-338.

c859 *Haiman* Mordechai, Agriculture and nomad-state relations in the Negev Desert in the Byzantine and early Islamic periods: BASOR 297 (1995) 29-53; 18 fig.

c860 **Hughes** J. Donald, Pan's travail; environmental problems of the ancient Greeks and Romans: AncSocH. Baltimore 1994, Johns Hopkins Univ xii-276 p. $ 48. -- [R]A(mer)HR 100 (1995) 501s (Susan E. *Alcock*); ÉtCL 63 (1995) 191s (D. *Donnet*).

c861 **LaBianca** Øystein S., Sedentarization and nomadization; food system cycles at Hesban [< diss. Brandeis] 1990 → 9,15457; 10,13747: [R]A(ndr)USS 32 (1994) 284-6 (G. L. *Mattingly*).

c862 **Maisels** Charles K. [→ c698], The emergence of civilization from hunting and gathering to agriculture, cities, and the State in the Near East. NY 1993, Routledge. xx-395 p.;

ill. $ 28.50. 0-415-09659-6 [RStR 22,56, D.I.*Owen*: challenging new models, does not say against what].

c863 **Sallares** Robert, The ecology of the ancient Greek world. L 1991, Duckworth. x-588 p. -- [R]VDI 213 (1995) 221-6 (Y.N. *Litvinenko*).

c864 **Staubli** Thomas, Das Image der Nomaden im Alten Israel .. : OBO 107, 1991 → 7.e822; 10,13751: [R]BZ 39 (1995) 301-3 (S. *Beyerle*).

c865 *Van der Steen* Eveline J., Aspects of nomadism and settlement in the central Jordan valley [perhaps reflecting LB-EI transition]: PEQ 127 (1995) 141-158; 2 maps.

U5.8 **Urbanismus**

c866 **Bailey** Wilma Ann, The contributions of the Israelite city to the shaping and preserving of the religion of Israel: diss. Vanderbilt, [D]*Harrelson* Walter. Nv 1995. 184 p. 95-41775. -- D(iss)AI 56 (1995s) p. 3164.

c867 [E]**Bassett** Steven, Death in towns; urban responses to the dying and the dead. Leicester 1992, Univ. 258 p.; 35 fig.; 23 pl. 0-7188-1418-1.

c868 *Battini* L., La città quadrata; un modello urbano nella Mesopotamia del II e I millennio a.C.?: *OrExp 3 (1994) 98s; 1 fig.

c869 *Baudry* Marcel, L'urbanisation à l'époque du Fer: → 10,30, [F]COUTURIER G., Maison 1994, 31-51.

c870 **Böhme** Christian, Princeps und Polis; Untersuchungen zur Herrschaftsform des Augustus über bedeutende Orte in Griechenland: Quellen & FaW 17. Mü 1995, Tuduv. 307 p. 3-88073-512-3.

c871 *Casalegno* Alberto, A cidade entre realidade e simbolo; duas perspectivas do Apocalipse: PerTeol 27 (1995) 7-26.

c872 [E]**Cornell** T.J., *Lomas* Kathryn, Urban society in Roman Italy [London, July 1991]. L 1995, Univ. College. xii-221 p. 1-85728-033-4.

c873 *Demont* Paul, Â propos de la démocratie athénienne et de la cité grecque: RÉG 108 (1995) 198-210.

c874 **Dobbs-Allsopp** F.W., Weep, O daughter of Zion; a study of the city-lament genre in the Hebrew Bible [diss. Hopkins]: BibOrPont 44. 1993 → 9,3719: [R]A(ndr)USS 33 (1995) 115s (P.D. *Duerksen*: ivory-tower sans pathos); ZAW 107 (1995) 527 (U. *Becker*).

c875 *Finkelstein* Israel, Two notes on Early Bronze Age urbanization and urbanism: *TAJ 22 (1995) 47-69.

c876 *Franzmann* Majella, The city as woman; the case of Babylon in Isaiah 47: A(ustrl)BR 43 (1995) 1-19.

c877 *Freyne* Seán, Jesus and the urban culture of Galilee; → 79, [F]HARTMAN L., Texts & Contexts 1995, 597-622.

c878 **Fritz** Volkmar, The city in ancient Israel: Biblical Seminar 29. Shf 1995, Academic. 197 p.; 60 fig. £ 20. 1-85075-477-2.

c879 *Fritz* Volkmar, Die Stadt als Lebensform im alten Israel: → 10,31*, [F]DAUTZENBERG G., Nach 1994, 219-233.

c880 *a) Gesché* André, Le croyant dans la cité; -- *b) Chéza* Maurice, L'inculturation, défi pour toutes les communautés chrétiennes: FoiTe 24 (1994) 246-255 / 256-274.

c881 **Grainger** John D., The cities of Seleukid Syria 1990 → 7,e829 ... 10,13762: [R]HZ 260 (1995) 521s (W. *Orth*).

c882 *Gruen* Erich S., The polis in the Hellenistic world: → 143, [F]OSTWALD M., Nomodeiktes 1993, 339-354.

c883 [E]**Hansen** Mogens H., *Raaflaub* Kurt, [Copenhagen] Studies in the ancient Greek
'polis ': HistEinz 95. Stu 1995. Steiner. 219 p. 3-515-06759-0.

c884 [E]**Hoepfner** Wolfram, *Zimmer* Gerhard, Die griechische Polis; Architektur und Politik:
F.Univ. Berlin Sem.Klas.Arch. 1. Tü 1993, Wasmuth. 139 p.; ill. 3-8020-1041-1.

c885 *a) Israel* Felice, La ville dans les sociétés de Palestine et de Transjordanie; -- *b)*
Rouillard-Bonraisin Hedwige, Les relations villes-rois en Juda et en Israël des débuts à la
chute de la monarchie: → 730, Semitica 43s (1992/5) 37-52 / 53-62.

c886 *Jacobson* D., The city in the Bible; implications for urban ministry: *WW(StP) 14
(1994) 395-401 [NTAb 39, p.267].

c887 *Jones* David C., The multiracial city: Presbyterion 21 (St.Louis 1995) 67-72.

c888 **Kasher** Aryeh, Jews and Hellenistic cities in Eretz-Israel 1990 → 7,e832: [R]JQR 84
(1993s) 517-520 (A. *Mittleman*).

c889 *Le Guen* B., Théâtre et cités à l'époque hellénistique; 'mort de la cité' -- 'mort du
théâtre': RÉG 108 (1995) 59-90.

c890 *a) Lemaire* André, Villes, rois et gouverneurs au Levant d'après les inscriptions
monumentales ouest-sémitiques (X[e]-VIIe siècles); -- *b) Lozachmeur* Hélène, Un exemple
de ville-garnison judéo-araméenne au Ve siècle: Yeb [Éléphantine], la forteresse; -- *c)*
Briquel-Chatonnet Françoise, Palmyre, une cité pour les nomades: → 730, Semitica 43s
(1992/5) 21-36 / 67-74 [75-78, *birtâ*'] / 123-134.

c890* **Lonis** Raoul, La Cité dans le monde grec; structures, fonctionnement, contradictions.
Tours 1995, Nathan. 320 p. 2-09-19037-5.

c891 *a) McSwain* Larry L., Urban mission and ministry in the 21st century; -- *b) D'Amico*
David D., Ethnic ministry in the urban setting: RExp 92 (1995) 9-17 / 39-56.

c892 *Martínez Montoya* Josetxu (p.283, 447, 541s: front cover outside and inside wrong),
a) Ruralidad y sacralidad; -- *b)* Religión y medio rural en el territorio histórico de Araba
[en título (no palestinense); en texto Alava, País Vasco] ; retos y perspectivas : Lum(Vt)
44 (1995) 261-284 / 429-447.

c893 *Marty* François, La ville, creuset de l'humanité; la diversité, une bénédiction: Christus
42,3 ('Chrétiens dans la ville' 1995) 163-172.

c894 [E]**Murray** Oswyn, *Price* Simon, La cité grecque d'Homère à Alexandre [1990 → 6,759],
[T]*Regnot* F., 1992 → 10,13773; 432 p.: [R]RÉG 108 (1995) 603-5 (D. *Rousset*).

c895 *Nicolet* Claude, Les 'mégapoles' méditerranéennes: → 706*, *JAT/RTA 4 (1994) 7s;
Eng. 213.

c896 **Owens** E.J., The city in the Greek and Roman world 1991 → 7,e844 ... 9,15488:
[R]EM(erita) 62 (1994) 379-381 (M. *Mayer*).

c897 **Polignac** François de, Cults, territory, and the origins of the Greek city-state [La
naissance de la cité grecque 1994], [T]*Lloyd* Janet. Ch 1995, Univ. xvi-187 p. $ 17.25 pa.
0-226-6734-0. -- [R]Antiquity 69 (1995) 1031 (C. *Broodbank*).

c898 [E]**Pozzi** D.C., *Wickersham* J.M., Myth and the polis: Myth and Poetics, 1991 →
8,k388;$ 29; pa. $ 9: [R]CLR 45 (1995) 81-83 (Christiane *Sourvinou-Inwood*).

c899 **Robertson** Noel, Festivals and legends; the formation of Greek cities in the light of
public ritual. Toronto 1993, Univ. xii-287 p. 0-8020-5988-0.

c900 *a) Robinson* James J., Breaking down church/community barriers; transforming the
dream of sanctuary into a safe space of another kind; -- *b) Bohl* Robert W., 'Our cities cry

out to you, O God': [Presbyterian (NY)] Church & Society 86,2 ('Seeking the peace of the city' 1995) 47-55 / 41-46.

c901 **Robinson** Olivia F., Ancient Rome; city planning and administration 1992 → 8,k390 ... 10,13779: [R]Gnomon 67 (1995) 648s (W. *Nippel*).

c902 *Sancho Rocher* Laura, TUCIDIDES y el tema de la polis-tyrannos: Q(uad)St 40 (1994) 59-83.

c903 **Schofield** Malcolm, The Stoic idea of the city 1991 → 10,13780; £ 28: [R]CLW 89 (1995) 77 (Victoria T. *Larson*); Gnomon 67 (1995) 99-103 (K. *Abel*).

c904 **Storoni Mazzzolani** Lidia, L'idea di città nel mondo romano; l'evoluzione del pensiero politico di Roma: Vie della Storia 16. F 1994, Lettere. 162 p.

c905 **Tomlinson** Richard, From Mycenae to Constantinople: the evolution of the ancient city 1992 → 8,k398; 10,13786: [R]HZ 260 (1995) 831s (F. *Kolb*).

c906 **Wharton** Annabel J., Refiguring the post classical city; Dura Europos, Jerash, Jerusalem and Ravenna. C 1995, Univ. xviii-238 p.; ill.; map. $ 80. 0-521-48185-6 [NTAb 40, p.567].

c907 [E]**Whitehead** David, From political architecture to Stephanus Byzantinus; sources for the ancient Greek *polis*: HistEinz 87. Stu 1994, Steiner. 124 p.; 11 fig. DM 56. -- [R]GaR 42 (1995) 231s (H. van *Wees*).

c908 **Winter** Bruce W., Seek the welfare of the city. GR/Carlisle 1995, Eerdmans/Paternoster. 245 p. /£ 15. 0-8028-4091-4 / 0-85364-633-3. -- [R]ET 106 (1994s) 310 (N. *Clark*); *TBR 8,1 (1995s) 39 (Judith *Lieu*); TS 56 (1995) 813s (A.C. *Mitchell*).

c909 **Zaccaria Ruggiu** Annapaola, Spazio privato e spazio pubblico nella città romana: Coll. Éc.Fr. 210. R 1995, École Française. ix-607 p.; bibliog. 411-462. 2-7283-0349-5.

U5.9 *Demographia*, **population-statistics**

c910 **Bagnall** Roger S., *Frier* Bruce W., The demography of Roman Egypt: Cambridge Studies in Population, Economy, and Society in Past Time 23, 1994 → 10,13788; £ 35: [R]Aevum 49 (1995) 278s (Loisa *Casarico*); CÉg 70 (1995) 320-3 (J.A. *Straus*); JRS 85 (1995) 310s (A.K. *Bowman*); *Prudentia 27,1 (1995) 62-66 (M. *Sharp*); SCI(sr) 14 (1995) 176s (J. *Schellekens*).

c911 *Bordreuil* Pierre, Métropoles et métrologies poliades; → 706*, Semitica 43s (1992/5) 9-20; 8 fig.

c912 *Kislyi* A.E., [R] Palaeodemography and the possibilities of the ancient population modelling: RossA (1995,2) 114-122; 2 fig.; Eng. 122.

c913 *LoCascio* E., The size of the Roman population; BELOCH [K.J. 1886 based on preconceptions] and the meaning of the Augustan census figures: JRS 84 (1994) 23-40 [NTAb 39, p. 459].

c914 **Parkin** Tim G.,Demography and Roman society; AncSocH. 1992 → 9,15504; 10,13793: [R]CLR 45 (1995) 351-3 (A.K. *Bowman*); Latomus 54 (1995) 163s (P. *Salmon*).

c915 *Renger* J., Landwirtschaftliche Nutzfläche, Einwohnerzahlen und Herdengrösse: → 10,81, [F]MEYER L. de, 52 Réflexions 1994, 251-4.

c916 *Scheidel* Walter, Incest revisited; three notes on the demography of sibling marriage in Roman Egypt; BASPAP 32 (1995) 143-155.

U6 **Narrationes peregrinorum et exploratorum;** *Loca sancta*

c917 *Abdallah* T., Jean-Pierre MAFFEI et sa présentation de l'Asie orientale à la fin du xvie siècle; ChH 40 (1995) 229-237 [RHE 91,112].

c918 ^{TE}**Arrowsmith-Brown** J.H., *Pankhurst* Richard, PRUTKÝ's travels 1991 → 8,k407 ... 10,13800: ^RBSOAS 58 (1995) 116-8 (E. *Hammerschmidt* †, deutsch).

c919 *Azim* Michel, La Notice Analytique [1829] des voyages de Jean-Jacques RIFAUD: GöMiszÄg [135 (1993) 33-45, PATANÉ M.] 143 (1994) 7-19.

c920 **Behdad** A., Belated travellers; orientalism in the age of colonial dissolution. Durham NC 1994, Duke Univ. 165 p. $45; pa.$16. -- ^RBuCanadMesop 30 (1995) 39-41 (S.C. *Brown*).

c921 **Bermejo Cabrera** Enrique, La proclamación de la Escritura en la liturgía de Jerusalén; estudio terminológico dell''Itinerarium Egeriae': SBF 37 → 10,13816; J 1993, Franciscan. $ 60. -- ^REO(rans) 11 (1994) 121s (M. *Augé*); POrC 45 (1995) 296-8 (D. *Attinger*).

c922 *Beyer* Jeorjios M., Die Orientreise des Louis-François CASSAS (1756-1827): AW(elt) 25,3 (1994) 354-8; 9 fig.

c923 *Cignelli* Lino, La grazia dei Luoghi Santi; più che verso un Luogo, camminiamo verso Qualcuno: *TSa 71,1 (1995) 14-16 (17-19, *Provera* Mario, chiesa del primato).

c924 *Crane* Howard, EVLIYA ÇELEBI, journey through Pamphylia: → 70, ^RGRABAR O., Muqarnas 10 (1993) .. [< JRAS (1994) 414].

c925 *Crowther* Charles, Lord DUFFERIN's grand tour and the collection of Greek inscriptions at Clandeboye: *JAncCiv 9 (Changchun 1994) 14-32.

c926 *Cunz* Martin, 'Un uomo apprende in base alle vie che egli percorre'; il viaggio di Rabbi NACHMAN nella Terra d'Israele 1798/99 [deutsch 1994 → 10,13803*]: Qol 51s (Reggio Emilia 1994) 6-10 [< Jud(aica) 51 (1995) 61].

c927 **Denon** Vivant, Voyage [1802 ^E*Vatin* J. 1989s → 8,k451; Travels 1989 → 6,g865]: RJRAS (1994) 275s (R. *Irwin*).

c928 **Drori** Joseph, ^H IBN EL ARABI of Seville -- journey to Eretz Israel (1092-1095). Ramat-Gan 1993, Bar-Ilan Univ. 201 p. -- ^RRÉJ 154 (1995) 184s & 513s (J. *Shatzmiller*).

c929 ^E**Droulia** Loukia, ^G On travel literature and related subjects. Athens 1993, Institute of Neohellenic Research. 558 p. -- ^RWZKM 85 (1995) 405 (Gisela *Procházka-Eisl*).

c930 EGERIA (→ c921; c942): **Natalucci** Nicoletta, Egeria, pellegrinaggio in Terra Santa: BtPatr 17, 1991 → 7,e875; 9,15524: ^RSalesianum 57 (1995) 587s (S. *Felici*).

c931 **Frank** Katherine, A passage to Egypt; the life of Lucie Duff GORDON. Boston 1994, Houghton Mifflin. xiv-399 p. 0-395-54688-5 [*OIAc 11,23].

c932 **Gibb** H.A.R. † [Hakluyt 2,110.117; 1962], *Beckingham* C.F., Travels of Ibn Battuta. 1994. -- ^RArOr 63 (1995) 380 (L. *Kropáček*).

c933 **Greenberg** Gershon, The Holy Land in American religious thought, 1620-1948; the symbiosis of American religious approaches to Scripture's sacred territory. Lanham MD 1994, UPA. xiv-370 p. $ 59; pa. $ 35. -- ^RChH 64 (1995) 516s (E.L. *Queen*).

c934 *Heid* S., Das Heilige Land; Herkunft und Zukunft der Judenchristen: Kairos 34s (1992s) 1-26 [→ 10,12346; NTAb 39, p.118: how Christianity might have developed within an undestroyed Jerusalem].

c935 **Heid** Stefan, Chiliasmus und Antichrist-Mythos; eine frühchristliche Kontroverse um das Heilige Land 1993 → 9,5674; 10,5557: ^RBLE 96 (1995) 234 (S. *Légasse*); *CritRR 7 (1994) 340-2 (G.C. *Jenks*).

c936 *Hen* Yitzhak, GREGORY OF TOURS and the Holy Land [Jordan mouth: De gloria martyrum 588]: OCP 61 (1995) 47-63; map 64.

c937 *Hennessy* Anne, Holy Land pilgrims and ministry to them: RfR 53 (1994) 605-616.

c938 *Horn* Jürgen, Kleine Bibliographie zur Erschliessung der Literatur der Reiseberichte über und Landesbeschreibungen von Ägypten (vom Spätmittelalter bis zum Ende des 18. Jahrhunderts): → 10,145, ᶠWINTER E., Aspekte 1994, 171-7.

c939 *Kupczyk-Lewin* Lola, Benjamin fra TUDELA, Rejsedagbogen i dansk oversïttelse I: *NordJud 14 (1993) 125-143 [< Jud(aica) 51 (1995) 60].

c940 **Mabro** Judy, Veiled half-truths; western travellers' perceptions of Middle Eastern women. L 1991, Tauris. x-275 p. £ 20. 1-85043-355-0. -- ᴿBiOr 52 (1995) 484-6 (Wiebke *Walther*).

c941 **Mackowski** Richard M., Cities of Jesus; a study of the 'three degrees of importance' in the Holy Land. R 1995, Pontifical Oriental Institute. 114 p. -- ᴿOCP 61 (1995) 631s (M.G. *Thomas*).

c942 ᴱ**Martín-Lunas** Teodoro H., Peregrinación de EGERIA; itinerarios y guías primitivas a Tierra Santa: Ichthys 17. S 1994, Sígueme. 151 p. -- ᴿLum(Vr) 44 (1995) 184s (F. *Ortiz de Urtaran*).

c943 *a) Oliverius* Jaroslav, Alois MUSILs Reisebücher; -- *b) Kropáček* Luboš, Alois Musil [Catholic priest] on Islam]: → 731*, ArOr 63 (1995) 410-418 / 401-9.

c944 *Pennec* Hervé, La mission jésuite en Éthiopie au temps de Pedro PAEZ (1583-1622) et ses rapports avec le pouvoir éthiopien: RSEt 36 (1992) 77-115 / 37 (1993) 135-165; maps.

c945 ᴱ**Price** Michael, *Taylor* William, Christians in the Holy Land. L c.1995, World of Islam Festival Trust. £ 10. -- ᴿTablet 249 (1995) 289s (M. *Adams*).

c946 **Rich** Anthony (& ᵀ*Cheruel* M., aussi c.1900). P 1995, Payot. xix-740 p. -- ᴿRÉL 73 (1995) 312-4 (C. *Nicolas*).

c947 *Roberts* Paul W., River in the desert; modern travels in ancient Egypt. NY 1993, Random. xiv-394 p. xiv-394 p. 0-679-42104-1 [*OIAc 11,39].

c948 *Roos* Johan de, Early travellers to Boğazköy : → 84, ᶠHOUWINK TEN CATE, H., Studio (1995) 261-269.

c949 **Schur** Nathan, Twenty centuries of Christian pilgrimage to the Holy Land. TA 1992, Dvir. 257 p.; (color.) ill. [*OIAc 11,40].

c950 *Stadnikov* Sergei, Die Wanderungen des deutsch-baltischen Orientreisenden Alexander von Üxküll in Ägypten und Nubien 1822-1823; GöMisz 146 (1995) 71-92; 3 fig. (map)

c951 *Starowieyski* Marek, ᴾ I pellegrini in Terra Santa dal secolo II al IV e la Bibbia: Bobolanum 4 (1993) 146-160: ital. 161.

c952 *a) Stopford* J., Some approaches to the archaeology of Christian pilgrimage; -- *b) Coleman* Simon, *Elsner* John, The pilgrim's progress; art, architecture and ritual movement at Sinai; -- *c) Petersen* Andrew, The archaeology of the Syrian and Iraqi Hajj routes: WA 26 ('Archaeology of pilgrimage' 1994) 57-72; 3 fig. / 73-89; 4 pl. / 47-56; 3 fig.; maps.

c953 **Taylor** Joan E., Christians and the Holy Places; the myth of Jewish-Christian origins 1992 → 9,15533; 10,13824*: ᴿRB 102 (1995) 627s (J. *Murphy-O'Connor*: unconvincing).

c954 *Teensma* B.N., Palestina aan het begin van de zeventiende eeuw; levensbeschouwelijke en toeristische notities van Jerónimo CALVO: Studia Rosenthaliana 28 (Assen 1994) 144-155 [< Jud(aica) 51,196].

c955 **Turner** Victor W. & Edith L.B.. Image and pilgrimage in Christian culture; anthropological perspectives: History of religions 11. NY 1995 = 1978, Columbia. 281 p. $ 16 pa. 0-231-04286-8; pa. -7-6. -- ᴿ*TBR 8,2 (1995s) 36 (C. *Moody*).

c956 **Wilken** Robert L., The land called holy 1992 → 9,15536; 10,13826: ᴿ*CritRR 7
(1994) 378-380 (E.D. *Hunt*); JAAR 63 (1995) 146-9 (W. *Harrelson*); Speculum 70 (1995)
446s (K.G. *Holum*); TorJT 11 (1995) 114s (T.M. *Rosica*).

c957 *Wright* Denis, James Baillie FRASER; traveller, writer and artist 1787-1856: Iran 32
(1994) 125-134 [34,101-115, in Mashhad, *Farmanfarmaian* Fatema S.].

U7   *Crucigeri* -- **The Crusades**

c958 *Auffarth* Christoph, Die Makkabäer als Modell für die Kreuzfahrer; Usurpationen und
Brüche in der Tradition eines jüdischen Heiligenideals; ein religionswissenschaftlicher
Versuch zur Kreuzzugseschatologie: → 42, ᶠCOLPE C., Tradition (1994) 362-390.

c959 *Baraz* Daniel, The incarnated icon of Saidnaya [Crusade pilgrimage site] goes west;
a re-examination of the motif in the light of new manuscript evidence : Muséon 108 (1995)
181-191.

c960 **Barber** Malcolm, The new knighthood; a history of the Order of the Temple. C 1994,
Univ. xxi-441 p. $ 70. 0-521-42041-5 [RStR 22,74, A. *Thompson*: much needed].

c961 **Beck** Andreas, La fine dei Templari. CasM 1994, Piemme. 252 p.; ill. Lᵐ 32. -- ᴿCiv-
Catt 146 (1995,3) 98-100 (G. *Forlizzi*).

c962 **Bull** Marcus G., Knightly piety and the lay response to the First Crusade; the Limousin
and Gascony, c.970-c.1130. Ox 1993, Clarendon. xiv-328 p. $ 65. 0-19-820354-3 [ThD
42,358].

c963 **Cardini** F., Studi sulla storia e sull'idea di crociata. R 1993, Jouvence. 505 p. --
ᴿStMdv 35 (1994)480-2 (G. M. *Cantarella*) < RHE 90 (1995) 272*.

c964 **Cole** Penny, The preaching of the Crusades to the Holy Land, 1095-1270: 1991 →7,e887
... 9,15540: ᴿ*JMdvLat 3 (1993) 213-6 (Beverly M. *Kienzle*).

c965 ᴱ**Coli** Enzo, *al.*, Militia sacra; gli ordini militari tra Europa e Terrasanta [convegno
Magione/Perugia 1989]. Perugia 1994, San Bevignate. 248 p. -- ᴿOCP 61 (1995) 281s (G.
Traina).

c966 *Derksen* John, Deus non vult; opposition to the Crusades in Europe 1049-1274:
(NES)ThRev 16 (1995) 98-125.

c967 **Epp** Verena, FULCHER von Chartres; Studien zur Geschichtsschreibung des ersten
Kreuzzuges. Dü 1990, Droste. 404 p. DM 72 pa. -- ᴿE(ng)HR 110 (1995) 145 (A.V.
Murray).

c968 *Fiorella* Danila A.R., La Terrasanta e il crepuscolo della crociata; oltre Federico II e
dopo la caduta di Acri [Bari -- Matera -- Barletta, 19-22 maggio 1994]: Nicolaus 22,2
(1995) 163-177.

c969 **Forey** Alan, Military orders and crusades: CS 432. Aldershot/Brookfield 1994,
Variorum/Ashgate. viii-318 p. $ 99.50. 0-86078-398-7 [ThD 43,168].

c970 **France** John, Victory in the East; a military history of the First Crusade 1994 →
10,13833: ᴿChH 64 (1995) 459s (T. *Renna*).

c971 *Heers* Jacques, La première Croisade: Le Figaro magazine (30 sept. 1995) et livre
(Perrin): E(spr)eV 105 (1995) 662-4 (J. *Daoust*).

c972 **Jotischky** Andrew, The perfection of solitude; hermits and monks in the Crusader
states. Univ.-Park 1995, Penn State. xviii-198 p. $ 35. 0-271-01346-X [ThD 43,71]. --
ᴿ*CritRR 8 (1995) 465-7 (T. *Pulcini*).

c973 *Jotischky* Andrew, Gerard of Nazareth, John Bale and the origins of the Carmelite order: JEH 46 (1995) 214-236.

c974 *Káldy-Nagy* Gyula, Kleinasien im Spannungsfeld von vier neuen Machtzentren um 1260 [... Baibars]: WZKM 85 (1995) 117-146.

c975 **Kedar** Benjamin J., The Franks in the Levant, 11th to 14th centuries: CS 423. Aldershot / Brookfield VT 1993, Variorum / Ashgate. xii-322 p. £ 49.50. -- ᴿBSOAS 58 (1995) 622 (P.M. *Holt*).

c976 **Lilie** Ralph-Johannes, Byzantium and the Crusader states 1096-1204 [1981, ²1988], ᵀ*Morris* J.C., *Ridings* Jean E. Ox 1993, Clarendon. xiv-342 p. $ 59. -- ᴿByzantion 65 (1995) 539s (Despoina *Mai*); C(ath)HR 81 (1995) 424s (G.T. *Dennis*).

c977 **Maier** Christopher T., Preaching the Crusades; mendicant friars and the cross in the thirteenth century [< diss. London 1990]: StMdvLife. C 1994, Univ. x-202 p. £ 25. 0-521-45246-5 [RStR 22,74, A. *Thompson*]. -- ᴿ*TBR 8,1 (1995s) 50 (Anna S. *Abulafia*).

c978 *Matzukis* C., Latin attitudes in Constantinople and the Aegean Islands after the Fourth Crusade (1204) (ecclesiastical and cultural): AcPatrByz 5 (Pretoria 1994) 101-112.

c979 *Mayer* Hans Eberhard, Herrschaft und Verwaltung im Kreuzfahrerkönigreich Jerusalem: HZ 261 (1995) 695-738.

c980 **Naumann** Claudia, Der Kreuzzug Kaiser Heinrichs VI. [Diss. Tübingen 1988]. Fra 1991, Lang. 305 p.; foldout. -- ᴿRHE 90 (1995) 525s (J. *Richard*).

c981 **Platelle** Henri, Les croisades: BtHistChr 33. P 1994, Desclée. -- ᴿMélSR 52 (1995) 343 (J. *Heuclin*).

c982 **Pringle** Denys, The churches of the Crusader kingdom I: A-K, 1993 → 7,e902 ... 10,13839*: ᴿBiOr 52 (1995) 816s (R.B.C. *Huygens*); Speculum 70 (1995) 671=3 (R. *Ousterhout*).

c983 **Richard** Jean, Saint Louis, crusader king of France [1983], ᵀ*Birrell* Jean, abridged by *Lloyd* Simon, 1992 → 8,k481; 9,15551: ᴿJRAS (1994) 92-94 (P. *Jackson*).

c984 **Rogers** Randall, Latin siege warfare in the twelfth century. Ox 1992, UP. 292 p. -- ᴿClio 31 (R 1995) 334s (P. *Morpurgo*).

c985 **Schein** Sylvia, Fideles crucis; the Papacy, the West, and the recovery of the Holy Land, 1274-1314: 1991 → 7,e911a ... 10,13841: ᴿChH 64 (1995) 464s (T. *Renna*).

c986 ᴱ**Shatzmiller** Maya, Crusaders and Muslims in twelfth-century Syria: The Medieval Mediterranean; peoples, economies and cultures 400-1453, 1. Lei 1993, Brill. xii-235 p. ƒ 140. 90-04-09777-5 [Islam and Christian-Muslim Relations 6 (1995) 295]. -- ᴿWZKM 85 (1995) 304-6 (H. *Eisenstein*).

c987 *Tyerman* C.J., Were there any Crusades in the twelfth century ?: E(ng)HR 110 (1995) 553-577.

c988 *Vannini* Guido, *Vanni Desideri* Andrea, Petra in the territorial fortification system of Crusader Transjordan; .. al-Wu'ayra: ADAJ 39 (1995) 509-540; 20 fig.

c989 **Vatin** Nicolas, L'Ordre de Saint-Jean-de-Jérusalem, l'Empire ottoman et la Méditerranée entre les deux sièges de Rhodes (1480-1522). Lv 1994, Peeters. 571 p. Fb 2400. -- ᴿWZKM 85 (1995) 351-3 (S. *Bono*).

c990 **Wickens** Karen A.L., Military ethics for Christians, knights, and soldiers: diss. Harvard: HThR 87 (1994) 479-481.

c991 **Winkelmann** F., Die Kirchen im Zeitalter der Kreuzzüge, xl.-xiii. Jht. KGE 1/10. Lp 1994, Ev.-VA. 158 p. DM 21,50 [< RHE 90 (1995) 276*].

U8 *Communitates Terrae Sanctae* -- **The Status Quo**

c992 **Abou el-Haj** Rifa'at A., Formation of the modern state; the Ottoman empire, sixteenth to eighteenth centuries: SocEcME. Albany 1991. suny. 156 p. $ 15. 0-7914-0894-9. -- ᴿBiOr 52 (1995) 496-9 (Sina *Akşin*).

c993 **Aburish** Said K., The forgotten faithful; Christians of the Holy Land: Quartet Books .. Tablet (1.VIII.1994) [< *TSa 71,1 (1995) 29s].

c994 **Akarli** Engin, The long peace; Ottoman Lebanon 1861-1920. NY/L 1993, Center for Lebanese Studies / Tauris. xviii-288 p. £ 34.50. -- ᴿBSOAS 58 (1995) 126-8 (Stephanie *Cronin*); JRAS (1995) 282-4 (E. *Rogan*).

c995 ᴱ**Andrews** Peter A., *Benninghaus* Rüdiger, Ethnic groups in the Republic of Turkey [Map A-VIII 14, 1987]: TAVO B-60. Wsb 1989, Reichert. 636 p.; 2 maps. DM 220. -- ᴿBSOAS 58 (1995) 37-9 (R. *Tapper*).

c996 *Belt* Don, Living in the shadow of peace; Israel's Galilee: National Geographic 187,6 (1995) 62-87; color.ill.

c997 **Ben-Rafael** Eliezer, *Shariot* Stephen, Ethnicity, religion and class in Israeli society 1991 → 10,13844: ᴿBSOAS 58 (1995) 547 (L. *Glinert:* convincing, but there have been dizzying developments since then).

c998 **Benvenisti** Meron, Intimate enemies; Jews and Arabs in a shared land. Berkeley c. 1995, Univ. California. 260 p. $ 25. -- ᴿ*CWeal 122.19 (1995) 25s (Jo-Ann *Mort*).

c999 **Bin Talal** (Jordan Crown Prince) Hassan, Christianity in the Arab world: Royal Institute for Interfaith Studies. Amman 1994, Arabesque. 120 p. -- ᴿ(NES)ThRev 16 (1995) 68-71 (G. *Sabra*).

g000 **Chacour** Elias, Auch uns gehört das Land; ein israelischer Palästinenser kämpft für Frieden und Gerechtigkeit. Fra 1993, Knecht. 287 p. 3-7820-0663-1. -- ᴿActuBbg 31 (1994) 320.

g001 **Cohn-Sherbok** Dan, Israel, the history of an idea 1992 → 8,k502: ᴿIrBSt 15 (1993) 44-47 (E.A. *Russell*).

g002 *Cousin* Hugues, Le pays de la Bible aujourd'hui: Supp(VSp) 148 (1994) 371-7.

g003 **Cragg** Kenneth, The Arab Christian 1991 → 7,e925 ... 10,13848: ᴿChH 64 (1995) 333s (C.B. *Paris*: obtuse verbiage); M(uslim)W 85 (1995) 176s (R.M. *Speight*); ScoBuEv 11 (1993) 56s (R.W. *Thomas*).

g004 **Denœux** Guilain, Urban unrest in the Middle East; a comparative study of informal networks in Egypt, Iran, and Lebanon: SocEconME. Albany 1993, SUNY. x-210 p. $ 18. -- ᴿA(mer)HR 100 (1995) 928s (M.C. *Hudson*).

g005 **Dick** Ignace, Les Melkites; Grecs-Orthodoxes et Grecs-Catholiques des Patriarcats d'Antioche, d'Alexandrie et de Jérusalem. Maredsous 1994, Brepols. 222 p.; 16 pl. -- ᴿPOrC 45 (1995) 321s (P. *Ternant*).

g006 *Dick* Ignace, Évolution du statut légal et sociologique des Chrétiens en Syrie: POrC 45 (1995) 64-78: the *dhimmi* 'protection (by law)' has its exceptions, but we should set aside the rancors of the past. -- *al.,* 151-161, Iraq, Chrétiens entre 'église' et 'nation'; 164-198, Jérusalem; 199-104, Jordanie; 204-277, Liban.

g007 **Donno** Antonio, Gli Stati Uniti, il sionismo e Israele (1938-1956). R 1992, Bonacci. 213 p. -- ᴿClio 19 (1993) 381-4 (M. *Toscano*); p. 461-474, Donno.

g008 *Echeverría* José Ángel, La presencia española en la misión capuchina de Mesopotamia (1841-1886): EstFr .. 96 (1995) 33-70.

g009 **Ellis** Marc H., Über den jüdisch-christlichen Dialog hinaus; Solidarität mit dem palästinensischen Volk[2]: Kleine Schriftenreihe. Trier 1992. 21 p. -- [R]TIC(context) 12,2 (1995) 108 (H. *Suermann*).

g010 **Emmett** Chad F., Beyond the basilica; Christians and Muslims in Nazareth: Geog.Research 237. Ch 1995, Univ. xix-303 p. $ 22. 0-226-20711-0 [ThD 42,365].

g011 **Erlich** Avi, Ancient Zionism; the biblical origins of the national idea. NY 1995, Free Press. 227 p. $23. 0-02-902352-1 [RStR 22,152, M.A, *Sweeney*].

g012 [E]**Feinberg** Anat, Kultur in Israel; eine Einführung. Gerlingen 1993, Bleicher. 240 p. — [R]FrRu NF 1 (1993s) 292-4 (Elisabet *Plünnecke*).

g013 [E]**Gerhards** Albert, *Brakmann* Heinzgerd, Die koptische Kirche; Einführung in das ägyptische Christentum; Urban-Tb 451. Stu 1994, Kohlhammer. 240 p. -- [R]O(stk)S 212-4 (O.F.A. *Meinardus*).

g014 *Girod* Stefania, Il kibbutz tra realtà e utopia; un'analisi della sua evoluzione secondo la teoria di Talcott PARSONS: RasIsr 61,1 (1995) 104-126.

g015 *a) Greenberg* Moshe, On the political use of the Bible in modern Israel; an engaged critique; -- *b) Falk* Ze'ev W., A peace of compromise between Israel and the Arabs: → 130. [F]MILGROM J., Pomegranates 1995, 451-471 / 473-8.

g016 **Hartman** David, Conflicting visions; spiritual possibilities of modern Israel. NY 1990, Schocken. xi-292 p. -- [R]*A(sn)JS 20 (1995) 256-260 (G. *Tucker*).

g017 **Hess** Moses, The revival of Israel; Rome and Jerusalem; the last nationalist question. Lincoln 1995, Univ. Nebraska. xvii-265 p. 0-8032-7275-8.

g018 *Holes* Michael, Community, dialect and urbanization in the Arabic-speaking Middle East: BSOAS 58 (1995) 270-287.

g019 **Holthaus** Alexander, Italienische Nahostpolitik; Genese einer mediterranen Variante westlicher Nahostpolitik 1946-1956: IKU 171. B 1993, Schwarz. 365 p. -- [R]OLZ 90 (1995) 546-8 (G. *Barthel*).

g020 *Hurwitz* David L., CHURCHILL and Palestine: Judaism 44 (1995) 2-25.

g021 *a) Khalidi* Rashid, Ottoman notables in Jerusalem; nationalism and other options;-- *b)* *Caplan* Neil, Zionist visions of Palestine 1917-1936: M(uslim)W 83 (1994) 1-18 / 19-35.

g022 **Landau** Jacob M., The Arab minority in Israel 1967-1991: 1993 → 9,15583; 10, 13864: [R]A(mer)HR 100 (1995) 199s (Lourie A. *Brand*).

g023 **Laskier** Michael M., The Jews of Egypt 1920-1970, in the midst of Zionism, anti-Semitism, and the Middle East conflict 1992 → 8,k522: [R]*A(sn)JS 20 (1995) 245-8 (Rachel *Simon*); JQR 86 (1995) 243s (L. *Nemoy*).

g024 **Layne** Linda L., Home and homeland; the dialogics of tribal and national identities in Jordan. Princeton 1994, Univ. xvi-188 p. $ 30. -- [R]A(mer)HR 100 (1995) 1635 (R.T. *Antoun*).

g025 *Le Coz* Raymond, Histoire de l'Église d'Orient; Chrétiens d'Irak, d'Iran et de Turquie [... Chine; diaspora USA]. P 1995, Cerf. 442 p. -- [R]OCP 61 (1995) 650-2 (V. *Poggi*); POrC 45 (1995) 315-8 (P. *Ternant*).

g026 **Lewis** Bernard, The shaping of the modern Middle East. Ox 1994, UP. xiv-186 p.; 2 maps. £ 22.50. -- [R]JRAS (1995) 417s (D.O. *Morgan*).

g027 *Mahfouz* José, bispo dos Maronitas no Brasil, O maronitismo; história e relaciones com o Líbano : Teocomunicação 25 (1995) 691-7.

g028 **Minerbi** Sergio I., The Vatican and Zionism; conflict in the Holy Land, 1895-1925, [T]*Schwartz* Arnold, 1990 → 7,e942; 8,k524: [R]JQR 85 (1994s) 431s (C. *Klein*).

g029 **Morris** Benny, Israel's border wars, 1949-1956. Ox 1993, Clarendon. 451 p. -- ᴿZion 60 (1995) 234-6 (Y. *Gelber*, ᴴ).

g030 ᴱ**Naff** Thomas, Paths to the Middle East; ten scholars look back. Albany 1992, SUNY. 360 p. $ 17. -- ᴿBSOAS 58 (1995) 556s (M.E. *Yapp*).

g031 **Near** Henry, The kibbutz movement, a history; 1. Origins and growth, 1909-1939: Littman Library. Ox 1992, UP. xvii-431 p. -- ᴿ*A(sn)JS 20 (1995) 248-250 (Sara *Reguer*); JJS 45 (1994) 327s (N. *Lucas*, also on REINHARZ J., BERKOWITZ M., SHAPIRA A.).

g032 **Otto** E., *Uhlig* S., Bibel und Christentum im Orient; Studien zur Einführung der Reihe: OrBC 1 / OBO 85. FrS/Gö 1991. 215 p. Fs 54, -- ᴿVT 45 (1995) 140 (P. E. *Satterthwaite*).

g033 ᴱ**Pallath** Paul, Catholic Eastern Churches; heritage and identity. R 1994, Mar Thoma Yogam. 397 p. -- ᴿOCP 61 (1995) 628-639 (B. *Petrà*).

g034 *Parlato* Vittorio, Oriente cristiano; stato [civile] e realtà etnico-religiose: Nicolaus 22,2 (1995) 145-162.

g035 **Qleibo** Ali H., Wenn die Berge verschwinden; die Palästinenser im Schatten der israelischen Besatzung. Heid 1993, Palmyra. 276 p. DM 40. -- ᴿJ(unge)K 56 (1995) 59s (Elisabeth *Adler*).

g036 **Raheb** Mitri, I am a Palestinian Christian. Mp 1995, Fortress. x-164 p. $ 12 pa. -- ᴿIBM(iss)R 19 (1995) 178s (J.M. *Bailey*).

g037 **Raheb** Mitri, Ich bin Christ und Palästinenser; Israel, seine Nachbarn und die Bibel: Tb 1307. Gü 1994. 125 p. -- ᴿTIC(ontext) 12,1 (1995) 98 (H. *Suermann*).

g038 *Reinharz* Jehuda, Old and new yishuv; the Jewish community in Palestine at the turn of the twentieth century: Jewish Studies Quarterly 1 (Tü 1993s) 54-71.

g039 *Rösch-Metzler* Wiltrud, Ein mühsamer Weg zum Frieden; Christen in Palästina: Orien(tierung) 59 (1995) 20-23.

g040 **Salibi** Kamak, The modern history of Jordan. L 1993, Tauris. 298 p. £ 29.50. -- RBSOAS 58 (1995) 365s (Stephanie *Cronin*).

g041 **Satloff** Robert B., From Abdullah to Hussein; Jordan in transition. Ox 1994, UP. xii-251 p. $ 40. -- ᴿA(mer)HR 100 (1995) 1636 (Linda B. *Layne*).

g042 **Schoenbaum** David, The United States and the State of Israel 1993 → 10,13882: *A(sn)JS 20 (1995) 486s (Donna R. *Divine*).

g043 **Setian** Nerses M., Gli armeni cattolici nell'impero ottomano; cenni storico-giuridici (1680-1867). R 1992. xv-170 p. -- ᴿOCP 61 (1995) 263s (V. *Poggi*).

g044 *Sharkansky* Ira, Religion and politics in Israel and Jerusalem: Judaism 44 (1995) 328-340; 3 fig.

g045 *Shaw* Roy, Whistle-blower in solitary [18 years for revealing that Israel was secretly making nuclear weapons]: Tablet 249 (1995) 9.

g046 *Stephanous* Andres Z., The Coptic Evangelical organisation for social services, Egypt: Transformation 11,3 (1994) 18-20.

g047 ᴱ**Stone** Russell A., *Zenner* Walter P., Critical essays on Israeli social issues and scholarship. Albany 1994, SUNY. vi-268 p. -- ᴿ*A(sn)JS 20 (1995) 499. titles sans pp.

g048 *Sullivan* Antony T., Palestinian universities in the West Bank and Gaza Strip: M(us-lim)W 83 (1994) 168-188.

g049 **Valognes** Pierre, Vie et mort des Chrétiens d'Orient [islamique], des origines à nos jours. P 1994, Cerf. -- ᴿOCP 61 (1995) 656-660 (V. *Poggi*).

g050 **Wagaw** Teshome G., For our soul; Ethiopian Jews in Israel. Detroit 1993, Wayne State Univ. xi-293 p. -- ᴿ*A(sn)JS 20 (1995) 481-3 (E. *Tabory*).

g051 *Yapp* M.E., Two great British historians of the modern Middle East [HOURANI Albert, KEDOURIE Élie]: BSOAS 58 (1995) 40-49.

g052 ᴱ**Zürcher** Erik J., Turkey; a modern history. L 1993, Tauris. xii-381 p. £ 35. -- ᴿBSOAS 58 (1995) 155s (H. *Poulton*).

XX. Historia scientiae biblicae

Y1 History of exegesis .1 General

g053 ᴱ**Aland** Kurt, *Rosenbaum* Hans-Udo, Repertorium der griechischen christlichen Papyri, 2. Kirchenväter-Papyri 1. Beschreibungen: PTS 43. B 1995, W. de Gruyter. cxxix-580 p. DM 338. 3-11-00698-6 [RHE 91,9*].

g054 ᴱ**Alberigo** G., *al.*, Les conciles œcuméniques 1, 2/1, 2/2, 1994 → 10,13892: ᴿE(xp)T 107 (1995s) 14 (G. *Wainwright*); ÉTRel 70 (1995) 284s (H. *Bost*).

g055 ᴱ**Alberigo** Giuseppe, Geschichte der Konzilien, vom Nicaenum bis zum Vaticanum II [1990], ᵀ. Dü 1993, Patmos. 482 p. -- ᴿAHC 26 (1994) 179-181 (O. *Engels*).

g056 **Alkier** Stefan, Urchristentum; zur Geschichte und Theologie einer exegetischen Disziplin [ev.Diss.Bonn]: BHTh 53. 1993 → 9,15612: ᴿZRGG 47 (1995) 189s (F.W. *Horn*).

g057 **Allison** C.FitzSimons, The cruelty of heresy. .. 1991. Morehouse. 0-8192-1513-9. — ᴿSewaneeT 38 (1994s) 196s (D.S. *Armentrout*).

g058 ᴱ**Altendorf** H.-D., Orthodoxie et hérésie dans l'Église ancienne 1983/92 → 9,15613: ᴿRevB(Arg) 57 (1995) 190-2 (J.P. *Martín*).

g059 **Amis** Robin, A different Christianity; early Christian esotericism and modern thought: Western Esoteric Traditions. Albany 1995, SUNY. xxi-388 p. 0-791-2572-X.

g060 **Andresen** Carl, *Ritter* Adolf M., Geschichte des Christentums 1/1. Altertum: TWiss 6. Stu 1993, Kohlhammer. xiv-219 p. DM 28. 3-17-011710-6. -- ᴿBijdragen 56 (1995) 98s (M. *Parmentier*, Eng., also on HALL S. 1991; ᶠFREND W., ᴱHAZLETT I. 1991).

g061 **Beatrice** Pier Franco, L'intolleranza cristiana 1993 → 9,15616; 10,13896: ᴿBLE 96 (1995) 144s (H, *Crouzel*); JEH 46 (1995) 547 (T.D. *Barnes*); NRT 117 (1995) 146s (A. *Harvengt*); RCatT 30 (1995) 199 (J.M. *Escudé*).

g062 *a) Beaude* Pierre-Marie, Christianisme et modèles d'appartenance au Iᵉʳ siècle [NTAb 40, p.460]; -- *b) Joncheray* Jean, Les institutions et la mémoire croyante: RICP 56 (< Metz 17-19 mai 1995) 67-83 / 95-106.

g063 **Beck** Hans-Georg, Vom Umgang mit Ketzern; der Glaube der kleinen Leute und die Macht der Kirche. Mü 1993, Beck. 198 p. DM 48. 3-406-37618-5. -- ᴿByZ 88 (1995) 157 (K. *Onasch*).

g064 **Becker** Jürgen, Das Urchristentum als gegliederte Epoche: SBS 155. Stu 1993, KBW. 144 p. DM 35,80. 3-460-04551-5. -- ᴿZkT 117 (1995) 230s (R. *Oberforcher*).

g065 **Becker** Jürgen, Annäherungen; zur urchristlichen Theologiegeschichte und zum Umgang mit ihren Quellen: BZNW 76. B 1995, de Gruyter. viii-495 p.; Becker Bibliog. 471-484. 3-11-014551-0.

g066 *Benoît* André, Militia Christi; remarques sur les images militaires utilisées dans le christianisme ancien: → 60, ᶠFRÉZOULS E. II, Ktema 19 (1994) 299-307; Eng. 299.

g067 **Beyschlag** Karlmann, Grundriss der Dogmengeschichte, 2/1. Das christologische Dogma: Grundrisse 3. Da 1991, Wiss. xii-210 p. 3-534-08088-2. -- ᴿAug(ustinianum)R 34 (1994) 489-500 (B. *Studer*).

g068 **Bof** Gianpiero, Teologia cattolica; duemila anni di storia, di idee, di personaggi: Universo Teologia 35. CinB 1995, S. Paolo. 288 p. Lᵐ 22. -- ᴿVivH 6 (1995) 412s (S. *Dianich*).

g069 **Bosio** Guido † [c. 1963], ²ʳᵉᵛ*Dal Covolo* Enrico, *Maritani* Mario, Introduzione ai Padri della Chiesa, secoli III e IV: Corona Patrum Strum.3, 1993 → 9,15618; 10,13898: ᴿAnCL 64 (1995) 341s (J. *Schamp*); Asprenas 42 (1995) 442-4 (G. *Trettel*); Orpheus 16 (1995) 501-4 (A. *Gallico*); Salesianum 57 (1995) 572-4 (F. *Bergamelli*); Vox Patrum 29 (Lublin 1995) 466-474 (S. *Longosz,* ᴾ , also on CONTRERAS E & DROBNER H. 475-482-492).

g070 **Brox** Norbert, A history of the early Church [Kirchengeschichte 1983, ²1992], ᵀ*Bowden* John. L 1994, SCM. viii-184 p. £ 10. 0-334-02576-1 [NY 1995, Continuum: 'A concise history ..' $ 19]. --   ᴿET 106 (1994s) 281 (W.H.C. *Frend*); SewaneeTR 39 1995s) 204.206 (R.W. *Prichard*); *TBR 8,1 (1995s) 47s (V.H.H. *Green*).

g071 *Burini* Clara, Comunione e comunità nella *ecclesia* delle origini: PSV 31 (1995) 221-230 (-317, *al.:* dopo).

g072 **Callan** Terrance E., The origins of Christian faith. NY 1994, Paulist. viii-147 p. $ 10. -- ᴿRestQ 37 (1995) 51s (J.T. *Fitzgerald*).

g073 **Cameron** Averil, Christianity and the rhetoric of empire; the development of Christian discourse 1991 → 9,15621; 10,13899: ᴿRS(to)LR 30 (1994) 182-5 (Adele *Monaci Castagno*).

g074 **Carcione** F., Le eresie; Trinità e Incarnazione nella Chiesa antica 1992 → 10,13901: ᴿAsprenas 42 (1995) 121-3 (E. *Dovere*).

g075 **Carmichael** Joel, The unriddling of Christian origins; a secular account. Amherst NY 1995, Prometheus. 425 p. 0-87975-952-6.

g076 *Castro* Carlos, La recepción en la historia de la Iglesia: TeolBA 30 (1993) 115-140.

g077 **Chadwick** Owen, A history of Christendom. L 1995, Weidenfeld & N. £ 25. — ᴿTablet 249 (1995) 1584 (R. *Runcie*).

g078 **Chau Wai-Shing**, The letter and the spirit; a history of interpretation from Origen to Luther: AmUSt 7/167. NY 1995, P. Lang. vii-250 p.; bibliog. 225-250. 0-8204-2328-9.

g079 **Comby** Jean, Duemila anni di evangelizzazione. T 1994, SEI. 370 p. Lᵐ 35. -- ᴿCiv-Catt 146 (1995,4) 635s (I.M. *Ganzi*).

g080 *Conniry* Charles J.ᴶ, Identifying apostolic Christianity; a synthesis of viewpoints: JETS 37 (1994) 247-261.

g081 *Corsato* Celestino, Alcune 'sfide della storia' nel cristianesimo delle origini; GIUSTINO, CIPRIANO, GREGORIO MAGNO: → 168, ᶠSARTORI L., StPat(av) 42 (1995) 231-251.

g082 *a) Covito* Antonio, La vita cristiana come risalita al Padre nella tradizione patristica.— *b) Làconi* Mauro, La preghiera al Padre, dati biblici: RivLi 82 (1995) 9-44 / 63-79.

g083 **Dal Covolo** Enrico, Chiesa società politica; area di 'laicità' nel cristianesimo delle origini: Ieri oggi domani 14. R 1994, LAS. 187 p. Lᵐ 18. -- ᴿRA(sc)M 20 (1995) 211s (C. *Burini*).

g084 *De Clerck* Paul, 'Lex orandi, lex credendi'; the original sense and historical avatars of an equivocal adage: StLi(turgica) 24 (1994) 178-200.

g085 **Deschner** Karl, Historia criminal del Cristianismo I (-4, 1986-94). Barc 1990, Martí-nez Roca. -- ᴿREB 55 (1995) 992-7 (E. *Hoornaert*: 'iconoclasta e irreverente, mas por outro lado irrefutável na sua base documental'; desmitiza Gregório Magno, Bonifácio, Carlos Magno).

g086 **di Berardino** Angelo, *Studer* Basil, Storia della teologia, epoca patristica 1, 1993 →
9,15626; 10,13909: RAtK(ap) 124 (1995) 459-461 (N. *Widok*); CivCatt 146 (1995,1) 516-
8 (G. *Capizzi*); C(olc)Th 64,1 (1994) 171-3 (J. *Slomka*) & 64,4 (1994) 166s (A. *Żurek*).

g087 **Doran** Robert. Birth of a worldview; early Christianity in its Jewish and pagan context:
Explorations. Boulder 1995, Westview. xv-183 p. 0-8133-8745-0.

g088 **Drobner** Hubertus R., Lehrbuch der Patrologie 1994 → 10,13910; DM 78: RÖR 44
(1995) 399s (W.A. *Bienert*); R(öm)Q 90 (1995) 256-262 (M. *Durst:* eine Leistung, kein
ALTANER); ScrT(Pamp) 27 (1995) 1059s (A. *Viciano*).

g089 EFelici Sergio, Esegesi e catechesi nei Padri 1992/3 → 9,448*: RCivCatt 146 (1995,3)
437s (G. *Cremascoli*).

g090 **Ferraro** Giuseppe, L'evangelizzazione nella Chiesa primitiva. CasM 1994, Piemme.
127 p. L^m 20. 88-384-2225-7. -- RCivCatt 146 (1995,2) 330s (D. *Scaiola*); Div 39
(1995) 86s (E.P.)

g091 **Floristan** C., *Tamayo* J.J., Conceptos fundamentales del cristianismo: Estructuras y
procesos. M 1993, Trotta. 1524 p. -- RNRT 117 (1995) 129s (A. *Toubeau*).

g092 **Fouilloux** Étienne, La collection 'Sources chrétiennes'; éditer les Pères de l'Église au
XXe siècle. P 1995, Cerf. 238 p. F 120. -- RÉtudes 383 (1995) 426s (P. *Vallin*).

g093 **Frede** Hermann J., Kirchenschriftsteller; Verzeichnis und Sigel^4rev: Vetus Latina 1/1.
FrB 1995, Herder. 1049 p. 3-451-00120-9.

g094 **Gamble** Harry Y., Books and readers in the Early Church; a history of early Christian
texts. NHv 1995, Yale Univ. xiv-312 p $ 32.50. 0-300-06024-6 [RStR 22,244 (F.W.
Burnett].

g095 **Gillespie** Thomas W., The first theologians; a study of early Christian prophecy
[... 1Cor 12] 1994 → 10,5918: P(rinc)SB 16 (1995) 338-341 (D.P. *Moessner*).

g096 **Gillieron** Bernard, Cette Église qui vient de naître; histoire et vie quotidienne des premiers chrétiens 1993 → 10,15635: RFV 92,6 (1993) 96s (G. *Vahanian* → 9793).

g097 **Gnilka** Christian, *Chresis* II. Kultur und Konversion 1993 → 10,13913*: RNZM(iss)W
51 (1995) 146s (J. *Baumgartner*).

g098 **Grant** Robert M., Heresy and criticism 1993 → 9,15637; 10,13914*: RCLW 89 (1995s)
74s (T.M. *Teeter*); *CritRR 7 (1994) 338s (B.E. *Daley*); Interpretation 49 (1995) 216, 218
(T.S.L. *Michael*); *JEarlyC 3 (1995) 361-3 (F.W. *Norris*).

g099 **Hall** Stuart G., Doctrine and practice in the early Church 1992 → 7,e983 ... 10,13916:
R*JEarlyC 3 (1995) 68-70 (Kelley M. *Spoerl*); JThS 46 (1995) 689-691 (Frances M.
Young).

g100 **Hamman** Adalbert, How to read the Church Fathers. TBowden John, *Lydamore* Margaret, 1993 → 9,15641 (SCM; also NY, Crossroad, $ 20): RLuthQ 9 (1995) 94s (J. T.
Voelker); RExp 92 (1995) 120 (C.J. *Scalise*).

g101 **Hauschild** Wolf-Dieter, Lehrbuch der Kirchen- und Dogmengeschichte 1. Alte Kirche und Mittelalter. Gü 1995, Kaiser. xvii-693 p. 3-579-00093-4 [ThRv 92,78].

g102 **Hinson** E. Glenn, The Church triumphant; a history of Christianity up to (→ y3)
1100. Macon 1995, Mercer Univ. xxi-495 p.; bibliog. 473-484. 0-86554-436-0.

g103 TEHoffmann R.Joseph, PORPHYRY, Against the Christians. Amherst NY 1994, Prometheus. 181 p. £ 28. 0-87975-889-9. -- RE(xp)T 107 (1995s) 27 (G. *Bostock*, not
satisfied); *TBR 8,1 (1995s) 25 (H. *Chadwick*).

g104 **Hultgren** Arland J., The rise of normative Christianity 1994 → 10,13919: RCBQ
57 (1995) 815s (Sheila *McGinn*); *CritRR 8 (1995) 229-231 (L.T. *Johnson*); JRel 75
(1995) 558-560 (H.W. *Attridge*).

g105 **Illanes** José Luis, *Saranyana* Josep I., Historia de la teología: Sapientia Fidei 9. M 1995, BAC. xxv-404 p. -- [R]*Carthaginensia 11 (1995) 442s (P. *Chavero Blanco*); Salmanticensis 42 (1995) 461-4 (I. *Vázquez Janeiro*: algunas confusiones); Ter(esianum) 46 (1995) 609 (A. *Alvarez-Suárez*).

g106 **Jacobs** Philip W., A guide to the study of Greco-Roman [right-hand pages] and Jewish and Christian [corresponding, on left] history and literature. NY 1994, upa. 132 p. $ 23.50. -- [R]BS 152 (1995) 242s (H.W. *Bateman*: an excellent resource, despite unacceptable datings).

g107 **Kennel** G., Frühchristliche Hymnen ? Gattungskritische Studien zur Frage nach den Liedern der frühen Christenheit [ev. Diss. [D]*Hahn* F., Mü 1993]: WMANT 71. Neuk 1995. xv-334 p. DM 128. 3-7887-1514-6 [NTAb 40, p.511].

g108 **Kinzig** W., Novitas christiana; die Idee des Fortschritts in der Alten Kirche 1994 → 10,13921: [R]C(ath)HR 81 (1995) 629s (R.B. *Eno*); TTh 35 (1995) 80s (A. *Lascaris*).

g109 [E]**Klein** Richard, Das frühe Christentum: TFo 60.62, 1993s → 10,13922: [R]HZ 261 (1995) 523-5 (E. *Mühlenberg*).

g110 *a*) *Koester* H., Jesus' presence in the early Church; CrSt 15 (1994) 541-557; -- *b*) *Legrand* L., Jésus et l'Église primitive; un éclairage biblique: *Spiritus 36 (P 1995) 64-77 [NTAb 39, p.444 both].

g111 **Kraft** Heinrich, Einführung in die Patrologie 1991 → 7.e989 ... 10,13922*: [R]JEH 46 (1995) 127s (C. *Stead*); Vox Patrum 29 (1995) 463-6 (N.*Widok,* [P]).

g112 **Ladner** Gerhart B., God, cosmos and humankind; the world of early Christian symbolism [Handbuch der frühchristlichen Symbolik, Stu 1992], [T]*Dunlap* Thomas. Berkeley 1995, Univ. California. viii-334 p.; 138 fig.; 10 color.pl. 0-520-08549-3.

g113 **Lafont** Ghislain, Histoire théologique de l'Église catholique; itinéraire et formes de la théologie: C(og)Fi 179, 1994: [R]E(xp)T 107 (1995s) 14s (G. *Wainwright*); ETRel 70 (1995) 297s (A. *Gounelle*); StPat(av) 42 (1995) 565-8 (L. *Sartori*).

g114 **Lietzmann** H., A history of the early Church [1942, [T]1951]. C 1992. Clark. 1121 p. (2 vol.) -- [R]PEQ 127 (1995) 174s (M.W. *Elliott*).

g115 **Lüdemann** G., Ketzer; die andere Seite des frühen Christentums. Stu 1995, Radius. 320 p. DM 68. 3-87173-063-7 [NTAb 40,p.368].

g116 *Maier* Harry O., Religious dissent, heresy and households in late antiquity: VigChr 49 (1995) 49-63.

g117 [E]**Manners** John, The Oxford illustrated history of Christianity 1990. -- [R]Churchman 108 (L 1994) 181s (H. *Rowdon*).

g118 **Marcovich** Miroslav, Patristic textual criticism I: ILCLST.s 6. At 1994, Scholars. x-171 p. -- [R]VigChr 49 (1995) 307-9 (J. van *Winden*).

g119 *a*) *McEvoy* James, The patristic hermeneutic of spiritual freedom and its biblical origins; -- *b*) *Ó Fearghail* Feargus, PHILO and the Fathers; the letter and the spirit; -- *c*) *Watson* Gerard, ORIGEN and the literal interpretation of Scripture; -- *d*) *Finan* Thomas, St. AUGUSTINE on the 'mira profunditas' of Scripture: → 504, Scriptural 1995, 1-25 /39-59 / 75-84 / 163-199.

g120 **McGinn** Bernard, The presence of God; a history of western Christian mysticism 1-5 c., 1992 → 8,k567; 10,15650; [R]CrSt 16 (1995) 172-4 (M. *Paparozzi*); TorJT 11 (1995) 109-111 (P.J. *Fedwick*).

g121 **Moreschini** Claudio, *Norelli* Enrico Storia della letteratura cristiana antica greca e latina, I. da Paolo all'età costantiniana. Brescia 1995. Morcelliana. 619 p.; bibliog.17-25.

g122 **Nagler** Norbert, Frühkatholizismus; zur Methodologie einer kritischen Debatte:

RSTh 43. Fra 1994, Lang. 209 p. DM 64. 3-631-46634-X [ThRv 92,84].

g123 **Nardi** Carlo, Il millenarismo; testi dei secoli I-II: BPat 27. F 1995. Nardini. 274 p.; bibliog. 47-51; 116-128. 88-404-2031-2.

g124 *a) Norelli* Enrico, Fin d'un temple, fin d'un Dieu ? La réflexion suscitée par la destruction du Temple de Jérusalem chez les auteurs chrétiens du IIe siècle; -- *b) Grappe* Christian, D'un Temple à l'autre; l'Église primitive de Jérusalem: → 486, Temple lieu de conflit 1991/4, 151-169 / 139-150.

g125 ^{E}**Norelli** E., La Bibbia nell'antichità cristiana 1993 → 9,292a: ^{R}VetChr 32 (1995) 471-3 (Immacolata *Aulisa*).

g126 *Noro* Harlei A., As origens da inculturação do Evangelho: Teocomunicação 24 (1994) 311-329 (631-648).

g127 **Orbe** Antonio, Estudios sobre la teología cristiana primitiva: FP.e 1. M/R 1994, Ciudad Nueva / Pont. Univ. Gregoriana. viii-918 p. -- ^{R}RevAg 36 (1995) 624s (L.A. *Sánchez Navarro*); Salmanticensis 42 (1995) 458-461 (R. *Trevijano*); ScrT(Pamp) 27 (1995) 1061s (D. *Ramos-Lissón*).

g128 **Ostriker** Alicia S., The nakedness of the Fathers; biblical visions and revisions. New Brunswick 1994, Rutgers Univ. xi-260 p. $ 22. -- ^{R}CrossCur 45 (1995s) 541-3 (Amy B. *Brown*).

g129 *Paulsen* Henning, Aufgaben und Probleme einer Geschichte der frühchristlichen Literatur: → 536, ^{F}STRECKER G., Bilanz 1995, 170-185.

g130 **Pawlowsky** Peter, Christianity, ^{T}*Bowden* John: Basics. L/Ph 1995, SCM/Trinity. 103 p. £ 10. 1-56338-112-5. £ 6. -- ^{R*}TBR 8,1 (1995s) 47 (R.A. *Burridge*: reliable, informative, but with 17-18th century gap).

g131 **Peinado Peinado** M., La predicación del Evangelio en los Padres de la Iglesia; antología de textos patrísticos: BAC 519, 1992 → 9,15654; 10,13930: ^{R}Burgense 35 (1994) 294s (M. *Guerra Gómez*).

g132 **Pelikan** Jaroslav, Christianity and classical culture 1993 → 10.13931: ^{R}A(mer)HR 100 (1995) 503s (S.A. *Stertz*); SV(lad)SQ 39 (1995s) 99-103 (P.C. *Boutaneff*); SvTK 69 (1993) 35s (B. *Hoffman*); VDI 213 (1995) 240-2 (A.V. *Muraviev* ^{R}).

g133 **Pelikan** Jaroslav, La tradition chrétienne, 1. L'émergence de la tradition catholique 100-600; -- 2. L'esprit du christianisme oriental 600-1700; -- 3. Croissance de la théologie médiévale 600-1300; -- 4. La Réforme de l'Église et du dogme 1300-1700; -- 5. Doctrine chrétienne et culture moderne depuis 1700 [Eng. 1973-89], ^{T}*Quillet* P. P 1994, PUF. I. xxxii-413 p.; II. xxxvi-360 p.; III. xxxiv-350 p..; IV. lxiv-424 p.; lxix-362 p. 2-13-045610-3; -611-1; -612-X; -912-9; -913-7. F 2250. -- ^{R}E(spr)eV 105 (1995) 561-8 (P. *Jay*); ÉTRel 70 (1995) 448-450 & 595-8 (H. *Bost*); Études 383 (1995) 715s (P. *Vallin*).

g134 **Pierrard** Pierre, Histoire de l'Eglise catholique$^{3\ [peu]\ rev}$ 1991 → 8,k574b: ^{R}RHE 90 (1995) 495s (R. *Aubert*).

g135 **Quacquarelli** Antonio, Retorica patristica e sue istituzioni interdisciplinari. R 1995, Città Nuova. 430 p.; bibliog. 398-403. 88-311-9232-9.

g136 **Reventlow** Henning, Epochen der Bibelauslegung 1. Vom AT bis Origenes 1990 → 6,k10 ... 9,15659: ^{R}AHC(onc) 26 (1994) 391-9 (K. *Limburg*); TPQ 143 (1995) 429s (F. *Hubmann*). -- 2. 1994 → g777 infra (10,13934).

g137 *Ribeiro* Ari L. do Vale, A leitura da Bíblia na era patrística: Teocomunicação 25 (1995) 117-130.

g138 *Rius-Camps* Josep, Ortodóxia o ortopraxi ? El concepte d'heretgia en els primers segles del cristianisme: QVidaC 176 (1995) 7-18.

g139 **Ryken** Leland, Realms of gold; the classics in Christian perspective. Wheaton IL
1991, Shaw. x-230 p. -- ᴿJETS 38 (1995) 114s (D.T. *Williams*).

Salzmann J.C., Lehren und Vermahnen; zur Geschichte des christlichen Wortgottesdienstes in den ersten drei Jahrhunderten: WUNT 2/59, 1994 → 4531.

g140 **Schmithals** Walter, Theologiegeschichte des Urchristentums; eine problemge-
schichtliche Darstellung 1994 → 10,13938: ᴿStPat(av) 42 (1995) 763s (G. *Segalla*); TTh
35 (1995) 288 (A. van *Diemen*); ZkT 117 (1995) 370s (L. *Lies*).

g141 **Sesboüé** Bernard, *Wolinski* Joseph, Histoire des dogmes, 1. Le Dieu du salut. P 1994,
Desclée. 544 p. -- ᴿEeV 105 (1995) 138s (P. *Jay*); RThom 95 (1995) 341-3 (G. *Emery*).

g142 -- *Tihon* Paul, Les problèmes d'une histoire des dogmes [ᴱSᴇsʙᴏüé B. 1s, 1994s]:
RTL 26 (1995) 307-325.

g143 **Simonetti** Manlio, Biblical interpretation in the Early Church; an historical
introduction to patristic exegesis [Profilo 1981], ᵀ*Hughes* John A., 1994 → 10,13940
[NTAb 40, p.330]: ᴿTS 56 (1995) 397 (J.J. *O'Keefe*: useful; some dissents).

g144 **Simonetti** Manlio, Ortodossia e eresia tra I e II secolo: Armarium 5. Soveria
Mannelli CZ 1994, Rubbettino. 351 p. -- ᴿOrpheus 16 (1995) 500s (F.E. *Sciuto*).

Smith Jonathan Z., Drudgery divine ... early Christianities 1990 → 8217 supra.

g146 **Thils** Gustave, Les doctrines théologiques et leur 'évolution'; RTL.c 28. P 1995,
Procure. 72 p. -- ᴿE(spr)eV 105 (1995) 303 (H. *Wattiaux*).

g147 **Trevijano Etcheverría** Ramón, Orígenes del cristianismo; el trasfondo judío del
cristianismo primitivo: Plenitudo Temporis 3. S 1995, Univ. Pontificia. 475 p.; bibliog.
403-444.

g148   **Trevijano Etcheverría** Ramón, Patrologia: BAC Sapientia Fidei 5, 1994 →
10,13944; 84-7914-137-9: ᴿAng 72 (1995) 593-5 (B. *Degórski*); Burg 36 (1995) 564s (M.
Guerra Gómez).

g149   **Trombley** Frank R., Hellenic religion and Christianization: ÉPR 115, 1993s· →
10,14060: ᴿJRS 85 (1995) 341-4 (G. *Fowden*).

g150 **Urban** Linwood, A short history of Christian thought. Ox c.1995, UP. xviii-461 p.
£ 32,50; pa. £ 13. 0-19-509347-X; -8-8. -- ᴿ*TBR 8,1 (1995s) 27 (R. *Hannaford*).

g151 **Wallis** Ian G., The faith of Jesus Christ in early Christian traditions: SNTS.mg 84.
C 1995, Univ. xix-281 p. $ 60. 0-521-47352-7 [ThD 43,191].

g152 *a) Walter* Nikolaus, Hellenistic Diaspora-Juden an der Wiege des Urchristentums; --
b) Pilgaard Aage, The Hellenistic *theios aner* -- a model for early Christian Christology ?
-- *c) Nissen* Johannes, The distinctive character of the New Testament love command in
relation to Hellenistic Judaism: → 487, NT & Hellenistic 1992/5, 37-58 / 101-122 /
123-150.

g153   **Winden** J.C.M. van, De ware wijsheid; wegen van vroeg-christlich denken:
Bronnen van de Europese cultuur 10. Baarn 1992, Ambo. 315 p. *f* 65. 90-263-4477-9.
— ᴿBijdragen 56 (1995) 100 (M. *Parmentier*: Dogmengeschichte).

g154 *Young* Frances, Interpretative genres ['commentaries' in the Fathers] and the
inevitability of pluralism [< Manchester Manson lecture 1993]: JSNT 59 (1995) 93-110.

Y1.4 *Patres apostolici et saeculi II* -- **First two centuries**

g155 *Castelli* Giovanni, Cristo nei Padri Apostolici: → 142, ᶠOROZ RETA II, Helm 45
(1994) 349-371.

g156 **Francis** James A., Subversive virtue; asceticism and authority in the second-century pagan world. Univ. Park 1995, Penn State. xviii-222 p. $ 32.50. 0-271-01304-4. -- D(iss)AI 56 (1995s).

g157 **Grant** Robert M., Jesus after the Gospels; the Christ of the second century 1990 → 6,k35 ... 10,12954: ᴿJETS 37 (1994) 446s (B. *Nassif*).

g158 *Grant* Robert M., Old Testament saints and sinners of the second century: → 42, ᶠCOLPE C., Tradition (1994) 356-361.

g159 ᴱ**Holmes** Michael W., The Apostolic Fathers; Greek texts and (LIGHTFOOT J.B. 1869-85 = Baker 1981 + Nachlass completed by HARMER J.R.) English translations²ʳᵉᵛ. GR 1992, Baker. x-609 p. $35. -- ᴿ*JEarlyC 3 (1995) 81-83 (C.N. *Jefford*).

g160 **Neymeyr** Ulrich, Die christlichen Lehrer im zweiten Jahrhundert; ihre Lehrtätigkeit, ihr Selbstverständnis und ihre Geschichte: VigChr.s4, 1989 → 6,k30; 7,g23: ᴿMThZ 45 (1994) 80-83 (R. *Hanig*).

g161 **Orbe** Antonio, La teologia dei secoli II e III; il confronto della Grande Chiesa con lo Gnosticismo; 1. Temi veterotestamentari; 2. Temi neotestamentari [Introducción 1987], ᵀ*Gilli* M., ᴱ*Zani* A. CasM/R 1995, Piemme/Pont.Univ.Gregoriana. 606 p.; 654 p. 88-384-2283-4; -4-2 / [NTAb 40, p.183]. -- ᴿVivH 6 (1995) 413s (C. *Nardi*).

g162 **Osborn** Eric, The emergence of Christian theology 1993 → 10,14046: ᴿJRel 75 (1995) 129-132 (J.P. *Kenney*).

g163 *Ramos-Lissón* Domingo, La novità cristiana e gli apologeti del II secolo: SR(ic)OC 15,1 (1993) 15-34.

g164 **Ridings** Daniel, The Attic Moses; the dependency [of PLATO ..] theme in some early Christian writers : diss. Göteborg 1995. 270 p. -- ᴿRPh(lgLH) 69 (1995) 351s (B. *Pouderon*).

g165 **Rizzi** Marco, Ideologia e retorica negli 'exordia' apologetici; il problema dell''altro' 1993 → 9,15687: ᴿJThS 46 (1995) 306-311 (W. *Kinzig*).

g166 *a) Siniscalco* Paolo, Lo stile biblico nella riflessione di scrittori cristiani del II e III secolo; -- *b) Quacquarelli* Antonio, Gli schemi retorici dell'espressione verbale: → 119, ᶠMARA M.Grazia = Aug(ustinianum)R 35 (1995) 215-230 / 259-266.

g167 **Torrance** Tom, Divine meaning [CLEMENT, IRENAEUS ..]. E 1995, Clark. 439 p. £ 25. 0-567-09709-9. -- ᴿE(xp)T 107 (1995s) 120s (G. *Bostock*).

g168 **Vögtle** Anton, *Oberlinner* Lorenz, Anpassung oder Widerspruch ? Von der apostolischen zur nachapostolischen Kirche. FrB 1992, Herder. 155 p. DM 27. 3-451-22623-5. -- ᴿMüTZ 45 (1994) 79s (T. *Böhm*).

g169 **Wagner** Walter H., After the Apostles; Christianity in the second century 1994 → 10,13959: ᴿChH 64 (1995) 86s (R.B. *Eno*); *CritRR 8 (1995) 422-4 (G.F. *Snyder*); ET 106 (1994s) 186s (G. *Huelin*); NewThR 8,2 (1995) 99s (K. *Madigan*); RestQ 37 (1995) 119s (E. *Ferguson*).

g170 *a) Wilson* Stephen, The apostate minority; -- *b) Räisänen* Heikki, The clash between Christian styles of life in the book of Revelation: → 88, ᶠJERVELL J.: ST 49 (Oslo 1995) 201-211 / 151-167.

-----

g171 ATHENAGORAS: *Pouderon* Bernard, *a*) Le 'De resurrectione' d'Athénagore face à la gnose valentinienne: RechAug 28 (1995) 145-183; -- *b*) Apologetica ... De resurrectione: RevSR [67,3 (1993) 22-40 → 9,15689] 69 (1995) 194-200 ; Eng. 271.

g172 *Zeegers-van der Vorst* Nicole, Adversaires et destinataires du De resurrectione attribué à Athénagore d'Athène: Salesianum 57 (1995) 75-117: bibliog. 117-122 . 199-250

. 415-442 . 511-656.

g173 BARNABAS: **Hvalvik** Reidar, The struggle for Scripture and covenant; the purpose
   of the Epistle of Barnabas and Jewish-Christian competition in the second century: diss.
   Oslo 1994 [WUNT 2/82, 1996]; favorable 'objections' of *Müller* Mogens: TT(og)K 66
   (1995) Norwegian 247-259; Eng. 260. [NTAb 40,p.501s, also NTS 97,49, *Sandnes* K.].

g174 *Draper* Jonathan A., Barnabas and the riddle of the Didache revisited: JSNT 58
   (1995) 89-113.

g175 **Paget** James C., The Epistle of Barnabas; outlook and background [< diss.
   Cambridge 1992]: WUNT 2/64, 1994 → 10,13962; DM 88: ᴿJAC 38 (1995) 170-2 (A.
   Lindemann); JThS 46 (1995) 696-8 (L.W. *Barnard*); RHE 90 (1995) 619 (J.-M. *Auwers*);
   SNTU 20 (1995) 248s (A. *Fuchs*); *TBR 8,1 (1995s) 25 (R. *Morgan*); TTh 35 (1995) 291s
   (F. van de *Paverd*).

g176 *Vinzent* Markus, Ertragen und Ausharren -- die Lebenslehre des Barnabasbriefes :
   ZNW 86 (1995) 74-93.

g177 CLEMENS A.: *Bregliozzi* Annarita, I comici greci moralisti e poeti; considerazioni
   sulla presenza dei comici greci nel Pedagogo di Clemente Alessandrino: SMSR 61 (1995)
   327-347.

g178 **Buell** Denise K., Procreative language in Clement of Alexandria: diss. Harvard,
   ᴰ*Brooten* Bernadette J. CM 1995. 229 p. 96-09903. -- DissA 56 (1995s) p. 4818.

g179 *Canfora* Luciano, Clemente di Alessandria e Diogene LAERZIO: → 10,42, ᶠGIGANTE
   M., Storia 1994, 79-81.

g180 *Criddle* A.H., On the Mar Saba letter [Morton SMITH 1973; Mk 14,51] attributed to
   Clement of Alexandria: *JEarlyC 3 (1995) 215-220.

g181 *Kuyama* Munehiko, Klemens von Alexandrien und heidnische Philosophie: → 129,
   ²ᶠMIKASA T., Orient 30s (1995) 158-170.

g182 *Leyerle* Blake, Clement of Alexandria on the importance of table etiquette:
   *JEarlyC 3 (1995) 123-141.

g183 *Martens* John, *Nómos émpsychos* in PHILO and Clement of Alexandria: -→ 10,322,
   Hellenization 1991/4, 323-338.

g184 ᵀᴱ**Merino** M., *Redondo* T.E., Clemente, El pedagogo 1994 → 10,13965: ᴿEstAg 30
   (1995) 156s (P. de *Luis*); TE(spir) 39 (1995) 143-6 (E. *Pérez Delgado*).

g185 *Termini* Cristina, Il profilo letterario delle sezioni storiografiche nel primo libro
   degli Stromati di Clemente Alessandrino: SMSR 60 (1994) 219-242.

g186 *Vergōti* Y.T., ᴳ The pedagogical *antilepseis* of Clement of Alexandria in
   Paidagogos I: Kler 23 (1991) 157-205

g187 CLEMENS R; *Bowe* Barbara E., 1 Clement 59,3-61,3; epistolary prayer in Clement
   of Rome; → 512, SBL Seminars 34 (1995) 221-5.

g188 **Cola** Silvano, Pseudo-Clemente, I ritrovamenti (Recognitiones) 1993 → 9,15699:
   ᴿCivCatt 146 (1995,4) 630-2 (G. *Cremascoli*).

g189 *Gieschen* Charles A., The seven pillars of the world; ideal figure lists in the
   Christology of the Psuedo-Clementines: JSPE 12 (1994) 47-81.

g190 **Henne** Philippe, La christologie .. Clemens/HERMAS ᴰ1992 → 9,7489.15699*;
   10,7444: ᴿ*CritRR 7 (1994) 342-4 (Barbara E. *Bowe*).

g191 **Jeffers** James S., Conflict at Rome 1991 → 7,4087; 8,4892: ᴿChH 64 (1995) 83s
   (K. B. *Steinhauser*).

g192 **Jones** F. Stanley, An ancient Jewish Christian source on the history of Christianity: Pseudo-Clementine recognitions 1,27-71.   Atlanta 1995, Scholars.   xiii-208 p. $ 40. 0-7885-0013-9 [E(xp)T 107 (1995s) 155].

g193 *LeBoulluec* Alain, Les citations de la Septante dans l'homélie XVI pseudo-clémentine, une critique implicite de la typologie ? : → 78, ᶠHARL M., Katà toùs o' 1995, 441-461.

g194 **Lindemann** Andreas,   Die Clemensbriefe 1992 → 8.k616 ... 10,13969:   ᴿJAC 38 (1995) 167-170 (H.-J. *Vogt*).

g195 *Lona* Horacio E.,   Rhetorik und Botschaft in 1Clem 49: ZNW 86 (1995) 94-103.

g196   *Martín* José P.,   La cultura romana y la Prima Clementis: → 635, 2° Patrología 1993, TeolBA 30 (1994) 55-71.

g197 **Strecker** Georg, Die Pseudoklementinen 1989 → 8,k621: ᴿNT 37 (1995) 196 (J.K. *Elliott*).

g198 DIDACHE: *Cayón* Avelino, Los capítulos IX y X de la Didajé sobre la Eucaristía; hipótesis o intento de interpretación: Phase 35 (1995) 195-208.

g199 *Damme* Dirk Van, Bekenner und Lehrer; Bemerkungen zu zwei nichtordinierten Kirchenämtern in der Traditio apostolica; → 96, ᶠKRAUSE M., Divitiae Aegypti 1995, 321-330.

g200 *Del Verme* Marcello, Medio giudaismo e *Didaché;* il caso della comunione dei beni (Did.4,8): VetChr 32 (1995) 293-320.

g201   ᴱ**Jefford** Clayton N.,   The Didache in context; essays on its text, history and transmission: SpNT 77 → 10,248: Lei 1995, Brill.   xviii-422 p., bibliog. 383-399. 90-04-10045-8. -- ᴿSalmanticensis 42 (1995) 449-451 (R. *Trevijano*).

g202 *Milavec* Aaron, The social setting of 'turning the other cheek' and 'loving one's enemies' in light of the Didache: BThB 25 (1995) 131-143.

g203 **Schöllgen** Georg, Didache / *Geerlings* Wilhelm, Traditio apostolica: FC 1, 1991 → 7,g42 ... 10,13977: ᴿZkT 117 (1995) 256-8 (L. *Lies,* also on Fontes Christiani 3, 6, 7).

g204   *Methuen* Charlotte,   Widows, bishops, and the struggle for authority in the Didascalia Apostolorum: JEH 46 (1995) 197-213 [NTAb 40, p.123].

g205 HERMAS: **Ayán Calvo** J.J., El Pastor, edición bilingüe: FP 6.   M 1995, Ciudad Nueva. 310 p. -- ᴿSalmanticensis 42 (1995) 452s (R.*Trevijano*).

g206 **Henne** Philippe, L'unité du Pasteur 1992 → 8.k639 ... 10,13980: ᴿ*CritRR 7 (1994) 344-6 (Carolyn *Osiek*); NT 37 (1995) 305-7 (A. *Kirkland*).

g207 **Vezzoni** Anna, Il Pastore di Erma, versione palatina 1994 → 10,13983: ᴿOrpheus 16 (1995) 495-9 (P. *Santorelli*).

g208 **Wilson** John C.,   Five problems in the interpretation of the Shepherd of Hermas; authorship, genre, canonicity, apocalyptic, and the absence of the name 'Jesus Christ': Biblical Series 34. Lewiston NY 1995, Mellen. ix-101 p. $ 60. 0-7734-2392-6 [NTAb 40, p.567: continuing his 1993 book, finds Hermas theologically superior to Rev, 2 Pt, 2-3 Jn, Jude].

g209 IGNATIUS: *Bakke* Odd M., The rhetorical genre of the letters of Ignatius; TT(og)K 66 (1995) Norwegian 275-291; Eng. 291 ['deliberative rhetoric'; NTAb 40, p.499].

g210 **Haley** Judy R., The politics of unity; envoy and audience in Ignatius's letters to Smyrna: diss. Harvard. -- : HThR 87 (1994) 476.

g211 **Neri** U., Ignazio di Antiochia: Conversazioni bibliche Monteveglio.   Bo 1994,

Dehoniane. 90 p. L^m 10. 88-10-70947-0 [NTAb 40, p.180].

g212   *Rius-Camps* Josep,   *a)* Indicios de una redacción muy temprana de las cartas auténticas de Ignacio (c. 70-90 d.C.) : → 119, ^FMARA M.Grazia = Aug(ustinianum)R 35 (1995) 199-214; -- *b)* 'Realitat' o 'aparença'; el ser o no ser del cristianisme. segons Ignasì, el bisbe de Síria: → 41, ^FCOLOMER E., RCatT 29 (1994) 67-77; Eng. 78.

g213   *Thomassen* Einar, *Lógos apò sigês proelthōn* (Ign.Mag.8:2); → 79, ^FHARTMAN L., Texts & Contexts 1995, 847-867.

g214   **Trevett** Christine, A study of Ignatius of Antioch in Syria and Asia: SBEC 29, 1992 → 8,k652; 0-7734-9495-2: ^RJEH 46 (1995) 167s (C.P. *Bammel*).

g215   *Wesche* K.P.,   St. Ignatius of Antioch; the criterion of orthodoxy and the marks of catholicity: *ProEccl 3,1 (1994) 89-109   [NTAb 40, p.503].

g216   IRENAEUS   **Brox** Norbert, Irenaeus von Lyon, Adversus haereses 3: FC 8/3. FrB 1995, Herder. 336 p.; DM 58; pa. 48 [RHE 91,30*] -- ^RZkT 117 (1995) 371s (L. *Lies*: 1s, 1933).

g217   **Bingham** Dwight J.,   Irenaeus' use of Matthew's Gospel in 'Adversus haereses': diss. Dallas Theol. Sem., ^DBlaising C., 1995. 474 p.   95-31273. -- DissA 56 (1995s) p. 1844.

g218   **Fantino** Jacques, La théologie d'Irénée; lecture des Écritures en réponse à l'exégèse gnostique; une approche trinitaire: C(og)Fi 180, 1994; F 170: ^RE(xp)T 107 (1995s) 15s (G. *Wainwright*);R(ech)SR 83 (1995) 141 (Madeleine *Scopello*); TTh 35 (1995) 192 (F. van de *Paverd*).

g219   **Hauke** Manfred, Heilsverlust in Adam; Stationen griechischer Erbsündenlehre: Irenäus, ORIGENES, Kappadozier: KkKSt 58, 1992 → 8,2332; 9,1914: ^RForKT 11 (1995) 203-7 (L. *Scheffczyk*: ökumenischer Brückenschlag); RTPh 127 (1995) 298 (F. *Siegert*).

g220   *Leśniewski* Krzysztof,   The Adam-Christ typology in St. Irenaeus of Lyons: R(ocz)TK 41,7 (1994) 63-74; ^P 74s.

g221   *Löhr* Winrich A.,   [Iren 1,25] Karpokratianisches: VigChr 49 (1995) 23-48.

g222   **Minns** Denis, Irenaeus: Outstanding Christian thinkers 1994 → 10,13994; £ 25; pa. £ 10: ^RFurrow 46 (1995) 127 (A. *Goodison* prefers to sr. Mary CLARK's Augustine).

g223   *Orbe* Antonio, *a)* Sobre los 'Alogos' de san Ireneo (adv.haer.III,11,9): Greg 76 (1995) 47-68; franç. 68; -- *b)* El Espíritu en el bautismo de Jesús (en torno a san Ireneo): Greg 76 (1995) 663-699; franç. 699; -- *c)* (Haer,III,3,4) En torno a una noticia sobre POLICARPO : → 119, ^FMARA M.Grazia = Aug(ustinianum)R 35 (1995) 507-604.

g224   *Quantin* Jean-Louis, Irénée de Lyon entre humanisme et Réforme; les citations de l'Adversus haereses dans les controverses religieuses, de Johann Fabri à Martin Luther (1522-1527): RechAug 27 (1994) 131-175 (-184, *al.*).

g225   *Ribeiro* Ari Luis do Vale,   S. Irineu de Lião; teología, tradição e profetismo : Teocomunicação 25 (1995) 525-544.

g226   ^TE**Rousseau** Adelin, Irénée de Lyon, Démonstration de la prédication apostolique: SC 406. P 1994, Cerf. 412 p. F 293. 2-204-05110-1. -- ^RNRT 117 (1995) 590s (A. *Harvengt*).

g227   *Slate* C.Philip,Two features of Irenaeus' missiology: Miss(iology) 23 (1995)431-42

g228   **Tiessen** Terrance L., Irenaeus on the salvation of the unevangelized: ATLA mg 31, 1993 → 10,13998: ^RE(v)RT 19 (1995) 201-3 (D. *Parker:* cannot be claimed as precursor of RAHNER'S 'anonymous Christian'); EThL 70 (1994) 508-510 (V. *Neckebrouck*).

g229 JOSIPPON: ^{TE}**Grant** Robert M., *Menzies* Glen V., Joseph's Bible notes 'Hypomnestikon': SBL.TT 41. At c. 1965, Scholars. xi-372 p.; bibliog. 351-360. 0-7885-0195-X.

g230 JUSTINUS: *Edwards* M.J., Justin's Logos and the Word of God: *JEarlyC 3 (1995) 261-280.

g231 *Hamman* Adalbert-G., Essai de chronologie de le vie et des œuvres de Justin : → 119, ^FMARA M.Grazia = Aug(ustinianum)R 35 (1995) 231-240.

g232 *Henne* Philippe, Justin, la Loi et les Juifs: RTL 26 (1995) 450-462: Eng. 609.

g233 ^E**Marcovich** Miroslav, Pseudo-Justinus, Cohortatio ad Graecos: De monarchia: Oratio ad Graecos: PTS 32, 1990 → 6,k85; 7g63: ^RSalesianum 57 (1995) 145 (F. *Canaccini*).

g234 **Markovich** M., Patristic textual criticism [JUSTIN, *al.*]: *ILCL.s 6. Atlanta 1994, Scholars. x-171 p. $ 25. 1-7885-0046-5 [NTAb 39, p.355].

g235 **Merlo** Paolo, Liberi per vivere secondo il Logos; principi e criteri dell'agire morale in San Giustino filosofo e martire: BSRel 111. R 1995, LAS. 373 p., bibliog. 333-352. 88-213-0284-9.

g236 **Munier** Charles, L'apologie pour les Chrétiens de Saint Justin philosophe et martyr; Paradosis 38 [39,1995, éditions et traduction; 2-8271-0682-5], 1994 → 10,14003: ^RRHPhR 75 (1995) 233s (P. *Prigent*).

g237 *Tabory* Joseph, The crucifixion of the paschal lamb [... Justin]: JQR 86 (1995s) 395-406.

g238 POLYCARPUS: **Bauer** Johannes B., Die Polykarpbriefe, übersetzt und erklärt: KAV 5. Gö 1995, Vandenhoeck & R. 112 p. DM 58 3-525-51678-9 [NTAb 40, p.373; RHE 91,29*].

g239 **Buschmann** Gerd, Martyrium Polycarpi -- eine formkritische Studie; ein Beitrag zur Frage nach der Entstehung der Gattung Märtyrerakte: BZNW 70, 1994 →10,14006; DM 178: ^RJThS 46 (1995) 698-701 (H.O. *Maier*).

g240 PTOLEMAEUS: *Löhr* Winrich A., La doctrine de Dieu dans la lettre à Flore de Ptolémée: RHPhR 75 (1995) 177-191 . 701-727.

Y1.6 Origenes

g241 **Benjamins** Hendrik S., Eingeordnete Freiheit; Freiheit und Vorsehung bei Origenes: VigChr.s 28, 1994 → 10,14010: ^RSalmanticensis 42 (1995) 453-8 (R. *Trevijano*).

g242 *Berchman* Robert M., The categories of being in Middle Platonism; PHILO, CLEMENT, and Origen of Alexandria: → 132*, Mem. MOEHRING H., School of Moses 1995, 98-140.

g243 **Clark** Elizabeth, The Origenist controversy 1992 → 8,k669 ... 10,14012: ^RIst(ina) 39 (1994) 432s (B. *Dupuy*); JEH 46 (1995) 548s (E.D. *Hunt*); US(em)QR 48,3 (1994) 158-161 (Virginia *Burrus*).

g244 **Crouzel** Henri., Origen 1989 → 8,k689; 9,15755: ^RA(ustrl)BR 41 (1993) 92s (J. *Painter*); JAAR 63 (1995) 383s (S. *Pollett*).

g245 **Crouzel** Henri, Origène et PLOTIN, comparaisons doctrinales. P 1991 → 10,15756; Croire et savoir; F 185; 2-7403-0097-2: [RStR 22,305, J.W. *Trigg* shows Crouzel's development since 1962, amid 16 other books on 'Origen and Origenism in the 1990s']. - - ^RBijdragen 56 (1995) 460s (J. *Haers*); Ist(ina) 39 (1994) 430-2 (B. *Dupuy*).

g246 **Crouzel** Henri, Bibliographie critique d'Origène, supplément I-II: IP 8. Steenbrugge 1982-96. S.Pietersabdij. I. 339 p.; II. xxiii-363 p.; 2-503-50480-9.

g247 *Crouzel* Henri, Chronique origénienne: BLE 96 (1995) 309-312.

g248 [F]CROUZEL Henri, Recherches et tradition; mélanges patristiques, [E]*Dupleix* André: THist 88, 1992 → 8,35: [R]BLE 96 (1995) 47-53 (P. *Force*, détaillé sur les 21 art., 11 sur Origène); *JEarlyC 3 (1995) 64-66 (P.J. *Gorday*).

g249 [E]**Daly** Robert J., Origeniana quinta 1989: BEThL 105, 1992 → 8.532 ... 10,14016: [R]RTL 26 (1995) 77-82 (J.-M. *Auwers*).

g250 *Edwards* M.J., Origen's two resurrections [one (or both) figurative, 'as certain as any deduction from his writings']: JThS 46 (1995) 502-518.

g251 **Fédou** Michel, La sagesse et le monde; le Christ d'Origène: JJC .. P 1995, Desclée. 450 p. -- [R]BLE 96 (1995) 311s (H. *Crouzel*).

g252 **Fernández Lago** José, 'La montaña' en las homilías de Orígenes 1993 → 9,15764; 10.14019: [R]Aug(ustinianum)R 34 (1994) 237 (M.Grazia *Mara*); CBQ 57 (1995) 178s (J.T. *Forestell*); E(st)E 70 (1995) 417s (J. A. *Alcaín*); OCP 61 (1995) 311s (V. *Ruggieri*); Salesianum 57 (1995) 581 (M.K. *Sebastien*).

g253 *Florovsky* Georges, Origène, EUSÈBE et la controverse iconoclaste [< ChH 19 (1950) 77-96], [T]*Chantal* Anne: Ist(ina) 39 (1994) 341-357.

g254 **Küng** Hans, Great Christian thinkers (Origen p. 41-67) 1994 → 10,14021: [R]ET 106 (1994s) 90s (G. *Slater*: a sparkling introduction); Tablet 249 (1995) 113s (A. *Louth*).

g255 *Lamberigts* Mathijs, Het vroege Christendom; een godsdienst [religion] voor armen en vrouwen ?: TTh 35 (1995) 323-337; Eng. 357: CELSUS rightly: earliest Christians mostly impoverished; wrongly: they were too uneducated to understand the Gospel correctly; anyway in 2d-3d centuries included many well-to-do, some (also women) of high-level intellectual training.

g256 *a) Lefebvre* Philippe, Origène et l'Écriture; -- *b) Bianchi* Enzo, Lectio divina et vie monastique: VSp 149 (1995) 117-133 / 145-161.

g257 *Lettieri* Gaetano, In spirito o/e verità da Origene a Tommaso d'Aquino: ASEs 12,1 ('Il culto in spirito e verità' 1995) 49-83 (+ 4 *al.* su Gv 4,23).

g258 **Lies** Lothar, Origenes' 'Peri archon', eine undogmatische Dogmatik 1992 → 8,k687; 10,14022: ThLZ 120 (1995) 1012s (C.P. *Bammel*); ThRv 91 (1995) 395-7 (B. *Studer*).

g259 *Meis* W. Anneliese, Teología patrística y pastoral según el Cantar de los Cantares de Orígenes, y el De doctrina christiana de AGUSTÍN : TyV 36 (1995) 31-50.

g260 *Meredith* Anthony, Origen's *De principiis* and GREGORY OF NYSSA's *Oratio cate-chetica*: HeythJ 36 (1995) 1-14.

g261 *a) O'Leary* Joseph S., Le destin du Logos johannique dans la pensée d'Origène; -- *b) Moingt* Joseph, La réception du Prologue de Jean au IIe siècle: → 106, [F]LÉON-DUFOUR X., R(ech)SR 83 (1995) 283-292 249-282; Eng. 179s.

g262 *Prinzivalli* Emanuela, Aspetti esegetico-dottrinali del dibattito nel IV secolo sulle tesi origeniane in materia escatologica: → 488, ASEs 12 (1995) 279-325

g263 **Rubenson** Samuel, The letters of St. Anthony; Origenist theology .. 1990 → 7,g86; 9,15779: *JEarlyC 3 (1995) 493-5 (D. *Barton-Christie*).

g264 *a) Schockenhoff* Eberhard, Kirchliche Autorität als Hilfe zum Christsein ? Zwei Antworten der frühen Kirche; -- *b) Markschiess* Christoph, Was bedeutet *ousía* ? Zwei Antworten bei Origenes und AMBROSIUS und ihre Bedeutung für ihre Bibelerklärung und Theologie: → 539, Origenes 1995, 83-93 / 59-82.

g265 *Scholten* Clemens, Die alexandrinische Katechetenschule: JAC 38 (1995) 16-37.

g266 *Scognamiglio* Rosario, Grazia o profitto ? La parabola dei talenti (Mt 15,14-30) nell'esegesi di Origene: Nicolaus 21 (1994) 239-261.

g267 **Strutwolf** H., Gnosis als System; zur Rezeption der valentinianischen Gnosis bei Origenes: FKDG 56, 1993 → 9.15783; DM 130; 3-525-55164-9: [R]TTh 35 (1995) 81 (A. *Davids*).

g268 *Trigg* Joseph W., EUSTATHIUS of Antioch's attack on Origen; what is at issue in an ancient controversy ? : JRel 75 (1995) 219-238.

g269 *Williams* Rowan, Origenes/Origenismus, [T]*Schäferdiek* Knut: → 772, TRE 25 (1995) 397-420.

g270 **Witte** Baernd, Das Ophitendiagramm nach Origenes' Cels VI 22-38,1993 → 9,15788; 10,14029: [R]ThLZ 120 (1995) 725-7 (M. *Westerhoff*).

g271 **Ziebritzki** Henning, Heiliger Geist und Weltseele; das Problem der dritten Hypostase bei Origenes, PLOTIN und ihren Vorläufern: BHTh 84, 1994 → 10.14029*: [R]Greg 76 (1995) 771 (G. *Pelland*).

Y1.8 **Tertullianus**

g272 **Braun** René, Tertullien, Contre Marcion 3: SC 399,1994 → 10.14031*: [R]Greg 76 (1995) 619s (G. *Pelland*).

g273 **Braun** René, Approches de TERTULLIEN 1992 → 9,15793; 10,14032: [R]RB(elg)PH 73 (1995) 158s (M. *Testard*).

g274 **Daly** Cahal P., Tertullian the puritan and his influence; an essay in historical theology 1993 → 9,15795; £ 30: [R]Ang 72 (1995) 100s (B. *Degórski*); ZKG 106 (1995) 126s (H.G. *Thümmel*).

g275 *Drink* Ali, Cerès, les *Cereres* et les *sacerdotes magnae* en Afrique; quelques témoignages épigraphiques et littéraires (Tertullien): → 10,73, Mém. LE GLAY M., L'Afrique 1994, 174-184.

g276 *Gramaglia* Pier Angelo, Note sul 'De pudicitia' di Tertulliano [SC 394s, MICAELLI C., MUNIER C.]: RSLR 31 (1995) 235-258.

g277 **Harnack** Adolf von, MARCION, the gospel of the alien God, [T]*Steely* John E., *Bierma* Lyle D 1990 → 7,g97*; 8,k711: [R]JHiCrit 2,1 (1995) 154-7 (R.M. *Price*).

g278 *Helleman* Wendy E., Tertullian on Athens and Jerusalem: → 10,322, Hellenization 1991/4, 361-391.

g279 **Hoffman** Daniel C., The status of women and gnosticism in IRENAEUS and Tertullian: SW(omen)R 36. Lewiston NY 1995, Mellen. x-240 p.; bibliog. 219-234. 0-7734-8996-7.

g280 *Kirkland* A., Liturgical time in Tertullian: AcPatrByz 6 (Pretoria 1995) 69-85.

g281 *Kirkpatrick* Lawrence, Baptism, Scripture and the problem of the Christian sinner in Tertullian's De Paenitentia and De Pudicitia: I(rish)BSt 17 (1995) 75-85.

g282 **Lüdemann** Gerd, Concerning the history of earliest Christianity in Rome; I. Valentinus and Marcion; II. Ptolemaeus and Justin : *JHiCr 2,1 (1995) 112-141.

g283 [TE]**Micaelli** Claude, intr. *Munier* Charles, De pudicité: SChr 394s. P 1993, Cerf. -- [R]Greg 76 (1995) 410s (G. *Pelland*); ScrBru 49 (1995) 162-5 (P. *Hamblenne*).

g284 *Micaelli* Claudio, Tertulliano nel quarto secolo; VITTORINO di Pettau e Vittricio di Rouen: SC(las)O 43 (1993) 251-262.

g285 [E]**Munier** Charles, La pudicité: SC 394s. P 1993, Cerf. -- [R]Greg 76 (1995) 410s (G. *Pelland*).

g286 *Pastor* Félix-Alejandro, El discurso del método en teología: Greg 76 (1995) 69-93;

g287 **Rankin** David I., Tertullian and the Church. C 1995, Univ. xvii-229 p. £ 35. 0-521-48067-1 [ThD 43,285; RHE 90,308*]. -- [R]CLit 44 (1994s) 383-5 (G. C. *Roti*); *TBR 8,2 (1995s) 43 (G. *Gould*).

g288 *Rapalino* Edoardo, In margine ad una nuova edizione del trattato De monogamia di Tertulliano [UGLIONE R. 1993]: SMSR 60 (1994) 389-398.

g289 **Robeck** Cecil M., Prophecy in Carthage; Perpetua, Tertullian, and CYPRIAN 1992 → 9,15804; $ 30: [R]C(alvin)TJ 30 (1995) 499-501 (R.A. *Muller*); Pneuma 17 (1995) 138-141 (S.M. *Burgess*).

g290 **Ruggiero** Fabio, Tertulliano, De corona 1992 → 9.15804*; 10,14048: [R]Gnomon 67 (1995) 561-3 (R. *Braun*).

g291 **Schmid** U., MARCION und sein *Apostolos*: Rekonstruktion und historische Einordnung der marcionitischen Paulusbriefausgabe: ANTT 25. B 1995, de Gruyter. xvii-381 p. DM 214. [RHE 91,29*].

g292 *Trevett* Christine, Fingers up noses and pricking with needles; reminiscences of revelation in later Montanism: VigChr 49 (1995) 258-269.

g293 *a) Ugenti* Valerio, Norme prosodiche delle clausole metriche nel De idololatria di Tertulliano; -- *b) Norelli* Enrico, Note sulla soteriologia di MARCIONE; -- *c) Osborn* Eric, The conflict of opposites in the theology of Tertullian: → 119, [F]MARA M.Grazia = Aug(ustinianum)R 35 (1995) 241-258 / 281-305 / 623-639

g294 **Uglione** R., Tertulliano, Le uniche nozze; CP 15,1993 → 10,14050: [R]AtenR 40 (1995) 43-46 (A.V. *Nazzaro*); Greg 76 (1995) 187-190 (G. *Pelland*: trois obscurités du texte original, d'importance doctrinale).

g295 *Uglione* Renato, Gli *hapax* tertullianei di matrice fonica: BSL(at) 25 (1995) 529-541.

g296 *Uribarri Bilbao* Gabino, Arquitectura retórica del Adversus Praxean de Tertuliano: E(st)E 70 (1995) 449-487.

g297 *a) Winden* J.C.M. van, The adverbial use of *cum maxime* in Tertullian; -- *b) Buschmann* Gerd, Martyrium Polycarpi 4 und der Montanismus: VigChr 49 (1995) 209-214 / 105-145 (-164 *al.*).

Y2 *Patres graeci* -- **The Greek Fathers**

g298 *Dorival* G., La mutation chrétienne des idées et des valeurs païennes: *BICL 106 (Lyon 1994) 33-49 [NTAb 39, p.486].

g299 **Margerie** Bertrand D., The Greek Fathers, [T]*Maaluf* Leonard: Introduction to the History of Exegesis 1 [2. AUGUSTINE 1993 → 9,15995] Petersham MA 1993, St. Bede. iv-173 p. $ 20 pa. 1-879007-05-3 [NTAb 40, p.329; ThD 43,278].

g300 **Meredith** Anthony, The Cappadocians: Outstanding Christian Thinkers. L 1995, Chapman/Cassell. xiv-129 p. £ 25; pa. £ 10. 0-225-66705-3; -7-X. -- [R]E(xp)T 107 (1995s) 155s (G. *Bonner*: high praise); *TBR 8,2 (1995s) 49 (Jill D. *Harries*: concise, learned and accessible).

g301 *Neuner* Peter, Die Hellenisierung des Christentums als Modell von Inkulturation: StZ 213 (1995) 363-376.

g302 [E]*Oort* J. van, *Wickert* U., Christliche Exegese zwischen Nicaea und Chalcedon 1991/2 → 8,484*: [R]ChH 64 (1995) 641s (G.T. *Armstrong*); *JEarlyC 3 (1995) 228 (R.L. *Wilken*); RSLR 31 (1995) 121-5 (M. *Simonetti*).

g303 **Orbe** A., La teologia dei secoli II e III; il confronto della Grande Chiesa con lo gnosticismo [1987], [TE]*Zani* A. CasM 1995, Piemme. 608 p.; 656 p. L[m] 85 + 85.

g304 **Ortiz de Urbina** Ignacio, Storia dei concili ecumenici I. Nicea e Costantinopoli [c. 1965], ᵀ. Vaticano 1994, Editrice. 302 p. Lᵐ 32. 88-209-1880-3. -- ᴿAng 72 (1995) 345s (T. *Stancati*).

g305 *a) Patsavos* Leis J., Ecclesiastical reform; at what cost ? -- *b) Timiadis* Emilianos, Focusing emphasis on true metanoia rather than on penitential canons; -- *c) McManus* Frederick R., The Council in Trullo; a Roman Catholic perspective : → 627, GOTR 40,1s [Holy Cross Conference, The Council "in Trullo" (= Quinisext = Penthekte, 6th Ecumenical 692: 1995) 1-10 / 97-114 / 79-96.

g306 **Pelikan** Jaroslav, Christianity and classical culture; the metamorphosis of natural theology in the Christian encounter with Hellenism (Aberdeen Gifford lectures 1992s) 1993 → 10,14057; $ 40; 0-300-05554-4: ᴿAsbTJ 50 (1995) 93-95 (D. *Bundy*); Interpretation 49 (1995) 293-5 (Rebecca H. *Weaver*); JRel 75 (1995) 414-6 (D.L. *Balás*); SewaneeT 38 (1994s) 172-181 (R.J. *Schoeck*); SV(lad)TQ 39 (1995) 99-103 (P.C. *Bouteneff*).

g307 *Rordorf* Willy, Bedeutung und Grenze der altkirchlichen Glaubensbekenntnisse (Apostolicum und Nicaeno-Constantinopolitanum): ThZ 51 (1995) 50-64.

g308 *a) Rudolph* Kurt, Das frühe Christentum in Ägypten; zwischen Häresie und Orthodoxie; -- *b) Gelzer* Thomas, Heidnisches und Christliches im Platonismus der Kaiserzeit und der Spätantike: → 732, Begegnung 1991/3, 21-31 / 33-48.

g309 **Shaw** Gregory, Theurgy and the soul; the Neoplatonism of [pagan] Iamblichus: Hermeneutics. Univ. Park 1995, Penn State. x-268 p. $ 45. 0-271-01437-7 [ThD 43,388].

g310 *Starowieyski* Marek, ᴾ De Concilio Ephesio et Nestorii doctrina; fontes: Mea(nder) 50 (1995) 23-35: lat. 35.

g311 **Trombley** Frank R., Hellenic religion and Christianization: ÉPRO 115, 1993 → 10,14060: ᴿThRv 91 (1995) 483s (M.-Barbara von *Stritzky*).

g312 *Valevičius* Andrius, The Greek Fathers and the 'coats of skins' [Gen 3,21]: Logos 36 (Ottawa 1995) 163-175.

g313 **Vogel** Cornelia J. de, Platonismo e cristianesimo; antagonismo o comuni fondamenti ? ᵀ*Reale* G., ᴱ*Peroli* E.: Platonismo e filosofia patristica 2. Mi 1993, VP. 161 p. -- ᴿTer(esianum) 46 (1995) 295-7 (M.D. *Sánchez*, también sobre VÖLKER, G.Nissa 1993); VetChr 32 (1995) 219-221 (Immacolata *Aulisa*).

g314 **Watson** Gerard, Greek philosophy and the Christian notion of God 1994→10,14061: ᴿET 106 (1994s) 249 (G. *Bostock*).

g315 *Yeago* D.S., The New Testament and the Nicene Dogma; a contribution to the recovery of theological exegesis: Pro Ecclesia 3 (1994) 152-164 [< ZIT 95, p.131].

g316 **Young** Frances M., The making of the creeds 1991 → 7.g17; 8,k588*: ᴿWW 15 (1995) 378s . 382 (G.M. *Simpson*).

------

g317 ARIUS: ᴱ**Barnes** Michael R., *Williams* Daniel H., Arianism after Arius; essays on the development of the fourth century trinitarian conflict 1993 → 9,310a; £ 20: ᴿJETS 38 (1995) 629s (K.R. *Calvert*); JThS 46 (1995) 333-347 ! (T.A. *Kopeček*); Theol 97 (L 1994) 466s (Averil *Cameron*: rarely has a rival been so successfully blackened).

g318 *Studer* Basil, Zu einer neuen Untersuchung der Theologie des Arius [BÖHM T. 1991]: MüTZ 45 (1994) 329-325 (593-9, Böhms Replik).

g319 ASTERIUS: ᴱ**Vinzent** Markus, Asterius von Kappadokien [dem der Psalmkommentar ist nicht zuzuschreiben]; die theologischen Fragmente: VigChr.S 20, 1993: ᴿJThS 46 (1995) 331-3 (S.G. *Hall*: one of the best 'Arian' thinkers).

g320 ATHANASIUS: **Bartelink** J.M., Vie d'Antoine: SC 400, 1994 → 10,14074: [R]RÉByz 53 (1995) 339s (G. *Wolinski*); RHPhR 75 (1995) 347s (P. *Maraval*).

g321 **Brakke** David, Athanasius and the politics of asceticism [< diss. Yale]. Ox 1995, Clarendon. xviii-356 p. $ 65. 0-19-826816-5 [ThD 43,159].

g322 **Camplani** Alberto, Le lettere festali 1989 → 6.k164: [R]OL(ov)P 25 (1994) 281-5 (H. *Hauben*).

g323 *Kannengiesser* Charles, Die Sonderstellung der dritten Arianrede des Athanasius: ZKG 106 (1995) 18-55.

g324 **Tetz** Martin, Athanasiana; zu Leben und Lehre des Athanasius: BZNW 78. B 1995, de Gruyter. [viii-] 324 p. 3-11-014611-8.

g325 BASILIUS **Backus** I., Lectures humanistes de Basile de Césarée; traductions latines (1439-1618). Antiquité 125, 1990 → 7,g129; 8,k749: [R]RHE 90 (1995) 241s (P.-A. *Deproost*).

g326 **Coffigny** D., Basile le Grand: EdH&A. P 1995, Atelier. 172 p.; map. F 85 [RHE 90 (1995) 95*].

g327 **Drecoll** Volker, Basilius von Caesarea als Trinitätstheologe; sein Weg vom Homöiousianer zum Neonizäner: ev. Diss. [D]*Hauschild* W. Münster/Wf 1995.

g328 **Fedwick** Paul J., A study of the manuscript tradition of the works of Basil: BtBasUniv CC. Turnhout 1993, Brepols. xlii-755 p. Fb 10,400. -- [R]*JEarlyC 3 (1995) 97s (M. *Slusser*) .

g329 **Gain** Benoît, Édition des lettres de Basile de Césarée, Laurentianus San Marco 584: EurHH 15/64. Berne 1994, Lang. xiii-536 p. F 352. -- [R]RHE 90 (1995) 116-9 (J.R. *Pouchet*).

g330 *Girardi* Mario, Fra esigenze di perfezione e rapporti con I fratelli; Basilio di Cesarea e le beatitudini: Nicolaus 21 (1994) 95-132.

g331 **Hauschild** Wolf D., Briefe [I c.1973]; II (1-94), III (214-368): BGrL [3;] 32; 37: 1990/3; DM 190; 220: [R](Tü)TQ [154 (1974) 89] 175 (1995) 67-70 (H.J. *Vogt*).

g332 **Pouchet** Robert, Basile le Grand et son univers d'amis; correspondance 1992 → 8,k758; 9,15856: [R]Aug(ustinianum)R 34 (1994) 227-235 (E. *Cavalcanti*).

g333 **Rousseau** Philip, Basil of Caesarea: TransfClasHer 20, 1994 → 10,14085 [RStR 22,72, R.L. *Wilken*]. -- [R]GaR 42 (1995) 252 (P. *Walcot*).

g334 *Vogt* Hermann J., Zum Briefwechsel zwischen Basilius und APOLLINARIS; Übersetzung der Briefe mit Kommentar: (Tü)TQ 175 (1995) 46-60.

g335 CHRYSOSTOMUS: *Allen* Pauline, *Mayer* Wendy, *a)* Chrysostom and the preaching of homilies in series; a re-examination of the fifteen homilies In ep.Phlp. (CPG 4432): VigChr 49 (1995) 270-289; -- *b)* The thirty-four homilies on Hebrews; the last series delivered by Chrysostom in Constantinople: → 100, [F]LAFONTAINE-DOSOGNE J., Byzantion 65,2 (1995) 309-348.

g336 [TE]**Kacynski** Reiner, Taufkatechesen 1-11 gr.-dt.: FC 6,1s, 1992 → 9,15865; je DM 40, pa. 29. -- [R]*JEarlyC 3 (1995) 72-75 (A. *Shippee*: erudite, with concordance to varying citation-numbers).

g337 **Kelly** J.N.D., Golden mouth, the story of John Chrysostom -- ascetic, preacher, bishop. L 1995, Duckworth. x-310 p. £ 35. 0-7156-2643-4. -- [R]E(xp)T 107 (1995s) 64 (C.S. *Rodd*); *TBR 8,2 (1995s) 51 (G. *Gould*: a masterpiece).

g338 **Kertsch** Manfred, Exempla chrysostomica; zu Exegese, Stil und Bildersprache bei

Johannes Chrysostomos: GrazTSt 18. Graz 1995, Univ. Inst. Ök. xxiii-221 p. Sch 240. 3-900797-18-8 [ThRv 91].

g339 *Krupp* Robert A., Golden tongue and iron will: ChrHist 13,44 [→ 10,14090] ('John Chrysostom, the great preacher who paid for his convictions with his life'; 1994) 6-11 (-39, *al.*).

g340 *Leroy* F., Comment travaille un éditeur patristique parisien du XVIe siècle ? Le p. G. TILMAN, chartreux, et les Chrysostomi opera de Chevallon en 1536; sondage dans la collection Arsenal du Chrysostome latin: SE(rud) 35 (1995) 45-53.

g341 *Leyerle* Blake, John Chrysostom on almsgiving and the use of money: HThR 87 (1994) 29-47.

g342 **Malingrey** Anne-Marie, .. Anoméens Vii-XII: SC 396, 1994 → 10,14091*: [R]JThS 46 (1995) 725-7 (L.R. *Wickham*).

g343 *Mitchell* Margaret M., John Chrysostom on Philemon; a second look: HThR [86 (1993) 357-376, CALLAHAN A.] 88 (1995) 135-148.

g344 [E]**Dattrino** Lorenzo, PALLADIUS H., Dialogo sulla vita di Giovanni Crisostomo: CTePa 125. R 1995, Città Nuova. 316 p. 88-311-3125-7. [Eng. [T]*Meyer* R. 1985 → 9,15870].

g345 **Papageorgiou** Panayiotis E., A theological analysis of selected themes in the homilies of St. John Chrysostom on the epistle of St. Paul to the Romans: diss. Catholic University of America, [D]*Young* R. Washington D.C. 1995. 301 p. 95-28264. -- D(iss)AI 56 (1995s) p. 1401.

g346 *Vannier* Marie-Anne, L'influence de Jean Chrysostome sur l'argumentation scripturaire du De incarnatione de Jean CASSIEN: RevSR 69 (1995) 453-462; Eng. 533.

g347 *Zincone* Sergio, La funzione dell'oscurità delle profezie secondo Giovanni Crisostomo: → 488, ASEs 12 (1995) 361-375.

g348 CHRYSOSTOMUS (PSEUDO): *Backhuizen* J.H., *a*) Pseudo-Chrysostom's homily 'On the four-day [dead] Lazarus'; an analysis; -- *b*) Homily 3 of Amphilochius of Iconium, 'On the four-day [dead] Lazarus'; an essay in interpretation: AcPatrByz 6 (Pretoria 1995) 1-14 / 5 (1994) 1-11.

g349 CYRILLUS A.: *Wilken* Robert L., St. Cyril of Alexandria; the mystery of Christ in the Bible: *ProEc 4 (1995) 454-478.

g350 CYRILLUS H.: [TE]**Röwekamp** Georg, Cyrillus von Jerusalem, Mystagogische Katechesen / Mystagogicae catecheses; FC 7, 1992 → 9,15887: *JEarlyC 3 (1995) 232-4 (K. *Anderson*).

g351 CYRILLUS S.: [T]**Price** R.N., [E]*Binns* John, Cyril of Scythopolis, Lives of the monks of Palestine: CistSt 114, 1991 → 8,k779; 0-87907-714-X. -- [R]Bijdragen 56 (1995) 87s (M. *Parmentier*, Eng.)

g352 DAMASCENUS: *Armitage* Nicholas, The Eucharistic theology of the 'Exact exposition of the Orthodox faith' (De fide orthodoxa) of Saint John Damascene: OS(tk) 44 (1995) 292-308.

g353 [T]**Darras-Worms** Anne-Lise, Jean Damascène, Le visage de l'invisible: CPF 57. P 1994, Migne. 189 p. 2-908597-16-5.

g354 **Le Coz** Raymond, Écrits sur l'Islam: SC 383, 1992 → 8.k781 ... 10,14099: [R]Greg 76 (1995) 413s (E. *Farahian*).

g355 DIDYMUS: **Doutreleau** Louis, Didyme l'Aveugle, Traité du Saint-Esprit: SC 386, 1992 → 10,14100: ᴿJAC 38 (1995) 183-5 (W.A. *Bienert*).

g356 **Nelson** Anne B., The classroom of Didymus the Blind: diss. Michigan, ᴰ*Koenen* L. AA 1995. 96-10207. -- D(iss)AI 56 (1995s) p. 4758.

g357 EPIPHANIUS: *Camplani* Alberto, Epifanio (Ancoratus) e GREGORIO DI NAZIANZO (Epistulae) in copto; identificazione e status quaestionis : → 119, ᶠMARA M.Grazia = Aug(ustinianum)R 35 (1995) 327-347.

g358 **Stewart** Columba, 'Working ..' Messalian 1991 → 7,g156; 8,k786*: ᴿJRel 75 (1995) 113s (B. *McGinn*).

g359 ᵀᴱ**Williams** Frank, The Panarion of Epiphanius of Salamis: NHSt 36, 1987/94 → 10,14102: ᴿR(ech)SR 83 (1995) 143-5 (Madeleine *Scopello*: un grand service malgré les défauts).

g360 EUSEBIUS: ᴱ**Attridge** H.W., *Hata* G., Eusebius, Christianity and Judaism [30 art.]: StPB 42, 1992 → 8.k790; 9,15901: ᴿRS(to)LR 31 (1995) 334-8 (M. *Simonetti*).

g361 **Hoornaert** Eduardo, The memory of the Christian people [distorted by Eusebius and other early fathers from a small-communities network into a Roman Empire model], ᵀ*Barr* Robert R: Theology and Liberation. Mkn 1988, Orbis. 268 p. -- ᴿA(sia)JT 8 (1994) 191-4 (D.E. *Wingeler*).

g362 *Manns* Frédéric, Une tradition judéo-chrétienne rapportée par Eusèbe de Césarée [→ 10,14104]: CrSt 15 (1994) 145-8; Eng. 148 [NTAb 39, p.119: the Rechabites are called priests].

g363 **Places** Édouard des, La préparation évangélique VIII-X (avec *Schroeder* G.) & IX; SC 369, 1991 → 7,g160 ... 10,14104: ᴿKL(eronomia) 26 (1994) 375-382 (I.M. *Foudoulis*, ᴳ on SC 369-386; 14 earlier volumes on p. 382-9 of vol. 25, 1993); RHE 90 (1995) 259s (P.-A. *Deproost*).

g364 *Springborg* Patricia, HOBBES, heresy and the Historia Ecclesiastica: JHId 55(1994)553-71

g365 EVAGRIUS: **Bunge** Gabriel, Paternité spirituelle; la gnose chrétienne chez Évagre le Pontique; SpOr 61. Bellefontaine 1994. 115 p. -- ᴿRHPhR 75 (1995) 236s (J.-C- *Larchet*).

g366 *Maier* Barbara, Apatheia bei den Stoikern und Akedia bei Evagrios Pontikos -- ein Ideal und die Kehrseite seiner Realität: OrChr 78 (1994) 230-249.

g367 GREGORIUS A.: ᴱ**Nadal Cañellas** Juan, Gregorius Acindynus, Refutationes duae: CCG 31. Turnhout 1995, Brepols. cxc-486 p. 2-503-40311-5.

g368 GREGORIUS NAZ.: **Bernardi** Jean, Saint Grégoire de Nazianze; le théologien et son temps (330-390): Initiations aux Pères de l'Église. P 1995, Cerf. 367 p. F 150. 2-204-05099-7. -- ᴿMuséon 108 (1995) 430s (B. *Coulie*, dont le CCG 28 est recensé par G. *Uluhogian* p. 431-4).

g369 ᴱ**Calvet-Sebasti** Marie-Ange, Grégoire de Nazianze, Discours 6-12: SC 485. P 1995, Cerf. 418 p. 2-204-05194-2.

g370 **Coulie** Bernard, S.Gregorii Nazianzeni opera, versio armeniaca, I. orationes II, XII, IX: CCG 28. Turnhout 1994, Brepols. xlix-233 p. Fb 4500. -- ᴿMuséon 108 (1995) 431-4 (G. *Uluhogian*).

g371 ᵀᴱ**Crimi** Carmelo, Sulla virtù; carme giambico [I, 2,10]: Poeti cristiani 1. Pisa 1995, ETS. 459 p.; bibliog. 7-22. 88-7741-818-4.

g372 *Maritz* P.J., Logos articulation in Gregory of Nazianzus: AcPByz 6 (Pretoria 1995) 99-108.

g373 **Mossay** Justin, Repertorium Nazianzenum, Orationes, Textus graecus Cypri 4/2. Pd 1995, Schöningh. 246 p. DM 58. 3-506-79011-0 [ThRv 92,78; RHE 90 (1995) 204*].

g374 *Schmitz* Dietmar, Schimpfwörter in den Invektiven des Gregor von Nazianz gegen Kaiser Julius: Glotta 71 (1993) 189-202.

g375 *Van Dam* Raymond, Self-representation in the will of Gregory of Nazianzus: JThS 46 (1995) 118-143, Text 143-8

g376 *Wesche* Kenneth P., 'Mind' and 'self' in the Christology of St. Gregory [Naz] the Theologian. contribution to .. Christian anthropology: GOTR 39 (1994) 33-61 (1-278, *al.*).

g377 GREGORIUS NYSS.: De oratione dominica; de beatitudinibus, ᴱ*Callahan* John F.: Opera 7/2. Leiden 1992, Brill. lii-180 p. ƒ 170. 90-04-09598-5. -- ᴿJThS 46 (1995) 349-352 (A. *Meredith*).

g378 ᴱ**Drobner** Hubertus R., *Klock* Christopher, Studien zu Gregor von Nyssa und der christlichen Spätantike [7. Kolloquium seit 1969]: VigChr supp. 12. L 1990, Brill. x-418 p. 21 art: 7 Eng.; 7 deutsch. -- ᴿ*JEarlyC 3 (1995) 76-78 (G.C. *Berthold*).

g379 **Kees** Reinhard J., Die Lehre von der Oikonomia Gottes in der Oratio catechetica Gregors von Nyssa: VigChr supp. 30. Lei 1995, Brill. x-339 p.; bibliog. 323-336. ƒ 160. 90-04-10200-0. -- ᴿThLZ 120 (1995) 1009-12 (M. *Vinzent*).

g380 *Le Boulluec* Alain, Corporéité ou individualité ? La condition finale des ressuscités selon Grégoire de Nysse : → 119, ᶠMARA M.Grazia = Aug(ustinianum)R 35 (1995) 307-326.

g381 *Marxer* Fridolin, Gregor von Nyssa -- Vater der christlichen Mystik: GuL 67 (1994) 347-358.

g382 **Peroli** Enrico, Il Platonismo e l'antropologia filosofica di Gregorio di Nissa con particolare riferimento agli influssi di PLATONE, PLOTINO e PORFIRIO. Mi 1993, Univ. Sacro Cuore. 364 p. Lᵐ 34. 88-343-0566-3. -- ᴿAng 72 (1995) 591-3 (B. *Degórski*); DoC(om) 48 (1995) 200-2 (D. *Composta*).

g383 *Preez* D.J. du, Die vas [fasting] in die vroeë Kerk soos gesien deur Gregorius van Nyssa: AcPByz 6 (Pretoria 1995) 36-46; Eng. 36.

g384 ᴱ**Terrieux** Jean, Grégoire de Nysse, Sur l'âme et la résurrection: Sagesses chrétiennes. P 1995, Cerf. 220 p. 2-204-05136-5.

g385 HERMIAS: ᴱ**Hanson** R.P.C., (ᵀ*Joussot* D.), Hermias, Satire des philosophes païens: SC 388, 1993 → 10,14005: ᴿAnCL 64 (1995) 342-4 (J. *Schamp*); JAC 38 (1995) 181-3 (C. *Riedweg*).

g386 ISIDORUS P.: **Évieux** Pierre, Isidore de Peluse: ThH 99. P 1995, Beauchesne. xxvii-444 p.; bibliog. xv-xxvii. 2-7010-1301-1.

g387 JOHANNES SCYTH.: **Suchla** Beate R., Verteidigung eines platonischen Denkmodells einer christlichen Welt; die philosophie- und theologiegeschichtliche Bedeutung des Scholionwerks des Johannes von Skythopolis [c. 540] zu den areopagitischen Traktaten: NAWG.ph 1995/1. Gö 1995, Vandenhoeck & R. 28 p.

g388 MACRINA: *Beagon* Philip M., The Cappadocian Fathers, women, and ecclesiastical politics: VigChr 49 (1995) 165-179.

g389 MARCELLUS A.: **Riedweg** Christoph, Ps.JUSTIN (Markell von Ankyra ?) ad Graecos de vera religione (bisher 'Cohortatio ad Graecos'); Einleitung und Kommentar: SBA 25. Ba 1994, Reinhardt. 711 p. (2 vol.) Fs 128. - ᴿJThS 46 (1995) 720-2 (H. *Chadwick*).

g390 **Seibt** Klaus, Die Theologie des Markell von Ancyra [< ev. Diss. Tübingen 1991] : AKG 59. B 1994, de Gruyter. xiv-557 p. DM 258. 3/-11-014027-6. -- ᴿJThS 46 (1995) 716-720 (A.H.B. *Logan*); RS(to)LR 31 (1995) 259-269 (M. *Simonetti*); VigChr 49 (1995) 198-201 (K. *Fitschen*).

g391 MAXIMUS C.: **Karayiannis** Vasilios, Maxime le Confesseur, Essence et énergies de Dieu: ThH 93,1993 → 9,15936; 10,14129*: ᴿJEH 46 (1995) 494 (A. *Nichols*).

g392 **Nichols** Aidan, Byzantine gospel: Maximus the Confessor in modern scholarship 1993 → 9,15937; $ 22: ᴿI(r)ThQ 61 (1995) 321s (N. *Madden*); *ProEc 4 (1995) 375-8 (P.M. *Blowers*); *TBR 8,1 (1995s) 52 (H. *Chadwick*).

g393 MAXIMUS T.: ᴱ**Koniaris** George L., Maximus Tyrius, Philosophoumena / dialexeis: TK 17. B 1995, de Gruyter. lxxxiii-527 p. 3-11-012833-0.

g394 NILUS A.: *Guérard* Marie-Gabrielle, Testimonia christologiques et pédagogie monastique: la notion de prophétie chez Nil d'Ancyre; → 78,ᶠHARL M., Katà toùs o' 1995, 381-91.

g395 PAULINUS P.: **Marcone** Arnaldo, Paolino di Pella, Discorso di ringraziamento, Eucharisticos: BPat 26. Fiesole 1995, Nardini. 133 p. 88-404-2029-0.

g396 PETRUS C.: ᵀᴱ**Ebied** Rifaat Y., Petri Callinicensis patriarchae Antiocheni tractatus contra Damianum II (3,1-19): CCG 32. Turnhout c. 1995, Brepols. lviii-568 p.

g397 PROCLUS C.: *Constas* Nicolas P., Weaving the body of God; Proclus of Constantinople, the Theotokos, and the loom of the flesh: *JEarlyC 3 (1995) 169-194.

g398 SEVERUS: *Beatrice* Pier Franco, Pagan wisdom and Christian theology according to the Tübingen Theosophy [Byzantine epitome of appendix to a lost treatise of 500 A.D.,, here claimed attributable to Severus of Antioch]: *JEarlyC 3 (1995) 403-414.

g399 *Nin* Manel, Monaci e monachesimo nella predicazione di Severo di Antiochia a proposito dell 'Omelie cattedrali' LV e LXI : Aug(ustinianum)R 34 (1994) 207-271.

g400 SYNESIUS: *Gericke* J.D., *Maritz* P.J., Synesius of Cyrene's dependence on and adaptation of PLATO's Republic: AcPByz 6 (Pretoria 1995) 47-56.

g401 THEODORETUS: **Bishop** David L., The doctrine of Providence in selected writings of Theodoret of Cyrus: diss. Southern Baptist theol. sem., ᴰ*Weber* T., 1995. 290 p. 95-20632. -- D(iss)AI 56 (1995s) p. 595.

g402 ᴱ**Gallico** Antonino, Teodoreto di Cirro, Storia di monaci siri: CTePa 119. 324 p. 88-311-2119-2.

g403 **Guinot** Jean-Noël, L'exégèse de Théodoret de Cyr: ThH 100. P 1995, Beauchesne. 880 p. F 360. 2-7010-1303-3. -- ᴿE(spr)eV 105 (1995) 704 (P. *Jay*); Muséon 108 (1995) 428-430 (F. *Petit*); ScEs 47 (1995) 344s (G. *Pelland*).

g404 *Guinot* Jean-Noël, Théodoret de Cyr; une lecture critique de la Septante; → 78, ᶠHARL M., Katà toùs o' 1995, 394-407.

g405 *Tompkins* Ian G., Problems of dating and pertinence in some letters of Theodoret of Cyrrhus: Byz(antion) 65 (1995) 176-195.

g406 THEODORUS: *Abramowski* Luise, Über die Fragmente des Theodor von Mopsuestia in Brit.Libr. add. 12.156 und das doppelt überlieferte christologische Fragment [KÖBERT R., PIB Rom 1985 ?? an GRILLMEIER]: OrChr 79 (1995) 1-8.

g406⁀ **Bruns** Peter, Den Menschen mit dem Himmel verbinden; eine Studie zu den katechetischen Homilien des Theodor von Mopsuestia; CSCOr 549, subs. 89. Lv 1995, Peeters. xviii-444 p.; Bibliog. vii-xviii. 90-6831-718-0.

g407 **Guida** A., Teodoro di Mopsuestia, Replica a Giuliano: BPat 24, 1994 → 10,14135: [R]ASEs 12 (1995) 160-3 (L. *Lugaresi*).

g408 *Guida* Augusto, La prima replica cristiana al Contro i Galilei di GIULIANO: Teodoro di Mopsuestia: → 561, Pagani 1993/5, 15-33.

g409 *Wickham* L.R., Aspects of clerical life in the early Byzantine church in two scenes, Mopsuestia and Apamea: JEH 46 (1995) 3-18.

Y2.4 **Augustinus**

g410 **Alexander** David C., The emergence of Augustine's early ecclesiology (386-391): diss. [D]*Wright* D. Edinburgh 1995. xxx-328 p. -- RTLv 27.p.539.

g411 **Arteaga Natividad** Rodolfo, La creación en los comentarios de San Agustín al Génesis: Mayéutica mg. 2. Marcilla (Navarra) 1994. 374 p. -- [R]Lat 61 (1995) 229s (I. *Sanna*).

g412 **Askoul** Michael, The influence of Augustine of Hippo on the Orthodox Church 1990 → 9,15952: GOTR 39 (1994) 379-381 (G.C. *Papademetriou*).

g413 *a) Ayres* Lewis, Agustín y TICONIO sobre metafísica y exégesis; -- *b) Steinhauser* Kenneth R., Ticonio ¿ era griego ? [T]*Cruz Lacarra* Juan (dos); -- *c) Tilley* Maureen A., Agustín ¿ interpretó mal a Ticonio ?, [T]*Anoz* José: → 623, AugM 40 (1995) 13-30 / 283-289 / 297-301.

Barnes Michel R., Augustine on contemporary Trinitarian theology 1995 → 3603 supra

g414 **Bauerschmidt** J.C., The relationship of men and women in the theology of St. Augustine: Diss. Oxford 1995. -- RTLv 27.p.540.

g415 *Bavel* Tarsicio J. van, La mujer en san Agustín [< AugLv 39 (1989) 5-53]: EstAg 29 (1994) 3-49.

g416 -- *Capilla González* R.A., La herencia de San Agustín según el P. Tarcisio van BAVEL [jornadas Madrid 9s.X.1993]: EstAg 29 (1994) 353-365.

g417 *Bok* N. den, Wat God wil volvoert Hij; een systematische analyse van AUGUSTINUS' visie op Gods (verkiezende) wil in relatie tot de menselijke wilsvrijheid: NedThT 49 (1995) 24-41; Eng. 70.

g418 *Bok* Nico den, In vrijheid voorzien; een systematisch-theologiese analyse van Augustinus' teksten over voorkennis en wilsvrijheid: Bijdragen 56 (1995) 40-60; Eng. 60.

g419 **Bourke** Vernon J., Augustine's love of wisdom; an introspective philosophy. West Lafayette 1992, Purdue Univ. viii-234 p. $ 13.75. -- [R]AugM 40 (1995) 399-401 (J. *Oroz*).

g420 *Campo del Pozo* Fernando, El P. LOPE CILLERUELO y las nuevas cartas de San Agustín [< DIVJAK J. 1981: traducción RevAg 33 (1992), antes suprimida de EstAg 'en corrección de pruebas']: RevAg 35 (1994) 1067-1095.

g421 [T]**Chiarini** Gioacchino, Confessioni III (libri 7-9), ed. critica. Mi 1994, Mondadori.152 p. L[m] 44. -- [R]VP(ens) 78 (1995) 236-9 (G. *Cristaldo*).

g422 *Cipriani* Nello, Le fonti cristiane della dottrina trinitaria nei primi Dialoghi di S. Agostino: Aug(ustinianum)R 34 (1994) 253-312.

g423 [E]**Clark** Gillian, Confessions I-IV. C 1995, Univ. x-198 p. $ 60; pa. $ 22. 0-521-49763-9 [< ThD 43,355].

g424 **Cooper** R.H., *al.*, Concordantia in libros XIII Confessionum .. Skutella (1969) edition: Alpha-Omega-A124. Hildesheim/Z 1991, Olms/Weidmann. 2 vol. -- [R]AugLv 45 (1995) 319s (M. *Lamberigts*).

g425 ^T**Cosgaya** José, Confesiones[3]: BAC minor 70. M 1994. 506 p. -- ^RRevAg 36 (1995) 1123s (R. *Lazcano*).

g426 **Dassmann** Ernst, Augustinus, Heiliger und Kirchenlehrer 1993 → 10,14148: ^RZKG 106 (1995) 139-141 (M. *Vinzent*).

g427 **Dodd** Kevin, A transcending presence; four pre-modern Christian positions on the hiddenness of God -- Augustine, Pseudo-DIONYSIUS, AQUINAS, LUTHER: diss. Vanderbilt, ^D*Forstman* J. Nv 1995. -- RStR 22,273.

g428 **Drobner** Hubertus R., 'Für euch bin ich Bischof'; die Predigten Augustins über das Bischofsamt 1992 → 10,14151: ^RTPQ 143 (1995) 206s (R. *Zinnhobler*).

g429 *a) Estal* Gabriel del, San Agustín y su concubina de juventud; el problema y la herida sangrantes; separación de la mujer amada, que legalmente no puede ser su esposa; -- *b) Luis* Pío de, Señor, siervo tuyo soy (Conf. 9,1,1): → 162, ^FRUBIO L., Semitica: CDios 208 (1995) 883-974 / 811-829.

g430 *Falque* Emmanuel, Saint Augustin ou comment Dieu entre en théologie; lecture critique des livres V-VII du 'De Trinitate ': NRT 117 (1995) 84-111.

g431 *Fendt* Gene, Confessions' bliss; postmodern criticism as a palimpsest of Augustine's Confessions: HeythJ 36 (1995) 30-45.

g432 *a) Ferrari* L.C., Young Augustine, both Catholic and Manichee; -- *b) Lienhard* J.T., ORIGEN and Augustine, preaching on John the Baptist: AugSt 26 (1995) 109-128 / 37-47.

g433 *Folliet* Georges, Deux grandes éditions de Saint Augustin au 19e siècle, GAUME (1836-1839) et MIGNE (1841-1842): AugLv 45 (1995) 5-44.

g434 *Genosko* Gary, Augustine gives us the finger [his works show special interest in hands]: Semiotica 104 (1995) 81-97.

g435 **Girard** Jean-Michel, La mort chez saint Augustin; grandes lignes de sa pensée, telle qu'elle apparaît dans ses traités: Par 34. FrS 1992, Univ. 251 p. Fs 48. 2-8271-0594-2. -- ^RAng 72 (1995) 101-3 (B. *Degórski*); RevAg 35 (1994) 1198-1200 (J. *Sepulcre*).

g436 *Girardet* Klaus M., Naturrecht und Naturgesetz; eine gerade Linie von CICERO zu Augustinus ?: R(hein)MP 138 (1995) 266-298.

g437 **Godet** Jacques-Marie, L'image de Dieu dans l'homme dans les Enarrationes in Psalmos de saint Augustin [< diss.]. R 1995, Inst Patr. Aug. ii-[+ 4-p. bibliog.]-100 p.

g438 *a) Gordon* Barry, Producción, distribución y cambio en el pensamiento de san Agustín, ^T*Arroyo* C.; -- *b) Weaver* Rebecca H., Los avisos escriturarios contra el orgullo en san Agustín, ^T*Anoz* J.: → 623, AugM 40 (1995) 95-103 / 319-326.

g439 ^{TE}**Green** R.P.H., De doctrina christiana. Ox 1995, Clarendon. xxv-293 p. $ 80. 0-19-826334-1 [< ThD 43,256].

g440 **Groeschel** Benedict, Augustine, major writings: Spiritual Legacy. NY 1995, Crossroad. xiv-178 p. $ 13 pa. 0-8245-2505-1 [ThD 43,168].

g441 *Grünbeck* Elisabeth, Augustins ekklesiologische Christologie im Spiegel seiner Hermeneutik; die Bildstruktur der Enarratio in Ps 44: VigChr 49 (1995) 353-378.

g442 **Harmless** William, Augustine and the catechumenate: Pueblo. ColMn 1995, Liturgical. xii-406 p. $ 35 pa. 0-8146-6132-7 [< ThD 43,368].

g443 **Harrison** Carol, Beauty and revelation in the thought of Saint Augustine 1992 → 8.k863 ... 10,14517: ^RChH 64 (1995) 455s (R. *Mackenzie*); *JEarlyC 3 (1995) 225s (D.H. *Williams*); JRel 75 (1995) 417-420 (J.P. *Kenney*, also on WETZEL J., MILES Margaret, both 1992).

g444 ^T**Hill** E., ^E*Rotelli* J., Sermons I (1-10) on the Old Testament: Works 3/1. Brooklyn 1990, New City. 399 p. 0-911782-75-3. -- ^RRHE 90 (1995) 260s (P.-A. *Deproost*).

g445 **Hoffmann** Andreas, De utilitate credendi; Über dem Nützen des Glaubens: FC 9, 1992 → 9,15983; 10,14158: [R]*JEarlyC 3 (1995) 502-5 (F. *Van Fleteren*).

g446 *Kendeffy* Gábor, Pourquoi AUGUSTIN a-t-il écrit le Contra academicos?: AAH(ung) 36 (1995) 177-183.

g447 **Klein** Richard, Die neugefundenen AUGUSTINUS-Predigten in der Mainzer Stadtbibliothek: Gym 100 (1993) 370ss; 192 (1995) 242-262.

g448 **Kotila** Heikki, Memoria mortuorum; commemoration of the departed in Augustine: StEphAug 38. R 1992, Augustinianum. 218 p. -- [R]Greg 76 (1995) 421 (F.-A. *Pastor*).

g449 *Langa* Pedro, San Agustín y la cultura: RevAg 36 (1995) 3-33; .. y la cultura cristiana, 685-732.

g450 **Lanzi** Nicola, La Chiesa Madre in Sant'Agostino: BStR 19. Pisa 1994, Giardini. 189 p. -- [R]Ang 72 (1995) 588-591 (B. *Degórski*); Div 39 (1995) 91-93 (A. *Quacquarelli*); E(spr)eV 105 (1995) 46 (Y-M. *Duval*).

g451 *Lanzi* Nicola, La Chiesa-comunione in S. Agostino: DoCom 46 (1993) 132-149.

g452 *Lazcano* Rafael, Información bibliográfica sobre San Agustín en castellano (VI) : RevAg [29 (1988) 235-259 ...] 36 (1995) 1095-1121.

g453 *Lössl* Josef, Augustinus -- Exeget oder Philosoph; Schriftgebrauch und biblische Hermeneutik in De uera religione: WiWei 56 (1993) 97-114.

g454 [E]**McWilliam** Joanne M., *al*, Augustine, from rhetor to theologian [15 papers for 1600th anniversary of his conversion: Trinity College, Toronto] 1992 → 8,588; 9,15991: [R]*JEarlyC 3 (1995) 85-87 (J.C. *Cavadini*).

g455 **Mallard** William, Language and love; introducing Augustine's religious thought through the 'Confessions ' story 1994 → 10,14165; 0-271-01038-X. -- [R]E(xp)T 107 (1995s) 27s (Carol *Harrison* condemns severely especially the deliberate total exclusion of books 10-13); *TBR 8,3 (1995s) 45 (P. *Sheldrake*).

g456 **Marafioti** Domenico, Sant'Agostino e la Nuova Alleanza; l'interpretazione agostiniana di Geremia 31,31-34 nell'ambito dell'esegesi patristica: Aloisiana 65. R/Brescia 1995, Pont.Univ.Gregoriana / Morcelliana. 400 p.; bibliog. 339-366. L[m] 55. -- [R]*AnT 9 (1995) 477-480 (M.A. *Tábet*); CivCatt 146 (1995,3) 443s (G. *Pelland*); VetChr 32 (1995) 476s (Immacolata *Aulisa*).

g457 **Margerie** Bertrand de, St. Augustine: Introduction to the history of exegesis 3, 1993 → 10,15995: [R]Thom 59 (1995) 506-8 (W.G. *Most*).

g458 **Marie-Ancilla** o.p., La charité et l'unité; une clé pour entrer dans la théologie de saint Augustin: *CahCathéd 6. P 1993, Mame. 72 p.

g459 **Marrou** Henri-Irénée, Augustinus und das Ende der antiken Bildung, [T]*Wirth-Poelchau* Lore, *al*. Pd 1995, Schöningh. xxxix-613 p. 3-506-75339-8 [ThRv 92,79].

g460 **Martin** Thomas F., Miser ego sum; Augustine, Paul, and the rhetorical moment: diss. Northwestern, [D]*Groh* D. Evanston 1994. 495 p. 95-21764. -- D(iss)AI 56 (1995s) p. 987.

g461 *a) Mayer* Cornelius, Kenntnis und Bewertung der Zeichen als Voraussetzung der Bibelhermeneutik nach Augustinus; -- *b) Müller* Christof, Geschichte, heilige Geschichte, Heilsgeschichte -- zum Begriff 'historia ' bei Augustinus: → 10,31*. [F]DAUTZENBERG G., Nach den Anfängen Fragen 1994, 719-738 / 739-764.

g462 *Moda* Aldo, Bibliografia per uno studio di S. Agostino: Nicolaus 22,2 (1995) 179-239.

g463 [E]**Neuhaus** Richard J., Augustine today. GR 1993 → 9,337: LuthQ 9 (1995) 349s (J. T. *Voelker*).

g464 **O'Donnell** James, Confessions I-III, 1992 → 8,k881 ... 10,14173: [R]ChH 64 (1995)

453-5 (B. *McGinn*); JRS 85 (1995) 344-6 (G.J.P. *O'Daly*); RStR 21 (1995) 201-3 . 206-8- (J. C. *Cavadini*); S(cot)JTh 48 (1995) 275-7 (L. R. *Wickham*).

g465 **Oort** J van, Jerusalem and Babylon ..: VC.s 14, 1991 → 7.g284 ... 10,14174: ᴿRHE 90 (1995) 123s (P.-A. *Deproost*).

g466 *Orbán* A.P., Augustinus en CASSIODORUS; twee pogingen om het heidens Latijns onderwijs te kerstenen: → g781, Scholing 1995, 37-56.

g467 *Pani* Giancarlo, L'eredità di Agostino nella Römerbriefvorlesung di Martin LUTERO ... : SMSR 61 (1995) 82-87.

g468 *Papageorgiou* Panayiotis, CHRYSOSTOM and Augustine [divisive procreation-transmission] on the sin of Adam and its consequences: SV(lad)TQ 39 (1995) 361-378.

g469 *Pérez Velázquez* Rodolfo Víctor, El De doctrina cristiana: ¿ una obra catequética ?: AugM 40 (1995) 327-387.

g470 *a) Pizzolato* Luigi F., L' 'induramento' del cuore del Faraone tra GREGORIO DI NISSA e Agostino; -- *b) Pollastri* Alessandra, Note su De doctrina cristiana; un riferimento biblico per l'*intellegere* e per il *proferre* -- *c) Studer* Basil, Zur Pneumatologie des Augustinus von Hippo (De Trinitate 15, 17,27 -- 27,50) : → 119, ᶠMARA M.Grazia = Aug(ustinianum)R 35 (1995) 511-525 / 527-536 [549-565, *Simonetti* Manlio] / 567-583.

g471 **Rees** B.R., Letters of PELAGIUS and his followers 1991 → 8,k890 ... 10,14179: ᴿBijdragen 56 (1995) 95 (M. *Parmentier*. Eng., also on his Pelagius reluctant); JEH 46 (1995) 355s (Judith *McClure*).

g472 ᵀ**Rettig** John, Augustine, Tractates on the Gospel of John 112-24; Tractates on the First Epistle of John: Fathers [78s, 88s] 92. Wsh 1995, Catholic University of America. xvi-301 p. $ 35. 0-8132-0092-X [ThD 43,56]

g473 **Rist** John M., Augustine; ancient thought baptized 1994 → 10,14180: ᴿCanadCath 13,8 (1995) 20s (P. *Jones*); ET 106 (1994s) 249 (C.S. *Harrison*); RelSt 31 (1995) 542-4 (D. *Farrow*); TS 56 (1995) 361-3 (R.J. *Teske*); TTh 35 (1995) 292 (A. *Davids*).

g474 **Scott** T. Kermit, Augustine; his thought in context. NY 1995, Paulist. iv-253 p. $15 pa. 0-8091-3566-3 [ThD 43.288].

g475 **Siebach** James L., Self-knowledge in Socrates and St. Augustine; a consideration of 'Alcibiades I' and 'Confessions' Book 1: diss. Texas, ᴰ*Mackey* L. Austin 1995. 195 p. 95-34958. -- D(iss)AI 56 (1995s) p. 2270.

g476 *Simonetti* Manlio, L'ermeneutica biblica di Agostino: ASEs 12 (1995) 393-418.

g477 *Staubach* Nikolaus, Christiana tempora; Augustin und das Ende der Alten Geschichte in der Weltchronik FRECHULFs von Lisieux: FM(ittelalt)St 29 (1995) 167-206.

g478 **Stead** Christopher, Philosophy in Christian antiquity. C 1994, Univ. 261 p. £ 37.50; pa. £ 13. 0-521-46553-2; -955-4. -- ᴿE(xp)T 107 (1995s) 26s (S.G. *Hall*: genuinely only Augustine).

g479 **Studer** Basil, Gratia Christi, gratia Dei bei Augustinus 1993 → 9,16013; ᴿTHGL 85 (1995) 135s (H.R. *Drobner*).

g480 **Sumruld** W.A., Augustine and the Arians; the Bishop of Hippo's encounters with Ulfilan Arianism. Toronto 1994, Susquehanna Univ. £ 28. -- ᴿCLR 45 (1995) 469 (R.P.H. *Green*).

g481 *Tauer* Johann, Neue Orientierungen zur Paulusexegese des PELAGIUS: AugR 34 (1994) 313-358.

g482 *Teske* Roland, Ultimate reality according to Augustine of Hippo: URM 18 (1995) 20-33.

g483 *a) Teske* Roland J., Herejía e imaginación en San Agustín, ᵀ*Cruz Lacarra* Juan; -- *b) Shibata* Mimiko, San Agustín y la 'voluntas Moysi' (Conf. 12), ᵀ*Oroz* J.; -- *c) Bonner*

Gerald, Reconsideración del Pelagianismo, ^T*Cruz*: → 623, AugM 40 (1995) 291-6 / 267-271 / 47-52.

g484 ^{TE}**Teske** Roland J., Arianism and other heresies: Works 1/18. Hyde Park NY 1995, New City. 486 p. $39. 1-56548-038-4 [< ThD 43,355].

g485 *Tortorelli* Kevin M., LONERGAN as a point of reference for reading The Confessions: D(owns)R 113 (1995) 111-8.

g486 ^FTRAPP Damasus: Via Augustini; Augustine in the later Middle Ages, Renaissance and Reformation, ^E**Oberman** Heiko A., *James* Frank A.: StMdvRT 48, 1991 → 7,155; *f* 115; 90-04-09364-8: ^RLatomus 54 (1995) 458s (N. *Adkin*).

g487 *a) Turrado* Argimiro, El problema del mal y la responsabilidad moral de las personas especialmente en la 'Ciudad de Dios' de S. Agustín; -- *b) Dolby Múgica* María del Carmen, San Agustín y KIERKEGAARD; dos filósofos religiosos: RevAg 36 (1995) 733-789 / 791-807.

g488 **Vannier** Marie-Anne, Saint Augustin et le mystère trinitaire: Foi vivante 324. P 1993, Cerf. -- ^RE(spr)eV 105 (1995) 29s (Y.-M. *Duval*).

g489 **Vannier** Marie-Anne, 'Creatio', 'conversio', 'formatio' chez S. Augustin: Paradosis 31, 1991 → 7,1780 ... 10,1686: ^RRTPh 127 (1995) 90s (J. *Borel*).

g490 *Vinel* Françoise, Une étape vers l'affirmation du salut universel; PROSPER d'Aquitaine, Lettre à RUFIN [contre Augustin] sur la grâce et le libre arbitre; introduction et traduction: RHE 90 (1995) 367-394; Eng. deutsch 395.

g491 **Wetzel** James, Augustine and the limits of virtue 1992 → 9,16021; 10,14190: ^RJAAR 63 (1995) 184-6 (G.W. *Schlabach*).

g492 *Wetzel* James, Time after Augustine: RelSt 31 (1995) 341-357.

g493 **Wiles** James W., A Scripture index to the works of St. Augustine in English translation. Lanham MD 1995, UPA. xx-223 p.; bibliog. 217-223. 0-8191-9848-X.

g494 *a) Ziolkowski* Eric J., St. Augustine, Aeneas' antitype, Monica's boy; -- *b) Pfatteicher* Philip H., Plashing pears in Augustine and BUNYAN: : [J]LTh(Ox) 9 (1995) 1-23 / 24-29.

Y2.5 **Hieronymus**

g495 *Adkin* Neil, ALAN of Lille, Walter of Châtillon and Jerome; the prose preface of the 'Anticlaudianus': RCCM(dv) 37 (1995) 141-151.

g496 *Adkin* Neil, *a)* An echo of EVAGRIUS of Antioch in Jerome: SIF(g)C 12 (1994) 118-22; -- *b)* Is the Marcellina of Jerome Ep. 45,7 AMBROSE's sister ?: Phoenix 49 (Tor 1995) 68-70; -- *c)* Plato or Plautus ? (Jerome. epist. XXII, 30.2: EM(erita) 61 (1994) 43-56; -- *d)* Self-imitation in Jerome's Libellus de virginitate servanda (epist. xxii): At(henaeum) 83 (1995) 469-485; -- *e)* Tobit and Jerome: → 142, ^FOROZ RETA III, Helmantica 46 (1995) 109-114.

g497 *Alcacer* José M., Itinerario bíblico de S. Jerónimo (I): TE(spir) 39 (1995) 219-245.

g498 *Allen* Mont, The martyrdom of Jerome: *JEarlyC 3 (1995) 211-3.

g499 *a) Booker* Courtney M., 'Vermiculatus' as scarlet in Jerome; -- *b) Löfstedt* Bengt, [Paulinus A., Hieronymus in Ezech:] Nicht identifizierte Bibelzitate: Orpheus 16 (1995) 124-6 / 140s.

g500 **Brown** Dennis, Vir trilinguis 1992 → 8,k906; 10,14195: ^RBijdragen 56 (1995) 220s (L.H. *Westra*); *JEarlyC 3 (1995) 83-85 (L. *Frizzell*); JSJ(ud) 26 (1995) 244-6 (J. van *Ruiten*); NT 37 (1995) 194-6 (J. *McGuckin*); RHE 90 (1995) 121-3 (J.-C. *Haelewyck*).

g501 *Buschmann* Gerd, [epist. 41,3, ad Marcellam] *Christoû koinōnós* (MartPol 5,2; das Martyrium und der ungeklärte *koinōnós*-Titel der Montanisten: ZNW 86 (1995) 243-264.

g502 *Clausi* Benedetto, Storia sacra e strategia retorica; osservazioni sull'uso dell' 'exem-

plum' biblico nell'Adversus Iovinianum di Gerolamo: CrSt 16 (1995) 457-485; Eng. 485
[.. → VetChr 32 (1995) 21-50].

g503   *Dolbeau* François,   Nouvelles recherches sur le De ortu et obitu prophetarum et
apostolorum [dont sept chapitres empruntés à Jérôme]: Aug(ustinianum)R 34 (1994) 91-107.

g504   *Donohue* John W.,   Holy terrors [vexing saints, Jerome ...]:   America 172,17   (1995)
10-15.

g505   *Fechtinger* Barbara,   Konsolationstopik und 'Sitz im Leben'; Heronymus' ep. 39 ad
Paulam de obitu Blesillae im Spannungsfeld zwischen christlicher Genusadaption und
Lesermanipulation: JAC 38 (1995) 75-90.

g506   *Guillaumont* Antoine, Les 'remnuoth' [? copte transcrit, ép.22] de saint Jérôme: →
10,27, ᶠCOQUIN M.-G. 1994, 87-92.

g507   ᵀᴱHayward C.T.R.,   Saint Jerome's Hebrew Questions on Genesis. Ox 1995, Clarendon. xiii-274 p.; bibliog. 247-253. 0-19-826350-3.

g508   *Hennings* Ralph, Correspondencia entre AGUSTÍN y Jerónimo, ᵀ*Eguílaz* M.A.: → 623,
AugM 40 (1995) 111-118.

g509   **Hennings** Ralph, Briefwechsel Aug/Hieronymus.. Kanon 1994 → 10.14200: ᴿZKG 106
(1995) 137-9 (E. *Mühlenberg*).

g510   *Jay* Pierre,   Saint Jérôme et L'un et l'autre Testament: → 14, ᶠBEAUCHAMP P., 'Ouvrir
les Écritures' 1995, 361-379.

g511   **Kamesar** Adam, Jerome, Greek scholarship, and the Hebrew Bible 1993 → 9,1777;
10,1622: ᴿEThL 71 (1995) 199s (J. *Lust*); JSSt 40 (1995) 153S (A. *Louth*); Latomus 54
(1995) 894-9 (Y. *Burnand*); Orpheus 16 (1995) 160-2 (A. *Sanfilippo*); Speculum 70 (1995)
160-2 (C. *Witke*).

g512   **Krumeich** Christa, Hieronymus und die christlichen feminae clarissimae: Diss. AltG
36. Bonn 1993, Habelt. xi-408 p. DM 98. -- ᴿJAC 38 (1995) 199-201 (Griet *Petersen*);
VigChr 49 (1995) 83-85 (G.J.M. *Bartelink:* noch 'Aetheria'); VizVrem 56 (1995) 341-4
(A.S. *Kozlov*).

g513   **Lardet** P., L'apologie de Jérôme contre RUFIN; un commentaire, VC.s 15, 1993 →
9,16033; 10,14202: ᴿJAC 38 (1995) 190-8 (N. *Pace*); RHE 90 (1995) 261s (P.-A.
Deproost); RPh(g) 68 (1994) 344S (R. *Braun*).

g514   **Maraval** Pierre, Petite vie de Saint Jérôme. P 1995, D-Brouwer. 136 p F 56. 2-220-
0352-7. -- ᴿRHPhR 75 (1995) 259 (*ipse*).

g515   *Milazzo* Vincenza, 'Etsi imperitus sermone ...' ; Girolamo e i solecismi di Paolo nei
commentari alle epistole paoline: → 488, ASEs 12 (1995) 261-277.

g516   **Mirri** Luciana, La vita ascetica femminile in San Girolamo; diss. Angelicum. R 1992,
Pont.Univ.S.Tommaso: ᴿ(R)*StEc 13 (Venezia 1995) 530 (T. *Vetrali*).

g517   **Moreschini** Claudio, Dialogus adversus Pelagianos: Opera 3/2, CCL 80, 1990 →
7,g254 ... 10,14204: ᴿLatomus 54 (1995) 413-8 (P. *Hamblenne*).

g518   **Oberhelman** Steven M., Rhetoric and homiletics in fourth-century Christian literature;
prose rhythm, oratorical style, and preaching in the works of AMBROSE, Jerome, and
AUGUSTINE: AmerPgAsn, ClasSt 26, 1991 → 8,k935 ... 10,14219: ᴿGnomon 67 (1995) 17-
22 (W. *Blümer*).

g519   *a) Perrone* Lorenzo, Motivi paolini nell'epistolario di Gerolamo; -- *b) Pesce* Mauro,
Destro Adriana, La 'Ekklesia' di fronte a 'quelli di fuori'; -- *c) Ghiberti* Giuseppe,
Questione sul 'Destinatario' della missione negli Atti degli Apostoli: 521, Tarso 3, 1994/5,
171-201 / 87-105 / 107-117.

g520   *Ratzinger* Joseph, The new covenant; a theology of covenant in the NT, ᵀ*Shrady* Maria

[Jerome substituted *foedus* or *pactum* for Old Latin *testamentum*, which nevertheless remained our title for the biblical books]: Com(US) 22 (1995) 635-651.

g521 **Rebenich** Stefan, Hieronymus und sein Kreis 1992 → 9,16040; 10,14207: [R]Latomus 54 (1995) 662-5 (Y.-M. *Duval*).

g522 **Schmid** J., Index in S. Hieronymi epistulas; Alpha-Omega 140. Hildesheim 1994, Olms. 588 p. [RHE 90 (1995) 235*].

g523 **Scourfield** J.H.D., Consoling Heliodorus, .. letter 60. 1993 → 9,16043; 10,14208: [R]*JEarlyC 3 (1995) 223s (P.L. *Buck*).

g524 **Steininger** Christine, Virgo -- vidua -- nupta; eine Studie zum Bild der idealen christlichen Frau bei Hieronymus und PELAGIUS: kath. Diss. [D]*Hübner*. München 1995. -- ThRv Beilage 92/2, xii.

g525 **Valero** Juan Bautista, S. Jerónimo, Epistolario, bilingüe 1s: BAC 530 (1993 → 10,14210) 549. M 1995. (910 p.); 800 p. -- [R]Ang 72 (1995) 96-100 (B. *Degórski*, 1); ATG(ran) 58 (1995) 382s (C. *Granado*).

g526 *Weingarten* Susan, *Postliminium* in Jerome; a Roman legal term as a Christian metaphor: SC(Isr) 14 (1995) 143-150.

g527 **White** Carolinne, Christian friendship in the fourth century 1992 → 9,16022: [R]*JEarlyC 3 (1995) 234-6 (D. *Trout*); Speculum 70 (1995) 222s (J. *Lienhard*).

g528 **Wissemann** Michael, Schimpfworte in der Bibelübersetzung des Hieronymus: BtKlasAW 2/86. Heid 1992, Winter. x-211 p. -- [R]Gnomon 67 (1995) 122-6 (S. *Rebenich*); GrazB 21 (1995) 234-6 (T. *Polański*, Eng.).

Y2.6 **Patres Latini** *in ordine alphabetico*

g529 **Contreras** Enrique, *Peña* Roberto, El contexto histórico eclesial de los Padres latinos, siglos IV-V, 1993 → 9,16048; 10,14212*: [R]TeolBA 30 (1993) 87-89 (D. *Krpan*).

g530 **Daniélou** Jean, Le origini del cristianesimo latino; storia delle dottrine cristiane prima di Nicea [postumo 1978], [T]. Bo 1993, Dehoniane. 478 p. L[m] 32. -- [R]RasT 36 (1995) 245-7 (U. *Parente*).

g531 *Fredouille* Jean-Claude, L'apologétique chrétienne antique; métamorphose d'un genre polymorphe: RÉAug 41 (1995) 201-210.

g532 [E]**Herzog** R., Restauration et renouveau; la littérature latine de 284 à 374, [TE]*Nauroy* G. Turnhout 1993, Brepols. xxxi-614 p. -- [R]VigChr 49 (1995) 100-3 (J. den *Boeft*).

g533 **Mathisen** R.W., Roman aristocrats in barbarian Gaul; strategies for survival in an age of transition. Austin 1993, Univ. Texas. -- [R]At(henaeum) 83 (1995) 564s (A. *Marcone*).

g534 *Shanzer* Danuta, Date and identity of the centonist Proba [Anicia Faltonia c.388]: RechAug 27 (1994) 75-96.

g535 *Simonetti* Manlio, Tra Noeto, Ippolito e Melitone: RS(to)LR 31 (1995) 393-414.

-----

g536 AMBROSIASTER; *a) Perrone* Lorenzo, Echi della polemica pagana sulla Bibbia negli scritti esegetici fra IV e V secolo; le Quaestiones Veteris et Novi Testamenti dell'Ambrosiaster: -- *b) Vinchesi* Maria Assunta, Il rapporto tra cristianesimo e cultura pagana in PAOLINO di Nola: → 561, Pagani 1993/5, 149-172 / 299-310.

g537 AMBROSIUS M.: *Bonney* Gillian, L'esegesi di sant'Ambrogio in relazione alle figure femminili dell''Expositio secundum Lucam': Salesianum 57 (1995) 123-130.

g538 *Burrus* Virginia,Reading Agnes; the rhetoric of gender in Ambrose:*JEarC 3(1995)23-46.

g539 **Corsato** Celestino, La Expositio euangelii secundum Lucam di sant'Ambrogio: St43. R 1993, Inst. Patr. Augustinianum. 306 p. -- ᴿSalesianum 57 (1995) 575s (Katarzyna *Dobrawolska*).

g540 *Davidson* Ivor J., Ambrose's De officiis and the intellectual climate of the late fourth century: VigChr 49 (1995) 313-333.

g541 **Fontaine** Jacques, Ambroise, Hymnes 1992 → 8,k931 ... 10,14219: ᴿEThL 71 (1995) 239-243 (J. *Verheyden*).

g542 **Franz** Ansgar, Tageslauf und Heilsgeschichte; Untersuchungen zum literarischen Text und liturgischen Kontext der Tageszeithymnen des Ambrosius von Mailand [Diss. Mainz 1991]. St. Ottilien 1994, EOS. xxii-541 p. DM 98. 3-88096-289-8 [ThRv 91,276].

g543 **Pasini** Cesare, Le fonti greche su sant'Ambrogio 1990 → 6,k117 ... 8,k936: ᴿAugR 34 (1994) 518-521 (M. *Navoni*).

g544 *Savon* Hervé, Saint Ambroise a-t-il imité le recueil de lettres de PLINE le Jeune ?: RÉAug 41 (1995) 3-17.

g545 *Testard* Maurice, Le De officiis de saint Ambroise; observations philologiques et historiques sur le sens et le contexte du traité: RechAug 28 (1995) 3-35.

g546 **Williams** Daniel H., Ambrose of Milan and the end of the Arian-Nicene conflicts. Ox 1995, Clarendon. xi-259 p.; bibliog. 244-252. 0-19-82646-2.

g547 *a) Williams* D.H., Polemics and politics in Ambrose of Milan's *De fide*; -- *b) Winterbottom* Michael, The text of Ambrose's *De officiis* [some forty bolder readings for conservative TESTARD M. 1984-92]: JThS 46 (1995) 519-531.

----

g548 ARATOR: **Schwind** Johannes, Sprachliche und exegetische Beobachtungen zu Arator: Abh g/soz 1995,5. Mainz 1995, Akademie. 130 p. 3-515-06792-2.

g549 ARNOBIUS: **Mora** F., Arnobio e I culti di mistero: analisi storico-religiosa dell'Adversus Nationes: Storia delle religioni 10. R 1994, Bretschneider. 217 p. -- ᴿVetChr 32 (1995) 465-8 (N. *Biffi*).

g550 CASSIANUS: *Frank* Karl S., Johannes Cassian über Johannes Cassian: R(öm)Q 90 (1995) 183-197.

g551 CASSIODORUS: **Santiago Amar** Pio B., La iniciación a la Biblia en las 'Institutiones divinarum letterarum' di Cassiodoro: diss. Santa Croce, ᴰ*Tábet M.* R 1995. 246 p. -- RTLv 27, p.541.

g552 COELESTINUS: Epistolario, ᴱ**Gori** Franco: CTPat 127. R c, 1995, Città Nuova. 200 p. 88-311-3127-3.

g553 CYPRIANUS: *Adkin* Neil, The use of Scripture in the pseudo-Cyprianic 'De duplici martyrio': GitFg 47 (1995) 219-248.

g554 **Adolph** Anneliese, Die Theologie der Einheit der Kirche bei Cyprian: EHS 23/460, 1993 → 9,16063, Lang. 263 p. Fs 74: ᴿHZ 261 (1995) 522s (H.R. *Seeliger*).

g555 *Braun* René, *al.*, Chronica Tertullianea et Cyprianea 1994: RÉAug 41 (1995) 325-355.

g556 **Mazières** J.-P., *al.*, Pontius, Vie de Cyprien; Paulin, Vie d'AMBROISE; Possidius, Vie d'AUGUSTIN: Les Pères dans la foi 56. P 1994, Migne/Brepols. 193 p. F 90. 2-908587-15-7. -- ᴿRHE 90 (1995) 620 (B. *Coulie*).

g557 *Tornatora* Alberto, Diabolus eloquens, l'archetipo letterario di un 'nuovo' *locus a fictione* (Op.Eleem. 22): SMSR 59 (1993) 21-34.

g558 EUCHERIUS: **Skibiński** Tomasz, L'interpretazione della Scrittura in Eucherio di Lione: diss. R 1995, Pont. Univ. Lateranense. 182 p.; bibliog. 165-182.

g559 GREGORIUS M. *Bentivegna* Giuseppe, I carismi nella vita spirituale dei credenti secondo San Gregorio Magno: CivCatt 146 (1995,2) 26-39.

g560 **Fiedrowicz** Michael, Das Kirchenverständnis Gregors des Grossen; eine Untersuchung seiner exegetischen und homiletischen Werke [Diss. Pont. Univ. Lateran, [D]*Siniscalco*, Rom 1990] : RQ.s 50. FrB 1995, Herder. 416 p.; bibliog. 391-406. DM 174. 3-451-22699-5. - - [R]ForKT 11 (1995) 157s (S. *Heid*).

g561 **Markus** R.A., The end of ancient Christianity 1990 → 6,g379 ... 10,14230: [R]Bijdragen 56 (1995) 95-97 (L.H. *Westra*, deutsch).

g562 **Cusack** Pearse, An interpretation of the second dialogue of Gregory the Great. Lewiston 1992, Mellen. iii-191 p. 0-7734-9272-0. -- [R]MilltSt 35 (1995) 161-4 (T. *O'Loughlin*).

g563 HILARIUS 315-357: *Bertrand* Dominique, l'impassibilité du Christ selon Hilaire de Poitiers, De Trinitate X : → 119, [F]MARA M.Grazia = Aug(ustinianum)R 35 (1995) 350-8.

g564 *Doignon* Jean, Le goût de l'équilibre dans la culture morale, exégétique et théologique d'Hilaire de Poitiers: JAC 38 (1995) 67-74.

g565 **Smulders** Peter, Hilary of Poitiers' Preface to his 'Opus historicum': VigChr.s 29. Lei 1995, Brill. xi-169 p. 90-04-10191-8. -- [R]Greg 76 (1995) 771s (L.F. *Ladaria*).

g566 *Pelland* Gilles, La Loi dans le tr. ps. 118 de saint Hilaire: Greg 76 (1995) 575-583. --

g567 [E]**Jacob** Paul-A., HONORAT de Marseille, La vie d'Hilaire d'Arles: SC 404. P 1995, Cerf. 182 p. 2-204-05119-5.

g568 HIPPOLYTUS: **Brent** Allen, Hippolytus and the Roman church in the third century; communities in tension before the emergence of a monarch-bishop: VivChr.s 31. Lei 1995, Brill. xxxviii-611 p.; 24 pl.; bibliog. 541569 *f* 250. 90-04-10245-0.

g569 *Brent* Allen, *a)* Was Hippolytus a schismatic ?: VigChr 49 (1995) 215-244; -- *b)* Hippolytus' see and EUSEBIUS' historiography: → 9,465: StP 28 (1991/3) 28-35 [< RHE 90 (1995) 267*].

g570 *Hill* C.E., [Hippolytus] Antichrist from the tribe of Dan: JThS 46 (1995) 99-117.

g571 JUVENCUS: **Fichtner** Rudolf, Taufe und Versuchung Jesu in den Evangeliorum libri quattuor des Bibeldichters Juvencus [Diss. Regensburg 1993]: Beit.Altertumskunde 50. Stu 1994, Teubner. 222 p. 3-519-07499-0.

g572 LACTANTIUS: [E]**Heck** E., *Wlosok* A., Epitome divinarum institutionum. Stu/Lp 1994, Teubner. xlviii-128 p. -- [R]RPh(lgLH) 69 (1995) 225s (P. *Monat*).

g573 LEO M.: Sermons: Fathers 92. Wsh 1995, Catholic University of America. cii-436 p.

g574 OPTATUS: [E]**Labrousse** Mireille, Optat de Milève, Traité contre les donatistes I (livres 1-2): SC 412. 312 p.; bibliog. 146-169. 2-204-05335-X.

g575 PACIANUS: [E]**Granado** Carmelo, Pacien de Barcelone, Écrits: SC 410. 393 p,; bibliog. 13-20. 2-204-05239-6.

g576 PAULINUS: **McLynn** N.B., Paulinus [of Pella, born 376] the Impenitent; a study of the Eucharisticos: *JEarlyC 3 (1995) 461-486.

g577 PRUDENTIUS **Kah** Marianne, 'Die Welt der Römer mit der Seele suchend ...': Hereditas 1990 → 6,k259 ... 8,k969: ᴿRHE 90 (1995) 120s (P.-A. *Deproost*); ThRv 91 (1995) 319-323 (R. *Henke*).

g578 -- *Petruccione* J., The martyr's death as sacrifice; Prudentius, Peristephanon 4, 9-72: VigChr 49 (1995) 245-257.

g579 RUFINUS: *Murphy* F.X., Rufinus of Aquileia and Gregory the Theologian: GOTR 39 (1994) 181-6.

g580 ᴱ**Veronese** Maria, Rufino di Concordia, Le benedizioni dei Patriarchi: CTePa 120. R 1995, Città Nuova. 121 p. 88-311-3120-6.

g581 SIDONIUS c. 470: *Prévot* Françoise, ORIGÈNE, LACTANCE, JÉRÔME et les autres; la culture chrétienne de Sidoine Apollinaire: BuSAntF (1995) 215-228.

g582 VALERIANUS: ᵀᴱ**Fatica** Luigi, Valeriano di Cimiez, Le venti omelie: CTePa 122. R 1995, Città Nuova. 194 p. 88-311-3122-2.

g583 VINCENTIUS L.: *Ferreiro* Alberto, Simon Magus and Priscillian in the Commonitorium of Vincent of Lérins: VigChr 49 (1995) 180-8.

Y2.8 Documenta orientalia

g584 ᴱ**Albert** Micheline, *al.*, Christianismes orientaux; introduction à l'étude des langues et des littératures 1993 → 9,16090; 10,14240: ᴿOrChr 79 (1995) 286-8 (H. *Kaufhold*).

g585 ᵀᴱ**Bausi** Alessandro, Il Sēnodos Etiopico: CSCR aeth.101s. Lv 1995, Peeters, 2 vol. 90-6831-694-X.

g586 *Brakke* David, The problematization of nocturnal emissions in early Christian Syria, Egypt, and Gaul [as impediment to Eucharist; rare case of discourse on purity focusing male rather than female body]: JEarlyC 3 (1995) 419-460.

g587 *Brock* Sebastian, St. Theodore of Canterbury [BISCHOFF B.†. LAPIDGE M. 1994]. the Canterbury school and the Christian East: → 134, ᶠMURRAY R., HeythJ 36,4 (1995) 431-8.

g588 *Edakalathur* Louis, The theology of marriage in the East Syrian tradition [survey of the documents ...]. R 1994, Mar Thomas Yogam. xliii-200 p. -- ᴿOL(ov)P 26 (1995) 216-8 (L. van *Rompay*).

g589 *Egron* Agnès, La prière de feu dans la tradition monastique des premiers siècles chrétiens. P 1995, Cerf. 172 p. -- ᴿRThom 95 (1995) 700 (sr. M. *Ancilla*).

g590 *Fiey* Jean Maurice, Pour un Oriens Christianus novus; répertoire des diocèses syriaques orientaux et occidentaux [LE QUIEN M. diocese-list 1740, reprinted 1958]: BeiruterTSt 49,1993 → 9,16097: ᴿJRAS (1995) 264s (S. *Brock*: in his 80th year unsurpassed, despite FEDALTO G. 1988 and obvious need of continued updating); OrChr 79 (1995) 247-263 (H. *Kaufhold*: 300 konstruktive Addenda).

g591 **Frankfurter** David, [Apocalypse of] Elijah in Upper Egypt 1993 → 8,a261 ... 10,9610: ᴿ*JEarlyC 3 (1995) 237-9 (J.O. *Gooch*).

g592 **Johnson** Maxwell E., Liturgy in early Christian Egypt: Alcuin/GROW 33. Nottingham 1995, Grove. 51 p. £ 4. 1-85174-305-7 [TBR 8,2 (1995s) 45],

g593 **Khoury** R.G., Chrestomathie de papyrologie arabe; documents relatifs à la vie privée, sociale et administrative dans les premiers siècles islamiques. Lei 1993. x-262 p.; XXXIV pl. -- ᴿAION 55 (1995) 487 (S. Noja *Noseda*).

g594 *Koshelenko* G., *al.*, The beginnings of Christianity in Merv: → 174, ᶠSCHIPPMANN K. II, IrAnt 30 (1995) 55-70.

g595 **Palmer** Andrew, The seventh century in the West-Syrian chronicles 1993 → 9,16103: [R]*JEarlyC 3 (1995) 95-97 (E.C. *Mathews*); JRAS (1995) 97-101 (C.F. *Robinson*); JRS 85 (1995) 339s (J. *Haldon*); OrChr 77 (1995) 245-7 (H. *Kaufhold*).

g596 **Paprocki** Henryk, Le mystère de l'eucharistie; genèse et interprétation de la liturgie eucharistique byzantine 1993 → 9,16104: [R]OrChr 79 (1995) 233-6 (R.F. *Taft*).

g597 *Poirier* Paul-H., Note sur le nom du destinataire des chapîtres 44 à 54 de la Caverne des Trésors: → 10,27, [F]COQUIN M.-G. 1994, 119-122.

g598 **Roca-Puig** Ramón, Anunciació, acròstic copte en dialecte bohairic[2]. Barc 1995. 11 p.

g599 [E]**Samir Khalil** Samir, *Nielsen* Jørgen S., Christian Arabic apologetics during the Abbasid period (750-1258): Numen.s 63. Lei 1994, Brill. xiv-250 p. *f* 150. -- [R]OLZ 90 (1995) 415-7 (W. *Hage*); POrC 45 (1995) 306-8 (P. *Ternant*).

g600 *Story* C. I K, A Coptic Christmas story, and more: Princeton Univ. Library Chronicle 55 (1993s) 43-62; 4 facsim. < RHE 90 (1995) 42*.

g601 [F]TAFT Robert, Eulogēma 1993 → 9,149: [R]M(aison)D 198 (1994) 155s (I.-H. *Dalmais*); O(stk)S 43 (1994) 67s (H.M. *Biedermann*).

g602 **Teixidor** Javier, La filosofía traducida; crónica parcial de Edesa en los primeros siglos: EstOr 4. Sabadell 1991, AUSA.210 p.; bibliog. 179-195. 84-86329-73-6.

g603 *Tubach* J., Eine christliche Legende syrischer Herkunft in der Prophetenbiographie IBN HIŠĀMs: [R]OL(ov)P 26 (1995) 81-99.

g604 *Winkler* Gabriel, Die Licht-Erscheinung bei der Taufe Jesu und der Ursprung des Epiphaniefestes; eine Untersuchung griechischer, syrischer, armenischer und lateinischer Quellen: OrChr 78 (1994) 177-229.

-----

g605 ABU ZAYD Shafiq, Ihidayutha 1993 → 9,8659: [R]Sefarad 55 (1995) 393-5 (N. *Fernández Marcos*).

g606 ADDAI: **Gelston** Anthony, The Eucharistic prayer of Addai and Mari 1992 → 8,k985; 9,14248: [R]JSSt 40 (1995) 157-160 (G. *Rouwhorst*); S(cot)JTh 48 (1995) 528s (K. *Stevenson*).

g607 BARDESANES: **Teixidor** Javier, Bardesane d'Edesse; la première philosophie syriaque 1992 → 8,k9898 ... 10,14252*: [R]RB(elg)PH 73 (1995) 235-8 (J. *Schamp*); RTPh 127 (1995) 71 (J.*Borel*).

g608 BARHEBRAEUS: *Teule* Herman, Juridical texts in the Ethicon of Barhebraeus: OrChr 79 (1995) 23-47.

g609 BARLAAM: *Kolbaba* Tia M., Barlaam the Calabrian; three treatises on papal primacy; introduction, edition, and translation: RÉByz 53 (1995) 41-115.

g610 BASILIUS: [E]**Thomson** Robert W., The Syriac version of the Hexaemeron: CSCOr syr.222s. Lv 1995, Peeters. I. syr.; II. Eng. 90-6831-704-0.

----

g611 EPHRAEM: **Brock** S.,Hymns on Paradise 1990 →6,k390;[R]CrSt 16 (1995)161-3(E.*Vergani*).

g612 *Baarda* Tjitze, Nathanael, 'the scribe of Israel'; John 1,47 in Ephraem's commentary on the Diatessaron: EThL 71 (1995) 321-336.

g613 *Botha* P.J., *a)* The significance of the senses in St. Ephrem's description of Paradise; — *b)* Ephrem the Syrian's treatment of Tamar in comparison to that in Jewish sources: AcPatrByz 5 (1994) 28-37 / 6 (1995) 15-26.

g614 [TE]**McCarthy** Carmel, Saint Ephrem's commentary on TATIAN's Diatessaron, Beatty Syriac 709: JSS supp 2. Ox 1993, UP. vii-381 p. -- [R]BoL (1995) 155s (R.P.R. *Murray*);

DocLife 45 (1995) 198s (W. *Riley*).

g615 *McCarthy* Carmel, Allusions and illusions; St. Ephrem's verbal magic in the Diatessaron commentary: → 504, Spiritual 1995, 143-162 [ThRv 92,78].

g616 ᵀᴱ**Mathews** Edward G.ʲ, *Amar* Joseph P., Ephraem, selected prose works; commentary on Gn/Ex; homily on our Lord; letter to Publius: Fathers 91. Wsh 1994, Catholic University of America. xxx-393 p. $ 40. 0-8132-0091-1.

g617 **Amar** Joseph P., A metrical homily on Holy Mar Ephrem by Mar JACOB of Sarug: PO 209 [or 47.1]. Turnhout 1995, Brepols. 76 p.

----

g618 GABRIEL: ᴱ**Samir Khalil** Samir, Le nomocanon du patriarche copte Gabriel II Ibn Turayk (1131-1145): Patrimoine arabe chrétien12s. Beyrouth 1993, CEDRAC.

g619 ISAACUS N.: ᵀᴱ**Brock** Sebastian, Isaac of Nineveh (Isaac the Syrian), 'The second part ', chapters IV-XLI: CSCOr 224s [syr. 224s]. Lv 1995, Peeters. 2 vol. 90-6831-708-3.

g620 JACOBUS E.: *Drijvers* Han, The Testament of our Lord; Jacob of Edessa's response to Islam: → 712, Aram 6 (1993/4) 104-114.

g621 MACARIUS: ᵀᴱ**Maloney** George A., Pseudo-Macarius, the fifty spiritual homilies [= 1978] and the Great Letter 1992 → 9,16120: ᴿRStR 21 (1995) 148 (A. *Golitzin*).

g622 PETRUS A.: **Pearson** Birger, *Vivian* Tim, Two Coptic homilies attributed to Saint Peter of Alexandria on riches, on the Epiphany 1993 → 10,14260: ᴿBiOr 52 (1995) 671-5 (R.-G. *Coquin*).

g623 PHILOCALIA: *a)* **Clément** Olivier, La Philocalie, les écrits fondamentaux des Pères du désert aux Pères de l'Église (ivᵉ-xivᵉ siècle). P 1995, Lattès / D-Brouwer. 692 p. F 220. - - *b)* **Touraille** Jacques, Le Christ dans la Philocalie: CJJC 63. P 1995, Desclée. 104 p, -- ᴿE(spr)eV 105 (1995) 414 (O. *Perru*) / 408 (P. *Jay*).

g624 PHILOPONUS: *MacCoull* L.S.B., A new look at the career of John Philoponus (490 575 Egypt; papyrus relevance): *JEarlyC 3 (1995) 47-60.

g625 -- **Scholten** Clemens, Antike Naturphilosophie und christliche Terminologie in der Schrift 'De opificio mundi ' des Johannes Philoponos: P(atr)TS 45. B 1995, de Gruyter. xi-498 p.; Bibliog. 429-448. 3-11-014834-X.

g626 SERAPION: **Johnson** Maxwell E., The prayers of Sarapion of Thmuis; a literary, liturgical and theological analysis: OCA 249. R 1995, Pont. Inst. Orientale. 299 p.; bibliog. 11-20. 88-7210-307-X.

g627 -- *Sims-Williams* Nicholas, Christian Sogdian texts from the Nachlass of Olaf HANSEN, I. Fragments of the [Syriac] Life of Serapion; II. Fragments of polemic and prognostics: BSOAS 58 (1995) 50-68 / 288-302.

g628 SHENUTE: **Young** Dwight W., Coptic manuscripts from the White Monastery; works of Shenute: Rainer 23, 1993 → 10,14263*; Sch 835: ᴿBASPAP 32 (1995) 21-94 (T.S. *Wilfong*, also on HASITZKA M. 1993); CÉg 70 (1995) 354-6 (Anne *Boud'hors*); Orientalia 64 (1995) 151-5 (A. *Shisha-Halevi*); WZKM 85 (1995) 276-281 (K. *Schüssler*).

g629 -- **Emmel** Stephen L., Shenute's literary corpus: diss. Yale. 5 vol.; bibliog. p.1278-1316.

g630 SYMEON † 1022: *Ginter* Mark E., Conscience and the Holy Spirit; moral foundations in the writings of St. Symeon the new theologian: Logos 36 (Sask 1995) 7-29; 29s, Ukrainian summary.

Y3 **Medium aevum,** *generalia.*

g631 **Armstrong** Karen, Visions of God; four medieval mystics and their writings. NY 1994. Bantam. xxv-228 p. $ 11. 0-553-35199-0.

g632 *Bachrach* Bernard S., Anthropologists and early medieval history; some problems: Cithara 33,2 (1993) 3-10.

g633 *Baert* Barbara, Sethof de terugkeer naar het Paradijs: bujdragen tot het kruishoutmotif [wood of the Cross] in de middeleeuwen: Bijdragen 56 (1995) 313-336 + 4 fig.; Eng. 228s.

g634 **Baldwin** John W., The language of sex; five voices from northern France around 1200: Series on Sexuality, History. and Society 1994 → 10,14268: ᴿTS 56 (1995) 366s (E.C. *Vacek*: fascinating diversity, at a time when the Church was trying to universalize its control over marriage, but the wed were no longer restricted to coitus one day in nine).

g635 **Bartlett** Robert, The making of Europe; conquest, colonization and cultural change, 950-1350. L 1993, A.Lane/Penguin. xvi-432 p.; ill.; maps. £ 22.50. 0-713-99074-0. -- ᴿJEH 46 (1995) 139s (D. *Matthew*).

g636 **Beckwith** Sarah, Christ's body; identity, culture and society in late medieval writings. L 1993, Routledge. xii-199 p. £37.50. -- ᴿ[J]LitTOx 9 (1995) 105s (Marion *Glasscoe*); Speculum 70 (1995) 337-9 (Clarissa W. *Atkinson*).

g637 **Beer** Frances, Women and mystical experience in the Middle Ages. Woodbridge 1992, Boydell & B, vi-174 p. £ 29.50. -- ᴿTorJT 11 (1995) 224-8 (Kate P. *Crawford Galea*).

g638 **Bell** David, What nuns read books and libraries in medieval English nunneries. Kalamazoo 1990, Cistercian. 300 p. 0-87907-558-9. -- ᴿMagistra 1/2 (1995) 375s (D. *Vess*).

g639 a) *Biffi* Inos, Teoretica della teologia e teologia medievale; -- b) *Marabelli* Costante, Storia della storiografia o storia critica della teologia medievale ?: TeolBr 20 (1995) 261-9; Eng. 269 / 270-7; Eng. 277.

g640 *Blamires* Alcuin, Women and preaching in medieval orthodoxy, heresy and saints' lives: Viator 26 (1995) 135-152.

g641 **Bloch** R. Howard, Medieval misogyny and the invention of western romantic love 1991 → 8,m11: ᴿSalesianum 57 (1995) 764s (G. *Gentileschi*).

g642 **Bornstein** Daniel E., The Bianchi [anti-violence marchers] of 1399; popular devotion in late medieval Italy. Ithaca 1995, Cornell Univ. 232 p. $ 32.50. -- ᴿJRel 75 (1995) 567-9 (T. *Tentler*)

g643 *Borobio* Dionisio, Iniciación cristiana en la Iglesia hispana de los siglos VI al X: Salmanticensis 42 (1995) 29-61; Eng. 61.

g644 **Bosl** Karl, Gesellschaft im Aufbruch: die Welt des Mittelalters und ihre Menschen. Rg 1991, Pustet. 252 p. 3-7917-1281-0. -- ᴿSalesianum 57 (1995) 765 (P.T. *Stella*: lode; tit.pp. dei 10 capitoli).

g645 *Bosworth* Lucy E., The two churches typology in medieval heresiology: Heresis 24 (1995) 9-20; franç. 9s, deutsch 11s.

g646 **Boureau** Alain, L'événement sans fin 1993 → 10,14276: ᴿÉTRel 70 (1995) 450s (M. *Bouttier*).

g647 *Bredero* Adriaan H., Christendom and Christianity in the Middle Ages; the relations between religion, church and society, ᵀ*Bruinsma* Reinder, 1994 → 10,14278: ᴿHeythJ 36 (1995) 83s (R.N. *Swanson*); RRelRes 37 (1995s) 175-7 (R.A. *Wortham*).

g648 **Brenon** Anne, Petit précis du catharisme. Toulouse c. 1995, Loubatièrers. 143 p. -- ᴿHeresis 25 (1995) 147s (Françoise *Chaffaud*).

g649   *Brenon* Anne, Les hérésies de l'an mil; nouvelles perspectives sur les origines du catharisme: Heresis 24 (1995) 21-36.

g650   **Brieskorn** Norbert, Finsteres Mittelalter ? Über das Lebensgefühl einer Epoche 1991 → 8,m12; 3-7867-1569-6: ᴿSalesianum 57 (1995) 766s (F. *Meyer*).

g651   ᴱ**Brown** Virginia, *al.*, Catalogus ... Medieval and Renaissance Latin translations [from Greek] and commentaries [on Greek and Latin texts, vol.1-6 since 1960] 7. [... PLOTINUS, IRENAEUS]. Wsh 1992, Catholic University of America. xxi-356 p. -- ᴿ*JEarlyC 3 (1995) 67s (M. *Vessey*).

g652   **Buc** Philippe, L'ambiguïté du livre; prince, pouvoir et peuple dans les commentaires de la Bible au Moyen Âge: ThH 95, 1994 → 10,14279; F 270. 2-7010-1298-8: ᴿChH 64 (1995) 273s (T.F.X. *Noble*); JEH 46 (1995) 709s (Lucy *McGuiness*).

g653   **Burton** Janet, Monastic and religious orders in Britain, 1000-1300: 1994 → 10,14380: ᴿHeythJ 36 (1995) 239s (R.N. *Swanson*); JRel 75 (1995) 563s (E. Rozanne *Elder*); TS 56 (1995) 364-6 (J.F. *Kelly*).

g654   **Bynum** Caroline, Jeûnes et festins sacrés, les femmes et la nourriture dans la spiritualité médiévale, ᵀ*Pergnier* Claire F., *Saint-André* Eliane U., 1994 → 10,14282: ᴿBLE 96 (1995) 154-6 (Rolande *Vélut*).

g655   **Caciola** Nancy, Discerning spirits; sanctity and possession in the later Middle Ages: diss. Michigan, ᴰ*Hughes* Diane O. AA 1994. 433 p. 95-13310. -- D(iss)AI 56 (1995s) p. 315.

g656   *Cadden* John, Science and rhetoric in the Middle Ages: the natural philosophy of William of Conches: JHI(d) 56 (1995 1-24.

g657   **Cantor** Norman F., Inventing the Middle Ages ... medievalists of the twentieth century 1992 → 8.m18; 9,18151: ᴿHeythJ 36 (1995) 360s (R.N. *Swanson*: not for scholarship).

g658   **Carruthers** Mary J., The book of memory; a study of memory in medieval culture: StMdvLit, 1990 → 9,16152; 10,14285: ᴿSalesianum 57 (1995) 140s (P.T. *Stella*).

g659   **Caspers** Charles M.A., De eucharistische vroomheid en het fest van sacramentsdag in de Nederlanden tijdens de late middeleeuwen (diss.): MiscNeerl 5. Lv 1992, Peeters. xiv-320 p.

g660   *Cescon* Everaldo, Decadência y renovaço espiritual na Idade Média, numa perspectiva milenarista: Teocomunicaço 25 (1995) 131-140.

g661   **Chance** Jane, Medieval mythography from Roman North Africa to the school of Chartres, A.D. 433-1177. Gainesville 1994, Univ. Press of Florida. xxxvii-731 p. $ 85. -- ᴿCithara 34,2 (1994) 43-45 (J. *Mulryan*, also on her Mythographic Chaucer, Mp 1995).

g662   **Chélini** Jean, L'aube du Moyen Âge; naissance de la chrétienté occidentale; la vie des laïcs dans l'Europe carolingienne (750-900). P 1991, Picard. 548 p. -- ᴿAST(arr) 68 (1995) 433s (V. *Serra*).

g663   *Cluse* Christoph, Stories of breaking and taking the Cross; a possible context for the Oxford incident of 1268: RHE 90 (1995) 396-441; franç. deutsch 442.

g664   *Cobban* Alan R., John ARUNDEL, the tutorial system, and the cost of undergraduate living in the medieval English universities: BJRL 77,1 (1995) 143-159.

g665   **Constable** Giles, Three studies in medieval religious and social thought; the interpretation of Mary and Martha, the ideal of the imitation of Christ, the orders of society. C 1995, Univ. 423 p. £ 40. 0-521-30515-2. -- ᴿE(xp)T 107 (1995s) 121 (Valerie *Eden:* encyclopedic erudition).

g666   **Cramer** Peter, Baptism and change in the early Middle Ages 1993 → 9,16157; 10,14293: ᴿJEH 46 (1995) 130-2 (R.W. *Pfaff*); JRel 75 (1995) 416s (P.F. *Bradshaw*).

g667 ᴱ**Cremascoli** Giuseppe, *Leonardi* Claudio, La Bibbia nel medioevo: Bibbia nella Storia 16. Bo c.1995, Dehoniane. 485 p. Lᵐ 62. 88-10-40262-6.

g668 ᴱ**Dagron** Gilbert, *al.*, Die Geschichte des Christentums, 4. Bischöfe, Mönche und Kaiser (642-1054). FrB 1994, Herder. xviii-982 p. ᴅᴍ 248. 3-451-22254-X. -- ᴿTTh 35 (1995) 293s (J. van *Laarhoven*).

g669 ᴱ**Dagron** Gilbert, *al.*, Évêques, moines et empereurs (610-1054): Histoire du christianisme 4, 1993 → 10,14294: ᴿC(ath)HR 81 (1995) 421-3 (T. *Head*); JEH 46 (1995) 135s (C. *Morris*).

g670 **Dahan** Gilbert, Les intellectuels chrétiens et les Juifs 1990 → 6.k430 ... 10,14295: ᴿJQR 84 (1993s) 102s (W.C. *Jordan*).

g671 ᴱ**Davril** A., *Thibedeau* T.M., Guillaume Durand, Rationale divinorum officiorum I-IV: CChr.CM 140. Turnhout 1995, Brepols. xxvi-601 p.

g672 *Demy* Timothy J., *Ice* Thomas D., The rapture and an early medieval citation [Pseudo-Ephraim]: BS 152 (1995) 306-317.

g673 *Deswarte* Thomas, Rome et la spécificité catalane; la papauté et ses relations avec la Catalogne et Narbonne (850-1030): RH 294 (1995) 3-43.

g674 *Dette* Christoph, Kinder und Jugendliche in der Adelsgesellschaft des frühen Mittelalters: AKuG 76 (1994) 1-34.

g675 ᴱ**di Rosa** Gabriele, *al.*, Storia dell'Italia religiosa, I. L'antichità e il medioevo. R 1993, Laterza. xvi-612 p.; 20 pl.; 17 maps. Lᵐ 50. 88-420-4318-4. -- ᴿJEH 46 (1995) 353-5 (Patricia *Skinner*).

g676 ᴱ**Dinzelbacher** Peter, *Bauer* Dieter R., Volksreligion im hohen und späten Mittelalter: QFGesch 13. Pd 1990, Schöningh. 494 p. 3-506-73263-3. -- ᴿSalesianum 57 (1995) 776s (E. *Fontana*).

g677 **Dohar** William J., The Black Death and pastoral leadership in the diocese of Hereford in the fourteenth century, Ph 1995, Univ. Pennsylvania. xvi-198 p £ 31. 0-8122-3262-3.— ᴿET 106 (1994s) 377s (G.R. *Evans*).

g678 ᴱ**Drijvers** Jan W., *MacDonald* Alasdair A., Centres of learning; learning and location in pre-modern Europe and the Near East: StIntelH 61. Lei 1995, Brill. xiv-340 p. 90-04-10193-4.

g679 ᴱ**Dykema** Peter A., *Oberman* Heiko A., Anticlericalism in Late Medieval and early modern Europe 1990/3 → 10,356*: ᴿGGA 247 (1995) 112-130 (T. *Kaufmann*).

g680 **Eamon** William, Science and the secrets of nature; books of secrets in medieval and early modern culture. Princeton 1995, Univ. 490 p. $ 50. -- ᴿCanadCath 13,4 (1995) 29 (M. *Doughty*).

g681 *Eberhard* Winfried, Klerus- und Kirchenkritik in der spätmittelalterlichen deutschen Stadtchronistik: HJ(b) 114 (1994) 349-380.

Eleuteri P., *Bigo* A., Eretici .. XII sec. 1993 → 9975 supra.

g682 ᴱ**Emmerson** Richard K., *McGinn* B., The apocalypse in the Middle Ages 1992 → 28,5949: ᴿJRel 75 (1995) 275-7 (P.D. *Krey*).

g683 *Evans* G.R., Philosophy and theology in the Middle Ages. ɴʏ 1993, Routledge. vii-139 p. $ 15. -- ᴿ*CritRR 8 (1995) 458s (V.E. *Taylor*).

g684 *Fedalto* Giorgio, Le Chiese d'Oriente 2. Dalla caduta di Costantinopoli alla fine del cinquecento. Mi 1993, Jaca. xiii-202 p. -- ᴿOCP 61 (1995) 288-290 (E.G. *Farrugia*).

g685 **Fichtenau** Heinrich, Ketzer und Professoren; Häresie und Vernunftglaube im Hochmittelalter 1992 → 9,16171: ᴿActuBbg 31 (1994) 267s (A. *Boada*).

g686 ᴱ**Follon** J., *al.*, Actualité de la pensée médiévale: PhMéd 31. LvN 1994, Inst.Sup.Ph. / Peeters. 90-6831-607-9 / 2-87723-1372. -- ᴿAng 72 (1995) 611-4 (Margherita Maria *Rossi*).

g687 **Fossier** Robert, Hommes et villages d'Occident au Moyen-Âge 1992 → 8,m33: ᴿClio 31 (R 1995) 633-6 (L. *Gatto*).

g688 **Frank** Isnard W., Storia della Chiesa 2. Epoca medioevale, ᵀ*Limiroli* Mariarosa, ᴱ*Mezzadri* Luigi. Brescia 1989. Queriniana. 168 p. Lᵐ 20. 88-399-0076-4. -- ᴿETL 70 (1994) 484s (R. *Wielockx*).

g689 **Frank** Isnard W,, A history of the medieval church². ᵀ*Bowden* John. L 1995, SCM. v-153 p. £ 10. 0-334-02593-1. -- ᴿE(xp)T 107 (1995s) 121 (G.R. *Evans*: unsatisfying beside Sᴏᴜᴛʜᴇʀɴ R.); *TBR 8,2 (1995s) 51 (M.S. *Kempshall*).

g690 *Froehlich* Karlfried, The significance of medieval biblical interpretation: LuthQ 9 (1995) 139-151.

g691 *Gatto* Lorenzo, L'Europa nell'età di mezzo: Clio 30 (R 1994) 5-21.

g692 **Gatto** Ludovico, L'atelier del medievista. R 1992, Bulzoni. 265 p. -- ᴿClio 31 (R 1995) 333s (Eleonora *Plebani*).

g693 *a) Gaus* Joachim, Die Lichtsymbolik in der mittelalterlichen Kunst; -- *b) Herrmann* Botho, Die Lichtmetapher in biblischen Schriften; -- *c) Schaeffler* Richard, Licht und Sonne -- Bemerkungen zu Sachproblemen und Wirkungsgeschichte eines platonischen Gleichnisses: Symb 12 (Fra 1995) 107-118 / 149-163 / 137-148.

g694 **Georgedes** Kimberly, The serpent in the tree of knowledge; enjoyment and use in fourteenth-century theology: diss. Wisconsin, ᴰ*Courtenay* W. Madison 1995. 323 p. 95-27292. -- D(iss)AI 56 (1995s) p. 2813.

g695 **Gibson** Margaret T., The Bible in the Latin West: The Medieval Book 1, 1993: ᴿSpeculum 70 (1995) 619-621 (Laura *Light*).

g696 **Gilbert** Paul, Introducción a la teología medieval 1993 → 10,1430: ᴿScrT(Pamp) 37 (1995) 1064s (S. *Martínez Sarrado*).

g697 **Goetz** Hans-Werner, Life in the Middle Ages, from the seventh to the thirteenth century, ᵀ*Wimmer* Albert, ᴱ*Rowan* Steven. ND 1993, Univ. ix-316 p. $ 45; pa. $ 20, -- ᴿChH 64 (1995) 655s (T. *Renna*).

g698 **Grandjean** Michel, Laïcs dans l'Église; regards de Pierre Dᴀᴍɪᴇɴ, Aɴsᴇʟᴍᴇ de Cantorbéry, Yᴠᴇs de Chartres: THist 97. P 1994, Beauchesne. 434 p. F 120. 2-7010-1302-X. -- ᴿE(spr)eV 105 (1995) 148-152 (P. *Jay*); ÉTRel 70 (1995) 286s (J.-F. *Zorn*); TS 56 (1995) 780s (K.B. *Osborne*); TTh 35 (1995) 293 (J. van *Laarhoven*).

g699 **Gregory** T., Mundana sapienza; forme di conoscenza nella cultura medievale. R 1992, StoLett. 481 p. -- ᴿCrSt 16 (1995) 182-7 (O. *Capitani*).

g700 ᴱ**Grotans** Anna A., *Porter* David W., The St. Gall Tractate; a medieval guide to rhetorical syntax: MdvTTGerman. Columbia sc 1995, Camden. ix-149 p.; bibliog. 143-9. 1-87951-19-4.

g701 **Hage** Wilhelm, Das Christentum im frühen Mittelalter: ZugängeKG 4, 1993 → 10,14309: ᴿO(stk)S 43 (1994) 224 (M. *Tamcke*).

g702 *Halverson* James, Franciscan theology and predestinarian pluralism in Late-Medieval thought: Speculum 70 (1995) 1-26

g703 **Harvey** Barbara, Living and dying in England 1100-1540; the monastic experience. Ox 1993, Clarendon. xviii-291 p. £ 30. 0-19-820431-4. -- ᴿHeythJ 36 (1995) 86s (T.M. *McCoog*).

g704 **Harvey** Margaret, England, Rome and the Papacy, 1417-1464; the study of a relationship 1993 → 10,14310: ^RChH 64 (1995) 471s (A.D. *Frankforter*).

g705 **Hinson** E.Glenn, The Church triumphant; a history of Christianity up to 1300. Macon GA 1995, Mercer Univ. xxi-492 p.; 19 maps. $ 45. 0-86554-436-0 [NTAb 40, p.175; ThD 42,370].

g706 **Horowitz** Jeanine, *Menache* Sophian, L'humour en chaire, le rire dans l'Eglise médiévale 1994 → 10,14311: ^RBLE 96 (1995) 152 (G. *Passerat*); RHPhR 75 (1995) 240s (M. *Arnold*).

g707 **Hughes** Andrew, Medieval manuscripts for Mass and Office. Toronto 1995 pa. = 1982, Univ. xvii-470 p.; ill. 0-8020-7669-6. -- ^R*TBR 8,3 (1995s) 41 (B. *Spinks*: a uniquely useful tool despite undue remotely-relevant reliance on JUNGMANN).

g708 *Hull* Caroline S., Rylands MS French 5; the form and function of a medieval Bible picture book: BJRL 77,2 (1995) 3-24; 8 fig.

g709 **Hunt** Tony, Teaching and learning Latin in thirteenth-century England. C 1991, Brewer. I. Text, ix-453 p.; II. Glosses, 175 p.; III. Indexes, 365 p. -- ^R*JMdvLat 3 (1993) 230-3 (A.G. *Rigg*).

g710 **Jaeger** C. Stephen, The envy of angels; cathedral schools and social ideals in medieval Europe, 950-1200. Ph 1995, Univ. Pennsylvania. xvi-515 p. £ 38. 0-8122-3246-1. -- ^RET 106 (1994s) 311s (G. R. *Evans*).

g711 **Jansen** Katherine L., Mary Magdalen and the mendicants in late medieval Italy: diss. Princeton 1995. 440 p. 96-07703. -- D(iss)AI 56 (1995s) p. 4519.

g712 ^E**Jedin** Hubert, The medieval and Reformation Church, vol.4-6 (1962-79) ^T*Dolan* John, abridged by *Holland* D.L., 1993 →10,14315*: ^RRStR 21 (1995) 58 (D.R. *Janz*).

g713 **Kaeppeli** Thomas [† 1984], *Panella* Emilio, Scriptores Ordinis Praedicatorum Medii Aevi [I. 1970; II. 1975; III. 1980] IV, T-Z. R 1993, Ist. Storico Domenicano. 720 p. -- ^R*FrSZ 42 (1995) 213s (J.-P. *Torrell*)

g714 *Kido* T., The state of research; the study of the medieval history of Europe in Japan; JMeditH 21 (1995) 79-96 < RHE 90 (1995) 203*.

g715 *Kieckhefer* Richard, The office of Inquisition and medieval heresy; the transition from personal to institutional jurisdiction: JEH 46 (1995) 36-61.

g716 **Kieckhefer** Richard, La magia nel Medioevo [1990 → 7,g372], ^T*Corradi* Federico: Storia e Memoria. Bari 1993, Laterza. viii-302 p. 88-420-4292-7. -- ^RSalesianum 57 (1995) 557 (M. *Müller*).

g717 **Körntgen** Ludger, Studien zu den Quellen der frühmittelalterlichen Bussbücher: QFRechtMA 7, 1993 → 10,14319; 3-7995-6088-2: ^RZkT 117 (1995) 349 (R. *Messner*).

g718 **Kruger** Steven F., Dreaming in the Middle Ages. 1992. -- ^RBijdragen 56 (1995) 108s (M. *Parmentier*, Eng.).

g719 **Landes** R., Relics, apocalypse, and the deceits of history; Ademar of Chabannes, 989-1034: HistSt 117. CM 1995, Harvard Univ. xii-404 p.; 15 fig.[RHE 91,111*].

g720 **LaRoncière** Charles M. de, Religion paysanne et religion urbaine en Toscane (c.1250 - c.1450): CS 458 [8 art. + 1 Eng., 1973-1992]. Brookfield VT 1994, Ashgate. x-319 p. $ 95. 0-86078-445-2 [< ThD 42 (1995) 276].

g721 **Lawrence** C.H., The Friars; the impact of the early mendicant movement on western society: The Medieval World. L 1994, Longman. x-245 p. £ 11 pa. -- ^RA(mer)HR 100 (1995) 505s (R.E. *Lerner*); Speculum 70 (1995) 647-9 (Nancy *Spatz*); Theol 98 (L 1995) 144s (C. *Harper-Bill*).

g722 **Lawrence** Clifford H., Il monachesimo medievale; forme di vita religiosa in Occidente. T 1993, S. Paolo. 403 p. L^m 35. -- ^{R}CivCatt 146 (1995,4) 311 (G. *Cremascoli*).

g723 ^{E}**Lees** Clare A., Medieval masculinities; regarding men in the Middle Ages. Mp 1994, Univ. Minnesota.

g724 **Le Goff** Jacques, Intellectuals in the Middle Ages [1985 = 1957], ^{T}*Fagan* Teresa L. CM 1992, Blackwell. 194 p. $ 45; pa, $ 18. -- ^{R}JI(ntd)H 26 (1995) 482-5 (W.J. *Courtenay*).

g725 *Le Goff* Jacques, Économie, morale et religion au XIIIe siècle: RicStoSR 23,46 (1994) 7-20.

g726 [*Le Goff* J. (non^E), *al.*]. Le travail au Moyen Âge [Lv 21-23 mai 1987]: LvN Publ. 101. LvN 1990, Univ. viii-440 p.; 33 fig. -- ^{R}Salesianum 57 (1995) 367 (P.T. *Stella*).

g727 ^{E}**Lewis** Bernard, *Niewöhner* Friedrich, Religionsgespräche im Mittelalter [25. Wolfenbütteler Symposion, 11.-15. Juni 1989]: W MA-St 4, 1992 → 8,531; DM 148; 3-447-03349-5: ^{R}WZKM 85 (1995) 389s (H. *Bobzin*).

g728 **Lewis** Suzanne, Reading images; narrative discourse and reception in the thirteenth-century illuminated Apocalypses. C 1995, Univ. xxvii-459 p.; bibliog. 402-426. 0-521-47920-7.

g729 **Linehan** Peter, History and the historians of medieval Spain. Ox 1993, Clarendon. xvii-748 p. 0-19-821945-8. -- ^{R}JEH 46 (1995) 136-9 (R.B. *Tate*).

g730 **Little** Lester K., Benedictine maledictions; liturgical cursing in [1000 A.D.] Romanesque France. Ithaca 1993, Cornell Univ. xx-296 p. $ 31.50. 0-8014-2876-9 [RStR 22,74, T.F.X. *Noble*].

g731 ^{E}**Lomas** F.J., *Devís* F., De Constantino a Carlomagno, disidentes 1992 → 10,14328: ^{R}At(henaeum) 83 (1995) 295-8 (G. *Mazzocchi*).

g732 **McGinn** Bernard, The growth of mysticism; Gregory the Great through the 12th century: Presence of God 2. L/NY 1995, SCM/Crossroad. 630 p. $ 49.50; £ 20 pa. 0-334-02572-0; pa. -966-6. -- ^{R}ChrCent 112 (1995) 823.5 (Anne L. *Clark*); ET 106 (1994s) 347s (C. *Thompson*); *TBR 8,2 (1995s) 35 (G. *Mursell*); TS 56 (1995) 782-4 (H.D. *Egan*).

g733 **McLaughlin** Megan, Consorting with saints; prayer for the dead in early medieval France. Ithaca 1994, Cornell Univ. x-306 p. $ 32.50. 0-8014-2648-0 [< ThD 42 (1995) 278].

g734 *McNamara* Martin, Hiberno-Latin bulletin: PIBA 16 (1993) 114-124.

g735 *Macy* Gary, Demythologizing 'the Church' in the Middle Ages: JHispLat 3,1 (1995s) 23-41.

g736 *Madigan* Kevin, Ancient and high-medieval interpretations of Jesus in Gethsemane; some reflections on tradition and continuity in Christian thought: HThR 88 (1995)157-73

g737 **Marsden** Richard, The text of the Old Testament in Anglo-Saxon England: StudiesASEng 15. C 1995, Univ. xxviii-506 p.: bibliog. p.452-471.

g738 **Martin** Nell G.. Reading the Huntingfield Psalter (Pierpont Morgan library manuscript M. 43); devotional literacy and an English psalter preface: diss. North Carolina, ^{D}*Folda* J. Chapel Hill 1995. 418 p. 95-38449. -- D(iss)AI 56 (1995s) p. 2454.

g739 *a) Martínez Pizarro* Joaquín, Images of Church and State, from Sulpicius Severus to Notker Balbulus; -- *b) Blamires* Alcuin, *Marx* C.W., Women not to preach; a disputation in MS Harley 31: *JMdvLat 4 (1994) 25-38 / 3 (1993) 34-63.

g740 *Mateo Seco* Lucas F., Adopcionismo hispánico y concilio de Frankfurt (en la conmemoración de su XII centenario): *AnVal 20 (1994) 99-120.

g741 **Maurin** Krystel, Les Esclarmonde; la femme et la féminité dans l'imaginaire du catharisme. Toulouse 1995, Privat. 238 p. -- [R]Heresis 25 (1995) (Françoise *Chaffaud*).

g742 [E]**Mayeur** J. *al.*, Apogée de la papauté (1054-1274): Histoire du christianisme 5, 1993 [deutsch 1994 → 10,14337*]: [R]Ang 72 (1995) 341-5 (S. *Krasić*).

g743 *Mier Vélez* Antonio de, Supersticiones y horóscopos entre los cristianos visigodos y francos [siglos IV -- VII]: Rel(y)Cult 41 (1995) 811-839.

g744 [E]**Miethke** J., *Schreiner* K., Sozialer Wandel im Mittelalter; Wahrnehmungsformen, Erklärungsmuster, Regelungsmechanismen. Sigmaringen 1994, Thorbecke. 452 p. -- [R]*DAEM 51 (1995) 313-5 (G. *Schmitz*) [RHE 91,139*].

g745 **Mills** Ludo J.R., Angelic monks and earthly men [... influencing European society] 1992 → 8.m63; 10,14339: [R]HeythJ 36 (1995) 78-80 (B. *Hamilton*).

g746 *Mitre Fernández* Emilio, Muerte, veneno y enfermedad, metáforas medievales de la herejía: Heresis 25 (1995) 63-84; franç. 63s.

g747 **Moranski** Karen R., Predicting the past and recounting the future; prophecy and propaganda in Late Medieval Britain: diss. Univ. N. Carolina, [D]*Wittig J.* Chapel Hill 1995. 218 p. 95-38455. -- D(iss)AI 56 (1995s) p. 2672.

g748 **Muir** Lynette R., The biblical drama of medieval Europe. C 1995, Univ. xxiii-320 p.; bibliog. 292-300. 0-521-41291-9.

g749 Natura, scienze e società medievale, I. I discorsi del corpo: Micrologus. P 1993, Brepols. 346 p. [RHE 91,112*].

g750 **Nebbiai-Dalla Guardia** Donatella, I documenti per la storia delle biblioteche medievali (sec. ix-xv): Univ.Venezia MatRic 15. R 1992, Jouvence. 146 p. -- [R]Speculum 70 (1995) 182s (M.L. *Colker*).

g751 **Nekrasov** G.A., [R] Tausend Jahre russisch-schwedisch-finnische Kulturbeziehungen, IX-XVIII Jht. Moskva 1993, Nauka. 268 p. JGO 43 (1995) 410-2 (S. *Troebst* [RHE 91,53*].

g752 **Nineham** Dennis, Christianity medieval and modern; a study in religious change 1993 → 9,16216; 10,14341: [R]JEH 46 (1995) 504-8 (H.E.J. *Cowdrey*).

g753 *Noble* Thomas F.X., Morbidity and vitality in the history of the early medieval papacy: C(ath)HR 81 (1995) 505-540.

g754 **Nodes** Daniel L., Doctrine and exegesis in biblical Latin poetry: Arca 31, 1993 → 10,14342; 0-905205-86-3: [R]AnCL 64 (1995) 346 (J. *Wankenne*).

g755 *Odenthal* Andreas, Zwei Formulare des Apologientyps der Messe vor dem Jahre 1000: AL(tg)W 37 (1995) 25-44.

g756 *O'Keeffe* Dunstan, *a)* The via media of monastic theology; the debate on grace and free will in fifth century southern Gaul III; -- *b)* Dom Jean LECLERCQ and the concept of monastic theology: DR 113 (1995) 157-174 / 271-281.

g757 *O'Loughlin* Thomas O., Seeking the early medieval view of the Song of Songs: P(Ir)BA 18 (1995) 94-116.

g758 **Ortenberg** Veronica, The English Church and the Continent in the tenth and eleventh centuries; cultural, spiritual, and artistic exchanges 1992 → 9,16217: [R]JThS 46 (1995) 379-382 (Rosamond *McKitterick*); ZKG 106 (1995) 248s (H. *Lutterbach*).

g759 *Ortenberg* Veronica, 'Angli aut angeli'; les Anglo-Saxons ont-ils sauvé la papauté au VIIe siècle ?: RMab 67 (1995) 5-32.

g760 [E]**Osborne** K.B., The history of Franciscan theology. NY 1994, St. Bonaventure Univ. ix-345 p. -- [R]CFr 65 (1995) 699s (B. *Vadakkekara*) [RHE 91,111*].

g761 *Otten* Willemien, Nature and Scripture; demise of a medieval analogy: HThR 88 (1995) 257-284.

g762 **Palazzo** Eric, Le moyen âge, des origines au XIII⁶ siècle: Histoire des livres liturgiques 1993 → 10,14345: ᴿJEH 46 (1995) 356 (R.W. *Pfaff*).

g763 *Pastoureau* M., Jésus teinturier; histoire symbolique et sociale d'un métier reprouvé: *Médiévales 29 (1995) 47-63 [RHE 91,140*].

g764 **Payer** Pierre J., The bridling of desire; views of sex in the later Middle Ages. Toronto 1993, Univ. vi-285 p. -- ᴿSR 24 (1995) 221s (J.J. *Snyder*).

g765 **Podskalsky** Gerhard, Griechische Theologie in der Zeit der Türkenherrschaft 1453-1521: 1988 → 3,g733 ... 6,k781: ᴿAKuG 75 (1993) 228-231 (G.D. *Metallinos*).

g766 **Price** B.B., Medieval thought; an introduction. Ox 1992, Blackwell. ix-261 p. 0-631-17508-3; pa. 9-1. -- ᴿRHE 90 (1995) 522-5 (P. *Cramer*, Eng.).

g767 **Reventlow** Henning, Epochen der Bibelauslegung, 2. Von der Spätantike bis zum Ausgang des Mittelalters 1994, Beck. 324 p. ᴅᴍ 58. 3-406-34986-2. -- ᴿE(xp)T 107 (1995s) 180s (R. *Mason*); LM(on) 32,3 (1995) 41 (E. *Lohse*); RHE 90 (1995) 619s (P.-M. *Bogaert*); TPQ 143 (1995) 430-2 (F. *Böhmisch*)/ ᴡᴢᴋᴍ 85 (1995) 392s (G. *Stemberger*); ZkT 117 (1995) 105 (R. *Oberforcher*).

g768 *Reynolds* Philip L., Same-sex unions [in pre-modern Europe [→ 10,14275]; what Boswell didn't find: ChrCent 112 (1995) 49-54 [on p.10 is discreetly mentioned the ᴀɪᴅs death of Yale medievalist John E. Boswell at 47, 12.XII.1994].

g769 **Reynolds** Philip L., Marriage in the Western church: the Christianization of marriage during the patristic and early medieval periods: VigChr supp. Leiden 1994. Brill. xxx-438 p. -- TS 56 (1995) 777-9 (D.G. *Hunter*).

g770 **Riché** Pierre, *Alexandre-Bidon* Danièle, L'enfance au Moyen-Âge [... exposition 1994]. P 1994, Seuil / Bibliothèque Nationale. -- ᴿCRAI (1995) 60s (B. *Guenée*).

g771 ᴱ**Ridder-Symoens** Hilde de, Universities in the Middle Ages: [ᴱ*Ruegg* Walter], History of the university in Europe 1. 1992 → 8,440: ᴿE(ng)HR 110 (1995) 162s (J. *Catto*).

g772 *Ritter* Adolf M., Das Mittelalter als Zeitalter der Missionsgeschichte: ZM(iss)R 79 (1995) 97-110.

g773 **Rubin** Miri, Corpus Christi; the Eucharist in late medieval culture 1991 → 9,16226; 10,14352: ᴿ*CritRR 7 (1994) 366-8 (T.M. *Finn*).

g774 ᵀᴱ**Ruello** Francis, Hugues de ʙᴀʟᴍᴀ † 1304, Théologie mystique, Tome I: SC 408. P 1995, Cerf. 280 p. 2-204-05111-2.

g775 **Ruh** Kurt, Geschichte der abendländischen Mystik, I. Die Grundlegung durch die Kirchenväter und die Mönchstheologie des 12. Jahrhunderts 1990 → 8,8386: ᴿSalesianum 57 (1995) 775s (E. *Fontana*).

g776 *Rusconi* Roberto, Modelli di santità e religiosità femminile in età medievale [École Française de Rome, 30.I.1995]: RS(to)LR 31 (1995) 503-517.

g777 **Sebastián** Santiago, Mensaje simbólico del Arte Medieval; arquitectura, liturgía e iconografía. M 1994, Encuentro. 437 p. -- ᴿScrT(Pamp) 37 (1995) 681s (J.L. *Gutiérrez-Martín*).

g778 ᴱ**Souza** José A, de, O Reino e o sacerdócio; o pensamento político na Alta Idade Media [10 estudos]: Filosofia 33. Porto Alegre 1995, ᴇᴅɪᴘᴜᴄʀs. 234 p. -- ᴿTeocomunicação 25 (1995) 734s.

g779 **Spencer** H. Leith, English preaching in the late Middle Ages 1993 → 10,14359: ᴿJRel 75 (1995) 569s (J.A. *Alford*); JThS 46 (1995) 382-4 (Christina von *Nolcken*).

g780 **Stoyanov** Yuri, The hidden tradition in Europe; the secret history of medieval Christian [Bogomil/Cathar] heresy. L 1994, Arkana Penguin. xix-309. -- ᴿOCP 61 (1995) 298s (E.G. *Farrugia*).

g781 **Stuip** R.E.V., *Vellekoop* C., Scholing in de middeleeuwen: Utrechtse bijd.mdv. Hilversum 1995, Verloren. 256 p.; 28 fig. -- p. 9-36, *Sancisi-Weerdenburg* H., 'Qui a inventé l'école ?'; -- p.87-125, 9 fig., *Mostert* M., Kennisoverdracht in het klooster; over de plaats van lezen en schrijven in de vroegmiddeleeuwse monastieke opvoeding [RHE 91,108*].

g782 **Swanson** Robert N., Religion and devotion in Europe, c.1215-c.1515: Medieval Textbooks. C 1995, Univ. xv-377. xv-377 p. $ 70; pa. $ 19. 0-521-37076-0; -950-4.

g783 **Tellenbach** Gerd, The Church in Western Europe from the tenth to the early twelfth century [1988], **Reuter** Timothy, 1993 → 10,14360: **ChH 64 (1995) 265s (F. *Oakley*); C(ath)HR 81 (1995) 255s (Uta-Renate *Blumenthal*); Churchman 108 (L 1994) 86s (H. *Rowdon*: excellent; Gregory VII).

g784 **Thompson** Augustine, Revival preachers and politics in thirteenth-century Italy; the Great Devotion of 1233. Ox 1992, Clarendon. xiv-244 p. $ 50. -- **JRel 75 (1995) 118s (D. *Bornstein*).

g785 **Tomea** Paolo, Tradizione apostolica e coscienza cittadina a Milano nel Medioevo; la leggenda di San Barnaba: BtErudita 2. Mi 1993, Vita e Pensiero. xvii-702 p. -- **RS(to)LR 31 (1995) 338-340 (G. *Penco*).

g786 **Turner** Paul, Source of confirmation from the Fathers through the Reformers. ColMn 1993. 64 p. $ 7 pa. -- **R*JEarlyC 3 (1995) 61s (Joanne M. *Pierce*).

g787 **Ullmann** Reinholdo, *a)* A Reforma e as Universidades: -- *b)* A Reforma católica e a atividade intelectual dos Jesuitas: Teocomunicação 24 (1994) 139-154 / 289-309.

g788 **Valentin** Frédérique, Les hommes du Moyen Age; constitution physique, alimentation, maladies; les découvertes de la paléo-anthropologie: Les Dossiers d'Archéologie 106 (c.1995). 87 p. F 48.

g789 **Van Dam** Raymond, Saints and their miracles in late antique Gaul. Princeton 1993, Univ. xii-349 p. $ 49.50; pa. $ 17. -- **JEarlyC 3 (1995) 239-241 (P.J. *Potter*).

g790 **Vauchez** André, The laity in the Middle Ages; religious beliefs and devotional practices, [→ 7,g401; essays interlocked], **Bornstein** Daniel E., **Schneider** Margery J., 1993 → 9,16245; 10,14266; $ 37; 0-268-01297-0: **CScR 25 (1995s) 241-4 (R. *Sweetman*) ; RRelRes 36 (1994s) 87 (J. *Kroll*).

g791 **Vauchez** André, *al.*, Apogée et expansion de la chrétienté (1054-1274): Histoire du Christianisme 5, 1993 → 9,16243; 10,14367: **Speculum 70 (1995) 439-442 (K. *Pennington*).

g792 **Vauchez** André, Textes prophétiques ... en Occident 1988/90 → 8,679*b*: **Speculum 69 (1994) 304.

g793 **Vereno** Ingolf, Studien zum ältesten alchemistischen Schrifttum, auf der Grundlage zweier erstmals edierter arabischer Hermetica: IKU 155. B 1992, Schwarz. v-414 p. 3-87997-206-0. -- **WZKM 85 (1995) 307 (H. *Eisenstein*).

g794 **Vitz** Evelyn B., Medieval narrative and narratology; subjects and objects of desire. NYU 1989. x-228 p. $ 40; pa. $ 19.50. -- **Cithara 33,1 (1993) 36s (L. S. *Crist*).

g795 **Wei** Ian P., The self-image of the masters of theology at the University of Paris in the late thirteenth and early fourteenth centuries: JEH 46 (1995) 398-431.

g796 **Wessels** Anton, Europe; was it ever really Christian ? 1994 → 10,14599*; 0-334-02569-9: **E(xp)T 107 (1995s) 185 (C. *Holdsworth*).

g797 **Wessels** Anton, Kerstening en ontkerstening van Europa; wisselwerking tussen evangelie en cultuur. Baarn 1994, Ten Have. 271 p. 90-259-4492-2. -- **VSVD 36 (1995) 460s (H. *Rzepkowski*).

g798 **Wippel** John F., Mediaeval reactions to the encounter between faith and reason (1995 Aquinas lecture). Milwaukee 1995, Marquette Univ. 113 p. $ 10. 0-87462-162-3 [ThD 43,94].

g799 **Wittern** Susanne, Frauen, Heiligkeit und Macht; lateinische Frauenviten aus dem 4. bis 7. Jahrhundert: Ergebnisse der Frauenforschung 33. Stu 1994, Metzler. 220 p. -- ᴿChH 64 (1995) 260s (A.D. *Frankforter*).

g800 **Wroe** Ann, A fool and his money -- life in a partitioned medieval town [Rodez 14th c.]. L 1995, J. Cape. 244 p. -- ᴿHeresis 25 (1995) 161s (J. *Duvernoy*).

g801 ᴱ**Zutshi** Patrick, Medieval Cambridge: essays on the pre-Reformation university: HistUnivC 2. Woodbridge/Rochester 1993, Boydell & B. viii-198 p., map. $ 63. -- ᴿRHE 90 (1995) 641s (D.B.); Speculum 70 (1995) 991 (titles and pages).

Y3.4   **Exegetae mediaevales** [Hebraei → κ7]

g802 ABELARDUS: ᵀᴱ**Gandillac** M. de, Dialogue d'un philosophe avec un juif et un chrétien. P 1993, Cerf. 295 p. -- ᴿCrSt 16 (1995) 179 (María Isabel *Méndez Romano*).

g803 -- **Jussila** Päivi H., Peter Abelard on imagery; theory and practice with special reference to his hymns: Annales 8/280. Helsinki 1995, Suomalainen Tiedeakatemia. xviii-237 p. 951-41-0787-X.

g804 -- *Strothmann* Jürgen, Das Konzil von Sens 1138 und die endgültige Verurteilung Abaelards 1140: ThGL 85 (1995) 238-253 . 396-410.

g805 AELRED; **McGuire** Brian P., Brother and lover 1994 → 10,14374: ᴿC(ath)HR 81 (1995) 425-7 (T.J. *Heffernan*); *CWeal 122,7 (1995) 28 (L. S. *Cunningham*); JRel 75 (1995) 420s (M.K. *Shawn*); TS 56 (1995) 398 (D.M. *La Corte*).

g806 -- *a) McGuire* Brian P., Sexual awareness and identity in Aelred of Rievaulx (1110-67); -- *b) Vess* Deborah, Continuity and conservatism in the cathedral schools of the twelfth century; the role of monastic thought in the so-called intellectual revolution of the twelfth century: ABenR 45 (1994) 184-226 / 161-183.

g807 -- ᵀ**Powicke** F.M., DANIEL WALTER (lat.), The life of Aelred of Rievaulx: Cistercian Fathers 57. Kalamazoo 1994, Cistercian. 172 p. -- ᴿCiteaux 46 (1995) 181s (Colette *Friedlander*).

g808 D'AILLY: **Smoller** Laura A., History, prophecy and the stars; the Christian astrology of Pierre d'Ailly, 1350-1420: 1994 → 10,1442: ᴿCanadCath 13,3 (1995); TS 56 (1995) 399s (I. *Murdoch*).

g809 ANSELMUS: **Bencivenga** Ermanno, Logic and other nonsense; the case of Anselm and his God. Princeton 1993, Univ. 152 p. $ 20. -- ᴿJRel 75 (1995) 296s (G.L. *Goodwin*).

g810 *Clayton* John, The otherness of Anselm: NZSTh 37 (1995) 125-142: Eng. 143.

g811 **Eckhardt** Burnell F.ᴶ, Anselm and LUTHER on the Atonement; was it 'necessary'? 1992 → 9,16248: ᴿC(alvin)TJ 29 (1994) 556-8 (R. *Kolb*: 'cheap shots unbecoming a scholar').

g812 **Gäde** Gerhard, Eine andere Barmherzigkeit; zum Verständnis der Erlösungslehre Anselms von Canterbury. Wü 1989, Echter.

g813 *Grandjean* Michel, Hors du cloître pas de salut ? Note sur l'ecclésiologie d'Anselme de Cantorbéry et de son milieu: ÉTRel 70 (1995) 349-357.

g814 **Southern** Richard W., Saint Anselm, a portrait in a landscape[2] 1991 [[1]1990 → 7,g416 ... 10,14382: [R]FilTeo 8 (1994) 161s (G. *Garelli*); RTL 26 (1995) 97s (J.-M. *Counet*); RTPh 127 (1995) 72s (F. *Schoch*); Salesianum 57 (1995) 366s (P.T. *Stella*).

g815 **Werlin** Steven, How faith seeks understanding in Anselm's 'Proslogion': diss. Loyola, [D]*Peperzak* A. Chicago 1995. 153 p. 95-17211. -- D(iss)AI 56 (1995s) p. 224.

g816 AQUINAS **Aillet** Marc, Lire la Bible avec S. Thomas: StFrS 80, 1993 → 9,16251: [R]DoC(om) 48 (1995) 199s (B. de *Margerie*).

g817 [R]**Bonino** Serge-Thomas, Saint-Thomas au XXe siècle 1993/4. -- [R]RTPh 127 (1995) 278s (Tiziana *Suarez-Nani*).

g818 *Boyle* John F., St. Thomas Aquinas and Sacred Scripture: *ProEc 4 (1995) 92-104.

g819 **Gaboriau** Florent, Thomas d'Aquin penseur dans l'Église: Réfléchir. P 1992, FAC. 200 p. -- [R]CiTom 121 (1994) 427-9 (A. *Osuna); DoCom 46 (1993) 199-201 (D. *Vibrac*).

g820 **Geisler** Norman L., Thomas Aquinas, an evangelical appraisal 1991 → 7,g420 ... 10,14338: [R]JETS 37 (1994) 604-6 (D.L. *Russell*).

g821 **Gilson** Étienne, The Christian philosophy of St. Thomas Aquinas [Le Thomisme, 1948 ed.], [T]*Shook* L.K. ND Univ 1994 = Random 1956. x-502 p £ 15.50. 0-268-00801-9. [R]*TBR 8,1 (1995s) 5s (A. *McCoy*).

g822 **Harak** G. Simon, Virtuous passions; the formation of Christian character [Summa I-II 6-48]. NY 1993, Paulist. viii-180 p. 0-8091-3436-5. -- [R]Salesianum 57 (1995) 379-381 (G. *Abbà*).

g823 **Hood** John Y.B., Aquinas and the Jews: Middle Ages. Ph 1995, Univ. Pennsylvania. xiv-145 p. $ 30; pa. $ 15. 0-8122-3305-0 [ThD 43,172]

g824 *Lang* David P., Aquinas' proofs for the nature and existence of angels: Faith & Reason 21 (1995) 3-16.

g825 **Pesch** Otto H., Thomas d'Aquin; limites et grandeur de la théologie médiévale; une introduction, [T]*Hoffmann* J.: CFi 177, 1994 → 10,14391: [R]DoC(om) 48 (1995) 91-93 (D. *Vibrac*); ÉTRel 70 (1995) 130s (H. *Bost*); RTL 26 (1995) 82-84 (J. *Étienne*).

g826 *Rikhof* H., Een kwestie van lezing [Utrecht-group way of reading Aquinas]; een antwoord an J. AERTSEN: Bijdragen [55 (1994) 56-71] 56 (1995) 429-449; Eng. 450.

g827 **Sarale** Natalino, San Tommaso d'Aquino, oggi. Brescia 1990, Civiltà. L[m] 25. -- [R]RA(sc)M 20 (1995) 204-8 (I. *Agostini*).

g828 *Saranyana* Josep-Ignasi, Tommaso D'Aquino e le origini dello spirito laico: *AnT 9 (1995) 89-106.

g829 **Selman** John, Saint Thomas Aquinas ('quite briefly'). E 1994, Clark. iv-103. £ 9. 0-567-29245-2. -- [R]ET 106 (1994s) 187 (G.R. *Evans*).

g830 *a) Spiazzi* Raimundo, Il Catechismo della Chiesa Cattolica e San Tommaso d'Aquino; — *b) Elders* Leo J., Veritatis splendor et la doctrine de saint Thomas d'Aquin; DoCom 47 (1994) 107-120 / 121-146 [215-239, *Lucas* Ramón].

g831 **Torrell** J.P., Magister Tomas; Leben und Werk des Thomas von Aquin [1993 → 9,16265; 10,14395]. FrB 1995, Herder. 412 p. -- [R]Communio (Sev) 28 (1995) 390-2 (M. *Sánchez*); TS 56 (1995) 162-4 (T.F. *O'Meara*).

g832 **Weisheipl** James A.. Frère Thomas d'Aquin [1975, Friar Thomas Aquinas; his life, thought, and work], [T]*Lotte* Christian, *Hoffman* Joseph. P 1993, Cerf. 460 p. -- [R]RTPh 127 (1995) 279s (R. *Imbach*: vivant; pas exactement dépassé).

g833 **Williams** Anna N., Deification in Thomas Aquinas and Gregory PALAMAS; diss. Yale, [D]*Lindbeck* G. NHv 1995 [< RStR 22, p.271].

g834 BERNARDUS: EBertrand D., .. Histoire, mentalité .. : SChr 380, 1992 → 8,513;
9,16269: RMelSR 52 (1995) 185-8 (J.-L. Solère).

g835 Bell Theo M., a) LUTHER's reception of Bernard of Clairvaux: ConcordiaTQ 59 (1995)
245-277; -- b) Bernhard von Clairvaux als Quelle Martin LUTHERs: Bijdragen 56 (1995)
2-17; Eng, 18.

g836 Casey M., Bernard's biblical mysticism: Studies in Spirituality 4 (Kampen 1994) 12-30
[< ZIT 95, p.267].

g837 Hendrix Guido, Saint Bernard et son historiographie: RHE 90 (1995) 80-103.

g838 Tamburello D.F., Union with Christ; John CALVIN and the mysticism of St Bernard.
LVL 1994, W-Knox. vii-167 p. $ 16. 0-664-22054-1. -- RET 106 (1994s) 348 (P.N,
Brooks: altogether peripheral to Calvin's priorities, though less than SNITS' AUGUSTINE);
*TBR 8,2 (1995s) 35 (G. Mursell).2

BONAVENTURA: Carpenter David, Revelation, history, and the dialogue of religions; a
study of BHARTRHARI [c.480 A.D.] and Bonaventure 1995 → 9118 supra.

g839 Schepers Kees, Ps.-Bonaventura super Cantica Canticorum and its source text Glossa
tripartita super Cantica: AF(ranc)H 88 (1995) 473-496.

g840 CAESARIUS (470-542): Klingshirn William E., Caesarius of Arles; the making of a
Christian community in late antique Gaul: StMdvLT 4/22. C 1994, Univ. xi-317 p. £ 40.
0-521-430955-X. -- RAnCL 64 (1995) 352s (Jeanne-Marie Demaroll); TS 56 (1995) 779s
(C. Leyser).

g841 CASSIANUS: Russell Kenneth C., Healing the heart; desert wisdom for a busy world.
... c.1994, Novalis. 93 p. $ 8. -- RCanadCath 13,4 (1995) 20s (E. Skublics).

g842 CASSIODORUS; Meyer-Flügel Beat, Das Bild der ostgotisch-römischen Gesellschaft
bei Cassiodor; Leben und Ethik von Römern und Germanen in Italien nach dem Ende des
weströmischen Reiches [Diss. Zürich 1992]: EurHS 3/533.   Fra 1991, Lang. 771 p. Fs 134.
-- RGnomon 67 (1995) 528-532 (C. Schäfer).

g843 CUSANUS: Vannini Marco, La visione di Dio; Cusano ed IBN ARABI: RA(sc)M 20
(1995) 159-177.

g844 Krämer Werner, Das Subjekt der Gesellschaft; Anthropologie und Menschenrechte bei
Nikolaus von Kues: → 41, FCOLOMER E., RCatT 29 (1994) 141-151; Eng. 152 (129-139.
Domínguez Rebeiras Fernando, on Cusa manuscripts).

g845 Nicholas of Cusa, The Catholic Concordance: Texts in the history of political thought.
C 1995, Univ. xlvii-326 p. 0-521-56773-4.

g846 DAMIANI: a) Russell Kenneth C., Who really knows -- the monk or the scholar ?
Peter Damian's defense of experiential knowledge; -- b) Theisen Wilfrid, The attraction
of alchemy for monks and friars in the 13th-14th centuries: ABenR 46 (1995) 3-23 / 239-
253.

g847 Leyser C., Cities of the plain; the rhetoric of sodomy in Peter Damian's Book of Gomorrah: Romanic Review 86 (1995) 191-211 [RHE 91,42*].

g848 DIONYSIUS C.; Emery Kent, Dionysii cartusiensis opera selecta 1. Studia
bibliographica: CCMdv 121. Turnhout 1991, Brepols. I. 360 p.; II. p. 370-386; 16 pl.
2-503-04211-2; -3-9. -- REThL 71 (1995) 244-7 (R. Wielockx).

g849 DIONYSIUS PS.-A.: **Rorem** Paul, Pseudo-Dionysius. a commentary 1993 → 10,14410: ^RAug(ustinianum)R 34 (1994) 514-8 (W.J. *Hankey*); CCurr 44 (1994s) 127-9 (Mary E. *Giles*); Horizons 22 (1995) 149s (J.C. *Cavadini*); JEH 46 (1995) 125-7 (A. *Louth*); JRel 75 (1995) 115-7 (T.A. *Carlson*); LuthQ 9 (1995) 221-3 (A. *Golitzin*); RExp 92 (1995) 530s (C.J. *Scalise*).

g850 -- *Casarella* Peter J., On the 'reading method' in [1993 Paul] ROREM's Pseudo-2Dionysius: Thom 59 (1995) 633-644.

g851 *Boland* Vivian, On naming God; the theological vision of the Ps.-Dionysius: MilltSt 35 (1995) 5-18.

g852 *Vives* Josep, 'Bonum est diffusivum sui'; el depassament cristià del neoplatonisme en els escrits areopagítics: → 41, ^FCOLOMER E., RCatT 29 (1994) 79-90; Eng. 91.

g853 ECKHART: *Corduan* Winfried, A hair's breadth from pantheism; Meister Eckhart's God-centered spirituality: JETS 37 (1994) 265-274.

g854 *Kovacs* George, The way to ultimate meaning in Meister Eckhart's mysticism.

g855 *Stachel* Günter, Meister Eckhart, `Vom edlen Menschen'; Übersetzung, Interpretation, Redaktionskritik: ZkT 117 (1995) 167-190: Eng. 191.

g856 *Vannier* Marie-Anne, Déconstruction de l'individualité ou assomption de la personne chez Eckhart ?: RHPhR 75 (1995) 399-418; Eng. 439.

g857 *Wackernagel* Wolfgang, Eckhart et son double; mythographie comparative d'un nom emblématique: RevSR 69 (1995) 216-226; Eng. 272.

g858 ERIUGENA east and west 1991/4, ^E**McGinn** B., *Otten* W. → 10,368: ^RChH 64 (1995) 263s (E.Ann *Matter*).

g859 *Beuchot* Maurice, La hermenéutica de Juan Escoto Eriúgena: AnáMnesis 5,2 (1995) 49-59.

g860 FERRER: **Cátedra García** P.M., Sermón, sociedad y literatura en la Edad Media; San Vicente Ferrer en Castilla (1141s). Valladolid 1994, Junta. 714 p. -- ^RCommunio (Sev) 28 (1995) 393-5 (M. *Sánchez*).

g861 FICINUS: *Buzzi* Franco, I 'motivi di credibilità' del cristianesimo nell'apologetica di Marcello Ficino (1433-1499) e Girolamo SAVONAROLA (1452-1498): S(cuola)C 123 (1995) 723-764.

g862 FIORE: *Cescon* Everaldo, Joaquim de Fiore, o escatologista da nova era: Teocomunicação 25 (1995) 627-635.

g863 **McGinn** Bernard, Apocalypticism in the Western tradition [4 art. on Joachim + 8] 1994 → 10,203*d*: ^RChH 64 (1995) 462-4 (D. *Bornstein*).

g864 FLODOARDUS: **Sot** Michel, Un historien et son église au Xe siècle, Flodoard de Reims 1993 → 9,14414; 30 fig.; F 260; 2-213-03184-3. -- ^RRHE 90 (1995) 136-140 (A.J. *Stoclet*).

g865 GERSON: **Grosse** Sven, Heilsungewissheit und Scrupulosität im späten Mittelalter; Studien zu Johannes Gerson und Gattungen der Frömmigkeitstheologie seiner Zeit: BHTh 85. Tü 1994, Mohr. ix-289 p. DM 158. -- ^RHeythJ 36 (1995) 354-6 (R. *Schniertshauer*).

g866 *Grosse* Sven, Existentielle Theologie in der vorreformatorischen Epoche am Beispiel Johannes Gersons; historische Überlegungen zum ökumenischen Disput: KuD 41 (1995) 50-111; Eng. 111.

g867 GROSSETESTE: ^EMcEvoy James, Robert Grosseteste; new perspectives on his thought and scholarship: I(nstr)P 27. Steenbrugge 1995, S. Pietresabdij. 438 p.; bibliog. 415-431. 2-503-50541-4.

g868 GULIELMUS A.: *Teske* Roland J., William of Auvergne *a*) and the Manichees; -- *b*) on the individuation of human souls: Traditio 48 (1993) 63-75 / 49 (1994) 77-93.

g869 HAUVILLA: **Wetherbee** Winthrop, Johannes de Hauvilla's Architrenius^{TE} (12th c.). C 1994, Univ. 288 p. £ 35. 0-521-40543-2. -- ^RE(xp)T 107 (1995s) 28 (Valerie *Edden*, welcoming also two other volumes of this new series of offbeat medieval Greek and Latin texts with English on facing pages).

g870 HILDEGARD: *Fox* Matthew, Creation spirituality; 300 years from Hildegard to Julian: *CreSp 11,3 (1995) 10-15.

g871 *Gössmann* Elisabeth, Zu de neuesten Ergebnissen der Hildegard-Forschung: ThRv 91 (1995) 195-215.

g872 **Lautenschläger** Gabriele, Hildegard von Bingen; die theologische Grundlegung ihrer Ethik und Spiritualität. Stu-Bad Cannstatt 1993, Frommann-Holzboog. 423 p. -- ^RT(rier)ThZ 104 (1995) 320 (H. *Weber*).

g873 HONCALA: **Fuente Adánez** Alfonso de la, Una exégesis para el siglo XVI; Antonio de Honcala (1484-1565) y su 'Comentario al Génesis': BtSalmEst 167. S 1994, Univ. Pontificia. 312 p. 84-7299-336-1. -- ^REstB 53 (1995) 402s (P. *Barrado*).

g874 HRABANUS: *Perrin* Michel, La composition de l'In honorem sanctae crucis de Raban Maur: possibilités et limites de l'explication de la structure de l'œuvre: RÉL 73 (1995) 199-212.

g875 ISIDORUS: **Cazier** Pierre, Isidore de Séville et la naissance de l'Espagne catholique: ThH 96, 1994 → 10,14419; 2-7010-1299-6: ^RComM(Sev) 28 (1995) 115-7 (M. *Sánchez*); MelSR 52 (1995) 183-5 (M. *Spanneut*); TTh 35 (1995) 282s (L. *Goosen*); VigChr 49 (1995) 413s (G.J.M. *Bartelink*).

g875* JONAS: ^E**Debreucq** Alain, Jonas d'Orléans (c.900; ^D1992, ^D*Rouche* M.), Le métier de roi (De institutione regia): SC 407. P 1995, Cerf. 304 p.; bibliog. 139-145. 2-204-05225-6

g876 JULIANA: **Baker** Denise Nowakowski, Julian of Norwich's Showings: from vision to book. Princeton 1994, Univ. 215 p. 0-691-03631-4. -- ^RET 106 (1994s) 378 (R. *Howe*).

g877 **Nuth** Joan M., Wisdom's daughter (Julian) 1991 → 9,16300: ^REThL 71 (1995) 243s (R. *Wielockx*).

g878 LANGTON: **Quinto** Riccardo, 'Doctor nominatissimus', Stefano Langton († 1228) e la tradizione delle sue opere [diss. (destinata a) Milano S.Cuore]: BGPTMA 19. Müns 1994, Aschendorff. xxxiv-326 p. DM 98. -- ^RCivCatt 146 (1995,3) 92s (A. *Di Maio*); StPat(av) 41 (1994) 708s (R. *Battocchio*).

g879 LULLIUS: *Bonner* Antoni, Possibles fonts musulmanes de les deu regles i qüestions de Ramon Llull: → 41, ^FCOLOMER E., RCatT 29 (1994) 93-98; Eng. 98 (p.99-107, *Llinarès* Armand, on Llull's early 'Doctrina pueril').

g880 **Perarnau i Espelt** Josep, El 'Llibre contra Anticrist' de Ramon Llull: Arxiu de Textos Catalans Antics 9 (1990) 7-182. -- ^RRCatT 30 (1995) 203-7 (D. *Escuder*).

g881 *a) Reinhardt* Klaus, Ramón Lull und die Bibel; -- *b*) *Euler* Walter A., De adventu Messiae; Ramón Lulls Beitrag zur christlich-jüdischen Messiaskontroverse; -- *c*) *Walter* Peter, Jacobus Faber STAPULENSIS als Editor des Raimundus Lullus dargestellt am Beispiel des 'Liber natalis pueri parvuli Christi Jesu': → 112, [F]LOHR C., Aristotelica et Lulliana 1995, 311-331 / 429-441 / 545-559.

g882 *a) Bonner* Antoni, Ramon Llull; relació, acció, combinatòria ii lògica moderna; -- *b) Gayà* Jordi, *Ascensio, virtus*; dos conceptos del contexto original del sistema luliano: (E)StLul 34 (Mallorca 1994) 51-74 / 3-49.

g883 LYRANUS: **Klepper** Deeana C., Nicholas of Lyra's 'Questio de adventu Christi' and the Franciscan encounter with Jewish tradition in the late Middle Ages: diss. Northwestern, [D]*Lerner* R. Evanston 1995. 322 p. 95-37457. -- DissA 56 (1995s) p. 2813.

g884 *Krey* Philip, Many readers but few followers; the fate of Nicholas of Lyra's 'Apocalypse commentary' in the hands of his late-medieval admirers: ChH 64 (1995) 185-201.

g885 OCKHAM: *Leppin* Volker, Mit der Freiheit des Evangeliums gegen den Papst; Wilhelm von Ockham als streitbarer Theologe: FrSZ 42 (1995) 397-406.

g886 *Leff* Gordon, Ockham, Ockhamismus, [T]*Leppin* Volker: → 772, TRE 25 (!995) 6-18.

g887 OLIVI: **Burr** David, Olivi's peaceable kingdom; a reading of the Apocalypse commentary 1993 → 9,5682: [R]M(dv)eH 22 (1995) 213-7 (R.K. *Emmerson*).

g888 *Packull* Werner, Olivi, Petrus J.: → 772, TRE 25 (1995) 239-242.

g889 PATRICIUS: [E]**Howlett** Daniel, The book of letters of Saint Patrick the bishop. Dublin 1994, Four Courts. 135 p. £ 17.50. 1-85128-136-8 [ThRv 91].

g890 PETRIĆI c. 1200: *Xaranauli* Ana, Die Bibel in den Kommentaren Ioane Petrićis; Georgica 19 (1996) 71-76.

g891 PICO DE MIRANDOLA: [E]**Viti** Paolo, Pico, POLIZIANO e l'umanesimo di fine quattrocento [mostra Biblioteca Medicea 1994]: Centro Studi Pichiani 2. F 1994, Olschki. 376 p. 88-222-4272-6.

g892 SACHSEN Ludolph von: [TE]**Greiner** Susanne, *Gisi* Martha, Das Leben Jesu Christi; ausgewählte Texte: Christliche Meister 47. Fr 1994, Johannes. DM 25. 3-89411-324-3 [ThRv 91,276].

g893 SAVONAROLA: *Buzzi* Franco, 'Religione' e 'cristianesimo' nel pensiero politico di MACHIAVELLI; un confronto con Savonarola: TeolBr 20 (1995) 331-358; Eng. 358.

g894 *Centi* Tito S., Invalida la scomunica di Savonarola ?: StCatt 39 (1995) 699-702.

g895 SCOTUS: *Giustiniani* Pasquale, Due cattedrali del pensiero; Tommaso d'AQUINO e Duns Scoto: RasT 36 (1995) 447-462.

g896 **Broadie** Alexander, The shadow of Scotus; philosophy and faith in pre-Reformation Scotland [< 1994 Gifford Lectures]. E 1995, Clark. viii-112 p. $ 34. 0-567-09734-X [< ThD 43,356: Clark's USA outlet is Box 605, Herndon VA 22070]

g897 SEDULIUS: *Bertola* Ermenegildo, Il commento paolino di Sedulio Scoto; un caso di pelagianismo nel secolo nono ?: Div 39 (1995) 41-54.

g898 **Springer** C.P.E., The manuscripts of Sedulius: a provisional handlist: *TAPS 85,5 (1995). xxii-244 p.; 2 fig. [RHE 91,9*].

g899 VILLANOVA; **Gerwing** Manfred, Vom Ende der Zeit; der Traktat des Arnald von Villanova über die Ankunft des Antichrist in der Auseinandersetzung zu Beginn des 14. Jahrhunderts; kath. Hab.-Diss. [D]*Knoch*. Bochum 1995. -- ThRv Beilage 92/2, iii.

Y4 **Luther**

g900 **Altmann** Walter, Lutero e libertação. São Leopoldo / São Paulo 1994, Sinodal/Atica 353 p. -- [R]PerTeol 27 (1995) 387-393 (P.A. *Maia*).

g901 *Asheim* Ivar, Luther's way of arguing in ethics: TT(og)K 66 (1995) Norwegian 159-176; Eng. 176.

g902 [E]**Bielfeldt** Dennis D., *Schwarzwäller* Klaus, Freiheit / Freedom as love in Martir Luther; 4th international congress, St.Paul MN 1993, I., 12 papers. NY 1993, Lang. 181 p $38. 3-631-47787-2 [RStR 22,75,76, R. *Kolb*: uneven].

g903 *Bienert* Wolfgang A., The patristic background of Luther's theology: LuthQ 9 (1995 263-279 [< [F]SCHNEEMELCHER W. 1989 [T]*Schweider* Carolyn].

g904 **Blaumeiser** Hubertus, Martin Luthers Kreuzestheologie, Schlüssel zu seiner Deutung von Mensch und Wirklichkeit (Oper.Pss. 1519-21 [Diss. Gregoriana 1993 → 9,16320] KkKSt 60. Pd 1995. 570 p. DM 98. 3-87088-809-2. ThRv 92,81.

g905 **Brecht** Martin, M. Luther, I. sein Weg; II. Ordnung; III. Erhaltung [1987] Studienausgabe. Stu 1994, Calwer. 1520 p.; 68 fig.; 52 pl. DM 98. 3-7668-3310-3. -[R]RevAg 36 (1995) 288s (I. de la *Viuda*).

g906 **Brendler** Gerhard, Martin Luther; theology and revolution [1983], [T]*Foster* Claude R.[J] 1991 → 7,g746 ... 9,16325: [R]ChH 64 (1995) 282s (H.J. *Hillerbrand*: the 1983 German got through communist censorship which favored MÜNTZER over Luther); S(cot)JTh 48 (1995) 537-541 (W.P. *Stephens*, also on BRECHT II).

g907 **Burandt** Christian B., Luthers Sicht der Geschichte auf Grund der Operationes in Psalmos 1519-1521; ev. Diss. [D]*Lohse*. Hamburg 1995. -- ThRv Beilage 92/2, ix.

g908 *Buzzi* Franco, Martin Luther (1483-1546), motivi di interesse e perplessità: Sc(uola)C 122 (1994) 263-288.

g909 **De Michelis Pintacuda** Fiorella, Lutero, Il servo arbitrio: Opere scelte 6. 1993 → 9.16327; 472 p. 88-7016-176-5: [R]Salesianum 57 (1995) 581s (M. *Müller*).

g910 *a) Drewery* Benjamin, Was Luther a heretic ? ; -- *b) Stupperich* Robert, Luther's *itic spiritualis*: → **5**, [F]ATKINSON, J., Bible, Reformation, Church: JSNT.s 105 (1995) 109-123 / 245-257.

g911 *a) Ebeling* Gerhard, Luthers Gebrauch der Wortfamilie 'Seelsorge'; -- *b) Wenger* Timothy J., Martin Luther's movement toward an apostolic self-awareness as reflected ir his early letters: LuJ 61 (1994) 7-44 / 71-92.

g912 **Edwards** Mark U.[J], Printing, propaganda, and Martin Luther. Berkeley 1994, Univ California. xiii-225. 0-520-08462-4 [RStR 22,76, R. *Kolb*: message conveyed largely ir Bible translation prefaces and margins]. -- [R]ChH 64 (1995) 479-481 (H.A. *Oberman*); JEH 46 (1995) 724-6 (D.V.N. *Bagchi*).

g913 **Gherardini** Brunero, Creatura Verbi; la Chiesa nella teologia di Martin Lutero. R 1994, Vivere In. 378 p. L[m] 30. -- [R]Sc(uola)C 123 (1995) 138-140 (F. *Buzzi*).

g914 *Gherardini* Brunero, Lutero nel Concilio di Trento: Div 39 (1995) 168-182.

g915 **Grane** Leif, Martinus noster; Luther in the German reform movement 1518-1521; *Veröff. Inst. Europ. Gesch 153. Mainz 1994, von Zabern. xii-326 p. DM 78. 3-8053-1652-6 [ThRv 92,81].

g916 **Guicharrousse** Hubert, Les musiques de Luther: histoire et Société 31. Genève 1995, Labor et Fides. 324 p. 2-8309-0747-7. -- [R]RHPhR 75 (1995) 242-4 (M. *Arnold*).

g917 **Hagen** Kenneth, Luther's approach to Scripture .. Gal 1993 → 8,6502 ... 10,5988: [R]CrSt 16 (1995) 648-650 (G.*Pani*); LuthQ 9 (1995) 191-9 (U.*Asendorf*, also on BAYER O.)

g918 *Hagen* Kenneth, It is all in the et cetera; Luther and the elliptical reference: Luther-Bulletin 3 (Kampen 1994) 57-67.

g919 *Hart* Ian, The teaching of Luther [and CALVIN] about ordinary works: EvQ 67 (1995) 35-53 [121-135] (195-309, ... of the Puritans).

g920 *Hasse* Hans-Peter, Die Lutherbiographie von Nikolaus SELNECKER: ArRefG 86 (1995) 91-122; Eng. 123.

g921 **Henkel** Annegret, Geistliche Erfahrung und Geistliche Übungen bei Ignatius von LOYOLA und Martin Luther; die ignatianischen Exercitien in ökumenischer Relevanz. Fra 1994, Lang. 402 p. -- ^RManresa 67 (1995) 293-6 (I. *Iglesias*).

g922 *Hoffmann* Fritz, Magister Martin Luther -- die Ursprünge seines Lehrens und Wirkens an der abendländischen Universität .. zu WHITE G. 1994 [→ 10,14449*: ThLZ 120 (1995) 611-6.

g923 **Hong Ji Hoon**, Luthers Auseinandersetzung mit dem täuferischen Taufverständnis: ev. Diss. ^D*zur Mühlen*. Bonn 1995. -- ThRv Beilage 92/2,vi.

g924 **Jordon** Sherry E., The patriarchs and matriarchs as saints in Luther's lectures on Genesis: diss. Yale, ^D*Lindbeck* G. NHv 1995. 367 p. 95-38687. -- D(iss)AI 56 (1995s) p. 367 [RStR 22.273 somewhat differently: 'Jordan' 'Shirley', 'Abraham and Sarah as saints', '^D*Wandel* L.'].

g925 **Köpf** Ulrich, Lateinisches Register zu Band 1-60: Luthers Werke 66/1. Weimar 1995, Böhlau. 635 p. DM 180. 3-7400-0171-2 [ThRv 91,276].

g926 ^E**Landkammer** Joachim, La libertà del cristiano. T 1994, La Rosa. -- ^RFilTeo 9 (1995) 181-3 (F. *Piro*).

g927 *Lienhard* M., Luther et le monachisme: FV 93,2 (1994) 9-28.

g928 **Lohse** Bernhard, Luthers Theologie in ihrer historischen Entwicklung und in ihrem systematischen Zusammenhang. Gö 1995, Vandenhoeck & R. 378 p. DM 78 pa. 3-525-52196-0; -7-8 [ThRv 92,81].

g929 **Maaser** Wolfgang, Luthers Wort- und Naturverständnis vor dem Hintergrund rhetorik-dialektischer Traditionen und die Konsequenzen für die ethische Urteilsbildung: Hab.-Diss. ^D*Frey* C. Bochum 1995. -- ThLZ 120 (1995) 1146.

g930 **McGoldrick** James E., Luther's Scottish connection 1989 → 6,k565 ... 8,m194: ^RJETS 38 (1995) 122s (E. *Schupbach*).

g931 *Mannermaa* Tuomo, Theosis as a subject of Finnish Luther research: *ProEc 4 (1995) 37-48.

g932 **Ngien** Dennis, The suffering of God according to Martin Luther's 'theologia crucis' [< diss. Toronto]: AmUSt 7/181. NY 1995, P. Lang. xii-289 p. $ 47. 0-8204-2582-6 [ThD 43,281].

g933 *a) Pani* Giancarlo, L'Expositio/Rom di AGOSTINO e la Röm/Vorlesung di M. Luther; - - *b) Agnoletti* Attilio, Considerazioni sull'umanesimo luterano tedesco cinquecentesco; la giudeofobia : → 119, ^FMARA M.Grazia = Aug(ustinianum)R 35 (1995) 885-906 / 907-917.

g934 *Ringleben* Joachim, Wort und Rechtfertigungsglaube; zur Horizontauffächerung einer Worttheologie in Luthers Disputation 'De fide': ZThK 92 (1995) 28-53.

g935 *Rogge* Joachim, LUTHERs Kirchenverständnis in seinen Spätschriften: TLZ 120 (1995) 1051-8.

g936 *Spinks* Bryan D., Luther's timely theology of unilateral baptism: LuthQ 9 (1995) 23-45.

g937 *Taylor* Stephen M., Sharing within the community of saints; a study of Luther's ecclesiology: AB(ap)Q 14 (1995) 260-9.

g938   *Wendland* E.R., Martin LUTHER, the father of confessional, functional-equivalence Bible translation: *NoTr 9,1s (1995) 16-36 (2) 47-60 [NTAb 40, p.404].

g939 **Wicks** Jared, Luther's reform; studies on conversion and the Church 1992 → 8,m208; 9,16348: ᴿBijdragen 56 (1995) 101-3 (T. *Bell*).

g940 *Yeago* David S., The bread of life; patristic Christology and evangelical soteriology in Martin Luther's sermons on John 6: StVlad 39 (1995s) 257-279.

g941 **Zachman** Randall C., The assurance of faith .. in Luther & CALVIN 1993 → 9,16349: ᴿA(ngl)ThR 77 (1995) 101s (J.A. *Carpenter*); TorJT 11 (1995) 285-7 (H. *McSorley*).

g942 **Zambruno** Elisabetta, La 'Theologia deutsch' [anon., ᴱLutero 1518] e la via per giungere a Dio; antropologia e simbolismo teologico: Scienze filosofiche 48, 1991 → 9,16350: ᴿEThL 71 (1995) 247s (J.E. *Vercruysse*).

Y4.3   Exegesis et controversia saeculi XVI

g943   **Allison** Gregg R., The Protestant doctrine of the perspicuity of Scripture; a reformulation on the basis of biblical teaching: diss. Trinity Evangelical Divinity School, ᴰ*Grudem* W., 1995. 601 p. 95-33040. -- D(iss)AI 56 (1995s) p. 2287.

g944 **Andrés** M., Historia de la mística de la Edad de Oro en España y América: BAC. M 1994, Católica. xix-490 p. -- ᴿArTGran 57 (1994) 372 (A. *Navas*).

g945 *a) Arend* Charles P., *Voelz* James, *al.*, The Lutheran Confessions as normative guides for reading Scripture; -- *b) Doterding* Paul E., The NT view of time and history: Con(cordia)J 21 (1995) 366-384 / 385-389.

g946 **Bagchi** David V.N., Luther's earliest opponents 1525: 1992 → 7,g503 ... 10,14450*: ᴿBS 152 (1995) 120s (S.R. *Spencer*: their arguments were convincing but only to those who shared their ground-rules).

g947 ᴱ**Birmelé** André, *Lienhard* Marc, La foi des Églises luthériennes; confessions [1530, 1537, 1577 .. , déjà séparément en français] et catéchismes [1529], ᵀ*Jundt* A. & P. 1991 → 7,g505; 8,m217: ᴿRTL 26 (1995) 100s (E. *Brito*).

g948 *Blickle* Peter, Reformation und kommunaler Geist; die Antwort der Theologen auf den Verfassungswandel im Spätmittelalter: HZ 261 (1995) 365-402.

g949 *Bodenmann* Reinhard, La Bible et l'art d'écrire des lettres; pratiques dans l'aire germanique du XVIᵉ siècle: BuHProt 141 (1995) 357-381; Eng. 382.

g950 *Bottigheimer* Ruth B., Publishing, print, and change in the image of Eve and the apple 1470-1570: ArRefG 86 (1995) 199-220; dt.220; 13 fig.

g951 ᴱ**Brady** Thomas A.ᴶ, *Oberman* Heiko A., *Tracy* James D., Handbook of European history, 1400-1600; Late Middle Ages, Renaissance and Reformation, I: Structures and assertions 1994 → 10,14451: ᴿRHE 90 (1995) 608s (J.-F. *Gilmont*).

g952 ᴱ**Bray** Gerald, Documents of the English reformation. Mp/.. 1994, Fortress / J. Clarke. 674 p. £ 20. 0-8006-2907-8 / 0-2276-7930-X [ThD 43,63]. -- ᴿET 106 (1994s) 281s (P.N. *Brooks*).

ğ953 ᴱ**Campi** Emidio, Protestantesimo nei secoli; fonti e documenti 1. Cinquecento e seicento 1991 → 7,g508 ... 10,14454: ᴿFilTeo 8 (1994) 519s (F. *Ferrario*).

g954 **Caponetto** Salvatore, La Riforma protestante nell'Italia del Cinquecento 1992 → 8,m225; 9,16360: ᴿProtest(antesimo) 50 (1995) 158s (Laura *Ronchi de Michelis*).

g955 **Christin** Olivier, Les Réformes; Luther, Calvin et les Protestants: Découvertes 237. P 1995, Gallimard. 160 p.; 151 fig. 2-07-053228-3. -- ᴿÉTRel 70 (1995) 600s (J. *Cottin*: documentation visuelle); Études 383 (1995) 132 (P. *Lécrivain*, bref, admirant, critique).

g956 **Darowski** Roman, Filozofia w szkołach jezuickich w Polsce w XVI wieku. Kraków 1994, Wydział filozoficzny T.J. 450 p. -- ᴿBobolanum 6 (1995) 184-190 (F. *Sieg, P*).

g957 *David* Zdenek V., The strange fate of Czech Utraquism; the second century, 1517-1621: JEH 46 (1995) 641-668.

g958 **Denis** P., Il Cristo conteso; le rappresentazioni dell'Uomo-Dio al tempo delle Riforme 1500-1565: Gesù dopo Gesù. Brescia 1994, Morcelliana. 215 p. Lᵐ 25. -- ᴿAsprenas 42 (1995) 125s (P. *Pifano*).

g959 **Díez** Karlheinz, 'Ecclesia -- non est civitas platonica'; Martin Luthers Anfrage an die 'Sichtbarkeit' der Kirche und Antworten katholischer Kontroverstheologen des 16. Jahrhunderts: kath. Hab.Diss. Mainz 1994. -- ThRv Beilage 92/2, iv.

g960 **Duffy** Eamon, The stripping of the altars 1992 → 8.m232 ... 10,14459: ᴿChH 64 (1995) 118s (Fredrica H. *Thompsett*); JAAR 63 (1995) 149-151 (John *Dillenberger*); RHE 90 (1995) 167-171 (C. *Fitzsimons*); SewaneeT 38 (1994s) 182-8 (D.J. *Grieser*); S(cot)JTh 48 (1995) 137s (R.N. *Swanson*).

g961 *Duffy* Eamon, The Reformation revisited {first in a series entitled 'Prejudice unmasked '): Tablet 249 (1995) 280-2.

g962 **Ehrstine** Glenn E., From iconoclasm to iconography; Reformation drama in sixteenth-century Bern: diss. Texas, ᴰPrice D. Austin 1995. 364 p. 96-03835. -- DissA 56 (1995s) p. 3983.

g963 **Elwood** Christopher L., The body broken; the Calvinist doctrine of the Eucharist and the symbolization of power in France, 1530-1570; diss. Harvard. -- HThR 88 (1995) 521s.

g964 *Esch* Arnold, Rom in der Renaissance: seine Quellenlage als methodisches Problem: HZ 261 (1995) 337-364.

g965 **Evans** G. R., Problems of authority in the Reformation debates 1992 → 8.234 ... 10,14460: ᴿJRel 75 (1995) 278s (D.V.N. *Bagchi*); ProEccl 4 (1995) 116-9 (C.S. *Farmer*: 'never' omitted p. 117, corrected p.380).

g966 **Freiberg** Jack, The Lateran in 1600; Christian concord in counter-reformation Rome. C 1995, Univ. $ 75. 0-521-46057-3 [ThD 43,168].

g967 *García Oro* José, Los reyes y los libros; la política libraria de la Corona en el Siglo de Oro (1475-1598): VyV 53 (1995) 7-141.

g968 **Garstein** O., Rome and the Counter-Reformation in Scandinavia [1. 1963; 2. 1980] 3. Jesuit educational strategy 1553-1622: 1992 → 8,m236: ᴿCrSt 16 (1995) 196-8 (R. *Burigana*).

g969 **Garstein** Oskar, Rome and the counter-reformation in Scandinavia [4 (last)]; the age of Gustavus Adolphus and Queen Christina of Sweden 1622-1656: 1992 → 9,16374, Brill. xviii-833 p.

g970 **Gentili** M., *Regazzoni* M., La spiritualità della riforma cattolica; la spiritualità italiana dal 1500 al 1650. Bo 1993, Dehoniane. 414 p. -- ᴿLaur 36 (1995) 511s (R. *Cuvato*).

g971 **Gerl-Falkovitz** Hanna-Barbara, Die zweite Schöpfung der Welt; Sprache, Bekenntnis, Anthropologie in der Renaissance. Mainz 1994, Grünewald. 240 p. DM 56. 3-7867-1782-6 [ThRv 91,296].

g972 *Gilmont* Jean-François, La Réforme et le livre 1990 → 6,411* ... 8,m239: ᴿSalesianum 57 (1995) 364s (F. *Meyer*).

g973 **Goertz** Hans-Jürgen, Antiklerikalismus und Reformation; sozialgeschichtliche Untersuchungen. Gö 1995, Vandenhoeck & R. 140 p. DM 22.80. -- ᴿLuthQ 9 (1995) 463-6 (C. *Lindberg*).

g974 ^E**Grell** Ole P., The Scandinavian Reformation: from evangelical movement to institutionalisation of religion. C 1994. Univ. 218 p. £ 30. 9-521-44162-5. -- ^RET 106 (1994s) 282 (Í. *Chetwynd*).

g975 **Haigh** Christopher, English Reformations; religion, politics, and society under the Tudors. Ox 1993, Clarendon. 367 p. $ 55; pa. $ 20. -- ^RJRel 75 (1995) 277 (C.M. *Gray*).

g976 **Harrington** Joel F., Reordering marriage and society in Reformation Germany. C 1995, Univ. xv-315 p. $ 50. 0-521-40483-8 [ThD 44,68].

g977 *a) Heimann* Heinz-Dieter, Antichristvorstellungen im Wandel der mittelalterlichen Gesellschaft; zum Umgang mit einer Angst- und Hoffnungssignatur zwischen theologischer Formalisierung und beginnender politischer Propaganda; -- *b) Hillerbrand* Hans J., Von Polemik zur Verflachung; zur Problematik des Antichrist-Mythos in Reformation und Gegenreformation: ZRGG 47 (1995) 99-113 / 114; → 7666, *Ley* M., *al.*

g978 ^E**Hunter** Michael, *Wootton* David, Atheism from the Reformation to the Enlightenment 1992; $ 60: ^RChH 64 (1995) 127-9 (R.G. *Clouse*); SR 24 (1995) 115-7 (R.T. *McCutcheon*).

g979 ^E**Johnson** W.S., *Leith* J.H., Reformed reader, a sourcebook in Christian theology, 1. Classical beginnings, 1519-1799: 1993: → 9,16384: ^RRExp 92 (1995) 122s (W.L. *Hendricks*).

g980 **Jones** Martin D.W., The Counter Reformation; religion and society in early modern Europe: Topics in History. C 1995, Univ. 171 p. $ 16 pa. 0-421-43993-0 [ThD 44,72].
Kuri Sami, Monumenta Proximi Orientis III. Palestine -- Liban -- Syrie -- Mésopotamie (1583-1623) 1994 → a936 supra.

g982 **Liechty** Daniel, Sabbatarianism 1993 → 10,14474: ^RA(ndr)USS 33 (1995) 307s (K.A. *Strand*).

g983 *a) Lienhard* Marc, La Réforme de Luther et l'Europe; succès ou échec ?; -- *b) Delafosse* Marcel, Événement et images au temps des guerres de religion; l'exemple de La Rochelle: RHPhR 75 (1995) 113-121 / 123-9; Eng. 150s.

g984 *Lindberg* Carter, Modern *fanatici* and the Lutheran Confessions: ConcordiaTQ 59 (1995) 191-217 [the word there means 'enthusiastic', itself also a danger today].

g985 *Lobato* Abelardo, Presencia e influjo de Santo Tomás de AQUINO en la evangelización de América : DoC(om) 46 (1993) 3-39.

g986 **Louthan** Howard, Johannis Crato and the Austrian Habsburgs; reforming a counter-reform court: StRefT 2/3. Princeton 1994. Univ. 44 p.

g987 **McGinness** Frederick J., Right thinking and sacred oratory in counter-reformation Rome. Princeton 1995, Univ. xii-337 p. $ 49.50. 0-691-0342-5 [ThD 43,177].

g988 **McGrath** Alister E., Il pensiero della Riforma^T 1991 → 7,g530 ... 10,14477: ^RProtest(antesimomo) 50 (1995) 86s (S. *Manna*).

g989 **Maiello** Francesco, Storia del calendario; la misurazione del tempo, 1450-1800. T 1994, Einaudi. 235 p.; 8 fig. -- ^RR(ic)SS(oc)R 47 (1995) 258-261 (G. *Cassiani*).

g990 *Maillard* J.F., Apocryphes et pseudépigraphes; le goût des faux au cœur de l'humanisme de la Renaissance ? BuSAntF (1995) 93-106.

g991 **Mandziuk** Józef, ^P History of the Catholic Church in Silesia; times of the Protestant Reformation, the Catholic reform, and the counter-reformation 1520-1742, vol. 2. Wsz 1995, Akad. Teol. Katolickiej. 264 p.; bibliog. 229-243. 83-7072-056-0.

g992 **Mannu** Maria, I Francescani sulle orme di Cristoforo Colombo. R 1992. -- ^RSMSR 59 (1993) 166-175 (Anna *Unali*).

g993 *Markschies* Christoph, Die eine Reformation und die vielen Reformen: ZKG 106 (1995) 70-97.

g994 **Marshall** Peter, The Catholic priesthood and the English Reformation. Ox 1994, Clarendon. vii-271 p. $ 55. 0-19-820448-5. -- ᴿChH 64 (1995) 286s (J.J. *LaRocca* gives a rather subtle alternative to the 'anticlericalism' of the populace); *TBR 8,1 (1995s) 43 (V.H.H. *Green*).

g995 *Martín Ortega* Mariano, 450 años del Concilio de Trento (1545-1563) : Rel(y)Cult 41 (1995) 245-279.

g996 **Metzler** Josef, America pontificia primi saeculi evangelizationis 1493-1592, documenta. Vaticano 1991. 2 vol. -- ᴿCrSt 16 (1995) 521-55i; Eng. 552 (Bruna *Bocchini Camaiani*).

g997 *Mignolo* Walter, The darker side of the Renaissance; literacy, territoriality, and colonization. AA 1995, Univ. Michigan. 426 p -- ᴿJHispLat 3,4 (1995s) 79-84 (E. *Mendieta*).

g998 **Mittermeier** Otto, Evangelische Ordination im 16. Jahrhundert; eine liturgiegeschichtliche und liturgietheologische Untersuchung zu Ordination und kirchlichem Amt [Diss.]: MüThSt 11/50. St. Ottilien 1994, EOS. 269 p. 3-88096-250-2. -- ᴿForKT 11 (1995) 227-230 (R. *Bäumer*).

g999 *Navas Gutiérrez* Antonio M., Trento; algunas lecciones de un gran concilio: Proyecciòn 42 (1995) 259-271.

k000 **O'Malley** John W., The first Jesuits. CM 1993, Harvard Univ. viii-457 p.; 5 fig. $ 35. -- ᴿJRel 75 (1995) 122s (W.V. *Hudon*: brilliant; disproves 'dominated by militaristic outlook', 'founded for demolition of Protestant heresy', 'defensive of and controlled by the Papacy').

k001 **Orabona** Luciano, Chiesa e società moderna; istituzioni figure problemi [1/i. Riforma cattolica, il 'buon pastore' e BELLARMINO, p. 9-39]. R/N 1995. LSR. 153 p. + Orabona bibliog.

k002 **Packull** Werner O., Rereading Anabaptist beginnings. Winnipeg 1991, Mennonite Bible College. 78 p. -- ᴿ(NES)ThRev 16 (1995) 135s (J. *Derksen*).

k003 **Pearse** Michael T., Between known men and visible saints; a study in sixteenth century English dissent. Cranbury NJ 1994, Assoc.Univ. 280 p. £ 32.50. -- ᴿ*TBR 8,1 (1995s).

k004 ᴱ**Pettegree** Andrew, The early Reformation in Europe. C 1994, Univ. 250 p. $ 16. —- ᴿLuthQ 9 (1995) 456-6 (W.R. *Russell*: to the question 'why more impact in some parts than others ?'); Zwingliana 2 (1995) 136-8 (A.C. *Gow*).

k005 *Pozo* Cándido, Repercusiones del descubrimiento de América en las Universidades de Salamanca y Alcalá: ATG(ran) 58 (1995) 9-22.

k006 **Raitt** Jill, The [Lutheran-Calvinist] Colloquy of Montbéliard; religion and politics in the sixteenth century 1993 → 9,16414; 10,14487* [JETS 39,41s, S. *Clark*]: ᴿJRel 75 (1995) 121s (D.E. *Tamburello*: superb).

k007 **Roper** Lyndal, The holy household; women and morals in Reformation Augsburg: StSocHist. Ox 1989, Clarendon. ix-296 p. 0-19-821769-2. -- ᴿAKuG 77 (1995) 231s (A. *Classen*).

k008 **Rummel** Erika, The humanist-scholastic debate in the Renaissance and Reformation: HistSt 120. CM 1995, Harvard Univ. 249 p. $ 45. 0-674-42250-3 [ThD 43,85].

k009 ᴱ**Scribner** R., *al.*, The Reformation in national context. C 1994, Univ. 236 p. £ 30; pa. £ 11. 0-521-40155-0; -960-8. -- ᴿET 106 (1994s) 152 (P.N. *Brooks*).

k010 **Self** Charles E., The tragedy of Belgian Protestantism; subversion and survival: diss. California. Santa Cruz 1995. 423 p. 95-30096. -- D(iss)AI 56 (1995s) p. 1492.

k011 **Shuger** Debra K., The Renaissance Bible; scholarship, sacrifice, and subjectivity: New Historicism. Berkeley 1994, Univ. California. xv-197 p. $ 40. 0-520-08480-2. -- ᴿCLIT 44 (1994s) 227-230 (Julienne H. *Emprie*).

k012 *Sommer* Wolfgang, Die Stellung lutherischer Hofprediger im Herausbildungsprozess frühmoderner Staatlichkeit und Gesellschaft: ZKG 106 (1995) 313-328.

k013 **Sommerville** C.John, The secularization of early modern England; from religious culture to religious faith 1992 → 8,m280; 9,16425: ᴿChH 64 (1995) 123-5 (K.L. *Parker*).

k014 **Strehle** Stephen, The Catholic roots of the Protestant gospel; encounter between the Middle Ages and the Reformation: StHCT 60. Lei 1995, Brill. xii-248 p. -- ᴿRThom 95 (1995) 358s (G. *Emery*).

k015 *Strickland* Ernest, The English Reformers' teaching on Scripture: Churchman 107 (1993) 38-53.

k016 **Sullivan** Carl, Dismembered rhetoric; English Recusant writing, 1580 to 1603 [... CAMPION, SOUTHWELL]. Cranbury NJ 1995, F. Dickinson Univ. 184 p. $ 37.50. 0-8386-3577-6 [ThD 43,291].

k017 *Thompson* John L., 'So ridiculous a sign'; men, women, and the lessons of circumcision in sixteenth-century exegesis: AR(ef)G 86 (1995) 236-256; deutsch 256.

k018 **Tolley** Bruce, Pastors and parishioners in Württemberg during the late Reformation, 1581-1621. Stanford 1995, Univ. xii-198 p. $ 39.50. 0-8047-1681-1 [ThD 43.92].

k019 **Tourn** Giorgio, I Protestanti, una rivoluzione, I. Dalle origini a Calvino (1517-1564). T 1993, Claudiana. 400 p.; 89 fig. Lᵐ 39. -- ᴿCivCatt 146 (1995,1) 518s (S. *Mazzolini*); StPat(av) 41 (1994) 709s (L. *Sartori*).

k020 **Trueman** Carl R., Luther's legacy; salvation and English Reformers 1525-1556. Ox 1994, Clarendon. xii-308 p. £ 35. 0-19-826352-X. -- ᴿJEH 46 (1995) 567s (D. *MacCulloch*).

k021 **Venard** Marc, Réforme protestante, réforme catholique dans la province d'Avignon, XVIᵉ siècle: HistRelFrance 1. P 1993, Cerf. 1281 p. -- ᴿMélSR 52 (1995) 193-6 (G. *Mathon*).

k022 ᴱ**Venard** Marc, De la réforme à la Réformation (1450-1530): Histoire du christianisme [8. 1992 → 9,16431s] -- 7. P 1994, Desclée. 926 p. 2-7189-0624-3. -- ᴿÉTRel 70 (1995) 451s (H. *Bost*).

k023 *Wagner* Christine, Le profil sociologique et théologique des Protestants dénoncés à l'Inquisition de Tolède au XVIᵉ siècle : RHPhR 75 (1995) 289-308; Eng. 384.

k024 **Wandel** Lee P., Voracious idols and violent hands: iconoclasm in Reformation Zurich, Strasbourg and Basel. C 1995, Univ. 205 p. £ 30. 0-521-47222-9. -- ᴿET 106 (1994s) 378 (Karin *Maag*).

k025 **Weir** David A., The origins of the federal theology in sixteenth-century Reformation thought 1990 → 6,k643 ... 9,16435: ᴿSBET 12 (1994) 55-57 (J.L. *Duncan*).

k026 **White** Peter, Predestination, policy and polemic [against 1987 N. TYACKE claim of how England's installed Calvinism was ousted by Arminianism after 1600] 1992 → 9,16437; 10,14496: ᴿS(cot)JTh 48 (1995) 523-5 (B.D. *Spinks*).

k027 **Willis-Watkins** David, The Second Commandment and Church reform; the colloquy of St. Germain-en-Laye, 1562. StRefT 2/2. Princeton 1994, Univ. 80 p.

k028 **Wilson** N.G., From Byzantium to Italy; Greek studies in the Italian renaissance. Baltimore 1993, Johns Hopkins Univ. xi-200 p. $ 50. -- [R]*JEarlyC 3 (1995) 509s (M. *Vessey*).

k029 *Wright* David F., Sixteenth-century reformed perspectives on the minority church: [R]S(cot)JTh 48 (1995) 469-488.

k030 *Zimmermann* Gunter, Gottesbund und Gesetz in der Westminster Confession [1647]: ZKG 106 (1995) 179-199.

Y4.4 Periti aetatis reformatoriae

k031 ANDREWES: **Lossky** Nicholas, Lancelot Andrewes the preacher (1555-1626); the origins of the mystical theology of the Church of England, [T]*Louth* A., 1991 → 8,m296: [R]C{oncordia)TQ 59 (1995) 137-9 (C.A. *MacKenzie*); StVlad 39 (1995s) 305-312 (C. *Lock*: T.S. ELIOT took from him).

k032 ARGULA: **Matheson** Peter, Argula von Grumbach [c.1520], a woman's voice in the Reformation. E 1995, Clark. 212 p. £ 17. 0-567-09707-2. -- [R]E(xp)T 107 (1995s) 186s (Penny *Roberts*).

k033 BARNES: *Trueman* Carl R., 'The Saxons be sore on the affirmative' [from letter to imprisoned English Reformer J. FRITH from TYNDALE fearing for English Protestant unity if an English Reformer were to compose a tract on the Eucharist which upset the Lutherans]; Robert Barnes [Lutheran with Reformed leanings] on the Lord's Supper : → **5**, [F]ATKINSON, J., Bible, Reformation, Church: JSNT.s 105 (1995) 290-307.

k034 DE BILLY: **Backus** Ilon, La Patristique et les guerres de religion en France .. de Billy 1993 → 9,16445; 10,14501*: [R]EThL 71 (1995) 237-9 (J. *Verheyden*); JThS 46 (1995) 390-3 (B. *Hall*); RTPh 127 (1995) 303s (M. *Engammare*).

k035 BRUNO 1548-1600: **Drewermann** Eugenio, [Giordano] Bruno o El espejo del infinito, [T]*Gancho* Claudio. Barc 1995, Herder. 363 p. -- [R]Lum(Vr) 44 (1995) 525s (U. *Gil Ortega*).

k036 BUCER: **Greschat** Martin, Martin Bucer, ein Reformator und seine Zeit 1990 → 7,g557 ... 10,14502: [R]C(alvin)TJ 29 (1994) 228-231 (J.R. *Payton*).

k037 *Burnett* Amy N., Confirmation and Christian fellowship; Martin Bucer on commitment to the Church: ChH 64 (1995) 202-217.

k038 [E]**Krieger** Christian, *Lienhard* Marc, Martin Bucer and sixteenth-century Europe. 1991/3 → 9,462: [R]ÉTRel 70 (1995) 131s (Marianne *Carbonnier-Burkard*).

k039 [E]**Wright** D.F., Martin Bucer, reforming Church and community 1994 → 10,410: [R]JThS 46 (1995) 769s (J.C. *MacClelland*); Zwingliana 22 (1995) 152-7 (A. *Gäumann*).

k040 BUDÉ: [TE]**La Garanderie** M. de, *Penham* D.F., Guillaume Budé, Le passage de l'hellénisme au christianisme [lat.1535]. P 1993, BLettres. 294 p. -- [R]Études 382 (1995) 281 (M. *Fédou*).

k041 BUGENHAGEN: *Gummelt* Volker, Bugenhagens Handschrift von KARLSTADTs Jeremiavorlesung aus dem Jahre 1522: AR(ef)G 86 (1995) 56-66; Eng. 66.

k042 **Kötter** Ralf, Johannes Bugenhagens Rechtfertigungslehre 1994 → 10,14508: [R]RHPhR 75 (1995) 246s (M. *Arnold*).

k043 BULLINGER: **McCoy** Charles S., *Baker* J. Wayne, Fountainhead of federalism 1991
→ 7,g561 ... 10,14509: ᴿJETS 37 (1994) 451s (D.W. *Hall*); 38 (1995) 124-6 (M.I. *Klauber*).

k044 CAJETANUS: **Morerod** Charles, Cajetan et Luther en 1518; édition, traduction et
commentaire des opuscules d'Augsbourg de Cajetan: CahOec 26. FrS 1994, Univ. 424 p.;
p. 425-676. Fs 95. 2-8271-0686-8 [TR 91,276]. -- ᴿETRel 70 (1995) 598s (H. *Bost*:
précision intellectuelle).

----

k045 CALVIN: **Butin** Philip W., Revelation, redemption and response; Calvin's trinitarian
understanding of the divine-human relationship. NY 1995, Oxford-UP. 232 p. £ 30. 0-19-
508600-7. -- ᴿE(xp)T 107 (1995s) 58 (J. *Thompson*: anticipated BARTH & RAHNER, but
does not support current church/worship/society paradigms); RStR 21 (1995) 245s (D.K.
McKim).

k046 *Budé* J., *Joinviller* C., notes of Calvin's 1561 lectures on Daniel I. GR/Carlisle 1993,
Eerdman/Paternoster. xii-300 p. 0-85364-573-6. -- ᴿThLZ 120 (1995) 541 (Irene *Dingel*).

k047 **Dowey** Edward A.ᴶ, The knowledge of God in Calvin's theology. GR 1994, Eerdmans.
283 p.

k048   **Duke** Alastair, *al,*, Calvinism in Europe, 1540-1610; a collection of documents.
Manchester 1992, Univ. ix-246 p. $ 60; pa. $ 25. -- ᴿChH 64 (1995) 675s (W.F. *Graham*:
makes a useful triad with his own and R. MENTZER's).

k049 *Engammare* M., Calvin connaissait-il la Bible ? Les citations de l'Ecriture dans ses
sermons sur la Genèse: BSHPF 141 (1995) 163-184; deutsch 184: trifles easily explainable
[RHE 90 (1995) 259*].

k050 **Gallars** Nicolas Des, [ᴱ**Gounelle** Jean-François], Jean Calvin, Défense de Guillaume
FAREL et de ses collègues [devant tribunal Réformé c. 1542 contre les calomnies de Pierre
CAROLI]: ÉtHPR 73. P 1994, PUF. 148 p. F 198. 2-13-045769-X.-- ᴿÉTRel 70 (1995)
134s (H. *Bost*); RTPh 127 (1995) 301s (P.-Y. *Ruff*).

k051 **Gerrish** Brian A., Grace and gratitude; the Eucharistic theology of John Calvin 1993
→ 9,16457*: ᴿBS 152 (1995) 231s (S.R. *Spencer*); JRel 75 (1995) 119-121 (R.A. *Muller*);
RefTR 54 (1995) 87s (K.J. *Cable*).

k052 **Greef** Wulfert de, The writings of John Calvin, an introductory guide [1988], ᵀ. /GR
1993, Apollos/Baker. 254 p. £ 15. -- ᴿET 106 (1994s) 90 (A. *McGrath*).

k053 *a) Hesselink* John, John Calvin on the Law and Christian freedom: -- *b) Taylor* Robert,
Ricci Ronald, Three biblical models of liberty and some representative laws; -- *c) Pierard*
Richard V., Natural law or God's law ? a historian's perspective: → 127, MEYER B. mem.,
ExAu 11 ('Biblical law and liberty' 1995) 77-89 / 111-127 / 129-144.

k054 **Hesselink** I. John, Calvin's concept of the Law; Princeton ThMg, 1992 → 9,16458;
10,14514: ᴿChH 64 (1995) 667s (W.Fred *Graham: simpatico* i.e. 'sympathetic').

k055 **Holtrop** Philip C., The BOLSEC controversy on predestination, 1. Theological currents,
the setting and mood, and the trial itself. Lewiston NY, Mellen. xxviii-1033 p. 0-7734-
9248-8. -- ᴿC(alvin)TJ 29 (1994) 581-9 (R.A. *Muller*); S(co)BET 13 (1995) 85-87 (C.R.
Trueman).

k056 **Jones** Serene, Calvin and the rhetoric of piety: Columba series in Reformed theology.
LVL 1995, W-Knox. ix-238 p. $ 18. 0-664-22070-3 [*TBR 9/1,25, M. *Elliott*]

k057 *Kayayan* Éric, Accommodation, incarnation et sacrement dans l'Institution de la réligion chrétienne de Jean Calvin; l'utilisation de métaphores et de similitudes: RHPhR 75 (1995) 273-287: Eng.384.

k058 **Kelly** Douglas F., Emergence of liberty ... Calvin 1992 → 8,m333: [R]S(cot)BET 12 (1994) 58s (C. *Campbell-Jack*).

k059 **Kingdon** Robert M., Adultery and divorce in Calvin's Geneva. CM 1995, Harvard Univ. ix-214 p. $ 40. 0-674-00520-1 [ThD 43,72: some death penalties].

k060 **McGrath** Alister E., Johann Calvin, eine Biographie [1990 → 6,k666 ... 10,14516], [T]*Burkhardt* Gabriele. 1991. -- [R]Zwingliana 21 (1994) 163-6 (E. *Saxer*).

k061 *Muller* Richard A., Calvin and the 'Calvinists'; assessing continuities and discontinuities between the Reformation and orthodoxy: C(alvin)TJ 30 (1995) 345-375.

k062 *Naphy* William G., Calvin's letters; reflections on their usefulness in studying Genevan history: ArRefG 86 (1995) 67-89; dt. 90.

k063 [E]**Neuser** Wilhelm H., Calvinus Sacrae Scriptor professor .. as confessor 1990/4 → 10,379: [R]ET 106 (1994s) 312 (Karin *Maag*); ÉTRel 70 (1995) 133s (H. *Bost*); JETS 38 (1995) 456s (M.I. *Klauber*); JThS 46 (1995) 770s (T.H.L. *Parker*).

k064 [F]NEUSER Wilhelm, Calvin, Erbe und Auftrag, [E]**Spijker** Willem van 't 1991 → 7,110a: [R]Zwingliana 21 (1994) 172-4 (E. *Saxer*).

k065 **Parker** T.H.L., Calvin's preaching 1992 → 8,m329 ... 10,14520: [R]E(cu)R 47 (1995) 505-8 (Jill *Schaeffer*).

k066 **Parker** T.H.L., Calvin; an introduction to his thought: OutstCT. L 1995, Chapman. 192 p. £ 15; pa. £ 10. 0-225-66575-1: -43-3 [Westminster/Knox 0-664-25602-3: RStR 22,334, R.W. *Holder*]. -- [R]E(xp)T 107 (1995s) 156 (Karin *Maag*).

k067 **Puckett** David L., [Judaism-related tensions in] John Calvin's exegesis of the Old Testament: ColumbiaRef. LVL 1995. W-Knox. vii-179 p. $ 17. 0-664-22044-4 [OTA 19, p.148]. -- [R]E(xp)T 107 (1995s) 117s (R.P. *Carroll*).

k068 *Riggs* John W., Emerging ecclesiology in Calvin's baptismal thought, 1536-1543: ChH 64 (1995) 29-43.

k069 **Schreiner** Susan E., The theater of his glory 1991 → 8,m331; 9,16469: [R]JETS 38 (1995) 123s (M.I. *Klauber*).

k070 [E]**Schreiner** Thomas R., **Ware** Bruce A., The grace of God, the bondage of the will, 1. Biblical and practical perspectives on Calvinism; 2. Historical and theological perspectives .. [21 art.] GR 1995, Baker. 521 p. $ 17 each. 0-8010-2002-6; -3-4 [NTAb 40, p.370; ThD 43,269].

k071 **Summa** Gerd, Geistliche Unterscheidung bei Johannes Calvin: SSST 7. Wü 1992, Echter. xi-266 p. DM 42. 3-429-01468-9. -- [R]JEH 46 (1995) 550s (P. *Rousseau*).

k072 **Thompson** John L., John Calvin and the daughters of Sarah ... : THR 159, 1992 → 9,16471; 10,14523: [R]JEH 46 (1995) 172s (R. *Bauckham*); P(rinc)SB 16 (1995) 90-92 (P.D. *Miller*).

k073 *Thorson* Stephen, Tensions in Calvin's view of faith; unexamined assumptions in R. T. KENDALL's Calvin and English Calvinism to 1649: JETS 37 (1994) 413-424.

k074 *Tonkin* J., The Calvin enigma revisited: JRelH 18 (1994) 219-... [< ZIT 95,p.168]

k075 *Westhead* Nigel, Adoption in the thought of John Calvin: S(co)BET 13 (1995) 102-115.

k076 **Zillenbiller** Anette, Die Einheit der katholischen Kirche; Calvins CYPRIANrezeption 1993 → 10,14523*: [R]JRel 75 (1995) 421-423 (Barbara *Pitkin*).

----

k077 CANO: **Tapia** Joaquín, Iglesia y teología en Melchior Cano 1989 → 6,k678: ᴿMélSR 52 (1995) 345s (J.-C. *Matthys*).

k078 CHEMNITZ Martin, Loci theologici, ᵀ*Preus* Jacob A.O. St. Louis 1989, Concordia. -- ᴿC(oncordia)TQ 59 (Fort Wayne 195) 125-8 (R. *Preus*).

k079 CISNEROS: **García Oro** José, El Cardenal Cisneros, vida y empresas 1992s → 9,14657; 10, 14526: ᴿBLE 96 (1995) 74s (J. *Darrabat*); RHE 90 (1995) 175-181 (G.M. *Columbás*).

k080 COLUMBUS: *Avalos* Hector Ignacio, The biblical sources of Columbus's Libro de las profecías: Traditio 49 (1994) 331-5 [RHE 90 (1995) 260*].

k081 ᵀ**Melczer** William, Christopher Columbus, Libro delle profezie. Palermo 1992, Novecento. 367 p. Lᵐ 50. -- ᴿCithara 33,1 (1993) 38 (J. *Mulryan*).

k082 CRANMER: *Ayres* Paul, Destroying the monasteries. where was Thomas Cranmer during this unscrupulous chapter: Christian History 14,4 ('Cranmer and the English Reformation' 1995) 20s.

k083 *a) Galli* Marc, Courage when it counted; Thomas Cranmer was the most cautious, even indecisive, of reformers -- until his final hour; -- *b) Loades* David, Why Queen Mary was 'bloody' and why her persecution of Protestants failed; -- *c) Martin* Dennis, Catholic counterpoint: ChrHist 14,48 (1995) 8-15 / 16-19 / 28-30.

k084 *Jeanes* Gordon, A Reformation treatise on the Sacraments: JThS 46 (1995) 149-190.

k085 CUEVAS: *Jericó Bermejo* Ignacio, Fides christiana a Deo revelata et ab Ecclesia proposita; la enseñanza de Domingo de Cuevas en 1551: AVal 21 (1995) 1-50 (in 1994).

-----

k086 ERASMUS: **Asso** C., La teologia e la grammatica; la controversia tra Erasmo ed Edward LEE: StT'500, 4. F 1993, Olschki. 262 p. -- ᴿCrSt 16 (1995) 650s (S. *Giombi*).

k087 **Dickens** A.G., *Jones* Whitney R.D., Erasmus the reformer. L 1994, Methuen. 367 p. £ 25. 0-413-33480-5. -- ᴿ*TBR 8,2 (1995s) 55 (Alastair H.B. *Logan*).

k088 **Gielis** Marcel, Scholastiek en Humanisme; de kritiek van de Leuvense theoloog Jacobus [Masson = !] LATOMUS op de Erasmiaanse theologiehervorming [diss. ᴰ*Borne-wasser* J.A.] Tilburg 1994, Univ. 149 + 399 p. -- TTh 35 (1995) 72. -- ᴿEThL 71 (1995) 471-4 (J.E. *Vercruysse*).

k089 **Halkin** Léon-E., Erasmus, a critical biography 1992 → 9,16489; 10,14534: ᴿZwingliana 21 (1994) 191-3 (Christine *Christ-von Wedel*).

k090 **Huizinga** J., Erasmus, eine Biographie. Ha 1993, Rowohlt. DM 15. 3-499-13181-1. — ᴿGym 102 (1995) 567 (H.-U. *Berner*).

k091 **Jardine** Lisa, Erasmus, man of letters; the construction of charisma in print. Princeton 1993, Univ. xii-284 p.; 26 fig.; $ 30. -- ᴿRenQ 48 (1995) 183s (Laurel *Carrington*).

k092 *Knox* Delwyn, Erasmus' De civilitate and the religious origins of civility in western Europe: AR(ef)G 86 (1995) 7-47; dt. 47s; 7 fig.

k093 *Krüger* Friedhelm, Erasmus aus evangelischer Sicht: Thomas Morus Jb 1993, 68-80 [< NZSTh 37 (1995) 118s*].

k094 *Lasala* Fernando de, Una carta inédita de Erasmo de Rotterdam: AST(arr) 68 (1995) 105-123.

k095 **Letis** Theodore P., From sacred text to religious text; an intellectual history of the impact of Erasmian Lower Criticism on dogma as a contribution to the English Enlightenment and the Victorian crisis of faith: diss. ᴰ*Wright* D. Edinburgh 1995. 429 p. -- RTLv 27.p.543.

k096 [F]MARGOLIN Jean-Claude: Langage et vérité. [E]**Céard** Jean: THR(en) 272, 1993 →9,95: [R]RenQ 48 (1995) 806 (Barbara C. *Bowen*: 4 articles on Erasmus; Margolin had 114).

k097 **Olin** John C., Erasmus, Utopia, and the Jesuits; essays on the outreach of humanism. NY 1994, Fordham Univ. xvii-105 p. $ 16. 0-8232-1601-2. -- [R]RStR 21 (1995) 337 (M. *Hoffman*).

k098 *Ozaeta* José M., Erasmo de Rotterdam enjuiciado por fray Lucas de Alaejos: → 162, [F]RUBIO L., Semitica: CDios 208 (1995) 663-688.

k099 **Shantz** Douglas H., CRAUTWALD and Erasmus; a study in humanism and radical reform in sixteenth century Silesia: BtDissid 4, 1992 → 8,m538 ... 18,14539: [R]ChH 64 (1995) 670s (J.C. *Godbey* agrees, correcting R. MCLAUGHLIN).

k100 *Walton* Robert C., Erasmus and MARSILIUS of Padua [Defensor Pacis 1324] :→ 5, [F]ATKINSON, J., Bible, Reformation, Church: JSNT.s 105 (1995) 308-325.

k101 **Wolgast** Eike, ERASMUS von Rotterdam über die Weltmission: ZM(iss)R 79 (1995) 111-9.

k102 **Wozniak** Judith T., The 'Ecclesiastes' of Erasmus; a cry for unity: diss. SUNY, [D]*Stinger* C. Buffalo 1995. 329 p. 95-25637. -- DissA 56 (1995s) p. 1493.

------

k103 FICINUS: *Mojsisch* Burkhard, Epistemologie im Humanismus; Marsilio Ficino, Pietro POMPONAZZI und Nikolaus von KUES: FrSZ 42 (1995) 152-171.

k104 FISHER: **Bradshaw** Brendan, *Duffy* Eamon, Humanism ... John Fisher 1989 → 5,638; 6,k701: [R]RThom 95 (1995) 705s (G.-T. *Bedouelle*).

k105 **Carpenter** Edward, Archbishop Fisher, his life and times. Norwich 1991, Canterbury. xx-520 p.; 33 pl. £ 35. 1-85311-016-7. -- [R]*TBR 8,1 (1995s) 53 (D.M. *Thompson*).

k106 **Rex** Richard, The theology of John Fisher 1991 → 8,m362 ... 10,14541: [R]RThom 95 (1995) 706s (G.-T. *Bedouelle*).

k107 **Strauss** Paul, In hope of heaven; English Recusant prison writings of the sixteenth century [Fisher, MORE, SOUTHWELL ..]: AmUSt 4/166. NY 1995, P. Lang. 156 p. $ 36. 0-8204-2099-9 [ThD 43,188].

k108 GÓMEZ: **Sakuma** Tsutomu, Holy Scripture in 'Compendium catholicae veritatis' of Pedro Gómez S.J. (1533-1600): diss. Pont. Univ. Gregoriana, [D]*Gilbert* M. Rome 1995. 534 p.; extr. N° 4114. vi-126 p.; bibliog. 114-122. -- RTLv 27.p.543.

k109 GOUGH: *Britnell* Jennifer, John Gough [[T]1541] and the Traité de la différence des schismes et des conciles [de l'Église 1511] of Jean LEMAIRE de Belges; translation as propaganda in the Henrician Reformation: JEH 46 (1995) 62-74.

k110 HENRICUS VIII: **Rex** Richard, Henry VIII and the English reformation. L 1993, Macmillan. x-205 p. £ 30; pa. £ 9. -- [R]S(cot)JTh 48 (1995) 150s (R.N. *Swanson*).

k111 HUSS: **Seibt** Ferdinand, Hussitica; zur Struktur einer Revolution[2] [=[1]1965 + foreword & 7 Latin texts]. Köln 1990, Bohlau. xvii-267 p. -- [R]E(ng)HR 110 (1995) 166s (G. *Leff*).

k112 JORIS; **Waite** Gary K., David Joris and Dutch Anabaptists 1524-1543. Waterloo 1990, W.Laurier Univ. xi-235 p. US$ 32.50. -- [R]C(ath)HR 81 (1995) 445s (J.M. *Stayer*, also on Waite's 1993 translation of Joris).

k113 KNOX: *a) Felch* Susan M., The rhetoric of biblical authority; John Knox and the question of women; -- *b) Kelter* Irving A., The refusal to accommodate Jesuit exegetes and the Copernican system: S(ixt)CJ 26 (1995) 805-822 / 273-283.

k114 *Halliday* bp. R.T., Will the real John Knox please stand up?: [R]ET 106 (1994s) 169-172.

k115 **Johnson** Dale W., Prophecy, rhetoric and diplomacy: John Knox and the struggle for the soul of Scotland: diss. Georgia State, ᴰ*Armstrong* B., 1995. 279 p. 95-35248. -- D(iss)AI 56 (1995s) p. 2370.

k116 *Jones* R. Tudur, Preacher of revolution: ChrHist 14,46 ('John Knox, the thundering Scot' 1994) 8-16 (-46, *al.*).

------

k117 LAS CASAS: **Dahms** Bernd, Bartolomé de Las Casas (1484-1566); Indio-Politik im 16. Jahrhundert und ihre Rezeption in lateinamerikanischer Literatur [Diss.:] Dü Univ, Kultur und Erkenntnis 9. Tü 1993, Francke. 303 p. DM 68 [RHE 90 (1995) 284*]. -- ᴿNZM(iss)W 51 (1995) 232s (J. *Baumgartner*).

k118 *Eggensperger* Thomas, El 'paraíso terrenal' de Cristobal COLÓN y la interpretación de Fray Bartolomé de Las Casas, ᵀ*Chico* Gabriel: AnáMnesis 5,1 (1995) 39-47.

k119 **Gillen** C., Bartolomé de Las Casas, une esquisse biographique: Histoire. P 1995, Cerf. 252 p.; map. F 140 [RHE 90 (1995) 284*].

k120 *Goizueta* Roberto S., Bartolomé de Las Casas, modern critic of modernity; an analysis of a conversion: JHispLat 3,4 (1995s) 6-19.

k121 **Gutiérrez** G. In search of the poor of Jesus Christ 1993 → 10,14451: E(cu)R 47 (1995) 393-5 (J.W. *de Gruchy*); I(nd)TS 32 (1995) 357-360 (A.R. *Ceresko*); Miss(iology) 23 (1995) 216s (S.P. *Judd*); MoTh 11 (1995) 388-390 (R.S. *Goizueta*); P(rinc)SB 16 (1995) 258-260 (A. *Neely*); TS 56 (1995) 367-9 (T.G. *Walsh*).

k122 **Gutiérrez** Gustavo, Alla ricerca dei poveri di Gesù Cristo; il pensiero di Bartolomé de Las Casas [1992 → 9,16510]: BtTContemp 80. Brescia 1995, Queriniana. 673 p. Lᵐ 80. 88-399-0380-1. -- ᴿAsprenas 42 (1995) 452-4 (B. *Forte*); Greg 76 (1995) 612-4 (F.P. *Sullivan*, also on the English and the 1993 Sígueme reedition → 9,16510).

k123 *Mahn-Lot* Marianne, Las Casas et les cultures païennes: RÉTM = Le Supplément 193 (1995) 5-24 (& 195, 107-114).

k124 ᴱ**Parish** Helen R., The only way [1518], ᵀ*Sullivan* Francis P. NY 1992, Paulist. 281 p. $ 23. -- ᴿPresbyterion 18 (St.Louis 1992) 117-121 (D.C. *Jones*).

k125 **Parish** Helen R., *Weidman* Harold E., Las Casas en México; historia y obra desconocidas. México/San Diego 1992, Fondo de Cultura Económica. 409 p. $ 23. -- ᴿC(ath)HR 81 (1995) 470s (J.B. *Warren*).

k126 *Pérez* I., Bartolomé de LAS CASAS, máximo representante del humanismo sustantivo; ¿ Último episodio del Medioevo o principio de la Modernidad ?: Studium 34 (1994) 59-84 [< ArTGran 57 (1994) 45s, E. *Moore*).

k127 *Sievernich* Michael, Der unbewaffnete Prophet; die Brevísima relación de Las Casas als 'Fürstenspiegel': ZM(iss)R 79 (1995) 193-206; Eng. 206.

k128 **Sullivan** Francis P., Indian freedom; the cause of Bartolomé de las Casas, 1484-1566; a reader. KC 1995, Sheed & W. 371 p. $ 25. 1-55612-717-0 [ThD 43,59].

------

k129 MARPECK: **Boyd** Stephen B., Pilgram Marpeck; his life and social theology 1992 → 9,16520; 10,14556: ᴿJRel 75 (1995) 423 (J.C. *Godbey*).

k130 MELANCHTHON: **Kisukawa** Sachiko, The transformation of natural philosophy; the case of Philip Melanchthon: Ideas in Context. C 1995, Univ. xv-246 p. $ 60. 0-521-47347-0 [ThD 44,74].

k131 MILTON (→ 1891-9 supra): **Lieb** Michael, Milton and the culture of violence. Ithaca 1994, Cornell Univ. xii-273 p. $ 32.50. -- ᴿCithara 34,2 (1994) 46s (R.K. *Wickenhauser*).

k132 MORÉLY: **Denis** Philippe, *Rott* Jean, Jean Morély (ca 1524-ca 1594) et l'utopie d'une démocratie ecclésiastique [Traité de la discipline et police chrétienne 1562]: THR(en) 278, 1992 → 10,14561; 13 fig. Fs 132: [R]JEH 46 (1995) 148-150 (G.F. *Nuttall*).

k133 MÜNTZER: **Bubenheimer** Ulrich, Thomas Müntzer, Herkunft und Bildung 1989 → 6,k723; 7,g607: [R]ThLZ 120 (1995) 1095 (S. *Bräuer*).

k134 **Goertz** Hans-Jürgen, Thomas Müntzer, apocalyptic mystic and revolutionary [1989 → 9,16525, [T]*Jaquiery* Jocelyn. E 1994, Clark. xxi-229 p. 0-567-09606-8. -- [R]JThS 46 (1995) 767-9 (A. *Bradstock*).

k135 *La Rocca* Tommaso, Esperienza religiosa ed esperienza politica; misticismo e rivoluzione nei movimenti eretici a partire da Thomas Müntzer: FilTeo 8 (1994) 61-73.

k136 OECOLAMPADIUS: *Gäbler* Ulrich, Oekolampad: → 772, TRE 25 (1995) 29-36.

k137 OSIANDER, Andreas (1496-1552): → 772, TRE 25 (1995) 507-515 (G. *Seebass*).

k138 PAULUS III: *Gleason* Elizabeth, Who was the first counter-reformation Pope ? [presidential address]: C(ath)HR 81 (1995) 173-184; portr.

k139 PÉREZ: *Cortés Soriano* Agustín, La teología como supuesto y resultado de la interpretación de la Escritura en Jaime Pérez de Valencia: *AnVal 20 (1994) 1-97.

k140 RHEGIUS: **Zschoch** Hellmut, Reformatorische Existenz und konfessionelle Identität; Urbanus Rhegius als evangelischer Theologe in den Jahren 1520 bis 1530 [ev. Hab.-Diss. Mü]: BeitHisT 88. Tü 1995. Mohr. x-390 p. DM 160.

k141 RIVAUDEAU: *DiMauro* Damon, André de Rivaudeau [1540-80] et la Bible: BuHProt 141 (1995) 207-219; Eng. 219.

k142 SCHWENCKFELD: **Hiller** Michael [† 1557, Silesia-Zo(b)ten successful supporter of his wife's relative C. Schwenckfeld] Froehlich KARLFRIED, A [tattered Speer Library] Reformation manuscript yields its mystery: P(rinc)SB 16 (1995) 80-82.

k143 SOTO: *Belda Plans* Juan, Domingo de Soto (1495-1560) y la reforma de la teologia en el siglo XVI: *AnVal 21 (1995) 193-221 (-297, *al.*).

k144 STAUPITZ: *Posset* Franz, Preaching the Passion of Christ on the eve of the Reformation [1512]: C(oncordia)TQ 59 (1995) 279-300.

k145 STEPHANUS: *Gilmont* Jean-François, Le sommaire des livres du vieil et nouveau Testament de Robert Estienne, ou l'étrange périple d'une confession de foi: RHR 212 (1995) 175-218.

k146 STURM: **Brady** Thomas A.[J], Protestant politics; Jacob Sturm (1489-1553) and the German Reformation. Atlantic Highlands NJ 1995, Humanities. xix-447 p.; 11 fig.; 5 maps. $ 65. 0-391-03823-0 [ThD 43,58]

k147 TYNDALE: **Daniell** David, William Tyndale, a biography 1994 → 10,14568: [R]ET 106 (1994s) 128 (C.S. *Rodd*); I(rish)BSt 17 (1995) 86-88 (R.B. *Knox*); [J]LT(Ox) 9 (1995) 229s (D. *Fuller*) JThS 46 (1995) 765s (P.N. *Brooks*).
[E]**Dick** A., *Richardson* A., Tyndale and the law 1991-4 → 570 supra.

k148 **Trueman** Carl R., Luther's legacy; salvation and English Reformers, 1525-1556 [Tyndale & 4 others:diss. Aberdeen]. Ox 1994, Clarendon. 307 p. £ 35. 0*-19-826352 - - [R]ET 106 (1994s) 89s (P.N. *Brooks*).

k149 VALDÉS: **Fanlo y Cortés** T., Juan de Valdés, Il dialogo della dottrina cristiana; Testi della Riforma 17, 1991 → 9,16534: [R]CrSt 16 (1995) 194-6 (K. *Ganzer*).

k150 VERMIGLI: ᵀ**Di Gangi** Mariano, ᴱ*McLelland* Joseph C., Peter Martyr Vermigli, early writings: creed, scripture, church: SixtCEs 30. Kirksville MO 1994, Jefferson Univ./S(ixt)CJ. x-244 p. $ 35. 0-940474-32-8 [ThD 42,392].

k151 WITZEL: **Henze** Barbara, Aus Liebe zur Kirche, Reform; die Bemühungen Georg Witzels (1501-1573) um die Kircheneinheit: RefGStT 133. viii-430 p. DM 138. 3-402-03795-5 [ThRv 91].

k152 WYCLIF: *Hankey* Wayne J., *Magis ... pro nostra sententia*; Wyclif, his mediaeval predecessors and Reformed successors, and a Pseudo-Augustinian eucharistic decretal: AugLv 45 (1995) 213-245.

k153 ZWINGLI: *Koch* Ernst, Z. und die Berner Reformation: ThR(u) 60 (1995) 131-151.

k154 **Stephens** W. Peter, Zwingli 1992 → 8,m407; 9,16540: ᴿChH 64 (1995) 481s (J.W. *Baker*); *CritRR 7 (1994) 376-8 (M.L. *Klauber*); Zwingliana 21 (1994) 190s (E.J. *Furcha*).

k155 *Stephens* W.P., Zwingli and the salvation of the Gentiles [heathens, but also bad Christians]: → 5, ᶠATKINSON J., Bible, Reformation, Church: JSNT.s 105 (1995) 224-244.

Y4.5 *Exegesis post-reformatoria* -- **Historical criticism to 1800**

k156 *Acheson* Alan, The evangelical revival in Ireland [50 years after England]; a study in Christology: Churchman 108 (L 1994) 143-153.

k157 **Allan** David, Virtue, learning and the Scottish enlightenment; ideas of scholarship in early modern history. E 1993, Univ. viii-276 p. -- ᴿJEH 46 (1995) 156-160 (J.G.A. *Pocock*, also on KIDD C. 1993).

k158 **Baird** William, History of NT research I. From Deism to Tübingen 1992 → 8,m411; 0,14573: ᴿA(ndr)USS 33 (1995) 105s (M.M. *Kent*: wary of 'conservatives'); *CritRR 7 (1994) 138-140 (J. *Riches*: more an anthology than an analysis).

k159 **Ball** Bryan W., The seventh-day men; sabbatarians and sabbatarianism in England and Wales, 1600-1800. Ox 1994, Clarendon. xi-402 p.; 4 fig.; 7 maps. $ 65. 0-19-826752-5 [ThD 42 (1995) 256]. -- ᴿJThS 46 (1995) 778-2 (R. *Brown*).

k160 **Barrie-Curien** Viviane, Clergé et pastorale en Angleterre au XVIII siècle, le diocèse de Londres. P 1992, CNRS. 442 p. F 280. -- ᴿRHR 212 (1995) 237-240 (B. *Cottret*).

k161 ᴱ**Brecht** M., Geschichte des Pietismus, 1. [aus 4] vom siebzehnten bis zum frühen achtzehnten Jahrhundert. Gö 1993, Vandenhoeck & R. xi-584 p. DM 120. 3-525-55343-9. -- ᴿCrSt 16 (1995) 437-440 (B. *Bianco*); TTh 35 (1995) 413s (E.G.E. van der *Wall*).

k162 **Burkard** D., 'Oase in einer aufklärungssüchtigen Zeit ?' Die katholisch-theologische Fakultät der Universität Heidelberg zwischen verspäteter Gegenreformation, Aufklärung und Kirchenreform [Diss.]; Contubernium 42. Sigmaringen 1995, Thorbecke. 254 p. [RHE 91,109*].

k164 **Butler** Jon, Awash in a sea of faith; Christianizing the American people 1990 → 6,k770 ... 9,16456*: ᴿCScR 25 (1995s) 92-96 (R.A. *Wauzzinski*).

k165 *a) Carbonnier-Burkard* Marianne, Protestantisme et tolérance (XVIᵉ-XVIIIᵉ siècles); — *b) Collange* Jean-François, Protestantisme, tolérance et intolérable; -- *c) Stucki* Pierre-André, Assertion, reconnaissance et tolérance: BCPÉ 47,4 (50 ans, 1995) 21-30 / 31-42 / 43-54 9-68 débat).

k166 **Champion** J.A.J., The pillars of priestcraft shaken; the Church of England and its enemies 1660-1730: 1992 → 9,16548: ^RChH 64 (1995) 299s (Marcella Biro *Barton*).

k167 **Cogliano** Francis D., No king, no popery: anti-Catholicism in revolutionary New England: CAmH 164. Westport CT 1995, Greenwood. xii-173 p. $ 53. 0-313-29729-0 [ThD 43,360].

k168 *Collinson* Patrick, No Popery; the mythology of a Protestant nation ('Prejudice unmasked', 4): Tablet 249 (1995) 384-6.

k169 **Cubitt** Geoffrey, The Jesuit myth, conspiracy theory and politics in nineteenth century France. Ox 1993, Clarendon. viii-346 p. £ 40. 0-19-822868-6. -- ^RJEH 46 (1995) 161s (W. *Doyle*).

k170 **Cummins** J.S., A question of rites; Friar Domingo NAVARRETE and the Jesuits in China. Aldershot 1993, Scolar. xv-349 p.; 2 fig.; 2 maps. £ 39.50. -- ^RJRAS (1994) 147s (W.J. *Peterson*: 'aiming to correct the pervasive pro-Jesuit bias').

k171 *D'Arelli* Francesco. La Sacra Congregatio de Propaganda Fide e la Cina nei secoli XVII-XVIII; le missioni, la Procura ed i Procuratori nella documentazione dell'Archivio storico di Roma: AION 55 (1995) 217-231 . 326-352.

k172 **Davies** Julian, The Caroline captivity of the Church: Charles I and the remoulding of Anglicanism. Ox 1992, UP. xx-400 p. £ 45. 0-19-820311-X. -- ^RJThS 46 (1995) 398-401 (C. *Hatch*).

k173 **De Nardis** Luigi, Antoine LE MAISTRE, 1608-1658; Port-Royal e la retorica. N 1995, Bibliopolis. 43 p. 88-7088-347-7.

k174 **Ehrhardt-Rein** Susanne, Zwischen Glaubenslehre und Vernunftswahrheit; Natur und Schöpfung bei Hallischen Theologen des 18. Jahrhunderts: Diss. ^D*Beintker* M. Halle-Wittenberg 1995. -- ThLZ 120 (1995) 1177.

k175 **Fineham** Kenneth, The early Stuart church, 1503-1642, Stanford 1993, Univ. 301 p. $ 42.50. -- ^RAThR 77 (1995) 410-2 (W:H. *Petersen*).

k176 ^E**Force** James E., *Popkin* Richard H., The books of Nature and Scripture 1994 → 10,14579*: ^RJThS 46 (1995) 772 (M. *Wiles*).

k177 *Galli* Marc, Gifted founders; the first generation of American Puritans .. five leading examples: ChrHist 13,41 (1994) 28-21.

k178 **Gibson** William, Church, state and society, 1760-1850: British History in Perspective. L /NY 1994, Macmillan / St. Martin's. x-209 p. £ 9 pa. 0-333-58757-X. -- ^RJEH 46 (1995) 571s (I.R. *Christie*).

k179 ^E**Goldman** Shalom, Hebrew and the Bible in America; the first two centuries 1993 → 9,281; 10,14580*: *A(sn)JS 20 (1995) 271s, titles sans pp.; *Gordon* Cyrus H., The ten lost tribes.

k180 *a) Gooch* Leo, 'What shall we do with the wanton student ?', tutoring the Catholic gentry in the eighteenth century; -- *b) Morris* Kevin L., Rescuing the Scarlet Woman; the promotion of Catholicism in English literature, 1829-1850; -- *c) Birrell* T.A., English counter-Reformation book culture: Re(cus)H 22 (1994s) 63-74 / 75-87 / 113-122.

k181 **Greaves** Richard L., Secrets of the kingdom; British radicals from the Popish Plot to the Revolution of 1688-89. Stanford 1992, Univ. xviii-465 p. $ 49,50. 0-8047-2052-5. -- ^RJEH 46 (1995) 339s (J. *Scott*).

k182 *Harvey* Graham, The suffering of witches and children; uses of the witchcraft passages in the Bible : → 170, ^FSAWYER J., Words; JSOT.s 195 (1995) 113-134.

k183 **Haydon** Colin, Anti-Catholicism in eighteenth-century England, c. 1714-80; a political and social study. Manchester UK 1993, Univ. xi-276 p.; 10 pl. £ 40. 0-7190-2859-0. — [R]JEH 46 (1995) 342-4 (S. *Taylor*).

k184 **Heyberger** Bernard, Les Chrétiens du Proche-Orient au temps de la Réforme catholique (Syrie, Liban, Palestine, XVIIe-XVIIIe siècles) [diss Nancy 1993, [D]*Châtellier* L.]: BtÉcF 284. R 1994, École Française. v-666 p.; 4 pl.; 6 maps. -- [R]IslChr 21 (1995) 249-151 (M. *Borrmans*); OCP 61 (1995) 648-650 (V. *Poggi*); POrC 45 (1995) 313-5 (P. *Ternant*).

k185 **Hill** Christopher, The English Bible and the seventeenth-century revolution 1993 → 9,16555; 10,14584; [R]AmHR 100 (1995) 1248 (H. *Davies*); RExp 92 (1995) 109s (J.D.W. *Watts*).

k186 *Hotson* Howard, Irenicism and dogmatics in the confessional age; PAREUS & COMENIUS in Heidelberg, 1614: JEH 46 (1995) 432-456.

k187 *Jaspert* Bernd, Theologische Mystikforschung vor der Aufklärung: ThLZ 120 (1995) 203-218.

k188 **Jori** Giacomo, Le forme della creazione; sulla fortuna del 'Mondo creato' (secoli XVII e XVIII): BRSLR 6. F 1995, Olschki. [iv-] 159 p.; bibliog. 145-154. 88-222-44319-6.

k189 **Kaplan** Benjamin J., Calvinists and libertines; confession and community in Utrecht 1578-1620. Ox 1995, Clarendon. xv-347 p. $ 65. 0-19-820283-0 [ThD 43,372].

k190 *Kranemann* Benedikt, 'Liturgie nach den Grundsätzen der Vernunft und der Heiligen Schrift'; Überlegungen zur Prägung der Liturgie des deutschen Aufklärungskatholizismus durch die Bibel: AL(tg)W 37 (1995) 45-67 (227-303).

k191 *Kurzke* Hermann, Kirchenlied und Literaturgeschichte; die Aufklärung und ihre Folgen: JLH(ymn) 35 (1994s) 124-135.

k192 [E]**Lamberigts** Mathijs, (*Kenis* Leo) L'Augustinisme à l'ancienne Faculté de Théologie de Louvain [... JANSENIUS 1640]: BETL 111, 1990/4 → 10,366: [R]EstAg 30 (1995) 354 (C. *Moran*); EThL 71 (1995) 248-250 (J. *Étienne*); RevAg 36 (1995) 1127-9 (J. *Sepulcre*).

k193 **Laplanche** François, La Bible en France entre mythe et critique 1994 → 10,14588: [R]ÉTRel 70 (1995) 599s (H. *Bost*); Études 383 (1995) 138 (P. *Gibert*).

k194 **Longenecker** Stephen L., Piety and tolerance; Pennsylvania German religion, 1700-1850: Pietist & Wesleyan Studies 6. Metuchen NJ 1994, Scarecrow. xv-195 p. $ 27.50. 0-8108-2771-9 [ThD 43,74].

k195 **MacIntyre** Alastair, Justicia y racionalidad. Barc 1994, Edic.Int Univ. 387 p. -- [R]E(st)E 70 (1995) 397-403 (L. *Vela:* Tres tradiciones: HOMERO Y ARISTÓTELES y hasta HUME; a través los árabes a ALBERTO-AQUINATE; desde la Biblia por medio de AGUSTÍN al Aquinate; una quarta sería 'El liberalismo transformado en tradición').

k196 **McIntyre** Patricia Q., The ordinary care of Providence; how religious discourse colonial theologies produced the moral roots of the First Amendment: diss. Southern California, [D]*Orr* J. 1994 (No AA photocopy.) -- DissA 56 (1995s) p. 975.

k197 *Maier* Hans, Aufklärung, Pietismus, Staatswissenschaft; die Universität Halle nach 300 Jahren: HZ 261 (1995) 769-791.

k198 *Meier* Johannes, Nordwestdeutsche Jesuiten in den mexikanischen Missionen um 1750: ZM(iss)R 79 (1995) 259-289; 5 fig. (maps); Eng. 289.

k199 **Milton** Anthony, Catholic and reformed; the Roman and Protestant churches in English Protestant thought, 1600-1640. C 1995, Univ. 599 p. £ 50. 0-521-40141-0 [ThD 44,79]. — [R]E(xp)T 107 (1995s) 58 (Claire *Cross*); Month 256 (1995) 449 (T. *Clancy*).

k200 **Misiurek** Jerzy, [P] Historia i teologia polskiej duchowości (spirituality) katolickiej I, saec. X-XVII. Lublin 1994, KUL. 422 p. -- [R]AtK(ap) 125 (1995) 145s (I. *Werbinski*); R(ocz)T(Lub) 42,5 (1995) 155s (A.J. *Nowak*, [P]).

k201 **Neveu** Bruno, L'erreur et son juge [... Jansénisme] 1993 → 10,991: [R]JEH 46 (1995) 363s (A. *Bellenger*); TS 56 (1995) 371-3 (J.M. *Grès-Gayer*).

k202 **Petersen** Rodney L., Preaching in the Last Days; the theme of 'two witnesses' in the seventeenth and eighteenth centuries 1993 → 9,16563; £ 37.50: [R]JThS 46 (1995) 395s (R. *Bauckham*).

k203 *Pitassi* Maria-Cristina, La théologie au XVIIe siècle; violence ou modération ?: BuH-Prot 141 (1995) 341-354; Eng. 353 [on Jean LE CLERC].

k204 **Pitassi** Maria-Cristina, De l'orthodoxie aux Lumières; Genève 1670-1737: HistSoc 24. Genève 1992, Labor et Fides. 88 p. -- [R]RTL 26 (1995) 241s (J.-F. *Gilmont*: how J.-A. TURRETTINI undid Calvin).

k205 **Rohrer** James R., Keepers of the covenant; frontier missions and the decline of Congregationalism, 1774-1818: Religion in America. NY 1995, Oxford-UP. x-201 p. $ 35. 0-19-509166-3 [ThD 42.184].

k206 **Ross** Andrew C., A vision betrayed; the Jesuits in Japan and China, 1542-1742. Mkn 1994, Orbis. 216 p. 0-7486-0472-3. -- [R]VSVD 36 (1995) 192s (T. *Krosnicki*).

k207 **Roussos-Milidonis** Markos N., [G] Jesuits on Greek soil (1560-1773-1915]. Athena 1991, KEO. 407 p. -- [R]CivCatt 146 (1995,1) 93s (C. *Capizzi*); Kler 23 (1991) 356-363 (D.N. *Kasapidis*).

k208 **Shain** Barry A., The myth of American individualism; the Protestant origins of American political thought. Princeton 1995, Univ. xix-394 p. $ 39.50. 0-691-03382-X [ThD 42,387].

k209 *Sorg* Theo, Die Bibel als Lebensbuch; die Treue des Pietismus zur Heiligen Schrift: BiKi 50 (1995) 60-63.

k210 **Spellman** W.M., The Latitudinarians and the Church of England, 1660-1770. Athens GA 1993, Univ. Georgia. x-228 p. $ 40. -- [R]JRel 75 (1995) 279 (R.M. *Grant*).

k211 **Tabraham** Barrie, The making of Methodism. L 1995, Epworth. xiii-130 p. £ 10. 0-7162-0499-1.

k212 **Terray** Emmanuel, Une passion allemande: LUTHER, KANT, SCHILLER, HÖLDERLIN, KLEIST: Librairie XXe siècle. P 1994, Seuil.

k213 *Todd* Marco, 'All one with Tom Thumb'; Arminianism, popery, and the story of the Reformation in early Stuart Cambridge: ChH 64 (1995) 563-579.

k214 **Vander Sluijs** C.A., Puritanisme en Nadere Reformatie; een beknopte vergelijkende studie. Kampen 1989, DeGroot Goudriaan. 82 p. *f* 13 pa. -- [R]C(alvin)TJ 30 (1995) 493s (H.D. *Schuringa*).

k215 *Walsh* M., Profession and authority; the interpretation of the Bible in the seventeenth and eighteenth centuries: JLT 9 (1995) 383-398 [NTAb 40, also p.398].

k216 **Walsham** Alexandra, Church papists; Catholicism, conformity and confessional polemic in early modern England: Royal Historical Society 68. Woodbridge 1993, Boydell. xiii-142 p. £ 29.50. 0-86193-225-0. -- [R]JEH 46 (1995) 151-3 (C. *Haigh*).

k217 *Werbick* Jürgen, Toleranz und Vernunft; die Entstehung der Toleranz aus dem Geist der Aufklärung: → 589, Mit dem Anderen 1995, 15-38.

k218 **Zakai** Avihu, Exile and kingdom; history and apocalypse in the Puritan migration to America. C 1992, Univ. x-262. £ 30. -- [R]E(ng)HR 110 (1995) 178s (W. *Lamont*: strives to stem the trend away from Perry MILLER*).

Y4.7 **Auctores 1600-1800 alphabetice**

k219 BAYLE: **Bost** Hubert, Pierre Bayle et la religion. P 1994, PUF. 128 p. F 45. -- ᴿMélSR 52 (1995) 107 (D. *Lecompte*); Protest(antesimo) 50 (1995) 327s (P. *Ribet*).

k220 ᴱ**Gros** Jean-Michel, De la tolérance; commentaire sur ces paroles de Jésus-Christ 'Contrains-les d'entrer'. .. 1993, Pocket. 433 p. -- ᴿL(aval)TP 51 (1995) 201-4 (Marie-Anne *Solasse*).

k221 BOSSUET: *Costigan* Richard F., Bossuet and the consensus of the Church: TS 56 (1995) 652-672.

k222 BOUVET 1656-1730: **Collani** Claudia von, Eine wissenschaftliche Akademie für China; Briefe des Chinamissionars Joachim Bouvet S.J. an G.W. LEIBNIZ & J.P. BIGNON. Wsb 1989, Steiner. 136 p. -- ᴿNZM(iss)W 51 (1995) 69-72 (H. von *Senger*).

k223 BRACHET: **Schoor** R.J.M.Van de, The irenical theology of Théophile Brachet de la Milletière (1588-1665): SHCT 59. Lei 1993, Brill. xii-279 p. $ 74.50. 90-04-09961-1 [RStR 22,256, Susan *Rosa*: ignored because of opprobrium against ecumenists among both Protestant and Catholic orthodox].

k224 CANTEMIR D. 1700: *Mitescu* Adriana, Il libro come 'specchio' del secolo e della sapienza divina -- sul giudizio del Mondo col Sapiente o 'la disputa tra l'anima e il corpo' [Cantemir D.]: Ter(esianum) 46 (1995) 459-499.

k225 CHERBURY: *Tadie* Andrew, Lord Herbert of Cherbury's idea of 'ultimate reality and meaning' and a note on the popularization of Deism: URM 18 (1995) 264-274.

k226 COMENIUS: *Campi* Emidio, Johann A. Comenius (1592-1670) und die protestantische Theologie seiner Zeit: Zwingliana 22 (1995) 67-83.

k227 DESCARTES: **Philonenko** Alexis, Relire Descartes: Ouverture. P 1994, Grancher. 457 p. -- ᴿRTPh 127 (1995) 168s (D. *Christoff*).

k228 -- *Soffer* Walter, DESCARTES' secular paradise; the Discourse on Method as biblical criticism: *PhTh 8,4 (Milwaukee 1994) 309-346 [199-212, *Conley* John, Silence of Descartes (on mystery of God)].

k229 EDWARDS: **Conforti** Joseph A., Jonathan Edwards, religious tradition, and American culture. Chapel Hill / Boston 1995, Univ. N. Carolina / Colonial. xiv-267 p. $ 30; pa. $ 14. 0-8078-2224-8; -4535-3 / [RStR 22,262, G.R. *McDermott*, also on LESSER's bibliog. 1994].

k230 *Jinkins* Michael, The 'true remedy'; Jonathan Edwards' soteriological perspective as observed in his revival treatises: S(cot)JTh 48 (1995) 185-209.

k231 **Morimoto** Anri, Jonathan Edwards and the catholic vision of salvation. Univ. Park 1995, Penn State. viii-178 p. $ 33.50. 0-271-01453-9 [RStR 22,262, G.R. *McDermott*].

k232 ᴱ**Oberg** Barbara B., *Stout* Harry S., Benjamin FRANKLIN, Jonathan Edwards, and the representation of American culture. NY 1993, Oxford-UP. vii-230 p. $ 35. -- ᴿJRel 75 (1995) 281s (R.M. *Payne*).

k233 **Schröder** Caroline, Der Mensch vor Gott; die religiöse Selbsterkenntnis in der Erweck-ungstheologie Jonathan Edwards': ev. Diss. ᴰ*Sauter* G. Bonn 1995. -- ThLZ 120 (1995) 1146.

k234 FAIRFAX: *Holt* Geoffrey, The seventeenth-century Hebrew scholars: Thomas Fairfax and Edward SLAUGHTER: R(ecus)H 22 (1994s) 482-490.

k235 FÉNELON: *Sansen* Raymond, Fénelon, un penseur toujours actuel: MélSR 52 (1995) 235-262; Eng. 262.

k236 FOX: **Ingle** H.Larry, First among friends; George Fox and the creation of Quakerism. Ox 1994, UP. ix-407 p. £ 12.50. 0-19-507803-9. -- ᴿC(ath)HR 81 (1995) 285s (T.L. *Underwood*); ET 106 (1994s) 96 (C.S. *Rodd*).

k237 GILL: *Ella* George M., John Gill [1697-1771] and the charge of hyper-Calvinism: B(ap)Q 36 (1995s) 160-177.

k238 GROTIUS: ᴱ**Nocentini** Lucio, Ugo Grozio, Il potere dell'autorità suprema in ordine alle cose sacre [1613]. Pisa 1993, Cerro. -- ᴿProtest(antesimo) 50 (1995) 251-3 (Debora *Spini*).

k240 HELMONT: *Vismara* Paola, Tra Quaccheri, millenaristi e inquisitori, F[ranciscus] M[er-curius] van Helmont [1662; Seder Olam 1693]: Acme 48,3 (1995) 65-84.

k241 HERDER: ᴱ**Bultmann** Christoph, *Zippert* Thomas, Johann Gottfried Herder, Theolo-gische Schriften: Werke 9/1. Fr 1994. Dt. Klassiker. 1239 p. DM 172. 3-618-60793-8.

k242 **Federlin** Wilhelm L., Kirchliche Volksbildung und bürgerliche Gesellschaft; Studien zu Thomas ABBT, ... J.G. Herder *al.* [Hab.-Diss. Frankfurt 1989]: Theion 1. Fra 1993, Lang. vii-236 p. DM 65. 3-631-46165-8 [ThRv 91].

k243 **Zippert** Thomas, Bildung durch Offenbarung; das Offenbarungsverständnis des jungen Herder als Grundmotiv seines philsophisch-literarischen Lebenswerks [Diss. Mainz 1992]: MarburgTSt 39. Marburg 1994, Elwert. 339 p. DM 68. 3-7708-1028-7 [ThRv 91].

k243* HOUDRY: **Varachaud** Marie-Christine, Le père [Vincent] Houdry (1631-1729); prédication et pénitence [Bibliothèque des prédicateurs, 22 vol., 1711-25]: TH 94. P 1993, Beauchesne. 454 p F 297. 2-7010-1273-2. -- ᴿJEH 46 (1995) 569s (T. *Worcester:* she does not explain his lack of interest in Exodus and merely hints that he was willing to accommodate Jansenism).

k244 JANSENIUS: *Hogan* Edmund M., Jansenism; towards a definition: I(r)ThQ 61 (1995) 289-289.

k245 *Quantin* Jean-Louis, Ces autres qui nous font ce que nous sommes; les Jansénistes face à leurs adversaires: RHR 212 (1995) 397-417.

k246 *Roegiers* J., Van 'Unigenitus' (1713) tot 'Mirari vos' 1832; Noord- en Zuidnederlandse katholieken tussen jansenisme en ultramontanisme; Trajecta 1,1 (Nijmegen 1992) 49-66 [< RHE 91,276, R. *Aubert*).

k247 JUNOT: **MacKay** Charles H., 'The Tempest'; the life and career of Jean Andoche Junot. 1771-1813: diss. Florida State, ᴰ*Mackay* C., 1995. 470 p. 96-12127. -- DissA 56 (1995s) p. 4908.

k248 LACORDAIRE: **Margerie** Bertrand de, Lacordaire semi-traditionaliste; la pensée de Lacordaire sur les origines du langage et de la société dans le contexte de la révélation et de la préhistoire: Ang 72 (1995) 63-81.

k249 LEIBNIZ: *a) Adams* Robert M., Leibniz's 'Examination of the Christian religion'. -- *b) Sleigh* Robert, Leibniz on divine foreknowledge [*al.,* LOCKE, SPINOZA, PASCAL]: Faith & Philosophy 11 (1994) 517-546 / 547-571 [572-662].

k250 LESSING: *a) Schilson* Arne, '... auf meiner alten Kanzel dem Theater'; über Religion und Theater bei G.E. Lessing; 2. Nathan der Weise als poetische Predigt über die wahre Religion; -- *b) Frühwahl* Wolfgang, Zwischen Märtyrerdrama und politischem Theater;

vom spannungsvollen Verhältnis der Kirche zur Theaterkultur: THGL 85 (1995) 12-34 . 518-532 / 35-46.

k251 MALEBRANCHE: *Nadler* Steven, Choosing a theodicy; the LEIBNIZ-Malebranche-ARNAULD connection: JHId 55 (1994) 573-589.

k252 MENDELSSOHN: *Breuer* Edward, Rabbinic law and spirituality in Mendelssohn's *Jerusalem*: JQR 86 (1995s) 299-321.

k253 OLIVEIRA, *Max* Frédéric, Un écrivain français des Lumières oublié, Francisco Xavier de Oliveira (1701-1783) [... tolérance pour les Juifs] : RHPhR 75 (1995) 193-8.

------

k254 PASCAL: **Adamson** Donald, Blaise Pascal; mathematician, physicist and thinker about God, NY 1995, St.Martin's, xii-297 p. $ 60. 0-312-12502-X [ThD 43,55].

k255 *Groothuis* Douglas, Proofs, pride, and incarnation; is natural theology theologically taboo ? : JETS 38 (1995) 67-76.

k256 **Horner** Jerry L.[J], Pascal prophet: diss. [D]*Apostolides* J. Stanford 1955. 315 p. 95-35698. -- D(iss)AI 56 (1995s) p.2258.

k257 [E]**Jordan** Jeff, Gambling on God; essays on Pascal's wager. .. 1993, Rowman & L. 168 p. $ 49; pa. $ 20. 0-8476-7833-4. -- [R]ET 106 (1994s) 252 (J.K. *Ryan*'s essay shows the idea was far from original).

k258 **Kolakowski** Leszek, God owes us nothing; a brief remark on Pascal's religion and on the spirit of Jansenism ['Why did the Catholic Church condemn the teaching of St. AUGUSTINE ?']. Ch 1995, Univ. x-238 p. $ 22.50. 0-226-45051-1 [ThD 43,275; RStR 22,256, E. *Radner*: lucid].

k259 *Meskin* Jacob, Secular self-confidence, postmodernism, and beyond; recovering the religious dimension of Pascal's Pansées: JRel 75 (1995) 487-508.

k260 **Morodo González** Patricia, El itinerario de la conversión [Original sin, anthropology and Christology] en los 'Pensées' de Blaise Pascal: dis. Navarra, 1994.   (No AA photocopy.) -- DissA-C 56 (1995s) p. 580.

k261 **Wetsel** David, Pascal and disbelief; catechesis and conversion in the Pensées. Wsh 1994, Catholic University of America. xvii-409 p.; 16 pl. $ 70. 0-8132-0808-4 [ThD 43,93; RHE 90 (1995) 259*]. -- [R]I(r)ThQ 61 (1995 514-6 (M. *O'Dwyer*).

------

k262 POIRET: **Chevallier** Mariolaine, Pierre Poiret (1646-1719); du protestantisme à la mystique 1994 → 10,14637: [R]P(rinc)SB 16 (1995) 106-8 (Elsie *McKee*).

k263 RÁVAGO: **Alcaraz Gómez** J.F., Jesuitas y reformismo; el Padre Francisco de Rávago (1747-1755): Valentina 35. Valencia 1995, Fac. Teol. 795 p. -- [R]ATG(ran) 58 (1995) 330s (E. *Olivares*).

k264 REIMARUS: **Schmidt-Biggemann** W., Hermann S. Reimarus, Kleine gelehrten Schriften, Vorstufen zur .. Schutzschrift: Jungius 79. Gö 1994, Vandenhoeck & R. 652 p. DM 165. -- [R]SNTU 20 (1995) 249s (F. *Weissengruber*).

k265 REINHOLD 1757-1823:   *Lazzari* Alessandro, Zwischen Illuminatismus und Vernunftkritik; neue Literatur zu Karl Leonhard Reinhold: *FrSZ 42 (1994) 416-424.

k266 ROUSSEAU: *Cladis* Mark S., Tragedy and theodicy; a meditation on Rousseau and moral evil: JRel 75 (1995) 181-199.

k267 SEMLER 1725-91: **Lüder** Andreas, Historie und Dogmatik; ein Beitrag zur Genese und Denkentfaltung von Johann Salomo Semlers Verständnis des Alten Testaments [Diss. Marburg 1994, [D]*Kaiser* O.: BZAW 233. B 1995, de Gruyter. x-259. 3-11-014627-4 [OTA 19,p.147] k268 SPENER: **Chi Hyeong-Eun**, Philipp Jacob Spener und seine Pia desideria; die Weiterführung der Reformvorschläge der Pia desideria in seinem späteren Schrifttum: Diss. [D]*Wallmann* J. Bochum 1995. -- ThLZ 120 (1995) 1146.

k269 -- **Kim Moon-Kee**, Das Kirchenverständnis Philipp Jakob Speners in seiner Evangelischen Glaubens-Lehre von 1688: Diss. [D]*Sommer* W. Neuendettelsau 1995.

k270 SPINOZA: *Preus* J. Samuel, A hidden opponent in Spinoza's Tractatus [MEYER Ludwig, Philosophia S. Scripturae interpres 1666]: HThR 88 (1995) 361-388.

k271 -- *Rougemont* Jean-Daniel, Spinoza et le totalitarisme; fiction et réalité: RTPh 127 (1995) 127-141; Eng. 208.

k272 TAYLOR: **McAdoo** H.E., First of its kind; Jeremy Taylor's Life of Christ. Norwich 1994, Canterbury. xii-136 p. £ 10. 1-85311-083-3. -- [R]*TBR 8,1 (1995s) 28 (P. *Sheldrake*).

k273 TOLAND: *Palmer* Gesine, Die mosaische Republik; eine Konstruktion von John Toland, entworfen zum richtigen Verständnis und Gebrauch jüdischer, griechischer und christlicher Traditionen im England des frühen 18. Jahrhunderts: → 42, [F]COLPE C., Tradition (1994) 230-243.

k274 TURRETIN Francis, [T]**Giger** G., [E]*Dennison* J., Institutes of elenctic theology 1, 1992 → 8,m478; 10,14631: [R]JETS 37 (1994) 609s (T.R. *Phillips*).

k275 VOLTAIRE: **Lepape** Pierre. Voltaire le conquérant. P 1994, Seuil. 392 p. F 149. -- [R]Études 382 (1995) 121-3 (J. *Mambrino*, aussi sur POMEAU R. [2]1994).

---

k276 WESLEY J.: **Abelove** Henry, The evangelist of desire; John Wesley and the Methodists. Stanford 1990, Univ. xii-136 p. $ 25. -- [R]E(ng)HR 110 (1995) 208s (V.H.H. *Green*).

k277 **Brown-Lawson** Albert, John Wesley and the Anglican evangelicals of the eighteenth century. E 1994 → 10,14636; 1-85821-095-X. -- [R]ET 106 (1994s) 58 (J.A. *Vickers*); I(r)ThQ 61 (1995) 87s (W.J. *Marshall*).

k278 **Butler** David, Methodists and Papists; John Wesley and the Catholic Church in the eighteenth century. L 1995, Darton-LT. xiv-240 p. £ 13. 0-232-52110-7. -- [R]ET 106 (1994s) 348 (J. *Newton*); I(rish)BSt 17 (1995) 88-90 (D. *Cooke*); OneInC 31 (1995) 184-8 (D. *Carter*).

k279   *Carter* Kelly D., The High Church roots of John Wesley's appeal to primitive Christianity: RestQ 37 (1995) 65-79.

k280   *Haas* J.W.[J], John Wesley's vision of science in the service of Christ: PerspSCF 47 (1995) 234-243 (-254, *Malony* H.N.).

k281 **Heitzenrater** Richard P., Wesley and the people called Methodists. Nv 1995, Abingdon. xiv-338 p. $ 15. -- [R]*CritRR 8 (1995) 409-411 (R.L. *Maddox*).

k282 **Jones** Scott J., John Wesley's conception and use of Scripture. Nv 1995, (Abingdon-) Kingswood. 268 p. $ 17. 0-687-20466-6 [ThD 43,274].

k283   *a) Maddox* Randy, Reading Wesley as theologian; -- *b) Bundy* David, The historiography of the Wesleyan/Holiness tradition: WeslTJ 30,1 (1995) 7-54 / 55-77 [-231, *al.*]

k284 **Rataboul** Louis J., John Wesley, un Anglican sans frontières 1703-1791: 1991 → 10,14635; F 160: [R]RHR 212 (1995) 237s (B. *Cottret*).

k285 WESLEY C.: *Newport* Kenneth G.C., Charles Wesley's interpretation of some biblical prophecies according to a previously unpublished letter dated 15 April 1754: BJRL 77,2 (1995)31-52.

Y5 *Saeculum XIX* -- **Exegesis** -- **19th century**

k286 **Abzug** Robert H., Cosmos crumbling; American reform and the religious imagination
[c.1800-1850].   Ox 1994, UP. $30.   0-19-503752-9.   -- [R]CScR 25 (1995s) 230-2
(J.E.*Johnson*).

k287 **Addinall** Peter, Philosophy and biblical interpretation, a study in nineteenth century
conflict 1991 → 7,g706 ... 9,16612: [R]RHR 212 (1995) 140-3 (B.E. *Schwarzbach*).

k288   **Bechtoldt** Hans-Joachim,   *a)* Die historische Bibelkritik im Judentum des 19.
Jahrhunderts; ausgewählte Vertreter und ihre Werke; ev. Diss. [D]*Meyer* G.   Mainz 1995
[ThRv Beilage 92/2, xii → 10,14642]. -- *b)* Die jüdische Bibelkritik im 19. Jahrhundert.
Stu 1995, Kohlhammer.   485 p.   DM 128.   3-17-013912-2 [ThRv 92,77; OTA 19, p.143;
NTAb 40, p. 319].

k289 *Beckwith* Roger, Essays and reviews [F. TEMPLE and B. JOWETT periodical] (1860); the
advance of liberalism: Churchman 108 (L 1994) 48-58.

k291 *Binfield* Clyde, Jews in evangelical dissent; the [19th c.] British Society, the Herschell
Connection and the pre-millenarian thread: → [E]*Wilks* M., Prophecy and eschatology 1994,
225-270, singled out in [R]JJS 46 (1995) 320s (I.M. *Resnick*).

k292 *Blaschke* Olaf R., Der Altkatholizismus 1870 bis 1945; Nationalismus, Antisemitismus
und Nationalsozialismus: HZ 261 (1995) 51-99.

k293 **Boles** John B., The irony of southern [U.S. evangelical] religion: Rice Univ. Rockwell
Lectures 4.   NY 1994, P.Lang.   118 p. $ 32.   0-8204-2584-2 [ThD 42,357].

k294 *Bolt* John, Nineteenth- and twentieth-century Dutch Reformed Church and theology Af-
scheiding 1834 ([E]BAKKER W., al. 1984), Doleantie 1886 (same[E], 1986); these two united as
Gereformeerde in 1892 ([E]WOLTHUIS L. 1992)]; a review article: C(alvin)TJ 28 (1993) 434-
442.

k295 [E]**Borgman** Erik, *Harskamp* Anton van, Tussen openheid en isolement; het voorbeeld
van de katholieke theologie in de negentiende eeuw: Kerk en theologie in context 16, 1992
→ 9,16613: [R]Bijdragen 56 (1995) 464 (A. van *Eijk*).

k296 *Briese* Olaf, Wie unsterblich ist der Mensch ? Aufklärerische Argumente für
Unsterblichkeit in der Zeit von 1750-1850: ZRGG 47 (1995) 1-16.

k297 BRIGGS: **Christensen** Richard L., The ecumenical orthodoxy of Charles Augustus
Briggs (1841-1913) [diss. 1992 → 8,m515].   Lewiston NY 1995, Mellen.   236 p. $ 90.
0-7734-2273-0 [ThD 43,261].

k298 **Briggs** J.H.Y., The English Baptists [3d volume of 4] of the nineteenth century. Did-
cot 1994, Baptist Hist.   432 p.   £ 20 pa. £ 15.   0-903166-19-6. -- [R]ET 106 (1994s) 187s
(D.M. *Thompson*).2

k299 BUSHNELL: **Edwards** Robert L., Of singular genius, of singular grace; a biography of
Horace Bushnell.   Cleveland 1992, Pilgrim.   xi-c.400 p. $ 25. -- [R]*CritRR 7 (1994) 331s
(G.A. *Hewitt*); Horizons 22 (1995) 155s (Margaret M. *McGuinness*); P(rinc)SB 16 (1995)
105s (K.P. *Minkema*).

k300 **Butler** Diana H.,   Standing against the whirlwind; Evangelical Episcopalians in
nineteenth-century America: Religion in America. NY 1995, Oxford-UP. xiii-270 p. $ 45.
0-19-508542-6 [ThD 42,159].

k301 CAMPBELL: *Holloway* Gary, Alexander Campbell [movement c. 1850 with 100,000
adherents] as a publisher: RestQ 37 (1995) 28-35.

k302 CANINA Luigi (1785-1856), architetto e teorico del classicismo, ᴱ*Sistri* Augusto. Mi 1995, Guerini. 194 p. 88-7802--599-2.

k303 **Chadwick** Owen, The secularization of the European mind in the nineteenth century; Canto pa. C 1991 = 1975, Univ. 286 p. £ 7. -- ᴿThRv 91 (1995) 492s (K. J. *Rivinius*).

k304 COLENSO: *Rogerson* John W., J.W. Colenso's correspondence with Abraham KUENEN, 1863-1878 : → 5, ᶠATKINSON J., Bible, Reformation, Church: JSNT.s 105 (1995) 190-223.

k305 *de Bie* Linden J., Real presence or real absence ? The spoils of war in nineteenth-century American eucharistic controversy [HODGE Charles; NEVIN John W.]: ProEccl 4 (1995) 431-441.

k305* **Dekker** C.D., Gereformeerd en evangelisch; ontstaan en geschiedenis van de Buddings-gemeinte te Goes en haar plaats in het Nederlandse Protestantisme in die periode 1839-1881. Kampen 1992, Kok. 818 p. *f* 97.50. 90-24267-55-2. -- ᴿNedThT 49 (1995) 77s (P.L. *Schramm* †).

k306 DELITZSCH: **Lehmann** Reinhard, Friedrich Delitzsch [1850-1922] und der Babel-Bibel-Streit [Vorträge 1901s] < Diss. Mainz 1989: OBO 133, 1994 → 10,14651: ᴿAfO 42s (1995s) 308-311 (W. von *Soden*: Diss. Marburg, nicht = ebenda 1988 fast gleichnamig JOHANNING K., fehlend in den Orientalia- und AfO-Bibliographien); OTA 18 (1995) p. 149s (C.T. *Begg*); ThLZ 120 (1995) 905-7 (W. *Wiefel*); ZAW 107 (1995) 534 (C. *Bultmann*).

k307 DREY: ᴱ**Kustermann** A., Revision der Theologie, Reform der Kirche; die Bedeutung des Tübinger Theologen Johann Sebastian Drey (1777-1853) in Geschichte und Gegenwart [Symposium Stuttgart März 1992] 1994 → 10,355b: ᴿTTh 35 (1995) 295 (L.*Kenis*) [& 32 (1992) 185s, N. *Schreurs*]; (Tü)TQ 175 (1995) 362-4 (R. *Reinhardt*).

k308 -- **Himes** Michael J.ᵀ, Brief introduction to the study of theology with reference to the scientific standpoint and the Catholic system, by Johann Sebastian Drey. ND 1994, Univ. xxxv-185 p. $ 33. 0-268-01171-0 [RStR 22,225, W. *Madges*; ThD 42,364].

k309 EDDY; **Knee** Stuart E., Christian Science in the age of Mary Baker Eddy (1821-1910): CAmH 154. Westport CT 1994, Greenwood. xii-158 p. $50. 0-313-28360-5 [< ThD 42 (1995) 276].

k310 EMERSON: **Robinson** David M., Emerson and the conduct of life; pragmatism and ethical purpose in the later work. C 1993, Univ. ix-232 p $ 45. -- ᴿJRel 75 (1995) 286s (W.C. *Gilpin*).

k311 *Forbes* Alexander M., Ultimate reality and ethical meaning; theological utilitarianism in eighteenth-century England: URM 18 (1995) 119-139.

k312 FORBES: **Strong** Rowan, Alexander Forbes [bishop] of Brechin. Ox 1995, Clarendon. 281 p. £ 35. 0-19-826357-0. -- ᴿET 106 (1994s) 289 (C.S. *Rodd*).

k313 FORSYTH: ᴱ**Hart** Trevor, Justice the true and only mercy: essays on the life and theology of Peter Taylor Forsyth [Aberdeen colloquium 1993]. E 1995, Clark. xvii-333 p. £ 29. 0-567-09703-X. -- ᴿE(xp)T 107 (1995s) 115s (A.H.B. *Logan*).

k314 **Franchot** Jenny, Roads to Rome; the antebellum Protestant encounter with Catholicism 1994 → 10,14657: ᴿA(mer)HR 100 (1995) 1682s (P.W. *Carey*); *CritRR 8 (1995) 404-6 (Tracy *Fessenden*).

k315 *Fuller* Donald, *Gardiner* Richard, Reformed theology at Princeton and Amsterdam in the late nineteenth century; a reappraisal: Presbyterion 21 (St.Louis 1995) 89-117.

k316 GALURA Bernard (1764-1856): **Hell** Leonhard, Reich Gottes als Systemidee der Theologie; historisch-systematische Untersuchungen zum [katholisch-] theologischen Werk

B. Galuras und F[riderich] BRENNERs [Diss. Tübingen]: TSTP 6, 1993 → 9,16649: [R]MThZ 45 (1994) 223 (G. *Rottenwöhrer*).

k317 *Garhammer* Erich, Die 'unmodernen' Katholiken [STOLBERG F. 1800; DOBLIN A. 1941]: ThGL 85 (1995) 386-395.

k318 GONZÁLEZ C. 1831-1894: *a) López de Las Heras* Luis, 'La Biblia y la ciencia' del cardenal Ceferino González; -- *b) González Pola* Manuel, El cardenal Zeferino González, filósofo, restaurador de la filosofía escolástica: Studium 35 (M 1995) 29-52 / 267-308.

k319 [E]**Hall** Donald, Muscular Christianity: embodying the Victorian age. C 1994, Univ.

k320 **Hanley** Mark Y., Beyond a Christian commonwealth; the [mainline] Protestant quarrel with the American republic, 1830-1860. Chapel Hill 1994, Univ. N.Carolina. 210 p. $ 35. - - [R]JRel 75 (1995) 282s (Catherine A. *Brekus*).

k321 HAYDOCK: *Ohlhausen* Sidney K., The last [(George L. &) Thomas] Haydock Bible: Re(cus)H 22 (1994s) 529-535.

k322 *Haymes* Dan, 'To honor the God of the Bible '; J.W. MCGARVEY [Disciples of Christ c.1890] and the 'Higher Criticism': L(ex)TQ 29 (1994) 159-187.

------

k323 HEGEL: *Badcock* Gary D., Divine freedom in Hegel [not recognized, says BARTH]: I(r)ThQ 61 (1995 264-271.

k324 **Bialas** Wolfgang, Von der Theologie der Befreiung zur Philosophie der Freiheit; Hegel und die Religion: ÖB 23, 1993 →10,14660*: [R]TTh 35 (1995) 415 (P.A. van *Gennip*).

k325 **Bradt** Raymond K.[J], Hegel's word 'God': diss. Yale, [D]*Dupré* L. NHv 1995. 393 p. 95-38677. -- D(iss)AI 56 (1995s) p. 2734.

k326 **Burbidge** John W., Hegel on logic and religion; the reasonablenes of Christianity [2 inedita + reprints]. Albany 1992, SUNY. x-184 p. $ 49.50; pa. $ 17. -- [R]*CritRR 7 (1994) 448-451 (Ardis B. *Collins*).

k327 *Di Giovanni* George, Hegel's Phenomenology and the critique of the Enlightenment: L(aval)TP 51,2 ('Hegel aujourd'hui', 1995) 251-270 [*al.* 229-419].

k328 *Jamros* Daniel P., Hegel on the Incarnation; unique or universal: TS 56 (1995) 276-301.

k329 **O'Donohue** John, Person als Vermittlung. Mainz 1993, Grünewald. 492 p. DM 62. — [R]JRel 75 (1995) 427s (A. *Kyongsuk Min*).

k330 **Olson** Alan, Hegel and the Spirit; philosophy as pneumatology 1992 → 9,16656; 10,14660 [RStR 22,28-33, A. *Kyongsuk Min*, also on 5 cognates].

k331 **O'Regan** Cyril, The heterodox Hegel. Albany 1994, SUNY. xv-517 p. -- [R]MoTh 11 (1995) 385s (P.C. *Hodgson*: magnificent).

k332 **Pagano** Maurizio, Hegel; la religione e l'ermeneutica del concetto: BtFT 2. N 1992, Scientifiche. 245 p. L[m] 32. 88-7104-488-6. -- Protest 50 (1995) 172s (S. *Rostagno*).

k333 **Splett** Jörg, La dottrina della Trinità in Hegel, [TE]*Sansonetti* Giuliano: GdT 222. Brescia 1993 → 10,7590; L[m] 35: [R]EThL 71 (1995) 480s (E. *Brito*).

------

k334 HEINE: **Wirth-Ortmann** Beate, Heinrich Heines Christusbild; Grundzüge seines relgiösen Selbstverständnisses. Pd 1995, Schöningh. 244 p. DM 68. 3-506-73442-3 [TR 91,445].

k335 **Hempton** David, *Hill* Myrtle, Evangelical Protestantism in Ulster society 1740-1890. L c.1994, Routledge. £ 40. -- [R]Furrow 46 (1995) 53-55 (R. *Dunlop* : one of the most important books on Ireland to appear for a long time).

k336 HESS: **Lundgren** Svante, Moses Hess on religion, Judaism and the Bible. Åbo 1992, Akademis. 206 p. -- ᴿZRGG 47 (1995) 191 (J. *Neusner:* first rate; Hess as theorist was in the shadow of MARX and HERZL, but in some ways superior).

k337 *Hitchin* Neil, Probability and the Word of God; William PALEY's Anglican method and the defense of the Scriptures: A(ngl)ThR 77 (1995) 392-407.

k338 **Hodges** Graham R., Black itinerants and the Gospel; the narratives of John JEA and George WHITE. Madison WI 1993, Madison House. viii-200 p. $ 27. -- ᴿChH 64 (1995) 500-2 (M.C. *Sernett*).

k339 **Holzem** Andreas, Weltversuchung und Heilsgewissheit; Kirchengeschichte des Katholizismus des 19. Jahrhunderts: MThA 35. Altenberge 1995, Oros. 247 p. DM 40. 3-89375-106-8 [ThRv 91,276].

k340 **Holzem** Andreas, Kirchenreform und Sektenstiftung; Deutschkatholiken, Reformkatholiken und Ultramontane am Oberrhein (1844-1866): Komm.ZGesch B-65. Pd 1994, Schöningh. xlvi-460 p. DM 98. 3-506-79968-1 [ThRv 91,276].

k341 **Hope** Nicholas, German and Scandinavian Protestantism, 1700-1918: Oxford History of the Christian Church. Ox 1995, Clarendon. xxvii-685 p. $ 120. 0-19-826923-4 [ThD 43,273].

k342 **Hylson-Smith** Kenneth, High Churchmanship ... 16th-20th century 1994 → 10,14886: ᴿJThS 46 (1995) 398s (J. *Garrard*).

k343 ILGEN †1834: **Seidel** Bodo, K.F. Ilgen und die Pentateuchforschung .. BZAW 213, 1993 → 9,16658: ᴿCBQ 57 (1995) 790s (J.W. *Rogerson*); *CritRR 8 (1995) 150 (N.P. *Lemche*).

k344 KÄHLER Martin, Il cosiddetto Gesù storico e l'autentico Cristo biblico [1892], ᵀᴱ*Sorrentino* S., 1992 → 8,4301: ᴿFilTeo 8 (1994) 142s (G. *Zarone*).

k345 KEIL: **Siemens** Peter, Karl Friedrich Keil (1807-1888), Leben und Werk [Diss. Tü] 1994 →10,14669*; DM 49: ᴿThR(und) 60 (1995) 349s (L. *Perlitt*); ZAW 107 (1995) 366 (C. *Bultmann*).

k346 **Kenis** Leo, De theologische faculteit te Leuven .. 1834-1889: 1992 → 10,14670: ᴿRTL 26 (1995) 55-61 (G. *Thils*; Eng.143); TTh 35 (1995) 295-7 (T. *Schoof,* ook over ᴱLAMBERIGTS M. 1994).

------

k347 KIERKEGAARD: *Abraham* Matin, Søren Kierkegaards 'bewaffnete Neutralität', zur Kirchenkritik eines 'christlichen Schriftstellers': NZSTh 37 (1995) 308-323; Eng. 323 [242-287, *Steiger* Lothar: 286-307, *Schulz* Heiko].

k348 *Crouter* R., KIERKEGAARD's not-so-hidden debt to SCHLEIERMACHER: ZnTg 1 (1994) 205-225 [< ZIT 95,p.176].

k349 **Ferguson** Harvie, Melancholy and the critique of modernity; Søren Kierkegaard's religious psychology. L 1995, Routledge. xvii-286 p. £ 40; pa. £ 15. -- ᴿRelSt 31 (1995) 537-540 (M.J. *Ferreira*).

k350 *a)* **Ferreira** M. Jamie, Transforming vision; imagination and will in Kierkegaardian faith. Ox 1991, Clarendon. 160 p. -- ᴿS(cot)JTh 48 (1995) 266s (A. *McFadyen*). -- *b) Law* David R., How Christian is Kierkegaard's God ? : S(cot)JTh 48 (1995) 301-314.

k351 **Fonk** Peter, Zwischen Sünde und Erlösung; Entstehung und Entwicklung einer christlichen Anthropologie bei SK [Diss.]. Kevelaer 1990, Butzon & B. 463 p. DM 64. -- ᴿMThZ 45 (1994) 95-97 (B. *Irrgang*).

k352 ᵀᴱ**Hong** Howard V. & Edna H., Kierkegaard, Works of love [1847 ²1852]: Kierkegaard's Writings 16. Princeton 1995, Univ. xvi-561 p. $ 65. 0-691-03792-0 [ThD 43-174].

k353 **Rosas** L. Joseph[III], Scripture in the thought of Søren Kierkegaard 1994 → 10,14675: [R]C(alvin)TJ 30 (1995) 299-301 (C. *Brown*); ET 106 (1994s) 90 (S. *Plant*); RExp 92 (1995) 531-3 (D.R. *Stiver*).

k354 *Torralba Roselló* Francesc, Cristologia de Kierkegaard: RCatT 30 (1995) 103-153; Eng. 153.

k355 *Ward* Rodney A., The reception of Søren Kierkegaard into English: E(xp)T 107 (1995s) 43-47.

------

k356 **Knight** George R., Millennial fever [1844] and the end of the world; a study of Millerite Adventism. Boise 1993, Pacific. 384 p. -- [R]ChH 64 (1995) 308-310 (D. *Morgan*).

k357 KUHN: **Wolf** Hubert, Ketzer oder Kirchenlehrer ? [kath. Diss. Tü 1990 → 8,m543]. Mainz 1992, Grünewald. lvii-395 p. DM 86. 3-7867-1624-2. -- [R]EThL 71 (1995) 250-2 (L. *Kenis*): *ZnTg 2 (1995) 315-7 (W. *Madges*).

k358 MACDONALD: **Hein** Roland, George MacDonald, Victorian mythmaker. Nv 1993, Star Song. xxv-453 p. $23. 1-56233-046-2. -- [R]CScR 25 (1995s) 221-3 (K.J. *Fielding*, also on his 1994 anthology).

k359 **McLeod** Hugh, European religion in the age of the great cities 1830-1930. L 1994, Routledge. x-398 p £ 40. 0-415-09522-0. -- [R]ET 106 (1994s) 282 (R. *Gill*).

k360 MENDELSSOHN: *a) Kaus* R. Jeremy, Moses Mendelssohn als Psychologe der Ambivalenz; die psychoanalytische Aktualität seiner Theorie der 'gemischten Empfindungen'; -- *b) Schoeps* Julius H., Auf dem Weg zur Glaubensfreiheit; die Herausbildung des Intoleranzbegriffes in Brandenburg-Preussen im Zeitalter Moses Mendelssohns: ZRGG 47 (1995) 17-35 / 193-204.

k361 MIGNE: **Bloch** R. Howard, God's plagiarist 1994 → 10,14681: [R]C(ath)HR 81 (1995) 450s (R.F. *Costigan*).

k362 MÖHLER J.A.: Vorlesungen über die Kirchengeschichte [1823s], [E]**Rieger** R.: Wewelbuch 179. Mü 1992, Wewel. xli-716 p. DM 128. -- [R]CrSt 16 (1995) 203-6 (A.P. *Kustermann*).

k363 **Murphy** Terrence, *Stortz* Gerald, Greed and culture; the place of English-speaking Catholics in Canadian society, 1750-1930. Montreal 1993, McGill-Queens Univ. xxxix-253 p. -- [R]SR 24 (1995) 117s (D.F. *Campbell*).

k364 NEALE: **Litvack** Leon, John Mason Neale [1818-1866] and the quest for sobornost. Ox 1994, Clarendon. xi-295. £ 35. 0-19-826351-1. -- [R]ET 106 (1994s) 59 (Ann *Shukman*: uneven); StVlad 39 (1995s) 428-431 (N. *Birbs*).

k365 *Niehoff* M.R., [H] [Leopold] ZUNZ's concept of *Aggada* as an expression of Jewish spirituality: Tarbiz 64 (1994s) 423-459; Eng. 3,viii: based on HERDER.

k366 NIETZSCHE: **Heidegger** Martin, Nietzsche [lezioni 1936-46], [T]*Volpi* Franco. Mi 1994, Adelphi. 973 p. L[m] 125. -- [R]RasT 36 (1995) 107-9 (O. *Di Grazia*).

k367 -- *Sambou* Ernest, La critique nietzschéenne de la vérité: RICAO 10 ('Critique nietzschéenne et regards bibliques', Abidjan 1995) 19-49.

k368 **O'Meara** Thomas F., Church and culture; German Catholic theology, 1860-1914: 1991 → 8,m567: [R]JThS 46 (1995) 789-791 (G. *Jones*); TTh 35 (1995) 297 (T. *Schoof*).

k369 OVERBECK: **Henry** M., Franz Overbeck: theologian ? Religion and history in the thought of F.O.: EHS 23/536. Fra 1995, Lang. xvi-312 p. [RHE 91,111*].

k370 **Palmer** Bernard, Reverend rebels; five Victorian clerics and their fight against authority [R. DOLLING → 9,16645, and others like TOOTH R., romanizing but) aiming mainly to help the poor]. L 1993, Darton-LT. £ 15. -- ᴿI(rish)BSt 17 (1995) 45-48; JEH 46 (1995) 533s (Sheridan *Gilley*)

k371 PARKER: **Teed** Paul E., 'A very excellent fanatic, a very good infidel and a first-rate traitor'; Theodore PARKER and the search for perfection in antebellum America [Transcendentalism]: diss. Connecticut, 1994. 402 p. 95-25688. -- D(iss)AI 56 (1995s) p. 1501.

k372 **Paul** Jean-Marie, Dieu est mort en Allemagne; des Lumières à NIETZSCHE: BtScientifique. P 1994, Payot. 320 p. -- ᴿRTPh 127 (1995) 383s (F. *Félix*).

k373 ᴱ**Paz** D.G., Nineteenth-century English religious traditions, retrospect and prospect [8 art.]: Contributions to the study of religion 44. Westport CT 1995, Greenwood. xiv-232 p. $ 55. 0-313-29476-3 [ThD 43,379].

k374 PEIRCE: *Ward* Roger [*al.*], C.S. Peirce and contemporary theology; the return to conversion: A(mer)JTP 16 (1995) 125-148 [-197],

k375 RITSCHL: ᴱ**Jodock** Darrell, Ritschl in retrospect; history, community, and science [AAR seminar]. Mp 1995, Fortress. xvi-199 p. $ 24 pa. 0-8006-2606-0 [ThD 43,184]. -- ᴿ*CritRR 8 (1995) 480-3 (J.C. *Livingston*).

k376 **Rogerson** J.W., The Bible and criticism in Victorian Britain; profiles of F.D. MAURICE and William ROBERTSON SMITH [Aberdeen Gifford Lectures 1994; London Maurice Lectures 1992]: JSOT.s 201. Sheffield 1995, Academic. 188 p. £ 30. 1-85075-553-1 [OTA 19, p.148].

k377 -- ᴱ**Johnstone** William, William ROBERTSON SMITH; essays in reassessment [† 1894 age 47; Aberdeen Univ. congress April 1994; 34 art.]. Shf 1995, Academic. 403 p. £ 45. 1-85075-523-X. -- ᴿE(xp)T 107,4 top choice (1995s) 97s (C.S. *Rodd* on his view of the place of the Bible within Christianity).

k378 ROSMINI: *a) Lorizio* Giuseppe, Ricerca della verità e 'metafisica della carità' nel pensiero di Antonio Rosmini; -- *b) Bof* Giampiero, 'Credere pensando'; a proposito di un convegno sulla teologia rosminiana [Rovereto 3-5.V. ..]: RasT 36 (1995) 527-552 / 470-6.

k379 -- **Quacquarelli** Antonio, Le radici patristiche 1991 → 9,16676: ᴿRHE 90 (1995) 331s (R. *Aubert*).

k380 SABATIER: *a) Reymond* Bernard, Il protestantesimo liberale di Paul Sabatier nella sua 'Vita di San Francesco d'Assisi'; -- *b) Bertalot* Renzo, Paul Sabatier et l'ecumenismo: (R)*StEc 12,2 (Venezia 1993s) *55-*72 / 153-9 (*al.* *5-*191).

k381 **Sachs** William L., The transformation of Anglicanism; from state church to global communion 1993 → 9,16879: ᴿJRel 75 (1995) 280 (Ellen K. *Wondra*: chiefly on 19th century).

k382 SCHAFF (1819-93): *a) Shriver* George H., Philip Schaff, Christian scholar and ecumenical prophet. Macon 1987, Mercer Univ. -- ᴿC(oncordia)TQ 59 (1995) 139s (L.R. *Rast*). -- *b) Meyer* John C., Philip Schaff as an ecumenical prophet; a fresh look at an old plan for Christian reunion: E(cu)R 47 (1995) 52-59.

k383 ᴱ**Schieder** Wolfgang, Religion und Gesellschaft im 19. Jahrhundert: Industrielle Welt 54. Stu 1993, Klett-Cotta. 331 p. 3-608-91632-6. -- ᴿRHPhR 75 (1995) 356s (M. *Lienhard*: 13 art. de réaction contre la confessionalisation de l'histoire religieuse).

----

k384 SCHLEIERMACHER, Le statut de la théologie [1811, ²1830], ᵀ*Kaempf* B.: Passages. Genève/P 1994, Labor et Fides/Cerf. 194 p. F 120. 2-8309-0729-9 / 2-204-05036-9. -- ᴿÉTRel 70 (1995) 140s (A. *Gounelle*).

k385 *Blaser* Klauspeter, Les études de théologie selon Schleiermacher, [ᵀ*Kaempf* B. 1994]: RTPhil 127 (1995) 155-162; Eng. 208.

k386 **Brito** Emilio, La pneumatologie de Schleiermacher: BETL 113,1994 → 10,14696: ᴿBLE 96 (1995) 249s (A. *Dartigues*); EThL 71 (1995) 185-200 (É. *Gaziaux*).

k387 -- *Gaziaux* Éric, Philosophie et théologie à la lumière de Schleiermacher; à propos de [BRITO E., Pneumatologie 1994]: RTL 26 (1995) 484-493; Eng. 609.

k388 **Curran** Thomas H., Doctrine and speculation in Schleiermacher's 'Glaubenslehre'. B 1994, de Gruyter. xx-390 p. -- ᴿModern Believing [continuing the numbering of Modern Churchman] 36,1 (1995) 40-42 (G. *Pattison*).

k389 *Gerrish* B.A., The doctrine of faith [< awaited 1994 Warfield Lectures]: P(rinc)SB 16 (1995) 202-215.

k390 **Hübner** Ingolf, Wissenschaftsbegriff und Theologieverständnis; eine Untersuchung zur Dialektik Schleiermachers; Diss. ᴰ*Krötke*. Berlin 1995. -- ThRv Beilage 92/2, v.

k391 *Hübner* Ingolf, Schleiermachers epistemologischer Ansatz und die Erkenntnistheorie des amerikanischen Pragmatismus: BThZ 12 (1995) 58-73 (95-108, *Reich* Andreas).

k392 *Schock* Werner, Abhängigkeitsgefühl und Sinneinheit; zum Gottesbegriff in Schleiermachers Glaubenslehre: NZSTh 37 (1995) 41-56; Eng. 56.

k393 **Schröder** Markus, Die kritische Identität des neuzeitlichen Christentums; Schleiermachers Wesensbestimmung der christlichen Religion: ev. Diss. ᴰ*Fischer*. Hamburg 1995. -- ThRv Beilage 92/2, ix.

k394 *Steiger* Johann A., Friedrich Schleiermacher, das Alte Testament und das Alter; zur Geschichte einer überraschenden Alterseinsicht: K(er)uD 40 (1994) 305-326; Eng. 327, 'History and drama of a surprising devotion '.

k395 **Vance** Robert L., Sin and self-consciousness in the thought of Friedrich Schleiermacher: NABPR.ds 1. Lewiston NY, Mellen. 219 p. [RStR 22,334. W.E. *Wyman*].

----

k396 *Smend* Rudolf, The interpretation of wisdom in nineteenth-century scholarship; → 55, ᶠEMERTON J., Wisdom 1995, 257-268.

k397 **Smith** Helmut W., German nationalism and religious conflict; culture, ideology, politics, 1770-1914. Princeton 1995, Univ. xiii-271 p. $ 39.50. 0-691-03624-1 [ThD 43,89].

k398 **Snay** Mitchell, Gospel of disunion; religion and separatism in the antebellum South. C 1993, Univ. 265 p. $ 50. -- ᴿJRel 75 (1995) 283-5 (C. *Grasso*).

k399 ᴱ**Stroup** George w., Contemporary trajectories, 1799 to the present: Reformed Reader 2. LvL 1993. W-Knox. 369 p. $ 25. 0-664-21958-6. -- ᴿInterpretation 49 (1995) 326 . 8 (E. *TeSelle*).

k400 *Vilar* Juan B., Propaganda protestante en Asturias a mediados del siglo XIX; difusión en Gijón en 1857, por un colportor prusiano, de folletos contra el recién definido dogma de la Inmaculada: DiEc 30 (1995) 341-350.

k401 **Warner** William W., At peace with their neighbors; Catholics and Catholicism in the national capital, 1770-1860. Wsh 1992, Georgetown Univ. xi-307 p. -- ᴿChH 64 (1995) 502s (F.M. *Perko*).

k402 **Watts** Michael R., The Dissenters [in Britian, I, 1978; from the Reformation to the French Revolution]; II. The expansion of Evangelical Nonconformity [to 1869]. Ox 1995, Clarendon. xxi-911 p. $ 120. 0-19-822968-2 [ThD 43,192].

k403 **Wauzzinski** Robert A., Between God and gold; Protestant evangelicalism and the industrial revolution, 1820-1914. Rutherford NJ 1993, F.Dickinson Univ. 224 p. $ 39.50. 0-8386-3481-8. -- ᴿCScR 25 (1995s) 225-7 (A C. *Guelzo*).

k404 DE WETTE: *Ohst* Martin, De Wette als theologischer Ethiker neben SCHLEIERMACHER: ThZ 51 (1995) 151-173.

k405 -- **Rogerson** John, W.L.M. de Wette, founder of modern biblical criticism: JOTS.s 126, 1992 → 8,m488 ... 10,14712: [R]BiOr 52 (1995) 104s (M.J. *Paul:* supplants A. WIEGAND 1879, unduly pious); JSSt 40 (1995) 96 (R.E. *Clements*); VT 45 (1995) 417s (J.A. *Emerton*).

k406 -- *Rogerson* John W., Synchrony and diachrony [DE SAUSSURE 1916] in the work of de Wette [† 1849] and its importance for today: → 515, Synchronic ? 1994/4, 145-158.

k407 WUNSCH Ernst † 1828: *Kempski* Jürgen von, Apokalypse, 'Horus' und Wunsch [der letzte Rektor der Univ. Frankfurt an der Oder]: ZRGG 47 (1995) 304-319.

k408 **Zorn** Jean-François, Le grand siècle d'une mission protestante; la Mission de Paris de 1822 à 1914. P 1993, Karthala. 791 p.; 14 pl.; 10 maps. F 250. 2-85304-106-9. -- [R]RHPhR 75 (1995) 366s (M. *Chevallier*).

Y5.5 *Crisis modernistica* -- **The Modernist Era**

k409 **Malusa** Luciano (I), *Cornoldi* Giovanni M., Neotomismo e intransigenza cattolica, I. Il contributo; II. Testi: Univ. Verona, Ric. Filos. 3.6. Mi 1986/9, Ist. Propaganda Libreria. xxxii-510 p.; xiv-487 p. -- [R]RHE 90 (1995) 567-571 (R. *Aubert*).

k410 *Meyer* Wendel W., The phial of blood controversy and the decline of the liberal Catholic movement [CAPES J., The Rambler 1846 ... WISEMAN 1848]: JEH 46 (1995) 75-94.

k411 *Nicolas* J.-H., Les rapports entre la nature et le surnaturel dans les débats contemporains: RThom 95 (1995) 399-416.

k412 **O'Connell** Marvin B., Critics on trial ... Catholic modernist crisis 1994 → 10,14720: [R]*CanadCath 13,9 (1995) 23 (L.A. *Kennedy*); Month 256 (1995) 315s (E. *Birmingham*).

k413 [E]**Rowell** Geoffrey, The English religious tradition and the genius of Anglicanism (for 1792 KEBLE birthday) 1992 → 479*; 8010: [R]Churchman 108 (L 1994) 91s (G. *Bray:* excellent).

k414 **Schatz** K., Vatikanum I (1869-1870) I-II 1992s→ 10,14724; -- III. Unfehlbarheitsdiskussion und Rezeption. Pd 1994, Schöningh. 300 p.; 405 p.; 358 p. 3-506-74695-2. -- [R]E(st)E 70 (1995) 262-4 (J.A. *Estrada*).

k415 **Schultenover** David G., A view from Rome on the eve of the Modernist crisis 1991 → 9,16699: [R]*CritRR 7 (1994) 368-370 (R. *Burke*).

----

k416 BLONDEL: The letter on apologetics [1896] and History and dogma [1904 on LOISY], [T]*Dru* Alexander, *Trethowan* Illtyd. GR 1994, Eerdmans. 301 p. $ 19. 0-8028-0819-0 [ThD 42,357; RStR 22,51, Jean S. *Liddell:* unduly tamed; no updated bibliography].

k417 **Antonelli** M., L'Eucaristia nell' 'Action' (1893) di Blondel, la chiave di volta di un'apologetica filosofica [diss. Gregoriana]: Pont. Sem. Lombardo di Roma. Mi 1993, Glossa. xvi-271 p. L[m] 45. -- [R]StPat(av) 42 (1995) 571-4 (L. *Sartori*).

k418 [E]**Coutagne** Marie-Jeanne, L'Action; une dialectique du salut, colloque Aix-P 1993. P 1994, Beauchesne. 296 p. -- [R]ScrT(Pamp) 27 (1995) 1022-6 (M. *Martorell*).

k419 *Long* Fiachra, Blondel's religious postulate in Action (1893): I(r)ThQ 61 (1995) 57-69.

k420 *Reimão* Cassiano, A problemática da Acção na filosofia de Maurice Blondel: → 27, [F]BRAGANÇA J., Didask 25 (1995) 453-468.

------

k421 BOUQILLON: *Curran* Charles E., Thomas Joseph Bouqillon [Belgian-born Catholic U. moralist best known for his defense of Archbishop IRELAND's 'Faribault plan' for deprivatizing Catholic education]: Americanist, Neo-Scholastic, or manualist ? → 564, CTS 50 (1995) 156-173.

k422 HECKER: **O'Brien** David J., Isaac Hecker, an American Catholic 1992 → 8,m580; 9,16714: ^RChH 64 (1995) 313-5 (T.M. *Keefe*); IBM(iss)R 18 (1994) 93s (C.J. *Kauffman*).

k423 LAGRANGE [→Y6]: *Nicolas* Jean-Hervé, Un grand serviteur de l'Église au temps du modernisme, le Père Lagrange : NV 70 (1995) 43-60.

----

k424 NEWMAN: **Achten** Rik, First principles and our way to faith; a fundamental theological study of J.H.Newman's notion of first principles: EHS 23/539. NY 1995, P.Lang. 309 p. $ 58. 0-8204-2912-0 [< ThD 43,353].

k425 ^E**Allsopp** Michael E., *Burke* Ronald R., J.H. Newman; theology and reform 1992 → 8,505c: ^RNewThR 8,4 (1995) 111s (M.A. *Testa*).

k426 **Biehl** Vincent F., The white stone; the spiritual theology of J.H. Newman 1994 → 10,14750 [RStR 22,51. J.T. *Ford*]: ^RAmerica 173,25 (1995) 25s (G.E. *Griener*, also on PAGE J.R., on infallibility).

k427 ^E**Biehl** Vincent Ferrer (SJ), J.H. Newman, Sermons 1824-43, II [all the modifications and modulations and Anglican pre-formulations carefully noted] 1993 → 10,14750*: ^RET 106 (1994s) 187 (S. *Gilley*).

k428 -- **Murray** Placid (I), J.H.Newman, Sermons on the liturgy and sacraments and on Christ the mediator: 1824-43: 1991; xx-384 p.; $ 89; 0-19-920088-2: ^RCScR 25 (1995s) 244s (M.A. *Testa*); *CritRR 7 (1994) 353s (R. *Penaskovic*).

k429 **Boudens** Robrecht, Two Cardinals: John Henry Newman -- Désiré Joseph MERCIER: BETL 123. Lv 1995, Univ. 362 p.; p. 135-167. Newman bibliog. 1990-4. 90-6186-717-7.

k430 *Boudens* Robrecht, Irony and humor in Newman: → 40, ^FCOLLINS R. : LouvSt 20 (1995) 254-264.

k431 *Boyce* Philip, Newman's reception into the Catholic Church; its message and relevance: Ter(esianum) 46 (1995) 521-542.

k432 **Britt** John F., Newman's use of Sacred Scripture in texts on the Incarnation and Mary [< diss. 1992-5]: Marian Library Studies 24. Dayton 1995, Univ. P. 197-264; Newman bibliog. 204-210.

k433 *Cooper* Austin, Ireland and the Oxford Movement: JRelH 19 (1995) 62-74.

k434 *Gilley* Sheridan, The end of the Oxford movement ('Prejudice unmasked' 3): Tablet 249 (1995) 352-4.

k435 **Griffin** John R., A historical commentary on the major Catholic works of Cardinal Newman. NY 1993, P.Lang. $40.-- ^RFaith & Reason 21 (1995) 277-280 (A. *Andres*).

k436 *Guarino* Thomas, Vatican I and dogmatic apophasis [revelation even as received by faith remains shrouded in darkness]: I(r)ThQ 61 (1995) 70-82.

k437 *Harskamp* Anton van, Zoeken naar gegeven eenheid; akademische vorming volgens J.H. Newman: TTh 35 (1995) 339-356; Eng. 356s.

k438 **Lackner** Bernhard, Segnung und Gebot: J.H. Newmans Entwurf des christlichen Ethos [Diss. Regensburg 1993, ^D*Schockenhoff* E.] . RgStTh 41. Fra 1994, Lang. 355 p. DM 95. 3-631-46840-7. -- ^RThGL 85 (1995) 139-141 (M. *Rieger*).

k439 ^E**Magill** Gerard, *a)* Discourse and context 1993 → 9,468; / *b)* [12 art.] Personality and belief; interdisciplinary essays on John Henry Newman [both from St.Louis Univ. (1990) centenary conference]. NY 1994, UPA. xviii-210 p.; $39.50 [RStR 22,257, J.T. *Ford*].

k440 *Morales* José, The personality of John H. Newman as seen through his theology: PhilipSa 30 (1995) 99-112.

k441 *Morales* José, Experiencia religiosa; la contribución de J.H. Newman: ScrT(Pamp) 37 (1995) 69-87.

k442 ᴱNicholls David, *Kerr* Fergus, J.H. Newman; reason, rhetoric and romanticism 1991 → 7,g821; 8,m611: ᴿA(ngl)TR 77 (1995) 244 . 246s (M.A. *Testa*).

k443 Nockles Peter B., The Oxford movement in context 1760-1857: 1994 → 10,14764: ᴿA(ngl)ThR 77 (1995) 247s (Rowan A. *Greer*); JThS 46 (1995) 782-6 (H.D. *Rack*); Theol 98 (L 1995) 399s (J. *Garrard*).

k444 *a) O'Connell* Marvin R., *Tillman* Mary Katherine, Development; the context and the content (1839-1845); -- *b) Norris* Thomas, The development of doctrine: 'a remarkable philosophical phenomenon'; -- *c) Callam* Daniel, Christopher DAWSON on the Oxford movement; the relationship of development to authority: Com(US) 22 (1995) 446-469, 470-487: 488-501.

k445 *O'Regan* Cyril, Newman and von BALTHASAR: the christological contexting of the numinous: É(gl)eT 26 (1995) 165-202.

k446 Pattison Robert, The great dissent 1991 → 7,g824 ... 10,14765: ᴿC(ath)HR 81 (1995) 297-9 (S. *Gilley*).

k447 Selén Mats, The Oxford Movement and Wesleyan Methodism in England 1833-1882: 1992 → 8.m617: ᴿChH 64 (1995) 506s (C.I. *Wallace*); SvTK 69 (1993) 192s (S. *Hidal*).

k448 *Tercic* Hans, Doordenken is door-denken; Newmans visie op de dynamiek van het dogma als uiting van de vitaliteit van de Kerk: CVl 25 (1995) 387.-410.

k449 Terril Stephanie. A study of Newman's epistemological thought in light of a model of conception; diss. Graduate Theological Union. Berkeley 1995. 332 p. 95-36449. -- D(iss)AI 56 (1995s) p. 2738.

k450 *Tolhurst* James, 'A blessed and ever-enduring fellowship'; the development of J.H. Newman's thought on death and the life beyond:Re(cus)H 22 (1994s) 424-457.

-----

k451 RENAN: *Montagnes* J., Ernest Renan selon le Père LAGRANGE: RThom95 (1995) 273-283.

k452 TYRRELL George, Medievalism [1908 reply to MERCIER, who had earlier tried to mediate for him]; pref. *Daly* Gabriel.. Tunbridge Wells 1994, Burns & O. 173 p. £ 8. -- ᴿET 106 (1994s) 223 (C.S. *Rodd*); *ModBlv 36,2 (1995) 65s (M.R. *Dorsett*); *TBR 8,2 (1995s) 53.

k453 -- ᴱLivingston James C., Tradition and the critical spirit.. Tyrrell writings 1991 → 8,m626: ᴿChH 64 (1995) 508s (D.G. *Schultenover*: already out of print !).

Y6 *Saeculum XX* -- 20th Century Exegesis

k454 *Baasland* Ernst, Neutestmentliche Forschung in Skandinavien (und Finnland): BThZ 12 (1995) 146-166.

k455 Beilner Wolfgang, Dem Evangelium dienen; 35 Jahre Neutestamentler: Vermittlung 54-56. Salzburg 1995. 3 vol.

k456 Carter Robert L., The 'message of the Higher Criticism'; the Bible renaissance and popular education in America, 1660-1925: diss. North Carolina, ᴰ*Wacker* G. Chapel Hill 1995. 476 p., 95-38380. -- DissA 56 (1995s) p. 2731

k457 ᴱ**Felder** Cain H., Stony the road 1991 → 7,433 ... 10.14800: ᴿJITC 22 (1994) 110-169 (J. *Chopp* + 5) [NTAb 39, p.372]; SWJT 37,1 (1994s) 53s (J.E. *Massey*).

k458 -- *Sanders* Boykin, On the track of African American biblical scholarship [FELDER C.]: JRT 49 (1992s) 87-96 [NTAb 36, p.103; 39, p.186].

k459 *a) Fusco* Vittorio, Un secolo di metodo storico nell'esegesi cattolica (1893-1993); -- *b) Grech* Prosper, L'ermeneutica biblica nel XX secolo : StPat(av) 41 (1994) 341.398. Eng. 398 / 399-411; Eng. 411 (457-490 *al.*).

k460 **Harrisville** Roy A., *Sundberg* Walter, The Bible in modern culture; theology and historical-critical method from Spinoza to Käsemann. GR 1995, Eerdmans. 292 p. 0-8028-0873-5 [Word&World 16,382, C.R. *Koester*]

k461 *Marguerat* D., L'exégèse biblique; éclatement ou renouveau: FV 93,3 (1994) 7-24 [NTAb 39, p.189].

k462 ᴱ**Ochs** Peter, The return to Scripture in Judaism and Christianity; essays in postcritical Scripture interpretation 1993 → 9,292*b*: ᴿCrossCur 45 (1995s) 253-7 (L.L. *Edwards*).

k463 *O'Ferrall* Fergus, Catholics, Protestants, and the Bible today: DoLi 35 (1995) 672-680.

k464 **Riches** John K., A century of New Testament study 1993 → 9,16788: ᴿA(ndr)USS 33 (1995) 320s (E.E. *Reynolds*); *CritRR 8 (1995) 285-7 (W. *Baird*); ET 106 (1994s) 308s (J.A. *Ziesler*); ZnTg 2 (1995) 313s (M.D *Chapman*).

k465 ᴱ**Segalla** Giuseppe, Cento anni di studi biblici (1883-1993); l'interpretazione della Bibbia nella Chiesa [convegno Padova 17-18 febb. 1994: StPatav supp (1994). 186 p. Lᵐ 30. -- ᴿB(bb)eO 37 (1995) 61-64 (G. *De Virgilio*).

k466 **Seidel** H.W., Die Erforschung des ATs in der katholischen Theologie seit dem Jahrhundertwende, ᴱ*Dohmen* C. 1993 → 9,16766: ᴿZAW 107 (1995) 543s (C. *Bultmann*).

k467 **Smith** Theophus H., Conjuring culture; biblical formations of black America 1994 → 10,14777: ᴿMoTh 11 (1995) 394-6 (D.N. *Hopkins*: important, creative).

k468 **Sperling** S. David, *al.*, Students of the Covenant; a history of Jewish biblical scholarship in North America 1992 → 8,m637; 10,14778: ᴿEThL 70 (1994) 135s (A. *Schoors*); RB 102 (1995) 471 (É. *Nodet*).

k469 *Stein* Stephen J., America's Bibles; canon, commentary and community [1995 presidential address]: ChH 64 (1995) 109-184.

k470 *Thompson* Thomas L., Offing the Establishment [DIEBNER B., LEMCHE N.]; DBAT 38 [or ? 28, dated 1994 in note 19] and the politics of radicalism: BN(otiz) 79 (1995) 71-87.

k471 *Vanhoye* Albert, ᴳ Past and present of the Biblical Commission [= Passé et présent, Gregorianum 74 (1993) 261-270]: DeltBM 22,2 (1993) 35-48 [NTAb 38, p.14; 39, p.199].

k472 *West* Gerald, Reading the Bible [formerly used to support apartheid, then liberation ..] and doing theology in the new South Africa: → 159, ᶠROGERSON, J., Bible/Society; JSOT.s 200 (1995) 445-458.

k473 *Wyssenbach* J.P., La Biblia y el Dios de la vida: T-IUSI 14 (Caracas 1995) 47-60.

k474 BEA: *Cassidy* Edward, The ecumenical legacy of Augustin Cardinal Bea: Mid-Str 34 (1995) 157-175.

k475 -- **Schmidt** Stjepan, Augustin Bea the Cardinal of unity 1992 → 10,14781: ᴿObnŽiv 49 (1994) 394-6 (I. *Koprek*).

k476 BLOCH: *Disse* Jörg, Espérance et individu chez Ernst Bloch: RTPh 127 (1995) 217-233; Eng. 320.

-----

k477 BUBER M., Jo i Tu. Barc 1994, Claret. 143 p. -- ᴿEstFr 96 (1995) 276s (J. *Llimona*).

k478 *Ben-Chorin* Schalom, Martin Buber, 8.II.1878 -- 13.VI.1965: FrRu 2 (1995) 311-4.

k479 **Kepnes** Steven, The text as thou 1992 → 9,16776: [R]*A(sn)JS 20 (1995) 253-6 (T. *Weinberger*).

k480 *Kovacs* George, God as the ultimate thou and meaning of life in Martin Buber: URM 17 (1994) 33-49.

k481 ['Carol Publishing Group'], Martin Buber's ten rungs; collected Hasidic sayings. NY 1995, Carol. 127 p. 0-8065-1593-7.

k482 *Repges* W., Martin Buber und der Glaube der Christen: Renovatio 51,1 (Rg 1995) 31-42 [< Judaica 51,196].

k483 **Rotenstreich** Nathan, Immediacy and its limits; a study in Martin Buber's thought. Chur 1991, Harwood. 118 p. -- *A(sn)JS 19 (1994) 104-6 (S.D. *Breslauer*).

k484 *Tyldesley* Michael, Martin Buber and the Bruderhof communities: JJS 45 (1994) 258-272.

------

k485 BULTMANN: *Anz* Wilhelm, Die existentiale Theologie Rudolf Bultmanns: WuD(ienst) 23 (1995) 8-22.

k486 **Fergusson** David, Bultmann 1992 → 9,16783; 10,14790: [R]S(cot)JTh 48 (1995) 122s (J. *Macquarrie*).

k487 *Hübner* Hans, Rudolf Bultmanns Her-Kunft und Hin-Kunft; zur neueren Bultmann-Literatur: [R]ThLZ 120 (1995) 3-21.

k488 **Jaspers** K., *Bultmann* R., Il problema della demitizzazione [1953/63], [E]*Celada Ballanti* R. Brescia 1994, Morcelliana. -- [R]Studium 91 (R 1995) 969-971 (G. *Penzo*).

k489 *Krallis* Charis, [G] The meeting of R. Bultmann with M. HEIDEGGER -- the vicissitude of Protestant theology and of existential ontology: D(elt)BM 14,2 (1995) 5-20.

k490 *a)* *Perrot* Charles, Bultmann et l'exégèse d'aujourd'hui; -- *b)* *Gisel* Pierre. R. Bultmann's illustration d'un 'destin protestant' ?: → 120, Mém. MARLÉ R., Présence de Bultmann: R(ech)SR 83 (1995) 543-555 / 585-606; Eng. 516 . 518.

k491 *Schmithals* Walter, Zum Problem der Entmythologisierung bei Rudolf Bultmann: ZThK 92 (1995) 166-206.

k492 **Valerio** K. de, Altes Testament und Judentum im Frühwerk R. Bultmanns: BZNW 71, 1994 → 10,14798; DM 172: [R]SNTU 19 (1994) 256s (A. *Fuchs*).

------

k493 DĄBROWSKI: *Łach* Jan, Ks. Prof. Eugeniusz Dąbrowski jako interpretator Pisma Świętego: STV(ars) 33,2 (1995) 139-145.

k494 FINKELSTEIN L.: *Greenbaum* M.B,. Finkelstein and his critics [he transformed NY Jewish Theological Seminary from a local rabbinical school in 1940 into a major center of Jewish scholarship and outreach by 1995]: CJud 47,4 (1995) 3-78 [NTAb 40, p.406].

k495 **Grelot** Pierre, Combats pour la Bible en Église 1994 → 10,14802: [R]BLE 96 (1995) 136 (S. *Légasse*); I(nd)TS 31 (1994) 178-180 (L. *Legrand*); RB 102 (1995) 309 (R.J. *Tournay*); RThom 95 (1995) 324 (X. *Perrin*); Salesianum 57 (1995) 568s (R. *Vicent*).

k496 HARNACK: **Hübner** Thomas, Adolf von Harnacks Vorlesungen über das Wesen des Christentums unter besonderer Berücksichtigung der Methodenfragen als sachgemässer Zugang zu ihrer Christologie und Wirkungsgeschichte [Diss. Bonn 1992]: EurHS 23/493. Fra 1994, Lang. 421 p. 3-631-46604-8. -- ZkT 117 (1995) 222.

k497 **Harnack** Adolf von, Histoire des dogmes [1881, ^{T}1893]. P 1993, Cerf. 430 p. -- ^{R}BLE 96 (1995) 159s (J.J. *Péré*).

k498 -- *Murrmann-Kahl* M., Nestor der Wissenschaften, Adolf von Harnack (1851-1930): EK 28 (Stu 1995) 728-731 [NTAb 40, p.208].

k499 -- *a) Rowe* William V., Adolf von HARNACK and the concept of Hellenization [response *Henaut* Barry W.]; -- *b) Williams* Daniel H., Harnack, MARCION and the argument of antiquity: --→ 10,322, Hellenization 1991/4, 69-98 [99-106] / 223-240.

k500 HESCHEL: **Merkle** John C., The genesis of faith; the depth of theology of Abraham J. Heschel. L 1995, Macmillan. 292 p. $ 17.50. 0-02-920990-0. -- ^{R}*TBR 8,1 (1995s) 61 (N.R.M. *de Lange*).

k501 **Hildebrandt** Wilf, An Old Testament theology of the Spirit of God. Peabody MA 1995, Hendrickson. xviii-238 p. $ 15 pa. 1-56563-051-3 [< OTA 19, p.548].

------

k502 LAGRANGE: **Montagnes** Bernard, Le Père Lagrange (1855-1938); l'exégèse catholique dans la crise moderniste. P 1995, Petits Cerf-Histoire. 246 p. F 125. 2-204-05131-4. -- ^{R}Ang 72 (1995) 579-582 (S. *Jurić*); E(spr)eV 105 (1995) 377-9 (É. *Cothenet*); Études 383 (1995) 5693 (P. *Gibert*); PensCath 279 (1995) 88s (D. *Vibrac*).

k503 *Montagnes* Bernard, La correspondance du Père Lagrange avec l'abbé BARDY: MélSR 52 (1995) 65-86; Eng. 86.

k504 ^{E}**Gilbert** Maurice, Exégète à Jérusalem 1991 → 7,g684 .... 10,14804: ^{R}RTL 26 (1995) 87s (J. *Ponthot*).

k505 **Guitton** Jean, Retrato del Padre Lagrange; él que reconcilió la ciencia con la fe [1992 → 8,m667*], ^{T}*Villar Ponz* Mercedes. M 1993, Palabra. 185 p. pt 2650. 84-7118-902-X. -- ^{R}*ActuBbg 31 (1994) 102 (J. *O'Callaghan*).

k507 **Scott** Timothy, The contribution of M.-J. Lagrange O.P. to Catholic biblical studies (1890-1903): diss. Pont. Univ. Gregoriana, ^{D}*Conroy* C. Rome 1995. 308 p.; Extr. N° 4254, 186 p. -- RTLv 27.p.548.

------

k508 LE ROUX J.H., A story of two ways: thirty years of Old Testament scholarship in South Africa: OTEs.s2. Pretoria 1993, Verba vitae. 383 p. 0-9583-8051-1.-- *SeK 15 (1994) 391-413 (J.A. *Loader* claims that he and other scholars are belittled); 16 (1995) 82-101 (Le Roux's respectful but critical answer) [< OTA 19, p.149; p.3].

k509 -- *Loader* J.A., Adrianus VAN SELMS, *responsum* [to LE ROUX J.H.]: → 218*, ^{F}WEST-HUIZEN J., *J/TydSem 7,2 (1995) 240-250.

k510 MARTINI: **Ghidelli** Carlo, Comunicare; note bibliche per la vita sulla lettera pastorale 'Effatà, apriti' del Cardinale Carlo M. Martini [Mi 1990]. R 1991, Paoline. 141 p. -- ^{R}PaVi 40,2 (1995) 64 (G. *De Virgilio*).

k511 **Martini** Carlo M., Communicating Christ to the world; the pastoral letters 'Ephphatha, be opened', 'The hem of his garment', and 'Letters to a family about TV'. Kansas City MO 1994, Sheed & W. xvi-192 p. 1-55612-655-7.

k512 SCHWEITZER Albert, Reich Gottes and Christentum. ^{E}*Luz* U., *al.*: Werke/Nachlass. Mü 1995, Beck. 508 p. DM 118. 3-406-93131-1. -- ^{R}ThLZ 120 (1995) 823-5 (H.H. *Jenssen*).

k513 STRATHMANN: **Hass** Otto, Hermann Strathmann; christliches Handeln und Denken in bewegter Zeit 1993 → 10,14821: ^{R}EThL 70 (1994) 453s (F. *Neirynck*).

k514 STRAUSS: **Orr** Susan, Jerusalem and Athens; reason and revelation in the work of Leo Strauss. Lanham MD 1995, Rowman & L. iv-245 p.; bibliog. 227-236. 0-8476-8010-X.
k515 VINAY: ^E**Spreafico** A., Valdo Vinay († 1990), Commenti ai Vangeli. Brescia 1992, Morcelliana. 336 p. -- ^RPaVi 40,2 (1995) 63s (G. *De Virgilio*).

Y6.3 *Influxus Scripturae saeculo XX* -- Surveys of current outlooks

k517 *a) Adriani* Maurilio, L'orizzonte spirituale del XX secolo / Fallimento dell'utopia e neogenetica religiosa; -- *b) Morandi* Franco, Crisi della teologia o teologia della crisi ?: CiVi 50 (1995) 15-s . 127-132 / 119-126.
k518 **Airhart** Phyllis D., Serving the present age; revivalism, progressivism, and the Methodist tradition in Canada. Montreal 1992, McGill-Queens Univ. 218 p. $ 20. -- ^R*CritRR 7 (1994) 308-310 (M.A. *Knoll*).
k519 **Altermatt** Urs, Le Catholicisme au défi de la modernité: l'histoire sociale des catholiques suisses aux XIXe-XXe siècles [Katholizismus 1990 → 7,g883].^T. Lausanne 1994, Payot. 396 p. -- ^RASSR 92 (1995) 89s (É. *Poulat*).
k520 *a) Artus* Walter W., The value and limits of modern technology within an authentic humanism; -- *b) Duch* Lluís, Notes sobre la inculturació: → 41, ^FCOLOMER E., RCatT 29 (1994) 297-307 / 355-364; Eng. 365.
k521 **Bacik** James A., Tensions in the Church; facing the challenges, seizing the opportunities. KC 1993, Sheed & W. xx-171 p. $ 10. -- ^RÉ(gl)eT 26 (1995) 403 [A. *Peelman*].
k522 *Barry* William A., U.S. culture and contemporary spirituality: RfR 54 (1995) 5-21.
k523 *Baxter* Michael J., *Bauerschmidt* Frederick C., *Eruditio* without *religio*; the dilemma of Catholics in the academy: Com(US) 22 (1995) 284-302.
k524 *Beaudin* Michel, Cette idole qui nous gouverne; le néo-libéralisme comme 'religion' et 'théologie' sacrificielles: SR 24 (1995) 395-413.
k525 *a) Beem* Christopher, American liberalism and the Christian Church; Stanley HAUER-WAS vs. M.L. KING Jr. [Hauerwas reply]; -- *b) Wilson* Jonathan R., From theology of culture to theological ethics; the [Julian] HARTT-Hauerwas connection: JRE(th) 23 (1995) 119-133 [135-148] / 149-164.
k526 *a) Bentué B.* Antonio, Panorama de la teología en América Latina desde el Vaticano II a Santo Domingo; -- *b) Adolfo Galeano* A., Desafíos de la postmodernidad a la teología en América Latina: → 651, TyV 36 (1995) 159-191 / 291-306.
k527 *Berg* Thomas C., 'Proclaiming together ?' Convergence and divergence in mainline and evangelical evangelism: R&AC(u) 5 (1995) 49-76.
k528 **Berger** P., Una gloria lejana; la búsqueda de la fe en época de credulidad, ^T*Iglesias* Juan Andrés. Barc 1994, Herder. 267 p. 84-254-1836-4. -- ^RPerTeol 27 (1995) 254-7 (J.B. *Libanio*).
k529 *a) Bertrand* Michel, Visibilité et témoignage du Protestantisme; -- *b) Mottu* Henry, Force et faiblesse de l'ecclésiologie Réformée aujourd'hui: BCPÉ 46,6 (1994) 5-21 / 23-39.
k530 **Blaser** Klauspeter, Les théologies nord-américaines: LieuxTh 26. Genève 1995, Labor et Fides. 165 p. -- ^RRThPh 127 (1995) 187a (A. *Gounelle*).
k531 **Blumhofer** Edith L., Restoring the faith; the Assemblies of God, Pentecostalism, and American culture. Urbana 1993, Univ. Illinois. x-320 p. $ 42.50; pa. $ 20. -- ^RA(ndr)USS 33 (1995) 106 (G. *Knight*).
k532 **Bogović** Milan, Riflessioni sociologiche sul fenomeno religioso nella società Jugoslava contemporanea. Rijeka 1994. 90 P. -- ^R*RijT 3 (1995) 332s (M. *Žagar*, Croatian).

k534 **Bothwell** John, Old-time religion or risky faith. Toronto 1993, Anglican. 107 p. C$ 11. 1-55126-073-5. -- [R]ET 106 (1994s) 31 (W.D. *Horton*).

k535 **Bourgeois** Henri, *a)* Foi et cultures: quelles manières de vivre et quelles manières de croire aujourd'hui ? : Parcours. P 1991, Centurion. 151 p. 2-227-30150-3. -- *b)* Fede e culture; in che modo vivere e in che modo credere oggi, [T]*Crespi* Pietro, [E]*Laurita* Roberto: Percorsi 15. Brescia 1993, Queriniana. 162 p. L[m] 16. 88-399-2780-8. -- [R]EThL 70 (1994) 211s (J. *Étienne*).

k536 **Boyer** Paul, When time shall be no more; prophecy belief in modern American culture 1992 → 9,16817; 10,14831 ('Beyer'): [R]*CritRR 7 (1994) 314-6 (W, *Martin*).

k537 **Brereton** Virginia L., Training God's army; the American Bible school 1990 → 6,1233* ... 10,14832: [R]JETS 37 (1994) 458s (D.L. *Russell*).

k538 *a) Brinkman* M.E., Onwil en onmacht tot het formuleren van een gereformeerde identiteit; -- *b) Augustijn* C., Historisch pleidooi: G(ereformeerd)TT 95 (1995) 59-68 / 51-59.

k539 **Brooke** Christopher N.L., A history of the University of Cambridge IV. 1870-1990. C 1993, Univ. xxv-652 p.; 22 fig.; map. £ 50. 0-521-34350-X. -- [R]JEH 46 (1995) 344-6 (J.H. *Prest* personalizes theologically even the chapters beyond the four on religion).

k540 *Bruce* Steve, The truth about religion in Britain [STARK R., INNACONE R. 1994]: JSSR 34 (1995) 417-429.

k541 **Brueggemann** W., Biblical perspectives on evangelism 1993 → 9,868: [R]A(ndr)USS 33 (1995) 108s (R. *Burrill*).

k542 **Büchele** Herwig, SehnSucht nach der schönen neuen [technologischen] Welt. Thaur 1993, [2]1994. Kulturverlag. 426 p. Sch 206. -- [R]TPQ 143 (1995) 83s (J. *Niewiadomski*).

k543 *Byrne* Patricia, American ultramontanism: TS 56 (1995) 301-326.

k544 *Cabella* Alberto, Radici storiche e culturali del nazionalismo; la sacralizzazione dello Stato: Protest(antesimo) 50 (1995) 258-265.

k545 *Carrasco* Alfonso, Considerations on theology's difficulty in gaining the interest of reason today, [T]*Reimers* Adrian, *Walker* Adrian: ComI-US 22 (1995) 265-283.

k546 **Carroll** John, Humanism, the wreck of western culture. L 1993, Fontana. 232 p. + index. -- [R]L(ex)TJ 29 (1995) 137s (J.G. *Strelan*).

k547 **Carter** Stephen L., The culture of disbelief 1993 → 9,16822; 10,14839: [R]CCurr 44 (1944s) 260-7 (J. W. *Skillen*); CScR 25 (1994s) 85-87 (M. *Baer*); HeythJ 36 (1995) 103s (J.H. *McKenna*); Pneuma 17 (1995) 123-7 (D. *McNutt*).

k548 **Chenu** Bruno, *Neusch* Marcel, Théologiens d'aujourd'hui; vingt portraits. P 1995, Bayard/Centurion. 171 p. F 110. -- [R]ÉTRel 70 (1995) 453s (A. *Gounelle*: mostly Catholic, nothing on process or DREWERMANN); Spiritus 36 (1995) 385s (G. *Reynal*).

k549 **Cherry** Conrad, Hurrying toward Zion; universities, divinity schools, and American Protestantism. Bloomington 1995, Indiana Univ. xiii-373 p. $ 25. 0-253-32928-0 [< ThD 43,260].

k550 **Choper** Jess H., Securing religious liberty; principles for judicial interpretation of the religious clauses. Ch 1995, Univ. xiii-198 p. £ 20. 0-226-10445-1. -- [R]*TBR 8,1 (1995s) 64 (M. *Fielding*).

k551 **Clouse** Robert G., *Pierard* Richard, *Yamauchi* Edwin, Two kingdoms; the Church and culture through the ages [redressing the unconcern with Protestant Evangelicals in Church histories ..]. Ch 1993, Moody. 689 p. $ 30. -- [R]Pneuma 17 (1995) 128-131 (A.L. *Clayton*).

k552 **Coalter** Milton J., al., The Re-Forming tradition; Presbyterians and mainstream Protestantism. LvL 1992, W-Knox. 355 p. $ 17. -- [R]ChH 64 (1995) 745s (B.J. *Longfield*).

k553 *Copeland* F. Shawn, The exercise of black theology in the United States: JHispLat 3,3 (1995s) 5-15 [43-58, *Phelps* Jamie T.].

k554 **Crews** Clyde F., American and Catholic; a popular history of Catholicism in the United States 1994 → 10,14846: [R]Church 11,2 (NY 1995) 53 (T.J. *Shelley*).

k555 *Daiber* Karl-Fritz, Evangelical churches and the Catholic Church in Germany: JE(mp)T 7,2 (1994) 5-20 (21-47 in the Netherlands, *al.*).

k556 **Davie** Grace, Religion in Britain since 1945; believing without belonging. Ox 1994, Blackwell. xiii-226 p. 0-631-18444-9, -- [R]*TBR 8,1 (1995s) 63 (L. *Houlden*); JEH 46 (1995) 581 (K. *Robbins*); *ModBlv 36,3 (1995) 50-52 (M.R. *Dorsett*).

k557 **Davies** D., *Watkins* C., *Winter* M., Church and religion in rural England. E 1991, Clark. 504 p. £ 12.50. -- [R]S(cot)JTh 48 (1995) 526-8 (R. *Jeffery*).

k558 **Davies** Horton, Worship and theology in England [I. 1534-1690; II. (Princeton 1961-75, 5 volumes reprinted, with a new volume on] III. The ecumenical century; 1900 to the present. GR c.1995, Eerdmans. 788 p. $ 50 [all three $ 150: 0-8028-0891-3; -2-1; -3-X [ThD 43,163].

k559 **Davis** Walter, Shattered dream; America's search for its soul. Ph 1994, Trinity. 193 p. -- [R]US(em)QR 48,1 (1994) 191-4 (D.W. *Shriver*).

k560 **Day** Thomas, Where have you gone, Michelangelo ? The loss of soul in Catholic culture 1993 → 10,14850: [R]Horizons 22 (1995) 162s (Sandra Y. *Mize*).

k561 **Dean** William, The religious critic in American culture. Albany 1994, SUNY. xxiii-256 p. $ 49.50. -- *a)* [R]JRel 75 (1995) 578s (J.A. *Stone*: important).

k562 -- *b) Cady* Linell E., [Dean's] The religious critic and the negotiation of collective identities; -- *c) Crosby* Donald A., Construction, convention, and conviction; -- *d) Suchocki* Marjorie H., An American myth, or, conventional wisdom commentary, caveat, and construction; -- *e) Roth* John K., Dean's dilemma; -- *f) Brown* Delwin, History, country, and God; on the role of the religious critic; -- *g) Dean* response: AmJTP 16,1 (1994 Highlands Institute Seminar, 1995) (a) / 3-20 / 21-32 / 33-47 / 49-67 / 69-86 / (Dean) 87-109.

k563 *Devčić* Ivan, Die Kirche vor der Herausforderung des praktischen Atheismus: RijT 2 (1994) 3-18 kroatisch; deutsch 19.

k564 [E]**Díaz-Salazar** Rafael, *Giner* Salvador, Religión y sociedad en España. M 1993, Cis. 382 p. -- [R]SalTer 82 (1994) 839s (R. *Bilbao*).

k565 [E]**Dockery** David S., Southern Baptists and American Evangelicals; the conversation continues. Nv 1993, Broadman. $ 11. 0-8054-6041-1. -- [R]CScR 25 (1995s) 108-111 (F. *Humphreys*); RExp 92 (1995) 237-9 (M.J. *Erickson*).

k566 **Donegani** J.-M., Catholiques sans église; que reste aujourd'hui de 'l'intransi-geantisme'? P 1993, Fondation Nationale des Sciences Politiques. -- [R]RicStoSR 23,46 (1994) 117-125 (É. *Poulat*, citant:) Catholica 41 (P? ...) 76s (C.*Barthe*).

k567 **Dupré** Louis, Metaphysics and culture: Aquinas Lecture 1994. Milwaukee c. 1994, Marquette Univ. -- [R]L(aval)TP 51 (1995) 216-8 (Suzie *Johnston*, Leslie *Armour*).

k568 **Dupré** Louis, Passage to modernity; an essay in the hermeneutics of nature and culture 1993 → 10,15141: [R]L(aval)TP 51 (1995) 671-8 (L. *Valcke*); MoTh 11 (1995) 272-4 (R.P. *Scharlemann*).

k569 **Dupront** Alphonse [† 1990, Il presente cattolico; potenza della religione, latenza del religioso [1993 → 10,14861], [T]*Salemi Cardini* Maria. T 1993, Bollati B. -- [R]RS(to)LR 31 (1995) 271-292 (F. *Bolgiani*).

k570 *Edwards* David, Roman Catholics as others see them ('Prejudice unmasked'): Tablet 249 (1995) 452s.

k571 **Edwards** David L., What is Catholicism ? An Anglican responds to the official teaching of the Roman Catholic Church. L c.1994, Mowbray. -- [R]Tablet 249 (1995) 18s (R.P. *McBrien*).

k572 **Eller** Vernard, Christian anarchy. GR 1987, Eerdmans. -- [R]Forefront 1,1 (1994) 26-28 (E. *Haarer*).

k573 **Ellwood** Robert S., The sixties spiritual awakening; American religion moving from modern to postmodern 1994 → 10,14863: [R]ChrCent 112 (1995) 791.3 (D.C. *Hackett*)

k574 *Emmons* Sherri W., How to welcome single-parent families [to church]: Disciple 133,10 (St. Louis 1995) 6s.

k575 [E]**Encrevé** André, Les Protestants: Dictionnaire du monde religieux dans la France contemporaine. P 1992, Beauchesne. 534 p. F 330. -- [R]ChH 64 (1995) 722s (G.R. *Stotts*).

k576 *a) Estrada* J.A., Crítica materialista del cristianismo; -- *b) Quinzá* H., Revendicar el placer ¿ gracia o idolatría ? (crítica hedonista del cristianismo): Igl(esia)V(iva) 172 (Valencia 1994) 319-334 / 397-412 [< RET 55 (1995) 417].

k577 **Estruch** Joan, Santos y pillos; el Opus Dei y sus paradojas. Barc 1994, Herder. 478 p. -- [R]ScrT(Pamp) 27 (1995) 1034-41 (J.-L. *Illanes*).

k578 **Fisher** James T., The Catholic counterculture in America, 1933-1962. Chapel Hill 1989, Univ. N. Carolina. xv-305 p. $ 32.50. -- [R]*CritRR 7 (1994) 334-6 (Margaret S. *Thompson*).

k579 **Flegg** Columba G., 'Gathered under apostles' church 1992 → 8.m497: [R]S(cot)JTh 48 (1995) 405-7 (K. *Stevenson*).

k580 **Foster** Patrick, The paradigm of the symbol; the loss of 'truth' in twentieth-century thought: diss. California, [D]*Capps* W. Berkeley 1995 [< RStR 22, p.270].

k581 *France* R.T., The Ramsden sermon [Oxford 1992, endowed 1847 to be annual on 'Church extension over the colonies and dependencies of the British Empire']; a shift in the centre of gravity of Christian mission: Theol 98 (L 1995) 338-344: A.WALLS parable: researcher from Mars finds the colonial church in 1592 as a religion of pink-skinned northerners; confirmed 1692, 1792, though some have moved to retain their identity among tribes elewhere; only 1892 forces change and 1992 abandonment of this appraisal).

k582 **Fuller** Robert C., Naming the Antichrist; the history of an American obsession [... Kissinger; John Paul II ..]. NY 1995, Oxford-UP. vi-232 p. $ 25. 0-19-508244-3 [RStR 22,204, J. *Fea*; up to recent evangelicals' 'tribalist assaults'; ThD 42 (1995) 269].

k583 **Gabriel** Karl, Christentum zwischen Tradition und Postmoderne: QD 141. FrB 1992, Herder. -- [R]ZNKUL 37,1 (1994) 155-7 (J. *Mariański*, [P]).

k584 *Galantino* Nunzio, *Lorizio* Giuseppe, Le 'scuole' di teologia oggi in Italia: RasT 36 (1995) 63-9.

k585 **Gallagher** Michael P., What are they saying about unbelief ? NY 1995, Paulist. iii-84 p. $ 10. 0-8091-3596-5 [ThD 44,65].

k586 *García Gómez* Matías, El anuncio de la fe en una sociedad en crisis económica y política: Proyección 42 (1995) 3-20.

k587 *a) García Rojo* Ezequiel, Cultura y cristianismo, hoy, un fenómeno de extrañamiento; -- *b) Goya* Benito, La fe, fuente de madurez humana: REsp 54 (1995) 455-490 / 491-521.

k588 *Garhammer* Erich, Literaten und die Kirche; Bemerkungen zu einem Spannungsverhältnis: ThGL 85 (1995) 5-11.

k589 *Gay* Craig, Evangelicals and the language of technopoly: Crux 31,1 (1995) 32-40.

k590 *Geffré* Claude, La modernité, une chance, pas une menace: Metanoia 4 (Praha 1994) 106-111; Eng.111.

k591 **Gelpi** Donald L., The turn to experience in contemporary theology 1994 → 10,14870: [R]C(alvin)TJ 30 (1995) 562s (H.I. *Lederle:* 'one of the leading philosophical theologians of our day').

k592 **Gibellini** Rosino, Panorama de la théologie au XXe siècle, [T]*Mignon* Jacques: Théologies, 1994 → 10,14872: [R]EstTrin 29 (1995) 135 (X. *Pikaza*); ETRel 70 (1995) 298s (A. *Gounelle*: bon, dépassant les premières impressions); RTPh 127 (1995) 95 (K. *Blaser*); ScrT(Pamp) 27 (1995) 1027-30 (J.-L. *Illanes*); ZkT 117 (1995) 374s (K.H. *Neufeld*).

k593 *González Faus* José Ignacio, *a)* Del ateísmo postcristiano a la increencia postmoderna; génesis de una situación cultural: RCatT 30 (1995) 37-53; Eng. 54; -- *b)* Dogmática cristológica y lucha por la justicia: RCatT 30 (1995) 345-365; Eng. 365.

k594 *Gross* Engelbert, Religiöse Unterweisung in Solidarität mit der verweltlichten Welt: ThGL 85 (1995) 365-385.

k595 **Gründer** Horst, Welteroberung und Christentum; ein Handbuch zur Geschichte der Neuzeit 1992 → 9,8121: [R]NZM(iss)W 51 (1995) 74-77 (K.J. *Rivinius*); ThRv 91 (1995) 328-333 (auch K.J. *Rivinius*).

k596 *Guarino* Thomas, 'Spoils from Egypt' [ORIGEN]; contemporary theology and non-foundationalist thought [HEIDEGGER, WITTGENSTEIN, GADAMER]: LavalThP 51 (1995) 573-587.

k597 **Guinness** Os, The American hour [failure of cultural authority]. NY 1993, Free Press. 458 p.$25.-- [R]BS 152 (1995) 248s (K.O. *Gangel*); Churchman 108 (1994) 277-9 (P.*Moore*).

k598 *a) Hall* Douglas J., The future of Protestantism in North America; -- *b) Winter* Gordon, America in search of its soul; -- *c) Callan* Carnegie S., Building a visionary Church; an organizational theology for the congregation: ThTo 52 (1995s) 458-475 / 476-484 / 485-93.

k599 **Hall** Douglas J., Professing the faith; Christian theology in the North American context. Mp c.1995, Fortress. 553 p. $35. -- [R]ChrCent 112 (1995) 58s (L.E. *Snook*).

k600 **Hastings** Adrian, A history of English Christianity[3] [→ 6,m68* ... 9,16845: to] 1920 − [extended to] 1990. L 1991, SCM. xxix-720 p. -- [R]ChH 64 (1995) 532-4 (W.L. *Sachs*).

k601 **Hatch** Nathan O., The democratization of American Christianity 1989 → 6,m69 ... 10,14880: [R]C(oncordia)TQ 59 (1995) 141s (L.R. *Rast*).

k602 **Hauerwas** Stanley, Unleashing the Scriptures 1993 → 9.203b: (Reformed) Perspectives 9,8 (1994) 21s (S.D. *Hoogerwerf:* Is sola scriptura heresy ?).

k603 *Heilbronner* Oded, Wohin verschwund das katholische Bürgertum ? Der Ort des katholischen Bürgertums in der neueren katholischen Historiographie: ZRGG 47 (1995) 320-337.

k604 *a) Herms* Eilert, Die Bedeutung der Kirchen für die Ausbildung sozialer Identität in multikulturellen Gesellschaften; eine systematisch-theologische Betrachtung; -- *b) Smolik* Josef, Die christliche Identität in Mitteleuropa; -- *c) Wilson* Bryan, Religious toleration, pluralism and privatization; -- *d) Repstad* Pål, Civil religion in modern society; some general and some Nordic perspectives: KZG 8 (1995) 61-89 / 90-98 / 99-116 / 159-175.

k605 **Hildreth** Thomas P.[III], Contemporary contextualism and relativism; the justification and advocacy of religious beliefs: diss. Southern Baptist Theol. Sem., [D]*Cunningham* R., 1995. 206 p. 95-30695. -- D(iss)AI 56 (1995s) p. 1399.

k606 **Hillis** Bryan V., Can two walk together unless they be agreed ? American religious schisms in the 1970s: Chicago StHistAmRel. Brooklyn 1991, Carlson. xvii-247 p. $ 50. — RTorJT 11 (1995) 106 (Phyllis *Airhart*).

k607 *Hindmarsh* D. Bruce, The 'Toronto Blessing' and the Protestant Evangelical awakening of the eighteenth century compared: Crux 31,4 (1995) 3-13.

k608 *Hitchcock* James, Conservative bishops, liberal results [... the conservative bishops steadily appointed give a mantle of respectability to liberal policies]: *C(ath)WR 8,5 (May 1995) 21-27.

k609 **Hoeksema** Gertrude, A watered garden; a brief history of the Protestant Reformed Churches in America. GR 1992, Reformed Free. vi-417 p. $ 20. -- RChH 64 (1995) 739-741 (J. R. *Beeke*).

k610 **Hoge** Dean R., *al.*, Vanishing boundaries; the religion of mainline Protestant baby boomers. LVL 1994, W-Knox. viii-254 p. $ 18. -- RP(rinc)SB 16 (1995) 98-100 (R. *Fann*).

k611 **Holloway** Richard (Anglican bishop), The stranger in the wings; affirming faith in a God of surprises. L 1994, SPCK. xvi-154. £ 8. -- *ModBlv 36,1 (1995) 45s (J. *Lewis-Anthony:* unusually good in its genre, but weak on social issues).

k612 **Howard** Philip K., The death of common sense; how law is suffocating America. NY c.1995, Random. 202 p. $ 18. -- RCommentary 100,1 (1995) 56-58 (M.M. *Arkin*)

k613 **Hunt** Michael J., College Catholics; a new counter-culture. NY 1993, Paulist. 172 p. $ 10. -- RC(alvin)TJ 29 (1994) 287s (D. *Cooper*).

k614 *a) Ingram* John A., Contemporary issues and Christian models of integration; into the modern/postmodern age; -- *b) McCullough* Michael E., Prayer and health; conceptual issues, research review, and research agenda: JPsT 23 (1995) 3-14 / 15-29.

k615 **Jewett** Robert, St. Paul at the movies; the Apostle's dialogue with American culture 1993 → 9.5871; 10,5666: RC(oncordia)TQ 59 (1995) 133s (G.E. *Veith*: sanitized politically-correct 'inclusive').

k616 **J o h** [sic], Reformed fundamentalism in America; the Lordship of Christ, the transformation of culture, and other Calvinist components of the Christian Right: diss. Florida State, PSandon L., 1994. 341 p. 95-16733. -- D(iss)AI 56 (1995s) p. 225.

k617 *Johnson* Paul, God and the Americans: Commentary 99,1 (1995) 25-46: a short history of religion in the US.

k618 **Jüngel** Eberhard, L'Évangile et les églises protestantes en Europe: FV 92,2 (Assemblée de Budapest 24-30 mars 1992: 1993) 41-62.

k619 *Killen* Patricia O., Geography, denominations, and the human spirit; a decade of studies on religion in the western United States [SCHOENBERG W. & 8 others]: RStR 21 (1995) 277-284.

k620 *a) Koester* Nancy, The future in our past; post-millennialism in American Protestantism; -- *b) Nestingen* James A., The end of the end; the role of apocalyptic in Lutheran reform : WW 15 (1995) 137-144 / 196-205 (+ *al.*, 7 art. on the Book of Revelation).

k621 *Komonchak* Joseph A., U.S. bishops' suggestions for [before] Vatican II: CrSt 15 (1994) 313-371.

k622 **Kreeft** Peter, The Snakebite letters [how Catholic behavior and schools got so sidetracked]. SF 1993, Ignatius. 121 p. -- RC(alvin)TJ 29 (1994) 288-293 (C. *Van Reken*).

k623 *Krötke* Wolf, Gestalten christlicher Freiheit in der Kirche -- Wirkungen christlicher Freiheit in der Gesellschaft: ZThK 92 (1995) 238-250 (251-277, *Preul* Reiner; 278-286, *Huber* W.).

k624 **Küng** Hans, Das Christentum, Wesen und Geschichte. Mü 1994, Piper. 1056 p. DM 88. -- ᴿEntschluss 50,4 (1995) 37 (H. *Brandt*).

k625 **Küng** Hans, The religious situation of our time, 2. Christianity, its essence and history. L/NY 1995. SCM/Continuum. xxvi-936 p. £ 35; pa. £ 20. 0-334-02571-0: -84-2 / US 0-8264-0807-9; $ 44.50 [RStR 22,255, D.R. *Janz*]. -- ᴿET 106,11 top choice (1994s) 321 (C.S. *Rodd*); Modern Believing [continuing the numbering of Modern Churchman] 36,4 (1995) 61-63 (I. *Bradley*): *TBR 8,2 (1995s) 23 (R. *Fernandez*).

k626 **Lafont** Ghislain, Imaginer l'Église catholique: Théologies. P 1995, Cerf. 286 p. F 150. -- ᴿÉtudes 383 (1995) 717 (M. *Fédou*).

k627 *La Russa* Antonino, Il neotomismo in Italia ed il contributo della Compagnia di Gesù; quale 'pensiero cristiano' ? : FilTeo 8 (1994) 323-333.

k628 *Lenk* Hans, Universität oder Multiversität [... Zersplitterung der Bereiche]: Univ 47 (1992) 38-47.

k629 ᴱ**Lesch** Walter, *Schwind* Georg, Das Ende der alten Gewissheiten 1993 → 9,333: ᴿE(st)E 69 (1994) 551s (A. *Tornos*).

k630 *Letham* Robert, *Macleod* Donald, Is evangelicalism Christian ? : EvQ 67 (1995) 3-33.

k631 **Lienesch** Michael, Redeeming America; piety and politics in the New Christian Right. Chapel Hill 1993, Univ. N.Carolina. x-332 p. $ 45; pa. $ 18. 0-8078-2089-X. -- ᴿCScR 25 (1995s) 249-251 (R. *Zwier*).

k632 *Limouris* Gennadios, Christian and religious education, a priority for the Eastern Orthodox churches: Kl(eronomia) 26 (1994) 29-45.

k633 **Little** Joyce A., The Church and the culture war; secular anarchy or sacred order. SF 1995, Ignatius. 207 p. $ 13 pa. 0-87870-547-9 [ThD 43,277].

k634 **Lück** Wolfgang, Lebensform Protestantismus; Reformatorisches Erbe in der Gegen- wart: PrakTHeute 9. Stu 1992, Kohlhammer. 159 p. DM 40. 3-17-012198-7. -- ᴿBijdragen 56 (1995) 225s (A.H.C. van *Eijk*).

k635 **McBrien** Richard P., Report on the Church 1992 → 8,m976; 10.14901: ᴿ*CritRR 7 (1994) 346-8 (P. *Hegy*).

k636 **McCool** Gerald A., The Neo-Thomists. Milwaukee 1994, Marquette Univ. vi-166 p. [RStR 22,224, B.E. *Hinze*]. -- ᴿTS 56 (1995) 816s (J.P. *Dougherty*). -- [On McCool's 1989 From unity to pluralism ... Thomism → 6,m174* (not 147 as in l0,14389) and also 10,279].

k637 *McGreevy* John T., Racial justice and the people of God; the Second Vatican Council, the civil rights movement, and American Catholics: R&AC(u) 4 (1994) 221-254.

k638 *Maron* Gottfried, Papsttum und Päpste in der neuzeit: ThR 60 (1995) 404-429.

k639 **Marsden** George, The soul of the American university; from Protestant establishment to established nonbelief 1994 → 10,14903: ᴿBS 152 (1995) 489-491 (S.R. *Spencer*); Horizons 22 (1995) 298s (W.M. *Shea*); JRel 75 (1995) 442s (J. *Findlay*); P(ersp)Ref 9,9 (1994) 19s (D.A. *Hoekema*); P(rinc)SB 16 (1995) 94-96 (J.F. *Wilson*: tough title worth treating, but softened suggestions).

k640 ᴱ**Marsden** G.M., *Longfield* B.J., The secularization of the Academy 1992 → 8,m506; 10,14902: ᴿChH 64 (1995) 319-321 (W.C. *Gilpin*).

k641 **Marshall** David B., Secularizing the faith; Canadian Protestant clergy and the crisis of belief. Toronto 1992, Univ. viii=325 p. $ 55; pa. $ 20. -- ᴿTorJT 11 (1995) 108s (G.A. *Rawlyk*).

k642 *Martínez Medina* F. Javier, Patrimonio cultural y evangelización: Proyección 42 (1995) 91-110.

k643 **Marty** Martin E., A short history of American Catholicism. Allen TX 1995, Thomas More. 231 p. $ 11 pa. 0-88347-329-8 [ThD 43,278: up to the lively laity of the 1990s].

k644 *Matijević* Pavica, The increase of the tendency towards general neurosis [postwar 15-year-olds, chiefly boys, but not more noticeably in refugees]: ObŽ 50 (1995) 487-498; Eng. 499.

k645 *Menozzi* Daniele, Regalità sociale di Cristo e secolarizzazione; alle origini della Quas primas [Pio XI 1925, → gesuita RAMIÈRE H, 'pur conservando il paradigma intransigente medievale, non vi attribuisce un valore normativo']: CrSt 16 (1995) 79-113: Eng.113 (115-135, *Verucci* Guido, su Menozzi, Secolarizzazione 1993).

k646 *Miller* J. Michael, The Pope's challenge to the Church in America [from his 1993 allocutions to U.S. bishops in eleven groups]: FaR 21 (1995) 29-53.

k647 **Mitchell** Joshua, Not by reason alone; religion, history, and identity in early modern political thought [LUTHER, HOBBES, LOCKE, ROUSSEAU]. Ch 1993, Univ. xi-252 p. $ 32. - - [R]JRel 75 (1995) 125-7 (D. *Sturm*: forces toward radical revision, but bypasses MÜNTZER, PAINE, process theology).

k648 **Montefiore** Hugh, Credible Christianity; the Gospel in contemporary society. L 1994, Mowbray. 304 p. £ 12; pa. £ 10. 0-264-67300-X; -2-3. -- [R]ThR(und) 77 (1995) 413-5 (D.W. *Haddorf*).

k649 *a) Moreno Muñoz* Miguel, Implicaciones éticas, sociales y legales del proyecto 'Genoma Humano'; -- b) *López Azpitarte* Eduardo, Exigencias ecológicas y ética cristiana: Proyección 42 (1995) 179-200 / 273-286.

k650 **Moses** John, A broad and living way. .. 1995, Canterbury. 260 p. £ 12. 1-85311-112-0. -- [R]E(xp)T 107 (1995s) 91 (J. *Reader*: disestablishment is no way forward).

k651 [E]**Müller** Hans M., Kulturprotestantismus 1992 → 8,410: [R]NedThT 49 (1995) 78s (A.L. *Molendijk*).

k652 *Muscato* Franco, Il cristianesimo russo contemporaneo: Asprenas 42 (1995) 355-370.

k653 **Nazé** Ghislain, Les images du protestantisme et de l'anglicanisme dans 'La libre Belgique' de 1945 à 1985; étude de l'information religieuse dans un quotidien confes-sionnel: diss. Paris-Sorbonne 1995. -- [R]*BuHProt 141 (1995) 613s (Édith *Weber*).

k654 *Neuhaus* Richard J., *Novak* Michael, and 70 others invited (mostly prominent Jews), The national prospect: Commentary 100,5 (50th anniversary, 1995) 89-91 (23-116.

k655 **Neville** Robert C., The highroad around modernism. Albany 1992, SUNY. xvi-339 p. $ 20 pa. -- [R]CCurr 44 (1944s) 123-7 (J. *Grange*).

k656 **Nicholls** David, Deity and domination; images of God and the State in the nineteenth and twentieth centuries. L 1994 pa., Routledge. xi-321 p. £ 13. -- [R]*ModBlv 36,1 (1995) 48s (M.R. *Dorsett*: very fine).

k657 **Nichols** Aidan, The panther and the hind .. Anglicanism 1993 → 9,16869*: [R]Thom 59 (1995) 666-670 (W.B. *Soule*).

k658 [E]**Nickle** Keith F., *Lull* Timothy E.. A common calling; the witness of the Reformation churches in North America today. Mp 1993, Augsburg. 88 p. $ 5. -- [R]P(rinc)SB 16 (1995) 96s (D.W.A. *Taylor*).

k659 *Nikkel* David H., Discerning the spirits of modernity and post-modernity: JRelSt 19 (Cleveland 1995) 99-122.

k660 **Noll** Mark, The scandal of the evangelical mind 1994 → 10,14912*: [R]ChrCent 112 (1995) 488-490 (D. *Heim*: 'in the shadow of fundamentalism'); CScR 25 (1995s) 203-7 (T.A. *Askew*); ET 106 (1994s) 315 (J. *Kent*); JETS 38 (1995) 110-112 (C.F.H. *Henry*); NOxR

62,3 (1995) 27s (P. *Blosser*); (Reformed) Perspectives 10,2 (1995) 22s (R.J. *Mouw*); P(rinc)SB 16 (1995) 375-7 (D.G. *Bloesch*); RefR 49 (1995s) 71s (P.R. *Meyerink*).

k661 **Noll** Mark A., A history of Christianity in the US and Canada 1992 → 8,m723 ... 10,14912: [R]JETS 37 (1994) 453s (D.L. *Russell*) & 38 (1995) 108-110 (J. *Fox*).

k662 *Noll* Mark, *Kellstedt* Lyman, The changing face of evangelicalism: ProEccl 4 (1995) 146-164.

k663 **Nowak** Kurt, Geschichte des Christentums in Deutschland; Religion, Politik und Gesellschaft vom Ende der Aufklärung bis zur Mitte des 20. Jahrhunderts. Mü 1995, Beck. 389 p. DM 58. -- [R]KZG 8 (1995) 226s (G. *Ringshausen*: Juden eingeschlosssen).

k664 **Osborn** Lawrence, Restoring the vision: the Gospel and modern culture. L 1995, Mowbray. 176 p. £ 11. 0-264-67330-1. -- [R]ET 106 (1994s) 315 (Rod *Garner*).

k665 *Pattel-Gray* Anne, Gender and race relations in Reformed churches in Australia; an aboriginal perspective: R(ef)W 45 (1995) 16-26.

k666 *Peckham* Mary L., Women religious and the nineteenth century transformation of Irish Catholic culture: Magistra 1,2 (1995) 288-321.

k667 **Pesch** Otto H., Das Zweite Vatikanische Konzil; Vorgeschichte -- Verlauf -- Ergebnisse -- Nachgeschichte[3] [[1]1993]. Wü 1994, Echter. 443 p. DM 48. -- [R]BiKi 50 (1995) 142-4 (R. *Russ*).

k668 **Poulat** Émile, La galaxie Jésus; un Évangile et des Églises 1994 → 10,4119: [R]ÉTRel 70 (1995) 128s (J.-M. *Prieur*: suite annoncée, Le christianisme à l'aube du troisième millénaire).

k669 **Poulat** Émile, L'ère postchrétienne; un monde sorti de Dieu → 10,15166. P 1994, Flammarion. 320 p. F 140. 2-08-066744-0. -- [R]Greg 76 (1995) 434s (J. *Joblin*); R(ic)SS(oc)R 48 (1995) 184-6 (G. *De Rosa*).

k670 **Poulat** Émile, L'antimaçonnisme catholique (p.103-190; avec Mgr de SÉGUR, Les Francs-Maçons [1867, [62]1884], [T]*Laurant* Jean-Pierre. P 1994 Berg. 203 p. F 120. 2-900269-83-0. -- [R]Greg 76 (1995) 433s (J. *Joblin*).

k671 *Provencher* Norman, Catholicisme et modernité au XXe siècle; du modernisme à aujourd'hui: É(gl)eT 26 (1995) 361-393.

k672 **Pyle** Ralph E., Persistence and chamge in the Establishment; religion, education and gender among America's elite, 1950 and 1992; diss. Purdue, [D]*Davidson* J., 1995. 310 p. 95-40300. -- D(iss)AI 56 (1995s) p. 2633.

k673 **Ravitch** Norman, The Catholic Church and the French nation, 1589-1989. L 1990 [→10,14917], Routledge. ix-214 p. £ 30. -- [R]HZ 261 (1995) 134 (Ilja *Mieck*).

k674 **Reese** Thomas J., A flock of shepherds; the National Conference of Catholic Bishops. KC 1992, Sheed & W. 416 p. $ 20. 1-55612-557-7. -- [R]GOTR 39 (1994) 377-9 (J. *Gros*).

k675 *Reinert* Paul C., *Shore* Paul, The Catholic university's recognition of mystery: America 172,19 (1995) 17-20 . 32.

k676 ROBERT Dana L., From missions to mission to beyond missions; the historiography of American Protestant foreign missions since World War II: IBM(iss)R 18 (1994) 146-162.

k677 *a) Robertson* John C.[1], The challenge of secular humanism to Christianity; -- *b) Chethimattam* John B., Secular humanism in Catholic theology; -- *c) Greenspan* Louis, Judaism and secular humanism; -- *d) Lash* Nicholas, Religion and the public order beyond modernity; -- *e) Desmond* William, Equivocal being; the mathesis of nature and the poiesis of naturing: JDh 10 (1995) 352-367 / 380-393 / 368-379 / 334-351 / 321-333.

k678 **Roman** Carol, Left/right dualization as symbol of human cultural values: diss. Union Institute, [D]*Sells* H., 1995. 263 p. 95-24672. -- D(iss)AI 56 (1995s) p. 1411.

k679 *Romanowski* William D., John Calvin meets the creature from the black lagoon; the Christian Reformed Church and the movies 1928-1966: CScR 25 (1995s) 47-62.

k680 **Rouner** Leroy S., To be at home; Christianity, civil religion, and world community. Boston 1991, Beacon. viii-151 p. $20. -- [R]RStR 21 (1995) 39 (J.A. *Stone*).

k681 **Rubin** Julius H., Religious melancholy and Protestant experience in America 1994 → 10,14921: [R]Horizons 22 (1995) 299 (E.G. *Hinson*)

k682 **Russ** Jacqueline, La marche des idées contemporaines; un panorama de la modernité. P 1994, A.Colin. 479 p. 2-206-21416-2. -- [R]ÉTRel 70 (1995) 461s (O, *Bauer*: devrait plaire aux théologiens).

k683 **Sachs** William L., The transformation of Anglicanism, from state church to global communion 1993 → 9,16879: [R]ChH 64 (1995) 732s (D.B. *McIlhiney*); EvQ 67 (1995) 272-4 (P. *Cook*); JThS 46 (1995) 415-8 (A. *Hastings*) [→ k381 on 19th century].

k684 **Sack** Daniel E., Disastrous disturbances; Buchmanism and student religious life at Princeton, 1919-1935: diss. Princeton Univ., 1995. 340 p. 95-27858. -- D(iss)AI 56 (1995s) p. 1390.

k685 *Sauer* Hanjo, Abschied von der säkularisierten Welt?: TPQ 143 (1995) 339-349[-401,*al*]

k686 **Saxbee** John, bp., Liberal evangelism. L 1994, SPCK. 118 p. £ 8. 0-281-045691-3. — [R]ET 106,2 top choice (1994s) 33s (C.S. *Rodd*).

k687 **Schaeffer** Frank, Dancing alone; the quest for orthodox faith in the age of false religions. [Boston ? 1994], Holy Cross Orthodox. 327 p. -- [R]NOxR 62,10 (1995) 28s (P. *Blosser*: by Orthodox-convert son of prominent Evangelical).

k688 **Schmied** Gerhard, Kanäle Gottes? Katholische Kirche in der Medienzange. Opladen 1991, Leske & B. 137 p. DM 24,80 pa. 3-8100-0916-4. -- [R]TPQ 143 (1995) 297s (H. *Haslinger*).

k689 **Schmitz** Robert E., The disenchantment of American Catholicism; profiles of active Catholics in a changing Church: diss. Columbia, [D]*Lindt* Gillian. NY 1994. 279 p. 95-16174. -- D(iss)AI 56 (1995s) p. 227.

k690 *Sedgwick* Timothy F., The new shape of Anglican identity: A(ngl)ThR 77 (1995) 187-197 [212-231, *Mues* Stephen W.]

k691 **Sell** Alan P.F., Commemorations; studies in Christian thought and history. Calgary 1993, Univ. xi-394 p. -- [R]TorJT 11 (1995) 135-7 (W.O. *Fennell*: clear and interesting, but largely on in-house Protestant debates since 1700).

k692 **Shelley** T.J., Dunwoodie; history of St. Joseph's Seminary, Yonkers NY. Westminster MD 1993, Christian Classics. xx-416 p. $ 40. -- [R]CrSt 16 (1995) 447451 (R. *Burigana*).

k693 *Sherwin* Byron L. (Jewish), *Brown* Robert M. (Christian), Toward a just and compassionate society: CrossCur 45 (1995s) 149-164-175.

k694 **Sloan** Douglas, Faith and knowledge; mainline Protestantism and American higher education. LVL 1994, W-Knox. xv-252 p. $ 20. 0-664-22035-5.

k695 **Sochan** George S., The cultural role of Christianity in England, 1918-1931; an Anglican perspective on state education: diss. Loyola, [D]*Hays* Joy. Chicago 1995. 235 p. 95-17204. -- D(iss)AI 56 (1995s) p. 317.

k696 **Spykman** Gordon J., Reformational theology; a new paradigm for doing theology. GR 1992, Eerdmans. 584 p. $ 30. -- [R]C(alvin)TJ 30 (1995) 501-6 (G. *Haas*: only Neo-Calvinist systematics in English).

k697 **Stackhouse** John[J], Canadian Evangelicalism in the twentieth century, an introduction to its character. Toronto 1993, Univ. xii-319 p. -- [R]SR 24 (1995) 229-231.

k698 *Stackhouse* John G.[J], The historiography of Canadian Evangelicalism; a time to reflect: ChH 64 (1995) 627-634.

k699 **Stewart** Robert J., Religion and society in post-emancipation Jamaica. Knoxville 1992, Univ. Tennessee. xxi-254 p.; 6 fig.; 2 maps. $ 20. 0-87049-748-0. -- [R]JEH 46 (1995) 346-8 (H. *Johnson*).

k700 **Stibbe** Mark, O brave new Church. L 1995, Darton-LT. 163 p. £ 9. 0-232-52054-2. -- [R]E(xp)T 107 (1995s) 124 (W.D. *Horton*, also on CLARKE J., MIDDLETON A.).

k701 **Sykes** Stephen, Unashamed Anglicanism. L 1995, Darton-LT. 233 p. £ 10. 0-232-52103-4. -- [R]E(xp)T 107 (1995s) 91 (J. *Macquarrie*: but not uncritical).

k702 **Thils** Gustave, Les doctrines théologiques et leur évolution ['Le mouvement théologique au xxᵉ siècle de RTL 25 complété']: RTL Cah 28. LvN 1995, Fac. Théol. 70 p. Fb 200. 90-6831-660-5. -- [R]RTL 26 (1995) 242 (P.-M. *Bogaert*).

k703 [E]**Tilly** Terrence W., Postmodern theologies; the challenge of religious diversity [FlaSt Univ. seminar 1993]. Mkn 1995, Orbis. x-182 p. $ 19. 1-57075-005-X [ThD 43,190].

k704 *Timm* Hermann, Formation des Geistes; protestantische Theologie, Religiosität und neuzeitliche Lebenswelt: ThLZ 120 (1995) 859-866.

k705 *Tornos* A., Del giro antropológico al giro textual; hombres y textos [< Cuando hoy vivimos la fe, de próxima aparición]: E(st)E 70 (1995) 191-210.

k706 **Tornos** Andrés, *Aparicio* Rosa, ¿ Quién es creyente en España hoy ? M 1995, PPC. 157 p. -- [R]SalTer 83 (1995) 409-411 (J.A. *García*).

k707 *Torrens* James S., The Catholic Church in France; an interview with Jean-Robert ARMOGATHE: America 173,4 (1995) 15-19.

k708 **Urquhart** Gordon, The Pope's armada; unlocking the secret of mysterious and powerful new sects in the Church [rightist Focolari, Neocatechumenate, Communion & Liberation]. ... 1995, Bantam. 419p. -- [R]Creation Spirituality 11,4 (Oakland 1995) 59 (unsigned: 'Ratzinger claims they represent the only positive accomplishment of Vatican II').

k709 **Vahanian** Gabriel, L'utopie chrétienne. P 1992, D/Brouwer. -- [R]FV 92,1 (1993) 100-2 (E. *Jacob*).

k710 *a) Valadier* Paul, Veiller sur le monde dans l'actualité historique; -- *b) Lamarche* Paul, La vigilance dans le Nouveau Testament; le message originel et son évolution: Christus 41 (1994) 264-274 / 293-300.

k711 **Vaneigem** Raoul, The movement of the free spirit .. some brief [heterodox] flowerings of life in the Middle Ages ..[1986 diatribe against the morbid Bible, all religion, and all modern ideologies], [T]*Cherry* Randall, *Patterson* Ian. NY 1994, Zone. 302 p. $ 25. 0-942299-70-1 X [RStR 22,254, D.D. *Martin*].

k712 **Veith** Gene E.[J], Postmodern times; a Christian guide to contemporary thought and culture: Turning Point Christian Worldview Series. Wheaton IL 1994, Crossway. 256 p. $ 11 pa. 0-89107-768-5. -- [R]CScR 25 (1995s) 216-221 (D. *Diepbouse*).

k713 *Vilar* J.B., Intolerancia y libertad en la España contemporánea. M 1994, Itsmo. 452 p. -- [R]Communio (Sev) 28 (1995) 117s (M. *Sánchez*).

k714 *Volf* Miroslav, Christliche Identität und Differenz; zur Eigenart der christlichen Präsenz in den modernen Gesellschaften: ZThK 92 (1995) 357-375.

k715 *Wagner* Falk, Geht die Umformungskrise des deutschsprachigen modernen Protestantismus weiter ?: *ZnTg 2 (1995) 235-254; Eng. 235.

k716 **Waldenfels** Hans, [P] *O Bogu* .. fundamental theology in the context of current trends, [T]*Paciorek* Antoni. Katowice 1992, sw. Jacka. 531 p. -- [R]PrzPow 881 (1995) 119-122 (H. *Seweryniak*); STV(ars) 32,2 (1994) 269-273 (J. *Krasiński*).

k717 **Ward** Keith, A vision to pursue 1991 → 7,k134; 8,m993: [R]S(cot)JTh 48 (1995) 126-130 (B. *Hebblethwaite*).

k718 **Ward** W.R., The Protestant Evangelical awakening. C 1992, Univ. xviii-370 p. £ 40. 0-521-41491-1 (E.G.E. van der *Wall*).

k719 *Ward* W.R., Established churches, free churches, religious communities; their contemporary social setting: ET 106 (1994s) 110-3.

k720 **Wargny** Christophe, Die Welt schreit auf, die Kirche flüstert; Jacques GAILLOT, ein Bischof fordert heraus, [T]*Eichelberger* Hanns-W. FrB 1993, Herder. 189 p. -- [R]NZM(iss)W 51 (1995) 149s (O. *Eckert*).

k721 **Watson** Francis, Text, Church and world. E/GR 1994, Clark/Eerdmans. viii-360 p. £ 25. -- [R]S(cot)JTh 48 (1995) 507-517 (C. *Rowland*; response 518-522).

k722 [E]**Weaver** Mary Jo, *Appleby* R. Scott, Being right; conservative Catholics in America [Lilly Foundation four-year study]. Bloomington 1995, Indiana Univ. xiv-352 p. $ 40; pa. $ 19. 0-253-33922-1 [< ThD 43,257].

k723 *a) Weber* Timothy P., Evangelicalism north and south: -- *b) Hull* William E., Doctoral studies at Southern [Baptist] Seminary, 1944-94; RExp 92 (1995) 299-317 / 359-371.

k724 *Weston* P., Evangelism; some biblical and contemporary perspectives: *Anvil 12 (1995) 243-253 [NTAb 40, p.283].

k725 **Willaime** Jean-Paul, La précarité protestante; sociologie du protestantisme contemporain; Histoire et société 25, 1992 → 9,16889; 2-8309-0684-5: [R]ActuBbg 31 (1994) 319s (J. *Boada*); FV 92,6 (1993) 95s (Solange *Wydmusch*).

k726 *Wilson* John F., A new denominational historiography ? [mainline numbers down, publicizing up]: R&AC(u) 5 (1995) 249-263.

k727 **Wittberg** Patricia, The rise and decline of Catholic religious orders; a social movement perspective. Albany 1994,SUNY. xii-432 p.$20 pa.--[R]RfR 54 (1995) 467s (Elizabeth *Kolmer*).

k728 **Witten** Marsha G., All is forgiven; the secular message in American Protestantism. Princeton 1993, Univ. 179 p. $ 20. -- [R]JRel 75 (1995) 575s (A.E. *Farnsley*: she toes an orthodox line while professing 'methodological atheism' p.16).

k729 *Wolterstorff* Nicholas, Does truth still matter ? Reflections on the crisis of the postmodern university: Crux 31,3 (1995) 17-28.

k730 **Wright** Robert, A world mission; Canadian Protestantism and the quest for a new international order, 1918-1939. Montreal 1991, McGill-Queen's Univ. x-337 p. -- [R]SR 24 (1995) 231s (Phyllis D. *Airhart*).

k731 **Wuthnow** Robert, God and mammon in America. NY c.1994, Free Press. 364 p $ 23. -- [R]ChrCent 112 (1995) 22s (D. *Benne*).

k732 **Yates** Timothy, Christian mission in the twentieth century. C 1994, Univ. xvi-275p. £ 35. 0-521-43493-9. -- [R]ET 106 (1994s) 61 (K. *Cracknell*); JThS 46 (1995) 413-5 (A. *Hastings*); Theol 98 (L 1995) 243 (P.B. *Price*).

k733 *Yonnet* Paul, Aspects du neo-antiracisme [... son livre de 1993]: Catholica-Paris 48 ('Excursus: politiquement correct', 1995) 53-69.

k734 **Young** Frances, Dare we speak of God in public ? [1993s Birminghmam Cadbury lectures]. L 1995, Mowbray. 161 p. £ 15. 0-264-67366-2. -- [R]ET 106,12 3d-top choice (1994s) 336 (C.S. *Rodd*).

k735 **Zilles** Urbano, A modernidade e a Igreja. Porto Alegre 1993, EDIPUCRS. 94 p. -- [R]Teocomunicação 25 (1995) 194-6 (A.L. *Parzianello*).

Y6.5 **Theologi influentes** *in exegesim saeculi XX*

k736 ADAM: **Krieg** Robert C., Karl Adam; Catholicism in German culture 1993 →
9,16893: [R]TorJT 11 (1995) 107s (D. *Donovan*).

k737 ALSZEGHY; *Osculati* Roberto. Zoltán Alszeghy (1915-1991) e la teologia romana;
CrSt 16 (1995) 127-139: Eng. 139.

k738 ALTHAUS: **Christensen** Kurt, *a)* Hvordan erkjennes Guds vilje ? [Erkendelsen av
Guds vilje. en studie i Paul Althaus' teologi, diss. Oslo 1994]: MenighedsfK. 6. Århus
1994, Kolon. 429 p. -- [R]Ichthys 22 (1995) 87-93 (Gunnar *Heiene*). -- *b)* The
acknowledgment of God's will; a study in the theology of Paul Althaus; Århus diss. 1994;
evaluators *Austad* Torleiv / *Bakkevig* Trond: TT(og)K 66 (1995) 27-37; Eng. 38 / 39-49;
Eng. 49 -- Replikk 51-56.

k739 -- **Meiser** Martin, Paul Althaus als Neutestamentler [D]1993 → 8,m638; 9,16767:: [R]EThL
70 (1994) 454s (P. *Neirynck*).

k740 ALTIZER Thomas J.J., The genesis of God; a theological genealogy. LVL 1993,
W-Knox. 200 p. $ 22. 0-664-21996-9. -- [R]ET 106 (1994s) 29 (G. *Pattison*: a lexical
thinker, not by argument or evidence but 'by incantation in which names and concepts are
grouped'; ultimately The Death of God refigured in an apocalyptic mode).

----

k741 BALTHASAR: La dramatique divine [iii. 1990 → 9,16914], IV. Le dénouement 1993
→ 10.14964: [R]RTL 26 (1995) 223-5 (É. *Gaziaux*).

k742 -- Balthasar, Theo-Drama; theological dramatic theory, IV. The Action, [T]*Harrison*
Graham. SF 1994, Ignatius. 511 p. $ 40 [RStR 22,49, F.C. *Bauerschmidt*].

k743 **Gawronski** Raymond, Word and silence; Hans Urs von Balthasar and the spiritual
encounter between East and West. E 1995, Clark. xiv-233 p. £ 20, 0-5676-09744-7. --
[R]*TBR 8,3 (1995s) 17s (A. *McCoy*).

k744 *Lochbrunner* Manfred, H.U.von Balthasars Trilogie der Liebe; vom Dogmatikentwurf
zur theologischen Summe: ForKT 11 (1995) 161-181.

k745 [E]**McGregor** Bede, *Norris* Thomas, The beauty of Christ [Maynooth conference, May
1992] 1994 → 10,14959: [R]I(r)ThQ 61 (1995) 160-3 (Vivian *Boland*).

k746 *Meis W.* Anneliese, H.U. von Balthasar y K. RAHNER, coincidencias y divergencias:
TyV(ida) 35 (1994) 259-280.

k747 **Oakes** Edward T., Patterns of redemption; the theology of H.U.von Balthasar. NY
1994, Continuum. xii-334 p. $ 29,50. 0-8264-0685-8 [ThD 43,79]. -- [R]*CWeal 122,7
(1995) 24s (R. P. *Imbelli*); TS 56 (1995) 787-9 (J.R. *Sachs*).

k748 **Scola** Angelo, H.U.v.B., a theological style [1991 → 9,16909][T]: Resourcement. E/GR
1995, Clark/Eerdmans. xii-111 p. £ 9. 0-567-29297-5 / 0-8028-0894-8. -- [R]*TBR 8,3
(1995s) 19 (Elizabeth *Lord*: an invitation, but not for beginners; strongly philosophical and
counter to current thinking).

k749 **Wallner** Karl J., Gott als Eschaton; trinitarische Dramatik als Voraussetzung göttlicher
Universalität bei H.U. von Balthasar [Diss. Wien] 1992 → 9,16912; 10,14964: [R]MüTZ 45
(1994) 227s (O. *Meuffels*).

----

k750 BARTH: *Armstrong* A. Hilary, Karl Barth, the Fathers of the Church, and natural theo-
ology: JThS 46 (1995) 191-5.

k751 *Aubert* Philippe, Barth et SCHWEITZER; pour dépasser le conflit entre orthodoxie et libéralisme: FV 94,1 (1995) 61-72.

k752 **Barth** Karl, The theology of John CALVIN, [T]*Bromiley* Geoffrey W. GR 1995, Eerdmans. xxiv-424 p. $ 25. 0-8028-0696-1 [*TBR 9/1,24, M. *Elliott*; RStR 22,340, D.K. *McKim*].

k753 **Biggar** Nigel, The hastening thàt waits 1993: → 9,16923; 10,14967: [R]MoTh 11 (1995) 277-9 (N.M. *Healy*).

k754 *Busch* Eberhard, Weg und Werk Karl Barths in der neueren Forschung: ThR(und) 60 (1995) 273-299 . 430-470.

k755 *Cremer* Douglas J., Protestant theology in early Weimar Germany; Barth, TILLICH, & BULTMANN; JHI(d) 56 (1995) 289-307.

k756 **Cunningham** Mary Kathleen, What is theological exegesis ? Interpretation and use of Scripture in Barth's doctrine of election. Ph 1995, Trinity. 95 p. $ 10. 1-56338-115-X [RStR 22,166, W.T. *Dickens*; ThD 43,162].

k757 *a) Egmond* A. van, Zu lebendes Drama ? Bemerkungen zu Barths Rechtfertigungslehre; -- *b) Dulk* M. den, Die pastoriale Dynamik der Rechtfertigungslehre Karl Barths: ZD(ialekt)T 11 (1995) 7-27 /

k758 *Finke* Anne-Kathrin, Karl Barth and British theology: *ZnTg 2 (1995) 193-224; deutsch 193.

k759 **Goud** Johan F., Emmanuel LEVINAS und Karl Barth; ein religionsphilosophischer und ethischer Vergleich: AbhPPP 234, 1992 → 9,16926*: [R]ETL 70 (1994) 495s (E. *Brito*); FilTeo 8 (1994) 354-7 (S. *Sorrentino*).

k760 *Hart* Trevor, The word, the words, and the witness; proclamation as divine and human reality in the theology of Karl Barth: TynB 46 (1995) 81-102.

k761 *Hielema* Syd, Searching for 'disconnected wires'; Karl Barth's doctrine of creation revisited: C(alvin)TJ 30 (1995) 75-94.

k762 **Hunsinger** George, How to read Karl Barth 1991 → 6,m100* ... 10,14972]]: [R]SvTK 69 (1993) 195-9 (Ola *Sigurdson*, svensk, also on MACKEN J. 1990; NIELSEN B.).

k763 **Klimek** Nicolaus, Der Begriff 'Mystik' in der Theologie Karl Barths: KKTS 56, [D]1990: [R]RTL 26 (1995) 109s (E. *Brito*).

k764 **Kraege** Jean-Denis, L'Écriture seule; pour une lecture dogmatique de la Bible; l'exemple de LUTHER et Barth: L(ieux)Th 27. Genève 1995, Labor et Fides. 304 p. 2-8309-0789-2.

k765 **McCormack** Bruce, Karl Barth's critically dialectical theology; its development, 1909-1936. Ox 1995, UP, xvii-499 p. £ 50. 0-19-826337-6. -- [R]E(xp)T 107 (1995s) 88s (G. *Ward*); *TBR 8,1 (1995s) 26 (C. *Gunton*: 'definitive').

k766 **Matheny** P.D., Dogmatics and ethics; the theological realism and ethics of Karl Barth'a Church Dogmatics [D]1990 → 7,g94: [R]S(cot)JTh 48 (1995) 544-7 (T.J. *Gorringe*, also on BIGGAR).

k767 *Molnar* Paul D., Some problems with PANNENBERG's solution to Barth's 'faith subjectivism': S(cot)JTh 48 (1995) 315-339.

k768 *Nichols* Aidan, Barth's theology of revelation, II -- theology and Church: D(owns)R 113 (1995) 20-30.

k769 **Roberts** Richard H., A theology on its way 1992 → 8,m775: [R]JETS 38 (1995) 131-3 (W.A. *Detzler*).

k770 *Roberts* Richard H., Barth, BLOCH and the 'end of history': Metanoia 1 (Praha 1992) 26-28; franç. 29.

k771 *Roy* Louis, Karl Barth et les expériences de transcendance: SR 24 (1995) 323-330.

k772 **Sonderegger** Katherine, That Jesus Christ was born a Jew 1992 → 8,a789 ... 10,14985: RP(rinc)SB 16 (1995) 103-5 (Ellen T. *Charry*).

k773 **Taxacher** Gregor, Trinität und Sprache; dogmatische Erkenntnislehre als Theologie der Sprache; eine systematische Befragung Karl Barths: BDS 18. Wü 1995, Echter. 540 p. DM 64. 3-429-01637-1 [ThRv 92,84].

k774 **Ward** Graham, Barth, DERRIDA and the language of theology. C 1995, Univ. xvi-258 p. £ 35. 0-521-47290-3. -- RE(xp)T 107 (1995s) 89 (Esther *Reed*).

k775 **Webster** John W., Objectivity after Barth; Barth's ANSELM book and the problem of objectivity in a postmodern age; diss. Theol. Sem., DMcClain-Taylor M. Princeton 1995. — RStR 22,p.271.

k776 **Webster** John, Barth's ethics of reconciliation [the Church Dogmatics is a work of moral theology]. C 1995, Univ. 238 p. £ 35. 0-521-47499-X. -- RE(xp)T 107 (1995s) 122 (Brian *Haymes:* superb).

----

k777 BATAILLE: **Kate** L. ten, De lege plaats; revoltes tegen het instrumentele leven in [1943 G.] Bataille's atheologie: een studie over ervaring, gemeenschap en sacraliteit in 'De innerlijke ervaring' [diss. Utrecht]. Kampen 1994, Kok Agora. 639 p. *f* 80. -- RG(ereformeerd)TT 95 (1995) 41s (W. *Stoker*).

k778 BAYER: *Korsch* Dietrich, Das rettende Wort; zu Gestalt und Entwicklung der Theologie Oswald Bayers: ThR 60 (1995) 192-203.

779 BERDYAEV: *Dietrich* Wolfgang, 'Löscht den Geist nicht aus!'; Nikolai Berdjajews freie christliche Philosophie: ThZ 51 (1995) 65-86.

k780 BOFF: Leonhard, Christentum mit dunklem Antlitz; Wege in die Zukunft aus der Erfahrung Lateinamerikas, THermans Karel. FrB 1993, Herder. 157 p. DM 22,80. -- RLebZeug 50 (1995) 305s (Regina *Kaufmann*).

----

k781 BONHOEFFER: *Barker* H. Gaylon, Bonhoeffer, Luther and theologia crucis: Dialog 34 (1995) 10-17.

k782 EBethge Eberhard, Friendship and resistance; essays on Dietrich Bonhoeffer. Geneva 1995, WCC. 120 p. Fs 15. 2-8254-1153-1. -- RET 106 (1994s) 378s (E. *Robertson*).

k783 EBismarck Ruth-Alice von, *Kabitz* Ulrich, Love letters from cell 92; the correspondence between D. Bonhoeffer and Maria von Wedemeyer, 1943-45 [year of his final arrest; she was 18], TBrownjohn John. Nv 1995, Abingdon. 378 p. $ 35. 0-687-01098-5. -- RRStR 21 (1995) 212 (P.C. *Hodgson:* lyric praise).

k784 *Bobert-Stützel* Sabine, 'Kirche für Andere' oder 'Spielraum der Freiheit?': EvTh 55 (1995) 534-557 (*al.* 489-533 . 558-574).

k785 *Carey* George [abp. Canterbury], Faith in resistance 1933-1945; a tribute to the BELL-Bonhoeffer tradition: Theol 98 (L 1995) 424-431: Bonhoeffer's last known words were a message to his 15-year-long friend George Bell, bishop of Chichester, 'an outspoken supporter of the Confessing Church and a powerful critic of some aspects of his own Government's policy'.

k786 *Galantino* Nunzio, Bonhoeffer: teologo cattolico ? Confessione e chiesa in Dietrich Bonhoeffer: RasT 36 (1995) 261-283.

k787 *Krötke* Wolf, Der zensierte Bonhoeffer [subject to state censorship]; zu einem schwierigen Kapitel der Theologiegeschichte in der DDR: ZThK 92 (1995) 329-356.

k788 **Marsh** Charles, Reclaiming Dietrich Bonhoeffer; the promise of his theology 1994 →
10,14996: R*CritRR 8 (1995) 487-493 (G.B. *Kelly*); C(omm)V 37 (1995) 143-160 (P.
Macek); ET 106 (1994s) 188 (S. *Plant*); *ModBlv 36,2 (1995) 71s (also S. *Plant*);
P(rinc)SB 16 (1995) 254s (C.C. *West*); SewaneeT 38 (1994s) 371-4 (J.C. *Rochelle*).

k789 *Rochelle* Jay C., Bonhoeffer and biblical interpretation; reading Scripture in the Spirit:
CThMi 22 (1995) 85-95.

k790 *Schild* Maurice E., [b.1885 Hermann] SASSE and Bonhoeffer, churchmen on the brink:
LTJ 29 (1995) 3-10 (-32, *al.*).

k791 *Scilironi* Carlo, Bonhoeffer o il domandare radicale: Asprenas 42 (1995) 323-354.

k792 **Soosten** Joachim von, Die Sozialität der Kirche; Theologie und Theorie der Kirche in
Dietrich Bonhoeffers 'Sanctorum communio': Öffentliche Theologie 2, 1992 → 8,m792
(Index!): RZEE(th) 39 (1995) 81-84 (D. *Korsch*).

k793 **Wüstenberg** Ralf-Karolus, Glauben als Leben; *a*) Religionskritik und nichtreligiöse
Interpretation bei Dietrich Bonhoeffer: Diss. DWirsching. Berlin 1995. -- ThRv Beilage
92/2, v. -- *b*) FrSZ 42 (1995) 367-381.

----

k794 BROWN Raymond E., Death of the Messiah 1994 → 2103 and 3926 supra; 10,4634:
RChurchman 108 (L 1994) 370-2 (R.S. *Ascough*: magisterial); P(rinc)SB 16 (1995) 360-3
(D.M. *Smith*: awesome accomplishment); RefR 49 (1995s) 139s (D.W. *Jurgens*: a resource
by which relevant works will be measured); US(em)QR 48,1 (1994) 187-190 (R. *Scroggs*:
called by the popular press 'radical', but to scholars 'conservative': both merited by his
common-sense).

k795 BRUEGGEMANN Walter, Biblical perspectives on evangelism; [→ k541 supra] living in
a three-storied universe 1993 → 9,868: P(rinc)SB 16 (1995) 114-6 (J.W. *Stewart*).

k796 BURGHARDT W., Autobiography in search of meaning; on turning 80: Origins 24
(1994s) 486-493.

k797 BURHOE; *Godbey* John C., Ralph Wendell Burhoe in historical perspective: Zygon
30,4 ('A new look at [Zygon-founder' 1965] Burhoe 1995) 541-543.

k798 **Ciani** John L., S.J., 1951 -- 22.XII.1994 ('CivCatt from Americanism to Modernism'
awaited at Catholic Univ.Press): RC(ath)HR 81 (1995) 306 (G.P. *Fogarty*).

k799 CONE: *Chopp* Rebecca, Beyond narratives [and four other comments on] Cone's
Martin & Malcolm & America: US(em)QR 48,1s (1994) 19-27 {1-50}; Cone response 52-
57; -- further on Cone's KING, JB(lack)St 26 (1995s) 217-9 (Cynthia L. *Lehman*).

----

k800 CONGAR: **Blakebrough** D.S. (autora), El Cardenal Congar o la libertad teológica;
ensayo sobre su comprensión del Espíritu Santo; ¿ Femineidad del Espíritu ? S 1995,
Varona. 305 p. -- REstTrin 29 (1995) 360s (M. *Ofilada Mina*).

k801 **Bosch** Juan, A la escucha del Cardenal Congar: Vida y misión. M 1994, Edibesa.
280 p. -- RRET 55 (1995) 107-9 (J.L. *Larrabe*).

k802 **Brown** Susan Mader, Faith and history; the perspective of Yves Congar; Diss.
St.Michael, DDonovan D. Toronto 1994. -- RTLv 27, p.546.

k803 *Duval* André, Regards sur la bibliographie du P. Congar pendant ses années
strasbourgeoises (1957-1967): RevSR 69 (1995) 130-134.

k804 *Famerée* Joseph, *a*) Aux origines de Vatican II; la démarche théologique d'Yves
Congar: EThL 71 (1995) 121-138; -- *b*) Orthodox influence on the Roman Catholic
theologian Yves Congar, O.P.; a sketch: SV(lad)SQ 39 (1995s) 409-416.

k805 *Lago Alba* Luis, Yves M.-J. Congar, O.P., teólogo del diálogo y de la tolerancia: CiTom 121 (1994) 599-618.

k806 *Larrabe* José Luis, Aportación sacramental del Cardenal Congar (situándola en el contexto de sus obras): Lum(Vt) 44 (1995) 121-134.

k807 **Muñoz i Durán** M., Yves-M. Congar; su concepción de teología y de teólogo [dis. Roma, Pont. Univ. Gregoriana]: Fac.Teol. Catalunya. Barc 1994, Herder. 365 p. - [R]CDios 208 (1995) 287s (J.M. *Ozaeta*); MélSR 52 (1995) 352s (J.-C. *Matthys*); Rel(y)Cult 41 (1995) 428s (P. *Langa*).

k808 *Neufeld* Karl-Heinz, Theologe und Kardinal der Kirche; zu Y. Congars Buch 'Église et Papauté'; Dank eines Schülers: ZkT 117 (1995) 447-452.

k809 **Nichols** A., Yves Congar, [T]. Mi 1995, Paoline. 295 p. -- [R]EstTrin 29 (1995) 508 (M. *Ofilada Mina*).

k810 **Okashoko Nkoy Mukanga** Daniel, La dynamique de la catholicité dans l'ecclésiologie du P. Yves Congar: diss. [D]*Halleux* A. de. LvN 1994. xxv-367 p.

k811 *Tangorra* Giovanni, L'itinerario e l'opera di Yves Congar: Ter(esianum) 46 (1995) 445-458.

----

k812 CROSSAN: *a)* [E]**Carlson** J., *Ludwig* R., A conversation 1994 → 10,315: [R]I(nd)TS 32 (1995) 289s (B.J. *Francis*); -- *b)* *Halstead* James, The orthodox unorthodoy of John Dominic Crossan; an interview : CrossCur 45 (1995s) 510-530.

k813 CUPITT Don, After all; religion without alienation 1994 → 10,15007: [R]Modern Believing [continuing the numbering of Modern Churchman] 36,3 (1995) 28-33 (Joan *Crewdson:* faith at sea ?).

k814 -- **Cupitt** Don, Solar ethics [against 'no morality without God' and future life]. L 1995, SCM. 71 p. £ 8, 0-334-026180. -- [R]*TBR 8,2 (1995s) 21 (M. *Oakley*).

k815 -- **Cupitt** Don, The last philosophy. L 1995, SCM. vii-149 p. £ 10. 0-334-02586-9. — [R]E(xp)T 107 (1995s) 29 (R. *Burns*: self-contradictory throughout); Modern Believing 36,4 (1995) 54s (S. *Shakespeare*); *TBR 8,2 (1995s) 20s (Esther *Reed*: reader-friendly style).

k816 -- *a)* *Spearritt* Gregory, Don Cupitt, Christian Buddhist ?: RelSt 31 (1995) 359-373; — *b)* **White** Stephen R., Don Cupitt and the future of Christian thinking 1994 → 10,15006: [R]ET 106 (1994s) 92 (G. *Slater*).

k817 DANIÉLOU: Carnets spirituels [pubblicazione impedita dalla famiglia 1978]. P 1993, Cerf. 406 p. F 150. -- [R]CivCatt 146 (1995,1) 194s (B. *Van Hove*).

k818 DAY: *a)* **Merriman** Brigid O., Searching for Christ; the spirituality of Dorothy Day. ND 1994, Univ. xi-333 p. $ 30. -- [R]Horizons 22 (1995) 156s (Mary *Milligan*). -- *b)* *Mize* Sandra Y., Dorothy Day's Apologia for faith after MARX [The long loneliness 1952]: Horizons 22 (1995) 198-213.

k819 DE LUCA: **Ossicini** Adriano, Il 'colloquio' con Don Giuseppe De Luca, della resistenza al Concilio Vaticano II. R 1992, Storia e Lett. -- [R]RHPhR 75 (1995) 190-216 (É. *Goichot,* aussi sur ANTONAZZI G. 1992).

k820 DIX: **Bailey** Simon, A tactful God; Gregory Dix, priest, monk and scholar. Leominster 1995, Gracewing. xi-268 p. £ 16. 0-85244-340-4. -- [R]*TBR 8,3 (1995s) 48 (Maxine *West*).

k821 DOOYEWEERD: *Dengerink* Jan D., *a)* Herman Dooyeweerd (1894-1977), philosophe chrétien, Réformé, œcuménique : RRéf 46,4 (1995) 1-18; 19-38, sa Sécularisation de la science 1953; -- *b)* Herman Dooyeweerd (1894-1977); filosofo cristiano, riformato, ecumenico: STEv 6,12 (1994) 103-120 (121-198, Dooyeweerd, Il nuovo compito 1959, ᵀ*Coletto* R.; bibliog. 199-201)

k822 DUCHESNE: **Waché** Brigitte, Msgr Louis Duchesne (1843-1944), historien de l'Église: ÉcFrR 167. P 1992, École Française. xii-757 p. 2-7283-0259-6. -- ᴿGreg 76 (1995) 405-8 (F. de *Lasala*).

k823 ECO: *Cavalleri* Cesare, I goliardici sofismi di Umberto Eco [L'isola del giorno prima 1994]: StCatt 39 (1995) 108-111.

k824 ELLUL: **Troude-Chastenet** Patrick, Lire Ellul; introduction à l'œuvre socio-politique de Jacques Ellul. Bordeaux 1992, Univ. 302 p. F 90. -- ᴿFV 92,6 (1993) 85s (S. *Dujan-court*).

k825 FLOROVSKY: ᴱ**Blane** Andrew, Georges Florovsky, Russian intellectual and Orthodox churchman. Crestwood NY 1993, St. Vladimir. 444 p. $ 20. -- ᴿSV(lad)SQ 39 (1995s) 103-7 (R. *Slesinski*).

k826 **Ford** David F., Theologen der Gegenwart; eine Einführung in die christliche Theologie des zwanzigsten Jahrhunderts [The modern theologians], ᵀᴱ*Schwöbel* Christoph. Pd 1993, Schöningh. 359 p. 3-506-72599-8. -- ᴿActuBbg 31 (1994) 226s (J. *Boada*).

k827 FOSDICK: *Camroux* Martin F., Liberalism preached: ᴿET 106 (1994s) 44-47.

k828 FOX: *a) Echeverri* Alberto, Matthew Fox e Ignacio de LOYOLA; para una espiritualidad de la creación: TX(av) 109 (1994) 459-472; -- *b) West* Angela, Matthew Fox, blessing for whom ?: SewaneeT 38 (1994s) 329-350.

k829 GAILLOT: *Legrand* Hervé (interview), 'Autorität anders ausüben' [.. synodal; 'Subsidiarität' klingt formalistisch]: HerKor 49 (1995) 185-190 [347s; 680; -- 445 adv., **Gaillot**, Ihr seid das Volk; Brief an meine Freunde in der Wüste; Herder, 114 p., DM 22,80; 3-451-23889-6].

k830 GIUSSANI Luigi [dir. Comunione e Liberazione], Warum Jesus Christus?; Theologia Romanica 19, 2d to appear. FrB 1994, Johannes. 171 p. 3-89411-322-7. -- ᴿZkT 117 (1995) 351s (K.H. *Neufeld*).

k831 GOLLWITZER: **Orth** Gottfried, Helmut Gollwitzer; zur Solidarität befreit: Theologische Profile. Mainz 1995, Grünewald. 194 p. DM 38. 3-7867-1828-8. -- ᴿThLZ 120 (1995) 1028 s (G. *Haendler*).

k832 GRAHAM: **Randall** Ian M., Conservative constructionist; the early influence of Billy Graham in Britain: EvQ 67 (1995) 309-333.

k833 GREEN: **Yates** Timothy, Bryan Green; person -- evangelist. L 1994, B,Green Soc. 186 p. £ 11. 0-9524625-0-8. -- ᴿET 106 (1994s) 224 (C.S. *Rodd*: a remarkable book).

k834 HABERMAS: ᴱ**Arens** Edmund, Habermas et la théologie [sélection de ᶠ1989 → 6,384; 10,15017], ᵀ*Trierwiler* Denis: CFi 178. P 1993, Cerf. 162 p. F 130. 2-204-04722-8. -- ᴿRTL 26 (1995) 368 (P. *Weber*).

k835 -- *Jespers* F.P.M., De theologische receptie van de latere Habermas: TTh 35 (1995) 176-185.

k836 -- ᴱ**White** Stephen K., The Cambridge companion to Habermas. C 1995, Univ. ix-354 p. £ 30; pa. £ 13. 0-521-44120-X; -666-X. -- ᴿE(xp)T 107 (1995s) 188 (R. *Burns*).

k837 HÄRING Bernhard, Las cosas deben cambiar; una confesión valiente, ᵀ*Villanueva* Marciano. Barc 1995, Herder. 153 p. -- ᴿLum(Vt) 44 (1995) 521s (F. *Ortiz de Urtaran*).

k838 **Harries** Richard (bishop of Oxford), The real God [reply to Anthony FREEMAN's 1993 God in us, his conversion to Christian humanism, 'which cost him his job']. L 1994, Mowbray. 90 p. £ 7. 0-264-67384-0. -- ᴿET 106,6 top-choice(s)(1994s) 193-6 (C.S. *Rodd* assesses points on which the bishop's clarity and insight do not face directly enough some valid points raised by Freeman).

------

k840 HEIDEGGER: *Brito* Emilio, *a)* Le sacré dans les 'Éclaircissements pour la poésie de Hölderlin' de M. Heidegger: EThL 71 (1995) 337-369; -- *b)* Le sacré dans le cours de Heidegger sur 'La Germanie' de HÖLDERLIN : ScEs 47 (1995) 33-68.

k841 *Dartigues* André, Saint Thomas d'AQUIN et Heidegger d'après quelques étudesthomistes: RThom (1995) 137-149.

k842 *Grünfeld* Joseph, Heidegger's hermeneutics: ScEs 47 (1995) 141-152.

k843 **Kulueke** Heinrich, Die Bedeutung der 'Beiträge zur Philosophie' Martin Heideggers für die Gottesfrage; Impulse des 'seynsgeschichtlichen Denkens': Diss. Pont. Univ. Gregoriana. Rom 1994. 268 p. (No AA photocopy). -- D(iss)AI-C 56 (1995s) p. 827.

k844 **Lotz** Johannes B., Dall'essere al sacro; il pensiero metafisico dopo Heidegger. Brescia 1993, Queriniana. -- ᴿFilTeo 9 (1995) 191s (F.S. *Festa*).

k845 **Macquarrie** John, Heidegger and Christianity 1994 → 10,15025: ᴿET 106 (1994s) 190 (W.D. *Hudson*: not conformed but compatible); JThS 46 (1995) 791-4 (F. *Kerr*).

k846 *Riedel* Manfred, Verwahrung und Wahrheit des Seins; Heideggers ursprüngliche Deutung der Aletheia: → 182, ᶠSIMON J., Denken 1995, 275-293.

k847 *Sánchez de Murillo* José, El desarrollo de la fenomenología moderna, II. de HUSSERL à HEIDEGGER: Ter(esianum) 46 (1995) 51-89.

k848 **Tommasi** Roberto, 'Essere e Tempo' di Martin Heidegger in Italia (1928-1948): Roma Sem. Lombardo. Mi 1993, Glossa. 330 p. Lᵐ 45. 88-7105-022-3. -- ᴿEThL 71 (1995) 481s (E. *Brito*).

k849 **Ziegler** Susanne, Heidegger, HÖLDERLIN und die *alētheia*; Martin Heideggers Geschichtsdenken in seinen Vorlesungen 1934/35 bis 1944: PhS 2. B 1991, Duncker & H. 403 p. -- ᴿA(nz)AW 48,1s (1995) 49-51 (E. *Thurnher*).

------

k850 JOHANNES XXIII: ᴱ**Melloni** Alberto. G. Roncalli (Giovanni XXIII), La predicazione a Istanbul; omelie, discorsi e note pastorali (1935-1944): BRSLR 15. F 1993, Olschki. 418 p. -- ᴿRevSR 69 (1995) 109-114 (R. *Rusconi* -- p.517: non G. *Alberigo*).

----

k851 JOHANNES PAULUS II: Karol Wojtyla -- John Paul II's idea of ultimate reality and meaning: URM 18 (1995) 102.

k852 **Hebblethwaite** Peter †, Pope John Paul II and the Church. KC 1995, Sheed & W. (Fowler Wright £ 17). -- ᴿTablet 249 (1995) 1305s (A. *Woodrow*).

k853 *Lefebure* Leo D., John Paul II, the philosopher pope: ChrCent 112 (1995) 171-6.

k854 ᴱ**Messori** Vittorio, Crossing the threshold of hope, ᵀ*McPhee* Jenny & Martha. NY 1994, Knopf. 244 p. $ 20. -- ᴿCanadCath 13,2 (1995) 22s (G. *Trudel*); CrossCur 45 (1995s) 275s (J. *Cunneen*: the Pope peels away much of Messori's 'obsequious bordering on blasphemous'); DunwoodieR 18 (1995) 169-172 (J.J. *Higgins*).

k855 *Miller* J. Michael, The Pope's challenge to the Church in America: Faith & Reason 21 (1995) 29-53.

k856 **Schmitz** Kenneth L., At the center of the human drama; the philosophical anthropology of Karol Wojtyla 1993 → 10,15030: ᴿNOxR 62,3 (1995) 22.24 (J.G. *Hanink*).

k857 **Szulc** Tad, Pope John Paul II, the biography. NY 1995, Scribner. 542 p. $ 27.50. — ᴿAmerica 173,1 (1995) 26s (R.E. *Sullivan*); C(ath)HR 81 (1995) 621-3 (G.G. *Higgins*: truly *the* biography, far surpassing all others).

k858 **Walsh** Michael, John Paul II, a biography. L 1994, HarperCollins. ix-310 p. £ 20.
0-00-215993-7. -- ᴿET 106 (1994s) 256 (C.S. *Rodd*); Month 256 (1995) 108-110 (D.
Robinson).

----

k859 JONAS: *Boissinot* Christian, La réception française de l'œuvre de Hans Jonas: RÉTM
= Le Supplément 194 (1995) 180-206.

k860 JOURNET: *Mougel* René, La correspondance MARITAIN-Journet [vol 1, 1920-9, 850
p.], un renouveau libérateur de la théologie de l'Église : NV 70,4 (1995) 66-84.

----

k861 JÜNGEL: **Cislaghi** Alessandra, Interruzione e corrispondenza; il pensiero teologico di
2 Eberhard Jüngel: GdT 225. Brescia 1994, Queriniana. 266 p. Lᵐ 27. -- ᴿAsprenas 42
(1995) 130s (P. *Pifano*); RasT 36 (1995) 499-501 (P. *Gamberini*).

k862 **Gamberini** Paolo, Nei legami del Vangelo: l'analogia nel pensiero di Eberhard Jüngel;
Aloisiana 27, 1994 → 10,15035: ᴿAng 72 (1995) 615-7 (A. *Lobato*).

k863 *Kappes* Michael, 'Natürliche Theologie' als innerprotestantisches und ökumenisches
Problem; die Kontroverse zwischen Eberhard Jüngel und Wolfhart PANNENBERG und ihr
ökumenischer Ertrag: Cath 49 (1995) 276-309.

k864 **Rodríguez Garrapucho** F., La cruz de Jesús y el ser de Dios; la teología del
Crucificado en Eberhard Jüngel ᴰ1992 → 10,15036: ᴿEstTrin 29 (1995) 128s (A.
Llamazares Ugena).

k865 *Webster* John, Jesus' speech, God's word; an introduction to Eberhard Jüngel: ChrCent
112 (1995) 1174-8 . 1217-9 (2. Who God is, who we are).

k866 **Zimany** Roland D., Vehicle for God; the metaphorical theology of Eberhard Jüngel
1994 → 10,15036*: ᴿE(xp)T 107 (1995s) 122s (K. *Clements*); *TBR 8,2 (1995s) 24 (C.
Gunton).

k867 KASPER: **Madonia** Nicolò, Ermeneutica e cristologia in W. Kasper: Theologia 2,
1992 → 7,7480; 8,7538: ᴿFilTeo 8 (1994) 378s (P. *Giustiniani*).

k868 KATTENBUSCH: *Deuser* Hermann, Dass und wiefern es 'glaublich' sei; Ferdinand Kat-
tenbuschs historisch-systematische Theologie: ZThK 92 (1995) 54-70.

k869 KAUFMAN G.: *Irwin* Alec, Face of mystery, mystery of a face; an anthropological
trajecory in WITTGENSTEIN, CAVELL, and Kaufman's biohistorical theology: HThR 88 (1995)
389-409.

k870 -- *Jehle* Frank, Vor dem Geheimnis leben; zum Gesamtentwurf des amerikanischen
Theologen Gordon Dester Kaufman: FrSZ 42 (1995) 425-436.

k871 KÜNG: *Carroll* Denis, Hans Küng's vision of Christianity [Religious situation 2, 1995
→ k625 supra]: DoLi 45 (1995) 681-5: vision, lucidity, scholarliness, openness; unlike
ecclesiastical theologians, who march to another drum.

k872 KUITERT H.: **Murphy** David G., Debates on God and experience in the Netherlands
1965-1989 [diss.]. SF 1993, Catholic Scholars. 193 p. $ 60; pa. $ 40. -- ᴿC(alvin)TJ 30
(1995) 532-4 (J. *Bolt*: illuminating and helpful).

k873 LAVIGERIE: **Renault** François, Cardinal Lavigerie; churchman, prophet, and
missionary, ᵀO'Donohue John. L 1994, Athlone. $ 60. -- ᴿIBM(iss)R 19 (1995) 85s (A.
Hastings).

k874 LECLERCQ: *Penco* Gregorio, Jean Leclercq e il concetto di tradizione monastica: Ben
41 (1994) 317-339.

k875 LEHMANN: **Duff** Nancy J., Humanization and the politics of God 1992 → 9,17008; 10,
15042: ᴿInterpretation 49 (1995) 220 . 222 (A.J. *McKelway*).

k876 LEVINAS: *Purcell* Michael. Nec tamen consumebatur; Exodus 3 and the non-consumable other in the philosophy of Emmanuel Levinas: S(cot)JTh 48 (1995) 79-95.

k877 LEWIS C.S., An experiment in criticism. C 1995, Univ. viii-143 p. 0-521-42281-7.

k878 -- *Abraham* William J., C.S. Lewis and the conversion of the West: P(ersp)Ref 10,1 (1995) 12-17.

-----

k879 LONERGAN: **Crowe** F.J. Lonergan: Outstanding Christian thinkers 1992 → 8,m833 ... 10,15046: ᴿMilltSt 35 (1995) 146-9 (R. *Moloney*); TorJT 11 (1995) 125s (M. *Vertin*).

k880 **Crowe** Frederick E., Bernard F.J. Lonergan; progresso e tappe del suo pensiero, ᵀᴱ*Spaccapelo* Natalino, *Muratore* Saturnino. R 1995, Città Nuova. 192 p. Lᵐ 25. -- ᴿAng 72 (1995) 619-622 (A. *Lobato*); DoC(om) 48 (1995) 312s (D. *Vibrac*).

k881 ᴱ**Farrell** Thomas J., *Soukup* Paul A., Communication and Lonergan; common ground for forging the new age. KC 1993, Sheed & W. 416 p. $ 23 pa. -- ᴿCrossCur 45 (1995s) 272s (Moira T. *Carley*).

k882 **Liddy** Richard M., Transforming light; intellectual conversion in the early Lonergan 1993 → 9,17016: ᴿTS 56 (1995) 170 (W.E. *Conn*).

k883 **McEvenue** Sean E., *Meyer* Ben F,. Lonergan's hermeneutics; its development and application 1989 → 6,650*; 8,m837: ᴿNewThR 8,1 (1995) 94s (R. *Viladesau*),

k884 *Matthews* William, On Lonergan and John Stuart MILL: MilltSt 35 (1995) 39-50.

k885 **Meynell** Hugo A., Bernard Lonergan [The theology of .. 1986]. CinB 1994, S. Paolo. 270 p. Lᵐ 32. 88-215-2788-3. -- ᴿGreg 76 (1995) 408s (G. *Ferraro*).

k886 *Sala* Giovanni B., Da Tommaso d'*Aquino* a Bernard Lonergan; continuità e novità: RasT 36 (1995) 407-425.

k887 **Stebbins** J. Michael, The divine initiative; grace, world-order, and human freedom in the early writings of Bernard Lonergan. Toronto 1995, Univ. xxii-399 p. US$ 73. 0-8020-0464-4 [ThRv 92,84; ThD 43,90.].

k888 **Steenburg** David J.F., Nature and history in the knowledge of value; a study in Bernard Lonergan's account of value: diss. McMaster (Canada), ᴰ*Robertson* J., 1994. 298 p. NN93425 (ISBN 0-315-93425-5). -- D(iss)AI 56 (1995s) p. 227.

----

k889 DE LUBAC: **Bertoldi** Francesco, De Lubac, Cristianesimo e modernità. Bo 1994, Studio Domenicano. 322 p. -- ᴿVPens 78 (1995) 554-8 (A. *Frigerio*).

k890 *Ciola* Nicola, Il contributo di Henri de Lubac alla teologia sistematica: Lat 61 (1995) 79-106; Eng. 106.

k891 *Dessì* Gianni, Una biografia di Henri de Lubac [RUSSO A, (Mi 1994, San Paolo) 261 p.]: Studium 91 (R 1995) 136-142.

k892 **Moretto** Giovanni, Destino dell'uomo e corpo mistico, BLONDEL, de Lubac e il Concilio Vaticano II. Brescia 1994, Morcelliana. 160 p. Lᵐ 20. -- ᴿProtest(antesimo) 50 (1995) 166s (M. *Fabris*).

k893 **Russo** Antonio, Henri de Lubac, Teologia e dogma nella storia; l'influsso di BLONDEL: La cultura 40. R 1990, Studium. 433 p. Lᵐ 142. -- ᴿRTL 26 (1995) 110 (É. *Brito*: lacune comblée par des inédits).

k894 **Russo** Antonio, Henri de Lubac: I teologi del 20° secolo 3. CinB 1994, Paoline. 261 p. Lᵐ 32. 88-215-2756-5. -- ᴿZkT 117 (1995) 117 (K. H. *Neufeld*).

------

k895 **McGrath** A., Bridge-building 1992 → 9,7184: ᴿSTEv 6 (1994) 100s (V. *Bernardi*).

k896 MACHEN: **Hart** D.G., Defending the faith; J, Gresham Machen and the crisis of conservative Protestantism in modern America 1994 → 10,15058: [R]CrossCur 45 (1995s) 269-272 (J.H. *Moorhead*); PerspSCF 47 (1995) 282s (R. *Ruble*); P(rinc)SB 16 (1995) 377-9 (G.S. *Smith*).

k897 MARÉCHAL: **Matteo** Anthony M., Quest for the absolute; the philosophical vision of Joseph Maréchal 1992 → 9,17030: [R]JRel 75 (1995) 134s (K. L. *Willumsen*).

k898 MAURICE: **Young** David, F.D. Maurice and Unitarianism 1992 → 9,17032: [R]HeythJ 36 (1995) 95s (P. *Butler*).

k899 MEN: **Hamant** Yves, Alexandre Men [assassiné 9.XI.1990], un témoin pour la Russie de ce temps: Actes de la foi. P 1993, Mame. 206 p. F 185. -- [R]Christus 41 (1994) 337-341 (Marguerite *Lena*).

k900 MERCIER: *Carcel Ortí* Vicente, Le cardinal Mercier et les études ecclésiastiques en Espagne: RHE 90 (1995) 104-112.

k901 MERTON [→ 4474 supra]: *O'Connell* Patrick F., Thomas Merton and the multiculturalism debate; cultural diversity or transcultural consciousness ?: Cithara 34,2 (1995) 27-36.

k902 -- **Reese** Daniel B., The feast of wisdom; Thomas Merton's vision and practice of a sapiential education: diss. Theol.Sem., [D]*Loger* J. Princeton 1995 [< RStR 22, p.270].

k903 MOLNÁR: *a) Gonnet* Giovanni, Amedeo Molnár, studioso del valdismo est-europeo; — *b) De Michelis* Cesare G., Una fonte rutena inedita su Jan HUS: Protest(antesimo) 50 (1995) 178-187 / 188-194.

------

k904 MOLTMANN: **Bauckham** Richard, The theology of Jürgen Moltmann. E 1995, Clark. xii-276 p. £ 13. 0-567-29277-0. -- [R]E(xp)T 107 (1995s) 89 (J. *Macquarrie*).

k905 *Clutterbuck* Richard, Jürgen MOLTMANN as a doctrinal theologian; the nature of doctrine and the possibilities for its development: S(cot)JTh 48 (1995) 489-505.

k906 *Larsen* Peter K., Jürgen Moltmanns syn på lidelsen: Ichthys 22,4 (1995) 147-154.

k907 **Moltmann** Jürgen, Jesus Christ for today's world [Wer ist Christus für uns heute?], [T]*Kohl* Margaret. £ 1994, SCM. vii-152 p. £ 7. 0-334-00814-X. -- [R*]TBR 8,2 (1995s) 27s (A. *Warren:* sprinkled with Nazi-era anecdotes).

k908 *Schweitzer* Don, Jürgen Moltmann's theology as a theology of the Cross: SR 24 (1995) 95-107.

k909 **Trouillez** P., De vele bronnen en de ene stroom; onderzoek naar continuiteït en vernieuwing in de theologie van Jürgen Moltmann: diss. [D]*Mertens* H. Leuven 1994. xlix-527 p. -- TTh 35 (1995) 173.

----

k910 MONTEFIORE Hugh, Credible Christianity; the Gospel in contemporary society. GR 1994, Eerdmans. 287 p. $ 20. -- [R]Encounter 56 (1995) 402s (B. *Epperly*).

k911 DE MONTREMY: **Léon-Dufour** Xavier, Dieu se laisse chercher; dialogue d'un bibliste avec Jean-Maurice de Montremy. P 1995, Plon. 187 p.   2-259-18368-9.

----

k912 MURRAY J.C.: Religious liberty; Catholic struggles with pluralism [1955-68, one ineditum], [E]*Hooper* J.Leon, 1993 → 9,17035: 159s (W. D. *Lindsey*).

k913 **Gonnet** Dominique, La liberté religieuse à Vatican II: la contribution de J.C. Murray [diss. P Centre Sèvres]:CFi 183. P 1994, Cerf. 410 p. -- [R]ATG(ran) 58 (1995) 393-5 (I. *Camacho*); EThL 71 (1995) 504s (L. de *Fleurquin*).

k914 **Hughson** Thomas, The believer as citizen; John Courtney Murray in a new context 1993 → 10,15063: [R]NewThR 8,1 (1995) 106-8 (J.H. *McKenna*).

k915 ^E**Hunt** Robert P., *Grasso* Kenneth L., John Courtney Murray and the American civil conversation. GR/Leominster 1992, Eerdmans / Fowler Wright. x-298 p. £ 16. -- ^RHeythJ 36 (1995) 99s (B. *Aspinwall*).

k916 **Pavlischeck** Keith, John Courtney Murray and the dilemma of religious toleration. Kirksville 1994, T. Jefferson Univ. 260 p. $ 58; pa. $ 22.50 [JETS 39, 301s, M. *McKenzie*].

----

k917 NEILL: *Jackson* Eleanor M., The continuing legacy of Stephen Neill: ^RIBM(iss)R [11 (1987) 62-66, LAMB C.] 19 (1995) 77-80.

k918 NEWBIGIN: *Conway* Martin, *a)* God-open, world-wide, and Jesus-true: Lesslie Newbigin as an ecumenist of our time: *Mid-Str 34 (1995) 21-33; -- *b)* Dios-Abierto, Mundo-Amplio y Jesús-Verdad; la peregrinación de fe de Lesslie Newbigin: DiEc 30 (1995) 51-66.

k919 NICHOLS Aidan, A grammar of consent 1991 → 10,15066: ^RS(cot)JTh 48 (1995) 110s (P. *Helm:* from Newman's 'illative sense = primacy of unreflective experience' Nichols 'tends to turn time-worn arguments for God's existence into descriptions of experience').

k920 NIEBUHR: *Brown* Charles C., Niebuhr and his age; Reinhold Niebuhr's prophetic role 1992 → 10,15067: ^RT(or)JT 11 (1995) 71-76 (G. *Harland*, also on four cognates).

k921 -- **Lovin** Robin, Reinhold Niebuhr and Christian realism. C 1995, Univ. x-255 p. £ 35. pa. £ 12. 0-521-44363-6; -7932-0. -- ^RET 106 (1994s) 316s (B. *Haymes*).

k922 NOUWEN: **Henderson** Kyle L., The reformation of pastoral theology in the life and works of Henri J. M. Nouwen: diss. SW Baptist Theol. Sem., ^D*Brister* C., 1994. 330 p. 95-17950. -- D(iss)AI 56 (1995s) p. 231.

k923 NYGREN *al.:* **Gerhardsson** B.. FRIDRICHSEN .. fyra theologer 1994 → 10,15074: SvTK 70 (1994) 184s (B. *Olsson*); TT(og)K 66 (1995) 321s (V.L. *Haanes*).

2k924 OMAN: **Bevans** Stephen, John Oman [1860-1939] and his doctrine of God C 1992, Univ. 173 p. £ 18. -- ^RS(cot)JTh 48 (1995) 543s (T. *Bradshaw*).

k925 OTTO, Rudolf (1869-1937): → 772, TRE 25 (1995) 559-563 (C.H. *Ratschow*).

k926 PANIKKAR: **Frost** Stephen W., Interstates; an investigation in the interphase between discursive and non-discursive perception according to pertinent criteria in the works of Raimundo Panikkar: diss.G.Theological Union, ^D*Empereur* J. Berkeley 1994 -- RStR 22, p.272.

------

k927 PANNENBERG: **Brena** G.L., La teologia di W. Pannenberg, cristianesimo e modernita 1993 → 9,17045; 10,15075: ^RCivCatt 146 (1995,2) 95s (G. *Pirola*) [487-499 & 4,366-378, *Brena*]; StPat(av) 41 (1994) 650-2 (L. *Sartori*).

k928 **Hasel** Frank M., Scripture in the theologies of W. Pannenberg and D.G. BLOESCH; an investigation and assessment of its origin, nature, and use: diss. Andrews, ^D*Canale* F. Berrien Springs 1994. -- A(ndr)USS 33 (1995) 285. -- 386 p. 95-22614. -- D(iss)AI 56 (1995s) p. 598.

k929 **Martínez Camino** J.A., Recibir la libertad .. Pannenberg, JÜNGEL [dis. Frankfurt S.Georgien]. M 1992, Univ. Comillas. 392 p. -- ^RRET 55 (1995) 105-7 (G. del *Pozo Abejón*).

k930 *Martínez Gordo* Jesús, La verdad como anticipación de lo último; la teología fundamental de Wolfhart Pannenberg: Lum(Vt) 44 (1995) 193-219.

k931 PAULUS VI: **Gloder** Giampiero. Carattere ecclesiale e scientifico della teologia in Paolo VI: diss. Lombardo Roma 5. Mi 1994, Glossa. xiv-275 p. L^m 45. 88-7105-123-1.— ^RZkT 117 (1995) 354s (K.H. *Neufeld*).

k932 **Hebblethwaite** Peter, Paul VI, the first modern Pope 1993 → 9,17053; 10,15084: ^RDunwoodieR 18 (1995) 173-5 (M.T. *Martine*).

k933 **Molinari** F., *Trebeschi* M., G.-B. Montini maestro di religione: Preti bresciani 1. Brescia 1994, Fond. Civiltà. -- ^RRHE 90 (1995) 209-211 (R. *Aubert*).

------

k934 PETERSON: **Nichtweiss** Barbara, Erik Peterson, neue Sicht 1992 → 10,15084: ^RMüTZ 45 (1994) 93 (G.L. *Müller*); TS 56 (1995) 168s (M.J. *Hollerich*).

k935 PINNOCK: **Roennfeldt** Ray C.W., Clark H. Pinnock on biblical authority; an evolving position; pref.Pinnock: Andrews diss. 16. Berrien Springs 1993, Andrews Univ. xxiv-428 p. $ 20. -- ^RA(ndr)USS 33 (1995) 322-4 (G. *Chartier*).

k936 POLANYI: **Crewdson** (Miss) Joan. Christian doctrine in the light of Michael Polanyi's theory of personal knowledge. Lewiston 1994, Mellen. xii-445 p. £ 60. 0-7734.9150-3. — ^RET 106 (1994s) 250 (J. *Macquarrie*).

k937 *Poupard* Paul, Pédagogie chrétienne et culture moderne [invité Angers 1995]: E(spr)eV 105 (1995) 609-616.

k938 PREUSS: **Conley** Rory, Arthur Preuss, journalist and voice of German and conservative Catholics in America, 1871-1934: diss. ^DTrisco R. Washington D.C. 1995. -- ^RRTLv 27, p.545: Catholic Univ.?

----

k939 RAHNER: **Ackley** John B., The Church of the Word; a comparative study of Word, Church, and office in the thought of Karl Rahner and Gerhard EBELING: AmerUnivSt. NY 1993, P. Lang. xviii-381 p. $ 60. -- ^RTS 56 (1995) 789-781 (R. *Masson*).

k940 *Batlogg* Andreas, Karl Rahner; Jesus lieben ? Zum Schicksal einer Veröffentlichung aus der 80er Jahren: GuL 67 (1994) 90-101.

k941 **Conway** Eamonn, The anonymous Christian -- a relativized Christianity; an evaluation of H.U.v.BALTHASAR's criticisms of Karl Rahner's theory: EurUnivStud 23, 1993 → 10, 15089: ^RZkT 117 (1995) 93-96 (A, *Batlogg*).

k942 *a) Crowley* Paul, Rahner's Christian pessimism; the problem of perplexity; -- *b) Kelly* Geffrey B., 'Unconscious Christianity' and the 'anonymous Christian' in the theology of Dietrich BONHOEFFER and Karl Rahner: *PhT 9 (Milwaukee 1995) 151-176 / 117-149 (177-243 *al.* on Rahner).

k943 **Dych** William V., Karl Rahner 1992 → 8,m881; 9,17056: ^RHorizons 22 (1995) 140s (Mary E. *Hines*).

k944 **Dych** William V., The mystery of faith; a Christian creed for today [centered on the Last Supper]. ColMn 1995, Liturgical/Glazier. 99 p. $ 8. 0-8146-5514-9 [ThD 92,364].

k945 **Guenther** Titus F., Rahner and METZ; transcendental theology as political theology [i.e. fully engaging contingent history]. Lanham MD 1994, UPA. xxiii-366 p. [RStR 22,50, Mary V. *Maher*].

k946 ^EKelly Geffrey B., Karl Rahner, theologian of the graced search for meaning → 9, 17061. E/Mp 1992, Clark/Fortress. 372 p. £ 10. 0-567-29238-X / . -- ^RFurrow 46 (1995) 734-6 (E. *Conway*. also on SCHILLEBEECKX); *TBR 8,2 (1995s) 29 (E. *Lord*}.

k947 *Lamadrid* Lucas, Anonymous or analogous Christians ? Rahner and VON BALTHASAR on naming the non-Christian: MoTh 11 (1995) 363-384.

k948 *Leijssen* Lambert, Grace as God's self-communication; the starting point and development in Rahner's thought: LouvSt 20 (1995) 73-78.

k949 **Lennan** Richard, The ecclesiology of Karl Rahner. Ox 1995, Clarendon. vi-289 p. £ 32.50. 0-19-826358-9-- ᴿTablet 249 (1995) 1206 (R. *Moloney*: 'balancing act').

k950 *Marucci* Corrado, Ancora sulla riforma degli studi teologici; il contributo di K. Rahner: RasT 36 (1995) 743-751.

k951 **Neufeld** Karl-Heinz, Die Brüder Rahner [Karl, Hugo], eine Biographie. FrB 1994, Herder. 416 p. DM 78. 3-451-23446-1. -- ᴿEntschluss 50,6 (1995) 33 (O. *Schulmeister*); STV(ars) 33,1 (1995) 215-8 (I. *Bokwa*); THGL 85 (1995) 423-8 (G. *Fuchs*).

k952 **Peters** Carmichael C., Through grace to freedom; a GADAMERIAN reading of Karl Rahner and the tradition: diss. Graduate Theological Union, ᴰWelch C. Berkeley 1995. 500 p. 95-36441. -- D(iss)AI 56 (1995s) p. 2737; RStR 22, p.271.

k953 *Schmalz* Mathew N., Transcendental reduction; Karl Rahner's theory of anonymous Christianity: Vidyajyoti 59 (1995) 680-692 . 741-752.

k954 *Skowronek* Alfons, ᴾ La théologie et la pastorale des sacrements selon Karl Rahner: AtK(ap) 125 (1995) 43-53.

k955 **Tourenne** Yves, La théologie du dernier Rahner; 'aborder au sans-rivage'; approches de l'articulation entre philosophie et théologie chez 'le dernier Rahner' suivi de Considération sur le méthode de la théologie par Karl Rahner: CFi 187. P 1995, Cerf. 461 p.; bibliog. 451-8. F 190. 2-204-05088-1. -- ᴿÉtudes 383 (1995) 572 (Gwendoline *Jarczyk*).

k956 *Vorgrimler* Herbert, Rahner-Literatur rund um das Gedenk-Jahr 1994: TR 91 (1995) 113-122.

----

k957 RAMSEY: ᴱGill Robin, *Kendall* Lorna, Michael Ramsey as theologian. L 1995, Darton-LT. 199 p. £ 9. 0-232-52081-X. -- ᴿE(xp)T 107 (1995s) 18 (L. *Houlden*); *TBR 8,1 (1995s) 58 (also L. *Houlden*).

------

k958 RICŒUR: *Grossi* Stefano, Possibili risposte al problema del male secondo Paul Ricœur: VivH 6 (1995) 395-410; Eng. 410.

k959 *Russell* Kenneth C., Paul Ricœur on Lectio Divina: E(gl)eT 26 (1995) 331-344.

k960 *Salvi* Marco, Ricœur, oltre la dispersione dell'alterità; S(cuola)C 123 (1995) 191-215.

------

k961 RORTY R.: **House** Vaden D., Without God or his doubles. Lei 1994, Brill. 194 p. — ᴿSR 24 (1995) 501s (T. *Penelhum*; temperate analysis of the erudite iconoclast).

k962 ROUSSELOT: *Bellandi* Andrea, Les yeux de la foi di Pierre Rousselot; un'opera da rileggere -- ancora attuale: VivH 6 (1995) 279-312: Eng. 313.

k963 RUIZ GARCÍA: *Kruip* Gerhard, Krise des Selbstvertrauens; nicht nur in Chiapas kommt Mexiko nicht zur Ruhe ['Bischof Ruiz bleibt Schlüsselfigur des Friedens']: HerKor 49 (1995) 267-271.

----

k964 SCHILLEBEECKX: *Engel* Ulrich, Gotteserkenntnis und Gotteserfahrung; eine Skizze zu Biographie und Werk E.Schillebeeckx': Orien(tierung) 59 (1995) 243-6 . 263-6.

k965 **Kennedy** Philip, Deus humanissimus; the knowability of God in the theology of E. Schillebeeckx [Diss. ᴰVergauwen G.]: ÖB 22. FrS 1993, Univ. xxi-435 p. Fs 75. 2-8271-0620-5. -- ᴿTTh 35 (1995) 300 (E. *Borgman*).

k966 **Kennedy** Philip, E. Schillebeeckx, Die Geschichte von der Menschlichkeit Gottes [ᵀomitting S. preface]: *TProfile. Mainz 1994, Grünewald. 225 p. DM 32. 3-7867-1789-3 [TTh 35,317].

k967 **Procario-Foley** Elena, Orthopraxis or orthodoxy ? An analysis of the relationship between experience and thought in Edward Schillebeeckx's trilogy 'Jesus, Christ, Church': diss. ᴰ*Carr A.* Chicago ... [no date or school, RTLv 27.p.548].

k968 **Rochford** Dennis H., The appropriation of hermeneutics in the theological works of Edward Schillebeeckx; an historical textual evaluation of the theological project to bridge Christian faith with modern culture: diss. Leuven 1995, ᴰ*Schrijver G. de.* lxxv-538 p. -- LouvSt 20 (1995) 418.

k969 **Schillebeeckx,** Colloqui [autobiografici] con Francesco *Strazzari.* Bo 1993, Dehoniane. 115 p. -- ᴿREB 55 (1995) 465-9 (F.L. Couto TEIXEIRA).

k970 **Schillebeeckx** (avec) *Strazzari* Francesco, Je suis un théologien heureux, ᵀMIGNON Jacques: Parole présente. P 1995, Cerf. 155 p. -- ᴿRevSR 69 (1995) 412s (M. *Deneken*). [Eng. español 1994 → 10,15015s].

----

k971 STRINGFELLOW: *Wink* Walter, William Stringfellow [ᴱKELLERMANN B. 1994], theologian of the next millennium: CrossCur 45 (1995s) 205-216, < Radical Christian and exemplary lawyer, ᴱ*McThenia* A. (Eerdmans 1995).

k972 STUDER: ᴱ**Orazzo** O. (in dialogo), I Padri della Chiesa e la teologia: Library 1. CinB 1995, San Paolo. 286 p. 88-215-3013-2.

k973 SUBILIA: *Conte* Gino, Vittorio Subilia († 1988; SAMPIETRO A., ᴰ1992; BETTETO F., ᴰ1992): ETRel 70 (1995) 557-565.

----

k974 TEILHARD: *Cowell* Sión, Re-review, The phenomenon of man (1959): *ModBlv 36,4 (1995) 2-8.

k975 *Daecke* Sigurd M., Christus-Omega; das Geschichtsverständnis von Teilhard de Chardin: Entschluss 50,9s (1995) 35-37 [2-46, *al.*]

k976 *King* Ursula, Apostle of the cosmic Christ: Tablet 249 (1995) 455.

k977 *Masiá* Elvira, Un pensador profético: Teilhard de Chardin, cuarenta años después: SalTer 83 (1995) 825-834.

k978 *Molari* Carlo, Futuro del cosmo, futuro dell'uomo; rivisitazione di un modello problematicamente significativo, Teilhard de Chardin: RasT 36 (1995) 479-491.

k979 **Trennert-Helwig** Mathias, *a)* Die Urkraft des Kosmos; Dimensionen der Liebe im Werk Pierre Teilhards de Chardin: FrTSt. FrB 1993, Herder. xiv-551. DM 78. -- ᴿTS 56 (1995) 382s (K. *Schmitz-Moormann*). -- *b)* Die Kirche lieben -- die Kirche erleiden; zum 40. Todestag von P. Teilhard de Chardin: GuL 68 (1995) 289-303.

k980 *a) Trennert-Helwig* Mathias, The Church as the axis of convergence in Teilhard's theology and life; -- *b) King* Ursula, Teilhard's reflections on eastern religions revisited: Zygon 30,1 (1995) 73-85 / 47-72.

k981 *Wojciechowski* Tadeusz, Teilhard de Chardin und die neue Auffassung des Todes; → 98, ᶠKUMOR B., AnCr 27 (1995) 35-42; ᴾ 43.

----

k982 THIELICKE Helmut, Notes from a wayfarer; autobiography, ᵀ*Law* David R. NY 1995, Paragon. xxi-422 p. $ 30. 1-55778-708-5 [ThD 43,190].

k983 THURNEYSEN: *Raschzok* Klaus, Ein theologisches Programm zur Praxis der Kirche; die Bedeutung des Werkes Eduard Thurneysens für eine gegenwärtig zu verantwortende Praktische Theologie: ThLZ 120 (1995) 299-311.

k984 TILLICH; **Albrecht** Renate, *Schüssler* W., Paul Tillich; sein Leben. Fra 1993, Lang. 187 p. Fs 54. 3-631-46487-8. -- ᴿTTh 35 (1995) 299 (W. *Stoker*).

k985 **Barron** Robert E., A study of the 'De potentia' of Thomas AQUINAS in light of the 'Dogmatik' of Paul Tillich; creation as discipleship [< diss. Paris, Institut Catholique]. SF 1993, Mellen Univ. xix-493 p. £ 49. 0-7734-2238-2. -- ᴿ*TBR 8,1 (1995s) 29s (A. *McCoy*).

k986 *Hort* Bernard, Le démonique chez Paul Tillich: ÉTRel 70 (1995) 571-4.

k987 **Lai Pan-Chui**, Towards a trinitarian theology of religions; a study of Paul Tillich's thought [< diss. King's College London, ᴰ*Gunton* C. 1991]. Kampen 1994, Kok Pharos. 181 p. -- ᴿC(alvin)TJ 30 (1995) 573-8 (R.W. *Vunderink*).

k988 *Lata* Jan A., ᴾ L'existence solitaire de l'homme et sa caractéristique dans la théologie de Paul Tillich: AtK(ap) 125 (1995) 12-23.

k989 *Schüssler* Werner, Metaphysik und Theologie; zu Paul Tillichs 'Umwendung' der Physik in der 'Dogmatik' von 1925: ZkT 117 (1995) 192-201; Eng. 202.

k990 TRACY: **Neumann** Klaus, Wege amerikanischer Theologie; Gordon D. KAUFMANN, David Tracy und Edward FARLEY fragen nach Gott: Diss. ᴰ*Ritschl*, Heidelberg.

k991 TROELTSCH; **Drescher** Hans-Georg, Ernst Troeltsch; his life and thought, ᵀ*Bowden* J. 1993 → 9,17103; 10,15119: ᴿET 106 (1994s) 32 (C.S. *Rodd*); Interpretation 49 (1995) 98-100s (C.J. *Kinlaw*).

k992 **Gisel** P., Histoire et théologie chez Ernst Troeltsch 1992 → 8,m911; 10,15120: ᴿRHE 90 (1995) 335s (A. *Minke*: 'Gistel').

k993 ᴱ**Graf** Friedrich W., Liberale Theologie; eine Ortsbestimmung: Troeltsch-Studien 7. Gü 1993, Gü-V. 209 p. DM 98. 3-579-00257-0. -- ᴿBijdragen 56 (1995) 465s (A.L. *Molendijk*).

k994 **Troeltsch** Ernst, Protestantisme et modernité, ᵀ*Launay* M, B. de. P 1991, Gallimard. 167 p. -- ᴿL(aval)TP 51 (1995) 678-680 (A. *Dumais*).

k995 *Trupiano* Antonio, Sociologia e teologia in E. Troeltsch; quale possibile integrazione? RasT 36 (1995) 753-762.

k996 **Yamin** George J.ᴶ, In the absence of fantasia; Troeltsch's relation to HEGEL. Gainesville 1993, Univ.Press of Florida. xiii-183 p. $ 30. -- ᴿJRel 75 (1995) 291s (W.E. *Wyman*).

k997 VAN TIL: *Edgar* William, L'apologetica di Cornelius Van Til [1895-1987; USA dal 1905: STEv 7.13 (1995) 5-20 (21-47, Van Til, Il mio credo 1977, ᵀ*Terino* J.; 49-52. bibliog.)

k998 VERWEYEN: *Smith* Joseph J., Hansjürgen Verweyen [since his 1977 Brennpunkt: now he is at FrS] and the ground of Easter faith: Landas [8 (1994) 147-181] II. Testimony of NT, Mt Lk Jn. III. Mk: 9 (1995) 72-120 . 181-208.

k999 VOEGELIN: **Morrissey** Michael, Consciousness and transcendence; the theology of Eric Voegelin. ND 1994, Univ. 353 p. $ 42. -- ᴿAmJTP 16 (1995) 233-6 (G. *Mann*).

q000 WALDENFELS Hans, Gott; auf der Suche nach dem Lebensgrund. Hildesheim 1995, Benno-BM. 119 p. DM 14,80. -- [R]GuL 68 (1995) 395 (J. *Sudbrack*).

q001 WARFIELD B.B.: **Ruthven** John, On the cessation of the charismata; the Protestant polemic on postbiblical miracles. Shf 1993, Academic. 270 p. 1-85075-405-5. -- [R]RExp 92 (1995) 119s (W.L. *Hendricks*).

q002 WEIL: *a) Bori* Pier Cesare, 'Ogni religione é l'unica vera'; l'universalismo religioso di Simone Weil; -- *b) Forni* Guglielmo, Simone Weil e il cristianesimo: FilTeo 8 (1994) 393-403 / 404-417.

q003 WELTE (1906-1983): **Godzieba** Anthony J., Bernhard Welte's (3-phase Neo-Scholasticism critique and] fundamental theological approach to Christology: AmUSt 7/160. NY 1994. P.Lang. [RStR 22,48, B.E. *Hinze*].

------

q004 WITTGENSTEIN; **Kerr** Fergus, *a)* La théologie après W: CFi 162, 1993: [R]LV(itF) 50 (1995) 237 (M.M.). -- *b)* La teologia dopo Wittgenstein 1992 → 9,17109; 10,15126: [R]FilTeo (1995) 666-9 (R. *Cortese*).

q005 **Phillips** D.Z., Wittgenstein and religion. L 1993, Macmillan. xxi-259 p. £ 40; pa. £ 15. -- [R]RelSt 31 (1995) 111-122 (B.R. *Clack*); reply 121-7.

q006 *Pinkas* Daniel, Suivre une règle; Wittgenstein et les sciences cognitives: RTPh 127 (1995) 1-25; Eng. 111.

------

q007 WOBBERMIN, *al.*: **Pfleiderer** G. Theologie als Wirklichkeitswissenschaft: BeitHisT 82, 1992 → 9.11262: [R]Bijdragen 56 (1995) 103s (H.J. *Adriaanse*).

Y6.8 *Tendentiae exeuntis saeculi XX* -- **Late 20th Century Movements**

q008 [E]**Alberigo** Giuseppe, *al.*, Verso il Concilio Vaticano II (1960-1962); passaggi e problemi della preparazione conciliare. Genova 1993, Marietti. 504 p. L[m] 65. -- [R]CivCatt 146 (1995,1) 89s (S. *Mazzolini*).

q009 [E]**Alberigo** Giuseppe, Storia del Concilio Vaticano II. Bo 1995-, Mulino. I. 549 p.; II. 664 p.; 2 maps. 88-15-05146-3; -654-8.

q010 *a) Aubert* Roger, Come vedo il Vaticano II; -- *b) Burgalassi* Silvano, Tradizioni e tradizione; esiste il rischio della loro scomparsa ? -- *c) Brena* Gian Luigi, Pensare il futuro: anticipazione, previsione e responsabilità; -- *d) Masani* Alberto, Verità scientifica e verità religiosa; la voce della cosmologia; -- *e) Muratore* Saturnino, Formazione teologica; alla ricerca di nuovi modelli: RasT 36 (1995) 133-148 / 149-166 / 167-184 / 185-194 / 195-202.

q011 *Barbieri Masini* Eleonora, Studio del futuro; metodi e prospettive: RasT 36 (1995) 339-348 (351-6, *Sanna* Ignazio).

q012 **Barcellona** P., Postmodernidad y comunidad; el regreso de la vinculación social [Torino 1990], [T]. M 1992, Trotta. 141 p. -- [R]E(st)E 70 (1995) 269s (O. *França-Tarrago*).

q013 *a) Barth* Hans-Martin, Teologia della secolarizzazione oggi; teologia post-secolare; -- *b) Rizzi* Armido, Alleanza e secolarizzazione; -- *c) Molinaro* Aniceto, Filosofare/secolarizzare; modernità e postmodernità; -- *d) Filoramo* Giovanni, Fondamentalismo e modernità; -- *e) De Vitiis* Pietro, Hans BLUMENBERG e il dibattito sulla secolarizzazione: FilTeo 9 (1995) 475-490; Eng. 475 / 491-500; Eng. 491 / 501-511; Eng. 501 / 512-528; Eng. 512 / 529-542; Eng. 529.

q014 *Becht* Michael, Ecclesia semper purificanda; die Sündigkeit der Kirche als Thema des II. Vatikanischen Konzils: Cath 49 (1995) 218-237 . 239-260.

q015 *Berlis* Angela, Amt und Autorität im ausgehenden 20. Jhdt: IK(i)Z 85 (1995) 243-261.

q016 **Biser** E., Hat der Glaube eine Zukunft ? Dü 1994, Patmos. 236 p. DM 29,80. 3-491-77954-5. -- ᴿTTh 35 (1995) 195s (A. *Brants*).

q017 **Biser** Eugen, Pronóstico de la fe; orientación para la época postsecularizada [Glaubensprognose 1991 → 9,17113], ᵀ*Gancho* Claudio, 1993 → 10,15132; 85-254-1836-4: ᴿEE 70 (1995) ll2-4 (R. *Franco* †); PerTeol 27 (1995) 398-401 (R.J. *Gottardo*).

q018 *Brasher* Brenda E., The Christian Church (Disciples of Christ) into the third millennium: Discipliana 55,3 (Stone-Campbell Historians Seminar 2, Nashville May 5s, 1995) 81-92.

q019 **Bühlmann** Walbert, A Igreja no limiar do terceiro milênio. São Paulo 1994, Paulus. 268 p. -- ᴿREB 55 (1995) 475-8 (H. *Lepargneur*).

q020 **Bühlmann** Walbert, Ojos para ver ... Los cristianos ante el tercer milenio. Barc 1991, Herder. 270 p. -- ᴿIter 5,2 (1994) 133-5 (F. *Moracho*).

q021 *Bulhof* Ilse, Die postmoderne Herausforderung der ökumenischen Bewegung: UnSa 50 (1995) 15-29.

q022 *Burggraff* David L., Fundamentalism at the end of the twentieth century: C(alv)BTJ 11,1 (1995) 1-32.

q023 *Burrows* William R., Reasons to hope for reform; an interview with David TRACY: America 173,11 (1995) 12-18.

q024 **Capra** Fritjof, *Steindl-Rast* David, Wendezeit im Christentum; Perspektiven für eine aufgeklärte Theologie [Belonging to the universe] , ᵀ*Matus* Thomas. Bern 1991, Scherz. 286 p. 3-502-17105-8. -- ᴿActuBbg 31 (1994) 223-5 (J. *Boada*).

q025 **Carrier** Hervé, Evangelizing the culture of modernity 1993 → 10,15135: ᴿCatholic World 238 (1995) 283 . 287 (M.P. *Kerrigan*).

q026 **Chandler** Russell, Facing toward 2000; the forces shaping America's religious future. GR 1992. 367 p. -- ᴿRefR 49 (1995s) 70 (M. *Draffen*).

q027 **Cousins** Ewert H., Christ of the 21st century 1992 → 10,4129: ᴿUS(em)QR 48,3 (1994) 178-182 (R.T. *Cornelison*).

q028 **Cox** Harvey, Fire from heaven; the rise of Pentecostal spirituality and the reshaping of religion in the twenty-first century. Reading MA 1995, Addison-Wesley. 321 p. $ 24. — ᴿCrossCur 45 (1995s) 257-261 (Carol *LeMasters*); JHisp 2,4 (1994s) 65s (D.H. *García*).

q029 Cristianismo y cultura en los años 90, ᵀ*Gabalda Irujo* Alberto: GS 4. M 1993, PPC. 211 p. pt 975. 84-288-1106-7. -- ᴿActuBbg 31 (1994) 55s (C. *Sarrias*).

q030 *Dagens* Claude, Une certaine manière de faire la théologie; de l'intérêt des Pères del'Église à l'aube du III millénaire: NRT 117 (1995) 65-83.

q031 *a) Dammert B.* José, El aire fresco del Concilio Vaticano II; -- *b) Gutiérrez* Gustavo, El Concilio, una pauta espiritual; -- *c) Tornos* Andrés, La sensibilidad cultural en el Vaticano II: Páginas 20 (136) 9-16 / 17-28 / 29-35.

q032 **Doty** William G., Picturing cultural values in postmodern America. Tuscaloosa 1995, Univ. Alabama. xiii-247 p. 0-8175-0733-8. -- ᴿRStR 21 (1995) 311 (R-H. *Seager*).

q033 **Drane** John, Evangelism for a new age. L 1994, Marshall-P. 223 p. £ 7. 0-551-02843-2. -- ᴿET 106 (1994s) 154 (bp. J.C. *Saxbee*: fine except that the 'Putting into Practice' is mostly embarrassing anecdotes).

q034 *Ferraro* Giuseppe, Il cammino ecumenico nella preparazione e nella celebrazione del giubileo del 2000: CivCatt 146 (1995,2) 3-16.

q035 **Forte** Bruno, La Chiesa della Trinità; saggio sul mistero della Chiesa, comunione e missione. CinB 1995, Paoline. -- ᴿRasT 36 (1995) 493-7 (M. *Semeraro*: immagine della Chiesa 30 anni dopo Vaticano II).

q036 **Foster** Douglas A., Will the cycle be unbroken ? Churches of Christ face the 21st century. Abilene 1994. 1188 p. -- ᴿRestQ 37 (1995) 247s & 249s (R. *McRay*).

q037 ᴱ**Fouilloux** Étienne, Vatican II commence ... approches francophones. Lv 1993, Fac. Godgeleerdheid. 392 p. -- ᴿBLE 96 (1995) 161s (R. *Cabié*).

q038 **Geering** Lloyd, Tomorrow's God. (NZ) 1994, Bridget Williams. 249 p. $ 35. 0-908912-66-8. -- ᴿE(xp)T 107 (1995s) 123s (T.J. *Gorringe*: POPPER-JASPERS 'non-realist liberal').

q039 **Gellner** Ernest, Postmodernism, reason and religion [... Islam]. L 1992, Routledge. ix-108 p. £ 10. -- ᴿJRAS (1994) 83-85 (V. *Choueiri*: postmodernism by a long detour continues Marxism, and 'abhors reference to the real world'); MuslimW 83 (1994) 345-7 (W.S. *Bodman*).

q040 **Goldstein** Jürgen, Die beschleunigte Moderne und der Verlust des Subjekts; über eine Lücke in der Akzelerationstheorie Hermann LÜBBEs: ThGL 85 (1995) 271-9.

q041 ᴱ**Gourgues** Michel, *Laberge* Léo, 'De bien des manières'; la recherche biblique aux abords du XXIᵉ siècle; Association Catholique des Études Bibliques au Canada: LD(iv) 163. P 1995, Cerf. 491 p. 2-204-01592-6.

q042 **Grenz** Stanley, Revisioning evangelical theology ... 21st century 1993 → 9,17132; 10,15148: BS 152 (1995) 361s (R.A. *Pyne*).

q043 **Gutiérrez Martín** Dario, El hombre futuro y la nueva sociedad. M 1994, Atenas. 235 p.-- ᴿBurg 36 (1995) 246s (J. *Yusta Sainz*).

q044 *Häring* Bernhard, La mia partecipazione al Concilio Vaticano II [su richiesta del Card. Wetter], ᵀ*Turbanti* G.: ᴿCrSt 15 (1994) 161-181: Eng. 181.

q045 **Harmer** Catherine M., Religious life in the 21st century; a contemporary journey into Canaan. Mystic CT 1995, Twenty-Third. 136 p. $ 10. -- ᴿRfR 54 (1995) 779s (Patricia *Wittberg*).

q046 **Hastings** Adrian, Modern Catholicism; Vatican II and after: 1991 → 7,348*a*.k100 ... 10,15150: ᴿC(alvin)TJ 29 (1994) 248-251 (J.H. *Kromminga*).

q047 **Hawkins** Charles T., Implications for postliberal theology of the encounter of poststructuralism and critical theory: diss. Southern Baptist Theol. Sem., ᴰ*Stiver* D., 1995. 95-30693. -- DissA 56 (1995s) p. 1399.

q048 **Hebblethwaite** Peter, The next Pope; an enquiry. L 1995, Collins Fount. 146 p. £ 6 pa. -- ᴿTheol 98 (L 1995) 495-7 (H.E. ROOT: at life's end he became more appreciative of JOHN PAUL II).

q049 *a) Hulshof* Jan, Balansrekening; de kerk in Nederland 30 jaar na Vaticanum II; -- *b) Berghe* Eric Vanden, Vaticanum II en zijn erfenis; een internationaal colloquium in Leuven (25-27 april 1995): CVL 25 (1995) 291-307 / 309-315.

q050 **Ingraffia** Brian D., Postmodern theory and biblical theology; vanquishing God's shadow. C 1995, Univ. xvi-284 p.; bibliog, 270-280. 0-521-56840-4.

q051 **Introvigne** Massimo, Mille e non più mille: millenarismo e nuove religioni alle soglie del Duemila. Mi 1995, Gribaudi. 253 p. -- ᴿBurg 36 (1995) 582s (M. *Guerra Gómez*).

q052 *Jurčević* Marijan, Superstition and faith [the world has slipped from secularization into superstition]; *RijT 3 (1995) 229-249 Croatian; Eng. 249.

q053 *Kelley* Shawn, Poststructuralism [DERRIDA and ASANTE, 'violence of the West'] and/or Afrocentrism [... postmodern anti-imperialism]: → 512, SBL Seminars 34 (1995) 226-249.

q054 **Kennedy** Paul, In Vorbereitung auf das 21. Jahrhundert, [T]*Hörmann* Gerd. Fra 1993, S. Fischer. 527 p. 3-10-039324-4. -- [R]ActuBbg 31 (1994) 187-192 (J. *Boada*: problemas muy reales y urgentes).

q055 **Küng** Hans, Christianity; essence, history, future [→ k625; k871]. NY/L 1995, Continuum/SCM. 936 p. $44.50. -- [R]America 173.12 (1995) 23s (R.P. *Imbelli*: 'future' added to English title, though announced for a further volume); Tablet 249 (1995) 1202-4 (R. *McBrien*).

q056 **Laurentin** André, *Dujarier* Michel, Il catecumenato; fonti neotestamentarie e patristiche, la riforma di Vaticano II [1969], [TE]*Di Nola* Gerardo. R 1995, Dehoniane. 516 p. L[m] 49. -- [R]Asprenas 42 (1995) 462s (A. *Di Donna*: ormai classico).

q057 *a) Libanio* J.B., A trinta anos do encerramento do Concilio Vaticano II; chaves teológicas de leitura; -- *b) Palácio* Carlos, O legado da 'Gaudium et spes'; riscos e exigências de uma nova 'condição cristã'; -- *c) Barreiro* Alvaro, Superação do dualismo entre fé cristã e compromisso terrestre; atualidade de um tema central da Gaudium et spes: PerTeol 27,3 ('Para uma segunda recepção do Vaticano II, 1995) 297-332 / 333-353 / 355-368.

q058 **Lindbeck** George A., The nature of doctrine; religion and theology in a postliberal age (1994 deutsch → 10,15045): [R]MThZ 45 (1994) 1-10 (M. *Knapp*, zitiert] Thomist 49 (1985) 392-472 (D. *Tracy*, al.).

q059 **Louchez** E., Concile Vatican II et Eglise contemporaine 4. Inventaire des fonds J. DUPONT et B. OLIVIER: RThLv Cah 29. LvN 1995, Fac.Théol. 131 p. [RHE 90 (1995) 203*].

q060 **Lundin** Roger, The culture of interpretation ['therapeutic': not what is right and true, but what satisfies]; Christian faith and the postmodern world 1993 → 9,17146; 10,15159: [R]C(alvin)TJ 29 (1994) 293-5 (J. *Cooper*).

q061 **McCarthy** Timothy G., The Catholic tradition, before and after Vatican II, 1878-1993: 1994 → 10,15160: [R]ChH 64 (1995) 325s (A.W. *Novitsky*).

q062 **McGrath** Alister E., Evangelicalism and the future of Christianity. DG 1995, InterVarsity. 209 p. $ 17. 0-8308-1694-4 [ThD 43,76].

q063 *Mendieta* Eduardo, From Christendom to polycentric oikonumē [there seems to be no explanation for this repeated spelling, though on p. 73 is found 'oikoumenē (ecumene)']; modernity, postmodernity, and liberation theology: *JHispT* 3,4 (1995s) 57-76.

q064 *Meynell* Hugo, Archdeconstruction and postpostmodernism: HeythJ 36 (1995) 125-139.

q065 **Middleton** J. Richard, *Walsh* Brian J., Truth is stranger than it used to be; biblical faith in a postmodern age. L 1995, SPCK. 250 p. 0-281-04938-6.

q066 **Moore** Stephen D., Poststructuralism and the NT; DERRIDA & FOUCAULT at the foot of the Cross 1994 → 10,4177: [R]JRel 75 (1995) 581s (D. *Bartlett*); Theol 98 (L 1995) 138s (D.A. *Templeton*); *CritRR 8 (1995) 498-502 (E.V. *McKnight*).

q067 *Natal* Domingo, La aventura posmoderna: EstAg 29 (1994) 97-153 (postm-); 30 (1995) 437-490 (posm-).

q068 **O'Brien** John, Seeds of a new Church. Dublin 1994, Columba. 244 p. £ 9. 1-85607-089-1. -- [R]ET 106 (1994s) 61 (A.D. *Falconer*: in Ireland the familiar model is in decline, but a new model is emerging in diversified small groups).

q069 *Ochs* Peter, Scriptural logic; diagrams for a postcritical metaphysics: MoTh 11 (1995) 65-92.

q070 *Orlando* Pasquale, Ricostruzione critica del postmoderno; l'intelligenza riflette su se stessa: DoC(om) 48 (1995) 233-255.

q071 **Pérez Aguirre** Luis, Glaubwürdigkeit zurückgewinnen! Die Kirche und ihre ungelö-

sten Probleme an der Schwelle zum Dritten Jahrtausend. Luzern 1994, Exodus. 176 p.
DM 27,50 pa. 3-905575-88-4. -- ᴿJE(mp)T 8,2 (1995) 108s (H. *Mendl*); StZ 213 (1995)
859 (M. *Maier*).

q072 *Poli* Gian Franco, La donna consacrata nella Chiesa del terzo millennio; fatti -- testi
— questioni: VitaCons 31 (1995) 260-275 . 387-396 . 646-700.

q073 *Rausch* Thomas P., The unfinished agenda of Vatican II: America 172,21 (1995) 23-27.

q074 **Ricca** Paolo, Un incontro pancristiano nel 2000 ? : Protest(antesimo) 50 (1995) 77-82.

q075 **Roberts** W. Dayton, Patching God's garment; environment and mission in the twenty-
first century. Monrovia CA 1992, World Vision. 168 p. $ 14 pa. -- ᴿIBM(iss)R 19 (1995)
34s (B.A. *Anderson*).

q076 **Routhier** Gilles, La réception d'un concile [Vatican II dans une église locale, diss.
Sorbonne 1991]: CFi 174, 1993 → 9,12172; 10,15168: ᴿRTL 26 (1995) 505-8 (J.
Famerée); SR 24 (1995) 362-4 (D. *Hurtubise*); TorJT 11 (1995) 132-4 (J.T. *Ford*).

q077 **Salom Clement** F., Una lectura teológica del Concilio Vaticano II en le frontera del
protestantismo y mundo de hoy; catolicidad y justificación: Valentina 28. Valencia 1992,
Fac. Ferrer. 195 p. -- ᴿSalmanticensis 42 (1995) 153-5 (A. *González Montes*).

q078 *Sanders* James A., Scripture as canon for post-modern times: BThB 25 (1995) 56-63.

q079 *a) Sauer* Hanjo, Abschied von der säkularisierten Welt; Fundamentaltheologische Überlegungen; -- *b) Klein* Stephanie, Der tradierte Glaube in der modernen Gesellschaft: TPQ
143 (1995) 339-349 / 351-360.

q080 *Scabini* Pino, Le vie della Chiesa; la comunità cristiana è pronta per una nuova società?: RasT 36 (1995) 589-600.

q081 **Scotland** Nigel, Charismatics and the next millennium; do they have a future? L 1995,
Hodder & S. £ 9. -- ᴿTablet 249 (1995) 1204s (Kristina *Cooper*).

q082 *Smith* Huston, The religious significance of postmodernism; a rejoinder: FAP(hil) [10,4
(1993) ..] 12 (1995) 409-422.

q083 **Straelen** Henry van, L'Église et les religions non-chrétiennes au seuil du XXIᵉ siècle;
étude historique et théologique 1994 → 10,15172: ᴿMélSR 52 (1995) 348-350 (J.-C.
Matthys).

q084 **Thiel** John E., Nonfoundationalism: GTI. Mp 1994, Fortress. 123 p. $ 10. -- ᴿThTo
52 (1995s 521s . 524 (J. *Wentzel van Huÿssteen*).

q085 **Touraine** Alain, Critique de la modernité. P 1992, Fayard. -- ᴿFV 92,1 (1993) 89-99
(Pascale *Gruson*).

q086 *Tracy* David, Theology and the many faces of postmodernity: TTod 51 (1994s) 104-114.

q087 *Verhaar* John, Aspetti del postmoderno [...RORTY R.]: CivCatt 146 (1995,1) 135-142.

q088 *a) Viana* Mikel de, Postmodernidad y fe cristiana; -- *b) Mujica Ricardo* Michel,
Globalización y postmodernidad; -- *c) Trigo* Pedro, Apertura de la Iglesia al mundo actual
según el Concilio Vaticano II: → 544, Iter 6,1 (1995) 55-76 / 82-88 / 8-34.

q089 **Vogels** Walter, Interpreting Scripture in the third millennium; author -- reader -- text.
... Novalis. 108 p. $ 12. -- ᴿCanadCath 13,7 (1995) 24 (F. *Wagner*).

q090 *Weinberger* T., *a)* Solomon SCHECHTER's (postmodern) [d.1915] conservative Jewish
theology: CJud 46,4 (1994) 24-26; -- *b)* Fructifying S.Schechter's traditional Jewish
theology: MoTh 10 (1994) 271-9 [NTAb 39, p.114].

q091 **Wuthnow** Robert, Christianity in the twenty-first century; reflections on the challenges
ahead 1993 → 9,17191; 10,15179*: ᴿJE(mp)T 8,1 (1995) 119s (F. *Lechner*); JRel 75
(1995) 128s (J.W. *Lewis*); PhilipSa 30 (1995) 264s (N.M. *Castillo*); TTod 51 (1994s) 444.6
(J.M. *Mulder*).

q092 *Zecca* Alfredo H., Las antecedentes y las raíces filosóficas de la posmodernidad: TeolBA 30 (1993) 141-156.

q093 *Zuberbier* Andrzej, [P] Trente ans après le Concile: PrzPow 892 (1995) 285-295.

Y7 *(Acta) Congressuum* 2. *biblica*: **nuntii**, rapports, Berichte

q094 *Agourides* S., [G] *a)* International and interdisciplinary symposium on the 19th centenary of the writing of John's Apocalypse, Athens 17-22 September 1995; -- *b)* Ecumenical biblical conference of Orthodox and Roman Catholic scholars [ALETTI J.-N., TAYLOR J., VIVIANO B. ...], Athens 25-29 October 1995; -- *c)* Colloquium ecumenicum paulinum, Rome 15-30 September 1995: D(elt)BM 14,2 (1995) 85-88 / 89-100 / 101-112.

q095 *Aulisa* Immacolata, Paolo di Tarso nell'esegesi cristiana antica (Trani, 24-29 aprile 1995): VetChr 32 (1995) 453-7.

q096 *Barbaglia* Silvio, I convegni dell'Aquila [11-13.IX]: PaVi 40,6 (1995) 56-58.

q097 *Bieringer* Reimund, The Corinthian correspondence; Colloquium Biblicum Lovaniense XLIII (1994): EThL 71 (1995) 266-277.

q098 *a) Cardellini* Innocenzo, XXXIII settimana biblica nazionale A.B.I., 'Lo straniero nella Bibbia; aspetti storici, istituzionali e teologici' (Roma, 12-16 settembre 1994); -- *b) Marucci* Corrado, Convegni simultanei del XLIII Colloquium Biblicum Lovaniense e della SBL a Lovanio (7-10 agosto 1994) / Un convegno sul Codice di Beza (Lunel-Montpellier, 27-30 giugno 1994); -- *c) Mazzarone* Angelo, Archeologia, esegesi biblica e storia; convegno di studi in memoria di P. Virgilio CORBO (Potenza-Avigliano, 5-6 dic. 1994): RivB 43 (1995) 309-311 / 312s.313s / 314s.

q099 *Chmiel* Jerzy, *a)* [P] Sin and liberation from sin in the NT: Strasbourg meeting [April 3-7] 1995; -- *b)* [P] Międzynarodowe kolokwium 'Pentecostes' w Angers [1-3.VI] (1995); *c)* [P] Sesja kumranologiczna (Kraków 1994): R(uch)BL 48 (1995) 137-9 / 217s / 214.

q100 *García Martínez* F., La salvación como revelación del mecanismo victimal de la cultura de la violencia; en torno a la soteriología de R. GIRARD: EstTrin 28 (1994) 63- ... [< ZIT 95, p.173].

q101 *Heimerdinger* Jenny, International colloque, le Codex de Bèze, 27-30 June 1994, in Lunel, France: RCatT 30 (1995) 401-9, in English.

q102 *Hoppe* Rudolf, Tagung der deutschsprachigen katholischen Neutestamentler in Straßburg vom 3.7. April 1995: BZ 39 (1995) 210s.

q103 *Kaiser* Walter C., *al.*, The Bible; yesterday, today, and tomorrow; 11th annual symposium on exegetical theology, Fort Wayne Concordia Seminary, January 1966 [program]: ConcordiaTQ 59 (1995) 241s [242s, *Hagen* Kenneth, *al.*, Luther symposium].

q104 *Karavidopoulus* Ioannis D., Chronicle (Lausanne 22-25 March 1995) [on Christian apocrypha]: D(elt)BM 14,1 (1995) 80-83.

q105 *a) Klauck* Hans-Josef, 49. General Meeting der Studiorum Novi Testamenti Societas vom 1. bis 5. August 1994 in Edinburgh; -- *b) Schwank* Benedikt, Vor vierzig Jahren; die Entwicklung der Arbeitsgemeinschaft deutschsprachiger katholischer Neutestamentler: BZ 39 (1995) 156-8 / 158s.

q106 *Klein* Nikolaus, Zum 26. Deutschen Evangelischen Kirchentag in Hamburg, 'Die prophetische Herausforderung des Micha': Orien(tierung) 59 (1995) 151-5.

q107 **Magí** Joan, *al.*, La Bibbia e il Mediterraneo. Barc 18-22 sett. 1995. -- [R]*AnT 9 (1995) 470-3 (M.A. *Tábet*).

q108 *Passoni dell'Acqua* Anna, Septuaginta; libri sacri della Diaspora giudaica e dei cristiani

(Milano 28 nov. 1995): Henoch 17 (1995) 370s.

q109 *a) Pisarek* Stanisław,[P] Colloquium biblicum [Wien 1993]; -- *b) Fitych* Tadeusz, [P]Chrześcjanie zgromadzeni w 'Terzym Rzymie' [Moskva, 21-23.VI. 1994]; nienawisci przeciwstawiaja miłośč: AtK(ap) 124 (1995) 453s / 455-7.

q110 *Prinzivalli* Emanuela, Cronaca del II Corso di Specalizzazione in 'Storia dell'esegesi cristiana e giudaica antica' (Trani, 11-16 aprile 1994); ASEs 12 (1995) 419-421.

q111 *Segalla* Giuseppe, 50° Congresso della Studiorum Novi Testamenti Societas (Praga 1-4.VIII.1995): StPat(av) 42 (1995) 857-861.

q112 Studiorum Novi Testamenti Societas, 50th General Meeting, Prague 31.VII-4.VIII.1995: EThL 71 (1995) 526s, titles of 5 longer and two shorter Main Papers; also of six offered papers and eighteen seminars

q113 *Tuckett* C.M., Studiorum Novi Testamenti societas, the forty-ninth general meeting, 1-4 August 1994 : NTS 41 (1995) 298s, 300-320, membership list [with postal addresses].

q114 *Vervenne* Marc. The Book of Exodus; Colloquium Biblicum Lovaniense XLIV (1995): EThL 71 (1995) 512-8.

q115 *Walsh* Jerome T., Report of the 59th General Meeting of the CBA [Albany August 12-15, 1995]: CBQ 57 (1995) 747-750; 751-4, names only of members present.

q116 *Warzecha* Julian, Sympozjum biblijne -- 4.04.1995: STV(ars) 33,2 (1995) 137s.

Υ7.4　*(Acta) theologica,* **nuntii**

q117 *Ancona* Giovanni, Il peccato originale: quinto corso di aggiornamento dell'ATI [2-4.I.1995]: RasT 36 (1995) 91-96.

q118 Bericht uber den 26. Internationalen Altkatholiken-Kongress in Delft, 22.-26. August 1994: IK(i)Z 85 (1995) 1-8.

q119 *Botella Cubella* Vicente, Una teología eucarística renovada; del santo sacrificio de la Misa a la memoria sacramental de la Cena del Señor: TE(spir) 39 (1995) 379-401.

q120 *Bottino* G. Claudio, *Manns* Frédéric, Un simposio delle tre fedi monoteistiche; l'interpretazione del sacrificio d'Isacco nel giudaismo, nel cristianesimo e nell'Islam [2° SBF] (Gerusalemme, 16-17 marzo, 1995): RivB 43 (1995) 561-7.

q121 *Bouwen* Frans, VIe assemblée générale du Conseil d'Églises du Moyen-Orient [Limassol], 15-21 nov. 1994: POrC 45 (1995) 111-130 (-142); Eng. 131; 142.

q122 *Brunetti* Aury Azelio, I Congresso nacional de diáconos permanentes: REB 55 (1995) 418-425.

q123 *Carroll* Eamonn E., 46th annual convention of the Mariological Society of America (Dayton, May 24-27, 1995): Marianum 57 (1995) 387-9.

q124 *Ceresko* Anthony R., The XVIIIth annual meeting of the Indian Theological Association [Jharsuguda/Orissa, April 20-24, 1995 'Toward a Christian vision of the Indian']: I(nd)TS 32 (1995) 259s (261-277, Final Statement).

q125 *a) Chéza* Maurice, Le 15e colloque du CREDIC [26-29 août 1994] -- Les cadres locaux et les ministères consacrés dans les jeunes Églises. -- *b) Soetens* C., Le colloque de Chevetogne [29 août -- 2 sept. 1994]: -- *c) Louchez* Eddy, Colloque internationale [5° sans dates] de Lv-LvN; Les commissions conciliaires à Vatican II: RTL 26 (1995) 126-9 / 129-131 / 132-5.

q126 *Chmielewski* Alfred, [P] Polski słownik [Leksykon p.282] duchowości [katolickiej:

project-meeting Piaseczno 21-22.IV]: AtK(ap) 125 (1995) 280-2.

q127 *Collins* R.F., Catholic Theological Society of America, 49th, June 9-12 (?1994): ETL 71 (1995) 288; Francis A, SULLIVAN award for insisting on non-definitive versus definitive magisterium decisions.

q128 *Courth* Franz, Marienerscheinungen im Widerstreit [Augsburg] (14.-16. März 1994]: Marianum 56 (1994) 461-3 (-476, other meetings).

q129 *Dolby Múgica* María del Carmen, Crónica del II Congreso Nacional de Filosofía Medieval (Ética y política en el pensamiento medieval, fundamentos de la modernidad; Zaragoza, 15-16 diciembre 1994): RevAg 36 (1995) 267-282.

q130 *Domínguez Morano* Carlos, Psicoanálisis y religión; anotaciones a un simposio [Santiago de Chile 5-6 de mayo, Univ. Católica / Asoc. Psicoanalítica]: Proyecciòn 42 (1995) 137-240.

q131 *a) Giemza* Bogdan, ᴾ Międzynarodowe sympozjum duchowości (Wrocław 5-8.XII.1994): -- *b) Dragula* Andrzej ᴾ Sługa Słowa (III Sympozjum Homiletyczne, Kraków 21-22.X.1994 r.: AtK(ap) 125 (1995) 127s / 130-5.

q132 *Grafinger* Christine M., Aspekte der Gegenreformation, Darmstadt 11.-13. Febr. 1994: RHE 90 (1995) 679-682.

q133 *Heidemanns* Katja, Dritte nationale Tagung der Deutschen Sektion der European Society of Women in Theological Research (ESWTR) vom 23.-25. September 1994 in Gelnhausen: NZM(issW) 79 (1995) 43-50.

q134 **Igwegbe** Isidore Okwudili O., Sacramental theological thinking in the African symbolic universe; affinities with John Henry NEWMAN: EurUSt 23/525. NY 1995, P.Lang. 206 p. $ 43. 3-631-48130-6 [ThD 43,370].

q135 International colloquium on Vatican II and its heritage, Leuven 25-27 April 1995 [titles of 16 main papers and 14 others]: EThL 71 (1995) 284s.

q136 *Langella* Alfonso, La verginità di Maria fra storia e teologia; un convegno di studi mariologici a Capua [19-24 maggio 1992]: Asprenas 42 (1995) 263-8.

q137 *Miguel* José M. de, Crónica del XXVIII Simposio de Teología Trinitaria, Salamanca, 25 al 27 de octubre de 1993: : EstTrin 28 (1994) 87-90.

q138 *Moore* Susan H., 'Towards koinonia in faith, life, and witness'; theological insights and emphases from the Fifth World Conference on Faith and Order, Santiago de Compostela 1993: E(cu)R 47 (1995) 3-11.

q139 *Peerlinck* Frans, Het tweede congres van de europese vereniging voor katholieke theologie, Freising/München, 27-31/8/1995: CVI 25 (1995) 425-432.

q140 *Peña* Nicanor, Congreso internacional mariológico Loreto 22-25.III.1995: EphMar 45 (1995) 435-442 [-453, al., otros congresos].

q141 *Rostagno* S., al., Teologia negli incontri estivi [ATI; Mendola 33° ecumenico; *Genre* E., 'Arte e teologia; convegno delle Facoltà protestanti di teologia dei paesi latini d'Europa', Roma 22-26 sett., p. 296-8]: Protest(antesimo) 50 (1995) 296-302.

q142 *Ruggieri* Giuseppe (ᴱActa),Koinonia, Bologna 13-14 aprile 1993; CrSt 16 (1995) 237-43.

q143 *Sakowicz* Eugeniusz, ᴾ Religious tolerance as a challenge for the contemporary world, Vilnius, Oct. 4-6, 1993: C(olc)Th 64,s (1994) 179-181.

q144 *Salzano* Teresa, Semi nascosti di dialogo fra ebrei e cristiani in due mila anni; tracce per il futuro; XV colloquio ebraico-cristiano, Camaldoli (Arezzo) 7-11 dicembre 1994: St-Pat(av) 42 (1995) 853-6.

q145 *Suerman* Harald, Colloquium over de vernieuwing van het samenleven in Libanon (Antélias 12-14 mei 1994): TTh 35 (1995) 66.

q146   a) *Tisnes* Roberto,   Congreso mariano nacional [15-17.VIII. 1992], Colombia V centenario; -- b) *Arnaiz* José M., X simposio internacional mariológico [Roma 4-7.X.1994] : EphMar 44 (1994) 533s / 553-560.

q147   *Turbanti* Giovanni, 'Il contributo dei paesi di lingua tedesca e dell'Europa orientale al Concilio Vaticano II', quarto convegno internazionale Würzburg 17-19 dic. 1993: CrSt 16 (1995) 141-159; Eng. 159s.

q148   *Völker* Alexander, Zur zukünftgen Gestalt des Gottesdienstes; XV. Kongress der Societas Liturgica, 14.-19. August 1995 in Dublin : JLH(ymn) 35 (1994s) 81.

Y7.6   *(Acta) congressuum philologica*: **nuntii**

q149   *Ankum* Hans, *Michel* Jacques-Henri, La XLVIIIe session de la Société internationale Fernand De Visscher pour l'histoire des droits de l'antiquité (Vienne, 19-23 septembre 1994): RIDA 42 (1995) 475-511; index 512.

q150   *Motte* André, *Loucas-Durie* Éveline, Chronique des rencontres scientifiques: Kernos 8 (1995) 287-297.

Y7.8   *(Acta) congressuum orientalistica et archaeologica*, **nuntii**

q151   a) *Richard* Y., Seconde conférence européenne des études iraniennes, Bamberg 30 septembre -- 4 octobre 1991; -- b) *Gignoux* Philippe, Symposium 'Bilingualism in Iranian cultures' [Univ. Bamberg 17-20.VII.1992]: StIr 21 (1992) 125-7 / 22 (1993) 123s. en français.

q152   *Salles* Jean-François, The archaeology of death in the Ancient Near East, Manchester 16-20 Dec. 1992: TopO 3 (1993) 373-380.

q153   *Shanks* Hershel, Long-winded in the Windy City [Chicago 1994 SBL-AAR & (now in a different hotel) ASOR meeting; 7500 participants: BArR 21,2 (1995) 74-76.

q154   Société Asiatique 1993s / 1994s: JA 282 (1994) 457-470; liste des membres 471-507 / 283 (1995) 505-518.

q155   *Suerman* Harald, Die dritte syrische Weltkonferenz in Kottayam [4.-10- Sept. 1994]: OrChr 79 (1995) 228s.

q156   *Zayadine* Fawzi, ^A The thirteenth conference of the Arab archaeologists held at Tripoli, Libya: ADAJ 39 (1995) ^A 37-39; phot.

Y8 *Periti*; **Scholars, personalia, organizations**

q157   *Alichoran* Joseph, Du génocide à la diaspora; les assyro-chaldéens au XXe siècle: Ist(ina) 39 (1994) 363-398 [40 (1995) 191-202, *Yacoub* Joseph].

q158   **Barrios** Marciano, Facultad de Teología de la Pontificia Universidad Católica de Chile; sesenta años de historia al servicio de Chile y de su Iglesia. Santiago 1995, Soc.Hist.Igl. 218 p. -- ^RTyV 36 (1995) 457 (L. *Celis Muñoz*).

q159   *Beuken* W.A.M., [some 50 Netherlands] Promotions: EThL 71 (1995) 296-8.

q160   *Brister* C.W., The making of a Southwesterner [Baptist seminary 75th anniversary: 'our student body is aging ': 1000 of the 4600 over 30!]: SWJT 37,3 (1995) 4-8.

q161   *Buetubela* Balembo, Les Instituts supérieurs catholiques en Afrique: Telema 81 (1995) 45-51.

q162   *Caquot* A., al., Naissance de la méthode critique 1990/2 → 8,462: ^RRB(elg)PH 73

(1995) 168s (J. *Klener*, Eng.)

q163 *Casado Orcajo* Felicísimo, Memoria del curso 1992-1993: Burgense 35 (1994) 259-292.

q164 *a) Courthial* Pierre, La foi Réformée en France; la Faculté Réforméee d'Aix, raison d'être et origines [1974]; -- *b) Berthoud* Pierre, Pour une 'apologie' biblique de la foi; — *c) Kallemeyn* Harold, Drames et découvertes; pour une lecture vivifiante des récits de l'Ancien Testament [*al*.]: RRéf 46,2 (1995) 1-24 (-30) / 43-52 / 53-68.

q165 [E]**Doré** Joseph, Les cent ans de la Faculté de théologie UER (Unité d'Enseignement et de Recherche) 1992 → 9,17257; 10,15226: [R]C(ath)HR 81 (1995) 128 (J. *Grès-Gayer*); MélSR 52 (1995) 217-9 (J.-C. *Matthys*).

q166 **Mateo-Seco** L.F. (*Rodríguez Ocaña* R.), Sacerdotes en el Opus Dei; secularidad, vocación y ministerio. Pamplona 1994, EUNSA. 329 p. -- [R]*AnT 9 (1995) 178-185 (P.0 *Goyret*).

q167 *Olivares d'Angelo* E., Cien años del 'Colegio Máximo' de Cartuja (Granada): *Proyección 41 (1994) 227-236 [< RET 55 (1995) 541].

q168 *Palumbo* Claudio, Gli ottant'anni del Pontificio Seminario Regionale abruzzese e molisano: Pianum (1995) 13S (-28, *al*.).

q169 **Sauvé** M., L'Institut supérieur de sciences religieuses de la faculté de théologie de l'Université de Montréal. M 1995, Bellarmin. 227 p. [RHE 91,111*].

q170 *Suchy* Jerzy, [P] Chronicle of KUL [Lublin] biblical studies for the academic year 1993/4: RTK 42,1 (S.Scr. 1995) 119-122.

q171 **Taft** Robert F., *Dugan* James L., Il 75° anniversario del Pontificio Istituto Orientale 1992: OCA 244, 1994 → 10,15235: [R]OrChr 79 (1995) 287s (H. *Kaufhold*); POrC 45 (1995) 322-4 (P. *Ternant*); ScEs 47 (1995) 348-350 (J. *Lison*); SV(lad)TQ 427s (P. *Meyendorff*).

q172 *Teixidor* Javier, Antiquités sémitiques; *Yoyotte* Jean, Égyptologie; *Veyne* Paul, Histoire de Rome; *al*.: ACFr Résumé des cours et travaux 1995s, 761-771 / 759 / 823-7.

q173 **Vesco** Jean Luc, Cent'anni di esegesi .. École Biblique, I. AT [**Murphy-OConnor J.** NT]: RivBib.s 25s, 1992 → 9,17272/62; 10,15236: SBF*LA 45 (1995) 650s (E. *Cortese*) [651s].

Y8.5 *Periti*, **in memoriam**

q174 Necrologia: AnFratPraed 102 (1994) 115-130 . 281-293 . 394-428; RHE 90 (1995) 134* . 350*; REB 55 (1995) 223-233 . 457-464 . 699-709. 960-969.

q175 Abramek, Rufin Józef, OSPPE, 13.Xii.1937 -- 20.IV.1990: R(uch)BL 48 (1995) 61-72 (Z.S. *Jabloński*, bibliog.).

q176 Adams, James L., aet. 92, 26.VII.1994; Harvard Divinity prof.: EThL 71 (1995) 292 (R.F. *Collins*).

q177 Ahern, Barnabas Mary, C.P., 1915 -- 9.I.1995; CBA president 1964s, Vatican II peritus: CBQ 57 (1995) 114s (D. *Senior*); founding editor, Bible Today.

q178 Åkerberg, Hans † 1994: SvTK 70 (1994) 200 (N.G. *Holm*).

q179 Aland, Kurt [→ 10,15239], aet. 79, 13.IV.1994: Luther Jb 62 (1995) 9-12 (M. *Brecht*).

q180 Alfaro, Juan, aet. 79, 5.VIII.1993: Marianum 56 (1994) 71-94 (J.M. de *Miguel González*: aportación a la mariología).

q181 Alvarez Sáenz de Buruaga, D. José, 1917 - 21.VIII.1995: ArchEspArq 68 (1995) I (J.

Arce).

q182 Anawati [for Qanawati], Georges Chehata [→ 10,15239], 6.VI.1905 -- 28.I.1994: BÉtOr 47 (1995) 9-14 (E. *Platti*); JA(siat) 282 (1994) iv-ix, phot. (C. *Gilliot*).

q183 Andrzejewski, Bogumił Witalis, 1.II.1922 -- 2.XII.1994; RSEt 36 (1992 !) 143-150 (-160, bibliog.).

q184 Anz, Wilhelm, 23.XII.1904 -- 23.V.1994: WuD(ienst) 23 (Bethel 1995) 330 (H. *Braun*).

q185 Azevedo, Thales de, † 5.VIII.1995: REB 55 (1995) 923-7 (E. *Hoornaert*).

q186 Baird, J. Arthur, aet. 71, 2.V.[?1994], founder-editor of The Computer Bible: EThL 71 (1995) 292 (R.F. *Collins*).

q187 Bajsić, Vjekoslav, 11.II.1924 -- 20.V.1994: *BogSmot 65 (1995) 175-177 (S. *Kušar*, Croatian; 178-186 bibliog.).

q188 Baker, William, 1917 -- 19.IX.1994, ecumenist: Mid-Str 34 (1995) 187-191 (D.M. *Thompson*).

q189 Balmas, Enea, 23.VI.1924 -- 30.XII.1994: Acme 48,1 (1995) 177s (Anna M. *Finoli*).

q190 Balout, Lionel, 18.IV.1907 -- 1992: AntAfr 29 (1993) 13-15 (G. *Souville*).

q191 Barry, Colman J., O.S.B., [→ 10,15243] 21.V.1921 -- 7.I. 1994: Collegeville president, Catholic U. dean: EThL 71 (1995) 291 (R.F. *Collins*).

q192 Barth, Markus, 1915 -- 1.VII.1994: FrRu 2 (1995) 72 (C. *Thoma*: b.1920?); HBT (→ 12 supra) 17,2 (1995) 93-95 (D.E. *Gowan*) & 96-116 (C. *Dickinson*).

q193 Battenhouse, Roy Wesley, 9.IV.1912 -- 17.II.1995: *ChrLit 43 (1993s) 115s (R.G. *Collmer*).

q194 Beletsky, Andrey Aleksandrovich, 12.VIII.1911 -- 10.IV.1995: VDI 215 (1995,4) 230s, phot.

q195 Bénisti, Mireille, 10.X.1909 -- 11.XII.1993: JA 282 (1994) 215-8 (Colette *Caillat*).

q196 Berchem, Denis van [→ 10,15247], 19.XII.1908 -- 7.V.1994: At(h-Pavia) 83 (1995) 274s (M.A. *Levi*).

q197 Berghe, Louis Vanden [→ 9,17286], 24.XII.1923 -- 17.IX.1993: Iran 34 (1994) v-vi; phot. (J.*Curtis*).

q198 Bianchi, Ugo, 13.X.1922 -- 14.IV.1995; presidente: Numen 42 (1995) 225-7 (K. *Rudolph*); SMSR 18,1 (1994) 7-9 (P. *Siniscalco*).

q199 Biedermann Alfons (Hermenegild O.S.A.) [→10,15250*], 15.XII.1911 -- 26.X.1994: OrChr 79 (1995) 231s (J. *Assfalg*); OS(tk) 44 (1995) 3-7; portr. (J. *Hofmann*; b.1913?); bibliog. 8-10 (Hannelore *Tretter*).

q200 Black, Matthew, 3.IX.1908-2.X.1994; first editor: NTS 41 (1995) 161-3 (R. M. *Wilson*).

q201 Bläser, Peter, 1910 -- 4.IX.1994: ThGL 85 (1995) 1-3 (A. *Klein*).

q202 Blumenkranz, Bernhard, c.1990: RÉJ 154 (1995) 209-217 (G. *Dahan*, G. *Nahon*).

q203 Bohemen, Frans (Nicolaas OFM), aet. 77, 13.XI.1994: EThL 71 (1995) 524-6 [F. *Neirynck*].

q204 Boling, Robert G., 1930 -12,XII.1994, with wife Jane in auto accident near 'Aqaba: BASOR 298 (1995) 1s; phot. (E. F. *Campbell*).

q205 Boswell, John Eastburn, 24.XII.1994; Yale historian of same-sex unions: EThL 71 (1995) 292 (R.F. *Collins*).

q206 Bothmer, Bernard V., 13.X.1912 -- 24.XI.1993: JA(m)RCE(g) 32 (1995) i-iii (R.A. *Fazzini*); ZÄS 122 (1995) 1-3; portr. (D. *Wildung*).

q207 Bradshaw, Brendan, ... ed.1979-94: JEH 46 (1995) 1.

q208 Breydy, Michael, 16.XI.1928 -- 11.IX.1994: OrChr 79 (1995) 231 (J. *Assfalg*).

q209 Briand, Jean-Marie, O.F.M., 1921-1994: : *TSa 71,4 (1995) 44s.

q210 Brink, Charles Oscar, 13.III.1907 -- 2.III.1994; dir. Thesaurus Linguae Latinae: Gnomon 67 (1995) 650-5; portr. (H.D. *Jocelyn*).

q211 Bronkhorst, Alex J., 1914 -- 8.XII.1994 : NedThT 49 (1995) 66-69 (A. *Houtepen*, 'een leven en dienst van kerk en oecumene' à la KÜNG H.).

q212 Broughton, Thomas R. S., 17.II, 1900 -- 17.IX.1993: Gnomon 67 (1995) 91-93 (J. *Linderski*).

q213 Bruce, Frederick Fyvie [→ 6,m442 ... 9,17301], 12.X.1910 -- 11.IX.1990: *ABW 1,1 (1991) 46 (J.J. *Scott*).

q214 Burgmann, Hans, 1914-1992: *QumC 4,1 (Kraków 1994) 125-8 (A. van der *Woude*).

q215 Burns, Tom, aet.89, † XII.1995, editor 1967-82: Tablet 249 (1995) 1633-5 (D. *Milroy, al.*).

q216 Butler, J. Donald, 1908 -- 20.IX.1994; seminary professor (Princeton 1944-58) and dean: PrincSemBu 16 (1995) 225-7 (J.F. *Armstrong*).

q217 Cahen, Claude, 26.II.1909 -- 1991; StIr 21 (1992) 257-261 (G. *Lazard*, M. *Rodinson*).

q218 Calmeyer, Peter, 1930 -- 22.XI.1995, Iranische Archäologie; AfO 42s (1995s) 329, phot. (W. *Kleiss*); AMI(ran) 28 (1995s) 1s (W. *Kleiss*): 3-10 Bibliog. (Ursula *Seidl*).

q219 Caminos, Ricardo Augusto [→ 9,17302; 10,15259], 11.VII.1915 -- 26.V.1992: ZÄS 120 (1993) iii-v (J. *Osing*).

q220 Campana, Augusto, 22.V.1906 -- 7.IV.1995: Epigraphica 57 (Faenza 1995) 173-185; fot. (Ginette *Vagenheim*).

q221 Chéhab, Maurice, 27.XII. 1904 -- 24.XII. 1994: fouilles de Tyr; directeur des antiquités du Liban: CRAI (1995) 1s (J. *Marcadé*).

q222 Congar, Yves, 13.IV.1904 -- 22.VI.1995, card.: America 173,4 (1995) 6s, phot. (A.*Dulles*) & 4,23-28 (W.*Henn*); *ArFrPraed 103 (1995) 267-282 (T. *Radcliffe*); Asprenas 42 (1995) 281-3 (B. *Forte*); CW(orld) 238 (1995) 284s (M.E. *Ginter*); *CWeal 122,21 (1995) 15-17 (J.A. *Komonchak*: 'a hero of Vatican II'); DocLife 45 (1995) 511s; phot. (D. *Cadrin*) & 468-473 (T. *Radcliffe*); EThL 71 (1995) 523; Études 383 (1995) 211-8 (J.-P. *Jossua*); PrPeo 9 (1995) 340-2 (T. *Radcliffe* funeral sermon); RasT 36 (1995) 517-526 (E. *Cattaneo*); RSPT 79 (1995) 379-404 (E. *Fouilloux*); Studium 91 (R 1995) 845-850 (B. *Forte*); Tablet 249 (1995) 854s (A. *Woodrow*); TTh 35 (1995) 271-3 (E. *Schillebeeckx*). Corbato, Carlo, 1921 -- III.1996: Aeg 75 (1995) 243 (S. *Daris*).

q223 Corrigan, Daniel aet. 93, IX.1994: A(ngl)ThR 77 (1995) 131-3, phot. (G.W. *Barrett*).

q224 Cronin, John F., aet. 85, 2.I. (1994?), labor relations: EThL 71 (1995) 291.

q225 Deblaere, Albert, S.J. 5.VI.1916 -- 31.VII.1994, Gregorian Univ. historian of spirituality: EThL 71 (1995) 294 (J.E. *Vercruysse*): OGE(rf) 68 (1994) 3-7; phot. (J. *Alaerts*).

q226 Deichmann, Friedrich Wilhelm [→ 9,17313], 17.XII.1909 -- 13.IX.1993: Gnomon 67 (1995) 477s (P. *Grossmann*).

q227 Delcor, Mathias, 1919-1992: BLE-c (1994,1) 17-34 (P. *Grau*: 'la fidélité aux sources' [NTAb 39, p.198].

q228 Della Casa, Adriana, 1925-1993: BSL(at) 25 (1995) 206-9 (M.Franca *Buffa Giolita, al.*).

q229 Desroche, Henri, 1914 -- 1.VI.1994, sociologie des religions: RHE 90 (1995) 362s (D. *Pelletier*).

q230 Devos, Roger, 10.V.1927 -- 30.VII.1995; historien de la Savoie [RHE 91,367, M. *Fox*].

q231 Dijk, Johannes Jacobus Adrianus van, 28.I.1915 -- 14.V.1996; Sumerologo al

Pontificio Istituto Biblico [Or 66,89-97 (D.O. *Edzard*); VO 10,3-6 (A. *Archi*)].

q232　Dijk-Hemmes, Fokkelien van [→ 9,15274]　1943-1994:　Mara 7,3 (1994) 5-8 (A.*Brenner*).

q233　Donceel, Joseph, S.J., aet. 88, 15.XII. (1994?), Fordham Univ.: EThL 71 (1995) 292.

q234　Dow, Sterling, 19.XI.1903 -- 9.I.1995, re-founder: GRB(yz)S 36 (1995) 3 (W.H. *Willis*); AJA 99 (1995) 729s, phot. (E. *Vermeule*); CLW 88 (1994s) 473 (A.L. *Boegehold*, M. *Chambers*).

q235　Drerup, Heinrich, 31.VIII.1908 -- 10.II.1995: MiDAV 25,2 (1994 !) 1.

q236　Dumoulin, Heinrich, 1905 -- 21.VII.1995: J(ap)JRS 22 (1995) 459-461 (J. *Van Bragt*).

q237　Durán y Gudiol, Antonio. 1918 -- 6.XI.1994, archiviste de la cathédrale de Huesca [RHE 91,360, T. *Moral*].

q238　During Caspers, Elizabeth C.L. (Inez), † 31.I.1996: Persica 15 (1993-5 !) 4-6: phot. (C. *Nijland*); 7-21, 20 fig., her article on Harappan seals.

q239　Dworakowska, Angelina, 4.VIII.1913 -- 26.VII.1994: Arch 46 (Wsz 1995) 127-130; portr. (M. *Nowicka*); 131s bibliog.

q240　Eberhardt, Newman Charles, 10.VII.1912 -- 26.V.1995: C(ath)HR 81 (1995) 658s (F.J. *Weber*).

q241　Eborowicz, Wacław, 29.V. (= 11.VI.) 1915 -- 11.XI.1994: Vox Patrum 24-29 (Lublin 1992-5) 24-28 (A. *Eckmann*, [P]).

q242　Eggermont, Pierre Herman Leonard, 4.II.1914 -- 11.IV.1995: Persica 15 (1993-5) 1s, phot. (J.T.P. de *Bruijn*).

q243　Ellul, Jacques [→ 54 supra], aet. 82, 19.V.1994: ed. 1969-86: FV 93,5s ('Le siècle de Jacques Ellul' 1994) 1-8 (G. *Vahanian*).

q244　Ennis, Arthur John, O.S.A., 22.X.1922 -- 27.III.1994: Catholic Univ., Villanova [RHE 91,361]: C(ath)HR 81 (1995) 157 ...

q245　Enright, Derek: Tablet 249 (1995) 1491 (K. *McNamara*; no †).

q246　Enrique y Tarancón, Vicente, card., 1907 -- XI.1994: EThL 71 (1995) 287; RF 231 (1995) 91-98 (J.M. *Díaz Moreno*).

q247　Ergardt, Jan, ... Buddhism: SvTK 69 (1993) 84s (T. *Olsson*).

q248　Fabro, Cornelio, 1911 -- 4.V.1995: Studium 91 (R 1995) 221-4 (P. *Prini*).

q249　Firet, Jaap, † 8.II.1994; redacteur 1978-92: G(ereformeerd)TT 45 (1994) 3s (W. *Stoker*).

q250　Folgado Flórez, Segundo, 28.VIII.1931 -- VIII.1994: EstMar 61 (1995) 310-3 (F. *Ochayta Piñeiro*, bibliog.).

q251　Franchini, Vincenzo, † 7.X.1995: RSEt 37 (1993 !) 177-182 (L. *Ricci*).

q252　Franco, Ricardo, S.J., 19.VI.1920 -- 7.II.1995, colaborador : Proyección 42 (1995) 220-238 (E. *Borrego*, con selecciones).

q253　Fransen, Gérard, chanoine, 26.I.1915 -- 20.IV.1995; droit canon: EThL 71 (1995) 519 (G.T.); RHE 90 (1995) 682s (A. *García y García*: plusieurs doctorats d'honneur); RTL 26 (1995) 416s (J.-M. *Sevrin*).

q254　Freudenberger, Theobald, 23.III.1904 -- 29.IX.1994: AHC(onc) 26 (1994) 174-8 (R. *Bäumer*).

q255　Frezouls, Edmond, 1925 -- 14.V.1995: Ktema 16 (1991 !) i (E. *Lévy*).

q256　Frostin, Per [→ 10,15280], aet. 48, 8.VI.1992: SvTK 68 (1992) 143s (P.E. *Persson*).

q257　Gabain, Annemarie von [→ 9,17328] 4.VII.1901 -- 15.I.1993] : zDMG 143 (1993) 239-149; portr. (P. *Zieme*, bibliog.[R]

q258　Gargan, Edward, 25.II.1922 -- 10.I.1995, president 1970: C(ath)HR 81 (1995) 306s.

q259　Gaster, Theodor H., 1906-1992, A biographical sketch and a bibliographical listing of

identified published writings: UF 27 (DIETRICH 60. Gb. 1995) 59-114; 2 phot. (R.H. *Hiers*).
q260 Genicot, Léopold, 18.III.1914 -- 11.V.1995, médiéviste: CRAI (1995) 515-7 (J. *Marcadé*); RHE 90 (1995) 345s (J. *Pycke*).
q261 Gerleman, Gillis [→ 10,15284], 27.III.1912 -- 25.VII.1993: SvTKv 70 (1994) 77 (S. *Hidal*).
q262 Ghrab, Saâd, 18.XII.1940 -- 16.VII.1995: Islamochristiana 21 (1995) 9-13 (A. *Ferré*, bibliog.
q263 Gollwitzer, Helmut [→ 9,17335; 10,15287], aet. 84, 17.X.1993: FrRu NF 1 (1993s) 153; phot.
q264 Grantovsky, Edvin Arvidovich, 16.II.1932 -- 28.VI.1995: VDI 215 (1995,4) 227-9;phot.
q265 Greenfield, Jonas Carl, 20.X.1926 -- 13.III-1995; exegesis, comparative Semitics; AfO 42s (1995s) 439-441; portr. (J.H. *Tigay:* born 20.X); BASOR 298 (1995) 3-5; phot. (Z. *Zevit*); Henoch 17 (1995) 278 (Jan A. *Soggin:* b. 30.X ?).
q266 Grzegorzewski, Karl [→ 10,15289], 21.II.1908 -- 10.IX.1994: WuD(ienst) 23 (Bethel 1995) 332s (H. *Braun*).
q267 Hänggi, Anton, mgr., 17.I.1917 -- 21.VI.1994: EO(rans) 12 (1995) 11-13 (A. *Nocent*).
q268 (von Fürer-) Haimendorf, Christoph, 27.VII.1909-11.VI.1995: MitAnthW 125s (1995s) 313s (A. *Gingrich*).
q269 Halleux, André de [→ 10,15290], 18.I.1929 -- 30.I.1994: Aram 6 (1994) 449-456 (S. *Brock:* contributions to Syriac studies): OrChr 78 (1994) 254 (J. *Assfalg:* † 15.II ?).
q270 Hapgood, John, 1905 -- 4.VII.1995; 50 years artwork for: America 173,13 (1995) 22s (D.M. *Linehan*).
q271 Harrison, Roland Kenneth, 4.VIII.1920 -- 2.II.1993: *ABW 2,2 (1994) 57s (R.N. *Longenecker*).
q272 Haugen, Einar ...: Lg 71 (1995) 558-564 (J.A. *Fishman*).
q273 Hay, Denys, 1915-1994; editor 1959-65 : E(ng)HR 110 (1995) 1-3 (G. *Holmes*).
q274 Hebblethwaite, Peter [→ 10,15295], 1930 -- 18.XII.1994: editor 1967-73: Month 256 (1995) 73s; phot. (M. *Barnes*); C(ath)WR 8/2 (Feb. 1995, p. 12 phot.('persistent critic of Pope John Paul II'): DocLife 45 (1995) 251 (D. *Keogh*); EThL 71 (1995) 294 (: S.J. 1948-74); Orien(tierung) 59 (1995) 11s (N. *Klein*); Tablet 249 (1995) 14; p. 68, his lecture 'The Vatican and the mystery of Israel'; p, 80, review of his The next pope by J. *Cornwell*).
q275 Hemmerle, Klaus, † 23.I.1994, Bischof von Aachen: LebZeug 50 (1995) 91-100 (Hans *Waldenfels*, Theologie der Nachfolge; zum theologischen Weg Klaus Hemmerles).
q276 Hermaniuk, Maxim, CSSR, aet. 84, 3.V.1996; founder-editor: Logos 36 (Ottawa 1995) inside cover.
q277 Heurgon, Jacques, 25.I.1903 -- 27.X.1994: CRAI (1995) 881-3 (J. *Favrier:* † 1995?); RÉL 73 (1995) 19s (J.-C. *Richard*).
q278 Higuera, Gonzalo, † 17.IV.1995: E(st)E 70 (1995) 211-238 (V. *Gómez Mier*, bibliog.
q279 Hill, Archibald A., 5.VII.1902 -- 29.III.1992: Lg 70 (1994) 132-140 (R.D. *King*).
q280 Horgan, Paul, 1.VIII.1903 -- 8.III.1995; president 1960: C(ath)HR 81 (1995) 484s.
q281 Hrbek, Ivan, 20.VI.1923 -- 20.III.1993, Islamologe: ArOr 62 (1994) 79s (L. *Kropáček*).
q282 Hu Houxuan, 20.XII.1911 -- 16.IV.1995; excavations, scapulimancy: *JAncCiv 10 (Changchun 1995) 1s, phot. [3-20, his Oracle Inscriptions; reviewed here p. 147s (*Ri Zhi*)].
q283 Hulin, Peter, 11.VII.1923 -- 29.III.1923, Assyriologist; AfO 42s (1995s) 332; phot. (O.R. *Gurney*).
q284 Huntington, Ronald P., †15.V (1994?): EThL 71 (1995) 292.

q285 Hurk Alphonsus van den, 1911 -- 25.VII.1994: AnPraem 71 (1995) 221-235 (H. van *Bavel*, bibliog.).

q286 Iglesias, Angel Luis, 17.I.1909 -- 2.V.1994: EstMar 61 (1995) 303-9 (E. *Llamas*, bibliog.)

q287 Kapelrud, Arvid S., 14.V.1912 -- 23.X.1994: [R]NTT 96 (1995) 127 (H.M. *Barstad*); TT(og)K 66 (1995) 77s (A. *Tångberg*).

q288 Karouzou, Semni, 1898-1994: RAr (1995) 333-5 (C. *Rolley*).

q289 Kasparova, Ksenija Vasiljevna, 8.XII.1929 -- 1994: RossArkh (1995,4) 230-3; phot. (S.A. *Pletneva, al.* bibliog.).

q290 Kastenbein, Renate Tülle, 27.I.1937 -- 29.III.1995: MiDAV 25,2 (1994) insert.

q291 Kilmartin, Edward J., S.J., 31.VIII.1923 -- 16.VI-1994; Baghdad; Weston College; Pont.Oriental Inst.: OCP 61 (1995) 5-14 (M.A. *Fahey*), bibliog. 19-35.

q292 Klawek, Aleksy, 1890-1969, biblista i orientalista: R(uch)BL 48 (1995) 51-55 (J. *Chmiel*) & Archutowski A. jako religioznawcy 55-58 (S. *Cinal*).

q293 Krautheimer, Richard [10,15318], 6.VII.1897 -- 1.XI.1994: MDAI-R 102 (1995) 1-3 (O.F.)

q294 Krefter, Friedrich, 15.X.1898 -- 25.I.1995: AMI(ran) 28 (1995s) 11-27; 33 fig. (W. *Kleiss*).

q295 Kribl, Josip, 12.I.1924 -- 9.V.1994: *BogSmot 65 (1995) 167-170 (J. *Kolarić*; 171-4, *al.*, bibliog.).

q296 Kromminga, John H., 1918-1994: C(alvin)TJ 29 (1994) 339-345 (H. *Zwaanstra*).

q297 Kümmel, Werner-Georg, 16.V.1905 -- 9.VII.1995: ThLZ 120 (1995) 945s (O. *Böcher*).

q298 Kunze, Emil, 18.XII.1901 -- 13.I.1994; Olympia, DAI Athen: Gnomon 67 (1995) 570-4; portr. (H.-V. *Herrmann*).

q299 Kuschke, Arnulf, aet. 83, 2.XI.1995: ThLZ 120 (1995) 1151.

q300 Laarhoven, Jan C.P.A. van, 3.VIII.1926 -- 28.XI.1995 [RHE 91,368, J. *Goossens*].

q301 Labourdette, Marie-Michel, 28.VI.1908 -- 26.X.1990: DoCom 46 (1993) 75-84 (D. *Composta*).

q302 Land, Philip, S.J., aet. 82 (1994?); 'social justice think tank': EThL 71 (1995) 292.

q303 LaSor, William Sanford, 1911 -- 11.I.1991: *ABW 1,2 (1991) 54 (F.W. *Bush*).

q304 Lavelle, Michael J., 1934 -- 25.III.1995, Jesuit provincial, university president, and collaborator: America 172,15 (1995) 4-6; portr. (V.M. *Cooke*).

q305 Lavery, Hugh, † I.1995, writer, preferred pastoral among the poor to brilliant academic career: Tablet 249 (1995) 239 (K. *Nichols*).

q306 Le Glay, Marcel, 7.V.1920 -- 14.VIII.1992: AntAfr 29 (1993) 7-11, phot. (J.-M. *Lassère*, bibliog).

q307 Leclercq, Jean [→ 9,17380; 10,15328], 31.I.1911 -- 27.X.1993: AL(tg)W 37 (1995) 89-92 (E. von *Severus*); E(spr)eV 105 (1995) 49s [J. *Daoust* < MSR 1994, M. *Platelle*].

q308 Leeuwen, Arend Theodoor van, 1918 -- 27.VI.1993: Exchange 23 (1994) 207-220 (T. *Salemink*: 'prophet in a secular world').

q309 Lehmann, Paul L. [→ 10,15329], 10.IX.1906 -- 27.II.1994: EThL 71 (1995) 291 (J.F. *Collins*).

q310 Leibowitz, Yeschayahu, 1903 -- 18.VIII.1994: FrRu 2 (1995) 74s; phot. (C. *Thoma*: hart gegen Christentum, aber auch gegen alle Magie: Westmauer 'die religiös-nationale Diskothek').

q311 Levin, Harry, 1912 -- 29.V.1994: ed. board 44 years: JHI(d) 56 (1995) 161 (J. *Engell*).

q312 Liedtke, Antoni, 29.IX.1904 -- 26.VII.1994: Vox Patrum 24 (1995) 729-732 (A. *Eck-*

mann, [P], bibliog.).

q313 Lindsey, Robert Lisle, 19.VIII.1917 -- 31.V.1995: *JPersp 49 (1995) 24-34 (D. *Flusser, al.*); 35s bibliog.); 10-17.38, his 'Unlocking the Synoptic Problem'.

q314 Luckner, Gertrud, 26.IX.1900 -- 31.VIII.1995: Orien(tierung) 59 (1995) 193-5 (E.L. *Ehrlich,* K. *Weber*).

q315 Lundin, Avraam Gregorievich, 25.XII.1929 -- 12.X.1994: VDI 213 (1995) 251-3 (M.A. *Rodionov,* [R]).

q316 Lurker, Manfred, 17.III.1928 -- 11.VI.1990: Symbolon 11 (Fra 1993) 7s (H. *Jung*).

q317 Luschey, Heinz [→ 6,r209; 9,17388] 3.XII.1910 -- 1.I.1993, Dir. DAI Istanbul, Teheran: ZDMG 144 (1994) 1-4, portr (H. *Gaube*).

q318 Macintyre, Angus, 1935 -- 21.XII.1994: E(ng)HR 110 (1995) 829-831 (P. *Williams*).

q319 MacKinnon, Donald [10,15340*], 1913 -- III.1994: ScotJR 16 (1995) 141-152 (A. *Millar*); Theol 98 (L 1995) 2-9 (G. *Steiner*).

q320 McNaspy, Clement J., S.J. aet. 79, 3.II.1995, polymath (Scripture, music, Russian) and associate editor 1960-70: America 172,5 (1995) 4 (G.W. *Hunt*).

q321 Mannucci, Valerio, mons., 10.V.1932 -- 27.II.1995: *VivH 6 (1995) 5-7 (B.*Marconcini*).

q322 Marlé, René [10,15342 'b.1920'], † 17.II.1994: RSR 83 (1995) 499-506 ('b.1919': J. *Moingt*; bibliog. 509-513) + 521-532 (J. *Joncheray*) + 533-542 *al*.

q323 Martínez Gómez, Luis: 9.II.1911 -- 1995: MCom 53 (1995) 207-9 (J. *Masiá Clavel*).

q324 Mauris, Édouard, 28.IV.1908-22.VI.1995, collaborateur: RTPh 127 (1995) 209-212 (D. *Müller*).

q325 Mazar, Benjamin, 1906 -- 8.IX.1995, 'world's greatest living Biblical archaeologist and historian': BArR 21,6 (1995) 22s . 77 (L.E. *Stager*); Qadm 28 (1995) 65s, phot. (A. *Biran, al.*[H] '9.IX').

q326 Meinecke, Michael, 6.XI-1941 -- 10.I.1995; Dir. des Islamischen Museums, Berlin: ADAJ 39 (1995) 11s (T. *Weber*); *DamaszM 8 (1995) vi-ix; phot. (K.S. *Freyberger*).

q327 Mendes Atanazio, Manuel, † 15.VII.1992 : RAHAL(ouvain) 26 (1993) 193 (R. Van *Schoute*).

q328 Meyer, Ben(jamin Franklin) [→ 127 supra], XI.1927 - 28.XII.1995: ExAud 11 (1995) iii-v; phot (D.Y. *Hadidian*); SR 24 (1995) 491-3 (S. *Westerholm*, bibliog.).

q329 Michel, Otto, 1903-1993: FrRu NF 1 (1993s) 235 (H. *Schmelzer*).

q330 Monaco, Giusto, 15.XI.1915 -- 14.II.1994: A(ten)eR 39 (1994) iii (F. *Bornmann, al.*).

q331 Moore Candelera, Eduardo, S.J. 26.VII.1920 -- 9.IV.1994: ATG(ran) 58 (1995) 3-8; fot.; bibliog.

q332 Moubarac, Youakim, 20.VII.1924 -- 24.V.1995: Islamochristiana 21 (1995) 1-8 (M. *Borrmans,* bibliog.); RICP 56 (1995) 225 (R. *Lebrun*).

q333 Munro, Winsome, aet. 68, 2.VI (1994?): EThL 71 (1995) 299 (R.F. *Collins*).

q334 Mveng, Engelbert, S.J.,, 1930 -- 24.IV.1995 (Yaoundé, Cameroun, 'par un acte de banditisme'), 'authentique théologie africaine': EThL 71 (1995) 520s (A.*Vanneste*).

q335 Nasrallah, Joseph, mgr.; exarque [→ 9,17406]: 10.X.1911 -- 19.XI.1993; littérature melchite: OrChr 79 (1995) 230 (J. *Assfalg*); Syria 72 (1995) 267-9; phot. (P. *Canivet,* R. *Haddad*).

q336 Nolan, Hugh Joseph, 8.VII.1911 -- 1.II.1995: C(ath)HR 81 (1995) 657s (R.H. *Schmandt*).

q337 Nyssen, Wilhelm Peter Ägidius, 19.IV.1925 -- 16.VII.1994;: OrChr 79 (1995) 230s (J. *Assfalg*).

q338 Oesterreicher, Johannes M. [→ 9,17408; 10,15354*]: 1904 -- 18.IV.1993: FrRu NF 1 (1993s) 68-70; phot. (C. *Thoma*).

q339 Otero, Miguel, O.F.M.,, 28.X.1941 -- 28.VI.1994: Anton 70 (1995) 707.

q340 Otte, Bernardo, S.V.D., 20.XII.1912 -- 11.VII.1995: RevBib(Arg) 57 (1995) 129s.

q341 Pallottino, Massimo, 9.XI.1909 -- 7.II.1995: ArchEspArq 68 (1995) 2 (J. *Arce*); Gerión 13 (1995) 11-16 (J.M. *Blázquez*; J. *Martínez-Pinna*); MDAI-R 102 (1995) 525; Prospettiva 77 (gennaio 1995) 191s (Marina *Martelli*); StRo 43 (1995) 107-110, phot. (R.A. *Staccioli*).

q342 Parsons, Frederick William, 9.II.1908 -- 2.XI.1993, (N.Niger) Hausa language: BSOAS 58 (1995) 109-112; portr. (P.J. *Jaggar*).

q343 Pavan, Pietro, card., 30.VIII.1903 -- 26.XII.1994, Rettore dell'Univ. Lateranense 1969-1974; Lat 61 (1995) 5-9.

q344 Pax, Wolfgang Elpidius O.F.M , 22.IV.1912 -- 14.IV.1993, Biblist in Jerusalem: WiWei 57 (1994) 295-301 (O. *Mund*, Bibliog.).

q345 Perelli, Luciano, 1916 -- 24.VII.1994: BSL(at) 25 (1995) 210-3 (G. *Bonelli, al.*).

q346 Pesaresi, Raimondo, aet. 81, 3.II.1994: A(ten)R 39 (1994) i-ii (M. *Gigante*).

q347 Petuchowski, Jakob J., 1925-1991: FrRu NF 1 (1993s) 231-5 (C. *Thoma*).

q348 Pietrangeli, Carlo † 23.VI.1995: MDAI-R 102 (1995) 525.

q349 Piskaty, Kurt, SVD, 26.XI.1932 -- 24.I.1995: VSVD 36 (1995) 109s (H. *Rzepkowski*) & 110-4 (J.*Mitterhöfer*); ZM(iss)R 79 (1995) 240-4 (H. *Rzepkowski*).

q350 Poliakova, Sofia Viktorovna, † IV.1994: VizVrem 56 (1995) 373s; fot. (Ya.*Lyubarski*)

q351 Polotsky, Hans Jacob [→ 7,k347; 9,17420] 13-IX-1905 -- 1991, 'linguistic genius': JRAS (1994) 3-13 (E. *Ullendorff*, lecture 13 May 1993).

q352 Popper, Karl Raymond, 1902 -- 17.IX.1994: EstAg 30 (1995) 99-115 (F. *Rubio C.*: 'antiutópico, pragmático, conservador, reaccionario' ?); FrRu 2 (1995) 76 [Ursula *Blum*].

q353 Porada, Edith [→ 10,15361], 22.VIII.1912 -- 24.III.1994: AJA 99 (1995) 143-6, 2 phot. (Holly *Pittman*); Iran 33 (1995) v-vi. portr. (Dominique *Collon*).

q354 Rawlyk, George A., 1935-1996: SR 24 (1995 !) 494-6 (J.G. *Stackhouse*, bibliog.).

q355 Reinbold, Ernst Thomas, 4.III.1907 -- 14.V.1994: Symbolon 12 (Fra 1995) 7-10; portr. (J. *Gaus*).

q356 Rennings, Heinrich [→ 10,15369], 9.VI.1926 -- 2/3.X.1994: L(tg)J 44 (1994) 193s.

q357 Riley, William [→ 156 supra], 4.IX.1948 -- 21.VI.1995: PI(r)BA 18 (1995) 9-13 (Carmel *McCarthy*, bibliog.).

q358 Robijns, Jozef , 1920 -- 1993 : RAHAL(ouvain) 26 (1993) 195 (N. *Meeüs*).

q359 Rössler, Otto, 6.II.1907 -- 9.VII.1991: ZDMG 145 (1995) 1-6, port. (R. VOIGT, bibliog).

q360 Rogers, David McGregor, 29.V.1917 -- 31.V.1995, Oxford Bodleian: RHE 90 (1995) 691 (J.-L. *Quantin*).

q361 Rubinstein, Eliezer, 5.V.1926 -- 29.VII.1989: Te'uda 9 (1995) 9-12; phot. 7.; bibliog. 13-15.

q362 Ryan, John F. †7.IV (1994?): ETh 71 (1995) 292.

q363 Scano, Gaetano, 12.I.1922 -- 23.II.1995: StRo 43 (1995) 113s (G. *Batelli*).

q364 Schaerer, René, 1901-1995, philosophe: RTPh 127 (1995) 213-6 (C. *Gagnebin*. D. *Schulthess*).

q365 Schindler, Jochem, 8.XI.1944 -- 24('am Heiligen Abend').XII.1994: Die Sprache 36 (1994) i; Kratylos 40 (1995) 216-8 (H. *Eichner*, Bibliog. 219-221).

q366 Schmaus, Michael [→ 10,15376*], 17.VII.1897 -- 8.XII.1993: MThZ 45 (1994) 115-119-123-7 (F.Card.*Wetter*, W. *Steinmann*, R. *Heinzmann*).

q367 Schmitz, Walter J., S.S., aet. 87, 20.X.(1994?): Catholic U. liturgist: EThL 71 (1995)

292 (R.F. *Collins*).

q368 Schneerson, Menachem M., rabbi, 1902, aet. 92: CrossCur 45 (1995s) 234-140 (Susan *Handelman* > Wellsprings).

q369 Schröger, Friedrich, 1.XII.1931-6.V.1994, NT Eichstätt/Passau; Heb 1Pt; Assistent von O.KUSS: BZ 39 (1995) 308s (J. *Ernst*, J. *Hainz*).

q370 Schwyzer, Hans-Rudolf, 8.III.1908 -- 23.X.1993; PLOTINUS; : Gnomon 67 (1995) 379-381 (W. *Beierwaltes*).

q371 Selb, Walter, 22.V.1929 -- 2.VI.1994: ZS(av)RG.r 112(1995) lxiii-lxxx, phot. (G. *Thür*, H. *Kaufhold*).

q372 Sersale, suor Celina, 22.III.1920 -- 2.IX.1995: Anton 70 (1995) 707.

q373 Sherrard, Philip, aet. 72, 30.VI.1995: SV(lad)SQ 39 (1995) 432s (J. *Chryssevgis*).

q374 Shore, Arthur Frank (Peter), 14.XI.1924 -- 1994: Catholic; Coptic studies [→ 9,118]: JEA 81 (1995) 197-200 (C.J. *Eyre*).

q375 [Karamanli-] Siganidou, Maria, 29.III (? 1994); Makedoniká 29 (1993s) 423s (A. *Papaefthymiou-Papanthímou* & A. *Pilali-Papastiriou*).

q376 Smits, Edmé Renno, 17.V.1950 -- 19.V.1992: JMdvLat 3 (1993) v.

q377 Soares-Prabhu, George, S.J., 1929 -- 22.VII.1995: I(nd)TS 32 (1995) 192; Vidyajyoti 59 (1995) 707-710 (K.R. *D'Souza*).

q378 Sontheimer, Günther-Dietz, 21.IV.1934 -- 2.VI.1992: ZDMG 143 (1993) 248-254 (J. *Lütt*).

q379 Spätling, Luchesius, 15.IX.1912-15.VIII.1995: Anton 70 (1995) 707.

q380 Starr, Richard Francis Strong, 1900 -- 9.III.1994, Nuzi excavator; AfO 42s (1995s) 337-9; portr. (D. I. *Owen*, < Starr mem., Nuzi 8, 1996).

q381 Stępień Jan, 23.VI.1910 -- 8.I.1995: R(uch)BL 48 (1995) 142-8 (S. *Mędala*, [P], bibliog.).

q382 Stockwood, Mervyn, † I.1995; Anglican bishop of Southwark: Tablet 249 (1995) 126s (< 'the dean of Westminster').

q383 Strecker, Georg [→ 10,14381*], 15.III.1929 -- 11.VI.1994: D(elt)BM 14,1 (1995) 84s (S. *Agouridis*, [G]) '11.VII'].

q384 Stuhlmueller, Carroll, C.P. [→ 10,15383] 2.IV.1923 -- 21.II.1994: EThL 71 (1995) 291; LiLi 31,1 (1994) 58-61 [NTAb 39, p.199].

q385 Tanenbaum, Marc [→9,17459], 1926 -- 3.VII.1992: FrRu NF 1 (1993s) 72.

q386 Tedeschi, Salvatore, 4.I.1914 -- 19.I.1996: RSEt 37 (1993 !) 183-5 (L. *Ricci*, bibliog.)

q387 Theisen, Jerome, O.S.B. (Collegeville MN), 30.XII.1930 -- 11.IX.1995; Abbas Primas dal 1992: Ben 42 (1995) 510; EO(rans) 12 (1995) 321-4 (A. *Nocent*).

q388 Théodoridès, Aristide [→ 10,15387], 30.VI.1911 -- 4.II.1994: CÉg 70 (1995) 5-8 (A. *Mekhitarian*).

q389 Turbin, Dora, 1912 -- 28.I.1955, founder of feminist 'Dorcas', consulted and outspoken e.g. on church-charity finance-accounts: Tablet 249 (1995) 193s (Marysia *Owsianka*).

q390 Vagner, Georgy Karlovitch, 19.X.1908 -- 25.I.1995: RossArkh (1995,3) 249; phot. (B.A. *Rybakov*, V.P. *Darkevitch;* bibliog. S.V. *Mesniankipa*).

q391 Vallet, Georges, 1922 -- III.1994: StRo 43 (1995) 111, phot. (M. *Colesanti*).

q392 Vattioni, Francesco, msgr. † 13.XII.1995: AION 55 (1995) 463.

q393 Vélez Chaverra, Neftalí, 3.VIII.1948 -- 1994: TX(av) 109 (1994) 357-366 (G.*Neira F.)*

q394 Venturi, Franco, 16.V.1914 -- 14.XII.1994: encyclopédistes: RHE 90 (1995) 364 (R. *Aubert*).

q395 Wattel, Jean-Marie, 1933 -- 23.III.1994: RICP 56 (1995) 223s (J. *Milet*).

q396   Weil, Raymond,   29.X.1923 -- 26.III.1995:   CRAI (1995) 359-361 (P. *Toubert*);
RPh(ilolog) 67 (1993) 195s, phot. (J.-L. *Perpillou*).
q397   Wenger, John Christian, 1910 -- 26.III.1995: MennQR 69 (1995) 215 (L. *Gross*).
q398   Wieacker, Franz [→ 10,15398],   5.VIII.1908 -- 17.II.1994; Rechtsgeschichte:
Gnomon 67 (1995) 473-7 (D. *Liebs*); ZS(av)RG.r 112 (1995) xiii-lxii, phot. (O. *Behrends*).
q399   Williams, Ronald J. [→ 10,15402], 9.V.1917 -- 19.XI.1993: *JSStEg 21s (1991s !)
iv-vi. phot.
q400   Wolfram, Richard,   16.IX.1901 -- 30.V.1995: MitAnthW 125s (1995s) 317s; portr.
(Ulrike *Kammerhofer-Aggermann*).
q401   Yunis, Najat, 1943 -- 5/6/1994: Sumer 47 (1995) A 68.
Žabkar, Louis V., 7.XII.1914 -- 15.VIII.1994:   JA(m)RCE(g) 32 (1995) iv.v (L.
Lesko, F. Friedman).

Index Alphabeticus

A u c t o r u m   [sic] & *s i t u u m* [sic, omisso *al, tell, abu* ..]

Ddissertatio vel director - Eeditor,publisher - FFestschrift, memorial - Mmentio, de eo - Rrecensio - † obit

Alfonseca M 0915
Alfonsi P ^M7458 7736
Alfonso E ^R342 438 7348
-Troncoso V c788
Alford J 1788 ^Rg779
Algaze G b362 b870
Algeria a088
Ali M 6140*b* a819*a*
Alichoran J q157
Ali Khan M 9044*b*
Alişar b807
Alison J 3916*a*
Aliti A 5377
Alizadeh A ^Rb473
Alkier S ^Dg056
Allam S 9355 ^R8766
Allan D k157 **E** 751 a835
  b237*b* **N** 5785
Allatson W ^E843
Allegro J 7050
Allen D ^R2384 **J** 4417 6152*b*
  ^E713 **M** g498 **P** 916 g335 **R**
  1518 **S** b872 **W** 2678
-da P ^Ra640
Alles G ^R7970
Alliata E a952 b039 b205
  ^Ea948
Alliet M g816
Allison C g057 **D** 2226 **G**
  ^Dg943
Allsopp M ^E1879 4582 k425
  ^R1880
Alma H 3721
Almond P 5378 7963 ^R9106
d'Aloia F ^Ra076
Alon D b030 **I** ^E392
Alonge A 6261
Alonso J ^M8938
-Díaz J ^R3168 4422
-Schökel L 1076 1261 1789
  2065 2497 2667 2745 2843
  4418 5749
-Turienzo T ^R2670
Alpers M ^Dc789
Alram-Stern E b988
Alroth B ^Da633
Alster B 6000 r^R6021
Alston R ^Dc564 ^R308 326*a* **W**
  6680 7980
Alszeghy Z ^Mk737
Alt F 2089 **K** 8514
Altaner ^Mg088
Altemeyer F 8127
Altendorf H ^Eg058
Altenmüller H ^Rb601
Alter P ^R7521 **P** 5786 ^M2038
Altermatt U k519
Althann R ^R5755
Althaus P ^Mk738s

Altheim-Stiehl R 5985
Althoff J 9565
Altìn b808
Altizer T 2804 ^Mk740
Altmann W g900 ^T1764
Altschuler G ^R7538
Alvar J 457 ^E0662
Alvarez A 3005 **C** ^R4859 **E**
  ^R5197
-Bolado A 4035*a*
-Cineira D ^D3917 ^R278 2181
  b644 c662
-Gómez M 2935
-Pereyre F 7247
-Sáenz de Buruaga J †q181
-Suárez A ^R4054 g105
-Valdés A 223 1077 2457
  3802 a953
Alves de Melo ^R4901
Alviar J ^R3708 4387
Amadasi Guzzo M 5909*b*
  c283
Amaladass A 1262
Amaladoss M 3643*a*
Amandry P a136 b877
Amante Sánchez M a778
  b258
Amar J ^Eg616s ^R9978
Amarelli F ^R8353
Amarna 6012 6017 6020 6058
  a034*b* b571-b596
Amata B ^R5439 a786 a857
Amathus b912-4
Amberg E ^F116 ^M1014 ^R96
Ambros A 6060 ^R5835s 6069
  6097
Ambrosiaster ^Mg536
Ambrosius M g537-47 g556
  ^M2242 5425 c217 g518
Amedick R a626
Ameling W b243
Amersfoort J van 7578 ^R9998
Amery C 393
Amico E ^R1746
Amiet P 7880 a686*a* b363
  b481*a* ^Ra221 a332 a511
  b437
Amigues S c284 ^Ra385
Amín Q 5260
Aminoah N ^R7296
Amiran D c167
Amirim b082
Amirov S ^Rb396
Amis R g059
Amit Y ^R1389
Amitai P c406
Amman b138-141
Ammermann A ^Rb999 **N** 7881
Ammianus M ^M9843 9857

9874 9911
Ammon 5896 c533
Amorai-Stark S 9680
Amorós P 8515
Amorth G ^M3852
Amos C ^R8638
Amouretti M a205 ^E207 c28
Amphoux C ^R2168 2488
Amsler F 6728
Amstutz M 4728
Anagnostou-Canas B 9356
Anamur b809
Anandam L ^D9112
Anastasiadis A 8618
Anastasio S 1057
Anastasius P a967
Anastos M ^F4*
Anati E a788 b738
Anatolia 6228-6256 6462
  9517-28 b741-b891 c09
  c114
Anatrella T 5261
Anawati G 8991 †q182
Anaximenes M ^Mc118
Anazarbo a913
Anbar M b339 b342*c*
Anbeek C ^D5379
Anchukandam T 4247*b*
Ancilla M ^Rg589
Anckaert L ^R8521
Ancona G 5380 q117 ^R606
  5381
Ancyra b810
Andersen F 5750 ^R5755 **H**
  b449 **O** b880 **P** 6557
Anderson A ^R4954 **B** a028
  ^M2424 ^Rq075 **C** 4362
  ^D3722 **G** 5805 6791 7045
  8350 8578 9838 ^R822 261
  6278 6742 9845 **H** 5102
  1885 ^E530 ^Ra574 **K** ^Rg35
  L 4330 **P** 3430 **R** 538
  c523*a* ^R7595
Andersson S 7971
Andiñach P 1332 ^Ra926
Andorlini I ^Rc478
Andouche I c407
Andrae W ^Mb399
Andrassy P c810*c*
André J 9265 9779 c546*
  ^R9751
Andreae B a628s b934 ^Ea62
  ^Fa837
Andreas B 2936
Andreau J c790*a* ^R9942
Andreev Y b976
Andres A ^Rk435
Andrés M g944
-R de ^R0794 2785 2789 c56

(Artola ..) [E]1078
Arts H 8129
Artson B 7523
Artus W k520a
Artzi P b596b
Arubas B b039
Arundel J [M]g664
Arzt P 6421
Asad T 224 8993
Asante M [M]q053 [R]7679
Asbury B [R]7751
Ascalon a212 b023 b065
Aschim A 6972
Ascione A 1971
Ascough R [R]4647 5188 a839
    c699 k794
Ascuitto L 1703
Asen B [R]0361 [E]3001 4907
    [T]1453 3765 4571 7623
Ash J 7695b P [R]9186
Ashanin C [R]2133
Asheim I g901
Asher R [E]840
-Grève J a481
Ashley B 4419
Ashmole B a137
Ashton D 7524 [R]7520
Ashworth M [R]1541
Asia Minor 1069 b741-b891
    c974
Asimov I [M]2396
Askani H [D]2715
Askew T [R]k660
Askoul M g412
Aslanoff C 5694 6582 [T]7440
    7452
Asmussen J c212
Aspegren K 5161
Aspinwall B [R]k915
Asraf M [M]c398
Assaël J [R]6410
Assfalg J q199 q208 q269
    q335
Assman H 225
Assmann H 4710 J 6661
    8736-8 9187 9267 [E]542 734
Asso C k086
Aššur a098 b399 c838a
Assyria a453 a518b
Astell A 1851
Asterius [M]g319
Asti F 4420 [R]7964
Aston B a498 M 226
Astor C [D]7273
Astour M b276
Åström P b986
Asurmendi J 1972
Aswan b663
Atallah N 6061a

Athanasius A [M]1635 2866
    9946 g320-4
Athanassiadi P 8517
Athappilly S [R]9116
Athenae 736 a388 a665 a682
    a894 b934-b949 c204 c729
    c803 c831
Athenagoras g171s
Atherton J 4731
Athos a904
Atij b309s
Atkinson C [R]g636 D [E]801
    [R]2337 5395 P [F]5
Atlan H 2287
Attias J 7471 7475 [T]6927
Attinger D [R]c291 P 6001
    [R]6042
Attridge H [E]6966b g360
    [R]2561 6845 7805 9696 g104
Atwan R 1817
Atwood R [R]4743 5162
Atzler M [R]b668
Auberger J c332
Aubert J [D]c792 [T]7238 P k751
    [R]3758 R 4168 q3944 [R]760
    763 4106 g134 k246 k379
    k409 k933 q010a
Aubet M b224
Aucker W 2288
Auden [M]8545
Audinet J 8131b c568a
Auer J 3876 [M]4148
Auerbach E [D]a630
Auffarth C c598 [R]6584 8435
    8481
Aufrecht W a687 [R]a727 b229
Augé M [R]c921
Augello A 2227
Augros R 2389b
Auguet R a398
Augustijn C k538b
Augustinovich A 775
Augustinus g410-g494 g556
    g933a [M]354 446 482 573
    623 757 3456 3603 3636b
    3677 3828 4453c 4800 5437
    5455 6657 7621 7808 7829b
    9279 9325 a442 c218 c383
    c731 g119d g259 g299
    g508s g518 k258
Augusto Tavares A 2498
Aujac G c094
Auld A 2076 [R]c521
Aulisa I [R]g125 g313 g456 q095
Aumann J [F]6
Aumont M 1921s 5265
Aune D 1790 6830e [R]368 8441
Auneau J 1150 3737b
Aupert P [R]b911 b918

Aura Jorro F 6485 [R]6497
Auroux S 6612
Ausejo S de [E]0779
Ausín S [R]3362
Austad T k738b
Austin N b874 [R]a306 R 300◖
Auwers J [R]5962 6882 g175
    g249 J van der [E]688
Avalos H c408s k080
-Cadena B [T]c714
Avanzini A 8880 b445 b462◖
    [R]8887
Avemarie F 7169 7191b 727◖
Averincev S a955
Avery-Peck A 7573 [R]7309
Aviam M c333
Avicenna 8962 [M]7403
Avidov A [R]a383
Aviezer N 2289s
Aviram J a030
Avis P [E]2346 [R]4336
Avi-Yonah M c120
Avner M b340 R a741
Avotri S 4946a
Avraham N 2417
Avram A 8458
Axcelson J [D]1818
Axe T [R]1083 6481
Axum b670
Ay K c569
Ayalon D 227 E b022
Ayán J [R]3107
-Calvo J [E]g205
Ayestarán J 1404 [E]544
Aylward W a291
Ayoub M 8894 8945
Ayoun R 7496 [R]7349 7412
    7596
Ayres L g413a P k082
Ayrookuzhiel A 4947
Azar M 5787 5828
Azarnoush M b474
Azevedo M 4948 T de ±q18◖
Azim M c919
Aziz K b404
Azraqi al- 8935
Azzali Bernardelli G 3570
Azzi R [R]4852

Baalbaki R 6062
Baar M 9721
Baarda T 2604 7848 g612
    [E]7170
Baasland E k454
Baatz D a305
Babalola E 2418
Babcock R 4496
Babinet R 2128
Babington B 1791

Blickle P g948
Bliquez L c416
Bloch ᴹk770 **A** c293 **E** ᴹk476
    R g641 k361
-Hoell N ᴿ4173
-Smith E a821 ᴹa855
Blocher F a692 **H** 3807
Block P 2717
Blockley R 9953
Bloedhorn H a957 b093
Bloedow E 9616a
Bloesch D 1086 1588 4204
    ᴰk928 ᴿk660
Blohm D 5789 ᴿ5910 6100
Blois F de 6511
Blok J 8328
Blokland A ᴰ5700
Blomberg C 390 1267
Blomé B a636
Blomqvist J ᴿ8497 **K** 1708
    9842
Blondel M k416-20 ᴹk892s
Bloom H 1633
Bloomquist L 861
Blosser P ᴿk660 k687
Blottière A c178
Blough N 4539 4560b 8235
Blount B 1268 2093
Blowers P 1407 ᴿg392
Blue J ᴿ4209
Blümer W ᴿg518
Blum E 8645a ᴿ9224 c739 **R**
    b634 **U** q352
Blumenberg H ᴹ5387 q013e
Blumenkranz B †q202
Blumenthal D 3165 ᴹ7751
    ᴿ2767 2966 7278 **U** ᴿg783
-Clark ᴹ8517
Blumhardt C ᴹ3527
Blumhofer E k531
Blumin S ᴿ7505
Blunt W c294
Blyskal L 5271
Blyth D ᴿ8553
Boada J 1016 1925 3514 ᴿ779
    1945 2763 2982 3858 3949
    4633* 4816 5458 5676 7063
    7078 7655 8336 g685 k725
    k826 q024 q054
Boadt L ᴿ1097
Boardman J a523s ᶠ22
Boatwright M ᴰ9768 ᴿb949
Bobert-Stützel S k784
Bobrinskoy B 3604
Bobzin H ᴿg727
Boccaccini G 7106b 7173-5
Boccara E 2230
Bocchini Camaiani B g996
Bochinger C 8236

Bock D 3315 ᴿ455 **S** 9193
    c525
Bockmuehl M 2094 3220 4594
    c676 ᴿ379 483 2274 3915
    7005 7052
Bocquet É 7989
Bodan G c179
Bodelot C 6527
Bodemann M 1031
Bodendorfer-Langer G 1269
Bodenmann R g949
Bodéüs R 9539
Bodine W ᴱ1980 5701
Bodman W ᴿq039
Bodson L ᴱ0667
Børtnes H ᴿ1810
Böcher O 925 q297 ᴰ2871
Boëdec F c180
Boeft J den 9843 9954 g532
    ᴱ668
Boegehold A 9540 q234 ᴱ669
Böhl F 2535
Böhler D 2231 **H** 4540
Böhlig A 6265 7810
Böhm S a635 **T** 3455 ᴹg318
    ᴿ2049 g168
Böhme C c870
Boehmer R b438 ᶠ23
Böhmisch F 862a 910b ᴿ860
    1146 9068 g767
Boehrer P 6290
Bömer F ᴿ755
Böning A 3166
Boeotia c366b
Boer J 1873b 4734 **J** de 1061
    M de ᴰ5392
Børresen K 5170 ᴱ1709 ᴿ433
Boers H ᴿ2117
Börsig-Hover L 5272
Bösch M ᴿ1923 5387
Boespflug E ᴿ7887 **F** 7990
    a556 ᴿ8296 8338 **S** ᴿ8050
Boethius 1851
Böttrich C 3167a 6752 6754
    ᴰ6753
Boeve L 2899b 6683
Bof G g068 k378b
Boff L 232 3013-5 ᴱ405 ᴹ3504
    3576 4227 4860 k780
Boffo L 5428s a394
Bogacki H ᶠ24
Bogaert P 2647c ᴿ1934 2602
    6733 6912 g767 k702 **R** ᶠ25
    ᴿc803
Boğazköy b764-b780 c948
Bogović M k532
Boha G 6065
Bohak G 6796 9667
Bohan G 6585

Bohas G 5922
Bohemen F/N †q203
Bohl R c900b
Bohrmann M 9668
Boisjoly R a430
Boismard M 2605 539.
    7074b
Boissinot C k859
Boissonneault J a463
Boitani P 8459
Bójd I 7143
Bojesen S 7131
Bok N den 3456 g417s
Bokser ᴹ7291
Bokwa I 3781 ᴿk951
Bolado A ᴹ3734
Boland V 4806a g851 ᴿk74.
Bolatti Guzzo N 1069
Bolelli C 1872
Boles J k293
Bolewski J 3808a 5111
Boley P 6237b
Bolger D ᴿa762
Bolgiani F ᴿ1641 k569
Boling R †q204
Bollansée J 9844
Bologna G 2462
Bolognesi P 863 6361 ᴿ575
    8232
Bolsec ᴹk055
Bolshakov A 6104 b492 b54
Bolt J 3016 k294 ᴿ1554 k87
    ᵀ4171 **M** ᴿ2291 2305
Boman T ᴹ5679
Bomann A 8746 b572
Bombeck S 2536
Bombonatto V ᴿ9338
Bommas M b663
Bommelaer J b930
Bompaire J ᴱ9845
Bompois C 2741
Bona I c217
Bonamente G ᴿa365
Bonanate U 8999
Bonaventura g839   ᴹ294
    3484 3628 5339 9118
Bondì R 4453b **S** c046 ᴿb36
Bonechi M c149 ᴹb292
Bonelli G q345
Bonfante G b875 ᴿ6519
    a472 ᴿa635
Bonfil R 7176 7341
Bongard-Levin G ᴿ9914
Bongioanni A a081 b493
Bonhême M 9360
Bonhoeffer D ᴹ2974 k942
    k781-93
Boni A 4541 **G** ᴹc033 **L** d
    ᴱ109

Bowering G ᴿ6074 8903
Bowersock G 9274 9542
  9847s ᴱ297 ᴹa413
Bowker J 2301 5395 9001
  ᴱ8083
Bowkett L b96
Bowman A c910 ᴱ550 9362
  ᴹ9590 ᴿc914 R ᴿ390 2403
  S ᴱc418 ᴿ8907 T 4960a
Bown T a181
Bowser E ᴿa059
Boyano M ᴿ4361
Boyarin D 5171 7278-80
  ᴿ7294 7320
Boyce J ᴿ372 M 8861-3 P
  k431 ᴿ3901
Boyd G 2808 J 1914 2942
  S k129 ᴹ1676
Boyer M 3783 P k536
Boyle J 234 g818
Boyne D ᴿ1318
Boys M 2025f 3923
Braaten C 2100 ᴱ489*
Braccesi L 9617a
Bracchi R 2738 ᴿ32 782
  843 6292 6534 6540 6549
  6562 6568 6600 6623
Brachet R 8522 T
  ᴹk223
Bracken J 2810 ᴿ4992
Bradbury S 3924 9957
Bradley 7906 ᴹ2828 I
  3019 ᴿ9306 J 3925 K
  c582-4 ᴿc673 c746 L
  ᴿk625
Bradshaw B k104
  †q207 J 6107 P 3169
  4499-4501 ᴱ87 ᴿ4531
  ᴿg666 T ᴿ3705 k924
Bradstock A ᴿk134
Bradt R ᴰk325
Brady T k146 ᴱg951
Braemer F b316 ᴿa244
  a918
Brändle R 7587 ᴿ757
  W 3119 ᴱ108
Bräuer S ᴿk133
Bragança de Oliveira
  J ᶠ27
Bragt J van †q236
Brahms T ᴰa525
Braine D 2943 ᴿ2834
Brajčic R 4596
Brakelmann G ᴰ4844
Brakke D 1635 g586
  ᴰg321 ᴿ9436
Brakmann H ᴱg013
Brancazio P 2302
Brand L ᴿg022

Brandão J 8460
Brandenburg H a241
Brandenburger E
  ᴰ2839
Brandt H ᴰc798 ᴿ5449
  8371 c335 k624 K 1270
  1981
Brann R 7342
Brannen N ᵀ6359
Brants A ᴿq016
Brashear W 6431 845s
  c585 ᴿ8476
Brasher B q018
Brashler J b203
Bratcher R 2697 ᴿ2686
  2716
Brattinga T ᴿ4283
Brauch T 9958 ᴿ8516
Brauer 7488 7531 M
  ᴰ9275
Braulik G 634 1147
  4497b 4502 ᴱ128 490
Braun H q184 q266 J
  b995 R g555 ᴱg272s
  ᴿ2639 g290 g513 W
  ᴿa503 c737
  -Holzinger 8828 ᴿa692
  a713* b484
Braund D 9849 c526 G
  b743
Braungart K ᴰ4736
Bravo B 8380 E 3683
  -Aragón J 1261
Brawley R 3948 ᴱ1370*
  ᴿ3948
Bray G 1626 3810 ᴰg952
  ᴿ2561 6864 k413
Braybrooke M 7588 ᴿ837
  7739
Bréard L ᴿ5132
Brears P ᴿa040 a062
Brech-Neldner R a794
Brecht B ᴹ1852 M 235
  k161 g905 q179 ᴹg906
Breck J 1982 4597 5112
  ᴿ5150
Breckwoldt T c338
Bredero A 236 g647
Brees M 1410
Breeze D a306
Bregliozzi A g177
Bregman M 7589
Brehm H ᴿ3597
Breid F ᴱ551
Breitenberg V ᴱ2303
Breitsching K ᴰ4598
Breivik N 4961 ᴿ5059
Brekus C ᴿk320
Bremen R van ᴿb792

Bremer I 5396 J ᴱ552 T
  ᴿ9010
Bremmer J 886 8461 ᴰ8841
Brena G k927 q010c
Brendler G g906
Breniquet C ᴿb407
Brenk B b170 F ᴹ9733
Brennan B 9959 W 5113
  ᴿ5115
Brenner A 1711 q232 ᴿ1762
  ᴹ3655 k316
Brenon A g648s
Brent A g568s
Brentjes B 9618 a307
  a537b
Brereton V 5172 k537
Bresciani E c220 ᴱ714
  b518 ᴿ8764
Breslauer S 7528 W
  ᴿk483
Breton J b447 ᴿb456
Bretscher P 2102
Brett M 529 1271 6066
  b067 ᴱc586
Brettler M 9276
Bretzke J 4599 ᴿ4642
Breuer C ᴰ4600 E k252
  ᴿ7506 S c587a
Breuil P du 8864
Breuning W 4337
  ᴹ3608*
Breuvart J ᴿ8199
Brewer D 7177 c295
  ᴿ6315 E ᴰ2304
Brewster H b744
Breydy M †q208
Bria I 4962
Briand J †q209
Briant P 8865 9491-3
Brice W 6432
Brickhouse T 8523
Bridger F ᴹ4722
Briel J ᴹ7638
Briend J 2769s a242
  a296 b192 ᴱ770
Brienen T 1523 ᴿ7614
Brier B ᴱa082
Briese O k296
Brieskorn N g650
Briggs C ᴹk297 J k298
  ᴹ3146
Bright J 9196 ᴹ840 P
  ᴱ482
Brill R a184 a187
Brillante C ᴿ6667
Brilliant R 237
Brin G 3222a 5852
  7015a 7093 7477 ᴿ3203
  7046

Chéhab M †q221
Cheikh N el- [R]8924
Chélini J g662
Chelliah R 4741
Chemnitz M k078
Chen D b043 T [R]2298
Chénard G [R]3573
Cheneaux P 4742
Chenu B 8144a k548 M [M]3099
Chen Xu 6232a
Cherbury H [M]k225
Cherchi Chiarini G a563
Cherix P 7838
Chernick M [E]7281
Chernykh Y a209a
Cherry C k549 J b999 R [T]k711
Cheruel M [T]c946
Chesnutt R [D]6797 [R]7186 7226
Chesson M b198
Chester A [R]1641 b822
Chethimattam J 3096b k677b
Chetwynd L [R]g974
Cheung L 5180
Chevallier M k262 k408 R a210 c012 c424 [F]36 [R]a000a a213 c285 c402
Cheyette B 7597
Cheynet M b203
Chéza M c880b q125a
Chial D 3022
Chiarini F [R]397 G [T]g421
Chiat M a796
Chico G [R]3733 3956 T [T]k118
Chiera G b247
Chiesa B [R]8923 C 2938 G 9756
Chi Hyeong-Eun [D]k268
Childe V [M]a146s
Childress J [D]4812
Childs B 1636 5647s [E]282 [M]1324 5657 5679
Chilton B 2233 3927s 3982 7694 [R]2542
Chimelli C [R]4042
Chimera b951
Ching J 9137
Chinitz J 3224
Chiodi M 6688 S 8750 8830
Chios b992
Chirban J [E]4602
Chirichigno G c599
Chisholm R 2817 [R]1999 5766

Chittick W 8952
Chmiel G 7057b 7061 J 1481b 6070 q292 L q099
Chmielewski A q126 M 4427
Choe Joon Soo [D]1718
Choi Jongtae [R]5977
Cho Kah Kyung [D]9159
Cholidis N a297
Cholvy G 1414 5181 9283
Chomsky N [M]6635 6658
Choper J k550
Chopp J [R]k457 R k799 [E]403
Choueiri V [R]8943 q039 Y [E]719
Chouraqui A 2721
Chow J c600 S 2234
Chowcat D [T]9238
Christ K 9728
Christakis C 4554
Christen E [E]441 5146 5493
Christensen K 2947 [D]k738 L [R]4040 R [D]k297
Christians C 4743
Christiansen E [D]3120
Christidis A 6256a 6509
Christie I [R]k178 N [R]a036
Christin O g955
Christmann-Franck L [E]1154
Christoff D [R]k227
Christophe P 809
Christ-Von Wedel C [R]k089
Chrostowski W 2228b 7598-7600 [E]494 [T]2268b
Chrupcala L [R]3558 6710 9314
Chrysostomus D [M]1708 9842 J 7587 [M]3476 c678 g335-48 g468
Chryssevgis J q373
Chung Hyung Kyung [M]3576
Chung Song-Tae [D]4968
Chupungco A 4969 4970b [D]5487
Church Bytes 866
Church History, Amer.Soc. 979
Churchill W [M]g020
Chuvin P 8586 9542
Chyutin M 6981 a961
Cialowicz K [R]a400
Ciampini E b573
Ciani J k798
Ciccarese M c225
Cicero M [M]3929 8440 9748 c396 g436
Cifola B 6003 a921
Ciggaar K b838
Cignelli L 6272 c923

Cilicia b745
Cilleruelo A 8227c 8261b
Cimmerii c528 c534s c541
Cimmino F 9367
Cimosa M 6273 6732 [E]1235 [R]1383 2582
Cinal S q292
Cini M 2311
Ciniello N [R]1206
Ciola N 3606 4896 k890 [E]20
Cioli G [R]4636 4639
Cipriani A [E]310 N g422 S 1415 [R]575
Ciprotti P 5703
Cirelli G 123 2984b
Cislaghi A k861
Cisneros [M]k079
Citrin P [E]5746
Citroni Marchetti S 8364
Cittadini R a675b [R]2399
Civil M c341
Cizek E 9822 9857 [R]9800 9808
Clack B [R]192
Clackson J [R]6299
Cladis M k266 [R]8046
Clagett M 9284 b496 c425
Clague J [R]5264
Clairmont C a823
Claman E [T]283
Clancy F [R]4382 T [R]k199
Clangio R 4019b
Clare A 8066 J 2749
Claret B [D]3813
Claringhall D 4744
Clark A [R]g732 B [R]6713 D b201 [R]4619 E 5182 g243 [R]1582 4647 G 5183 5821 9968 [E]g423 [R]462 958 J 9812 [E]b396 L [R]83 M 3278 5184a [M]g222 N [R]1564 2105 4342 c638 c908 S [R]k006
Clarke A c601 [R]2897 E 2546 a245 J [M]c055 k700 K [R]c111 W [F]241
Clarkson S 6684
Claros b821 b993
Clarus I 5454d
Clarysse W 6436s c801 [R]a510
Classen A [R]k007 C [M]a035 [R]807
Claudel G [R]2249
Clausi B g502 [R]c101
Clauss M 8448s [R]a306 c374
Claussen M 9969
Clayton A [R]k551 C 1318 J

Congar Y 242 4350 ^{M}4065
  4242 k800-11 †q222
Congourdeau M ^{R}9975
Conigliaro F 4050
Coninck F de 1675
Conio C 9121 ^{E}720
Conley J k228 **R** ^{D}k938
Conn J ^{R}5368 **W** ^{R}k882
Connelly D 5405
Connery ^{M}4637
Conniry C g080
Connor W 679
Connors R 3647 4637
Conrad C ^{R}8525 8547 8571
  D a033 **L** ^{E}8897 8923
Conroy C ^{D}3239 k507
Conser W 2313
Conso D ^{E}92
Constable G g664
Constantelos D 4187
Constantinidis A c793
Constantinopolis 5138 b838
  b841 → *Ist-,Byz-*
Constas N g397
Contardo ^{M}7667
Conte G 8366 k973
Contenson H de b317 ^{R}457
  6678 b908 b911 c340
Conti G b278
Contini R 5925
Contreni J ^{R}2637
Contreras E g529 ^{M}g069
Conus H 5406
Conway E k941 ^{R}k946 **M**
  k918 ^{R}4234 5058 7896
  8028
Conybeare F 6274
Conzelmann H 2154
Cooey P 5279 ^{R}3090
Coogan D 1537 **M** a034*a*
  ^{E}1113 **R** 2635
Cook A ^{R}8367 **B** ^{R}8122 **E**
  6914 8330 ^{R}5969 6958
  6962 **G** ^{E}4859 ^{R}413 **J**
  2584*a* 5926 6820 6915 **M**
  ^{R}3525 8904 **P** ^{R}k683 **R**
  5407 b614*b* b616 ^{M}5440
  ^{R}2912 **S** c603
Cooke B 628 3404 ^{R}3552 **D**
  ^{R}k278 **V** q304
Coolsaet W m9567
Cooper A a824 k433 ^{R}8918
  D ^{R}k613 **J** ^{D}2327 ^{R}3587
  6043 8145 q060 **K** ^{R}q081
  R g424 **W** 7939*a*
Coote R 1200
Copan P ^{R}2395 4149 8016
Cope L ^{R}2258
Copeland F k553 **M** 4973*a*

N 3866 **W** 4747
Copenhaver B 7758
Copher C c604
Copley A ^{R}729
Copon P ^{R}3705
Coquin M ^{F}43 ^{R}g622
Corbato C †q223
Corben T 2887
Corbett J c185
Corbier M ^{M}6435
Corbin H 8953s
Corbo R 4547 **V** ^{M}q098
Corcoran L a826*a*
Cordes P c426
Cordier P ^{R}9731
Corduan W g853
Corell J 5756
Corely J ^{R}2472 9251
Coren M ^{R}5357
Coreth ^{D}6699
Corey M 1917 2314
Coriden J ^{R}4399
Corinthus 8592 a405 b952s
  c600s
Corkery J 4860
Corley K 5187 c605 ^{R}5241
Cormie L ^{R}4927
Corneanu N 4428
Cornelison R ^{R}5477 q027
Cornelius F 9517 **I** 3279
  8650 a638
Cornell T 9859 ^{E}c606 c872
  ^{T}297
Corner M 4915
Cornes A 4604
Cornette K ^{E}562
Cornick D 2910 ^{R}4813
Cornille C ^{E}8170
Cornman R ^{T}7212
Cornoldi G k409
Cornwall R 4051s
Cornwell J q274 **P** 4188
Corona R 2099*b*
Corradi F ^{T}g716
Correll C 5927 ^{R}5918
Correns D 7251
Corrigan D †q223* **K** a565
Corrington G 5188 ^{R}5255
Cors i Meya J b209
Corsani B 2168 6275
Corsato C g081 g539 ^{R}b644
Corsten T ^{R}a827
Cortès E ^{R}779
Cortes R 1592
Cortés Fuentes D ^{E}5073
-Soriano A k139
Cortese E 5498*b* ^{R}2424
  3175 8734 q004
Cortey M 1183b

Cory C ^{R}1589 1593
Cosand J ^{D}8651
Cosgaya J ^{T}g425
Cosgrove B 7941
Costa C 8368 ^{R}8381 **R**
  ^{E}4877 ^{T}4862
Costabel B ^{R}2719
Costamagna G 2494*d*
Costas N ^{R}5138
Coste R 3023 7885 ^{R}1921
Costen M 4974
Costigan R k221 ^{R}k361
Côté A 8349*c*
Cothenet E 2115 6916 ^{R}110
  3558 6869 k502
Cotter J 6360 **W** ^{R}5108
Cottier G 9285
Cottin J a566 ^{R}1253 2803
  3428 a583 g955
Cotton H b046 b179
Cottret B ^{R}k160 k284
Couchoud C ^{R}c508
Couliano I ^{M}7798 **J** ^{M}7764
Coulie B ^{E}g370 ^{R}g368
Coulot C 1278
Couloubaritsis L 8588
Coulson W ^{E}736
Counet J ^{R}2359 g814
Countryman L 1593 2116
  4604*
Courbin P b312
Cournelis J 243
Court J 5408 ^{R}5390
Courtenay W ^{D}g694 ^{R}g724
Courtés J ^{M}1371
Courth F 3607 q128 ^{R}5102
Courthial P 1973*b* q164*a*
Courtils J des b930 c226
Courtine-Denamy S ^{T}7357
Courtright N c013
Cousar C ^{R}3937
Cousin H 1199*c* 2585 g002
  ^{R}5482 7152
Cousins E q027
Coutagne M ^{E}k414
Couto A ^{R}c466
-Teixeira F ^{R}k969
Couture A 5409 **P** 5280
Covell R 4975
Coviello D ^{R}2976
Covington M ^{R}28
Covito A g082*a*
Cowan C c342 **T** 3608
  8068
Coward H 4198*c* 9075
Cowdin D ^{R}3047
Cowdrey H ^{R}g752
Cowell S k974
Cowen J c227

Derchain P b534 [R]6108
b695
-Urtel M 6116 [R]b540
D'Ercole M a642
Derda T 6443
Derenbourg H [M]6079
Dericquebourg R 8245
[R]8266
Derksen J c966 [R]1585 k002
Derkuš b320
Dermange F 4613
Der Manuelian P 9373
[D]b499
Dermience A 5191a [R]5183
5211
Der Nersessian S a568
Derosa E [D]1821
De Rosa G 9288 [R]k669
de Rossi G [M]a138 a162a
a165
de' Rossi A [M]2739
De Rossi Filibeck E 1045
Derousseaux L 7607
Derrenbacker R [R]c600
Derrett J 249 9124 [M]363
Derrida J [M]3948 k774 q053
q066
Derroitte H 4981
Derville A [E]763
De Salvo L a365
Desanges J c549 [R]8786
b255
Descamps S [R]a645
Descartes R [M]2938 k227s
Descat R c790b [R]9508
Deschamps L [R]9938
Deschner K cg085
Desclès J 6650
Descœudres J [E]82
Descy S 4195
Deselaers P 1539
Desforges G [D]2070
Deshen S 7501 [E]408
De Siano F 4057a
Desideri P b745
de Silva D 6775b 7062
8526
De Simone G 5036c
Desjardins M 7757c 7761
[R]3970 7788 7839
DeSmet [M]5026 5096 9177 P
[E]107 [R]6107
Desmond W ck677e
De Souza C 1418 4196a
Desreumaux A 5988 6882
[E]c102
Desroche H †q229
Desroches-Noblecourt C
b696

Desroussilles F [E]a570
Dessel J [R]a821 P van 1062
Dessi G [R]k891
Destro A 8673c c615 g519b
Deswarte T g673
Desy P [R]9830
Detienne M [E]8071
Dette C g674
Dettenhofer M 9729 [E]0462
Dettling W [R]1139 2149
Dettori E r0306
Detweiler R [D]1819 [F]46
Detzler W [R]k769
Deun P van [E]0633
Deurloo K 1388c [R]9255
Deuser H k868
Deutsch N 7814 [D]3786 R
5758 a872
Devauchelle D 6117 [E]b687
Devčić I 4197 [R]k563
Develin R 9548 [R]c353
Dever W 8657 a037s a761a
[E]0463 [M]9242 a945 [R]9186
a168 b074 b144
Devijver H a312 [R]a328
c184 c640 c798
Deville R 4433
Deviller O 9760
Devillers L [R]0317 O 9783b
[R]8364
Devine A 6277 [R]9654
De Virgilio G 6367 [R]5652
c713 k465 k510 k515
Devis F [E]g731
Devisch R [E]409
De Vitiis P q013e
De Vito R 6005
Devos R †q230
de Vries B b203
DeVries S 2237
de Waal E 3025
Dewan L 3701
De Weese D 9014
De Wette [M]k404
Dewey A 6871 J 5192 7919
De Witt C 3026
Deyo S 1062*
De Young D 2320
De Zan R 3122
Dharmaraj J 4058
Dhavamony M 4198a
4982a
Diakonoff I a039
Diamond E 3358 4557c
[R]7284
Dianich S 3879 4059 [R]1510
2909 4067 g068
Diano C 9549
Díaz Esteban F 7348 [E]7417

Díaz Marcos C 3977b
-Mas P 7349
-Moreno J q246
-Salazar R [E]7997 k564
Dibble H a195 a201
Di Berardino A 8382 g086
[E]762 4340
Dicen D a434
Dicenso J 6719
Dick I g005s J [E]570
Dickens A k087 C [M]1853
W [R]1323 k756
Dickinson C q192 E [M]1865
O a923
Dicou B b152 c527
Didache g198-g204 [M]g174
Diderot [M]2938
Di Donna A [R]q056
Didyma b856a
Didymus A g355s [M]3575
Diebner B 2617 7146 7849a
[M]k470
Dieckmann B [R]3271 7742 E
[D]3610
Diedrich F 597
Diego Lobejón M de 2670
-Sánchez M 3591 [R]b644
Diem W [R]5068
Diemen A van [R]g140
Diepbouse D [R]k712
Dierken J 4606
Diethart J 6479
Dietrich G 3080c M 2428
5891 8658-8661 b323
[E]738 b262 [E]185 [F]47 W
1823 k779 [E]2772
Dietz E [E]769 S b931
Díez K [D]g959
-del Río I [R]8006
-Fernández M b126
-Macho [M]2544
-Merino J 5928 L 2506
5119a
-Presa M 4201
Di Gangi M [T]k150
Di Gennaro T 8833 b433
Di Giovanni G k327
Di Giovine P 6240b [R]6606
Di Grazia O [R]k366
Dihle A 6278 9550 [R]c549
Dijk F van a366a J van
†q231
-Hemmes F van 1711 †q232
Dijkstra K 8834 [R]8838 M
[M]5899
Dik H 6279
Dilanni A 4549
Di Lella A [R]875 2529 2684
7302

Doret E 6120
Dorff E ^{E}3228
Dorian N ^{R}6660
Doriani P 6281
Dorin R ^{T}c738a
Dorival G 2587 g298 ^{E}78
    571
Dorman W 1285
Dormeyer D 2125 ^{R}c661
Dorner I 2818
Doron C ^{R}a206
Dorrell P ^{R}b193 c123
Dorrfuss E 4727
Dorrien G 4753s ^{R}267
Dorsett M ^{R}k452 k556 k656
Dorsey D ^{D}c550
Dorsz W ^{R}3728
Dossetti J 4435
Dossin G ^{M}5882
Dostal W ^{F}49
Dostálová R ^{E}208 ^{R}9916
Dotan A 7407 7422a ^{E}161
Doterding P g945b
Dothan 463
Dothan M a924 T a924
    b049 ^{M}a926
Dotolo C ^{T}2967
Doty W q032
Douch b679s
Doudna G ^{M}a135b
Doughty M ^{R}g680
Douglas J ^{E}811s M 3177
    5285 7957 c620
-Klotz N 8956
Doukellis P 9863
Doukhan J 5711
Doumet C a696
-Serhal C c805
Doutreleau L 3575 ^{E}g355
Dovere E ^{R}3458 g074
Dow S †q234
Dowd S ^{R}1709
Dowden K 8471 ^{E}8411
Dowey E k047
Downes D ^{E}1879
Downet M ^{E}153
Downey M 4436 S b322
Downing F 2126 4607 5420
    8372 8594 ^{R}2098 P ^{E}6628
Downs F 4985
Doxey D ^{D}9375
Doxiadis E a826b
Doyle D ^{R}5351 W ^{R}k169
Dozeman T ^{R}9256 c513
Dra' Abu Naga b568
Dräger O a797 P ^{D}8472
Draffen M ^{R}q026
Dragula A q131b ^{R}1547
Drake A 9973 H ^{R}a018

Drane J 3027 8247 q033 ^{R}2
Draper J g174
Drechsel J ^{E}787 W 1239
Drecoll V ^{D}g327
Drees W 2322s
Drehem 9478 b408
Dreher M 9974
Drenkhahn R ^{R}b603
Drerup H †q235
Drescher H k991
Dresen G ^{R}178
Dresher B 2508
Dresken-Weiland J b837
Drewermann E 1931 1942-5
    4354 8070 k035 ^{M}1920-
    41 k548
Drewery B g910a
Drews R a925 ^{M}9544a
Drey J ^{M}k307s
Dreyer E ^{R}188 4656
Dreyfus ^{M}7606 7645 7733
Dreytza ^{D}5868
Driessche V van ^{R}a870
Driessen J b997
Drijvers H ^{R}2607 8885 J
    a965 ^{E}g678 ^{R}b354
Drink A g275
Drinkard J ^{R}2424 5755 c712
Drioton-Vandier ^{M}9428
Dritsas D ^{E}871
Drobner H g088 g428 ^{E}g378
    ^{M}g069 ^{R}g479
Droge A 3229 ^{R}4647
Dromey F 3700
Drori J c928
Drory R 57737408
Droste zu Hülshoff V a728
Droulia L ec929
Drower M a145
Dru A ^{T}k416
Druet P 3028
Drury C ^{R}1113
Dryer E ^{R}4437
D'Sa F 645 ^{E}140
D'Souza C 8248a K q377
Dubielzig U c231
Dubois G ^{R}2612 J 475
    7866a ^{R}809 L 6444 8473
Dubourdieu A ^{R}9875
Dubuisson D 8331
Duby G ^{E}1722
Ducat J 8474
Duch L 1618 k520b
Duchemin J 8332
Duchesne L a165 ^{M}k822
-Guillemin J 6512
Duchet-Suchaux G c145*
Duchini F ^{E}4755
Duchrow U 4756

Duckworth R 9202
Dudek R ^{T}2065
Dudley J 8529 R ^{R}4396
-Smith T ^{E}1005
Duduit M ^{E}1533
Dünnbier W 4757
Duerksen P ^{R}3726 c874
Dürr H ^{E}29
Dufay F 3689
Duff N k875 P 3930
Duffe B ^{E}7
Dufferin ^{M}c925
Duffy E g960s k104 S ^{R}348
Duft J 2468 ^{F}50
Dugan J q171
Duggan P ^{T}395
Duhaime J 7021 7714 8249
    ^{R}3798 7105
Duhoux Y 6282s ^{R}c381
Dujancourt S ^{R}4174 4593
    k824
Dujarier M q056
Duke A ^{E}k048 E ^{E}8530
Dulaey M a569
Duling D 1240
Dulk M den k757b ^{R}1523
Dulles A 2869 2890s 3598
    3732 4986a 5360b q222
    ^{M}5669 ^{R}3766 8122
Dulley D a868
Dumais A ^{R}k994 M ^{M}4699
Dumas A 4101a F 4101a
Dumbrell B ^{R}2272 W 3123
    5421
Dumézil G 7911s ^{M}8331
Dumm D ^{R}4546
Dumont J ^{F}51
Dumortier J ^{T}2173
Dumoulin H 9126 †q236
Dunand F b679
Dunayevsky I ^{F}a246
Duncan J 6984 ^{R}k025
-Jones R a873 a900b c806
Dunde S ^{E}8250
Dunham S ^{R}8828 b439
Dunkel G 6400
Dunkly J ^{R}2098
Dunlap T ^{T}g112
Dunlop R ^{R}1113 k335
Dunn J 3120 3427 4607*
    7182 7691 9761 ^{E}7609
    ^{M}2251 ^{R}9823 O ^{T}2994 P
    6893
Dunnett W ^{R}2112
Dunstan A ^{R}1583 4487
Dupleix A ^{E}g248
Dupont F a299 J 250 3437
    ^{M}q059
-Roc R 6284

Eigner D ^{R}a247
Eijk A van k634 ^{R}1625
    4238 k295 **P van der**
    c438 ^{R}c468
Eiland M ^{R}752
Eilberg-Schwartz H ^{R}2849
Einstein A ^{M}2763
Eisele J a196
Eisenman R 6925 ^{M}6909
    6916 6922
-/Wise ^{M}7026 7070 7085
    7111
Eisenstein H ^{R}842 8959
    9349 c211 c986 g793
Eissa A b535
Ekeland I ^{M}3146
Ekenberg A 2819
Ekstrom R 814
Elam a321 a686a b469
    b481b b483
Elanskaya A 6203
Elath M 9291
Elayi A a874 **J** a874 b300
Elazar D 3124
El'azar W ^{M}7363
Elberfelder 2704
Elberti A ^{M}4119
Elbogen I 3178
Eldamaty M b678
Elder C 7921 **E** ^{E}103 ^{R}g653
Elderen R van ^{D}7613
Elders D ^{R}8210 **L** 2951
    5424 g830b
Elephantine 5931 8722
    b663-b670 c890b
Eleusis 8595
Eleuteri P 9975
Elford R 7998
Elgvin R ^{M}7035 **T** 6985
Eliade M 7916-8 ^{M}423 8084
    8331 9101
Elias J ^{D}9377
Elior R 3787a 7429
Eliot G ^{M}1853 **T** ^{M}1862
    1870 5096 k031
Elitzur Y c068 c152
Elizondo V ^{E}405
Elkab b681
Ella G k237
Ellacuria I 9292 ^{E}4870
Ellenburg B 1373
Ellens J ^{R}2762
Ellenson D 7537
Eller C 5286 **V** k572
Ellero G 6219
Elliger W b783
Ellingsen M 4758
Ellington J 2722
Ellingworth P ^{T}5081

Elliott C ^{R}4822 **D** ^{M}c731 **J**
    2562-4 6863 c625s ^{R}889
    1113 2258 2556s 2569
    2604 2612-two 2633 2682
    5121 6879 6912 6933
    g197 **M** ^{R}5655 9314 g114
    k752 **N** ^{R}3970 **T** ^{R}9995
Ellis E 1639 **M** 7615 g009
    R 3104b **W** 9378
Ellison J ^{D}1849
Elluin J 5425
Ellul J 4759 ^{F}54 ^{M}4827
    4895 k824 †q243
Ellwood R k573
Elm S 4550 ^{M}5185
Elman Y 7252 ^{R}7270 7298
Elsas C ^{R}42
Elsbernd M 4760
Elsdon R 3032
Elsner J 8067 a040 a522
    a523 c952b ^{E}9786 ^{R}5138
    a637
Elwanger J b693
Elwell W 815
Elwolde J 5801 ^{E}5755
    ^{R}1261 7364 7446 c457
    ^{T}5741
Elwood C ^{D}g963
Elzey W 8084b
Emar 474 8658 8666 8702b
    b323-6
Emberling G ^{D}b374
Emeis D ^{R}1448
Emerson R ^{M}7919 k310
Emerton J 5929 ^{D}2542 ^{E}501
    ^{F}55 ^{R}1126 1328 2060
    2699 3798 5845 6296
    6968 7362 9246 k405
Emery G ^{R}g141 k014 **K**
    c172 ^{E}g848
Emmel S 7867 8758 ^{D}g629
Emmerick R 6513
Emmerson G ^{M}379 **R** 7886
    ^{E}g682 ^{R}g887
Emmett C g010
Emmons S k574
Empedocles ^{M}8550
Empereur J ^{D}k926
Empiricus S 8516
Emprie J ^{R}k001
Encrevé A ^{E}816=k575
Enderle G ^{E}4761
Enders M 8531 ^{R}3882
Endesfelder E 9379
Endres F ^{M}8106
Endruweit A a247
Enermalm A 3283
Engammare M k049 ^{R}k034
En Gedi b028

Engel D ^{R}7664 **U** k964
    ^{E}3733
Engelhardt H ^{R}594
Engell J q311
Engelmann H b784 c439
Engels J ^{R}9597 c803 **O**
    ^{R}g055
Engen C Van ^{E}68
Engineer A 9024b
England J ^{R}3599
English E ^{E}573
Englund G ^{R}8787 **R** 6007
    c234 c347 ^{R}c153
Ennabli A b249
Ennis A †q244
Enns P ^{R}1288
Ennulat A 2131
Eno B ^{R}g108 g169
Enright D †q245
Enrique y Tarancón V
    †q246
Epalza M de 3463
Ephesus 520 8365 b783-
    b797
Ephraem S g611-7 ^{M}c470
    g672
Ephraïm f 2241 7616
Epicurus 8548 ^{M}8387
Epidaurus 6466
Epiphanius S g357-9 ^{M}b132
Epp ^{M}2455 **E** 2565 **V** c967
Epperly B ^{R}k910
Eprem m 3462b
Epstein C b110 **M** ^{R}8240
Equiza J 4871
Erasmus D 6269 ^{M}1304
    2635 k086-k102
Erbse H 6370 9551 ^{E}8532
    ^{R}9583
Erdel T ^{R}812 **Y** 7158
Eretz-Israel Byz 739ss
Ergardt J †q247
Erğili b824
Erhart A ^{R}6607
Erickson M 255 1288 2893
    3506 3532*b 3611 3880
    ^{M}3446 c590 ^{R}k565
Eriksson K a762
Eriugena J ^{M}g858s
Erkanal A b281
Erlemann K ^{D}5426
Erler M ^{D}1821 ^{R}8569
Erlich A g011 **V** c528
Erling B ^{R}7911
Erndl K 9078
Ernest J ^{T}6324
Ernst H ^{D}5877 ^{E}195 **J** q369
    M 5643 ^{R}1163 **R** 6204 **W**
    4752

.. (García) -de Paredes J
   5123
-Estebanez E 5197
-Gómez M k586
-Hernández B 6535*b* 6538
-Hirschfeld C 4443
-Jurado F 6539*a*
-López F 1427 [R]666
-Martinez F 3931 5939
   6933s 7026 7102s q100
   [M]6912 [R]5920 6925 6949
   9422
-Monge J c709*b*
-Moreno A 1428*a* [R]1141
   3778 6366
-Murga Vázquez J 5433
   [R]5393
-Oro J g967 k079
-Recio J 9449 c234
-Roca J 4767
-Rojo E k587*a*
-Sánchez J 8382
-Santos A r1157
-Trapiello J 1329 [R]9209
-y García A q253
Garcin J 8960
Gardeil P [R]3934
Gardin J a052 [E]b486
Gardiner A c852 R k315
Gardner E 4614* I 7815s J
   c639 [R]c659 c746 P [E]788
Garelli G [R]g814 P 9450*a*
Garelli-François M a437
Garfi S b582
Gargan E †q258
Garhammer E k317 k588
   [R]1832
Garijo-Guembe M 4068
   4213 [D]3610
Garizim b072
Garland D r7054 L [E]464 R
   8480s [M]a380
Garner R [R]k664
Garofalo I c444
Garrard J [R]k342 k443
-Burnett V [E]413
Garrett A 6247 6254*b* C
   [R]5400 J 5650
Garrigues J 2776
Garrison R [D]3884
Garrudo C [R]4013
Garsiel M 1099
Garstein O g968s
Garsur b412
Gartner J 4547
Garuti A 4355s
Garvey J 4214 [R]4021
Gascoigne R 2339
Gascou J [R]9800 9814 9855

Gaseltine K [R]8020
Gasparri C a644 F 6666
Gasper H [R]8117
Gaspert-Sauch G [R]1418
Gasse A 8766 b525 [R]b556
Gasslein B [E]80
Gassmann G [R]4313 L 1928
Gaster T [M]3800*b* †q259
Gasti F c445 [R]668
Gaston L [R]7726
Gates B 8053*b* M b747
Gatier P b035*c* [R]a811
Gattermann G [F]63
Gatti E [T]7703 G 4768
   [R]4612* S c057
Gatto L g691s [R]g687
Gatz E [R]a987
Gaube H q317
Gaudemans W 7846
Gaudemet J 4215
Gauer H a576
Gauger J 9616*b*
Gaume [M]g433
Gaus J g693*a* q355
Gauthier N [E]c042 P 6430
   6450 a402s
Gautier P c101
-di Confiengo E a250
Gaventa B 5124s
Gavrilovic Z 1948
Gawlikowski M 8882 a318*d*
   b350s [R]a322 b355
Gawronski R k743
Gay C 4769 k589 D 1896*a*
Gayá J g882*b* [R]7601
Gaza 6023 b029
Gazajca W 7600*a*
Gaziantep b826
Gaziaux E 4615 4615*
   k387 [R]3571 k386 k741
Geach P [F]64
Gebara I 5293
Gebelein a183
Gebhardt G 4220*c*
Geckle R [D]9792
Geer N [R]5328
Geerard M [E]25
Geering L q038
Geerlings W [E]152 539 g203
   [R]a446
Geernaert D 4216*a*
Geffen R [E]3181
Geffré C 1296 1299b 3746*b*
   4307*c* 5000 8144*b* 8163*a*
   9017 k590
Geffroy C 2128
Gehrke H [D]9433
Geider M 9881
Geiger J b046[M]7542 7572

[R]8578
Geis M 6630 S 5198
Geisen R 7768 [R]4818
Geisler N 9018 g820
Geist L 946
Geivett D 2777 R 8164
Gelabert Balester M 5001
Gelb I [M]6024 c360
Gelber Y [R]g029
Gelder A [R]5306 G van
   6073
Gelinas M 9206
Gelio R a969
Geller M c469 [E]506 681
   [R]5932 5941 6031 9454
   b285 b389 c154 c458
   c574 S [D]1394 c391
Gellian J 3992*b
Gellner E 8001 [M]8943 q039
Gelpi D k591
Gelston A g606 [R]3169 8677
Gelzer T g308*b* [R]8596 9596
Gempeler R b665
Genderen J van 5651
Genest O 1771*b* 3932
Genette G 1378
Gengler D [R]8488 O [R]b990
Genicot L †q260
Gennep A van 7905 [M]7981
Gennip P van [R]k324
Genosko G g434
Genot-Bismuth J 7160 7472
Genre E 1929 8165 [M]q141
Gensichen H [M]947 [R]4166
   8995
Gentileschi G [R]7240 g641
Gentili B [F]65 M g970
Genton P [R]5482
Gentry K 3651
Genz H b158
Geoffroy B a091*a*
Geoghegan J b107
Geoltrain P [D]5142
Geominy W a369
George A b377 [D]c154 C
   4069 D 2136 J 1836*c* K
   4444 M 1165
Georgedes K [D]g694
Georges P 9553s
Georgi D 7198*b*
Georgia 6257 6259 b743
   c526
Georgiadou A 9296*a*
Gera L [D]8162
Geraci G [R]6434
Gerard N [M]c973
Gerardi P 9442*b*
Gerasa a852 b035 b170
   c555*a*

Girlanda A 1167
Girod S g014
Girón L r2523
Gischala b122
Gisel P 2244 7973c 9295
    k490b k992 ᴹ3986
Gisi M ᴱg892 ᵀa240
Gismondi G 2333
Gispert-Sauch G 3513b
    ᴿ720 1652 2861
Gitay Z a580
Gitin S b065 ᴱa094
Gittin S b049
Gittins A 9127a ᴿ4967
Gittlen B ᴿa777
Giussani L 8169 ᴹk830
Giustiniani P 1340b g895
    ᴿk867
Give B de 4198e
Giversen S ᴱ487 ᶠ67
Giza a092a b612-b633
Gizzi E ᴿa000b
Gjongecaj S a877
Glaeser Z ᴰ4218
Gläser G ᴱ58 M ᴿ773
Glässer A 597
Glanzmann W ᴰb463 ᴿc547
Glare P 1504d
Glasner R 7470
Glass J ᴹb739 W 1431a
Glasscoe M ᴿg636
Glasser A ᶠ68 ᴿ7636
Glassner J 9498 c360
Glatt D 1379
-Gilad D ᴿ9260
Glaz M ᴱ415
Glazier M ᴱ818 S ᴿ5051
Gleason E k138 M 8385
Gleixner H 4617*
Glen-Doepel W ᵀ1295
Gless D 1909
Glessmer E 2541 U 6986
Glickler-Chazon E 3182
Glinert L 5791s ᴿ5732 5795
    7287 c997
Glinka L ᴿa608
Gliściński J 9981
Glob P ᴹb449
Globig C 5257
Gloder G ᴰk931
Glueck N ᴹb144 b154
Glünz M 874a
Gnanapragasam V 3011
Gnilka C g097 J 5652s
    ᴰ7851 ᴹ858
Gnoli G 8869a 8887 ᴿ9057
Gnomon Bibliog./zu erwar-
    ten 1019
Gnuse R 1950 ᴿ4469 9256

Godart L 6489 6492 6667
    b975 b977 b984 c070
Godbey J k797 ᴿk099 k129
Goddard A 9020
Godden M 1844a
Godel E ᴹ3526
Godet J ᴰg437
Godey J 4670b
Godlove T 8041d
Godoy A 896 R 6313
Godron G 8768
Godwin J ᵀ7763
Godzieba A 1298 2779
    3408 3510 ᴿ3552
Göbl R a878
Goebs K 6129
Goecke-Seischab M a581
Goedegebuure J 1826
Goedicke H 6130 9384a
    b504 b552 ᴿ8810
Goeltring J ᴿ4546
Goenaga J ᴿ5496
Göreme b827
Görg M 2245 3285 5815
    5822 5849 5857 6131
    7770 b117 c155s c529
Görgemanns H 8541
Goergen D 3511 P 1827
Görman U 2344
Goertz H 9297 g973 k134
Goerwitz R 2511 5717 5720
    5853
Goes J ᴿ6618
Gössmann E g871
Goetschel R 7606 ᴿ7448
Goetz H ᴿg697
Götzelt T 6013
Goff B 8595
Goffart W ᴿ167
Goffi J 3041 T 9128
Gohary J b541
Goichot É ᴿk819
Goizueta R k120 ᴱ5006
Golan A 8077
Golan b110-2
Golb N 6935 ᴹ7096b
Gold A 3042 D 8004a
    ᴿ7550 V ᴱ2684 ᴿ7054
Goldberg A 3323 C 9683 E
    7550 I 6988 9386 J 7544
    a932 ᴿ1189 7704 c148 T
    ᴱ371
Goldenberg D ᴱ507 G 6592
    ᴿ5944 N 5295 R ᴿ7177
    7293
Goldfus H b039
Goldhill S a532 ᴹa536
    ᴿa531
Goldin O ᴿc273

Goldingay J 580 1298*
    1599 ᴿ1310 2759 5296
Goldish M ᴿ7495
Goldman B a506 E ᴿ7309
    7312 S ᴱk179
Goldmann M ᵀ4592
Goldsmith J 6635 S 1828
    a973
Goldstein B a825 J 9628
    q040
Goldwasser O 6132s
Goldwurm H ᴱ7287
Golemon L ᴿ5206
Golenko V a879
Golinkoff R 6634
Golitzin A ᴿ245 9970 g621
    g849
Gollinger H 7625 ᴿ7718
Gollwitzer B ᴿ4702 H
    ᴹk831 †q263
Golomb D ᴿ2544
Golovina V c808
Gomaà F b723 c071
Gombault A 5196b
Gomes ᴿ104 A 3615 M
    8260
-Barbosa M 4071
Gómez B a755b P ᴹk108
-Acebo I 2850
-Aranda M 7419 ᴿ7466
-de Castro A 8382
-Kelley S r5262
-Mier V cq278
-Ortiz M 1678b
Gonçalves F 9208
Gong Y d6014
Gonnet D ᴰk913 G k903a
Gonur b472
González ᴹ1105 A 4879a C
    5126 ᴹk318 I 8227b
    8261a J 4878 4937 5007
-Blanco A 9982 b332 ᴱ221
    b227 ᴿb319
-Caballero A 1531b
-Carvajal Santabarbara L
    4770s
-de Cardedal O 1432 5438
-Echegaray J a047 c072
-Faus J 261 3512-4 4357s
    4879b 9298 k593 ᴿ4941
-García F ᴿ9698
-Lamadrid A 9209
-Montes A 2898 3736
    ᴿq077
-Núñez J 5990
-Pola M ck318b
-Salazar J b766
Gooch J ᴿ6808 g591 L
    k180a

Hegedus T 8774
Hegel G ᴹ3524 7925-8
 9271*a* k323-ᵐck333 k996
Hegemann P ᴿb302
Heger P 5864
Hegesippus ᴹ9711
Hegy D 8556*b* **P** ᴿk635
Hehmeyer L c191
Heid S c934s ᴿg560
Heide A van der 7190
Heidegger M k366 k840-9
 ᴹ648 6698 6719 7964
 9159 k489 k596
Heideking J ᴿ9889
Heideman E 5014 ᴿ7654
Heidemanns K q133
Heider G ᴿ8654
Heidermanns F 204
Heidorn L ᴰb716
Heidt P 7632
Heiene G ᴿk738*a*
Heijke J ᴿ19
Heijst A van 5204
Heil S 3894
Heilbronner O k603
Heilman S ᴹ7537
Heim D ᴿk660 **F** 3288 8389
 9989 **S** 4367 8013 8175
 ᴿ2345 3760 8122 8153
 8184
Heimann H g977a **N** ᴰa586
Heimerdinger J q101 ᴿ6863
Hein I a646 ᴿa187 **R** k358
Heine B 6566 **H** ᴹk334
Heinegg P ᵀ1942*
Heinemann H 4143*b* **O** a132
Heinen H c240 ᴿ6425 b531
Heinrichs J c622
Heintz J b337 b575s
Heinzelmann M 9304
Heinzer F ᴱ2640
Heinzmann R q366
Heipp-Tamer C a884
Heisel J a254
Heiser R ᴿ4639* **W** ᴿa610
 and all ThD citations
Heitink G 3721
Heitsch E 8546 ᴹ8577
Heitzenrater R k281
Helberg J 9305
Helck W 6138s 9393 b508
 c810*a*
Held S a198
Helden J b967
Helderman J ᴿ7785
Helfta G ᴹa455
Helgeland J ᴱ3289
Heliopolis aeg. b627
Hell L ᴰ3655 k316

Hellamo G ᴰ5444
 Hellegouarc'h **J** ᴿ9760
 9772 9809
Helleman A 4228 **W** g278
 ᴱ587
Hellemo G 3739
Heller M 2348*b*
Hellestam S b613*b*
Hellholm D 7774*a* ᴱ88 ᶠ79
Hellmann M a255*a*
Hellwig M ᴱ818
Helm A van der 4368 **P**
 3129 ᴿk919
Helmis A 8776*a*
Helmont F van ᴹk240
Helms ᴹb202
Helsper M ᴿc715
Heltzer M 5758 5881 9501
 b232*a* ᴿ5774 8694 c379
 c777
Helve H c657
Helwing B a769
Hemann C ᴿa571
Hemelrijk J b885* ᴿb751
 b783 b885*
Hemker C c192 **E** 7713*b*
Hemmerle K 4337 ᴹ3608*
 †q275
Hempel C 7028 **W** 6016
Hemphill K 4083
Hempton D k335
Hemrick E 1440
Hen Y c936
Henaut B k499*b*
Hendel R 2433 3969*c* 6900
 6937 9215 ᴿ3945 6043
Henderson F 5205*a* **I** 1277*c*
 K ᴰk922 **L** 5066*b*
Hendricks F 957 **O** 2020**b* **S**
 1065 **W** ᴿ789 818 1210
 3888 g979 q001
Hendrix G g837 ᴿ9347 **R**
 a919
Hengel M 268 3469 7191s
 9636 ᴱ2591
Hengsbach F 4765*b* 4803*b*
Hengst K ᴱ139
Hengstl J 6455 c241
Henig M a483 **R** ᴿg577 **W**
 a050
Henkel A g921 **W** ᴱ958
Henkelman W a484
Henking S 1951 c658
Henn V ᴿ173 **W** 3740 q222
Henne P 3470 7607 g190
 g206 g232
Hennelly A 4885 ᴰ3562
Hennesey J 454
Hennessy A c075 c937 **J** ᶠ82

Hennings R g508s ᴹ1641
Henrich R 7135
Henrici P ᴹ3569
Henrickson R b768*a*
Henricus VIII ᴹk110
Henrivaux O ᴿ1497
Henrix H 3324
Henry C 3886 ᴿ2911 4186
 8044 k660 **G** 2821 **M**
 k369
Henshaw R 1736 8677
Henson J 3992 **K** ᴿc712
Henten J van 9700 ᴱ6456
Hentschel F a442
Henze B k151 **K** 959
Heper M b748
Hepper F c300
Heraclitus ᴹ6420
Heraty J ᴱ820
Herbermann C ᴱ6571
Herbert ᴹ1850 **A** 4369 **E**
 ᴿ6960
Herbordt S a702
Herborn W ᴱ132
Herbst S ᴿ4885*a*
Herbut J 5497*b*
Herculaneum a114 c054
 c773
Herden H ᴿ9420
Herder J ᴱ3685 ᴹ7683 k241-
 k243 k365
Herdt J 7935
Heredia J ᴿ798* 830
Heriban J 2711
Herion G ᴱ754
Herklots H 2701*b*
Herman Z ᴿ2710*
Hermaniuk M †q276
Hermans K ᵀk780
Hermansen S 6865
Hermary A b907 ᴿb820 b913
Hermas ᴹ3470 6798 c205-8
 g190
Hermelink J 1548
Hermias ᴹg385
Hermopolis 5956 6422 a311
 b686
Herms E 8124 k604*a*
Hermsen E ᴹ8755*a*
Hernández M c811 **R** ᴿ3899
Herodotus 8747*a* ᴹ6279 6279
 6339 6352 6518*c* 8806*b*
 8857 8865 9261 9473
 9507 9551 9554-7 9564
 9566 9580s 9585-7 9593
 9602-4 9748 a174 b029
 c546 c786
Herr B 8678 **L** b200 c367 **M**
 a401 ᴱ2229

888 Elenchus of Biblica 11/2, 1995

Hoek A W van den [E]81
Hoekema D [R]k639
Hoeksema G k609
Hölbl G 9395
Hölderlin [M]k212 k840*b* k849
Hölscher U b617
Hönig W 8777
Hoenkamp-Bisschops A 274
Hoepfner W 685 c884
Hoeps J [R]1232
Hörmann G [T]q054
Hoerth A [E]c532
Hoeschke R 7485
Hoet H [R]1180
Höver G 3064*b* [R]316
Höyücek b834
Hoezee S [R]3848
Hofer P [R]436
Hoff R von den [D]a649
Hoffken P 7195
Hoffman B [R]g132 C [T]g832 D
  g279 [D]5207 [R]68 J 3325 L
  3130 3169 [R]3205 M [R]k098
  Y 8679 [E]3256
Hoffmann A [E]g445 F g922 J
  1181*b* 4843*c* [T]g825 M
  1304 P 2143 4370*a* c661
  [D]9694 R 6398 [E]g103 T
  2958 4624* [E]182 Ü [R]1717
Hoffmeier J b102
Hoffmeyer J [T]3594 4583
Hoffner H 6233 6235*a*
  b768*b* [R]6244
Hofius O 3862 4509
Hofmann I [R]9376 J q199
Hofreiter P a443
Hofrichter P [E]4498
Hoftijzer J 1976*c* 5895 [R]5806
Hogan E k244 L 5309 [R]1518
  4642 M 2959
Hoge D k610
Hoglund K 9216 a933
Hoheisel K [D]8699
Hohlfelder R b920
Hohmann F a588*a* J 4371
Hohnjec N 1682
Hoitenga D 3741
Holbert J 1518 1550
Holbrook N [R]a276
Holder R [R]k066
Holdrege B 9131
Holes C [R]5856 6059 6068
Holgate R [R]3732
Holladay C 7187 7196 8598
  W 1175 2247
Holland D [E]g712 G [R]5495
Hollander H 6763*a*
Holleman J 877
Hollenbach D 4682

Hollerich M [R]k934
Holliday P [E]470 a536
Hollis S 6137*b*
Holloway G k301 H c019 R
  k611 S [R]3204
Hollstein W a885s
Holm H [R]b645 K [E]8083 N
  q178
Holman J 3376
Holmberg B 2144 7635 c662
Holmes [M]2509 G q273 M
  [E]126 g159 [R]2689 [R]2744
  6336 W [R]2568
Holmgren F e1551
Holoubek A 3941 c453 3941
  J c453
Holscher L [T]8565
Holt G k234 P [R]227 c975
Holthaus A g019
Holton G 2339
Holtrop P k055
Holtz T 5660
Holtzmann B [R]a648 H [M]383
Holum K c076 [R]c956
Holwerda D 3131 7636
  [R]c725
Holze H 6341
Holzem A k339s
Holzer V 3618
Holzhausen J 8391*a* 8775*a*
Hombergen D 6938
Homerski J 3656
Homerus [M]6879 8509 9562
  9971 a105 c775
Homès-Fredericq D a485
  b174
Honcala A de g873
Honderich T 2960
Honders C [F]83
Honea S [R]8479 8495
Honecker M 4779
Hong E [E]k352 H [E]k352
Hong Ji Hoon [D]g923
Honings M 8625
Honoratus M g567
Hood J 7334*b* 7636 g823 S
  b882*a*
Hoogendijk F 6457
Hoogerwerf S 8178 [R]k602
Hoogstraeten J [M]7702
Hook D 2853
Hooker M 3942 [R]754 P 9214
Hooley D [R]9647
Hooper J [E]k912
Hoopes J a752
Hoornaert E 4886 c663 g361
  q185 [R]4862 9974 g085
Hoose B 4625* [R]4619*
Hoover R [E]2135

Hope N k341
Hopf M c330
Hopkins D [R]5061 5089 k467
  G [M]1879s J 3521 5310
  [R]3043
Hopkinson N [E]8599 [R]9882
Hoppe L 1441 3789 [R]6804
  a503 R q102 [R]c661
Hopper S 270
Hopwood K [R]b862
Horak U a486
Horatius [M]9727 a416
Horbury W 6458s 7638
  [D]7877 [R]6807 7226
Horgan P †q280
Horn [D]1628 F 4626 [E]536
  [R]7609 g056 H [M]8451 J
  c938
Hornblower S 9307 [E]693
Horne B [R]3542 L b466
Horner J [D]k256
Hornsby S [R]1807
Hornung E 5446 6142s 8778
  8809 b545 b570 b578
Horom b901
Horowitz J g706 N 7639 W
  9453 b090
Horrell D [R]3447 6324
Horrocks G 6288
Horsfall N c454
Horsley G 1027 6459 9637
  R 9764 b077s b122 c664
Horsmann A a320
Horst P van der 4449 6460
  6763*b* 7197 [D]7254 [E]591
  6456 8729 9757 [R]1737
  2275 5633 6928 b128
  c632
Horstmanshof M b203
Hort B k986 [R]3534
Hortal J 1442 8284
Horton F b034 b059 [R]77 M
  [R]a393 R 271 W [R]k534
  k700
Hoskier H [M]2578*a*
Hoskin M 751 a835 b237*b*
Hoskins J [R]5314 S 5467*b*
Hoško F b123
Hosp I [E]2303
Hossenfelder M [R]8520
Hossfeld F [D]8667
Hostetter E 878 a258 [D]9217
Hotson H k186
Houdu L 9689*b*
Houlden J 1443 [E]785 [R]2208
  L [E]805 [R]16 59 2130 3545
  3855 4093 4644 5689
  9139 a594 c089 k556 k957
Hourani A [M]g051

Ibn Ezer A ᴹ5769
Ibn Ezra ᴹ7417-20
Ibn Hazm ᴹ7335 7424
Ibn Hišām ᴹg603
Ibn Janah ᴹ7421
Ibn Khaldun ᴹ6066
Ibn Lev J ᴹ7481
Ibn Rabban ᴹ7335
Ibn Rushd ᴹ7470
Ibrahim A ᴰ8914
Ice T g672
Icenogle G 4086 4372
Iconium b837
Idalion 6486 b915
Idel M 3326 7414 7426
	7439s 7508 ᴹ7435 7542
Idfu 6157 b687-b690 → *Edfu*
Idinopulos T 8084*a* ᴱ423
Idrisi b618
Idumaea 500 8656 b151-4
Iersel B van ᴰ884
Iglesia J ᵀ1177
Iglesias A †q286 **I** ᴿg921 **J**
	ᵀk528
Ignatius A g209-15 ᴹ3471
	4043 4102 5498*c* **L** ᴹ4739
	k828*a* **M** ᴹg921
Igwegbe I q134
Ihnatowicz J ᴿ4375
Ikram S c369
Ilan T 1737s 7198*a* ᵀ7120
Ilgen K ᴹk343
Iliescu M 6540
Ilisch L a889
Illanes J g105 ᴿk577 k592
Imbach J 4233 **R** g832
Imbelli R ᴿk747 q055
Imhof A ᴱ594 **P** ᴿ3166
Imhoof S ᴿ8419 8555 9549
	c118
Inbody T 4946*c*
India 8100 8184 8591 9069-
	9175 c108 c549 c795 c819
Indus c078
Informatica 857 859s 879
	884-6 899s 905ss 915 929
	966s 970 1007 1020 1026
	1029 1035 1038s 1041
	1043 1046 1050s 1053
	1055 1061s 1062* 1064
	1073s 1607 2742 2744
	5721
Ingle H k236
Inglebert H 9734 ᴿ9895
Ingoglia R da890
Ingraffia B 5663 q050
Ingram B ᴿ1962 **J** k614*a*
Innacone R ᴹk540
Innes D ᴱ163

Innocente L 6250
Instone S ᴿ8477 c426
Internet 872 915
Introvigne M 8266-8 8284*b*
	q051
Invernizzi A a537*a* a704
	b380 b432 ᴿ9515
Inwood B ᵀ8548
Ioanita I ᵀ3422
Ionopolis a886*a*
Ioppolo A 8392*a*
Ippolito A a162*b*
Iraburu J 4888
Iran 6510-23 6749 7123
	7127 7807 8861-79 9490-
	9514 a097 b464-b485 c190
	c196
'Iraq 1057 7552 a093 b362-
	b443
'Iraq/Amîr b166
Irarrázaval D c456
Irbid-Marû b167
Ireland abp ᴹk421 **R** 8279
Irenaeus L g216-28 ᴹ1632
	3107 5207 7757*d* g167
	g279 g651
Iriarte A ᴿ460 6267
Irigoin J 2474
Irmscher J 7882 9991 c003
Irrgang B ᴿk351
Irshai O 9892
Irvin D 4234
Irwin A k869 **R** c927 **T**
	8549 ᴱ707 **W** ᴿ8716
Isaac B a322 c812 ᴿa310
	c856 **J** ᴿ1763
Isaacs H c457
Isaacus N g619
Isager J a650*a*
Isasi Díaz A 5018
Isherwood L 5311
Ishida M 5019*a*
Ish-Shalom B 7547
Isichel E 5020
Isidorus H ᴹa444 c445 c448
	g875 **P** g386
Işìk F b223 b902
Isin b416
Iskandar/Wala b168
Isman F a102
Isnardi Parente M 8393 8600
Ispérian G 4468
Israel F b035*b* c885*a* ᴿ5760
Isser N 7642 ᴿ7231
Istanbul b838-b842
Iten M 7065
Ito A c169
Ivanchik A 9499
Ivanov V 6589

Ivantchik A c534
Ivatte R de 1103
Iver W ᴱ4963
Iversen E 6145 b510 ᴹa519
	b525
Ives C ᴱ9111
Ivo C ᴹg698
Ivry A 7402
Iwanowski T 4510
Iwersen J 7775
Iyer V 9024*a*
IZBG 880
Izmir b867
Izquierdo C ᴿ 2915 2924
	3728
Izre'el S 6020 b596*c* ᴱ5773
Izydorczyk Z 6867

Jabès E ᴹ1881
JabloNski Z q175
Jack S a980
Jackendorff R 6636
Jackman D ᴱ115
Jacks P 9893
Jackson A c668 **D** 2435 **E**
	k917 ᴱ302 **H** 6146 **P**
	ᴿb015 **R** c416
Jacob C 8339 ᵀ4545 **E** 3116
	7642 ᴿk709 **I** ᶜ458 **M**
	ᵀ283 **P** g567 **W** ᴱ458 **X**
	9025
Jacobs E 2678 **I** 7292 ᴿ3205
	L 7293 7548s ᴿ7253 7737
	M ᴰ7199 **P** 1028 g106 **W**
	9308
-Brown T 260
-Malina D 5209
Jacobsen T 6021 8840
Jacobson A ᴿ2160 **D** a175
	a972 c886 **E** a538 **H** 6829
	W ᴰ1552
Jacobsson I b703
Jacobus E g620 **S** ᴹg617
Jacoby R a800
Jacquemin A 6352 b954 **D**
	3034b
Jacques R 3826
Jacquet J ᴿa236
Jacquinod B ᴱ686
Jaeger B a705 **C** g710
Jäger A 4373 ᴿ4766
Jähnichen T ᴿ4756
Jaffee M 7255 ᴿ344 376
Jagersma H 9218
Jaggar P q342
Jaher F 7644 ᴹ7524
Jahnow H ᶠ1739
Jaki S 2341s 3695 4626*a*
	ᴹ2327 2343

Kempshall R ^{R}g689
Kempski J von k407
Kendall L ^{E}k957 **R** ^{M}k073
Kendeffy G g446
Kenis L k346 ^{E}k192 ^{R}k307
  k357
Kennedy D a318c b301 b826
  c134 c195 c555b **E** 5454a
  H ^{T}9249 **J** 2007 3084 **L**
  ^{R}k412 **P** q054 ^{D}k965s **T**
  ^{R}4619* 4795
Kennel G ^{D}g107
Kennell N ^{R}587
Kenneson P ^{R}3616
Kennett D b458
Kenney J 7650 ^{D}6833 **J**
  ^{R}g162 g443
Kenny J 5455
Kenrick P ^{E}b713
Kent J ^{R}k660 **M** ^{R}k158
Kenyon K ^{M}a966 a968a
Keogh D 4806b q274
Keos b999
Keown D 9133 ^{R}9099
Kepel G 9030
Képinski-Lecomte C b407
  b329
Kepnes S k479
Kerber W ^{E}425 7889 8085
  9031
Kerkhofs J 5456
Kerlouégan F ^{F}92
Kerma b691
Kern ^{D}2833 **I** 9134 **K** 4452
  U ^{D}3501 **W** ^{R}3569
-Ulmer B 5814
Kerr F 2815 q004 ^{E}k442
  ^{R}1511 k845 **W** ^{D}9898
Kerrigan M ^{R}q025
Kertelge K 1451 ^{D}3329
Kertész I 9631 b799
Kertsch M g338
Kervran M c078
Kesel J de ^{R}8129
Keshavjee S ^{D}7917
Keshgegian F ^{R}5369
Keshishian A ^{D}4218
Kessler A ^{E}44 **D** 4239 8776c
  b686 ^{R}c071 **G** ^{R}8563 **H**
  ^{D}2008 ^{R}2637 **M** ^{R}2782 **R**
  9219
Kesten E ^{T}7561
Kettel J a150s
Kettenbach G a376
Kettler C 3891
Kettner E 8182
Keveny M 4698d
Kevers P 1180
Kevorkian R ^{R}a810

Keynes ^{M}4800
Keyser J ^{E}28
Khabur b331
Khairi A b405
Khalidi R g021a
Khalil L b146
Khan G 2512 5725 6075
  ^{R}b761
Khanoussi M a407
Kharaneh b171
Kharaz b172s
Kharbteng J 190
Kharga 6441 b710
Kharusi N ^{D}6084
Khayma b458
Kheleifeh b144
Khorasan b475 c393
Khorsabad b417
Khosroyev A 7841s
Khoury A 8916 9032 ^{R}9038
  P 9033s **R** g593 ^{E}6075
Khraysheh F 6061b
Khurramshāhi B 8917
Khursheed A 2347
Kidd C ^{R}k157
Kido T g714
Kieckhefer R g715s
Kieffer R 2009a ^{M}93
Kienast B 6024s 6596a **D**
  ^{R}9731 a878
Kienzle B c964
Kierdorf W 9800
Kierkegaard S ^{M}1937 5277
  6402 g487b k347-55
Kiernan-Lewis J ^{R}2799
Kiessig M ^{R}1448
Kijas Z ^{R}309
Kilgallen J 4982b 8183
Kilise b846
Kill D 3111
Kille D ^{R}359
Killen ^{M}4822 **G** a301 **P** 2905
  k619
Killet H ^{D}a765
Killick J ^{R}419 3049
Killingley D ^{R}9143
Killoren J 5026 9177
Kilmartin E †q291
Kilmer A a431
Kilner J ^{E}600
Kim C 5316
Kimball S 6237-9
Kimel A 2853 2855
Kim Jongwoo ^{D}3829
Kim Kyoung Jae ^{D}5027
Kim Moon-Kee ^{D}k269
Kim Young-Dong ^{D}9135
Kinast R 1452a
Kinberger M 4559

Kindler A a892
Kinet D c147
King A 3135 **E** 4378 **F**
  ^{R}4092 4953 **G** ^{E}725 **H**
  ^{R}c433-5 c476 **J** ^{R}4336 **K**
  7804b 7862 **L** a104 **ML**
  ^{M}1559 2915 k525a **N** 5028
  P ^{R}a071 b063 **R** q279 **T**
  2348a U k976 k980b ^{E}426
  5317s
Kingdon R k059
Kingsbury J 1331
Kingsley P 8550 8872 9502
Kinlaw C ^{R}k991
Kinnamon M ^{R}339
Kinnard J ^{R}9102
Kinnear M 3892
Kinney D a591
Kinsley D 3058
Kinukawa H 5216
Kinzig W g108 ^{R}9034 g165
Kipp D ^{T}1493 5308
Kippenberg H 8622 ^{D}427
Kiraz G 2608s 5991
Kirby J 5029
Kirchberg J ^{R}2239 7725 7747
Kircher Durand C ^{E}118
Kirchschläger W 277 2148s
  3697 4096
Kirjanov A ^{T}39
Kirk A ^{R}2224 **J** ^{R}4082 **P**
  5319a
Kirkland A b750 g280 ^{R}g206
Kirkpatrick F 4097 8018 **L**
  ^{E}g281 ^{R}1641
Kirmani H al- ^{M}8979
Kirsch T ^{T}4374
Kirschenbaum A 7360
Kirschner R ^{M}7257
Kirste R 8395
Kirwan C ^{R}8516 **M** ^{R}339
Kislyi A c912
Kiss Z ^{R}a637
Kissel T ^{R}a342
Kissonerga b917
Kister D 9083 **M** 2437
  7037c ^{M}8927
Kisukawa S k129
Kitagawa J 5030
Kitchell K 6289
Kitchen K 6153 9220 b450s
  ^{M}6162 ^{R}8809 9411 a401
  a703 a925 b597
Kition b918
Kittel G 3943 **R** ^{M}9257
Kjesbo D 5200=5301
Klaghofer W 5457
Klaiber W 4185b 4453a
Klaine R 3698

Lagerquist L ^R5172
Lagerwerf L ^E187 ^R5081
Laghi P 1457
Lago Alba L k805 ^R3507
Lagorio V ^F101
Lagrange M ^Ma157 k423 k451 k502-7
Lagrée M ^R3297
Lahey S 7399
Lai Pan-Chui ^Dk987
Lake P ^R3158
Lakeland P ^R3658a 5659
Laks A ^E691
Lala Comneno M b487
Lalich J 8305
Lalou E ^Ea510
Lamadrid L k947
La Maisonneuve D de 7300
Lamarche P k710b
La Matina M 1313
Lamb C ^Mk917 M 6705b
Lambdin D 5728
Lamberigts M g255 ^E633 k192 ^Mk346 ^R1497 g424
Lambert J 8090 ^Rb008 P b630 W 374 6029s 8666 9459 a518a ^M6054 ^R6017 6020 8835 9468 a702 a736 Y ^R4957
-Millard ^M5813
Lamberterie C de ^R692 6595 I de 970
Lamberth D ^D7946
Lamberti M 6223
Lambery-Zielinski H 3007
Lambiasi F ^R3606 5137
Lamblin J ^R1120
Lamboley J ^R9589
Lambrecht J ^R6377 U 9802 ^R9724
Lambrechts R ^Rc424
Lambropoulos V 1314
Lambton A 9505a
Lami G 9311
Lamont W ^Rk218
La Mothe R ^D8021
Lamoureux J 4381 P 5219
Lampe P 7780
Lamprichs R 9460
Lamy B ^M6613
Lana I ^R6530
Lancaster L c022
Lancel S b251 ^Mb250
Land J van der 9221 P †q302
Landau J g022
Landels J a218
Landes G ^R2524 5753 R g719

Landkammer J ^Eg926
Landman C r^R3521
Landurant A 2643
Landy F ^R2077 T ^R1417
Lane B 3062 b735 D 3700 8274 T 4382
-Fox R 9904
Laney J 1176
Lang B 458 1108 1934s ^Dc753 ^E880 D g824 M 9137
Langa P g449 ^Rk807
Langdon S ^Ea105
Lange A 881 ^D3134 7107s D 4633* 7954b F ^E91 F de 6692 8188a H de ^R4756 J b384 c058 N de 2499b 6291 ^R1141 3194 3716 7301 k500
Langella A 5134 q136 V ^F102
Langendoen D ^R6646
Langenhorst G 1804
Langenhoven P Van ^Rc402
Langer J ^R2890 M ^D7659 ^R3178 R ^R3205
Langermann Y c471
Langevin G 3746a 5035 ^R3558
Langhade J 6085
Langholm O c821
Langhorst P 4634a
Langhoven P Van ^Ra398 a425
Langin H 9567
Langkammer H 5667
Langlamet F 1
Langland ^M1885s
Langmuir G 7660
Langnas S ^R3185
Langsfeld P ^R3432
Langslow D 6548
Langton S ^Mg878
Lanithottam G ^R6
Lanzetti R 5036a
Lanzi N g450s
La Penna A 8397 c251
Laperrousaz E 6943 8022 ^Ea937
Lapide P 2726
Lapidge M g587
Lapini W 9568 c170
Laplanche F ^Rk193
La Porte J 6835 ^T6834
La Potterie I de 2128 2260c 4456 5135s ^R6384
Lapp E a782 G a840 N a710
Lapschy G ^E6641
Lapsley J 282

Laqueur R 9905
Lara Polaina A 4515
Larché F b166
Larchet J c472 ^R4318 g365
Lardet P ^Eg513
Lardinois A ^D2001
Largo Dominguez P 3831
Larkin D 971 K ^R1105 3381 3384
Larmour D 9296a
La Rocca E c050 J ^Rg994 T k135
-Pitts E ^D8693
Laroche E ^Ma158
La Roche R 8398
La Roncière C de g720
Larrabe J k806 ^Rk802
Larsa b419s c338
Larsen D 1557 P k906 ^T6675
Larson E 7029 7109 ^D6756 ^M7035 G 5037 V ^Rc903
Larsson E 7774b
Lartraud ^M2716
La Russa A k626
Las Casas B de ^M4849 k117-k128
Lasala F de k094 ^Rk822
Lascaris A ^R198 1509 g108
La Serna E de 1747
Lash N 3622 k677d
La Shell J ^R3446
Lasic H 7955
Laskier M g023 ^R7516
La Sor W †q303
Lassner J 8918s 9222
La Stella T 6568
Lata J ^Rk988
Lategan B 2012a 2062b
Latkin C 8301
Latmos b851
Latomus J ^Mk088
Latorre J ^D3377 ^R2089s
La Torre Vargas R de ^R2969
Latpusek P ^R1039
Lattanzi G b089
Lattke M ^R44 9106
Laube M 7890
Lauer S ^E195 ^T7639
Lauffer S eb926
Lauffray J b215 b536
Launay M de ^Tk994
Laurance J 4517
Laurant J ^Ek670
Laurence R c051 ᵎ
Laurentin A q056 R 3831 5137
Laurier D 6642
Laurita R ^Ek535b
Laut J ^R6154

Léonard J ᴿ7441
Leonardi C g667 ᴿ7059 a984
   L 3528
Leong K 9141
Leonhard C 5953
Leontis A 9640
Leontopolis 9705
Lepape P k275
Lepargneur H ᴿ109 4064
   4339 q019
Lepenies W 9312
Lepicard E 3246
Leppin V g885 ᵀg886
Leprohon R a654
Leptis b711-3
Le Quien M g590
Lera J 4102
Lerberghe K van 9461 b313
   c686a ᴱ110
Lerer S ᴿ1851
Leriche P ᴱa327
Le Rider G a106 a895 b866
   ᴿa874
Lerner B 2354 7957 D 7445
   G ᴹ1749 7554 R ᴰg883
   ᴿg721
Leroux N 2013
Le Roux J 5025b k508s M
   9223 P 8400 ᴿa306 c740
Leroy F g340 J 2488 M
   ᶠ107
Le Salix H ᴹ9121
Le Saux H ᴹ8156 9168
Lesbos 8616
Lesch W ᴱk629
Leschhorn W 9521 ᴿ9588
Lescow T 1369
Lesinng E ᴰ4242
Lesko H 1050 L q402 ᴱb565
Leśniewski K g220
Lesser ᴹk229
Lessing E ᶠ108 G ᴹ1888
   7619 k250
Lester A 5465
Leszko L ᴿ8807
Lete → Olmo
Letellier J 1623
Letham R k630
Letis T ᴰk095
Létoublon F ᴱ6292 ᴿ207 686
   8463
Letta C 8626b b803b ᴿ8422
Lettieri G g257
Leuba J ᴱ5466
Leukart A 6293
Leung B 5039
Leuze R 9038
Levallois N b513
Levene D 8401

Levenson A ᴿ1314 J 1407
   2014 3945 ᴿ3844
Lévêque P 3995 9570 ᴿ8590
Levey S ᴿ7309
Levi D ᶠ743 E ᴹ7570 G
   ᴱ9571 J c697 M 9741
   9803 q196
Lévi-Strauss ᴹ8331
Levick B ᴱ683 b753 ᴿc798
Levin B ᴰ6572 C 9224 ᴹ888
   H q311 S 6294 6598
   ᴿ5715 b874
Levinas E 284 1315 2025e
   ᴹ4738 8161 k759 k876
Levine A ᴿ9869 B 5820
   b150 H 7664 L a801 b079
   M 4906
Levinson B 6026b N a447 P
   7204
Levison J 5040 6837 7205
   9695 P 5040
Levoratti A 1458 9313 ᴿ223
   1077 1290 5187 5214
   6320 a937 c605 c712 c737
Levy A 285 7491 ᴱ7492 L
   3246 R ᵀ7724 T 9225
   a055 c080 ᴱa054 c687
   -Yadun S c308b
Lévy E q255
Lewerentz A ᴰa655
Lewicki T ᶠ727
Lewin I ᴱa107
Lewis B 9039 b841 g026
   ᴱ688 g727 C k877s ᴱ3357
   ᴹ1873 4484 D ᶠ693 G
   2907 3893 H ᴱ604 J 7665
   8023 ᴿ955 q091 K ᴿ296 N
   286 6369 6465 S g728
Lewis-Anthony J k611
Lewit T c375
Ley D ᴿ3754 M 7666a
Leyerle B g182 g341 ᴿc628
Leypunskaya N b965
Leyser C g847 ᴿg840
Lhoest F ᶠ4261 a002
L'Hôte N b506
Liang Chin-Hsien J ᴰ9142
Liau Yongxiang T 3048
   3292
Libanio J q057a ᴿ225a 4780
   4832 9027 c663 k528
Libanius ᴹ6295 9863 a001
   a007
Libanus 719 b207-b224 c994
   g027 q145
Liberati A 2477 c023
Libero L de ᴿ383
Libya b704-9
Liccardo G ᴱ5134

Liccione M 3701
Licht J 1383
Lichtenberger H 2259b 7110
   ᴰ3134 7107
Lichtheim M 8787 ᴹ8755b
   ᴿ6187
Lickona L 2971b
Liddell J ᴿk416
Liddle R ᴰ8958
Liddy R k882
Li Donnici L 6466
Lieb M k131
Lieberman S 7305 ᴹ3262
Liebermann D ᴿa192
Liebers R 2251
Liebes Y 3334 7446 ᴹ5733
   7542 ᴿ7457
Liebeschuetz J 9996 ᴿb755
   W ᴿ8401
Liebowitz H ᴿa544
Liebs D q398
Liechty D g982
Liedtke A †q312
Lienhard J 1649 g432b
   ᴿg527 ᵀ4552 M 4121b
   4960a g927 g983a ᴱg947
   k038 ᴿ4810 k383
Lienisch M k631
Lierke R a186
Lies L 3894 3996 4199 g258
   ᴰ4087 ᴿ3607 3699 4217
   g140 g203 g216
Lietzmann H g114
Lieu J 7206 c908 ᴱ9907
   ᴿ3194 6895 9822 S 7696
   7819 ᴿ7820 7826 9652
Lifschitz D 3832 ᴱ7512
Light L ᴿg695
Lightfoot C a185 ᴱa864 D
   6569 J ᵀg159
Lightner R 3451 ᴿ5654
Lightstone J 3193 7301
Ligorio P ᴹc010
Ligt L de c822
Lilie F 3702 R c976
Lilienfeld F von 4250
Lillback P 3135a
Lilley J ᴰ9804
Lilli B 1749
Lilliu G a841
Lilyquist C a187
Lim R 9908 T ᴿ6968
Lima C ᶠ109
Limberis V ᴰ5138 c771
Limburg J ᴿ1599 3200 4470
   K ᴿg136
LIMC 848
Limet H ᴿc265
Limiroli M ᵀg688

Longobardi M 1835
Longosz P ^Rg069 S ^E598
Longrée D ^R6533 6541
Longrigg J c476
Lœnning I 3769
Lonsdale S 8488 a448
Loon M van b327 b476
Loonbeek R 4104*a*
Looy H van ^F25
Looz-Corswarem C von ^R63
Lope Cilleruelo ^Mg420
López A ^R7951 ^T2785 **D**
　^E9087s **J** 2970 8788 ^Ra713
-Aparicio ^R7364
-Azpitarte E k649*b*
-Campuzano M c554
-de la Osa J 5041
-de las Heras L k318*a*
-Eire A 6295
-Férez J c477 ^Rc444
-Martínez J 4518 **N** 7669
　^R488
-Melús F 4457
Lopik T van 2578*b*
Loprieno A 6152*c* 6158s
Lorberbaum M ^R7246
Lorcin N ^F113
Lord A 289 **E** ^R3851 4101
　k748 **M** ^E289
Lorenz R 9998 **T** ^Rc018
Lorenzen T 2156
Lorenzin L ^R2719
Loretan A 4384
Loretz O 8659s 8695 9315
　^Eb262 ^R5802 5907 8667
　a703 a706 b577
Loritus G 6269
Lorizio G k378*a* k584 ^E431
　606 2909 5622 ^R3564 7533
Lorscheider A 4105
Lorton D 8789 9361
Łoś A c790*d*
Losada L ^R9595
Lossky N k031 ^E4253
Losveld G a467
Lothers J 2372
Lothrop G 4516*a*
Lott J ^D9743
Lotte C ^Tg832
Lotz J k844
Loucas-Durie É b927 q150
Louchez E q059 q125*c*
Loughlin G 1110s 1317*a*
　^R7934
Louis A ^R2373
Lourdaux G ^F114
Lourenço J 7209*b*
Louth A ^E3637 ^R1295 3999
　6708 8897 9946 9978

a578 g254 g511 g849
^Tk031
Louthan H g986
Love J c823 **S** 5220
Lovell N b648
Lovering E ^E512
Lovibond S ^R8564
Lovik E 9227
Lovin R k921
Lowden J 2593
Lowe M ^E607
Lowell R ^M1878
Lowerson J ^R7334
Lowery K ^R907 **M** 4637
Loyola I ^Mg921 k828*a*
Loza J ^T3916*b*
-Vera J 1459
Lozachmeur H c890*b* ^E728
Lozoya T de ^T2118
Lubac H de ^M2941 3999
　k889-k894
Lubich C 290
Lubin T ^R9091
Lubrano di Ciccone C 1063
　1068
Lucas D ^F115 **F** ^E116 **L** ^F116
　N ^Rg031 **R** g830
Lucas Lucas R 2970*
Lucchesi-Palli E a712
Luce T 9805 ^R9277
Lucianus S ^M666 9296*a* 9845
　9930
Luckert K 8790
Luckmann ^M8014
Luckner G †q314
Lucretius 8369 8381 8383s
　8397 ^M8360 8366s 8387
　8403 8407 8413 8417
　8419 8424 8432 c251
Ludwig M ^M6051 **R** ^Ek812*a*
　T ^R4988
Ludwisiak T 4666
Lübbe H ^Mk040
Lück U 3064*a* **W** k634
Lückhoff M ^Da989
Lüddeckens E 1050* 6160
Lüdemann G 536 7782 g115
　g282 ^M1945
Lüder E ^Dk267
Lüling D 8922
Lüllsdorff R 5388*b*
Luengo Vicente A ^R3736
Lütt J q378
Luft U 6161 9399*b* ^M9402
Lugaresi L ^Rg407
Luginbühl M 2442
Lugo Rodríguez R 4891
Luibl H 4458
Luis P de g429*b* ^Ra446

g184
-Carballada R de ^R4756
　5653
Luisier P ^R643 6896 6906
　7827 7841
Luke H c693 **K** 3833
Lukken G 291
Lull T ^E4268 k658
Lullius R ^M9023 g879-882
Lulof P a656
Lumpp D ^R4034
Lund J b252 ^R2607
Lundberg M ^E6949
Lundgren S k336
Lundin A b453 †q315 **R**
　2024 q060
Lupieri E 7821
Luria M ^E7426
Luristan b476
Lurker M 794 †q316
Luschey H †q317
Lusitania a270
Lusnia S a898
Lust A ^R6725 **J** 6296 8727
　^R346 515 1379 2591 2595
　3253 3342 6761 6949
　8652 8699 8702 a937
　c527 g511
Lustig J ^D694
Lustiger J ^M7586 7639
Lutfi M b404
Luther M 2963 4560*a* g835
　^M354 410*b* 1580 2707
　2973 3676 3828 4810
　5500 a440 g427 g467
　g811 g900-42
Lutterbach H ^Rg758
Luttikhuizen G ^R7785
Lutz N db962
-Bachmann M ^E215 568
Lutzeier P ^E6571
Lux R ^R7750
Luxon T 1856
Luxor b533-b570
Luz A ^Ek512
Luzi A b554
Luzini G ^E6219
Luzzati M 6795 7670
　^E7483
Lyapustinoi E ^Ta209*c*
Lycia 6247-54 6482 a884
　b742 b751*a* b763 b850
Lydamore M ^Tg100
Lydia 6252s 9834 a258
　b882*b*
Lydus J ^M9999
Lyman J 3474
Lynch J 7373 **K** a784
Lyon D ^M3754

Macken J ^Mk762
McKenna J ^R4605 4687
 k547 k914 **M** 1751
Mackenzie R ^Rg443
MacKenzie C 4378 ^Rk031 **I**
 2829
McKenzie M 3026 4790
 ^Rc421 k916 **S** ^R9217 a942
McKeon R ^M4927
Mackey J 4791 **L** ^Dg475
McKim D ^R1564 k045 k752
MacKinnon D †q319
McKinsey C 1603
Mackintosh M a540
McKitterick ^Rg758
McKnight E 1991*b* 2017
 ^Rq066 **S** ^R3396 c737
Mackowski R c082 c941
 ^R6553 9374
MacLachlan B 6418
McLachlan E ^D2644
McLain M ^E1316
McLaren J c697 ^D9744
McLaughlin J ^R3218 9234
 c712 **M** g733 **R** ^Mk099
MacLean N 3024
McLean B 2253 **P** 5372
McLelland J ^Ek150
MacLennan R ^Rc526
Macleod D k530
MacLeod D 4385
McLeod D ^R4876 **H** k359
 W c328
McMahon A 6643 **G** 8623
 9319*d*
McManus D 3795*a* (*not*
 MAc) **F** g305*c*
McMichael S 7674
McMillan D ^R1807
McMinn M 6693
McMullen M ^R1466 **R** a000
McMullin E ^R2324
Macnair J ^R1855
McNamara M 2546 g734
 ^E2532 **W** 1186 2971*a*
McNaspy C †q320
McNichols W ^Ea592
McNutt D ^Rk547 **P** 3971*b*
McPartlan P 3999 4107
McPhee J ^Tk854 **M** ^Tk854
Macquarrie J 485 3749
 5139 5669 8024 k845
 ^M3435 4402*a* ^R3414 3732
 k486 k701 k904 k936
McQueen E ^R76
McRay J a042 a842 ^Ra245
 R ^Rq036
Macrina ^Mg388
McSorley H ^Rg941

McSwain L c891*a*
 7675
McThenia A ^Ek971
Macuch R 7822
Macumber P b155*b*
Macuñana A ^Rc562
McVann M 4507
McVeigh T 4639*
McVey C 8191
McWilliam J ^Eg454
Macy G 4000 g735
Madaba a034*a* b176 c103
Madangi Sengi J 5043
Madany B ^R9003
Madden N ^Rg392
Maddox R k283*a* ^Rk281
Madelung W ^E722 ^R8914
Madey J 5044
Madges W ^Rk308 k357
Madigan D 9040 **K** g736
 ^R7886 g169 **P** 4463 ^T3981
 4068 a625
Madinat Habu 8819s b567
Madonia N k867
Madrid P ^E1187 **T** 4108
Madrigal A ^R4310 **S** ^R1621
 4131
Madzaridis Y 3068
Maecenas ^M9841
Maeckelberghe E ^D5140
 ^R5292 5299
Maehler H ^E681
Maekawa K c376
Männchen G ^Da154
März C ^R2125
Maffei J ^Mc917
Maffeis A 4257
Mafico T 2028*d*
Mafraq/Ajib b178
Magara b332
Magašš b146
Magdala b117
Magdalena M m5162 5167
 5203 5217 5230 5232
 5249*b* 5252
Magee D ^R26 **P** 638*
Magen Y b041 b042*b* b072
Magesa L 5325
Maggi S ^Rc032 c055
Magí J q107
Magill G ^Ek439
Magna Graecia 694
Magne J 2161 4001
Magnelli L 2972
Magnesia a119
Magness J 6945 7112 a767
 b080 b129 ^Ma798 ^Rb017
-Gardiner B ^Da731
Magonet J 1188s 1319 2787

Magris A 7784
Maguire D 4640 ^R4753
Mahdi M ^F117
Mahé J 6257 7866*b*
Maher M 1461 3195 ^Rk945
Mahfouz J g027
Mahnke A ^T7441
Mahn-Lot M k123
Mahoz(a) b179
Mai D ^Rc976
Maia P ^Rg900
Maidl L 7676
Maidman M c824 ^Ra732
Maiello F g989
Maier B g366 **C** ^Dc977 **G**
 900* 5470 **H** g116 k197
 ^Rc239 **J** 3296 7208 ^E7447
 7677 ^R3203 3387 6743
 6954 7046 **M** ^Rq071 **W**
 ^Rb468
Mailberger P 1190
Maillard B ^E169 **J** g990
 ^E850
Maimon S ^M7493
Maimonides ^M7388-7404
 9807 c471
Main A ^F2
Mainardi P a586
Maine de Biran 2938
Mainville O 2016 ^E375
Maisels C c698 c862
Maitland S ^R1248
Majdańaki K ^E610
Majdansky V 4258
Majercik R 6907 ^R7789
Majorano S 4641
Mak H 7478
Makarov J b955
Makhortykh S ^Rc542
Makowski J ^R8361
Makselon J ^E98
Maksoud M el- b649
Malaise M c309
Malamat A a264 b306
 ^R9466
Malatya c389*b*
Malavolta M 2494*e*
Malbon E ^E2017 ^Ma589
Malbran-Labat F 6033 b483
 ^Rc164
Malcolm J ^M9505*a*
Malcolmson P 2353*d*
Maldamé J 2558 3531
 3795* ^R3534 4711
Maldonado J 1752
Malebranche ^M3494 k251
Malek H a899 **J** ^Eb514
 ^R9427 b561 b612 b622

Melchin K 4794*a*
Melczer W ^Tk081
Melebiya b344
Melena J 6497
Mélèze-Modrzejewski J 7212 9403
Melita 6102 b236s c046
Mello A 7213
Mellon C ^R3023
Melloni A ^Ek850
Mellor E ^R1197 1236 R 9809 ^Dc724
Melotti L ^R3198 4480
Melson R ^R7753
Meltzer E 6163 ^E6481 b588 ^R748 6126 T ^R748
Melville C c254
Melzi R 7365
Memiş E 9523
Memphis a317 b597-b611 c355
Men A ^Mk899
Menache S g706
Menasce J de 7514
Mendecki N a993
Mendel M ^M9035
Mendels D 9747 9810 ^R8582 9686
Mendelssohn M ^M7488 k252 k360
Mendes b648
Mendes Atanasio M †q327
Mendes-Flohr P ^E7558
Méndez Dosuna J 6302 6470 6498
-Fernández B 3138 3899
-Romano M ^Rg802
Mendieta E q063 ^F253 ^R4866 4918 g997
Mendl H ^Rq071 J ^D1837
Mendoza Ríos M 5046
Meneses R de 9085*b*
Menestrina G e2729
Menges T ^E179
Menichetti M c024
Menin G ^R761
Menke K 3947
Menn S 8554
Menninga C ^R2381
Menozzi D k645
Mensch J 1806
Mentzer R ^Mk048
Menu B 9384*b* c999*c* ^Rc815 M a179
Menze E 7683
Menzies G ^Eg229
Mercadante L ^R2858 3845 8243
Mercier D ^Mk429 k900

Mercogliano F ^Ra324
Meredith A g260 g300 ^R3481 4202 g377 P 1838*a*
Merhav R a487 a807
Merimdé b693
Merino M ^Eg184
Merk O 5672*a* ^Dc365 ^R5692
Merkelbach R 8451 8792
Merkle J k500 ^R4068
Merklein H 8697
Merkur D ^R5395
Merling D b163 ^R853 a777 a924
Merlini C 5768
Merlo P g235 ^R1777 2148
Mernissi F 89o7
Meroe b714
Merras M 4521
Merriell D 3625
Merrigan T ^R2874 5140 8180
Merrill A 1322 E a941 ^R5647 8635
Merriman B k818*a*
Mertens D c047 H ^Dk909 ^R2142
Merton T 4474 ^M9059 k901s
Merv b478 g594
Merwe C van der ^R5744
Méry S b459
Meskell L a808
Meskin J k259
Mesle C 2830
Meslin M ^D9470
Mesniankipa S q390
Mesopotamia 1057 8823-60 9437-89 b362-b443 c868 g008 → *'Iraq*
Mesquita R ^E140
Messadié G 3838
Messenia b959
Messing M 7855
Messner R ^E128 ^R4461 g717
Messori V ^Ek854
Mesters C 1191
Metallinos G ^Rg765
Metapontus a758
Methuen C ^Rg204
Mettinger T 2789 8698 a541 ^R8686
Metwally E El- a541 a843
Metz J 393 5047 ^D5387 ^E434 ^M3341 k945
Metzger B 1192 B 1651 2568 5645 ^E1113 ^F126 ^R1141 1641 H a158 M 4522 b219s ^R4350 T 2513
Metzler J g996 K 5813
Metzner G ^R8680
Meuffels O ^R3522 k749

Me(y)uhas Ginio A 7366 7684
Meulder M 9811
Meulenaere H de ^R8787
Meunier B 3466 3482 ^M3503
Mey P De ^R3504 3774
Meyboom P a744
Meye Thompson M 2025*h*
Meyendorff J 4261 4388 a002 P ^Rq171
Meyer B 1323 k883 ^F127 †q328 C c828 ^E757 E ^Mc587*b* F ^R2468 g650 g972 G ^Dk288*a* H ^R196 3186 4498 4536 4576 a590 J 4610*b* k382*b* ^Rb304 J von 6739 K b878 L ^Mk270 M ^E472 696 ^Ra659 R 2514 ^E9889 ^Tg344 W 7922 k410
-Flügel B ^Dg842
-zu Schlochtern J ^R4062
-Zwiffelhofer E a901 ^Rc628
Meyerink P ^R8298 k660
Meyers C 3969*b* b130 ^R8724 a924 a970 E 1070 b078 b122 b130 ^Dc040
Meyes-Schlögl C a673
Meyfart J 1577
Meyjes C 3706
Meynell H 2166 2916 3752 k885 q064
Meynet R 1193 2018s ^E14 ^M1278
Meyr-Blanck M 6695
-Wilmes H ^R5211
Meyuhas Ginio A 7366 7684
Meyvaert P 2647*b*
Meywe H ^F128
Mezzadri L ^Eg688
Me'iri M ^M7395
Micaelli C g284 ^Eg283 ^Mg276
Miccoli P 6696
Michael S 5048*a* T ^R3203 6735*a* 6864 9316 g098
Michalowski P 8837*b* 8844 b342*a*
Michaud J 2167 2188
Michel ^D5781 A 8407 C c829 ^Rb848 E ^M3875 H ^Tb808 J q149 O †q329 S c255 T 9042
Michiels R ^R3621
Michl J ^M3800*b*
Mickelsen A 1194
Micks M 3753
Midant-Reynes B ^Ra085
Middleburgh C 7633 ^R3133

Moir I 2563
Moise J 2168*
Moitel P 1199e
Moitrieux G ᴿ8371
Mojsisch B k103 ᵀ5494
Mojsov ᴰa657
Mojzes P ᴱ4262
Molari C k978 ᴱ3876
Molendijk A ᴿk651 k993
Moles J 9915
Molette C ᴱ618
Molière ᴹc420
Molin G 6993
Molina E ᴿ4721 J 4717 M
   6035 9469
-Gómez J ᴿ4544
Molinari F k933
Molinaro A q013c
Molinier A 9643
Moll H ᴿ4576 4733
Mollat de Jourdin M a106
Mollenkott V 2856
Molnar P k767 ᴿ3638
Molnár A ᴹk903
Moloney F 168 ᴿ2017 R
   ᴿ3432 3915 k879 k949
Moltmann J 3073s 3538-40
   3587s 3626 4263 4718b
   4899 5477 7687a 7708
   ᴱ434 ᴹ1382 1832 3017
   3576 3608* 4813 5055
   5485 k904-9
-Wendell E 2975
Momani A al- b203
Momen M ᴿ8974
Momigliano A 297 9320
Mommsen T ᴹ9623 W c718
   ᴰ4652
Monaci Castagno A ᴿg073
Monaco G q330
Monat P ᴿg572
Moncelon C 8316
Mondin B 827 2976s 5478
   5673 ᴹ2980
Mondrain B 9580
Monelli A a268 N a268
Monloubou L 1216 2173
   3098 ᴿ1934 2362 3051
   3270 3803 5199
Monmonier M c085
Monnot G 8964 ᴿ9047
Monsacré H b385
Monsarrat J 1199f ᴿ6861 V
   1199f
Mons Claudianus 6427 b694
Monserrat D 6472 ᴿ6205
Monshouwer D 4497c
Monson J ᴿa298
Montagnes B k502s J k451

Montagnini F ᴿ766
Montague G ᴿ8100
Montanari E 7916 F 6303 G
   ᴿa294
Montchamp J a653b
Montefiore H k648 ᴹk910
Monteil P 1692a
Montenat C 2362
Montero D 1196 S 8408
   ᴿa021
-Carrión D 6740
Montet P 9404
Montevecchi O 6405 ᴿ6436
   6442s 6473
Montgomery I ᴿc611
Montini G ᴹk933
   → Paulus VI
Montoya Sáenz J 9321a
Montremy J de ᴹk911
Montserrat D a269 ᴿc628
Moo D 2112
Moody C ᴿc955 L 5319b
Moon C ᴿ4956 W ᴱ697
Moonan L 2831
Moor J de 2548 8700s ᴱ515
Moore D 5479s E ᴿ4916 G
   ᴿ3235 J 2363 M b941
   ᴿ8721 b943 P 7894 ᴿ597
   R 269 6723 S 1370 2020
   2020*a 3948 c483 q066
   q128 ᴰ1756 ᴹ1372 ᴿ2001
   2204 T a411
-Candelera E †q331
Moorehead C b879
Mooren T 8027
Moorey P a059 a220 ᴿa511
Moorhead J a003 ᴿk896
Mopsik C ᴱ7368
Mopsuestia 8421 g409
Mor M 9701
Mora C ᴱ717 ᴿ8402 F 8409
   8491 8605 g549
-Lomeli R 4797a
Moracho F ᴿq020
Morag S 5733
Moral A ᴿ4873 T q237
Moraldi L 2631 6870 ᴿ6922
Morales J 3708 k441
Moran C ᴿk193 J 9147 W
   b585-7
Morandi F k517a ᴿ7977
-Bonacossi D ᴿb310
Morandini S 2364 ᴿ3091
   3670 4253 4590 5091
   8135 8176b
Morani M 6417
Moranski K ᴰg747
Morard F 7866d
Mordecai H 3900

More T ᴹ5244 k107
Moreau A ᴱ8410 P ᴿc631
Moreen V ᴿ7568
Moreira A 1936
Moreland J ᴱ390 2365
Morell S 7481 V a200
Morelli G ᴿ4602
Morély J ᴹk132
Moreno A 4643b J 9322 P
   a663
-Muñoz M k649a
Morenz L 6164 ᴿa840
Morerod C ᴱk044
Moreschini C 3627 g121
   g517 ᴱ2729 D 9335b
Moret J a717 P a270 c045
Moretti J a271 ᴿb819
Moretto G k892
Morfill G ᴹ3146
Morgan D 9505b ᴿ4870 c123
   g026 k356 F ᴿ3228 7292 J
   ᴿ8578 M 7559 9323 P
   8098 R 2256 ᴿ528 2255*
   3525 3663 5687 g175 S
   5330
Morganti C 8289 ᴿ7229
Moriarty F ᴿ1652 M 8290
Morimoto A k231
Morin T a852
Moriya A ᴰ5956
Morla V ᴱ5749
-Asensio V 1114
Morodo González P ᴰk260
Moroney J 3795d
Morony A ᴿ74 M ᴿc688
Morpurgo P ᴿ7378 7495
   7736 c984
-Davies A 6304
Morrice W 6305
Morris B g029 C ᴱ38 ᴿg669
   I a844 b945 c719 ᴱ473
   b928 ᴿ9582 a776 J 2169
   ᵀc976 K k180b L 211 M
   ᴿa594 S ᴰ9089 ᴱ212 ᴹb925
   ᴿ473
Morrison C ᴰ2611 D 3756 J
   ᴿ2821 5610 6719 K ᴿ2766
   M b429 T 1900 ᴹ1859
Morrissey M 9324 k999
Morrone F ᴱ3901
Morschauer S 8793
Morscher E 2983b
Morse C 3757
Mort J ᴿc998
Mortel R 8969
Mortensen B ᴰ2549 V 4653
Mosca A a272
Moscati S 298 a060s a753
   b230 b238 b240s ᴱ744 ..

Mysia a827
Naab E ᴱ5486
Na'aman N 5770 9231 b095c
  ᴿb018
Nabataea 5965 5993 8892
  c348
Nabk b346
Nachman r ᴹc926
Nachmanides 7412-5
Nachtergael G a664 ᴿ6260
  6475 b683
Nadal Cañellas J ᴱg367
Naddaf G 6415
Nadler S k251
Nadolski B ᴱ982 ᴿ765 3212
Nádor G 7304
Näf B a004 ᴿ9828
Naeh S 7258
Näsström B a005 ᴿ8497
Naff T g030 ᴱa159
Nagel T 8970 W a718 ᴿa715
Nag" Hammadi 7836-7879
Nagler N g122
Naguib S 6166 9406
Nagy G ᴹ6586
Nahman B ᴹ7504
Nahon G 6943 7497b q202
Najock D 9820
Nakanose S ᴰc723
Nakata I b338
Namita sr ᴿ9160
Namyslo M 5491c
Naphy W k062
Napiórkowski S 4221 4264a
  8291
Naqš/Rustam b480
Narayanan V 9090
Nardi C g123 ᴿg161
Nardo D ᴿ9655
Nardoni E 8795 9407
Naredi-Rainer P von a994
Narithookil J 9044a
Narmer ᴹ9225
Narr K ᴿ8077
Narramore B 4547
Nash K ᴿa477 R 4851 8195
Nasr S 8971 ᴿ8106
Nasrallah J †q335
Nassif B ᴿg157
Natal D q067
Natalucci N c930
Nathan G ᴰc724
Nau E 6241*b
Naudé J 5961 ᴿ5741
Nauerth C 6216b ᴿa475
Nault F ᴿ8199
Naumann C ᴰc980 S ᵀ1189
Nauroy G ᵀg532

Nautin P ᴿc447
Navarrete D ᴹk170
Navarrini C ᴿ5473
Navarro M 2023
-Girón M 2870 4005 ᴿ4310
-Puerto M 3141
-Suárez F 9321d
Navas A ᴿg944
-Gutiérrez A g999
Naveh J 5884d 5962-4 b097
  ᴿ5979
Navia L ᴹ8543
Navoni M ᴿg543
Nawas J ᴿ9249s
Nayak A ᴿ8050
Nazareth b123-8
Nazé G ᴰk653
Nazir-Ali M 299
Nazzaro A rcg294
Ndigi O 6167
Ndi-Okalla J ᴿ5024
Neale J ᴹk364
Neall B ᴿ5711
Neame A ᵀ4466
Near H g031
Nebbiai-Dalla Guardia D
  g750
Nebe G 7163
Nebehay S ᴿa889
Nebeker G ᴿ2423
Nebelsick H 2370
Nebes N 6088 ᴱ133
Nebo b180-3
Neckebrouck V 5053s ᴱ8170
  ᴿ2338 4479 4979 5045
  8153 g228
Need S 3480 ᴿ1343
Needham H ᵀ1604
Needleman J 8252
Neef H 3797 8702 ᴰc518
Neely A 8042 ᴿ9157 k121
Neev D c172
Neeve P de ᶠc380
Negahban E a332 b473
Negbi O c006
Negeb a074 b050s c859
Negenman J ᴿ2199 9221
  c627 c717
Negev A 5965
Negri M 6500
Nehmé L b187
Nehorai M 7400
Neidhart W 2355 ᴿ1567 7082
Neill S ᴹk917
Neils J 8493
Neira F.G q393
-Faleiro C ᴿ8386
Neirab b347
Neirynck F 7602 q203 ᴿ228

.. 365 760 2154 2199 2555
  2565 6324 k513 k739
Nekrasov G g751
Nel P 2012b ᴱ517
Nelson A ᴰg356 E 9148 J
  4656 M ᴹa035 R 4392
  4800
Nemat-Nejat K b385s
Nemer L ᴿ4166-two
Németh G 8556a a333
Nemoy L ᴿ7159 g023
Nemrut Dağ b857
Nenci G ᶠ1350
Nenna M a222
Neri C ᴿ467 U 1198 g211
  ᴱ2551 V a006
Nerlich B 6603
Nersessian V b894
Nesbitt M c311
Nessan C ᴿ9058
Nessana b052
Nesselrath H 9581 ᴿ8578
Nessim Y 6212
Nestingen J k620b
Nestle-Aland ᴹ2564
Nestori A c039
Nestorius ᴹ3462a 9961b
Netanyahu B 7370
Netland H 8196 J 2024
Nettler R ᴱ438
Netton A ᴿ8954 I ᴿ8946 J
  8962 ᴿ8951
Netzer N 2482
Neu E 6231d 6235d 6241*b
  6243s
Neubauer A ᴹ2502
Neuchterlein J ᴰ6698
Neudecker R 7689
Neufeld E 3202 K 2978
  k808 ᴿ175 431 2876 2889
  2954 3322 3554 3558
  3759 4350 4952 7882
  8015 8085 8143 8219
  9005-7 9173 k592 k830
  k894 k931
-Fast A ᵀ275
Neugebauer F 3839a
Neuhaus G 2921 3142 3759
  R 4657 4986b k654 ᴱ4186
  g463 ᴹ4790 4836 8188a
Neuheuser H ᴱ4523 ᴿa622
Neumann B 4265a G 6381
  6432 ᴿ6242 H 9471 b387
  c385c K k990
Neuner J 4325b 4658 P 4118
  4393 g301
Neunheuser B 955a
Neusch M k548
Neuser W ᴱk063 ᶠk064

Rey-Coquais J 8626a 8707
E8898
Reydams-Schils G 6850d
Reyes A Rb224
Reymond B a280 k380a
R1542 a240 a612 P 5775
Reynal G Rk548
Reynolds C R1561 D E350 E
K2155 k464 F E8036 L
M9806 P 5339 c843 g768s
T 2786 V 7896
Rhegius U Mk140
Rhem R 4284
Rhoads D R9818
Rhodes E T2529 P 6445b
R6477 R 3446 4788 b946
Rhodus a344 c003
Rhosos 9707
Riaud J R6836
Ribbat E R0791
Ribeiro A g137 g225 R1994
Ribera J R1141 2512
Ribet P Rc466 k219 T331
Ribichini S 8343 8708 R8640
b207
Ricca P 4285 q074 M4253
Ricci C 9821 9926 a339
E5230 L 6224 q251 q386
R6217 6219 6221 R k053b
Ricciardi A R1519
Rice E 1962a G 2797a 8709
M b455
Rich A 4816 c946 J Ea340
c740
Richard J c983 q277 D4751
R758 8442 9900 c032 c980
L 1693 M4959 M 2572 P
2028e 4884b M4940 R8212
3903 S b168 Y q151a
Richards F a724 I M1862 J
5601 K 1332 E201 5954 M
1212a 4124
Richardson A E570 C Tb291
J 2926 3853 4527 4960b
8301 9927 M3871 L c029
M 5766 R5895 R6046 N
R6317 P D3884 c728 R9914
W R2355
Riché P g770
Riches J k464 k158
Richler B 898 2486
Richter K E634 P 1961
M2178 R 6225 R341 6222
S 7827 W 899a 6653
E2519 M5739
Rickheit G E2037
Ricks C M1878
Rico C c844
Ricœur P 14 1337s 3854 ..

..4704 6700 M1289* 1552
1573 1972 2050 6688
6694 6699 6704 6719s
k958-60
Ridder-Symoens H de Eg771
Ridgway B a668 R470 848
9588s
Ridings D Dg164 J Tc976
Ridley W Rb312
Riebe-Estrella G R4880
Riebers R M858
Riede P c267
Riedel M k846
Riedlinger D2388
Riedweg C Eg389 R6845
g385
Rieger M D3553 Rk438 R
8207a Ek362
Riennecker F 900 M6287
Rienstra D D1907 M 4481a
R3874
Riera I Ec179
Ries J 7787b 7809d 7828-
7830 7968 E7969
Riesebrodt M Rc684
Riesenhuber H 2349b
Riesner R 7053-6 E312 6993
M6962
Riess J a606 R E445
Rietz H 7018
Rifaud J Mc919
Rigal J 4125
Rigg A Rg709
Riggans W a225
Riggs J k068
Righini V Rc009
Rigo C 7465
Rijk L de F702
Rike J E8180
Rikhof H g826
Riley D c134 G 5602 7854
M c109 W F156 Rg614
†q357
-Smith J 545
Rilinger R c741 R9723 c721
Rimaud D 1571b
Rimedio V 2989
Rimon O Ea117
Rin S 5902
Rindner M R3174
Ringe S T3912 4936
Ringgren H 7116 E774 M5830
Ringleben J g934
Ringshausen G Rk663
Rinsveld B Van Rc769
Riordan C 2081c P R3951
Rippin A 8931 8974 R8918
8928
Rist J g473

Ritchie T R2077
Ritner R 8804 c482
Ritschl Dk990 Mk375 A
M3829 D 1938 3613*
D3052 F157
Ritter A 3089 3555 g060
g772 R3455 H 5996 T
6178s 9365b
Ritterband P 7562
Rius-Camps J g138 g212 E41
Rival M a385
Rivas L 635 P T3019
Rivaudeau A de Mk141
Rivera E R4865 L 4912 R
D4914
-de Ventosa E 4912
Rives J 8415s
Rivier D R2394
Rivinius K Rk303 k495
Rix H F158
Rizakis Y b933
Ri Zhi Rq282
Rizk S 6093
Rizza G 4817 R658
Rizzi A 8037 q013b G 2538
2582 R2606 M g165
Rizzo F 9921 Rc742 G c030
T 1574
Robb G R5175 K 9590 P
E1729
Robbe M E8975
Robbins G 3714 J 2835*
R3824 7923 K k556
Robeck C g289
Roberge M 1485 7876c R
E632 R8436
Robert D k676 R4260 M
4528a P b003 Ra460 P de
3116 R3270 3679 R 317
a547 Ra460
Roberts A R410 D b516 J
9591 R1105 2419 P c947
Rk032 R k769s E636 W
q075
Robertson E Rk782 J k677a
Dk888 Rb336 M a774 N
c899
Robijns J †q358
Robin C 8887 8890 b189
b461 Eb456
Robins G 9417 a519 b517
b592d R a013
Robinson B R1052 9186 C
Rg595 D c520 k310 Rk858
E a607 J 2191 3665 7709
c900a E902 7845 M3435 N
R7362 O c901 P 6472 R
2038 D1870 S R4688 T 995
Robles R 4840b

Serra A 5151 ^M5096
Serrano Delgado J 9422
-Gómez E c752
Sersale C †q372
Servais P 4692
Serzisko F ^R688
Sesboüé B 3482 3558
  3636a 3910s g141 ^M3503
  g142
Sessions W 3766
Sestieri L ^R7367 7571
  7703a
Setian N g043
Setzer C 7236 9713
Seumois A 4137
Seurin J 4827
Sevegrand M 4693
Sevenich-Bax E 2269
Severus A ^Mg398s **E von**
  955b q307
Sevin M 1133 1142b 1199b
  V a288
Sevrin J 7857a q253
Seweryniak H ^R2401 ^Rk716
Sexton J 1904a
Sextus E 8516
Seybold M ^R2852
Seyfried K b559
Sfameni Gasparro G 8108a
Sgarbossa R 4293a
Sgarlata M c044
Sguaitamatti M c248b
Sguazzero T ^R4172
Sha'ban F 9053
Shadur J ^Tb098
Shafer B ^E8810 ^R3235
Shafter A 2451 6052
Shahbazi A 9511
Shaheen A ^E271
Shahid I b457 ^R9914
Shahrastani 8964
Shai D ^R1769
Shain B k208
Shaked S 3787b 5962 7123
  8863b 8877s ^R8861
Shakespeare W ^M1903-5
  1910
Shaki M ^R854
Shakova N c819
Shalem A b009
Shalev V ^Ra971
Shamir O a473
Shammai ^M7230
Shanahan T 4101
Shanks A ^R4813 **H** 1072
  6953s a017 a135 b010-2
  q153 ^E387 532 7237
  9242s a120 a143 ^R813
  6939 6966b 7104

Shanley M ^R5363
Shannon T 5354 **W** 1496
  ^R292
Shantz D k099
Shanzer D g534
Shapira A ^Mg031
Shapiro H 8587b 9598 a550
  ^R7565 **M** ^D7517
Shareef A ^E722
Shariati M ^D4926
Shariot S c997
Sharkansky I g044
Sharma A 8042 9101 ^E7934
  9157s
Sharon a787 b057-b067
Sharon D ^D1394 ^Dc391
Sharp G 6121 **M** ^Rc910
Sharpe W ^Mc448
Sharvit S 5779b
Shatz D ^R7547
Shatzman I a344 ^Rb111
Shatzmiller J ^S5960 c928 **M**
  c986
Shavit Y 9651
Shavitsky Z 5769
Shaw B 9714 ^R3844 9864 **G**
  g309 **I** b522 b591 **M** 9102
  b654a **R** g045 **S** 7518
  ^D9159
Shawcross J 841
Shawn M ^Rg805
Shea J ^R203 **N** ^E3690 **W**
  ^Rk639
Shear J a388
Shechem b071
Sheehan M ^R4587
Sheeley S ^R3659 c701
Sheffer A a474
Shehadeh H 7150
Sheldrake P ^R4463 g455
  k272
Shelke C 5084
Shellard B 2205
Shelley B 1906 **P** ^M1824
  1906 **T** k692 ^Rk554
Shelmerdine C 6505
Shenk D 8109
Shennan S ^Ra066
Shenute g628s
Shepard R 1996b 4694
Shepherd J 8110 **L** 5355 **N**
  1770 **R** a228 **W** ^R3416
Sheppard G ^R1507
Sheres I 7124
Sheridan J 6423 **S** ^M712
Sherira r ^M7270
Sherk K ^M9707
Sherrard L ^T8954 **P** †q373
Sherratt A ^Ea075 ^Rb311

Sherry P ^R3757
Sherwin B 4754c k693
-White S 9652
Sherwood J ^R464
Shibata M g483b
Shields K 6607s
Shifman Y 7403
Shikhin b133
Shillington V 1346
Shiloh b073s
Shiloh Y ^Ma954
Shinan A 2553 5975 ^E904
Shinnie P b719 ^R6200
Shinoff S c322
Shipley G ^Ea340 c740
Shippee A ^Rg336
Shirock R ^R2117
Shirun-Grumach I ^R6143
Shisha-Halevi A 6134b
  ^Rg628
Shishin a729
Shivtiel A ^E577 ^R6093
Shlesinger Y ^R5788
Shmeruk H 7380
Shmueli E 7566
Shoaff M 9672
Sho'ala A al- 9044c
Shofner R ^R8010
Shook L ^Tg821
Shore A †q374 **P** k675
Shorter A 5085s
Shortz J ^D4294
Shotter D 9826
Shoulson J ^D1899
Showalter R 8246
Showers R 3451
Shrady M ^Tg520
Shriver D ^Rk559 **J** k382a
Shtober S c161
Shubert S b648
Shuger D k001
Shukman A ^R4444 k364
Shupak N 6187
Shute M 9340
Siat J 9827 ^D8426
Sibley J 2206 ^R4848
Sicard S von ^R9063
Sicari A 2207
Sicario A 3450
Sichem b071
Sichtermann H a853
Sicilia 9621 a271 c044 c143
  c397
Sick F ^T7707
Sicking T ^E6709
Sicre J 3345 3420 4138
  ^R2118 7054s 9687-dos
  c566 c662
Side b861s

Vahanian G k709 q243
	^R781 1942 7917 9793
Vaillancourt M 3672 4836
Vajda Criado G 342
Valadier P 4711 k710*a*
	^Rc637
Valantasis R 7858 ^E659
	4575
Valbelle D 9396 9426 c769
Valdés J de ^Mk149
Valdrini P 4317
Valencia Hernández M
	c396*a*
Valen-Sendstad A 8226
Valensi M ^T9549
Valenti P ^R1824
Valentin F 1425**b* ^Eg788
Valentini C ^T1154
Valentinus ^M7760 7762
	7780 7782 7785 7789
	7810
Valenziano C a619
Valera C de ^M2672
Valerianus g582
Valerio K de k492 ^D7741
Valero J g525
Valevičius A 8314 g312
	^R2840
Valignano A ^M9147
Valkenberg P ^R1616 9171
Vall H ^R2785 3019
Valla F a192
Vallarino J ^R4111 4646
	8258
Vallat F c164 ^Eb467
Vallauri E 9774
Valle F del ^D1876 **L del**
	^R1426 **R** c770
-Rodríguez F de 3591
Valler S 7326
Vallet G †q391
Vallin P 1697*c* ^E4693 ^R3976
	a027 a010 g133
Valloggia M a858
Valls Lobet C 5366
Valognes J 4318 **P** g049
Van b464*b*
van: for Dutch scholars →
	final element
Van Allen R 1011 1505
	^R1474
Van Asselt W ^R2920
Van Bask E ^R5049
Van Buren P ^M772
Vancamp A ^R8566 **B** c492
	^Rc478
Vance D 5913 **R** k395
Van Dam C 3968 **R** g375
	g789 ^R3288

Vandana (Mataji) ^E9168
Vander Hart M 3156
Vanderhooft D b151*b*
VanderKam J 3343*b* 6762
	6788s 6962 7012 7044
	9717 ^E538 7126 ^R3362
	6803 6968 7005 7120
	8672 9679
Vandermeersch C c397 **P**
	^R1943
Vandersleyen C 9427 b214
	b529 c093 ^R9364 9425
	a924
Vander Sluijs C k214
Van der Steen E c865
Vandervelde G 1626
Vander Weele M ^R1861
Vandevelde G ^D3913
Vandiver E 9504
Van Dop S ^R4086 5666
Vándor J ^R7375
Vandorpe K c801
Van Dyk L ^R403 3066 3622
	W 1581 ^R1557
Vaneigem R k711
Van Elderen B 9656
Van Engen J ^R3835
Van Hamersveld M ^R1310
Vanhetloo W 3592 ^R2702
Vanhoozer K 1664 5690
	^R1361
Van Horn R 1581
Van Hove B ^Rk817
Vanhoye A 1456*b* 1506
	4319 4493 k471 ^D3917
Van Inwagen P 343
Van Kampen R 5629
Vankatakrishna B ^R9108
Van Keuren F ^Ra661
Van Leeuwen C 2277 **M**
	1780
Van Lepp J c206
Van Minnen P c165
Van Ness P ^R8606
Vanneste A q334 ^R5649
Vanni Desideri A c988
Vannier M g346 g488s
	g856
Vannini G c988 **M** g843
Vanoni G 2863 3265
Van Reken C ^Rk622
Vanschoonwinkel J 9605
	b990 ^R8493 b931
Van Seters J 535 9255s
	^M9244 ^R1379
Van Siclen C b589
Vanstiphout H 6054 8853
	9481
Van Til C ^Mk997

Van Till H 3024*b* ^R2365
Van Toorn P 1913
Van Voorst R ^D6885
Vanzan P ^M8165
Varacalli J r7994
Varachaud M k243*
Vardy P 3417
Varella E a023
Varène P b993
Vargas-Machuca A ^R5607
Varghese R ^E615
Vargyas P b269
Varias García C 6507s
Varisco D c398
Varner E a681
Varo D 9257 ^R9254 **F**
	1428*e* 7384 **P** ^R9209
Varone F 5630
Vasse D 1321*c* 3272
Vassileva M b823
Vassilika E a123 b528 b695
Vath A ^M5060
Vatin C ^F207 **J** b530 ^Ec927
	N c989
Vattioni F 1054 5892*b* 5914
	b194 b415 †q391
Vauchez A g790-2
Vaughn A a688
Vaux R de 387
Vavouranakis G b916
Vavrinek V ^F208
Vavrousek P ^E94 469
Vaz A 3720 ^R6428
Vazhuthanapally J ^Da813
Vázquez R 7327 **U** 8200
-Janeiro I ^Rg105
Vecsey C ^R5026
Vedder B ^R519 3039 9308
Veenhof K 6048*b* b848
Veerkamp T ^R4748
Vega Santoveña F ^R3591
Vegas Montaner L ^E6961
Vegetius F a329s
Vegetti M c506
Veh O ^E9609
Veijola T 535
Veissière M ^F209
Veith G k712 ^Rk615
Vela L ^R4648 k195
Velasco F 7997 8227*a* **J**
	4970
Velati M ^R4279
Veldhuijsen P van ^R5494
Veldhuis N 6054 8854s
	^R6007
Velema W 5651
Vélez Chaverra N †q393
Veliath D 1507 ^R4246 5063
Veligianni C ^Rb978

Vitz E g794
Viuda I de la ^Rg905
Vivante A b393
Vivaro c061
Vivekananda ^M9097
Vives J 4713 4840*a* 8230
  g852
Vivian T g622
Viviano B 3674 ^Mq094*b*
  ^R3993
Viviers D a682 ^R9504
Vlastos G ^F707
Vleeming S 6193 6480 ^E750
  b564
Vliet J 6216*a* **J Van** 1845
Vlieth Cornelis van ^D4158
Voegelin E 9311 9347
  ^M9286 9324 k999
Vögtle A 3675 g168
Voegtli H b804
Voelke A 8614
Voelker J ^Rg100 g463
Völker A q148
Voelz J 1160*b* 1357 g945*a*
Vössing K ^Rc721
Voet G b313
Vogel A 4028 **C de** g313
  M ^R7751
Vogels W 1358 3001 c772
  q089 ^R2839 3353 3726
  5707 9314
Vogelsang W 9512
-Eastwood G a480
Vogler W 7743 ^R777
Vogt E e9650 **H** 4412 a620
  g334 ^F214 539 ^R3595
  g194 g331
-Spira G ^E708
Vogüé A de 4573 ^R2660
Voicu S ^T7472
Voigt H ^T7740 **R** 6018*c*
  q359
Voigts M 3349
Vokotopoulou I 6509
Volf M 1700 5631 k714
Volgger D ^D5745
Volk K 6025 9485
Volker G ^Mg313
Vollenweider S 6362
Vollkommer R ^R8448
Volokhine Y ^R8791*a* 8810
Volpe F ^E33 **G** 7264 ^R2776
Volpi F ^Tk366 **I** 123
Volsenet J c277
Voltaire ^Mk275
Volz C c088 ^R236
Von Waldow H 7744
Voorwinde S 3872
Vorgrimler H 1448 4029

5632s k956 ^E2997 ^F215
  ^R3904
Vororéva-Desjatovskaya M
  6513
Vorster J 2058
Vos H ^Ea043 **J** ^R5662 c755
Voss C 8102 **H van** 6192
  → Heerma; **J** 8730 a815
  K 8253
Vree D ^R1187
Vries A de ^D2710
Vriezen K a816 ^Ra404 b038
Vroom H 1359 5098 9171
Vunderink R ^Rk987
Vyas C 9108
Vycichl W 6194
Vyhmeister N 190
Vyvere Y Vande 2709

Waabel T 1580
Waal E de 3025 **V de**
  ^R4537
Waansbrough H 2749
Waard J de ^D5751
Waardenburg J 8050 ^E9062
Waardt P Vander ^M8523
Wace H ^E835 **R** b532
Waché B k822
Wachinger L 1224
Wacholder BZ 7013 ^D5919
  ^M7015 **S** 7013
Wachsmann G ^T7494 **S**
  a366*b* a395
Wacht M ^F196
Wachtel K 2577*a* ^E6332
Wachtmann C ^D7918
Wackenheim C ^R5686
Wacker G ^Dk456 **M** 1765
  3365 3378*c* 5173*b* ^E2864
Wackernagel W g857
Wacome D ^R2365 2381
Wada H b171
Waddleton F ^R4777
Wadell P ^R3010
Wadsworth M 9300
Wächter L ^R552 3095
Waelkens M b863
Wagaw T g050
Wagener U 5256
-Rau U 5257
Wagner A ^D5781 **C** c401
  ^Rk023 **F** k715 ^R1358 q089
  G 6440 **H** 7992 ^E819 **S**
  ^E1701 ^R5239 **W** 2865
  g169
-Hasel B ^Rc575
Waheeb M b138
Wahrmund ^M6098
Waines D 8936 ^T9250

Wainwright A ^R5403 **G**
  4322 ^R321 a566 a613
  g054 g113 g218
Waite G k112
Wajntraub E c132 **G** c132
Wajsberg E 7329
Wakefield G 1878 1912
  ^R605 1909
Wakker G 6333
Wal A van der ^R1723
Walbank F 9718
Walbrunn P ^D5634
Walcot P 5138 8489 ^R5185
  8328 8480 9570 9599
  9849 a820 b224 b879
  c380 c612
Wald B ^R3484
Waldenfels H 2933 8051
  8121 8181*b* 8231 k716
  q275 ^E5639 ^E836 ^Mq000
  ^R5448
Waldmann H 8869*b* c708*b*
  ^D8879
Waldren W ^E751
Waldron T ^R7536
Waldstein M 6888 7865 **W**
  ^Rc741
Walfish B ^R7283 7477
Walford A ^E762
Waliszewski T a745 ^Ra948
  b205
Walker A c248*c* ^Tc738*a*
  k545 **C** b394*a* ^Rb894 **E**
  ^D9430 **G** ^T1555*a* **P** 8982
  R ^Ec431 **S** 8346 ^R1879
  T ^M5077
Walkusz J ^E9765
Wall E van der ^Rk161 k718
  J ^D1815 **P** c327 **R** 1360*a*
Wallace C ^Rk447 **D** 2578*a*
  2579 7086 ^D6334 ^R7081 **H**
  ^R1723 **M** 1361 **R** 9606
  ^R8381 8518 **W** ^R2307
-Hadrill A 9776 c054 c773
Wallat K ^R1020
Wallinga H a394 ^E337
Wallis I 2218s 3567 4494
  g151 ^R2132 c430 **J** 3771s
Wallmann J ^Dk268
Wallner K ^Dk749
Walls A 1012 ^Mk581 **J** 2220
  5635
Walmsley A b155*c*
Walser G ^F216
Walsh B 3754 q065 **J** q115
  ^R1155 c527 **M** 1110*b*
  1317*b* k215 k858 ^E1511
  ^M1413 ^R824 **T** k122
Walsham A k216

(.. Welker M) 4718*a*
Weller P [E]837
Wellesley K [E]9940
Wellhausen J [M]7962 m8668
Wells C 9941 **D** 3773 8232
  [R]3520 **P** 1151*b* 1973c
  2004*c*
Welscher C [T]8050
Welser W a911
Welsh F b595 [R]b549s
Welte B [M]3510 q003
Welten B [M]6734 **P** [M]3204
Welwei K [R]685 700 758
Wendebourg D 4323
Wendland E g938
Wenger J <q397 5373
Wengert T g911*b* [E]454
Wengst K 3309
Wenham G 3969*a* [R]3235
  3253 **J** [R]5410
Wénin A 346 3002 3267
  [R]6305
Weninger S [R]2628
Wenskus O 6539*b* 9607
Wente E [D]8753 9430 [T]6481
Wentz R 3300*b*
Wentzel van Huÿssteen J
  [R]q084
Wenz G [R]3522 3897
Wenzel S [F]217
Wenzelmann G [D]4574
Werba C [R]6521
Werbick J 1513 1616 3774
  k217 [E]554 589 [R]8136
Werbiński I [R]k200
Werblowski R 4324*a* [R]9094
Weren W [R]2709
Werlin S [D]g815
Werman C 5816 6790 7331
Werner E [F]218 **F** [R]5789 **J**
  [R]9650 **K** 9172 [R]9129 **P**
  c192
Wernicke H [F]173
Wertheimer J [E]1630
Wertz S [R]a415
Wes M 9700 9942
Wesche K g215 g376 [R]a020
Wesch-Klein G a860 [R]a312
Wesley C [M]k285 **J** [M]3878
  5467 5485 5668 k276-84
Wesselius J 9261
Wessels A 8348 g796s
Wessely C 0910
Wessinger C [E]8320
West A 3873 k828*b* **C**
  8167*b* [R]5079 k788 **D** 8510
  G 1259 k472 **N** c278
  [R]k820 **W** [R]9590
Westendorf W c279 c508

[R]c410
Westenholz A [R]8835 **J** 8857
  b420
Westerdahl C a396
Westerhoff M [R]g270 [T]3637
Westerholm S q328
Westermann C 1145s [M]2038
  3376
Western A c328
Westerwelt B 4325*a*
Westhead N k075
Westhelle V 2413
Westhuizen J b596*a* [F]218*
Weston A [T]8459 **P** k724
Westphal M 3775 [E]410
Westra L 2878 3776 [R]7130
  [R]g500 g561
Weszeli M 1067 [R]715
Wetherbee W [E]g869
Wetsel D k261
Wetter F q366
Wetzel C [E]2653 **J** g491
  [M]g443
Wever A 4326
Wevers J [R]2594 6307
Wewers G 7332
Wexler P 5793
Whalen M [R]4499
Wharton A b321 c906 **E**
  [M]1859
Whealey A 9719
Wheeler B [R]832 4729 **G**
  [R]2960 3395 **S** 2453 4719
  4838
Whidden W 5485*d* [R]255
  [R]8272
Whie H [R]1885
Whipple [M]5096
Whiston W 9236
Whitby M [R]9914 9963 c856
Whitcomb D b142 b145*a*
White A [R]3082 **C** g527 **D**
  b708 **G** [M]g922 k338 **H**
  [M]9301 **J** 2702 4537 [R]3247
  K a233 c403*a* **L** 3041
  4720 a294 c128 [M]3007 **M**
  [E]125 **P** 3158 k026 **S** 5154
  k816*b* [E]k836
Whitehead A 2841 [E]c907 **R**
  [M]2806 2821 2828
Whitehorn J [R]9356
Whitehorne J 9434 9657
Whitelam K 9262 c780
  [R]1379 9316
Whitely M [E]437
Whitfield S [R]1514
Whiting R 9468 [E]b381
Whitley J a776 b945 [R]a820
  c763

Whitney B [R]1658 2832
  3835 6703 8030
Whitt W b271 [D]b270 [R]8666
Whittaker C c856 [M]9330
Wiame B 1142
Wichrowicz J [R]920
Wickede A von [R]a708
Wickenhauser R [R]k131
Wickens C [R]7228 **K** [D]c990.
Wicker B [E]3310
Wickersham J 9608 [E]c898
Wickert U [E]g302
Wickham L g409 [R]g342
  g464
Wicks J g939 **K** [D]1842
Widdicombe P 2866 [R]3534
Widengren G 7127
Widok N [R]g086 g111
Widowson P [E]2043
Wieacker F <q398
Wiebe D 347 8053*a* 8084*c*
  [R]7898s **R** [E]7839 [M]1913
Wieck R a595
Wiedemann T 349 [R]9886
  9899 a003 a025 c792
  c806 c845 c856
Wiedenhofer S 4162
Wieder L 1817 1843
Wiederkehr D 1631
Wiefel W [R]k306
Wiegand A [M]k405
Wiegers G 8938
Wielockx R [R]453 g688
  g848 g877
Wiener M [M]7572
Wier J 3847
Wieringen A van 911
Wierschowski L [R]a365 c793
Wiese A a737
Wiesehöfer J 9497*b* 9513s
  [R]9658 9905 c087
Wiesel E 7333 [F]219
Wiessner G 8124
Wiest J [E]5093
Wietheger C b602
Wiggins S 8731 [R]555 1736
  8675 8847
Wight C a189
Wightman G a968*b* b016
Wijk-Bos J van [E]2867
Wijnkoop M van [D]8321
Wilcken J 4828*b*
Wilckens U 5155
Wild S 8939
Wildung D q206
Wileituer J 9420
Wiles J g493 **M** [R]k176 **V**
  [R]1810
Wilfong G [R]6205 **T** b567

(Wolfson E) ^{R}7456
Wolgast E k101
Wolinski G ^{R}g320 **J** 3911
  g141 ^{R}3475s
Wollaston I ^{R}5311 7237
Wollbold A 4030
Woloch I ^{D}c762
Wolohojian S ^{D}a623
Wolski J 9515
Wolsky F b924
Wolsza J 9352
Wolter M r3676
Wolters A 6830c ^{R}5169
Wolterstorff N 1613 2881
  4031 k729
Wolthuis L ^{M}ck294
Wondra E 5369 ^{R}5350 k381
Wong J 9174
Won Jong Ji ^{R}3504
Wood B a777 **D** ^{E}456 600
  7754 **I** ^{R}9965 **J** 7972 **K**
  ^{R}5341 **S** 4328 ^{R}5350
Woodall C ^{T}a299
Woodard R ^{R}693
Woodford S b885*
Woodhead L ^{R}c611
Woodhouse R 6611
Woodman A 9805
Woodrow A q222 ^{R}k852
Woodrum E 3110
Woods C 4724 **R** 8324a
Woodward J ^{R}5465
Wooler E ^{T}5444
Woolf G 9943 ^{E}550 9362 **V**
  ^{M}7972 **W** ^{M}9590
Wootton D ^{E}g978 **J** 5370
Worcester T ^{R}k243*
Worgul G ^{R}3732
Worley L a351
Worp K 6483s c079b
Worrell A ^{T}3705
Worth F ^{R}3094 **R** ^{R}3817
Wortham R g647
Worthing M ^{T}3858
Worthington E ^{D}4294 **I**
  ^{R}9654 **J** ^{E}76
Woschitz K ^{R}2239 5643
Woude A van der 2528
  6939 7129 q214 ^{R}370 376
  538 3332 6911 7009 7098
  7609
Woudenberg A 9353
Woytowitsch E a358
Wozniak J ^{D}k102
Wray D ^{R}2317
Wren T 9562
Wright C 351 1614 2278
  3268 **D** c957 k029 ^{D}g410
  k095 ^{E}130 806 k039 **F**

^{E}203 ^{T}c298 **G** 8715b
^{M}5679 ^{R}a246 b918 c192 **H**
^{D}b374 **J** 1360c ^{R}745 8012
M 2454 **N** 3111 3427
^{D}6798 **O** a461 ^{R}6097 **R**
3112a c282a k730 ^{D}8439
8617 **T** 1840 **W** 5371a
Wroe A g800
Wrogemann H 947
Wucketits F 2414 c784
  ^{R}2295
Wuellner W 2061s ^{F}2224
Würthwein E 2529 ^{M}888
Wüstenberg R ^{D}k793
Wulff D 1786*
Wunenberger J 8349a
Wunsch C 9488 c404 c857
  ^{E}732* **E** k407
Wurst G 7835
Wurzburger W 1363b
  1365a
Wuthnow R 8054 k731
  q091 ^{E}8325
Wu Yi ^{D}9089b
Wu Yuhong 6056 9486s
Wyatt N 1074 5858 b020
  ^{R}2421 2445 5907 8724
  c141
Wybrew H ^{R}333 a607
Wyckoff D 1015
Wyclif J 4639* ^{M}1788 k152
Wydmusch S ^{R}k725
Wyman W ^{R}k996
Wynveen B ^{R}3891
Wyper G ^{R}3129 3895
Wyschogrod E 7960b ^{M}4578
  ^{R}318 **M** 3526b 7755
  ^{M}7586
Wyss D ^{M}3146
Wyssenbach J k473

*X*anthos 5951 b890s c226
Xaranauli A g890
Xavier A ^{R}307
Xella P 5858 5916 8708
  8733 ^{E}5638 ^{R}5891
Xenophon ^{M}a337 b865
  b900c c176 c284 c394

*Y*acoub J q157
Yadin Y 6465 6965 b114
  ^{M}a168
Yaeko M 2713
Yakobson A 9759
Yalman B b858
Yamada S 5983
Yamagata N 8511
Yamauchi E 7088 7806a
  9319b b468 b709 c559
  k551 ^{R}7812

Yamin G k996
Yandell K 7900 ^{R}5635
Yanes E 4725a
Yankélévich V ^{M}1252
Yannai E a787
Yao Xinzhong 9175
Yapp M g051 ^{R}g030
Yarbrough O c785 ^{E}125 **R**
  ^{R}390 3187 4429
Yardeni A 5967 6980a
  7027 ^{M}5940
Yardenna A a749
Yarkho V ^{R}6452
Yarmuth b075
Yarnold E r3915
Yaron R 5747
Yarshater E ^{E}854
Yaseen G b328
Yates J 1366a 4726 **T** 4166
  k732 k833
Yavetz Z ^{F}220
Yavné 9668
Yazìlìkaya b782a
Yeago D g315 g940
Yee M r7907
Yekutieli Y b030
Yelo Templado D ^{F}221
Yemen 7510 b453 b463
  c191
Yener K b762
Yeniso Ganci V a871
Yeoh Siok Cheng d8986
Yerushalmi Y 7385
Yeskel F 5303b
Yevics P ^{R}4389
Yiannis J ^{R}a625
Yifrach E 5782
Yisrael Y b031
Ylvisaker R ^{R}8606
Yocum G 8987
Yoder J 352 ^{R}2120 3276
  4723 **P** ^{R}3299
Yoffe A ^{R}b071
Yoffee N ^{E}a075 b396 ^{R}9462
Yon M b272s ^{E}753 b911
Yonan E 8041c 8055a ^{E}423
Yonge C 6855
Yonnet P k733
Yoonprayong A ^{D}5156
Yoshida D 8631
Yoshikawa M 6057
Yoshinori T ^{E}9110
Young B 2279 ^{R}5378 **D**
  2415 7901 k898 ^{E}g628 **F**
  1367s 1977c 3777 3933
  g154 g316 k734 ^{M}2040
  ^{R}1741 5412 g099 **I** 5748 **J**
  5783 ^{R}5367 7527 **M** 8988
  P ^{R}5305 **R** 3113 ^{D}g345

sāpôn 5858
sārap 5860
saraq 5859
sedeq 5854
şinnor 5857

Qof

qades, q°desâ 5861
qûm 5862s
qātar 5864
teqnItu c838b
†*qnoma* 5995
q°pîsat ha-derek
　7242
qārôb 5865

Res

rîšôn 5852
reba', arba'îm
　5866
r°gî'a 5867
rûah 5868
rûm 5869
rô' 5853
marzeah b069
rîb 5870
RMH, *mirma* 5882
RP', Shadrapha 5873
rapasu 5842
raq 5871

Šin

š°'ôl 3352b 4534
šad 5872
šadday 5873
šaw 5874
šûah 5875
šûp 5846
šôt 5859
šākab îm/et 5876
šikkum 6016
š°kînâ 2783 5877
šālal, m°sillâ 5847
šālôm 5878
‡*sela"* 5949
‡*šelia* 5995
*šm, *surinnu* 5885
šm, °ism 6063
Simdat Sarrim
　c580s
š°mayim 5879
šumma 6018c
sāma' 5880
supalu c310
šārap a212

Tau

tubqum a264
‡*tmk* 5881
torma 5882

Genesis

-: 1899 2625 3677
　6999a 7004 7314
　g507 g873
1-11: 3037
1-4: 5296
1-3: 1783 4707
1: 2440a 3685 a596
1,28: 3007
2-11: 3155
2s -: 8933
2: 535 5637
2,4-3,24: 3720
3: 2057 3862 6717
　8726
3,14: c268
3,21; g312
3,23: 6409
4: 8948
6: 8726
6,3: 6978
7s: 6991
12: 1779
12,10-20: 1763
14:1,17: 2550
15,11: 6785
16: a554
17,20: 5726
20,1-18: 1763
21: 2445 a554
21,9: a418
21,13-20: 9041
22: 513 3197 3921
　3928 7589
22,1s: 8673d
22,1-19: a569
23,2-20: b033
24,63: 5875
28,11-22: 6805
29,32-35: 2535
32,22-33: 1887
37-50: 9674
37s: 1800 a469
37: 6817
37,3: c711
39,12: c711
47,13: c609

Exodus

-: 243* 1565 k876
　q114
3s: c065
7: 9681
10,3: 6840
15,3.11: 7148
15,26: c503

19: b340b b342c
21s: c706
23,21s: 3797
24,12-18: 6787
32,34: 3797
33,22: 3797

Leviticus

-: 7022
4s: 3963
8: 8689
10,6: 5853
11,29: c225
16-26: 3191
17,7: 8486
19,1-27: 4475
23,10: 2498
25: 3033b 4727
　c517 c630 c809
26,1: 7113

Numeri

-: 2587 3177 c620
1: 535
6,22-27: a991
6,24: a034b
15,30s: 3805
18,20-29: 7332
23,28: 2034
24,17: 5726
26: 535
33,18-36: b733

Deuteronomium

-: 1123 1762 5824
　9691a
1,2: b733
6,4: 8695
13,10: 6026b
16: 7113
16,1-8: 535
17,8.12: 9684a
21s: 7113
23,19: c236
36,20-24: 6027c

Josue, **Joshua**

-: 7283
14-21: c091
15,52: c152

Judicum, **Judges**

-: 535 2028d 2554
2,1-5: 3797
5,23: 3797
14,14: c247
19-21: b018

Ruth

-: 3338

1 Samuel

-: 484 2503 3346
1.9-17: 2231
1,24: 3969b
3: 0535
3,9: 4482a
6: a356
13s: 9291
13,19: a225
14,4: b020
15,27: a477
24,4s: a477

2 Samuel

2,18: c753
12-19: 2057

3 Regna, **1 Kings**

-: 535 2712 5783
　9690b
2,39; c624
3,16-28: 5204
10: 8918
12-22: 9659
12,26-28: 9204
18-21: 1223

4 Regna, **2 Kings**

-: 535 9690b
1: 9660a
9: b109a
12,24G: 9252
14,5: c753
15,22s: 9662
17: 8706
20,1-19: 9662
21: 2057
23,21s: c723

Esdras b', **Ezra**

-: 2646 6768-6772
　9506
3,10s: 2590
4: 6798
6,16-18: 2590
7,12-26: 9497a(-c)
9s: c671

Nehemias

1,3: 9191
11,23s: 9497
13,30s: 9497

1 Chronica
-: 3306 3365* a451
22,37: 5819

2 Chronica
3,1: 8673*d*
11,15: 8486
16,15: a341

Tobias
-: 6801 g496*e*

Judith
8,18: c753
9,l-14: 8589

Esther
-: 6801 7008 7317
9290

Machabaeorum
-: 1844*c* 3283 3355
c9581
I: 9,15-41: c536
II: 4,9: a997
III: -: 6773-5
2,2-20: 6774
6,1-15:6774
IV: -: 6775*b*

Psalmi
-: 535 634 1843
1907s 2500 2618
2640 2670 2708
3195 3363 5612
6099 6975s 6981
a457 a565 g738
7: 3862
19: 8732
44: g441
61: 535
79: 1344
92,15: 1678*a*
100: 1344
104: 3112
118V: g566
119: 7003
137,5: 8732
155: 7001

Canticum
-: 2617 3233* g757
g839
6,12-7,1: a356

Job
-: 254 1699 1851
1917 2646 3869

8902 c275
2,9: a580
15,7: 2422
28: 3161
40s: c218

Proverbia
-: c785
7: 3233*
7,5-27: 8642
8,30: 6793

Eces, **Qohelet**
-: 2617 2661 5695
7419 k102

SapientiaSalomonis
-: 3355 3798 5459
5475 6349
1-6: 3359

Ecus, **Sirach**
-: 5782 6750 7302
a451 c785
7,30-11,35: 2652
17,1-4: 3155
24,15: c310
38,1-15: c503
50,2: a968*b*

1-Isaias
-: 1847 7416 c235
5: c748*b*
5,13: 5726
7,14: 2697
9,1-5: 5726
10,28: 5726
10,34: 3314 3321
7089*b*
13,21: 8486
38s: 9662

2-Isaias
40,41-20: 2639
43,14: 5726
46,13-50,3: 2639
47: c876
52,13-53,12: 7209*b*
53: 7384
54,9: 5841
60,16: 5872
63.16: 2863

Jeremias
-: 373 509 2249
k041
31: 7110

31,31-34: 3126
g456
31,31-36: 3116
36: b343
40s: 9662
46,7: c194
48,41: 5726
51,30: 5726
Lam -: 7273
Bar 1,15-2,8; 6776
2 -: 6778

Ezekiel
-: 2522
1s: c065
28,11-19: 2422
37.1-10: c315

Daniel
-: 535 1836*c* 3140
5977 6801 9305
1638
1: k046
7,27: 5726

Amos
-: 899a 2538 b806
2,8: 5942

Osee, **Hosea**
-: 1565
1-3: 5296
2: 8642*c*
4,17-19: 8668
5,7: 3155

Jonas
-: 1917 2234 3370

Michaeas, **Micah**
-: q106
1,8: 5697
4,14H: b040
5,1s: 6986

Nahum
-: 2542 6997
2,9-12: 9664

Habakkuk
-: 6988

*Zacharias***Zechariah**
-: 3316
7,4s: 7076

Malachi
-: 3236

Matthaeus
-: 2025*g* 2109 2208
2226 2249 2265
2570 2577 7464
g217
5,1-48: 2662
5,13-16: 4141
5,32: 4699
7,12: 4704
8,1-16: c503
10: 6860
11,28-30: 5463
15,14-30: g266
16,13-20: 3669
21,13-45: 7058
24,51: 7087

Marcus
-: 1373 2088 2145
2215*b* 2449 3141
3938 4743 6359
6396 6399 6736
2,5: 3862
2,22-3,6: 3718
3,20-35: 5156
6,52: 7049
6,52s: 7074*b*
11,15: 2124
13: 5386
14,51: cg180
14,61: 1272

Lucas
-: 340 1556 2205
6367 6848 7285
9715 9804 b741
c674 g537 g539
1s: 3445
4,16-30: 4911
5,39: 7854
6,31: 4704
7,36-50: 5338
9,22: 4530
11,14-26: 3657
12,14: 7854
12,46; 7087
16,1-8: 3644
18,1.6: 3644
24,18-27: 9683

Johannes
-: 890 1963 2025*h*
2205 3420 4151
4887 5180 5602
6384 6416 7626
7648 7681 b741
g472

Joh 1: 3430 6888
  a556 g261
1,47: g612
2,21: a990
2,5: a503
2,6: a513
4,23: cg357
5,46: 2264
6: g940
19,5: 2231
19,13: a990

Actus Apostolorum
-: 2115 2601 b795
  c592
2,42: 4127
4,33: 1758
15: 7755
28,17s: 9704

Ad Romanos
-: g345 g933a
1,25: 4524*
1,26: 4722
2,28: 2573
5: 5392
8,18-22: 2820
9-11: 3937

1 ad Corinthios
-: 2636 4352 c728
  q097
5,1-6: 3930
10,16s: 3154
12: g095
12,3: 1272
14: 5220
15: 5392 5467e
15,29: 8592
15,35-49: 5619
15,49: 3751

2 ad Corinthios
-: q097
5: 5467e

Ad Galatas
-: 5171
-: g917
2,1: 7073
2,20: 9098c

Ad Ephesios
-: 3284
1,10 3107

Ad Colossenses
1,15-18: 7432
1,15-20: 3097
1,16: 2411

Ad Philemonem
-: g343

1 Thessalonians
-: 2114

2 Thessalonians
3,11: 2616

Ad Timotheum
-: 2088 5256

Ad Hebraeos
-: g335b
1,5-13: 6973
3,19-26: 3496
3,7-4,11: 5463
3,19-26: 3496
10,1-8: 3917
10,26s: 3805

1 Petri
1,1-12: 6284
2,11: c633
2,5.9: 6849

1 Johannis
-: 2550
4,11: 3747

Judae
(1,) 5-7: 7432

Apocalypsis,
Revelation
-: 1901 1933b
  2260b 2663 3399
  5382 6798 9813
  a044 a953 a973
  g170b g728 g884
  g887 k620 q094a
1-3: b750
1,20-3,22: 3799
3,20: 4300
7,4-8: 7134
16,16: b121

FINIS -- THE END

Pubblicazioni periodiche dell'Editrice
Pontificio Istituto Biblico

BIBLICA

rivista trimestrale di Studi Biblici
abbonamento 1999: L.80.000 - US $ 75.00

ORIENTALIA

rivista trimestrale di Studi sull'Antico Oriente
abbonamento 1999: L.120.000 - US $ 110.00

ROBERT   ALTHANN

STUDIES IN
NORTHWEST SEMITIC

(BIBLICA ET ORIENTALIA, 45)

1997, pp. XII-208   L.36.000

EDITRICE PONTIFICIO ISTITUTO BIBLICO - ROMA

GIORGIO GIURISATO

STRUTTRA E TEOLOGIA DELLA PRIMA LETTERA DI GIOVANNI

Analisi letteraria e retorica,
contenuto teologico

(ANALECTA BIBLICA, 138)

1998, pp.720 e 2 pieghevoli   L.98.000

EDITRICE PONTIFICIO ISTITUTO BIBLICO - ROMA

CRAIG G. BARTHOLOMEW

READING ECCLESIASTES

Old Testament Exegesis and
Hermeneutical Theory

(ANALECTA BIBLICA, 139)

1998, pp. VIII-320   L.45.000

EDITRICE PONTIFICIO ISTITUTO BIBLICO - ROMA

JAMES SWETNAM

An Introduction to the Study of New Testament Greek
Part One: Morphology

Volume I: Lessons

(SUBSIDIA BIBLICA, 16/I)

Volume II: Key, Lists, Paradigms, Indices

(SUBSIDIA BIBLICA, 16/II)

Second, Revised Edition

1998, pp. LIV-800   L.75.000
The two volumes cannot be separated.
I due volumi non possono essere venduti separatamente.

EDITRICE PONTIFICIO ISTITUTO BIBLICO - ROMA

AMMINISTRAZIONE PUBBLICAZIONI PIB/PUG

Piazza della Pilotta, 35 00187 Roma - Italia
Tel.066781567 Fax 066780588

Kenrick-Glennon
Seminary Library

Charles L. Souvay Memorial

Finito di stampare nel mese di febbraio 1999
Tipografia " Giovanni Olivieri "
Via dell'Archetto, 10 - 00187 Roma

ISBN 88-7653-611-6 (= vol.